WITHDRAWN

WORLD AUTHORS   1980–1985

Biographical Reference Books from
The H. W. Wilson Company

Greek and Latin Authors 800 B.C.–A.D. 1000
European Authors 1000–1900
British Authors Before 1800
British Authors of the Nineteenth Century
American Authors 1600–1900
Twentieth Century Authors
Twentieth Century Authors: First Supplement
World Authors 1950–1970
World Authors 1970–1975
World Authors 1975–1980

The Junior Book of Authors
More Junior Authors
Third Book of Junior Authors
Fourth Book of Junior Authors and Illustrators
Fifth Book of Junior Authors and Illustrators
Sixth Book of Junior Authors and Illustrators

Great Composers: 1300–1900
Composers Since 1900
Composers Since 1900: First Supplement
Musicians Since 1900
American Songwriters

World Artists 1950–1980
World Artists 1980–1990

American Reformers
Facts About the Presidents

Nobel Prize Winners

World Film Directors: Volumes I, II

WORLD AUTHORS
1980–1985

_____

A Volume in the Wilson Authors Series

_____

Editor
VINETA COLBY

THE H. W. WILSON COMPANY
NEW YORK
1991

93-418

Library of Congress Cataloging in Publication Data

Main entry under title:

World authors, 1980–1985 / editor, Vineta Colby.
    p. cm. — (Wilson authors series)
  Includes bibliographical references.
  ISBN 0-8242-0797-1 : $80.00
    1. Literature, Modern—20th century—Bio-bibliography.
  2. Literature, Modern—20th century—History and criticism.
  I. Colby, Vineta. II. Series.
  PN451.W672 1991
  809'.04048—dc20   90-49782
                                       CIP

Acknowledgments for the use of copyrighted material and credits for photographs appear at the end of the volume.

PRINTED IN THE UNITED STATES OF AMERICA

CONTENTS

List of Authors vii

Key to Pronunciation x

Preface xi

List of Contributors xii

Biographical Sketches 3

List of Authors by Nationality...925

Acknowledgments...929

Picture Credits..936

LIST OF AUTHORS

Abbey, Edward 3
Ackroyd, Peter 5
Adams, Alice 8
Adler, Renata 11
Ai Qing 13
Aickman, Robert 15
Allende, Isabel 18
Alter, Robert 23
Amadi, Elechi 25
Amis, Martin 28
Anagnostakis, Manolis 31
Anderson, Jessica 34
Anthony, Michael 36
Apple, Max 37
Ariès, Philippe 40
Ariyoshi Sawako 42
Arnheim, Rudolf 45
Ashton, Dore 47
Astley, Thea 51
Auster, Paul 54
Baghio'o, Jean-Louis 58
Bailey, Anthony 60
Bakhtin, Mikhail Mikhailovich 63
Banks, Russell 65
Barnes, Julian 68
Barthelme, Frederick 72
Becker, Jurek 75
Benedikt, Michael 77
Bernstein, Jeremy 81
Bester, Alfred 84
Bhattacharya, Bhabani 86
Billington, Rachel 89
Birmingham, Stephen 92
Bok, Sissela 95
Bombal, Maria Luisa 97
Boyd, William 100
Boyle, T. Coraghessan 102
Briggs, Asa 104
Bringhurst, Robert 107
Brodkey, Harold 110
Brombert, Victor H. 112
Bronk, William 115
Bruner, Jerome S. 117
Brutus, Dennis 120
Cao Yu 125
Caputo, Philip 128
Caraion, Ion 130
Carey, Peter 133
Carpenter, Humphrey 135
Carter, Angela 139
Chappell, Fred 144
Chedid, Andrée 146

Chen Rong 151
Churchill, Caryl 152
Clampitt, Amy 155
Clarke, Gillian 157
Cobb, Richard 160
Cohen, I. Bernard 163
Colegate, Isabel 166
Comyns, Barbara 169
Condé, Maryse 172
Conrad, Peter 176
Conroy, Frank 180
Cook, Robin 182
Cornelisen, Ann 184
Costantini, Humberto 186
Crane, Ronald S. 188
Crevel, René 192
Csoóri, Sándor 194
Darnton, Robert 197
Davidson, Donald 200
Davis, Natalie Zemon 202
de Man, Paul 204
Denby, Edwin 208
Dick, Philip K. 210
Djebar, Assia 212
Dodson, Owen 217
Douglas, Ellen 220
Dourado, Autran 223
Dove, Rita 225
Dovlatov, Sergey 228
Drew, Elizabeth 230
Dubie, Norman 233
Durang, Christopher 236
Dyson, Freeman J. 238
Eagleton, Terry 241
Edmond, Lauris 245
Ehle, John 247
Ellis, Alice Thomas 249
Emin, Gevorg 253
Enchi Fumiko 255
Ende, Michael 258
Ephron, Nora 262
Epstein, Joseph 264
Erdrich, Louise 266
Etzioni, Amitai 269
Evans, Stuart 271
Federman, Raymond 273
Federspiel, Jürg 277
Feng Jicai 279
Fenton, James 281
Figes, Eva 285
Findley, Timothy 287

Fisher, Roy 290
Fitzgerald, Frances 293
Flanagan, Thomas 296
Fo, Dario 297
Follett, Ken 301
Forché, Carolyn 303
Ford, Richard 306
Forster, Margaret 310
Fox, Paula 313
Friedlander, Saul 316
Fulton, Robin 321
Furbank, P. N. 323
Gadamer, Hans-Georg 326
Gallagher, Tess 330
Gardner, Howard 333
Gardner, Martin 336
Geertz, Clifford 338
Ghiselin, Brewster 341
Ghose, Zulfikar 344
Gilchrist, Ellen 346
Ginzburg, Carlo 348
Girouard, Mark 351
Glendinning, Victoria 354
Głowacki, Janusz 357
Goldbarth, Albert 360
Goodman, Ellen 362
Gray, Alasdair 364
Gregor, Arthur 367
Grossman, Vasily 368
Grumbach, Doris 372
Gurney, A. R., Jr. 376
Guy, Rosa 379
Haavikko, Paavo 381
al-Hakim, Tawfiq 384
Hampton, Christopher 389
Hannah, Barry 392
Hare, David 394
Harrison, Tony 396
Heilbroner, Robert L. 402
Henley, Beth 405
Herbert, Xavier 408
Hewitt, John 410
Highwater, Jamake 414
Himmelfarb, Gertrude 417
Hine, Daryl 420
Hoffman, Alice 422
Hofmann, Gert 424
Hofstadter, Douglas R. 428
Hood, Hugh 431
Hood, Stuart 435
Hope, Christopher 437
Hughes, David 439
Hughes, Robert 441
Hulme, Keri 444
Ibuse Masuji 446

Ingalls, Rachel 449
Innaurato, Albert 451
Inoue Yasushi 454
Jandl, Ernst 458
Johnson, Denis 460
Jolley, Elizabeth 463
Josipovici, Gabriel 467
Keane, Molly 469
Keegan, John 473
Kelly, Robert 476
Kempowski, Walter 478
Kerman, Joseph 481
Kincaid, Jamaica 484
King, Stephen 486
Klíma, Ivan 489
Konwicki, Tadeusz 491
Kristeva, Julia 496
Kunze, Reiner 500
La Guma, Alex 502
Lacouture, Jean 504
L'Amour, Louis 508
Le Goff, Jacques 512
Le Sueur, Meridel 516
Leithauser, Brad 520
Leonard, Elmore 522
Lerner, Laurence 525
Lettau, Reinhard 530
Levi, Primo 531
Liddell, Robert 535
Lispector, Clarice 538
Liu Binyan 542
Longley, Michael 544
Lopate, Phillip 547
Lopez, Barry Holstun 549
Lu Wenfu 552
Ludlum, Robert 554
Lyall, Gavin 556
MacEwen, Gwendolyn 558
Mack, Maynard 561
Mack Smith, Denis 563
Maclean, Norman 566
Mahapatra, Jayanta 571
Malcolm, Janet 574
Mandel, Eli 577
Mándy, Iván 579
Mano, D. Keith 583
Marechera, Dambudzo 586
Mason, Bobbie Ann 588
Mathews, Harry 591
Matthews, William 596
McGinley, Patrick 599
Mellers, Wilfred Howard 602
Mewshaw, Michael 605
Miller, J. Hillis 607
Morgan, Frederick 611

Morris, Richard B. 614
Motion, Andrew 617
Munro, Alice.....................................621
Murray, Les A....................................627
Muschg, Adolf 630
Naipaul, Shiva 634
Naylor, Gloria 636
Newby, Eric.......................................639
Nichols, John.....................................642
Niedecker, Lorine 645
Nkosi, Lewis......................................647
Norman, Marsha 650
O'Brien, Tim 652
Ōe Kenzaburo.....................................655
O'Faolain, Julia 658
Olds, Sharon......................................661
Oliver, Mary......................................664
Osborn, Paul......................................667
Padilla, Heberto.................................669
Palmer, Michael S..............................671
Pastan, Linda.....................................673
Patterson, Orlando..............................676
Pavlović, Miodrag 680
Perec, Georges 683
Petrakis, Harry Mark..........................686
Phillips, Jayne Anne 688
Plimpton, George...............................691
Popescu, Dumitru Radu 694
Portis, Charles 697
Prose, Francine 698
Rakosi, Carl......................................700
Ratushinskaya, Irina 704
Rendell, Ruth 707
Rezzori, Gregor von 710
Rhodes, Richard 713
Roa Bastos, Augusto 715
Rodgers, Carolyn M............................718
Rubens, Bernice.................................721
Rumens, Carol...................................723
Russell, Peter 727
Rybakov, Anatoly Naumovich 730
el-Saadawi, Nawal..............................733
Sacks, Oliver.....................................737
Sanford, John....................................740
Sánta, Ferenc 744
Schaeffer, Susan Fromberg..................748
Schickel, Richard 750
Schwartz, Lynne Sharon 753
Scliar, Moacyr...................................756
Segal, Lore 758
Semprun, Jorge 761
Seton, Cynthia Propper.......................764
Shabtai, Yaakov.................................766
Shapiro, Harvey.................................768
Sharpe, Tom 771

Sheehan, Susan 773
Simmons, James.................................776
Simon, Kate......................................778
Smith, Dave......................................781
Souster, Raymond 784
Spence, Jonathan D. 787
Spinrad, Norman 791
Stander, Siegfried..............................794
Steel, Ronald 796
Stone, Lawrence.................................800
Strauss, Botho...................................802
Sukenick, Ronald...............................805
Swift, Graham 808
Szabó, Magda 810
Szymborska, Wisława 815
Takamura Kōtarō 817
Tanikawa Shuntarō.............................820
Taylor, Charles 822
Taylor, Henry 825
Tennant, Emma..................................828
Thompson, E. P..................................832
Thompson, Flora 835
Thompson, Hunter S. 838
Tindall, Gillian 842
Todorov, Tzvetan...............................844
Tomkins, Calvin.................................848
Toulmin, Stephen 851
Tsaloumas, Dimitris 854
Turner, Fred 856
Valenzuela, Luisa...............................860
Vliet, R. G...863
Walker, Margaret...............................865
Walser, Robert Otto............................869
Wang Meng 873
Wasserstein, Wendy...........................875
Welch, James.....................................877
White, Edmund 880
Whitman, Ruth...................................882
Wideman, John Edgar 885
Wieners, John 888
Wilcox, James....................................890
Williams, Thomas 894
Wilson, A. N......................................896
Wilson, August 901
Wilson, William S...............................904
Wittkower, Rudolf..............................908
Wolfe, Gene......................................911
Yang Jiang 913
Yasuoka Shōtarō................................914
Yoshiyuki Junnosuke..........................918
Zhang Jie 921
Zhang Xianliang 923

KEY TO PRONUNCIATION

ā	āle	ō	ōld	ü	Pronounced approximately as ē, with rounded lips: French u, as in *menu* (mə·nü); German ü, as in *grün*
â	câre	ô	ôrb		
a	add	o	odd		
ä	ärm	oi	oil		
		o͞o	o͞oze		
ē	ēve	o͝o	fo͝ot		
e	end	ou	out		
				ə	the schwa, an unstressed vowel representing the sound that is spelled
g	go				
					a as in sofa
ī	ice	*th*	the͡n		e as in fitted
i	ill	th	thin		i as in edible
					o as in melon
ĸ	German *ch* as in *ich* (iĸ)	ū	cūbe		u as in circus
		û	ûrn; French eu, as in *jeu* (zhû), German ö, *oe*, as in *schön* (shûn), *Goethe* (gû′te)	zh	azure
ɴ	Not pronounced, but indicates the nasal tone of the preceding vowel, as in the French *bon* (bôɴ)			′	= main accent
				″	= secondary accent
		u	tub		

PREFACE

As *World Authors* moves into the last decade of the twentieth century, it may be useful to re-examine its goals. Now that *world* has assumed truly global dimensions, no longer primarily Europe and the northern half of the Western hemisphere, *World Authors 1980–1985* includes an even larger number than had its predecessors of writers from Latin America, Africa, the Middle East, and Asia. And as in earlier volumes in this series, the word *authors* stretches to many areas besides fiction, poetry, drama, and belles lettres to include authors who, while specialists in their professional disciplines, have also written books of interest to the general reader: journalists, historians, philosophers, and social, political, and natural scientists.

World Authors strives to represent the most significant writing produced during the five-year period that each volume covers and to offer not only a biographical account but also a comprehensive survey of each author's achievement. To attempt this within the limits of a single volume means, inevitably and regretably, that there will be omissions in coverage. These, however, will be corrected in later volumes, just as the present volume includes some writers whose major works were published as long as forty or fifty years ago, but who have come into current prominence through new editions or recent English-language translations (Mikhail Bakhtin, René Crevel, Vasily Grossman, Meridel Le Sueur, John Sanford, Flora Thompson, Rudolf Wittkower).

We are grateful to the many authors who supplied us with autobiographical sketches and/or biographical and bibliographical material and to the contributors to this volume listed on page xii. We also acknowledge with warm thanks those who made substantial contributions to the planning, editing, and production of this volume: Howard Batchelor, Laurie Brown, Bruce R. Carrick, Andrew C. Kimmens, Henrietta Koffi, Diane Price, Norris Smith, and John Stone.

V. C.
December 1990

CONTRIBUTORS

Leslie A. Adelson
Stephen Akey
Steven Anzovin
David Bellos
Basil M. Boland
Tom Clyde
Robert A. Colby
Adam Czerniawski
Marcella Driscoll
S. Eile
Caryl Emerson
Suzanne Erena
Tamara S. Evans
Van C. Gessel
M. E. Grenander
Lucia Guerre-Cunningham
James V. Hatch
George Held
Ruth Herschberger
C. Kanaganayakam
Takis Kayalis
Alan F. Keele
Rolf Kieser
Andrew C. Kimmens

Lawrence Klepp
Rosette C. Lamont
Neil Lazarus
Robert E. Long
Lev Loseff
Catharine Nepomnyashchy
Rob Nixon
David H. Richter
Martin Robbins
Miriam Rosen
Natalie Ross
Hiroaki Sato
Shen Jun
Norris Smith
Stephen Stepanchev
Stefan Stoenescu
Robert R. Sullivan
Albert Tezla
Peter N. Thomas
John W. Treat
Timothy Tung
John Wakeman
Michiko N. Wilson

WORLD AUTHORS   1980–1985

WORLD LEADERS 1900-1965

WORLD AUTHORS 1980–1985

ABBEY, EDWARD (January 29, 1927–March 14, 1989), American novelist, essayist, and environmentalist, was born in Home, Pennsylvania, the son of Paul Revere (a farmer) and Mildred Postlewaite (a teacher) Abbey. Raised on a farm in the Appalachian mountains of Pennsylvania, Abbey served in the U.S. Army in Italy in 1945–1946. He received his B.A. (1951) and M.A. (1956) degrees from the University of New Mexico, and also attended the University of Edinburgh and Stanford University. In 1965 he married Judith Pepper, by whom he had two sons; following his wife's death in 1970 he remarried, and had three other children. From 1956 to 1971, Abbey worked as a park ranger and fire lookout for the National Park Service in the Southwest, an experience fundamental to his career as a naturalist and commentator, in novels and essays, on the wilderness areas of Arizona, New Mexico, and Utah.

Although Abbey's first novel, *Jonathan Troy*, was set in Pennsylvania, it foreshadows his later fiction since its young hero, in his conflicts and disappointments in the industrialized East, constantly dreams of the American West as a place of escape and freedom. His second novel, *The Brave Cowboy*, later adapted for the screen as *Lonely Are the Brave*, is set in New Mexico, but in it the radical freedom of which Jonathan Troy has dreamed is shown to be anachronistic. A kind of embodiment of frontier anarchic freedom, the young cowboy, John Burns, defies constraints of various kinds, refusing to accommodate himself to the demands of modern urban civilization. Escaping from jail, he is pursued by a vast posse, equipped with cars and radios, helicopters and airplanes. Burns successfully eludes the mechanized posse only to be killed accidentally, crossing a new superhighway on his horse, by a truck loaded with bathroom fixtures. His story becomes an elegy for an earlier-day romantic freedom that can no longer exist in a cramped technological society in which the value and importance of the individual have been scaled down almost to the vanishing point. *The Brave Cowboy* was followed by *Fire on the*

EDWARD ABBEY

Mountain, also made into a film, concerned with similar conflicts and themes. In *Fire on the Mountain*, the tough old rancher John Vogelin fights a losing battle against the encroachments upon his land of the expanding White Sands missile range. Martin Levin, in the *New York Times Book Review*, remarked that "if Mr. Abbey oversimplifies the twentieth century a bit by making White Sands a locus of pure evil, he states his case with a lyricism that is highly persuasive."

Abbey's next book, *Desert Solitaire*, a collection of autobiographical essays, attracted widespread praise and was perceived by some reviewers as a "minor classic." In *Desert Solitaire*, Abbey relates his experience as a park ranger and fire lookout in southeastern Utah, and reflects upon the spoliation of the wilderness by tourism. "His strongest polemic," Alan Ternes remarked in *Audubon* magazine, "is against the National Park Service's catering to the 'indolent millions born on wheels and suckled on gasoline who expect and demand highways to lead them in comfort, ease and safety' to every nook and corner of the national parks. The writer is brash and biased, but ever sensitive to the beauties and wonders of nature." In a similar vein Freeman Tilden, in *National Parks Magazine*, considered the book strongly biased, but acknowledged that "we need angry young men to remind us that there is plenty we should be angry about, and scattered all through his volume are just, biting statements we shall do well to heed. . . . Abbey is an artist in words. There are pages and pages of delicious prose, sometimes almost magical in their evocation of the desert scene." A. C. Ames, in the *Washington Post Book World*, observed that "from now on, no one should visit southeastern Utah without first reading this book but, informative as it is, *Desert Solitaire* is literature, not just a guide book. It is an eloquent expression of tense, vehement, joyous being." The noted naturalist Edwin Way Teale, in the *New York Times Book Review*, endorsed the book as "passionately felt" and "deeply poetic," an account "set down in lean, racing prose, in a close-knit style of power and beauty."

Abbey's fourth novel, *Black Sun*, is a curious love story set on the Grand Canyon's North Rim. Like Abbey himself in *Desert Solitaire*, Will Gatlin, the hero, is a fire warden who lives alone in a cabin under a tower that overlooks the forest land. Thirty-seven and divorced, an ex-college teacher who became disaffected with the classroom, Gatlin meets a young girl, Sandy, and they have a brief love affair before she disappears into the Canyon country. Edward Hoagland, in the *New York Times Book Review*, observed that *Black Sun* "is not a masterpiece [like *Desert Solitaire*]. It's a treat, a light, indeterminate book, a stopover, almost perfectly written but with the beginning and the end left untold." Other critics found the novel self-indulgent. The reviewer for the *New Yorker* called it an "embarrassingly bad novel . . . a kind of pipedream . . . the ranger, a broken-hearted social dropout, meets a girl—a sweet little wide-eyed nineteen-year-old virgin who likes to bathe by candlelight—deflowers her in the Lawrencian thou art-a-good-lass style, and then loses her somewhere down in the Grand Canyon. Pretentious, witless, sentimental, it has but one virtue—its length, which is a scant fifty thousand words."

The Monkey Wrench Gang, on the other hand, was highly praised. On a white-water float trip down the Colorado River, four maverick individuals meet—Seldom Seen Smith, an outcast Mormon; Bonnie Abbzug, an exile from the Bronx; Doc Sarvis, M. D., whose hobby is the destruction of billboards; and George Washington Hayduke, a foul-tongued ex–Green Beret and Viet Cong medic with a formidable knowledge of explosives. Comparing notes, they decide to team up as eco-raiders, declaring war on strip miners and highway, dam, and bridge builders. The result is chaos and comedy. The reviewer for *Audubon* magazine called Abbey's crew "raunchy, courageous, and a delight." Similarly, the reviewer for the *New York Times Book Review* described the work as an "extravagant, finely written tale," and David Robinson, in the *Times Literary Supplement*, called it "compulsively readable and extremely funny: a must for any eco-freak's reading list." Sheldon Frank, in the *National Observer*, had mixed feelings about the novel but was on the whole positive in his reactions. It is, he wrote, "a sad, hilarious, exuberant, vulgar fairy tale filled with long chase sequences and careful conspiratorial scheming. As in all fairy tales, the characters are pure cardboard, unbelievable in every respect. But they are delightful. . . . [Abbey] is a good man and a superb prose stylist, and he has written an entertaining, infuriating book." A sequel, *Hayduke Lives*, was published posthumously.

After *The Monkey Wrench Gang*, Abbey published further fiction dealing with environmental themes, and a large number of essay collections concerned with his experiences in the Southwest and other areas. *Abbey's Road* describes a personal odyssey through the Rio Grande Country in Texas and Canyonlands National Park in Utah, as well as his excursions to Scotland, the interior of Australia, and the Sierra Madre in Mexico. *Beyond the Wall* ranges widely from the deserts of the Southwest and the Baja peninsula of Mexico to the Kungakut River of Alaska. *Slumgullion Stew* includes both fiction and essays from thirty years of his writing. Reviewing the book in *Sierra* magazine, Don Scheese remarked that it "seems safe to say that Abbey is today's most well-known nature writer."

Abbey died at sixty-two at his home in Oracle, Arizona. He was survived by his second wife, Clarke, and five children. In a memorial piece in the *New York Times Book Review*, Edward Hoagland recalled Abbey: "Personally, he was a labyrinth of anger and generosity, shy but arresting because of his mixture of hillbilly and cowboy qualities, and even when silent he appeared bigger than life. . . . He was uneven and self-indulgent as a writer and often scanted his talent by working too fast. But he had about him an authenticity that springs from the page and is beloved by a rising generation of readers."

PRINCIPAL WORKS: *Fiction*—Jonathan Troy, 1956; The Brave Cowboy, 1958; Fire on the Mountain, 1962; Black Sun, 1971; The Monkey Wrench Gang, 1975;

Good News, 1979; The Fool's Progress, 1988; Hayduke Lives, 1990. *Non-fiction*—Desert Solitaire, 1968; Appalachia, 1970; Sunset Canyon, 1971; Slickrock, 1971; Cactus Country, 1973; The Journey Home, 1977; The Hidden Canyon, 1978; Abbey's Road, 1979; Desert Images, 1979; Down the River, 1982; Beyond the Wall, 1984; In Praise of Mountain Lions, 1984; One Life at a Time, Please, 1987; Rock Salt & Cherry Pie, 1988; Vox Clamantis in Deserto: Some Notes from a Secret Journal, 1989. *Collections (short stories and essays)*—Slumgullion Stew, 1984; The Best of Edward Abbey, 1988.

ABOUT: Abbey, E. Desert Solitaire, 1968; Contemporary Authors New Revision Series 2, 1981; Contemporary Literary Criticism 36, 1986; McCann, G. Edward Abbey, 1977. *Periodicals*—Audubon March–April 1968; National Observer September 6, 1975; National Parks Magazine February 1968; New York Review of Books August 18, 1988; New York Times March 15, 1989; New York Times Book Review September 30, 1962; January 28, 1968; June 13, 1971; November 14, 1976; February 28, 1988; December 18, 1988; May 7, 1989; February 4, 1990; New Yorker April 6, 1968; July 17, 1971; Newsweek January 5, 1976; Progressive July 1976; Times Literary Supplement December 1, 1978; October 20, 1989; Washington Post Book World March 27, 1968.

ACKROYD, PETER (October 5, 1949–), British novelist, biographer, poet and critic, writes: "I was born in London in 1949, went to a Catholic school—St Benedict's—in that city and then in 1968 was accepted at Clare College, Cambridge, where I studied English literature. I graduated with double first class honours and then in 1971 travelled to Yale University as a Mellon Fellow; I remained there for two years and, in 1973, returned to England. In that year I became literary editor of *The Spectator*—at which post I remained until I became managing editor of that magazine in 1977. I resigned from the post in 1981 in order to take up a career as a full time writer—a career I am currently (1987) pursuing. I have won the Somerset Maugham Prize (1984), the Guardian Fiction Award (1985), the Whitbread Prize for Best Biography (1984/1985), and the Whitbread Prize for Best Novel (1986). I am a Fellow of the Royal Society of Literature. Apart from my work as a novelist and a biographer, I am chief book reviewer for *The Times.*"

Peter Ackroyd's terse account of his career outlines but does not emphasize his remarkable versatility as a writer. Within one year, 1984–1985, he produced a major literary biography, *T. S. Eliot*, and a major novel, *Hawksmoor.* He

PETER ACKROYD

is also a poet, a literary critic, and a film and book reviewer. It would be disingenuous to suggest that Ackroyd has had equal success in all these endeavors. His poetry has attracted attention more for its eccentricity than for its intellectual and/or emotional appeal. "Peter Ackroyd makes not only an odd poetry, but a poetry out of the oddness of the world, which is much more difficult and a good deal more entertaining," the *Times Literary Supplement* wrote of his *London Lickpenny*, a small (35-page) collection of literary collages, found poetry, and short prose essays; "for the most part total incomprehensibility on a rational level . . . [that here yields] many rather beautiful effects as well as some agreeably comic ones." An engaging example—certainly not incomprehensible—is "Among School Children," its title borrowed from Yeats but the poem uniquely Ackroyd's:

And everyone heard the wrong story
   my terrific love-cries
   are probably for sale
the technician said, "these poems are a wounded
   fawn":

oh the strange story of the quantum!
   if I smile will she smile
   no one smiles, your eyes
   are like broken glass are
   you unemployed?

What do these words mean? (a) love-cries
(b) quantum (c) unemployed.
Have you ever met anyone with eyes
like broken glass? If you have, write about it.
If not, would you like to? Why?
Read the poem again, and think about
the last lines. Why was nobody smiling?

Try to explain in your own words how
the writer felt when he saw the girl
with eyes like broken glass.

As a critic Ackroyd has displayed a wide-ranging perspective. Reviewing books and films for the *Spectator* and the London *Times*, he can appreciate a popular American film star like John Travolta ("The discothèque dancing, the hair drenched in Brylcreem, the hoola-hoop lyrics, all concealed his facility before the camera," he wrote in the *Spectator*, November 24, 1979). He can also attack the entire canon of academic English studies and "the impoverishment of a national culture," as he does in *Notes for a New Culture: An Essay on Modernism*. Here his targets are the traditional humanism and literary realism of much contemporary English writing. Describing his book as "a polemic and an extended essay against our declining national culture," Ackroyd turns to European modernism, the post-structural and deconstructionist movement in France, in particular the writings of Roland Barthes and Jacques Derrida, for a revitalization of language based on "the affirmation of difference and incongruity." He faults much modern English writing—critics like F. R. Leavis and Raymond Williams, novelists like John Braine and Kingsley Amis, poets like Ted Hughes and Sylvia Plath—for seeking values and imposing interpretation and meaning. He favors instead the "new" novel of Alain Robbe-Grillet, which rejects moral-rational visions of reality for pure form, and the poetry of the New York School (Frank O'Hara, John Ashbery), which creates "a unique space for the experience of subjectivity."

Notes for a New Culture had a generally unfavorable critical reception, even from writers who are not unsympathetic to the modernism Ackroyd advocated. David Lodge, for example, wrote in the *New Statesman* that the book "makes it easy to understand why literary criticism is falling into neglect and disrepute as a mode of humane discourse." Lodge agreed that England "has much to gain from Continental theory and practise," but he found Ackroyd's approach intimidating and obscure. "A prime inspiration for [this] book is Nietzsche, who said, 'There are no facts, only interpretations'—a suggestive but easily abused proposition." Ackroyd himself seems to have moved away from his extreme position in his subsequent work. *Ezra Pound and His World*, profusely illustrated with photographs of Pound, his friends, and the places where he lived, is a highly condensed biography and critical introduction to the poet. Considering the limitations of space and the controversial character of its subject, the book is remarkably thorough and even-handed. Ackroyd writes lucidly on Pound's poetry, describing its "disconnectedness" as "a deliberate technique to exert the maximum strength from the words on the page . . . a transcript of the workings of the possessed imagination," but observes that the poet failed to impose the same discipline on his life and his political prejudices. "Pound's commitment to Fascism is not easy to explain . . . [his] temperament was an obsessive one . . . he was impatient with anything other than neat and speedy solutions: Fascism offered them." The tragic result was that he "retreated into a private world of fantasy from which he never fully escaped."

Writing a full-length biography of T. S. Eliot posed even greater challenges, not least of which were the restrictions imposed by the Eliot estate on quoting from unpublished material or—except only briefly within a critical context—from his published works. Ackroyd had access to a large number of letters and unpublished records but could only summarize their contents and allude in general terms to information on which the reader craves specific details. Nevertheless he produced a comprehensive and fair-minded book that is likely to remain the definitive biography for some years to come. John Updike, in the *New Yorker*, noted its "virtues of solidity and fairness"; A. Walton Litz, in the *New York Times Book Review*, called it "as good a biography as we have any right to expect"; Rosemary Dinnage, in the *New York Review of Books*, felt that the book fulfilled Eliot's own criteria for a poet's biography: "the biographer of an author should possess some critical ability; he should be a man of taste and judgment, appreciative of the man whose biography he undertakes." In 1989 Ackroyd was working on a biography of Charles Dickens and considering, as a future prospect, a biography of William Blake.

Biography is always to some degree a reinvention of its subject. Much of Ackroyd's fiction extends that function of biography. His characters often have their roots in historical reality or in works of imaginative literature, but they are transformed into fictional characters. Ackroyd's first published novel, *The Great Fire of London*, deals with the re-invention in film of Charles Dickens's novel of prison life, *Little Dorrit*. A director is shooting his film about a modern-day London prison, but little by little the characters who weave in and out of his tangled professional and personal life become submerged in the past and possessed by Dickens's characters. The parallels are not forced and exact, but they evoke a haunting Dickensian spirit. More daring, perhaps, was Ackroyd's re-invention of a famous literary-historical personality in *The Last Testament of Oscar Wilde*, written in the form of a journal kept by Wilde in the last years of his life in Paris. Assuming Wilde's voice in what one commentator called "consummate ventriloquism," Ackroyd attempts to probe the mind of the now humiliated and impoverished exile: "Like Semele who longed to see God and was wrapped in fire which consumed her, so I longed for fame and was destroyed by it. I thought, in my days of purple and gold, that I could reveal myself to the world and instead the world has revealed itself to me." Ackroyd's Wilde reviews his life candidly and without self-pity: "I thought I could mingle in the sensuous world without shame or loss, and come back from it with fresh perceptions," but he discovers that his contemporaries angrily reject him: "They did not wish to see their sins in any light—not even one which refined them, and made them the elements of a new spirituality in which the fine instinct for beauty was the dominant characteristic." The critics received both these novels as virtuoso exercises. "The book is as well done as it might be," the *Virginia Quarterly Review* observed of *The Last Testament of Oscar Wilde*, "given the need to do it at all." Galen Strawson, in the *Times Literary Supplement*, summed up *The Great Fire of London* as "an oddly artless novel" without a strong design, "often curiously perfunctory in its details," but fascinating for "some very poignant sketches of people together . . . simply failing to think properly about each other, failing to take each other seriously."

Strawson also noted that "Ackroyd is clearly intrigued by the idea of past fiction working great changes in present (fictional) reality." Nowhere is this idea better demonstrated than in *Hawksmoor*, the time of which shuttles back and forth from late seventeenth–early eighteenth century to contemporary London. The two principal characters are fictitious—Nicholas Dyer, an architect who designs churches for the historical Christopher Wren, and a modern-day detective, Nicholas Hawksmoor, the namesake of the historical architect (and assistant to Wren) Nicholas Hawksmoor, who lived from 1661 to 1736. The fictional Hawksmoor, a Scotland Yard inspector, is trying to solve a series of contemporary murders apparently committed by the eighteenth-century Dyer. Ackroyd told an interviewer: "I am not sure whether it's a historical novel set in the present or a contemporary novel set in the past. That's one of the puzzles the book sets for itself." One certainty, however, is that the novel is haunting, indeed hallucinatory. Nicholas Dyer is a Satan-worshipper living in the filth and squalor of superstition- and plague-ridden London and writing his memoir in a re-

markably faithful style: "My Inke is very bad; it is thick at the bottom, but thin and waterish at the Top, so that I must write according as I dip my Pen. These Memories become meer shortened Phrases, dark at their Beginning but growing faint towards their End, and each separated so, one from another, that I am not all of a peece." The sinister, murky atmosphere of East London past and present, the alienation and ultimately the obsessions of both characters, draw them together into a mysterious but inevitable confrontation. Several reviewers noted echoes of T. S. Eliot's mordant vision of "a purgatorial London." Allan Hollinghurst, in the *Times Literary Supplement*, wrote: "There is an Eliotic mood to it . . . What Ackroyd may be saying is that time present and time past are both present in time future." But Hollinghurst concluded that the novel "does not, alas, sustain that conviction; for all its sporadic brilliance and intricacy it has a lowering effect. It is a dark, cold novel, almost wholly untouched by altruism or responsibility." Joyce Carol Oates, in the *New York Times Book Review*, also detected "an unmistakably Eliotic tone" in the book, but concluded more favorably that "*Hawksmoor* is an unfailingly intelligent work of the imagination."

Chatterton, published two years after *Hawksmoor*, is another example of the serio-comic semiotic games that Ackroyd plays in his fiction. Again he weaves back and forth in time and mingles imaginary characters with historically real people. The "real" here is the eighteenth-century Thomas Chatterton, who won brief fame as a forger of medieval poetry and immortality as a gifted poet who committed suicide at eighteen when his forgery was discovered. Ackroyd imagines a Chatterton who forged not only medieval poetry but his own suicide and lived on to forge other poems for profit. His fictitious twentieth-century central character makes this discovery and becomes involved in a network of fakery and deceit. Like *Hawksmoor*, *Chatterton* is a demonstration of deconstruction at work, undermining its complicated plot even as it develops. It is simultaneously intriguing as an intellectual exercise and exasperating as a novel. Reviewing the book in the *Times Literary Supplement*, Martin Dodsworth praised its "inventive power" but confessed to impatience and frustration in reading it: "*Chatterton* sustains itself perfectly as an idea; but if art is about feeling as well as ideas . . . then *Chatterton* is vulnerable to criticism. Its stylistic strategy, so brutal in its treatment of the reader, while it may be justified as an idea may not prove tolerable in practice. Its refusal of representation may, if the reader neglects or even rejects the novel's idea, look suspiciously like the alibi for a failure to represent what in a slipshod way could be called reality."

Ackroyd's next novel, *First Light*, was advertised as "a giant leap away from the urban worlds of *Hawksmoor* and *Chatterton*." It takes place entirely in the present and appears to have no dominating literary or artistic motif in its background, as his earlier novels all had. However, the reader is not far into the novel before discovering a conspicuous literary ghost—Thomas Hardy. Set in Dorset, with characters named Clare, Damian, and a dog named Jude, incidents that frequently recall Hardy's novel *Two on a Tower*, a few characters who speak in Wessex dialect, a larger number of characters of distinctly eccentric habits, and a plot that involves an archaeological dig on the site of neolithic ruins of a prehistoric Britain, *First Light* is a virtuoso display. Claude Rawson, reviewing the book for the *Times Literary Supplement*, wrote: "One sometimes suspects in Ackroyd the Oscar Wilde penchant for building a whole scene or paragraph for the sake of a piece of phrase-making or a nugget of observation"; but, Rawson continues, "Ackroyd is probably the funniest reporter of both male and female camp now in business." His characters neither act nor speak like "real" people. But his eye and ear for the manners, mannerisms, eccentricities and jargon of his contemporaries—lesbians, homosexuals, the pompous and pretentious of both sexes—are sharp. And if his characters strike some of his readers as artful constructions rather than as genuinely realistic, he has a ready answer: "I know people say I can't create 'real' characters. But I'm not interested in writing moral tracts about human behaviour. I'm not interested in being realistic. Television can give you all the realism you want. TV and cinema have co-opted so much of the territory once available to the novelist. Now it is paramount for the novelist that he find other ways of dealing with reality than the merely human."

PRINCIPAL WORKS: *Poetry*—London Lickpenny, 1973; Country Life, 1978; The Diversions of Purley, 1987. *Novels*—The Great Fire of London, 1982; The Last Testament of Oscar Wilde, 1983; Hawksmoor, 1985; Chatterton, 1987; First Light, 1989. *Non-fiction*—Notes for a New Culture: An Essay on Modernism, 1976; Dressing Up: Transvestism and Drag: The History of an Obsession, 1979; T. S. Eliot; A Life, 1984; Ezra Pound and His World, 1989; Dickens, 1990.

ABOUT: Contemporary Novelists, 4th ed., 1986; *Periodicals*—New Statesman March 19, 1976; New York Review of Books December 20, 1984; April 14, 1988; New York Times Book Review December 16, 1984; September 19, 1986; January 17, 1988; September 17, 1989; New Yorker March 25, 1985; Spectator January 30, 1982; September 29, 1984; (London) Sunday Times Magazine April 9, 1989; Times Literary Supplement May 3, 1974; December 7, 1979; January 29, 1982; September 21, 1984; September 11–17, 1987; April 28, 1989; August 31, 1990.

ADAMS, ALICE (August 14, 1926–   ), American novelist and short-story writer, was born in Fredericksburg, Virginia, where she spent her childhood and adolescent years. Her father, Nicholson Barney Adams, was a professor of Spanish at the University of North Carolina at Chapel Hill, and her mother, Agatha Erskine Boyd Adams, had writing aspirations that, according to Alice Adams in a 1980 interview in *Story Quarterly,* were unfulfilled. Her mother, Adams said, "was depressed, unhappy, and peripherally involved with the literary world." The Adams farmhouse near Chapel Hill had a tennis court and swimming pool, and her parents "entertained a lot"; but Adams and her parents remained "three different, isolated people." Of herself Adams remarked: "[I] was one of those rotten little kids who write poetry. I grew up in a semi-intellectual atmosphere and I was encouraged. . . . I was bright in school and ran into trouble because of that Southern thing that women are supposed to be stupid." At sixteen, she entered Radcliffe College in Cambridge, and after graduating in 1946 moved to New York City where she worked briefly in publishing.

In 1947 Adams married Mark Linenthal, Jr., and the couple went to France where her husband did graduate work at the Sorbonne. After returning to the U.S. they moved to California, where Linenthal studied and taught English, joining the faculty at San Francisco State University in 1954 and completing his doctorate at Stanford in 1957. Adams' only child, Peter Adams Linenthal, was born in San Francisco in 1951. During the 1950s Adams wrote short stories, and attempted novels without success, and her marriage ended in divorce in 1958. In the mid-1960s, Adams met Robert K. McNie, an interior designer, with whom she has lived since that time. During the 1960s Adams's stories began to be published in "women's magazines," and by 1969 in the *New Yorker.* "Success came late," she has said. "I wasn't even earning a living at writing until I was over forty. I always had some kind of part-time job, the sort only available to women, which is to say secretarial."

Adams' first novel, *Careless Love,* published in England as *The Fall of Daisy Duke,* depicted the disappointing affairs of a divorced woman

ALICE ADAMS

and was better received abroad than in the U.S. The *New York Times Book Review,* however, was quite favorable. "Miss Adams," the reviewer observed, "renders Daisy's ordeal faithfully—even in its stretches of boredom—and with considerable wit . . . a fetching first novel." Adams' successes at this time were chiefly in the short story. Indeed, from 1971 to 1982 a story of hers was included in each consecutive issue of the short-story annual *Prize Stories: The O. Henry Awards.* It was not until 1975, with the publication of *Families and Survivors,* nominated for a National Book Critics Circle Award, that Adams came into prominence as a novelist. *Families and Survivors,* dealing with Adams' persistent theme of women who are "survivors," chronicles the lives of two friends, Louisa Calloway and Kate Flickinger, from their early adolescent years in the South in 1941, through the 1950s and 1960s, to a New Year's Eve party they attend in California at the commencement of the 1970s.

The reviewer for the *New Yorker* called *Families and Survivors* a "beautifully written, generous book. . . . As the girls go on to college, take lovers, marry, move to California, bear children—we see how youthful misconceptions, fantasies, grudges, missteps, and illusions gradually, subtly become definitions of a life. . . . Adams's sense of timing . . . is acute and her eye for detail is unvaryingly sensitive." Annie Gottlieb, in the *New York Times Book Review,* also commented on the observant and generous vision of the work. "Despite a slight tendency to idealize the young," she wrote, " to see in them the ice

onciliation, freedom, honesty Alice Adams wishes for her grownups—I can't think of a more perceptive, ironic and *kind* novel about the way we live now."

In 1976, following the success of *Families and Survivors,* Adams received a National Endowment for the Arts Fiction Grant, and in 1978 a John Simon Guggenheim Memorial Fellowship. However, her third novel received less than enthusiastic reviews. *Listening to Billie,* concerns Eliza, whose quest for herself takes her to California, where she becomes a successful poet. In the *New York Times Book Review,* Jane Larkin Crain began by praising Adams as a stylist. "Powered by the author's cool, spare prose," she remarked, "this novel creates beautiful surfaces—tableaux composed of sleek creatures perfectly arranged in elegant rooms, romantic, exquisitely detailed landscapes—that have an almost tactile quality for the reader, like fine wood and fabric." But she went on to complain of a "curious lifelessness" in the novel—and in Eliza herself. "The heroines of such novels," she observed, "eventually find 'fulfillment' in a kind of sanctified selfishness, with a total devotion to self and its 'needs' held up as salvatory. . . . [The novel] ultimately succeeds in banishing genuine feeling from its pages." R. Z. Sheppard, in *Time,* found Eliza unfocused. "The author's gelid, hearsay prose," he commented, " . . . tells but rarely shows us what happens. Most of the characters are sacrificed to vague sociological stereotypes. As a poet, Eliza is barely credible. Her special qualities of mind remain a secret that Novelist Adams seems unwilling to share."

The novel was quickly followed by *Beautiful Girl,* Adams' first collection of short stories, with settings ranging from Chapel Hill to New England to San Francisco. The collection was widely praised. James N. Baker, in *Newsweek,* remarked: "Instead of trying to dazzle us with verbal acrobatics or hammering away at ugly truths about society in the manner of many of her contemporaries, she writes elegant short stories that recall such past masters of the form as Flannery O'Connor and Katherine Mansfield. Like them, she offers fleeting, melancholy glimpses of ordinary people made extraordinary by her perception. These are old-fashioned stories, artfully simple in structure, rich in precise language and consistently moving in their examination of imperfect human relationships." Katha Pollitt, in the *New York Times Book Review,* observed that "the typical Alice Adams short story announces itself in the very first sentence as a thing of edgy wit and compressed narrative power. . . . [She] writes with a seductive grace that burnishes even a slight tale." But Pollitt also felt that "while deft and careful . . . her stories do not always dig deep enough into their subject to satisfy the interest their craftsmanship arouses."

Rich Rewards, Adams' fourth novel, is a first-person narrative recounting the experiences of Daphne White, a forty-year-old survivor of a divorce, numerous troubled love affairs, and the 1970s, who is offered a chance to start a new life with a Frenchman in Paris. Reviews of the novel were mixed. Victoria Glendinning, in the *Washington Post Book World,* for example, found much to admire in the work and much to object to. She thought *Rich Rewards* "often carelessly written" and Daphne never fully created. "Daphne has a literary bent," she pointed out, "and her 'intuitive flashes' are made much of. But the banality of most of her insights about life and behavior [does not] merit the importance they seem to be given." *To See You Again*, Adams' second collection of stories, with settings in California, Mexico, Europe, the South, and Washington, D. C., received many favorable notices. Rhonda Brammer, in the *Saturday Review*, remarked that "the best of these stories are charmingly precise—more deftly executed than Adams's novels . . . and more delicately complex than her first collection, *Beautiful Girl."* And Stephen Goodwin, in the *Washington Post Book World,* was impressed by the "formidable worldliness" of the tales.

Superior Women, Adams' novel of five Radcliffe girls and their subsequent experience of life, was widely regarded as a failure. Peter Prescott, in *Newsweek*, observed that "the superiority of these . . . young women derives principally from what their author is pleased to call their 'extreme intelligence.' Never in this novel does any woman exhibit anything more than a flicker of intuition—certainly not a shred of intelligence. . . . for two-thirds of her novel's course, Adams tells us what becomes of these women as the years roll by. For the readers, this means plodding through a formulaic sequence of vicissitudes. The experience might not be so dispiriting, had Adams been able to distance herself from her characters, had she developed some irony, some satire, some wit. *Superior Women* lacks all of these." A number of critics compared the novel unfavorably to Mary McCarthy's *The Group,* from which it was felt to derive. Yet Adams' next work, *Return Trips*, her third collection of short stories, was warmly received. Susan Schindehette, in the *Saturday Review,* spoke of Adams' "subtlety" and "quiet perception," making her an "absolute master of craft. . . . Characters learn things about themselves and the people they have loved— sometimes with stunning emotional impact. Throughout, there is a deep resonance of truths, large and small, told with glistening accuracy."

In several of her earlier short stories and in her novel *Superior Women* Alice Adams has explored the theme of maturing and aging. This subject finds its fullest development in her novel *Second Chances,* which Benjamin DeMott described in the *New York Times Book Review* as "a touching, subtle, truth-filled book." Her main characters, comfortably well-to-do and uncommonly articulate, are a group of friends who live in northern California. They are in their late sixties and early seventies—a generation rarely receiving justice and attention in modern fiction. "I have the perception that people talk about old age in two ways," Adams told an interviewer for the *New York Times Book Review.* "One is to focus on the horrors of it, not that they should be underestimated, and the other is to romanticize it." She does neither in this novel. Instead she recognizes their need for love and commitment and their reluctance to detach themselves from the vital issues of their times. The novel moves between their past, when they were actively engaged in the business of living, and their present, where they struggle to adjust to the realities of aging. DeMott considers *Second Chances* Adams' strongest book to date: "The strength flows partly from Ms. Adams' capacity to evoke fellow feeling, kindness and devotion as entirely natural inclinations of the heart. Her people care intensely for one another, and, although not beyond rage, seem beyond meanness."

Adams received a "Special Award for Continuing Achievement" in 1982 from the editors of *Prize Stories: The O. Henry Awards*—a prize given only twice before, to Joyce Carol Oates in 1970 and to John Updike in 1976. In 1980, Adams taught a writing course at the University of California and has since taught at Stanford. She lives today, as she has for many years, in San Francisco, the evocative setting of many of her tales.

PRINCIPAL WORKS: *Novels*—Careless Love, 1966 (in U.K. The Fall of Daisy Duke, 1967); Families and Survivors, 1974; Listening to Billie, 1978; Rich Rewards, 1980; Superior Women, 1984; Second Chances, 1988. *Short stories*—Beautiful Girl, 1979; To See You Again, 1982; Return Trips, 1985; After You've Gone, 1989.

ABOUT: Contemporary Authors 81–84, 1979; Contemporary Literary Criticism 6, 1976; 13, 1980, Dictionary of Literary Biography Yearbook: 1986, 1987; Who's Who in America, 1989–1990. *Periodicals*— New York Times September 7, 1984; New York Times Book Review May 22, 1966; May 16, 1985; February 26, 1978; January 14, 1979; September 1, 1985; May 1, 1988; October 8, 1989; Newsweek February 3, 1975; January 8, 1979; September 24, 1984; Saturday Review May 4, 1978; March 1982; November/December 1985; Story Quarterly #1, 1980; Time December 26, 1977; Washington Post Book World September 14, 1980; May 19, 1982.

ADLER, RENATA (October 19, 1938–), American novelist and non-fiction writer, was born in Milan, the third child and only daughter of Frederick L. Adler, a lawyer, and the former Erna Strauss, refugees from Nazi Germany. The Adler family immigrated to Danbury, Connecticut, when Renata was a small child. She graduated from Danbury High School, and in 1959, *summa cum laude*, from Bryn Mawr College. Two years later she earned a diploma in philosophy from the Sorbonne, where she studied under the philosopher Jean Wahl and the anthropologist Claude Lévi-Strauss. She then began work on a doctorate in comparative literature at Harvard University, but abandoned this course of study in 1962, when she was hired as a staff writer by the *New Yorker* magazine, a post she held until 1982. She has a master's degree from Harvard as well as a law degree from Yale, the latter obtained in 1979.

Adler's first book, *Toward a Radical Middle: Fourteen Pieces of Reporting and Criticism*, consists entirely of articles, all previously published in the *New Yorker*, on such varied topics as the march for nonviolence from Selma, Alabama, in April 1965, the Six-Day War between the Arab states and Israel in June 1967, and some typically incisive, opinionated reviews of books as different as J. P. Donleavy's *A Singular Man*, Herbert Gold's *Salt*, and the works of Jean Genet and Nathalie Sarraute. In her introduction, Adler sounds very much like a radical of the 1960s, demonstrating an unfocused anger, a disillusioned alienation, and a strong tendency toward generational generalization: "What I am trying to say is that if there is any age group that should loathe what is called the System in its bones that group is us. . . . I think the first post-war jolt the System had in its complacency, in our time, was not social or humanitarian, but technological: in 1957, when Sputnik went up. After that, there began to be a little room for change and mavericks, who, when there is not a desperate community lie at the heart of things, are the rule. . . . We have lived all through two sunny periods of lies, and seen some of the truth in both of them: the Eisenhower lie that the noble American experiment was complete, that all was well, that there was no need to move; and the Kennedy era lie that with glamour, image, and the instantaneous application of power you can gratify immediately, totally, those human concerns that are, in reality, met by inches, by years of work and suffering. I believe that the generation gap

RENATA ADLER

is in part an almost meteorological collision of those airs, the two lies of those years."

Wilfred Sheed, calling this collection "gracefully phrased, ardently intelligent," remarked that Adler's "literary criticism is always at the service of her general ideas, which means that esthetic judgments tend to come in at a slightly irregular angle." The *Newsweek* reviewer thought the articles "of reporting and criticism vibrate with control [and] confidence. . . . But if Miss Adler finally seems to be slightly repelled by almost everything and inclined to think of most people's performances as second rate, from this niggling and probably correct position she sees with chilling clarity."

Adler's *A Year in the Dark: Journal of a Film Critic* was a collection of reviews that had appeared in the *New York Times*. Upon the retirement in 1967 of Bosley Crowther, the *Times'* venerable film critic, Adler, to the surprise of many, was hired to replace him. From her first reviews in January 1968, her uncompromising critical posture led her into controversy. It was apparent from the start that she liked very few movies, and those she disliked she often disapproved of on moral grounds. She was, for example, implacably opposed to nudity and violence in films. Reviewing *In Cold Blood* and *The Dirty Dozen*, which later earned considerable success at the box office, she wrote, "Dwelling on pain or damage to the human body can [never] be morally or artistically valid." She quickly found herself the target of Hollywood's fury: in March 1968, only a little over two months after her critical debut in the *Times*, Lopert Pictures Corporation, a subsidiary of United Artists, took a full-page ad in the paper to condemn her, ironically contending that because of her dismissal of so many successful films, her negative review of its latest release, *Here We Go Round the Mulberry Bush*, was tantamount to an augury of success. The *Times'* editorial management supported her, and Adler, for neither the first nor last time in her career, found herself widely discussed: "I like movies," she told a reporter from *Newsweek* in April 1968, "and I like bad movies but that doesn't mean I have to say they're good. I'm not supposed to be drumming up trade for movies that I like or closing down movies that I don't like." Critical response to *A Year in the Dark* was generally favorable: she "writes uncommonly well," observed the *Newsweek* reviewer, " . . . the reviews, taken together and in sequence, unfold as a very special kind of drama: can an uncommonly sensitive young lady trained in the lofty art of philosophical argument and used to the leisurely craft of extruding *New Yorker* prose stoop to the harried business of clothing snap judgments about pop culture in the off-the-peg language imposed by daily deadlines, all the while managing to conquer her own loathing for the job enough to bring it off? More often than not, yes." Yet finally, bored with the sameness of the films she had to review, Adler quit the *New York Times* in late February 1969 and returned to the *New Yorker*.

She used her reacquired freedom from the pressure of deadlines to concentrate on writing fiction. The *New Yorker* published all she produced, including a story called "Brownstone," which appeared in January 1973 and won first prize in the O. Henry Short Story Awards for 1974. It is the narrative of an unnamed woman journalist who lives in New York and who attempts, over many disconnected paragraphs, to explain her life. She writes for a newspaper, lives off and on with a political scientist; her friends tend to annoy her; chance encounters bemuse or occasionally amuse her. Only her quirky, dry sense of humor never fails her, and she concludes, after much free-association, "When I wonder what it is that we are doing—in this brownstone, on this block, with this paper—the truth is probably that we are fighting for our lives." The story was praised by William Abrahams, editor of the O. Henry Prize Stories series, as a "realistic evocation of the serio-comic tone and detail of metropolitan life in the 1970s in America." Along with six other quite similar stories, "Brownstone" was revised and published in 1976 as a novel, *Speedboat*, which elicited widely divergent critical opinions. Calling Adler "a realist in miniature," Robert Towers remarked in the *New York Review of Books*, "the cumula-

tive effect of her book is dizzyingly surrealistic—and to my mind the impact is far greater than the deliberate, though perfunctory, surrealism to which so many contemporary 'serious' novelists resort. . . . Her style is luminiously exact, subtle in its rhythms, capable of both concrete immediacy and arresting generalizations. . . . *Speedboat* is neither boring nor dehumanized." Peter Prescott thought it "the quintessential 'New York book.' It's hard to imagine anyone west of the Hudson or south of Langley, Va., reading it with anything but indifference, or perhaps hostility. In fact, it's hard to imagine anyone at all being able to understand it twenty years hence—and yet if it were stashed in a time capsule and dug up a century from now it would be worth deciphering—a latter-day Linear B that would show how some of us lived and what passed for thought in the '70s."

Adler's second novel, *Pitch Dark*, is remarkably similar to *Speedboat* in tone and style. In three 50-page interconnected stories, the narrator, a woman journalist named Kate Ennis, recounts the protracted end of her love affair with an older married man and a disastrous escape on a holiday to Ireland, where a minor car accident leaves her feeling guilty, disgusted, and miserable. In her review, Anne Tyler described "the effect of an intelligent, wry, rather quirky woman lying awake in the small hours, staring at the ceiling and sorting over her life. There's the same reflectiveness, the same insomniac earnestness in her voice, the same eerie immediacy in the recollected voices of others. Curious and sometimes comical questions snag her attention. . . . As the fragments collect, the situation emerges. . . . If you read these fragments in hope of some forward motion—some conclusive final goal—you'll be disappointed. But if you simply allow them to settle in their own patterns, flashing light where they will, you'll find *Pitch Dark* a bright kaleidoscope of a book." Gary Giddens, on the other hand, called the novel "tiresome [and] foolish": "Adler can't be bothered with specifics. She wants something more, a mood; she arrives at something less, a sentimental accretion of generalizations, trivia, injokes, newspaper items, anecdotes and disquisitions (some clever, others sophomoric) on Homer, football, euthanasia, libel cases, newspaper bylines and computerized typewriters."

Armed with her new law degree, Adler next plunged headlong into the reporting of two of the most famous and contentious civil trials of the 1980s. The book she produced in 1986, *Reckless Disregard: Westmoreland v. CBS et al; Sharon v. Time*, became her most controversial. General William C. Westmoreland, commander of Allied forces during the Vietnam War, brought a case for libel in September 1982 against CBS for having aired the previous January a 90-minute documentary, "The Uncounted Enemy," a program purporting, in Adler's words, "to describe, for the first time, certain events in 1967, which, according to the program's opening statement, reflected 'a conspiracy at the highest levels of American military intelligence'—specifically, within the command and upon the orders of General William C. Westmoreland—'to suppress and alter critical intelligence on the enemy,' and to deceive the American people, Congress, the Joint Chiefs and the President of the United States about the strength, in numbers, of the North Vietnamese Army and the Vietcong." In June 1983 Ariel Sharon, then the Israeli defense minister, brought suit for libel in New York against *Time* magazine for suggesting, in its cover story of February 21, 1983, that Sharon, during a condolence visit to the family of Bashir Gemayel, the assassinated president-elect of Lebanon, told the family of the Israeli army's impending advance into West Beirut and that he expected the Christian Phalangist forces to go into the Palestinian refugee camps south of the city and there take revenge for Bashir's assassination.

The stories of both CBS and *Time* were widely reported throughout the world. They were, however, in Adler's view, false: the press, she held, acted with gross irresponsibility. "If there is a moral to be drawn from both cases . . . it seemed rather this: that received ideas, as so often upon examination in detail, happened to be wrong. The received, the right-minded, the liberal position in both cases was that the press defendants were protecting some valued and fragile Constitutional right against the assaults of whatever ideology was personified by two former military men. The reality had to do, rather, with the fragility, under the combined assault of modern newsgathering and contemporary litigation, of the shared sense of historic fact." *Reckless Disregard* caused an angry storm of critical and legal reaction; it was highly praised by the right and excoriated by the left. The book was "both fascinating reading and a formidable indictment," wrote Christopher Buckley. "Miss Adler's confluence of talent was well suited to these two trials, which, as she notes, 'brought together, in an almost astrological configuration, four immense and powerful constellations within the American system: the courts; the military; the lawyers; and the press.' One comes away from the book utterly dismayed by the latter two, and admiring of the first. The military falls somewhere in between." In John L. Hess's opinion, however, the author "goes beyond the paranoid right in assailing the media as a hateful

monolith whose nature the framers of the Bill of Rights could not have contemplated."

Adler was a Guggenheim Fellow in 1973–1974. *Speedboat* won the American Academy and Institute of Arts and Letters Award and the Ernest Hemingway Prize in 1976. In 1987 she was elected to the American Academy and Institute of Arts and Letters. She has very occasionally used the pseudonym Brett Daniels in contributions to publications other than the *New Yorker*. From January to August 1974, during the House Judiciary Committee's investigation into the impeachment of President Richard M. Nixon, Adler served as speech writer for the committee's chairman, Rep. Peter W. Rodino of New Jersey.

PRINCIPAL WORKS: *Non-fiction*—Toward a Radical Middle, 1969; A Year in the Dark, 1969; Reckless Disregard, 1986. *Fiction*—Speedboat, 1976; Pitch Dark, 1983.

ABOUT: Contemporary Authors New Revision Series 22, 1987; Contemporary Literary Criticism 8, 1978; 31, 1985; Current Biography 1984; Who's Who in America 1989–1990. *Periodicals*—America April 7, 1984; Atlantic October 1976; Choice March 1987; Columbia Journalism Review November–December 1986; Commentary June 1984, March 1987; Commonweal June 1, 1984; Harper's November 1976, February 1984; Library Journal February 15, 1970; March 1, 1970; September 15, 1976; December 15, 1983; February 1, 1987; Ms. November 1976; Nation November 6, 1976; February 18, 1984; November 29, 1986; National Review April 7, 1970; April 10, 1987; New Republic October 16, 1976; November 27, 1976; December 5, 1983; New York December 12, 1983; New York Review of Books November 25, 1976; August 14, 1980; March 15, 1984; February 26, 1987; New York Times January 28, 1970; September 23, 1976; December 5, 1983; December 27, 1983; August 28, 1986; October 25, 1986; November 6, 1986; New York Times Book Review March 29, 1970; September 26, 1976; January 2, 1977; December 18, 1983; November 9, 1986; Newsweek April 15, 1968; February 2, 1970; October 11, 1976; December 19, 1983; November 10, 1986; Saturday Review April 4, 1970; October 2, 1976; Spectator September 10, 1977; Time February 16, 1970; October 11, 1976; December 5, 1983; Times Literary Supplement August 26, 1977; July 20, 1984.

*AI QING (also rendered as AI CH'ING, pseudonym of Jiang Haicheng, formerly Chiang Hai-Cheng) (March 27, 1910–   ), Chinese poet, was born into a landlord's family in Jinhua county, Zhejiang province. Because of a fortune-teller's declaration that it was his fate to harm his parents, he was sent away to be nursed by a poor peasant woman until he was five. Not even having a name of her own, the woman was

AI QING

only known by the name of her village Da Yan He (Da Yan River). Ai Qing was to grow up to detest fortune-telling and all other feudal superstitions, but he has since harbored a special compassion for the poor, particularly his wet-nurse. Later, his poem "Da Yan He, Wo Di Bao Mu" (Da Yan He, My Wet-Nurse), dedicated to the peasant woman, was to establish his place firmly in modern Chinese literature.

While he was in primary school, he was already influenced in his thinking by the May 4th Movement of 1919. He loved painting as a boy. In 1928, he enrolled in the painting department of the West Lake National Institute of Fine Arts in Hangzhou. His talent discovered, at the urging of the Institute's director, his father dug up a thousand Mexican silver dollars from his savings and sent him to Paris the next year to further his study of painting. It was in Paris that he began to take an interest in literature, Soviet as well as Western. In poetry, Whitman, Rimbaud, Mayakovsky, and the Belgian poet Verhaeren were his idols. He stayed in Paris for three years, earning a living by working in a small lacquer factory run by Chinese. His first poem, "Gathering," was inspired by a meeting of the Great Anti-imperialist League he attended. When Japan invaded Manchuria in 1931, his patriotism was aroused, and, since his family could no longer afford to support him abroad, he decided to return home, arriving in Shanghai in March, 1932.

The now worldly youth was not happy in his hometown Jinhua. In May he went back to Shanghai, became active in radical politics and joined the League of Leftwing Artists. With friends he organized the Spring Soil Art Society to sponsor an exhibit. For his political activities he was arrested by the French police in the city's French Concession and thrown in jail, thus effectively ending his career as a painter. He began to write poetry to while away time. One of his first published poems was "Lu Di" (The Reed Pipe), printed in a magazine called Xiandai (The Modern Age). It was in prison that he wrote the widely acclaimed poem "Da Yan He, Wo Di Bao Mu," using plain and powerful language to speak to his love for the poor suffering common people. To avoid the suspicion of the prison authorities, he used a pen name, and Ai Qing the poet was thus born. He spent three years and three months in prison. In 1939, at his own expense, he published his first collection of poems entitled Da Yan He. It promptly aroused the attention of the novelist Ba Jin, who arranged to have it published by his successful Cultural Life Publishing House.

On July 6, 1937, the eve of Japanese invasion in Shanghai, he wrote Fuhua Di Tudi (The Land Reborn), extolling patriotism. Like many writers and artists, he later left Shanghai and started a nomadic life, stopping first at Wuhan, then moving on to the north. He taught at the National Revolutionary College in Shanxi province, and in Guilin he edited the literary supplement of the Guangxi Ribao (Guangxi Daily) for one year. In 1940 he arrived in Chongqing (the wartime capital, then known as Chungking) to head the literature department of Yucai College. During the war years, with his rich life experience, he had no lack of inspiration and wrote many more poems. The epic poem Xiang Taiyang (Facing the Sun) and his earlier Huoba (The Torch) are considered his representative works of the period. His style and technique having matured, his poetry became an effective force in persuading the young to participate in the war and the revolution. Other collections published in this period were Ta Sizai Dierci (He Dies a Second Time, 1939), Kuang Ye (The Desolate Wilds, 1940), and Bei Fang (The North, 1942).

While in Chongqing Ai Qing was the target of Kuomintang surveillance, but with the help of Zhou Enlai he succeeded in getting to Yanan in 1941. He was shortly after elected a member of the Shanxi-Gansu-Ningxia Border Area Congress, a sort of people's representative body in the Communist-controlled region. In the spring of 1942 he was summoned by Mao Zedong several times to discuss literary subjects with the chairman. He took part in the famed Yanan Forum on Literature and Art chaired by Mao and later became a member of the faculty of the Lu

Xun Academy of Art and Literature. He was also the editor of *Shai Kan* (Poetry) a magazine published locally. The Yanan Forum had a profound effect on him as a poet, and his poetry underwent great changes both in content and in style. He began to utilize the form of folksongs and his themes were largely patriotism and the war of liberation. His poetry had by then become an effective propaganda tool. His long adulatory poem "Mao Zedong" was finished in this period. Other collections included *Yuan Chuntian Zaodian Lai* (Wishing an Early Arrival of Spring, 1944), *Xianji Xiangcun Di Shi* (Poem to a Village, 1945), *Fan Faxisi* (Anti-Fascism, 1945), and *Duoshou Song* (Ode to the Helmsman, 1948). Ai Qing joined the Communist party in 1945.

After V-J Day he was appointed Associate Dean of the College of Art and Literature of the North China Union University in the city of Zhangjiakou. In 1949, when the People's Republic was established, he returned to Beijing and was put in charge of the Central Academy of Fine Arts. In the following years he was elected to various societies of artists and writers and was at a time deputy editor-in-chief of the prestigious *Renmin Wenxue* (People's Literature). In 1950 he went on a four-month visit to the Soviet Union and was inspired to write a series of poems *Baoshi Di Hongxing* (Red Star of the Precious Stone) which he regretted later. In 1954 he visited Chile and Brazil, making friends with Pablo Neruda and Jorge Amado. It was in May 1958, when he was accompanying Neruda and Amado on a tour of China that he first learned he had become a victim of Mao's Anti-Rightist Campaign. He was relieved of his hosting duties without even having a chance to say goodbye to the distinguished visitors.

A target of denunciation, he was first sent to a state farm in Heilongjiang in the northeast (Manchuria) for a year and a half, then transferred to Xinjiang in the northwest to do physical labor. Both places were known for cold weather and hardships and were dreaded by the exiled intellectuals. He was in Xinjiang for most of the duration of the Cultural Revolution (1966–1976). His home was searched and many of his manuscripts were lost; he was denounced, criticized publicly, and paraded in the streets. By 1975, his eyes failing, he got permission to return to Beijing for treatment.

Ai Qing himself claimed he was silenced for twenty-one years. It was not until May, 1978, shortly after his "rehabilitation," when Shanghai's *Wen Hui Bao*, a newspaper for intellectuals, published his poem "Hong Qi" (The Red Flag), was he heard again. Within the same year,

he published "Yuhuashi" (Fish Fossil), "Zai Langjian Shang" (On the Crest of a Wave), and "Guang Di Zange" (Song in Praise of Light).

He also began to travel abroad. In 1979 he visited Europe and wrote "Qiang" (The Wall) while in Berlin and "Gu Luoma Di Da Douji Chang" (The Great Cockpit of Ancient Rome) while in Rome. In June of 1980 he returned to Paris after an absence of forty-eight years to take part in the international forum on Chinese literature during the War of Resistance and wrote a history covering sixty years of Chinese poetry. He found Paris changed but recognized the hotel where he had lived, although "with a new facade." In September of that same year he visited the United States for the first time at the invitation of the Iowa International Writers' Workshop. While in New York he met a number of American writers including Elizabeth Hardwick, Bernard Malamud, Hortense Calisher, Stanley Kunitz, Robert Payne, none of whom he had read before. He visited Japan in 1982, Singapore in 1983, lecturing and attending conferences. In his advanced years he has slowed down both in writing and in travel. In the January 1984 issue of *Chinese Literature* he published an article about his life in which he concluded:

> Many who are younger than I have died before me. But I have lived on. If I had died seven or eight years ago, my death would have been no more important than a dog's. Half a century has passed since I published my first poem, "Gathering," in 1932. Often my creative life has seemed like a long tunnel, dark and damp. And sometimes I wondered whether I could live through it.
>
> But I did.

WORKS IN ENGLISH TRANSLATION: Selected Poems of Ai Qing was edited by Eugene Chen Eoyang, 1982: his work also appears in *Literature of the People's Republic of China*, edited by Kai-yu Hsu, 1980; also, in *Literature of the Hundred Flowers*, edited by Hualing Nieh, 1981.

ABOUT: Boorman, H. L. and R. C. Howard (eds.) Biographical Dictionary of Republican China, 1971; Encyclopedia of World Literature in the 20th Century, 1981; Literature of the People's Republic of China, 1980; Literature of the Hundred Flowers, 1981.

AICKMAN, ROBERT (FORDYCE) (June 27, 1914–February 26, 1981), British writer of supernatural tales, was born in London, the only child of William Arthur Aickman, an architect, and the former Mabel Violet Marsh. His maternal grandfather was Richard Marsh (d. 1915), author of the famous occult novel *The Beetle* and other similar tales. In Aickman's autobiography, *The Attempted Rescue*, he gives an account

ROBERT AICKMAN

of his grandfather's literary career: Marsh wrote "comic sketches of lower middle class life . . . [and] detective stories, with a female detective, named Judith Lee; a great innovation at the time. . . . Most of all, in terms of quantity, there are the popular romances, of which the writing mainly filled Marsh's later days. . . . The books are full of invention, indeed an education in how to be dashing without being sadistic, but their main interest now is in their matter-of-fact representation of a daily social paradise. Here, in my opinion, they better the novels of E. F. Benson, currently being re-read by the collectors of wax fruit."

Although Aickman's parents were of relatively modest means, many of their friends, some of his father's clients, and a few of his relatives were very rich indeed; much of his childhood was spent visiting large, imposing residences, the like of which find their way into a great many of his fictions. He attended London's Highgate School, but, though his school days were eminently successful, he never progressed to university. In the main, his early life was marked, according to his own reckoning, by unending mental suffering and misery. "For years," he writes in *The Attempted Rescue*, "I seem to have regarded myself as what F. R. Rolfe called a Nowt: a being without independent volition, directed wholly by circumstances and the will of others. If the circumstances were right (which was very infrequently), I could shine in a moment, and rise too, but I could do nothing to generate or to discover these circumstances. I was as the clown in a French mime; with wild hair in

place of long sleeves. I turned almost all of my suffering inwards, until it became unbearable, because nothing ever happened, neither breakout nor breakdown, so that I never ceased to bear it. Doubtless the suffering was consciously purposive, in the true neurotic idiom. The only possibility in my mind was that I might become an author."

In the mid-1930s, he goes on, he "spent just over a year producing a book named *Panacea*." It was never published. While still at Highgate he "sent a toy pagoda of words, 'What Is a Flounce?', to A. R. Orage's famous *New Age*, which accepted and printed it, but made it clear that it could not pay for it." He wrote no more fiction for a decade, but began writing regularly for publication as drama critic for the relentlessly highbrow but low-circulation monthly *The Nineteenth Century and After*. He came to feel that the English theater had sadly declined from its former greatness; the same feeling overcame him when he considered most of the other manifestations of modern culture. He was a Tory of the old school; he hated Socialism and in his later stories poked fun at Socialists. Only opera, the most classically conservative of the arts, held his interest throughout his life.

Aickman's autobiography ends in 1939; he saw no military service in World War II. One of the revelations of his life, however, occurred in 1946. "I chose," he writes in the "Proem" to his autobiography, "or was led by destiny (i.e. temperament), to find a field of activity, the navigable rivers and canals of Britain, where a counter-demonstration seemed possible; where a redoubt, big enough and various enough to be worth bothering about, might be captured and held indefinitely by a few like-minded people, and whence, just conceivably, the word might spread, not too hopelessly mangled. I failed; but I set up some powerful idols en route, and picked many pretty thorns. I learned much about the interaction of public life and private character, to me one of the most fascinating themes, the theme of 'Coriolanus'; even a little about their interaction in myself." In May 1946 Aickman joined with five other people to form The Inland Waterways Association. Within twenty years membership had grown to some 3,000. Aickman wrote that its success was "because the Association has uniquely deep roots in history, imagination, and the quest for happiness in a world where happiness is impossible. From the centre of the battle, I, the priest and the sacrifice, cry out against the horror of the world."

Such solemn, hieratic language is very characteristic of all Aickman's writing. It is evident even in his influential booklet *Know Your*

Waterways, which was certainly the bestselling work on the subject, and in his more discursive *The Story of Our Inland Waterways.* His career in fiction was about to begin. With Elizabeth Jane Howard—each writing three stories independently—Aickman published *We Are for the Dark.* Despite the quiet critical reception accorded this volume, he apparently felt that he had found a mode of expression that suited him. He had become a connoisseur of the genre of supernatural short fiction, and soon turned into a recognized expert in the field as well. In 1964 he edited with great success *The Fontana Book of Great Ghost Stories* and by 1972 had produced seven similar volumes for the same publisher, Collins.

Dark Entries, containing six stories, was Aickman's first book of short fiction all his own. He was fifty years old at the time of its publication, and his somewhat old-fashioned literary style—which critics have compared to those of M. R. James and Walter de la Mare—had by then become established. His supernatural themes, as well, did not greatly increase in number, though his exploration of them deepened in significance as his career progressed. "Bind Your Hair" stands out from his first collection in its serio-comic exploration of the theme of rite of passage. In this fantasy, Dudley's engagement to Clarinda has been thrown into doubt because of their evident lack of sexual compatibility. She unexpectedly finds herself within a sacred grove, in which an ancient fertility rite takes place with her more or less at its center. The end of the story finds Clarinda still attached to the unexciting Dudley, but possibly on the brink of a meaningful rite of passage away from him to a fuller life. Yet the reader is left to wonder—as often with Aickman's characters—whether she is really capable of saving herself.

"Larger Than Oneself," from *Powers of Darkness,* shows a similarly perplexed heroine-victim at a turning point in her life. Mrs. Iblis, a self-possessed woman with no evident purpose in life but many powers of observation, arrives at a large country house where a "Forum" of spiritualists is under way—a gathering to which she has not been invited. "My invitation was postponed on account of the Forum," she explains to her host, Vincent Coner, a wealthy publisher of "popular journalism," who has become "known for his advocacy of a synthesis between the best of this world and the best of the next." She is asked in an offhand manner to stay anyway, and proceeds during the course of the day to have numerous baffling conversations with rude, self-absorbed people. The story, which is all told from Mrs. Iblis's uninformed point of view, continues in increasingly hallucinatory

fashion; its climax, which takes place in front of the house, is the disappearance or "merging" of the hysterical guests—the participants in the Forum—with "a vast shining figure which filled the entire visible earth and sky." Mrs. Iblis, having emerged unscathed from witnessing this event, then escapes from the house by an open back window. Yet even her immediate future is notably unclear.

A similar character in a more conventionally eerie story with no elements of farce is Rosa, in "The Real Road to the Church" from *Cold Hand in Mine: Eight Strange Stories.* She is a sad, dispirited woman who in her late middle age had moved from a life of grief and disappointment in London to a small stone house on one of the Channel Islands (which one is never specified). Aickman, who is very good at describing the foibles of his female characters, catches perfectly Rosa's uneasy relationship to her surroundings—the fact that she has not yet come to terms with any aspect of her life. She often attempts self-assessment by looking at her reflection, as she does here in the glass of her sitting-room window: "Even her face was still pretty, she thought, beneath the grey hair. At least she had the decency to keep her grey hair short. . . . And my skin is amazingly good for my age, Rosa thought to herself. (She had long ago made a decision to defer *talking* to herself for as long as she could.) She attempted a smile, though she knew it could only be a bitter one, at least for the most part. But it proved to be not so much a bitter smile, as a timid and frightened smile. She was smiling like a shaky adolescent. And then the image in the dirty window lost shape and identity. Rosa turned away once more depressed." The reader develops the jumpy sense that at any moment in the story something devastating might occur to Rosa, who despite her testiness is always a figure of considerable sympathy. She finally experiences a vision of her own soul being borne past her house by ghostly porters. It strangely energizes her, and she resolves to return to London and change her life. She is one Aickman character who may well have enough self-possession to do so.

One who does not, who fails at the crisis to invest meaning in his life, is Delbert Catlow, in "No Time Is Passing" from *Intrusions: Strange Tales.* This is a classic Aickman story of the type which the critic John Clute has called "tales of failed transcendence, [in which the] protagonists are compelled by their sense of inward crisis to attempt to change their lives, perhaps utterly," but fail to do so. Delbert one day discovers a "wide river behind the thick hedge at the bottom of the garden." He immediately sets out to explore it in a small boat, rowing to an island,

where a strange creature called Petrovan—
perhaps a river god, perhaps an ogre—hails him,
invites him to his "burrow," and asks him elemental questions about his life. He is unhappily
conscious that he is not giving the requisite answers. He rests there for a time, only minutes by
Petrovan's reckoning, but when he finally is able
to return to his home he finds it has been invaded by squatters, sealed off by the police, and
apparently several years have passed. "There are
coincidences everywhere," he concludes, "and
likelihood is often linked with them." Yet nothing has changed for Delbert; he is still lost in the
ridiculous shambles of his life.

The implicit suggestion of the legend of Rip
Van Winkle in Delbert's story points to another
characteristic of several of the most admired of
Aickman's nearly fifty published works of short
fiction: the faint reiteration of a theme, situation, or character familiar from other fictional
works. "Mark Ingestre: The Customer's Tale,"
from the posthumous collection *Night Voices:
Strange Stories*, is a story quite old-fashioned in
structure, in which an old man tells the young
narrator of a visit when he was a youth to a
strange barber shop off Fleet Street and of waking up afterwards in a hot cellar. The propri-
etress of the place, after making love to him,
obviously means to kill him, but he shoots her
and escapes. He learns on leaving that he has
been imprisoned in a pie shop. There is much in
the story that recalls the legend of Sweeney
Todd—even the name of the pie shop propri-
etress, Mrs. Lovat.

Aickman's most admired story, which won
him the World Fantasy award for 1973–1974, is
"Pages from a Young Girl's Journal" from *Cold
Hand in Mine*. It is a tour de force of the macabre, deftly combining a virtuoso command of
period diction with an intimate view of lycan-
thropic possession. Elements from Jane Austen's
Northanger Abbey and from the works of Mrs.
Radcliffe are subtly infused throughout, and Byron and Shelley even make a brief appearance.
The story is set in 1819, in a crumbling palazzo
in Ravenna, where a young Englishwoman, on
holiday with her fussy mother and aged father,
has come to stay with their friends, a contessa
and her young daughter. At a ball she meets a
handsome, fatally attractive vampire, who immediately recognizes her as another "visitant
from a world that is not this one." She willingly
falls under his spell and begins to waste away, to
the obvious (and, to her, the comic) consternation of her parents and hostess. Her approaching
demise only thrills her; in the end, in a decrepit
hotel in Rimini—they have been forced by the
scandalized contessa to leave her palazzo—she
writes, "I am very tired, but it is the tiredness

that follows exaltation, not the vulgar tiredness
of common life. I noticed today that I no longer
have either shadow or reflection. . . . How I rejoice when I think about the new life which
spreads before me into infinity, the new ocean
which already laps at my feet, the new vessel
with the purple sail and red oars upon which I
shall at any moment embark! . . . Soon, soon,
new force will be mine, fire that is inconceivable; and the power to assume any night shape
that I may wish, or to fly through the darkness
with none. What love is his! How chosen among
all women am I; and I am just a little English
girl! It is a miracle, and I shall enter the halls of
Those Other Women with pride."

Aickman was an inveterate founder and joiner
throughout his maturity. He was director and
chairman of the London Opera Society in 1954–
1969, and chairman of the production company
administering the traveling Ballets Minerva in
1963–1968. He was a member of the council of
the National Council on Inland Transport, the
World Wildlife Fund, and the Lower Avon Nav-
igation Trust. In addition to his founding work
for the Inland Waterways Association, he was
vice president on the Railway Development Association, the Stratford-upon-Avon Canal Society, the Kennet and Avon Canal Trust, the River
Stour Trust, the Great Ouse Restoration Society,
the Leeds University Waterways Society, and
the Northampton Drama Club. He was also
chairman in 1969–1975 of the Upper Avon Nav-
igation Trust and president of the Residential
Boat Owners Association.

PRINCIPAL WORKS: *Novel*—The Late Breakfasters, 1964,
repr., 1978; *Collected short stories*—(with Elizabeth
Jane Howard) We Are for the Dark, 1951; Dark Entries, 1964; Powers of Darkness, 1966; Sub Rosa:
Strange Tales, 1968; Cold Hand in Mine, 1975; Tales
of Love and Death, 1977; Painted Devils, 1979; Intrusions, 1980; Night Voices, 1985. *As editor*—The Fontana Book of Great Ghost Stories, in eight volumes,
1964–1972. *Autobiography*—The Attempted Rescue,
1966. *Non-fiction*—Know Your Waterways, 1955 and
6 eds.; The Story of Our Inland Waterways, 1955, rev.
ed., 1967.

ABOUT: Contemporary Authors 7–8, 1969, and New Revision Series 3, 1981; Supernatural Fiction Writers,
1985.

*ALLENDE, ISABEL (August 2, 1942–   ),
Chilean novelist, writes: "It is difficult for me to
write about my life without repeating many
things from my books. My father left when I was
so small that I have no memories of him. He is
the model for the Count de Satigny in *The*

°ä yen´ dä

ISABEL ALLENDE

House of the Spirits. My mother was the most important person in my childhood and, together with my daughter, is now my best friend. We have a tradition of strong female bonding in our family. My grandmother was an extraordinary lady, spiritual, detached from earthly matters, with great sense of humor and compassion. She could speak with the dead and move objects without touching them. After my parents divorced, my mother went to live in the house of her father, a patriarch like Esteban Trueba, the main character of my first novel. I grew up in that extravagant home, surrounded by benevolent ghosts.

"My mother says that when I was a little girl I invented stories for my brothers, horrible truculent long stories that filled their heads with bad dreams at night and with unexplainable fears during the day. Yet nobody thought that this inclination could be useful. I was a girl and therefore my education was not directed toward creativity. I was supposed to get married, be a mother and work in a second-rate job, as women usually do, specially in the continent where I was born. But my love for story-telling did not vanish with my first menstruation, as my Nani predicted; on the contrary, it grew and when I got married and had my own children, they had to stand the same ordeal that my poor brothers did.

"My love for words induced me to work as a journalist since I was seventeen, but my vicious imagination was a great handicap. I could never be objective, I exaggerated and twisted reality, I would put myself in the middle of every feature. At that time I also wrote humor articles,

short stories for children, and theater plays. I suppose that all these were peripheral approaches to my real vocation. Deep in my heart I wanted to become a writer, but was too busy coping with my children, a husband, a house and a very demanding job. I also was too timid to try literature. I thought that nothing written by me could be of any interest to anyone else, much less to a publisher. Finally, at an age when women knit pullovers for their grandchildren, I fell upon literature, taking it by assault.

"My experience and my land have determined my writing.

"I am Chilean and for a long time I considered my beautiful country the beginning and the end of the universe, there was no other place where I would like to be; there I would bring up my family, work, get old and someday be buried. But then, something happened that changed the destiny of Chile. In September 1973, the military, supported from the outside by the government of the United States and from the inside by the political enemies of the socialist president Salvador Allende, put an end to our long democracy. After a year and a half living in the dictatorship, my husband and I decided to leave. We extended a map of the world to see where we could go. We chose Venezuela because it was a democracy. We have lived in that warm, green and generous country since then.

"I believe that one writes because one cannot avoid doing so. The need to do it is an overwhelming passion. If I don't write, words accumulate in my chest, grow and multiply like carnivorous flowers, threatening to choke me if they don't find a way out. Journalism, television, and theater satisfied that need while I lived in Chile, but in Venezuela I could not find a job of the type I had before, and for a long time that torrent of words stayed inside me. For years I felt paralyzed as most exiles do at the beginning, but finally in 1981 I took a sheet of paper and began a long letter to my grandfather, which later became a novel.

"For me the impulse to start a book comes from a great emotion that has been in my heart for a long time. *The House of the Spirits* was the result of nostalgia. In that book I intended to save the past, to gather again the loved ones, to bring the dead back to life. I wanted to recover all that I had lost, my land, my family, the objects that had been with me during all my life, my memories and the memories of those who were no longer with me. My second novel, *Love and Shadows*, was written in fury and pain. I wanted to speak up for those that are kept in silence. The inspiration came from those hundreds of men, women and children that are murdered, impris

oned and tortured and that "disappear" in my
continent, victims of political repression. My
third book, *Eva Luna*, is about being a woman
and about story-telling.

"When I write two obsessions appear constantly in my lines: love and violence. Two antagonist forces, light and darkness, good and evil,
always present in my stories and in my life."

————

Isabel Allende was born in Lima, Peru, where
her father, Tomás Allende, held a diplomatic
post in the Chilean embassy. Her parents were
divorced when she was three years old, and she
returned with her mother, Panchita Llona Bar-
ros Allende, to Santiago, Chile. She grew up in
the home of her maternal grandparents, Isabela
and Augustine Llona. This was her "house of the
spirits," and although she has always been on
friendly terms with her father's family—her uncle and godfather was Salvador Allende Gossens,
the president of Chile, who died in the military
coup of 1973—her closest ties were to her mother and her grandmother ("a luminous and transparent being," as she describes her) who became
the model for the matriarchal Clara in *The
House of the Spirits*, and her strong-willed
grandfather who inspired the colorful and turbulent Esteban Trueba of that novel. Growing
up in their large old house, crammed with memories, "inhabited by tenuous ghosts," with a library in which she could read freely everything
from Shakespeare to Jules Verne, Freud, and the
Marquis de Sade, she early cultivated her literary imagination. She was educated in private
schools in Chile and, on her mother's second
marriage to a diplomat whose duties took him to
Europe and the Middle East, she traveled widely
abroad.

Returning to Santiago at the age of fifteen, Isabel Allende spent another two years in school,
then dropped out to work briefly for a United
Nations agency in Chile. Drawn to journalism by
both her background and her commitment to social causes, especially feminism, she began writing for women's and children's magazines. In
the years between 1964 and 1973 she had a successful career as a television news reporter and
interviewer, a news filmmaker, and a writer of
plays and café sketches. She balanced all this activity with marriage in 1963 to Miguel Frias, an
engineer, and motherhood—a daughter, Paula,
and a son, Nicolas.

In 1970 Isabel Allende's uncle Salvador Allende was elected president of Chile, heading a
coalition government dedicated to democratic
Marxist socialism. The violent overthrow of this
government by General Augusto Pinochet in

1973 and the subsequent establishment of a military dictatorship made inevitable the exile of
many Chilean artists and intellectuals. A year
later, after seeing many of her friends jailed or
forced to leave the country, Isabel Allende and
her family emigrated to Caracas, Venezuela. In
recent years there has been some relaxation of
censorship in her native land; *The House of the
Spirits*, first smuggled into Chile in a Spanish
edition and distributed underground, became a
best-seller there, and some members of President Allende's family have returned. But Isabel
Allende now divides her time between her home
in Venezuela and the United States, where she
has taught and lectured in recent years.
"Officially I can go back," she told an interviewer for the *New York Times*. "But I don't think
it would be wise."

La casa de los espiritos (1982; translated as
The House of the Spirits) was conceived as a very
personal memoir. As Allende is quick to acknowledge, many of its characters were inspired
by her own family; and its plot, at least in the last
quarter of the novel, clearly follows the tragic
political events of recent Chilean history. But its
stunning success in other Latin American countries as well as in Europe and the United States
suggests that it has far wider resonance. Allende
says in an autobiographical memoir that it was
her intention to draw "a fresco of Latin
America." She sets her novel in no particular
country, although her allusions to an unnamed
"President" and "Poet" unmistakably are to
President Allende and the Nobel Prize–winning
poet Pablo Neruda, thus identifying the country
as Chile. Nevertheless, the story of the fortunes
and misfortunes of the Trueba family might indeed have taken place in any part of the modern
world that has seen the violence of political
revolution and dictatorship.

Like many other novels produced in twentieth-century Latin America, *The House of the
Spirits* is a heady mixture of raw political realism
and surrealistic fantasy—a technique that has
become known as "magic realism." Its characters, even when they are directly inspired by living people, are larger than life. The patriarch
Esteban Trueba has superhuman energy and uncontrollable passions. His wife Clara, her mother
Nivea, her daughter Blanca, and granddaughter
Alba—a quartet of women who constitute the
real center of this long novel—are united by
bonds of spirituality. Clara, in particular, haunts
the novel. She has supernatural powers—to fore-
see the future, to will objects to move, to play
Chopin on the piano without lifting the lid.
Though they live in a grand house with servants
and all the luxuries that wealth can offer, they
are at only one remove from the fierce jungles,

the burning deserts, the superstitions of primitive Indian tribes and descendants of slaves—the whole complex culture of South America. When young Alba observes to her grandmother that there are no lunatics in their family, Clara replies: "No. Here the madness was divided up equally, and there was nothing left over for us to have our own lunatic." That such a family will self-destruct in modern society is as inevitable as is the survival of their indomitable spirit. At the end of the novel, Alba, who has moved from her sheltered girlhood into the horrors of a modern political dictatorship, surviving torture, rape, and the deaths of loved ones, cannot hate her enemies: "It would be very difficult for me to avenge all those who should be avenged, because my revenge would be just another part of the same inexorable rite. I have to break the terrible chain." She resolves to collect her family history, "to reclaim the past and overcome terrors of my own."

Translated into many languages and an overnight best-seller wherever it appeared, *The House of the Spirits* was hailed for its passion and its richness of narrative invention. The book is crowded with eccentric characters and incidents that range from grisly violence to near slapstick comedy, guaranteeing "a good read." Its critical reception included both unqualified praise—especially from feminists who appreciated its sensitive recognition of the plight of women in a society rife with machismo—and stinging criticism of its loose structure, "one-dimensional characters of excessive good or evil," "patches of simplistic writing" (Christopher Lehmann-Haupt in the *New York Times*), and its abrupt switch, in the last chapters, from imaginative narrative to something like political journalism. Even the harshest critics of the novel, however, acknowledged its merits. Lehmann-Haupt concluded his review with praise: "But judged by the standards of the mainstream of historical fiction, *The House of the Spirits* has to be considered powerful and original. . . . I began by wanting to kill the book and ended up with deep respect for it." Enrique Fernandez, who dismissed the novel in the *Village Voice* as "radical chic," superficial and imitative of other and greater Latin American fiction, a "shameless cloning of [Gabriel García Márquez's] *One Hundred Years of Solitude*," conceded: "Her book is as engaging as most on the market, and it calls attention to the unresolved plight of her country."

Fernandez was only one among many readers of *The House of the Spirits* to note its resemblance to Márquez's great novel *One Hundred Years of Solitude* (1970), also a panoramic family history that treats the political history of a

South American country (in Márquez's novel Colombia) within the framework of magic realism. Although Allende did not deliberately model her work on his, there are undeniable similarities between the novels. Jonathan Yardley offered a balanced comparison in his review of *The House of the Spirits* in the *Washington Post Book World*: "Like García Márquez, she has created a world that interweaves the real and the fantastic, she has devised a colorful, ironic language with which to describe it, and she has addressed herself to the contemporary Latin American political and social situation. But her narrative method is more conventional, her prose is less flamboyant, and her politics are less insistent. She is most certainly a novelist in her own right and, for a first novelist, a startlingly skillful, confident one."

In the two novels that followed *The House of the Spirits*, Isabel Allende has narrowed her focus, working with fewer characters and a more compact narrative structure. But she continues to pursue what she sees as her mission as a novelist, writing in an autobiographical memoir: "All of us who write and are lucky to be published must assume the responsibility of serving the cause of freedom and justice. We have a mission to fulfill in the vanguard. We must oppose the darkness which burdens several countries in our continent with words, reason and hope. Literature must be used to serve man."

Both *De amor y de sombra* (1984; translated as *Of Love and Shadows*) and *Eva Luna* (1987) have revolution and politics—an unnamed South American state falling under dictatorial rule—as background and are centered on strong and independent women. Following closely upon the phenomenal success of her first novel, *Of Love and Shadows* disappointed many of its reviewers. John Updike, in the *New Yorker*, found it "smaller, paler, and less magical than her first [novel]." What appeared minor flaws in the massive *House of the Spirits*—an occasionally heavy-handed treatment of political subjects, "purple passages" describing love-making, lapses into inflated rhetoric and cliché—were more apparent here. The tone is set in an Author's Note at the opening: "This is the story of a woman and a man who loved one another so deeply that they saved themselves from a banal existence." The lovers are a beautiful young woman journalist from a patrician family and a handsome young photographer-journalist, the son of a political exile from Franco's Spain. The heroine Irene, Allende writes, "had lived surrounded by the gales of hatred, but remained untouched behind the high wall that had protected her since childhood." The hero Francisco has liberal thinking but old-fashioned parents:

"From them there were only three reasons why a son would leave home: war, marriage, or the priesthood. Later they would add a fourth: flight from the police." Brought together by their work and their ideological commitment to freedom and social justice, they uncover the bodies of a number of victims of the totalitarian government under which they live—among them a fifteen-year-old girl who appeared to have psychic or supernatural powers. Their determination to expose these crimes leads to a machine-gun attack on Irene and to their desperate escape over the border, pledging, "We will return, we will return." For Antony Beevor in the *Times Literary Supplement*, Allende here "does not seem to have achieved enough emotional distance in writing the novel; it badly lacks a clear perspective and a consistent voice." But Sonia Gernes, in *Commonweal*, found only minor flaws in the novel. She described it as one "that takes the risks of combining love story, adventure story, comic episode, and morally serious political event. Allende has struck her target with little margin of error."

Though the picaresque adventures of the heroine-narrator of *Eva Luna* are not even remotely related to the life of Isabel Allende, Eva Luna is in one respect at least a mirror reflection of her creator. A born storyteller who literally invents her own life in this novel, Eva is the daughter of one of those typically wise and enigmatic women who people Allende's novels—a waif of unknown origin who had "spent her childhood in an enchanted region where for centuries adventurers have searched for the city of pure gold the conquistadors saw when they peered into the abyss of their own ambitions." Eva's father was an Indian who, after surviving a venomous snakebite thanks to her mother's nursing, disappeared. His daughter says: "I do not have fangs, or reptilian scales—at least no visible ones. The somewhat unusual circumstances of my conception had, instead, only positive consequences; these were unfailing good health and the rebelliousness that . . . in the end saved me from the life of humiliations to which I was undoubtedly destined." Early orphaned and destitute, Eva drifts from adventure to adventure, from the life of a servant to a successful career as a writer of soap operas for television and a participant in the guerrilla war against her country's oppressive government. Along the way she meets an assortment of colorful characters—a Turkish emigré shopkeeper with a cleft palate, a transvestite, a leader of the guerrilla forces whom she passionately loves, and a handsome young Austrian photographer with whom she finally finds happiness. What preserves and sustains Eva throughout her tumultuous adventures is not simply her inherited stamina but her native skill at storytelling. Allende dedicates the novel to her mother, "who gave me a love of stories," and cites Scheherazade in an epigraph. Eva does not have time to write until fairly late in the novel, but once launched, stories flow from her. Allende herself did not begin to write until she was in her early forties, so Eva's experiences here confronting a typewriter have special relevance:

> Then I felt something odd, like a pleasant tickling in my bones, a breeze blowing through the network of veins beneath my skin. I believed that the page had been waiting for me for more than twenty years, that I had lived only for that instant. . . . I could see an order to the stories stored in my genetic memory since before my birth, and the many others I had been writing for years in my notebooks . . . . Little by little, the past was transformed into the present, and the future was also mine; the dead came alive with an illusion of eternity; those who had been separated were reunited, and all that had been lost in oblivion regained precise dimension.

Eva Luna received mixed reviews. John Krich, in the *New York Times Book Review*, called it "a confessional saga" and placed Allende somewhere between García Márquez and Judith Krantz as "a popularizer who performs a valuable service by making general audiences aware of the rich milieu and timeless fatalism captured by prior practitioners of the new Latin American fiction." Abigail Lee, however, in the *Times Literary Supplement*, found "attractive characterization" and "interesting structure" in the book and considered it "an accomplished novel blending humor and pathos." In July 1989 Isabel Allende was named one of eighteen winners of the 10th Annual American Book Awards for *Eva Luna*, the judges welcoming the opportunity to "provide wider recognition for outstanding achievements of authors representing the breadth of America's literary and cultural traditions."

WORKS IN ENGLISH TRANSLATION: Magda Bogin's translation of *The House of the Spirits* was published in 1985. Margaret Sayers Peden translated *Of Love and Shadows* in 1987 and *Eva Luna* in 1988.

ABOUT: Contemporary Authors 125, 1989; Contemporary Literary Criticism 39, 1986; Current Biography 1988; Hart, P. Narrative Magician: The Fiction of Isabel Allende, 1990. *Periodicals*—Commonweal August 14, 1987; Nation July 20, 1985; New York Review of Books July 18, 1985; New York Times May 9, 1985; February 4, 1988; September 2, 1988; July 2, 1989; New York Times Book Review May 12, 1985; July 12, 1987; October 23, 1988; New Yorker August 24, 1987; Observer June 7, 1985; Publishers Weekly May 17, 1985; Times Literary Supplement July 15, 1985; July 10, 1987; Village Voice June 4, 1985; Vogue June 10, 1985; Washington Post Book World May 12, 1985.

ALTER, ROBERT (BERNARD) (April 2, 1935–), American educator and critic, can be described as a literary man of two worlds, being equally at home in the Western tradition, particularly English and continental fiction, and in Hebrew literature, ancient and modern. Alter was born in New York City to Henry and Tillie (Zimmerman) Alter. He received his Bachelor of Arts degree from Columbia University in 1957, his graduate degrees from Harvard University (M.A., 1958; Ph.D, 1962), and he also studied at the Hebrew University in Jerusalem. While pursuing his doctoral studies at Harvard, he was a teaching fellow there as well as an instructor in Judaic studies at Brandeis University. His first post-doctoral teaching post was in the English department of Columbia University (1962–1966). In 1967 he joined the faculty of the University of California at Berkeley and he was named a professor of Hebrew and comparative literature in 1969. From 1970 to 1973 he was chairman of the comparative literature department. Berkeley has remained his academic base, with interruption for visiting appointments. While teaching at Columbia, Alter reviewed current books for *Commentary,* the beginning of a long association with this magazine devoted to Jewish thought and opinion, published under the auspices of the American Jewish Committee. From 1968 to 1973 he reported intermittently on the current cultural scene in the column called "In the Community" and remained a contributing editor through 1986.

Rogue's Progress. Studies in the Picaresque Novel, Alter's first book, grew out of his doctoral dissertation at Harvard under the joint direction of the comparatist Harry Levin and Harold Martin, a professor of English. Exploring what was fundamentally distinctive about "the picaresque way of looking at the world," Alter traces the genre from its beginnings in sixteenth-century Spain through such modern "heirs of the tradition" as Saul Bellow (*The Adventures of Augie March*), Thomas Mann (*Felix Krull*), and Joyce Cary (*The Horse's Mouth*), illustrating both its evolution from rogue tale to bildungsroman, and the socialization of the vagabond hero. His next book, *Fielding and the Nature of the Novel,* was in a way an offshoot of the first since it concentrates on the panoramic 'road' novels *Joseph Andrews* and *Tom Jones.* By his fundamental emphasis on what their author "reveals through his own artistic practice of the inherent possibilities of the genre [of the novel]," Alter's intention was to reverse the denigration of Fielding as a serious writer by modern critics, among them F. R. Leavis.

Leavis' rather solemn *The Great Tradition* is more specifically behind *Partial Magic: The*

ROBERT ALTER

Novel as a Self-Conscious Genre in which Alter deplores the lack of critical appreciation for the novel "that expresses its seriousness through playfulness, that is acutely aware of itself as a mere structure of words, even as it tries to discover ways of going beyond what words seek to indicate." His chosen examples begin with Cervantes but are drawn mainly from the eighteenth century (Sterne, Diderot) and the twentieth (Joyce, Broch, Gide, Nabokov). While reviewers were impressed with his breadth of reading and critical acuity, some reservations were expressed about Alter's setting apart of the nineteenth century as a unique period when the self-conscious novel went into "eclipse," with the interest of writers shifting from the creative mind to the surrounding world. Stendhal, who figures in passing in both *Rogue's Progress* and *Partial Magic* occupies center stage in Alter's one literary biography (written in collaboration with Carol Cosman), *A Lion in Love,* commended for its painstaking scholarship combined with empathy for its subject.

Erudite and well written as are Alter's critical investigations along these beaten paths of the literary canon, his unique contributions to humanistic culture undoubtedly lie in his assessments of contemporary Israeli literature and particularly in his ensuing groundbreaking work in Bible interpretation. *After the Tradition: Essays on Modern Jewish Writing,* dealing with the so-called "Jewish renaissance," is a gathering of articles mainly from *Commentary* (along with others from *Hadassah Magazine, Judaism, Daedalus,* and *Saturday Review*). This book includes noteworthy essays on such world figures as Franz Kafka and the Nobel Prize–winning novelist S. Y. Agnon, but is mainly concerned with comparing and contrasting the literature currently being produced by Jews in America with native Israeli fiction and poetry, on the assumption that the two literary societies have much to learn from each other owing to "their different yet complementary cultural predicaments." The double entendre in the title—"after" signifies both a search and a later point in time—links these widely separated cultures for Alter: both engaged in a quest for ethnic identity, and both struggling to reconcile an ancient creed with the modern world. In America Alter noted the "sudden new ascendancy" during the 1950s and 1960s of writers of Jewish origin, notably Saul Bellow and Bernard Malamud, which had been interpreted in some circles as a displacing of a long established "WASP hegemony" in this part of the world. By the time of writing, this wave had already spent itself, Alter himself concluded, and was actually falling into "a declining phase of unwitting self-parody." The "Israeli scene," as Alter characterizes it, was then beset by a conflict of ethnic loyalties. The essay "The Two Generations" in particular defines the cleavage between novelists like Haim Hazaz, who emerged out of the folksy East European world of Peretz and Sholem Aleichem, and those, represented by Yizhar Smilansky, who were part of the Sabra generation nourished in violence and upheaval.

Poetry, on the other hand, has more successfully united the reading public of Israel, according to Alter, because it is rooted in Biblical Hebrew, a language which has undergone little change since ancient times, so that the younger poets have more in common with Bialik than the younger novelists have with Agnon. For this reason, he concludes, "Israel is probably one of the few remaining countries where verse . . . has managed to stay at the vital center of literary culture." John Gross, reviewing *After the Tradition* for *Commentary*, admired the gentle reasonableness with which Alter exposed the "tacit conspiracy afoot to foist on the American public as peculiarly Jewish admired characteristics which in fact belong to the common humanity of us all." Meyer Levin, writing in the *New York Review of Books*, also reviewed the book favorably, but considered the Israeli section more original in its perceptions than the American section.

Subsequent essays from *Commentary*, eked out by papers delivered at scholarly meetings, make up the content of *Defenses of the Imagination: Jewish Writing and the Modern Historical Crisis*, conceived by Alter as "the complementa-

ry opposite" of *After the Tradition*. Where the earlier book is concerned with the problems posed, for Jewish writers, by different literary and cultural traditions, the later volume is focused on the literary response to twentieth-century events. Here writers such as Walter Benjamin, Hermann Broch, Saul Tchernikovsky, Osip Mandelstam, and Lea Goldberg, "wandering from one crossroads of historical disaster to the next," collectively serve as "an acutely sensitive index of Western culture's disturbances and confusions." Although, as Alter reminds us, many non-Jewish writers of the twentieth century have been jeremiahs and naysayers, the surprise of this book is that Jewish writers, despite the sufferings that they have witnessed, tend to affirm the regenerative powers of the imagination, what Alter calls the "anti-apocalyptic stance."

The Art of Biblical Narrative, which received the Jewish National Book Award for Jewish Thought, is the culmination of Alter's experience in teaching the literary study of the Bible, beginning with a colloquium in the department of religion at Stanford in 1971, continued by lectures, institutes, and seminars at various universities. Applying modern critical methods to ancient texts, in opposition to the so-called "excavative" approach of historians and linguists, Alter persuasively demonstrates that their authors, far from mere scribes or replicators of oral traditions, were conscious and sophisticated literary artists. In the chapter titled "Sacred History and the Beginnings of Prose Fiction" he points out that while these writers were circumscribed by the eschatological teachings of Judaism, the "double dialectic between design and disorder, providence and freedom" left them leeway for the exercise of individual "artful determinations" in the representation of character and in the deployment of language. Although the writings that make up the Hebrew Bible were composed over nine centuries (a time-span, as Alter reminds us, analogous in French literature to the stretch from *The Song of Roland* to the novels of Alain Robbe-Grillet), he conceives of it as, not the stitching together of disparate texts envisaged by some scholars, but a unified work linked by recurring Type-Scenes, leitmotifs, and subtle verbal echoes. Frank Kermode, in his enthusiastic review of this book (*New York Times Book Review*), referred to the author as "a true descendent of the Midrashic exegetes." Alter, however, probes beyond exegesis, concerned with the expounding of doctrine, to the poetics of scriptural writing.

A pendant volume to *The Art of Biblical Narrative* is *The Art of Biblical Poetry*, begun while Alter was a fellow at the Institute for Advanced Studies of the Hebrew University of Jerusalem (1982–1983). In this group of studies, Alter applies his critical skills, enhanced by his intimate knowledge of the original Hebrew, to verse portions of the Hebrew Bible—specifically the psalms, the prophetic poems, the Song of Songs, and the Book of Job. The analyses of such devices as the "dynamics of parallelism" and "structures of intensification," while sometimes tediously technical and philological, penetrate to the roots of Hebrew prosody and demonstrate the verbal virtuosity of the poets. His method is not original—he acknowledges indebtedness to such predecessors as Benjamin Hrushkovski and James L. Kügel—but he goes further than they to show that Hebrew poetry is "one of the wellsprings of Western literature." *The Art of Biblical Narrative* won the Present Tense Award for Jewish Thought in 1986.

Alter's biblical criticism was distilled for a larger audience in *The Literary Guide to the Bible*, jointly edited with the British scholar-critic Frank Kermode. This composite book brings together essays on such topics as the canon and translations, and expositions of specific books by scholars, Catholic, Protestant, and Jewish, from the United States, Canada, England, the Netherlands, Italy, and Israel. Alter supervised the Old Testament section to which he contributed the Introduction and the essays on the psalms and on "The Characteristics of Hebrew Poetry"; Kermode was responsible for the New Testament half, which he introduced as well as writing the essays on John, Matthew, and the canon. This enterprise was truly ecumenical inasmuch as emphasis was placed on the indebtedness of St. Paul and the Gospel writers to the Old Testament (or Hebrew Bible), which they frequently echo. Although some of the chapters get mired in textual minutiae, *The Literary Guide to the Bible* was widely welcomed as an up-to-date authoritative vade mecum to the Judaeo-Christian scriptures for the non-specialist of general culture. Among reviewers, Harold Bloom (in the *New York Review of Books*) observed that few of the other contributors match the editors for learning combined with critical sensitivity.

Concurrently with his studies of Hebrew literature, sacred and secular, Alter has maintained his interest in Western literature, as indicated by *Motives for Fiction* and the more recent *The Pleasures of Reading in an Ideological Age*, in which he addresses some of the post-modernist trends in creative writing and criticism. In the first book he upholds the representational function of the novel in reaction against the *nouveau roman*; in the second book he reaffirms the referential character of language, *pace* the deconstructionists.

Alter's literary worlds mingle and impinge upon one another through his eclectic use of examples to illustrate his critical principles as well as by occasional cross references. His concept of "serious play" introduced in *Partial Magic*, for example, is applied to the craft and deviousness of biblical narrators and poets, and the Bible for him is viewed as a "self-conscious genre." The situation of modern Israeli novelists is likened to the plight of writers with the disposition of Bellow, Malamud, and Styron caught in a literary world dominated by Fielding, Smollett, and Goldsmith. Fundamentally his literary criticism is informed by his fascination with what he refers to in his introduction to *The Literary Guide to the Bible* as "the poised choreography of words." His versatility is reflected in the diversity of literary honors he has received, which include the English Institute Prize (1965), two Guggenheim Fellowships (1966–1967; 1979–1980), a National Endowment for the Humanities Senior Fellowship (1972–1973), and an honorary Doctorate in Hebrew Letters conferred by the Hebrew Union College in 1985.

Alter has been married twice. From his marriage to Judith Berkenbilt in 1961 he has two children, Morris and Dan. Following his divorce in 1973 he married Carol Cosman, an editor and translator. The two children from this marriage are named Gabriel and Micha.

PRINCIPAL WORKS: Rogue's Progress, 1964; Fielding and the Nature of the Novel, 1968; After the Tradition, 1969; Partial Magic, 1973; Defenses of the Imagination, 1977; (with C. Cosman) A Lion in Love, 1979; The Art of Biblical Narrative, 1981; Motives for Fiction, 1984; The Invention of Hebrew Prose, 1988; The Pleasures of Reading in an Ideological Age. *As editor*—Modern Hebrew Literature, 1975; (with F. Kermode) The Literary Guide to the Bible, 1987.

ABOUT: Contemporary Authors New Revision Series 1, 1981; Contemporary Literary Criticism 34, 1985; Who's Who in America, 1988–1989. *Periodicals*—Commentary April 1969; Georgia Review Spring 1969; Los Angeles Times October 19, 1979; New Republic July 9, 1984; New York Review of Books March 31, 1988; New York Times Book Review January 26, 1969; October 7, 1979; July 9, 1981; June 25, 1989; Nineteenth-Century Fiction March 1977; Quill and Quire June 1981; Times (London) Literary Supplement May 7, 1976; Washington Post Book World September 16, 1979.

*AMADI, ELECHI (May 12, 1934–   ), Nigerian novelist, dramatist, and educator, was born into an Ibo family in the village of Aluu in the Delta region of Eastern Nigeria. Like other major Nigerian writers including Nobel laureate

°ä mä´ dē, el´ e kē

ELECHI AMADI

Wole Soyinka, Chinua Achebe, John Okigbo, John Pepper Clark, and Kole Omotoso, he was educated at the prestigious University College of Ibadan, where he completed a Bachelor of Sciences degree in physics and math in 1959. Returning to the Delta after graduation, he worked as a land surveyor in Enugu for a year, then became a science teacher in Protestant mission schools in Oba and Ahoada. In 1963 he joined the Federal army with the rank of captain (he was one of the few graduate officers) and was assigned to teach his native Ekwerri language at the military school in Zaria; two years later he resigned his commission and took a teaching post at the Anglican Grammar School in Port Harcourt. Amadi is best known for his depictions of traditional African society not yet under colonial rule but subject all the same to the workings of supernatural fate.

His first novel, *The Concubine*, published in 1966 six years after Nigerian independence, seemingly turned its back on the political and social dramas of the moment to recreate a timeless tale of village life. Notwithstanding the title, the central character, Ihuoma, is a young woman whose virtues are equaled only by her misfortunes—and the misfortunes she brings to others: her husband dies prematurely; she falls prey to an abusive suitor who later commits suicide, and when she is about to remarry, her husband-to-be is accidentally killed while preparing a sacrifice. The narrative is developed with an abundance of descriptive detail and psychological depth rooted in the inner workings of the society. Introducing his central character, for example, Amadi tells readers that

Ihuoma's complexion was that of the ant-hill. Her features were smoothly rounded and looking at her no one could doubt that she was "enjoying her husband's wealth." Nothing did a husband greater credit than the well-fed look of his wife. In the first year of her marriage, Ihuoma had been slim and quite a few of her more plumpy mates had remarked that food was being wasted on her. Now she shamed her critics.

But in fact, the key to the unfolding of events in the novel is to be found neither in the material world nor in human behavior, but in the supernatural: as Amadi reveals only at the very end of the story, the hapless Ihuoma is really the wife of the Sea-King, who reluctantly granted her wish to assume human form for a time but took his revenge on all of her admirers. In the words of the medicine man, Anyika,

You see, Ihuoma is is a little unusual. . . . Ihuoma belongs to the sea. When she was in the spirit world she was a wife of the Sea-King, the ruling spirit of the sea.

Look at her . . . have you ever seen anyone quite so right in everything, almost perfect? I tell you only a sea goddess—for that is precisely what she is—can be all that.

Some years later, Amadi himself was to elaborate on his particular mix of realism and the supernatural in the context of African literature and society: "I think the novel, the so-called Western novel, is really a universal form. It is story-telling," he commented in 1976. But, he continued, "our problem is: Are we exploiting this universal form enough from the African point of view? . . . an African writer who really wants to interpret the African scene has to write in three dimensions at once. There is the private life, the social life, and what you may call the supernatural."

The Concubine was widely praised for its engagingly simple style and its universal vision: in the words of Alastair Niven: "It is as though Amadi were distilling some of the essential elements of his society—family obligations, religious rites, social laws, river mythology—and then rendering them into an English prose which is sturdy enough to support these archetypes and make them relevant to other cultures. . . . " But what also struck critics about this novel (and the two that followed) was Amadi's insistent departure from the political vision that informed the writings of his contemporaries. "He was not alone in attempting to convey the day-to-day texture of traditional, pre-colonial life in an African village," notes Gerald Moore in *Contemporary Novelists*, but "he distinguished himself by not offering any explicit contrasts between that traditional world and the one that replaced it." Unlike Chinua Achebe's *Things Fall Apart* and other contemporary African novels, which address themselves to the impact of colonialism, Moore explains, Amadi's world remains timeless and self-contained: "the dilemmas which confront and finally destroy his heroes or heroines derive entirely from the beliefs, practices, and events of their indigenous culture." And indeed, Amadi himself has made it quite clear that he eschews any activist role as a writer: "I consider commitment in fiction a prostitution of literature. The novelist should depict life as he sees it without consciously attempting to persuade the reader to take a particular viewpoint. Propaganda should be left to journalists."

During the civil war, Amadi was virtually the only East Nigerian writer to support the Federal cause. He was twice arrested and detained by the Biafran government—as he later wrote in *Sunset in Biafra*, "They would be fools to let a former officer of the Nigerian army wander around freely at this time"—and after his second release, he rejoined the Federal army for a year. From this period came a second novel, *The Great Ponds*, which again depicted traditional village life in the Delta region, but here, if there were no ostensible connections to contemporary life, the story of a feud between two groups over fishing rights to the local pond was certainly not without resonances of civil war. Like *The Concubine*, *The Great Ponds* drew praise for its meticulous rendering of daily life: "Elechi Amadi's achievement," wrote David Sebukima in *Mawazo*, was that "he depicts the naivety and superstition of a simple community without making the community in any way look ridiculous."

With the war's end in 1970, Amadi went to work for the government of the newly constituted Rivers State, eventually becoming head of Ministry of Information and then the Ministry of Education. In 1973 he published *Sunset in Biafra: A Civil War Diary*, which, he insisted, was "not a story of the war. It is an intimate, personal story told for its own sake." Indeed, the work was appreciated for much the same qualities as his novels: documentary accuracy anad narrative form. Dan Agbese, for example, told readers of the Lagos *Sunday Times*, "To read Amadi's *Sunset in Biafra* is to be in Biafra . . . Above all, it is to read a master of prose at his magnificent best."

In the late 1960s Amadi also turned to writing plays, which, in contrast to his novels, addressed increasingly topical issues. The first of these, *Isiburu*, was the story of a wrestler; written for teenagers (and in verse), it was first performed at Port Harcourt in 1969. *Pepper Soup*, which was staged in 1971, was a light comedy about a

jobless musician trying to choose between two girlfriends, one Nigerian and the other English, while *The Road to Ibadan*, performed in 1977, took a more serious look at love with the story of a battle-front romance between a Federal Army captain and a refugee student nurse during the civil war. The last of these stage ventures, *Dancer of Johannesburg*, performed in 1979, was a mystery about a Nigerian diplomat in love with a nightclub dancer who turns out to be a spy for the South African regime.

With *The Slave*, Amadi returned to the novel and completed what is generally regarded as a loose-knit trilogy of village tales. The title character, Olumati, attempts to change the course of his life by leaving the shrine where his parents had served as slaves to a local god and returning to his ancestral village. There, he is considered to be an *osu*, or outcast, because of the long time he spent at the shrine, and he encounters one disaster after another until he finally decides to go back to the shrine and assume his destiny. As Randall L. Davenport suggests in *World Literature Today*, Amadi once again presents a hero "whose life is more limited than others in the village," but, in the tradition of the story-teller, he does not really give an explanation of events. Amadi, writes Davenport, "is an anthropologist, a historian and a novelist," and, he concludes, "In Nigeria, only Achebe looms larger."

Eight years elapsed before Amadi published another novel: in the interim, he completed a study of ethics in Nigerian culture and also continued a long-term project of translating Protestant prayers and hymns into Ikwerri. With *Estrangement* in 1983 he returned to the civil war and its aftermath as the setting for the intimate drama of a woman refugee, the Hausa major who saves her from rape and then falls in love with her, and her husband, who repudiates her after the war. A seeming departure from his earlier village themes, this "unusual love story," as *Choice* described it, is nonetheless immersed in the workings of tradition and again, the inability of individuals to control their fates: after innumerable intrigues of politics, passion, and commerce, Alekiri's major comes back to marry her and, in another one of Amadi's concluding twists, tells her, "Blame the war, not men."

In *Africa and the Novel*, Neil McEwan comments that Amadi's tales of traditional village life "are told as though by a villager but written by an exceptionally intelligent scientist, teacher and administrator." This implicit balance between immediacy and reflection, the insider's and outsider's eye, is amply apparent in a passage like the following from *Estrangement*, which weaves together the personal relations of one of the three protagonists (the husband, now in search of a second wife to bear him a child), longstanding marriage customs, and the actuality of the civil war:

It was not easy finding a woman to fit Ibekwe's prescription. The younger women rejected him because they did not want to be second wives. Older ones who liked him made it quite clear they would come to stay with him and Ibia in town. But Oyia, Elei's sister, accepted without any preconditions. Still in her twenties, her husband had been conscripted into the Biafran army and killed. She had not remarried, and some said she was still mourning her husband and two children who died in Biafra. Oyia was quiet. Her beauty was a little roughened by much farm work, but Ibekwe guessed that she would blossom if she enjoyed some comfort and security. . . .

Amadi himself indicates that "I like to think of myself as a painter or composer using words in the place of pictures and musical symbols . . . In my ideal novel, the reader should feel a sense of aesthetic satisfaction that he cannot quite explain—the same feeling he gets when he listens to a beautiful symphony." But he adds, in seeming confirmation of McEwan's appraisal, "For those readers who insist on being taught, there are always things to learn from a faithful portrayal of life in a well-written novel."

PRINCIPAL WORKS: Novels—The Concubine, 1966; The Great Ponds, 1969; The Slave, 1978; Estrangement, 1986. Published plays—Isiburu, 1973; Peppersoup, 1973; The Road to Ibadan, 1973. Essays—Sunset Biafra: A Civil War Diary, 1973; Ethics in Nigerian Culture, 1982.

ABOUT: Booth, J. Writers and Politics in Nigeria, 1981. Contemporary Authors New Revision Series 16, 1986; Contemporary Novelists, 4th ed., 1986; McEwan, N. Africa and the Novel, 1983; Niven, A. The Concubine: A Critical View, 1981; Zell, H. M., C. Bundy, V. Coulon. A New Reader's Guide to African Literature, 1983. Periodicals—Choice, October 1973, September 1979, February 1987; Journal of Commonwealth Literature July 1967; Presence Africaine 98, 1976; Times Literary Supplement December 21, 1973; World Literature Today Spring 1980, Winter 1980.

*AMIS, MARTIN (LOUIS) (August 25, 1949–   ), British novelist and critic, was born in Oxford, the second son and the second of three children of the novelist Kingsley Amis and the former Hilary Ann Bardwell. He attended more than thirteen schools in Britain, Spain, and the United States, then a series of crammers (intensive university-preparation schools) in London and Brighton. He read English at Exeter College, Oxford, working for the most part extremely hard and in the end gaining a formal first-class honors degree—the third best in his subject in the entire university—in 1971.

MARTIN AMIS

Amis wrote evocatively of his time at university in the compendium My Oxford (1977, edited by Ann Thwaite): "even during my relatively in-demand periods at Oxford, most of my life there was to consist of me alone in a study, reading books pressed calmly out on the blotting-paper, or writing malarial, pageant-like, all-night essays, or listening to records, or playing moronically simple forms of patience, or having soul-sessions, or having crying-jags. And, however self-pitying I was about it at the time, this segment of my life I regret not at all: a relative latecomer to literature, I was a contrite pilgrim on the path towards its discovery. Many poignant and humbling moments were passed with assorted masterpieces staked out on my lap; over those three years 'the friction, the sense of pregnant arrest' which accompanies fresh intimacy with an oeuvre (the glamorous phrase is F. R. Leavis's) was a regular guest at Tower 1, my romantic room facing the stained glass of the chapel windows ten yards opposite, which were warmly illuminated from within at dusk."

Thanks to his famous father, young Amis knew his way about literary London. After a year (1971) reviewing books for the London Observer, he joined the staff of the Times Literary Supplement (1972–1974), rising from editorial assistant to fiction and poetry editor. In 1975–1979 he was assistant literary editor, then literary editor of the New Statesman. He has often visited America, especially New York. Since 1980 he has been a special writer for the Observer, at one time contributing a much-admired column, "Letter from New York," which covered, in his words, "preferably the most vulgar and lurid things" he could find to write about. The attraction of the tawdry was apparent in all his early fiction.

Amis made an auspicious literary debut with *The Rachel Papers*, a novel wittily narrated in the first person by Charles Highway, which takes place the day and night before he turns twenty and concerns his endlessly anguished adolescent amorous adventures. He aspires to be a writer, has just passed his Oxford entrance examination, and the woman of the title, an extremely willing sexual conquest, is to be the subject of his first novel. The author said in 1981 that this first novel owed a great deal to his father's influence. It "is very like my father, stylistically—writing about low events in a rather pompous, mock-heroic style. It's sort of *Lucky Jim* twenty years on. And by doing it I got rid of the whole problem [of paternal influence]—I wasn't tempted to look at my father's stuff and do something entirely different." The elder Amis, however, has always been unable to read his son's published works. "I like his stuff," said Martin in 1981, "a lot more than he likes mine—that's how it should be. He thinks my stuff is much too tricksy and mannered." In 1985 he added, in the same vein, "He can't finish my stuff. I tell him he carries incuriosity to fanatical extremes." *The Rachel Papers* won the Somerset Maugham Award in 1974.

Dead Babies takes place in the near future in a rented house, Appleseed Rectory, in Hertfordshire, near London. It is the grotesque story of nonstop joyless drug-taking, unconsummated sexual fever, and wanton violence, indulged in by the six residents of the rectory and their visitors, three of them American and one English, over the course of a weekend. The cruelties and sexual horrors go on and on, and the author's enthusiasm for describing them in cleverly original ways never flags either: his satiric exhilaration makes the novel memorable. James Price, writing in *Encounter*, pays tribute to its "violently aggressive high spirits. With so much wilting, anemic writing about, it's good to have a little mayhem." Amis' satiric misanthropy is as much in evidence here as in any of his works; in particular, writes Michael Mason in the *Times Literary Supplement*, the novel "is fueled by a hatred of libertarian practices for which . . . Amis can find no adequate vehicle. A sense of the horrific is carefully fostered, but no atrocities occur that quite justify it until the spectacularly brutal final one."

The crucial link of utter egos in the shocking denouement of *Dead Babies* finds a sequel in *Success*. Gregory, languid, verbally elevated,

materially and sexually successful, shares a London flat with his nearly cretinous foster brother, the foul-mouthed Terry, a man tensely aware of his own failure in respect to girls and money. The novel covers a year in their lives and is narrated alternately by them; ever so gradually, their situations begin to be reversed, as the reader becomes aware that the story is a satiric parable about, as Paul Ableman put it in the *Spectator*, "the decline of the old order in England and the new raj of the yobs." As Gregory says in one of his more down-to-earth moments, "The world is changing; the past is gone, and from now on all is future tense." "Central to Amis's vision," wrote Tom Paulin in *Encounter*, "is a sense of deprivation which annihilates the past and makes the present moment seem an exhausted bundle of vicious, fetid and desperate energies. . . . The only constants in this dead secular world are 'self-pity, self-disgust, and self-love' . . . life has a scratchy, scurfy texture that infests the rhythms of Amis's prose."

Other People: A Mystery Story tells of the pitiful fate of Mary Lamb, an extremely naive amnesiac who used to be a knowing and vicious girl called Amy Hide. Mary's progress through the sordid underside of London lowlife is minutely and painfully detailed by the author, as she slowly accomplishes a fabulous rise from the world of whores, drunks, criminals and psychopaths to the giddy heights of bourgeois bohemia. All the while wondering at the ambiguous power of the ordinary events encountered during her picaresque journey, Mary never loses her unnatural innocence, which is always strongly contrasted with the depravity and violence occurring all around her. Her story ends as it begins, with an awakening and perhaps with violence. Victoria Glendinning in the *Listener* thought it "quite hard to understand . . . a very literary and word-mongering novel . . . it is, in its sad, funny and sidelong way, peculiarly interesting and effective. But you could be a deal less intelligent and aware than [Amis] is and be a better novelist."

John Self, the self-indulgent and self-loathing hero of *Money: A Suicide Note*, is by all odds Amis' most rebarbative character, and he is roundly reviled by the author throughout the story. He has just arrived in New York to direct a big-money feature film called *Good Money*, a stature he has attained because of his small reputation for some scandalous British television commercials selling junk food, cigarettes, and pornography. "He is one of the new men," wrote Ian Hamilton in the *London Review of Books*, "the uneducated media slicksters who took over in the Sixties, a practitioner and a product of junk culture." Quite helpless to make the film good, Self sees it falling to pieces before his eyes. He hires one Martin Amis, a London writer of his slight acquaintance, to rewrite the script (for lots of money) and pacify thereby the film's maniacal and money-grubbing stars. Amis the character comes across as a high-minded, ascetic prig, forever maundering on about the art of fiction and the phenomenon of "gratuitous [i.e., money-free] crime." He accomplishes the rewrite, but the film is a failure and Self is ruined. Amis recognizes his responsibility, in the end, for destroying Self, but incurs no blame for the act. Hamilton confesses that he is "already persuaded that *Money* will be thought of for years to come as one of the key books of the decade." "The comedy and horror of the untrammeled self," wrote John Gross in the *New York Times*, "make a more powerful theme in Mr. Amis's hands than the theme of money. . . . *Money* remains a highly original and often dazzling piece of work."

Amis shows himself an engaging, exact, and perceptive critic in *The Moronic Inferno and Other Visits to America*, a collection of reviews, interviews, and pieces of reportage from the *Observer*, the *New Statesman*, the *London Review of Books*, *Tatler*, and *Vanity Fair*. The title, which comes from Wyndham Lewis via Saul Bellow, "is not," he says in the introduction, "a peculiarly American condition. It is global and perhaps eternal. It is also, of course, primarily a metaphor, a metaphor for human infamy: mass, gross, ever-distracting human infamy. One of the many things I do not understand about Americans is this: what is it like to be a citizen of a superpower, to maintain democratically the means of planetary extinction? I wonder how this contributes to the dreamlife of America, a dreamlife that is so deep and troubled. . . . Perhaps the title phrase is more resonant, and more prescient, than I imagined. It exactly describes a possible future, one in which the moronic inferno will cease to be a metaphor and will become a reality: the only reality." He is wonderfully apt about American writers, especially those who, like Amis himself, are wittily vicious and misanthropic satirists. Gore Vidal, he says, is "probably the cleverest book-reviewer in the world . . . the unchallengeable master of the droll stroll. . . . When writing about the real world, Vidal sounds like the only grown-up in America—indeed, his tone is that of a superevolved stellar sage gazing down on the globe in pitying hilarity. There are two reasons for this. First, Vidal was born into the governing classes, and has never regarded them with anything but profound suspicion. . . . The second and closely related reason for Vidal's bracing hauteur is that he is incorrigibly anti-American.

My, is Gore unpatriotic! No pomaded Hanoverian swaggerer could have such natural contempt for that coarse and greedy colony."

Something of Vidal's acidic vision of America seems to have infused Amis' vision of his own country in *London Fields*. Published in 1989, the novel was a best-seller in Britain and was well received by reviewers in the United States. Its failure to win a Booker Prize nomination clearly had less to do with its artistic quality than with the bitterness of its satire on contemporary England. "His pitch-black humor springs from a bristling arsenal of outrage, despair and fear," Mira Stout wrote in a profile of the author in the *New York Times Magazine*. "Amis's laughter is vengeful, vigilante humor." With characteristic ironic reversal there is nothing pastoral about these London fields. It is a bleak London of 1999 awaiting an ominous eclipse of the sun as its (anti-)heroine awaits her own murder (and indeed seems to invite it by making sexual victims of her male lovers). Not suprisingly *London Fields* managed to shock and offend many readers, particularly women. Nevertheless, it was generally conceded that men came off no better than women in this novel and that the real object of Amis' attack was the materialism of Thatcherite England. As Amis told Stout: "Money is a more democratic medium than blood, but money as a cultural banner—you can feel the whole of society deteriorating around you because of that. Civility, civilization is falling apart."

The dark mood of *London Fields* is considerably relieved by its rich comic invention. Like Vladimir Nabokov and Saul Bellow—both of whom have influenced his work—Amis has what Bette Pesetsky described in the *New York Times Book Review* as "a virtuoso's ear" for dialect and a gift for language that give his often caricature-like figures "a vitality and an erotic intensity seldom found in current fiction." She continues: "*London Fields* is not a safe book; it is controlled and moved not by plot but by the density of its language. The author freely offends sensibilities. Indeed, it's difficult to think of anything he spares us when it comes to the concerns of the flesh. But his language is demonically alive."

Amis is also the author of *Invasion of the Space Invaders*, a coffee-table book about video games, and *Einstein's Monsters*, a collection of five stories for the nuclear age which are preceded by a long introductory essay, "Thinkability," about his reactions to living under the threat of nuclear destruction. "In this debate," he writes, "in this crap game, I do want to get my chip on the table, however thin, however oddly coloured, however low its denomination. 'Einstein's

Monsters,' by the way, refers to nuclear weapons, but also to ourselves. We are Einstein's monsters, not fully human, not for now."

Amis married Antonia Phillips, a professor of aesthetics, in 1984. They live with their two sons in North London. He also maintains a flat where he writes in Notting Hill Gate, the setting of *London Fields.*

WORKS: *Fiction*—The Rachel Papers, 1973; Dead Babies, 1975; Success, 1978; Other People, 1981; Money, 1984; Einstein's Monsters, 1987; London Fields, 1989. *Non-fiction*—Invasion of the Space Invaders: An Addict's Guide, 1982; The Moronic Inferno and Other Visits to America, 1986.

ABOUT: Contemporary Authors New Revision Series 8, 1983; Contemporary Literary Criticism 38, 1986; Current Biography 1990; Mars-Jones, A. Venus Envy, 1990; Thwaite, A. (ed.) My Oxford, 1977, rev. ed., 1986; Who's Who, 1989. *Periodicals*—Book World March 24, 1985; Books and Bookmen April 1974; Encounter February 1974, February 1976, September 1978; Listener October 30, 1975; April 13, 1978; March 5, 1981; September 27, 1984; London Magazine February–March 1974; London Review of Books September 20–October 3, 1984; New Leader May 13, 1974; New Statesman November 16, 1973; October 17, 1975; March 13, 1981; New York April 29, 1974; New York Review of Books July 18, 1974; New York Times January 16, 1976; October 21, 1980; October 28, 1980; August 20, 1981; March 15, 1985; New York Times Book Review May 26, 1974; February 8, 1976; April 5, 1981; July 26, 1981; March 24, 1985; May 17, 1987; September 6, 1987; March 4, 1990; New York Times Magazine February 4, 1990; New Yorker June 24, 1974; Newsweek May 6, 1974; Observer (London) April 16, 1978; October 19, 1980; October 26, 1980; Saturday Review June 1, 1974; Spectator November 24, 1973; April 15, 1978; March 21, 1981; October 20, 1984; Sunday Times (London) April 13, 1978; September 26, 1982; Times Educational Supplement July 12, 1974; Times Literary Supplement November 16, 1973; October 17, 1975; October 17, 1976; April 14, 1978; March 6, 1981; October 5, 1984; May 1, 1987; September 29, 1989; Village Voice January 26, 1976; June 10–16, 1981.

*ANAGNOSTAKIS, MANOLIS** (March 9, 1925–   ), Greek poet and cultural critic, was born in Thessaloníki, where he lived and practiced medicine until 1978, when he settled in Athens. A major representative of the first postwar generation of Greek poets (sometimes called "the generation of defeat," with reference to the Left's defeat in the Greek civil war), Manolis Anagnostakis has been involved in the political and social life of his country in an unusually active and risky manner.

At the age of eighteen Anagnostakis joined

MANOLIS ANAGNOSTAKIS

EPON, the youth branch of the broad, Communist-supported resistance movement EAM. Shortly afterwards he was arrested by the German authorities and spent time in a concentration camp. He continued to be politically active during and after the occupation; this activity included the editorship of the leftist student journal *Xekinima* (Beginning) in 1944. In 1948 Anagnostakis was court-martialed and sentenced to death for his participation in the civil war (1945–1949). He was released in 1951, having spent three years in prison.

In the postwar period, Anagnostakis was critical of the Communist party, challenging its dogmatic attitude and undemocratic methods on literary as well as on social issues. His influential cultural and social criticism in the 1950s and 1960s provoked broad revaluations and contributed significantly to the development of a humanist Marxist culture in Greece. From 1959 until 1962 Anagnostakis published *Kritiki* (Criticism), a journal devoted to the democratic reform of Greek Marxism. He participated in the struggle against the military dictatorship (1967–1974) and, after the 1968 split of the Communist party, he joined the Greek Communist Party of the Interior (KKE Es.). After the restoration of democracy in Greece, Anagnostakis was a candidate of that party in many national elections.

A staunch moralist, Anagnostakis never wished to separate his poetry from his political and ethical commitments. His poems are those of an uncompromising radical humanist who seeks to express, and thus restore, the moral integrity of the Left in art and society. Anagnostakis' work is often topical and, in its later phase, sarcastic, strongly critical of the petit bourgeois spirit which he considers the major threat to human decency and social progress. While Anagnostakis' lifelong commitment to Marxism alienated conservative critics, who preached a doctrine of non-engaged art, his relentless anti-dogmatism was met with forceful attacks from the Communist leadership which would not tolerate any expression of dissent.

Although his poetry sometimes leans toward didacticism, Anagnostakis rarely adopts a pose of self-righteousness. His indignation is usually combined with painful self-criticism and sympathy for the victims of a rapidly deteriorating society, who are themselves its daily executioners. Thus he has won the admiration and respect of many readers who find in Anagnostakis a voice of rare honesty and integrity and read his work as a powerful body of poems which, in the words of D. N. Maronitis, "translate political protest into personal confession, and vice versa." His poetry, according to Yannis Dallas, "has the significance of a unique document, [it is] the chronicle of an individual as well as of a generation in the continuous 'Eras' and 'Sequels' of his collections' titles."

Anagnostakis has never been a prolific writer; his total literary output over a period of thirty years amounts to only eighty-seven poems. This concise oeuvre falls into three cycles. An early period consists of three small volumes under the common title *Epoches* (Eras), published between 1945 and 1951. The middle period consists of three volumes under the common title *I Sineheia* (The Sequel), published between 1954 and 1962. Anagnostakis' final period consists of thirteen poems under the title *O Stohos* (translated as *The Target*), written during the dictatorship (1970–1971). Most of these later poems were first published in the important collective volume *18 Keimena* (the American edition of the book, translated as *Eighteen Texts*, includes the entire work). A book of prose poems and fragments written in the same period (*To Perithorio '68 – '69*, The Margin '68–'69) has been excluded from Anagnostakis' collected poems, *Ta Poiimata 1941–1971* (Poems 1941–1971).

The cycle *Epoches*, written during the occupation and the civil war, begins as an elegy for the lost adolescence of young men and women growing up in the midst of war. Anagnostakis' chronicle of the era has two dimensions: in a general sense, the hard reality of war deprives his generation of the youthful carelessness it is entitled to and forces it into premature adulthood. In a more personal sense, the era thwarts the poet's desire to express himself in the soft, confessional mode of love poetry.

In a 1944 review Anagnostakis complains that "the reality of our time is so alien to dreamy and sentimental moods, [that aestheticism] can not satisfy us today as it would in other, peaceful times. . . . We do not see life, our life, in it. There is no answer to our questions." But this complaint is not addressed so much against aestheticism as against the era that deems it irrelevant. In his early work, Anagnostakis, overwhelmed by sorrow for "our lost ignorance, our lost wings," longs for precisely those "dreamy and sentimental moods" he feels obliged to repudiate in his criticism: "Still, it might be beautiful, like an open book, if hours would pass in silence, surrounded by security / And we could forget death, we who envied butterflies in our summer recollections."

While the dominant mood in the first book is soft melancholy, there are occasional optimistic notes, too. "Haris 1944," an elegy for a lost companion, ends with the affirmation that the young martyr's voice "shows us like a radiant sun the golden cities / Which spread before us bathed in Truth and clear light." But these positive visions do not seem to express Anagnostakis' real feelings. To a large extent, they are mandated by a powerful leftist critical credo, which considered excessive sorrow a sign of bourgeois decadence and demanded that socialist writers balance it with visions of the illustrious postrevolutionary future. For Anagnostakis, the promise of future social change can neither revoke nor justify the actual loss, whether it be the companion's spilt blood or the speaker's wasted youth.

The sense of loss deepens in Anagnostakis' second book, *Epoches 2*, which appeared near the end of the civil war, when the hope of social change has been irrevocably cancelled. As the poet's chronicle fills with images of a wounded, disintegrating society beyond the hope of healing, he tries to find strength by keeping the dream of love alive. This last resource is cancelled in the opening line of his next book, *Epoches 3*, written in prison after the end of the war: "Love is the fear that holds us close to others." Anagnostakis now finds a sterner voice: images of social decay mingle with those of political prisoners waiting for execution, to evoke not only sadness, but also anger and indignation.

At this stage Anagnostakis begins to develop a new poetic method: the poem incorporates specific, local memories and details in an attempt to capture the truth of actual, lived experience and save it from being leveled down by the progress of time. While this theme, resistance to time and forgetting, is Proustian, Anagnostakis' new method was inspired by Cavafy (whom Anagnostakis calls in a 1963 essay "the most accomplished, personal, and conscious figure" in Greek poetry). Yet this poet differs from both predecessors in an important respect; time, for Anagnostakis, devours and debases all that is valuable in human life, in a process that is not metaphysical and cannot be accepted as ordinary. Time is a material and malignant moral enemy, facilitated, as D. N. Maronitis observes, by "the guilty timidity or the hypocritical expedience of men too weak or too arrogant to preserve their personal memories alive." The struggle with such a powerful enemy is lonely and taxing, a romantic agon taking place in the context, and with the painful material, of hard reality. This agon dominates Anagnostakis' next cycle, I Sineheia.

Linos Politis has noted that, while "in Epoches [the poet's] target is the adversary political situation of the age, what is expressed in Sineheies is the internal struggle of the left. . . . " The early cycle occurs in an environment of companionship and political agreement; most poems are spoken in the name of a harmonious community of persistent dreamers, a valiant, cherished "we." The first two collections of the new cycle dramatize the disintegration of this community (the end of a heroic age), which is caused not only by the political defeat but, more significantly, by the ethical inadequacy of hypocritical survivors, who now appear eager to redeem the lost companion's blood with power. The poet finds himself "Upright and lonesome, in the terrible desert of the crowd" and assumes the duty of rescuing and guarding a heritage of precious values, the true history of his age. He reprobates the massive sellout of this heritage by the Party's leadership and undertakes to preserve, in his poetry, "what Elias was / Claire, Raoul, Egypt Street / The 3rd of May, streetcar no 8, 'Alcynoe' / George's house, the Infirmary."

In launching such a formidable attack against the ethics of his former comrades, Anagnostakis surely anticipated the resentment with which his work would be met. The official criticism of the dogmatic Left immediately branded it "decadent poetry" and spoke of Anagnostakis' "self-abandon" and "self-annihilation," even hinting at the author's "biological incapacity" as a reason for his failure to carry on with "active resistance." Yet this period of Anagnostakis' poetry includes some of his best work, the poems which later established him as a major representative of his generation.

The problem of this generation's cultural contribution is a major concern in Anagnostakis' criticism of the early 1960s. In 1960 he closed his journal Kritiki with a memorable statement:

"Our generation gradually passes leaving no decisive traces behind it, failing to establish its presence, its capital ideals, abandoning the arena to bankrupt figures of dubious history, or to younger bawlers who 'rebel,' 'get angry' and shout without ever suspecting the true meaning of revolution. In a suffocating space deprived of the oxygen of freedom, in the odorous conditions that have long become permanent in our land, our generation, battered from all sides, with its best sons decimated, was essentially confined to marginal columns, or handed over its 'representation' to its weakest members who, at best, falsify the true meaning of its struggle. In a land where mediocrity, slavishness, and hypocrisy are deified, our orphaned generation, unable to play the leading role it was historically entitled to, faces the danger of being buried silent, constantly promising, while time's merciless clepsydra is running out."

A few months later Anagnostakis published Sineheia 3, a collection of poems expressing, above all, fatigue; the middle-class ethic dominates his country completely, forming a reality too strong to be upset by either poetic or political struggle. The poet questions the relevance of his art and can find no strong argument to defend it. He starts looking for a final verse, "Intransigent, inaccessible, always ready. / With no potential for flowering / With no potential for corruption." After Sineheia 3 Anagnostakis stopped writing for eight years. Then, in 1970, O Stohos appeared as part of an important collection (Eighteen Texts), which ended the Greek intellectuals' refusal to publish during the dictatorship.

O Stohos, as D. N. Maronitis comments, is Anagnostakis' "fighting exodus," a work that "puts him back on the track of political cooperation, under extraordinary circumstances." As another critic, G. Lyciardopoulos, observes, referring to the poet's problems in Sineheia 3, this work is also "the violent solution which [Anagnostakis'] poetic will provided to a dead-end in poetic expression." In this final collection, Anagnostakis leaves behind him the wounded sensibility of his lost generation. He writes in a strong, confident voice, balancing sarcasm with mirth; his target is the Greek middle class whose members, including many ex-leftists, have conveniently and happily fit in the dictatorship. Anagnostakis' wrath is reserved for this class' intellectual representatives, timid, self-seeking aesthetes who accuse concerned poets of betraying "poetry, man's holiest expression." Anagnostakis' decisive response is that "Words must be hammered in like nails / so the wind won't take them." His last poem ends with an effective apology for political poetry: "So be it. / Crippled, show your hands. Judge so that you may be judged."

O Stohos completes Manolis Anagnostakis' poetic oeuvre. Since 1971 he has continued to write critical essays but, according to his own statements, no more poems. Yet this is not entirely true; in 1987 Anagnostakis published a critical biography of a fictional figure, Manousos Fassis, the poet's own satirical persona. This delightful parody of a scholarly monograph includes many poems (attributed to Fassis) which mock the style of a number of Greek poets, including Anagnostakis himself. Although the book is written in a playful manner, it is not free of a serious purpose: through Manousos Fassis, Anagnostakis exposes and undermines high seriousness in poetry, criticism, and literary scholarship. Writing has always been for Anagnostakis a confessional experience, a process whose aim is absolute liberation from every sort of illusion. The final stage of this stripping process is liberation from the illusion of poetry itself.

In an important 1985 article, published in the French newspaper *Libération*, Anagnostakis confesses why he stopped writing. He began to write very young, he says, when poetry was simply a way to compete with friends who excelled in things he could not do as well, like football. As he matured he realized that through poetry he could say what he was not allowed to express directly, that he could write about his personal experiences and his ideological adventures in a codified, elliptical idiom. But now he feels removed from poetry, his own as well as that of others. Although he is pleased by the fact that he is considered a good poet and that his work is still read, he is not flattered, nor does he seek the title or the halo of "poet." Poetry, Anagnostakis concludes, is a tool for youth, "for the age of voracious, abundant dreams." When it is prolonged after this period, the illusion it offers can become a substitute for action, a "flight from the essential encounter with action."

WORKS IN ENGLISH TRANSLATION: English translations of Anagnostakis' poetry include Edmund and Mary Keeley's "The Target" in *Eighteen Texts: Writings by Contemporary Greek Authors* (Willis Barnstone, ed., 1972) and Kimon Friar's *The Target: Selected Poems*, 1980.

ABOUT: Friar, K. *Introduction to* The Target. *Periodical*—Journal of Modern Hellenism 3, 1986.

ANDERSON, JESSICA (MARGARET QUEALE) (1917–   ), Australian novelist and short-story writer, was born in Gayndah, Queensland, Australia, the daughter of Charles James Queale, a livestock inspector, and the former Alice Hibbert. In a short interview with

JESSICA ANDERSON

Jane Perlez published in the *New York Times Book Review* on November 29, 1987, the writer compared Queensland, the remote, northeastern Australian state, to the American South: "It produces a disproportionate number of novelists. I think it might be the boredom, the quiet pace. The people I speak of are old enough to have benefited [from] or been affected by the quietness. But strangely, they all leave. It produces, but it doesn't nourish."

In 1935, having completed her schooling in the Queensland capital of Brisbane, where her family had moved, Jessica Queale left for Sydney, where she found work and began, in her free time, to write stories—she now calls these early efforts "trashy." She did not begin what she considers her serious work until twenty years later. *An Ordinary Lunacy*, her first published novel, takes place in the sharp, greedy, and hypocritical world of fashionable Sydney society. It is the story of a barrister, David Byfield, whose reputation at thirty-five "was beginning to be brilliant"; he "was being groomed," and "had a great future in politics." He is also shallow, careless, and impressionable. His mother, Daisy, is portrayed as a ruthless and ambitious woman, whose comprehensive dominance over others so fascinates the author that early on this character quite dominates the novel: Daisy is "one of those charming bullies whom it seems rather churlish to resist." The story finally and fully becomes David's own as he falls in love with a beautiful married woman, Isobel Purdy, who soon after they meet is charged with murdering her husband. Despite his mother's condemnation and at the steep cost of public approbation and, in all probability, his future political success, David wholeheartedly takes up her cause. He loses Isobel in the end, along with all the smart certainties of the life he has been bred to. The novel is primarily an intricate study of several flawed characters; the moral judgments Anderson makes, and the spiritual values she affirms, are universal ones. There is very little examination of Australian peculiarities: David and his mother would not be thought out of place in the equivalent social stratum of London or Boston. Anthony West in a review in the *New Yorker* called the book "an acutely sensed, intelligent, and discerning account of a genuinely troublesome, and most important, aspect of the psychosexual relationship between men and women"; he also felt, however, that it was "written in the terms of a commonplace piece of pulp fiction." Anderson herself continues to regard the book with affection: "I wouldn't write like that today," she remarked in 1987 soon after *An Ordinary Lunacy* was republished in the United States, "but I'm not ashamed of it. Some of it's a trifle purple."

After publishing *The Last Man's Head*, a psychological thriller about a Sydney police detective who comes to suspect a distant relative of murder, and *The Commandant*, a historical recreation in fictional form of the final days of Patrick Logan, the early Australian settler who was the flogging commandant of the penal colony at Moreton Bay near Brisbane, Anderson produced what many consider her finest novel, *Tirra Lirra by the River*. This slender volume comprises the first-person reminiscences of Nora Porteous, who is witty and lively at seventy years of age but who remembers her past only with great selectivity. Earlier in her life, we learn, Nora had suffered a good deal: she nearly died in an epic battle with pneumonia, lived through an intermittently happy marriage, then a bitter divorce, after which she escaped Australia for London and a sort of career, and finally managed, after yet another struggle, to return home to Australia. She is a brave and resourceful woman and always tells her story in an interesting way. Nora's is evidently not an important life, except of course to herself, yet it may well be exemplary of the lives of many Australian women who have, all this century and before, been doggedly intent on wresting independence and a sense of personal space from their often harsh, male-dominated society. Australia is strongly presented in this novel, and this is one of its most attractive features; there are well-drawn contrasts between conditions during Nora's youth and during her old age, between the small town she grew up in and the sophisticated sylling mo-

tropolis. Clifford Hanna, reviewing the novel in the Australian journal *Southerly*, thought it "a study of a mind haunted by a failed life, [and] an intimate view of life in suburban Australia between the wars, . . . a mood piece that takes great delight in resurrecting the past, and shows great skill in evoking atmosphere."

The Impersonators, which was published in the United States in 1985 as *The Only Daughter*, is a novel of only medium length, which nonetheless manages to tell the complex tale of a large Australian family, the Cornocks, with unerring grace, unforced detail, and an unhurried tempo. It begins by recounting the death of Jack Cornock, the patriarch, analyzing the feelings this event has generated throughout the family; the vexed question of the division of his considerable estate brings together the family's disparate members, all of whom the reader comes to know in considerable detail, in all their contrariness and contradictions. There seems hardly to be a wasted paragraph in the entire novel. Although Australia is vividly depicted throughout, this is finally a comedy of manners, in which well-drawn, rounded characters are made to relate to one another in exactly the way people do in real life, in delight and distress, in happiness and anger. "It takes . . . some fierce concentration," wrote Hilma Wolitzer in the *New York Times Book Review*, "to sort out the enormous cast of this book, but it's well worth the time and effort. Through Miss Anderson's artistry, her gifts for observation, insight and humor, each character comes to life and proves essential to the complex story."

Anderson has also published a two-part collection of exceptionally fine short stories, *Stories from the Warm Zone and Sydney Stories*. The five stories "from the warm zone" are told in the first person by Beatrice, a young girl growing up in rural and suburban Brisbane during the 1920s. She is the youngest of three daughters of a sickly father and a practical, no-nonsense mother. Her eldest sister, Rhoda, is the source of the greatest excitement and reassurance in Bea's life, from the time she is four (in "Under the House"), and Ro assumes the role of a thrillingly omniscient maker of magic, to the time, four years later, when (in "The Appearance of Things") the eight-year-old Bea is introduced by Ro to the much more sedate mysteries of the Anglican church. The stories have several themes, from the innocence and dependency of childhood to the conflict between the desire to please parents and siblings and the need to feel free and to express the rebelliousness in one's nature. The adults in the "Sydney stories" live in a considerably more complicated and circumscribed world; Marjorie, for example the central character in "The Milk," has finally found the courage to leave her husband, and because of her straitened circumstances must come to terms with living in a tiny flat in a poor suburb of Sydney. Her rueful self-awareness and calm acceptance of the newly difficult conditions of her life are recounted by Anderson in a steady, straightforward, and constantly illuminating prose. "The necessary backdrop of all Jessica Anderson's work," writes Hannah Pakula in the *New York Times Book Review*, "is the family. She delights in dissecting its subtle relationships—the natural alliances and enmities, the interplay within and between the generations. Her dialogue, devilish in its characterization, captures the diverse and wildly conflicting agendas beneath the surface of dinner table conversation."

Anderson has twice won the Miles Franklin award, her country's most important literary prize: in 1978, for *Tirra Lirra by the River*, and in 1981, for *The Impersonators*. She lives in Sydney in an apartment overlooking the harbor; like many of her characters, indeed like many Australians, she feels drawn to the sophistication of Europe but believes that for her "Australia is inescapable." She is "never at home away from the place, nor ever quite at home in it." Twice married and twice divorced, she has a daughter from her first marriage.

PRINCIPAL WORKS: *Novels*—An Ordinary Lunacy, 1963; The Last Man's Head, 1970; The Commandant, 1975; Tirra Lirra by the River, 1978; The Impersonators (U.S. title The Only Daughter), 1980; Taking Shelter, 1990. *Collected short stories*—Stories from the Warm Zone and Sydney Stories, 1987.

ABOUT: Contemporary Authors New Revision Series 4, 1982; Contemporary Literary Criticism 37, 1985. *Periodicals*—Book Week March 29, 1964; Library Journal February 15, 1964; December 1, 1983; Listener May 1, 1975; Ms. July 1984; New Republic February 25, 1985; New York Times March 5, 1964; New York Times Book Review March 1, 1964; February 19, 1984; February 24, 1985; November 29, 1987; March 11, 1990; New Yorker August 8, 1964; Newsweek January 23, 1984; Observer (London) July 20, 1975; Southerly December 1978, September 1980; Spectator August 22, 1970; The Times (London) August 22, 1970; Times Literary Supplement August 30, 1963; September 14, 1990; Village Voice May 22, 1984.

ANTHONY, MICHAEL (February 10, 1932–), Trinidadian novelist and travel writer, was born in Mayaro, a village on the southeast coast of Trinidad, the son of Nathaniel Anthony, a farmer, and Eva Jones Anthony. His primary and secondary schooling was in Trinidad; he never attended university. In 1955 he went to live in Britain, where he remained until 1968, working part time for the Reuters News Agency and concentrating on his writing, which in those early days was primarily poetry. He became friends with V. S. Naipaul, a fellow Trinidadian and his exact contemporary, who was for a time editor of the influential BBC program "Caribbean Voices." Naipaul persuaded Anthony to give up verse in favor of prose fiction. In 1968 he left Britain for Brazil, where he remained for two years. He returned home in 1970, finding a job as editor in the publications department of Texaco Trinidad. In 1972 he became an official of the Trinidad and Tobago Ministry of Culture.

Michael Anthony has never written about his life in Britain; his inspiration, except for his Brazilian book, has always been his home island, and particularly its southwest and southeast corners, areas little known even to Trinidadians, and unknown to foreigners who have visited Trinidad.

His first novel, *The Games Were Coming*, was a modest success. It is the story of Leon, a young man in anxious training for the cycling event of the Southern Games, to be held in Trinidad about the same time as the famous Carnival. There is a kind of matter-of-factness to the third-person narration of this novel which does not detract from its agreeably lively characterizations; the delineations of Leon, his father, his pregnant girlfriend Sylvia, and Leon's various fellow competitors have a rounded, lifelike quality. Leon's loss of the race, and its consequences for his life, is unexpected but, on reflection, possesses a strong sense of inevitability—the boy has thereby grown into a man. The novel was published in an expanded edition, with an introduction by the literary critic Kenneth Ramchand, and issued in Heinemann's Caribbean Writers Series in 1977.

The Year in San Fernando is another novel of self-discovery, told in a vivid first-person narration by twelve-year-old Francis, who is selected to leave his mother's home in Mayaro and to go to the small city of San Fernando, on the island's southwest coast, there to live in a large house as the companion of an ill, elderly woman. During his year in San Fernando Francis learns about life: he comes to terms with his awesome employers, he comes to understand the various faces of love and death, he touches and exploits his own inner resources. The novel was adversely criticized in sectors of the West Indian press for its lack of "any strong or profound philosophy"—by which was intended a political position. Yet its innocence of the endless political wrangling so typical of much West Indian literature is its very strength, in the opinion of Kenneth Ramchand, who devotes a chapter to the novel in his influential book *The West Indian Novel and Its Background* : "Anthony wishes primarily to establish our faith in the pure experiencing quality of the boy's mind; and the village is sensuously presented as the known and loved place, soon to become the place in memory." The novel mirrors, perhaps, a year Anthony himself spent in San Fernando in 1944, when he was also twelve. Yet this is not a novel of conventional recollection; in Ramchand's opinion: "Anthony's art of memory is so vivid and his artistic control so tight that never once does the mature man impose an adult's perception on his adolescent narrating character; nor does the author at any point allow the older man he has become to break into the narrative, either directly or with anticipatory devices."

Green Days by the River is another first-person narrative of growing up, told by Shellie, whose father is dying and who is struggling to help support his mother. He begins to work for Mr. Gidharee, whose daughter, Rosalie, becomes the beautiful object of the young man's first feelings of romantic tenderness. His passage to a kind of self-awareness, through various dark aspects of adult life, is told with unaffected simplicity and ease of narration. The reviewer for the *Times Literary Supplement* called Anthony's writing "limpid, clear to the point of ruthlessness, luminously single-minded. His style is all pace, colour, movement and purposeful gaiety. . . . Sometimes the facility and vivaciousness of it all get a bit too young and easy under the cashew trees, but mostly the tale is admirably judged, relaxed but urgent, unsentimentally passionate."

Anthony's non-fiction is also mainly about Trinidad. *Glimpses of Trinidad & Tobago with a Glance at the West Indies* was the first publication of a National Cultural Council program aimed at inculcating among the young a greater awareness of their country's history and culture. He included a dozen chapters, including those on the watercolorist Jean-Michel Cazabon, on the mountain village of Lopinot, on the glory days and final extinction of the old Trinidad & Tobago Government Railway, on the great calypso singer Lord Beginner, on the huge asphalt lake at La Brea, on offshore oil exploitation, on the national symbol the Bird of Paradise, and on the devastation caused the islands by Hurricane Flora in the autumn of 1963.

With Andrew Carr, Anthony edited another book of a tourism-promotional nature, bearing the somewhat incongruous title *David Frost Introduces Trinidad and Tobago*. Along with a brief introduction by Frost, the British television

entrepreneur, the book consists of chapters mostly by eminent Trinidadians, including Derek Walcott on Port-of-Spain, the capital, and C.L.R. James on cricket. Carr writes on the yearly Carnival celebrations, and Anthony contributes one of the book's most memorable chapters, "In a South-eastern Village," about a day in his birthplace, Mayaro, still an out-of-the-way village, even at the time of writing far off the usual tourist track. He evokes the simple existence of the place, the slow, ideal pace of life of the fishermen and the regular routine of schoolchildren, with a simplicity and ease that only long familiarity can produce.

PRINCIPAL WORKS: *Fiction*—The Games Were Coming, 1963 (U.S. 1968); The Year in San Fernando, 1965; Green Days by the River, 1967; King of the Masquerade, 1974; Streets of Conflict, 1976; All that Glitters, 1981; Bright Road to El Dorado, 1982. *Collected short stories*—Michael Anthony's Tales for Young and Old, 1967; Cricket in the Road, 1973; Sandra Street and Other Stories, 1973; Folk Tales and Fantasies, 1976. *Non-fiction*—Glimpses of Trinidad & Tobago with a Glance at the West Indies, 1974; Profile Trinidad: A Historical Survey from the Discovery to 1900, 1975; The Making of Port-of-Spain, 1757–1939, 1978; First in Trinidad, 1985; Heroes of the People of Trinidad & Tobago, 1986; A Better and Brighter Day, 1987; Towns and Villages of Trindad and Tobago, 1988. *As editor*—(with A. Carr) David Frost Introduces Trinidad and Tobago, 1975.

ABOUT: Black Writers, 1989; Caribbean Writers: A Bio-Bibliographical-Critical Encyclopedia, 1979; Contemporary Authors New Revision Series 10, 1983; Contemporary Novelists, 4th ed., 1986; Ramchand, K. The West Indian Novel and Its Background, 2nd ed., 1983. *Periodicals*—Best Sellers August 15, 1967; Books and Bookmen February 1971; Choice February 1971; Library Journal September 15, 1967; London Magazine April 1967; New Statesman November 9, 1973; New York Times Book Review August 6, 1967; April 14, 1968; Observer (London) February 22, 1976; July 26, 1981; Spectator February 21, 1976; Times Literary Supplement March 4, 1965; April 13, 1967; March 1, 1974; World Literature Today Spring 1984.

APPLE, MAX (ISAAC) (October 22, 1941–), American novelist, short-story writer and essayist, writes: "I've tried to live a quiet life which is good for a writer, but I live in a noisy world and I like to listen. I'm the son of working class parents, immigrants. My first language was Yiddish, an oddity in Grand Rapids, Michigan. My two older sisters and I all became English majors at college, but I was never quite sure where one language stopped and the other began.

"I've spent fifteen years teaching at Rice Uni-

MAX APPLE

versity in Houston. I have two children, Jessica and Sam, and am married to Tayla Fishman, a historian."

One of the generation that came to literary maturity in the America of the early 1970s, an era of rage, protest, and iconoclasm, Max Apple has made a unique place for himself among American satirists. He is troubled rather than angry, tolerant rather than rebellious, critical but never cynical, worried but never despairing. In one of Apple's semi-autobiographical stories, "Pizza Time," he takes his two children to a shopping mall near Houston where they become mesmerized by video games. The piece begins with a game plan: "Directions: You are a parent. Your mission is to raise your two children to become reasonably sane, decent, compassionate, capable adults. You must overcome all the obstacles on the board." At the end, caught up himself in the electronic frenzy of the game, he receives these directions: "You are the last human family. The robitrons conclude that human life is inefficient and therefore must be destroyed. Save Daddy, save Mommy, save Mickey. . . . " To which he replies: "We do not answer. Jessica and Sam pull me toward home. We will not be the last human family. Your turn."

Larry McCaffrey and Sinda Gregory write: "Part of Apple's fascination with American culture lies in the fact that he grew up under circumstances that tended to set him outside that culture." Like many children of immigrants, he dreamed the American Dream, focussing partic-

ularly on two of its most conspicuous elements—business success and sports. Born in Grand Rapids to Samuel and Betty (Goodstein) Apple, he lived in a large Yiddish-speaking family, close to his immigrant grandparents, especially to his story-telling grandmother. "My grandfather," Apple writes, "wanted me to be a rabbinic scholar, my grandmother thought I should own at least two stores, my sisters and my mother groomed me for a career as a lawyer or 'public speaker.' My father knew that I wanted to play second base for the Tigers." Having discovered the public library, however, Max Apple had no problem in choosing his career: "The books all in order, the smiling ladies to approve me, the smooth tables, even the maps on the walls seemed perfect to me. The marble floors of the library were the stones of heaven, my Harvard and my Yale, my refuge in the English language."

Apple completed his B.A. at the University of Michigan in 1963 and went to Stanford in 1964 for graduate study. In 1970 he received a Ph.D. from the University of Michigan with a dissertation titled "Arabism, Hermeticism, and the Form of *The Anatomy of Melancholy*," a study of influences on Robert Burton's Jacobean prose work. Remote as all this seems from the American pop culture that is the subject of most of Apple's published work, it is not without certain affinities—at least in the mysticism and myth and the often melancholy tone that inform his satires. After teaching for a year as assistant professor of literature and the humanities at Reed College in Oregon, he joined the English faculty of Rice University where he has been a full professor since 1980.

Apple's first book, *The Oranging of America*, was a collection of imaginative short stories about very real characters—among them Howard Johnson, Norman Mailer, Walt Disney, Fidel Castro, and Apple himself. The stories belong to the relatively new literary genre sometimes called "faction" that mingles reality and fantasy, not necessarily with political or sociological intent, but in the interests of portraying the quality, the quintessential spirit, of contemporary America. His "real" characters, Apple told McCaffrey and Gregory in an interview some years later, are not based on research but on free imagination. They are shortcuts: "If I use J. Edgar Hoover in a work, it seems to me that everyone in our culture who has done his job has already created Hoover in their minds . . . My interests aren't in the literal stuff but in what these figures represent, what arises from these institutions, the characters who evolve from them . . . I wanted to present that image of understanding human limits and needs."

The Oranging of America was an immediate success. "Apple's humor is entirely effective," Celia Betsky wrote in the *Saturday Review.* "From political morality to private hang-ups, he hits things right on target by making the familiar into a parody of itself, by letting spoofs show how serious our zany realities are . . . Apple pokes fun at high culture and appreciates low, but his own art shades more to the transcendental than the pop. It transforms while it impersonates, changing not only what we see but the way we see it." What we see is a visionary Howard Johnson dotting the American landscape with his orange roofs and providing comfort for the hungry, weary American motorist; Walt Disney creating an American myth with Mickey Mouse while his business-like brother builds Disneyland American enclaves. In one story the narrator, a mirror reflection of Apple, engages in a boxing match with Norman Mailer who has all the advantages, not only of height and weight but also of best-selling books, money, and fame. "My weapons," Apple writes, "are desperation, neglect, and bad form." The humor of *The Oranging of America* is satirical but not black. As Apple told McCaffrey and Gregory: "Since I like the stories and the people in them, I usually want to give my work a happy ending. That's the child's wish for good behavior that I have carried wholly with me into adult life."

Zip: A Novel of the Left and the Right, Apple's first novel, found less favor with reviewers. His central character is a lonely, apathetic young man in Detroit in 1968. He dismantles dead batteries for a living and faces a bleak future because, as his ambitious grandmother tells him, he lacks "zip." His life changes radically when he meets and takes over the management of a middle-weight boxer; through him he begins to live vicariously. He meets Jane Fonda and becomes involved in a conspiracy to kidnap J. Edgar Hoover and hold him hostage in Fidel Castro's Cuba, a wild scheme that just skirts the edges of nightmare. Nicholas Delbanco, writing in the *New Republic,* found the novel flawed by a split between the seriousness with which the characters take the world and the author's comic sense which "produces a kind of vertigo . . . Apple is most effective when he goes for the sidelong effect . . . But it's hard to know what this novel's about, or who's kicking whom for a loop." Delbanco conceded, however, that the writing is "sprightly" and that "Apple's imagination is fecund; if the book leaves the aftertaste of cotton candy, it's nevertheless been a well-spun sweet roll." The problem apparently was in sustaining the wildly imaginative conception through a full length novel. As Tony Tanner-Gultonick wrote in *Partisan Review, Zip* "mates thou a humanal of the

Jewish novel of the fifties with the whimsy and politics of the pop novels of the sixties, and the result is a hybrid that should be palatable but is curiously uninteresting as an entire book."

In 1987 Apple published a second novel, *The Propheteers,* that brought back some of the characters from *The Oranging of America* and added some new ones—the wealthy Margery Post Merriweather, her father the cereal maker C. W. Post, and the frozen-food inventor Clarence Birdseye. Wildly absurd as the plot is— involving the struggles of Howard Johnson and Mrs. Merriweather to foil plans to build a Disneyland in Florida—the book has a sounder structure than *Zip.* Described as "a mock-epic treatment of entrepreneurial capitalism," *The Propheteers* (the title of course a pun) presents a now aging Howard Johnson, accompanied by his faithful assistants, driving back and forth over an America in which he is being superseded by a younger generation of corporate executives. The old man's dream of a "Johnsonland, a nature-lover's park, an Audubon Society version of Disneyland where there were no waiting lines, only a large-scale game preserve dotted with small restaurants and lodges," is doomed. The era of propheteers as human beings is dying. Impersonal corporate business is taking over their names "without wholly taking them over." "Despite a convoluted imagination," Cyra McFadden wrote of the book in the *New York Times Book Review,* "he [Apple] writes straightforward prose, no sly asides, cheap shots or nudge-nudge wink-wink witticisms . . . No one's funnier, in his own singular fashion." That there is, however, considerable depth to Apple's gentle satire was suggested by Alan Wilde in his book on satire and irony in literary modernism and postmodernism. Wilde believes that Apple's work represents "a distinctly postmodern art. Neither reductive nor, on the other hand, hopeful of establishing in art or in life an aesthetic of total order endorsing modest pleasure in a world accepted as making no ultimate sense, it is a vision that lacks the heroism of the modernist enterprise but that, for a later and more disillusioned age, recovers its humanity."

Fiction and more recognizable reality come together in Apple's essays and short stories collected in *Free Agents.* Shimon Wincelberg, in the *New Leader,* found this book "a cheerful mixture of Apple's deceptively bland sense of fantasy and airy humor—a humor free of malice, aggression, or sly nudges to share a laugh at another's expense." In *Free Agents* his targets are once again pop culture, Washington lobbying, Hollywood, the jargon of corporate business, but, as Walter Clemons wrote in *Newsweek*: "He is a satirist without scorn, an affectionate ironist." Apple dedicates this book to his children, "who are as real as they can be," and acknowledges that some of the pieces are "obviously biographical." Among these is the essay "The American Bakery," first published in the *New York Times Book Review* as "My Love Affair with English." Here Apple traces his development as a writer discovering the English language and its power to transform his whole immigrant heritage into a new language, a means of communication that links worlds and cultures. At the end of the essay he addresses his readers: "Believe me, reader, I would like to know you . . . I wish I could tell you more, and I will perhaps in stories and novels. there I'll tell you more than I know. There I'll conjure lives far richer than mine, which is so pedestrian that it would make you seem heroic were you here beside me. Take comfort, though, in these sentences. They came all the way from Odessa at the very least and have been waiting a long time. To you they're entertainment; to me, breath."

PRINCIPAL WORKS: *Collected short stories*—The Oranging of America and Other Stories, 1974; Free Agents, 1984. *Novels*—Zip: A Novel of the Left and the Right, 1976, The Propheteers, 1987.

ABOUT: Contemporary Authors New Revision Series 19, 1987; Contemporary Literary Criticism 33, 1985; McCaffrey, L. and S. Gregory (eds.) Alive and Writing, 1987; Wilde, A. Horizons of Assent: Modernism, Postmodernism, and the Ironic Imagination, 1981. *Periodicals*—New Republic June 24, 1978; New York Times Book Review July 16, 1978; March 1, 1987; Newsweek June 25, 1984; Partisan Review 47, 1980; Saturday Review January 22, 1977.

*ARIÈS, PHILIPPE (July 21, 1914–February 8, 1984), French historian, was born in Blois to a conservative, monarchist family, some of whom had been planters in Martinique. He attended the Sorbonne, where during the late 1930s he continued to espouse Roman Catholic and royalist beliefs and was furthermore a devoted follower of Charles Maurras, the intellectual leader of Action Française, an antisemitic, deeply disreputable, far-right-wing group that eventually welcomed and collaborated in the Nazi occupation of France. Ariès wrote frequently for *L'Etudiant français*, the organization's student journal. He was called up for military service at the very end of the 1930s, but accepted demobilization following the German seizure of Paris in June 1940; he never joined the Resistance, but returned to take part in the attenuated intellectual life of the occupied capital.

Ariès' first book, *Les traditions sociales dans les pays de France* (Social Traditions in the Regions of France, 1943), was put out by a collaborationist publishing house, Editions de la Nouvelle France. It is an anodyne volume, quite unlike the historian's later work, and purports to examine "how very different social types have been able to localize themselves in France"; "We shall see," he writes in the introduction, "how these stable social states may be disturbed by exterior influences, [such as] the attraction of the great cities, but these very influences act with such a periodicity that they constitute a permanent element of differentiation and permit one to pick out well-defined social types."

Ariès never qualified to be a university teacher; he spent most of his working life as a civil servant, a tropical-plant specialist for the Institut Français de Recherches Fruitières d'Outre Mer, a job substantially connected with the old family business. He eventually became the Institut's director of publications and of its documentation center. He continued to write history, however: in his autobiography, *Un historien du dimanche* (A Sunday Historian, 1980), he explained, "I began to write history the way other people spend their Sundays painting." His next book was the vast compendium *Histoires des populations françaises et leurs attitudes devant la vie depuis le XVIIIe siècle* (History of the French Population and Their Attitudes to Life since the Eighteenth Century, 1948; rev. ed., 1971), which eventually won the Gabriel Monod Prize of the Académie des Sciences Morales et Politiques.

His first book to appear in English translation was *L'Enfant et la vie sous l'ancien régime* (1960; translated as *Centuries of Childhood: A Social History of Family Life*, 1960). Challenging the prevailing belief "that the family constituted the ancient basis of our society, and that, starting in the eighteenth century, the progress of liberal individualism had shaken and weakened it," Ariès argued that "on the contrary the family occupied a tremendous place in our industrial societies, and that it had perhaps never before exercised so much influence over the human condition. . . . The idea of the family appeared to be one of the great forces of our time. I then went on to wonder, not whether it had ever been as strong before, even whether it had been in existence for a long time. . . . The aim of this book is to reply to this question on the modernity of the idea of the family." The book's conclusions, in the opinion of Peter Gay writing in the *Saturday Review,* "are a little too curt to be wholly convincing, but they are congruent with [Peter Laslett's] work on English social structure in the seventeenth century. . . . [The book] deserves a wide public not merely for its own sake—for its wealth of anecdotes, its illumi-

°ä rē ·ez ´, fē lēp´

nating portraits and its far-reaching suggestions, but also because it is a model of a new kind of history."

A series of four lectures delivered at Johns Hopkins University led to the essays in *Western Attitudes toward Death: From the Middle Ages to the Present*. Ariès was convinced by his research that it was the culture of the United States which has played the principal role in transforming Western attitudes toward death in the twentieth century. Death appeared to be omnipresent during the nineteenth century and earlier, as he writes in the introductory essay: "Funeral processions, mourning clothes, the spread of cemeteries and of their surface area, visits and pilgrimages to tombs, the cult of memory. But did this pomp not hide the weakening of old familiarities, which alone were really deeply rooted? In any case, this eloquent decor of death toppled in our day, and death has become *unnameable*. . . . Technically, we admit that we might die; we take out insurance on our lives to protect our families from poverty. But really, at heart we feel we are nonmortals. And surprise! Our life is not as a result gladdened! . . . Must we take for granted that it is impossible for our technological cultures ever to regain the naive confidence in Destiny which had for so long been shown by simple men when dying?" Robert Darnton, in the *New York Review of Books*, called the work "important and challenging. . . . [Ariès] has fused his insights into one eloquent synthesis—and he covers almost two millennia in one hundred pages. . . . He has enriched history with a supply of hypotheses that will reorient research, even if many of them prove to be false."

Ariès's exploration of Western attitudes toward death continued in *L'Homme devant la mort* (1977; translated as *The Hour of Our Death*, 1981). His original plan for the 651-page book, the author writes in the preface, "was modest. I had just finished a long study on the sense of family, in the course of which I had discovered that this sense, which was said to be very old and to be threatened by modern life, was, in fact, recent and was associated with a specific phase of modern life. I wondered whether this represented a general tendency, in the nineteenth and early twentieth centuries, to attribute remote origins to collective and mental phenomena that were really quite new. This would be tantamount to recognizing, in this age of scientific progress, the capacity to create myths." Surveying ancient funerary practices, he noted "marks of indifference toward the dead," reflecting an attitude quite different from our own. And what attributed the piety associated with death since the late eighteenth century to "a new

sensibility [that] rejected the traditional indifference . . . a piety was invented which became so popular and so widespread in the romantic era that it was believed to have existed from the beginning of time." "Who would have thought," asked J. S. Allen in the *Saturday Review*, "death has a history, that it has worn a different cloak in every age and rattled its sack of bones to different tunes? Who, that is, but Philippe Ariès? . . . [He] meanders through the long, mazelike corridors of his theme like an insatiable collector, relishing every suggestive find, taking turns at random, and spinning interpretations of everything he sees. Exhausting (if not exhaustive), the book is a monument to its subject: our culture's obsession with death."

Images de l'homme devant la mort (1983; translated as *Images of Man and Death*, 1985) is a briefer work than its predecessor, a sort of terse iconographic history of its subject. The book consists of 397 illustrations arranged alongside an integrated text describing the changing image of death through two thousand years of Latin Christianity. "Death loves to be represented," Ariès wrote in his preface just a year before his own death, which he had been expecting for some time. "That not only was true of the long periods before the invention of writing but remained so thereafter. Despite the body of discourse on death which has flourished ever since the existence of writing and therefore of (initially sacred) literature, the image is still the richest and most direct means that man has of expressing himself, faced with the mystery of the end of life. The image can retain some of the obscure, repressed meanings that the written word filters out. Hence its power to move us so deeply."

Ariès was general editor, along with the medieval historian Georges Duby, of the massive five-volume series, *Histoire de la vie privée* (A History of Private Life, 1986), which began with the publication of two 630-page volumes: *De l'Empire romain à l'an mil* (translated as *From Pagan Rome to Byzantium*), edited by Paul Veyne, and *De l'Europe féodale à la Renaissance* (translated as *Revelations of the Medieval World*), edited by Duby (1986). In an introduction to the first volume, Duby intends the series as a memorial to his coeditor, whom he calls a distinguished historical pioneer, one of the very first "to discover how to penetrate the apparently impenetrable sectors . . . of childhood, the life of the family, and death." Unfortunately, Ariès wrote no major section of the work before he died. Another book, which he edited with André Béjin, constitutes the remainder of his work in English translation. *Sexualité occidentale* (1982; translated as *Western Sexuali-*

ty: Practice and Precept in Past and Present Times, 1985) grew out of a seminar given by Ariès in 1979-1980 at the Ecole des Hautes Etudes en Sciences Sociales. It was the last book he himself saw through the press, a remarkably coherent and wide-ranging collection of sixteen essays, of which the four most historically provocative are by the master himself: "St. Paul and the Flesh"; Thoughts on the History of Homosexuality"; Love in Married Life"; and "The Indissoluble Marriage."

WORKS IN ENGLISH TRANSLATION: *Centuries of Childhood* was translated by Robert Baldick in 1962; Helen Weaver translated *The Hour of Our Death* in 1981; and *Images of Man and Death* was translated by Janet Lloyd in 1985. *Western Sexuality*, which Ariès co-edited with André Béjin, was published in Anthony Forster's translation in 1985. The first two volumes of his *Histoire de la vie privée* were translated by Arthur Goldhammer as *From Pagan Rome to Byzantium* in 1987 and *Revelations of the Medieval World* in 1988. Ariès' *Western Attitudes toward Death* was published in 1974.

ABOUT: Annual Obituary 1984; Contemporary Authors 89–92, 1980; *Periodicals*—America May 1987; American Scholar Autumn 1974; Choice May 1981, June 1987; Christian Science Monitor March 11, 1987; Contemporary Sociology July 1986; Critic June 1981-I; Economist March 28, 1987; History February 1987; Library Journal December 1, 1962; February 1, 1981; January 1986; February 15, 1987; Nation June 27, 1981; New Republic August 23, 1974; March 7, 1981; June 29, 1987; New York Review of Books June 13, 1974; New York Times Book Review July 21, 1974; February 22, 1981; May 3, 1987; March 20, 1988; New Yorker December 1, 1962; June 22, 1981; Newsweek July 8, 1974; April 6, 1981; Psychology Today August 1975, March 1981; Saturday Review March 23, 1963; February 1981; Scientific American April 1963; Time December 28, 1962; March 9, 1981; Times Literary Supplement September 14, 1962; September 5, 1986.

*ARIYOSHI SAWAKO (January 20, 1931–August 30, 1984), Japanese novelist and playwright, was born in Wakayama City at the home of her maternal grandparents. She was the only daughter and second of three children of her mother, Akizu, and her father, Masatsugu. At the time of her birth, Ariyoshi's father, an employee of the Yokohama Specie Bank (the forerunner of Tokyo Bank), was on assignment at the New York branch. He did not return to Japan until 1935, when his daughter was already four years old. At that time, the family moved from Wakayama to Tokyo, but in 1937 they accompanied Masatsugu on his next assignment, to Batavia on the island of Java (present-day Djakarta, Indonesia). Ariyoshi was enrolled in a Japanese

ARIYOSHI SAWAKO

elementary school that had been established for overseas workers. But further transfers between Java and Tokyo until 1941 resulted in Ariyoshi's changing elementary schools five times before she graduated. In addition, poor health kept her attendance record low. She returned to spend the war years in Japan, first in Tokyo, then back to Wakayama after the attacks on Tokyo commenced. Altogether she attended five higher schools before graduating in 1949. In 1947, she was baptized into the Catholic Church.

In April of 1949, Ariyoshi was admitted into the English Literature department of Tokyo's Women's College, but illness forced her to take a leave of absence the following year. While she was recuperating, her father died unexpectedly. The financial shock to the family meant for Ariyoshi that, when she was well enough to return to school, she had to rematriculate into the two-year English program at the women's college. While at school she became interested in the classical Japanese arts, particularly the theater, and for a time it was her ambition to become a drama critic. She joined the Kabuki study club at her college, and in June of 1951 won an essay contest sponsored by the theater journal *Engekikai* for her piece on actors. At school she also joined the Catholic student union and literary clubs devoted to the study of the proletarian writers Kobayashi Takiji and Miyamoto Yuriko. Before graduation she joined the editorial staff of the theater journal, and after receiving her degree in March of 1952 she took an editorial job with the Okura Publishing Company. She also became affiliated with two small coterie journals

°a rē ō′shē

that were publishing the works of unknown writers. There she met several budding authors who would later become major figures, including Yoshiyuki Junnosuke and Miura Shumon.

In 1954 Ariyoshi became associated with a theatrical dance troupe, Azuma Kabuki, headed by the dancer Azuma Tokuno, and from July of that year until May of 1956, she performed a variety of functions for the group, from serving as traveling correspondent and secretary on the troupe's tour of the United States to assisting in the direction of their stage pieces.

In January of 1956 her associates at one coterie magazine, without seeking her approval first, submitted a story Ariyoshi had written to a literary competition sponsored by the important journal *Bungakkai*. The story, "Jiuta" (Ballad), was one of the finalists for the Newcomer's Prize and was published in the journal. It subsequently was nominated for the Akutagawa Prize, the most important award for serious literature to which a new writer can aspire. This unexpected—and unsolicited—success prompted Ariyoshi to write further short stories, but her interest in the drama did not wane. She wrote both a dance play, *Aya no Tsuzumi* (The Damask Drum), and a play for the puppet theater, *Yuki Konkon Sugata Mizuumi* (Snow Falling Thick Over the Lake) in 1956. The latter play was performed at the Osaka Bunraku Theatre, an auspicious introduction into the professional theatrical world. Both plays deal with artists who work within the traditional forms, thereby confronting the conflicts between orthodoxy and the changing nature of contemporary society. Generational conflicts are added to the formula, but in each instance a final resolution is reached between the unyielding past and the unsettled present, between parent and child.

The reception for Ariyoshi's next short story, "Shiroi Tobira" (The White Door, 1957), suggests some of the ambivalence which surrounded her work. The border lines between "serious" and "popular" literature are clearly drawn in modern Japan, and few authors cross over once they are defined as belonging in one category or another. In addition, the boundaries between male and female writers were closely preserved until the 1970s, and few women were considered fit for the "serious" classification. Ariyoshi was one of a small group of female authors to challenge those boundaries in her career, and though she was not always successful, her contributions in the demolition of these artificial walls were significant. Although she was nominated for the "serious" Akutagawa Prize, she never received it. Likewise, "The White Door" in 1957 was nominated for the "popular" Naoki Prize, but

again did not win. Her script for the television drama *Ishi no Niwa* (Rock Garden, 1957), however, was awarded a citation in that year's Arts Festival.

The short story "Eguchi no Sato" (The Village of Eguchi, 1958) is one of the few Ariyoshi stories to deal overtly with Christian themes. It centers on the conflict that develops between a foreign priest and his Japanese congregation when a young geisha presents herself for baptism. The prejudices and reactionary shortsightedness of the majority are motifs in this story that spill over into the novels of social consciousness that Ariyoshi would later write.

In January of 1959 Ariyoshi began serialization of her first important novel, *Ki no Kawa* (*The River Ki*). A partially autobiographical work, this novel traces the lives of three women who live along the banks of the Ki, which flows through Wakayama Prefecture. Hana, a woman of the late nineteenth century, is brought up to believe that her purpose in life is to forget herself in service to her husband, an important local landholder who is intent upon introducing new agricultural techniques to the region. She is the character most strongly identified with the title image: "You can compare her to the River Ki. Its blue waters, flowing leisurely, appear tranquil and gentle, but the river itself swallows up all the weak rivers flowing in the same direction." But their daughter Fumio is brash, rebellious, and contemptuous of the old ways; once she becomes a mother herself, however, she finds herself reverting to some of the family traditions. The granddaughter, Hanako, has been raised overseas, and her perceptions of Japan are all fresh and newly-learned rather than inherited. The novel, spanning these three generations, is necessarily episodic, and the interplay of old and new is sometimes obvious, but like many other Ariyoshi works the individual story parts are solidly told, and the ambitious structure of the novel renders it ultimately compelling.

From November of 1959 to August of the following year, Ariyoshi studied at Sarah Lawrence College in New York on a fellowship from the Rockefeller Foundation. At the completion of her studies, she spent three months touring Europe and the Middle East before returning to Japan. In June of 1961 she joined a group of Japanese writers who were invited to visit China at the invitation of the communist government. Her 1962 novel *Kōge* (Incense and Flowers), depicting the complex emotional relationship between an entertainer in the pleasure quarters and her mother, captured two literary prizes and attracted a popular audience in adaptations for the stage and in film.

In March of 1962 Ariyoshi married a promoter for an art patrons' society; they were divorced in 1964, only six months after the birth of a daughter. In 1963 Ariyoshi published the second of several panoramic novels set in her native Wakayama, *Sukezaemon Yondaiki* (A Chronicle of Four Generations in Sukezaemon's Family). These popular works were balanced by novels centered on major social concerns: the first, *Hishoku* (Without Color, 1964), treating the question of racial discrimination through the story of a Japanese woman married to an American black.

One of the distinctive features of Ariyoshi's fiction, particularly her social novels, is the detailed field research she conducted prior to the actual writing. She was a tireless foreign traveler, dedicated to the accurate observation and recording of information. The precise details she wove into her narratives added to their effectiveness as social documents as well as literature. In 1965 she planned a lengthy, complex one-year study of Chinese Catholicism and set out for China in May of that year, but had to cut her visit short in November. The following two months were spent gathering materials in Hawaii and other parts of the United States.

One of Ariyoshi's best-known novels, and certainly the literary peak of her Wakayama epics, is *Hanaoka Seishū no Tsuma* (The Wife of Hanaoka Seishū, 1967; translated as *The Doctor's Wife*), which received the Women's Literature Prize the year it appeared. At the center of the work is an historical drama, the story of the nineteenth-century Japanese surgeon, Dr. Hanaoka Seishū, who was the first physician to perform experimental surgery for breast cancer using general anesthetic. But it is the personal drama of the women surrounding Hanaoka, particularly the conflict for the doctor's attentions between his mother and wife, that is Ariyoshi's true concern in the novel. The stifling restrictions which the traditional Japanese family structure placed upon the daughter-in-law, the unchecked authority of the matriarch, and the resulting power struggles are described in clinical detail. The pressures emanating from the home, combined with the selfless dedication with which the doctor's wife supports his research, eventually impel her to volunteer to be the first patient to undergo the untried surgical techniques. By placing her own life in jeopardy, she is able to achieve a moral victory over her mother-in-law and assure herself of Hanaoka's gratitude and indebtedness. The work was popular not only in novel form, but also in the dramatic version which Ariyoshi herself wrote and directed for the Tōhō Geijutsuza Theatre in 1967. Extending her interest in the theater, that

same year Ariyoshi composed a ballad drama for her former dance colleague, Azuma Tokuho; in its performance at the National Theatre, it was awarded a prize from the Minister of Education. In 1968, Ariyoshi's novel about the female originator of Kabuki drama, *Izumo no Okuni* (Okuni of Izumo), received the readers' prize from Fujin Kōron publishing company. Ariyoshi expanded the work in 1969 and it received the Geijutsu Senshō Prize.

Another ambitious journey commenced in January of 1968. After traveling through Cambodia and Indonesia, Ariyoshi visited the uncharted interior wildernesses of New Guinea with a Japanese anthropologist as her guide. After her return to Japan in April, she serialized an account of her travels, *Onna Futari no Nyū Giniya* (Two Women in New Guinea, 1968). Shortly after she commenced the serialization, she was hospitalized for treatment of malaria, which she had contracted in New Guinea.

Ariyoshi's popularity among her contemporaries is attested to by the fact that her collected works were published in thirteen volumes in 1970; a second series was brought out in 1977. In November 1970 she traveled to Honolulu, where she lectured for one semester at the University of Hawaii on Japanese literature of the late Edo period (ca. 1750–1868). At the conclusion of her lecture duties, she spent six months touring the U.S. and Europe; she visited nineteen Broadway theaters while in New York City.

Ariyoshi was appointed a member of the tenth Central Council for Education in June of 1972. That same month saw the publication of her most widely-read novel, *Kōkotsu no Hito* (The Enraptured; translated as *The Twilight Years*). Ariyoshi was the first to give literary expression to what has come to be recognized as the key social problem of Japan in the 1980s: the graying of the population. The problem is, of course, acute for Japan, with the highest longevity rates in the world and a long tradition of children living with and catering to every need of their aging parents. By the time Ariyoshi's novel was published, however, a breakdown of the traditional system, a proliferation of nuclear families no longer willing or financially capable of nursing the elderly, and a consumerist ethic that was redirecting the resources of younger families— all these factors combined to make the issues Ariyoshi raises in her novel of vital concern to a large sector of the Japanese populace. That interest was reflected in sales figures for the novel; it sold more than a million hardback copies in less than a year, and over two million before the wave had crested. The plot of the novel is everyday, mundane, tracing the decline and advanced senility ("enrapturement") of Shigezō, an elderly man who loses his wife to death and struggles toward the same end himself. The problems, frustrations, and tears he brings to his family, especially his daughter-in-law Akiko, are detailed with the same painstaking care that Ariyoshi took with all her historical and field research. The result is a work about which Donald Keene has written, "I know of no Japanese novel available in English translation which gives so convincing a picture of what daily life is actually like for most people living in Tokyo today."

Ariyoshi followed up the success of *The Twilight Years* by collaborating on a translation into Japanese of Daniel Berrigan's anti-war play *The Trial of the Catonsville Nine*; she directed a stage version at the Kinokuniya Hall in Tokyo in October of 1972. Yet another novel, *Fukugō Osen* (Compound Pollution), dealing with the everyday impact of large social dilemmas, this time environmental pollution, was published in 1975. Although it was criticized for its incessant use of documentary evidence, graphs and statistics unbecoming a work of popular literature, Ariyoshi had once again succeeded at stirring widespread public discussion of major problems connected with life in the modern period, and once again the reading public made the book a best-seller.

Ariyoshi's health began to fail in 1977, and her literary output was slowed for a time. By the following year, however, she had begun to concern herself increasingly with feminist political and social issues, and it became clear that the role of women, which had been one of the motifs in her Wakayama novels, would come increasingly to the fore in her writings. That was certainly the case with her novel *Akujo ni Tsuite* (Concerning an Evil Woman, 1978), which in a unique cross-media experiment was serialized in a weekly magazine and simultaneously dramatized on national television. The novel takes the form of interviews which a reporter conducts with a variety of people who had known the central figure, a vastly wealthy woman of obscure background, after she has died in a fall from the tall office building named for her. The interchange of characters who regarded her as a pure, idealistic young woman and those who saw her as a conniving, money-grubbing opportunist create a dramatic tension in the novel, and though Ariyoshi prepares the reader for a simplistic, melodramatic conclusion to the work, she betrays that expectation and leaves the question of her protagonist's "evil" image open.

Ariyoshi produced another best-seller in *Kazunomiya Sama Otome* (Her Highness Princess Kazu, 1978) which received the Mainichi

Cultural Prize for the following year. In April of 1978 she traveled to France to hold consultations regarding her translation of a feminist work by Benoite Groult. From June through July she lived in seven people's communes and labored alongside the workers on mainland China in preparation for her *Chūgoku Repōto* (China Report, 1978).

Ariyoshi's last important novel, *Kaimaku no Beru wa Hanayaka ni* (The Splendor of the Bell at Curtain Time), was published in 1982. She had become single-mindedly involved in women's causes, and her public outbursts at the international PEN club conference held in Tokyo in May of 1984 caused considerable embarrassment. She died, an apparent suicide from drug overdose, just three months after the conference.

WORKS IN ENGLISH TRANSLATION: "The Village of Eguchi" and "Jiuta" were translated by Yukio Sawa and Herbert Glazer in 1971 and 1975, respectively; *The Doctor's Wife* was translated by Wakako Hironaka and Ann Siller Kostant in 1978; *The River Ki* and *The Twilight Years* were both translated by Mildred Tahara, in 1980 and 1984.

ABOUT: Contemporary Authors 105, 1982; Kodansha Encyclopedia of Japan, 1984; Nihon Kindai Bungaku Daijiten, 1984. *Periodicals*—Japan Book News October 1, 1984; New York Times Book Review January 20, 1985; Observer April 8, 1984; World Literature Today Summer 1981, Summer 1988.

ARNHEIM, RUDOLF (July 15, 1904–), American (German-born) psychologist, writes: "I am by nature a sedentary person, and if the twentieth century had not buffeted me around in Europe, America, and Asia, I probably would still be sitting in Berlin and doing my writing in the language and in the manner of what I did until 1933. I had been born at the center of the then undivided German capital as the son of a businessman, who would have liked me to enter his small piano factory by the time I finished my secondary education. But my father was soon persuaded that business was not for me. I became absorbed instead in the work at the Psychological Institute of the University of Berlin. The Institute, which after the revolution of 1918 had been located on two floors of the Imperial Palace, became the breeding place of Gestalt psychology. Much experimental work in the psychology of perception fitted my developing interest in the psychology of the visual arts. My doctoral degree in psychology and philosophy, together with studies in the history of art and that of music, was granted in 1932. Rather than

RUDOLF ARNHEIM

pursue my academic career, however, I was attracted at that time by editorial and journalistic work. I edited the cultural part of the weekly periodical *Die Weltbühne*, whose courageous editor in chief, Carl von Ossietzky, later received the Nobel Peace Prize while dying in a Nazi concentration camp. I myself left my native country in 1933, less than a year after my first major book, dealing with psychology and art of the film, had been published in Berlin. For about six years I worked in Rome as an editor for an institute of the League of Nations dedicated to educational film. The privilege of spending decisive years of my development in the Eternal City gave me standards of what is noble and lasting in Western culture; it created a kind of internal home base that remained with me wherever I went to live thereafter. The language of Dante and Petrarch has been a cherished possession of mine ever since.

"Before emigrating to the USA I spent the first months of the Second World War in London working as a translator for the news service of the British Broadcasting Corporation. Unforgotten are the night shifts, the walks through the blacked-out city with the moonlight reflected from the Georgian colonnades near Regent's Park. Finally, arriving on an equally blacked-out ocean steamer in America I saw the splendidly lit skyline of New York City for the first time in the autumn of 1940.

"America brought me back to my academic career. Generous grants from the Rockefeller Foundation and the John Simon Guggenheim Foundation helped me over the first few years in this truly new world. Teaching appointments at Sarah Lawrence College and the New School for Social Research in New York acquainted me with two very different facets of American education—a small suburban college with its highly individualized care for small groups of selected students and an evening university for city people of any age and class working during the day and eager to study at night. For many years I taught courses in psychological theory and the psychology of art at both institutions.

"In 1968 Harvard University established its Department of Visual and Environmental Studies—an ambitious attempt to put studio work in a broad social, psychological, and historical context. Six years later I reached retirement age and moved with my wife, who had been brought up in the Detroit area, to Ann Arbor, Michigan, where I enjoyed teaching as a Visiting Professor for another ten years.

"As I look over my work of the last sixty-five years or so I find it devoted essentially to one broad theme, the human mind's coping with the experience of living in a complex world with the help offered by an intelligent use of the senses. My analysis of the silent film had made me describe the image of a world obtained by entirely visual means, and, a few years later, a book on radio as an art of sound presented the counterimage of an exclusively audible world. This led me after my move to America to a comprehensive survey of visual perception in its application to the arts. *Art and Visual Perception,* first published in 1954, is now available in fourteen languages. There followed later books with more particular investigations of composition, architecture, the creative process in a painting by Picasso, and others. A particularly adventurous excursion into a broader range of human cognition produced a study of visual thinking, an attempt to show that not only does art always involve penetrating thought; but conversely, all truly creative reasoning in the sciences and elsewhere is based on the handling of perceptual imagery. A great reconciliation of thought and image is what I hope to have promoted during the work of a lifetime."

In 1954 a reviewer of Rudolf Arnheim's *Art and Visual Perception* described his work as an attempt "to bridge the gap between art and science as methods of understanding man and his world." Thanks to his broadly based education in the humanities and his continuing interest in literature, philosophy, and music as well as in the visual arts, Arnheim has been able to realize his ambitious aims. His training in Gestalt psychology which, he has said, "deals with the problem of wholeness, of field processes, situations in which the whole is entirely determined by its parts, and the other way around," gave him a solid foundation for his life's work. Gestalt psychology, he wrote in *Art and Visual Perception*, holds that "we know reality by creatively projecting meaning into whole configurations of detail, rather than by mechanically recording visual details that are later put together by reason."

Perception, Arnheim argued in *Toward a Psychology of Art*, is not an unconscious, mechanical function but "the eminently active and creative grasping of structure." It is an activity of both the creator-artist and the viewer. "The human mind receives, shapes, and interprets its image of the outer world with all its conscious and unconscious powers, and the realm of the unconscious could never enter our experience without the reflection of perceivable things. There is no way of preserving one without the other." We assume a gap between perception and thinking when in fact the two are complementary. Perception gathers the material of thought: "Unless the stuff of the senses remains present, the mind has nothing to think with." Arnheim called one of his books *Visual Thinking* because he believes that the act of looking itself "is an intelligent process—as complex as any 'purely' mental operation."

In his many writings on the psychology of art, Arnheim has drawn on a variety of sources—not only painting and sculpture but graphology, film (he began his career in Germany as a film critic), radio (his first job in the United States was a study of radio soap operas for Columbia University), music, children's drawings, which reflect spontaneous perception, and literary manuscripts, because these reflect, in the conscious efforts of poets to revise their work, "the stages of the creative process." He rejects what he calls "Freud's outmoded *l'art pour l'art* idea of artistic form," sublimation, the idea that the unconscious prevails in the conception of a work of art. He also rejects what he calls "the dazzling obscurity of arty talk, the juggling with catchwords and dehydrated aesthetic concepts." Complex as his ideas are, Arnheim writes lucidly: "Art is the most concrete thing in the world, and there is no justification for confusing the minds of people who want to know more about it."

Interviewed on the occasion of his retirement from the University of Michigan in 1984, Arnheim was asked for his impressions of the contemporary art scene. Noting that he had been born at the beginning of the twentieth century, "just about the time when Picasso painted the *Demoiselles d'Avignon*," and that he had been

witness to the major and most exciting developments of modern art from the Weimar Republic, the careers of Picasso, Matisse, Henry Moore, to Jackson Pollock, he confessed to a sense that today's art was less interesting to him because of "a lack of content. A work of art has to be about something . . . A man like Cézanne was a wise man. A man like Matisse was a wise man. A man like Jackson Pollock had a way of looking at the world which was very striking and which nobody had ever had before. And that's what his pictures are about. But if you're only interested in 'This is a shape,' and 'This is a color,' and 'This goes together,' and if your life otherwise is determined . . . by looking at television, you're not going to make it. Because none of them was that way."

Arnheim has received many academic honors and awards, including a Guggenheim Fellowship in 1942–1943, a Fulbright lectureship in Tokyo in 1959–1960, and a fellowship of the U.S. Office of Education, 1966–1968. Since 1976 he has been a Fellow of the American Academy of Arts and Sciences. Now emeritus professor of the Psychology of Art at Harvard, he has honorary doctorates from the Rhode Island School of Design, Bates College, Marquette University, the Kansas City Art Institute, Massachusetts College of Art, and Sarah Lawrence College. He married Mary Frame, a librarian, in 1953, and they have one daughter. His home is in Ann Arbor, Michigan.

PRINCIPAL WORKS: Film, 1933; Radio, 1933; Art and Visual Perception, 1954, 1974; Film as Art, 1957; The Genesis of a Painting (Picasso's *Guernica*), 1962; Toward a Psychology of Art, 1966; Visual Thinking, 1969; Entropy and Art, 1971; Radio: An Art of Sound, 1971; The Dynamics of Architectural Form, 1977; The Power of the Center: A Study of Composition in the Visual Arts, 1982; New Essays on the Psychology of Art, 1986; Parables of Sun Light: Observations on Psychology, the Arts, & the Rest, 1989. *Essay*—"Psychological Notes on the Poetical Process" *in* Poets at Work, ed. C. D. Abbott, 1948.

ABOUT: Arnheim, R. "My Life in the Art World," School of Art, University of Michigan, 1984; Contemporary Authors, New Revision Series 3, 1981; Thinkers of the 20th Century, 1983. *Periodicals*—Salmagundi Spring–Summer 1988; Studies in Art Education Spring 1984; Times Literary Supplement January 16, 1987.

ASHTON, DORE (May 21, 1928–   ), American art critic, writes: "When I was nine years old my parents were divorced. My father was a physician and my mother a working journalist. My mother loved books and my father loved the theater. My cultural exposure until their separation

DORE ASHTON

consisted of my father's taking me to theater
whenever he could (frequently having to leave
me alone when he was called to some sick child's
bedside), and my mother's making sure I had
plenty to read. They both came from Jewish
families that revered learning. I went to public
school and once, when there was an exhibition
of Dutch seventeenth-century painting at the
Newark Museum, the entire class was marched
through it. I was astounded by a painting of lem-
ons with tear-like moisture on their glistening
skins. As soon as I could, I tried to paint. My parents were pleased. The following year my father
took me on a cruise to Havana which seems to
have inspired me, as I have never forgotten the
huge panorama I painted, complete with palm
trees and cathedral and balconies and waterfront. On a visit last year to Havana I recognized
the streets my father and I had explored. Soon
after I was admitted as a special student in a Saturday art class for high school students in Newark, although I was at least four years underage.

"My mother gave me an old typewriter when
I was ten years old. I wrote little stories, and
eventually, a book for children which I illustrated myself. Still, if I think of it, I probably spent
more time reading than painting, and my two
interests vied all through my childhood and adolescence. I had the misfortune to attend a high
school where art meant bunny rabbits for Easter
and Santa Claus for Christmas, but I did have
one teacher who encouraged my reading and
gave me a copy of *War and Peace* as a reward.
Since most of the children in the school were not
interested in college, I found myself becoming

a star athlete in order not to be a total pariah. I
used to resent the long hours of practice on the
hockey field (I had made the first team) when
I could have been lying in my room reading Russian novels. I was in a hurry to get to college and
entered the University of Wisconsin just after
my seventeenth birthday.

"I could read as many novels as I liked there
and did, having managed to become a comparative literature major in a very liberal department. Meanwhile, a friend, who later became a
major art historian and who, like me, was divided in his loyalties, began to tell me about a professor of renown in the art history department.
I delayed for two years but finally sat in on Oskar Hagen's lectures. My friend, Fred Licht, had
not exaggerated. Hagen was superb and I was almost hooked. In my last year (after an absence
which took me to Paris to study painting for a
brief interlude with Fernand Léger, and to New
York to attend the New School, where I studied
with Rudolf Arnheim, a great influence in my
life), I went to Hagen and asked to take his graduate seminar. He was stunned by my audacity.
I hadn't even taken a survey course. But, typically for him, he sternly but cordially invited me
to try. I did two semesters and won his approval
to such a degree that he probably singlehanded-
ly won me a fellowship to Harvard's Fogg Museum in art history. (I had also applied to Yale in
comparative literature but they balked because
I had no Latin or Greek.)

"By the time I got to graduate school I was
very much interested in contemporary painting
and sculpture—an area for which the mandarins
in Cambridge had little respect. When once I
suggested that I might want to be an art critic,
even perhaps on a magazine or newspaper, they
quickly informed me that Fogg graduates didn't
indulge in such vulgar activities. Meanwhile, I
had asked the editor of the Art Students' League
magazine (I had attended classes desultorily
there since my fourteenth year) if I could occasionally send reports from Boston. With their assent, I became a fledgling art critic, writing
about contemporary art and discovering exhibitions at the Boston Institute of Contemporary
Art.

"My inauguration into the New York art
world was not auspicious. I worked for a time as
a receptionist in an art gallery, where I was fired
when the boss discovered I could not do simple
arithmetic and could not translate British
pounds into dollars. Then I worked in a book factory that produced indexes and very unhappy
employees, many of whom had Ph.D.s. I kept
trying to break into art writing and after a year
succeeded in landing a job as a reviewer for *Arts*

magazine at something like four dollars a review.

"So, at last, I was settled into what is called a profession. Or somewhat. I soon began to visit studios at a time when there was plenty of excitement about the "new American painting." I had the luck to meet artists who would soon be world-acknowledged, such as Willem de Kooning, Philip Guston, James Brooks, Jack Tworkov, Robert Motherwell, and scores of others, in their studios. Meanwhile, I had moved in with a European painter, Adja Yunkers, whom I would marry in 1954. My life, then, was totally saturated with contemporary art and studios and the art magazine's informal editorial meetings in a bar on E. 58th Street. Late in 1953 I met Howard Devree of the *New York Times* who had noticed my short reviews and asked if I would like a part-time job at the *Times*. I could scarcely believe my good fortune and, despite my Fogg background, felt it would be the best education possible for me. Two things happened after a few months: Devree offered me a full-time job and my husband won a Guggenheim grant to go to Italy. The dilemma was painful but I decided to sacrifice the *Times*. (Once again my luck held. Devree actually kept the job open and when I returned to New York in the Fall of 1955, I became a critic on the *Times*.)

"My five years at the newspaper were fraught with struggles. As a young writer, I began exploring the vanguard which, by then, was known as the Abstract Expressionist school, or the New York School. I tried to cover their exhibitions and persuaded the night managing editor to permit me to write a new kind of column which combined an interview with a review of contemporary artists' current exhibitions. Within two years I had been told of Mr. Sulzberger's (the owner) negative views of these wild artists and warned off. I was, and still am, a fighter, and refused to understand the messages I kept getting obliquely from fellow journalists and editors. Finally I was called 'upstairs' and roundly denounced by the highest authority. Perhaps I already knew that I never meant to be a journalist all my life, or perhaps I was just too young to understand how huge and powerful institutions work. In any case, my quarrel with the *Times* reached epic proportions, eventually became a public scandal, and ended with my resignation in 1960.

"I have often thought that my brush with real power was probably the most educational experience of all at the *Times*. I was active politically in both the campaign against nuclear armament and the civil rights struggle and never hesitated to sign my name to petitions and letters of pro-

test. The newspaper did not like its employees to be politically active, especially in those Cold War days, and especially on what they regarded as 'the left.' Once, Clifton Daniel, managing editor, even told me: 'Miss Ashton, you take care of art, I'll take care of politics.' I mention this only to stress the importance, at least in my life, of total commitment. I made no separation between my professional and my private life, and still don't. My views were undoubtedly partly shaped by the vivid philosophical discussions I heard amongst older intellectuals many of whom were pondering the writings of the European Existentialists. I regard myself as extremely fortunate to have been a member of a generation that could respond to the idea of being *engagé*, and the notion that there is inevitably an ethical increment in the pursuit of those activities we designate as art.

"After my debacle, I turned to academe to make a living. I have been a professor ever since, and have used the fortunate schedule to pursue my interests in articles and some twenty-three books. I don't really believe that being an 'art critic' or even an art historian, is a profession. I think that it is generally a means of inquiry; a means to pursue, for oneself, answers to those imponderable questions that proliferate in the arts. I have shunned ideology and attempted to broaden my personal culture in the interest of my work. I hope, still, to succeed."

––––––

At a seminar at Columbia University in 1981 Dore Ashton described herself as "a working art critic . . . not a theoretician or an aesthetician." However, she claims no critical methodology: "I am a fusion of many methods. I am an *activity* of my culture, a culture that I not only inherited but also shaped. I am, I hope, what Northrop Frye called 'a well tempered critic.'" Specializing in the contemporary visual arts, she has in fact written knowledgeably on art from pre-Columbian sculpture to the paintings of Fragonard and the French Impressionist school. Nor has Ashton confined her work to the visual arts. Widely read in literature and philosophy, she seeks in her writings a common ground on which painting, music, and poetry can meet. "He who talks about must *know* about a great deal. No amount of technical expertise can make up for a cultural narrowness," she writes, deploring narrow specialization as "a ghetto-izing of the arts . . . a symptom of a failing culture." In 1987 Ashton collected eighty-three of her essays, reviews, and introductions to art exhibition catalogues in *Out of the Whirlwind: Three Decades of Art Commentary*. In his preface to this volume Donald Kuspit noted the sophistication and independence of her work. As an advocate of the intellectual as well as the esthetic appeal of the visual arts, he wrote, "she is always looking for art which, whether or not it openly uses language, 'expands the boundaries of visual art into the general intellectual climate of our time.'"

Ashton's wide personal acquaintance with working artists has enriched her criticism. While some of her best known books—*American Art since 1945; The New York School: A Cultural Reckoning*—are wide-ranging surveys, others are close, sensitive readings of individual artists—*Yes, But . . . : A Critical Study of Philip Guston; About Rothko; A Joseph Cornell Album.* As early as 1969, in *A Reading of Modern Art*, she argued that the critic must see the work of art "in a double perspective," as a unique work of the individual artist and in its "expansiveness" to the viewer's mind, "emotionally, morally, psychologically, intellectually, historically, depending on a host of subtle considerations." The artist, she wrote, "is in a sense a delicately balanced compass needle, going back and forth from points of interior reconnaissance to points of exterior rapport. In our century the needle quivers ceaselessly."

Some art critics have found Ashton's judgments on individual artists too highly colored by her personal sympathies. Peter Schjeldahl, reviewing *Yes, But . . .* in the *New York Times Book Review*, suggested that her book on Philip Guston lacked critical perspective: "The kinds of traps Ashton falls into are not easy to evade when one is writing about an artist one reveres and feels to be misunderstood, but they are lethal." Norbert Lynton, on the other hand, in his review of the book in the *Times Literary Supplement*, felt that "it is Dore Ashton's responsiveness, her willingness to be led in her thinking by the work she admires rather than by theoretical restrictions that makes *Yes, But . . .* an unusually convincing account of a living artist." Hilton Kramer responded somewhat in the same way to her *Joseph Cornell Album*, noting that her "affectionate reconstruction of the esthetic universe in which her subject lived and worked . . . is the best possible guide to Cornell's magical inventions."

Ashton's eighteen-year friendship with Mark Rothko produced a book that, as its title suggests, is "about" Rothko—"because in both senses—all around and approximately—writing of painting is always 'about.'" Characteristic of her approach, and her writing style, is her description of the sense of "expectation" that his later paintings evoked in her:

The movement Rothko created was always hovering, re-

spiring, pulsing, but never wholly described. He teased his viewer into a state of receptivity and inquiry. Unaccustomed juxtapositions of huge areas of color (or sometimes merely one) challenged not only the eyes of the beholder but his entire psychological and motor being. Rothko's uncanny command of these often baffling juxtapositions and subtle movements transformed his viewer into more than a collaborator. If his soul was almost undecided whether to communicate or reveal itself, its movements were nonetheless suggestive. It was this very equivocation that gave back so much that had been banished from painting—a chance for metaphor, a chance for indeterminate feeling, a chance for mystery.

Peter Schjeldahl, reviewing *About Rothko* in *Art in America*, responded more favorably this time: "Ashton has many strengths, all of them apparent here: intimate personal acquaintance, a passionate response to the art and the artists, and an encyclopedic command of relevant art history, literature, and philosophy." He objected, however, to "an elusive point of view and a style of argument that is all elaboration of theses curiously unstated." John Russell, art critic of the *New York Times*, suggests perhaps a reason for the elusiveness some readers find in Ashton's writing. He was reviewing Ashton's *A Fable of Modern Art*, an extended essay on Balzac's *The Unknown Masterpiece* (1837). In that novel a famous artist's long awaited masterpiece appears to its viewers as a bewildering mass of colors piled on each other, a work which curiously anticipates modern abstract painting. Russell was impressed with how densely packed the book is, tracing relationships between Balzac's fictional painting and the work of Cézanne, Picasso, the poet Rilke, and the composer Arnold Schoenberg: "Mrs. Ashton has read a lot, thought a lot. On every page there are pregnant ideas that flash before we have time to see them born." In order to cover so wide an area, Russell says, Ashton's book should have been much longer. "But if it sometimes reads like notes for a seminar, at least we know that the seminar would be a major experience."

Ashton faced similar problems of compression with her study of the New York School, a "loose community" of painters mainly associated with abstract expressionism who flourished from the 1930s through the 1950s. Her purpose in *The New York School: A Cultural Reckoning* was an investigation and survey of the whole cultural climate of America during this period: "In this book I am not dealing with works of art, as I have in my other writings. Rather, I have pursued the problems that cultural historians have always raised in the hope of answering at least partially a simple question that occurred to me years ago: Why did painting take such a long time to make its force known in American culture? In trying to answer the question for myself, I have written a book that is not about art, nor about artists individually, but about artists in American society." Similarly, *American Art since 1945* covers a vast area, moving swiftly over the political, economic, and cultural history of America in the first half of the twentieth century. The book concludes with the observation that in the cultural "renaissance" of the 1960s—with the opening of many new museums and the inflation of prices paid for art—the role of the artist has changed from the neglected "loner and pioneer" to Establishment figure. Ashton is wary of the influence of private corporations, funding what she calls "art for banks" and the general commercialization of art. Reviewers noted, and some objected to, the subjective quality of *American Art since 1945*, but most praised the combination of factual survey and personal criticism. John Perreault, in the *Nation*, admired the insights Ashton offered: "What makes her book so much better than others of its kind is that she manages to balance the sociological and the esthetic deftly indicating their connection."

Ashton was born in Newark, New Jersey to Ralph Neil and Sylvia (Smith) Ashton. She received a B.A. from the University of Wisconsin in 1949 and an M.A. from Harvard in 1950. She has written on art and other subjects for many journals—among them *Arts Magazine, Art and Architecture, Studio International,* and the *Kenyon* and *Evergreen* reviews—and has received grants from the Ford Foundation (1960), the Grant Foundation (1963), the Guggenheim Foundation (1964), and the National Endowment for the Humanities (1980). She has taught at Pratt Institute (1962–1963), the School of Visual Arts (1956–1968), and since 1968 she has been professor of art history at Cooper Union, all in New York City. By her first husband, Adja Yunkers, who died in 1983, Ashton has two daughters. In 1985 Ashton married Matti Meged.

PRINCIPAL WORKS: Abstract Art before Columbus, 1957; (with J. Rewald) Redon, Moreau, Bresdin, 1961; The Unknown Shore, 1962; Modern American Sculpture, 1968; A Reading of Modern Art, 1969; Richard Lindner, 1970; Pol Bury, 1970; The New York School: A Cultural Reckoning, 1972 (in U.K. The Life and Times of the New York School, 1972); A Joseph Cornell Album, 1974; Yes, But . . . : A Critical Study of Philip Guston, 1976; A Fable of Modern Art, 1980; Rosa Bonheur, 1981; American Art since 1945, 1982; About Rothko, 1983; Out of the Whirlwind: Three Decades of Art Commentary, 1987; Fragonard in the Universe of Paintings, 1988.

ABOUT: Ashton, D. Out of the Whirlwind, 1987; Contemporary Authors New Revision Series 2, 1981; Who's Who in America 1986-87. *Periodicals*—Art in America October 1982, December 1983; Nation July 10, 1982; New York Times April 24, 1980; New York Times Book Review November 9, 1973; December 2, 1973; December 29, 1974; July 4, 1976; Times Literary Supplement January 7, 1977; March 19, 1982.

ASTLEY, THEA (BEATRICE MAY) (August 25, 1925–   ), Australian novelist and short-story writer, was born to Cecil and Eileen (Lindsay) Astley, in Brisbane, Queensland. Although she has lived in other parts of Australia, northern Queensland—its provincial towns, its rain forests and dusty plains—has been the scene of most of her fiction. A graduate of the University of Queensland (1947), she taught English in local schools from 1944 until her marriage to Edmund John Gregson in 1948. From 1948 to 1967 she taught in schools in New South Wales, raised her son, and began her writing career with poems, short stories, and in 1958 her first novel, *Girl with a Monkey*. In 1968 she became senior tutor in the English department of Macquarie University in Sydney, where she remained until her retirement in the mid-1980s when she returned to Queensland and settled in Kuranda.

Although Thea Astley early on received recognition as a novelist in her native Australia, with fellowships from the Commonwealth Literary Fund in 1961 and 1964, and the distinguished Miles Franklin Award three times (in 1962 for *The Well-Dressed Explorer,* in 1965 for *The Slow Natives,* and in 1973 for *The Acolyte*), she did not come to the attention of readers in England and the United States until the 1980s. With the publication in the United States in 1988 of two of her earlier novellas, *The Acolyte* and *A Kindness Cup,* under the title *Two by Astley,* she won many new readers who, like Bret Lott in the *New York Times Book Review,* wondered why "these two superbly intelligent, compassionate novels weren't published in an American edition sooner."

A writer of pungent social satire and a sensitive observer of human character, Astley bridges the vast distances between the continents. Her settings are remote, and her dialogue is often sprinkled with regionalisms unfamiliar to her non-Australian readers. But whether writing about the sterility of life in the outback, the long and painful history of the white Australian's relationship with the native Aboriginal population, or the failure of human beings simply to connect with each other, Astley transcends geography. "My subject," she wrote in a comment on her fiction in 1972, "is self-delusion . . . Whether the delusion is that of being conformist or nonconformist, the end result is that such delusion

THEA ASTLEY

does create an outsider. I don't think in anything I have written is there a main character who does not suffer from such delusion."

Astley's background in Roman Catholicism gives her fiction an added dimension. Her principal characters—some religious, others not—suffer deep crises of conscience in which religion (or their private sense of morality) offers no easy answers. Still, it is through their questioning, their suffering, their very weaknesses of character, and their sometimes tragic errors of judgment that Astley affirms a faith. Critics often cite Graham Greene and Muriel Spark as influences on her work, but if she is to be compared to contemporary writers, it may well be, as Kerryn Goldsworthy suggested in *Meanjin*, to American Southern women: "Flannery O'Connor, in her relentless retributions and Eudora Welty, in her knowledge of small-town life and her delight in the physical texture of any given day, are two names which spring most readily to mind."

Astley's earliest fiction was very much the product of her years of teaching in small-town schools where her central characters come into conflict with the philistinism of provincial life. The heroine of *Girl with a Monkey*, a refined and well-educated young teacher who has drifted into a relationship with a rough laborer, finds herself trapped. Not only does she recognize the impossibility of marrying a man who is her intellectual inferior, but she also confronts the hopelessness of her job:

> There was the school, the oldest in town, festering with bird lice and blistered paint, where the classrooms in the February days simmered like an oven, or filled up with

great sound waves from the frenetic drumming of the monsoon rains; each class antipathetic to learning and each teacher cowed before the rotund tyrant who guarded each sub-clause of each day's work. There lay no room for imagination with this inflexible syllabus and none for affection when the entire process of education became a holocaust to the headmaster, who in turn sacrificed it to the inspectorial system peopled by bizarrely ignorant men who knew half a dozen tricky ways of wording a mental problem and all the hardest spellings for children under fourteen.

In *A Descant for Gossips* two teachers—a married man with a wife who is a helpless invalid and a young widow—find themselves trapped not only by the mindless bureaucracy of the school system, but by the gossip of the small town which destroys their relationship and, more tragically, the life of a young schoolgirl whom they befriend. Both novels were praised for their freshness and their close observation of provincial life. "She shows up this life with all its snobberies, petty jealousies and hatreds, its narrowness and its ghoulish glee in vilification," R. G. Geering wrote in *Southerly* in 1961. Some reviewers, however, found Astley's satire more superficial than soundly based. Her sympathetic intellectuals are so self-consciously superior to the other characters that they emerge as intellectual snobs. The social-satirist author does not probe the characters who live outside this charmed circle. What Astley needs, J. F. Burrows suggested in *Southerly* in 1963, is charity: "not the charity which weakly forgives, but that which seeks patiently to understand." Burrows was here also reviewing Astley's third novel, *The Well-Dressed Explorer*, where her satirical target was not a community but a successful journalist—an intelligent, well-meaning man who is a total egoist. In this novel Astley's sharp wit was directed less at her hero's male chauvinism (though she makes that abundantly clear) than at the social conditioning that made him what he is—the parents who "had discovered God . . . in a spiritual rigidity that absolutely precluded warmth and love," the teachers who rewarded flattery and conformity, even his patient wife who accepts "his real need to be constantly admired by women."

In her next novel, *The Slow Natives*, Astley moved from social satire to a larger, more humane study of personal relationships within a comfortably middle-class family, relationships that reflect the breakdown of communication between parents and children and the inability of people to express their quite genuine love for each other. More than a study of the generation gap, *The Slow Natives* depicts the inner conflicts of a sensitive father, who has lost faith in both his wife and his God, and his equally troubled teen-aged son, who can find neither faith nor love in his sterile bourgeois surroundings. It also introduces a group of Roman Catholic nuns and a priest who questions his vocation: "But he was a nothing-man this year, a priest with his vocation askew, no other object in view but a detailless desert whose wells of prayer had dried up." In another novel, *A Boatload of Home Folk*, a priest performs his duties mechanically: "He was not a deeply religious man despite the outward conformities his job demanded, for job it was; and he was now a rather tired businessman in his master's service, with the capabilities and many of the attitudes of a public service inspector. He had so little sense of humour and such a plenitude of stuffy attitudes he might have been Protestant."

The loss of faith—in religion and, with even more serious consequences, in one's fellow human beings—is the source of the torment that many of Astley's characters suffer. They move from apathy to cynicism to self-loathing, carrying with them the baggage of their guilt for failing those who love them. In *The Acolyte,* her central character, Paul Vesper, deliberately abases himself to serve as amanuensis to a blind composer, Jack Holberg. Vesper worships Holberg's musical genius, but he loathes his demanding egoism—"his complete involvement in his own darkness." Vesper correctly defines his ambivalence as love-hate, writing of the man he serves: "His arrogance, his impatience, his rudeness to fawners are mitigated by the private man who is funny and generous and at times tender. I am overcome with love." But living as he does, a "fringe dweller in the suburbs of the great man's genius . . . the natural tick parasite necessary for preserving the ecology of culture," and watching Holberg's reckless disregard for the lives of the women who love him, Vesper can only finally explode in violence, acknowledging the hopelessness of his situation. Of himself and Holberg he writes: "We both munch the eucharist and no grace enters our soul."

Inaction or misdirected action is responsible for the unhappiness of others among Astley's central characters. The narrator of *An Item from the Late News* watches passively while her ignorant, greedy neighbors in an outback town systematically torment and finally murder an outsider—a "hippie" who has come to this remote community to find a refuge from the threat of nuclear war. In the historical novel *A Kindness Cup* the protagonist, Tom Dorahy, does act. He seeks retribution for a crime perpetrated on the natives some years earlier—but with disastrous consequences for himself and for those he enlists in his cause, Dorahy is a schoolteacher who, twenty years before the novel begins, had left the rugged frontier town of The

Taws in horror and disgust at the slaughter of a group of Aborigines by a posse of white settlers. Astley based her story on an actual incident that occurred in 1867; a hearing was held on the atrocity but the perpetrators went unpunished. In the book, Dorahy returns just as the town is celebrating a reunion and proceeds to carry out his own plan of retribution. He believes he is a righteous man, Astley wrote of the book, "but he failed to see the disaster that accompanies righteousness." At the beginning of the novel one of the residents of the town accuses him of madness. "You become that which you do," Dorahy almost prophetically replies. Assuming the role of avenger, he becomes increasingly obsessed with hatred and is deaf to the words of a townsman who attempts to reason with him: "There are things I regret. Naturally. Every man has those. But I—all of us—have been trying to live these moments down. No one's proud of them. They just happened in a natural cause of events. It's part of history." It is the moral ambiguity of Dorahy's quest that fascinates Astley and, in turn, her readers. Nicola Jane Tareha, who studied the historical background of *A Kindness Cup*, observes: "The novel demonstrates that Dorahy's bitterness and hatred are greater than his own sense of charity."

Astley's despairing view of the human condition is usually balanced by her wry humor and a gift for elegant phrasing that can turn a potentially maudlin or melodramatic episode into comic irony. Describing an elderly, overripe traveller on a cruise to the South Pacific islands in *A Boatload of Home Folk,* she writes: "For her it was a traveller's joy. Every significant ploy of the gaudy tourist folders she was determined to enjoy and de-juice for rapture. She was geared to receive the devices of another people's domestic exigencies with all the wonder of a Marco Polo." In some of her books, however, Astley's prose has struck reviewers as idiosyncratic—"highly charged," "waver[ing] into incoherence," "full of ambiguous dualities." Surveying her work in 1969, L. J. Clancy wrote, in *Meanjin:* "Miss Astley then remains an exasperating novelist. She has possibly the sharpest eye and most biting tongue of almost any contemporary Australian novelist, but none of her novels stands as a fully achieved work of art in itself."

As her talent matured, Astley's prose became less self-conscious. However, she continues to demand the close attention and concentration of her readers, shunning conventional linear narrative, switching scenes and characters abruptly, introducing flashbacks and passages of dialogue in which it is sometimes difficult to identify the speakers. For example, *It's Raining in Mango,* one of Astley's most interesting novels, com presses a family history of three generations stretching from 1861 to the late twentieth century—into a mere two hundred pages. Though rich in incident and full of colorful characters, the novel fails to cohere. As Rosellen Brown wrote, in the *New York Times Book Review*: "Each generation fills the frame as if it were the only one. But before we've mastered its faces, it is pulled out from under our still-adjusting gaze. In fact, rural Australia turns out to be the tragic heroine—Australia's is the only face Ms. Astley renders with real conviction."

Similar problems arise in her short but ambitiously conceived *Beachmasters,* but here they are resolved in a fashion that suggests that Astley has achieved full mastery over her craft. The scene is an imaginary South Pacific island still under colonial rule some time after World War II, where a group of half-caste Melanesians are organized under the leadership of an idealistic native in a rebellion for their independence. The leader, Tommy Narota, is a gentle man—"light skinned enough to show promise but too dark, of course, to get anywhere on an island with a long white memory of planter picnics and drinks on verandahs and the cocktail gabble of the ruling classes." Dreaming of a new life cut out of the jungle "with the violence of love," he sees his "*aeland* wiped clean of colonial settlers, unless they, too, were prepared to swing on the lianas of custom. Then, oh then, the whole *aeland* would assert the pride of its myths." *Aeland* is a word from Astley's invented pidgin to which she gives the name "Seaspeak," and her use of it in passages of the novel is less confusing than it would appear. Sounded aloud, Seaspeak imitates a native dialect: *hapkas* is a half caste, *gavman* is government, *wai'te basat* is white bastard, etc. More challenging to the reader is Astley's use of shifting points of view. As Vernon Young described it, in the *New York Times Book Review:* "Each chapter is dominated by the monologue or indirect discourse of the islander who is upstage; in short, her novel is a sequence of near soliloquies that reveal each character from another person's viewpoint as well as from her own. The method . . . is a fruitful one; it circumvents an unaccountable know-all."

The revolution itself is more comic-pathetic than menacing: "Pardon, Madame," the natives announce to a colonial, "tomorrow we make protest march. Tomorrow there will be revolution." When tomorrow comes, dreams are crushed but little blood is shed. Recognizing his failure, Narota waits quietly for the colonial soldier to come to arrest him: "In the sleepless after-midnight with the crack of falling water on the broad leaves of the banana thatch and the taro, Narota wept a little for a crumbled kingdom. Weep?

The doors had been held up only by vines, the floors cracked by ant colonies, the windows the fragile panelling of spiders." *Beachmasters,* Sally Dawson wrote in the *Times Literary Supplement,* "shows Astley's talent blossoming into a more expressive and imaginative medium." It appears to fulfill the promise of her earlier work and to confirm Judith H. McDowell's judgment in *World Literature Today* in 1981 that Thea Astley is "one of the major novelists currently writing in Australia."

PRINCIPAL WORKS: *Novels*—Girl With a Monkey, 1958; A Descant for Gossips, 1960; The Well-Dressed Explorer, 1962; The Slow Natives, 1965; A Boatload of Home Folk, 1968; The Acolyte, 1972; A Kindness cup, 1975; An Item from the Late News, 1982; It's Raining in Mango, 1987; Beachmasters, 1988; Two by Astley (A Kindness Cup, The Acolyte), 1988; Reaching Tin River, 1989. *Collected short stories*—Hunting the Wild Pineapple, 1979.

ABOUT: Blake, L. J. Australian Writers, 1968; Contemporary Authors New Revision Series 11, 1984; Contemporary Literary Criticism 41, 1987; Contemporary Novelists, 4th ed., 1986; Oxford Companion to Australia Literature, 1985; Tareha, N. J. The Legend of the Leap, 1986. *Periodicals*—Meanjin September 1969, December 1983; New York Times Book Review June 22, 1986; November 22, 1987; July 31, 1988; Southerly 21, 1961, 23, 1963; Times Literary Supplement November 15, 1985; World Literature Today Autumn 1981.

AUSTER, PAUL (February 3, 1947–), American novelist, essayist, poet, and translator, was born in Newark, New Jersey to Jewish parents of East European–Austrian descent. He grew up in a large and comfortable suburban home, went to local schools, and played Little League baseball. He attended Columbia University, where he took his B.A. in 1969 and his M.A. in 1970.

Shortly before Auster entered college his parents were divorced. Although he kept in touch with his father, he became increasingly aware of an estrangement between them. They were friendly, but his father remained always distant, unreachable ("devoid of passion, either for a thing, a person, or an idea, incapable or unwilling to reveal himself under any circumstances. . . . "). Some fifteen years later the sudden death of this "invisible man," as he calls his father, caused Auster, by this time married, a father himself, and a publishing writer—to review their relationship in a prose memoir, *The Invention of Solitude.* While the book offers only scanty factual information about Auster's life, and in part of it he writes of himself in the more

PAUL AUSTER

distant third person, it fully and richly chronicles his creative life and poses the paradox of
much of his fiction and his poetry: "Like everyone else he craves a meaning. Like everyone
else, his life is so fragmented that each time he
sees a connection between two fragments he is
tempted to look for a meaning in that connection. The connection exists. But to give it a
meaning, to look beyond the bare facts of its existence, would be to build an imaginary world
inside the real world, and he knows it would not
stand."

Auster's search for "connections" between the
fragments of experience began early. Instead of
settling down in a job when he finished his
studies at Columbia, he shipped out as a seaman
on an oil tanker in the Gulf of Mexico. Eventually he drifted to France where his real literary apprenticeship began. He lived in France for four
years, writing poetry and an occasional film
script, ghostwriting, translating, acting as caretaker for a farm in Provence, and for a time, now
fluent in French, working as a telephone operator for the Paris bureau of the *New York Times*.
During this period he began publishing his
translations of French poetry and prose (some of
the latter in collaboration with his first wife,
Lydia Davis), as well as his own poetry and essays, in literary journals in the United States. By
the mid-1970s, having returned to New York,
Auster had won some reputation as a writer. He
received a grant from the Ingram Merrill Foundation in 1975 (and another in 1982) and from
the PEN Translation Center (1977) and in 1979
he had a fellowship from the National Endow-

ment for the Arts. Nevertheless, when Auster
tried to publish his first novel, *City of Glass*, he
had many rejections before a small publisher in
Los Angeles, Sun and Moon Press, accepted it.
That novel, the first in his New York Trilogy,
brought him immediate favorable attention, and
he now has a small but steadily growing audience of enthusiastic readers.

Auster's translations from the French include
poems and prose by Mallarmé, Sartre, and Maurice Blanchot. As editor of *The Random House
Book of Twentieth-Century French Poetry* he
faced problems of selecting from an enormous
quantity of excellent verse ("the unhappy situation of trying to fit an elephant into a cage designed for a fox," he wrote in his Introduction),
and of judging the quality of the translations he
included. There his own gifts as a poet were
helpful because in the end he recognized that he
had to rely on his ear, his common sense, and his
instinct for language:

> Whenever I was faced with a choice between literalness
> and poetry, I did not hesitate to choose poetry . . . The
> experience of a poem resides not only in each of its
> words, but in the interactions among those words—the
> music, the silences, the shapes—and if a reader is not
> somehow given the chance to enter the totality of that
> experience, he will remain cut off from the spirit of the
> original. It is for this reason, it seems to me, that poems
> should be translated by poets.

In the second part of *The Invention of
Solitude*—a long, meditative essay that he calls
"The Book of Memory"—Auster finds an analogy between the translations of others' writing
and his own act of writing. Translating, he reflects, "is as though he were entering that man's
solitude and making it his own." A memoir is the
translation of moments of the author's life, entering his solitude, the language itself unleashing
memory: "He imagines an immense Babel inside
him. There is a text, and it translates itself into
an infinite number of languages. Sentences spill
out of him at the speed of thought, and each
word comes from a different language, a thousand tongues that clamor inside him at once, the
din of it echoing through a maze of rooms, corridors, and stairways, hundreds of stories high. In
the space of memory, everything is both itself
and something else."

The Babel image recurs in Auster's work. In
his novel *City of Glass* a madman seeks to recreate the original "language of innocence" spoken
in Eden: "If the fall of man also entailed a fall
of language, was it not logical to assume that it
would be possible to undo the fall, to reverse its
effects by undoing the fall of language, by striving to recreate the language that was spoken in
Eden!" In his poem "Scribe" Babel is the home

of the writer translating his memories and unleashing his creative imagination:

> The name
> never left his lips: he talked himself
> into another body: he found his room again
> in Babel.
>
> It is spring,
> and below his window
> he hears
> a hundred white stones
> turn to raging phlox.

Auster writes a lean, imagistic poetry that is
not imitative of but certainly reflects his wide
knowledge of modern French poetry. Like his
novels, his poems envision a bleak and meaningless world, an existential void through which the
poet stumbles despairingly in a bleak, surrealist
landscape:

> Nothing less than nothing.
>
> In the night that comes
> from nothing,
> for no one in the night
> that does not come.
>
> And what stands at the edge of whiteness,
> invisible
> in the eye of the one who speaks.
>
> Or a word.
>
> Come from nowhere
> in the night
> of the one who does not come
>
> Or the whiteness of a word,
> scratched
> into the wall
>   —"Wall Writing"

In both poetry and prose Auster seems obsessed with the negation of personality, the drift
toward oblivion that governs the lives of the central characters of his fiction:

> Against the facade of evening:
> shadows, fire, and silence.
> Not even silence, but its fire—
> the shadow
> cast by a breath.
>
> To enter the silence of this wall,
> I must leave myself behind.
>   —"Shadow to Shadow"

The novels that comprise Auster's New York
Trilogy—*City of Glass, Ghosts,* and *The Locked
Room*—are short and make swift, suspenseful
reading. On the surface they are detective stories—intellectual private-eye fiction with distinct echoes of Raymond Chandler and Dashiell
Hammett. But even the most casual reader will
suspect that the smooth surface of the text is a
slippery trap that plunges one into the metaphysical paradoxes of the *nouveau roman* in
which the act of writing the story becomes the
story itself. Each of the novels introduces a different set of characters (though there is significant cross-referencing) and a different kind of
mystery. In fact, however, the action is always
the same: the pursuit of one writer by another
writer. Toby Olson's description of the plot of
City of Glass, in the *New York Times Book
Review,* serves for all three: "the descent of a
writer into a labyrinth in which fact and fiction
become increasingly difficult to separate." The
text always rests on a nest of subtexts and literary
allusions. While the literary influences on the
novels may be traced to Alain Robbe-Grillet,
Samuel Beckett, and Jean-Paul Sartre, the larger
frame of reference in the New York Trilogy is
classic American literature. *City of Glass* develops the doppelganger motif of Edgar Allan Poe
(the central character uses the pen name William Wilson); characters in *Ghosts* read Thoreau,
live in self-created urban Waldens, and walk
through the streets of Brooklyn Heights rich
with memories of Walt Whitman; the object of
the hero's quest in *The Locked Room* is named
Fanshawe, the eponymous hero of Hawthorne's
first novel, and his wife Sophie echoes the name
of Hawthorne's wife Sophia. In some fiction literary allusions like these appear self-conscious
and pretentious, but in the New York Trilogy
they deepen and enrich the crime novel genre.
As Stephen Schiff observed, in his review of *The
Locked Room* in the *New York Times Book
Review* : "Mr. Auster has hit upon something. By
changing the nature of the clues from the physical to the metaphysical, he harnesses the inquir-
ing spirit any reader brings to mystery,
redirecting it from the grubby search for a
wrongdoer to the more rarefied search for self."

The New York City of the trilogy is itself an
example of transformation from the physical to
the metaphysical. The setting is the real city that
Auster knows at first hand from having lived
there for many years—the Lower East Side, the
Upper West Side, Brooklyn. The hero of *City of
Glass,* Daniel Quinn, a detective story writer by
profession whose wife and three-year-old son
died some years before the novel begins, walks
its streets—"a labyrinth of endless steps, and no
matter how far he walked, no matter how well
he came to know its neighborhoods and streets,
it always left him with the feeling of being lost.
Lost not only in the city, but within himself as
well." In a metropolis like this, individual identities are confused and often lost. Quinn receives
a series of telephone calls for one Paul Auster, a
private detective. Intrigued by the urgency of
the calls, he pretends to be Paul Auster, under-

takes the job of following a man who appears to be a threat to his client, then seeks out the real Paul Auster, who is not a detective but a writer with a wife and three-year-old son. Quinn follows his man through a maze of New York streets and engages him in several conversations, only to realize that the man is hopelessly demented. By now, however, Quinn is so obsessed with his quest that he loses all sense of self-identity. The detective mystery proves in the end irrelevant, but the mystery of human identity is haunting. "It is a mystery," Gary Gach wrote in the *American Book Review*, "more of ripples forming in a still pond." Though full of the tension and suspense of conventional detective fiction (it was a nominee for the Edgar Award for mystery novels in 1986), it moves into the realm of the philosophical novel. Gach wrote: "drawing deeply upon the solitude of the act of writing, he [Auster] has communicated the great solitude of great cities. In sharing so generously with us his daily act of placing a blank rectangle of paper on the cleared rectangle of his desk, he elicits from us the most intimate experiences of our daily urban aloneness."

In *Ghosts* Auster strips the conventions of the detective genre down to minimal details: "This is how it begins. The place is New York, the time is the present, and neither one will ever change," the first of the novel's ninety-six pages announces. The characters are identified by single names, all of them colors: "White wants Blue to follow a man named Black and to keep an eye on him for as long as necessary." Blue is a businesslike private-eye. He moves into an apartment in Brooklyn Heights that his employer has rented for him and spends what may be years at a window observing Black in his apartment across the street. He follows Black on long city walks, observes him writing at his desk and reading *Walden*, and gradually submerges his own life in Black's. He drifts apart from his fiancée and experiences the acute loneliness of the abandoned, discovering "that he has been thrown back on himself, with nothing to grab hold of, nothing to distinguish one moment from the next. He had never given much thought to the world inside him, and though he knew it was there, it had remained an unknown quantity, unexplored and dark, even to himself." The plot of *Ghosts* itself is "an unknown quantity." Rebecca Goldstein, reviewing the novel in the *New York Times Book Review*, raised a number of questions about its meaning and concluded: "In any case, what does one call a seamless little detective story that forces one to ask questions such as these? I call it nearly perfect."

Other readers felt, however, that in *Ghosts*, and in some degree in its predecessor, intriguing

as they are, Auster was stretching his metaphysics and his literary allusiveness rather tenuously. Colin Greenland commented in the *Times Literary Supplement*: "There is a deliberate minimalism at work here, a desire to strip things down not to bare forked mortality but to simple formal relations, which Auster intermittently decorates with masks and mannerisms that no longer constitute personality. In this twilit, undifferentiated context there is finally no subject or object, only a free-standing, self-devouring text." Stephen Schiff, in the *New York Times Book Review*, called the novels "glassy little jigsaws," and confessed to longing for more substantial characters. For him the publication of *The Locked Room* marked "a brilliant leap forward, a beguiling entertainment that accomplishes nearly everything the first two books set out to do and provides a diverting main character as well."

The Locked Room is narrated in the first person by a writer who reluctantly agrees to write a biography of a brilliant writer, Fanshawe, who has disappeared and is apparently dead. He and Fanshawe had been close boyhood friends and drifted apart in later years, but he had always admired his friend. When he learns that Fanshawe has left behind him several unpublished manuscripts, as well as a beautiful wife and a charming baby, the narrator not only arranges for the publication of the writings but eventually marries the wife and adopts the child. Thus again one man's identity is submerged in another's life:

> I had stumbled onto a cause, a thing that justified me and made me feel important, and the more fully I disappeared into my ambitions for Fanshawe, the more sharply I came into focus for myself. This is not an excuse; it is merely a description of what happened. Hindsight tells me I was looking for trouble, but at the time I knew nothing about it. More important, even if I had known, I doubt that it would have made a difference.

Although the setting is a real New York, the worlds of Auster's characters in the trilogy are intensely private and subjective. In the same year that *The Locked Room* appeared, Auster published a novel set in an unnamed American city of the future. It might be New York or any other large urban center in which the characters are engaged in the more objective problem of physical survival. *In the Country of Last Things*, like many future-prophecy novels, projects a city of ruin and devastation. This is, in Padgett Powell's phrase, "post-apocalyptic" fiction—a vision of a future of food shortages, lawlessness, total breakdown of public services: "Slowly and steadily," the narrator writes, "the city seems to be consuming itself even as it remains." The novel is in the form of a letter written by Anna Blume, newly arrived on the shores of this country, to a friend back in her homeland. Anna has come here to search for her brother, a journalist, who has disappeared. But this is not a mystery-quest novel. Like everyone else in this city, Anna is absorbed in the struggle for mere physical survival. Ravaged as the city is, however, Anna discovers that not all its citizens are completely demoralized. She meets a feeble old bag-woman, Isabel, who allows Anna to share her wretched quarters with herself and her deranged husband Ferdinand. Later, after a series of harrowing escapes from injury and death, Anna meets a few more rational people; but in this futuristic city rationality itself is an incongruity. At the end of the novel Anna is reunited with the man she loves and with some friends, all of them dreaming of escaping to the country to perform magic shows. This is clearly an act of desperation, yet Anna closes her letter with a pathetic hope: "The only thing I ask for now is the chance to live one more day. This is Anna Blume, your old friend from another world. Once we get to where we're going, I will try to write to you again, I promise."

Anna's written account of her experiences and her pledge to go on writing is an affirmation, however faint, of her faith in the power of language. In Auster's post-apocalyptic vision, it is language itself that is in mortal danger and that survives only in the seemingly futile struggles of Anna and a few of her friends. "In *Country of Last Things*," Daniel Max wrote in the *Boston Review*, "language is dying with its people . . . Here is the true power of Auster's dark age vision—not only has horror replaced all the good of our society but the good can no longer even be remembered because the words are gone with which to think of it." Padgett Powell, however, found the conclusion of the novel less despairing. In Anna's resilience, her courage in the face of an even more terrible future, she remains hopeful. "If in the beginning there was only the Word," Powell observed, "she wants to say that in the end it will still be."

A real New York City, principally the Upper West Side, is again the scene of Auster's *Moon Palace* (a Chinese restaurant that does in fact exist near Columbia University). As in the earlier novels of the New York Trilogy, however, the reader is taken into the interior world of the novel's hero, the young Marco Stanley Fogg, an explorer of his own subjectivity. Like Marco Polo, Phileas Fogg, or Henry Stanley—more celebrated travelers into remote and unexplored territory—Auster's Marco embarks on a picaresque journey through the city. He meets an assortment of bizarre characters and has a series of nightmarish adventures, all rich with literary and philosophical echoes. Michiko Kakutani, in the *New York Times*, found the book "a sad-funny tale of coming of age . . . [that] reads like a composite of works by Fielding, Dickens and Twain, with a faint 20th-century gloss of Ionesco and Camus."

Auster lives with his second wife, Siri Hustuedt, and his son in Brooklyn. In 1985 he received a second National Endowment of the Arts grant for creative writing.

PRINCIPAL WORKS: *Novels*—City of Glass, 1985; Ghosts, 1986; The Locked Room, 1987; In the Country of Last Things, 1987; Moon Palace, 1989; The Music of Chance, 1990. *Poetry*—Unearth: Poems 1970–1972, 1974; Wall Writing, 1976, Fragments from Cold, 1977; Facing the Music, 1980; Ground Work: Selected Poems and Essays, 1990. *Non-fiction*—White Spaces, 1980; The Invention of Solitude, 1982; The Art of Hunger, 1982; Ground Work, 1990. *As editor*—The Random House Book of Twentieth-Century Poetry, 1982.

ABOUT: Auster, P. The Invention of Solitude, 1982; Contemporary Authors New Revision Series 23, 1988; Contemporary Literary Criticism 47, 1988. *Periodicals*—American Book Review September–October 1986; Boston Review April 1987; New York Review of Books August 17, 1989; New York Times March 7, 1989; New York Times Book Review November 3, 1985; June 29, 1986; January 4, 1987; May 17, 1987; March 19, 1989; Times Literary Supplement December 11, 1987; July 22, 1988; April 27, 1990.

AYDY, CATHERINE. See **TENNANT, EMMA**

BACHMAN, RICHARD. See **KING, STEPHEN**

*BAGHIO'O, JEAN-LOUIS (December 21, 1910 –), expatriate Guadeloupian storyteller and novelist whose tales and poems interweave his personal history with the lore of the French West Indies, was born Vishnou (later Victor) Jean-Louis in Fort-de-France, Martinique. He came from a family rich in tradition and creativity: "I the mulatto," he describes himself in *Le Colibri blanc*, "descendant of Blacks, Indians, Caribbeans, Spaniards, Bretons, Alsatians, or Germans—what do I know? In my blood, all the colors of the rainbow."

His maternal grandmother, Marie de Virel, was a Creole musician and storyteller who raised him on the repertoire of poetic legends he later incorporated into his writings; his mother, Fer-

°bä gē´ ō

nande de Virel, was an accomplished violinist. His father, Henri Jean-Louis, was the magistrate celebrated in Senegalese novelist Cheikh Hamadou Kané's *L'Aventure ambigüe* (The Ambiguous Adventure, 1961); an author in his own right (best known for a dictionary of African medicine), he was the one who first adopted the pseudonym Baghio'o, the name of a slave from Timbuktu. Finally, his sister, Moune de Rivel, is a well-known singer and journalist who has also published collections of tales and legends.

As a child, Baghio'o had little interest in school and frequently skipped classes to go off to the woods and chase birds. In 1923, when his father took a post in Brazzaville, in the Congo, Baghio'o was sent to Paris to continue his schooling but promptly ran off to Burgundy and took up the mechanic's trade. Brought back to Paris by one of his uncles, he eventually completed a degree in engineering and began working for French radio as a telecommunications engineer in 1934.

A friend of such future giants of the Négritude movement as Léopold Sédar Senghor, Léon Gontran-Damas, and Jacques Rabemananjara, he shared their anticolonialist views, although he remained a supporter of union with France rather than complete independence. During World War II, he served as a lieutenant in a radio company and was taken prisoner but escaped and took refuge in Switzerland for a year. Active in the Resistance within French radio, he helped to prepare the first "Free Radio" broadcasts after the Liberation. Following the war, he was appointed technical director of French broadcasts to the overseas departments and continued to work as a telecommunications engineer until his retirement.

Strictly speaking, Baghio'o's writing activity began with the technical work he published for the radio—most notably, *L'Ingenieur du son* (The Sound Engineer, 1949)—and even his first fiction, *Issandre le mulâtre* (Issandre the Mulatto, 1949), grew out of his broadcasting activity, in the form of a long poem for the radio. Composed while he was in Switzerland during the war, it was broadcast following the Liberation as "Les Chants des Îles" (Songs of the Islands), then transformed into prose and published as *Issandre the Mulatto*. Written in celebration of both the West Indies and the mother continent Africa, this "string of crazy themes" (as Catherine Dunham characterizes it in her preface), is basically a fairy-tale adventure about the ill-fated romance of Issandre the Mulatto and Blanche the Creole. "By definition," writes literary historian Jack Corzani, "such a text defies description: these are tableaux superimposed on the shifting fragility of a dream." But, he insists, for all of the

fantasy elements, the intangible ingredients, the work is clearly inspired by a strong devotion to the West Indies and the island culture, without a trace of exoticism. "There is no enumerating, inventorying, or describing of superstitions here: they are lived. We are *in* the dream, *in* the legend, rather than studying them."

According to Corzani, Baghio'o drew much of his inspiration for *Issandre* from the legends told him by his grandmother. A decade later, he turned to the writings of his father (who died in 1958) and reworked them into a book of poems which he called *Les Jeux du soleil* (The Sun's Games, 1960). Here, in Corzani's view at least, the results were less successful: notwithstanding the atmosphere of sensuality and mystery that clearly intrigued the son, the father's legacy of classic metaphors, mythological allusions, and "yellowed clichés," served up in standard meter and rhyme, yielded a collection which was "slightly antiquated."

Another literary silence ensued—thirteen years this time—and in 1973 Baghio'o reemerged with another work of fiction, this time adding to the repertoire of fantasy and legend a quasi-historical dimension in the form of a generational saga. *Le Flamboyant à fleurs bleues* (translated as *The Blue Flame-tree*, 1984), recounts the story of the O'O family, which boasts a corsair as its eponymous ancestor, followed by a long and consistent line of mixed marriages and a pair of twins in every generation (thus the significance of the name, beyond the obvious allusion to Baghio'o). In and among the generations appear the myths and fantasies—sorcerers, genies, sirens, great doses of violence and sexuality—and the emblematic event of the title, when the red flowers of the flame-tree turned blue from the mixing of blood at the marriage of a freed slave and a Creole woman: "The races could fuse! And nature could rejoice over it. . . . Who would have thought that a tree could turn from red to blue, or a slave become free?"

The Blue Flame-tree brought Baghio'o the 1975 Caribbean Literary Prize awarded by the Association of French-Language Writers, and when it was reissued in 1980, it bore the enthusiastic preface of celebrated Guadeloupian writer-critic Maryse Condé. Placing Baghio'o in the larger context of West Indian literature, Condé stressed the significance of his hybrid historical fiction as a kind of modern mythology, reconstituted from the fragmented remains of the colonial past, rooted in oral tradition, and thus giving voice and image to those who are excluded from "official" history. But other critics were less convinced—Jack Corzani, for example, contended that Baghio'o had not succeeded in retrieving the style of *Issandre*, with the result that "his tale is never anything but a pseudohistorical work cruelly lacking in the supernatural," while Patrick Lindsay Bowles, citing some of the flashier local color in the novel, told readers in the *Times Literary Supplement* that "sadly, this rather earnestly mythic performance is far more dreary than juicy passages suggest."

Baghio'o spent the 1970s in Africa as a technical counselor for radio and television broadcasting. On his return to France, he published *Le Colibri blanc* (The White Hummingbird, 1981), where he worked with yet another melange of fantasy, history, and autobiography, but this time clearly placed the autobiographical elements in the fore. Taking up, in effect, where *The Blue Flame-tree* left off—the departure of the youngest generation of O'O twins for Paris—he opens this "memoir in two voices," as it is subtitled, with his father's account of his 1923 journey from Fort de France to Le Havre, two sons in tow, on his way to the Congo. But after this first chapter based on the recollections of the father, the son takes over the narrative to fill in the gaps, not only as they might have been lived but also as they might have been fantasized by a teenage boy whose father has gone off to the unknown continent of Africa—encounters with the Amazon, the Serpent-women, the Antelope Girl—and finally, the grown-up Vishnou's return to the West Indies that he had left nearly thirty years before.

Jean-Louis Baghio'o has enjoyed a mixed reputation as a writer. In the militant climate of the postwar years, his use of family legends and fairy tales was seen as apolitical, and even after the emergence of an abundant Caribbean literature of folklore and fantasy, Baghio'o's version is still sometimes dismissed as excessively exotic and aimed primarily at a European audience. In his review of *The Blue Flame-tree*, for example, Oruno D. Lara wrote of the "bitter taste" the book left, "the same one I get when I see West Indians mammies gyrating on the stage of the Hotel Meridien in Guadeloupe or Martinique, dressed up like maids in Sunday best, covered with rings and necklaces and bracelets and lace and desperately trying to show passing tourists the antiquated charm of the West Indies fossilized in its colonial corset."

But in the preface to a new edition of the very same novel, Maryse Condé, Guadeloupe's most distinguished writer and critic, speaks out strongly in Baghio'o's defense: "Certain readers who are used to 'militant' or 'didactic' literature will be disturbed because they're not going to find . . . their usual grazing territory. The descriptions will strike them as reeking of exoticism. They'll be surprised to find the lives of the colonizers depicted with so much indulgence. They'll have a hard time identifying the author's 'cause.' But they can't remain indifferent to the love for the West Indies embedded in these pages." And, reminding her readers of Baghio'o's personal history as a member of the French Resistance, a vociferous critic of French colonialism, and a friend of the pioneers of Négritude, she concludes that "in his own manner, and with the others, he paved the way for our awareness."

WORKS IN ENGLISH TRANSLATION: *The Blue Flame-tree* was translated by Stephen Romer in 1984.

ABOUT: Corzani, J. La Littérature des Antilles-Guyane Françaises, 6, 1978; Rouch, A. and G. Clavreuil. Littératures nationales d'écriture française, 1986. *Periodicals*—Observer, March 4, 1984; Présence africaine no. 98, 1976, 147, 1988; Times Literary Supplement May 11, 1984.

BAILEY, ANTHONY (January 5, 1933–), British novelist and essayist, writes: "The fact that I am not a naval officer or a naval architect I can explain mostly by fear of seasickness and a failure to grasp mathematics beyond the basics. Otherwise much of my early life seems to have been influenced by the proximity of water and attraction to it. My first memories are of objects floating: a yellow plastic duck bobbing happily in the bath alongside me; a toy white yacht ghosting across a municipal pond; gray warships moored in the harbor. My father worked in a bank in Portsmouth, one of Britain's then great naval ports, where I was born. My mother hailed from Southampton, the seaport for transatlantic liners a dozen miles to the west. Both ports were sheltered from the open Channel by the benign green hills of the Isle of Wight, to which we went by steam-powered paddle-wheel ferries for summer holidays. My mother, before marriage, had been a secretary at the United States Consulate in Southampton, and that American connection made a difference to my life in 1940, when many British children were being evacuated to safer places at home and abroad. More excited than afraid, I was shipped away from Hitler's bombs aboard a small Cunarder in convoy to the New World, and for four charmed years enjoyed an Ohio boyhood before being shipped home again, this time on an escort carrier. I went on growing up in the village of Portchester, at the head of Portsmouth harbor, where I spent a lot of time clambering about the walls of the Roman-Norman castle and even more time mucking about in small boats.

ANTHONY BAILEY

"At some point late in adolescence, I recognised that I was more interested in the seaside than the sea, a land-loving sailor fonder of shallow creeks and intricate marshes than of the full-fathomed expanses of ocean. I was also a walker, for whom the turfed chalk of the South Downs provided the buoyant springboard not just for ambulatory exercise but for thought and—once in a while—inspiration. It may be that one reason I took to writing was in order to get close and stay close to the elements by preserving in words my sense of contact with the fabric of creation. Pen in hand, I could attempt perhaps to recapture what I had seen, felt, or thought as I traversed land and water. Or was it that, at my desk, I tried to express as well all that I *couldn't* reach by simple contact with the elements?

"Various influential strands in my life now apparently arise from those years. After my wartime childhood in Dayton, I have remained entangled with America. Sometimes I feel myself stretched between two lives—one led in Stonington, a coastal village in Connecticut, where with my wife (who is from Yorkshire) and eventually four daughters I lived year round from 1961 to 1971, and where my wife and I still spend several months every autumn; the other in Greenwich, an urban village of sorts in southeast London, where we live most of the year. We returned from Stonington to dwell in England for many reasons, but the most important were familiar: feeling that we should be closer to our parents, and our children closer to their grandparents. Educational and cultural opportunities also figured in the move back, and so too did a

sense of leading a slightly over-privileged existence in Connecticut, away from city problems that affect so many. There was also a nudging thought that I should be looking at the situation of people who had greater difficulties with division and bifurcated lives than I, for example in Northern Ireland and in Central Europe along the Iron Curtain.

"Other strands, at once intertwined but opposing, that I'm now aware of are a persistent restlessness and a profound need for a particular place. Since that first westward journey at the age of seven I am often impelled to set forth on expeditions or excursions. Yet I am more often compelled to stay put and look intently at where I am and work out what this or that locality means to me. Certainly I now find myself at home in Stonington and Greenwich, loving both and infuriated by some things in both, occasionally missing one when in the other, and seeing both now and then with a foreign eye. My four daughters were born in the United States and educated for the most part in London schools; at this moment, three are in Britain, one in the USA, but the positions might be reversed; the entanglement continues. Although at moments this doubled life produces a melancholy sensation of not being entirely whole-hearted wherever I am, it generally makes me feel fortunate, granted enhanced choice and enlarged prospect, for which—may it enter my writing!—I am immensely grateful."

———

The "doubled life" that Anthony Bailey describes in his sketch has given him unique advantages not only as a travel writer but as a novelist and essayist who observes and reflects on the whole human habitat. "Mr. Bailey is imaginative as well as observant, thoughtful as well as venturesome," John Gross wrote of his *Spring Jaunts*, a collection of essays that range from England and Ireland to New Hampshire and Nice. "He knows how to hit off a scene with a few rapid strokes; he is equally alert to the quiddity of a place or of a personality, and he imparts information so neatly that you scarcely realize how much he has packed in."

American readers know Bailey best from his impressionistic reportorial pieces in the *New Yorker* and from his memoir of his boyhood years in Dayton, Ohio, *America, Lost & Found.* One of several thousand English children evacuated during World War II and sent to temporary homes in America, Bailey displayed even then the adaptability and aplomb of the ideal travel writer. His four-year stay in the United States left him with happy memories which he recalled for his book—a warm, almost idyllic picture of a sheltered midwestern boyhood in a prosperous, hospitable American family. Returning to his English home and family in 1944 at age eleven, he experienced only a few gentle cultural bumps but no dramatic traumas. His account of his return, his adjustment to his family, to wartime and postwar food shortages, to public school, then on to military service (1951-1952) as a lieutenant in West Africa, are described in *England, First & Last*, another quiet, unassuming, gently humorous and perceptive book.

The transatlantic character of his life already firmly established, Bailey returned to the United States after receiving his B.A. from Merton College, Oxford in 1955 (M A in modern history, 1959). He joined the *New Yorker* as a staff writer in 1956, an association he has maintained to the present time; he has also written for the London *Times* and the *Observer*, for *Die Zeit*, and other periodicals. Bailey's first books were poetry (a small volume, *The Fool and Fancy*, 1955) and two novels—*Making Progress*, a light-hearted spoof involving international intrigue, British Intelligence, and a secret trip to Poland, and *The Mother Tongue*, a satire on the New York literary scene, public relations, fund raising, television talk shows in the 1950s. He did not publish another novel until 1987. This was *Major André*, an historical novel based on the life of the British army officer in the Revolutionary War who was convicted of spying in a conspiracy with Benedict Arnold and hanged. Bailey lets André tell his own story and presents a sympathetic, thoroughly human and vulnerable character. "Mr. Bailey tells a good yarn well," Esmond Wright commented in the *New York Times Book Review*. "He catches André's alternating moods of gay optimism and total despair; and André's code of honor, his charm, his talents as a versifier and artist all come through."

In another work of imaginative historical reconstruction, the nonfiction *Rembrandt's House*, Bailey pursued a fascination, born twenty years earlier, with the self-portrait of Rembrandt that hangs in the Frick Museum in New York. "Wherever one stood in that long rectangular room of the Pennsylvania coal baron's mansion, his gaze had to be met . . . In that self-portrait, painted in 1658, when he was fifty-two, Rembrandt was evidently a man who had found such a balance: the need to describe himself and the duty to be himself had become one." In the intervening years Bailey made several visits to Amsterdam with the intention of writing a biography of Rembrandt. Realizing, however, that he lacked the specialized scholarship for such a task, he wrote instead a book about Rembrandt's city as he knew it. The contents of the creditors'

inventory of Rembrandt's house taken when the artist declared bankruptcy is the basis for Bailey's informed and informal essays. Walking the streets that Rembrandt walked, Bailey reconstructs the life and clutter of seventeenth-century Amsterdam—its houses, its people, its churches and ghetto, its food and games. Profusely illustrated, the book is a rich compendium of art, history, and simple human life—"a profligacy of information, reflection and appreciation," the *New Yorker* described it, "but [the author], for all his addiction has himself under control and there is not a word too much."

As a reporter Bailey makes no pretense of journalistic invisibility. The reader sees through his eyes—whether the scene be sailing the coastal waters of New England, life in the village of Stonington whose inhabitants he knows as friends and neighbors, or traveling through violence-torn Northern Ireland. The pieces he wrote for the *New Yorker* and other journals over half a dozen years collected in *Acts of Union: Reports on Ireland, 1973–1979* were intended not "as a comprehensive picture of the Troubles that have once again beset Ireland. I offer them rather as aspects of my own education in Irish things." In profiles of a primary school continuing its activities amid the danger and devastation of street bombings; a young working class couple, one Catholic, one Protestant, trying to reconcile their parents to their marriage; of a journey with the poet Seamus Heaney from Dublin to Belfast in 1977, he was a sympathetic but nonpartisan observer. "There are no villains in his narrative," Thomas Flanagan wrote, "but there is indeed a villain, and that villain is history . . . He offers no explanations but only asks us, and by implication, his fellow-countrymen, to see what is happening."

Bailey was born in Portsmouth, in Hampshire, to Cowper Goldsmith Bailey and Phyllis (Molony) Bailey. He is married to Margot Spaeth, a writer and illustrator.

PRINCIPAL WORKS: *Novels*—Making Progress, 1959; The Mother Tongue, 1961; Major André, 1987. *Non-fiction*—The Inside Passage, 1965; Through the Great City, 1967; The Thousand Dollar Yacht, 1968; The Light in Holland, 1970; In the Village, 1971; A Concise History of the Low Countries, 1972; Rembrandt's House, 1978; Acts of Union: Reports on Ireland, 1973–1979, 1980; America, Lost & Found, 1981; Along the Edge of the Forest, 1983; England, First & Last, 1985; Spring Jaunts, 1986.

ABOUT: Bailey, A. America, Lost & Found, 1981; England, First & Last, 1985; Contemporary Authors New Revision Series 3, 1981. *Periodicals*—Connecticut January 1987.

*BAKHTIN, MIKHAIL MIKHAILOVICH
(November 16, [November 4, Old Style] 1895–
March 7, 1975), philosopher of language, theorist of literature and culture, was born in Orel
(south of Moscow), grew up in Vilnius and Odessa, and earned a degree at the University of Pet-
rograd in classics and philology, 1913–1918.
After graduation, to avoid the terrible privations
in the capital during the Civil War, Bakhtin
moved to the small town of Nevel in Western
Russia, where he worked as a schoolteacher and
participated in lecture series and study circles
devoted to the relationship between philosophy,
religion, and politics. In 1920 Bakhtin resettled
in Vitebsk (the home town of Marc Chagall and
a center for the artistic avant-garde), where
the"Bakhtin Circle," now including Valentin
Voloshinov and Pavel Medvedev, continued to
meet. During the early 1920s, defining himself
against the neo-Kantianism of his own mentors,
Bakhtin worked on a massive treatise on the nature of moral responsibility and aesthetics. His
central concerns in these early writings were
two: the possibility of ethics without system, and
the types of obligation authors bear toward their
characters. In 1924, with the country more stabi-
lized economically and politically, Bakhtin and
his wife, Elena Aleksandrovna (who quickly became indispensable to her impractical, often ailing and yet astonishingly productive husband),
moved back to Leningrad.

Most of Bakhtin's associates in his circle were
able to find official and stable employment during the 1920s (for reasons of their Marxism or
their versatility); Bakhtin was not. This was due
in part to his health, a bone disease that left him
frequently bedridden and resulted in the amputation of his right leg in 1938; partly it was due
to Bakhtin's lack of political credentials under
the new regime. To be sure, Bakhtin shared with
his Marxist associates an opposition to certain
current ideological trends (Formalist, Freudian,
structuralist-linguistic), but available evidence
indicates that Bakhtin himself was *not* a Marxist
and could not create effectively within that ideology. This question is of some importance, because the case has been made (although not
persuasively) that Bakhtin in fact wrote three
quite remarkable and indisputably Marxist texts
signed by two associates in his circle:
Voloshinov's *Freudianism: A Critical Sketch*
(1927) and *Marxism and the Philosophy of
Language* (1929)—the latter also being a fine sociological study in the semiotics of language, and
Medvedev's *The Formal Method in Literary
Scholarship* (1928). Bakhtin's disciples in the Soviet Union first attributed these texts to Bakhtin
in 1970. The attribution is currently widespread
in the English-speaking scholarly community,

and has encouraged incorporations of "Bakhtin"
into ideologies as disparate as Marxism, structuralism, and deconstruction.

A careful reading of the disputed texts suggests an orientation there heavily influenced by,
but very different from, Bakhtin's own work.
Bakhtin's critique of the Formalists, "The Problem of Content, Material, and Form in Verbal
Art" (1924; first published 1975), is cast in abstract Kantian categories quite different from
Medvedev's more practical criticism aimed at
the early "mechanical" Formalists (such as Viktor Shklovsky). And the seminal idea of polyphony, as outlined in Bakhtin's first major published
work, *Problems of Dostoevsky's Art* (1929), owes
nothing to Marxism. Polyphony, perhaps the
least understood of Bakhtin's major concepts,
does *not* imply "heteroglossia," social diversity,
or social stratification, nor does it investigate issues of social coding or decoding. It is, rather, a
special approach to the creative process, a speculation on possible multiple positions for the author in a text and on modes of sharing "authorial
surplus" with heroes in the construction of a non-
Aristotelian plot. In contrast, Voloshinov's and
Medvedev's works of the late 1920s are sociological and Marxist: that is, they take Bakhtin's concepts of interpersonal dialogism and radical
individual responsibility for events and incorporate them into a dialectical system based on class
and community. Confronted with a sophisticated sociological version of his own ideas, Bakhtin
appears to have responded in the 1930s with theories of language and literature that were sociological without being Marxist, dialectical, or
"systematizing."

In 1929 Bakhtin was arrested. In these mass
raids on intellectuals in the early Stalinist years,
almost any political eccentricity could serve as
pretext; Bakhtin's particular charge concerned
his activity in the underground Orthodox
Church. He was imprisoned and sentenced to
ten years on the Solovetsky Islands, a death camp
in the Soviet Far North. Thanks to the intervention of influential friends and to his own precarious health, Bakhtin's sentence was commuted to
six years internal exile in Kazakhstan. During
the 1930s, working as a bookkeeper and at other
odd jobs in exile, Bakhtin wrote his most famous
essays on the theory of the novel ("Discourse in
the Novel," "The *Bildungsroman* and Its Significance in the History of Realism," "Forms of
Time and of the Chronotope in the Novel,"
"Epic and Novel," "From the Prehistory of Novelistic Discourse"). He also did research for a major work on Rabelais, which he was to submit as
his doctoral dissertation in 1941 to the Gorky Institute of World Literature in Moscow. The Rabelais project—with its irreverence, celebration

of carnival and sexuality, and utopian, philosophical anarchism—became something of a scandal. A degree (although not the *doktorat*) was eventually granted to Bakhtin, but the book was not published until 1965 (as *The Work of François Rabelais and Popular Culture of the Middle Ages and the Renaissance*).

In 1936, Bakhtin took up a professorship at the fledgling Mordovia Pedagogical Institute in the town of Saransk, east of Moscow. There he taught courses in Russian and world literature until rumors (and soon the reality) of new political purges—always a danger to former exiles—prompted him to resign and retire to a less conspicuous place. After the Germans invaded, Bakhtin was recruited to teach German in the local schools; at the end of the war he returned to work at the Pedagogical Institute. His relative obscurity and low profile in print during this time of mass repression doubtless saved his life.

Bakhtin's final years are the story of rediscovery and rising fame. In the 1950s , on the other side of the Stalinist night, a group of graduate students in Moscow discovered Bakhtin's 1929 Dostoevsky book. They also learned, to their astonishment, that its author was still alive, teaching at what had by then been upgraded to the University of Saransk. Bakhtin was persuaded to rework the book for a second edition. Once this book was reapproved for print (1963), other long-delayed Bakhtin manuscripts were quickly published. By the early 1970s, Bakhtin was already the object of a cult in the Soviet Union. Various approaches to literary studies (structuralist, semiotic, Marxist-Leninist humanist) continue to compete for his legacy, in his homeland and in the West.

In retrospect, Bakhtin's intellectual development appears to coalesce around three major ideas and divide into four periods. These three "global concepts" are prosaics, dialogue, and unfinalizability. *Prosaics* (which is not his term) refers to that deep preference Bakhtin had for the obligations and complexities of prose as opposed to the regularities of a poetics (and of poetry generally); it also privileges messy, particular everyday events over the abstract or the systematic. By *dialogue*, Bakhtin meant a model of creativity based on the assumption that genuine consciousness requires the interaction of at least two embodied voices or personalities; because all words bear traces of earlier users and contexts, language is the most dialogic of human forms. *Unfinalizability* refers to Bakhtin's conviction that messiness and dialogue, taken together, make the world an open place where real creativity is an ongoing and everyday event.

These three global concepts emerged at different times, sometimes complementing, sometimes contradicting one another. Bakhtin's first period (1919–1924) begins with his earliest published article "Art and Responsibility" and ends with his 1924 essay "The Problem of Content, Material and Form in Verbal Art." At this time, the *word* as such was not yet central for Bakhtin: true to his neo-Kantian origins, what concerned him were ethical and aesthetic *acts.* When the Formalists advanced "literariness" as their own special marker of aesthetic value, Bakhtin countered in 1924 with a critique of their "material aesthetics," their tendency to reduce art to material and devices acting upon it. He called for an "aesthetics of content," but at this point his critique was still largely negative. The central question seemed to be: can there be a "non-material aesthetics" that possesses the rigor, analytical precision and objectivity promised by Formalism in its structuralist (Jakobsonian) phase?

The second period, 1924–1930, started with this question and ended with its provisional solution: the typology of "double-voiced words" (words serving more than one voice-center) offered in the fifth chapter of *Problems of Dostoevsky's Art* (1929, revised 1963). The major event of this period was the discovery of the potential of the word. This discovery led to a redefinition of language—not as understood by structural linguists or Russian Futurists, but as dialogue, as uttered discourse. Traditional stylistics has been "monologic," Bakhtin argued, analyzing texts as if a single voice were in control. But in fact real understanding and real uttering—Bakhtin makes no crucial distinction here between speaking and writing—are always oriented *toward* a listener who thus participates in shaping the utterance as it is being formed. Likewise, words themselves are endowed with "inner dialogicality," a potential for "loopholes" and "sideways glances" that forever reassess the authority of other utterances.

The discovery of the dialogic word made possible a third period, lasting from the early 1930s until the 1950s, in which the novel itself becomes the hero. Two related but distinct lines of thought can be said to issue from the Dostoevsky book. In the first line, Bakhtin expanded his focus from Dostoevsky, progenitor of the polyphonic novel, to "novelness" in general. The double-voiced word and the "word with a loophole" (that is, the chance always to reorient itself) become characteristic of all truly novelistic prose. But language use was not the only criterion for novels: in his essays of the early 1930s, Bakhtin also speculated provocatively on the history of "novelistic consciousness" in terms of various conceptualizations of time and space (the "chronotope"), which in turn legitimized certain sorts of events and personalities. Throughout these essays runs the idea that genres of speech and literature are finalized *not* as closed wholes or as systems, but more as clusters or complexes of events, thus providing a relative freedom to both authors and their characters.

Bakhtin then succumbed to exaggerating and idealizing "novelization" in a second line of thought that reached its peak during the 1930s and 1940s. He appears to have experimented by taking one of his global concepts, "unfinalizability," to an extreme, even to the point where it contradicted the other two. This line became the "ambivalent carnivalesque," and it was its most extravagant in the book on Rabelais. For all its current vogue and critical productivity, carnival is arguably one of Bakhtin's weaker formulations. Under carnival conditions, unfinalizability becomes the only and supreme value; anything closed or defined is declared to be dogmatic and repressive. Carnival laughter overcomes death and dialogue is reduced to an explosion of obscene epithets. Under pressure of this carnival imperative, the novel itself is redefined. Literary history becomes a battlefield between the spirit of "finalized" genres, with their repressive canon, and the joyously outcast novel. Wherever the novel appears, other more conservative genres appear hopelessly inadequate and go into decline. Bakhtin begins to sound like his fellow countryman Bakunin—rejoicing in the undoing of rules for its own sake, celebrating the novel as nothing but loophole and the sole locus of human freedom. It is no surprise that during these years of maximalist rhetoric, political terror, and High Stalinism, carnival utopia is linked with novel imperialism.

Bakhtin's fourth and final period, stretching from the early 1950s until his death, was a time of recapitulation and a return to the earlier ethical themes of the 1920s. His last essay concerned the role of the humanities in contemporary culture. In the "posthumous" stage of his career, Bakhtin's texts migrated to France in the 1960s (filtered originally through French structuralism) and then to the United States in the 1970s. There they have been annexed by Marxists and semioticians (who tend to ascribe authorship of the disputed texts to Bakhtin), as well as by certain deconstructionists (usually emphasizing the subversive potential of carnival, or misreading polyphony as authorial indifference to value or abdication of authority). Bakhtin is peculiar among literary theorists today in that he is an opponent of *both* system and "relativism"—that is, an opponent of the idea that, in literary as well as real life structures, either there is system or there is nothing. Although his ideas of dialogism

and the carnivalesque have proved very attractive to critics, Bakhtin's importance as an ethical philosopher, and as a spokesman for the ethical aims of literature, has yet to be thoroughly explored.

WORKS IN ENGLISH TRANSLATION: A collection of four Bakhtin's essays and lectures on the novel was translated by Caryl Emerson and Michael Holquist as *The Dialogic Imagination* (1981) and a selection of his writings on art and aesthetics is available in *The Architectonics of Answerability*, edited by Michael Holquist and translated by Vadim Liapunov, scheduled for publication in 1990. The first edition of Bakhtin's book on Dostoevsky has not been translated, but Caryl Emerson translated his revised and expanded edition of 1963 as *Problems of Dostoevsky's Poetics* (1984). Other translations include Helene Iswolsky's *Rabelais and His World* (1968, 1984) and Vern McGee's *Speech Genres and Other Late Essays* (1986).

ABOUT: Clark, K. and M. Holquist. Mikhail Bakhtin, 1984; Morson, G. S. (ed.) Bakhtin: Essays and Dialogues on His Work, 1986; Morson, G. S. and C. Emerson. Rethinking Bakhtin: Extensions and Challenges, 1989. *Periodicals*—New York Review of Books October 23, 1986.

BANKS, RUSSELL (EARL) (March 28, 1940–), American novelist and short-story writer, was born in Newton, Massachusetts, the oldest child of Earl and Florence Banks. Banks' father was a plumber, as was his grandfather, as was Banks himself for a time. His parents divorced when he was twelve and his mother took a job as a bookkeeper in Barnstead, New Hampshire to support her four children. This hardscrabble, blue-collar upbringing is very much a presence in Banks' fiction. Like many of his characters, he experienced in his youth family disintegration, economic deprivation, and the many varieties of rural discontent and restlessness. After eight unhappy weeks on a scholarship at Colgate University in Hamilton, New York (where he felt like "a poor kid" among "the sons of the captains of American industry"), he drifted to Mexico and Florida with the naive idea of joining Castro's glamorous revolution in Cuba. Instead he ended up in a trailer in Islamorada Key, pumping gas, fishing, and writing stories. Also in this period he married and had a daughter, but his two-year marriage to Darlene Bennett ended in divorce in 1962. These were "terrible years," Banks later said. Almost the only thing he knew with any certainty about himself was that he wanted to be a writer.

After a series of odd jobs (including his stint as a plumber back in New Hampshire), Banks enrolled at the University of North Carolina at

RUSSELL BANKS

Chapel Hill in 1964, graduating Phi Beta Kappa in 1967. At Chapel Hill he and William Matthews founded a literary magazine called *Lillabulero;* this involvement helped him to focus his literary energies and to familiarize him with contemporary writing. He continued to edit the magazine after he had returned to New England in 1968 and taken teaching posts at Emerson College in Boston and at the University of New Hampshire in Durham. Over the next several years his short stories began to appear in such publications as *Ploughshares, Shenandoah,* and *Partisan Review,* and he brought out his first collection, *Searching for Survivors,* in 1975.

Although not without its "journeyman stuff and . . . Barthelmean oddments," in the words of Thomas LeClair, *Searching for Survivors* revealed a talent that had been ripening for years. In the best stories, LeClair wrote, "invention seems offhand and natural, artifice and circumstance one. Without being small, Banks's stories have an assurance few younger—or established—writers can match." This was much more than could be said for Banks's first novel, *Family Life,* published also in 1975. A fable set in an imaginary kingdom with characters given names like King Egress, Orgone, and Dread, *Family Life* failed to amuse just about anyone. Still, it did demonstrate Banks's willingness to take chances, a willingness that paid off in his next work of long fiction, *Hamilton Stark.*

No less experimental than *Family Life* but certainly more controlled, *Hamilton Stark* is a sort of anti-novel about a mysterious New Hampshire eccentric. The eponymous Stark,

who never actually appears in the book, may or may not be insane, may or may not be alive, may or may not be, Banks teasingly suggests, the anonymous narrator himself. Complicating these questions of identity is the book's collage-like structure. Banks gives us footnotes, learned digressions, tape-recorded transcripts, monologues by secondary characters, and excerpts from a novel in progress about Stark by his daughter, with whom the narrator—who is also trying to write a novel about Stark—happens to be in love. "Sometimes all this works, and sometimes it doesn't," was the assessment in the *New York Times Book Review,* yet most critics were persuaded that Banks's complex techniques were an appropriate means for his exploration of the enigma of individual identity.

In *The New World,* a short story collection published the same year as *Hamilton Stark,* Banks separated his more experimental stories from his more traditional ones by dividing the book into halves. Although well received, the more "innovative" second half was generally considered less successful than the more "realistic" first half. In general, Banks's work has evolved from an ironic post-modernism to a relatively straightforward realism. Certainly his next collection of short stories, *Trailerpark,* was a more thorough-going exploration of literary realism than *The New World* or anything he had written until that time. Set in the Granite State Trailerpark in Central New Hampshire, the book consists of thirteen interrelated stories, each focusing on one or more of the inhabitants of the dozen or so trailers on the edge of town by the lake. These are, one senses, up-to-date versions of the kind of people Banks grew up with: "widows and widowers, divorcées and bachelors and retired Army officers, a black man in a white society, a black woman there, too, a drug dealer, a solitary child of a broken home, a drunk, a homosexual in a heterosexual society." The longest and one of the most successful pieces, "The Guinea Pig Lady," concerns Flora Pease, a gentle, not-quite-sane, former Air Force steward of uncertain sexual orientation, whose forbidden menagerie of ever-multiplying guinea pigs forces a crisis in the trailerpark community. "These are bleak stories set in a bleak place, yet there is a wicked comic edge to them," Jonathan Yardley wrote, and he noted that for all her neighbors' failure to tolerate or understand her, Flora "emerges at the end oddly triumphant." The book as a whole he considered "less than a novel and more than a short-story collection, and very good work all the way through."

Banks has been slower to embrace realism in his longer fiction than in his shorter, and the two novels that followed *Hamilton Stark* continued his investigation of disparate narrative modes and subjects. *The Book of Jamaica*, which begins in the first person, moves to the second, and ends in the third, is about an unnamed New Hampshire novelist and professor who receives a grant to study a Jamaican people known as the Maroons. Banks himself was the recipient of such a grant in the 1970s and his love and knowledge of Caribbean culture is clearly reflected in his sympathetic portrayal of the horribly exploited yet resourceful Maroons, descendants of escaped African slaves. Yet Banks does not presume to describe this culture from the inside, and, as Darryl Pinckney observed, "being an outsider is the subject of the novel." Whether the narrator succeeds in shedding his western identity and embracing the alien Other is very much an open question at the book's end.

The Relation of My Imprisonment, by contrast, turns to seventeenth-century Puritanism and to an entirely different form to consider some of the same questions about the relationship between self and community. The book is modeled on the "relation," a confessional genre used by jailed Puritans to recount their sins and testify acceptance of the prescribed orthodoxy. Banks's narrator (once again unnamed) is a death-obsessed coffin-maker imprisoned for twelve years when his trade is suddenly deemed heretical; he eventually retreats to the sanctuary of his own coffin to compose his "relation." This was, to say the least, an odd subject for a contemporary American novel, and no two reviewers seemed to agree on what it was fundamentally *about*. Yet it, like *The Book of Jamaica*, earned more than respectful reviews while selling very modestly indeed.

With *Continental Drift*, Banks finally broke through to a large, general readership. This success was no accident, for *Continental Drift* was his longest, most ambitious, and, by critical consent, best book to date. It also marked his belated acceptance of realism (several critics detected the influence of Dreiser) as a guiding principle for his long fiction. In *Continental Drift* he synthesized the two milieus he had used most frequently in the past: that of hard-pressed, blue-collar New England, in the person of Bob Dubois, a thirty-year-old oil-burner repairman from Catamount, New Hampshire who tries—disastrously—to make a new life for himself and his family by relocating themselves to Florida; and that of the Caribbean, in the person of Vanise Dorsinville, a young Haitian woman who, fleeing poverty and violence with her infant son and nephew, sails desperately and erratically northward, parallelling Bob's movement south. Although their paths converge off the coast of

Boca Raton in a shocking and tragic climax, Bob, not Vanise, is the central character, and indeed some critics considered the Haitian scenes a little worked up—the voodoo episodes, in particular, thought the reviewer in the *Nation*, "give off the gentlest whiff of something cooked up from a stack of *National Geographics*." No one was prepared to argue that *Continental Drift* was flawless. "It is unremittingly, grindingly grim, unleavened by hope, humor, or wit," wrote Garrett Epps, yet he maintained at the same time that it "has many of the strengths and weaknesses of the very best American fiction." And for all its shortcomings, James Atlas did not cavil at calling it "a great American novel." "The tragedies in this novel," he wrote in the *Atlantic*, "are so awesome, so wrenching, so terrible, that it's hard to believe they're happening to real people. Real-estate speculators who get in over their heads, dope dealers who get mixed up with the wrong crowd, liquor-store clerks who get held up by men willing to kill for a few dollars: these are the kinds of anonymous disasters you read about in the newspaper. In *Continental Drift* Banks has brought them to life, given them reality."

Banks followed *Continental Drift* with *Success Stories*, short stories set mostly in working-class New England but with a few excursions into the third world. After the tragic reverberations of its predecessor, the small-scale, tight-lipped life-histories of *Success Stories* struck many readers as somewhat disappointing. In a harsh appraisal in the *New York Times Book Review* John W. Aldridge described the whole collection as merely "precise and coldly objective delineations of reality, black-and-white prose photographs with virtually no shading or dramatic emphasis." Yet even Aldridge could concede that Banks "writes a fine, clear prose—some of the best, in fact, now being written by anyone."

The critical reception of *Affliction*, Banks' sixth novel, was by contrast almost uniformly favorable. This somber, relentlessly tragic novel is set in a bleak small town in New Hampshire and records the life and death of Wade Whitehouse, a coarse, uneducated, violent and self-destructive man who is frustrated at every turn in his feeble but well-meaning efforts to turn his life around. Reverberating through the novel is the theme of domestic violence. Wade's childhood, not unlike Banks' own, was scarred by an alcoholic father who beat him. Wade has a brother, the narrator of the story, who has managed to break the pattern of violence, get an education, and become a teacher. Reconstructing his and Wade's life in *Affliction*, he is exorcising the ghosts of his own past, as Banks seems to be exorcising his. "I was trying to understand my own life, and also my father's and grandfather's," he told an interviewer for the *New York Times Book Review.* In a review of *Affliction* in the same issue Elizabeth Tallent observed that in Banks' fiction "every awakening mind is immediately at risk. Not to be aware of the implacable forces bent on keeping one down is to be, in the most absolute way, a victim—used, mute, manipulated and finally, in what seems a rather minimal step, dead. To be alive, then, to try for some sense of meaning in life, is to be deeply vulnerable from within as well as without—to be, in essence, a tragic figure." A novel of obsession that has the power "to implicate the reader in its own warped and passionate view of the world," *Affliction*, Tallent wrote, "is magnificently convincing." For Robert Towers in the *New York Review of Books* the novel was "almost unremittingly grim; the passages of grotesque comedy are shot through with pain." Nevertheless, Towers finds, Banks brings so much compassion to his portrait of Wade "that the reader in turn is made to care for an unlikable man and to believe that others have loved him. Banks's dour vision is realized intensely and impressively in this novel, and it should strengthen the reputation he earned with *Continental Drift.*"

In addition to his fiction, Banks has published several volumes of small-press verse, but these predate his published fiction and properly belong to his literary apprenticeship. He has continued to teach throughout his career and is currently on the faculty of the Writing Program at Princeton, where he finds the contact with other writers congenial. "We aren't just eyeing each other across a crowded room with drinks in our hands," he told the *New York Times Book Review.*

Banks has one daughter from his first marriage and three daughters from his second marriage, which ended in 1977. His third wife was Kathy Banks, an editor, from whom he was divorced in 1988. He is now married to the poet Chase Twichell. They divide their time between a townhouse in Princeton and a house in Keene, New York, in the Adirondack Mountains. In a 1985 *Publishers Weekly* interview Banks described his literary goals and incidentally answered those critics who have accused him of obtrusiveness in his use of the narrator. "I'm really interested in re-inventing the narrator," he said. "It's a convention that went out the window in the 20th century. I want to feel I have my arm around a shoulder of this reader and I'm explaining, narrating, telling a wonderful story to this person that I've stopped, like the wedding guest in Coleridge's *The Ancient Mariner.* I'm like the ancient mariner stopping the wedding guest in his rush to tell this wonder to him. And I want to have that sense of intimacy, a face-to-face, arm-around-the-shoulder contact."

PRINCIPAL WORKS: *Novels*—Family Life, 1975; Hamilton Stark, 1978; The Book of Jamaica, 1980; The Relation of My Imprisonment, 1983; Continental Drift, 1985; Affliction, 1989. *Collected short stories*—Searching for Survivors, 1975; The New World, 1978; Trailerpark, 1981; Success Stories, 1986. *Poetry*—15 Poems, 1967; 30/6, 1969; Waiting to Freeze, 1969; Snow: Meditations of a Cautious Man in Winter, 1974.

ABOUT: Contemporary Authors, New Revision Series 19, 1987; Contemporary Literary Criticism 37, 1986; Contemporary Novelists, 4th ed., 1986. *Periodicals*—Atlantic February 1985; Nation April 27, 1985; New Republic April 1, 1985; New York Review of Books December 7, 1989; New York Times April 29, 1985; New York Times Book Review May 18, 1975; July 2, 1978; June 1, 1980; March 24, 1985; June 22, 1986; September 17, 1989; New York Times Magazine September 10, 1989; Publishers Weekly March 15, 1985; Washington Post Book World October 4, 1981.

BARNES, JULIAN (PATRICK) (January 19, 1946 –   ), British novelist, was born in Leicester. Both his parents were teachers of French. He studied French literature at Magdalen College, Oxford University, receiving a B.A. with honors in 1968. After spending some time in Paris, he worked as a lexicographer on the *Oxford English Dictionary Supplement* from 1969 to 1972. Since 1972 he has made his living in writing, first becoming known in England as a television critic, a job he has performed for the *New Statesman* (1977–1981) and, since 1982, for the London *Observer.* He has also served as assistant literary editor for the *New Statesman* (1977–1979), contributing editor of the *New Review* (1977–1978), and deputy literary editor of the London *Sunday Times* (1979–1981).

Barnes first won high critical acclaim as a novelist in 1984 with the appearance of his witty, tangential meditation on Flaubert, *Flaubert's Parrot,* a novel that takes the shape of whimsical and obsessive scholarship. But he had already published two solidly accomplished novels in England, *Metroland,* a coming-of-age story, and *Before She Met Me,* a darkly comic tale of obsessive jealousy. After the success of *Flaubert's Parrot,* both books were issued in the United States and earned him further critical praise. He had also launched a pseudonymous career as a crime novelist, publishing under the name Dan Kavanagh two books, *Duffy* and *Fiddle City,* featuring a tough homosexual ex-policeman and the seamier side of London.

JULIAN BARNES

A major reason for Barnes' growing reputation is that he has managed to combine the traditional strength of the English novel, polished social comedy, with philosophical and formal concerns more characteristic of Continental European fiction. In acknowledgment of its caustic wit and formal playfulness, *Flaubert's Parrot* was frequently compared to Vladimir Nabokov's mischievous novel in footnotes *Pale Fire*. The plot of *Before She Met Me* turns on the same sort of erotic obsession that Nabokov and many Continental novelists have made use of. *Staring at the Sun* concerns itself with the questions of meaning and purpose that can be put to life and the elusiveness and mysteriousness of its replies. Throughout his work and especially in *Flaubert's Parrot*, Barnes has also been preoccupied with the ambiguous commerce between art and life. *A History of the World in 10 Chapters* ponders questions of conscience—i.e. human judgment—and final judgment. The "half" chapter is an essay on love, a frail but life-saving raft in the perilous seas of human existence. As Michael Wood writes in the *Times Literary Supplement* in 1989: "Barnes is not an essayist who writes novels, but a novelist who uses his imagination as an instrument of thought." Among contemporary British novelists, perhaps only Iris Murdoch has displayed a comparable philosophical curiosity and ambition.

Barnes' first novel, *Metroland*, is conventional in form and in its coming-of-age subject, but in tracing the divergence between two schoolboy friends, it reveals an acute moral concern with questions of integrity, vocation, and fidelity.

The narrator, Christopher Lloyd, and his best friend, Toni Barbarowski, are precocious, irreverent boys full of private jokes and literary ambitions. In the middle section of the book, Christopher goes to Paris and loses his virginity with an intellectual French girl named Annick; it is May 1968, but Christopher is so self-conscious and absorbed by his love affair that he misses out completely on the famous *événements*, the student rebellion that nearly paralyzes France. He then loses Annick, simultaneously falling in love with the very level-headed English girl whom he eventually marries. In the final section, Christopher, who has turned thirty and settled in suburban Metroland with wife, baby daughter, and mortgage, confronts an embittered Toni, now an unsuccessful, politically militant writer, who directs his sarcasms at marriage, middle-class compromise, and Christopher's notions of fidelity. What emerges from this confrontation is a tender and perceptive portrayal of marriage and maturity.

Critics found each part of *Metroland* evocative. The British critic Frank Kermode, writing in the *New York Review of Books*, called it "a *Bildungsroman* without the solidity or the desperation the term may seem to imply. It records the private jokes and amusements of a bright London schoolboy and his bright friend, and it does so with such accuracy that other ex-clever school-kids who hated sports, built a secret repertory of jests and allusions, and baffled adults by their choice of reading matter, will have the pleasure of self-recognition." In the *New York Times Book Review*, Jay Parini wrote that the novel is "a moving account of friendship between two precociously erudite and *witty* adolescent boys (a type almost inconceivable in American fiction)" and praised the Paris episode: "One would have to look hard to find a wryer, more lovingly detailed account of intellectual and sexual innocence abroad." But *Metroland* "is, finally, a meditation on the meaning of fidelity within the context of marriage in an age of crushing cynicism."

When Barnes' second novel, *Before She Met Me*, first published in England in 1982, was reviewed in the United States several years later, critics, already primed by the oddity of *Flaubert's Parrot*, emphasized its originality. Frank Kermode called it "a remarkably original and subtle book" which is "horribly funny, and idiosyncratic without seriously departing from the tradition of the modern English farcical novel. If we want evidence that Barnes is an original artist we can find it in the inexplicit links and echoes that declare themselves only on a second reading, or in small acts of observation that turn out not to be marginal but of the real substance of the book." In the *New York Times*, Michiko Kakutani wrote, " . . . it's rare to come across a novel that's so funny and odd, and at the same time, so resonant and disturbing."

The hero of *Before She Met Me*, a tranquil, witty historian named Graham Hendrick, escapes a ghastly marriage and settles into a happy second marriage with a sensible, suitable woman who had once been a movie actress. Uninterested in movies, he is tricked by his ex-wife into seeing one of his wife's old films which has an adulterous theme. He gradually becomes obsessively jealous of his wife's past, putting his skills as a historian to work in tracking down all her old films and all the films of her on-screen lovers, eventually confusing her possible real-life affairs with her cinematic ones. His relentless interrogation of his increasingly distressed wife finally pushes this comic obsession toward a tragic denouement.

One reviewer, Gary Krist, writing in the *New York Times Book Review*, found this sudden plunge into obsession contrived: " . . . while Mr. Barnes makes us feel genuine pity for his protagonist, Graham's transition from lovesickness to pathological jealousy ultimately seems forced. As the book hurtles toward its sensationalistic end, we feel more and more that we're being pulled along by sheer authorial will . . . But we are pulled along nonetheless, and Mr. Barnes has at least succeeded in writing one of those books that keep us up until 2 A.M. reading just one chapter more. *Before She Met Me*, despite its flaws, is an intelligent and addictive entertainment."

In 1984 Barnes published *Flaubert's Parrot*, which was greeted by a chorus of praise on both sides of the Atlantic. Most critics were not troubled by the fact that the novel contains only a few hints of a story involving its almost invisible narrator, a retired English doctor named Geoffrey Braithwaite, who, after the somewhat mysterious death of his unfaithful wife, has developed an obsession with Flaubert and has gone to Rouen in Normandy to pursue it. On this tenuous fictional framework Barnes erects an eccentric assemblage of facts, lists, reflections, speculations, and critical rejoinders concerning Flaubert. Critics were especially impressed by the unflagging formal playfulness of the novel; much of *Flaubert's Parrot* is parody. There is a chapter called "Braithwaite's Dictionary of Accepted Ideas," with entries on various aspects of Flaubert's art and people in his life, modeled on Flaubert's own *Dictionnaire des idées reçues*. There is a "Flaubert Bestiary" tracing the appearances of assorted animals in Flaubert's work and life, a "Flaubert Apocrypha" listing books he

planned to write and didn't, a "Train-spotter's Guide to Flaubert" cataloging his allusions to and opinions of trains. There is an "Examination Paper" asking the reader to discuss quotations expressing Flaubert's hatred of critics or the significance of one of his dreams.

The result, as John Updike wrote in the *New Yorker*, is a book of "dashing originality" which imparts a great many odd and entertaining facts about Flaubert: "his statue in Trouville has lost some of its thigh and moustache; . . . his novel *Salammbô* provided the name for a new brand of petit four; . . . he found a business card from Rouen at the top of the Great Pyramid of Cheops in 1849; . . . he couldn't dance; he assured Louise Colet that he was thinking seriously of becoming a bandit in Smyrna; he did not appear on a French stamp until 1952; and in 1876, to facilitate the writing of *A Simple Heart*—which deals, of course, with a servant woman who in dying confuses a beloved pet parrot with the Holy Ghost—he borrowed from the Museum of Rouen a stuffed parrot, which can now be seen on exhibit in two separate sites, the Hotel-Dieu in Rouen and Flaubert's writing pavilion in Croisset, both relics identified as the actual bird borrowed over a century ago."

"All this scattered, avid attention," Updike wrote, "fleshes out an image of 'the first modern novelist' rather more heroic and lovable than the haughty customary daguerreotype," a conclusion echoed by Martha Duffy in *Time*: "By the adroit use of such detail, Barnes builds a warmer personality for the novelist than his glacial public image." But besides being a portrait of Flaubert, *Flaubert's Parrot* is also, in word and deed, a defense of his aestheticism and stylistic subtlety. Braithwaite is made to deliver a devastating refutation of Enid Starkie, the late French literature scholar, who had complained that Flaubert was carelessly inconsistent about the color of Emma Bovary's eyes; he caustically answers the "case" against Flaubert that might be made by a late-twentieth-century critic seizing upon Flaubert's pessimism, dislike of democracy and politics, and questionable treatment of his mistress, Louise Colet. Braithwaite also casts Flaubertian (or Nabokovian) scorn upon certain hackneyed themes in contemporary fiction, calling for quotas on novels about civilized people who revert to savagery, incest novels, campus novels, surrealistic South American novels. Braithwaite, a victim of an adulterous wife, drawn to the creator of a famous adulterous wife, himself becomes Flaubert's parrot, his delegate to the late twentieth century, and makes his own story a story that Flaubert might have written. The book implies that the transmutation of life into art makes it livable.

This formal and thematic intricacy was enough for most critics. In the *Times Literary Supplement* David Coward wrote that the book is "sober, elegant, and wry. It works as literary detection, literary criticism and literary experiment. . . . The modern British novel finds it easy to be clever and comic. Barnes also manages that much harder thing: he succeeds in communicating genuine emotion without affectation or embarrassment." American reviewers were no less emphatic. Terrence Rafferty of the *Nation* called it a "minor classic," and Peter Brooks in the *New York Times Book Review* declared it "a great success, humane and generous, full of insight and wit, rich and even prodigal in its verbal inventiveness. . . ."

The main dissenting note was registered by John Updike. Conceding the book's wit and brilliance, he went on to say: "Too many epigrams on art and life—'The past is autobiographical fiction pretending to be a parliamentary report,' 'Books are where things are explained to you; life is where things aren't'—keep reminding us that we are only reading a book. While the novel as a form certainly asks for, and can absorb, a great deal of experimentation, it must at some point achieve self-forgetfulness and let pure event take over. In *Flaubert's Parrot*, that point arrives too late, and brings too little. . . . So much artifice in establishing the priority of the 'real' feels artificial, and leaves us cold. Whatever we want from novels, we want more than conversation with the author, however engagingly tricksome." But other reviewers, such as Frank Kermode, explicitly defended the book's eccentricity of form: "*Flaubert's Parrot* is a very unusual novel; people who think they know exactly what a novel is tend to say this isn't one, just an eccentric essay on Flaubert. That's nonsense; the book does feel disorderly at times, but it is true to the laws of its own being."

Barnes began *Staring at the Sun* before *Flaubert's Parrot*, but while turning *Flaubert's Parrot* from a short story into a novel, he set the earlier work aside and did not finish it until 1986. More conventional in form than *Flaubert's Parrot*, *Staring at the Sun* is also more directly philosophical and speculative in intention. By tracing the long life of Jean Serjeant, an ordinary, innocent, but persistently inquisitive Englishwoman, it raises questions of the meaning of life. The book divides into two parts: the first third describing Jean's childhood in the 1920s and her unhappy marriage to a policeman; the latter two-thirds following her decision to leave her husband, taking her young son Gregory with her, in pursuit of a "first-rate" life. This leads her to travel around the world—a trip to China, an almost mystical experience contemplating the

Grand Canyon, and finally, well into the twenty-first century, a plane ride in which she is able to watch the sun set twice, echoing the book's opening, in which an R.A.F. pilot during World War II watches the sun rise twice. The latter part of the book also contains something of the playful speculative quality of *Flaubert's Parrot*—for instance, in a list, compiled by Gregory, of fourteen possible solutions to the question of God's existence: "7. That God didn't actually create Man and the Universe: he merely *inherited* them. He was quietly sheep-farming out in some celestial Australia when a panting cub reporter from a local newspaper tracked him down. . . . 8. That God did exist, doesn't exist at the moment, but will exist again in the future. . . . 13. That there is a God, and that he did create the world, but that it is only a first draft. . . . "

Some reviewers found the difference between the earlier and later parts of the book a sign of failed inspiration. The British novelist David Lodge, writing in the *New York Review of Books*, argued that "*Staring at the Sun*, charming and effective as it is in parts, is a broken-backed whole, a book that starts out as one thing and ends up as another. . . . It is full of questions, fundamental questions about the meaning of life and death, posed by very ordinary people . . . and answered in very private and personal ways. The enterprise is risky, always hovering on the edge of the sentimental and banal, but for the first third of the book, at least, it achieves a precarious success. Once Jean Serjeant has left her husband, however, Mr. Barnes doesn't seem to know what to do with her. He sends her around the world. . . . He makes her the object of a rather improbable lesbian passion on the part of her son Gregory's girlfriend, the fanatical feminist Rachel. . . . He introduces Gregory as an alternative point of view in the novel, but unfortunately he is a singularly colorless character, a mere mouthpiece for philosophical speculations that can't plausibly be attributed to his mother."

Christopher Lehmann-Haupt, in a *New York Times* review, complained that the novel "bogs down a bit" as it enters the twenty-first century. But he found that it overcomes its weaknesses: " . . . if this new book lacks the artistic trickiness of its predecessors, there is a quieter game being played on its pages. That game lies in the language, with words and phrases echoing musically throughout the novel until the homeliest of phrases is raised up to a kind of poetry." And most reviewers thought that the novel amply confirmed Barnes' reputation as an important younger novelist. Ann Hulbert, in the *New Republic*, found the discontinuity occasioned by Jean's leaving her husband and embarking on travels an appropriate symbol of her spiritual rebirth: "Flight is the reigning image in the narrative and also of the narrative, which itself skims over expanses of space and time, doubles back, lands smoothly in unusual places, then takes off again to follow Jean's runic observations." Anne Duchêne in the *Times Literary Supplement* spoke of the book's "teasing fullness, its wit, incisiveness, gentleness and generosity," and Carlos Fuentes praised it as "a miracle, a marvelous literary epiphany" and saluted "the universal English voice of Julian Barnes, as he breaks barriers of conventional time and genre, creates characters from ideas and language, and stares not only at the sun but at the reader's intelligence."

Although published as a novel, Barnes' *A History of the World in 10 Chapters,* is a collection of prose pieces—part fable, part history, part philosophical *conte*—"a playful, witty, and entertaining gathering of conjectures by a man to whom ideas are quite clearly crucial, a quintessential humanist, it would seem, of the pre-postmodernist species," Joyce Carol Oates wrote in the *New York Times Book Review.* Barnes makes his readers work hard, but the book does finally articulate his theory of the relationship between fiction and history. He writes: "We make up a story to cover the facts we don't know or can't accept; we keep a few true facts and spin a new story around them. Our panic and our pain are only eased by soothing fabulation; we call it history." A recurring theme or, more accurately, leitmotif here involves sea voyages, beginning with "Genesis" (the story of Noah and the Ark as witnessed by a woodworm stowaway) and moving to a series of variations on voyages real and imaginary. These include stories of the takeover of a luxury liner by Middle East terrorists; the historical tragedy of the *St. Louis,* a ship carrying hundreds of Jewish refugees that in 1939 was refused a port in America or anywhere else and finally returned its passengers to almost certain death in Europe; the historical wreck of the French ship *Medusa* in 1816, immortalized by Géricault in his painting "The Raft of the *Medusa*"; stories of a latter-day Jonah, an astronaut who is looking for the remains of Noah's Ark on Mt. Ararat; a woman who deliberately drifts off to sea because she fears an atomic war. *A History of the World in 10 Chapters,* critics agreed, is a daring and intriguing book. But Michiko Kakutani, in the *New York Times,* though praising the "intelligence and fluency" of Barnes' writing, detected in it a kind of academic exercise quality, a series of rhetorical challenges to which Barnes rises, but at the sacrifice of deeper feeling—a novel "that reads like a hodgepodge of non-sequiturs . . . the sum is smaller, not greater than its parts." For Robert Adams, in *New York Review of Books,* however,

"Barnes is an accomplished equilibrist; a reader who appreciates being made to work for his sense of balance will find in *A History of the World* special pleasure, special perils."

PRINCIPAL WORKS: Metroland, 1980; Before She Met Me, 1982; Flaubert's Parrot, 1984; Staring at the Sun, 1986; A History of the World in 10 Chapters, 1989.

ABOUT: Bayley, J. The Order of Battle at Trafalgar, 1987; Contemporary Authors New Revision Series 19, 1987; Contemporary Literary Criticism 42, 1987; Contemporary Novelists, 4th ed., 1986. *Periodicals*—Nation July 6, 1985; New Republic May 11, 1987; December 4, 1989; New Statesman October 12, 1984; October 3, 1986; New York Review of Books April 25, 1985; May 7, 1987; October 1, 1989; October 26, 1989; New York Times November 29, 1989; New York Times Book Review December 28, 1986; April 12, 1987; October 1, 1989; New Yorker July 22, 1985; Times Literary Supplement October 5, 1984; September 19, 1986; June 30, 1989.

*BARTHELME, FREDERICK (October 10, 1943–   ), American novelist and short-story writer, was born in Houston, Texas, the son of Donald and Helen Bechtold Barthelme. Perhaps because his father was an architect interested in all forms of contemporary art, Frederick, like his older brother the writer Donald Barthelme (d. 1989), gravitated toward the visual arts. After undergraduate study at Tulane University, the University of Houston, and the Museum of Fine Art in Houston, he began working as an architectural draftsman in 1965. Moving to New York from Houston in 1967, he became involved in the conceptual art movement while working as an assistant at a gallery. In a 1988 article in the *New York Times Books Review,* Barthelme remembered this as "a great and silly time. You could put dirt in the work, a bag of dirt, staple it in there, and argue that it recontextualized the prose." During this period his own artwork was exhibited in galleries in New York, Houston, Seattle, Buenos Aires, and elsewhere. He returned to Houston in 1971 and spent the next five years as an advertising writer, while honing his own prose at night. He had already written one book, *Rangoon,* a collection of short stories interspersed with cartoons and blurry snapshots, which, like its successor, *War and War,* had more to do with conceptual art than with literature. These casual experimental fictions failed to win Barthelme any admirers; most critics regarded them as put-ons, and not very amusing ones at that.

After several years of "woodshedding," Barthelme enrolled in the writing program at Johns

°bär′ thul mē

FREDERICK BARTHELME

Hopkins University in 1976, earning his M.A. the following year. Ironically, Barthelme's two most important teachers, John Barth at Johns Hopkins and older brother Donald at home, influenced him most by counter-example: he knew that he couldn't possibly write like them. In his *New York Times Book Review* piece (April 3, 1988), "On Being Wrong: Convicted Minimalist Spills Beans," Barthelme described a humble epiphany that fundamentally altered his literary goals:

> So then, if you were a trained post-modern guy, sold on the primacy of the word, on image, surface, sound, connotative and denotative play, style and grace, but short on sensitivity to the representational, what you did was drive from Texas to Mississippi and realize, while crossing the 20-mile bridge over the swamp outside Baton Rouge, that people were more interesting than words.

It was not, as he went on to say, as simple as that, and yet he had discovered a subject and a style which, with practice, would make him sound like himself and not someone else. His first characteristic short stories began appearing in literary reviews in the early 1980s, then in magazines like the *New Yorker* and *Esquire. Moon Deluxe*, for all practical purposes his "first" book, was a collection of seventeen of his more recent and accomplished stories.

Like all his subsequent work, *Moon Deluxe* is set in the "New South" of shopping malls, condominiums, and fast food restaurants. Barthelme's boutique owners, ad writers, and low-level executives drift aimlessly from attachment to attachment, victims of "fall out" from the sex wars and

of a pervasive anomie. Their predicaments are narrated in a studiously unadorned prose, as neutral and detached as the "relationships" they so casually form.

An example is "Rain Check," in which a man just turned forty goes on a date with a woman much younger than he. They eat at a restaurant called Red Legs, drive around town, argue about whether they should break into the zoo, get in a minor car crash, and end up standing in front of the woman's apartment, with the man undecided about whether he should accept her invitation to come in and take a shower.

"What's going on with stories like this?" Margaret Atwood asked in her review. "It's difficult at first to tell. One might glibly say, 'Not much,' but although that in a way is the point, it's not the whole point. Although it is by turns funny, weird and sad, *Moon Deluxe* makes sinister suggestions." Like the works that followed, *Moon Deluxe* tended to polarize critics. Atwood praised Barthelme's "totally believable" dialogue and "impeccable textures" and maintained that it was "impossible to conceive of any writer doing what he does any better than he does it." To Richard Eder the book was an expert and "scary" delineation of "mildewed emotion." "In the world," he wrote, "that Barthelme evokes with so much wit, such an acute ear and so large a desolation, it is not childhood that is lost, nor empires and passions that rise and decline. It is consumer brands."

On the other hand, many critics were repelled by what they took to be the moral poverty and glib tone of the book. Deborah Gimelson, who thought Barthelme representative of the worst trends in contemporary American fiction, put the case like this: "Barthelme reflects . . . infantilism in both his incessant use of first-person narrative and the emptiness of his content. The sort of passionate human connections that draw a reader in are absent; a detached elegance of tone seems to be the primary concern." Barthelme has answered such criticism by casting doubt on the concept of literature as a container of ideas and by arguing for a fiction that allows its characters to be "skeptical about language and its use." Nevertheless, his detractors persist in seeing his work as a facile response to complex social and literary problems.

Barthelme's next book, the novel *Second Marriage*, had all the earmarks of his by-now familiar world: feckless men, aggressive women, quirky, laconic dialogue, and myriad allusions to television shows and brand names. However, there was a lighter, almost jaunty tone that distinguished it from *Moon Deluxe.* The narrator, patient, passive Henry, does, after all, prevail and win back his second wife even after she has "disinvited" him from their home and installed Henry's first wife in his place. This "domestic-unit-of-the-eighties" is born when Clare, Henry's former wife, flees from her current boyfriend, Joel, seeking solace from her friend Theo, Henry's current wife. Eventually the two women decide they like each other more than Henry, who obligingly moves into another apartment until Theo can sort things out, which she does when she gives up on Clare and takes Henry back. This resolution suggests that Barthelme's male protagonists are not necessarily the benumbed automatons that some critics have taken them to be; Henry, at least, seems closer to Barthelme's conception of his men as "wised-up John Waynes, able to take a hit, which they do repeatedly."

Although *Second Marriage* ends "happily," it provides no greater sense of rootedness or connection than did *Moon Deluxe*. This is still, as Ron Loewinsohn wrote in the *New York Times Book Review*, "a world of surfaces, all of which are either disposable or easy-to-clean—nothing will take or leave a lasting impression. Most of the people who live here are no thicker than Formica, yet they hunger obscurely for some continuity with the place and with each other." Loewinsohn was not alone in thinking the novel a stronger achievement than the collection that preceeded it, maintaining that in "some of his short stories published last year in *Moon Deluxe*, [Barthelme] got facile, occasionally gaining a gratuitous weirdness simply by detaching his incidents from any explanatory context. But in *Second Marriage* . . . he provides the context that naturalizes these understated events."

Tracer was a briefer, harsher, more rapidly-paced novel than *Second Marriage* : "a nasty and sad and unhappy story," as Barthelme called it in an interview in *Contemporary Authors*. Its protagonist and narrator is Martin, who, recently divorced from his wife Alex, travels to the Sea-Side hotel and condominium on the Gulf Coast of Florida, obscurely seeking consolation from his wife's younger sister Dominica, the owner of the hotel. Martin and Dominica fall into an affair, which is complicated by the arrival of Alex, whose motives in coming to the SeaSide are no clearer to her than Martin's are to himself. Indeed, nobody in the novel, including the subsidiary characters who live or just hang out at the hotel, seems to know what he or she wants. One thing that does become clear by the novel's end is that neither Dominica nor Alex has much more use for Martin, and he is dumped, rather unceremoniously, at the airport where he had arrived on the first page of the novel.

Susan M. Dodd, in the *New York Times Book Review*, dismissed *Tracer* as "this really contemporary novel, see," full of new-wave mannerisms and flat one-liners. Roz Kaveney thought it "a coherent picture of the randomness of contemporary American life" and "a moderate advance over [the] already impressive *Second Marriage*." By this point in Barthelme's career it had become evident that what most pleased some critics in his work was just what made others so unhappy. *Chroma*, a further collection of short stories, elicited a predictably divided critical response, and yet despite some fine pieces, no one could have called it an advance upon his previous work. Criticism of Barthelme's abrupt, indeterminate endings and his use of the second-person narrative voice seemed more to the point this time out.

Two Against One is longer, denser, and possibly deeper than any of Barthelme's earlier books. (It is significant that for the first time he grants his protagonist a surname.) Edward Lasco, though not any happier than Barthelme's other fortyish men, has a greater capacity to feel and to express his feelings; so do the other characters in the novel: Edward's younger wife Elise, currently undergoing a painful separation from Edward, whom she still loves despite his sexual coldness; Elise's lover Roscoe, quiet and polite but unrecovered from his wife's death a year before; and Kinta, a sexy ex-girlfriend of Edward's also having problems with *her* husband. It is not so much that these characters *want* to feel as that they can't stop themselves from feeling. Edward, in particular, would rather sit down with a copy of *InfoWorld* and a snack of Oreos and skim milk than deal with the presence of Elise when she shows up on his porch in the first scene of the novel. It is Elise's proposition that she not give up Edward *or* Roscoe. This proposition is debated for the rest of the novel, between trips to the supermarket, meals in shopping-strip restaurants, and long drives on the highway to "the Gulf" (of Mexico). A complex combination of inertia, fear, and resentment decides the outcome, and the novel ends with Edward lying in bed next to his girlfriend, quietly sobbing for his wife:

> There in the dark in the bed he felt how much he missed her, how much he had *already* missed her, and he had tears in his eyes, gathering there but not coming any further, and he felt his life was smaller than it used to be, that it would get only smaller, and then Kinta rolled over beside him, kissed his arm, and moved to her pillow, and she said, when she was resettled, "Edward. She loves you. I promise."

There was general agreement that *Two Against One* was something of a departure for

Barthelme, and one that repaid the risks taken. Francine Prose noted how Barthelme's "palette has darkened, how his sense of possibility seems drastically to have diminished. His loopy humor and trenchant social observation are still very much in evidence. Yet *Two Against One* is by far the most powerful, disturbing and interior of Mr. Barthelme's fictions."

Frederick Barthelme lives in Hattiesburg, Mississippi, where he is director of the Center for Writers at the University of Southern Mississippi and editor of *Mississippi Review*. In his *Times Book Review* piece he described "what's going on with this new fiction"—meaning his own as well as that of Raymond Carver, Ann Beattie, Mary Robison, and other "minimalists" with whom he is often compared—as "people rolling down the windows, trying to get a good whiff of what's out there." The objective, he said, is not to capture "*the* world on the page," but "*a* world, palpable, compelling, frightening."

PRINCIPAL WORKS: *Novels*—War and War, 1971; Second Marriage, 1984; Tracer, 1985; Two Against One, 1988; Natural Selection, 1990. *Collected short stories*—Rangoon, 1970; Moon Deluxe, 1983; Chroma, 1987.

ABOUT: Contemporary Authors 122, 1988; Contemporary Literary Criticism 36, 1986; Contemporary Novelists, 4th ed., 1986; Dictionary of Literary Biography Yearbook, 1985. *Periodicals*—Los Angeles Times Book Review July 31, 1983; New Leader November 28, 1983; New York Times Book Review July 31, 1983; September 30, 1984; August 11, 1985; April 3, 1988; November 13, 1988; August 19, 1990; Times Literary Supplement March 21, 1986.

BECKER, JUREK (September 30, 1937–), Polish-German novelist, was born to Jewish parents in the ghetto of Lodz (Poland) and grew up in the concentration camps of Ravensbrück and Sachsenhausen. He learned German only in 1945 after moving to Berlin with his parents. He writes in German. After completing *Gymnasium* in Berlin and serving in the army of the German Democratic Republic (GDR), he studied philosophy. Between 1960 and the end of 1977 he lived in East Berlin as a writer. Michael Butler writes, in the *Times Literary Supplement* : "It was perhaps as natural for such an archetypal victim of fascism to settle in the German Democratic Republic as it was inevitable that he would come to share the frustration of many East German writers and intellectuals in the mid-1970s. Not surprisingly, therefore, literature and politics are closely interwoven in Becker's work, the central theme of which is the problem of reconciling the

JUREK BECKER

claims of the individual with the demands of society." From 1957 until 1976 he was a member of the Socialist Unity Party, the Communist party of the GDR. He was expelled in the spring of 1977 after having protested Reiner Kunze's expulsion from the Writers' Union of the GDR and having signed the so-called "Biermann Petition" in the fall of 1976. In 1977 Becker left the Writers' Union and, in the same year, the GDR, making his home in West Berlin. With an exit visa he went in February 1978 to Oberlin College, Ohio, as a writer-in-residence. Becker has since traveled extensively. In 1982 he was appointed *Stadtschreiber* (writer-in-residence) by the town of Bergen-Enkheim in the Federal Republic.

Becker's first novel, *Jakob der Lügner* (1969, translated as *Jacob* [or *Jakob*] *the Liar*), was an immediate success. The "liar" is Jakob Heym, an inmate of the Polish ghetto, who is driven to invent good news about the rapid approach of the Red Army—news he has allegedly heard on a radio which does not exist. This (invented) ownership of a radio, prohibited by the punishment of death, is nevertheless more credible than Jakob's explanation of how he managed to leave the headquarters of the German ghetto commander alive, since no Jew ever managed to do that before. While being forced to develop a network of more and more sophisticated lies, Jakob keeps up the hope and life spirit of his fellow Jews. The story has two possible endings, leaving the identity of Jakob and the narrator wide open. Thus it reflects the author's helplessness in confronting his own disturbing life story.

This novel, which established Becker's literary

national reputation as a powerful new German narrator of a painful past, clearly shows a strong influence of the Yiddish narrative tradition represented by such writers as Sholem Aleichim and Mendele Moicher Sfurim as well as of Becker's older compatriot, the writer Johannes Bobrowski. Becker's narrative technique, wit, and melancholy humor are used dialectically as counterpoint to the horror and despair in the Polish ghetto. The triumph of the human spirit surviving inhumanity and the cold efficiency of the Nazi extermination machine makes this novel one of the most moving literary statements in contemporary German literature dealing with the Holocaust. Eva Figes observed in the *New York Times Book Review*. "Those with any kind of personal involvement in the destruction of Europe's Jews usually feel a profound distaste for the way in which the subject has become part of the entertainment business. As time goes by, the amount of crass and insensitive exploitation steadily increases. But the work of writers like Jurek Becker provides an antidote to this nasty trend." *Jacob the Liar* received the Heinrich Mann Prize in 1971, and a film version, for which Becker wrote the script, won an award in the West Berlin Film Festival of 1974.

Becker's somewhat weaker second novel, *Irreführung der Behörden* (Misleading the Authorities, 1973), plays on a remotely similar concept. The protagonist is another liar. Only this time his lying is not life-supporting but destructive. He is depicted as a successful GDR author whose rapid career is a result of total moral submission to the party line. The law student Gregor Bienek loves and lives without any commitment. He tells many stories; he publishes a few. His law studies turn out to be a front to fool the authorities, for he really wants to become the author of the Great East German Novel. When success suddenly arrives, he joins the conformists. It is a novel of disillusion, frustration, and compromise, reflected in Gregor's career and in his once idyllic marriage. Reviewers of the novel mainly noticed its ambiguity and inconclusiveness. The story, starting auspiciously as a tale of rebellion against social supression, fizzles out into a rather banal marriage melodrama and resignation. Although the critical reception was not enthusiastic, Becker was awarded the Literary Prize of the City of Bremen in 1974 and the National Literature Award of the GDR in 1975.

In his novel *Der Boxer* (The Boxer, 1976), which was made into a TV movie (1980), Becker describes the terrible difficulties a former concentration camp inmate has in adjusting to a "normal" life (in West as well as East Berlin). Aaron Blank, a boxer, has lost his family in the Holocaust. His wife has been murdered. His children have vanished. Through a search organization he eventually finds a boy who could be his son, although no one can prove it. Aaron is no longer capable of starting a loving relationship with other people. When Mark, his alleged son, becomes attached to a nurse, Aaron decides to marry her, though he does not love her, and establish a "normal" home for the boy. He also resolves to raise Mark as a German, teaching him how to box and defend himself so that he may fit into society. Ironically, however, Mark asserts his identity as a Jew. He goes to Israel and is killed in the Six Day War. In *Der Boxer* Becker shows the terrible psychological damage that Nazism inflicted upon its victims and on the whole German people. Critics acknowledged the book's authenticity, but some faulted the complex narrative form used by Becker: Aaron, who is relating the story to the apparent author, at times undermines the credibility of what he is saying and what the narrator is reporting.

Becker's fourth novel, *Schlaflose Tage* (1978; translated as *Sleepless Days*), appeared in West Germany only. It describes a model case of renunciation. Simrock, a GDR teacher, aged thirty-six, is warned by chest pains that he has a heart condition. He decides "to go straight," i.e., to leave his wife and his child and to start a new life outside the narrow confine of his seemingly secure existence. From now on he conducts his lessons at school in such a way that he is warned and eventually fired, allegedly "unfit to do educational work in the interest of the state." Rather than trying to win back his old position by undergoing the expected process of public self-criticism, Simrock prefers to get a humble job in a bakery. Of what is officially expected of him, he says: "How would people think of a teacher willing to accept this kind of offer?" Instead he accepts a lower living standard, thus defying manipulations from without.

In this tale Becker demonstrates how an individual's instinct of survival and self-preservation can be misused by a totalitarian regime. However, it can also be modified by the individual to serve his self-respect, so that he becomes a thorn in the flesh of a cynical bureaucratic system. Again some critics faulted the rather abstract protagonist of Becker's novel as a pure "head birth" and thought the story itself too smooth, dry, and artificial to allow for much reader involvement. Paul Ableman, in the *Spectator*, for example, felt "merely depressed by the robot nature of the society that can just be discerned through the ponderous narrative." But Irving Howe, discussing the novel in the *New York Times Book Review*, was impressed with Becker's skill in evoking "the daily grind of an authoritarian society, the psychic drabness of it all. . . . his book tells us what it is like to live in the airless world of authoritarianism."

In his novel *Aller Welt Freund* (Friend of the Whole World, 1981) Becker relates in ironic style some episodes from the life of a news editor whose suicide attempt ("I cannot stand any news anymore.") is unsuccessful. "The bulk of the novel," Michael Butler writes in the *Times Literary Supplement*, "consists of the bewildered reactions of family, girl-friend and officials whose inability to communicate on any other plane but the trivial is matched only by their determination to uncover an 'explanation' for his eccentric behavior." Gradually the journalist discovers that there is no possibility of real communication and, Butler writes, he "is forced to recognize that others remain strangely untouched by the catalogue of world-wide horrors which it is his job to describe and evaluate." At the end of the novel the journalist is transferred to the sports page and accepts with irony the banality of his existence.

The novel *Bronsteins Kinder* (translated as *Bronstein's Children*), published in 1988, is set in East Berlin in 1973. A Jew, born a decade after the end of the war and living in the GDR, discovers by accident that his father is keeping a former concentration camp warden as prisoner in his weekend cottage, submitting him to the kind of torture he has experienced himself. Eva Figes writes: "Most of the narrative concerns the boy's response to the situation. He knows he must eventually set [the prisoner] free—for his father's sake, as much as for the other man's—but it takes him some time to reach the point of decision, and when he finally arrives, what he finds suggests that the victim and persecutor were inextricably bound to each other." When does one stop acting like a victim? All the figures of Becker's novels deal with this question. The answer is: Never. The dramatic qualities in this novel about victimization and the need to lie in the face of reality are obvious. Becker narrates in precise images. He develops carefully constructed suspense. With this novel Becker once again won the unmitigated critical praise he had received for *Jacob the Liar*.

Nach der ersten Zukunft (After the Immediate Future, 1980) is a collection of twenty-five stories which could not be published in the German Democratic Republic. With a few exceptions, they all describe the conditions of living in a society that calls itself "socialist." Two of the stories, "New Yorker Woche" (New York Week) and "Ohio bei Nacht" (Ohio at Night) reflect the author's experiences in the United States. In the story "Der Nachteil eines Vorteils" (The Advantage of a Disadvantage) Becker urges a man none

ble to explain the existence of GDR writers like himself:

> Penguins, so I have read, are extremely hard to keep outside of their home region, for example in zoological gardens. The conditions of their natural environment are such that there are hardly any germs of disease. The result is that the organism of the penguin, since it hardly ever has to fight such germs, is practically unprepared for resistance against them. Only against the cold does the penguin have great powers of resistance.
>
> In zoos, however, where there are billions of germs from all over the world, the situation for penguins is fatal. Almost defenseless, so it is said, they are exposed to deadly germs at which the other animals only smile, so to speak. And even the tiniest dangers, not even noticed by the organisms of others, can be deadly for penguins. It takes a long time for them to accommodate, and extraordinary patience must be asked from the animal attendants.
>
> —trans. R. Kieser

WORKS IN ENGLISH TRANSLATION: *Jacob the Liar* was translated by Melvin Kornfield in 1975; *Sleepless Days, Bronstein's Children*, and *Jakob the Liar* were translated by Leila Vennewitz in 1979, 1988, and 1990 respectively.

ABOUT: Cassell's Encyclopedia of World Literature, 1973; Columbia Dictionary of Modern European Literature, 1980; Contemporary Authors 85–88, 1980; Contemporary Literary Criticism 7, 1977; 19, 1981; Demetz, P. After the Fires, 1986; Dictionary of Literary Biography 75, 1988. *Periodicals*—New German Critique Winter 1980, Spring 1980; New York Times Book Review September 16, 1979; November 27, 1988; Spectator December 8, 1979; Times Literary Supplement October 7, 1983; August 3, 1990.

BENEDIKT, MICHAEL (May 26, 1935–   ), American poet, critic, editor, and translator, writes: "There are probably two perspectives in my mind when I sit down—or even stand up—to write. One is 'Willed'; the other isn't, and by and large is more or less 'Involuntary.'

"Regarding the 'Willed' aspect: I try, of course, to do the best work that I can do (what writer doesn't?). There really is not only 'inspiration, but also perspiration,' involved in writing poetry. Thus, although sometimes a poem will come to me rather quickly, at other times it's necessary, in order to get the poem to come out right, to work on it for years and years. (In recent years I've particularly found that to be the case—perhaps partly because lately I've been writing some longer poems than I used to.)

"On the 'Involuntary' side of things: My work has changed a lot, so far, over the years. I sometimes tend to be rather surprised, even myself, by the various unwilled, relatively involuntary stylistic changes which have already taken place

periments for their own sake than I am in experiments that succeed, and which thus may cease to be regarded in the long run as experiments at all! Above all, I try to make my impulses towards exploratative work, to, in fact, actually 'work.' As a writer, I seek the genuinely authentic, and hopefully esthetically viable, 'Eureka!'"

MICHAEL BENEDIKT

in it. Those changes, on a from-book-to-book basis, sometimes startle even me. (My first 'slender sheaf' of poetry, a chapbook issued by a small press in 1960 of short and rather extremely experimental poems for their time, was in fact actually entitled *Changes*.) I guess I saw that changes of some kind would be coming.

"Probably what has happened is that as my life I've always led has changed—sometimes in the extreme—my poetry has too. I've never striven to become that relatively rare phenomenon, a kind of literary 'chameleon'—any more than a musician I admire, Stravinsky, or a painter I admire, Picasso, actually planned to have their work fall into definite 'periods.' The changes, both stylistic and in terms of content, have taken place largely in tandem with, and, at least to some extent, in direct reflection of, the Life. Not that I, especially, don't agree that 'Variety Is One of the Spices of Life'!

"Indeed, I think that the desire I've always deeply felt to explore what seem to me to be the seemingly limitless possibilities of the medium of poetry is something which, in me, keeps the desire to write poetry itself alive. Hopefully, of course, that is something that will keep one's poetry alive not only for the writer, but for the reader as well.

"So, I suppose, writing, for me, is something akin to 'Process'—the learning process especially, I always like to think, a process for which I have a long-standing respect and admiration.

"Although I know of course that the processes of Change involve risk, in Art as well as in Life, I know also that I'm far less concerned with ex-

Michael Benedikt was born in New York City to John Benedikt, an electronics engineer, and Helen (Davis) Benedikt, a teacher. Self-described as "a lifetime New Yorker" who makes his home on the Upper West Side of Manhattan, he has a B.A. in English and journalism from New York University (1956) and an M.A. in comparative literature from Columbia University (1961), where he wrote his master's thesis on Wallace Stevens. Benedikt served with the U.S. Army from 1958 to 1959 and in the Army Reserve from 1959 to 1964 with the rank of SP-4. He has taught literature and creative writing at a number of colleges—Bennington from 1967 to 1968, Sarah Lawrence from 1968 to 1973, Hampshire from 1973 to 1975, Boston University, where he had the Anne Sexton Chair in Poetry in 1975 and was visiting professor from 1977 to 1979, and Vassar College, where he was an associate professor from 1976 to 1977. While still a candidate for his M.A., he worked as an editor for Horizon Press, and he was for four years, 1974 to 1978, poetry editor of the *Paris Review*. He has also written art criticism for *Art News* and *Art International* and has published translations of contemporary drama and poetry from the French, German, and Spanish. He has received prizes and awards for his work from the Guggenheim Foundation (1968), *Poetry* Magazine (the Bess Hokin Prize in 1968), the National Endowment for the Arts (1970, 1979), and the New York State Council on the Arts (1975).

In *Benedikt: A Profile* Michael Benedikt characterizes his work as being "in some kind of motion; and that motion, change, both esthetic and psychological, has always been an issue with me in poetry." He has moved rapidly and apparently with ease from editing to teaching, from criticism to poetry, and—within his own poetry—from free verse to prose poems and back to verse, and from surrealism to realism. If there is a single literary quality that dominates his creative activities thus far, it is metaphor, in its original Greek sense of transformation from one shape or form to another. More than a figure of speech, metaphor represents for him the power "of relating internal truth to external manifestations, and vice versa. For me, metaphor is the broadest, most reality-spanning thing in poetry, the most important single element, much more important than considerations which are nevertheless still *there*, like music, rhythm, meter, cadence, linebreaks, and things like that. I see metaphor as a kind of container for them all. I still use metaphor a lot, but I'm now more interested in the leaps, the spontaneous jumps of consciousness, as they relate to surprises in logic."

The essence of the surrealism that figures so large in Benedikt's early poetry lies in these surprises and leaps in the logic of human consciousness because they represent his effort to unite the worlds of inner and outer reality, and of imagination and fact. In his introduction to *The Poetry of Surrealism*, which he edited, and which has become the standard anthology of French surrealist writings translated into English, Benedikt traces the influence of French surrealism on a diverse group of American poets ranging from "Beats" like Allen Ginsberg, Gregory Corso, and Lawrence Ferlinghetti to the New York School of Frank O'Hara, Kenneth Koch, and John Ashbery to poets such as W. S. Merwin, Louis Simpson, James Wright, Donald Hall, David Ignatow, and Robert Bly. Writing in 1970, Benedikt defined the "major theme" of his own work as "probably the relationship of matter and spirit, sometimes the sensual and the 'pure.'" For him poetry is "a way of knowing": "It is not so much 'knowledge' of the world in the final, conventional sense—valuable as that surely is—but knowledge of the world in process; and also, of course, of self-knowledge in process."

The process itself is liberating. It frees the poet to explore consciousness and his experience of the world randomly and fluidly with what Lewis Gallo, in *Benedikt: A Profile*, describes as "rational irrationalism." Benedikt's metaphors make connections which at first appear illogical, and which work as a kind of dialectic, bringing together opposites or contradictions in the process. In this sense Benedikt reflects another literary stream—the English romantic poets, especially Wordsworth and Coleridge, whose influence he acknowledges, and who were also concerned with dealing with the interplay of inner and outer, subjective and objective, realities. He said in an interview in 1977 that surrealism "is no longer the central issue with me. I simply feel, with surrealism, and many other movements in contemporary thought . . . that it's a question of relating your mind to what's out there and responding to it; and then hoping that what's out there will respond to your mind, so that seeming contradictions cease. It's a matter of having a loving dialogue, not a monologue, with the world."

If some of Benedikt's poems defy easy explica-

tion, they nevertheless communicate the inner logic of our dreams. His imagination unleashed, beginning early on, Benedikt writes with a freedom and humor that is striking and original:

> Our window is covered by the beard
> Of the man overhead
> Leaning out of the window
> Watching the jewel-thieves:
> The door is useless as a hatch.
> The house is moving slowly
> Toward Victoria Falls
> Place of melancholy and humor and destruction.
> Will you comfort me with the soddenness
> Of your cheeks at night,
> Of your eyes,
> Of your harmless, webbed feet.
>   "Victoria Falls" (in *Changes*)

As Laurence Lieberman writes in *Poetry* in 1969 (reprinted in his *Unassigned Frequencies*): "Michael Benedikt's surrealist poems are a highly serious form of play in which easily recognizable chunks of human and non-human reality are re-ordered in enchanting and luminous fantasies." The result of such freedom is, however, sometimes preciousness and self-indulgence. Lieberman finds some of his poems "mere intellectual curios, clever exercises in . . . a vivacious display of technique . . . . His best poems [In *The Body*] are parodies of intellectual self-consciousness and moral decadence. They are compact allegories, or narrations, which project with the stunning clarity of animated cartoons the de-spiritualization of all beings into gadgets, self-imitating inventions."

Still, in "Country Living," a poem written in the late 1960s and collected in *Sky*, Benedikt appears to define his dialogue-oriented poetic credo:

> If all the finest perceptions in the world were to be
>   dropped
>   into the feet of a diving suit, or space suit
> As sole weight
> How we would laugh to see a gentleman in a diving
>   suit
>   floating
>   outstretched upon the water, signaling for help;
> or
> a
>   gentleman in a space suit with an astonished
>   look,
>   floating
>   off at the end of a tether!
> If all the keenest ideas were placed in a prescription
>   bottle
>   beside bad butter at a barbeque table
> All the guests would go home anyway and hiccup
>
> Everything is in its place, everything is now in its place
>
> Still, to face the southwest and watch streetlights
>   against
>   sunsets
> Or to observe star reflections in a dying aunt's

lorgnette
Or the sea sucking in and out between two rocks
Or the feeling of sand in my sneakers
Is to listen, to think to hear
Little dialogues of spirit and matter.

The long lines of "Country Living" anticipate a trend toward the prose poetry to which Benedikt devoted himself in the 1970s. In his introduction to *The Prose Poem: An International Anthology* he links the development of the prose poem with surrealism's emphasis on the unconscious and traces the form back to its French origins in Baudelaire. More liberating even than free verse, the prose poem legitimizes the free fluid expression of the human consciousness. Yet, as Benedikt uses the form, it has a design of its own. Discussing metaphor in 1977 Benedikt said: "In the prose poem I'd take a single metaphorical statement and develop that metaphor slowly, logically;—that's where my feeling about the unconscious as being, metaphorically speaking, 'mole-like'—both all-pervasive in its workings, and *gradual* in its development— probably comes from."

The prose poems in *Mole Notes* and in *Night Cries* reflect Benedikt's "fascination with contradiction." They are filled with puns and wordplays, which are also, as Benedikt sees it, "a minor form of metaphor." The speaker in *Mole* digs through his experience busily, like a mole, and is "a trembling antenna, straining to hear what will be . . . But how can he go in this condition—how can he proceed without seeing? And how is it that I can see him, since he is obviously invisible from where I live, here on the earth? Mole can go on because his eyesight is famous for excluding the visual as a necessary component of vision; and as for me, I admit I am feeling my way."

For Lewis Gallo, Mole is an alienated artist, identified of course with the poet himself, "digging through the tunnels of metaphor." Benedikt sees himself not with self-pity but with a gleeful, if sometimes rather rueful humor:

A mole finds the subject of "taxidermy" a very delicate subject indeed. Before he stamps his foot and disappears down the Mole-hole, he announces, shouting: "Everybody knows that everything on earth will have to become more 'Open.' This of course includes poetry. And when poems are 'Open' enough, people may be able to fit inside of them more comfortably, as if inside the skin of some original and novel animal."
            "Taxidermy" (in *Mole Notes*)

Gallo hailed *Mole Notes*, in which individual prose poems are linked as in a narrative, as unprecedented in American literature, "although certainly it belongs to the tradition of our modern epics, beginning with, say, Walt Whitman's *Leaves of Grass* and continuing with texts like Charles Olson's *Maximus Poems.*" Jerome J. McGann, in the *Times Literary Supplement*, was somewhat more qualified in his praise of Benedikt's second collection of prose poems, *Night Cries.* For McGann, also, Benedikt writes in the romantic tradition revitalized by the symbolist and surrealist movements. However, some of the poems, he finds, are self-consciously manipulated. Nonetheless, overall he admires the work: "His book is important—it is also enjoyable—because it offers a fine, a clear opportunity to understand the craftsmanship of poetry . . . Like all poetry, this sort of work is neither to be believed (romantically) nor disbelieved (critically). One must either respond to it selfconsciously (if one is inclined to be Romantic) or follow one's understanding of its forms until one appreciates the grace of its art. . . . "

Demonstrating once again what Deno Trakas, in the *Dictionary of Literary Biography*, cites as "his adaptability, a readiness to change," Benedikt returned in 1980 to verse with *The Badminton at Great Barrington; or, Gustave Mahler and the Chattanooga Choo-Choo.* The eccentricity of this title conceals a cycle of love poems which add up—almost as in a sonnet sequence—to what is, in effect (like *Mole Notes*), a book-length narrative poem, which is probably more accessible to readers than some of his earlier works. The dust jacket describes the poem as "the story of two lovers crossed not only by their stars but by their psychologies." With his characteristic flair for opposites, Benedikt identifies his narrator with the great and serious composer Gustave Mahler and the woman he loves with the popular song "Chattanooga Choo-Choo," and introduces musical references from the classical to Bruce Springsteen and rock:

Am I doomed to a future of lonely domestic muzak
Now that I have abandoned the Gustave Mahler
Records I use to love, long since.
            —from "Teenybopper Soliloquy"

The poet traces a passionate but if tragi-comic love affair, taking for his theme Catullus' line "Odi et amo" ("I hate and I love"). "Was she crazy?" he asks at the beginning of the poem:

        . . . All I can say is
Although I was her lover, her then current shrink
Used to call me up and ask *me* for advice,
And finally urged me to take up a practice!

One section of the poem is set in the Massachusetts summer resort town of Great Barrington where Choo-Choo has a cottage with a badminton court. The abandoned badminton game is a metaphor for the failure of their relationship. Sadly the poet acknowledges:

. . . I would have táken your hand,
Charming Choo-Choo, except that we were joined more
Already, by metaphor; as for making love that very last
                                                      time
Together, it would have been too much like literature.

Benedikt has said that his later poetry is moving "towards a more literally realistic direction." *The Badminton at Great Barrington* seems to be a step in that direction. Whatever the direction Benedikt will move in his future writing, he is likely to remain, as Lewis Gallo writes, a poet who "will either excite or incite readers. He takes chances . . . What Benedikt fights against is the kind of closed arena he himself has encountered in the Eliotic tradition. A *good* poet should be able to do anything he wants and readers should not mechanically reject work because it fails to conform to accepted norms."

PRINCIPAL WORKS: *Poetry*—Changes: A Chapbook, 1961; The Body, 1968; Sky, 1970; Mole Notes, 1971; Night Cries, 1976; The Badminton at Great Barrington; or Gustave Mahler and the Chattanooga Choo-Choo, 1980. *Prose*—Benedikt: A Profile, 1977. *As editor and translator*—(with G. E. Wellwarth) Modern French Theatre: The Avant-Garde, Dada, and Surrealism, 1964; (with G. E. Wellwarth) Postwar German Theatre: An Anthology of Plays, 1967; Ring around the World: Selected Poems of Jean L'Anselme, 1967; Theatre Experiment: New American Plays, 1967; (with G. E. Wellwarth) Modern Spanish Theatre: An Anthology of Plays, 1968; 22 Poems of Robert Desnos, 1971; The Poetry of Surrealism: An Anthology, 1974; The Prose Poem: An International Anthology, 1976.

ABOUT: Benedikt, M. Benedikt: A Profile, 1977; Contemporary Authors 15–16, 1966; Contemporary Literary Criticism 4, 1975; 14, 1980; Contemporary Poets, 4th ed., 1985; Dictionary of Literary Biography 5, 1980; Lieberman, L. Unassigned Frequencies: American Poetry in Review, 1964–1977, 1977; Turner, A. T. (ed.) Fifty Contemporary Poets: The Creative Process, 1977; Who's Who in America 1988–1989; Who's Who in the World, 1988. *Periodicals*—American Poetry Review September–October 1977; Modern Poetry Studies Winter 1976; Spring 1977; Poesis 1987; Poetry August 1977; Times Literary Supplement July 23, 1976.

BERNSTEIN, JEREMY (December 31, 1929–), American writer on science, was born in Rochester, New York, the eldest of three children of Rabbi Philip Sidney Bernstein and the former Sophy Rubin. His father, born in Rochester in 1901, returned to the city in 1926 to become the assistant rabbi and then the rabbi of a large and old Reform congregation, Temple B'rith Kodesh, founded in 1848. Philip Bernstein's parents had emigrated as very young people from a *shtetl* in Lithuania Jeremy Bernstein's maternal ancestors are of Russian descent.

Bernstein was educated first in the Rochester public schools, where he was a good student but not particularly gifted in science or mathematics. Later, when the family moved to New York City, he attended and graduated from Columbia Grammar School, where his chief interests were playing the trumpet, attending jazz sessions all over Manhattan, and interviewing musicians and other celebrities for the school newspaper. He became especially friendly with Duke Ellington and members of his orchestra.

Bernstein wrote in his autobiography, *The Life It Brings: One Physicist's Beginnings*, that his years at Harvard University "transformed my life." He took his bachelor's degree in 1951, his master's in mathematics in 1953, and his doctorate in physics in 1955. At the beginning of his career at Harvard College, however, he was determined, after a none-too-happy high-school experience, "not to take any more science courses." Yet he was obliged to fulfill an undergraduate requirement in science, and so enrolled in Natural Sciences 3, "taught by I. Bernard Cohen, the historian of science. This course, it was said, was for people who were basket cases in science. That sounded just right for me." The turning point for the young student came during this course when Cohen began to talk about the theory of relativity, certain aspects of which Bernstein found "absolutely mind-boggling." When Cohen remarked, probably jokingly, "that only nine, or twelve, people in the world understood the theory of relativity," Bernstein took him entirely seriously and "decided, with the bravado characteristic of a Harvard freshman, that I would become the tenth, or thirteenth, person to understand relativity." The future course of his life was set, and over the next several years, after Harvard courses with Philipp Frank, George Mackey, Julian Schwinger, Percy Bridgman, and Wendell Furry, Bernstein became a theoretical physicist, with a specialty in the study of elementary particles and weak interactions. He worked at first as a research associate at Harvard's Cyclotron Laboratory (1955–1957); a junior physicist at Princeton's Institute for Advanced Study (1957–1959), where he came to know the theoretical physicist J. Robert Oppenheimer, then the director; and an associate in physics at the Brookhaven National Laboratory (1960–1962). He began his teaching career as associate professor at New York University (1962–1967), after which he went as full professor to the Stevens Institute of Technology in Hoboken, New Jersey, a position he still holds.

Bernstein's other profession, that of professional writer on science, got started in 1959 when the *New Yorker* accepted a piece he had written about teaching physics at an idyllic summer school on the island of Corsica. He wrote several other articles for the magazine, and in 1962 was hired as a staff member, the first physicist to be offered such a position. He has remained there ever since, and much of the dozen-odd books he has published first appeared in the pages of the *New Yorker*. His first really important article was a profile of Tsung Dao Lee and Chen Ning Yang, who won the Nobel Prize in 1957 for their work on the so-called nonconservation of parity—the violation of symmetry between left and right in physics. "I think," Bernstein wrote in 1982 of the article, "it set a sort of milestone, at least at the *New Yorker*, for the sophistication of the science writing." Martin Gardner, in *Commentary*, described the article as "a masterpiece of science writing" when it was reprinted in *A Comprehensible World: On Modern Science and Its Origins*. After the extensive work Bernstein carried out with members of the magazine's editorial staff in order to make the article fit for publication in a popular periodical, he developed "an informal understanding" with William Shawn, then the magazine's greatly respected editor: "I would make everything as simple as I could without falsifying anything, and if not everything was understandable to every reader even then, so be it. This agreement has often entailed rewriting things many times in response to editorial questions. It is sometimes difficult for a scientist to realize just how much has to be spelled out, for we scientists tend to speak in codes. I have never resented this editorial process, though at times I have been ready to fly out the window in frustration. People have told me they find my science writing fairly accessible, and, believe me, despite appearances, this is the end product of a lot of work."

Bernstein's first book, *The Analytical Engine: Computers—Past, Present and Future*, was one of the earliest literary explorations of the subject, then not at all understood even by most well-read Americans. The author confessed in the preface to his own incomplete grasp of the subject: "There is a part that I have come to understand on my own; . . . there is a part that computer experts have explained to me; and, finally, there is a part that involves things on the frontier of research and not yet completely understood. I have tried to warn the reader when things become speculative—and often these were for me among the most fascinating things to learn and write about—by sprinkling the appropriate sections liberally with 'probably's' and 'perhaps's.'" The book, which seems very dated today when computers have found their way into millions of ordinary households, is divided into five untitled chapters: on the language of computers, then chiefly FORTRAN; on the

computing proto-pioneers Charles Babbage and the poet Byron's daughter, Ada Countess Lovelace; on the modern background to the building of computing machines; on the complex relationship between the computer and the human brain; and on Alan Turing, the brilliant British mathematician, who asked and answered many of the most profound questions about computers years before any of them were built. *The Analytical Engine* was generally very well received. "For those people," wrote Arnold Beichman in the *Christian Science Monitor*, "who look upon the computer as the menace of the century, who are affected by horrendous magazine articles written by more literate versions of Dickens' Fat Boy, Dr. Bernstein's book is recommended as a salubrious antidote."

Bernstein's next book was on the history and current practice of mountaineering, a subject not so far removed as it might appear from the concerns of a physicist. In the introduction to *Ascent: Of the Invention of Mountain Climbing and Its Practice*, he writes, "To most Americans, mountaineering is, at best, an extremely eccentric sport. Among Europeans, on the other hand, climbing is quite a popular sport. . . . It is especially popular with intellectuals." He dedicates the book to a French physicist, Georges Bonnevay, whom he met in 1960 and who was killed three years later climbing "a beautiful ice peak near Mont Blanc. . . . His death made a deep impression on me. Apart from anything else, it convinced me once again of the extreme dangers involved in climbing, even for climbers as skilled and experienced as Georges was. I decided that I myself would never climb anything really difficult without a guide." He tries to describe how the cultural change occurred, about a century and a half ago, when mountains—especially snow-covered ones—stopped being "despised, loathed, and dreaded, and their inhabitants regarded as cursed and doomed" and began to be looked at as beautiful, attractive places to be explored by intelligent people in their leisure time. Other books on mountaineering by Bernstein are *The Wildest Dreams of Kew: A Profile of Nepal*, a kind of climbing tourist's introduction to the Himalayan country, and *Mountain Passages*, which contains, among other pieces, an account of a journey by Land Rover from Paris to Pakistan.

The most difficult book for Bernstein to write was *Three Degrees Above Zero: Bell Labs in the Information Age*. He describes the problems it posed for him in the preface, noting that he was asked in July 1982 by Philip W. Anderson, one of Bell Labs' seven Nobel Prize–winning physicists, "if I had ever thought of writing anything about Bell Labs. I had to confess that I had not—

for several reasons, not the least of which is the fact that those areas of physics for which Bell Labs is most noted are just the areas of physics with which I am least acquainted." In the fall of 1982 Bernstein began to commute to Murray Hill, New Jersey, the branch of Bell Labs most directly concerned with basic research. The vastness of the place awed him—"essentially one gigantic building, housing some four thousand people, the majority of whom are engaged in research in almost every known discipline." The complex of laboratories to him resembled "a gigantic technology warren within which, at least at first sight, everything resembles everything else. Until I got used to the place, I had a menacing fantasy that, in the process of going from one laboratory to another, I would take the wrong turn and never find my way out."

Bernstein decided to concentrate on writing about the individuals he encountered daily, and those whose careers were made at Bell Labs. The book's first section, entitled "Bits," comprises profiles of people whose work is related to computers and computation. The second section, called "The Solid State," describes "the crown jewel of Bell Labs research. Four of the seven Nobel Prizes in physics awarded to Bell Labs scientists have gone to solid-state physicists—the most famous of whom are the three who were awarded the prize for the invention of the transistor." This section includes a complete account of this invention and concludes with a long profile of Philip Anderson. The next section, "Telephony," explains the business that occupies ninety percent of laboratory effort at Bell Labs: communications, or, specifically, the art and science of the telephone. The book's final section is "Three Degrees Above Zero," referring to the average temperature of the universe (three degrees above absolute zero), one of the "remarkable series of discoveries that began with, and followed on the heels of, a serendipitous observation in 1964 by two Bell radio astronomers, Arno A. Penzias and Robert W. Wilson, of the cosmic static that is caused by the bath of low-energy light quanta in which we are all immersed." The section consists of a dual profile of these scientists, who won the Nobel Prize in 1978.

As with most of Bernstein's books, reviewers received *Three Degrees Above Zero* with warmth and admiration. "Bernstein's true subject," wrote D. D. Guttenplan in the *Nation*, "is the nuts and bolts of the scientific process—not just how scientists think and talk but how they solve real-world problems. Chapters . . . are heavy going at first, but are ultimately exhilarating. . . . [He] is not a flashy writer, but his subjects talk to him as a fellow scientist, and the

reader benefits from their respect for his intelligence." Norman Sondak, in *Library Journal*, called the book "important and well written. . . . The story of Bell Labs at the crossroads is very much a metaphor for American science and engineering in this time of increasing foreign pressure and competition."

Two *New Yorker* profiles that subsequently became full-length biographical studies were *Einstein*, published as part of the "Modern Masters" series edited by Frank Kermode, which was nominated for the National Book Award in 1974, and *Hans Bethe: Prophet of Energy*. The former book is organized around the three basic themes in Einstein's work: the special theory of relativity, the general theory of relativity and gravitation, and the quantum theory. The biographical information on the century's greatest theoretical physicist is interpolated within the three basic sections. The biography of the astrophysicist Bethe, who won the Nobel Prize in 1967 for his work on stellar energy production, begins with an account of his early studies in Germany under the renowned theoretical physicist Arnold Sommerfeld, then traces his career at Cornell University, where he taught from his arrival in the United States in 1934 until his retirement in 1975. The two major aspects of Bethe's work recounted in the book are his help in developing both the atomic and hydrogen bombs and his passionate defense of nuclear reactors—especially "fast breeders"—as the solution to the global energy crisis. Other notable magazine profiles by Bernstein collected in book form are those of the Nobel Prize–winning developer of radar, Isidor I. Rabi (*Experiencing Science*), and of J. Robert Oppenheimer and the artificial intelligence expert Marvin Minsky (*Science Observed: Essays Out of My Mind*). The last-named book also contains an entertaining article, reprinted from the *American Scholar* (for which Bernstein writes a semiannual column, "Out of My Mind"), on the subject of pseudoscientific cranks and how to deal with them.

Bernstein has produced two books that might be termed science for specialists. The first was his only textbook, *Elementary Particles and Their Currents*, on the recondite, though to scientists thoroughly fashionable, subject of particle physics. It unsuccessfully ran "the risk," as he put it at the beginning of Chapter 1, "of having the material out of date before the book appears in print." The textbook was never kept up to date by issuing subsequent editions, despite its detailed treatment of "one subject of fundamental importance—currents— . . . electromagnetic currents, weak currents, and the currents conserved by the strong interactions." The other contribution to "straight science" was his edition, with Gerald Feinberg, of *Cosmological Constants: Papers in Modern Cosmology*, a collection of twenty-five papers by various physicists (none of them the book's editors), including Einstein, Edwin Hubble, George Gamow, and Andrei D. Sakharov.

In an article in 1982 in the *New York Times Book Review* on how he became a writer, Bernstein is candid about the fact that his popularizing writing "has been done at some cost to my scientific career, something I have understood and accepted. I was once discussing this with Hans Bethe. . . . He told me that the wonderful thing about physics is that it is always there: 'It won't go away.' One can always go back to it. Furthermore, I was always honest enough with myself to know I would never be a great physicist—a good one, perhaps, but not a great one. My writing has given me the perspective to deal with this realization without rancor. It has enriched my life, and I have never regretted doing it." Although Bernstein may never win the Nobel Prize, he has received several highly coveted science-writing awards, including the Westinghouse-AAAS Writing prize (1964), the American Institute of Physics-U.S. Steel Foundation Science Writing prize (1970), and the Brandeis award (1979). He is a fellow of the American Physical Society.

PRINCIPAL WORKS: The Analytical Engine, 1964; Ascent, 1965; A Comprehensible World, 1967; Elementary Particles and Their Currents, 1968; The Wildest Dreams of Kew: A Profile of Nepal, 1970; Einstein, 1973; Experiencing Science, 1978; Mountain Passages, 1978; Hans Bethe, 1980; Science Observed, 1982; Three Degrees Above Zero, 1984; Cosmological Constants, 1986; The Life It Brings, 1987.

ABOUT: American Men & Women of Science, 15th ed. 1982; Contemporary Authors 13–14, 1965.
Periodicals—Book Week June 28, 1964; Choice October 1970, February 1979, October 1982, January 1985, August–September 1987; Christian Science Monitor July 2, 1964; October 23, 1984; Commentary October 1967, December 1973; Economist September 15, 1973; Library Journal July 1964; September 1, 1964; September 15, 1964; December 15, 1965; June 1, 1967; October 15, 1967; April 15, 1970; July 1973; June 15, 1978; March 15, 1979; October 1, 1980; February 15, 1982; September 15, 1984; April 1, 1987; Nation November 17, 1984; Natural History August–September 1978; New Republic October 3, 1964; June 24, 1978; New York Times Book Review November 21, 1965; September 23, 1973; August 6, 1978; March 4, 1979; September 28, 1980; February 28, 1982; October 14, 1984; April 5, 1987; Newsweek October 20, 1980; Saturday Review January 9, 1965; Science May 1, 1973; Scientific American August 1964.

BESTER, ALFRED (December 18, 1913– September 30, 1987), American science-fiction writer, was born in New York City, the son of James J. Bester and the former Belle Silverman. "I was born a Jew," he wrote in an essay, "My Affair with Science Fiction," in 1975, "but the family had a *laissez-faire* attitude toward religion and let me pick my own faith for myself. I picked Natural Law. . . . I went to the Little Red Schoolhouse in Manhattan (now preserved as a landmark) and to a beautiful new high school on the very peak of Washington Heights. . . . I went to the University of Pennsylvania in Philadelphia where I made a fool of myself trying to become a Renaissance man. I refused to specialize and knocked myself out studying the humanities and the scientific disciplines." Bester earned his bachelor's degree in 1935, then studied law at Columbia University and zoology at New York University, taking no degree from either institution.

Bester had been an avid reader and admirer of science fiction from its earliest days; in the late 1920s he read as many as he could find of the ephemeral magazines, notably *Amazing Stories*, produced by Hugo Gernsback, suffering, he recalled, "through the years of space opera when science fiction was written by the hacks of pulp Westerns." He was intrigued and delighted by the arrival on the scene of *Astounding*, an innovative magazine (later renamed *Analog*) edited by John Campbell, which "brought about the Golden Age of science fiction." His story "The Broken Axiom" won the fifty-dollar first prize in the *Thrilling Wonder Stories* contest in 1939. He was a professional writer from then on, turning out several published stories during the 1940s, as well as working for the *Superman* group of magazines writing comic-book scripts and for network radio writing scripts for the popular shows "Nick Carter," "Charlie Chan," and "The Shadow." He also worked as script writer in the early days of television and was senior editor and a prolific contributor to *Holiday* magazine from 1956 until its closing in 1972.

Bester's exalted reputation in the genre of science fiction rests on only two novels, works of considerable stylistic originality and psychological acuity. *The Demolished Man* takes place in a world run by an elite of telepathic mind readers who have revolutionized society by putting their talents to work in such fields as business, psychiatry, and especially crime detection. The protagonist, police prefect Lincoln Powell, one of the planet's most advanced telepathics, struggles against the evil represented by the charismatic villain, Ben Reich, a murderer apparently without a motive and one of the solar system's most powerful businessmen. The novel becomes

ALFRED BESTER

a complex psychological battleground in which the main characters come to stand for antithetical world views; the (psychological) demolition of the title eventually destroys the villain. The novel was serialized during 1952 in *Galaxy* magazine, and published in book form the following year in both London and New York. It won one of the earliest awards ever given in American science fiction (later called the Hugo Award) at the World Science Fiction Convention in Philadelphia in 1953. Mark Reinsberg, reviewing the book in the *Chicago Sunday Tribune*, called it "terrifically exciting . . . just about the best [of its kind] ever written. . . . it is likely to attract readers who have never before taken science fiction seriously."

Almost as successful as *The Demolished Man*, and at least as influential, was *The Stars My Destination* (published in the United Kingdom as *Tiger! Tiger!*). It is the story of Gully Foyle, a Gulliver figure and a kind of amoral Renaissance man, a shipwrecked space traveler who finds himself early in the novel marooned on an asteroid inhabited by a race of beings who have made a religion of science. His driving passion, once he is able to return to Earth, becomes a hunger for revenge for the wrongs done him, and his immense strength of will and drive for self-awareness finally present the world with a challenge it will have to meet in order to survive. "For some time," Bester explained in "My Affair with Science Fiction," "I'd been toying with the notion of using the 'Count of Monte Cristo' pattern for a story. The reason is simple; I'd always preferred the anti hero and I'd always found

high drama in compulsive types." Discussing the novel with the science-fiction critic Charles Platt in *New Worlds Quarterly* 4, the author referred to another classic antecedent: "I've always been attracted to the Henry V protagonist—the man of direct action. . . . I'm a great believer in *people*, and their untapped potential. It's obvious we can't all be a Gully Foyle, but most of us energize at such a low level, so far short of our real capabilities, we could all be more, do more."

The novel, according to the science-fiction authority Samuel R. Delany, "is considered by many readers and writers, both in and outside of the field, to be the greatest single science-fiction novel. . . . In this book man, both intensely human and yet more than human, becomes, through greater acceptance of his humanity, something even more. It chronicles a social education, but within a society which, from our point of view, has gone mad. In the climactic scene, the protagonist . . . saves himself and attains a state of innocence and rebirth." Charles Platt agrees, terming the novel "probably the best science fiction of its kind ever written; by definition, this also means that it is the best that ever will be written, for the worth of such science fiction lies in its ideas, and the number of possible new ideas within the self-imposed strictures of the field really is limited. *The Stars My Destination* is a summation of what had been so far achieved. . . . After it, everything seems at least a little derivative."

Bester neither wrote nor read any science fiction during his employment on *Holiday*—he always, he maintained, considered himself an "amateur" in the field in any case. He returned to the genre, beginning in the mid-1970s with two novels, neither of which captured anything like the popular or critical esteem of his two great works of the 1950s. *The Computer Connection* (published in the United Kingdom as *Extro*) is an extremely complicated story involving time travel, cryonics, and computer-generated transformation; *Golem*[100] is a dark, sardonic tale about a culture of death and demonic possession, in which musical notation and unconventional typographics are frequently and confusingly used and demonstrate the author's impatience with traditional form. Such technical experimentation had long intrigued Bester; his influence in this regard can be seen in the work of, and has been acknowledged by, such writers as Robert Silverberg, Clifford Simak, and Kurt Vonnegut, Jr.

Another early novel, Bester's only one on a non–science-fiction theme, was *Who He?* (published in the United Kingdom as *The Rat Race*), a bitter satire on the television and advertising industries as they existed in New York City in the early days of television. The author's selected short science fiction appeared in two volumes, *The Light Fantastic* and *Star Light, Star Bright.* His only non-fiction published in book form was *The Life and Death of a Satellite*, a report on NASA in its glory days as a high-powered, well-funded scientific organization.

WORKS: *Fiction*—The Demolished Man, 1953; Who He?, 1953; The Stars My Destination (U.K., Tiger! Tiger!), 1956; Starburst, 1958; The Dark Side of the Earth, 1964; An Alfred Bester Omnibus, 1967; The Computer Connection (U.K., Extro), 1975; The Light Fantastic, 1976; Star Light, Star Bright, 1976; Golem[100], 1980. *Non-fiction*—The Life and Death of a Satellite, 1966.

ABOUT: Aldiss, B. W. and H. Harrison (eds.) Hell's Cartographers, 1975; Aldiss, B. W. Trillion Year Spree, 1986; Ash, B. Who's Who in Science Fiction, 1976; Clareson, T. D. (ed.) SF: The Other Side of Realism, 1971; Contemporary Authors New Revision Series 12, 1984; Davenport, B. (ed.) The Science Fiction Novel: Imagination and Social Criticism, 1959; Dictionary of Literary Biography 8, 1981; Gunn, J. (ed.) The New Encyclopedia of Science Fiction, 1988; Knight, D. In Search of Wonder, 1967; Magill, F. N. Survey of Science Fiction Literature, 1979; Moskowitz, S. Seekers of Tomorrow, 1966; New Worlds Quarterly No. 4, 1972; Scholes, R. and E. Rabkin. Science Fiction: History, Science, Vision, 1977; Spinrad, N. Modern Science Fiction, 1974; Twentieth-Century Science-Fiction Writers, 2nd ed., 1986; The Writers Directory, 1986–1988; Wendell, C. Alfred Bester, 1982. *Periodicals*—Chicago Sunday Tribune March 22, 1953; November 15, 1953; Christian Science Monitor March 3, 1967; Extrapolation May 1975; Kirkus Bulletin March 1, 1953; Library Journal December 15, 1966; New York Herald Tribune Book Review March 10, 1953; New York Times November 1, 1953; New Yorker December 5, 1953; Publishers Weekly September 6, 1952; Riverside Quarterly August 1972; Saturday Review August 29, 1953; Times Literary Supplement May 23, 1975.

*BHATTACHARYA, BHABANI (November 10, 1906–), Indian novelist, short-story writer, and essayist, was born in Bhagalpur, in the Bihar state of northeast India, to Promotho and Kiranbala Bhattacharya. His father was a judge. After completing a degree with honors at Patna University in 1927, Bhattacharya went abroad to study at the University of London, where he received another B.A. with honors in 1931 and a Ph.D. in history in 1934. He began his literary career at the remarkably early age of fourteen writing for a Bengali children's magazine and continued to write for Bengali and English-language journals during his student days in Patna and in London.

°bā tä chär´ ēä

BHABANI BHATTACHARYA

Living in London and traveling whenever he could on the continent, Bhattacharya never lost touch with his Indian roots. It had been his plan at first to study literature at the University of London, but he switched to history because it offered him a wide perspective not only on western civilization but also on contemporary Indian affairs. In classes at the London School of Economics he studied with the noted Socialist theorist Harold Laski and was for a while strongly impressed with Marxism, even to the extent of joining the Marxist League against Imperialism, which was led by his fellow-Indian Jawaharlal Nehru. In London in 1931 he met Mahatma Gandhi, on whom he was later to write two books. Bhattacharya also read widely in Western literature—Whitman, Ibsen, Shaw, Romain Rolland, Dos Passos, Sinclair Lewis, John Steinbeck. But the writer who had the greatest influence upon his work was the great Indian poet and humanitarian Rabindranath Tagore whom he had read first in his boyhood and later met in London in 1930. Tagore encouraged Bhattacharya to write in English and arranged for him to publish translations of some of his own writings in *The Golden Boat* (1930). Many years later, working on a Ford Foundation grant in 1961, Bhattacharya collected and translated Tagore's essays under the title *Towards Universal Man.*

When he completed his doctoral studies in 1934, Bhattacharya returned to India where he worked as a journalist in Calcutta. In 1935 he married Salila Mukerji, to whom he has since dedicated several of his books. They had three children, a son and two daughters. In 1937 Bhattacharya settled with his family in Nagpur, which has remained his principal home ever since. He has lived elsewhere in India and abroad, however—in Washington, D.C. from 1949 to 1950, where he was press attaché to the Indian Embassy; in Bombay from 1950 to 1952 as assistant editor of the *Illustrated Weekly of India*. With the publication of his novels in the late 1940s, some of them translated into more than twenty languages, Bhattacharya became internationally known and was invited to teach and participate in conferences all over the world. He was at the Harvard International Seminar in Cambridge in 1959 and in Tokyo in 1960; he has lectured in Australia, New Zealand, Germany, and England; and in 1971 he was in Hawaii as a fellow of the Institute of Advanced Projects of the East-West and professor at the University of Hawaii. In 1973 he lectured at the University of Washington in Seattle. Since the mid-1970s Bhattacharya has suffered from a heart ailment that has slowed but not altogether curtailed his activities.

In *Perspectives on Bhabani Bhattacharya*, B. S. Goyal wrote that Bhattacharya "belongs to the category of those Indian English novelists who, instead of dwelling in a world of metaphysical abstractions and transcendental speculations, are devoted to the exploration of the various facets of social reality." This is not to suggest, however, that he has rejected those aspects of Indian culture that constitute its rich spiritual heritage. The major influences on his life and writing have been Tagore and Gandhi—both mystics but both also strong partisans for humanitarian and social welfare causes. In an essay "Literature and Social Reality" of 1955 Bhattacharya declares himself a writer of social realism but acknowledges that social realism "cannot be cut apart, isolated, as though it were an entity by itself. It cannot be taken out of context of the general cultural pattern of a period." Folklore, mythology, fairy tales are all part of that cultural pattern and have their place in art. "Art must teach," he writes, "but unobtrusively, by its vivid interpretation of life. Art must preach, but only by virtue of its being a vehicle of truth."

Bhattacharya writes in English—winning thereby, says Dorothy Shimer in her study of him, a larger reading public in India than if he wrote in Bengali, his native language, or Hindi, or any other of the many native languages of that country. His novels are contemporary in setting, spanning the period from the outbreak of World War II, the drought and famine in Bengal in 1943, and the struggles for Indian independence through the Chinese invasion of northern India in 1962. His characters range from nation al leaders to simple country folk

conflicts that they are only beginning slowly to understand. Although the clash of East-West cultural values figures in some of his novels, Bhattacharya's main emphasis is on the internal struggles of the Indian people to adapt themselves to the profound social and spiritual challenges of their times. He chronicles in graphic and sometimes painfully realistic detail the suffering they have undergone—the poverty, corruption, ignorance and superstition in which they have been forced to live. But Bhattacharya presents an ultimately hopeful view of his country's future. He shows an indomitable people, in what K. K. Sharma describes as "a transparently positive vision of life . . . [an] unflinching faith in life and its invincibility, indestructability, and worthiness."

Bhattacharya's first published novel was *So Many Hungers!*, a compelling portrait of the ravages of the Bengali famine of 1943. World War II was raging in Europe and elsewhere in Asia, but the Indian populace was at first relatively untouched. As the threat of Japanese conquest increased, the movement for Indian independence from Britain accelerated. The combination of civil unrest in the large cities like Calcutta and the suffering of the Bengali peasants whose crops had been destroyed by drought provides the dramatic background for Bhattacharya's story of a prominent Calcutta family and a starving rural family whose destinies curiously and tragically intersect. The agent who brings these two together is a mystic, the grandfather of the young, Cambridge-educated hero Rahoul, who rejects his Western training to fight for his country's independence. His grandfather has renounced his wealth and elected to live in poverty among the peasants whose lives are ravaged by hunger and war. At the end of the novel Rahoul is arrested for his political activities but goes to prison proudly, recalling Tagore's lines: "The more they tighten the chains, / The more the chains loosen!" As Bhattacharya writes of Rahoul: "He was alone and in enemy hands. Yet he was far from alone. He was a ripple in the risen tide of millions for whom prisons enough could never be devised, nor shackles forged."

Thank to the enthusiastic reception of *So Many Hungers!* in India and abroad, Bhattacharya was encouraged to complete and publish an earlier novel, *Music for Mohini*. Described as his "most light-hearted novel," this book reveals another side of Bhattacharya—his humor and his taste for romance. Mohini is a beautiful, carefully reared young woman living with her family in Calcutta where she has already won fame for her singing of folksongs on the radio. She is high spirited but still loyal to the customs and traditions of Indian family life. As a result, she enters willingly into an arranged marriage with a young Vedic scholar and writer who lives quietly in a remote country village. How she adjusts to this totally new kind of life, to her oldfashioned mother-in-law and her loving but sometimes remote husband, provides the plot; but the main interest of the novel is the dilemma of the scholar-husband who studies the culture patterns of East and West and sees himself as "a projection of his scholarly ancestors, a continuation of their lives," even as he struggles to meet the problems of everyday life in what is rapidly becoming a modern India: "How could he pause and give himself to his private life at this great moment of history when India, proud with the freedom of which he had often dreamed, must re-orient her national life on a new social basis?" Both husband and wife are drawn with sympathy and gentle humor. It has in fact been suggested that in some degree the scholar was a projection of Bhattacharya himself at the time of his marriage, and the charming Mohini was modeled upon his own wife. *Music for Mohini* was well received by reviewers in the United States. Eunice Holsaert, in the *New York Times*, found it "a quiet, unassuming novel that has moments of true lyric charm and infectious humor." The reviewer for the *New York Herald Tribune Book Review* wrote: "The author has worked to further American understanding of Indian culture, and his novel is a welcome contribution to that end."

Probably Bhattacharya's most ambitious novel, and certainly his most colorful one, is *He Who Rides a Tiger*. Its central character is a blacksmith in a remote village—physically powerful, good-humored, a widower devoted to his lovely young daughter whom he has educated generously in spite of their low social position. War and the 1943 famine shatter their placid lives, and he is forced to seek work in Calcutta, leaving his daughter in the care of an old woman. Unable to find a job and starving, he steals some bananas and is sent to jail for three months. On his release he returns to the city which "bulged with riches, glittered with loveliness, throbbed with life and joy, but alongside it were unspeakable misery, revolting ugliness, the creeping horror of slow death." Now desperate, he becomes a procuror for a brothel to which, he discovers, his daughter has been lured by trickery. He rescues her and resolves to make money and avenge himself on society. This he does with amazing success by posing as a Brahmin holy man and winning a large, devoted following. Satirizing religious charlatans and exploiters of the poor, Bhattacharya writes a powerful indictment of materialism and opportunism. He leads his hero into a trap—"He rode a lie as if it were

a tiger which he could not dismount lest it would pounce upon him and eat him up." Ultimately he finds the courage to dismount and redeem himself, but not before Bhattacharya has had the opportunity to indict a society that tolerates so much corruption. Reviewers in the United States hailed the novel as lively and compassionate, humorous and tragic, though some objected to what Joseph Hitrec, in the *Saturday Review*, called its "pronounced moralizing." Nevertheless, Hitrec felt, Bhattacharya is "not a tendentious writer . . . he has important things to say about his country and his people and he has his heart in the right place." In the *New York Times*, Orville Prescott observed of the novel that Bhattacharya "writes of Indians and the social and cultural world in which they live with an authority and understanding that no Western writer could hope to match. . . . Its indignation is warm and generous; its material is fresh; its writing is blessed with vigor and charm."

The humor of *He Who Rides a Tiger* reflected a cynical view of the world, though much mixed with compassion and genuine indignation. In *A Goddess Named Gold* the humor is undiluted. The target is once again materialism and the superstition which persists even in modern-day India. Set in a small rural community, this is the story of how a rumor about a plain amulet that can magically turn copper into gold transforms the peaceful villagers into greedy, jealous opportunists. But because it is set in contemporary times, *A Goddess Named Gold* introduces other issues that are awakening the village from its ancient customs and traditions—especially the independence of the women who are beginning to rebel against the domination of their men.

Far more serious in intent but not without touches of humor is *A Shadow from Ladakh*—dedicated to Millen Brand, the American novelist and editor who was instrumental in publishing Bhattacharya's novels in the United States. This novel, set in 1962 when the Chinese crossed the border into India and threatened a major war, poses against each other a devout ascetic follower of Gandhi, who seeks to organize a peace march, and a vigorous young Indian engineer, trained in the United States, who is building a steel mill that will bring modern technology into this quiet and remote region of northern India. Both are idealistic in having as their goal the betterment of the Indian people, and both are sympathetic characters. Western reviewers generally found the book didactic and less appealing than his earlier novels. The characters tend to speak in set speeches rather than in natural dialogue. A romantic scene thus loses credibility when the engineer says to the heroine, who is the daughter of the Gandhi follower:

Voluntary poverty is no answer to our country's problems. True, as things stand, we have nothing to give to the people, nothing to distribute except poverty. With industrial progress we'll attain higher standards within a short span of time. We have big resources in men, materials. What we need is application, energy. We've been sitting tight over the ages. Let's start moving along!

In India, however, *A Shadow from Ladakh* was highly praised, and Bhattacharya received the Sahitya Akademi Award of India's National Academy of Letters in 1966.

Bhattacharya did not publish another novel for the next fourteen years although during that interval he published short stories and books on Gandhi and Indian history. The novel that finally appeared in 1980 was *A Dream in Hawaii*—in many ways a departure from everything he had written earlier. It is the first of his novels to be set outside of India, to introduce many Western characters, and to confront directly the clash of Eastern and Western values. Its central character is a youthful and idealist swami, leader of a cult that has gained a large following in the United States. Earlier on he had been a professor of Indian philosophy, and he is still torn between his spiritual calling and the temptations of a free secular life. Around him cluster a group of Americans who are very much the product of the sexually liberated generation of the 1960–1970s. Returning to India with some of his followers, the swami stops off in Hawaii where an enterprising American seeks to exploit him and his sect in a World Center for Yogic Disciplines, described by one character as "a Supermarket of Religion, a Department Store of Religion with Seven Counters." The novel is lively, but the characters are largely one-dimensional. Its interest lies mainly in what it reveals about Bhattacharya's own perceptions of the nature of modern society. In an essay on "The Sensuous and the Sublime in *A Dream in Hawaii*" in *Perspectives on Bhabani Bhattacharya*, B. S. Goyal writes: "Bhattacharya's handling of his theme reveals that he can take a hard and unblinking look, with an ironic incisiveness, at what may be described as spiritual charlatanism. He also presents a critique of the bourgeois value-system which believes in making a profitable business venture out of even personal human needs like sex and yoga."

PRINCIPAL WORKS: *Novels*—So Many Hungers!, 1947; Music for Mohini, 1952; He Who Rides a Tiger, 1954; A Goddess Named Gold, 1960; A Shadow from Ladakh, 1966; A Dream in Hawaii, 1980. *Short stories*—Steel Hawk and Other Stories, 1968. *Non-fiction*—Some Memorable Yesterdays, 1941 (expanded as Indian Cavalcade, 1948); Gandhi the Writer: The Image as It Grew, 1969 (in U.K. Mahatma Gandhi, 1976); Glimpses of Indian History, 1971; So-

cio-Political Currents in Bengal: A 19th Century Perspective, 1980.

ABOUT: Contemporary Authors New Revision Series 9, 1983; Chandrasekharan, K. R. Bhabani Bhattacharya, 1974; Mehta, P. P. Indo-Anglican Fiction, 1968; Sharma, K. K. Bhabani Bhattacharya: His Vision and Themes, 1979; Shimer, D. B. Bhabani Bhattacharya, 1975; Srivastava, K. K. (ed.) Perspectives on Bhabani Bhattacharya, 1982. *Periodicals*—Indian Literature 12, 1969; Library Journal September 15, 1954; New York Herald Tribune Book Review August 3, 1952; August 28, 1960; New York Times June 15, 1952; October 24, 1954; June 1, 1966; New York Times Book Review August 21, 1960; Saturday Review November 20, 1954.

BILLINGTON, RACHEL (MARY) (May 11, 1942–   ), British novelist, playwright, and children's writer, was born in Oxford. The daughter of Francis Aungier Pakenham, 7th Earl of Longford, and Elizabeth Pakenham, Countess of Longford, Billington belongs to a family of writers often referred to as "the writing Pakenhams." Her father, a former leader of the House of Lords, is the author of several books on politics, banking, and philosophy. Her mother, under the name Elizabeth Longford, has written historical biographies of Queen Victoria, the Duke of Wellington, and others. Billington's siblings include biographer Antonia Fraser, historian Thomas Pakenham, and poet Judith Kanzantzis. After graduating from Oxford University with a degree in English in 1963, Billington worked as a researcher for ABC-TV in New York City. There she met Kevin Billington, a BBC director, whom she married a year later. Although she had kept "the odd sort of teen-age diary" as a girl, Billington claims "I never took my writing very seriously until my husband did. I started my first book on my honeymoon and I wrote a book a year for the first five years we were married."

She based her first novel, *All Things Nice*, on her experience as a researcher for an ABC program on drug addiction. The novel is set in New York City, where the heroine Kate, a young upper-class Briton, dabbles in New York society and in philanthropy, trying to help a drug addict and his girlfriend. Eventually, however, she returns to her posh English environment. Billington paints a grim, drab, metropolitan backdrop against which she exposes Kate's facile lack of involvement in either New York's social scene or genuine charity. Reviewers praised the novel for displaying Billington's comedic and stylistic flair. The book's content fared less well: the *Times Literary Supplement* reviewer called it

RACHEL BILLINGTON

"squalid and unfeeling not for what it reveals about New York but for what New York reveals about its heroine: an empty, glumly swinging chick, who blames her dabbling on a world which accepts her bleakness as fashionable and English and rewards her appropriately."

The Big Dipper, Billington's second novel, also focuses on a discontented Briton. Ian, an aging television executive, has just been left by his wife. Unlike the elegiac tone of Kate's story, Ian's has a grotesque quality. At first he seems minimally affected by his wife's departure, filling his days with obsessive eating and casual sexual affairs. His behavior is symptomatic of his mental deterioration, however, which eventually leads to premature senility. As in *All Things Nice*, Billington presents her protagonist as an object of ridicule, underscoring both Ian's foolishness and the justice of his deserts. The novel received equivocal reviews that commended Billington's sense of humor and polished prose style but faulted her shaky plot and venomous characterizations. The *Times Literary Supplement* reviewer found *The Big Dipper* "more controlled and accomplished" than *All Things Nice*, but cautioned that Billington's derision of her characters diminishes her books. "Rachel Billington is quite funny and is a good observer and certainly should be able to make her wit and perceptiveness work for her more successfully," Mark Helborne wrote in *The Tablet*.

Billington again adopted an elegiac tone in *Lilacs Out of the Dead Land*. Her main character, April, an insecure, well-to-do young teacher, has an affair with an older, married publisher. In between a Sicilian weekend and London trysts, April has an identity crisis. Her introspection, which she relates in the first person, foreshadows the psychological dimension of Billington's later novels. Reviewers found the novel unconvincing but somewhat amusing. John Keates remarked in the *New Statesman* that "Lady Rachel fails to arouse our sympathy for her heroine's narrow vision of the colour supplements." In the *Times Literary Supplement* Aubrey Waugh located the problem with Billington's novel in April's tedious search for identity, otherwise finding the book fluently and vividly written, witty, and sexually evocative.

In *Cock Robin; or, A Fight for Male Survival* Billington tells the story of Robin, a diffident Oxford scholar who becomes enamored of three female undergraduates, one upper-class, one working-class, and one American. Although these highly sexed but elusive young women initially get the better of Robin, by the novel's end their fortunes have declined and he has avenged his male pride. Billington's well-styled prose and flair for social comedy impressed reviewers. Her exploration of the pathological impulses of her characters, however, prompted the *Times Literary Supplement* critic to remark that this sophisticated novelistic treatment calls for greater talent. "Anybody can write from the heart; writing from the head is a good deal harder."

Billington's *Beautiful* explores the manipulative power a woman derives from her extraordinary beauty. The heroine, Lucy Trevelyan, is an interior designer and socialite with a passive husband, adoring children, and countless lovers. Billington lays bare the secrets of Lucy's success: her self-made beauty, her great talent for small talk, her ability to order her life and those in it. It becomes clear to the reader, if not to Lucy, that this success depends on exploitation, manipulation, and most importantly, self-deception. *Beautiful* received widely varying reviews. One reviewer admired the author's finely controlled writing and the lightness of tone that overlies the dark psychological drama of the book. Others labeled the novel silly and malicious. Peter Prince, in the *New Statesman*, failed to see any beauty or charm in Lucy or any redeeming features in the novel. The *Times Literary Supplement* reviewer faulted the novel's telescopic narration and Billington's blatant lack of sympathy for her characters: "She seems to regard novel-writing as an exercise in punitive candour about people she must, after all, take responsibility for. Until she lets them speak and act for themselves she will find it hard to enlist the reader's support for her strictures."

The author delved into the darker side of egotistical passion in *A Painted Devil*. Edward Aubrey, a highly successful painter, receives total support and admiration from his family and friends and yet gives nothing in return. His ruthless behavior has tragic consequences for the people around him and finally for himself. The disparity between the novel's refined veneer and the bloody, tragic fates of its characters left reviewers cold. Anne Barnes referred to it as "a rather empty unattractive novel" in the *Times Literary Supplement*. In the *New York Times Book Review* Katha Pollitt recommended that Billington populate her elegant landscapes with characters better able to enjoy them.

Billington ventured into new territory with her next novel, *A Woman's Age*. The book's heroine, Violet Hesketh, lives from 1905 to 1975 and thus witnesses many of the social revolutions of the twentieth century. Billington, who spent five years researching and writing the novel, examines the changes time has wrought on women's roles and lives by creating and contrasting vitally different female characters. *A Woman's Age* garnered positive reviews for its ambitious theme and partial success. One critic lauded it as a "superb novel," a "far-reaching dramatization of a time and an era, all seen . . . through women's eyes." The *Listener* reviewer praised Billington for skillfully maneuvering a large and complex cast and for writing some "felicitous descriptions of people and places." Overall, however, he graded it as "a civilised, comfortable read, but no more than that." Novelist Anne Tyler, discussing *A Woman's Age* in the *New York Times Book Review*, mildly disapproved of Billington's slavish devotion to historical events, comparing the book to a stilted and overcrowded battle-scene painting.

Billington drew on her Catholic faith and on her reading of Tolstoy's *Anna Karenina* in *Occasion of Sin*. Like Tolstoy's heroine, Billington's Laura jeopardizes her comfortable family life for a lover. Laura, Catholic and generally perceived as a paragon of virtue, reminds herself that according to Church teachings, allowing oneself an "occasion of sin" is a sin itself. Nevertheless, Laura can't resist the temptation and falls from grace. Moreover, she ultimately falls from the certainties of either life with her husband or passion with her lover. The book generated disparate responses from reviewers. One called it a well-crafted narrative, somewhat overburdened with "emotional minutiae," that wanders into "weary melodrama." In the *New York Times Book Review*, Abigail McCarthy praised the work as "a memorable novel" in terms of Billington's "uncanny ability to pin down the moment-to-moment shifts of feeling of

a woman in love." *Times Literary Supplement* reviewer Lindsay Duguid was far more critical of the novel and its premise: "The introduction of serious themes—the religious dimension—and the way the narrative keeps breaking into the present tense to convey intensity show that the book is meant to be taken seriously, but like the many echoes of *Anna Karenina*, only serve to emphasize its emptiness."

The Garish Day, Billington's eighth novel, revolves around Henry and his father Lionel, both career diplomats. Billington follows Henry from his birth in India in 1940 through his Oxford days in the early 1960s, a failed marriage, an unfulfilling career, and suicidal episodes around the world. Henry's problems arise when he tries to retrace his father's ambassadorial tracks but finds that the world has radically changed since his father's day and now poses new, seemingly unsurmountable difficulties. Although he seeks meaning through his vaguely Catholic religion throughout the book, Henry doesn't achieve any sort of release from his psycho-religious trauma until the end of the novel. Clancy Sigal, in the *New York Times Book Review*, called *The Garish Day* a "funny, playful novel about deeply serious matters." Other reviewers, however, discovered faults in the novel's psychological groundwork. "I would like to see Rachel Billington's next novel concentrating less on the setting and shifting of the scenes and more upon—horrible term—character motivation," Miranda Seymour noted in the *Times Literary Supplement*. Giles Gunn, writing in the *Los Angeles Times Book Review*, suggested that the novel failed because Henry's search for salvation achieves only "cheap grace," rather than the real thing. Geoffrey Trease, *British Book News* reviewer, found Billington "less [than] successful in the persuasive elucidation of an internal conflict demanding our sympathetic entry into the thought process of a tormented individual."

Billington has said that her interest "in the secret life of ordinary people" has provided the raw material for her novels. She exposes the secret lives of several such people in *Loving Attitudes*. Mary Tempest, a married forty-year-old BBC executive, rediscovers her feelings for her former lover when the pair's illegitimate daughter, Elizabeth, shows up unexpectedly. The resulting emotional havoc reverberates in the lives of the lovers and their spouses, and extends to the Tempests' daughter, her boyfriend, the neighbors, and Elizabeth herself. The novel impressed reviewers as "novelettish" but generally well-written. Lindsay Duguid of the *Times Literary Supplement* found Billington's prose "informal and intimate" and the style of the material suited to its subject. Another reviewer ro marked that "although its style often seems breezy, *Loving Attitudes* does something startlingly sophisticated and surprisingly seductive: it calls all the assumptions of conventional morality into question." In the *Listener* Wendy Brandmark reproved it as a "novel that never jelled," its writing "pallid and banal," its plot forced and mechanical.

In addition to her novels, Billington has written three children's books and several radio plays. She reviews regularly for the *Financial Times* and also contributes to the London *Times* and the *New York Times*. She and her husband Kevin, a film and theater director, have four children, Nathaniel, Catherine Rose, Chloe, and Caspar. They live in London and spend weekends in Dorset at their fourteenth-century country home.

PRINCIPAL WORKS: All Things Nice, 1969; The Big Dipper, 1970; Lilacs out of the Dead Land, 1971; Cock Robin, 1972; A Painted Devil, 1975; A Woman's Age, 1979; Occasion of Sin, 1982; The Garish Day, 1985; Loving Attitudes, 1988.

ABOUT: Contemporary Authors 33–36, 1978; Contemporary Literary Criticism 43, 1987; Contemporary Novelists, 4th ed., 1986. *Periodicals*—Best Sellers June 1983; British Book News November 1985; Listener November 29, 1979; March 3, 1988; Los Angeles Times Book Review June 29, 1986; New Statesman May 21, 1971; May 3, 1974; New York Times Book Review December 28, 1975; February 10, 1980; May 1, 1983; June 15, 1986; Newsweek February 25, 1980; People March 24, 1980; Publishers Weekly December 31, 1979; Tablet July 11, 1970; Times Literary Supplement May 29, 1969; May 28, 1970; June 26, 1971; April 20, 1973; May 31, 1974; September 19, 1975; October 29, 1982; September 6, 1985; January 29, 1988.

BIRMINGHAM, STEPHEN (May 28, 1932?–), American novelist, biographer, and chronicler of wealthy American society, was born in Hartford, Connecticut, the only son of Thomas J. Birmingham, a lawyer and sometime assistant district attorney in the Connecticut capital, and the former Editha Gardner. He and his sister were brought up in the small farming community of Andover, a few miles east of Hartford, and Stephen attended Hotchkiss, a fashionable preparatory school in Lakeville, Connecticut. He went from there to Williams College, where he majored in English, was elected to Phi Beta Kappa, and graduated *cum laude* in 1953. After a period of study at an institution called the Graduates' School for Extra-Mural Study in Oxford, England, he returned to America and went to work in New York City, where his first job, which he held only briefly, was writ-

STEPHEN BIRMINGHAM

ing advertising copy for Gimbel's department store. After two years of service with the U.S. Army Signal Corps (1953–1955), he returned to the New York advertising world, where he wrote copy for the Needham, Harper & Steers agency for the next dozen years, finally leaving the business in 1967.

Birmingham's first novel, *Young Mr. Keefe*, was read and approved in manuscript by the "society" novelist John P. Marquand, who was given it to read by Carol Brandt, the wife of their mutual agent, Carl Brandt. The older and younger novelist met and became friends, frequently discussing in the few years before Marquand's death in 1960 their shared interest in the peculiarities of East-coast moneyed society. Marquand not only gave Birmingham a great deal of advice on how to improve the first novel and suggested the title, he actually arranged for its publication by Little, Brown, his own publisher, and even produced a a blurb for the jacket ("one of the best first novels I have read in years"), a thing he almost never did and, Birmingham later confessed, "disapproved of authors' doing." *Young Mr. Keefe* is the story of the marital and emotional difficulties faced by two young couples, who, although they live in California, are products of wealthy New England society. The novel was widely reviewed and generally faintly praised for its characterizations: it was "altogether too obviously a very young man's novel," according to Walter Allen in the *New Statesman*; the author "has captured the flavor of the region nicely," wrote Leland Windreich in *Library Journal*, "and . . . knows how to hold one's attention, [which] makes up for whatever immaturities are evident in the style."

The title character of Birmingham's second novel, *Barbara Greer*, also comes from a wealthy New England family. The novel tells the soap-operatic story of her dissatisfaction with her marriage, her planned affair with her brother-in-law, and the growing self-awareness, after his accidental death, that makes her marriage seem more meaningful. John Coleman in the *Spectator* called the book "an upper exurbanite gavotte"; V. S. Naipaul, in the *New Statesman*, thought it "exceedingly verbose. . . . [Birmingham's] purpose is partly to expose; but like so many American writers, he takes his characters at their own valuation. So that if one does not share the writer's awe at the swimming pool, the ritual of the cocktail hour, . . . and if one sees the characters as dreary and unenviable, exposure becomes pointless."

Birmingham's other fiction explored very much the same social and emotional territory and received the same captious, rather dismissive critical receptions. *The Towers of Love* was judged by one critic fit only for publication in slick women's magazines. *Those Harper Women* was called by R. D. Spector in *Book Week* "trite, . . . stereotyped, . . . contrived, . . . designed for some purpose other than literature." The characters in *Fast Start, Fast Finish* "remain wooden, middle class and pedestrian," in the opinion of Charles Dollen in *Best Sellers*. The fourteen stories in *Heart Troubles* were termed "drearily familiar" by C. A. Hough in *Library Journal.* They "have an air of being formula-written for the mass readership of women's magazines where most of them first appeared." After a hiatus of fifteen years, Birmingham returned to fiction writing in 1983 with *The Auerbach Will* and, three years later, *The LeBaron Secret*, which sold well but were not widely reviewed.

Birmingham's reputation as a writer has come mainly from his nonfiction, especially that very extensive series of breezily written, anecdotal sketches of various cross-sections of America's elite, the very rich. They are not serious sociology or ethnology, nor were they meant to be; scholarly reviewers and others have consistently derided the books as gossipy and suffused with trivia, but the author has simply justified himself as an "entertainer." Most of these popular ethnographs have sold very well. His most notable and original contribution to this minor genre—which he has virtually made his own—are his three books on Jewish immigrants to America: *Our Crowd: The Great Jewish Families of New*

York, about the Ashkenazim, the German-Jewish bankers and merchant princes; *The Grandees: America's Sephardic Elite*, which treats the old, reticent, private Sephardic families who constitute "the nobility of Jewry, with the longest, richest, most romantic history"; and *The Rest of Us: The Rise of America's Eastern European Jews*, which tells the story of the Russian-Polish immigrants of the late nineteenth century, who "are now, barely a hundred years later, people of prominence and influence in every major American city, and in nearly every walk of life. . . . Theirs has been a success story in what the sociologists call assimilation."

The Right People: A Portrait of the American Social Establishment is a book which some critics dismissed as "bloodless" and "vulgar." It is filled with photographs of so-called establishment figures; its constituent chapters were for the most part originally published in the now-defunct *Holiday* magazine and were worked at over and over at the insistence of its editor, Harry Sions, who, the author says at the end of the preface to the book (which is dedicated to Sions), "taught me two things. He taught me how to write nonfiction. And he taught me that the American upper-class surroundings and training (including The Right School) and institutions (including the 'junior dances') which I had grown up with . . . were both interesting and exceptionally worth writing about."

At the beginning of *Real Lace: America's Irish Rich*, Birmingham allows himself a minor autobiographical note: "I grew up in a small New England city where Irish Catholics, or those of 'Irish extraction,' were not asked to join the country club, and so—being of that extraction myself [though Episcopalian]—I have long been aware of the strong, and at the same time vulnerable, position of the Irish in American life." He proceeds to chronicle in exhaustive detail the growing fortunes and the many marriages—especially those to rich Protestants—of a group of people who actually called themselves the "First Irish Families of America" (or "FIF's"). *Real Lace* annoyed several critics by its rigid stress on money and (some form of) social standing. The book was not, in the opinion of J. R. Moran in *Library Journal*, a "serious study. [It] is anecdotal and poorly organized organized. . . . The result is like an extended society column from the Hearst press, with the same biases and emphasis on marital problems."

Birmingham was even more sharply criticized for *Certain People: America's Black Elite*, in which, with no change in tone or approach from his earlier works, he recounts anecdote after anecdote about America's wealthy blacks, their habits, schools, clubs, accents, charities, and obsession about skin tones. Some critics thought the book insensitive, even racist. Roger Wilkins, in the *New York Times Book Review*, wrote: "Painfully ignorant of the complexities of his project, Birmingham galloped past them, flinging behind him snippets of elementary psychology, flawed sociology, half-baked history and, to spice it all up, bits and pieces of plain mean gossip." Le Anne Schreiber in *Time* called the author "insensitive to the tragic involutions of identity that make the black elite very different from—and much more vulnerable than—its white counterpart. . . . By substituting gossip for insight, Birmingham has produced a book that lacks not only a thesis but also a heart."

Birmingham has continued regularly to produce books of gossip about the wealthy. *California Rich* recounts the histories of the founding families of America's most populous state, the country's El Dorado, a place to live "a life of riches and pleasures, without work and without care, . . . a land of perpetual youth and sunshine." *The Grandes Dames* treats "that special and increasingly rare breed of [American] women who flourished between the Mauve Decade of the nineteenth century and the Second World War as high priestesses of upper-case Society, Culture, Philanthropy and Civic Duty." *America's Secret Aristocracy* is something of a reprise of much of the material found in Birmingham's earlier books. It concerns the "First Peers of the Realm," as he calls them, the rich men who founded the United States and then governed it for generations, the "Brahmins, Knights of the Chivalry, and California Grandees" who came after them, and their "Heirs Apparent."

Of Birmingham's three biographies, *The Late John Marquand*, on his friend and mentor, is widely considered to be his best—even the best of his numerous books. It is an admiring exploration of the literary career and tangled private life of the acerbic novelist, which, although uniformly sympathetic in its treatment and conclusions, was written without the cooperation of Marquand's five children and without access to much of his correspondence and personal papers, which were housed at Harvard. Victor Howes in the *Christian Science Monitor* called Birmingham "the ideal chronicler of Marquand's life-in-fiction. . . . Read [him] for the same pleasures you find in Marquand, for a Marquandian tale the master raconteur left unwritten." The other Birmingham biographies, *Jacqueline Bouvier Kennedy Onassis* and *Duchess: The Story of Wallis Warfield Windsor*, are considerably less generous in their treatment of their subjects: Mrs. Onassis is seen as insecure,

snobbish, and obsessed with possessions; the Duchess of Windsor as insecure, snobbish, and obsessed with having been badly treated by her in-laws.

Birmingham also wrote two books which, although in part about the rich, are in their subjects unlike the popular works described above. *The Golden Dream: Suburbia in the Seventies* is a brief study of the historical and cultural aspects of the phenomenal American flight to the suburbs, which "began before the turn of the century, encouraged at first by the coach and ferry, then spurred by the development of the railroad and the automobile. By 1925, suburbanization had become [a] national trend. But it was not until the economically booming days of the 1960s that the trend became a roaring phenomenon. . . . The escapees to the suburbs have found many of the things they were looking for . . . they have also discovered that curious anomie, that sense of disorientation, that indefinable 'feeling of separation,' which living in suburbia so often seems to convey." *Life at The Dakota: New York's Most Unusual Address* traces the history of the glamorous apartment building and its rich and famous (and poor and unknown) residents from the time, in 1880, when a new millionaire named Edward Clark "was building, of all things, a luxury apartment house at a location that wasn't even an address— Seventy-second Street and Eighth Avenue—so far out of the swim of city life that it seemed like the North Pole—or like Dakota." The book consists mainly of thumbnail sketches of various people who have lived in the building. It is, wrote Hillary Johnson in the *Christian Science Monitor*, "both a laboriously researched history and present-day account of Manhattan's oldest, most famous and celebrity-laden apartment building. . . . Birmingham's method is to be comprehensive and, more often than not, he turns up information that does fascinate. He has fashioned the Dakota's story into a microcosm of New York social history."

Birmingham has lived in Cincinnati since the early 1970s. He continues to think, he told an interviewer in *Publishers Weekly* in 1984, that "rich people are more interesting than poor people."

PRINCIPAL WORKS: *Fiction*—Young Mr. Keefe, 1958; Barbara Greer, 1959; The Towers of Love, 1961; Those Harper Women, 1964; Fast Start, Fast Finish, 1966; Heart Troubles, 1968; The Auerbach Will, 1983; The LeBaron Secret, 1986. *Non-fiction*—Our Crowd, 1967; The Right People, 1968; The Grandees, 1971; The Late John Marquand, 1972; The Right Places, 1973; Real Lace, 1973; Certain People, 1977; The Golden Dream, 1978; Jacqueline Bouvier Kennedy Onassis, 1978; Life at the Dakota, 1979; California Rich, 1980; Duchess, 1981; The Grandes Dames, 1982; The Rest of Us, 1984; America's Secret Aristocracy, 1987.

ABOUT: Contemporary Authors New Revision Series 20, 1987; Current Biography 1974; Who's Who in America, 1988–1989. *Periodicals*—Atlantic August 1964, January 1968, July 1968, April 1971, July 1971, November 1973; Best Sellers June 15, 1964; May 15, 1966; October 15, 1967; June 1, 1968; September 15, 1968; June 15, 1972; March 15, 1973; January 1, 1974; September 1977; September 1978; December 1979; Booklist March 1, 1958; September 15, 1959; Book Week July 5, 1964; July 16, 1967; Catholic World May 1958; Choice January 1968, July 1971, November 1972, November 1977; Christian Science Monitor July 8, 1967; May 21, 1968; April 29, 1971; May 21, 1972; July 13, 1972; December 19, 1973; September 14, 1977; August 2, 1978; September 12, 1979; Commentary January 1968; Commonweal February 28, 1958; November 17, 1967; October 25, 1968; September 27, 1974; Economist May 18, 1968; Library Journal January 15, 1958; July 1959; October 1, 1961; June 15, 1964; May 1, 1966; July 1967; June 15, 1968; December 1, 1968; February 1, 1971; July 1972; February 1, 1973; November 1, 1973; June 1, 1978; September 1, 1979; October 15, 1980; June 1, 1981; June 1 1982; July 1984; September 15, 1987; Nation May 10, 1958; May 5, 1979; National Observer October 7, 1968; National Review July 13, 1971; June 17, 1972; April 13, 1973; March 15, 1974; September 16, 1977; New Republic June 17, 1972; June 11, 1977; New Statesman July 26, 1958; January 9, 1960; New York May 13, 1968; New York Herald Tribune February 23, 1958; August 4, 1959; August 9, 1959; New York Post December 18, 1973; New York Review of Books August 4, 1977; New York Times March 2, 1958; August 2, 1959; New York Times Book Review June 21, 1964; May 22, 1966; July 2, 1967; June 9, 1968; September 1, 1968; April 18, 1971; August 20, 1972; November 18, 1973; May 15, 1977; September 16, 1979; January 4, 1981; July 26, 1981; October 14, 1984; September 27, 1987; New Yorker August 8, 1959; Newsweek June 19, 1967; April 22, 1968; June 19, 1972; Publishers Weekly August 19, 1984; Saturday Review March 1, 1958; August 8, 1959; January 13, 1968; November 2, 1968; March 20, 1971; June 17, 1972; June 11, 1977; Spectator August 1, 1958; January 8, 1960; Time February 24, 1958; August 3, 1959; June 21, 1968; May 16, 1977; August 27, 1979; Times Literary Supplement August 22, 1958; January 8, 1960; April 6, 1967; May 30, 1968; August 14, 1969.

BOK, SISSELA (ANN) (December 2, 1934–   ), American philosopher, was born in Stockholm, one of three children of Gunnar and Alva Reimer Myrdal. Bok's family background is distinguished. Her parents were Nobel Prize winners (Gunnar Myrdal in Economics, Alva Myrdal in Peace), and her husband is Derek Bok, president of Harvard since 1971. They met in Geneva when she was a student at the Sorbonne and he a Harvard Law graduate in Paris on a

SISSELA BOK

Fulbright scholarship. Nine months later, in 1955, they were married. Bok continued her education in the United States, receiving her B.A. and M.A. degrees in psychology from George Washington University in 1957 and 1958. (She became a naturalized citizen in 1959.) Throughout much of the sixties she worked on a Ph.D. in philosophy at Harvard, all the while raising three children, Hilary, Victoria, and Tomas. Although she has admitted to being "very tired towards the end" and wondering "how it would all work out," she received her doctorate in 1970 and began lecturing at Simmons College the following year. Since then she has taught at Harvard and the Massachusetts Institute of Technology and is currently professor of philosophy at Brandeis University.

Bok's specialty is moral philosophy, and her major contributions to this field are *Lying: Moral Choice in Public and Private Life* and *Secrets: On the Ethics of Concealment and Revelation.* In undertaking a systematic study of lying for the first book, Bok was surprised at the relative paucity of modern commentary— troubling evidence in itself of the degree to which lying is taken for granted in our world. And she quotes alarming statistics in her introduction about the lack of trust Americans in recent years have expressed in their leaders and institutions. It is with some urgency, then, that she frames questions such as the following: "Should physicians lie to dying patients so as to delay the fear and anxiety which the truth might bring them? Should professors exaggerate the excellence of their students on recommendations in order to give them a better chance in a tight job market? Should parents conceal from children the fact that they were adopted?"

Bok's answers to most of these questions is a qualified no. Rejecting the absolutist prohibitions against lying of Kant and Augustine, she nevertheless argues that "truthful statements are preferable to lies in the absence of special considerations." This is so because "trust in some degree of veracity functions as a *foundation* of relations among human beings; when this trust shatters or wears away, institutions collapse." Thus, an initial negative weight attaches to all lies, and this negative weight can be counterbalanced only in cases where a lie is able to prevent a harm greater than the telling of the lie itself. As Bok shows again and again, such cases do not occur as frequently as most of us would like to believe.

A memorable illustration is given in the chapter on "Lies for the Public Good." In the 1964 election campaign President Johnson portrayed himself as the candidate of peace and his opponent, Barry Goldwater, as a dangerous warmonger certain to escalate the war in Vietnam. Unbeknown to the public, however, Johnson and his advisers were already considering a massive escalation of the war, which in fact took place early in 1965. Believing that they alone knew what was best for the country, Johnson and his advisers, by their deception, "denied the electorate," as Bok writes, "any chance to give or refuse consent to the escalation of the war in Vietnam. Believing they had voted for the candidate of peace, American citizens were, within months, deeply embroiled in one of the cruelest wars in their history."

Bok makes similar points about the insidious danger of lying to enemies, to peers and clients, to the sick and dying, and to subjects in social science experiments. Her method is to take examples of lying that have been or can be defended, and by showing the damage done to public trust, to the integrity of the liar, and to the self-respect of the deceived, reveals such defences as, in the majority of cases, self-serving and, in the end, self-defeating. In the weight of such evidence her conclusion seems unassailable: "Trust and integrity are precious resources, easily squandered, hard to regain. They can thrive only on a foundation of respect for veracity."

Lying was well received by most critics and earned Bok the George Orwell Award from the National Council of Teachers of English. "It is pleasant," wrote J. M. Cameron in the *New York Review of Books*, "to find a work of such analytical power devoted to a set of severely practical problems and to find it so well written . . . It

is also refreshing, and uncommon, to find a contemporary philosopher who is prepared to consider as possibly usable the resources of the entire philosophical tradition."

A few critics, finding in Bok's reasoning a fatal lack of realism, rejected the fundamental premises of *Lying*. "For the sake of our sanity and essential shrewdness," wrote David Bazelon in the *Times Literary Supplement*, "we must resist many moral impulses . . . , especially those leading immediately to richly fulfilling fantasies in which we master vast tracts of human difficulty—like lying, or sleeping late in the morning." And he implied that in Bok's methodology "no real analysis is taking place, since the conclusion is foregone."

Bok begins her second book by noting the close connection between lying and secrecy. Yet they differ, she maintains, "in one important respect. Whereas I take lying to be *prima facie* wrong, with a negative presumption against it from the outset, secrecy need not be. Whereas every lie stands in need of justification, all secrets do not. [Secrecy] may accompany the most innocent as well as the most lethal acts; it is needed for human survival, yet it enhances every form of abuse." The question raised by secrecy, then, are inherently more complex and ambiguous than those raised by lying, and *Secrets*, in the view of some critics, went deeper into its subject than did *Lying*.

Throughout the book, Bok distinguishes between secrets in the public and private realms. In general she views a certain amount of secrecy as indispensable to the individual's sense of self. Some control over secrecy, she writes, "may be needed to guard solitude, privacy, intimacy, and friendship. It protects vulnerable beliefs or feelings, inwardness, and the sense of being set apart: of having or belonging to regions not fully penetrable to scrutiny." She is much less disposed to accept the need for secrecy in public affairs. Her objection to secrets of this type, like her objections to lying, is two-fold: such secrets are impractical *and* unethical—impractical because it is naive to believe that in an open society government and business officials can ever achieve the level of secrecy that they deem optimal, and unethical because of the corrupting influence powerful secrets can have on character and moral judgment. She quotes approvingly C. P. Snow's warning about the "euphoria of secrecy" in public life: "It takes a very strong head to keep secrets for years and not go slightly mad. It isn't wise to be advised by anyone slightly mad."

Representative of Bok's even-handed approach to secrecy is her chapter on gossip (there are others on confessions, military secrecy, secrets of state, and investigative journalism). Once again rejecting unyielding proscriptions (notably those of Kierkegaard and Heidegger, who abhorred all gossip as an idle and false knowledge), she distinguishes between gossip that provides information and acts as a social bond and that which is unduly invasive, knowingly false, or a breach of confidence. An example of such reprehensible gossip was the FBI's effort to destroy the career of the actress Jean Seberg, a well-known supporter of black nationalist causes, by planting stories in the press about her alleged sexual relationship with a member of the Black Panther Party. Such uses of gossip, Bok notes, are not rare, and yet their obvious malice is balanced by the attention gossip can bring to human complexity. In any case, the extraordinary variety of gossip cannot be ignored, and the view of it as necessarily "trivializing human lives is itself belittling if applied indiscriminately."

Richard Sennett was one of several critics who considered *Secrets* a significant advance upon *Lying*. The earlier book, he wrote in the *New York Times Book Review*, "was a brisk, efficient analysis. As the rationales for lying were toppled one after the other, certain nagging but important problems were pushed to the side, like the relationship between a lie and a fiction. There are no such evasions in *Secrets*; the problems raised are examined from many sides. Indeed, the book is almost maddeningly fairminded." Of special importance, Sennett believed, was "the author's acknowledgement that legal definitions of proper and improper secrecy will always miss the psychological and, indeed, theological rationales for secrecy."

A minority of critics thought that *Secrets* contributed little to the study of applied ethics. "Mrs. Bok is thoughtful, but she is rarely bold," wrote Paul Robinson in the *New Republic*. "There is a wearisome predictability about her judgments. She is on the right side of every issue: she opposes forced confessions, she has not a single good word to say for brainwashing, and she thinks secret societies that discriminate on ethnic or religious grounds are a bad thing. Such soporific probity makes one yearn for the moral audacities of an Oscar Wilde or a Friedrich Nietzsche, or even a Marquis de Sade."

Some of the same ethical considerations that shaped Bok's studies of secrecy and of lying are applied to the subject of world peace in two lectures she gave at Harvard in 1985 and subsequently expanded into her book *A Strategy for Peace*. The exercise of what Daniel Schorr sums up, in the *New York Times Book Review*, as "moral restraint against deceit, betrayal, exces-

sive secrecy—and violence" is the only strategy for world peace, she argues. Such a strategy would begin by rejecting all forms of pressure from terrorism, assassination, and the restoration of trust and confidence in a nation's domestic as well as its foreign affairs. Published almost four years after these lectures were originally delivered, in an era of *glasnost* and a less belligerent climate, Bok's *A Strategy for Peace* struck Schorr, along with other readers, as less visionary than it might have appeared in 1985. Schorr wrote: "It is refreshing, if not customary, to see the issue of international conflict addressed in unashamedly moral terms. Who is to say whether 'moral constraints' represent a more naive approach to the threat of war than pragmatic hostility? In any event, it appears that since Mrs. Bok formulated her 'strategy,' some of her hopes for easing distrust have begun to be realized."

Sissela Bok had contributed articles to a variety of scholarly publications on such topics as the administering of placebos, the ethics of abortion, the prospects for world peace, and the philosophy of Sartre, Mill, Montaigne, and Kant. She is co-editor (with John A. Behnke) of *The Dilemmas of Euthanasia* and (with Daniel Callahan) of *Ethics Teaching in Higher Education*. Since 1974 she has been a fellow of the Hastings Institute and during the Carter administration she served on the Ethics Advisory Board of the Department of Health, Education, and Welfare. Her only full-length non-philosophical work is a memoir of her mother, *Alva: Ett Kvinnolov*, published in Stockholm in 1987.

PRINCIPAL WORKS: Lying: Moral Choice in Public and Private Life, 1978; Secrets: On the Ethics of Concealment and Revelation, 1982; A Strategy for Peace: Human Values and the Threat of War, 1989. *As editor*—(with John A. Behnke) The Dilemmas of Euthanasia, 1975; (with Daniel Callahan) Ethics Teaching in Higher Education, 1980.

ABOUT: Contemporary Authors 112, 1985; Who's Who in America, 1988–1989. *Periodicals*—New Republic February 21, 1983; New York Review of Books June 1, 1978; New York Times March 6, 1983; December 19, 1987; New York Times Book Review February 20, 1983; March 19, 1989; Times Literary Supplement August 11, 1978.

*BOMBAL, MARIA LUISA (June 8, 1910– May 6, 1980), Chilean novelist, short-story writer, and essayist, was born in Viña del Mar, Chile, one of three daughters of Martin Bombal Videla and Blanca D'Anthes Precht. She was educated by a governess at home and at a Catholic school run by French nuns. After her father's death, the

*bom bal´

MARIA LUISA BOMBAL

family moved in 1922 to Paris where she continued her education at the Lycée la Bruyère, and took a degree in philosophy and literature at the Sorbonne. Her early years in France had a significant influence on her artistic and intellectual development. From 1924 to 1931 she attended lectures given by Paul Valéry, studied violin with Jacques Thibaut, performed at L'Atelier, the famous acting school directed by Charles Dullin, and joined Fortunat Strowsky's literary workshop, where she won her first prize as an author with a short story written in French.

By 1931 she was back in Santiago de Chile befriended by writers who later became famous: Rosamel del Valle, Marta Brunet, and Pablo Neruda. She fell hopelessly in love with an aviator, Eulogio Sánchez, and, after an unsuccessful suicide attempt, she shot but did not kill him. The notoriety forced her to leave Santiago and move to Buenos Aires, Argentina, where Neruda was now Chilean consul. She lived in Neruda's house writing her first novel, *La última niebla* (The Final Mist, published in English as *The House of Mist*), while at the same time Neruda was writing his masterpiece *Residencia en la tierra* (1946, translated as *Residence on Earth*). As Amado Alonso has pointed out, *The House of Mist* was almost as significant a landmark in Latin American prose as Neruda's book was in Latin American poetry. Published during a period in which the predominant literary trend was *criollismo*—a realistic and naturalistic depiction of Latin American prototypes and their environment—*The House of Mist* was an avant-garde vision of reality through the use of new lit-

erary techniques—subjective, impressionistic, deliberately ambiguous. The book was quickly recognized as an outstanding example of the emerging avant-garde in Latin American writing, as well as a precursor of the Latin American novel of the 1960s. In a moving testimony to her innovations Carlos Fuentes once stated that "Maria Luisa Bombal is the mother of us all."

The protagonist of *The House of Mist* is a married woman who seeks fulfilling love. Reality is important only in terms of her agony and hidden wishes; the rain and the cold on her wedding night, for example, symbolize her husband's indifference to love. Time is measured in the context of the feminine experience of approaching old age—the source of an ever-increasing anxiety that the opportunity for love is inexorably receding. Her encounter with a man who makes love to her in a mysterious house is tinged with ambiguity arising from the convergence of common domestic details as well as from her lover's supernatural qualities: his silence, the halo of light surrounding his body, his uncanny appearance. The absence of a transition between the love scene and the moment the protagonist finds herself in bed beside her husband leaves the reader in doubt as to whether the lover really existed or was part of a dream. This doubt is never resolved: the reader enters a three-dimensional world whose landscape is simultaneously concrete, dreamlike and supernatural. At the same time, however, *The House of Mist* makes a powerful statement about the social predicament of Latin American women in a world dominated by masculine values. This basic conflict is illustrated by an unresolved conflict between the protagonist's intimate desires and the social conventions which prevent her from attaining love. Social values have forced her into marriage with a man she does not love in order to escape the stigma of spinsterhood in a society that makes marriage woman's only goal in life. Burdened by spiritual dissatisfaction and erotic frustration, she is forced into an anguished search for love.

With the publication of her first novel, Bombal found herself very much at home in Buenos Aires, in close touch with Jorge Luis Borges, Norah Lange, Oliverio Girondo, and García Lorca (who was touring in Argentina and Uruguay at that time). She was especially close to Victoria Ocampo, the editor of the vanguard magazine *Sur* which in 1939 published her novel *La amortajada* (*The Shrouded Woman*) and her short stories "Las islas nuevas" ("The New Islands"), and "El arbol" ("The Tree") in 1939 and "Las trenzas" "(The Tresses") and "Mar, cielo y tierra" ("Sea, Heaven, and Earth") in 1940. In *The Shrouded Woman* Bombal explores another mysterious facet of reality: the unknown and supernatural realm of Death. Her preoccupation with the mysterious is evident in a statement she made shortly after the publication of this novel: "I think people have willingly ignored that we live on the surface of the unknown. We have organized a logical system on a well of mystery. We have chosen to ignore what is primordial to Life: Death."

The novel begins with a static event easily recognized as part of empirical reality: Ana Maria lies dead and is surrounded by those who once had relationships with her. This static event irradiates supernatural dimensions. Although she is dead, Ana Maria can still hear and see those who are mourning her. She recapitulates her past life while at the same time undergoing an archetypal journey to Death. The ambivalence between past and present, the factual and the marvellous, the visible and the invisible, is elaborated in the novel through the techniques of counterpoint, perspective, and montage. As in *The House of Mist*, love in *The Shrouded Woman* is conceived as the only gratification for women, a concept Simone de Beauvoir defined in *The Second Sex* in terms of the subordinate relation of women (the Other) to men (the Absolute). Therefore, the protagonist, a prototype of Latin American women in the 1930s, has no active participation in history, and her restrictive role of wife and mother compels her to search for love. Her relations with three men reveal three crucial stages in her life: sexual initiation, the passive acceptance of society's conventions symbolized by marriage, and erotic sublimation in unconsummated adultery. Significantly, these three stages mark the progressive degradation of those instinctive and primordial elements in feminine character. Ana Maria represents a tragic view of women and their place in society. As though literally shrouded, the protagonist ends up alienated, forced into passive acceptance of the status quo. Ironically, the solution to this dilemma lies not in changing her historical role but in accepting the supernatural realm of death. Only when dead is she able to unveil the intrinsic nature of those she knew in life. Moreover, death allows her to penetrate the secrets of nature: the intensity of night, the sounds of rain, the beauty of tree bark.

In her short stories and essays, as in her novels, Bombal formulated a conservative feminist ideology which was dominant among Latin American upper classes during the 1930s and 1940s. Feminine and masculine are conceived as static and generic qualities not subject to change by the influence of social and historical factors. Where the essence of masculinity is rationality, activity, and power, the roots of feminity are intuition, passiveness, and love. Although Bombal

was conscious of the predicament of women in Latin American society, she did not postulate a concrete solution which would modify the historical situation. On the contrary, she viewed women as alienated from politics, as human beings imprisoned in their restricted roles; by presenting her women characters as totally dependent on love, their relationship with men, she reinforced the traditional role of women.

In her later work, however, there is a significant change. Instead of centering the conflict on the opposition between marriage and feminine aspirations, Bombal expanded her Latin American social context to a more universal level, exploring the archetypal feminine through the use of more traditional literary genres such as fairy tale and legend. She presented the characteristic female archetype of matriarchal societies but made an important modification to the ancestral myth by presenting these positive qualities as essential attributes of women which have been annulled by the triumph of reason, science, and technology in the modern world. This concept is evident in the short, poetic story entitled "Sea, Heaven, and Earth." Here women emerge as possessors of the ancestral mysteries of water and earth—two realms inhabited by supernatural beings described in highly poetic language. Heaven, on the other hand, is the domain of masculine consciousness, a fragment of the universe which is subject to mathematical calculation and scientific theories. Her emphasis on the dehumanizing effects of science and technology was accentuated by her experiences in the United States, where she lived from 1940 to 1973. Her poetic essay "Washington, City of Squirrels" is highly revealing, emphasizing the thematic conflict between masculine rationality (culture) and feminine intuition (nature). She describes Washington as a place governed by "the Big World's Machine"—a feverish monster which demands to be fed by constant labor, bureaucratic files, and political affairs. In this microcosmos enslaved to the clock no one has time to look at the sky, "to watch a beautiful dawn, or think of love—natural laws which are always postponed." As a way to reaffirm fantasy and imagination in a pragmatic society, Bombal focuses her description on the squirrels—wild little animals who are ignored by everybody in the busy city. In the wide parks of Washington, these mysterious animals live in close contact with the earth and are a testimony of innocence and natural life.

With the exception of "La maja y el ruisenor"—a memoir of her childhood published in 1960, Bombal stopped publishing in 1946, although she wrote two plays, *El Canciller* (The Foreign Minister) and "Dolly and Jeckill and

Miss Hyde," as yet unpublished. A full-length novel on which she worked for many years was never finished, possibly because of her problems with alcoholism. Small as her output was, Bombal's voice is unique in Latin American letters. She was a pioneer, a daring innovator who took chances exploring the possibilities of language, the complex potential of structure, the multiplicity of narrative modes.

Bombal was married twice—first, in 1934, to the Argentinian painter Jorge Larco who died some years later. From her second marriage in 1944, in New York City, to the French Count Raphaël de Saint-Phalle, she had a daughter, Brigitte. She spent her last years in Santiago de Chile in near poverty. Ironically her country now offers a $10,000 literary prize named in her honor.

WORKS IN ENGLISH TRANSLATION: *La última niebla* was published in Buenos Aires in 1935. In 1947 Bombal published her English version of this novel as *The House of Mist*. An English version of *La amortajada*, on which she had worked in 1940 with Angel and Kate Flores, was published in 1948 as *The Shrouded Woman*. A collection of her short fiction, *The New Islands and Other Stories*, was translated by Richard and Lucia Cunningham in 1982.

ABOUT: Adams, M. I. Three Authors of Alienation: Bombal, Onetti, Carpentier, 1975; *In Spanish*—Alonso, A. *Introduction to* La última niebla, 1941; Goíc, C. La novela chilena, 1968; Guerra-Cunningham, L. La narrativa de Maria Luisa Bombal, 1980. *Periodicals*—Christian Science Monitor October 25, 1983; Hispania 44, September 1961; Nation December 11, 1982; New York Times Book Review December 19, 1982; Saturday Review of Literature May 3, 1947; World Literature Today Summer 1983. *In Spanish*—Atenea 1942; Sur 47, August 1938.

BOYD, WILLIAM (March 7, 1952–   ), British novelist, short-story writer, and playwright, was born in Accra, in Ghana, Africa, son of Alexander Murray and Evelyn (Smith) Boyd. His early years were spent in Ghana and Nigeria, where his father was a physician and specialist in tropical medicine and his mother was a teacher. At the age of nine, he was sent to the Gordonstoun School in Morayshire, Scotland (both of his parents were born in Scotland), returning to Africa only on vacations. Boyd received a diploma in French studies at the University of Nice in 1971, and an M.A. (with honors) from the University of Glasgow in 1975. In the same year he married Susan Anne Wilson, who today is publicity director with a British publishing company. He pursued postgraduate study at Jesus College, Oxford University, 1975–1980; and

WILLIAM BOYD

was Lecturer in English at St. Hilda's College, Oxford, 1975–1980, after which he became a full-time writer. In addition to contributing stories to magazines, he was television critic for the *New Statesman*, 1981–1983, and fiction reviewer for the *London Sunday Times*, 1982–1983.

In 1982, Boyd published his first novel, *A Good Man in Africa*, which won both the Whitbread Literary Award for best first novel and the Somerset Maugham Award. The novel deals with a British junior diplomat in a West African outpost, Morgan Leafy, who is prone to endless blundering and humiliation. This comic work was favorably compared with the writings of Evelyn Waugh and Tom Sharpe, and particularly with Kingsley Amis' novel *Lucky Jim*. Alan Hollinghurst in the *New Statesman* remarked that "Overwriting is the only thing that occasionally spoils *A Good Man in Africa* . . . which is in every other respect highly controlled; Boyd is clearly a comic writer with a very successful career ahead of him." Frances Taliaferro in *Harper's* stressed particularly the resemblance between Morgan Leafy and Amis' Jim Dixon, commenting that "*Lucky Jim* and *A Good Man in Africa* represent a minor and undignified art form . . . they are too funny to be ennobling." To Robert Towers in the *New York Review of Books*, however, the indebtedness to Amis' novel was one of the novel's limitations. "The book," Towers wrote, "seems to me . . . heavily imitative in tone and farcical incident, of the early novels of Kingsley Amis. . . . Boyd makes his anti-hero, Morgan Leafy, too abjectly contemptible to win even the sneaking sympathy we regularly accord to rogues; one derives little exhilaration from his mischief-making and small satisfaction from his repeated humiliations."

An Ice-Cream War, which received the John Llewelyn Memorial Prize and a Booker Prize nomination, was inspired by a reference in a book he was reading to the World War I campaign in East Africa. Boyd spent a year researching the campaign, perusing archival material including unpublished diaries, and discovering incident after incident that confirmed his conviction that wars are "chaotic and absurd." Concerned chiefly with two brothers, Gabriel and Felix Cobb, *An Ice-Cream War* makes use of interweaving narratives that contribute to the sense of the war's disjunction and folly. "The only real problem," Michiko Kakutani observed in the *New York Times*, "is that Mr. Boyd's narrative fluency lets him get away with a handful of characters, who seem like two-dimensional exiles from an old English comic novel. . . . Felix, however, is one of those characters who insidiously grows in the reader's mind as he, himself, matures. . . . By the end of this fine novel, death is no longer merely comic, but terrible and senseless and suddenly very personal as well." Almost all the reviewers agreed that *An Ice-Cream War* marked an advance over his first novel, James Wolcott in *Harper's* remarking that it was "psychologically thicker than *A Good Man in Africa* ; its depiction of colonial misrule "bolder and more acute." Harriett Gilbert in the *New Statesman* summed up the novel by calling it an extremely skillful re-creation of the war in Africa, striking a "fine balance of satire, black comedy, and horror."

On the Yankee Station, a collection of fifteen of Boyd's short stories published in the United States in 1984, was an expanded version of the collection of the same title published three years earlier in England. The volume includes tales set in Africa, as well as others in Southern California, France, England, and Vietnam. "The impression they convey," Paul Abelman observed in the *Spectator*, "is of an aspiring author exploring his talent by setting it a variety of literary challenges. So far, so good, and there is no doubt that Mr. Boyd, not yet thirty, is set fair for a dazzling career. And yet there is something about these stories that disturbs me. They are imbued with a fashionable sense of disenchantment. The author appears to be blasé before he has lived long enough to be genuinely disillusioned."

On the Yankee Station was quickly followed by Boyd's third novel *Stars and Bars*, a comic work about a young Englishman who comes to America hoping to free himself from the constriction bred in him by Britain. What follows are a series of misadventures taking him to the Deep South, depicted as a world of preposterous incoherence. Reviews of the novel were mixed. Jonathan Yardley in the *Washington Post Book World* commented that Boyd "has firmly established himself as a writer of impressive, original achievement. . . . he is heir to an established tradition of English comic fiction . . . yet he regards his characters with an affection that is too rare in such fiction. There's hardly a writer around whose work offers more pleasure and satisfaction." Like many reviewers, Martha Duffy in *Time* liked the early section set in New York, but felt that once Boyd ventured into the South "the story tends to unravel, and the picaresque incidents verge on cartoons. . . . Because he's English and revels in satire, Boyd has often been compared to Evelyn Waugh. The comparison does not really work; he has neither Waugh's masterly style nor his fine-floating malice." *Stars and Bars* was made into a film in 1988, with Boyd writing the screenplay.

The two short plays that make up *School Ties*, about the comic-horrible rites of passage in an English boarding school, were written for British television and were considered slight. But Boyd's fourth novel, *The New Confessions*, was widely regarded as his best work to date. While a prisoner of war during World War I, the protagonist, John James Todd, reads Rousseau's *Confessions* and subsequently adapts the book as a silent screen epic. This is completed, however, at the very moment when talking pictures appear, so Todd's masterwork is consigned to oblivion. His subsequent experiences, in part as a writer of Hollywood westerns and then as a victim of the House Un-American Activities Committee, testify to a life of misdirection and failure. Writing in the *Times Literary Supplement*, Antony Beever remarked that *The New Confessions* "is Boyd's most ambitious and most successful novel. . . . The writing is often brilliant in his impressively economic vignettes . . . and the narrative as a whole possesses a compelling rhythm." Michiko Kakutani in the *New York Times* was impressed by the scope of the work, and by Boyd's ability "to combine the comic with the tragic fluently . . . we are meant to see John James Todd's life—with all its discontinuities and calamities—as a kind of metaphor for the 20th century and its nervous discontents. . . . his closely observed descriptions of people and places lend even the most improbable incidents the weight and density of real life."

In an interview in the *New York Times* in 1983, Boyd discussed his work habits. "I try to put in a good eight hours a day," he said. "Often I write in libraries. I don't have to be inspired

I don't need total silence. I don't worry about writer's block, which I think is a self-fulfilling prophecy. . . . I do enjoy writing. I know some writers enjoy the invention but find the writing an endless night of the soul. I don't. I think, if you can earn your living writing fiction, it's very agreeable."

PRINCIPAL WORKS: *Novels*—A Good Man in Africa, 1982; An Ice-Cream War, 1983; Stars and Bars, 1985; The New Confessions, 1987; Brazzaville Beach, 1990. *Collect short stories*—On the Yankee Station, 1984. *Plays*—School Ties: "Good and Bad at Games" and "Dutch Girls," 1986.

ABOUT: Contemporary Authors 120, 1987; Contemporary Literary Criticism 28, 1984; Contemporary Novelists, 4th ed., 1986. *Periodicals*—Harper's June 1982, March 1983; New Statesman January 30, 1981; New York Review of Books June 2, 1983; New York Times April 5, 1983; May 21, 1983; April 27, 1988; Spectator August 8, 1981; Time May 20, 1985; Times Literary Supplement September 25, 1987; September 14, 1990; Washington Post Book World August 17, 1986.

T. CORAGHESSAN BOYLE

BOYLE, T. *CORAGHESSAN (1948–), American novelist and short-story writer, was born in Peekskill, New York, where he attended local public schools. His early years, according to an account he has given, were aimless and rebellious. Later he attended college, indifferently, and then taught English in a "tough" high school in Peekskill. When he became excited by literature, however, he entered the graduate program at the University of Iowa, where he earned his doctorate in nineteenth-century English literature and was drawn to writing short stories.

Boyle's first book, *The Descent of Man*, a collection of seventeen of his tales, was published to enthusiastic reviews. David Emblidge called *Descent of Man* an "impressive collection" in which "beautiful words in artful combinations make even the hideous, obscure, and terrifying a mysteriously beautiful experience for the imagination." Many of the stories, he pointed out, have the quality of "absurdist black humor, with . . . echoes of Kafka, Pynchon, Sartre, and Ionesco" that make Boyle "a writer to savor and to watch." Steven Crist compared Boyle's tales with those of Roald Dahl and Donald Barthelme. "At his best," he observed, "he effectively combines the wonderfully perverse twists of Dahl's plots with Barthelme's disjointed use of language." While conceding that "too often, he merely ends up being unpleasantly odd," he concluded that Boyle "is a legitimate, major talent who can be forgiven his excess for the clear promise of better things to come."

The Descent of Man was quickly followed by Boyle's first novel, *Water Music*, a send-up of the picaresque novel. The work employs two protagonists, Mungo Park, based on the actual Scottish explorer who charted the Niger River in Africa in the decade between 1795 and 1805; and Ned Rise, a London rogue and con man, a purely fictional creation. Their paths cross in a series of wild and preposterous adventures captured in a style that crosses over from the elegantly archaic to the colloquial and modern. "Boyle is delightfully shameless," Jay Tolson commented, "in his exploitation of melodramatic devices—cliff-hangers . . . coincidences . . . and miraculous resurrections. He pulls his most implausible inventions with wit, a perfect sense of timing, and his considerable linguistic gifts. He treasures the apt word, the earthy Anglo-Saxonism or the precise Latinate term, and his ear for cockney, brogue, pidgin English and other dialects is sure. If this is the historical novel and the Victorian novel transformed into comic book fiction, it is High Comic Book Fiction, in the manner of John Barth's *The Sot-Weed Factor*."

Many reviewers compared Boyle's novel to the "new fiction" of John Barth, Robert Coover, Thomas Pynchon, and William Gass. Ken Tucker commented on the work particularly in relation to the picaresque/experimental novel. "Written in a slangy high style," he observed, "Boyle parodies every one he's read—and he's read everyone. Like Pynchon, he includes song lyrics and reams of useless information. . . . Like Barth, Boyle is always eager to stop pro-

*cô rä´ ge sen

ceedings to reprint letters and diary entries, or to discourse on some fine point of historical etiquette." But other critics were less enthusiastic. Alan Friedman remarked that the "intention of such writing is, I think, not precisely humor; its intention is to limn the characters of another century with the most colorless expressions of our own in order to make them recognizable, to make them look and feel like ourselves. But that's not the effect. Cobbled together out of such banalities, Mungo Park and his wife Ailie, Ned Rise and Ned's true love Fanny exist neither here nor there. . . . Throughout the novel Mr. Boyle seems to want to establish an equality and fraternity with the past both for himself and for the reader. But unfortunately the effort too often serves as an extended occasion for comic-strip pathos."

Boyle's second novel, *Budding Prospects*, deals with a young man named Felix who teaches freshman English at a community college in San Francisco and is inveigled by his friend Vogelsang into a scheme to harvest a profitable crop of marijuana. The comic incidents on the remote mountain farm—ranging from fire, flood, bears, suspicious neighbors, blackmail, and threats of a police raid—culminate in Vogelsang's enrichment but Felix's exasperation and disillusionment, so that he finally adopts a conventional, hard-working, and more purposeful life. Reviews of the novel were mixed. Richard Eder called it a "shrewd and funny novel" in which Boyle "handles the day-to-day misadventures, the befuddled relationship of the three city hicks with each other and with the wilderness they are turned loose upon, with superb control and timing." Michael Gorra, however, felt that Boyle tended to settle "for one liners like small fireworks, rather than working toward a more sustained comic structure. Mr. Boyle's raw ability to make one laugh reminds me of Kingsley Amis and the early Evelyn Waugh as well as Thomas Berger. If he can match that verbal agility with a mastery of their larger and more self-conscious comic structures, he could become an important contemporary novelist."

Greasy Lake & Other Stories, Boyle's next book, received a number of remarkably favorable reviews. Dennis Drabelle, for example, wrote that Boyle "is one of the most gifted writers of his generation (he is still in his thirties), and in *Greasy Lake & Other Stories* he has moved beyond a prodigy's audacity to something that packs even more of a wallop: mature artistry." And Charles Champlin observed that Boyle "owns a ferocious, delicious imagination, often darkly satirical and always inflated with language in the best Irish way. . . . These stories have a sort of undergraduate exuberance,

though it is carried off with a postgraduate control that suggests the harder feelings detectable beneath the surface of the stories."

Greasy Lake was greeted by Larry McCaffrey as "a brilliant new collection." "Mr. Boyle's literary sensibility," he went on, "like that of Robert Coover and Stanley Elkin, thrives on excess, profusion, pushing past the limits of good taste to comic extremes. He is a master of rendering grotesque details of rot, decay and sleaze. . . . Despite some unevenness in execution, the stories in *Greasy Lake* display a vibrant sensibility fully engaged with American society." But reservations were also expressed. The reviewer for the *New York Times* admired Boyle's sense of the absurd, and called him a "master of overstatement and hyperbole," but felt that he frequently substituted "cleverness for felt emotion, one liners for sustained comedic effects—he seems more comfortable making jokes or dazzling the reader with his verbal pyrotechnics than working through the consequences of his characters' actions and beliefs."

Boyle's next work, *World's End*, a vast 400-page novel that spans four centuries, was considered the most ambitious work he had yet undertaken and won the Pen/Faulkner award for fiction in 1988. Set in the Hudson River Valley, it moves back and forth in time from contemporary events occurring in the life of Walter Van Brunt to much earlier but analogous occurrences in the experience of his Dutch ancestors. The early Van Brunts, indentured to the big landlord Van Wart, are introduced in a tale of intermarriage and betrayal that also involves a tribe of Kitchawank Indians who live on the same land. *World's End* was hailed by Benjamin DeMott as a "smashing good book, the peak achievement thus far in a career that seems now to have no clear limits." In this work, it seemed to DeMott, Boyle had "powerfully challenged his own disengagement—the constraints of automatic knowingness and habitual irony. And this movement of mind creates space for moral and emotional as well as esthetic reality, producing a narrative in which passion, need and belief breathe with striking force and freedom."

Michiko Kakutani, however, although acknowledging that *World's End* gave Boyle more room than ever before "to work all sorts of magical variations on literature and history," felt that the result was disappointing. Many of the points Boyle makes, she wrote, "that white men stole the Indians' land, that the upper classes have always distrusted the left—are simplistic and poorly delineated. Worse, there's something mechanical and cumbersome about Mr. Boyle's orchestration of time past and present: his subsidiary characters (in both the 17th and 20th centuries) proliferate in such profusion that we never really get a chance to know them as recognizable individuals, and even Walter's tale begins to sound increasingly contrived. Instead of feeling that he's living out some inexorable family destiny, we end up suspecting that he is just another pawn in the author's elaborate chess game."

Boyle's penchant for bizarre situations and literary pyrotechnics gets a full showcase in his short-story collection *If the River Was Whiskey.* Here once again the *New York Times'* Michiko Kakutani was ambivalent, acknowledging Boyle as "this gifted and highly versatile young writer" capable of producing some powerful and persuasive fiction. But most of these stories—though she concedes that they are ingenious, daring, and often witty—disappointed her: "his disparate talents are used, singly, for showy but shallow effects." More enthusiastic was Elizabeth Benedict, in the *New York Times Book Review,* who singled out the final, title story, a poignant account of a young boy's relationship with his alcoholic father, for special praise: "Humor and exaggeration have served Mr. Boyle well. He is a consummate entertainer, a verbal showman, an explosively gifted satirist. If he uses humor to provide 'quick cover' for his 'alarm and bewilderment,' and for other more powerful feelings, it's refreshing now and then—it's almost a relief—when he ditches his cover, as he does in the last story, and allows us a peek at his heart."

Boyle is a tenured professor in the English department at the University of Southern California in Los Angeles, and lives with his wife Karen in a large ranch house in nearby Woodland Hills. He spends every morning into the early afternoon at his typewriter. He teaches classes twice a week, hikes, chops wood, and whenever possible goes drinking with his friends. Paul Ciotti, in a feature article on Boyle in the *Los Angeles Times Magazine,* describes him as intense, witty, and self-assured. His first two novels have already been optioned by Hollywood studios, but he has shown no inclination to write screenplays himself. As Ciotti writes: "Although Boyle could write screenplays if he wanted to, he says he's not interested in playing distant third fiddle to directors and actors. 'I don't like the loss of control. I don't like to collaborate. I'm very egotistical. I want to be the guy who's profiled on the front cover.'"

PRINCIPAL WORKS: *Novels*—The Descent of Man, 1979; Water Music, 1981; Budding Prospects: A Pastoral, 1984; World's End, 1987; East Is East, 1990. *Collected short stories*—Greasy Lake and Other Stories, 1985; If the River Was Whiskey, 1989.

ABOUT: Contemporary Authors 120, 1987; Contemporary Literary Criticism 36, 1986; Dictionary of Literary Biography 1986. *Periodicals*—Carolina Quarterly Fall, 1979; Christian Science Monitor June 29, 1979; Los Angeles Times Book Review May 6, 1984; June 30, 1985; Los Angeles Times Magazine August 3, 1986; New York Times September 23, 1987; May 2, 1989; September 7, 1990; New York Times Book Review December 27, 1981; July 1, 1984; June 9, 1985; September 27, 1987; May 14, 1989; September 9, 1990; Times Literary Supplement August 26, 1988; Washington Post Book World February 7, 1982.

BRIGGS, ASA (Lord Briggs) (May 7, 1921-   ), British historian, writes: "I was born in the North of England in an industrial town on the edge of the moors. No one in my family had been to University: no one talked much of history. Nonetheless, experience of my early years strongly influenced the kind of history that I began to write after the end of the Second World War—social and political history with a strong economic thrust and with an explicit human concern for the implications of technological change. In the meantime I had studied history at Cambridge and, in parallel, economics at the University of London, and I had worked as a young soldier in the team deciphering Ultra at Bletchley.

"My first academic appointment was at Worcester College, Oxford, where I became a Fellow in 1944 before I had left the Army. I was to be there until 1955 and after a long interval I have been back there for ten years as Provost of the College. It is a College with a strong sense of place which I love. Yet the organised study of history at Oxford has had far less influence on the development of my own kind of history or my ways of writing it than my own experiences outside Oxford. Cambridge, however, made me interested in historiography, and Leeds, where I was Professor of History from 1953 to 1961, was on the edge of the industrial region that I had known as a boy. I wrote my *Age of Improvement* there and in the United States: it was published in 1959 and I regard it as my most important work of synthesis.

"America, particularly Chicago and the people who were then teaching at Chicago University, had a big impact on me. I visited it for the first time in 1953, one year after I had published a history of Birmingham, an industrial city in the Midlands which I had not known as a boy. My *History of Birmingham* I thought of as 'total history.' I set out to look at the whole life of the city and to explain how and why it changed. In a sense this was local history—and I have retained my interest in local history—but it was broadly

ASA BRIGGS

interpreted. Chicago drew me more deeply into 'urban studies,' comparative and 'general,' as it had drawn many people before me, and from history into sociology. I have never believed, however, that the only way to study history is through the social sciences. I have always attached much importance to the relationship between the study of literature (and more recently the study of art, aesthetics and music) and the study of history. Clio I believe to be a Muse, and increasingly I have come to think of myself as a cultural as much as a social historian. Among historians who have influenced me are some outside the British or the American tradition: I attended the eightieth birthday celebrations of Gilberto Freyre, the Brazilian historian, and have written a paper on him. The British historian who has most influenced me has been G. M. Young.

"I have never restricted myself to one field. I believe everything is grist to the historian's mill and that he should seek to communicate with a broad audience and not just with other professional historians. I have interested myself particularly, however, in Victorian history, have written *Victorian People* and *Victorian Cities* and am now writing a book called 'Victorian Things.' I have also worked hard in the field of communications history, examining not only British but world-wide experience of broadcasting. I have written more than a million words in five volumes—on the history of the British Broadcasting Corporation. I have tried as far as possible to write in this field as much for future as for present readers, trying above all to get the

record straight. My interest have gone back in time, too, to earlier changes in communications.

"My *Social History of England*, which has sold more copies than any other book of mine, I see as a major venture in communications. We all carry round versions of our national history, true or false. I hope that my own version will endure."

In the preface to his two-volume *Collected Essays* published in 1985, Asa Briggs reviewed his career and concluded that the motto for his life's work might be the comment by the French historian Georges Duby that human attitudes toward their times are determined "not so much by actual economic conditions as by the image in the minds of the individual groups." Describing himself as a "cultural as much as a social historian," Briggs has explored in his many books and essays what another historian, F. M. Martin, has called "the mental maps of the social scene." The journey has taken him through fields far beyond the traditional annals of history into urban sociology, science, art, literature, communications, indeed the entire realm of human experience. The ideal social historian, he wrote in the preface to his *Social History of England*, "is an explorer who does not stay in his study; he will use his eyes and his feet as much as his brain. We learn through things as well as through ideas, and through reminiscences as well as through documents—or statistics." The result of such an approach has been not only an impressive bibliography of scholarly works but books that have also enjoyed a wide popular readership.

Asa Briggs was born in Keighley, Yorkshire, to a working class family, the son of William Walker and Jane (Spencer) Briggs. "I was brought up in the North of England in a district where moorland and industry met. The Brontës were not strangers, they were almost neighbours. And I always learnt as much from landscape and townscape as from books." After receiving his Bachelor of Arts degree from Sidney Sussex College, Cambridge, in 1941 (and in the same year a Bachelor of Science from the University of London), he joined the intelligence service of the British Army as a cryptographer, serving from 1942 to 1945. Since then his entire career has been in higher education, mainly at Worcester College, Oxford, where from 1945 to 1955 he was a fellow and university reader in recent social and economic history. He returned to Oxford in 1976 as provost of Worcester College after six years (1955–1961) as professor of modern history at the University of Leeds and four years (1961–1965) at the University of Sussex where he was a founder and the first dean of the School of Social Studies as well as vice-chancellor. Briggs was also a member of the Institute for Advanced Studies at Princeton University from 1953 to 1954, a visiting professor at the Australian National University in 1960 and at the University of Chicago in 1966 and in 1972. An ardent advocate of continuing education for older and non-traditional students, he has been chancellor of the Open University since 1978.

Briggs began his career as an urban historian in the late 1940s with a thoroughly documented history of the industrial city of Birmingham that concentrated on the decades from the 1840s through the 1870s. While studying Birmingham history, he wrote in his later book *Victorian Cities*, he realized that one city's uniqueness could be appreciated only when it was compared with other cities not only in England but in every country where cities were going through comparable development. He found parallels, for example, between Manchester of the 1840s and Chicago of the 1890s—both "shock" cities, rapidly growing centers of social and ethnic problems. By the close of the Victorian era, he wrote, "It was in the United States, indeed, that the real new cities of the world were located." But cities are a human phenomenon toward which the humans who build and live in them feel an ambivalence of love and hate that is reflected in their culture, their art and imaginative literature as well as in their politics. "I am as much drawn to the study of language and literature as to the social sciences . . . I am writing for readers outside my own country as well as for fellow-Englishmen, and I have tried to take nothing for granted."

Briggs cites as the major influences on his career the English historian G. M. Young whose masterful *Victorian England: Portrait of an Age* was published in 1934, and the Brazilian Gilberto Freyre whose *The Masters and the Slaves* appeared in 1933 (translated into English in 1946). Both Young and Freyre were cultural historians, assimilating anthropology, psychology, sociology, and literature with the disciplines of strict historical research. For them, as for Briggs, historical time is not simply chronology but a social dynamic—a view sometimes described as left-wing but never Marxist, doctrinaire, radical. Such an approach imposes challenges not only of research but of writing, of assimilating and presenting material in a lucid, readable style. Here, the reviewers of Briggs's books would agree, Briggs has been eminently successful. Richard D. Altick found his *Victorian People* "a warm and vivid book, as readable as it is well informed." R. K. Webb praised his *A Social History of England*, a generously illustrated book

that covers his subject from prehistory to the present, as "an array of delights in little things . . . a remarkable summary of a generation of scholarship." Of Briggs's *The Age of Improvement*, which covers English history from 1783 to 1867, the *Times Literary Supplement* reviewer wrote: "Indigestible as Professor Briggs's material is—and, in a sense, should be—he fits it with considerable skill into his running commentary which, if not always inspiring, is uniformly apt and often, especially at the beginning and end of his book, rises to passages of real contemplative power and historical insight."

With the publication of *Victorian Things* in 1989 Briggs completed the trilogy on which, as David Cannadine wrote in the *New York Review of Books*, "Briggs's reputation rests as the foremost interpreter of the Victorian age since G. M. Young himself." The earlier *Victorian People* had brought the age to life with profiles of notable personalities like Thomas Hughes and Benjamin Disraeli. *Victorian Cities* focused on the emergence of industrial urban centers in the nineteenth century. In *Victorian Things* Briggs turns to the products, the artifacts of the age that measure its material achievement from such seemingly humble objects as needles, steel pens, and matchboxes to machine technology, photography, and the internal combustion engine. Once again he places these phenomena in their broad historical and cultural contexts.

Although most of Briggs' studies have been in nineteenth-century history, he has also written a massive five-volume study of the British Broadcasting Company, *A History of Broadcasting in the United Kingdom*. Drawing on the archives of the BBC, Briggs organized his complex and detailed material in what one reviewer called "a flowing, narrative style . . . entertaining, factual, historical, and stimulating," and another hailed as "a task that will put the sociologist as well as the future historian permanently in his debt."

In 1976 Asa Briggs was created a Life Peer with the title Baron. Peter Scott, who interviewed him for the (London) *Times Higher Education Supplement* in 1986, described him as genial, relaxed, "an activist, a doer, a public man . . . a happy exception" to the supposed rule that high achievers are often tense and maladjusted: "As a Keighley boy from a lower middle class home who today sits in the House of Lords he should display all the proper socio-psychological symptoms of personal displacement. But he displays none of them. The various parts of his life have flowed together; they are not held in tension by a determination to be rec-

ognized and to succeed." He has received many
academic honors, among them doctorates from
the universities of Leeds, Liverpool, York (Canada), Cincinnati. He has been married since 1955
to Susan Anne Banwell; they have four children.

PRINCIPAL WORKS: History of Birmingham, 1952; Victorian People, 1954, 1973; Friends of the People, 1956;
The Age of Improvement, 1783–1867, 1959 (in U.S.
The Making of Modern England, 1965); Chartist
Studies, 1959; Victorian Cities, 1963; William Cobbett,
1967; Iron Bridge to Crystal Palace: Impact and Images of the Industrial Revolution, 1979; The Power of
Steam: An Illustrated History, 1982; A Social History
of England, 1983; Karl Marx, the Legacy, 1983; Toyn-
bee Hall, 1984; Collected Essays (2-vols.), 1985; A History of Broadcasting in the United Kingdom (5 vols.),
1961–1985; Victorian Things, 1989. As editor—The
Nineteenth Century: The Contradictions of Progress,
1970; (with J. Saville) Essays in Labour History, 1886–
1923, 1971; (with Susan Briggs) Cap and Bell: Punch's
Chronicle of English History in the Making, 1841–61,
1972.

ABOUT: Contemporary Authors New Revision Series 7,
1982; Who's Who 1990. Periodicals—New York Re-
view of Books February 15, 1990; (London) Times
Higher Education Supplement November 18, 1977;
July 4, 1986; (London) Times Literary Supplement
September 13, 1986.

BRINGHURST, ROBERT (October 16,
1946–), Canadian poet, was born in Los Angeles, the son of George Heber Bringhurst and
Marion Jeanette Large Bringhurst. In an essay,
"Breathing through the Feet: An Autobiographical Meditation," which first appeared in
Canadian Literature (1985) and then, revised,
was published in book form in his collection of
poetry and prose *Pieces of Map, Pieces of Music*,
he described his origins: "I was born in the post-
Depression diaspora at the close of the Second
World War, the only child of itinerant parents—
ambitious father, obedient mother—and raised
in the mountains of western North America,
moving often and liking it well. I remember especially the Absaroka Ranges in Montana, the
Valley of the Little Bighorn and the Wind River
Mountains and the Southern Absarokas in Wyoming, the Maligne Mountains and the Goat
Range in Alberta, and the Virgin River country—my Mormon great-grandfather's mountains—in southern Utah. In later years, I've felt
myself at home in a thousand named and nameless places in that long spine of mountains,
steppe and desert which I've walked, in bits and
pieces, most of the way from the Yukon to Peru.
Much as I've loved the few cities I've lived in—
Boston, Beirut, London, Vancouver. I've never

ROBERT BRINGHURST

been at ease for long in urban spaces. Premoni-
tions of doom come over me readily in the large,
self-confident capitals of eastern North America,
where so many decisions that touch the world I
prefer to live in are now made."

Bringhurst received a varied university education: he attended the Massachusetts Institute
of Technology in 1963–1964 and 1970–1971, the
University of Utah in 1964–1965, and Indiana
University in 1971–1973, from which he finally
received a bachelor's degree in comparative literature. He also received a master's degree in
fine arts from the University of British Columbia
in 1975. In 1966–1969 he served with the United
States Army in California, Israel, and the Panama Canal Zone. In Israel he functioned as, in his
words, a "dragoman," or Arabic interpreter. He
has always enjoyed a great facility for languages,
a fact constantly reflected in his poems: he seems
at home with classical Greek, with modern European languages, and even, more lately in his
career, with Native American tongues. "I was
thirty years old before I began the serious study
of the languages and cultures native to the hemisphere I called home. . . . I'm still very glad of
my little Greek and less Chinese—but the ten
years I spent learning Arabic would, I now
know, have been far better spent learning Hopi
and Navajo." He served as editor of the Arabic
and Greek issues of *Contemporary Literature in
Translation* (no. 19, 1974 and no. 23, 1976).

Bringhurst has nearly two dozen poetry publications to his credit, mostly short pamphlets,
chapbooks, and broadsides produced by small
presses. Occasionally, as with the early *Cadastre*

and *Bergschrund*, his books have been somewhat longer, subsuming much previous work. His first comprehensive collection was *The Beauty of the Weapons: Selected Poems 1972–82*, published as part of the Modern Canadian Poets series. "Most of the poems," he writes in a prefatory note, "are products more of oral composition than of writing, and have survived into this selection only with repeated performance as a test. Some of them have changed a good deal in the process. It seems to me they exist in the voice, to which the page, though we enshrine it, is in the right order of things a subservient medium. On this view, a man's selected poems ought to mean not his washed and dressed historical record but his living repertory: not a catalogue of the animals he has named but a festival of those who are still speaking. A book, like a performance or recording, no matter how illustrious the audience or how formal the occasion, is only one more draft."

This collection contains some of the author's earliest published works, including the hundred-line poem "Deuteronomy," from the grouping of the same name that appeared in 1974. The poem is an interior monologue spoken by Moses, not a reverential but nevertheless a deeply moving self-portrait of a powerful man, a kind of proto-poet and magician, helpless in the hands of his all-demanding Voice.

> The bush. Yes. It burned like they said it did,
> lit up like an oak in October—except
> that there is no October in Egypt. Voices
> came at me and told me to take off my shoes
> and I did that. That desert is full of men's shoes.
> And the flame screamed *I am what I am.*
> *I am whatever it is that is me,*
> *and nothing can but something needs to be*
> *done about it. If anyone*
> *asks, all you can say is, I sent me. . . .*
>
> Once I used to sing them
> a song about an eagle and a stone, and each time
> I sang it, somehow the song seemed changed
> and the words drifted into the sunlight. I do not
> remember the song now, but I remember
> that I sang it, and the song was the law and the law
> was the song. The law is a song, I am certain. . . .

Also in this collection are Bringhurst's versions of other early earth-poets, the pre-Socratics, "men who knew no distinctions between physicist, philosopher, biologist and poet, and who were, each in his own way, all in one. . . . They have in common that their work survives in fragments, if at all. But if it is true that for us the fragment is the atom of the form, this brokenness is one more bond between them and ourselves." Among these is "Parmenides," an account of a pedestrian poet surprised one day by the strength of his own creation:

> Thirty-odd years, and thirty lines wasted
> on wagonaxles, doorhinges, horses, veils
> and the sun's girls, and suddenly
> then
> Parmenides
> hummed to himself, caught an idea clean
> in his teeth and bit into it, singing:
>
>   . . . things which appear to be,
> even though they all exist, actually
> have to be there
> always. Everywhere. . . .
>
> And this revelation
> distressed and dumbfounded
> Parmenides.
> Nevertheless he pushed into it,
> choked on exhaustion, swallowed, piled into it:
> the whole bill of lading,
> everything intermingling into
>
> finally, only
> the endless, full,
> indivisible stillness:
> the lock
> on the safe of creation. . . .

"I have lived and worked with the discontinuous ghosts of the old philosopher-poets of Greece for a long time," writes Bringhurst in the autobiographical essay referred to above, "and I admire about those poets in particular their refusal to be compartmentalized. . . . I admire, in other words, their moral and spiritual and intellectual integrity. And I admire, by the way, the fact that they were good ecologists, good environmentalists, though they'd have made no sense of that compartment either." One of his favorite quotations—it could be the motto of his work—is the famous maxim of Herakleitos: "All things think," or "Thinking is the thing that links all things."

Bringhurst's other major collection is *Pieces of Map, Pieces of Music*, the most striking section of which is a fifty-page sequence of meditations, "The Book of Silences," written in the styles and encapsulating the thought of various Oriental poet-sages from the Jain master Parśvanatha, who "was, or may have been, a contemporary of Homer," to the seventeenth-century Zen teacher Hakuin. "The speakers between are the ghosts of other thinkers and singers, most of them from China, most of them students of the Tao and of the Buddhadharma." One of his most significant discoveries is the eighth-century Buddhist philosopher-poet Saraha, who affirmed the ultimate virtue of perfect silence, which modern readers might consider to be a potentially dangerous position for a poet to be in. This teacher's essential message is contained in the last two stanzas of "Saraha":

> There is no something, no nothing,
> but neither. No is

and no isn't, but neither. Now,
don't defile the thought
by sitting there thinking.
No difference exists
between body and mind, language
and mind, language and body.
What is, is not. You must love,
and let loose of, the world.

I used to write poems,
and like yours, they were made
out of words, which is why
they said nothing.
My friend, there is only one word
that I know now, and I have somehow
forgotten its name.

"I want," writes Bringhurst in his introduction to the sequence, "a poetry of knowledge and thought, not of opinion—and not of belief, which is merely dead thought, severed from the thinking. Poetry is the musical density of being, but sometimes it is *silent*, and sometimes that silence is musically still. Those whom I hoped to make speak here spoke for its sake. For themselves, they mostly listened." To aspire to silence is not a foolish or self-defeating aim for a poet, in Bringhurst's opinion. He lives alone on an island off the coast of British Columbia and has learned to look for the integrity he so respects "in some of the quiet, cornered voices of the native American tradition. It is there to be read in the salvaged scraps of oral literature, and it is still there to be heard in the mouths of a steadily shrinking number of native gardeners, hunters and herders who live in the steadily shrinking real world—the lean tracts not yet consumed by an insatiable white society with the stupidest goals in the world: money and jobs." As to the surrounding, impending silence, he is not worried: "A man who turns his back upon his fellows severs himself from the wellsprings of eloquence, but not from the sources of meaning." He believes in, and often quotes, the Rinzai masters' admonition that "the true man has no name and no address."

In a survey article, "Recent Canadian Poetry," which appeared in *Poetry* magazine, Robin Skelton praises Bringhurst's poems which "for all their learning, are neither obscure nor pedantic; they have the lucidity and wit of true authority, . . . there is often a simplicity born of a deep awareness and understanding of the mythopoeic instinct in the center of man. . . . He may well be the poet we have all been waiting for, one who can reclaim for poetry the dignity, wit, brilliance, and wisdom it has recently appeared to have mislaid. He is without doubt a major poet, not only in the context of Canadian letters, but in that of all writing of our time."

Bringhurst has also edited *Visions: Contemporary Art in Canada*, which he describes in the Foreword as "a multiple cross-section, not a survey, not a history, of Canadian art since the Second World War. . . . The focus is on attitudes and meanings, on the issues which contemporary art in Canada addresses, not the careers which it has spawned." With the Haida artist and storyteller Bill Reid, he published *The Raven Steals the Light*, comprising ten illustrated stories from the Haida mythology about the exploits of the Raven, "most powerful of all the creatures who lived during mythtime, whose whim could light the world and bring the lakes and rivers to Haida Gwai [the Queen Charlotte Islands, off the northern coast of British Columbia] and fill them with fish, the great transformer of himself and of the universe, the final distillation of the essence of the clever, complex, ingenious, restless Haidas—and, for that matter, of all the contradictory human race." Both volumes were designed by Bringhurst, who has long been interested in typography. One of the poet's greatest moments is in scholarship and is directly connected to his life and work among the Haidas: "In the summer of 1984, I found in a Philadelphia library unpublished transcripts, in Haida, of performances by the great Haida mythteller Walter McGregor of the Qaiahllanas, recorded in 1901 in the Queen Charlotte Islands. And I felt then an excitement such as I think Gian Francesco Poggio Bracciolini felt in 1417, when, poking through manuscripts in a monastery in Italy, he uncovered the lost text of Lucretius' *De rerum natura*."

PRINCIPAL WORKS: *Poetry*—The Shipwright's Log, 1972; Cadastre, 1973; Deuteronomy, 1974; Eight Objects, 1975; Bergschrund, 1975; Jacob Singing, 1978; The Stonecutter's Horses, 1979; Tzuhalem's Mountain, 1982; The Beauty of the Weapons, 1982, U.S. ed., 1985; Tending the Fire, 1985; The Blue Roofs of Japan, 1986; Pieces of Map, Pieces of Music, 1986, U.S. ed., 1987; Conversations with a Toad, 1987. *History and criticism*—Ocean/Paper/Stone, 1984; Shovels, Shoes and the Slow Rotation of Letters, 1986; (coeditor) Visions: Contemporary Art in Canada, 1983. *Narrative prose*—(coauthor) The Raven Steals the Light, 1984.

ABOUT: Contemporary Authors New Revision Series 6, 1982; Contemporary Poets, 4th ed., 1985; Canadian Who's Who, 1988. *Periodicals*—Books in Canada August–September 1983, January 1984, December 1986; CM September 1983, September 1984; Choice October 1976, December 1984, January 1988; Kayak February 1977; Library Journal March 15, 1976; September 1, 1984; New York Times Book Review September 28, 1986; Poetry August 1984; Quill & Quire February 1983, December 1983; Saturday Night (Toronto) March 1984; Western American Literature Fall 1983.

BRODKEY, HAROLD (October 25, 1930–), American novelist and short-story writer, writes: "I think of what I write as an amalgam of language and the politics of moral procedure sifted through common life. By *common life* I mean something along the lines of what in experience might be commonly known by readers—the portrayal of the real making full acknowledgement of time as reality—rather than literary evasions of the reality of time—so that statements and the evidence in events and actions for those statements is recognizable in one's own experience; and the relation of writer and reader is changed, making it more nearly equal. The reader in his or her life has more access to the real than the author does, which counters the author's hauntedly more practiced access to language. This is *Momentism*—an experiment with the sayable in regard to what is overwhelmingly present but has usually been held to be unsayably relegated to silence—or to be lied about: i.e, distorted for the sake of a personal advantage of some sort.

"Since the evidence for statements of opinion lies in how what is observed, is observed, a sort of prose is created which is not propaganda. If reality is, in fact, presented, in a way heretofore held to be impossible, then truths of a more complete and interesting order can be dealt in. The literal reality of American lives including that of the narrator is proposed; and this is done as an antidote, or counterweight, to the stale misunderstandings of American life when American existence is looked at in stale and unsuitable frames and is not taken for what it is (or for any one true thing it is of the many things it is).

"So, the events pictured are accessible but are not laid out in the techniques or familiar shapes and forms of old or recent literary tradition. The safe, and largely idle keys, of satire and lament are avoided; and the author behind the narrator is not assumed to be a scion of language with some sort of artificial claim to rightness as a matter of course in the claim of being a narrator in more or less intellectually stylish English. When that privilege is laid aside, the obstreperous falsity of false auctorial claims (of knowledge, of ascription of character, even of sequences) becomes much harder: one is less likely to be bearing false witness.

"The work, the text, then becomes an open subject with some kind of meaning required as the purpose of the work other than that of claiming the American right to hold the rank of author, or knower, because you have had some sort of American as a writer. The meaning, then, that is offered is the grounds for the licence for the privilege—even for writers who claim to be nihilistic solipsists or religiously devout or who use

HAROLD BRODKEY

any of those dodges rather than take the responsibility for meaning something—and is necessary morally and esthetically once silence has been broken by an attempt at narration.

"Politics and psychology depend on the use of language so that one becomes, with such a program as the above, a political writer and a psychological theoretician—and every man's enemy.

"In the 1950s, I wrote simpler, younger, somewhat lyrical versions of the above. In the 1960s, I wrote third person narratives in which the same questions were addressed but the element of the truth-proposition was placed in relation to some identifiable and unarguable element of illusion—movie-making, drug-taking, projections of personal happiness as daydream—(the subject being false and real emotions, felt, or known, to be such). In the 1970s, the truth element became the active element of narration—that is, the core of each narrative was scandal, usually multiple—that is to say, scandals—of tone and of language and of subject and of event and of truthfulness. (These stories were misread as being in opposition to The New Novel and the Post-Modernist effort because so much of American Post-Modernism relished and flaunted untruth as evidence of honesty as such whatever the merit of the truth as story-telling or as fantasy or as symbol.)

"The purpose of what I do is a more equitable and flexible language, and a just world, of course, an increase in the spirit of charity among us, and greater happiness for a widening number of people, an enlargement of one's sense of amusement and interest in life, more of which can be spoken about sensibly, more of which can find its way into language and thought."

The facts about Harold Brodkey's life can be briefly stated. He was born in Staunton, Illinois, to Ceil and Max Weintraub. He was adopted in 1932 by Joseph and Doris Brodkey of Alton, Illinois, after the death of his mother, and grew up in the St. Louis suburb of University City, Missouri. He received a B.A. from Harvard in 1952 and began publishing short stories, poetry, and essays in the *New Yorker, Esquire, Partisan Review, American Poetry Review,* and other periodicals. In 1958 his first book, *First Love and Other Sorrows,* was published. He has taught at the University of Arizona, Cornell, and City College, and received a number of literary honors including O. Henry First Prize awards (1975, 1976), a Prix de Rome award (1959–1960), a National Endowment award (1984–1985), and a Guggenheim Fellowship (1987). He is married to the novelist Ellen Schwamm and lives in New York City.

Infinitely richer than these biographical details is the ongoing life of Harold Brodkey in his writing. Critics have somewhat uneasily compared him to writers as oddly matched as Walt Whitman (Harold Bloom) and Marcel Proust (Dennis Donaghue), who have in common perhaps only the obsessiveness of their self-consciousness. Leon Wieseltier, reviewing Brodkey's *Women and Angels,* has suggested that a better comparison is to Ralph Waldo Emerson, "America's true pioneer in the salvaging of God by the swelling of the self." Brodkey has worked painstakingly for nearly three decades over the material of his literal and spiritual life. The culmination of that work will be his long-awaited novel "A Party of Animals," which has yet to appear. In spite of his long silence in the intervening years, or possibly because of it, he has become a kind of legend among his contemporaries. In 1986, Christopher Hitchens, in the *Times Literary Supplement,* suggested that he is a victim of "a Penelope syndrome" and others have voiced the suspicion that he will never finish defining his life or refining his eccentric prose style. Nevertheless, in 1985 three fragments from the work-in-progress were published with the title *Women and Angels,* not by a trade publisher but in a limited edition by the Jewish Publication Society. Two of these pieces, "Ceil" and "Lila" had appeared earlier in the *New Yorker.* The book received little critical attention in the popular press, but it did not pass unnoticed. And in 1986 Vintage Press re-issued his *First Love and Other Sorrows.*

A comparison of these early stories with his later work is instructive. The fiction he published in the 1950s, much of it in the *New Yorker,* was a series of vignettes of youth and adolescence. Some centered on a young boy growing up in a midwest suburb, bright, self-consciously Jewish, awakening to sex, going to Harvard, traveling in France. Some centered, in almost parallel fashion, on a young girl going to Wellesley, dating, marrying, and trying to cope with motherhood and domesticity. All the stories have a quality of bittersweet innocence and ultimate compromise and conformity typical of much fiction of the 1950s. A British reviewer in the *New Statesman* observed: "For all its charm—and Mr. Brodkey writes with a light engaging sympathy which one has no wish at all to resist—this is the terrifying tribal American world of compulsive dating and marriage. Among its natives, scholar, rake or recluse, there isn't a place for a rebel." The writing was appropriately simple and sensitive. "Mr. Brodkey writes well," William Peden commented in the *Saturday Review,* "in a clear, uncomplicated, unaffected prose. He sees well, too; more important, he thinks about what he sees and understands its meanings and implications."

The striking changes not only in the subject matter but also in the prose of Brodkey's later work reflect long, slow, laborious effort, a passion for endless revision. Anatole Broyard, who interviewed him in 1981 for the *New York Times Book Review,* was intrigued with "the exhaustiveness of his determination. His work is like a revenge on carelessness. Nothing is left to chance. He is at the opposite end of the spectrum from those writers who concede part of the decision, part of the finishing of the work, to the reader." Even punctuation, or its lack in many sentences that run on for paragraphs, becomes an element of his style. The novelist D. Keith Mano, who read parts of this work-in-progress in the mid-1970s, wrote in *Esquire*: "The style is a rational instrument for getting at once-felt emotion. And that emotion . . . is gotten at. I have never read so many pages as consistently successful and arresting at the level of prose-craft, which were enfused as well with a powerful, magical thereness."

The women in *Women and Angels* are his two mothers—Ceil, the Jewish immigrant mother who died when he was a small child but whom his persona, Wiley Silenowicz, recalls in vivid imaginative detail, and Lila, his nagging and demanding adoptive mother for whom he has ambivalent feelings of hate and pity. "The Angel," however, is a total departure from the stark and bitter realism of the first two stories. It is an esoteric, near-cabalistic account of a vision that anpears to Wiley and a group of other people at 3 P.M. on October 25, 1951 in front of Harvard Hall. There is no plot, no characterization—only a confrontation with a divine presence. The Angel does not speak ("There is no equivalent of speech in the Seraphic appearance, no silence or stillness imposed by the dignity of what one has seen and by one's wonder"); it cannot be described (" . . . a face-like thing that was also a figure . . . a Countenance not human, not exactly—or entirely—inhuman"). Its presence and its transcendence cannot be denied, and it communicates: "It said to love incomplete and complex meanings and One speechless and apparently not Omnipotent God and to struggle toward a new idea of idea, therefore." After an hour, the apparition vanishes, leaving Wiley and the others "bathed in the afternoon's ordinary rivers of white light, yellow light, its faint heat and the damp coolness near the ground and struggling to grow, an invisible harsh corn, into the ice fields of winter."

"The Angel" evokes strong and usually conflicting reactions in its readers. D. J. Enright, in *New York Review of Books*, found passages of "impressive" writing in it but was exasperated by Wiley's self-absorption even in the presence of the Divine: " . . . it needs a saint to stand very much of the self-indulgent playfulness, the self-regarding exegesis in Brodkey's narrative." Leon Wieseltier was staggered by the sheer daring of Brodkey's vision: "I know of nothing like it in literature. It takes courage to write about God . . . Brodkey's attempt to describe the numinous object of the vision, and to name it, are awkward and frantic, which is fitting for a work written under the shock of such a communication." But he too found Wiley's resistance to the Angel an act of "massive vanity" typical of much modern spirituality and was disturbed by Brodkey's introduction to the book in which, describing himself as a "non-observant Jew," he wrote that "observance is a great help in ethical matters and as communal discipline but . . . it interferes with sacredness." Nevertheless, Wieseltier concedes that *Women and Angels* is "a book of substance, and perhaps of consequence," and that "The Angel" is "one of the most astounding pieces of prose I have been blessed to discover."

In the autumn of 1988, while readers still waited patiently for "A Party of Animals," Brodkey published *Stories in an Almost Classical Mode*. These included "The Angel" and other stories previously published. Once again reviewers were sharply divided—as much on the personality of the author as on his work. In a long article in *New York* Dinitia Smith reported that some believe "A Party of Animals"—of which

Brodkey has allegedly written several thousand pages—does not exist at all. A reviewer in one journal even suggested that "the cult buildup of Harold Brodkey has become a bit of a con job." Smith quotes Brodkey himself: "I'm nowhere. I'm part of a tradition of failure, another version of the mad Delmore Schwartz or James Agee." Nevertheless, his work continues to intrigue readers. Frank Kermode, reviewing *Stories in an Almost Classical Mode* in the *New York Times Book Review*, described Brodkey's writing gifts as "certainly remarkable, though often a cause of pain to the reader"—sentences of interminable length, "a prose of painful abundance." Smith finds his writing "characterized by a lush and rigorous prose of an almost suffocating intensity." If for such critics reading Brodkey is an act of near masochism, it is also aesthetically rewarding. Quoting one of Brodkey's characters—"A poet is a man whose words ring true—non-counterfeit"—Kermode concludes his review: "Mr. Brodkey wishes to be and is a poet, never counterfeit, though not always current coin."

PRINCIPAL WORKS: First Love and Other Sorrows, 1958, 1986; Women and Angels, 1985; Stories in an Almost Classical Mode, 1988 (half the stories in this volume were published in Britain in 1989 under the title The Abundant Dreamer).

ABOUT: Contemporary Authors 111, 1984; Contemporary Novelists, 4th ed., 1986. *Periodicals*—Esquire January 1977; New Republic May 20, 1985; New York September 19, 1988; New York Review of Books February 15, 1990; New York Times Book Review April 26, 1981; September 18, 1988; Times Literary Supplement May 2, 1986; November 3, 1989; Vanity Fair March 1985.

BROMBERT, VICTOR H(ENRI) (November 11, 1923–   ), American literary critic, was born in France, the son of Jacques and Vera Brombert. He came to the United States in 1941 and became a naturalized citizen two years later. He entered Yale University, where he earned a bachelor's degree (1948), a master's degree (1949), and a doctorate (1953). He joined Yale's romance languages and literature department in 1951 and remained there until 1975; from 1969 to 1975 he held the Benjamin Barge chair of Romance literatures. In 1975 he became the Henry Putnam university professor of romance and comparative literature at Princeton University; from 1984 he served as director of the Christian Gauss seminars in criticism.

Brombert's senior thesis as an undergraduate at Yale was published as volume seven in the

VICTOR H. BROMBERT

university's series of undergraduate prize essays. *The Criticism of T. S. Eliot: Problems of an "Impersonal Theory" of Poetry* examines the distinction made by Eliot in his critical works between "minor uses" of literary works and "the major use which consists of an appreciation of intrinsic values." In general, transforming literature "into a philosophical or ideological document" is "particularly dangerous and indicates an inability to distinguish between two fundamentally different activities: that of the poet and that of the philosopher." The aim of the essay is to show that Eliot's criticism may properly be accepted by the New Critics, who were at the time just beginning to make their mark on American academic literary criticism, and on that produced at Yale in particular. (Brombert's faculty adviser for his senior thesis was William K. Wimsatt, a pioneer New Critic.)

Brombert's next book was his doctoral thesis, written under the direction of Jean Boorsch. *Stendhal et la voie oblique: L'auteur devant son monde romanesque* attempts to examine the peculiar stance adopted by the French novelist Stendhal before his readers; it is a study of the novelist's irony and sensibility as revealed through his many authorial intrusions in his novels. Brombert focusses on the complexity of Stendhal's thought—"his attitude and reactions to the work at the very moment of composition—in a word, his living and complex presence as it shows itself in the very text of the work." Fascinated by what he perceived as "the art of lying and dissimulation," Stendhal Brombert argues, early recognized how people use hypocrisy "as

a defensive weapon." Assuming himself the mask of cynicism and hypocrisy, "Stendhal's presence in his novelistic works is infinitely more complex and mysterious than one would have at first believed. . . . This false cynic, this hypocrite by vocation does not allow himself to be discovered so easily." Brombert's two other works on Stendhal are *Stendhal: Fiction and the Themes of Freedom* and, as editor, *Stendhal: A Collection of Critical Essays.*

The Intellectual Hero: Studies in the French Novel 1880-1955 examines the hero as intellectual in the novels of, among other French writers, Émile Zola, Anatole France, Roger Martin du Gard, Louis Guilloux, André Malraux, Jean-Paul Sartre, Simone de Beauvoir, and Albert Camus. "The twentieth-century novel in France," he writes in his introduction, "has been literally invaded by intellectuals. Never before in fiction has the experience of living been so unremittingly filtered through the *minds* of the protagonists." Brombert sees this "proliferation of intellectual heroes" as "symptomatic of a general invasion of all branches of literature by scholars, teachers and professional philosophers." The intellectual hero thus becomes representative of the epoch itself.

"Persistent readers of *The Intellectual Hero*," wrote Kathleen Cannell in the *Christian Science Monitor*, "may learn much that will enlarge their understanding of French literature, of the French character, and of the modern world." The critic for the *Yale Review* called the book "a clear picture of the transformation of the intellectual-in-fiction . . . confronted with 'the highest, and often conflicting, exigencies of his own mind.'"

Brombert was invited to give the Christian Gauss seminars at Princeton in 1964; he subsequently published his lectures as *The Novels of Flaubert: A Study of Themes and Techniques.* In the book's opening section, treating Flaubert's literary temperament, Brombert writes that the author "always considered that the highest and purest pleasure of literature is its power to liberate those who practice it from the contingencies of life. Art was for him quite literally an escape. Its superiority over life was precisely its ability to transcend the conditions of living." He writes of Flaubert's "quest . . . after a higher, more general truth," of his obsession with "exoticism and orgiastic dreams," of "the monastic urge"—his "ascetic, monastic disposition," of his innate pessimism, his beliefs in the writer's vocation and in salvation through art. Flaubert, he concludes, "proudly viewed himself as the last of the troubadours. He sensed that he was one of the late, but most imposing manifestations of the literary phenomenon known as Romanticism. . . . But if he is, in a sense, a splendid crepuscular figure, he also stands at the threshold of modern literature, as a direct link between Romanticism and our own visions of reality." The reviewer for *Choice* called *The Novels of Flaubert* "the definitive analysis of Flaubert's creative techniques and of his principal themes." The *Times Literary Supplement* critic thought it "a highly intelligent analysis of each of Flaubert's works of fiction."

The place and function of the prison metaphor in a great deal of premodern French literature is the subject of Brombert's next work, *La prison romantique: Essai sur l'imaginaire*, translated into English by the author as *The Romantic Prison: The French Tradition*. "Prison haunts our civilization," the author writes in his introduction. "Object of fear, it is also a subject of poetic reverie. The prison wish does exist. The image of immurement is essentially ambivalent in the Western tradition. Prison walls confine the 'culprit,' victimize the innocent, affirm the power of society. But they also, it would seem, protect poetic meditation and religious fervor." The prison experience and the idea of prison are then examined in the works of Pascal, Pétrus Borel, Stendhal, Victor Hugo, Gérard de Nerval, Baudelaire, J.-K. Huysmans, and Jean-Paul Sartre. The author acknowledges at the end, however, that what finally separates modern readers most sharply from the romantic heritage is the recurrent twentieth-century nightmare: "The dream of a happy prison has become hard to entertain in a world of penal colonies and extermination camps, in a world that makes us fear that somehow even our suffering can no longer be our refuge." Jacqueline Tavernier-Courbin wrote in *Library Journal* that *The Romantic Prison* "is an interesting book which offers fresh insight into an old theme and deepens our understanding of Romanticism." "At every point," wrote the reviewer for *Choice*, "the breadth of Brombert's scholarship is as evident as its depth."

When Brombert began his serious study of literature after World War II, Victor Hugo, the subject of the masterful study he was to publish in 1984, was not generally considered a subject for close critical analysis. As he read and later taught the major nineteenth-century French novels, however, Brombert came increasingly to appreciate the profound significance of Hugo's work. His aim in *Victor Hugo and the Visionary Novel* was to account for the novelist's interest and originality "by clearly analyzing forms, themes and techniques, and also by relating individual works to a larger vision." Brombert works his way through all of Hugo's many novels and attempts to relate some of the novelist's

many extraordinary drawings to the themes of his fiction. He describes the "surprisingly modern nature" of Hugo's fiction, which "undermines and decenters the subject, using character and plot to achieve the effects of visionary prose narrative . . . The dramatic and psychological power of Hugo's novels depends in large part on the creation of archetypal figures. Their poetic and thematic unity derives from his ability to conceive the linguistic analogue for larger forces at work. . . . [His] supreme talent was essentially of a mythopoetic nature. He was able to convert personal experiences into a destiny, and then relate this destiny to the disturbing configurations of contemporary history."

Hayden White, writing in the *New York Times Book Review*, called Brombert's readings of Hugo's novels "uniformly patient, generous, subtle and nonreductive." R. S. Stowe in *Choice* thought the author "makes a persuasive case for the underlying ambiguity and 'subversiveness' of Hugo's vision and for its surprising modernity."

Brombert has been visiting professor at many universities, including the Scuola Normale Superiore in Pisa, Italy (1972), the University of California (1978), Johns Hopkins University (1979), Columbia University (1980), New York University (1980, 1981), the University of Puerto Rico (1983, 1984), and the University of Bologna, Italy (1984). His awards and prizes include the French Ordre des Palmes Académiques, the Harry Levin prize in comparative literature (1978), the Howard T. Behrman award for distinguished achievement in the humanities (1979), and Yale's Wilbur L. Cross medal for outstanding achievement (1985). He has been a grantee of the American Council of Learned Societies (1966) and a Fulbright fellow (1950–1951), a Guggenheim fellow (1954–1955, 1970), a National Endowment for the Humanities senior fellow (1973–1974), and a Rockefeller Foundation resident fellow in Bellagio, Italy (1975). He is a fellow of the American Academy of Arts and Sciences, and a member of the American Association of Teachers of French, the American Comparative Literature Association, the Société des Études Françaises, the Academy for Literary Studies, the Société d'Histoire Litteraire de la France, and the Società Universitaria per gli Studi di Lingua e Letteratura Francese.

PRINCIPAL WORKS: The Criticism of T. S. Eliot, 1949; Stendhal et la voie oblique, 1954; The Intellectual Hero, 1961; The Novels of Flaubert, 1966; Stendhal: Fiction and the Themes of Freedom, 1968; Flaubert par lui-même, 1971; La prison romantique, 1975; The Romantic Prison: The French Tradition, 1978;

Victor Hugo and the Visionary Novel, 1984; *As editor*—Stendhal: A Collection of Critical Essays, 1962; Balzac's La peau de chagrin, 1962; The Hero in Literature, 1969.

ABOUT: Contemporary Authors New Revision Series 9, 1982; Who's Who in America 1988–1989. *Periodicals*—Booklist July 1, 1961; Choice September 1967, January 1979, January 1985; Christian Science Monitor June 15, 1961; Commonweal May 2, 1969; Economist July 1, 1967; Kirkus Reviews February 15, 1961; Library Journal April 15, 1961; March 15, 1967; April 15, 1969; February 15, 1979; New Statesman August 24, 1962; September 1, 1967; New York Review of Books April 20, 1967; November 6, 1969; January 17, 1985; New York Times Book Review April 27, 1969; December 23, 1984; San Francisco Chronicle August 13, 1961; Saturday Review May 13, 1961; Spectator May 4, 1962; Times Literary Supplement June 22, 1962; July 6, 1967; June 26, 1969; October 11, 1985; Yale Review October 1961, October 1967, June 1969.

WILLIAM BRONK

BRONK, WILLIAM (February 17, 1918–   ), American poet and essayist, was born in Fort Edward, New York, the son of William M. Bronk and the former Ethel Funston. He was educated at Dartmouth College, taking his bachelor's degree in 1938. During World War II, from 1941 to 1945, he served in the U.S. Army, ending his military service as a lieutenant.

For many years Bronk has lived in Hudson Falls, two miles north of Fort Edward on the Champlain Canal, north of Albany, New York, where he owns and operates a lumber mill. There is little record of close literary friendships or even associations with other poets. He has rarely given readings; he belongs to no school; the influences on his work are hard to place, although one can catch glimpses of the dense imagism of Wallace Stevens and William Carlos Williams and the sharp metaphysicality of Emily Dickinson.

Bronk's first notable book of poetry to be published was *The World, the Worldless*, brought out by New Directions—The San Francisco Review Press. It contains some of his finest poems, compact pieces in which the poet is able, by his taciturn sense of awe, to let the reader share directly in the sense of his own profound discovery. "The Tree in the Middle of the Field" is such a poem of greatly understated power:

The tree in the middle of the field stands round, stands
     tall
as though the sun hung just above forever,
and every wind were always favoring wind.

Elm branches fall with pure contemplative grace;
oak asserts without sound; a maple tree
holds a whole summer's green in one rich green.

This tree! This tree! Look, there are parts of the world
not ever wounded, within whose light, the world
is always changed with light. This tree, this tree.

Bronk's interest in and deep commitment to the uniqueness and particularity of experience are well attested in this poem and others in the collection. Richard Elman, in the *New York Times Book Review*, described his poems as "engraved with terse statement, a high seriousness and strong uncluttered feeling." Frequently the endings of his poems point sharply to the lesson they have intended to teach, a lesson of deliberate disillusion, of existential finality:

           . . . Sight
is inward and sees itself, hearing, touch,
are inward. What do we know of an outer world?
           ("How Indeterminacy Determines Us")

How strange that after all it is rarely space
but time we cling to, unwilling to let it go.
           ("The World in Time and Space")

A possible name for the country whose colony
we were could be Truth, wherever that is.
Who knows it, or remembers? It lies so unreachably far
     distances away. Let it be.
           ("Truth as a Far Country; as a Piteous Ogre")

This ringing, lapidary quality of statement does not seem, strangely enough, part of a philosophy that Bronk would have us learn, but rather forms a singularity of poetic purpose for us to feel. Robert D. Spector, in *Saturday Review*, talked about Bronk's poems' "unbroken thematic unity . . . . his poetry of statement impresses with its clarity and precision of language; it manages to make metaphysics a subject of human emotion rather than a grand abstraction."

Bronk had published, with small presses that specialize mainly in poetry, more than a dozen short collections of verse, beginning with *Light and Dark* in 1956, before North Point Press published a volume of his collected works, *Life Supports: New and Collected Poems* in 1981. This book, which won the American Book Award for poetry in 1982, was remarkable among collections of contemporary poets' works for several reasons. Each and every poem from previous collections was included, with not the slightest excision, revision, or variation; even the order in which poems had been presented in previous collections was rigorously observed. This order of presentation, some critics thought, was almost certainly the order in which the poems had been written. Samuel French Morse, writing in *Poetry*, suggested that those who knew Bronk's work would go first to the new poems, those grouped together at the end under the subtitle *Life Supports*, "but having done so should then begin at the beginning and read straight through to the end. . . . Such a reading will provide some surprises. One follows the shifting but recurrent patterns of the poetry with a growing awareness of Bronk's achievement and an occasionally ambiguous feeling of anticipation, and, finally, a conviction that the encompassing title he has chosen for the work of more than forty years is as telling as it is precise." Morse goes on to remark on the increasing abstraction and syntactical complexity of the later poems, in which "language . . . becomes plain almost to the point of being purely denotative, stripped of color, in order not to interfere with the statement as it emerges, or seems to emerge, from the matrix of rumination." Such a startling effect is especially evident in the collection *Silence and Metaphor*, which consists of forty-nine eight-line poems with starkly abstract titles, many of which reiterate the questions of what "we say" or what "we are" or what "we know," a sense of the "possible as true, or not":

Wanting the significance that cause and effect
might have (we see it in little things where it is)
not seeing it in any place
important to us (it is in our lives but in ways

that deny each other) and the totality,
I suppose, is what I mean—it isn't there—
we look around: the possibilities,
dreams and diversions, whatever else there is.
                              ("The Effect of Cause Despaired")

Such poetry as this, resolutely unmetrical, even unmusical, memorable only on its own severe terms, and calculated not to be appealing but to assert a hard nugget of meaning, can have only a small coterie of admirers. In his two short collections published after *Life Supports*, Bronk seems to have drawn back from the brink of total abstraction to become more accessible, even amusing (he has always seemed amused at the work he has done). From *Manifest; and Furthermore*, a substantial collection from North Point Press, a poem like "Getting Older" reprises a theme—the complexity and unknowableness of aging—which the poet has often treated, but in a manner quite light-hearted and funny:

When I was young I didn't drink alcohol.
Well, yes, I did but I didn't drink much. I went
for days and weeks without it—money partly
I guess—but I didn't think in those terms as such
because everything is money when you haven't it
and it isn't a particular term; it's just part
of the basics.
                    Now, I don't remember what
it was I started to say but that may be age
and have nothing at all to do with alcohol.

Bronk's essays, almost as dense and rigorous as his poetry, originally appeared collected in limited editions by the Elizabeth Press. *The New World* comprises six pieces of pre-Columbian Inca and Maya civilizations, and the ways they measured and took account of those aspects of living they considered important. *A Partial Glossary* contains only two short essays, one of which, "Costume as Metaphor," is not only about the subject in its title—the idea that dress is mainly surface decoration—but also about knowledge, belief, the world's concreteness, and dying. The author's most sustained effort in prose, however, is *The Brother in Elysium: Ideas of Friendship and Society in the United States*, which consists of three essays on "Silence and Henry Thoreau," two on "Walt Whitman's Marine Democracy," and two on "Herman Melville; or, The Ambiguities." In an "epistle dedicatory" to his friend Sidney Cox, written in 1946, "several years . . . since this book was started in and around your house," he discusses the lack of awareness of most people of the truths he proposes to talk about: "Most men live in the social body as unconsciously as cells live in the physical body. Or they are like the multitude of fish in the sea, which cry out to the glory of God, but not in a voice which fish can understand or readily discourse in." In a coda, he turns the hoary idea of the brotherhood of man neatly upon its ear: "How often when we are on our best behavior, and moved by generosity or loneliness, we are led to speak of society in terms of brotherhood. We are told that all men are brothers, and the inference has sometimes been that a simple acceptance of that dictum leads to no further problems. Are there then no family quarrels, no bitterness in the blood? How complex and ambiguous is the problem of brotherhood is shown in the tragic frustration of Thoreau, Whitman's erotic phantasy, and Melville's hard-won wisdom. Read, mark, therefore, learn and inwardly digest; here, as some of our contemporary devils might say, are the scriptures."

In 1983, following the success of *Life Supports*, North Point Press brought out a collected edition of all of Bronk's previously published prose, *Vectors and Smoothable Curves: Collected Essays*. The title comes from a line in a difficult and typically dichotomous early poem, "My House New-Painted," which holds that houses, "the measured entities," have sometimes been held in a kind of contempt: "They fade and sag. They fall away." But, in truth, an opposite opinion or view often prevails:

This was man did this, and thought to do well
when he turned away to say, on the contrary, all
the world was what we measured: houses, sums
and angles, vectors and smoothable curves. We turn,
and turn again another way to find
some way to state the world, dissatisfied
none answers.

There is, as these essays make clear, no way to mediate between these points of view, but they can be analyzed, and one can even choose between them. Andrea Barnett, writing of this austerely metaphysical essay collection in the *New York Times Book Review*, marvelled "at the rigor and philosophical reach of [Bronk's] intelligence." The *Choice* reviewer commented: "In tone and style these essays resemble old-fashioned nineteenth-century meditations. . . . In intention, they are experiments in form, eschewing explicit judgment, evading or avoiding 'the language of history, or sociology, or criticism.'"

PRINCIPAL WORKS: *Poetry*—Light and Dark, 1956; The World, the Worldless, 1964; The Empty Hands, 1969; That Tantalus, 1971; To Praise the Music, 1972; Utterances, 1972; Looking at It, 1973; Silence and Metaphor, 1975; The Stance, 1975; My Father Photographed with Friends and Other Pictures, 1976; The Meantime, 1976; Finding Losses, 1976; Twelve Losses Found, 1976; That Beauty Still, 1978; The Force of Desire, 1979; Life Supports, 1981; Light in a Dark Sky, 1982; Careless Love and Its Apostrophes, 1985; Manifest; and Furthermore, 1987. *Essays*—The New World, 1973; A Partial Glossary, 1974; The Brother in Elysium, 1980; Vectors and Smoothable Curves, 1983.

ABOUT: Contemporary Authors New Revision Series 23, 1988; Contemporary Poets, 4th ed, 1985; Corman, C. William Bronk: An Essay, 1976; Who's Who in America, 1988–1989. *Periodicals*—Choice September 1977;

June 1984; Commonweal December 24, 1965; Contemporary Literature 23, 1982; Library Journal November 1, 1976; October 15, 1981; April 15, 1987; New York Times Book Review January 17, 1965; March 9, 1975; September 18, 1977; December 13, 1981; January 1, 1984; Parnassus Spring–Summer 1977; Poetry July 1965, November 1982; Saturday Review February 13, 1965; July 8, 1978; Virginia Quarterly Review Winter 1965; World Literature Today Winter 1988.

BRUIN, JOHN. See **BRUTUS, DENNIS**

BRUNER, JEROME S(EYMOUR) (October 1, 1915–   ), American cognitive and developmental psychologist, was born in New York City and brought up in Far Rockaway, New York, the youngest of four children of Herman and Rose Glücksmann Bruner, both immigrants from Poland. His father died when he was twelve, and he spent several years moving about the country with his mother, he recalls in his autobiography, "in search of health and company, back and forth to Florida, to California, to 'the country.'" He became a freshman at Duke University in the autumn of 1933, and began to study neuropsychology there under Karl Zener and comparative psychology under Donald Keith Adams, both "fresh from Berlin," where they had worked with Wolfgang Köhler and "the budding young Kurt Lewin, apostles of the still 'new' Gestalt psychology. . . . I was caught by the idea of the evolution of mind." Bruner took his bachelor's degree in 1938, having made a name for himself in Durham as "a 'troublemaker,' . . . I was a bumptious and self-important young man."

Accepted to do graduate work in psychology at both Yale and Harvard, he chose the latter, fitting in quickly to the intensely fast-paced intellectual life of prewar Cambridge, going "to Kurt Goldstein's seminar on brain and behavior, to Bob White's on 'lives in progress,' to Gordon Allport's on life history, to Smitty Stevens's on operationism, to Köhler's William James lectures, to Professor [Edwin Garrigues] Boring's on sensation and perception, [and] to Kurt Lewin's on topological psychology." He earned his master's degree in 1939 and his doctorate in 1941. He wrote his thesis on the nature of propaganda broadcasting of belligerent nations; within a week of finishing it, in June 1941, he was on his way to Washington to work for the brand-new Foreign Broadcast Monitoring Service of the Federal Communications Commission.

In 1942–1944 Bruner was associate director, under the psychologist Hadley Cantril, of the

JEROME S. BRUNER

Office of Public Opinion Research in Princeton,
New Jersey, in which he organized, participated
in, and wrote about governmental public-
opinion surveys on war problems; the importance of the public's understanding and support
of the country's foreign policies was a high priority for the wartime government. Bruner's earliest publications date from this time: *Public
Thinking on Post-War Problems*, the results of
a questionnaire which attempted to ascertain the
concerns of the American people for the economic and social future of the country once the
war had ended; and *Mandate from the People*,
also "a book about the future—about the
peace. . . . The first part traces the outlines of
American public opinion on international issues
crucial for winning the peace. . . . The second
half . . . looks to the post-war home front." The
author's conclusion is that "there is a long way
to travel before Americans become responsible
citizens of the world." Bruner was also editor in
1943–1944 of *Public Opinion Quarterly*.

After a brief overseas-service stint in France
following D-Day with a "gallant little band" of
psychological-warfare experts "out of the theater of the absurd," he was delighted to return
to Harvard, where he taught as a member of the
psychology department from 1945 to 1972. He
was professor of psychology from 1952 and
founder-director from 1961 of the university's
Center for Cognitive Studies.

It is as a pioneer in cognitive psychology that
Bruner has made his greatest contribution to his
discipline. The concept of perception was the
first to be permanently altered by his efforts.

During the 1950s he and several colleagues, most
especially Leo Postman, showed in a series of
brilliantly conceived experiments that perceptions were not mental photographs but rather
images shaped by the meaning given them by
the individual. "We started to see perception as
active," he remarked in 1987 in an interview
with the *New York Times*, "rather than passive,
as had been assumed. I was a visiting scholar at
Princeton's Institute for Advanced Studies about
that time [1951], and found physicists deeply interested in the same question. As one put it,
physics was 5 percent observation and 95 percent speculation. They saw that the models you
build determine what you look for, how you interpret what you see, and what you do not see."
His work and that of his collaborators gave rise
to a psychological movement called the "New
Look," which focused on such questions as how
emotions or intentions formed human perception. Although bitterly assailed at the time by the
behaviorists and experimental psychologists then
firmly entrenched in power, the New Look's direct descendant, cognitive psychology, is today
the most thriving branch of the discipline. The
concepts of intelligence and language were also
challenged and renewed by Bruner's work. As
David R. Olson writes in the preface to Bruner's
festschrift, *The Social Foundations of Language
and Thought*, "When it was conventional to treat
perception   as   sensation   determined,
Bruner . . . showed that it was expectancy or
knowledge driven. When intelligence was treated as a quality of an organ, Bruner treated it as
a set of strategies and procedures for solving
problems, and when language was seen as the
gradual unfolding of semantic and syntactic
structures from an innate base, Bruner treated it
in terms of its uses as an expression of intention
and as a means of constructing and maintaining
a social relationship between infant and adult."

Bruner's work on infantile cognition in the
mid-1960s was the link to the other great preoccupation of his career, the issue of education,
and the necessity for marshalling American public opinion behind its improvement. In his first
Heinz Werner lecture (at Clark University) he
outlines the work done to analyze what he
calls the "four great issues in human infancy:
1. Through what processes does voluntary control of behavior develop?; 2. Through what
means does the child gain control of his own attention?; 3. Through what form of learning does
the infant progress from being a 'one-track' enterprise, capable seemingly of one activity at a
time, to a capacity for carrying out several lines
of activity jointly or synergistically?; and 4. How
does the infant manage to begin a career of re-
ciprocation and exchange that prepares him in

such a degree for culture using in general and language using in particular?" He discovered in a key experiment on the sucking mechanism in infants that they possess a directing sense of intention guiding their intellectual development: babies were thereby shown to be active participants in their own learning. "Infants were assumed," he said in 1987, "to be blank slates, who had to learn even the most basic distinctions. Their world was supposed to be a buzzing, blooming confusion."

The insight gained from this and allied experiments was the seed that was to blossom into the Head Start program for preschool children; Bruner was chief among the psychologists and educators who originated the program and served on the presidential commission that implemented it. The key to successful learning in childhood, he believes, is the encouragement and rewarding of natural curiosity: "When kids live in an impoverished environment that gives them little or nothing back for their efforts to learn, they give up." Bruner's major contributions to educational theory and practice are: *The Process of Education*, the proceedings of the famous Woods Hole Conference in September 1959, a ten-day gathering called by the National Academy of Sciences under Bruner's direction to assess science education in the U.S. school system: *Man: A Course of Study*, an extremely popular textbook and curriculum for secondary-school instruction in the behavioral sciences; *Toward a Theory of Instruction*; and *The Relevance of Education* (1971).

Among Bruner's most generally accessible works are the eleven pieces in *On Knowing: Essays for the Left Hand*. These are divided into three groups: The Shape of Experience, on the connections between cognition and the various modes of art; The Quest for Clarity, on methods of learning; and The Idea of Action, on Freud and common sense, behaviorism, and the concept of fate. The author remarks in the preface to the revised edition on his affinity for the essay form, which "posits for itself a topic and a set of constraints that limit the forms of comment one can make upon it. [It] is the literary counterpart of the 'possible world' of the logician or like the 'thought experiment' of the scientist. As with each of these, it begins with a set of connected familiars and seeks by rearranging them to leap to the higher ground of novelty, a novelty rooted in what was previously familiar." The essays were for the "left hand," remarked Jeremy Anglin in the introduction to the collection *Beyond the Information Given*, "because [the book] was concerned with the intuitive and creative aspects of knowing which complement the more orderly, rational, and mathematical skills of

the 'right hand.' It dealt with knowing through art and poetry, through myth and man's image of himself. The essays in this book again reflected Bruner's persistent effort to achieve a more integrated conception of human cognition, in this case by viewing man not only as a scientist and logician but also as humanist and artist."

Also revealing and accessible is Bruner's autobiography, *In Search of Mind*, an urbane, candid, even chatty commentary on his life and career, written at the request of the Alfred P. Sloan Foundation, which had commissioned several scientists to explain their lives and their commitment to science. He describes his decision to leave Harvard in 1972 to take up a newly established chair in psychology at Oxford, the Watts professorship, which included a fellowship at Wolfson College, a new graduate institution. He was, he writes, "attracted to a new start in a new setting, wearied of the familiar outlines of Harvard's political squabbles and of the back-and-forth of the behavioral sciences there." Yet despite his "nonadministrative" chair (entailing no head-of-department duties) and his strong liking for the social diversions afforded by English university life, he had determined within five years of his arrival there to leave Oxford. His department of experimental psychology was to blame: it "was sadly compartmentalized. . . . Its members were fiercely hardworking, both as teachers and as researchers, but one had the strong impression that the atmosphere of criticism kept them prudently turned in on their own specialties." The department was "institutionally appalling! I have rarely seen an unhappier one. Its unhappiness was, I think, brewed from several bitter roots. For one, psychology is not much appreciated or admired in Britain, and certainly not much in Oxford. . . . There is . . . more than a little self-hatred among British psychologists, and it is usually displaced into dismissiveness toward specialties down-market in rigor from one's own. Some British psychologists, indeed, are never so flattered as when taken for a physiologist or pharmacologist or geneticist. This curious turn of mind . . . may, historically, be an echo of the hopeless struggle of psychology to fight free of philosophy, to achieve a unique 'methodology' untainted by philosophical presuppositions." Bruner left Oxford in 1980.

In 1984, at nearly seventy years of age, Bruner was appointed to the George Herbert Mead university professorship at the New School for Social Research, New York City. At the same time he became a fellow, and two years later the director, of the New York Institute for the Humanities at New York University. In this post he has hoped to promote a cross-fertilization of cognitive psychology—which he believes has become as a subdiscipline somewhat narrow and sterile—with philosophy, literature, and the arts. The ten essays in *Actual Minds, Possible Worlds* represent Bruner's attempt, based on his research into anthropology, philosophy of language, literary theory, and linguistics, as well as philosophy, to formulate the kinds of mental processes involved in our creation of world-versions. He makes the radical claim that there are two distinct "modes of cognitive functioning, two modes of thought, each providing distinctive ways of ordering experience, of constructing reality. The two (though complementary) are irreducible to one another." The first is the "paradigmatic mode": it proceeds via causal explanation and is most usually and successfully realized in the sciences. The second is the "narrative mode"; it proceeds via storytelling and concerns "the vicissitudes of human intention." He has no patience with those cognitive psychologists who devote themselves to creating computer-like models of cognition—such people impoverish psychology. "Basing a view of the mind on compute-ability leaves too much out of the story," he said in 1987. "It rules out things like beliefs, desires, emotions, expectations, and intentions."

Bruner is a fellow of several professional societies: of the American Psychological Association, which he served as president in 1964–1965 (he had won its Distinguished Scientific Contribution Award in 1962); of the American Academy of Arts and Sciences; of the Society for the Psychological Study of Social Issues, of which he is also past president; and of the American Association of University Professors. He holds U.S. honorary degrees from Lesley College (1964) and from Northwestern (1965), Temple (1965), Cincinnati (1966), Northern Michigan (1969), Duke (1969), and Yale (1975) universities. His foreign honorary degrees include those from New Brunswick (1969), Sheffield (1970), Oxford (1972), Bristol (1975), Leuven (1976), and Ghent (1977) universities, and from the Sorbonne (1974).

PRINCIPAL WORKS: Public Thinking on Post-War Problems, 1943; Mandate from the People, 1944; (with J. Goodnow and G. Austin) A Study of Thinking, 1956, repr., 1977; (with M. Smith and R. White) Opinions and Personality, 1956; The Process of Education, 1960, repr., 1977; On Knowing, 1962, repr., 1979; Man: A Course of Study, 1965; Toward a Theory of Instruction, 1966; Processes of Cognitive Growth: Infancy, 1968; The Relevance of Education, 1971, rev. ed., 1973; Communication as Language, 1982; In Search of Mind, 1983; Child's Talk, 1984; Actual Minds, Possible Worlds, 1986. *As editor*—(with D. Krech) Perception and Personality, 1950, repr., 1968; Learning about Learning, 1966; (with K. Connolly) The Growth of Competence, 1974; (with A. Jolly and K. Sylva) Play: Its Role in Evolution and Development, 1976; (with A. Garton) Human Growth and Development, 1978; Under Five in Britain, 1980. *As contributor*—Contemporary Approaches to Cognition, 1957; Logique et perception, 1958; (H. Murray, ed.) Myth and Mythmaking, 1959; Studies in Cognitive Growth, 1966; (V. Denenberg, ed.) Education of the Infant and Young Child, 1970; (R. Leeper, ed.) Dare to Care/Dare to Act: Racism in Education, 1971; (M. Meyer and F. Hite, eds.) The Application of Learning Principles to Classroom Instruction, 1971; (J. Anglin, ed.) Beyond the Information Given, 1973.

ABOUT: Bruner, J. In Search of Mind, 1983; Contemporary Authors New Revision Series 1, 1981; Olson, D. R. (ed.) The Social Foundations of Language and Thought: Essays in Honor of Jerome S. Bruner, 1980; Who's Who, 1989. *Periodicals*—America January 7–14, 1984; Booklist June 1, 1962; Book Week February 20, 1966; Choice October 1967, September 1966, November 1971, March 1977, February 1984, March 1984, September 1986; Christian Science Monitor June 15, 1962; Commentary July 1966; Educational Studies Fall 1977; Harvard Educational Review Summer 1966, Summer 1967; May 1977, Library Journal May 1, 1962; February 1, 1966; May 15, 1971; August 1983; September 15, 1983; July 1986; Nation November 15, 1971; National Review May 22, 1966; New Republic December 26, 1983; June 9, 1986; New Statesman April 13, 1984; New York Review of Books April 14, 1966; New York Times October 20, 1987; New York Times Book Review November 18, 1962; February 20, 1966; January 8, 1984; March 23, 1986; Psychology Today October 1983; Quill & Quire February 1984; Saturday Review June 16, 1962; Science April 8, 1966; May 18, 1984; Science Books and Films January–February 1987; Teachers College Record October 1966, April 1967; Times Literary Supplement July 13, 1984; November 21, 1986.

BRUTUS, DENNIS (pseudonym JOHN BRUIN) (November 28, 1924–   ), South African poet, writes: "Born of South African parents in Salisbury, Southern Rhodesia (now Harare, Zimbabwe) and moved at a very young age, due to a change in parents' teaching positions, with my older brother Wilfred and sisters Helena (older) and Dolly (younger) to a ghetto township in Port Elizabeth, South Africa, designated for coloureds under apartheid law. I grew up imbued with a sense of fair play: a yearning for justice and sympathy for the exploited. I believe that this has animated my activities in sport, poetry and academia and explains my battle against apartheid, racism and injustice, which began in college.

"Through the good fortune of qualifying for a merit scholarship, I was able to attend Fort Hare University, the only university in South Africa for non-whites, and earned teacher certifi-

DENNIS BRUTUS

cation with majors in English (Distinction) and psychology. My interest in sport brought me into contact with the black athletes on campus who I discovered were exceptionally talented with the best records in the country, but who were ineligible for the Olympic team. My letter writing on behalf of two weight lifters, whose strength should have qualified them for the all-white Olympic team, led to being elected secretary of the local sports association.

"After graduation in 1947, I returned to Port Elizabeth and taught English at St. Thomas Aquinas High School from 1948–1949 and then worked as a social welfare officer with the Social Welfare Department of Port Elizabeth from 1949–1950. From 1950–1961 I taught English at Paterson High School, and from 1962–1983 at Central High School. In 1950, I married May Jaggers and we gave birth to eight children over the next eighteen years: Jacinta, Marc, Julian, Antony, Justina, Cornelia, Gregory and Paula. The urgency and allegiance of my mission against apartheid was not displaced through my marriage and growing family: *My continental sense of sorrow drove me to work and at times I hoped to shape your better world.*

"While teaching, I saw the inequities between black and white education and attacked them. Through the Social Welfare Department I saw the same inequities between black and white housing, and attacked them as well. I was committed to helping and inspiring my students to become as well educated as possible to take their place as equals in a society that dictated their inequality and inferiority. I challenged these un-

just prejudices and joined with like-minded teachers and parents to offer classes to students underground in garages and after hours at various homes.

"While teaching, I remained active on the question of why black athletes who were scoring the best records in the country were ineligible for the Olympic team and was told by the South African Olympic team that they couldn't qualify for the team because they are black. I pointed out that Clause One of the Olympic Charter states that any country that discriminates on the grounds of race, religion, or politics cannot be included in the Olympics, and asked if they were aware of that. Sure, they said. I told them that they might get expelled, and their response was to go ahead and try. It was on the grounds of that invitation that SASA (South African Sports Association) was formed in 1958. I became Founding Secretary and we launched an international campaign to have South Africa excluded from the Olympic Games. Determined to stifle antiapartheid organizing, the government issued its first banning order against me in 1961, which made it a crime for me to write. The moment I realized that a man or a woman's creative talent could be destroyed by law, it infuriated me to such an extent that as an act of defiance, I began taking up writing seriously, which I had not done previously. I began to seek publication opportunities outside of South Africa. Another consequence of my banning was that I applied for and received a scholarship from Leeds University in England and began to study for an LL.B. (Law) Degree at Witwatersrand University in Johannesburg from 1962–1963.

"Meanwhile, interesting developments were occurring on the sport front as well. Correspondence from SASA to Avery Brundage, President of the International Olympic Committee (governing body of the Olympic Games), was being returned unanswered and at times even unopened. We were informed that no correspondence pertaining to the Olympics was relevant unless it was from an Olympic organization. Accordingly, SASA became SAN-ROC (South African Non-Racial Olympic Committee) in 1963. Our campaign started to gain momentum and I was served with further banning orders from the Secret Police which made it a crime for me to teach, attend any meeting, belong to any organization, attend a sporting event, or to be with more than two people other than my family at any one time. In defiance of this attack against me, I was spontaneously elected to the Honorary Position of Founding President of SAN-ROC, in recognition of establishing sport as an area of activism against apartheid.

"I continued my work against racism in sport despite the two bannings, to the point of going to the office of the Olympic Association in Johannesburg to raise the question of the black athlete with Olympic officials before their meeting began, as my banning order prohibited my attendance or participation at the meeting. While I was talking with the officials, two members of the Secret Police jumped out of the big cupboard in the wall where the Gestetner duplicating equipment and stencils were kept, and arrested me. I was charged with the crime of attending a sports meeting, despite the fact that the meeting had not yet begun when I was arrested. I was sentenced to eighteen months in jail and released on bail. While on bail pending trial, I fled to Mozambique but was recaptured at Nkomati and returned to South Africa by the Portuguese Secret Police through their reciprocity agreement with the South African Secret Police. Under guard of two South African Secret Police marksmen, driving me to prison, I knew, while riding in the car, that I must make a second attempt to escape, and let my friends, who were celebrating my escape, know that I had been recaptured, convicted and returned to South Africa for imprisonment.

"When the car stopped to let me off to walk to the prison at McClean Square, one of the policemen went to the trunk of the car to remove my suitcase. When I got out of the car, I was carrying my suitcase, the same one I had escaped to Mozambique with. I walked along carrying it, as if it were very heavy, and when I got to the sidewalk in front of the prison, I put it down on the sidewalk. I was in a crouching position, like a sprinter, took off from that position, and dashed off into the crowd, before the guards realized what had happened. I knew they were armed, but I thought that in that Tuesday afternoon, end of the work-day rush hour crowd, they would not shoot, simply because there were too many people. But, when I turned a corner, I ran into one of the Secret Police assigned to guard me, and was shot at such close range that the bullet entered through my back and exited through my chest (a through-and-through wound). I leaned against the wall, and was ordered by the policemen to walk back to prison. Bleeding heavily, I collapsed on the sidewalk. Lying in a pool of my own blood, I looked up, saw the skyscraper headquarters of the Anglo-American Corporation towering over me, and understood with a blinding clarity my role to help end corporate investment's bondage of my people. The ambulance that arrived to transport me to hospital drove off, upon realizing I was a 'coloured' and another ambulance for non-whites had to be called.

"While in hospital, I managed to successfully write my first year law exam, amidst seemingly insurmountable mental and physical pain. Not yet having recovered from my bullet injury, I was transferred from hospital to the notorious Robben Island Prison where I remained from March 1964 to July 1965. I broke stones on a rockpile with, among other leading political prisoners, Nelson Mandela and Walter Sisulu. We were subjected to spirit-breaking mental and physical abuse, hard labor and beatings by our wardens, who were common law criminals. We were also forced to run and exercise until we dropped. When I requested an appointment with the prison doctor to inform him that I was being made to exercise and to run until I drop and that I couldn't do it with the bullet injury that still was not healed, his reply to me was: 'Brutus, aren't you the man who was so keen on the Olympics? You should be grateful for the opportunity to exercise.'

"While I was on Robben Island, news came of South Africa's expulsion from the Olympic Games. Fellow prisoners and I cheered aloud at this victory, knowing that brutal reprisals awaited us after this Kafkaesque celebration. Also while imprisoned, publication of my first book of poetry *Sirens, Knuckles, Boots*, was completed and straightaway banned in South Africa. I was confronted in prison with a copy of the publication and asked if I was responsible for the work. I readily admitted that I was and a prosecution was initiated, but dropped for lack of sufficient charging evidence. The banning against me was expanded to the point where it became illegal to own a book of my poetry, to be found in possession of a book of my poetry owned by someone else, to recite my poetry in public, or even to quote my poetry in a review.

"Released from prison in 1965 with my spirit steeled instead of broken, I lived under house arrest for one year in Port Elizabeth and departed from South Africa for England on July 30, 1966 as an exile on an exit-permit document. Though issued to me, the government retained the document, stamped CANCELLED, as evidence to imprison me immediately if I attempted to return. Upon arrival in England, I became director of the World Campaign for the Release of South African Political Prisoners and served as representative to the United Nations for the International Defense and Aid Fund from 1966–1971. After working with IDAF in England for approximately one year, they brought my wife and seven children, who were still in South Africa, over as well. Our eighth child, Paula, was born in England. While working with IDAF I was also busy organizing my second book of poetry, *Letters to Martha*, consisting of poems recounting experiences as a political prisoner on Robben Island, which had been written as letters to my sister-in-law, Martha, after my brother Wilfred, who was also active against apartheid, had been sent to Robben Island for a term of imprisonment. His term began upon my release, utterly confusing the guards and prison officials!

"In 1970, I was offered a Visiting Professorship in the English Department at the University of Denver in Colorado for Winter Quarter and accepted it. In 1971, I was offered a teaching position, which I accepted, as a specialist scholar in African literature at Northwestern University's English Department in Evanston, Illinois, which I maintained with tenure, until 1985.

"Shortly after being hired at Northwestern, I organized a successful, widely publicized civil disobedience action at the Wimbledon Games in London. This protest took place because the English Lawn Tennis Association (ELTA) refused to take any action of its own against South Africa, whose government continued to participate in the games. I was the only one to be arrested, and was filmed on British national television, being carried off of the court. Samuel Hines, chairman of Northwestern's English Department, who had just hired me as the new professor in his Department, was in London at the time, saw this action recapped on television, was startled, and subsequently testified on my behalf at the trial to follow! Several days before the demonstration and arrest, my brother Wilfred had been arrested and charged with disturbing the peace after he tossed a rotten tomato in the face of South Africa's visiting Defense Minister. He was convicted, fined, and released on probation. After my arrest, however, they confused me for my brother and charged me with the additional crime of violating my probation. The police later discovered the mistake, but decided not to disclose their error and scheduled the case for trial.

"At the initial trial, the female magistrate dismissed the charges. The government appealed, noting that Scotland Yard had been thoroughly embarrassed as they were in charge of security at Wimbledon. The appeal went to the Queen's Bench which reversed the magistrate's decision in favor of the government's. Funded by IDAF for a second trial, I decided to appeal the government's decision to the House of Lords, the final appeal court in England. They ruled in my favor, setting a legal precedent in England known as Cousins v. Brutus, establishing the right to protest in public places and defining Wimbledon as a 'public place'.

"Returning to Northwestern University for teaching, I continued my mission of service against apartheid. In addition to teaching, I accepted literally cross-country speaking invitations to universities, churches, legislative testimonials, and community groups anxious to learn more about apartheid and the crucial role divestment plays in its dismantling. I also helped to organize principled campus and community outcries of conscience for divestment at the universities where I was teaching. I made the commitment, however, to keep my work against apartheid and teaching of African literature as two separate entities, as I feel this is the honest format to follow as a professor.

"In 1981, I was served with a deportation order from the Immigration and Naturalization Service and waged a relentless battle over the next three years, without relinquishing my South African citizenship, for political asylum in the United States. I became an asylee in September of 1983 on condition that *I cannot trade security for silence. If I had been offered political asylum on condition that I remained silent, I would have rejected it.* I consider the asylum victory a people's victory. It was only through the support of a dedicated legal team, and thousands of people internationally from all walks of life, who opposed my deportation, seeing it as a symbol of constructive engagement's destructiveness, that the victory was realized.

"As an exile and an asylee, I remain driven to serve the cause of freedom and peace in my country, South Africa, so inextricably interwoven with action against apartheid and for divestment in this country, the United States; with a prayer that *pain will be quiet, the prisoned free and wisdom sculpt justice from the world's jagged mass.*

Dennis Brutus began writing poetry in the 1950s. The first of his volumes, *Sirens, Knuckles, Boots*, was published in Nigeria in 1963, while he awaited the sentence that was to confine him to Robben Island. The volume resonates with the poets who were to remain the major influences on his work: Yeats, Hopkins, Donne, and Browning. But if his work is stylistically indebted to European models, it is thematically rooted in the distinctively South African violence and anguish which he knew so intimately from the country's jails and ghettoes. The title poem of *Sirens, Knuckles, Boots* provides the first hints of Brutus' sense of himself as speaking for apartheid's silent sufferers:

importunate as rain
the wraiths exhale their woe
over the sirens, knuckles, boots;
my sounds begin again

However, despite the directness of Brutus' political commitments, he shuns the label of protest poet:

> By reporting a simple experience I ask people to make up their own minds. . . . I don't think I myself would call this protest. I would say it functions as protest; it has the effect of protest. But I think it's poetry and not protest; it's not propaganda. The politics is not imported into it.

A lyrical version of this sentiment surfaces in "I must speak":

> . . . when your heart answers
> some strong assertion of the truth
> in blood, or action or belief and seeks for words
> let then my echoes rise
> unbidden
> in the tunnels of your mind.

While in solitary confinement, Brutus rethought many of the poetic directions he had taken in the first volume. Retrospectively, much of the language seemed too congested, ornamental, and inaccessible. He has described how he decided thereafter to seek a sparer, more direct language and to write with ordinary people in mind rather than students of poetry. Certainly, in his second and finest collection, *Letters to Martha, and Other Poems from a South African Prison*, he writes with a crisp control that avoids verbosity. These poems are both thematically and literally about survival. He wrote many of them during the six months after his release from Robben Island when, however, he was still restricted from traveling and forbidden to engage in literary or political writing. By casting his poems as letters to his sister-in-law, Brutus circumvented the literary proscription. As his brother had now been jailed on the Island, Brutus' letter-poems also helped console his sister-in-law by evoking the physical and emotional conditions of the prisoners.

Some of these early poems focus on the psychological battles between warders and prisoners, battles which become symbolic of the racial conflicts in the society at large. Despite the extremity of Brutus' circumstances, the tone of *Letters to Martha* is remarkably free of bitterness. It is, moreover, quite inward and self-effacing. Brutus reflects modestly on his own

> vague heroism
> mixed with self-pity
> and tempered by the knowledge of those
> who endure much more
> and endure . . . .

The forcefulness of his finest poems derives from a talent for negotiating his way between the public anger that shapes his activist self and a more reserved, meditative lyrical self. ("I cut away the public trappings to assert / certain private essentialities"). Even in the most politically motivated of his poems, one discerns a readiness to explore poetically his own vulnerabilities and the full range of human passions. The gulf between his innate poetic gentleness and the brutality of his society prompted the critic Ursula Barnett to remark that: "When reading Dennis Brutus's work, more than that of any other black South African writer, one becomes aware of the contrast between the essential nature of the poet and what the South African situation has forced him to become."

Brutus' work has always been marked by his sense of isolation. There are several reasons for this. First, he began writing poetry in the fifties and sixties, a period when almost all black South African writers preferred to work in prose. (By the seventies, the era when black South African poetry really burgeoned, Brutus was irremediably stranded abroad.) His sense of literary loneliness as a black South African lyricist sharpened the sense of isolation he endured first as a prisoner and subsequently as an exile. The themes of exile and homelessness surface in Brutus' third collection, *Poems from Algiers*. This very slender volume conveys his increasingly traumatic struggle to belong and to remember, his homesickness and his battle to sustain, through all his prodigious traveling on political and literary assignments, a sense of a directed, purposeful existence. From here on, these themes were to dominate his poetry. *Poems from Algiers* was occasioned by a visit to North Africa which, because of a climate and a quality in the light similar to Cape Town's, brought on waves of nostalgia, allowing him a restored if tenuous sense of identity. In 1970 Brutus published a further brief collection, *Thoughts Abroad*, under the pseudonym John Bruin, in the hopes that the volume would thereby circulate more freely in South Africa.

A Simple Lust contains selected lyrics from the four earlier volumes supplemented by unpublished work. The bulk of the poems are drawn from Brutus' London years, the period between 1966 and 1970 when he was traveling incessantly as a global campaigner against apartheid. The volume reflects deeply on the condition of exile and, particularly, on the contrast between England and South Africa. After the raw trauma of life under apartheid, he now finds himself surrounded by "efficient unhostile people" and worries that he may be seduced into a life of purposeless tranquility. Yet *A Simple Lust* suggests that he is in no danger of losing poetic contact with his memories of Robben Island. "Flying to Denmark," for instance, finds the poet, characteristically itinerant and self-questioning, urging that he may be

> armed with such passion, dedication, voice
> that every cobblestone would rear in wrath
> and batter down a prison's wall
> and wrench them from the island where they rot.

Brutus' American years have seen a falling in his poetic output and the intensity of the work. *Strains* gathers together poems from the previous fourteen years, while *China Poems* is devoted primarily to experiments with minimalist forms in the tradition of *haiku* and *Chueh chu*. Published in cursive script with Chinese translations, the poems are Brutus' response to an official visit to China. *Stubborn Hope* is more diffuse than Brutus' early volumes. The poetic mood is frequently one of fatigue and bewilderment yet with an overriding commitment, as the titular poem suggests, to political and poetic endurance. As the critic Ken Goodwin has remarked, "the later poems about South Africa and the campaign on which he is engaged tend to be more prosaic, oratorical and bare of imagery." This decline in the calibre of the works seems, to some extent, to reflect Brutus' growing ambivalence toward the value of the poetic craft when confronted with the scale of South African injustices. By contrast, much of the poet's more youthful work, especially *Letters to Martha*, stands as a spare, passionate, and closely crafted testament to human resilience in the face of great suffering. As the critic Gerald Moore has observed: "It is not so much the call to action that he is uniquely qualified to give, as the call to see, to hear and to know. Dennis Brutus has measured the difficulty of this task . . . and he has achieved in some poems a control which masters horror without diminishing its impact."

During his tenure at Northwestern University Brutus had visiting professorships at the University of Texas in Austin, Amherst, Dartmouth, and Swarthmore colleges. Since 1986 he has been chairman of the University of Pittsburgh's Department of Black Community Education Research and Development. He has traveled to poetry festivals in India and in Nicaragua, and he has received honorary Doctor of Humane Letters degrees from Worcester State College and the University of Massachusetts at Amherst.

PRINCIPAL WORKS: Sirens, Knuckles, Boots, 1963; Letters to Martha, and Other Poems from a South African Prison, 1968; Poems from Algiers, 1970; A Simple Lust, 1973; Strains, 1975; China Poems, 1975; Stubborn Hope, 1978, As *"John Bruin"* Thoughts Abroad, 1970

ABOUT: Barnett, U. A Vision of Order, 1983; Contemporary Authors New Revision Series 2, 1981; Contemporary Literary Criticism 43, 1987; Goodwin, K. L. Understanding African Poetry, 1982; Pieterse, C. and D. Duerden, African Writers Talking, 1972; Zell, H. M., C. Bundy, V. Coulon (eds.) A New Reader's Guide to African Literature, 2nd ed., 1983. *Periodicals*—Ariel 13, 1982, 17, 1986; World Literature Today 55, 1981.

*CAO YU (formerly TS'AO YÜ, pseudonym of Wan Chia-pao) (September 24, 1910–   ), Chinese playwright, writes in 1986: "I was born into an old-fashioned, feudal family. My father, a graduate from an army school in Japan, served the Qing Dynasty as an officer. My mother died three days after she gave birth to me. When I was quite young, my father went to find a family tutor for me, teaching all the traditions of the Four Books and the Five Classics. However, in my family there is a rich collection of classical works of ancient Chinese literature. As a result, soon after I could read and write, I began to immerse myself in reading such novels as *The Dream of the Red Chamber*, *Journey to the West*, and *Water Margins*. To a boy who lost his mother from infancy, and who had become lonely and melancholy, these books offered me a spiritual calmness. For this, I will pay perpetual gratitude to my father who didn't forbid me to read these books. Some senior officials at that time considered those books evil.

"Though my father was very kind and generous to me, I still felt suppressed by my life in this feudal family. An enslaved society completely ignores the nature of humanity and this made me feel even more angry and rebellious. I began to sympathize with the common folk living in poverty and ignorance. I had an aged nursemaid at home, whom I called Mama Duan. She often told me what happened in the rural areas, about the miserable death of her son and then of her husband, and about how her mother-in-law finally committed suicide. She was a good nursemaid for me, enlightening my road through life.

"At the age of eleven, I was sent to a government-run school of translation in Tianjin to study English. There I began to read foreign literature, eg. Shakespeare, Dickens, and Maupassant. 'The Last Lesson' by Alphonse Daudet touched me deeply, and I felt the immense power of literature. Another novel, *The Adventures of Robinson Crusoe*, also cast a spell upon me. In a later essay 'My Life as Well as Career in Literary Creations,' I wrote that the work 'excited my imagination, and made me dream all day long about making voyages out to sea.'

"In 1924, when I was fourteen, I read for the

°sô yū

CAO YU

first time a collection of short stories by Lu Xun. The ultimate fate of ordinary people living under a feudal system, as Lu Xun depicts, touched me greatly. I remembered the stories Mama Duan told me, and I felt sympathetic for the working people. At the same period of time, I also read the works of Kuo Mo-jo and others. In those dark and suffocating days, this new literature of anti-feudalism broadened my horizon. I formed the belief that our decadent social system would finally be shattered. I felt my blood boiling for a fight with evil.

"My interest in plays can be traced back to my childhood. According to the memories of some of my relatives, I was lost at the age of four while watching the Peking Opera and other, local plays. One day I had even said, 'It is really a wonderful thing to watch plays.' Of course, it wasn't until after I entered Nankai Middle School that I really began to perform on stage, and sometimes even write plays myself. I joined Nankai Troupe of New Plays, quite well-known then, with a repertoire including many progressive plays. I soon became its leading member. This experience of performing on stage showed me what audiences like or dislike, and what they need and do not need. Though I was obsessed with the dream of becoming an actor, my performance proved that I was not a born actor. As a result, I decided to give it up. Nevertheless, my stage experience was of great benefit to me when I turned to writing years later.

"In 1933, when I was twenty-four, I was a graduate student in the Western Literature department in Qinghua University. I started to write *Thunderstorm* (*Lei-yu*), an idea I had conceived five years before. I finished it within four months. *Thunderstorm* was not my first writing, but it proved to be the first of importance. Government authorities at that time imposed a ban on it, claiming that it advocated incest. The play stirred up wide attention and strong social response.

"From *Thunderstorm* to *Sunrise* (*Jih-ch'u*) to *Wilderness* (*Yuan-yeh*) to *Peking Man* (*Pei-ching-jen*), every play of mine was written under accumulated pressures of intense emotions. In those years, wandering in this transformed society, I had encounters with events and people that loomed like nightmares. I will never forget these things till my death. They crystalized into serious issues that attacked my brain relentlessly. The events set my emotion on fire and intensified my desire to seek justice. Finally, out from my pen flowed my protest and desire to seek justice.

"In 1949, a new China was founded and from then on, I read many works by Karl Marx. I also wrote several plays, before the Cultural Revolution, including *Ming-lang-ti-t'ien* (*Bright Skies*), *Danjian pian* (A Story of Courage and Sword), and "Lady Wang Zhojun." The latter was only finished in 1978. Looking back on ten years of cultural catastrophe, I now feel that these plays, though they have some merits, are greatly handicapped by the political tide of that time.

"As a writer, I am fortunate in that I have experienced events big or small in Chinese modern history. I underwent ups and downs and saw many twists and turns. Now I am seventy-six years old, in poor health. But still I feel the impulse to write, before my life ends, more works with my pen—not those cheap plays shackled by political slogans, but works of art condensed from life itself."

————

The following note was written for *World Authors 1980–1985* by Shen Jun, a staff writer for China Features in Beijing and a close friend of Cao Yu's:

"When *Thunderstorm* first appeared in the *Literary Quarterly* in July 1934, it did not stir up much notice. The play became a hit, however, in April 1935 when a group of Chinese students studying overseas put it on stage in Japan. Owing to time limits and trouble with the Japanese police, the performers omitted part of the original script. Even so the play was widely acclaimed. A Japanese critic praised it for completing the leap of Chinese stage plays from the era of Mei Lanfang to that of the vernacular. Chinese critic Cao Juren punned on the play's title:

'In the perspective of the history of Chinese drama, 1935 marks the date when plays in China entered the time of thunderstorm.' Soon after, every kind of stage performance, from local Shanghai opera to Yue opera to so-called 'civilized' plays, put on their own version of *Thunderstorm*.

"Soon after publishing *Thunderstorm*, Cao began his second major work, *Sunrise*. To gather raw material for this play, he went into poverty-stricken areas to interview the 'insulted and injured' poor. In early 1936, Lu Xun, the representative writer of the 'New Culture' movement, told American journalist Edgar Snow that the 'best playwrights living in China now include Kuo Mo-jo, Tian Han, Hong Shen, and a newly emerged left-wing writer, Cao Yu.' *Sunrise* was published in installments in the *Literary Quarterly* beginning in June 1936.

"Often asked about the symbolic meaning of *Thunderstorm*, Cao Yu wrote: 'I cannot point it out clearly, but I have made efforts to let the audience feel it.' In the preface to his 1936 edition of the play he wrote that at first 'I did not sense clearly what I wanted to correct, satirize and attack. Perhaps it was near the end that I vaguely felt a kind of emotion rushing out to push me on, and I gave vent to a long pent-up fury. I cursed both the family and society in China.' But the writer stressed that 'I was mainly writing a poem, a narrative one . . . there may have been some concrete events in it, such as workers' strikes, but it was by no means a mere play of social problems.'

"As plays exposing reality, *Thunderstorm*, *Sunrise*, as well as his later plays *The Wilderness* and *Peking Man* were inevitably condemned by the corrupt governments of the time. The Nationalist authorities charged that *Thunderstorm* taught incest and they arrested the actors playing in it, forcing them to acknowledge that they were Communists. Between 1937 and 1945 Cao wrote several plays about the Chinese resistance to their Japanese aggressors. *Shui-Pien* (Metamorphosis), published in 1939, is probably the most important. Cao wrote that the play's keynote shows 'the tendency to transform the old into new in our nation's war against Japan.' The play met with the interference of Chiang Kai-shek's government and was at one time banned because at the end, the protagonist doctor waves a red body bag, as if waving a red flag, to say goodbye to a wounded soldier. Owing to pressure from the public, the ban was finally lifted.

"With the founding of the People's Republic of China in 1949, Cao continued to write plays, prose, and poetry. During the Cultural Revolution, however, he was labeled a reactionary and

beaten. It was only after 1978 that he was restored his public position. He is now head of the Beijing People's Art Theatre as well as honorary Dean of the Central Drama Institute."

————

Internationally recognized today as one of the major Chinese playwrights of the twentieth century, Cao Yu has been a pioneer in the development of the dramatic genre *huaju* or "speech drama." His early plays, written in spoken dialogue, broke with the traditional song pattern of Chinese drama and dealt boldly with modern issues of family and social conflict. Influenced by the Western dramatists he had read—Aeschylus among the ancients, and the moderns Ibsen, Chekhov, and O'Neill—"he was able to objectify his own people's dreams for fulfillment during a time of momentous national change," as Christopher C. Rand writes.

Cao's first three plays—*Thunderstorm*, *Sunrise*, and *The Wilderness*—form a tragic trilogy of the downfall of Chinese bourgeois society through family feuding, corruption, and greed. Fatalistic, even nihilistic, they reach beyond political ideology to depict "cosmic cruelty." In *Thunderstorm* the secret past of a wealthy and respected mine owner is unfolded with stark and violent tragedy for his whole family. In *Sunrise*, set in the economic depression of the 1930s, a poverty-stricken young girl is forced into prostitution while a wealthy and privileged young woman who finds herself powerless to save her commits suicide in despair. In her death Cao symbolizes the destruction of an entire social system. As he told an interviewer in 1980: "Those gentlemen and gentlewomen who are fond of *Sunrise* . . . don't understand the sentences in the play which expose their lives as parasites." In *The Wilderness* a man who has been railroaded to prison escapes to avenge the ruin of his family by a greedy landlord. The third act of this play shows the direct influence of O'Neill's expressionist play *The Emperor Jones* with the protagonist, now a fugitive in the forest, haunted by visions of the people he has killed. Another of O'Neill's expressionist dramas, *The Hairy Ape*, influenced the characterization in Cao's *Peking Man*, whose protagonist, though living in the modern world, is a primitive, "almost a purely biological phenomenon," as David Y. Chen describes him in an essay in the journal *Modern Drama*.

In spite of a clearly affirmed political ideology, Rand and Joseph Lau point out in their Introduction to *The Wilderness*, these plays were criticized during the period of Maoist repression not only for showing European/Western influence but also for being too mystical and fatalistic and not sufficiently "social." In 1952 Cao was obliged to repudiate this early work, but with the end of the Cultural Revolution his works have been widely published, produced on stage, and made into films.

WORKS IN ENGLISH TRANSLATION: *Thunderstorm* was first translated into English as *Thunder and Rain* by Yao Hsin-nung and published in *T'ien Hsia Monthly* from October 1936 to February 1937. In 1958 it was translated as *Thunderstorm* by Wang Tso-liang and A. C. Barnes. *Sunrise* was translated by Wang Tso-liang and A. C. Barnes in 1960. Chang Pei-chi translated *Bright Skies* in 1960. *The Wilderness* was translated by Christopher C. Rand and Joseph S. M. Lau in 1980. *Peking Man* was translated by Leslie Nai-kwai Lo, with Don Cohn and Michelle Vosper, in 1986.

ABOUT: Biographical Dictionary of Republican China 3, 1967–1971; Bowers, F. Theatre in the East, 1956; Encyclopedia of World Literature in the 20th Century 4, 1984; Frenz, H. (ed.) Asia and the Humanities, 1959; Hu, J.Y.H. Ts'ao Yü, 1973; Lau, J.S.M. Ts'ao Yü, 1970; Rand, C. C. and J.S.M. Lau. *Introduction to* The Wilderness. *Periodicals*—Comparative Drama 2, 1968; Modern Drama 9, 1967; Yearbook of Comparative and General Literature 15, 1966.

CAPUTO, PHILIP (JOSEPH), (June 10, 1941–), American novelist, journalist, and non-fiction writer, writes: "I may be one of the last American novelists to have achieved some measure of literary success without first taking a Master of Fine Arts in creative writing. I owe this piece of good fortune to my parents and Italian immigrant forebears, who, though they respected higher education, believed that experience was indeed the best teacher. My father, a machinist and carpenter, a craftsman of the highest order, taught me the importance of care, precision, and attention to detail in performing one's work. To watch him build a room, repair a machine, or overhaul an automobile was to learn more about the qualities needed in the writer's craft than could be gained in the classrooms of literary theoreticians. My father did not go to school to study his trades; he learned them by practicing them, using the two things God gave us to set us apart from the rest of creation: the human hand and the human brain.

"When I was in high school, he set himself the task of converting our attic into a bedroom for me. It was quite difficult, as the room was irregular in shape, and had a ceiling that dropped in two places into sloping double angles. As I recall, the job took him nearly a year to complete. Doubtless, he could have finished sooner if he'd cheated. He could have used pre-fabricated pan-

PHILIP CAPUTO

elling instead of tongue-in-groove knotty pine, each board cut, sanded and fitted by hand. He could have hidden the rough corner and ceiling joints with molding instead of finishing them so carefully that you could run a finger over them without feeling the slightest imperfection. Why did he put himself through such trouble? It certainly wasn't for money or fame—they didn't pay tradesmen a lot in those days, and didn't hand out prizes for doing good work. He didn't do it to earn praise from others. I think he had the now-antiquated notion that if you were given a talent or an ability, then you were required to use it to the fullest. The knowledge that you had done something as best as you could was its own reward, and did not need confirmation in the form of bonus checks or slaps on the back from the boss.

"I try to work with words the way my father worked with wood and steel. I want my sentences to fit together as seamlessly as his planks, my paragraphs to be as rock-solid as his studs and cross-braces. I want to do what he did— make things that last."

———

Philip Caputo was born in Chicago, Illinois, the son of Joseph (a plant manager) and Marie Ylonda (Napolitan) Caputo. He received his B.A. degree from Loyola University (Chicago) in 1964 and served as a second lieutenant in the U.S. Marine Corps from 1964–1967, a tour of duty that included combat experience in Vietnam. After his discharge from the Marine Corps, he became a journalist in Chicago, reporting on city news for the *Chicago Tribune* from 1969–1972. In 1972, with William Hugh Jones, he received a Pulitzer Prize for coverage of primary election fraud. Beginning in 1972 Caputo served as a foreign correspondent for the *Tribune*. He was head of the paper's Rome bureau from 1972–1974, during which time he covered the October 1973 war in the Middle East, and he received the George Polk Award (1973) from the Overseas Press Club for his reporting on his capture by Palestinian guerrillas. During 1974–1976, he was assigned to Beirut, where he covered the Lebanese civil war, as well as the Ethiopian civil war, and the Turkish invasion of Cyprus. He also returned to Vietnam to cover the fall of Saigon in 1975 and was among the last reporters to leave the city. While reporting on the Lebanese civil war in the same year, he was shot in the left ankle and right foot by Moslem gunmen but managed to crawl to safety. After six weeks in hospitals in Beirut, Germany, and Chicago, he spent the next year convalescing, during which time he received word of the acceptance of his Vietnam war memoir, *A Rumor of War*.

A Rumor of War, a Book-of-the Month Club selection, was widely regarded as one of the important new books on Vietnam from the point of view of those who participated in it. As a twenty-four-year-old officer, Caputo landed at Da Nang on March 8, 1965 with the 9th Marine Expeditionary Brigade in the earliest stage of American involvement in the war. His recollections in the memoir include both candid admissions of exultation in combat (virtually as an orgasmic experience) and of exhaustion, dehumanization, and disillusionment—a sense of the war's brutal pointlessness. His experience also included an incident in which two villagers were killed as Viet Cong suspects, though actually innocent, and for which Caputo was court-martialed, although charges were eventually dropped and Caputo later honorably discharged. The reviewer for the *Virginia Quarterly Review* remarked that *A Rumor of War* "is unquestionably the very best book to appear on the Vietnam war and one of the finest pieces of American writing on war from the ground in this century." Also reviewing the book in superlatives, William Styron, in the *New York Review of Books,* remarked that "Some of Caputo's troubled, searching meditations on the love and hate of war, on fear, and the ambivalent discord that warfare can create in the hearts of decent men, are among the most eloquent I have read in modern literature. . . . In this book Philip Caputo writes so beautifully and honestly about fear and courage, writing with such knowing reticence about death and

men's confrontation with the abyss, that we cannot doubt for an instant that he is a brave man who fought well after that 'splendid little war' became an obscene nightmare in which he nearly drowned."

Although Caputo claimed in the book that he was writing of one man's personal experience only, some reviewers felt that his experience formed an indictment of the war for his generation. Theodore Solotaroff, in the *New York Times Book Review,* for example, observed that "the ultimate effect of the book is to make the personal and the public responsibility merge into a nightmare of horror and waste experienced humanly by the Caputos and inhumanly by the politicians and generals. Out of the force of his obsession with the war and his role in it, Caputo has revealed the broken idealism and suppressed agony of America's involvement. *A Rumor of War* is the troubled conscience of America speaking passionately, truthfully, finally." Some reviewers, although admiring the book, expressed reservations of one sort or another. William J. Bennett, in *Commentary*, noted that "Much of the first half of the book is overwritten, and the neat, consecutive recall of the raising of Caputo's consciousness is more likely an invention after the fact than a report." And C.D.B. Bryan, in the *Saturday Review,* commented that "if I were to pick the major fault of his book, it would be that the understanding he brings to himself in his prologue is missing in his portrayal of the others with whom he served. Caputo is a reporter, with a reporter's aversion to characterization, but a book of this sort demands more than just the name-rank-and-serial-number details he gives us if we are to share his sense of loss over the death of his comrades." Caputo's large overview of the American combat experience, nevertheless, struck Bryan as an "extraordinary accomplishment."

Caputo was the *Chicago Tribune*'s foreign correspondent in Moscow in 1976-1977, and in 1980 he covered the Soviet invasion of Afghanistan for *Esquire* magazine. Since then he has devoted himself entirely to fiction. His first novel, *Horn of Africa*, a large, 500-page work, became a bestseller. Drawing on his first-hand experience of the region, Caputo creates a complicated and harrowing tale of several U.S. intelligence agents who undertake a secret mission in Ethiopia, the purpose of which is to smuggle arms to a warlike Islamic tribe and to help them fight the central Ethiopian government. It develops, however, that Nordstrand, the central figure, is really interested in pursuing his own murderous impulses beyond the restraints of civilization. Randall Kennedy, in the *New Republic*, remarked that *Horn of Africa* "is an ambitious work meant to last beyond the vagaries of a single literary season and to say something of permanence about the human condition. Caputo succeeds when he describes the psychological effect of violence upon its perpetrators and victims. . . . [He] runs into trouble, however, when he too obviously strives to make *Horn of Africa* weighty. He puts Nietzsche into his narrative by propping a paperback copy of *Beyond Good and Evil* into Nordstrand's hands and filling his mouth with drivel about supermen. And while Caputo never expressly mentions Conrad, his influence hovers over *Horn of Africa*." Anthony Astrachan, in the *Nation,* remarked that "the Nietzschean character is sophomoric so often (and keeps his author in the same condition) that the moral conflict never rouses us to real agony, to the true horror of evil."

Horn of Africa was followed by *Del Corso's Gallery*, about a Vietnam veteran and photojournalist who returns to Vietnam ten years after his initial tour of duty, to witness the fall of Saigon in 1975. Later, in Beirut, covering the Moslem-Christian conflict, he carries a burden of guilt for not having shown the atrocity of war in its full brutality; through the novel he seeks expiation. *Del Corso's Gallery* attracted less attention than Caputo's two previous books, and critics tended to feel that he was effective chiefly in scenes of action and violence. Joe Klein, in the *New York Times Book Review*, observed that Caputo "writes with all the subtlety of a punch in the gut, but his descriptions of combat photographers and correspondents at work are right on the money. Like his hero, though, the author seems far more comfortable in ravaged Beirut than in the putatively civilized world of New York." Writing in the *Christian Science Monitor,* Regina Millette Frawley remarked that *Del Corso's Gallery* is authentic. "Yet, the personal flavor of Vietnam is mysteriously missing. Instead, *Del Corso's Gallery* seems novel-writing-by-headlines—familiar events and stereotypes strung together as a plot."

Caputo's third novel, *Indian Country*, about a returned Vietnam veteran suffering from post-traumatic stress disorder, received mixed reviews. Michiko Kakutani, in the *New York Times,* remarked that "much of the novel is familiar from news reports, and there are portions of *Indian Country* where Mr. Caputo's hero, Christian Starkmann, seems more like a representative man—a neatly packaged set of problems—than like a character with a psychology and history of his own. The people in his past—including the cold, judgmental father he defied by going off to war and the best friend he joined by signing up—are too sketchily defined to ever become more than broad, Freudian symbols,

and the people in his present can seem similarly opaque." She conceded, however, that "in cutting back and forth between Chris's memories of the war—recreated with frightening, dreamlike power—and his current paranoia, Mr. Caputo does a brilliant job of communicating his increasingly crazed state of mind." John Byrne Cooke, in the *Washington Post Book World,* felt that "the narrative of Starkmann's struggle rarely equals the standard set by Caputo's previous work" but was strongly impressed by the "unexpected power of the ending." "Although in many ways a less capable narrative than those that preceded it," he concluded, "it is by far the most moving."

Caputo married Jill Esther Ongemach in 1969, and from this marriage, ending in divorce in 1982, he has two sons, Geoffrey Jacob and Marc Anthony. In 1982 he married Marcelle Lynn Besse; they were divorced three years later. In 1988 he married Leslie Blanchard Ware, an editor.

PRINCIPAL WORKS: *Non-fiction*—A Rumor of War, 1977. *Fiction*—Horn of Africa, 1980; Del Corso's Gallery, 1983; Indian Country, 1986.

ABOUT: Biden, P. American Literature and the Experience of Vietnam, 1982; Contemporary Authors 73–76, 1978; Contemporary Literary Criticism 32, 1985; Meyers, T. Walking Point 1988; Who's Who in the World 1986, 1987–1988. *Periodicals*—Christian Science Monitor January 4, 1984; Commentary October 1977; Nation December 20, 1980; New Republic October 25, 1980; New York Times May 30, 1987; June 5, 1988; New York Times Book Review May 29, 1977; November 2, 1980; November 13, 1983; Saturday Review June 11, 1977; Times Literary Supplement February 26, 1988; Virginia Quarterly Review Winter 1978; Washington Post Book World May 10, 1987.

*CARAION, ION (pseudonym of Stelian Diaconescu) (1923–July 21, 1986), Romanian poet and translator. The following sketch, translated from the French, was written for *World Authors* by Valentina Caraion, Ion Caraion's widow, and his daughter Marta Caraion:

"Ion Caraion was born in the village of Rusavat to a family of peasants. Although an atheist, his father came from a family of generations of orthodox priests who, in the mid-nineteenth century, had fled Transylvania, a Romanian province that had been occupied by Hungary for six hundred years during which orthodox religion had been persecuted. The poet's father, Mihai Diaconescu (the poet adopted the pseudonym of Ion Caraion at sixteen when he began publishing his poems in reviews), was a strong-

°cä rī´ ŏn, ē´ on

ION CARAION

willed peasant, passionately fond of hunting and fishing. Later, having finished a course in viti-culture, he began planting fruit trees and vine-yards in all the neighboring villages of the dry hilly countryside. Unusual for a peasant, he owned a fine library covering most of the books that had been published in Romanian. An enthu-siastic reader, he often kept his oil lamp (elec-tricity was then unknown in the villages) burning in his bedroom until dawn. For the young child his father's hunting rifle inspired as much terror as his multitude of books lining the shelves of the library fascinated him.

"At the age of seven, when he was ready for school, Ion Caraion was put into the care of a great uncle who lived in a little town, Rîmnicu-Sarat. During his four primary school years he was on one side persecuted by his great aunt and on the other encouraged by his teacher for his studiousness and thirst for learning. He then returned to his family home because his fa-ther had decided to enroll him in military school to prepare for a career as an army officer. For that purpose he took his son to Jassy, capital of Moldavia, where he passed his admissions exam-ination. Satisfied, his father returned home leav-ing his son in the boarding school. At eleven little Stelian did not know exactly what he wanted to do when he grew up, but he knew definitely that he did not want a military career. For that rea-son he ran away from school to the town of Bu-zau, capital of the canton, where several of his aunts lived. He found refuge with one of them and was taken in the direction of the college in Buzau to explain his case and apply for admis-

sion to the first class of the *lycée*. He was not able to pay the tuition, but by chance he met a gener-ous spirited man who immediately recognized in him a gifted child, hungry for learning. He was excused from the fee and admitted to the school with a small stipend. During his eight years there, because his parents were too poor to assist him, he had to manage with the stipend and money earned from privately tutoring younger pupils. From the age of twelve he wrote poetry, bad poetry (according to his own testimony), but at fourteen he had his first poems published in a variety of literary reviews in his country. About the same time he edited his first review.

"In 1942, having completed his studies at the *lycée* and passed his baccalaureate, he left for Bucharest with twenty *lei* in his pocket. He slept in railroad stations and parks until he found the courage to seek out other young writers in the capital who had published in the same reviews. Shortly after, he entered a competition for a proofreading job on one of the most important newspapers of the period. He won out over about forty other contestants. But he did his work at night to keep it secret from his friends. After several months he published an essay in this paper on the then leading poet Tudor Ar-ghezi, who so admired the article that he tele-phoned the director of the paper to find out who the author was. The director called Caraion into his office and appointed him chief editor of the literary supplement of the paper, which was the most important and the most democratic of that time.

"Thus Caraion directly entered the world of the press. In the same year, 1942, he enrolled in the departments of literature and philosophy at the University of Bucharest, but in 1943 he was expelled because of his anti-Fascist convictions. He continued his studies after the war, complet-ing his degree in 1947.

"World War II was raging by this time. Allies of the Germans, the Romanians fought on the eastern front. Of this period Caraion later wrote: 'I have published in Romania, always under cen-sorship, in despite of three successive dictator-ships (King Carol II, Fascism, Communism), nearly twenty volumes of poetry, numerous translations and anthologies of lyric poetry and prose, as well as five collections of essays. When the Romanian Fascist rulers of 1939–1944 were in power I was anti-Fascist, and they pursued and tried to kill me. I escaped miraculously from the hands of the Gestapo murderers, fled and went into hiding. In 1943 the head of the Bucha-rest censorship office put his revolver to my tem-ple threatening to shoot because of my anti-Fascist articles.'

"On August 23, 1944 the leaders of the democratic political parties, with the connivance of King Michael I, took over power and turned the army against Germany, joining the side of the Allies. Following the Yalta conference, the countries of southeastern Europe were turned over to the influence of the U.S.S.R. Until that time these countries had never had a leftist government. Caraion wrote: 'In 1944 I participated in the legal establishment of the Communist-party journal *Scinteia* (The Spark) and I became secretary of the editorial board of *Scinteia tineretului* (The Spark of Youth), a publication of the Union of Young Romanian Communists. After several months I handed in my resignation, declaring pointblank that Communism was nothing else than the cause of the birth of Fascism and that the victorious Western powers had, at the end of the war, made the grave, unpardonable error of destroying the effects of an evil (Fascism) without touching the cause of the evil, the Communist peril, although the cause as much as the effect demanded to be destroyed simultaneously and definitively. My resignation statement was published in two challenging articles on the crisis of culture and the crisis of mankind, in five languages and 300 pages of an international journal, *Agora*. Accusations against this journal, of "cosmopolitanism," anti-Zhdanov-ism [Andrei Zhdanov, 1896–1948, member of the Politburo and President of the Supreme Soviet of the U.S.S.R.], and other crimes against the state, led to my arrest and imprisonment between 1950 and 1955 and again between 1958 and 1964 in the most savage prisons or extermination camps. Condemned to death a second time, I was freed at the same time as all political prisoners.'

"In his eleven years in prisons and concentration camps, Caraion composed hundreds of poems. Denied paper or anything to write with, he, along with his fellow prisoners, memorized these poems. As soon as they were released, they wrote them down and thus saved a great many of them. After his liberation and an absence of fifteen years from the Romanian press, Caraion worked seventeen or eighteen hours a day to make up for lost time. Then came the years of exile. Caraion wrote: 'My first book of poems protesting the war, *Panopticum*, had been banned by censors in 1943 under the Fascists. My last book of essays protesting the laxity, corruption and betrayal of conscience, *Journal I*, was banned by censors in 1981 under the Communists. I have thus been forced by months and months of threats and chauvinistic attacks to leave my country, taking, at the age of fifty-eight, the road of the wanderer with my wife, my child, and two valises. I was part of a vast political movement that numbered 22,000,000 members. That political movement calls itself the people of Romania.'

"Caraion and his family settled in Lausanne, Switzerland, where he promptly received the status of political refugee. He was at last able to realize his old dream editing an international review on the model of *Agora*. At the price of great material sacrifice he published three numbers of the journal *Correspondances*, eleven numbers of another journal *Don Quichotte*, and then an annual of international writing with beautiful graphics *2 PLUS 2*, thanks to his friend and patron James Gill. In his native language he published a polemical pamphlet against the totalitarian Romanian regime, as well as three volumes of poems, one translated into English and two in French.

"Ion Caraion died in 1986 after a long and painful illness attributed directly to a neglected case of hepatitis that he had contracted during his imprisonment and forced labor in a lead mine. The sadness of leaving his native land never abated."

––––––

Ion Caraion is recognized as "the major voice of his generation" in Romanian poetry. That generation, struggling to write under severe economic and political restraints, was noted for experimentation in the arts, much of it either in protest against repression or in bitter disillusionment at the crushing of their ideals of freedom. Caraion's poetry is difficult to classify. One of his translators, Marguerite Dorian, writes: "Called in turn an existentialist and a surrealist, Caraion is, in fact, something of both and at the same time neither one." Ovid S. Crohmalniceanu, who translated Caraion's Romanian poems into French in *Le chant de l'unique* (Song of the Unique, 1979), agrees, in his preface to that volume, that these influences appear in his work—"but only to a degree and assimilated in a completely personal form." He converted, as it were, all the troubled elements of his life into the substance of his poetry with results Crohmalniceanu describes as "a frightening force, concise and masterly, terrible and mysterious . . . a tragic testimony of living history." An example is his "Song from the Occupation Time":

What I would not give for this century, were it only to change!
How deep would my heart plow its field with life!
Had you ever felt the pains of an army in retreat,
you would not have imprisoned joy in any city.

I ask you: where is freedom for which the cities have burned
and where are the joys for which
our children, charred, have multiplied the carcasses of war?

Caraion's early poetry, however, was characterized by exuberant and eclectic imagery, daringly imaginative and individual. As Robert Hudzik wrote in *Library Journal*: "Essentially an intellectual and cynical poet, cool, distant, impersonal, Caraion is capable of expressing the most personal and tenderest of feelings." He writes, for example, in a long love poem "She Who Tarries in the Land of Winds":

Oh, when you were smaller than the sweet briar of the field,
     hiding in the wolf pelts,
with hair like a black flame, unreal, inebriant,
without ever thinking that one day I shall love you,
I drew you, with a potter's rye-straw, astonished, on a jug.

Your body like a compass rose, which would
come back each night from a warm love-song, since then,
I heard it crumble under the herald cloaks
in the tumbling of the worlds toward miracles.

Star lint, lace of diaphonous little bells
soars above the far-offness words unfinished
and I hold close your hair spread like the light on Eskimo huts,
my darling like an effigy effaced by so many rememberings.

Marguerite Dorian detects a change in his work after 1969: "The luxurious, mad underbrush of his earlier poems thins out; a 'de-ornamentation' seems to take place. The pleasure in words appears lost; speech becomes 'these sad little inventions: the words.'" In "De-ornamentation" Caraion writes despairingly:

No one discovers anything for you, alone
you discover the miracles you can believe in.
All other miracles have died a thousand times
in a thousand people
and no one wonders about them any longer
but to lie again, and again.

This weariness was needed, needed
these solitudes to surround me,
to be without splendor, to hear
as before the symmetrical air—
. . . not to be able to tell anything.

In spite of the political persecution he suffered in his native land, Caraion received several Romanian literary honors, including a prize from the Romanian Academy in 1969 and from the Association of Bucharest Writers in 1977. He won a prize from the Union of Romanian Writers in 1968 for his translation of Edgar Lee Masters's *Spoon River Anthology*. He also published a Romanian translation of Ezra Pound's *Cantos* in 1975 and of collections of French and Swiss poetry.

WORKS IN ENGLISH TRANSLATION: In 1981 Marguerite Dorian and Elliott B. Uradang translated Caraion's *Poems*. All quotations from his poetry above are from that volume.

ABOUT: Dorian, M. *Preface to* Poems, 1981; Encyclopedia of World Literature in the 20th Century, rev. ed., I, 1981. *Periodicals*—Library Journal March 15, 1982; World Literature Today Summer 1982.

CAREY, PETER (May 7, 1943–), Australian novelist and short-story writer, was born in Bacchus Marsh, Victoria, Australia. He was educated at Greelong Grammar School, and studied for a year at Monash University, Clayton, Victoria. After leaving the university, he worked in advertising in Australia, 1962–1968; in London, 1968–1970; and again in Australia, from 1970 onward. He currently divides his time between advertising (as a partner in McSpadden Carey Advertising Consultants) and writing. His first three novels went unpublished, and he made his debut as a short-story writer in two collections published in Australia in the 1970s, *The Fat Man in History* and *War Crimes*, the latter of which won the New South Wales Premier's Award, 1980. *The Fat Man in History* that was published in London in 1980 contains stories from both Australian collections and made a decidedly favorable impression on reviewers.

"His work," Page Edwards wrote in *Library Journal*, "is magical and surreal. . . . In 'Peeling' we are treated to a graphic description of a man trying to get to know an abortionist's assistant slowly by peeling away layer after layer. What's left is her obsession—a white doll. . . . It's Carey's ability to make the most implausible fact become a heightened reality that makes this collection fascinating." In the *Times Literary Supplement*, Peter Lewis elaborated on the peculiar nature of the tales by remarking that "Carey looks to the Americas for his literary models; the debt is chiefly to Borges and to such American 'new fiction' writers as Donald Barthelme. Carey's nonrealistic stories, which tend toward fable, owe something to surrealism, something to science fiction, and something to an older tradition of the imaginative and Gothic tale (especially Poe). Yet the fantasy is also rigorously controlled, so that once the imaginary context is established . . . the narrative proceeds with quasi-realistic attention to precise detail." Sandra Katz in the *Saturday Review* expressed the sentiments of many reviewers when she wrote that the stories in the collection "are as brilliant as they are bizarre."

In the opening pages of Carey's first novel *Bliss*, which received the Miles Franklin Award,

PETER CAREY

an Australian advertising man named Harry Joy
floats above his own dead body lying on the lawn
of his house after a coronary. Dead for nine minutes, he comes to life again, has a heart operation, dies briefly again and revives to the sense
that Heaven and Hell do exist and that the life
he has known is in fact Hell. His wife, he understands now, is having an affair with his American business partner; his clients poison the
environment with carcinogens; his drug-dealing
son and Communist daughter are having incestuous relations. Judith Chettle in the
Washington Post Book World commented that
"Carey is a writer of power and imagination.
Harry Joy's descent into Hell and his trip back
is a masterful amalgam of black humor, satire,
perceptive observation and empathy for Harry,
his damned family and his friends." The one reservation reviewers expressed was that the ending, in which Harry finds peace in a tropical
rain-forest with a girl named Honey Barbara, is
sentimental and simplistic. "Nevertheless," Neil
Philip observed in *British Book News*, "this is a
rich, rewarding novel: crisply written. Daringly
conceived, brilliantly achieved."

Carey received Australia's National Book
Council Award in 1982; and in 1985 published
his second novel *Illywhacker*, which was short-
listed for England's coveted Booker Prize and in
Australia won the Victorian Premier's Literary
Award. A work of over 600 pages, *Illywhacker*
was described by Curt Suplee in the *Washington
Post Book World* as a "huge and hugely
rewarding" novel. "The grander comic vision,"
Suplee wrote, "from Rabelais to Dickens,

Huckleberry Finn to *Garp*, is ultimately compassionate, its protagonists worth our sympathy,
its purport auspicious. It gives our vanities and
failings a wholesome thrashing, but in the end
refreshes our sense of human possibility. . . .
Such a book is *Illywhacker*." *Illywhacker*, a word
meaning trickster or confidence man, relates the
life of Herbert Badgery, a 139-year-old car salesman who loves to attract crowds with his prodigious lies. His adventures reflect at the same
time upon the history of Australia, implied in his
"Best Pet Shop in the World," a giant menagerie
of Australiana surmounted by a winking eye
that, although located in Sydney and run by his
grandson, is actually owned by the Mitsubishi
Company of Japan.

As Nicholas Spice commented in the *London
Review of Books*, Badgery "finds little in life to
recommend, and even less as it is lived in Australia. Wherever he looks he sees lies, and Australia
is the biggest lie of all: the people pretending to
be English or American, the buildings pretending to be European, and his own history based
upon the lie 'that the continent at the time of the
first settlement, was said to be occupied but not
cultivated'—justifying the eviction of the
aborigines." Spice found Carey a master of the
tall tale related in an "irresistable and addictive
style." Not all the reviewers were wholly pleased
by the novel, however. Andrew Hislop in the
Times Literary Supplement, for example, felt
that the novel "overreaches itself. . . . [It] has
many brilliant moments but . . . the performance cannot be sustained, and there is something unsatisfactory about the reduction of the
broad canvas . . . [depriving Australia] of its vibrant identity by imposing his symbolic interpretation on it."

Illywhacker was followed by another large
novel, *Oscar and Lucinda*, set in England and
Australia in the nineteenth century and once
again incorporating elements of fable and fantasy. The novel received generally glowing reviews, and won the Booker Prize for 1988.
Typical of the unusually strong praise of the
novel, Paul Taylor in *Punch* declared that Carey
"has more gifts as a novelist than it seems altogether decent for a single man to possess and one
of them is his ability, demonstrated . . .
throughout this huge and brilliant novel, to fuse
his instinct for the fairy-tale side of fiction with
his absorbing and intricate curiosity about how
things actually work. . . . Genius is a devalued,
overworked word, but make no mistake about it,
in that department Peter Carey has been richly
blessed." Very briefly put, the work concerns the
life of Oscar Hopkins, his rearing in England in
the mid-nineteenth century, and his removal to
Australia on a ship aboard which he meets and

falls in love with Lucinda, an Australian heiress returning from England where she has met, among others, the novelist George Eliot (introduced as a character). Lucinda bets her inheritance that Oscar cannot deliver a glass church to a missionary's post in the outback, providing the plot for the latter part of the work.

Lorna Sage in the *Times Literary Supplement*, impressed by the many layered dimensions of the novel, compared Carey's "tricksiness and literariness" to the work of "contemporary *pasticheurs* such as John Fowles (*The French Lieutenant's Woman*), John Barth (*The Sot-Weed Factor*), even, at moments, Salman Rushdie." And Carolyn See in the *Los Angeles Times Book Review* was struck by Carey's use of "image and metaphor, and amazing feats of prose style." The case for those with reservations about the novel was expressed by John Gross in the *New York Times*. "Peter Carey is already one of the most highly acclaimed contemporary Australian novelists," he remarked, "and this latest novel . . . will undoubtedly confirm his reputation as a writer of force and originality. . . . And yet for all the energy that has gone into it, the book only works by fits and starts. . . . In the end *Oscar and Lucinda* seems to me impressive but imperfect, poised halfway between being a genuinely big book and a merely large one."

Carey has also adapted his novel *Bliss* as a film, which earned him the Australian Film Institute Award for screenplay, 1985. He has married twice, the second time to Alison Summers, a theatrical director, in 1985. They live in Balmain, overlooking Sydney Harbor. In 1988, he was interviewed by the *New York Times* about the nineteenth-century flavor of *Oscar and Lucinda*. "I've never really read Dickens," Carey responded. "I quit *Bleak House* after I encountered this nauseatingly good little girl. But I will read Dickens one day, I promise."

PRINCIPAL WORKS: The Fat Man in History, 1980; Bliss, 1981; Illywhacker, 1985; Oscar and Lucinda, 1988.

ABOUT: Contemporary Authors 123, 1988; Contemporary Literary Criticism 40, 1986; Contemporary Novelists, 4th ed., 1986; The Oxford Companion to Australian Literature, 1985. *Periodicals*—British Books News May 1982; Library Journal October 1, 1980; London Review of Books April 18, 1985; New York Times May 24, 1988; New York Times Book Review May 14, 1989; Punch April 1, 1988; The Spectator December 12, 1981; Times Literary Supplement October 31, 1980; May 3, 1985; April 1, 1988; Washington Post Book World May 2, 1982; September 14, 1986

CARPENTER, HUMPHREY (WILLIAM BOUVERIE) (April 29, 1946–), British biographer and expert on children's literature, was born in Oxford, where he has lived most of his life. He read English at Keble College of Oxford University, from which he holds a master's degree and a diploma in education. The latter degree is a prerequisite in Britain for secondary-school teaching, but Carpenter never followed that career. He worked in 1968–1974 as a radio producer and staff broadcaster for the British Broadcasting Corporation; since 1974 he has been a writer, occasionally doing radio broadcasts on subjects of special interest to him.

During his years as a resident of North Oxford, Carpenter came to be friends with the family of John Ronald Reuel Tolkien (1892–1973), a distinguished Oxford professor of philology, an authority especially on certain Old and Middle English texts, and the internationally famous author of the "heroic romances" (as he called them) *The Hobbit* (1937) and *The Lord of the Rings* (1954–1955). Carpenter was chosen by the family to write the authorized biography after Tolkien's death, and his *J.R.R. Tolkien* is a highly readable, short account (only 287 pages, including four appendixes and an index) of a life that was no more eventful than one would have supposed, beginning with Tolkien's early childhood in the Orange Free State and in Birmingham, his student years at Oxford, then his experience as a British Army officer serving on the Somme, and concluding with his many years as an academic, first at Leeds, then at Oxford universities. The subject did not himself, writes Carpenter in an author's note, "entirely approve of biography. . . . 'One of my strongest opinions,' he once wrote, 'is that investigation of an author's biography is an entirely vain and false approach to his works.' . . . Yet he was undoubtedly aware," Carpenter continues, "that the remarkable popularity of his fiction made it highly likely that a biography would be written after his death; and indeed he appears to have made some preparation for this himself, for in the last years of his life he annotated a number of old letters and papers with explanatory notes or other comments. He also wrote a few pages of recollections of his childhood. It may thus be hoped that this book would not be entirely foreign to his wishes."

Carpenter deferred to Tolkien's wishes to the extent that he made no critical judgments on his fiction. He did, however, give attention to "some of the literary and other influences that came to bear on Tolkien's imagination, in the hope that this may shed some light on his books." Carpenter's first attempt at literary biography garnered mixed reviews. "Not very exciting but entirely

HUMPHREY CARPENTER

competent," Doris Grumbach called it in the *New York Times Book Review.* "Repetitious at times, at others doggedly dull in its strict attention to every detail, the book is still, because of its conversational tone, a readable biography of special interest to devotees of Tolkien's elves, dwarves and malevolent orcs." T. A. Shippey, writing in the *Times Literary Supplement,* wrote that the biographer's "greatest achievement, . . . is to have found his way through tangles of reminiscence, confusion, unordered manuscripts. His book ends with a complete bibliography containing many forgotten published works; his index offers a list of unpublished ones, each threaded into the line of a narrative complicated both by the intensity of his subject's inner life and by the uneventfulness of his public career."

Carpenter's highly selective edition *Letters of J.R.R. Tolkien* followed upon his biography of the philologist and romancer. With the cooperation and assistance of Christopher Tolkien, an Oxford English don and the professor's youngest son, Carpenter presents selections, usually in excerpted form, from 354 letters written from 1914 to 1973: the book is nearly twice the biography's length. Nicholas Walter, writing in the *New Statesman,* called the letters volume "one of the most interesting contributions to Tolkien studies, especially for anyone who is not entirely convinced by the claims for or of his work. There are particularly impressive items on his political and religious ideas and especially on what he was trying to do in his main work."

The Inklings: C. S. Lewis, J.R.R. Tolkien,

Charles Williams, and Their Friends is Carpenter's sympathetic and spirited account of an Oxford literary club, whose members were Tolkien, an inveterate founder and joiner of all-male language-and-literature societies, and Lewis, his close friend and fellow committed Christian, and a tutor in English at Magdalen College. The group gathered with perfect regularity every Tuesday in term time for lunch at the Eagle and Child public house, then on Thursday evenings in Lewis' college rooms. Initially they met to read and discuss Norse sagas and Middle English poetry, but over time the members began to talk about their own works in progress, particularly Tolkien's heroic romances and Lewis's mythological "Narnia" series of tales. In addition to the three principal members named in the book's title, Carpenter gives brief accounts of the other Inklings: Nevill Coghill, H.V.D. Dyson, Father Gervase Mathew, John Wain, and C. L. Wrenn, all of them well-known Oxford figures. "All," wrote C. E. Lloyd in the *Sewanee Review,* "including those [the author] did not know, come to life under his pen. He is an appreciator by nature; he reads letters and records with a quick imagination and a warm heart. We get a clear picture of men who encouraged one another to produce works of the imagination that will outlive our time." Kingsley Amis in the *New Statesman* called *The Inklings* "oddly vivid, as if the author must have known at first hand what he described." The book received the Society of Authors' Somerset Maugham award in 1979.

W. H. Auden: A Biography was Carpenter's next project. He is at pains to point out at the outset in an author's note that the work is "not an 'authorised' or 'official' biography of Auden, and it was undertaken on my own initiative rather than under the auspices of his Estate." Once again Carpenter eschews literary criticism: "I have not," he wrote, "usually engaged in a critical discussion of Auden's writings. But I have tried to show how they often arose from the circumstances of his life, and I have also attempted to identify the themes and ideas that concerned him. I hope I have also managed to convey my own huge enthusiasms for his poetry." In the succeeding preface, Carpenter had once again to justify his book's reason for being, because Auden was another figure who, like Tolkien, disliked and mistrusted literary biography. Yet most of Auden's friends preserved their letters and some, as Carpenter says, "far from doing anything to hinder the writing of a life," published in various periodicals their own memoirs of him. The author believes that "here, as so often in his life, Auden adopted a dogmatic attitude which did not reflect the full range of his opinions, and which he sometimes flatly contradicted." The poet usually welcomed in his reviewing all manner of newly published literary biographies, and was equally friendly as a reviewer to collections of writers' letters, being censorious only "when he thought that something private had been included which was merely personal and threw no light on the writer's work." He also left a great deal of authobiographical writing. "I do believe . . . ," Auden once wrote, "that more often than most people realise, [an artist's] works may throw light upon his life."

The life Carpenter describes was indeed a full one, and he gives considerable attention to Auden's private life with pages of description of his sexual habits and encounters. Carpenter attempts, none too successfully even by his own criteria, to connect episodes in Auden's sexual life to specific poems. The main problem of the biography, however, is that in refraining from critical discussion of the poetry and in concentrating so much upon personal matters hardly touching upon the works, it seems to risk leaving the reader with little sense of W. H. Auden as one of the greatest poets of the twentieth century: "It is only too possible," wrote Alan Brownjohn in *Encounter*, "to put down [this] book with the feeling that Auden's poetry has been unwittingly diminished. . . . [Carpenter's] discussion of Auden's writing is always lucid and accurate, and frequently very helpful, but it is mainly rather ordinary." "Carpenter's forthrightness," complained Andrew Motion in the *New Statesman*, "sometimes seems too blunt an instrument to investigate Auden's emotional and artistic complexities. . . . [His approach] provides circumstantial evidence more often than psychological insights. We're always told when and where Auden cried, and yet the book still seems a portrait of a poet without real tears."

Carpenter's wife Mari Prichard was her husband's coauthor for his next project, a major work of reference, *The Oxford Companion to Children's Literature*, a 558-page, alphabetically arranged treasure trove of biographical and bibliographical information, notable for its integral inclusion of short, concise biographies of every major writer of children's literature as well as summaries of plots and critical comment on all important works of imaginative literature for children or read as such by them. The work is dedicated to the memory of the pioneer student of children's literature, Peter Opie (1918–1982), who with his wife Iona (authors of, among other classics, *The Oxford Dictionary of Nursery Rhymes*, 1951, and *The Lore and Language of Schoolchildren*, 1959) had originally proposed to the Oxford University Press that they should produce a companion to children's literature.

The authors describe in their preface how the status of children's literature has changed over the past few decades: "From being the concern of a few brave individuals, who were often on the defensive against charges of triviality and were as likely to be collectors as critics, children's books became the focus of countless courses, conferences, centres of study, and works of scholarship. It might be said that the subject reached maturity." The book, like most Oxford companions, was written entirely by its two compilers, rather than made up of contributions by a large number of hands. The scope of the work was enlarged to include foreign language children's literature as well. The compilers departed from their primary model, Harvey's *Oxford Companion to English Literature*, in that they frequently indulged in remarks of criticism or praise. As they explain, "The popular and the classic are especially hard to keep separate in the field of children's literature, and a book might often rate more space as a phenomenon than it could for literary merit. So, since the length of entries for particular works could not do the work of criticism for us, we have often had to be more explicit in our judgements, and have made brief comments on what seem to us the qualities or failings of many of the authors and books included."

The reviews of this long-awaited book were generally favorable. The *Economist* critic thought it "a wonderful book [that] deserves to become a classic." Hugh Brogan, writing in the *Times Literary Supplement*, considered that its "greatest strength . . . is probably its comprehensive and sensitive coverage of the whole topic of pictures and picture-books. . . . Another undoubted asset is the Carpenters' prose style. . . . [They] have also done their best to ignore the fact that the definition of children's literature is even more difficult than the definition of children, who are at least human beings of a certain age." However, Eudora Welty, in the *New York Times Book Review*, pointed to what she considered a major failure of the work: "And now—to whom will it be a companion? The librarians, the collectors, the rare book dealers, the thesis writers—yes, all of these from now on. But hardly for the children. It is a reference book, but if a book concerns children, it should be theirs to consult. One hoped for a book they could read and live with that would nourish their love for reading. Perhaps it's my failure to recognize it in the *Companion*, but I felt the absence of some central love of literature that would have warmed the whole."

In 1985, only a year after the appearance of the massive *Oxford Companion*, Carpenter brought out two books both of which must have necessitated considerable time to research and write. *OUDS: A Centenary History of the Oxford University Dramatic Society, 1885–1985* is the official history of the famous theatrical club, a lively, well-written narrative filled with gossipy anecdotes as well as the names of the leading lights of British theater, art, and literature. *Secret Gardens: A Study of the Golden Age of Children's Literature* follows up on some of the interests in that literature Carpenter was unable to develop fully in the *Oxford Companion*. It consists of an extended and connected critical reading of the relevant works of Charles Kingsley, Lewis Carroll, George MacDonald, Louisa May Alcott, Kenneth Grahame, E. Nesbit, Beatrix Potter, J. M. Barrie, and A. A. Milne. Carpenter writes in his preface that the book underwent many changes as it was written. His original notion had been to concentrate on the biographies of the writers he was dealing with, "but again and again the links between these authors proved to be not in their lives, but on the deeper levels of the books themselves." He was determined to discover why so many British writers of this period "had chosen the children's novel as their vehicle for the portrayal of society, and for the expression of their personal dreams." Jonathan Cott, in the *New York Times Book Review,* thought some of Carpenter's appraisals of the writers in *Secret Gardens* "curmudgeonly": "One might be tempted to dismiss [the book] as some sort of petulant aberration. That would be a mistake. In the second part of his study, Mr. Carpenter reduces his polemical speed and moves into constructive gear in order to examine—with a more leisurely style and with greater percipience, irony and intelligence—the literary and emotional worlds of Beatrix Potter, Kenneth Grahame, Barrie and Milne." In the *Times Literary Supplement,* Isabel Quigly wrote: "The trouble with this stimulating book is that there is simply too much material. Each chapter seems skimpy because (and it is a compliment to Carpenter's suggestiveness and close-knit writing) one wants more. Some of the most memorable things about it are its oddments and asides: never again shall I meet the flamboyant Mr. Toad without remembering the man Carpenter suggests as his possible godfather, Oscar Wilde."

In 1988, after five years of painstaking research, Carpenter published his massive (over 1,000 pages) biography *A Serious Character: The Life of Ezra Pound.* It is impossible for any writer on Pound to evade controversy; but, while some reviewers expressed reservations on certain aspects of his book, Carpenter achieved the near-impossible—a detailed and even-handed account of the poet's turbulent life and career.

He records with candor Pound's virulent anti-Semitism and pro-Fascism, telling a *New York Times Book Review* interviewer that "in the interests of free speech nothing was changed. And Pound's children could have withheld or censored material, but they gave me carte blanche." Carpenter's announced intention was neither to defend or condemn Pound nor to re-evaluate his poetry. Rather, by culling the huge amount of writing about him and principally by drawing on Pound's own words in his writings (his letters as well as his books) and his broadcasts from Italy during World War II, he presented Pound as "a serious character."

In the opinon of some reviewers, the sheer weight of Carpenter's research overloaded the book. Michiko Kakutani, in the *New York Times,* objected that "Mr. Carpenter seems less interested in analyzing the verse than in giving the reader a blow-by-blow account of the poet's daily life . . . [he] appears to be gathering information for its own sake . . . [his] faith in the mechanical recitation of detail points to a reluctance to fully assess his subject: an unwillingness or inability to make sense of his life and art." Writing in the *New York Times Book Review,* however, William H. Pritchard pronounced the book the best of all earlier biographies of Pound. Conceding that "Poundians will, I think, be disturbed at what may be for them a too dispassionate or merely dutiful rehearsal of the march of poems, essays, and books," he nevertheless praised Carpenter for his fair-mindedness and a flair for writing "that keeps his narrative alive and on the move—a good thing for narrative to be if its subject is, in Mr. Carpenter's words, 'so agile and slippery a creature' as the outrageous Ezra." For Christopher Ricks, in *New York Newsday,* Carpenter's is a "resourceful and humane life of this astonishing figure . . . a serious character study and not less so for being hilarious, bizarre, poignant and myriad-minded." Even more enthusiastic was William Gass, in the *Times Literary Supplement,* who praised Carpenter for "being neither mealy-mouthed nor serpent-toothed but by making certain that when he is confronted with an aesthetic judgment, he makes one; and when he is faced with a moral judgment, he makes that; and by not harping or playing prosecuting attorney, and by not shovelling loads of unpleasantness under acts of generosity or rhymes of genius; by refusing every special plea, and, above all, by keeping calm. He sees through Ezra without, on that account, failing to see him. It is a feat worthy of salute."

Carpenter's fascination with brilliant and eccentric literary personalities is reflected once again in *The Brideshead Generation: Evelyn*

Waugh and His Friends. The television success of *Brideshead Revisited* created a ready audience for information, a good deal of it racy literary gossip, on the upperclass, public-school and Oxford educated young men who emerged as wits and pundits in the 1930s and, Peter Kemp noted in his review in the *Times Literary Supplement,* "dominated English culture for almost half a century." Although Carpenter discusses a number of these figures, including Anthony Powell, Cyril Connolly, Graham Greene, and John Betjeman, the center of his book is Evelyn Waugh. He traces the roots of Waugh's tragi-comic satire back to the novelist's psychological vulnerability, demonstrating—as David Cannadine wrote in the *New York Times Book Review*—that "he was driven by one of the most powerful and self-destructive of all human feelings: bitter and unassuageable social resentment." The picture that Carpenter draws of the Brideshead generation is overall a gloomy one, in spite of the fact that these were ostensibly the "Bright Young Things," young men who began their professional lives with glittering promise. "For all the zest and geniality and enlivening perceptiveness of Humphrey Carpenter's approach," Kemp writes, "one is left . . . with the dispiriting sense that this group of privileged associates were, in the last resort, each other's most pernicious enemies of promise."

PRINCIPAL WORKS: (with Mari Prichard) A Thames Companion, 1975; J.R.R. Tolkien: A Biography, 1977; The Inklings, 1978; Jesus, 1980; Letters of J.R.R. Tolkien, 1981; W. H. Auden: A Biography, 1981; (with Prichard) The Oxford Companion to Children's Literature, 1984; OUDS, 1985; Secret Gardens, 1985; A Serious Character: The Life of Ezra Pound, 1988; The Brideshead Generation, 1989. *Juvenile*—The Joshers, 1977; The Captain Hook Affair, 1979; Mr. Majeika, 1984.

ABOUT: Contemporary Authors New Revision Series 13, 1984. *Periodicals*—American Scholar Autumn 1982; Antioch Review Summer 1982; Choice October 1977, February 1982, February 1985, November 1985, December 1985; Christian Century August 15, 1979; March 31, 1982; Christian Science Monitor November 9, 1981; September 7, 1984; August 2, 1985; Commonweal November 6, 1981; Economist May 11, 1984; Encounter September 1981, September–October 1985; Library Journal June 1, 1977; September 15, 1981; November 15, 1981; April 15, 1984; May 15, 1985; Nation October 24, 1981; New Statesman May 13, 1977; October 20, 1978; April 4, 1980; July 3, 1981; October 30, 1981; May 18, 1984; New York Newsday December 11, 1988; New York Review of Books December 17, 1981; New York Times December 14, 1988; New York Times Book Review August 14, 1977; April 8, 1979; October 4, 1981; November 15, 1981; August 19, 1984; July 21, 1985; December 18, 1988; January 7, 1990; Saturday Review June 25, 1977; September 1981; Se-

1982; Times Literary Supplement May 13, 1977; May 9, 1980; July 3, 1981; August 28, 1981; May 4, 1984; March 15, 1985; June 21, 1985; January 13, 1989; September 8, 1989.

CARTER, ANGELA (OLIVE) (May 7, 1940 –   ), British novelist, short-story writer, and critic, was born in Eastbourne, Sussex, the daughter of Hugh Alexander and Olive (Farthing) Stalker. She studied English at the University of Bristol, receiving a B.A. in 1965. Her father was a journalist, and she began her own writing career as a journalist in Croydon, Surrey, from 1958 to 1961. In 1960 she married Paul Carter (divorced, 1972). Since the late 1960s she has devoted most of her time to writing fiction, but she has also frequently contributed cultural criticism and book reviews to many publications, including the *New Statesman, New Society,* and the *New York Times Book Review.* In the early 1970s she lived in Japan, an experience that inspired some of her stories, and she has been a visiting professor of creative writing at Brown University in Providence, Rhode Island (1980 – 1981), and writer-in-residence at the University of Adelaide, Australia (1984). She has received a number of literary awards, including the Rhys Memorial Prize (1968), the Maugham Award (1969), the Cheltenham Festival Prize (1979), and the James Tait Black Memorial Prize (1985). Since the early 1980s she has lived in South London with her second husband Mark Pearce and their son Alexander.

Carter's fiction is characterized by a daring, extravagant imagination and a lush, vividly poetic and allusive style. Her stories and novels take the form of fables, allegories, sophisticated fairy tales, Gothic melodramas and historical and futuristic fantasies. They are thus a major British contribution to the international revival of literary fantasy and fable that has taken place since the 1960s. Carter has acknowledged the crucial influence on her of the Argentine writer of metaphysical fables, Jorge Luis Borges. But it is clearly the speculative freedom of Borges, not his dry, ironic elegance, that interested her; her own work is far more feverish and fanciful. Displaying a conspicuous eroticism, peopled with eccentrics, archetypes, hermaphrodites, and sadists, it draws heavily on the Gothic tradition of literature. Carter herself has written, in an afterword to her collection of stories *Fireworks,* about her early admiration for Poe and E.T.A. Hoffmann and her affinity for the Gothic: "The Gothic tradition in which Poe writes grandly ignores the value systems of our institutions, it deals entirely with the profane. Its great themes

ANGELA CARTER

are incest and cannibalism. Character and events are exaggerated beyond reality, to become symbols, ideas, passions. Its style will tend to be ornate, unnatural—and thus operate against the perennial human desire to believe the word as fact. Its only humor is black humor. It retains a singular moral function—that of provoking unease."

This is a fair description of Carter's own work. Incest is a recurrent theme, and even her most realistic stories have dark undercurrents of violence and perverse eroticism, especially sadomasochism, sometimes accompanied by a reversal of roles. Yet however horrific at times, Carter's fiction is also informed by a robust comic spirit, and not all her humor is black humor; it is often fanciful or farcical. Nevertheless it is clear that a major aim of her fiction is that of "provoking unease." Often the provocation has a political or feminist edge to it, but she is not primarily a political writer. The unease comes from her blurring of the distinctions between conscious and unconscious, contemporary and archaic, civilized and savage, adult and child, masculine and feminine, the innocent and the erotic.

Critics have generally applauded the bold, anarchic freedom of Carter's imagination, while conceding that the literary results are uneven. Ann Snitow, writing in the *Nation*, evoked the experience of reading Carter with an arresting metaphor of her own: "Reading a lot of Angela Carter at once is like being galloped on a child's hobbyhorse through the culture attic. You're choking on the fumes of greasepaint; you're star-

tled as a bunch of waxwork Bluebeards, beasts and beauties blunder into you; you're tangled in string by some grand puppeteer who jerks you around, then cuts the connection, leaving you free to play with whatever toy you want. . . . Sometimes called a pornographic writer, she is one only in a very special sense. Pleasure—and the fear that is so often pleasure's sauce—are her subjects, but the most exciting moments in her fiction are literary: the splendid verbal coups, the sensuous unfolding of the story line. . . . "

Critics have expressed a similar reservation about Carter's prose style—that it is sometimes too much of a good thing. Quoting a passage from Carter's story "Reflections," in which the narrator is commanded to kiss himself "in the mirror, the symbolic matrix of this and that, hither and thither, outside and inside," Victoria Glendenning, writing in the *New Statesman*, complained that "the mirror-kiss and its weird consequences had their own force. Talk of symbolic matrices belongs to American Ph.D. theses." And William Hjortsberg, reviewing *The War of Dreams* in the *New York Times Book Review*, remarked: "A tendency toward wordiness, then, and a baroque texture, which at times becomes almost impenetrable, seem the main faults. The devious and complex nature of fantasy demands a simple style. Consider fairy tales and folk stories. A frog turning into a prince is cause enough for wonder without embellishing the event with rhetoric . . . But at her best Angela Carter has created a grotesque and sensual world that calls to mind the texture of Fellini's film *Satyricon* and the violent poetics of Kenneth Patchen's *The Journal of Albion Moonlight*."

Hjortsberg isn't the only critic to range outside of literature in search of comparisons. James Brockway, in *Books and Bookmen*, likened Carter's work to that of one film director (Roman Polanski) and two artists (Aubrey Beardsley and Gustav Moreau) as well as invoking Poe and Hoffmann and "the decadence, the hysteria and the preciosity" of Huysmans and Maeterlinck. What is undisputed is that Carter's prolific and bizarre imagination and sensuous, mannered style set her apart from the main English fictional tradition and from most contemporary English-language writers.

Carter's first novel, published in England in 1966 as *Shadow Dance* and in the United States in 1967 as *Honeybuzzard*, is set in a squalid English slum populated by grotesque characters. The despotic, demonic Honeybuzzard runs a scavenging operation and lives with the beautiful, blond, promiscuous Ghislaine, whose face he casually mutilates with a knife. There is an inexorable descent into madness and violence. Some critics found Carter's approach fashionably sensationalistic, while praising her powers of description and imagination. In the *New Statesman* Edwin Morgan wrote: "There is something a little too fashionable about Angela Carter's first novel, with all its Victoriana, Pop Art, Beardsleyesque rooms, dark glasses, casual lust and violence, but she shows a decided talent for the grotesque scene, the nightmarish atmosphere, the alarming uncertainties of human relationships." P. L. Sandberg, in the *Saturday Review*, complained that Carter's outlook "is the fashionable one of utter despair. Life, as the author views it, is brutal, cannibalistic, and doomed by depravity. . . . the book suffers at times from a lack of restraint, as though the author were not quite sure if she had shocked us sufficiently to drive her point home." But, he went on, "Miss Carter is an exceptionally talented and imaginative writer. . . . She sets up outrageous tensions between her people and suggests many layers of meaning. The reader is suspended between belief and disbelief, crying yes and no with an equal voice."

The Magic Toyshop has a setting even more intensely Gothic. An orphaned fifteen-year-old girl named Melanie and her brother and sister are sent to London to live with a cruel uncle, the proprietor of a mysterious toyshop. In this strange household, in which mirrors are forbidden and her aunt has been struck dumb, Melanie is a virtual prisoner. A nightmarish atmosphere, compounded with guilt, incest, and rape, envelopes the characters. John Wakeman, writing in the *New York Times Book Review*, found the plot "grossly implausible," but concluded that the intensity of Carter's imagination allowed the book to overcome its flaws: "It leaves behind it a flavor, pungent and unsettling, which owes as much to its imperfections as its virtues."

Two subsequent novels, *Several Perceptions* and *Love*, retain Carter's Gothic penchant for eroticism and violence while depicting the alienated, bohemian young people of the 1960s. Sounding a familiar critical note, Richard Boston in the *New York Times Book Review* declared that *Several Perceptions* is "marred by some unconvincing dialogue and a good deal of overwriting." But he added that in portraying a young man prone to nightmarish hallucinations, the book "gives a powerful account of the horror, the logic and the poetry of the schizophrenic's world." The novel won the Somerset Maugham Award for 1969.

Between these two books, Carter published a futuristic fable called *Heroes and Villains*, set in the desolate aftermath of a nuclear war. Its six-

teen-year-old heroine, Marianne, flees the arid rationalism of an enclave of civilized people known as the Professors and goes to live with the Barbarians who occupy the surrounding ruins, marrying a brutal marauder named Jewel who had previously killed her brother and raped her. Critics were sharply divided over the book. Boston, again in the *New York Times Book Review*, described it as "a strange, compelling book." What Carter had succeeded in doing, he wrote, was "to take her images from a variety of sources, and assemble a fable that discusses the roles of reason and imagination in a civilized society." The reviewer for the *Times Literary Supplement* found the world Carter created in the novel "richly imagined, never whimsical and extraordinarily believable," though "occasional pretentiousness" in the latter part of the book spoiled "what is in many ways a remarkably effective novel." But James Fenton in the *New Statesman* found the pretentiousness more than occasional: "the novel is pretentious to a degree and suffers from all the common faults of the Gothick novel which is at present such a booming trade."

The Infernal Desire Machines of Dr. Hoffman, published in the United States in 1974 as *The War of Dreams*, is another fantasy that resolves itself into a fable of civilization and imagination. The mad scientist figure Hoffman has discovered a secret which allows him to replace reality with illusion—transforming, for instance, an opera audience into a flock of peacocks—and the hero, Desiderio, sets out in search of him, encountering along the way, as Hjortsberg wrote in the *New York Times Book Review*, "a macabre traveling carnival, an Indian tribe living on river-barges and speaking a kind of birdsong, a troupe of Moroccan acrobats who juggle the dismembered parts of their own bodies," and similar marvels. In the end, by destroying Hoffman's machine, which relies on the exploitation of erotic energy, Desiderio, as J. D. O'Hara wrote in the *Washington Post Book World*, "chooses the real, chooses contentment rather than ecstasy, reason rather than passion. And so does Carter."

In *The Passion of New Eve* and *Nights at the Circus*, feminist allegory lurks just beneath the surrealistic surface of the narratives. The earlier book follows an Englishman who, having abandoned a pregnant girlfriend, is captured, while passing through the Southwestern desert on his way to California, by a group of Amazons, who surgically transform him into a woman so that he may experience rape. *Nights at the Circus*, set at the end of the nineteenth and beginning of the twentieth centuries, tells the story of a girl raised in a brothel who mysteriously sprouts wings and becomes a celebrated circus performer and the skeptical American journalist who follows her around the world. The heroine, called Fevvers, and the journalist, Walser, eventually find themselves in love. It was widely reviewed and did much to establish Carter's reputation in the United States. Critics were quick to see the feminist moral to the story: "the 19th-century woman giving way to the larger, more powerful, altogether enchanting 20th-century Winged Victory," as Carolyn See put it in the *New York Times Book Review.* "In her wacky invincibility," wrote Amy E. Schwartz in the *New Republic,* "Fevvers serves as an obvious figure of feminist mythology, a miracle of nature who can't make love except female-superior because her wings get in the way. . . . But it's Walser's comic reeducation that provides the more interesting feminist legend." The latter point was echoed by Michiko Kakutani in the *New York Times,* where she spoke of the novel's "standard-issue feminist concerns: how women are used and abused by men, and how their imaginative and intuitive gifts are debased by the rationalist, male world. The women in *Nights at the Circus* are all victims . . . whereas the men emerge as either sex fiends or unfeeling dopes. Even nice Jack Walser suffers from the nasty male commitment to logic: he has to survive a string of terrible adventures before he can fall in love with Fevvers and appreciate her specialness—that is, accept the marvelous on faith."

Critics were unanimous in praise of the early part of the book, and nearly unanimous in finding that it declined in interest toward the end. Kakutani stressed the way in which Carter, through "her ability to nail down the wondrous with details that are visually precise," made the strange events of the novel seem real: "Not only Fevvers, but her whole world—at once mundane and grotesque—come brilliantly into focus. It's like watching the unveiling of a canvas by Bosch. . . . Unfortunately, as *Nights at the Circus* progresses, Fevvers and Walser become less and less important, and Miss Carter's narrative gradually loses both its focus and its drive." Carolyn See compared the experience of reading the book to that of a child who has spent his entire allowance on chocolate chip cookies and eaten every one: "Page by page, even chapter by chapter, *Nights at the Circus* is delicious, a sweet for the mind, but after a while, it's hard not to get a little queasy. . . . Mrs. Carter . . . might have remembered that at the circus, or in a book, the real trick is to quit while you're ahead, to get off stage with the audience begging for more." "As the story moves from St Petersburg to Siberia," Adam Mars-Jones wrote in the *Times Literary Supplement,* "Angela Carter piles on the prodigies until everything is equally miraculous—except that a miracle needs a humdrum context, or at least a whiff of the mundane, to set it off. . . . *Nights at the Circus* starts off in full commanding cry, and later disappoints the towering expectations it has created for itself." Even Amy Schwartz, who recommended giving the novel a second and third reading, conceded that "at times the odyssey becomes a rather exhausting trudge."

Carter has published three collections of short stories: *Fireworks, The Bloody Chamber,* and perhaps her most acclaimed book, *Black Venus,* published in the United States as *Saints and Strangers.* Discussing *Fireworks* in the *Listener,* John Mellors wrote: "Angela Carter's 'nine profane pieces' in *Fireworks* are set either in Japan, where she has lived, or in dreamscapes, where she considers herself equally at home. . . . I remained immune to, though admiring of, most of her Gothic blood-and-thunderstorms; but 'Reflections,' a horrifying tale in which the male narrator is forced at gunpoint to seek the mirror-world through the glass, and is raped by a girl whose eyes 'were the eyes justice would have if she were not blind,' came near to destroying my sleep. . . . On the other hand, the story-tales of Japan enthralled me." Ann Snitow, commenting on the tension between the fairy-tale form and the sophisticated authorial consciousness, found several stories "moving precisely because the narrator wants so much to be authentic, to feel directly, and suffers the fate of the ironic and self-conscious, the fate of alienation from anything simple and sentimental. Carter's sophistication is a curse and a blessing. She can't go naked, no matter how many layers she strips off; a postlapsarian Eve, she is infernally knowing."

Some critics found that the ironic knowingness of Carter's reworked fairy tales in *The Bloody Chamber* seriously damaged them. Alan Friedman, in the *New York Times Book Review,* complained of "cutesy mannerisms," "comical overwriting," and "cloying cleverness." And Paul Gray, while conceding that the eroticized fairy tales "titillate and amuse," concluded that "the stories are a bit too calculated and playful to do justice to the dangerous materials they raise. They tick perfectly well but they do not explode." Nevertheless, Friedman found that the volume was redeemed by several "direct and intense" stories toward its end. And contrary to Gray, Susan Kennedy, writing in the *Times Literary Supplement,* was struck precisely by the stories' unsettling power "not only to cause us to think again, and deeply, about the mythic source of our common cultural touchstones, but to plunge us into hackle-raising speculation about aspects of our human / animal nature."

The stories in *Saints and Strangers* retain Carter's characteristic preoccupation with sex, sexual roles, and power, but the most distinguished of them depart from her earlier fiction by addressing themselves to actual historical figures rather than mythical archetypes. Nevertheless, as Lorna Sage pointed out in the *Times Literary Supplement*, this distinction hardly matters, for Carter treats history as myth. The stories are about "everyday life among the mythic classes. Real people—Baudelaire's Creole mistress Jeanne Duval, Edgar Allan Poe and his mother, and Lizzie Borden, who unpicked her domestic problem with an ax—rub shoulders with entirely imaginary beings. But then of course these particular people are real only in quotation marks: in their different ways they made it into mythology, splendid inversions of nineteenth-century enterprise, and what Angela Carter is up to here is figuring out how they did it, or had it done to them." Or as Jennifer Krauss put it in the *New Republic*, Carter "takes apart the accepted morality tales that constitute the sacred cow called History, and exposes, through her manipulation of them, the cultural conventions that shape our view of the past."

Krauss sees these stories as conveying a direct political meaning, exposing the "sexism, racism, and classism" that have been insinuated into our received histories, but Charles Newman, in the *New York Times Book Review*, sees them simply as parables of the "insubstantiality of history," as "fantasies in the guise of historical meditations." What he finds most admirable about them is Carter's "absolutely unique voice, intensely literary without being precious, deep without being difficult, indifferent to formulas without being 'experimental,' and funny without being superficial or cruel." A sharp dissenting note, however, was registered by D. J. Enright in the *New York Review of Books*: "Angela Carter's use of language, her large, eclectic, and glittering vocabulary, . . . is undeniably impressive. Whether you always admire the workings of her imagination is another matter; the new wine she puts in these old bottles can be peculiarly sour. Some readers will be ready to sink down on their knees in awed obeisance; others will feel like throwing up at times."

Carter's engagement with sadomasochistic and pornographic fantasy and feminist themes in her own work led her to write a study of the Marquis de Sade and pornography called *The Sadeian Woman: An Exercise in Cultural History*, published in the United States as *The Sadeian Woman and the Ideology of Pornography*. She finds in Sade both an accurate picture of woman in traditional Western society

tine), and, in the tyrannical Juliette, the possibility of a new pornography in which women are sexually dominant. But Sade, she concludes, ultimately fails to imagine a sexuality which cannot be reduced to power. "Just when he seemed to Carter so close to being a revolutionary pornographer," wrote Ann Snitow, "one who can see that everyone, even the mother, is sexual, and that everyone can cross the boundaries of gender and taboo, he lapses into the myths common in most pornography, reinstating the old rigidity, reasserting the safe laws of transgression." Richard Gilman, in the *New York Times Book Review*, argued that by taking Sade as the prototype of pornography, Carter has willfully misunderstood the subject: "For all her intelligence, Miss Carter is a rigid ideologue, fervidly feminist, furiously antireligious and against transcendence of any kind. . . . At the heart of what's wrong with her assault on pornography and her related critique of Sade is her inability or refusal to see that pornography, like any form of imagination, is an effort at compensating for finiteness, at getting past limitations. It deals with the possible, not the actual, and imaginative possibility at that. If she could see this, she wouldn't be likely to construe pornography as treating only of violence." But whether or not Carter is right in understanding pornography (and the society which produces it) in terms of an equation of sex and power, it is clear that she believes this equation must be transcended in art and in life, and that this aim is central to her work.

PRINCIPAL WORKS: *Novels*—Shadow Dance (U.S., Honeybuzzard), 1967; The Magic Toyshop, 1968; Several Perceptions, 1968; Heroes and Villians, 1969; Love, 1971; The Infernal Desire Machines of Dr. Hoffman (U.S., The War of Dreams), 1972; The Passion of New Eve, 1977; Nights at the Circus, 1985. *Collected short stories*—Fireworks: Nine Profane Pieces (U.S., Fireworks: Nine Stories in Various Disguises), 1974; The Bloody Chamber and Other Stories, 1979; Black Venus (U.S., Saints and Strangers), 1985. *Plays*—Come Unto These Yellow Sands (radio plays), 1984. *Verse*—Unicorn, 1966. *Juvenile*—Miss Z, the Dark Young Lady, 1970; The Donkey Prince, 1970; Comic and Curious Cats, 1979; The Fairy Tales of Charles Perrault, 1977; Moonshadow, 1982; Sleeping Beauty and Other Favorite Fairy Tales, 1983. *Non-fiction*—The Sadeian Woman: An Exercise in Cultural History (U.S., The Sadeian Woman and the Ideology of Pornography), 1979; Nothing Sacred: Selected Writings, 1982.

ABOUT: Contemporary Authors New Revision Series 12, 1984; Contemporary Literary Criticism 5, 1976; 41, 1987; Contemporary Novelists, 4th ed., 1986; Dictionary of Literary Biography 14, 1983. *Periodicals*—Books and Bookmen February 1975; Lis-

New Republic May 20, 1985; December 22, 1986; New Statesman July 8, 1966; August 16, 1974; July 10, 1981; New York Review of Books February 26, 1987; New York Times January 30, 1985; New York Times Book Review February 25, 1968; March 2, 1969; September 13, 1970; September 8, 1974; February 24, 1985; September 7, 1986; Saturday Review February 18, 1967; Times Literary Supplement November 20, 1969; February 8, 1980; September 28, 1984; October 18, 1985; Washington Post Book World August 18, 1974.

CHANG CHIEH. See **ZHANG JIE**

CHANG HSIEN-LIANG. See **ZHANG XIANLIANG**

*CHAPPELL, FRED (May 28, 1936–), American poet, novelist, and short-story writer, writes: "Almost as soon as I understood that poems and stories and books were written by actual people who were living or who had lived in the actual world, I decided that I would write. The mountains of western North Carolina were, in the 1940s, not particularly hospitable to this kind of ambition, but I was lucky in my parentage. Both my parents were schoolteachers; they respected education and there was a variety of books in our house—as there was in comparatively few of the houses of our neighbors.

"Because they taught, they had to spend a great deal of time grading papers. I remember being jealous of the hours they gave to reading this writing on Blue Horse notebook paper and tried to attract their attention with my own 'writing': squiggles, dots, and doodles I drew painstakingly between the lines. I was heartbroken to be told that these hieroglyphic scrawls were not real writing, not at all.

"This incident was symptomatic of my whole career to come.

"In high school I wrote hundreds of poems and scores of what I thought were science-fiction stories. At Duke University, under the astute tutelage of Dr. William Blackburn and Mr. Reynolds Price, I learned to think of writing more seriously, in terms of a vocation. That was what it was for me, though I hadn't realized this fact until then.

"All my reading up to this point had been very traditional: Shakespeare, Sir Walter Scott, Tennyson, a little Browning, Homer and Virgil in translation. At Duke modern literature burst upon me like a sudden summer downpour. I neglected my classes in order to spend my days

FRED CHAPPELL

puzzling at Pound, Eliot, Auden, Joyce, Gide, Valéry, Baudelaire, and—especially—Rimbaud. The nights I spent discussing them with friends similarly afflicted. These two years were a whole education in one intoxicating dose, and I have never quite recovered from it.

"My first three novels were written in a sort of fever brought on by this dazzled exposure. I hardly remember the composition at all; it was as if those books were merely using me in order to get themselves written. Though employing raw materials I was familiar with—'folk' materials, if you will—*It Is Time, Lord* and *The Inkling* and *Dagon* are relentlessly and almost helplessly experimental in nature. Experiment was necessary simply because I didn't know what I was doing. I am mystified now when I remember that these books drew, for the most part, favorable criticism.

"I got it all backwards. Two later novels, *The Gaudy Place* and *I Am One of You Forever*, are quite traditional in tone, treatment, and organization. But for me the traditional was an experiment, and I was not surprised to discover how difficult the traditional is. The experimental proceeds from obsession, the traditional from ordered compulsion; and this latter requires some measure of maturity to attain to.

"I would prefer not to speak of my poetry at all. My first book, *The World Between the Eyes*, strikes me as being very bad. Which is not to say that the later ones are better. But they are certainly less calculating and arise from inner necessities that I do not care to look at closely. I am willing to say, though, that my poetry is first

°chá pel

conceived of in terms of whole books, the design appearing to me in a single flash and the individual poems set into it painfully one at a time.

"I teach for a living. If my first personal duty after my family is to my writing, my first professional duty is to my students. I don't teach particularly well because I am too earnest about it, but I always hope to do well.

"And I hope to begin to write better too."

———

The son of James Taylor and Anne (Davis) Chappell, Fred Chappell was born in Canton, a small town in North Carolina where he grew up close to the mountain people and country setting of most of his books. Labeled with the overused and not always meaningful epithet "Southern Gothic," his work is indeed Southern regional and often emphasizes the tragedy and violence that dominate so much of that writing. But as with his most celebrated peers—Eudora Welty, Flannery O'Connor, and William Faulkner—his work is enriched by a breadth of vision, a humanity and compassion, and a degree of earthy humor alien to that sensational genre.

At Duke University where he took his B.A. in 1961 and his M.A. in 1964, Chappell prepared for an academic career and planned to take a Ph.D. in English literature. His master's thesis was a 1,000-plus page concordance to the English poems of Samuel Johnson. But exposure to the teaching of William Blackburn, Reynolds Price, William Styron, and to fellow students Anne Tyler and Mac Hyman (author of *No Time for Sergeants*) drew him almost inevitably to creative writing. With the encouragement of a sympathetic editor, Hiram Haydn, and the financial needs of a young family, he developed a workshop short story into a first novel, *It's Time, Lord* and took a job teaching creative writing at Greensboro College in North Carolina. Although he has taught courses in English and American literature as well as in science fiction and film, writing has remained his primary concern as teacher and practitioner.

Chappell's fiction has won him an appreciative but small reading public. Something of a writer's writer, he is perhaps more widely read in England and in France (where a translation of his *Dagon* was awarded the Prix Meilleur des Lettres Étrangers of the French Academy) than in the United States. Reviewers are usually impressed with the quality of his writing. He has been called "a fine technician," a precise craftsman who writes a sensitive, often beautiful prose. But the complex philosophical nature of his novels, dense sometimes murky symbolism involving questions of alienation, disaffection,

loss of will, have troubled readers. In *It Is Time, Lord,* for example, a mature man who has lost all free will and sense of moral purpose confronts his past. Chappell himself describes the protagonist's crisis as one in which "the human will is as helpless as a foetus under the ruthless pressure of time itself." The disturbed consciousness of the protagonist, the shifts backwards and forwards in time, the obscure nature of his philosophical dilemma, do not make for easy reading. Even the simpler point of view of the child-protagonist of his second novel, *The Inkling*, is complicated by grim philosophical fatalism, the helplessness and passivity of the characters in the face of violence and tragedy. While acknowledging the excesses of the plot and the writing, Orville Prescott, in the *New York Times*, concluded that "his book holds one's attention and inspires respect." Similarly, writing of *Dagon*—a starkly tragic story of a clergyman who, in the course of writing a book on "elements of paganism in American Puritanism," becomes involved with a loathsome mountain girl who may well be a witch and ends a sacrificial victim to a satanic cult—the *Virginia Quarterly Review* observed: "Whatever defects the story may possess in a technical sense are far outweighed by the brilliance and sureness of the writing"

In the short stories that comprise *Moments of Light*, perhaps better than anywhere else in his fiction, Chappell articulated his philosophy. These are highly imaginative stories, some set in the eighteenth century, some set outside of time completely, all dealing with the theme of moral discovery, what Annie Dillard describes in her Foreword to the book as "man's hope of a just moral order and his responsibility to things as they are; man's longing for transcendence and the obdurate difficulty of the temporal destiny he faces instead; and man's art . . . which reconciles, if anything, man's hope of harmony with his experience of chaos."

Chappell's later fiction has shown a distinct lightening of spirit and tone. *The Gaudy Place*, a realistic picture of street life, prostitution and pimping in a small North Carolina town, evoked, according to Jonathan Yardley in the *New York Times Book Review*, "an accurate feeling for the new urban South." Then, after twelve years during which Chappell wrote only short stories and poetry, he published *I Am One of You Forever*, a portrait of a young boy growing up in the North Carolina mountains in the 1940s, his family, friends, neighbors, with flashes of whimsy and some real humor. "I can easily grow tired of reading about the Southern boy-man and his idea of a wild time, but just as I was gritting my teeth at yet another stupid prank, Mr. Chappell woke me up with a superb pitt of writing." commented David Guy in the *New York Times Book Review.*

During his ten-year sabbatical from novel writing, Chappell wrote some of his most impressive poetry, much of it narrative and dramatic and therefore closely linked to his fiction. His major poetic work is *Midquest*, a collection of four earlier volumes named for the elements—*River, Bloodfire, Wind Mountain, Earthsleep.* As he explains in his preface to *Midquest* : "It is an odd sort of performance, something like a verse novel, each of the four parts focusses upon one of the classical four elements, each book made up of eleven longish poems and together covering four times the same twenty-four hours of the speaker's life. These twenty-four hours occur on his thirty-fifth birthday, but not every hour here is in present time; many hours are given to reminiscences of the same hour at an earlier period of his life." Complex as this sounds—and even more complex are the symbolic references to Dante (who, like the speaker in the poem, was thirty-five in his *Divine Comedy*); the use of a variety of verse forms (Dantean terza rima, rhymed couplets, free verse, blank verse); and a structure in which the order of the poems is repeated in circular fashion—the poems are lucid and emotionally appealing. *Midquest* is a kind of *Prelude* with Chappell, like William Wordsworth, tracing "the Growth of the Poet's Mind" in a series of memories of his childhood, the North Carolina mountains where he grew up, his family, friends and neighbors, and his discovery of his vocation as a poet. He recalls, for example, his freshman year at college when he discovered Baudelaire and Rimbaud and began to write:

> I had a wish, 'Mourir aux fleuves barbares'
> And to fulfill it could have stayed at home.
> But down at Duke in 1954
> (*I like Ike*) it carried weight with some
> Few wild men and true who wanted to write
> And even tried to write—God bless them
> Everyone!—and who scheduled the night
> For BEER and the explication of a POEM.

There are love lyrics, intellectual games, folk humor, and poems of warm, homely realism. In "My Grandmother Washes Her Feet," he observes her sitting on the rim of an old-fashioned bath tub:

> Her cracked toes thumped the tub wall, spreading
> Shocklets. Amber toenails curled like shavings.
> She twisted the worn knob to pour in coolness
> I felt suffused her body like a whiskey.

"Part of Chappell's power," Robert Morgan wrote in *American Poetry Review*, "is his willingness to put all of himself into this work. He

gives to his poetry a great reservoir of learning, lyric hymning alternating with science fiction and fantasy, country music. . . . That he is willing to invest so many facets of himself is our gain. For we come to feel the wholeness of a human being."

In 1959 Chappell married his childhood sweetheart Susan Nicholls. They have one son and live in Greensboro. Among his honors are a Rockefeller grant which enabled him and his family to spend a year, 1967–1968, in Florence. He also received a National Institute of Arts and Letters grant, the North Carolina Award in Literature, and in 1985 he was named co-winner, with John Ashbery, of the Bollingen Prize in Poetry.

PRINCIPAL WORKS: *Novels*—It Is Time, Lord, 1963; The Inkling, 1965; Dagon, 1968; The Gaudy Place, 1972; I Am One of You Forever, 1985. *Collected short stories*—Moments of Light, 1980. *Poetry*—The World Between the Eyes, 1971; River, 1975; The Man Twice Married to Fire, 1977; Bloodfire, 1978; Awakening to Music, 1979; Wind Mountain, 1979; Earthsleep, 1980; Driftlake: A Lieder Cycle, 1981; Midquest, 1981; Castle Tzingal, 1984; Source, 1985.

ABOUT: Contemporary Authors Autobiography Series 4, 1986; Contemporary Authors New Revision Series 8, 1983; Dictionary of Literary Biography 6, 1980; Jackson, R. Acts of Mind, 1983; Stuart, D. *Introduction to the Fred Chappell Reader,* 1987. *Periodicals*—American Poetry Review July–August 1982; Chicago Review Summer 1981; Mississippi Quarterly Winter 1983–1984; Sewanee Review Spring 1988.

*CHEDID, ANDRÉE (March 20, 1920–   ), French-language poet, novelist, short-story writer, and playwright, was born in Cairo. Her parents, Alice Khoury-Haddad and Selim Saab, were of Lebanese Christian origin; her father was a comfortable landowner, and she recounts childhood memories of "a large house along the Nile. A brother a little bit younger. Receptions, balls at night." French was the language spoken at home, and so, as she acknowledged to Bettina Knapp in a 1983 interview, "in a certain way, I lived on the margins of the real body of the country." Nonetheless, she realized many years later, she was still profoundly marked by the Egyptian culture teeming around her.

Chedid's parents separated while she was young, and she was sent to French boarding schools, first in Cairo and then, at the age of fourteen, in Paris. Returning to Egypt four years later, she enrolled in the American University of Cairo, where she studied journalism and also did some acting. The year after her graduation, she

°chā dēd´

married Louis Chedid, then a medical student, and the two of them went to Lebanon so that he could continue his studies. In 1946 they made the decision to settle in Paris, which has been Chedid's home ever since. "I was attracted by the anonymity of the big city. I loved all of Paris," she told Knapp, adding, "I still love it." Her husband, a distinguished scientist who worked for a time at the Institut Pasteur, is now director of the Centre National de Recherche Scientifique.

Chedid recalls that she began writing very young, not out of any design to become a writer but because "the desire to express myself, a kind of thirst, was pushing me." While still at the American University in Cairo in 1940, she published a collection of poems in English, *On the Trails of My Fancy*. After her arrival in Paris, she sent a group of poems in French and in English to an editor, who published the French works, without her knowledge, in *La Revue des deux mondes*. From then on, she opted to write exclusively in French, because, she explained to Knapp, in contrast to the lyricism of English, it afforded her a "rigor" that balanced "my wholly Oriental facility for expressing myself lyrically."

In 1946 Chedid had a daughter, Michèle, followed by a son, Louis, two years later, but throughout their infancy and childhood, she continued to write. "The choice between a literary career and family life never really occurred to me," she later explained to a newspaper inquiry on "How to Be a Woman of Letters?" "Art and family life are reconcilable if it's worth it. Which is to say, if you act out of conviction and not just convention or a sense of obligation." And indeed, in 1949 she published her first French poetry collection, *Textes pour une figure* (Texts for a Figure), followed by *Textes pour un poème* (Texts for a Poem, 1950), *Textes pour le vivant* (Texts for the Living, 1953), and *Textes pour la terre aimée* (Texts for the Beloved Land, 1955). These are generally short, free-verse poems (plus a few prose-poems in *Textes pour le vivant*) with no specific place or time or setting; rather, as Jacques Izoard wrote of *Texte pour un poème*, they express "an internal elan, the will to be present among trees, children, mountains." For Marcel Hennart, they are reminiscent of Lorca while attesting to a "sensual attachment to vision, a taste for the image" that he, like others, associates with the East.

For Chedid herself, these poems were a means of getting at essentials: "I've always been attached to a compact, concise style," she told Knapp. But, she went on, after ten years of writing in this way, she had a desire to open up some-

at the essential by other means, "by the very flesh of existence, the fragility of time, the sequence of events, the entrenchment in a place, a society, historical circumstances." As a result, she turned to the novel, even though, she later acknowledged, she found it more difficult than poetry: "It's necessary to construct, to reckon with time, to be intelligible to a larger number of people."

In marked contrast to the poems, Chedid's novels draw directly on her own cultural heritage—Egypt, Lebanon, the Mediterranean—for their settings and situations. Thus *Le Sommeil délivré* (1952; translated as *From Sleep Unbound*) is set in Egypt and tells the story of a long-suffering wife literally paralyzed by her situation. Within the frame of a narrator's introduction and conclusion, Samya, the central character, recounts the painful story of her life from the time she was married, at the age of fifteen, to a man twenty-five years her senior. After years of a relationship devoid of human caring, she has a brief respite with the birth of a daughter, but the husband is indifferent to the female child, even refusing, when she falls ill, to call the doctor; the baby dies. It is at this point that Samya is struck by paralysis. After two more years of even greater indignity, there is nothing left but the terrible rage of desperation, and in the end (which is the beginning of the novel), she shoots her husband to death.

As R. M. Desnues pointed out in a 1969 appreciation of Chedid's work, this first novel, couched in the form of a murder mystery, might have remained fairly banal except for the "exotic flavor we call (naively perhaps!) the magic of the Orient," but what was even more important, he quickly added, was the sensibility of the poet so evident in the way the story was told, whereby "the sun transforms everything it touches, even ragged clothing or squalid little huts." As for the Egyptian setting, in this and later novels, Chedid indicates that it was more than a mere backdrop but never entirely realistic, and certainly not autobiographical; rather, she explained to Knapp, it serves both to "root and uproot" the narrative: the setting, the people, the sensibility are familiar to her, yet always seen from a distance. "It's an attempt to probe particular places, times, characters, but also to bring out the *common basis* of all humanity." And indeed, this is the sentiment expressed so clearly by Samya with regard to her condition as a woman: "Others, like myself, must have felt their lives crumble away in the course of an existence devoid of love. If I cry, I cry a little for them."

In the novels that follow this dead woman's

pation with the temporal and the timeless takes on the stylized cadence of myth. *Jonathan* (1955), for example, hovers somewhere between *Bildungsroman* and Greek tragedy with the story of a religious youth's coming to consciousness in the turbulent political climate of an unnamed Middle Eastern country (which is Egypt in the wake of the 1952 Free Officer's Revolt). And with *Le Sixième jour* (1960, *The Sixth Day*), Chedid combines the historical circumstances of the 1948 cholera epidemic in Egypt with the mythic dimension of resurrection to fashion an exemplary tale of faith and the struggle for survival.

Her protagonist in this most acclaimed of her novels is an old washer-woman named Saddika, who ekes out a living in Cairo while caring for her orphaned grandson. In spite of the threat of cholera, she decides to pay a visit to her village after an absence of seven years, but on her arrival, her nephew tells her she is too late: "Here there are only the dead to greet you." Cholera, he insists ruefully, "isn't for the city-folk, just for us!" In fact, the city-folk aren't to be spared either, and when Saddika returns to Cairo, she learns that her grandson Hassan's teacher has also been stricken. Declining her offer to care for him, he assures her, "In six days I'll be OK. Don't forget what I'm telling you: on the sixth day, either you die or you get better. The sixth day . . . that's a veritable re-sur-rec-tion!" When the day arrives, Hassan and his grandmother dutifully return to the school, but there is no one there.

Then Hassan also begins to show signs of the disease. Recalling what the teacher said, Saddika frantically seeks a safe place to shelter him during the fateful six days. The river, she finally decides, will be their refuge—"The water cures, the water is holy"—and she carries him to a felucca on the Nile. The days take their toll on both of them, and as she waits out the last night before the sixth day, the boatman realizes she is no more likely to survive than the child. In the morning, Hassan is dead, but the boatman reassures Saddika that "You have given him your last breath . . . the child will see the sea." And with her last breath, she murmurs "Life, the sea."

As Chedid has often remarked, her novels generally evolve not from an idea but from a single image, one or more "characters in motion"—like a film, she says. The details of events, places, characters emerge in what she describes as a "splashing" of very free writing (sometimes the whole book, sometimes just a few pages), from which, she explained to Knapp, she finds the sense of her story "like a sculptor before an uncut stone or a lump of clay." In the case of *Le Sixième jour*, the initial image was that of an old woman pushing her sick child in a cart. It was, she recalls, a long time before she knew what the end would be, but the story that finally evolved—one that "sings out hope in the struggle against death," in the words of R. M. Denues—has had an enduring success: the novel has been reissued several times, and in 1986, more than twenty-five years after the original publication, it was brought to the screen by one of Egypt's foremost directors, Youssef Chahine.

In retrospect, it is with *Le Sixième jour* that the elements of Chedid's thematic universe, long implicit in her poems and novels, assume a coherent dynamic, where the injustices of life and the inevitability of death are countered with the resilience of human nature and the indomitable hope for the future. In her next novel, *Le Survivant* (The Survivor, 1963), the central character is a woman who refuses to believe that her husband has been killed in a plane crash and spends two years searching for him until she finally joins him in death; in *L'Autre* (The Other, 1969), it is an old man who, by his sheer determination, saves the life of a stranger buried in the rubble of an earthquake. As she writes in an introduction for the paperback editions of these and other works, "I want to keep my eyes open to the world's sufferings, unhappiness, cruelty, but also to the light, its beauty, all that helps us to transcend, to live better, to bet on the future."

Throughout this period of her early novels, Chedid continued to write poetry as well, and by the mid-sixties, first with the collection entitled *Double pays* (Double Country, 1965) and then with *Contre-chant* (Countermelody, 1968), critics had begun to recognize the voice of a mature poet. Her earlier poems, observed fellow poet Alain Bosquet, had been like "tender and sweet projections into the mystery of the soul . . . a garden of delectable words, delicately arranged, made for the reader's pleasure." But with *Contre-chant*, he noted approvingly, her poetry had become "more direct, more austere, punctuated with the challenges she directs at herself and would like to share with others."

During this same prolific period (perhaps not uncoincidentally, after her children were grown up), she also turned to writing plays. These were close to her poems in their language, reminiscent of the novels in their core of myth and ritual, and considerably more experimental than either in their form. Two of her earliest plays go back to ancient sources—the history of Ptolemaic Egypt for *Bérénice d'Egypte* (Berenice of Egypt, first produced for French radio in 1964), and the biblical story of Deborah from the Book of Judges for *Les Nombres* (The Multitudes, also aired on the radio in 1966)—while *Le Montreur* (*The Show-Man*, performed at the Comédie Française in 1971 and the Berliner Ensemble in 1972, was conceived as a "spectacle" for puppeteer and four (human) puppets.

The innovations in these works in turn had echoes in both the style and the themes of her novels, beginning with *L'Autre*, where entire sections are presented in scenario form. In the highly successful novel that followed, *La Cité fertile* (The Fertile City, 1972), an elusive character named Aléfa, aging but ageless, or, in Chedid's words, "at once very incarnate and millennial," unfolds in alternating passages of narration and interior monologue reminiscent of *Le Survivant*. But now each section is composed of a rapid succession of scenes or acts, identified by brief titles in the margins, as in the first chapter's "Rivers . . . Aléfa dances . . . Aléfa's metamorphoses . . . Entry of four characters . . . The shipyard, the river bank . . . The games, the sluice." As critic Michel Bourgeois conceded with admiration, the novel effectively defies summary, but underlying this fanciful (and often humorous) literary exercise is the same "anguished search" that informs the rest of Chedid's novels: "Obviously an ambiguous work," he wrote, "but incredibly open, borrowing the royal paths of the imagination and [utilizing] the irrational to express the potentialities of all human beings, of all eras."

With *Nefertiti et le rêve d'Akhnaton* (Nefertiti and the Dream of Akhnaton), which followed in 1974, Chedid pursued another dimension first explored in the plays, namely recourse to the ancient past, here going back some 3300 years to the reign of the Egyptian pharoah Akhnaton. The use of such a historical setting, she had already advised her readers in the preface to *Les Nombres*, was "in no way an attempt to escape from the present;" rather, "it seemed to me that some bits of our common profile would emerge more freely from an unpolished universe, stripped bare, escaping memories." And as in the two historical plays, it is a mixed moment that she invokes—the triumph of an ideal (Akhnaton's unification of Egypt under the religious banner of monotheism) followed by its reversal and defeat. Once again, she uses a dual narrative structure to negotiate disparate realities—the intimate recollections of Nefertiti transmitted, and commented upon, in journal form by her scribe, Boubastos. Echoing the remarks of R. M. Desnues several years earlier, writer-critic Claude Michel Cluny pointed out that the story was not original "except that the journal is in two voices and invented by a poet." The novel never reaches the level of tragedy, he thought, because this is not its purpose; rather, "this 'poem' is bathed

in an immense melancholy, but one that sparkles nonetheless with the brilliance of life's joy."

In 1975 Chedid received the Africa Mediterranean Prize for *Nefertiti* and her work as a whole; this was not her first award—she had already won the Louise Labé Prize (1966), the Golden Eagle of Poetry (1972), and the Grand Prize of the Royal Academy of Belgium in French Letters (1975) for her collected works—and it was soon to be followed by the Mallarmé Prize for one of her finest books of poetry, *Fraternité de la parole* (Fraternity of the Word, 1976). Here, the poet's métier becomes a mission: "Through wafts and falls, obstacles and outbursts," writes Chedid in the introduction, "these texts—following others in poetry or prose—persist in forging a path of resemblances, in enumerating the proofs of a common land, of unveiling the traces of a fraternity. In spite of our enclosures, our Babels, our devastations, *somewhere* the word converges and binds us together."

As Alain Bosquet remarked, these poems, "purified, bare, practically hostile to the flamboyant image," marked a turning point in abandoning "their former tendernesses to go straight to the painful evidence." In this volume, published when the war in Lebanon was barely under way, Chedid had reserved a section for the "Cérémonial de la Violence" (Ritual of Violence), an impassioned outcry against war and destruction. As the war continued, her personal anguish generated a separate collection of poems under the same name, *Cérémonial de la violence* (1976). This "vast text-cry," in the words of Jacques Izoard, opens with the question "How to name you, Lebanon? / How not to name you? / How to cry from the depths of your chasms / Outside the camps and the clans / Far from the catechisms of discord?" Here, wrote Izoard, "pain and revolt weave a poem of unprecedented intensity," and under its surface "runs the history of our time; through the war in Lebanon, Andrée Chedid voices her reproaches for all the violence in the world, whether in Chile or Palestine or elsewhere."

During this period, Chedid found that once again she had "more taste" for poetry than for novels, and *Cérémonial de la violence* was followed by two more volumes of sober reflections on life and art, *Cavernes et soleils* (Caverns and Suns, 1979) and *Epreuves du vivant* (Proofs of Living, 1983). But as she frequently points out, moving from one form of writing to another is a vital part of her artistic activity—"a sort of perpetual rebellion . . . against any attempt at definition," she told Bettina Knapp. And indeed, alongside her poems, novels, and plays, she pub lished a travel guide to Lebanon (*Le Liban*, 1974), several collections of short stories, including *Le Corps et le temps* (Body and Time, 1978), for which she received the Goncourt short-story prize in 1979, and a number of poems and illustrated stories for children.

When she returned to the novel with *Marches de sable* (Steps of Sand, 1983), the setting was once again Egypt (early Christian this time) and the theme, the familiar reflection on life and death developed through a stark tale of three women whose paths of flight and self-searching cross in a desert retreat. Not necessarily one of her best novels—Renée Linkhorn, for example, found the structure awkward, the mix of tenses in the narrative "disconcertingly casual," and the ending rather disjointed—it was nonetheless recognized as a timely parable on violence and confessional strife. Chedid herself indicated that Lebanon was on her mind as she wrote, and that for several years she had been trying to work another one of her "images" into a novel treating the contemporary situation directly. This second project, growing fitfully out of a short story in *Le Corps et le temps*, eventually became *La Maison sans racines* (The House without Roots, 1985), Chedid's most visual, filmic novel, which interweaves narrative and flashback around a kind of slow-motion playback of a pivotal event: an abortive peace demonstration turned massacre. Once again the protagonists are women— grandmothers and granddaughters, and two unrelated women whose gesture of reconciliation ends in still more bloodshed—and once again, Chedid insists on distilling a message of hope out of a tragic situation. The last image is that of the symbolic yellow scarf of reconciliation, now stained with blood but continuing to bob up and down in the breeze. "You have to have the sense of the moment and that of the long term, which for me is the bearer of hope," she told Josyane Savigneau. "In spite of everything, I have a very positive view of history."

As various critics have pointed out, neither Chedid's novels nor her poems fall into any "school," but she is well recognized on the French literary scene; in 1986 she received the Pierre Régnier prize of the Académie Française, and the same year, she was named a chevalier of the French Legion of Honor. "Under her pen," wrote Conrad Detrez in the *Magazine littéraire*, "our language takes on a warm coloring, a singular tone." Her work is much less widely read in Egypt and the rest of the Arab world, but she seems to share none of the regrets often voiced by other Arab francophone writers. Rather, she stresses that she writes in French, and lives in France, by choice: she is not an exile. She returns to Egypt every few years for a short visit, but has no need to search for her past: "I don't feel like I've cut my roots because I carry them with me," she explained to Amina Saïd and Ghislain Ripault. "It's an internal Orient that doesn't seem incompatible with what I live here."

In order to write, she indicates, she needs solitude—which at times has meant going to a local bistro or renting a room outside of her home— and although she insists that she's "not very disciplined," she acknowledges that she sometimes works ten hours a day. But even if her writing is important to her, she says, it is not the whole of her life: "I need other people, their love, loving them; I need to look at life and to love it too," she told Saïd and Ripault. "Maybe writing is a way to multiply the feeling of life."

> First,
> erase your name,
> unravel your years,
> destroy your surroundings,
> uproot what you seem,
> and who remains standing?
> Then,
> rewrite your name, restore your age,
> rebuild your house,
> pursue your path,
> and then,
> endlessly,
> start over, all over again.
>
> (from *Contre-chant*,
> tr. Samuel Hazo and Mirène Ghossein
> in *Women of the Fertile Crescent*)

Now a grandmother, Andrée Chedid has also become the mother of a celebrity: her son Louis is a popular singer-composer whose music seems to be appreciated for the same "lucid concision" as her poetry and prose, and the two of them discuss their work and exchange manuscripts. "I don't love her because she writes," says her son, "but she's certainly influenced me." As for the elder Chedid, she suggests that "if it were possible to live three hundred years, for example (without growing too old!), I would undoubtedly try film, painting, and dance as well." As she wrote in her poem, "Qui reste debout?" (Who remains standing?).

WORKS IN ENGLISH TRANSLATION: Andrée Chedid's first collection of poems, *On the Trails of My Fancy*, was published in English in 1940, and some of her poems have been translated in K. Boullata (ed.) *Women of the Fertile Crescent*, 1978, and in the periodicals *Mundus Artium*, August 2, 1974, and the *French-American Review* June 1, 1982. Her play *Le Montreur* was translated in 1984 by Felicia Londre as *The Show-Man* for the Ubu Repertory Company. English translations of her novels include *The Sixth Day* by Isobel Strachey, 1962, and *From Sleep Unbound* by Sharon Spencer, 1983.

ABOUT: Beaumarchais, J.-P. de et al. Dictionnaire des littératures de langue française, 1984; Izoard, J. Andrée Chedid, 1977; Knapp, B. Andrée Chedid, 1984; Knapp, B. French Novelists Speak Out, 1976; Royer, J. Ecrivains contemporains vol. 3, 1985; Who's Who in France 1987–1988. Periodicals—L'Ethnie française April 1977; French Review March 1984; Livres et lectures January 1969; Magazine littéraire November 1972; Présence francophone Spring 1982.

*CHEN RONG (also rendered as SHEN RONG and SHEN JUNG) (August 18, 1935–), Chinese short-story writer and novelist, was born in Hankou into an upper-middle-class family. Her father was a judge in the Beijing (then Peiping) court under the Kuomintang rule and her mother a schoolteacher and a painter. Such family background did not serve her well later. When the Communists came into power in 1949, Chen Rong, at the age of thirteen, like all other youngsters, was stirred by the revolutionary fervor and quit junior middle school to become a salesclerk in a bookstore set up for workers. "We were full of enthusiasm," she recalled later. Groups of youngsters with packs of books on their backs went to mines and factories to teach workers to read. In 1952, at sixteen, she was assigned to work at the *Xinan Gongren Ribao* (The Southwestern Workers' Daily) as a clerk. It was at the newspaper that she became interested in writing. For the next two years she also studied Russian by following radio broadcast lessons, as was the trend then. She was doing so well with the Russian lessons that by 1954 she was admitted to the Russian Language Institute in Beijing. She was then eighteen. Before long she met, fell in love with, and married a journalist.

Upon graduation, she was hired as a translator at Radio Beijing. Too young to be affected by the 1957 Anti-Rightest Campaign, she nevertheless was sent down to a people's commune in Shanxi province to learn to work with her hands in 1963. A year later she returned to Beijing but did not get her old job back. It was then she began to do some writing and painting. Among her first works were plays. Her dream of becoming a playwright was quashed by the start of the Cultural Revolution, when of one of her plays was cancelled in rehearsal. She and her colleagues in the writing profession were *xiafang* (sent down) to Tongxian, where she again lived with a peasant family and joined in the field work. Later she claimed she enjoyed the farm work and that hard labor improved her health. Intellectuals like Chen Rong were regarded as political suspects during the Cultural Revolution and, humiliated, they often took comfort in the notion that physical hardship was good for their physical well-being. Chen Rong was no exception and, still with revolutionary fervor, she joined a propaganda team which went from village to village explaining to the peasants the Party's policies at the time.

In Tongxian she also found time to finish her first novel *Wan Nian Qing* (Perpetual Youth), which saw publication in 1975. Her subsequent works included *Yongyuan Shi Chuntian* (Eternal Spring) and *Bai Xue* (White Snow), both novelettes, and a number of short stories.

It was her short novel *Ren Dao Zhongnian* (At Middle Age), first appearing in the January 1980 issue of the Shanghai bimonthly *Shouhuo* (Harvest), that established her fame among her readers. Particularly moved were fellow intellectuals, who saw themselves in the story's protagonist, a woman doctor who, after years of devotion to her profession, suddenly discovers she cannot be also a good wife and an attentive mother. Not only must she bear the brunt of housework and child-rearing after long hours in the hospital, she must also make ends meet, which, on the meager salary accorded professional work in China, she cannot do. This novel is by no means a work of feminist ideology. It is a subtle cry for help on behalf of overworked and underpaid intellectuals who yearn for an improvement in the material conditions of their lives. Chen Rong had long been indignant at the treatment of the nation's "middle-aged" intellectuals, those who were educated after the Liberation, had high ideals, and were eager to serve the people. She said she chose doctors as her central characters instead of, say, schoolteachers because she believed that in curing the sick, doctors came into contact with people from all walks of life. Before writing *At Middle Age*, she had familiarized herself with a hospital in Beijing. After days of observation, she said: "The sacrifices our middle-aged professionals make are no less than those on the Long March." The novel was made into a hit movie soon after it was published. It was translated into several languages.

Chen Rong resides in Beijing and is now at work on a large-scale novel with an industrial setting.

WORKS IN ENGLISH TRANSLATION: *At Middle Age*, translated by Yu Fanqin and Wang Minjie, was published in 1987; "Not Your Average Girl," translated by Geremie Barme, is in Renditions, Spring and Autumn 1987; another translation, entitled "A Freakish Girl," by G. Yang, appears in the Antioch Review, Spring 1988.

ABOUT: Chinese Literature October 1980.

CHURCHILL, CARYL (September 3, 1938–), British playwright, was born in London, the only child of Robert Churchill, a political cartoonist for the London *Daily Mail*, and his wife, a fashion model, secretary, and minor film actress who had left school at fourteen. The Churchills emigrated to Canada in 1948, and Caryl was educated at the Trafalgar School, Montreal. In 1957 she returned to Britain to attend Lady Margaret Hall, a women's college of Oxford University, where she read English, taking her degree in 1960. Her three earliest plays, the one-act *Downstairs*, the full-length verse play *Having a Wonderful Time*, and *Easy Death*, were produced in 1958, 1960, and 1962, respectively, by Oxford-based dramatic groups.

Her dramatic career thus well begun by the time she left university, Churchill spent the 1960s and early 1970s raising a family and writing, in her spare time, a number of mostly one-act radio plays; during much of the 1970s she wrote plays for British television. *The Ants* (1962), *Lovesick* (1967), *Identical Twins* (1968), *Abortive* (1971), *Not . . . Not . . . Not . . . Not Enough Oxygen* (1971), *Schreber's Nervous Illness* (1972), *Henry's Past* (1972), and *Perfect Happiness* (1973) were all produced and broadcast by BBC radio. *The Judge's Wife* (1972), *Turkish Delight* (1974), *The After Dinner Joke* (1978), and *Crimes* (1982) were seen on BBC-TV. The author once characterized much of this apprentice work as "depressed plays about depression." In a 1987 interview with Mel Gussow in the *New York Times*, she qualified this statement: "I was fed up with the situation I found myself in in the 1960s. I didn't like being a barrister's wife and going out to dinner with other professional people and dealing with middle-class life. It seemed claustrophobic. Having started off with undefined idealistic assumptions about the kind of life we could lead, we had drifted into something quite conventional and middle-class and boring. By the mid-60s, I had this gloomy feeling that when the Revolution came I would be swept away."

Churchill's first major theatrical venture was *Owners*, a two-act, fourteen-scene play set in Islington, then an up-and-coming residential area of London (Churchill has lived there since the 1960s), where the poor were being displaced from their cheap rental flats to make way for the gentrification of the neighborhood. It concerns Marion, a grimly ambitious and very successful property developer who pursues Alec, the unhappy man she wants, almost as passionately as she buys up old houses and drives out the sitting tenants. She is obsessed with power, specifically the power to rule utterly the lives of everyone with whom she comes into contact. The ancillary

CARYL CHURCHILL

characters include her husband; Clegg, a loutish butcher who is being forced out of his shop by rising real-estate prices and who speaks often of wanting to kill Marion; Worsely, Marion's suicidal assistant who does the very dirty work of her evictions; and Alec and Lisa, the sitting tenants in question, a married couple whose baby is taken away from them by the rapacious Marion in exchange for allowing them to stay in their dingy flat. By the end of the play Marion has caused a fire to be set that kills Alec and a baby. But she declares herself just before the final curtain to be "not sorry at all. Not at all. I never knew I could do a thing like that. I might be capable of anything. I'm just beginning to find out what's possible." Marion is a character whose like Churchill has often drawn, a powerful, self-centered woman who outdoes all the men about her—indeed all the men anyone could imagine—in rapacious greed and overbearing malice. By the end of her story she is self-revealed as entirely monstrous. Martin Esslin, writing in *Plays & Players*, commented, "What is remarkable is that this play, which has such deep undertones, is on the surface a highly amusing folk-comedy, full of brilliant observation, witty lines, a truly Dickensian zest in creating richly eccentric characters and a wealth of telling theatrical images." *Owners* was presented at the Royal Court's Theatre Upstairs in December 1972.

Churchill was resident dramatist at the Royal Court Theatre in 1974; during this period she wrote *Objections to Sex and Violence*, which the theater produced in January 1975. Set on a stretch of almost deserted beach, it is a polemical work about a group of unhappy holiday-makers who expatiate upon and demonstrate various forms of aggressiveness, sexuality, and cravings for power. These include a middle-aged couple who quarrel constantly, a bitter divorced woman and her dithering lover, and a furiously angry female terrorist. The play was not especially favorably reviewed, but it marked the end of solitary dramatic labor for Churchill: by the time of its production she had become involved with two dramatic companies, David Hare and Max Stafford-Clark's Joint Stock Company and a feminist group, Monstrous Regiment. Joining with actors, directors, and technicians in workshop conditions, she completed two historical dramas set in seventeenth-century England, *Light Shining in Buckinghamshire* (1976), about religion and revolution during the Commonwealth, and *Vinegar Tom* (1976), about the murderous scapegoating of witches during the 1640s.

Clearly thriving on this collaborative form of theater, Churchill next worked with another Joint Stock Company workshop to fashion *Cloud Nine* (1979), a major commercial success on both sides of the Atlantic. The play is a kind of farce about sexual oppression and sexual politics, the first act of which is set in nineteenth-century colonial Africa, the second in present-day London, when the same family of characters seem to have aged only twenty-five years rather than a century. The author's tricks with time are coupled with tricks of casting and sex-roles: in act one, the mother is played by a man, her son by a girl, her African servant by a white man; in act two a little girl is played by an adult man. One of the play's themes, Churchill told Bernard Weiner in a 1983 interview for the *San Francisco Chronicle*, is "the parallels between the way colonizers treat the colonized and the way men tended to treat women. . . . I meant to show the way people move away from the rigid ways of the past and open themselves to new ways." The play had two respectable runs at the Royal Court in March 1979 and September 1980 and a long run off-Broadway at the Theatre de Lys beginning in May 1981 in a production directed by Tommy Tune, which won rave reviews and an Obie award in 1982 as best play of its year.

Top Girls is a two-act, five-scene play in which Churchill once again treats the theme of powerful women who must give up their humanity to succeed in a male-dominated world. The opening scene, the one for which the play is best known, is a fantastical dinner party in the Prima Donna restaurant celebrating Marlene's ascension to managing director of the Top Girls employment agency. Seated around the table are her guests—various historical, quasi-historical and fictional "top girls," all of whom

tell their stories to one another in overlapping dialogue. They include the nineteenth-century Scottish traveler Isabella Bird; Lady Nijo, a thirteenth-century courtesan to the Japanese emperor, who halfway through her life became a Buddhist nun; Pope Joan, the putative female pope of the ninth century; Dull Gret, from the Breughel painting of the same name, a woman dressed in an apron and armor who led a female army against the devils of hell; and Patient Griselda, the obedient wife from Boccaccio's *Decameron* and Chaucer's "Clerk's Tale," who accepted even the sacrifice of her children to her husband's whim. Most of the guests relate the climactic moments of their lives and careers. Pope Joan, for example, who has lived as a male cleric all her life, vividly and affectingly describes the fatal consequences of giving birth to a baby in the middle of a papal procession on a Rogation day; Gret, a peasant housewife, tells in her rough, honest way of leading her town's women in a raid on hell: "I'd had enough, I was mad. . . . I come out my front door that morning and shout till my neighbours come out and I said, 'Come on, we're going where the evil comes from and pay the bastards out.'" This dinner scene ends in weeping, drunkenness, and vomiting; the rest of the play is divided between scenes in Marlene's office, where she turns out to be the callous, scheming boss of underlings no less cruel and thoughtless than she, and scenes in her childhood home near Ipswich, in East Anglia, where she has left an illegitimate, somewhat retarded daughter in the care of her slatternly elder sister, Joyce. As revelation is piled on revelation, Marlene is shown by the end of the play to despise her origins—she has visited her daughter, whom she does not acknowledge as her child, only once in six years; she declares her hatred for the working class and trade unions and her love for fast cars, monetarism, and Margaret Thatcher. She looks forward to the 1980s, which she feels will be "stupendous for me. I think I'm going up, up, up. . . . This country needs to stop whining." Churchill told Michael Coveney in an interview published in the *New York Times* in January 1983, "I wanted to write a play about the unpleasantness of the sort of careers a capitalist society offers to both men and women. Mrs. Thatcher, for instance, has succeeded because she has taken on male values and has not, by her success, done anything for the oppressed women in Britain. Women achieving things isn't success if it entails the exploitation of men and women." *Top Girls* received two successful Royal Court productions in 1982 and 1985 and a New York production, off-Broadway at Joseph Papp's Public Theater, in 1982–1983. It won the author another Obie as best play of 1983.

Churchill's overall themes, which she itemized for Mel Gussow in 1987 as "power, powerlessness and exploitation; people's longings, obsessions and dreams," found increasingly intense expression during the 1980s. *Fen*, another work created under the auspices of the Joint Stock Company, presents the bitterly hard lives of East Anglian tenant-farm women, literally the peasants of our own day, who have become virtual slaves to the land and the hard, uncaring men in their lives. Their lives, almost unbelievably unrewarding, are spent cultivating and picking potatoes in the desolate, fog-shrouded marshlands of the English fen country. The only respites from this backbreaking work are tranquilizers, alcohol, and furtive sexual affairs. The play was first produced at the University of Essex Theatre, in East Anglia, in January 1983; its London opening was the following month at Islington's Almeida Theatre. Two months later the original English cast traveled to New York as part of the Britain Salutes New York Festival, then returned to London for a season at the Royal Court beginning in September 1983. An American cast presented the play at New York's Public Theater in March 1984. *Fen* won for Churchill the sixth annual Susan Smith Blackburn award for 1984, given to a woman playwright for "a work of outstanding quality in the English-speaking theatre."

Churchill's interest in methods of social coercion, state control, and the ensuing lack of human freedom resulted in the play *Softcops*, a surreal historical fantasy set in nineteenth-century France. The twelve members of the all-male cast discuss various coercive methods, including public execution and various forms of torture, public atonement and penance, and solitary confinement within a "garden of laws." Overall, the treatment of criminals is presented as a form of public entertainment, and as a sign of the state's urgent need to depoliticize the process of crime. In preparation for this play, Churchill wrote in the *RSC News* (Winter 1983), she read memoirs of the notorious Inspector Vidocq, an erstwhile criminal turned police officer; of Lacenaire, an equally notorious thief and murderer turned romantic hero; and Michel Foucault's *Surveiller et punir* (1975; translated as *Discipline and Punish*), "which fascinatingly analyses the change in methods of control and punishment from tearing the victim apart with horses to simply watching him. Jeremy Bentham comes in here, the inventor of the panopticon, the tower from which one person can watch and control many, an idea that goes right through the way society is organised."

Softcops, Churchill wrote, "was to be about the soft methods of control, schools, hospitals, social workers, when I came across the Foucault book, and was so thrilled with it that I set the play not here and now but in nineteenth-century France, where Vidocq puts on half a dozen disguises and Lacenaire is feted by the rich in his cell, while the king's assassin is quietly disposed of. There is a constant attempt by governments to depoliticise illegal acts, to make criminals a separate class from the rest of society so that subversion will not be general, and part of this process is the invention of the detective and the criminal, the cop and the robber." *Softcops* was staged by the Royal Shakespeare Company at the Barbican Pit in January 1984 in a production directed by Howard Davies.

By far Churchill's most successful and timely play was *Serious Money*, her coruscating comedy of the financial world, which was produced at the Royal Court Theatre in March 1987 and the following December, two months after the Wall Street collapse of that year, at New York's Public Theater. Another of the author's mordant studies of greed, corruption, and total self-interest, this work is set in the world of the City, London's financial center, and specifically reveals the empty lives of the men and women who work for LIFFE (pronounced "Life"), the London International Financial Futures Exchange. The play begins with a curtain-raiser, a scene from Thomas Shadwell's 1692 comedy *The Volunteers; or, The Stock-Jobbers*, then opens on the main event, with the audience left to reflect how little has changed in the brutal, cut-throat London financial world over three centuries. In the play, which is written in roughly rhyming verse, everyone is driven by greed or fear or both. These are narrow, narrowly focused people, free-market monsters with no culture or education, who know, down to the nearest penny, how much money they can make in a day and hence how much they are worth to their bosses. The play treats current topics—there is reference to the Guinness-Distillers scandal in Britain, to the Boesky scandal in New York; there is even a Peruvian version of Imelda Marcos, sweating to invest her country's overseas-aid money in Eurobonds for her own benefit and her people's ruin. "If Churchill is right," wrote Gordon Rogoff in the *Village Voice*, "Marx didn't dream the half of it. In little more than two hours, *Serious Money* bombs supply-siders out of their bunkers. Churchill has found out that capital is not about need, product, or sensibility—it's only about money, paper, and the endless supply of horror in the human heart."

With *Icecream*, produced at London's Royal Court Theatre in the spring of 1989, Churchill attempted to explore Anglo-American stereotypes. Setting off a visiting American couple, "improbably innocent," as Stephen Fender wrote in the *Times Literary Supplement*, against an unsavory pair of East Londoners in a series of short "blackout" scenes, *Icecream* exposes both the illusions of the visitors and the moral vacuum in which the British pair live. What does the play mean? "Best (for our enjoyment) not to ask," Fender concluded. He was satisfied, however, that the dramatist had composed another teasing, unconventional work: "Churchill's plays do not provide a metaphor for an underlying reality so much as demonstrate a tension between various models of representation—others as well as her own. The dialectical energy is all on the surface. It is all very post-modern, no doubt. It is also a lot of fun."

Having at last, at the age of fifty, found a resonance to her voice and a considerable amount of respect from her theatrical colleagues, Churchill has no intention of abandoning play-writing for fiction or Hollywood. "I believe in the magic of theater," she told Coveney in 1983, "but I think it is important to realize that there is nothing magical about the work processes behind it. I spend ages researching my plays and sitting alone writing them. I love going to rehearsals, but I never feel proprietorial about the text I've supplied. I love seeing actors bending and shaping what I've given them." "The attraction of theater," she said to Gussow in 1987, "is that plays are not the same every time. They can be done differently by different people and that makes it more exciting. The reason for being in the theater is the pleasure of the medium itself. . . . I [first] thought of plays as poetry and novels as prose. I thought Sophocles and Shakespeare were better than Dickens and Jane Austen. It was the greater thing to do; it was more exciting. That's why I did it, and probably why I still do it."

PUBLISHED DRAMATIC WORKS: Owners, 1973; Light Shining in Buckinghamshire, 1978; Vinegar Tom, 1978; Traps, 1978; Cloud Nine, 1979; Fen, 1983; Top Girls, 1984; Softcops, 1984; (with David Lan) A Mouthful of Birds, 1986; Serious Money, 1987.

ABOUT: Betsko, K. and R. Koenig (eds.) Interviews with Contemporary Women Playwrights, 1987; Contemporary Authors New Revision Series 22, 1988; Contemporary Dramatists, 1977; Contemporary Literary Criticism 31, 1985; Current Biography 1985; Findlater, R. At the Royal Court, 1981; Itzill, C. Stages in the Revolution, 1980; Who's Who in the Theatre, 1981. *Periodicals*—Drama Spring 1975, Summer 1979; Guardian December 12, 1972; January 2, 1975; Hudson Review Winter 1981–1982; London Times January 0, 1975; J_____, 10, 1075; J___ 19, 1980; September 10, 1980; February 10, 1983; February 18, 1983; August 1, 1983; January 17, 1984; _____ ___ 7

1986; March 30, 1987; Ms. May 1972; New Statesman September 20, 1982; February 25, 1983; January 27, 1984; New York June 13, 1983; New Yorker May 26, 1973; New York Times May 20, 1981; August 8, 1982; December 29, 1982; January 9, 1983; February 25, 1983; March 13, 1983; March 17, 1983; May 31, 1983; March 5, 1984; March 25, 1984; November 22, 1987; Plays & Players March 1973, March 1975, November 1976, February 1977, March 1977, November 1982, January 1984; Spectator January 21, 1984; Times Literary Supplement September 24, 1982; December 12, 1986; April 3, 1987; April 21, 1989; Village Voice December 15, 1987.

CLAMPITT, AMY (June 15, 1920–   ), American poet, was born in New Providence, Iowa, to Ray Justin and Pauline (Felt) Clampitt and grew up on a 125-acre farm. She graduated from Grinnell College in 1941 with a B.A. (Honors in English) and was elected to Phi Beta Kappa. Clampitt told an interviewer for *New York* magazine that at this time her goals were to get a job in publishing and to live near the ocean, with no serious thought of poetry as a career. Coming to New York in 1941 on a graduate fellowship to Columbia University, she dropped out before the academic year was finished and took a job as a secretary and later promotion director at Oxford University Press. She won a trip to England by entering an essay contest. "Growing up in the Midwest, I didn't get a sense of history," she has said. "England changed my perspective on life." After her return to the United States, Clampitt worked at the Audubon Society as a reference librarian from 1952 to 1959. She has also been an editor, for E. P. Dutton, from 1977 to 1982.

In 1975 Amy Clampitt published a book of poems, *Multitudes, Multitudes*, at her own expense. The *New Yorker*'s publishing of a poem in 1978 was her "first real appearance in a magazine," she has said. Clampitt was then in her late fifties, and this was the first significant money she had ever earned as a writer. Her first full-length collection, *The Kingfisher*, appeared in 1983. Both its title poem and its epigraph acknowledge her indebtedness to Gerard Manley Hopkins ("As kingfishers catch fire, dragonflies draw flame"). The volume was highly praised and had, for poetry, unusually large sales. In the *New York Review of Books* Helen Vendler wrote: "A century from now, this volume will still offer a rare window into a rare mind, it will still offer beautiful objects of delectation . . . it will, I think, still be read for its triumph over the resistance of language, the reason why poetry lasts." Nature appears to be the source of Clampitt's richest inspiration. Like numerous writers,

AMY CLAMPITT

to whom she is often compared, she tends (in J. D. McClatchy's phrase) "to view the [natural] world through the spectacles of language." In "Fog," for example—

A vagueness comes over everything,
as though proving color and contour
alike dispensable: the lighthouse
extinct, the islands' spruce-tips
drunk up like milk in the
universal emulsion; houses
reverting into the lost
and forgotten; granite
subsumed, a rumor
in a mumble of ocean.

Varied as is the subject matter of the poems in *The Kingfisher*, they are unified, one reviewer wrote, "by one persona, the passionate, vigorous, precise observer." Clampitt observes a truckload full of wrecked automobiles in "Salvage":

I like it; privately
I find esthetic
satisfaction in these
ceremonial removals

from the category of
received ideas
to regions where pigeons'
svelte smoke-velvet
limousines,taxiing

in whirligigs, reclaim
a parking lot . . .

Or she listens, in "Beethoven, Opus 111," to "Beethoven ventilating, / with a sound he cannot hear, the cave-in / of recurring rage" and remembers

In the tornado country
of mid-America, my father,
might have been his twin—a farmer
hacking at sourdock, at the strangle-
roots of thistles and wild morning glories,
setting out rashly, one October,
to rid the fencerows of poison ivy.

Richard Tillinghast, in the *New York Times Book Review*, commented: "It is hard to think of any poet who has written as well about the natural world as Amy Clampitt does. *The Kingfisher* opens with nine splendid poems about the New England seashore—its weather, its tidal flora and fauna, and its effect on the observer. One is led to imagine the writing of an expert naturalist with a poet's virtuoso command of vocabulary, gift for playing the English language like a musical instrument and startling and delightful ability to create metaphor." The English edition of the book, published in 1984, was widely acclaimed. It comprised a selection of thirty-two poems from the original fifty. In eliminating the social and public concerns of the final section, as well as Clampitt's notes, one British reviewer felt that the edition imposed a uniformity that did not do justice to her breadth and depth.

What the Light Was Like, published two years after *The Kingfisher*, received extensive analysis and high praise. Many reviewers noted the poet's preoccupation with death. The book was dedicated to the memory of her brother, who had died in 1981, and contained two elegies for him: "one of them, 'Urn-Burial and the Butterfly Migration,'" wrote Neil Corcoran, "is one of the best poems in the book, an intricate, finely tuned piece which tenderly yokes its heterogeneous ideas together to make its inquiry of death." In the poem she writes:

O drifting apotheosis of dust
exhumed, who will unseal
the crypt locked up within
the shimmer of the chromosomes,
or harvest, from the alluvial
death-dance of these wrecked
galaxies, this risen residue
of milkweed and honey,
rest for the body?

The title poem concerns the death of a Maine lobsterman and is characteristic of Clampitt's empathetic, sensuous attitude:

Every year in June—up here, that's the month for
    lilacs—
        almost his whole front yard,
with lobster traps stacked out in back, atop the rise
        that overlooks the inlet
would be a Himalayan range of peaks of bloom,
        white or mauve-violet . . .

A sequence of poems on John Keats stresses the

brevity of Keats' life, his brother's death, and memorializes Hart Crane's suicide and Osip Mandelstam's unknown end in Russia. "Nearly every poem in this book," Alfred Corn wrote, "has a carefully constructed 'argument,' a significant form dovetailed with a controlling metaphor."

Clampitt told an interviewer that she often spends months composing a poem, and critics have cited the need for patient study and re-reading of her poems. Occasionally objection is made to their complexity and erudition. In fact she often supplies notes to her poems on the sources of her allusions, revealing an amazing breadth of interests ranging from the natural sciences, psychology, history, music, mythology, to the New York City subway system ("Times Square Water Music") and the Beatles ("The Dakota" is an elegy for John Lennon). "When you read Amy Clampitt, have a dictionary or two at your elbow," Richard Tillinghast advised. "Her curiosity and lovingly precise attention to the world, both natual and manmade, have their logical extension in her knowledge and choice of words." Commenting on the acclaim that has greeted Clampitt's work, Alfred Corn wrote in 1985: "[It] is the more surprising in that its special characteristics are among those routinely disparaged by mainstream contemporary taste. Instead of 'natural speech' and Hemingway terseness she gives us baroque profusion, the romance of the adjective, labyrinthine syntax, a festival lexicon. She is as 'literary' and allusive as Eliot and Pound, as filled with grubby realia as William Carlos Williams, as ornamented as Wallace Stevens and as descriptive as Marianne Moore . . . All of this amounts to saying that Miss Clampitt is found among the famous eccentrics of style, like Milton, Dickinson, Mallarmé and Stevens who write in a special poetic dialect of their own confection."

While living mainly in New York, in a Greenwich Village apartment she has had for many years, Amy Clampitt enjoys traveling abroad and has crisscrossed the United States many times, usually by bus. Her work has many landscapes—Maine, Iowa, Greece, Italy—with, as J. D. McClatchy observed in *Poetry*, "the local color of each place freshly seen through anecdote and detail." Clampitt avoids parties and literary circles and focuses on work. "I had to accept that writing is hard work, and that it will *always* be hard work," she told Patricia Morrisroe. She has also stated: "As a poet, I'm trying to sort out values. To discriminate between the authentic and the phony—to preserve what's worth preserving." Among her honors has been the nomination of *The Kingfisher* for a National Book Critics Circle award, a Guggenheim Fellowship (1982), a doctorate from Grinnell, and an award in literature from the American Academy and Institute of Arts and Letters. She has also taught, as writer-in-residence, at the College of William and Mary (1984–1985) and at Amherst College (1986–1987).

PRINCIPAL WORKS: Multitudes, Multitudes, 1975; The Isthmus, 1983; The Summer Solstice, 1983; The Kingfisher, 1983; A Homage to John Keats, 1984; What the Light Was Like, 1985; Archaic Figure, 1987; Westward, 1990.

ABOUT: Contemporary Authors 110, 1984; Contemporary Poets, 4th ed., 1985; McClatchy, J. D. White Paper: On Contemporary American Poetry, 1989. *Periodicals*—Library Journal January 15, 1983; New York October 15, 1984; New York Review of Books March 3, 1983; New York Times Book Review August 7, 1983; May 19, 1985; Parnassus Spring–Summer 1983; Poetry, December 1983; Times Literary Supplement June 10, 1983; March 14, 1986; June 3, 1988; Washington Post Book World July 22, 1990.

CLARKE, GILLIAN (WILLIAMS) (June 8, 1937–), Welsh poet and editor, the daughter of Penri Williams and the former Ceinwin Evans, was born in Cardiff. Her Welsh-speaking father went to sea as a boy, became a radio engineer, and eventually settled in Penarth as an employee of BBC Wales, newly established in Cardiff. Her mother was the daughter of a poor Welsh farmer. Gillian Clarke herself was not taught Welsh as a child but learned the language later. She was educated at St. Clare's Convent, Porthcawl, Glamorgan, and at University College, Cardiff, where she received her B.A. in English in 1958. From 1958 to 1960 she worked in London as a news researcher for the BBC. She married Peter Clarke on April 21, 1960 and over the following six years had three children, Catrin, Owain, and Dylan. Interviewed by Adam Hopkins in the *Guardian* in 1983, she said: "It's what caused me the greatest distress of my life. I feel as if I had no time to be grown-up. Within eighteen months of having my first job I was married and pregnant. That was the end of full-time work. I was trapped by a pram, and have been trapped ever since." She nevertheless worked when she could as a writer, lecturer, and broadcaster on BBC and Radio Wales poetry programs. She has also appeared on television.

Gillian Clarke's own poems began to appear in magazines in 1970, when she was already thirty-three. Her first small collection, *Snow on the Mountain*, was published by a Christmas press in 1971 and warmly received. Her work was represented in the 1974 Carcanet Press collection *Ten*

Anglo-Welsh Poets and in Faber's *Poetry Intro-duction 3* (1975). In 1974, meanwhile, she had received a grant to give a series of poetry readings in Ireland from Yr Academi Gymreig (the Welsh Academy).

In 1975, with the demands of motherhood diminishing a little, she was able to take a part-time post as a lecturer in art history at Gwent College of Art and Design in Newport. The following year, after a stint as reviews editor of the *Anglo-Welsh Review*, she was appointed editor of that respected literary quarterly. She published more poetry and fewer reviews than her predecessor, and more women writers. Of this last development she has said that it was not "deliberate policy but the natural prejudice of a woman editor, a redressing of the balance towards a poetry which spoke the perceptions, experience, tone of voice which rang truest to me."

Gillian Clarke's marriage ended in divorce in 1976. Again sponsored by Yr Academi Gymreig, she visited the Soviet Union in 1977 and Yugoslavia in 1979. Her first major collection, *The Sundial*, was published in 1978 by the Gomer Press of Llandysul. It received the Welsh Arts Council Prize for 1979 and established hers as an important new voice in Anglo-Welsh poetry. It has been twice reprinted. Jeremy Hooker, reviewing the collection in *PN Review*, wrote that the poet's world "is composed of simple elements—seeds and skulls, sun and darkness, earth and water, birds, beasts and flowers—but indeed composed: as an order sustaining, and sustained by, forms of essential labour and primary human relationships. . . . The best poems in *The Sundial* . . . enact the creation of their world, by using traditional forms to contain its natural and human energies. They are remarkable for being both immediately accessible and not wholly fathomable, and, at times, [for achieving] the effective celebration of fullness of being in words that are simple and direct."

In the title poem, the speaker's young son, burning with fever and assailed by nightmares about lions, makes a paper sundial and with it is able to measure and contain the fierce sun—the emblem both of his fever and predatory nature. "In Pisgah Graveyard" is a homage to the Welsh poet Dewi Emrys:

And all around the living corn concedes
Fecundity to him. They're proud of him
Here, where full barns count as much as poetry.
He, who, they say, knew women as well as words,
Lies in the blond fields blowing to seed
With the threshing machine and the chapel clock.

Linden Peach, in an essay on Gillian Clarke's poetry in the *New Welsh Review*, speaks of her "concern with the 'feminine principle' of hold-ing opposites together," and says that "'In Pisgah Graveyard' puts together the two dimensions of Dewi Emrys's life: the earth and the chapel. . . . The whole thing is handled with grace, tact and wry humour."

The same ability to perceive connections between things apparently disparate is visible in "Lunchtime Lecture," one of the most admired poems in *The Sundial*. Here a modern woman reflects upon the excavated skull of a woman of the Bronze Age and recognizes their sisterhood. As Jeremy Hooker wrote, the poem "progresses in a way characteristic of Gillian Clarke, through stages of increasing resonance, at the same time as the description—never used only for decorative effect in her poems—becomes an extended metaphor connecting, across time and in place, particular lives through the dynamic forces they express":

She's a tree in winter, stripped white on a black sky,
Leafless formality, brow, bough in fine relief.
I, at some other season, illustrate the tree
Fleshed, with woman's hair and colours and the
   rustling
Blood, the troubled mind that she has overthrown.
We stare at each other, dark into sightless
Dark, seeing only ourselves in the black pools,
Gulping the risen sea that booms in the shell.

Mary Fitzgerald, writing about Gillian Clarke in the *Dictionary of Literary Biography*, quotes the same passage. She finds that this and other poems "present a confident and secure womanhood. . . . Her accuracy in giving voice to womanly experience, both ancient and modern, accounts in some measure for her rapid success: she can put men and women in touch with the core experiences in life from a perspective some have never imagined." Some reviewers had reservations, however. John Mole thought "too many of her vivid, sensuous nature poems [are] marred by neat, moralistic codas" and Jo Lloyd, similarly, found a tendency for some of these poems "to fall away into a limp banality.

In the late 1970s two of Gillian Clarke's poems were broadcast by the BBC. These were "Talking in the Dark," about a pair of lovers in the Welsh hills, and "Letter from a Far Country." In 1982 she gave a series of poetry readings in the United States, and the same year her second major volume of verse was published. This was *Letter from a Far Country*, taking its title from the radio poem that begins the volume. The title poem had been commissioned jointly by the Welsh Arts Council and BBC Radio Wales. According to Adam Hopkins in the *Guardian*, it was "a task . . . which seemed easy enough when the deadline was twelve weeks off. In the event, though, it was composed entirely

during the final week of the commission and delivered by hand, steaming, on the day it was
due." It was written, Gillian Clarke says, "in a
terrible rage, in great anger against the things
and people that stopped me having enough time
to write—the children, the house, the need to
earn a living. I'd just had twelve people for
Christmas and it was rage that gave me the energy to sit up five nights in a row. I started each
night where I'd left off the night before but
without knowing what I was going to write. It
was only when I finished that I realised I had not
made a protest but a celebration. . . . I would
write in anger, but I could hear the voice that
was writing the poem becoming tender with the
memories of real life."

"Letter from a Far Country" is for Gillian
Clarke "my apologia, my / letter home from the
future, / my bottle in the sea which might / take
a generation to arrive." It is a meditation on the
life of women in a rural community—the household drudgery of her grandmothers and mother
and of herself. She has called it "an epic of
housework," and in Susan Butler's anthology
Common Ground asks "why not? If the work of
raising the generations is not epic, what is? If
trenches, guns, blood are fit for poetry, as in the
work of David Jones, why not kitchens, jam,
nappies, birth!" "Where are your great works?"
the men ask the woman scornfully: this poem is
the only answer she has had time to make. There
are forty-three stanzas, one for each year of her
life, so her poem will not be done until her life
is. When that happens, she says, she will post it
home from "a far country."

According to Linden Peach, women's lives are
seen in the poem "as being concerned traditionally with ordering and counting and with the
problem of being . . . the one who stays behind,
waiting. . . . Both these roles are fixed . . . by
a frame of reference which includes psychological, historical and socio-cultural perspectives.
The eclectic nature of the poem itself shows, for
example, how the role of women as the ones who
wait is legitimised by culture and custom on
many levels. . . . Clarke, however, does not
simply delineate the strength of women which
has come from coping with traditional roles and
situations. She is interested in what all women
share as a result of these":

We are hawks trained to return
to the lure from the circle's
far circumference. Children sing
that note that only we can hear.
The baby breaks the waters,
disorders the blood's tune, sets
each filament of the senses
wild. Its cry tugs at flesh, floods
its mother's milky fields.
Nightly in white moonlight I wake

from sleep one whole slow minute
before the hungry child
wondering what woke me.

Speaking of the collection as a whole in the
Powys Review, Anne Stevenson wrote: "I don't
think there exists a book of poems today so abundant in its imagery or so generous in its acceptance of the world as it is. If there is a fault to
be found in these poems, it is perhaps that there
is too much abundance, too much acceptance . . . [and] little room to deal with evil in
her vision of the world. Of sorrow, however, she
is unsparing. In one of her finest poems, 'White
Roses,' a boy is dying in a 'green velvet sitting
room' outside of which 'white roses bloom after
rain.' It is a scene painted by Bonnard, bright,
domestic in its details. . . . The final stanza
withdraws from the scene with heartbreaking
tact":

The sun carelessly shines after rain.
The cat tracks thrushes in sweet
dark soil. And without concern
the rose outlives the child.

As Mary Fitzgerald points out, the structure
of Gillian Clarke's poems "is always far more
complex than it first appears. The verbal patterning derives from traditional Welsh metrical
devices" which "work well, and even surreptitiously—on an English-trained ear. Gillian
Clarke's poetry is . . . rich in these complex as-
sonantal patternings. . . . They result in a more
tightly unified poem, replete with subtle repeti-
tions and variations of vowels and consonant
groupings from line to line. The effect is more
complete than mere rhyme, working more like
harmony in music by suggesting connections
among words throughout the poem, not just at
the ends of lines. Its visual equivalent is the complex interlacing motif found in ancient Celtic
illumination."

A number of poems in Letter from a Far
Country explore Celtic mythology. "Sheila na
Gig at Kilpeck" is about the notorious figure of
a fertility goddess, labia grossly spread, at an ancient church at Kilpeck in Herefordshire. Male
poets as various as Jonathan Williams and Seamus Heaney have characterized this figure as a
devouring sex goddess. For Gillian Clarke she is
mother to the church's other ancient sculpted
figures; mother of us all; sister to all women:

Not lust long labouring
absorbs her, mother of the ripening
barley that swells and frets at its walls.
Somewhere far away the Severn presses
alert at flood-tide. And everywhere rhythms
are turning their little gold cogs, caught
in her waterfalling energy.

Gillian Clarke gave up the editorship of the *Anglo-Welsh Review* in 1984 and the same year left Gwent College of Art and Design to spend a year as Welsh Arts Council Writing Fellow at St. David's University College in Lampeter, Dyfed. Her *Selected Poems* of 1985 draws upon *The Sundial* and *Letter from a Far Country*, adding about twenty new poems, and confirmed her reputation as Wales' "leading woman poet." She is not a prolific one, however, and it was not until 1989 that her next substantial volume of poems, *Letting in the Rumour*, appeared. Carol Ann Duffy wrote of it that "Gillian Clarke's outer and inner landscapes (Wales, womanhood) are the sources from which her poetry draws its strengths. Her confident deployment of language—sometimes to quite extraordinary effect—gives her, mostly, a warm toughness which it has been fashionable to disassociate from such areas of concern. . . . Clarke's zest for language occasionally leads her to go over-the-top" but "otherwise this is a strong, rewarding collection, culminating in the long, moving biography 'Cofiant' which is so good it should be longer."

Gillian Clarke has said that "my main occupation here in Wales seems to be the public performance of my own and other people's poetry and teaching creative writing in various ways." It is mostly in primary and secondary schools that she teaches creative writing, and in 1989 she was working on a book about the practice and importance of such teaching. She is also preparing a book on Shakespeare for secondary school students and a book for younger children of translations from Welsh folk stories by T. Llew Jones. Clarke is a member of the executive committee of Yr Academi Gymreig.

In spite of the rage she has expressed about being "trapped by a pram," she told Adam Hopkins in her *Guardian* interview that she has "an important and close relationship with each of her three children. . . . They had me, not the other way round. They are all in my mind all the time." She has been "a Socialist since the day that I was born" and, Hopkins says, "believes in God without the trappings and rules of organised religion. What she mostly feels, she says, is a yes to life, no matter how terrible."

In *Common Ground*, interviewed by its editor Susan Butler, she said: "I do not need to be hurt into poetry, as Yeats put it. Neither do I need ideas, as such. I store things in memory. . . . I have kept journals and diaries since I was fifteen, and I re-read them and things spring to life and poetry from those pages. I take photographs and make what I call my picture books. Looking at them reminds me there are things I want to write about when the image/energy/idea meet at the right force."

PRINCIPAL WORKS: Snow on the Mountain, 1971; The Sundial, 1978; Letter from a Far Country, 1982; Selected Poems, 1985; Fires on Llŷn, 1987; Letting in the Rumour, 1989.

ABOUT: Butler, S. (ed.) Common Ground: Poets in a Welsh Landscape, 1985; Contemporary Authors 106, 1982; Contemporary Poets, 4th ed., 1985; Dictionary of Literary Biography 40, 1985.
3Periodicals—Guardian August 26, 1983; August 11, 1989; New Welsh Review Summer 1988; Planet (Welsh Internationalist) August–September 1985; PN Review 6, 1979; Poetry Wales 21 1985; Powys Review 17, 1985; (London) Sunday Times July 9, 1989; Times Literary Supplement September 29, 1989.

COBB, RICHARD (CHARLES) (May 20, 1917–), British historian, was born in Tunbridge Wells, Sussex, the only son of Francis Hills Cobb, an officer in the Sudan Civil Service, and the former Dora Swindale. He attended Shrewsbury School in Shropshire, and in 1930 won a scholarship to Merton College, Oxford; he took a first-class degree in modern history in 1934.

Cobb was a distinctly reluctant soldier during World War II, and on leaving the British Army in 1946 returned to live in Paris, a city he had loved from his undergraduate days. He describes his Paris years in many of his works; in *Tour de France*, a collection of articles and reviews, he recalls: "Although I have been described . . . as only an 'occasional tourist' in Paris (and one who could enjoy the luxury of observing the city and its inhabitants from *outside*, though not presumably *sous les ponts*) I was in fact fortunate enough to acquire a base in the city in which I was able to write, and from which I could set out, on repeated *tours de France*, for exactly twenty years. It was the rue de Tournon that enabled me to get a new start, on writing, on research and on living."

In 1955 Cobb left France to take up a lectureship in history at the University College of Wales in Aberystwyth, where he remained until 1961. After a year as Simon Research Fellow at Manchester University, and another lecturing at Leeds, he was elected fellow and tutor in modern history at Balliol College, Oxford. In 1969 he became the university's reader in French Revolutionary history, and in 1973 took up the professorship of modern history and its accompanying fellowship at Worcester College. He resigned the chair in 1984, since when he has been senior research fellow of Worcester.

RICHARD COBB

As a historian, Cobb has made a specialty of the French Revolution, particularly the Thermidorean and Directorial periods, which when he began his work were relatively underdeveloped areas of study. He had so integrated himself into France, its language and society that his first five books were written in French. These concern the revolutionary armies that wreaked havoc on much of France, especially the south, during the 1790s. Some historians believe *Les Armées révolutionnaires* to be Cobb's best work; it was translated into English by Marianne Elliott as *The People's Armies* in 1987. In Martyn Lyons' opinion, it "illustrates all Cobb's positive characteristics as a historian: the insistence on local variations, the individual case-histories, the wealth of evocative detail of violent popular protest, the vigor and color of his writing. . . . It is, in other words, the product of a fertile and erudite historical imagination, combined with the discipline and organization imposed by the demands of a French doctoral thesis."

Cobb's first major book in English was *The Police and the People: French Popular Protest 1789–1820*, a work which grew, the author writes in the introduction, "out of lectures and discussions on subjects which are not evidently related, and it does not possess any clear central theme, other than 'popular history.'" He divides the book into three sections: the first, "The Sources of French Popular History and Their Interpretation 1789–1818"; the second, "'Popular Movements,' Popular Protest, and Repression in France 1793–1818"; the third and most important, "Dearth, Famine, and the Common

People." Cobb's main concern throughout was, he writes, "to allow people to speak for themselves and to give as much license as possible to individual behavior and popular habit. I am writing about people, not about movements; about attitudes, prejudices, and mentalities, not about thought." The author appends to this introduction a personal view of his subject, the *petit peuple* of France: "Since 1935 I have walked French popular history, drunk it, seen it, heard it, participated in it, walking hand in hand with fraternity and liberty, both first discovered by me in Paris. I have been deeply involved in every event affecting the French people during the last thirty-two years. I make no claim to impartiality, for I am inside, not outside, my subject; I have acquired a new nationality—a fact which, I fear, may be apparent to the reader, as this is my first book in English—and I do not merely believe, I know that the *sans-culottes* are still with us, though they are fast disappearing in the France of the *Plan* and of the super-technocrats."

Critical reaction to *The Police and the People* was not, in general, especially favorable. "The author," wrote Judah Adelson in *Library Journal*, "calls it an impressionistic and not an exhaustive work; it is quite evident that it is, but as such it makes poor reading." C.B.A. Behrens, writing in the *New York Review of Books*, thought Cobb "so much preoccupied by the uniqueness of every individual and historical situation that generalizations, even though of course he cannot avoid them, seem to him a sin against the truth." Morris Slavin, however, reviewing the book in *Social Studies*, was considerably more favorable: "The author's remarkable knowledge of archival sources gives him an insight into the daily lives of the struggling poor, the starving artisan, or the hunger-maddened virago. . . . He understands both revolutionaries and counterrevolutionaries, the left as well as the right, and he presents them as they reveal themselves in their racy words and in their violent acts. All this is done without employing elaborate statistical tables and sociological charts."

Cobb's *Reactions to the French Revolution* covers essentially the same period as *The Police and the People* and displays in similar fashion his vast knowledge of French local history. It attempts to evaluate how the revolution was experienced by individuals, as opposed to classes or collectivities, and how events initiated in Paris by the revolution's political leadership either affected or failed to affect established patterns of private social behavior. William Slate, in *Library Journal*, called the book a "scholarly, lyrical' . . . account of selected events 'from be- low,' emphasizing the tenacity of seasoned behavior during a nonetheless epochal revolutionary period." "It is clear," wrote the reviewer for the *Times Literary Supplement,* " . . . that what [Cobb] himself seeks in history is not so much information as reassurance . . . what he seems to be looking for is confirmation that the familiar, the everyday, the idiosyncratic and the individual will survive the assaults of an invasive society moving towards technocratic and dehumanized uniformity."

Paris and Its Provinces 1792–1802 focuses on the public and private attitudes that informed the idea of Paris and its relations with the villages that surrounded it during the immediate postrevolutionary period. Cobb followed this with a tour de force of historical research and invention, *Death in Paris: The Records of the Basse Geôle de la Seine October 1795– September 1801 Vendémiaire Year IV– Fructidor Year IX.* This work is the result of the study of a single archive, "Box D4 U1 7, in the *fonds* of the *justices de paix* of Paris," which lists the particulars of "404 persons . . . who met violent deaths through suicide, accidents, murder, and natural causes." Cobb deepens the study in various ways: by noting the differences between the sexes and among the ages of the victims; by delving into the records of their clothing and jewelry; by writing as extensively as he can about "the problem of loneliness," "the provincial origins of the suicides," "the social analysis" of them "by occupation," etc. The passionate interest which Cobb feels for his subjects is evident in his description of "the harlequin colors of the very poor, as they walked in rainbow clothing, as if to defy death, always so close behind them, always dogging their brave footsteps, either in harmony with sun, shadow, and light, or in cheeky defiance of a Parisian November. . . . Dying was an important business two hundred years ago, as it must always be in a civilized society. It is consoling to discover that an urban society as allegedly brutal as that of eighteenth-century Paris should never have become habituated to suicide, regarding it, on the contrary, as something worse than murder." Later in this short yet extremely dense book, entire chapters are devoted to "The calendar of suicide and sudden death: emulation and opportunity," "The network of neighborhood, work, and leisure," "The language of clothing and livery," and "Habituation to death."

"Cobb has an extraordinary eye," wrote D. H. Fischer in the *New Republic,* "for interpretative possibilities, a gift for discovering the truths which his documents betray." Douglas Johnson in the *New Statesman* called *Death in Paris* "a fascinating work of exploration. . . . Professor Cobb shows his typically delicate insight as his reading of the documents reveals the small and intimate societies created by ordinary people in order to protect themselves against the violent and the unexpected."

In several other books, Cobb has dealt more lightly and personally with aspects of French history at some remove from the Revolution. *A Sense of Place,* which consists of three essays, "ranges," in the author's words, "from the geography of my childhood—Tunbridge Wells, Sussex and Shrewsbury—to the border between the French Empire and the Kingdom of Holland, north of Antwerp, and to the central areas of Lyon in the early days of the Revolution." *A Second Identity* and *Tour de France* each contain dozens of occasional pieces, most previously published in such British periodicals as the *Times Literary Supplement,* the *Listener,* the *Guardian,* the *Spectator,* and the *New Statesman. The Streets of Paris,* a book of photographs by Nicholas Breach with captions and accompanying text by Cobb, shows the fast-disappearing Paris of the walker: "Paris *should* be walked, because much of it, the most secret, the most modest, the most bizarre, the tiniest, is only discoverable by the pedestrian who is prepared to push behind the boulevards and the long straight streets of the Second Empire and the early confident years of the Third Republic. It is as if a different city, made up of tiny courtyards and diminutive houses, were prepared to reveal its unpretentious and endearing proportions only to the walker, still clinging to nineteenth-century forms of transport and the itineraries imposed by the amount that two legs can tackle."

Promenades: A Historian's Appreciation of Modern French Literature is a series of very personal reflections on writers as varied as Maxence van der Meersch, Louis Guilloux, Jules Roy, Hervé Bazin, and Raymond Queneau. *People and Places* included twelve essays on people, among them Christopher Hill, Cobb's fellow historian at Balliol College and later Master of Balliol; Pierre Loti; the great Resistance figure Robert Lageat ("Robert des Halles"); Georges Simenon; Raymond Queneau; and a long "tribute" to Albert-Marius Soboul, widely admired historian of the French Revolution. Ten essays follow on topics such as "Bastille Day 1944," "21 July 1945," "Bourgeois Ladies from the North-East of France," appreciations of Paris aroused by the films of René Clair and the photographs of Brassaï, and finally "The Assassination of Paris," a far from lugubrious meditation on the very dirty work accomplished, in Cobb's opinion, by generations of Paris urban planners. Cobb's two volumes of autobiography are *Still Life* and *A Classical Education.*

Cobb was visiting professor in the history of Paris at the Collège de France in 1971, and was the Ralegh lecturer at the British Academy (1974), the Zaharoff lecturer at Oxford (1976), and the Helmsley lecturer at Brandeis University (1981). He holds an honorary doctorate from the University of Essex (1981) as well as several French decorations, including Chevalier de la Légion d'Honneur (1985). His *festschrift* is *Beyond the Terror: Essays in French Regional and Social History, 1794–1815* (1983), edited by Gwynne Lewis and Colin Lucas; of the eight essays the most interesting is Martyn Lyons's "Cobb and the Historians"; it clearly demonstrates just how modern a historian he really is. "It is no exaggeration to describe Cobb as a historian of *mentalités*, a historian of mental attitudes and assumptions. . . . Cobb . . . remains a law unto himself, an idiosyncratic figure, admired by a wide public for his human approach to history, while his very personal preoccupations make his work harder and harder to absorb into the mainstream of historiography. . . . Cobb, one might say, is our greatest historian of France *malgré lui*. Great for his human sympathy, his eloquence, his effervescent historical imagination, his unparalleled archival knowledge; *malgré lui* because of his adamant refusal to build structures, to make syntheses, to refer to historical problems others wrestle with, because for him everyday details are all. Is Cobb a novelist *manqué*? Such a question could only be asked by someone who mistakenly assumes the novelist to be necessarily more creative than the historian. It is hard to see how the novel could offer Cobb a better medium for his incomparable talents."

WORKS: *In French*—L'armée révolutionnaire à Lyon, 1952; Les armées révolutionnaires du Midi, 1955; Les armées révolutionnaires, vol. 1 1961, vol. 2 1963; (The People's Armies, 1987); Terreur et subsistences, 1965. *In English*—A Second Identity: Essays on France and French History, 1969; The Police and the People, 1970; Reactions to the French Revolution, 1972; Paris and Its Provinces 1792-1802, 1975; A Sense of Place, 1975; Tour de France, 1976; Death in Paris 1795–1801, 1978; Streets of Paris, 1980; Promenades, 1980; French and Germans, Germans and French, 1983; Still Life, 1983; A Classical Education, 1985; People and Places, 1985.

ABOUT: Cobb, R. Still Life, 1983; A Classical Education, 1985; Contemporary Authors 116, 1986; Lewis, G. and C. Lucas (eds.) Beyond the Terror, 1983; Who's Who 1987–1988. *Periodicals*—American Historical Review December 1971, April 1973, December 1979, February 1984; American Journal of Sociology September 1971; American Scholar Summer 1976, Summer 1984; Annals of the American Academy January 1973, September 1981; Choice November 1971, January 1973

October 1983; Economist June 14, 1975; May 24, 1980; August 6, 1983; Encounter November 1973, January 1976; English Historical Review October 1976; Library Journal November 1, 1970; November 1, 1972; November 15, 1975; May 15, 1980; May 1, 1983; New Republic December 9, 1978; May 17, 1980; August 15–22, 1983; New Statesman May 2, 1975; December 1, 1978; New York Review of Books May 25, 1971; April 5, 1973; June 16, 1983; New York Times Book Review December 18, 1983; New Yorker February 5, 1979; Social Studies November 1971; Times Literary Supplement November 27, 1970; June 16, 1972; March 17, 1976; August 12, 1983; April 26, 1985; January 17, 1986; Virginia Quarterly Review Autumn 1979.

COHEN, I. BERNARD (March 1, 1914–   ), American historian of science, was born in Far Rockaway, New York, the son of Isidor Cohen and the former Blanche Bernstein. Virtually his entire academic career has been at Harvard University. He entered as a freshman in 1933 at the age of nineteen, received his undergraduate degree *cum laude* in 1937, then became a graduate student under the auspices of the Committee on Higher Degrees in the History of Science on Learning. His principal mentor was George Sarton. From 1938 to 1941 he was a fellow in the department of the history of science at the Carnegie Institution in Washington, D.C., but returned to Harvard to teach physics and mathematics during World War II under a program arranged for the Navy. In 1947 he received his doctorate and took up a post teaching physical science and the history of science in the university's general education division. He was made a professor in 1959 and in 1977 was named to the Victor S. Thomas chair in the history of science, becoming emeritus in 1984. Cohen married Frances Parsons Davis in 1944; they have a daughter.

Cohen has specialized throughout his career in the history of the physical sciences in the seventeenth and eighteenth centuries, and has examined in particular the structure of the processes of change and transformation that occurred in early modern science as a result of the Newtonian revolution. He is among the premier experts on the works of Sir Isaac Newton and is the coeditor of the *Principia*, the pioneering physicist's most important work.

The famous electrical experiments of Benjamin Franklin were the basis for Cohen's first significant book, *Benjamin Franklin's Experiments: A New Edition of Franklin's Experiments and Observations on Electricity*. His lengthy introduction examines Franklin's work on electricity, but the main portion of the book also covers other subjects: meteorology, heat,

I. BERNARD COHEN

and light. Cohen writes that "Franklin's scientific reputation was based largely on his electrical research, which forms his most permanent and lasting contribution to scientific thought." Cohen continued his examination of Franklin with a general biographical study, *Benjamin Franklin: His Contribution to the American Tradition*, in which Franklin's "inventions and applications of science" formed only one aspect of the overall treatment; others included Franklin's opinions and writings on self-improvement, mutual aid, community service, and "the style of being American." Franklin the scientist, however, remained at the forefront of Cohen's mind and scholarly commitment; his next book, *Franklin and Newton: An Enquiry into Speculative Newtonian Experimental Science and Franklin's Work in Electricity as an Example Thereof*, was one of his most important and influential works. The study's major aim, he writes in the preface, "is to illuminate the nature of scientific thought by considering the interaction between the creative scientist and his scientific environment. I have chosen the physics of the eighteenth century as a field of inquiry primarily because it provides an example of the profound influence exerted by the work of a single man, Isaac Newton, to a degree that is unique in the development of modern science. . . . The choice of Franklin as an eighteenth-century Newtonian scientist presents a special challenge in that Franklin was without mathematical training and thus appears to be wholly outside the Newtonian tradition as usually conceived today. The very fact that Franklin was referred to as a 'Newton'

indicates that the concept of 'Newtonian' science in the eighteenth century had a connotation quite different from that which is generally found in our present-day histories. Thus the burden of the monograph may be said to be a search for the connotations of 'Newtonianism.'"

The careful exploration in *Franklin and Newton* of the eighteen-century experimental tradition and its direct descent from seventeenth-century experimental sources encouraged the emergence of several themes that have remained important in Cohen's later work. These are summarized by Everett Mendelsohn, the editor of Cohen's *festschrift, Transformation and Tradition in the Sciences* (1984), as: "his interest in the 'scientific personality' of key figures in science . . . and an explicit concern for the conditions of the emergence of novelty, treated in [*Franklin and Newton*] as an appendix. If it was Benjamin Franklin who captured Bernard Cohen's imagination in the first phase of his career, it became clear with this book that Isaac Newton would dominate the next phase." Indeed, Cohen disclosed at the conclusion of the preface that he had agreed to collaborate with the French historian of philosophy and ideas Alexandre Koyré on a variorum critical edition of the *Principia*.

The work of the two historians was fruitful and productive, and most of the detailed labor on the edition was complete when Koyré died in 1964. It fell to Cohen then, with the assistance of Anne Whitman, to see the work through the press. The two large volumes of *Isaac Newton's "Philosophiae Naturalis Principia Mathematica," the Third Edition (1726) with Variant Readings* (1972) were preceded by Cohen's own *Introduction to Newton's "Principia"* (1971), a 380-page book in the same large format, in which Cohen explains how the edition enables "the reader to see at a glance the successive alterations made by Newton during the span of about four decades from the completion (in 1686) of the manuscript of the first edition [London, 1687, through the second edition, Cambridge, 1713] up to the printing of the third and ultimate authorized edition in 1726." The new edition "displays for comparison the variants uncovered by a *verbatim et litteratim* collation of the three authorized editions, . . . thus presenting Newton's concepts, biases, tastes, knowledge, and mastery of the subject." The *Choice* reviewer called the edition "a chef-d'oeuvre which is certain to become an indispensable item for Newtonian scholars in the generations to come. It will also provide much intellectual delight to the general reader of science and history."

Other book-length contributions by Cohen to

Newtonian studies, supplementing his dozens of scholarly articles, include his edition of *Isaac Newton's Papers and Letters on Natural Philosophy*, in which, with the assistance of Robert E. Schofield, William B. Todd, Thomas S. Kuhn, Marie Boas, Perry Miller, and C. C. Gillispie, he brought together, he writes in the introduction, "for the first time Newton's scattered papers and letters on natural philosophy (excluding mathematics, pure theology, and biblical chronology) as they were actually available *in print* during most of the 18th century, that is, prior to Horsley's edition of Newton's works in 1779–1785." He also edited, and wrote a lengthy introduction for, a pioneering study by the British mathematician Walter William Rouse Ball (1850–1925), *An Essay on Newton's "Principia."*

In 1966 Cohen was invited to give the Wiles Lectures at Queen's University, Belfast. It was an opportunity for the Newtonian editor to take a step back from his painstaking labor and consider the broader meaning of Newton's work. The lectures were expanded and revised over the next dozen years with special attention to the themes of the development of Newtonian science and the idea of scientific change. *The Newtonian Revolution: With Illustrations of the Transformation of Scientific Ideas* centers on the scientific life of Newton, "but does so," he explains in the preface, "as a key to the understanding of an aspect of Newtonian Science and as a means of understanding scientific change generally." The book concerns the Newtonian revolution "in the ways in which I believe Newton's contemporaries and immediate predecessors in the exact sciences conceived him to have made a 'revolution.'"

Cohen had refined his ideas regarding scientific change, moving from the word "transformation" to the word "revolution" in acknowledgement of the Newtonian impact. In his next book he went further, adding many comments on the concept of revolution as it refers to the sciences in general. *Revolution in Science* is a massive 711-page tome which assesses the idea of revolution throughout scientific thought, inquiry, and experimentation. In the preface, he describes the work as "a historical and analytic study of [the] concept through the course of four centuries." He makes a clear distinction between "the historical perception of revolution and the historian's perception. The former comprises the judgments made at the time of the revolution and during successive ages and are the objective facts or data of history; but the latter are present-day subjective judgments. . . . In almost every case there is a confluence of the two; those revolutions that pass the test of historical evidence tend to be those that in the judgment of today's

historians (and scientists) are also revolutions." The book examines the Copernican revolution of the seventeenth century, the Newtonian and chemical revolutions of the eighteenth, the Darwinian and Freudian revolutions of the nineteenth, and the Einsteinian and earth-science revolutions of our own century. "There is not," wrote Tom D'Evelyn in the *Christian Science Monitor*, "a dull page, or an awkward sentence in the book. . . . [It] is animated by a radical faith in science. . . . The general reader . . . can only be grateful to Professor Cohen for writing his big book, his magnum opus, with us in mind. Generations will be diverted and no doubt instructed by this book."

George Sarton, Cohen's teacher at Harvard, founded and edited for many years *Isis*, the official journal of the History of Science Society. Cohen served as the journal's managing editor (1947–1952) and then as its editor and chairman of its editorial committee (1953–1958). He was long active in the general affairs of the Society, serving as a member of its executive council (1945–1958), as vice-president (1959–1960), and as president (1961–1962). He was also chairman of the National Committee on the History and Philosophy of Science (1961–1962), and president (1968–1971) of the International Union of the History and Philosophy of Science. He has been a frequent visitor to the United Kingdom, where he was special university lecturer at University College, London (1957) as well as Wiles lecturer at Belfast (1966). He spent perforce a good deal of time at Cambridge University, where many of Newton's manuscripts are housed, and was visiting fellow of Clare Hall (1965) and visiting overseas fellow of Churchill College (1968). He is a fellow of the Royal Astronomical Society and the Royal Society of Art.

PRINCIPAL WORKS: Benjamin Franklin's Experiments, 1941; Roemer and the First Determination of the Velocity of Light, 1944; Physical Laboratory Manual, 1944; Science, Servant of Man, 1948; Some Early Tools of American Science, 1950; Ethan Allen Hitchcock, 1952; Benjamin Franklin, 1953; Franklin and Newton, 1956; The Birth of a New Physics, 1960, rev. ed., 1985; Introduction to Newton's "Principia," 1971; The Newtonian Revolution, 1980; From Leonardo to Lavoisier, 1450-1800, 1980; Revolution in Science, 1985; Benjamin Franklin's Science, 1990. As editor—(with F. Watson) General Education in Science, 1952; Benjamin Franklin's Account of the Pennsylvania Hospital, 1954; Isaac Newton's Papers and Letters on Natural Philosophy, 1958; (with Howard Mumford Jones) A Treasury of Scientific Prose, 1963; Jean - Baptiste-Joseph Delambre's "Histoire de l'astronomie moderne," 1969; (with A. Koyré and A. Whitman) Isaac Newton's "Philosophiae Naturalis Principia Mathematica," 1972; W. W. Rouse Ball's "An Essay on Newton's Principia," 1972; Stephen Peter Rigaud's "Historical

Essay on the First Publication of Sir Isaac Newton's 'Principia,'" 1972; William Whiston's "Sir Isaac Newton's Mathematick Philosophy More Easily Demonstrated," 1972; Isaac Newton's Theory of the Moon's Motion (1702), 1975; (with K. E. Duffin and S. Strickland) Puritanism and the Rise of Modern Science, 1990.

ABOUT: Contemporary Authors 69–72, 1978; Who's Who in America 1980–1981. *Periodicals*—Booklist July 1, 1971; Choice February 1972, April 1981, July–August 1981, November 1985, April 1986; Christian Science Monitor April 24, 1985; Library Journal December 1, 1980; December 15, 1980; June 1, 1985; July 1985; New Republic April 21, 1986; New York Review of Books February 27, 1986; New York Times Book Review April 21, 1985; Science July 28, 1972; Scientific American June 1972, January 1981; Times Literary Supplement December 17, 1971; September 13, 1985.

ISABEL COLEGATE

COLEGATE, ISABEL (September 10, 1931–), British novelist and critic, is the daughter of Lady Colegate Worsley and Sir Arthur Colegate, a businessman and member of Parliament. She and her three older sisters grew up in Lincolnshire, Yorkshire, and Shropshire. Educated at home until she was eleven, she next attended two boarding schools before convincing her parents that she should leave school. Colegate describes her younger self as "overwhelmingly shy" and her school experiences as "agony." She began writing as a child to compensate for feeling "outside of the real world. . . . I think that did contribute to the fact that I went on writing and wrote more than I might have if I had found it easier to communicate."

Following a short interval of private tutoring, Colegate abandoned the idea of pursuing a university degree and took a secretarial job in London. Shortly after, she starting working for Anthony Blond, who had just opened a literary agency. Blond soon started his own publishing business and published Colegate's first novel, *The Blackmailer*, in 1958. The book concerns Judith Lane, the widow of an alleged war hero, Anthony Lane. Baldwin Rees, a soldier Lane commanded in Korea, extorts money from Judith by threatening to reveal that her husband was actually a coward and maybe even a traitor. By these perverted means, Rees hopes to forcibly enter the Lanes' upper-class society. He and Judith find themselves bound together in a bizarre and grotesque relationship until a weekend with Anthony's snobbish, aristocratic family shows Rees that his underhanded scheming is no match for the more subtle iniquities of his social betters. As a result, his strange association with Judith dissolves, along with its attendant immorality.

Throughout the novel, Colegate explores the nature of power, both in terms of Rees' blackmail and Lane's mythic heroism. She also begins to question the post–World War II upheaval that caused wealthy families like Anthony's to lose their bearings as well as their social prominence. *The Blackmailer* was a critical success. While reviewers discerned some flaws—a mechanical quality and overzealous writing and plotting— they attributed them to inexperience. A *New Yorker* reviewer praised the author's "stunning perception of character." "Colegate is as astute about the psychological underpinnings of her characters' behavior as she is about their comic potential," Dorothy Wickenden observed in the *New Republic*. In the *Hudson Review* Wendy Lesser labeled *The Blackmailer* "Pinter-like" in its abrupt realism.

Colegate's third novel, *A Man of Power*, similarly examines the attempt of a nouveau-riche man to penetrate aristocratic circles. The protagonist Lewis Ogden divorces his wife and woos Lady Essex Cowper, an aging aristocrat. Lady Cowper and her friends tolerate Ogden in order to spend his money. He finally realizes that his attraction for them is purely monetary when he discovers Lady Cowper with a lover. Vanessa, Lady Cowper's daughter, serves as the book's narrator. Like Colegate, she is both a member and a critic of the upper classes, struggling to reorient her position in rapidly a changing world. *A Man of Power* generally earned praise from reviewers. Oswell Blakeston called it "as satisfying as an Edwardian piece of storytelling . . . informed with the insight of modern realism."

The *New Yorker* described the novel as "a kind of English *The Great Gatsby*." "Unlike her clumsy heroes and youthful heroines," another reviewer observed, "[Colegate] intuitively understands all about the 'hateful little sounds' that social creatures make as they scrabble after the unattainable."

Colegate's most autobiographical novel, *The Great Occasion*, follows the fortunes of five sisters as they become adults and set forth from their well-to-do home. All of them face the insecurity of a changing world in which the role of women is no longer rigidly defined. Penelope marries a conventional upper-class man; the couple's conventionality is shaken, however, by the husband's older brother, Lord Trent, who lives at the family estate, now also housing a zoo, with his male lover, the former bear-keeper. Susan devotes herself completely to her husband and has a nervous breakdown as a result of her self-repression. The beautiful Angel, rendered a sexual object by the men in her life, finds a meaningful role in motherhood; nevertheless, Colegate suggests that this solution is a temporary one. Charlotte attempts to find fulfillment in her art and marriage to an artist. She forfeits her career for his, however, and eventually dies of cancer. The youngest daughter, Selina, devotes herself to writing in the henhouse, much as Colegate herself had done as a girl. At the end of the novel, Selina appears to have achieved self-realization. Reviewers acclaimed *The Great Occasion*'s strong characterization and astute portrayal of the social disruptions of the 1960s. They criticized the book for its dim view of human existence and its tendency to ramble but found Colegate an adept and witty stylist. "The treatment varies when necessary from the deadpan to the poignant but there is never any forced brightness," Maurice Richardson noted in the *New Statesman*.

Although these three novels enjoyed critical successes, they failed to attract a wide readership. In response, Colegate decided to experiment at the risk of offending conventional tastes. The ensuing book, *Statues in a Garden*, is set during the ironically splendid summer of 1914, the eve of World War I. It centers on the Westons, a liberal, aristocratic family whose own domestic tragedies, including a quasi-incestuous relationship and a suicide, presage the havoc soon to be wreaked by the war. Colegate highlights the tension of the plot by concealing the identity of the narrator until the end of the book. Colegate's experiment won her praise for economical writing, confident handling of a historical setting, and skillful unfolding of the story. Statues in a Garden has, despite its slight self-consciousness, a resonance which is the mark of

an achieved work of art," Stephen Wall wrote in the *Listener*. Frank Littler, in the *New York Times Book Review*, compared Colegate favorably to Ivy Compton-Burnett: "Where she differs is in weaving documentary details so adroitly into her story that the century in its teens is given a reality at once recognizable and fresh."

Colegate's next work, the Orlando trilogy, has been called her most ambitious. The first book, *Orlando King*, is a modern version of the Oedipus story. It follows the rising and falling fortunes of Orlando King from 1930 to 1940. Orlando gets his first job with a man who, unknown to them both, is his real father. He achieves great wealth and a cabinet position and then accidentally triggers his father's death. He marries his stepmother, who has a mental breakdown. After learning the truth about his father and being partially blinded in the Blitz, Orlando goes into exile in Tuscany. The second book in the trilogy, *Orlando at the Brazen Threshold*, takes place in 1951, the era of the Suez Canal crisis. The novel chronicles the relationship between Orlando and his seventeen-year-old daughter Agatha. In the last book, *Agatha*, the heroine's stepbrother Paul is convicted of treason. Agatha helps him escape from prison and ends up in prison herself, but she passionately maintains her conviction that loyalty to a brother overrides loyalty to a country.

The Orlando trilogy received uneven reviews. The first book was criticized for its "almost unreadable opening" and obscure closing. However, critics admired Colegate's handling of historical detail and "sharply outlined characters." *Orlando at the Brazen Threshold* struck reviewers as more conventional, less astute and courageous. *Agatha*'s reviewers praised Colegate for confronting the novel's final issue, the heroine's responsibility for her actions. John Mellors of *London Magazine*, however, noted that he was "left cold and puzzled by this story of half-siblings, homosexual traitors, property tycoons, and Cabinet Ministers at the time of Suez."

The trilogy was not a commercial success; the first two books went out of print by the time *Agatha* appeared. Colegate decided that this freed her to continue experimenting with her writing. Her next book, *News from the City of the Sun*, concerns a secular community built by the Whitehead brothers in the early 1930s. Although the three brothers have very different visions of the community's mission, it endures until the 1970s. Colegate provides the historical context for the stream of characters who people the community in the course of forty years and draws her characters to match social and political changes. The novel earned Colegate commendation for a confident tone, wit, and acuity. Gillian Wilce in the *New Statesman*, found Colegate's description of one of her characters applicable to the author: "[she has a] detached way of looking at things which you might expect to be cold but is somehow the opposite, all bright awareness and sympathy." Francis King observed in the *Spectator* that "Miss Colegate has the kind of deep-breathed, long-paced style that suggests a pen being dipped into an ink-pot rather than the clatter of an electric typewriter." Nevertheless, he criticized the work for uneven historical development, an overabundance of characters, and a tendency to overreach.

In *The Shooting Party*, her best known and most acclaimed novel, made into a successful film in 1985, Colegate revisits England a year before the outbreak of World War I. She chose to return to this period because

> I think that the period that's just going out of living memory is always rather fascinating. And for Europeans, the first World War was such an enormous cataclysm. From the point of view of social history, nearly *all* the problems which are still besetting us and which we go on worrying away at, were coming up then. . . . It wasn't a peaceful golden age. Everything was there, beginning to agitate, and then the war accelerated the processes of change.

The novel is set at the Nettleby estate, where aristocrats have gathered to engage in games they take "too seriously" in the absence of "proper functions." Colegate demonstrates all their rigid and sometimes effete standards, such as good sportsmanship and paternalism. The preoccupied pleasure of the aristocrats is shattered at the end when one of the working-class men helping to rouse the pheasants in the brush is accidentally shot. At the end of the book, the narrator off-handedly remarks, "By the time the next season came round a bigger shooting party had begun, in Flanders."

Some reviewers faulted *The Shooting Party* for its thin, somewhat predictable plot. In general, however, the novel received high praise. *Spectator* reviewer Francis King called it "a marvelous evocation of a period that Miss Colegate is far too young to have lived through." Other reviewers commented on her gentle irony, deftness, and "subtle rendering of manners." The book won the W. H. Smith Literary Award, the first novel to do so in nine years.

Colegate published her first collection of short stories, *A Glimpse of Sion's Glory*, in 1985. In "The Girl Who Lived among Artists," an arty young woman creates social chaos when she joins a motley household in interwar Bath. In the second story, "Distant Cousins," a science-fiction writer's story about a Russian tribesman, whose superhuman yet sweet race could have salvaged life on earth, comes true. The title story concerns Raymond, an Oxford graduate who dwells on his life's empty achievements in a lengthy, disturbing letter to Alison, a stodgy diplomat's wife. Reviewers found the collection problematic. The length of the stories struck Toby Fitton of the *Times Literary Supplement* as "awkward," given their content and intrinsic interest. "They are loosely connected by the theme of how particular moments of revelation—anthropological, intellectual and artistic-sexual—affect the very varied characters," Fitton noted, "but there is wisely no forced attempt at linkage." In the *New York Times Book Review*, Anne Bernays acknowledged Colegate's range of "interests, style and powers"; Bernays called the first story very good, the second merely interesting, and the third "a mistake." "We don't care what happens to Raymond and I suspect Miss Colegate doesn't much care either."

Colegate once referred to her eleventh novel, *Deceits of Time*, as "much more concerned with contemporary life" than her earlier novels. It centers on Catherine Hillary, a mediocre biographer who is chosen, for reasons beyond her ken, to write the life of Neil Campion, a war-hero and member of Parliament who died in a mysterious car crash in 1941. Her inability to get to the bottom of Campion's story makes her doubt the value of biography and her own talents. As Catherine continues research on the book, however, she discovers that Campion was involved in a plot to make peace with Germany. The revelation restores both her faith in biography, tempered by an acceptance of its limitations, and her self-esteem. Thomas Mallon noted in the *New York Times Book Review* that *Deceits of Time* "offers a good mystery." There are, however, some social situations "beyond the descriptive powers of Miss Colegate." *Times Literary Supplement* reviewer Lindsay Duguid listed among the pleasures of the book the historical background that does not "unbalance the present-day interest." She also admired the sensitivity with which Colegate handles Catherine's personal struggle. The author fails, though, "to make something serious . . . of the class comedy of the first half of the novel . . . ."

Colegate lives with her family at Midford Castle, an eighteenth-century "gothic-folly" style building, just outside of Bath. She has been married since 1953 to Michael Briggs, who has directed engineering firms. They have three grown children, Emily, Joshua, and Barnaby.

PRINCIPAL WORKS: *Novels*—The Blackmailer, 1958; A

Man of Power, 1960; The Great Occasion, 1962; Statues in a Garden, 1964; Orlando King, 1968; Orlando at the Brazen Threshold, 1971; Agatha, 1973; News from the City of the Sun, 1979; The Shooting Party, 1981; Deceits of Time, 1988. *Short stories*—A Glimpse of Sion's Glory, 1986.

ABOUT: Contemporary Authors New Revision Series 8, 1983; Contemporary Literary Criticism 36, 1986; Contemporary Novelists, 4th ed., 1986; Dictionary of Literary Biography 14, 1983. *Periodicals*—Hudson Review Autumn 1984; Listener August 27, 1964; London Magazine February 3, 1974; New Republic April 18, 1981; May 28, 1984; New Review Spring 1978; New Statesman May 4, 1962; July 13, 1979; New York Times Book Review November 17, 1985; December 11, 1988; New Yorker May 7, 1984; Publishers Weekly December 13, 1985; Punch September 18, 1968; Spectator July 21, 1979; September 13, 1980; Times Literary Supplement June 21, 1985; July 2, 1988.

BARBARA COMYNS

*COMYNS (-CARR), BARBARA (BAYLEY) (December 27, 1909–   ), British novelist, was born in Bidford-on-Avon, Warwickshire, to Albert Edward and Margaret (Fenn) Bayley. In an autobiographical introduction to the Virago reprint of her 1959 novel *The Vet's Daughter*, she writes a candid account of her early life that reads remarkably like almost any of her novels. One of six children in a shabby-genteel family, she recalls a childhood that was at once idyllic and chilling. Her father, a semi-retired businessman, "was an impatient, violent man, alternatively spoiling and frightening us." Her mother, a delicate woman considerably younger than her husband and evidently exhausted by so many childbirths, suddenly lost her hearing at the age of twenty-five and thereafter communicated with her family in sign language: "We really had little contact with our mother even before she went deaf and were brought up by our formidable grandmother, governesses and the servants." The children created their own little world, boating on the nearby river, playing in the garden, and wandering freely in the beautiful Warwickshire countryside.

Young Barbara's education was irregular at best. After the governesses ("who had few qualifications to teach," she writes), she attended a boarding school briefly, but her formal schooling ended at fifteen when she returned to the family home. She had been writing and illustrating her own stories since the age of ten, and it was her interest in art that finally took her, after her father's death, to London where she studied at Heatherly's Art School until her meagre funds were exhausted. Adrift in London, barely twenty years old, she supported herself with office work and copy writing in an advertising agency,

and lived in a small shabby bed-sitter in Mornington Crescent: "It was a decaying, gritty district but central, and it pleased me to know that Dickens had once lived there, also several of the characters in his books." Thanks to her discovery of public libraries her education progressed. She read, she says, "until I was almost drunk on books." Her writing, however, was not progressing—at least in her own critical judgment. Finding her work "imitative and self-conscious," she destroyed everything and did not resume writing for many years.

There would in fact have been little time for writing. In 1931 she married a fellow art student, and there were soon two children to provide for. Just as she was later to record her childhood memories in her first novel, *Sisters by a River*, she describes the struggles of an improvident and impoverished young couple much like herself and her husband in *Our Spoons Came from Woolworths*. In that novel, as in her own life, the marriage could not bear the strains of poverty and broke up. To support her little family Barbara Comyns modeled, often posing with her children, tried property management, restoring old houses into small flats, and even for a while ran a garage "where I sold elderly, unusual cars." When World War II broke out she lost most of her tenants and there was no market for vintage automobiles, so she moved to the country with her son and daughter to work as a cook-housekeeper for a family. "The children were happy, which pleased me," she writes, "but I felt lonely and frustrated until I borrowed a typewriter and started writing again." Her manuscript was a fictional memoir of her childhood; once written, it was packed away in a suitcase and forgotten. She returned to London in 1942 where she re-established herself as a business-woman. In addition to real estate management, she sold old pianos and antique furniture and she bred poodles. All this provided her with enough income to pay the children's school fees and enough self-confidence to resume writing, with the novel that was to be *Our Spoons Came from Woolworths*. By 1950 Comyns was an estab-lished author with a small but appreciative audi-ence.

Reviewers early on recognized that Comyns' novels were not the lightweight romantic fare that a superficial reading would suggest. Though disturbed by her "sometimes irritatingly simple style," most of them recognized that hers was a deceptive simplicity that cloaked an undercur-rent of nightmare reality—a world in which be-nign nature sometimes turns wildly destructive, lovers disappoint and betray, parents brutalize their children, and children torment animals and each other. Among her early admirers was Graham Greene, himself an expert on the depths to which human character can sink even in the midst of a so-called humane and civilized soci-ety. Although one of her early novels, *The Vet's Daughter*, had some popular success in BBC a radio serialization and in a musical adaptation staged by Sandy Wilson as *The Clapham Wonder*, it was not until the early 1980s when Virago Press began reissuing her novels in paper-back with introductions by the novelist Ursula Holden that readers in the United States as well as in Great Britain became aware of the peculiar pleasures of her work. "These are strange little books," Lou Ann Walker observed in the *New York Times Book Review* in 1987, "veering as they do from the sweetly comforting to the gris-ly. They're about childhood and growing up. And . . . that means initiation into the horrors of life."

Like the classic tales of the Brothers Grimm—one of which directly inspired her novel *The Ju-niper Tree*—Barbara Comyns' works enchant by their curiously amoral mixture of innocence and evil. Modern fairy tales, they only narrowly es-cape the traps of romantic sentimentality, and they do so by setting their own traps for the un-wary reader. *Sisters by a River*, as Ursula Holden points out, had difficulty finding a publisher in the post-war era because "readers needed reas-surance, non-violence, soothing, and *Sisters by a River* deals succinctly with cruelty and misun-derstanding between children and adults in a middle-class family—that bastion of English society." The child-narrator of the book ob-serves, in her eccentric spelling and punctuation,

that her eldest sister is plain and "bossy": "I have often noticed the eldist in a family isnt so pretty as the others, usually the youngest is best, it is so in fairy stories too, it must be because the parents haven't had enough practice at making babies." Commenting on her mother's sudden loss of hearing, she writes: "After she had six babies at eighteen monthly intervals Mammy suddenly went deaf, perhaps her subconscious mind just couldn't bear the noise of babies crying any more." While the children revel in the joys of country living, they also learn to take in stride a father who beats them in fits of rage and once threw one of the babies down a flight of stairs: " . . . fortunately a cook called Harriat caught her at the bottom and saved her life, after that Harriat kept her in her bedroom at night so that he couldn't hear her crying which was a good thing in case there hadn't been anyone to catch her next time, but Harriat had to leave soon after because her feet smelt."

Comyns' simplicity of style sometimes betrays her into a false naiveté that reviewers have found disturbing. Writing in the *Spectator* Ste-phen Brook's objections to the style of *The Vet's Daughter*, another first-person narrative by a teen-aged girl, are characteristic: "The bleak simplicity of her narrative is supposed to reflect her own innocence, steeling itself against the buffetings of a hard world—but it doesn't come off." He detects "patches of sophistication that ring false." In *Sisters by a River*, for example, we are abruptly reminded from time to time that the little girl narrator is a grown woman: "I hat-ed dancing class so much and had a kind of sick feeling in the pit of my stomach before I went, I called it dancing class feeling, and still have it sometimes, when I'm applying for a job, or get-ting married and similar occasions." And the child recalls a fourteen-year-old boy: "for some time I wondered if he was dead yet, but he wasn't, in fact he is still alive today, this I know because some years later I married him."

Ursula Holden singles out as Comyns' unique-ness "her surreal eye and Chagallian viewpoint." Like Chagall she converts barnyard realism into enchantment, and some of her characters experi-ence a sense of lightness that defies gravity. At the age of five or six two of the children in *Sisters by a River* pretend to be riding horses by strad-dling the branches of a tree: "then we found our-selves slowly raising from the ground, soon we were floating through the sky, we were not at all afraid." The narrator of *The Vet's Daughter*, an older girl, actually levitates—creating a disas-trous panic in the crowds who watch her. The su-pernatural, however, figures only rarely in Comyns' work. Rather, as Patricia Craig pointed out in a *Times Literary Supplement* review of

The Juniper Tree, she is a writer "whose imagination is drawn to the odd, the macabre, and the picturesque." Like the Brothers Grimm she is fascinated by the juxtaposition of good and evil in a world in which conventional moral values are suspended. With the exception of *The Vet's Daughter*, her novels have happy endings. Her heroines are cruelly buffeted by fate, suffer poverty and humiliation, but in the end marry and presumably live happily ever after.

In Barbara Comyns' third published novel, *Who Was Changed and Who Was Dead* (the title from Longfellow's lines: "Of what has been and might have been / And who was changed and who is dead"), the elements of stark and terrible realism almost upset the balance that her other books achieve. Though some reviewers hailed the work as a masterpiece, others, Ursula Holden writes in her Introduction, found it "too unpleasant to stomach," and it was banned in Ireland not for blasphemy or obscenity but "for its power to disgust . . . Barbara Comyns' ruthless eye defies squeamishness; nothing is too raw for her consideration." Drawing again on her childhood memories, she introduces in this novel three motherless children growing up in a country village. Their father, an unemployed journalist, is idle, indifferent, self-centered, and the children are ruled by a tyrannical and half-mad grandmother. The novel opens with a devastating flood of the nearby river which seems enchanting to the eyes of the child Emma, the central character: "The ducks swam through the drawing-room windows. The weight of the water had forced the windows open; so the ducks swam in. Round the room they sailed quacking their approval, then they sailed out again to explore the wonderful new world that had come in the night." But horrible images follow—peacocks floating in the garden, "a new-born pig all pink and dead," the body of a drowned child. And horrors pile on horrors as the village is ravaged by an epidemic of ergot poisoning (an incident Comyns based on an actual outbreak in a French village in 1951). Madness, sexual license, and mob violence dominate the second half of the book. Nevertheless, the subtext is one of lyrical innocence—of children, pet animals, gardens, and a happy ending.

In none of her other novels has Comyns gone to such extremes, although in *The Skin Chairs* she introduces a grisly image of a set of chairs covered in human skin that a retired army officer had brought back to England after the Boer War. That novel, however, is redeemed by a charming young narrator, Frances one of six children of an impoverished widow. The family is impoverished too, hounded by overbearing relatives but, in fairytale fashion, the good are rewarded,

the bad gently punished. Spunky little Frances is an innocent but uncommonly articulate child ("It was green where we lived and like living in the heart of a lettuce"), and the novel shows considerable advance in Comyns' command of narrative structure. Her more recently published novels—notably *Mr. Fox* (written some forty years earlier but "mislaid"), *The Juniper Tree*, and *The House of Dolls*—center on adult heroines who confront some very sordid realities. In *Mr. Fox* the heroine, struggling to support herself and her young child, is befriended by a seedy and often surly black marketeer and swindler and works for a time as a dance hall hostess. But she survives these experiences—and the London blitz—with her cheerful innocence undamaged. Abandoned by her lover and left with her half-black child to care for, the heroine of *The Juniper Tree* steps into a near fairytale world of good fortune until a terrible accident destroys it. Fortunately she recovers from a nervous breakdown and finds a new husband and home. In *The House of Dolls* a respectable widow finds herself the madam of a brothel, but like most Comyns' women, she is a born survivor.

Barbara Comyns has written one work of nonfiction, *Out of the Red into the Blue*, from which she emerges as much a survivor as any of her heroines. In 1945 she married a journalist, Richard Comyns-Carr. They lived happily in London in a house in Kensington taking in lodgers, but when her husband lost his job they found themselves "in the red" and settled on the island of Ciriaco, off the Spanish coast, where they could live cheaply. Her struggles with unheated houses, friendly but alien neighbors, dwindling finances, and her inability to speak Spanish are described with lively humor. By the end of the year her husband had found a job in London, and they left Spain with regrets. Since then she has continued her writing and her painting (she has exhibited her paintings in London). In 1982 when Ursula Holden visited her at her house in Richmond where she was living with her husband, several cats, and a greyhound, "I was struck with her sense of fun. In her work she drives her characters around hairpin bends of disaster and mishap, but she says, 'I like to be happy.' Her garden is packed with plants and the pictures in her home (her own and those painted by friends) testify to her love of colour."

PRINCIPAL WORKS: *Novels*—Sisters by a River, 1947; Our Spoons Came from Woolworths, 1951; Who Was Changed and Who Was Dead, 1954; The Vet's Daughter, 1959; The Skin Chairs, 1962; Not for Me the Wilds, 1963; Birds in Tiny Cages, 1964; Cherries on My Plate, 1966; A Touch of Mistletoe, 1967, The Juniper Tree, 1985; Mr. Fox, 1987; The House of Dolls, 1988. *Non Fiction*—Out of the Red into the Blue, 1960

ABOUT: Contemporary Authors 5–8, 1969; Comyns, B. Out of the Red into the Blue, 1960; Comyns, B. Introduction to The Vet's Daughter (Virago, 1981); Holden, U. Introductions to Virago editions: Our Spoons Came from Woolworths, 1983 and Sisters by a River, 1985; The Skin Chairs, 1986; Who Was Changed and Who Was Dead, 1987. Periodicals—New York Times Book Review March 22, 1987; Spectator February 7, 1981; Times Literary Supplement May 10, 1985; June 5, 1987; February 24, 1989.

*CONDÉ, MARYSE (November 2, 1937–), Guadeloupian novelist, literary historian, and critic, has emerged in the 1980s as the foremost woman writer of the French-speaking West Indies. Combining an intimist eye for detail with an epic sense of history, she has developed an idiom of historical fiction that probes both the personal and political dimensions of black identity in the wake of the colonial experience.

Born Maryse Boucolon in Point-à-Pitre, Guadeloupe, she grew up in a comfortable milieu that was, in her words, "too conformist, with countless fears about what other people would say." She always liked to write and produced her first novel at the age of eleven. Five years later, in 1953, her parents, Auguste and Jeanne (Quidal) Boucolon, sent her to Paris to continue her studies at the prestigious Lycée Fénélon; at the time, she recalls, the black communities in France were caught up in the fervor of the anticolonialist movement; but "for me, the West Indies were just a setting that didn't confer any identity. I was just a little French girl. . . . " Ironically, she told Madeleine Mukamabano in 1984, it was the "real" French girls at the Lycée Fénélon who introduced her to the writings of the Négritude poets—notably Aimé Césaire—and took her to her first anticolonialist meetings. Césaire in particular, she acknowledges in another interview, "completely changed my adolescence. Thanks to him I learned that I wasn't a French girl like the others but a Black West Indian."

Continuing her studies at the Sorbonne, she majored in English literature, but her main preoccupation was Africa: "I was swallowed up by this unknown Africa," she recalls, "completely oriented toward it." In 1961 she married Guinean artist Mamadou Condé ("to the scandal of my family"), and went with him to Guinea. "It was," she told Mukamabano, "a way of concretizing a ten-year search for identity." As it turned out, the experience was far from what she expected: as she was to acknowledge many years later, "I know now just how badly prepared I was to encounter Africa; I had a very romantic vision, and

I just wasn't prepared, either politically or socially." Not only did her marriage fall apart, but the post-independence regime of Sekou Touré soon showed its repressive colors with waves of arrests and exiles. Condé herself fled to Ghana with three young daughters and began teaching at the Winneba Ideological Institute. She also published an anthology of French-language African literature. With the fall of Kwame Nkrumah in 1966, Condé was arrested and expelled from the country. After two years in London, where she worked for the French service of the BBC, she went to teach in Senegal but after two more years, decided to return to Guadeloupe.

Looking back on this chaotic sequence of events, Condé comments, "Until the age of thirty-four, my life was a total failure: broken marriage, studies abandoned, could hardly support my children. I was totally marginal." The turning point, she indicates, came when she decided to resume graduate studies in Paris, and after completing a thesis on black stereotypes in West Indian literature, she started teaching African literature at the Sorbonne. At the same time, and in a conscious effort to reach a broader public, she began writing essays and reviews for various African newspapers and magazines, including Africa, Demain l'Afrique, and Présence Africaine, and also produced programs on African culture for Radio France International.

In her critical essays, as in all of her subsequent writing, Condé took strong and often provocative positions. The venerable Négritude movement was an early and consistent target: as she argued in a conference paper published in 1973 ("Pourquoi la négritude? Négritude ou révolution?"), the root causes of the exploitation of Africans were not racial but economic and political, and, she pointed out, the slave trade itself was carried on with the complicity of African rulers. Similarly, while she often chose to write about women, she avoided any notions of inherent gender differences: "I simply believe," she declared in a 1972 article on three women writers from English-speaking West Africa "that the personality and the inner reality of African women have been hidden under such a heap of myths, so-called ethnological theories, rapid generalizations and patent untruths that it might be interesting to study what they have to say for themselves when they decide to speak." Nor did she mince words where individual writers were concerned: in a 1972 review, for example, she characterizes her compatriot Simone Schwartz-Bart's novel Mulâtresse solitude as "an elegant, exotic product very visibly intended for the non-local market," and similarly, in her essay on West African women writers, she dismisses one of her subjects as a "sub-product of the West."

°cōn da, mar ēs´

Parallel to her return to academia and her entry into journalism, Condé also tried her hand at writing for the theater, beginning with a "pre-first play," as she calls it, *Le Morne de Massabielle* (The Mournful One of Massabielle), which was performed at the Théâtre de Puteaux in 1971. This "experience I don't like to think about anymore," in her words, was followed by two published plays, *Dieu nous l'a donné* (God-given, 1972) and *La Mort d'Oluwemi d'Ajumaki* (The Death of Oluwemi of Ajumaki, 1973). Both of these were stylized tragedies offering bitter commentary on the contemporary political scene in the West Indies and Africa respectively: in *Dieu nous l'a donné*, a European-trained doctor who comes back to the Islands to lead an idealistic revolution becomes its first and only martyr, while *La Mort d'Oluwemi d'Ajumaki* is about a traditional ruler who finally comes to accept the necessity of his death but, again, without any great hope for the future.

While these plays struck a resonant note with the critics—*Dieu nous l'a donné* was subsequently performed in Paris and the West Indies, and *La Mort d'Oluwemi d'Ajumaki* in Haiti—Condé herself soon dismissed the entire venture. She had become a playwright, she told Mukala Kadima-Nzuji in a 1977 interview, not by taste but "because I was the victim of an illusion," namely that the theater, like journalism, would provide her with a means of reaching popular audiences; and at the same time, she admitted, she made the "grave error" of thinking that writing for the theater was less complex than writing a novel. "In the world we live in, I think theater is the most difficult form of expression there is," and it could not "change anything about anything. Whether a play is performed or not, it's only a piece of literature, and I don't think it has a great influence on sociopolitical events, regardless of what anybody says." Nor, she added, did she have any plans to write more plays.

Instead, she finally plunged into the novel, and in 1976 published *Heremakhonon*, the story of a young Guadeloupian woman who goes to Africa in search of roots and identity, gets caught up in the tumult of politics and romance, and winds up back in Paris telling herself: "I made a mistake about my ancestors, that's all. I looked for my salvation in the wrong place." The setting, she explained in a foreword to the 1988 edition, was inspired by what she had lived through in Guinea in 1962—"events that left me permanently traumatized," she indicated more than twenty-five years later—but, she insisted, the main character, Véronique, was hardly autobiographical; rather, "narcissistic, egotistical, indecisive, sometimes even weak," she was intended as a "negative heroine." Furthermore,

she explained, she originally wrote the novel in the third person but found it didn't have the immediacy she wanted and rewrote it in the first person "as a literary device, pure and simple."

In practice, many people identified Condé with Véronique and reproached her for all of her protagonist's shortcomings. Still others found the style too "hermetic," beginning with a title taken from the Malinke language. ("Hermetic for whom?" she shot back in a 1979 interview. "Malinke is spoken in almost all of West Africa.") And nearly everyone, she indicates, was disappointed with her negative image of Africa (which, according to one African reviewer, "Play[ed] the game of the neocolonialists"). The net result, she acknowledged in the 1988 preface, was "a total lack of success."

It was six years before she published another novel, but in the interim—while continuing to teach, write for the magazines, and produce radio programs—she compiled two short anthologies of West Indian literature (*Le Roman antillais* and *La Poésie antillaise*, 1977) and a critical essay on Aimé Césaire's *Cahier d'un retour au pays natal* (*Profil d'une oeuvre/Césaire*, 1978), as well as studies on the oral literature of Guadeloupe and Martinique (*La Civilisation du Bossale*, 1978) and women writers from the French-speaking West Indies (*La Parole des femmes*, 1979). As Jonathan Ngate points out, her study of *Cahier d'un retour au pays natal* successfully avoided the two common pitfalls of Césaire criticism: excessive adulation of his poetry and equally excessive condemnation of his political stand. "What is striking about Condé as a critic first of all," Ngate writes, "is her tough-mindedness, her clear sense of history, and as a corollary, the way she seems to have her feet planted firmly on West Indian soil."

These qualities emerge even more clearly in *La Civilisation du Bossale* and *La Parole des Femmes*, where, in effect, she uses literary analysis to come back to the question of West Indian identity that she had indirectly addressed through her "anti-heroine" Véronique in *Heremakhonon*. The civilization of the *bossale*, or newly arrived slave, Condé reminds her readers, was a product of oppression, and thus, she argues, its oral tradition was chiefly the internalization of a stereotype inherited from the white slave masters. Analyzing the transformation of African traditions within the slave society, she shows how collective social values gave way to individualism, cunning, and deceit, and in a final chapter devoted to the emergence of written literature, she offers the no less trenchant observation that the first generation of educated blacks in turn broke with the only indigenous tradition available to them. As Ina Césaire wrote in *Notre librairie*, this "brilliant and very personal essay" was likely to elicit both enthusiasm and dissent, but its thesis "will not leave anyone indifferent." Self-image was also the focus of *La Parole des femmes* (The Word of Women), where Condé turned to the writings of West Indian women to examine their attitudes toward basic life experiences from childhood to death in order to "define the image they have of themselves and approach the problems they may face," an investigation that led her to focus, no less controversially, on the difficulty of man-woman relations and what she saw as a resulting rejection of motherhood.

When Condé resumed fiction writing in 1981 with *Une saison à Rihata* (A Season in Rihata), this personal dimension of women's experience was much more fully developed. As in *Heremakhonon*, *Une saison à Rihata* was the story of a Guadeloupian woman in Africa, but family relations, in all of their Freudian complexity, are now the focus of the drama, and the channel through which social and political conflicts are played out. The central character, Marie-Therèse, is a Madame Bovary of the Sub-Sahara, living with her husband and six children in the timeless town of Rihata. Like Véronique, she has made the trek from Guadeloupe via Paris, but her itinerary is laced with far more drama: a possible murder (of her mother), seduction (of her sister's lover), suicide (of her sister), adultery (with her husband's brother), and finally political assassination (of same). Nonetheless, the subtle development of the characters and the skillful depiction of the milieu, transmitted through a deliberately understated third-person narrative, avoid any false notes of melodrama. As Jacques Chevrier wrote in *Jeune Afrique*, "avoiding the trap of Manicheanism in this way, Maryse Condé offers us a complex and nuanced image of contemporary Africa permeated with the drama of uprootedness, which is at once that of the West Indian in search of a mythical homeland and that of the African haunted by the memory of a glorious past."

By the time *Une saison à Rihata* appeared, Condé had in fact renewed her ties with Africa and, under considerably different circumstances, was immersed in a vast project of historical fiction. As she recalled in a 1984 interview, ten years after her first "adventure" in Africa, she was invited to Niger for a colloquium and took the opportunity to visit Mali as well: "It was love at first sight," she told Frédéric Ferney in the *Nouvel observateur*; but, she continued, she then returned to Paris to discover that Mali was currently ranked among the thirty-one least developed nations of the world, and shocked by

this discrepancy between standard of material wealth and that of its culture, she set out to recapture the grandeur of Mali's precolonial past. Five years and five visits later, she published *Ségou: Les Murailles de terre* (1984; Ségu: The Ramparts of Earth, translated as *Segu*), the first of a two-part historical novel set in Segu, the capital of the ancient Bambara kingdom.

In the five hundred pages of this first volume, she traces three generations of the Traore family in its collective and individual encounter with the forces of change overtaking traditional society: Islam, the slave trade, and French colonialism. Following the death of the family patriarch, Dousika Traore, one of his four sons, Tiekoro, becomes a Muslim missionary and, following his execution by the animists, a Muslim saint. The second son, Naba, is taken into slavery and dies in Brazil just at the point when he and his wife were about to buy their freedom. The third son, Siga, makes his way back to Segu after various adventures in Timbuktu and Fez, while the fourth son, Mobbali, a staunch anti-Muslim, becomes a mercenary, then a servant to a white missionary, and dies from smallpox on the way back to Segu. The second volume, translated as *The Children of Segu*—nearly another five hundred pages—continues the saga with the descendants of Dousika Traore's eldest son, Tiekoro, but here the historical element looms much larger, with increased numbers of real-life characters integrated into the fiction and with greater emphasis on the collective destiny. But common to both parts of the novel is a meticulous and caring attention to detail (not the least of which is devoted to the women of the story) that breathes new life into a forgotten past.

Ségou, Condé explained to Marie-Clotilde Jacquey in 1985, "was an homage to a land that revealed to me a dimension of my past that I didn't know. . . . I wasn't at all trying to dress myself up as a Bambara or a Malien; I was simply looking to relive, in my own way, with my personality, the events that greatly concerned me: the dissolution, the disappearance of these great empires, these great families, all this great African dream." And, contrary to a number of critics who saw the book as a French version of Alex Haley's *Roots*, she stressed that "*Ségou* is not about a return to the source; it's a reflection on the fact that, finally, after all that Africa has undergone, it could not become anything other that what it is, a reflection on the confrontations, the power plays, the myths that simplify history on the pretext of reasserting the value of the African past."

From the beginning, Condé had intended *Ségou* as a mass-audience book: "It was necessary to break out of a double ghetto," she explained to Denis Constant, "the deluxe ghetto of the university and the non-deluxe one of African literature, which isn't even read. To break down the barriers between the whites, who think Africa has no past, has nothing interesting to offer, and the Blacks, who say wonderful things but keep them all to themselves. That's how *Ségou* was born." In fact, with some 200,000 copies sold, the novel represented the first major commercial success of a black French-language writer, and it met with equal enthusiasm from the critics. "If the two novels of Maryse Condé have all the necessary ingredients for a popular success," wrote *Notre librairie*, they are no less the happy result of a skillful blend of knowledge and imagination, erudition and creativity, where fiction joins fact to yield two books in which historical detail never disrupts the flow of the plot."

Emerging from the relative obscurity of a university professor who wrote an occasional novel, Condé the best-selling author suddenly found herself making the rounds of the popular press, radio, and television, including the pinnacle of literary achievement, Bernard Pivot's weekly program *Apostrophes*. But in the midst of this recognition, Condé made it increasingly clear that what she really wanted was to return to Guadeloupe. "I'm here in France because I can't live anyplace else," she told Denis Constant in 1985, explaining that she had never been able to find work in the West Indies, but "I need to put down my roots again, and that becomes more and more imperative, to go back to my own country."

In the wake of *Ségou*, Condé was invited to spend a year teaching at the University of California at Los Angeles and, somewhat by accident, wound up writing yet another historical novel, this one rooted in American history. *Moi, Tituba Sorcière* (I, Tituba the Witch, 1986) recreates the story of a black slave from Barbados who was among the women tried for witchcraft in Salem, Massachusetts. According to Condé, the way the book came about was itself "a case of magic": a book about the Salem witch trials literally fell on top of her in the university library, and when she tried to put it back on the shelf, it fell again and opened to Tituba's testimony. "I just took a quick look," she recalls, "and when I saw that it was about a West Indian Black woman, I was hooked."

Setting out on the trail of the historical Tituba—the daughter of an Ashante slave-woman, born in Barbados, sold to a pastor in Salem and accused of bewitching his daughters but acquitted at her trial—Condé went to Salem to read

her deposition, consulted with specialists, read other documents from the period, and even got access to a CBS film series to see how the details of daily life had been reconstituted. But working around this historical core, she developed a highly charged work of fiction that once again resonated as much through the individual characters as through the events they were involved in: Tituba's childhood in Barbados; an invented mother; a real-life husband named John the Indian (who betrayed her to the witch-hunters); a proto-feminist cellmate who, like Nathaniel Hawthorne's heroine, is named Hester; an aging Jewish lover in Boston after her trial ("to show that it wasn't just the Blacks who were rejected by America, the land of freedom"); and finally a much younger lover with whom she meets her death in an abortive slave rebellion. "Tituba and I," she tells readers in the prologue, "have lived in close intimacy for an entire year, and during our endless conversations, she told me things that she'd never confided to anyone else."

For Condé, the challenge of completing the historical record was also a means of addressing the present. "I gave Tituba all my preoccupations, freedom, the failure of freedom, revolution and the failure of revolution, and of course, the struggles and efforts to arrive at something in spite of it all," she told the monthly *Jeune Afrique*, explaining that "of course it deals with the Puritan period, but since America is still Puritan, that was a way for me to talk about America today. I lived there for a year, and I found the same intolerance."

Awarded the 1986 Grand Prix Littéraire de la Femme, *Tituba* met with widespread approval. If some critics such as Claude Wauthier in the *Quinzaine littéraire* found this New World tableau of race relations too jarring or "Manichean," others felt that it rang perfectly true: "Written in an intimist mode, with a merciless portrait gallery of the era, *Tituba* comes off like a novel of astonishing modernity," wrote Elisabeth Nicolini in *Jeune Afrique*.

At the time of *Ségou II* and somewhat in its shadow, Condé had published in 1985 two novellas set respectively in Guadeloupe and Jamaica, *Pays-mêlé* and *Nanna-ya*, and for her, these stories were above all "a draft, a summoning of courage, to see if I can go farther, if I can write about my country, my family, my friends." Following *Tituba*, she not only plunged into the task but, after more than thirty years abroad, went back to Guadeloupe to do it. "I needed thirty years to understand that the West Indies is my country," she remarked after her return. "I needed to travel, to get rid of the craving for elsewhere in order to finally realize that I could find my identity at home."

Indeed, her first Guadeloupian novel, *La Vie scélérate* (The Wicked Life, 1987), was an appropriate reflection of both the wandering and the homecoming, an irreverent family history following four generations of Guadeloupians through their lives, loves, mixed marriages, and insistent upward mobility, from Albert Louis, the impoverished cane cutter who goes off to build the Panama Canal in 1904, to his great-granddaughter Coco who tells the story in 1987. For Condé, this colorful parade of family skeletons (including a number from her own family) was her "most important" work to date; for the critics, such as Pierre Demeron of *Marie-Claire*, the story of great-grandfather Albert and his innumerable offspring marked both "the social ascendancy of one family and the political and cultural awakening of the Caribbean world and even the entire Afro-American world. But because she's an experienced novelist, it's through the loves, the mishaps, the voyages—which, as is often the case with the disinherited, turn out to be exiles—the illusions, the dreams and aborted hopes, the failures of her characters that she makes us piece it all together."

Since July 1986, Condé has been living with her second husband, translator Richard Philcox in, the wooden house they built in Montebello, Guadeloupe, but she also teaches one semester a year at Occidental College in California. "My thirty-four disorganized years gave me a tremendous amount of experience," she told Lili Réka just before her return home. "I think that I write to clarify all that I've been through, so that I can better understand my heart, my head, my body. I write first of all for myself, and I'm very happy if, afterwards, people feel involved." She is, she indicates, "very feminist without flags or slogans, because I know that it's hard to be a woman and essential to realize one's femininity," but she disclaims any connection with "feminist lines that want to attribute that realization to success in the intellectual domain at the expense of what I see as a woman's real beauty: the gift of sharing." Likewise, she considers herself a supporter of the Guadeloupian independence movement but believes that the most important contribution she can make is her writing: "That's a writer's work, not planting bombs." And while Aimé Césaire remains one of her two major influences (the other one she cites is Philip Roth, because of his ironic portraits of Jewish family life), she has come to believe that literature doesn't necessarily have to serve a cause: "Literature is there to make people think, reflect, translate the anguish that individuals carry inside of them. It is also there to make you dream . . . which we've forgotten too much."

WORKS IN ENGLISH TRANSLATION: *Heremakhonen* was translated by Richard Philcox in 1983. Part I of *Ségou* was translated by Barbara Bray as *Segu* and published in 1987 (paperback edition 1988); Part II, translated by Linda Coverdale as *The Children of Segu*, was published in 1989.

ABOUT: Dictionnaire des littératures de langue française, 1984; Rouch, A. and G. Clavreuil, Littératures nationales d'écriture française, 1986. *Periodicals*—Books Abroad Spring 1973; Current Biography on African Affairs 19/1, 1986–1987; L'Esprit créateur Summer 1977; French Review October 1982; L'Humanité March 4, 1985; L'Humanité Dimanche April 1982, November 1987; Jeune Afrique November 11, 1981; February 19, 1986; October 15, 1986; Marie-Claire December 1985; New York Times Book Review May 31, 1987; Notre librairie July–September 1979, April–June 1984; World Literature Today Spring 1985, Winter 1985, Summer 1986, Fall 1986, Spring 1987.

CONRAD, PETER (February 11, 1948–   ), British cultural critic, was born in Hobart, Tasmania—"an offshore island off the shore of an offshore continent," as he describes it in his memoir *Down Home: Revisiting Tasmania*. From early life he shared with many of his fellow Australians a sense of alienation from the cultural mainstream of Europe. His father, a builder who worked in the Tasmanian housing department and read American Westerns for relaxation, and his mother, who patiently planted flowers in a stubbornly unyielding garden, "made themselves at home in the country and with the land by virtue of their daily, soiling struggle with it. I lacked their courage and ran away." Before he was old enough to run away, however, Conrad found refuge from what he considered his drab, claustrophobic confinement in the free exercise of his imagination. When he was thirteen, his ability to project emotions of fear that he had never actually felt won him a role in a film, *They Found a Cave*, being shot in Tasmania. But literature, not the make-believe of acting, gave him the surest escape from his surroundings. "Once I began to read, I discovered somewhere else to live: the Noddyland or Neverland or wonderland or secret garden of English books. Art even at its most naive could colonise the hostile world; it freed you from facts by inventing alternatives. Thus I became unassuageably homesick for a place I had never seen, which existed only in writing. That fantasy was my home." Escape came with a Rhodes scholarship that took him to Oxford at the age of twenty for graduate study in English literature. Since that time, except for periods of travel and teaching in the United States, Oxford has been his home, although he also maintains residences in New York's Greenwich Village, in London, and in Lisbon. In 1970 Conrad became a Fellow of All Souls College; since 1973 he has been Fellow of Christ Church, Oxford. He has also taught at Princeton and at Williams College.

When Peter Conrad revisited his family home some twenty years after he had left it, he discovered new interest and a raw, vital energy in its landscape and history. Perhaps more significant were the insights the visit gave him into himself. "Everything that constituted me had been made by the place I left long ago, where I would never live again. It was the landscape inside me, the space where I spent my dreaming time. . . . The home you cannot return to you carry off with you: it lies down there at the bottom of the world, and of the sleeping, imagining mind."

Conrad's memoir, like his critical writing, reflects an intense subjectivity. Reviewing the American edition of *Down Under*, retitled *Behind the Mountain*, in the *New York Times Book Review*, Carolyn Kizer noted its meditative quality: "To meditate means to contemplate, to ponder, to swell in thought, it is an exercise that requires no company, no direct communication, no reaching out from the cave of the mind." The book "is virtually unpeopled," she wrote—only the barest mention of his parents, no mention of friends or neighbors. Yet Conrad's critical writing is dense with detail, overwhelming with allusions to literature, music, art, and popular culture. His reviewers have often responded to his books with amazement at the range and extent of his reading ("The man must have started reading in the womb, and carried on from breakfast to midnight," Pat Rogers wrote in the *Times Literary Supplement* of his *Everyman History of English Literature*); but many of them have also responded with distinct reservations to the subjectivity of his work which is always provocative and often provoking. Characteristic is Jean-Pierre Barricelli's comment on Conrad's *Romantic Opera and Literary Form* in *Drama, Dance and Music*: "This is an author who has thought a lot and gets carried away a lot. But this is also an author who thoroughly enjoys his own provocative richness."

Conrad's first book, published when he was only twenty-five, is an ambitious study, *The Victorian Treasure House*, a sweeping survey of the literature, art and architecture of the age. His thesis is an expansion of Henry James' comment on a single Victorian novel, George Eliot's *Middlemarch*: "a treasure house of detail, but it is an indifferent whole." Conrad writes: "The same might be said of the entire Victorian period . . . Paintings and novels and even poems

have a chaotic fullness, a superabundance, which James thought to be their weakness, but which is perhaps their glory." In Victorian narrative painting particularly—arguably not the "glory" of Victorian culture—Conrad finds an evasiveness from the troublesome reality of life: "The realism of the Victorians has an anxious, preoccupied quality; they feel an obligation to tell the truth but back nervously away from its implications, retreating, for instance, into the picturesque, the soothing resolution of antagonisms and conflicts into a picture." He sums up: "Victorian art and literature are, like life, crowded, contradictory, growing and spreading in an energetic anarchy, a riot of detail uncontrolled by the whole."

Published in 1973, when Victorian literature and art were undergoing searching reassessment from scholars and critics, *The Victorian Treasure House* offered many generalizations so broad and unsupported that they were challenged by reviewers. Conrad writes, for example: "If romanticism is the youth of the nineteenth century, Victorianism is its middle age; romance is appropriate to the one, realism to the other—youth is poetic but maturity turns to prose." While acknowledging that the book raises "pertinent questions about the function of the past in diverse forms of nineteenth century art," and is "useful in proposing that an awareness of context might enrich understanding of nineteenth century fiction," Karl Kroeber, in *Victorian Studies*, continued: "Not that Conrad's journalistic spirit will itself guide us to profundity. The book is full of mistakes and sophomoric judgments." Richard D. Altick, surveying the writings on the relationship between romanticism and Victorianism in *Victorian Fiction: A Second Guide to Research* (1978), found the book "facile." "Conrad maintains a patronizing attitude towards Victorian fiction, as well as Victorian art." Altick conceded, however, that "his book is full of matter for thought," and journals of more general outlook received it favorably. The *Times Literary Supplement*'s reviewer, though regretting the absence of a bibliography and noting that Conrad's "lack of sympathy with the principles [of Victorian art] makes him a dubious guide," found the book overall "a treasure house of brilliant, sensitive, and adventurous observations." And John Bayley wrote enthusiastically in the *Listener*: "This is an ambitious book, which thoroughly justifies its inclusiveness."

Conrad's *Shandyism: The Character of Romantic Irony*, like *The Victorian Treasure House*, is a study of the cultural contexts of literature. Beginning with a single work, Laurence Sterne's eccentric and brilliant eighteenth-century novel *Tristram Shandy*, Conrad writes in his preface: "This is a book less about than around *Tristram Shandy*. I have set out to find various interlocking contexts for it in the art of its period, and in relating it to its aesthetic surroundings have attempted to suggest its romantic quality." Conrad traces the roots of romanticism back to Shakespeare, and in the mercurial character of Tristram he finds links to eighteenth-century theories of romantic art—among these the theories of Fuseli, Hogarth, Burke, and the German aesthetic philosophers of the eighteenth century.

The risks and rewards of cross-cultural study are strikingly demonstrated in Conrad's controversial books on the relationship of literature and opera. An ardent opera fan himself, Conrad writes in *A Song of Love and Death: The Meaning of Opera* of opera's almost religious power of acquiring converts: "for like a religion it changes the lives of those it wins over, transforming them into acolytes and partisans who will queue all night in a blizzard to buy tickets or cross continents for a performance—who think, talk, read and dream about the art that is their avocation." Developing directly from Conrad's study of the literature and art of romanticism, his *Romantic Opera and Literary Form* proposes a controversial thesis: that romantic opera, though it draws its librettos from dramatic literature, is not dramatic but is closer in form to the novel, which he defines as "a private, self-soliloquizing form": "Drama is limited to the exterior life of action, and romanticism increasingly deprecates both the tedious willfulness of action and the limits of the form which transcribes it. The novel, in contrast, can explore the interior life of motive and desire and is naturally musical because mental. It traces the motions of thought, of which music is an image. Opera is more musical novel than musical drama."

In the great nineteenth-century operas of Wagner, Verdi, and Berlioz, Conrad argues, the dramatic literary sources from which they worked are converted, turned inward as it were, into lyrical novels and symphonic poems. Citing *Macbeth* as an example, he writes that in terms of dramatic action "Macbeth is an unscrupulous hell-hound," but in romanticism's reading of Shakespeare ("Shakespeare is virtually a creation of romantic criticism. Though he may not be romantic in himself, he is the cause of romanticism in others"), Macbeth's inward debates, his crises of will and conscience, turn the work into a "lyrical novel," and the romantic composers "tend to adapt the plays most successfully not as operas but as symphonic poems in which the characters can meditate musically without the interference of action or the intermediary of

words." Even Wagner, who described his works as "music dramas," in his Ring cycle converted epic drama "to a novelistic study of the evasive and guilt-ridden society which looks to the hero for its redemption and finally reaches . . . the most modern of its forms, the abstract, ideological morality play." Conrad draws on the theories of Nietzsche and, in more recent years, of W. H. Auden, who wrote opera librettos himself, to conclude that music "is essentially antagonistic to the verbal text." Because he assumes the incompatibility of music and words—"jealous of one another because each longs for the privileges of the other while resenting intrusions on its own territory"—Conrad sees romantic opera as moving toward such purity of form that the librettos of early twentieth-century operas like Richard Strauss' *Ariadne auf Naxos* and *Capriccio* become virtually "disquisitions on the operatic idea."

By frankly acknowledging the paradoxes and contradictions of opera, Conrad disarms his critics. "He forges a tool for dealing with romantic art by pushing romantic theory to its most provocative, dogmatic, paradoxical extreme," Joseph Kerman wrote in *New York Review of Books*. "The result is a brittle instrument which will shatter at the first critical pressure . . . but it does throw up some good sparks when held up against the grindstone of modern literary criticism." For Kerman, Conrad has built "a sophisticated critical structure [on] simplistic foundations." For Jean-Pierre Barricelli, *Romantic Opera and Literary Form* is "as ingenious and provocative as it is glib and inconclusive"; and Calvin S. Brown, in *Comparative Literature*, while suggesting that Conrad is here "not so much interested in his subject as in his own performance, for which the subject is merely raw material," concluded: "Though sometimes infuriating, he is never dull."

A similar reception awaited *A Song of Love and Death: The Meaning of Opera*. A collection of essays and reviews that Conrad had written for the *Times Literary Supplement*, the *New Statesman*, the *Observer*, *Harper's*, *Vanity Fair*, and other journals, and material from his BBC documentary on opera direction, the book ranges widely over the field of opera. Conrad's theories and personal tastes in opera may bemuse or antagonize the reader, but they are notable for their liveliness and for the sheer amount of miscellaneous knowledge of opera that he displays. From its origins in mythic Orphic and Dionysian rites to contemporary works by Philip Glass and Karlheinz Stockhausen, from its pure aesthetics to the practical problems of staging and performance, all opera is his domain. "Opera," he writes, "is a sport, a display of physical and technical prowess. At the same time it is a form of almost religious aspiration, reaching for the sky from which music first poured down like Apollo's sunlight." Conrad's own dazzling performance—his wit, his epigrammatic style, his bold leaps in logic—impressed even the most disapproving of his reviewers. Edward Downes, in the *New York Times Book Review*, cited numerous errors of fact but overall confessed astonishment: "I know of no other opera survey in English (or any other language) tossed off with such exuberant verbal virtuosity, such a constant stream of hyperbole, simile, metaphor, aphorism, epigram, paradox—the works." John Rockwell, in the *New York Times*, noted the absence of any comment on music itself: "For Mr. Conrad, music seems to be little more than an excuse to spin his own fantasy subtexts to opera's librettos." Still, he found Conrad's insights "arrestingly fresh, sometimes . . . idiosyncratic, but illuminating."

Conrad's cultural criticism extends to the popular arts as well. In *Television: The Medium and Its Manners* he meditates with wit and imagination on the impact of television on our daily lives. "Why are we so apologetic about owning one? . . . Granting it entry into our houses as furniture, we've allowed it to take over those houses." As familiar with television in America as he is with British television, he discusses everything from news coverage (the Kennedy assassination and funeral, the on-screen shooting of Lee Harvey Oswald, the 1968 Chicago Democratic Convention) to soap operas ("a world of fidgety existential dubiety, in which a multitude of happenings of arbitrary and inane comings and goings . . . covers the absence of anything which would qualify as action: a resolution of the will, a purposeful expenditure of energy"), and concludes: "I, for one, won't stop watching television. Nor, I suppose, will I stop feeling guilty about doing so."

In both *The Art of the City: Views and Versions of New York* and *Imagining America* Conrad again ranges freely over the cultural scene. He first visited New York in 1969 and reacted with characteristic subjectivity to "the perils of the place" and "the skyline and the dazzling sky [that] pardon and transfigure it." As Edward Mendelson wrote in the *Times Literary Supplement*: "Conrad's New York is implicitly a projection of himself rather than a city shaped by those who live there." Though he has walked its streets and knows the city at first hand, Conrad is mainly concerned in his book with its image in paintings, photographs, and films. He offers an exhaustive survey of the literature of New York beginning with Whitman, Henry James, Howells, Wharton, Stephen Crane and

O. Henry, of painting from post-Impressionists like Childe Hassam and Maurice Prendergast to twentieth-century surrealists and the New York School, of photography from Weegee to Walker Evans, Berenice Abbott and André Kertesz.

Imagining America confines itself to literature and the impact of the American experience on English writers, from nineteenth-century visitors like Dickens, Frances Trollope, and Oscar Wilde to the many English who temporarily at least adopted America as home—D. H. Lawrence, Aldous Huxley, Christopher Isherwood, W. H. Auden. "Before America could be discovered, it had to be imagined," Conrad writes. For British visitors the image of America was strikingly varied, each imposing his or her own vision: "The Victorians see Niagara as a prodigy of nature, but their successors either refine that wayward nature into aesthetic form (like [Henry] James and [Rupert] Brooke), or commandeer it for scientific use (like [H. G.] Wells). . . . The later subjects of this book . . . go there to construct private mental shelters for themselves, and in so doing are insulated from their environment." Not surprisingly, Conrad again challenged and even antagonized some reviewers. Elizabeth Hardwick found the book "easy to read yet a torture to unravel." She objected to Conrad's "moralizing tone," what struck her as the accusatory, almost belligerent attitude he takes toward some of his subjects, judging them for their lives rather than their works. She finds him especially judgmental on Wilde, Huxley, and Auden, producing "a text that bristles like the quills on a pestered porcupine." A fellow visitor and sometimes critic of America, Anthony Burgess, writing in the *Times Literary Supplement*, however, could find no fault with the book. Comparing it to his "admirable" *Romantic Opera and Literary Form*, in which Burgess felt that "his prose, witty, chiselled, tending to the epigrammatic, was becoming an object for admiration in itself and not a mere transparent vehicle for the exposition of ideas," he observed that in *Imagining America* "Conrad writes even more brilliantly."

In 1985 Conrad published a work that could serve as the culmination of many another writer's career but was for him simply another challenge. This was his massive (over 700 pages) *The Everyman History of English Literature*, published in the United States as *The History of English Literature: One Indivisible, Unending Book*. Conrad acknowledges that the project was "a risky business," and he approaches it with the distinct, if questionable, thesis: that there is a continuity in English literature from the *Beowulf* poet through Seamus Heaney whose poems of the dark bogs of Ireland serve as "a reunion at long last with the beginning." The "indivisible, unending book" begins with epic and evolves in a continuous stream of words— epic transformed into medieval romance transformed into nineteenth-century romanticism and reshaping itself in contemporary literature: "Raymond Chandler writes detective fables which are versions of the Grail narrative, Graham Greene anti-heroically revises the *Song of Roland.*" Conrad's broad sweep across the canon, catching fragments of European literature along the way, leaves the reader breathless: "If Joyce is modernism's Chaucer, D. H. Lawrence is its Langland, worrying as fanatically as his precursor in *Piers Plowman* about the letter's fidelity to the spirit, and recurring in *The Rainbow* to the biblical commentary and translation from which in the Middle Ages our literature initially grew." He follows the chronology of English literary history and exhaustively covers not only major figures but manages to cite obscure or farfetched references from the entire corpus of world literature and from popular culture. For example, he writes that the spirit of Beowulf found a host in America with Paul Bunyan, "Melville's Ahab the Whaler, Cooper's Deerslayer, and Michael Cimino's deer hunter." He is at home with Lessing, Ezra Pound, and contemporary figures like Len Deighton, Howard Brenton, and David Hare.

For the student seeking specific information or solid critical evaluations of writers, the book can be frustrating and mystifying (e.g. "Nonsense is decadence under the frivolous sign of comedy"; "The novel is invented as a device of literary history. . . . In every generation, it pretends to reject a past it is merely revising"). But for the reader who enjoys Conrad's dazzling virtuosity as a prose stylist, it has its rewards. Pat Rogers, in his *Times Literary Supplement* review, is just such a reader, delighting in Conrad's mastery "of the unexpected collocation: none of his chapters sticks rigidly to the authors nominally under discussion, but rather each leaps out toward parallels from elsewhere. . . . There is a constant surge of life passing from one book to another, as Conrad exposes to view the unregarded consanguinity of creative minds." For Rogers, "the virtues of this astonishingly rich and thought-provoking account of literary history far outweigh any defects."

PRINCIPAL WORKS: The Victorian Treasure House, 1973; Romantic Opera and Literary Form, 1977; Shandyism: The Character of Romantic Irony, 1978; Imagining America, 1980; The Art of the City: Views and Versions of New York, 1980; Television: The Medium and Its Manners, 1982; The Everyman History of English Literature (in U.S. The History of English Litera-ture: One Indivisible, Unending Book), 1985; A Song of Love and Death: The Meaning of Opera, 1987; Down Home: Revisiting Tasmania (in U.S. Behind the Mountain), 1988; Where I Fell to Earth: A Life in Four Places, 1990.

ABOUT: Conrad, P. Down Home, 1988; Conrad, P. Where I Fell to Earth, 1990; Hardwick, E. Bartleby in Manhattan, and Other Essays, 1983; Redmond, J. (ed.) Drama, Dance, and Music, 1981. *Periodicals*—Comparative Literature Spring 1979; Hudson Review Autumn 1984; Journal of American Studies August 1986; Listener July 5, 1973; London Review of Books March 21, 1985; New Republic March 22, 1980; New Statesman July 7, 1978; New York Review of Books February 9, 1978; October 13, 1988; New York Times September 8, 1987; New York Times Book Review November 8, 1987; April 9, 1989; Review of English Studies February 1987; Times Literary Supplement July 6, 1973; May 30, 1980; September 21, 1984; November 13, 1985; January 29, 1988; October 21, 1988; March 2, 1990; Victorian Studies September 1975.

CONROY, FRANK (January 15, 1936–), American memoirist and short-story writer, was born in New York City, the son of Francis Philip and Helga (Lassen) Conroy. Conroy's unconventional, erratic upbringing is the subject of the first and best known of his two books, *Stop-time*. Though hardly a conventional autobiography, *Stop-time* follows the basic outline of Conroy's youth. His father was a formerly successful literary agent who spent "most of his adult life . . . as a patient in various expensive rest homes for dipsomaniacs and victims of nervous collapse." He died of cancer when his son was twelve; by then his wife (called "Dagmar" in the book) had divorced him and was shortly to marry Jean Fouchet, "the ne'er-do-well son of a collapsed aristocratic New Orleans family." Most of *Stop-time* concerns Conroy's childhood, from his ninth through eleventh years at an "experimental" and faintly ludicrous boarding school in Pennsylvania to his enrollment in Haverford College at the age of eighteen or nineteen. Though not strictly chronological or even committed to fact, the book describes the salient experiences of his youth: a joyous year with a twelve-year old neighbor in the Florida scrub, where Jean and Dagmar built a house for themselves "for no money down and a few dollars a month"; a sullen, rebellious adolescence in which "the fact of being alive became synonymous with the fact of being in trouble"; a hapless education at Stuyvesant High School in Manhattan; an attempt to escape the chaos of his home life by running away from New York to Florida (he gets as far as Maryland); a year spent in a

FRANK CONROY

very lax international high school in Denmark
(his mother's homeland), where he ignores his
studies and falls in love with a Swedish girl; and
finally, an exceptionally high score on a college
entrance exam which makes possible his acceptance at Haverford College and a decisive break
with his past.

Framing the main story are a brief prologue
and epilogue in which the adult Conroy describes a drunken, suicidal drive ritualistically
taken in his Jaguar while living in England and
writing *Stop-time*. Although smacking of a
glamorous, Maileresque existentialism, the
frame serves obvious structural purposes and
subtly undermines the "happy" ending of Conroy's welcome into the fostering environment of
Haverford. Has he really left behind his past?
Has he avoided the taint of madness that marks
so many of the characters in the book? Is it possible to draw a line between the past and the present, to "stop time" merely by writing about it?

The frame is especially needed because of the
loose, episodic structure of the book. Each chapter is conceived of as an individual unit, relating
to the other chapters but able to stand on its own.
Nor do the chapters necessarily relate the outwardly significant events of traditional autobiography. One of the most widely praised, for
example, is given over to Conroy's infatuation
with yo-yoing for a brief period in his early teens
when his family had returned temporarily to
Florida. Yet this seemingly inconsequential episode draws forth some of Conroy's bravura writing, faithfully captures the serio-comic banality
of adolescence, and prefigures the writer that

the boy is to become (discovering rhythmic patterns in a yo-yo that he will later discover in
words). In an oft-quoted passage Conroy writes:

> I practiced the yo-yo because it pleased me to do so,
> without the slightest application of will power. It wasn't
> ambition that drove me, but the nature of yo-yoing. The
> yo-yo represented my first organized attempt to control
> the outside world. It fascinated me because I could see
> my progress in clearly defined stages, and because the in-
> timacy of it, the almost spooky closeness I began to feel
> with the instrument in my hand, seemed to ensure that
> nothing irrelevant would interfere. I was, in the language
> of jazz, "up tight" with my yo-yo, and finally free, in one
> small area at least, of the paralyzing sloppiness of life in
> general.

Tony Tanner, in *City of Words: American Fiction 1950–1970*, thought this chapter
"beautifully fresh and original, and [it] gives the
impression of being totally unforced." "What
makes the book remarkable," he wrote, "is the
combination of absolute lucidity in the description of each separate episode, and the feeling of
an emerging *forma*, some possible shape which
links the apparent randomness of the detached
events. Each chapter is itself beautifully and
subtly structured without any apparent thematic
manipulation of each unique detail of the life
under recall."

Despite rare moments of triumph and transcendence, *Stop-time* is a harsh and radically unsentimental memoir. The boy is everywhere
surrounded by selfish, dazed, and irresponsible
adults, from his mother's favored "boarder,"
Donald, "a bitter and sarcastic man, unable to
get along with anyone except at the greatest
effort," to his stepfather's psychotic mistress,
who installs herself in the apartment while Dagmar is on a visit to Denmark. Indeed, madness
in its many varieties is one of the central motifs
of *Stop-time*, even claiming for a while Frank's
older sister Alison, whose surface calm throughout most of the book is bought only at a "terrible
price." Early on, after running in terror from a
screaming uncle and crashing into a parked car,
Frank has an epiphany that his experience of the
world is to bear out: "it came to me that the
world was insane. Not just people. The world."

Stop-time was greeted with nearly unanimous
acclaim upon its publication and in the years
since has taken its place as a key work in the hybrid genre of novelistic autobiography. (Other
recent examples are *A Fan's Notes* by Frederick
Exley and *The Woman Warrior* by Maxine
Hong Kingston.) After *Stop-time*, however,
there was an eighteen-year gap before Conroy
brought out a rather slim volume of short stories,
Midair, in 1985. Inevitably, there was speculation about the long delay, and at least one story
"The Mysterious Core of B," in which a sympa-

thetic but uncomprehending psychiatrist is taught that there is no such thing as "writer's block," seemed to allude indirectly to this circumstance. It was also inevitable that many readers would interpret *Midair* in the light of Conroy's life since the publication of *Stop-time*. There was little doubt, at least, that some of the stories were strongly autobiographical. The title piece, for instance, concerns a middle-aged man who recalls a harrowing incident from early childhood with his affectionate, maniacal father and is obviously based on Conroy's memories of his own father's abrupt visits home from various mental institutions. Similarly, in "The Sense of the Meeting" the narrator returns to his "old Quaker college" in Pennsylvania, sounding very much like Haverford, to meet with former roommates and watch his son (Conroy has two, Daniel and Will) play basketball. "Gossip," about a creative writing teacher's attraction to a beautiful and talented student, just as clearly draws on Conroy's stint as a creative writing teacher at the University of Iowa. But fundamentally *Midair* is straight and, with two or three exceptions, realistic fiction, different in kind from the genre-transgressing *Stop-time*. For some critics straight, realistic fiction, however skillfully done, was not enough—not after the startling, ground-breaking debut of *Stop-time*. Comparing the use of memory in the title story to that of the earlier book, John Haegert, in *Modern Fiction Studies*, wrote that the protagonist's "memory of his father acquires an initiatory prestige that mobilizes the entire narrative, infusing it with a relevance that is both beautiful and tyrannous. At the same time, however, the memory itself exists only for the sake of its required resolution; it has no narrative purpose apart from its anticipated end . . . Very different is *Stop-time's* free-ranging use of memory where people, places, and events are recalled in all their original immediacy and plenitude, largely unencumbered by any commanding relevance or ulterior end."

That was only one view, however. While conceding the unevenness of the collection, Terrence Rafferty nevertheless considered *Midair's* existence "a kind of victory" over a Salinger-like paralysis. What has perhaps saved Conroy, Rafferty wrote in the *Nation,* "is a kind of childlike dedication to getting things just right, a meticulousness that ruined his writing in the 1970s [when a few of the stories first appeared in the *New Yorker*] but gives his new stories their special tension, their scary balancing of emotion and formal precision. And this collection may not fully resolve the suspense of *Stop-time*, but in some ways it completes the earlier book, makes Conroy's work tell an oddly coherent and satisfying story."

In addition to his two published books, Frank Conroy has written music criticism (he has performed as a jazz pianist) and other journalism for a variety of publications. For several years beginning in 1981 he served as director of the literature program of the National Endowment for the Arts; as the *New York Times Book Review* put it, he was "the man to see" for "poets, prose writers, small press editors and other literary dreamers seeking money from the Government." Conroy married Margaret Davidson Lee in 1975; his earlier marriage, to Patty Monro Ferguson, ended in divorce. In recent years he has lived in Watertown, Massachusetts, Washington, D.C., and Nantucket Island. Asked by the *New York Times Book Review* in 1985 why it took eighteen years between books, he replied, "I was out doing errands."

PRINCIPAL WORKS: *Autobiography*—Stop-time, 1967. *Collected short stories*—Midair, 1985.

ABOUT: Contemporary Authors 77–80, 1979; Tanner, T. City of Words: American Fiction 1950–1970. *Periodicals*—Critique Spring 1986; Modern Fiction Studies Winter 1987; Nation January 11, 1986; New Republic November 11, 1967; November 18, 1985; New York Review of Books December 21, 1967; New York Times Book Review September 22, 1985; New Yorker February 3, 1968; Village Voice September 24, 1985; Washington Post Book World September 15, 1985.

COOK, ROBIN (May 4, 1940–), American novelist, was born in New York City, son of Edgar Lee and Audrey (Koons) Cook. His father was an artist and businessman. He received his B.A. from Wesleyan University in 1962, and his M.D. from Columbia University in 1966. From 1966 to 1968, Cook was a resident in general surgery at Queen's Hospital, Honolulu, Hawaii; from 1969 to 1971 he served in the U. S. Navy, becoming Lieutenant Commander. In idle periods on submarine duty, Cook began writing a novel based on his internship in Hawaii that was published in 1972 as *The Year of the Intern.* Tracing the experiences of a Doctor Peter, the novel demonstrated how the long hours and intense pressures of the assignment militated against the young protagonist's initial idealism; it can be seen as part of a growing protest against the processes of depersonalization built into medical training.

From 1971 to 1975 Cook was a resident in ophthalmology at the Massachusetts Eye and Ear Infirmary, affiliated with the Harvard Medical School in Boston; and in 1975 he became a staff member and opened a private practice

ROBIN COOK

north of Boston. He continued, however, to be interested in writing fiction. *The Year of the Intern* had sold well (250,000 copies), but Cook now set his sights on a work that would have even broader appeal. For six months, in 1975, he read through a hundred bestsellers to decide what would "capture the interest of the largest number of people," and determined to write a medical mystery-thriller. The result (the writing took only six weeks) was his novel *Coma*, which indeed became a bestseller and was made into a movie in 1978, directed by Michael Crichton and starring Genevieve Bujold and Michael Douglas.

The action of *Coma* takes place within a period of three days, during which a young medical student, Susan Wheeler, discovers an unusually high incidence of brain death at Boston Memorial Hospital and, investigating on her own, uncovers a shocking black market in human organs. She spends much of the novel attempting to convince incredulous police and hospital officials of the conspiracy, and in the process attracts the attention of the conspirators. Mel Watkins in the *New York Times Book Review* praised Cook's skillful plotting, which thrusts the heroine "into an escalating cycle of terrifying events that keep the action moving. . . . [It is] a gripping, scarifying novel." Rather similarly, Charles J. Keffer in *Best Sellers* characterized *Coma* as "an absolutely fascinating story. . . . I do not think anyone can beat the suspense of the story line developed throughout this novel." Although David Brudnoy in the *National Review* complained of the "formulaic quality" of the

novel, he too was impressed by *Coma* as a thriller, "a horror story of the first order." Walter Clemons in *Newsweek* found the novel and its endangered heroine full of "movie clichés," but conceded that it was often "unnerving" and played skillfully on the reader's fears of "impersonal hospital bureaucracy."

Coma was followed by *Sphinx*, which draws on Cook's interest in archaeology. Again his protagonist is a young woman, an Egyptologist in Cairo who witnesses the murder of an antiques dealer and becomes involved in a complicated black market intrigue. The novel was not well received by reviewers, some of whom wrote of it scathingly. Henri C. Veit in *Library Journal* remarked that "the writing is so bad that it seems a quibble to complain that there is not a speck of life in this expensive agglomeration of words." Writing in the *New York Times Book Review*, Jack Sullivan described the novel as "inert as its many mummies. . . . Even Mr. Cook's sense of place and history, the novel's one strength, is compromised by triteness." *Sphinx* was filmed in 1981.

Reviews were much better for *Brain*, a novel set like *Coma* in an urban medical center and concerned with disturbing occurrences and sinister intrigue. In this case, Martin Phelps, a brilliant assistant chief of neuroradiology, and his colleague and lover Denise Sanger investigate— and run afoul of the F.B.I. and the C.I.A. William A. Nolan in the *Washington Post Book World* remarked: "Shall I say 'I couldn't put the book down'? Why not? It's true. Even though *Brain* is low-grade formula fiction . . . [it's] a damn fast read [and has] a plot with enough twists and turns to satisfy any reader." Rosalind Smith in the *Los Angeles Times Book Review* found the novel "unnervingly plausible, deeply frightening. . . . The milieu of a large university medical center is rendered with exquisite accuracy, from the bureaucratic regulations victimizing both patients and personnel to the atmosphere of the operating rooms and the laboratories. . . . Medical procedure assumes the importance of character."

Fever is another variation on Cook's theme of medical misdoing and the threat posed to a solitary individual who seeks to expose corruption, but in this work Cook has related the mystery to cancer research and environmental pollution. Charles Martel, a struggling doctor-scientist, finds that his cancer research project will be terminated; a dubious rival project financed by a large pharmaceutical company has received institutional backing instead. At the same time, he learns that his daughter's fever, a particularly virulent strain of myeloblastic leukemia, is linked to the presence of benzene in the river that runs by his house. Before long Martel finds himself the embattled adversary of ruthless corporate interests. Stephen MacDonald in the *Wall Street Journal* commented that Cook "is blatant in his exploitation of reader alienation. In *Fever* the villains are a familiar roster of nasty American stereotypes: greedy businessmen, mindless bureaucrats, venal lawyers, icy doctors and rednecked cops." Yet critics again praised Cook's ability to create reader interest. Writing in the *New York Times*, Christopher Lehmann-Haupt remarked that "Cook has the storytelling skill to seduce us away from intelligence. By the time *Fever* began to deteriorate into absolute absurdity, I was having too good a time to be willing to notice."

In *Godplayer*, another male-female team of doctors investigate the unexplained deaths of patients at Boston Memorial Hospital. Although some reviewers felt that Cook's medical thriller formula was "wearing a bit thin" and that his characters were mere stereotypes, others admired his ability to draw the reader into his narrative and his authoritative recreation of medical centers. Jonathan Coleman in the *New York Times Book Review* commented that "Dr. Cook is marvelous when he reveals the mysteries of the medical world. So, while the novel is plodding and the reader, unfortunately, will figure out who is responsible for these medical murders much too soon, there is enough going on here to engage one until the end." Cook's later novels include *Mindbend*, about the machinations of a giant corporation with physicians themselves as its victims; *Outbreak*, dealing with a viral plague and a sinister cabal of ultraconservative doctors who attempt to undermine the public's faith in prepaid health-maintenance facilities; and *Mortal Fear*, concerned with a furtive research project at a large Boston hospital.

In addition to his medical practice and writing, Cook has a variety of other interests—he is a painter and a proficient diver, surfer, and skier. In 1979 he married Barbara Ellen Mougin, an actress.

PRINCIPAL WORKS: The Year of the Intern, 1972; Coma, 1977; Sphinx, 1979; Brain, 1981; Fever, 1982; Godplayer, 1983; Mindbend, 1985; Outbreak, 1987; Mortal Fear, 1988; Harmful Intent, 1990.

ABOUT: Contemporary Authors 108, 1983; 111, 1984. *Periodicals*—Library Journal May 1, 1979; Newsweek April 18, 1977; New York Times Book Review May 8, 1977; May 13, 1979; July 24, 1983; Time June 13, 1977; Wall Street Journal April 29, 1982; Washington Post Book World March 8, 1981.

***

*CORNELISEN, ANN (November 12, 1926–   ), American essayist and novelist, writes: "All of my adult life, more than thirty years now, has been spent in Italy, much of it in the unknown Italy of the south where even today life has an oddly Biblical quality. The landscape is desolate, cruel and beautiful. The villages are isolated from the world and each other, as the people who live in them are isolated from each other by suspicion. Progress is a rumor, prosperity something that happens on television, elsewhere. Spells are still cast, the evil-eye is an ever-present, though little talked of, danger. Poverty, like typhoid, is endemic. And yet . . . and yet by 1066 the Normans had built walls and defense towers around 'Torregreca.' It was an important center. Already in 966 it was a diocese and the local Synod of Bishops had outlawed paid wailers at funerals as uncivilized, pagan.

"A thousand years later there had been few dramatic changes. Paid wailers were still a feature of funerals. To most Italian was a foreign language. The *lingue franche* were three dialects, each a mysterious garble of dipthongs, distorted Greek and pure local inventions. To the outside world the South in general was a statistical disaster, boasting the highest infant mortality in Italy (in Europe for that matter), the lowest income, consumption of meat and sugar, the highest unemployment, the highest illiteracy, the lowest number of cars and radios per capita. It was medieval. Why? What could be done? When? How? As a social worker, in charge of training centers for nursery teachers and expected to follow them up once they went to work in even more remote villages, I asked myself those questions every day. And never found satisfactory answers. Finally I admitted to myself that one person, or a hundred, could not, alone, change what centuries of invaders, bureaucracy and inertia had wrought. I quit. Maybe by writing about the limbo, lost, after all, in Italy, not the Himalayas or Africa, I could help the people who had so moved me. Knowledge brings change, no? I was a true innocent.

"The book business is a field mined with myths. One is the 'over the transom' manuscript, an ungainly bundle of paper no one has asked to see, indeed, no one wants to see, that miraculously is dredged out of the sludge pile and more miraculously still, is published. Only the naive and the self-deceivers could believe in such fantasy—but—I am proof that it *can* (and does) happen. Twenty years ago William Abrahams' assistant at the Atlantic Monthly Press discovered me, lurking by her desk, on what I have always imagined to be a gray, snowy day when the office was semi-closed. Or more probably she did not so much discover me as she stumbled

ANN CORNELISEN

over me, because my masterpiece, encased in a large blue billing ledger, was something of a traffic hazard. So *Torregreca* set off on its wobbly way. She insisted Mr. Abrahams read it and he has read every word since, puzzling over my erratic spelling, which, with time, has become slightly more orthodox, and my sentences, crocheted into interminable paragraphs, that neither God nor man can put asunder.

"What started as a passion to interest one reader, even two, if a second could be found, in the unknown, deceptive world that had held me fascinated, in the original 'bewitched' sense of the word, has spawned a second passion—for writing itself: why and how do words, sentences, paragraphs and pages in certain elusive combinations take on a life of their own that can be shared? At times, it seems, every word is a warlock, every sentence a mutation of intention. I have not understood, and so I do not understand how 'writing' can be taught. One day I am going to take a course. But not yet."

———

Ann Cornelisen went to Italy in 1954 to study archaeology at the University of Rome. Born in Cleveland, Ohio, to Ralph White and Ydoine (Rose) Cornelisen, educated at the Girls Latin School, the Baldwin School in Bryn Mawr, Pennsylvania, and Vassar College where she majored in English, Latin, and Greek, she had no knowledge of Italian and no background in Italian culture other than that acquired in a general education. A three month crash course in the language was her only preparation, and that

would hardly have prepared her for the challenges she was to confront as a worker for the British-sponsored Save the Children Fund in the impoverished south of Italy. Her job—and it soon became her mission—was to supervise the building and then administration of a nursery school in a small country town in Lucania, a farming community in many ways unchanged from feudal days. That town, and the many others that she came to know in the mountains of the Abruzzi, Lucania, and Calabria, was the model for her first book, *Torregreca*, a fictional name for an all too real community. (She also describes it in her memoir *Where It All Began: Italy 1954*.) In the following years she established other demonstration nurseries, supervised housing relief, contended with a vast and nearly always frustrating bureaucracy, with superstition and sometimes the suspicions of the people she (a foreigner, a Protestant, a lone woman) was serving, with the rigors of hot, dry summers, cold, wet winters, earthquakes, often near-primitive living conditions. As she described her work in *Torregreca*: "We could not be theoretical. Everything had to work every day and on the simplest possible basis . . . I cannot honestly say special talents were needed. It was enough to know how to wash without water, how to delouse children or dose them for worms, how to cope with fleas and eat gratefully whatever was offered."

Torregreca, however, is not an account of her personal trials and triumphs. Like her other nonfiction books on Italy, it speaks through the lives of individual Italians, people who came to know and trust her as a sympathetic listener and friend. "Fascinated with the rediscovery of themselves, they were not curious about me. It was enough that I was there, an outsider who seemed to understand their world. I was that unique person: I could not hurt them, would not judge them, no matter what they told me." Like Oscar Lewis' now classic portrait of Mexican slum dwellers *The Children of Sanchez* (1961), to which several reviewers compared it, *Torregreca* was widely praised for its honesty. Thomas Bergin, writing in the *Saturday Review*, found it "an authentic and engaging record of a unique experience . . . written in sturdy, unpretentious prose."

Ann Cornelisen resigned from the Save the Children Fund in 1964 to devote her time to writing about the people she by then knew so well. Many of them emigrated from the hopeless poverty of the south to the industrial cities of northern Italy and Germany. She continued the record of their struggles in *Women of the Shadows* and *Strangers and Pilgrims*. The first failure of the social welfare reforms in the South, the inability of distant bureaucrats to understand the people they were seeking to help. "In a few words," Robert Coles observed of *Women of the Shadows* in the *New Yorker*, "she provides a textbook's worth of comment on the psychology of social observation." In that book, portraying five peasant women who stayed at home struggling to keep their families alive while their husbands went off to seek work, she argued impressively against the belief that Italian peasant societies were patriarchal. Rather, it was "the absence of the men and the women's discovery that they could manage their decisions" that convinced her that "the social structure of Southern Italian villages, archetypal peasant societies, is matriarchal." As Jane Kramer wrote in the *New York Times Book Review* : "Ann Cornelisen knows these women so well, and her regard for them is so loving, complicated and despairing that her book is worth a shelf of dissertations on Italian village life or the effect of labor migration on the southern peasantry."

The effect of migration on the personal lives of these men and women and their families is the subject of *Strangers and Pilgrims*. Traveling to Frankfort, Dusseldorf, Offenbach, Milan and Turin, she visited the families she had known in the South. Most of them had fared well materially. They had jobs and far better living conditions, but none of this had been achieved without pain and bitterness. While northern Italy thrives, Torregreca and the South that it represents remains hopeless, in Ann Cornelisen's view. Emigration is the only answer: "No matter what the moral bleatings of politicians . . . emigration suits the government concerned too perfectly for reform. Mediterranean countries, overpopulated, without industries and never the most stable, must siphon off their hordes of unemployed . . . or explode."

The same barren South is the scene of Ann Cornelisen's first novel, *Vendetta of Silence*. Like her non-fiction it portrays realistically the life and passions of the people of the South, but its narrative, centering on a forbidden love between a young priest and a schoolteacher, is complicated by the oblique and laborious device of the narrator's diary interspersed with letters, the priest's journal, tape recordings, newspaper clippings. This "collage," as Herbert Mitgang described it in the *New York Times Book Review*, obscures an otherwise interesting story but is redeemed by the book's authentic color. More successful with reviewers and the public in general was her second novel, *Any Four Women Could Rob the Bank of Italy*. All of Cornelisen's books, grim as much of their subject matter has

been, display a lively sense of humor. This novel is a "romp." Its title gives away its outrageous plot—a group of Anglo-American women bored with their lives in a Tuscan town and with the chauvinism of Italian men, successfully bring off robbery of a mail train only to find that their own sensitive consciences, not the police, have foiled them. Phoebe-Lou Adams, in the *Atlantic*, judged it "a witty, satiric novel . . . The drop of bitters in Ms. Cornelisen's champagne merely increases its sparkle."

Ann Cornelisen lives most of the year in a fifteenth-century farmhouse in Tuscany. In addition to her writing, she is a photographer; her work illustrated *Torregreca* and *Women of the Shadows*. She has received an award for excellence in literature from the National Institute of Arts and Letters (1974), a Guggenheim Fellowship (1977), and a Christopher Award (1981). In 1979 she was Patten Foundation Lecturer at Indiana University.

PRINCIPAL WORKS: Torregreca: Life, Death, Miracles, 1969; Women of the Shadows, 1976; Strangers and Pilgrims: The Last Italian Migration, 1980; Where It All Began: Italy 1954, 1990. *Novels*—Vendetta of Silence, 1971; Any Four Women Could Rob the Bank of Italy, 1984.

ABOUT: Contemporary Authors New Revision Series 17, 1986; Cornelisen, A. Torregreca, 1969. *Periodicals*—New York Times Book Review April 4, 1976; February 18, 1990 Newsweek April 14, 1980; Publishers Weekly November 1, 1971.

CORNWELL, SMITH. See **SMITH, DAVE**

*COSTANTINI, HUMBERTO (April 8, 1924–June 7, 1987), Argentinian novelist and short-story writer, sent the following sketch to *World Authors* in January 1986: "My father, an Italian-Jewish immigrant, arrived in Buenos Aires in 1905, in second class. I was brought up in a neighborhood where all my friends were also sons of immigrants, generally workers who had traveled in third class. I do not hesitate to say that the physical place where I spent my childhood was beautiful, vital, and the best school of life one could wish for a boy: dirt streets, kerosene lights, almost no cars, joyful jingling sounds of the milk wagon, peddlers and maybe a horseback rider. Two ditches, about one and one half meter wide, separated the dirt street from the brick sidewalk. These ditches, fringed by weeds, foul-smelling, covered by weeds and aquatic plants, were for us, the children, a fabulous

°kō′ stän tē′ nē, ōom ber′ tō

HUMBERTO COSTANTINI

world. We caught frogs, an activity at which we had acquired a certain virtuosity; there we challenged each other to jump the meter and one half ditch in the most diverse and inconceivable ways; there we or our rivals landed more than once in the course of a fight. Since there was no danger of traffic, our parents did not watch us much, and we spent almost the whole day on the street. We learned to respect and to demand respect in the same way adults learn to do it in life. I always felt sorry for the children who are born in apartments. My first book, not lightly called *De por aqui nomas* (Just From Around Here), which was received by the critics and the public, especially the young people, with particular enthusiasm, appeared in 1958 and related to this world.

"Later, naturally, my world became larger, and this expansion was also reflected in my books. I was born to political life under the fascist military coup of 1943. All my secondary and university student life was marked by the daily struggle against that type of native fascism called Peronism. I think that marked me politically forever. In one way or another, denunciation of repression, torture, violations of human rights, appear frequently in my work. It was therefore logical that the bloody military dictatorship established in 1976 would persecute me and invade first my paternal home and then my small private apartment. I saved my life, somewhat miraculously, and went to exile in Mexico. There, in Mexico, I stayed for seven years, seven months and seven days (I arrived on June 0, 1076 and returned to Buenos Aires on January 16,

1984) and, naturally, my literature during this endless period of separation from all that was mine could not fail but refer to that long and painful night of Argentina. The dictatorship ended; since 1983 there is a democratic government in my country. I could then live in the city I love and to which I feel culturally indebted: Buenos Aires. After a long honeymoon of re-acquaintance with every inch of my beloved city, I am now again completely integrated with it. I live modestly from the royalties produced by my books, especially those published abroad, and I work arduously, laboriously, on a novel that I'm sure will be my most important work, the one that will 'justify me in the eyes of God', so to say. Of the four books, and about 1500 pages, which will constitute my *Rapsodia de Raquel Liberman* (Raquel Liberman's Rhapsody) (this is the name of the novel), I have already finished the first book and am working on the second.

"I have three children and six grandchildren who, although they did not know the ditch of the dirt street or the jingling milk wagon, I can assure you are the loveliest and best brought up kids in the world."

———

Born in Buenos Aires in 1924, Humberto Costantini is frequently cited as one of the most notable examples of the contemporary generation of authors who "prove that Argentine literature is more than Borges and Cortázar." Costantini is likewise identified as one of the most important contemporary novelists and short story writers to have effectively portrayed the brutal political reality known as the "dirty war" in their native country during the 1970s and who, though disillusioned and exiled, managed to keep in touch with a public suffering under repressive political rule. Mixing comedy with suspense, his novels show how, by the sheer whim of fate, the lives of average, non-political citizens become tangled with the power structure of a dictatorship. "He's Argentina's Milan Kundera," American novelist Russell Banks observed in *Mother Jones*, "highly ironic, subtle, formally inventive, and brave."

Although Costantini is known internationally almost exclusively for the two novels he wrote while in exile in Mexico from 1977 until 1983, he had begun his career as a writer in his native country in the late 1950s. Before the advent of the military dictatorship in Argentina in the mid-70s, he had established himself in literary circles in Buenos Aires as a successful dramatist poet, and short story writer as well as a novelist. True of his works, *Una vieja historia de caminantes* (An Old Story about Travelers, 1967), and *Háblenme de Funes* (Talk to Me about Funes, 1970) won the Municipal Prize of the City of Buenos Aires, and his efforts as a short-story writer were likewise acknowledged in Mexico when he received special recognition from the "Casa de la Cultura" in the city of Puebla. He also won the National Theater Prize in Mexico in 1981 for his play for children *Una pipa larga, larga, con cabeza de jabalí* (A Long, Long Pipe with a Boar's Head).

De dioses, hombrecitos y policías (1979; translated as *The Gods, the Little Guys and the Police*) was Costantini's first major international success. The novel, loosely constructed in forty short chapters in a variety of narrative styles, mingles poetry, mythology, and contemporary politics. It introduces a group of harmless amateur poets calling themselves "The Poetry Circle of Polimina," who meet weekly in Buenos Aires to recite their innocuous verses to each other. In a police state, however, any gathering invites suspicion, and they are put under surveillance. Also watching the group, from the lofty distance of Mt. Olympus, are the gods Aphrodite, Hermes, and Athena. Juxtaposed against the bureaucratic language of the police are the flowery poetic language of the mortal poets and the rich mythological language of the gods. With the arbitrariness that characterizes divine manipulation, the gods save the poets from the firing squad, but other victims replace them. "The book is absorbing, moving, and often sadly funny," Kristin Helmore wrote in the *Christian Science Monitor*. For Lydia Hunt, in the *New York Times Book Review*, "this funny yet serious novel" raises challenging questions about moral responsibility. It is the randomness of political repression—the helplessness of its victims who are arbitrarily chosen—that is terrifying. "If," Mac Margolis notes in *Newsweek*, "Gabriel García Márquez and Mario Vargas Llosa have succeeded in rendering fantastic the mundane side of life, then Costantini has managed in this slim book to make the fantastic chillingly mundane. The disarming, almost circus-like, tone of this novel is in fact a searing portrait of the terror, paranoia and vainglory that once gripped his country." *The Gods, the Little Guys, and the Police* was awarded first prize for narrative by Cuba's Casa de las Américas in 1979.

Costantini's second novel to be translated into English, *La larga noche de Francisco Sanctis* (1984; translated as *The Long Night of Francisco Sanctis*) was equally well received by reviewers in the United States and Great Britain. In this novel Costantini confronts his central character, an accountant living quietly in Buenos Aires, uninvolved in politics and content in his marriage

and routine job, with a glamorous former girlfriend who seeks his aid in rescuing two fugitives from the secret police. The novel covers the ten hours in which Sanctis must decide whether he will risk his life and make this commitment. For John Updike in the *New Yorker*, *The Long Night of Francisco Sanctis* had distinct Borgesian qualities—a Buenos Aires of "practically endless, undistinguished streets that gather to themselves a mysterious maziness wherein a specific address becomes charged with some unspeakable spiritual burden." Reviewing the book in *Newsday*, James Polk also noted an echo of Borges.

Costantini, he writes, works in a "complex style that is part mystery and part cautionary tale, all told with generous amounts of humor and humanity. The parts all mesh and, as they do, draw us deeper into the narrative. . . . The author has taken us inside the mind of a quite average man as he takes arms against a hostile world and, often, against himself. We see in Francisco Sanctis the heroism of the ordinary—a sometimes Borgesian theme—where fate and circumstances have been hastily piled atop a life ill-prepared to bear the weight. But bear it he does, and by the end of his night the fate of this ordinary man has assumed a decided grandeur."

Humberto Costantini returned to Argentina in 1984. He continued to live and write in Buenos Aires until his death from cancer in 1987.

WORKS IN ENGLISH TRANSLATION: *The Gods, the Little Guys, and the Police* was translated by Tony Talbot in 1984. Norman Thomas di Giovanni translated *The Long Night of Francisco Sanctis* in 1985.

ABOUT: Contemporary Authors 122, 1988; Contemporary Literary Criticism 49, 1988.
Periodicals—Christian Science Monitor May 23, 1984; Latin American Literary Review Fall–Winter 1981; Mother Jones January 1986; New York Times Book Review April 29, 1984; October 6, 1985; New Yorker September 22, 1986; Newsday September 19, 1985; Newsweek July 23, 1984.

CRANE, RONALD S(ALMON) (January 5, 1886–August 27, 1967), American scholar and critic, was hailed by the poet-critic John Crowe Ransom as the first of the great professors to give criticism prior status in American departments of English. Actually Crane came to criticism in mid-career after pursuing traditional disciplines of academic scholarship—literary history, textual editing, and bibliography. In these studies, however, he established the rigorous methodology that he brought to criticism.

Crane was born in Tecumseh, Michigan to

Theodore H. and Bricena (Chadwick) Crane. He received his Bachelor of Arts degree from the University of Michigan (which honored him as Doctor of Humane Letters in 1941). His Ph.D. was earned at the University of Pennsylvania in 1911 with a dissertation on "The Vogue of the Medieval Chivalric Romance during the English Renaissance." He began his academic career in the English Department of Northwestern University, and taught there until 1924, when he was appointed associate professor of English at the University of Chicago, where he remained until his retirement in 1951. As chairman of the English Department from 1935–1947 Crane gained wide eminence through his reform of the literature curriculum and as leader of the circle that became known as the Chicago Critics.

Following collaboration with colleagues on two textbooks intended for composition classes—*The English Familiar Essay: Representative Texts* (1916, with William F. Bryan); *The English of Business* (1921, with Franklyn Bliss Snyder)—Crane established a reputation as a meticulous scholar. His first publications grew out of the field of his doctoral dissertation, after which he moved into the then relatively uncultivated area of eighteenth-century literature and intellectual history with *A Census of British Newspapers and Periodicals, 1620–1800* (1927, with F. B. Kaye); *New Essays by Oliver Goldsmith* (1927); and *A Collection of English Poems, 1660–1800* (1932). This last book was noteworthy for its painstaking work in dating and establishing texts and its inclusion of poets who tended to be scanted by other anthologists.

During this period Crane probably made his greatest impact as editor (from 1926 to 1931) of the bibliographies headed "English Literature, 1660–1800" that appeared annually in the *Philological Quarterly*. His trenchant, sometimes mordant, critiques exposing deficient scholarship made him legendary throughout academia. ("One sometimes wondered how he dared," a colleague once remarked.) However, during these years, indicative of his abiding interest in ideas, he welcomed such landmark books as John Livingston Lowes' *The Road to Xanadu*, Emile Bréhier's *Histoire de la Philosophie*, Carlton Hayes' *The Historical Evolution of Modern Nationalism*, and Richard Henry Tawney's *Religion and the Rise of Capitalism*. (On Tawney's now classic study he demurred that its style "is perhaps too brilliant in places," a fault, however, which "after a prolonged diet of dissertations and articles in learned journals, one is easily tempted to forgive.") He continued to contribute to these annual bibliographies after he stepped down as their editor, and the series kept up his practice

of lengthy comment on significant items. Concurrently, from 1930 to his retirement, he was managing editor of *Modern Philology*, the scholarly journal published by the University of Chicago, and occasionally reviewed books for other journals. A primary concern of Crane's as editor and reviewer was refuting the so-called "Pre-romantic Fallacy" which viewed Neo-Classicism as a dry stretch between the Renaissance and Romanticism. He also urged a firmer mental discipline and intellectual sophistication on students of the eighteenth century.

Crane's "conversion" to criticism (as his bibliographer John C. Sherwood puts it) was openly proclaimed in 1935 in a landmark article "History and Criticism in the Study of Literature" that appeared in the *English Journal*. The immediate occasion for this article was a controversy then raging between two leading English professors, Howard Mumford Jones and John Livingston Lowes. Jones had contended through the pages of the *English Journal* in 1934 that the primary purpose of the student of literature should be "historical, not aesthetic," in response to John Livingston Lowes' presidential address before the Modern Language Association of America in December, 1933 which elevated criticism "in the fullest sense of an often misused word" to the pinnacle of scholarly investigation. Mediating these positions, Crane distinguished between the understanding of *why* an author says what he says, which the historian recovers, and *what* the author says and his reasons for saying it ("the artistic rationale"), which the critic discovers. Reacting against both antiquarianism in history and impressionism in criticism—at the time the twin bugaboos of English departments to his mind—Crane stressed the central importance of "aesthetic education" for English majors.

Shortly thereafter, word got around the University of Chicago campus that English was "hard." Aesthetic education for Crane essentially meant the careful and close reading of literary *texts* (as against subjective "appreciation") in order to determine what makes them cohere as artistic structures. Because Crane, influenced by the eminent classicist Richard P. McKeon, drew on Aristotle's *Poetics* as a prototype, this approach to literature was called "Neo-Aristotelian" by the critic Kenneth Burke, but this label never really caught on. The term more frequently used among Crane's students was "Formal Analysis." In his Preface to *Critics and Criticism* (1952), a collection of essays by Crane and colleagues (McKeon, Elder Olson, Rea Keast, Bernard Weinberg and Norman Maclean), which constituted a manifesto of the Chicago School, Crane made clear that the *Poetics* served them as guide rather than dictate. He pointed out that Aristotle's treatise was the only work of theoretical criticism that treated literary forms ("imitations" in Aristotle's terminology) *literally*—as things unique to themselves— rather than *analogically*—in relation to other mental activities such as philosophy or politics. Inasmuch as nobody had yet attempted such a task, the aim of criticism as Crane conceived it was to apply Aristotle's method of analysis of the form and affective power of Greek tragedy to modern literary genres. Among his colleagues, Elder Olson analyzed Yeats' "Sailing to Byzantium," and Norman Maclean a speech from *King Lear*. Crane himself illustrated this method with his most impressive piece of practical criticism, "The Concept of Plot and the Plot of *Tom Jones*."

Critics and Criticism was widely greeted as a significant book, but some reviewers resented what they felt was its intolerance of other critical positions. Crane and some of his associates were particularly harsh towards the so-called New Critics who they thought placed undue weight on language and symbolism to the scanting of the larger holistic analysis they advocated. In a famous essay "The Bankruptcy of Critical Monism," which first appeared in *Modern Philology* in 1947, and was reprinted in *Critics and Criticism*, Crane aimed his barbs at Cleanth Brooks as one of those critics who start out with preconceived notions of what poems should be rather than analyzing each as a unique work—a fallacy he was later to dub the "High Priori Road."

The title of this essay is actually premonitory of what was to be Crane's fundamental critical position—pluralism—as set forth in a lecture titled "Questions and Answers in the Teaching of Literary Texts," presented before a regional conference of English teachers at Carleton College in 1953. Here the concern of Aristotle with structure—"the ordering of elements into wholes"—was presented as one of five groups of critical questions, corresponding to the various aspects under which literature can be examined. According to the scheme that Crane outlined, a full investigation of a literary work should also encompass its language (*explication de texte*); its quality or personality (the approach of Longinus' *On the Sublime*); the circumstances under which it was written (source and influence studies); and its moral, social, political, and religious values (the concern of Plato's dialogues dealing with the arts, Shelley's "Defence of Poetry," Arnold's "The Function of Criticism at the Present Time," and T. S. Eliot's critical essays).

The Carleton College lecture belongs to Crane's post-retirement career—a period of great personal satisfaction to him when, as he confided to friends, he could enjoy the "essence" of the academic life and scholarly colleagiality unburdened by editorial and administrative tasks. Following his becoming Professor Emeritus of English Literature at the University of Chicago in 1952, he widened his audience and reputation with visiting professorships at a number of institutions—notably Stanford, Cornell, New York University, the University of Rochester, and the University of Toronto.

In *The Language of Criticism and the Structure of Poetry,* which grew out of the Alexander Lectures delivered at the University of Toronto, Crane viewed poetry generically as standing "for the whole range of artistic creation in words" and attempted to set the enterprise of criticism "in the context of humanistic learning." While emphasizing that criticism is essentially a practical activity, he recognized that theory of some sort is necessary even when dealing with specific works. At the same time he signified his own distrust of "abstract theorizing about the concrete phenomena of human life," allying himself with empirical philosophers like David Hume. His concern in the fields of his interest, he reiterated, "has not been in the patterns of ideas which particular things reflect, but the immediate causes in the literal sense of the word, which have made things what they are, and rendered them capable of affecting our minds as they do." In these lectures Crane also advanced his conception, introduced in earlier writings, of the critic as an aid to the maker of literature. He envisaged the study of the literary *product* as a bridge to the literary *process,* providing insight into the choices, conscious or unconscious, that the writer makes in groping towards perfection of form and achieving appropriate emotional effects.

The Idea of the Humanities, a miscellany published in the year of Crane's death which brings together essays, some never before published, and lectures from various stages of his career, is a summation of his critical credo. In the title essay, first published in 1953, Crane defines what he regarded as the distinctive humanistic disciplines—linguistics, historiography, criticism, and the analysis of ideas. His massive erudition is most fully displayed in the monograph-length "Shifting Definitions and Evaluations of the Humanities from the Renaissance to the Present" (a revision of lectures first delivered in 1943), which traces the concept of humanism from the ancient preoccupation with rhetoric to the nineteenth-century debate on literature versus science.

Undoubtedly the pivotal essay in this culminating volume is the lengthy "Critical and Historical Principles of Literary History" that had been written back in 1950, allegedly for Crane's "own use," and not intended for publication. Always critical of the traditional "external" type of literary history—the chronicling of lives and works of authors—and of cultural histories based upon "relations of ideas" unconnected with their context, Crane designed a more inward-turning "narrative history of literary forms." For Crane, this ideal history should represent literary works as "unique works in their own right," syntheses of the forms, materials, and techniques which the author took over from his age, with his individual achievement. Such terminology as "hypotheses" and "variables" suggest that, even though he demarcated a distinct province for the humanities, Crane was trying to transfer the precision of the physical sciences to literary scholarship. By his own testimony he hoped to emulate political and military historians who investigated the dynamics of change and discovered causal sequences in events. (He acknowledged intellectual indebtedness to his teacher of medieval history at the University of Michigan, Earle Wilbur Dow.) This prospectus for a literary history proved as tantalizing as it was provocative. Crane's arguments are "hard to refute," as John C. Sherwood has commented, "yet their consequences are hard to live with."

At any rate this ideal never reached fruition, for Crane eventually abandoned the grand history of eighteenth-century literature he was long rumored to be working on, and one eagerly awaited by fellow scholars (some with knives sharpened). Some inkling of his procedure in operation is provided by such pieces as "English Criticism: Neo-Classicism," (contributed to Shipley's *Dictionary of World Literature*); his classic analysis of *Tom Jones*; along with his "Suggestions toward a Genealogy of *The Man of Feeling*," and "The Houyhnhnms, the Yahoos, and the History of Ideas." A whole history carried out on a proportionate scale might have been overwhelming indeed, but Crane's body of writing as it stands remains a series of prologomena to a work in progress.

Nevertheless his influence on the world of humane letters is palpable, if ultimately incalculable. It is true that his idea of the humanities, however capacious, was limited to the verbal arts. (Close associates have observed that he ignored music and the graphic arts.) Some have found his emphasis on form constricting, and his view of the creative process over-intellectualized. He has been faulted even as an interpreter of Aristotle, some of the terminology he adapted from the *Poetics* not having been entirely

out by discerning reviewers, owing more to the Renaissance than to the classical age. Furthermore his orotund style of writing, all too easily caricatured by Frederick C. Crews in *The Pooh Perplex* (under the guise of "Duns C. Penwiper"), does not make for easy reading. But there is no gainsaying his effectiveness in the classroom and on the platform. Many a student was stimulated by his penetrating Socratic mode of inquiry; others recall him as a commanding lecturer, despite his short stature. The poet-critic Elder Olson, one of Crane's students at the University of Chicago in the early 1930s, eventually his colleague, office mate, and intimate friend, has left a vivid impression in the journal *American Scholar* of the sparks struck by his "constantly active critical intelligence" on those with whom he achieved a meeting of minds. Since then, Crane's critical principles have been filtered through numerous books, notably Olson's *Tragedy and the Theory of Drama* and *The Theory of Comedy*, and Wayne C. Booth's *The Rhetoric of Fiction*. His was undeniably the most learned and the most incisive philosophical mind of his generation to grapple with literary texts, and the method of systematic analytic reading that he taught and practiced continues to be replicated by the students of his students.

Ronald S. Crane died at his home in Chicago at the age of 81 on August 27, 1967, after a long illness, survived by his wife Julia Fuller Crane, whom he married in 1917, a daughter Barbara, who married William M. Gibson, a professor of English, and a son Ronald Fuller, a professor of English at the University of Wisconsin, Oshkosh. He is buried in Tecumseh, Michigan. According to report, when a friend visiting him shortly before his death remarked that he was looking better, Crane set up in bed and inquired, "What is your evidence?"

PRINCIPAL WORKS: The Languages of Criticism and the Structure of Poetry, 1953; The Idea of the Humanities and Other Essays Critical and Historical, 2 vols., 1967; Critical and Historical Principles of Literary History, 1971. *As editor*—Critics and Criticism, 1952.

ABOUT: Booth, W. C. *Introduction to* The Idea of the Humanities, 1967, *also* The Powers and Limits of Pluralism, 1979; Borklund, E. Contemporary Literary Critics, 1977; Burke, K. A Grammar of Motives, 1945; "Chicago Critics" *in* Princeton Encyclopedia of Critics and Criticism, 1965; Contemporary Authors 85–88, 1980; Contemporary Literary Criticism 27, 1984; Crews, F. C. The Pooh Perplex, 1963; Dictionary of Literary Biography 63, 1988; Graff, G. Professing Literature, 1987; Sacks, S. *Foreword to* Critical and Historical Principles of Literary History, 1971; Sherwood, J. C. R. S. Crane, An Annotated Bibliography, 1904; Wimsatt, W. K. The Verbal Icon, 1954; *Period-*

icals—American Scholar Spring 1984; Listener 78, 1967; Michigan Quarterly Review 8, 1969; Modern Philology 50, 1952; New York Times August 29, 1967; Sewanee Review 61, 1953; Times Literary Supplement September 10, 1954; September 14, 1967; Virginia Quarterly Review 13, 1937.

*CREVEL, RENÉ (August 10, 1900–June 18, 1935), French surrealist novelist and essayist, was born in Paris. He attended lycée in the capital, then the Sorbonne and the Faculty of Law. In 1921, while doing his military service part-time (as was then permitted for students) at the barracks of La Tour–Maubourg in Paris, he made friends with other young conscripts of exactly his age: Marcel Arland, François Baron, Georges Limbour, Max Morise, and Roger Vitrac. With Vitrac and Baron, Crevel soon attended a conference organized by the dadaists at Saint-Julien-le-Pauvre, where they met Louis Aragon, who introduced them to the other members of the somewhat older group that was active in the journal *Littérature*: André Breton, Philippe Soupault, and Paul Éluard. Inspired by these meetings, the young men of the barracks decided to found a review of their own. This was *Aventure*, in the pages of which Crevel published his first literary efforts.

Crevel had begun the research for a doctoral dissertation on the novels of Denis Diderot. His new circle of friends caused him, as he wrote in an autobiographical notice appended to his third novel, *La mort difficile* (Difficult Death, 1926), "to forget the eighteenth century in favor of the twentieth. . . . and one day, before a picture by Giorgio de Chirico, he [Crevel] finally had the vision of a new world. He neglected from that time on the old logico-realist attic, understanding that it was cowardly to confine oneself within a ratiocinating mediocrity, and that in the work of true poets are found neither word nor image games, but that he loved them—and among them most particularly Rimbaud and Lautréamont—for their liberating power."

The dadaist movement was coming to an end. The preparation for the literary Paris Congress was notable for prolonged quarrels between Breton and Tristan Tzara, the grand old man of dada. This dispute put an end to *Aventure*; Vitrac took the review's editorial policy into Breton's camp, but he was not followed by the young group's other members. Crevel then contributed a sketch, "Acceuil" (Welcome), to the sole issue (April 1922) of *Dés* (Dice), publication of which had been begun by Marcel Arland immediately after the collapse of *Aventure*.

Continuing his short autobiographical ac-

RENÉ CREVEL

count, Crevel recalled having "participated in the first hypnotic experiments from which André Breton drew his arguments for his [first] *Surrealist Manifesto* [of 1924]. He was able thus to witness for himself that surrealism was the least literary and the most disinterested of movements; persuaded that there is no possible moral life for someone who is not susceptible to subterranean passageways or who refuses to recognize the reality of obscure forces, he decided once and for all, at the risk of being taken for a Don Quixote, an arriviste, or a fool, to try, both by his acts and by his writings, to leap over the barriers which limit and do not sustain man." The hypnotism was accompanied by other experiments, notably dream transcriptions and various forms of automatic writing and language. Crevel soon became a philosopher of surrealism, publishing treatises and militant tracts in *La révolution surréaliste* beginning in 1924. He was solidly a man of the Left, a Communist and also a homosexual. The extent to which surrealism allied itself to proletarian aspirations and attempted, with occasionally stunning success, to affront conventional morality owed much to Crevel's efforts as polemicist and publicist.

His first novel, *Détours* (1924), according to Crevel, "was a preliminary promenade in which the critics, notably Benjamin Crémieux, Edmond Jaloux, and Albert Thibaudet, recognized the attitudes, wanderings, and rages characteristic of the actual young man." *Mon corps et moi* (My Body and I, 1925) was "a novel the hero of which carries within himself all his adventures, and in which the gestures and characters are

°krə vel´

only pretexts—it is an interior panorama." His other novels include the aforementioned *La mort difficile, Etes-vous fous?* (Are You Crazy?, 1929), *Babylone* (1929; translated as *Babylon*, 1985), and *Les pieds dans le plat* (Feet in the Dish, 1933). His non-fiction writings include *L'esprit contre la raison: Cahiers du Sud* (Spirit against Reason: Notebooks of the South, 1928); two art monographs, *Paul Klee* (1930) and *Dali or l'anti-obscurantisme* (Dali, or Anti-obscurantism, 1931); and the collected essays in *Le clavecin de Diderot* (Diderot's Harpsichord, 1932). His novels are practically indescribable in conventional fictional terms, in that they have no plots to speak of and their characters are changeable, difficult to fix in the reader's mind. His narrative form is free-associative: Angelo Rinaldi, literary critic of *L'Express*, commenting on the integral republication of Crevel's works in the 1980s, claimed that although he was "the author of a half-dozen true works, [he] really wrote only a single sentence, the long sentence of a feverish monologue, as if Proust had dipped an L.S.D. biscuit into his tea instead of his unctuous madeleine." Claude Prévost, writing in the Communist daily *L'Humanité*, noted: "Not respecting the rather dogmatic counsels of Breton, who forbade the surrealists to write 'bourgeois' novels, Crevel left several superb ones. His prose covers an immense register, from the burlesque to the macabre. It is rapid and supple, occasionally pierced with astonishing metaphors. It accommodates derision, as well as the liveliest movements of the heart and all the nuances of passion and the most naked despair, and is subject to the temptation of voluntary death, which is always there, welcoming."

Crevel was a shining personality to his friends, who eventually included nearly everyone of importance in the French literary world between the wars. His friend Marcel Jouhandeau, in his introduction to the 1969 republication of the essay collection *L'esprit contre la raison*, recalled that "his perpetual adolescent beauty, which he kept until his death, . . . the ashen blond of his hair, the light which constantly escaped from his laughing eyes could not but attract attention. René by himself was a spectacle, the rhythm of his step had about it something of a dance. . . . One could not compare him to anyone else. His élan made one think of that of a young horse and his smile evoked the expressions of the horsemen of the Acropolis, whose ardor accentuates their anguish. . . . As I write these words, I see the three of us, Gide, René, and I, walking the streets of Paris one summer's day. We were about to take the Metro, and as we were walking along looking for a cheap restaurant, André Gide brought us up short, claiming that people cast

shadows colored with their various auras, my own violet, René's haloed with gold."

Ezra Pound, who could not have been more unlike Crevel politically, published a curmudgeonly but admiring critical memoir of the younger man—he was already half forgotten—four years after his death in the very last number of T. S. Eliot's quarterly *The Criterion*:

> Joyce wrote in the slither of corrupt usuriocracy. Crevel revolted but knew nothing else. . . . His sheer talent *as writer* more than justifies the present effort on my part, even though I think each generation should provide its own critics and announcers. The date of my writing is, let me say it in my own defense, due to the failure of René's own time-group to broadcast him efficiently. I don't take it as my function to review current novels by the young. Some at least of Crevel's were worth it. Apart from Cocteau's productions I think they are the only productions by my French juniors that have given me a first class, as distinct from second or 4th or nth rate, literary delight. . . . Crevel was a writer, born, more born, I should have conjectured, a writer than born to programaticality. Any how, and damn it, he is dead. And I am not to put off with "You go and discover things after everyone else has forgotten them." A great many people haven't even forgotten it. As long as Crevel was alive, there was no need of my introducing him, any more than there is ever any need of anyone writing in English introducing any french writer, because any french writer whom any of us can read with respect is always known to a great many more people than we are. . . . The "after everyone has forgotten" examination is necessary to sort out the real from the book-stall flush.

In the mid-1920s Crevel contracted tuberculosis. His doctor put him into a sanatorium in Davos, Switzerland, hoping that time away from the tyranny of his careless, fast-paced life in Paris, a few months of breathing mountain air and eating regular meals, might improve his health. He wrote to a friend from Davos in 1927: "Here always the same life. . . . I have too much time ahead of me and not enough hope. In taking care of oneself, one becomes an egoist, an egoism of the dullest kind. And youth so quickly spent, so badly spent."

He was often sent to Switzerland in the years that followed. The hospital in Davos must have been very similar to the institution so exhaustively described by Thomas Mann in *The Magic Mountain*. In 1935, on the very eve of the Congress of Writers for the Defense of Culture, having failed in his effort to effect a reconciliation between surrealists and the Stalinist directorship of the conference—they had voted not to permit Breton to speak—Crevel committed suicide. His death produced a great shock in literary and political circles; it was a cry of pain and of protest, the ultimate surrealist act, echoing his work's theme of self-immolation, and very much in the rebellious spirit of his models, Rimbaud and Lautréamont. As one of his earliest friends, the surrealist Philippe Soupault, wrote of him after his death, "He was born a rebel the way others are born with blue eyes."

WORKS IN ENGLISH TRANSLATION: *Babylon* was translated in 1985 by Kay Boyle, who had in 1931 translated an excerpt from the novel as *Mr. Knife and Miss Fork*, published in Paris by the Black Sun Press in a limited edition with photograms by Max Ernst.

ABOUT: Columbia Dictionary of Modern European Literature, 1980. *Periodicals*—Choice December 1985; Criterion January 1939; Kirkus Reviews May 15, 1985; Library Journal May 1, 1985; Los Angeles Times Book Review August 4, 1985; New York Times Book Review September 22, 1985; Publishers Weekly April 26, 1985.

SÁNDOR CSOÓRI

*CSOÓRI, SÁNDOR (February 3, 1930–), Hungarian poet, essayist, and screenwriter, was born in Zámoly, "right in the middle of a teeth-chattering hard winter and the similarly severe economic crises." His parents were peasants and Protestants who were defenseless against the desperate economic situation but stubborn in their faith and convictions. His father, always stirred by historical events and questions of social justice, picked up every scrap of newspaper to inform himself about such issues; his mother, on the other hand, was, according to Csoóri, a peasant who lived solely within "the world of oral tradition," and it was she who not only ran the household but assigned all the tasks on the family's seven-acre farm, and who served the portions at meal times but, in keeping with village custom, never sat at the table to eat with the family. Csoóri often pays tribute to his parents for the hardships they endured throughout his boyhood and youth. His mother, he says, suffered "enough anguish, fear, and apprehension for five lives," because "whatever [burdens] she couldn't share with others weighed down upon her." He also tells how his father risked being killed by poachers or soldiers at Christmas in 1945 by walking the 120 kilometers from Zámoly to Pápa through woods and snowstorms to fetch him home from school.

The small farm and the poverty of the village made it difficult for Csoóri to obtain an education past the six years of elementary school. Before him, only one other village youngster had managed to go on to high school. Csoóri was fortunate, in 1942, to be included among six hundred peasant children recommended for a free education by the National Village Talent Search Institute, probably founded at the instigation of Hungary's populist writers. Surviving a series of screening examinations, he passed the final test at Pápa and, after some administrative delay,

entered the famous Protestant College there. His studies at the college shaped his life so significantly that he questions the wisdom of the state's dissolution of this ancient school, as well as those at Debrecen and Sárospatak, "like some ruined castle haunted by owls." Before he attended school at Pápa, he had only a peasant's view of the world, "unable to imagine the summer without the crackling of straw, without dusty acacias and sleepy hens." Much later, when standing on the ocean shore in Mexico, he heard "the startled horde of starlings crackling in the froth of waves striking high." The war initiated him into "manhood," or "let me say bitterly rather—modernity, universality. I arrived in the vicinity of physical catastrophes from alongside oxen. Within the period of three and one-half months, my village changed hands seventeen times. After the front passed by, we spent two weeks burying human beings and animals. After that came trenches and underground bunkers."

Hired by the *Pápai Néplap* (Pápa Popular News) in recognition of his writing potential even before he graduated from high school, he toured the country for stories and often wrote highly enthusiastic articles about the changes taking place under the socialism of the Rákosi government that had come to power in 1949. This newspaper also published his first poem on May 1 of that year. After graduation he became the editor of a column for *Veszprém Megyei Népújság* (Veszprém County Popular Newspaper). In 1950, growing ever more discontent with village life, he went to Budapest, with which he had become enamored on a visit with

*chó ri, shän´ door

a student delegation in 1948, to study Russian history, Marxism, and, chiefly, the art of translating at the Lenin Institute. He was soon chosen a member of the board of directors of the newly established Young Writers' Association, where in debates he addressed aesthetic problems in literary expression, already taking issue with the vigorous imposition of schematism on poetry by governmental arbiters, even as he later, as a member of the Writers' Union, continued to raise urgent questions about relations between literature and society, to his own political disadvantage. He left the Lenin Institute after "three-fourths of a year of fakery," a time followed by "a fleeing from all kinds of dogmatism and strictly directed pedagogy." The first of many serious illnesses, that continue to trouble him and permeate A félig bevallatott élet (The Half-Acknowledged Life, 1981), forced him in the winter of 1952 to return to Zámoly and spend the spring with his family.

His life and activities, growing increasingly literary, took him to Budapest again, where he served on the staff of Szabad Ifjúság (Free Youth) in 1952 and of Irodalmi Újság (Literary News) from 1953 to 1954 and then became the head of the poetry section of Új Hang (New Voice) from 1955 to 1956. Csoóri considers these early years of the 1950s, especially his familiarity with the hardships of village life, critical to his development. Singled out as a promising young author by the Literary Foundation, he was awarded an annual stipend to write, but he used the income primarily to support his parents. When asked in 1976 what impact the Rákosi years had upon him, he replied that if he can be grateful to Rákosi for one thing only: "he taught me to have faith in myself. In my own desires, in my own experiences." And that recognition of the necessity to defend individuality from destruction was more recently stressed in his commitment "to preserve the significance of the individual in the great war against impersonality. For in vain would wonders be occurring on earth if these wonders no longer mattered to us. In vain would the ocean come up to my window if I, the host, no longer knew anything about myself."

Csoóri won the Attila József Prize for his poetry in 1954, the year he published Felröppen a madár (The Bird Takes Wing), a slender collection of five years of poems. This early work was inspired by folk poetry and the poems of Sándor Petőfi, a revolutionary who died in 1849 fighting the Austrians in the unsuccessful war of independence and one of Hungary's greatest poets. The poems reveal a love of country, a joy of building socialism in Hungary, and a feeling of fulfillment at being one with the community.

Csoóri's early lyrics are not personal in tone but are pitched, rather, in the sphere of Hungary's national development. However, some signs of his peasant origin and a personal awareness of domestic difficulties were already present in poems published in the fall of 1952 in Új Hang. After he observed some of the troubling consequences of land reform during his convalescence in Zámoly, his poems, some of them published in Irodalmi Újság and Csillag (Star) in 1953, took on a critical tone in describing the economic dislocation and psychological suffering experienced by the peasants. "Indignation," he says, "gave birth to my first writings. Understandably, they contained more moral than aesthetic value," and, he candidly adds, "occasionally even today, the continuing struggle between these two is observable in my poems and in the texts of my lyrically masked prose."

His second book of poems, Ördögpille (Devil's Moth, 1957) still resembled the Petőfi model but considerably differed in outlook. Reflecting the dilemma of the new generation of writers who found their home in the socialism of the Rákosi period but felt the need for a new birth as a result of the 1956 uprising, Csoóri turned from political and social conflicts and submerged himself in his private world, no longer feeling a kinship with his village and tormented by apathy and anxiety. From this point on, his poems changed in style and substance. His careful study of Apollinaire, Éluard, García Lorca, and modern European poetry generally helped to shape poetic means suitable to his intimate and restless effort to validate amid human dilemmas the uniqueness of his own personality: a less restricted structure, a wider range of imagery, a freer imagination. The fruits of self-examination first appeared in his next book, Menekülés a magányból (Flight from Solitude, 1962), and were further cultivated in Második születésem (My Second Birth, 1967), Párbeszédek, sötétben (Dialogue in the Dark, 1973), and A látogató emlékei (The Visitor's Remembrances, 1977)— all four titles reflecting his states of mind during a period of more than fifteen years. In these works, as one critic observes, Csoóri emerges as an "athlete" in lonely competition with himself and the world around him, never knowing rest, casting his victories aside, ever taking new risks, and, his rebellion and discontent having hardened into a permanent attitude, running headlong, unable to stop. His lyric poems, widely viewed as his most effective form of poetic expression, are distinguished by the candid self-revelation of his most intimate thoughts and emotions in the form of memories suddenly reviving themselves in verse. These lyrics tend to become extremely intimate as a major expression his innermost experiences by interweaving recollections that touch basic human situations, sometimes unexpectedly, through imagistic rather than conceptual means and a natural, simple language acquiring its energy from the intensity of his passion. As Csoóri states in a postscript to *Menekülés a magányból*, the function of lyric poetry is not simply "to provide abstract beliefs or even resolute ideas but a zest for life, so that, besides fear, which is as much a part of human culture, say, as the yearning for freedom, it will teach man to love this Earth." He constructs his lyrical world sensitively and sincerely on the dialectics of loneliness, defeat, hope, affiliation, indignation, love, and fidelity, drawing, says a critic, on "his sweet and acerbic, gentle and thorny, homely and shocking experiences" and conveying that reality "mostly as a dream: sharply, very discernably but still with vibrant, volatile outlines."

Csoóri constantly tries to understand the basic situations human beings have always faced. *Kezemben zöld ág* (A Green Branch in My Hands, 1985) includes in its first pages the songs of grief and farewell in *Elmaradt lázálom* (Cancelled Nightmare, 1982), in which he mourned the death of his lover, whom he had tended during her terminal illness. The poems, built on thoughts of death and renewal, grief and consolation, eventually lead him to accept death as a tragic event fixed by inexorable laws of human nature. Elegiac feelings and philosophical resignation permeate the verses:

> I don't think death is more gifted than I.
> I don't think death can take you from me.
> I see myself in you, as if seated on a lovely wound:
> a green bough in my hand and behind me, oh, behind me
> boundless expanses: a hereafter darkening over me.
> —trans. by A. Tezla

Poems like this, illuminating his spiritual torment and revealing his effort to alleviate his deep feeling of isolation and loneliness, offer a fulcrum to comprehend a fundamental and ancient existence, a taste, however slight sometimes, of that happy and natural condition out of which, according to Csoóri, technology and civilization have wrenched mankind since the end of World War II.

After the publication of *Ordögpille* in 1957, Csoóri turned to other genres as well to reach, as he reports, an audience larger than the one for poetry. He has written several successful filmscripts that are credited with elevating Hungarian film writing to new heights, including *Tízezer nap* (Ten Thousand Days), which won a major Cannes Festival award in 1964, and he has served as dramaturge at the renowned Hun-

garian Film Studio since 1971. Of more literary significance are his sociographic writings, which, he feels, give him the room to expound principles and concepts "I couldn't cram into verse." *Tudósítás a toronyból* (Report from the Tower, 1963), in which Csoóri wrote passionately on the plight of peasants uprooted by forced collectivization, and *A költő és a majompofa* (The Poet and the Monkey Face, 1966) and *Faltól falig* (From Wall to Wall, 1969), both containing mainly sketches on various aspects of Hungarian folk culture, were followed by *Utazás, félálomban* (Journey While Half-Asleep, 1974), a collection of forty-two essays whose subjects shift to the consideration of fundamental human attitudes and behavior.

In that collection Csoóri began his work in a genre, the sociographic essay, which he fine-tuned in successive writings and which, according to some reviewers, resemble Montaigne's essays. Csoóri's essays are not specialized articles but accounts of his own personal experiences and opinions on matters dealing with vital questions of Hungarian and East European culture. Anthologized in *Nomád napló* (Nomad's Journal, 1979), which sold out in days, these essays, though personal, are precise and concrete in the hands of a self-taught sociographer. In general, the structuring of Csoóri's "lyrically masked prose" is similar to the technique present in many of his poems. There, as Balázs Lengyel points out, Csoóri begins with "a simple perception of a situation, a momentary observation or experience perceived by a receptive, 'soft lyrical temperament'" and "rises to the higher levels of thought and consciousness, without losing its receptivity and reaches subjects which permeate our world today." Here, as several critics note, Csoóri recalls something, envisions it, and, reflecting upon it, tries to confirm what he envisions with substantive arguments, ending most of the essays with a question mark. There, he aims at the self in search of meaning beyond the particulars of the here and now. Here, he makes an equally monumental effort to lay a cultural and historical foundation for a universality that will furnish coordinates for Hungary's intellectual life and, beyond that, for Central and Eastern Europe to bestow on the region its rightful place alongside the nations of Western Europe.

By building on this model in "Tenger és diólevél" (Ocean and the Leaf of a Nut Tree), which closes the anthology and was also published separately in New York in 1982, Csoóri finds the distinctive literary form that forcefully conveys a distillation and real-life portrayal of his life view. Called a "master essay" that supplies "authoritative evidence of the spiritual maturing of a committed Hungarian intellectual" and also considered by many among the most important four or five books written in present-day Hungary, this work is a synthesis of every motif probed in his earlier essays, and, according to one critic, Csoóri's personal "evolutionary novel," squarely facing "the disordered, divided world" to recover "the right to live and the possibility of an order-creating, all-embracing spirit." To Csoóri the path to this end lies in helping the human personality to find its home directly in the present age, "not despite the confused state of the world nor outside it but within it."

In keeping with this aim, Csoóri views today's technological civilization with a jaundiced yet hopeful eye. To correct its mistakes and to preserve and restore values that can sustain human relationships in the alienating present, he advocates reliance on the ethical values inherent in mankind's past, in the human traditions, especially those preserved in folklore, and in the historicity of human events. To him the past is needed to stabilize and correct the invidious effects of knowledge and technology on the inner life of humanity. Supporters of civilization, he maintains, would gladly destroy human sensitivity to the historical past with their firm belief that technological solutions can be found for all social ailments. Admittedly, some problems can be solved in this manner, but, he insists, even as they are being solved by these means, many other elements are being destroyed. In his view, the basic flaw is that the laboratory ideas of scientific learning are thought capable of solving human problems that have evolved historically. That approach cannot work because what to the mind may seem a perfect solution is very possibly not so to the emotions. Csoóri urges "twentieth century man [to] cling ever more tightly to a knowledge of history at least to the extent he once did to religion." By doing so, humanity would have an orientation toward existence in today's world as Western man once had from religion in the Middle Ages.

Using literary means and values extensively even in his prose writings, Csoóri, of course, considers imaginative literature as a special means of linking humanity to a direct perception of the most ancient and supportive essentials of life. "Look about the world," he urges, "and everywhere you will find confusion and despair, outer or inner,—in the worst instances, degradation. You see that the night of human relationships will arrive sooner than their dawn." He is convinced that human beings have become "social creatures" far too much, that "if long ago the issue was for man to triumph over nature, now it is for him to rule over society." It is poetry, the drama, and the novel that direct human attention to human reality "which has polluting out our

distortions" or mixing "suffering and freedom together," and "the good writer is one who, like history, makes us wiser but doesn't explain. . . . Good works must be as suggestive as reality is suggestive." And to him, poetry—like all the arts—helps human beings to create an order within their inner world, restoring them to a direct and primary relationship with the earth that civilization has stripped away from them.

WORKS IN ENGLISH TRANSLATION: Selected poems by Csoóri were translated into English by I. L. de Beky, 1981, with the title *Wings of Knives and Nails* and by Nicholas Kolumban, 1983, with the title *Memory of Snow*. Translations of other poems and a short prose piece were published in Albert Tezla's *Ocean at the Window: Hungarian Prose and Poetry since 1945*, 1980. In 1989 Csoóri's *Barbarian Prayer: Selected Poems* was published in Budapest by Corvina.

ABOUT: Tezla, A. Hungarian Authors: A Bibliographical Handbook, 1970; Tezla, A. Ocean at the Window, 1980. *Periodicals*—New Hungarian Quarterly Winter 1980; Booklist March 1, 1984.

DARNTON, ROBERT (CHOATE) (May 10, 1939–   ), American historian, was born in New York City, the son of Byron Darnton and the former Eleanor Choate, both journalists. He graduated from Harvard University in 1960, won a Rhodes scholarship and spent the next four years at Oxford University, earning a B.Phil. degree in 1962 and a D.Phil. in 1964. After a few years' work as a journalist—he was a stringer for the *New York Times* during his years at Oxford—Darnton returned to Harvard in 1965 as a junior fellow in the history department. In 1968 he went as assistant professor of history to Princeton University, where he has remained ever since; he has been full professor since 1972. In his career as historian, Darnton has concentrated on pre-Revolutionary eighteenth-century France, in particular the period of the Enlightenment with special reference to the events surrounding the publication of the era's greatest work, Diderot and Alembert's *Encyclopédie*.

His first book, *Mesmerism and the End of the Enlightenment in France*, "attempts to examine," in the words of the introduction, "the mentality of literate Frenchmen on the eve of the Revolution, to see the world as they saw it, before the Revolution threw it out of focus." Darnton limited this study to what seems to have been "the hottest topic—science in general, mesmerism in particular." The Viennese physician Franz Mesmer and his somewhat mystical ideas concerning the benefits to be derived from "animal magnetism" caused an immense sensa-

ROBERT DARNTON

tion in the Paris of the 1770s and 1780s. "Mesmerism," Darnton continues, "offered a serious explanation of Nature, of her wonderful, invisible forces, and even, in some cases, of the forces governing society and politics. They absorbed mesmerism so thoroughly that they made it a principal article in the legacy of attitudes that they left for their sons and grandsons to fashion into what is now called romanticism." Later generations have not adequately recognized Mesmer's importance and influence in his time, and it was Darnton's intention to "restore him to his rightful place, somewhere near Turgot, Franklin, and Cagliostro in the pantheon of that age's most-talked-about men . . . [and] to help one to understand how the Enlightenment ended, not absolutely . . . but historically, as a movement characterizing eighteenth-century France." Included are chapters on mesmerism and popular science, its status as a movement, its connections to eighteenth-century radicalism, and its links to romanticism. J. H. Young thought the book "excellent and exemplary. . . . Based on a thorough study of manuscripts, pamphlets, and journals, learned in its broad setting and persuasive in its internal logic, . . . [it] provides a commendable model for those interested in the way . . . ideas interact and broadly influence behavior."

In the late 1960s, in pursuit of information about a French revolutionary named J.-P. Brissot, Darnton came upon a cache of 50,000 letters in the Municipal Archives of Neuchâtel, Switzerland, concerning the Société Typographique de Neuchâtel, an important French-language publishing house of the eighteenth century, and publishers and distributors of a later edition of the *Encyclopédie*. The letters, which had never before been systematically studied, revealed much about the publishing industry in pre-Revolutionary France, a time when powerful ideas were principally disseminated by means of books. The first study by Darnton to come of this line of research he entitled *The Business of Enlightenment: A Publishing History of the Encyclopédie 1775–1800*. In his introduction the author addresses the implications of his historical method. He has written, in effect, "a book about a book: the subject seems arcanc, and it could contract into the infinitely small, like a mirror reflected in a mirror." Yet in France *l'histoire du livre* (literally, "history of the book") "opens onto the broadest questions of historical research. How did great intellectual movements like the Enlightenment spread through society? How far did they reach, how deeply did they penetrate? What form did the thought of the *philosophes* acquire when it materialized into books, and what does this process reveal about the transmission of ideas? Did the material basis of literature and the technology of its production have much bearing on its substance and its diffusion? How did the literary market place function, and what were the roles of publishers, book dealers, traveling salesmen, and other intermediaries in cultural communication? How did publishing function as a business, and how did it fit into the political as well as the economic systems of prerevolutionary Europe?" All these questions Darnton attempts to answer in this lengthy work, which Robert Lindsay called "intellectual, economic, business, and social history at its best." Darnton also completed his biography of the writer-publicist Brissot, but has not yet published it.

The wider world of literary production in pre-Revolutionary France was Darnton's next subject. *The Literary Underground of the Old Regime* attempts, in the author's words, "to bring together pieces of a world that fell apart in the eighteenth century. It was a world, or underworld, that lived from the production and diffusion of illegal literature in prerevolutionary France." The world consisted of "Grub Street hacks, pirate publishers, and under-the-cloak peddlers of forbidden books." The underground was especially important in the eighteenth century, "when censorship, the police, and a monopolistic guild of booksellers attempted to contain the printed word within limits set by the official orthodoxies. . . . Most of what passes today for eighteenth-century French literature circulated on the shady side of the law in eighteenth-century France. . . . During the eighteenth century, a general reading public emerged in France; public opinion gathered force; and ideological discontent welled up with other currents to produce the first great revolution of modern time. Books contributed a great deal to this ferment." Along with the material from the Neuchâtel Archives, the author's principal sources were a collection of documents kept by the French secret police, records of incarcerations in the Bastille, and papers of the booksellers' guild. The book's chapters exist virtually as separate pieces, yet are thematically linked in that all are concerned with "the book as a force in eighteenth-century Europe"; they treat a Grub Street spy, a renegade pamphleteer, a clandestine bookseller, a printing shop across the border, and an attempted answer to the question of what Frenchmen read in the later eighteenth century. Norman Hampson remarked on the author's "enviable gift for reading between the lines, extracting meaning and life from unpromising material, and finding relations between things that have no obvious connection with each other. Whatever he writes is stimulating to read. . . . Thanks to [Darnton] we know a good deal more about the ecology of ancien régime society. His attempt to impose a rather rigorous classification on the flora that it produced is less persuasive, but even here there is much to learn from him."

Several more discrete contributions to a history of eighteenth-century *mentalités* comprise *The Great Cat Massacre and Other Episodes in French Cultural History*. Much of the force behind this book's genesis came from a course Darnton regularly teaches at Princeton with the anthropologist Clifford Geertz. Historians, Darnton has come to believe, can better grasp the "otherness" of earlier periods if they allow an anthropological methodology to enter their work. He discussed this point in an interview in 1984: "By learning to think his way into alien ways of thinking, the anthropologist can provide an example to the historian. If we study people who are separated from us by two wars, an Industrial Revolution, a French Revolution, and a transformation in health, diet, demography, family relations, communications, and many other things that shape our daily life, we must be dealing with human beings whose experience is quite different from our own. . . . I think there is a growing trend among historians to turn to anthropology and among anthropologists to turn to history. We recognize that we are studying the same thing, namely culture. . . . So I see a growing body of literature in the two subjects which indicates that they are moving together." Chapters in *The Great Cat Massacre* concern the brutal fairy tales told by peasants, the great cat

massacre of the rue St.-Séverin, Paris, in the late 1730s as a prototype of a workers' revolt; the complete description of his city written in 1768 by a Montpellier *bourgeois*; a police inspector's description during the period 1748–1753 of his attempts to control the traffic in forbidden books; the intensity with which the works of Rousseau were greeted by the reading public; and the epistemological (and editorial) strategies of the *Encyclopédie*. Stanley Hoffmann commented, "Darnton has the inquisitiveness of a first-rate investigative reporter, the thoroughness of a rigorous scholar, and the sensitivity of a novelist. Rarely have these very different gifts been so deliciously combined." Mavis Gallant thought the book "eccentric and original. . . . Mr. Darnton encloses his essays between an introduction and a conclusion, raised like umbrellas to war off a hail of objections about method, treatment, extrapolation, confusion about academic territory and even the use of the first person singular. The clear language of the text derails into academic thistle-talk only when its author appears to address himself to fellow academics."

Darnton has been an active member of several U.S. and international societies for the study of eighteenth-century history, and in 1982 was awarded the much-coveted prize of the John D. and Catherine T. MacArthur Foundation. He was George Eastman visiting professor at Oxford in 1986–1987. He next plans a more complete history, "a systematic treatise" as he calls it, of the trade during the old regime of private publishing houses in illegal, forbidden books. In the bicentenary commemorations of the French Revolution, Darnton coedited and wrote the Introduction to *Revolution in Print: The Press in France 1775–1800*, a collection of essays developing out of the New York Public Library's major exhibition (Spring 1989).

PRINCIPAL WORKS: Mesmerism and the End of the Enlightenment in France, 1968; The Business of Enlightenment: A Publishing History of the Encyclopédie 1775–1800, 1979; The Literary Underground of the Old Regime, 1982; The Great Cat Massacre and Other Episodes in French Cultural History, 1984. *As coeditor*—(with D. Roche) Revolution in Print, 1989.

ABOUT: Contemporary Authors 16, 1986. *Periodicals*—America August 18–24, 1984; American Journal of Sociology November 1985; American Historical Review October 1969, October 1980, June 1983; Annals of the American Academy November 1969; Atlantic February 1984; Best Sellers September 1979; Business History Review Winter 1981; Choice November 1969, January 1980; History June 1985; History Today February 1980; Journal of Interdisciplinary History Spring 1980; Journal of Modern History September 1970,

June 1981; Library Journal October 15, 1979; December 1, 1983; London Review of Books December 2, 1982; Modern Language Review January 1984; National Review June 8, 1979; New Republic April 16, 1984; New York Review of Books February 7, 1980; October 7, 1982; New York Times February 15, 1983; April 14, 1983; New York Times Book Review November 21, 1982; February 12, 1984; Newsweek February 27, 1984; Quill & Quire October 1984; Science March 21, 1969; Time February 13, 1984; Times Literary Supplement December 14, 1979; Virginia Quarterly Review Summer 1969, Spring 1980.

DAVIDSON, DONALD (HERBERT) (March 6, 1917–   ), American philosopher, was born in Springfield, Massachusetts, the son of Clarence Herbert Davidson, an engineer, and the former Grace Anthony. He was educated in public schools and attended Harvard University, receiving his bachelor's degree in philosophy in 1939 and his master's degree two years later. He served in the United States Navy in the Mediterranean theater during World War II, then returned to Harvard for more philosophical study, in particular under the noted logician W. V. Quine. He received his doctorate from Harvard in 1949. Davidson's teaching career has included positions at Queens College in New York City, where he was instructor (1947–1950); Stanford University (1951–1967), where he rose to the rank of full professor; Princeton University (1967–1975); Rockefeller University in New York City (1970–1976), where he was adjunct professor; the University of Chicago (1976–1981); and the University of California at Berkeley, the faculty of which he joined in 1981 and where he has been emeritus professor since the mid-1980s.

In common with those of several influential philosophers, Davidson's high reputation in his field rests as much upon inspired teaching and the impressions made upon his peers in personal contacts as upon his published work. He has published only two books entirely under his own name, and both of these have consisted of disparate articles ("designed," he wrote, "to be more or less free standing") that had appeared in philosophical journals over a couple of decades. *Essays on Actions and Events* comprises fifteen pieces on the general topic of human action, evenly divided into three groups among the themes intention and action, event and cause, and philosophy of psychology. Davidson argues here, as he has throughout his career, in favor of an ontology that includes events along with persons and objects. The essays are thus, he maintains in his introduction, "unified in theme and general thesis. The theme is the role of causal

DONALD DAVIDSON

concepts in the description and explanation of human action. The thesis is that the ordinary notion of cause which enters into scientific or common-sense accounts of non-psychological affairs is essential also to the understanding of what it is to act with a reason, to have a certain intention in acting, to be an agent, to act counter to one's own best judgment, or to act freely. Cause is the cement of the universe; the concept of cause is what holds together our picture of the universe, a picture that would otherwise disintegrate into a diptych of the mental and the physical." Although the essays represent thirteen years of work by a philosopher near the peak of his powers, he did not, in assembling them for joint publication, conceal the discrepancies between earlier and later views; he did, however, eliminate inadvertent blunders and stylistic infelicities, and he reduced redundance. "Redundance in plenty remains," he concluded, "but the points that are worked over most are usually the ones that gave me trouble, and so there is, I hope, instruction or interest in what may seem, and probably was intended as, mere repetition." He then goes on to analyze each essay in turn in terms of both its contribution to the book's overall thesis and its position in the body of his work.

The collection was described by Ted Honderich, in the *New Statesman*, as "an exemplar of philosophy as it is in English at this moment, and he is one of three or four active candidates in the running for being the philosophers' philosopher. . . . The book is an absolutely admirable one. Struggle and learn." According to Sir Peter Strawson in a full-page review in the *Times Literary Supplement*: "Each essay is strictly argued, and the whole collection forms a tightly interlocking set of theoretical positons in metaphysics and the philosophy of mind. . . . This is one of the most impressive works of analytical philosophy to appear for a good many years. It is also one of the least casual. The positions adopted are argued for with an extraordinarily sustained seriousness and determination. Whether or not these positions win general acceptance, the work will become, and deserves to become, a classic in its field."

Inquiries into Truth and Interpretation is Davidson's other collection of disparate pieces, this one consisting of eighteen essays written between 1965 and 1982 and roughly divided among the five topics: truth and meaning, applications, radical interpretation, language and reality, and limits of the literal. "What is it," the author asks in the introduction, "for words to mean what they do? In the essays collected here I explore the idea that we would have an answer to this question if we knew how to construct a theory satisfying two demands: it would provide an interpretation of all utterances, actual and potential, of a speaker or group of speakers; and it would be verifiable without knowledge of the detailed propositional attitudes of the speaker. The first condition acknowledges the holistic nature of linguistic understanding. The second condition aims to prevent smuggling into the foundations of the theory concepts too closely allied to the concept of meaning. A theory that does not satisfy both conditions cannot be said to answer our opening question in a philosophically instructive way."

Ian Hacking wrote in a long review of this collection (significantly entitled "On the Frontier") in the *New York Review of Books*: "there is no more creative or systematic philosopher at work in America today than Donald Davidson. . . . [He] proceeds by composing small talks that he delivers over and over again in lectures and seminars. Their first publication may be nearly anywhere. . . . After Davidson's work has had its long and careful larval life, it passes into a dormant chrysalis stage of obscure publication. *Inquiries into Truth and Interpretation* is the occasion for the final metamorphosis into a readily available sequence of sustained arguments. . . . [He] is not posing the practical questions of a linguist or psychologist about the processes by which people learn and deal with words. He is putting an abstract question about how to represent the knowledge that a person must have in order to understand another person." Hacking went on to point out that Davidson is not a philosopher content to let things rest. In an article

"A Nice Derangement of Epitaphs," which appeared in *Philosophical Grounds of Rationality: Intentions, Categories, Ends* (1986), edited by Richard E. Grandy and Richard Warner, a *festschrift* for the philosopher Paul Grice, Davidson permits himself to doubt that there *is* such a thing as language, at least as commonly understood by philosophers, psychologists, and linguists. Hacking concludes: "That would seem to put the cat among Davidson's own pigeons. Such complex issues are a matter for long, hard, cautious thinking. Whatever conclusions we shall finally reach, it is evident that Davidson has already constructed one of the most remarkable pillars of sustained philosophical reasoning to be found in any era."

Davidson's life's work is the subject of a remarkable volume edited by the philosophers Bruce Vermazen and Merrill B. Hintikka, *Essays on Davidson: Actions and Events*. In this book fourteen philosophers present thirteen essays on the three main categories of Davidson's work: intention and action, event and cause, and the philosophy of psychology. Davidson himself, in chapters occupying the final fifth of the book, provides responses and replies to each of the contributions, and in a postscript to the replies revealed a little of his philosophical and literary method: "Before one starts to write one thinks one knows what one is going to say. But in my case at least it is only as I write that I discover what I think, and this is almost never what I thought when I began. . . . I suppose it is natural when reading comments and criticisms of one's own work to suppose one knows how to respond; on this supposition I have generally avoided public answers to my critics. This volume has changed my attitude. . . . There is not one essay in this book to which I found it easy to reply."

Reviewing *Essays on Davidson* in the *Times Literary Supplement*, Paul Snowdon wrote that Davidson's pre-eminence among the philosophers of his time rests upon "a group of striking, highly general, interconnected and developing ideas. . . . The most famous proposal was captured in the slogan that 'a theory of meaning for a language should be a truth-definition for that language.' A truth-definition for a language is an assignment of properties to the semantic units within it, from which can be deduced, for each complete sentence, a statement of the conditions in which it is true. This proposal was the conclusion of a complex line of thought which purported to identify what we want of a theory of meaning, and tried to show that a truth-definition provides it."

Davidson has been winning praise in the

merous institutions throughout the world, including the universities of Tokyo (1955), Adelaide (1968), Sydney (1968), Pittsburgh (1972), and Capetown (1980). He has been the John Locke lecturer (1970) and the George Eastman professor (1984–1985) at Oxford, the John Dewey lecturer at the University of Minnesota (1975), the Matchette Foundation lecturer at the University of Wisconsin (1976), the José Gaos lecturer at the Federal University of Mexico (1980), the Kant lecturer at Stanford (1986), the Keeling lecturer at University College, London (1985), the Selfridge lecturer at Lehigh University (1986), and the Thalheimer lecturer at Johns Hopkins (1987). He is a longtime member of the editorial boards of the journals *Philosophia, Theoretical Linguistics, Theory and Decision, Erkenntnis,* and *Current Commentary in the Behavioral and Brain Sciences.* His fellowships have included: Rockefeller (1945–1946; 1948), Ford (1953–1954), Guggenheim (1973–1974), All Souls College, Oxford (1973–1974), and the American Academy of Arts and Sciences. He is a member of the American Philosophical Society and the American Philosophical Association. Davidson married Marcia Cavell in 1984. He has one child from a previous marriage.

PRINCIPAL WORKS: (with P. Suppes) Decision Making, 1957; Essays on Actions and Events, 1980; Inquiries into Truth and Interpretation, 1984. *As coeditor*—(with J. Hintikka) Words and Objections, 1969; (with G. Harman) Semantics of Natural Language, 1972, and The Logic of Grammar, 1975.

ABOUT: Contemporary Authors New Revision Series 2, 1981; Vermazin, B. and M. B. Hintikka (eds.) Essays on Davidson, 1985; Who's Who in America, 1988–1989. *Periodicals*—American Economic Review December 1958; American Journal of Sociology September 1958; Choice April 1981, February 1985; New Statesman April 3, 1981; New York Review of Books December 20, 1984; Times Literary Supplement February 6, 1981; December 27, 1985.

DAVIS, NATALIE (ANN) ZEMON (November 8, 1928–), American historian, was born in Detroit, the daughter of Julian Leon Zemon, a businessman, and the former Helen Lamport. She received her bachelor's degree from Smith College in 1949, a master's from Radcliffe the following year, and a doctorate in history from the University of Michigan. Her thesis, "Protestantism and the Printing Workers of Lyon: A Study in the Problem of Religion and Social Class during the Reformation," was completed in 1959. Its topic foreshadowed much of her most important historical work, which she

NATALIE ZEMON DAVIS

has described as growing out of an interest "in the 'people,' the artisans and poor of sixteenth-century French cities, and also in the culture of peasants." She has become one of the foremost American practitioners of the "new social history," which has attempted to bring within the purview of modern historical study the lives of the largely illiterate artisans, laborers, and peasants of preindustrial Europe. To do so she has enlisted the help of anthropological research, thereby demonstrating the extent to which the new social historians rely on interdisciplinary methods in their work.

After a decade and a half of teaching and of contributing influential articles on her specialty to scholarly journals—in particular the British *Past and Present*—Davis produced her first book, a collection of eight of these essays, *Society and Culture in Early Modern France.* The essays, she remarks in her preface, "are about peasants and even more about artisans and the *menu peuple* of the cities. The very rich, the powerful, the learned, and the priestly are described primarily in relation to the lives of the 'modest'—as they reacted to them, conflicted with them, or shared their activities or beliefs. The interaction between Society and Culture and the balance between tradition and innovation are thus explored only for certain segments of the social order, and then through a set of case studies rather than systematically." Her research, she notes, was "not simply a matter of scouring libraries for popular playlets, poems and pamphlets and of sifting criminal and judicial records, welfare rolls, notarial contracts, and militia and financial lists for mentions of artisans and the poor. It was also a matter of recognizing that forms of associational life and collective behavior are cultural artifacts, not just items in the history of the Reformation or of political centralization. A journeyman's initiation rite, a village festive organization, an informal gathering of women for a lying-in or of men and women for storytelling, or a street disturbance could be 'read' as fruitfully as a diary, a political tract, a sermon, or a body of laws." The topics of the first three essays are, generally speaking, aspects of social protest and religious change; of the next three, the folklore of social and religious strife; of the last two, the relationship between the printed word and popular culture. Several of the essays are concerned with the role of women in illiterate, preindustrial society. The historian Theodore Rabb greatly praised "the benefits of the historian's interaction with the anthropologist. . . . Professor Davis not only appreciates the actions and beliefs of ordinary men and women, but also finds in them a significance, a purpose, and a coherence which earlier scholars considered either inconceivable or insignificant. . . . There are approaches which allow the sympathetic inquirer to glimpse the assumptions, the values, and the ambitions of seemingly inaccessible historical actors. An entire style of life, with its special rituals and symbols, can come to the surface."

Davis' next book, *The Return of Martin Guerre*, grew out of her interest in a story of peasant imposture that was discussed throughout France at the time of its occurrence in the southwestern part of the country during the middle of the sixteenth century. She briefly sketches its outlines in the preface: "In the 1540s in Languedoc, a rich peasant leaves his wife, child, and property and is not heard from for years; he comes back—or so everyone thinks—but after three or four years of agreeable marriage the wife says she has been tricked by an impostor and brings him to trial. The man almost persuades the court he is Martin Guerre, when at the last moment the true Martin Guerre appears. Two books were immediately written about the case, one by a judge of the court. All over France there were comments on it, by the great Montaigne among others." Soon after her own rediscovery of the story, Davis found that a film of it was being planned by two Frenchmen, the scenarist Jean-Claude Carrière and the director Daniel Vigne. The three decided to collaborate on the film, which was released to international acclaim in 1982 with Gérard Depardieu as the impostor. In the course of her work with Carrière and Vigne, she explains, she "was prompted to dig deeper into the case, to make

historical sense of it." At the same time, the film, as films are wont to do, "was departing from the historical record: . . . the Basque background of the Guerres was sacrificed; rural Protestantism was ignored; and especially the double game of the wife and the judge's inner contradictions were softened. . . . Where was there room to reflect upon the significance of identity in the sixteenth century?" The story's most essential aspect to her was that it revealed "the hidden world of peasant sentiment and aspiration." The fact that it was an unusual case was all the better for the historian, "for a remarkable dispute can sometimes uncover motivations and values that are lost in the welter of the everyday." She decided to write a book that would deepen and broaden the story's most salient aspects, and intended to show "that the adventures of three young villagers are not too many steps beyond the more common experience of their neighbors, that an impostor's fabrication has links with more ordinary ways of creating personal identity. I also want to explain why a story that seemed fit for a mere popular pamphlet—and indeed was told in that form—became in addition the subject for a judge's 'one hundred and eleven beautiful annotations'; and to suggest why we have here a rare identification between the fate of peasants and the fate of the rich and learned."

The book's most influential reviewer was the French social historian Emmanuel Le Roy Ladurie, whose own best-known work *Montaillou* concentrated on the peasants who lived in the same area of southwestern France two centuries before Martin Guerre. "One can only admire Natalie Davis," he wrote, "for the major work of historical reconstruction she has performed without any kind of ideological bias. . . . Comparing her learned work with the screen images of Daniel Vigne and Jean-Claude Carrière, my own preferences are no doubt biased. I once asked a woman if she knew of *War and Peace*, and she replied ingenuously, 'Yes, I've read the book, but I prefer the movie.' About Martin Guerre, I would say, without any hesitation, the movie was great, but Natalie Davis's book is even better."

Drawing again from what Robert M. Adams described in *New York Review of Books* as "the raw stuff of popular culture," Davis collected a number of pardon tales or *lettres de remission* in *Fiction in the Archives: Pardon Tales and Their Tellers in Sixth Century France*. These were legal documents submitted by defendants accused, usually, of murder, explaining, justifying and apologizing for their actions and pleading for mercy. Presented in the form of narrative—"storytelling under pressure," as it were—they were lively and often amusing reading. More significant is their value as social history, especially in documenting the lives of the poor and working classes of the period. They also cast light on the evolution of narrative fiction in the Renaissance, much of which reads like these pardon pleas. Stephen Greenblatt wrote, in an endorsement for the book: "[Davis'] original and detailed exploration of the stories French men and women told to save their lives challenges the conventional boundaries between fiction and truth. She had decisively altered the landscape of the Renaissance imagination." For Robert M. Adams, however, the main value of the book was in the letters themselves: " . . . the rough stuff of the letters is a pleasure in its own right; it is meticulously presented, fully documented, and authenticated by transcriptions of seven letters in their vernacular origins."

Davis has taught in the history departments of Brown University (1959–1963), the University of Toronto (1963–1971), and the University of California at Berkeley (1971–1978). Since 1978 she has been on the faculty of Princeton University. She is a member of the American Historical Association, the Society for French Historical Studies, the Society for Reformation Research, and the Renaissance Society of America.

PRINCIPAL WORKS: Society and Culture in Early Modern France: Eight Essays, 1975; The Return of Martin Guerre, 1983; Fiction in the Archives: Pardon Tales and Their Tellers in Sixteenth Century France, 1988.

ABOUT: Contemporary Authors 53–56, 1975. Periodicals—American Historical Review June 1976, October 1985; Choice March 1986; Commonweal September 21, 1984; Encounter January 1976; Library Journal April 15, 1975; September 1, 1983; New Statesman April 19, 1985; New York Review of Books December 22, 1983; March 16, 1989; New York Times Book Review October 2, 1983; Newsweek October 10, 1983; Times Literary Supplement November 21, 1975; June 15, 1984.

DE MAN, PAUL (December 6, 1919–December 21, 1983), Belgian-born critic and literary theorist, was born in Antwerp. His father, Robert de Man, was a well-to-do manufacturer of x-ray equipment, a man of culture, descended from the Flemish poet Jan van Beers. His uncle, Hendrik de Man, with whom Paul strongly identified, was celebrated in his own right as the head of the Belgian Workers Party. When Paul de Man was about eighteen, his family circle disintegrated: his elder brother was killed in a railway accident and his mother subsequently committed suicide. De Man was educated at the Free University of Brussels, receiving a degree

PAUL DE MAN

in science and philosophy, but he moved in literary and artistic circles, where he met Anaïde Baraghian, who became his first wife. When the German armies invaded Belgium in 1940, de Man and Anaïde fled through France to Spain, but were unable to get a visa to cross the Spanish border and were forced to return to Belgium.

In 1941, now married and the father of a son, de Man began working for the Brussels paper Le Soir, a journal that had been taken over by the Nazis. He may have owed this employment to his uncle Hendrik, who had entered into active collaboration with the Nazis. Most of de Man's articles for Le Soir were interviews, book reviews, and notices of cultural activities; few had anything to do with politics in general or Nazism in particular. But one article welcomed the Germans as "civilized invaders," while what has become his most notorious essay, "Les Juifs dans la littérature actuelle" (Jews in Modern Literature), published in Le Soir, March 4, 1941, examining the Jewish influence on modern literature, takes the position that, "despite the ingrained Jewish influence upon all aspects of European life," modern literature has not been very much affected by Jews. De Man concludes by considering a "final solution" to the "Jewish problem": "it would seem that a solution to the Jewish problem which envisaged the creation of a Jewish colony isolated from Europe would not bring with it any deplorable consequences for the literary life of the West. That life would lose a few personalities of mediocre value and would continue as in the past to develop according to its own great laws of evolution." The sudden virulent anti-Semitism of "Les Juifs dans la littérature actuelle" is not easy to explain; it does not appear to have been an ingrained part of de Man's personality; he is not known to have made anti-Semitic remarks in later life, and during the occupation itself he took into his home a Jewish pianist and his wife who had been locked out on the streets after curfew. In November of 1942, when the Jews of Belgium were forced to wear yellow armbands and the deportations to Auschwitz began, he resigned from *Le Soir* and spent the rest of the wartime period working on translations, including one of *Moby Dick* published in 1945.

After the war, de Man organized a publishing house to print art books, Editions Hermés; the venture failed in 1947, and the bankruptcy ruined not only de Man himself but his father, whom Paul had convinced to invest heavily in the enterprise. Anaïde de Man and their three children left for Argentina, where some of her relatives were living. During the final struggle to recoup his losses, de Man engaged, according to Belgian sociologist Georges Goriely, in shady financial dealings and was on the point of being arrested for fraud when he left Brussels for New York.

There, in 1948, de Man became a clerk at Doubleday's bookstore, where he met the writer Mary McCarthy; McCarthy was so impressed with de Man's encyclopedic knowledge of modern literature that she recommended him as a lecturer to Bard College in Annandale-on-Hudson, New York, where he taught from 1949 to 1951. There de Man caused another scandal by marrying in 1950 a former student, Patricia Kelley, without obtaining a divorce from his first wife. When Anaïde de Man appeared at Bard, together with one of their children, de Man was forced to leave for Boston, where he taught at Berlitz before becoming a graduate student in the comparative literature department at Harvard University.

For the last thirty years of his life, from the early 1950s on, de Man's life became that of the exemplary critic and theorist. He worked under Harry Levin at Harvard, earning his Ph.D. in comparative literature in 1960. From there he moved on to teach at Cornell (1960–1967), at Johns Hopkins (1967–1970), and at Yale (1970 – 1983), where he was Sterling professor of French and comparative literature until his death from cancer in 1983.

Arguably the most inventive and influential literary critic writing in America in the 1970s, Paul de Man did not publish an academic book until he was fifty-one, and his lifetime output was not voluminous. As of 1980, Paul de Man's

published writings consist entirely of a few dozen essays gathered into four slim volumes: *Blindness and Insight*, *Allegories of Reading*, *The Rhetoric of Romanticism*, and *The Resistance to Theory*. Several further posthumous volumes have been published, however, including translations of his wartime journalism.

De Man's best known writings are an important part of the wing of poststructuralist criticism known as deconstruction, whose founder and leader is the Algerian/French philosopher Jacques Derrida. Using ideas derived from the later works of Nietzsche and the more recent philosophical speculations of Edmund Husserl and Martin Heidegger, Derrida mounted in the late 1960s a skeptical critique of the central structuralist assumption that the elements of human culture could be analyzed as codes analogous to natural languages and could be understood through the total analysis of their lexicon and syntax. Derrida adhered to the structuralist notion that all culture, indeed all human thought, was necessarily inscribed in language, but he attempted to demonstrate that, far from possessing the solidity and clarity structuralists ascribed to the relation of sign and meaning, signifier and signified, language was always radically ambiguous, fraught with "free play," impossible to systematize. In a sense, Derrida's critique was analogous to that of the Austrian mathematician Kurt Gödel, who demonstrated in the 1920s that any mathematical system complicated enough to be useful (like arithmetic) must either be incomplete or contain contradictions. Derrida's deconstructive critiques are close readings of philosophers, searching for the points of privilege lurking within their writings that lead to fatal paradoxes.

In 1967, Derrida brought deconstruction across the Atlantic. Invited to Johns Hopkins University for a structuralist conference on "The Languages of Criticism and the Sciences of Man," he outlined a deconstructive critique of one of the fathers of structuralism, Claude Lévi-Strauss ("Structure, Sign, and Play in the Discourse of the Human Sciences") that provoked outrage. De Man, then professor at Johns Hopkins, met Derrida at this time. It was an important confluence: de Man, who is now thought of as the disciple, was by some years the older of the two; but both men were working on the same text of Rousseau, and both were at once disciples and critics of Martin Heidegger, admirers of his critique of metaphysics who nevertheless feared that that critique had not gone far enough. In 1955, while still a fellow at Harvard, de Man had published an essay paradoxically praising Heidegger's misreadings of the German poet Hölderlin; the next year he published

"Impasse de la critique formaliste," an exposition and critique of Anglo-American New Criticism from the point of view of Heidegger's concept of temporality. De Man's essay is an attempt to rebut the premises of what he calls "salvational poetics"—the romantic attempt to achieve redemption through the poetic imagination—and "naive poetics"—the formalist notion of unity grounded on the contact poetry achieves between matter and form. As Jonathan Culler has noted, the essay is prophetic of de Man's later combats with "new and apparently sophisticated forms of naive poetics that surface in the debates of contemporary criticism."

These notions, that "true" reading was always misreading and that one must always distrust the reconciliations and unities constructed by romantic or formalist poetics, are central to de Man's first major collection of essays, *Blindness and Insight*. The individual chapters were written between 1966 and 1969, all but one as separate lectures or as contributions to journals and *festschriften*, but while they certainly do not comprise a coherent and linear argument, they form a pattern: everywhere, de Man finds, "a paradoxical discrepancy appears between the general statements [critics] make about the nature of literature (statements on which they base their critical methods) and the actual results of their interpretations. . . . Not only do they remain unaware of this discrepancy, but they seem to thrive on it and owe their best insights to the assumptions these insights disprove." The central essay, "The Rhetoric of Blindness," was the only one written especially for *Blindness and Insight*. It is a critique of Derrida's reading of Rousseau in *Of Grammatology* (1967); de Man agrees with Derrida that Rousseau's argument in the *Essay on the Origin of Language* undermines his metaphysics, but argues that Rousseau's rhetoric (if not Rousseau the man) is fully aware of this, that Rousseau's language is in effect deconstructive *avant de la lettre*. This rather subtle difference illustrates the main discrepancy between the views of de Man and Derrida: that Derrida deconstructs texts while de Man prefers to demonstrate how texts deconstruct themselves. The other important difference is in the texture of their prose: Derrida's language is punningly playful, as though he cannot resist demonstrating at every moment the free play of the signifier; de Man's style, to the contrary, is blandly straight-faced, his slashing paradoxes announced with pomp and dignity.

Blindness and Insight made de Man's national reputation: it was a book treating with lucidity and intellectual power avant-garde topics just beginning to take center stage within an academic scene that was coming to terms with structuralism. It was not universally praised, even by those who understood it. Jonathan Culler's long and respectful analysis of de Man's theoretical premises and arguments in *Yale Review* conceded de Man's brilliance but concluded that "blindness does not necessarily produce insight; more often it prevents one from asking the questions that would yield to insight. De Man's book fails as a study of the complexities of reading because of the deliberate blindness of misinterpretation and a less deliberate willingness to be blinded by the splendors of ontology." Robert Martin Adams' more gossipy and enthusiastic notice in *Hudson Review* singled out de Man's "devious Belgian mind . . . as one of the more vicious players of dirty croquet," marvelled at the paradoxes and difficulties de Man was able to generate, and prophetically suggested that de Man's method was bound up with the romantic movement and was unlikely to find much paydirt earlier than Rousseau. In *Comparative Literature*, Frederick Garber struck a balance, terming *Blindness and Insight* "the imperfect, unsystematic product of a considerable critical intelligence," and calling for de Man to produce "an organized and coherent poetics, its parts systematically related, its radical . . . positions acknowledged and . . . defended."

By 1979, however, when *Allegories of Reading* appeared, the need for such a poetics had passed, in the sense that deconstruction, which de Man had largely introduced to America, had become a *succès de scandale* with strongly established connections. De Man was recognized as the most original and rigorous of a quartet that also comprised Harold Bloom, Geoffrey Hartman, and J. Hillis Miller, which had become known as the Yale School of Critics (or less reverently, as the "Gang of Four"). In addition, younger disciples of de Man such as Cynthia Chase, Barbara Johnson, and Carol Jacobs had already published their own theoretical essays and books of practical criticism. And if *Allegories of Reading* took another step away from Derrida by practicing deconstructive technique primarily upon imaginative rather than philosophical texts, that step had already been taken by de Man's disciples.

If deconstruction was still enormously controversial, it was also beginning to be more widely understood, and the appearance of *Allegories of Reading* generated respect from non-deconstructionists but mild disappointment from the devotees of the movement. George McFadden, generally sympathetic, suggested that "de Man . . . seems to set too much store upon discoveries of a purely doctrinaire sort, amounting only to a Q.E.D." and judged the book "too unrelenting in its returns to the Derridean model . . . and too far-fetched in its choice of 'exorbitant' side-texts as levers to be poised in the abyss." De Man's notion that every text was an allegory of its own reading had become practically standard, and readers had begun to become aware that all deconstructions, wherever they chose to begin, led to the identical *paradoxes*, the same aporias, the small hall-of-mirrors of textuality. *Allegories of Reading* contains de Man's most widely-reprinted essay, "Semiology and Rhetoric," which demonstrates swiftly, almost effortlessly, that the grammatical structure of an utterance may be at odds with its meaning, particularly in the trope known as the rhetorical question. As a general position, this attacks a form of structuralism that had long ceased to be current, but de Man's application of deconstruction to three short texts (including a routine from the television show "All in the Family") had exemplary clarity.

De Man's first posthumous book, *The Rhetoric of Romanticism*, collected all his writings on romanticism that had not already been published in his first two books; it runs the gamut of de Man's academic career from a section of his 1960 doctoral dissertation to the preface, which may have been one of the last things he wrote. But, as David Simpson remarked, "twenty years or so does not so much change de Man's mind as lead him to explore different facets of his basic insights into Romanticism as marked by a nostalgia for a lost object and a corresponding discomfort with (or exhilaration at) the irreducible superficiality of the figural, linguistic alternatives." But de Man's deconstructive program demands a blindness to all and any such unifying insights, and the book denies "either dialectical progression or, ultimately, historical totalization" and remains—tragically, in de Man's own view—a collection of fragments on Hölderlin and Wordsworth, Shelley and Yeats, bricolage celebrating the "breaks and interruptions that the readings disclose."

By 1984, the vogue of deconstruction may have peaked, and many critics not hostile to its fragmentizing intent from the first had begun to become disappointed with the never-changing vistas into the void that it revealed. As a result, critical reception was not always kind to *The Rhetoric of Romanticism*. Northrop Frye's notice was appreciative and elegiac but tended to read de Man through Frye's own system and so made little contact with de Man's characteristic ideas. David Simpson said that "what we have here and elsewhere in his writings in no sense meets the standards for 'critical reading.'" Theodore Ziolkowski pounced upon a lapse in German grammar that undercut one of de Man's most "brilliant and seductive" readings. Julian

R. Furst was dismayed by the book's "quintessential negativity." Peggy Kamuf, however, found a noble heroism in the fact that "de Man finds no easy way to read, only hard ones," and in de Man's continual willingness to start out, not from an extrinsic ideology, but from the words and tropes of the literary text itself; this sort of hermeneutical heroism is analyzed in J. Hillis Miller's *Ethics of Reading* (1988).

It is the primary subject as well of de Man's second posthumous book, *The Resistance to Theory*, whose title essay examines at length the ways in which theory is felt as threatening by the majority of humanist scholars and critics. The central issue is that humanist scholars presume that texts achieve meaning and that they can seek that meaning without risk, while theory turns a skeptical eye on the production of meaning and on the ideological screens which predetermine the sort of meaning the reader may find. *The Resistance to Theory* also contains discussions of Walter Benjamin, Mikhail Bakhtin, Michael Riffaterre, and Hans Robert Jauss. In a move that recalls those of his first book, *Blindness and Insight*, de Man praises Benjamin and Bakhtin for not allowing Marxist ideology to predetermine their insights, while Riffaterre and Jauss are used as examples of theorists whose chosen modes (structuralism and reception-aesthetics, respectively) allow them (as Jonathan Culler has put it) to "evade . . . the rhetorical nature of language and the problem of reading in presuming a phenomenality of language-form or meaning given to perception."

In the summer of 1987, following the publication of *The Resistance to Theory*, the news began to break over the literary world that Ortwin de Graef, a Belgian graduate student writing a thesis on de Man, had identified over 100 articles in *Le Soir* and *Het Vlaamische Land*, including the anti-Semitic and pro-Nazi pieces mentioned above. Even de Man's closest friends at Yale were clearly astonished to hear of this discovery from his past. De Man had been one of the most private of men, but he had not only kept silence about this episode, he had actively misled acquaintances about where and how he had spent the wartime years. It was clear that de Man's posthumous reputation would be tarnished by his wartime collaboration; but it was not de Man's reputation alone that was at stake. It was also that of the theories of deconstruction with which he was indelibly associated.

When it began in France in the late 1960's, deconstruction was associated with the leftist critical journal *Tel Quel*, and the politics of its founder, Jacques Derrida, in so far as they were intelligible, leaned vaguely to the left as well.

But in the intense rivalry that grew in the 1970s between deconstruction and Marxist or New Historicist criticism, deconstruction was shifted into the political right wing as a movement whose obsession with textuality blinded it to the significance of lived experience and historical change. And not only Marxists but liberals who (like the structuralist Tzvetan Todorov) had found de Man's theories anti-humanistic might seek to find all deconstructionists guilty by association.

As journalists raked the scandal, former students like Chase, colleagues like Hartman and Miller, even Derrida, all wrote elaborate and tormented defenses of de Man and, implicitly, of themselves. Thirty-eight of these essays were collected in 1988 as *Responses: On Paul de Man's Wartime Journalism*. This still unresolved controversy, a Dreyfus case in reverse, is fraught with paradoxes of the sort de Man himself would have approved: that many of de Man's defenders are Jews (including Derrida and Hartman); that the focus of the waves of forensic rhetoric had been dead for half a decade; and that de Man's offense in 1942 predated his adoption of deconstruction by over twenty-five years. It is difficult to make out any strong connection between de Man's collaboration and his literary theories, but if there was one it is most likely to be negative. De Man's deconstructionist theories seem a more rigorous extension of his attacks in the 1950s against "salvational poetics"—of which Nazi cultural imperialism would be one crude version. If this is so, then de Man's career as a critic and theorist might be viewed as a long atonement for his juvenile sins.

PRINCIPAL WORKS: Blindness and Insight, 1971, 1983; Allegories of Reading, 1979; The Rhetoric of Romanticism, 1984; The Resistance to Theory, 1986; Aesthetic Ideology, 1988; Fugitive Writings, 1988; Critical Writings: 1953–1978, 1988; Wartime Journalism 1939–1943, 1988.

ABOUT: Derrida, J. Mémoires: for Paul de Man, 1986; Dictionary of Literary Biography 67, 1988; Hamacher, W., N. Hertz, T. Keenan (eds.) Responses: On Paul de Man's Wartime Journalism, 1988; Norris, C. Paul de Man: Deconstruction and the Critique of Aesthetic Ideology, 1988; Waters, L. and W. Godzich (eds.) Reading de Man Reading, 1989. *Periodicals*—Comparative Literature Summer 1974, Winter 1981, Fall 1986; Criticism Spring 1980; Hudson Review Winter 1971–1972; Journal of Aesthetics and Art Criticism Winter 1981; New Republic July 7, 1986; New York Review of Books June 29, 1989; New York Times December 31, 1983; New York Times Magazine February 9, 1986; August 28, 1988; Times Literary Supplement February 29, 1980; January 17, 1986; June 17, 1988; September 30, 1988; May 26, 1989; World Literature Today Spring 1987; Yale French Studies 69 1985; Yale Review Summer 1980.

DENBY, EDWIN (ORR) (February 4, 1903–July 12, 1983), American poet and dance critic, was born in Tientsin, China, the son of Charles Denby, Jr., a diplomat, and Martha (Orr) Denby, and named after his uncle, who was Secretary of the Navy under Warren G. Harding. He was raised in China, Austria, and the United States. After attending the Hotchkiss School, where he was class poet, he went on to Harvard but dropped out in 1922 to go to New York. In 1923 Denby travelled to Austria and studied for a time at the University of Vienna. With a colleague of Freud he began psychoanalysis, which continued for several years. Beginning in 1925 he enrolled in the Hellerau-Laxenburg School, a dance academy whose teachings were based on the work of Jacques Dalcroze. After three years he received a diploma in gymnastics, which led to his specializing in *Grotesktanz* ('eccentric dancing'), a form of modern dance. From 1928 to 1933 Denby was part of a group that toured Germany. His satirical dances were suspect under Hitler, and he went to Paris. Here he saw a performance of George Balanchine's work, which struck him as "the most wonderful thing I had seen in my life" and he began to take a serious interest in ballet. Returning to New York, in 1935, he collaborated with Orson Welles on a translation of a French farce, *The Italian Straw Hat*, which they called *Horse Eats Hat*. It was produced at the WPA Theater (1936). Denby wrote several librettos. Through his friends Virgil Thomson and Aaron Copland he began a dance review column in *Modern Music*. During World War II he was the dance reviewer for the *New York Herald Tribune* (1942–1945).

In 1949 a collection of Denby's articles appeared as *Looking at the Dance*. Stark Young declared it "some of the most distinguished, luminous, tactful and penetrating criticism in any field of the arts that we have ever had in this country." The reputation of the book has grown with the years; indeed the *New Yorker* critic Arlene Croce has said that it "may be the most universally admired book of dance criticism in American publishing history." Lincoln Kirstein called *Looking at the Dance* and Denby's collected notices from the Forties and Fifties, *Dancers, Buildings and People in the Street*, "basic theatrical history." In an article in the *New York Review of Books* in 1983, Kirstein wrote that Denby's essay on Stravinsky and Balanchine's *Agon* is the most telling and comprehensive technical appreciation of a dance work that has been written. "He loved every tribe of dancer, traditional, ethnic, experimental, popular. . . . He tended to lean eagerly toward pioneers."

In the article on Dance Criticism that he contributed to *The Dance Encyclopedia* in 1949 (reprinted with minor revisions in 1967), Denby expressed at some length his own conception of dance criticism. He began with the premise that "in recent years ballet has been the liveliest form of poetic theatre we have had" and that ballet performance should be judged with the same serious attention given any other work of the artistic imagination. "An intelligent reader," he wrote, "learns from a critic not what to think about a piece of art but how to think about it." The critic's function is to educate the reader about the history and technique of classic ballet, no easy task considering how elusive and ephemeral dance is. "It is difficult to see the great dance effects as they happen, to see them accurately, catch them so to speak in flight and hold them fast in memory." Dance aesthetics, he noted, "is vague and clumsy," in only the pioneering stage of its development. The dance critic must therefore work backwards, from the actual performance: "He tries to deduce from it a common denominator in what he saw—a coherent principle, that is, among uncertainly remembered, partly intense, partly vague, partly contradictory images. It takes boldness to simplify his impressions so they add up clearly to a forthright opinion; and it sometimes takes a malicious sense of fun, too, to trust his instinct where he knows he is risking his neck." The critic must give the reader "the illusion of being present at a performance." To this end the critic must know the history and the general principles of dance, the merits of the choreographer as well as of the dancer. The critic must also be a gifted writer with a command of language and an ability to describe "dancing in its own terms," without pedantry or academicism, "to suggest how the flavor or the spell of it is related to aspects of the fantasy world we live in, to our daily experience of culture and of custom."

That Denby's excellence as a dance critic was allied to his excellence as a poet was often cited. In 1926 two of his poems appeared in *Poetry*. *In Public, In Private*, his first book, was financed by the poet and others. It received mixed reviews, the British critic Nicolas Moore and the American critic Dudley Fitts complaining that the poems lacked "control," though Moore found the language and imagery striking. Frank O'Hara, a friend of Denby's, once characterized the volume as "a kind of 'Poet in New York' with its acute and painful sensibility, its vigorous ups and downs and stubborn tone."

Denby's second book of poems, *Mediterranean Cities*, was also subsidized in part by the poet. It contained photographs by Rudy Burckhardt, Denby's lifelong friend. Ron Padgett found this cycle of sonnets milder, less vio-

lent, more classical than the first book. Its publication went all but unnoticed. In the 1950s Denby appeared in several of Oscar Williams's anthologies, and recorded a poem in *An Album of Modern Poetry*, which was released by the Library of Congress in 1960.

In the early 1960s recognition began to come in from a new wave of younger poets. Ted Berrigan brought out a special Denby issue of his magazine *C*. When *Collected Poems* appeared in 1975, the notices were highly favorable. "This is not the incidental poetry of an eminent dance critic, or the work of an underground cult figure, but the work of a unique and major voice in contemporary poetry," wrote the *Washington Post Book World*. Posthumously published in 1986, *The Complete Poems* solidified Denby's reputation. A long laudatory review by George Dickerson in the *New York Times Book Review* described "the gentle wit and mature grace that makes reading his poetry a delight. . . . Indeed, Denby is a reticent, lonely prowler in the cityscape. There he observes mundane things—a naked light bulb in a rented room, the way men carry their shoulders, the bustling city streets, the air between the buildings, the aimless talk of weather—and builds from them his pithy, compassionate insights into the nature of man and man's place in the landscape." Denby once commented on his verse: "Theme: city. Form: sonnet." He wrote in "City Without Smoke":

> For to city people the smudgy film of smoke
> Is reassuring like an office, it's sociable
> Like money, it gives the sky a furnished look
> That makes disaster domestic, negotiable.
> Nothing to help society in the sky's grace
> Except that each looks at it with his mortal face.

Denby was the recipient of a Guggenheim Fellowship in 1948 for comparative study of ballet in the United States and Europe; of a Poets' Foundation Award in 1965; and of the *Dance Magazine* Award in 1966. A sociable man, with a wide circle of friends, he lived from 1935 on in a fifth-floor walk-up loft on West 21st Street, in Manhattan. It was his habit to attend performances and then stay up all night alone in his loft, thinking, writing, and sleeping at dawn, to wake in the afternoon. When he died at the age of eighty, after taking a combination of sleeping pills and alcohol at his summer home at Searsport, Maine, a memorial was held for three days, the poets, painters, dancers, and critics who revered him participating. Speakers included Virgil Thomson, Merce Cunningham, John Ashbery, Jerome Robbins, and others. "The dancers who performed ranged from luminaries of the avant-garde to a stately pair from the New York City Ballet," reported *Harper's* in prose

that was rich in wit and metaphors," commented the obituary in *Newsweek*, "he captured the beauty, rhythm and movement of dance."

PRINCIPAL WORKS: *Poetry*—In Public, In Private, 1948; Mediterranean Cities, 1956; Snoring in New York, 1974; Collected Poems, 1975; The Complete Poems, 1986. *Criticism*—Looking at the Dance, 1949; Dancers, Buildings and People in the Streets, 1965. *Librettos*—The Second Hurricane, 1957; Miltie Is a Hackie, 1973. *Fiction*—Mrs. W's Last Sandwich, 1972.

ABOUT: Contemporary Authors 110, 1984; The Dance Encyclopedia, 1949, 1967; Haggin, B. H. *Introduction to Looking at the Dance*, 1968; Kirstein, L. *Essay in* The Complete Poems, 1986; Murphy, R. (ed.) Contemporary Poets of the English Language, 1970; O'Hara, F. *Essay in* The Complete Poems, 1986; Padgett, R. *Introduction to* The Complete Poems, 1986. *Periodicals*—Bookletter March 15, 1976; Harper's February 1984; New York Herald Tribune Weekly Book Review May 29, 1949; New Republic May 14, 1966; New York Review of Books September 29, 1983; New York Times June 5, 1949; New York Times Book Review October 17, 1976; November 2, 1986; Newsweek July 25, 1983; Partisan Review April 1949; Poetry February 1957, December 1976, April 1987; Poetry Quarterly (London) Autumn 1948; Saturday Review of Literature April 30, 1949; Washington Post Book World February 8, 1976.

DICK, PHILIP K(INDRED) (December 16, 1928–March 2, 1982), American novelist and short-story writer, was born in Chicago, Illinois, the son of Joseph Edgar Dick, a Federal government employee, and Dorothy Kindred. As a child he moved with his family to California, where he attended Berkeley High School and, from 1945 to 1946, the University of California at Berkeley. Dropping out after a year to avoid ROTC service, Dick worked as a classical disk jockey for the KSMO radio station and as manager of a record store while writing short stories, mostly science fiction, in his spare time. Dick's first published work, a science-fiction tale titled "Beyond Lies Wub," was sold to the pulp magazine *Planet Stories* in 1952. His first novel, *Solar Lottery*, a fairly conventional space-opera in the mode of A. E. Van Vogt, was published in paperback by Ace in 1955, back-to-back with a novel by another science-fiction writer.

For most of his career, Dick lived in poverty, subsisting on the meager income from his writing. In the 1950s and early 1960s, the science-fiction pulps paid a half cent a word for short fiction, and advances on Ace Doubles often did not cover the month's expenses. The genre as a whole was held in derision by the literary and publishing world. Dick said himself that to select science-fiction writing as a career at that time was "an act of self-destruction." (Dick, who sought recognition as a serious writer outside the science-fiction ghetto, labored on several "mainstream" novels, none of which was published during his lifetime.) He managed to survive by writing constantly; between 1955 and 1970 he published an average of two paperback novels a year under incredibly tight deadlines, plus more than one hundred short stories in such science-fiction magazines as *Galaxy, Amazing, Fantasy and Science Fiction*, and *Worlds of If*. This hasty output, and the lack of editorial attention to his work—the science-fiction paperback houses were anxious to publish his work as fast as he could write it—accounts for some hack writing in his oeuvre. Most of his novels have dangling plot threads that lead nowhere. But his best works—including *The Man in the High Castle, Martian Time-Slip, The Three Stigmata of Palmer Eldritch, Do Androids Dream of Electric Sheep?, A Scanner Darkly*, and *Valis*—have an improvisational edge that links them to the best writing of the 1950s and early 1960s. They are fully mature novels, with realistic dialogue, deftly drawn and sympathetic characters, and ingenious plotting supported by an eclectic web of ideas drawn from Buddhism, Kabbalism, Gnosticism, Taoism, and other philosophies.

Dick chose science fiction because, as he wrote, "Writing science fiction is a way to rebel. . . . It needs writers and readers with bad attitudes—an attitude of, 'Why?' Or, 'How come?' Or, 'Who says?' This gets sublimated into such themes as appear in my writing as, 'Is the universe real?' Or, 'Are we really all human or are some of us just reflex machines?'" (For its part, the science-fiction community, with its tolerance for outrageous notions and unconventional plotting, was the only place Dick could gain a literary foothold.) The author typically used the conventional apparatus of science fiction—space ships, robots and androids, ESP, extraterrestrials, alien planets, parallel universes—to present some Kafkaesque ideas about the uncertain nature of reality. Abrupt disjunctions of time, space, and meaning, or successions of hallucinations and fake worlds (as in *The Three Stigmata of Palmer Eldritch* and *Ubik*) present Dick's protagonists with difficult, often impossible choices. Brian Aldiss wrote in his critical history of science fiction, *Billion Year Spree*: "In [Dick's] novels, things are never what they seem. Between life and death lie the many shadowlands of Dick, places of hallucination, artificial reality, dim half-life, paranoid states . . . full of disconcerting artifacts, scarecrow people, exiles, robots with ill consciences. . . . He is one of the masters of present-day discontents."

Camouflaged as conventional science fiction, Dick's best work is in fact as far from the standard adolescent science-fiction power fantasy as could be imagined. His characters are flawed adults, scarred with their experiences (which were often based on Dick's own life or lives of his friends). His heroes may succeed in saving the universe, but they are never certain of their personal salvation. As Colin Greenland noted in the *Times Literary Supplement* in 1986: "In Dick's fiction generally, the world of rational materialism seems no more than a little lighted room, traveling at speed through a deadly vacuum. Only the precarious, ridiculous rigmarole of human relations offers any hope of surviving the journey." Leavening the oppressive paranoia in Dick's work is a strain of satiric humor—what Dick called "the mustard seed of the funny in the core of the horrible and the futile."

Dick first achieved general recognition in the field with *The Man in the High Castle*. In an alternative universe, the Axis powers have won World War II and jointly occupy the United States. The Nazis symbolize the imposition of evil on the world; Mr. Tagomi, a Japanese official, lives by the more benign laws of the *I Ching* (which Dick also used to help him write this novel). In a moment of irritation, Tagomi saves a Jew, Frank Frink, from the Nazis and begins to realize he can thwart their evil in small but significant ways. Later, inspired by silver jewelry created by Frink, Tagomi steps for a moment into the 1960s San Francisco of our world, but sees in it only "a dreadful gliding among shadows." A fugitive American writer, Hawthorne Abendsen, is writing a novel-within-a-novel (also using the *I Ching*) entitled "The Grasshopper Lies Heavy," in which Hitler loses the war. At the end of *High Castle*, Abendsen's novel is revealed to be the true reality—but that novel does not describe the world we live in. The Barthian metafictions of *High Castle* were second nature to Dick, who employed them in several novels. In 1962, however, they were new for science fiction, and earned Dick the 1963 Hugo Award for best novel.

Martian Time-Slip takes place on Mars, where a fragile society has been largely abandoned by Earth and scarce water supplies are controlled by the head of the plumbers' union. The precognitive powers of an autistic boy, Manfred Steiner, cause a "temporal dislocation" whose psychological effects are seen from the points of view of, among others, the boy himself, a suicide, and a Martian named Heliogabalus, whose point of view is outside time itself. The survivors of the time-slip are those who live within or accept the paranormal understanding of the Martians. Those who worship the past or the future are doomed.

Fear of political or social repression, secret police, and loss of personal integrity is omnipresent in Dick's fictional worlds. The heroes of *The Variable Man*, *The World Jones Made*, *The Man in the High Castle*, *Galactic Pot-Healer*, *Ubik*, *A Scanner Darkly* and *Flow My Tears, the Policeman Said*, are among those who face arrest and interrogation by the authorities for their "antisocial" activities, which are misunderstood, unintentional, or engineered by the state for its own purposes. (Dick himself was under scrutiny by the FBI and Air Force intelligence for his tenuous connection to the American Communist party and his public opposition to the Vietnam War.) In *The Man in the High Castle*, *Martian Time-Slip*, and other novels, the old order of repression is destroyed or abandoned, and the protagonists build a new order based on freedom, communality, and compassion. In *Galactic Pot-Healer*, for example, the hero, Joe Fernwright, escapes the lethal bureaucracy of Earth and helps save another planet by joining his healing skills with those of other refugees within the body of a vast being, the Glimmung. The others decide to become permanent parts of the Glimmung, but Fernwright does not, choosing instead to try creating his own works, with no guarantee of success.

The strain of paranoia in Dick's work increased as he immersed himself in the drug culture of the 1960s and early 1970s, ruining his health by heavy use of psychedelics and living a rootless existence on the street. Instead of many characters attempting to cope with a multidimensional and chancy universe, Dick's introverted novels of the 1970s and early 1980s describe the philosophical dilemmas of one or two central characters who fractionate into multiple personalities. *A Scanner Darkly*, one of the best of his later novels, is a devastating picture of a future drug culture secretly controlled by the state. Bob Arctor, like much of the population of 1994 California, is addicted to the deadly "Substance D." Hired by the police to inform on himself, Arctor splits into three personas and ultimately becomes a human vegetable to serve the mysterious purposes of the makers of Substance D, who may be extraterrestrials. Based in part on Dick's own drug experiences, *A Scanner Darkly* is full of the authentic horrors of addiction, mental deterioration, and squalid death.

Drugs may also have led to a 1974 experience in which Dick claimed to have been contacted by an extraterrestrial, godlike force. His last novels, the trilogy *Valis*, *The Divine Invasion*, and *Valis Regained* (unfinished), draw on this experience and its religious ramifications. Dick himself, or rather various aspects of his personality, are the main characters of *Valis*, which questions the nature of revelation within a science-fiction framework heavily influenced by Gnostic metaphysics. Dick makes clear that there is no way for his protagonist, Phil, to be sure of the validity of the revelation he has experienced of an extraterrestrial god (which parallels Dick's own). At the end of the novel, Phil can only wait faithfully in front of his television, hoping for a further sign.

Dick died of a stroke in 1982 at the age of fifty-three. He was survived by his fifth wife, Tessa Busby, a son Christopher, and two daughters, Laura and Isolde, from previous marriages. His papers, which include many unpublished novels and stories, are collected at the California State University in Fullerton. Since his death, Dick's reputation has blossomed, especially in France, where he is considered a leading American novelist. *Blade Runner*, a 1982 film, was based on his novel *Do Androids Dream of Electric Sheep?*. In the book and film, a retired policeman is assigned to kill a group of replicants— powerful androids who have escaped illegally to earth in search of their own origins—and discovers his own lost humanity in the process. Directed by Ridley Scott and starring Harrison Ford, the film was visually stunning, with a convincing cyberpunk look (principal special effects were by Douglas Trumbull). However, the script, which Dick did not write, was an update of 1940s *film noir* and detective movie clichés and lacked the playfulness and philosophical sophistication of the novel. In June 1988 *Flow My Tears, the Policeman Said* was adapted for the stage by Linda Hartinian for the Mabou Mines company in New York City. *New York Times* critic Mel Gussow thought that this was an effective adaptation, heightened by the use of appropriate visual effects. "In a final striking touch," wrote Gussow, "the text is projected on a screen, enlarged, and then blurred into Pointillist patterns, through which pass the actors. Words and characters symbolically merge until, in this eerie space-time continuum, it is impossible to differentiate one from the other."

PRINCIPAL WORKS: *Fiction*—Solar Lottery (in U.K. World of Chance), 1955; A Handful of Darkness (story collection), 1955; The World Jones Made, 1956; The Man Who Jaded, 1956; Eye in the Sky, 1956; The Variable Man and Other Stories, 1956; The Cosmic Puppets, 1957; Time Out of Joint, 1959; Dr. Futurity, 1960; Vulcan's Hammer, 1960; The Man in the High Castle, 1962; The Game-Players of Titan, 1963; Martian Time-Slip, 1964; The Simulacra, 1964; The Penultimate Truth, 1964; Clans of the Alphane Moon, 1964; The Three Stigmata of Palmer Eldritch, 1965; Dr. Bloodmoney, or How We Got Along after the Bomb, 1965; The Crack in Space (Cantata 140), 1966; Now Wait for Last Year, 1966; The Unteleported Man, 1966 (republished as Lies, Inc. in 1985); Counter-Clock World, 1967; The Zap Gun, 1967; The Ganymede Takeover, 1967; Do Androids Dream of Electric Sheep?, 1968 (also published as Blade Runner, 1982); Ubik, 1969; Galactic Pot-Healer, 1969; The Preserving Machine and Other Stories, 1969; A Maze of Death, 1970; Our Friends from Frolix 8, 1970; The Philip K. Dick Omnibus (story collection), 1970; We Can Build You, 1972; The Book of Philip K. Dick (in U.K. The Turning Wheel and Other Stories), 1973; Flow My Tears, the Policeman Said, 1974; Deus Irae (with Roger Zelazny), 1976; A Scanner Darkly, 1977; The Best of Philip K. Dick (story collection), 1977; Confessions of a Crap Artist, 1978; The Golden Man (story collection), 1980; Valis, 1981; The Divine Invasion, 1981; The Transmigration of Timothy Archer, 1982; Valis Regained (unfinished); Warwick, Patricia S. and Martin S. Greenberg (eds.) Robots, Androids, and Mechanical Oddities: The Science Fiction of Philip K. Dick (story collection), 1985; I Hope I Shall Arrive Soon (story collection), 1985; Radio Free Albemuth, 1985; Puttering About in a Small Land, 1985; Mary and the Giant, 1987; The Broken Bubble, 1988.

ABOUT: Aldiss, B. Billion Year Spree: A True History of Science Fiction, 1973; Gillespie, B. (ed.) Philip K. Dick, Electric Shepherd, 1975; Levack, D. PKD: A Philip K. Dick Bibliography, 1981; Olander, J. D. and M. H. Greenberg (eds.) Philip K. Dick, 1983; Rickmann, G. Philip K. Dick: In His Own Words (interviews), 1983; Spinrad, N. Modern Science Fiction, 1974. *Periodicals*—New Republic October 30, 1976; Christianity Today May 20, 1977; Times Literary Supplement January 18, 1985; February 2, 1986.

*DJEBAR, ASSIA (August 4, 1936–   ), Algerian fiction writer, translator, and filmmaker, was born Fatma-Zohra Imalayène, the eldest of three children in a middle-class family from the coastal town of Churchell, about thirty miles west of Algiers. Her father, Taher Imalayène, taught in the French grade school at Mouzaïa; her mother, Baya Sahraoui, belonged to a family of notables that included several heroes from the first period of resistance to French colonization. As a child, Fatma-Zohra attended Qur'an school and the grade school where her father taught; when she was ten, he enrolled her in the French *lycée* at Blida so that she could encounter "modernity"—the episode that opens her 1984 novel, *L'Amour, la fantasia*. One of a dozen Algerian boarders in the predominantly French school, she quickly distinguished herself as a brilliant student who read continuously and walked off with all the prizes. After completing her *baccalauréat* in classics and philosophy, she spent a year studying in Algiers and then left for Paris, where she became the first Algerian woman to gain admission to the elite École Normale Supérieure of Sèvres.

°ju bär´, äs´ yä

Djebar had arrived in France just before the outbreak of the Algerian War in November 1954; at the end of her first year at the École Normale, the Algerian Students Union called a strike, and in solidarity with them, she refused to take her exams. It was during this unexpected break from her studies that she turned to writing fiction and in a period of two months produced her first novel, *La Soif* (The Thirst, translated as *The Mischief*). By her own account, this third-person story of a self-absorbed young woman who tries to seduce her friend's husband in order to make her own boyfriend jealous was mainly a "stylistic exercise" intended as "the caricature of a westernized Algerian girl." She thought about it for a long time, she explained in a 1957 interview, and "One fine day, I set to work, prompted by the need to write. I created the characters without any particular aim, but then they came alive and carried me along with them."

When the manuscript was accepted by the French publisher Julliard, the twenty-year-old student, faced with the problem of hiding this non-scholarly success from her father, adopted the pen-name Assia Djebar. In Paris, anonymity proved more difficult to maintain, and she was expelled from the École Normale Supérieure, not only because of the strike but also because students there were not permitted to publish. While Djebar herself maintained at the time that she did not take this first novel—or herself—seriously, French critics were quick to hail her as "the Françoise Sagan of Muslim Algeria." Among Algerians, the response was much less favorable, mainly because the novel ignored the political reality of the day. Djebar—whose younger brother was at that time imprisoned in France for his pro-Algerian activities—subsequently explained that her decision to ignore the war was quite conscious, and already bound up in her complex relationship to the French language: "At the time," she recalled in a 1968 essay,

I was absolutely convinced that it would have been indecent on my part to use this life as a theme . . . A mistake perhaps? I don't know. On the one hand, I distrusted—I still distrust—a literature that bears witness. On the other hand, because I was writing in French, I thought I shouldn't let the 'others' see beyond the surface, with regard to myself and my people. In sum, the passage to another language meant that for me, the making of the novel began with dissimulation, something like, 'I write to hide what seems the most important to me,' not to express things simply, naturally.

Immediately following the publication of *La Soif*, she began to work on a second novel, *Les Impatients* (The Impatient Ones, 1958), which again dealt strictly with the life and loves of the

traditional Algerian bourgeoisie. The central character in this first-person narrative is a young woman, Dalila, who feels herself trapped in a family environment of domineering men and frustrated women: fearing that her father's second wife is going to steal her boyfriend, she follows him to Paris, only to discover that he too has a jealous, domineering side. On their return, the stepmother is safely remarried, but her new husband now becomes jealous of the boyfriend and kills him.

"What I wanted to show here," Djebar later explained to Jean Déjeux, "was the awakening of Dalila, a young Algerian woman revolting against tradition, her environment, her family." But as in *The Mischief*, she insisted that there was no autobiographical connection, which she avoided "for fear of indecency, a horror of a certain intellectual striptease." For the critics, there was a general recognition that this second novel—written in six months—was, as A. Nataf wrote in *Présence africaine*, "of a quality well above that of the preceding one" in both its language and its character development. But as Nataf went on to point out (and the reaction was even more vehement in Algeria), both novels "are disconcerting in that they portray an Algeria whose very existence seems enigmatic . . . Because ultimately, isn't the primary Algerian reality that of war, misery, courage? And what is most astonishing is that no trace of these events is to be found in the world related in *The Mischief* and this last *Impatient Ones*."

By the time the second novel was published, Djebar was living the reality of the war as she never had before: in 1958 she married Ahmed Ould-Rouï, a member of the Resistance, and together they went to Tunis, which was then an outpost for Algerian refugees. There, while continuing her studies with the renowned French scholar-mystic Louis Massignon, she conducted a series of interviews with women refugees that were published in *El-Moujahid*, the newspaper of the National Liberation Front. She also began writing short stories about the exile experience, as well as the first of the poems that were to be published after Independence as *Poèmes pour l'Algérie heureuse* (Poems for a Happy Algeria, 1969). Moving to Morocco the following year, she pursued her work in history as a teaching assistant at the University of Rabat and participated in various Algerian cultural activities. In 1960, she collaborated with her husband (who used the pen-name Walid Garn) on the French version of a play about revolution, *Rouge l'aube* (Red Is the Dawn), which was intended to be performed in colloquial Arabic for the refugee communities on the Algerian frontiers. (Nine years later, Garn's adaptation in Arabic was performed at the first Panafrican Festival in Algiers, but Djebar disavowed the "epic" staging which, she felt, betrayed the original intention of the work.)

During her stay in Morocco Djebar also wrote her third novel, *Les Enfants du nouveau monde* (Children of the New World, 1962), and here, not surprisingly, the charged reality of the war replaced her earlier preoccupation with the timeless world of the bourgeois family. Writing in a single "burst" of two or three months, she drew on her encounters with refugee women in Tunisia and Morocco to create a vivid fresco of village life, where domestic drama was interwoven with the exigencies of a war of liberation. One woman, Cherifa, leaves the businessman she didn't love to marry the local political leader and join him in the struggle against the French; another, Touma, is murdered by her brother for betraying the cause; a sixteen-year-old, Hassiba, joins the guerrillas as a nurse; the schoolteacher Salima is denounced and imprisoned by the French; and the central character, Lila, struggles to break with tradition in her private life, but has difficulty accepting her husband's political decision to join the guerrillas.

The title, Djebar explained in a 1962 interview, referred to "the birth of a people, their discovery of themselves. Rather than 'Third World,' I think that Africa represents the New World, like America before." The unidentified setting for the novel was in fact Blida, the village where she had attended French *lycée* and where three of her friends had become the first women imprisoned by the French. Of her women characters, she commented, "I knew them and loved them," adding that a certain amount of time had to elapse before she could recount their stories: at first, she explained, "It was too close, you understand, too painful. It was necessary to act, help, share. Being interested wasn't enough."

As the Paris weekly *Témoignage chrétien* noted, Djebar's engagement nonetheless avoided didacticism: "The arabesques that the story follows through past and present . . . these ingenious detours of a skilled novelist throw into relief faces that are singularly alive; common to the purest and the most corrupt alike is their humanity and the affection they receive from the novelist." Also apparent in this third novel was an increasingly complex use of language, a "very personal style" yielding a "rich, tumultuous thought that wants to say everything, express everything, not leave anything in the shadows . . . ," as Paul Buttin wrote in *Confluent*. For Buttin, the markedly overloaded syntax and tendency to invert the order of the sentences suggested that "the author does not seem to be completely in control." Yet as Djebar herself made clear, these apparently uncommon usages reflected her growing preoccupation with Arabic and a conscious attempt to "arabize" French. "I often jump from one language to the other," she remarked to *Jeune Afrique* at the time. "My images, my memories, concrete things, demand the use of Arabic, but I reason in French."

The publication of *Les Enfants du nouveau monde* coincided with the end of the Algerian War. Following independence, she and her husband returned immediately to Algiers, where she taught North African history at the Faculty of Letters and worked with the Algerian press and radio. She also began working on a new novel, but in contrast to the first three, which were written in a matter of months, *Les Alouettes naïves* (The Innocent Larks, 1967) was two years in the writing alone, preceded and followed by long periods of reflection. Like *Les Enfants du nouveau monde*, it is set among the refugee communities that she knew firsthand, but instead of individual women, it attempted to portray the couple and the larger, collective memory of the nation through different viewpoints and different moments in time. Divided into three sections—"Another Time," "Beyond [Time]," and "Today," the novel pieces together the lives of two young Algerians, Nfissa and Rachid, in war and love. As Djebar explained in a 1967 interview with *Jeune Afrique*, her title came from the name the French soldiers used for a famous group of dancers known in Arabic by the name of their tribe, the OuledNaïl. There were, she acknowledged, no dancers in the novel, and practically no fighters, but, she explained, "I think I was trying to restore a rhythm [between past and present] like that dance, with its ambiguity."

Appearing just five years after the end of the Algerian War, the novel was welcomed for its evocation of what one reviewer called "the drama of a lost generation that is conscious of the difficulty of regaining its equilibrium." But even more striking was Djebar's treatment of the intimate life of the Algerian couple—their language of love and in particular, the woman's interior monologues expressing her own sexual awakening.

As many critics have noted, her candid depiction of women's sentiment and sexuality was unprecedented in North African literature, and for Djebar herself it marked a momentous "turning point" in her writing. "I'd say that my first three novels were youthful works," she told Raymond François at the time, "and that for me, *Les Alouettes naïves* marks the end of one period—and one style—and the beginning of another." As she has frequently acknowledged since then, this change was not without anxieties: "I understood that I had still not written about myself . . . never," she recalled to Philippe Gardenal nearly twenty years later. "All of a sudden, I was afraid . . . afraid of unmasking myself. Afraid as an Arab woman."

At times, Djebar has offered this fear as an explanation of the long (literary) silence that followed—in a 1984 interview, for example, she said, "When I realized that the heart of this book was starting to brush against my own life, I stopped publishing. . . . " But another, related factor that apparently played an even greater role in the trajectory of her writing career was the question of language, and the difficulty of expressing her own Arab identity in French. "I couldn't say 'I love you' in French, and I didn't know how to say it any other way," she told Gardenal. "I couldn't write about love in French because the blood hadn't dried yet. If I had to unveil myself, I suddenly realized that I could only do it, that I had to do it, in Arabic."

During the second half of the 1960s, she was deeply committed to becoming an Arabic-language writer. Throughout the decade she had been writing poetry in both Arabic and French; she studied classical Arabic with the hope of using it for prose works as well, and she immersed herself in the spoken language, the sound of which, she told Gardenal, was "deeply, essentially feminine." But she also continued to write in French: by 1969 she had completed another novel, *Les Mille Nuits* (The Thousand Nights), which she never published; she worked on short stories and poems, and she contributed book reviews and film criticism to Algerian and French magazines.

In the early 1970s she and her husband were back in Paris, where, among other things, she acquainted herself with the new currents of European feminism. She deepened her involvement with the theater, working as assistant director on a number of productions and, in 1973, directed her own adaptation of Tom Eyen's play about Marilyn Monroe, *The White Whore and the Bit Player*. When she returned to the University of Algiers the following year, she began teaching theater and film, including courses on direct cinema and the semiology of film. This increasing interest in non-literary art forms coincided with her recognition that she was not going to become an Arabic-language writer: by the mid-1970s she had virtually decided to stop writing because French would never be accessible to the audience that was now most important to her—Algerian women. As an alternative she decided to turn to filmmaking, and in 1977 began working on *La Nouba des femmes de Mont Chenoua*

(The Nouba of the Women of Mount Chenoua, 1979) for Algerian television. A meditation on history and memory, the film combines a dramatic narrative about a young professional woman returning to her village with documentary footage of aging village women from Djebar's own region of Mount Chenoua. Here fact and fiction are woven into five movements modeled on the Andulasian musical composition called a *nouba,* but which also recall the rhythmic structure of *Les Alouettes naïves.* "For me," she told Josie Fanon in 1977, "making film doesn't mean abandoning the word for the image. It's making an image-sound. It's going back to the sources on the level of language."

In Algeria, the film proved controversial, especially because of its almost exclusive focus on women—the only male character is the fictional protagonist's husband, who is literally immobilized in a wheelchair. As one of the film's defenders, Ahmed Bedjaoui, wrote in the Algerian film magazine *Les Deux écrans,* "*La Nouba* is a film of a rare intelligence, where there is always a search for form and new ideas," but, he continued, "It is easy for me to imagine that the viewer trained in the school where the hero is the super-male would have a hard time accepting this vision of a universe that revolves around the castration of the man." Resistance to the film was such that it was excluded from the official competition at the Carthage film festival in Tunisia, but when it was shown at Venice in 1979, it received the International Critics Prize, and it was similarly acclaimed on its release in France.

For Djebar, in addition to the mix of notoriety and praise that the film brought her, it permitted her to resolve her ambivalence about writing in French. "My work in film puts me in a creative relationship with Arabic as a living language, a language in space," she told writer-critic Tahar Ben Jelloun in 1987. "My confrontation with the language of my childhood came in making films. Now I can write in French without feeling cut off, without any bad conscience."

This new posture was soon confirmed with the publication of *Les Femmes d'Alger dans leur appartement* (Women of Algiers in Their Apartment, 1980), a collection of six short stories offering in Djebar's words, "a few landmarks on a journey of listening between 1958 and 1978. Conversations that have been fragmented, recalled, reconstituted . . . fictitious accounts, faces and murmurs from a nearby imagination, from a present-past revolting under the intrusion of an abstract newness." Presented in two sections, "Today" and "Yesterday" (in that order), the stories, written between 1958 and 1978, seem to be saying that progress too has remained a male domain, and that the closed world of the harem has not necessarily been improved upon by that of the high-rise. In a provocative afterword titled "Forbidden Glance, Sound Off," Djebar returned to the Delacroix painting that gives its name to the collection and contrasts the closed world of the harem as Delacroix represented it just after the French invasion of Algeria in 1830 to the "variations" executed by Picasso 120 years later at the time of the Algerian War. "Only in the fragments of ancient murmurs," she concludes, "do I see a way of restoring the womanly conversations that Delacroix has frozen on the canvas. Only in the door left open to the streaming sun, what Picasso was later to impose, can I place my hope for a concrete, lasting liberation of women."

Coming after an ostensible silence of ten years, *Les Femmes d'Alger* was enthusiastically welcomed in critical circles. For Hedi Abdeljaouad, this small volume represented "a landmark in her career as a writer and in Maghrebine esthetics in general." Writing in *World Literature Today,* he compared Djebar's literary reworking of Delacroix to Picasso's variations and suggested that her "painter's perspective" brought a new dimension to North African literature. "Although the general tone is tragic," he noted, "there is no pleading and no sensibility. She simply recounts the humdrum of women's daily life." In the late 1970s Djebar once again settled in Paris. While preparing *Les Femmes d'Alger* for publication, she began working on another film which, like the "variations" on Delacroix, sought to retrieve the "signs and echoes" of Algerian women from under layers of colonial history. *La Zerda et les chants de l'oubli* (The *Zerda* and Songs of Forgetting, 1982) combined French archival photographs and documentary footage with traditional women's songs and poems and Djebar's own commentary in order to "decolonize and feminize" the history of Algeria. First screened on Algerian television in July 1982, it was presented at the Berlin film festival the following year and like *La Nouba,* continues to be shown in conferences and festivals throughout North Africa, Europe, and the United States.

As Hedi Abdeljaouad wrote in his review of *Les Femmes d'Alger,* Djebar, at the age of forty-four, had not only "reached the peak of her intellectual maturity," but had also "tried her hand at every conceivable genre." In the first half of the 1980s, while organizing several exhibitions in Paris, co-translating two Arabic novels into French, and attempting to mount a succession of fiction film productions, she seemingly brought together all of her interests—literature, history,

music, film, and the culture of women—into a monumental novel, *L'Amour la fantasia* (1985; translated as *Fantasia: An Algerian Cavalcade,* 1989).

Carrying over the rhythmic structures of *The Nouba* and *The Zerda,* the *Fantasia* is constructed around an alternation of voices and visions, beginning with a ten-year-old Algerian girl about to encounter "modernity." Juxtaposed with this autobiographical thread are epic historical accounts of the French conquest of Algeria that got underway with the attack on Algiers in June 1830. Exactly halfway through the novel, this literary counterpoint of feminine and masculine history gives way to a composition of "Buried Voices" divided into five movements variously interspersed with "Clamoring," "Whispers," "Murmurs," and the like. These are the voices of Algeria's women warriors, the living archives of the War of Liberation who, as in *La Nouba,* preserve collective memory in the spare prose of oral tradition:

> My oldest brother, Abdelkadir, joined the maquis; that was a while ago. France came to where we were . . . France came and burned us out. We stayed just like that, in the middle of the blackened stones . . . My second brother, Ahmed, was the next to go. I was thirteen years old. The soldiers came back again, they burned us out again.

What holds the times, places, and voices together is the rhythm, the tone, and ultimately the music of the language. Commenting on her increasingly paradoxical relationship to French, she told *Jeune Afrique* just after the novel was published, "French is my stepmother, this language that used to be my people's tomb. I carry it like a messenger would carry the sealed letter condemning him to silence, or the dungeon." But in the view of critics and public alike, this personal struggle for expression yielded a literary and social document of the highest quality. A bestseller in both France and Algeria, it brought Djebar the Franco-Arab Friendship Prize for 1985.

Fantasia was conceived as the first part of a quartet, and in 1987, Djebar published the second volume, *Ombre sultane* (The Sultana's Shadow; translated as *A Sister to Scheherazade*). Here, through the voice of a narrator who speaks alternately for herself and for another woman who cannot speak—her husband's second wife—Djebar stages the drama of modern Algerian women in the intimate setting of the household. There is no rivalry because the first wife has left the husband, and indeed, has chosen her own replacement. What the two women come to share is the sisterhood of suffering, and once again, as in *The Women of Algiers,* Djebar concludes on a melancholy note:

My sister, I, who thought I'd awaken you, I'm afraid that
the two of us, the three of us, all of us—except for the
midwives, the mothers standing guard, the death-
bearing grandmothers—will find ourselves shackled
again in this "west of the East," this corner of the earth
where the dawn has risen so slowly that dusk is already
settling around us on all sides.

As reviewers were quick to recognize, *A Sister
to Scheherazade* offered Western readers a singular opportunity to enter the harem, or its mod-
ernday equivalent, without the typical trappings
of exoticism. For some, notably in Algeria, there
was still an element of voyeurism at play, but for
others, such as *Libération*'s Philippe Gardenal,
Djebar's vision served to ennoble, not to betray:
"Through her long, sisterly pursuit, the crude,
drab fates of these cloistered women attain the
grandeur usually reserved for princesses:
through the voice of someone who knew how to
speak in their place, the shadows and the sultan's
wives aspire to another fate."

In contrast to the rapid-fire novels of her
twenties, Djebar's recent works have been written over extended and overlapping periods of
time—in the case of *A Sister to Scheherazade*,
four distinct intervals between 1981 and 1986.
As she commented in a 1987 interview, "I don't
behave like an intellectual and I separate my life
as a writer from the rest." Divorced from Ahmed
Ould-Rouïs in 1975, she married poet Malek Al-
loula in 1980; she has a daughter and a son from
her first marriage.

WORKS IN ENGLISH TRANSLATION: Frances Frenaye translated *The Mischief* in 1961. Djebar's "Forbidden
Glances, Sound Off" appears in E. W. Fernea's anthology *Women and the Family in the Middle East*, 1985,
in J. M. McDougal's translation. Dorothy S. Blair translated *A Sister to Scheherazade* in 1988 and *Fantasia:
An Algerian Cavalcade* in 1989.

ABOUT: Dictionnaire des littératures de langue
française, 1987; Mortimer, M. Assia Djebar, 1988.
Periodicals—Afrique artistique et littéraire 3, 1969;
Arabies (Paris) February 1987; Contemporary French
Civilization Spring–Summer 1985; Europe October
1968; Jeune Afrique June 4, 1962, October 1, 1967,
June 27, 1984; Jeune Cinéma February 1979;
Libération May 6, 1987; Le Monde August 8, 1980,
May 29, 1987; Research in African Literatures Sum-
mer 1980; Times Literary Supplement June 24, 1988.

DODSON, OWEN (VINCENT) (November
28, 1914–June 21, 1983), American poet, playwright, and novelist, was born at home, 309 Ber-
riman Street, Brooklyn, New York, the ninth
child of a poor black family. His parents had migrated to Brooklyn from their birthplace, Boyd-
ton, Virginia. The father, Nathaniel Barnett

OWEN DODSON

Dodson, worked as a freelance writer for black
newspapers, and his mother, Sarah Elizabeth
Goode, served her church and community as a
volunteer social worker.

From such a modest beginning, one might not
anticipate that Dodson would write three volumes of poems which would be anthologized in
sixty-five texts, and translated into Japanese,
Italian, German, Czech, and Dutch, nor that
Dodson would be invited to read his poems before the Library of Congress (1973). Richard
Eberhart, Pulitzer Prize poet, at the 1968 Dartmouth College Black Arts Festival introduced
Dodson as "the best Negro poet in the United
States." The next year, *Time* magazine wrote
that Dodson's poetry "stands peer to Frost, Carl
Sandburg and other white American poets."

George Plimpton awarded Dodson's story
"The Summer Fire" a Paris Review Prize and
published it in his collection *Best Short Stories
from the Paris Review* (1959). Dodson, a Phi
Beta Kappa, received two honorary doctorates
and was recipient of Guggenheim (1953), Rosenwald (1944), and Rockefeller (1968) grants; his
friends included W. H. Auden, Countee Cullen,
Langston Hughes, Richard Wright, and Thornton Wilder, all of whom influenced his writing.

These achievements, and others, began modestly enough in Brooklyn with Dodson's discovery of the joy of poetry under the tutelage of
Elias Lieberman, principal of Thomas Jefferson
High School (1928). Here Dodson achieved acclaim in oratory and declamation. Awarded a
scholarship, he enrolled at Bates College in Lew-
iston, Maine where he began to write traditional

sonnets and to direct plays under the mentorship of Professor Robert Berkelman. By the year of his graduation (1936), the young black poet had published verse in the *New York Tribune*, and in the journals *Opportunity* and *Phylon*.

Entering the Yale Drama School on a General Board of Education scholarship, Owen Dodson received main-stage presentations of his verse plays. *Divine Comedy* (1938), the initial production, was a poetic examination of the messiah phenomenon as incarnated by the character of Father Divine, a black evangelist who had claimed to be God. This play received the Maxwell Anderson Award for verse drama. Dodson's second production, *The Garden of Time* (1939), set partially in the South, retold the classic Medea story in terms of American racism. An element of fatalism, a motif woven through Dodson's work, perhaps taken from his love of the Greek drama, appears in his lyrics:

Nothing happens only once,
Nothing happens only here,
Every love that lies asleep
Wakes today another year.

Why we sailed and how we prosper
Will be sung and lived again;
All the lands repeat themselves,
Shore for shore and men for men.

In 1939, graduating with an MFA, Dodson left the North to teach speech and drama at Spelman College of Atlanta University; he remained there for three years before accepting a position with the Communications Department at Hampton College in Virginia, where he taught before enlisting in the U.S. Navy in November of 1942. At Great Lakes Naval Training Station, he was appointed by Commander Armstrong, along with artist-dancer Charles Sebree, to write and to produce a series of naval history plays for the black seamen. Two of these plays were published by *Theatre Arts*, the most prestigious theatre monthly in America at the time. *The Ballad of Dorrie Miller* (1943), a verse chorale, portrays the heroism of the black seaman, Miller, who shot down several Japanese planes during their attack on Pearl Harbor. *Freedom, the Banner* (1943) praises the struggles of Chiang Kai-shek in nationalist China's war against the Japanese.

In 1943, a major race riot broke out in Detroit, and Dodson composed "Black Mother, Praying," a poem that was to become his most popular. The thrust of the poem is a black mother imploring God to end racial discrimination against black servicemen. The poem concludes:

I ain't never gonna hush my mouth or lay down this
    heavy, black, weary, terrible load
Until I fights to stamp my feet with my black sons

On a freedom solid rock and stand there peaceful
And look out into the star wilderness of the sky
And the land lyin about clean, and secure land,
And people not afraid again.
Lord, let us all see the golden wheat together,
Harvest the harvest together,
Touch the fullness and the hallelujeh together.
                                        Amen.

Immediately following his medical discharge from the service for asthma, Dodson, with the help of a Rosenwald Fellowship composed and directed *New World A-Coming,* a pageant of Negro history designed to demonstrate black Americans' contributions to the war effort. The pageant, presented at Madison Square Garden, New York City in 1944 to an estimated 25,000 people, so impressed Edwin Embree, the head of the Rosenwald Foundation, that he nominated Dodson to the position of Executive Secretary of the newly formed Committee for Mass Education in Race Relations at the American Film Center, a prestigious body of writers and film producers whose charge was to produce films that would present America's ethnic minorities in roles other than stereotypes.

August 1946 saw the publication of Dodson's first book of poetry, *Powerful Long Ladder*, a book which established his national reputation as a poet. The poetry, divided into five sections, focuses around the epigram for the book, "It takes a powerful long ladder to climb to the sky / and catch the bird of freedom for the dark," and concludes with this final verse from the poem, "Open Letter": "Brothers, let us enter that portal for good / When peace surrounds us like a credible universe. / Bury that agony, bury this hate, take our black hands in yours." M. L. Rosenthal wrote in the New York *Herald Tribune Weekly Book Review*: "The positive achievements of *Powerful Long Ladder* are its vividness, its solid strength in picturing pain and disgust without losing the joy of life which marks the best artist, its ethical force." Dodson said several times that he would like to write one line of poetry that would enter the language as Keats' line, "A thing of beauty is a joy forever," has. In this slim book of verse, Dodson may have come near his wish with "Sorrow is the only faithful one."

Dodson's attempts to make manifest his dream of brotherhood in the real world often led to frustration. After three years of unsuccessful attempts to persuade Hollywood and the white establishment to produce new ethnic image films, Dodson resigned his position with the American Film Committee and moved to Washington, D.C., to join Howard University's newly established drama department; here he would remain for the next twenty-three years.

His first Howard triumph came in September

1949, when he, along with Professors Anne Cooke and James Butcher, led the Howard Players on a tour of Norway, Denmark, Sweden, and Germany. Their performances of Ibsen's *The Wild Duck* and Heyward's *Mamba's Daughters*, received wide praise from the European press. A review in *Børsen*, a Copenhagen daily, was typical of the European press: "The Howard players played with heart and affection and carried the audience with them." The three-month tour concluded with Drew Pearson awarding the troupe the American Public Relations International Award. The Howard Players had been the first American college theater troupe to tour Europe, and their success influenced the U.S. Congress to establish a nationally funded policy of cultural exchange abroad.

In February, 1951, *Boy at the Window*, Dodson's first and best novel, was published to nearly unanimous praise. Review headlines caught the essence. From the *Washington Star*: "A Sensitive Writer Gives New Color to an Old Theme," and from the *Washington Post* "Eloquent Writing: Child's Eye View of the Adult World." The semi-autobiographical story concerns a sensitive black lad named Coin and his confrontation with the death of his beloved mother, a death he feels he should have been able to prevent. The prose, rich in image and metaphor, captures a working-class neighborhood of Brooklyn in the 1920s where West Indians, Jews, Italians, and blacks lived a vital and integrated life.

Dodson's second novel, *Come Home Early, Child*, a sequel to the first, did not appear until 1967; Coin, in this novel, leaves home, joins the navy, has a love affair in Italy, and returns to Brooklyn to discover that you can't go home again. His passage into manhood is again conceived in a rich poetic structure that often borders on the surreal.

Teaching at Howard University consumed much of Dodson's energy and time, and it was not until his retirement that he was able to publish another book of verse. Camille Billops, a visual artist, had contracted the Harlem photographer, James Van Der Zee, to publish a series of his funeral photographs taken during the 1920s, 1930s, and 1940s. Dodson agreed to write poems as captions to the photos. The result, *The Harlem Book of the Dead*, appeared in 1978. In this unique volume, poems like "Allegory of Seafaring Black Mothers" reveal Dodson's talent for combining idea with startling image: "How many mothers with their grit / with their bony and long dreams / have dared to splash with us out to sea?"

Although Dodson wrote thirty-seven plays

and operas, and twenty-seven of them saw production, his best work remains his verse plays, *Divine Comedy* (1938) and *Bayou Legend* (1948) (a black Louisiana version of Ibsen's *Peer Gynt* drama). His opera, *Til Victory Is Won* (1965), written with composer Mark Fax to celebrate Howard University's centennial, was produced at the Kennedy Center (1974). A collage of Dodson's poetry and plays, *Owen's Song*, was produced at the Center in December of that same year.

He considered *The Confession Stone* (1970), a series of monologues spoken by the Holy Family concerning the life of Jesus, to be his masterpiece. Often performed as a play at Easter services, the cycle has developed a devoted following. The simplicity of the language denotes the humanity of the Holy Family. Mary speaks to her boy Jesus:

> Don't pay attention
> to the old men in the Temple:
> they have given up.
> Tell them what you told me:
> cast the sinners out.
> Clean the house of God.
> Load the rich with grief,
> prepare the poor with hope . . .
>   . . . and Jesus,
> don't stop to play
> with Judas and his friends
> along the way.

Dodson was once asked by an editor to write "a few Negro poems." He countered by replying that he did not "feel Negro" that day. This exchange catches an important attitude Dodson held about himself and his art. He considered himself a writer, a poet, a humanist who happened to be black. He never married and was the last surviving member of his immediate family. Until his fatal heart attack the morning of the summer equinox in 1983, Dodson continued to write and publish poetry.

PRINCIPAL WORKS: *Poetry*—Powerful Long Ladder, 1946; The Confession Stone, 1970; Harlem Book of the Dead, 1978. *Novels*—Boy at the Window, 1950; Come Home Early, Child, 1967. *Plays*—Bayou Legend, 1971; Divine Comedy, 1974.

ABOUT: Contemporary Authors 28, 1988; Dictionary of Literary Biography 76, 1988; Hatch, J. V. and O. Abdullah, Black Playwrights, 1823–1977, 1977; Redman, E. Drumvoices: The Mission of Afro-American Poetry, 1976; Rush, T. B., C. F. Myers, E. S. Arata. Black American Writers Past and Present, 1975; O'Brien, J. Interviews with Black Writers, 1973. incl. Black American Literature Forum Summer 1980.

DOUGLAS, ELLEN (pseudonym of JOSE-PHINE AYRES HAXTON) (July 12, 1921–), American novelist and short-story writer, sends the following to *World Authors*: "Ellen Douglas is the penname of Josephine Ayres Haxton, American novelist, born in Natchez, Mississippi, daughter of Richardson and Laura (Davis) Ayres. Douglas, one of four children of a civil engineer, has lived in small towns in Louisiana, Arkansas, and Mississippi for most of her life. She graduated from the University of Mississippi in 1942 and worked for three years at various jobs (for the army, as a disk jockey, in the Gotham Book Mart) before marrying Kenneth Haxton of Greenville, Mississippi, in 1945. She has three sons and five grandchildren and is presently divorced and living in Jackson, Mississippi.

"She has said of herself that she began writing poems (mostly about God and Mother) at an early age, turned to short stories in her adolescence, and after marriage put writing aside during the years when she had small children at home. In the mid-fifties she began to write again and finished her first novel, *A Family's Affairs*, in 1960. In 1961 *A Family's Affairs* won the Houghton Mifflin 25th Anniversary Fellowship. That same year her novella, 'On the Lake,' was published in the *New Yorker*, and later included in the O. Henry Collection.

"Orville Prescott of the *New York Times Book Review* said of her earlier books, 'There can be no question about it, Miss Douglas is one of the best of our contemporary novelists . . . an artist who sees, who understands and who grieves over the sorrows of life.' Eudora Welty wrote of *A Lifetime Burning*, 'Ellen Douglas has always been a writer of strength and substance with the power to move her readers to fresh awareness and feeling. *A Lifetime Burning* marks a deeper penetration. . . . It is a rare novel; I tremendously admire its achievement.' And of her latest book, *Can't Quit You, Baby*, Michael Dorris wrote in the *San Francisco Chronicle*, 'Her language is full of the cadence, rhythm and startling clarity of true regional idiom. She can spin a story with a narrative that is reminiscent of the best of Gail Godwin . . . and demonstrates a mastery of technique that brings to mind the exquisite texture of Philip Roth. But finally, she is like nobody else.'

"Living as she has, in the Deep South through the years of upheaval—the fifties, sixties and seventies—Douglas inevitably concerns herself with the tangled and bloody relationships between black and white people. *The Rock Cried Out* explores lives that were formed or destroyed in the crucible of the civil rights struggle and the Vietnam War. *Black Cloud, White Cloud* and

ELLEN DOUGLAS

Can't Quit You, Baby are both preoccupied with the ways that black and white people—individuals—reach out to, reject, and hate and love each other. Douglas has also written about family life and the raveling of family ties in our time in *Apostles of Light* and *A Family's Affairs*. She has been concerned, too, particularly in *Where The Dreams Cross* and *A Lifetime Burning*, with the lives of individual women in the modern South, a world where old stereotypes die hard."

———

Like her sister-Mississippian Eudora Welty, Ellen Douglas has taken full advantage of the special Southern delight in narrative. Everybody has a story and, like Welty, Douglas has absorbed local story into her creative life. Like another Mississippian, William Faulkner, she has set her fiction in an imaginary but, reality-based county in the Mississippi Delta. Hers is Homochitto—rural, but in the mid- and late-twentieth century when her novels take place, rapidly transforming itself into high-tech, modern middle America. The theme of social change and individual displacement and/or adjustment to it informs her novels. A passage from *A Family's Affairs* epitomizes Douglas' vision of her region and her characters. She is describing a lively, imaginative little girl:

Like the world, the child, Anna, spun in her place. Her grandmothers' houses, her family, the lovers, the summer days, floated in a circular succession. Strange astral bodies flew off in unforeseen directions and collided with one another and exploded, but she observed everthing with godlike interest and detachment, and the unconscious conviction that, whatever the new orbits into which they finally settled, she would still be at the center of the universe.

Anna grows up and figures in several other of Douglas' stories. She is a sympathetic observer but also fully engaged in life, serving in many ways as a persona for Ellen Douglas herself. While her work is not autobiographical, it is certainly drawn deeply and fully from her experience of life in the New South. Anna McGovern's family history is the subject of *A Family's Affairs*. That novel chronicles the lives of three generations, beginning during the First World War and moving on to contemporary times. Observed mainly through Anna's eyes are "the strands of family life"—parents and children, uncles and aunts, the very old and the very young:

> Gathering, separating, gathering again, they came together with glad cries of recognition; and almost without pausing to say hello, to touch cheeks in the accepted gesture of reserved affection, began anew old conversations, old quarrels, the settling of old problems, the retelling or finishing of jokes and stories that had patiently awaited these occasions through months of separation. And all of it, every word they said to one another, rested lightly on the mysterious base of shared experience.

A Family's Affairs has none of the violence and horror associated with the so-called "Gothic" Southern novel. Some reviewers indeed found its pace too leisurely, its voice too soft, to sustain steady interest. F. H. Lyell, in the *New York Times Book Review*, while acknowledging that "the interplay of personalities and emotions in the final chapter [is] as beautiful and affecting as anything of its kind in recent fiction," nevertheless judged that "the novel as a whole lacks vigor and excitement." R. C. Healey, in the *New York Herald Tribune Book Review*, agreed that it was "long on character and short on plot," but praised Douglas as "a fine new writer [who] is steadily transcending the ordinary and familiar in a sensitive and penetrating study of the meaning of family."

In subsequent novels Douglas has introduced more plot, with some occasional violence and lurid detail, but essentially it is human character—people of good will who blunder but persist in their efforts to live by a code of simple decency and morality—that most engages her. The central character of *Where the Dreams Cross*, a strong-willed divorcée of easy virtue, returns to her family home and in her own unconventional but morally committed way saves her aged foster parents from disaster. There are some sinister and unsavory characters in the novel, but they are far less interesting than its overall picture of small-town Southerners struggling to preserve

their values in a rapidly changing society. Far more ambitious and serious in theme is *Apostles of Light*, a troubling novel about the exploitation and abuse of the elderly. The title is ironic, referring to the biblical false apostles who, like Satan, could transform themselves into angels of light. Her central characters, their victims, are an old woman whose lovely but now shabby family home is converted into a nursing home for the aged by a ruthless and hypocritical distant relative, and her lifelong lover, a doctor who struggles desperately to rescue her and the other victims of the callous indifference of society to the needs of the aged.

Although Douglas' subject in *Apostles of Light* is timely, her resolution of the problems in a violent climax and the unmitigated nastiness of the nursing home manager and his head nurse were found by some reviewers to have seriously weakened what was otherwise an intelligent and emotionally compelling novel. Walter Sullivan, in *Sewanee Review*, suggested that the ending of the novel was gratuitous and morally ambiguous although he found the book otherwise highly effective: "She gives us a sense of the past, of life having been lived and now coming to its close, of the agonies and glories that mold our humanity." The strongest feature of *Apostles of Light* is its projection of the states of mind of its principal characters—the gentle old Martha Clarke slipping between the unhappy present and her memories of a gracious, genteel past, her doctor-lover fighting off the numbing effects of the tranquilizing drugs administered to silence him, her loyal black gardener-servant torn between his desire to help her and his need to protect his own family, her well-meaning but obtuse relatives who fail to see what is really happening to these old people. "The emotional impact of her novel is undeniable," the *New Yorker* wrote. And V. S. Prescott, in *Newsweek*, judged it "a fine, strong novel about fundamental human conditions."

Violence, implicit and explicit, also figures in *The Rock Cried Out*. Set in the South of the civil rights movement of the 1960s and the post-Vietnam traumas of the 1970s, it is narrated by a young man who returns in 1971 to his family's farm after a long absence in the North. Only a boy in 1964 when the civil rights movement turned violent in Mississippi, he now reconstructs his memories of that period even as he struggles to make a place for himself in the South of the present. What was most striking about the novel to Jonathan Yardley, writing in the *New York Times Book Review*, was its treatment of "a theme that so far has received little attention in Southern fiction: the corrosive effect upon whites and their families of massive, violent reaction to the civil rights movement. It is this theme, and Miss Douglas's admirably sensitive treatment of it, that gives *The Rock Cried Out* its true distinction."

The first-person point of view in *The Rock Cried Out* reflects Douglas' interest in literary technique. Although she has always worked with shifting points of view, moving between direct narrative and interior monologue, she has more recently experimented in other techniques. *A Lifetime Burning* is a more concentrated and intense study of the mind of its central character. It is written as the diary of a sixty-two-year-old woman, a professor of English literature in a small Southern college. Long married, the mother of grown children, she is seemingly secure, but her revelations in the diary expose a bitterly frustrated and unhappy woman seeking some meaning in her life and drifting between illusion and reality. Susan Isaacs, in the *New York Times Book Review*, observed that *A Lifetime Burning* is self-consciously literary in spots—"technique overpowers characterization . . . [and] diffuses the impact of the novel." Nevertheless, she found the book "for the most part a beautifully constructed work of fiction. Ellen Douglas has all the qualities a reader could ask of a novelist: depth, emotional range, wit, sensitivity, and the gift of language."

Though now recognized as a sensitive and candid observer of the vast social changes sweeping the American South, Ellen Douglas' major achievement in fiction is in her portrait of Southern women, black and white, who long before the civil rights campaigns establish a unique bonding that almost—but not completely—obliterates the barriers between them. Her Southern white women enjoy warm, intimate friendships with Southern black women. They gossip together, cook together, even go fishing and picnicking together. What continues to hold them apart is a vestigial but subtly powerful community pressure. When white Anna, in the novella "Hold On" (originally published in the *New Yorker* as "On the Lake"), saves her black friend and former housemaid Estella from drowning at the risk of her own life, it is the casually brutal remark of a police officer that reminds her and a few other like-thinking white people of their own alienation from the white community.

In *Can't Quit You, Baby*, Douglas writes as a self-conscious narrator and addresses the reader directly from time to time:

There is no getting around in these stories of two lives that the black woman is the white woman's servant. There would have been no way in that time and place—the nineteen-sixties and seventies in Mississippi—for

them to get acquainted, except across the kitchen table from each other, shelling peas, peeling apples, polishing silver. True, other black and white women became friends under other circumstances, but such friendships, arising out of political crisis—revolution—were rare. In this house the white woman had to choose to sit down to set the tone of their conversation.

Can't Quit You, Baby—its title taken from a blues song—is the story of the parallel lives of a sheltered white Southern woman and her black servant. The white Cornelia has grown up in a comfortable and traditional Southern family (in her youth "a World War II Rapunzel," as one reviewer described her). She has had what to every appearance was an idyllic marriage and happy family. Although she has lost her hearing—a condition as symbolic of her insulation from reality as it is real—she is serene and secure. Her life is shattered, however, when her husband suddenly dies and her son makes what she considers a bad marriage. Suffering an emotional breakdown, she drifts to New York where she has a brief love affair. Counterpointing Cornelia's story is the narrative of her black servant Tweet who has managed to survive a tragic childhood, marriage to an unfaithful husband, and attempts by her cruel father and a white farmer to steal her inheritance, a little plot of land. Almost simultaneously with Cornelia's breakdown, Tweet suffers a disabling stroke. The novel ends with Cornelia recovering her mental health as she nurses Tweet back to physical health, and the two women finding solace in each other. For Alfred Uhry, in the *New York Times Book Review*, the novel was "a haunting examination of two memorable women." In *Library Journal* Edward C. Lynskey wrote of the book: "Douglas's sure diction, natural idiom, emotional complexity, and feminine sensitivity render this an exceptional novel. Despite the tangible themes of rage, guilt and sorrow, the narrative is refreshing for its redemptive powers."

Ellen Douglas lives in Jackson, Mississippi. In addition to the Houghton Mifflin Award that she received for *A Family's Affairs*, she has twice received grants from the National Endowment for the Arts—for *The Rock Cried Out* and *Can't Quit You, Baby*. *Apostles of Light* was nominated for the National Book Award in 1973. Since 1983 she has been writer-in-residence at the University of Mississippi. She has also been professor of creative writing at the University of Virginia (1984) and at Millsaps College (1988).

PRINCIPAL WORKS: *Novels*—A Family's Affairs, 1961; Where the Dreams Cross, 1968; Apostles of Light, 1973; The Rock Cried Out, 1979; Can't Quit You, Baby, 1988. *Short fiction*—Black Cloud, White Cloud,

1963. *Children's books*—The Magic Carpet: Fairy Tales Retold, 1987.

ABOUT: Contemporary Authors 115, 1985. *Periodicals*—America April 14, 1973; Best Sellers October 1, 1963; Book Week September 19, 1963; Choice June 1973; Christian Science Monitor October 31, 1963; Library Journal June 15, 1988; New York Herald Tribune Book Review July 8, 1962; New York Times Book Review February 18, 1973; September 23, 1979; October 31, 1982; July 10, 1983; New Yorker March 3, 1973; Newsweek March 5, 1973; Sewanee Review Winter 1974.

AUTRAN DOURADO

*DOURADO, AUTRAN (WALDOMIRO)
(January 18, 1926–   ) Brazilian novelist, short-story writer, and essayist, writes: "With the exception of *A Barca dos Homens* (The Ship of Men), the scene of which is an island off the Brazilian coast, and *A Serviço del-Rei* (At the Service of the King), which deals with the theme of the intellectual and power, the product of my experience as President Juscelino Kubitschek's press secretary in Rio de Janeiro and Brasília, I divide my work into two groups: the historical novels and the Duas Pontes stories. The novels in the first group make up a view of the history of Minas Gerais; they include *Ópera dos Mortos* (*Opera of the Dead*, also translated as *The Voices of the Dead*), which is set in the beginning of the present century, and *Lucas Procopio*, set in the late nineteenth century, as well as *Os Sinos da Agonia* (*The Bells of Agony*), the Greek myth of Phaedra in an eighteenth-century setting during the Portuguese colonization of Brazil. In *Os Sinos da Agonia* I try to portray the implacable Portuguese authoritarianism in its most brutal period, in the last decade of the century, which reaches its climax with the hanging of the national hero Joaquim José da Silva Xavier, called Tiradentes, who was the leader of the liberation movement in Villa Rica and who was executed in Rio de Janeiro with great and exemplary pomp. This book cannot be considered entirely as a historical novel in the way Georg Lukács defines the term in his *The Historical Novel*, which is nothing more than a branch of Realism. My goal was to write a symbolic novel set in the past as a metaphor of the authoritarianism of the Brazilian military dictatorship in its darkest period of the 1970's. (In order to evade dictatorial censorship, I set it in the eighteenth century). In *Os Sinos da Agonia* I always speak of the King, when at that time the monarch was Queen Mary I.

"The second group of works is set in Duas Pontes, the mythical city that I created based on Minas Gerais, where I spent my childhood and

early youth and where my father was a judge and my mother belonged to the decadent rural aristocracy, whose past prosperity derived from coffee growing and slave labor. The same characters and their descendants reappear in novels and short stories. Duas Pontes is similar to [William] Faulkner's Jefferson due to the sociological, historical and economical similarities between the American South and the south of Minas Gerais, both regions characterized by slavery and one-crop farming. The novels *Lucas Procopio* and *Opera dos Mortos*, although part of the historical saga of Minas Gerais, somehow are part of the Duas Pontes group since they are historical landmarks of the city's foundation.

"I am neither a realistic writer (Realism was a literary school whose time has come and gone; the death-blow was given by Dostoevski, whose characters laugh when they should be crying and cry when they should be laughing), nor a neo-realist—I am not a follower of Spanish-American magical (or fantastic) realism—least of all a neo-naturalistic writer: my realism is symbolic realism, where things are what they are and what they mean."

———

Autran Dourado was born in Patos, Minas Gerais, Brazil. He attended elementary school in Monte Santo de Minas and high school in São Sebastião do Paraíso and Belo Horizonte, the state capital, where he graduated in law and worked as a newspaperman. Dourado lived in Belo Horizonte till 1954, when he moved to the de Janeiro, to work as press secretary in President Juscelino Kubitschek's government. Out of that experience he wrote the novel *A Serviço del-Rei*. In 1975, he was invited as a guest writer to give a course on his own works at the Pontifical Catholic University of Rio de Janeiro. Out of those lectures came the work *Uma Poética de Romance: Matéria de Carpintaria*.

Autran Dourado has been publishing short stories, novels, and essays since 1947. His books have been translated into several languages, and his novel *Os Sinos da Agonia* was chosen as one of the books for the *agrégation* examination at the French universities. More than twenty university dissertations have been written about his works. He has been awarded eight literary prizes in Brazil and one in Germany, the Goethe Prize for literature. His novel *Ópera dos Mortos* was included by UNESCO in its Collection of Representative Works. Dourado married Maria Lucia Christo in 1949. They have four children.

Autran Dourado has been described as "the most important storyteller" of the key generation of Brazilian writers to emerge in the years immediately following the end of the Second World War. As John M. Parker notes in the introduction to his translation of Dourado's *Ópera dos Mortos* (*The Voices of the Dead*), this was the generation of Brazilian novelists who began to define themselves by "turning their backs on the regionalist social-realist fiction dominant in the thirties and forties, avoiding overt political orientation and following rather the introspective fiction of the same period, with its roots in Symbolism and the spiritual revival of the 1920s". It was, therefore, precisely as one of the first Brazilians to establish himself as "a creator of a narrative form both realistic and poetical, always searching for the symbolic power of things and events" and as a writer "capable of changing the confined milieu of the Minas [Gerais] hinterland [of his youth] into universal parables" that Autran Dourado is viewed as one of the most exemplary authors of this generation. In the words of Günter Lorenz: "What is powerfully seductive in Dourado's prose is his poetical language, which, with its powerful resonance and multiplicity of meanings, confers upon the nonstop action surprising touches." Because of his use of interior monologues and an "indirect free" style of narration, he is likewise often classified, along with certain other Brazilian authors of this period, as a "master stylist of psychological fiction."

Dourado's earliest work is described as revealing "Existentialist tendencies." After the appearance of a series of short stories in the 1950s, Dourado published the novel which, according to Parker, marked "the beginning of his maturity as a writer," and which resulted in his gaining an international reputation. *A Barca dos Homens* (The Ship of Men, 1961) is, in the words of Malcolm Silverman in *Revue des Langues Vivantes,* "conceivably the author's best work." It is, he explains, "immersed as much in poetic symbolism and allegory as it is in the ubiquitous sea, surrounding the setting: the island of Boa Vista. Personal discord oscillates, at once, among collective, epic, mythical and even mystical confrontations." *A Barca dos Homens* has been translated into French, Spanish, and German.

In identifying Autran Dourado as a practitioner of "new regionalism" in Brazil, Parker points out that his "works are steeped in the atmosphere of what we might call 'old Minas': the gloomy baroque of the eighteenth-century churches and . . . the sluggish uneventful monotony of life in the sleepy little towns of the interior, where gossip seems to be the main activity, yet which can be the scene of tragedies of almost Aeschylean proportions. This has been the case more specifically since the publication, in 1964, of the short novel *Uma vida em segredo* (*A Hidden Life*), which was acclaimed as a minor masterpiece by Brazilian critics." According to Silverman, this novelette "has a certain bitter sweetness to it, like a kind of adult fairy tale: happiness finally comes but it is *not* everlasting."

A Hidden Life was followed by *Ópera dos Mortos* (*The Voices of the Dead*) in 1967. For its translator, Parker, this novel is one "whose baroque nature starts with its very title. . . . The opening section calls attention specifically to the baroque nature of the architecture of the manor house, which is itself the key to the book: as the past speaks through the building, so the voices of the dead control the destinies" of the main characters. In commenting on this novel, Peter Lewis in the *Times Literary Supplement* compares Dourado with William Faulkner both in terms of the mythic proportions of his "regionalism" and his "complex and elaborate prose." He elaborates by adding: "In *The Voices of the Dead,* third-person (sometimes first-person) narration, dialogue, and internal monlogue flow into each other without the usual signs of demarcation, but with disturbingly unexpected changes of tense. One effect is to break down normal chronological assumptions so that past and present virtually co-exist. Another is to introduce relativism into the main narration, since the narrator is not a static, omniscient presence but a shifting, chameleon one: sometimes detached, sometimes involved, sometimes choric." Lewis concludes that the novel is open to "a variety of interpretations. Even the characters are conceived symbolically as well as realistically. . . . However, what makes this novel so difficult for British readers is not its symbolism as such but its baroque idiom, pace, and intensity, which are far removed from our novel traditions."

In 1970, Dourado published *O Risco do Bordado* (translated as *Pattern for a Tapestry*) in which "the narrator returns to the scene of his adolescence to seek, in family and other relationships, explanations for an apparently fated past." In his introduction to this work, Parker is careful to warn the reader that "the narrative is to be viewed not as horizontal and linear, but as vertical and multiple, allowing not merely a straight reading through from Unit I onwards, but [one] somewhat like [Julio] Cortázar's suggested reading of *Hopscotch*." The "historical" tragedy *Os Sinos da Agonia* appeared in 1974 and was followed by a number of minor novels and novellas, as well as a volume of literary criticism. Dourado's most recent efforts, yet to be published outside his native country, include *As Imaqinacoes Pecaminosas* (The Sinful Fantasies, 1981) and *A Servico Del-Rei* (In His Majesty's Service, 1984), based on his experience as press secretary to Brazilian President Kubitschek.

WORKS IN ENGLISH TRANSLATION: John M. Parker translated *The Voices of the Dead* in 1980, *Pattern for a Tapestry* in 1984, and *The Bells of Agony* in 1988. *A Hidden Life* was translated by Edgar H. Miller, Jr. in 1969.

ABOUT: Contemporary Authors 25–28, 1977; Contemporary Literary Criticism 23, 1983; Dictionary of Contemporary Brazilian Authors, 1981; Parker, J. M. *Introductions to* The Voices of the Dead, 1980, and The Bells of Agony, 1988. *Periodicals*—Revue des Langues Vivantes 42, 1976; Saturday Review March 29, 1969; Times Literary Supplement January 30, 1981; January 20, 1989; World Literature Today Autumn 1979.

DOVE, RITA (August 28, 1952–   ), American poet, writes: "I was born in Akron, Ohio in 1952. The year of birth indicates I was old enough to witness the phenomena of social protest that characterized the Sixties yet too young to participate; this peculiar vantage point has played a significant role in my development as a writer. The characters portrayed in my poems and fiction often exist outside the larger sweep of history; they are relatively ordinary persons whose quiet struggles are moot, historically speaking, but who for all their unimportance are nonetheless heroic.

"I grew up in a first generation middle-class Black family. My mother had had to fight through a scholarship to Howard University when she

RITA DOVE

was seventeen because her parents were afraid to let her out 'into the world' by herself. My father, the only child from ten who had gone to college, became the first Black research chemist in the American rubber industry's history. He scarcely talked about the years he spent (after earning a master's degree) running a service elevator; but we children knew somehow (there were four of us) and decided not to disappoint him. Education was everything in our house. Books lined the sunroom, and we were allowed to read anything we thought we could understand. This eclectic upbringing is responsible for my catholic curiosity; no subject is essentially boring, and no topic unfit for a poem. I have written poems on fossils ('The Fish in the Stone'), math ('Geometry'), slavery ('The Slave's Critique of Practical Reason'), archeology ('The Hill Has Something to Say'), horticulture ('The Copper Beech'), and household chores ('Dusting'); short stories deal with everything from grafitti ('The Spray Paint King') to bag ladies ('Zabriah') and musical composition ('The Vibraphone').

"Although I've written since childhood, it wasn't until my junior year in college that I admitted I wanted to be a writer. Telling my parents (who dreamed I would become the family's first lawyer) was one of the hardest things I've ever done. Between undergraduate and graduate school I went to West Germany on a Fulbright Fellowship. For the first time in my life I was immersed in a language and culture quite different from my own, and I had a year to study American foreign policy from a non perspective.

"*The Yellow House on the Corner*, like many first books of poems, is a miscellany; my second full-length poetry collection, *Museum*, is a concentrated attempt to portray the underside of a museum—the politics behind the artifacts, the stories behind the legends. My third book of poems, *Thomas and Beulah*, is based loosely on my maternal grandparents' lives. The first section follows the husband's life, and the second section recounts the wife's story. This book, then, carries on the notion of telling the underside of history that *Museum* began. It also applies the pressure of two variant viewpoints on the same slice of time.

"My foremost commitment to poetry is to the language that creates it—molds it, really, like a sculptor finding the ibex in the marble. It is by language that I enter the poem, and it's language that leads me forward. That doesn't exclude perceptions and experience and emotions; it simply defines the way I go about connecting with emotion and experience. And the language must have music, it must sing. (Ever since I was ten I have played some kind of musical instrument—cello, viola da gamba, recorder—and I've performed everything from Bach's Suites for Unaccompanied Violoncello to Baroque ensemble music to progressive jazz.)

"My second commitment—so essential that the first cannot exist without it, though it might sound pious and starched—is to moral necessity. I simply mean that poetry must be about something. After all, the poem must live *in* the world, not above it.

"I have many favorite poets; I can never choose one, or present a Top Forty list when asked that inevitable question of Major Influences. There's a measure of self-protection in this, just as in trying to stay unaware of what 'my style' is, since categorizations are limiting. Frequent mention has been made of my use of color and a near surreal juxtaposition of images. The latter description baffles me, but I don't worry about it. Indeed, if I think too much about what I *have* written, I'd be inhibited in what I have *yet* to write. Let the critics come to their own conclusions."

The conclusions to which critics have come on Rita Dove's poetry are almost uniformly favorable. What has especially impressed them is Dove's breadth of vision and range of interests. One of a growing number of distinguished black women poets, she is unique among the group in expressing what Calvin Hernton, reviewing her book *Museum* in *Parnassus*, called "a European sensibility"—writing poems, that is, that "do not fall within the aesthetic frame of reference of the black tradition, either personally or collectively." This is not to suggest, however, that Dove's poems ignore her black cultural heritage. In her first two volumes, for example, poems about the black experience in America are carefully balanced with poems inspired by her travels in Europe, Africa, and Asia. *The Yellow House on the Corner* is a collection of personal poems that frame a series of American slave narratives, some presented as pure narrative, some as dramatic monologues. To Linda Gregerson in *Poetry* the structure of the volume was initially puzzling, but she came to recognize a link between the two groups of poems—a meditative dialogue, as it were, between the uprooted tourist and the captured slave. Both share a sense of displacement and each, with its contrasting point of view, lends depth and heightened perception to the other.

Museum even more strikingly juxtaposes Europe and black America, past and present, black and white. There are poems inspired by Boccaccio, by hagiography (poems on St. Catherine of Siena and St. Catherine of Alexandria), by a medieval tapestry that hangs in a hall in Munich as an ironic backdrop to a contemporary German writers' conference. Alien as the subjects may appear, Dove manages to mediate and synthesize these impressions, as she does in "Receiving the Stigmata":

There is a way to enter a field
empty-handed, your shoulder
behind you and air tightening.

The kite comes by itself,
a spirit in a fluttering string.

Back when people died for
the smallest reasons, there was
always a field to walk into.
Simple men fell to their knees
below the radiant crucifix
and held out their palms

in relief. Go into the field
and it will reward. Grace

is a string growing straight
from the hand. Is
the hatchet's shadow on the
rippling green.

In the same volume Dove celebrates her personal memories of a childhood in the American midwest—a Memorial Day when the family visited a cemetery, then came home to eat grape sherbert prepared by her father—"Everyone agrees—it's wonderful! / It's just how we imagined lavender / would taste." And she writes a powerful narrative on the slaughter of thousands of blacks in the Dominican Republic in 1957 under the dictator Trujillo ("Parsley"—the title alluding to the word *parejil* which non-Spanish speaking people could not pronounce), and a poem on the little-known eighteenth-century American black scientist Benjamin Banneker who helped to plan the city of Washington, D.C. but died a lonely, unappreciated man:

> But who would want him! Neither
> Ethiopian nor English, neither
> lucky nor crazy, a capacious bird
> humming as he penned in his mind
> another enflamed letter
> to President Jefferson—he imagined
> the reply, polite and rhetorical.

Thomas and Beulah, for which Dove received the Pulitzer Prize for poetry in 1987, is by far her most intimate and personal expression—a chronicle not of her own experience but of the lives of two black people modeled closely on her grandparents who met, married, raised a family, and died—ordinary lives distinguished less by their skin color than by their simple humanity. "Dove has learned," Helen Vendler wrote in *New York Review of Books*, "how to make a biographical fact the buried base of an imagined edifice." The circumstantiality of their lives is meticulously noted in a chronology printed at the end of the poem—their dates of birth and their moves from the South to Akron, Ohio where they spent their lives, the dates of birth of their children, the background of their lives—the Depression, unemployment, World War II, the Civil Rights movement—and the dates of their deaths. Fleshed out in a two-part narrative, more accurately a series of what Vendler describes as dramatic, cinematic "takes," momentary insights of the two protagonists, *Thomas and Beulah* "forms an elegant cycle of poems," wrote the *Virginia Quarterly Review*: "More than a mere tribute (of sorts) to Dove's own heritage, it is a fascinating exploration of the process in which we shape metaphors about 'the course' of life. In a certain sense the key word of Dove's title is *and*, for it is the nature of human relation and the formation of identity that is, for her, at issue."

Part I, "Mandolin," centers on Thomas who had left Tennessee "with nothing to boast of / but good looks and a mandolin":

> He used to sleep like a glass of water
> held up in the hand of a very young girl.
> Then he learned he wasn't perfect, that
> no one was perfect. So he made his way
> North under the bland roof of a tent
> too small for even his lean body.

He marries and works hard to support his family, four daughters and the much wanted son:

> He gave up fine cordials and
> his hounds-tooth vest.
>
> He became a sweet tenor
> in the gospel choir.
>
> Canary, usurper
> of his wife's affections.
>
> Girl girl
> girl girl.

He suffers unemployment, humiliation, ill health and sometimes despair, an embodiment of the universal mystery of human life:

> They were poor then but everyone had been poor.
> He hadn't minded the sweeping,
> just the thought of it—like now
> when people ask him what he's thinking
> and he says *I'm listening*.

Beulah's section, "Canary in Bloom," provides a kind of counterpoint in a softer feminine voice. In courtship, motherhood, work as a seamstress, or in domestic chores Beulah lives up to her name ("Promise, then / Desert-in-Peace"). In "Dusting" Beulah is

> patient among knicknacks,
> the solarium a rage
> of light, a grainstorm
> as her gray cloth brings
> dark wood to life.

In "Weathering Out" she revels in her pregnancy—"Past the seventh month she couldn't see her feet / so she floated from room to room, houseshoes flapping, / navigating corners in wonder." Exhausted by her duties, she yearns, in "Daystar," for a quiet private place of her own "where / she was nothing, / pure nothing, in the middle of the day." In "Wingfoot Lake" she attends a company picnic—"white families on one side and them / on the other, unpacking the same / squeeze bottle of Heinz. . . ." And in "The Oriental Ballerina," long widowed and now dying, she contemplates a china ornament near her bed:

> The head on the pillow sees nothing
> else, though it feels the sun warming
>
> its cheeks. *There is no China*,
> no cross, just the papery kiss
> of a kleenex above the stink of camphor,
>
> the walls exploding with shabby tutus.

It is the simplicity, the sheer ordinariness of the lives of Thomas and Beulah that the poem illuminates. The language, the imagery, the quiet lyric line all move naturally and seemingly without art. "The brilliance lies in her arrangement of context," Vendler writes, "as the elements of meaning find their one inevitable form, juxtaposition alone takes on the work of explanation . . . Dove has planed away unnecessary matter: pure shapes, her poems exhibit the thrift that Yeats called the sign of a 'perfected manner.'"

Rita Dove is the daughter of Ray and Elvira (Hord) Dove. She received her B.A., summa cum laude and Phi Beta Kappa, from Miami University in Oxford, Ohio in 1973, and an M.F.A. in 1977 from the University of Iowa. She has also studied as a Fulbright fellow at the Universität Tübingen in West Germany, and she is married to a German writer, Fred Viebahn. They have one child. Dove has taught creative writing at Arizona State University in Tempe since 1981. In 1982 she was writer-in-residence at Tuskegee Institute. She has received grants from the National Endowment for the Arts, the National Endowment for the Humanities, and in 1983 she was named a Guggenheim fellow.

PRINCIPAL WORKS: The Yellow House on the Corner, 1980; Museum, 1983; Thomas and Beulah, 1986. Collected short stories—Fifth Sunday, 1985.

ABOUT: Contemporary Authors 109, 1983; Hernton, C. C. The Sexual Mountain and Black Women Writers, 1987. Periodicals—Georgia Review Summer 1984, Winter 1986; Hudson Review Spring 1984; New York Review of Books October 23, 1986; Parnassus Spring 1985; Poetry October 1984; Virginia Quarterly Review Spring 1987.

*DOVLATOV, SERGEY (September 3, 1941–August 24, 1990), Russian short-story writer and essayist, was born in Ufa, Bashkiria, into a family of what is called in the Soviet Union the "creative intelligentsia": his father, Donat Mechik, was a variety show director, a playwright in the same genre, and a satirical poet; his mother, Nora Dovlatova, whose maiden name he adopted, was an actress turned proofreader. The close-knit family, of mingled Armenian and Jewish roots, also included a book editor, a film director, and another writer. Raised in Leningrad, Dovlatov briefly attended the University of Leningrad, where he studied the Finnish language. After dropping out of school he was drafted and assigned to a prison camp guard unit in the Komi Autonomous Republic.

Upon his return to Leningrad in 1965, he joined the group of aspiring young writers called Gorozhane (The Townsmen)—a group that included Vladimir Maramzin, Valery Popov, Boris Vakhtin, and Igor Yefimov. The group was only loosely associated with the official Writers Union, and its members seldom had an opportu-

SERGEY DOVLATOV

nity to have their works published. Like his fellow Townsmen, Dovlatov supported himself through various para-literary activities: reviewing books, writing pieces for TV and radio shows and articles for children's magazines, and editing a factory newspaper. In his free time, he worked on a novel and short stories. Dovlatov's unpublished prose circulated among Leningrad intellectuals, and his reputation as a witty and sensitive young author was soon established. However, all attempts to publish individual stories in magazines or in a book failed. Dovlatov's subject matter—prison camps, life in the "lower depths" of a big city—could not pass the censorship. In 1974 the frustrated author decided to try a new start. He moved to Tallinn, Estonia, the most "Western" of Soviet cities, and for three years worked as a journalist for the local Russian-language press. A collection of his short stories was prepared for publication by a local publishing house, but the project miscarried when the KGB accused him of associating with Estonian dissidents. After his Tallinn fling Dovlatov returned to Leningrad. His jobs were part-time: editor of a children's magazine, tour guide at the Pushkin memorial museum, journalist. The state security went on harassing him, and when his works began to appear in emigré magazines in the West, he was briefly detained and then "offered an opportunity" to emigrate.

Dovlatov made his new home in New York City, where he lived from 1978 until his death in 1990. He had married Elena Ritman in 1963, and she joined him in exile with their young daughter; their second child—a son—was born

°dov lä´ tof

in New York. In America Dovlatov published ten books of prose in Russian and five in English. Translations of his short stories appeared in the *New Yorker, Partisan Review,* and *Grand Street,* and with the advent of *glasnost* in the Soviet Union, some of his work saw publication in literary magazines there as well. Dovlatov served as an essayist for Radio Liberty Russian broadcasting after his emigration; from 1979 to 1983 he was also editor-in-chief of the Russian language weekly *Novy Amerikanets* (The New American).

Dovlatov's genre of choice was the short story. He tended to unify his collections either thematically (prison camp stories in *Zona* [1982; *The Zone*], stories about a single family in *Nashi* [1983; *Ours*]), or by using a single autobiographical narrator: a freelancer in Leningrad (*Nevidimaya kniga* [1977; *The Invisible Book*]), a Russian journalist in Estonia (*Kompromiss* [1981; *The Compromise*]) , and an emigré editor in New York ("Nevidimaya gazeta" ["The Invisible Newspaper"], published in 1985 as Part II of *Remeslo* [Trade], with "The Invisible Book" as Part I).

All the vicissitudes of Dovlatov's life are reflected in his strongly autobiographical fiction, but, unlike many other writers who explore their personal experiences, Dovlatov seems never to have been tempted to mythologize them, or turn his life story into an epic. Although he sometimes felt obliged to invent some spurious "framework" for his stories (e.g., in *The Zone* and in *The Compromise*), each of the tales could stand on its own. A born storyteller, Dovlatov usually required an anecdote as a nucleus for a piece of fiction: an official funeral oration delivered over the wrong corpse, convicted thieves and rapists made to play Lenin and other Soviet "saints" in a prison camp's amateur theater, an old party faithful who turns virulently anti-Soviet when he thinks that he is dying, only to return to his old loyal ways after recovery—it is the rare Dovlatov story that does not contain an absurdist situation of this kind. He even published, in *Solo na Undervude* (Solo for Underwood—that being the brand name of the author's old American typewriter), a collection of jokes and anecdotes heard or observed; publication of the notebook of a living author (which in effect this was) is quite uncommon in Soviet literature.

It is obvious that Dovlatov's great model was Chekhov, whose process of creation—going from sketched anecdote to carefully crafted short story—was essentially the same as his own. Dovlatov's other literary mentors were those twentieth-century American short-story masters whose works were widely translated and read in

the post-Stalinist 1950–1960s, Dovlatov's formative years: from Sherwood Anderson, Faulkner, and Hemingway to John O'Hara, Cheever, and Updike. To Dovlatov's Russian readers, his style—with its irony, understatement, and ostensibly emotionless tone—as well as his constant motifs of macho self-pity and drunken rebellion against a conformist society bear the recognizable imprint of *amerikanskaya proza* (American fiction). The latter features explain, incidentally, why Dovlatov, who used language as colorful and subject matter as exotic as any other modern Russian writer, is more "translatable" than most of them: the psychological foundation of his prose is familiar to English-speaking readers.

For those readers Dovlatov's "satire with a light touch," as one reviewer described it, is a refreshing change from the heavier black humor of some of his contemporaries—Vladimir Voinovich, for example. But the casual, offhand manner, the anecdotal style, and the digressive, seemingly pointless drift of his stories are part of a carefully calculated art. Sally Laird observed, in the *Times Literary Supplement,* that "his books are always elegant; many of them often build on a symmetrical theme-and-variations form that has neatly served to schematize his disparate material." In *The Compromise* his persona, an unemployed Soviet journalist named Dovlatov, reviews his career in a series of stories, numbered from "The First Compromise" to "The Eleventh Compromise." Each begins with a brief "news" item as the journalist officially reported it—bland and banal examples of the correct Communist party line—and proceeds to the real story behind the assignment: "Yellowed pages," he writes. "Ten years of lies and dissembling. And yet, some people stood behind them: conversations, feelings, things that actually happened. Not on the pages themselves but beyond them. It's a hard road from the reported facts to the truth." From the carefully engineered birth of a baby who is to symbolize a Soviet anniversary to a ludicrously botched funeral of "a Hero of Socialist Labor," Dovlatov pinpoints the absurdities of a repressive political system: "with a light, lyrical touch," Karen Rosenberg wrote in the *Nation,* "he sketches a society in which horrors are simply part of the scenery." In *The Zone* it is again the Dovlatov persona, now in America but recalling his experiences as a prison guard, who announces characteristically in an opening disclaimer: "The names, dates given here are all real. I invented only those details that were not essential. Therefore, any resemblance between the characters in this book and living people is intentional and malicious. And all the fictionalizing was unexpected and accidental." No disclaimer is needed for *Ours* (subtitled "A Russian

Family Album," it is a concise (133 pages), candid, often hilarious account of himself, his mother, father, uncles, aunts, cousins—"a mini-saga of the Russian psyche of today," Jerzy Kosinski wrote of it. The subtext of this little book, however, is dark—an uncle who has a small portrait of Solzhenitsyn hanging over the head of his bed ("He took it down whenever guests came"); Dovlatov's own imprisonment ("I don't much feel like writing about it in detail. I'll say only this about it: I didn't like being in jail"); his emigration with his mother, his wife and daughter having left earlier ("I didn't even ask my mother if she was ready to make the journey out with me. I was amazed to learn that there were families who took months to make up their minds, sometimes with tragic results"). Dovlatov left the Soviet Union with one valise, containing a few personal possessions and some unpublished writings. Eight of his Leningrad stories were eventually collected and translated as *The Suitcase*, but just as the book was going to press, he died unexpectedly at the age of forty-eight.

He was also the author of three novellas, as yet untranslated into English. Two of them were published as books: *Zapovednik* (The National Park, 1983) and *Inostranka* (A Lady Foreigner, 1986), and the third, *Filial* (The Branch Office, 1987), was serialized in an emigré magazine.

WORKS IN ENGLISH TRANSLATION: Katherine O'Connor and Diana Burgin translated *The Invisible Book* in 1979. Ann Frydman translated *The Compromise* in 1983, *The Zone: A Prison Camp Guard's Story* in 1985, and *Ours: A Russian Family Album* in 1989. Antonina W. Bouis translated *The Suitcase* in 1990.

ABOUT: Brown, E. Russian Literature since the Revolution, 1982; Contemporary Authors 115, 1985; Modern Encyclopedia of Russian and Soviet Literature 5, 1981. *Periodicals*—Harper's Summer 1983; Nation November 5, 1983; New York Times August 25, 1990; New York Times Book Review August 30, 1983; October 27, 1985; April 30, 1989; Slavic and East European Journal Winter 1984; Times Literary Supplement February 12, 1988.

DREW, ELIZABETH (November 16, 1935–), American journalist, was born in Cincinnati, the second of two children of William J. Brenner, a furniture manufacturer, and Estelle Jacobs Brenner. Drew had a conventional midwestern upbringing, attended the local schools, and enrolled in Wellesley College in 1953. At Wellesley she majored in political science and graduated Phi Beta Kappa in 1957. Surprising as it may seem, Drew's long and distinguished career as a political journalist has

ELIZABETH DREW

been something of an accident. Drew has said that most of her classmates at Wellesley got married shortly after graduation or took any job that offered itself until marriage and that she herself seemed to fall into the latter category. For two years after college she worked as a secretary in Cambridge, Massachussetts before getting a lucky break on a small Boston magazine, *The Writer*. Still not intending to become a writer, she worked as an editorial assistant, a position considered acceptable for women at that time. After two years with *The Writer*, she moved to Washington, where she had once spent a memorable summer as a college intern on Capitol Hill. From 1959 to 1964 Drew worked for *Congressional Quarterly*, beginning as a temporary office assistant and ending up as a senior editor. The experience proved invaluable. "I learned how to read a bill, understand the federal budget—all the technicalities of how the Congressional system really works," she told *Publishers Weekly* in 1979. Drawing on this newly acquired expertise, Drew spent the next three years writing free-lance articles for the *New York Times Magazine*, the *New Republic* and other publications on such subjects as gun control, the cigarette lobby, and public housing. Now an experienced journalist and Washington insider, Drew was hired by the *Atlantic* in 1967 as its Washington editor.

While continuing to write articles for the *Atlantic* on an ever broader array of subjects (e.g. the medical lobby, the Army Corps of Engineers, hunger in America), Drew branched out into broadcast journalism. Her first broadcasting endeavor was *Thirty Minutes With . . .* , a weekly, prime-time interview program which ran on public television from January 1971 to June 1973. Drew's "guests" included Edmund Muskie, George McGovern, Indira Gandhi, and then-governor of California Ronald Reagan, all of whom were treated respectfully but not slavishly. It was generally agreed that Drew was a most effective television interviewer and in 1973 she received the Alfred I. duPont–Columbia University Award for her "informed and incisive" questioning.

Drew left the *Atlantic* in 1973 and joined the staff of the *New Yorker*, where, at the suggestion of editor William Shawn, she began to keep a journal of the momentous events then unfolding in the nation's capitol. These dramatic dispatches were to form the basis of *Washington Journal: The Events of 1973–1974*, still considered one of the best books about Watergate. Drew began the journal on September 4, 1973, about five months after the first in a series of major revelations about the break-in at the Democratic party headquarters had begun to shake the Nixon White House. It was already clear to Drew in the first journal entry that "our Constitutional system [was] being tested," yet one of the virtues of her book is that it shows how uncertain the outcome was until the very end of that epochal period. When the full extent of President Nixon's involvement in the cover-up was revealed in the transcript of a tape released on August 5, 1974, Drew describes the shock that a nation felt:

There is an inexplicable difference between the experiences of suspecting a lie and being whacked in the face with the evidence of one. Many Americans had become accustomed to thinking of the President as a liar, and had alternately suspended belief in, scoffed at, or become enraged at his statements. But I wonder whether the enormity of his lying has sunk in yet —whether we have, or can, come to terms with the thought that so much of what he said to us was just noise, words, and that we can no longer begin by accepting any of it as the truth.

Washington Journal ends, fittingly, on August 9, 1974, the day that Richard Nixon tearfully bade goodbye to his staff and became the first president of the United States to resign his office.

Again at the urging of William Shawn, Drew kept a journal for the *New Yorker* of the political events of 1976, focusing on the Bicentennial celebration and Jimmy Carter's defeat of Gerald Ford in the less-than-inspiring presidential campaign of that year. The result was *American Journal: The Events of 1976*, a chronicle that inevitably lacked the immediacy and drama of Drew's Watergate reporting. *American Journal* also marked the beginning of a critical divide among Drew's readers. In one camp were those who admired her methodically researched re-

porting, her concentration on political events from the inside, and her circumspection in making judgments about political figures; in the other were those who faulted her writing for almost the very same reasons. In the latter camp was Richard Reeves, who complained that *American Journal* was "without passion; chances are not taken; it is edited as if readers had no other sources of information, sometimes reducing copy to a style reminiscent of 'see Spot run.'" Godfrey Hodgson was in the opposite camp. For him *American Journal* was "one of the more intelligent and readable books I have ever read about an American presidential election, written by a reporter who combines, in a way that is sadly rare, access to accurate information about what is going on with some sense of what this means to those who are not insiders."

It is also noteworthy that Drew's critics tend to divide along ideological lines. This was especially true of the reaction to her third book, *Senator*, in which she followed for ten days Senator John C. Culver, a liberal Democrat from Iowa (subsequently defeated in his bid for reelection in 1980), as he met with constituents and reporters, planned strategy with aides, flew to Iowa for meetings with local officials and voters and a brief respite with his family, and returned to Washington to push through a modified version of the Endangered Species Act. Drew gives an almost blow-by-blow account of Culver's impossibly hectic comings and goings and she portrays the legislative process in all its tedious and fascinating detail. Nor does she make a secret of her admiration for Culver, who impresses her as "a man with firm principles and beliefs who is also a practical politician—one who gets in there and does the hard work of legislating, of putting together coalitions, of mediating among the conflicting interests in this country, of making the whole thing go." Writing in the conservative *Commentary*, Joseph W. Bishop, Jr. derided both Culver for his "protypical [sic] Left-Liberal" stance and Drew for her "worshipful tone." Yet even Drew's admirers on the other end of the political spectrum seriously questioned her judgment in seeming to write so uncritically of Culver. Robert Sherrill put it rather bluntly in the *New York Times Book Review*. "My, my," he wrote, "this is certainly a beautiful big valentine. Which is O.K. with me. But when a reporter of Mrs. Drew's caliber carves her initials on the tree with 'J.C.C.,' I expect to be supplied some persuasive reasons. Very few are in evidence here." Nevertheless, Sherrill agreed with the near-unanimous opinion that the book gave "probably a very accurate impression of the day-to-day life of any member of Congress."

With *Portrait of an Election: The 1980 Presidential Campaign*, Drew returned to the descriptive, narrative style of her first two books. *Portrait of an Election* and its successor, *Campaign Journal: The Political Events of 1983–1984*, received mixed reviews, to some extent reflecting the ideological biases of Drew's critics. Yet reviewers of quite different political persuasions bemoaned what they considered an increasing lack of selectivity in Drew's writing. This charge was leveled especially against *Campaign Journal*, a book of nearly eight hundred pages. The problem, wrote Eileen Shanahan in the *Washington Post Book World*, is that "the book is, quite simply, much too long, much too daily, much too full of minutiae that have lost whatever importance they may once have had. Is there really any point in our knowing now whether pollster Patrick Caddell was in or out of the Hart campaign's inner circle in a given week?" Still, both books were characteristic of Drew's unflashy, painstaking approach to politics, and to critics like Tom J. Farer in the *New York Review of Books,* such an approach was its own reward. Speaking of the earlier book, Farer said, "Drew neither makes claims to special insight, nor attempts to give a general analysis, and she writes with such unself-conscious grace that the election story, from the first primary to Reagan's victory, seems almost to tell itself. Nevertheless, her *Portrait* contributes generously to our sense of what actually happens in the frantic comedy of contemporary political life."

In between these two big books Drew published a much briefer and very different one, *Politics and Money: The New Road to Corruption.* Unusually impassioned for Drew, *Politics and Money* is a protest against the role that money plays in contemporary politics. Drew believes that this role is "different both in scope and in nature from anything that has gone before," and in her closely reasoned analysis she shows how the financial influence of special interest groups, political action committees, lawyer-lobbyists, as well as ineffective campaign-finance laws and an enfeebled Federal Election Commission have endangered the very idea of representative government. Drew concludes the book by offering several proposals that she believes would restore the democratic process to the people. The most important of these are the public financing of congressional campaigns, and, since television advertising is the most expensive commodity in any campaign, the allotment of free broadcasting time to all candidates. It was not to be expected that conservatives would approve of such a book and indeed Robert J. Samuelson wrote an eight-page article in the *New Republic* in which he attempted to show

that Drew's "argument fails—utterly" and even that the spending limitations that she and other campaign reformers advocate strike at the basic right of free speech. Reviewers closer to Drew's liberal viewpoint, however, were sufficiently convinced. "*Politics and Money,*" wrote Morton Mintz in the *Washington Post Book World*, "is the best single contemporary work of reporting and commentary in its field, partly because Drew's opinions emerge as if by iron logic out of her reporting."

In all of this time Drew had not scanted her broadcasting career. In 1973 she became a commentator of public television's *Agronsky & Company* and she has appeared periodically as a panelist on *Meet the Press* and *Face the Nation.* She had the distinction of being chosen as one of the three questioners in the first of the Ford/Carter debates in 1976, although her doubts about the value of those debates are expressed in *Campaign Journal.* Drew's commentary for public television during the Iran-Contra hearings earned her acclaim in the summer of 1987. The *Christian Science Monitor* noted that Drew and her colleagues Judy Woodruff and Cokie Roberts were "being hailed as the only straightforward, no-nonsense commentary in town, shorn of the breathless wonderment for which the commercial networks have been criticized."

Elizabeth Drew's numerous awards and honors include a Literary Lion Award from the New York Public Library (1985), an award for excellence from the Society of Magazine Writers (1971), a Wellesley Alumnae Achievement Award (1973), as well as honorary degrees from Yale, Williams, Georgetown, and other universities. Her first husband, J. Patterson Drew, a Washington lawyer whom she married in 1964, committed suicide in 1970. Since 1981 she has been married to David Webster. Aside from glancing references to her fondness for gardening and tennis, Drew reveals little of herself in her writing. She told *Contemporary Authors* that she tries to keep her balance and her sanity "by taking breaks, getting out of Washington, traveling out of the country, to the extent that's possible . . . I make it a point to lead as normal a life as I can."

PRINCIPAL WORKS: Washington Journal: The Events of 1973–1974, 1975; American Journal: The Events of 1976, 1977; Senator, 1979; Portrait of an Election: The 1980 Presidential Campaign, 1981; Politics and Money: The New Road to Corruption, 1983; Campaign Journal: The Political Events of 1983–1984, 1985; Election Journal: Political Events of 1987–1988, 1989.

ABOUT: American Women Writers 1, 1979; Contemporary Authors 104, 1982; Current Biography, 1979; Who's Who in America, 1986–87. *Periodicals*—Book World September 25, 1977; September 4, 1983; March 17, 1985; Christian Science Monitor July 26, 1987; Commentary October 1979; New Republic September 5, 1983; New York Review of Books January 21, 1982; New York Times Book Review September 11, 1977; May 13, 1979; Publishers Weekly May 7, 1979.

DUBIE, NORMAN (EVANS, JR.) (April 10, 1945–), American poet, was born in Barre, Vermont, the son of Norman Evans Dubie, a businessman and later a clergyman, and Doris Dubie, a registered nurse. He recalled in an interview published in 1978 in *American Poetry Review* various ways in which nineteenth-century modes of life—with their, for him, inevitable literary associations—influenced his own 1950s childhood: "While we lived on this peninsula off Bath, Maine, we were in another culture and in another time. There were still kerosene lanterns in the houses of the fishermen. Many houses were without electricity and their ways were dated too. Also, leaving that peninsula was hard. There I was, a twelve-year-old, realizing I had a longing for this place that shouldn't have existed at all. I would never again find the 19th century. Anyway I was really being raised in the manner of the 19th century, where it was a popular convention to bother children with great literature. . . . I write a narrative poem often, and I'm confident that I employ many of the strategies of a Chekhov, a Turgenev, or Thomas Mann; those three were perhaps most important to me."

Dubie attended Goddard College in Plainfield, Vermont, taking his bachelor's degree in 1969, and obtained a master's degree in fine arts in 1971 from the University of Iowa, where he was a member of the Writers' Workshop. He was subsequently lecturer at the workshop (1971–1974) and taught in the English departments of Ohio University (1974–1975) and Arizona State University, in the latter successively as writer-in-residence (1975–1976), lecturer (1976–1983), and professor of English (1983 on). He was director of the graduate writing program there from 1976 to 1977. In 1977 Dubie traveled in Mexico on a Guggenheim fellowship.

Dubie's first collection of poetry appeared in 1969 under the title *The Horsehair Sofa*. Some of the poems contained in that small volume were the only translations he has so far published, several lyrics by the Soviet poet Osip Mandelstam. Imitation continued as his main source of inspiration in his longer second volume "I took to John Berryman early on," he said in 1978, "and it was his masterpiece, *Homage to*

NORMAN DUBIE

Mistress Bradstreet, that won me over. My affection for Berryman perhaps did a great harm to me as I was writing *The Alehouse Sonnets*. I think that book is imitative . . . people imitate Berryman all the time." The fifty poems are Dubie's attempt, using a rigorously adhered-to fifteen-line sonnet form, to combine and merge his own experience with what is known of the biography of the early-nineteenth-century English critic William Hazlitt. In these poems he sometimes seems to be addressing Hazlitt, sometimes to be taking on his personality, although the narrator's exact persona is never fixed, or even fixable. There is much reference made to some of the in-jokes of English literary history (four of the poems are entitled "Sonnets from the Portsmouth Geese") and there is throughout a fair amount of "Romantic" poetic diction. At their best, the sonnets convey a fondness for and familiarity with their testy subject and an insistent desire to impose order upon a novel literary experiment. A simple example is the second of the two poems entitled "Noli Me Tangere":

> We are nude so that our clothes may dry,
> reading the *New Eloise* at the inn at Llangollen;
> sucking a bottle of sherry, and a cold chicken.
> You say that Wordsworth first awakened you
> to the beauty of a sunset. You're mixing
> your metaphors, again.
> And what am I doing here with you
> in this cold inn. You can have your China orange.
>
> William, I want to return to Vermont
> and walk three miles to a winter farmhouse.
> In January, in Vermont, no one thinks
> to criticize a hedgerow or blank mile,
> And furthermore within this farmhouse,

there's a friend, a Jew, who awakened me
to you; and sure, why not, to winter sunsets also.

Dubie's next major collection, *In the Dead of
the Night*, marked a liberation of form and a
widening of subject matter. This is a very rich
and disparate group of thirty-eight poems, of
which few are sonnets and some run well over
a hundred lines. The poet attempts, in a much
more pervasive and generous way than in the
previous collection, the imaginative projection
of his personality into those of other people, often such famous ones as Paul Klee, Thomas
Traherne, Paul Eluard, Charles Baudelaire, or
the Russian futurist Vladimir Mayakovsky, as in
this excerpt, from "Anima Poeta. A Christmas
Entry for the Suicide, Mayakovsky":

. . . Think of yourself with your black fingers
In the flowerpots, in the candlelight,
The double violets and scarlet Anthus
Of a narrow window.
You were trying
To remember the French word
For a hedgerow sparrow that soldiers
Made captive for its song. You thought
The kingfisher
Was so slow when in the vicinity of winter
That even a bureaucrat
Would distinguish all its colors. Mayakovsky,
You watched a snail one afternoon eat twice
Its length in brooklime.
When you were young

You could list all the birds of passage,
Much later in your life you joined them.

Some critics, such as Sandra M. Gilbert in
Poetry, objected to the demanding erudition revealed in these poems and found Dubie's brand
of poetry "so elaborately learned and/or metaphysical that I'm left feeling completely inferi-
or. . . . When I read such verse I close the book,
thick-headed with fatigue." She concluded,
however, that "when he resists the temptation to
rely upon erudition rather than vision, his poetry
is striking, accurate, visionary." And Paul Ramsey, in the *Sewanee Review*, found the "obscure
essencing images" of the poems in *In the Dead
of the Night* "packed with varied detail [that
gives] a strong sense of complex and completed
structure." In such poems, he suggested,
"coherent narrative or understanding is impossible because experience is too mysterious."

The poet gave an account of his preference for
this kind of poetry in his 1978 *American Poetry
Review* interview. He writes narrative poems
and likes to put himself in others' shoes:
"Because I'm reluctant to be myself in my poems
and to speak about my life [and] because I don't
have the instinct to be autobiographical, I have
to acquire another kind of authority. So I did discover early on that I could adopt a persona and
then, somehow, superimpose my life, my primary voice, against the endearment of this adopted
persona, and arrive at a transcending voice that
doesn't really conform to the idea of what a persona is, as we know it, say, in the work of Robert
Browning."

In *The Everlastings*, the poet's imagination is
again most fired by his reverence for the past, by
his fascination for stories never fully told, or by
those that his active imagination can expand
upon. "The Composer's Winter Dream" is a series of sharp vignettes surrounding the death of
Beethoven, in which the composer imagines a
Viennese Christmas:

. . . In the sinks the gall bladders
Of geese are soaking in cold salted water.
Walking in the storm this evening, he passed
Children in rags, singing carols; they were roped togeth-
er
In the drifting snow outside the palace gates.
He knew he would remember those boys' faces.

The soaking goose gall bladders and roped-
together children are touches only a poet with a
vivid and accurate historical imagination could
bring to the recreation of an historical event. In
"There Is a Dream Dreaming Us" the reader is
asked to reflect on what the reality must have
been for the last one left alive of a retinue of
slaves buried with a dead Egyptian pharaoh:

I am alone as I had planned.
I'm a girl who was favored in the market by the King.
I've eaten the grapes that the slaves carried in for him:
If someone breaks into this tomb in a future time how
Will they explain the dead having spit grape seeds
Onto a carpet that was scented with jasmine?
The arrogance of the living never had a better monu-
ment
Than in me. I am going to sleep
In a bed that was hammered out of gold for a boy
Who was Pharaoh and King of Egypt. . . .

This clearly is a poetry which has as its core
the beauty and mystery of the historical moment
deftly recaptured. Once again, the collection
aroused diametrically opposed critical opinions.
"His poems," wrote Katha Pollitt in the *Nation*,
"are highly erudite, or perhaps recondite is a
better word, . . . at once mannered and hallucinatory, histrionic and elliptic, they are surrealist
costume dramas in which *something* of great urgency seems to be communicated—but with
each new book it becomes harder to say
what. . . . I found most of *The Everlastings*
incomprehensible." But Peter Stitt in the
Georgia Review admired the mystery and allusiveness: "The suppleness of Dubie's imaginative
intellect is complemented by his wonderful abilities to turn a phrase and tell a story. His mind

is enormously inventive; over and over we find enticing images practically tumbling over one another in their rush to get onto the page, into the poem."

Dubie's *Selected and New Poems* reprints work from some of his previously published collections, along with a dozen new poems. This collection showed that he had changed little as a poet over the years: there was always in his work the same easy empathy for unusual historical circumstances, the same almost grim seriousness of purpose. There is much meditating on death, final things, and, even in the new poems, as little laughter and joy as ever, as in "To a Young Woman Dying at Weir":

> . . . Sometimes her spirit grows and she remembers
> A mountain dulcimer being played
> While a woman sews. When the fear is largest
> She remembers the old hermit poling his boat
> Back along the cooling pond, he's taken burlap bags
> Of the whitest sand from the cove
> For plastering the walls of his autumn shack:
> This comforts her,
>   errand and prospect,
> A freshened sense of snow
> Feathering over the frozen pond. She says
>   in a hush
> That she loves something she has not found.

Dubie in his 1978 interview acknowledged the darkness palpable in his poetry, surmising that it comes from "the manner of a Romantic tradition which I certainly belong to."

Something of a break with long-established poetic norms was apparent for the first time in *The Springhouse*. These thirty poems are more lyrical in inspiration than any of his previous work; some, in their brevity and imagistic intensity, seem almost haiku-like. There is much less evidence here of his previously characteristic and jealously defended historical imagination, and more recounting of direct poetic experiences, even those of his own childhood. There are even glimpses of something quite new for Dubie, an unalloyed curiosity about and even a certain delight taken in nature, as in "Hummingbirds":

> They have made a new statement
> About our world—a clerk in Memphis
> Has confessed to laying out feeders
> Filled with sulphuric acid. She says
>
> God asked for these deaths . . . like God
> They are insignificant, and have visited us
>
> Who are wretched.

Yet even here, evidently, there is the darkly cautionary at the center of his vision. Life has little in it of the joyful, and Dubie does not write about even being surprised by happiness; of suf-

fering and the macabre, however, he has become, in poetic terms, past master. *The Springhouse*, to Jorie Graham, writing in the *New York Times Book Review*, "is concerned with compassion—how, as a form of reunion with the world, it saves while reason and knowledge fail. The act of imagination itself is seen as an act of compassion, perhaps the ultimate one."

Norman Dubie has a daughter, Hannah, from his first marriage, in 1968, to Francesca Stafford. They were divorced in 1973, and in 1978 he married the poet Pamela Stewart. After their divorce in 1980 he married the poet Jeannine Savard in 1981. They live in Tempe, Arizona. In 1989 Dubie told James Green, in an interview for the *American Poetry Review*, that he was working on a trilogy of lyric poems, of which *The Springhouse* and the more recently published *Groom Falconer* are the first two parts. Questioned by green about his fascination for "three-part invention"—many of his earlier books having been divided into three sections—Dubie replied: "I think it's sort of an *eccentric* rendering of properties that we've found traditionally in poems that argue. I'm thinking of 'turn, counter-turn, and stand,' which is the patterning of emotions and thoughts perhaps in my individual poems as well as in my books."

PRINCIPAL WORKS: The Horsehair Sofa, 1969; The Alehouse Sonnets, 1971; Indian Summer, 1974; The Prayers of the North American Martyrs, 1975; Popham of the New Song and Other Poems, 1975; In the Dead of the Night, 1975; The Illustrations, 1977; A Thousand Little Things and Other Poems, 1978; Odalisque in White, 1978; The City of the Olesha Fruit, 1979; The Everlastings, 1980; Window in the Field, 1981; Selected and New Poems, 1983; (with Robert Cornfield and William MacKay) Dance Writings, 1986; The Springhouse, 1986; Groom Falconer, 1989.

ABOUT: Contemporary Authors New Revision Series 12, 1984; Contemporary Literary Criticism 36, 1986; Contemporary Poets, 4th ed., 1985. *Periodicals*—American Book Review December 1977; American Poetry Review July–August 1978, May–June 1982, September–October 1984; November–December 1989; Book World August 19, 1979; Choice April 1976, December 1977; Georgia Review Spring 1980, Fall 1980, Summer 1984; Library Journal December 15, 1975; February 15, 1977; May 15, 1980; November 1, 1983; April 1, 1986; Nation July 5, 1980; New York Review of Books April 29, 1982; New York Times Book Review April 15, 1984; September 28, 1986; Parnassus 1980; Poetry August 1976, August 1978, November 1984; Sewanee Review Summer 1976, Yale Review Spring 1976.

DURANG, CHRISTOPHER (FERDI-NAND) (January 2, 1949–   ), American playwright, was born in Montclair, New Jersey, the only child of Francis Ferdinand Durang, an architect, and Patricia Elizabeth Durang. He was brought up in Berkeley Heights, like Montclair an upper-middle-class New Jersey town, and for twelve years was educated in Roman Catholic parochial schools. His first play, a two-page adaptation of the having-the-baby episode of *I Love Lucy*, was—somewhat unaccountably, he feels, given the nuns' general prudishness about all matters dealing with human reproduction—put on by his second-grade class. He was, by his own account, a devout and well-behaved pupil. By his mid-teens he had become politically militant, taking part in protests against U.S. involvement in Vietnam. Uncertain as to whether to enter the monastery straight from his Benedictine prep school, he chose instead to go to Harvard, becoming a freshman in 1967.

Durang immediately sought out whatever Roman Catholic society that a secular university might offer, but those Catholics he found did not appeal to him. "I assumed," he told Chet Flippo in an interview for *New York* magazine in 1982, "that I would find all these radical Catholics all over the place, like the Berrigans. I just presumed that's who'd be at Harvard. The Catholic society I found there was very traditional and very kind of clubby. I really hated it. And found it stultifying." In short order, by the end of his freshman year, he left the church: "I stopped believing for all the various reasons one does stop believing." He then entered upon a period of personal crisis: "I just sort of didn't do anything. Just went to the movies obsessively." He stayed in his room, failed to attend classes, but faithfully performed his college job, which he had been assigned to help pay for his board: for two hours a day, five days a week, he cleaned bathrooms, work he later claimed to find "very contemplative." This peculiar secular version of the monastic existence ended in his senior year, after a course in playwriting with William Alfred. On the strength of one play, *The Nature and Purpose of the Universe*, he was accepted at Yale Drama School. In this play, one of his suburban satires, a housewife suffering at the hands of her brutally cruel family is offered deliverance from her misery by a heavenly messenger in the form of a Fuller Brush salesman. When she is finally able to welcome death by sacrifice as an end to her misery, she is spared by a "God of Gods" who declares Himself "merciful." The one-act plays ends with the housewife screaming, "I don't want to live. Please kill me. Kill me!" This play eventually received a New York production in 1979, but was first staged at Smith

CHRISTOPHER DURANG

College, Northampton, Massachusetts, in 1971. "My mother brought some of her friends to see it," Durang told Flippo. "After they saw it, their faces were so funny to see. They really looked as if they had both just been slapped and as if someone had come up and defecated right in front of them. It made me sort of giddy."

The young playwright found the Yale Drama School a relatively productive experience. No fewer than seven of his short works were staged there, including *The Idiots Karamazov*, one of three plays he wrote with his classmate Albert Innaurato. This sendup of the Dostoevsky novel was produced at the Yale Repertory Theater in 1974, with another Yale classmate, Meryl Streep, in the pivotal role of the translator Constance Garnett and with Durang himself in the role of the saintly Alyosha. Another success in New Haven, which went on to be staged in New York in 1976, was *Das Lusitania Songspiel*, a parody of a Brecht-Weill revue which he had co-written and performed with yet another drama school classmate, Sigourney Weaver. "One of the conceits of the piece," the playwright explained in *Hollywood Drama-logue* for 1982, "is we played a couple who thought they were Brecht experts. She was in an evening gown and I was in a tuxedo. We had all our facts wrong. . . . Some of [it] is a satire on Brecht and some of it just uses the structure to go off onto other topics." New York reviews of the piece, which in its 1976 version appeared on a double bill with the author's *Titanic*, a parody of disaster films, were uniformly good. Clive Barnes, who saw the revised and expanded version produced in 1980 with the same principals, called it "very good . . . and deliciously outrageous. . . . For my money these two are as funny as Nichols and May." One final collaboration with a classmate should be noted. With Wendy Wasserstein, Durang wrote the revue *When Dinah Shore Ruled the Earth*, which received a performance at the Yale Cabaret.

The two-act play *The Vietnamization of New Jersey*, another suburban satire by Durang, was produced by the Yale Repertory Theater in 1977. It makes fun of the anguished anti–Vietnam War dramas that were then fashionable and frequently encountered, and tells about the bizarre welcome home offered a veteran and his Vietnamese wife by his violent and unpleasant family in New Jersey. At about the same time, *A History of the American Film* was receiving regional productions at the Hartford Stage Company, the Arena Stage in Washington, and the Mark Taper Forum in Los Angeles. Durang in this play attempts to recapitulate American cinematic history: five typical moviegoers, who occasionally also portray movie actors, take part in watching and enacting several classic films, proceeding from the innocence of the early days of Hollywood to the intense self-absorption of the contemporary cinema. The play's regional productions received excellent reviews, but, as the author explained later, "things didn't come together on Broadway. . . . My rewrites went off-kilter, the ANTA Theater was much too large for us, and . . . the reviewers were cranky and harsher on the show than I felt it deserved, flawed though it was." Indeed, John Simon in *New York* magazine called the play "bloated, . . . drawn out and overproduced, . . . self-indulgent, repetitious, and sophomoric."

The playwright's mild expression of regret at this failure conceals what several of his friends described as his devastation and ensuing deep depression. This was compounded by the slow death from cancer of his mother, which occurred in 1979. He recalls in the introduction to the collection of six of his plays, *Christopher Durang Explains It All for You*, how his mother tried and failed during her protracted agony "to use her Catholic religion to help her face death and find some comfort." Watching this brought back "recollections of the doctrines I had been taught." During the last year of his mother's life he began his most successful, famous, and controversial play, *Sister Mary Ignatius Explains It All for You*, concluding it a few months after her death. "I was nostalgic for belief," he recalls, "since it offered comfort, and yet I was also made angry by the illogic of the Church's muddy teachings on how suffering fits into God's Grand Plan. From thoughts on suffering I

moved on to remembering the dizzying intricacies of some of the dogma—limbo, the Immaculate Conception, mortal and venial sin, papal infallibility, etc. Because ten years had passed since I'd thought about all this, I felt like a tourist in my own past, and what I'd accepted as a child and forgotten about as a young adult now seemed on a new viewing as the sincere ravings of a semi-lunatic."

The semi-lunatic became personified in Sister Mary Ignatius, a teaching nun for whom the quirky and, by her only half understood, dogmatic tenets of pre–Vatican Council II Roman Catholicism are a source of glorious certainty in a profoundly corrupt world. She veers dizzily from stern reprimands to rewards of cookies for a good recitation of the catechism to assurances of eternal damnation in hell for many, including Zsa Zsa Gabor, Brooke Shields, Betty Comden and Adolph Green. The ultimate gangster nun, she is not only arbitrary and extremely authoritarian, she is also, as is evident by the end of the play, quite insane—she shoots and kills two of her former pupils who return to her classroom to dispute the simplistic and ultimately destructive nature of her teaching.

The play caused a furor among traditionalist Roman Catholics. Richard Gilman, a convert to the church, reviewing the play in the *Nation*, called it tasteless, vicious, and splenetic. The archbishop of St. Louis, John May, who like many traditionalist critics never actually saw the play, condemned it as a "vicious diatribe . . . [that] caricatures and ridicules every Catholic doctrine and every Catholic virtue." Most critics, however, appreciated the play as a consistently funny piece of very effective theatre. Although it was only moderately successful in its original showcase production (beginning in December 1979 at Ensemble Studio Theater), another production opened in October 1981 to great critical praise; the play enjoyed an extremely successful thirty-month run Off-Broadway. It won Durang an Obie award for best Off-Broadway play of its year.

Sister Mary Ignatius was the iconoclastic playwright's unique *succès de scandale* ; his succeeding plays enjoyed no such accolades during the rest of the 1980s. *Beyond Therapy*, a farce about psychotherapy, was called "delightful" by Brendan Gill in the *New Yorker*, but all other critics savaged it and its run on Broadway in the spring of 1982 was very brief. (It subsequently became an unsuccessful film, directed by Robert Altman with a screenplay by Durang.) *Baby with the Bathwater*, on the insanities of parenthood, was moderately well received on its short Off-Broadway run in the fall of 1983. *The Marriage* of *Bette and Boo* had a two-month run in 1985 at Joseph Papp's New York Shakespeare Festival-Public Theater. A bitter, only intermittently funny vision of American marriage and parenthood, it features onstage deaths from cancer and stroke. Durang, who performed in the play as Bette's son, Matt, received an Obie for his acting, but the play was poorly received by virtually all the New York critics. Frank Rich, in the *New York Times*, described Durang's "special knack for wrapping life's horrors in the primary colors of absurdist comedy. . . . His jokemaking is becoming more mannered and repetitive—an automatic, almost compulsive reflex. [The play] has a strangely airless atmosphere, and it says little the author hasn't said with greater wit and emotional ferocity before." Two further plays, *Laughing Wild* and *For Whom the Belle Tolls*, received regional productions in 1987 but were not brought on to New York.

Durang told *Newsday* in 1986 that he has come to consider himself an Off-Broadway playwright: "I used to feel that I was an Off-Broadway playwright who might flukishly have a success on Broadway. Now I feel that that's less likely and that all the doomsayers about Broadway are right. Broadway seems to have room for one or two comedies a year if Mike Nichols directs them and if there's a star or two, and even then they just barely make it. And then there are musicals, particularly if there's no plot and it looks like a Las Vegas show. And then a play, perhaps, by Peter Schaffer. And that's it. I don't see anything else there at all. It's really depressing."

PRINCIPAL WORKS: A History of the American Film, 1978; The Vietnamization of New Jersey: An American Tragedy, 1978; The Nature and Purpose of the Universe; Death Comes to Us All, Mary Agnes; 'dentity Crisis, 1979; (with Albert Innaurato) The Idiots Karamazov, 1981; Sister Mary Ignatius Explains It All for You and The Actor's Nightmare, 1982; Christopher Durang Explains It All for You (six plays: The Nature . . . , 'dentity Crisis, Titanic, The Actor's Nightmare, Sister Mary Ignatius . . . , Beyond Therapy), 1983; Baby with the Bathwater, 1984; The Marriage of Bette and Boo, 1985.

ABOUT: Contemporary Authors 105, 1982; Contemporary Literary Criticism 27, 1984; 38, 1986; Current Biography 1987. *Periodicals*—America December 26, 1981; American Film September 1977, April 1983; Backstage June 10, 1988; Commonweal January 29, 1982; Dramatists Guild Quarterly Summer 1986; Film Comment January–February 1982; Hollywood Drama-logue September 30–October 6, 1982; Interview October 1982; Nation April 15, 1978; December 11, 1981; February 18, 1984; New Republic April 22, 1978; December 9, 1981; New York April 17, 1978; March 15, 1982; June 7, 1982; November 21, 1983;

June 3, 1985; New York Newsday July 31, 1986; New York Post January 11, 1980; November 9, 1983; May 17, 1985; New York Times November 11, 1974; May 11, 1976; February 13, 1977; March 21, 1977; February 8, 1980; January 6, 1981; October 22, 1981; December 8, 1981; May 23, 1982; November 9, 1983; May 17, 1985; May 26, 1985; June 25, 1985; November 17, 1985; September 4, 1987; Saturday Review May 27, 1978; Theater Spring 1978; Time May 23, 1977; Village Voice December 2–8, 1981; November 10, 1987.

DYSON, FREEMAN J(OHN) (December 15, 1923–), American physicist and writer, writes: "The world of science and the world of literature have much in common. Each is an international club, helping to tie mankind together across barriers of nationality, race and language. I have been doubly lucky, being accepted as a member of both. As a scientist I have professional friends and colleagues, people I know and feel at home with, in thirty countries around the earth. As a writer I have pen-friends, people who write me eloquent and personal letters, spread over an equally wide range. It is wonderful to discover that, in this age which is supposed to be dominated by television and computers, people still read books and write letters.

"My mother used to say that life begins at forty. That was her age when she had her first baby. I say, on the contrary, that life begins at fifty-five, the age at which I published my first book. So long as you have courage and a sense of humor, it is never too late to start life afresh. A book is in many ways like a baby. While you are writing, it is curled up in your belly. You cannot get a clear view of it. As soon as it is born, it goes out into the world and develops a character of its own. Like a daughter coming home from school, it surprises you with unexpected flashes of wisdom. The same thing happens with scientific theories. You sit quietly gestating them, for nine months or whatever the required time may be, and then one day they are out on their own, not belonging to you any more but to the whole community of scientists. Whatever it is that you produce, a baby, a book, or a theory, it is a piece of the magic of creation. You are producing something that you do not fully understand. As you watch it grow, it becomes part of a larger world, and fits itself into a larger design than you imagined. You belong to the company of those medieval craftsmen who added a carved stone here or a piece of scaffolding there, and together built Chartres Cathedral.

"I was born in 1923 in Crowthorne, a village in the South of England without pretensions to scientific fame. My parents' interests were artis-

FREEMAN J. DYSON

tic and literary rather than scientific. My mother [Mildred Atkey Dyson] was a lawyer, my father [George Dyson] a musician. Our only connection with professional science was Sir Frank Dyson, who held the exalted position of Astronomer Royal. Sir Frank was not related to us, but he came from the same village in Yorkshire as my father. We were proud to share his name. His glory helped to turn my infant thoughts toward astronomy.

"When my mother died at the age of ninety-four, I found among her papers a long-forgotten manuscript, an unfinished novel with the title 'Sir Phillip Roberts's Ero-Lunar Collision,' which she had preserved among the relics of my childhood. I wrote it at the age of nine. My hero Sir Phillip is clearly based on Sir Frank Dyson, the literary style is borrowed from Jules Verne's story 'From Earth to Moon and a Trip Round it,' and the theme of a collision between the asteroid Eros and the Moon must have been suggested by the close approach of Eros to the Earth in the year 1931. Sir Phillip, having successfully predicted the collision by calculating the orbit of Eros ten years in advance, organizes an expedition to the Moon to observe the event in detail, just as Sir Frank had organized the expeditions to Africa and Brazil to observe the gravitational bending of light by the Sun during the solar eclipse of 1919. Unfortunately the narrative stops abruptly before Sir Phillip's expedition has left Earth. When I rediscovered this fragment forty-two years later, I was amused to see how little I had changed. I was a writer long before I became a scientist. And I was always in love with spaceships.

"I resumed my career as a writer in 1979 with a book called *Disturbing the Universe*, attempting to give to non-scientists a picture of the human passions, misadventures and dreams that constitute the life of a scientist. Another book, *Weapons and Hope*, appeared in 1984. It tries to put the big problems of war and peace into a humanly comprehensible framework. The people, after all, are more important than the weapons. In 1985 came *Origins of Life*, a slim volume explaining what we know and what we do not know about one of the central mysteries of science. In all my writing, the aim is to open windows, to let the experts inside the temple of science see out, and to let the ordinary citizens outside see in."

———

Freeman Dyson is one of a growing number of scientist-writers who have attempted, as he says of himself in *Disturbing the Universe*, "to describe to people who are not scientists the way the human situation looks to somebody who is a scientist." As a physicist working in the most complex and—to the lay reader—the most obscure of the sciences, and as an expert on nuclear warfare who has spoken out unequivocally on problems of international disarmament, Dyson writes with authority. As a humanist widely read in classical and modern literature, he also writes with skill and distinction and with a passionate belief that "because I live in two worlds, the world of the warriors and the world of the victims . . . I am possessed by an immodest hope that I may improve mankind's chance of escaping the horrors of nuclear holocaust if I can help these two worlds to understand and listen to each other."

Dyson came to this conviction through long experience in both theoretical science and practical action. A Cambridge undergraduate in the early years of World War II, he became a civilian technician with the Royal Air Force Bomber Command in 1941. Witnessing the bureaucratic bungling of the Command and the appalling loss of life, both military and civilian, he confronted the first of the many moral crises he would confront in his later career. "Bomber command was an early example of the new evil that science and technology have added to the old evils of soldiering," he wrote. "Technology has made evil anonymous. Through science and technology, evil is organized bureaucratically so that no individual is responsible for what happens."

Dyson returned to Cambridge for his B.A. in 1945. In 1947 he came to the United States on a Commonwealth Fellowship as a graduate student in physics at Cornell University. Los Alamos and the nuclear bomb were already history. Physicists who had worked on the project, among them Hans Bethe with whom Dyson was studying, were now working on quantum electrodynamics, trying to reconcile theories about the behavior of electrons into a general system of calculation. With his background in mathematics as well as in physics, Dyson solved this problem—the solution striking him, after months of effort, on a Greyhound bus trip in the West: "As we were driving across Nebraska on the third day, something suddenly happened. For two weeks I had not thought about physics, and now it came bursting into my consciousness like an explosion." Without pencil or paper, he put all the diagrams and equations together. "Then I knew that they all fitted." At Bethe's suggestion Dyson went for a year (1948–1949) to the Institute for Advanced Studies at Princeton to work with J. Robert Oppenheimer, who shared his sensitivity to the moral and ethical issues involved in their scientific research. He returned to the Institute in 1953, and although he has taught and worked elsewhere (Cornell, the University of Birmingham, the General Atomic Company of General Dynamics Corporation), the Institute has been his home base ever since. In 1957 he became a naturalized American citizen.

Dyson's research in space travel began in the late 1950s. On leave from the Institute in 1958 he worked on the Orion project which was to have developed a propulsion system for spacecraft through a series of precisely controlled atomic explosions. The project was ultimately abandoned, but Dyson has remained an enthusiast for space exploration, arguing, in *Disturbing the Universe,* that in addition to its potential for practical enhancement of the universe, there is a spiritual need for an open frontier in space: "The ultimate purpose of space travel is to bring to humanity, not only scientific discoveries and an occasional spectacular show on television, but a real expansion of our spirit." He sees the exploration of the universe not as an end in itself but as a beginning: "At the same time as life is extending its habitat quantitatively, it will also be changing and evolving qualitatively into new dimensions of mind and spirit that we cannot imagine."

Over the years Dyson has shaped and clarified his thinking on disarmament—a process he describes in detail in his two books *Disturbing the Universe* and *Weapons and Hope.* He has given long and thoughtful consideration to both the practical questions of international politics and the moral and ethical questions of nuclear war, offensive or defensive. In *Disturbing the Universe* he wrote eloquently of his faith in nu-

clear power for peaceful purposes. At one time opposed to the ban on nuclear bomb testing, he reversed his opposition in 1963. But he does not favor total disarmament: "It is important for long-range stability that peaceful countries be well armed and well organized in self-defense." But he sees in the development of "small and sophisticated defensive weapons" an effective alternative to the costly and perilous policy of Mutual Assured Destruction, "the strategy that has led the United States and the Soviet Union to build enormous offensive forces of nuclear bombers and missiles, sufficient to destroy many times over the cities and industries of both countries, while deliberately denying ourselves any possibility of a defense." Six years later, in *Weapons and Hope*, Dyson argued again for non-nuclear, precision-guided defense weapons: "Morally, we must arouse the conscience of mankind against weapons of mass murder as we roused mankind against the institution of slavery years ago. Politically, we must negotiate international agreements to reduce offensive deployments and strengthen defensive capabilities."

Understandably Dyson's books have had mixed reactions from reviewers. Lord Solly Zuckerman, writing of *Weapons and Hope* in *New York Review of Books*, called him "a romantic—even a fantasist" and challenged his arguments: "He supports his prescriptions with sweeping, but often dubious, generalities . . . And unlike Freeman Dyson the scientist, Dyson the savior has failed to check many of his presumed 'facts.'" A reviewer in the *Library Journal* commented that "Dyson's faith in the humane progress of military technology and his tolerance of dangerous conventional weapons will not please dovish readers, while his denunciation of 'military idolatry' and his support of a nuclear freeze will disappoint some hawks." On Dyson's writing, however, there is no dispute. Jim Miller, in *Newsweek*, called *Weapons and Hope* "a meditation of lyrical beauty, striking wisdom and steady moral passion . . . At once a realist and a visionary . . . Dyson is a man of conscience."

In 1985 Dyson delivered the Gifford Lectures at the University of Aberdeen under the title "In Praise of Diversity." These were collected and expanded in *Infinite in All Directions*. The theme of the book is the infinite diversity of creation. He writes: "I hope that the notion of a final statement of the laws of physics will prove as illusory as the notion of a formal decision process for all of mathematics. If it should turn out that the whole of physical reality can be described by a finite set of equations, I would be disappointed. I would feel that the Creator has been uncharacteristically lacking in imagination." Dyson finds support for diversity in biology and the theory of genetic drift but extends his arguments to embrace social issues such as technology and arms control and even theology. He does not deny the unifying influence of great scientific thinkers like Newton, Darwin, Maxwell, and Einstein, but he argues that life is based on complicated "homeostatic systems" in which internal stability remains constant although external conditions are subject to disruption and change:

> I have been trying to imagine a framework for the origin of life, guided by a personal philosophy which considers the primal characteristics of life to be homeostasis rather than replication, diversity rather than uniformity, the flexibility of the cell rather than the tyranny of the gene, the error tolerance of the whole rather than the precision of the parts.

Scientists like Stephen Jay Gould, who reviewed *Infinite in All Directions* in the *New York Review of Books*, challenged Dyson's thesis while praising the book itself as thoughtful and eminently readable. For Gould, however, Dyson's justification of diversity by affirming it "as the highest of nature's laws" is inconsistent and illogical—"the fobbing off of human hope upon nature by investing the universe with intrinsic purpose, defined as predictable and progressive movement toward human intelligence." For Roger Penrose, in the *New York Times Book Review*, there is an element of paradox in Dyson's argument: "Despite his avowed love of diversity, that he is himself a unifier is exemplified by his very striving to comprehend so much in terms of one unity-diversity polarity." But, Penrose concludes, "Whether one sympathizes fully or partially with his grandiose and highly stimulating ideas—or even if one is totally of another mind—this is a book to be read, savored and appreciated."

Dyson has received many honorary degrees and other academic honors. He is a Fellow of the Royal Society of London and a member of the United States National Academy of Sciences. In 1982 he delivered the Tanner Lectures at Brasenose College, Oxford; these were later incorporated into *Weapons and Hope*. His home is in Princeton, New Jersey. From his first marriage in 1950 to Verena Esther Huber, Dyson has a son and a daughter. After a divorce in 1958 he married Imme Jung with whom he has four daughters.

PRINCIPAL WORKS: Disturbing the Universe, 1979; Weapons and Hope, 1984; Origins of Life, 1985; Infinite in All Directions, 1988.

ABOUT: Munroe, L. Full Solution and the Jorns with

Contemporary Authors New Revised Series 17, 1986; Current Biography 1980; Dyson, F. Disturbing the Universe, 1979; Weintraub, P. (ed.) The Omni Interviews, 1984; Who's Who 1990; Who's Who in America 1988–1989. *Periodicals*—Library Journal February 15, 1984; New York Review of Books June 14, 1984; October 27, 1988; New York Times Book Review July 24, 1988; Newsweek April 16, 1984; Times Literary Supplement December 16, 1988.

EAGLETON, TERRY (TERENCE FRANCIS) (1943–), British literary critic, novelist, and playwright, was born in Salford, England and educated at local schools. He attended Trinity College, Cambridge, where he became a student and disciple of Raymond Williams, then the premier Marxist literary critic writing in England. He shared with Williams a rural upbringing and a Celtic background (Eagleton is of Irish extraction, Williams Welsh). Eagleton took his master's and doctoral degrees at Trinity, and became a fellow of Jesus College, Cambridge, at the age of twenty-one. In 1969, Eagleton moved as fellow to Wadham College, Oxford, where, as of the late 1980s, he is Tutor in English.

With the death of his mentor Raymond Williams in 1988, Terry Eagleton is without serious rival the premier Marxist literary critic born in Great Britain. Enormously productive, his thought has evolved through several phases in the more than two decades since he first began to publish—phases that, like the eras of history in Marxist thought, have seemed not to evolve but rather to change through a process of revolutionary catastrophe. Since his first books (especially *The New Left Church* and *The Body as Language*, both 1966), Eagleton's publications, according to Richard Aczel, "seem to form three distinct periods, each divided by an interval of five years," though all of them can be placed within the dialectical framework of Marxist criticism and scholarship. In the first phase, roughly from 1966 to 1970, Eagleton's work consisted of four books, each of which, in its own way, attempts to reconcile the humanist Marxism which he had absorbed under the influence of Raymond Williams with the values of his Roman Catholic background. After a five-year hiatus (1970–1975), Eagleton rapidly published three more books in 1975–1976, which essentially reject the humanist Marxism of Williams in favor of a post-Althusserian "science of the text" based on the critical theory of Pierre Macherey. After another five year hiatus (1976–1981), Eagleton's position shifted once more. Though he has not explicitly repudiated the "scientific" theorizing of *Criticism and Ideology*, his books since *Walter Benjamin* in 1981 have called for a

TERRY EAGLETON

"revolutionary criticism" which explicitly seeks practical social goals as the end of literary study rather than a mere knowledge of the text.

The first Terry Eagleton, the humanist Marxist, the disciple of Raymond Williams, is the author of simply written and accessible books such as *Shakespeare and Society*, essentially an analysis of the relation between the individual and society in some of the major tragedies and romances. In *Hamlet*, for example, Eagleton sees a "deadlock" consisting of the "incompatability of authentic and responsible action, of action-for-self and action-for-others." On the one hand spontaneous self-expression (as we see it in Ophelia and Laertes) is dangerous self-exposure; on the other, "men have to stifle themselves in the interest of the State," like "Guildenstern, the hollow man, who seals Hamlet's death-warrant." As Eagleton suggests in his conclusion, his interest in "the tension between spontaneous life and society" that he explores in Shakespeare is generated by the similar problems of his own age, which are shaped by the very different "lived experience" of "an industrial society" where "spontaneous living is crippled by industrial capitalism." Eagleton's emphasis here on literature as the distillation of lived experience reflects the social humanism of Raymond Williams' best work.

The same emphasis can be seen in Eagleton's *Exiles and Emigrés*, which covers much of the same ground as the latter chapters of Williams' *Culture and Society 1780–1950*. Here Eagleton contrasts those writers of the nineteenth century (such as Blake and Wordsworth, Dickens and El-

iot) who were able to "fuse the profoundest inwardness with the specific life of their own times with a capacity to generalise that life into the form of a complete vision." In the early twentieth century, by contrast, the alienation caused by advanced capitalism has largely prevented that fusion, with the ironic result that it is by and large only aliens and expatriates who can understand Britain and reproduce its society in art: the major modernists in Britain, for Eagleton, are "a Pole, three Americans, two Irishmen and an Englishman [Conrad, James, Eliot, Pound, Yeats, Joyce, and Lawrence]." Meanwhile English writers with attachments to the upper classes, like Woolf, Forster, Huxley, and Waugh, are able to create art only by adopting a stance of metaphorical "exile" centering on "a disorientated, isolatedly traditionalist, 'underground' or individualist subculture within English society itself."

In the mid-1970s Eagleton broke decisively with the humanist-socialist position he had inherited from Williams—even at a time when Williams himself was in the process of reconsidering his own position in favor of a more rigorous and dialectical Marxism based on the ideas of the Italian thinker Antonio Gramsci. The first break appeared in 1976 in a short (87-page) book addressed to the student as much as the scholar and entitled *Marxism and Literary Criticism*. Here Eagleton attempts to survey the powers and limitations of Marxist aesthetics from Marx and Engels' own essays and letters to the Continental neo-Marxists of the 1960s. In doing so, Eagleton perhaps inevitably presents that history as a long decline from the insights of the original master until its post-Althusserian renaissance in his own day. He attacks not only the anti-artistic repressions of Stalin and Zhdanov but also the British Marxists of the 1930s, like Christopher Caudwell and Arnold Kettle, and contrasts the broad world-historical issues favored by George Lukács (for Eagleton a "stiff-necked Stalinist") with the more subtle questions about the social determinants of art which post-Althusserian Marxists like Pierre Macherey were enabled to ask.

Though ostensibly a neutral analytic history, Eagleton's survey of Marxism distinctly took sides in a battle within Marxism, and its reception reflected this. Some old line socialists, such as the Australian critic Michael Wilding in *Modern Language Review*, decried Eagleton's neglect of "the crucial Marxist concept of praxis" and attacked him for an "academic" and "partial" approach. But those less committed to a particular stance within Marxism were usually appreciative of the clarity and concision of Eagleton's survey. Stephen Zelnick, writing in

Journal of Aesthetics and Art Criticism, for whom Marxists like Kettle and Lukács seem "foreign, dogmatic and wooden," was impressed by the "healthy testing and adapting spirit" of Eagleton's work: "this new Marxism is a growing set of hypotheses emerging in a world shaped differently from Marx's, Lenin's or the 'thirties." Similarly, Stanley Mitchell, in the *Times Literary Supplement*, praised Eagleton's book as "amazingly comprehensive," and if Eagleton dismissed too rapidly for his tastes the Marxists of the 1930s, he praised him for demonstrating in brief but telling critiques of Conrad and T. S. Eliot that "Marxist criticism, used well, is a complex instrument and not a means of reducing literature to its economic base."

Properly speaking, *Marxism and Literary Criticism* is only the pendant to Eagleton's much longer study, *Criticism and Ideology*, which provides not only a fuller explanation of post-Althusserian literary theory but also the practical criticism whose absence Wilding had decried. *Criticism and Ideology* also contains Eagleton's declaration of independence from Raymond Williams, whose shifting allegiances—from "left-Leavisite" social criticism to the "genetic structuralism" of Lucien Goldmann—Eagleton subjects to sharp but ultimately generous scrutiny. For most readers trying to learn how to read or write neo-Marxist criticism, however, the most important sections are the second and third chapters. Here Eagleton presents the literary work as determined not solely by the "economic base" as in classical Marxism but in addition by a large number of interrelated factors, including the "literary mode of production" (is the text transmitted orally, through handwritten manuscripts, printed books, periodicals), the "general ideology," the "aesthetic ideology" of the time, and the "authorial ideology"—the writer's particular slant on the social conflicts of his day. Here also Eagleton presents the Althusserian thesis that ideology, far from being a coherent and unified mode of social consciousness (as Lukács, for example, had conceived of it), was actually fragmented and inconsistent: the artistic work, as a production of ideology, foregrounds these incoherencies and makes them visible to the reader. In this way art, regardless of the social views of the artist, has revolutionary effects.

Eagleton's commitment to praxis as well as theory here might well have satisfied his earlier critics—he includes a history of "organicism" as an element in ideology in writers from Arnold through Joyce. But the scientific element in *Criticism and Ideology* was not well received by aestheticians like John Casey, who complained in the *Times Literary Supplement* that Eagle-

ton's book seemed innocent of aesthetic theory from Kant through Collingwood, and that it failed to provide the approach to the idea of the beautiful in human affairs that traditional aesthetic theory has usually centered on. Instead, Eagleton "treats the novels of George Eliot and the poetry of T. S. Eliot simply as objects of ideological decipherment. . . . The question remains—and is not faced—of how [the ideological patterns Eagleton finds] make sense of our appreciation of literature." Casey finds all Marxist aesthetics crude and reductive, however, not just Eagleton's.

If Eagleton the humanist Marxist emerged out of the relatively ecumenical 1960s, and if Eagleton the scientific post-Althusserian came out of the more dialectical spirit that followed the failed social revolution of 1968, we might see the Eagleton of the 1980s as an oppositional product of the Thatcher years in Britain, during which most social policies ran retrograde to the Labour gains of the previous decades. As Eagleton himself put it in his Preface to *Walter Benjamin, or Towards a Revolutionary Criticism* :

> What seemed important when I wrote my earlier book [*Criticism and Ideology*], at a time when "Marxist criticism" had little anchorage in Britain, was to examine its prehistory and to systematize the categories essential for a "science of the text." [This] is perhaps no longer the focal concern of Marxist cultural studies. Partly under the pressure of global capitalist crisis, partly under the influence of new themes and forces within socialism, the centre of such studies is shifting from narrowly textual or conceptual analysis to problems of cultural production and the political use of artefacts. . . . This shift in direction was in turn obscurely related to certain deep-seated changes in my own personal and political life since the writing of *Criticism and Ideology*.

One index to these "deep-seated changes" may be the dedication of *Walter Benjamin* to the post-structuralist feminist critic Toril Moi, whose intellectual influence he gratefully acknowledges, and which may be seen in Eagleton's vision of a "revolutionary criticism" based primarily on the "paradigm" of "feminist criticism." Like the contemporary feminist critics, attempting to make patriarchy visible in order to dismantle it, Eagleton proposes to "dismantle the ruling concepts of 'literature', reinserting 'literary' texts into the whole field of cultural practices." He proposes further to "deconstruct the received hierarchies of 'literature,'" to reevaluate the canon, and to reveal the role of literature "in the ideological construction of the subject."

Eagleton's synthesis of poststructuralist feminism with Marxism appeared in its purest form in *The Rape of Clarissa*. Here Eagleton argues that in their distaste for the suburban soul of

Samuel Richardson, most modern commentators have failed to take seriously the two crucial events in Richardson's novel, the rape of the heroine and her death, the points where she loses and where she regains control over her body and spirit. He thus attacks critics like V. S. Pritchett and Dorothy van Ghent for misreading Clarissa in the very way Lovelace misreads her, as a masochistic tease, as well as deconstructionists like William Warner for turning the cruelty of the rape into a linguistic trope. In her *Times Literary Supplement* review, Marilyn Butler admires his "fondness for epigram" and his self-effacing habit of joking "to unsettle cherished notions." Still, she senses that the eighteenth century is alien territory for Eagleton, and that, surprisingly for a Marxist, he is "perfunctory about history" and "very imprecise about contemporary culture" and, lacking genuine knowledge of the period, relies too heavily on a few secondary sources. For Merritt Moseley in *Sewanee Review*, however, Eagleton had done Richardson "a great service" by showing that *Clarissa* "is modern in confronting the most important social problems," and because of this he is willing to overlook the "unsatisfactory exegesis" of some of the book's sections.

In 1983 Eagleton published his single most popular book—its worldwide sales undoubtedly have surpassed the rest of his productions combined—*Literary Theory: An Introduction.* This book is, like his *Shakespeare and Society,* dedicated to Raymond Williams, which perhaps signals Eagleton's return to an *engagé* if not a "humanist" Marxism. The immense popularity of *Literary Theory* was undoubtedly due to its time of arrival: at a moment when the English-speaking world was deluged with new literary theories, mostly derived from difficult Continental philosophers, Eagleton had crafted a lucid, witty, and apparently balanced overview of most of the major new approaches: structuralism and semiotics, deconstruction, hermeneutics and reception theory, and post-Freudian psychoanalysis.

Those using *Literary Theory* as a study-guide to their courses in literary criticism undoubtedly noticed that two major "schools"—Marxism and feminism—were left out. In fact this was demanded by the rhetoric of the book, which operates in three stages. The first chapter, "The Rise of English," views the academic establishment as having operated before the 1960s by ground rules—the New Criticism or Leavisite social ideas—that paid attention to the social role of literature but were crippled by allegiance to a "bankrupt" liberal humanism. The central chapters, on the new theories that have come in during the past two decades, consistently make the point that these theories are *literary* in a strict sense: they define literature in such a way as to isolate it from social practices and politics; in doing so, criticism defuses the revolutionary potential of culture and tacitly upholds the status quo. In the final chapter, "Political Criticism," Eagleton presents a manifesto for—but does not discuss in detail—Marxist and feminist criticism as the only antidotes to the ostensibly apolitical but actually reactionary modes of theory. Though Eagleton does not admit this here, it is clear that any detailed consideration of either Marxism or feminism as practiced up to 1983 would doubtless have revealed that the two movements have been riddled with both liberal humanists and fetishizers of the literary text.

The critical reception of *Literary Theory* was an index of both the political commitments of the reviewers and their awareness of Eagleton's rhetorical scheme. Those like Wallace Jackson, who agreed in *South Atlantic Quarterly Review* that "the liberal humanist position" is "both theoretically and politically bankrupt," tended to like the book from beginning to end, complaining only about Eagleton's "neglect of the old warriors" like Caudwell, Kettle, and Lukács. More conservative theorists like Paul H. Fry were irritated by Eagleton's offhand tendency to accuse theories he doesn't like of "reification" or "fetishism." While Fry in *Yale Review* concedes Eagleton's "knowledge and understanding" of his subject and his "witty and relaxed" style, he feels that for all his commitment to politics, Eagleton has lost touch with the human: "Eagleton lacks the charitable, concretely detailed attention to people and pursuits of every kind that one finds in [Raymond] Williams."

Eagleton's more recent books have come out at the rate of nearly one per year, but few of these have made the impression of *Literary Theory. The Function of Criticism* argued that, just as Continental literary criticism came into existence in the eighteenth century "born of a struggle against the absolutist state," so literary criticism must struggle against capitalism to maintain its *raison d'être. Against the Grain: Selected Essays 1975–85* collects some of Eagleton's fugitive pieces of the crucial decade in which he embraced, then pointedly reacted against, the academic dandyism and social irresponsibility of Althusserian Marxism.

Eagleton's *Saints and Scholars* is a novel rather than a book of criticism, a swerve which aligns him further with his mentor/opponent Raymond Williams, who also combined historical studies with fiction. Unlike Williams' heartfelt and autobiographical *Border Country,* however, Eagleton's novel is a *roman à thèse,* an ideological romp set in 1916 with characters that include philosopher Ludwig Wittgenstein, linguist Nikolai Bakhtin (Mikhail's smarter brother), Irish revolutionary James Connolly, and Joyce's Leopold Bloom. In the *New York Times Book Review*, Matthew Flamm wrote that "Eagleton's novella of ideas reads quickly and has its humorous moments," but that "this is less a work of fiction than the kind of entertaining concert . . . an enterprising professor might use to liven up his class."

Eagleton has also written a play, *Saint Oscar*, in which Oscar Wilde's unhappy fate in England becomes emblematic of the age-old colonial domination of England over the Irish. The play was produced in Derry, Northern Ireland, in the autumn of 1989 by Field Day, a group of Northern Irish writers and critics who, as Edna Longley writes in the *Times Literary Supplement*, "[have] sought to open up cultural issues relevant to the current political situation in Northern Ireland and between Ireland and Britain." Longley found the play witty but lacking in "theatricality": "Eagleton's effort to conflate Wilde's story with Ireland's severely strains drama as well as credulity."

PRINCIPAL WORKS: *Criticism*—Shakespeare and Society: Critical Studies in Shakespearean drama, 1967; Exiles and Emigres: Studies in Modern Literature, 1970; Myths of Power: A Marxist Study of the Brontës, 1975; Marxism and Literary Criticism, 1976; Critisicm and Ideology: A Study in Marxist Literary Theory, 1976; Walter Benjamin; or, Toward a Revolutionary Criticism, 1981; The Rape of Clarissa: Writing, Sexuality and Class Struggle in Richardson, 1982; Literary Theory: An Introduction, 1983; The Function of Criticism: From the Spectator to Post-Structuralism, 1984; William Shakespeare, 1986; Against the Grain: Selected Essays 1975–85, 1986; The Ideology of the Aesthetic, 1990; The Significance of Theory, 1990. *Novel*—Saints and Scholars, 1988. *Play*—Saint Oscar, 1989.

ABOUT: Contemporary Authors New Revision Series 23, 1988. *Periodicals*—American Book Review May–June 1985; British Book News February 1985; Commentary March 1984; Comparative Literature Fall 1986; French Review March 1985; German Quarterly Summer 1985; Journal of Aesthetics and Art Criticism Summer 1977; Library Journal February 15, 1987; London Review of Books February 7, 1985; Modern Fiction Studies Summer 1984; Modern Language Review January 1979, April 1985; Modern Philology August 1985; Nation December 24, 1983; January 21, 1984; New Left Review 1985; New Republic November 10, 1986; New Statesman June 3, 1983; October 5, 1984; New York Review of Books July 21, 1983; December 8, 1983; November 6, 1986; New York Times April 10, 1986, New York Times Book Review September 1, 1988, Observer (London) March 21, 1985; Poetics Today 5:1, 5:2, and 7:1; Sewanee Review Fall 1978; South Atlantic Quarterly 108A; Spring 1989;

Southern Humanities Review Summer 1985; Spectator August 21, 1986; Thought December 1984; Times Literary Supplement July 13, 1967; January 23, 1969; August 14, 1970; October 23, 1970; May 20, 1977; November 12, 1982; February 4, 1983; June 10, 1983; November 23, 1984; July 4, 1986; October 6, 1989; March 30, 1990; Victorian Studies Summer 1985; Washington Post Book World October 2, 1983; Village Voice Literary Supplement June 1983, March 1985; Yale Review Summer 1984.

EDMOND, LAURIS (DOROTHY) (April 2, 1924–), New Zealand poet and novelist, writes: "I grew up in a small country town where being 'like everyone else' mattered enormously; my family, to my constant chagrin, was definitely unlike them. It was odd; it had cranky notions, and not many friends. My parents believed—in turn, or all together—in reincarnation, extrasensory perception (they called it 'thought transference'), diet reform (an endless series of new ideologies) and, by far the longest lasting and most compelling, Douglas Social Credit. I enjoyed these family obsessions and indeed became moderately obsessed myself, but I felt the embarrassment of them too. We were all shy—two parents, four children—and all the expansive part of our lives was lived at home, with the rest of the town out there behaving in the way other people do, a way we could never quite master.

"I began to write poems and keep them in a notebook with a shiny black cover when I was about nine or ten, reading them aloud to my mother who was, of course, very proud. She also believed however (and in this respect *was* like everyone else), that clever girls don't get boyfriends unless they learn to pretend they're not. I was to get married to a nice man and have a family, and that, in my twenty-second year, is exactly what I did. Twenty-five years and six children later, I looked in the drawers where my 'poetry' was stuffed in heaps of scrawled unfinished fragments and realized that something had to change. My marriage was already doing so, in preparation for breaking up a few years later; it was the end of the sixties, I'd just read Betty Friedan, the new wave of awareness was seizing New Zealand women, and me amongst them. My second life was due to begin.

"It didn't happen easily. Growing up for the second time was frightfully turbulent, euphoric and devastating by turns; the one constant aspect of it was that I kept on writing. Having at last begun to give poetry room in the foreground as it were, I found it took over everything. In the last twelve years I have published eight volumes of poetry including a *Selected Poems*, a novel and several plays, as well as which we found invaluable

LAURIS EDMOND

graphical writings. There has been a strange compulsiveness about all this, as though it had been waiting throughout the domestic years, and now it has its head it can not be stopped.

"The obsessiveness I grew up with has its uses, it would seem. So does that intense private family life, which taught me a profound knowledge of relationships and the behavior that occurs within them. It was a microcosm, an enclosed world in which I fought, raged, laughed, sang, played, and above all talked, through my childhood and adolescence. The strong sense of relationship that informs all my poetry I am sure has its source there; I do not think I ever write as an observer, always as a participant. It's often remarked that my poems sound like conversations—'as though you are talking to an intelligent friend,' as one critic puts it. That quality too I think I learnt in the days when what you really meant you said at home; with outsiders you pretended. Poetry says what I mean.

"My later life too has been a mixture of the populated and the private. It has mattered to me to learn how to write of deeply felt emotion, in particular of love and of grief, in a way that makes my experience available to others without unsuitably exposing myself or people near me. A good deal of my life has been spent in small towns, in a country that has astonishing physical beauty. It is impossible not to respond powerfully to this environment; nevertheless I do not write 'nature poetry.' My landscape is always populated. In a small remote country perhaps human conflicts and contradictions are writ large—they seem so to me.

"Since I am now something of a matriarch, with new children continually extending my tribal network, the tragi/comic perplexities of life continue close at hand, and my awareness of them grows and perhaps mellows a little. My old sense of dislocation, of never quite belonging, is still with me, but differently. I have travelled a lot in the last few years and acquired a kind of global neighborhood, writers and others, friends who have this same consciousness of always being on the edge of other people's worlds. Their work, like mine, is an attempt to reach beyond the walls that enclose and divide us from one another."

A relative latecomer to writing, Lauris Edmond produced within the decade 1975 to 1985, as if to compensate for lost time, a large number of poems, two radio plays, a novel and several short stories. By the time she received the inaugural British Airways Commonwealth Poetry Prize in 1985, her name was prominent among Australian and New Zealand women writers— from Katherine Mansfield to Judith Wright, Fleur Adcock, and Judith Rodriguez—who have won international recognition. Her *Selected Poems* of 1984, collected from her earlier as well as later volumes, established her, wrote Simon Rae in the *Times Literary Supplement*, as "one of New Zealand's leading poets." Readers in England and in the United States are discovering her, however, not as a regional author but as an uncommonly sensitive and appealing writer on the common human condition, a poet who brings to her work a uniquely warm and mature feminine sensibility.

While many of Edmond's poems stress themes of childbirth, motherhood, aging and loss, there is a balancing sense of consolation and serenity and even, sometimes, ironic humor. Janet Wilson, who has lectured and written on Edmond's work in West Germany and Australia, describes much of it as "strongly experiential," not so much autobiographical as retaining the immediacy of living experience. In "Before a Funeral," from her first volume, for example, the speaker is putting in order the room of a loved one who has just died:

Mechanically useful, I make
preparations for some possible
impossible journey no one
will ever take; work will help
they tell me, and indeed
your room is now nothing
but things, and tidy.
I have put away your life.

But it is the recognition and acceptance of mortality that links the poet to the rest of humanity, that confirms her relationship to and kinship with others. In late afternoon Sunday twilight as a family gathers for tea:

> there is a time when time itself comes to nothing,
> light on the wall stares without expression,
> a mere absence of darkness; chair, table,
> flower become outlines as words repeated lose
>   meaning
>
> I too am weightless, a leaf's skeleton, dry
> and pale, all green flesh eaten by worms that came
> to the autumn garden and turned the pear tree to
>   paper.

Isolated, alienated from each other, the family members sense the inevitability of death:

>   . . . we tremble, and are saved by our fear.
> Now we can hurry in to stand together
> and talk with quick hopefulness, waiting
> for evening to fall, remembering what we are
> and peering into the shadows to try to make out
> the tremulous existences of others.
>   "Turning the Pear Tree to Paper"

As a New Zealander, Edmond has a realistic sense of the remoteness of her country:

> Let me tell you of my country, how it
> suffers the equivocal glories, the lean
> defeats of a discontented not a tragic
> people.

But she is also conscious of its beauty:

> I tell you too of the tiny jewelled
> orange trees of the north and the cloudy
> vineyards, grape bloom mornings of summer . . . .
>   —from Wellington Letter, XVI

Her travels abroad, especially the year she spent in Menton, France, on a Katherine Mansfield Fellowship (1981) writing a novel about small-town New Zealand life, High Country Weather, have enlarged and enriched the scene and focus of her poetry. She has read her poems to audiences in Australia, West Germany, England, and the United States and has received recognition at home and abroad in the form of fellowships, prizes (the International PEN–New Zealand Centre Poetry Prize, 1987) and honors (the O.B.E. for services to poetry and literature, 1986). Those services include a career in teaching and in editorial work. She holds a teaching certificate and a speech therapy diploma.

Lauris Edmond was born in Dannevirke, in the district of Hawkes Bay in the North Island of New Zealand. Her father was Lewis Herbert Scott; her mother Fanny (Price) Scott. She married Trevor Edmond in 1945 and has four daughters and a son. In 1968 she returned to school to complete her B.A. degree at the Uni-

versity of Waikato. While studying for her M.A. (1972, Victoria University, Wellington) she taught in secondary school. From 1974 to 1981 she was an editor for the Post-Primary Teachers Association in Wellington, a group which encouraged creative writing among young students. In 1979 she edited for the PEN New Zealand Centre a collection of their work—Young Writing. Her works in progress include poetry and a second novel.

PRINCIPAL WORKS: Poetry—In Middle Air, 1975; The Pear Tree and Other Poems, 1977; Wellington Letter: A Sequence of Poems, 1980; Seven, 1980; Salt from the North, 1980; Catching It, 1983; Selected Poems, 1984; Seasons and Creatures, 1986; Summer near the Artic Circle, 1989. Novel—High Country Weather, 1984. Autobiography—Hot October: An Autobiographical Story, 1989.

ABOUT: Contemporary Poets, 4th ed., 1985; Edmond, L. Hot October, 1989. Periodicals—CRNLE Reviews Journal (Flinders University, South Australia) No. 2, 1986; Landfall (Christchurch, N.Z.) September 1983; New Zealand Listener June 11, 1983; Times Literary Supplement August 1, 1986.

*EHLE, JOHN (December 13, 1925–), American novelist and non-fiction writer, was born in Asheville, North Carolina, son of John M. and Gladys (Starnes) Ehle. Ehle grew up in Asheville, and served in the United States Army as an infantry rifleman from 1942 to 1946. He received his B.A. from the University of North Carolina, Chapel Hill, in 1949 and began teaching creative writing at Chapel Hill in 1951. He was the author of twenty-six plays in the series "American Adventure," which were broadcast on the NBC network and carried by Radio Free Europe, the Voice of America, and the Armed Forces Network, 1952–1953. In 1953 Ehle received his M.A. from Chapel Hill. With the exception of a year in which he was visiting associate professor at New York University, 1957–1958, Ehle was on the faculty at Chapel Hill steadily until 1963. For the next two years, 1963–1964, he was special assistant to North Carolina Governor Terry Sanford, developing programs for the improvement of the state's educational system. In 1964–1965, he was program officer for the Ford Foundation, New York City. Ehle has received numerous awards and prizes, including the Walter Raleigh Prize for fiction five times (1964, 1967, 1970, 1975, 1984); State of North Carolina Award for Literature, 1972; Governor's Award for distinguished meritorious service, 1978; Distinguished Alumnus Award, University of North Carolina, Chapel Hill, 1984; and the Thomas Wolfe Prize, 1984.

°ē´ lē

JOHN EHLE

Among his other books, Ehle has published a number of works of non-fiction, beginning in 1958 with *The Survivor*, an account of the life of Eddy Hukov, a German born in Poland who became a Storm Trooper at seventeen, survived the war, joined the French Foreign Legion to avoid capture by the Russians, and deserted from the Legion in Indochina to find himself, after incredible adventures, a man without a country. *Shepherd of the Streets* told the dramatic story of an Episcopalian rector who became a fighting advocate for the rights and better treatment of the Puerto Rican community in New York City. *The Free Men*, Ehle's best-known work of non-fiction, describes and analyzes the movement for civil rights for blacks in Chapel Hill, which was led by two students who faced jail and disenfranchisement in order to bring about change. In 1988 Ehle published *Trail of Tears*, about the destruction of the Cherokee aspiration for nationhood in the South during the time of Andrew Jackson.

Ehle is best known, however, as a regional novelist who in a series of works has focused on the mountain people of North Carolina. *Move Over, Mountain*, his first novel, is striking in that it is a work about a black farmer written by a white man with fidelity and without resorting to stereotypes. "The fact that the central character and nearly all the rest are Negroes," Paul Flowers wrote in the *New York Times Book Review*, "is incidental. . . . [Ehle] writes from a deep knowledge of his subject, and an understanding of technique rare in a first novelist." Coleman Rosenberger in the *New York Herald Tribune*

Book Review praised Ehle particularly for his "insight and humor and . . . fine narrative sense." Also well received was *Kingstree Island*, about a community of fishermen on an isolated island off the coast of North Carolina in 1938. *Lion on the Hearth* is set in Asheville and was frequently compared by reviewers to the writing about the same community by Thomas Wolfe (in fact, Ehle was born on the same street in Asheville as Wolfe). Betty Anne Stanback in the *Saturday Review* observed that *"Lion on the Hearth* is certain to call forth comparisons with Thomas Wolfe's *Look Homeward, Angel.* Though a generation apart in time, both books have their settings in Asheville, North Carolina. Both were written by young men who were natives of that city. And both are stories of young men growing up amid the tensions that exist within a big, complex, alive family. . . . Ehle is not the poet that Wolfe was, but he is, happily, a more disciplined novelist, and his story is well told and highly readable. He writes with affection for and deep insight into the mountain people."

Ehle's next novel, *The Land Breakers*, is set in the historical past, in 1779–1783, and deals with the desperate efforts of land-hungry pioneers to establish a community in the mountains of western North Carolina. It received exceptionally favorable reviews. Robert W. Henderson in *Library Journal* remarked that to "call this a historical novel would not do it justice. . . . This is the work of a novelist of importance, regardless of historical setting." Hal Borland in the *New York Times Book Review* commented that *"The Land Breakers* is one of the best recreations of our pioneer past that we have had in years. . . . His characters are full-dimensioned, wholly credible. . . . *The Land Breakers* has a rare degree of greatness." *The Road*, a companion novel to *The Land Breakers*, is concerned with the effort to extend the Western Carolina Railroad over a mountain barrier in the 1870s. Ruth R. Gambee in *Library Journal* described the novel as an "absorbing historical novel," and praised Ehle's presentation of the mountain people and "the ancient wilderness with its menace and beauty."

A Time of Drums extends Ehle's chronicle of the Wright family, members of which had appeared in *The Land Breakers* and *The Road*. The setting this time is the Civil War, in which thirty-year-old Colonel Owen Wright fights for the Confederacy at Chancellorsville and Gettysburg. The reviewer for *Publishers Weekly* remarked that "Ehle writes of it all without frills or frippery, portraying in strong masculine style, not the glories of the day but the hardships." James Boatwright in the *New York Times Book*

Review had mixed reactions. He began by calling the novel "a likable book—sober, honest, unpretentious," but he faulted Ehle's craftsmanship. "Reading it," he commented, "is hard going—there's no narrative thrust, no urgency, no sustained rhythm." Ehle's next novel, *The Journey of August King*, had a uniformly favorable reception. Set in North Carolina in 1810, it concerns a pioneer farmer who, with inner misgiving and at personal risk, assists a young slave girl to escape. The reviewer for *Publishers Weekly* noted that the book "is a tender, moving, but wholly unsentimental story that comes across like a folk tale. . . . The conclusion is not only satisfying but uplifting, in a healthy, old-fashioned way. The novel is full of poetry and beauty in the style of its telling. It is also a brutal tale about human nature at its worst, and in August's case, at its best."

Like Ehle's three previous novels, *The Winter People* is a chronicle of the Wright family, set now in the Depression, during Franklin Roosevelt's first term, and focusing upon the entanglement of two rival clans, the Wrights and the Campbells. Edmund Fuller in the *Wall Street Journal* called it "a splendid story. . . . The cast is large, with memorably delineated personalities. . . . There is a 39-page bear hunt in which the slight and gentle Wayland is tested, foreshadowing a graver testing he will face. Of bear-hunt stories William Faulkner is king, but Mr. Ehle can claim a dukedom." *Last One Home* is set in turn-of-the-century Asheville, and according to the reviewer for *Booklist* draws its strength from the mountain life, "which Ehle re-creates lovingly and lyrically." James B. Hemesath in *Library Journal* characterized *Last One Home* as "regional writing at its best."

In 1952, Ehle married Gail Oliver; they were divorced in 1967, and later that year Ehle married the celebrated English actress Rosemary Harris, by whom he has a daughter, Jennifer Anne. The Ehles live, as a 1982 profile in *Publishers Weekly* described it, in a "rambling, eclectically furnished home in a leafy suburb of Winston-Salem." Ehle also owns a number of rental properties, "a tiny real-estate empire," and has a mountain cabin in Penland with a spectacular view where he does much of his writing. His novels have not been bestsellers, but have been consistently well reviewed. Commenting on them, Ehle remarked: "In a sense I like to feel the people in my books are timeless. . . . It's the sense of place that's important. Most of my books start with that, then the people come in, and out of them comes the action. These are people rooted to their place."

PRINCIPAL WORKS: *Novels*—Move Over, Mountain, 1957;

Kingstree Island, 1959; Lion on the Hearth, 1961; The Land Breakers, 1964; The Road, 1967; A Time of Drums, 1970; The Journey of August King, 1971; The Changing of the Guard, 1974; The Winter People, 1982; Last One Home, 1984; The Widow's Trial, 1989. *Non-fiction*—The Survivor, 1958; Shepherd of the Streets, 1960; The Free Men, 1965; Trail of Tears: the Rise and Fall of the Cherokee Nation, 1988.

ABOUT: Contemporary Authors, 1974; Contemporary Literary Criticism 27, 1984; Who's Who in America: 1988–1989. *Periodicals*—Booklist September 1, 1984; Library Journal February 1, 1964; December 15, 1966; September 1, 1984; New York Herald Tribune Book Review April 28, 1957; New York Times Book Review April 21, 1957; February 23, 1964; September 27, 1970; Newsweek June 1, 1964; Publishers Weekly March 5, 1982; May 4, 1970; August 9, 1971; Saturday Review September 30, 1961; Wall Street Journal April 20, 1982.

ELLIS, ALICE THOMAS (pseudonym of ANNA MARGARET HAYCRAFT)

(September 9, 1932–), British novelist and journalist, is the daughter of John and Alexandra Lindholm. She was educated at Bangor County Grammar School for Girls, in Gwynedd, Wales, and at Liverpool School of Art. Her parents were members of the Church of Humanity, based on the positivistic philosophy of Auguste Comte, but at nineteen she rebelled against so much rational humanism and became a convert to Roman Catholicism.

In 1956 she was married to the publisher Colin Haycraft, then a director of Weidenfeld & Nicolson Ltd. He moved in 1968 to Gerald Duckworth & Co. Ltd., a small but distinguished publishing house established in 1898. She joined him there as Duckworth's fiction editor. Haycraft is now the company's chairman, managing director, and chief shareholder. They have four sons and a daughter. Another son and daughter are deceased, and bereavement is a persistent theme in her work.

According to John Walsh in *Books and Bookmen*, Alice Thomas Ellis is at the center of "the Duckworth gang," whose other members include Beryl Bainbridge, Caroline Blackwood, and Patrice Chaplin. These novelists, all women writing mostly about women and their emotional problems, share an ironic detachment from the sometimes macabre sufferings of their characters, a lucid and witty style, and a talent for what Walsh calls "devilish entertainment."

Harriet Waugh, writing in the *Spectator*, says that Ellis herself writes "short, edged comedies of human failure in the face of some ultimate good, . . . [she] manoeuvres to pit the world against the spirit and then stands back to see

ALICE THOMAS ELLIS

which will win. Her stories are domestic in nature, her protagonists often women taking an understandable interest in the oddities they inadvertently manage to collect around themselves." Her work has earned comparison with that of Ivy Compton-Burnett, Malcolm Bradbury, and Kingsley Amis, as well as of other Catholic writers like Evelyn Waugh and, above all, Muriel Spark.

The author published her first two books in 1977, when she was forty-five. One was a guide to infant nutrition: *Natural Baby Food: A Cookery Book* ; the other a novel about spiritual malnutrition: *The Sin Eater*. Both appeared under pseudonyms: the first as by Brenda O'Casey; the second under the name Anna Haycraft has continued to use for most of her work, Alice Thomas Ellis.

The Sin Eater posits an old English landowner dying in his Welsh mansion and explores the interactions within his dreadful family and between them and an equally unattractive Welsh proletariat. Jeremy Treglown, unsure which of these repellent characters is the eponymous "sin eater," suggests that the "the first suspect must be Rose," the old man's daughter-in-law, "whose relish of her reactionary intolerance becomes almost carnivorous." In his *New Statesman* review, Treglown found in this first novel "some of the satirical malice, the implacable cruelty of plotting and the snobbish humour of early Waugh, and a lot of Virginia Woolf's narrative method—the fluid movement from one centre of awareness to another among the characters. . . . Forster is recalled too, not only in her alertness to

repressed sexuality but in what is at the same time the novel's most original feature. It is a fiction about the British Empire, satirizing both the pretensions of the rulers and the inadequacies of the ruled. . . . The story's gothic ending has been a shade too clearly signalled. . . . But it's an impressively self-confident novel, full of uncomfortable jokes and sharp perceptions."

The Birds of the Air, which followed in 1980, is set at Christmas in an English village quaintly named Innstead. It centers on the widowed Mrs. Marsh and her two grown daughters. Mary, grieving for the death of her illegitimate son Robin, hardly knows what is going on around her; she waits numbly for Robin's resurrection or her own death. Her sister Barbara is obsessed by the infidelity of her husband Sebastian, an academic whose "insistence on ordinary language and absolute clarity of expression rendered his discourse unintelligible to the ordinary person." Their son Sam shares some of his aunt Mary's intensity of feeling and, in protest against the hypocrisies of an English Christmas, dyes his hair green.

Penelope Lively called the novel "brief and very good indeed. She is one of those admirable economic writers who can reduce characterization to a line, a phrase, an action, and use the same words to tell a story, point a moral and set a scene." Jennifer Uglow wrote that "beneath its elegant, and often very funny surface, this short novel is densely packed, strengthened by a network of imagery, almost overburdened by urgent blasts against modern society. One is buffeted by changes of mood and left with a disconcerting impression of mingled comedy and pain. . . . One is confronted by the forces of death, love, hatred and sex in the suggestive context of Christmas, a feast at once pagan, Christian, and capitalist."

When the book reached the United States in 1981, Ronald Nevane similarly found in it "an unexpectedly radical rejection of the cozy middle-class values of a debased society. . . . At the heart of the story is an imagery that evokes a more primitive and more religious Britain (with the bird as a symbol of the Holy Ghost). As in Shakespeare's *A Winter's Tale*, there are the mysteries of birth, death, and resurrection . . . but without the magical healing. There are no easy reconciliations in this novel, which sparkles in the cold light of a brilliant and pitiless comedy." Not quite everyone was so enthusiastic, however, and Anatole Broyard thought the novel "curiously gratuitous. Perhaps its people are too preoccupied with themselves to occupy us."

A combination of "low comedy and exalted meditation" also characterized *The 27th Kingdom*, which was short-listed for Britain's most sought-after literary award, the Booker-McConnell Prize. The novel is set in Chelsea in the 1950s and has at its hub Aunt Irene, an eccentric *poseuse* whose good looks have "disappeared under waves of creamy, curdling flesh." Her bizarre extended household includes her wicked nephew Kyril and is joined by Valentine, a saintly black postulant nun from the West Indies. Back at the convent, an apple picked by Valentine from an unreachable branch refuses to rot, an emblem of her "worrying flawlessness." As Linda Taylor wrote, Valentine is sent by her Mother Superior to Aunt Irene in the hope that she will "provide sufficient imperfection to tempt Valentine into normality." In fact, Valentine rises triumphantly and literally above these machinations, levitating away over the Thames. Nicholas Shrimpton, in his *Sunday Times* review, described the book as "eschatology with pratfalls. . . . Reflections on the nature of good and evil combine effortlessly with bad puns, wild farce and excellent comic dialogue. . . . " Linda Taylor demurred a little, suggesting that "the trouble with this diet of singular originality is that it becomes a bit indigestible." In retrospect, a number of reviewers have placed *The 27th Kingdom* as the best or among the best of Ellis' novels so far.

In her next novel, *The Other Side of the Fire* Ellis turned from sacred to profane love. After fifteen repressed and boring years of suburban marriage, Claudia Bohannon becomes passionately enamored of her stepson Philip, who as it happens is homosexual. Not a great deal can be or is done about this, and Claudia emerges from the fire barely singed. Others involved are Claudia's tedious husband Charles; her bohemian friend Sylvie, whom life had "cured of love"; and Sylvie's daughter Evvie, a romantic novelist. For Sebastian Faulks, Ellis here exhibited the same "cruel glee" at her characters' discomfiture that had distinguished the earlier novels, as well as hints of a "mythic purpose." Sylvie may be in communion with the spirits of the dead and "Evvie, as well as writing her silly romance, is in some strange way the 'author' of Claudia's real-life lovesickness. There is a deliberate blurring of the lines between fiction and reality, complicated by the fact that this book is itself a variant of romantic 'women's fiction.'" In this case, however, it seemed to Faulks that "the suggestions don't really add up to anything. The novel doesn't give the impression of having been really thought through." Other reviewers had different but related reservations about *The Other Side of the Fire*. T. O. Treadwell thought that it "ultimately falls victim to a case of creeping

decorum," the author retreating "from the demands of her book," and Marcia Pally considered that, in this "slight" novel, "too many sentences stop long after they should, too many metaphors spin out overly far. Add to that a leading character who is somewhat implausible and a confusion about the author's view of life, and you have a novel with a tendency to veer off course."

Unexplained Laughter was more warmly received. Lydia, a snobbish and selfish London journalist, retreats to her cottage in a small Welsh town to lick the wounds of a failed love affair. She is accompanied by her dowdy but good-hearted foil Betty. Exploring the local community, anatomizing in caustic one-liners its eccentric denizens, Lydia begins a potentially redemptive friendship with Beuno, the parish priest. Meanwhile the holy idiot Angharad, roaming the Welsh hills, provides a kind of chorus to the proceedings. Neither Angharad's ramblings nor Lydia's icy rationality explains the mysterious laughter, unheard by some, that emanates from a wooded valley and offers another response to Lydia's arrogance or human folly in general.

It seemed to Isabel Raphael that *Unexplained Laughter* "is, quite simply, brilliant. It will not be to everyone's taste, being dominated by a character who will arouse the same mixture of emotions in the reader as she does in the book. But I defy anyone to remain indifferent, or to put down this novel unread. . . . The book is most elegantly and economically written, and I can't think of a writer who catches more accurately the flavour of contemporary conversation." Harriet Waugh called it "an elusive novel teetering on the edge of comedy but remaining faintly and unexpectedly sombre. Its awful, wise-cracking heroine deserves none of the reader's sympathy but mysteriously wins it."

Margaret, the nineteen-year-old heroine of *The Clothes in the Wardrobe*, has returned from a traumatic visit to Egypt. Back home in the London suburb of Croydon, she allows her bourgeoise mother to drive her into an engagement with Syl Monro, a middle-aged bachelor who likes young girls. It emerges that in Egypt she had participated in something so dreadful that she had lost her sense of herself as someone blessed by God with special grace. Margaret no longer cares what becomes of her, but an improbable guardian angel appears in the shape of Lili, her mother's old school friend, exotic, licentious, hard drinking but life affirming. Harriet Waugh wrote that *The Clothes in the Wardrobe* "has all the right ingredients for enchantment but something has gone very slightly amiss in the distillation. Margaret, whose five senses articulate the story, is not a very interesting central character. It hardly seems to matter if she is saved from the ghastly fate of marrying Syl. Instead, the pleasure and energy of the novel reside in the peripheral characters, the ghastly mother, Lili and Lili's artist husband and Syl and Syl's malevolent mother with whom he lives. . . . It could be that the novel is slightly undernourished."

If that last observation is justified, it may be because *The Clothes in the Wardrobe* offers a deliberately partial and monocular perception of the events described. They are seen very differently in *The Skeleton in the Cupboard*, which tells the same story again from the point of view of Syl's widowed mother. Seen through her own eyes, Mrs. Monro is more sinned-against than malevolent. In a long and unrewarding life, she, rather like Margaret herself, "fell into the habit of sadness and gave up the practice of hope. It made existence easier." Again like Margaret, she finds a comforter in Lili, even though Lili had once seduced Mrs. Monro's husband. Under Lili's raffish influence, she turns cheerfully to drink. We now see that Mrs. Monro's opposition to Syl's marriage proceeds not from malevolent possessiveness but, quite reasonably, from the recognition that Margaret loathes him. Or does it? As Cressida Connolly wrote, "the subtlety of the writing is such that we never know for certain whether Mrs. Monro is disingenuous. . . . The most readable novels are seldom the best-written, but those of Alice Thomas Ellis are an exception. Her style is succinct, her humour dry. . . . If *The Skeleton in the Cupboard* has a fault, it is that it is more forlorn than creepy, lacking the cutting edge of *Unexplained Laughter*." Seen through still another point of view, Lili's, Margaret's proposed wedding is the subject of a third novel, *The Fly in the Ointment*. The three novels, Patricia Craig observed, in the *Times Literary Supplement*, "are not so much parts of a trilogy as a story told in triplicate." Though the novels share a single subject, each in turn challenges and finally enlarges our understanding of the characters. Lili's sparkling if trouble-making presence considerably lightens the spirit of *The Fly in the Ointment* and, Craig writes, "affords scope for the author to exercise her capacity for light-handed abrasiveness to the full. . . . *The Fly in the Ointment*, like its two predecessors, is notable for its vivacity and elegance."

A few years earlier, Ellis had edited another novel dominated by a very different sort of widow, *Mrs. Donald*. It had been written in the 1950s by "Mary Keene," who was Ellis' own mother, and was published posthumously in 1983. *Mrs. Donald*, set in the East End of London in the 1920s, has as its antiheroine a woman who is, wrote Grace Ingoldby, "a bully, a braggart and child-beater," but so "roundly drawn" as to achieve "a hideous but undeniable dignity."

Alice Thomas Ellis has also produced a sizable body of non-fiction. In 1980, three years after her early treatise on *Natural Baby Food*, came a somewhat less serious cookery book, *Darling, You Shouldn't Have Gone to So Much Trouble*, written by Ellis in collaboration with her friend Caroline Blackwood. It offers guidance on home entertaining of the sort where visiting children are fed fast foods in the kitchen while their elders get so smashed as not to notice what they are eventually given to eat. On the other hand, Ellis' friend Jeffrey Bernard has testified to the fact that she "runs one of the best lunch and afternoon drinking clubs in London in the kitchen of her house in Camden Town."

Bernard's "Low Life" column in the *Spectator* adjoins Ellis' own column on "Home Life," which has appeared every week since January 1985. It draws a sometimes melancholy humor from the ordinary exigencies of domestic life in a large family in a large London house. Cressida Connolly reports that she knows people who "buy the *Spectator* for the 'Home Life' column alone," although she is "worried by its relentless pathos. Perhaps it is simply too like life. But surely one of that big family should notice when she is down in the dumps and offer some gesture of comfort, or at least mend her washing machine?" Harriet Waugh, who calls the column "rivetingly entertaining," nevertheless wrote (in the *Spectator*) that "I rather wish she would give up writing for *The Spectator*." Reviewing *The Clothes in the Wardrobe*, she maintained that Lili's "recognisable tones" were "familiar to 'Home Life' readers," and suggested that Ellis' "journalistic persona is beginning to infiltrate her fiction." A collection of these columns was published in 1986 as *Home Life*, and two more such volumes have followed.

The death of two of her children is a continuing part of the author's life, and is not excluded from the "Home Life" columns. When her grief was least manageable, she turned for help to the psychiatrist Tom Pitt-Aikens, with whom she has since collaborated on several books. The first of these, *Secrets of Strangers*, is the case-study of "Geoffrey Hutton," delinquent from the age of six, a thief, arsonist, and transvestite. The theory Pitt-Aikens advances in this book is that Hutton is a scapegoat for unadmitted, indeed unrecognized, conflicts within the family going back at least a generation. Therapy for the family as a whole had at least alleviated his symptoms and his parents' anxieties. Anthony Storr found that "some of the accounts of the family meetings . . . chaired by Tom Pitt-Aikens make tedious reading," but Ellis' account, "rightly intolerant of psychiatric jargon," made Storr "wish that psychiatric case-conferences were more often attended by critical non-professionals. . . . nothing drowns either Mrs. Ellis's sense or her sensibility."

The same theory is developed further in *Loss of the Good Authority*, where Pitt-Aikens proposes that "the parent(s) of a delinquent will *always* be found to have lost his own parent's (or parents') authority during childhood." He goes on to associate obesity, alcoholism, and even cancer with this "loss of the good authority," and, having discussed such loss in the family of Adolf Hitler, asks: "Should we allow . . . the grandsons of divorcees, widows or widowers to become president or prime minister or king?" Reviewing the book in the *Observer*, Anthony Burgess wrote that Pitt-Aikens' "scientific frigidity is warmed by the collaboration of Alice Thomas Ellis, who is a novelist and a Christian. She would be capable of imputing delinquency not just to the collapse of authority in grandparents but to that primordial catastrophe in the garden of Eden."

Duckworth & Co. have their offices, along with other companies, at the Old Piano Factory in Gloucester Crescent, in the Camden Town district of London. The Haycrafts live two hundred yards away on the same street. Duckworth has published most, though not all, of Ellis' books, for reasons adumbrated by Alan Franks in a *Times* profile (October 13, 1982). When Cape wanted to publish her second novel, Colin Haycraft reportedly said: "No; why should I cultivate the oyster and you get the pearl?"

Anna Haycraft remains a high and traditional Roman Catholic, and is far from happy with the Church's liberal tendencies. She told Alan that "I have not left the Catholic Church as much as the Catholic Church has left me." It follows that she favors a celibate priesthood and opposes the ordination of women. She is nevertheless "extremely feministic. . . . I agree that women have a really lousy time" because society sees them not as individuals "but as appendages. It's most insulting and wasteful, and women are right to kick up a terrific fuss about it." However, "what I couldn't stand was when, about five years ago, there was all that appalling wingeing. . . . I felt women did themselves no service by the adoption of such a 'Poor Me' posture."

PRINCIPAL WORKS: *Fiction*—The Sin Eater, 1977; The Birds of the Air, 1980; The 27th Kingdom, 1982; The Other Side of the Fire, 1983; Unexplained Laughter,

1985; The Clothes in the Wardrobe, 1987; The Skeleton in the Cupboard, 1988; The Fly in the Ointment, 1989. *As editor*—Mrs. Donald, by Mary Keene, 1983. *Non-fiction*—(as Brenda O'Casey) Natural Baby Food: A Cookery Book, 1977; (with Caroline Blackwood) Darling, You Shouldn't Have Gone to So Much Trouble, 1980; Home Life, 1986; (with Tom Pitt-Aikens) Secrets of Strangers, 1986; More Home Life, 1987; Home Life Three, 1989; (with Tom Pitt-Aikens) Loss of the Good Authority, 1989.

ABOUT: Contemporary Authors 122, 1988; Contemporary Literary Criticism 40, 1986; Who's Who, 1989. *Periodicals*—Books and Bookmen February 1983; Contemporary Review April 1978; Encounter November 1980; New Statesman December 16, 1977; September 16, 1983; New York Magazine October 15, 1984; Observer July 30, 1989; Saturday Review August 1981; Spectator August 31, 1985; October 24, 1987; Sunday Times June 27, 1982; Times (London) October 13, 1982; August 22, 1985; Times Literary Supplement August 15, 1980; July 2, 1982; September 17, 1988; September 23, 1988; November 10, 1989; Village Voice November 27, 1984.

*EMIN, GEVORG (October 30, 1919–), Armenian poet, essayist, and translator, was born Karlen Muradian, the son of a school teacher, in the then small but historically important village of Ashtarak (Ashtarag), from which Mt. Ararat can be seen. In 1927 his family left Ashtarak and moved to Yerevan (Erevan), the capital of Soviet Armenia. In 1936 he finished secondary school, and in 1940 he graduated from the local Polytechnical Institute as a hydraulic engineer. After graduation he designed and supervised the building of a hydroelectric power station which is still producing electricity.

That power station was his only engineering accomplishment. While still in school, the young Emin met Armenia's leading poet Yegishe Charentz (Charents), who died in 1937 in a Soviet prison, and "became his son in poetry." Emin recalls in his preface to *For You on New Year's Day*: "Today if I write instead of build canals and power plants it is due to two things: the impact of meeting the poet Eghishe Charents, and second, the touch of the ancient manuscripts at the Madenataran library where I worked as a student and could read and hold the magnificent old manuscripts from the fifth through the eighteenth centuries." Emin's roots as a poet are deeply embedded in the culture and the physical landscape of the country in which he grew up. "The source and beginnings of my poems are in Ashtarak and particularly the river which flows in the deep valley of Kasakh. From my childhood I came and listened to the mysterious murmuring of the river." To this is added his

°e mēn´

GEVORG EMIN

extensive reading in modern poetry, especially the French symbolist poets, and his enduring faith in the power of poetry: "I am one of those poets who believe in the strength of the word and who have the noble naiveté to think that poetry can change something in human life."

From 1941 to 1945 Emin fought (and was wounded) in World War II. His poetry makes no specific references to his own war experiences, but it often refers to the genocide practiced by the Turks against the Armenians and the Nazis against the Jews. He writes, for example:

> . . . I would also court martial
> the flower blooming at the Gestapo door
> and the dainty crescent moon
> illuminating the scimitar
> cutting Armenians down.
>
> Yes, and the canary that sang
> near the crematorium at Auschwitz.
> And the piece of paper that allowed
> lies printed on its face.
> And the thing, the unnamed thing that
> allows all the above to the repeated. . . .

Because Emin writes in Armenian, a language little known even within the Soviet Union, most of his poetry has been published in Russian translation. It was in Russian that the poet Yevgeny Yevtushenko read him and immediately hailed his work. Yevtushenko wrote the Introduction to the collection of Emin's verse translated into English as *For You on New Year's Day*; here the Russian poet contrasted Emin to his fellow Armenian poets who emphasized emotion in their work. "Gevorg Emin," Yevtushenko writes,

"has an entirely opposite conception of the craft. He takes pride in revealing the rational armature of poetry and the details of its construction. Some of his poems remind us of transparent watches where the movements and direction of each gear and lever are visible. But it is a watch that keeps perfect time." Perhaps as a result of his training in science Emin writes in a simple, straightforward language. ("I believe the exact sciences have endowed me with the discipline and sense of form and construction, plus an abhorrence of the superfluous and the hazy.") Edmond Y. Azadian, in an Afterword to *For You on New Year's Day*, suggests that Emin freed Armenian poetry "from the restrictions that followed Charents' time, the bleak Stalin era," reinvigorating it after a long period during which experimentalism had been discouraged. Martin Robbins suggests, in *Ararat Quarterly*, that his poetry reflects "the tough compression of an engineer's mathematically trained mind," and cites as a representative example his poem "Small," in which he acknowledges the defenselessness of the Armenian people but affirms their strength:

> Yes, we are small,
> the smallest pebble
> in a field of stones.
>
> But have you felt the hurtle
> of pebbles pitched
> from a mountain top?
>
> Small
> as the pinch of salt
> that seasons the table.
>
> Small, yes,
> you have compressed us,
> world, into a diamond.

In many of his poems Mt. Ararat itself serves as an emblem of the endurance of his people. In "Song of Songs" he writes: "I am an Armenian, ancient as this Biblical Ararat / my feet still wet from the waters of the flood." He remembers his proud heritage although

> Every century has cut a frown into my soul,
> scattered my children over the skin of the world,
> uprooted tree and reed and left the lowly bush,
> plunged Ararat into new tides of blood.

But his people survive "with the stubborn orphan's will," and will return to their land, "waiting to greet / a Golden Age once more."

Collections of Emin's poetry in Russian translation began to appear in 1940. He has twice won the Soviet State Prize for Poetry, in 1951 and again in 1976. Two of his books, a collection of essays (*Seven Songs of Armenia*) and of poems

(*Songs of Armenia*), were published in English in Moscow in 1974 and 1979 respectively. In 1972 he toured the United States with Yevtushenko giving poetry readings. At that time Yevtushenko said: "He spoke to the Americans from the power and truthfulness of his spirit in representing Armenia and its culture to them. Emin's mastery lies not only in the smoothness of his lines, but also in a spiritual mastery, a mastery of passionate conviction." His American experience is reflected in some of his later poems, published in *Land, Love, Century*, including "Gravestone in a Negro Cemetery," "First Night in New York," and "In the Streets of Boston."

In the Foreword to *Songs of Armenia* in 1979, Emin wrote candidly about his conviction that poetry must directly confront political realities, the "red news of massacre and blood. . . . To say nothing about certain periods of history, to keep silent about . . . rampant evil, escaping into so-called 'pure' poetry is tantamount to complicity in crime." Deceptively simple, his poems often use wit and the folklore of his native Ashtarak to mask a bold comment on the predicament of Iron Curtain writers. He writes in "Political Funeral":

> As if he never crawled,
> as if he did not bite,
> he lies here in state,
> even dignified,
>
> exactly like the snake
> or like the worm
> who never could go straight
> until the day it died.

Emin's first wife was the daughter of the distinguished Armenian poet Vahan Derian. After her death he married a writer, Armenouhi Hamparian. He has three sons. He says that he is proud of his sons' generation because it has a "noticeably higher culture and a working knowledge of foreign languages." Emin himself is a translator of note in Eastern Europe: he is especially admired for his translations of Polish poets ranging from the eighteenth-century poet Adam Mickiewicz to the contemporary poet Tadeusz Rozewicz. In Poland's long struggle for independence and national identity he identifies some of his own feelings about Armenia and he has hailed "the proud spirit of the Polish people, their fanatical attachment to their land, language, literature, tradition." Emin, who has been in poor health in recent years, lives in Erevan.

WORKS IN ENGLISH TRANSLATION: Two collections of Emin's poetry are available in English translation—Diana Der Hovanessian's *For You on New Year's Day* (1985) and *Land, Love, Century: New and Selected Poems* (1988), translated by Martin Robbins and Tatul Sonentz-Papazian. Selections of his poems in English translation appear in Ararat Quarterly, Summer 1972. *Seven Songs of Armenia* was published in the U.S.S.R. in 1970 in Isabel Chookaszian's translation and in 1983, translated by Mkrtich Soghikian.

ABOUT: Aragon, L. Littératures Soviétiques, 1955. *Periodicals*—Ararat Quarterly Summer 1972, Autumn 1987; Literary Review Spring 1980; New York Times November 18, 1971.

***ENCHI FUMIKO** (October 2, 1905–November 14, 1986), Japanese novelist, playwright, and short-story writer, was born in the Asakusa district of Tokyo. She was the last of three children born to the Kazutoshis—her mother Tsuruko and her father Ueda, who was professor of Japanese language and linguistics at Tokyo Imperial University. Kazutoshi had orignally intended to study drama (an interest he passed on to his daughter), but under the guidance of the British linguist Basil Hall Chamberlain, who taught at the Tokyo university from 1886 to 1890, he became interested in linguistics, and after advanced training in Germany he returned to teach in Japan and lay the foundation for the modern study of language. He was active in attempts to preserve the special qualities of the Japanese language, another feature which is echoed in his daughter's fiction. And when Chamberlain left Japan for the last time in 1911, he left his library of Japanese and Chinese classics to his prime pupil Ueda; those books were kept in the family's attic, where young Fumiko spent much time reading and familiarizing herself with a literary heritage that was to become the core of her own writing.

Though plagued by ill health and thus frequently absent from class, Fumiko completed four years of higher school in 1922. Although her formal education ended there, the family hired tutors to continue her training in English, French and classical Chinese. She was also taken frequently by her mother to see Kabuki plays, and her grandmother entertained her by relating the plots of seventeenth- and eighteenth-century novels and plays. When she was only ten years old, Fumiko picked up a copy of the eleventh-century novel *The Tale of Genji*, a work many adult Japanese could decipher better in English translation than in the original classical Japanese, and read the entire work. That experience sparked her interest in the Japanese classics, and she read many other volumes over the next few years. But Fumiko was also a child of her surroundings, and while she maintained an interest in the Japanese literary heritage, she also

*en´ chē foo´ mē kō

became absorbed in such decorative modernists (all of whom shared her fascination with classical writings) as Tanizaki Jun'ichirō, Nagai Kafū, and Izumi Kyōka. The foreign authors who appealed to her most in her formative years were Wilde, Poe, and Hoffmann.

In 1926, she first tried her hand at playwriting; her one-act, "Furusato" (Hometown), was singled out for recognition by two of the most important theater figures of the day, Okamoto Kidō and Osanai Kaoru. The play depicts the homecoming of the beloved nineteenth-century poet Issa and his attempts to smooth over the strained relationship with his stepmother and stepbrother. Okamoto found the play particularly effective in depicting the weak aspects of Issa's personality, and in the characterization of the stepbrother's new wife, the only character who shows warmth and sympathy toward Issa.

The young author's one-act play, Banshun Sōya (A Noisy Night in Late Spring, 1928) was performed at Osanai's Tsukiji Little Theatre, at the time the most important stage for modern drama in Japan. In the play, two women who have been close friends finally walk separate paths. When one decides to devote her life to leftist political activism, the other clings to art as her form of personal expression. Osanai described the play as "depicting personality very ably, but still not an adequate portrayal of human life." The sympathy for left-wing political views, not unusual for this period in Japan, came to Fumiko through her friendship with several women authors who became actively involved in writing proletarian literature. She herself never took strident political stances in her writings, though she remained sympathetic to the leftist movement.

In 1930 she married Enchi Yoshimatsu, a reporter for the Tokyo Nichinichi newspaper. She gave birth to a daughter in 1932, and in 1935 her first collection of plays, titled Sekishun (Lamenting the Passing of Spring), was published. Her dramaturgy derived largely from her readings of Hauptmann and Galsworthy. Enchi Fumiko also began writing short stories in 1935, and her first collection, Kaze no Gotoki Kotoba (Words Like the Wind) appeared in 1939. But her writing was often interrupted by ill health: in 1938 she underwent surgery for mastitis. Later diseases and surgery also seemed to involve her female organs, and it is worth noting that her postwar fiction deals predominantly with women who have been deprived of the pleasures and travails of sexual association and childbearing, and whose attendant frustration often erupts in acts of vengefulness, both against men who retain their virility and women who still enjoy their youth.

In 1941, Enchi joined several other writers to tour south China and Hainan Island on behalf of the Japanese navy. After the outbreak of fighting on the Chinese mainland, most established writers were persuaded to join patriotic associations and to lecture in various parts of the Japanese empire on the virtues of Japanese culture and the need for Asian cooperation. Her wartime literary activities largely consisted of writing children's adaptations of the indigenous classics.

Enchi's family lost their home and all their material possessions in a fire bomb raid on Tokyo in 1945, and they were evacuated to a summer cottage in Karuizawa until the surrender. After their return to Tokyo in 1946, Enchi again went into the hospital, this time for uterine cancer complicated by pneumonia. She continued in poor health for over two years. No sooner had she begun to recover than she started writing pulp novels for juvenile readers in an attempt to stave off poverty. But many of the manuscripts which she hand-delivered to publishers were rejected. It was during this difficult period that she completed the first chapter of her novel Onnazaka (Female Slope; translated as The Waiting Years).

It was not until 1953 that a short story finally broke the hex of failure and obscurity for Enchi; it was, appropriately, titled "Himojii Tsukihi" (Days and Months of Hunger). A largely autobiographical story, it treats a housewife who struggles to keep her family from starvation while she is ignored and abused by her apathetic, palsied husband. The shock of her son's announcement that they ought to arrange his father's death increases the intensity of her ministrations to her husband, but she drops dead one day while washing his clothes in the bathroom. The story received the Women's Literature Prize for 1954, invited both praise and "shudders" from important male authors, and established Enchi as an important figure in postwar fiction. Her reputation was further enhanced with the appearance of Ake o Ubau Mono (The Vermilion Pilferer, 1955), the first volume in an autobiograpical trilogy of novels which center on an intelligent, sensuous woman trapped in an unsatisfying marriage but determined to act out the role of the obedient housewife. Eventually she concludes that the only way to maintain her identity as a woman is to begin to write. The motif spills over into one of her finest short stories. "Yō" (translated as "The Enchantress," 1956).

In 1957, the novel Enchi had struggled over for many years, The Waiting Years, was completed. It was widely hailed, awarded the important Noma Prize for fiction, and described by novelist Mishima Yukio as an "enduring classic."

The structural outline of the novel shows an indebtedness to *The Tale of Genji* : a male character, an important political figure in the early years of the Meiji period, is placed at the center of the work, and is surrounded by a principal wife and several mistresses. But in Enchi's modern work the husband is relegated to a minor role, and the chief focus in upon the wife, Tomo, an intelligent, vibrant woman who quietly endures a great deal of philandering by her husband. She eventually is reduced to the role of selecting new mistresses for him, bringing them to live in the same house with her; she looks on wordlessly as he sleeps with the maids and even their own daughter-in-law. Tomo's impeccable management of the household earns her the respect if not the love of her husband, but she is unable to attain either of her final wishes: to outlive her husband, and to have her ashes cast upon the ocean rather than buried in his family crypt.

Another important short story, "Nise no en—Shūi" (A Bond For Two Lifetimes—Gleanings, 1957), highlights Enchi's ability to intermingle classical texts with modern situations. Here again a stark contrast is drawn between the enduring passions of the mind and the debilitation of the body. The central female character is drawn into an intellectual bond with an aged, physically decrepit scholar when she serves as scribe for his translation of a seventeenth-century tale into modern Japanese. There are indications throughout the story that the scholar, who is so shrivelled and impotent that he can scarcely rise from his bed, would like to turn the relationship into a romantic liaison, even though he no longer has the capacity. Ironically, the old tale he is translating is about a Buddhist priest who is restored to life after many years in the grave; he has lost all traces of religious devotion and has become fanatically absorbed in carnal fulfillment. Enchi proposes in this story that the bonds of lust are the most enduring ties between men and women, and her heroine is able to feel a degree of forgiveness for the "inevitable sexual aggressions of men."

Perhaps nowhere in Enchi's writings are the frustrations of unfulfilled passion and the power struggle between men and women more forcefully and frighteningly portrayed than in her novel *Onnamen* (Masks, 1958). The ties to *The Tale of Genji* are overt in this work: the heroine Mieko, a beautiful, mysterious widow who has gone through an unhappy marriage and a tragic love affair with a man who was killed in the war, devotes herself to a study of spirit possession and compares herself to the Rokujō Lady in *Genji* whose spirit attacks and kills her rivals for the prince's affections. Accumulating images from *Genji*, the Noh plays, classical poetry and mythology, Enchi describes the elaborate plot which Mieko conceives, involving cruel manipulation of her widowed daughter-in-law and her own retarded daughter, as a means of achieving revenge upon the men who have used her.

The ensuing decade was a highly productive and successful one for Enchi. She published several volumes of short stories, as well as a number of plays and novels. In 1958, at the invitation of the Asia Foundation, she joined her close friend, Hirabayashi Taiko, one of the early proletarian women authors, on a three-month excursion through Europe and the United States. Her account of that experience was published as *Obei no Tabi* (Journey through Europe and America, 1959). The major novels from this period are *Kizu Aru Tsubasa* (Crippled Wings, 1962), the second volume of her autobiographical trilogy, and the work which some critics regard as her best, *Namamiko Monogatari* (Tale of a False Shamaness, 1965). This novel, according to critic and writer Takenishi Hiroko, "combines the motifs of 'Days and Months of Hunger' and *The Waiting Years* with those of 'The Enchantress' and 'A Bond For Two Lifetimes,'" in the sense that it is a distillation of Enchi's sympathy for frustrated modern women and her attraction to the elegant world depicted in classical texts by female authors. It is an elaborately constructed narrative, merging the present with a central story line set in the tenth-century court of Emperor Ichijō. The powerful regent, Michinaga, plots various stratagems to drive a wedge between Ichijō and the empress Teishi, so that he can install his own daughter as the favored consort. He employs a false shamaness to stir up rumors about the malignant "living ghost" that resides within Teishi, but Teishi's love for Ichijō is so strong and pure that her spirit is able to overpower the false shamaness and force her to speak the truth. Enchi casts the fairytale-like story in such convincing terms, even employing classical diction to relate portions of the narrative, that the reader is drawn into accepting it; at the same time, a separate, more cynical narrative voice from the modern period through which the story is filtered suggests that the idyllic, untainted love between Ichijō and Teishi is an impossibility in our present world. The virtuosity with which Enchi balances and intertwines these separate narrative voices attracted the praise of many critics and readers and earned the novel the Women's Literature Prize for 1966.

Just a year after she completed *Namamiko Monogatari*, Enchi followed in the wake of a handful of other twentieth-century writers and commenced a six-year labor of translating *The Tale of Genji* into modern Japanese. She supplemented her translation with two volumes of essays on the *Genji*, including several analyses of the female characters who play prominent roles in the classical novel. In 1968, Enchi finished her autobiographical trilogy with the publication of *Niji to Shura* (Rainbows and Carnage); the completed trilogy received the Tanizaki Prize for literature.

Enchi remained productive through several more bouts with illness, including surgery for a detached retina in 1969 and chronic heart disease. In 1970, she spent the summer semester at the University of Hawaii, where she presented lectures on modern Japanese female writers. That same year, she was elected to membership in the Geijutsuin, the Japan Academy of Arts.

She remained productive and vigorous to the end of her life. The finest literary products of her late years were the short-story collection, *Haru no Uta* (Song of Spring, 1971), with a chilling title story about a decrepit grandmother who remains convinced of her sexual attractiveness to young male relatives; the collection *Yūkon* (Free-floating Spirit, 1971), which received the Grand Prize for Japanese Literature; and her final novel, *Kikujidō* (Chrysanthemum Child, 1984), in which she ironically employs the central image, from Chinese legend, of a lady-in-waiting at the court of the Chinese emperor who attained eternal youth by drinking the dewdrops from a chrysanthemum; this classical legend she counterpoises against several characters who wander in the blind delusions of old age. In 1985, the year before her death, she became the second female author to receive the Bunka Kunshō, the Order of Cultural Merit, the highest official honor bestowed upon Japanese creative artists.

WORKS IN ENGLISH TRANSLATION: *The Waiting Years* and "The Enchantress" were translated by John Bester, in 1958 and 1971, respectively; "A Bond For Two Lifetimes—Gleanings" was translated by Phyllis Birnbaum in 1982; *Masks* was translated by Juliet Winters Carpenter in 1983.

ABOUT: Encyclopedia of Japan, 1984; Vernon, V. Daughters of the Moon: Wish, Will, and Social Constraint in Fiction by Modern Japanese Women, 1988. *Periodicals*—World Literature Today Summer 1988.

*ENDE, MICHAEL (ANDREAS HELMUTH) (November 12, 1929–   ), is a German author of fiction, plays, and songs. His publisher Edition Weitbrecht, in Stuttgart, sends the following: "Michael Ende was born in Garmisch-Partenkirchen. His father Edgar Ende, one of the first German surrealist painters (1901–1965),

MICHAEL ENDE

who was prohibited from pursuing his vocation by the Nazis, continued to paint in secret. During this period, his mother Luise, née Bartholomä, provided for the family by working as a physiotherapist and masseuse. Michael Ende grew up in bohemian Schwabing, amidst painters, sculptors, and writers. There he went to elementary school, had to join the Hitler Youth, and, from 1940 on, attended the Maximilian Gymnasium. In the final year of the war when fourteen- and fifteen-year-olds were called up, three classmates died on the very first day of their tour of duty. Michael Ende ripped up his draft orders. Shortly after the end of the war his father returned from an American POW camp. In 1946 Michael returned to his Schwabing school for one year; his last two years were spent at the Free Waldorf School in Stuttgart. In 1943 Ende began writing poems and short narratives. For financial reasons a university education was out of the question. In Munich he attended the Otto Falckenberg School for actors from 1948–1950; following his graduation he was employed at the Landesbühne Schleswig-Holstein for one season. He returned to Munich subsequently.

"In 1951 he met Ingeborg Hoffmann, his future wife and an actress through whom he was able to establish connections with the political-literary cabarets. He wrote sketches and songs; he also directed performances at the Munich Volkstheater and wrote film reviews for the Bavarian Broadcasting Company. In the meantime his parents had separated; the financial situation became more and more difficult, and there was barely enough money to pay the rent for himself and his mother.

"As a consequence of his exposure to [Bertolt] Brecht's aesthetics and theories of dramaturgy, Michael Ende went through an artistic and literary crisis. Although he had decided to give up writing, he gave himself one last chance. At the request of a graphic artist he wrote the text for a picture-book, which—by 1958—had become a very thick manuscript, *Jim Knopf und Lukas der Lokomotivführer* (translated as *Jim Button and Luke the Engine Driver*). He contacted more than ten publishers; nobody was interested. Finally Lotte Weitbrecht, then chief editor at Thienemann's, accepted the manuscript. It was revised to appear in two volumes. The first volume received the German Jugendbuchpreis (an award for adolescent literature); upon the publication of the second volume there followed radio- and TV-series based on the book as well as translations into many languages. In 1964 Michael Ende and Ingeborg Hoffmann were married in Rome. They bought a villa in Campagna, south of Rome, where he lived from 1971 until the late 1980s. There he wrote his fairy-tale novel *Momo* in 1972, although initially considered quite controversial, the book was awarded the German Jugendbuchpreis in 1974. In 1979 he published *Die unendliche Geschichte* (translated as *The Neverending Story*) which established his international reputation.

"Other publications were to follow: *Das Gauklermärchen* (The Juggler's Fairy Tale, 1982), a play in seven scenes with a prologue and an epilogue, which was staged several times; *Phantasie/Kultur/Politik: Protokolleines Gesprächs* (Fantasy/Culture/Politics: The Protocol of a Conversation, 1982); *Der Spiegel im Spiegel: Ein Labyrinth* (1984; translated as *The Mirror in the Mirror*); *Der Goggolori* (1984), a Bavarian legend, accompanied by Wilfried Hiller's musical composition and performed in Munich; *Archäologie der Dunkelheit* (Archaeology of Darkness, 1985), conversations about art and the oeuvre of the painter Edgar Ende (with a view to a monograph about his father); *Trödelmarkt der Träume* (Rag-fair of Dreams, 1986), midnight songs and ballads. *Die Spielverderber* (The Spoilsport, 1967), a play, remains unpublished. Ende's books have been translated into twenty-eight languages and have reached an edition totaling over five million copies. For his literary works he received numerous German and international prizes and awards.

"Ende's wife Ingeborg died in March 1985. Michael Ende returned to Germany and is living in Munich once again."

— FRANK THOMAS J. EVANS

Without any question Michael Ende has been one of the most successful German writers in recent years. Ever since the 1979 publication of *Die unendliche Geschichte* (*The Neverending Story*) his reputation, along with the sales figures of his books, has soared. For months and months *The Neverending Story* was at the top of best-seller lists in respectable German weeklies; there is a constant demand for new editions, and the circulation of his books in public libraries continues to be brisk. Besides the television adaptations of *Jim Knopf*, *The Neverending Story* was adapted to the screen by Wolfgang Petersen (better known for his film *Das Boot*) in 1984; an adaptation of *Momo* by the avant-garde director Johannes Schaaf followed in 1986. Many of Ende's stories and plays are also available on records and cassettes. Michael Ende himself admits that not in his wildest dreams had he ever dared to imagine such a breakthrough.

What accounts for such popularity? First of all, Ende is a superb storyteller who holds the attention of readers from the beginning to the end of his typically quite voluminous novels that introduce us into a fantasy world reminiscent of such classics of children's literature as *Alice in Wonderland*, *The Wizard of Oz*, *Treasure Island*, *The Grinch Who Stole Christmas*, and *Where the Wild Things Are*. At times, the reader also finds himself strongly reminded of movie productions by either Walt Disney or Stephen Spielberg. Ende's appeal to children and young adolescents is not surprising since the protagonists of his novels and picture books are frequently children themselves, speaking their language—precocious and yet delightfully unself-conscious—while simultaneously transcending their everyday world in the most charming, at times touching manner.

To the four inhabitants of Lummerland in *Jim Knopf und Lukas der Lokomotivführer* the arrival of Jim, a tiny black boy delivered in a mysterious package off a mail ship, amounts to a population explosion. In order to create space for the growing boy, the King eventually demands that Lukas, the engine driver, get rid of his locomotive Emma. Instead Lukas decides to leave with Emma, and Jim, who does not want to lose his fatherly friend, joins them on a voyage which takes them to Mandala (China) where they hear of the abduction of the Emperor's young daughter. As they attempt to find and free her, Lukas, Emma, and Jim undergo many adventures, e.g., coming up against a halfdragon and a giant who grows smaller upon approach. Eventually they penetrate into Sorrowland, the dragon city, where they find the princess and 1100 her from the clutches of her devilish teacher, Mrs. Grindtooth. On their return trip to Lummerland they catch a floating magnetic island which they will attach to Lummerland, thus solving their country's space problems. Jim gets his own locomotive and celebrates his engagement to the princess of Mandala. In the sequel to the novel, *Jim Knopf und die Wilde 13* (Jim Knopf and the Wild 13), Jim and Lukas set out for new adventures, visit old friends, discover the origin of the foundling Jim, and defeat the Wild 13, a gang of pirates who had kidnapped Jim as well as other children in order to sell them to Mrs. Grindtooth. In the end, the outsiders and misfits will be integrated into the social fabric of Lummerland. The giant works as a lighthouse, the half-dragon is the guardian of the magnet island, a very much mellowed Mrs. Grindtooth will lecture on the Blossoms of Wisdom, and the Wild 13 become Jim's bodyguards. According to one German critic, Jim Knopf represents the symbiosis of technology and fantasy. He works as an engine driver and yet, as prince of a legendary empire, he wears a crown of myrrh.

Momo and *The Neverending Story* are fairytale novels, children's books for adults. Rooted in the tradition of German romanticism (Novalis, E.T.A. Hoffmann) Ende's young heroes criticize the course of history and represent a still innocent state of being. Momo, a ten-year-old girl with no family, lives in the ruins of an ancient amphitheater at the periphery of a large city. She has the very rare gift of being able to listen to her friends, to make them "aware of ideas whose existence they had never suspected," and thereby to help them solve their problems. A ghostly society of "men in grey" about town coerce people to save more and more time. In reality, however, they cheat people out of their time, and the more people "save" time and quantify everything they do, the more alienated, hectic, and ruthless they become. Most of the children are the victims of this ever increasing loss of love and life. At a time when the world has been nearly taken over by the men in grey, Master Hora, the mysterious manager of time, decides to interfere, but he needs the help of Momo, who agrees to take up the fight against the time-thieves—all alone with a flower in her hands and the turtle Cassiopeia under her arm. In the end all the time out of which people had been cheated is returned to its owners. The world is healed again: the principle of "time is life" triumphs over the notion that "time is money." As Ende explains in *Phantasie/Kultur/Politik: Protokoll eines Gesprächs*, Momo represents a new type of hero, i.e., someone who is heroic in her passivity as opposed to "the Arthurian knights ranging from John Wayne to Gary Cooper (and Che Guevara too)."

The romantic blending of dream and reality

that Ende practiced and advocated in *Momo* is developed further in *The Neverending Story*. The land of Fantastica is in great danger: the Childlike Empress suffers from a terminal illness: her country and its inhabitants are disappearing into nothingness. Only a new name invented by a human child can save her and her empire. But humans have long ceased to come to Fantastica—until Bastian Balthasar Bux, a fat little boy whose mother died and who is constantly laughed at and beaten up by his classmates, steals a book with the title "The Neverending Story" from Mr. Koreander, the owner of an old book store. Hiding in the attic of his schoolbuilding Bastian begins to read about the problems of Fantastica and gradually realizes that he alone can help. With Auryn, the sign of the Childlike Emperess, he penetrates deeper and deeper into the land of gnomes, good-luck dragons, will-o'-the-wisps, etc. and into the stream of untamed fantasy which makes him almost forget his origins and his ultimate destination. The image of his father that appears before him finally moves Bastian to seek his return to his own world. *The Neverending Story* is a very carefully constructed novel. It is divided into twenty-six chapters whose opening letters follow the alphabet. According to a comment made in the novel, all stories consist of twenty-six letters. "The letters remain the same, only their composition changes. You make words out of letters, sentences out of words, chapters out of sentences and books out of chapters." The combinative possibilities are neverending. After the thirteenth letter, exactly in the middle of the novel and as the clock strikes midnight, Bastian invents a new name for the empress, thus saving Fantastica from annihilation. Bastian learns to overcome his diffidence and to develop his self-esteem in the first part of the novel; in the second part he has to overcome his own vanity, his love of power and his arrogance in order to find his way out of Fantastica and return to reality where his lonely father longs for affection.

The blending of reality and fantasy, of reading and acting, is reflected in the design of the book: the plot of the frame in which Bastian functions as recipient of the book he is reading is printed in red, whereas the accounts of Fantastica's history, its current predicament and Bastian's adventures once he enters the land of Fantastica are printed in green. The typography with its complementary colors reflects not only Bastian's dual role as recipient and agent but also Ende's message that his young protagonist must learn to negotiate between fantasy and reality in order to be able to cope with everyday life and to become a giving, fully responsible human being. To the extent that Bastian develops a new conscience and a new self-awareness, *The Neverending Story* is a *Bildungsroman* charting the inner development of a young person, as Ende himself stated in *Phantasie/Kultur/Politik*.

A number of themes central to Ende's work reappear in the thirty surrealist prose pieces collected in *Der Spiegel im Spiegel: Ein Labyrinth*, illustrated with lithographs and etchings by Ende's father. A single word or a mythological motif leads the reader from one text to the next; sometimes a marginal figure in one story will assume a central role later in the collection. Plots dissolve into visions, dreamscapes, and nightmares. The narrator's sobriety of tone, contrasting sharply with the absurdity of the situations described, is at times oddly reminiscent of Kafka's parables. However, in contradistinction to Kafka's world, which offers no way out, Ende's labyrinth is not so much a maze as a symbol of self-discovery. In order to find your way out, you must turn around, conquer the Minotaur within yourself and—a difficult proposition to say the least—"change once again into the reversed mirror image of your own mirrored mirror image."

While he is best known for his children's books and novels, Ende's love of the theater has stayed with him through the years. Not only the theater versions of his novels, but also his picture book, *Ophelias Schattentheater* (translated as *Ophelia's Shadow Theater*) and his various plays and librettos have been moderately successful. In *Gauklermärchen*, a group of circus artists are about to be driven away from a vacant lot by a chemical corporation in the process of expanding its plant. The management offers the circus people an income provided they agree to travel and advertise the corporation's products. However, a retarded girl whom the artists find lying deadly ill in a ditch following an environmental catastrophe, must be institutionalized since her presence would do damage to the corporation's promotional campaign. Although the circus people all love Eli, they almost give in to the pressure. Clown Jojo tells his fellow artists a fairy tale which, in their imagination, carries them off into the better world of Morrowland. Back in reality, as the construction machines are moving in on them, they decide to tear up and burn their contract with the corporation. "Do you believe that fantasy is not real," Jojo asks and, echoing Ende's thoughts, he adds: "Out of fantasy future worlds do grow: In what we create, we are free." Ende's libretto *Der Goggolori* is an adaptation of a sixteenth-century Bavarian legend. Goggolori, a goblin, would have to live for ever if it were not for the self-sacrifice of a peasant maiden who renounces her own mortality so that Goggolori can finally die and thus gain the blessing of his resurrection. Here, too, as in Ende's fairy-tale novels and in *Gauklermärchen*, good triumphs over evil once again. Most recently Michael Ende wrote a libretto for clowns, a translation with variations on Lewis Carroll's nonsense poem "The Hunting of the Snark."

The reasons for Ende's appeal to adult readers appear rather complex. Undeniably his books offer escape and entertainment; they are "fun" reading especially when one keeps in mind that so much contemporary German literature is politically committed and purposefully disquieting, addressing such issues as Germany's national guilt and what social psychologist Alexander Mitscherlich diagnosed at his country's "inability to mourn." Michael Ende, however, takes issue with the proposition that his work is escapist in nature. His goal is more serious and ambitious than merely to provide fuel for the entertainment industry. According to him, the task of the writer consists in creating social awareness, not in offering concrete solutions to the problems of industrial society. As he explained in *Phantasie/Kultur/Politik* our century is characterized by an alarming absence of positive utopias and happy visions of the future. Ende considers it crucial for the survival of our species that we create positive images of the world we wish to live in. Furthermore, technocratic positivism constitutes a system of terror. Ende is against the preponderance of one-dimensional Cartesian thinking. Without condemning quantifying thought altogether, he postulates the need for a mutation of thinking, for a leap of consciousness. We ought to push forward towards what Ende (somewhat vaguely) terms "multidimensionality." "We must not reverse the Enlightenment but enlighten the Enlightenment concerning itself and its consequences." For man to feel at home in this world, the inner and the outer world need to converge. Once again man wishes to find himself in a larger, different context. Not only has Ende discovered a new yearning for spirituality in his readers; he also concedes that his own quest for a new reality is in essence religious. Michael Ende is not simply a latterday German romantic; he also proves to be a successful popularizer of recent theories that made a case for postmodern pluralism and launched virulent attacks against the New Frankfurt School (especially Jürgen Habermas) with its indebtedness and commitment to the traditions of Enlightenment thought.

WORKS IN ENGLISH TRANSLATION: *The Neverending Story* was translated by Ralph Manheim in 1983. J. Maxwell Brownjohn translated *Momo*, 1985, and *The Mirror in the Mirror*, 1986. An earlier translation of

der the title *The Grey Gentlemen* was done by Frances Loeb in 1974. *Ophelia's Shadow Theater* was translated by Anthea Bell in 1989, and in 1990 *Jim Knopf* was translated by Bell as *Jim Button and Luke the Engine Driver.*

ABOUT: Contemporary Authors 118, 1985; Contemporary Literary Criticism 31, 1985; Dictionary of Literary Biography 75, 1988; Something About the Author 42, 1986. *Periodicals*—Christian Science Monitor November 9, 1983; Library Journal October 15, 1983; New York Times Book Review November 6, 1983; February 17, 1985; Newsweek November 14, 1983; Seminar 23 1987; Times Literary Supplement November 25, 1983.

EPHRON, NORA (May 19, 1941–   ), American journalist, essayist, and screenwriter, was born in New York City, the daughter of Henry and Phoebe (Wolkind) Ephron, playwrights and Hollywood screenwriters, and grew up in the affluence of Beverly Hills. In the early 1960s, Ephron made her mark precociously on the theater when her parents based their play *Take Her, She's Mine* on her letters home from Wellesley College. After receiving her B.A. from Wellesley in 1962, she became a reporter for the *New York Post*; and in 1968–1972 was a freelance journalist. In 1973–1974 she was a contributing editor for *New York* magazine, and in 1974–1978 was senior editor and columnist at *Esquire*. Ephron married the writer Dan Greenburg in 1967; they were subsequently divorced. Her second marriage in 1976 to Carl Bernstein, who achieved fame through his coverage of the Watergate scandal for the *Washington Post*, also ended in divorce. She has two sons by Carl Bernstein—Jacob and Max.

Wallflower at the Orgy collects pieces Ephron wrote for *Vogue, Harper's Bazaar, New York, Esquire*, and the *New York Times Magazine* during 1968–1969, mostly on such celebrities and trend-setters as Craig Claiborne, Jacqueline Susann, Bill Blass, and *Women's Wear Daily*. The book was well received by reviewers. Henry S. Resnik in the *Saturday Review* commented that Ephron "captures the true spirit of the popular arts in America perfectly. . . . Ephron is at her best when probing and exposing the mass-cult sensibility, for she brings to the subject just the right combination of camp playfulness and shrewd intelligence." The reviewer for *Booklist* praised her "entertainingly sophisticated, tongue-in-cheek profiles," and the critic for *Library Journal* characterized the book as "urbane and sophisticated journalism . . . a fine collection for those 'in the know.'"

Wallflower at the Orgy was followed by

NORA EPHRON

Crazy Salad: Some Things About Women, another collection of her magazine articles. Barbara Zelenko in *Library Journal* praised the book as "witty and absorbing. . . . At her best, Ephron brings a great deal of herself to her writing . . . but she is good at thoroughly researched, impersonal reporting as well. Her feminist consciousness is evident throughout, but Ephron is a far too perceptive and original writer to take the usual movement line on every occasion." The reviewer for *Booklist* observed that Ephron "has an admirable taste for the outrageous as her feminist consciousness has been raised . . . these collected articles record with a waggish perception the trials and rewards, pleasures and tribulations of growing up as a woman in America." Susan Braudy in *Ms.* noted, similarly, that "if you've ever heard Nora Ephron hold forth on television, or read her excellent pieces in *Esquire* and *New York* magazine—many of which are collected in *Crazy Salad*—you know her unpredictable and trenchant take on any subject and her unique voice: smart, witty, and confidential. And her voice—written or verbal—is backed by a brilliant, restless mind."

Ephron's third collection, *Scribble Scribble*, centering on the media, was also well received. The reviewer for *Booklist* remarked that Ephron "subjects the print medium (principally) and fellow journalists to her hard-edged wit. . . . With a few restrained exceptions, the pieces in this collection exemplify the caustic cleverness that has gained their author a measure of celebrity." John Leonard in the *New York Times Book*

Review wrote that Ephron "can write about anything better than anybody else can write about anything. . . . She is that peculiar phenomenon, the blithe moralist, the mistress of the steely clause, a brilliant scourge." John Deedy in the *Critic*, however, found the pieces sketchy and less thoughtful than Ephron's work at its best. The question, he marked, "is how long she can hold her book audience with reprinted 1500-word columns. One of these days her audience is going to insist on something more substantive."

In the early 1980s, Ephron collaborated with Alice Arlen on the screenplay of *Silkwood*, released in 1983, which dramatizes the life of Karen Silkwood, her involvement with certain incidents at the nuclear plant at Crescent, Oklahoma, and the mysterious circumstances surrounding her death in a car crash. Directed by Mike Nichols, and starring Meryl Streep and Kurt Russell, *Silkwood* proved to be one of the most commercially successful and talked-about movies of the year. Several reviewers, however, found fault with Ephron's script, accusing her of taking liberties with supposedly factual material. Richard Schickel in *Time* remarked that "Unable to prove a corporate conspiracy against Silkwood . . . the movie must content itself with showing, without comment, mysterious headlights appearing behind her car just before the crash. And then admit, on a concluding title card, that an autopsy revealed large amounts of tranquilizers as well as a small amount of alcohol in the system of this demonstrably unstable woman. This is the most significant set of contradictory implications in a movie that is a tissue of them. And they leave the viewer about where he began, free to consult his own paranoia, or lack of it, for an interpretation of her life and death." Stanley Kauffmann in the *New Republic* raised similar objections, complaining that "The script by Nora Ephron and Alice Arlen is a compound of compromise, alteration, and misleading implication—all serious matters in what purports to be a true story."

Heartburn, Ephron's first novel, draws on her marriage to Carl Bernstein and its breakup. Reviewers immediately noted the autobiographical basis of the novel, and had mixed feelings about it as a fictional entity. "Let's face it," Grace Glueck commented in the *New York Times Book Review*, "this dishy *roman à clef* is not a novel to make Virginia Woolf fans change their allegiances. It is not to be read for its penetrating insights into their character—and maybe it's not a novel at all." Christopher Lehman-Haupt in the *New York Times* remarked that the "question is why any woman, real or imaginary, would attach herself and then reattach herself to a man who could cheat on her compulsively and

promise to stop and then continue cheating on her when she was foolish enough to believe him. . . . For a while, she fends off the question with wit and comedy, and we collaborate happily in the evasion by laughing. . . . [But] we really want her to achieve a glimmer of self-understanding." The autobiographical nature of the novel was a problem for several reviewers. "Is *Heartburn* a good novel?" Stuart Schoffman asked in the *Los Angeles Times Book Review*. "It is innocent, to be sure, of literary pretensions, resembling in style an endless but entertaining phone call from a college roommate not heard from in years. . . . Lit professors and coy novelists will tell you it is a dangerous mistake to confuse author and narrator. Here, such a caveat is laughable, and Ephron of course knows it. It is impossible to separate this novel from its own publicity." *Heartburn* was adapted by Ephron herself for the screen, but the resulting film, released in 1986, was not particularly successful, despite the contributions of Mike Nichols, Meryl Streep, and Jack Nicholson; Ephron's bittersweet comedy *When Harry Met Sally . . .*, directed by Rob Reiner and released in 1989, had greater "audience appeal."

Ephron lives in New York City with her two small sons, and earns a living by writing screenplays. Interviewed in *Vogue* in 1983, shortly after the publication of *Heartburn*, and asked if she was still "optimistic about the institution of marriage," she replied in the frank, funny, and wry manner that marks her prose. "I don't know," she commented, "what I think any more. It seems to me, looking back on the last twenty years of my life, that my happier times were as a single person. And you know the statistics are that the happiest people are married men and the second happiest are single women. But I'm not in much of a position, that's for sure. I mean, it's really like asking Ann Boleyn what she thought of marriage."

PRINCIPAL WORKS: *Essays*—Wallflower at the Orgy, 1970; Crazy Salad, 1975; Scribble Scribble, 1978. *Novel*—Heartburn, 1983.

ABOUT: Contemporary Authors New Revision Series 12, 1984; Contemporary Literary Criticism 17, 1981; 31, 1985; Who's Who in America, 1988–89; Who's Who of American Women, 1989–90; *Periodicals*—Critic August 15, 1978; Los Angeles Times Book Review April 17, 1983; Ms. November 1975; New Republic January 23, 1984; New York Times April 8, 1983; New York Times Book Review April 18, 1970, April 24, 1988; Saturday Review November 21, 1970; Time December 19, 1988.

EPSTEIN, JOSEPH (January 9, 1937–),
American essayist, was born in Chicago, the son
of Maurice Epstein, a businessman and salesman, and the former Belle Abrams. After attending public schools in his native city, he
entered the University of Chicago, where he
earned a bachelor's degree in 1959. He has
worked as associate editor of the *New Leader*
magazine and as senior editor of the
Encyclopaedia Britannica ; he was once director
of the anti-poverty program in Little Rock, Arkansas. In 1973 he was a fellow in urban journalism at the University of Chicago, and he has
been a visiting lecturer at Northwestern University. He has two children from his first marriage,
and in 1976 married Barbara Maker, an editor.

Epstein has written for the *New Yorker*,
Harper's, the *Atlantic*, *Commentary*, the *New
York Review of Books*, and *Dissent*, but is perhaps best known as the author, under the pseudonym Aristides, of a regularly appearing column
in the *American Scholar*, the Washington-based
quarterly published since 1932 by the United
Chapters of Phi Beta Kappa. Epstein has been
chief editor of the magazine since 1974. In an
early column, he admitted his identification
with Aristides the Just, "the early fifth-century
Athenian leader who was finally ostracized by
the citizens of Athens because they grew tired of
always hearing him called the Just."

The first collection of his *American Scholar*
pieces appeared under the title *Familiar Territory: Observations on American Life*. In his introduction, he terms his essays "of the type known
as 'familiar.' . . . The familiar essayist lives,
and takes his professional sustenance, in the everyday flow of things. Familiar is his style and
familiar, too, is the territory he writes about."
Epstein has no difficulty in finding subjects for
his essays. "For the familiar essayist in America,
every day is like Christmas morning in a wealthy
and loving Christian home; subjects, like gifts,
are strewn about everywhere. In the end the true
job of the familiar essayist is to write what is in
his mind and in his heart in the hope that, in doing so, he will say what others have sensed only
inchoately." Essays are included on, among other topics, the proper way to begin and end letters
and, by extension, the proper way to address others; the need for a Secretary and Department of
Language; what Alexis de Tocqueville ought to
see on visiting America a second time; "Boutique
America!"; ethnic jokes; "Marlboro Country," on
publishing and remaindering books; jogging;
and watching (black and white) television.

Although offering "several quiet satisfactions
to its reader," wrote Benjamin DeMott in the
New York Times Book Review, *Familiar
Territory* as a collection "is less impressive. One

JOSEPH EPSTEIN

problem is the author's apparent conviction that
opinions shopworn to begin with . . . gain vitality when developed in full-length essays. . . .
Still another is the author's passion for sounding
unpretentious; it sometimes makes him sound
abject." Charles Fenyvesi, writing in the *New
Republic*, thought, however, that Epstein's columns "reveal a man of exemplary sobriety, understated scholarship, and balanced judgment."

In *The Middle of My Tether: Familiar Essays*,
Epstein writes on dedications and acknowledge-
ments in books ("In and Around Books"); the
kinds of letters he, as a published writer, is apt
to receive ("A Man of Letters"); clichés ("The
Ephemeral Verities"); the attractions and repul-
sions of life in New York ("You Take
Manhattan"); the pleasures and pains of reading
("Bookless in Gaza"); the myriad expressions of
vulgarity in American life ("What Is Vulgar?");
memory and its foibles ("Disremembrance of
Things Present"); and an inordinate love for
fountain pens ("Penography").

Earl Rovit, in *Library Journal*, likened Epstein to Lewis Thomas as "one of the contemporary masters of the *causerie*, . . . [a form which]
gives the reader the illusion of listening to an urbane, intelligent person who is informed, witty,
capable of self-deprecation, somewhat skeptical,
but usually buoyant with curiosity and belief in
conversation itself." Russell Jacoby, in the
Nation, wrote that if Epstein's "name does not
spark recognition, it is because he keeps a low
profile, paying no heed to headlines or Yale literary theorists, quietly monitoring the daily life of
the urban intellectual." Yet in Jacoby's view,

"conservatism distorts his vision. Unlike other vigorous professor-baiters, such as H. L. Mencken, whom he frequently honors, Epstein shoots only to the left. He dumps on a Herbert Marcuse or a Michael Harrington; he has nothing to say about a Milton Friedman or an Irving Kristol."

Once More Around the Block is yet another collection of familiar essays from the *American Scholar*. This time, among the sixteen pieces are essays on work and the work ethic ("Work and Its Contents"); on reading with a failing memory ("Joseph Epstein's Lifetime Reading Plan"); on damning with faint praise ("Let Us Now Praise Famous Knuckleheads"); on being satisfied to live in Evanston, Illinois ("Unwilling to Relocate"); on his lifelong love of bookstores ("New & Previously Owned Books & Other Creampuffs"); on jokes and humorlessness ("What's So Funny?"); and on turning fifty ("An Older Dude").

Earl Rovit, again writing in *Library Journal*, termed this collection of essays "one too many. . . . Epstein's prose succumbs to a kind of flatulence, while a pervasive tone of smug complacency allows for self-indulgence, repetition, premature nostalgia, and a general slackening of wit, bite, and willingness to explore new perspectives." To David Bromwich in the *New Republic*, "Epstein writes about style so constantly, with so ponderous an air of staking his claim, that his essays seem one long entreaty for a judgment of his own worth as a stylist. The truth is, he writes well enough to be read, sometimes, with pleasure, for paragraphs at a stretch, but not well enough to set up as an authority on writing." Joel Conarroe, in the *New York Times Book Review*, attributed some of what he felt was padding or the attenuation of essentially slight subjects to the demands of the format of the journal for which most of the essays were written. He admired Epstein's "lively, lucid style," though he confessed to irritation with many of his opinions: "As in his previous collections, the subject of these pieces, whatever the announced topic, is Joseph Epstein, and one gets a thorough sense of his tastes and prejudices. To read him is to sit in the company of a bookish, witty, abrasive individual with a liberal education and conservative views."

Epstein has also published several works of nonfiction on individual subjects. The earliest of these is *Divorced in America: Marriage in an Age of Possibility*. His subject, he writes in his introduction, is one "rich in chaos, squalor, and mean feeling." The author nevertheless "presumes to justify [the book] at least in part on the limits of his own small talent for facing unpleasant facts. . . . The argument in this book,

insofar as it has an argument, is that divorce is often necessary yet is seldom accomplished without sadness, pain, and significant loss." Reverting to autobiography, Epstein writes from personal experience of divorce: " . . . a graduate so to say, it seemed to me that my own experiences, feelings, and thoughts were of sufficient interest to be described in some detail. Second, I wished to avoid . . . the method . . . of the case study." He concentrates on the divorce experience of the American middle class because it is his own class and because he believes it is the class most "vulnerable" to the traumas of divorce. He ends by proclaiming his book as one "by a divorced man whose bias is on behalf of the nuclear family, a man who, despite all its flaws, really cannot imagine any other arrangement being any better. God, as the sages suspected, must love a good joke."

Sara Sanborn, in the *New York Times Book Review*, found *Divorced in America* "generally perceptive and sometimes enlightening, dense with the experiences and observations of a comprehensive intelligence." Sonya Rudikoff, in the *Washington Post Book World*, thought the book "has all the nuance of domestic poetry about it, the poetry of making do and making the best of it with rueful dignity."

In *Ambition: The Secret Passion*, Epstein defines ambition in his introduction as "the fuel of achievement," but goes on to ask, "What order of achievement does it propel?" In Epstein's view, ambition has become clouded—a source of grief and frustration for many, especially among the educated. "It appears that the more educated a person is, the more hopeless life seems to him. This being so, ambition, to the educated class, has come to seem pointless at best, vicious at worst. Ambition connotes a certain Rotarian optimism, a thing unseemly, in very poor taste, rather like a raging sexual appetite in someone quite elderly. None of this, of course, has stopped the educated classes from attempting to get their own out of the world—lots of the best of everything, as a famous epicure once put it— which they continue to do very effectively. To renunciation is thus added more than a piquant touch of hypocrisy." The degradation of ambition, in Epstein's opinion, has hit America particularly hard: "All that American energy, placed exclusively in the service of getting on, getting in, getting ahead—of sheer getting—was viewed as crass in the extreme in the nineteenth century and scarcely less so in the twentieth. . . . The American hustler/pusher/self-starter is taken not to be universal but representative of a national type: a fish indigenous to American waters, a distinctly American species." One of Epstein's main contentions is that "ambition in America has been unrelievedly, almost systematically, discouraged by men and by conditions. In the process a natural appetite has nearly lost its justification, although that does not mean that the appetite itself has disappeared. Ambition cannot be altogether suppressed, although it can be twisted and perverted. But always at a high cost." In the process of exposing his subject, the author tells the stories of the ambitions of well-known Americans, including Benjamin Franklin, Henry Adams, Edith Wharton, John D. Rockefeller, Henry Ford, Henry Luce, Joseph P. Kennedy, and Adlai Stevenson.

All the twenty-six literary essays in *Plausible Prejudices: Essays on American Writing* were previously published in the *New Criterion*, *Commentary*, the *Times Literary Supplement*, and *Book World*. The author divides the book into parts: "The Scene" is first, with articles on the modern literary life, on literary reviewing and reviewers, and on literary culture; "Portraits of Novelists" treats, among others, John Irving, Bernard Malamud, John Updike, Norman Mailer, Philip Roth, and Cynthia Ozick; "The Older Crowd" contains more general and expansive considerations of Van Wyck Brooks, Maxwell Perkins, A. J. Liebling, Willa Cather, John Dos Passos, and James Gould Cozzens; and there is finally a miscellaneous section, "Amusements and Disasters (Essays on Language)," which contains essays on the new American vogue for language criticism, on sexual euphemism, on the foolishness and futility of compiling lists of books for others to read, and on essay writing as an amiable, even ideal way to waste time.

"It is hard to disagree," wrote L. S. Klepp in the *Christian Science Monitor*, "with [Epstein's] bleak assessment of our literary climate. The evidence of cultural inflation can be acquired at any newsstand. What makes these mostly pessimistic essays palatable and plausible, though, is that they are triumphs of style and wit." A less favorable judgment was Stephen Fender's in the *Times Literary Supplement*, "The way to argue" the book's case is "to set about it with both rigour and vigour, not to impute bad faith to almost everything interesting, engaging, intriguing, funny and even moving that has been written since the war, and not lazily to subsume every innovation under the general trope of degeneration."

Soon after becoming editor of the *American Scholar*, Epstein had the idea for a series of articles, all to be modeled on Edmund Wilson's fine essay on Christian Gauss, his teacher at Princeton. He commissioned articles from such people as Sidney Hook, Robert Nisbet, John Wain, Anthony Hecht, Suzanne Hoover, George Brock-

way, and Jeremy Bernstein. The teachers these and other writers describe include Alfred North Whitehead, C. S. Lewis, Ruth Benedict, Hannah Arendt, Yvor Winters, Leo Strauss, John Crowe Ransom, I. A. Richards, J. Robert Oppenheimer, and Nadia Boulanger. After publishing the essays in the magazine, Epstein included 16 of them in *Masters: Portraits of Great Teachers*. For Benjamin DeMott, writing in *Psychology Today*, "the book's value lies in its recreation of moments of significant encounter, processes of personal and moral development. . . . The remembered encounters between teacher and student— . . . when people seemed to discover, on the spot, through a teacher's example, what they most wanted—are absorbing."

PRINCIPAL WORKS: Divorced in America, 1974; Familiar Territory, 1979; Ambition, 1980; The Middle of My Tether, 1983; Plausible Prejudices, 1985; Once More Around the Block, 1987; Partial Payments: Essays on Writers and Their Lives, 1989. *As editor*—Masters, 1981.

ABOUT: Bunzel, J. H. (ed.) Political Passages, 1988; Contemporary Authors 119, 1987; Contemporary Literary Criticism 39, 1986; Who's Who in America, 1988–1989. *Periodicals*—American Scholar Summer 1984, Spring 1985; American Spectator June 1985; Chicago Tribune November 11, 1979; February 24, 1985; Christian Science Monitor March 11, 1981; April 17, 1985; Commentary August 1976, July 1978, June 1980, February 1981, April 1981, March 1982, September 1985; Commonweal July 3, 1981; Harper's November 1977; Library Journal September 1, 1979; January 15, 1981; February 15, 1981; November 15, 1983; February 1, 1985; May 15, 1987; Los Angeles Times Book Review February 24, 1985; Nation May 30, 1981; November 19, 1983; New Republic November 10, 1979; January 24, 1981; March 7, 1981; June 8, 1987; New York Times December 29, 1979; January 16, 1981; April 25, 1981; October 20, 1983; New York Times Book Review June 16, 1974; November 4, 1979; January 18, 1981; April 5, 1981; February 24, 1985; June 7, 1987; March 12, 1989; New York Times Magazine November 24, 1985; Newsweek July 1, 1974; Psychology Today April 1981; Publishers Weekly December 16, 1983; March 1, 1985; Quill & Quire September 1981; Saturday Review January 1981; Time January 19, 1981; Times Literary Supplement January 13, 1984; August 2, 1985; October 13, 1989; USA Today March 15, 1985; Wall Street Journal April 2, 1985; Washington Post Book World June 30, 1974; December 16, 1979.

ERDRICH, (KAREN) LOUISE (June 7, 1954–), American novelist, was born in Little Falls, Minnesota, the eldest of seven children of Ralph and Rita Gourneau Erdrich, both teachers in the Bureau of Indian Affairs boarding school in Wapheton, North Dakota. Like many of the

LOUISE ERDRICH

characters in her novels, Erdrich is of mixed ancestry—mostly Chippewa on her mother's side,
German on her father's. It was not until she entered Dartmouth College, however, and enrolled in the Native American Studies program
there (taught by her future husband, Michael
Dorris), that she began to think seriously about
her heritage. Until then, she told *Publishers
Weekly* in 1986, she had never thought about
"what was Native American and what wasn't. I
think that's the way a lot of people who are of
mixed descent regard their lives—you're just a
combination of different backgrounds."

She also began to think seriously about writing. At Dartmouth she won literary prizes in poetry and prose and after graduating in 1976
worked at a variety of odd jobs (waitress, teacher, life-guard, and flag signaler on a construction
site) in order to store up experience for her writing. In 1979 she received an M.A. in creative
writing from Johns Hopkins and while there
wrote many of the poems that were to comprise
her first book, *Jacklight*. *Jacklight* was for the
most part well received, but it was clear to a
number of critics that Erdrich's gift was for the
narrative rather than the strictly lyrical, and in
any case she had been publishing short stories in
anthologies and little magazines for several
years. One of these stories, "The World's Greatest Fisherman," which won the Nelson Algren
fiction competition in 1982, was the genesis of
her first novel, *Love Medicine*.

Set on and around a Chippewa reservation in
North Dakota in the years between 1934 and the
present, *Love Medicine* describes the interlocking fates of several generations of Kashpaws, La-
martines, and two or three other Indian and
part-Indian families. Since the fourteen chapters
function rather like closely related short stories,
Love Medicine depends as much on tone, imagery, and moments of sustained intensity as on
traditional novelistic continuity. Nevertheless,
certain characters—Nector Kashpaw, the put-
upon tribal chairman, admired for his sense of
responsibility by some, scorned as a turncoat by
others; his wife Marie, who raises a large family
under trying circumstances and keeps Nector in
line with a mixture of convent Catholicism and
old tribal medicines; and Lulu Lamartine, Nector's old flame and the unrepentant mother of
eight children by as many men—appear in almost every chapter, and most of the other characters are forced to respond to them in one way
or another. From all of these stories a portrait of
modern Indian society emerges: a society blighted by alcoholism, government betrayal, and
general demoralization, redeemed only in part
by the tenuous survival of Native American traditions and bonds.

The publication of a first novel by a young
writer with Erdrich's apparent gifts was one of
the literary events of 1984, and *Love Medicine*
won the National Book Critics Circle Award for
fiction for that year. Writers like Peter Matthiessen and Kay Boyle acclaimed Erdrich on
the jacket of the book, and Philip Roth pronounced her "the most interesting new American novelist to have appeared in years." Yet even
her admirers conceded that Erdrich's handling
of the many complicated relationships between
her three generations of five Indian families was,
at the least, extremely confusing. Robert Towers
thought *Love Medicine* very much "a poet's
novel," with the strengths and weaknesses such
a description implies. "At times," he wrote in the
New York Review of Books, "the language becomes overwrought to the point of hysteria or
else so ecstatic that the reader may feel almost
coerced into accepting a romanticized version of
a situation—a version that the hard facts belie.
But at its best, the writing is admirably graphic,
full of unexpected and arresting images and brilliantly dramatized small scenes. Louise Erdrich
is in any case a notably talented writer whose
first novel, despite its structural problems and
stylistic excesses, clearly merits much of the
praise it has received."

A few of the characters from *Love Medicine*
turn up in *The Beet Queen*, the second volume
in a projected tetralogy. Yet unlike its predecessor, *The Beet Queen* is a fully formed novel with
a plot elaborate enough to suggest ironic parallels to the "foundling fiction" of Fielding and
Dickens. The story begins in 1932 when Mary

and Karl Adare, along with their baby brother, are abandoned by their unwed and overburdened mother, who impulsively flies off with an aerialist at a country fair, never to return. The baby is kidnapped and fourteen-year-old Karl and eleven-year-old Mary hop a freight train to the town of Argus, North Dakota, where relatives take in Mary. Karl never gets that far, yet his and Mary's paths intersect over the years as she stays in Argus running a butcher shop and becoming stolidly eccentric and he drifts in and out, a traveling salesman and amoral seducer of men and women. Two of Karl's conquests are Celestine James, a mixed blood Chippewa and Mary's long-suffering best friend, by whom he had a daughter, Dot, and Wallace Pfef, the town booster, secret homosexual, and godfather of Dot. All of these lives are marked by emotional deprivation and personal betrayal, from Adelaide Adare's abandonment of her three children to Dot's adolescent rebellion against her absent father and defeated mother. Indeed, *The Beet Queen* might be quite depressing were it not for Erdrich's gentle irony and her constant juxtaposition of the comic and the potentially tragic.

To Russell Banks, the strength of the novel was in Erdrich's placement of personal grief in sources beyond the personal. The story, he wrote in the *Nation*, "is played against a view of history in which decent folks are victimized not by their dopey and amusing gullibility but by economic and social forces too powerful to overcome with wile or guile." It was, he thought, "a Dickensian story, an angry comedy about abandonment and survival, pluck and luck (ambition and coincidence), common sense and pretension, and wise children and foolish adults." Although a few critics detected a diminishment in poetic force from *Love Medicine*, others saw advances on every front. "This is a rare second novel," wrote Josh Rubins in the *New York Review of Books*, "one that makes it seem as if the first, impressive as it was, promised too little, not too much."

Tracks takes the story back to the winter of 1912 and the following decade, when the North Dakota Chippewa were decimated by cold, starvation, epidemic disease, and the loss of their native land. Although several of the characters from *Love Medicine* appear as children or young adults, the focus is on their elders: Fleur Pillager, the young mother and lover who embodies her people's fierce pride and mysticism; Nanapush, Fleur's worldly old guardian who has lived to see his tribe "unraveled like a coarse rope, frayed at either end as the old and new among us were taken"; and Pauline Puyat, whose morbid pride and sexual jealousy of Fleur lead her to an increasingly reckless and fanatical embrace of Catholicism. In alternating chapters Nanapush and Pauline tell the story of Fleur's heroic but doomed resistance; throughout, his warm, humorous, but weary voice contrasts with her perfervid imaginings.

"This book is no mere catalogue of past injustices," wrote a reviewer for the *New Yorker*. "In it the author captures the passions, fears, myths, and doom of a living people, and she does so with an ease that leaves the reader breathless." One repeated criticism of *Tracks*, however, was that its rhetoric, particularly in Pauline's chapters, was overheated, lacking the grace and suppleness of Erdrich's earlier prose. In the *New York Review of Books*, Robert Towers offered this mixed assessment: "Louise Erdrich's gift for vivid descriptive writing is everywhere in evidence, and many of the episodes are almost blinding in their hallucinated brilliance. But the novel has, I think, serious problems in addition to its rhetorical inflation. For one thing, the narration of events is kept at such a pitch that finally one wishes to stop one's ears. Credence is exhausted." Erdrich was perhaps most successful in conveying the tragedy of Native American experience through the more modulated, elegiac cadences of Nanapush, as in this passage from the first chapter:

> I guided the last buffalo hunt. I saw the last bear shot. I trapped the last beaver with a pelt of more than two years' growth. I spoke aloud the words of the government treaty, and refused to sign the settlement papers that would take away our woods and lake. I axed the last birch that was older than I, and I saved the last Pillager.
> Fleur, the one you will not call mother.

All of Erdrich's novels have been close collaborations with her husband, Michael Dorris, himself a novelist and part Native American. They were married in 1981 and have five children, three of whom Dorris adopted as a single father from Indian reservations in the midwest (he has written movingly of one of these children—a victim of fetal alcohol syndrome—in *The Broken Cord*, 1989). The family lives in Cornish, New Hampshire, near Dartmouth, where Erdrich has taught as a writer in residence and Dorris continues as professor of anthropology and Native American studies. "My characters choose me," she told the *New York Times Book Review* in 1986, "and once they do it's like standing in a field and hearing echoes. All I can do is trace their passage."

PRINCIPAL WORKS: *Poetry*—Jacklight, 1984. *Novels*—Love Medicine, 1984; The Beet Queen, 1986; Tracks, 1988.

ABOUT: Bruchac, J. Survival This Way: Interviews with American Indian Poets, 1987; Contemporary Authors

114, 1985; Contemporary Literary Criticism 39, 1985; Who's Who in America, 1988–1989. *Periodicals*—Life April 1985; Nation November 1, 1986; New York Review of Books April 11, 1985; January 15, 1987; November 10, 1988; New York Times October 13, 1986; New York Times Book Review August 31, 1986; October 2, 1988; New Yorker November 21, 1988; Publishers Weekly August 15, 1986; Times Literary Supplement February 27, 1987; October 28, 1988.

*ETZIONI, AMITAI (January 4, 1929–), American sociologist and educator, writes: "The book, of the fifteen I have authored, that best captures what I am trying to say (and be) is *The Active Society*. It provides an analysis of what it takes for a society to come to terms with its fate; to guide its future rather than be subject to its whim. Born in Germany (1929), I escaped in 1935 and was raised in Palestine. I dropped out of high school in 1946 to actively participate in the Israeli War of Independence. While in combat, I wrote my *Diary of a Commando Soldier*. After the war, I was a student-activist at the Hebrew University and a frequent contributor to newspapers, magazines, and the Israeli Labor party (*MAPAI*). I got my Ph.D. in Berkeley (University of California) in 1958 when it was on the verge of exploding with action, and found my first job at Columbia University. Here, as activism turned into violence, I parted ways with the youth but continued to participate in the peace movement (*The Hard Way to Peace, Winning Without War*) and published one of the very first articles against the war in Vietnam (*Washington Post,* 1964).

"In the two decades that followed, I moved on two tracks: attending to my scholarship, which led to one of the ten most often cited books in social science (*A Comparative Analysis of Complex Organizations*); and much recognition (Guggenheim Fellowship, Social Science Research Council Faculty Fellowship, Center for Advanced Study in the Behavioral Sciences Fellowship). At the same time I maintained my active role as a writer on public affairs (*The Moon-Doggle*, against the space race; *Genetic Fix*, on bioethics). I served for several years as a member of the National Board of the Americans for Democratic Action, testified frequently before Congress, took my case before the public on the editorial pages of the *New York Times*, the *Washington Post* and the *Wall Street Journal*, and network TV ("60 Minutes," "Firing Line," "Phil Donahue"). For a year I served as senior advisor to the White House (1070 1080). As an immigrant I was proud to be awarded a certificate of recognition for my contribution to the Bicentennial Commemoration of the American

AMITAI ETZIONI

Revolution and to be consultant for the President's Commission on the Causes and Prevention of Violence.

"My interest in the bridges between social sciences and public life led me to study, teach, and write about the ways public policy is formulated and to found and direct, since 1968, the Center for Policy Research. It is also the reason I moved from New York to live in Washington, D.C., spending a year at the Brookings Institution, a year in the government, and seven years at the George Washington University, as University Professor.

"My last area of interest brings together my sociology and activist interests. I am working on a new economic theory, one that I hope is more realistic and more inductive than neoclassical economics; I refer to it as socio-economics. The endeavor took me into ethics (socio-economics is deontological or Kantian, not utilitarian), psychology (the view of the self as conflicted rather than as unitary) and, of course, my field, sociology (the view of the market as a sub-system).

"Meanwhile, I have brought up four fine sons and am bringing up the fifth, on my own since 1985. My day is never long enough, but I would not want it any other way."

In 1984 Amitai Etzioni opened his *Capital Corruption: The New Attack on American Democracy* with a personal note: "This book is an expression of my concern for, and dedication to, American democracy." Although in a profes

° et´ zē ō nē, á mi tī

sional sociologist and social psychologist he practices a strictly disciplined analytical approach to the problems of modern society, he is also a deeply committed and passionate believer in the values of a free democratic society. This commitment has given his writings a wide circulation outside the academic community. His frequent contributions to newspapers and magazines as well as several of his books on subjects like nuclear warfare, genetic engineering, space exploration, and abuses of political power have examined problems that are of concern to the general American reading public.

Etzioni defined his several roles—an academic, a social theorist, a political and social critic, and an activist—as early as 1968 in his large and ambitious book *The Active Society: A Theory of Societal and Political Processes:* "Our theory seeks to reconcile three approaches to the study of society. We wish to illustrate that a social science theory can be scientifically valid, can be intellectually relevant, and can serve as a springboard for active participation." He envisions, therefore, a society which knows itself, is committed to moving toward a fuller realization of its values, one that would reduce the problems of social alienation because it would be responsive to its members. Such a society remains purely theoretical, but Etzioni has converted theory into practice in his own career. *The Active Society* is densely reasoned, heavily documented, dotted with technical language, but, as Carl Dreher observed in the *Nation*, "a good deal of the text is as pellucid as the popular articles he has written, or his lectures . . . [This book] will make the lay reader realize how naive and inchoate the ideas subsumed under 'social consciousness' usually are, and how much we stand in need of the sharply focussed thinking that professionals like Etzioni bring to bear on social problems."

Etzioni's prose can be vigorous and hardhitting. In an article in the *New York Times* in 1982 he wrote flatly that "Washington is corrupt to the core"—a statement that evoked considerable criticism. But he expanded his thesis in *Capital Corruption: The New Attack on American Democracy* in 1984, his target the political action committees with their power and special interests: "the old interest groups equipped with a new set of computer-age tools for cracking public safes." Etzioni sees these groups as a problem of both major political parties. The real issue, he writes, "is nothing less than who has the power to guide the government. If you believe that in contemporary America it is the people, each person having an equal say, as in 'one person, one vote' you probably also believe in the tooth fairy."

Born in Cologne, Germany, Etzioni emigrated to Israel with his parents, Willi and Gertrude Falk Etzioni, in 1935. After active service in the Israeli army, he completed his undergraduate education in 1954 and took an M.A. in sociology at the Hebrew University in 1956. His first book, an account of his military experiences, was written in Hebrew. He did his doctoral work in the United States, at Berkeley, with a dissertation on the organizational structure of the kibbutz. The study of organizational structure was subsequently the basis of his first major book on sociology, *A Comparative Analysis of Complex Organizations*, in 1961. Etzioni's teaching career began at Columbia University in 1958, where he also founded and directed the Center for Policy Research. He rose the rank of full professor of sociology and was chairman of his department from 1969 to 1971. In the spring of 1968 he headed a committee negotiating with the students who had seized and shut down several university buildings in protest against the war in Vietnam. Etzioni described the negotiations in "Confessions of a Professor Caught in a Revolution," an article in the *New York Times Magazine.* Sympathetic to student demands for reform and a voice in university governance, he nevertheless recognized the danger of universities becoming political: "I personally had been long interested in the question of how a liberal handled himself in a radical confrontation." What he discovered from this experience was the necessity for reason and compromise, the need for what he called "differentiation," defining clearly the areas of responsibility of students and faculty, giving students full control over their lives outside the classroom but preserving the autonomy of the faculty on academic standards and course content.

In 1978–1979 Etzioni was a guest scholar of the Brookings Institution in Washington, D.C.; since 1980 he has been on the graduate faculty of the George Washington University in Washington, D.C. From his first marriage, to Eva Horowitz in 1953, he has two sons. In 1965 he married Minerva Morales, a political scientist, who died in 1985. He has three sons from that marriage.

PRINCIPAL WORKS: A Comparative Analysis of Complex Organizations, 1961, 1975; The Hard Way to Peace: A New Strategy, 1962; Winning Without War, 1964; Modern Organizations, 1964; The Moon-Doggle: Domestic and International Implications of the Space Race, 1964; Political Unification: A Comparative Study of Leaders and Forces, 1965; Studies in Social Change, 1966; The Active Society: A Theory of Societal and Political Processes, 1968; Genetic Fix: New Opportunities and Dangers for You, Your Child and the Nation, 1975; An Immodest Agenda: Rebuilding

America before the Twenty-first Century, 1983; Capital Corruption: the New Attack on American Democracy, 1984.

ABOUT: Contemporary Authors New Revisions Series 5, 1982; Current Biography 1980; Paloma, M. Contemporary Sociological Theory, 1979; Who's Who in America, 1988–1989. *Periodicals*—Nation May 26, 1969; New York Times Magazine September 15, 1968; Time February 17, 1975.

EVANS, STUART (October 20, 1934–), British novelist and poet, writes: "I was born in Swansea, South Wales, and brought up in a village in the Swansea Valley. When I was four, we moved into a house, built by my great-great-grandfather, in which my grandparents lived. Both of them came from large families and as an only child I was therefore in the company of adults, most of whom were elderly. My early recollections are of this considerable family living in different parts of the village but concentrated in two big houses. I was, consequently, more a watcher than a participant in what went on though some of my happiest times were spent in naughty collusion with my grandmother in such matters as illicit dumplings, concealed broken crockery, quick swigs of 'pop' and the like.

"My grandmother and her brothers and sisters all talked Welsh. My parents could not speak the language. This, together with the fact that we were a bourgeois, Anglican clan in a predominantly working-class, non-conformist community, perhaps accounted for a certain isolation of which I became increasingly aware but the full extent of which I only realized when, one by one, the last surviving members of the immediate family died. Allegedly my health was delicate, so I was forbidden to play football, swim, ride bicycles and join in the scores of rapscallion enterprises of my contemporaries. So I invented football teams—indeed, a whole league of them—and played off scrupulously fair games between them, on my own, in our yard. In the evenings I would write up accounts of the 'matches' with selective biographies of the outstanding players. Of course I had school-friends, but while not unhappy, I was for the most part solitary.

"This all changed overnight, as it were, when I went up to Jesus College, Oxford, where the joys of gregariousness, good talk and not-so-small beer led, in part, to the not-so-outstanding degree that I took. The other part of the distraction from purer academic pleasures was an increasing urge to write. I had written poems and some extraordinarily opulent prose from the age of fifteen. Now, introduced to college and university

STUART EVANS

revues, I aspired to be Lorenz Hart, though never Frank Loesser—I knew that was beyond me. I became more serious about my verse, however, when I was awarded the Newdigate Prize for my 'Elegy for a Dead Clown' in 1955. At this time I intended to devote most of my writing to verse, although my next published poems were in *Imaginary Gardens with Real Toads* in 1972, part of a longer sequence which has yet to appear in its entirety. My collection *The Function of the Fool* was published in 1977.

"After leaving Oxford, I was conscripted into the Royal Navy and liked it enough to apply for a commission and longer service. A very lucky decision, since it was in the navy that I met my wife, then a W.R.N.S. officer, some twenty-eight years ago. I continued to write steadily. Although I gradually turned to prose fiction, it is still within the discipline of various poetic forms adapted to the structure of the novel. The strict, precise frame which I impose upon my work is intended both as a discipline for myself and to give strength and thrust to the content. While the linear continuity of each novel is consistent, all the books are experiments in multiple narrative, different prose (and verse) conventions, in which the interpretation of character and event is seldom straightforward.

"*Meritocrats*, my first published novel, is a satire on the self-admiring elite in British society whose public lives are above reproach but whose private lives may be beneath contempt. Critics regarded it as a demanding but very funny book. My second novel *The Gardens of the Casino* is my purest fiction, owing little to room or life torical events during the time in which it is set. The third, *The Caves of Alienation* (awarded a Welsh Arts Council prize), is a portrait of a tormented Welsh writer—most emphatically *not* an idealized study of myself.

"Since then I have written five novels in the 'Windmill Hill' sequence. The epigraph which is central to this series of books, each one complete in itself, is taken from an article by Professor Stuart Piggott about the Windmill Hill site, near Avebury in Wiltshire: "The occupational debris implies temporary hearths and there is no evidence of permanent houses on the site." This line set in movement a train of thought which suggested an experiment in literary archaeology, uncovering and chipping away at aspects of our contemporary society as it proceeds, so that fictional events occur in parallel (or possibly parallax) with actual events of the time. *Centres of Ritual*, the first novel in the sequence, was written day by day to include a chronicle of current events alongside a multiple account of the lives of the central characters. Politician friends have told me that they recognize in this book a prediction of the formation of the Social Democratic party some three years before it was founded and the Liberal-SDP Alliance was agreed.

"A conviction that Western society is in a condition of irreparable decline underlies both my prose and verse. My work tends to reflect a genuine pessimism induced by the ever-diminishing regard for ethics and morals—political, social, literary and intellectual—often using comic techniques. Most of my books have a mythic basis, since I believe that the same themes have obsessed, motivated, corrupted or inspired people throughout the ages. My characters are often themselves writers, so that extracts (sometimes lengthy) from their work are included in the novels. I also make occasional use of parody. Such devices make the books vulnerable to slovenly reviewers who thumb through and mistake such passages for lapses in style or rank imitation, not appreciating that they are part of a carefully conceived over-all plan.

"I do not expect ever to become a 'popular' author, because what the form dictates the book will demand. But those who begin at page one and read through to the end may anticipate some surprises and, I hope, some delights."

Describing his novels as "experiments in multiple narrative," Stuart Evans tacitly acknowledges what he openly admits at the end of the autobiographical sketch above—that he is not a "popular" novelist. Admired but not widely read in England, he is even less accessible to readers in the United States—partly because so much of his recent writing deals with contemporary British politics, but mainly because, as Peter Lewis wrote in the *Times Literary Supplement* in 1984: "Evans is one of the most intellectual novelists now writing; his work is artistically uncompromising and demands intense concentration." It also demands, on the part of his readers, familiarity with a range of writers from T. S. Eliot to Wallace Stevens to Jorge Luis Borges to Iris Murdoch, as well as a host of philosophers, sociologists, historians and archaeologists. With all this erudition, however, Evans manages to sustain narrative interest, often with suspense and humor. What he is striving to achieve in fiction may be something like the aim of his novelist character Michael Caradock in *The Caves of Alienation*, who writes in a critical essay that the modern novelist has a special challenge: "After the enormous labours of Proust, Thomas Mann, and most of all Joyce, the unproved writer is under an obligation to try to contribute to the development or expansion of the form: the novel did not end with *Finnegans Wake*." This means that the novelist must take chances, "must attempt to do things which are technically daring, if not in language then in structure." He must induce his reader to read not just his text but what is beneath and beyond the text. "The novelist must surprise and startle, he must make efforts to achieve an imaginative state of excitement which will awaken responses in the reader (from his own experience) that the novelist cannot know anything about, but which he guessed must be possible."

Evans' method subverts traditional narrative, linear story-telling. From *Meritocrats* through the latest of his Windmill Hill sequence, his novels are a series of fragments—letters, journals, excerpts from the characters' novels-in-progress, radio and television scripts, random passages of monologue and dialogue in which the speakers are not always identified. The technique can be exasperating, and reviewers often complain that Evans' ingenuity "leaves the reader feeling like an ignominious eavesdropper in the corridors of the elite" (*Spectator*). Especially vulnerable to this charge is *The Gardens of the Casino* which explores the whole question of the "reality" of fiction by forcing the reader to wonder which of the characters are "real" or whether episodes in the plot ever really "happen." Dealing with the experiences of an Anglo-French painter and a British novelist with whose wife the painter is having an affair, it introduces a subplot involving a woman who may or may not be involved in a gangster-spy intrigue which may or may not be happening. This kind of "rococo elaboration," in a novel peopled by rich, elegant, articulate and very remote characters, led David Wilson in the *Times Literary Supplement*, to conclude that Evans "is an intelligent, imaginative, skillful writer; it is a pity he is so insistently preoccupied with the problems of being one."

The novels of the Windmill Hill series, while employing the same complex narrative structure, have generally had a more favorable reception. Their subject is contemporary England, mainly the political scene from the late 1960s through the 1980s. Evans calls them "an experiment in literary archaeology," viewing the current scene in the perspective of a distant past history that we uncover in fragments. As his English historian, an Oxford don, in *Centres of Ritual* writes: "How we piece together the ordinary activities of vanished generations from scraps of metal or clay or bone and try to guess at their social structures, their politics, their early instincts for art and why they needed it, their first attempts at rudimentary technology . . . and in our time, these same fragments are the lives or what we see of the lives, of the people we know, or observe, or simply glimpse." This sequence of novels, Peter Lewis wrote in 1984, "stands out among recent fiction as the most ambitious project undertaken by a British writer. It embodies a confidence in the novel form as a way of understanding contemporary reality, perhaps even a belief in the cultural centrality of the genre, that is increasingly hard to find."

Evans' poetry is more formal and traditional than his fiction, though almost equally as erudite and allusive. The title poem of his first full collection, *The Function of the Fool*, identifies the modern poet-artist with the fool of literature and legend who represented "reason in madness." But, the poet asks, "Who needs the fool" today when rulers "spell out their own acrostic of doom?" The poems are reflective, sometimes melancholy, sometimes ironic. "There is a bitter awareness of human pain throughout which is unlike that of any other poet known to me," Peter Porter wrote in the *Observer*. "There are undoubted faults of wordiness at times, but they count for little against the power of feeling present." The feeling, in some of the poems, is deeply personal, expressing Evans' delight in travel, his interests in art and literature, his religious and philosphic uncertainties. Others—including a remarkable series of Shakespearean sonnets on six of Shakespeare's plays—show him in his more characteristic role as critic and historian of contemporary society. A group of poems called "An Anglo-Saxon Reader" comments with wry humor but deep feeling on "the condition of England":

Certainly no longer the noblest its fair fields

And sweep of green forest now furrowed with autoroutes,
Concessionairies in the greenwood pull-ups,
Coke and Skol and Cuba Libre.

Nevertheless, in the beauty of what is left of the countryside, in parish churches where "the effortless purity of English music" manages to survive, in English gardens ("You are expected to walk on the grass, trusted / Not to steal the roses or scare the ducks"), in "the endless grumbling of the English conscience"—

It is still possible to imagine rising again
Harmonies that are a delight, traditional sounds
That rise aloft in brightness under the stars.
—"The Happy Land"

PRINCIPAL WORKS: *Poetry*—Elegy for a Dead Clown, 1955; Imaginary Gardens with Real Toads, 1972; The Function of the Fool, 1977. *Novels*—Meritocrats, 1974; The Gardens of the Casino, 1976; The Caves of Alienation, 1977. *Windmill Hill* sequence—Centres of Ritual, 1978; Occupational Debris, 1979; Temporary Hearths, 1982; Houses on the Site, 1984; Seasonal Tribal Feasts, 1987.

ABOUT: Contemporary Authors 118, 1986. *Periodicals*—Listener December 5, 1974; April 29, 1976; March 17, 1977; May 11, 1978; August 16, 1979; October 11, 1984; New Statesman April 30, 1976; April 28, 1978; June 29, 1979; Observer December 15, 1974; April 25, 1976; March 13, 1977, February 12, 1978; April 23, 1978; Spectator March 12, 1977; May 15, 1982; Times Literary Supplement April 30, 1976; March 11, 1977; August 18, 1978; April 28, 1978; June 25, 1982, November 9, 1984.

FARRELL, M. J. See **KEANE, MOLLY**

FEDERMAN, RAYMOND (May 15, 1928–), American novelist, poet, and critic, writes: "I often wonder if being a writer, becoming a writer, is a gift one receives at birth, or if it happens accidentally in the course of one's life? Even today, after the millions of words I have scribbled over the past twenty-five years, with six novels in print, one more in progress, two volumes of poems, several books of essays and criticism, I often doubt that I am a writer. I do not think I was born a writer. I believe I am still working at becoming a writer, and perhaps shall die never knowing whether or not I was a real writer. It seems to me that everything I write, and very few days pass that I do not sit at my desk to write, is a preparation for the great book that someday I shall write which will make of me a real writer. Meanwhile my books are published, reviewed, discussed, analyzed, trans

RAYMOND FEDERMAN

lated, praised and attacked, a couple of them were awarded literary prizes, and still I am not sure I am a writer. The other day my best fan, my lovely daughter (who having graduated from college now lives in New York where she works as a waitress before becoming the great whatever she will be), on the phone from the Big City (collect of course), says to me, oh without malice, lovingly in fact: 'Hey Pop, I think I know what your epitaph will be, I mean, you know, what should be written on your tombstone: OUT OF PRINT.' What gentle brutality! She's got it right though, there is brutality in what writers are doing. Writing is such a brutal and inhuman thing to be doing, so brutally asocial, unnatural. So much against nature. No wonder writers suffer fits of doubts and despair. No, I don't think I was born a writer, but the accidents of my life may have helped make of me a writer. If I was given a gift at all which helped me write, it was what happened to me, in spite of myself, during the first twenty years of my life. I lived these first twenty years almost oblivious to myself and to the sordid affairs of the world around me, unaware that the experiences I was living, or perhaps I should say enduring, would someday make of me a writer.

"I was born in Paris, France, in 1928, May 15 (a Taurus, which means someone who lives in the world with his feet on the ground and his head in the clouds). My parents were poor, very poor. And worse, in France, they were foreigners (*des étrangers*), Jews who had come from some eastern part of Europe. They had three children—my sisters and I. My father was an artist, a starving artist, a surrealist painter who never achieved recognition. He was thirty-nine years old when his body (along with those of my mother and my two sisters) was reduced to ashes in the furnaces of Auschwitz. My mother washed clothes for other people. For a while I was a schoolboy, until my parents were arrested with my sisters (I managed to escape when my mother hid me in a closet); after that I worked, first for three years until the end of the war on a farm in southern France, then after the war in a factory in Paris. Having been given an excess of life, I managed to survive. I got involved in black-marketing—everybody did that then. I was living a day-to-day life with nothing ahead of me. I had stopped school at the age of twelve, and here I was eighteen, nineteen years old, a total ignorant. I read books, but without any sense of order. In 1947, I went to America, my head full of dreams and illusions. Two weeks after I arrived I started working on the line in a factory in Detroit, at Chrysler. I worked the nightshift. So during the day, after I slept a few hours, I would wander in the streets of Detroit. In 1947, Detroit was a rather depressed and depressing city. One day, on Woodward Avenue, next to the Jewish Center where I would sometimes go to swim, I noticed the word SCHOOL on a building. By then I had enough English to manage to make myself understood (with a rather thick French accent which, I must confess, I have carefully cultivated over the years for social and sentimental reasons) and went into that school. It was an all-black high school, but in my state of obliviousness that meant nothing to me. The next day, after a conversation with the principal of the school, I attended my first class at Northern High School in Detroit. My first class (English) was in the afternoon. The principal, a very nice white man, had understood that because I worked all night at Chrysler I needed some sleep in the morning and therefore could only attend classes later in the day. I graduated from Northern High School in 1949. I was then twenty-one years old, a bit older than most high school kids, but what the hell. I had learned a great deal in that school—English of course, which I spoke then like a black kid in the ghettos of Detroit but with a French accent, American history, government, but especially music. Yes, at Northern High School I became a jazz musician. I played the tenor saxophone. Some of the kids I played with were called Tommy Flanagan, Kenny Burrell, Frank Foster, Roland Hannah, some of them today are giants in the world of jazz. I even jammed once at the Blue Bird in Detroit, on Dexter Avenue, a jazz joint, with Charlie Parker who was in town for a concert.

"In the winter of 1950, I moved to New York.

I was fed up with Detroit, and besides, the country was in a recession and I had been laid off from Chrysler. In New York I starved for a while. I had to pawn my overcoat, my watch, and even one day my tenor saxophone. That was the end of my career as a jazz musician, but then, even though I played well, I was not good enough, not as good as my buddies from Northern High School. Eventually I found a job in a lampshade factory in Brooklyn (what irony!), and took night classes at City College. I would do most of my sleeping on the subway after class going back to Brooklyn where I had a little room near Flatbush Avenue not far from the lampshade factory. In 1951, I was drafted into the U.S. Army. I volunteered for the paratroopers. I wanted to explore high altitude. I made forty-seven jumps out of an airplane. Two in combat, in Korea where I was shipped in 1952. I didn't stay in Korea very long; the army needed someone to serve as a French interpreter for the French speaking U.N. forces. I was qualified. I found myself in Tokyo having a great life with the money I and my fellow soldiers were making on the blackmarket. I became a U.S. citizen in Tokyo in 1953. I was discharged in March 1954. In Tokyo, one day, I wrote something. I think I was trying to write a poem but I was not sure then what it was; it was something about the prostitutes in the streets of Tokyo. In the fall of 1954, I was admitted as a freshman at Columbia University under the G.I. Bill. I was then twenty-four years old. I read Shakespeare for the first time, and Joyce, and Flaubert, and Proust, and everything I could get my hands on. I went wild reading. During my second year at Columbia I started writing my first novel. It is called AND I FOLLOWED MY SHADOW. It is a very badly written novel which I will never allow to be published, but it is perhaps in 1954 that I began to be a writer. I am still trying. . . . "

Raymond Federman completed his B.A., Phi Beta Kappa, in 1957 and his M.A. in 1959, at Columbia University, and his Ph.D. in French in 1963 at the University of California in Los Angeles. From 1959 to 1964 he taught French and comparative literature at the University of California in Santa Barbara. Since 1964 he has been teaching at the State University of New York in Buffalo where he is now professor of English and comparative literature and director of the creative writing program. He has been a visiting professor at the University of Montreal (1970) and at the Hebrew University in Jerusalem (1982–1983) and has held Guggenheim (1966), Fulbright (1982), National Endowment for the Arts (1985), and New York State Foundation for the Arts (1985) fellowships. In 1960 he married Erica Hubscher. They have one daughter.

All this conforms to the pattern of a successful and conventional academic career. But Federman's writings explode any such notions. "Experimental"—a term he rejects—does not adequately describe them, nor does "post-realistic" (a phrase used by a fellow novelist, Ronald Sukenick), nor "post-modern," nor any other word in the critical lexicon. Federman himself coined the word "Surfiction"—on the analogy of surrealism—as the name for "the only fiction that still means something today . . . the kind of fiction that challenges the tradition that governs it; the kind of fiction that constantly renews our faith in man's imagination and not in man's distorted vision of reality—that reveals man's irrationality rather than man's rationality." Radical as Federman's fiction is, it is in fact in a tradition of non-linear narrative, picaresque, spontaneous, improvisatory, digressive, that goes back at least to Rabelais, found its first expression in the English novel in the eighteenth century with Laurence Sterne's *Tristram Shandy*, and its fullest development in the twentieth century with James Joyce and Samuel Beckett.

It is indeed to Beckett that Federman owes his first allegiance. The bilingual Irish-French writer was the subject of Federman's doctoral dissertation and of his first published book, *Journey to Chaos: Samuel Beckett's Early Fiction* ; he even appears as "sam" in one of his novels. Like Beckett—and a number of others including Jorge Luis Borges, Julio Cortazar, Italo Calvino, Claude Simon—and in the United States John Barth, William Burroughs, Donald Barthelme, and Ronald Sukenick—Federman assumes an irrational, chaotic universe in which truth and reality do not exist except as the fictions we create. In practice he carries his theory beyond the text itself to the very processes of creating and reproducing it. Writing becomes a verbal and visual "performance." The so-called story or plot does not imitate reality, as traditional narrative claims to do, but creates it by reflecting upon itself. Conventional typography, punctuation, the arrangement of words upon the printed page, the habit of reading from left to right and from top to bottom of the page, are "boring and restrictive," Federman declares in his essay "SURFICTION." "If we are to make the novel an art form, we must raise the printed word as the medium, and therefore, *where* and *how* it is placed on the printed page makes a difference in what the word is saying." Similarly, characters in fiction must be liberated from their defined roles and become as changeable, in unstable, as illusory, as nameless, as unnamable, as fraudulent, as unpredictable as the discourse that makes them." The new fiction will be "deliberately illogical, irrational, unrealistic, non sequitur and incoherent," its meaning to be "extracted" only by the joint efforts of reader and writer. The author will no longer be omniscient, authoritative, but on equal footing with the reader who becomes a collaborator rather than a passive audience.

Federman's theory articulates what is implicit in his eccentric, iconoclastic, but surprisingly readable novels. In each of them he transforms the experience of his own past into a "verbal performance." In his first published novel, *Double or Nothing*, a man is writing the story of another man who is locked in a room in New York City for one year to write a novel about a third man—a young immigrant from France who has lost his parents and sisters in the Holocaust—an experience so unimaginable that it defies language and is expressed as "X°X°X°X°." Each page is designed: some single columns, some double, some single spaced, some double:

FABULOUS!   AMAZING!
Who ever thought of that?
- A NOODLE MAP OF AMERICA -
°
°
°

This whole story is getting
more and more
SYMBOLIC

One page is simply an arrangement of the word "noodles" (the novelist's only food during this year of incarceration) repeated endlessly around some blank spaces in the shape of a cross, two triangles, a rectangle. Others, like "concrete" poetry, which Federman writes, are printed in shapes—an hourglass, for example. There are parallel columns of French and English, including an essay, "Some Reflexions on the Novel in Our Time" ("Quelques Reflexions sur le Roman Aujourd'hui"), with margins strictly justified:

> The   history   of   the   novel   is—one
> must   admit   it—nothing   else   but   the   succes
> sion   of   its   efforts   to   "appresent"   a   reali
> ty   which   always   evades,   always   substitutes
> for   vulgar   mirrors   finer   mirrors,   more   sel
> ective   mirrors.   But,   in   another   sense,   th
> e   novel   is   nothing   else   but   a   denounciatio
> n,   by   its   very   reality,   of   the   illusion   wh
> ich   animates   it.

Take It or Leave It, an English version of his French *Amer Eldorado*, continues what Federman describes as "a coherent project which is an effort on my part to come to terms with both my personal experiences (especially during World War II and as an immigrant in America) and the recent historical events in which I have participated as a writer and a human being." Here "Frenchy," his immigrant central character, is drafted into the United States army during the Korean War and has a series of wildly picaresque and comic adventures trying to get back to an army base after a leave. *The Voice in the Closet* is a more serious attempt to come to terms with his past. In highly condensed form, with only 5,000 words (French and English texts), the narrator, named "federman," listens to the voice of a boy hiding in the closet from the Nazis who are storming his home. Physically—each page a square box of eighteen lines and sixty-eight characters per line with no punctuation—the book gives the reader a sense of enclosure that the child in the closet experienced. Less immediately personal but certainly an imaginative reconstruction of his experiences is *The Twofold Vibration*. The time is the future, 1999, and the central figure is an old Jewish refugee from France, once a minor writer, who is awaiting exile to an outer planet (the fate of the elderly in 1999). Fighting to save him are his friends Namredef (the mirror spelling of Federman) who is half-deaf, and Moinous (I/We), who is half-blind. Both tell the story to the narrator, who is "Federman."

Moinous is the center of perhaps the most accessible of Federman's novels to date, *Smiles on Washington Square*. Here, in what on the surface is almost a conventional romantic love story, Moinous, a lonely refugee, penniless in New York, meets a beautiful and wealthy young woman, Sucette (the French for "lollipop"), who is a student in a writing workshop course at Columbia. There are few special effects of typography here, but neither is there anything like a conventional linear narrative. At the end the lovers separate and the story may or may not begin again. As he writes at the opening of the novel:

> The story of Moinous & Sucette
> Their love story. It should be told.
> The intensity of its hope. The fury of its
> conditional disappointment. It should be told,
> one way or another. . . .

Probably because his novels have not been published by major trade publishers but by small presses (including the Fiction Collective of which Federman was codirector from 1979 to 1980), they are rarely reviewed in the popular press. But Federman has been the subject of a number of critical essays and, along with Ronald Sukenick, of a full-length book by Jerzy Kutnik. His writings have been translated into German, Polish, Hungarian, Italian, Japanese, Spanish, and Portuguese.

PRINCIPAL WORKS: *Fiction*—Double or Nothing, 1971; Amer Eldorado (in French), 1974; Take It or Leave It, 1976; The Voice in the Closet (French and English), 1979, 1985; The Twofold Vibration, 1982; Smiles on Washington Square, 1985. *Poetry*—Among the Beasts/Parmi los Monstres (French and English), 1967; Me Too, 1975. *Criticism*—Journey to Chaos: Samuel Beckett's Early Fiction, 1965; (with J. Fletcher) Samuel Beckett: His Works and His Critics, 1970. *As editor*—SURFICTION: Fiction Now and Tomorrow, 1976; Samuel Beckett: Cahier de l'Herne, 1976; Samuel Beckett: The Critical Heritage, 1979.

ABOUT: Caramello, C. Silverless Mirrors: Books, Self and Post-Modern American Fiction, 1983; Contemporary Authors New Revision Series 10, 1986; Contemporary Novelists, 4th edition, 1986; Dictionary of Literary Biography Yearbook, 1980; Klinkowitz, J. Literary Disruptions, 1975; Klinkowitz, J. The Self-Apparent Word, 1985; Kutnik, J. The Novel as Performance: The Fiction of Ronald Sukenick and Raymond Federman, 1986; Nagel, J. (ed.) American Fiction, 1977; Pearce, R. The Novel in Motion, 1983; Waugh, P. Metafiction, 1984; Wilde, A. Horizons of Assent: Modernism, Postmodernism, and the Ironic Imagination, 1981. *Periodicals*—Antaeus 20 Winter 1976; Chicago Review 28 Fall 1976, 29 Summer 1977, 30 Autumn 1978; Chicago Tribune Book World September 26, 1982; December 29, 1985; Indian Journal of American Studies 14, 1984; New York Times Book Review October 1, 1972; November 7, 1982.

JÜRG FEDERSPIEL

*FEDERSPIEL, JÜRG (June 28, 1931–   ), Swiss novelist, essayist, poet, playwright and short-story writer, who writes in German, was born in Kempthal near Winterthur. He attended elementary school in Davos and continued his education at the Rudolf Steiner School in Basel. At twenty Federspiel was a reporter and film critic, and he has worked for several Swiss and German newspapers. Short stories and news reports are his favorite literary art forms. He has lived in Berlin, Paris, Basel, and Zürich and over the years has spent considerable time in New York, his city of imagination. He is one of the most widely traveled of the Swiss writers of his generation. The many literary prizes awarded Federspiel include the prizes of the cities of Basel and Zürich, the Swiss Schiller Prize, the Georg-Mackensen-Prize for the best German short story, and the C.-F.-Meyer-Prize.

Asked about his favorite topics and his literary tastes, Federspiel pointed to his contemporary the late Thomas Bernhard and the latter's morbid obsession with death and dying. In fact, Federspiel represents the total opposite of what could be expected of a member of a wealthy, optimistic, growth-oriented society such as his. His basic literary idea is a reverse look at life, seen from death toward birth rather than the opposite.

way. Asked in an interview about his often violent and passionate metaphors, he responded: "I am a sensuous man. If there are no oranges anymore, I am for death. Mine." This statement, of course, refers to his first volume of short stories, *Orangen und Tode* (Oranges and Deaths, 1961), with which he established himself instantly as a significant narrative talent. His first novel, *Massaker im Mond* (Massacre on the Moon, 1963), however, disappointed his critics, perhaps because Federspiel had not yet found his energetic and colorful personal style but contented himself with comments on the behavior of middle-class society types from the point of view of a cynical party guest. In his next book, a collection of seven short stories under the title *Der Mann, der Glück brachte* (The Man with a Lucky Star, 1966), Federspiel appeared at his best. The literary figures in this book have one thing in common: they all deal in one way or the other with the question of how one would document adequately (and authentically) one's existence in a time that has long forgotten the difference between reality and fiction. Federspiel, the narrator, finds his own solution for that problem by "taking shapshots" of his characters at the salient points of their existence. In fact, "picture taking," photography, and film are at the center of Federspiel's narrative art.

Federspiel is altogether visual in his literary approach. His near obsession with vision is demonstrated in one of his most beautiful poems, about a collection of eyes kept in a hatbox. Paradoxically, in his successful book *Die beste Stadt für Blinde* (The Best City for the Blind, 1980) he

°féd er zhpēl, yürg

turns his love-hate relationship for his favorite place, the city of New York, into an Odyssey for blind beggars who knowingly lead a seeing reader through the maze of that monstrous metropolis. Two more of Federspiel's novels deal explicitly with New York: his first major success, *Museum des Hasses. Tage in Manhattan* (Museum of Hatred. Days in Manhattan, 1969), a literary diary, written probably under the influence of Max Frisch, who wrote similar semi-fictional accounts, and *Die Ballade von der Typhoid Mary* (1982; translated as *The Ballad of Typhoid Mary*).

Federspiel's New York books display the visions of an entirely untraditional, wild, emotional and deeply compassionate narrator who watches the human comedy with a great sense of humor that quickly gives way to streaks of horror and to a notion of the approaching apocalypse. While Federspiel is indebted to the tradition of Rabelais and Villon, the religious undercurrent of his writings reveals a distant relationship with Dante. Federspiel's journeys through hell, however, lack revelation and are without the elements of faith that dominate the medieval poet's work. All that is left from Dante's world of faith is a host of angels that inhabit Federspiel's stories and poems. For his *Museum des Hasses* and for *Paratuga kehrt zurück* (Paratuga's Return, 1973) Federspiel invents his own Virgil—a fat, obnoxious, querulous, and perfidious person called Paratuga, a perfect guide through Manhattan and a visionary to boot.

Paratuga's literary sister is the notorious Typhoid Mary, the immigrant cook who dished out death with all the food she prepared. Based on a historic figure named Mary Mallon, his Maria Caduff is a Swiss immigrant whose ability to prepare the most exquisite specialties of her homeland launches her career as a master cook in the most exclusive households of New York. *The Ballad of Typhoid Mary* was a considerable success in the United States. It was recognized as a thriller with far deeper implications than its subject would suggest. Federspiel's version was indeed read as an allegory of the American dream. Richard Eder, in the *Los Angeles Times Book Review*, described Mary/Maria as "the dark side of the Gilded Age, the hidden bill for a decades-long orgy of accumulation and spending, the crack in the edifice." By calling the book a "ballad," Federspiel was suggesting not only its folk origins but also its open-endedness. Just as one adds verses to a ballad endlessly amplifying the original story, he has several narrators telling Mary's story. "Mary's stolid, tumbril-like passage through life was epically destructive," Mark Caldwell wrote in the *Voice Literary Supplement*, "but morally and psychologically flat, the same thing happening over and over again." But Federspiel's imaginative inventiveness keeps the book constantly fascinating. We meet the cook's victims and watch with horror what Caldwell calls "the hair-raising grotesqueness of her fate." Maureen Howard, in the *Yale Review*, found Brechtian elements in the novel: "The years flash by in headlines, history is a quick take of triumphs and disasters, yet the song goes by with its overkill, affronts us and entertains us."

Yet another relative of Paratuga is Kilroy, that famous phantom of the American GI in World War II, who always had already been there when everybody else arrived and whose graffitti were written on the ruins of bombed-out European cities. Kilroy appears in one of Federspiel's more recent collections of short stories, *Stimmen aus der Subway* (Voices from the Subway, 1988), a new version of a 1981 radio play. The three "guides" have one thing in common: they appear and exist in the great wastelands of history, battlefields, slums, metastatic cities and decaying cultures. Federspiel knows them all from personal experinces. He has traveled to the European battlefields of World War II; he went to the Vietnam War as a reporter (in the uniform of a United States Army Major), to the New York City morgue, and to the city's Potter's Field.

Wahn und Müll (Illusions and Garbage, 1983) is the title of one of Federspiel's collections of stories and poems. It is also his definition of history. Relentlessly he analyses our *Träume aus Plastic* (Dreams of Plastic, 1972), as he called a collection of his essays on literature, art, and film. It is hardly surprising that Federspiel prefers gargoyles and freaks, the horrid and the macabre, as objects of observation and speculation. In New York's "Museum of Forensic Medicine" he contemplates on the many grisly ways a person might be killed or commit suicide (*Die beste Stadt für Blinde*). In *Wahn und Müll* he follows in the footsteps of Madame Tussaud, who started her famous wax cabinet by duplicating the heads of the victims of the guillotine and exhibiting them for money to the public.

Mme. Tussaud also appears as a figure in Federspiel's successful play *Brüderlichkeit* (Brotherhood, 1979), a drama about the life of Eng and Chang, the "original Siamese twins" whose real-life story Federspiel, in his usual precise and meticulous manner, recovered and documented. In this case he found, as usual, reality to be far more grotesque and fantastic than the wildest fiction. The story of the exotic twins, who spend their life in a circus freak-show, who both marry and have children, is historic fact. It is Federspiel's special merit to have rediscovered it and to have turned it into a fable of human bondage, of suffering and fear of death. (The twins cannot be surgically separated; as one of the brothers dies, he drags his twin brother with him into death.)

Like Thomas Bernhard, Jürg Federspiel is a master of black humor. He often hides his dark and desperate tales behind the colorful but deceptive wrappers of yesteryear's romantic literary traditions: the fairytale (*Die Märchentante*; The Fairytale Teller, 1971) the ballad (*Die Ballade von der Typhoid Mary*), and the fable. A collection of his later tales carries the operetta title *Die Liebe ist eine Himmelsmacht* (Love Is a Heavenly Power, 1985). Needless to say, these and other stories could not be further away from their romantic models. They are narrative endgames in the tradition of Samuel Beckett, but also influenced by such writers as Raymond Chandler, Hemingway, B. Traven, and Melville. They deal with wrecked marriages, broken promises, murder, disease, and visits of extraterrestrial freaks making love to the schoolteacher, Miss Davenport, who finds out that love can really be "a heavenly power," to which the author adds: "You never know."

Die Geographie der Lust (The Geography of Desire, 1989) is Federspiel's most recent novel, a tour de force of wild fantasy and grotesque humor. It deals with the art of tattooing and its transcendental dimensions. "Skin is the deepest thing about a human being," says Federspiel. The story introduces Primo Antonio Robusti, a powerful Milan tycoon with the features of Mussolini, who intends to celebrate his seventieth birthday by "giving the world" to nineteen-year-old Laura Granati. This "world" turns out to be a masterful tattoo of the two global hemispheres carried out on Laura's behind, in color and with spheric sound effects (echoing Vivaldi's *Four Seasons*) by the master tattoo artist Omai O'Hara of Santa Fe. The moment Laura Granati has become a living piece of art ("a posterior for posterity," Anthony Vivis wrote in the *Times Literary Supplement*), she goes on world tour together with her friend Lucia Florestano. The elderly members of the National Geographic Society, the International Dermatologists' Association, senile ex-dictators and the mighty and the powerful from all over the globe come rushing together to inspect "the geography of desire" presented by this latterday "lady world." It is inevitable that the Yukuzas, Japanese mafiosi, eventually want to get hold of that *peau de chagrin*, first through a deal, then by the use of a scalpel. As she falls in love with a blind man in New York, angels come to Laura Granati's aid. "We'll never know whether there is a heaven," says Federspiel in the end, "but wo mun lu llı uı lu angeli."

WORKS IN ENGLISH TRANSLATION: *The Ballad of Typhoid Mary* was translated by Joel Agee in 1963. Evelyn Kaues' *An Earthquake in My Family*, published in 1986, is a translation of fourteen stories of Paratuga originally published in the 1960s and 1970s. The title story, translated by Joachim Neugroschel, was also published in *Fiction* 6, 1978. Other short stories by Federspiel in translation are Charles G. Horne's "The Dogs of Salonika," in *Dimension* 2, 1969; Thomas O'Hare's "Hitler's Daughter," *Dimension* 7, 1974, and "The Turk," *Dimension* 10, 1977. Another story, "Swiss Watching Mishap," appeared in the Australian journal *Western Magazine* in 1981.

ABOUT: Cassell's Encyclopedia of World Literature, 1973; Columbia Dictionary of Modern European Literature, 1980; Contemporary Literary Criticism 42, 1987. *Periodicals*—Los Angeles Times Book Review December 18, 1983; Times Literary Supplement January 12, 1990; (Village) Voice Literary Supplement February 1984; Yale Review January 1985.

*FENG JICAI (also rendered as FENG CHI-TSAI) (February 9, 1942–), Chinese short-story writer and novelist, was born in Tianjin, a coastal city near Beijing, which as the birthplace of the Boxer Uprising forms the background to many of his stories. His father was a merchant who had come originally from Ciqi, Chejiang province, not far from Shanghai. In his childhood he vowed to become an artist because he found philistinism repugnant. He began to read traditional and modern fiction and classical Chinese poetry at an early age. Later his curiosity and thirst for knowledge extended to history (especially of the late Qing period), sports, classical Western music and, above all, traditional Chinese art and Chinese folklore. Tall and agile, he was a natural athlete in middle school. He was admiringly labeled by his schoolmates *wenwu shuangquan* ("adept with both the pen and the sword") because he painted well and excelled in sports competitions. After graduation from middle school in 1960, he was recruited to become a member of the Tianjin basketball team, playing the game professionally until he broke his ankle in a fall. He then devoted his time to painting and before long was good enough to be hired as a teacher at the Tianjin Painting and Calligraphy Studio. His early writing was confined to art criticism and appeared in local newspapers. When the Cultural Revolution came he, like many others, was denounced. His house was raided by Red Guards, and he and his wife had to live in a shabby room with no furniture but beds made of bricks and boards. When the studio was converted into a printing mill, he was forced to give up teaching and work as a traveling salesman. Having the opportunity

°foong chi ts'ai

of meeting ordinary people of all trades, he began to hear horror stories of the suffering of the "masses" whom Mao Zedong had regarded as the backbone of the Communist Revolution. In one of his interviews he confessed he could not rid his mind of images of women tying small children to their waists before plunging into the river.

It was such vivid images that gave him the urge to write. He felt a need to put down these tragic occurences on paper, and he was confident he knew the characters as well as if they had been old friends. He wrote in secret, locking himself in a room and hiding his manuscripts away whenever there was a knock on the door. He claimed that he had written about a million words before he finally began to publish. When asked how he could continue without an audience, he said he had two readers: "God and myself." The voluminous writing in secret undoubtedly served as useful training for his later works. Today he recalls those confining days with satisfaction because as a writer he had complete freedom of expression, having neither to consider publishability (and therefore financial gain) nor to kowtow to the prevailing Party line.

In 1973, his interest in history and traditional Chinese folkways intensified. He started collecting folktales and studying the local history and customs of Tianjin. The next year he was allowed to teach painting again at the Tianjin Workers' College of Arts and Crafts. With his livelihood assured, he spent his spare time making a concentrated study of the Boxer Movement at the turn of the century when peasants rose up, at the instigation of Dowager Empress Cixi (also known as Tz'u Hsi), attempting to drive out foreigners and Western influence. Known in the West as the Boxers, the Yi He Quan (literally "righteous and harmonious fists") believed that martial arts training ("fists") and magical practices would make them invulnerable to attack. Among the Tianjin locals, even after the Communist Revolution, folktales of miraculous fighting ability in the face of foreign gunfire continued to circulate, largely because Tianjin, a city with foreign concessions, had seen many bloody encounters toward the end of the Qing dynasty. Feng was to use much of this material for his story-telling.

In 1977, his first novel *Yi He Quan* (The Boxers), a collaboration with another young writer, Li Dingxing, was published by the People's Literature Publishing House. It is a story with strong local color and a keen sense of the period, blended with a sustained attack on foreign imperialism. It contains sixteen chapters, 550,000 words, and was written from a Marxist point of view, combining mythical legends with modern ideology, reflecting the Communist doctrine of class struggle and of national conflicts of the time. In 1977, the year after the death of Mao and the downfall of the Gang of Four, the country was hungry for entertaining reading. *Yi He Quan*, a historical novel that reminded readers of the old-fashioned, martial arts fiction they could no longer obtain, became an instant hit. Feng was formally inducted into the Tianjin branch of the Writer's Union as a *zhuanyi zuojia* (professional writer). Since 1979 he has written prolifically. Stories of the same genre have included "Shendeng" (The Magic Lantern), "Shenbian" ("The Miraculous Pigtail"), and "Sancun Jinlian" (Three-inch Golden Lotus). It is Feng's intention to write a series of stories using the late Qing period as background under the general title *Guaishi Qitan* (Strange Tales in the Strange World).

"Shendeng" is a story about the legendary Hongdeng Hui (the Red Lantern Society), a branch of Yi He Tuan (the Society of Righteousness and Harmony). "Sancun Jinlian" is a harrowing story about the cruel practice of footbinding. "Shenbian" won an award for the best novelette of 1984 and is perhaps the best known of Feng's works. It paints a vivid picture of old Tianjin and its underworld, where an unpretentious man uses his pigtail, because he is an expert in martial arts, as a miraculous weapon to ward off foreign devils.

Feng's other stories include the novellas "Ah!" and "Ganxie Shenghou" (Thanks, Life), both award-winning, and "Diaohua Yandou" (three times translated, as "The Carved Pipe," "Figure-carved Pipe," and "Chrysanthemums"), judged as one of China's best short stories in recent years. His interests being varied, he has also written, besides fiction, essays and criticisms on social topics, history, literature, art, and folklore. In fiction he is one of the most original and colorful among modern Chinese writers. His fascination with the Qing period notwithstanding, he also addresses himself to current subjects of nationwide significance. His new work is *Bairen Shinian* (A Decade According to a Hundred People), recording the nightmares of the Cultural Revolution as revealed by a hundred ordinary men and women. He believes that it is wrong to forget such atrocities, committed by misled Communists who started out as idealistic do-gooders, and that the nation must probe into the cause of such horrors so as to prevent any repetition of those nightmares in the future.

In a recently published volume of literary essays, *Wo Xinzhong De Wenxue* (Literature to

Me), he admits that his writing has greatly benefited from his skill in painting and that he consciously blends symbolism, fantasy, allegory, and
realism in his tales with historical backgrounds.
Yet many of his stories are about modern-day
life; one good example is "Gao Nuren He Tadi
Ai Zhangfu" (The Tall Woman and Her Short
Husband), which is almost comical. His interest
in traditional folklore is so strong that a few
years ago when he first visited the United States
he specifically requested a trip to an Indian reservation.

WORKS IN ENGLISH TRANSLATION: *Chrysanthemums and
Other Stories* was translated by Susan Wilf Chen in
1985. *The Miraculous Pigtail and Other Stories* was
published in 1987; translators were Gladys Yang, John
Moffet, Stephen Fleming, Susan W. Chen, and Hu
Zhihui.

ABOUT: Who's Who in the People's Republic of China,
2nd ed., 1987.

JAMES FENTON

FENTON, JAMES (MARTIN) (April 25,
1949–   ), English poet, journalist, and critic,
was born in Lincoln, where his father, the Reverend J. C. Fenton, was then chaplain of Lincoln
Theological College. Fenton's mother is the former Mary (Ingoldsby) Hamilton. He was educated at the Durham Choristers School and at
Repton, an ancient public school in Derbyshire.

Interviewed by Andrew Motion in *Poetry
Review*, Fenton said that at Repton "I read Auden, and Auden was *the* hero, and for me in all
sorts of different ways still is." By then he was
writing poetry of his own, but "in a certain kind
of way. I always wrote frivolously. I used to
write to take the piss out of the other people in
school who were writing very serious kinds of
poetry." This habit has persisted, and Fenton
told Motion that "an enormous number of bits in
my poems have an element of practical joke."

After Repton, Fenton spent six months studying in Florence and then went up to Magdalen
College, Oxford University. He read English for
his first two terms, but meanwhile developed an
interest in anthropology. Since Oxford at that
time offered no undergraduate course in the
subject, he switched to the PPP tripos (Philosophy, Psychology, Politics), which was considered
a suitable preparation.

In 1968, when he was nineteen, Fenton won
Oxford's Newdigate Poetry Prize for *Our Western Furniture*. This is a precocious sequence of
twenty-one poems in a variety of sonnet forms
about Commodore Perry and the economic
opening-up of Japan in the 1850s. The sequence

was published in Oxford by the Sycamore Press
and broadcast by the BBC in 1968. Julian Symons later described this in the *London
Magazine* as "an astonishing piece of work"
showing "Japanese and American reactions to
each other, Perry's dreams of the distant country
after his return, his death, and in the final
sonnet a non-moral reflection on history's
contradictions." Another small pamphlet of
verse, *Put Thou Thy Tears into My Bottle*, followed in 1969.

Fenton graduated from Oxford in 1970 with
a third-class honors degree. By this time he knew
that he wanted to be a poet, but not as "a means
of earning a living," which would have involved
"putting a tremendous financial pressure on
something which should feel tremendously free.
So I thought, well, I'll do journalism. . . . so I
went into literary journalism, and then after six
months I went on to the *New Statesman*." This
was in 1971. Fenton worked for that influential
left-wing weekly "first on the literary side," but
after six months he "switched to the political
side, and did much more reporting." *Terminal
Moraine*, published in 1972, contained *Our
Western Furniture* and poems from *Put Thou
Thy Tears*, along with newer work, and was welcomed by Douglas Dunn in *Encounter* as "one
of the most interesting debuts for many years."

The newly collected work in *Terminal
Moraine* includes the title poem, spoken by one
who lives alone in a mountain valley and describes his life there in terms pervaded by an
anxious awareness of the uncertainties of perception and expression. "The Kingfisher's Box-

ing Gloves" is a sophisticated nonsense poem describing the adventures of a motley group of travelers. It was reportedly written by Fenton in French and then "translated" into English. Full of literary jokes and echoes, it seemed to Douglas Dunn the work of "a cross between a Parisian dandy and the heavyweight champion of Oxford." Dunn was better satisfied by "The Pitt-Rivers Museum, Oxford," an amusing poem cataloguing some of the bizarre "primitive" artifacts in an anthropological museum that suddenly becomes a serious poem about "self-delusion through imagination."

"Open Letter to Richard Crossman," in *ottava rima*, is both witty and hard-hitting. Fenton writes in the letter as a socialist disillusioned by the fall of Harold Wilson's Labour government in 1970 and equally disenchanted with the *New Statesman*, whose "ultimate commitments are the same" as the Tories'. The letter is dated November–December 1970 and, since Crossman had served in the Wilson goverment and was by then editor of the *New Statesman*, it is perhaps surprising that Fenton was hired the following year as a *New Statesman* employee.

Terminal Moraine also includes a number of "found" poems, including a cautionary one quoting at length from a book about fruit-growing and the use of pesticides. In his *Poetry Review* interview, Fenton explains that his "found" poems are "examples of poetic language from non-poetic contexts. . . . One of the things I found particularly seductive was scientific language, the way it used familiar words in an unfamiliar way, or familiar concepts in an unfamiliar way, or completely unfamiliar words—great clusters of them, so that the mind would just have to ride for a while, while these sounds just came. That's obviously a way towards finding, in non-poetic language, what can be the poetic language of the future. It's a way of drawing on the great richness of prose language as opposed to poetic language. Poetic language is very much denatured and overworked, and it needs a lot of new fertilizer."

Douglas Dunn concluded that "Fenton is clearly 'influenced' by Auden, especially later Auden. . . . He has immense potential, but . . . his talent seems to me the kind that could be swindled out of fulfilment by too much journalism, of which light verse can be a part," and by "his displays of erudition, the cultural glee with which he seizes the recherché or historical." Julian Symons, reviewing the same collection, said that "such a writer gives the impression of being so accomplished that he has nothing to learn. It is true that with all this ingenuity and inventive power goes a certain quirki-

ness, a determination to have fun, which is exhilarating but has its dangers. . . . The thing to emphasize is the real achievement of 'Our Western Furniture,' and the promise of development implicitly in almost everything Fenton has written since then."

The political journalism Fenton did for the *New Statesman* interested him in working as a foreign correspondent. When he received an Eric Gregory Award for his poetry, he decided to use the prize money to go abroad, spending the years from 1973 to 1975 in Vietnam and Cambodia. He explained to Motion that "1973 was just the time that the Americans were withdrawing, and so it was obviously going to be a crucial period to see whether the regimes that they left behind—the Lon Nol regime in Phnom Penh and the Thieu regime in Saigon—were going to last. So there was obviously going to be a great deal of change. I wanted to see that. I wanted to see a war, and what it was like." This adventure may also be seen as renewed evidence of Fenton's interest in Western interference in Far Eastern affairs, already revealed in *Our Western Furniture*.

Working as a freelance, Fenton reported on what he saw for a number of British newspapers and journals, most often the *New Statesman*, establishing himself as a humane, accurate, and stylish correspondent, with an eye for the telling detail. He says that after about a year "I came home for an abortive attempt at a job, then went back to Cambodia again with private help, and stayed there, and saw the two regimes collapse, and was evacuated from Phnom Penh by the Americans. Then I went to Saigon and watched the Americans leave Saigon, and stayed there for a while, while the new regime fitted itself in." Fenton is deprecating about the dangers of the war correspondent's life, but admits that "you seek out the danger in a rather meaningless way." In 1989, Fenton collected his reportage in *All the Wrong Places: Adrift in the Politics of Asia*. The book includes, in addition to his pieces on Vietnam, reports on his observations on civil strife in Korea and the Philippines during the 1980s.

Back in England in 1976, Fenton became the *New Statesman*'s political columnist, and in 1978 was a strongly backed candidate for the journal's editorship. However, as he told Motion, "my camp lost," and "at that point one always feels like a change." He went to Germany as the *Guardian*'s correspondent there (1978–1979) but found it "a very difficult country to write about, particularly in a daily paper. In journalistic terms it was a failure, and I got to the end, at that point, of my ambitions of being a foreign correspondent or a journalist. . . . There was only one job that could interest me, which was theatre criticism. And quite by chance that job came up on the *Sunday Times.*"

Fenton had written very little poetry during his years as a journalist, but as drama critic of the *Sunday Times* (1979–1984) he found "I could write and it's partly that doing theatre criticism is a very stimulating job. You're watching other people's writing in action all the time, and having this large input of artistic experience, and you feel challenged by it."

The pamphlet collection *A Vacant Possession* (1978) was followed by two more in 1981: *A German Requiem* and *Dead Soldiers.* Work from all of these, together with new and uncollected poems, made up Fenton's second major collection, *The Memory of War*, published in 1982.

The collection begins with the poem-sequence "A German Requiem," whose theme is Germany's attempt to wipe the losses and horrors of the recent past from the national memory:

It is not what they built. It is what they knocked down.
It is not the houses. It is the spaces between the houses.
It is not the streets that exist. It is the streets that
no longer exist.
It is not your memories which haunt you.
It is not what you have written down.
It is what you have forgotten, what you must forget.

As several critics have pointed out, this process of omission and suppression operates in the poem itself, and indeed in many of Fenton's poems: "It is not what they say. / It is what they do not say." Jonathan Raban wrote in the *Times* (London): "With its rapidly shifting locations and its large family of characters, 'A German Requiem' creates the illusion of extraordinary space and inclusiveness within a very tight form. In fewer than eighty lines, Fenton manages to build something that feels cathedral-like, vaulted, tall, full of echoes and dark cloisters of implication." Fenton himself says that "the poem expresses one's experience and memory of history in a country which is Germany but not just Germany: i.e., a country which has been through a traumatic experience of that kind."

Fenton lived for a time in a Cambodian village—perhaps the village that is the subject of "In a Notebook." We see it first as pastorally idyllic, almost undisturbed by "the pleasant war," a place where "one by one there came into the clearing / Mothers and daughters bowed beneath their sheaves." Then, after "the pleasant war" has "brought the unpleasant answers," the village is described again in almost identical phrases, but this time with a tragic sense of loss: "And I'm afraid, reading this passage now, / That everything I know has been destroyed / By

those whom I admired but never knew." It is both a technical tour de force and another and very moving poem about "self-delusion through imagination."

Seamus Heaney, writing in the *New York Review of Books*, suggested that Fenton is "at his most characteristic in secluded, hinting narratives of repression and isolation." *The Memory of War* contains several of these. "Nest of Vampires" is about a country house being sold off, a family dispersed, seen through the eyes of the young son. But, as Blake Morrison has said (*Yearbook of English Studies*, 1987), "the poem proceeds by hints (hints of madness, loss, and guilt especially) so that for all the precise details of place the ambience remains Gothic and murky." Rather similar is "A Vacant Possession," another country house poem, though this time a family is moving in, guests are arriving and "I hear my name being called, peer over the bannister / And remember something I left in my bedroom. / What can it have been? The window is wide open. / The curtains move. The lights sway. The cold sets in."

As Morrison says, "the chief vacancy of 'A Vacant Possession' may be meaning itself. . . . But against this absence is its presence of mind, its perfect command of pacing and technique." For Stephen Spender in the *New Republic*, such poems are "in the manner of Auden's poetry of psychoanalytic parables mixed with an ominous sense of the neurotic forces moving through contemporary history. . . . Fenton, like Auden, seems to be drawing strongly on memories of his own Anglican upbringing in Yorkshire." The poet himself concedes that his poems are often "more rooted in specific experience than would be apparent."

The Memory of War also includes a group of Fenton's nonsense poems. ("The Empire of the Senseless") and a number of found poems. "Chosun," using bizarre details taken from a nineteenth-century book on Chosun (Korea), is to that extent a found poem, and a brilliantly sustained one, building up a picture of a society at least as monstrous and absurd as our own. A long verse-letter to Fenton's friend and fellow poet John Fuller employs the stanza form invented by Robert Burns. It makes fun of the critic A. Alvarez—his campaign against "gentility" in English verse, and his advocacy of the "confessional" poets whose painful lives so often ended in suicide. Fenton invites Fuller to join him in a suicide pact, since "If poets want to get their oats / The first step is to slit their throats." Seamus Heaney thought that this poem marked "the desire of [British] poets" to reject extremism and "to regroup around the aesthetic of 'common sense and understatement.'"

In 1982 Fenton provided a new libretto for a London production of Verdi's opera *Rigoletto*; it was published in that year and also staged in New York in 1984. In 1983 Fenton edited a collection of short humorous pieces by the playwright Michael Frayn, and the same year published a selection of his own theater reviews, *You Were Marvellous*. Hilary Spurling, reviewing the latter in the *Observer*, wrote that "evocation is not his forte. His verdicts, often just and sometimes memorably offensive . . . are always magisterial. His style is high-minded, heavy-handed and, when it comes to performance, direction, and design, so uninformative that this column reads at times like an end-of-term report. . . . But the great virtue of this eccentric critic is precisely the seriousness with which he takes himself, his trade and the theatre which it is his delight to study and evaluate. He thinks, reads, compares, weighs and judges, in a word he ponders; and, in an age so conditioned by and to snap judgments, ponderousness has its point."

Another pamphlet of poetry, *Children in Exile*, appeared in 1983, and the same year Penguin published as a single paperback volume *The Memory of War and Children in Exile: Poems 1968–1983*. (Rather confusingly, this was called simply *Children in Exile* in the United States, where Random House published the composite volume in 1984). The title poem "Children in Exile" is one of the most movingly direct of Fenton's poems, universally praised. It is about three children and their mother, refugees from Pol Pot's Cambodia, who have been taken in by an American family in Italy and who, as the poet observes them, begin to "unfurl," to "relax and learn, and learn about happiness," transcending though not forgetting the suffering and the deaths, the "five years of punishment for an offence / It took America five years to commit."

In 1984 Fenton accepted a post as chief book reviewer of the London *Times*. He soon tired of life behind a desk, however elegant, and in 1986 became Far East correspondent of the *Independent* newspaper. That same year he edited *Cambodian Witness*, the autobiography of Someth May. *Partingtime Hall*, published in 1987, is a volume of light verse, much of it rude, written in collaboration with John Fuller. The title poem is a "film script" in ironic but sometimes oddly touching verse. It tells the story of a greedy and ambitious public schoolteacher, Mountgracechurch McDiarmid, whose seduction of a schoolboy and then of his rich mother costs three lives, including his own. Another serio-playful venture was the privately printed, limited edition *Manila Envelope*, a collection of

thirteen poems by Fenton, illustrated and packaged with a poster and a fold-out manifesto proclaiming his independence of and impatience with current academicism in British, French, and especially American poetry and criticism. The manifesto is addressed to the American critic Helen Vendler ("In Madame Vendler's Chamber of Horrors I saw seven American poets. . . .) and calls for "a new recklessness" in poetry. Blake Morrison described the volume, in the *Times Literary Supplement*, as "just the sort of whimsical product—inspired, eccentric, unobjective and unfair—which will madden the professors even more," but he found it a spirited challenge, "making it difficult for the professors to write off contemporary British poetry just yet."

Michael Carlson has criticized Fenton's poetry on account of the "distance between the poet and the poem, which is created by artifice, and which robs his most accomplished verses of their effect." Julian Symons, on the other hand, maintains that he "fulfils what the socially conscious poets of the Thirties intended but hardly ever achieved. They wanted to write about war but not to experience it, and ended up producing poems chiefly about their own feelings. Fenton's work, ironic, elegant, aware of yet always a little detached from the suffering it deals with, is the truest social poetry of our time."

Fenton himself says in the *Poetry Review* interview that "writing a poem is very much working into the unknown. . . . One should always be prepared to entertain strong ideas about what kind of thing constitutes a good approach to poetry. But as soon as the idea becomes unhelpful, chuck it, absolutely chuck it." He has been described as a formalist, and allows that "I've always enjoyed the possibilities of poetic form," while working towards "a kind of free verse." He disagrees with poets who believe that "treatment is all-important," and thinks that "a poem that's intrinsically interesting has a tremendous advantage over others. . . . But of course you have to find your own method. . . . You have to begin everything afresh, fundamentally, with each poem."

When he is in England, Fenton lives in Oxford. He is a Fellow of the Royal Society of Literature.

PRINCIPAL WORKS: *Poetry*—Our Western Furniture, 1968; Put Thou Thy Tears Into My Bottle, 1969; Terminal Moraine, 1972; A Vacant Possession, 1978; A German Requiem, 1981; Dead Soldiers, 1981; The Memory of War, 1982; Children in Exile, 1983; The Memory of War and Children in Exile: Poems 1968–1983 (published in the U.S. as Children in Exile: Poems 1968–1984, 1984); (with John Fuller) Partingtime

Hall, 1987; Manila Envelope, 1989. *Journalism*—All the Wrong Places: Adrift in the Politics of Asia, 1989. *Theater criticism*—You Were Marvellous, 1983. *Opera libretti*—Rigoletto, 1982; Simon Boccanegra, 1985. *As editor*—Cambodian Witness: The Autobiography of Someth May, 1986.

ABOUT: Contemporary Authors 102, 1982; Contemporary Literary Criticism 32, 1985; Contemporary Poets, 1985; Dictionary of Literary Biography 40, 1985; Fenton, J. All the Wrong Places, 1989; Who's Who, 1988. *Periodicals*—Encounter November 1972; London Magazine August–September 1972; New Republic May 14, 1984; New York Review of Books October 25, 1984; Observer July 31, 1983; Poetry Review June 1982, September 1983; The Spectator October 9, 1982; Times (London) October 10, 1982; Times Literary Supplement April 28, 1989; June 30, 1989; Yearbook of English Studies 1987.

EVA FIGES

*FIGES, EVA (UNGER) (April 15, 1932–   ), British novelist and social critic, writes: "My earliest memories of childhood are, ironically, as idyllic as childhood memories are supposed to be. This all changed from the time my father was arrested and taken to Dachau in November 1938. I did not know what had happened, but the bubble of protection in which I had been nurtured burst, forever. My father got out of the camp and I left Germany with my parents in the spring of 1939.

"My childhood from then on was dominated by the war which, in London, was never far away; by my father's absence as a soldier in the British army; and by parental anxiety about missing relatives in Europe. Perhaps even more important for me was the fact that I had social difficulties at school, where I was often pilloried for being German at a time when we were at war with Germany. Later I was also pilloried for being Jewish—and did not know what the word meant. The discovery of what the word meant in real terms during the rest of the war was very painful.

"I also, at the age of six, had to begin to learn a new language. Children do this very quickly, but the process certainly gave me a heightened awareness of language, which I think helps to make a writer. I made an effort not to lose my German (a taboo language during the war) and the quality of difference has stayed with me.

"Having to learn both a new language and a new script delayed my reading and writing. I was eight before I could read fluently, but then I never stopped. I knew instantly what I wanted to be when I grew up—the idea of collecting words in a book seemed pure magic to me.

"During my later school years and my time as a university student, my overriding interest was in poetry, and I saw myself as a poet. It was only after I left the university that I began to see the poetic possibilities of prose. I saw prose as a form of liberation from the restrictions of prosody, as a way of opening things out. It seemed to me that my own poetry had got stuck in a groove of verbal cleverness, of small statements, and that this was a disease that seemed to be affecting modern poetry as a whole.

"So I began with an overriding passion for language. I suppose it is natural that when I began to think seriously of writing prose, I began very much in opposition to traditional narrative, or what I saw as traditional narrative at the time. The insight which allowed me to begin writing prose was the realization that experience is fragmentary, and that we impose a narrative structure on those fragments.

"I am working on my tenth novel (for want of a better term) at the moment. Each book is different from the last, and I go for difference, for change. Some have quite a lot of narrative, and I have come to realize that all the writer does is to change the nature of the narrative. But I have remained true to my two first insights—a passion for the magic of language, and the need to question the nature of experience.

"My feminism is a different strand in my life, and has only gradually fused with the mainstream of my writing. Growing up, I knew that life was deeply unfair to women. It was unfair to me, in the sense that I was expected to make impossible choices. After my divorce, when I faced the hardships of bringing up two children on my own, my feminism became much more coherent and aggressive. But I still kept it separate from my 'creative' self. It was only after I had written and published *Patriarchal Attitudes*, after women's discontents had been more widely aired, that I really came to grips with women's experience in my novels. It is not the only theme in my books, or even the most important one, since I think that there are many areas of human experience which override gender, but I write as a woman, and nowadays I allow this to come through."

Like Virginia Woolf, to whom she has often been compared, Eva Figes is fascinated with what she calls "the fragmentary nature of remembered experience." In the personae of a variety of characters, most of them women, she reconstructs her own past and explores the feminine sensibility in novels that have been described as "prose poems." She is a novelist of the inner self—a self that is distinctly feminine and passionately feminist. She is also an outspoken feminist social critic and historian. Sexual politics and polemics are the subject of most of her non-fiction; the subordination, alienation and disaffection of women the subject of most of her fiction.

Patriarchal Attitudes is now regarded as a pioneering work. By 1970, when it was published, the demands of the women's movement for social and economic equality with men had been widely recognized, but, Figes argued, the central facts of a male-dominated society remained unchallenged. Patriarchal attitudes continue to prevail in religion, in the economy, in the whole structure and culture of society. "The voice of God is the voice of man," she writes; and in this world: "Man's vision of woman is not objective but an uneasy combination of what he wishes her to be and what he fears her to be, and it is to this mirror image that woman has had to comply." Citing the injustices against women in all our major social institutions and in the Freudian-dominated psychology of our society, Figes wrote what most critics judged a telling, succinct and intelligent book. More tendentious and controversial were *Tragedy and Social Evolution*, a study of the anthropological bases of our views of women in tragic drama, in which she argued that woman is the true tragic victim because she can assert herself only by defying the power structure, thereby becoming a victim or a pariah; and *Sex and Subterfuge: Women Novelists to 1850*, in which she argues that "If there is such a thing as the classical novel in English literature, and I think there is, then women were responsible for defining and refining it."

Figes' novels are short and densely concentrated. Most of them—notably *Days, Nelly's Version, Waking, The Seven Ages, and Ghosts*—focus on a woman reviewing a life of struggle and frustration. These are intensely personal but at the same time emblematic lives. In *Days* a woman lies ill in a hospital bed, as rigidly confined in her lonely narrow space as one of Samuel Beckett's characters: "I am not unhappy. My situation being what it is, I concentrate on its limitations." In the fragments of her memory and her consciousness she dimly recalls her empty past—her complex but emotionally unfulfilling relationships with her mother, the men in her life, her daughter. Past and present converge and sometimes merge. Although he found the writing "always lyrical and often perceptive," Peter Ackroyd, reviewing the book for the *Spectator*, objected that "Miss Figes has wrapped her subject within a cocoon of false self-consciousness." Valentine Cunningham, in the *Listener*, objected to "the intrusive polemical moments"; to Figes' attempt "over-ambitiously to embrace the plight of all women."

Waking, a book Cynthia Ozick in the *New York Review of Books* characterized as "a kind of rhapsody of the self," is a series of monologues describing the consciousness of a woman in the moments between sleeping and waking: the five-year-old child waking to play, the adolescent waking to her sexuality, the mother, the divorcee, the lonely, dying old woman. "The atmosphere of silence; the relationship of the woman to her body, tender and wondering in youth, bitter in age; one's sense of the changing, darkening season of life—these are beautifully evoked," D. M. Thomas wrote in the *New York Times Book Review*. The amnesiac central character of *Nelly's Version* is even more alienated, a symbol perhaps of the "liberated" woman who can find no identity in a world which remains male-dominated. Lovers, family and children exist, but no valid relationships can endure. Ackroyd again objected to the polemical tone of the novel but praised her descriptive writing, her picture of "the sad paraphernalia of Britain: the schools, the insane hospitals, the little shops, the houses that coalesce into a prospect of grey, the skies always threatening rain." More ambitious in its scope but in the critical consensus less successful was *The Seven Ages* in which seven women, all midwives spanning nearly a thousand years of English history, testify to the oppression of women. The governing metaphor is childbirth, generations of women suffering to bring life into a world in which male-dominated "progress" has meant war and death. "It is Ms. Figes' insistence on hammering home a message that weakens an otherwise ambitious, innovative, stunningly poetic work," Angeline Goreau wrote in the *New York Times Book Review.* Nevertheless she praised "the fascinating detail" and "the admirably original framework of the book."

The narrator of *Ghosts* is a sensitive, mature woman with grown children. She has so submerged herself in the monotony of her existence that she has no sense of her own identity. We do not even learn her name. At the end of this short novel she writes: "I have nothing to say. I see only the door marked EXIT." For Tracey Warr, reviewing *Ghosts* in the *Times Literary Supplement*: "At times the repetitive style and relentlessly melancholic mood of the novel become irritating and its form constricting." But because Figes writes so movingly and so vividly describes nature and the woman's reponses to her environment, Warr concludes that *Ghosts* "represents achievement of a high order, drawing on and referring to similar themes and moods in the Elizabethan sonnets, Joyce's 'The Dead' and Hardy's poetry."

Even where Figes' central characters are men, they are isolated and alienated—a victim of the Holocaust in *Konek Landing*, a deaf and dying old man in *Winter Journey*. A single exception is her portrait of the French Impressionist painter Claude Monet in *Light*. While Monet's large family and visiting friends are all introduced in this brief but sharply focussed novel, it is the unique quality of his art that Figes most remarkably captures. As in Virginia Woolf's *To the Lighthouse*, in which painting is the central motif and family life and routine domestic activities form a kind of canvas for the background, the theme (and the essence of Monet's painting) is mutability: "We live in a luminous cloud of changing light," he reflects, "a sort of envelope. That is what I have to catch." The novel begins with the first streaks of morning light awakening the painter and summoning him to work and ends with nightfall, the disappearance of light, on the same day. Told from the point of view of several characters (including his five-year-old daughter, who discovers the fascinations of light in soap bubbles and the transparency of a red balloon), *Light* has a texture not unlike Monet's paintings. Joyce Carol Oates, in the *New York Times Book Review,* called it "a luminous prose poem of a novel. . . . Its prose is unhurried, richly descriptive, rarely ornamental or excessive—indeed, a kind of Impressionism in words." There is "no strain, no self-conscious sensibility operating here," Linda Taylor wrote in the *Times Literary Supplement,* and "Figes manages to avoid any real sense of preciosity. Instead we are struck by the aptness of her untroubled thoughts and feelings, the detail and lucidity of her prose."

Eva Figes was born in Berlin to Emil Eduard and Irma (Cohen) Unger, a comfortable upper-middle-class family who escaped to England before the Holocaust. While her father served in the British army in a special unit for alien refugees, her mother worked as a seamstress to support her and her younger brother. Figes' early years in English schools, especially at a boarding school in Cirencester run by two kindly but eccentric spinsters, are described with humor and vivid detail in *Little Eden: A Child at War.* She attended Queen Mary College of the University of London on a scholarship and received a B.A. with honors in 1953. Her marriage to John George Figes, by whom she has two children, ended in divorce in 1963, and she supported herself and her children by translating novels from German and French and working in publishing until 1967 when her second novel, *Winter Journey*, won the *Guardian* Fiction Prize. Since then she has devoted full time to writing.

PRINCIPAL WORKS: *Novels*—Equinox, 1966; Winter Journey, 1967; Konek Landing, 1969; B, 1972; Days, 1974; Nelly's Version, 1977; Waking, 1981; Light, 1983; The Seven Ages, 1986; Ghosts, 1988. *Non-fiction*—Patriarchal Attitudes: Women in Society, 1970; Tragedy and Social Evolution, 1976; Little Eden: A Child at War, 1978; Sex and Subterfuge: Women Writers to 1850, 1982.

ABOUT: Contemporary Authors New Revision Series 4, 1981; Contemporary Novelists, 4th ed., 1986; Dictionary of Literary Biography 14, 1983. *Periodicals*—The Listener January 24, 1974; New York Review of Books May 13, 1982; New York Times Book Review February 2, 1982; October 16, 1983; March 22, 1987; August 16, 1987; September 25, 1988; Spectator January 12, 1974; September 30, 1977; Times Literary Supplement August 26, 1983; May 16, 1986; June 3, 1988.

FINDLEY, TIMOTHY (October 30, 1930–), Canadian novelist and playwright, was born in Toronto, the son of Allan Gilmour Findley and the former Margaret Mary Bull. He was educated in public and private schools in Ontario until the age of sixteen, when, after suffering for the better part of a year from mononucleosis, he was permitted to drop out of school, which he had hated, and to attempt to educate himself. He was strongly drawn to the theater and at seventeen was earning money as a member of Earle Gray's Shakespeare Company in Toronto. He appeared in some early Canadian television productions, notably as Marchbanks in Shaw's *Candida.* His success in that production led to his being recruited in 1953 for the first season of Tyrone Guthrie's Shakespeare Festival in Stratford, Ontario. "I'll never forget," Findley

TIMOTHY FINDLEY

told Alison Summers in an interview published in *Canadian Literature* (Winter 1981), "that first meeting at Stratford, when about eighty-five actors, drawn from across the country, sat down in a room with Tyrone Guthrie, Alec Guinness, and Irene Worth, and read through *Richard III*, the first play done there. The feeling was absolutely electric. It was as though in one moment we realized that a new kind of theatre was being born. And it was going to happen because we were ready: we had done our work."

Alec Guinness, one of the stars of that season, invited Findley to return with him to England, where he studied for a while at London's Central School of Speech and Drama. He became a contract player to the dramatic impresario H. M. Tennant and in 1953–1956 toured in the United Kingdom, on the Continent, and in the Soviet Union and the United States with several productions, in particular as Osric in the Paul Scofield *Hamlet*, with Guinness in *The Prisoner*, and in two plays by Thornton Wilder, *A Life in the Sun* and *The Matchmaker*. During the long run of the last play, the actress Ruth Gordon suggested he write a short story. The result was "About Effie," which he recast after receiving encouragement from Wilder, to whom Gordon had sent it. The story appears along with six others in his collection of short fiction, *Dinner along the Amazon*. He began writing full time in 1962.

Findley's first published novel was *The Last of the Crazy People*, the story of eleven-year-old Hooker Winslow, who is ignored by his deranged mother, his preoccupied older brother, and his obsessed father, finding the affection he craves only from the family's black maid, the amiable Iris, and from the numerous cats he cares for in the cellar of the family house. Left to his own devices during a long, stiflingly hot summer, Hooker determines upon a solution to the family's careless, loveless plight which involves a tremendous act of violence against them. "I think Hooker is a saviour figure," the author told Donald Cameron in *Conversations with Canadian Novelists*, "by which I don't mean at all anything Christ-like. There are people who come to save and people who come to destroy, and it's funny how Hooker winds up killing the family. . . . At first I thought that perhaps he went downstairs into the cellar and killed his cats, and then about two days after that I realized that that isn't what he did, that he has to save the family by ending their lives, ending their misery. It was the only thing he could do—and all the other things in the book pointed to it." Charles Dollen wrote in *Best Sellers*: "It is difficult to believe that this is a first novel because it is so well written with characters so true to life and so sensitively handled."

The Butterfly Plague followed hard upon the warm reception accorded Findley's first book and continued his imaginative exploration of the moral dilemmas facing modern man. The novel is set in the Southern California film world of the 1930s—it takes place from August 28, 1938 to April 1, 1939—and concerns the doomed Damarosch family: the father, George, a once-successful film director; Naomi Nola, his former wife, once a star and now dying of cancer; their son, Adolphus (called Dolly), a currently successful director, a homosexual, and inheritor of the family's hemophilia; and their daughter, Ruth, a swimming champion in the 1936 Berlin Olympics, who stayed in Germany, married her coach, and became a Nazi. The parallels and contrasts between Germany and California—their political and natural disasters, their exaltation of physical perfection, and their lack of true spirituality—are insisted upon, though not to the exclusion of character analysis. Joan Coldwell, writing in *The Oxford Companion to Canadian Literature*, takes Findley to task for overworking the "rich lode of symbolism and analogy. . . . One is almost suffocated by significance, as if by a plague of monarch butterflies that are beautiful and fragile individually, but in their masses bring destruction." Discussing with Cameron the significance of his novel's title-motif, Findley said: "I got into the greatest hassle when the editor kept saying, But you must explain what the butterflies mean. And I got in the most terrible panic about that, because of course they meant everything. They were the people who flocked to California, they were fascists, they were the people who were being destroyed by the fascists, both the Jews and the Germans, they were *everything*. They were anything you wanted them to be. Please don't make me put that on paper, I said, don't pin it down for God's sake, but I wrote two sentences, at their demand, and it ruined the whole book for me."

Many critics consider *The Wars* Findley's most artistically successful novel to date. It recounts the World War I career of Robert Ross, a young artillery subaltern in the Canadian army, whose strong reaction against the horror of the trenches led to an act that is variously considered by the other characters as treasonous or life-affirming. The novel's narrator, reconstructing the events many years later with the aid of newspaper clippings, personal letters, and interviews, ensures the reader's close identification with Ross and hence with the overall antiwar theme of the novel. T. R. Edwards wrote in the *New York Times Book Review* that the author's method, "reconstructing what can be known of [Ross] from incomplete evidence, . . . stresses the human strangeness that even war can't break down. . . . [It] is an impressively sustained meditation on how war crystallizes an unfinished personality even while destroying it." *The Wars* was made into a film in 1982, directed by Robin Phillips to a script by Findley.

Famous Last Words, like *The Butterfly Plague*, treats the historical reality of the spread of fascism in Europe before and during World War II. The main character is Hugh Selwyn Mauberley, borrowed from Ezra Pound's 1920 poem of that name. Various historical "fascists" also appear in the novel, including Pound himself, the Duke and Duchess of Windsor, Rudolf Hess, Joachim von Ribbentrop, and Charles Lindbergh. As in *The Wars*, the novel's narrator, in this case one Lieutenant Quinn of the U.S. Army, controls what the reader learns of Mauberley, even what the reader is allowed to read of Mauberley's work, which he has scrawled with a silver pencil on the walls of the deserted Grand Hotel Elysium in the Austrian Tyrol. The complex interplay between fact and fiction, between actual and perceived reality, may be seen as the overall theme of the book. Mauberley recalls how, one evening, "Wallis told the story of her life and left out China [where they had met]. I was very hurt. Then the Duke told the story of his life and left out having abdicated. Wallis was very pleased. Nonetheless these stories told the temper of the times and the motto we had adopted: *the truth is in our hands now.*" Another of Mauberley's characteristic mottoes is, "All I have written here is true: except the lies." The novel attempts to answer the central question of the relationship between aestheticism and fascism:

how could one (Mauberley, Pound) "whose greatest gift had been an emphatic belief in the value of imagination" have been so deluded as to "join with people whose whole ambition was to render the race incapable of thinking"? Paul Roberts in *Quill & Quire* called *Famous Last Words* "a landmark in Canadian literature [which] will place Findley where he deserves to be, alongside the best writers of our time. . . . This whole book is excessive, and mad, and marvellous, puzzling, disturbing, and utterly brilliant."

Findley's other novels include *Not Wanted on the Voyage*, a theatrical tale with Biblical overtones about the megalomania of its main character, the pseudo-scientist Dr. Noah Noyes, and *The Telling of Lies: A Mystery*, a meditation on the murder of the odious pharmaceutical magnate Calder Maddox, "who owned half the world and rented the other half." As a dramatist, Findley has been much less prolific (and is less widely published) than as a novelist. His most widely appreciated work has been written for television and, to a lesser extent, for radio. He wrote five of the scripts for the Canadian Broadcasting Company's dramatization of Mazo de la Roche's *The Whiteoaks of Jalna* (1971–1972) and two of the plays for the CBC's series about immigrants to Canada, *The Newcomers* (1978–1979): "Island," about the Scots, and "A Long Hard Walk," about the Danes. Story versions based on the dramatizations appeared in *The Newcomers*, a book based on the series. His radio play *The Journey* (1971) won the Armstrong award for radio drama. He has also, in collaboration with his friend William Whitehead, a CBC science reporter, written documentaries, including *The National Dream* (1974) and *Dieppe 1942* (1979).

For the theater, Findley's best-known work is undoubtedly *Can You See Me Yet?*. Set in The Asylum for the Insane in Britton, Southern Ontario, in 1938, its protagonist is Cassandra Wakelin, who confuses her fellow inmates with members of her ill-fated, loveless family. She repeatedly raises the issue of the relativity of madness and sanity and her central question, the one of the title, which she repeatedly asks of God, seems by turns bitterly ironic and mildly hopeful. Margaret Laurence, in her introduction to the printed version of the play, called it "an astonishing work, richly textured, sombre, and yet possessing a relieving wit. It's angry and impassioned about people's maltreatment of one another, and yet in places it not only speaks of the possibility of gentleness—it shows gentleness happening. . . . [It] is a play which will, I believe, continue to be performed in our theatres for a very long time to come." In September

1989 *Mute Court*, Findley's play about censorship, was performed in Toronto for an international congress of PEN. Here he introduces a variety of authors and literary characters who were condemned by censors, from Beatrix Potter (there is radish stealing in *Peter Rabbit*) to Jean Genet, from Emma Bovary to Molly Bloom and Lady Chatterley.

Speaking to Alison Summers in the *Canadian Literature* interview (Winter 1981—the issue is devoted to his work), Findley readily admitted that he regrets very much having given up his acting career·

> . . . knowing the kind of actor that I was—and I think it's dumb not to acknowledge that I was a good actor—I could have had a career. I'd never have been a star, not in a thousand years, but I would always have been a useful actor, a good second string—which in a sense is the best thing to be, because you do go on forever—not being dependent on star stuff, you can play anything.
> The playwrights I missed out on altogether were Pinter and Albee. I have an instinct for that kind of playwriting. I know I had the talent to deliver something of what they're writing about. I would have loved to play George in *Who's Afraid of Virginia Woolf?*. I'd love to be able to do plays like *No Man's Land* when I'm older. The other aspect of my acting career is that I had just begun to flower. If I had continued acting, it would have been the next ten years—between fifty and sixty—that I would really have hit what was naturally mine. That's when you're learning, building in terms of who you are. And I regret that terribly. But I don't regret having made the choice to write at all. There's nothing negative about that decision. I'm not big enough to encompass both things. I don't know how Coward managed to do it.

Findley's fiction has won several prizes. *The Wars* received the Governor-General's Award for fiction in 1977 and the City of Toronto Book Award. He has also received awards from the Canada Council (1968), the Ontario Arts Council (1977–1978), the Canadian Booksellers (1984), and the Canadian Authors Association (1985). He has been writer-in-residence at the University of Toronto (1979–1980) and Trent University (1984), and has received honorary degrees from Trent (1982) and the University of Guelph (1984). In 1986 he was made an officer of the Order of Canada. In 1986–1987 he was the elected president of the English-language chapter of PEN Canada, an organization working for the release and freedom from political persecution of writers throughout the world.

PUBLISHED WORKS: *Fiction*—The Last of the Crazy People, 1967; The Butterfly Plague, 1969; The Wars, 1977; Famous Last Words, 1981; Not Wanted on the Voyage, 1984; Dinner along the Amazon, 1984; The Telling of Lies, 1986; Stones, 1990. *Play*—Can You See Me Yet?, 1977. *Non-fiction*—The Newcomers, 1979.

ABOUT: Cameron, D. Conversations with Canadian Novelists, 1973; Contemporary Authors New Revision Series 12, 1984; Contemporary Literary Criticism 27, 1985; Canadian Who's Who, 1988; Dictionary of Literary Biography 53, 1986; Gibson, G. Eleven Canadian Novelists, 1973; Harger-Grinling, V. and T. Goldie (eds.) Violence in the Canadian Novel since 1960, 1980; Hutcheon, L. The Canadian Postmodern: A Study of Contemporary English-Canadian Fiction, 1988; Kroetsch, R. and R. M. Nischik (eds.) Gaining Ground: European Critics on Canadian Literature, 1985; Ripley, G. and A. Mercer. Who's Who in Canadian Literature 1987–88, 1987; Toye, W. (ed.) The Oxford Companion to Canadian Literature, 1983. *Periodicals*—Best Sellers June 1, 1967; Body Politic October 1984; Books in Canada December 1981; Canadian Forum February 1982; Canadian Literature Winter 1981, Autumn 1982, Spring 1984; Chatelaine February 1983; Choice October 1982; CM no. 2, 1982; Essays on Canadian Writing Winter 1984–85; Etudes Canadiennes June 1983; Fiddlehead Summer 1968; Journal of Canadian Fiction 1981–82; Journal of Canadian Studies Fall–Winter 1981; Kirkus Review February 15, 1969; Kunapipi vol. 6, no. 1, 1984; Library Journal May 1, 1967; April 15, 1969; New York Times Book Review July 16, 1967; July 9, 1978; August 15, 1982; October 9, 1988; New Yorker August 21, 1978; August 9, 1982; Newsweek July 19, 1982; Queen's Quarterly Winter 1982; Quill & Quire November 1981; Saturday Night May 1967, January 1985; Saturday Review August 5, 1967; Time August 2, 1982; Times Literary Supplement March 5, 1970; April 24, 1987; WLWE Autumn 1982, Spring 1984, Winter 1984.

FISHER, ROY (June 11, 1930–), British poet, was born in Birmingham, the son of Walter Fisher, a jewelry maker, and the former Emma Jones. He was educated at local state schools (until he was thirteen he never spent a single night away from his native city) and earned both bachelor's and master's degrees at the University of Birmingham. He has worked as a teacher and lecturer at various colleges and universities in the Midlands: at Dudley College of Education in Worcestershire (1953–1963); at Bordesley College of Education in Birmingham, where he became head of the department of English and drama (1963–1971); and at the University of Keele in Staffordshire, where he was until 1982 senior lecturer in American studies.

As a child Fisher was intensively involved with drawing and painting, and the poetry of his adult life is often startlingly visual and color-oriented. Since the mid-1940s, he has played jazz piano with various groups. His poetry's associative freedom, its deliberate and careful avoidance of the conventional in form or imagery, both owe a good deal to his musical affections.

The most remarkable accomplishment of Fisher's early poetic career is *City*, a combina-

ROY FISHER

tion of poetry and prose, an assemblage which was, in the poet's own words, "carved from half a dozen notebooks, poems written in various towns or about various towns or no town at all." Even so, the images of bombed-out desolation, nightmarish distortion, mutant and unhealthy nature, and drab meanness strongly convey the unitary image of one city, not pretty or happy, but a single place nonetheless, of powerful and surreal intensity. A few of the component poems recall childhood experiences overlaid with mature reflection, as well as much wartime devastation, as in "The Entertainment of War," a hallucinatory recollection of wartime bombing:

I saw the garden where my aunt had died
And her two children and a woman from next door;
It was like a burst pod filled with clay.

A mile away in the night I had heard the bombs
Sing and then burst themselves between cramped
    houses
With bright soft flashes and sounds like banging doors;

The last of them crushed the four bodies into the
    ground,
Scattered the shelter, and blasted my uncle's corpse
Over the housetop and into the street beyond. . . .

Those were the things I noticed at ten years of age:
Those, and the four hearses outside our house,
The chocolate cakes, and my classmates' half-shocked
    envy.
But my grandfather went home from the mortuary
And for five years tried to share the noises in his skull,
Then he walked out and lay under a furze-bush to
    die

These were marginal people I had met only rarely
And the end of the whole household meant that no

grief was seen;
Never have people seemed so absent from their own
    deaths. . . .

This is a city of alienation, where even in memory, even among relatives, there is no closeness, identity, or warmth, and love is nowhere in evidence. The poet's spirit is as tortured as his landscapes; he feels incapable of making a unity: "I come quite often now," runs one of his prose passages, "upon a sort of ecstasy, a rag of light blowing among the things I know, making me feel I am not the one for whom it was intended, that I have inadvertently been looking through another's eyes and have seen what I cannot receive."

Fisher at first made *City* "a symmetrical assemblage," in the words of A. Kingsley Weatherhead in *The British Dissonance*, "but this symmetry was disorganized by Michael Shayer and thus published by the Migrant Press in 1961." Fisher subsequently reorganized the first version into a tidier one (*Then Hallucinations: City II*), which is the version that has been reprinted and become widely admired. Alan Brownjohn, reviewing in the *New Statesman* Fisher's *Collected Poems 1968: The Ghost of a Paper Bag*, called *City* "surely one of the most consistently interesting experimental poems to come out of the little magazine activity of the last decade."

Fisher has written, "In my poems there's seldom /any *I* or *you*." He does not mean this literally, of course, but in the figurative sense that one will not find many love poems among his works, or much metaphysical exposition. He offers instead "the music of the generous eye" (a telling line from "Five Morning Poems from a Picture by Manet"), in which the world of events and phenomena can be captured and described as precisely and clearly as possible. His poetry can seem resolutely antimetaphorical, but it is never cold or unfeeling, and when he comes to describe the lineaments of human pathos there is calmness and a sureness of touch that many more overtly emotional poets must certainly envy. In "As He Came Near Death," for example, from the collection *Ten Interiors with Various Figures*, he is obviously describing the death of a loved one, capturing the pungent, poignant sense of the essence of life coming in a crisis to the surface:

As he came near death things grew shallower for us:
We'd lost sleep and now sat muffled in the scent of
    tulips, the
                medical odours, and the street sounds
    going past,

And he, too, slept little, the morphine and the dark
    light the

                    curtains let through floating him with us,
So that he lay and was worked out on to the skin of his
    life and
                    left there,
And we had to reach only a little way into the warm
    bed to scoop
                    him up. . . .

Donald Davie, in *Thomas Hardy and British Poetry*, considers this "one of the finest short poems to come out of England these many years," and finds in the next-to-last line cited above a reminder of the conclusion of Philip Larkin's poem "Afternoons" (from *The Whitsun Weddings*, 1964), about the mothers who bring their children to the playground: "Their beauty has thickened. / Something is pushing them / To the side of their own lives." "Behind 'worked out on to the skin of his life,'" writes Davie, "and 'pushing them to the side of their own lives,' the act of imagination is identical." "The best moments in Fisher, as in Larkin, are moments of piercing pathos." Fisher, Davie believes, "has opted for pathos and compassion as his objectives."

Before the publication of the prose poems in *The Cut Pages*, Fisher experienced a few years of blockage. "Until I was nearly forty years of age," he explained, "it was a source of mingled compulsion and excruciating pain to publish, in that I could never feel I had got the thing right, that I had the power of design which I might be expected to have." In *The Cut Pages* he feels "more the theorist," and able "to give the words as much relief as possible from serving in planned situations; so the work was taken forward with no programme beyond the principle that it should not know where its next meal was coming from. It was unable to participate, but it could have on the spot whatever it could manage to ask for." Such an agonized attitude to the affective and self-affective quality of his own words has persisted in Fisher's work to the present day. He has become solidly anti-rhetorical, ever suspicious of the cajoling and persuasive power of poetry. A two-stanza poem, "It Is Writing," from the collection *The Thing About Joe Sullivan: Poems 1971–1977*, might serve as the terse summmum of his poetic:

    Because it could do it well
    the poem wants to glorify suffering.
    I mistrust it.

    I mistrust the poem in its hour of success,
    a thing capable of being
    tempted by ethics into the wonderful.

Over the years Fisher has developed a warily acerbic attitude toward the business of reviewing, a field he has entered extremely rarely, and never except kindly, with no discernible animus. The activity of comparing poets and their gifts he has likened to "a civilization: or just / the dirtiest brawl you ever saw— / the choice isn't yours." ("Sets," from *Joe Sullivan*). In a memorable poem, "The Making of the Book," an *envoi* of sorts to the difficult collection *Matrix*, he vents much sardonic anger at the shape the "brawl" has taken:

    Let the Blurb be strong,
    modest, and true.
    Build it to take a belting;
    they'll pick on that. . . .

            set up an interesting
    tension between the acknowledgements
    and the resemblances; but in the photograph keep
    the cut of your moustache equivocal. . . .

    And remember, though you're only a poet,
    there's somebody, somewhere, whose patience

    it falls to *you* finally to exhaust.
    For poetry, we have to take it, is essential,
    though menial; its purpose
    constantly to set up little enmities. . . .

Early in his career, through diffidence or by design, Fisher published all his work only in little magazines and with small presses. The brief, seemingly grudging, or perfunctory attention (or no attention at all) received by his first dozen and a half books was for some British observers, admirers of his work, a disgrace. Donald Davie, for one, remarked caustically in 1973 that "the blindness or condescension of the metropolis to writing which is provincial in its origins or its subject matter is not much less scandalous now . . . than it was forty years ago. . . . And, indeed, though 'underground' and 'counterculture' are both words too fashionably theatrical to be accurate, it cannot be doubted that there are in literary England two distinct circles or systems of literary activity and literary reputation, and that there is a sometimes rancorous rivalry between them." Such ignorance, whether willful or not, was largely dispelled by the publication in 1980 by Oxford University Press of *Poems 1955–1980*, a book that garnered Fisher just about all the attention most poets nowadays could ever hope to expect. The metropolitan critics were at last full of admiration, though there was no hint in their praise of contrition for past slighting. Reading the collection was for Michael Hulse, writing in *London Magazine*, "an eye-opener. . . . Fisher's is very much a painter's perception, not only of colour, which he deploys carefully, but also of light. . . . If [he] is to be judged by his best he deserves to be rated highly." The poet is to Peter Porter in the *Observer* "strongly bound to experiment and to

certain avant-garde expectations. . . . [The po-
etry] is difficult, compacted and surreal; yet it
has charm and many flashes of brilliant writing. . . . I have not stressed sufficiently how
witty and humane Fisher is. His is a 'Collected'
to hang on to."

A Furnace was the first major work produced
by Fisher after Poems 1955–1980. Divided into
seven discrete parts, each subdivided into
shorter untitled sections, it bears a title that is,
strangely enough for this poet, metaphorical in
its significance. He explains this in the preface:
"A Furnace is an engine devised, like a cauldron,
or a still, or a blast-furnace, to invoke and assist
natural processes of change; to persuade obsti-
nate substances to alter their condition and show
relativities which would otherwise remain hidden by their concreteness. . . . Some of the substances fed in are very solid indeed: precipitates,
not only topographical, of industrial culture in
its rapid and heavy onset, when it bred a new
kind of city whose images dominated people's
intelligences in ways previously unknown." Thus
evoking City, his triumph of a quarter-century
before, Fisher bids us return to Birmingham, but
in this new vision concentrates on the chronic in-
stability of the industrial culture pre-eminently
represented for him by that place, always rebuilding, always destroyed. The new adumbra-
tion of his native city owes a good deal to the
novelist John Cowper Powys (author of Atlantis),
to whose memory A Furnace is dedicated, and
who constructed a "profound, heterodox and
consistent vision" of preindustrial culture, a vision which retains its power to move us only because of our awareness of the intervening
industrial reality. Section VI of the poem, entitled "The Many," comprises the poet's final realization of the endlessly repeating and resonant
message of the ages, one directly relevant even
to the British Midlands:

> Landscape superimposed
> upon landscape. The method
> of the message lost
> in the poetry of Atlantis
> at its subsiding to where all
> landscapes must needs be
> superimpositions on it. All landscapes
> solid, and having transparency
> in time, in state.

Fisher won the Andrew Kelus Prize in 1970,
and the Cholmondeley Award in 1981 for Poems
1955–1980. He has received bursaries from the
West Midlands Arts Council (1982) and from the
Arts Council of Great Britain (1983). He lives in
the countryside just south of Birmingham.

PRINCIPAL WORKS: City, 1961; Then Hallucinations. City
II, 1962; The Ship's Orchestra, 1966; Ten Interiors

with Various Figures, 1967; The Memorial Fountain,
1967; Titles, 1969; Collected Poems 1968, 1969; Corre-
spondence, 1970; Metamorphoses, 1970; Matrix, 1971;
The Cut Pages, 1971; Also There, 1972; Bluebeard's
Castle, 1972; Cultures, 1975; Nineteen Poems and an
Interview, 1975; Neighbours We'll Not Part Tonight!,
1976; Four Poems, 1976; Barnardine's Reply, 1977;
Scenes from the Alphabet, 1978; The Thing About Joe
Sullivan, 1978; Comedies, 1979; Poems 1955–1980,
1980; Consolidated Comedies, 1981; The Half-Year
Letters, 1983; A Furnace, 1986.

ABOUT: Contemporary Authors New Revision Series 16,
1985; Contemporary Literary Criticism 25, 1983; Da-
vie, D. Thomas Hardy and English Poetry, 1973; Dictionary of Literary Biography 40, 1985; Jones, P. and
M. Schmidt (eds.) British Poetry since 1970: A Critical
Survey, 1980; Silkin J. (ed.) Poetry of the Committed
Individual, 1973; Weatherhead, A. K. The British Dis-
sonance, 1983. Periodicals—Atlantic Review no. 2,
Autumn, 1979; Choice July–August 1981; Encounter
February 1970, March 1979, September 1981; Kulchur
vol. 7, 1962; Library Journal March 15, 1970; London
Magazine April–May 1981; New Statesman November
4, 1969; October 1, 1971; February 6, 1981; Observer
(London) November 22, 1981; Poetry April 1970;
Spectator October 27, 1967; Stand vol. 2, no. 1, 1969–
1970; Times Literary Supplement July 24, 1969;
March 20, 1981; April 2, 1982.

FITZGERALD, FRANCES (October 21,
1940–   ), American historian and journalist, was
born to a wealthy family in New York City. She
is the daughter of Desmond FitzGerald, who was
a specialist in covert action—he was in the early
1960s director of the fantastically elaborate attempts by the U.S. government to assassinate Fidel Castro—and was from 1965 until his death
two years later deputy director of plans at the
Central Intelligence Agency. Her mother was
Mary Endicott Peabody FitzGerald, who, as
Marietta Tree, was a member of the U.S. delegation to the United Nations, sometimes with the
rank of ambassador, from 1961 to 1967 and was
afterwards an urban planner. Frances FitzGerald was educated in private schools and received
her bachelor's degree magna cum laude from
Radcliffe College in 1962.

FitzGerald began working as a journalist soon
after graduation from college. She has written
for newspapers, including the New York Herald
Tribune, the New York Times, and the Village
Voice, and for the magazines Atlantic, Vogue,
and the New York Review of Books. Since the
late 1960s she has been on the staff of the New
Yorker, where the major parts of all her books
originally appeared.

Fire in the Lake. The Vietnamese and the
Americans in Vietnam grew out of FitzGerald's
first-hand reportorial assignments in Vietnam,

FRANCES FITZGERALD

which she first visited in 1966 at the time of fast-growing U.S. involvement in the war which had by then lasted for more than two decades. Her first visit also coincided with the beginning of the most intense phase of the Buddhist rebellion. She writes in her preface: "The succeeding political crisis within the Saigon government dramatically exposed the rift between the Vietnamese political reality and the American ambitions for the anti-Communist cause in the south. In the following months my attempt was to follow this rift and to try and understand the politics of Vietnam and the effect of the American presence and the war on Vietnamese society." Her excellent command of French and her natural persistence and inquisitiveness paid off with several insightful articles during her initial nine-month stay: in 1967, at the age of only twenty-six, she won the Overseas Press Club Award for the best interpretation of foreign affairs.

Shortly after arriving in Vietnam, FitzGerald happened to read Paul Mus' *Viêt-Nam: Sociologie d'une guerre* (1952), one of the central documents in the attempt by some Western intellectuals to fathom the political, economic, and social issues at stake for the Vietnamese in their struggle. "The book," she adds, "not only answered a great number of questions the American experience raised, but it indicated an entirely new way of asking them." She came to know Mus on her return to the United States, and much of *Fire in the Lake* is informed with the mature fruits of her continuing consultation and friendship with him. The book's title comes from the *I Ching*, the Chinese book of changes:

Fire in the lake: the image of REVOLUTION.
Thus the superior man
Sets the calendar in order
And makes the seasons clear.

In FitzGerald's opinion, the man in question was Ho Chi Minh, the nature of whose struggle was to bring order to his country by ridding it of the foreign-inspired turmoil and corruption suffusing it. After more than four hundred pages detailing the destruction brought upon Vietnamese society by the American intervention, the author in a prophetic passage looks forward to the moment when "the narrow flame of revolution [will] cleanse the lake of Vietnamese society from the corruption and disorder of the American war. The effort will have to be greater than any other the Vietnamese have undertaken, but it will have to come, for it is the only way the Vietnamese of the south can restore their country and their history to themselves."

The book was widely praised. FitzGerald, wrote S. R. Davis in the *Christian Science Monitor*, "constructs her case by a narrative of intricate facts which sharply cuts through the typical self-deceptions about the war that have been built up by official righteousness. . . . [She] has caught the sweep of the subject as well as the context." D. D. Buck in *Library Journal* called it "one of the best descriptions and analyses of Vietnam ever published in English. . . . She has been able to combine a basic understanding of the nature of peasant society, Confucianism, French colonial rule, and the impact of modernization to produce an exceptionally clear account of the problems of South Vietnam." *Fire in the Lake* won many major prizes, including the Bancroft Award for history, the George Polk Award, the Sidney Hillman Award, the National Institute of Arts and Letters Award, the National Book Award, and the Pulitzer Prize (all 1973).

FitzGerald's next book was timely, important, and based on much research, but hardly the stunning document her first book became. *America Revised: History Schoolbooks in the Twentieth Century* begins on a personal note. What the author remembers from the history textbooks she used in the 1950s is "not any particular series of facts but an atmosphere, an impression, a tone. . . . now the texts have changed, and with them the country that American children are growing up into. . . . The system that ran so smoothly under the guidance of benevolent conductor Presidents is now a rattle-trap affair. The past is no highway to the present; it is a collection of issues and events that do not fit together and that lead in no single direction. The word 'progress' has been replaced by the word 'change': children, the modern texts insist, should learn history so that they can adapt to the rapid changes taking place around them. History is proceeding in spite of us." She reviews the popular texts of the past, in particular David Saville Muzzey's *American History*, which, from its first publication in 1911 through the 1930s, was far and away the most popular history text in use. Her central thesis is the rather conservative one that, given all the rewriting of history encouraged by changing pedagogical fads and political interest groups, no clear, central idea is left, as the publisher's note has it, of "what the American dream ever was or is supposed to be." The "intellectual reductiveness" of pedagogical thinking has led to the teaching of history "with the assumption that students have the psychology of laboratory pigeons." To follow this approach "is not only to close off the avenues for thinking about the future; it is to deprive American children of their birthright."

America Revised was well received. A "strong, incisive and long overdue indictment," wrote Milton Meltzer in *Library Journal*. "Our history textbooks," in the words of P. S. Prescott in *Newsweek*, "have not only distorted our past, but erased whole hunks of it. . . . From her examination of a great many of these unconscionably dull and uninformative books FitzGerald has made a fascinating and important book. How can it not be important when we Americans, more than any other people, insist that our government can function only through the efforts of an informed citizenry?"

Cities on a Hill: A Journey through Contemporary American Cultures is an attempt to understand social change in the United States; it gives an account of a heterogeneous set of mid-twentieth-century American groups: the gay activists in the Castro district of San Francisco; the fundamentalist Christians surrounding the Reverend Jerry Falwell in Lynchburg, Virginia; the retirement community of Sun City, south of Tampa, Florida; and the group of rich devotees surrounding Bhagwan Shree Rajneesh who had taken over the central Oregon town of Antelope. "On the individual level," FitzGerald writes, following the lead of the American historian-sociologist Richard Hofstadter, "rootlessness and the search for self-definition were permanent and characteristic features of American life. It was a consequence of occupational and geographic mobility and the loose weave of the society." At two specific periods in the country's history—during the Age of Jackson and the Second Great Awakening of the 1830s and 1840s, and again during the 1960s and 1970s— Americans invented new religions and new social movements as a way of restitching the fabric for themselves." In the latter period, in-

deed, "the dominant sector—the white middle class— . . . transformed itself quite deliberately, and from the inside out, changing its costumes, its sexual mores, its family arrangements, and its religious patterns. . . . Jerry Falwell, the Rajneeshees, gay activists, and Sun Citians laid claim to the American tradition—not the tradition of the Founding Fathers but that of the Puritans." This notion gives the book its title, from John Winthrop's admonition to the Puritan elect: "We shall be a city upon a Hill, the eyes of all people are upon us."

Because of the author's thoughtful, intelligent, detached, and learned attitude, wrote Diane Johnson in the *New York Review of Books*, "she is a reliable observer and her method [of repeatedly visiting each of the communities she describes] seems admirably adapted to the complex subject." FitzGerald chose communities for what she termed their "prismatic quality": that by their structures and content they were able to say a great deal about the wider society in which they existed. "This assumes," concludes Johnson, "that they all somehow express in various ways quintessentially American behavior and values, and one senses from FitzGerald's account that they do. But what they say about America is more difficult to decide." Richard Wightman in *Commonweal* termed *Cities on a Hill* "virtuoso cultural commentary. . . . We are all products of the inherited American myth of 'starting over,' a myth that gives our life its distinctive frenzy, its unique hopefulness, and its special poignancy."

PRINCIPAL WORKS: Fire in the Lake, 1972; America Revised, 1979; Cities on a Hill, 1986.

ABOUT: Contemporary Authors 41, 1979; Who's Who in America, 1988–1989. *Periodicals*—Best Sellers September 15, 1972; Choice January 1980; Christian Century January 7–14, 1987; Christian Science Monitor August 23, 1972; November 11, 1979; April 9, 1987; Christianity Today April 3, 1987; Commentary February 1980; Commonweal April 11, 1980; February 27, 1987; Critic June 1980—II; Harper's May 1980; Library Journal June 15, 1972; September 1, 1979; January 1987; Nation October 27, 1979; National Review September 29, 1972; December 7, 1979; New Republic September 16, 1972; October 20, 1986; New York Review of Books October 5, 1972; December 20, 1979; January 29, 1987; New York Times Book Review August 27, 1972; October 14, 1979; October 12, 1986; Newsweek October 15, 1979; November 3, 1987; Phi Delta Kappan September 1980; Psychology Today December 1986; Saturday Review August 19, 1972; December 1979; Time August 28, 1979; Times Literary Supplement September 18–24, 1987.

FLANAGAN, THOMAS (November 5, 1923–), American novelist and critic, was born in Greenwich, Connecticut, son of Owen de Salus and Mary (Bonner) Flanagan. He served in the Pacific in the United States Naval Reserve from 1942 to 1944, and received his B.A. from Amherst College in 1945. He did his graduate work at Columbia University, taking his M.A. in 1948 and his Ph.D. in 1958. In 1949, he married Jean Parker, by whom he has two daughters, Ellen Treachy and Caitlin Honor. Flanagan's professional life as a scholar has been spent as a teacher in the English departments of several universities. He was instructor, 1949–1952, and assistant professor, 1952–1959, at Columbia University; assistant professor, 1960–1967, associate professor, 1967–1973, and professor of English, 1973–1978, at the University of California, Berkeley. Flanagan was also chairman of the English department at Berkeley from 1973 to 1976. Since 1978 he has been professor of English literature at the State University of New York, Stony Brook. His first book, *The Irish Novelists: 1800–1850*, was a critical study of five nineteenth-century writers from the perspective of historical forces in Ireland affecting their fictional visions and presentations of their characters. In 1962, Flanagan was the recipient of a grant from the American Council of Learned Societies, and in 1962–1963, a fellowship from the Guggenheim Foundation.

Flanagan's career as a novelist began when he was past fifty, with the publication of *The Year of the French*, a Book-of-the-Month Club selection, and winner of the National Book Critics Circle Award for fiction in 1979. A large historical novel set in Ireland, it deals with the Irish rebellion against the British, partly in County Mayo, in the summer of 1798. In that year the French dispatched an expedition of a thousand men to rouse the Mayo peasants into an armed insurrection—an insurrection that failed when confronted by the British army regulars led by General Cornwallis. The French surrendered, and were allowed to return to their homeland, but the Irish insurgents were driven into the bogs and mercilessly bayoneted to death. In all, thirty thousand people were killed in Ireland during that year. Flanagan's narrative method in the novel is complex, playing off an omniscient survey of the events against the partial views of five major contemporary witnesses—a Church of Ireland minister, a Catholic village schoolmaster, a youthful aide to General Cornwallis, a solicitor and member of the Society of Irishmen, and the solicitor's English wife. The cast of the novel is large, involving over a hundred characters, and Flanagan brings to the drama a sense of the epic.

THOMAS FLANAGAN

The Year of the French received exceptionally favorable reviews. Julian Moynahan in the *Washington Post Book World* called the work "an astonishing and terrible story. It is certainly the finest historical novel by an American to appear in more than a decade. . . . As he masterfully traces the course of this most brutal and eccentric military campaign, Flanagan avoids partisan myths while deploying his ironies, wryly, compassionately, authoritatively." Denis Donoghue in the *New York Review of Books* emphasized the way in which Flanagan's concern with narrative affected the shape and nature of the work. "Mostly," he remarked, "we come upon the events when their form and consequence have already been assessed. There is a loss of immediacy, for our interest is not allowed to fasten upon a character as distinct from his role in the story as a whole. . . . But there is a gain in the depth and resonance of the characters; when we meet them, they have already been changed by their experience. . . . It is my impression that Flanagan organized the novel in this way not chiefly for the pleasure of managing several viewpoints and styles but to ensure that the conflicts of class, religion, tradition, and self-interest would be disclosed and interrogated."

Writing in the *Observer*, Conor Cruise O'Brien also called attention to Flanagan's concern with the social dimensions of the rebellion. The novel's "main and absorbing interest," he commented, "is its picture of society, or societies, into which the French landed. . . . [Flanagan's] special academic interest is Anglo-Irish literature and he puts this interest to good use in this novel, much of which is built of brilliant pastiche extracts from various 'diaries' and 'work-books.' It is the work of a man learned in Irish history . . . but also emotionally involved in it, tied to it by a strange sardonic yearning. . . . *The Year of the French* is a magnificent and beautifully written historical novel. It can be read with pleasure and profit by people who have no particular interest in Ireland."

Flanagan's second historical novel of Ireland, *The Tenants of Time*, is also a large work (of over 800 pages), written from a panoramic perspective. The novel centers upon the Irish revolt against British rule in the 1867 Fenian uprising in the town of Kilpeder, a disastrous affair; but its time frame spans the period to the first decade of the 1900s. The work begins in 1904 when a young historian, Patrick Prentiss, arrives in Kilpeder to research the battle of Clonbrony, scene of the ill-fated uprising of 1867. As in *The Year of the French*, the novel involves a number of principal characters—the young terrorist Edward Nolan, schoolteacher Hugh MacMahon, and politician Robert Delaney, all veterans of Clonbrony whose paths to freedom from British domination take different directions and create a tapestry of Irish history.

Digby Diehl in the *Los Angeles Times Book Review* called *The Tenants of Time* "a masterful historical novel, a rich tapestry of life in the nineteenth century, and it is also a novel about the processes of history. . . . As a confident historian/novelist with a purpose, Flanagan whips us backward and forward through the decades of complicated events as seen by more than half a dozen narrators. The effect is a marvellous roller-coaster ride that is full of thrills and surprises." But Diehl faulted the novel in certain respects, finding it "overwritten—beautifully overwritten to be sure—but also bulky, talky and repetitive to a degree that burdens the story. . . . What he does not pull off are lengthy sections of dialogue chocked full of wordy historical exposition and . . . fulsome descriptions of settings. . . . By treating us to excesses of his own research, Flanagan often distances us from empathizing with these men 'ensnared in history.'"

Yet in the main, reviews of the novel were strongly favorable. R. Z. Sheppard in *Time* commented that Flanagan's "settings from Ardmor Castle to the local pub, are natural and unforced; the language of his characters hints at hidden poetry without breaking into showy lyricism or stage Irish . . . For all its size and sweep, *The Tenants of Time* is an intimate book. . . . [the] best historical novel to be pub-

lished in the U.S. since Thomas Flanagan's *The Year of the French*." Marcus Gee in *Maclean's* observed that, considering the situations that are dealt with "—dark Fenian plots, illicit love, the tragic sweep of Irish history—many writers would descend to literary blarney. Not Flanagan. *The Tenants of Time* is a complex novel, written with restraint and grace. . . . With *The Tenants of Time*, Flanagan proves once again that an original mind can shape good history into brilliant fiction."

Flanagan, whose four grandparents emigrated from Ireland to the United States, is a quiet man who avoids publicity. During the last twenty years or more, he has spent a good deal of time in Ireland, and has many friends who are Irish writers. Asked in a 1983 interview if the Irish people considered him "Irish" because of his Irish descent, Flanagan replied: "No, certainly not. People with Irish names who are Americans are simply considered Americans by the Irish, and Americans who go over to Ireland speaking of themselves as Irish are really making a hard time for themselves. However, I think maybe I've become a bit Irish myself, though not for ancestral reasons, but because I've lived there so long, because I go there so often."

PRINCIPAL WORKS: *Novels*—The Year of the French, 1979; The Tenants of Time, 1988. *Non-fiction*—The Irish Novelists: 1800–1850, 1959.

ABOUT: Contemporary Authors 108, 1983; Contemporary Literary Criticism 25, 1983; Contemporary Novelists, 4th ed., 1986; Dictionary of Literary Biography Yearbook, 1980. *Periodicals*—Los Angeles Times Book Review February 14, 1988; Maclean's April 18, 1988; New York Review of Books June 14, 1979; Observer July 22, 1979; Time January 11, 1988; Washington Post Book World May 13, 1979.

FO, DARIO (March 24, 1926–), Italian playwright, was born in Sangiano, a fishing village in Varese province on Lake Maggiore in northern Italy, the eldest of three children of Felice Fo, a Socialist, a railway stationmaster, and an amateur actor, and Pina Rota Fo, who came from a peasant family and is the author of *Il paese delle rane* (Land of Frogs, 1978), reminiscences of life in the Lake Maggiore area between the wars. Dario recalled one aspect of his childhood during a workshop given by him and his wife at London's Riverside Studios in May 1983: "I started in the theater when I was a little boy. I began with puppet theaters (not marionette puppets). I and my brother and sister used to make our own puppets, because we couldn't buy them in those days. Puppets weren't part of

DARIO FO

the world of toys. Particularly because we made great big ones. Then we began to write little plays. Now I enjoyed a great advantage, because around where I lived there were a lot of story-tellers. The fishermen, for example: they used to get the children to come and hold up their fish-ing nets for them, so that they could mend them. During this work, in order to keep the kids amused, they would tell all kinds of stories. Only afterwards did I realize that these stories were very old. And also it was only afterwards that I realized that these people were great actors. It was from them that I learned how to tell stories."

His family believed that Dario's schooling should promote his evident artistic talent, but when it came time for him to enter art school, World War II had broken out. The young man spent four years with his father in the Resistance, helping Allied prisoners of war to escape across the Alps into Switzerland. After the war he was finally able to leave for Milan, where he enrolled to study art and architecture in the school at-tached to the Brera Gallery and at the Milan Polytechnic. Almost immediately, he felt him-self drawn to the theater, first as set designer and then as performer. He was strongly attracted to revue, the escapist entertainment *per eccellenza* of postwar Italy, which combined showgirls in scanty costumes, stand-up comics, and glamor-ous *chanteuses*. It was not, as a rule, a socially or politically daring genre, and for that reason it was favored by the ruling Christian Democratic politicians, pro-clerical and anti-Socialist, who themselves were repelled by the burgeoning so-cial consciousness of the postwar Italian cinema.

In 1950 Fo joined a small theatrical troupe run by the well-known radio comedian and actor Franco Parenti, which staged improvisatory rou-tines for local audiences. His monologues were so well received that Italian State Radio, RAI, in-vited him in 1951 to broadcast a series, *Poer Nano* (Poor Dwarf), based on a character he had created. Poer Nano is the wise fool who habitual-ly and with a sly perversity turns historical and Biblical stories upside down, preferring, for ex-ample, Cain to the unbearable prig Abel.

In 1952 Fo, Parenti, and the comic actor Gius-tino Durano formed their own revue company, I Dritti (The Straight Men). Their first major production, *Il dito nell'occhio* (Finger in the Eye), was a hit from its opening in 1953, both at Milan's Piccolo Teatro and later, when it toured the country. It represented groundbreaking pop-ular theater of the left, a comic "anti-revue," whose aim, to Fo and his collaborators, was clear: to attack those myths of Italian life "which Fas-cism had imposed and Christian Democracy had preserved." The participation on the tour of the great French mime Jacques Lecoq was crucial; Fo learned much from him technically. I Dritti's next production, *I sani da legare* (Lock Up the Sane), was a pointed satire on the fanatical, knee-jerk anti-Communism then triumphant in both Italy and the United States. The company's successes made the authorities nervous: the cen-sors ordered the police to attend each perfor-mance, following the prepared script with flashlights to ensure there were no unauthorized departures or improvisations.

In 1954 Fo married Franca Rame, a young woman who came from a family of travelling players and whose stage debut had occurred at the age of eight days. They soon founded the Compagnia Dario Fo–Franca Rame. Through-out the 1950s Fo's stature as an inventive comic virtuoso grew apace, as he learned how to exploit his immense range of gestures, movements, and facial expressions, his rich stock of voices and ac-cents, and his unrivalled skill as a storyteller.

In 1959 Fo-Rame mounted its first season in Milan's famous Teatro del Odeon. They chose Fo's *Gli arcangeli non giocono a flipper* (Arch-angels Don't Play Pinball), a farce about a wise fool (Fo's Poer Nano figure again) who triumphs over bureaucracy and other absurd excesses of Italian society. It was an enormous hit with its middle-class audiences, securely establishing both Fo and Rame as leading performers and personalities in the public eye. In their occasion-al pieces they were able to exploit their abilities at comedy, music, mime, and farce. Fo, for ex-ample, would in one piece play two roles, of ab-sent-minded priest and bandit, leaving the audience to wonder whether they were not, perhaps, the same personage. Both principals of the company were close to the Italian Communist Party and eager to single out for satirical treatment the political tensions in society. The wonder of it was that their paying audiences of Milanese *borghesi* loved it. In the period of industrial and social unrest leading to the general strike of 1960, the authorities threatened repeatedly to ban the company's performances.

In 1962, with the accession to power of Italy's first center-left Christian Democratic government, the firm conservative hold over the state television apparatus began to weaken. Fo-Rame were invited to appear on "Canzonissima," one of the system's most popular shows, a kind of variety revue with many singing acts. Their contributions to the program's rather tired format electrified the country. In one memorable sketch, a worker's aunt, visiting a processing company, falls into a meat grinder which cannot be switched off for fear of holding up production. He then piously takes her home as canned meat. Right-wing press and politicians were incensed, censorship was called for and immediately imposed by the political appointees of state television, and the Fos walked out on the show. An immense national scandal ensued, with questions in parliament and threats of lawsuits. It was clear from the outset that the Fos had public opinion squarely on their side, but state power nevertheless banned them from television for fourteen years. Fo explained that he had intended to explore the reality behind the Italian postwar "economic miracle" which took the (to him) outrageous view that "we were all one big happy family now," and to show how scandals flourished as exploitation increased.

During the 1960s, Fo had become deeply interested in what might loosely be called "medieval" material, determining, in his own words, "to look at the present with the instruments of history and historical culture in order to judge it better." His first production in this area was *Isabella, tre caravelle, e un cacciaballe* (Isabella, Three Caravels, and a Dreamer, 1963), in which Columbus is presented as a sort of earnest, easily befuddled intellectual who is defeated at power politics. This was followed a few years later by the first versions of Fo's one-man show, *Mistero Buffo* (1969), one of his enduring triumphs both in Italy and abroad. This "medieval revue" drew heavily on the author's growing understanding of the counterculture of the Middle Ages and was performed in a language called grammelot, part north Italian dialect, part medieval pastiche, "an Esperanto of the poor and disinherited." Mistero Buffo changed, refined, and expanded considerably

from year to year; Fo included in it apocryphal gospel stories, little-known tales and legends, as well as unusual versions of well-known tales from the Bible. Fo's intention throughout has been to ensure the survival of the subversive nature of medieval and religious culture; this intention has not always been appreciated by the guardians of orthodoxy: a version of the piece performed in Italy in the late 1970s was condemned by the Vatican as "the most blasphemous show in the history of television."

The Compagnia Fo-Rame disbanded in the late 1960s. Its principals considered that it had become primarily an antiprogressive association, set up to perform like "jesters to the bourgeoisie." In Fo's words, "it was becoming more and more difficult to act in a theater where everything, even down to the seating sections, reflected class divisions. The choice facing honest intellectuals was to leave this gilded ghetto and to put themselves at the disposal of the movement." The Fos joined with other committed theater types to form Nuova Scena, a short-lived cooperative which attempted to dispense with traditional decision-making roles in a stage company by substituting collective for individual responsibility wherever possible. Political arguments tore apart the new group, but the Fos persevered, forming another new troupe, Il collettivo teatrale La Comune (The Commune Theatrical Collective), by which they intended, in Rame's words, "to put our work at the service of the class struggle."

It was in the early days of his working with La Comune that Fo performed for the first time his most famous play, *Morte accidentale di un anarchico* (1970; *Accidental Death of an Anarchist*). In his introduction to the English version, Fo recounts the story of the bombing in December 1969 of the Agricultural Bank in Milan in which sixteen people died. Anarchists were immediately blamed for the act and one of them, a railway worker named Giovanni Pinelli, "flew," according to the police report, from a fourth-floor window of the police commissariat. "He was said to have jumped out a wide-open window—past seven policemen, all witnesses, and on a freezing midwinter night." Ten years later, the trial of those later accused of complicity in the bombing came to an end, and three Fascists—rightist terrorists, not people of the left—stood convicted of material responsibility for the crime. One of these, to no one's great surprise, turned out to be an agent of the Italian secret police. "The great and provocative impact of the play," Fo continues, "was determined by its theatrical form: rooted in tragedy, the play became farce... the farce of power... the audience gradually came to see that they were laughing the whole time at real events, events which were criminal and obscene in their brutality: crimes of the state. . . . This tragic farce . . . was repeated all over Italy for more than two years on end. It was seen by more than half a million people. . . . In the daily debates [among the audience] which took place after performances it was the public itself which jogged us toward greater clarity about the new struggles which were growing daily and developing throughout the country." Fo speaks of how the English version "may have produced some erosion of the satirical level, that is to say in the relationship of the tragic to the grotesque, which was the foundation of the original work, in favor of solutions which are exclusively comic." The Italians, in his opinion, have a more highly developed taste for satire than other European peoples. "By good fortune our Italian bourgeoisie has always shown itself to be more stupid than its counterparts in the rest of Europe. It didn't devote as much effort to destroying the cultural forms peculiar to the lower classes and to replacing their traditions, their rituals, their language—in short their 'vulgar' powers of expression and creativity—with the ruthlessness and thoroughness used by the French, German and English bourgeoisie. . . . We Italians 'enjoyed' the Industrial Revolution after a long time-lag. So we are not yet a sufficiently modern nation to have forgotten the ancient feeling for satire. That is why we can still laugh, with a degree of cynicism, at the macabre dance which power and the civilization that goes with it performs daily—without waiting for carnival."

Fo's and Rame's effective political involvement deepened following the international success of *Morte accidentale*. They became prime movers behind Soccorso Rosso Militante (Red Aid), an organization founded to provide assistance to the thousands of political prisoners detained in Italy without trial and under harsh conditions. Their farce *Pum, pum! Chi è? La polizia!* (Knock, Knock! Who's There? The Police!, 1972) was sharply satirical about the heavy-handed, criminal activities of the several Italian police forces. The Fascist supporters of the police came close to making the Fos pay with their lives for such effrontery. In the spring of 1973 Rame was kidnapped from their home in Milan by a Fascist gang, brutally assaulted, and finally, days later, thrown out of a car, bleeding badly, in the middle of the city. No one was ever arrested for this crime. Fo was arrested in Sardinia later that year for banning the police from his rehearsals, and was released only after nationwide protests and demonstrations.

The Fo-Rame collaborations, from this watershed year on, have kept their typical sharp, satirical edge, but they have become slightly less politically overt as Italy has moved away from intense left-right political confrontation to a situation in which pluralism has been more or less accepted, even by the die-hard right. *Guerra di popolo in Cile* (People's War in Chile, 1973) was written after the right-wing coup toppled the Allende regime and murdered the president. *Non si paga! Non si paga!* (1974; *Can't Pay? Won't Pay!*), about a proletarian-consumer boycott in southern Italy, has become one of Fo's most-performed works abroad. *Storia di una tigre* (1980; *The Tale of a Tiger*) is an allegorical monologue based on a story Fo heard in Shanghai; its moral is that if you are a "tiger" you must never delegate responsibility, never expect others to solve your problems, and never place your trust in a party—the enemy alike of reason and revolution. *Clacson, trombette e pernacchi* (1981; *Trumpets and Raspberries*) grew out of the kidnapping and murder in 1980 of the former Christian Democratic premier, Aldo Moro. In the Italian production, Fo played the double role of Gianni Agnelli, the boss of FIAT, and a shop steward in the company, whose identities become confused. The play pokes bitter fun at the police, who after the kidnapping were as ever ready to arrest every radical in the country without a scintilla of evidence, and at the political establishment, who were themselves prepared, with indecent haste, to abandon Moro, their former leader, to his bloody fate.

One of Fo's most interesting works of the 1980s has a Renaissance English theme. *Quasi per caso una donna: Elisabetta* (1984; *Elizabeth: Almost by Chance a Woman*) opens in its English version with a tongue-in-cheek introduction by the author, who insists that practically everything in the work is a forgery: "sentences attributed to Shakespeare, . . . allusions to historical facts; . . . certain characters who appear on stage are downright forgeries, to say nothing of those who are referred to from time to time. Yet the body of the text is, I assure you, laden with authenticity." The play is essentially a piece for two virtuoso players, and was written in fact for Franca Rame, who took the part of Elizabeth, the Virgin Queen, a love-sick monster of unbridled power and cruelty, and for Fo, who created the transvestite part of Dame Glosslady, a bawdy dealer in patent medicines who sees deeply into the truth of things and who speaks in his extraordinary stage language, grammelot. Fo is interested in the authenticity of the heart, "in the terrible nature of power wielded by persons who can send others to their deaths. Allied to that is the theme which gives the play its driving force: how in a world where she is a rare exception among men, a woman of strength and beauty, endowed with a passionate nature, faces age, fears over the loss of sexual power, and fears of death."

Franca Rame during the 1980s established herself as one of the most outspoken feminists in Italy—indeed in Europe. She produced a number of one-woman plays, some in collaboration with her husband. Four of these extraordinarily powerful one-act plays were translated by Margaret Kunzle and Stuart Hood in 1981 as *Female Parts*. These are stories of women's oppression and of the characters' realization in their monologues of the reality of that oppression. Hood in his introduction to the English versions spoke of them as "a direct political intervention by Franca Rame in a society where the role of women is notably restricted by the Roman Catholic Church, by the state and by male society. But they have a reference beyond Italy. . . . In performance there is produced in the audience a kind of astonishment which finds its expression in laughter but behind which there is the shock of recognition: this is how women are, in our society this is how they are treated."

Although much sought after throughout Europe as theatrical geniuses whose workshops were international attractions to people interested in the theater, Fo and Rame were repeatedly denied visas to visit the United States under the State Department's rigid application of the ideological exclusionary provisions of the anti-Communist McCarran-Walter Immigration Act of 1952. Finally, however, in November 1984 the visas were granted and Fo and Rame arrived for their first visit, just in time for the Broadway opening of *Accidental Death of an Anarchist*. "America is the myth," Fo said on arrival, "but New York is the capital of the empire." He offered effusive thanks to President Reagan "for the magnificent publicity campaign he organized for our Broadway debut"—the president "gave us the visa on the day he was reelected—a show of solidarity with two of his colleagues" in the acting profession. In early 1986 Fo returned to perform in *Mistero Buffo* at the Kennedy Center in Washington, D.C., and at New York's Joyce Theater.

WORKS IN ENGLISH TRANSLATION: Lino Pertile's translation of *Can't Pay? Won't Pay!* was published in 1978. *Accidental Death of an Anarchist*, translated by Gillian Hanna and adapted by Gavin Richards, appeared in 1980. Gillian Hanna also translated *Elizabeth: Almost by Chance a Woman*, 1987. *Female Parts* was translated by Margaret Kunzle and Stuart Hood in 1981. *Trumpets and Raspberries* and *Archangels Don't Play Pinball* were translated by R. C. McAvoy and A.-M. Giugni in 1984 and 1987 respectively. Ed Emery's translations include *The Virtuous Burglar*, 1984; *The Open Couple*, 1984; *The Tale of a Tiger*, 1984; *One Was Nude and One Wore Tails*, 1985; and *Mistero Buffo: Comic Mysteries*, 1988.

ABOUT: Contemporary Literary Criticism 32, 1985; Current Biography 1986; Mitchell, T. Dario Fo: People's Court Jester, 1984; Valentini, C. La Storia di Dario Fo, 1977; Who's Who in Italy, 1987. *Periodicals*—Drama Summer 1979; Drama Review September 1972, June 1975, March 1978; Guardian March 1, 1980; April 26, 1983; New Republic December 17, 1984; New Society May 13, 1980; New Statesman March 14, 1980; July 3, 1981; August 7, 1981; New York Times December 18, 1980; August 5, 1983; August 14, 1983; October 31, 1984; November 14, 1984; May 25, 1986; November 27, 1987; New Yorker February 23, 1981; Playboy December 1974; Plays and Players May 1979; Sunday Times (London) May 1, 1983; Theater Winter 1982, Summer–Fall 1983, Summer–Fall 1984; Theatre Quarterly Autumn 1979; Times Literary Supplement December 18, 1987; Village Voice December 17, 1980; August 2, 1983.

FOLLETT, KEN(NETH) (MARTIN) (June 5, 1949–), British novelist and non-fiction writer, was born in Cardiff, Wales, son of Martin D. (an internal revenue clerk) and Lavinia C. (Evans) Follett. In 1968, while a student at the University of London, Follett married Mary Emma Elson, by whom he has two children, Emanuele and Marie-Claire. After graduating from the university with a degree in philosophy in 1970, he worked as a reporter and rock music columnist for the *South Wales Echo* in Cardiff; and from 1973 to 1974 was a crime reporter for the *Evening News* in London. It was as a reporter in London that Follett began writing novels. The first of them, *The Big Needle*, a mystery about drug dealers, was written very quickly to pay for the repair of his car and was neither an artistic nor a commercial success. Convinced that he could do better, he joined the staff of Everest Books, a small London publishing house, with the intention of learning how best-sellers are made.

At Everest Books from 1974 to 1977, Follett before long became deputy managing director, but at the same time, and with almost incredible rapidity, published nine more books—mysteries, thrillers, and two children's thrillers. Follett's first two spy novels, *The Shakeout* and *The Bear Raid*, appeared under his own name; for the other books, however, he used pseudonyms (Martin Martinsen, Simon Myles, Bernard L. Ross, and Zachary Stone) "because my agent suggested I might write better books later." In 1977, Follett left the publishing house to become a full-time writer, and in the following year published *Eye of the Needle*, which catapulted him to fame and sold five million copies, and became a best-seller

KEN FOLLETT

in twenty languages. Not yet thirty, Follett was called "the world's youngest millionaire author." Since then his sales have continued to break records. Following a bidding "war" among some of the major trade publishers in June 1990 all earlier records were shattered when the Dell Publishing Company bought the rights to two as yet unwritten novels by Follett for $12.3 million. The president of Dell was quoted in the *New York Times* (June 28, 1990) as describing the purchase as a "prudent investment."

Eye of the Needle, which was made into a United Artists film in 1981 that starred Donald Sutherland and Kate Nelligan, deals with a manhunt for a German spy in England during World War II. In early 1944, the Allies attempted to deceive the Nazis into believing they were preparing an invasion at Calais rather than Normandy by building a dummy fleet (plywood airplanes and rubber troop ships) in southeastern England. The German's top spy, Heinrich von Müller-Güder, code name *Die Nadel* (for the needle-like stiletto strapped to his left arm) penetrates security and races to rendezvous with a German submarine to report the imposture to Hitler; but a storm off the Scottish coast washes him up on a small island, where the denouement and defeat of Müller-Güder's desperate mission is enacted. Writing in *Newsweek*, Peter Prescott remarked that Follett "seems to rejoice in the clichés he has inherited from [Frederick Forsyth's international best-seller of 1971] *The Day of the Jackal*, yet his story, though ultimately as rubbishy as its canine progenitor, improves upon it by virtue of its remarkable pace, its astute use

of violence, its sense of particular environments and its occasionally felicitous prose." The reviewer for *Time* also found the novel "a crackling good yarn. . . . Follett's plotting is crisp, but it does not get in the way of his people— nicely crafted, three-dimensional figures who linger in the memory long after the circumstances blur."

Triple, Follett's second best-seller, revolves around a mysterious disappearance of uranium and the spy networks of the Soviets, Egyptians, Israelis, and Palestinians. The central figure is Nathaniel Dickstein, the Israelis' most resourceful spy, who devises the theft of the uranium with which to build a nuclear bomb at a time when the Israelis are most endangered by their enemies. Michael Demarest in *Time* called *Triple* "one of the liveliest thrillers of the year. . . . Follett is a master of crafty ploy and credible detail. . . . a sizzling narrative." Many reviews referred to the high level of tension sustained in the work. Robert Lekachman in the *Nation* characterized *Triple* as "a readable adventure story, a success in a form quite different from that of Le Carré. No ambiguities, just good guys versus bad ones."

In *The Key to Rebecca*, which was made into a television miniseries in 1985, Follett returned to World War II—specifically to the African campaign in 1942 in which a German spy, Alex Wolff, intercepts and relays British intelligence information to General Rommel. In another Follett manhunt, one of General Montgomery's intelligence officers tracks down Wolff and alters the course of the African campaign. Allan J. Mayer in *Newsweek* remarked that "Follett is no literary stylist, but his clean, purposeful prose is more than adequate to the demands of his tightly plotted, fast-moving story. More to the point, he knows his people and his territory; his evocation of wartime Cairo is a marvel of atmospherics." William Demarest in *Time* concurred. "Follett's true strength," he remarked, "remains an acute sense of geographical place, and the age-old knowledge that character is action. . . . The most romantic of all the top espionage thriller writers, he understands and sensitively portrays the women who come in and out of his cold. When the belly dancer and the courtesan appear onstage, Rommel seems almost irrelevant."

Follett's next novel, *The Man from St. Petersburg*, drops back further in time to the eve of World War I. The setting is London, where a military treaty between Russia and Great Britain is about to be negotiated, but where a Russian anarchist, Feliks Kschersinsky, is bent on the assassination of Prince Orlov before the treaty can be signed. Susan Jeffreys in *Punch* found the novel "thoroughly well-researched. . . . [But] though he's obviously done his homework [Follett] never gets bogged down with period detail. . . . For your money you get a rich brew of aristocrats and anarchists, society and suffragettes, a strong plot with some surprising twists and four well-portrayed main characters." The reviewer for the *New Yorker* also emphasized the brisk, involving pace of the narrative, remarking that Follett "for all his soapy plotting, is a good, straight-forward writer in the Maugham mode." Roderick MacLeish in the *Washington Post Book World*, however, thought that Follett's sympathy with all his characters prevents "the tension which comes from the true thriller's art of presenting us with heroes and villains." MacLeish was more impressed by the book's sense of time and place, the "evocation of an era" that makes *The Man from St. Petersburg* "endearing and absorbing."

In *On Wings of Eagles*, adapted for the screen in the following year, Follett turned to nonfiction. The book relates how Ross Perot, chairman of Electronic Data Systems, engineered a guerrilla-style rescue of two of his employees imprisoned in Iran during the upheaval just before the Shah fled the country. The book drew extremely favorable reviews. Hubert Herring in *Business Week* described it as "a remarkable telling" of escape in the Mideast. "Follett," he commented, "takes a hundred loose ends and false trails and weaves them into a book that flows like the best of well-made fantasies. . . . Perot, it seems, worked magic on Follett. The first chapter, an account of the arrest, drags on methodically, but the book springs to life in the second chapter as if Perot's energy were flowing through the author." Don G. Campbell in the *Los Angeles Times Book Review* thought the book "sometimes too finely detailed," but conceded that it was a "painstaking job of reporting" reading at times like one of Follett's own thrillers.

Lie Down with Lions, another Follett bestseller, is set in Afghanistan where Russian forces are pitted against Afghan rebels; agents of the CIA and KGB also become involved. Jane Lambert, who provides the romantic interest, is torn between two men who turn out to be opposing intelligence operatives, and before long her personal experience becomes part of current history. The reviewer for *Time* thought that the novel offered "little respite from treachery" and no truly sympathetic characters. Rory Quirk in the *Washington Post Book World* found the first third of the novel painful, slow, but added, "Lapses and slowish start notwithstanding, Follett has woven a highly readable story, rich in

detail and full of surprises." John Rubins in the *New York Times Book Review* took a dimmer view of the novel, maintaining that Follett shuffles "implausibilities and clichés. . . . Those who welcomed Mr. Follett as a true master of espionage fiction will be mildly entertained—and ultimately disappointed."

Among Follett's other novels are *The Modigliani Scandal* and *Paper Money*, which first appeared under the pseudonym Zachary Stone, and, in a distinct change of subject matter, *The Pillars of the Earth*, a long (close to 1,000 pages), action-packed story of the building of a Gothic cathedral in strife-torn twelfth-century England. Follett lives today in the Chelsea section of London, in a 200-year-old house overlooking the Thames River, with his second wife Barbara "and a varying assortment of children by previous marriages." His main interest apart from writing is music, and he is a keen amateur rock-and-roller who plays the electric guitar.

PRINCIPAL WORKS: Eye of the Needle, 1978; Triple, 1979; The Key to Rebecca, 1980; The Man from St. Petersburg, 1982; The Modigliani Scandal, 1985; Lie Down with Lions, 1986; Paper Money, 1987; The Pillars of the Earth, 1989. *Non-fiction*—On Wings of Eagles, 1983.

ABOUT: Contemporary Authors New Revision Series 13, 1984; Contemporary Literary Criticism 18, 1981; Dictionary of Literary Biography Yearbook, 1981. *Periodicals*—Business Week September 19, 1983; Los Angeles Times Book Review September 11, 1983; Nation April 26, 1980; September 29, 1980; New York Times June 28, 1990; New York Times Book Review January 26, 1986; New Yorker August 16, 1982; Newsweek August 7, 1978; Punch June 16, 1982; Time October 30, 1978; November 5, 1979; September 29, 1980; February 24, 1986; Washington Post Book World April 25, 1982; February 2, 1986.

*FORCHÉ, CAROLYN (LOUISE) (April 28, 1950 –   ), American poet and translator, was born in Detroit, the eldest of seven children, to Michael Joseph and Louise Nada (Blackford) Sidlosky. Her father was a tool and die maker; her mother, a journalist before her marriage, returned to college to complete her degree in the same year as her daughter. From her father's East European background, and particularly from her Slovak paternal grandmother Anna who died when Carolyn was eighteen, she acquired a strong sense of her ethnic identity, of the rootedness of the present in the past, and of a common bond of human experience that links people of all races and cultures. "Kinship is the theme that preoccupies Carolyn Forché," Stanley Kunitz wrote in the Foreword to her first col-

°for shā´

CAROLYN FORCHÉ

lection of poems, *Gathering the Tribes*. The "tribes" are literally her own people but also include the people she has encountered in her travels in the United States and abroad—the Native Americans of New Mexico and the Pacific Northwest, the victims of civil war and political oppression in Central and South America and in Lebanon and Greece.

Carolyn Forché began writing poetry with her mother's encouragement at the age of nine. At Justin Morrill College of Michigan State University in East Lansing, where she completed her B.A. in 1972, she studied creative writing, foreign languages, history, and international politics. While still an undergraduate she won several poetry prizes and began publishing her poems in journals like *Antaeus* and the *Chicago Review*. In 1973 she enrolled at Bowling Green State University in Ohio as a graduate student and received an M.F.A. in 1975. From that point on, Carolyn Forché has had spectacular success as a poet. Her first book of poems, collected when she was only twenty-four, was published in the Yale Younger Poets Series in 1976; her second collection, *The Country Between Us*, a Lamont selection of the Academy of American Poets, broke records for poetry with sales of about 17,000 copies. She has held teaching and writer residency appointments at Michigan State (1974), San Diego State (1975, 1976–1978), the University of Arkansas (1980, 1981), the University of Virginia (1979, 1982–1983), Vassar (1984), New York University (1985), the State University of New York at Albany (1985), Columbia University (1984–1985), and has given

poetry readings and lectured on many campuses. She has received many fellowships and awards, including the Emily Clark Balch Prize (1979),the Poetry Society of America's Alice Fay di Castagnola Award (1981), and fellowships from the National Endowment of the Arts (1977) and the Guggenheim Foundation (1978). In 1985 Russell Sage College awarded her an honorary doctorate.

Forché's first book assembles and epitomizes the major themes of all her work. Though not as immediately political as the poems in her later *The Country Between Us*, *Gathering the Tribes* establishes her as a poet of witness, one who exposes herself to the widest possible range of experience in order not so much to report as to testify. Her quest is for empathy: "I am spirit entering / the stomach of the stones," she writes in "Song Coming Toward Us," a kind of ritualistic chant shared with the Indians of the American West:

> You walk where drums are buried.
> Feel their skins tapping all night.
> Snow flutes swell ahead of your life.
> Listen to yourself.
>
> You live
> like a brief wisp
> in a giant place.

Even more personal and intimate are the poems on her East European grandmother who taught her to cook ("I am damn sick of getting fat like you") and to dance ("but I'm glad I'll look when I'm old / Like a gypsy dusha hauling milk"). In "Burning the Tomato Worms" she grows into sexual maturity in terms of metaphors of domesticity, learning to bake bread from her grandmother, sharing with her the chores of burning the worms as part of her own rite of initiation:

> She was asking me to go with her
> To the confrontation of something
> That was sacred and eternal
> It was a timeless, timeless thing
> Nothing of her old age or my childhood
> Came between us.

"Forché's poems give an illusion of artlessness because they spring from the simplest and deepest human feelings," Stanley Kunitz writes, "from an earthling's awareness of the systemic pulse of creation. The poems tell us she is at home any place under the stars, wherever there are fields or mountains, lakes or rivers, persons who stir her atavistic bond-sense." Her instinct for bonding transcends personal relationships and stretches to what links us to strangers— languages. She has some knowledge of the Tewa language of the Indians of New Mexico, as well as of Spanish, Russian, and French. "Aiming at wholeness, strength, and clarity, she works at language as if it were a lump of clay or dough in her hands."

Her bonding with women is strikingly articulated in these poems. Probably the most noticed of these in *Gathering the Tribes* is "Kalaloch," a long narrative poem centering on a weekend the poet and a woman friend spend alone on the Olympic Peninsula. Their intimacy with nature serves as a kind of parallel to their intimacy with each other, resulting in a poem that is both erotic and spiritual. "In its boldness and innocence and tender, sensuous delight it may well prove to be the outstanding Sapphic poem of an era," Kunitz writes. "The strongest influences in my life have been women—" Forché told an interviewer for *Rolling Stone* in 1983, "my grandmother, my mother, many older women. With one exception, everyone who taught me in El Salvador was female—*compagnêras*—it's a word in Spanish that means something more than companion."

It was through her friendship with a woman, the Salvadoran poet Claribel Alegría, then living in Mallorca in exile from her native land, that Forché became a witness to and an activist in the tragic civil strife in El Salvador from 1978 to 1980. Forché published her translation of Alegría's *Flowers from the Volcano* in a bilingual edition. As a translator she was praised for "bringing the essence of this passionate poetry to an English-speaking audience," although reviewers noted an "idiosyncratic" quality in the translation (*Choice*) and "sometimes hard-to-justify liberties with Alegría's diction, punctuation, and point of view" (*Library Journal*). At their first meeting Alegría was wearing a dress decorated with tiny pieces of reflecting glass, and though the women were physically and culturally vastly different, Forché found a mirror reflection of herself in the Salvadoran poet:

> . . . When I look for myself
> in her, I see the same face
> over and over.
>
> I have the fatty eyelids
> of a Slavic factory girl,
> the pale hair of mixed blood
>
> —from "The Island"

Through Alegría, Forché met other Latin Americans, among them the poet Leonel Gómez Vides, who urged her to go to El Salvador, "to learn about it because our country is your country's next Vietnam." Because her former husband, James Turner, and some of her friends had served in the Vietnam war, and although many friends warned her against travelling in so dan-

gerous a place, she went: "I knew I was ignorant about the situation there, and that it would be a worse ignorance to refuse this offer." Forché's political and spiritual education in Salvador from 1978 to 1981 was a crash course, unsparingly rigorous and taken at great personal risk. She went there first as a journalist, visiting clinics and hospitals, farms, factories, homes of wealthy landowners and of starving peasants; She returned there several times to work as a hospital aide and for Amnesty International. As she wrote in "El Salvador: An Aide Memoir" in *American Poetry Review* in 1981: "A young writer, politically unaffiliated, ideologically vague, I was to be blessed with the rarity of a moral and political education—what at times would seem an unbearable immersion, what eventually would become a focussed obsession. It would change my life and work, propel me toward engagement, test my endurance and find it wanting, and prevent me from ever viewing myself or my country again through precisely the same fog of unwitting connivance."

It cannot be said, however, that this experience converted Forché into a political poet. "All poetry is both pure and engaged," she wrote in that article, "in the sense that it is made of language, but it is also art. . . . What matters is not whether a poem is political, but the quality of its engagement." Reviewers of *The Country Between Us*, which contains eight poems growing out of her Salvadoran experiences, were impressed with her ability to transform the horrors of this war into the material of poetry itself, into metaphor and lyric. Although the war poems comprise only a small portion of *The Country Between Us*, they received the widest attention and no doubt account for the remarkable sales of the volume. Certainly they have an intensity, a passion and conviction that are rare in contemporary poetry. Dedicated to the memory of the assassinated Archbishop Romero, they reach out beyond the borders of El Salvador to embrace other tragic conflicts in Latin and South America. In "The Memory of Elena," for example, the mixture of shells and seafood in a lunchtime dish of paella is transformed into a grisly reminder of human violence and mutilation:

> This is not *paella*, this is what
> has become of those who remained
> in Buenos Aires. This is the ring
> of a rifle report on the stones,
> her hand over her mouth,
> her husband falling against her.

The most horrific of this group is a short prose vignette, "The Colonel." He is the poet's host at an excellent dinner in his comfortably furnished home in 1978, who flaunts his savage treatment of his countrymen by displaying before her a sackful of human ears. "Something for your poetry, no? he said." Such atrocities are not easily erased from the memory. Forché writes in her long poem "Return" that even in the safety and security of the United States:

> . . . I was afraid more than
> I had been, even of motels so much so
> that for months every tire blow-out
> was final, every strange car near the house
> kept watch and I strained even to remember
> things impossible to forget.

She reflects bitterly on Americans' fascination with horror, reports of terror ("the cocktail conversation"), and ignorance of the reality of El Salvador's politics, and concludes, reflecting on herself:

> Your problem is not your life as it is
> in America . . . .
> . . . It is
> that you were born to an island of greed
> and grace where you have this sense
> of yourself as apart from others. It is
> not your right to feel powerless. Better
> people than you were powerless.
> You have not returned to your country,
> but to a life you never left.

Other poems in *The Country Between Us* deal with her travels in Eastern Europe, Yugoslavia, Czechoslovakia, Turkey; and the book ends with "Ourselves or Nothing" a powerful poem of tribute to Terrence Des Pres, author of a memorable book on the Holocaust and the gulags, *The Survivor: An Anatomy of Life in the Death Camps*, who died in 1987. Des Pres had also been in El Salvador; like Forché he understood that all human atrocities are the same—"Belsen, Dachau, Saigon, Phnom Penh / and the one meaning Bridge of Ravens, / Sao Paulo, Armagh, Calcutta, Salvador . . . ." The poem ends:

> There is a cyclone fence between
> ourselves and the slaughter behind it
> We hover in a calm protected world like
> netted fish, exactly like netted fish.
> It is either the beginning or the end
> of the world, and the choice is ourselves
> or nothing.

Terence Diggory observed in a review of *The Country Between Us* in *Salmagundi* that for all her sympathy with the sufferings of others in foreign countries, especially in Latin America, Forché remains a North American writing in "the Anglo-American literary tradition": "One of the great strengths of *The Country Between Us* is that, unlike so many of her reviewers, Forché does not allow herself the illusion that a cultural perspective or a literary tradition can be, or should be, simply wished away." Others, like Katha Pollitt in the *Nation*, question whether Forché has found a poetic language adequate for the intensity of the feelings she seeks to communicate—in Pollitt's words "the incongruity between Forché's themes and her poetic strategies." As with her earlier collection, this volume evoked qualified responses—essentially, that Forché, still young, is a poet of greater future promise than present achievement. Nevertheless, she is a considerable artist who, on the merits simply of these two books, deserves her reputation as an important contemporary American poet. As Rochelle Ratner wrote in the *American Book Review* in 1982, Forché has an "astute sense of observation and a tendency to describe things in a way slightly out of the ordinary, so that our heads turn sharply around to look."

In the years immediately following her return from El Salvador, Carolyn Forché published no poetry. It was a period of personal reassessment. Writing in 1987 a preface to Olga Broumas' translation of *The Little Mariner* by the Greek poet Odysseus Elytis, she said: "It had been my intention to know the world as if it were apart from myself, and to become more fully conscious, as if consciousness were a repository of experience and wisdom, rather than an analog of the world itself." She has also been teaching, giving poetry readings, and lecturing on Latin American conditions, and she wrote the text for a collection of photographs, *El Salvador: The Work of Thirty Photographers* (1983). Married since 1984 to Henry E. Mattison, a photographer, she lives in Greenwich Village in New York City.

PRINCIPAL WORKS: *Poetry*—Gathering the Tribes, 1979; The Country Between Us, 1981. *As translator*—C. Alegría's Flowers from the Volcano, 1982.

ABOUT: Contemporary Authors 117, 1986; Contemporary Literary Criticism 25, 1983; Contemporary Poetry, 4th ed., 1985; Dictionary of Literary Biography 5, 1980; Kunitz, S. Foreword to Gathering the Tribes, 1976. *Periodicals*—American Book Review November–December 1982; American Poetry Review July–August 1981; Choice June 1982; Library Journal November 15, 1982; Nation May 8, 1982; New York Times Book Review August 8, 1979; April 4, 1982; Rolling Stone April 14, 1982; Salmagundi Fall 1983.

FORD, RICHARD (February 16, 1944–   ), American novelist and short-story writer, was born in Jackson, Mississippi. His father, Parker Carrol Ford, was a salesman. After his father de-

RICHARD FORD

vcloped heart problems, Ford spent much of his time with his grandparents in Little Rock, Arkansas, where they ran a hotel. His mother, Edna Akin Ford, joined him there after his father's death in 1960. In 1962, he enrolled at Michigan State University in East Lansing, where he studied literature and began to write stories. After graduating in 1966, he taught school for a year and then entered law school at Washington University in St. Louis. After a semester, however, he decided against a law career, and in January 1968 he made up his mind to become a writer. Later that year he married Kristina Hensley, whom he had met at Michigan State. After working briefly as an editor in New York, Ford studied literature and writing with the novelists Oakley Hall and E. L. Doctorow at the University of California, Irvine. He has taught writing at the University of Michigan, Princeton University, Goddard College, and Williams College, and in the early 1980s he worked as a writer for *Inside Sports* magazine. He was a Guggenheim fellow in 1977–1978 and held a National Endowment for the Arts fellowship in 1979–1980. Since 1983, he and his wife have lived most of the time in a remote cabin in the Highwood Mountains of Montana, about thirty miles from Great Falls.

Ford's first two novels, *A Piece of My Heart* and *The Ultimate Good Luck*, received some scattered high praise, but *The Sportswriter* was the book that established his reputation, which was enhanced by his collection of stories, *Rock Springs*; several of these had already been acclaimed when they appeared in *Esquire* and the

New Yorker. Ford's fiction is searching, profoundly sympathetic, and morally serious. A number of critics have seen it as an antidote to the shallowness and passivity of minimalist fiction. His hard-luck characters struggle toward understanding, acceptance, and hope rather than receding into apathy and aimless distraction. His style is not neutral and flat but intense and lyrical. Along with such contemporaries as Russell Banks and André Dubus, Ford has conveyed through marginal and working-class characters a sense of moral and spiritual engagement that is rare in recent American fiction.

In Ford's case, the tragic depths of his work may owe something to his Southern background. His first novel, *A Piece of My Heart*, is saturated with the influence of Southern literature, especially Faulkner, and for some critics it was too much. The novel, Larry McMurtry wrote in the *New York Times Book Review*, "shows obvious promise, but it also exhibits all the characteristic vices of Southern fiction. . . . If the vices . . . could be squeezed into one word, the word would be neo-Faulknerism. It reads like the worst, rather than the best, of Faulkner. . . . Portentousness, overwriting, pronouns drifting toward a shore only dimly seen, a constant backward tilt toward a past that hasn't the remotest causal influence on what is actually happening, plus a more or less constant tendency to equate eloquence with significance: these are the familiar qualities in which Mr. Ford's narrative abounds. From the tone, one might think that something of great moment is happening, but one would be wrong." Summarizing the plot, McMurtry complained, "What we have here is a fairly mundane story of working class adultery, in which the adulterer gets shot, not by the husband he has cuckolded, but by an indifferent youth who happens to be guarding a boat he makes off in. It would have made a creditable spare short novel. It does not, however, lend itself well to constant overtones of the fall of man." Yet McMurtry concluded by saying that Ford's "minor characters are vividly drawn, and his ear is first-rate. If he can weed his garden of some of the weeds and cockleburrs of his tradition, it might prove very fertile."

In contrast, it was precisely Ford's feel for the South and the Southern literary tradition that Victor Gold, himself of Southern background, praised in the *National Review*: "His poet's vision of a Mother Region littered with decay and deformity, where violence and death are shrugged off as integral to the life-force itself, is clear and unsentimental. The book may indeed be a classic of the genre, first novel or tenth. Ford is a superb storyteller who can relate a vignette of pure horror or a comedy of rustic manners with equal brilliance." Gold found Ford's use of symbolism masterful and the novel's structure flawless: the two main characters "are mirror images: their fates interwined, to be resolved during a brief and surreal stay on a river island between Arkansas and Mississippi." In the middle of these two polar critical reactions was Walter Clemons of *Newsweek*, who found in the novel promise of "a career that could turn out to be extraordinary," but who also found it frustrating: "Richard Ford is a writer of strong talent who doesn't make things easy. . . . Having established at the start an air of menace and heartsickness, he is in no hurry to rush the book to its violent climax. The water torture of leisurely, anecdotal southern talk is part of his plan." But Clemons praised the sharpness of the novel's observation and summed up: "Its power is mysterious and unmistakeable. At his best Ford is able to combine sardonic comedy with an enfolding apprehension of doom."

Reviewing Ford's second novel, *The Ultimate Good Luck*, in 1981, Clemons again found it promising but thought that Ford's obvious talent had not been fully realized. Comparing it to *A Piece of My Heart*, he wrote: "*The Ultimate Good Luck* is a tighter, more efficient book, and a good one, though Ford has jimmied himself into the confines of the existentialist thriller with a conspicuous sacrifice of his robust gift for comedy." The novel, set in Oaxaca, Mexico, is about a Vietnam veteran, Harry Quinn, a rootless, detached loner, and his efforts to free his girlfriend's brother from the jail where he has been sent for drug-dealing. C.D.B. Bryan, in the *New York Times Book Review*, praised the "taut cinematic quality" of Ford's prose: "It is a style that bathes his story with the same hot, flat, mercilessly white light that scorches Mexico, and it captures exactly that disquieting sense of menace one often feels lurking there just off the road."

The Mexican setting inspired Raymond Carver in the *Chicago Tribune Book World* to compare the novel with two classics that take place in a similar Mexico, stark and menacing. Ford's novel, he wrote, "belongs alongside Malcolm Lowry's *Under the Volcano* and Graham Greene's *The Power and the Glory*. I can't give this novel higher marks." Carver, like Bryan and Clemons, singled out Ford's sense of place and the exceptional power of his prose style in evoking it. *The Ultimate Good Luck* was not published in England until 1989. Maureen Freely, reviewing that edition for the *Times Literary Supplement*, added literary comparisons: "Richard Ford has learned as much from [Raymond] Chandler as he has from Hemingway. He is a brilliant technician when it comes to build-

ing tension and suspense. But what he is best at is getting under the reader's guard—using careful, stripped-down sentences that promise dullness and then deliver unexpected insights."

After the publication of *The Sportswriter* in 1986, Ford's reputation could no longer be described as quiet. The book was widely reviewed and almost as widely acclaimed; it sold well; and articles on Ford appeared in publications like the *New York Times Magazine*. The narrator-hero of *The Sportswriter* is Frank Bascombe, a middle-aged man living in an affluent New Jersey suburb. He has suffered several losses: his nine-year-old son died from a rare disease, and soon afterward his wife divorced him. He has also had to give up writing fiction after being unable to follow up the success of a book of short stories. He has taken a job writing about sports for a weekly magazine and has found an agreeable girlfriend; retreating into a kind of dreamy detachment and harmony with his ordinary suburban surroundings, he professes contentment. The novel, taking place over Easter weekend, consists of Bascombe's reflections about his life and the events of that weekend which may undermine his precarious disengaged contentment.

The critics who most emphatically approved the novel were those who found its immersion in the hero's consciousness rewarding in itself. "One of the chief pleasures of reading the novel comes from its sense of lively absorption in the varied details of contemporary American life that it conveys," wrote Robert Towers in the *New York Review of Books*. "Frank's embrace of these details—including the most banal—reaches beyond acceptance to something approaching active celebration. Drive-ins, bars, airports, a glitzy hotel room in Detroit, New Jersey housing developments, even the hodgepodge landscape of New Jersey itself—all of these receive Frank's rapturous attention. He relishes the lives of lower-middle-class people without even a hint of condescension. . . . *The Sportswriter* is not a 'big' novel. It is slow-paced and, like its protagonist, lacks a clear sense of direction; it arrives nowhere, so to speak. The book is, instead, a reflective work that invites reflection, a novel that charms us with the freshness of its vision and touches us with the perplexities of a 'lost' narrator who for once is neither a drunkard nor a nihilist but a wistful, hopeful man adrift in his own humanity."

In the *New York Times*, Michiko Kakutani compared the book as "a devastating chronicle of contemporary alienation" to Walker Percy's *The Moviegoer* and Richard Yates' *Revolutionary Road*. Although she found that Bascombe's "discursive monologue on his life, past and present" became at times "long-winded and overly meditative," Kakutani, like Towers, praised the "pliant and persuasive" quality of the novel's narrative voice: "It is a journalist's voice—observant of people and places, astringent in its attempt to eschew the sentimental—and quite clearly the voice of someone attuned to the random surprises of daily life, its discontinuity and its capacity to startle and wound." Yet Ford managed to avoid too close an identification with Frank Bascombe: "he writes with a great deal of compassion for his hero, but his affection is tempered by a certain toughmindedness; and so we come to see Frank not only as he sees himself (hurt, alienated, resigned to a future of diminishing returns) but as he must appear to others—essentially kind and decent, but also wary, passive and unwilling to embrace the real possibilities for happiness that exist around him." Thus the events of the novel have a cumulative significance, as Frank Bascombe "is forced to reassess his own image of himself and the readers of *The Sportswriter*, too, are made both to see and experience the gathering sense of loss and disorder in his life."

Other critics, however, concluded that Ford failed to distance himself from his narrator clearly enough to make the moral import of the novel accessible to the reader. The book, wrote Alice Hoffman in the *New York Times Book Review*, "suffers from a lack of compelling action and an emphasis on Bascombe's dry meditations that obscures and minimizes the complex domestic structure the author initially presents. Mr. Ford is a daring and intelligent novelist, but in choosing Bascombe as his narrator he has taken a risk that ultimately does not pay off. The authorial voice is so weakened that we are left only with the observations of an emotionally untrustworthy narrator. . . . Mr. Ford's admirable talents, which include an extraordinary ear for dialogue and the ability to create the particulars of everyday life with stunning accuracy . . . , are not well served in a novel given to abstract analysis. . . . Certainly, what is at the heart of Frank Bascombe's sorrow remains, for the reader, a mystery."

The same point was made by Christopher Hitchens in the *Times Literary Supplement*. Ford, Hitchens wrote, "really catches the limited, tedious, repetitive agony of much modern American 'conversation.'" But his success in capturing Bascombe's muddled voice obscures his own point of view. "*The Sportswriter*," Hitchens summed up, "is a rather well-wrought account of the rewards and punishments for letting go, and of the temptations of indifference and mo diocrity. It also illustrates some of the dangers and paradoxes that attend the effort to bring

these overlooked qualities to life." Ultimately, critical opinion of the novel seemed to depend on the critic's degree of sympathy with the narrator. Thus Jonathan Yardley, in the *Washington Post Book World*, declared, "*The Sportswriter* is intelligent and compassionate, but it's terribly difficult to sustain the reader's interest in a narrator/protagonist who is not himself interesting. Though there are lively passages here and there . . . most of the novel simply drones along just as Bascombe does, maintaining an amiable curiosity about things but never getting fully engaged with anything." But Walter Clemons, returning to Ford once again in *Newsweek*, called the book's "casual, flexible" narrative voice a "superlative achievement," which led the reader to identify with the narrator: "Only a scrupulously honest novelist could make us sympathetic to such an unheroic nature. Ford makes us feel we're more like Bascombe than we often care to admit."

The question of sympathy also arises in connection with the stories in *Rock Spring*, which take place, David Klinghoffer wrote in the *National Review*, "in Montana and Wyoming, on the frontier between America and Canada, between the Eastern and Western United States, a land 'half-wild,' not quite civilized yet," and which feature characters who are "helpless and unstable," "living perpetually 'in between,'" and "easy prey for chance." "The characters," wrote Alfred Kazin in the *New York Review of Books*, "even when married and intimate, are remarkably out of sync with each other. . . . These are people who break out of their loneliness—when they do—only to commit some mistake that sends them reeling back." Yet Kazin found that Ford managed to make these people who are "silenced and crippled by their precious 'privacy'" dramatically compelling. Writing in *Time*, Paul Gray also made the point that Ford "has the ability to convey the drama of aimless, drifting, passive people, the suspense entailed in waiting each day to see what new misfortunes the world has in store."

In a dissenting opinion, John Clute, in the *Times Literary Supplement*, found the stories deficient in sympathy, intrusively ironic, and thus too heavy-handed to engage the reader deeply: "There can be no questioning Ford's ambition, the craftsmanlike construction of his tales, even the cogency of some of the lessons he derives from the terrible lives he describes. What is missing is a sense that author and protagonist are bound together in the same story . . . Ford is incapable of conveying an empathetic identity between himself and his damaged cast. . . . In his hands, they become objects of commiseration."

A similar disengagement with his characters was noted by some of the reviewers of Ford's fourth novel, *Wildlife*. This is a reminiscential book, narrated by Joe Brinson, a mature man, recalling from the point of view of a sixteen-year-old the disintegration of his parents' marriage. So youthful a witness is obviously incapable of interpreting what he saw, although he is sensitive and intelligent enough to recognize the profound importance of what is happening in his life. But he remains essentially inarticulate: "And there are words, significant words, you do not want to say, words that account for busted-up lives, words that try to fix something ruined that shouldn't be ruined and no one wanted ruined, and that words can't fix anyway." The main action of the novel is compressed into three days during which the boy's father goes off to fight a forest fire and his mother begins an affair with another man. The title *Wildlife*, Christopher Lehmann-Haupt suggested in the *New York Times*, has "oblique reference" to the domestic events in the novel. With a setting in the still rugged country around Great Falls, Montana, "wildlife" evokes images of the destructive forces of nature—forest fires, for example—that suggest the terrible inevitability of loss, just as the boy must confront the loss of his parents and his boyhood innocence. Lehmann-Haupt, however, found the characters enigmatic and their actions unconvincing: "But is it really in the nature of things for Joe's father to abandon his mother, and for her to lack the understanding not to inflict her frustration on her child? Is her doing so just a coincidence? A mere specimen of wildlife? . . . And if this drama is not a random incident, if Mr. Ford intends it to have universal resonance, then he owes the reader more than the sort of sententious baby talk that too often mars his writing." Sheila Ballantyne expressed similar reservations in the *New York Times Book Review*: "*Wildlife* is a thin book rather than a rich one. It is shot through with nuance and minute observation involving four people who have moved from other places to this particular place. Yet these people seem to have no friends; they are present only to one another." The writing too, she finds, "seems loose, even skimpy when compared to the densely elegant prose of his earlier works." Yet in the overall assessment of his work to date, even Ford's most severe critics agree that he has won himself a prominent place in contemporary American fiction by evoking with considerable power and precision the muted tragedies of the marginal and disconnected.

PRINCIPAL WORKS: A Piece of My Heart, 1976; The Ultimate Good Luck, 1981; The Sportswriter, 1986; Wildlife, 1990. *Collected short stories*—Rock Springs, 1987.

ABOUT: Contemporary Authors New Revision Series 11, 1984; Contemporary Literary Criticism, 46, 1988. *Periodicals*—Antaeus Autumn 1987; Chicago Tribune Book World April 19, 1981; National Review November 12, 1976; December 4, 1987; New York Review of Books April 24, 1986; November 5, 1987; New York Times February 26, 1986; June 1, 1990; New York Times Book Review October 24, 1976; May 31, 1981; March 23, 1986; September 20, 1987; June 17, 1990; New York Times Magazine April 10, 1988; Newsweek February 14, 1977; May 11, 1981; April 7, 1986; Time March 24, 1986; November 16, 1987; Times Literary Supplement November 7, 1986; May 13–19, 1988; August 4, 1989.

FORSTER, MARGARET (May 25, 1938–   ), British novelist and biographer, writes: "For me, writing sprang out of reading—there wouldn't have been one without the other. Yet in our house there was virtually nothing to read. I was born and brought up on a council estate in Carlisle, a small border town between Scotland and England. My father was a fitter in a metal factory. My mother, who was much cleverer and socially slightly superior in class (very important in England then) was a housewife. I had an elder brother and a younger sister and we all squashed into a very small house with an outside lavatory—a typical working-class set-up. We had bibles and prayer books (my mother was religious) and a medical dictionary and that was that. Our newspaper was the worst kind of tabloid. Yet from the age of four I was an avid reader. God knows where I got the books from at that stage—from neighbors and relatives I suppose—but get them I did. My mother got me into school six months before the statutory age on the strength of my ability to read.

"School was heaven. There was no stopping me. Through school came libraries—I was a book-a-day girl with Sundays hell because I couldn't change a book. I read a strange mishmash of junk and things far too old for me. When I found something I loved—this is around the age of seven—I'd feel excited in a physical way (I still do). But I never then thought of writing. It was something entirely outside my experience. I wrote 'compositions' at school which were always extravagantly praised but I didn't write for myself. All my energies went into reading and living in those books I loved so much.

"At eleven, I passed what was known as the 11-plus exam and went to the local grammar school. I was extremely ambitious, passionately wished to get out of my environment and leave the kind of life my mother led behind. I saw all her talents disappear in a grinding routine of cleaning, cooking, and general slavery and I re-

MARGARET FORSTER

sented it on her behalf bitterly. She shouldn't have let it happen was my opinion—I certainly wouldn't. I would never marry because marriage led to children and children to the total abnegation of self. Not for me.

"From school I won a history scholarship to Somerville College Oxford. I was still reading voraciously, still not writing but by then I'd begun to think that this thrill I got when I read a book that inspired me—like *Vanity Fair* or *Wuthering Heights*—was a kind of signal to try to write myself. I didn't try until I left Oxford by which time I'd married and gone back on my original vow. Marriage as I saw it in Oxford was no feminist trap—it was only in working-class terms that it was. I wrote my first novel in 1960. It was a long Balzac-type saga, rejected by the only agent I sent it to. He said it was promising, come and see me, but I took that as thumbs down and tore it up. Next I wrote *Dames' Delight* in direct imitation of Salinger and in a fit of petulance: if this is what they want, let them have it. After that came *Georgy Girl*, in much the same vein. I was established.

"For the next ten years I played around. Not a single thing I wrote during the whole decade meant a damn thing. I just enjoyed myself, fiddling around, writing traditional novels in a traditional style, all about human relationships in a one dimensional sort of way. After eight novels I veered off at a tangent and wrote a biography (on Bonnie Prince Charlie) which pleased me very much; it was proper work. My standards perceptibly lifted. When I went back to fiction I tried harder to make it mean more (but failed).

Back to nonfiction and another "autobiography" on Thackeray upon which I worked like a slave. When I returned to fiction after *that* I wrote *Mother Can You Hear Me?*, the first decent novel I'd written. I was no longer fiddling about—this was for real, exposed my own nerve ends. I am ashamed to say I followed it with two more nonentities, before starting a feminist history book, but there won't be any more. I am reformed. At forty-eight I can't afford to write anything more that is not serious in intent and execution. Writing isn't a game any more. Curiously, I need to write now in a way I never did in my childbearing years (I have three children). I can't shove it aside any more and then pick it up like knitting. More and more I see myself as a feminist writer, more and more I see it as worthwhile to be writing about women's experience of life and the world. I'm over the trivializing of it, finished with being self-deprecating. I'm fascinated by *how* a novel is written more than what it is about—shape, structure, style are supremely important—but it has to have some meaning in it too. Entertainment, for writer or reader, isn't enough. That's why biography appeals to me more and more—the crafting is more satisfying. Only thing is, reading biography doesn't give me that charge, that mysterious thrill which fuels the writing. Writing biography is work, hard and rewarding in a very obvious way; writing fiction is magic and I want to be a very good magician before I finish."

———

A reviewer of one of Margaret Forster's later novels, *Private Papers*, wrote that she is "a very sympathetic writer [who] is good on the details of failure to live happily ever after." To the extent that most of her characters (and these are mainly women) live relatively uneventful lives in familiar patterns of middle-class domesticity, they are doomed to frustration. Brilliantly successful careers, romantic love affairs, adventure and intrigue in exotic foreign lands are denied them. Endowed only with the saving grace of common sense and enough toughness to survive, they usually manage pretty well for themselves. A representative Forster novel is *Georgy Girl*, in which her gawky, confused, love-starved and genuinely appealing heroine is a kind of perverse Cinderella. She is used, if not abused, by a selfish girlfriend and her lover, left stranded with her girlfriend's unwanted baby, and rescued by a fat, unappealing, but rich and kind older man who marries her. He is no Prince Charming, and the London scene of the mid-1960s is no fairyland. But Forster is, all told, one subtle writer, as "a skilful chronicler of the lifestyles of our times." *Georgy Girl* was more successful commercially in its film version than as a novel. With a screenplay by Forster and the playwright Peter Nichols, with Lynne Redgrave, James Mason, and Alan Bates in the leading roles and a catchy theme song, it became a kind of emblem for the rootless, swinging generation of the sixties.

Forster is somewhat dismissive of her early novels. Reviewers too have tended to regard them as light-weight entertainments. But in recent years her readers have come to recognize and appreciate them as wry and very telling portraits of contemporary manners and morals. Underneath the humor, the misunderstandings, and even the clowning in some of them is what Hana Sambrook describes as Forster's preoccupation with love: "even today love, whether within or outside marriage, or between those tied by the unbreakable blood knot, remains all-important to women." It is an ambitious theme, demanding intense probing of the psychology of the characters, and here Forster's lightness of touch often proves inadequate to the challenge. In *Marital Rites*, for example, where a marriage survives despite the wife's discovery of her husband's infidelity, the *Times Literary Supplement*'s reviewer Patricia Craig found the characters shallow: "Margaret Forster makes no attempt to devise consistent psychological motivations for her characters." But in the later novel *Mother Can You Hear Me?* Forster apparently identified more closely with her central character. She told an interviewer for the *Guardian* : "This time I have exposed some nerve ends. I began by doing the book as a stream of consciousness and the result was very honest but not a good novel. I rewrote it and there is a less direct comparison to be made between my central character and myself, but it's honest enough to have a few . . . neighbors pointing fingers." The result is what the *Times Literary Supplement* described as "a carefully written story of a modern woman trying to cope with the problems of an aging mother and a difficult teenage daughter. The book is honest and very painful; the same unflinching view is turned on everyday domestic pressures and the deeper pull of maternal love, duty, and memory." Ten years later Forster took up the theme of aging again in *Have the Men Had Enough?*. This is the most serious of her novels to date, inspired by her own witnessing of the senility and slow death of her mother-in-law and its effects on the family who loved her. It does not argue a thesis about the need for better geriatric care, but it presents the problem honestly and affectingly. "Perhaps this book may nudge the question a little closer to the public domain," Anne Duchêne wrote in the *Times Literary Supplement*.

American readers probably know Forster better for her non-fiction than for her fiction. Her first biography, a study of Charles Edward Stuart (Bonnie Prince Charlie), *The Rash Adventurer*, gave her rigorous training in historical research. "I am far from being obsessed by Charles Edward Stuart," she wrote in her preface. "What made me settle on him after close scrutiny of many other possibles was the symbolic nature of his life. Here was a man groomed for stardom who performed in blazing limelight for two short years and then was yanked off the stage protesting all the way. What does this kind of rejection do to a man?" To answer her question Forster had to go through microfilm of some 700 volumes of the Stuart Papers as well as numerous secondary sources. The result is a brisk, sound, and readable biography. The *Economist*'s reviewer observed that while she makes no discoveries or significant revisions to history's view of the prince, "she throws a bright and very cold light on him." *Library Journal* found it fresh and honestly told: "Pedants may object to Forster's light vernacular prose, but her book reads delightfully and should appeal to a wide audience interested in truth rather than legend." That truth, Forster concludes, is that Charles was a tragedy "of a common enough kind . . . an arrested adolescent [who] never for one moment showed any signs of true greatness." Yet she finds the real Charles more human and therefore more pardonable than the legends that grew up around him.

Less formal research was involved in Forster's fictionized "autobiography" *William Makepeace Thackeray: Memoirs of a Victorian Gentleman*. On the title page she identifies herself as "editor" of these memoirs, but because she drew her factual material entirely from Thackeray's letters and private papers she is more accurately a fictionizing biographer. She makes no pose of objectivity. In her "Author's Note" at the end of the book she confesses: "I wanted to be prejudiced . . . I had no desire whatsoever to know how far Thackeray was telling the truth about himself." Identifying herself so closely with her subject that she writes in imitation of his chatty, informal, genial style, Forster produced what J.I.M. Stewart, in the *Times Literary Supplement*, hailed as a "highly original book." In spite of many anachronisms in tone and language (enough for Jonathan Keates in the *New Statesman* to complain that "the illusion that we are reading the novelist's own work becomes a depressing embarrassment") and a tendency to ramble ("behavior that the author of *Vanity Fair* would surely have scorned," the *New Yorker* commented), the book is an entertaining labor of love. It is richly illustrated with Thackeray's own delightful drawings.

No such whimsy or self-indulgence figures in Forster's collection of profiles of some remarkable women, *Significant Sisters: The Grassroots of Active Feminism 1839–1939*. Her novels had shown a strong though not tendentious feminism, and *Significant Sisters* is a natural extension of that interest. She writes in her introduction: "In many ways, I myself am the product of everything the eight women in this book fought for . . . I have the best of both worlds even if I am also bound to admit this happy state is not maintained without effort." It has indeed been a struggle, she continues, "to be everything—wife, mother, housekeeper, writer." The purpose of her study of feminist history is to lighten that struggle by showing women that they are not isolated: "There *is* a joint purpose, and this brings not just comfort but hope . . . [for] a better balance between the sexes in our society." The lives of the women in her book—Caroline Norton, Elizabeth Blackwell, Florence Nightingale, Emily Davies, Josephine Butler, Elizabeth Cady Stanton, Margaret Sanger, and Emma Goldman—demonstrate, she argues, that in spite of their struggles against formidable obstacles, "there has been a continuous if not easily identified development which has succeeded in substantially redressing the balance between the sexes." The struggle is not ended; the demands of marriage and motherhood remain compelling. But, Forster concludes, "real progress has been made." Even those critics who objected that *Significant Sisters* failed to put the subject into sufficiently wide socio-historical contexts—like Sheila Rowbotham who wrote in the *Times Literary Supplement*: "As an analysis of feminist dilemmas or as an historical perspective, *Significant Sisters* is a disappointment"—found it eminently interesting and informative; and Rowbotham continued: "As a collection of lively character sketches of women who refused the common destiny of their sex and battled courageously through prejudice, heartache and conflict it is often inspiring." Carolyn Heilbrun, in *Ms.*, praised Forster's sensitivity: "Her book is particularly to be recommended to those who are made uncomfortable by the word 'feminist,' but who can recognize courage when they encounter it and summon gratitude where it is due."

Forster confronted the issue of feminism once again in her biography of the Victorian poet Elizabeth Barrett Browning, whose life and work, especially her long narrative poem about a strong-minded woman *Aurora Leigh*, have been closely studied by feminist critics in recent years. Her *Elizabeth Barrett Browning* is a substantial, sympathetic, but in no way partisan biography. Robert Bernard Martin wrote of it in

the *Times Literary Supplement* : "Margaret Forster faces the problem directly, but her opinions are so judicious that she probably will not give much comfort to extremists of any complexion . . . In its understated manner, this new biography is a daring book, for it shows us a far more complex woman than we have seen before. I am not sure she is more lovable because of what we learn about her, but she is infinitely more interesting." Forster also avoids the traps of romantic sentimentally into which many writers on the Brownings have fallen. She presents a woman who was brilliant but self-centered even in her devotion to her husband and her child. In connection with the biography Forster also published an edition of the poet's *Selected Poems*.

Margaret Forster lives in London with her husband, the writer Hunter Davies, whom she married in 1960. They have three children.

PRINCIPAL WORKS: *Novels*—Dames' Delight, 1964; Georgy Girl, 1965; The Bogeyman, 1965; The Travels of Maudie Tipstaff, 1967; The Park, 1968; Miss Owen-Owen Is at Home (in the U.S. Miss Owen-Owen), 1969; Fenella Phizacherly, 1971; Mr. Bone's Retreat, 1971; The Seduction of Mrs. Pendlebury, 1974; Mother Can You Hear Me?, 1979; The Bride of Lowther Fell: A Romance, 1980; Marital Rites, 1982; Private Papers, 1986; Lady's Maid, 1990. *Biography*—The Rash Adventurer: The Rise and Fall of Charles Edward Stuart, 1974; William Makepeace Thackeray: Memoirs of a Victorian Gentleman, 1978; Significant Sisters: The Grassroots of Active Feminism 1839–1939, 1984; Elizabeth Barrett Browning, 1988. *As editor*—Elizabeth Barrett Browning: Selected Poems, 1988.

ABOUT: Contemporary Novelists, 4th ed. 1986. *Periodicals*—Economist October 22, 1973; Guardian September 18, 1979; Library Journal April 1, 1974; Ms. June 1985; New York Times Book Review February 17, 1985; New Yorker May 14, 1979; Times Literary Supplement January 28, 1965; May 8, 1969; September 29, 1978; November 23, 1979; July 24, 1981; September 28, 1984; March 7, 1986; August 19, 1988; March 24, 1989; July 20, 1990.

FOX, PAULA (April 22, 1923–   ), American novelist and author of children's books, was born in New York City, the daughter of Elsie de Sola, a Cuban native, and Paul Hervey Fox, a playwright who took part in the founding of the Provincetown Theatre and was later a scenarist for MGM in Hollywood and for Gaumont studios in England. Fox has described herself as a "traveling child" who seldom lived in any one place longer than a year or two and rarely saw either of her parents. She went to elementary schools in New York and Cuba and to high schools in New Hampshire and Montreal. "I at-

PAULA FOX

al for the body of her work for children. Other honors include a National Book Award nomination (1979) for *The Little Swineherd and Other Tales* ; the American Book Award (1983) for *A Place Apart* ; and, in 1985, both a Christopher Award and a Newbery Honor Book Award for *One-Eyed Cat.*

Particularly striking about Fox's books for children is her ability to enter a young person's mind and imagination while at the same time preserving a refined and mature sensibility. Her sensitively crafted and at times morally complex tales introduce youthful protagonists beset by problems arising both from within themselves and from the settings in which they exist. "In her best children's books," Anita Moss commented in the *Dictionary of Literary Biography*, "Fox manages to discover what it is to be a vulnerable child struggling for a sure sense of self in a bewildering and often alien world. . . . They need to use all of their human faculties . . . to endure the world and to make sense of it." Typical of her early books, *A Likely Place* explores the condition of isolation, a generation and communication gap, as a small boy attempts to come to terms with the confining restrictions of overly protective parents. *How Many Miles to Babylon?* was a milestone both for Fox and for the modern children's book in its use of minority children. James Douglas, a black child in the inner city, is forced to deal with the conflicts that arise from his ethnic background, as well as from the loss of family contacts. *Blowfish Live in the Sea*, one of her best-known works, has as its central character a thirteen-year-old girl, Carrie, whose relationship with her eighteen-year-old half-brother Ben leads to a trip they take together to Boston. There they find Ben's alcoholic artist father, through whom Ben searches for a sense of relation, while at the same time Carrie recognizes that Ben's growth to maturity must cost her the one human tie that has been most crucial to her. Fox's most controversial children's book, *The Slave Dancer*, is cast in the form of a historical romance, in which thirteen-year-old Jessie Bollier is kidnapped aboard a slave ship. The book was scorned by critics concerned with ethnicity for its depiction of the blacks held in bondage as being merely helpless and passive; but other reviewers were impressed by the horror with which the slave experience is evoked and by the bond formed between white Jessie and the black boy Ras that leads to a new growth of awareness in Jessie.

Although perhaps best known as the author of award-winning children's books, Fox has also published adult novels that have earned her considerable prestige. Her first, *Poor George*, concerns a George Mecklin, who teaches in a private

tended nine schools before I was twelve," she has said, "by which time I had discovered that freedom, solace, and truth were public libraries."

At seventeen Fox began a working career that led in a variety of directions. She worked for a newspaper, for the British publisher Victor Golancz, was a reader for a movie company, and a reporter for a British news service in Paris and Warsaw. After leaving the news service, she returned to New York and in 1948 married Richard Sigerson, by whom she has two sons, Adam and Gabriel. Divorced from Sigerson in 1954, she attended Columbia University from 1955–1958 but left without finishing her degree. She then taught at a school for emotionally disturbed children in Dobbs Ferry, New York, and at the Ethical Culture Schools in New York City. In 1962 Fox married Martin Greenberg, formerly editor of *Commentary* and professor of English at C. W. Post College, where she herself had taught since 1963. At various times, she has also conducted writing workshops at the University of Pennsylvania.

Although considering herself a late-starter as a writer, Fox has proved remarkably prolific and has received numerous awards. She was a finalist in the National Book Award Children's Book Category for *Blowfish Live in the Sea*, and in 1972 received both a National Institute and American Academy and a Guggenheim Fellowship. In 1974 she was the recipient of a grant from the National Endowment for the Arts and the American Library Association Newbery Medal for *The Slave Dancer*. In 1978 she was honored with the Hans Christian Andersen Med-school in Manhattan and lives with his nagging wife in Westchester. It becomes, in effect, a scrupulously observed study of alienated suburban lives. Bernard Bergonzi, in the *New York Review of Books*, called it "the best first novel I've read in quite a long time. . . . she writes with great accuracy and control in a prose whose symbolism is always unobtrusive. Whether Miss Fox will bring off this kind of success a second time remains to be seen; but she has, certainly, the required gifts." Irving Howe, in the *New Republic*, was also favorably impressed by Fox's craftsmanship. "What interested me most about the book," he wrote, "is that while Miss Fox is entirely caught up with the experience of the contemporary, she is largely free of its cant and bravado. It is something of a miracle that a new and sophisticated writer should be so unstained by the nihilism . . . of the sixties."

Fox's next novel, *Desperate Characters*, later made into a film starring Shirley MacLaine, made a still stronger impression. A severely-observed and rapidly-paced study of the stress-filled marriage of Otto and Sophie Bentwood, who live in a renovated brownstone in Brooklyn, *Desperate Characters* was described by Pearl K. Bell, in the *New Leader*, as "a small masterpiece, a revelation of contemporary New York middle-class life that grasps the mind of the reader with the subtle clarity of metaphor and the alarmed tenacity of nightmare." The reviewer for the *New Yorker* commented that "these nice, bitterly disappointed people become understandable and sympathetic in Miss Fox's kind, ironic, dispassionate vision of them and their city. She is one of the most attractive writers to come our way in a long, long time."

The Western Coast focuses upon the life of Annie Gianfola, whose drifting, curiously passive existence takes her in the late 1930s and through the World War II years from a failed marriage in the East to a series of thwarted encounters in California. A number of critics praised the novel for its sheer observation and evocation of a period. Sally Cunneen, in *Commonweal*, remarked that "Miss Fox revisits the time and place of *The Day of the Locust* and even shares certain talents with Nathanael West: she has an encyclopedic knowledge of the sadness and incoherence of American lives, and her belligerent, intense characters are seen utterly without false romance." Vivian Gornick, in the *New York Times Book Review*, called *The Western Coast* "a haunting novel. Spare . . . alive with the calm of dread: even as our lives are"; and Thomas R. Edwards, in the *New York Review of Books*, noted that "what is impressive here is Fox's ability to remain almost frighteningly remote and noncommittal, without any sympathy for her heroine."

The Widow's Children, however, was generally found disappointing. An account of two days in the life of the Maldonado clan in which hardly anything happens but the bitterness and estrangement of its members is vividly evoked, the novel was regarded by some reviewers as an "exercise." "On the stage," Thomas R. Edwards wrote in *Harper's*, "where such as Pinter have taught us not to look for explanation or 'larger meanings,' *The Widow's Children* could be shattering. As a novel it leaves me puzzled and oddly resentful." William McPherson, in the *Washington Post Book World*, found it "well-made" and "elegantly written," but went on to say that "it is quite possible to admire Paula Fox's style and to appreciate her talent without feeling much more affection for this novel than its characters feel for one another or for themselves, which is very little indeed. Estranged from the world and abandoned to one another, they seem unable to fulfill either their own needs or the needs of anyone else. In the same way, the reader, too, is estranged; his own expectations, heightened by the form of this very formal novel, unfulfilled."

The more recent *A Servant's Tale* deals with another of Fox's passive women who are buffeted by the world about them and whose experience is a kind of testament to life's disorder. From the Caribbean island of San Pedro, Luisa de la Cueva is the daughter of a kitchen servant seduced and later married by the landowner's son, who is then disinherited. In New York the outcast family finds only poverty and further dislocation. Reviews of the novel were mixed. Blair T. Birmelin, in the *Nation*, called Fox "one of our most intelligent (and least appreciated) novelists," and Darryl Pinckney, in the *New York Review of Books*, found the novel's conception "original, daring, and unnerving." He added, however, that Luisa's motives for remaining a servant were abstract and unclear. Paula Giddings, in the *New York Times Book Review*, thought much the same. "Despite Paula Fox's excellent prose," she remarked, "Luisa does not evolve. She fails to transcend the stereotype of a women—and one of color at that—who submits to a station in life preordained by others."

Fox lives with her husband in the Brooklyn Heights section of New York, and prefers privacy to public visibility. Her occasional statements about her writing reflect her allegiance to observation and an understanding of others. In receiving the Newbery Award she remarked: "Because writers have sovereignty over their own inventions, they appear to make an outrageous claim: they will tell you everything about the characters in the stories. . . . In real life, we stammer, we dissimulate, we hide. In stories, we are privy to the secrets, the evasions, the visions of characters in a fashion which real life permits us during periods of extraordinary sensibility, before habit has made us forget that the cries behind the locked doors are our own."

PRINCIPAL WORKS: *Children's books*—Maurice's Room, 1966; A Likely Place, 1967; How Many Miles to Babylon?, 1967; The Stone-Faced Boy, 1968; Dear Prosper, 1968; Portrait of Ivan, 1969; The King's Falcon, 1969; Hungry Fred, 1969; Blowfish Live in the Sea, 1970; Good Ethan, 1973; The Slave Dancer, 1973; A Place Apart, 1980; The Little Swineherd and Other Tales, 1981; One-Eyed Cat, 1984; The Moonlight Man, 1986; Lily and the Lost Boy, 1987. *Novels*—Poor George, 1967; Desperate Characters, 1970; The Western Coast, 1972; The Widow's Children, 1976; A Servant's Tale, 1984.

ABOUT: Children's Literature Review, 1976; Children's Writers, 1978; Contemporary Authors New Revisions Series 20, 1987; Contemporary Literary Criticism 2, 1974; 8, 1978; Dictionary of Literary Biography 52, 1986; Townsend, J. R., A Sense of Story: Essays on Contemporary Writers for Children, 1971; revised and enlarged as A Sounding of Storytellers, 1979; Twentieth Century Children's Writers, 1978. *Periodicals*—Harper's October 1976; Nation November 3, 1984; New Leader February 2, 1970; New Republic March 18, 1967; November 11, 1972; New York Review of Books June 1, 1967; October 5, 1972; October 28, 1976; June 27, 1985; New York Times Book Review October 8, 1972; November 18, 1984; New Yorker February 7, 1970; October 28, 1972; November 1, 1976; Newsweek March 16, 1970; September 25, 1972; Washington Post Book World October 31, 1976.

FRIEDLANDER, SAUL (October 11, 1932–), Czech-Israeli historian and political analyst, is the only son of Jan and Elli (Glaser) Friedlander. Pavel (as he was named at birth) spent his first seven years in the sheltered environment of Prague's German-speaking Jewish community. In the first sentence of his 1978 memoirs, *When Memory Comes*, Friedlander encapsulates the real-life drama that was to circumscribe his childhood: "I was born in Prague at the worst possible moment, ten months before Hitler came to power." His father, who had served as an artillery officer in the Austro-Hungarian army during World War I, was an insurance executive in a German company. At home, Friedlander recalls, "everyone felt German," and their Jewish identity did not go beyond a few colorful Yiddish expressions: "In sum, we were typical representatives of the assimilated Jewish bourgeoisie of Central Europe."

On the eve of the 1938 Munich Pact (which delivered the Sudetenland to Germany), the six-year-old boy was enrolled in an English private

SAUL FRIEDLANDER

school; less than six months later, anticipating Hitler's imminent occupation of Czechoslovakia, his parents made an abortive attempt to flee to Hungary, but the German army was already at the border, and they were forced to return to Prague. They subsequently made their way across Germany to Paris, where Pavel, now called Paul, was placed in a home for Jewish children, only to be bullied and battered by his Orthodox peers, who targeted him as a non-Jew and made him a scapegoat for all their sufferings. A second foster home followed, and then, with the German Occupation of Paris in June 1940, the family fled south to a small resort town called Néris-les-Bains. After the roundup of some thirteen thousand persons at the Vel' d'Hiv in July 1942, Friedlander's parents took the dubious step of sending him again to a home for Jewish children; another roundup ensued almost immediately after his arrival, and the ten-year-old child barely escaped with his life.

At that point, he was sent into hiding at the Catholic boarding school of Saint-Béranger in Montluçon. With his father's permission, he was baptized Paul-Henri Ferland, and after an initially difficult period of transition, he threw himself into his new life: not only did he become an outstanding student, but he decided to enter the priesthood. "I had passed over to Catholicism body and soul," he writes in his memoirs, adding, "I had the feeling, unstated but quite clear, of having entered the compact, invincible majority, of no longer belonging to the camp of the persecuted but, potentially at least, to that of the persecutors . . . Paul Friedlander had disappeared; Paul-Henri Ferland was someone else."

During this time at Montluçon, Friedlander had no word from his parents. In fact, they had attempted to flee to Switzerland in 1942 but were turned over to the French police at the border; arrested on September 30, 1942, they were deported to Auschwitz. Friedlander learned of their fate only at the war's end, when he was about to enter the priesthood. The Jesuit priest assigned to counsel him explained the extent of the Holocaust and the particular nature of the anti-Semitic campaign that had led to his parents' deaths. "For the first time," he recalls in his memoirs, "I felt Jewish—not in spite of myself or secretly, but with a sensation of total loyalty."

On his return to Montluçon, he took back his real French name, Paul Friedlander, and a few months later, left Saint-Béranger for a middle school in the provinces. Placed in the care of a Russian Jewish family whose religious enthusiasm and *shtetl* culture were hardly more familiar than French Catholicism, he found himself "completely uprooted." But through his guardian, he became aware of the Zionist movement, and this soon provided him with an all-consuming focus for an admittedly tortured sense of identity: by autumn 1947, he writes, the project to create a Jewish state in Palestine had become his "main preoccupation." At the time, he was attending the prestigious Lycée Henri IV in Paris where, among other things, he dabbled in communism with future Marxist economist Samir Amin, but simultaneously joined Betar, the youth movement of Menachem Begin's right-wing independence movement, the Irgun. On June 4, 1948, instead of taking his final exams, he set out for the newly created state of Israel. "To leave for [Israel] meant joining my personal destiny to a common fate; it was also a dream of communion and community; it meant dissolving my particular anxieties in the spirit of the group."

On his arrival in Israel, he changed his name for the fourth time and became Saul Friedlander (in Hebrew, Shaul). He learned Hebrew while completing high school and once again found himself surrounded by an alien Jewish culture. Three years of military service behind a desk (because of a heart murmur) allowed him to resume his own intellectual pursuits which, he acknowledges, remained firmly in the European orbit: "It never occurred to me to read a novel or a poem in Hebrew, even though my new language had become just as familiar to me as French, because the little bit that I knew of this literature convinced me I wouldn't find anything in it. But more important, it was the other culture, the one I got from my own books, mainly French, that I wanted like a fish on the beach misses water.

In the early 1950s Friedlander returned to Paris to study at the Institut d'Etudes Politiques. Following his graduation in 1955, he worked for the World Zionist Organization and the Israeli government and spent a year in Sweden working at his uncle's school for mentally disturbed children. In 1961 he resumed his studies, completing a doctorate in political science at the Graduate Institute of International Studies in Geneva.

His first book was a revised version of his dissertation, *Hitler et les Etats-Unis 1939–1941*, first published in Geneva in 1963, reissued in Paris in 1966, and translated into English in 1967 as *Prelude to Downfall: Hitler and the United States 1939–1941*. Working with documents from the German Foreign Ministry in Bonn, Friedlander attempted to explain the Third Reich's attitude toward the United States in the period prior to American entry into the war. As the *Times Literary Supplement* noted, the selection of those documents dealing with Hitler's pronouncements on the United States perhaps exaggerated the importance of the issue, but nonetheless, by bringing together the Reich's Atlantic and Pacific policies, the study closed "an important gap in our overall picture of Nazi diplomacy."

Reflecting on the personal evolution that led him to such research, Friedlander candidly acknowledges: "Through the changing prism of witnesses, accounts, archival documents, I was trying to recapture the sense of an era and reestablish the coherence of a past—my own." While this private mission was hardly apparent in the straightforward diplomatic history that resulted, the initial venture into the wartime past was to lead Friedlander to a second project that was unmistakably closer to his personal experience. *Pie XII et le IIIe Reich: Documents* (1964; translated as *Pius XII and the Third Reich: A Documentation*), was, in the author's words, "born of chance and circumstance." While pouring over the Foreign Ministry archives for his dissertation, he came across a document from Pope Pius XII requesting that the Berlin National Opera perform at the Vatican in March 1941. This initial discovery of the Pope's apparently compromising relationship to the Third Reich was followed by hundreds of other, similar indications. Yet, as Friedlander explained in a 1964 interview, "For more than two years, I kept these documents without making up my mind to publish them in book form— hesitations born of the debt of gratitude I feel for the Catholics, who saved my life."

Ultimately, it was not Friedlander but German prosecutors and journalists who first made a public issue of the Pope's conduct during the war, with his play *The Deputy*, first performed in West Berlin in February 1963. In the midst of the controversy that immediately erupted, Friedlander decided to publish his documents as well, "in an attempt," he insisted, "beyond any personal experience, to contribute some new elements to the historical research of the stages of this drama." The resulting book complemented the German Foreign Ministry documents with material from United States, British, French, and Israeli sources—but not those of the Vatican archives, which remained closed at the time. Apart from a methodological introduction, in which Friedlander argued his case for the reliability of the documents at hand, his own comments were virtually absent; even his conclusions were limited to observations about the Pope's longstanding "predilection" for all things German, plus a deep-rooted fear of Communism that made him receptive to a German-Anglo-Saxon alliance against the Soviet Union.

Notwithstanding his unpolemical approach, the book was immediatley caught up in the debate surrounding *The Deputy* and enjoyed an enormous success. Excerpted in popular magazines such as *Look*, *L'Express*, and *Der Spiegel*, it was subsequently published in German, Italian, Spanish, Dutch, Serbo-Croatian, Czech, Slovak, and Hungarian. By the time of the English translation in 1966, the Vatican had also begun to publish its documents, and in the view of the *Times Literary Supplement*, Friedlander's failure to update his selection compromised his claims to objectivity. But as Albert Grosser suggested in his postscript to the original French edition, the book went beyond the "documentation" of the subtitle: "A contribution to history, *Pius XII and the Third Reich* is also a contribution to the understanding of today's political and moral reality."

In any event, Friedlander himself was soon to take a more personal approach to the same events with *Kurt Gerstein, ou l'ambiguité du bien* (1967; translated as *Kurt Gerstein, The Ambiguity of Good*). The enigmatic Kurt Gerstein (one of the characters in *The Deputy*) was a German mining engineer who volunteered for the Waffen SS in order to give first-hand testimony about the horrors of the death camps to the outside world; in the course of carrying out his duties, he also managed to sabotage shipments of poison gas to the camps. At the end of the war he was arrested and apparently hanged himself in his prison cell while preparing testimony for his war crimes trial.

Drawing once again on the German archives, on Gerstein's own reports to the war crimes commission, and material supplied by Gerstein's family, Friedlander attempted to explain the logic of his life—and death. At the same time, he notes in the introduction, he hoped "through the story of one man, to grasp the dilemmas of a whole society," and ultimately, in terms reminiscent of *Pius XII*, "to examine not only the attitude of the Nazi executioners in the face of the Jewish victims, but also that of the 'spectators' whom Gerstein tried to alert: the German churches, the Allies, the Holy See." The result, wrote Arthur A. Cohen in the *New York Times Book Review*, was "a fascinating, exhaustive, and brutally deadpan historical essay."

By the time that he wrote *Kurt Gerstein*, Friedlander was internationally recognized as a leading authority on the German war archives, but with his new book he stepped outside his academic specialization to address the immediate reality of his adopted homeland. Written in the wake of the June 1967 war, *Réflexions sur l'avenir d'Israël* (Reflections on the Future of Israel, 1969) argued the dangers of military expansion and surveyed the options for peaceful alternatives which would guarantee the security of Israel while respecting the Palestinian right to self-determination. The future of Israel, as he saw it, lay not in the manipulation of Western power politics, but in its role as "spiritual center of the Jewish people."

While his proposals were hardly revolutionary—among other things, he condoned a "strategic" occupation of Gaza, the eastern Sinai, Transjordan, and the Golan Heights for anywhere from ten to thirty years—they represented an undeniably pioneering effort. Hailing *Réflexions sur l'avenir d'Israël* as "a burning book, always courageous, often contradictory," Francis Monheim wrote in *Le Monde*: "Never, perhaps, has an Israeli citizen made such a critical analysis of the weaknesses and errors of the Jewish State; never has a Jewish writer taken such a comprehensive stance with regard to the Palestinian Arabs, who have also been shattered by the drama they are undergoing."

Following this topical venture, Friedlander picked up the thread of his historical researches with *L'Antisémitisme nazi* (1971), an inquiry into the psychosocial evolution of anti-Semitism from the late nineteenth century to the Third Reich. As he told *Le Monde*'s Pierre Sorlin at the time, when he first began researching the Nazi period as a graduate student, his interests were much broader, "but along the way I understood that behind a diplomatic question, I was looking to throw some light on Nazi attitudes toward the Jews." In this study, like the others, he commented, "I was looking for a response to that fundamental anxiety of the persecuted Jew who doesn't understand what they have against him."

In place of standard attempts to explain anti-Semitism in terms of cultural traditions, political and economic circumstances, or broader theories of fascism or totalitarianism, Friedlander advanced the hypothesis that "the Nazi persecution and extermination of the Jews is above all the product of a collective psychopathy." The motor force behind the evolution of modern anti-Semitism, he argued, was the interaction of social forces with the individual personality—notably that of Adolf Hitler—to create a "veritable collective madness."

In general, French reviewers balked at this psychohistorical approach, which seemingly reduced anti-Semitism to a function of Hitler's Oedipal conflict. For Leon Poliakov, the doyen of studies on anti-Semitism, Friedlander's analysis appeared to make cultural and ideological factors an "epiphenomenon" of individual emotions, and his attempt to separate these external and internal domains "seems to sacrifice some of the richness of nuances to the precision of the schema." Nonetheless, there was widespread recognition that Friedlander's exploration of collective psychology offered a new approach to the subject: "Those who believe in [psychohistory]," wrote Victor Malka in *Les Nouvelles littéraires*, "will find in Saul Friedlander the most rigourous of analysts and a historian who sheds new light on Nazi anti-Semitism."

Following the October 1973 War, and while he was preparing a lengthy theoretical essay on psychohistory, Friedlander again turned to the contemporary political scene for what was at the time a fairly unorthodox venture in Arab-Israeli reconciliation. At the instigation of his journalist friend Jean Lacouture, he met with two young Egyptian journalists (writing collectively under the name of Mahmoud Hussein) in order to discuss the past, present, and future of the Arab-Israeli conflict. From their three days of tape-recorded conversation, Lacouture then distilled *Arabes et Israéliens: Un premier dialogue* (1974; translated as *Arabs and Israelis, A Dialogue*).

In practice, the "dialogue" turned out to be something of two parallel monologues, and as several reviewers pointed out, the pronounced differences between participants were not simply a function of nationality but also one of ideological perspective: Friedlander's liberalism vs. Hussein's Marxism. Predictably, the performances of the two sides were evaluated in terms of the observers' own political predispositions. Anna Francos, for example, interviewing Mahmoud Hussein in the progressive Paris weekly *Jeune Afrique*, was struck by the "weakness of Friedlander's line of argument," while *Commentary*'s Ruse C. Lewis dismissed Hussein

as "altogether self-righteous and arrogant," but also went on to fault Friedlander for being "tolerant, didactic, defensive, and finally weary." True to her hawkish convictions, Lewis contended that Friedlander was "apologetic and therefore defenseless, and in this he demonstrates all too well the ideological weakness of that 'liberal current of thought' which he represents." Nonetheless, in France, where the book was followed by a joint TV appearance on the literary magazine show "Apostrophes," along with various newspaper articles and interviews, there was a feeling that, as Xavier Grall wrote in *Hebdo TC*, the Friedlander-Hussein duo manifested "an effort at comprehension and an intellectual courage that the political leaders of both camps would do well to share."

The year after *Arabs and Israelis*, Friedlander provoked yet another controversy, albeit of a more academic nature, with his *Histoire et psychanalyse (History and Psychoanalysis)*. For Friedlander, who was by this time also recognized as one of the leading European psychohistorians, psychohistory represented an invaluable tool for probing otherwise unexplained phenomena; in his view, the Final Solution, for example, did not "belong" to social or economic history but rather, was "an insane tragedy with mad, mysterious causes that psychohistory attempts to comprehend." Thus, in *History and Psychoanalyis*, he set out to determine "to what degree the historian can already go beyond the description of psychological facts and attempt a theoretical interpretation, which is both a practical necessity and a theoretical possibility for historical research." While acknowledging the key weakness of the psychohistorical approach, namely the impossibility of verifying evidence directly, he argued for three principal benefits: the new light psychohistory promises to shed on traditional subjects; the new areas it opens up for investigation (e.g., family history or the history of sexuality), and, in the largest sense, the possibility of a more encompassing "total history."

Once again some reviewers found Friedlander's approach overly schematic and specifically noted the minimal role accorded to social struggles and ideology, but as Peter Loewenberg wrote in the *American Historical Review*, *History and Psychoanalysis* "presents for the first time a coherent summary of the extant literature of psychohistory and particularly the current European contributions to the field."

In making his case for psychohistory, Friedlander duly acknowledged the paradoxical situation of the psychohistorian, whose claim to objectivity is clearly undermined by his or her emotional involvement. Indeed, the tension between a hypothetically objective norm and the subjectivity of personal experience runs through much of Friedlander's own writings, beginning with *Pius XII and the Third Reich*, which is presented as straightforward "documentation," but at the same time dedicated to the memory of his parents, who died at Auschwitz. With *Quand vient le souvenir* (1978; translated as *When Memory Comes*), he embarked on the autobiographical reworking of the same historical moment he had attempted to pass through the prism of historical objectivity for nearly two decades. In place of official documents and testimonies, there are his parents' letters, conversations recalled, fragments of memories scattered over two continents and forty-five years. Citing the string of name changes that marked his childhood displacements, he comments that it was "impossible, in short, to find myself, which, all in all, seems the proper expression of a real, profound confusion," and adds a few pages later, "It took me a very long time before I found the route of my own past."

Unlike his historical studies, *When Memory Comes* is free of any overriding schema—even the flow of years is interrupted by a parallel series of diary entries from 1977, not to introduce any note of certainty, but to inject further doubts. "Even today," he observes at one point, "the Jews are the people of obedience, no longer to the injunctions of God, but to those of a mysterious destiny. Why this fidelity? In the name of what?" As Leon Wieseltier wrote in the *New York Review of Books*, "Dissolution triumphs," adding, "*When Memory Comes* is a significant work partly because of this failure."

For Wieseltier, the book was "a major document of Jewish bitterness in this century," and one that held particular lessons for American Jewry, not only in terms of the Holocaust ("for they tend to be much too enthusiastic in their sorrow") but also with regard to Israel, "for the melancholy argument of his book is that, if things did not work out for the Jews in Europe, they are not exactly working out for them in Israel either." Yet, as David Pryce-Jones noted in the *Times Literary Supplement*, the book's message reached a level of universality as well: in addition to "a concrete and very moving experience of what it is to be Jewish," he sees in the haunting image of "the child who reaches out to parents lost to him for reasons never ultimately understandable . . . some generalized metaphor for human loneliness."

Among the winding threads of consciousness in *When Memory Comes* is the lingering aura of Nazism today. In a diary entry near the end of the book, for example, he comments on a recent German film, *Hitler, a Career* : "Dazzling ascent, titanic energy, demonic fall: it's all there. As for the Holocaust, a few words in passing, barely . . . For anyone who doesn't know, what remains is the power and the glory, followed by a veritable wrath of the gods." This theme is pursued in turn in *Reflets du nazisme* (1982; translated as *Reflections of Nazism: An Essay on Kitsch and Death*), where Friedlander offers neither a historical study nor an essay in the traditional sense, but what he calls a "re-presentation" of contemporary culture. While material circumstances hardly seem ripe for a Nazi revival *per se*, he argues that the "psychological dimension" has been transmuted into a spate of epic films, novels, historical literature, and TV mini-series that unconsciously glorify the very ethos they seek to exorcise—"Not so much through what one person or another wanted to say, but through what is said, outside of them, in spite of them." As Alan Mintz pointed out in the *New Republic*, this psychological argument, "as brilliant as it may be, remains largely unsusceptible to proof," yet he was appreciative of Friedlander's "tightly argued essay in cultural analysis." For the *New York Times*' Christopher Lehmann-Haupt, meanwhile, it was "a much-needed, thought-provoking thesis that Mr. Friedlander has offered," for (quoting Friedlander's conclusion): "We know that the dream of total power is always present, though dammed up, repressed by the Law, even at the risk of destruction. With this difference . . . This time, to reach for total power is to assure oneself, and all of mankind as well, of being engulfed in total and irremediable destruction."

Throughout his career, Friedlander has combined research and writing with university teaching. In 1964 he obtained his first post at the Graduate Institute of International Studies in Geneva, where he was to hold a professorship in the history of international relations until 1987. Between 1967 and 1975 he taught international relations and history at the Hebrew University of Jerusalem as well; in 1975 he became professor of modern history at Tel Aviv University, and since 1987, he has divided his time between Tel Aviv University and the University of California at Los Angeles, where he holds a chair in the history of the Holocaust. He has also had visiting appointments at the University of Montreal, the University of Lausanne, the Massachusetts Institute of Technology, the Institut d'Etudes Politiques and the Ecole des Hautes Etudes in Paris, Dartmouth College, and the Wissenschaftskolleg in Berlin.

In addition to his historical monographs, political reflections, and autobiographical writing, Friedlander has published numerous articles in scholarly journals and has coedited three volumes of collected essays, *L'Histoire et les rélations internationales* (1981), *La Politique étrangère de General De Gaulle* (1985), and *Visions of Apocalypse, End or Rebirth* (1985). In 1983 he received the Israel Prize in History.

WORKS IN ENGLISH TRANSLATION: Aline B. and Alexander Werth were the translators of *Prelude to Downfall: Hitler and the United States 1939–1941* in 1967. Charles Fullman translated *Pius XII and the Third Reich: A Documentation* in 1966 and *Kurt Gerstein, The Ambiguity of Good* in 1969 (published in U.K. as *Counterfeit Nazi*). *Arabs and Israelis: A Dialogue* was translated by Paul Auster and Lydia Davis in 1974, *History and Psychoanalysis* in 1978 by Susan Suleiman. *When Memory Comes*, in Helen R. Lane's translation, appeared in 1979. Thomas Weyr translated *Reflections of Nazism: An Essay on Kitsch and Death* in 1984.

ABOUT: Contemporary Authors 117, 1986. *Periodicals*—Commentary January 1976; Foreign Affairs October 1969; New York Times May 28, 1984; New York Review of Books October 25, 1979; New York Times Book Review July 15, 1979.

FULTON, ROBIN (May 6, 1937–), Scottish poet and translator, writes: "I spent my childhood on the Island of Arran, off the southwest of Scotland: despite its latitude, Arran's landscape and history are more highland than lowland, and the mild wet climate gives the sheltered parts of the island a lushness not found so easily on the chillier eastern side of the country. The manse and its large garden made a world in themselves; the front windows looked out across a shallow green valley whose little fields were divided by hawthorn hedges. Warships came to rest in the bay off Blackwaterfoot; Spitfires and Hurricanes frolicked just above the roof, and Avro Ansons droned across at a great height. On a few occasions German bombers came over us. My father, the Reverend John S. Fulton, was Church of Scotland minister of Shiskine. During the war he ran the local Royal Aircraft Observation Corps (R.A.O.C.), using an ingenious home-made magic-lantern to train his colleagues in plane-spotting: many hours were spent in a dug-out up on the moor behind the house, watching the sky. (I found out only recently that he spotted Rudolf Hess on the way in.) One day when I set off to visit him I got lost: I thought I was walking in a straight line but in fact I was wandering in a circle and eventually arrived back on the road not far from home. Unknown to me, father had all the time been watching me, from the center of the circle! and this of course made a suitable topic for one of his

ROBIN FULTON

children's sermons. Considering what was happening to so many other children at that time, I must admit that my childhood was lucky and happy; I recall intense experiences of weather and close contact with plants and animals, while the world outside was haunted by deadly anxieties I couldn't understand.

"My father's family were Border people (they included Francis George Scott, the composer); my mother, Margaret Macpherson, came on the other hand from the opposite end of Scotland, from Thurso in Caithness (that branch of the Macphersons seems to have come from around Kinbrace in Sutherland, in the moors near the source of the Helmsdale River, and it is possible they were moved during the Clearances). After a short period in the outskirts of Glasgow (1944–1948), a period when the wartime and postwar shortages really hit us, we moved north, to Helmsdale, where my father came to serve as minister of Loth and Kildonan for the next thirty years. I think this move was his idea rather than my mother's; he loved the landscape and seemed to get on well with country people. I lived in Helmsdale and commuted daily to school in Golspie for six years: busy at school, rather lonely out of it. I took to the piano and practiced with an ambition and on a scale that was quite professional, except that I lacked the necessary basic professional training. Music became the only thing I wanted to know about—a single-mindedness which doubtless did little to encourage clear thinking on the subject of what to do with myself as I grew up. A school-time aptitude for maths and science was not followed. At Edinburgh University I read English, thinking it would be a reasonable substitute for music, which it wasn't. The school pattern repeated itself: busy terms in Edinburgh, solitary vacations in Sutherland. As a student I worked hard but not very intelligently and it was only much later that I realized how with the right kind of guidance and stimulation I could have made more lasting use of those years. My schooldays had taught me the value but not the limitations of methodical plodding. Graduation as a brand-new M.A. (Hons) brought me a choice: two years in the army or at least two years in schoolteaching, and I took the lesser evil. In fact I taught for nine years, five of them at the Edinburgh Academy. I did my best but found the process irksome and repetitive: so much energy was needed just to keep going and I never lost the sense of captivity.

"By the late 1960s I was quite active in Scottish literary life, and I had also started on a Ph.D. degree (this was completed by 1972). I was most grateful to Edinburgh University for giving me their Writer's Fellowship for two years (1969–1971). This was followed by two years in which I could have been described either as an unemployed person or as a free-lance writer, two classes which in Scotland particularly are uneasily close to each other. Hopes of a university post—half-hearted anyway, since the academic approach to literature attracts me little—were fading fast as the cut-backs started, and in 1973 I moved to Stavanger in Norway to a college teaching post. This was meant to be a temporary expedient, but such things have a habit of lasting . . .

"I have been writing poems since my late teens, and publishing poems since my early twenties. Since the late 1960s I have been regularly active as a translator, of poetry and prose, mostly from Swedish to English. My main editorial work took place between 1967 and 1976, chiefly as editor of *Lines Review* and the associated book-series, Lines Review Editions; my most recent editorial task was the preparation of Robert Garioch's poems, and a selection of his letters.

"How much of this autobiographical information is relevant to or apparent in my writing is not for me to say. I would imagine that directly or indirectly most of it should be, since one writes out of a total situation. There are only two aspects I would want to comment on briefly here. First, my upbringing in a Presbyterian manse gave me no problems of the kind we often hear about in such a context: the Christianity of my parents, while definitely Protestant, was undogmatic and humane; goodness was a matter of doing things, not of talking about them. Later contact with a wiser and richer Catholic tradition made me realize how impoverished Scottish Protestantism in many respects is, but still I am grateful to have been brought up on the assumption that materialistic and rationalistic ways of seeing life leave much to be desired.

"Second, the pattern of my life has given me a sense, not of rootlessness, but of having roots that are scattered or widespread (if one can say so of roots). When I lived in Scotland I felt divided by the Highland Line, belonging fully neither north nor south of it; and now I feel divided by the North Sea as well. If I think about this, it is uncomfortable. If some of my poems reflect this, the cause is not metaphysical but quite simply geographical."

———

A reviewer of Robin Fulton's *Fields of Focus*, Marlo Relich, described him as "an objective solipsist" whose poems "probe a self-sufficient mind in its painful isolation, a not uncommon dilemma." His work reflects two different but not dissimilar landscapes—Scandinavia, where he has lived since 1973, and Scotland, his native land, where he began his literary career. Both landscapes have a quality of isolation, of time frozen into moments of vision, of mystery, mist and darkness. Yet within these landscapes Fulton has found a poetic voice that speaks not only for himself but, as Christopher Rush writes in *Books in Scotland*, for "the frailty of the human ego, surrounded by the imponderables of time and space."

Fulton received the prestigious Gregory Award in 1967 for his first volume of poems, *Instances*. He published his second volume, *Inventories*, two years later while on a writer's fellowship at Edinburgh University. By this time he had become an influential figure in Scottish poetry as editor of the literary quarterly *Lines Review*, publishing the work of both new poets and older established poets in the journal and in their press, *Lines Review Editions*. Very much in the center of the Scottish literary scene, Fulton noted that although Scottish poets had been highly productive in recent years, there had been no critical writing on contemporary Scottish poetry. To supply that need he wrote *Contemporary Scottish Poetry : Individuals and Contexts* in which he studied the works of three major poets—Edwin Morgan, Iain Crichton Smith, and Norman MacCaig—in their regional and social as well as their personal contexts and a number of promising but lesser known poets. Fulton has also edited the *Complete Poetical Works* (1983), of the distinguished translator and poet Robert Garioch who wrote in Scots and he collected Garioch's prose writings in *A Garioch Miscellany* (1983).

Like Garioch, Fulton has won distinction as a poet-translator who captures not only the letter but also the voice of the poet he is translating. His translations of Swedish poets, notably Lars Gustafsson, Gunnar Harding, and Tomas Tranströmer, have made these writers accessible to English-language readers. Among other Swedish poets he has translated Östen Sjöstrand, Werner Aspenström, Kjell Espmark, Gunnar Ekelöf, and Olav Hauge; he also translated Pär Lagerkvist's novel *Guest of Reality*. In 1966 he published *An Italian Quartet*, "free versions" of the poets Umberto Saba, Giuseppe Ungaretti, Eugenio Montale, and Salvatore Quasimodo. For his Swedish translations he received the Artur Lundkvist Award in 1977 and the Swedish Academy Award in 1978.

With the publication of his own *Selected Poems 1963 to 1978* and *Fields of Focus*, Fulton has established himself as one of the leading contemporary Scottish poets, and his work has become known in England and in the United States. Martin Booth writes in the *Dictionary of Literary Biography*: "His is not a poetry concerned with word games; he is not a poet who loves language for its own sake, but one who uses it simply as a means of intellectual expression." Disciplined in form, cool and controlled in expression, his poetry is nevertheless deeply personal. Most of his poems are short lyrics, distant yet revealing. Though he lives abroad, his native Scotland remains a living presence for him:

If I were to return now after
'an absence'? But while absent I have gained
too much presence. It's where I live.

I add years, change houses, keep
track of myself. I post letters to the past
and answers come, always up to date.

The generations are always catching up.
The tall historic houses will still be leaning
forward like runners waiting for the starting-gun.

It's dusk—but for a pin-hole in the clouds:
a ray of sunlight glares on an empty field.
Something I can't see is being interrogated.
                                        —"Home Thoughts"

Sometimes the link between past and present, home and self-imposed exile, is music. While a winter storm rages outside, he listens to a Rachmananov recording:

A resinous house then with no smell of the past,
The dead wood will live through generations
not mine. At night I listen to the forest in my head
and christen the new house with music written in
vrnlu.
                —from "Listening to Rachmananov in a New House"

George Szirtes writes of Fulton's "lyric gift which flowers quietly and unobtrusively." Even when he writes in the first person, Szirtes continues, "It is, after all, a universal experience that Fulton is describing . . . These are contemplative poems, perhaps even monastic, but their quietness is illuminating. They reject anything that smacks of glitter; they work beneath the skin." As a poet Fulton is probably best described by the title of one of his poems—"A Meticulous Observer," striving for what Marlo Relich calls "constant definition of what is perceived." Michael Hoffman writes in the *Times Literary Supplement* that Fulton "shows and makes us believe that he is actually in the grip of the things he is writing about." Although the experience is uniquely his, it reaches out to the reader compellingly:

Spring: behind us evenings quietly open,
spaces between houses and trees dilate.

I see an old newspaper in a corner:
It's full of hard facts that have softened and dried
hard again after weeks of change.

Suddenly it makes a dash across
open ground scaring a pigeon up—
then lies deceptive as a jumping-jack
whose lit fuse seems to have failed.
I keep an eye on it till I'm out of range.

As the days widen I notice
I'm walking further just to get home.
                                        —"Passing Events"

PRINCIPAL WORKS: *Poetry*—Instances, 1967; Inventories, 1969; The Spaces between the Stones, 1971; The Man with the Surbahar, 1971; Tree-Lines, 1974; Between Flights, 1976; Following a Mirror, 1980; Selected Poems 1963–1978, 1980; Fields of Focus, 1982. *Prose*—Contemporary Scottish Poetry: Individuals and Contexts, 1974.

ABOUT: Contemporary Authors New Revision Series 16, 1986; Contemporary Poets, 4th ed., 1985; Dictionary of Literary Biography 40, 1985. *Periodicals*—Ancrastus Spring 1983; Books in Scotland Spring 1983; Lines Review March 1983; Poetry Review March 1983; Times Literary Supplement April 8, 1983; World Literature Today Spring 1981, Winter 1984.

FURBANK, P(HILIP) N(ICHOLAS) (May 23, 1920–   ), British biographer and critic, son of William Percival and Grace (Turner) Furbank, was born in Cranleigh, Surrey. He attended Emmanuel College, Cambridge, earning an M A in English literature in 1947, and then served as a fellow of the College until 1953. Furbank worked as an editor at Macmillan & Co., Ltd., in London from 1963 until 1970, when he returned to Cambridge for two years as a research fellow of Kings College. Since 1972, he has taught at the Open University in Milton Keynes.

Furbank wrote his first book, *Samuel Butler, 1835–1902*, while a student at Cambridge. The original version of the study won the university's Le Bas Prize in 1946. The slightly shorter published version consists of seven loosely integrated essays on such topics as Butler's earlier detractors, his writings on evolution, and the Butler collection at St. Johns' College, Cambridge. Initially, Furbank states his purpose as a defense of Butler, especially from Malcolm Muggeridge, who had written a vituperative biography of the novelist in 1936. His focus soon shifts, however, to a sensitive and detailed explication of Butler's texts. In the second chapter, Furbank interprets the "real nature of Butler's talent," specifically "a capacity for sharpness and penetration, of quick combination of the elements of unremarked everyday experience, which makes the success of the best things in his controversial writings such as the Notebooks." Of Butler's attack on Darwinian evolution, Furbank writes that his embellished theory is "quite fun, but it has nothing to do with biology." Moreover, "the theory has ceased to be a refutation of Darwinism; the world of writing is too different."

Samuel Butler received very good reviews, although several found that Furbank's defense of Butler often backfired. Largely for this reason, the *Saturday Review* pronounced the study "muddled and obscure." Gordon Haight, in the *Yale Review*, likewise noted that Furbank's work occasionally degrades Butler as much as Muggeridge's did. Nevertheless, Haight wrote, the book is "free from the absurd idolatry of the cult and the sensationalism of the debunkers, [and] marks the beginning of an objective statement of Samuel Butler and his works." According to the *Times Literary Supplement*'s reviewer, "Mr. Furbank's attempts to enter into his subject's feelings are the more effective for their restraint and for his ability to see the contortions of a repressed personality from different angles."

In *Italo Svevo: The Man and the Writer*, Furbank presents a writer little known in his own lifetime. A businessman who lived in Trieste, where he met James Joyce, Svevo wrote numerous short stories and several novels including *A Life, As a Man Grows Older*, and *The Confessions of Zeno*. Furbank interprets Svevo's novels as distorted autobiography and consequently devotes two-thirds of the study to the writer's life and one-third to his work. As Furbank explains, Svevo's innovative writing helped shape the direction of the modern novel, yet he remained a literary failure for most of his life, publishing books at his own expense and having little or no readership outside of Trieste. Svevo finally achieved literary stature as an old man in Paris, mostly due to James Joyce's belief in his genius as a writer. In the second part of the book, Furbank analyzes Svevo's novels and stories, demonstrating their autobiographical quintessence. For example, the author drew heavily on his own experience as a bank clerk in *A Life* and used his brother Elio as a model for the protagonist of *The Confessions of Zeno*. According to Furbank's analysis, Svevo's writing functions as autobiography at a much deeper level in that the novelist's ironic awareness of his bourgeois milieu permeates all of his work. Furbank further interprets the novels as "studies in weakness," pointing out that death and senility are both recurring themes.

Critics commended Furbank for having written a sensitive study of a long-neglected writer. "Given the sort of claims Mr. Furbank might have made for the sort of pioneering work he has done, he is to be praised and respected for the self-effacing and unpretentious way in which he introduces us to Italo Svevo," Tony Tanner noted in the *Spectator. Saturday Review* critic Walter Guzzardi, Jr., declared the book "competent and thorough," but felt that Furbank's self-effacement rendered the study merely a "useful addition" to English works on Svevo. While Guzzardi found the division of the book into biography and analysis distracting, other reviewers praised this method in light of the autobiographical nature of Svevo's work. Denis Donoghue, in the *New York Review of Books*, regretted that the book lacked more idiosyncrasy, detail, and literary analysis, but recommended it as "an ideal introduction, guide, manual."

In contrast to his first two books, Furbank's *Reflections on the Word "Image"* is theoretical. Like his earlier works, however, it aims to right a literary wrong. Furbank's reflections on "image" focus on the dominance of the word in literary criticism, particularly as synonymous with "metaphor" and "simile." This usage, he argues, obscures the sense of comparison implicit in "metaphor." Furthermore, "the word 'image,' unlike the word 'metaphor,' suggests no connection with the *medium* of poetry, which is words, syntax, and rhythm; and that should make us suspicious of it." Critics, Furbank asserts, have pilfered "image" from art historians, who use it in the sense of pictorial image. In doing so, these critics treat the verbal medium as if it were paint—brush strokes with which a writer creates "a world." Words, Furbank insists, cannot create concrete images. "Tree," for example, could refer to any one of hundreds of different species, rather than an individual specimen.

Citing the works of Milton, Ezra Pound, Ted Hughes, and William Carlos Williams, among others, Furbank explores the development of "image" and "imagery" as tools for literary criticism. He expounds on their current misuse and on the similar misuse of the terms "concreteness" and "world." Much of the confusion results, Furbank maintains, from a twentieth-century aversion to dualism and writers' misguided attempts to make art and reality one and the same.

The study provoked both admiration and skepticism among critics. Martin Seymour Smith, reviewing it in the *Spectator*, lamented Furbank's monolithic treatment of poetry of the "Imagist" school. He nevertheless agreed with Furbank's general argument and concluded that the book was "eminently sensible and sane: as good as a book of critical theory can be." *Listener* critic Denis Donoghue was not totally convinced by the argument, siding with the benighted critic who must work with "blunt instruments." "Mr. Furbank is a vivid writer," Donoghue added, "and his polemic is lively, sometimes perhaps too jaunty to be exactly fair, but never dull." The argument was praised as "very finely woven," by Jonathan Bryant in the *New Statesman*. However, "having, most plausibly, traced the fascinating history of a potent fallacy in critical discourse, he proceeds to use it as a stick with which to beat the literature of which he disapproves for its irresponsibility." Furbank was also accused of borrowing too heavily from critics like F. R. Leavis and Donald Davie.

Furbank returned to biographical writing with *E. M. Forster: A Life*. The two men were friends for twenty-three years and Forster himself asked Furbank to be his official biographer. In one chapter, "E. M. Forster Described," Furbank provides an intimate portrait of the novelist, including this description of their meeting:

I got to know Forster myself early in 1947, a few months after he had arrived in Cambridge. I was then twenty-seven and had just become a fellow of Emmanuel College. We met at the Apostles [a select group of Cambridge intellectuals], and a day or two after our first encounter he called on me in my rooms uninvited. It was a sort of "apostolic" visit, very charmingly conducted on his part, and on the strength of it, during the coming year, we got on to terms of friendship. I left Cambridge a few years later, to work in London, but we continued to meet and to correspond; and eventually, a year or two before his death, he asked me if I would like to write a book about him.

Even before Forster's death in 1971, Furbank had access to his unpublished writings, private papers, and correspondence. These sources, combined with Furbank's personal knowledge

of his subject, enabled him to relate the story of Forster's life in frank detail, including his sheltered childhood, his latent and then active homosexuality, and his creative highs and lows. Furbank notes that a major motif in Forster's novels, as well as his life, was the deliverer, come "to rescue the hero or heroine from muddle and self-deception." As to why Forster never wrote another novel after *A Passage to India*, Furbank explains that Forster received "his whole inspiration—a vision, a kind of plot, a message—all at once, in early manhood." Another explanation, Furbank suggests, may be the demise of the Edwardian world that Forster's characters inhabited.

Critics gave the biography an enthusiastic reception, many hailing it as the "definitive" life of Forster. The *Chronicle of Higher Education*'s Paul Piazza praised Furbank as sympathetic and judicious, "as tolerant and wise as Forster himself." He wished only that Furbank had further distilled the abundant, detailed information he drew on. John Carey, reviewing the first volume of the work in the *New Statesman*, wrote, "Graceful, intimate, evocative, it is that rare thing, a study of a major writer by a major critic who was also a close friend. We shall not be brought so near to the young Forster again."

Furbank addresses a much broader subject in *Unholy Pleasure: The Idea of Social Class*. Focusing on England, Furbank traces the history of social class in terms of both thought and reality. He dates its emergence to circa 1830 and traces its development throughout the Victorian, Edwardian, and interwar eras. Furbank contends that after World War II, when domestic servants all but disappeared, *actual* class distinction disappeared as well. After establishing his thesis, Furbank offers a multidisciplinary critique of scholarship on class. Sociologists such as Max Weber and Alain Mousnier, and historians, notably E. P. Thompson, are rebuked for their inconsistent treatment of the subject. In a discussion of English literature, Furbank argues on the one hand that the idea of class distorted the vision of novelists like Thackeray and Trollope. On the other hand, he maintains that writers like Dickens, Proust, Joyce, and Kafka transcended class feeling in their work. Their writing, therefore, demonstrates a way of thinking about people in terms independent of class.

While critics found Furbank's argument intriguing, they also perceived it as limiting. Anthony Quinton, in the *Times Literary Supplement*, noted that "the book is written by a member of the upper-middle class and will be read only by people of the same kind." *Spectator* reviewer Sarah Bradford commended the skill and scholarship with which Furbank "scored his academic points" but wondered what Furbank would "suggest in place of concepts which in one form or another have always existed as a human reaction to the complexity of existence and the desire to make order out of chaos?" According to the *New Statesman*'s Jon Cook, the study contains "local insights" into literature and language. However, many critics ultimately doubted the effectiveness of Furbank's prescribed reading to overcome such a pervasive social condition.

In *The Canonisation of Daniel Defoe* Furbank again takes the literary offensive. He and his co-author W. R. Owens launch an attack against the accepted canon of Defoe's works, suggesting that "from the very beginning, something may have gone wrong—that some error crept in, begetting over the years a long series of further errors, or that the basic principles of attribution adopted have somehow been faulty." To rectify this error, the authors propose the deletion, at least until further proof, of over 300 of the 570 works on the Defoe list. They do not question his authorship of major works like *Robinson Crusoe* and *Moll Flanders*, but of various lesser works. Since Defoe wrote a prodigious amount, often anonymously, the authors contend, it was easy for bibliographers and booksellers to assign books and pamphlets to him incorrectly. Furbank and Owens develop their argument in three parts: biographies of the six men responsible for this inflated bibliography, a proposal for new principles of author-attribution, and a discussion of Defoe's characteristics as a person and an author.

Although some critics questioned the feasibility of completing Furbank and Owens' assignment, they endorsed the need for such an undertaking. Robert Adams, writing in the *New York Review of Books*, remarked that the book "seems at moments like a manifesto nailed to the cathedral door of English studies." He characterized Furbank and Owens' principles of attribution as astringent and practical but hard to apply consistently. *Times Literary Supplement* reviewer David Trotter acclaimed the authors' "exemplary account of this extraordinary process of accretion. They have destroyed, once and for all, the authority of the Defoe canon: the bibliographer has no clothes."

In addition to his full-length works, Furbank contributes regularly to the *Listener* and also writes for the *Manchester Guardian*, the *Observer*, and *Encounter*.

PRINCIPAL WORKS: Samuel Butler, 1948; Italo Svevo: The Man and the Writer, 1966; Reflections on the Word Image, 1970; E. M. Forster: A Life, 1978; Unholy Plea-

sure: The Idea of Social Class, 1985; The Canonisation of Daniel Defoe, 1987.

ABOUT: Contemporary Authors New Revision Series 18, 1986. *Periodicals*—Chronicle of Higher Education January 8, 1979; Listener August 27, 1970; New Statesman August 14, 1970; July 22, 1977; July 5, 1985; New York Review of Books May 4, 1967; December 22, 1988; Saturday Review January 29, 1949; June 10, 1967; Spectator May 13, 1966; August 15, 1970; July 6, 1985; Times Literary Supplement December 4, 1948; September 13, 1985; May 20, 1988; Yale Review Summer 1949.

*GADAMER, HANS-GEORG (February 11, 1900–   ), German philosopher, was born in Marburg (West Germany), the son of Johanes and Johanna (Geweise) Gadamer. His father taught chemistry, first at Marburg and later as a professor at Breslau (Wroclaw). Gadamer grew up in Breslau and graduated from the classical *Gymnasium* there. He studied philosophy, German, ancient philology, and art history in Breslau, Marburg, Freiburg, and Munich. Gadamer completed his doctorate in 1922 as one of Paul Natorp's last students, and in 1929 he "habilitated"—or qualified for the German professoriat—as one of Martin Heidegger's first students. He and Karl Löwith were Heidegger's first *Assistenten*, or graduate assistants, in Marburg in the mid-1920s. Less formally, Gadamer's years as a graduate assistant included close contact with the theologian Rudolf Bultmann, the art historian Ernst Robert Curtius, and the classical philologist Paul Friedländer.

Gadamer became a professor in Leipzig in 1938 and rector (president) of that university in 1945. He accepted a position at Frankfurt in West Germany in 1947, where he remained until becoming Karl Jasper's successor at Heidelberg in 1949. He remained there until his retirement in 1968. Thereafter Gadamer taught occasionally at American universities and regularly at Boston College from the early 1970s to the mid-1980s. He lives with his second wife in Heidelberg-Ziegelhausen and has two daughters, one from each of his marriages.

The key year in Gadamer's intellectual career was 1960, when he published his first widely acclaimed book, called *Truth and Method*. Nothing Gadamer had done before that year had gained for him any intellectual acclaim; everything he did thereafter was received with avid attention. Hence, before reconstructing the before-and-after of his intellectual career, it is worth while to grasp the argument of Gadamer's *opus magnum*.

One school of the counter-enlightenment has

°ga′da mer

HANS-GEORG GADAMER

been *hermeneutics*, the aim of which has always been to restore the legitimacy of traditional approaches to knowledge and truth. It strives to do this by means of understanding ancient texts. Originally a matter of trying to understand the truth claims of the Bible, hermeneutics took secular form in the German nineteenth century and became an effort to reconstruct mainly classical Greek texts in order to understand their truth claims. Schleiermacher, Nietzsche, and Dilthey were the leaders of nineteenth-century literary hermeneutics in Germany.

The problem was how a modern person, equipped with scientific reason, understands an ancient text, written from the point of view of a traditional form of reason. Either we understand in terms provided by our modern, western, scientific rationality, which was the model for Wilamowitz's classical philology in nineteenth-century Germany, or we "go native" and understand in terms of a different model of reason, in which case we lose our modern identity as, for example, Nietzsche does in *The Birth of Tragedy*. Neither solution is attractive, and the third option—of having it both ways, of being a participant observer—has for the most part struck philosophers as being a case of wishful thinking.

It was toward this problem-situation that Gadamer keyed *Wahrheit und Methode* (1960; translated as *Truth and Method*). There Gadamer argued that the beginning points of what knowledge we have and the irreducible elements of consciousness are "prejudices," which are footholds of certainty from which we argue but which we are ready to submit to question. Even the crudest Cartesian scientific reason is formed this way, insofar as it has a bias against tradition, that which Gadamer calls the enlightenment prejudice against prejudices. A dialogue between modernity and tradition that begins by suspending the privileging of scientific reason thereby lifts the chief barrier to understanding. Put slightly differently, an admission of the irreducible prejudice of reason lays aside the universality claim of scientific reason and opens the way for pluralism in philosophy. Looked at this way, Gadamer is defining philosophy as an unfounded discipline. That is to say, where physics, psychology, chemistry, sociology, or political science exist as disciplines only insofar as they proceed from a body of established and reliable knowledge, philosophy is a discipline only insofar as it proceeds from a claim to ignorance. The model of this practice of hermeneutic philosophy is the Platonic Socrates, with his profession of ignorance.

The appropriate philosophical consciousness, aware of its own irreducible prejudices, is called by Gadamer *effective historical consciousness*, and this is characterized by him as a consciousness that is always "more being than consciousness." Taken at face value, this term is a compressed argument against enlightenment philosophy. It is diametrically opposed to all enlightenment claims about scientific reason being value-free, that is to say, purged of all traditional prejudices, as Descartes claimed. On the contrary, the ideal philosopher is one who is aware of the degree to which reason is constructed of valuations, or prejudices drawn from past experiences or history. In this sense, effective historical consciousness is very close to being another name for practical reason.

The result of a philosophical discourse based on an awareness of irreducible prejudice is not truth or knowledge but rather *agreement*. That is to say, the result is a matter of judgment, and with the passage of time, every judgment becomes a prejudgment, or prejudice. To the classical question: is agreement reached because it is true or is truth what is agreed upon, Gadamer strongly implies that the latter is the case. This is not to say that there is no truth-as-such, but at least in the human condition, there is only truth-for-us. This is the only knowable truth, and it boils down to a matter of knowing our prejudices, or the conditions for producing truth-for-us.

And so, how is cross-cultural understanding achieved? How does a modern scholar understand an ancient text, or how does a western anthropologist understand an Azandi witchdoctor?

Quite simply, by repeating for philosophy what Copernicus did for astronomy or Darwin for biology: by decentering the world. That is to say, the condition of the possibility of any understanding worth having is a withdrawal from the unwarranted belief that modern western scientific rationality is the sole means to attain reliable knowledge and truth. We must decenter, or relativize, modern western scientific rationality. This, of course, does not guarantee that understanding will result, but it at least makes it possible.

Gadamer's *Truth and Method* might have languished as an interesting but curiously cryptic book if it had not been for subsequent developments in western thinking. In 1962, Thomas Kuhn published his *Structure of Scientific Revolutions*, in which he argued that scientific activity was itself carried out in terms of paradigms, or models of the world, and that there was no algorithm (or universal standard) by which to judge competing paradigms. Theory-choice, as Kuhn described it, was a matter of persuasion and conversion, and this finally was a matter of arguing in terms of basic values, such as adequacy or simplicity, which were themselves subject to differing interpretations. Overnight, as it were, modern western science itself began to look like the world Gadamer had described. Kuhn himself admitted in the preface to his most recent book that he was practicing something like hermeneutics.

In social and political theory, the key event for the reception of Gadamer's ideas was a review of *Truth and Method* by Jürgen Habermas, followed by a prolonged debate with this leading contemporary German political and social theorist. But where Habermas' thinking peaks to come to direct confrontation with Gadamer's, is at that point where the younger man holds that truth will prevail in an ideal, undistorted discourse, a claim which Gadamer—keyed to a 'truth' which is not a *telos* of nature or a transcendent entity of any type—cannot accept. Therefore Gadamer would not eliminate the so-called 'distortions' of discourse. He would rather own up to them as prejudices and take them as irreducible, inescapable starting points of philosophical conversation.

Finally, in literary theory, the writings of former students of Gadamer—Hans-Robert Jauss and Wolfgang Iser—have helped to establish the so-called Constance School and thereby occupy a strategic corner of an expanding and very fashionable academic discipline. At the time of this writing, it appears as though Gadamer has more influence in literary and aesthetic theory than in social and political theory. In order to avoid an overly narrow interpretation of Gadamer's thinking, one restricted to the sciences and epistemology, it therefore might be well to see how the same line of thinking has been worked out in literary theory and, more generally, art criticism.

For more than a century, since Schleiermacher, the problem of understanding in literary hermeneutics was a matter of grasping what the author was saying, or intended to say, in the text. Gadamer was one of the earliest to argue that the *meaning* of a text is not determined by its author. This is the case for simple but compelling reasons. The author is also a "prejudiced" human being and, in any case, the text has an effective history, knowledge of which is unavailable to the author during writing. Therefore the meaning of a text is reader-determined as well. In this sense, meaning is no more than the agreement of a community of readers with each other, with tradition, and with the author. What *Huckleberry Finn* means is not solely determined by the intentions of Mark Twain but is rather more determined by the curious effective history—of which Twain was of course unaware—and by the "prejudices" we readers bring to bear on it. The text gains it own life, greater than that of its author or readers. In this sense, to paraphrase Gadamer, language speaks us before we speak it.

Does this kind of hermeneutics relativize meaning? Yes, insofar as it denies that there is one fixed meaning, to be found out by means of scientific reason. But then again, no, insofar as it argues that a text, even an Azandi witchdoctor, is open to interpretation and hence remains meaningful, insofar as meaning is completed by us. Hence *meaning* is an ongoing, fluid process of interpreting the world. Texts serve us as reference points for thought. They are mirrors over against which we can measure ourselves and in terms of which we talk to each other.

Now apply this kind of thinking to a painting, or any work of art, to get a sense of its role in aesthetic criticism. The meaning of Picasso's *Les demoiselles d'Avignon* is not limited to Picasso's intentions. He painted a painting, not a meaning. The meaning is rather more to be found in its reception history, which is something very much like its effective history. This is a roundabout way of saying that a true work of art is incomplete. It receives its completion in the act of interpretation, as (for example) the United States Constitution from that community of interpreters called the Supreme Court. Indeed, one might even argue that Picasso, like the American framers, did not understand his own work of art as well as we do (a contemporary prejudice!), else he would not have departed from the immense potential of cubism as completely as he did. The only end to argumentation set up this way is agreement, for there is no truth-as-such about Picasso, just as there is no truth-as-such about the United States Constitution.

After the publication of *Truth and Method*, Gadamer published several more books, but no one of them broke new ground. Many of them, in fact, were collections of articles that had been published before *Truth and Method*. Nonetheless, some of them were suggestive in respect to the problem of applying Gadamer's ideas, and hence have proved to be of value. In this respect, perhaps the two most important books have been collections of his essays: *Philosophie Hermeneutik* (1975; translated as *Philosophical Hermeneutics*) and *Vernunft im Zeitalter der Wissenschaft* (1976; translated as *Reason in the Age of Science*). Gadamer also published something of a memoir-autobiography, *Philosophische Lehrjahre* (1977; translated as *Philosophical Apprenticeships*), which sheds light on the development of his career. Gadamer is at work on the production of his *Gesammelte Werke* (Collected Works) which will appear in ten volumes when the set is complete in the 1990s.

An overview of the projected *Gesammelte Werke* provides something of an authorized sketch of how Gadamer categorizes his own intellectual life. Volume one is *Truth and Method*, thereby alerting us that Gadamer is not organizing things chronologically. Volume two is made up of writings on hermeneutics and hence is a supplement to the first volume. Volume three deals with modern philosophers and problems of modern philosophy. Volumes four, five, and six include Gadamer's writings on ancient Greek philosophy. Volumes eight and nine incorporate literary criticism and art criticism, and volume ten will include writings that Gadamer is doing now. It will be published after his death.

One feature of the *Gesammelte Werke* that calls for comment is its large amount of writing—three volumes—on ancient Greek philosophy. For the most part, these writings were published before *Truth and Method*, and almost without exception they comprise all of the writings Gadamer did in the interwar period, which is to say, in the first two decades of his intellectual career. What those writings reveal is not simply the working out of the concepts of *Truth and Method* but also the working out of a hermeneutics different from the one contained in the 1960 book.

Under the influence of the thinking of members of the Stefan George Circle, the young Ga-

damer adopted the position that Plato's moral philosophy was not determined by a doctrine of objective ideas or founded knowledge. Ethical questions were rather to be decided by means of the dialectic, which meant that ethical norms were agreements arrived at in philosophical discourse. This of course describes a society distinctly modern in its self-reliance, one in which the gods are not actively handing down moral values.

This was the basic theme of Gadamer's habilitation thesis, done under Heidegger's supervision and called *Platos dialektische Ethik* (1931), a title which hardly needs translation. This theory of an unfounded ethics led Gadamer into the second major work of his youth, a monograph called "Plato and the Poets" in which Gadamer defended Plato's expulsion of the poets from the city. This was even then an unorthodox interpretation of Plato, but it makes sense when viewed in terms of Gadamer's later thinking about language. Poetry produces what Gadamer then called "aesthetic consciousness," by which he meant a consciousness distracted by the beauty of language from the issues of practical philosophy. What Plato wanted was a "philosophical conversation," by which Gadamer means a prosaic discourse which was not distracted by its own language from the problems of life it had to confront. Gadamer finally capped off his early career with a study called "Plato's Educational State," in which he argued on behalf of the moral role of the state in shaping the individual soul.

Gadamer's early writings constitute a kind of political hermeneutics and hence may be juxtaposed against the philosophical hermeneutics in his later writings. The concept of the political here is clearly classical: politics is a macrocosmic continuation of ethics, and so "Plato and the Poets" was a logical continuation of the thinking of *Platos dialektische Ethik*. But the converse is also true: ethics is a microcosmic continuation of politics, and hence the argument of "Plato's Educational State" represented is the logical counterpart of Gadamer's earlier argumentation.

WORKS IN ENGLISH TRANSLATION: There is a longstanding problem with the English translation of *Truth and Method*, a problem which has given a comparative advantage to those Anglophone scholars fluent enough in German to work with the original text. After years of complaints and criticisms, a new translation has been commissioned and was scheduled to appear in 1989. This will no doubt create an upsurge of interest in Gadamer as reviewers compare the translations and the original and discover new meanings or, quite possibly, new and unexpected mistranslations. This planned event will provide yet another chapter in Gadamer's own effective history. The existing translation of *Truth*

and Method (1975) was "edited by Garrett Barden and
John Cumming," wording which leaves it some-
what unclear whether they were the translators.
Philosophical Hermeneutics was translated by David
E. Linge (1976) and *Reason in the Age of
Science* by Frederick G. Lawrence (1981). Three
books—*Dialogue and Dialectic* (1979), *Hegel's
Dialectic* (1980) and *The Idea of the Good in Platonic-
Aristotelian Philosophy* (1986)—were translated by P.
Christopher Smith. *The Relevance of the Beautiful*
was translated by Nicholas Walker (1986) and
Philosophical Apprenticeships by Robert R. Sullivan
(1985). *Platos dialektische Ethik* is being translated by
P. Christopher Smith, and the new edition of *Truth
and Method* is being done by Don Marshall and Joel
Weinsheimer.

ABOUT: Contemporary Authors 85–88, 1980; Bernstein,
R. J. Beyond Objectivism and Relativism, 1983; Palm-
er, R. E. Hermeneutics, 1969; Sullivan, R. R. Political
Hermeneutics, 1989; Warnke, G. Gadamer, Herme-
neutics, Tradition, and Reason, 1987; Weinsheimer,
Joel. Gadamer's Hermeneutics, 1985.

TESS GALLAGHER

GALLAGHER, TESS (BOND) (July 21,
1943–), American poet, short-story writer,
and essayist, was born in Port Angeles, Washington. Although she has lived in many other parts
of the United States, including the south, midwest, and upstate New York where she teaches
one semester every year at Syracuse University,
the green and rainy Pacific Northwest remains
her home for most of the year. "It is the climate
of my psyche," she wrote in an autobiographical
essay in *A Concert of Tenses*. There she recalls
her parents—her father, Leslie Bond, a hearty,
heavy-drinking logger and longshoreman who
had come west from Oklahoma, and her mother,
Georgia Marie (Morris) Bond. Both parents
worked in logging camps, sharing their outdoor
life with their five children, of whom Tess was
the eldest. Her father later bought a farm, "so as
to teach his children something 'not learned in
books.'" Hers was a rough and turbulent but not
unhappy childhood: "My father's drinking, and
the quarrels he had with my mother because of
it, terrorized my childhood . . . And if coping
with terror and anxiety are necessary to the psychic stamina of a poet, I had them in steady
doses—just as inevitably as I had the rain. I
learned that the world was not just, that any balance was temporary, that unreasonableness
could descend at any minute, thrashing aside everything and everyone in its path." Balancing
that, however, was the freedom of her life in nature. She recalls a moment from her childhood,
out in the open fields, when it suddenly rained,
at first slowly, then heavily:

> . . . Until I'm looking up
> to let my eyes take the bliss.
> I open my face. Let the teeth show. I
> pull my shirt down past the collar-bones.
> I'm still a boy under my breast spots.
> I can drink anywhere. The rain. My
> skin shattering. Up suddenly, needing
> to gulp, turning with my tongue, my arms out
> running, running in the hard, cold plenitude
> of all those who reach earth by falling.
>   —"Sudden Journey"

In later years Gallagher came to recognize
that what she calls an "invisible love" existed in
her family—"a rawness of impulse, a sharpness,
a tension, that complicates the emotion, that
withholds even as it gives." Her parents figure
in many of her poems. Her relationship with her
mother is recalled with sadness at the distance
that until recent years existed between them.
"She is visiting / the daughter never close / or
far enough away to come to," she wrote in "My
Mother Remembers That She Was Beautiful":

> . . . Who
> she must have been
> is lost to me through some fault
> in my own reflection and we will have to go on
> as we think we are . . . .

Yet they also share moments of communion—
as in "With Stars" when she remembers one
night her mother wrapping her in a quilt and
standing with her at a window:

> . . . I am four years old and
> a star has the power of wishes.
> We stare out together, but she sees past
> their fierce shimmering sameness, each

point of light the emblem
of some lost, remembered face. What
do they want? I ask. "Not to be
forgotten," she says and draws me close.

Gallagher writes about her father without bitterness and with no trace of sentimentality. In "3 A.M. Kitchen: My Father Talking" he reviews his life of hard labor in the oil fields, logging, fishing:

It's winter. I play a lot of cards
down at the tavern. Your mother.
I have to think of excuses
to get out of the house. You're
wasting your time, she says. You're wasting
your money.

You don't have no idea, Threasie.
I run out of things
to work for. Hell, why shouldn't I
play cards? Threasie,
some days I just don't know.

At sixteen she went to work as a reporter for the *Port Angeles Daily News*, earning money for her college expenses. At the University of Washington in Seattle she was in the last poetry class that Theodore Roethke taught there. Full of awe in the presence of so major a poet, she appreciated not only his own work but the way he taught, "his seriousness about poetry." In Roethke's class she first read the poems of Stanley Kunitz, whom she later met at a writers' workshop at the University of Iowa. His poetry and his translations of the Russian poet Anna Akhmatova were very influential on her later career: "His faith in my own endeavors to write poetry and to teach has been a guiding force at the very heart of my writing and living." Gallagher left the University of Washington without completing her degree in 1963 when she married Lawrence Gallagher, who served in the Marine Corps. She lived with him in training posts in South Carolina and in Missouri until he was sent overseas during the Vietnam war as a pilot. Deeply troubled by the war and by the break-up of her marriage, she went abroad and traveled alone in Europe, England, and Ireland, an experience she later wrote "that put me firmly in possession of my own life." In Northern Ireland especially, and in Galway, she discovered that poetry was more than an absorbing interest for her; it had become her vocation. On her return to the United States she went back to the University of Washington to complete her B.A. in 1968. She went on to take an M.A. in 1970, then studied at the University of Iowa where she received an M.F.A. in 1974. Since then, except for leaves for travel and writing, Gallagher has taught English literature and creative writing at St. Lawrence University in Canton, N.Y. (1974–1975), Kirk-

land College in Clifton, N.Y. (1975–1977), at the University of Montana in Missoula (1977–1978), and at the University of Arizona (1979–1980). Since 1980 she has been on the English faculty of Syracuse University. Her poems began appearing in literary magazines and her first volume, *Stepping Outside*, was published in 1974. She is now widely acknowledged to be one of the most accomplished of younger American poets, with awards from the National Endowment for the Arts (1976, 1981) and the Guggenheim Foundation (1978–1979); she has also received an award from Syracuse University for distinguished teaching.

Although Gallagher's language is simple, often colloquial, and her subjects are usually drawn from ordinary domestic life, she is not an "easy" poet to read. Commenting on her first collection, Robert Ross, in *Prairie Schooner*, noted its subtlety: "one thinks, somehow, of underground passages that recurve on themselves, so that the adventurer is expelled at the exact spot he entered the maze, retaining the conviction of hidden treasure." Of her second volume, *Under Stars*, Peter Davison wrote in the *Atlantic*: "The apparent simplicity of Gallagher's way of speaking turns out to be difficult to follow because she is dodging through the most intricate of alien entanglements, the movements of the human mind itself." Because her poems embody these movements of mind, it is not surprising that, as Dawson noted: "Poetry is most sublimely, for her, the subject of the poem."

Gallagher sees the poem as a dialogue not between separate individuals but between the poet's two selves, the real self and the one who lives vicariously in the poem itself. The title poem of her volume *Instructions to the Double* proclaims her passionate dedication to poetry. Sending her double out into the world of reality, she instructs her:

Don't stop for anything, not
a caress or promise. Go
to the temple of the poets, not
the one like a run-down country club,
but the one on fire
with so much it wants
to be done with

It's a dangerous mission. You
could die out there. You
could live forever.

All the more because she came relatively late to it, the urgency of her poetic vocation seems to possess her. "I admit / I delayed. I was the Empress / of Delay." But now she no longer has a choice: "In the sacred branch / of my only voice—I insist":

```
        . . . Else
what am I for, what use
am I if I don't
insist?
There are messages to send.
Gatherings and songs.
Because we need
to insist. Else what are we
for? What use
are we?
```
—"Refusing Silence"

Gallagher's poems have been praised for their "mesmerizing rhythms" (Joyce Carol Oates in the *Ontario Review*), but in fact it is their irregularity, their power to startle the reader, that creates their lyrical effects. "I like a sense of expectancy and tend to stop the line before it answers itself," she has said. The abrupt breaks in her poetic lines reinforce the sense of rapid movement and change that is characteristic of modern life. The poem, she writes in her essay "The Poem as Time Machine," "is in a state of perpetual formation and disintegration as it lives in the poet's mind and in the consciousness of each reader." H. G. Wells' time machine could carry one into the past or the future. "The poem, on the other hand, is like a magnet which draws into it events and beings from all possible past, present, and future contexts of the speaker."

Early on in her career Hayden Carruth, writing of *Under Stars* in *Harper's*, singled out for praise the "verbal finesse" of her work. "I am tempted to call it feminine," he said with proper reluctance to mark gender distinctions in literature. Carruth was referring to a delicacy of sensibility that is combined with "the feminine strength of a clear view." Gallagher is not a feminist poet, but her poems explore her identity as a woman in ways to which women can especially respond. Traveling alone in Ireland after the break up of her marriage, she finds herself in a large commercial hotel where she feels "end of season like a somebody / who's hung around the church / between a series of double weddings":

```
Friend, what you said about the terror
of American Womanhood,
I forget it already, but I know
what you mean. I am so scary some days
I'd run from myself. It's hard work
having your way, even
half the time, and having it,
know what not to do with it. Who
hasn't thrown away a life or two
at the mercy of another's passion,
spite or industry?
```
—"On Your Own"

Gallagher finds sisterhood with many women because, as she told an interviewer in *At the Field's End*, one function of fiction and of poetry is "to give voice, to give witness to lives that otherwise won't be recorded." Among those voices are the struggling poor women of Ireland, seen metaphorically in "Women's Tug of War at Lough Arrow," who compete in a contest against each other for the possession of their men. And she identifies with a crippled old woman neighbor who offers to teach her how to sew an elaborate coverlet:

```
       . . . Sunlight dazzles
her spectacles and in the chromium glint
of her walker she is bright royalty
on an errand of magnitude. An effort to
stand, an effort to step the pain
carefully around invisible parameters
and still to say: effort is nobility.
```
—"Some with Wings, Some with Manes"

For Gallagher narrative—in fiction or in verse—is a medium for giving voice to otherwise inarticulate people. Writing of her collection *Willingly* in the *New York Times Book Review*, William Logan observed that "increasingly her poems have become minor fictions, with beginnings, middles, and ends." They tend to frame an episode, a moment in time that is a little story in itself. The most gripping of these is "Two Stories," first collected in *Instructions to the Double*, addressed "To the author of a story taken from the death of my uncle Porter Morris, killed June 7, 1972." Gallagher visited this uncle, a Missouri farmer, some years before his brutal murder by two drifters in a robbery. His death, she wrote in *A Concert of Tenses*, "has caused violence to haunt my vision of what it is to live in America." His murder, she reflects, can be dismissed as one of many crimes, but for her it has deep personal significance:

```
I say it matters
that the dog stays by the chimney
for months, and a rain
soft as the sleep of cats
enters the land, emptied
of its cows, its wire gates pulled down
by hands that never dug
the single well, this whitened field.
```

The writing of short stories was a natural transition for Gallagher and *The Lover of Horses and Other Stories*, her first collection of fiction, carries over many of the features of her poetry—its discipline, what Michiko Kakutani in the *New York Times* called its "tensile quality," and its delicacy of observation. In "Beneficiaries," for example, a wife who is shocked to learn that her husband plans to leave his estate to his children from an earlier marriage, experiences a chilling sense of betrayal. As she walks downstairs into the lobby of her office building:

There was a white gloom of light falling from an arch

of glass panes above the entranceway, illuminating the marble pattern on the floor. She took her time going down the steps. When she reached the lobby she stood in the core of light and waited for Stanley. She looked up through the cold glaze and saw that it had begun to snow again. The sky seemed to be hurling itself in steady bits of matter at the glass.

Most of the stories involve epiphanies, moments of revelation and self-discovery in which her central characters, usually women, confront the perils of their routine domestic lives—loneliness, the breakdown of communication between lovers, fear of aging and death. In her review of *The Lover of Horses* in the *New York Times Book Review*, Bette Pesetsky wrote that while reading the stories she tried "to forget what a fine poet the author is. And the reward was to find an excellent writer of prose who savors the elegance of simplicity and whose stories resonate and linger." But it is difficult to forget the poet in the title story of the volume. A lover of horses from her childhood, Gallagher writes a story, she says, about "the difficult and complex relationship between men and horses." More fundamentally the story is about her difficult and complex relationship with her father. It begins with her discovery of her great-grandfather whom she never knew but whose history she learned when she visited the west of Ireland where he had lived: "They say my great-grandfather was a gypsy, but the most popular explanation for his behavior was that he was a drunk." Fascinated by horses and capable of exercising strange powers over them, at fifty-two he deserted his wife and family to join a circus and work with performing horses. Seven years later he returned home with a saddle blanket and some plumes from a dancing horse's headdress. For Gallagher his story was emblematic of her whole family's history: "Ever since my great-grandfather's outbreak of gypsy necessity, members of my family have been stolen by things—by mad ambitions, by musical instruments, by otherwise harmless pursuits from mushroom hunting and childbearing or, as was my father's case, by the more easily recognized and popular obsession with card playing." Just before he died he had a winning streak at cards and returned home from the local tavern where he played; he was deathly ill but jubilant. She spent the night he died out-of-doors under the open sky and experienced her own epiphany: " . . . that the vastness he was about to enter had its rhythms in me also. . . . That so far I had denied the disreputable world of dancers and drunkards, gamblers and lovers of horses to which I most surely belonged. But from that night forward I vowed to be filled with the first unsavory desire that would have me. To plunge

myself into the heart of my life and be ruthlessly lost forever."

Gallagher's first marriage ended in divorce in 1968. She married the poet Michael Burkard in 1973; they were divorced in 1977. From 1977 until his death in August 1988 she lived with the short-story writer and poet Raymond Carver. They built a home overlooking the Straits of Juan de Fuca and the Olympic Mountains in Washington where she spends most of every year. Carver's influence on Gallagher's work—and hers on his work—was considerable. They collaborated on several screenplays. One of these was on the life of Dostoevsky which the director Michael Cimino planned to film with Carlo Ponti as producer. Though the film was never made, excerpts from the Carver-Gallagher scenario were published in 1985. Carver strongly encouraged Gallagher to write prose fiction. "I wouldn't have written this book of short stories," she said of *The Lover of Horses*, "if it hadn't been for him." They were married in June 1988, only three months before his death from lung cancer.

PRINCIPAL WORKS: *Poetry*—Stepping Outside, 1974; Instructions to the Double, 1976; Under Stars, 1978; Portable Kisses, 1978; On Your Own, 1978; Willingly, 1984; Amplitude, 1987. *Collected short stories*—The Lover of Horses, and Other Stories, 1986. *Screenplay*—(with R. Carver) Dostoevsky, 1985. *Essays*—A Concert of Tenses: Essays on Poetry, 1986.

ABOUT: Contemporary Authors 106, 1982; Contemporary Literary Criticism 18, 1981; Contemporary Poets, 4th ed., 1986; Gallagher, T. A Concert of Tenses, 1986; O'Connell, N. At the Field's End: Interviews with Pacific Northwest Writers, 1987. *Periodicals*—Atlantic Monthly June 1979; Harper's May 1979; New York Times September 6, 1986; August 3, 1988; New York Times Book Review August 26, 1984; September 28, 1986; Ontario Review Spring–Summer 1980; Prairie Schooner Winter 1975–1976.

GARDNER, HOWARD (July 11, 1943 –   ), American psychologist, writes: "Until now I have made my living as a research psychologist, carrying out studies of brain-damaged adults at the Boston Veterans Administration Medical Center as well as investigations of normal and gifted children at a Harvard University research site improbably called Project Zero. The life of the 'soft-money' researcher is not one which would have been familiar to our ancestors (and not one which I would have recommended to them either). I spend between one-third to one-fifth of my time writing grant applications to the government and to private foundations, describing experiments and observational studies which

HOWARD GARDNER

colleagues and I propose to carry out with our 'subjects.' The 'hit-rate' of grant applications is not high and so one must always apply for more grants than one wishes to have. Once received, the money is quickly put to work, as we hire research assistants, purchase computer time, pay subjects, travel to conferences, and the like. My colleagues and I write up our findings for technical journals, argue with reviewers and editors when our views do not jibe with theirs, and then hope that our publications will affect what subsequent researchers in psychology think and what they do. The greater the impact of our work, the greater the likelihood for additional funding and the opportunity to carry on work which we value—studies of the ways in which the mind develops in normal and gifted individuals and how it breaks down under conditions of brain disease.

"In one way I differ from the vast majority of my scientific colleagues. I enjoy writing for a non-technical audience and do so during much of my spare time. Perhaps surprisingly, this 'writing tic' does not endear me to colleagues: when I was invited to contribute a monthly column to *Psychology Today*, nearly all of my colleagues strongly urged me not to do so. I listened instead to the advice of one older friend and colleague who said 'Of course, all of us would do it too if we were asked.' Whether or not his assessment was correct, it ended up carrying the day.

"For as long as I can remember, I have always enjoyed writing. I cannot remember a sustained attack of writer's block. Indeed, as has been said of more than one inveterate scribbler, I have not fully digested an experience until I have written about it. In second grade I began a newspaper for my class and, ever since, I have been issuing one or another type of broadside to whoever would read it (and probably for myself in the absence of any readers). My busiest time was probably in high school, where I edited a news magazine called *The Opinator*, highly unusual in that it featured an equal amount of news and fictional-poetic material each week. Not surprisingly, the editorial board ended up writing most of the content and I learned to compose on command.

"I early overcame any incipient inhibitions about writing books. The year after I graduated from college I sat down in Switzerland and wrote a 1,000 page novel. The novel was so bad that I didn't even bother to bring it back home with me—it sits unlamented in a cousin's house in Paris. The novel served one purpose: it cured me of any latent urge I might have to write fiction. Then the following year, I was approached by a psychologist with a writer's block who asked me to help him write a textbook. This time, in the course of a summer I drafted an entire textbook which was subsequently published. My sponsor was gracious enough to convert my 'ghost status' to co-authorship.

"Since that time, I have never been very far from a typewriter or word processor. About half of my writing is for technical journals, though recently nearly all of this scientific writing has been co-authored. I like to help younger colleagues with their writing and am told that I am sometimes successful. The rest of my time at the keyboard is devoted to describing scientific work in language which non-experts can understand and may find engaging. I would like to think that this work has some originality and even, upon occasion, constitutes a scientific contribution in its own right. This represents a minority point of view, however: many of my scientific colleagues believe that anything written in plain language must be derivative or 'mere popularization.'

"My books cover a broad range within social science, from a study of structuralism (*The Quest for Mind*) to brain damage (*The Shattered Mind*) to children's drawings (*Artful Scribbles*). My occasional essays are collected in *Art, Mind, and Brain* and my best known (and controversial) work is *Frames of Mind*, in which I claim that humans are capable of developing seven different forms of intelligence. For many years my intellectual hero has been Edmund Wilson, an unbelievably wide-ranging author who had little patience for technical jargon and even less regard for psychology! I would like to think that he would nonetheless have admired William James, my favorite among psychologists who write for a wider public.

"I was born in 1943 in Scranton, Pennsylvania, the son of recent immigrants from Nazi Germany. While lacking in formal education, my parents are hard working and productive individuals. They are also lovers of learning— my father in history and politics, my mother in the arts, particularly music. In certain respects at least, Scranton was not as bad a place to grow up as I used to believe: I studied piano with good teachers, was allowed to roam the library, and had good friends ranging in age up to eighty or so. But my education began in earnest when I arrived as a freshman at Harvard in 1961. Since then, with the exception of one year in London and three months in China, I have remained happily in Cambridge, Mass. My first marriage, to Judy Gardner, produced three children (Kerith, born 1969; Jay, born 1971; and Andrew, born 1976). I am now remarried, to Ellen Winner, a close colleague, and we have a young son (Benjamin, born 1985). In 1987, I joined the Harvard faculty as a full time professor of education and the second half of what has so far been a good life commenced."

A working scientist who has also won recognition as a writer, Howard Gardner is neither a popularizer nor a publicist for any cause other than the widest possible dissemination of vital knowledge. Cognitive science, the area in which he has done major work, embraces all human culture. It is, as he defines it in *The Quest for Mind*, "a contemporary, empirically based attempt to address some longstanding questions in the area of philosophy . . . the nature of mental representation, the status of mind and body, the relationship between language and thought, the source of novel ideas." For Gardner such a definition includes not only the study of how humans think but also how they create. The ultimate goal of cognitive science, he suggests in *The Mind's New Science*, should be "to provide a cogent scientific account of how human beings achieve their most remarkable symbolic products: how we come to compose symphonies, write poems, invent machines . . . or construct theories."

The Mind's New Science traces the history of the "cognitive revolution" from Plato to Descartes to the emergence in the present age of the computer—"artificial intelligence." While acknowledging the indispensability of the computer ("the computer serves as the most viable model of how the human mind functions"),

Gardner is aware of its limitations, what he calls "the computational paradox"—its inability to account for human thought and behavior in all its subjectivity and irrationality. The computer has facilitated and accelerated the work of cognitive science, but its progress depends on the pursuit of a broad base of disciplines ranging from anthropology and linguistics to neuropsychology.

Gardner's interest in the cognitive sciences began with his undergraduate and graduate training in philosophy and social psychology. His early research was with young children, studying their developing use of language. He moved from here to the study of the effects of brain injury or brain disease on language use, working with the Aphasia Unit of Boston's Veterans Administration Hospital. Out of this experience he wrote *The Shattered Mind: The Person after Brain Damage*. Having studied both the mentally damaged and the mentally developing, he became convinced that human intelligence is not a single faculty but a complex of multiple intelligences. In *Frames of Mind* he explores seven broad categories of intelligence, adding to the traditional verbal, mathematical, and spatial, four more intelligences—musical, physical, social, and self-knowledge. With his emphasis on multiple intelligences, Gardner has challenged the traditional measurement of intelligence by examinations like the Stanford-Binet I.Q. tests, which have been under challenge for many years as culturally biased. Gardner rejects a single measurement. Studying the musical and artistic skills of children in nursery school as part of Harvard's Project Zero, he is continuing to investigate other methods of measuring human intelligence.

Gardner's contributions to cognitive science have won him many honors including a Mac-Arthur fellowship (1981–1986) and an award for excellence from the American Psychological Association for *Frames of Mind* in 1984. His books, heavily documented and based on impressive bibliographies, make no compromise with serious scholarship, but his ability to write lucidly and gracefully, with a minimum of technical language, makes them interesting and sometimes exciting reading. Jonathan Sharp, writing in the *San Francisco Chronicle*, describes his books as "advocacy scholarship of the highest order." Richard M. Restak, a neurologist himself, reviewing *The Shattered Mind* in the *New York Times Book Review*, wrote that "ground-breaking neuropsychologists like Howard Gardner are helping to bring about in our own lifetime a synthesis that has been years in the making. the final reconciliation between brain scientists on the one hand and a potpourri of psychiatrists, psychologists, and psychothera-pists—all sharing a common interest in behavior, but lacking the communality of concept neces-sary to achieve a final synthesis of the mind-brain problem."

PRINCIPAL WORKS: (with M. Grossack) Man and Men: So-cial Psychology as Social Science, 1970; The Quest for Mind: Jean Piaget, Claude Lévi-Strauss, and the Struc-turalist Movement, 1973, 1981; The Arts and Human Development, 1973; The Shattered Mind, 1975; De-velopmental Psychology: An Introduction, 1978, 1982; Artful Scribbles: The Significance of Children's Draw-ings, 1980; Art, Mind, and Brain: A Cognitive Ap-proach to Creativity, 1982; Frames of Mind: The Theory of Multiple Intelligences, 1983; The Mind's New Science; A History of the Cognitive Revolution, 1985; To Open Minds: Chinese Clues to the Dilemmas of Contemporary Education, 1989. As editor—(with J. Gardner) Classics in Psychology, 1973, 1975; (with E. Winner) Fact, Fiction, and Fantasy in Childhood, 1979; (with H. Kelly) Viewing Children through Tele-vision, 1981.

ABOUT: Contemporary Authors New Revision Series 9, 1983. Periodicals—Discover Magazine October 1985; New Republic February 24, 1986; New York Times Book Review March 2, 1975; April 6, 1980; October 13, 1985; Newsweek November 14, 1983; Psychology Today June 1984; San Francisco Chronicle Review Oc-tober 6, 1985; Times Literary Supplement January 20, 1978; U.S. News and World Report March 19, 1984.

GARDNER, MARTIN (October 21, 1914–), American writer on science and edi-tor, was born in Tulsa, Oklahoma, the son of James Henry Gardner and the former Willie Spiers. He has never in any of his voluminous writings described in detail his parents or his childhood, except to refer once (in his personal philosophical accounting, The Whys of a Philo-sophical Scrivener) to being brought up with "an ugly Protestant fundamentalism," which he "outgrew . . . slowly." He also loved the Oz books as a small child and was interested in mu-sic and chess from an early age. Each of these as-pects of his life received attention from him as an adult writer.

After earning his bachelor's degree from the University of Chicago in 1936, Gardner re-turned to Tulsa, where he found work as a cub reporter on the Tribune. He spent World War II in the U.S. Naval Reserve (1942–1946), then joined the public relations staff of the University of Chicago. While in that position, in 1946, he attended a seminar given by the renowned theo-retical physicist Rudolf Carnap. Twenty years later, after more than a decade's worth of exact-ing editing by Gardner, Carnap (who rarely

MARTIN GARDNER

published on science for the general reader) brought out Philosophical Foundations of Phys-ics: An Introduction to the Philosophy of Science, a book widely considered a masterful summary of an abstruse and demanding subject.

As an editor, Gardner was to accomplish a great deal more, far removed from the field of science. He can fairly be said to have originated a particular kind of popular edition, the annotated reprinting of beloved literary classics. He turned his attention first to L. Frank Baum, and with a coeditor, Russell B. Nye, published The Wizard of Oz & Who He Was, a rather lightly annotated edition, with an introductory essay by each of the coeditors, of the most cen-tral of the Oz books. In his own essay, Gardner calls Baum "America's greatest writer of chil-dren's fantasy, . . . as everyone knows except li-brarians and critics of juvenile literature. . . . By and large, the critics have looked upon Baum's efforts as tawdry popular writing in a class with Tom Swift and Elsie Dinsmore; . . . fortunately, children themselves seldom listen to such learned opinion. . . . [Baum's books are] well written, rich in excitement, humor, and philosophy, and with sustained imaginative in-vention of the highest order."

Gardner's next editorial project became what is undoubtedly his single best-known book. The Annotated Alice: Alice's Adventures in Wonder-land & Through the Looking Glass by Lewis Carroll is a reprinting, with a helpful and illumi-nating introduction, of the widely read (though not perhaps very fully understood) fantasy by C. L. Dodgson, the nineteenth-century Oxford mathematician and pedophile. In his introduction, the editor calls *Alice* "a very curious, complicated kind of nonsense, written for British readers of another century, and we need to know a great many things that are not part of the text if we wish to capture its full wit and flavor. It is even worse than that, for some of Carroll's jokes could be understood only by residents of Oxford, and other jokes, still more private, could be understood only by the lovely daughters of Dean Liddell." Further work on Dodgson resulted in *The Annotated Snark: The Full Text of Lewis Carroll's Great Nonsense Epic The Hunting of the Snark and the Original Illustrations by Henry Holiday*, an edition of what Gardner calls the "surrealist poem . . . over which an unstable, sensitive soul might very well go mad," and *The Wasp in a Wig: A "Suppressed" Episode of Through the Looking-Glass and What Alice Found There*. Other "annotated" volumes by Gardner include *The Annotated Ancient Mariner; The Annotated Casey at the Bat: A Collection of Ballads about the Mighty Casey*, an edition of "the nation's best known piece of comic verse—a ballad that began a native legend as colorful and permanent as the legend[s] of Johnny Appleseed or Paul Bunyan and his blue ox"; and *The Annotated Innocence of Father Brown*, a well-received version of twelve stories featuring G. K. Chesterton's amiable little priest, described by Gardner as "by all odds the second most famous mystery-solver in English literature, and he has always had a devoted following, not just in England, but throughout the world."

Gardner worked for a decade as contributing editor of *Humpty Dumpty's* magazine, an endearingly old-fashioned publication for which, each month, he wrote a short story (about Humpty Junior), none of which have been reprinted, and a poem of moral advice, twenty of which were revised and reprinted as *Never Make Fun of a Turtle, My Son*. In his next regular writing assignment, for *Scientific American*, the author produced each month from December 1956 until he stopped in 1981 a column, "Mathematical Games," which became a popular although by the end somewhat predictable feature of the magazine. Through 1988, no fewer than twelve book-length collections of these columns have appeared, with the original pieces often corrected, updated, or expanded by Gardner on the basis of letters from knowledgeable and alert readers. In addition, since 1976 the author has been a regular contributor to *Isaac Asimov's Science Fiction Magazine*, composing each month a puzzle clothed in a science-fiction or fantasy story line. The first thirty-six of these were published as *Science Fiction Puzzle Tales*, the next thirty-seven as *Puzzles from Other Worlds*.

Among Gardner's more extended writing on scientific subjects should be noted *Logic Machines and Diagrams*, a brief but penetrating study of that ancient branch of scientific discovery, the mechanization of thought. He begins his narrative in thirteenth-century Europe with a disquisition on the *Ars Magna* of Ramon Lull, in which he describes the mechanical devices and systems of an inspired Catalonian madman. He then pursues the idea through the intervening centuries to our own, considering the systems devised by Charles, Earl Stanhope (1753–1816), William Stanley Jevons (1835–1882), and Allan Marquand (1853–1924), through early electrical machines to the leading edge of today's computer-based work on machine intelligence. In another full-length book, *The Ambidextrous Universe: Mirror Asymmetry and Time-Reversed Worlds*, he examines the idea of mirror-reflection symmetry and the relatively new doctrine of parity nonconversion in physics. The book seeks to answer three questions: What is parity? How was it overthrown? Why are physicists so excited? "We begin with a deceptively simple question about mirrors. After examining the nature of mirror reversals in one, two, and three dimensions, followed by an interlude on left and right in magic and the fine arts, we plunge into a wide-ranging exploration of left-right symmetry and asymmetry in the natural world. This exploration culminates in an account of the fall of parity and an attempt to relate its fall to some of the deepest mysteries in modern physics."

For several years Gardner has been an active member of a group known as the Committee for Scientific Investigation of Claims of the Paranormal. This committee has made what are widely considered valuable contributions to society in general and science in particular by carefully investigating and debunking popular (and, especially in contemporary America, very widespread) pseudoscientific frauds and delusions. He has been writing about pseudoscience since *Fads and Fallacies in the Name of Science* (which is a revised edition of his earlier *In the Name of Science*); his more recent articles and reviews on the subject are collected in *Science: Good, Bad and Bogus* and its more philosophical and literary sequel, *Order and Surprise*, volumes in which he attacks such phenomena as ESP, parapsychics, psychokinesis, precognition, UFOs, faith healing, psychic surgery, the orgone box sex theories of Wilhelm Reich, the synchronicity theories of latter-day Jungians, and the biorhythmics.

Dealt by Gardner not easily classifiable into any of the already mentioned categories are *The Whys of a Philosophical Scrivener*, whose introduction reads, in toto, "This is a book of essays about what I believe and why." In twenty-one chapters and in an easy, almost chatty style, he treats such vast subjects as the world, truth, beauty, goodness, science, the state, faith, prayer, evil, and immortality. *The Wreck of the Titanic Foretold?* examines and debunks as many aspects as the author can find of "the amazing mystique that has developed around the sinking of the *Titanic.*" This mystique has lasted so long, Gardner supposes, because "it springs from the ironic juxtaposition of a titanic pride—the belief on the part of everyone concerned that this floating museum of conspicuous waste could not be sunk—and the unexpected suddenness with which that belief was shattered. . . . Like the fall of Babylon, the *Titanic*'s sinking can be taken as a symbol of the crumbling of proud empires with their similar mix of the rich, the middle class, and the poor—all going down together." He reprints several examples of seeming precognition—stories, poems, and other accounts of coincidence and clairvoyance, including "the single most impressive example," Morgan Robertson's short novel, *Futility* (1898), which tells of the wreck of a ship called the *Titan* and has many other parallels of its own with the actual story of the disaster which occurred fourteen years later.

Gardner's only work of fiction, *The Flight of Peter Fromm*, is a novel of ideas exploring conflicting aspects of Protestant theology. The narrator is a secular humanist, the protagonist a "persistent theist." "I tried to explain," the author recalled in a chapter of *The Whys* . . . , "why I think it more honest to call oneself a non-Christian than to continue to call oneself a Christian after abandoning belief in the historicity of those myths that support the central doctrines of the Church."

WORKS: *Non-fiction*—In the Name of Science, 1952; Mathematics, Magic and Mystery, 1956; Fads and Fallacies in the Name of Science, 1957; Logic Machines and Diagrams, 1958; The Scientific American Book of Mathematical Puzzles and Diversions, 1959; The Arrow Book of Brain Teasers, 1959; Science Puzzlers, 1960; The Second Scientific American Book of Mathematical Puzzles and Diversions, 1961; Mathematical Puzzles, 1961; Relativity for the Million, 1962; The Ambidextrous Universe, 1964, rev. ed., 1979; Archimedes, Mathematician and Inventor, 1965; New Mathematical Diversions, 1967; The Numerology of Dr. Matrix, 1967; Logic Machines, Diagrams, and Boulean Algebra, 1968; The Unexpected Hanging, and Other Mathematical Diversions, 1969; Perplexing Puzzles and Tantalizing Teasers, 1969; Never Make Fun of a Turtle, My Son, 1969; Space Puzzles, 1971; The Sixth Book of Mathematical Games from Scientific American, 1971; Codes, Ciphers, and Secret Writing, 1972; The Snark Puzzle Book, 1973; Mathematical Carnival, 1975; The Incredible Dr. Matrix, 1976; Mathematical Magic Show, 1977; More Perplexing Puzzles and Tantalizing Teasers, 1977; Aha! Insight, 1978; Mathematical Circus, 1979; Science Fiction Puzzle Tales, 1981; Science: Good, Bad and Bogus, 1981; Aha! Gotcha, 1982; Wheels, Life, and Other Mathematical Amusements, 1983; The Whys of a Philosophical Scrivener, 1983; Order and Surprise, 1983; Puzzles from Other Worlds, 1984; Knotted Doughnuts and Other Mathematical Entertainments, 1986; The Wreck of the Titanic Foretold?, 1986; Time Travel and Other Mathematical Bewilderments, 1988; The New Age: Notes of a Fringe Watcher, 1988; Gardner's Whys & Wherefores, 1989. *As editor*—(with R. B. Nye) L. Frank Baum, The Wizard of Oz & Who He Was, 1957; Great Essays in Science, 1957; Sam Loyd, Best Mathematical Puzzles of Sam Loyd, vol. 1, 1957, vol. 2, 1960; Lewis Carroll, The Annotated Alice, 1960; C. C. Bombaugh, Oddities and Curiosities of Words and Literature, 1961; Lewis Carroll, The Annotated Snark, 1962; Samuel Taylor Coleridge, The Annotated Ancient Mariner, 1965; Rudolf Carnap, Philosophical Foundations of Physics, 1966, rev. ed., 1974; Ernest L. Thayer, The Annotated Casey at the Bat, 1967, rev. ed., 1984; Henry E. Dudeney, 536 Puzzles and Curious Problems, 1967; Boris Kordemsky, Moscow Puzzles, 1971; Koban Fujimura, Tokyo Puzzles, 1978; Lewis Carroll, The Wasp in a Wig, 1978; The Annotated Innocence of Father Brown, 1987. *Fiction*—The Flight of Peter Fromm, 1973.

ABOUT: Contemporary Authors 73–76, 1978. *Periodicals*—American Scholar Autumn 1977; Choice December 1967, December 1981, April 1982, December 1983; Christian Science Monitor February 23, 1960; January 10, 1963; February 2, 1963; October 28, 1981; February 24, 1982; Commonweal November 18, 1960; April 20, 1984; Harper August 1963; Library Journal September 1, 1958; January 15, 1960; May 1, 1960; January 15, 1961; October 1, 1961; October 1, 1962; November 1, 1966; September 15, 1967; September 15, 1973; October 1, 1975; April 15, 1981; October 15, 1981; September 1, 1983; May 15, 1985; Nation June 25, 1960; September 10, 1973; New York Review of Books February 4, 1982; December 8, 1983; New York Times March 14, 1986; New York Times Book Review August 13, 1981; November 18, 1962; April 7, 1963; September 10, 1967; October 1, 1967; December 23, 1973; November 7, 1976; February 14, 1982; May 26, 1985; New Yorker December 20, 1952; October 8, 1979; Saturday Review January 24, 1953; December 17, 1960; October 6, 1962; Science Books & Films May–June 1962; January–February 1983; March–April 1984; Scientific American December 1982; Time April 9, 1979; August 10, 1981; January 11, 1982; Times Literary Supplement February 15, 1963; December 25, 1981; December 2, 1983; August 4, 1988; Yale Review October 1973.

*GEERTZ, CLIFFORD (August 23, 1926–   ), American anthropologist, writes: "I think I became a writer, and quite possibly an anthropological writer, because my parents' di-

CLIFFORD GEERTZ

vorce when I was about three projected me immediately into an unfamiliar, and somewhat unpalatable, world I had to understand if I was going to prosper at all. I was sent to live with a foster mother, no relative, in a small village in northern California, and soon learned, especially after I got into a small rural school at the age of six, that if I was ever going to get out of a difficult situation my best bet was by using my head, and the best thing I was good at using my head with was writing. The first notion was to be a newspaperman, the second to be a novelist, only the last—in college in the late forties—to be a scholar.

"I remained in that village, full of solitude and fantasy, until the Second World War liberated me by taking me into the Navy. After the war, I had the GI Bill and went to Antioch College, about as far from 'home' as I could at the time, where I was first an English major and then a philosophy major. A few weeks before I graduated, anxious to go to graduate school in something or other, someone suggested to me anthropology might be a good idea, which, after talking to some anthropologists—Margaret Mead, Clyde Kluckhohn—I decided (as did my then wife, who was also an English major) I too thought it might.

"I don't know what that makes me: an unfulfilled newspaperman or novelist, or someone who finally found the place where he could be a writer. I think the latter, and as an anthropologist, I have been always concerned with it as a form of writing as well as a field of study. This irritates some people, who think social science

that is readable can't be serious, but it pleases me. I get to go to other villages I don't understand and try to make sense of them for myself and to do so in prose; I get to read just about anything that interests me, for anthropology has only the fuzziest of intellectual boundaries; and I get to think of my life as having had some sort of coherence. The last is not so, but I have at least, this way, a plausible story to tell."

In the intellectual self-scrutiny characteristic among many academic disciplines in recent years, social scientists have debated a central question: Where is the "science" in the social sciences? Can the study of human society be based on the same principles of objective research as the study of the physical universe? As an anthropologist whose career has been equally divided between field work (in Indonesia and North Africa) and theory (teaching and research), Clifford Geertz has given that question close examination. His answer is that anthropology is not an experimental science in search of laws of the universe, but an interpretive study in search of the meaning of human activity, what he calls "the informal logic of actual life."

Born in San Francisco to Clifford James Geertz, an engineer, and Lois (Brigger) Geertz, he had his early schooling in California and served in the U.S. Navy from 1943 to 1945. He attended Antioch College in Ohio, from which he received his B.A. in 1950. Geertz began his career in anthropology as a graduate student at Harvard. Appointed a research assistant at the Center for International Studies at the Massachusetts Institute of Technology in 1952, he began preparing for his field work by studying the Javanese language. He continued his study of Javanese in the Netherlands and lived for a year (1953–1954) in a rural Indonesian town, Modjokuto, with his wife, Hildred Storey Geertz, herself now a distinguished anthropologist. Divorced in 1981, they had married while still undergraduates at Antioch in 1948, and they collaborated in their field research. During their year in Modjokuto they lived with a native family and, without the aid of an interpreter, participated actively in community life. In his book *The Religion of Java*, he recalls their experiences: "This total sink-or-swim commitment to Javanese fairly soon led to at least a relatively high degree of fluency and comprehension, and the knowledge of the language thus attained proved to be by far the single most important research tool in the investigation of religious beliefs and practices." Not only religion, but every aspect of life in Modjokuto was of interest to the

Geertzes and prepared them for their future careers.

After receiving his Ph.D. from Harvard in 1956 and spending a year there as research associate and instructor in social relations, Geertz returned to Indonesia in 1957 as research associate in the Center for International Studies based at MIT. From 1958 to 1959 he was a fellow at the Stanford Center for Advanced Study in Behavioral Sciences, and in 1958 he became an assistant professor of anthropology at the University of California in Berkeley. From 1960 to 1970 he taught at the University of Chicago. Since 1970 he has been professor of social science in the Institute for Advanced Study at Princeton University. He has also had an appointment, since 1975, as visiting professor in Princeton's Department of History.

Geertz began publishing essays in scholarly journals as early as 1956. His first book was *The Religion of Java* reporting the results of his six years of field work in that country. He organized his study around "the three main social-structural nuclei in Java today." These are the village, the market, and the government bureaucracy. His aim, he writes, was "good ethnographic reporting" in which "the ethnographer is able to get out of the way of his data, to make himself translucent so that the reader can see for himself something of what the facts look like and so judge the ethnographer's summaries and generalizations in terms of the ethnographer's actual perceptions." In what was to become characteristic of his later work, Geertz focussed on single customs or rituals for in-depth study, showing the rich texture, the depth and complexity of human social activities. Social structure, as he perceives it, is "a network" of inter-acting forces. A whole culture cannot be defined, he acknowledges, by study of any single cultural institution, but study of representative social activities reveals the interdependency of culture and social structure. As he wrote in his second book, *Agricultural Involution: The Process of Ecological Change in Indonesia*, a study of the economic problems of a society emerging from Dutch colonial rule: "In most general terms, this book is an attempt to apply to the interpretation of—in this case economic—history, some concepts and findings of social anthropology, to utilize the insights derived from microsociological analysis for understanding macrosociological problems, and to establish a fruitful interaction between the biological, social, and historical sciences." Thus a single rural town like Modjokuto offers a case history revealing basic elements common to other areas of the underdeveloped third world.

In other books based on his field work in Indonesia, Geertz has traced the developing history of communities not as a chronological series of events, but in terms of "the changing forms of a particular sort of human community . . . an attempt not so much to re-create the past as to discover its sociological character" (*The Social History of an Indonesian Town*). From ritual practices to everyday customs to individual perceptions—a religious feast, a cockfight, a street bazaar in a Moroccan town, the way the Balinese define each other by name and title—all these "patterns of cumulative activity" are to Geertz "significant symbols" through which "man makes sense of the world in which he lives."

Clifford Geertz first came to the attention of a non-specialist readership with a collection of his essays written over a fifteen-year period, *The Interpretation of Cultures*. The first of these essays, "Thick Description: Toward an Interpretive Theory of Culture," presents his fundamental belief that "the aim of anthropology is the enlargement of the universe of human discourse." Writing in a prose that Ronald G. Walters described in *Social Research* as "grammatically correct, fairly jargon-free and intelligible to normal human beings," and others have praised as lucid and often witty, Geertz appeals to the general reader who can appreciate his wealth of philosophical, historical, and literary allusions (he does not name-drop but refers appositely to writers ranging from Burckhardt and Marc Bloch to Wittgenstein and Ryle, to Flaubert, Faulkner, and Robert Lowell), and the thoroughly humanistic character of his work.

For Geertz, writing anthropology is analogous to making fiction. An interpretive approach to anthropology does not work from or toward rigid laws but "reads" or interprets the symbols by which a society operates. He is indebted to sociologists like Max Weber and Talcott Parsons for recognizing that a culture and the social structure in which it exists are interdependent: "The concept of culture I espouse . . . is essentially a semiotic one. Believing, with Max Weber, that man is an animal suspended in webs of significance he himself has spun, I take culture to be those webs, and the analysis of it to be therefore not an experimental science in search of law but an interpretive one in search of meaning. It is explication I am after, construing social expressions on their surface enigmatical." Geertz studies "the anthropologist as author" in *Works and Lives*—an analysis of the writing, in terms of its form and rhetoric, of such well known anthropologists as Bronislaw Malinowski, Ruth Benedict, Claude Lévi-Strauss and E. E. Evans-Pritchard.

Widely acknowledged today as, in Richard Schweder's words, "America's most renowned cultural anthropologist," his work cited often by social historians and literary critics, Geertz has been the subject of considerable controversy within his own field. Several issues of the journal *Current Anthropology* carried a debate on his interpretive theory that grew out of a seminar held at the University of Colorado in Boulder in 1982. Here Paul Shankman hailed Geertz as a figure "of strategic importance in the rebirth of an American cultural anthropology" and described his work as "an attempt to refocus anthropology—indeed all of social science—away from the emulation of the natural sciences and toward a reintegration with the humanities." Some anthropologists, however, criticized his work as lacking in exactness, too "inward," "imaginative but often flawed," while others questioned whether his ideas are really revolutionary since many of them can be traced back to the writings of Franz Boas and his disciples.

Like his essay "Thick Description," Geertz's "Blurred Genres: The Refiguration of Social Thought" (first published in the *American Scholar* in 1980, reprinted in his collection *Local Knowledge*) was a fresh and discerning look at the whole field of the social sciences, the identity of which he finds to be a "seemingly anomalous state of affairs." He urges social scientists and historians alike to look to the humanities—to cultural history, law, linguistics, aesthetics, and literature—"for illumination, rather than they used to do, to mechanics or physiology." Noting the "enormous amount of genre mixing in intellectual life in recent years and the consequent blurring of borders—novelists who introduce real life characters, philosophers who write literary criticism, scientists who write belles lettres, historians who work with graphs and equations"—he concludes: "one waits only for quantum theory in verse or biography in algebra." Geertz is sanguine about such developments because he feels that they have given social scientists freedom "to shape their work in terms of its necessities rather than according to received ideas as to what they ought or ought not to be doing." But he cautions that "the relation between thought and action in social life can no more be conceived of in terms of wisdom than it can in terms of expertise. How it is to be conceived, how the games, dramas, or texts that we do not just invent or witness but live have the consequence they do remains very far from clear. It will take the wariest of wary reasonings, on all sides of all divides, to get it clearer."

In 1986 Geertz revisited Indonesia, returning to the town where he had done his first major field work thirty years earlier. It was an occasion for reflection on his career and on the changing nature of anthropology itself. He was more than ever convinced that anthropology could not follow the disciplines of the physical sciences if it was to arrive at knowledge of other cultures, nor could it continue to assume vast cultural gulfs between the anthropologists and the peoples who are being studied. In *Works and Lives*, winner of the National Book Critics Circle Award for non-fiction in 1987, he even questions whether Western observers can really understand those "enigmatical others on the grounds that you have gone about with them in their native habitat." So much has changed, he observed in a lecture at New York University in May 1988—in substance and in subtle matters like emotional, moral and personal tonalities—"that some flickering vision of what might be going on and where over all, we might be going, comes uncertainly into view, soon to dissolve again into a ragged multiplicity."

PRINCIPAL WORKS: The Religion of Java, 1960; Agricultural Involution: the Processes of Ecological Change in Indonesia, 1963; Peddlers and Princes: Social Change and Economic Modernization; The Social History of an Indonesian Town, 1965; Person, Time and Conduct in Bali: An Essay in Cultural Analysis, 1966; Islam Observed: Religious Development in Morocco and Indonesia, 1968; The Interpretation of Cultures: Selected Essays, 1973; (with H. Geertz) Kinship in Bali, 1975; (with H. Geertz and L. Rosen) Meaning and Order in Moroccan Society, 1979; Negara: The Theatre State in Nineteenth Century Bali, 1980; Local Knowledge: Further Essays in Interpretive Anthropology, 1983; Works and Lives: The Anthropologist as Author, 1988.

ABOUT: Contemporary Authors 33–36, 1978; Devine, E. (ed.) Thinkers of the Twentieth Century, 1983; Who's Who in America 1988–1989. *Periodicals*—Current Anthropology June 1984, August 1984, December 1984, April 1985, December 1985; New York Times May 11, 1988; New York Times Book Review February 28, 1988; Social Research Autumn 1980; Times Literary Supplement, August 26, 1988.

GHISELIN, BREWSTER (June 13, 1903–), American poet, writes: "The founder of my family in America, the Huguenot goldsmith and silversmith Cesar Ghiselin, came through England before the end of the seventeenth century to settle in Philadelphia. His descendants, artisans and men of regional affairs, lived in the tidewater regions of Maryland and Virginia until, at the end of the Civil War, my grandfather, newly married after his return from the battlefields, settled in Webster Groves, a town on the outskirts of St. Louis, where after the turn of the century I was born. My maternal

°gēz´ lin

BREWSTER GHISELIN

grandfather, of older New England ancestry, married the daughter of a fiercely partisan Southerner. As a child, looking to that past, I was educated by divergent loyalties.

"The language spoken at home, and often read aloud, was that of the American midlands, qualified by the accents of New England and the Virginian South. It was supplemented by the Negro dialect of those days, remarkable in economy and force and great in ebullience and rhythmic charm. My parents were readers of literature, talented in use of words, my mother a graduate of the school of speech at Northwestern University. Shakespeare was read to me before I was old enough to sense more than the wonder of it. I memorized poems of Tennyson for the delight of repeating them. Living with little thought of the future, between the wide and wild countryside and one of the older centers of commerce and culture, knowing waterfront and markets and libraries and museums, I rarely felt any pressure of enclosure.

"But when I was nearly seventeen the family moved to California, across the long west, by train. The deserts provided sensory comprehension of a widening perspective. Coming to the ocean, I found new images of distance unbounded and depths virtually fathomless. That opening of the visible world was of the subjective sphere also. Swimming the surf, I found rhythmic energies relevant for life and art. Living the next year in Marin County, north of San Francisco, a sparsely settled, wildly beautiful region, reached by ferryboats plying the Bay, I finished high school. After a term at the University of California, crossing the Bay in delight of water and winds, but disappointed by plod and constriction of freshman classes, I worked a while as a newspaper reporter, before going south to take a degree in English, with a minor in philosophy, 1927, then north again for the M.A. at Berkeley, 1928.

"During a year as a graduate student at Oxford I learned more of academic life, but found compensations in encounter with some of the men there, in particular Sir Michael Sadler, Master of University College, a generous collector of works of art, and on the Continent through contact with such men as Llewelyn Powys, and most at length and especially, D. H. Lawrence. Writing some of the poems that are in my first book, *Against the Circle*, I began to see what I was about. The poems described by that title adumbrate more clearly the insight I had phrased for myself as an undergraduate: 'The precincts of the mind must be also the courts of the sun.'

"Thinking to shape my life in that realization, I went in 1929 to teach at the University of Utah. There I learned at length to accord scholarly duties with the passions of life—and to neglect neither. The outgrowth of that discipline, learned partly through teaching others, was a mode of behavior advanced in my courses, particularly 'The Creative Process,' introduced in 1941, and through The Writers' Conference which I founded in 1947 and directed for two decades.

"My 'Foreword, 1985' in the new paperback edition of my book *The Creative Process*, in print now for a third of a century, cites testimony of a noted psychologist in emphasis upon the scope and centrality of my characterization of creativity. I believe all the insight I have tried to reveal in prose is most fully exhibited, however, concretely and with richest implications, in my poetry."

————

Brewster Ghiselin's first volume of poetry was not published until he was over forty, but the quality of his work had already been recognized by the small audience who read poetry journals and by the students and professional writers who had known him at the University of Utah. The poet and critic Allen Tate, who met him in 1946 at one of the series of writers' conferences which Ghiselin directed, attributed his relative obscurity to his reticence: "It has never occurred to Brewster Ghiselin, in the course of what is now a long life, that three-fourths of a literary reputation is the result of self-dramatization. For Ghiselin the total job of the poet is to write the poems, and then the poet withdraws." A score of other distinguished writers who contributed to

The Water of Light: A Miscellany in Honor of Brewster Ghiselin made similar observations. His lifelong dedication to teaching and writing, the quiet, meditative nature of his poetry, his almost classical vision of a harmonious, transcendent universe, and his painstaking concern with form have kept Ghiselin out of the mainstream of contemporary poetry. Yet few poets span the history of modern poetry more completely. He began writing poetry as a contemporary of D. H. Lawrence, T. S. Eliot, and John Peale Bishop, and his career has moved steadily through all the revolutionary movements of twentieth-century literature. In "Answering a Letter from a Younger Poet" he reflects on those who will come after him:

> What shall I say but, having written for use,
> I am glad, hearing that others shape, with words
> Made for my ear and stride, a life like mine.

The poets he admires, he writes, are those like Lawrence and Bishop "Because they made of momentary ways / Their being." Out of the very transitoriness of nature, "Those men divined a measure, then a thought." His own resolution has an almost classical stoicism—

> Twenty-five years ago alone in foam
> Between the brown and blue of noon I climbed
> The hill of change in instantaneous flame
> Up the thrown slope of an enormous wave
> To a height toppling like a bathing swan.

tempered with a faith in the brotherhood of man and the purity of art:

> I have found no definition of a man
> But in that change, where now you hear and move
> Even in that loneliest wave we are not alone.

Fascinated with the creative process, which he describes in the introduction to his collection of essays on that subject by artists, writers, composers, dancers, mathematicians, and scientists as "the process of change, of development, of evolution, in the organization of subjective life," Ghiselin emphasizes "understanding, discipline, and hard work"—"the concentration of a life"—as the essential demands of creativity. But above and beyond all that is the need for experimentation, invention, risk-taking: "The alien, the dangerous, like the negligible near thing, may seem irrelevant to purpose and yet be the call to our own fruitful development." Like nature, the creative process is subject to constant change and growth, and it is constantly assimilating and shaping. In a poem, as in the human body, "the parts tend to merge into one another without absolute demarcation, often have multi-

ple functions, are at the same time one thing and another thing, escaping the outlines of any one pattern applied in abstract analysis."

The central images of Ghiselin's poetry are drawn from nature—in sensitive descriptions of both the grandeur and the minutiae of natural forms and of animal life, and in myths that themselves grew out of nature. Kathleen Raine describes his work, in *Sewanee Review*, as "a poetry of modern, complex man's re-confrontation with virgin Nature, with the myth of Eden." In the long poem "Sea," which is generally regarded as his masterpiece, his perception of man's alienation from but ultimate reunion with nature has its expression in a passage in which the poet, walking along the seashore, finds a human skull washed up on the beach:

> . . . Dead or alive,
> Brimming ambiguous music like a shell—
> What is it but a husk of whispers. Breathless,
> It sighed to me: "I grieve to think how I wasted,
> When I was dressed in delight, my dearth of hours
> In being so careful to shun both pain and filth.
> I would be glad, having the brown dung
> Daubing my flesh or blood flowing from it—
> Now I am a clicking system of reminders."

Although he has written in a variety of metrical forms, Ghiselin has never written free verse. The measure he favors is accentual, "a strongly stressed and syllabically various flow that I first heard clearly when I read *Beowulf* in Old English and turned to my own freer use, long before I read any of Gerard Manley Hopkins." A passage from "The Catch," a poem about a hunt for a rattlesnake that leads to the capture of a badger who fights back desperately, is representative of his long line, his use of assonance and alliteration:

> A badger strap-throttled, flipping like a marlin,
> battling
>   like a bull on a gaff
> And snoring anger till over his bravery and
> scuffling the
>   door of a cage clapped.

But the animal continues to fight

> . . . He never slept—
> Daylong, nightlong. His furious freedom resounded. At
> starlit dawn
> Jaws and claws rasping and thudding thump of his
> thunder drummed once. Long
>
> Silences rang for him, cage-eater greedy of snakes,
> abroad in the dawn.

Ghiselin has received awards for his work from the Ford Foundation (1952–1953), the National Institute of Arts and Letters (1970), and the Utah Arts Council (1982), as well as *Poetry* magazine's Blumenthal-Leviton-Blonder Prize (1973) and the Levinson Prize (1978). Now professor emeritus at the University of Utah, Ghiselin lives in Salt Lake City. He has been married since 1929 to Olive Franks. They have two sons. In addition to writing poetry, he is continuing his studies in the creative process and in twentieth-century literature. His collection of verse from 1929 to 1979, *Windrose*, won the William Carlos Williams Award in 1981. Among the more recently written poems in that volume is "For the Eighth Decade":

> Darkness and cold sweeten the wild persimmons.
> Up to my hundredth year,
> I thought, I would take my fill of that ripe harvest.
>
> But now that the withered rounds
> of the rich substance sag on the tree in the great
> square of the bull's pasture
>
> I stand by the barbed wire we sprinted from
> across long frosts of autumn
> to climb and feed close to that hot bull-back
>
> till dusk or animal peace
> swayed him away. Avid and glad, I taste
> the tightening bite of the green
>
> fruit: bitter, astringent, pungent, sweetening the feast
> with sweet of the feast complete.

PRINCIPAL WORKS: *Poetry*—Against the Circle, 1946; The Nets, 1955; Country of the Minotaur, 1970; Light, 1978; Windrose: Poems, 1929–1979, 1980. *Prose*—Writing, 1959, 1963; The Creative Process: A Symposium, Edited and with an Introduction, 1952, 1985.

ABOUT: Contemporary Authors New Revision Series 13, 1984; Contemporary Literary Criticism, 1983; Contemporary Poets, 4th ed., 1985; Taylor, Henry (ed.) The Water of Light: A Miscellany in Honor of Brewster Ghiselin, 1976; Who's Who in America 1988–89. *Periodicals*—Concerning Poetry Fall 1970; Counter Measures 1974; Nation January 25, 1971; Sewanee Review Spring 1971; Michigan Quarterly Review Fall 1971, Winter 1977; Poetry March 1972; Western Humanities Review Summer 1981.

*GHOSE, ZULFIKAR (March 13, 1935–), Indo-Pakistani poet, novelist, short-story writer and critic, was born in Sialkot (a city in East Punjab, close to the Indo-Pakistani border, which became part of West Pakistan after the Partition of India in 1947). Ghose spent his first seven years in Sialkot, in relatively prosperous circumstances, in the midst of an extended family. He often refers to this period in terms that suggest the memory of having lived in the midst of an organic community which retained a

ZULFIKAR GHOSE

strong sense of continuity. His family moved from Sialkot to Bombay in 1942 and Ghose spent the next ten years in this metropolitan, predominantly Hindu city, a Muslim in a Hindu environment at a time when the conflict between the two communities was becoming increasingly violent. The Partition and Independence of India only confirmed his growing sense of alienation, and in 1952 Ghose and his family left for England. In his autobiography *Confessions of a Native-Alien*, referring to this crucial moment, Ghose writes: "When we left Bombay in 1952 for England, we were leaving two countries, for in some ways we were alien to both and our emigration to a country to which we were not native only emphasized our alienation from the country in which we had been born."

The next seventeen years in England were a period of shifting fortunes, of recognizing his predicament as outsider and discovering his vocation as a writer. Ghose studied at Sloane School in Chelsea and took a degree in English and philosophy at the University of Keele. He then worked as a correspondent for the *Observer*, served as a teacher and wrote literary reviews for the *Western Daily Press*, the *Guardian* and the *Times Literary Supplement*. In 1964 he married Helena de la Fontaine, a Brazilian artist. In 1969 he left for the United States to accept a teaching appointment with the University of Texas at Austin, where he now serves as a professor of English. Apart from periodic trips to Brazil and England, the last eighteen years have been spent in Texas, surrounded by a landscape that is reminiscent of "home," one that emphasizes the dilemma of native-alien experience which has been his formal preoccupation these last two decades.

During the last two decades Ghose has produced an impressive collection of novels, short stories and poems, and yet he remains relatively unknown except in academic circles. This literary obscurity is in many ways a self-imposed one, for his persistent attempt to find a form that would adequately express the complexity of double exile and a language that would retain its experiential component while detaching itself from a referential surface have led him to a species of writing that bears very little resemblance to his biographical or historical circumstances of exile, thus providing very little signposting for the casual reader.

Ghose's early works are probably the easiest to comprehend, for they belong quite clearly to the Anglo-Indian tradition of writing. His collections of poems *The Loss of India* and *Jets from Orange* are largely biographical and anecdotal, and they deal with themes that are familiar in the context of Commonwealth writing: alienation, nostalgia, conflict of cultures, family, and home. Their form too is traditional and stanzaic. His collection of short stories *Statement Against Corpses*, written in conjunction with the British postmodern writer B. S. Johnson, despite its thin veneer of modernism, is traditional in its concern with rural displacement and the predicament of Anglicized Indians in pre-independence India.

Ghose's early novels *The Contradictions* and *The Murder of Aziz Khan*, the former set in India and the latter in Pakistan, are referential works that rely heavily on causality and sequentiality to explore themes of alienation, quest, rural displacement, cultural conflict and identity. Successful as these works are, the author reveals on occasion a dissatisfaction with the diachronic reading that the form entails. His repeated attempts to provide a synchronic viewpoint by distorting chronology and introducing flashbacks are an indication that the mimetic form, by tempting the reader to read fiction as historical reality rather than imaginary construct, proves inadequate to express the author's personal vision. Hence it is no surprise that he moves away from this mode to another better equipped to capture what Robert Humphrey calls "pre-speech levels of consciousness."

Crump's Terms, written in 1968 and published in 1975, is a strikingly different work that belongs to the English tradition and locates its action in England and Europe. It deals with Crump, a cynical and disillusioned teacher in London whose frustrating attempts to impose a

sense of order and discipline at the Pinworth School are juxtaposed with the memories of his ex-wife Frieda, with whom he spent several vacations in Europe but who finally deserted him to seek asylum in East Germany. The novel does not eschew external reality, but the external and the objective are means to explore what lies below the surface, the non-verbal. The stream-of-consciousness mode is essentially a metaphoric one, and what Ghose attempts is to portray the native-alien experience as one that cannot be fully articulated, one that is private and atemporal. This work is not without its shortcomings, but it is obviously a necessary one in that it provides the theoretical framework for his trilogy, *The Incredible Brazilian*.

The three novels that constitute the Brazilian trilogy are puzzling, for their mimetic surface and linearity link these novels to the author's early works. In fact critics have often tended to view them as colonial novels that capture four centuries of Brazilian history. As historical or picaresque fiction the novels are certainly successful, but to ignore the nonrealistic underpinning of the works is to deny them their complexity. The choice of a reincarnated protagonist, the constant pattern of repetition, the description of events that closely resemble myth and the metafictional observations provide a vertical structure and compel a different mode of reading.

The trilogy remains a substantial work in Ghose's career because the author appears to have found a medium that teases and absorbs the reader by providing an illusion of referentiality but remains a work that draws attention to its artifice and retains its freedom as an authorial construct. Providing a convenient taxonomy for the trilogy is perhaps less important than being aware that it creates a mode which provides a wealth of historical material, retains the reader's involvement through sequentiality, but also accommodates a vertical axis that addresses the complexity of native-alien experience.

The next postmodern novel, *Hulme's Investigations into the Bogart Script*, must be seen in relation to his collection of poems *The Violent West* and his critical work *Hamlet, Prufrock and Language*, all of which are concerned with language, artifice and the creative function of the imagination. The poems that belong to this phase reflect a variety of influences, which include John Berryman, Theodore Roethke, William Carlos Williams and Elizabeth Bishop. Both the critical work and the novel often reveal the influence of Wittgenstein whose works the author appears to have re-read at this time. *Hulme* is more a collection of nine imaginary Bogart scripts, tenuously linked together, than a traditional novel. About *Hulme* Ghose remarks that he was "trying to produce . . . a text which was simply a structure of language, which was not based on preconceived ideas . . . which did not have a story or plot, but which was still fiction." In short, the attempt is to distance a fictive work as far as possible from referentiality in order to test its strength as a vehicle for expressing the native-alien experience. In relation to the author's career, this postmodern phase appears to have been an experimental one which provided the impetus for his next phase of magic realism.

Ghose's three novels *A New History of Torments, Don Bueno,* and *Figures of Enchantment* are probably his most competent works, and they establish him as a significant contemporary writer. Remarkably deceptive in their surface simplicity, these novels exhibit a union of form and content that has not been achieved before. Criticism often alludes to Jorge Luis Borges, Gabriel García Márquez, Alejo Carpentier and other magic-realist writers as possible comparisons, but for the reader an equally useful reference would be Ghose's collection of poems *A Memory of Asia* and his critical work *The Fiction of Reality.* Ghose himself is dismissive of "isms," and he remarks that although his recent novels might "contain elements of magical realism" for him "the creation of a new text is an investigation into those possibilities of language that have not been exhausted."

All three novels meticulously preserve the illusion of representational narrative but, as the author himself points out, the mimetic surface is flawed. In fact the metafictional comments often remind the reader of the danger of beginning with a preconceived image of a referent. The careful reader perceives a "well made" imaginary world, one which is constituted according to its own laws, although linked experientially to the objective world. And the freedom Ghose achieves through this form enables him to combine improbable incidents, coincidences and mythical parallels with a mimetic surface and probe the complexity of marginalization.

Ghose's novels recapitulate the evolution of the novel in order to seek a form that would express an intensely personal vision. Patterns of imagery, motifs, and situations keep recurring in all of his writing to remind the reader that reading by form is an essential aspect of comprehending meaning, and that his works achieve unity through thematic concerns. Despite all the diversity in mode and language Ghose's works retain a strong sense of coherence, for their objective is to explore the possibility of negating the torment of existence and creating a paradise, even if that paradise can be only a linguistic construct.

PRINCIPAL WORKS: *Autobiography*—Confessions of a Native-Alien, 1965. *Poetry*—The Loss of India, 1964; Jets from Orange, 1967; The Violent West, 1972; A Memory of Asia, 1984. *Fiction*—(with B. S. Johnson) Statement Against Corpses, 1964; The Contradictions, 1966; The Murder of Aziz Khan, 1967; The Incredible Brazilian: The Native, 1972; The Incredible Brazilian: The Beautiful Empire, 1975; Crump's Terms, 1975; The Incredible Brazilian: A Different World, 1978; Hulme's Investigations into the Bogart Script, 1981; A New History of Torments, 1982; Don Bueno, 1984; Figures of Enchantment, 1986. *Criticism*—Hamlet, Prufrock and Language, 1978; The Fiction of Reality, 1984.

ABOUT: Contemporary Authors 65–68, 1977; Contemporary Literary Criticism 42, 1987; Contemporary Novelists, 4th ed., 1986; Contemporary Poets, 4th ed., 1985; Ghose, Z. Confessions of a Native-Alien, 1965. *Periodicals*—American Book Review January–February 1982; New York Times January 25, 1969; New York Times Book Review January 26, 1969; November 12, 1972; Times Literary Supplement June 17, 1965; November 9, 1967; July 28, 1972; April 23, 1976; September 10, 1982; Twentieth Century Literature Summer 1986; World Literature Today Summer 1982, Spring 1985, Winter 1985.

GILCHRIST, ELLEN (February 20, 1935–), American novelist, essayist, and short-story writer, was born in Vicksburg, Mississippi, daughter of William Garth (an engineer) and Aurora (Alford) Gilchrist. She received her B.A. in philosophy from Millsaps College in Jackson, Mississippi in 1967. She married four times (the first and third times to the same man); spent her twenties and thirties raising three sons—Marshall, Garth, and Pierre Walker; and did not begin writing seriously until she was forty. In 1975, while living in New Orleans, she began writing poetry, and in the following year studied creative writing at the University of Arkansas at Fayetteville. A collection of her poetry, *The Land Surveyor's Daughter*, was published by a small press in Fayetteville in 1979; and in the same year Gilchrist received a prize for her stories from the Pushcart Press and was awarded a grant in fiction from the National Endowment for the Arts. Her first collection of stories, *In the Land of Dreamy Dreams*, was published by the University of Arkansas Press in 1981. Considering especially that *In The Land of Dreamy Dreams* was published by a small university press, without advertising or promotion, its reception was phenomenal, selling ten thousand copies in the Southwest alone shortly after publication. The book was widely reviewed, and was reissued in 1985 by Little, Brown.

A collection of fourteen stories, many set in New Orleans and focusing upon the lives of ado-

ELLEN GILCHRIST

lescents, *In the Land of Dreamy Dreams* was compared to the work of such Southern writers as Carson McCullers and Tennessee Williams. Miranda Seymour in the *Times Literary Supplement* noted that Gilchrist shared with these writers "the curious gift for presenting characters as objects for pity and affection," and characterized the tales as "elegant little tragedies, memorable and cruel." Susan Ward in the *Washington Post Book World* praised especially Gilchrist's luminous revelation of her characters. "Even the least attractive characters," Ward commented, "become known to us, . . . because Gilchrist's voice is so sure, her tone so right, her details so apt." Jonathan Yardley, also writing in the *Washington Post Book World*, was struck by Gilchrist's searing depiction of the emptiness of the lives of her affluent New Orleans characters. The "chief subject" of the book, he wrote, "is domestic life among the bored, purposeless, self-indulgent and self-absorbed. . . . the brutal realities that Gilchrist thrusts into these lives are chilling, and so too is the merciless candor with which she discloses the emptiness behind the glitter."

In 1982, Gilchrist received an award for fiction from the Mississippi Adacemy of Arts and Sciences, and in 1983 a prize for her stories for a second time from the Pushcart Press. Her first novel, *The Annunciation*, tells the story of Amanda McCamey from her childhood on a Mississippi Delta plantation and marriage to a wealthy New Orleans man to her divorcing of her husband to find her own identity and fulfillment in a university town in Arkansas. The novel

received mixed reviews. Myrna McCallister in *Library Journal* called *The Annunciation* a "fast-paced, often funny and touching novel," but regretted that it relied "so heavily on a now overused formula." Frances Taliaferro in *Harper's* found *The Annunciation* "a surprisingly likable novel" and described Amanda's story as "invigorating and sappy"; yet also felt that Amanda was "in some ways a receptacle for current romantic clichés." Like certain other critics, Rosellen Brown in the *Saturday Review* found the novel better in parts than as a whole. It is, she wrote, "an unevenly compelling book by a talented short story writer who hasn't quite maneuvered the leap from short form to long. . . . When Amanda moves off to the land of redemption in Arkansas, it is as if a kind of gratitude for all the tender virtues abroad in the world touches character and author alike, and the book goes soft and uncritical."

Gilchrist's second short-story collection, *Victory Over Japan*, however, met with conspicuous success, winning the American Book Award for fiction. Writing in the *New York Times Book Review*, Beverly Lowry remarked that those "who loved *In the Land of Dreamy Dreams* will not be disappointed. Many of the characters [from the first collection] reappear. . . . These crossovers are neither distracting nor accidental . . . Ellen Gilchrist is only changing costumes, and she can 'do wonderful tricks with her voice.' . . . Without much authorial manicuring or explanation, she allows her characters to emerge whole, in full possession of their considerable store of eccentricities and passion." Jonathan Yardley in the *Washington Post Book World* was also enthusiastic about the collection. "Not merely is this humdinger of a book as good as *In the Land of Dreamy Dreams*," Yardley commented, "it is even better. . . . Because many of the stories are connected in ways both obvious and subtle, you feel as though you are reading a novel; at the end you have that satisfied, contented feeling that only a good novel can give. . . . *Victory Over Japan* is an absolute knockout."

Reviewers were less enthusiastic about Gilchrist's third short-story collection, *Drunk with Love*. The reviewer for the *Times Literary Supplement* observed that the stories "are not as nasty, funny or sexy as their predecessors. . . . The collection creates a sense of *déjà vu*, of things done well because they have been done well before." Meg Wolitzer in the *Los Angeles Times Book Review* remarked that the book "is filled with strong, occasionally dazzling pieces of fiction, but felt that as a whole the collection was uneven. A similarly mixed response was apparent in Wendy Lesser's review in the *New*

York Times Book Review. Lesser remarked that Gilchrist creates a "world alive with distinctive characters," but far too often relies on social stereotyping. "Her Jews," she wrote, "tend to be smart, rotund and money-grubbing; Catholics, she suggests, are always viciously sanctimonious; mountain boys have unrestrained sex drives; Californians spend their time in hot tubs; and so on."

In the late 1980s, Gilchrist reached a large new audience by reading her journal entries on National Public Radio's "Morning Edition"; and in 1087 she published a collection of these pieces—on such diverse topics as Southern society, poetry, feminism, her grandchildren, and atomic physics—in *Falling Through Space.* Her second novel, *The Anna Papers*, published following the year, was considered a more ambitious effort. In this novel, Anna Hand, a famous writer, goes to North Carolina in her mid-forties to reconsider her life, learns that she has cancer, and drowns herself in the Atlantic Ocean. After her death her sister Helen reads through Anna's papers, discovering a rich inner life that is Anna's real legacy to others. The reviewer for *Publishers Weekly* noted that Gilchrist "excels in drawing the bonds of love and resentment in sexual and family relationships," and that this peculiar gift makes the Hand family spring "to quirky life." Maggie Paley in the *New York Times Book Review*, however, felt that the work was flawed at its center. *The Anna Papers* she observed, "has been contaminated by kindness; it reads like a huge inspirational journal entry."

In a 1986 interview in *Contemporary Authors*, Gilchrist explains herself in the following way: "I write to learn and to amuse myself and out of joy and because of mystery and in praise of everything that moves, breathes, gives, partakes, is. . . . What are we doing anyway, all made out of stars and talking about everything and telling everything. . . . A friend once wrote to me, and ended the letter by saying: 'Dance in the fullness of time.' I write that in the books I sign. It may be all anyone needs to read."

PRINCIPAL WORKS: *Novels*—The Annunciation, 1983; The Anna Papers, 1988. *Collected short stories*—In the Land of Dreamy Dreams, 1981; Victory Over Japan, 1984; Drunk with Love, 1986; Light Can Be Both Wave and Particle, 1989; I Cannot Get You Close Enough, 1990. *Non-fiction*—Falling through Space: The Journals of Ellen Gilchrist, 1987.

ABOUT: Contemporary Authors 116, 1986; Contemporary Novelists, 1986; Who's Who of American Women, 1987. *Periodicals*—Harper's June 1983; Los Angeles Times Book Review September 14, 1986; New York Times Book Review September 23, 1984; October 5, 1986; January 5, 1988; Publishers Weekly August 12, 1988; Saturday Review July 1983; Times Literary Supplement October 15, 1982; March 6, 1987; October 27, 1989; Washington Post Book World March 21, 1982; September 8, 1985.

GINZBURG, CARLO (1939–), Italian social, art, and intellectual historian, was born in Turin, the son of Leone Ginzburg, a teacher of Russian literature and cofounder of the publishing firm of Einaudi, and the writer Natalia Ginzburg, who had already begun to publish short stories before her son was born, and who is now one of Italy's best-regarded novelists and essayists. On account of the father's anti-Fascist activities, the family spent three years in "confinement" in a village in the Abruzzi, but were allowed to move to Rome in 1943. In November of that year Leone Ginzburg was arrested by the Germans, and three months later died in the Regina Coeli prison after having been tortured. Carlo was raised in Rome, Turin, and London in the highly intellectual milieu of his mother and stepfather, Gabriele Baldini, a professor of English literature. He studied history at Pisa's highly regarded Scuola Normale Superiore, where his mentor was the Reformation historian Delio Cantimore, whose greatest work, on Italian heretics of the sixteenth century, appeared in 1939. Ginzburg began his teaching career at Rome University, moving in 1970 to Bologna, where he became professor of modern history. He has been a visiting fellow at the Harvard Center for Italian Renaissance Studies, London's Warburg Institute, and Princeton's Institute for Advanced Study.

Ginzburg's specialty is early modern history; his several publications have concentrated particularly on sixteenth-century religious radicalism and witchcraft as well as iconography and historiography. He is an admirer of the French *Annales* school of social history and especially of the work of one of its spiritual fathers, Marc Bloch. He is impressed with Bloch's assertion that rigorous critical and analytical thinking make history into a genuine science, as well as with Bloch's emphasis on the kinds of detective work that are required to make sense out of such various "irrational" phenomena as rumors and mass hysteria. According to the historian Anne Jacobson Schutte, Ginzburg, whose politics, like his family's, are of the anticommunist left, values Bloch's defense of history as a science "because it provides a corrective to the cruder varieties of Marxist 'scientific history'" widely practiced in Western Europe. The interdisciplinary nature of the *Annaliste* approach to history, the study of psychological and social

CARLO GINZBURG

"facts," enables the contemporary historian to treat "collective mentalities" in a refreshingly productive and subtle way. In addition, this approach to history, in Schutte's words, "can enable the historian to understand and sympathize with the most humble and oppressed members of past societies without abandoning his commitment to objectivity."

Ginzburg's first major book was *I benandanti: Stregoneria e culti agrari tra Cinquecento e Seicento* (1966; translated as *The Night Battles: Witchcraft & Agrarian Cults in the Sixteenth & Seventeenth Centuries*). The *benandanti* ("good walkers") were a group of peasants in the Friuli region of northeastern Italy who were born with cauls; they believed that on certain holy days throughout the year their souls were able to leave their bodies and, traveling on the backs of various animals, do battle with witches. Armed with bunches of fennel, they followed a leader into these contests; they aimed to overcome the witches, who fought them with stalks of sorghum, and so ensure bountiful harvests. Because of these experiences, they also held themselves able to recognize witches at any time and so protect their neighbors from evil spells. Ginzburg's story begins with the discovery in 1575 by the Roman Inquisition in Udine of the existence of the *benandanti*. The disintegration of this manifestation of a very ancient popular cult began almost immediately; by the middle of the seventeenth century, as a result of much imprisonment, torture, and incessant interrogation, the benandanti were at last perceived to be largely unable to differentiate themselves from their erstwhile opponents, the witches.

The author argues that the cult of the *benandanti* was a fertility ritual once widespread throughout central Europe, but by this period flourishing only in marginal regions such as the Friuli—where German, Italian, and Slavic customs meet—or Lithuania, where a strikingly similar institution is recorded from the seventeenth century. The relevance of the story to the now widely studied "witch-cults" is clear: these popular ritual practices had long since established a *modus vivendi* with the dominant religion. The *benandanti* originally thought of themselves as champions of Christ against the forces of evil; it was the uncomprehending Roman church which forced them into opposition. Ginzburg's overriding aim in the book is to "reconstruct the peasant mentality of the period." The historian E. J. Hobsbawm, in the foreword to the English edition of the book, writes, "It is Ginzburg's merit to have recognized, long before Le Roy Ladurie's *Montaillou* [1975], that—contrary to what has often been assumed—the documents of the Inquisition allow us to catch the voices of its victims and to reconstruct their intellectual universe, public and private. It takes a highly skilled and, above all, an imaginative historian to do so."

Il nicodemismo: Simulazione e dissimulazione religiosa nell'Europa del '500 (Nicodemism: Religious Simulation and Dissimulation in Sixteenth-Century Europe), published in Italy in 1970 and as yet untranslated into English, was Ginzburg's next important work, the idea of which he borrowed from an interest explored by Cantimore toward the end of his career. The Nicodemists were those independent-minded seekers after religious truth who lived in Catholic countries. Rather than flee to Protestant lands, they developed in secret their notion of the ideal union of a reformed Catholicism with a vibrant Protestantism while continuing to pose as obedient Catholics. They acted thus like Nicodemus, who visited Jesus secretly by night, justifying their religious dissimulation on the grounds that it was wrong for them to seek martyrdom before they were called to it and that God, in any case, knew their hearts. Ginzburg's chief discovery is that the father of this movement was the former Carthusian Otto Braunfels, a German, whose major work of scriptural exegesis, published in 1527 (a much earlier date for Nicodemism than anyone had thought), justified through the words of Elisha, Christ, and Paul the doctrine of concealing one's beliefs when circumstances made revealing them useless. The author employs the iconographical method previously almost exclusively the province of art historians to prove his thesis. He shows, according to Schutte, "beyond the shadow of a doubt that . . . Nicodemism was promulgated by a particular individual; that it was a coherent doctrine, rather than a vague attitude adopted in the face of persecution; and that it spread in a fashion that can be traced analytically, rather than impressionistically."

One of the most attractive and accessible of the European studies of early modern popular culture is Ginzburg's *Il formaggio e i vermi: Il cosmo di un mugnaio del '500* (1976; translated as *The Cheese and the Worms: The Cosmos of a Sixteenth-Century Miller*), which was the first of his works to be published in an English edition. In a preface specially supplied for that edition, the author describes how he discovered his subject: "[It] came about by chance. In 1962 I spent part of the summer in Udine. In the extremely rich (and at that time still unexplored) deposit of inquisitorial papers preserved in the Archivio della Curia Arcivescovile of that city I was searching for trials against a strange Friulian sect [the *benandanti*] whose members were identified with witches and witchdoctors by the judges. . . . Leafing through one of these manuscript volumes of trials I came upon an extremely long sentence. One of the accusations against the defendant was that he maintained the world had its origins in putrefaction. This phrase instantly captured my curiosity; but I was looking for other things. . . . I wrote down the number of the trial. In the next few years that notation periodically leaped out from among my papers and from my memory. In 1970 I resolved to try to understand what that statement could have meant for the person by whom it had been uttered. At that time what I knew about him was only his name: Domenico Scandella, called Menocchio. This book tells his story. Thanks to an abundant documentation we are able to learn about his readings and his discussions, his thoughts and his sentiments—fears, hopes, ironies, rages, despairs. Every now and then the directness of the sources brings him very close to us: a man like ourselves, one of us."

One of the most extraordinary things about Menocchio's case—he was examined and tried twice, in 1584 and 1599, by the Inquisition, and ended by being burned at the stake late in the year 1600—is that his answers to his interrogators' questions revealed "a deeply rooted stratum of basically autonomous popular beliefs." The fact that many of his utterances "cannot be reduced to familiar themes permits us to perceive a previously untapped level of popular beliefs, of obscure peasant mythologies. But . . . these obscure popular elements are grafted onto an extremely clear and logical complex of ideas, from religious radicalism, to a naturalism tending toward the scientific, to utopian aspirations of so-

cial reform. The astonishing convergence between the ideas of an unknown miller of the Friuli and those of the most refined and informed intellectual groups of his day forcefully raises the question of cultural diffusion . . . ." Menocchio's ideas, in short, "belong within an autonomous current of peasant radicalism, which the upheaval of the Reformation had helped to bring forth, but which was much older."

The Cheese and the Worms, in the opinion of the historian J. H. Elliott, writing in the *New York Review of Books*, "is a wonderful book. Dr Ginzburg is a historian with an insatiable curiosity, who pursues even the faintest of clues with all the zest of a born detective until every fragment of evidence can be fitted into place. The work of reconstitution is brilliant, the writing superbly readable, and by the end of the book the reader who has followed Dr. Ginzburg in his wanderings through the labyrinthine mind of the miller of [the] Friuli will take leave of this strange and quirky old man with genuine regret."

Ginzburg's most extensive venture into the realm of art history is the complex and ingenious *Indagini su Piero: Il Battesimo, il ciclo di Arezzo, la Flagellazione di Urbino* (1981; translated as *The Enigma of Piero: Piero della Francesca— The Baptism, the Arezzo Cycle, The Flagellation*). Very little certain knowledge exists of the life and career of this extraordinarily fine fifteenth-century northern Italian painter; very few of his works, and none of the masterpieces mentioned in the title, have been dated with precision. Ginzburg's aim in this book is to date the works more precisely using iconographical methods. "My perspective," he remarks in the preface, "is twofold: I am concerned with their commissioning, and with their iconography. I say nothing on the strictly formal aspects of the paintings for, being a historian rather than an art historian, I lack the qualifications to do so." What he does, instead, is to suggest that as a result of his identifying certain of the subjects in the paintings with some of Piero's known patrons, the dates of the paintings themselves (because dates in the patrons' careers are known) can be strongly inferred. "As a 'plain' historian," Peter Burke remarks in an introduction to the English edition, "Ginzburg's advantage over his art-historian colleagues is that he has more pieces to play with. He has put the problem of Piero into a wider context, notably that of the theological and political conflicts of the time. . . . the link between art and politics is central to his study of Piero as it is not in those of his predecessors." Ginzburg's most essential rule in his rigorous iconographical method is that all the pieces should fit together, leaving no blank spaces between them. The author becomes perceptively philosophical about the unusual melding of disciplines at the conclusion of his preface: "It is some time now since historians ceased to feel obliged to work only with written evidence. Lucien Febvre has already invited us to take account of weeds, field formations, eclipses of the moon: why not paintings, then—for example, Piero's paintings? After all, they, too, are documents of political or religious history. . . . I have conducted myself rather like someone making a foray into what is certainly foreign, though by no means definitely hostile, territory. . . . the learned body of art historians . . . will probably take it amiss that I have outlined an image of Piero that differs from the familiar one, and I have even disputed the chronology of some of his major works. It will be surprising indeed if nobody advises me to stick to the trade I know best. As a matter of principle I believe that forays such as this should become more and more frequent. . . . Only in this way will it be possible to reopen real questions about the techniques, the scope and the language of the individual disciplines—beginning, of course, with historical research."

WORKS IN ENGLISH TRANSLATION: John and Anne Tedeschi translated both *The Cheese and the Worms* (1980) and *The Night Battles* (1983). *The Enigma of Piero* was translated by Martin Ryle and Kate Soper (1985).

ABOUT: John Tedeschi. "Preliminary Observations on Writing a History of the Roman Inquisition," pp. 232–249 *in* F. F. Church and T. George (eds.) Continuity and Discontinuity in Church History, 1979. *Periodicals*—America June 9, 1984; Choice December 1980; History October 1984; Journal of Modern History June 1976; Library Journal July 1980; New Republic February 25, 1985; March 31, 1986; New Statesman January 27, 1984; November 29, 1985; New York Review of Books June 26, 1980; February 28, 1985; Times Literary Supplement February 24, 1984; May 23, 1986.

*GIROUARD, MARK** (October 7, 1931–   ), British architectural and social historian, was born in Britain, the son of Richard D. Girouard and Lady Blanche Girouard. He was educated at Ampleforth, a British public school run by the Benedictine order, and at Christ Church, Oxford. Postgraduate studies gained him a diploma in architecture from University College of London University and a doctorate in architectural history from the Courtauld Institute of Art. He was employed on the staff of the British magazines *Country Life* (1958 1966) and *Architectural Review* (1971 1975). Since the

early 1970s he has been a full-time writer; his books, which have increased in frequency during the 1980s, are among the most knowledgeable and readable in a popular and somewhat crowded field: the British country house and the society that gave rise to and supported it.

Girouard's first book on the subject, *The Victorian Country House*, traces the development and building of the English country house from 1840, the approximate beginning of the Victorian era, to 1890, when the country-house work of the great architects Norman Shaw, Philip Webb, and William Nesfield was virtually complete "and the generation of [Edwin] Lutyens . . . was just beginning to get under way." The book deals, the author explains in his preface, "with country houses rather than with houses in the country. . . . Victorian country houses, because of their size, their complexity and their social background, the occasional masterpieces and many curiosities among them, and the mixture of piety, snobbery, romanticism, idealism and pretentiousness that contributed to their making, form a fascinating collection. Seldom can so much money and such extensive study have produced a group of buildings that, as private houses, became so soon and painfully obsolete." Exhaustive detail on twenty-nine of the most notable Victorian country houses follows, along with information on many dozens of others. Paul Johnson, in the *New Statesman*, called the book "an elaborate work of original scholarship, . . . an informed and sparkling commentary on how the British upper classes lived in the years 1840–1990. . . . Looking through this wonderful book, one is amazed not merely by the prodigious size of the houses, but their sheer numbers, and the speed with which new technologies were recruited." Noel Annan, writing in the *New York Review of Books*, agreed: "[Girouard] has written a masterly book discuss[ing] the social and technological conditions which shaped these buildings."

Girouard followed this very successful literary debut with a stylistic study on a subject that had never before been systematically considered. Defining his terms in the preface to *Sweetness and Light: The "Queen Anne" Movement 1860–1900*, he remarks, " 'Queen Anne' has comparatively little to do with Queen Anne. It was the nickname applied to a style which became enormously popular in the 1870s and survived into the early years of this century. 'Queen Anne' came with red brick and white-painted sash windows, with curly pedimented gables and delicate brick panels of sunflowers, swags or cherubs, with small window panes, steep roofs and curving bay windows, with wooden balconies and little fancy oriels jutting out where one would least expect them. It was a kind of architectural cocktail, with a little genuine Queen Anne in it, a little Dutch, a little Flemish, a squeeze of Robert Adam, a generous dash of Wren, and a touch of François Ier." The lively mixture of these and other elements gave "Queen Anne" a distinctive character that outraged purists but delighted the public.

Sweetness and Light was no less well received by critics than its predecessor. Noel Annan, in the *New York Review of Books*, thought it "detailed, scholarly and absorbing, . . . admirably written and illustrated. While it is partly a review of numerous buildings, some of them long since demolished, it is also full of social history. Girouard has an eye for a social as well as an architectural nuance." Peter Conrad wrote in the *Times Literary Supplement*: "Girouard is expert at suggesting the social and cultural implications which buildings acquire by personal collusion. He catches exactly the literary affiliations of the architects. . . . He is even more revealingly subtle in deciphering the character of houses, showing how they assume the qualities of the inhabitants. . . . As well as making houses adhere to their owners or designers, [he] is able to assimilate them to landscape. . . . [This work] will automatically establish itself as an indispensable book."

Life in the English Country House: A Social and Architectural History is the expansion into book form of Girouard's lectures as Slade Professor of Fine Art at Oxford University in 1975–1976. In his introduction, the author insists upon the nuanced meaning of "social" in his title: "Even the most knowledgable country-house enthusiasts tend to think in terms of architects, craftsmen or family history, but to know surprisingly little about how families used the houses which architects and craftsmen built for them. . . . Country houses . . . were not originally, whatever they may be now, just large houses in the country in which rich people lived. Essentially they were power houses—the houses of a ruling class." J. H. Plumb, in the *New York Review of Books*, paid tribute to Girouard's "exceptional knowledge of individual country houses, whose history he ha[s] explored over many years. So huge a canvas requires a careful structure and a delicate sense of proportion, and this is not always achieved. Similarly, sweeping from century to century invites bold generalization. Certainly there is nothing wrong with bold generalization so long as a wary eye is kept for the exceptions and the divagations, but although Professor Girouard is aware of this necessity, he sometimes stumbles. And although he has read widely in political and social history, he is less at ease in these fields than he is in architectural history."

Girouard's next work is virtually his only one which could fairly be called a "coffee-table" book, in that its text seems of distinctly less importance than its illustrations. *Historic Houses of Britain* shows considerable similarity in layout, content, and approach to other books of its kind, notably Nigel Nicolson's *Great Houses of Britain*, the revised edition of which had appeared the previous year. Girouard divides the houses he discusses into chapters: there are the "Royal Residences" (Hampton Court Palace, The Royal Pavilion, Sandringham House); "Family Homes" (a section which includes Penshurst Place, Hatfield House, Chatsworth, Castle Howard, and Syon House); "Personal Reflections" (including Hardwick Hall, Blenheim Palace, Stratfield Sage, Abbotsford, and Bateman's); and "In Trust for the Nation" (including Lacock Abbey, Cotehele, Little Moreton Hall, Uppark, and Lindisfarne Castle). In an informative introduction, the author notes that country houses "should not be confused with mere houses in the country." They were built as homes, actually vast estates, of powerful families—"the people who ruled the country."

Girouard's only book removed from architectural history is *The Return to Camelot: Chivalry and the English Gentleman*, which describes "how the code of mediaeval chivalry, and the knights, castles, armour, heraldry, art, and literature that it produced, were revived and adapted in Britain from the late eighteenth century until the 1914–1918 war. Once one starts looking for the influence of chivalry in this period one finds it in almost embarrassingly large quantities." Girouard attempts at the beginning of the second chapter a definition of the elusive concept of chivalry: "the code of conduct evolved for the knights of the Middle Ages, that is for an élite and increasingly hereditary class of warriors; it accepted fighting as a necessary and indeed glorious activity, but set out to soften its potential barbarity by putting it into the hands of men committed to high standards of behaviour." The book is extremely wide ranging in its references, and includes chapters on, among other subjects, Sir Walter Scott, Victoria and Albert, the public schools, the return of Arthur, modern courtly love, knights of the Empire, chivalry for the people, and the Great War. Jan Morris, in the *New York Times Book Review*, wrote of Girouard's "particular gift to extract from art clues to the meaning of behavior. He does this so tolerantly, so wryly, so learnedly, with such sympathy and yet with such detachment, that he has evolved a literary form all his own—part history, part connoisseurship, part imagination, all expressed in a clear and often very funny prose. *The Return to Camelot* suits his genius absolutely." J. M. Crook, in the *Times Literary Supplement*, disagreed. To him, the book "hardly ranks as intellectual history: its philosophical content is negligible. It takes the form of an essay—but not an essay of the belles lettres type: the writing is seldom more than workmanlike. No, what we have here is really a prime example of the higher journalism, professionally edited, beautifully packaged and brilliantly timed."

Robert Smythson & the Elizabethan Country House is Girouard's revision and expansion of *Robert Smythson and the Architecture of the Elizabethan Era*, a book published in Britain by *Country Life*; this was in turn a revision of the author's doctoral thesis, *The Smythson Family, Their Work and Drawings*, presented to London University in 1957. The book is really an attempt, very largely successful, to resurrect the careers and accomplishments of the Smythsons, who "spent their lives in obscurity, ignored by the writers and historians of their time; and for the next three centuries . . . failed to obtain any but perfunctory recognition." Paul Goldberger, writing in the *New York Times Book Review*, called *Robert Smythson* "splendid social and architectural history, as perfect a reminder as we could ask for that the story of buildings and the story of the people who made them need not be mutually exclusive." "It is good," wrote John Buxton in the *Times Literary Supplement*, "that so notable a contribution to architectural history has been reprinted. . . . The book and the illustrations are well produced, . . . and as always Mr. Girouard writes with stylish elegance."

Girouard's *Victorian Pubs* is a very serious, even exhaustive treatment of its subject. The author terms it "an attempt to treat Victorian pubs as buildings built or altered at identifiable dates by identifiable architects and craftsmen for identifiable clients, in order to deal with identifiable social, political and economic situations." To do this Girouard effectively recreates a pub walk through the streets of the London of about 1898. "A great proportion of London's working population still walked to and from work, often several miles a day. To solace them on their long and cold journey home, main thoroughfares . . . were studded and in places crowded with pubs. As the street lights dimly lit up in the twilight the pubs lit up far more brightly; long rows of monstrous lanterns stretched out into the street on coiling and caparisoned tentacles of wrought iron and underneath them walls of sinuously bending and elaborately engraved glass were lit from the inside by an inner row of blazing globes. As well as being a work of architectural reconstruction, it is also a social history,

treating in great detail the classes who frequented the public houses as well as giving an account of the temperance campaigns that raged throughout the country in the late nineteenth and early twentieth centuries. Peter Bailey, writing in the *American Historical Review*, thought Girouard "particularly good on the genial rapacity of the publican-speculators; he also treats with architects, brewers, contractors, barmaids, . . . drinkers, and drink. The whole is accomplished with wit and erudition. . . . And, though the author is plainly and correctly in love with his subject, unlike the Victorian tippler he stops short of sentimentality and excess."

Cities and People: A Social and Architectural History is probably Girouard's most wide-ranging and adventurous book to date. "All big cities," he writes in his introduction, "are romantic places in the sense in which William Morris used the word: 'by romantic I mean looking as if something was going on.'" The book is concerned with "Western cities from the Middle Ages up to the twentieth century, in terms of who did what, why, where and when. It aims to start with the functions which have drawn people to cities, and to work outwards from them to the spaces and buildings which grew up to cater for them." An inveterate city walker himself, Girouard writes: "At a certain stage I find that savouring cities in ignorance or drinking them in visually is not enough; I want to find out, not just who designed the buildings and when they were built, but why they were built." His curiosity extends far beyond England to Constantinople, Bruges, Venice, Rome, Amsterdam, Paris, and New York, as well as Manchester and London. Peter Partner, writing in the *New York Review of Books*, had great praise for the book and its author: "Unlike most historians of 'urbanism,' who tend to organize their work around a theory of society and technology, Girouard denies having a theory or message. He writes simply, his judgments are modestly expressed, he eschews enthusiasm, pretension and jargon. . . . [This] is a remarkable achievement by a writer whose earlier work . . . has been mostly concentrated on the history of the English country house. Girouard has been admired for his powers of synthesis. The present book shows him to be a writer of formidable range." David Cannadine, however, who reviewed the book for the *Times Literary Supplement*, objected that *Cities and People* "will seem, despite its undeniable breadth, a classic piece of Western parochialism: there is nothing on the ancient civilizations of China, the Americas, or the Near East; the great urban societies of Greece and Rome are ignored; and the contemporary Third World gets very short shrift." Girouard's next book, *The English*

Town, an illustrated history, was deliberately parochial in its focus but achieved considerable depth in its evocation and examination of the constituent parts of typical English towns; it was praised on both sides of the Atlantic.

Girouard was a founding member of the Victorian Society in 1958. He has served since 1972 on the Royal Fine Art Commission, and since 1984 on the Commission for Historic Buildings and Monuments. He served from 1976 to 1981 on the Royal Commission on Historic Monuments for England, and from 1978 to 1984 on the Historic Buildings Council for England. He was also chairman of the Spitalfields Historic Buildings Trust from 1977 to 1983. He was made an honorary fellow of the Royal Institute of British Architects in 1980, and received an honorary D.Litt. degree from Leicester University in 1982.

PRINCIPAL WORKS: Robert Smythson and the Architecture of the Elizabethan Era, 1966, 2nd ed. Robert Smythson & the Elizabethan Country House, 1983; The Victorian Country House, 1971, 2nd ed. 1979; Victorian Pubs, 1975, 2nd ed. 1984; Sweetness and Light, 1977; Life in the English Country House, 1978; Historic Houses of Britain, 1979; Alfred Waterhouse and the Natural History Museum, 1981; The Return to Camelot, 1981; Cities and People, 1985; The English Town: A History of Urban Life, 1990.

ABOUT: Who's Who 1989–1990. *Periodicals*—American Historical Review December 1979, October 1982, April 1985, October 1986; Atlantic November 1981; Choice February 1979, February 1982, February 1984, January 1986; Christian Science Monitor November 13, 1978; March 12, 1982; Economist November 6, 1971; December 17, 1977; September 2, 1978; Harpers December 1981; Library Journal October 1, 1978; October 15, 1981; November 15, 1983; October 15, 1985; New Republic December 9, 1978; New Statesman December 3, 1971; November 18, 1977; September 22, 1978; New York Review of Books May 18, 1972; February 23, 1978; October 26, 1978; November 19, 1981; December 5, 1985; New York Times Book Review December 3, 1978; October 11, 1981; December 11, 1983; July 29, 1984; September 23, 1990; New Yorker February 13, 1978; November 13, 1978; Newsweek December 11, 1978; October 12, 1981; Times Literary Supplement December 31, 1971; February 17, 1978; November 10, 1978; September 25, 1981; December 23, 1983; September 20, 1985; May 11, 1990; Virginia Quarterly Review Summer 1979; Yale Review Winter 1979.

GLENDINNING, VICTORIA (April 23, 1937–), British educator, journalist, biographer, and novelist, was born in Sheffield, Yorkshire, to Frederick and Eve Seebohm. Her father, Baron Seebohm, a prominent banker

VICTORIA GLENDINNING

with an active social service record, was created a Life Peer in 1972. Glendinning received her early education at St. Mary's School, Wantage, and Millfield School. She later earned a Master of Arts degree in modern languages from Somerville College, Oxford, and a diploma in social administration from Southampton University.

Acclaimed for her sensitive and insightful literary biographies of Elizabeth Bowen, Edith Sitwell, Vita Sackville-West, and Rebecca West, Glendinning actually began writing while pursuing careers in other fields. She taught part-time from 1960 to 1969 and, while living in Ireland in the early 1970s, combined part-time psychiatric social work with book reviewing for the *Irish Times*. In 1974, she became an editorial assistant for the *Times Literary Supplement*, a position she held until 1978. During her editorial tenure, she regularly contributed book reviews and articles to the *TLS* and other well-known newspapers and periodicals.

Glendinning's first biography, *A Suppressed Cry: The Life and Death of a Quaker Daughter*, recounts the short life of Glendinning's Quaker ancestor Winnie Seebohm. A naturally gifted scholar born into a wealthy, protective Victorian family, Seebohm fought her way to Newnham College, Cambridge, only to be forced home almost immediately by her worsening asthma and nervous cough. She died shortly after as a result, Glendinning argues, of suppressed frustration and conflict. Although not widely reviewed, *A Suppressed Cry* met with praise. The *Times Literary Supplement*'s reviewer readily accepted Glendinning's interpretation of Winnie's premature death. Noting that the author, herself a See-bohm, had graduated from Oxford, he added that "one is tempted to believe in progress."

Elizabeth Bowen: Portrait of a Writer appeared in 1977. Glendinning's interest in Bowen and other Anglo-Irish authors developed during her residence in Ireland. She attributes considerable importance to Bowen's heritage, maintaining that "when she died the Anglo-Irish literary tradition died with her." Writing only four years after the novelist's death, Glendinning does not attempt to determine Bowen's status in modern literary history. She does, however, assert that Bowen ranks with major twentieth-century writers and provides the "link that connects Virginia Woolf with Iris Murdoch and Muriel Spark," an assertion not all reviewers found tenable.

Rather than critically analyzing the novels of Elizabeth Bowen, Glendinning probes their connection to Bowen's rather undramatic life: her tenacious love for Bowen's Court, the family's Irish estate; her seemingly mismatched yet enduring marriage to Alan Campbell; her lively literary salons; her intense love affairs and friendships. Glendinning highlights this connection because Bowen "shared with her reader her inexhaustible capacity for amusement. She combined an emotional intensity second to none with a humour that ranges from the subtlest social comedy to Dickensian burlesque. She entertains in her books because she herself found life entertaining."

Reviewers of *Elizabeth Bowen* extolled Glendinning as a sensitive and witty biographer with strong powers of narrative and psychological insight. "If it is true that . . . most writers get the biographers they deserve," Rene Kuhn Bryant wrote in the *National Review*, "then having drawn Victoria Glendinning speaks awfully well for Elizabeth Bowen." The *New York Times Book Review* observed that Bowen's writing "has not been strung up on the gibbet of methodology, or otherwise tortured, and . . . the language of the biography is free from critical jargon and cant." Others, however, found Glendinning's analysis of Bowen's novels and her portrayal of Bowen's working life too superficial, and her conclusions too dependent on the word of Bowen's friends and visitors.

Glendinning next chronicled the life of a more dramatic and controversial writer in *Edith Sitwell: A Unicorn Among Lions*. As Glendinning emphasizes in the biography, the English poet's reputation remains dichotomous. Like her brothers Osbert and Sacheverell, Sitwell created her own reputation to a large degree. Quoting literary critic F. R. Leavis well known remark, "The Sitwells belong to the history of publicity

rather than of poetry," Glendinning contends that Edith Sitwell belongs to the history of poetry *and* publicity. Acknowledging that she developed "a very protective feeling" for Sitwell, Glendinning advises readers not to dismiss Dame Edith's poetry as merely fashionable and now out of vogue. Neither should they discount her self-advertisement, which she used as a defensive screen from her painful interior life. "The public person," Glendinning suggests, "drove the private woman futher and further into the shadows." Glendinning's sources included Sitwell's manuscripts, drafts, personal papers, notebooks, available correspondence, and perhaps most importantly the autobiographical components in Sitwell's work. Her poem "The Sleeping Beauty," for example, in which the prince never enters the castle to awaken the princess with a kiss, speaks to Glendinning of Sitwell's unrequited thirty-year love for the homosexual Russian artist Pavel Tchelitchew. Glendinning likewise interprets Sitwell's popular biographies, which she wrote to earn much-needed money, as a cathartic yet secret way of divulging her own experiences.

Edith Sitwell won both the Duff Cooper Memorial Prize and the James Tait Black Memorial Prize and earned Glendinning widespread critical commendation. "This sympathetic yet objective work," biographer Michael Holroyd wrote in the *New York Times Book Review*, "transmutes the personal into the universal in a way that Edith Sitwell believed was only possible in poetry, because it conforms to Robert Gittings' definition of what the best biography should be: 'Poetry with a conscience.'" Some reviewers, however, while recognizing Glendinning's fine writing and compassionate approach, faulted the work for failing to assess Sitwell's poetry critically.

Vita: A Biography of Vita Sackville-West confirmed Glendinning's standing as a first-rate biographer of women writers. Based on Sackville-West's prodigious correspondence, journals, family papers, and her son Nigel Nicolson's revealing *Portrait of a Marriage* (1973), the biography explores the English poet and novelist's turbulent life, encompassing her privileged yet emotionally stark childhood, her extremely open marriage to diplomat Harold Nicolson, and her love affairs with Virginia Woolf and Violet Trefusis. As in her earlier books, Glendinning depicts her subject's life with considerable psychological insight. According to her interpretation, self-interest directed Sackville-West's behaviour, just as her love of the place and "passionate pursuit" guided her writing and love affairs. Glendinning notes that "nearing forty [Vita] recognized the functional necessity to her of passionate love for relieving tension and depression." Sackville-West "wrote some good books and some good poems," Glendinning asserts, "but her 'one magnificent act of creation' was Sissinghurst," the country home whose gardens she filled with colorful waves of flowers and where she planted climbing roses beneath apple trees. A recreational gardener herself, Glendinning concludes her story of a troubled life with soothing imagery, "But the white roses dangle from the apple trees, and the loveliness she made there in the shelter of the rose-colored walls, in the flowers that bloom and die year after year are her memorial. . . . "

Vita garnered Glendinning the Whitbread Prize for biography and further praise for her sensitive biographical approach and witty, concise prose style. Kathleen Leverich, writing in the *Christian Science Monitor*, called *Vita* an "exemplary biography" and an "astute portrait." The book received negative comments from one reviewer, however, for failing to emphasize the paradox that Sackville-West's self-indulgence limited her enjoyment and even imagination. The *New York Times* reviewer praised Glendinning's prose and compassion but belittled her assessment of Sackville-West's marriage as merely "embellishing" Nigel Nicolson's *Portrait of a Marriage*. Like Glendinning's other books, *Vita* was faulted by some reviewers for lacking a critical assessment of the subject's writing.

Glendinning wrote her fifth biography, *Rebecca West: A Life*, at her subject's request. She had known West personally for the last ten years of West's life "and saw her often with pleasure." Nevertheless, the project initially "seemed too difficult," and Glendinning proceeded only with the encouragement of Alan Maclean, West's publisher at Macmillan. Despite their long acquaintance, Glendinning found West's life unexpectedly sad, "on account of the way she felt about the things that happened to her." West's unpublished memoirs, correspondence, papers, books, and articles, plus others' writings, provided Glendinning with abundant biographical information. In addition, she drew on the remembrances of West's personal friends and acquaintances, including herself.

Glendinning views West as a "twentieth-century woman. . . . both an agent for change and a victim of change." She attributes some of her subject's personal difficulties, notably her destructive relationships with H. G. Wells and their son Anthony, to West's inability to reconcile what she herself perceived as the warring forces of her "masculine" interests and her "feminine" nature. "She was thus fighting against herself a lot of the time." West worked

in so many genres that she defies classification as a writer; Glendinning instead presents her in many roles: novelist, journalist, feminist, anti-communist, lover, mother, wife, and grande dame. She identifies West's overriding concerns as art, morality, history, and politics. *Black Lamb and Grey Falcon* (1941), her 5,000-page book about Yugoslavia, provided West with a format for articulating many of these concerns. "As such," Glendinning writes, "it is required reading for any understanding of her." Extending the music metaphor that West employed in her best-known novel, *The Fountain Overflows* (1956), Glendinning comments, "Rebecca West lived her life operatically, and tinkered endlessly with the story-line, the score, and the libretto."

Most critics commended Glendinning for writing a neutral, unsensational, and humorous book. "It is significant," a reviewer in *Contemporary Review* noted, "that Rebecca West, who had part consciously and part unconsciously obfuscated and fudged the sensitive areas of her life, ultimately chose a talented biographer who is psychologically skilled, accurate, and fair. . . " Some found Glendinning's sections on West's anti-communism and *Black Lamb and Grey Falcon* fascinating and perceptive. The *Wall Street Journal* reviewer, however, pronounced her "completely dense" about West's politics.

In addition to writing biographies, Glendinning regularly reviews contemporary literature and reports on literary figures and events. She contributes to the *Times Literary Supplement*, the *New York Times Book Review*, the *Washington Post*, and the *New Statesman*, among other newspapers and magazines. She has also written "Speranza: A Leaning Tower of Courage," a biographical essay on Oscar Wilde's mother, published in *Genius in the Drawing Room: The Literary Salon in the Nineteenth and Twentieth Centuries* (1980), as well as the afterword to Rebecca West's posthumously published novel *Sunflower* (1986).

In 1989 Victoria Glendinning published her first novel, *The Grown-Ups*, a switch, as Michiko Kakutani observed in the *New York Times*, "from writing about the lives of literary women to creating three idiosyncratic heroines of her own." These are three former schoolmates who once shared a flat in London and now are in love with the same man, a selfish and self-serving author and television host unworthy of anyone's love. While some reviewers suggested that Glendinning had set up a straw man here ("the man women love to hate," as Charles Dickinson described him in the *New York Times Book Review*), most agreed that the book offered shrewd insights into human character. "What sets the novel apart is Ms. Glendinning's easy familiarity with her characters and their inner lives, her ability to combine the sort of sociological observation practiced by a Margaret Drabble with the comic invention of a Kingsley Amis or a Fay Weldon."

Glendinning married her first husband, Oliver Nigel Valentine Glendinning, professor of Spanish, in 1958. The couple, who have four sons, Paul, Hugo, Matthew, and Simon, divorced in 1981. Glendinning now lives in London and Hertfordshire with her second husband, Terence de Vere White, an Irish solicitor, author, and journalist who served as literary editor of the *Irish Times* from 1961 to 1977. Since 1982, Glendinning has been a fellow of the Royal Society of Literature.

PRINCIPAL WORKS: *Biography*—A Suppressed Cry: The Life and Death of a Quaker Daughter, 1969; Elizabeth Bowen: Portrait of a Writer, 1977; Edith Sitwell: A Unicorn Among Lions, 1981; Vita: The Life of Vita Sackville-West, 1983; Rebecca West: A Life, 1987. *Novel*—The Grown-Ups, 1989.

ABOUT: Contemporary Authors 120, 1987; Contemporary Literary Criticism 50, 1987; Who's Who, 1986. *Periodicals*—Christian Science Monitor, December 30, 1983; Contemporary Review June, 1987; National Review May 26, 1978; New Statesman October 3, 1969; New York Times December 29, 1989; New York Times Book Review January 15, 1978; June 14, 1981; January 7, 1990 Times Literary Supplement, December 18, 1969; Wall Street Journal October 16, 1987.

*GŁOWACKI, JANUSZ (September 13, 1938–), Polish playwright, novelist, essayist and screenwriter, who has lived in the United States since 1982, was born in Poznan to Jerzy and Helena (Rudzka) Głowacki. His father was a writer and his mother an editor. Janusz early learned the bitter lessons of life in Eastern Europe during and after World War II. "When I was six years old," he wrote in the *PEN Newsletter* in 1983, "I escaped with my mother from a burning, German-occupied Warsaw. My mother kept explaining to me what I must do if they killed her. I saw dead people for the first time. I remember it all my life." At the age of ten, he recalls, "I stood in a long procession with other children waving a red flag, and a red-and-white one, while chanting, 'Long Live Comrade Stalin, the best friend and greatest teacher of Polish children!'"

Later, as a student at the University of Warsaw from which he received a master's degree in literature, Głowacki read Kafka and George

JANUSZ GŁOWACKI

Orwell. For him their writings were not remote political allegories but faithful portraits of the totalitarian system under which he lived. In Kafka he found a precise image for the dehumanizing effects of bureaucracy: the narrator of his novel *Give Us This Day* comments on the hovel where he lives with his family: "Cockroaches crackled merrily under my feet, and I thought to myself, if they've survived here by sheer willpower, why shouldn't we?" In the "Newspeak" of Orwell's *Nineteen Eighty-Four* he found confirmation of his belief in the power of language: "The language in which my characters speak is important to me. It comes from the sad Polish streets, from nostalgic, foodless restaurants, from corrupted life." The language of his narrator in *Give Us This Day*, Głowacki writes, "suddenly stops being an instrument of conversation, is transformed by TV statements, newspaper slogans, lumpen-proletariat talk. It resembles contemporary Eastern European tragicomic newspeak."

Głowacki's early literary career in Poland was a series of battles with the censors. He recalled some of these with wry humor in an article in the *New York Times* ("Polish Odyssey: Warsaw to Off-Broadway," February 15, 1987). While still a student he wrote a play for a university theater group, one act of which was challenged by the censors as lacking "social value." After long discussions with the official, he compromised and made a few revisions, but he learned then, he wrote, the difference between "an almost honorable agreement and a regular honorable agreement . . . almost honorable means not honorable." That play was never produced, but it launched Głowacki on an active if stormy writing career in Poland. By 1978 he had published more than half a dozen collections of short stories; he had also written several plays that were produced and several others that were rejected by the censors; four screenplays, including one for the well-known Polish director Andrzej Wajda—*Polowanie na muchy* (Hunting Flies) in 1970, and a number of radio dramas broadcast in Poland, West Germany, Belgium, and Sweden.

In August 1980 Głowacki was in Gdansk observing at firsthand the week-long strike of the workers in the Lenin shipyards and the formation of the Solidarity movement. This was not the first act of open defiance against the Communist party's control of Polish labor: an earlier strike in 1970 had been ruthlessly suppressed by the authorities. But its impact upon the workers and the emergence of a charismatic leader, Lech Walesa, marked the beginning of a sustained battle for freedom which reached its climax in the Polish elections of 1989. Głowacki was so moved by what he had witnessed in Gdansk that he wrote a short novel, *Moc truchleje* (1981; translated as *Give Us This Day*) describing that epoch-making strike through the eyes of one worker, a stolid and politically indifferent man who is swept up in the events and emerges almost accidentally as an activist in the movement. (Lech Walesa, incidentally, appears in the novel briefly but is identified only by his thick mustache; the narrator names him "the Walrus.") Not surprisingly the book was banned by the Polish censors, but it was published in Warsaw by an underground press and widely circulated in Western Europe. Published in France, England, West Germany, Switzerland, Turkey, and Greece, it won praise not only for the faithfulness of its account of the strike but even more for its wit and irony. For Hermione Lee in the *Observer*, *Give Us This Day* "is a vigorous, affecting, and—remarkably—*comic* novel about the start of the 1980 strikes in Poland." Lewis Jones, in the *Times Literary Supplement*, judged the book "an effective documentary, a humorous, personal and matter-of-fact supplement to the frequently bombastic coverage given by the media."

Głowacki's is not a black humor. Peter S. Prescott described it more accurately in *Newsweek* as "dark humor"—a mixture of innocence (on the part of the narrator), pathos, and cynicism. A widower with ailing parents and three young children to provide for, Głowacki's narrator plods away at his dangerous and exhausting job in the shipyard without self-pity. When asked by a reporter whether he is for or against socialism,

he replies: "I don't know. . . . All I know is I don't want to be thrown out of work, or locked up, or beaten up, or worse. And I want to have enough to eat for me and my family. And a place to live, maybe with running water. And I want to be able to afford medicine for my father, and maybe even have one kid in kindergarten." At the end—the strike a tenuous and temporary victory—he is cautiously hopeful: "Who knows? The government might even keep its promises. And I'll be sure to have something to burn in the stove in winter: not four, not five, but say seven crates. And anyway, . . . [it's] still a long time till winter; might be a mild one this year."

Such cautious optimism prevailed briefly in Poland. In 1981 Głowacki's play *Kopciuch* (translated as *Cinders*) was produced in Warsaw to critical and popular acclaim. *Cinders* is as imaginative in its form and style as *Give Us This Day* is realistic—a play within a play, a political fable framed in a fairytale. The scene is a reformatory for young women to which a filmmaker has come to produce a documentary about a dramatization of *Cinderella* that the inmates have performed. Pitted against the girls themselves and the well-meaning but powerless principal of the reformatory are the coldblooded official inspector of reformatories, a scheming deputy principal, and the exploitive and self-serving film director himself. The heroine of Głowacki's play is the girl who is cast as Cinderella, but her efforts to retain her self-respect and protect her sister inmates are doomed. Like his novel *Give Us This Day*, *Cinders* attracted considerable attention outside Poland. In 1981 it was produced in an English translation at the Royal Court Theatre in London, where it was well received. Rosalind Carne, in the (London) *Financial Times*, hailed it as "a defiant and intelligent play [that] compounds its relevance with every trickle of news from his [Głowacki's] beleaguered country." The playwright himself came to London for the premiere in mid-December, little realizing that he would not return to his homeland until eight years later. His wife, Ewa Zadrzynska, a journalist and writer of children's books, and his young daughter were still in Poland. On the morning of December 13, three days before the play was scheduled to open, Głowacki awoke to the news that martial law had been declared in Poland and that no planes were flying to Warsaw. What little news he could get was heavily censored, and he found himself in a hopeless maze of confusion and despair. As he recalled these troubled times in his article "Polish Odyssey": "I bought supplies of food for my family in Poland and was about to go back when martial law was declared. It was clearly impossible to go back for the moment.

Fortunately *Cinders* was a great success, so I calculated that by eating the food I had intended for Christmas in Poland, I should have enough money to last three weeks." Those weeks passed and, unable to reach his family, his funds now depleted, Głowacki candidly admits that "the only solution was to turn to alcohol." Though he soon stopped drinking, life remained "a heavy dark hangover." In the early spring of 1982, however, he received an unexpected invitation to lecture at Bennington College in Vermont. Paul Engle, head of the International Writing Program at the University of Iowa where Głowacki had been a fellow in 1977, sent him money for the plane ticket, and Głowacki became an emigré and an alien in America. After a semester at Bennington and another at the University of Iowa as a visiting professor, he found himself in New York, virtually penniless again but full of hope that he would begin a new career as a playwright.

Głowacki's struggles to survive in New York were only slightly less harrowing and hilarious than his imaginative rendering of them in his later play *Hunting Cockroaches*. His family in Poland needed money, but he was cheered by what little news he had from them: "My wife was dismissed from her job, but wasn't arrested, and my little daughter was growing harmoniously and was a very verbal child. At age three, she already knew such words as 'tear gas,' 'tank,' 'gun,' and 'passport.' To top off my good fortune, a very well known agent agreed to represent me and promised to make me rich and famous."

It was a hollow promise. Some of his one-act plays, translated into English—*Journey to Gdansk* (about a Polish journalist covering the shipyard strike), *Flashback* (also concerned with the moral dilemma of a writer in Poland), *A Walk Before Dawn*, and *Tea with Milk*—were produced off-off-Broadway at the Westside Mainstage Theatre in 1982. From these, Głowacki reports, he made $250. By 1983 he found himself in what he has described as "an archetypal refugee nightmare"—homeless, hopelessly entangled in bureaucratic red tape with the Immigration Service, and with no prospects of having another play produced. At that lowest point in his career, Joseph Papp, producer and director of the New York Shakespeare Festival, decided to produce *Cinders* at the Public Theatre in early 1984. No meteoric rise to fame and fortune followed, but *Cinders* marked a happy turning point in Głowacki's career. Frank Rich, in the *New York Times*, hailed it as "extremely clever and provocative writing," adding: "Mr. Głowacki has keen ability to mine the dark absurdist humor in the language of terror and

makes elegant Kafkaesque comedy out of his nation's ongoing nightmare of repression." In *New York* magazine John Simon found "strong, "funny-frightful stuff" in the play, although he had reservations about its artistic effectiveness. *Cinders*, he wrote, "offers pure political allegory, with every major character an archetype. Though his writing is peripherally splendid, the center lacks multiple resonance."

Produced for a limited engagement, *Cinders* had its run extended twice. It was later produced in Belgrade, Seoul, and Buenos Aires, where it received an award as the best play of 1986. In the era of *glasnost* in 1988 it was even produced in Moscow and in Leningrad. Głowacki was invited to lecture at a number of American universities; he received a grant from the New York Shakespeare Festival in 1985 to work on a new play; he was finally able to bring his family to the United States and he found an apartment on New York's Lower East Side. Here, he says, "I hopefully invested in four sets of window bars and eight locks." His first play to be written in America was a two-act tragi-comedy, *Fortinbras sie upil* (translated as *Fortinbras Gets Drunk*). It had several staged readings in New York in 1984. Głowacki describes the play as "a macabre retelling of *Hamlet* from the Norwegian point of view." In Głowacki's version the ghost of Hamlet's father is a Norwegian spy caught up in his country's plans to subjugate the small country of Denmark. As James Leverett wrote of the play in the *Village Voice*: "Bureaucrats and thugs run the country while Fortinbras, the only remaining heir to kingship, stays alive by staying drunk, thus a threat to nobody. The significance of the work as metaphor for the East European power bloc is obvious, but one wonders if the parable might not apply elsewhere." Głowacki responded to Leverett's comment, that the humor of the play was "dark," by admitting, "I know this 'dark.' The play is as funny as our lives at the end of the century."

Głowacki continued to have bruising experiences with Broadway producers. As of 1989 *Fortinbras* has not had a full-scale production; one potential producer dismissed it with the observation "How many people in New York care about a Norwegian prince? A minor character who appears on stage only after Hamlet is dead?" Another rejected his next play, *Hunting Cockroaches*, with the question "Would *you* go to see a play with insects in its title? Anyway, what are you going to say about cockroaches?" More imaginative producers, however, had no such qualms about *Hunting Cockroaches* Staged first in Woodstock, N.Y., by the River Arts Repertory Company, then opening in New York off-Broadway at the Manhattan Theatre

Club in 1987, *Hunting Cockroaches*—"a Polish reverie about the American dream," as Frank Rich described it in the *New York Times*—was uniformly praised. It headed *Time*'s and *New York Newsday*'s lists of best plays of 1987. Produced at the Mark Taper Forum in Los Angeles it won the Hollywood Dramalogue Critics Award of 1987. It has had productions in American regional theater, including the Wisdom Bridge Theatre in Chicago, the Ashland Festival in Oregon, and the Alley Theatre in Houston, as well as productions in France, Switzerland, and Australia. In 1989 Głowacki was writing a film version of the play.

Hunting Cockroaches is certainly the most personal of his plays. Its central characters are a Polish emigré couple struggling to survive in a crumbling tenement apartment on New York's Lower East Side. In their homeland he had been a prominent writer, she a famous Shakespearean actress. In New York they are non-persons—aliens without national identity, tangling with the bureaucracy of the Immigration Service, trying to cope with the English language, to understand and assimilate to American customs and culture, and—perhaps their main problem—they are still having nightmares about the secret police and censors from whom they have fled. The action takes place during one night in which they literally hunt the cockroaches and mice that infest their bedroom, reminisce about their once good life in Poland, and, in moments of fitful sleep, have nightmares (all acted out) about Polish and American bureaucrats, the drug addicts and drifters who live all around them, and patronizing and hopelessly obtuse rich Americans who make feeble efforts to befriend them. All this might be the material of tragedy, but in Głowacki's clear-eyed vision it turns into genuine comedy. The spirit of the play is captured in a comment Głowacki made in a *New York Times* interview (August 25, 1985): "This play is about people living in two worlds, two languages. It is also a play about the different ways of being frightened. In Poland, you're scared of the police or prison, and here you're scared of the super or how to get a green card."

Głowacki wrote *Hunting Cockroaches* on a grant from the New York State Council on the Arts. He has also received a playwriting award from the Drama League of New York, and a fellowship from the National Endowment for the Arts. In 1988 he was awarded a Guggenheim fellowship. In recent years he has returned to Bennington College and to the University of Iowa as visiting professor. In 1989 he was playwright-in-residence at the Mark Taper Forum and he also taught a playwriting course at Columbia University. He returned to Warsaw in June 1989 to visit his mother and recorded his impressions in an article, "A Burned-Out Light Bulb and Other Tragedies," in the *New York Times Magazine* (July 30, 1989). In Poland he found a renewal of the hopeful spirit of 1981 when the Solidarity movement first emerged: "To everybody's astonishment, a strange creature whose name was democracy, human decency, or simply, freedom, was being born in Central Europe." That democracy survived for only a few months before it was crushed, but in recent events, Głowacki believes, "Poland has made considerable progress toward freedom." He is too experienced in European politics to be entirely sanguine, however. He reports a dizzying inflation, food shortages, a thriving black market, and at best only a cautious hope that this time democracy will survive. Commenting on the Polish "practically free elections of the present," he concludes: "What next? Wait, gain strength, rebuild union structures, Lech Walesa keeps saying. But who can wait when everything is falling apart? Who or what will hold back a restless people? Lech Walesa, the Pope or the new President of Poland?"

WORKS IN ENGLISH TRANSLATION: Konrad Brodzinski's translation of Głowacki's novel *Give Us This Day* was published in 1983. Christina Paul translated *Cinders* in 1981. His one-act plays *Journey to Gdansk, Flashback, A Walk Before Dawn*, and *Tea with Milk* were translated by Halina Filipowicz and Robert Findlay in 1982; the two-act *Fortinbras Gets Drunk* was translated in 1984 by Konrad Brodzinski and Jadwiga Kosicka. Kosicka also translated *Hunting Cockroaches* in 1986.

ABOUT: Contemporary Authors 116, 1986. *Periodicals*—Chicago Tribune March 23, 1987; Los Angeles Times November 8, 1987; Modern Drama March 1985; New York Magazine March 5, 1984; New York Newsday December 27, 1987; New York Times February 21, 1984; February 15, 1987; March 4, 1987; November 2, 1988; New York Times Magazine July 30, 1989; New Yorker March 18, 1987; Newsweek February 25, 1985; Observer March 27, 1983; PEN Newsletter Winter 1983; Times Literary Supplement June 3, 1983; Vanity Fair February 1987; Village Voice March 3, 1987; World Literature Today Spring 1983.

GOLDBARTH, ALBERT (January 31, 1948–   ), American poet, was born in Chicago, the son of Irving Goldbarth, an underwriter for a life-insurance company, and Fannie Seligman Goldbarth, a secretary. He was educated in local schools and attended the Chicago Circle campus of the University of Illinois, from which he received a bachelor's degree in 1969, and the University of Iowa Writers Workshop, where he

ALBERT GOLDBARTH

completed a master's degree in fine arts in 1971. He has taught English and creative writing at Elgin Community College, Illinois (1971–1972); at the University of Utah in Salt Lake City (1973–1974), where he also did further graduate work; at Cornell University, Ithaca, New York (1974–1976); at Syracuse University, New York (1976); and since 1977 at the University of Texas at Austin.

Goldbarth began publishing collections of his poems in book form in 1973, and from that year on an extensive number of such collections have appeared—nine during the 1970s, another seven during the following decade. His poems may be characterized as both erudite and self-centered; he has been described by various critics, not all of whom have been unqualified admirers of his work, as "witty and learned," "a born show-off and gabber," and "egocentric." In diction, he can vary, even within the scope of a single poem, from a fair approximation of Elizabethan grandiloquence to genuine, slangy, streetwise modernity.

Coprolites, the poet's second collection, contains several long poems of a hundred lines or more, and one sequence, called "Interstices," which includes two learned dialogues, one between William Harvey and Joan of Arc, the other between J. J. Winckelmann and Joseph Busch. One of the collection's longest poems, the painful, controlled, and moving "Hospital," has at its heart the shocking realization of the difference between the laughing, joking, careless land of the well, the walking upright, and the grimly serious kingdom of the sick—"we are hundreds of

prostrate bodies / lying alone / as if already underground":

The bed-pan is not funny.
The wooden leg is not a leg.
The iron lung is not a lung.
To lie in the hospital is to be a sheet
of skin and a urine stain.

Jan. 31, Goldbarth's fourth collection, contains fifty surprisingly disparate poems. They are meant to be read, he notes at the beginning, "as a diary-of-sorts kept through one metaphorical winter, and are concerned with ways of surviving through that period. . . . Some of the poems are intended to act as flashback, prophecy, and conjecture, to approximate a sense of spontaneous notation through difficult times." He is especially adept at remembering the feeling of childhood, its interests and obsessions. In "The Lost First Decade" he recalls being a Mouseketeer, then switches to a bizarre, improbable, hilarious scene of riding the Chicago el train wearing his Mickey Mouse Club hat:

Without a caption one might never know Mickey
for a mouse; . . .
I've still the hat: and don't I feel silly now,
a bearded 25, with huge black plastic ears
for a yarmulke. Except I *want* to whistle
on the el as if the whole rush-hour jam would nod
in time on its way to work and easily break

out harps strung from suspenders, drums
from gutted attache cases, or the girl in the corner
blow a ragtime clarion on her prosthetic leg.

Jan. 31 was nominated for the National Book Award in poetry.

In the late 1970s and early 1980s, Goldbarth published several important collections, including *Different Fleshes*, "a novel/poem" containing both prose and prose arranged like poetry, as well as a good deal of straightforward verse. The action—if such it could be called: there is no plot or sequential development to speak of in the book—takes place early in the century both in Austin, Texas, and among expatriate American culture-hero/exiles in Paris: Gertrude Stein, Ernest Hemingway, Sherwood Anderson. *Who Gathered and Whispered Behind Me* consists of three sequences of untitled poems, some of which have to do with stained-glass windows, both those at Chartres and those made by Marc Chagall for Jerusalem. *Faith* is another extensive collection comprising poems of family remembrance and poems about the varieties of belief. *Original Light: New and Selected Poems 1973–1983* (1983) was assembled and edited by Raymond Smith and brought out by his Ontario Review Press in Princeton, New Jersey.

Goldbarth has most frequently been criticized

for a lack of emotional depth in his poems, for their failure to convey authenticity. Philip Lopate, writing of *Original Light* in the *New York Times Book Review*, considered that many are not "successful as a coherent statement. . . . Reading some of these dialogues is as wearying as being locked in a room with a maniacal medievalist graduate student who won't shut up." To William Logan, reviewing the same collection in *Poetry*, "None of Goldbarth's poems seems much different from any other. . . . This is not a failure to feel but a failure to transmit feeling. . . . His cynicism is more compelling than his innocence, and the romantic effusions to which he is often susceptible seem only a nod toward a current dogma the poet acquiesces to but does not believe in." Charles Altieri, however, writing about *Faith* in *Contemporary Literature*, held that "there is in Goldbarth no illusion that poetry can save us from ourselves or our culture, but his inventing fresh ways to put pressure on language in order to capture and to play with our frustrations makes it possible to believe, for a little while at least, that there is in the imagination a power for preserving a sense of the freedom and dignity of the mind that may not be an illusion."

PRINCIPAL WORKS: Under Cover, 1973; Coprolites, 1973; Opticks: A Poem in Seven Sections, 1974; Jan. 31, 1974; Keeping, 1975; A Year of Heppy, 1976; Comings Back, 1976; Curve: Overlapping Narratives, 1977; Different Fleshes, 1979; Eurekas, 1980; Ink Blood Semen, 1980; Smugglers Handbook, 1980; Faith, 1981; Who Gathered and Whispered Behind Me, 1981; Original Light, 1983; Arts & Sciences, 1986.

ABOUT: Contemporary Authors New Revision Series 6, 1982; Contemporary Poets, 4th ed., 1985. American Poetry Review March–April 1980; Choice June 1975, June 1977, September 1980; Library Journal November 1, 1974; December 15, 1979; April 15, 1983; October 15, 1986; New York Times Book Review November 21, 1976; October 2, 1983; January 4, 1987; Poetry November 1984, April 1987; Virginia Quarterly Review Spring 1977; West Coast Poetry Review Winter–Spring 1975.

GOODMAN, ELLEN (April 11, 1941–), American journalist and columnist, was born in Newton, Massachusetts, the daughter of Jackson Jacob (a lawyer and politician) and Edith (Weinstein) Holtz. She graduated, cum laude, from Radcliffe College in 1963, and was married the same year to Robert Levey, a medical student at Harvard. From this marriage, which ended in divorce in 1971, she is the mother of a daughter, Katherine Anne. During 1963–1965, Goodman was a researcher for *Newsweek* magazine and

ELLEN GOODMAN

from 1965–1967 a general assignment reporter for the *Detroit Free Press*. Since 1967 she has been a feature writer and columnist (of "At Large") for the *Boston Globe*—a column syndicated in 1976 with the *Washington Post* Writers Group and reaching a large national audience. She was a commentator for CBS radio's "Spectrum" in 1978, and a weekly guest commentator for NBC-TV's "Today" show in 1979. Goodman's reporting early attracted recognition, and she has been the recipient of numerous awards. She was named New England Women's Press Association Woman of the Year in 1968, and Columnist of the Year in 1974. She has received the Catherine O'Brien Award, 1973; UPI New England Newspaper Award for Columns, 1976; Mass Media Award, American Association of University Women, 1977; and the American Society of Newspaper Editors Distinguished Writing Award, 1980. Also in 1980, capping these many awards, she received a Pulitzer Prize for commentary.

In 1973–1974, as a Neiman Fellow at Harvard University, Goodman studied the dynamics of social change in America, taking classes in law, government, and sociology—a period of study that led in 1979 to her first book, *Turning Points*, which examines the effect of feminism on the lives of American women. Katherine Evans, in the *Washington Post Book World*, remarked that "to me, the value of the book lies less in the calibration of change than in the raw research, the vivid anecdotes with which these women and men describe their lives. There's enough frontline reporting of the sexual revolution here to keep you thinking a long time about who is winning, who is losing, and who the casualties are." Victoria Musmann, in *Library Journal*, however, felt that the book lacked the impact of Gail Sheehy's *Passages*. "Only in the final section," she remarked, "does she live up to her potential. Her objective but sympathetic interviews with couples trying to revise roles and reallocate family responsibilities illuminate one aspect of the contemporary dilemma the book deals with—either to endure the tyranny of tradition, or to accept the burden of choice." In a restrained review in the *New York Times Book Review*, Doris Grumbach found "little new in what [those interviewed] have to report about their lives. . . . Somewhat humorlessly written (for Miss Goodman), and lacking a very clear focus at times, *Turning Points* will be one of the many source books from which the full social history of these revolutionary times will be written."

Close to Home, also published in 1979, is a selection of over a hundred of Goodman's columns from the previous several years, covering a range of domestic topics from the problems of parents to personal relationships. The reviewer for *Time* commented that "The book's . . . selections show Goodman at her evenhanded best, a cool stream of sanity flowing through a minefield of public and private quandaries." Molly Ivins, in the *New York Times Book Review*, was particularly impressed by Goodman's persuasive style. "If as a feminist with some sense of public relations," Ivins observed, "it were up to me to choose a Voice for the women's movement, I would select Miss Goodman instantly over *Ms.* magazine and Germaine Greer. . . . Miss Goodman is at her best when she addresses a particular case that arouses her compassion or ire or both. [She] is at her weakest when maundering on about the state of the nation in one generalization after another."

Close to Home was followed by *At Large*, Goodman's second collection of columns covering events and personalities of 1979–1981. Barry Gewen, in the *New Leader*, was clearly pleased by Goodman's handling of domestic issues: "by shaping her views with a keen political edge. . . . it involves her in some of the most contentious issues of the day: abortion, censorship, teenage sex, rape, children's rights. Where the Moral Majority is working one side of the street, she can be found working the other—with wit and good humor. . . . Goodman is a committed feminist and an unrepentant liberal. . . . She is rightly praised for her sanity and common sense, virtues she has constructed out of such fine personal qualities as a willingness to hear all sides . . . to see things whole." Lee Metcalf, in the *Saturday Review*, remarked that

"at their best, the columns take on the news, look behind the political rhetoric, and point out the bad side effects of laws and trends in this 'massive behavior-modification program called society.' That's what newspapers are supposed to do, and Goodman often does it for them with brains and compassion." Tamar Jacoby, in the *New York Times Book Review*, however, was obviously displeased by the book. Goodman, she wrote, "seems to make a virtue of being cranky and opinionated, and rarely takes the trouble to test or probe or develop the often slight observations at the center of her columns. She is firmly convinced that what she calls 'the questions' are more interesting than 'the answers,' and generally prefers to end her essays with punch lines. . . . somehow neither her wit nor her censure has the moral authority she would like them to carry, and finally Miss Goodman herself seems the prisoner of her own quick, clever prose."

Goodman's *Keeping in Touch*, a selection of her columns in the 1980s, had generally favorable reviews. Taffy Cannon, in the *Los Angeles Times Book Review*, referred to the book as "a treasury of clever and insightful pieces by a woman of substantial perception," and she especially admired her "unceasing curiosity and fresh perspective." Similarly, the reviewer for *Publishers Weekly* remarked that "With Goodman, . . . half the delight lies in anticipating where her inquisitive mind will take her next. She brings us from Liz Taylor's need for 'privacy,' to aerial burials, to the Nancy Drew books, to thoughtful examinations of AIDS and other topics of controversy and concern. This is vintage Goodman." Joseph Sobran, in the conservative *National Review*, conceded that Goodman "does have the gift of putting a voice on the page, which is not to be despised, no matter how little you like what the voice is saying." It seemed to him, however, that her columns presented attitudes rather than arguments. "Perhaps," he observed, "it's just that people get tired of thinking. And Miss Goodman knows her readers too well to reason with them. What she offers them is a role model of a certain middle-brow sensibility, liberal, feminist, upwardly mobile, reacting to the topics of the hour in an assuredly fashionable way. . . . a whole collection of her pieces becomes very, very predictable."

In a 1980 interview in *Contemporary Authors*, Goodman was asked if it would be fair to say that she wrote about "cozy" subjects, as opposed to what some might consider more important questions. She responded that "I think I write about much more important questions than the average columnist. . . . I think it is much more important to look at the underlying values by which this country exists. It is certainly not cozy to be talking about abortion, the vast social changes in the way men and women lead their lives and deal with each other. . . . These subjects are certainly not cozy; they are pretty uncomfortable." Goodman's column has been one of the fastest-growing in the United States; carried by 140 newspapers in 1978, it appears today in approximately 400. Goodman lives in suburban Boston, where her avocations include squash and Chinese cooking.

PRINCIPAL WORKS: Turning Points, 1979; Close to Home, 1979; At Large, 1981; Keeping in Touch, 1985; Making Sense, 1989.

ABOUT: Contemporary Authors 104, 1982; Who's Who in the East, 1986–1987, 1986; Who's Who of American Women 1987–1988, 1986. *Periodicals*—Library Journal March 1, 1979; December 1, 1981; Los Angeles Times Book Review January 12, 1986; National Review February 14, 1986; New Leader November 2, 1981; New Republic March 10, 1979; New York Times Book Review March 18, 1979; December 23, 1979; September 20, 1981; Saturday Review September 20, 1981; Time December 10, 1979; Washington Post Book World March 25, 1979.

GRAY, ALASDAIR (December 28, 1934–   ), Scottish novelist, short-story writer, poet, playwright, and painter, writes: "I was born in Riddrie, east Glasgow. I graduated in design and mural decoration from Glasgow Art School in 1957, lived by painting with the assistance of part-time teaching until 1962, became a scenepainter with two Glasgow theatres until 1963, lived on social security money through 1964, sold a play called *The Fall of Kelvin Walker* to London BBC television in 1965, and thereafter supported myself by a variety of portrait and mural commissions for radio and television plays. From 1953 I worked sporadically on a novel, eventually called *Lanark*, which I completed in 1976, also on a verse autobiography called 'Old Negatives' which I completed in 1982 and will have published when I have finished illustrations for it: probably in 1989. I plan to write no more prose fictions. Some anthologies, playscripts, filmscripts, the poem book and several paintings are being sporadically worked upon."

Alasdair Gray's fiction is brilliantly, often wildly, imaginative. Nevertheless, a good deal of it is autobiographical. Though perhaps not faithful in every factual detail, the following passage from his "Portrait of a Painter" (in *Lean Tales*),

the story of an artist named Alasdair Taylor who persists in his painting though he remains unrecognized and unrewarded, is a succinct self-portrait:

Since 1985 Alasdair is one of over 350,000 Scots whose work is not wanted and whose existence embarrasses administrators. He is not a tragic soul. He is not on the dole, his wife is the breadwinner, he labours at what he does best. He often feels lonely and useless, but we all have our troubles. Hardworking, salaried arts administrators and teachers have quite different troubles, and can dismiss him with a touch of envy. He creates what they are paid to promote. His work accumulates. One day more than five or six people will learn to love it.

As an artist Gray works on the grand scale even in the small illustrations that decorate his books. The most ambitious of these appear in *Unlikely Stories, Mostly* and in *Lanark*. They are bold and fanciful black-and-white drawings that display the imagination of a William Blake reborn in the age of Art Nouveau. Like Gray's writing, his art assimilates traditions of the past with the techniques of modernism but emerges stamped with his unique personality in what David Lodge, in the *New Republic*, called "an exuberantly eclectic style." Gray acknowledges an astounding variety of sources. He writes of his work in *Unlikely Stories, Mostly* : "Illustrations in this book are drawn from work by Paul Klee, Michelangelo, Raphael, Piranesi, G. Glover, W. Blake, E. H. Shepherd and a Japanese artist whose name has no agreed phonetic equivalent in Roman type."

Lanark: A Life in Four Books, Gray's first novel, is and—if his resolution to abandon prose fiction is kept—will remain his finest and most ambitious work of fiction. It was received in Scotland and in England with almost unqualified praise—"one of the greatest of Scottish novels," Douglas Gifford judged it, and Anthony Burgess pronounced Gray "the most important Scottish novelist since Sir Walter Scott." In *Ten Modern Scottish Novels* Isobel Murray and Bob Tait wrote that "arguably, Alasdair Gray's *Lanark* is, both in form and content, the most exuberantly unusual and inventive work of fiction to have appeared in Scotland during the entire period represented by our selection" (their book begins with Lewis Grassic Gibbon's *Sunset Song* of 1932). In a sense *Lanark* is a life's work since Gray claims that he began it at nineteen, and he was many years in the living and making of it. The subtitle "A Life in Four Parts" refers to the four sections of the book but in fact the "life" is at least two and possibly three lives combined.

With characteristic whimsy Gray opens the novel with Book III, introducing an amnesiac drifter named Lanark who finds himself in the perpetually sunless and threatening city of Unthank, a Glasgow of the future transformed into a Wasteland. He has a series of fantastic, nightmarish experiences that read like a blend of John Bunyan, Lewis Carroll, and Franz Kafka. But in Books I and II which follow, the protagonist is young Duncan Thaw, the child of working-class parents, growing up in a Glasgow that is as palpable as James Joyce's Dublin in his *Portrait of the Artist as a Young Man*. Sensitive and asthmatic, Duncan demonstrates his rebelliousness early on. He is a gifted painter, also a writer, but he is unable to love or to establish genuine and lasting relationships. At the end of the second book of Thaw's story he has painted a spectacular but unappreciated mural of the Creation on the walls of a provincial Scottish church and, loveless, sick, and penniless, he apparently commits suicide. The last segment of the novel reverts to Lanark, whom we begin to perceive as probably the spirit of Thaw, and to the city of Unthank, now less a bleak and cold Wasteland and more obviously a Dantean hell. Nevertheless, within that hell he falls in love, has a son, and makes positive moral commitments. Lanark's journey leads him finally to a necropolis, an apocalyptic vision, and death. Grim and despairing as all this sounds, *Lanark* is redeemed by the author's breathless exuberance—events almost tumbling over each other out of an endlessly fertile imagination—and by its affecting ending. Lanark, awaiting his death on a hill overlooking the necropolis, "propped his chin on his hands and sat a long time watching the moving clouds. He was a slightly worried, ordinary old man but glad to see the light in the sky."

In *Lanark* Book IV Gray introduces a "third" life, another facet of the Lanark/Thaw protagonist. This is the author himself, who turns up in the Epilogue which (characteristically for this novel) comes not at the end but four chapters earlier. Unnamed, identified only as "the conjuror," he patiently explains his rationale to Lanark:

> Your survival as a character and mine as an author depend on us seducing a living soul into our printed world and trapping it here long enough for us to steal the imaginative energy which gives us life. To cast a spell over this stranger I am doing abominable things. I am prostituting my most sacred memories into the commonest possible words and sentences. When I need more striking sentences or ideas I steal them from other writers, usually twisting them to blend with my own. Worst of all I am using the great world given at birth—the world of atoms—as a ragbag of shapes and colours to make this second-hand entertainment look more amusing.

The author's confession of plagiarism is documented with a lengthy list of sources he has used from Anonymous to Zoroaster, including

Blake, Bunyan, Burns, Carroll, Coleridge, Walt Disney (some of the physical transformations of the characters were inspired by Pinocchio's lengthening nose in the cartoon film), to Freud, Hobbes, Hume, Norman Mailer, Milton, and Shakespeare.

Whether *Lanark* is read as an anti-novel, in the current postmodernist fashion with the novelist undermining his text and himself as well, or as a work of science fiction superimposed upon a realistic novel, or as an allegory of the doom of the modern city—and all these readings have been suggested by the book's reviewers—it remains a uniquely Scottish, Glaswegian novel. The city of Unthank is "a sterile and Wasteland Glasgow," Douglas Gifford wrote, in *Studies in Scottish Literature*, "without parallel—harsh, bleak, yet horrifyingly and naggingly relevant and prophetic." Unemployment, urban blight, crime, polluted air—the real problems of the real Glasgow—receive extra dimension in Gray's vision of the city. Edwin Morgan, in his Preface to Moira Burgess' *The Glasgow Novel*, wrote: "Alasdair Gray is, in part, as realistic as anyone could wish, but he adds a science-fiction dimension which seems to be exactly what was needed to bring out the incongruously evolving, multifaceted, sometimes frightening, always aspiring urban spirit." Moira Burgess considered *Lanark* the quintessential Glasgow novel: "*Lanark* has become a cult novel; there is lot of it to read, and a lot to read into it. We can safely say that there has never been a Glasgow novel like it."

One can just as safely argue the uniqueness of *Unlikely Stories, Mostly* and *1982 Janine*, both of them "tricksy, eclectic and scintillating," Daniel Eilon wrote in *London Review of Books*. Gray's experiments in typography in both books include printing the text in as many as four parallel columns, or in large blocks of upper case, or in pyramids and inverted pyramids, or upside down, or interspersed with lines of asterisks or blank pages. "At its worst," Jonathan Baumbach wrote, in the *New York Times Book Review*, "*Unlikely Stories, Mostly* is an advertisement for its author, a showcase exemplifying the impressive range of his skills. What the stories share with the novel is a dazzling command of rhetoric, a willingness to take large risks, and a handful of obsessive themes."

The publication of *1982 Janine* evoked an impassioned response from British readers, though it received less attention in the United States. Characterized by Gray himself as "mainly a sado masochistic fetishistic fantasy," it describes in minute and, in the judgment of some readers, pornographic detail the nocturnal fantasies of a middle aged businessman (a supervisor of security installations), Jock McLeish. He is a bitterly frustrated and unhappy man trying to bury his memories of a failed and emotionally sterile life in alcohol, sleeping pills, and by spinning out an ongoing but never completed fable of male machismo and female victimization. Within the single night of tormenting insomnia in which the novel takes place, McLeish relives his life, and we discover in him a once creative and idealistic man who failed himself and those few who genuinely loved him because of his lack of moral courage. What redeems *1982 Janine* from any charge of pornography is its unmistakably redemptive conclusion. In his dark night of the soul, McLeish at last confronts his past and sees himself for what he is. He rejects the suicide he had contemplated and resolves to live: "Before I die I will make folk glad I exist again. How? . . . I will work among the people I know; I will not squander myself in fantasies; I will think to a purpose, think harder and drink less; I will be recognised by my neighbours; I will converse and speak my mind . . . I am not a massive man but I must be tough to have survived a night like this."

Reviewers traced literary influences from eighteenth-century Laurence Sterne to James Joyce in *1982 Janine*. (The *Janine* of the title is certainly an echo of the Marquis de Sade's notorious *Justine*.) For David Lodge the novel was typical of "a general trend in the contemporary novel"—a deconstruction of pornographic narrative "by parody, metafictional commentary . . . and the interpellation of another, more authentic discourse—the discourse of confession—which eventually dominates the book." As a story of conversion and redemption, Lodge pointed out, *1982 Janine* is "a venerable form of narrative that goes back to Augustine." But, he continued, "Gray does not seem merely derivative. . . . He is very much his own man."

The Fall of Kelvin Walker, which may be Gray's last work of prose fiction, is a novelization of his early television play. Readers have noted in all his novels a deeply rooted social conscience and concern with the problems of present-day British society. The subtitle of *The Fall of Kelvin Walker* is "A Fable of the Sixties," and in this short novel of a young "innocent"—a Scottish-Calvinist Candide who finds his fortune, and his fall, in British television—Gray has for his satirical target the whole power structure of mass communications in Britain today. This is a straight-forward narrative with no stylistic or typographical experiments. Young Kelvin, son of a fiercely religious father (clerk of the John Knox Street Free Seceders Presbyterian Church of Scotland) travels from the little town of Glaik to London, a city in which "money had accumulat-ed to a point where it flashed into wealth, and wealth was free, swift, reckless, mercuric." He arrives friendless and penniless, fortified only with his faith in Nietzsche, whom he has more or less accidentally discovered in a library, and profound self-confidence. Within a few weeks he has acquired a couple of impoverished young artistic friends and a high-paying, high-powered job as a talk show host on the BBC. As the title promises, Kelvin's meteoric rise to fame is only a prelude to his fall. In properly classic fashion it is his pride that is his undoing, for Kelvin cannot repress his basically Calvinist nature. He begins to attack the morality—or immorality—of the age. As D. J. Enright pointed out, in *New York Review of Books*: "The British public isn't ready for a revival of Victorian morality, and so Kelvin must be brought low." Humbled and humiliated on live TV by the sudden appearance of his father, Kelvin returns to Glaik to become in the end "the official spokesman for all that is most restrictive in Scottish religions and social opinion. The public, the press, and even his opponents love and respect him for the predictability of his utterances on any topic whatsoever." However, Enright cautioned, the novel should not be read as a humorless moral exposé of the British Establishment. "Alasdair Gray is enjoying himself, and if we are wise we shall enjoy ourselves too." For Larry McCaffery, in the *New York Times Book Review, The Fall of Kelvin Walker* confirms what Gray's earlier books had promised—"that he is emerging as the most vibrant and original new voice in English fiction."

PRINCIPAL WORKS: *Novels*—Lanark: A Life in Four Books, 1981; 1982 Janine, 1984; The Fall of Kelvin Walker: A Fable of the Sixties, 1985; Something Leather, 1990. *Short stories*—Unlikely Stories, Mostly, 1983; (with James Kelman and Agnes Owens) Lean Tales, 1985. *Novella*—McGrotty and Ludmilla: or The Harbinger Report, 1990.

ABOUT: Burgess, M. The Glasgow Novel: A Survey and Bibliography, 1986; Contemporary Literary Criticism 41, 1987; Malzahn, M. Aspects of Identity: The Contemporary Scottish Novel (1978–1981) as National Self-Expression, 1984; Murray, I. and B. Tait. Ten Modern Scottish Novels, 1984. *Periodicals*—London Review of Books May 3, 1984; New Republic November 12, 1984; New York Review of Books February 26, 1987; New York Times Book Review October 28, 1984; May 5, 1985; December 21, 1986; Studies in Scottish Literature 18, 1983; Times Literary Supplement March 29, 1985; July 6, 1990.

GREGOR, ARTHUR (Nov. 18, 1923–), American (Austrian-born) poet, playwright, and memoirist, writes: "The moments that have meant the most to me are those which have suggested the reality of something beyond statement, which have—either by means of artistic expression, human gesture or a display in nature—indicated a condition which, though not evident as such, is much to be desired. It has always seemed to me that it is this core of hidden evidence which art can provide and that we respond to because we need, need to absorb, what it provides. At any rate, this is the art that I have responded to, be it in music, literature, the individual person or in views of harmony that on occasion nature bestows. I have always, probably even long before I thought of it, considered this engagement to be the poetic reality and have attempted to reach it in my life and work. For that reason, the works of art that have spoken to me, the evidence of that poetic or spiritual reality in nature and, perhaps above all, in the individual, have had the most sustaining influence on me. Probably, this began early. For I was born in a city imbued with a sense of art's importance. Certainly in Vienna—where I lived until forced to leave in 1939 when I was fifteen and we immigrated to the United States—history with its gothic and baroque remnants fully intact, made permanence an almost palpable reality. Added to that was the longing for its undiminished vitality, for access to the source which, if indeed it ever existed within the cultural fabric, had long been lost.

"These then are the matters which have concerned me, which have caused my travels, the direction of my life and have determined the nature of my work. Much of this has been chronicled in my memoir, *A Longing in the Land*: *Memoir of a Quest* and the exhilaration, purpose, and anguish of this journey in my books of poems and other works."

———

A recurring motif in Arthur Gregor's memoir *A Longing in the Land* is "Something is missing." Like many other young Europeans driven from their sheltered environments by Nazism and thrust into the friendly but alien culture of America, he has spent much of his life in pursuit of what he describes as "the force within the environment that ignites the imagination and rests the soul." In one of the early poems in his first published volume, *Octavian Shooting Targets*, he recalls a war-torn Europe and his native Vienna from an American perspective:

Th.... ....th..... the disillusioned
the America pantomimed a sad pavane:

ARTHUR GREGOR

Justice dead, the Pure all lost;
and scuttling coffins planted tiny islands
for purity to prosper. It was here
that I looked in, scouting on my life-
boat's murdered rubbish, and it was here
I faced angels on rococo instruments,
saw the grand staircase where
fantastic shepherds rose wet from
a ridiculous sea, memory   memory.

—"Blackout"

Born to comfortable bourgeois parents, Benjamin and Regine (Reiss) Goldenberg in pre-war Vienna, Arthur Gregor (the name was legally changed) had a happy childhood and a solid classical education in a *Gymnasium* until, a few years after *Anschluss*, Austrian anti-Semitism drove his family into exile. They were fortunate enough to leave in September 1939 just on the brink of World War II, but they arrived in America to settle in Newark, New Jersey, penniless with years of struggle ahead of them. Young Arthur, who had learned English in Austria, went to work immediately—first delivering groceries, then training as a technician in a dental laboratory. He began writing poetry with the encouragement of a sympathetic high school English teacher, and after finishing college (B.S. 1945, Newark College of Engineering), he enrolled in a poetry workshop in Greenwich Village. By 1946 he was writing in earnest and publishing in little magazines.

Gregor worked as an engineer for an electronics company from 1947 to 1954. By that time he had won some recognition for his poetry, and he published his first volume of poems in 1954. That same year he became an editor in a technical publishing house; later he worked for Macmillan (where he prepared the 1967 edition of Marianne Moore's *Complete Poems*). Since 1974 he has been professor of English at Hofstra University, Long Island, New York, directing creative writing and publishing studies programs. Though best known as a poet, Gregor has also written children's books—two of them texts for the work of the celebrated photographer Ylla—and three plays—"Fire!" which was produced in 1952 at the University of Illinois in Urbana and "Continued Departure" and "The Door Is Open" which were produced by the Cubiculo Theatre in New York in 1968 and 1970 respectively.

In a section of *A Longing in the Land* entitled "The Cult of the Personal Life," Gregor describes his spiritual malaise during the 1950s. Though by this time a published poet with many friends in the arts—dance, music, literature—he felt "distressed, burdened by rifts, an unhealed split" and repelled by what seemed to him the self-centeredness of cultural life in New York. Attracted to Zen Buddhism and other Eastern philosophies, he went to India in 1955 and studied Vedanta for three months. This experience and further reflection in Italy and the south of France gave him—and his poetry—a new direction: *"Something is missing* : I sensed this more than forty years ago."* What was missing was an affirmation of the spirit, the inward self. "Expressions of power and energy, however attractive and stimulating—as I at first found them in America and still do—the hectic activities on life's surface, do not lead one inward. This the poet knows, not only the poet by practice but the poet alive within human consciousness."

It is precisely this quality of inwardness, of introspection and subjectitivy, that critics have found most striking in Gregor's poetry. Lawrence Lieberman, in the *Yale Review*, called him "one of the most deeply spiritual poets of our time." Because he is a poet of spiritual commitment, Lieberman continues, "it is easy enough to make the mistake of dismissing him as merely a philosopher-in-verse." But, Lieberman cautions, his poems are not doctrinaire: "Philosophy is subordinate to the stream of intensely devotional feeling running through most of the poems." Visionary poetry like his takes many risks, especially of obscurity and looseness of language—a charge Raymond Oliver brought against Gregor in the *Southern Review* in 1973 of an "associative, impressionistic manner . . . self-indulgence." Most of Gregor's critics, however, have found his mysticism lucid and moving largely because of what Hayden Carruth, in the *Nation* in 1967, characterized as the "simplicity and candor" of his language. According to Carruth: "For Gregor, metaphor remains all of poetry; psychedelic theory to the contrary notwithstanding, no direct re-creation of mystical intuition is possible. Hence most of his failures are poems in which he succumbs to the risk of metaphor and crosses over entirely into symbolism . . . his successes come from the times when his dream, his vision, has presented itself in sufficiently concrete terms. Given the abstractions of the human mind, such occasions are bound to be rare." Josephine Jacobson, also in the *Nation*, in 1976, noted that "the danger for poetry which has a strong spiritual force as its center is that the poems may become remote from the immediate and tangible. Gregor's most impressive accomplishment is his ability to make the spiritual intensely apprehended to the senses."

In his 1982 collection *Embodiments* Gregor includes a number of poems inspired by his travels in France and Italy all affirming his communion with nature as well as a deep inner peace. But this spiritual condition was not achieved without the kind of struggle he described in an earlier poem, "Words of the Pilgrim";

Nothing matters to me but
inner accord.
Come, beasts,
I'll face you if I must.
I'll walk through the dark with
the unfulfilled, the lost.
Let their terror be my cry.
What is hidden
shall come forth.
Light insists
nothing shall be missed.

PRINCIPAL WORKS: *Poetry*—Octavian Shooting Targets, 1954; Declensions of a Refrain, 1957; Basic Movements, 1966; Figure in the Door, 1968; A Bed by the Sea, 1970; Selected Poems, 1971; The Past Now: New Poems, 1975; Embodiment and Other Poems, 1982. *Memoir*—A Longing in the Land, 1983. *Children's books*—The Little Elephant, 1956; 1 2 3 4 5: Verses for Children, 1956; Animal Babies, 1959.

ABOUT: Contemporary Authors New Revision Series 11, 1984; Contemporary Poets, 4th ed., 1985; Something about the Author 36, 1984; Who's Who in America 1988–89. *Periodicals*—Crazy Horse April 1973; Modern Poetry Studies 2, 1971; Nation November 6, 1967; October 9, 1976; New York Times Book Review May 15, 1955; Poetry November 1970; Southern Review 9, 1973; Yale Review Summer 1968.

GROSSMAN, VASILY (December 12 [November 29, Old Style], 1905–September 14, 1964), Russian novelist, short-story writer, playwright, and essayist, was born in Berdichev in the Ukraine, the son of highly assimilated Russian Jews. Over a period of two and a half centu-

VASILY GROSSMAN

ries, until the annexation and partition of Poland by its neighbors in 1795, Berdichev had one of the largest and most diversified Jewish communities in Russia: manual workers, artisans, professional men (and later women), business entrepreneurs, a brilliant intelligentsia. During the reign of the last czar of Russia, Nicholas II, Berdichev remained untouched by the pogroms that devastated so many *shtetels* in Southern Russia. However, one of the worst raids took place in the independent Ukraine on January 5 and 6, 1919: seventeen men were killed, forty wounded, and thousands were severely beaten and robbed. Grossman was fourteen at the time. The Bolsheviks abrogated the Ukraine's independent status and put an end to the anti-Semitic raids that had decimated the Jewish population between 1917 and 1921. As a result many Ukrainian Jews were grateful to the new Bolshevik regime, but by the end of the civil war that followed the Revolution, the Jewish population of Berdichev had been reduced by fifty percent. Because it was still, however, considered "the most Jewish town in the Ukraine," it became a target of special interest to the German invaders of the U.S.S.R. in 1941. Grossman wrote a terrifying account of their systematic extermination of the Jewish population of his native city in the essay "Oubiïstvo evreev v Berdichev" (The Murder of Jews in Berdichev) that was published in *Chernaya Kniga* (translated as *The Black Book*, 1981), a collection of records of Nazi genocide suppressed by the Soviet government in 1948.

In 1921, at the age of sixteen, Vasily Grossman

entered the Kiev gymnasium, and then went on to Moscow University to study chemistry, becoming like his father a chemical engineer. For four years (1929–1933) he worked at the Institute of Pathology and Hygiene in the Donbass mining region. He left in 1933 to return to Moscow, where he was hired as an engineer by a pencil factory. By that time he had already started to write and had published some essays and stories; his first essay, "Berdichev, No More Joking!", had appeared in *Ogoniok* in 1928. He also contributed literary essays to journals and newspapers. He brought with him to Moscow the manuscript of a story, "Glückauf," dealing with the life of the Donbass miners. The novella was read by Gorky, who after his return to Russia (following years of exile) spent a good deal of time advising aspiring writers. Gorky realized that Grossman was highly gifted, but he did not like the story. In his comments he wrote: "What truth is the writer trying to affirm? What is his purpose in writing?" Responding to Gorky's criticism, Grossman rewrote his novella, which was published in 1934.

At first, and for many years to follow, Grossman's aesthetic adhered to the prevalent norms of Socialist Realism. "Glückauf" (the German exclamation can be translated as "Good luck coming back up!") deals with the world of miners. It glorifies the effort of production, the success of industrialization. The writer sketches the old guard of the engineering corps, most of whom join the Bolsheviks, and the undisciplined behavior of the entrenched working class against which both Lenin and Stalin struggled mercilessly. The hero of the story is a simple peasant who has joined the ranks of the proletariat. He is profoundly happy with his new activities. The rewritten version is a compendium of clichés, such as a "love scene" (Part II, Ch. 7) in which the woman speaks of tender feelings while her companion invests all his emotions into a discussion of the mine. However, even this conventional story reveals a ripening talent. The terror of the peasant when he finds himself underground in a mine shaft is almost palpable. There is also a colorful sketch of a celebration in which a rowdy drinking bout indulged in by most of the guests is followed by a delicate description of the nascent love of the young hostess for the newly arrived German locksmith. We have here, in the bud, all of Grossman's future characteristics: his ability to create a modern epic on a truly large scale, and his equally fine perception of the intimate, inner life of his characters.

Also in 1934, in April, Grossman's fifteen page story "In the Town of Berdichev" was published by *Literaturnaya Gazeta*. It depicts a thick-looking, low-voiced woman commissar,

Vavilova, who, like a latter-day Joan of Arc, wears breeches and carries a pistol. Finding herself pregnant, she is given a forty-day leave and requisitions a room to await the birth of her child. During that time, the Reds are assailed by a Polish regiment and prepare themselves for a retreat. Vavilova plans at first to wait out what appears to be a temporary occupation, but as the situation drags on she decides to leave Berdichev with the last Red detachment, and she entrusts her new-born infant to her landlady. Grossman's attitude is in no way critical of this decision, which is that of a patriot, a true Communist. The story is about the kinds of moral choices one has to make in times of crisis. Vavilova is moved by her memory of Lenin's Red Square address. During a civil war, a righteous struggle, maternal instincts must take second place, or perhaps be totally repressed. Having read this story, Gorky no longer questioned the young writer's motives. In fact, he invited Grossman to visit him.

The Berdichev Grossman depicts in this early work is not "the second Jerusalem" of the past. Rather, it is as the fulcrum of the final struggle between the Whites and the Reds. A new society, a new man, was supposed to emerge out of this struggle. As an adolescent, the writer had fervently believed that the Jewish problem had been eliminated from his country once and for all, that the Revolution would establish complete equality in an atmosphere of openness and responsible freedom. He was in effect signing a "social contract," the terms of which meant the erasure of marginality, of difference, and even, to some extent, of individuality. His own parents had never spoken Yiddish, and he himself hardly understood the language. It was essential, in his view, to become assimilated into the emerging new order, to be an active participant in the new society. Under these circumstances Jewishness, like all national identities, was irrelevant.

It took thirty more years and World War II for Grossman to rediscover that he was a Jew and to draw strength from his Jewish roots. During the war, this modest, self-effacing, nearsighted man played a heroic role as field-marshal of a tank division defending Stalingrad. In the epic passages of his major novels, he describes the collective spirit which infused the Russian people fighting on their own soil, defending every inch of ground, every life of the civilian population. In some ways, he saw this rallying spirit as one that had been forged by Communism in the early *kolkhozy*, the mines and the factories. He had described this spirit in the twelve short stories published in 1935 under the title *Schastie* (Happiness). These stories have two main themes: first, the emerging leadership of the country, drawn from the ranks of the old Bolsheviks, the

heroes of the civil war; second, the collectivization of farming. Although these themes conform to the ideology of the 1930s, Grossman was still able to introduce his unique sensibility. In a one-page sketch entitled "Still About Happiness," he describes the strange appearance in the train station at Lozovaya of a beggar woman, a homeless peasant wandering through the countryside as did so many victims of Stalin's enforced collectivization. Grossman does not breathe a word about the latter, but he depicts this old wanderer tenderly: "How dreadful is the evening solitude of one who in old age has nothing left! What was left for her to do but to lie down upon the tracks and die?" As the narrator walks out of the waiting room, he hears an odd laugh rising towards the star-studded sky, a young person's ecstatic sound. He sees the old crone sitting in the dust, "bathed by the azure and gold of a southern night, looking up in the direction of heaven." Thus Grossman's sensitive prose breaks the mold of strict Socialist Realism.

The love for one's work, its redeeming aspect, informs two other stories of this collection: "The Miner," first published in the review *30 Dney*, 7 1934, and "Comrade Fyodor," brought out in another issue of the same journal (*30 Dney*, 1 1935). "The Miner" depicts a dying man, ravaged by an incurable disease. He does not seem to care about his terminal situation, and even less about his wife's infidelity. All that he cares to do is to perform once more one of his daily tasks in the mine: "to light the fuse that will blow up the stony walls, revealing the heavy blocks of coal." There is nothing sentimental about Grossman's description of his hero; all he wishes to do is to make a statement about a simple, profoundly honest man, one of those people who may not change the world, but who insure its day-to-day operation.

There is a similar sense of dedication in "The Life of Ilya Stepanovich," first published in 1934 by the review *Znamya*. Ilya is an ex-revolutionary, an underground militant who was arrested and sent into exile. Now he is an important member of a production team. His mother, whom he has not seen for the past ten years, arrives in Moscow to see him. Because of his devotion to his work, he fails to meet her at the station. This is, in her view, a terrible slight, yet she does not utter one word of reproach. The following day, Ilya has to attend the installation of a new furnace. At the ceremony he undergoes a kind of epiphany and realizes that he ought to have invited his mother to share this experience with him. He sees the furnace as the lance he had dreamt of as a boy of ten, and he feels that he is one of the Knights of the Round Table, serving the new state with a glorious task.

"Comrade Fyodor" deals with an old revolutionary dying of tuberculosis. He has become a nonperson—nothing is left of the man he used to be, not even his real name. In this story for the first time Grossman writes philosophically with the kind of reflections and digressions which would become an integral part of his later novels.

Shortly before the outbreak of World War II, Grossman published some ten stories and two novellas (1935, 1937, 1938). Some of these stories testify to his descriptive talents, but they are marred by his strict adherence to party ideology. First published in *Znamya*, 8 1937, "Kuharka" (The Female Cook) is another tale about the glory of factory production. A woman who has spent the major part of her life working as a domestic discovers under the new regime the joy of factory collective work. Even her personal life—the choice of the right kind of man to admire—is affected by her new identity. She is now part of a group; above all she can no longer be labeled as "the cook," a kind of slave.

Two of the best stories in this collection are "The Dream," and "Four Days" (*Znamya*, 10 1935; *Znamya*, 1 1936). Neither of these two tales conveys an ideological commitment. "Four Days" is particularly significant in the light of Grossman's future development. It introduces a thoroughly unattractive yet deeply moving character, Faktorovich, one of three Red army officers who find themselves caught for four days in a small town occupied by the Poles. They will be saved by making contact with their friends in the underground. Faktorovich, a Jew, is a fanatical revolutionary, one for whom Marx is the true God, an ascetic who hates his own weak, hairy body and would be willing to sacrifice his life for the sake of the future. In his own way, he is a true descendant of the Hassids of the region. Although Grossman does not approve of his fanaticism, one senses that he also identifies with this mad idealist.

Grossman became conscious of his own Jewishness during World War II, mostly as a result of a devastating personal tragedy. His beloved mother, a teacher of French, was caught in the Ukraine in 1941, when the victorious German army was pushing its way eastward, deep into Russia. The Germans herded the Jews into new ghetto communities where they were either shot and cast into mass graves or dispatched to death camps. His mother's fate led Grossman to the realization—unthinkable for a loyal Communist—that all forms of totalitarianism are the same, that Stalin's genocidal practices were no different from those of Hitler and the Nazis. In his book *Le Cas Grossman* Simon Markish explains that Grossman was transformed by his mother's

tragic death into "l'écrivain du destin juif" (the writer of the Jewish destiny). One of his most moving works, a chapter from *Life and Fate* performed in the theater in both France and the United States, is the letter of Anna Semyonovna Strum to her son, a famous physicist. It is a testament written on the eve of a mass execution of the Jews by the Germans. Victor Strum is working on a very important experiment in the north of Russia, so that mother and son have been separated by circumstances. Anna Semyonovna entrusts her final message to a non-Jewish acquaintance who will mail it to the scientist.

Specifically Jewish characters had already appeared in Grossman's most flagrantly conventional realistic pre-war novel *Stepan Kol'chugin*. Written between 1936 and 1941, it was planned initially as a three-volume work. Finally published in 1955 as *Stepan Kol'chugin, Roman v dvukh knigakh*, it is the story of an orphan in czarist times who is put to work in a mine and then goes on to a factory. Having become a Bolshevik he is sent to Siberia, but he is freed on the eve of the February Revolution. World War II interrupted the composition of the work and the third volume was never completed, but the first two are carefully and lovingly written. There is no Jewish theme in this novel, Lenin and Stalin having decreed that no such theme ought to be introduced into a novel about a Russian workingman. However, the events take place in a zone inhabited by Jews, and Stepan inevitably comes into contact with a number of them. In fact, his ideal and mentor is one Abraham Bakhmutsky, an assimilated Jew, a true Russian revolutionary and a member of the intelligentsia.

Grossman's three major novels are *Za pravoe delo* (For a Just Cause), published in Moscow in four issues of *Novy Mir* (7 to 10, 1952), *Vse techet* (Everything Flows, translated as *Forever Flowing*), and *Zhizn' i sud'ba* (translated as *Life and Fate*). Both *Forever Flowing* and *Life and Fate* were "arrested" in manuscript by government officials. Grossman, however, was spared personal arrest and continued to serve on the presidium of the Soviet Writers Union until his death, in Moscow, in 1964. He even received an award, the Banner of Labor, for his work.

The first of these three novels, *Za pravoe delo*, was in no way controversial. Parts of it were published in newspapers and journals from 1945 to 1949, and it is a model example of Socialist Realism. Yet many of the characters find their way from this book into Grossman's second major novel, and plots and subplots straddle both volumes. But the political attitude reflected in the second novel could not be more at variance with that of the first: it is as though two different writers had composed the books. *Forever Flowing* concerns a former prisoner of a Siberian labor camp who is freed at last. On his way back, he travels through a good part of Russia, meeting relatives and former friends. They have continued to enjoy a comfortable lifestyle, and at the sight of the prisoner they experience the kind of guilt that is endemic to all survivors.

The same tone informs the third of Grossman's major novels, which was also suppressed. It is amazing that he should have thought that *Life and Fate* was publishable in the Soviet Union, even at the height of the Khrushchev thaw. Grossman took his thick manuscript to Vadim Kozhevnikov, the editor-in-chief of the review *Znamya* (Banner), which had published several of his earlier works. But the editorial board dispatched it directly to the Lubyanka prison. Grossman's apartment was searched and all his manuscripts confiscated. When he sought an explanation for the "arrest" of his manuscript, one of the members of the editorial board told him: "Your book couldn't be published for three hundred years." Nevertheless, someone managed to smuggle two microfilms of the manuscript out of Lubyanka. Grossman, however, never learned that his book had survived; it was finally published, in a French translation, in 1983, almost twenty years after his death.

Life and Fate is a great epic work in the Tolstoyan tradition. Its other presiding spirit is Chekhov, whom Grossman considered the great master of humanist realism. Grossman's novel is entirely free of inflated rhetoric and cliched posturing. The reader is taken into Russian trenches as well as behind enemy lines. The writer shows us German prisoner-of-war camps, death camps, and the recesses of KGB jails, ultimately opening for the interrogated victims—most of them loyal party members—onto the Siberian wasteland dotted with gulags. Grossman spares the reader no detail of what the French call "l'univers concentrationnaire." He writes graphically of German engineers planning the crematoria and depicts a private feast offered Adolf Eichmann within one of the future gas chambers. Like André Schwarz-Bart in *The Last of the Just* (1959; English translation, 1960) he follows the victims' *via dolorosa* directly into the gas chambers. Yet despite its lucid probing of horror, the breath of spiritual freedom moves through the entire novel. Although it appeared in print long after Alexander Solzhenitsyn's *Gulag Archipelago* (1973), *Life and Fate* is the first dissident novel written in the Soviet Union. While some reviewers in the mid-1980s found it dated, full of "old-fashioned simplicities," John Bayley reminded readers, in the *London Review of Books*, that Grossman's sensitivity and compassion transcend such criticism. "Only a man indifferent to the real voice of art, a man who insists that the novel must above all things be *novel*—aligned with whatever kind of Modernism is currently valid—could dismiss *Life and Fate* as merely 'noble, elevated, morally irreproachable.' It is a work whose greatest recommendation is that it has no need to be in time with the times."

WORKS IN ENGLISH TRANSLATION: John Glad and James S. Levine translated *The Black Book* in 1981. Thomas M. Whitney's translation of *Forever Flowing* was published in 1972, and Robert Chandler's translation of *Life and Fate* appeared in 1986.

ABOUT: *Biographical Dictionary of the Soviet Union 1917–1988*, 1989; *Contemporary Authors* 124, 1988; *Contemporary Literary Criticism* 41, 1987; (in Russian) Lipkin, S. *Stalingrad Vasiliya Grossmana*, 1986; (in French) Markish, S. *Le Cas Grossman*, 1983. *Periodicals*—Commentary April 1986; Encounter December 1986; London Review of Books September 19, 1985; New York Times Book Review March 26, 1972; Survey Spring 1985; Times Literary Supplement February 23, 1973; World Literature Today Winter 1985.

GRUMBACH, DORIS (ISAAC) (July 12, 1918–   ), American novelist, critic, and biographer, was born in New York City, the daughter of Leonard and Helen Isaac. She attended public schools in Manhattan, Hunter College High School, and Washington Square College, at that time the Greenwich Village branch of New York University, where she majored in philosophy, studying under Sidney Hook and Albert Hofstadter. She also studied medieval literature under Margaret Schlauch, a Chaucer scholar and linguistics expert. She graduated near the top of her class and Phi Beta Kappa in 1939 and, with the help of Professor Schlauch, entered the graduate English department at Cornell University in Ithaca, New York, where she pursued her "passion for medieval literature," receiving a Master of Arts degree in 1940. While at Cornell she met Leonard Grumbach, a graduate student in neurophysiology, whom she married on October 15, 1941. In the thirty-one years of what she has described as a "rich and rewarding" marriage (it ended in divorce in 1972), the couple raised four daughters.

After moving to New York City with her husband, Grumbach worked briefly for MGM, writing subtitles for movies being exported to foreign countries and as a proofreader and copywriter for *Mademoiselle*, a job she says she was fired from for "irrepressible frivolity." But the job was important to her, because she became

DORIS GRUMBACH

friends with the magazine's literary editor,
George Davis, and through him met such writers
as Carson McCullers, Christopher Isherwood,
and W. H. Auden. After a stint as proofreader
and then assistant editor at *Architectural Forum*
magazine, Grumbach, believing strongly that
World War II was "just and necessary," renounced the strict pacifism which she had
adopted during her student days (and which she
has since resumed); she joined the Navy and
served in the WAVES for the duration.

After the war, she and her husband, with their
growing family, lived in several upstate New
York towns before settling in Albany, where she
taught English at a private day school attended
by her daughters. From 1952 to 1973 she taught
English at the College of Saint Rose in Albany,
then a small Catholic women's college, where
she advanced from a night-school instructor to
full professor. During the early 1950s she began
her career as a book reviewer and literary essayist, writing at first for minor Catholic publications and eventually for the *New York Times
Book Review* and the *Saturday Review*, where
she had her own columns, and for the
Nation, Commonweal, the *New Republic,* the
Washington Post, the *Chicago Tribune,* the *Los
Angeles Times,* and other publications. She also
served as literary editor of the *New Republic*
from 1971 to 1973, and in 1982 she became a
book reviewer on the "Morning Edition" show
on National Public Radio. Following her divorce
she taught at Empire State College in Saratoga
Springs, New York, from 1972 to 1973. After
moving to Washington, D.C., where she still

lives, she served as professor of American literature at American University from 1975 to 1984,
when she retired to devote herself full-time to
writing. She has also taught at the Iowa Writers
Workship in Iowa City and at the University of
Maryland. Raised in a secular Jewish family, she
converted to Catholicism after her marriage and
later became a deeply committed member of the
Episcopal church.

In the early 1960s Grumbach published two
novels. *The Spoil of the Flowers* is based, she has
said, on her experiences as a teacher at a private
girls' school and presents "the little comedies and
large tragedies of adolescent life" at such a
school. *The Short Throat, the Tender Mouth*
draws on her experiences during the last three
months of the 1939 academic year at New York
University, when war was threatening and a
friend on a literary magazine committed suicide. Grumbach has said that she now regards
the novels as incompletely realized and immature, and they received little critical attention.

In 1967, however, her biography of Mary
McCarthy, *The Company She Kept,* received a
great deal of critical attention, much of it hostile.
Even before it was published it made news by
drawing threats of a lawsuit from McCarthy,
who had read it in galleys and objected to the inclusion of intimate biographical detail which she
had voluntarily disclosed to Grumbach in letters
and conversations. She claimed that these revelations were intended only as background to the
book and were never meant to be published in
the book itself. In an article for the *New York
Times Book Review* on the controversy, Grumbach confessed to having been naive. She had
been surprised and delighted by McCarthy's
cheerful cooperation (she even supplied the
book's title) and almost heedless candor. However, she did not realize that McCarthy, admittedly lacking discretion herself, was counting on her
to compensate with her own discretion. In the
end, Grumbach had to delete much of the material she had relied on to support her interpretation of McCarthy's fiction as thinly disguised
autobiography.

This interpretation was attacked by several
critics. In the *New York Times Book Review,* Ellen Moers sharply rejected Grumbach's view
that there is only a "faint line" between
McCarthy's life and her fiction: "This simply
cannot be true. The husbands in McCarthy fiction (those off-color Irishmen, pot-bellied Jews
and prissy Protestants) are such dreary mediocri-
ties, her artist colonies and political oases are so
bare of talent and distinction, her suites of college girls are so tediously thinluute—only a
powerful imagination could have made such

nonentities out of the very interesting company that Mary McCarthy actually kept." In *Commonweal*, Stephanie Harrington called Grumbach's tendency to reduce McCarthy's fiction to her life "a cliché." She also concluded that Grumbach had settled for a "disturbingly superficial cataloging technique" in her discussion of the fiction, lining up bits from other critics for and against the novels and adding little original of her own. Both Moers and Harrington charged that Grumbach had been negligent in relying so heavily on McCarthy's own information and failing to interview her former husbands and her friends and enemies, especially in view of Grumbach's autobiographical interpretation of the novels. The critics who praised *The Company She Kept* tended to be mild. Granville Hicks, in the *Saturday Review*, wrote: "Although there is nothing novel about finding Miss McCarthy in her books, critics are usually cautious about identifying characters in fiction with real people, and I am grateful for Mrs. Grumbach's refusal to beat around that particular bush." In the *New Statesman*, Desmond MacNamara called the book "stimulating" and commented on its "capacity to shock with candour often in some absurd prosaic juxtaposition." "I like it," he added; "some don't."

Critics were also divided over Grumbach's next book, the novel *Chamber Music*, but this time the dominant note was praise, if sometimes sharply qualified. The novel takes the form of the memoirs of a ninety-year-old widow named Caroline Maclaren, and the style in which her often shocking story is told is deliberately old-fashioned—clear, elegant, genteel. An innocent girl of seventeen, Caroline marries a promising composer named Robert Maclaren and goes with him to Germany, where he neglects her and where she learns that he has been sexually involved with his mother; later she finds out about a homosexual affair he has had with one of his students. They settle on a farm in upstate New York, where Robert, whose music had made him famous, treats her with cold contempt, as a mere adjunct to his work. But at the height of his fame he begins slowly to succumb to a mysterious disease which turns out to be syphilis, the gruesome details of which are described with unflinching candor. Caroline shares the burden of caring for her increasingly helpless husband with a young German nurse named Anna. After Robert's death, Caroline and Anna become lovers, and in this relationship Caroline, who publicly is occupied in establishing a colony for musicians in Robert's name, finds her fulfillment as a woman. The colony itself is apparently modeled on the MacDowell colony for artists in Saratoga Springs, New York.

Several critics praised the elegant style and careful composition of the novel as a formal realization of its musical motif. In the *New York Times*, John Leonard wrote that the characters in *Chamber Music* "are all stringed instruments. The music we hear occurs in the chamber of Caroline's heart. It is quite beautiful." Abigail McCarthy in *Commonweal* found that the novel has "the classical form, clarity, and brilliance of a composition for strings." The old-fashioned gracefulness of the style is, in the view of some critics, all the more effective for its contrast with the often grim subject matter. This "elegant" novel, wrote Peter S. Prescott in *Newsweek*, "succeeds in part because of the tension that Grumbach creates between her sexual drama and the measured formality of her narration." "What gives the main part of this book its polish and flavor is the contrast between matter and manner," wrote Victoria Glendinning in the *Washington Post Book World*. In the *Yale Review* Edith Milton found that Robert's disease is given "a clinical description so simply precise, so elegantly loathsome, that it would do nicely either in a medical text or in a book on style," and she amplified the point: "The novel is wonderfully written in a voice to evoke a time gone by, an era vanished. . . . The prose, understated, beautiful in its economies, supports a story of almost uncanny bleakness." Several British reviewers made similar observations. "The spartan freshness of tone in *Chamber Music*—its air of having been written, longhand, in one sitting—is extremely effective," wrote John Naughton in the *Listener*. Paul Ableman in the *Spectator* found that the restraint of the style allowed Grumbach to avoid the sensationalism pervasive in contemporary fiction and for that very reason made the book seem "more real than much modern realism."

A few critics, however, found the style limiting. Gail Godwin, for example, wrote in the *New York Times Book Review*: "Readers will no doubt vary in their opinions as to whether Caroline or her creator should be credited for the memoir's occasionally stifled tone, and for its stolid preference for essayistic recollections over vividly dramatized scenes." Godwin explicitly attributed what she regarded as the book's lack of dramatic vitality to Grumbach's "sticking so close to the biographical data of the late composer Edward MacDowell." There were also critical objections to the lesbian affair that concludes the novel. "At this point," wrote the anonymous *New Yorker* reviewer, "Doris Grumbach apparently feared that the theme of Man's Oppression of Woman in Love and Art had been too subtly drawn by her modest and meticulous narrator, for she has tacked on an implausible ending that reduces the memoirs to a feminist parable." Several reviewers thought that the episode threw Grumbach's style off-key, or as the anonymous *Time* reviewer put it: "the love that dare not speak its name eventually tends to drown out the delicate strains of Grumbach's musical prose."

Like *Chamber Music*, Grumbach's next novel, *The Missing Person*, is modeled on a real person. The novel traces the Hollywood career of a glamorous actress called Franny Fuller, who is clearly based on Marilyn Monroe, although Grumbach, in a prefatory note to the book, announced: "This novel is a portrait, not of a single life but of many lives melded into one, typical of the women America often glorifies and elevates, and then leaves suspended in their lonely and destructive fame." Thus, as Herbert Gold wrote in the *New York Times Book Review*, Franny is meant to represent those "missing persons" who are "above all, missing to themselves." But this symbolic function, he thought, undermined the character's reality: "Despite the deftness and delicacy of Miss Grumbach's touch, and the credible projection of a Marilyn Monroe aura, Franny does not offer us the sense of surprise that we expect of a fully created fictional character. . . . More interesting than the central character are the adroit structure of the novel and its peripheral characters. . . . Miss Grumbach manages a sober interlocking of anecdote that is reminiscent both of Sherwood Anderson and Nathanael West, though her melancholic lyricism is very much her own." Abigail McCarthy, writing in *Commonweal*, also thought that the Hollywood background eclipsed the somewhat two-dimensional quality of Franny Fuller: "It is hard for her to have a separate imaginary existence in the mind of the reader. But this flaw, if it is one, is more than compensated for by the writer's evocation of the scene against which Franny moves—tawdry, wonderful Hollywood at its peak."

The Ladies is a historical novel based on the lives of two Irish women who actually lived in eighteenth-century Wales. It is linked to her other work by its lesbian theme. Lady Eleanor Butler and Sarah Posonby struggle to escape repressive families and finally live together, as virtual recluses, in a large house in Wales, where they are known as the eccentric "Ladies of Llangollen." As in the case of Grumbach's previous fiction, critics praised her sense of concrete detail and expressed doubts about matters of style and tone. "Grumbach is acutely sensitive to the quiet hum of everyday living and the small acquired habits that bond lovers over long periods," wrote Diane Salvatore in *Ms.* magazine. "It is especially touching to watch the

women age as the pages turn, effecting a kind of time-lapse realism that doesn't diminish the Ladies' passion or love for each other. The quaintness is somewhat overdone, however, and in Grumbach's effort to portray a placid and harmonic lesbian household, she lets the story sink periodically into anaesthetized domestic oblivion. The reader may also grow irritated by Eleanor's increasing crankiness." In the *New York Times Book Review*, Catharine R. Stimpson echoed some of the critics of *Chamber Music* in finding that Grumbach's style faltered when confronted with the task of describing sexual passion: "Unhappily, the language of *The Ladies* is occasionally thin when Miss Grumbach describes sexuality, falsely archaic, even fey, when she describes passion." In spite of this, however, Stimpson described the novel as "boldly imagined, subtly crafted," and concluded that "Miss Grumbach has a serious purpose. Her Lady Eleanor and Sarah poignantly feel themselves to be alone. . . . *The Ladies* eloquently documents the existence of women who lived as they wished to, instead of as society expected them to."

The Magician's Girl tells the story of three women who meet as roommates at Barnard in the late 1930s, and again there is more than a suggestion of real persons in two of the characters, namely Sylvia Plath and Diane Arbus. Merle Rubin of the *Christian Science Monitor* found it the most "compelling" of Grumbach's novels and commented: "What is most poignant about this novel is that its special aura of serenity tinged with sadness comes not from the pains and losses the characters endure, although there are many of these, but from the conviction it conveys that life, for all its sorrows, is so rich with possibilities as to make any one life—however long—much too short." But again the critics were divided. Paula Deitz, in the *New York Times Book Review*, praised the "matter-of-fact plainness" of Grumbach's prose, which "shocks with its simple, quirky revelations," and the "rich images, informed with the magic conveyed by the small details that reveal the forming of these lives" that Grumbach offers in the early part of the book. "But, alas," she continues, "the promise of Part One goes unfulfilled as the three develop into stock figures amid a series of clichéd events that mar the freshness of their inner selves."

WORKS: *Novels*—The Spoil of the Flowers, 1962; The Short Throat, the Tender Mouth, 1964; Chamber Music, 1979; The Missing Person, 1981; The Ladies, 1984; The Magician's Girl, 1987. *Biography*—The Company She Kept, 1967

ABOUT: Contemporary Authors Autobiography Series,

2, 1985; Contemporary Authors New Revision Series 9, 1983; Contemporary Literary Criticism 13, 1980. *Periodicals*—America May 27, 1967; Atlantic Monthly March 1979; Christian Science Monitor July 13, 1967; February 22, 1987; Commonweal October 6, 1967; June 22, 1979; Harper's March 1979; Listener August 9, 1979; Ms. April 1979, January 1985; Nation March 28, 1981; National Review June 8, 1979; New Republic March 10, 1979; New Statesman December 1, 1967; August 17, 1979; New York Herald Tribune Book Week May 28, 1967; New York Times March 13, 1979; New York Times Book Review June 11, 1967; March 25, 1979; March 29, 1981; September 30, 1984; February 1, 1987; New York Times Magazine June 11, 1967; New Yorker April 23, 1979; Newsweek March 19, 1979; Saturday Review June 3, 1967; Spectator August 11, 1979; Time June 30, 1967; Times Literary Supplement November 30, 1979; September 11, 1981; June 19, 1987; Washington Post Book World March 18, 1979; April 5, 1981; Yale Review Autumn 1979.

A. R. GURNEY, JR.

GURNEY, A(LBERT) R(AMSDELL), JR.

(November 1, 1930–   ), American playwright and novelist, was born in Buffalo, New York, the second of three children of Albert Ramsdell Gurney, a prosperous real-estate broker and developer, and the former Marion Spaulding. He was sent to St. Paul's School in Concord, New Hampshire, and graduated in 1952 from Williams College. After three years (1952–1955) of service in the U.S. Naval Reserve, he attended Yale Drama School, earning his master's degree in fine arts in 1958. He was a member of the humanities faculty at the Massachusetts Institute of Technology in Cambridge from 1960, and professor of literature there from 1970, until 1982 when he gave up regular academic teaching and moved from eastern Massachusetts to New York City. He now lives on a farm in Connecticut with his wife, the former Molly Goodyear, whom he married in 1957. They have three children. "Liberated . . . from the oppressive obligations of academic life," as he wrote in 1986 in an article in the *New York Times*, he began writing plays at an accelerated rate, work which gave him the sense of "pushing against the traditional restrictions of drama." He remains a tenured professor at MIT, but teaches there only sporadically.

Gurney has been a consistently successful playwright since the mid-1970s, and has established a peculiarly solid niche for himself in the American theater. He is almost the only practicing playwright whose subject, lovingly and extensively treated, is the upper-middle-class white Protestant American family, a subject which might with approximate accuracy be considered not entirely fashionable but has nevertheless proved eminently popular. His plays

frequently enjoy Off-Broadway New York runs. His audiences are composed of more than their share of well-to-do suburban matrons, a group which has always constituted a strong basis for and assurance of any New York stage success. His drama has been succinctly described in the *Nation* by Richard Gilman, no great admirer of his work in general: Gurney writes "the most thoroughly American middlebrow plays of any of our dramatists. If 'middlebrow' is too strong a word, I'll call him the poet laureate of middle-consciousness. . . . Gurney speaks for, or to, or with the voice of what is still our largest population bloc. Gurney is a WASP—he has rather excessively been called the John Cheever of the theater—who celebrates the cultural and moral virtues of his heritage, . . . mourns their decline and pokes fun at their present perversions. He doesn't do any of these things with notable force or invention, true, but neither is he often flaccid or wholly derivative. His plays are usually about ordinary people to whom nothing extreme or spectacular happens; structurally, they combine traditional naturalism with some mildly avant-garde (or, more accurately, erstwhile avant-garde) techniques."

Gurney's earliest plays received mostly short-lived regional productions. Some of them were musicals: *Love in Buffalo* (Yale Repertory Theater, New Haven, Connecticut, 1958); *Tom Sawyer* (Starlight Theater, Kansas City, Missouri, 1960); and *Around the World in Eighty Days* (first solo published work, 1962). A one-act play he wrote at Yale, *The Rape of Bunny Stuntz*, was produced at the Image Theater, Cambridge,

Massachusetts, in 1966 and Off Broadway by the Albee-Barr-Wilder Playwrights Unit in 1967. *The Bridal Dinner* was produced in Cambridge in 1962; *The Comeback*, in 1964. All three treated upper-middle-class anxiety in the setting of a small American city not unlike Buffalo. A definite departure from this formula was *The David Show*, in which such Old Testament figures as David and Bathsheba, Ham, and Samuel were treated as characters on a television show; the play satirized 1960s political-social reality, including the New Left, the Great Society, and the changing relationship in America between Jew and Christian, black and white. The play received a summer-stock production in 1966 and opened Off Broadway in October 1968 at the Players Theater where it closed after one performance.

Gurney achieved his first genuine theatrical success with *Scenes from American Life*, a comedy about the WASP world he was coming to be expert at describing. Organized as a series of brief vignette-like scenes (a technique the author was often to use again), it examines the lives of the Buffalo well-to-do from the 1930s to (presumably) the mid-1980s, by which time the country has become a military dictatorship. The play was produced in April 1971 by the repertory company at Lincoln Center's Forum (later the Mitzi Newhouse) Theater. Reviewing it in the *New Yorker*, Edith Oliver wrote that Gurney's "underlying pessimism and apocalyptic outlook in no way dim his wit and his sense of fun; along with the comedy there is sadness, and even tragedy. . . . the play is never bleak, and heaven knows it is never dull." Gurney won the 1971–1972 Vernon Rice Drama Desk Award.

Children, loosely based on John Cheever's story "Goodbye, My Brother," received its premiere at the Mermaid Theatre, London, in April 1974. The two-act play concerns the emotional tensions within a WASP family vacationing at their summer home in Massachusetts, tensions which emerge during a Fourth of July weekend and threaten to pull the family apart for good. Apparent for the first time in this work are motifs later more thoroughly developed by Gurney, in particular the slow, anguished decline of family unity and direction and the discontent and malaise lurking just below the apparently placid surface of moneyed American family life. Much of the play's dramatic force comes from unspoken scenes and unseen characters—brooding offstage presences. This inferential technique was much praised by London reviewers but objected to by those in New York, where *Children* was produced by the Manhattan Theatre Club in November 1976. It was received in a New England summer-stock production in 1979 and received a German production, starring the late Lilli Palmer, in 1980.

One of Gurney's most subtle and disturbing works is *Richard Cory: A Play*, a one-act version of his earlier two-act *Who Killed Richard Cory?* (Circle Repertory Company, New York, March 1976). It is a dramatic treatment and extension of the powerful short poem by Edward Arlington Robinson about a handsome, genteel man, much admired by his neighbors, who suddenly and shockingly commits suicide. The play explores the reasons for his death: he was something of a prude, a bit too good a man for anyone to bear; a literal and spiritual hypochondriac, he is consumed by worries that because he's rich, his soul can't be saved. His marriage is in a shambles, his eldest son is turning bad, and his new mistress, after pursuing him at length, has decided she wants no more to do with him. All Cory's friends, colleagues, neighbors, and acquaintances think they know him, and are sure of the reason for his suicide, but none of them, it is apparent, knows the real, complex man. The play, especially in the one-act version, is notable for its fluid use of vignettes and, thematically, for its strong suggestions of cultural unease and decay among the upper middle class.

A two-act play, *The Middle Ages*, is another treatment of WASP decline which in manner and method harks back to *Scenes from American Life*. The action is confined to the trophy room of a men's club in a large American city over a span of time from the mid-1940s to the late 1970s. The play opens in the latter period on the day of the funeral of Charles, the long-time president of the decaying club. His elder son, the ne'er-do-well Barney, and Barney's sister-in-law Eleanor have loved one another since childhood. During the course of the play, their relationship is seen at various times from its inception to its climax, when Eleanor, who is unhappily married to Barney's brother, finally decides she will make a commitment to the irrepressible Barney. The couple joyfully stride from the room, arm in arm, as if to their own wedding, to attend Charles' funeral. The play was first produced at the Mark Taper Forum Laboratory in Los Angeles in January 1977 and had a three-week run in early 1978 at the Hartmann Theater in Stamford, Connecticut. Richard Gilman, writing in the *Nation*, called *The Middle Ages* "a fable about love and propriety, or the lack thereof, among [WASPs]. . . . Gurney has some sociological fun at the expense of aristocratic foibles and prejudices. . . . But the play, while never inept and seldom boring, hasn't much energy and offers no surprises. It's right in the middle."

Gurney's virtually patented vignette technique was pushed to its limits with *The Wayside Motor Inn*, a play which, according to an authorial note appended to the published version, "is composed of five separate subplots which take place simultaneously in one room of a suburban motor lodge outside of Boston during the late afternoon and early evening of a spring day in the late seventies." The play "is about ten ordinary people who find themselves at the wayside of their lives, wondering which turn to take. Their difficulties and conflicts are commonplace, but I have attempted to give a dimension and resonance to their situations by presenting them side by side, and in some cases, simultaneously on stage. It is my hope that in this way we can make the ordinary seem somehow extraordinary, just as several simple melodies enhance each other when they are interwoven in a musical ensemble piece." The characters include a traveling salesman, an ill and unhappy retired couple, a sexually confused student couple, an ambitious father and his unhappy son, and a divorcing doctor and his wife. The play had a short run, thanks to a Rockefeller Foundation grant, at the Manhattan Theatre Club in November 1977.

The Dining Room, a play in two acts, was not, the author notes in the published version, "about dishes, or food, or costume changes, but rather a play about people in a dining room." The work explores, in somewhat disjointed but interconnected scenes, the events occurring in several dining rooms in various houses over a span of perhaps fifty years. The single room setting represents, according to Gerald Weales in *Commonweal*, "not a particular home or family, but a host of such dining rooms peopled by families in varying degrees of stability or disintegration." The play shows the way the outside world impinges upon the dining room, "disrupts the family structure, renders the room obsolete, reveals the canker in the rose. It is a world in which adultery, homosexuality, heavy drinking, parental bullying, [and] youthful rebellion are recognized but not acknowledged, kept in their place which is certainly not in the dining room." Gurney's message is that WASPs are fading out as a distinct cultural group, and that places like the dining room, in which is centered a proper, sedate kind of domestic existence, are becoming unused, hence useless. The play was first produced in January 1981 at the Studio Theater of Playwrights Horizons in New York. John Simon, reviewing it in *New York* magazine, complained about its "excessive trickiness. In Thornton Wilder's *The Long Christmas Dinner*, from which this play seems to derive, there is, although stylized and accelerated, a consecutive progression and confinement to one family. Gurney, however, jumps back and forth in time, around in space (this only *seems* to be the same dining room), and ever onward with new dramatis personae. . . . Gurney has been in better form before . . . yet even at his second best he is observant, thoughtful, and, when most unflinchingly satirical, still unabatedly humane."

Gurney's move to New York in 1982 was almost immediately followed by a considerable increase in his rate of dramatic production. During the 1982–1983 theater season, three of his plays—*The Middle Ages*, *The Dining Room*, and *What I Did Last Summer*, about a boy's coming of age in the mid-1940s at a Lake Erie vacation resort—were produced in and around New York. Thereafter, he completed plays at a rate of more than one a year. *The Golden Age*, a contemporary adaptation of Henry James' *The Aspern Papers*, was produced Off Broadway in April 1984 at the Jack Lawrence Theater. *The Perfect Party*, about a WASP university professor's failed attempt to throw a party, was seen at New York's Playwrights Horizons in April 1986, then after favorable reviews moved in June 1986 to the Astor Place Theater. *Sweet Sue*, about a love affair between an older women and a younger man, ran briefly on Broadway at the Music Box Theater in December 1986. *Another Antigone*, concerning a conflict between a WASP professor and his Jewish student, was produced at Playwrights Horizons in January 1988. A longer-running success was *The Cocktail Hour*, which humorously details the worries of upstate New York WASP parents over an inflammatory autobiographical play written by their son. It began a long run Off Broadway in October 1988 at the Promenade Theater. In August 1989 Gurney's two-character play *Love Letters* opened at the same theater. Rotating casts (which have included William Hurt, Julie Harris, Jason Robards, Kate Nelligan, and a number of other prominent actors) simply sit at a table reading the letters they have written to each other over their lifetimes. *Love Letters* had a warm critical and popular reception and moved to another off-Broadway theater in the autumn of 1989.

Gurney's novels have not found nearly as large an audience as his plays. They also contain WASP characters and have the same intermittently amusing lightness of touch. *The Gospel According to Joe* is a contemporary narration of the life of Jesus. *The Snow Ball* exposes the foibles of Buffalo WASP society. His most consistently comic novel, *Entertaining Strangers*, has an academic setting. Professor Porter Platt "(known in the dorms as Professor Plattitude)," is an associate professor of humanities at a Boston institute of technology, "an ineffectually camouflaged MIT," as one reviewer put it, which is, according to Platt's own wry first-person narrative, "'polarized around science,' according to one of our presidents, 'paralyzed' around it, according to some of us who taught humanities there." Platt has always prized himself as being a tolerant, gentle man, yet the aim of his story is to explain how "I suddenly found myself seething with Satanic anger, contemplating mischief, committing rape, and attempting murder, all within a single second semester." This catastrophe occurs when he sponsors an Oxford-educated Rhodesian, who he thinks is an Englishman, for a minor temporary post in his department. He supposes, quite incorrectly, that the Oxonian will become his ally in the departmental wars. "Once the stray Englishman is hired," wrote P.-L. Adams in the *Atlantic*, "he precipitates a splendid confusion of academic incompetence, backbiting, and treachery. The frosting on this cyanide cupcake is the narrator, who presents himself as an abused innocent while revealing himself as a useless boob."

In addition to the Drama Desk Award, Gurney has also won the Rockefeller Playwrights Award (1977), the playwriting award of the National Endowment for the Arts (1981–1982), and the Award of Merit from the American Academy and Institute of Arts and Letters (1987). He is a member of the Authors League of America, the Writers Guild, and serves on the council of the Dramatists Guild.

PUBLISHED WORKS: *Drama*—The Comeback, 1967; The Golden Fleece, 1967; The David Show, 1968; The Open Meeting, 1968; The Problem, 1968; Scenes from American Life, 1970, rev. ed., 1976; The Old One-Two, 1971; Children, 1975; The Rape of Bunny Stuntz, 1976; The Love Course, 1976; Who Killed Richard Cory?, 1976; The Middle Ages, 1978; The Wayside Motor Inn, 1978; The Dining Room, 1982; Richard Cory, 1985; The Perfect Party, 1986. *Fiction*—The Gospel According to Joe, 1974; Entertaining Strangers, 1977; The Snow Ball, 1984.

ABOUT: Contemporary Authors 77–80, 1979; Contemporary Literary Criticism 32, 1985; Contemporary Dramatists, 1977; Current Biography, 1986; Who's Who in America, 1988–1989; Who's Who in the Theatre, 1981. *Periodicals*—Commonweal April 23, 1982; Nation April 30, 1983; New Republic May 12, 1982; New York March 8, 1982; February 14, 1983; April 4, 1983; New York Times October 26, 1976; May 30, 1982; July 27, 1986; January 10, 1988; February 4, 1988; October 16, 1988; October 21, 1988; New York Times Book Review May 26, 1974; February 10, 1985; New York Times Magazine November 12, 1989; New Yorker April 6, 1971, February 21, 1983; April 4, 1983; April 22, 1984; Plays & Players May 1974; Time April

4, 1983; Vanity Fair March 1986; Virginia Quarterly Review Autumn 1977; Women's Wear Daily March 26, 1971; April 4, 1983.

*GUY, ROSA (September 1, 1928–   ), American novelist and author of children's books, was born in Trinidad, West Indies, daughter of Henry and Audrey (Gonzales) Cuthbert. After coming to the United States with her parents in 1932, she was raised in New York City. She later married Warner Guy, now deceased, by whom she has a son, Warner. Her first novel was *Bird at My Window*, about a young black man, Wade Williams, who, brutalized by his upbringing on the streets of Harlem, is committed to the psychopathic ward of a New York City hospital following an outburst of rage in which he attacks his sister, his only real friend. The narrative moves forward in time while also moving back into the past to reveal the sources of Wade's frustration. The reviewer for *Booklist* summed up the book by commenting that the "author's intense feeling for the individuality of several of her characters saves them in the main from pawnlike roles in a passionately earnest novel." Miles Jackson in *Library Journal* remarked that the "devastating effects of life in Harlem as a subject of fiction runs the risk of becoming overworked" and that certain parts of the novel "smack of the sociological treatise"; yet conceded that at times the novel does "come off very well."

The Friends, written for a young audience, tells the story of a black girl, Phyllisia, who has recently moved from the West Indies to Harlem. Shunned by her classmates because of her dialect and her respect for her teacher, she forms a friendship with another girl, Edith Jackson, from a poor and disintegrating family. She has, however, an ambivalent feeling toward her, partly because of her sense of their social differences; Phyllisia's father Calvin, a hard-working member of the black middle class, harshly drives Edith away when she comes to their house. In the course of the story Phyllisia attempts to understand her feelings and to gain insight into her own life. Ethel L. Heins in *Horn Book* called *The Friends* a "strong, honest story—often tragic but ultimately hopeful—of complex, fully-realized characters and of the ambivalence and conflicts of human nature." The reviewer for *Booklist* commented that the "plot is nonexistent, the dialog awkward"; but went on to remark that "the main character's internal hardships, her difficult realizations of her own uncompassionate rigidity in her relationships with her sister, father and friend and her consequent value changes are unusual; the situation itself is starkly real."

°gē

ROSA GUY

Guy's next novel, *Ruby*, portrays a lesbian relationship into which the heroine, Ruby Cathy, enters in the course of her attempt to find herself. Some reviewers complained that Guy resorted at times to "rhapsodical overwriting," and Aubrey B. Eaglen in *Library Journal* found the lesbian relationship unrealized and "unbelievable." But most critics were struck by the strong realism of the novel. The reviewer for *Publishers Weekly*, for example, commented that "if Rosa Guy had taken a camera and put it down in 1970 (the year of the novel) on a completely believable black middle class family situation in any big city in America, she could not have achieved a more riveting picture of basically decent people, floundering because of the generation gap. Neatest of all, she has a sense of humor and hope for the future."

Edith Jackson, a sequel to *The Friends*, follows the life of the outcast title character, a seventeen-year-old girl whose parents are both dead and who attempts to hold her sisters together as a family. The novel received many favorable reviews. The reviewer for *Booklist* called it a "potent and moving first-person narrative of a strong willed but naive black girl's coming of age," and argued that the novel was "more convincing than *Ruby* . . . and more carefully developed than *The Friends.*" The reviewer for *Publishers Weekly* was also impressed by Guy's depiction of urban black life. "Guy's exquisite perceptions," the reviewer noted, "to say nothing of her skills at characterization, have created a world for her readers that evokes pity and understanding. There is the ring of truth in the in-

cidents, in her portrayal of all of the people, black and white, who touch the Jackson girls."

Having previously dealt with protagonists who are young girls, Guy changed her stride in *The Disappearance*, which relates the experience of a sixteen-year-old boy, Imamu Jones, who comes from a squalid Harlem apartment with an alcoholic mother, and is removed to the foster home of a middle-class family in Brooklyn. When the family's daughter disappears, however, Imamu is suspected of her murder, and it is only at the end that the actual murderer is found. To a number of critics, the revelation of the actual murderer seemed implausible and melodramatic. But otherwise critics tended to like the book. Ethel L. Heins in *Horn Book* called *The Disappearance* "a raw and powerful work. . . . the second half of the book is a shocking, suspenseful whodunit; but all of the book, transcending race and environment, is a remarkable, mature exposure—as clean and penetrating as surgery—of fear and loneliness, desperation and suffering, deception and pride."

A Mirror of Her Own, about a young girl's helpless emotions of love, and involving both black and white characters, received crushing reviews, Lillian L. Shapiro in *School Library Journal* calling it a "cliché-laden moralistic story about cardboard figures." But *A Measure of Time* was considered an arresting novel. It deals with a spunky, if not always well-guided, black girl who leaves behind an impossible situation of exploitation in Alabama to seek her fortune in Harlem in 1926. It was generally agreed among reviewers that the secondary characters were lacking in life and dimension, but that Guy's conception of Dorine Davis was a triumph. As the reviewer for *Booklist* put it, Dorine "is electrifyingly full of flavor and sass, even if the creaky plot provides this ebullient character with only spotty support." Almost all the reviewers were impressed by Guy's sense of place and period, her "poignant tribute to the great and glittering Harlem that was."

In *New Guys Around the Block*, Guy reintroduced her character Imamu Jones in a tale of violence on Harlem's streets. "Imamu is an appealing cross," the reviewer for *Booklist* commented, "between the defensively tough and genuinely caring in this hard-hitting sequel to *The Disappearance*. Not glossing over the violence of life on Harlem streets, Guy places the blame for bombed-out buildings and burned-out people squarely on society but ends the story on a note of hope." Also favorably impressed by the novel, Selma G. Lanes in the *New York Times Book Review* remarked that "if Ms. Guy's earlier trilogy (*The Friends*, *Ruby* and *Edith*

Jackson) was richer and more subtle, Imamu's story . . . is nonetheless absorbing and moving. The reader cannot resist rooting for Imamu, with his intelligence and growing self-awareness, as he negotiates the booby traps of a difficult life." *And I Heard a Bird Sing* brings Guy's trilogy of works centering on Imamu to a conclusion. Deborah Singmaster in the *Times Literary Supplement* remarked that "Rosa Guy has created a credible and appealing character in Imamu Jones. Her handling of his relationship with his foster family is at times sentimental but she is moving and perceptive about the disturbing mixture of concern and resentment that Imamu feels for his mother as she gropes her way out of dependence on him and her alcoholic past." The reviewer for *Publishers Weekly* remarked similarly that "Guy again proves her skill at creating stirring stories about real people—here not only Imamu but his mother, concerned foster family and everyone involved."

Although Rosa Guy is best known for the honest realism of her portraits of life in the black ghettos of America, she is also fascinated with the fables and folklore of West Indian cultures. *My Love, My Love, or The Peasant Girl*, as its title hints, is a fable drawn out of the poverty but also the rich imaginative tradition of the Caribbean islands. Its heroine is a poor and humble village girl who saves a prince from death and briefly wins his love. A poignant and enchanting story, *My Love, My Love* became the subject of a musical adaptation in a highly praised Off-Broadway production by Playwrights Horizon in April 1990, with book and lyrics by Lynn Ahrens and "a passionate calypso- and reggae-flavored score" (as Stephen Holden wrote in the *New York Times*) by Stephen Flaherty.

Rosa Guy was the founding president of the Harlem Writer's Guild, and has given lectures and readings in Africa, Europe, and Japan. She has traveled widely in pursuit of her interest in the history and culture of people of African descent—both in Haiti and Trinidad and in Africa itself, where she has visited Senegal, Gambia, the Ivory Coast, Nigeria, and Algeria. Guy, who speaks French and Creole as well as English, lives on Manhattan's Upper West Side.

PRINCIPAL WORKS: Bird at My Window, 1966; (as editor) Children of Longing, 1971; The Friends, 1973; Ruby, 1976; Edith Jackson, 1978; The Disappearance, 1979; A Mirror of Her Own, 1981; (translator-adapter Birago Diop) Mother Crocodile: An Uncle Amadou Tale from Senegal, 1981; A Measure of Time, 1983; New Guys Around the Block, 1983; Paris, Pee Wee and Big Dog, 1984; My Love, My Love, or the Peasant Girl 1985; And I Heard a Bird Sing, 1985.

ABOUT: Contemporary Authors New Revision Series 14, 1985; Contemporary Literary Criticism 26, 1983; Oxford Companion to Children's Literature, 1984; Something About the Author 14, 1978; Twentieth Century Children's Writers, 1983. *Periodicals*—Booklist February 6, 1966; January 15, 1974; April 15, 1978; July 1983; March 15, 1983; Horn Book April 1974, February 1980; Library Journal February 1, 1966; September 15, 1976; New York Times May 24, 1990; New York Times Book Review August 28, 1983; Times Literary Supplement June 12, 1987.

*HAAVIKKO, PAAVO (JUHANI) (January 25, 1931–   ), Finnish poet, dramatist, and fiction writer, was born in Helsinki to Heikki Adrian and Rauha (Pyykönen) Haavikko. His father was a businessman. In 1951, the year in which he published his first book of poems, Haavikko enrolled at the University of Helsinki, but after a year of military service (1951–1952) he did not return to the university. Instead he began a business career in real estate which he pursued until 1967. During that period he published some seven volumes of poetry, four novels, and four radio plays. In 1967 Haavikko joined the Otava Publishing Company in Helsinki as its literary director; he remained active in the firm until 1984, when he became an independent literary consultant, working at that time on a history of Finnish business. Though he has been an amazingly prolific writer, writing is a leisure time activity for Haavikko: "I think it's impossible to be just a writer," he told Philip Binham in an interview for *Books from Finland*. "That would mean isolating oneself completely from the outside world—so it's important to have other work."

Haavikko's first collection of poetry *Tiet etäisyyksiin* (The Ways to Far Away), published when he was only twenty, represented what the Swedish novelist Bo Carpelan called "the first breakthrough of Finnish modernism." It also expressed Haavikko's dedication to the art of poetry in a language that few people outside his country can read:

> Poem oh poem, my only birthplace, I speak of
> It is my beloved, flowering into song,
> But I also long for myself, for the place
>   where I am, an empty space,
> A soul in a field of flowers.
>   —trans. Anselm Hollo

The dominant literary language of Finland remained Swedish until well into the twentieth century. As Haavikko reflects sardonically:

> Finnish isn't a language, it's a local custom
> of sitting on a bench with hair over your ears,
> it's continual talking about the rain and the wind,
> it's inborn table-pounding,

°hä vík o, pä´ vo

PAAVO HAAVIKKO

Sure, it's the kind of language you can't speak,
it's nothing but endless talking.
—trans. A. Hollo

The modernist movement that swept through
Europe after World War I did not reach Finland
until the 1950s. Anselm Hollo observes in an introduction to his translation of Haavikko's poems
that "poets writing in Finnish during the first
four decades of the century had to contend with
the ideological demands and pressures of an
emergent country, to a much greater degree."
Haavikko, however, seemed born for modernism. Well read in European and American literature but with no commitments to literary
schools or movements, he "created his own
world of expression not only linguistically but
also in terms of ideas," Bo Carpelan said in nomi-
nating him for the 1984 Neustadt International
Prize for Literature. Writing in almost every
conceivable literary form from poetry and novels to radio and television plays and opera librettos, he is noted for his originality and candor. A
Finnish word that characterizes his work,
Carpelan suggests, is *hillitön*—"unrestrained,"
"unbridled"—or, "a freedom from restraint
which in his poetry also demands its own careful
patterns and involves the grotesque as well as the
contemplative, darkness as well as light."

Haavikko's striking independence and individuality have not made him an "easy" poet to
read. Like other modernist poets, notably
Pound, Eliot, and St.-John Perse, he has assimilated a vast body of traditional mythology and
history into a private, very personal vision that
demands from his readers not only erudition but
also sometimes wild imaginative leaps. He is also
a minimalist in language, switching suddenly
from one level of discourse to another, posing
more than ordinary difficulties for his translators. Jaakko Ahokas considers him "the poet of
his generation most difficult to describe or follow; we do not use the word *understand* which,
by its intellectual nature, is an anathema to the
new poets." Yet none of the many critics who
have written on him in recent years would describe Haavikko's poetry as hermetic. In embracing modernism and thereby breaking away
from the conventions that had dominated Finnish literature for generations, he extended its
range and significance for readers outside Finland. As Richard Dauenhauer writes in *Snow in
May* : "While the details of many of his poems
are drawn from and are therefore peculiar to
Finnish history and culture, most of his poetry
is truly international in concept. Haavikko's
style and thematic content combine in an attack
on positivism and national romanticism in particular, and on the irrationality of human perception and social and political ordering in
general." There is a sense of immediacy in his
poetry that transcends simple exposition. Anselm Hollo writes: "If the imagery in some parts
of his work seems 'closed,' extremely personal,
the over-all image-totality has unmistakable organic presence—it has breath, voice, is not silent,
though it may be quiet and often obsessed by the
possibility of silence." The illusion of arbitrariness in his work is in fact a reflection of the arbitrariness of the real world. Haavikko himself has
said that he aims "at a sentence that is as clear
and lucid as it can possibly be, and is the best
possible expression of what has to be said." It is
the duty of the poet, as a dedicated user of language, to be as zealous as possible in his efforts
to prevent language from turning into abstract,
meaningless symbols.

The most celebrated and influential of
Haavikko's major poems is "Talvipalatsi" (1959;
translated as "The Winter Palace"), which, like
Eliot's "The Waste Land," epitomizes the spirit
of its age and the culture in which it was produced. The American poet John Ashbery has
said that "it may be one of the great poems of
this century." The Winter Palace itself is real
and historical—the building erected for the
czars in then St. Petersburg in the middle of the
eighteenth century and now (with the adjoining
Hermitage) a museum:

In this white city,
Written by architects
In their perpendicular hand . . . .

As a building it celebrated the opulence of the czarist past:

> The old part (1754–1762) is known as
> The Winter Palace.
> Accordingly everything,
> Floor, ceiling, walls
> Is covered with these exalted beings:
> Venus, Jupiter, many ladies
> Of a full-bodied vintage.
> You can still see how many a man
> Lost head and hat
> By the Berezhina River,
> You can see that Borodino
> Was a victory . . . .

But as an edifice created by an architect/artist, it also has personal resonance for all who contemplate it, and thus it transcends time and history. Divided into nine short untitled sections, "The Winter Palace" moves within the poet's consciousness from the fact of the palace to the act of the poet himself writing about the palace:

> This poem wants to be a description,
> And I want poems to have
> Only the faintest of tastes.
> Myself I see as a creature, hopeful
> As the grass.
> These lines are almost improbable,
> This is a journey through familiar speech
> Towards the region that is no place,
> This poem has to be sung, standing up,
> Or read without voice, alone.

"The Winter Palace" thus becomes a poem about the enormous difficulties and frustrations involved in the making of poetry:

> I've come to the table, to hold the pen, and down, to
>   the sheet of paper,
> It is very northerly here, but my mind is a thicket,
> This is a poem I'm writing, in the fall, at night, alone
> And who is not I?
>
> I am only an image in this poem,
> Full of mind,
> Not wanting to know why the fruit does not flower,
> I ask myself who cares for these goods, this mind
> Thrown into the scale, it floats in the air, a round ship,
> Leisurely, running before the wind.

As he approaches the end of the poem the poet expresses his sense of duality—his "perforated soul": "A slow child, leading myself by the hand / Toward myself who is coming to meet me." One part of him is drawn to the business of life: "But let me go, I've deserved it, I don't feel at home here, / In this non-commercial world, constructed at random." The other part is the visionary poet who closes the poem with a benediction of sorts:

> Keep yourself warm
> When the pools are freezing,
> Here, at the bottom of the sky.

> When the sky is thin, and does not hold
> And the soul
>   is set free.

Consistent with his modernism, Haavikko writes "Absurdist" plays—unconventional, ambiguous, yet also witty and pointed in political and social satire. In 1984 Philip Binham wrote in *World Literature Today*: "The absurdist quality of the early Haavikko plays is still reflected today in his own brand of realism, in his ability to keep his ironic distance from the subject and in his tragicomic sense of life." From his earliest plays, *Munchhausen* (1958) and *Nuket* (The Dolls, 1960) onward he has used the medium for an oblique but penetrating criticism of society as he sees it. *Ylilääkäti* (*The Superintendent*), produced on Finnish television in 1968, is one of his few plays in English translation. It takes place in a mental hospital in 1960 with the superintendent arranging a dinner party for his wife's birthday that has as much logic as the Mad Hatter's teaparty, but the viewer cannot fail to see parallels between the madhouse and the inanities of modern life. Perhaps the most ambitious of Haavikko's dramatic works is the scenario for *Rauta-aika* (The Age of Iron, 1982), a four-part television film loosely based on the Finnish epic-lyrical collection of myths, the *Kalevala*. The *Kalevala* is generally known in the highly romanticized version of the Finnish poet Elias Lönnrot, published in 1835–1836. Haavikko's version, however, is a near-surrealistic, cynical "corrective" as it were, depicting the medieval Finns who travel eastward through Russia to Byzantium in search not of a magic token, a *sampo*, as in the original, but in pursuit of a machine that will manufacture money. It has been suggested that in *Rauta-aika* Haavikko is releasing his bitterness at what he sees as Finland's bureaucratic government and its failure to confront economic and political realities. A businessman and pragmatist, he has no faith in large schemes for reform. "In his view," Pekka Tarkka writes in *World Literature Today* (Autumn 1984), "one must not surrender the world to states, economic systems, economic organizations, parties, enterprises, cooperatives or banks, because 'you will get it back in even worse condition.' His world is ruthless, his people reified and his view of human nature skeptical." Much the same mood is manifested in Haavikko's collections of prose aphorisms—*Puhua, vastata, opettaa* (Speak, Answer, Teach, 1972) and *Ikuisen rauhan aika* (A Time of Eternal Peace, 1981):

> I've seen quite a few things in my time, I don't recall that
> a single one of them seemed reasonable.

Real delicacies are raw: oysters, salmon, and power.
I do not wish to change this system. It is bad enough already.

Haavikko has collaborated with Finnish composer Aulis Sallinen on two operas, writing the librettos for *Ratsumies* (1974, *The Horseman*) and *Kuningas lähtee Ranskaan* (1984, *The King Goes Forth to France*). Because, as Kirsti Simonsuuri wrote in *World Literature Today* (Autumn 1984), "Haavikko's poetic language is based on compelling rhythm . . . [emanating] from simple sounds, juxtaposition and frequent repetition," his work is especially suitable for musical adaptation. *The Horseman* is a tragedy of fate set in the Middle Ages. *The King Goes Forth*, subtitled "A Chronicle of the Coming of the New Ice Age," has for its subject both the past and the future—the historical English King Henry V's invasion of France in the fifteenth century and a new ice age that freezes the English Channel joining England and France "by a terrible bridge of ice, tough and elastic like a hangman's rope." The opera was produced in the United States in 1986 by the Santa Fe Opera Company. Haavikko's four novels (one written under the pseudonym Anders Lieksman) and many short stories remain largely untranslated. A novella, "Before History Begins," in Philip Binham's translation, is anthologized in *The Story Today*, 1967.

Haavikko married the poet and novelist Marja-Liisa Vartio Sairanen in 1955. She died in 1966. In 1971 he married Ritva Rainio Hanhineva, a university lecturer. He has a daughter from his first marriage. In 1984, on the occasion of his winning the Neudstadt International Prize for Literature, he visited the University of Oklahoma at Norman, where the award was presented. In his acceptance address he discussed the complex relationship between art and reality, pointing out the urgent need for a literature that always questions and challenges in the endless quest not for final answers but for knowledge and understanding:

It is easy to write when one knows that the significance of writing is in the work itself, in the examination of eternal issues. The inevitable consequence of this work is the realization that the only significant problems are those to which there are no answers or solutions. They must be examined constantly; they contain the limits of the possible and of human capacity. Only through the unanswerable questions can the world be depicted, constantly, unendingly.

WORKS IN ENGLISH TRANSLATION: A number of Haavikko's poems, including "The Winter Palace," were translated by Anselm Hollo in *Paavo Haavikko and Tomas Tranströmer: Selected Poems*, published in 1968 and reissued in paperback by Penguin in 1974. Philip Bin-

ham translated *The Horseman* in 1974, and *The King Goes Forth to France* was translated by Stephen Olivier and Erki Arni in 1984. Selections from his poetry in translation by various hands appear in *Snow in May: An Anthology of Finnish Writing 1945–1972*, edited by Richard Dauenhauer and Philip Binham, 1978. This volume also includes Binham's translation of *The Superintendent*. Additional and more recent poems are translated in *World Literature Today*, Autumn 1974, and *Books from Finland* 2, 1984.

ABOUT: Ahokas, J. A History of Modern Finnish Literature, 1973; Contemporary Authors 106, 1982; Contemporary Literary Criticism 18, 1981; 34, 1985; Dauenhauer, R. and P. Binham (eds.) Snow in May, 1978; Hollo, A. Translator's Note *in* Haavikko's Selected Poems, 1968. *Periodicals*—Books from Finland 2, 1984; World Literature Today Winter 1984, Spring 1984, Autumn 1984.

*AL-HAKIM, TAWFIQ (October 9, 1898–July 26, 1987), Egyptian dramatist, novelist, and essayist whose works, equally diverse in form, theme, and spirit, chart much of his country's political and cultural life in the twentieth century, was the last of a generation of literary pioneers that included Muhammad Husayn Haykal, 'Abbas al-Akkad, and Taha Husayn. He is the unquestioned founder of Egypt's dramatic tradition, with more than sixty plays spanning as many years of creative activity.

In spite of the very visible persona he maintained throughout his long career—the image of the cosmopolitan intellectual, complete, by the end, with beret and walking stick—Tawfiq al-Hakim was notoriously secretive about his personal life, the details of which are generally gleaned from his writings, notably his autobiographical novels and essays. As his English-language biographer Richard Long points out, dates are lacking in all of these works, and until quite late in his life, even the year of his birth was contested. His father, Isma'il al-Hakim Bey, was an influential rural magistrate (and amateur poet) with landholdings outside Damanhur, near Alexandria; his mother, Asma al-Bustani, was part of Egypt's Turkish elite—she was the daughter of an Ottoman army officer—and her disdain for all things Egyptian apparently caused a great rift in the household. The son, at any rate, grew up resenting her for trying to make him into a "little Turkish aristocrat," and these difficult relations are often placed at the root of the misogynistic currents that run throughout his work.

Tawfiq al-Hakim was born in Alexandria, but the family (soon to include a younger brother, Zuhayr) moved around continuously because of the father's judiciary post. A shy and retiring

°äl häkēm, too fik

child, he took an early interest in drawing and music but, he indicates, gave them up because of his parents' derision. He then turned to popular theater, which his father had taken him to see in the small town of Dusuq, and before the age of ten (his accounts vary) he had attached himself to an all-women road show, the Awalim, for which he eventually wrote some of his earliest plays.

Despite the fact that he was an avid reader, his studies suffered from the family's frequent moves—he repeated the first year of both primary and elementary school—and at the urging of his uncles and aunt in Cairo, he was sent to live with them in 1915 in order to complete his education properly. This arrangement suited him far more than the uncomfortable environment at home, and he spent the next three years there, belatedly graduating from high school in 1921 at the age of twenty-two. By this time he knew he wanted to become a writer and apparently had no other outside interests. His first play, *Al-Dayf al-thaqul* (The Unwanted Guest), dates from 1918–1919; probably written for al-Awalim, it was a thinly veiled allegory about the British occupation of Egypt and was promptly banned by the British censors. With the outbreak of the revolt of 1919, al-Hakim joined his uncles in protest activities and wound up briefly in jail with them. All of these experiences, from the Nile Delta to the jails of Cairo, were to be recounted in his first novel *'Awdat al-ruh* (The Return of the Soul, 1933).

Following high school, al-Hakim wanted to attend the College of Arts, but at his father's insistence, he spent the next four years in law school (here too he repeated the first year and finished third from the bottom of the graduating class). Throughout these studies, he continued to write plays, several of which were performed by the Akasha theater company in Cairo in 1924. In order to hide his double life, he took the pseudonym of Husayn Tawfiq (his full name was Husayn Tawfiq Isma'il Ahmad· al-Hakim), but he was found out by his family when the Akasha company performed in Alexandria. His father apparently remained calm but, in order to get him out of the theater environment, sent him to Paris to write a doctoral thesis in law.

Arriving in autumn 1925 with absolutely no program of study, al-Hakim predictably plunged back into an artistic milieu. He attended lectures out of curiosity (James Joyce on English poetry, for example), fed his voracious reading appetite at Sylvia Beach's Shakespeare & Co. bookstore, and quickly found his way to the theaters and concert halls, as well as the Louvre and the Paris Opera. "Paris was an open

book . . . " he wrote in an essay published in 1933, "the book of higher life." Among his own writings from this period were a small collection of poems, an operetta that he had begun in Egypt, and a story about the al-Awalim theater troupe. Negative reactions to some of his earlier plays, which were performed in Cairo during his absence, apparently discouraged him, and the only play he completed in Paris, apart from the operetta, was the one-act *Devant son guichet* (At the Booking Office, 1926) written in French and recounting his own failed romance with a young girl working at the Odéon theater.

By far the most important of his Paris writings was the five-hundred page *'Awdat al-ruh* (Return of the Soul), which, Egyptian critic Fathi Ridwan recalled, was immediately recognized as "a new page in our literary history." Drawing on the European novel form, al-Hakim wove personal and political history—another unhappy love story played out in the midst of the historic events that culminated in the 1919 revolt—to create a richly textured panorama of the period. At the time, it was greatly admired for its nationalist political message, and future Egyptian president Gamal Abdel Nasser, who read the novel as a high-school student, later claimed that he had been greatly inspired by the example of the 1919 revolt. Although completed in 1927, the book was not published until 1933 (several Egyptian authorities suggest that it was originally written in French and translated back into Arabic; in any event, a French version published in 1937 was highly successful in Europe).

In the interim, al-Hakim had been abruptly summoned home by his father after he failed his exams in Paris. Set to work as a public prosecutor in a succession of rural towns, he had little enthusiasm for this unchosen profession, but used it as a means of securing his livelihood. In letters exchanged with a friend in Paris after his return, published in 1943 as *Zahrat al-'umr* (Life in Bloom), he complained of the low level of intellectual life around him, as well as the economic problems faced by Egyptian theater companies, but he continued to write, turning out another five plays between 1929 and 1931. Mostly melodramas of a distinctly misogynistic tenor, these were, as Long indicates, "of little more than purely Egyptian social interest."

It was only with *Ahl al-kahf* (1933; translated as *People of the Cave*), which he had begun writing in Paris, that al-Hakim made his breakthrough from a theater of entertainment to a theater of ideas. One of the catalysts in this development was his discovery, in Paris, that European plays could be written for publication rather than performance. Taking this approach for the four-act *People of the Cave*, he used the Quranic version of the Seven Sleepers of Ephesus—now numbering three and transferred to nearby Tarsus—to develop a meditation on time: emerging from their cave after three hundred years, the sleepers soon realize that they cannot adapt to the changed world around them and return to their timeless retreat, which is death. According to al-Hakim, he chose this subject in order to write "an Egyptian tragedy on an Egyptian basis." "Read the *Book of the Dead* and you will be aware of this immediately," he explained to a journalist at the time. "With the Greeks, it is 'fate' and 'destiny'; with the Egyptians, it is 'time' and 'space'." A limited edition of the play circulated among writers and critics met with immediate success: the Egyptian novelist Taha Husayn wrote in his review that it was a "significant event" for all of Arabic literature, namely the beginning of modern theater.

The following year, al-Hakim wrote his second major play, *Shahrazad* (*Scheharezade*). A philosophical epilogue to the *1001 Nights*, it examines Scheharezade's relationships to the men in her life—the king (her husband), the vizier (her admirer), and the slave (her lover). Notwithstanding its dense symbolism, this play was also a critical success in its published form.

Considerably less favorable was the response of his superiors in the Legal Corps, who had asked for his resignation in the wake of the notoriety surrounding *People of the Cave*. Although his father was distressed, al-Hakim himself benefited from the situation to take a less demanding post as head of the Investigations Bureau at the Ministry of Education. But a real setback ensued in 1935 when this play was chosen to inaugurate Egypt's first official theater company; baffling audiences with its intricate language and singular absence of action, the staged version was a total failure. In the face of vociferous criticism from conservative playwrights and reviewers, al-Hakim contended that he had not written the play to be performed (although he also complained to the producer about the way it had been staged), and he effectively backed away from both live drama and the theater of ideas. His next major dramatic work, *Muhammad* (1937), was a vast historical tableau of the life of the prophet, elaborated in 95 scenes that totaled 485 pages in the published version and offered no possibility of performance because the prophet could not be represented on stage. As a historical approach to a religious subject, *Muhammad* was undoubtedly a bold venture, but as theater, modern critic M. M. Badawi has found its loose, episodic structure "Brechtian in a bad sense."

Later that year, al-Hakim published a second autobiographical novel, *Yawmiyat na'ib fi'l-aryaf* (Diary of a Country Magistrate). Even more than with *'Awdat al-ruh* (The Return of the Soul), his personal experiences here serve as an anchor for social analysis and criticism. From his tenure in the mixed courts of the Nile Delta, he distills twelve days of observations, presented in the form of narrative, memoir, and commentary and amounting to a graphic exposé of the plight of Egypt's rural population at the hands of a corrupt and insensitive bureaucracy. Much praised for its immediacy—Roger Allen ranks it as "one of the most memorable works of early modern Arabic fiction"—the book was a great popular success in Egypt and was subsequently published in French, German, Hebrew, Romanian, Spanish, and Swedish, as well as in an English version by Abba Eban called *The Maze of Justice* (1947). It was made into a film in 1969. A third autobiographical novel dealing with his student years in Paris followed in 1938, but *Al-'usfur min al-sharq* (*The Bird from the East*), is generally held to be the least original of the series, lapsing into a somewhat standard comparison between the "spiritual East" and the "material West" at the expense of the critical realism that enlivened the previous works. He was to write several more novels over the next decade or so, but none of these reached the stature of the first two.

For the remainder of the thirties, it was in his essays and plays that al-Hakim maintained what Long describes as the "reformist impetus" of his earlier autobiographical novel *Yawmiyat na'ib fi'l-aryaf*. The depiction of Muslim judges in that work had so angered the shaykh of al-Azhar, Cairo's preeminent mosque-university, that he publicly denounced al-Hakim at the Friday prayer service; al-Hakim then responded with a series of articles attacking al-Azhar's "repeated intrusions" into Egypt's intellectual life as "a danger that threatens freedom of expression and the country's development." Shortly afterwards, *Shagarat al-hukm* (The Tree of Ruling, 1938) a short satirical play aimed at the king and his entourage, brought angry demands for the author's dismissal from the Ministry of Education (he got off with forfeiting two weeks' pay), and a similar storm was created the following year by *Praksa aw mushkilat al-hukm* (Praksa, or The Problem of Ruling), a similar assault on the parliament presented in the guise of a classical comedy inspired by Aristophanes.

By this time, his own proposal for the creation of a ministry of social affairs had been implemented, and he was named director of its social orientation bureau, a post he held for the next four years. The confrontations continued, along with the demands for his dismissal, the forfeiture of pay, and the routine (if inaccurate) accusation that he was a communist. But by the beginning of the 1940s, apart from one collection of writings denouncing Hitler and the growing threat of fascism, al-Hakim himself pulled back from this social engagement into what he called the "ivory tower." At the time, he argued that a certain distance was necessary for intellectuals to rethink what was going on around them, but he later acknowledged that this distance had also been a refuge. His two major works of the early forties, *Pigmalyun* (Pygmalion, 1942) and *Sulayman al-hakim* (Solomon the Wise, 1943) were long, reflective dramas based on traditional sources and addressing the difficulty of choosing between fantasy and reality, whether in the form of art and life (Pygmalion and his sculpture) or love and politics (the fateful romance of Solomon and the queen of Sheba). By 1938 he had ceased writing plays for performance altogether (this was to be the case for the next fourteen years), and as he explained in the lengthy preface to *Pigmalyun*, "I set up my theater inside my mind and I make the actors [into] thoughts, moving freely amidst ideas, wearing the costumes of symbols."

In 1943—at the age of forty-five—al-Hakim finally left the civil service to write full-time; in order to support himself, he published his work in the Cairo newspaper *Akhbar al-yawm*, which, he indicated, also allowed him to reach a wider audience. Three years later, to the surprise of everyone, including himself, he married—his wife has been variously identified as a peasant from the region of Alexandria and the sister of a medical school dean—and subsequently had four children, three daughters and a son. His most important work of the mid-1940s was another long play cast in an antique mode, *Al-malik Udib*, which was published in 1949 (translated as *Oedipus the King*). As he explained in a long preface, added in 1959, he was again attempting to reinterpret Greek tragedy in Muslim terms, replacing fate with time and the search for truth. As had been the case with *People of the Cave*, the result did not have a great deal of mass appeal in Egypt.

With the appointment of his friend Taha Husayn as Minister of Education in 1950, al-Hakim again found himself back in the government service, this time as director of the National Library. As Long points out, with the growing popular discontent in the country, his political and social views became less and less marginal, and following the Free Officers Revolt of 1952 (which ended the monarchy), he moved rather easily into the official fold. In 1954 he was finally elected to the Arabic Language Academy and

in 1956, appointed to the newly created Higher Council of Arts, Letters, and Social Sciences as undersecretary for theater; he soon received two prestigious and well-remunerated awards, the State Prize for Literature and the Higher Council's merit award, and in 1958, he was presented with the Republican Chain, previously reserved for heads of state.

Al-Hakim in turn paid his dues to the Revolution in at least some of his writings—a critique of the previous regime in *Sahibat al-galala* (Her Majesty, 1954–1955), an endorsement of the present one's goals in *Al-Aidi al-na'ima* (Soft Hands, 1953), an allegorical tribute to President Nasser with *Izis* (Isis, 1955)—but his main preoccupations clearly lay elsewhere. Deeply affected by the invention of the atomic bomb and the resulting threat of nuclear war, he now infused his political vision with a global dimension that called into question the impact of science and technology on human relations. *Rihlat ila'l-ghad* (Journey to Tomorrow, 1957), for example, was a science-fiction fantasy about two condemned murderers who are granted a reprieve in exchange for undertaking a mission in outer space and, like the people of the cave, return to earth three hundred years later, in this case to find themselves in a futuristic dystopia. While this play, according to John A. Haywood, suffered from an excess of philosophizing, a more exotic and fanciful approach to problems of the social order, *Al-sultan al-ha'ir* (1960; translated as *The Sultan's Dilemma*). was an unequivocal success, performed at the National Theater in 1961 and revived eight years later.

In the artistic domain of theater, al-Hakim also devoted considerable attention to the issue of language, in terms of the particular problem posed by the split between classical, written Arabic and its colloquial variants (somewhat analogous to Latin and the Romance vernaculars during the European Middle Ages). From the beginning of his career as a playwright, he had alternated between the written and spoken languages, depending on the subject and its treatment, but by the 1950s he was seeking to create a "unified theatrical language" that would be comprehensible among all classes and in all regions of the Arab world. With *Al-Safqa* (The Deal, 1956) another colorful social microcosm, he introduced what he called a "third language," intended to give the impression of colloquial Arabic while following the logic of classical grammar and syntax. In fact, this "third language" failed to catch on, but the play itself met with great popular success and critic Mohammad Mandur placed it among the best of his social dramas.

In 1959 al-Hakim accepted a brief appointment as Egypt's permanent representative to UNESCO in Paris. As had been the case more than thirty years earlier, the encounter with contemporary European drama—now the Theater of the Absurd, as practiced by Beckett, Ionesco, Vauthier, Adamov, and others—proved decisive. On his return to Egypt in 1960, he embarked on what he called Irrationalism, "the presentation of the rational world in an irrational framework" (in contrast, theoretically at least, to the Europeans' depiction of an absurd world in an absurd framework) His first, bold work in this new vein was *Ya tali' al-shagara* (1962; translated as *The Tree Climber*), a stylized tale that revolves around a man and his disappearing wife, an orange tree, a dervish, and a lizard. One of his most successful plays, it was, according to the renowned Palestinian writer-critic Jabra Ibrahim Jabra, "as funny, as surprising, as dramatically effective as anything by Ionesco."

As al-Hakim explained in the preface to *The Tree Climber*, this new direction was not simply a response to the Theater of the Absurd, for he had long been aware of earlier irrational currents in European drama, such as Alfred Jarry and the dadaists. Rather, he argued, the real catalyst was his recognition that Egyptian folklore belonged to the same tradition and thus offered him an indigenous vocabulary of form. Drawing on these dual sources—the European avant-garde and popular tradition—al-Hakim proceeded to create some of his most acclaimed plays, including *Al-Ta'am li kulli famm* (Food for Every Mouth, 1963), *Shams al-nahar* (Morning Sun, 1965), and his last major dramatic work, *Masir sarsar* (1962; translated as *Fate of A Cockroach*),

Al-Hakim's own prestige, as Long suggests, was apparently aided by the fact that contemporary Western drama was now being produced in Egypt; at any event, in 1963 he had his own theater named after him in Cairo; in 1967 a Tawfiq al-Hakim festival was held at Cairo University to mark his fifty-year career, and in 1970, he was named lifetime honorary chairman of the Egyptian Drama Writers Association. He was also appointed to the board of directors of the semiofficial Cairo daily *al-Ahram*, where, installed in his own sixth-floor office with no official duties, he became a kind of resident sage for local and foreign journalists. Notwithstanding this recognition, he was increasingly disappointed with the Nasser regime, particularly after Egypt's military defeat in the 1967 war with Israel and its disastrous involvement in the Yemeni Civil War, and a few months before Nasser's death in 1970, he wrote him a letter protesting the removal of *Al-Ahram*'s editor, Muhammad Hasanan Haykal.

This political disaffection, coupled with personal grief over the deaths of his wife and son, brought on a period of severe depression in the early 1970s, but in the wake of the student demonstrations of December 1972–January 1973 he reemerged in public life with an almost unprecedented vigor, convening a public meeting of his fellow writers that resulted in a formal appeal to Nasser's successor Anwar al-Sadat to liberalize the government. This was followed by a long critical essay acknowledging the bankruptcy of the 1952 Revolution and decrying the abuses of the ensuing Nasser era, *'Awdat al-wa'i* (1974; translated as *The Return of Consciousness*), An immediate best seller in Egypt, it was eagerly welcomed by al-Sadat in his attempt to undo Nasserism, although a number of Egyptian intellectuals, including *al-Ahram* editor Haykal, found al-Hakim's attack on the dead president unseemly if not opportunistic, given his silence during Nasser's lifetime.

Al-Hakim's last play, a symbolic treatment of war and peace in the nuclear age appropriately entitled *al-Dunya riwaya hazliyya* (The World Is a Comedy), had been serialized in *Al-Ahram* in 1971 and several collections of essays and recollections were published in the course of the decade, but after *The Return of Consciousness* he again lapsed from view, apart from a lavish pronouncement in favor of President Sadat's peace initiative with Israel in 1978 (which he subsequently recanted). Then, in March 1983, the eighty-five year-old writer reappeared on the scene with a biting attack on Egypt's religious establishment published in *Al-Ahram* under the title of *Ahadith ma' Allah* (Conversations with God). Coinciding with the millenary celebrations for al-Azhar, the series generated hundreds of articles, interviews, and letters not only in Egypt but throughout the Arab world. Several months later al-Hakim suffered a heart attack, but notwithstanding the last respects paid him by scores of prominent Egyptians, he recovered and returned to his office at *Al-Ahram*, where he undertook a last volume of memoirs and tried to advance a plan for a new Arab League based on culture rather than politics. When he finally succumbed to another heart attack four years later, it was on the thirty-fifth anniversary of the 1952 Revolution, as if, in the words of French journalist Philippe Gardenal, "he was giving us a last wink before taking his place in eternal Egypt's great Kingdom of the Dead."

WORKS IN ENGLISH TRANSLATION: Two of Tawfiq al-Hakim's novels have been translated into English—*The Maze of Justice* by Abba Eban in 1947 and

Bird of the East by Bayly R. Winder in 1966. A collection of his plays (including *Scheharezade*) was translated by W. M. Hutchins and A. I. Abdulai under the title *Plays, Prefaces, and Postscripts*; Vol. I, subtitled *Theater of the Mind* which appeared in 1981; II, *Theater of Society*, in 1984. D. Johnson-Davies translated several of al-Hakim's plays—*The Tree Climber* in 1966, *Fate of a Cockroach and Other Plays*, 1972, and "The Donkey Market," published in *Egyptian One-Act Plays* in 1981. Riad Habib Youssef translated two plays—*A Conversation with the Planet Earth* and *The World Is a Comedy*—in 1985. A translation of *People of the Cave* by P. J. Vatikiotis was published in *Islamic Literature* 7, 1955, and 9, 1957. A translation of the first act of this drama by J. A. Haywood appears in *Modern Arabic Literature 1800–1970*, 1971. In addition to the prefaces and postscripts collected by Hutchins and Abdulai above, his essay *The Return of Consciousness* was translated by Bayly R. Winder in 1985, and his short story "Miracles for Sale," translated by D. Johnson-Davies, appears in *Modern Arabic Short Stories*, 1967. Al-Hakim's works have been somewhat more extensively translated into French, notably in three volumes of plays: *Théatre arabe*, 1950; *Théâtre multicoloré*, 1954; *Théâtre de notre temps*, 1960. The "Conversations with God" and accompanying debate appear in *La Revue de la presse égyptienne* (Aix) March 1983.

ABOUT: Awad, L. Problems of Egyptian Theater *in* Ostle, R. C. (ed.) Studies in Arabic Literature, 1975; Haywood, J. A. Modern Arabic Literature 1800–1970, 1971; Kilpatrick, H. The Modern Egyptian Novel, 1974; Landau, J. M. Studies in the Arab Theater and Cinema, 1969; Long, R. Tawfiq al-Hakim, Playwright of Egypt, 1979; Starkey, P. From the Ivory Tower: A Critical Analysis of Tawfiq al-Hakim, 1987; Tomiche, N. Histoire de la littérature romanesque de l'Egypte moderne, 1981; Who's Who in the Arab World 1986–1987. *Periodicals*—Journal of Arabic Literature 1971, 1977, 1978; Libération July 28, 1987; Le Monde July 28, 1987.

HAMPTON, CHRISTOPHER (JAMES) (January 26, 1946–   ), British playwright and scenarist, was born on Fayal Island, one of the Azores, the son of Bernard Patrick Hampton, a marine telecommunications engineer with the British company Cable & Wireless Ltd., and the former Dorothy Patience Herrington. He attended schools in Aden and Egypt before enrolling at Lancing College, where he was the exact contemporary of his fellow playwright David Hare, and at New College, Oxford, where he took a first-class degree in 1968 in modern languages (French and German). He recalled in 1987, in an interview with Jeremy Gerard for the *New York Times*, how after the Suez crisis in 1956 he was suddenly taken out of school in Alexandria, Egypt, and sent to England "which I at hardly visited, this very strange country in

CHRISTOPHER HAMPTON

which everybody ate cabbage and it was cold and they didn't turn the heat on. And nobody showed you for a second what they were thinking. And I was mysteriously impressed by this, as well as being deeply upset by it. I think that within a very short space, I became more English than the English. I thought there was something rather wonderful about it." Throughout his adolescence he felt like an outsider. "That's why I'm so interested in *émigrés*. I'm interested in outsiders who don't want to be outsiders; I'm also interested in outsiders who *do* want to be outsiders, and in the tension between the two."

Hampton's first play, *When Did You Last See My Mother?*, was written during a six-week period when he was eighteen, before he entered Oxford. "The entire plot," he recalled later, "came to me in fifteen minutes when I was sitting in a pub." It is a bleak play about youthful despair, telling the story of two young men, school friends who share a London "bed-sit" while waiting to go to university. They also share a sexual relationship, but claim to be interested in exploring heterosexuality. One of them enters upon a brief affair with his friend's mother, which ends tragically with her death in a car crash. Nothing is resolved by the play's end, but the well-drawn characters, intensely emotional dialogue, and general sense of hopelessness caused the play to be well received. It was produced in 1966 at the Royal Court and the Comedy theaters in London and had a short Off-Broadway run in early 1967 at the Young People's Repertory Theater in New York.

Total Eclipse was written in a year off from

Oxford, during which Hampton worked briefly as a reader for Hamburg's Schauspielhaus and as a translator in Paris. It is a romantic historical drama about the psychosexual relationship between the nineteenth-century French poets Arthur Rimbaud and Paul Verlaine. Verlaine, ten years Rimbaud's senior, speaks at the beginning of the play about his friend's strong attraction for him: "Sometimes he speaks, in a kind of dialect, of the death which causes repentance, of the unhappy men who certainly exist, of painful tasks and heart-rending departures. In the hovels where we got drunk, he wept looking at those who surrounded us, the cattle of poverty. . . . He pretended to know about everything, business, art, medicine. I followed him, I had to!" Rimbaud is hugely talented and self-centered, a magnificent outcast at the age of sixteen. Speaking to Verlaine, he says, " . . . what I needed, to be the first poet of the century, the first poet since Racine or since the Greeks, was to experience everything in my body. . . . It was no longer enough for me to be one person, I decided to be everyone. I decided to be a genius. I decided to be Christ. I decided to originate the future."

In this play, once again, well-written dialogue is Hampton's forte. With lyrical wit, he displays the crucial differences between the two main characters, especially in their conceptions of poetry. For Verlaine, poetry was merely a craft, almost a trade; for Rimbaud, it had either to change the world or was not worth writing (he ceased writing, in fact, before he was twenty-one). At the end of the play, some months after Rimbaud's death and years after the two poets last met, Verlaine, old and ill, sitting alone in a café in Paris, thinks about their past: "He's not dead, he's trapped and living inside me. As long as I live, he has some kind of flickering and limited life. . . . I remember him of an evening and he lives." *Total Eclipse* was produced in 1968 at the Royal Court Theatre, at the beginning of the playwright's two-year stint there as resident dramatist. It was revived in a revised version at the Lyric Theatre, Hammersmith, in 1981.

Hampton's next original play was *The Philanthropist: A Bourgeois Comedy*, which he saw as "a riposte to *Le Misanthrope*" of Molière. The action revolves around Philip, a bachelor and a philologist, who at the beginning of the play is discussing in his university rooms a play written by John, a younger man, with his colleague Don and the playwright himself. The young man is gradually made furious by Don's uncomprehending negativism, but even more by Philip's bland approval. Unlike Molière's Alceste, who decides to be brutally honest with everyone and expose thereby society's thorough hypocrisy, Philip likes everything and everyone so much he is unable to arrive at any of life's truths. He is obsessed by anagrams, with "individual rather than consecutive" words, in the young playwright's phrase. "Please take no notice of what I say," he tells John in complacent justification of his failure of judgment. "I always like things. I get pleasure from the words that are used, whatever the subject is. I've enjoyed every book I've ever read for one reason or another. That's why I can't teach literature. I have no critical faculties. I think there's always something good to be found in the product of another man's mind. Even if the man is, by all objective standards, a complete fool. So you see I'd like a play however terrible it was." Hearing this, John quickly acts out the conclusion to the play he has just finished reading: he puts a revolver in his mouth and blows his brains out. The rest of the play shows the almost equally disastrous consequences of Philip's inability to make critical judgments about anything; by the end he is reduced to utter despair. He is too indecisive to consider suicide himself, although he does take up smoking again. The play is cleverly constructed, with several scenes parallel to those in *Le Misanthrope*, stressing in addition the contrast between the active and contemplative life, between grasping worldly success and futile academic failure. It enjoyed a long run in London at the Royal Court and the May Fair theaters and a short run on Broadway in March 1971.

Savages, a one-act play in twenty-two scenes, had its origins in an article, "Genocide," by Norman Lewis in the London *Sunday Times Magazine* (February 1969), which dealt with the destruction of the Brazilian Indians. The play tells the story, only referred to in the article, of the murderous bombing of an Amazonian tribe with dynamite during a religious festival. It also concerns the simultaneous kidnapping and eventual murder of a British diplomat—an apologist to the Western world for the Indians—by Brazilian urban guerrillas. Hampton writes in the introduction to the British edition of the play, that the incident of the massacre of the Indians "forms . . . the climax of the play . . . it would be impossible to deal with the 'Indian problem' at all adequately without taking into account the current political situation. . . . the average urban Brazilian has far too many difficulties in his life to allow himself the luxury of worrying about the Indian of the interior, of whose existence he is in fact largely ignorant." The play's political message is overt, more so than any other of Hampton's works, but entirely inconclusive: the impotence of the contemplative world (that of the Indians and the diplomat) is strongly contrasted with the useless violence of the guerrillas' world of action, yet nothing is resolved by the play's end. *Savages* had a short run at the Royal Court, a longer one at the Comedy Theatre in London, then successful productions in Hamburg, Brussels, and Paris, and in a revised version was seen at the Mark Taper Forum in Los Angeles. It was joint winner (with Athol Fugard's *Sizwe Banzi Is Dead*) of the *Plays & Players* award for best play of 1973 voted by the London theater critics, as well as the 1974 Los Angeles Drama Critics Circle award for distinguished playwrighting.

Treats is a rather slight play in one act and nine scenes, a three-character drawing-room comedy which takes place in the mid-1970s. Ann and Patrick are living together, outwardly harmoniously; Dave, who used to live with Ann, reappears. The play concerns the loutish but witty Dave's attempts to insinuate himself back into the flat. He finally succeeds in driving off Patrick, and by the end of the play has Ann back to himself, but their old/new relationship is clearly just as stagnant and oppressive as ever to them both. The play is similar in its theme of lovelessness to *The Philanthropist*, and Patrick is very like Philip and like the diplomat in *Savages* in his ineffectual, helpless indecisiveness. The play ran briefly in the late winter of 1976 at the Royal Court and May Fair theaters.

Hampton said that he found *Treats* an unsatisfactory experience. He had, in fact, by the mid-1970s already found another successful theatrical career, that of translator and adapter of the established works of other dramatists. His dramatic adaptations include: Isaac Babel's *Marya* (Royal Court, 1967); Anton Chekhov's *Uncle Vanya* (Royal Court, 1970); four plays by Ibsen—*Hedda Gabler* (Shakespeare Festival Theater, Stratford, Ontario, 1970; Almeida Theatre, Islington, London, 1984); *A Doll's House* (Playhouse Theater, New York, 1971; Criterion Theatre, London, 1973); *Ghosts* (Actors Company, London, 1978); and *The Wild Duck* (National Theatre, 1979); two plays by Molière—*Don Juan* (Old Vic, Bristol, 1972) and *Tartuffe* (Royal Shakespeare Company, 1983); two plays by Ödön von Horváth—*Tales from the Vienna Woods* (National Theatre, 1977) and *Don Juan Comes Back from the War* (National Theatre, 1978); George Steiner's novel *The Portage to San Cristobal of A.H.* (Mermaid Theatre, 1982); and Choderlos de Laclos' novel *Les Liaisons Dangereuses* (Royal Shakespeare Company, 1985; Music Box Theater, New York, 1987).

The last-named play has been Hampton's greatest success to date. It is based on Laclos' novel of seduction, corruption, and betrayal among aristocrats during the French *ancien régime*, and had occasionally before been dramatized, most notably in a modern-dress film version (1959) by Roger Vadim. By staying faithful to the original in period and costumes, the playwright risked losing a large part of his audience, but in both a stage version and in a film (*Dangerous Liaisons*) directed by Stephen Frears the adaptation was an unexpected, runaway success. The play also won the *Plays & Players* award for best play of 1985, the Time Out magazine award for best production of 1986, and the *London Standard* and Laurence Olivier awards for best play of 1986. In the United States in 1988 it won the Academy Award for best screen adaptation. It had a very long run in London and was exported in nearly two dozen productions to, among other cities, New York, Rome, Tokyo, and even Paris.

Hampton's original historical fantasy, the one-act, twenty-two scene play *Tales from Hollywood*, was written especially for the Mark Taper Forum as a play set in Los Angeles. It was produced at the National Theatre in 1983 and won the *London Standard* award for best comedy of that year. The main character of the play is the Austro-Hungarian dramatist Ödön von Harváth, two of whose plays Hampton had adapted for the English stage. Here he imagines von Horváth (who died in Paris in 1936) as a guide to the sun-soaked boulevards and bizarre cultural collisions of wartime Hollywood, where among the immigrant characters are Thomas Mann and his brother Heinrich, Lion Feuchtwanger and his wife Marta, Helene Weigel, and Bertolt Brecht. Among the resident stars are Chico and Harpo Marx, Johnny Weissmuller, and Greta Garbo. The play has an unreal, Californian atmosphere throughout, as Horváth engages in conversations, all of them at least partly imaginary, with some of the most illustrious writers of continental Europe, who are, most of them, reduced to doing menial writing jobs for the film industry. Horváth himself at the end of the play (just before his death in a producer's swimming pool) turns down a job writing a sequel to *Bedtime for Bonzo*.

Notable among Hampton's other dramatic works are adaptations of Malcolm Bradbury's novel *The History Man* (1981), Graham Greene's novel *The Honorary Consul* (1983), and Anita Brookner's novel *Hotel du Lac* (1986), for BBC-TV.

PRINCIPAL WORKS: When Did You Last See My Mother, 1967; Total Eclipse, 1969, rev ed , 1981; The Philanthropist 1970, rev ed , 1985; Savages, 1974; Treats, 1976; Able's Will, 1979; Tales from Hollywood 1983; The Portage to San Cristobal of A.H., 1982; Les Liaisons Dangereuses, 1985.

ABOUT: Contemporary Authors 25–28, 1977; Contemporary Literary Criticism 4, 1975; Who's Who, 1988. *Periodicals*—Comparative Drama Summer 1979; Drama Summer 1976; Guardian March 14, 1977; Nation April 5, 1971; March 16, 1974; New Leader April 1, 1974; New York March 11, 1974; New Yorker March 27, 1971; March 11, 1974; New York Times December 12, 1979; January 26, 1986; April 26, 1987; May 1, 1987; August 15, 1988; Newsweek May 29, 1971; September 9, 1974; Plays & Players October–December 1973; Times Literary Supplement October 11, 1985; Transatlantic Review Winter 1968–1969.

BARRY HANNAH

HANNAH, BARRY (April 23, 1942–), American novelist and short-story writer, was born in Meridian, Mississippi, son of William (an insurance agent) and Elizabeth (King) Hannah. He grew up in Clinton, Mississippi, a town near Jackson, received his B.A. from Mississippi College in Clinton in 1964, and his M.A. and M.F.A. degrees from the University of Arkansas in 1966 and 1967. While writing fiction, he has earned his living chiefly by teaching literature and creative writing at a variety of colleges. He taught at Clemson University from 1967 to 1973; was writer-in-residence at Middlebury College from 1974 to 1975; taught literature and fiction at the University of Alabama from 1975 to 1980. He also, in 1980, worked as a scriptwriter with Robert Altman in Hollywood. Since then Hannah has been writer-in-residence at the University of Iowa, 1981, the University of Mississippi (University, Miss.), 1982, the University of Montana (Missoula), 1982–1983, and at the University of Mississippi (Oxford), from 1984 to the present.

Hannah made a very strong impression with his first novel, *Geronimo Rex*, which was nominated for a National Book Award. An initiation novel set in the 1950s and 1960s, it tells the story of Harry Monroe, as he grows up in Dream of Pines, Louisiana and comes of age. It was reviewed by a majority of critics as a brilliant first novel. Jim Harrison in the *New York Times Book Review* called *Geronimo Rex* "a stunning piece of entertainment, almost a totally successful book. . . . vulgar, sexual, ribald and wildly comic. . . . [the novel] is old fashioned in the sense that all the actions and characterizations are accelerated and energized, larger than life as it is ordinarily perceived by those who would settle for less. The characters are too lively to be likable, too possessed and frayed ever to the charming. A fine debut for Mr. Hannah and a very difficult act for him to follow." The movement of the work, as John Updike noted in the *New Yorker*, is toward "an accelerating incoherence. . . . The major weakness of a first novel like this is its limp susceptibility to autobiographical incident; its vitality must lie not in the shaping but in the language of the telling, and here Mr. Hannah is no mean performer."

Hannah's second novel, *Nightwatchmen*, is a bizarre and comic narrative taking the form in part of a murder mystery. Its narrator is a wealthy eccentric, Thorpe Trove, who investigates the strange goings-on occurring at a university in Mississippi. At the same time that a hurricane batters the surrounding Gulf country, a mysterious figure known as the "Knocker" clubs professors at their studies; later several campus guards are found decapitated. A number of characters are interviewed by Trove, and transcriptions of these interviews appear as chapters in the novel as he closes in on the killer. Reviews of *Nightwatchmen* were distinctly negative. John Skow in the *Washington Post Book World* found a disturbing lack of cohesion in the novel. "I think," he commented, "that Hannah's second novel . . . is a perverse and disappointing mistake. . . . the jolly killings . . . occur simply because Hannah's dark angel told him to write them into the novel." Jonathan Yardley in the *New York Times Book Review* remarked that "*Geronimo Rex* . . . has admirable energy, exuberant humor and a genuine feel for what it is like to grow up in the South. But *Nightwatchmen* is another matter altogether; it is simply a mess. . . . What we have here is dimestore philosophizing, uncertain satire and rambling story-telling. . . . The novel does not seriously shake my conviction that Hannah is a talented and promising novelist, but any admirer of *Geronimo Rex* is likely to wish that the author had kept *Nightwatchmen* to himself."

Hannah's third book, *Airships*, a collection of short stories, proved a conspicuous success, earning him the Arnold Gingrich Award for short fiction from *Esquire* and a special award in fiction from the American Academy of Arts and Letters. The book appeared with an array of strong jacket endorsements from writers and critics including Philip Roth, James Dickey, Cynthia Ozick, and Alfred Kazin. Frances Taliaferro in *Harper's*, in praising the book, noted Hannah's peculiar preoccupations: "The slow-moving good old boys, the greasers and their pregnant brides from the mobile homes, are outnumbered by the possessed: the randy and love-raddled, those who swoon from nostalgia and violence, who die of longing. Hannah often gratifies our national passion for the grotesque, nudges ordinary life into black fantasy. But he has a romantic streak, a fondness for Mercutio and Jeb Stuart, and his most memorable stories verge on heroic obsession. *Airships* is a book of tonic craziness and originality, a new seduction for readers who thought they had outlived the short story."

Many reviewers of *Airships* compared Hannah to other Southern writers. Paul Gray in *Time*, for example, remarked that "most young Southern writers resent being compared to such past giants as Faulkner and Flannery O'Connor. In embracing the Gothic mode, Hannah, 35, has planted himself firmly on their turf. On the evidence of *Airships*, their shadows are not stunting his growth." Writing in the *Nation*, Michael Malone remarked that "Hannah's tools (technical and thematic) come out of a Southern kit: the 'Gothic' humor . . . , the lush rhythmic, almost incantatory prose, the vocal quality of the writing. Point of view is almost always from a first-person narrator, or more precisely a raconteur. Hannah, in the Twain tradition, is what he calls 'a great liar,' a teller of 'big loose ones.' It is this oratory of hyperbolic Southern voices telling their largely luckless tales that reminds reviewers of O'Connor and Welty."

Hannah's third novel, *Ray*, centers on an alcoholic doctor in Tuscaloosa, Alabama. A former Vietnam jet fighter pilot, he is still an untamed spirit; his second marriage has foundered; and he has enjoyed "lust" with Sister Hooch, who has been shot dead by a religious fanatic. At the end of the novel he steals a Lear jet, crashes it, and convalesces from his alcoholism in a nearby hospital. John Romano in the *New Leader* remarked that the "postmoral protest against absurdity and violence, the exuberant sex and the mordant comedy work powerfully well in Hannah's . . . novel. *Ray* lacks the punch of his earlier collection, *Airships*, however. The protagonist's personal life is overdone, superficial

and boring. All too predictably, he winds up in the local asylum. It is only vis-à-vis the novel's small town citizens—the Hooch family, for instance, who are the most lovable white trash anyone has dared to portray in any medium—that Ray is a compelling character."

Ray was followed by *The Tennis Handsome*, involving a professional tennis player who becomes brain-damaged after attempting to stop his coach, the eccentric Dr. Word, from jumping off a bridge. Summing up the work, Jack Beatty in the *New Republic* remarked that *The Tennis Handsome* "is a lax drifting cloud of a book, full of casual mayhem. . . . There is no plot, no unfolding logic of development, no growth of character. These people are simply stewed together in a lurid gumbo of inconsequence—unwholesome, flavorless, and indigestible." "The trouble is," Christopher Lehmann-Haupt observed in the *New York Times*, "that . . . the manic language palls eventually, and there is little in the way of credible characterization to bring us relief. Finally, the only living thing . . . is the author's fierce determination to stun us with his zaniness. This works for a while, but it's simply not enough to sustain us for the length of a novel."

Captain Maximus, Hannah's sixth book and second collection of stories, was received unenthusiastically by reviewers. "It's distressing to see Hannah's work become so cryptic and spare," Terrence Rafferty remarked in the *Nation*, "as grudging in its revelations as his first novel, *Geronimo Rex*, was prodigal. This collection has the feel of those grim, creepy miscellanies that appear after an artist's death." Paul Gray in *Time* commented that *Captain Maximus* "is almost aggressively fragmentary," though he conceded that "Hannah's brand of disorderly conduct, even in bits and pieces, remains a welcome reminder that he is just as wild and unpredictable as daily life." A later novel, *Hey Jack!*, is narrated by a middle-aged Korean veteran named Homer who lives in a Southern town bearing a certain resemblance to Oxford, Mississippi. Richard Eder in the *Los Angeles Times Book Review* called the book "a lethal kaleidoscope . . . of grotesques, whose extravagant extremes are squarely in the Southern tradition of William Faulkner and Flannery O'Connor." Michiko Kakutani in the *New York Times*, however, felt that the novel failed to locate the larger meaning of the small town grotesquerie. "Amusing as they are," she observed, "the characters' dilemmas and attitudes . . . never open out—as in, say, Sherwood Anderson's *Winesburg, Ohio*—to give us an appreciation of the consequences of small town life. There is little affection, generosity, or understanding in

Homer's—or, for that matter, Mr. Hannah's—
depiction of these people; and as a result, they
seem a random collection of misfits whose eccentricity, selfishness and stupidity mean
nothing."

Hannah, who is divorced, has three sons—
Barry, Jr., Ted, and Lee. Approaching middle
age in the late 1980s, he has reviewed his life in
the semi-fictional *Boomerang*, which Joanne
Kennedy, in the *New York Times Book Review*
described as a "brief, minor but brilliant autobiographical novel. The book covers his Southern
boyhood, his early experiences in dating and trying to write, his marriages, up to his current life.
It introduces some real-life people like Robert
Altman, but the most striking character is fictional—an older friend who suffers great personal tragedy. For all its free-wheeling,
seemingly random account of a colorful and turbulent life, the book—boomerang-like—comes
back to its true subject. It has focus and emotional appeal. And in clear, spare prose and a distinctive raconteur's voice that could only be
Southern, there is originality, power, pain and
deadpan humor."

Hannah is writer-in-residence at the University of Mississippi at Oxford, the home town of
William Faulkner. Indeed, Hannah lives in a
small frame house in what was once the backyard of the Thompson house, through whose
fence in *The Sound and the Fury* Faulkner had
Benjy look out at the world.

PRINCIPAL WORKS: *Novels*—Geronimo Rex, 1972; Nightwatchmen, 1973; Ray, 1980; The Tennis Handsome,
1983; Hey Jack!, 1987; Boomerang, 1989. *Collected
short stories*—Airships, 1978; Captain Maximus, 1985.

ABOUT: Contemporary Authors 108, 1983, 110, 1984;
Contemporary Literary Criticism 23, 1983; Contemporary Novelists, 1986; Dictionary of Literary Biography 6, 1980; James, J. G. (ed.) Mississippi Writers
Talking, 1982. *Periodicals*—Harper's June 1987; Los
Angeles Times Book Review September 6, 1987; Nation June 10, 1987; June 1, 1985; New Leader December 15, 1980; New Republic April 18, 1983; New York
Times April 18, 1983; November 19, 1987; New York
Times Book Review May 14, 1972; November 18,
1983; New Yorker September 9, 1982; Time May 15,
1987; July 22, 1985; May 14, 1989; Washington Post
Book World December 23, 1973.

HARE, DAVID (June 5, 1947–   ), British
playwright and stage director, was born in the
seacoast town of St. Leonards, Sussex, the only
son of Clifford Theodore Rippon Hare, a ship's
purser, and the former Agnes Cockburn. He
grew up with his sister in nearby Bexhill-on-sea,

DAVID HARE

the most placid of English seaside resorts, then,
as now, filled mostly with old-age pensioners. He
attended Lancing College, a high-church Anglican public school, where he became head boy in
his final year and where his classmates included
the playwright Christopher Hampton and the
lyricist Tim Rice. Hare read English at Jesus
College, Cambridge, earning his bachelor's degree in 1968. He disliked the university intensely: "What did I learn at Cambridge?" he asked
rhetorically in a 1983 interview. "Not much. I
stayed three years at Cambridge, but the whole
climate got me down. Nothing but asthma: all
those fens and marshes." One of his friends there
was Germaine Greer, then a graduate student in
the English department. She acted in a production of *Oh What a Lovely War*, which Hare directed—one of his first theatrical ventures.

The year he left Cambridge, Hare founded,
with Tony Bicât, the Portable Theatre, a touring
group that intended, he recalled later, "to take
theatre where it normally didn't go." Among the
troupe's productions were *Inside Out*, an adaptation of Franz Kafka's diaries, which Hare co-
wrote with Bicât; Howard Brenton's *Christie in
Love*; David Mowat's *Purity*; and Hare's first
solo effort, *How Brophy Made Good*, a sharp satire about a leftist British intellectual utterly corrupted by his empty success as a television
celebrity—themes that were occasionally to recur in Hare's work. The playwright's association
with the Portable lasted until 1971.

From 1969 to 1971 Hare worked as literary
manager, then resident dramatist, of the renowned Royal Court Theatre, Chelsea, a very el-

evated position for a theatrical fledgling. Most of his playwriting during this period, however, was done for other groups. For the Portable in 1969 he wrote *What Happened to Blake?*, an enquiry into the thought processes of the visionary Romantic poet William Blake. In 1970 the Hampstead Theatre Club produced *Slag*, a savage and uninformed attack on feminism which the author has himself since repudiated as "a shameful piece of work." Set in a small, quite unsuccessful girls' public school, the play portrays the hateful, terminally nasty relations among three teachers who jointly swear to forgo sexual relations with men "in order to work towards the establishment of a truly socialist society." The play won Hare the award of the right-wing London *Evening Standard* as the most promising dramatist of the year. It was later produced at the Royal Court and New York's Public Theater (both productions, 1971) to indifferent success. The New York critics' reviews, in particular, were dismissive.

Hare's next three plays concentrated on exposing the hypocrisy of contemporary British society, giving vent, in particular, to the general popular disappointment at the half-hearted efforts of the Labour government to redeem its grandiose campaign pledges. *The Great Exhibition* (1972) showed a defeated Labour member of Parliament as a hollow shell of a man, vain and foolish. *Brassneck* (1973), written with Howard Brenton, depicted various formerly idealistic politicians up to their necks in municipal corruption. *Knuckle* (1974), the first work by Hare to receive a West End production, concerns the efforts of a British arms dealer to solve the mystery behind the disappearance of his sister, an attempt that exposes a vast amount of suburban corruption. For this, Hare won the John Llewellyn Rhys prize for the best literary work published by a British Commonwealth citizen under thirty—the first play to win the prize. *Knuckle* received two New York productions off Broadway, by the New Phoenix Repertory Company (1975) and by the Hudson Guild Theater (1981), but reviews of both were neither favorable nor encouraging.

Hare was resident dramatist at the Nottingham Playhouse, one of England's best regional repertory theaters, in 1973; he wrote and produced *Brassneck* while in that capacity. In 1975, with the director Max Stafford-Clark and the playwright David Aukin, he formed the Joint Stock Theatre Group, another short-lived experimental troupe. His only play for this venture was *Fanshen*, based on the well-received book of the same name by William Hinton about how the people of a remote Chinese village come to terms with communism. The play, which was produced in various places in the United Kingdom as well as in a film version for the BBC, "is much concerned," wrote Hare in a preface to the published version, "with political leadership, with the relationship in *any* society between leadership and led. In the political climate of Europe where the distrust between the people and their bureaucracy is now so profound, this seemed a subject of extreme urgency." At about this same time, Hare was increasingly busy as a director: he received favorable British reviews for his work on Snoo Wilson's *Pleasure Principle* (1973), Trevor Griffiths' *The Party* (1974), and Howard Brenton's *Weapons of Happiness* (1976). He later directed Christopher Hampton's *Total Eclipse* (1981) and a National Theatre production of *King Lear* (1986).

Hare's best-known work—many critics have contended it is also his best work—is *Plenty* (1978), about the degeneration and madness suffered by Susan Traherne, an idealistic Englishwoman: the hypocritical materialism of postwar Britain mocks the romantic and egalitarian political aspirations she had cherished as a British spy behind enemy lines during World War II. The work's wide popularity is probably due in large part to the intensity and mystery brought to Susan's characterization by the two actresses who have portrayed her, Kate Nelligan in the London and New York stage productions and Meryl Streep in the film version (1985), for which Hare wrote the screenplay. Critical response to both versions were generally favorable.

The author's plays since *Plenty* have been less well received. *A Map of the World* (1982) is a work full of passionate argument which treats such large subjects as world poverty, third-world nationalism, art and its expression, capitalism, Marxism, and the decline of Western civilization. *The Bay at Nice* (1986), a one-act play set in Leningrad in 1956, revolves around attempts to authenticate a suspect painting. *Wrecked Eggs* (1986), also one act in length and usually performed with *The Bay*, shows how the lives of three Americans in Rhinebeck, New York, are slipping wildly out of control. *The Knife* (1987), a musical about a sex-change operation, produced at the Public Theater in New York with Mandy Patinkin, had unfavorable reviews; and *The Secret Rapture* (1988), an anti-Thatcherite comedy, won critical acclaim in London, but the New York production, which Hare himself directed, closed after a brief run on Broadway in 1989. "I have been writing plays since I was twenty-two," Hare was quoted as saying in 1983 in the *New Yorker*. "At first the words just flowed out. I wrote practically on my knees—it seemed that easy. Now the writing itself has become more difficult, but once it is over I find the total experience fantastic, and I cannot imagine any other life, a life without it. I guess this gets back to my love of proscenium arches."

Yet his efforts for the conventional theater since the late 1970s have seemed to be at least partly subordinate to his dramatic work for other media. The freedom of films and television, in particular, have, in the opinion of some critics, allowed him the chance to expand his ideas, to take them out of the drawing-room. For the BBC he wrote *Licking Hitler* (1978), a drama about a British counterintelligence unit during World War II (it was voted best teleplay of its year by the British Academy of Film and Television Arts), and *Dreams of Living* (1980), about the relationship between an unconventional young woman and a struggling journalist. For Thames Television he wrote *Saigon: Year of the Cat* (1983), a play that sees the dissolution of South Vietnam in the mid-1970s through the eyes of a middle-aged British woman, a worker at a Saigon bank, who is involved with a young CIA agent. Hare's best-known work, after *Plenty*, is undoubtedly *Wetherby* (1985), a film he both wrote and directed. As told in a complicated and occasionally confusing series of flashbacks, it is the intriguing story of the suicide of a young man and the disturbed reactions of various people with whom he had come into contact. The film was made memorable by the brilliant performance in a pivotal role by Vanessa Redgrave. It won the Golden Bear Award at the 1985 Berlin Film Festival. "*Wetherby*," said Hare in a 1986 interview, "is my privet-hedge film. It's about what it's like to be brought up in suburban respectability, in which any kind of emotional outgoingness is frowned upon. . . . [It] may sound like Pinter, but what marks it out is its emotional flavor, and that stems from these people whose lives are apparently ordinary, and who indeed are ordinary, but who, by means of film, can be shown to be seething inside with passions and a sense of their own loss which they cannot express." Another unconventional film, the thriller *Paris by Night*, was released in London in 1989.

Hare has come during the 1980s to spend increasing amounts of time away from Britain: he calls himself "dreadfully restless," but it is clear that he is also disenchanted with the results of a decade of virtually unchallenged Conservative party rule. "England breaks my heart," he told Benedict Nightingale in a *New York Times* interview in 1982, relatively early in Mrs. Thatcher's tenure. "I find it almost impossible to live here. . . . It's a state of humiliation we never dreamed of, and it's very hard to know where change is going to come from." Yet he also clearly still loves the theater, even though his own

contributions to it as playwright may be in abeyance. "The kind of evening I enjoy in the theatre," he told William Harris in an interview in 1985 in *American Theatre*, "has lots of sets, big acting, good, firm left-wing politics, and lots of humor. It's difficult to keep going as a playwright. I only write when I actually have something to say. Luckily, I have another career to support myself—which is the one I began with, being a director."

PRINCIPAL WORKS: Slag, 1971; The Great Exhibition, 1972; Knuckle, 1974; (with Howard Brenton) Brassneck, 1974; Fanshen, 1976; Teeth 'n' Smiles, 1976; Plenty, 1978; Licking Hitler, 1978; Dreams of Leaving, 1980; A Map of the World, 1982; Saigon, 1983; The History Plays, 1984; Pravda, 1985; Wetherby, 1985; The Asian Plays (Fanshen, Saigon, A Map of the World), 1986; The Bay at Nice and Wrecked Eggs, 1986; The Secret Rapture, 1989; Racing Demon, 1990.

ABOUT: Ansorge, Peter. Disrupting the Spectacle, 1975; Craig, S. (ed.) Dreams and Deconstructions, 1980; Hayman, Ronald. British Theatre since 1955, 1979; Contemporary Authors 97–100, 1981; Contemporary Literary Criticism 29, 1984; Current Biography 1983; Dean, J. F. David Hare, 1990; Dictionary of Literary Biography 13, 1982; Oliva, J. L. David Hare: Theatricalizing Politics, 1990; Who's Who, 1988. *Periodicals*—American Theatre December 1985; Drama Winter 1975, Summer 1978, Autumn 1983; Guardian March 4, 1974; London Magazine July 1978; New Leader April 6, 1981; New Republic March 13, 1971; November 29, 1982; New York November 1, 1982; New York Times February 22, 1971; May 7, 1971; November 4, 1977; August 14, 1979; October 17, 1982; October 22, 1982; October 31, 1982; December 29, 1982; January 31, 1983; October 11, 1985; March 15, 1987; July 31, 1988; New York Times Magazine September 29, 1985; New Yorker January 24, 1983; Newsweek March 23, 1981; Plays and Players March 1970, July 1971, November 1971, February 1971, July 1974, November 1975, April 1978, January 1982, March 1983; Sunday Times (London) Magazine November 26, 1978; Theatre Crafts November 1985; Theatrefacts vol. II, no. 4, 1975; Times (London) May 22, 1971; April 23, 1975; August 30, 1975; Times Educational Supplement February 4, 1983; Times Literary Supplement January 25, 1980; February 11, 1983; September 26, 1986; October 14, 1988; February 16, 1990; Village Voice October 1, 1985.

HARRISON, TONY (April 30, 1937–   ), British poet, dramatist, translator, and librettist, was born in Leeds, Yorkshire, the only child of Harry Ashoton Harrison, a bakery worker, and the former Florrie Wilkinson-Horner. He attended Cross Flats Country Primary School in Leeds and at eleven won one of the scholarships that each year allowed six children whose parents could not afford the fees to enter Leeds Grammar School.

TONY HARRISON

His years there wrenched him from his milieu and deprived him, literally, of his "mother-tongue"—the speech of the Leeds working class that in "Wordlists II" he calls " . . . the tongue that once I used to know / but can't bone up on now, and that's mi mam's." These circumstances have provided the central theme of his poetry. They are also the subject of Ken Worpole's essay "Scholarship Boy: The Poetry of Tony Harrison" in *New Left Review* (September–October 1985). Britain's postwar grammar school system, long perceived as an enlightened assault on the rigidities of the class system, now seems to writers like Worpole "one of the most effective pre-emptive attacks on the possibility of a popular working-class socialist politics in this century." By identifying "the academically most able working-class children . . . and sending them to selective grammar schools," it "estranged [them] from their own families (and therefore their own class) and disinherited [them] from their political and cultural traditions. . . . Tony Harrison is pre-eminently the poet of that major cultural (and disintegrative) experience."

From Leeds Grammar School Harrison went on to read classics at the University of Leeds, at this time making his first experiments in the translation of classical literature. He graduated in 1958 and took a postgraduate diploma in linguistics—an early recognition, perhaps, that language was to be not only his vehicle but a crucial theme for him. Among his contemporaries at Leeds, albeit in the English not the classics department, were the poets Jon Silkin, James Simmons, and Wole Soyinka, the Nigerian who in

1986 received the Nobel Prize for Literature. Harrison's own first poems appeared in the university's magazine *Poetry and Audience*, which for a time he edited. In 1959 Harrison began his career as a teacher in Dewsbury, Yorkshire, and in January 1960 he married Rosemarie Crossfield. Their first child was stillborn; this was the subject of Harrison's only published short story, "The Toothache." It appeared in *Stand*, the now famous regional literary magazine launched by John Silkin and Ken Smith in 1952.

Harrison has recalled how, as the only bookish child in his working-class street, he was the recipient of "every kind of cultural throw-away from spring-cleaned attics and the cellars of the deceased." It was in this way that a copy of David Livingstone's *Travels* came into his hands, inspiring him with a passion for the idea of Africa. In 1962 he went there, with his wife and their small daughter Jane, as a lecturer in English at Ahmadu Bello University, newly established in Zaria, Northern Nigeria. During his four years there his son Max was born and Harrison brought out his first two books. *Earthworks*, published in 1964 in Leeds, is a pamphlet of nine competent but conventional poems. *Aikin Mata*, published a year later, was written in collaboration with another Leeds alumnus, the Irish poet James Simmons, for student actors at Ahmadu Bello. It exports Aristophanes' comedy *Lysistrata* to Africa, equating the Peloponnesian War with Nigerian tribal battles, and showing how politically powerless Nigerian women might follow the example of their Athenian predecessors, withdrawing conjugal rights until their men ended the bloodshed. The distinction in *Lysistrata* between Attic and Doric Greek is echoed in *Aikin Mata* by that between Standard and Pidgin English. Produced in Zaria in 1965, *Aikin Mata* played to capacity audiences both from the university and the town and was published in Ibadan by the Oxford University Press. It was the first of many adaptations from the theaters of a surprising range of cultures. In these plays Harrison has never limited his concern to the words of the page, instead working with actors and musicians to produce not merely a "readable" but an "actable" text. *Aikin Mata* 's enthusiastic reception in Zaria testifies to his ability to make the most ancient texts accessible and relevant to contemporary audiences from radically different cultures.

Harrison is a tireless devourer of cultures and languages. Leaving Nigeria in 1966, he taught for a year at Charles University in Prague, then spent another in England as the first Northern Arts Fellow in Poetry at the universities of Newcastle-upon-Tyne and nearby Durham. During this period, 1968–1969, he joined Jon Silkin and

Ken Smith in the editorship of *Stand*, which is published in Newcastle. That city became Harrison's base and is a theme in his long autobiographical poem *Newcastle Is Peru*, first published in the *London Magazine* in 1967. In twenty-one eight-line stanzas in octosyllabic rhyming couplets, the speaker, dizzy with drink, reviews a life that seems to reel in overlapping circles from Leeds to Nigeria to Prague and back again to Newcastle.

In 1969–1970 Harrison visited Cuba, Brazil, Senegal, and Gambia on a UNESCO Fellowship, and in 1971 was a delegate to the Conference on Colonialism and the Arts in Tanzania. His first full-length book of poems, *The Loiners*, was published in 1970 and brought him the Geoffrey Faber Memorial Prize. The collection is in five sections, the first containing poems about "Loiners"—citizens of Leeds—and recalling Harrison's own childhood and adolescence there. The second section deals with expatriate Loiners in Africa, the third with Eastern Europe, and the fourth and fifth with the poet's return to England. It is thus an extended exploration of material introduced in *Newcastle Is Peru* (which is reprinted in the fourth section). "Loiners" also suggests loins, and Harrison has quoted his mother's complaint that "You weren't brought up to write such mucky books!" She was not alone in finding his frankness about masturbation in Leeds, a homosexual Loiner in Africa, and extramarital sex in Prague gratuitous and excessive. Many reviewers nevertheless concluded that the wit, originality, and virtuosity of these poems paid their scatalogical way. An anonymous critic in the *Times Literary Supplement* defined *The Loiners* as "a single five-part poem," and found it "trenchant, pugnacious, hard-bitten." Its sexual preoccupations give it "at the very least, an above-average novelistic interest. Mr. Harrison has the rare knack of manipulating his ironically regular iambics to sustain a story-line or sketch a quick character. . . . it's a capacity to shackle within formal restraints what continually threatens to become a sprawling, turbulent naturalism which accounts for the book's limited success." For this reviewer, "the poem has little finally to offer beyond its ocean of immediate sensations. If it avoids a cultic toughness, it does so only because it sticks to a grimly empiricist level hostile to most kinds of meditation."

Harrison's anachronistic ability to deploy the rhyming couplet to both serious and ironic effect was a factor in John Dexter's decision to commission from him an adaptation of Molière's verse play *Le Misanthrope*. This was the National Theatre's contribution to the tercentenary of the dramatist's death. It was the first in a series of adaptations commissioned and directed by Dexter, and its great success enabled Harrison thereafter to earn his living as a translator of verse drama. The project was not without teething troubles. Harrison had set his adaptation in 1666, the year of the play's first performance, and had worked on it for a year when Dexter decided that he wanted a modern-dress production. Unable then to leave his text "marooned . . . in the seventeenth century," Harrison moved it forward three hundred years to the France of General de Gaulle, shortly before *les événements* of 1968. As he says in his introduction, he employs "a couplet similar to the one I used in *The Loiners*, running the lines over, breaking up sentences, sometimes using the odd half-rhyme to subdue the chime, playing off the generally colloquial tone and syntax against the formal structure."

Alan Young, in his essay on Harrison's poetry in *Critical Quarterly*, wrote that "as in Molière's French original, Harrison's verse for the [central] character of Alcèste performs a complex dramatic function. It is simultaneously an expressive vehicle for a vulnerable, frustrated sensibility and a method of distancing or critically placing that sensibility. Because of the way he rings all the changes of rhyme Harrison's couplets delight us continually with their conscious artifice. He is skilful too in using the verse simply at times to convey, for instance, the astonishment and anguish of idealism betrayed." Peter Buckley went so far as to call *The Misanthrope* "with all due reverence to Molière . . . , the best new play of the '70s," and in France also the piece was welcomed as "a brilliant adaptation."

In 1973–1974 Harrison was Gregynog Arts Fellow at the University of Wales. It was there that he wrote most of his second adaptation for Dexter and the National Theatre—a version of Racine's *Phèdre*, produced and published in 1975 as *Phaedra Britannica*. Harrison wrote in his learned and witty introduction that he has used "old material to make a new play" (as Racine himself had done), setting out "to rediscover a *social* structure which makes the tensions and polarities of the play significant again." Phaedra was famously the daughter both of Minos, the moralist and judge, and of Pasiphae, the sexually transgressing woman. Harrison found a social structure that embodied this conflict between order and passion in India under the British Raj. The repressed and repressive codes of the British rulers are threatened by the old lewd gods of the ruled.

John Weightman objected that, by translating the play to Victorian India, Harrison had destroyed "the naturalness of the continuity between the human and the divine." He nevertheless found the stage production "fascinating from beginning to end" and this, rather than the printed text, was after all Harrison's real concern. Oswyn Murray, in a major review in the *Times Literary Supplement* (June 6, 1986) of the writer's verse dramas, pointed out that his use here of rhyming iambic couplets "offset the passionate and uncontrollable emotions that are expressed through it, just as the controlled coolness of Racine's language heightened the violence of the original." Unlike Weightman, Murray thought that "the new setting . . . allows us to belive in the influence of the gods of India on the action, from the betrayal of the Memsahib's mother by lust to the final curse of the Governor, which brings forth Siva's monster to stampede his son's polo ponies and drag him to his death." Harrison's translations of seventy brief aphoristic poems by the fourth century satirist Palladas of Alexandria also appeared in 1975 and were generally admired. He found in these savagely witty poems "the authentic snarl of a man" trapped in poverty and "metaphysically in a deep sense of the futile"—a state of mind with which Harrison himself is only too familiar.

In 1976–1977 Harrison resumed the role of Northern Arts Fellow in Poetry, and then spent most of the next two years in London as the National Theatre's resident dramatist. Here, in close collaboration with actors and musicians, he wrote *The Passion* and *Bow Down*, both staged at the National's Cottesloe Theatre in 1977. *The Passion*, drawn from the Easter plays in the York cycle of fifteenth-century "mystery plays," was described in the *Guardian* as "one of the best things to come out the National to date." Most reviewers thought it perfectly appropriate that Harrison's version of these demotic medieval plays about the Crucifixion and Resurrection should employ Yorkshire dialect and make use of the proletarian conventions and techniques of music hall and pantomime.

The same influences are visible in *Bow Down*, a collaboration with the composer Harrison Birtwistle exploring traditional ballads. Music is central to Harrison's idea of performance, and it is so no surprise to find him assuming the role of librettist in a version of Smetana's *The Bartered Bride*, commissioned by the Metropolitan Opera Company of New York and premiered there in October 1978. According to C. E. Lamb, "this libretto is extraordinary in that Harrison did not change a single note value—'I was naive enough to think it was not allowed.' It is possible therefore to listen to a performance of the opera in Czech and to follow word for word and note for note Harrison's English version." In 1979–

1980 the poet spent a year in New York as UK/US Bi-Centennial Fellow.

Eight years earlier, in 1971, Harrison had embarked on the extended and ongoing sonnet sequence he calls "The School of Eloquence," employing the sixteen-line sonnet form devised by George Meredith for his verse novella *Modern Love*. *Ten Poems from "The School of Eloquence"* was privately printed in 1976; a rather larger selection, *From "The School of Eloquence" and Other Poems*, followed in 1978; and *Continuous*, collecting fifty sonnets, in 1981. *Continuous* is in three sections: the first contains poems about language; the second focuses on the death of Harrison's parents; the third deals with art and death. *Continuous* is so called because its central concern is to explore the continuities between Harrison's life and that of his parents. Its "special edge," as Blake Morrison wrote, "comes from Harrison's interest in the question of what it means to acquire language in a community which has had none." His determination to provide a voice for a class which had always been gagged by its exploiters is evident from the outset—in the four-line poem "Heredity" that serves as the book's epigraph:

> How you become a poet's a mystery!
> Wherever did you get your talent from?
> I say: I had two uncles, Joe and Harry—
> one was a stammerer, the other dumb.

The book's first section begins with "On Not Being Milton," a manifesto which trumpets that "Articulation is the tongue-tied's fighting." In "Them & [uz]" he remembers how at school he was condemned to play the drunken porter in *Macbeth* because of a "mouth all stuffed with glottals"; his teacher explains that "Poetry's the speech of kings. You're one of those / Shakespeare gave the comic bits to: prose!" Harrison's truculent response is to become that paradoxical thing a literate barbarian, a chewer-up of "Littererchewer," a rough-tongued marauder into territory preempted by speakers of "Standard English": "So right, yer buggers, then! We'll occupy / your lousy leasehold Poetry." And so he has.

The second section of *Continuous* open with the moving double sonnet "Book Ends" in which, sitting at home with his father on the evening of his mother's death, he remembers her words:

> You're like book ends, the pair of you, she'd say
> Hog that grate, say nothing, sit, sleep, stare . . .
>
> The "scholar" me, you worn out on poor pay,
> only our silence made us seem a pair.
>
> Book in our silences and sullen looks,

for all the Scotch we drink, what's still between's
not the thirty or so years, but books, books, books.

The education that has cut off from his family
does not make him better equipped than his father to compose an inscription for his mother's
memorial stone:

I've got the envelope that he's been scrawling,
mis-spelt, mawkish, stylistically appalling
but I can't squeeze more love into their stone.

As Ken Worpole wrote in *New Left Review*,
"one of the most evident strengths" of these poems "derives from the tension created between
the classical literary form of the sonnet and the
colloquial nature of the subject matter. It is precisely that tension which gives the poems their
sharp sense of irony and self-conscious dignity."
However, Worpole also finds Harrison guilty of
self-dramatization: "the whole sequence is about
his own class and cultural predicaments. . . .
there are no references to any other children or
friends of his own age, no evocation of children's
games, street life . . . or any of those 'collective
memories' which are usually the very stuff of the
literature of class or geographical exile."

Jeffrey Wainwright, on the other hand, reviewing *Continuous* in *Poetry Review*, found a
"profound contradiction in mounting this attack
upon 'owned language' in poetry, in *sonnets*
moreover, one of the very forms its owners have
appropriated as their own. . . . These poems
cannot solve the contradictions they embody,
but they are a passionate, sad, and heroic struggle with them. They speak of our culture in a
way that makes them some of the most important poems of the present day." It seemed to
Alan Ross that "no English poet has ever used dialect and the rhythms of working-class speech to
such powerful effect as Harrison in these
poems."

Such high praise was common, although Peter
Porter found the collection "full of hollow rhetoric and self-advertising guilt." For Blake Morrison, this "is a verse which coughs and splutters,
all fits and starts. . . . The clumping rhymes,
the all-too-iambic pentameters, the awkward
and repetitive abbreviated 's's' . . . the sheer
confusion of lay-out and typography, as capitals,
italics, Latin and Greek tags, brand-names,
songs, advertising jingles, dictionary symbols
and dialect rub shoulders on pages that have no
pagination—these must be some of the least fluent poems in the language. But they mean to be.
The poetry that comes as naturally as leaves to
a tree is, they imply, the poetry of the leisured
classes, whereas these are poems that must work
for their effects." Harrison's poetry "is written

with labour, and on behalf of labour, and out of
the labouring class."

The same year, 1981, saw the publication of
A Kumquat for John Keats—a celebration in
rhyming couplets of Harrison's "extra
days"—those by which the length of his life had
already exceeded Keats' twenty-five years—and
of *U.S. Martial*, a *tour de force* translation into
colloquial American English of the satirical and
frequently obscene verses of the Latin epigram-
matist Martial. Alan Young described the former
work as a "meditative love poem and elegy . . .
moving because it is a poem of celebration—a
mood which does not come easily to Tony
Harrison":

and being a man of doubt at life's mid-way
I'd offer Keats some kumquats and I'd say:
You'll find that one part's sweet and one part's tart:
say where the sweetness or the sourness start.

Also in 1981 Harrison's adaptation of *The
Oresteia* of Aeschylus opened at the National
Theatre, in an acclaimed production by Peter
Hall, with music by Harrison Birtwistle. Reviewing the play in the *Times Literary Supplement*,
Oswyn Murray said that it was "surely the best
acting translation of Aeschylus ever written. It
gives the impression of catching every image
and every nuance of meaning that is dramatically significant, while recreating Aeschylus' traditional grandeur and sonority." Re-reading the
play five years later, Murray wrote that "it is
easy to see how closely Harrison's achievement
is related to his technical skills as a writer of poetry. On this occasion he abandons rhyme (except in certain choruses) in order to appeal to a
far older tradition of English verse. He uses a variety of strongly stressed and regular metres often based on the dactyl or anapaest, to create a
poetry of pace and menace. . . . In the
Oresteia, Tony Harrison and Peter Hall showed
their understanding of the place of ritual in the
theater; and Harrison has always seemed close to
the ancient tragedians in his acceptance that poetry is part of this ritual context. Like them he
belongs to a verbal not a written culture: the
word is the spoken word." *The Oresteia* received
the first European Poetry Translations Prize in
1983.

In spite of the admiration of many critics and
of other poets, Harrison's poetry, as Ken Worpole wrote, "found it incomparably more difficult to gain access to the metropolitan literary
and cultural journals" than the work of less challenging contemporaries. Oswyn Murray suggests
that he was in fact best known as a playwright
until the publication in 1984 of his *Selected
Poems*. The collection includes work from all of

the earlier collections except the first, *A Kumquat for John Keats*, all of the Palladas translations, and about twenty-five uncollected poems.
Reviews of this very popular volume showed not
only what Harrison's admirers celebrated in his
work, but what offended adherents of the
"genteel" tradition in English poetry. Michael
Schmidt was reminded of Kipling by "the pace
of his poems, their lack of repose, the sudden
clarification in images brilliantly rendered," but
also by "the button-holing manner, the narrative
content, the insistent maleness of voice." Claude
Rawson found the poems "both thrusting and
coy" and "a striking mixture of emotional vigour
and patness." For David McDuff, however, Harrison had built in his poems "a cosmology that
throws into glaring relief, in a way not hitherto
attempted or achieved, those regions of the English psyche that are inhabited by the ghosts of
the dispossessed, the inarticulate and the
outlawed." It seemed to McDuff that Harrison's
voice had grown gentler in his more recent poems; that "what survives of the 'barbarian' persona in these later works is a deeply engaging and
engaged voice, serious without being earnest, the
voice of a scholar-poet. . . . " According to
Worpole, the *Selected Poems* moved Harrison
"from a largely unnoticed position to one in
which he is claimed to be among the most important English poets now writing."

Harrison's subsequent verse publications include *The Fire-Gap*, a snake poem with two alternative endings, produced as a poster book to
a design by Michael Caine, and *V*, a long poem
illustrated with gritty photographs of Leeds
slums by Graham Sykes. The setting is the van-
dalized cemetery where rest the ashes of Harrison's parents. Like Gray's *Elegy*, written two
centuries earlier in a very different kind of
graveyard, it ends with the poet's own rude epitaph. The "V" of the title stands for "versus,"
among other things, and this poem, written during the miners' strike of 1984, echoes the mounting class anger and frustration of Britain in the
mid-1980s. It provoked much protest in 1987
when Harrison read it on Channel 4 television.

As Christopher Reid wrote, the poem's
"central event . . . is a visionary encounter with
a graffito-daubing [Leeds] United supporter . . . who turns out to be . . . the personifica-
tion of Harrison's own vandalism." There are no
signs here of the growing moderation and gentleness that had been detected in the *Selected
Poems*, either in the content, the constant use of
Anglo-Saxon expletives, or in the "bellicose bad
behaviour" of the "rough versifying." The latest
installment in the continuing "School of
Eloquence" sequence was published in 1987 as
Ten Sonnets from "The School of Eloquence."

The Big H, a play with music by Dominic
Muldowney, was first shown on BBC Television
on Boxing Day (the day after Christmas) 1984.
It is a homage of sorts to Leeds Grammar School,
in which three schoolteachers share the role of
a modern Herod, instructing their pupils in the
desirability of massacring innocents and not
dropping their aitches (the other "big H" for
working-class children who would be upwardly
mobile in society). In 1985 a revised version of
The Passion was produced and published as a
trilogy under the title *The Mysteries*. The same
year saw the publication of Harrison's *Dramatic
Verse: 1973–1985*, which reached the United
States in 1986 as *Theatre Works*. The volume includes *The Misanthrope*, *Phaedra Britannica*,
The Bartered Bride, *The Oresteia*, *Bow Down*
and *The Big H*, as well as *Yan Tan Tethere*, a
collaboration for television with Birtwistle, and
Medea: A Sex-War Opera.

Harrison's has become an increasingly familiar face on British television. His lively interest
in death inspired in 1988 a much-praised series
of programs, *In Loving Memory*, introduced by
himself in a mixture of verse and prose, about
burial in various parts of the world. On July 31,
1989 he wrote and presented on BBC Television's "Byline" program a defense in verse of Salman Rushdie's novel *The Satanic Verses*, for
which Rushdie had been sentenced to death *in
absentia* by the late Ayatollah Khomeini of Iran
for blasphemies against the Muslim faith. The
program, called *The Blasphemer's Banquet*, is
set in a Bradford restaurant serving Indian food
to which Harrison had been "invited" and spoke
for writers who had been "damned by some
priest": Omar Khayyam, Lord Byron, Molière,
Voltaire, and Rushdie. Inveighing against all
forms of religious intolerance, Harrison celebrated all those condemned by the Koran for worldliness: "all who love this fleeting life" (a line sung
again and again by Harrison's wife, the soprano
Teresa Stratas). And, looking straight into the
camera, Harrison raised his glass to Rushdie and
his book: to its "brilliance and, yes, its
blasphemy." The Archbishop of Canterbury and
others tried without success to have the program
postponed to a less sensitive time, and it was condemned by Muslim and other religious leaders
in Britain. For many, however, it was a "brave
and inventive film," and evidence of the "sense
of gallantry" that Denis Donoghue has recognized in Harrison's poetry.

Harrison has been married to Teresa Stratas
since 1984. He was elected a Fellow of the Royal
Society of Literature in the same year, and in
1987–1988 served as President of the Classical
Association. He divides his time mostly between
his home in Newcastle, New York, and Florida,

and is someting of a recluse. "I don't socialize," he says. "I've too much poetry to write."

Rosemary Burton describes Harrison as a man of great intensity, with a "serious, utter commitment to writing" and a "measured, never casual, use of language, even in conversation. . . . There is darkness, despair and pessimism" in his character: "he says it has been with him since the age of eight and you can sense it as he speaks, but there is also an overwhelming warmth and openness—a sensual delight in and appetite for living." As he puts it himself, "the intellect despairs, the heart affirms." Tony Harrison has been described by Oswyn Murray as "our leading theatrical poet" and by Blake Morrison as perhaps "the first genuine working-class poet England has produced this century."

PRINCIPAL WORKS: *Poetry*—Earthworks, 1964; Newcastle Is Peru, 1969; The Loiners, 1970; Ten Poems from "The School of Eloqence," 1976; From "The School of Eloquence" and Other Poems, 1978; Continuous: Fifty Sonnets from "The School of Eloquence," 1981; A Kumquat for John Keats, 1981; Selected Poems, 1984; The Fire-Gap, 1985; V, 1986; Ten Sonnets from "The School of Eloquence," 1987; V. and Other Poems, 1990. *Plays and adaptations*—(with James Simmons) Aikin Mata, 1966; The Misanthrope, 1973; Phaedra Britannica, 1975; Bow Down, 1977; The Passion, 1977; The Bartered Bride, 1978; The Oresteia, 1981; Dramatic Verse: 1973–1985 (In the U.S., Theatre Works: 1973–1985, 1986) (contains The Misanthrope, Phaedra Britannica, The Bartered Bride, the Oresteia, Bow Down, The Big H, Yan Tan Tethera, Medea: A Sex-War Opera); The Trackers of Oxyrhynchus, 1989. *As translator*—Poems, by Palladas, 1975; U.S. Martial, 1981.

ABOUT: Contemporary Authors 65–68, 1977; Contemporary Literary Criticism 43, 1987; Contemporary Poets, 4th ed., 1985; Dictionary of Literary Biography 40, 1985; Who's Who, 1989. *Periodicals*—Critical Quarterly Spring & Summer 1984; Encounter December 1975; The Independent August 1, 1989; London Magazine March 1982; London Review of Books April 1–14, 1982; February 7, 1985; April 17, 1986; New Left Review September–October, 1985; New York Review of Books July 15, 1982; New Statesman July 24, 1970; Poetry Review July 1979; Stand 1 1985–1986; Sunday Times November 11, 1984; August 6, 1989; Times Literary Supplement September 11, 1970; December 11, 1981; April 4, 1985; January 4, 1985; June 6, 1986; Washington Post Book World July 22, 1990.

HAYCRAFT, ANNA. See **ELLIS, ALICE THOMAS**

HEILBRONER, ROBERT L. (March 24, 1919–), American economist and social critic, writes: "My start as a writer seems to have come under the guidance of that benign deity who, according to Adam Smith, presides over our economic destinies. I had studied economics in college, and after an Army stint, begun what I thought would be a career in business. Soon, however, I found myself powerfully drawn ('as by an invisible hand', in Smith's words) in quite a different direction, or rather, directions. A deep desire to continue my studies brought me to the New School for Social Research where I fell under the influence of a magnetic teacher. At the same time, a long-smouldering ambition to be a writer tempted me into the risky path of free-lance journalism. From the combination of scholarship and journalism, in so many ways at odds with one another, came the fortuitous origins of my writing career.

"The two pursuits came together at my first publisher's lunch, an invitation from an editor who had read a piece of mine and thought there might be a book in it. By the time salad came it was clear there wasn't, and my spirits fell considerably. But conversation veered around to my studies, and I found myself speaking with enthusiasm about the vision of economics projected by my professor—a vision that rejected the prevailing notion of economics as a long *gradus ad parnussum* from the error-filled past into the enlightened present, and that perceived it instead as a series of chapters of intellectual inquiry into the workings of society, the early chapters fully as interesting and often as relevant and illumining as the later.

"It was obvious by dessert time what my book was to be, and I hurried back to school to tell my teacher, Adolph Lowe, that I intended to write a history of the development of economic thought. Having since become a professor myself, I can understand why Lowe declared with magisterial finality, 'That you cannot do!'. I decided nonetheless that I would try it, as a journalist if not yet a scholar, and some months later, with considerable trepidation, showed the initial three chapters to my professor. It is a measure of the man that having read them he declared with equal authority, 'That you must do!'. Under his tutelage, that is what I did.

"The book was *The Worldly Philosophers*—an account of the great economists that wove together their ideas, their personalities, and the times in which they lived. Here is where the combination of my two interests made itself felt. My journalist's training prevented the account from bogging down in technicalities and abstractions, while the scholarly influence of my mentor prevented it from becoming mere re-

ROBERT L. HEILBRONER

portage. To the astonishment of my publishers and myself, the book quickly became a best-seller: I remember walking with my mother shortly after the book appeared, and coming on a total stranger reading it on a park bench. 'Tell him you wrote it!', said my mother. Despite—or perhaps because of—the fact that booksellers displayed it under Philosophy rather than Economics, the first edition of 2,500 copies disappeared overnight, and thirty-five years and six editions later, the *Worldly* still sails in orbit.

"Curiously enough, the initial success brought a problem along with its pleasures. The book gave me a reputation as an interpreter of economics, a translator of its hieroglyphics into the popular demotic. The problem was that my interest lay less and less in this kind of economic journalism, and more and more in projecting my own ideas of what economics was about. I suppose the truth of the matter is that I aspired to become a worldly philosopher myself—not for a moment that I ever ranked myself with Adam Smith or Karl Marx or John Maynard Keynes, but insofar as I wanted to continue in their tradition as a searcher for large unifying visions of the economic world.

"Hence my next major books took a very different tack from my first. In *The Future as History* and *An Inquiry into the Human Prospect* I wrote about the seismic forces of population growth, technological change, and ecological strain, and about the success or failure with which these forces could be contained within and controlled by the frameworks of social organization called Capitalism and Socialism. The

books were sober, even somber, and washed away the cheerful reputation that the *Worldly* had gained for me. I was now regarded as a prophet of doom, although in fact my prognostications were not predictions of disaster, but only warnings that the future seemed more likely than anything else to continue, perhaps to intensify, the tenor of our existing troubles. Given the capacity for world self-destruction, I would call that more of an optimistic than a pessimistic prognosis.

"These works, focused on the trend of things, were succeeded in 1985 by a more ambitious effort, *The Nature and Logic of Capitalism*. This was an attempt to search for the foundations in 'human nature' from which arose the drive for wealth and power, and to trace within the institutions of capitalism the manner in which these ancient and deep-seated propensities work their way with us. Neither cheerful nor pessimistic in its outlook, *The Nature and Logic* looked inward rather than backward, as did my first book, or forward as did its successors. Inward is not a direction to which economists normally direct their gaze. I suspect that not a few members of my profession regard this latest endeavor as being about as proper a sphere for economic inquiry as scientists might regard Jules Verne's project for a journey to the center of the earth. Quixotic or not, it is the direction in which my scholarly promptings now send me. My interest in the worldly philosophers has thus become an interest in the worldly philosophy itself, at its deepest and least explored roots. I have no illusion that I will map out the geological structures on which is raised the familiar landscape of worldly affairs, but it is in these caverns that I nonetheless expect to spend much of my time, sending up messages of a kind to anyone who is curious about what might lie beneath the surface of our economic life."

———

The nineteenth-century pundit who called economics the "Dismal Science" could not have foreseen the popularity of Robert L. Heilbroner's books with both college students and the general reading public. It is not because Heilbroner has simplified his complex subject that he is so widely read but because he has put economics into its social and historical context and shown its relevance to the major problems of modern society. The great economic thinkers who are his "worldly philosophers" (Adam Smith, Thomas Malthus, David Ricardo, Karl Marx, J. M. Keynes, Joseph Schumpeter) were worldly because, he writes "they sought to embrace in a scheme of philosophy the most world-

ly of all man's activities—his drive for wealth";
they were important because their work "was
more decisive for history than many acts of
statesmen who basked in brighter glory . . .
they swayed men's minds."

As a historian of ideas Heilbroner investigated
the roots of this acquisitive drive in *The Quest
for Wealth*. He also traced economic history
from Roman to modern times in *The Making of
Economic Society*, a book which was accepted
for his doctoral dissertation at the New School
for Social Research in 1963. Characteristic of
most of his later work, the book was short and
concise, but it was clearly, as L. M. Hacker wrote
in the *New York Times Book Review*, "the product of much reading and reflection." Robert
Lekachman, in the *New York Herald Tribune
Books*, placed Heilbroner among "a very select
company of economists who command their
subject, aspire to communicate its meanings to
a general public, and possess the gifts of exposition which translate aspiration into reality."
Widening his focus, Heilbroner surveyed the
economic development of the third world in *The
Great Assent: The Struggle for Economic Development in Our Time*, showing how American
foreign aid is instrumental in shaping and determining foreign policy.

Whether a "radical conservative," as he described himself some years ago, or a "liberal
idealist," as a reviewer of one of his books labeled him, Heilbroner sees capitalism as an
evolving system which is likely to survive in the
industrialized world for the next several decades
but is subject to formidable environmental and
energy problems as well as to the challenges of
the new technology and competing foreign economic systems. As early as 1966 in *The Limits
of American Capitalism* he suggested that traditional capitalism, with power centered in private
business dominated by the profit motive, would
inevitably change, moving in the direction of
some form of neo-Marxist socialism. In his
Marxism: For and Against Heilbroner describes
such self-styled Marxist states as the U.S.S.R.,
China, and Cuba as "evidencing, in their institutions and ideologies, attitudes that are abhorrent
to most Westerners, including the great majority
of Western Marxists," but regardless of political
ideology, Heilbroner has argued, the influence
of Marx is inescapable and still "germane and
relevant . . . if we are to understand the actual
processes of social existence."

By 1985, in *On the Nature and Logic of
Capitalism*, Heilbroner was raising an even more
fundamental question: not "What will become
of capitalism?" but "What is capitalism?" One
thing it is not, he points out, is the narrowly conceived equivalent of business or industry. These
represent what he calls "the outward-facing
reality of capitalism," its tangible manifestation.
But there is also an intangible "nether-
world"—the laws of motion of the system, principles of order and movement which direct the
balance and stability of an economy. The nature
of capitalism is rooted in human history, anthropology, and psychology: "For modern economics, the ordering impulses originate in the efforts
of individuals to acquire material wealth against
the counter-pressures of others within the confines of the social and physical world—a drama
of drive and constraint that impels the larger society toward a destination depicted as a 'general
equilibrium' of wants and capabilities."

Although some reviewers, notably Sidney
Hook in a review in *Commentary* of *Marxism:
For and Against*, have charged with Heilbroner
was writing an "apologia" for Marxism, most
have praised his balance, thoroughness, and lack
of bias. Raymond Williams, in the *New York
Times Book Review*, felt that while Heilbroner
had little new to offer in that book, he asks
"searching questions about political power" and
his discussions of the materialist interpretation of
history and the socio-analysis of capitalism
"are clear, careful expositions and critical
discussions." *The Nature and Logic of
Capitalism*, Kenneth E. Boulding observed in
the *New York Times Book Review*, lacks the
"brilliance and charm" of *The Worldly
Philosophers*. Far more complex in its approach
and in its attitudes, the book "does stimulate
some hard thinking," but in the end Boulding
detects "some ambiguity whether it is for capitalism or against it." Robert Kuttner, in the *New
Republic*, suggested that "it may be beyond the
talents of even a Heilbroner to make neo-Marxist
analyses respectable for American liberals, but
this is as worthy an attempt as we are likely to
see."

Because he sees economics as an integral part
of the structure of society, Heilbroner has also
written significant studies in social history. *The
Future as History: The Historic Currents of Our
Time and the Direction in Which They Are Taking America*, as its subtitle suggests, takes a hard
look at the challenges and the narrowing prospects confronting America. Though writing at
the end of the relatively euphoric 1950s, Heilbroner observed a "generalized anxiety for the
future" largely the result of our loss of a sense of
history and our historical identity: "Unlike our
forefathers who lived very much *in* history and
for history, we ourselves appear to be adrift in
an historical void." With a warning that Western
humanism is vulnerable to disillusion and the
loss of its vision of progress, Heilbroner urged an

intelligent and forthright reassessment of our values. Reviewers found the book challenging and disturbing. C. N. Degler, in the *American Historical Review*, judged that "its analysis of the implications of our economic growth is so stimulating and important that any historian interested in modern society, and America's position in the world will find the book compelling and sometimes frightening." Sidney Hook, in the *Saturday Review*, hailed it as "a masterly discussion of the revolutions of our century . . . excellently written in a sinewy and fast-moving style."

Some fifteen years later, in the context of the Vietnam War and Watergate, Heilbroner published *An Inquiry into the Human Prospect*. He described this period in a new Foreword to the 1980 edition as "a time when a great national illusion was gradually destroyed—the illusion that an invisible shield surrounded the United States. . . . This shield, we believed, held at bay the brutalities and irrationalities that seemed to be part of the life of other nations, but not our own. . . . During the period when this book was conceived, that shield gradually disappeared— or rather, our belief in it evaporated." A book that begins with the question "Is there hope for man?" and examines the potential sources of disaster—depletion of our national resources, a population explosion, a nuclear holocaust—is necessarily sobering reading. Some reviewers indeed, like M. J. Ulmer in the *New Republic*, found the book "an eloquent essay in unrelieved despair." Melvin Maddocks, in *Time*, wrote: "Here is no Spengler taking a sardonic pleasure in declines and falls. Here is a man of practical intelligence and good will, a man equipped by temperament and upbringing to hope. Yet his book is an epitaph on liberalism written with conspicuous pain by an author who includes himself in the epitaph." In the updated 1980 edition of *An Inquiry into the Human Prospect* Heilbroner did not alter his text, but he added an Afterword to each chapter examining the ideas from a current perspective. In the "Final Foreword" he answered his opening question, affirming his faith in "the transcendent importance of posterity." There is hope, provided society is prepared to sacrifice many of its material goals and rediscover "the self-renewing vitality of primitive culture without reverting to its level of ignorance and cruel anxiety."

Heilbroner's discovery of his vocation as an economist was, as he suggests in his sketch, almost accidental. The son of Louis and Helen (Weiller) Heilbroner, he was born in New York City; his father was a co-founder of a large chain of men's clothing stores. He was educated in private schools and at Harvard, where he received a B.A. in history, government, and economics in 1940, summa cum laude and Phi Beta Kappa. Brief experience in business convinced him that a business career was not in his future. After his service in military intelligence in the Pacific in World War II, however, he continued to draw on his business and economics background in free-lance journalism. It was largely under the influence of Professor Adolph Lowe that he was drawn into research and lecturing, and his association with the New School for Social Research has lasted for more than forty years—first as graduate student, then (beginning in 1968) as a member of the graduate faculty. Since 1972 he has been Norman Thomas Professor of Economics. He has two sons from his first marriage, in 1952, to Joan Knapp, an author of children's books. Divorced in 1975, he is now married to Shirley Elinor Taks Davis.

PRINCIPAL WORKS: The Worldly Philosophers (in U.K.: The Great Economists), 1953; The Quest for Wealth, 1956; The Future as History, 1960; The Making of Economic Society, 1962; The Great Assent, 1963; The Limits of American Capitalism, 1966; Between Capitalism and Socialism, 1970; An Inquiry into the Human Prospect, 1975; Marxism: For and Against, 1980; The Nature and Logic of Capitalism, 1985; Behind the Veil of Economics: Essays in the Worldly Philosophy, 1988.

ABOUT: Contemporary Authors New Revision Series 4, 1981; Current Biography 1975; Who's Who in America 1988–89. *Periodicals*—American Historical Review July 1960; Business Week September 30, 1972; Commentary July 1980; New Republic March 30, 1974; New York Herald Tribune Books August 19, 1962; New York Times Book Review October 28, 1962; April 13, 1980; Psychology Today February 1975; Saturday Review of Literature April 2, 1960; Time April 1, 1974.

HENLEY, BETH (ELIZABETH BECKER)

(May 8, 1952–), American playwright, was born in Jackson, Mississippi, the second of four daughters of Charles Boyce Henley, a lawyer and successively Mississippi state representative and senator, and the former Elizabeth Josephine Becker, who acted in the amateur productions of Jackson's New Stage Theater. She was educated in local public schools, but always considered herself an outsider, partly because of severe childhood asthma, which made her a semi-invalid for long periods of time, and partly because she failed to find a place in a high school "big on drill team and cheerleaders." She went on to study the dramatic arts at Southern Methodist University in Dallas, intending to become an actress. She received her bachelor's degree in fine arts in 1974.

BETH HENLEY

Henley's first play, the one-act *Am I Blue*, was written during a play-writing course she took in her sophomore year. A comedy set in New Orleans in 1968, it concerns the sexual and social maturation of a colorless college boy who meets and learns much from a sixteen-year-old high school girl, a young woman with the feckless, somewhat dizzy Southern charm possessed by many of Henley's female characters. The play was produced at SMU during her senior year, and so shy was she then of acknowledging authorship that she insisted that a pseudonym appear on the program. Years later, in early 1982, after her first New York success, it was produced under her own name along with two one-act plays by other authors as part of a bill called *Confluence* at the Circle Repertory Company in Manhattan. Walter Kerr in the *New York Times* called *Am I Blue* a "collegiate exercise . . . broad, buzzing, bittersweet. . . . you can see that even when Miss Henley was first writing about crazies at Southern Methodist U., the makings were there. They're still there, they just want a *little* more humanizing."

After some further dramatic study in 1975–1976 at the University of Illinois in Urbana, during which time she also taught beginners' classes in acting, Henley left for Los Angeles in late 1976 to try to break into the movies. She quickly found that her talent was unappreciated among the vast numbers of aspiring actors and actresses on the West Coast. She spent months with no jobs offers; then, she said in a *New York Times* interview in 1981, not liking "the feeling of being at everyone's mercy, . . . [I] decided to do something creative." Many of her acquaintances in Los Angeles were writing screenplays, usually with no hope whatever of their eventual production, "so I thought I would write a stage play that might at least get performed in a small theater somewhere. That's when I wrote *Crimes of the Heart*."

This three-act play, by far Henley's greatest success to date, takes place in the mid-1970s in the kitchen of the MaGrath family house in the small Southern town of Hazlehurst, Mississippi (which happens to be a real locale and Henley's father's birthplace). The three MaGrath sisters, Lenny, Meg, and Babe, have come together because of two crises: the approaching death of their grandfather, who is in a coma at the local hospital; and Babe's nonfatal shooting of her husband, the best-known lawyer in town, " 'cause I didn't like his looks." Combined with much talk about these family disasters are the revelations of other calamities: their father's past desertion of the family; their mother's more subsequent suicide, hanging herself and her favorite cat in the cellar of the house; the death by lightning that very day, Lenny's thirtieth birthday, of her favorite horse; the crippling of Meg's former lover, the town doctor, by an accident during a hurricane; and the shrunken ovary that not only prevents Lenny from achieving motherhood but makes her unnaturally shy and ashamed. These and other bizarre, somewhat distasteful events are revealed in a deadpan style by the characters (hence the play's designation as comedy), even as the desperation of their situations and the essential grimness of their stories constantly threaten to undermine the laughter. There is little pain sensed by the audience, however, since nearly every situation described, especially the grandfather's coma, provides the impetus for hysterical laughter on the part of the characters.

The play was the co-winner in 1979 of the Great American Play contest sponsored by the Actors Theater of Louisville, Kentucky, and was produced there in early 1979. After other regional productions at the California Actors Theater in Los Gatos (April 1979), the Loretto-Hilton Theater in St. Louis (October 1979), and the Center Stage, Baltimore (April 1980), it received an off-Broadway production for thirty-five performances beginning in January 1981 at the Manhattan Theater Club, which elicited a very favorable response from the New York critics. A Broadway production was quickly planned, and it opened on November 4, 1981 at the John Golden Theater. Before that occurred, however, *Crimes of the Heart* became indisputably the play of its year. In April 1981 Henley became the first woman in twenty-three years to win the Pulitzer Prize for drama. In June the New York Drama Critics Circle named *Crimes* best American play of the season. In August the author won the George Oppenheimer/*Newsday* Playwriting Award for 1980–1981. Critical response to the Broadway production was generally favorable. Walter Kerr called the play "clearly the work of a gifted writer . . . it does mean to arrive at an original blend of folkways, secret despairs, sudden fun. Given the giggling and wailing that overtake the girls regularly, it's a bit as though William Faulkner had tried his hand at writing *Little Women*." The play's plot, according to Brendan Gill in the *New Yorker*, has a "daffy complexity . . . that old pros like Kaufman and Hart would have envied, and it marches at a pace that keeps us from ever questioning the degree of clever manipulation that we are being made subject to." The play was a genuine hit, something rare enough on Broadway for a nonmusical in the 1980s; it ran for 535 performances before closing on February 13, 1983. Henley then wrote the screenplay for *Crimes of the Heart*, which, directed by Bruce Beresford, became a film in 1986. Her screenplay was nominated for an Academy Award.

Before winning the Pulitzer Prize, Henley had written two other plays that received both regional and New York productions. *The Wake of Jamey Foster*, like *Crimes of the Heart*, draws together a family facing a tragedy—in this case, the death of thirty-five-year-old Jamey Foster, a failed writer who had deserted his wife and children, and who was fatally kicked in the head by a cow. The mourners, gathering at his former house, are the usual Henley collection of grotesques and misfits. They have first names like Collard and Pixrose and they talk of others called Aunt Muffin and Papa Sweet Potato. Their jobs are as bizarre as they are—one works as a turkey jerker, another aspires to being a dog bather. There is little of the earlier play's hilarious urgency of situation; these figures come across more as Southern caricatures than as real people. The play was given its premiere at the Hartford Stage Company in a production directed by Ulu Grosbard. Despite indifferent reviews, it moved to Broadway, opening on October 14, 1982 at the Eugene O'Neill Theater. It closed after only twelve performances, having received unanimously unfavorable reviews, many strongly dismissive, which charged the playwright with repetitiousness and the play with being merely a reworking of her earlier success. Henley was publicly philosophical in her reaction to this failure. "It was good to go on that roller-coaster," she said in a 1986 interview, "It makes it makes life exciting instead of boring You kind of get to live the highs and lows and

see what your character is when things are going your way and . . . when things aren't."

The Miss Firecracker Contest is centered on a beauty pageant held each year on the Fourth of July in Brookhaven, Mississippi (also a real town, near Jackson, from which Henley's mother comes). The main characters are three dizzy but purportedly lovable Southerners, Carnelle Scott, the beauty queen, and her cousins, who are visiting her to help her through the contest. The work is full of typical Henleyisms and Henleyites: Uncle George falls to his death from the roof while trying to pull a bird's nest out of the chimney; Aunt Ronelle, a "famous medical case," recently died of cancer despite an implanted monkey gland that made her grow long black hair all over; Cousin Delmount is fresh from a lunatic asylum where he was put for cutting up a man's face with a broken bottle; Miss Popeye spent her childhood sewing "little outfits for the bullfrogs that lived out around our yard."

This two-act play had its premiere at the Victory Theater in Los Angeles and regional productions at the New Stage Theater in Jackson, the Studio Arena Theater in Buffalo, and the Steppenwolf Theater in Chicago. It then enjoyed a respectable run at New York's Manhattan Theater Club, opening on May 1, 1984 in a production directed by Henley's longtime companion, Stephen Tobolowsky. That production closed August 25 of the same year, but a return engagement at the same theater ran from October 15, 1984 to January 20, 1985. (It was released as a film in 1989.) Benedict Nightingale, writing in the *New York Times*, generally approved of *The Miss Firecracker Contest* as "a thoroughly beguiling addition to the Henley archives," but faulted the production as too "frantic, in tone and mood. . . . One consequence is that the play's events and characters seem slighter, sillier than they are. At times one begins to wonder if examples of Southern eccentricity aren't being paraded around the stage for the amusement of patronizing Yankees, something one imagines would be anathema to Miss Henley."

Henley's subsequent works have not fared so well. *The Lucky Spot*, which concerns an attempt to open a roadhouse in Pigeon, Louisiana, on Christmas Eve, 1934, had a twenty-four-performance run at the Manhattan Theater Club from April 28 to May 17, 1987. Reviews were few and unfavorable. *The Debutante Ball*, which the author described as "the Jacobean, underbelly side of *The Miss Firecracker Contest*, much more violent and darker," was scheduled for a production by the Manhattan Theater Club in 1988 but has not as yet been staged. Henley appears to be a victim, along with most of her

American playwright contemporaries, of early, stunning success, which has left her seemingly unable to replicate the dramatic urgency and surprise which fueled that first triumph.

In addition to the screenplay for *Crimes of the Heart*, Henley wrote the one for *Nobody's Fool*, which became a film in 1986; collaborated with the rock musician David Byrne on *True Stories* (1985); and wrote for Sissy Spacek (who played Babe in the film version of *Crimes*) a script, *Strawberry*, about the world of stand-up comedy in Los Angeles.

PRINCIPAL WORKS: Am I Blue, 1982; Crimes of the Heart, 1982; The Wake of Jamey Foster, 1983; The Miss Firecracker Contest, 1985; The Lucky Spot, 1987.

ABOUT: Betsko, K. and R. Koenig (eds.) Interviews with Contemporary Women Playwrights, 1987; Contemporary Authors 107, 1983; Contemporary Literary Criticism 23, 1983; Current Biography 1983; Who's Who in America 1988–1989. *Periodicals*—New Leader November 30, 1981; New York November 16, 1981; New York Post December 5, 1986; New York Times October 25, 1981; November 15, 1981; January 24, 1982; June 3, 1984; November 2, 1986; New Yorker January 12, 1981; November 16, 1981; Saturday Review November 1981, January 1982; Time February 8, 1982; Village Voice January 7–13, 1981; November 18–24, 1981; January 13–19, 1982.

HERBERT, (ALFRED FRANCIS) XAVIER (May 15, 1901–November 10, 1984), Australian novelist, was born in Port Hedland, Western Australia, the son of "T'othersiders" of Welsh, Irish, and English descent who had come to Western Australia from the other side of the continent. Soon after his birth, the family moved to another tiny port town, Geraldton. In his engaging yet imprecise autobiography, *Disturbing Element*, he describes Geraldton: "I first became aware of my existence in a tiny seaport on the long, lonely coast of Western Australia. As I knew the port, it consisted of a long jetty jutting out into the waters of the Indian Ocean, a struggling main street that crookedly followed the shore line, a little railway depot, and two or three cross streets that ended in a sandy scrubby waste in which there was a fringe settlement of Afghan camel drivers and the dispossessed aboriginal blacks."

The family moved again, in 1913, to Fremantle, just south of Perth, where Xavier was educated at state, technical, and Christian Brothers schools. He was first apprenticed as a pharmacist, then studied pharmaceutical medicine for two years (1923–1925) at Melbourne University, from which he took a diploma in pharmacy. In

XAVIER HERBERT

1926, on a trek up the east coast of Australia, he passed through Redlynch, a small settlement near the northeast coast of Queensland, on the Cape York Peninsula facing the Great Barrier Reef and the Coral Sea. He lived and worked there off and on for thirty-four years of his life in a weatherboard cottage opposite the railway station, dispensing in the local pharmacy on Saturday mornings. He worked by turns as pearl diver, sailor, bacteriologist, anthropologist, and farmer. In 1935, for a short time, he was even Superintendent of Aborigines at Darwin. He served with the Australian Imperial Forces in 1942–1943 in the southwest Pacific.

Herbert's first major published work was the novel *Capricornia*, an epic saga of nearly six hundred pages and more than a hundred characters which treats the Northern Territory from the 1880s to the 1930s. It is the story of, among others, Norman Shillingsworth, "a halfcaste aboriginal," whose long, difficult search for identity, self-worth, and a place in society forms much of the novel's foreground action. His education is accomplished through a series of journeys around northern Australia, during which he meets and is befriended by an extraordinary series of Aborigines who teach him about himself and his land. The novel is a passionate condemnation of Australian racism, of the base treatment meted out to the Aborigines by the pioneering Europeans, and of the hypocrisy and corruption of all the institutions of white society. Yet its vitality is such that it encompasses far more than social criticism; according to Herbert, "the greatest feeling expressed" in the book is "my love of this good earth." It is, nevertheless, a story permeated with the author's deep pessimism, which recounts, seemingly endlessly, searing human tragedies. It has become an indisputable Australian classic, winning on its publication both the Commonwealth sesquicentenary literary competition and the gold medal of the Australian Literature Society, and enjoying a reputation that has never slackened over the years. "His book," wrote Colin Roderick in his annotated anthology *20 Australian Novelists*, "is a human document, stained with blood, beflecked with ugly smudges of cruelty, misunderstanding and intolerance. It is . . . fearless and illuminating. Greed, selfishness, human weakness, official ineptitude, sanctimoniousness masquerading as religion, oppression, are exposed without reserve." Harry Heseltine, writing in Geoffrey Dutton's critical anthology *The Literature of Australia*, singles out for comment the novel's "outrageous comedy," which "exists in close alliance with a deeply serious (even pessimistic) theme. In episode after episode of *Capricornia* the best (and the worst) efforts of men are thwarted or even reversed by the operations of indifferent, possibly malign, fate. *Capricornia* is one of the few Australian novels of the twentieth century to suggest an imagination of such bursting energy that it is too big for the narrative in which it is more or less contained."

Seven Emus, Herbert's second novel, was published in 1959, more than twenty years after *Capricornia*. It is much shorter than its predecessor (less than 150 pages in length), yet it shares the earlier book's comic verve and major theme: racial conflict and exploitation. It is in the tall-story tradition of the Australian outback and concerns the increasingly frantic and ultimately unsuccessful machinations of two confidence tricksters—"Mr Malcolm Goborrow, B.A., Dip.Anth.," an ethnologist, and Appleby Gaunt, who calls himself "Baron," a land thief—who are deterimed to steal a very important artifact from an Aboriginal dreaming site. The site is part of a cattle-run, Seven Emus Station, which had been wholly owned (until he was swindled out of it by the Baron) by a half-caste, the amiable Bronco Jones. The crooks' plan to replace the priceless artifact with a fake encounters one comic failure after another; their final apparent success is met with a crushing ironic reversal.

Soldiers' Women is a much longer book. It is generally considered uncharacteristic of Herbert's work in that it is set in wartime, in the Sydney metropolis, and, although it has a certain comic inventiveness, possesses little of the irrepressible, tall-tale vitality of his other novels. In Herbert's view, the Australian home front during World War II was a place of unbridled vulgarity, sexual promiscuity, and perfidy. As Australian and American soldiers pass through in transit to South Pacific battle stations, seduction, drunken orgies, rape, and even murder rage side by side with that peculiar, old-fashioned, often hypocritical primness that Herbert always delights in poking fun at—and to a considerable extent shares himself. Several critics, notably Laurie Clancy in *Xavier Herbert*, have excoriated the author for the crude misanthropy of this book. Clancy refers to the "horrified and nauseated tone in which [Herbert] describes sexual misconduct (which in this novel equals sexual conduct of almost any kind) and the crudely moralistic tones he uses to describe and rebuke his characters. . . . Herbert is concerned to stress the sacramental nature of love but in his anxiety to do this he is led into language which at times falls little short of hysterical abuse." John K. Ewers suggests in *Creative Writing in Australia: A Selective Survey* that the reader, once the end of this compulsively readable novel has been reached, "feels he has been sharing a nightmarish experience that is a projection of the author's imagination rather than a balanced picture of women's reactions to the indisciplines of war-time conditions."

After a well-received volume of twenty short stories, *Larger than Life*, and his resolutely unrevealing autobiographical fragment, *Disturbing Element*, Herbert was silent for another dozen years. His last book was the massive, sprawling *Poor Fellow My Country*, at nearly 1,500 pages and 800,000 words the longest novel ever published in Australia, half again as long as *War and Peace*. In this huge, rambling story, filled with Herbert's characteristic driving, explosive energy, the author returns to his earlier interests: the nature of Australian nationhood, the beauty and attraction of the land, the corruption of the Aborigines, and the pervasiveness of racism. White Australia's hybrid and mongrelized "culture" is constantly compared unfavorably to the true, noble, Aboriginal culture downgraded and ravished by the ignorant invaders. Herbert shows throughout an astonishingly detailed grasp of the intricacies of Aboriginal lore and a deepened and reiterated understanding that it is only by finally coming to live in harmony with the land that Australians will ever be able to be accepted by, and to come to terms with, their beautiful yet demanding and difficult country. With its dozens of characters, rollicking plot, and the unalloyed delight it takes in scenery and folklore, *Poor Fellow My Country* has laid energetic claim to the title of Great Australian Novel, "a dirge," in Laurie Clancy's words, "in lament of the Australia that might have been." The title, however, is anything but undisputed. Adrian Mitchell, for example, in *The Oxford History of Australian Literature*, seems to speak for a strong minority of Australian literary critics in his claim that Herbert "sadly misjudges the sustaining interest of his narration. . . . Too much of the narration is flat dialogue or prosy exposition. The social anthropology is explained, not dramatized, the thesis of the white man's denial of the spiritual reality of this ancient land too relentlessly insisted on. The book is a vast jeremiad; . . . the passion of Herbert's convictions fails to sustain his creative energy, and the narrative proceeds only fitfully. The despondency at its core suggests glowering prophetic vision grounded in the thirties, rather than in the observed reality of contemporary Australia. Herbert, one feels, is writing exhaustively into the past, . . . stranded in attitudes, convictions and prejudices that are increasingly dated."

In July 1983 Herbert left Redlynch to make a final journey into the center of the continent in the hope of writing a final book. Sixteen months later he died at Alice Springs, Northern Territory, the almost mythical center of the Australian wilderness, his last work incomplete.

WORKS: *Fiction*—Capricornia, 1938, U.S. ed., 1943; Seven Emus, 1959; Soldiers' Women, 1961; Larger than Life, 1963; Poor Fellow My Country, 1975. *Autobiography*—Disturbing Element, 1963.

ABOUT: Blake, L. J. Australian Writers, 1968; Clancy, L. Xavier Herbert, 1981; Dunstan, K. Ratbags, 1979; Dutton, G. (ed.) The Literature of Australia, 1964; Ewers, J. K. Creative Writing in Australia, rev. ed., 1966; Green, H. M. A History of Australian Literature, Pure and Applied, rev. ed., 1962; Hadgraft, C. Australian Literature: A Critical Account to 1955, 1960; Hergenham, L. et al. (eds.) The Penguin New Literary History of Australia, 1988; Heseltine, H. Xavier Herbert, 1973; Johnston, G. (ed.) Australian Literary Criticism, 1962; Kramer, L. (ed.) The Oxford History of Australian Literature, 1981; Pierce, P. et al. (eds.) The Oxford Literary Guide to Australia, 1987; Roderick, C. 20 Australian Novelists, 1947; Wilde, W. H. et al. The Oxford Companion to Australian Literature, 1985. *Periodicals*—Bulletin March 8, 1961; October 19, 1963; January 5, 1974; Chicago Sun Book Week April 25, 1943; Commonweal May 28, 1943; Current History August 1943; New Republic May 24, 1943; New York Herald Tribune Book Review April 25, 1943; New York Times April 25, 1943; New Yorker May 1, 1943; Overland no. 50/51, 1972; no. 65, 1976; no. 67, 1977; Saturday Review May 1, 1943; Time May 10, 1943.

HEWITT, JOHN (HAROLD) (October 27, 1907–June 27, 1987), Northern Irish poet, essayist, art gallery curator, and critic, was born in Belfast. His father, Robert Telford Hewitt (a headmaster), and mother (the former Elinor Robinson) were both liberal Methodists, and he was neither baptized nor vaccinated: this combination of circumstances, he felt, made him "the ultimate protestant," a dissenter even from the Dissenters. After a conventional education at Methodist College, Belfast and Queen's University, Belfast, Hewitt was appointed art assistant at the Belfast Museum and Art Gallery. Over the next seventeen years he rose to the rank of deputy director; in 1957, due to his radical political views, the Protestant Unionist establishment closed ranks to deny him the directorship, so he left to become art director of the Herbert Art Gallery and Museum in Coventry, England. In 1972 he retired and returned to Belfast.

During the 1930s, Hewitt found himself drawn towards socialism, becoming a more or less orthodox Marxist; he and Roberta Black, whom he married in 1934, both supported the classic leftist causes of the period—the National Council for Civil Liberties, the Left Book Club, Republican Spain, and the Peace League. Geoffrey Taylor called one of Hewitt's "ancestors," William Allingham, "that almost impossible thing, an Irish liberal"; Hewitt himself was that even less likely creature, an Ulsterman without church or creed. Free from any of the nets which backgrounds like his cast so effectively over others, Hewitt was an inspiring example of the radical tradition in Ulster Protestantism, with its hatred of pomp and its elemental feeling for democracy and social justice, a tradition which has largely withered on the vine.

His early poems showed the strong influence of John Clare, Edward Thomas, and Robert Frost, although Hewitt's relationship with his countryside could never be so comfortable and confident as theirs; his chief influence, however, was Wordsworth. The most obvious characteristic of Hewitt's writing is its deliberate plainness; it is kept at a calm, low key, avoiding stylistic tricks and histrionic display. A superficial reader might sometimes regard him as simply dull, but this is rarely so; rather he belongs to a long tradition of poets, like Thomas Hardy, who eschew the heightened, "poetic" manner so that they may concentrate on intimate detail, exactness of imagery, precision of meaning. The quiet, measured tone allows him to release reserves of symbolic power or convey sincere emotion without straining. His work is deliberately aimed at those who shared his mistrust of the traditional Irish verbal profligacy:

JOHN HEWITT

> I write for my own kind
> I do not pitch my voice
> that every phrase be heard
> by those who have no choice:
> their quality of mind
> must be withdrawn and still,
> as moth that answers moth
> across a roaring hill.
>
>   "I write for . . . "

As so often in his verse, every phrase and image is gently loaded with resonance for anyone familiar with Ulster's divided society ("my own kind" has a bitter irony in this context). So too in "Neither an elegy nor a manifesto": "Bear in mind these dead / I can find no plainer words / I dare not risk using that loaded word, Remember." This is a man who believed that "a tree is truer for being bare," whose distrust of superficial, entertaining flashiness attains the level of a personal philosophy; clarity is a fundamental duty in this mindset, equated with truth and earnestness.

The slightly archaic diction and reluctance to conceal his meaning, perhaps incongruously, often carry a current of strongly-felt emotion which is not lessened by being tightly controlled, and the final impression is one of dignity. This is especially true in the long poems with which he regularly marked his progress, the discursive arguments of a stubbornly honest mind which John Montague described as that of "the first (and probably the last) deliberately Ulster, Protestant poet." In the context of his traditional meters, the unemphatic and decent exposition of his ideas, the sudden flaring up of passion which often occurs when he has his subject firmly pinned

down, can be deeply moving and can humanize his sometimes austere morality.

Hewitt's respect for craft was born partly out of the waste of talent he saw around him in the 1940s and 1950s, Patrick Kavanagh's slovenly abuse of his genius, and the timidly low standards set by too many of his contemporaries. For Hewitt craftsmanship was the outward sign of the poet's seriousness and his respect for himself and his audience; in his criticism he was fond of metaphors from traditional crafts and trades. Hewitt himself often worried why, as a Belfastman and a socialist, he could not make poetry out of city life. In this he was an example of the trend in English literature which culminated in the view of the country as vital and honest and of the city as the corrupt destroyer of the natural order; his most closely argued exploration of this is "Conacre," a long poem from 1943. Perhaps the subject matter was too close, his political views too fixed and dogmatic, to allow the tension which good poetry needs; certainly his early, urban short stories are weak, derivative, and shallow. By this time he had moved from Marxism to the anti-industrial Utopian socialism of William Morris, realizing that it lay closer to his heart.

Hewitt's approach to nature is the opposite of that of, say, Ted Hughes: he tends towards description of people and place, of the patterns of work and the seasonal cycle, moving logically from observation to reflection. What makes his rural verse different and interesting is his relationship with his subject matter. "Conacre" begins as a conventional nature poem in the English Romantic tradition: the structure is loose but stable, the poem marked by the freshness and variety of its observations of the natural world, and a climax is reached in the unexpected majesty of dawn at Garron Point. Thus far we have little more than an update of Wordsworth's vision of the cliff in Book 1 of *The Prelude*. But then there is a thoroughly modern, personal snarl, reminiscent of Yeats:

> I know my farmer and my farmer's wife,
> the squalid focus of their huxter life,
> the grime-veined fists, the thick rheumatic legs,
> the cracked voice gloating on the price of eggs,
> the miser's Bible, and the tedious aim
> to add another boggy acre to the name.

Hewitt's political education denied him the luxury of seeing country life as an idyll, but the awareness of distance between poet and subject goes deeper. A Northern Protestant poet, from the regional capital, writing of the Glens farmers in the English literary tradition, he treats of their rituals and customs, their work and the external details of their lives, but he cannot escape the fact that he cannot penetrate to their depths. And yet it is that very awareness and distance which makes much of Hewitt's poetry worth reading, the detachment which Terence Brown has described as "Ironic Pastoral," the observation of the primal rhythms of the country through the perplexed yet sympathetic eyes of the urban man. This is one reason why Hewitt never sentimentalizes his subject: more often his attitude is one of silent respect, and occasionally gentle humor:

You are coarse to my senses, to my washed skin;
I shall maybe learn to wear dung on my heel,
but the slow assurance, the unconscious discipline
. . . is beyond my mastery . . .
hand me a rake, and I at once, betrayed,
will shed more sweat than is needed for the task.

Of course, behind the unsatisfactory relationship with the (Catholic) farmers of the Glens is one of Hewitt's central preoccupations, the relationship of himself and his people to the rest of Ireland. Again and again (and this drive perhaps reveals the basic insecurity), he explores that relationship, producing as a consequence some of his finest work as he examines the colonial tragedy and attempts to establish the rights of his community to belong:

Once alien here my fathers built their house,
claimed, drained, and gave the land the shapes of
use . . .
The sullen Irish limping to the hills
bore with them the enchantments and the spells
that in the clans' free days hung gay and rich
on every twig of every thorny hedge . . .
So I, because of all the buried men
in Ulster clay, because of rock and glen
and mist and cloud and quality of air
as native in my thought as any here . . .
"Once Alien Here"

or in "The Colony," where he successfully blends the echoes of Ulster's current predicament with parallel colonial resonances from the Roman conquest of Britain, the Jacobean Plantations, or more contemporary horrors (the poem contains the first use of the word "ghetto" in this context). It ends with a moving plea for understanding and reconciliation in which the poet encapsulates the dilemma of his kind:

. . . the rain against the lips, the changing light,
the heavy clay-sucked stride, have altered us;
we would be strangers in the Capitol;
this is our country also, no-where else;
and we shall not be outcast on the world.

Such a poem makes it clear that Hewitt's alienation was but one manifestation of a universal modern *angst*, and that his work has relevance far beyond his own narrow ground.

Hewitt's real theme is the relation of people to their environment, the sadness of modern, cultivated humanity, shaped at the deepest level by their surroundings and history, yet cut off by intellect from any satisfying symbiosis. Other poems deal with the loss of friends, or evoke a chilling sadness from the contemplation of physicality, which separates our essences from one another ("The Distances").

Alienation, then, provides the vital tension in Hewitt's poetry, but he also explores possible escape routes; our intellects seek to dissolve isolation in social action; we are driven by the sense that there is a fundamental unity underlying all things, if only we could break through. Hewitt sought to achieve this in many ways; his socialism was an essential act of faith in this respect, but sometimes a more mystical strain surfaces in his writing. In "The Response" he assembles a delicate picture of a quiet night, child and dog asleep, their whimpers seeming to communicate:

[I] stood suddenly upon the shore
of a new continent of sense
that's mapped beneath our coarser world . . .
being, like water, finds its shape
no longer bottled into selves
but flowing, tidal, out of time,
and vast as ocean's unity.

This is as close as Hewitt comes to a faith, and this calm, accepting joy appears often—indeed, more than once there is a distinct sense of the pagan, though typically it is the open sunlight of Parnassus, rather than the strange pull of the blood which thrills him.

One of Hewitt's greatest contributions to the thought of the province was his experiment with Ulster Regionalism in the 1940s and early 1950s. Inspired by the ideas of Patrick Geddes and Lewis Mumford, and parallel developments in Scotland, Canada, and elsewhere, Hewitt felt that "we must seek for some grouping smaller than the nation, larger than the family, with which we could effectively identify . . . an area of size and significance that we could hold in our hearts"; this area was the Region, specifically the ancient, nine-county province of Ulster. As well as expressing the emergent twentieth-century rebellion against centralism and bureaucracy, Hewitt hoped that if they could set aside the national question for a while, and concentrate on exploring what they shared, their common culture and folklore, perhaps *all* the people of Ulster could find a political entity to which they could give their loyalty, and then go on to approach the bigger problems in harmony, not in conflict.

Hewitt and a small group of artists and historians set about laying the foundations of this Region, publishing long-forgotten poetry, resurrecting old political ideas, exhuming the myths, history, and folklore of the province. Hewitt himself produced the most satisfying and sophisticated poetic expression of the movement in poems like "Freehold," where he asserts his belief in the validity of the small community as a center of culture, fresher and healthier than the cosmopolitan centers. The regionalists were also attempting to establish a literary tradition, something which the North has always lacked, the prevailing ethos being provincial and philistine; they were the first, for example, to use the Ulster accent and vocabulary for effects other than comedy or pathos. They were also the first to directly confront the roots of Ulster's religious and political conflict in art. And in this respect they succeeded, although their victory was delayed until the outburst of artistic activity in the 1960s; James Simmons called Hewitt "the daddy of us all," and poets as diverse as Frank Ormsby and Paul Muldoon have expressed their debt. Seamus Heaney has confessed the influence of Hewitt's craftsmanship, his liberation of the local scene as fit subject for serious art, his celebration of the power of place name and the twists of language in a colony. If Hewitt had not cleared the way, done the research, and fought the preliminary battles, the subsequent course of Ulster poetry would have been very different.

Because he was a pioneer, Hewitt's project sometimes seems self-conscious and studied: he could never have the easy intimacy with myth and community of Heaney or Montague, although his careful awareness of the totality of the situation meant that he never slipped into the pernicious tribalism and racial theorizing of those poets' worst mistakes. Hewitt's unstated mission in all of this was reconciliation between the warring factions, a mission begun at a time when many in the province's establishment refused even to recognize that there was a problem. In "The Colony" his distancing device allows him to inject much irony into his speaker's descriptions of himself and "the natives," but there is no irony in his final plea for understanding:

I know of no vices they monopolise,
if we allow the forms by hunger bred,
the sores of old oppression . . .
and would make amends
by fraternising, by small friendly gestures,
hoping by patient words I may convince
my people and this people we are changed
from the raw levies which usurped the land,
if not to kin, to co-inhabitants

Hewitt's verse play *The Bloody Brae* confirms

tizes that mission with more urgency; recalling a past tribal massacre, he confronts us with the true horror of the situation in a way which makes the conventional liberal solution of virtue and goodwill seem painfully inadequate. In a scene which is a moving reminder of the irrevocability of our responsibilities to one another, the spirit of his victim forgives her murderer, but forces upon him the realization that that is far from enough; she exhorts him to fight for public justice:

I have said that I pardon you . . .
you should have stormed singing through this land,
crying for peace and forgiveness . . .
You built your world as a child its castle of sand.
You said to this and this 'I am kind and just' . . .
This is not a lack of pity. Truth is free
from pity or fear. Truth is a lightning flash.

Although he discovered his subject matter and basic style early, there was a gradual development in Hewitt's poetry, a characteristically careful refining of his art. From the early nature lyrics he moved through almost Augustan discursions to the political and Regionalist poems of his prime. Later his verse became harder and brighter, achieving a precision and spareness of expression. In his last years the role of the city in his writing began to change, from the negative and general references of his early work to the lyrics of *Kites in Spring* published in 1980, where he began to look at Belfast with something like the attention to detail he had applied to the country. Although he was anthologized as a simple nature poet, his poetic range was vast, from long discursive poems in heroic couplets that recall Goldsmith and Crabbe to brief unrhymed pensées like the untitled near-haiku

Grey sea, grey sky,
two things are bright;
the gull-white foam,
the gull, foam-white.

Hewitt's career could be seen as a failure: after all, the communities in Ulster are further apart than ever. A fundamental problem was his uniqueness: he was a very atypical Ulsterman. In Terence Brown's words: "He remains from first to last a man of liberal, humane sympathies, whose primary instinct is to live in harmony with nature and with his neighbours, earnestly debating with himself how on earth this can be managed in the province to which he gives his loyalty. Consequently much that is central to the Irish experience seems absent from his work, or comprehensible to him only as a spectator." Nevertheless, his influence inside his own province was significant, and for that that continual of public demand, his work quoted at the height

of the "Troubles" by the prime ministers of both
parts of Ireland; he was awarded honorary doctorates by both Ulster's universities, granted the
freedom of the city of Belfast; possibly the example of his own life affected his countrymen as
much as his work. He will also be remembered
for his academic and critical work in resurrecting writers like William Allingham and the peasant poets of the eighteenth century, his attempt
to give Ulster people pride and a sense of identity in a situation which is not conducive to such
things. Hewitt is not a great poet; his failure to
break through to the subliminal and psychological depths, his reluctance to experiment, his inability to *really* surprise the reader prevent that.
But a number of his poems approach greatness,
and the central core of one or two dozen are essential reading for anyone who has any pretensions to understanding the poets like Heaney
who have emerged since the 1960s, the Ulster
Protestant mentality, or the situation in the
North of Ireland today. In Heaney's words,
Hewitt enabled Ulster writers to use their province "as a hinterland of reference, should they
require a tradition more intimate than the
broad perspectives of the English literary
achievement."

PRINCIPAL WORKS: *Poetry*—No Rebel Word, 1948; Collected Poems 1932–1967, 1968; Out of My Time, 1974;
Time Enough, 1976; The Rain Dance, 1978; Kites in
Spring, 1980; Selected Poems, 1981; Mosaic, 1981;
Loose Ends, 1983; Freehold, 1986. *Prose*—The Rhyming Weavers, 1974; Colin Middleton, 1976; Art in Ulster: I, 1977; John Luke (1906–1975), 1978; Tom Clyde
(ed.) Ancestral Voices: Selected Prose, 1987.

ABOUT: Brown, T. Northern Voices: Poets from Ulster,
1975; Contemporary Authors New Revision Series 16,
1986; Contemporary Poets, 4th ed., 1985; Dawe, G. &
Longley, E. (eds.) Across a Roaring Hill, 1985; Dictionary of Literary Biography 27, 1984; Dunn, D. (ed.)
Two Decades of Irish Writing, 1975; Harmon, M. (ed.)
The Irish Writer and the City, 1984; Olinder, B. Papers from the First Nordic Conference for English
Studies, 1981: Warner, A. A Guide to Anglo-Irish Literature, 1981. *Periodicals*—Poetry-Ireland 3 Spring
1964; Canadian Journal of Irish Studies I 1975; Honest
Ulsterman 70, 1981; 84, 1987; Krino 4 1987; Threshold
38 Winter 1987; Fortnight 275 July/August 1989;
Times Literary Supplement May 14, 1982; September
8, 1989.

*HIGHWATER, JAMAKE ("J MARKS")
(February 14, 1942?–), Native American his-
torian, novelist, poet, and cultural critic, writes:
"I was adopted as a child and grew up as 'J
Marks' in Southern California, at a time when
adoption was still a covert matter. I do not know

°hī wă ter, jă mä´ ke

JAMAKE HIGHWATER

exactly where or when I was born. All records of
my birth were permanently sealed. In my home
we didn't talk about the past. My natural curiosity about my heritage was ignored or rebuffed.
When I did manage to prod a bit of information
from someone, what I was told usually contradicted something else I had been told earlier.
Nothing about my life seemed to match. And being the adopted son of a motion-picture family
that used four or five different professional
names also didn't help my sense of identity. By
the time I reached adolescence I urgently wanted to use my original name, Jamake Highwater.
My friends at school in the San Fernando Valley
were the offsprings of parents so often divorced
and remarried that they found my identity crisis
just a bit quaint. In Hollywood, wanting to be
called 'Jamake Highwater' smacked of something out of a cowboy-and-Indian movie.

"It is little wonder that so much of my writing
focuses upon the drama of familial and cultural
histories. The greatest mystery of my life is my
own identity. So I have always been fascinated
by people who recall the kind of intimate biographical information that is utterly alien to my
experience. About fifteen years ago I urged my
foster-mother to provide an affidavit containing
everything she knew about me. As I read that
document I was delighted by details that
matched my fragmented memories, and I was
astonished by incidents that made utterly no
sense to me. For a decade, as my foster-mother's
health declined, I gently urged her to clarify
those events of my life which would not fall into
place. She declined to talk about it. Then, in late

1986, she died, taking all of our family secrets with her to the grave.

"I have devoted myself to fiction because I have come to believe that in the post-modern world fiction is as close as we can ever come to the real truth about anything or anybody. Wallace Stevens understood what I mean. 'The final belief,' he wrote, 'is to believe in a fiction, which you know to be a fiction there being nothing else; the exquisite truth is to know that it is a fiction and that you believe in it willingly.' Quite apart from my confused history and the metaphysical stance produced by that confusion, I have also convinced myself that art is utterly final. As my friend, composer Ned Rorem, once said, art doesn't open doors; it closes them. Art exists as I do, without a history. Perhaps it is the inability of art to explain itself that makes it timeless. Art is not Anglo or Indian. It is just art."

In "A Cherished Alienation," his Prelude to *The Primal Mind* Jamake Highwater writes: "Some of us (and there are many more each generation) have stumbled into a newly forged sensibility made of irreconcilable values which, though never truly reconciled, have fused themselves into a new mentality." It is that new mentality, a product of his own "dual cultural orientation," that Highwater seeks to define in *The Primal Mind.* The lesson of the twentieth century, he writes, has been that neither assimilation nor genocide will blot out the vast cultural differences that exist among the peoples of the world. It is indeed these differences that Highwater celebrates: "Human diversity has not been vanquished by conformity and assimilation but has been magnified by our widening world perspective. What remains for all of us is a precious pluralism that is real—though it may seem to be less of a reality than we expected of the gods and goddesses who promised each of us absolute dominion." The urgent need is that we understand our differences and come to believe in one another. Quoting the Unicorn's dialogue with Alice in *Through the Looking Glass*, Highwater sums up: "If you'll believe in me, I'll believe in you. Is that a bargain?"

Jamake Highwater is of French Canadian, Cherokee, and Blackfeet heritage. He was born in Glacier County, Montana, to Jamie and Amana (Bonneville) Highwater. His father worked in carnivals and rodeos, and as a stuntsman in Hollywood Westerns. ("He died a hundred times for John Wayne," he writes.) His mother could not read or write, but she was richly educated in the folklore of her people, which she taught her son. "From my disinherited

mother I learned to stay alive by dreaming myself into existence—no matter how many forces attempted to negate or confine my sense of identity or pride." From this early background in Native American culture the boy was thrust into the vastly different society of upper-middle-class American life when, after his father's death in an auto accident, he was adopted by friends. In an essay in *Shadow Show* Highwater recalls his high school years in southern California (where a schoolmate was the writer Susan Sontag) and his early ambitions to become a writer: "While other children filled their days with friends and outings, I sat at an old typewriter in our home in the then rural [San Fernando] valley and spent my childhood trying to release the cry of rage that was buried within me." At the University of California at Berkeley and graduate school at the University of Chicago he studied music and anthropology.

His professional career began in San Francisco where he settled, determined to teach modern dance although he had had little experience in dance himself. With several other struggling young artists he set up a community arts center to encourage experimental work in music, theater, and dance as well as in the graphic arts. San Francisco was the home base of the counterculture movement of the early 1960s in which Highwater was both an observer and an active participant. As a journalist-reporter he covered the rock music scene and (under the name "J Marks") wrote two well received books—*Rock and Other Four Letter Words* and *Mick Jagger: The Singer not the Song.* In the same period of self-discovery he became more conscious of his ethnic background. "Indians find it incredible that a person must retain one identity, one name, one persona for his or her identity," he writes in *The Primal Mind.* Thus while openly embracing his own Indian ethnicity and adopting his natural family's name, he was accepting his duality as Native American and western American. His writing and his public career as lecturer and educator have successfully reconciled what might have seemed irreconcilable cultural heritages.

In 1967 Highwater moved to New York City: "I leaped directly out of San Francisco's so-called Summer of Love into a sultry and staggeringly aggressive Manhattan August." Although he has since traveled widely in Europe and the United States, New York remains his home. He supported himself with journalism, mainly writing about the cultural scene for a variety of journals and reference books including *Stereo Review*, the *New York Arts Journal*, and the *New Grove Dictionary of American Music.* For several years he reviewed classical music for the *Soho Weekly News.* He also wrote travel guide books for the popular Fodor's series—a *Student's Guide to Europe*, which gave him the opportunity to live abroad for several months, and *Indian America: A Cultural and Travel Guide*.

His Newbery Award-winning *Anpao: An American Indian Odyssey*, the first of a series of novels on Indian culture, was written for young adults although it has been widely read and admired by adults as well. Ambitiously conceived though direct and simple in its prose style, *Anpao* is a blend of history and folklore. The central character, a young Indian boy Anpao, wanders through North America on a mystical quest that brings together a wealth of tales of oral tradition and weaves them into a history of Native Americans from the creation through the coming of the white settlers. Highwater's aim, he writes in an Afterword to the book, was to create an Indian Ulysses "who could become the central dramatic character in the saga of Indian life in North America." In addition to the 1978 Newbery Honor Award, *Anpao* received the Horn Book Award and an American Library Association citation as the best book of the year for young adults. He has subsequently published The Ghost Horse Cycle: three novels, so far—*Legend Days*, *The Ceremony of Innocence*, and *I Wear the Morning Star*—that trace the life of an Indian, Amana, from her girlhood in the late nineteenth century into the twentieth- century lives of her daughter, by a white man, and her grandson—all of them witnesses to the exploitation of the Indians up through the 1940s and 1950s. He has drawn extensively on the history of the more distant past in novels like *Journey to the Sky*, which traces the expedition of James Lloyd Stephens and Frederick Catherwood in Mexico and Central America in 1839, and *Eyes of Darkness*, which is based on the life of the Sioux Charles Eastman who became a physician and treated the victims of the massacre at Wounded Knee. The most ambitious and best received of Highwater's historical novels to date is *The Sun, He Dies*, whose narrator is an Aztec who witnesses the destruction of that ancient civilization by the Spanish conquistadores. Although some reviewers found the characterization in that novel weak, they were in agreement that it was a vivid re-creation of the past—"a romantic book," Kurt Vonnegut, Jr. described it, "yet responsible and instructive at the same time."

Over the years Highwater has reached his largest audiences with his varied and usually beautifully illustrated books on Native American history, painting, and dance. *The Primal Mind*, which brings together his views on the diversity and richness of Native American culture in what is, as its title suggests, an anthropological study,

was the subject of a Public Broadcasting television documentary in 1985. Narrated by Highwater, the program was filmed on location in remote areas of the Southwest and in congested urban areas like New York City that graphically portray the cultural diversity of America. Highwater has also participated in the production of a television series on ethnic dance in America, in a program on mythology hosted by the late Joseph Campbell, in Bill Moyers' "A World of Ideas" series, and he has himself hosted a series of programs by and about Indians called "Native Americans." He has lectured throughout the United States and Canada and since 1979 has been on the graduate faculties of New York University's School of Continuing Education and Columbia University's School of Architecture. He is a founding member of the Indian Art Foundation and a consultant to the New York State Council on the Arts. In 1986 he received an honorary Doctorate of Fine Arts from the Minneapolis College of Art and Design. His proudest honor, however, came in 1979 when the Blood Band of the Blackfeet Nation of Alberta, Canada, conferred upon him the name Piitai Sahkomaapii, "Eagle Son," for his work in behalf of Native American culture.

PRINCIPAL WORKS: *Non-ficton*—Europe under Twenty-Five: A Young Person's Guide, 1971; Indian America: A Cultural and Travel Guide, 1975; Songs from the Earth: American Indian Painting, 1976; Ritual of the Wind: North American Indian Ceremonies, Music and Dances, 1977; Many Smokes, Many Moons: A Chronology of American Indian History through Indian Art, 1978; Dance: Rituals of Experience, 1978; The Sweet Grass Lives On: Fifty Contemporary North American Indian Artists, 1980; The Primal Mind: Vision and Reality in Indian America, 1981; Arts of the Indian Americas: Leaves from the Sacred Tree, 1984; Words in the Blood: Contemporary Indian Writers of North and South America, 1984; Shadow Show: An Autobiographical Insinuation, 1986; Native Land: Sagas of the Indian Americas, 1986; Myth and Sexuality, 1990. *As J Marks*—Rock and Other Four Letter Words, 1968; Mick Jagger: The Singer, not the Song, 1973. *Fiction*—Anpao: An American Indian Odyssey, 1977; Journey to the Sky, 1978; The Sun, He Dies, 1980; Legend Days, 1984; The Ceremony of Innocence, 1985; Eyes of Darkness, 1985; I Wear the Morning Star, 1986. *Poetry*—Moonsong Lullaby, 1981.

ABOUT: Contemporary Authors New Revision Series 10, 1983; Contemporary Literary Criticism 12, 1980; Dictionary of Literary Biography 52, 1986; Dictionary of Literary Biography Yearbook 1985; Highwater, J. Shadow Show: An Autobiographical Insinuation, 1986; Holtze, S. H. (ed.) Fifth Book of Junior Authors and Illustrators, 1983; Momaday, N. S. Literature of the American Indians, 1975; Something about the Author, 32, 1983; Who's Who in America 1986–1987. *Periodicals*—Catholic Library World December 1977;

Horn Book February 1978; New York Times Book Review December 4, 1977; July 27, 1980; Publishers Weekly November 6, 1978; Village Voice May 3, 1983.

HIMMELFARB, GERTRUDE (August 8, 1922–), American historian of ideas and professor of history, was born in New York City. She is the second child of Max Himmelfarb, a manufacturer, and Bertha Lerner Himmelfarb. Her older brother Milton is a well-known political observer and a contributing editor of *Commentary* magazine. After attending New Utrecht High School in Brooklyn, Himmelfarb studied history and philosophy at Brooklyn College and religion, history, scripture, and Judaic literature at the Jewish Theological Seminary. In 1942 Brooklyn College awarded her a Bachelor of Arts degree.

The same year, she entered the master's program in history at the University of Chicago, then known for its "conservative liberalism" school of thought. Her intellectual development was influenced by her adviser Louis Gottschalk and the work of sociologist Max Weber, economist R. H. Tawney, and psychoanalyst Sigmund Freud. She has also acknowledged her intellectual debt to the writings of Edmund Burke, Lord Acton, and Lionel Trilling.

Himmelfarb received her master's degree in 1944, having completed her thesis on French revolutionary Maximilien Robespierre. She wrote her doctoral dissertation on the nineteenth-century English historian Lord Acton after studying his papers at Girton College, Cambridge, while on a University of Chicago fellowship. On her return from England she edited a collection of Acton's works, *Essays on Freedom and Power*, before earning her Ph.D. in 1950.

For the first fifteen years of her career, Himmelfarb worked as an independent scholar, receiving funding from the American Association of University Women (1951–1952), the American Philosophical Society (1953–1954), the Guggenheim Foundation (1955–1956, 1957–1958), and the Rockefeller Foundation (1962–1963). In 1965 she began teaching at Brooklyn College and the Graduate School at the City University of New York.

Himmelfarb's first book, *Lord Acton: A Study in Conscience and Politics*, established her reputation as an incisive historian of ideas and accomplished stylist. "Not so much the biography of a life as the biography of a mind," the work traces Acton's intellectual career from his youthful studies in Germany in the 1850s to his final position as Regius Professor of Modern History

GERTRUDE HIMMELFARB

at Cambridge University in the 1890s. Himmelfarb contends that although as an historian Acton believed in the ideal of liberty, as a moralist he had very low expectations of people, as expressed in his famous epigram "power tends to corrupt and absolute power corrupts absolutely." This unresolvable tension between his understanding of history and his view of humankind prevented him from ever writing his long-planned "History of Liberalism." According to Himmelfarb, Acton's pessimism makes him more of the post-World War II era than the Victorian age: "He is, indeed, one of our great contemporaries." Himmelfarb's concern with the relationship among morality, history, and politics in Victorian England and its relevance for twentieth-century America is a recurring theme in her work. *Lord Acton* was well received by the critics as "the best [biography] of Acton yet written" and "a brilliant study of an unusual thinker. . . ."

Darwin and the Darwinian Revolution, Himmelfarb's second book, analyzes Darwin's role in and the true nature of the intellectual revolution instigated by evolutionary theory. Himmelfarb concludes that Darwin, by "dramatizing and bringing to a climax the ideas, sentiments, and conjectures of his age, may be thought of as the hero of a conservative revolution." The study established Himmelfarb as an authority on Darwin and Darwinism.

In addition to full-length studies, Himmelfarb has written a great number of articles, essays, and book reviews, many of which have been reprinted in collections. The first such collection,

Victorian Minds, consists of fourteen essays which examine inconsistency and duality in the way works or events have been interpreted or in terms of an author's own thinking. Ranging in subject from political philosopher Edmund Burke (1729–1797) to novelist John Buchan (1875–1940), the book explores proto-Victorians, High Victorians, and the Victorian ethos, which Himmelfarb defines as an "evolving," "absorbing," and widely varying entity that is nevertheless identifiable in contrast to earlier and later ages. Critics commended *Victorian Minds* as a "penetrating and refreshing book," but faulted it to different degrees for airing Himmelfarb's own opinion of the "inadequacy of orthodox Liberal assumptions about human nature and politics." The work was nominated for the National Book Award in 1969.

Several of Himmelfarb's short pieces have probed the Victorian "minds," or duality, of John Stuart Mill. In addition, she has edited two reprints of his treatises, *Essays on Politics and Culture* and *On Liberty*. Himmelfarb commented that Mill has fascinated and disturbed her; she abandoned an intellectual biography of him because she couldn't reconcile *On Liberty* with his other works. She eventually came to terms with Mill by writing *On Liberty and Liberalism: The Case of John Stuart Mill*, which is both textual analysis and semi-biography. After delineating the ways in which Mill's radical definition of liberty in *On Liberty* differs from both his earlier and later definitions, Himmelfarb argues that the deviation stems from his concerns about the subjection of women and from the ideas of his wife, Harriet Taylor Mill. It is his aberrant version of liberty, Himmelfarb asserts, that governs twentieth-century public issues: "The ambiguities and ambivalences that are to be found in him are those that have beset much of modern political thought and that continue to plague us today." While reviewers praised the book's lucidity and erudition, they questioned Himmelfarb's thesis (called "wrong-headed and mean-spirited" by Alan Ryan in the *American Historical Review*) and her emphasis on the dominance of Mill's radical idea of liberty in the twentieth century (deemed ideological commentary by another critic).

In *The Idea of Poverty: England in the Early Industrial Age*, Himmelfarb examines perceptions of poverty and their effect on the formulation of social policy from the mid-eighteenth to mid-nineteenth century. The large monograph, to which a sequel is planned, was described in the *Times Literary Supplement* as following poverty's transformation from "a natural, unfortunate, often tragic fact of life, but not necessarily a degrading fact" to "an urgent social problem." Dismissing "Whiggish" histories which interpret the Elizabethan poor laws as the origin of the post–World War II welfare state, Himmelfarb maintains that historians must look at the social ethos and the moral and intellectual climate of Victorian England to understand the Victorian idea of poverty. Himmelfarb was generally praised for the book, one critic, ironically, calling it "an invaluable guide to England's path from the Elizabethan Poor Laws to the Welfare State."

Himmelfarb's second collection of essays, *Marriage and Morals Among the Victorians*, was published in 1986. In the introduction she notes her embarrassment at discovering "how often— how obsessively, some might say—I have dealt on the same theme," that is, "the intellectual and moral nature" of nineteenth-century England, in her work. The theme of *Marriage and Morals* is the supersedure of religion by morality in the Victorian era and the subsequent replacement of morality by aesthetics, or style, in the Edwardian and interwar years. As in her other studies, Himmelfarb sees a direct relationship between her historical subject and the problems of the mid-to-late twentieth century. For example, she states that we cannot expect the humanities to provide the moral guidance necessary to sustain our endangered civilization because even they have "capitulated" to modernism, as witnessed by "the attempt of political philosophy to transform itself into political science, history into social science, literary criticism into semiotics, and, most recently, theology into semantics." *Marriage and Morals* received good reviews for its new insights into familiar and influential writers and thinkers. The book's weakness, according to Keith Thomas in the *New York Review of Books*, lies in its dual function as "historical exegesis and moral exhortation . . . one of them is bound to suffer when a writer attempts to carry out both tasks."

Himmelfarb further developes her criticism of what she calls deconstructed, desocialized, dehumanized, and demoralized scholarship in *The New History and the Old*. In this compilation of essays, articles, and reviews written between 1975 and 1984, she impugns "new history," which draws heavily upon the social sciences, and staunchly defends traditional "old" history. As an intellectual historian, she stresses that "the two modes of history reflect differences in subject and method which are tantamount to different conceptions of history, and that the new history has significant implications not only for the history of historiography but for the history of ideas as well."

The collection includes a highly controversial

essay, originally published in 1984, in which Himmelfarb considers the dire implications of the hegemony of social history, or "history with the politics left out," which "makes meaningless those aspects of the past which serious and influential contemporaries thought most meaningful." Himmelfarb criticizes Marxist historians for their politically-determined, ideological versions of history. She aims her most denunciatory remarks at quantohistory and psychohistory, calling the first inhuman and the latter "insidiously anti-intellectual" and accusing both of prohibiting communication even between historians of the same subject. In other essays, she laments the passing of a Macaulay readership, of respect for national history, and of the idea of progress, the last symptomatic of the current moral crisis "so deep that it may signal the end of Western civilizaton." Himmelfarb has commented elsewhere that higher education is also beginning to suffer from these demoralizing, dehumanizing trends.

Reviewers found *The New History and the Old* intelligent and well-written, accurate in some of its criticisms but exaggerated, "bitter and uncharitable" in others. In *New York Review of Books* Lawrence Stone (whose own work gets off "fairly lightly" in the book) likened Himmelfarb's convictions to those "shared by some liberals of the World War II period who were traumatized by the struggle against dogmatic Marxism during the cold war and became the neoconservatives of the Reagan era."

In a *Commentary* magazine symposium, "What is a Liberal—Who is a Conservative?" (September 1976), Himmelfarb has considered the term "neoconservative" and found it lacking. In America, she declares, the label "conservative" "has been so thoroughly vitiated that it is hopeless to try to rehabilitate it." "Neoconservative" is merely "an attempt to describe a reality that persists in spite of all the intellectual proscriptions against it." She advocates the abandonment of both "conservative" and "liberal," but admits that as an historian she would regret altering the traditional character of political debate in England and America. In another *Commentary* symposium, "Liberalism and the Jews" (January 1980), Himmelfarb asserts that Jews may question their commitment to a form of liberalism no longer congruent with valued aspects of Judaism, such as tradition, law, family, community, morality, religion. She does not find conservatism congenial either, however, and recommends that Jews take advantage of this "homelessness" to boldly define their own interests and principles.

As she herself noted in the introduction of

Marriage and Morals Among the Victorians, Himmelfarb has focused on moral and intellectual issues in Victorian England throughout her career and has drawn lessons for twentieth-century America in most of her studies. Her work has progressively become more overtly concerned with moral and political issues which affect late twentieth-century society, ideas, and learning. She has contributed to the history of ideas not by uncovering new subjects but rather by asking innovative, penetrating questions about well-known subjects like Charles Darwin and John Stuart Mill. Although consistently praised as well-written, erudite, and insightful, Himmelfarb's studies have often engendered historical and political controversy.

Since 1942, Himmelfarb has been married to Irving Kristol, editor of the journal *Dissent* and professor of urban studies at New York University. She is now Emeritus Professor of History at the Graduate School of the City University of New York, where she had been Distinguished Professor of History since 1978. Himmelfarb and Kristol have two children, William and Elizabeth.

Over the course of her career, Himmelfarb has been a fellow of the American Association of University Women (1951–1952), the American Philosophical Society (1953–1954), the John Simon Guggenheim Memorial Foundation (1955–1956, 1957–1958), the National Endowment for the Humanities (1968–1969), the American Council of Learned Societies (1972–1973), the Woodrow Wilson International Center (1976–1977), the Rockefeller Foundation Humanities Fellowship (1962–1963, 1980–1981) and a recipient of a Phi Beta Kappa scholarship (1972–1973). She has served on the Presidential Advisory Commission on the Economic Role of Women and the board of overseers of the Hoover Institute on War, Revolution and Peace (Stanford University), and has been a member of the American Academy of Arts and Sciences (fellow), the Royal Historical Society (fellow), the Society of American Historians, the National Humanities Center (trustee), the National Endowment for the Humanities (council member), the Woodrow Wilson Center (trustee), and the Council of Scholars, Library of Congress. She holds honorary degrees from Rhode Island College (1976), Smith College (1977), Lafayette College (1978), and Kenyon College (1985).

PRINCIPAL WORKS: Lord Acton: A Study in Conscience and Politics, 1952; Darwin and the Darwinian Revolution, 1959; Victorian Minds, 1968; On Liberty and Liberalism: The Case of John Stuart Mill, 1974; The Idea of Poverty: England in the Early Industrial Age, 1984; Marriage and Morals Among the Victorians,

1986; The New History and the Old, 1987. *As editor*—John Emerich Edward Dalton-Acton, Essays on Freedom and Power, 1949; Thomas R. Malthus, On Population, 1960; John Stuart Mill, Essays on Politics and Culture, 1962; John Stuart Mill, On Liberty, 1974.

ABOUT: Contemporary Authors 49–52, 1975; Current Biography 1985; The Writers Directory 1988–90, 1988; Who's Who in America 1984–85, 1984. *Periodicals*—New York Review of Books, March 28, 1968; May 28, 1987; December 17, 1987; New York Times Book Review, January 1, 1984; Times Literary Supplement May 25, 1984; Wilson Quarterly Spring 1984.

DARYL HINE

HINE, (WILLIAM) DARYL (February 24, 1936 –), Canadian-born poet, translator and playwright, writes: "Born and brought up in British Columbia that, while not perhaps as idyllic as I recall, had much of the flavour of an earlier century, at the age of eighteen I moved to Montreal as an undergraduate in Classics and Philosophy at McGill. My first poems had appeared in *Contemporary Verse* in 1951, and I was given the greatest encouragement, and the kindest criticism, by writers in the Vancouver area, whose informal get-togethers were the only poetry-writing classes I ever attended, at least until I had to teach such classes much later. My first book, a slim pamphlet, appeared in 1954, published by Jay MacPherson in Toronto; my next, more solid collection was the second in the McGill Poetry Series which began with Leonard Cohen and went on to Sylvia Barnard. Involved as I was increasingly in writing and in the production of my plays on and off campus, and the early recipient of a Canada Foundation travelling fellowship, I decamped without taking my B.A. degree, and spent the next fascinating and formative four years, more or less, in Europe, based in Paris. (See *Arrondissements*, etc.) There seems no need to repeat my bibliography here, except perhaps to say that *The Prince of Darkness & Co.*, my only prose fiction to date, written in London (1958/1959) deals with Robert Graves and his circle, visited in Majorca in Summer 1958: similarly *Polish Subtitles* arose out of a visit to Warsaw, with my illustrator and companion Virgil Burnett, who has since supplied the covers for all my books, in October 1960. Burdened with a persistent if fallible memory, I have never been able quite to invent in prose, though I do so all the time in verse, which is perhaps why I have written so much more of the latter: so *The Devil's Picture Book* is the purest fiction of these years. After supplementing my scholarships with radio plays and talks and occasional poems on the CBC and BBC Third Pro-

gram, I was enticed to New York at the end of 1961 by promise of steadier income as a freelance publisher's reader. In the next, eighteen-month period, perhaps the most sociable of an essentially solitary life, I made many lifelong literary friends, such as James Merrill, John Hollander, and W. H. Auden, all of whose work I had admired for years. But when offered a chance, through the agency of Anne Pippin Burnett, professor of Classics at the University of Chicago, to return to graduate studies there, I was happy to do so in 1963, taking my doctorate four years later, and in the meantime publishing *The Wooden Horse*, my first book, with Atheneum, my publishers for twenty years. I taught writing of poetry, for the first time and at an institution otherwise oriented, as well as Humanities at U. Chicago 1967/8, and left the University with genuine regret to take on the editorship of *Poetry* 1968–1978. I found I much preferred teaching to editing, and writing to either, but handled all three jobs as best I could in that interesting decade, doing part time lecturing at U. Chicago, U. Illinois (Chicago Circle), and Northwestern, and publishing five books in the same period. I had always been drawn to translation, and found it most compatible with the demands of a quasi-administrative position: since *The Homeric Hymns* through Theocritus and, now, Ovid's Heroides verse translation, largely from the ancient Greek (I admit to a sneaking feeling that the only perfect language is a dead language), has provided a kind of laborious recreation, and a rest, *mutatis mutandis*, from invention, though I have never ceased to write poetry. On leaving *Poetry* in 1968 I was able by means of a series of grants, culminating in the MacArthur Fellowship, and some part-time teaching here and there, and other literary odd jobs, to lead the life of the imagination even more fully and comfortably: this freedom and leisure, however busy (*otium negotiosum*) I owe chiefly to my friend and housemate of twenty-two years' standing, the philosopher S. J. Todes. Since 1971 we have lived in Evanston.

"Future projects include, in addition to Ovid: translations from the *Palatine Anthology*; a prose detective novel, complete but not yet ready for the press, "The Waste Basket", and an overdue new collection of poems, "Post Scripts."

"As for my poetics, I hope they can be deduced from my practice. Basically I believe merely in putting one foot before, after, or next to another, whichever comes first."

Having published his first volume of verse at the age of eighteen, Daryl Hine launched his career with the not always happy epithet of *Wunderkind*. His precocity, combined with what critics called the "preciosity" of his early work marked him as a brilliant but remote poet. His poetry, Louis Dudek wrote of Hine's *The Devil's Picture Book*, "is a series of extremely recherché, abstract, contrived word-forms, containing oblique and ambiguous philosophical essays and meditations." Richard Howard referred to the same collection as "that teratoid toybox of virtuosity," adding, "We are not aware in Daryl Hine's first poems of the nagging presence of anything so extranaeous or so impure as 'the real world.'" Northrop Frye, however, found distinct promise in young Hine's work, "a sense of powerful gathering forces," and the poet Eli Mandel wrote in *Canadian Forum*: "Whatever the dramatic pose, it issues in a poetry that is, for all the calculated echoes, wonderfully original: a stately and austere danse-macabre, always impressive in its restrained melancholy, its wry gloom, and its magical insights."

By 1976 there was a distinct shift in critical judgments of Hine's work. Harold Bloom, reviewing his long autobiographical poem *In & Out* in the *New Republic*, commented on the "amazingly good verse. . . . Hine, previously a classical lyricist with affinities to [James] Merrill, reveals himself as a natural story-teller and humorist. *In & Out* is one of the few poems I've read that has everything fresh and original to say about the quasi-identity of sexual and religious experience, but I suspect it will survive despite its length and complexity—because the reader,

once embarked, needs to know what will happen next." Still occasionally obscure, still marked—as Munro Blattie wrote in the *Literary History of Canada*—by "a baroque stateliness of utterance," his mature poetry is admired today for its purity, precision, "steely verbal elegance," wit and personal candor. In an article on Hine in *Modern Poetry Studies* in 1977 Robert K. Martin deplored the fact that though he is "among the sharpest, most original voices in Canada," he is a neglected talent. Martin found the confessional *In & Out* "one of the most important poetic documents of recent years . . . the history of a soul, a magnificent epic of the self in the great American tradition of 'Song of Myself' and 'The Bridge.'" In this 13,000-line poem, which describes the young poet's journey from his home in the Canadian West to Montreal and McGill University and his love for a young man who commits suicide, Hine comes to terms with his homosexuality in what Martin calls "an epic of gay liberation."

Probably not since William Wordsworth wrote his massively long *The Prelude* has a poet chronicled his spiritual and real life in such depth and detail as Hine. *Academic Festival Overtures*, published eleven years after *In & Out*, centers on only one year of his early adolescence. Written in classical form with long Alexandrine lines, though using the non-classical device of rhyme, the book is divided into the months of the school year, beginning in September:

> For me, as for anyone who was educated
>   In the same system, the year has always begun
> In effect with the first day of school in September,
>   Not, like the calendar, on January One.

The year is 1949. The poet, just entering junior high school, is already far beyond his years, surreptitiously reading Blake and Northrop Frye's *Fearful Symmetry* ("Reading had become my solitary vice"). In the course of the year, during which his mother dies, the boy explores his sexuality, his relationship with his reserved father ("Till we became like two incompatible convicts / Compelled to share the same inhospitable cell"), and discovers that he is an adopted child. Lonely and withdrawn, he falls in love with a handsome athletic boy:

> Unacquainted with the clinical nomenclature
>   Which would seem to me irrelevant anyway,
> I could not accept the glib vernacular verdict
>   That might have labelled me as queer (no one said
>   'gay'),
> In those days; a charge I must have repudiated
>   Insofar as my crush was innocently chaste

We follow, as we do in Wordsworth, "the growth

of the poet's mind"—his wide ranging reading, his growing interest in classical languages, his first efforts—encouraged by a sympathetic librarian—at writing poetry, and his grief when the boy he idolized was crippled in an automobile accident. The book ends some years later when at eighteen he leaves home for college. "It is a virtuoso achievement," Harold Beaver wrote in the *New York Times Book Review*, "as remarkable in its way as anything by Auden. It is also a remarkable record of a yearning, bookish and inhibited boyhood."

Hine is not, however, exclusively an autobiographical or confessional poet. Much of his work deals with the artifices of language and with the clashes of reality and sensibility. Parable, paradox, conceits, and puns are not merely tricks of virtuosity in his poetry but means of discovery. In his volume *Daylight Saving*, for example, he teases grammar into philosophical speculation:

Morning like a dangling participle,
Noon the present tense indicative
Moods of the irregular verb to be
Whose lack of subject is itself a subject. . . .

One of his best known poems is "Bluebeard's Wife" (in *The Wooden Horse*) in which the doomed woman wanders through her husband's castle opening the locked doors that lead into, first, "the room of artifice" ("Not a thing that grew there but was made") where she encounters art ("Each was at once an image and a deathless mould"); then nature where she

Saw greater good than any she had seen:
A window open on the sacred text
Of natural things, whose number had not been
Created or conceived, nor did they mean
Other than what they were, splendid and strange.

And at the end she comes to "the final door":

. . . There hung the past,
Putrid and crowned. And thinking, 'Love survives
The grave,' she stepped inside to join the other wives.

Hine's highly regarded translations of Greek poetry are a natural complement to his own poetry because his classical learning, as John Robert Colombo wrote in *Contemporary Poets*, "reverberates rather than echoes with Greek, Roman, Christian and even Celtic references throughout all his poetry." Using dactylic hexameters he attempts to capture as closely as possible the diction and meter of the original. The only liberty he takes is to provide rhymes for Theocritus' epigrams, observing that "an unrhymed epigram in English is an insipid thing, like an egg without salt." In his own "Epilogue: To Theocritus" he prays that his translation may

. . . prove a not wholly unworthy example
Not of pedantic myopia nor of impertinent freedom
But of inspired fidelity, such that a trifling departure
From the original only results in a fair reproduction.

Hine has also written a number of plays, some produced at McGill University and the University of Chicago, some broadcast over the CBC and the BBC. One of his plays, *The Death of Seneca*, was published in the *Chicago Review* in 1970.

PRINCIPAL WORKS: *Poetry*—Five Poems, 1955; The Carnal and the Crane, 1956; The Devil's Picture Book, 1960; The Wooden Horse, 1965; Minutes, 1968; Resident Alien, 1975; In & Out, 1975, rev. ed., 1989; Daylight Saving, 1978; Selected Poems, 1980; Academic Festival Overtures, 1985; Arrondissements, 1988. *Translations*—The Homeric Hymns, and The Battle of the Frogs and the Mice, 1972; Theocritus: Idylls and Epigrams, 1982. *Novel*—The Prince of Darkness and Co., 1961. *Non-fiction*—Polish Subtitles, 1962.

ABOUT: Contemporary Authors New Revision Series 1, 1981; Contemporary Literary Criticism 15, 1980; Contemporary Poetry, 4th ed., 1985; Dudek, L. Selected Essays and Criticism, 1978; Frye, N. The Bush Garden: Essays on the Canadian Imagination, 1971; Howard, R. Alone in America: Essays on the Art of Poetry in the United States since 1950, 1969; Klinck, C. F. (ed.) Literary History of Canada, 2nd ed., 1976; Who's Who in America, 1988–89. *Periodicals*—Modern Poetry Studies 8, 1977; New Republic November 20, 1976; New York Times Book Review March 2, 1986; Poetry June 1979; Times Literary Supplement August 15, 1975; October 20, 1978.

HOFFMAN, ALICE (March 16, 1952–   ), American novelist, was born in New York City. She received her B.A. from Adelphi University in 1973, and her M.A. from Stanford in 1975. Her first novel, *Property Of*, was published in 1977, when she was barely twenty-five. Characterized by reviewers as an "impressive debut" and a "taut and piercing first novel," *Property Of* deals with a young girl's infatuation with the leader of a juvenile youth gang known as the Orphans. The novel does not take place, however, within the inner city but at the edges of the suburbs, and the gang members are all WASPS. "The real magic," Edith Milton wrote in the *Yale Review*, "is heroin. The street fights, mortal, savage violence for abstract and distant principles, echo the Vietnam War. . . . The narrative is engrossing because Hoffman creates characters touched by legend; [she creates] lyrical parallels for a mindless state somewhere between violence and apathy." Richard Lingeman in the *New York Times* called *Property Of* "a remarkably envisioned novel, almost mythic in its cadences, hypnotic. . . . [Hoffman] imbues

ALICE HOFFMAN

her juvenile delinquents with a romantic intensity that lifts them out of sociology."

The Drowning Season is set on Long Island and involves a bizarre group of characters, including a tyrannical matriarch, Esther the White, who is dying of cancer; her son Phillip, who tries to drown himself every August (and eventually succeeds); and her stifled granddaughter Esther the Black. In one way or another these characters reflect upon Hoffman's theme of estrangement and the need for contact. Writing in *Newsweek*, Jean Strouse observed that a summary of the novel's plot "may sound contrived, but it works. Alice Hoffman's hallucinatory novel skims along just above the surface of the real like a finely wrought nightmare." Although Jerome Charnyn in the *New York Times Book Review* thought *The Drowning Season* flawed in some respects (Esther the Black resembling "a spook with too little flesh"), he praised Hoffman's "extraordinary sense of the fabulous," and called the novel "a fierce and wicked fairytale of these 'modern times.'"

Like *The Drowning Season*, *Angel Landing* deals with the theme of alienation and the effort to find redemption in human commitment. Its plot revolves around a set of characters in a small town on Long Island where a nuclear power plant is under construction. Chief among them are Natalie Lansky, a therapist at a counseling center who is adrift in her life, and Michael Finn, a disaffected welder who deliberately causes an explosion at the plant. Reviews of the novel were generally favorable. The reviewer for *Booklist* found Hoffman's characters

"credibly developed," and Miriam Sagan in *Ms.* praised the work as "essentially a novel of character, in which individuals struggle for meaning and control." *White Horses*, Hoffman's fourth novel, drew less favorable notices. Another study of a young woman's alienation, *White Horses* is concerned with the protagonist's incestuous obsession with her brother and her effort to break free of him to find her own identity. The reviewer for the *New Yorker* commented that Hoffman "is a daring and able writer; she plots the conjunctions of mundane and magical events with such ease that the reader never dares to doubt her word." Yet other critics found the novel self-conscious. Barbara F. Williamson in the *Saturday Review*, for example, noted that Hoffman's striking imagery "should be hypnotic . . . but instead . . . becomes merely labored."

In *Fortune's Daughter*, Hoffman was again preoccupied by women's emotional losses, but in this novel she makes use of two central female characters of differing generations, bringing them into a close juxtaposition. Rae, who ran off with a drifter named Jessup in her teens, is now in her twenties and pregnant by Jessup, who has abandoned her for a life in the desert. In Los Angeles she meets Lila, a gloomy, introverted woman of forty-six who works as a fortune-teller and dotes on the memory of a daughter who disappeared. As Rae looks ahead to the birth of her baby, and Lila recoils from her losses as a mother, Hoffman explores the possibilities of healing for both characters. Jennifer Crichton in *Ms.* described the structure of the novel as "a magic circle" in which the two women interact. "Like Anne Tyler," she commented, "Hoffman spins a story enchantingly, with the undeniable force and vividness of a dream, and a dream's own logic." Perri Klass in the *New York Times Book Review* also compared Hoffman to Tyler. Hoffman's men, Klass remarked, "are sometimes reminiscent of those in the novels of Anne Tyler, some of whom have this same quality of watching the women around them with bewilderment—occasionally awed, occasionally resentful. *Fortune's Daughter* calls up other comparisons with Miss Tyler, who has at times combined folk tale with contemporary details in ways that are not so different from Hoffman's."

Illumination Night brings together another set of isolated characters, this time in Martha's Vineyard. One of the principal characters is a teenage girl named Jody whose sexual recklessness ignites reactions in the others. The reviewer for the *New Yorker* called *Illumination Night* a "marvelous novel" dealing with the marvels of change and self-recognition. All the characters, she observed, are "wrapped in Hoffman's strange, charmed lyricism." For Gwyneth Cravens in the *New York Times Book Review, Illumination Night* marked an advance over Hoffman's previous work, in which "the male characters were rather sketchy. In *Illumination Night*, women with their sexual longings and inexplicable fears also hold center stage, but the men are more of a presence." Hoffman's *At Risk* deals with a bright young girl who, as the result of a blood transfusion for an appendectomy, has contracted AIDS; and with the devastating effect of her illness on her close-knit family. Christopher Lehmann-Haupt in the *New York Times* believed that "the reader never escapes the sense of a blueprint behind [the story] . . . that tries too conscientiously to teach a lesson. One can't forget that Ms. Hoffman is writing the news." Most reviewers, however, found the book a deeply-felt and "wrenching work of fiction." *At Risk*, which appeared in a first printing of 100,000 copies, was a Book of the Month Club main selection, and was scheduled to be made into a 20th Century–Fox film, with screenplay by Hoffman.

Alice Hoffman, who lives in Brookline, Massachusetts, is married to Tom Martin and has one child, a son. In a symposium on writing in the *New York Times Book Review* in 1984, she discussed the influences on her work: "When I was a teenager, and began to write, I separated my stories into two distinct categories—fantasy and realism—but neither seemed any good without the other. Gabriel García Márquez's *One Hundred Years of Solitude* was the book that changed everything for me. It allowed me to see that a writer could take everyday realities and transform them into something fabulous. It helped me find a way to write, but what I write about has been influenced most by a list that circulated among my friends when I went to school in California, writers they had 'discovered,' whose names were passed on to one another like love letters—Doris Lessing, Jean Rhys, Margaret Drabble, Grace Paley, Marge Piercy, Anne Tyler. These were the writers who made it clear that a novel could be about friendship, family, love gone wrong, desire, faith. Without them, I can't imagine having found the courage to begin my first novel."

PRINCIPAL WORKS: Property of, 1977; The Drowning Season, 1979; Angel Landing, 1980; White Horses, 1982; Fortune's Daughter, 1985; Illumination Night, 1987; At Risk, 1988; Seventh Heaven, 1990.

ABOUT: Contemporary Authors 77–80, 1979; Contemporary Novelists, 4th ed., 1986. *Periodicals*—Ms. June 1985; New York Times July 14, 1977; May 13, 1984; July 25, 1987; New York Times Book Review July 15, 1979; March 24, 1985; August 9, 1987; August 8, 1990; New Yorker May 3, 1982; Newsweek August 20, 1979; Saturday Review April 1982; Yale Review December 1977.

HOFMANN, GERT (January 29, 1931–), German author of fiction, plays, and radio plays, grew up in the town of Limbach in Saxony. In 1950 he began his university studies in Leipzig where he took courses in German literature, foreign languages and literatures (Romance, Slavic, and English), philosophy, and sociology. He moved to the West the following year, continued his university education in Freiburg, and received his doctorate with a dissertation on Henry James and Thomas Mann in 1957. From 1961 to 1971 he taught German literature at various foreign universities (Toulouse, Bristol, Edinburgh, Yale, Berkeley, the University of Texas at Austin). Between 1971 and 1980 he lived in Klagenfurt (Austria) while teaching at the University of Ljubljana (Yugoslavia). In 1980 he moved to Erding near Munich. Gert Hofmann is married and has four children. In conversations with critics Hofmann typically avoids detailed information about his private life and his childhood.

He is the recipient of numerous prestigious prizes and awards: Harkness Award (1965); Internationaler Hörspielpreis Radio Prag (1968); Internationaler Hörspielpreis Ohrid (1973); Ingeborg-Bachmann-Preis (1979); Prix Italia/Prix de la RAI (1980); Preis der Förderaktion für zeitgenössische Autoren (1982); Alfred-Döblin-Preis (1982); Hörspielpreis der Kriegsblinden (1983); Das rote Tuch: Medienpreis (1986).

Hofmann, the author of dozens of radio plays, was close to fifty when he wrote his first prose works, *Die Denunziation* (The Denunciation, 1979) and *Die Fistelstimme* (The Falsetto, 1979; Ingeborg Bachmann Prize), which suddenly brought him wide recognition by critics and readers and established his presence in contemporary German literature. Since 1979 at least one volume of prose has appeared annually. In his novels and shorter narratives he often introduces themes and concerns that he first used in his earlier radio plays, notably his critique of language and knowledge, often combined with ethical and sociopolitical questions. Frequently these plays have treated communication problems; for example, in *Autorengespräch* (Conversation with an Author, 1970) pseudo-dialogues lead to misunderstandings, and the participants remain alien to one another. Elsewhere, as in *Verluste* (Losses, 1972), Hofmann has criticized the clichés of everyday speech; by overcoming the vapid jargon characteristic of her environ-

GERT HOFMANN

ment, an abused housewife is able to change her predicament and to leave her unloving husband. *Leute in Violett* (People in Violet, 1961) describes the development of National Socialism by tracing the growing social isolation of an elderly Jewish couple living in a small town in Germany. As in his 1986 narrative, *Veilchenfeld* (Mr. Veilchenfeld), Hofmann demonstrates the extent to which euphemisms and seemingly innocuous phrases result in a numbing of the citizens' guilty consciences.

To Gert Hofmann the transition from the dialogue form of his plays to prose did not come easily at all, and, as indicated, it happened relatively late in his career. As he pointed out in his 1983 acceptance speech for the Blind Veterans' Radio Play Prize, "Hörspiel und Literatur" (Radio Plays and Literature), his love of dialogue is as much a *need* for dialogue, i.e., the need for many voices and opinions pointing out the dichotomies of the world we live in. To counteract his difficulties in presenting the world from a specific, single narrative point-of-view, Hofmann resorts to a number of techniques: his prose continues to be full of dialogue, occasionally turning into a sequence of intertwined, obsessed monologues, as in his 1987 novel *Unsere Vergesslichkeit* (Our Forgetfulness). A multiplicity of perspectives, what in a different context Wolfgang Iser has called a "wandering point of view," characterizes some of his best texts (e.g., *Die Denunziation*); his first-person-plural narrator voice, by now a hallmark of his prose, is intentionally dispersive and highly elusive (e.g., *Our Conquest*, *The Parable of the Blind*).

In *Die Denunziation* Hofmann attempts to reconstruct and explain Germany's Nazi past insofar as it is reflected in the history of one family. Reminiscent of the autoreflexive texts by Thomas Bernhard in general and of his 1968 story *Ungemach* in particular, *Die Denunziation* is composed as a multilayered collage of fragments from a long letter written by Karl Hecht, a forty-five-year-old attorney. During one long night Hecht recounts to his friend Flohta, who is not identified any further, that he has just been notified of his twin brother's death at Bellevue Hospital (New York) and that he has received the notebooks and letters in which his brother Wilhelm had tried to piece together the family history during the Third Reich. These papers force Hecht to remember their childhood in Nazi Germany when their parents were denounced by neighbors, and especially their mother's suicide shortly before the end of the war. The excerpts from Wilhelm's papers together with Hecht's own recollections are intertwined with his comments concerning not only the case of a young teacher who—persecuted by reactionaries and about to be fired because of his leftist views—has sought his legal counsel, but also his relationship with his liberal student son, with whom he has not spoken in five years. Hecht, who decides to defend the teacher's opponent just before the case goes to court (although he had originally agreed to defend the teacher) betrays a shocking lack of feeling and love in all his relationships. He ducks his own responsibilities and denies all guilt. His inability to mourn, which sets him apart from his brother who went insane because he *did* remember, expresses itself typically in a series of physical symptoms (insomnia, chest pains, etc.). Besides the denunciation of Hecht's parents and of the young radical teacher, Hecht's letter to Flohta constitutes yet another case of betrayal: it denounces the tradition of the liberal opposition to fascist Germany as represented by his parents, his deceased brother, the young teacher, and his very own son.

The influence of Thomas Bernhard, whom Hofmann admires greatly, is also traceable in *Die Fistelstimme*, an uninterrupted soliloquy of 250 pages, full of panicked digressions, absurd language, Doppelgänger obsessions and delusions: "a mad pas de deux of grammar and despair," as one German critic put it very aptly. A lecturer in his mid-thirties arrives in Ljubljana where he is supposed to teach German. In the dense November fog he begins to fall to pieces; reality dissolves into a series of events that repeat themselves. To assure himself of his existence, he constantly takes notes. In the course of his hectic monologue, the lecturer, who takes a train back to Germany two days after his arrival in Yugoslavia, emerges as the type of intellectual who is doomed to go under in a world of academia that bears an uncanny resemblance to Kafka's nightmarish institutional settings. As in his other works, Hofmann, who had taught at the University of Ljubljana, is never directly autobiographical. He admits to his interest in esoteric and marginal characters—e.g., the four authors in Hofmann's following publication, the 1981 collection, *Gespräch über Balzacs Pferd. Vier Novellen* (translated as *Balzac's Horse and Other Stories*)—and his hapless lecturer undoubtedly represents what Hofmann once termed "analogues of himself."

While Hofmann treats the historical biographies in *Balzac's Horse* very freely, he succeeds admirably in adapting his language to each author and the particular period he lived in. J.M.R. Lenz, Casanova, Balzac, and Robert Walser are captured at a point in time when their careers and their lives are in decline. Upon his return to Riga, Lenz—mentally unstable and professionally unsuccessful—has to face his domineering and threatening father (resembling Kafka's father figure in *The Trial*). He desperately attempts to reintegrate himself into normalcy but fails in the end. Casanova is shown as an aging parasite, rejected by everyone, registering his own deterioration; in a confrontation with his dynamic, common mother (whom he had mistakenly tried to pick up), he is severely taken to task. Balzac on the day of his death, hallucinating about the première of his most recent play, realizes that the audience is no longer interested in bourgeois theater; instead they are attracted by bestiality on stage (e.g., a horse is slowly killed by rats—a bloody spectacle organized by the inspector of the Paris sewers for the benefit of the bored establishment). Robert Walser at the age of fifty, socially marginalized and utterly destitute, is reduced to spending an evening with a dull, petty merchant who is also president of the local literary society and has the gall to remind the poet that his public readings are failures and that he still owes the society its annual membership dues.

Auf dem Turm (1982; translated as *The Spectacle at the Tower*), for which Hofmann received the coveted Alfred Döblin Prize, is thematically linked to the title story of his previous publication. A German couple on a vacation in Sicily have car trouble, leave the autostrada in search of a mechanic, and end up in a village in the midst of Sicily's *zona morta*, a region struck by incredible poverty and deprivation, Hofmann's rendition of which has been compared to Gabriel García Màrquez' village of Macondo in *One Hundred Years of Solitude* as well as to the Mexican settings in Juan Rulfo's work.

A repulsive, yet ultimately perhaps also pitiful local caretaker takes the two travelers on a "sightseeing tour" through this village that has none of the typical tourist attractions to offer; instead, in an atmosphere of mounting suspense and terror, the narrator and his wife are confronted by variations of human depravity culminating in the sacrifice of a youth who jumps to his death to satisfy the greedy sensationalism of the assembled foreign guests. As in Thomas Mann's 1929 novella *Mario and the Magician*, Hofmann's narrator keeps remarking that they should have either left the village right away or else at least not stayed to the end of the spectacle at the tower; unlike Mann's innocent witnesses to the Magician's perversions and Mario's act of self-defense, Hofmann's narrator cannot expect any deliverance, for the bestialities he witnesses only mirror his own deplorable behavior towards his pregnant wife.

In his 1984 novel, *Unsere Eroberung* (translated as *Our Conquest*) as well as in *Veilchenfeld* (1986) Gert Hofmann returns to Germany's troubled history between 1933 and 1945 as it was experienced by schoolchildren. In *Our Conquest* the collective narrative voice ("we," i.e., the two boys of the Imbach family and, by extension, German children of that entire generation) recounts the events in a small Saxon town on the day following the German defeat in early May, 1945. Contrary to the children's and the reader's expectations, the Allied troops remain invisible; "there's no trace of our conquerors." Sent out by their ailing mother to fetch leftover bacon fat at the local slaughterhouse and to talk a war widow out of her late husband's suit, the Imbach boys, accompanied by "our poor Edgar," an older, infinitely wiser and sadder orphan, undertake a bizarre daylong odyssey about town. The boys vacillate between the prejudices and clichés taken over from their Nazi parents on the one hand and their determination to uncover the truth about their father's vicious role in the death of a Czech prisoner on the other; they register the symptoms of Edgar's brain tumor and know of his fierce hunger but are too insensitive to share their food with him. Their naive, matter-of-fact tone as they comment on the utterly grotesque situations in which they find themselves is in the tradition of Ludwig Thoma's hilarious *Lausbubengeschichten* (Tales about Little Rascals); but given the historical context of *Our Conquest*, it is a false tone, not meant to solicit the readers' laughter but rather to shock them out of their complacency. Ambiguities also characterize Hans in *Veilchenfeld* who, together with his sister Grete, observes the increasing nazification in the town of L. during the late 1930s. Once again, Hofmann provides us with a child's-eye view of history, concentrating on the mentality of the victim (Bernhard Israel Veilchenfeld, a Jewish professor of philosophy no longer permitted to teach at the University of Leipzig), his tormentors, their fellow travelers, and the intimidated, ever more silent dissenters. Hans' voice is the voice of a chronicler without pity; even innocent children become collectively "guilty": the narrator provides, Professor Veilchenfeld with the poison he needs to commit suicide in the face of imminent deportation. Several critics have recognized Hofmann's hidden references to *Hänsel and Gretel*. As in the fairy tale, Hans and Grete are "abandoned" children, i.e., children betrayed by their parents' strategy of appeasement. It comes as no surprise that Hofmann has also been attacked for this approach to Germany's past; by studiously avoiding all references to Nazi insignia and never directly referring to Veilchenfeld as a Jew, Hofmann—no doubt contrary to his intentions—runs the risk of mystifying the "banality of evil" and of transplanting the Holocaust from history to the archetypal realm of myths and fairy tales.

Gert Hofmann's 1985 narrative, *Der Blindensturz* (translated as *The Parable of the Blind*) was critically acclaimed in Europe as well as in the United States *The Parable of the Blind* is a brilliant yet chilling imaginative account of the experiences of six blind men on the day they "stood" model for Pieter Brueghel's painting of the same name. Brueghel wants "to sum up the fate of man; he'd like to put everything he had to say about the world" into a single painting and to portray the blind men (i.e., mankind) "on a bridge, over a slope, as a dark procession making a descent." The parabolic aspect of Brueghel's painting finds its narrative equivalent in Hofmann's use of the collective "we" that refers now to the six blind men, now to the two nameless ones in the middle and, by implication, to all of us. The blind have to reenact their stumbling and falling and screaming time and again, and meanwhile "the superfluous and hideous blind people are rapidly being transformed into their true and beautiful and terrible picture, which will grip every one of us." Stressing the dichotomy of art and life, Hofmann adopts neither the conciliatory manner of Goethe's *Dichtung und Wahrheit* (*Poetry and Truth*) nor the usually coquettish solutions of Thomas Mann. On the one hand, as a variation to *The Spectacle at the Tower* and "Balzac's Horse," *The Parable of the Blind* uncovers the ruthless exploitation of the six blind men for the sake of aesthetic satisfaction; on the other hand, harking back to *Die Fistelstimme* and anticipating some central issues in Hofmann's next novel, the sheer fact that the blind men were painted is proof that they existed.

Fuhlrott, the main character in the novel written by the narrator of *Unsere Vergesslichkeit*, is terrified of forgetting everything. He decides to share his life with other people only because they will then help him remember parts of his life: he marries and has a child. His formula, however, is doomed to fail: his wife betrays and leaves him; the son's memories will differ from the father's. Fuhlrott reaches the conclusion that only the act of writing can document his existence. Asking for directions to get to his publisher, the narrator (whose real life closely parallels Fuhlrott's) encounters Reizer (the name suggests that he functions as an irritant). Reizer turns out to be the exact opposite of the narrator and Fuhlrott, for he is haunted by wartime memories, especially the bombing of his home town—a catastrophe which the narrator and his protagonist have repressed altogether. The crisis of remembrance engenders the crisis of the novel: *Unsere Vergesslichkeit* is a novel about the novel. Its strength lies in its autoreflexivity as well as in its ironic treatment of the two men talking past each other: one obsessed by collective history, missing out on life in the present; the other obsessed by his private anxieties, neither caring about nor understanding history. This dual perspective is the way Hofmann establishes his characteristic balance between (and distance from) the literature of social criticism and protest on one hand and the total subjectivity of "New Inwardness" on the other.

In *Vor der Regenzeit* (Before the Rainy Season, 1988) Hofmann reintroduces themes and narrative strategies from his previous writings. Following World War II, Don Enrique (a former Wehrmacht officer) moved to Bolivia to escape the rumor of having commited atrocities against civilians in Russia. The narrator, the son of an old friend in Germany, and his fiancée are visiting Don Enrique a few hours after the brutal stabbing of his younger brother Hans, a member of the Bolivian antifascist underground, who escaped from a mental institution and returned to his brother's heavily guarded hacienda for a day of reckoning. During the burial ceremonies two comrades of Hans remind him of the old rumor and threaten to kill Don Enrique unless he commits suicide. Having run to the edge of civilization, there is no way out: he hangs himself. Comparable to Hofmann's practice in *Unsere Vergesslichkeit*, the narrator's voice obsessively returns to his fiancée's alleged infidelities whereas Don Enrique's discourses, although talking him back into family history, are prime examples of the repression of Germany's past and the role he played in it: "My memories, I keep saying, are my dogs; I trained them well. When I scold them, they slink away; when I whistle, they lie down at my feet. . . . I don't remember the war at all, for years I haven't thought of it. As far as I'm concerned, it was over after the last shot." At times *Vor der Regenzeit* reads like the hackneyed script for a movie thriller complete with revolutionary terrorism, Nazi criminals and bodyguards, nudity and sex; at times Hofmann's style is altogether intriguing, e.g., when his skillful layering of voices removes the truth from the reader by several levels, or when he captures something of the local spirit and thus opens new spaces for German fiction.

Gert Hofmann has been praised for the technical brilliance and the melancholic, stoic tenor of his books. He is neither an author who points to the state of the world with a moralizing gesture, assuming that conditions could be significantly changed and ameliorated; nor is he interested in presenting us an everyday world, but focuses instead on what people are capable of—for better and for worse—when they are confronted by illness, deprivation, guilt, fear, or death: "All *in extremis*," as Brueghel puts it in *The Parable of the Blind*. A virtuoso of metafiction, Gert Hofmann wishes above all to remind the reader that he ought to juxtapose his own thoughts to the fiction that he is consuming.

WORKS IN ENGLISH TRANSLATION: Hofmann's major novels have been translated by Christopher Middleton. These are: *The Spectacle at the Tower*, 1984; *Our Conquest*, 1985; *The Parable of the Blind*, 1986; *Balzac's Horse and Other Stories*, 1988.

ABOUT: Boston Globe April 18, 1984; Guardian March 20, 1987; Houston Chronicle March 9, 1986; Houston Post June 6, 1985; Kirkus Reviews (New York) May 18, 1985; Los Angeles Times March 28, 1984; New Statesman September 1985; New York Times Book Review May 15, 1984; April 14, 1985; January 26, 1986; May 8, 1988; New Yorker May 20, 1985; Oberlin Review April 20, 1984; Observer September 1985; Publishers Weekly February 8, 1985; Review of Books August 14, 1986; San Francisco Examiner-Chronicle March 16, 1986; Sunday Telegram (Worcester, MA) February 16, 1986; World Literature Today Spring 1981, Summer 1983, Spring 1986; Summer 1989.

HOFSTADTER, DOUGLAS R(ICHARD)

(February 15, 1945–   ), American computer scientist and educator, writes: "I was was born in Manhattan in 1945. My first two years were spent there, and then we moved to Princeton, where my father was a professor of physics. In 1950, my father decided to accept a job offer at Stanford, and so we moved to California, where I grew up.

DOUGLAS R. HOFSTADTER

"My early fascinations were with particles (I particularly loved contemplating massless, speed-of-light particles like photons and neutrinos) and numbers: I delighted in calculating powers of 2, playing with complex numbers, and discovering number patterns. At age twelve, studying French, I discovered I was equally fascinated with the patterns of languages. For instance, I was greatly intrigued when I learned that in French, the conditional tense mysteriously combines the future stem with past endings ('je serais'), but I was truly thrilled when I noticed that in English as well, the conditional is based on a strange fusion of future and past ('will' plus 'ed' makes 'would'). Our family spent a year in Geneva, Switzerland the next year, and my French rapidly improved, so that by the end of the year I was quite fluent.

"In high school and college (Stanford), I explored mathematics with passion, doing a great deal of original research in number theory, often with the help of computers. Logic—particularly the twisty self-reference at the core of Gödel's theorem—was another main pursuit. When I was 16, I even taught symbolic logic to the sixth-grade class at Stanford Elementary School. I also studied several other foreign languages, and wrote computer programs to produce long, strange, complex sentences in some of those languages. The hardest course I took was Electricity and Magnetism. In fact, I flunked it the first time through, but since it was a required course for math majors (of which I was one), I had to tackle it again. The second time, I worked harder than in any other course in my life, and got an A-, of which I was extremely proud.

"In 1966, after a year off, spent mostly in London and Sweden, I started graduate school in mathematics at Berkeley, but found it disturbingly arid and devoid of meaning. At that time, I was also studying piano with great intensity (practicing several hours a day), in the hopes of perhaps becoming a composer. Gradually, I realized that my musical talent was insufficient, and that somehow, I was fated to use my love of numbers and other abstract structures (logic, physics, languages) in finding my way professionally. I decided to turn towards physics, and went off to graduate school at the University of Oregon, hoping to make a new beginning. Physics, however, was still very hard for me, and it took me nearly eight years of work to find a small niche. I had to abandon my original aim of being a particle physicist, and turn to a very different area. My Ph.D. work, done under solid-state theorist Gregory Wannier, turned out very well: it involved a completely unexpected return to the mathematics I had done as an undergraduate, and the core of my thesis was a computer-plotted graph composed of nothing but distorted and shrunken copies of itself, nested *ad infinitum* inside one another in an amazing and beautiful way. I got my degree at the end of 1975.

"Despite having completed a Ph.D. in physics, I now saw clearly that physics was no more my cup of tea than mathematics had been, and that the thing that had actually been pulling me intellectually ever since my teen-age years was a deep desire to understand patterns of all sorts, particularly the patterns that the mind follows naturally—the patterns of thinking. Thus I returned to my earlier fascination with computer programs that model language and other aspects of mentality: the discipline of artificial intelligence.

"All these interests were brought together in a book I wrote with a consuming passion, first called 'Gödel's Theorem and the Human Brain,' but eventually retitled *Gödel, Escher, Bach*, because I had decided to use Escher pictures to illustrate abstract, nearly unvisualizable themes, and because I had written many dialogues imitating the form of contrapuntal pieces by Bach. This book was published in 1979, four years after I received my Ph.D. in physics, and made quite a splash. Most people didn't know what to make of it: was it a book about three individuals? or three disciplines? or logic? or the mind? or computers? It is still not easy to answer these questions, because *GEB* is a very complex book, but most of all it is probably about free will, creativity, consciousness, mechanization, and the elusive self.

"After my Ph.D., I worked hard at converting myself into a credible artificial-intelligence researcher, and in 1977 I was offered a job by the Computer Science Department at Indiana University in Bloomington. I was delighted to accept it, and once again made a fresh start. At Indiana University, I began in earnest to develop my own research projects, one concerned with discovery of patterns (called 'Seek-Whence'), another concerned with free shufflings of mental parts to make new wholes (called 'Jumbo'), a third concerned with subtle analogies (called 'Copycat'), and a final one concerned with visual style and pattern (called 'Letter Spirit'). A recurrent theme in all these projects is trying to mimic the way the human mind does these things, rather than trying to take advantage of special properties of computers that allow them to do things in different ways from the mind. Thus my research falls more under the rubric of 'cognitive science' than that of 'artificial intelligence'—a term whose meaning has drifted recently, so that it now stands for a kind of glorified engineering.

"My continuing fascination with the mysteries of self and free will brought me into contact with the philosopher of mind Daniel Dennett, and we hit it off very well. We both thought it would be fun and useful to pull together a collection of vivid, tantalizing, and disturbing stories, dialogues, and essays that would be suitable for lay people and for experts, and that would presumably have something to trouble any thoughtful person interested in the mind, free will, and related issues. This anthology, which featured writings by the two of us as well as many others, came out in 1981 under the title *The Mind's I*.

"At roughly this time, *Scientific American* offered me the chance to take over the famous column 'Mathematical Games' from Martin Gardner, who had written it for twenty-five years and was about to retire. The offer was irresistible, but rather than continuing directly along Gardner's trajectory, I decided to go off in my own directions in a new column, which, in homage to Gardner, I called "Metamagical Themas," the two titles being anagrams of each other. In my columns I explored artificial intelligence, structure in music, visual patterns, language, quantum mechanics, self-reference, creativity, and numerous others topics. Writing the column was fun, but after a couple of years, I found that the column and the correspondence it engendered were taking ever-increasing amounts of time, and it seemed advisable to bring it to a halt, which I did in 1983. The complete set of my twenty-five columns, augmented by postscripts and also containing several other articles written during the same period, came out in book form as *Metamagical Themas* a couple of years later.

"In 1984, the University of Michigan offered me the interdisciplinary Walgreen Professorship, and an appointment in the Psychology Department. Given the fertile atmosphere there, I decided to accept, and moved to Ann Arbor, where I started a small research group called FARG—Fluid Analogies Research Group. The mission of FARG is to work on understanding the fluid (i.e., highly flexible) nature of human concepts, and how concepts interact, allowing subtle discoveries and inventions to issue forth from the mind. Esthetic considerations play a large role in the FARG projects, and we hope someday possibly to shed some light on such difficult issues as how mathematical and scientific insights are created, and where visual beauty and musical meaning come from."

Considering the intellectual challenges that his work presents the reader—the complex and highly specialized nature of his subject matter and the deliberately paradoxical manner of his presentation—it is nothing less than astounding that Douglas R. Hofstadter's first book *Gödel, Escher, Bach: An Eternal Golden Braid*, described on the cover of its paperback edition as "A Metaphysical Fugue of Minds and Machines in the Spirit of Lewis Carroll," should have sold over 100,000 copies in its first year of publication alone and won both the American Book Award and the 1980 Pulitzer Prize for nonfiction. Part of the reason for its success is certainly Hofstadter's ability to communicate to his readers his enthusiasm for his abstruse research. One cannot passively absorb his books. Hofstadter demands that the reader accompany him in his search for patterns of intellectual activity. Over the years, he writes in *Metamagical Themas: Questing for the Essence of Mind and Pattern,* his attention has shifted away from formal mathematics to "those more subliminal patterns of memory and associations. . . . Thus my interest has turned ever more to Mind, the principal apprehender of pattern, as well as the principal producer of certain kinds of pattern." If he has turned this search into what sometimes seem like intellectual games, the effect has not been to reduce its complexity but to explore more fully the riddles, inconsistencies, and paradoxes one encounters along the way.

Son of the distinguished physicist Robert Hofstadter and the former Nancy Givan, Douglas R. Hofstadter had his B.S. by the time he was twenty. His background in mathematics, logic, and physics gave him a solid base for his advanced studies in computer science. In 1977, two years after receiving his doctorate from the University of Oregon, he joined the Computer Science Department of the University of Indiana. He has remained in education (with periods off for research, including a Guggenheim Fellowship in 1980–1981) ever since. In 1984 he joined the faculty of the University of Michigan.

Gödel, Escher, Bach reflects his humanistic as well as his scientific interest. In his Introduction, "A Musico-Logical Offering," as Hofstadter describes it, Bach's *Musical Offering* becomes the starting point. An improvisation, Bach's work develops a theme of musical inventions as Hofstadter develops his own improvisatory themes. His work is thus a "Metamusical Offering," amplified by mathematics (Kurt Gödel's "Incompleteness" Theorem that some axiomatic systems are based on true but unprovable mathematical assumptions) and graphic art (the Dutch artist M. C. Escher's intricate, symmetrical drawings of infinitely interlocking patterns). All three—musician, mathematician, artist—work in patterns of paradox, in self-references that invariably revert back to themselves—what Hofstadter calls Strange Loops. An example cited by Gödel is the paradox of Epimenides, the Cretan, who said "All Cretans are liars"—a self-referential statement which translates: "This statement is false."

Working on the analogy of Bach's two- and three-part inventions, Hofstadter writes dialogues (the Tortoise, Achilles, and Zeno who invented them to illustrate his theory of motion) that present metaphorically concepts he then develops in each chapter. Sprinkled through the text are puzzles, graphs, illustrations (some by Hofstadter himself), mathematical formulae, and at one point—in a chapter on the structure of the brain—Carroll's "Jabberwocky" printed with French and German translations. All this leads to the central question of Artificial Intelligence and, as Hofstadter writes at the end of his book, proves to be "one big self-referential loop."

Reviewers of *Gödel, Escher, Bach* in the more general periodicals were intrigued. Edward Rothstein, in the *New York Review of Books,* described it as "exhilarating, challenging, valuable and frustrating. Hofstadter writes directly and playfully for the lay reader, explaining the most abstract and wide-ranging arguments in short sections of great virtuosity. He is sophisticated in his understanding of the systems he explores and is adventurously speculative about their limits. But the book resists simple evaluation; it is at once surprisingly subtle and annoyingly naive, exuberantly clever and embarrassingly silly." Brian Hayes, in the *New York Times Book Review*, wrote that while the mathematical aspects of the book are not rigorous, "the reader is not asked to accept results on authority or on faith." The book is readable, according to Hayes, because "the author is always ready to take the reader's hand and lead him through the thickets." Some of the more specialized journals had qualifications about the book. Russell Hardin, for example, in *Ethics,* found Hofstadter "remarkably informative in that he discusses with clarity a rich array of others' works," but objected to the writing: "It is written in the style of the new journalism (with greater emphasis on the journalist's telling than on what is told) . . . variously intelligent, learned, clever, silly and pretentious and not so variously self-indulgent."

The Mind's I: Fantasies and Reflections on Self and Soul grew out of meetings between Hofstadter and Daniel Dennett at the Center for Advanced Study in Palo Alto, California. Designed, as the Preface states, "to provoke, disturb and befuddle its readers, to make the obvious strange and perhaps to make the strange obvious," the book collects essays, science fiction and fantasies by writers ranging from Jorge Luis Borges and Stanislaw Lem to Alan Turing, Raymond Smullyan, and Robert Nozick. Reviewers found the selections interesting but reserved their highest praise for the stimulating reflections and dialogues of Hofstadter and Dennett which follow each piece. The best thing in the book, according to Peter Wilsher in the *New Statesman,* is Hofstadter's "Conversation with Einstein's Brain," another dialogue between Achilles and the Tortoise that takes place in the Luxembourg Gardens in Paris. Here he confronts questions of intelligence, human and artificial, in the playful but thought-provoking style "that made *Gödel, Escher, Bach* a runaway bestseller."

The collection of Hofstadter's columns for *Scientific American* honors his predecessor Martin Gardner in its title *Metamagical Themas,* an anagram of Gardner's column "Mathematical Games." Its subtitle "Questing for the Essence of Mind and Pattern" once again defines Hofstadter's goal. The columns themselves, and his added commentary, cover a broad spectrum—self-referential constructions, sexist and racist language, artificial intelligence, Rubik's Cube, Chopin, the nuclear arms race. What Murray MacBeath, in the *Times Literary Supplement,* found "most strikingly new" in the book is its "vigorous engagement with moral issues." Hofstadter's central concern on the subject of artificial intelligence is his conviction that "genuine" artificial intelligence cannot be achieved without recognizing the "subcognitive structures" of the human mind: "it is time for some of the irrational and subcognitive to be recognized in its pivotal role."

Hofstadter's thesis that contemporary computer research has put too much emphasis on the rational and given too little attention to the "much deeper processes of myriads of interacting subcognitive structures" is highly controversial in the scientific community, many of whose members regard him as a philosopher or theoretician rather than a scientist. In an article on Hofstadter in the *New York Times Magazine* in 1983, the year in which he lectured at Oxford on the subject of free will, James Gleik wrote that he is "trying to program a computer to think in the way human beings do. In doing so, he is provoking philosophical speculation about the nature of the 'soul.'" Logic and rational thinking, Hofstadter has argued, do not explain those instantaneous activities of mind whereby, for example, he unscrambles letters in a game of Jumbles and "instantly, the whole word is built in my mind like that." There remain mysteries in human cognition to which the current trend in artificial intelligence research is not directed, and as a result questions of "the real meaning of consciousness" are evaded. "There seems to be no alternative to accepting some sort of incomprehensible quality to existence," Hofstadter told Gleik. "Take your pick."

PRINCIPAL WORKS: Gödel, Escher, Bach: an Eternal Golden Braid, 1979; (with D. C. Dennett) The Mind's I, 1981; Metamagical Themas, 1985.

ABOUT: Contemporary Authors 105, 1982; Who's Who in America 1988–1989. *Periodicals*—Ethics January 1980; Indiana Writes 4, Summer 1980; New Republic July 21, 1979; February 24, 1982; New Statesman November 18, 1981; New York Review of Books December 6, 1979; New York Times Book Review April 29, 1979; April 29, 1985; New York Times Magazine August 21, 1983; Scientific American July 19, 1979; Times Literary Supplement April 18, 1986; Yale Review Winter 1980.

HOLMES, JOHN; HOLMES, RAYMOND. See SOUSTER, RAYMOND

HOOD, HUGH (JOHN BLAGDON) (April 30, 1928–), Canadian novelist, short-story writer, and essayist, writes: "My father's family divided neatly into Dorset seafaring people on his father's side and Highland Scots, MacDonalds to a man, on his mother's side. I prize this line of descent very much. The Hoods of Dorset were to be found in the country south of the Somerset border all the way to the Channel coast; there are hundreds of them in the graveyards of Mosterton, Beaminster, and Nether-

HUGH HOOD

bury. Many served in the Royal Navy and those who didn't were often connected with the marine rigging industry, cordage, nets, sailcloth, of Bridport. My great-great-great-great-grandfather John Hood ran a sailcloth manufacturing business in Bridport in the 1790s, where he died in 1803. His grandson John Alexander Hood came to Nova Scotia in the 1830s, dying in Weymouth, Nova Scotia in 1892. His son, my great-grandfather Arthur Hood, married into a prosperous boatbuilding concern in Shelburne, Nova Scotia where my father was born in 1900. This aspect of family history supplies some of the background of my first novel, *White Figure, White Ground*.

"My father's mother, Katherine MacDonald, could speak some Scotch Gaelic, and *her* mother was almost monolingually a Gaelic speaker. These MacDonalds, from whom I get my first name, Hugh, were settled in Antigonish, Nova Scotia, where they preserved many of the qualities of the dreaming Celts of the Outer Isles.

"Strangely enough, my mother's father took his descent from very near Dorset and the paternal Hoods. He was a Blagdon. His father had been a sea-captain coming from the district of the Bristol Channel, where there is a town called Blagdon not far from the seacoast. My grandfather Alfred Blagdon grew up speaking French in Lévis, Québec, and eventually found his way to Montana where he was teaching school in the early 1890s. He eventually returned to Toronto where he married Eugénie Sauriol, of the Cornwall, Ontario family. My grandmother Eugénie was one of eleven or twelve children, a family

of modest size according to Québec standards in those days. Many of these Sauriol relations were living in Toronto as part of a tightly-knit French-speaking community when I was growing up there in the 1930s, a period evoked in the opening volume of my serial novel 'The New Age/Le nouveau siècle.' That opening novel, *The Swing in the Garden*, is a kind of repository of popular Canadian history of the thirties and includes much that a student of Canadian literature will want to have experienced.

"I attended a Catholic high-school in Toronto and then took my three academic degrees at the University of Toronto, B.A., 1950, M.A., 1952, Ph.D., 1955. I have never regretted the rich academic background I acquired as a preparation for the doctorate, and I have been a university teacher for thirty-five years. I decided while I was a graduate student that I would acquire the professional teaching qualification, the Ph.D., and then begin to write novels, short stories, and essays rather than literary history or literary criticism. This formula has worked out almost perfectly. I was hired as a junior professor in the summer of the year I received my Ph.D. at Saint Joseph College, West Hartford, Connecticut, where I taught English literature 1955–1961. I was joined by my bride, Noreen Mallory, a remarkable painter and lithographer, in 1957. Our first two children were born in Hartford, and they have retained dual citizenship as Canadian and U.S. citizens. I began to publish fiction at this time. My first published short story appeared in the Toronto literary quarterly *The Tamarack Review*, No. 9, 1958. Much of my earlier work appeared first in this distinguished magazine which dedicated a special issue to my work, Summer, 1975. Then in 1960 I sold a story to *Esquire*. I was invited to come and see the editorial staff when next in New York. I went down from Hartford to talk to the fiction editor, who offered me the job of Assistant Fiction Editor on a one-year temporary-replacement basis. I'd probably still be there if I'd accepted the job, but the same week I was invited to move to the Université de Montréal, as part of a program in hiring new young staff to revitalize the university's faculty of arts.

"My wife and I both wanted to live in Canada, so we accepted this move very readily, arriving in Montreal in May 1961. We have remained here, living very happily, ever since. Our third and fourth children were born in Montreal in 1963 and 1965. I have continued to act as a teacher of literature until the present.

"As soon as I moved to Canada I found my work much in demand, and although I was thirty-four years old when my first book appeared, the collection of stories *Flying a Red Kite*, I have never felt that I got a late start on my work. The stories in *Flying a Red Kite* have been anthologized all over the world, and the book has often been called the first modern collection of stories in Canadian literature. Our literature began a process of extraordinary development and expansion at this time. I think of writers like Mordecai Richler, Mavis Gallant, Robertson Davies, Alice Munro, Margaret Atwood, as those colleagues of mine who have helped to create contemporary Canadian literature as the very large structure it has become. My own contribution has consisted of seven collections of short stories, eleven novels, and a number of books of nonfiction, as well as numbers of uncollected stories and essays.

"About 1967, at the time of the Canadian Centennial, I started to think about a long *roman-fleuve* which would form a large image of Canadian life from the time of the end of the first World War to the end of the twentieth century. I worked my way towards a first volume from 1967 to 1975, when *The Swing in the Garden* appeared. In the fall of 1986 I reached the halfway point in this undertaking with publication of the sixth volume, *The Motor Boys in Ottawa*. Other books in 'The New Age/Le nouveau siècle' have included *A New Athens, Reservoir Ravine, Black and White Keys*, and *The Scenic Art*. A seventh volume (of twelve) is now complete and will appear in the fall of 1988 as *Tony's Book*.

"I should mention that my work throughout has been inspired and illuminated by Catholic Christianity."

"Perhaps more than any other writer now publishing in Canada," Kent Thompson has observed, Hugh Hood "is aware of the implications of the recurring problem of a 'Canadian identity,' yet his concern is seldom obvious and, inevitably, it seems, it is tied to both large and more particular human problems." Certainly Hood's pervasive Canadian-ness—his grasp of his country's historical past and its culturally divided present—have established him as one of the most respected writers in Canada today. It has also, however, isolated him from the larger English reading public in the United States and in Britain, where his work is little known. Yet, as Thompson points out, Hood is not a provincial writer. Though most of his work is set within the geographical borders of Canada, its concerns transcend nationality. Indeed, having undertaken in his ambitious "New Age" series a project of the dimensions of Proust's

Remembrance of Things Past or Anthony Powell's *A Dance to the Music of Time*, he has set himself the goal of writing a kind of twentieth-century "human comedy."

Hood's first published works were short stories produced out of no theory or school of fiction but "instinctively, making all the important artistic decisions as I went along, with no theoretical bias. . . . Instinctively, then, I turned out to be a moral realist." He recalls this in an essay, "The Ontology of Super-Realism," in which he traces his development as a writer from this kind of spontaneous natural expression through his discovery "that prose fiction might have an abstract element, a purely formal element, even though it continued to be strictly, morally realistic." That abstract element is Hood's religious faith. In another essay, "The Absolute Infant," written as a Christmas piece, he affirms: "I'm a writer not a metaphysician or a priest, but I can try to share their sense of the mysterious richness of all things—conscious human beings, sticks and stones, all things. All are rich, full of splendour, the radiance of their formal perfection given to them by the fact of the incarnation. Everything is full of God."

"Super-realism," the word Hood has chosen to characterize his fiction, involves minute observation of everyday reality, a documentary-journalistic base from which Hood attempts to explore the essence of reality. From his early short stories onward he has explored such profound themes as human redemption in the everyday lives of ordinary people. In the title story of *Flying a Red Kite*, for example, a father, frustrated by all the petty pressures of modern life, finds spiritual exaltation suddenly when he finally gets his little daughter's kite to fly. In "The Fruit Man, the Meat Man, and the Manager" three Jewish partners in a foodshop, who are being forced out of business by the expanding nearby university, are revealed as a kind of Holy Trinity enduring in a materialistic world. Similarly, in his first published novel *White Figure, White Ground*, the central character, a painter in mid-life exploring his past and his memories of his father, experiences rebirth when he discovers that he and his wife are going to have a child. "This rising young Canadian writer has here tackled a notoriously difficult subject and brought it off," Ernest Buckler wrote of the book in the *New York Times Book Review*. "Not with any frothing of the eyeballs over the agony and the ecstasy of it all . . . but with the simple leverage of insight the author casts fresh and searching light not only on the creative process itself but on the father son relationship, the dynamics of marriage, the barrens of unfulfillment and the black malignant loam of roots and growth.

Hood's second novel, *The Camera Always Lies*, is one of his few books set outside of Canada. Purportedly offering an "inside view" of American filmmaking, it is the story of an aging Hollywood star whose career is rapidly going downhill. The critical reception was unfavorable, reviewers finding it "a weak imitation of F. Scott Fitzgerald" and "mechanically contrived." Far more successful was *You Cant Get There from Here*, set in an imaginary African state, Leofrica, that is attempting to emerge as an independent Third World country. Described as "a demonic satire" on power struggles and political corruption, it was compared with John Updike's *The Coup*. Leofrica, Keith Garebian writes, is "a fictional paradigm of universal colonialism . . . not so much about Africa as it is about fallen man." The characters may well be simply "mouthpieces of ideas," but, a reviewer in the *Times Literary Supplement* noted, "the storyline is strong . . . the novel is both exciting and intelligent."

Canadian politics was the subject of *A Game of Touch*, the title alluding to touch football, a sport in which Hood is much interested, but the novel itself grapples with fundamental concerns of contemporary Canadian life. Its protagonist is an idealist and a man of conscience, a professor of economics, who becomes involved in government bureaucracy. (It was suggested by several reviewers that he was modelled on the former Canadian prime minister Pierre Trudeau.) Hood's insights into Canadian politics and his realistic picture of contemporary Montreal life were, Garebian writes, "thoroughly credible"; and the novel's strength was its "searching investigations into the problems of finding a place in a troubled society . . . richly funny at times, rigorously intellectual at others." Robert Fulford, in *Saturday Night*, felt that here at last "the quintessential Canadian hero comes to life . . . fighting his way to mythic stature not through Greek islands or western plains but through the thickets of federal-provincial relations."

Its bilingual title "The New Age/ Le nouveau siècle," Hood's ambitiously conceived cycle of novels, suggests the unifying grasp of Canadian culture that marks his work. His scene is the real country, but symbolically it is the realm of the human spirit. The biblical echoes of the title of the first novel in the series, *The Swing in the Garden*, and the name of its protagonist, Matt Goderich, are not accidental. This novel deals with the edenic boyhood of Goderich, but it is also the story of his father and his forefathers, moving backward and forward in time. An art historian by profession, Goderich is both actor in and observer of his country's real history; this is meant to be his—and mankind's—moral and spiritual history. The second novel in the series, *A New Athens*, takes him through the 1950s and 1960s, his student years at the University of Toronto, and his first experiences of love and marriage. Hallvard Dahlie, in *Essays in Canadian Writing*, found it more successful than *The Swing in the Garden*, "which suffered, I thought, from too much overt moralizing . . . Hood wins us over more by rational persuasion than by catering to our emotions, but our patience is rewarded by a new respect we gain for his disciplined aesthetic." The scene shifts back to the Canada of the 1920s and 1930s in *Reservoir Ravine*, then forward to World War II in *Black and White Keys* where the adolescent Goderich begins to emerge into maturity, and again ahead in *The Scenic Art* to the cultural flowering of the Canadian theater with the founding of the national theater in Stratford, Ontario. Ultimately the "New Age" will cover the entire century. On the basis of what it and Hood's other writings have achieved so far, Robert Lecker writes in the *Dictionary of Literary Biography*: "Hood's short stories and his New Age novels—in their exuberance, technical virtuosity, and profound metaphorical richness—constitute a literary achievement approached by few writers in this century."

PRINCIPAL WORKS: *Novels*—White Figure, White Ground, 1964; The Camera Always Lies, 1967; A Game of Touch, 1970; You Cant Get There from Here, 1972. *In "New Age" series*—The Swing in the Garden, 1975; A New Athens, 1977; Reservoir Ravine, 1979; Black and White Keys, 1982; The Scenic Art, 1982; The Motor Boys in Ottawa, 1986; Tony's Book, 1988. *Short stories*—Flying a Red Kite, 1962; Around the Mountain: Scenes from Montreal Life, 1967; The Fruit Man, the Meat Man and the Manager, 1971; Dark Glasses, 1976; Selected Stories, 1978; None Genuine without this Signature, 1980; August Nights, 1985; Five New Facts about Giorgione, 1987. *Non-fiction*—Strength Down Centre: the Jean Béliveau Story, 1970; The Governor's Bridge Is Closed, 1973; Scoring: Seymour Segal's Art of Hockey, 1979; Trusting the Tale, 1983.

ABOUT: Contemporary Authors New Revision Series 1, 1981; Contemporary Literary Criticism 15, 1980; 28, 1984; Contemporary Novelists, 4th ed., 1986; Dictionary of Literary Biography 53, 1986; Garebian, K. Hugh Hood, 1983; Klinck, C. F. (ed.) Literary History of Canada, 2nd ed., 1976; Morley, P. The Comedians: Hugh Hood and Rudy Wiebe, 1977; Struthers, J. F. (ed.) Before the Flood, 1979. *Periodicals*—Canadian Literature Winter, 1971; Essays in Canadian Writing Summer 1978, Winter–Spring 1978–1979; Journal of Canadian Fiction Winter 1974; New York Times Book Review August 16, 1964; Saturday Night November 1970; Studies in Canadian Literature Summer 1977; Times Literary Supplement March 30, 1973.

HOOD, STUART (1915–   ), Scottish novelist, translator, and writer on television, writes: "I was born and grew up in Edzell, in the northeast of Scotland, the son of a village schoolmaster, who in an old Scottish tradition was also a scholar of literature and history. After secondary school I took a degree in English literature at Edinburgh University, graduating a year before the outbreak of the Second World War. My student years were dominated by the Civil War in Spain and radical politics. After teaching briefly in a high school I volunteered for the army because it seemed to me that Fascism must be fought. My army career took me to Eritrea and Abyssinia and over most of the Middle East as driver in an armoured division, platoon commander in an infantry battalion and staff officer until capture in 1942 during Rommel's last offensive in the desert of western Egypt. There followed a year of captivity in Italy from which I was released by the Armistice of September 1943 to find myself in German occupied territory. I came through the lines a year later having lived with the peasants and partisans of the Northern Appenines and Tuscany. The experiences of that year during which I experienced much human solidarity as well as the dangers and exertions of life in a resistance movement, were crucial to my formation.

"I finished the war in Northwestern Europe as a liaison officer with the American Ninth Army at the Rhine crossing. A year in the British Zone of Germany was taken up with political intelligence work. During this period I began to translate *On the Marble Cliffs* by Ernst Jünger, with whom I was able to discuss his work. His novel is a very precise description—in allegorical form—of Fascism and of tyrannies in general.

"Demobilized, I found a job with the BBC as a sub-editor in its foreign language services. These were years in which I had to come to terms with my wartime experiences and my political radicalism. My first published fiction was from this time. *The Circle of the Minotaur* was an attempt to deal in fictional form with my experiences in Italy, the circle of the minotaur being the one to which Dante consigns the violent against others.

"Rising through the hierarchies I eventually became head of the BBC's television news service and then head of television programs. I became impatient with the BBC and its relationship to the establishment and resigned in 1964 and became—after a brief and catastrophic experience in commercial television—a free lance journalist, writer, scriptwriter and producer working mainly in the field of documentary and drama. I had meantime been able to come

STUART HOOD

to terms with my Italian experiences which I set out in *Pebbles from My Skull* (published 1963), an exercise in memory and an examination of memory's pitfalls. A novel followed, *In and Out the Windows* ; it deals with the impossibility—in emotional terms—of possessing another human being. I had meantime begun to work as a translator from French, German, Italian, and Russian. This work has over the years included Theodore Plivier's *Moscow, The Diaries of Ciano* (Mussolini's son-in-law and foreign minister), *The Mill on the Po* by Riccardo Bacchelli, *The Holiday* by Dacia Maraini, *Seminar on Youth* by Aldo Busi, *Lutheran Letters* by Pasolini, a volume of poems by the Austrian poet, Erich Fried, and work by [Yulï] Daniel, the Soviet dissident.

"After some ten years as a free lance I was appointed Professor of Film and Television at the Royal College of Art, London, where I was plunged by my students into the debates over French film theory and the polemics of the avant-garde: a fruitful and stimulating period. I resigned after four years and returned to freelance writing and lecturing in the field of media studies to which I have contributed three books and numerous articles and have played a prominent part in the continuing public debate on the use and social function of the broadcasting media. I am a Fellow at the University of Sussex where I give seminars on the politics of broadcasting in the Department of Education.

In 1985 I published *A Storm from Paradise* (the reference is to a quotation from Walter Benjamin), a novel which has won literary awards from the Scottish Arts Council and the Scottish Saltire Society—the first time that the award has gone to a work of fiction. Set in the Scottish countryside before 1914 it is a (partially) deconstructed work in which the Scottish Protestant tradition is represented by the main male figure—a country teacher—and the wider European radical culture is embodied in a Russian woman exile with whom he falls in love. Another novel *The Upper Hand* appeared in July 1987; it deals with the questions of loyalty, secrecy and surveillance in British society.

"Meantime, having appeared with Dario Fo during his London appearances as his on-stage interpreter, I am supervising an edition of his works in English."

Stuart Hood's experiences in World War II, the subject of his autobiographical *Carlino* (originally published as *Pebbles in My Skull*) shaped his identity as a novelist. An escaped war prisoner and fugitive from the Nazis, hiding in the remote rural areas of Northern Italy, he lived and worked under the name Carlino with peasants who risked their own lives to shelter him. Many years later, in 1981, revisiting the village where he had found refuge in early 1944, he discovered, as he writes in an Afterword to *Carlino*, "that in a world of cruelty and oppression, there are still people who have generous impulses, courage, and understanding. It is something that gives me, even in these dark and terribles times, when in so much of the world cruel and powerful forces have the ascendency, a certain hope."

A recurring theme in Hood's fiction is memory, the arbitrary yet profoundly significant qualities of our perception of the past. *Pebbles from My Skull*, the original title of his war memoir, is a metaphor for just such memory: "Some things we choose to forget," he writes in his opening chapter. "Some which we cannot forget, we make bearable. Life washes through us like a tide. In its ebb and flow the fragments of the past are ground smooth so that, with time, we can handle them like stones from a rock pool, admiring their colour, shape and texture. We do not know which of them will stir and rattle as the tide ebbs from us for the last time. There are pebbles from my skull."

Although the war does not figure directly in the novels that Hood has published, the concept of escape from the prison of our individual selves and the recognition of the community and communality of humanity, our mutual dependency on and responsibility for our fellow human beings, underlie his work. His first novel, *The Circle of the Minotaur*, is a story of an Italian who revisits the village where as a boy he had passed himself off as an assassin of an unpopular landlord. Hailed as a hero, he nevertheless finds himself caught in a tangled web of responsibility and vengeance. The simple memory of the past has complex and, in this case, fatal ramifications. In his later novels Hood has set his scene closer to home. *In and Out the Windows* draws heavily upon his experience as a television writer and producer. A free-flowing interior monologue by a Scottish TV film maker, the novel gives an impressively detailed and authentic picture of back-of-the-camera activities, but its real subject is the protagonist's exploration of his past in a series of visits to a psychoanalyst. A hopelessly confused sex life, an unhappy marriage, memories of his father's suicide, are only parts of his problem. He also confronts the pressures and politics of the television industry. Rambling as the novel appears to be, it is carefully constructed and impressed reviewers with its inside view not only of television but of modern life. "Stuart Hood manages well this claustrophobic Scottish breeding-ground, with its whiff of original sin," Anthony Thwaite wrote in the *Observer*. John Mellers, in the *Listener*, commented: "The author's skill in using the verbal equivalents of TV documentary television gives the book pace and power and removes entirely any taint of case-history. *In and Out the Windows* is as fascinating as Stuart Hood's best programmes—not least for its insight into pressures and politics inside a television company."

The award-winning *A Storm from Paradise* is perhaps the most personal of Hood's novels to date, its central character modeled on his own father, a Scottish schoolmaster. Told from the point of view of the son, the narrative is a memory piece, weaving fact and imagination as the narrator reconstructs his and his father's past. Going back to years before his own birth, he traces his father's life from his arrival in a Scottish village to teach school, his conflicts with a hidebound conservative schoolboard, his romance with a beautiful Russian emigrée who introduces him not only to sex but to the challenging world of ideas outside his narrow provincial background, and his ultimate compromise in a safe, conventional local woman who will become the narrator's mother. The title of the novel, taken from the philosopher Walter Benjamin's *Theses on the Philosophy of History*, hints at its theme—the "angle of history" flies backward against the "storm from Paradise" (progress) which propels him toward the future. His father's lack of courage to make a break and his ultimate yielding to Scottish puritanism is instructive for the son, who realizes that he cannot relive the past but must seek his "paradise" in the outside world. John Sutherland wrote in the *London Review of Books*: "*A Storm from Paradise* has little to offer in the way of pace or plot. What Hood offers is a series of densely remembered or imaginatively reconstructed scenes from early childhood, strung on a theoretical meditation about the nature of the past and our relationship to it." John Clute, in the *New Statesman*, called it a "fine dour, wise, cynical novel," and Margaret Walters, in the *Observer*, described it as "a quiet novel with . . . unexpected depths of feeling." In its realistic picture of Scottish rural and provincial life, *A Storm from Paradise* invited comparison with other Scottish regional works by James M. Barrie, Douglas Brown, Lewis Grassic Gibbon, and Alisdair Gray. An article in the *Glasgow Herald* observed: "Hood takes the dilemma of the educated, modern Scot and introduces a spellbinding set of tensions—conformity and individuality, parochial mores and external influences, ambition and retraction—and weaves a story which locks the reader in its embrace until its magical conclusion. It is an historical novel about the present, by an author whose compassion is equal to his intellect."

The first of Hood's books to be published in the United States was *Carlino*. Hood added an Afterword in which he explained that with the distancing of time he felt more free to speak of the Italian Resistance movement and of Italian Communism. In the intervening years, he writes, he came to understand the "hagiography of the Left"—the stories of men and women who had sacrificed their lives in the anti-Fascist and anti-Nazi resistance and "had become the object of ritual admiration" in the present-day Italian Communist party. From this perspective he could appreciate the "vast demonstration of political and human solidarity" that was the peasants' resistance. Charles F. Delzell, in the *New York Times Book Review*, called *Carlino* "a contribution to cultural anthropology through its vivid description of the social structure and mores of peasant life in Emilia and Tuscany," and *Publishers Weekly* praised "its shimmering prose and hard-won insights." Brian Morton, the *Times Literary Supplement*, found it "an ideal companion piece to *A Storm from Paradise*, which is simply the strongest and most achieved fictional work to come out of Scotland in years."

PRINCIPAL WORKS: *Novels*—Circle of the Minotaur, 1950; Since the Fall, 1953; In and Out the Windows, 1970; A Storm from Paradise, 1985; The Upper Hand, 1987; The Brutal Heart, 1989. *Autobiography* Pebbles from My Skull, 1963, reprinted 1985 as Carlino. *Non-fiction*—A Survey of Television, 1967; The Mass Media (Studies in Contemporary Europe), 1970; On Television, 1980; (with Garret O'Leary) Questions of Broadcasting, 1990.

ABOUT: Hood, S. Carlino, 1985. *Periodicals*—Glasgow Herald November 22, 1986; Listener August 1, 1974; February 13, 1986; London Review of Books November 7, 1985; New Statesman October 11, 1985; New York Times Book Review September 24, 1950; April 28, 1975; Observer June 23, 1974; October 20, 1985; Publishers Weekly February 15, 1985; September 20, 1985; Times Literary Supplement July 19, 1974; December 13, 1985; August 14, 1987; November 3, 1989; February 9, 1990.

HOPE, CHRISTOPHER (DAVID TULLY)

(February 26, 1944–   ), South African poet, short-story writer, and novelist, now living in London, writes: "I am the grandson of an Irish republican who left his hometown of Waterford at the turn of the century and sailed for South Africa where, like many Irish nationalists, he felt great sympathy for the Boers in their war of independence against the British who had colonized the southern sub-continent. I suppose I must have inherited from him his sympathy for the Boers in their fight for freedom against their Imperial masters, as well as his dismay at the angry tribalism into which the Afrikaners retreated once independence had been achieved.

"I have tried in my writing to explore a society unhinged by its strange religion—its obsessional pre-occupation with colour. South African politics for as long as anyone can remember has been enthralled by the single issue of race. I learnt early that everything came down to this question. It was the interrogator in all of life's departments. The mystical worship of skin-tones decreed which door you went in by, which grave you lay in and it even insisted that the dying be collected in separate ambulances. Its shadow fell across every human activity from love to golf. In general, members of the white community were expected to support the policy while members of the large black majority were expected to appreciate it; and everyone was commanded to obey it. When it is remembered that the obsession with separating people according to colour was relentlessly applied in the name of 'freedom' then I think something of the grimly hilarious nature of the South African condition begins to emerge. I grew up, as did many of my compatriots, being reminded by the tireless ideologues of apartheid that ethnic separation was not really unfair because it preserved the freedom of various racial groups to develop without fear of domination by other, larger groups. The custom of locking people up behind walls of racial legislation and presenting this as an adornment of liberty is one of the common, bizarre features of South African life.

"Naturally such conditions call for their chroniclers. The difficulty for the writer lies in the inventiveness of the country itself which has always been stranger than fiction. South Africa writes its own book, and it outwrites the most resourceful authors. However, all is not lost for the writer. There are things to be noticed and noted down. For example there is the realization that apartheid is a weapon which cuts both ways. The outrageous crudity of measures aimed at black South Africans has blinded some to the effects of these policies upon those in charge. The point about apartheid is not only that it demeans its victims, but that it also makes such fools of the white men who run it. I am fascinated by the terminal comedy of South African life and its strange ability to wound and amuse all at once.

"In the mid-seventies I decided that if I was to say anything about the certifiable folly of South African life then I needed to put some distance between myself and the hospital walls. I moved abroad, and when my first novel was published in South Africa it was promptly suppressed by the censors. Since my poems had, on occasion, fallen foul of the official government media—of the state broadcasting service in particular—I was to some extent prepared for the banning of A Separate Development. The ruling caste was perhaps resigned to being castigated, but it resented being ridiculed.

"Though I may live at a distance I do not delude myself that I have escaped the gravitational pull of Southern Africa. Indeed I am very conscious of the fact that I would be nothing without it. Though in exile, decamped, absent without leave—call it what you will, I remain a South African and I am implicated in the lethal folly of that place, as I am sure my work continues to show. After over a decade abroad I remain, in the words of the Viennese satirist Karl Kraus, 'a loyal hater'."

Born in Johannesburg and raised in Pretoria, the son of Dudley Mitford and Kathleen (McKenna) Hope, Christopher Hope grew up in a South Africa in which he was a member of a minority (Irish-Catholic) within a minority (English-speaking white). He was educated at the Christian Brothers College in Pretoria, at the University of the Witwatersrand in Johannesburg (B.A. 1965, M.A. 1970) and the University of Natal in Durban (B.A. with honors, 1969). Hope served for a year, 1962, in the South African navy and worked as an insurance underwriter, a copywriter, an editor, and an English teacher in Capetown, Durban, and Johannesburg from 1966 to 1973. He married Eleanor Klein in 1967; they have two sons. In 1974 he left South Africa as a voluntary exile and settled in London where he became a full-time writer and where he still lives. In 1978 he was writer-in-residence at the Gordonstoun School in Elgin, Scotland. He has received honors for his writings both in England and in South Africa—the English Academy of Southern Africa Award (1974), the Cholmondeley Award for Poetry (1978), the David Higham Prize (1981), the Petric Arts Award sponsored by the University of Natal (1981), the Silver Pen Award (1982), and the Whitbread Award for fiction (1985).

The "grimly hilarious" nature of apartheid, its bizarre mixture of racism, complacency and outrage, characterizes Hope's fiction, poetry, and journalism. In 1987 he revisited his native land and reported his experiences in White Boy Running. What he observed—from interviews with farmers, politicians, laborers, black, colored, and white, across the political spectrum—was a country "so absurd, so incredible, so terrifyingly funny," that he was left painfully aware of the impossibility of his ever being a part of it again. "Few South African writers have been able to capture the dark humour generated by this confusion better than Hope," Stephen Watson wrote of White Boy Running in the Times Literary Supplement, "and his constant awareness of the ways in which the ludicrous and the horrific go hand in hand makes for a unique vision of the country."

Hope described his first novel, A Separate Development, as "a kind of joke-book, because if apartheid is cruel, it is also ridiculous." The title is "the official euphemism" for apartheid, seen in this novel through the eyes of a young boy, Harry Moto, born into a white family but carrying the genes of a distant black ancestor which reveal themselves in his tan complexion and slightly frizzy hair. Harry tells his story from a prison cell in a probably futile effort to explain the series of grotesque yet often grimly funny adventures that follow on his failure to pass as white. A kind of worldly innocent, Harry runs away from home to live as a "coloured." His struggles to survive in a hostile society are recounted with what P. L. Adams described in the Atlantic as "a mixture of savage mockery and lunatic farce. The combination is daring and brought off with total success."

A similar mixture of laughter and outrage marked readers' reactions to Hope's next novel, Kruger's Alp. This is a far more ambitious undertaking, its framework a dream vision frankly indebted to The Pilgrim's Progress. Like Bunyan's pilgrim Christian who sets out on a journey from the corrupt and doomed worldly city in which he lives to the Celestial City encountering but (with heavenly grace) prevailing over formidable obstacles along the way, Hope's pilgrim, a lapsed Catholic priest, leaves South Africa on a quest not for the City of God but for the celestial mountain in the Swiss Alps where, according to legend, the exiled Boer leader Paul Kruger found refuge and built a city of gold. In Hope's narrative the dream is largely nightmare, taking his priest from South Africa to London's sleazy Soho to Geneva in a series of wild adventures that involve spies, counterspies, much sexual activity, and murder. For all its fantasy, however, *Kruger's Alp* is a timely and telling version of the reality of South Africa today. As he nears the end of his quest, the priest is told by his guides: "What you see here is the death of a nation. Civilisations have died of old age, of decadence, of boredom, of neglect, but what you are seeing, for the first time, is a nation going to the wall for its belief in the sanctity of separate lavatories." Like *A Separate Development*, the book maintains its balance of bawdy sex and ironic comedy with the most serious political and moral issues of our age, and it received critical acclaim in both Britain and the United States. "He is an intelligent and gifted writer," Ron Loewinsohn wrote in the *New York Times Book Review*, "with an eye for realistic detail and an incisive but fluent style that together give substance to his allegory and complement his mordant wit."

There is a nightmare quality, though this time framed in a more realistic scene, in *The Hottentot Room*. Assembled in the shabby Earls Court district of London are a group of South African exiles who gather regularly to share their loneliness in a pub called the Hottentot Room, its name commemorating a Hottentot boy who had been kidnapped and brought to London in 1665: "These clubs eased the shock which accompanied the discovery that although English might have been the home language of these visitors, England was not the home country," Hope writes. Its central character, a journalist blackmailed by South African authorities into spying on the activities of fellow refugees, moves among a motley group of fanatics, idealists, Marxists, liberals, opportunists, all of them homesick aliens in a cold, unwelcoming England, and redeems himself in an empty but heroic gesture at the end of the book. Some reviewers found the novel's black humor forced and the characterization too broad, but Robert Brain, in the *Times Literary Supplement*, summed up the consensus: "*The Hottentot Room* is an entertaining novel, elegantly written and intricately plotted. It is also more than that, since the

entertainment seduces us into coming to grips with dirty politics and ruthless power games."

In a different mood but with the same target, Hope's novella *Black Swan* is the story of a seventeen-year-old retarded South African black youth who is introduced to the ballet "Swan Lake" by a sympathetic woman missionary teacher. Fantasy again mingles with grim humor and cruel reality when the boy tries to live the story of the ballet. "Airborne by the coherence of its imagery, this exhilarating fable is, and is about, a triumph of the imagination over an obdurate and intolerable status quo," Julia O'Faolain wrote in the *Times Literary Supplement*, while Nancy Ramsey in the *New York Times Book Review* found it "a remarkable parable of a cruel state . . . [a] moving, lyrical novel."

Hope's poetry, like his fiction, gets its richest effects from irony—sometimes comic, as in a poem on the cartoon "Peanuts" ("Round head, raisins eyes / And when baulked, a mouth / Suddenly serrated— / Charlie Brown. A loser."), sometimes tragic, as in the terrifying vision of the future in "The Flight of the White South Africans," which sees the fulfillment of a prophesy made in 1856 by an African woman, Nongquase:

> We flounder about, flying fish that fail,
> Staring with the glazed eyes of seers
> At our plane, hauled from the sky, lying like dead
> Silver on the tarmac, feeling hooks bed
> Deep within our mouths, sand heavy in our scales.
> —from *Cape Drives*

PRINCIPAL WORKS: *Fiction*—A Separate Development, 1980; Kruger's Alp, 1984; The Hottentot Room, 1986; Black Swan, 1987. *Short stories*—Private Parts and Other Tales, 1982; My Chocolate Redeemer, 1989. *Non-fiction*—White Boy Running: A Book About South Africa, 1987. *Poetry*—Cape Drives, 1974; In the Country of the Black Pig, 1981; Englishmen, 1985. *Children's books*—(with Y. Menuhin) The King, the Cat and the Fiddle, 1983; The Dragon Wore Pink, 1985.

ABOUT: Contemporary Authors New Revision Series 106, 1982; Contemporary Novelists, 4th ed., 1986; Hope, C. White Boy Running, 1987. *Periodicals*—Atlantic Monthly February 1982; Critique Winter 1986; London Magazine October 1986; New York Times December 20, 1981; June 25, 1987; New York Times Book Review May 5, 1985; November 8, 1987; July 19, 1987; Times Literary Supplement September 28, 1984; September 19, 1986; March 11, 1988.

HUGHES, DAVID (JOHN) (July 27, 1930), British novelist and nonfiction writer, was born in Alton, Hampshire, the only son of

Gwilym Fielden Hughes and Edna Frances
Hughes. He was educated at Eggar's Grammar
School, Alton, and King's College School, Wimbledon, and read English at Christ Church, Oxford University, taking his degree in 1953. He
was editor of the university literary magazine
Isis. After graduating, he worked as editorial assistant on *London Magazine* (1953–1955), as a
reader for the publisher Rupert Hart-Davis
(1956–1960), and as editor of *Town* magazine
(1960–1961) before becoming a full-time writer.

Hughes' early fictional efforts were not popular but received mostly favorable reviews. *A
Feeling in the Air* (U.S. title, *Man Off Beat*) is
about a once-successful London advertising man
who has suffered a nervous collapse after his second wife's death. He goes to stay for a time in
Wender, a remote Welsh village, where he falls
in love with his landlady, an experience which
promises him new life for the future. Caroline
Tunstall, writing in the *New York Herald Tribune Book Review*, called the first novel "firm,
witty, unsentimental"; D. R. Bensen, in *Saturday
Review*, described being "soothed by the book's
muted charm and leisurely pace. . . . within
the bounds [Hughes] has set for himself, he has
done commendably well."

After *Sealed with a Loving Kiss* in 1958, about
a misanthropic former physician who works for
a Christian quarterly magazine, and *The Horsehair Sofa* two years later, a rather lukewarm sexual farce concerning an inexperienced couple's
bumbling attempts to consummate their marriage, Hughes received international acclaim
with *The Major*, the lively and well-written story
of Major Kane, who is recalled from a satisfactory posting in Germany to a tiresome job on the
Salisbury Plain. He is a violent, ingenious man,
and the novel describes his schemes to oust the
elderly tenants to whom he has let his nearby
house as well as to evict the inhabitants of a village the army needs for military exercises. After
he rapes at gunpoint the Swedish *au pair* girl, he
has a sudden, typically violent realization of his
own futility and turns his gun on himself. The
reviewer for the *Times Literary Supplement*
commended "the vitality of [Hughes'] writing
and the confidence of his attack. . . . He has
written an odd, disturbing book." F. J. Dempsey
in *Library Journal* called it "a taut, engrossing
story, skillfully described."

Although none of Hughes' nearly dozen novels has found a wide readership, he has never
stopped inventing new and dissimilar characters
and plots and extremely diverse settings. *The
Man Who Invented Tomorrow*, a satiric comedy
on the television industry, concerns an attempt
to make a documentary film for the centenary
of H. G. Wells' birth. *Memories of Dying* is
about the persecution fantasies of an Englishman who is convinced that his old history teacher is taking over his consciousness. *A Genoese
Fancy*, set in the lower-middle-class British suburban world of the late 1940s, examines how an
orphaned adolescent comes to feel close to his
uncle, his new guardian, who in turn helps him
reorganize his life. *The Imperial German Dinner Service* is, precisely, about a man's spending
much of his life collecting a set of Wedgwood
porcelain that was commissioned for Kaiser Wilhelm.

Hughes' *The Pork Butcher* and *But for Bunter*
were both published in the United States as well
as in England. *The Pork Butcher* is the brief story of Ernst Kestner, a German soldier during
World War II now dying of cancer, who as expiation for his wasted life revisits the French village where he had met the only woman he ever
loved; nevertheless he had assisted in the ruthless
massacre of her and the other innocent inhabitants. He confesses his crimes privately to his
daughter, who accompanies him on his visit, and
publicly to the mayor of the village, whose own
family had been among Kestner's victims. Finally, after repeatedly confronting the memory of
the horror of wartime atrocities, both father and
daughter are able to find a measure of salvation:
the one is given the opportunity to absolve himself before his death, the other finds in a love affair the passion that has always been missing
from her life. *The Pork Butcher* won Hughes the
Welsh Arts Council Fiction Prize (1984) and the
W. H. Smith Literary Award (1985). *But for
Bunter* (U.S. title, *The Joke of the Century*) revolves around the claims of one Archibald Aitken to be the model and original of the character
of Billy Bunter, a favorite in British schoolboy
fiction from about 1908 to 1940. Interviewed by
the first-person narrator, Aitken, diffident at
first, eventually claims to have known most of
the great men and influenced most of the great
events of the twentieth century.

Hughes' non-fiction work includes a volume
of literary criticism on one of his favorite authors, *J. B. Priestley: An Informal Study of His
Work*, a personal account of his long admiration
for the works of this most prolific of English authors from the time Hughes first became aware
of him, during Priestley's inspiring wartime
broadcasts, to his greatly famous and highly honored old age. *The Road to Stockholm and
Lapland*, a travelogue, amusingly recounts a
summer spent touring through Belgium, Holland, northern Germany, Denmark, Sweden,
and Lapland. *The Rosewater Revolution: Notes
on a Change of Attitude* is a highly experimental
book in which Hughes attempts to demonstrate

"that everyone could make a revolution in himself—in other words, clarify to good purpose the uneasy mix of violence and impotency, conservatism and rebellion, that simmered in most of us—if only he would find some means of releasing his imagination from bondage to what we call facts and letting it run riot."

With his first wife, the Swedish actress, writer, and director Mai Zetterling, Hughes wrote several scripts for feature-length and made-for-television films and documentaries on such subjects as Sweden, Iceland, and the gypsies of southern France. *The Seven Ages of England* was a cultural history of his homeland based on the series of the same name which Hughes wrote for Swedish television.

Hughes was editor of the New Ficton Society in 1975–1978 and 1981–1982, film critic for the London *Sunday Times* (1982–1983), and fiction critic for the *Mail on Sunday* (1982–1988). With Giles Gordon he has annually edited since 1986 a volume entitled *Best Short Stories.* He has been visiting professor at the University of Iowa Writers' Workshop (1978–1979, 1987) and at the universities of Alabama (1979) and Houston (1986). In 1987 he was elected a fellow of the Royal Society of Literature.

WORKS: *Fiction*—A Feeling in the Air, 1957; Sealed with a Loving Kiss, 1958; The Horsehair Sofa, 1961; The Major, 1964; The Man Who Invented Tomorrow, 1968; Memories of Dying, 1976; A Genoese Fancy, 1979; The Imperial German Dinner Service, 1983; The Pork Butcher, 1984; But for Bunter, 1985. *Non-fiction*—J. B. Priestley, 1958; The Road to Stockholm and Lapland, 1964; The Seven Ages of England, 1967; The Rosewater Revolution, 1971; Evergreens, 1976. *As editor*—Winter's Tales, 1985; (with G. Gordon) Best Short Stories, annually from 1986.

ABOUT: Contemporary Literary Criticism 48, 1988; Dictionary of Literary Biography 14, 1983; Who's Who, 1989. *Periodicals*—Best Sellers April 15, 1965; June 1985; Booklist March 1, 1958; Bookmark March 1958; Kirkus Reviews December 1, 1957; Library Journal February 15, 1958; April 15, 1965; June 1, 1985; Manchester Guardian December 24, 1957; New York Herald Tribune Book Review February 9, 1958; New York Times Book Review February 9, 1958; March 21, 1965; May 19, 1985; New Yorker January 5, 1987; New Statesman December 24–30, 1980; Saturday Review February 8, 1958; Spectator May 5, 1984; Times Literary Supplement June 4, 1964; September 20, 1985.

HUGHES, ROBERT (STUDLEY FORREST) (July 28, 1938?–   ), Australian art critic and historian, was born in Sydney, the son of Geoffrey Eyre Hughes and the former Margaret

ROBERT HUGHES

Vidal. He attended a Jesuit school, St. Ignatius College, and from 1956 to 1961 studied architecture at Sydney University. In 1961, having left Australia for London, he began a decade of work as a free-lance writer, mainly on artistic subjects. He compiled several exhibition catalogues, including *Recent Australian Painting* (1961) and *The New Generation* (1966), both for the Whitechapel Art Gallery, London; a monograph, *Donald Friend* (1965); and a history which is even today the best of its kind, *The Art of Australia: A Critical Survey*, first published in 1966, with a revised edition in 1970. He also contributed articles on art criticism to the London Sunday newspaper the *Observer*.

A lively book undertaken by Hughes during this period, the subject of which is far removed from his usual beat of modern art, was *Heaven and Hell in Western Art*. The book is filled with striking images tracing the evolving concepts of Paradise, Heaven, Hell, and Satan as they are revealed through painting, drawing, and sculpture from early Christianity to modern times. Hughes explains his intention in his introduction: "The prospect of Heaven and Hell was, for more than fifteen hundred years, the chief religious obsession for most of the population of Europe. It remains so today, but for a dwindling number of Christians. . . . [Yet] the art of the twentieth century, despite a fitful interest in demonic and ecstatic images among the Surrealists, includes no significant paintings on eschatological themes." Hughes limits his own study to "noting certain recurrent images and themes in paintings and carvings of Heaven and Hell, showing . . . how and why they changed their *basic* features, and thus constructing an elementary outline of the iconography of Heaven and Hell in the art of the Christian west." The book received a very diverse critical reception. M. R. Newland thought it "a rare sort of book that combines an erudite discussion of its scholarly theme with superb reproductions of great art and eye-opening excursions into exotic topics ranging from medieval cosmogony and the symbolism of haloes to Renaissance monsters and Dionysian rites." But the reviewer for the *Times Literary Supplement* asked: "For whom is this book intended? In spite of occasional untranslated quotations in Italian, and references to sources of interest to iconographers, the book can scarcely be meant for scholars. There is neither bibliography nor index. . . . The quality of most of the color plates is poor, and the location of certain works of art is inaccurate. . . . What Mr. Hughes has produced is highly entertaining but disposable art journalism."

Hughes joined the staff of *Time* magazine in 1970 as a writer on art, and has since become senior art critic. He concentrates on contemporary painting and, to a lesser extent, architecture, having little to say about sculpture and even less about the many untraditional forms of modern artistic expression. Known in art circles as a fiercely opinionated nay-sayer whom almost nothing pleases, his wit is never sharper than when it is turned against any one or all of the newly anointed bright young things constantly offered up as paragons of excellence in an omnivorous art market. Typical of his style is "Careerism and Hype Amidst the Image Haze," a jeremiad he wrote in June 1985 against the then recently concluded Biennial exhibition at the Whitney Museum of American Art in New York. "What finds favor here is young, loud and, except in its careerism, invincibly dumb. It wants to be winsomely outrageous as a form of ingratiation. Its mood is claustrophobic because its sense of history (i.e., anything that happened before Warhol, except for kitsch surrealism) is nil. Because its artists draw badly and compose worse, they simply doodle until the canvas is full, making wacky parodies of 'all-over' composition. . . . Their work is all pose and no position."

The Shock of the New constitutes an expansion of an eight-part series which Hughes wrote and narrated for BBC-TV and Time-Life Television, "The Shock of the New: A Personal View." The series, according to Hughes in the book's introduction, "ate up" three years of research, writing, and filming, during which he covered 250,000 miles of travel to locations for shooting. He intended "a formal history of mod-

ern art, . . . with every artist who did anything significant given his or her just place and explication." He proceeds thematically, considering this the best means "to give a fairly wide panorama of the relations of art to ideas and to life in the modernist century." He wants to convey "what it was in the siren voices of our century that caught me as a boy—when I first read Roger Shattuck's translations of Apollinaire, hidden from the Jesuits in the wrapper of a Latin grammar—and has never let me go." The book begins, as did the series, by discussing "The Mechanical Paradise," which Hughes describes as "the blossoming of a sense of modernity in European culture—roughly from 1880 to 1914—in which the myth of the Future was born in the atmosphere of millenarian optimism that surrounded the high machine age." It ends by recounting "The Future That Was": "how art gradually lost that sense of newness and possibility, as the idea of the avant-garde petered out in the institutionalized culture of late modernism." The themes analyzed in between represent "some of the great cultural issues of the last hundred years. How has art created images of dissent, propaganda, and political coercion? How has it defined the world of pleasure, of sensuous communion with worldly delights? How has it tried to bring about Utopia? What has been its relation to the irrational and the unconscious? How has it dealt with the great inherited themes of Romanticism, the sense of the world as a theatre of despair or religious exaltation? And what changes were forced on art by the example and pressure of mass media, which displaced painting and sculpture from their old centrality as public speech?"

By the end of the book, during his treatment of contemporary artists, Hughes gets in many deft jabs, such as his attack on "the middle-brow cult of art. In our time, this cult is fed by corporate gold-and-masterpiece shows, so that the art experience is replaced by the excitement of peering at inaccessible capital." He also condemns "the small ambitions of art, . . . and its lack of any effort towards spirituality. . . . its sense of career rather than vocation, . . . its frequently bland occupation with semantics at the expense of the deeper passions of the creative self. . . . Art discovers its true social use, not on the ideological plane, but by opening the passage from feeling to meaning—not for everyone, since that would be impossible, but for those who want to try."

Critics found *The Shock of the New* provocative and informative. Margot Karp thought that "some essays are better than others: the one on art in the service of politics and revolution is particularly fine, while one on modern architecture

and its failures seems almost gleefully nasty."
John Canaday was full of high praise for
Hughes' accomplishment: "There are other critics at work today who are as erudite, or as perceptive, or as skillful with language and even a
few who are as ready to go for the jugular of a
sacred cow or pay it reverence, as the case may
justify. But I can't think of another . . . who
combines these virtues to the degree Hughes
does in writing about art since 1900. . . . The
spice in his book comes partly from critical witticisms but they are sound critical observations in
the first place. . . . This is easily the best book
to date on 20th-century art." Hughes also contributed to several other television documentaries, of which the most notable have been the
ten-part "The Art of Australia" (1975) for the
Australian Broadcasting Commission and
"Bernini: Master of the Baroque" (1978) for
BBC-TV.

By all accounts the best-researched and most
carefully written of Hughes' books, as well as the
best received, has been *The Fatal Shore: A History of the Transportation of Convicts to Australia,
1787–1868*. He recalls the book's genesis in his
introduction: in 1974, while on location filming
in Port Arthur, Tasmania, "I realized that like
nearly all other Australians I knew little about
the convict past of my own country. . . . An unstated bias rooted deep in Australian life seemed
to wish that 'real' Australian history had begun
with Australian respectability—with the flood of
money from gold and wool, the opening of the
continent, the creation an Australian middle
class. Behind the bright diorama of Australia Felix lurked the convicts, some 160,000 of them,
clanking their fetters in the penumbral darkness.
But on the feelings and experiences of these men
and women, little was written. They were statistics, absences and finally embarrassments." Australians wanted to forget this stain on their past
in what Hughes calls "amnesia—a national pact
of silence." But there was a lingering "curiosity
about these 'dark' years in which so many of its
roots lay tangled; and a vivid, trashy Grand
Guignol, long on rum, sodomy and the lash but
decidedly short on the more prosaic facts about
how most convicts actually lived and worked,
sprang up to supply its demands." What was
missing, Hughes felt, were "the voices of the
convicts themselves. . . . Accordingly I have
tried, as far as possible, to see the System from
below, through convicts' testimony—in letters,
depositions, petitions and memoirs—about their
own experiences. . . . This book is largely about
what they tell us of their suffering and survival,
their aspiration and resistance, their fear of exile
and their reconciliation to the once-unimagined
land they and their children would claim as their
own."

Coming as it did on the eve of their Bicentennial celebrations, *The Fatal Shore* touched a
highly responsive chord in Australians newly
hungry for the unadorned truth about their national origins. The book was a sensational success
there, and also enjoyed respectable sales in both
Britain and the United States. The Australian
novelist Thomas Keneally praised the book's
"grandeur of spirit." Hughes, in this critic's opinion, "tells his vast story with his accustomed elegance and all his usual gift for making
resounding historical and cultural connections.
Although the story of the convict system has recently been covered by a number of Australian
historians, this account, richly peopled with bizarre and compelling characters, is probably the
most full-blooded and monumental treatment
the subject has been given." To Peter Porter, another Australian writer, *The Fatal Shore* was
long overdue: "Robert Hughes won't let us console ourselves about the past, whatever we
choose to do about the present. He rubs our noses
in the real torment suffered by 160,000 transported felons, male and female, and never lets
us forget that, whichever way we look at Australia, it could hardly have been established without the labour of those unwilling pioneers, its
despairing first white inhabitants. Hughes's book
is a magnificent document, moving and painstakingly researched. . . . It may not be orthodox history but it is a terrifying story, one the
historians should have given us years ago." David Malouf, yet a third Australian writer, saw in
the book the working of a high historical imagination: "Writing the truth of what happened in
history is a matter of taking the records and then
listening hard between the lines for the cries of
individual agony and protest. It demands the
highest imagination. The nineteenth century in
Australia produced no literature of the convict
experience from a man or woman who had actually known it. We have no *House of the
Dead*. . . . *The Fatal Shore*, then, is a timely
book."

For Hughes, who has described himself as "a
journalist who has had the good luck never to be
bored by his subject," writing *The Fatal Shore*
was an exhilarating experience. He plans to
write more in the future on historical subjects,
for "the book," he said in a 1987 interview, "gave
me a tremendous appetite to write about the real
world, as opposed to the art world."

PRINCIPAL WORKS: The Art of Australia, 1966, 1970;
Heaven and Hell in Western Art, 1968; The Shock of
the New, 1981; The Fatal Shore, 1986; Nothing If Not
Critical: Selected Essays on Art and Artists, 1990.

ABOUT: Contemporary Authors 112, 1985. *Period-*

icals—America November 14, 1981; American Artists December 1981; American Journal of Sociology July 1982; Apollo October 1969, December 1981; Atlantic January 1987; Choice June 1981; Christian Century May 13, 1981; Christian Science Monitor February 9, 1981; January 22, 1987; Economist March 3, 1987; Encounter April 1981; Journal of Aesthetics and Art Criticism Spring 1971; Library Journal November 15, 1968; February 15, 1981; November 1, 1986; Listener November 27, 1980; New Republic March 14, 1981; February 9, 1987; New Statesman November 14, 1980; New York Review of Books March 12, 1987; New York Times January 9, 1981; January 11, 1981; February 9, 1981; November 5, 1983; New York Times Book Review December 8, 1968; February 15, 1081; January 25, 1987; New Yorker January 25, 1982; March 23, 1987; Newsweek December 21, 1981; January 26, 1987; Progressive October 1981; Quill & Quire June 1981, April 1987; Saturday Review November 30, 1968; January 1981, February 1981, March 1981; Spectator February 7, 1981; Time November 29, 1968; December 18, 1980; January 5, 1981; June 17, 1985; February 2, 1987; Times Literary Supplement January 2, 1969; January 29, 1971; January 23, 1987.

KERI HULME

*HULME, KERI (March 9, 1947–), New Zealand novelist, short story writer, and poet, was born in Christchurch, New Zealand, daughter of John W. (a carpenter and businessman) and Mere (Miller) Hulme. She was educated at North Beach primary school and Aranui High School, and attended Canterbury University, Christchurch, 1967–1968. Hulme, whose ancestry is a mixture of Maori, Orkney Island Scottish, and English, worked at a variety of jobs in her earlier years—as a postwoman, New Zealand television director, fish and chips cook, tobacco picker, woollen mill worker, and whitebait fisher. In 1978, she was writer-in-residence at Otago University, Dunedin, New Zealand. She is the author of two volumes of poetry, published in New Zealand—*The Silence Between* and *Strands*; but is chiefly known as a fiction writer.

Hulme's first novel, *The Bone People*, was published by a small feminist collective, Spiral, after having been turned down by other publishing houses in New Zealand. The book, which had a large sale in New Zealand and was highly praised by critics, won the New Zealand Book Award and the Pegasus Prize for Literature, given by the Mobil Oil Corporation "to introduce American readers to distinguished works of fiction from abroad." Most notably of all, *The Bone People* received the prestigious Booker Prize in England. In 1985, it was republished in America by the Louisiana University Press and made a strong impression. An idiosyncratic novel, *The Bone People* combines poetry, dream, and tribal lore in a narrative that is salty, odd, and lyrical.

Its plot centers on three characters on a remote stretch of New Zealand—Kerewin Holmes, a painter; Simon, a strange boy of six or seven who survives a shipwreck and is washed ashore; and Joe, a Maori factory worker who becomes Simon's foster father but beats him so badly that the child is taken from him and put in an institution. In a manner suggestive of ritual and myth, the three characters come together, break apart, and at the end come together in a new union.

The Bone People was prasied lavishly by some reviewers and commented upon harshly by others. "The reason for the novel's fairtytale success," Elizabeth Ward remarked in the *Washington Post Book World*, "is that it is an original, overwhelming, near-great work of literature. . . . First novel it may be, but there is nothing timid or derivative about *The Bone People*. It is a work of immense literary and intellectual ambition, that rare thing, a novel of ideas which is also dramatically very strong. *The Bone People* does have its failings. The exuberant prose occasionally lapses into mawkishness or gush. The last third of the book, especially the semi-mystical invocation of the 'Maoritanga,' is too schematic. And Joe remains a tantalizingly underdeveloped character compared with Kerewin. But the sheer flow of language and ideas sweep you on. The novel might even be thought of as, itself, 'something perilous and new,' and therefore a very exciting event, in the field of New Zealand literature and beyond."

Bruce King in the *Sewanee Review* considered *The Bone People* a work that virtually reshapes New Zealand literature. It is, he

°hūm

commented, "one of the most impressive works of fiction written from a distinctly feminist position: it reflects a change in New Zealand society, a shift from provincial, colonial, imitation British culture, in which sports and male values predominated, to a post-sixties culture, open to new ideas, cosmopolitan, and with an increasingly prominent role for women and Maoris. . . . Hulme is excellent in the menaced way she shows evolving feelings and the subtleties of relationships; in balancing the subjective with the exterior, she has moved the novel form closer to an extended lyric poem in several voices." The reviewer for *Kirkus Reviews*, however, remarked: "Stylistically, it is a very homemade-feeling book, hippy-ish, filled with elaborate Maori references (a glossary in the back is indispensable, too indispensable), inner thoughts, goopy lyricism, and torrents of inner thinking that are clumsy and unconvincing. . . . In all, a slow slog through a good deal of self-congratulatory spiritual homeopathy, with only the smallest smidge of story thrown in."

Writing in the *New York Times*, Michiko Kakutani remarked that "with some judicious pruning, the book might well make a powerful visionary fable—about love and redemption, violence and renewal. As it is, though, *The Bone People* feels too much like a grab bag stuffed with weird dreams . . . intriguing talismans . . . and lots of willfully symbolic events. If such images attest to the prodigality of Miss Hulme's imagination, their rampant profusion also indicates a certain reluctance, on her part, to exercise the critical faculties of selectivity—to shape the design of her narrative with some vision in mind. Instead, the reader increasingly feels that strange incidents have been included simply for the sake of their strangeness, and a result begins to tire of the novel's italicized emotions."

The Windeater/Te Kaihu, a collection of Hulme's short stories, also drew a mixture of praise and censure. Tim Armstrong in the *Times Literary Supplement* remarked that there "can be few other writers of undoubted power whose work is so full of deformity, both as subject matter and in style. . . . The theme of children who are abused or abandoned, familiar from *The Bone People*, is present in many of the stories. So too are the stylistic grotesqueries and overwriting of that novel: dialogue no one would ever speak, gothic nonsense about Ancient Ones, anthropomorphic musings on the 'sea people' (whales). . . . [There are] stories which seem apprentice work . . . , but in other stories Hulme raises delicate questions of class and culture in New Zealand in a way that nobody else in New Zealand before. . . . It is often the speech of the

margins we hear: of bikers, hippies, right-wing thugs. The best of the stories have an admirable sharpness and social observation." Alison Fell in the *New Statesman* commented that "while the resonance of *The Bone People* shows here and there . . . , the stories lack that sheer commitment to a theme that drove the novel on through some self-indulgent writing." The reviewer for *Publisher's Weekly* remarked: "That [Hulme] is also a poet is in constant evidence. . . . The pieces, often enraptured by nature and at one with it in a kind of mystical fusion of self and world, are often fragmentary. . . . too often the pieces lack dramatic force and narrative focus." Kit Reed in the *New York Times Book Review* has a similarly mixed and puzzled reaction. Reed complained that much of Hulme's writing "seems arty," yet acknowledged that "this is a writer who works with enormous power and energy when engaged at the human, emotional level."

In a 1988 interview in *Contemporary Authors*, when asked about her critics, Hulme responded: "The most negative criticisms have come from England, where, I think, many people took it as a personal affront that a book from an erstwhile colony could sneak/grab/steal/purloin/be-given-as-a-political gesture—anything but win—their premier literary prize. (It was made worse by the fact that, in everybody's minds, an Aussie was runner-up!) On the other hand—and this is called 'choppin the tall poppies' in New Zealand—when the collection of short stories came out, most critics had a bone to pick." Hulme, who is unmarried, lives in a remote village in New Zealand. In a profile article on her in the *New York Times Book Review*, Hulme remarked: "I can walk on the beach for 20 miles, cross the mouths of four rivers and not see anybody. I've lived there for 12 years. The house, which I built myself, has eight walls. . . . I fish a lot. . . . One of the things—actually the only thing—I hate about this trip [to America] is that I'm missing the whitebait season."

PRINCIPAL WORKS: The Bone People, 1984; Lost Possessions, 1985; The Windeater/Te Kaihau, 1986. *Poetry*—The Silence Between, 1982; Strands, 1988.

ABOUT: Contemporary Authors 125, 1988; Contemporary Literary Criticism 39, 1986; Contemporary Novelists, 4th ed., 1986. *Periodicals*—Kirkus Reviews September 15, 1985; New Statesman April 3, 1987; New York Times November 13, 1985; New York Times Book Review December 1, 1985; March 8, 1987; Publisher's World, October 31, 1986; Saturday Review April 1986; Times Literary Supplement March 6, 1987; Washington Post Book World November 8, 1986.

*IBUSE MASUJI (February 15, 1898–   ), Japanese author, poet, and translator, regarded as one of his country's foremost writers and a candidate for the Nobel Prize, was born and raised in the village of Kamo in eastern Hiroshima Prefecture. Ibuse was the second son of Ikuta and Miya Ibuse, members of an established landowning family. Ibuse's youth was punctuated by the frequent and unexpected deaths of friends and relatives. His first recollection, according to his memoir *Keirokushū* (Miscellany, 1936), is of viewing a neighbor's funeral from the shoulders of a family servant who was himself soon to die. Perhaps due to these dark beginnings as well as the violence he was later to witness during World War II, Ibuse's works comprise, in the words of critic Kawakami Tetsutarō, "a history of sorrow." From *Sazanami Gunki* (*Waves: A War Diary*, 1930–1938), his epic account of the human and moral carnage of a twelfth-century civil war, through his numerous stories of such natural upheavals as floods, volcanic eruptions, and earthquakes, to finally his most renowned achievement, the novel of the atomic destruction of Hiroshima *Kuroi Ame* (*Black Rain*, 1965–1966), Ibuse's writing has been noted not only for its distinctive style and its use of humor and folk characters, but for its portrait of a Japan less characterized by a highly refined elite culture than by the frequent assaults of both nature and history upon the average citizen.

After attending local schools where he was trained in such modern subjects as English in addition to the Oriental classics, and after a brief flirtation with painting as a profession, Ibuse left Kamo in late summer 1917 to study literature at Waseda University in Tokyo. He was not a model student. Rather, he learned through frequenting cafés and joining informal literary clubs. Like the hundreds of other aspiring writers gathered in the city's student quarters, he was present at the exhilarating explosion of new ideas, from surrealism to Marxism, that swept through Japan after the First World War.

Ibuse's start as a professional writer is linked to the unique friendship he enjoyed with his gifted classmate Aoki Nampachi. Living in squalid student boarding houses, and intimidated by the immense city surrounding him, Ibuse looked to Aoki not only for companionship but inspiration. Ibuse recalls Aoki at length in another major memoir, *Hanseiki* (The First Half of My Life, 1970): "Nampachi encouraged me every day. He said that the practice of writing was the first obligation of anyone with literary ambitions. He regarded as sacred the practice of writing and its fruits."

In the summer of 1919 Ibuse embarked upon his literary career by drafting seven short stories as a gift for Aoki. One provided the basis of his most famous early story, "Sanshōuo" (1919,"The Salamander"), the tragicomic tale of a salamander trapped in an underwater cave but comforted by a frog who one day joins him in his solitude—a rather lyrical allegory of "the life he and Aoki Nampachi shared in Tokyo." A further reworking of this material appears in *Yū hei*, (Confinement, 1923), Ibuse's first book.

In 1921 Aoki suddenly took ill and died. Ibuse was greatly shocked—he had been distracted by trouble at school, and had not even known his friend was sick—and his grief is reflected in the story "Koi" ("Carp"), written a few years later, in 1926. The narrator of "Carp" has been entrusted with the care of a pet fish by his now-dead best friend. The story concludes with a winter scene suggesting the depth of Ibuse's longing for the absent Aoki:

> One morning a thin snow fell onto the ice. I picked up a long bamboo pole and drew a picture on its surface. It was a picture of a fish over eighteen feet long. I imagined it to be my white carp.
>
> When I finished the drawing I thought of writing some words by the carp's mouth, but gave up the idea. Instead I drew beside it a large number of roach and killifish. They were chasing after the carp, trying not to fall behind. But how foolish and pitiful they looked! They had neither fins nor eyes nor mouths. I was utterly satisfied.

After Aoki's death Ibuse threw himself into writing. He labored for the rest of the 1920s in relative anonymity as a writer of short stories regarded as either simple child-like allegories or derivative versions of Western works ("The Salamander," for example, owes a distant debt to Chekhov's "The Bet"). Ibuse later referred to these years as his "practice period," the decade in which he not only made important friends in the literary circles of Tokyo, but also perfected his controlled, spare, and sturdy style. Meanwhile he supported himself through a variety of jobs, some arranged for him by Tanaka Kōtarō, a writer and editor who promoted Ibuse among prominent authors and publishers, and who additionally obliged Ibuse by arranging his marriage in 1927 to Akimoto Setsuyo.

Soon thereafter Kobayashi Hideo, perhaps Japan's most influential modern critic, praised Ibuse's talent in a widely read review, elevating him into the higher ranks of younger writers. Unlike many of his generation, Ibuse owed no allegiance to the proletarian literature movement, and so the companionship and recognition of older and less political writers was especially important to him. In 1930 he remarked that he was largely content with his growing success. At this same point in his career Ibuse began the experi-

°ē boo se

ments with longer forms of prose that resulted in the novella *Kawa* (The River, 1931–1932) and, most significantly, his historical novel *Sazanami Gunki.*

Sazanami Gunki is the story of the uprising in the late twelfth century of the Minamoto military clan against the then-powerful Taira, the story already told in the Japanese classic epic *The Tale of the Heike.* Ibuse's rendition, however, assumes the form of a journal kept by a rather minor historical figure, the adolescent nobleman Taira no Tomoakira. By using Tomoakira as his narrator, Ibuse is able to describe the violence that disrupted an entire nation through its impact on just one of its hapless victims.

Sazanami Gunki charts one young man's disillusionment with a world he had once thought innocent and benign. Similar disillusionment pervades most of Ibuse's historical fiction and was to prove oddly prescient once he himself was drawn into a catastrophic war.

Ibuse was unexpectedly conscripted into the Imperial Army at the advanced age of forty-four in November 1941. He was part of the first wave of writers who were organized into propaganda units to be dispatched to the Southeast Asian nations Japan intended to occupy. Ibuse was aboard ship close to Hong Kong when war against the Allies was declared. That voyage— Ibuse's first and only outside of Japan—took him to Singapore, where he worked as a newspaper editor and teacher at a local colonial school. He was repatriated in November 1942 to serve as a propagandist within Japan itself. Meanwhile he continued to write fiction, producing works about wartime Singapore such as *Hana no Machi* (City of Flowers, 1942) and *Aru Shōjo no Senji Nikki* (A Young Girl's Wartime Diary, 1943).

Conditions in Japan steadily deteriorated, and in 1944 Ibuse and his family were evacuated from Tokyo, then subject to American bombardment, to a series of rural locations that eventually brought him back to Kamo. It was there, in August 1945, that Ibuse learned of the annihilation of nearby Hiroshima and witnessed the end of the war. It was not until well into 1946 that he resumed his career in earnest with such noted stories as "Wabisuke" ("Isle of the Billows"), and he remained in the countryside until mid-1947, when he returned to Tokyo. Soon his output was greater than ever, albeit changed—perhaps focused—by the impact of a war that had altered history for Japan as it had, perhaps, for no other nation.

His country's tragedy was compounded by one particular to Ibuse himself. After Aoki Namnachi Ibuse's closest friend was Dazai Osamu, author of the noted postwar novels *Shayō* (The

Setting Sun, 1947) and *Ningen Shikkaku* (No Longer Human, 1948). Ibuse first encountered Dazai when the latter, a young man only recently arrived in Tokyo, sent him a desperate letter threatening suicide should he not agree to meet. (Dazai had been deeply impressed by a radio reading of *Yū hei* years earlier.) Eventually the two became teacher and student, literary collaborators, and finally close friends, but Dazai's erratic behavior continued, and there were several suicide attempts. When Dazai finally killed himself in 1948, Ibuse was stunned and deeply hurt. These events deepened Ibuse's appreciation of how fragile human survival is; to have outlived first his fellow soldiers in a war and then his own protegé in the peace that followed seemed to impose on him a double obligation to chronicle the human wreckage of history.

Ibuse's postwar stories note, with characteristic understatement and even humor, the suffering that Japan—or rather, its individual citizens—had just experienced, and treat these as part of a larger historical pattern. "Yōhai Taichō" ("A Far-worshipping Commander," 1950), hailed by critic Usui Yoshimi as the "greatest masterpiece" of the "pure tragedy" of the Second World War, is the portrait of a zealous army officer who, as the result of a head injury, does not understand that the war is over and continues to conduct himself according to a now discredited militarist ideology.

Ibuse's affectionate satire in this story suggests how mercurial and even frivolous official rhetoric can seem when compared with what ordinary people stubbornly and wisely perceive to be the real issues of their lives. The dichotomy between the authority of the state and the resources of the individual surfaces regularly in Ibuse's postwar work. *Hyōmin Usaburō* (Castaway Usaburō, 1954), a fictionalized account of a nineteenth-century shipwrecked crew, describes the sailors' cavalier treatment by foreign and native authorities. Reiterating the ignominy Ibuse's simple folk suffer as nation-states contend, *Hyōmin Usaburō* also prominently displays an increased awareness of human resilience in the face of such adversity. Usaburō, the novel's main character, minimizes his loneliness in foreign exile by cultivating the handful of rice kernels he had jealously husbanded aboard ship. Usaburō's small private rites of planting and harvesting enable him to recreate a nurturing culture amid the chaos of his castaway experience, giving rise to a character termed Ibuse's "most important postwar hero."

Ibuse's faith in human powers of regeneration motivated him in the 1960s to begin work on *Kuroi Ame* (*Black Rain*), praised in a 1987 poll of leading Japanese intellectuals as the most important book written in Japan since 1945. Ibuse had had a Hiroshima book in mind ever since he witnessed the exodus of refugees pouring out of the city into the surrounding countryside. The result, *Kuroi Ame*, is today perhaps not only the world's best-known Japanese novel, but the world's most intimate literary look at what the first use of nuclear weapons wrought.

Ibuse chose to preserve the actual testimony of those in Hiroshima rather than invent, and risk distorting, the scale of the destruction. His novel skillfully intertwines survivor accounts to state collectively how average men and women are shattered by forces they do not even comprehend and yet draw on inner, hitherto unrealized resources to persevere.

Kuroi Ame unfolds like a conventional novel, pursuing the problem succinctly stated in the work's opening sentence: "For several years past, Shigematsu Shizuma, of the village of Kobatake, had been aware of his niece Yasuko as a weight on his mind." Shigematsu has the responsibility of finding a husband for Yasuko, rumored to have been exposed to the bomb. To prove that she was, in fact, on the outskirts of the city on the morning of August sixth, Shigematsu uses her diary—and later his own, his wife's, and others'—as documentation. These diaries, which make up the bulk of the novel, guarantee the raw testimonial quality of *Kuroi Ame*. Shigematsu's contribution, simply entitled "The Journal of the Bomb," describes the explosion and its aftermath in ways that are all the more powerful for refraining from the hyperbole and "pornography of death" common elsewhere in A-bomb literature. He recalls August sixth as a random process of dehumanization:

> The countless people who had blackish dried blood clinging to them where it had flowed from their faces onto their shoulders and down their backs, or over their chests and down their bellies. Some were still bleeding, but they seemed to have no energy to do anything about it. . . .
> The woman leading a child by the hand who realized that the child was not hers, shook her hand free with a cry, and ran off. And the child—a boy of six or seven—running, crying plaintively, after her.
> The father leading his child by the hand who lost hold of him in the crush. He pushed through the crowd calling the child's name over and again, till finally he was struck brutally and repeatedly by someone he had thrust out of the way. . . .
> A man who carried, held like an offering before him, a clock that emitted a dull, broken noise as he walked.
> A man who carried over his shoulder a fish-basket attached to the cloth case of a fishing rod.
> A bare-footed woman shading her eyes with both hands, who sobbed helplessly as she walked. . . .

Excerpts from Shigematsu's diary alternate with descriptions of his life in Kobatake some years later. Unable to work full-time because of the lingering effects of radiation, he spends his days raising carp in a small hatchery. It is typical of Ibuse to contrast and complement mass destruction with the possibility, however meager, of regeneration. But though Shigematsu's baby fish mature and Hiroshima grows verdant once more, such signs of life are not finally compensatory. Yasuko does indeed succumbs to radiation sickness, and by the novel's end is on the verge of death. *Kuroi Ame* ends with Shigematsu wistfully hoping for her recovery, but though it seems probable that he will survive, she is doomed to a death at least as horrible as that of the bomb's initial victims.

Kuroi Ame was an immediate critical and commercial success. It has sold over a million copies in Japan, where critic Etō Jun hailed it as "the first true work of A-bomb literature," and has been adapted for the screen by the director Shohei Imamura. C. P. Snow, commenting on the novel's 1969 English translation, claimed Ibuse had turned "Hiroshima into a major work of art." This work won Ibuse, in addition to his earlier literary awards, the Noma Prize and the Order of Cultural Merit. Still, uncomfortable as a non-victim enjoying such acclaim, Ibuse has declared the novel a failure, the smallest fraction of what could have been told, and at the same time already perhaps too much. Hiroshima has been, since *Kuroi Ame*, a theme he has declined to discuss further.

Nonetheless Ibuse continues to explore allied themes. In addition to more memoirs of himself and his generation, such as *Chōyōchū no Koto* (Under Arms, 1977–1980) and *Ogikubo Fudoki* (An Ogikubo Almanac, 1981), Ibuse's fiction pursues the violence of history, its human toll, and the need to console, even post-mortem, those killed. In "Kenkōji no ike" (The Pond at Kenkōji Temple, 1978) Ibuse visits a remote village during the annual religious services for its war dead, sons and husbands lost several decades ago but still remembered by the survivors. More than Japan's other modern authors, Ibuse writes with a belief in our capacity to cultivate what is most essential for individual and collective survival. These qualities have endeared him to Japanese readers; as his fellow writer Yasuoka Shōtarō once said in tribute, Ibuse's works uncannily impart the sensation of having come home after a long journey. For this reason above all, he is regarded with a respect and affection unequaled by any other Japanese writer of his generation.

Ibuse and his wife live in the Ogikubo section of Tokyo. They have three children.

WORKS IN ENGLISH TRANSLATION: John Bester translated *Black Rain* in 1969; it has since gone through several editions and is available in paperback. Bester also translated *Lieutenant Lookeast and Other Stories* in 1971, and *Salamander and Other Stories* in 1981. *Waves: Two Short Novels* and *Castaways: Two Short Novels* were translated by David Aylward and Anthony V. Liman in 1986 and 1987 respectively. Short stories by Ibuse are also collected in several anthologies—*Modern Japanese Short Stories*, 1961; *The Shōwa Anthology 1929–1961*, 1985; *The Crazy Iris and Other Stories of the Atomic Aftermath*, 1985.

ABOUT: Bester, J. *prefaces to* Black Rain, 1969, and Lieutenant Lookeast, 1971; Contemporary Literary Criticism 22, 1982; Kimball, A. G. Crisis and Identity in Contemporary Japanese Novels, 1973; Liman, A. V. *in* Approaches to the Modern Japanese Novel (eds. K. Tsuruta and T. Swann), 1976; Liman, A.V. *in* Essays on Japanese Literature (ed. T. Katsuhiko), 1977; Liman, A.V. *in* Approaches to the Modern Japanese Short Story (eds. T. Swann and K. Tsuruta), 1982; Rimer, T. J. Modern Japanese Fiction and Its Traditions, 1978; Treat, J. W. Pools of Water, Pillars of Fire: The Literature of Ibuse Masuji, 1988. *Periodicals*—New York Times Book Review September 8, 1985.

INGALLS, RACHEL (HOLMES) (May 13, 1940–   ), American short-story writer and novelist, now living in England, was born in Boston, Massachusetts. She spent her childhood in Virginia, South Carolina, California, Washington, D.C., and Massachusetts, where she attended schools in Cambridge and Weston. From 1958 to 1960 she lived in Germany, auditing courses at the Universities of Munich, Erlangen, Göttingen, and Cologne. She then matriculated at Radcliffe College, Harvard University, completing a bachelor's degree in English in 1964. A Shakespeare devotée, she moved to London in 1965 in order to have the chance of "seeing his plays and hearing those lines spoken by people who were trained to say them." In addition to writing, she has worked as a theater dresser, librarian, publisher's reader, ballet critic, and film critic.

From the start of her writing career, Ingalls has produced pieces of "a very odd, unsalable length," between 40 and 100 pages. Like much of her published work, her first book, *Theft*, is a collection of novella-length stories. The title story retells the crucifixion of Jesus from the point of view of Seth, a poor fruit-picker who has been imprisoned with his brother-in-law for stealing. Although Seth never describes the time and place, the reader learns that the two men share common backgrounds and a previous suspicion of the authorities but have divergent mo-

RACHEL INGALLS

ral outlooks. Their situation grows more and more serious as outside rioters wind up in the jail, including a religious fanatic, with whom Jake and Seth finally are condemned to die. *Theft* impressed reviewers with its concise prose and shocking conclusion. Janet Burroway of the *New Statesman* commented that "details that were merely colourful become part of an ingenious, not facile, pattern. This is a short book, and in some ways a young one. But there is more than promise in a first novel that is not decorated autobiography but a true fiction." Comparing Ingalls to Kafka, the *Times Literary Supplement* reviewer noted that although Seth and Jake sometimes sound like Butch Cassidy and the Sundance Kid, "Miss Ingalls writes with the kind of confidence and economy rare, and hopeful, in first novels by young women writers."

Ingalls' second book, *The Man Who Was Left Behind and Other Stories*, consists of three stories. All of them deal with human vulnerability and the isolation every person potentially faces. The title story is about an old man who has become a tramp in the North American town where he once enjoyed a loving family, popularity, and respect. The other two stories concern Americans vacationing on the island of Rhodes, where the imminent disintegration of their marriages slowly emerges. In "Something to Write Home About," for example, a young wife keeps sending her mother postcards, apparently cheerful missives that eventually form a bizarre and astonishing pattern. Reviewers applauded Ingalls' work for its powerful economy and confident style. The *Times Literary Supplement* called it an "excellent book. . . . The work of an author who is as sensitive as she is accomplished. . . . " However, Lorna Sage, in the *Observer*, described Ingalls' writing as "impatient" and lamented the author's technique of condensing the characters and their existence into the stories' climaxes. Still, Sage acknowledged the "distinctive, sinister inventiveness" that makes Ingalls "a force to be reckoned with."

Ingalls' best known novella, *Mrs. Caliban*, displays a new level of such inventiveness. At the story's opening, the heroine Dorothy faces a deteriorating marriage after the death of her only child and a miscarried pregnancy. She temporarily escapes her despair by having an affair with a gentle amphibious creature, Larry, who has escaped from the torturous research of oceanographers. The affair brings Dorothy happiness and a new sense of purpose. She and Larry have thoughtful discussions in which he describes sea-life in the southern hemisphere and she tries to explain why "civilized" human beings behave as they do. Their satisfying but highly unorthodox relationship is doomed, however, and ends in disaster. Reviewers praised Ingalls' light touch, deft portrait of affluent suburban America, and ability to convey the pleasantness and affection that Dorothy and Larry share. "It is difficult to imagine an odder or more strangely entertaining novel being published this year," Melvyn Bragg wrote in *Punch*. The *Spectator*'s Caroline Moorehead pronounced the novel "delicate and infinitely precise" and Ingalls "a remarkable writer, able to convey, in a single phrase or line of dialogue, an entire rounded scene." Moorehead also praised the author's faultless ear for speech. Alan Brownjohn, however, offered a dissenting view in the *Times Literary Supplement*: "Several readily identifiable fables lie behind *Mrs. Caliban*, supplying it with most of the little power and excitement it possesses as a sort of macabre moral fantasy." In 1986, the British Book Marketing Council named *Mrs. Caliban* one of the twenty best postwar American novels, an honor that Ingalls said left her "stunned, completely staggered."

Ingalls imbued her next novella, *Binstead's Safari*, with an even greater degree of fantasy. Stan Binstead, an American anthropologist, goes to Africa to research animal-worship cults. He reluctantly allows his clinging wife Millie to join him. As Stan becomes increasing anxious on the safari, looking for a rumored lion cult, Millie grows independent and adventurous. She begins a passionate love affair with an attractive lion-hunter, Harry Lewis, nicknamed "Lion" because he survived the initiation rite of fighting an enraged lion. In magical, dream-like sequences, Harry appears as a lion-god associated with the cult Stan is researching. In the end, the lion's supernatural power overcomes both Stan and Millie. On the whole, reviewers found *Binstead's Safari* less convincing but more provocative than *Mrs. Caliban*. Hermione Lee, writing in the *Observer*, commended Ingalls' ability to sustain varying levels of consciousness within the novel: "Millie's dream-like transformation takes place inside a 'frame' of ominous offstage feuds and killings, in a world where the idea of lion-hunting as a 'test' is vanishing. . . . It is an interesting novel about folklore and heroism, and, most strikingly, it is a beautiful and restrained celebration of the happiness of love." *Times Literary Supplement* reviewer Adam Mars-Jones criticized Ingalls for romanticizing Millie's liberation, endowing Stan with an unconvincing psychology, and failing to combine the different genres she utilizes. "As a whole," he summarized, "it fails to transcend its elements of adventure-story and of novelette." William Scammell of *London Magazine* similarly concluded that "the fantasy doesn't quite succeed in extricating itself from literary models, perhaps, but it promises interesting things to come, not least from a writer who can write."

Ingalls' next work, *Three of a Kind*, fulfilled Scammell's prophecy. In each of the stories, disruption occurs after some form of sexual divergence. "Blessed Art Thou" is the story of Brother Anselm, a Californian monk who claims he has had sex with the Archangel Gabriel and soon shows signs of pregnancy. In "I See a Long Journey," a well-to-do American wife traveling in the Far East tries to understand her passion for her chauffeur at the temple of a juvenile goddess. An undisclosed force finally shatters the triangle. "On Ice" chronicles the declining fortunes of Beverly, who goes skiing in Austria with her German lover. She is warned that her illicit relationship will bring her harm, but the ensuing horror comes from a wholly different and unexpected source. The stories earned enthusiastic reviews. "The fantastic or violent interruptions Ingalls describes are made especially cogent by the even tenor of her prose," Colin Greenland remarked in the *Times Literary Supplement*. Anne Bernays, in the *New York Times Book Review*, called "Blessed Art Thou" "extremely funny, singular, perhaps a masterpiece." Victoria Glendinning in the (London) *Sunday Times*, found Ingalls' characteristically spare writing too sketchy "for her unearthly imagination to take hold on the reader." Although the stories "are full of small brilliant bites they leave you hungry for something more substantial. But she's good, a true original, and we must be grateful for that."

Ingalls explores the theme of affliction in her third collection, *The Pearlkillers*. "Inheritance" deals with a young woman who belongs to a family with skin that causes pearls to rot (hence "pearlkillers"). When Carla's great aunt gives her a black velvet box holding a puckered brown blob hung on a gold chain, niece and reader alike can only guess its true properties. "Captain Hendrik's Story" relates the tale of a Scandinavian explorer who tells the official version of his adventure until his partner returns to blackmail him with the true story. In "Third Time Lucky," Lily, twice a Vietnam widow, who seeks consolation from the ancient Egyptian cult of Isis, ends up in Cairo on her third honeymoon. "People to People" concerns a group of university graduates who must confront the truth of a classmate's death twenty years ago, with unhappy results for five of them. Once again, Ingalls' stories received critical commendation. Jonathan Keats described them, in the *Observer*, as "possessed by a knowingness that at times is awing in its perspectives." Keats found "Captain Hendrik's Story" particularly interesting for revealing "all those moral shadowings and veiling that fiction itself involves." In the *London Review of Books* Patricia Craig noted that "Ingalls has a calm way of presenting her ornamental imaginings which is highly effective." "These four stories aren't just fables of destructiveness but narratives of umbrous depth," Peter Kemp wrote in the *Times Literary Supplement*.

Another collection of Ingalls' stories, *The End of Tragedy*, was published in 1987. As suggested by the title, the stories share conclusions of death and destruction. "Friends in the Country" involves young lovers who go to dinner at a peculiar house in the country and find themselves trapped there for the weekend. They suffer through an increasingly eerie night that leaves their relationship in tatters. "An Artist's Life" tells the story of two Finnish artists, one successful, the other a failure. Not until the very moment of his death does the failed artist finally receive a creative vision. In the title novella, an actress famous for little else besides her dramatic scream is hired to play a murdered woman in an attempt to reveal the suspected killer. "In the Act" features an inventor who has created the ideal sex partner in the form of a female doll. When his wife discovers his invention, she hides the doll and demands that he make a male one for her. Reviewers paid tribute to Ingalls' style and imagination in *The End of Tragedy* but felt she had stopped short of her true potential. Linda Taylor, in the *Times Literary Supplement*, found the framework of the stories somewhat flimsy, implausible and thematically diminished: "The eye-catching thrills make us read on

fast when it would be more rewarding to mull over details of motivation, manipulation and downright treachery." In the *New York Times Book Review* Stephen Dobyns mildly reproached Ingalls for avoiding profundity at times. Nevertheless, "she is a beautiful stylist and her sentences unwind splendidly. Her sense of pacing, her descriptions and dialogue and syntax, are all masterful. Her language is the window through which we see her world: a spotless wall of glass between us and a landscape both gorgeous and grotesque." Christopher Lehmann-Haupt of the *New York Times* noted that "you continue to get the sense from the collection that she is gathering herself for something. In various works of short fiction—'I See a Long Journey,' 'The Pearlkillers,' and 'Binstead's Safari'—she has developed considerably from the writer who became famous for *Mrs. Caliban*. . . . It only remains for her to find a song of equal power to sing. In the meantime she is perfecting her trills, her scales, her cadenzas. It is a pleasure to hear her practice. One awaits further developments."

PRINCIPAL WORKS: Theft, 1970; Mediterranean Cruiser, 1973; The Man Who Was Left Behind and Other Stories, 1974; Mrs. Caliban, 1982; Binstead's Safari, 1983; Three of a Kind, 1985; The Pearlkillers, 1986; The End of Tragedy, 1987.

ABOUT: Contemporary Authors 123, 1988; Dictionary of Literary Biography 14, 1983; *Periodicals*—London Magazine September 1983; London Review of Books June 5, 1986; New Statesman September 4, 1970; New York Times February 23, 1989; New York Times Book Review, August 31, 1986; December 28, 1986; March 5, 1989; Observer March 10, 1974; May 8, 1983; April 20, 1986; Punch February 3, 1982; Spectator January 9, 1982; (London) Sunday Times November 3, 1985; Times Literary Supplement September 25, 1970; February 15, 1974; January 8, 1982; May 13, 1983; October 25, 1985; May 9, 1986; October 16, 1987.

*INNAURATO, ALBERT (F.) (June 2, 1947–), American playwright, was born in Philadelphia, the son of Albert Innaurato and the former Mary Walker. He grew up in the Italian-American neighborhood of South Philadelphia, where much of his work is set, attended local parochial schools and went for a couple of years to Philadelphia's Temple University. He transferred to the California Institute of the Arts in Los Angeles, from which he received a bachelor's degree in fine arts in 1972. He then entered the Yale Drama School, earning a master's in fine arts in 1974. At Yale Innaurato recalled in 1977, he found himself opposed to "the fashion for nonverbal theater. . . . It was difficult to get

*in or ra to

ALBERT INNAURATO

performers or directors willing to work with my plays because they wanted to develop their own things, either through improvisations or through working over a classic. When I wanted to stage one of my plays I had to import a friend from Philly and use the wife of one of the directing students at Yale. I don't want to oversimplify things. Original plays do get put on, but it is very difficult because we are living in a nonverbal period when everyone is oriented to the visual, to movies and TV, and this has affected theater as well. The playwright has been quashed and the director glorified."

Innaurato loved music and opera as a child; he was taken by members of his family to see many operas, which seemed to him as real as life. By the age of twelve, under the guidance of professional teachers and with the aid of classes in operatic composition, he was composing operas to his own librettos, "in sort of a pastiche style," he remarked in a 1985 interview, with "no talent whatever but plenty of ambition and energy." His early operatic efforts bore the evocative titles "The Vampire" and "Mildred Vagina." At fifteen he composed an operatic version of *Anna Karenina* to his own libretto based on the Tolstoy novel. His composition teacher predicted no career for him as a composer, he recalled, but because his librettos were such fun to read, asked him the fateful question, "Have you ever thought about writing plays?" By the time he was sixteen the future course of his professional life was set.

At Yale Innaurato became friends with the playwright Christopher Durang, and together they wrote three plays, most notably *The Idiots Karamazov*, a comic spoof of Dostoevsky. When this play was produced at the Yale Repertory Theater in 1974, another Yale classmate, Meryl Streep, took the pivotal role of the translator Constance Garnett while Durang played Alyosha, the saintly brother. At the play's very first production, however, at Yale's Silliman College in 1973, Innaurato played Constance Garnett; he also directed.

During his first year at the Yale drama school, Innaurato began *The Transfiguration of Benno Blimpie*. He writes in the introduction to his *Best Plays of Albert Innaurato* that the play was "finished later that summer, while I was staying at Edward Albee's house for writers (sometimes called The Stable by cynics). Christopher Durang was also at The Stable. . . . Mr. Albee we glimpsed only at a distance that summer. But it strikes me as curious now that two young writers hatched their first distinctive plays in a house owned by the last American playwright to make a great dent in the awareness of the larger American public . . . and I am not forgetting Messrs. Shepard and Mamet."

At the very start of the play, Benno Vertucci announces to the audience, "I am eating myself to death." What follows is the horrific account of his loveless life, of the parents, especially his mother, who despise him, of the schoolmates who jeer at and torture him, of his attempts to study art, and of his crushing realization that "when he had finished a painting, Benno was still fat, ugly, and alone. Nothing makes a difference, nothing alters anything." At the end of the play, Benno is holding a meat cleaver high in the air, ready to bring it down on himself to end his misery. Walter Kerr in the *New York Times* called *Benno Blimpie* "such a disturbing play—I felt as though I'd been mauled in the playhouse, and by experts—because we have at last been willing to face up to the nature of the sensual beast inside us. . . . If our experiences when dealing with sex in the theater have grown more troubling . . . it is because the theater itself has grown more honest." The play had a short but critically successful run Off-Broadway in 1977 with James Coco in the title role.

Midway through one of his hallucinatory declamations on the futility and ugliness of his life, Benno declares his intention to blind himself, lock himself in a room with the rats he can see all around him, and eat rat poison. "I will be a sexual object to them," he says bitterly, knowing that as the rats gorge themselves on his dead body they will also be killing themselves. The image of an unloved fat boy who takes rat poison was carried over to Innaurato's second play,

Gemini, but in that work the boy, the neighbor Herschel, is unsuccessful at self-destruction. The play is set in early June 1973 in the Italian neighborhood of South Philadelphia. It is Francis Geminiani's twenty-first birthday, and two friends from Harvard, Judith Hastings and her brother Randy, have arrived unannounced to help him celebrate it. Francis is ashamed of his poor neighborhood, of his vulgar father, and of his earthy, uneducated neighbors, and he is especially uncertain about his sexual identity—he has slept with Judith but is perhaps in love with Randy. The play does not resolve any of these conflicts—they are in any case not completely expressed or explored, but are mainly hinted at—yet one feels at the end that Francis is a more authentic individual for having talked a little about his obsessions, and that he may well be able to come to terms with his life in a more open, satisfactory way. In any case, as Kerr remarked in his overview of Innaurato's early progress as a playwright, the student trio does not provide us "with the real body of the play: that comes from the sidelines, from the sometimes too extravagant but often very amusing portraits of family and friends."

Gemini, the author wrote in *Best Plays of Albert Innaurato*, "ran [on Broadway] for more than four years but was roundly despised by the Powers On Broadway, and was never nominated for any awards." He wrote the play on a Guggenheim grant at a time of stress and illness, but "derived enormous pleasure" from the experience. "It was not much liked when it first began to circulate in manuscript. . . . During its long run, [it] was probably rightly considered a 'back door' success. It snuck up on the New York Theater and embarrassed the mocking opinion-makers who had damned it early on. Of course, they punished it and its writer for years afterwards. It became the play that refused to die." *Gemini* moved from an Off-Broadway production at the Playwrights Horizon to the PAF Theater in Huntington, Long Island, and thence to its four-year run on Broadway.

None of Innaurato's later plays has enjoyed the success of his early work. *Earth Worms* (1974), in many ways the most ambitious and operatic of his plays, is a dreamlike work again set among the dingy row houses of South Philadelphia. The central characters form a bizarre triangle: a young man beset with problems about his sexual identity; his bride, a country girl brought in from "outside"; and a seventy-year-old homosexual. The old man and the girl form a kind of loveless alliance with one another. Mel Gussow, writing in the *New York Times*, faulted the play, which had a brief Off-Broadway run in 1977, for "wavering focus [and] cluttered

background," yet claimed it had "moments . . . that are pure Innaurato. . . . [It] is both a weird love story and a disturbing look at man's indifference to man."

The two-act play *Ulysses in Traction* had a short run Off-Broadway in late 1977. It is set at a drama school in Detroit, in the rehearsal hall of which are trapped various students and teachers while a fierce race riot rages in the city outside. These characters attack each other no less ferociously than do the rioters, and many points are made about cruelty, unhappiness, failure, and unsureness of sexual identity—all by that time virtual trademark themes of Innaurato. Edith Oliver in the *New Yorker* commented that the play "never jells. Its principal weakness . . . is that so much of what we learn about the characters has to be told in monologues— a not uncommon defect these days."

Verna: USO Girl concerns the 1944 tour of a USO show traveling by jeep around the various battlefields of Europe; the heroine is a stage-struck but talentless orphan who signed on in desperation. The play, really more of a deliberately awful amateur revue, had a very brief run Off-Broadway in early 1978.

Passione is a two-act play which harks back to the locale and the family-centered theme of *Gemini*: an Italian family in South Philadelphia comes together for a reunion. The characters are all antagonistic to one another, but also decide that they love and need one another. As they eat great quantities of food (eating is another firmly established motif in most of Innaurato's work) they vociferously fall out and reconcile—in John Simon's words, in *New York*, "eating and drinking become a physical and metaphysical consummation, with the thinnest of lines between passionate consuming and consuming passions." *Passione* had both Off-Broadway and Broadway productions in 1980.

More than four years then elapsed before another Innaurato play was produced in New York. *Coming of Age in SoHo* was first presented in 1984 at the Seattle Repertory Theater, where the playwright was impressed with the genuine interest shown by the theatergoing public, unlike the sham interest that prevails, he feels, in New York. Extensively rewritten for its New York run in early 1985 at Joseph Papp's Public Theater, *Coming of Age* concerns the familiar Innaurato subjects of sexual identity and family love; the author calls it, in his introduction to *Best Plays*, "more autobiographical than any I've written, though precisely how I'd rather leave a mystery: I have never been able to reconcile fantasy with reality."

The playwright wrote in the *New York Times*

in 1986 that after the closing of *Coming of Age* "I sincerely swore never to write another play. I had worked for two years on [the] play. . . . In production at the Public Theater I directed it, rewrote it extensively in previews, and then wrote what amounted to a new play. I directed *that* play, rewrote it in previews and lived through a disappointing opening. A few people straggled in to see it over an eight-week run. I made about $2,000 over the four-month period, and that was that. . . . The realistic frame of reference for American playwrights has shrunk. Broadway, the former lifeblood of theater in America, has become, at best, a platform for 'sure bets,' usually defined as largely synthetic musical imports and occasional cavalcade-of-stars extravaganzas. Off-Broadway—now very risky because of production expenses—is only marginally more promising. And these venues are the only ones that can provide playwrights with the 'killing' Robert Anderson once described as the American playwright's safest expectation in terms of a living."

Yet Innaurato retains his love of language, and especially his love of opera. ("I'm still writing operas," he said in 1985. "I think that's the only way to put it. Operas without music.") Critics have often linked the ideas of language and opera in his work. Walter Kerr thought his language "atonally musical, taut and tough as piano wire." The playwright in a 1985 article for the *New York Times* described his "especial love of voices. . . . I believe the human voice is the most perfect instrument, the most completely expressive sign of humanity. . . . I still trudge wherever I can to hear interesting new voices and pieces. I've spent a long time pining away, wishing somehow that I had been able to make a career in music. God knows I tried hard enough. But then again, perhaps I was lucky."

Music and language were literally linked in Innaurato's *Gus and Al*, staged in New York by Playwrights Horizon in early 1989. The Al of the title is Innaurato himself—a Philadelphia-born, New York–based playwright approaching middle age and trying to come to terms with his failures. Gus is the composer Gustav Mahler, whom Al meets in a time-machine type of journey which takes him to Vienna in 1901. At that moment Mahler is in the throes of a complicated domestic life and a mental block that has halted the composition of what is to be his great Fifth Symphony, suffering from a depression that does not yield even to the ministrations of Dr. Sigmund Freud, who is also a character in the play. The two frustrated artists discover that they have much in common, and by the play's end Al has found a kind of redemption in Gus' example of persevering for the sake of art. In-naurato wrote *Gus and Al*, he told Mervyn Rothstein in a *New York Times* interview, to reconcile himself to "the sense of failure that I think is inevitable." He did not intend an exact parallel between himself and Mahler: "Not that we're similar or equivalent in talent—just in the struggle and in dealing with your personal life while you struggle to keep yourself afloat." *Gus and Al* received generally friendly reviews. "Next to Mr. Innaurato's usual theatrical eruptions," Frank Rich wrote in the *New York Times*, "*Gus and Al* is decidedly a chamber piece. The jokes are mild (while sometimes very amusing), the emotions are muted, and the tone is often ruminative. . . . Al's self-pity isn't self-martyrdom so much as a rueful hypersensitivity to the modern world with which he is perpetually at odds." That Innaurato is coming to terms with the modern world is confirmed by his comment to Rothstein: "The play is a journey toward realizing that an artist is a little like a guerrilla fighter. You run out into the gunfire with your arms open and let them shoot at you. And it's very hard to embrace that idea, especially in our century. But I think that at the end of the play Al is able to say, 'Of course, that's what it is.'"

PRINCIPAL WORKS: Bizarre Behavior: Six Plays, 1980 (includes The Transfiguration of Benno Blimpie, Gemini, Ulysses in Traction, Earth Worms, Urlicht, and Wisdom Amok); (with Christopher Durang) The Idiots Karamazov, 1981; Passione, 1981; Best Plays of Albert Innaurato, 1987 (includes Coming of Age in SoHo, The Transfiguration of Benno Blimpie, and Gemini).

ABOUT: Contemporary Authors 122, 1988; Contemporary Literary Criticism 21, 1982; Who's Who in America 1988–1989. *Periodicals*—America April 16, 1977; Harpers May 1978; Nation October 18, 1980; April 6, 1985; New York January 3, 1977; June 6, 1977; June 9, 1980; October 6, 1980; New York Times May 8, 1976; February 13, 1977; March 14, 1977; March 27, 1977; May 27, 1977; May 29, 1977; December 9, 1977; January 25, 1978; May 23, 1980; September 22, 1980; September 24, 1980; September 28, 1980; October 23, 1980; September 5, 1981; March 21, 1983; April 2, 1983; February 4, 1985; February 10, 1985; February 24, 1985; November 24, 1985; July 20, 1986; February 28, 1989; March 20, 1989; New York Times Magazine December 17, 1978; New Yorker December 19, 1977; October 6, 1980; April 6, 1983; February 18, 1985; Newsweek October 6, 1980; Time March 28, 1977; June 2, 1980; Village Voice December 27, 1976; March 21, 1977; April 18, 1977; June 27, 1977.

*INOUE YASUSHI (May 6, 1907–), Japanese novelist and poet, was born in Asahikawa on the northern island of Hokkaidō, the first of four children of Hayao and Yae Inoue. At the time of Inoue's birth, his father, Hayao, was on

° i no͞o ā

INOUE YASUSHI

assignment in Hokkaidō as an army surgeon, but the family's official home was in the village of Kamikano, on the scenic Izu peninsula in Shizuoka Prefecture. Hayao had, in traditional Japanese fashion, been adopted as a son-in-law into the Inoue family when he married Yae, and had inherited the medical practice that the Inoues had followed for seven generations. Yae's father had studied under the surgeon general of the Japanese army and had been director of the prefectural hospital. The Inoue family was therefore of considerable status in the region, and the expectations for eldest sons to carry on the family profession were high.

Hayao was transferred several times after the birth of Yasushi, and finally, in 1913, hoping to bring some stability into their child's life, his parents sent him to live with his grandmother in Shizuoka. This grandmother was in fact a former geisha who had become the common-law wife of Inoue's grandfather. She was not accepted by the villagers, but she and Yasushi formed a close bond against the small society which surrounded them, and for six years the boy was almost constantly in her company. Characters based upon Inoue's memories of his grandmother appear in several of his short stories.

Inoue was enrolled in the local elementary school, but in 1920 his grandmother died and he was sent back to be with his parents, who at this point were living in Hamamatsu. The family remained together for two years, until his father was appointed head of the army hospital in Taipei. Once again Inoue was sent to live with relatives in Shizuoka and this time enrolled in the

Numazu Middle School. He became friends with several students at the school who were interested in literature, and under their tutelage began reading the short stories of Akutagawa Ryūnosuke and Tanizaki Jun'ichirō. He neglected his studies in order to devote himself to the reading of fiction and poetry. Still, the pull of familial duty remained strong, and when he graduated from middle school in 1926, Inoue moved to Kanazawa to be with his parents once again; he also enrolled in the science department of the Kanazawa Fourth Higher School with the intention of proceeding to medical school. It was not long, however, before he lost interest in his classes. He embarked upon a program of self-discipline and self-denial by joining the school's judo club and spending virtually every waking moment in training at the *dojo*. Inoue kept up this routine for three years, then dropped out of the judo club and began writing poetry. He had decided not to pursue a career in medicine, but did not make that decision known to his family until after he failed the entrance examination for the medical school at Kyushu Imperial University in 1930. He was accepted into the university's English literature department instead, but his father, deeply disappointed, resigned his commission and returned to his native region, where he went into semi-hermetic retirement and never practiced medicine again. Inoue soon lost interest in his university classes and left Kyushu for the more lively environs of Tokyo, where he took a room on the second floor of a plant nursery and idled away his time in the company of young dadaist poets and political anarchists. Never involved in political protest himself, he remained fundamentally an outsider—a solitary, like many of the figures in his poetry and prose.

In 1932 Inoue completed his second year at Kyushu Imperial University and then transferred to the philosophy department at Kyoto Imperial University, where he majored in aesthetics. Remarkably for a man who would later achieve fame for the dedicated research he put into his novels, Inoue continued to neglect his studies, leading a life of profligacy, cutting classes, and not even showing up for his graduation exams. He did not receive his degree from the university until 1936, when he turned in a thesis on Valéry's poetry. While enrolled at the university, he published poetry and short stories, took a job in the script department of a film company, wrote a play of his own, and got married (in 1935) to Adachi Fumi. She was the daughter of Adachi Buntarō, an esteemed professor of anthropology at Kyoto Imperial University, and the nephew of Inoue's physician grandfather. A dedicated scholar, Adachi became the model for the central figure in Inoue's short story, "Hira no Shakunage" (The Rhododendrons of Hira, 1950; translated as "The Azaleas of Hira" and "The Rhododendrons"). Several of the stories Inoue wrote received cash awards, which enabled him to sustain his somewhat desultory activities. But he eventually tired of writing for the sole purpose of winning prize money, and turned down requests for manuscripts.

In August of 1936 Inoue took a job at the Osaka office of the Mainichi Shimbun Newspaper Corporation and was assigned to the editorial staff of the weekly magazine *Sandē Mainichi.* He had scarcely settled into the journalistic routine when Japan went to war on the Asian continent. In September of 1937, Inoue was drafted in the wake of the China Incident that had occurred earlier that summer. He was sent to northern China, but he fell ill, was returned to Japan, and released from military service in April of 1938. Unlike most of his contemporaries, whether they saw active service in the Japanese military or not, Inoue has had very little to say about his brief war experience in any of his writings. As always, he has maintained a solitary detachment from much that has transpired in the world around him, focusing his energies instead upon the portrayal of isolated individuals in the present and the past, in both Japan and China.

Upon his return to Japan, Inoue was rehired by the culture department of the Mainichi newspapers, and he was placed in charge of the columns on religion and the arts. This afforded him the opportunity to forge a link with the culture of the classical age; he wrote articles on the Buddhist sutras and traveled frequently to Kyoto and Nara to view traditional paintings, sculpture, and lacquerware. A devotion to these art treasures and a curiosity about the individuals who were involved with them (as creators, patrons, or collectors) are persistent elements Inoue's fiction.

In August of 1945 Inoue was working in the local news section of the Mainichi, and he received the assignment to compose the banner article on the Emperor's surrender broadcast. It was an assignment he fulfilled with distinction, producing an article so rhetorically impressive that it became the talk of the newspaper office. After the end of the war, Inoue increased his production of poetry, but it was with the publication of two short stories in 1947 that he attracted the attention and admiration of the literary world. "Tōgyū" ("The Bull Fight") and "Ryōjū" ("The Hunting Gun") were both entered in a contest for new fiction at a literary journal, but did not achieve the top award. Their poetic introspection was out of line with the mainstream of postwar Japanese writing. But the stories came to the attention of the poet and novelist Satō Haruo, who was so impressed that he had them published in the important journal *Bungakkai.* The attention this brought to Inoue earned him the Akutagawa Prize for literature in February 1950 for "The Bull Fight." Although his recognition as a "newcomer" at the age of forty-two might have been considered paradoxical, critics such as Nakamura Mitsuo have suggested that Inoue's age enabled him to express the views of a mature artist even in these first postwar stories. "The Hunting Gun," an effective application of poetic sensibility to a tangled love relationship, takes the form of three letters written to the male protagonist by his wife, his secret mistress (who also happens to be his wife's cousin and dear friend), and his mistress' daughter, who discovers her mother's diary account of the liaison. The story opens with a poem about a solitary hunter carrying a rifle on his shoulder, but the stark realities of human betrayal and pain that are gradually revealed through the letters shatter the pastoral quality of that image and suffuse it with extraordinary loneliness and sorrow. Inoue here has, in the words of Sadamichi Yokoo and Sanford Goldstein, "gather[ed] fictional materials around the core of a poem; poetry and story are dramatically integrated."

The encouragement Inoue gained from his receipt of the Akutagawa Prize gave him the initiative in 1951 to resign from the newspaper firm, move to Tokyo, and devote himself exclusively to his creative writings. Over the next six or seven years his literary output consisted primarily of popular novels, many of them based on contemporary incidents, which Inoue treated in the journalistic style he had perfected in his fifteen years with Mainichi. The first such novel *Kuroi Ushio* (The Black Tide, 1950), speculated about the circumstances surrounding the mysterious death of the president of the national railways the previous year. The most important of these books is *Hyōheki* (The Ice Cliff, 1957), inspired by the death in a climbing accident of a well-known Japanese mountaineer; it received the Academy of Arts Prize in 1959.

The series of works for which Inoue is best known and admired, however, are his historical novels set along the silk road of China. Some of these works reflect Inoue's romantic fascination with the cross-cultural encounters that have occurred along that highway; others are minutely-researched accounts of the arduous journeys and hardships endured by the early cultural and religious pioneers of East Asia. One of the first and most successful of these writings is *Tempyō no*

Iraka (The Roof Tile of Tempyō, 1957), which received the Ministry of Education Prize for literature. Set in the early eighth century, at a time when the Japanese were intent upon importing and absorbing elements of Chinese society and culture in an attempt to renovate their own, the novel describes the travails of four young Japanese Buddhist priests who make the arduous ocean journey to China in order to escort the eminent Chinese monk, Ganjin, back to Japan, where he is to establish the rites of ordination and monastic discipline. The young priests are repeatedly delayed or thwarted by weather or bureaucratic red tape, but they remain firmly dedicated to their mission. Paralleling this saga is the story of another devout monk, Gōgyō, who has spent years hunched over his desk, copying scriptures to transport to Japan. The delicate ephemerality of these human endeavors, one of Inoue's most persistent themes, is described in the waking dream one priest has of Gōgyō's ship crossing the channel: "He saw the waves rising mightily and felt the ship being tossed about like a leaf. . . . He saw dozens of tightly wound scrolls sinking, one after another, into the deep azure—scroll after scroll, fluttering as if alive, sinking and disappearing among the undulating turquoise strands on the ocean floor. Emerging from this vision of the scrolls—from the image of scrolls sinking down and down, each following another—was the sense, a revelation perhaps, of a constant, infinite process; there was a realization of loss, of certain, irreparable loss. Each time his eyes returned to that scene, from somewhere the anguished cry of Gōgyō could be heard."

The same year that *The Roof Tile of Tempyō* was published, Inoue led a delegation of Japanese writers to China at the invitation of the Mao government. He produced further historical tales set in China in *Ro-ran* (Lou-lan, 1959) and *Tonkō* (Tun-huang, 1959), speculating in the latter over the reasons why a trove of Buddhist manuscripts came to be hidden away in the Thousand Buddha Caves of the Tun-huang region. He also produced several novels set in the ruling houses of Japan: *Yodo-dono Nikki* (The Diary of Lady Yodo, 1961), which describes the life of one of the more colorful medieval women, the consort of the great warrior Hideyoshi; and *Go-Shirakawa In* (The Retired Emperor Go-Shirakawa, 1972) are examples of this mode.

In 1964 Inoue was elected to membership in the Japan Academy of Arts. He continued to travel widely to gather materials for his books: a journey to Korea produced the novel *Fūtō* (1963, translated as *Wind and Waves*), about the attempts of the Korean empire to stave off the Mongol attacks, while his sojourn to the United States in 1964 eventually resulted in the long, complex account of Japanese immigration to America, *Wadatsumi* (The God of the Sea, 1977). In 1965 he spent two months traveling in Central Asia; his collection of essays *Saiiki Monogatari* (Journey Beyond Samarkand, 1969) draws upon these and other travels in the area. Inoue was appointed a summer scholar-in-residence at the University of Hawaii in 1967, and lectured there on Japanese literature. The materials he gathered on a trip to the Soviet Union in 1968 found fruition in *Oroshiya Kokusui Mutan* (A Bemusing Tale about Russia), a tale of several Japanese who are shipwrecked off the coast of Russia in the eighteenth century and wander the Siberian mainland; it received the first Grand Prize for Japanese Literature in 1969.

From 1969 to 1972, Inoue served as chairman of the board of directors for the Japan Literary Association, the primary association of writers in his country. In 1972, a thirty-two volume collection of his fiction was produced by Shinchōsha, the leading publishing house in Japan. That same year a memorial association was created in memory of the Japanese Nobel laureate, Kawabata Yasunari, and Inoue was appointed chairman of it. Inoue's sense of affinity with Kawabata is strong, and in his later career he has sometimes seemed to be following in Kawabata's footsteps. In 1973, an Inoue Yasushi Literary Library was built near his hometown, and a year later, while he was touring China, he was appointed to the committee which is charged with the protection of important Japanese cultural properties.

In 1975, two years after his mother's death, Inoue collected three essays he had written about her since 1964 into a memorial volume titled *Waga Haha no Ki* (Chronicle of My Mother). James Kirkup says of these memoirs, "They cover the ten years or so of his mother's decline into a senility that is at once pathetic, clinically factual and unexpectedly comic. Inoue records her gradual decline with great tenderness and concern, but quite without sentimentality. . . . Inoue has always written well about desolate and lonely figures, and in this extraordinary portrait of his own mother he has surpassed himself."

In 1976, at the age of sixty-nine, Inoue received the highest honor his country can afford a writer, the Order of Cultural Merit; he was simultaneously designated a "person of cultural merit," an official government classification. His travels to China continued unabated past his seventieth birthday. In 1981, he published one of his most sensitive novels, *Honkakubō Ibun* (Papers Left by the Priest Honkaku), a quiet, reflective study of the motivations behind the suicide of Japan's first tea master, Sen no Rikyū. Inoue was elected president of the Japan PEN club in 1983, and he organized the international conference of PEN, which was held in Tokyo in the spring of 1984. At the conference, he was elected an international vice president of that organization, once again treading in the tracks of his predecessor, Kawabata Yasunari. Since the early 1980s, Japanese newspaper reporters have clustered outside Inoue's house every year at the time the winners of the Nobel Prize are announced.

WORKS IN ENGLISH TRANSLATION: "The Azaleas of Hira" (later retitled "The Rhododendrons") was translated by Edward Seidensticker in 1955; "The Hunting Gun" was translated by Sadamichi Yokoo and Sanford Goldstein in 1961; *The Counterfeiter, and Other Stories* was translated by Leon Picon in 1965; *Journey Beyond Samarkand* was translated in 1971 by Gyo Furuta and Gordon Sager; *The Roof Tile of Tempyō* was translated in 1975 by James T. Araki; *Tun-huang* was translated in 1978 by Jean Oda Moy; *Loulan and Other Stories*, translated by James T. Araki and Edward Seidensticker, was published in 1979; Jean Oda Moy also translated *Chronicle of My Mother* in 1982. *Wind and Waves*, in James T. Aroki's translation, was published in 1988.

ABOUT: Encyclopedia of Japan, 1984. Nihon Kindai Bungaku Daijiten, 1984. *Periodicals*—Times Literary Supplement April 28, 1989.

*JANDL, ERNST (August 1, 1925–), Austrian poet, essayist, and playwright, writes in English: "I was born in Vienna, and I still live there. My mother Luise, very long after her death, gave her name to the title of my second book, *Laut und Luise*. This, of course, is a pun on 'loud and quiet,' for the book contains poems that have to be read aloud, as well as some very quiet ones, to be looked at in silence, 'leise.' There is a humorous touch to many of them, and only a few strictly observe the rules of the language—so why not give them a pun for their overall title. If it could only have made her smile once more, my mother Luise who taught me all about poetry in the last eight years of her life, when she began to write poems in a courageous response to myasthenia gravis, of which she was found to suffer shortly after the birth of her third child, my youngest brother.

"My father, Viktor Jandl, a romantic at heart, was a fine draftsman and painter of water-colors who, alas, had to earn his living as a bank clerk. He took me to the exhibitions and showed me the work of the masters. He took me out into the country. He took me to the church and to the

ERNST JANDL

cemetery. He made me aware of the beauty of nature, the dignity of art, and the transience of life.

"There were religious processions, and there were military parades, and then there were the German soldiers and the SA and SS in their uniforms and the flags with the swastika, and each year of growing up as a pupil at what still resembled a grammar school moved you nearer to the deadly threat of the war. Friends, such as I was fortunate in having, could confide to one another that unless Germany was defeated and the Nazis were wiped out and liberty and democracy restored there was no chance for any of us to become citizens of the modern world, which to us was the world of abstract painting, expressionist writing, atonality and jazz, psychoanalysis, imagination unlimited. I got out of the war as PW of the U.S. forces early in 1945, and this was freedom. When repatriated after eleven months in England, I started my studies of English and German at Vienna University. In 1949 I began work as a teacher.

"'You should write your poems, not play the piano,' said my very best friend Dietrich Burkhard, a boy of exquisite musical talent who was killed in the war; he was playing the oboe in a military band when I last saw him. Since those grammar school days I never really stopped writing poems, and, later, some prose, a play or two, radio-plays, lectures on poetry, essays. The piano has remained closed. In 1956 I had my first book of poems, here in Vienna, but the second, bearing a punning title, did not appear until ten years later, even though almost all the

*yahn´dl

funny and serious poems in it were written before 1960. They were, however, the result of a new way of writing that I had discovered, inspired by the bold and powerful style of Gertrude Stein. This made them unpublishable at the time.

"'Shall we never be published?' was the question, for years, on many long walks through the Vienna Woods, Friederike Mayröcker and I asking each other; 'Shall we never be published?' That was ages ago. Today we are both published in Germany, and welcomed in Austria. Friederike Mayröcker, my companion since 1954, and my intimate critic, has reached a supreme level of writing. She is my religion.

"In the early 1950s, Eugen Gomringer, Swiss, invented concrete poetry, which was to break down the barriers of national languages. What an ambitious goal. I tried it my own way, and succeeded, if only for minutes, with *Sprechgedichte* (poems to be spoken) and sound poems, before audiences in London and in Toronto. These were highlights in my days as a poet. Another unforgettable thing was the way to reach children, by some of my poems. Another, to have them combined with music, and offer them to a restless audience, my fleeting voice joined by the saxophone and the vibraharp and the beautiful timbre of Lauren Newton, or supported by the heavenly powers of the organ and the trombone. Really, neither jazz nor the angels were very far.

"I believe in poetry, as a form of art and, almost, a way of living, although I know that I shall not go on living, certainly not, and am not going to be deep-freezed, certainly not, and am not even sure if I deserve the word living."

If any single figure can be said to have defined German avant-garde literature since the end of World War II, it is Ernst Jandl. Identified primarily with the genre of concrete poetry (in which words and/or letters are used as design elements to explore the borderland between literature and the visual arts), his experimental work extends beyond this into all areas of linguistic invention. For German-language audiences Jandl is also a performer, a very effective one according to reports, both in personal platform readings of his work and in his recordings and video cassettes. Readers of his first published volume *Andere Augen* (Other Eyes, 1956) identified him with a group of young writers experimenting in dadaism, expressionism and surrealism known as the Wiener Gruppe, as he was later to become identified with another avant-garde group, the Graz Circle. Essentially, however,

Jandl works independently (though often in close collaboration with Friederike Mayröcker) exploring the mysteries and the absurdities of language. His premise is that language can be expressive even when it is meaningless, and his aim is to write "poetry without preconceived ideas." Still, there is method and purpose in what he is doing. Michael Butler, in an essay in *Modern Austrian Writing*, describes Jandl's poetry as a conscious and deliberate attempt "to jolt language (and thus perception) out of stereotyped modes of expression by using it in three dimensions—semantic, phonetic, and visual."

The results are always intriguing, sometimes baffling and grotesque, sometimes hilarious. His experiments, for example, in *Oberflächen übersetzungen* (surface translation) produce aural imitations, as in this German echo of Wordsworth's "My heart leaps up when I behold a rainbow in the sky": "mai hart lieb zapfen eibe hold / er renn bohr in sees kai." But the nonsense elements often take a serious, even grim turning. His mock "Ode auf n" uses the letters of "Napoleon," Siegbert S. Prawer points out, "to suggest the senselessness of drilling and killing in pursuit of glory":

```
lepn
nepl
lepn
nepl
lepn
nepl
o lepn
o nepl
nnnnnnnn
```

The poem builds to its climax until the name Napoleon sounds like a donkey's bray—"naaaaaaaaaaaa." Using the poetic device of onomatopoeia Jandl communicates with pure sound. Prawer also cites one of his *Lautegedichte* (sound poems) in which he plays on the word *Schützengraben* (military entrenchment) to convey the horror of war. Reducing the word to its consonants—schtzngrbn—he "proceeds to dismember the word, painting in sound the noise of the trenches under fire and ending with suggestions of the death of the soldier whose experience we had, by implication, shared."

Radical as Jandl's work often is, he has also written in traditional lyric form, as witness his "Bitte Keine Musik" ("No Music Please"):

On the cold grass of the stone tiles,
no giants grow.
If you blew into this horn—
alas, only a thin whimper would come.

On the cold lawn of stone
no lions walk.
If you blew into this flute—

no bird-whisper would answer you.

On this washbasin, rolled flat,
there are no grasshoppers.
If you tried this song again,
the tongue would stick in your shoe.

—trans. Georg Rapp

Even many of his experimental poems, Michael Hamburger points out, "can be seen as developments of recognized and time-honored media. Nor, unlike other Concrete poets, can Jandl be accused of narrowing the scope of lyrical poetry as such . . . observations, reflections, feelings and ingenuity contribute to its effect, even where his material has been reduced to the components of a single word . . . ."

Jandl's playfulness with language does not conceal the darker implications of his work—the threat of war, his frustration with what he perceives as the banality and decadence of much modern culture, and most of all his personal depression, his anxieties about his creativity as a writer and the coming of old age and death. Much of this despair is reflected in his witty and candid play *Aus der Fremde* (From Abroad, 1980). Subtitled *Sprechoper in 7 Szenen*, it may be either spoken or sung in production, but the form of the play is very precise. The speeches in each of the scenes are of exactly three lines of fewer than ten words, and the three characters—he and she, both middle-aged writers, and a third younger speaker—speak only in the third person subjunctive. The play appears to be autobiographical, the older writers representing Jandl and Friederike Mayröcker; and the older man is insecure about his creativity, suffering a critical case of writer's block. In spite of the formidable difficulties of staging such a work, it has been produced to critical acclaim in theaters in Austria and Germany. "The play is easy to follow," Robert Acker wrote in *World Literature Today* in 1981; "it is witty and entertaining. Rarely has a dramatist exposed his mental framework so openly on the stage."

Since the late 1970s Jandl's poetry has similarly reflected his increasing anxieties about himself. In such collections as *Die Bearbeitung der Mütze* (The Treatment of the Cap, 1978) and *Der Gelbe Hund* (The Yellow Dog, 1980) there have also been interesting stylistic changes, less emphasis on wordplay and more on the sheer difficulty of living, expressed in what Acker describes as "a reduced language in the form of *Gastarbeiter* (foreign worker) German or children's German which is characterized by the use of the infinitive of the verb and a simple grammatical structure . . . a reflection of the author's changed relationship to himself and to the world. . . . The poet's own feeling of inadequacy finds its equivalent in an inadequate, mistake-ridden language."

Jandl's apparent self-doubt is not the result of a lack of recognition. He has received many honors and awards—among them the esteemed Georg Träkl Prize for poetry (1974), the Vienna State Prize for literature (1976), and the Georg Büchner Prize (1974). He is the subject of several book-length critical studies in German and has published collections of his essays and lectures in two volumes: *Die schöne Kunst des Schreibens* (The Fine Art of Writing, 1976) and *Das Öffnen und Schliessen des Munde* (Opening and Closing the Mouth, 1985). He has also traveled abroad giving readings of his work, and in 1971 he was visiting professor at the University of Texas in Austin. Jandl has published German translations of American writers—among these Robert Creeley's *The Island* (1965), John Cage's *Silence* (1969), and Gertrude Stein's *Narration* (1971).

WORKS IN ENGLISH TRANSLATION: Because of the eccentric linguistic character of Jandl's writing, little of his work has been translated. In 1967 a small collection (eight short poems) appeared in a bilingual German-English translation *No Music Please* by Georg Rapp. Selections from his poetry are included in the anthology *Austrian Poetry Today*, edited and translated by Milne Holton and Herbert Kuhner, 1985.

ABOUT: Best, A. and H. Wolfschütz. Modern Austrian Writing, 1980; Columbia Dictionary of Modern European Literature, 1980; Contemporary Literary Criticism 34, 1985; Prawer, S. S., R. H. Thomas, L. Forster. Essays in German Language, Culture and Society, 1969. *Periodicals*—World Literature Today Autumn 1980, Autumn 1981.

JOHNSON, DENIS (1949–), American novelist and poet, was born in Munich, Germany, the son of a United States diplomat. He grew up in various countries, including the Philippines and Japan, as well as in the Washington, D.C., area, depending on his father's postings. He has released very little in the way of autobiographical information, but he is known to have attended school in Washington, and he spent several years at the University of Iowa Writers' Workshop.

Johnson's novels should be called experimental rather than popular in structure, characterization, and plot. They are not, however, especially difficult to read or recondite in their references; indeed, his characters often have little education and communicate in varieties of street language. His overriding theme—it occurs in each of his novels published so far—is that a minimum of hope and spare, meager human re-

DENIS JOHNSON

silience can sustain outcast members of a society that is *in extremis*, crumbling everywhere. *Angels* tells the realistic, almost unrelievedly grim story of two self-destructive drifters: Jamie Mays, on the run across America with her two children from an unfaithful husband, and Bill Houston, a former convict, three times divorced. They meet on a bus leaving Oakland, fall in love, spend time in a decrepit motel in Pittsburgh, then separate. Their reunion occurs in Chicago, a place, like the rest of Johnson's America, of nightmarish degradation and tawdry, unsatisfiable emotional and sexual urges. Jamie is raped while searching for Bill—an act of brutal senselessness which leads to her psychic breakdown. The couple go next to Phoenix, a blighted city in the desert, sick with pollution, where Bill resumes a life of crime, kills a bank guard, and is sentenced to death in the gas chamber, while Jamie becomes mired in alcoholism and drug addiction. But their separate ends are not as hopeless as their beginnings, and what salvation they receive they earn squarely on their own. "I'll be in therapy," says Jamie, "a halfway house, One Day at a Time, Attitude of Gratitude, the whole program. I mean to get my kids back, or die on the way." As for Bill, he is far from the stereotype of the killer, vicious and amoral; he is revealed as a man whose self-awareness, which comes to him at the very moment of his death, is life-affirming and deeply spiritual.

Angels won considerable praise from the critics for the simple truth of its characterization and the humanity of Johnson's intent. Philip

Roth, in the London *Sunday Times*, called it "a small masterpiece." Alice Hoffman, writing in the *New York Times Book Review*, thought Jamie and Bill "people who slip helplessly into their own worst nightmares" and the novel "a terrifying book, a mixture of poetry and obscenity, . . . a dazzling and savage first novel." The main characters, to Peter Prescott in *Newsweek*, "are naked save for their humanity. Without making a fuss, Johnson defines that humanity precisely." "It is," according to Speer Morgan in *Saturday Review*, "carefully wrought, line to line, and by the end of the book the reader achieves empathy with its characters. *Angels* is a fine first novel."

Johnson passed in his second novel from the sad realism of *Angels* to the surreal futurism of *Fiskadoro*, set in the Florida Keys in the mid-twenty-first century, some sixty years after a nuclear holocaust. The book is no less grim and gritty than its predecessor, but its characters' enlightenment is purchased somewhat more easily, and they are less rebarbative, more appreciably human from the beginning, even, in some respect, admirable and likable. The three principal characters are Fiskadoro, a teenage boy, who asks A. T. Cheung, a ragtime clarinetist whose book-study group is intent on reconstructing prenuclear society, to teach him to play the clarinet he has inherited. Mr. Cheung's Grandmother Wright, a mute woman more than a century old, is the group's and the novel's touchstone of reality, because she remembers childhood experiences during the Vietnam War. The book's other group, the more inchoate one, is composed of people who recall nothing of and care nothing for the past: many of them are mutant creatures who have inherited the poisoned genes caused by the holocaust; others are savages who inhabit a blighted jungle; all live by a primitive kind of fishing and by barter. Voodoo is standard medical practice and is miserably unsuccessful. Fiskadoro is a member of this latter group, and he has been violently deprived of any memory, but his relationship with Mr. Cheung, initiated by him, intrigues the thoughtful, kindly older man: it may be that only those without memory, unobsessed with sad fragments of the unrecoverable past, can shape the new world that must be created if mankind is to have any hope of survival. And survival, the rebirth of civilization, is the only path that can be taken.

Eva Hoffman, writing in the *New York Times Book Review*, called *Fiskadoro* "startlingly original . . . an examination of the cataclysmic imagination, a parable of apocalypse. . . . [Its] physical geography is gritty, lyrical, surrealistic, a landscape so densely remote, and so disjointed, that it affects one like a feverish dream whose symbols and images demand interpretation." Jill Neville, however, in the *Times Literary Supplement*, criticized Johnson for making "the reader flounder inside the strangeness of his apocalyptic vision. Too much is left unexplained for it to anchor firmly in the mind; we have to make too many assumptions" about the characters.

The Stars at Noon is set in war-torn Nicaragua in 1984, but its true locale, allegorically speaking, is Hell. The nameless narrator, a young American woman on the run, describes herself as "a contact person for Eyes for Peace," but appears to be a reporter for *Roundup* magazine. She is drunken, degraded, self-despising, not in control of any aspect of her life. No one in her story gets other than temporary names. "I thought," Johnson said in a publication interview, "it was appropriate that the people in hell wouldn't have any names. She refers to a couple of people with names, then withdraws them." She has amassed a great number of cordobas, the worthless local currency, from selling sexual services but needs dollars in order to escape from the country, and dollars are impossible to come by. She becomes reluctantly involved in the rescue of a British businessman, a man so helpless, so out of touch with his surroundings, that he is in danger of being annihilated by both sides for having once innocently spoken the truth about the war. They are thereafter on the run from both murderous antagonists. Their flight south from Managua through the pestilential jungle has a horrific quality, real and unreal at the same time, as they try to escape a repellent yet seductive American agent, while political difficulties mount for them and they seem even to fall in love. Their end is unclear, as is, of course, the entire Central American crisis through which they have traveled. He may well have been killed; she may well have survived only to have become an even more degraded prostitute in Costa Rica.

Using a person so out of touch to narrate such a spiritual parable of greed and exploitation seems to have displeased several reviewers. Caryn James, in the *New York Times Book Review*, while calling the author "one of our most inventive, unpredictable novelists," and *The Stars at Noon* "daring, this political novel that disdains politics, this philosophical work that rejects all philosophies," nevertheless singled out as the book's "most serious flaw" the fact that "the narrator is a cardboard mouthpiece for the author. With her religious imagery and taste for irony, her philosophical attitudes toward everything from her own prostitution to Managua's oppressive heat, it's not plausible that she could remain so willfully dazed. Mr. Johnson's first-rate soul-searching is trapped in her

second-rate mind, which frequently borrows the author's eloquence and intellectual rigor." Anthony Beevor, in the *Times Literary Supplement*, criticized "Johnson's mouthpiece's flip bravado when it comes to descriptions and similes. Filtering everything through her becomes, not just a distraction, but a liability."

Three of Johnson's four volumes of poetry had appeared before he began to publish his fiction. His poetic debut was generally considered extremely accomplished: at the age of twenty he produced *The Man Among the Seals*, published by Iowa City's Stone Wall Press. This is an elegantly printed book of thirty-two medium-length lyrics; there are few short impressionistic pieces, and only a couple of the longer poems he was later to specialize in. His theme is primarily the epiphanic moments of reality that are thrust upon one in the midst of quotidian existence. He can achieve an extraordinary, quiet poignancy, as in "Checking the Traps," a poem of almost Franciscan meditative intensity about a moment of realization by a man who has been made to kill two house mice by his pregnant wife, who is frightened of them:

> half
>
> the night i stayed awake and smoked
> and watched the mousetraps.
> the mice were there, nudging
> into cups and plates, one fell
>
> into the toaster, but escaped.
> they waited until i gave up and slept to die.
> for these mice
> the night will be long. i heard
>
> the iron snapping
> in my sleep and dreamed my wife was
> closing the door. . . .
>
>   i wonder, were they
> married? was she pregnant? they are
> going out together,
> in the garbage this morning. it was
> morning when we were married.
> it has been morning
>
> for a long time. that mouse, with his
> eye, did he hear the iron snapping,
> and dream it was his
>
> wife with her stretching, laden tits
> closing the door?

In Johnson's subsequent volumes his poems and their narrative lines have lengthened and seem in the process to have lost this deliciously sweet, lyrical immediacy and intimacy of fused expression and feeling. *The Incognito Lounge and Other Poems* contains a great deal of extended description of the down-and-out aspects and anomie of life in the contemporary United

States and along the way much cleverly and sensitively reproduced urban speech. "The Boarding" is the monologue of a poor, sick old woman for whom getting on a long-awaited bus is a kind of ascension:

> putting
> this left-hand foot way up
> on the step so this dress rides up,
> grabbing this metal pole like
> a beam of silver falling down
> from Heaven to my aid, thank-you,
> hollering, "Watch det my medicine
> one second for me will you dolling,
> I'm four feet and det's a tall bus
> you got and it's hot and I got
> every disease they are making
> these days, my God, Jesus Christ,
> I'm telling you out of my soul."

The Incognito Lounge was one of the five collection of poetry published for 1982 in the National Poetry Series, which had been established in 1978. Each collection was chosen by one older, more established poet; Johnson's was the choice of Mark Strand. Donald S. Share in *Library Journal* called the poems in *The Incognito Lounge* "as busy and alive as the urban places that inspired them. . . . City life, a 'honky-tonk of terror and delight,' is filled with fleeting revelations of joy and desolation." Alan Williamson, in the *New York Times Book Review*, claimed that Johnson's poems had persuaded him "that he suffers over the anomie he describes. He is hard on himself, as well as on the culture; and he is agonizingly aware that life can be, and has been, different from the life around him. . . . [He is] good at American voices, so good that I wish he wrote dramatic monologues more often."

The Veil continues Johnson's experimentation with longer poetic forms. The monologue becomes ever more central in his treatment of the sad disenchantment of his characters' vision; yet the device, with its colloquial chattiness, detracts somewhat from the compression and intensity his themes of alienation and desperation need for their perfect realization and expression. Reviewers were, by and large, not satisfied with this disharmony. "Johnson's language at times seems inflated," wrote Paul Breslin in *Poetry*, "his cosmic reverberations too vast for their occasion." His "loose, prosaic constructs lack resonance," according to Fred Muratori in *Library Journal*, "and though they sometimes amuse and surprise, one detects a glibness that belies the nightmare. It's all just too chic to be true." Stephen Dobyns, in the *New York Times Book Review*, detected "a lot of hokum" in *The Veil*. "When one sees how well [Johnson] can do some things, one feels particularly impatient if

he does something badly. He has great gifts as a poet. I wish he would use them to better advantage."

WORKS: *Poetry*—The Man Among the Seals, 1969; Inner Weather, 1976; The Incognito Lounge and Other Poems, 1982; The Veil, 1987. *Fiction*—Angels, 1983; Fiskadoro, 1985; The Stars at Noon, 1986.

ABOUT: Contemporary Authors 121, 1987; Contemporary Novelists, 1986. *Periodicals*—Booklist September 1, 1986; Books April 1987; Bulletin of the Atomic Scientists March 1986; Christian Science Monitor July 31, 1985; Commonweal August 9, 1985; Kirkus Reviews August 1, 1986; Library Journal April 1, 1982; August 1983; May 15, 1985; September 1, 1986; July 1987; Listener May 28, 1987; London Review of Books April 23, 1987; New Statesman May 31, 1985; New York Times Book Review October 10, 1982; October 2, 1983; May 26, 1985; September 28, 1986; October 18, 1987; Newsweek September 19, 1983; July 8, 1985; Poetry October 1988; Saturday Review October 1983; May–June 1985; Times Literary Supplement May 4, 1984; May 24, 1985; March 27, 1987; Village Voice October 28, 1986; Voice Youth Advocates October 1985.

JOLLEY, ELIZABETH (1923–), Australian novelist and short-story writer, was born in the industrial Midlands of England. She was brought up in a German-speaking household; her mother, the daughter of an Austrian general, met her English husband while he was engaged in famine relief work in Austria in 1919. Elizabeth Jolley was educated at home and in a Quaker boarding school. In 1959 she moved from England to western Australia with her husband, Leonard Jolley, a librarian, and their three children. While working as a nurse and at such jobs as door-to-door salesperson and real estate agent, she wrote on her own for twenty years before her first novel was published. She has taught part-time in the Department of English at the Western Australian Institute of Technology and has conducted writing workshops in community centers and prisons. In recent years she has lived in a suburb of Perth in western Australia, dividing her time between writing and tending her nearby orchard and farm, where she raises geese.

Jolley's unsettling, mordantly witty, but compassionate novels are populated by lonely or estranged women and men who are often caught between two irreconcilable worlds or visions of the world and who seek release through forbidden love or the imagination of such love. Her work is realistic in approach but formally inventive, frequently relying on interlocking stories and on self-reflexive anticipations and echoes. "Characters, situations, phrases, images recur

ELIZABETH JOLLEY

throughout the novels and stories until they come to seem like old friends," wrote A. P. Riemer in an essay on her work in the journal *Southerly*. "We observe their transformations, how they are expanded or contracted, the manner in which they are presented from various perspectives." Joanna Motion, in the *Times Literary Supplement*, wrote: "Her preoccupations recur: a passion for music and the natural world are constant elements. A related series of disappointed, more or less lesbian, professional women stalk her pages. The dense skirts of a Viennese inheritance swing through her rooms. But she reappraises these constituents from different and enlivening angles." But perhaps the most essential recurrent theme is what Riemer calls a "sense of displacement, or of half-belonging."

Jolley first attracted critical attention and acclaim in North America and Britain in 1982 for *Mr. Scobie's Riddle*, but she had already published two novels in Australia, *Palomino* and *The Newspaper of Claremont Street*. *Palomino* tells the story of a love affair between an older woman and the daughter of a woman she once loved, a love that is burdened with ironies and overtones of fatality. Riemer found it "the least successful of Mrs. Jolley's works," its "mixture of 'elevated' prose and melodramatic material unfortunate. . . . Yet the novel has some interest because it sharpens, and in a sense translates into metaphor, that clash of cultures which informs much of the other work." Josephine Hendin, in the *New York Times Book Review*, thought that the characters were "so limited to their love for each other that Ms. Jolley resorts to ever more

improbable, if witty, surprises to sustain involvement" and that "the mythic reverberations of the affair" were occasionally "too loud." But the character of the older woman, "blending tragic knowledge and absurd hopes, is an achievement of tragicomic art."

In *The Newspaper of Claremont Street*, Claremont Street is a suburban street in Australia and "the newspaper" is the nickname of a cleaning woman, Margarite Morris, also known as "Weekly," who goes from house to house along the street, dusting and vacuuming and spreading gossip and other news. She saves her money in order to buy a plot of land in the wilderness. Praising the novel's "controlled poignancy" Linda Taylor wrote, in the *Times Literary Supplement*, "A lasting image is that of Weekly, an anachronistic bride of nature, under the falling petals of her carefully planted pear tree, doing her primitive dance." The dance is made all the more triumphant because under the pear tree is buried an enemy, a Middle European aristocratic woman who had taken advantage of her. "It is," said Taylor, "sweet revenge for the kind of wryly tenacious figure who is seen to deserve all the prizes in Jolley's meanly grasping suburban universe."

Reviewing *Mr. Scobie's Riddle* in the *New York Times Book Review*, Thomas M. Disch called it "a satire of great verve and acerbity." It is set amid "the horrors of the grotesquely squalid and oppressive nursing home of St. Christopher and St. Jude" (as Disch put it), where the mild, wistful, long-suffering Mr. Scobie dreams of his former life and longs for escape while the predatory matron of the place schemes to get him to sign over his pension and property to the institution. Eventually he realizes that the only escape is death. The novel is given metaphorical resonance by a nocturnal poker game in which the nursing home itself is at stake and by the dilemma of its inmates, mostly demented or senile, who can't survive in the outside world and can't bear the oppressive regime of the matron. Apart from Mr. Scobie, another character embodies several of Jolley's familiar themes: Miss Hailey, devoted to German music and literature, who had been headmistress of a fashionable girls' school but had lost everything after a lesbian incident with a favored pupil whom she had taken to Bayreuth. According to Riemer, "it is through Miss Hailey and the playful seriousness with which she is depicted that this novel makes some not-at-all-unimportant statements about the predicament of the artist, the condition of the hopeless wayfarer in a world seemingly dedicated to the materialistic 'order' for which the hospital is a vital image." But for Disch it is Mr. Scobie who remains "the focus of our sympathy" as "someone at the very bottom of all pecking orders, an endlessly abused sufferer." The conflict between the matron and him is "as stark in its contrast between a farcical evil and a lyric, helpless good as the persecution of Little Nell by the dwarf Quilp in *The Old Curiosity Shop.*"

In *Miss Peabody's Inheritance*, Jolley created a particularly complex and elegant vehicle for her concern with the artist inhabiting a world in which imagination may be the only form of liberation. In an essay in the *New York Times Book Review*, the novelist Robert Coover summarized its ingenious convolutions: "Miss Peabody . . . is a lonely English spinster, well past her prime, who sends a timid fan letter to the exotic Australian romancer Diana Hopewell, thereby initiating an elaborate correspondence between the two women in which the novelist in effect seduces the spinster with details of her work-in-progress about three elderly lesbians traveling through Europe with a young schoolgirl. When Miss Peabody starts confusing fiction and reality, she is asked to take a leave from her secretarial job, whereupon she flies off to Australia to meet her idol. But too late. She has died ignominiously, a sick old woman, in a nursing home. Miss Peabody is left with the projected novel, her 'inheritance.'" But the inherited bawdy fantasy of the dead artist finally redeems Miss Peabody from her drab and constrained existence.

The consequence of Jolley's deft orchestration of narratives within narratives in the novel "is not, as one might fear, that of attending a seminar on postmodern fiction," Disch wrote in the *New York Times Book Review*. Jolley's "motive for exploring the complex, three-way bond between novelists and readers and the 'characters' of fiction would appear to spring from an old-fashioned concern for morality, in this case the morality of imaginative experience. At a time when feminists are urging that pornography be banned as a violation of their civil rights, Mrs. Jolley's concern is timely— a canny reminder that fantasy may be the last redoubt of freedom and, as such, should not be meddled with."

Like *Miss Peabody's Inheritance*, *Foxybaby* also contains a story-in-progress within the story and thus becomes "an exploration of the intricacies of the imagination," Lesley Chamberlain wrote in the *Times Literary Supplement*. At a remote, rundown Australian summer school called Trinity College, "Alma Porch, unmarried, unsure, ugly and indeterminately middle-aged, agrees to tutor a creative drama course for obese and aspiring women, and opens a Pandora's box of unsuppressed ill-chosen passions, midnight feasts and loneliness" by having the women act

out her drama-in-progress. The women, caught up in the tense drama about a lonely man's love for his drug-addicted daughter, become emotionally involved, urge the often despondent Miss Porch to keep creating, and finally in effect bring the story to life, fusing it with the story of the novel itself. The relationship between the lonely Miss Porch and Anna, the student she has chosen to act the leading role in her drama, not only carries the lesbian erotic theme found in Jolley's other novels but also becomes a parable of the author's connection to the characters she creates, resulting, as Chamberlain wrote, in "an unusual novel about the genderless erotic adventure of writing."

In her review of *Foxybaby* in the *New York Times Book Review*, the British novelist Angela Carter found the blending of comic tone and serious matter in the novel disturbing but successful: "Part of Mrs. Jolley's comic method is to juxtapose profound feeling with low farce, high camp with agonized lyricism. *Foxybaby* is a deeply and, I suspect, intentionally disorienting read." But in her *New York Times* review, Michiko Kakutani said that only the purely comic passages stood up: the "narrow, cartoon-like characterization lends the first portion of *Foxybaby* some very amusing, if broadly drawn, moments, but it creates problems when Mrs. Jolley makes it clear that she does not merely want to write a straightforward satire, that she also wants to make a sobering commentary on the consequences of loneliness and isolation." Calling the play within the novel a "lurid melodrama," Kakutani concluded that Miss Porch, her fictional creations, and her students were all too "flimsy" and "predictable and pat" to support the novel's metafictional ambitions. "To make matters worse," she added, "we don't ever really sympathize with the melancholia these people all experience at the end of the novel—we've grown so accustomed to laughing at their peccadilloes in the first portion of the book that we're never really persuaded to take them seriously later on."

Milk and Honey, published in 1986 but written much earlier, is a darker, more macabre novel than Jolley's others, without the usual patina of acerbic social comedy. Told as a monologue, it is the story of a frustrated young man who is drawn into a Central European family that has insulated itself from the surrounding Australian culture. A guilt-ridden marriage with the daughter of the family and his subsequent attraction to an Australian woman result in divided loyalties and tragedy. Writing in the *New York Times Book Review*, the British novelist Peter Ackroyd stressed the differences between *Milk and Honey* and Jolley's more comic novels:

"The abiding images of this novel are those of mortality and decay; its narrative is striated with emblems of burning, of sickness and death. If Elizabeth Jolley was once close to Barbara Pym, on this occasion she is even closer to Edgar Allan Poe, and the prose of the book is slow, mournful, incantatory. Hers is the poetry of the grotesque. . . . *Milk and Honey* seems closer to fable or folk tale than to the conventional novel— its European images have been placed in an Australian setting where their shadows become darker and longer, more difficult to understand but also more difficult to resist." In the *Times Literary Supplement*, Joanna Motion also praised the book's somber power, calling it "the richest, the darkest and the most unexpected" of Jolley's works, a "self-conscious and prescient novel, mysterious, disturbing and genuinely risk-taking."

Like *Milk and Honey, The Well* bears a resemblance to a stark, horrific fable, involving two women living together, the younger having been acquired by the older when an orphan, and their relationship to a corpse—the body of a man that the younger woman has run down in their car. The younger woman believes that the man, whom they have thrown into a well, is still alive and has proposed marriage. In a front-page *New York Times Book Review* article on Jolley, Robert Coover called it her "most spellbinding work to date." In the *Washington Post Book World* Bob Halliday predicted that readers, while "shuddering at the cruelty" of the book's ending, "will admire the deftness with which it weaves together the strands of symbolism which thread their way through the story." Also noting the echoes of fairy tales and nursery rhymes in the book, Patricia Craig in the *Times Literary Supplement* put Jolley in the company of Angela Carter and Barbara Comyns, writers who have "turned to folklore to procure their headiest effects," but she added that Jolley's manner remains "quite distinctive, accommodating frivolity and sprightliness" in her sometimes nightmarish vision.

Jolley's two novels of the later 1980s, *The Sugar Mother* and *My Father's Moon*, are quieter and more serene in tone. In *The Sugar Mother* a middle-aged Australian professor finds his life transformed by the prolonged visit, while his wife is away, of an uneducated woman and her daughter. It is, wrote Patricia Craig in the *Times Literary Supplement*, "an audacious undertaking, admirably controlled, and with many characteristic Jolley flourishes; it manages to seem comic and bleak and nerve-straining and sparkling all at once." *My Father's Moon*, Vivian Gornick noted in the *New York Times Book Review*, resembles a memoir—"a kind of episod-

ic remembrance of an adolescence and a coming of age that coincided with the bombing of London during World War II." The heroine, Veronica, working as a nurse with wounded soldiers, finds herself sexually attracted to the other nurses, but instead of approaching them falls in love with a married doctor who gets her pregnant and is then killed in the bombing. But the tone of the novel is less dramatic than retrospective. "*My Father's Moon*," wrote Gornick, "has less of a story to tell than a mood to develop. . . . The atmosphere is soft, gray, touching and gloomy. The inexperienced girl seems to be groping among adults who are themselves puzzled and depressed by the way it's all turned out. . . . The result is a piece of writing that is all quiet sadness. It touches, but does not penetrate. . . . The narrator never emerges from her own shadows."

Jolley has also published three volumes of short stories—*Five Acre Virgin and Other Stories, The Travelling Entertainer*, and *Woman in a Lampshade*. Several of the stories contain embryonic versions or episodes of later novels, and many others echo the theme of dislocation and "half-belonging" prominent in the novels, the clash of Central European cultivation and restraint with Australian bleakness and freedom. *Woman in a Lampshade*, as Robert Coover pointed out, is also full of "charmingly dotty lady writers, no doubt often meant as ironic self-portraits," including the lampshade-wearing one in the title story "who takes her typewriter and dance music to bed with her, along with her newest Muse in the form of a hiccuping young hitchhiker, in the hopes of resolving her current plot problem."

PRINCIPAL WORKS: *Novels*—Palomino, 1975; The Newspaper of Claremont Street, 1978; Mr. Scobie's Riddle, 1982; Miss Peabody's Inheritance, 1983; Foxybaby, 1985; Milk and Honey, 1986; The Well, 1986; The Sugar Mother, 1988; My Father's Moon, 1989. *Collected short stories*—Five Acre Virgin and Other Stories, 1976; The Travelling Entertainer, 1979; Woman in a Lampshade, 1983.

ABOUT: Contemporary Literary Criticism 46, 1988. *Periodicals*—New Statesman May 10, 1985; New York Times November 16, 1985; New York Times Book Review November 18, 1984; November 24, 1985; June 15, 1986; November 16, 1986; July 19, 1987; July 10, 1988; April 30, 1989; Southerly September 1983; Times Literary Supplement October 18, 1985; June 13, 1986; August 15, 1986; April 15, 1988; March 3–9, 1989; Washington Post Book World November 2, 1986.

*JOSIPOVICI, GABRIEL (October 8, 1940–), British critic, novelist, short-story writer, and playwright, writes: "I was born in France on 8 October 1940—the day that the last ship sailed which would have taken my parents, Jews born in Egypt, away from the continent of Europe and back to the safety of their country of origin. My father's grandfather and my mother's mother's grandfather had both come to Egypt to seek their fortunes in the nineteenth century, the first from Rumania, the second from Italy. My father's father was the author, with his brother-in-law, of *Goha le Simple*, a novel that took France by storm in 1919 and is still in print in paperback; my mother's father was a Russian doctor who had settled in Egypt after being wounded in the Russo-Japanese war, and married into an old-established Jewish family. After their marriage my parents settled in France, first as students at the University of Aix-en-Provence, then in Vence, where they were living when the war broke out.

"We survived.

"When the war ended my mother returned to Egypt, taking me with her. I was educated at an English school, Victoria College, Cairo, and then, in the summer of 1956, we once again set out on our travels, to England this time. After finishing my schooling at Cheltenham College I went up to Oxford in 1958, to read English at St. Edmund Hall. I graduated with a first in 1961 and in 1963 took up an appointment at the newly-formed University of Sussex. I have been there ever since, becoming Reader in 1974 and Professor in 1984. In 1980 I began to teach part-time so as to devote more of my time to my writing.

"I don't believe artists have anything to say, only a need to speak, to set free the many voices we all of us have clamoring away inside us. That is why it is not a bad thing to work in as many different genres as possible, and even, if one gets the chance, in different media. For, as every composer knows, it is the limits that provide the stimulus to creation.

"Thus I have written novels, stories, stage and radio plays, and critical essays. And though I have always felt deep down that it was novels which offered the greatest challenge and provided the most profound satisfactions, there have been a few works in other genres which have given me intense pleasure, the sense of having touched on something absolutely fresh and vital: the stage play *Flow*, a set of five intertwining monologues written for the Actors' Company and performed by them in Edinburgh, London and on tour, and later included in the volume *Mobius the Stripper*, the radio play *Playback*,

GABRIEL JOSIPOVICI

the monologue *Vergil Dying* which I wrote for Paul Scofield and he performed on BBC Radio 3 in 1977; an essay on Stravinsky's *The Rake's Progress*, included in *The Lessons of Modernism*, and one on Kafka's last jottings, which forms the final chapter of *Writing and the Body*.

"I have always felt that my aims and interests were more akin to those of painters and composers than to those of my writing contemporaries, at least in England. I dedicated my first critical book to Peter Maxwell Davies because his concerns at the time seemed so very close to what I was trying to articulate in that book about the relations between medieval and modern art; and recently I have collaborated with Jonathan Harvey on a radio 'play.' In the past few years though painting seems to have been more of a stimulus than music. I have written a number of short stories based on specific paintings, and two novels which have painters at their center. In *The Air We Breathe* I wove a web round a figure I imagined as a Monet who doesn't paint but only looks; and in *Contre-Jour* the starting-point was Bonnard and his wife Marthe. I used a lot of Bonnard material for this as well as phrases and ideas picked up from painter friends; but above all I used my imagination. The book is not about Bonnard. As with *Vergil Dying* I only took a figure who already existed because the imaginative recreation that entailed seemed to set free a voice which at that time was clamoring to have its way.

"It must be left to others to decide if the above account is a true summary of my work and for me

sess its value. For the maker, art has to do not with masterpieces but with a daily activity. As the painter says in *Contre-Jour*: 'When I have a pencil or brush in my hand I am confronting the lies, but the rest of the time I am simply living them.' And the epigraph of the novel, one of Bonnard's own remarks about painting, adds a further twist: 'Many little lies for the sake of one big truth.'"

———

In *The World and the Book: A Study of Modern Fiction* Gabriel Josipovici acknowledges as the key to much of his critical thinking this passage from Proust's *Remembrance of Things Past*: "Every reader is, while he is reading, the reader of his own self. The writer's work is merely a kind of optical instrument, which he offers to the reader to enable him to discern what, without this book, he would perhaps never have perceived for himself." Considered the best of his several well-received critical studies, *The World and the Book* challenges literary realism and affirms that the achievement of modern fiction is that it has liberated the novel from the burden of *expressing* and restored it to its function of *being*. Like the French critics and the novelists who write the "new novel" (*nouveau roman*)—Roland Barthes, Jacques Derrida, Alain Robbe-Grillet—Josipovici makes a break with tradition by rejecting plot and linear narrative and the authority of the narrator—the conventions of realism and the nineteenth-century novel in particular. He does so, however, not in the iconoclastic manner of radical critics who would totally reject the literary canon, but on the basis of wide and thoughtful reading in the canon itself. In an essay-review of *The World and the Book* published in *Critical Quarterly*, a fellow novelist and critic David Lodge writes: "I warmly recommend it to anyone interested in literature of any period between Dante and Robbe-Grillet. . . . Mr. Josipovici is intelligent, eloquent and formidably well-read. He cares passionately about literature and can communicate his enthusiasm infectiously to the reader."

Lodge nevertheless takes issue with Josipovici's rejection of the major nineteenth-century novelists and faults his critical method as selective and prejudiced. Examining two of Josipovici's own novels, *The Inventory* and *Words*—both of them written with minimal dialogue and characters who appear to exist in a solipsistic vacuum—Lodge writes that in *The Inventory* "the atmosphere is weakly reminiscent of Beckett." Of *Words*, with its "Pinteresque" dialogue, he says: "*Words* is a novel about nothing but itself, hence the title. The

words of the characters, flat and unpoetic in themselves, are arranged and counterpointed with subtle elegance. . . . The unremitting banality of the experience rendered leaves our attention free to observe the formal patterns into which casual conversation falls. . . . Inasmuch as it defeats criticism by the total absence of pretensions, *Words* must be accounted a success; but it seems to me something of a Pyrrhic victory."

The World and the Book traces what seems to Josipovici a profound change in sensibility between the Middle Ages and the Renaissance. In the Middle Ages writers and artists saw and depicted the world as the book of God (he cites Hugh of St. Victor: "This whole visible world is a book written by the finger of God"). Their task, therefore, was not to teach moral lessons but simply "to teach men to see by the accurate depiction of reality," that is, to read the world or Nature as God's creation. Since the Renaissance, writers have become increasingly mediators between the world and the reader— interpreting, explaining, deluded into the belief that a novel, or any work of art, is an image of the real world. The realist convention that emerged divided the artist/creator from the reader and assumed a reality that never existed. The modernist artist, however, who has broken from traditional realism in the arts, music, or literature (Josipovici writes authoritatively on all these fields), has restored to us "an understanding of the laws of existence, of the nature of human consciousness and human perception." In Proust, Kafka, and in some of the work of more contemporary novelists like Vladimir Nabokov, William Golding, and Saul Bellow we no longer have the illusion that the novel is an image of the real world: "Having made his work, the author is now both the book and outside the book. Outside not in any space-occupying place . . . but outside by virtue of the fact that he made the book. And the reader too can stand out there, with him, because experiencing the limits of his own world, he too is momentarily freed of his imprisonment within it."

Josipovici's plays, especially those he has written for radio, put his theories into practice. They are stripped of a visual scene; the dialogue is free of exposition and stands complete in itself. Collected with some of his short stories in *Mobius the Stripper*, they offer fragments of dialogue in a kind of skeletal form. The title story, for example (the mathematical Mobius strip being "a single-surfaced geometrical figure that consists of a rectangle twisted 180 adjoined end to end"), is printed on pages that are divided in half. The upper half is the story of a male stripper named Mobius, totally dedicated to his work which he believes is metaphysical, not sexual: "Take off the layers and get down to the basics." The lower part of each page introduces a dedicated writer struggling to write a story about Mobius. Echoed here perhaps is Roland Barthes' observation that form in the novel is not like an apricot which has a kernel at its center, but analogous to an onion where layer after layer is stripped away to nothingness.

While acknowledging the obscurity of Josipovici's novels, reviewers have usually commented appreciatively on their wit, freshness, and virtuosity. Writing of his first novel *The Inventory*, in which a young man is literally preparing a list of the contents of a flat occupied by a father and son, both dead now, the *Times Literary Supplement*'s reviewer observed that it is "concerned with the way in which past events are transmuted by memory, by the need to dissemble, and by guilt. . . . [There] is barely a superfluous line, nor, it should be stressed, is there any affected obscurity." His more recent fiction like *Conversations in Another Room*, while still highly stylized, has a human dimension beneath the glacial surfaces. Of the closing of this novella—a series of exchanges between an old woman invalid and her young niece—A. J. Fitzgerald wrote in the *Times Literary Supplement*: "The final short chapter comes back to the original anecdote, the unstoppable cycle, and an endlessly receding perspective which he [Josipovici] cuts off, not with a flurry of self-doubt, but a poised and beautiful tableau of terror and flight: the intent gaze, the moment of arrest and powerfully suggestive depiction releasing the trapped undercurrents of feeling and fascination that have given rise to the book." *Contre-Jour*, a wholly imaginary novel about the painter Pierre Bonnard, has a similar power of evoking emotional response in the reader, presenting the intimate relationship between a painter and his wife through the eyes of a daughter who feels rejected by them, and also through the wife who may or may not be mad. The artist himself remains neutral, speaking only in the end, in a letter announcing his wife's death. "The central preoccupation of the book" Elaine Feinstein wrote in the *Times Literary Supplement*, "is the relation between those who make art, and those who become victims of that obsession."

In a personal note contributed to the *Times Literary Supplement* in 1985, Josipovici wrote that he has been studying biblical Hebrew in recent years and reading, in addition to the Old Testament, contemporary Hebrew poets like Amir Gilboa and Yehuda Amichai. "These speak to me as do few English writers, past or present. Reading them in Hebrew gives me an added pleasure, the sense of confrontation with something wholly other yet mysteriously personal."

He contributed an essay on the New Testament Epistle to the Hebrews to *The Literary Guide to the Bible*, edited by Robert Alter and Frank Kermode (1987), and in 1988 he published *The Book of God: A Response to the Bible*, which Northrop Frye described as "fresh and energetic, scattering insights in all directions, making original and unexpected connections between the Bible and such modern authors as Proust, casting new light on the Bible's place in Western culture, the nature of its authority, the unity and discontinuities of the text, and the need for a perspective that at once transcends and unites historical-theological and aesthetic interpretation." Though a work of considerable scholarship, *The Book of God* is addressed to the general reader who approaches the Bible with intelligent curiosity and the desire to know it better: "Let us turn to it not as to an object but as to a person," Josipovici writes. Citing his description of the Bible as "that most complex yet most reticent of books," Denis Donoghue wrote in the *Times Literary Supplement* that Josipovici's response to the Bible "observes both of the qualities he attributes to it. He will not let go of its complexity till it has blessed his account of it . . . [his] general approach to the Bible is admirable, and in most of the instances he has studied his interpretation is convincing. Not that he really wants to 'convince'; he is persuasive, mainly, to the degree of his candour. If he is stumped, he doesn't pretend that he isn't."

PRINCIPAL WORKS: *Novels*—The Inventory, 1968; Words, 1971; The Present, 1975; Migrations, 1977; The Echo Chamber, 1979; The Air We Breathe, 1981; Conversations in Another Room, 1984; Contre-Jour, 1986; Distances, 1987. *Short stories and plays*—Mobius the Stripper: Stories and Short Plays, 1974; Four Stories, 1977; In the Fertile Land, 1987. *Criticism*—The World and the Book, 1971; The Lessons of Modernism, 1977; Writing and the Body, 1981; The Mirror of Criticism, 1982; The Book of God: A Response to the Bible, 1988. *As editor*—The Modern English Novel: The Reader, the Writer and the Book, 1975; Selected Essays of Maurice Blanchot, 1982.

ABOUT: Dictionary of Literary Biography 14, 1983; Contemporary Novelists, 4th ed., 1986. *Periodicals*—Critical Quarterly Summer 1972; London Review of Books July 3, 1986; New Statesman October 4, 1968; August 26, 1977; Times Literary Supplement October 31, 1968; February 25, 1972; January 7, 1983; November 30, 1984; May 3, 1985; July 25, 1986; May 13, 1988; March 31, 1989.

*KEANE, MOLLY (MARY NESTA **SKRINE) (pseudonym M. J. FARRELL)** (July 4, 1904–), Anglo-Irish novelist and play-

MOLLY KEANE

wright, the daughter of Walter Clarmont and Nesta Shakespeare (Higginson) Skrine, was born in County Kildare, Ireland. The middle child of five, she grew up in an environment much like the scene of her novels—a fine old country house in the rolling hills of County Wexford, where her English-born father pursued the dominant passions of his life—fox-hunting and horse-breeding—and her mother, who had earlier published folkloristic Irish poetry under the pseudonym of Moira O'Neill, "poet of the Seven Glens," wrote literary critiques and took little interest in the education of her children. The sons were sent to schools in England, and the daughters turned over to governesses often no better educated than their charges. As Molly Keane told an interviewer many years later, "I have no education. I never could learn my grammar—it was always the same to me as arithmetic." This was no handicap, however, to young women of her class. Indeed, when she began publishing novels in her twenties, she adopted the pseudonym M. J. Farrell (the name of a local pub) because, "for a woman to read a book, let alone write one, was viewed with alarm; I would have been banned from every respectable house in County Carlow." She recalled later that her parents probably never read her books: "They would have worried her," she said of her mother, "and she avoided worry where possible. I'm quite sure my father read none of them. He only liked Surtees and history."

As a writer Molly Keane has lived through two incarnations. In her first, she wrote novels and plays as M. J. Farrell, most of these sharply ob-

served portraits of the frivolous and self-indulgent Anglo-Irish gentry who lived in chilly isolation from the native Irish population and spent their time hunting and entertaining each other at teas and hunt balls. M. J. Farrell disappeared after the 1950s, and the Molly Keane who emerged in the 1980s found a new and enthusiastic audience in England and in the United States. Simultaneously Virago Press began reissuing some of the M. J. Farrell titles in paperback; a *New Yorker* profile of her was published; and Molly Keane became a cult figure.

Keane's novels, though not autobiographical, so richly depict her own background that they serve as a mirror of a vanishing ruling class, the Anglo-Irish whom Polly Devlin quite accurately compared to the British Raj in India. Keane writes with no trace of sentimentality, but it is clear that she was herself an active and generally happy member of her class. Nevertheless, she casts a cold eye on its narrowness of interests and outlook. What emerges in her novels is a society that is at once romantically attractive and realistically doomed. On the surface her early novels in particular appear romantic comedies, but a closer reading reveals deeper layers of jealousy, meanness, boredom, and frustration. As Polly Devlin noted in her introduction to the Virago edition of Keane's *Devoted Ladies*: "She writes of narrow horizons, elitist occupations, the preoccupations of money, . . . a curiously dislocated class of people floating as it were over the political, angry geographical reality that was Ireland." Yet Ireland was—and is—a country Molly Keane loves. She has never outgrown the enchantment of its natural beauty. In *Red Letter Days*, a lyrical celebration of fishing and hunting, she recalls the experience of withdrawing (uninjured) from a hunt after being thrown from her horse:

> So in my mind I see that moment again, clear as glass; the grey walls, the grey fields, the grey sky. And I hear the hounds' voices, abiding and lovely in the air, now that the strife to be with them for me is over. I see their huntsmen and one servant still taking the shortest way over the country, their distant effort apart from us now in the gentleness suddenly come upon us. To write the tale of a hunt well and truly requires that its end should be in the death of a fox, but I shall never know how this notable chase concluded . . . I left while hounds were still hunting their fox and while better men than I hold with them still. In place of that hot achievement of completing this hunt, I saw this romantical moment, and I may forever hold it mine.

Though she continues to cherish the values of the past and has lived in Ireland most of her life, Molly Keane regards herself as an iconoclast in her attitude toward her country and her personal life: "I was a great old breaker-awayer," she told Mary D. Kierstead who interviewed her for the *New Yorker*. "I don't know how I was as brave as I was in those days . . . I realized I must fight my way. I loved people, and people were inclined to like me, because I *was* rather sharp and funny." She wrote her first novel (never published) at seventeen to pass the time while recuperating from an illness. When she discovered that by publishing novels she could make some money for new clothes and for independence, she began writing in earnest. The earliest of these novels, *Young Entry*, and those that followed rapidly, were well received. Her lively descriptions of hunting and country houses and her ear for the dialogue of fashionable young people of the 1920s "caught the exact tone" of the period, a *Times Literary Supplement* reviewer wrote—"laconic, abrupt, illuminating, occasionally obscure owing to the quick, unheralded jump from subject to subject, and occasionally affectionate." She was her own best critic in her novel *Devoted Ladies* where a jaded Londoner reads *Young Entry* and remarks: "It's full of the lowing of hounds and every one stuffing themselves with buttermilk scones dripping with butter. Plenty of picturesque discomfort and cold bath water and those *incredible* Irish mountains *always* in the distance." In a passage of inspired self-parody Keane writes: "Such thoughts were rude and fit only for some hysterical Irish novelist, writing her seventy thousand words through which the cry of hounds reverberates continuously, where masters of hounds are handsome and eligible men and desirable young girls override hounds continually, seeing brilliant hunts on incredible three-year-olds; and all—after even the hardest day—are capable of strong emotion at night."

Even in these early novels Keane never deluded herself or her readers with romantic escapism. There is a hard-edged ruthlessness in some of her characters and vulnerable innocence in others that almost inevitably leads to bitterly unhappy conclusions. In *Taking Chances* a distinguished old Anglo-Irish family is victimized by a selfish and shallow visitor from London. In *Mad Puppetstown* an idyllic childhood in a beautiful country house is abruptly changed with World War I and the outbreak of Sinn Fein violence, but this time the balance is corrected when the younger characters return from their refuge in England to restore their home.

The truly hard edge of Keane's satire appears in *Devoted Ladies*, which begins in London and introduces a set of fashionable and sophisticated writers and artists. But its central characters are an alcoholic young widow and the "passionate friend" who dominates her. In 1934, when the novel appeared, lesbianism and homosexuality

were rarely treated openly in fiction, and Keane's candid presentation of these characters was daring. The scene of the novel shifts to Ireland where the love-hate relationship between the "devoted ladies" ends in violence. Generally regarded as Keane's best novel up to that time, *Devoted Ladies* was praised both for its "stinging wit and an extraordinarily acute and vital faculty of observation" (Margaret Wallace in the *New York Times Book Review*) and its dramatic power. That Keane could balance her shrewd social satire with genuine human interest became even more apparent in the last two novels that she published as M. J. Farrell—*The Rising Tide* and *Two Days in Aragon*. *The Rising Tide* centers on the rivalry between a powerful matriarch and her rebellious daughter-in-law. It begins in the Edwardian era, once again in a stately Irish country house, and moves into the unsettling post–World War I era of the 1920s, tracing the changes in manners and mores in the lives of these strong-willed women. *Two Days in Aragon* even more tellingly records the inevitability of change and loss. The grandest and loveliest of Keane's many Irish houses,

> Aragon stood high above a tidal river. So high and so near that there was only a narrow kind of garden between house and water. It was almost a hanging garden: as Spanish as the strange name Aragon . . . Beauty so correct and satisfactory since then there had never been; nor so much dignity with so little heaviness . . . It was the quietest, most solemn garden. The parliaments of rooks in the woods below, only an echo here, a ring for the circle of the quiet.

This quiet is rudely shattered in a bungled raid by a group of Irish fighting for independence in the civil war of the 1920s, an attempt to kill two British officers that leads to the death of a loyal Irish servant and the destruction of the house by fire. Keane writes, according to Polly Devlin in her introduction to the Virago re-issue of the novel, "a threnody, or lamentation, for the great houses of Ireland and the end of a way of life." Her Anglo-Irish characters remain always isolated from the mainstream of Irish life, clinging to their own frail way of life even in what in her non-fiction *Red Letter Days* she calls "the dark present." For this alienated group, "Fox hunting is the thing that matters, the thing of first and last importance . . . beauty in the lovely hills as a wild and fitting counterpart to the savage beauty of hounds hunting a fox." For Keane herself, the present had no doubt been darkened by the burning of her own family's house in 1920 in just such a raid as she describes in *Two Days in Aragon*.

In 1938 Molly Skrine married Robert Keane whom she had met at a hunt ball five years ear-er. It was a happy marriage. "Bobbie" Keane, as he was known, shared her background and interests in horses and hunting, and they lived in his family's large home in County Waterford. Here she wrote, in collaboration with John Perry, the first of several plays that enjoyed considerable popularity. *Spring Meeting*, a light-hearted comedy about a nest of impoverished Anglo-Irish gentlefolk, had a successful London run in 1938 in a production directed by John Gielgud and featuring Margaret Rutherford and Roger Livesey. It fared less well on Broadway in 1939. Her *Ducks and Drakes* also had a successful London run, and another of her plays, *Guardian Angel*, was produced in Dublin at the Gate Theatre. The genre of drawing-room comedy, however, lost much of its vogue after World War II. Although Keane's later comedy *Treasure House*, written with Perry, did well in London in 1949, her farce *Dazzling Prospect* of 1961 was, in her words, "a stunning failure."

Between 1940 and 1945 her marriage, the birth of two daughters, and the running of her large country house left Keane little time or inclination for writing. Even after her husband died in 1946 and she moved to a small cottage in Ardmore on the south coast of County Waterford, which has remained her home ever since, she did not resume her writing. It was not until her daughters were grown and married that, Kierstead reports, "she felt that she was being excessively idle, and . . . she suddenly thought, Money." Her second literary incarnation, this time as Molly Keane, produced her two finest novels. *Good Behaviour*, the first of these, returns to the scene of an Irish country house and a landed gentry so preoccupied with horses and hunting that they are oblivious to the changing scene around them. This novel is narrated in flashback by one of her most memorable characters, an elderly unmarried woman named Aroon St. Charles, living with her dying mother and an old family servant in a shabby cottage on the Irish coast. Aroon is a classic example of the "unreliable narrator," telling her life story as honestly as she can but unaware of the damaging things she is revealing about herself and her family:

And I do know how to behave—believe me, because I know. I have always known. All my life I have done everything for the best reasons and the most unselfish motives. I have lived for the people dearest to me, and I am at a loss to know why their lives have been at times so perplexingly unhappy. I have given them so much, I have given them everything, all I know how to give . . . At fifty-seven my brain is fairly bright, brighter than ever I sometimes think, and I have a cast-iron memory. If I look back beyond any shadow into the uncertainties and glories of our youth, perhaps I shall understand more about what became of us.

Aroon is absolutely correct—except in her last sentence. She will never understand her fate although at one point in the novel, writing of herself as an overweight, unloved girl in her twenties, she has a moment of terrible insight: "I knew that here stood the changeless me, the truly unwanted person." The brother she loves is killed in an auto crash, her father whom she adores ignores her in his preoccupation with horses and his pursuit of women, her self-centered mother despises her, and the man she hopes to marry is homosexual. Nevertheless she clings to her heritage. The family sinks into poverty, her father lies paralyzed by a stroke, and her totally ineffectual mother neglects the household. Still Aroon proudly recalls: "We kept our heads above the morass, stifled screaming despairs only by the exercise of Good Behaviour." The irony of the title reflects the distinctly black humor of the novel. "No one gets away with anything in Molly Keane's novels," Mary Kierstead writes, "and no one is going to live happily ever after; form is everything, on or off a horse." Hard and cruel as *Good Behaviour* is, it is written with such sparkle and relish that it dazzled its reviewers. A. N. Jeffares, in *British Book News*, found in it "a dash and brio that bring the characters and period vividly to life." Garrett Epps, in the *New Republic*, compared it to the wicked humor of Evelyn Waugh's early novels, commenting that "her formidable skills let her stay in the ring with an established master like Waugh, taking the jumps with ease."

An even more enthusiastic reception awaited *Time After Time*, which plays variations on the same theme as *Good Behaviour*. Here Keane widens her focus to embrace a whole family of aged, wasted, empty souls who struggle along in shabby gentility. Set in present-day Ireland in a once fine house now crumbling, dirty, and overrun with the pet dogs and cats of its occupants, *Time After Time* summarizes and epitomizes the fate of the Anglo-Irish ruling class: "The old breath of human dinners and dogs' dinners, chickens' and pigs' dinners too, combined with cats' earth and dogs' favorite urinals, all clung to the air like gray hairs to a comb." The family consists of Jasper Swift, an elderly bachelor with homosexual inclinations, and his three sisters—one a widow, the others never married. Near-destitution, not love, keeps them together, but they cling to their class code, dressing for the elegant dinners which Jasper cooks, keeping up the pretenses of upper-class society. The dubious harmony of their lives is shaken by the unexpected appearance of a cousin with whom they had grown up—the once beautiful Leda, who turns up penniless and blind, claiming to be a refugee from the Holocaust. Always a disturbing presence—and in flashbacks we learn about their earlier lives—Leda sets about the systematic demolition of the family. Described by her own daughter as one who "loves to charm and she lives to hurt," she is ultimately foiled but not until she has opened old wounds and made a few new ones. Once again Keane maintains her delicate balance between grim despair and outrageous humor. V. S. Pritchett wrote admiringly of the novel in the *New York Review of Books:* "No Celtic twilight here! Detached as her comedy is, it is also deeply sympathetic and admiring of the stoicism, the *incurable* quality of her people . . . [a] very imaginative and laughing study of the anger that lies at the heart of the isolated and the old, and their will to live."

Good Behaviour and *Time After Time* brought Molly Keane, now in her eighties, more attention than she had ever had in her youth. *Good Behaviour* was shortlisted for the prestigious Booker Prize and produced by BBC television in Hugh Leonard's dramatization. *Time After Time* was also dramatized for British television with John Gielgud in the role of Jasper. With frequent travel in England and abroad and television and newspaper interviews, Molly Keane has found little time for writing in recent years. Nevertheless she published another novel, *Loving and Giving*, in 1988. Less bleak and blackly comic than its two predecessors, the novel reverts to the early part of the century, 1904, the year of her own birth, and follows the life of another sheltered Anglo-Irish woman up through World War II. Again the decline of a family and a great house is traced, here with more humor than grimness, and again the novel is peopled with amusing eccentrics. Patricia Craig characterized it in the *Times Literary Supplement:* "A sardonic tone, wickedness tempered with charm: these are the attributes of the novelist, while her theme, as always, concerns a primary obligation of the Anglo-Irish—to stifle any acknowledgement of the untoward."

PRINCIPAL WORKS: *Novels*—(as M. J. Farrell) Young Entry, 1928; Taking Chances, 1929; Mad Puppetstown, 1931; Conversation Piece (in U.S. Point-to-Point), 1932; Devoted Ladies, 1934; Full House, 1935; The Rising Tide, 1937; Two Days in Aragon, 1941; Loving Without Tears (in U.S. The Enchanting Witch), 1951; (as Molly Keane) Good Behaviour, 1981; Time After Time, 1983; Loving and Giving (in U.S. queen Lear), 1988. *Plays*—(as M. J. Farrell) Spring Meeting, 1938 (with J. Perry); Treasure House, 1950 (with J. Perry); Dazzling Prospect, 1961. *Non-fiction*—(as M. J. Farrell and Snaffles) Red Letter Days, 1933.

ABOUT: Contemporary Authors 114, 1985; Contemporary Literary Criticism 31, 1985; Dawe, G. and D. Longley. Across a Roaring Hill: The Protestant Imagi-

nation in Modern Ireland, 1985. *Periodicals*—British Book News January 1982; New Republic June 6, 1981; New York Review of Books April 12, 1984; New York Times Book Review June 10, 1934; September 17, 1989; New Yorker October 13, 1986; Times Literary Supplement March 22, 1928; September 9, 1988.

KEEGAN, JOHN (1934–   ), British military historian, was born in London and educated at King's College, Taunton; Wimbledon College; and finally at Balliol College, Oxford, where he specialized in military history. In 1957 he received an Oxford scholarship for travel to American Civil War battle sites, and he subsequently worked in the United States Embassy, London. From 1960 to 1985 he was senior lecturer in military history and war studies at the Royal Military Academy, Sandhurst. In 1985 he became defense and military correspondent of the *Daily Telegraph*, the most conservative of the serious British daily newspapers. "I thought to myself," he told Herbert Mitgang in a 1985 interview in the *New York Times,* "if I don't do it now, I'll be an academic all of my life. So I left Sandhurst and I've been enjoying myself ever since as a journalist. I discovered to my satisfaction that I could write quickly. I write three or four times a week, usually including one big piece."

Keegan has published more than a dozen books on military history, ranging from factual compendia, dictionaries, and atlases to lengthy studies of various aspects of warfare. His main area of interest, based on the extent of his publications in the field, may be said to be World War II; in particular, he is among the English-speaking world's greatest authorities on the activities of the German Army.

The Face of Battle, published in 1976, is an account of great historic battles along with an exploration of the predicament of the individual on the battlefield. Keegan begins the first chapter in an engagingly personal way: "I have read about battles, of course, have talked about battles, have been lectured about battles and, in the last four or five years, have watched battles in progress, or apparently in progress, on the television screen. I have seen a good deal of other, earlier battles of this century on newsreel, some of it convincingly authentic, as well as much dramatised feature film and countless static images of battle. . . . But I have never been in a battle. And I grow increasingly convinced that I have very little idea of what a battle can be like." The rest of Chapter One is a leisurely excursion through the subject of military history as it has been practised in all periods by men as various as Caesar and Clausewitz. The rest of the book

JOHN KEEGAN

covers, chapter by chapter, and from the common soldier's point of view, the great battles of modern history: Agincourt, Waterloo, the Somme, and closes with an examination of the future of battle.

The book was a considerable popular success, which, in the words of Edward N. Luttwak in the *New York Times Book Review*, "reflected widespread approval for Mr. Keegan's depiction of war. By careful selection, [he] effectively conveyed a variety of intensely personal experiences of combat, many by literary men, most of whom were British, while leaving offstage the very idea that war might be purposeful, or even necessary." Luttwak expressed reservations on grounds that "the effect of this book on many readers could be more seriously misleading than traditional or official military historiography ever was. True, such writings reduce the groans, screams, bleeding and death itself to the cold enumeration of casualty figures, but on the other hand, they do set the human experience of battle in context—as a very rare, almost incidental, consequence of the preparation for war, rather than as its logical outcome."

Keegan's next in-depth work of military analysis was *Six Armies in Normandy: From D-Day to the Liberation of Paris, June 6th–August 25th, 1944*. It is the first of several visits by the author to the battlefields of Normandy, the scene of the great, conclusive struggle between the Allied and German armies at the close of World War II. "Armies," he writes in the Foreword, "are universal institutions which, in the dimension of purpose and authority, closely resemble each other. Yet each is also a mirror of its own society and its values: in some places and at some times an agent of national pride or a bulwark against national fears, or perhaps even the last symbol of the nation itself; elsewhere and otherwise an instrument of national power deprecated, disregarded and of very last resort. It seemed to me worth finding some episode through which the varying status of national armies might be exemplified. And in the Normandy campaign of 1944 I believed that I had stumbled upon it." He proceeds to examine the contributions to the many and various battles and to the overall result by the national combatants, Americans, Canadians, Scots, English, Poles, French, and Germans.

Six Armies was also enthusiastically received by the critics. The reviewer for the *Economist* wrote that Keegan "blends with almost uncanny skill the minutiae of what it was like to be behind that hedgerow or in that tank with an overarching view of the strategic and operational decisions that were taken." Drew Middleton, writing in the *New York Times Book Review*, called this "the best book written on the 1944 Normandy campaign, . . . a coherent, lucid view of a vastly complex operation, brilliantly written by a military historian who has a fine eye for the telling detail that can bring alive a battle or a staff conference."

The Mask of Command is a kind of companion to *The Face of Battle*. Whereas the earlier book took the perspective on battle of the common soldier, this one looks at battle from the points of view of the great generals who have conducted them. Keegan takes as models in the art of generalship Alexander the Great, the Duke of Wellington, Ulysses S. Grant, and Adolf Hitler, who represent, in his view, types of heroic leadership, "aggressive, invasive, exemplary, risk-taking." His book concentrates on exhaustive analyses of the personality, the technique in combat and effectiveness at staff use, and the leadership style of each of the protagonists. The author considers Alexander closest to the heroic ideal, but sees in his leadership many similarities and affinities to Hitler, who exemplifies for Keegan the false-heroic style. The two leaders resembled one another, in the words of Gordon A. Craig, writing in the *New York Review of Books*, "not only in the overvaulting nature of their ambitions, which, because they combined in their persons both supreme military and supreme political power, were subject to no external control, but also in the essential meaninglessness of their achievements. . . . Perhaps their greatest similarity was their theatricality, which was the most important component of their respective masks of command." For the author, the demands of leadership in the nuclear age have made such heroism obsolete: "Mankind," he concludes, "needs an end to the ethic of heroism for good and all. . . . An inactive leader, one who does nothing, sets no striking example, says nothing stirring, rewards no more than the punishes, insists above all in being different from the mass in his modesty, prudence and rationality, may sound no leader at all. But such, none the less, is the sort of leader the nuclear world needs, even if it does not know that it wants him." Keegan further points out, according to Jim Miller in *Newsweek*, "that in a nuclear war, the innocent would risk annihilation, while their leaders are expected to reach safety—a startling reversal of the traditional ethos of combat: . . . 'Today the best must find conviction to play the hero no more.'"

The Price of Admiralty: The Evolution of Naval Warfare is Keegan's fourth analytical book, and does for naval warfare what *The Face of Battle* did for fighting on land: he conveys the experience of battle at sea from the viewpoints of both the naval tactician and the ordinary sailor. The great naval leaders whose careers he analyzes include Horatio Nelson, Stephen Decatur, David Farragut, George Dewey, Chester Nimitz, Chuichi Nagumo, and Karl Dönitz. The battles examined in detail are Trafalgar, Jutland, Midway, and the Atlantic. In each case the author gives all relevant historical background, lively quotations from the participants, and analyses of their thinking. He ends by examining submarine warfare as the hallmark of today's naval strategy. The submarine to him is the "ultimate capital ship" fighting for control of a three-dimensional sea; he sees ballistic-missile subs as "war-decisive." To the *Economist* reviewer, Keegan "seems . . . happier with the days of sail than with those of steam and nuclear power, possibly because an element of the romantic lurks beneath the austere reasonings of the military historian. . . . In fewer than a hundred pages . . . he establishes Nelson's greatness more convincingly than most of the full-length biographies."

Keegan's other works comprise in the main atlases and encyclopedias of warfare. These are often profusely illustrated books, published in large format, often with the cooperation of coauthors. *Who's Who in Military History: From 1453 to the Present Day* (with Andrew Wheatcroft) is a fairly brief, much-illustrated, and highly selective biographical compendium. *The Nature of War* (with Joseph Darracott) is a study of how mankind has waged war through the ages. A.J.P. Taylor, in the *New Statesman*, claimed that it was composed of two books of different character. The first and most substantial is a picture book about war." Then there is

the text, "well worth reading even if its relation to the illustrations is not altogether apparent. The theme of war is divided into topics, not into chronological periods." *World Armies*, a massive factual compilation, provides a statistical analysis of all the world's national armies in their domestic, historical, social, political, as well as military contexts. *Zones of Conflict: An Atlas of Future Wars* (with Andrew Wheatcroft) examines twenty-eight political trouble-spots throughout the world where wars have either taken place or are likely to occur in the relatively near future. *Soldiers* (with Richard Holmes and John Gau), an "intellectually unpretentious" book, in the words of one reviewer, offers a general illustrated survey of land warfare, past and present, with separate chapters on the various components of a modern army. The book served as a companion for a BBC-TV series of the same name.

Keegan has also published two monographs on aspects of the German military machine: *Waffen SS: The Asphalt Soldiers* and *Rundstedt*, a biographical account of General Gerd von Rundstedt, the last of a peculiarly German military type, the Prussian general staff officer.

PRINCIPAL WORKS: Waffen SS, 1970; Rundstedt, 1974; The Face of Battle, 1976; The Nature of War (with J. Darracott), 1981; Six Armies in Normandy, 1982; Soldiers (with R. Holmes and J. Gau), 1986; Zones of Conflict (with A. Wheatcroft), 1986; The Mask of Command, 1988; The Price of Admiralty, 1989; The Second World War, 1989. *As editor*—Rand McNally Encyclopedia of World War II, 1977; Who Was Who in World War II, 1978; World Armies, 1979, rev. ed., 1983; The Times Atlas of the Second World War, 1989.

ABOUT: *Periodicals*—America February 12, 1977; September 30, 1978; September 4, 1982; Atlantic February 1977, August 1982, April 1984, November 1985, January 1988, April 1989; Booklist September 15, 1978; December 1, 1980; September 15, 1986; Choice March 1978, June 1980, November 1982; Commonweal September 2, 1977; Economist March 22, 1976; May 1, 1982; January 23, 1988; December 3, 1988; Encounter June 1977; History Today July 1984; Library Journal October 1, 1976; January 1, 1978; November 15, 1978; March 1, 1980; August 1981; July 1982; February 1, 1986; November 1, 1987; February 1, 1989; Nation December 12, 1987; New Republic November 30, 1987; New Statesman May 1, 1981; April 23, 1982; October 4, 1985; New York Review of Books December 9, 1976; August 12, 1982; March 14, 1985; July 17, 1986; April 28, 1988; New York Times December 1, 1987; April 6, 1989; New York Times Book Review November 7, 1976; August 15, 1982; March 23, 1986; April 16, 1989; New Yorker January 19, 1988; Newsweek November 15, 1976; August 2, 1982; December 14, 1987, April 3, 1989; Quill & Quire October 1982, June 1989; Saturday Review December 11, 1976;

Time November 9, 1987; Times Literary Supplement July 30, 1976; February 29, 1980; June 25, 1982; February 5, 1988; September 1, 1989; Virginia Quarterly Review Spring 1977; Yale Review Spring 1977.

KELLY, ROBERT (September 24, 1935–), American poet and fiction writer, sent the following statement to *World Authors* in 1988: "The closest to a thing like a poem was on the moors in Yorkshire, north, off the road to Whitby. The ground was like no ground. Not earth and not rock, it was age upon age of growing, peat or moss or grass or all of these, thick-twisted as a Tibetan carpet, deep as time leaves spindrift in the mind.

"We are consequences. That is the point. The song of it is the close tracking, by ear, of what the mind makes of where it has come to, this place of Now, out of all its geneses, its flowerings and failings.

"This thing a poem is, moorland under your feet.

"The place was where sheep made the way, have been making the way for hundreds of years, and all a word could do was follow, like a big oafish ram, their nimbler quiet passage. This noise is made our music.

"Poems are trying to find out how you sound. How you sound and how you suffer. The poem is an enactment of the common moment of mind.

"A means to know each other is language. Language is to know. Language is a behavior, one part of it is speech, and one aspect of speech is what can be written down, in words, they say.

"So when poems work, they work because the fingerprint of mental obscurations, confusions and aspirations ('me') shapes by its whorls the ever-moving current of what-there-is-to-be-heard ('language') into that gorgeous interrupted silence we call 'music.'

"Is the poet exchanging self-justifications with the unknown reader? Why aren't they all out working to liberate all beings from the sufferings of samsara, the never-ending torment of the 'natural'?

"Language is the intersection of the self and the other. In the heart of it, maybe the exact crossing point, a lucid doorway opens. Through it, to escape from both self and other. That is the hope of poetry, the journey 'in the yellow of the eternal Rose.'

"Poetry is the intersection of the body and the mind. Poetry rescues language from meaning, and rescues meaning from having no way to talk.

ROBERT KELLY

"In all my work, a striving for one content: to let language tell its own story, of which everything that happens to me, and happens in anyone like me, is a particular instance. If we could listen thoroughly enough to language, we could hear everyone. The High History of Everyone.

"So lyric pours into narrative into discourse into those sketchy myths that rise out of friction of words, thin smoke of new meaning rising in the clear air, what Whitman called 'the flanges of words' ever bearing, one on another."

———

As a poet Robert Kelly speaks for himself and leaves little room or excuse for critical commentary. Enormously prolific (well over forty books of verse, several works of fiction and non-fictional prose, at least one play), he defines a poet (in *In Time*) as one "to whom all data whatsoever are of use." The omnivorous quality of Kelly's work puts it somewhere in the American romantic tradition of Walt Whitman. The models he cites himself are fellow omnivorous poets who appear to consume all knowledge and all human experience in their work—Goethe, Coleridge, Ezra Pound. Because Kelly's poetry has been published mainly by small private presses, and because much of it makes strenuous demands on the reader, he has never had a large audience. But readers, critics, fellow poets who know his work, and the several generations of students he has taught, are widening his reputation. His influence extends beyond his writing, for he has founded and edited several important literary journals—*The Chelsea Review*, which he established with George Economou and edited from 1957 to 1960; *Trobar*, also established with Economou, which he edited from 1960 to 1964; and *Matter*, which he has edited since 1963. *Trobar* and *Matter* are magazines *cum* publishing firms, specializing in avant-garde literature.

Kelly was born in Brooklyn, New York, to Samuel and Rose (Kane) Kelly, and was educated in the local Catholic and public schools ("where nothing was ever read and we wrote essays on Fire Prevention"). In an interview in 1973, published in the journal *Vort*, he recalled that the first poem he ever read was Coleridge's "Kubla Khan," when he was five or six years old. At eleven he began writing his own poetry. A few years later he discovered T. S. Eliot, Pound, the French symbolist poets, and his vocation as a poet. At City College in New York, Kelly studied psychology, then switched to classics, then to German, and finally to English, receiving his B.A. in 1955. At Columbia University for graduate studies (1955–1958) he specialized in medieval and seventeenth-century literature while working part-time for a commercial service as a translator. During these years he met a number of poets who shared his interests. Among them was Jerome Rothenberg, who coined the phrase "deep imagism" to describe a poetic imagery rooted in the archetypal unconscious. Kelly also discovered the work of Charles Olson, whose essay on "Projectivist Verse"—advocating a poetry of open form, one that abandons traditional English metrical patterns for spontaneous expression of voice and breath—influenced many poets of the 1950s and 1960s, among them Robert Duncan, Robert Creeley, and Denise Levertov.

For Kelly the image is the fundamental source of the poem, out of which its form and substance seem almost spontaneously and intuitively to develop. "Why are poems so difficult?" he asks. "To answer that is to say only, austerely, what they are: Poems are thinking feeling its was along, feeling thinking its way along." They shape themselves. "Style is death," he writes in *Finding the Measure*:

> . . . Finding the measure is finding
> a freedom from that death, a way out, a movement
> forward.
>   Finding the measure is finding
> the specific music of the hour,
>   the synchronous
> Consequence of the motion of the whole world.

Always drawn to the mystical (what attracted him in his graduate studies of medieval literature was the legend of the Holy Grail), Kelly is an avid reader of occult literature and has produced a share of it himself. He began writing fiction in college and has published one novel, *The Scorpions*, that enjoyed a cult following in the 1960s. Told from the point of view of a doctor whom Kelly describes as "to me abhorrent," it involves all manner of dreamlike and nightmare episodes, including a journey to a mythical island. His shorter fiction, collected in *A Transparent Tree*, includes a variety of stories ranging from the macabre to the satirical (one a take-off on the tough-guy detective genre) to pure parable. In the Afterword to this volume, Kelly writes that he has a so-far 1900-page novel called "Parsifal" in progress. But he insists that his vocation is poetry. "What fiction I write, whether in grand forms or small, always seems free and fabulous and alongside."

In 1964 Kelly published *Lunes*, a small collection bound in a volume with Jerome Rothenberg's *Sightings*. In contrast to most of his poems, these are carefully structured—"small poems," he writes in a Foreword, "that spend half their lives in darkness and half in light. Each line has thirteen syllables, one for each month of the moon's year. Along about the middle, the dark of the moon comes. The full moon is the approximate splendor of the whole lune, provided the clouds do not fall too heavily on that poem." One such poem is "Of Winter's Birds":

> Blue jays not yet up
> the seeds grow
> silently outside
>
> A minute ago
> that tree was
> still full of blackbirds
>
> I chopped branch against
> tree wind blew
> it down from: no blame
>
> birds in fustian masks
> filching seed
> not so warm tonight
>
> plain soft little birds
> on what con-
> ditions do you sing
>
> easily snuffed out
> even now
> names would be a help
>
> but such birds as make
> wing by wing
> new orders of time

Almost every volume by Kelly is an experiment of one kind or another. He never plans his poems. He says, for example, of his long meditative poem about America, *The Common Shore*, that it began with a trip to Vermont—a rare exposure for him to rural life. A host of images and perceptions, called forth by this experience, grew into individual poems, which then gradually coalesced into one long, inclusive work. Attempting to embrace all America as Kelly perceives it—its history, landscape, and peculiar essence—as well as his own personal history in America, *The Common Shore* is rigorously demanding. In a passage that ponders the question or the image of Long Island, Kelly writes:

```
            suburbs
            of the one
            great city
   swung thighs of a human body
   sunday afternoon of the world
   long on the grass
            how the stretched
   tendons of Jericho full breasts of Hempstead
   the pool Ron-
   konkoma
                spreads legs of Montauk & Orient
   brains of Flatbush define a body
   Brooklyn old heart & throne of it
   great Northshore spine, south
   great belly of bay
                vulvary oysters of the Sound
                millions of years?
```

One of Kelly's earliest admirers was the late Paul Blackburn, who reviewed *Armed Descent* in 1962 in the journal *Kulchur*, hailing Kelly as the only poet under thirty he knew who had "already written great poems." In Kelly's work Blackburn found "a kind of mystique of the earth and the things of the earth." Other commentators find Kelly, like Creeley, Olson, and Duncan, "deliberately 'difficult' . . . the act of reading their work at all requires some kind of special orientation to the methods and assumptions employed." To this kind of commentary Kelly replies that "perhaps ultimately all my poems have to be turned inside out to find that single region that they refer to." Kelly demands a reader sympathetic to his approach. If he has not found a large public, he has at least found a small number of devoted readers. Among them is the poet Guy Davenport, who calls him (in *Vort*) "a master, a stylist, who for all his eclecticism is always distinctly himself." Davenport is intrigued with Kelly's play of mind and his open-endedness: "his poems are mysteries to be pondered, something to dream on rather than puzzle out . . . It will take a while to get used to its [his poetry's] newness, but you only need to read two lines together to see that it is alive."

Kelly began a long career in teaching in 1960 at Wagner College, on Staten Island. In 1961 he joined the faculty of Bard College in Annandale-on-Hudson, New York, as an instructor in German, then after a year instructor in English. Since 1974 he has been professor of English and, since 1981, director of creative writing in Bard's Milton Avery Graduate School of the Arts. In 1986 he was given the Asher B Edelman chair of literature. He has also taught at the State University of New York in Buffalo, at Tufts, and at the California Institute of Technology, and been poet-in-residence at several universities, including Yale and the University of Southern California. He frequently gives readings and lectures at American and Canadian universities and colleges. He has received awards from the National Endowment for the Arts (1976) and the National Academy and Institute of Arts and Letters (1986). He has been married several times. His first wife was Joan Elizabeth Lasker (1931–1989), who called him to his work. His second marriage was with Helen Ann Belinky (divorced 1977). His life companion Mary Moore Goodlett passed away in 1990, after a union of four years.

PRINCIPAL WORKS: *Poetry*—Armed Descent, 1961; Her Body against Time, 1963; Round Dances, 1964; Enstasy, 1964; (with Jerome Rothenberg) Lunes/Sightings, 1964; Words in Service, 1966; Weeks, 1966; Song XXIV, 1966; Devotions, 1967; Twenty Poems, 1967; Axon Dendron Tree, 1967; Crooked Bridge Love Society, 1967; A Joining: A Sequence for H. D., 1967; Alpha, 1967; Finding the Measure, 1968; Sonnets, 1968; Songs I-XXX, 1968; The Common Shore (Books 1–5), 1969; A California Journal, 1969; Kali Yuga, 1970; Flesh Dream Book, 1971; Ralegh, 1972; The Pastorals, 1972; The Mill of Particulars, 1973; The Loom, 1975; Sixteen Odes, 1976; The Lady Of, 1977; The Convections, 1977; The Book of Persephone, 1978; Kill the Messenger, 1979; Sentence, 1980; Spiritual Exercises, 1981; (ed. by Jed Rasula) The Alchemist to Mercury: an alternate opus, (Uncollected Poems 1960–1980), 1981; Mulberry Women, 1982; Under Words, 1983; Thor's Thrush, 1984; Not This Island Music, 1987; The Flowers of Unceasing Coincidence, 1988; Oahu, 1988. *Fiction*—The Scorpions, 1967; Cities, 1972; A Line of Sight, 1974; Wheres, 1978; The Cruise of the Pnyx, 1979; A Transparent Tree, 1985; Doctor of Silence, 1988. *Non-fiction prose*—In Time (essays and manifestoes), 1972; (with P. Leary) A Controversy of Poets, 1965.

ABOUT: Contemporary Authors 17–20, 1976; Contemporary Poets, 4th ed., 1985; Dictionary of Literary Biography 5, 1980; Malkoff, K. Crowell Handbook of Contemporary American Poetry, 1973; Ossman, D. The Sullen Art: Interviews with Modern American Poets, 1963; Stepanchev, S. American Poetry since 1945, 1965. *Periodicals*—Kulchur Autumn 1962; New York Times Book Review September 15, 1985; Poetry June 1966, September 1966, November 1972; Vort no. 5, 1974.

KEMPOWSKI, WALTER (April 29, 1929–), German novelist, dramatist, and short-story writer, writes (in German): "I had the idea of becoming a writer very early on. My father owned a shipping business in Rostock and he warned me in my first childhood years that my older brother would inherit the firm. I began very soon to look about for another occupation. It happened that we had a boarder in our flat who was a writer. He lived in prosperity because his father was wealthy, something I did not know. I considered his prosperity to be the result of his writing, which also appeared to me to be a very pleasant activity: sitting in a warm room shuffling white paper and eating quails' eggs. (At this time I was about four years old.) Not until life 'hit me' or, more correctly, 'had hit me' did I realize my life's ambition, which happened in this way: In 1948, through excessive zeal and youthful idealism, I came into conflict with the Soviet Occupation Force in the eastern zone of Germany. I was arrested and sentenced to twenty-five years of forced labor. I was just eighteen years old at the time. I served eight of those twenty-five years, which the Russians referred to as a 'quarter,' in Bautzen prison. Although I had been sentenced to forced labor, I spent my years behind bars in almost total inactivity. I used my time studying foreign languages, writing poems, and composing plays for an illegal prison theater troupe. Immediately after the amnesty which brought about my release, I went to Göttingen in West Germany, where I studied German literature and history, later changing my major to pedagogy. During my student days I began working on a record of my imprisonment, thus sublimating my anxiety and my anger and becoming a writer.

"But because one cannot make a living in Germany by writing books, I moved to the country and became a teacher in a village school. In the mornings I taught reading and writing to the children and in the afternoons I wrote the account of my imprisonment. After eight years the record was complete and was published by Rowohlt under the title *Im Block* (In the Cellblock). Its critical reception varied from sympathetic to enthusiastic, but only slightly more than 1,000 copies were sold. I did not allow myself to be discouraged, however, by this relative lack of interest, and I formed a plan to write a multi-novel chronicle of the history of the German middle class in this century. I used my own family as the model for the chronicle, the important events and characteristics of whose lives I borrowed, but these were also chosen because they reflected the universal, all-encompassing dramatics of the political conflicts of our times: the Age of Imperial Germany, whose prosperity was based on borrowed capital; and the outbreak of the First World War due to a blindness born of imperialism (the catastrophic end of which already

bore within it the seeds of World War II). Then came the terrible inflation of 1923 (when a matchbook cost billions), which totally impoverished the middle class. And then the Nazis came to power, creating a kind of false prosperity for the upset and disoriented people, before casting them into an unprecedented inferno and entangling them in such guilt that their attempts to atone for it brought further collapses during the trying postwar period of resettlement: loss of family identity, denazification, black marketeering, and currency reform. Gradually six novels were completed, which have been a great success with critics and readers alike. Three of the novels have been filmed.

"In order to render an even more objective image of the last 100 years and of the most important events of this period, I supplemented the novels with a factual book about Hitler, one about concentration camps, and one about school experiences, since it was the failure of the schools, ultimately, which left people vulnerable to the great conflicts of this century. I placed all these books under the heading 'The German Chronicle.' Two publications have yet to be added before this chronicle can be considered finished. I have been working for several years on these capstones, which broaden the view to include the hemorrhaging and suffering in all of Europe and the world, because I consider this necessary to exorcise the troglodytes of the 'Third Reich.' The conclusion of the whole chronicle then will be the story of the young teacher, K., who moves to the country hoping to make children into critical thinkers, capable of avoiding future catastrophes. When he sees that he will fail at this, he begins to write a chronicle of the German past.

"Meanwhile I have a position at the University of Oldenburg, where I lecture and conduct seminars on literary and pedagogical topics. Teaching assignments have taken me to California and Utah in the USA; Mainz, Hamburg, and Essen in Germany. I have also founded an archive for unpublished biographies, in which almost 2,000 accounts have already been collected. Some of these life histories are being or have already been published. With them I wish to round out the full historical breadth and depth of my chronicle."

—trans. A. F. Keele

———

In 1969, when an unknown forty-year-old elementary school teacher in a tiny North German village published his first book, *Im Block* (In the Cellblock), almost no one realized how long the work had been in gestation, or that it represented the tip of a large, cohesive, and significant literary monolith yet to come, a complex symbol system describing the history of our century. Twenty years and over a dozen significant books later the full scope of Kempowski's "meganovel," the German Chronicle, has only just begun to become visible.

It is characteristic of Kempowski's grand concept that his chronicle of the history of our century is intended eventually to rest upon the solid foundation of no less than twenty-six previously unpublished book-length autobiographies personally edited by Kempowski and selected from his enormous private archive of diaries, photo albums, autobiographies, common objects of the period, and letters, all of which he keeps stored in a house especially constructed for the purpose. The published selections range from the perspective of a farm wife on the rise of fascism and the Holocaust to that of a German officer captured by Soviet troops on the eastern front to that of a young American bomber crewman shot down in an air raid over Germany and imprisoned in Stalag 17.

It is upon this projected foundation of broad universal human experience in our war-torn century that Kempowski's own "factional" (fact/fictional) novels are located. To date seven of these works have been published, along with three "factual" books (*Sachbücher*) containing answers by hundreds of people to Kempowski's three pointed questions: "Did you ever see Hitler?," "Did you know about the concentration camps?," and "What are your memories of your school-days (i.e. how did school fail to prepare you to live in a democratic society)?".

The factional novels about the Kempowski family are buttressed not only from without by the factual books but from within as well by recollections of other people. This serves to universalize the private experiences of Kempowski and his family, linking them to experiences shared by many others, thus making the Kempowskis into a kind of literary "everyfamily."

Chronologically first in the series is *Aus grosser Zeit* (*Days of Greatness*, 1978), which introduces Walter's grandparents and proceeds from the euphoric nationalism at the turn of the century to the defeat and collapse at the end of World War I. (It begins as Kempowski anticipates how the as-yet-unwritten last novel in the chronicle will end: with the elementary school teacher sitting down to write, three historical pictures of his home town of Rostock before him.)

Schöne Aussicht (A Nice View/Good Prospects, 1981) follows the fortunes of the Kempowskis, of Germany, and of the world from 1918 through the rise of Adolf Hitler. The title, a reference both to the Kempowskis' long-desired new apartment and to the new political system, is obviously ironic, as are the other titles in the series.

Tadellöser & Wolff (1971) picks up in 1938 where *Schöne Aussicht* left off: with the move into the new apartment. (The title is an oxymoronic pun on the name Löser & Wolff, a brand of cigar favored by Walter's father. It combines the image of wolf—the name Adolf also means wolf—with the comparative of *tadellos* meaning "even more blameless.") The novel treats World War II, the destruction of the Kempowski shipping business, and the death of Walter's father on the eastern front. It ends in 1945 as Soviet troops enter Rostock.

Uns geht's ja noch gold (We're Still Getting Along Great, 1972) covers 1945 to 1948. At the end of the war young Walter Kempowski leaves his hometown of Rostock in the Soviet zone and goes to Wiesbaden, in the American zone. In the hope of finding employment and a place to live, he foolishly follows a friend's advice and offers the American Counter Intelligence Agency (CIC) some information he has about what kinds of things the Soviets are shipping out of East Germany. When he returns home to Rostock for a visit, he, his brother, and his mother are all arrested and charged with espionage. "Everyfamily" finds itself trapped between the superpowers in the cold war.

It was the account of his eight-year incarceration that Kempowski had written in his first book, *Im Block*. Now he rewrote the history of that epoch to include more about his brother and his mother and to otherwise make the book better fit the universalizing pattern of the German Chronicle. It appeared in 1975 as *Ein Kapitel für sich* (One Humdinger of a Story). Between 1975 and 1979 *Tadellöser & Wolff, Uns geht's ja noch gold*, and *Ein Kapitel für sich* were filmed by Eberhard Fechner. They were a great success and were broadcast as a series on national German television.

Herzlich willkommen (A Hearty 'Welcome Home!', 1984) describes the Kempowskis' attempts to get on with their lives after they are released from prison by an amnesty and move to West Germany. During Walter's visit to Switzerland the problem of German guilt and the problems of alienation and of communication between peoples in the postwar world are symbolically treated. Walter eventually goes to the university, earns a teaching certificate in elementary education, and takes a post in a village school. It remains for the final projected novel to bring the chronicle full circle to the point where the schoolteacher begins to write.

The inverse complement of the grand structural scale of Kempowski's macroscopic "meganovel" is the unusual microscopic style in which it is written. Thus he writes not in long cohesive narrative strands, but in very small blocks of stream-of-consciousness prose, like verbal snapshots on the pages of photo albums, all seemingly unconnected. The author himself refrains almost entirely from using commentary and symbolism in the conventional sense. Only through the juxtaposition of the "snapshots" and through recurring motifs and language patterns (idioms and the titles of popular songs and films, for example, which reappear in disparate contexts) does he invest the work with symbolic meaning. Thus the recurring memory of a postage stamp collected by Walter's father as a boy which bears the inscription DEUTSCHES REICH misprinted as DFUTSCHES REICH ("das Reich ist futsch" the empire is down the tubes) reminds the reader—even as Walter's father denies it— that both Imperial Germany in 1918 and the Third Reich in 1945 are doomed.

One reason Kempowski has chosen to write his chronicle in this manner is that it allows him to draw his readers more fully into the events of the time by drawing them into the minds of the people of the time. Everything stated in Kempowski's books is a function of the subjective psychology of the persons from whose consciousness Kempowski "quotes." The tension between their often banal perceptions of momentous occasions as they unfold and our view of the same events with the advantage of hindsight demonstrates better than straight historical narrative ever could the degree to which good human beings allow themselves to be blinded by propaganda; by social, class, and economic pressures; or by common knowledge, by platitudes: "If these people weren't guilty the police wouldn't arrest them." At the same time Kempowski places these quotations in a web of subtle but ominous contexts, such as the one involving the fateful postage stamp, thereby demonstrating that his characters have in fact *chosen* to be blind to the awful realities of their world, and in so doing have chosen to overlook or repress the collusive implications of their own views.

Finally, though he had devoted himself with unprecedented energy to the vision of his lifework, the German Chronicle, Walter Kempowski has found time for many other projects as well. He has written nearly a dozen children's books out of his experiences as an elementary school teacher and composed nearly a dozen radio plays, including one in which Beethoven's Fifth Symphony is reconstructed from collective memory by a group of average people, a clear symbol of what Kempowski is attempting to do

in his chronicle: to reconstruct the past from the collective memory of the present. His "Moin Vaddr läbt" (My Father Is Alive, 1982) won the most prestigious German prize for radio drama. It is a gripping fantasy (written in a strange private dialect resembling Yiddish) in which the speakers' dead father lives on in a kind of limbo of the past, possibly another symbol of Kempowski's desire to bring history back to life. His novel *Hundstage* (Dogdays, 1988) is an ironic self-portrait of an author obsessed with his lifework. Like many of Kempowski's other books, it became a best-seller in Germany.

WORKS IN ENGLISH TRANSLATION: *Did You Ever See Hitler?* was published in paperback, translated by Michael Roloff, in 1975. Kempowski's novel *Days of Greatness* was translated by Leila Vennewitz in 1981.

ABOUT: Dictionary of Literary Biography 75, 1988; Keele, A. F. Word Concordance to the German Chronicle of Walter Kempowski, 1986; (in German) Dierks, M. Walter Kempowski, 1984; (in German) Neumann, M. Kempowski der Schulmeister, 1980. *Periodicals*—Books Abroad 48, 1974; 50, 1976; German Life and Letters 28, 1975; South Atlantic Review 47, 1982; World Literature Today 53, 1979; 55, 1981; 56, 1982; 59, 1985.

KERMAN, JOSEPH (WILFRED) (April 3, 1924–), American musical scholar and critic, was born in London, the son of an American journalist. He was educated at University College School, London, took his bachelor's degree from New York University (1943) and his doctorate from Princeton (1950), where his mentors were Oliver Strunk, Randall Thompson, and Carl Weinrich. Kerman was director of graduate studies at the Westminster Choir College in Princeton (1949–1951) before moving to the relatively new and rapidly developing faculty of music at the University of California at Berkeley. He has remained at Berkeley ever since, rising through the ranks of associate professor (1955) to full professor (1960). Chairman of the department in 1960–1963, Kerman has occupied the Jerry and Evelyn Hemmings Chambers chair in music since 1986. From 1972 to 1974 he held Oxford University's Heather professorship of music, concurrently with an honorary fellowship at Wadham College.

Joseph Kerman has been throughout his career an extraordinarily influential voice in American musicological circles, thanks both to the centrality of his scholarly pursuits to the main currents in music and to his fluid, graceful prose style. He has made his reputation as a serious scholar rather than as a reviewer or polemi-

JOSEPH KERMAN

cist; this earnestness of purpose has lent his critical pronouncements, when they have appeared in such publications as the *New York Review of Books* and the *Hudson Review*, a peculiar force unmatched by most of his musical contemporaries.

Opera as Drama, Kerman's remarkable and tough-minded first book, has always enjoyed great influence. The work was an expansion and revision of a series of articles he published in the *Hudson Review* beginning in 1948. He says in his introduction that he makes "no apology for the Wagnerian title"; the "point of view it develops is really the basic one celebrated by *Oper und Drama*, that astonishing volume of a hundred years ago [1851; rev. ed., 1868], Wagner's chief theoretical statement and the important opera tract of his time." Kerman is concerned to demonstrate "that the imaginative function of music in drama and that of poetry in drama are fundamentally the same. Each art has the final responsibility for the success of the drama, for it is within their capacity to define the response of characters to deeds and situations. Like poetry, music can reveal the quality of action, and thus determine dramatic form in the most serious sense." This idea is developed in the book with reference to the works of the great musical dramatists. For these men, "opera was not a mere concert in costume, or a play with highlights and an overall mood supplied by music, but an art form with its own consistency and intensity, and its own sphere of expression. Opera is a type of drama whose integral existence is determined from point to point and in the whole

by musical articulation. *Drama per musica*. Not only operatic theory, but also operatic achievement bears this out."

The book remains famous for some very pronounced critical verdicts: Kerman does not much like Puccini or Richard Strauss; their work, he feels, "will fade from the operatic scene"; by their flashiness and essential vulgarity they obscure "the true works of the operatic tradition." A particular bête noire is Gian-Carlo Menotti, much admired in the mid-1950s on account of the television presentation of his Christmas opera, *Amahl and the Night Visitors*. Kerman considers him "an entirely trivial artist" with his "own special level of banality" and "no kind of musical distinction." C. K. Miller in *Library Journal* called Kerman's style "flowing and polished; his argument scintillates. No one, in fact, can emerge from reading this book without a quickened sense of what opera can be." Harriett Johnson, writing in *Theatre Arts*, thought the book "provocative" and "maddening," the author "perceptive and sometimes brilliant in his probing beneath the surface of opera as an integrated, masterful musical entity that should be considered on its own terms."

Kerman's second book, *The Elizabethan Madrigal: A Comparative Study*, was similarly influential, although occupying a somewhat narrower field. Originally his Princeton doctoral dissertation, it was committed to book form with no "real revision in style and scope." The study is "devoted to an examination of the Elizabethan madrigal, and particularly the beginnings of the Elizabethan madrigal, in relation to the great Italian development which preceded and fathered it." It is basically "a secondary study, resting on the research already recorded by two of the most eminent musicologists of the last generation, Canon Edmund H. Fellowes [1870–1951] and Dr. Alfred Einstein [1880–1952]." Such disclaimers, however, understate the study's importance and originality. In his preface Kerman examines the large role played by each man in the study of sixteenth-century secular vocal music. He then moves on to quite original chapters treating: English madrigal verse and the position of poetry in the English madrigal; Italian music in Elizabethan England, its prestige and circulation; the native English traditions of secular song, with special reference to the work of William Byrd and Orlando Gibbons; a major re-evaluation of the work of Thomas Morley, the nearly forgotten late-sixteenth-century successor to Thomas Tallis and contemporary of Byrd, Tallis's pupil, and in particular of his three collections of *Canzonets* (1593, 1595, 1597) and his madrigal collection *The Triumphs of Oriana* (1601); and a final look at the "serious" madrigal and the works of Thomas Weelkes and John Wilbye, along with a study of chromaticism, or harmonic coloration, in the English madrigal.

The book was warmly received. W. L. Woodfill, in *Music Library Association Notes*, termed it "indispensable, a standard reference work." Everett Helm, in *Musical Quarterly*, thought Kerman's great strength was that "he sees the period, and understands it, as a whole. As a result, he is able to coordinate, relate, and synthesize his findings—to so order the details of his elaborate investigation that they contribute to the total picture." The qualities, coupled with Kerman's impressive gift for "natural but distinguished English," make the book "a joy to read, to reread, and to study. One senses in it the author's own enthusiasm for his subject."

The Beethoven Quartets is a rigorous, formal study, chronologically arranged, of the genesis, importance, and structure of the seventeen quartets composed by Beethoven from 1798, six years after his arrival in Vienna, to 1826, the year before he died, when, amid increasing illness, anxiety, and even a suicide attempt, he completed the great quartets in B^b, opus 130, in C$^\#$ minor, opus 131, and in F major, opus 135. Kerman's historical and social commentary owes everything to others' work on the great composer, in particular to Sir Donald Tovey's posthumous *Beethoven* (1945), but the solid, sensible musical analysis which informs the book is all his own. The book has remained the greatest one-volume work on the quartets, "a study," in the words of the reviewer for *Choice*, "of real depth . . . and contemporary in viewpoint. . . . The organization gives the volume an almost reference quality." For the *Times Literary Supplement*'s reviewer, the volume's chief virtues are scale and scope: "Mr. Kerman's actual knowledge is formidable, and he preserves a just balance between technical analysis and artistic result. As a handbook for the intelligent listener desirous of deepening his understanding, or of refreshing his mind about 'what happens,' the volume is important and the copious musical examples are excellently reproduced."

Kerman has contributed to the important collections of essays edited by Alan Tyson, *Beethoven Studies*. Volume 1, 1973, contains Kerman's article on the famous song of 1815–1816, "An die ferne Geliebte"; volume 2, 1977, has Kerman's article on Tovey (1875–1940), his own generation's most important interpreter of Beethoven's works and career. (Kerman also contributed to volume 3, 1982.) Kerman wrote, with Tyson, the forty-page text of the Beethoven entry for the *New Grove Dictionary of Music*

and *Musicians*, an entry widely regarded as among the most comprehensive and brilliantly written of the thousands in that multivolume work.

The book generally considered Kerman's greatest contribution to musical scholarship is *The Masses and Motets of William Byrd*, the second volume to appear in the three-volume series *The Music of William Byrd*, jointly published by Faber & Faber and the University of California Press. (Volume 3, by Oliver Neighbour, entitled *The Consort and Keyboard Music of William Byrd*, came out in 1978. Volume 2, by Philip Brett, on Byrd's sacred and secular vocal music in English, has yet to appear.) The project arose because of the three authors' friendship over the years, and the volumes share "certain assumptions," among them "that great music of the relatively distant past deserves the same degree of critical attention regularly accorded to that of the recent past or present." The authors wish, above all, to "address the music as music, mediating as best we can between historical vision on the one hand and contemporary aesthetic expectations and attitudes on the other. There is today and has been for many years much generous if somewhat unfocussed admiration for Byrd's genius. We have tried to lay the foundation for its fuller understanding and appreciation." The work is a mainly chronologically ordered study of all the composer's masses and motets, probably the most important part of the sacred music of this most unsecular Roman Catholic composer (1543–1623), from the early exercises in *cantus firmus* and the motets of praise and penitence printed in 1575 to the great works printed in his two volumes of *Gradualia* of 1605 and 1607. Kerman's conclusions on Byrd are typically large-spirited and enthusiastic, yet judicious: "It is the comprehensiveness of his art that commands, ultimately, the greatest wonder. The subtle, complex combination of old and new in his late music—what might be called its quality of historical texture—is only one aspect of this comprehensiveness. . . . Byrd's eye was not on history, however, but on eternity, and certainly in his own mind the music that he consecrated to his church was the most important. . . . Every text, being different from every other, offered a new technical challenge and suggested a new aesthetic solution."

Reviewers had high praise for Kerman's work on Byrd. "No short review," wrote *Choice*, "can do justice to this book, which is surely to seem definitive for some time." Richard Taruskin, in *Music Library Association Notes*, called the work "a compelling demonstration of 'connoisseurship'—that elusive quality that historians continually aspire to, but musicologists rarely"

According to Robert Donington in the *Times Literary Supplement,* "What we are getting in these [three volumes] is professional in the most solid sense—reliable, informative, and enthusiastic too." Kerman also wrote the Byrd entry— much shorter than his Beethoven, but no less magisterial—in the *New Grove.*

Perhaps Kerman's most invigorating and accessible work of musicology since *Opera as Drama* is *Contemplating Music: Challenges to Musicology,* in which he attempts, in little more than two hundred pages, to analyze, compare, and contrast the fields of musicology, music criticism, music theory, and ethnomusicology. "The way we think about music—as professionals or as amateurs; as critics, historians, theorists, whatever—is important at least partly because of the way it impinges upon music that is composed, performed, and listened to. Ideas can influence music: though it is just as glaringly obvious that the flow also runs in the other direction. Ideas about music come into being as a response to music that is already there. . . . What I would call serious music criticism . . . does not exist as a discipline on a par with musicology and music theory on the one hand, or literary and art criticism on the other. We do not have musical Arnolds or Eliots, Blackmurs or Kermodes, Ruskins or Schapiros. In the circumstances it is idle to complain or lament that critical thought in music lags conceptually far behind that in the other arts. In fact, nearly all musical thinkers travel at a respectful distance behind the latest chariots (or bandwagons) of intellectual life in general." In several chapters of quite disparate contents and aims, Kerman discusses, among other subjects, the current state of Verdi studies; the rise to eminent respectability of the historical-performance movement; the accomplishment and all-encompassing quality of the *New Grove*; and the career of Milton Babbitt and some of his colleagues on the Princeton faculty of music. Along the way he warmly exhorts his fellow musicologists to understand and embrace the field of philosophy as well as intellectual, social, and political history. The book contains passages of vintage Kerman, such as his lampoon of the business and frequent baseness of music journalism: "The folklore of journalism is rich in rascally tales of music critics who switched over one fine day from the sports pages to revel in a life of ignorance and spite."

With his wife, Vivian Shaviro Kerman, Kerman wrote a standard high-school or first-year college text on music appreciation, *Listen,* a lavishly illustrated work which deals with Western music only, covering the sixteenth century through the golden age in the late eighteenth and early nineteenth centuries, and which even includes a chapter on music since 1950. He has been coeditor since 1977 of the journal *19th-Century Music.*

Kerman has held Guggenheim (1960), Fulbright (1966–1967), and National Endowment for the Humanities (1982) fellowships. He has been a visiting fellow of All Souls College, Oxford (1966), the Society for the Humanities at Cornell University (1970), and Clare Hall, Cambridge (1971). In 1986 he was Walker-Ames visiting professor at the University of Washington. He is a fellow of the American Academy of Arts and Sciences and since 1984 has been a corresponding fellow of the British Academy. He is also an honorary fellow of the Royal Academy of Music and holds an honorary doctorate of humane letters from Fairfield University (1970).

WORKS: Opera as Drama, 1956, rev. ed., 1988; The Elizabethan Madrigal, 1962; The Beethoven Quartets, 1967; (with H. W. Janson) A History of Art and Music, 1968; (with V. S. Kerman) Listen, 1972, rev. eds., 1976, 1980; The Masses and Motets of William Byrd, 1981; (with A. Tyson) The New Grove Beethoven, 1983; Contemplating Music, 1985. As editor—Ludwig van Beethoven, Autograph Miscellany, 1786–99 (The Kafka Sketchbook), 2 vols., 1970; Mozart's Piano Concerto in C major, K. 503, 1970; (with W. Denny) Beethoven's Two Orchestral Minuets of 1790, 1973.

ABOUT: Contemporary Authors 65–68, 1977; Sadie, S. (ed.) The New Grove Dictionary of Music and Musicians, 1980; Who's Who, 1988; Who's Who in America, 1988–1989. *Periodicals*—Bookmark December 1956; Choice July 1967, February 1982, September 1985; Kirkus Reviews August 15, 1956; Library Journal November 1, 1956; December 1, 1966; Musical Quarterly April 1963, July 1967; Music Library Association Notes Summer 1963, June 1982; National Review May 23, 1986; New York Review of Books July 18, 1985; New York Times Book Review October 28, 1956; May 26, 1985; New Yorker December 15, 1956; Theatre Arts January 1957; Times Literary Supplement November 1, 1963; August 17, 1967; October 23, 1981.

KINCAID, JAMAICA (pseudonym of Elaine Potter Richardson) (May 25, 1949–), American novelist and short-story writer, was born in St. John's, Antigua, in the West Indies. Her parents figure prominently in her fiction, as indeed does her whole childhood. She has said that her father, a carpenter, was a critical, dignified man who could make an exact replica of a piece of furniture simply by looking at it; her mother, a descendant of Carib Indians and a literate, cultured woman, was, if Kincaid's fiction is any indication, formidable in every respect. Like the narrator of her second book, *Annie John,* Kincaid left behind the enclosing embrace of her

JAMAICA KINCAID

mother and the constricting opportunities of her
homeland at the age of seventeen. In 1966 she
arrived in America to work as an *au pair* and
pursue her education (Annie John goes to England to become a nurse), and by 1975 she had
published her first pieces in a national magazine
(*Ms.*). The following year she became a *New
Yorker* staff writer, submitting "Talk of the
Town" pieces and short fiction. Kincaid's work,
signed and unsigned, continues to appear in the
New Yorker and two of her three books carry
dedications to that magazine's former editor
William Shawn.

At the Bottom of the River, Kincaid's first
book, is a collection of ten interrelated short stories, most of which originally appeared in the
New Yorker and all of which concern an unnamed Caribbean girl on an unnamed Caribbean island. In the opening words of the opening
story, "Girl," Kincaid already reveals a distinctive literary voice, blending biblical cadences,
Caribbean folk rhythms, and Hemingwayesque
terseness:

> Wash the white clothes on Monday and put them on the
> stone heap; wash the color clothes on Tuesday and put
> them on the clothesline to dry; don't walk barehead in
> the hot sun; cook pumpkin fritters in very hot sweet
> oil . . . on Sunday try to walk like a lady and not like
> the slut you are so bent on becoming.

In form, "Girl" seems little more than an accumulation of harsh instructions from mother to
daughter, yet it is emblematic of Kincaid's
strange and hypnotic prose. This "elegant and
lucid piece," wrote Edith Milton in the *New

York Times Book Reivew,* "define[s] in a few
paragraphs the expectations, the limitations and
the contents of an entire life."

In fact, however, At the Bottom of the River
is a surprisingly difficult book, its narrative strategies depending on repetition, indirection, and
submerged psychological conflict, rather than
on plot or character development. The title
piece is a case in point. Obeying a logic of its
own, it shifts from realistic description to philosophical speculation to visionary experience.
The climactic scene is of a house and a naked
woman, glimpsed by the narrator, existing in
perfect harmony "at the bottom of the river."
After having this vision the narrator returns,
mysteriously strengthened, to the tangible world
of her bedroom, where everyday objects like pen
and chair and table now stand revealed in stunning clarity.

While writers like Susan Sontag and Derek
Walcott praised the book for its sumptuous and
"thrilling" prose, others had reservations. For
Anne Tyler, Kincaid's "poetic" style was just the
problem. The pieces, she wrote in the *New
Republic,* "are often almost insultingly obscure,
and they fail to pull us forward with any semblance of plot. Not once in this collection do we
wonder what happens next. Not once do we feel
that the writer is leaning forward and taking our
hands and telling us a story. Instead, she's spinning lovely, airy webs, with a sidelong glance in
our direction every now and then to see if we're
appreciative. For this reason, *At the Bottom of
the River* in its final effect seems curiously cold
and still."

The title of Kincaid's second book, *Annie
John*, is significant, for not only does her adolescent narrator now have a name, but she lives in
a specifically defined place: Antigua. And unlike
At the Bottom of the River, with its collage-like,
impressionistic vignettes, *Annie John* is a real, albeit loosely structured, novel. It traces the development of its protagonist from a petted and
precocious ten-year-old, fussed over by her adoring mother and teachers, to a willful and rebellious adolescent whose agonizing struggles to
win a measure of independence alienate her
from her family, her friends, and possibly from
herself. Finally she departs on a ship to England,
bidding a wrenching but liberating goodbye to
her mother, who stands on the pier waving her
handkerchief. And in a haunting shift of perspective, Annie's last sight of her mother becomes her mother's last sight of Annie: "just a dot
in the match-box-size launch swallowed up in
the big blue sea."

There is something parable-like in all of Kincaid's fiction, and *Annie John* has been read as

an enactment of the eternal fall from innocence into experience and alternately as a tale of spiritual death and rebirth. An exponent of the former view is Bryant Mangum. In his essay on Kincaid in *Fifty Caribbean Writers* he maintains that in the end Annie intuitively "understands the point that Kincaid has understood all along and has prepared the reader for in the allegory: she is escaping the pull of the world of prenatal union and harmony, a fact which makes the actual walk to the jetty and the boat that will carry her away from Antigua so painful." Taking note of the "metamorphic sickness" that Annie suffers for months before her departure, Paula Bonnell interpreted the novel's conclusion quite differently. "This psychic illness," she wrote in the *Boston Herald*, "and all the distortions with which it warps the narrator's world . . . is given in beautifully awful detail, language that cherishes the peculiar pains of the self. And out of the sickbed arises a new being: the young woman who will leave the island of her childhood behind and set sail to seek her fortune."

Many critics regarded *Annie John* as an advance upon the themes established in *At the Bottom of the River*. Without sacrificing her slow, hypnotic rhythms, Kincaid had gained in narrative coherence and control. "*Annie John* fills in between the bits," wrote Jacqueline Austin in the *Voice Literary Supplement*; "it gives the passions of *River* a rationale. The surreality, imagination, internal and external detail are still there, but they now flow in a single narrative wave." Yet after two books largely about an adolescent girl's relationship with her mother, there was some criticism of the relative insularity of Kincaid's preoccupations. Austin implied as much (other critics were more explicit) when she concluded that Kincaid's "wisdom, measured craft, and reticence" would "carry her on to more complicated and wider canvases, to larger geographies of the mind."

Little in Kincaid's previous work could have prepared readers for the ferocity of her third book and only work of non-fiction. *A Small Place* is an eighty-page jeremiad on the exploitation of her native land and its people by European colonials, North American tourists, and corrupt public officials. It is, as Kincaid plainly admits, an exercise in rage. "But nothing," she writes, "can erase my rage—not an apology, not a large sum of money, not the death of the criminal—for this wrong can never be made right, and only the impossible can make me still: can a way be found to make what happened not have happened? And so look at this prolonged visit to the bile duct that I am making, look at how bitter, how dyspeptic just to sit and think about these things makes me." Although Kin-

caid's finely-tuned prose was sharper than ever, her entirely subjective analysis struck some critics as unrealistic and reliant upon stereotype (especially in her castigation of white tourists). The *Library Journal* reviewer thought that "rather than interpret[ing] Antiguan experience for outsiders, Kincaid lays bare the limits of her own understanding" and the *New York Times Book Review* noted that "the writing is distorted by her anger." But even in this harsh and unforgiving book, traces of transfiguring lyricism remain. Towards the end Kincaid writes:

> Antigua is beautiful. Antigua is too beautiful. Sometimes the beauty of it seems unreal. Sometimes the beauty of it seems as if it were stage sets for a play, for no real sunset could look like that; no real seawater could strike that many shades of blue at once . . . and no real cloud could be that white and float just that way in the blue sky.

Jamaica Kincaid lives in Vermont with her husband Allen Evan Shawn and their two children, Annie and Harold. She is the recipient of the Morton Dauwen Zabel Award for fiction.

PRINCIPAL WORKS: *Short stories*—At the Bottom of the River, 1983. *Novel*—Annie John, 1985; Lucy, 1990. *Non-fiction*—A Small Place, 1988.

ABOUT: Contemporary Literary Criticism, 43, 1987; Contemporary Novelists, 4th ed., 1986; Cumber, D. (ed.) Fifty Caribbean Writers: A Bio-Bibliographical Critical Sourcebook, 1986. *Periodicals*—Boston Herald March 31, 1985; Library Journal July 1988; New Republic December 31, 1983; New York Times October 12, 1990; New York Times Book Review January 15, 1984; April 7, 1985; July 10, 1988; October 28, 1990; New York Times Magazine October 7, 1990; Times Literary Supplement January 13, 1989; Voice Literary Supplement April 1985.

KING, STEPHEN (EDWIN) (pseudonym RICHARD BACHMAN) (September 21, 1947–), American novelist and short-story writer, was born in Portland, Maine, of Scotch-Irish ancestry, the son of Donald and Ruth (Pillsbury) King. After the father, a merchant seaman, deserted the family in 1950, Stephen and his brother David were raised in Durham, Maine, by their mother, who took a succession of low-paying odd jobs to support her children. A rather introverted child, King became addicted to listening to horror tales on the radio and seeing science-fiction and monster movies. According to a 1986 cover story in *Time*, King as a boy "was oversized and ungainly, with a thick thatch of unruly black hair, buck teeth and thick glasses, the one who was predictably chosen last in sandlot games." He attended grammar school in Durham and Lisbon Falls High School, where

STEPHEN KING

he wrote offbeat stories and was rhythm guitarist in an amateur rock 'n' roll band. Following his graduation from high school in 1966, King attended the University of Maine at Orono on a scholarship, which he eked out by working as a dishwasher and gas station attendant. He took creative writing courses, contributed a weekly column to the campus newspaper, and sold his first short stories to magazines before receiving his B.S. degree in 1970. In 1971 he married Tabitha Spruce, a fellow student at the university, by whom he has three children—Naomi, Joseph, and Owen.

After graduating from college, King was at first unable to find a teaching position and worked in a laundromat for $60 a week. From 1971 to 1973, he was an instructor at the Hampden Academy, a private co-educational secondary school in Hampden, Maine; while teaching he continued to write stories, often in the school's boiler room, with a child's desk propped against his knees. In 1973, already a father and burdened with bills, King sold his first novel, *Carrie*, to Doubleday and was astounded when a Doubleday editor told him that paperback rights to the book had been sold for $400,000. He was now freed from teaching and could devote himself entirely to writing.

·*Carrie* is set in a Maine village and is concerned with a sixteen-year-old girl who is an object of scorn to her classmates and even to her religious fanatic mother, but who possesses formidable telekinetic powers (the ability to induce motion in objects simply by power of the mind). When Carrie is humiliated unforgivably at the

school prom, she wreaks telekinetic vengeance on all concerned. Reviews were not extremely favorable; the reviewer for *Booklist*, for example, remarked that "the novel as a whole requires a willing suspension of disbelief and taste." Sales of the novel, however, were phenomenal, passing the four million mark; and the subsequent screen version, directed by Brian De Palma and starring Sissy Spacek as the title character, became one of the top-grossing films of 1976.

Carrie was quickly followed by *Salem's Lot*, about another small Maine town. Salem's streets are deserted during the day but active at night, when the townspeople turn into vampires. The reviewer for *Booklist* commented: "Those caught up in supernatural tales à la *The Exorcist* will pore over every page"; but the reviewer for *Publishers Weekly* was less enthusiastic, remarking that "the sense of evil is almost palpable, but [the story is unnecessarily elongated], so that when the same ghastly, gruesome fate keeps on overtaking the Maine villagers . . . one does begin to wish things had been tightened up a bit. Enough is, after all, enough and there isn't that much variation in how one becomes a member of the 'undead.'" *Salem's Lot* became a CBS television miniseries in 1979. *The Shining*, King's next novel, is set in a snowy Colorado and centers upon the Overlook Hotel, where the writer Jack Torrance, accompanied by his wife and young son Danny, arrives to work as off-season caretaker. Danny is precognitive and telepathic, abilities that stand him (and the story) in good stead as Torrance descends into homocidal mania, possessed by the malign spirits that haunt the old hotel. Barbara Conaty in *Library Journal* remarked that "King is a masterful technician of suspense whose readers as well as characters are the victims of his relentless heightening of horror." *The Shining* was adapted for the screen in a 1980 film directed by Stanley Kubrick and starring Jack Nicholson.

In 1978, King published both *Night Shift*, a collection of stories of the supernatural, and *The Stand*, an 823-page novel taking the form of an apocalyptic fantasy about a flu-like plague that escapes from an experimental laboratory, devastates the country, and leaves only a few thousand immune people. The survivors all have a terrible dream in which good and evil are pitted against each other in the figures of the santanic Randall Flagg and the God-anointed Mother Abigail. Their followers come together in an Armageddon ending in which good finally prevails. The reviewer for *Publishers Weekly* called *The Stand* a "moral fantasy where gritty realism forms the basis for boldly imaginative raids upon the bizarre. . . . King's message is simple, but his characters are compellingly real." *The Dead*

Zone concerns a schoolteacher who, after an automobile accident, awakes from a coma with the ability to see into the future and read thoughts—powers that become horrifying when he is brought into a confrontation with a powerful and sinister political figure. The novel was made into a 1983 film starring Christopher Walken and Martin Sheen.

In *Firestarter*, made into a 1984 film starring Christopher Walken and George C. Scott, King focuses upon an eight-year-old girl named Charlie McGee, who possesses such pyrokinetic powers that she is judged capable of melting whole cities. A government agency known as "The Shop" seeks to eliminate her, but in the end she proves more than its match. Michael Demarest in *Time* wrote that despite its "pseudoscientific hokum," the work is "the most realistic, even credible novel [King] has written. . . . Firestarter Charlie McGee . . . is one of the most touching waifs in current popular fiction." *Cujo*, published in 1981 and filmed two years later, tells the story of a huge St. Bernard who becomes infected by rabies and terrorizes a small Maine town. Michael Bishop in the *Washington Post Book World* remarked that despite "the inordinate number of pages devoted to Cujo's siege, King's ability to draw character and to marshall a complex series of forward-moving scenes redeems the book. . . . Nineteenth-century England had Wilkie Collins for literate, headlong melodrama; we have Stephen King." *Pet Sematary* (1983), made into a film in 1989, is set in Ludlow, Maine, where a quaint graveyard for children's pets is located behind a pleasant white frame house (and beyond that another graveyard, from which the dead return). Annie Gottlieb in the *New York Times Book Review* felt that the novel "loses credibility toward the end, as it gains in gore. Loss of control, and perhaps interest in, his material after the midpoint is a recurrent flaw . . . that Mr. King has moderated but not entirely overcome. Nor is *Pet Sematary* his best book as a piece of writing. . . . It is, however, his grimmest. Through its pages runs a taint of primal malevolence so strong that on each of the three nights it took me to read it, both my companion and I had nightmares."

King's writing in the mid and late 1980s included *The Talisman*, written in collaboration with his friend and fellow explorer of the supernatural Peter Straub (author of the best-seller *Ghost Story*, 1979); *Skeleton Crew*, a collection of his previously unpublished fiction; five novels of horror written under the pseudonym of Richard Bachman; *It*, a novel of over 1,100 pages depicting a "thing" of terror besetting a small Maine town; and *The Tommyknockers*, which combines science fiction with terror. King has proved ever more prolific and is almost certainly the most popular of American writers today, his book sales numbering above the 25-million mark. In 1989 he signed a four-book contract with Viking Penguin, reportedly for between $30 and $40 million—a contract that has since been bought by the Book-of-the-Month Club for an even larger sum. The first of the new novels, *Dark Half*, was published in the fall of 1989. Dedicated to "the late Richard Bachman," it is the tale of a successful writer terrorized by his pseudonymous alter ego. *Four Past Midnight*, a collection of novellas, followed in 1990, and two more books—one a horror novel, the other a psychological thriller—are anticipated under the contract. In addition, the Book-of-the-Month Club has licensed eighteen King novels from several publishers for its Stephen King Library, a collection of twenty titles (initially) that the club will offer members in 1990.

King and his wife Tabitha, herself the author of three novels, continue to live in his native Maine. He owns an airy modern house in a Maine village and a 23-room 129-year-old Victorian mansion in Bangor, "surrounded by a black iron fence with interwoven designs of bats and spider webs, installed in an excess of whimsy by the owners," and located only a short distance from the poor neighborhood where he grew up. King writes 1,500 words every day without fail. An amateur guitarist, he still likes to get up in the morning and switch on rock 'n' roll.

PRINCIPAL WORKS: Carrie, 1974; Salem's Lot, 1975; The Shining, 1977; The Stand, 1978 (rev. ed. 1990); Night Shift, 1978; The Dead Zone, 1979; Firestarter, 1980; Cujo, 1981; Stephen King's Danse Macabre, 1981; Different Seasons, 1982; The Dark Tower: The Gunslinger, 1982; Christine, 1983; Pet Sematary, 1983; (with Peter Straub) The Talisman, 1984; Silver Bullet, 1985; Skeleton Crew, 1985; Cycle of the Werewolf, 1985; The Bachman Books: Four Early Novels, 1985; It, 1986; Maximum Overdrive, 1986; The Tommyknockers, 1987; Misery, 1987; The Eyes of the Dragon, 1987; The Dark Tower: The Drawing of the Three, 1987; Nightmares in the Sky, 1988; The Dark Half, 1989; Four Past Midnight, 1990. *As Richard Bachman*—Rage, 1977; The Long Walk, 1979; Roadwork, 1981; The Running Man, 1982; Thinner, 1985.

ABOUT: Beahm, G. (ed.) The Stephen King Companion, 1989; Collings, M. The Annotated Guide to Stephen King, 1986; Contemporary Authors New Revision Series 1, 1981; Contemporary Literary Criticism 26, 1983, 37, 1986; Current Biography 1980; Horsting, J. Stephen King at the Movies, 1986; Miller, U. Kingdom of Fear, 1986; The Science Fiction Source Book, 1984; Something About the Author 9, 1976; Supernatural Fiction Writers: Fantasy and Horror, 1985; Who's Who in America: 1988–1989; Who's Who in Horror and Fantasy Fiction, 1978; Winter, D. E. Stephen King: The Art of Darkness, 1984. *Periodicals*—Book List July 1, 1974; January 1, 1976; Kirkus Reviews June 15, 1982; Library Journal February 1, 1977; Maclean's September 24, 1978; New York Times Book Review November 6, 1983; Publishers Weekly August 11, 1975; September 25, 1978; September 28, 1984; Time September 15, 1980; August 30, 1982; October 6, 1986; Washington Post Book World August 23, 1981.

IVAN KLÍMA

*KLÍMA, IVAN (September 14, 1931–), Czech short-story writer, novelist, playwright, and essayist, was born in Prague, where his father was a scientist in the field of electric power and his mother was an administrative clerk. As a boy during World War II, Klíma spent three years in Terezín, the infamous Nazi concentration camp in Czechoslovakia. Following his graduation from high school in Prague in 1951 and after one semester at the University of Political and Economic Sciences, he studied Czech language and literature at Charles University. Upon graduating, Klíma became an editor of *Květy* (Flowers), a pictorial weekly with a popular audience, from 1956 to 1957. He then became an editor at the writers' union publishing house Ceskoslavenský Spisovatel (Czechoslovak Writer), from 1959 to 1963. From 1964 to 1969 he edited *Literární noviny* (Literary News), the weekly publication of the writers' union, read by most intellectuals of the time for its coverage of the Czechoslovak literary scene, until the repression following the Soviet-led invasion in 1968 forced its closing. Jobless, Klíma left Czechoslovakia to spend the academic year 1969 to 1970 as a visiting professor at the University of Michigan, then returned to Prague and the tenuous lot of a free-lance worker (*svobodné povolání*, the job description stamped in a Czechoslovak internal passport: a designation hard to obtain, hard to maintain, and hard to subsist on). During the 1960s Klíma received several Czechoslovak literary awards and was a member of the Union of Czechoslovak Writers, which was disbanded in 1970.

Klíma's first prose, dealing with his youthful experience in the concentration camp, was published in 1945, and thereafter he occasionally published in children's magazines. In 1955 his work began to appear in a host of other publications, including *Květen* (May), *Mladá fronta* (Youth Front), and *Divadelní noviny* (Theater News). His first book, *Mezi třemi hranicemi* (Between Three Borders, 1960), was a non-fiction work about Slovakia. His first novel, *Bezvadný den* (A Perfect Day, 1960), was adapted for the radio by Helena Klímová, the author's wife. Also in 1962 Klíma wrote the television play *Vavrrri*

chvost (The Squirrel's Tail), adapted from one of his short stories, and the script for the prize-winning *Kybernetická babička* (Cybernetic Grandma), an animated film by the puppeteer Jiří Trnka. In the sixties Klíma also wrote a series of stories for animated films, directed by Zdeněk Miler, about an adorable mole with a blue bib, wrote several afterwords for books by Karel Capek, edited a collection of Capek's essays, and was coeditor of a series of books, *Zivot kolem nás* (Life around Us), published by Ceskoslovenský Spisovatel. Also from this period are: the inverted socialist realist novel *Hodina ticha* (An Hour of Silence, 1963), the short stories in *Milenci na jednu noc* (Lovers for One Night, 1964), and the novel *Loď jménem Naděje* (1969), his first book to be translated into English, as *A Ship Named Hope*.

Perhaps Klíma's most important work of the sixties was *Zámek* (The Castle, 1964), which marked his debut as a playwright. In this drama he gave expression to two of his most important influences, the theater of the absurd and, as his title indicates, Franz Kafka. It was performed in the United States in December 1969 by the Professional Theatre at Ann Arbor, Michigan. His next play, *Mistr* (The Master, 1967), a detective story without a solution, was never performed in Communist Czechoslovakia because of its political subtext. In a question that alludes to the subversion of language by the regime, one of the characters asks, "What are . . . words in a world where words have been completely separated from deeds?" The third of Klíma's plays (and the last to be performed in Communist

Czechoslovakia) was *Porota* (The Jury, 1969), which contains absurdist elements and considers the question of man's guilt. It also reflects the impact on Klíma of reading Friedrich Dürrenmatt. Markéta Goetz-Stankiewicz has observed that "Klíma's particular closeness to Kafka and Dürrenmatt lies in his exploration of the secret, highly charged connection between 'right' and guilt and the way they can create or cancel each other." Though performed in Prague as late as 1969, *Porota* was subsequently banned as Klíma became part of what Goetz-Stankiewicz calls "The Silenced Theatre."

As a result of the government crackdown against intellectuals after the Soviet invasion of 1968, most of Klíma's work afterwards was outlawed in Czechoslovakia and appeared there in the original Czech only in so-called *edice petlice* (padlocked editions), the Czechoslovak equivalent of *samizdat*. Among his banned works are the children's book *Markétin zvěřinec* (Marketa's Animals, 1971), the story collection *Malomocní* (The Lepers, 1972), the one-act play *Hromobití* (Peals of Thunder, 1974), and the novel *Stojí, stojí šibenička* (Ready Stands the Gallows, 1978). Abroad, some of Klíma's books were published in Czech by émigré publishers. Klíma's position in creative limbo in his own country put him in the distinguished company of other Czechoslovak dissident authors, like the playwright Vaclav Havel and the novelist Ludvík Vaculík. In the view of Olga Carlisle, Klíma is "one of the more open and intrepid of the nonconformist writers who . . . [remained] in the country."

After the final performance of *Porota* in Czechoslovakia in 1969, Klíma's plays were produced only abroad, if at all. The one-act plays *Klára a dva páni* and *Zenich pro Marcelu*, both written in 1968, were presented in English translation as "Klara" and "A Bridegroom for Marcela" at La Mama Experimental Theatre Club in New York on a double bill in 1969. Later they were done in German on television in Austria and West Germany. With *Zámek* and two other one-acters, *Cukrárna Myriam* (Café Myriam) and *Pokoj pro dva* (The Double Room), they were published in one volume in German in 1971. In 1974 Klíma collaborated with the playwright Pavel Kohout to create a literal dramatization of Kafka's *Amerika*, which had its premier and was published in German in West Germany in 1978. While the German production of *Amerika* missed the essence of the play's psychological and philosophical import, a Viennese production later in 1978 came closer to realizing the two adapters' Kafka, according to Goetz-Stankiewicz.

Also influenced by Kafka is *Hry* (Games, 1975), Klíma's vision of man as an automaton guilty of either acquiescing or participating in the systematic murder of the human spirit. But this play, begun in 1973 and first performed in German in Vienna in 1975, owes its view of "the complex issue of man's rights and the forms of his guilt" (Goetz-Stankiewicz) equally to Dürrenmatt. In *Hry* the last of the six party games, to each of which a scene is devoted, is called *Poprava* (Execution), and in it the most obviously guilty of the guests, a murderer, avoids the gallows, while the most innocent, a gentle former revolutionary, ends up being hanged. However, the hapless victim-to-be, referring to his tied hands, gives a final speech that indicts the government that forbids the production of plays: "These are not the worst fetters. Power and false beliefs put us into much tighter chains. . . . I feel unified with all those who perhaps have not even a notion that their hands are tied too."

Despite the political subtext of many of Klíma's plays, he believes that the playwright's task is to engage an audience on a personal yet universal basis, to make his viewers feel that "whatever is happening on stage is about themselves, that each of their problems, emotions or words—no matter how insignificant—is familiar to the characters on stage." Klíma's success in achieving this aim is substantiated by the fact that his plays have been translated into Dutch, English, Finnish, French, German, Icelandic, Norwegian, and Swedish, and their stage, television, and radio versions have been performed in about a dozen countries.

Without a Czechoslovak audience for his theater pieces, however, Klíma increasingly turned to prose fiction in the early seventies. His collection of short stories *Má veselá jitra* (My Merry Mornings, 1979) was published in Czech by Sixty-Eight Publishers in Toronto, the leading Czechoslovak émigré publishing house. This work then appeared in a German translation in Switzerland in 1983 and in an English translation in England in 1985. The book contains seven tales, one for each day of the week and each bearing a title on the order of "Monday Morning: A Black Market Tale" or "Tuesday Morning: A Sentimental Story." All are narrated by a writer who seems to be Klíma's alter ego: he lives in Prague with his wife and two children, is forbidden to travel, is kept under surveillance, and has had a play produced in New York in which a critic has noted the influence of Dürrenmatt. Throughout these tales Klíma comments on and dramatizes the absurdity of the repressive life under his country's totalitarian regime. Yet this life in this country remains his primary subject, and with Ina Navazelskis we can "understand why he has chosen to remain in Czechoslovakia. His affection for and his commitment to his fellow countrymen come through."

Also in a Sixty-Eight Publishers edition is *Milostné léto* (1979), which Klíma wrote in 1972. It has been translated into German, Swedish, Norwegian, Danish, Dutch, French, Serbo-Croatian, Slovene, and English, in which it was published as *A Summer Affair* in London in 1987. This novel, about a dull married scientist in the throes of adultery with a crazy young woman, falls into the category of books Josef Skvorecký defines as those which in themselves were "not necessarily politically objectionable: it's their author's stance as citizen—his refusal to accept the ambush [the Soviet invasion of 1968] and the resulting neostalinist regime as legitimate"—that caused them to be banned.

As a novelist, according to William E. Harkins, Klíma belongs to a group of writers including Ludvík Vaculík and Josef Skvorecký whose work is "essentially ethical and political, and emphasizes the betrayal which Stalinism represented. . . . They are joined by a common concern for ideals and a disapproval of the betrayal of ideals by either extreme left or right." This ethical, political stance is also apparent in *Moje první lásky* (1985), which was published as *My First Loves* in London in 1986 and is the first of Klíma's works to be published in the United States (1988). The volume contains four linked stories set in Czechoslovakia during the decade from the middle of World War II to the Communist show trials of the early 1950s. In each the young male narrator has an unfulfilling experience with a woman who is the object of his sexual desire, and each of these women is associated with a particular idea that intrigues him. Walter Goodman calls the theme of these stories "a sensitive young man stoking his passions for an elusive woman in a world not made for lovers." That world is one of Nazi terror in the first tale, the short story "Miriam," and the world of Communist betrayal in the other three much longer stories, "Má vlast" ("My Country"), "Hra na pravdu" ("The Truth Game"), and "Provazolezci" ("The Tightrope Walkers").

Perhaps the most telling, and the most typically Czech, of these is the novella "Má vlast," in which the teen-aged narrator and his parents, who live in Prague, spend a summer holiday in the Bohemian countryside. Having been encouraged in his early literary efforts by an editor, the narrator determines to "constantly observe life, and the rest of the time . . . read the great masters of world literature. At the rustic Sterbak Inn he is exposed to a group of comical Czech

types and to a wide range of Czech music, including Smetana's patriotic "Má vlast," from which Klíma takes his title, as well as to an even broader sampling of verbal expression, including doggerel, advertising jingles, fishermen's ditties, limericks, the clichés of Marxist utopianism, and ironically appropriate passages from Gorky, Stendhal, Balzac, Sholokhov, and Maupassant. For Klíma the boy's infatuation with the young wife of a doctor in the room next door matters less than the multiple forms of verbal expression that represent his country (*vlast*) and shape his growing sense of a literary vocation. But like *My Merry Mornings* and *A Summer Affair*, *My First Loves* was banned in Czechoslovakia, presumably less for its contents than for its maker. Similarly smuggled out of his homeland, Klíma's fictions *Láska a smetí* (Love and Garbage, 1988) and *Soudce z milosti* (A Judge on Trial, 1988), a revised version of *Stojí, stojí šibenička*, were scheduled to be published in English in 1990.

On August 4, 1989, the *New York Times* reported that Klíma has been allowed to join the governing committee of the newly reopened Czech branch of PEN, the international writers' organization, which had been defunct since 1971. Also in 1989 arrangements were under way for the publication in Czechoslavakia of *Milostné léto* (*A Summer Affair*) and *Moje první lásky* (*My First Loves*).

WORKS IN ENGLISH TRANSLATION: English translations of Ivan Klíma's writings include Edith Pargeter's *A Ship Named Hope* in 1970; George Theiner's *My Merry Mornings* in 1985; and Ewald Osers' *My First Loves* in 1986, *A Summer Affair* in 1987, and *Love and Garbage* in 1990. Barbara Day translated *Games* for a London production in 1990.

ABOUT: Contemporary Authors New Revision Series 17, 1986; Goetz-Stankiewicz, M. The Silenced Theatre: Czech Playwrights without a Stage, 1979; Harkins, W. E. and P. I. Trensky (eds.) Czech Literature since 1956: A Symposium, 1980. *Periodicals*—Christian Science Monitor August 2, 1985; New Statesman May 3, 1985; January 2, 1987; New York Review of Books May 18, 1989; New York Times January 4, 1988; New York Times Book Review July 28, 1985; December 23, 1986; February 21, 1988; Times Literary Supplement July 5, 1985; January 23, 1987; August 25, 1987; March 30, 1990; August 3, 1990.

*KONWICKI, TADEUSZ (June 22, 1926–), Polish novelist, scriptwriter, and film director, was born in Nowa Wilejka, near Vilnius (then a part of Poland, now a part of Lithuania), into a rather poor family. When he was only three years old his father, Michał, died of tuberculosis. Since his mother, Jadwiga (Kimun), had

°kon' vit ski, ta de' ŏosh

TADEUSZ KONWICKI

saw but did not complete his degree. Instead, he successfully pursued a writing career, publishing book reviews, articles, and fiction in various newspapers and periodicals. Being on the editorial boards of leading literary magazines—first *Odrodzenie* (The Revival) and later *Nowa Kultura* (The New Culture)—he was one of those who pioneered the so-called Socialist Culture. His first published book, the short novel *Przy budowie* (At the Construction, 1950), won a state award and was put on the compulsory reading list in Polish schools, and his subsequent social-realist novels and propagandist journalism demonstrated his continuing commitment to Communist ideals (he joined the Party in 1951). When in 1956 Konwicki became literary chief in the film production team Kadr, his new career as a scriptwriter and film director began and has since paralleled his vocation as a novelist. Until the mid-sixties he was a writer recognized and appreciated by the state, but his refusal to act on behalf of the Party in its campaign against thirty-four intellectuals who signed an open letter questioning censorship (March 1964) paved the way for a new, rebellious stage of his life. After opposing the government's purge of intellectuals in 1968 and its notorious "anti-Zionist" campaign, he left the Party and was consequently dismissed from his post in Kadr. He then became active in the opposition movement. He was one of the founder-members of the Committee for Defense of Political Prisoners (December 1980) and after the imposition of martial law (December 1981) made clear to police interrogators that he also supported another independent organization, the Committee for the Defense of Workers. Between 1977 and 1984 all his literary works were published in London and only clandestinely in Poland, although more recently (since 1986) he has returned to the official state publishing house Czytelnik. Konwicki has traveled several times within Europe and abroad. His itinerary has included China, the United States, and Australia. He is married and has two grown daughters.

The author's early social-realist output belongs to a period despised and forgotten by contemporary Polish readers. Nowadays, it is resurrected only by critics settling accounts with Poland's Stalinist past. When pressed, Konwicki recalls those days reluctantly and not without a certain amount of self-pity: "After all, everybody took part in that, but I am the miserable one who is attacked and tormented day and night to make confessions." A sense of guilt, individual as well as collective, pervades his work and produces some of its more obscure and bizarre effects. Czesław Miłosz observed of one of his later novels that "the feeling of guilt oppress-

to work, the little boy was looked after by various relatives. In 1932 he and his mother moved to a house owned by Tadeusz's "grandparents"—his great aunt and uncle, the Blinstrubs—in Kolonia Wileńska, on the outskirts of Vilnius. The places where he was born and raised have reappeared as scenes of edenic happiness in Konwicki's work, but as he has observed, his situation was also a school of survival: "Oh no, I did not have a difficult childhood. My childhood was easy. Like a small fish I managed to glide between tragic consequences. I could breathe both in air and in water. I did well in the sea and on dry land."

Konwicki was in high school when the war started and the Red Army entered Vilnius. When, two years later, in 1941, the city came under German occupation, the teenaged boy managed to complete a clandestine education and join the Polish resistance movement, the Home Army. His underground group operated in the Lithuanian forests, waging guerrilla war against the Germans until the tide turned and Soviet forces recaptured Vilnius and the surrounding area. As Russian intentions became clear, remnants of the Home Army attempted to resist the new occupation as well, but without success. Konwicki's native province was restored to Lithuania, by then a part of the U.S.S.R., and he, along with many other ethnic Poles, was "repatriated" to postwar Poland in 1945. He went to Cracow and then, after a few years, settled in Warsaw, where he has lived ever since.

Konwicki specialized in Polish language and literature at the universities of Cracow and War-

es men with distorted, even monstrous recollections, everything bathes in an aura of torment:
situations, people, landscapes create a nightmarish web of metaphors." And Jerzy R. Krzya-
nowski, in *Books Abroad*, writes of Konwicki's
"haunted world," a paradise irreparably lost and
replaced by the nightmare reality of the here
and now: "Philosophically close to existential
thought, Konwicki, not as a moralist but as an accomplished artist, has put his finger on the very
source of the anxieties and fears of the modern
world, laying them bare in a relentless
exploration."

Rojsty (Marshes), a literary work of more lasting value than his social-realist writings, was
completed in 1948 and was thus actually his first
novel, but it was not released by the censors until
1956. In fact, at the time it was written, it could
have played into the government's hands by
voicing disillusion with the Home Army in the
days of its official denunciation and persecution.
Conversely, when public pressure brought about
its partial rehabilitation in the mid-fifties, *Rojsty*
introduced the image of an organization which
at the end of the war swiftly degenerated into
common banditry and the thoughtless killing of
friendly soldiers of the Red Army. Andrze-
jewski's famous *Popiół i diament* (*Ashes and
Diamonds*), representing a similar approach,
was released and officially welcomed in 1948.
Konwicki's problems with censors may well have
stemmed simply from the setting of his novel,
the Vilnius province, long a bone of contention
between Poland and Lithuania.

Dziura w niebie (A Hole in the Sky, 1959) was
the first of what is considered Konwicki's typical
narratives. Although this novel still recalls traditional realism, with its adherence to concrete,
everyday events, the artistic vision eventually
moves further towards metaphor and personal
mythology based on the strongly poeticized image of childhood in a fairy-tale valley. In its further development this tendency gave Konwicki's
fiction a definitely lyrical character. The ideological message of *Dziura w niebie* is vague. The
uncompromising search for truth represented by
the main character and his consequent opposition to any "Philistine" pursuit of personal career
or material gain place this story of suburban
youngsters within the well-known tradition of
Polish neoromanticism. Wacław Berent's novel
Zywe kamienie (Living Stones, 1918) about the
universal importance of the medieval quest for
the Holy Grail particularly comes to mind. If we
accept the author's later confession that the novel actually defended zealous commitment to the
ideological fictions of Stalinism, its interest and
satiric effects are broadened.

The next novel, *Sennik współczesny* (1963;
translated as *A Dreambook for Our Time*), was
much applauded in Poland and translated into
many languages. Marxist critics regarded it as
the writer's farewell to the past and his definite
approval of progress towards socialism. Even if
such an approach was somewhat simplified, the
obscure symbolism of the novel points in that direction. Due to a new dam on the river Soła the
graves of national heroes in a nearby forest will
be flooded, but the dam will generate electricity
and promote modern life in a backward countryside. The narrator himself will also wake up
from his past-oriented dreams and face common
reality with its everyday problems. *Sennik
współczesny* makes a further step towards Konwicki's typical blend of various styles: realistic
portraits, gushing lyricism in love scenes, romantic mystery, surreal flashbacks and then fashionable dialogues, excessively witty and allusive to
the point of obscurity. Instead of genuine plurality of representation, he ended with confusion
and discord, "a dreamlike haze of uncertainty,"
as Mark Shechnor wrote in the *Nation*.

In this respect even *Wniebowstapienie* (Ascension, 1967) has failed to strike a proper balance and that seems to be Konwicki's main
artistic problem. Considered by some as his
greatest achievement, the novel is the first in line
of nearly Kafkaesque nightmares, although this
is Kafka blended with Wiech, a popular narrator
of Warsaw urban folklore, or perhaps with
Marek Nowakowski, the bard of its underworld.
The hero, awakened with partial amnesia, finds
himself in the Polish capital at the time of the
traditional harvest festival, 'Dozynki'. As a man
without any but a hypothetical biography, or
rather with many potential biographies, he has
lost his identity and unable to find one. In a
hopeless search for the girl of his dreams, Anna,
he wanders aimlessly from one drinking den to
another and from the streets to prison in a dark
world of swindlers, prostitutes and social outcasts. Faceless crowds in the vast, hostile, and
sometimes monstrous city contribute to an image of oppressive helplessness, anticipating Konwicki's fiction of the late seventies.

Zwierzoczł ekoupiór (1969; translated as *The
Anthropos-Spectre-Beast*), ostensibly addressed
to children, gives, perhaps, Konwicki's most accomplished response to the problem of dreams
in their relation to reality. By implication it also
concerns the role of fiction or, in broader terms,
any attempt at artistic representation. In its plurality of coexistent worlds, which include a romantic adventure story, a science-fiction movie,
and a realistic portrayal of life in modern Warsaw, the novel demonstrates the relativity of perception, which only conforms to well-established

patterns and stock images. People play certain roles in this scheme, but these are reversible. The narrator, Peter, can be a good boy fighting with a bad one, Retep, in one story, to become Retep in another. In fact, "Peter is Retep spelt the other way round." The plot structure is also variable and subject to alternative conclusions. Therefore it is not surprising when we eventually learn that everything in the novel has been invented by a boy dying of leukemia in order to escape from the sole unquestionable reality, that of death. The world of dreams and fiction allowed him for a short while to enjoy freedom. All the rest has been dominated by the Anthropos-Spectre-beast, that is, by "everything that is not understood in nature and mankind."

Konwicki's next two novels illustrate well a danger inherent in his own lyrical art: a tendency towards loose structure accompanied by pompous and often empty rhetoric. Critics have cited the obsessive, monotonous recurrence of the same motifs, particularly of the fairy-tale valley of childhood, and unsuccessful attempts to suggest depth under actually trivial events, as well as self-indulgent emotionalism. *Nic albo nic* (Nothing or Nothing, 1971) certainly has philosophical ambitions. As some critics have pointed out, the novel is about human helplessness in the face of surrounding chaos and absurdity. This vague but then fashionable message is delivered in an experimental form where the author employs all three possible methods of narration: the first, second, and third person. With its paranoid hero suffering from mental dissociation, the novel creates a reality which is confusing and bizarre. *Kronika wypadków miłosnych* (The Chronicle of Love Events, 1974), although well-received by readers, introduces little more than a pastiche of romantic and neoromantic motifs. As a love story with a metaphysical background it is not a great success. Its symbolism—transforming for instance a common rail track into "the open abyss of destiny" or "the threshold of eternity"—seems forced.

The Polish social upheavals of the late 1970s inspired Konwicki with new ideas and certainly invigorated his talent. With the release of his books by independent publishers, i.e., outside censorship, his natural inclination towards catastrophism acquired political grounds. In the decadence of Communist-ruled Poland, which in his works includes not only the ruling elite, but also the majority of her population, *Kompleks polski* (1977; translated as *The Polish Complex*) portrays a society where apocalyptic images and old national messianism converge upon the triviality of everyday existence. The basic structural device depends on the parallel between people queuing for Russian jewelry in contemporary Warsaw and a forsaken party of insurgents fighting the Russians over a hundred years ago in one of the unsuccessful Polish uprisings. The latter also recalls much more recent guerrilla warfare waged by the Home Army. Due to the contrasts between the stories the foreground of the novel is dominated by former heroes drinking vodka with their former oppressors at the time of the so-called "small stabilization." The background, however, contains the morality play-style drama of the eternal struggle between God and Satan where Poles, whatever their sins, are placed on the right side for their traditional love of freedom and their opposition to Eastern tyranny. The problem with the novel, especially for readers in the Western world, Jaroslaw Anders wrote in *New York Review of Books*, is its allusive and cryptic language: "It is a code, a language reduced to symbols easily recognizable by those who share a similar experience, but an act of disdain toward those who were lucky enough to avoid it."

Mała apokalipsa (1979; translated as *A Minor Apocalypse*) is set in the indefinite future. It describes a world still suffering from the experience of World War II which "shattered the great palace of culture of European morality, aesthetics and custom." The narrator-protagonist is a unique person only slightly affected by the surrounding degeneration. With total annihilation of values even the oncoming apocalypse is a minor one, not so much terrifying as abominable to the point where real tragedy becomes impossible. Warsaw in the state of sordid disrepair and Poland in the process of incorporation into the Soviet Union are placed against the background of cosmic catastrophe where "the entire galaxy is hurtling off into an abyss, nothingness." While inert Polish society meekly accepts the Russian dominance, the protagonist's voluntary immolation, whether useful or futile in its romantic gesture, gains some meaning. In a world of empty words and actions whose grotesque face combines horror with absurdity, his act is hailed as the sole vestige of authenticity. "In spite of its bouncy absurdist surface," Irving Howe wrote in *New York Review of Books*, "*A Minor Apocalypse* is a novel saturated with weariness—weariness with falsity, weariness with having constantly to expose falsity, weariness with continuing nevertheless to live in a world of falsity."

Rzeka podziemna, podziemne ptaki (A Subterranean River, Subterranean Birds, 1984) is about Poland under martial law described in Konwicki's own personal way. Its lyrical character is unusually uniform, offering at its best that specific blend of romantic patriotism and modern skeptical, catastrophic approach which characterizes the writer's last works. The protagonist is surrounded once more by the inferno of overwhelming decadence. Mundane reality, dominated by General Jaruzelski's pledge of allegiance to the Soviet Union and by the spineless society of opportunists, approaches the brink of the abyss. Red helicopters, "the horses of Russian tzar," over Warsaw and the headquarters of the Warsaw Pact underground symbolize hell which, in the author's words, may soon engulf the whole world.

Konwicki's later novel, *Bohiń*, (translated as *Bohin Manor*) was described by Patricia Hampl in the *New York Times Book Review* as "a lyric antiphon, the call between Central Europe's 19th century and its lurid 20th." The central character is Konwicki's grandmother, who lived on a country estate, Bohin, in Lithuania in the last quarter of the nineteenth century. About to enter a loveless marriage with a neighboring landowner, she falls passionately in love with a young Jew, a fugitive from the oppressive government. From his own subjective point of view Konwicki seeks to discover his grandmother's history and relate it to his own existence. In some ways a romantic love story haunted by ghosts of the even more distant past (the poets Pushkin and Mickiewicz appear as characters), *Bohiń* is also haunted by more contemporary and terrifying ghosts, like Hitler and Stalin. "The great pleasure—and achievement—of the book," Hampl writes, "is that these calls and replies across the centuries are not arch literary gestures. They always feel urgent and as real as the imagination always makes memory."

In addition to his novels, Konwicki has published three books on the borderline between fiction and autobiographical essay: *Kalendarz i klepsydra* (A Calendar and an Hourglass, 1976), *Wschody i zachody księżyca* (1981; translated as *Moonrise, Moonset*) and *Nowy Świat i okolice* (Nowy Świat Street and its Neighborhood, 1986). According to his own account, these books freed him from the few conventions of narrative. Consequently, he produced literary works which include varied material and where what is fictitious and what is not has been purposely blurred. Thematically they cover almost everything, from the writer's beloved cat, Ivan, to his political and artistic opinions and his metaphysical unrest. They abound in autobiographical data and recollections of artists and writers. Like almost everything written by that author, they combine realistic observation with lyricism and sound judgment with rather obscure metaphysics.

Moonrise, Moonset takes the form of a journal written in 1980–1981 during the year of a major Solidarity crisis at the end of which martial law was declared and Konwicki was summoned for a police investigation. The book is described on its dust jacket as "a memoir, a confession spiced with gossip, a speculative essay on Poland's love-hate relationship with Russia—all woven into a 'real-life novel' whose narrator and central character is Konwicki himself," an aging man now, painfully aware of his own mortality. Rambling and anecdotal, it reviews not only the author's life but the life of Poland since World War II. At once the outsider-narrator and the insider-protagonist of the book, Konwicki shifts moods—satiric, witty, ironic, bitter—with dizzying results. As Ewa Kurylak noted in the *New York Times Book Review:* "The title, of a man's moody soul swinging back and forth between depression and exhilaration, boredom and irritation . . . about growing old, about the present falling to pieces and the past assuming an ever-greater significance." In one section of the book Konwicki describes his visit to his older daughter "in distant, legendary America." While in America he underwent surgery for throat cancer, and during his convalescence he experienced a kind of epiphany that suggests that his vision for the future is not as despairing as it had appeared to be:

> I had intended to speak of Poland, ours, mine, yours, which was reflected in short bursts of tragic light here in strange, ancient-modern-nouveau-riche America. Maybe that light isn't tragic, but at least it's somber, very dark. And in anthill New York, Poland has blossomed luxuriantly out of those brief, inanimate flashes of unhealthy light. Poland at every step, popping up everywhere, and speaking cautiously, one might say that Poland has run rampant. For the first time in this century we have crossed a certain essential boundary: intelligent attention paid to a cause, a problem, has begun to turn into sympathy for a certain geographic area and for a certain people.

Konwicki was both the scriptwriter and director of the following films: *Ostatni dzień lata* (The Last Day of Summer, 1958), *Zaduszki* (All Soul's Day, 1961), *Salto* (1965), *Matura* (Graduation, 1965), *Jak daleko stąd, jak blisko* (So Far Away, So Near, 1972), *Dolina Issy* (The Issa Valley, 1982, adapted from the work of Czesław Miłosz). Some of these films have been shown abroad and won film prizes.

WORKS IN ENGLISH TRANSLATION: David Welsh translated *A Dreambook for Our Time* in 1969; George and Andrzej Korwin-Rodziszewski translated *The Anthropos-Spectre-Beast* in 1977. Richard Lourie's translations of Konwicki include: *The Polish Complex*, 1982; *A Minor Apocalypse*, 1983, 1988; *Moonrise, Moonset*, 1988; and *Bohin Manor*, 1990.

Columbia Dictionary of Modern European Literature 1980; Contemporary Authors 101, 1981;

Miłosz, C. The History of Polish Literature, 1969, 1983; The Reader's Encyclopedia, 1988.
Periodicals—Books Abroad 48, 1974; Nation June 19, 1976; New York Review of Books, May 27, 1976; March 4, 1982; October 13, 1983; New York Times Book Review August 30, 1987; July 15, 1990; New Yorker January 2, 1984; Partisan Review 3, 1982; Polish Review 3, 1976, 2 1978, 3, 1984; World Literature Today 3, 1977, 4, 1982; World View 7, 1983.

KRISTEVA, JULIA (1941–), Bulgarian-born critic and literary theorist who writes in French, received her early education in Bulgaria in a school directed by French nuns. Her original ambition was a scientific career in physics or astronomy, but her middle-class parents were not sufficiently well-connected with the ruling elite of the Communist party to arrange for her to be educated in the research training centers of the U.S.S.R., so Kristeva shifted her field to philology. During the Eastern European cultural thaw in the early 1960s, Kristeva worked as a journalist, and she remained in contact with western ideas while taking her degree in linguistics at the Literary Institute of Sofia. When the cultural thaw ended with Khrushchev's fall in 1966, she emigrated to Paris.

Kristeva arrived in 1966 with a doctoral research fellowship and began working as research assistant to Lucien Goldmann, the "genetic structuralist" Marxist critic, author of *The Hidden God*. She was assisted in her career by her compatriot Tzvetan Todorov, the structuralist critic who had just translated the Russian formalists into French. Her primary mentor in the early part of her career, though, was the doyen of structuralism Roland Barthes. Kristeva took Paris by storm, publishing articles as early as 1967 in prestigious journals such as *Critique* and *Langages* and in the radical structuralist journal *Tel Quel*. (Kristeva later married its editor, the novelist and theorist Philippe Sollers.) During the late sixties, Kristeva submitted a *troisième cycle* doctoral thesis and then a separate thesis for her *doctorat d'état* in 1973. This doctoral thesis was published as *La Révolution du langage poétique* in 1974. Kristeva currently holds the chair in linguistics at Université de Paris-VII.

In a 1970 review of her work, Roland Barthes referred to Kristeva as "l'étrangère," and went on: "she always changes the places of things: she always destroys the *latest preconception,* the one we thought we could be comforted by." Literally, Barthes was alluding to Kristeva's status as a foreign woman, an immigrant to France, but he was also suggesting something perennially alien, or at least unorthodox, about the intellectual style in which she operates: Kristeva's politics are

JULIA KRISTEVA

Marxist, but not doctrinaire Marxist; her semiotic theory works against the grain of the contemporary structuralism of her teachers; her psychological theories owe much to Freud and to his French revisionist Jacques Lacan, yet Kristeva has made free to revise Lacan as well. Her feminist writings owe little to the specific ideas of any area of the movement. Like Jacques Derrida, who worked on the margins of philosophy to avoid being caught up in its antinomies, Kristeva too has preferred to work on the margins of the various schools and disciplines; her treatises have generally been primarily critiques of current theories and practices. For this reason, she has often been misunderstood, or understood but in part—a situation exacerbated at times by her playful French, which abounds in puns and coinages that presume a daunting range of reference and defy translation. The other general characterization of Kristeva's work is "eclectic." Though her thought is always original, she tends to combine elements from such diverse thinkers as Jacques Lacan, Roland Barthes, Michel Foucault, Mikhail Bakhtin, and Louis Althusser, usually with a considerable leap of faith about whether their divergent systems can work in harness as she insists they do. She sometimes seems unaware of the fact that texts which are linguistically revolutionary can be reactionary in every other respect.

The work of Julia Kristeva has two phases: an early structuralist-semiotic phase, followed by a psychoanalytic-feminist phase; in fact, both phases are deeply informed by psychoanalytic theory and practice. The early Kristeva is usually thought of as a structuralist literary theorist, but her first book, published in 1969, *Semeiotike: Recherches pour une semanalyse*, might be thought of as a critique of structuralism. Kristeva attacked the static conception of the signifier/signified relation within 1960s French structuralism, and attempted to replace it with a more fluid "semanalysis," which she hoped would do more justice to the historically shifting modes of representation. *Semeiotike* has not yet been translated into English as a whole, although two essays, "The Bounded Text" and "Word, Dialogue and Novel," are included in *Desire in Language*, a 1980 anthology. In "The Bounded Text" Kristeva seems to write as a fellow-traveler of the philosopher and historian Michel Foucault. "The Bounded Text" takes up the late medieval novel *Jehan de Saintré* as an *ideologème*—an example of the contemporary productions of language and thought—and Kristeva relates its peculiar semiotic practices, in particular its transitional uses of medieval symbolism, to the weakening of the bonds of feudal society and the approaching birth of the capitalism of the Renaissance. Kristeva's presentation of literature as an act of discourse, which is therefore, necessarily, a political act, shows some affinities to the readings of what is now called the New Historicism. "Word, Dialogue and Novel" is an exposition of the ideas of the Soviet literary theorist and critic Mikhail Bakhtin, whose books on Rabelais and Dostoevsky and essays on fiction, written as long ago as the 1920s and suppressed under Stalin, had in the early 1960s been released in Moscow. Just as her mentor Tzvetan Todorov had translated the Russian formalists into French, Kristeva was the major vector by which Bakhtin became influential in the West.

Kristeva's state doctoral thesis, published in 1974 as *La Révolution du langage poétique* (of which the first third has been translated into English as *Revolution in Poetic Language*), marks a turning point between pure linguistics and psychoanalysis, for the book was an application of psychoanalytic theory to language and literature. Kristeva's point of departure is the psychoanalytic theory of Jacques Lacan. In Lacan's revision of Freud, many of the psychological processes that Freud referred to as stages of physical development are given a purely symbolic or linguistic turn. The "Imaginary," a stage in the human infant's development in which desires are expressed as images and dreams, is the realm of the wordless image, characterized by Lacan as feminine; the "Symbolic" realm of the word, when the infant can speak and understand, is characterized as masculine, although both are obviously operative in individuals of ei-

ther gender. Nevertheless, for Lacanians literature is implicitly marked as a masculine domain. Kristeva's feminist revision of Lacan involves substituting what she calls the "semiotic" for the Imaginary. She posits that prior to its entry into language, the infant is the site of drives (*pulsions*) and primary processes: "discrete quantities of energy move through the body of the subject who is not yet constituted as such." These quanta of energy operate according to regulated bodily rhythms whose articulations are, like language, a signifying process, though they do not constitute a symbol system. Kristeva calls the "nonexpressive totality formed by the drives and their stases" the *chora*, after Plato's term in the *Timaeus* for "an invisible and formless being which receives all things and mysteriously participates in the intelligible, and which is most incomprehensible." For the child to learn language at all, the *chora* must be repressed. But as Terry Eagleton has put it, "the repression . . . is not total: for the semiotic can still be discerned as a kind of pulsional pressure within language itself, in tone, rhythm, the bodily and material qualities of language, but also in contradiction, meaninglessness, disruption, silence and absence." In all language, but particularly within poetic language (with its emphasis on sonority and on tropes), one may discern the irruption of the *chora*; like all productions of the subject—the self—poetic discourse is split between the pre-Oedipal semiotic and the Oedipal symbolic: "The very practice of art necessitates reinvesting the maternal *chora* so that it transgresses the symbolic order." The "revolution" to which Kristeva's title refers inheres in this "transgression": the semiotic is always subversive of the symbolic and sometimes, especially in poetic discourse, the semiotic manages to overrun the symbolic and to rule the signifying process. The important difference between Kristeva and Lacan is that, where for Lacan the Imaginary is *non*-linguistic, for Kristeva the semiotic operates as a continual pressure upon language. And where the Imaginary was identified with the feminine, the semiotic is identified with the pre-Oedipal mother, a figure who, as Toril Moi puts it, "looms as large for baby boys as for baby girls" and thus "cannot be reduced to an example of 'femininity' for the simple reason that the opposition between feminine and masculine does not exist in pre-Oedipality." The semiotic is not marked "feminine" as the Imaginary is; indeed, most of Kristeva's textual criticism in *La Révolution du langage poétique* is of male poets, primarily of Lautréamont, Mallarmé and Artaud.

The British and American response to *Revolution in Poetic Language* was mixed. Jonathan Culler, reviewing the 1974 French text fol-

fore his own conversion to poststructuralism, was primarily interested not in Kristeva's critique of Lacan but in what she would have to say about French avant-garde poetry. He found here "the tendency of a radical structuralism to denigrate and undermine those realms in which it might accomplish most. . . . An account of the revolutionary practice of texts cannot go far without reference to the conventions of literature as a social institution." Twelve years later, American critics were more familiar with Lacan and could appreciate Kristeva's revision of his theories. Nevertheless, Donald Morton's lengthy appreciation in *Western Humanities Review,* while finding Kristeva's model of language generally "a persuasive one," suggested that its feminism was suspect: "it is open to the charge of biologism" in that "the female . . . body becomes the 'ultimate signified.'"

Kristeva's collection of essays on literature and art written from 1966 to 1977, *Polylogue,* was in large part translated into English as *Desire in Language,* which was the first of her books to make a major impression on Anglophone audiences. The essays range from those on *Jehan de Saintré* and Mikhail Bakhtin from *Semeiotike* to new articles on theorists like Roland Barthes and Roman Jakobson, novelists like Louis-Ferdinand Céline and Philippe Sollers, and painters like Giotto and Bellini. By and large, Kristeva was respectfully received by the reviewers, but most of those who had not previously read *Revolution in Poetic Language*—then available only in French—were unable to make much sense of her method. Jonathan Arac noted only an "ambitious attempt to combine concern for the social world in its particularity, for the concreteness of the body, and for linguistic speculation"; Hayden White viewed Kristeva as a follower of Derrida (surely not her most important influence), though he found "many of her judgments scandalously implausible." White declared this "an important work for students of cultural processes" and admitted "there is no subject she introduces that does not force me to reconsider my own preconceptions." James Mall, with considerable awareness of her theories of language and the mind, however, was able to explain lucidly her view of art as an arena for the struggle between the symbolic and the semiotic; for Mall, Kristeva is "one of the major voices of the 'poststructuralist' era" and her book is "invaluable for the student of the contemporary critical climate."

Kristeva's distinctively feminist phase was inaugurated by her book *Des Chinoises* (*About Chinese Women,* 1974), and it was not an auspicious debut. China had been the Mecca of the New Left, particularly to the Parisian Marxists who participated in the events of May 1968, and Kristeva's three-week trip to China in April 1974 had the quality of a pilgrimage. But by the the time the book had been translated, the West was well aware of the repressive horrors of the Cultural Revolution, then drawing to its close. Sarah Jane Evans found the book behind the times and "short, interestingly speculative, but sadly uninformative." Kristeva's enthusiastic admiration for the Chinese social order seemed naive—or propagandistic. In general, as Edmund Leach wrote, the utopian tone of *About Chinese Women* told one more about "her feminist inner thoughts"—about Kristeva's desire to combine feminine eroticism with political power—than about "material reality in Eastern Asia." Though Kristeva certainly identifies herself as a feminist, her views on women's role in society, as on structuralism and Lacanian psychology, run counter to the movement's central direction, so much so that one cannot tell whether she is post-feminist or anti-feminist. In her introduction to the translation of Kristeva's important essay, "Women's Time," Alice Jardine admits that the essay "will be judged by many as antifeminist. I cannot possibly deny that it is." For Toril Moi, however, Kristeva is the French feminist who most deserves study and imitation.

Kristeva's prolific work in the 1980s consisted of four books centering on the emotions which occasionally touch upon literature but are written primarily in the psychoanalytic mode. These include one book on horror, or the more general quality of "abjection," two on love, and one on melancholy. As the analyst Otto F. Kernberg points out in the foreword to Kristeva's *In the Beginning There Was Love,* the common theme of these four books is a disengagement from her Lacanian training and a retracing of her steps back to the mainstream of psychoanalytic thinking. Kristeva "in contrast to Lacan, . . . places affects rather than language at the center of the contents of the Unconscious." *Powers of Horror* centers on the idea of abjection, an affect that includes physical disgust, spiritual repulsion, and religious renunciation. For Kristeva, the origin of abjection is co-terminous with the origins of the self when the infant separates as an individual from the pre Oedipal mother: it is the obverse side of the pleasure the infant took in fusion with the mother's body; in this moment of abjection Kristeva discovers the sources of fetish and taboo, and, more generally of language and culture. She explores the social ramifications of abjection through Eastern and Western societies, but her primary interest is the place of women— as objects of disgust and of religious taboo—in society. To deconstructionist Cynthia Chase, one primary interest of *Powers of Horror* was its congruence with Derrida's writings on Kant and Freud. For Toril Moi, "much of . . . *Powers of Horror* . . . could be valuably appropriated for feminism." The psychoanalyst Annette Lavers, on the other side, is skeptical about the relation of Kristeva's methods to her conclusions. Kristeva's method of semanalysis lays strong emphasis on the distinction between nature and culture, but "if one source of abjection is a feeling of emptiness springing from 'the mother's silent hatred for the father's word,' one could argue that a society where mothers don't have to use children to secure their own recognition might offer a better kind of welcome for the child. This might well be achieved if we put less stress on the dichotomy between nature and culture." Kristeva's way of theorizing a solution, in other words, may be part of the problem.

Tales of Love applies Kristeva's psychoanalytic method to the emotion at the other extreme from abjection. If anything, love seems more obviously constitutive of the individual and of society than abjection, and Kristeva traces the manifestations and myths about love (narcissism and idealization, decoy love and transference love, love of God and man and country and woman) throughout recorded culture. Interspersed with analyses of social structures and literary texts are analytic notes limning Kristeva's relationships with her analysands, though perhaps the most startling juxtaposition occurs within the chapter "Stabat Mater," where a shrewd and sober exposition of the history and psychology of the myth of the Virgin Mary is displayed in alternate columns with Kristeva's own inchoate feelings about her own first-time experience of motherhood. Of *Tales of Love*, Michael Ignatieff wrote, "the most exalted, overheated and least comprehensible passages . . . are perhaps best interpreted as a wild but exhausted pastiche of the original surrealist verve [which leaves] one longing for the conventions of clarity."

Melancholia, which Kristeva discusses in *Soleil Noir* (1987; translated as *Black Sun*), is the obverse side to religious faith, as she explains in essays on Holbein's *Dead Christ* and on Dostoevsky; its origin is the loss of the pre-Oedipal mother. Where melancholia and depression were similar in Freud, Kristeva posits a separate origin for narcissistic depression, where what is mourned is not the loss of the mother but the loss of the self. For Kristeva the obsessional nature of depression suggests that suffering is being embraced as a fetish—a substitute for the self that is lost. Of *Soleil Noir* Michael Ignatieff wrote, "Kristeva's contribution is to emphasize the relation between therapy and aesthetics, to tease out some of the reasons why beauty has the capacity to comfort. She is particularly concerned to understand why representations of depression or depressing subjects nevertheless retain their capacity to reassure and revive those who perceive them."

In 1990 Kristeva published a novel, *Les Samouraïs*, described by Elaine Showalter in the *Times Literary Supplement* as "a roman à clef about the theoretical and political fever that raged on the Left Bank after May 1968." The title alludes to the Japanese warrior class, Kristeva's characters being "intellectual warriors for whom living is a martial art, a stylized game of love and combat." Showalter found the novel "an interesting fictional début by an adventurous thinker who is always breaking new ground," but suggested that in her very deliberate effort to write a "popular" novel, Kristeva slipped too often into the conventions of stereotypical commercial fiction with lifeless characters and contrived incidents.

If Otto Kernberg's estimation is correct, Kristeva's most recent psychoanalytical books, though as ambitious as her earlier and more subversive work, have become less marginal to the field, just as her style has become less obtrusively inaccessible. Once a revolutionary squatter on the margins of discourse, Julia Kristeva has become a professor of linguistics, a psychoanalyst, a wife and a mother, and with her new sources of power and position, her discourse has moved toward the center. Roland Barthes' "étrangère" has found her homeland—and there are many readers who may find loss as well as gain.

WORKS IN ENGLISH TRANSLATION: Translations of full-length books by Kristeva include Anita Barrows' *About Chinese Women*, 1977; *Powers of Horror: An Essay on Abjection*, translated by Leon Roudiez, 1982; Roudiez also translated *Tales of Love*, 1987 and *Black Sun*, 1989; and Arthur Goldhammer's translation *In the Beginning Was Love: Psychoanalysis and Faith*, 1987. Parts of *Semeiotike* were translated as *Desire in Language* by Alice Jardine, Thomas A. Gora, and Leon Roudiez, 1980, which also includes parts of *Polylogue*. Katharine A. Jensen's translation of a chapter from *Soleil Noir*, "The Pain and Sorrow in the Modern World: The Works of Marguerite Duras," was published in PMLA, March 1987. Margaret Waller's translation of parts of *Revolution in Poetic Language* was published in 1984. Translations of shorter works include the essays "The System and the Speaking Subject," in the Times Literary Supplement, October 12, 1973; "Women's Time," translated by Alice Jardine and Harry Blake in Signs, Autumn 1981.

ABOUT: Eagleton, T. Literary Theory: An Introduction, 1983; Kernberg, O. F. *Foreword* to In the Beginning There Was Love, 1987; Moi, T. Sexual/Textual Politics, 1985; Roudiez, L. Introduction to Desire in Language, 1980. Periodicals—Choice September 1985, March 1987; Contemporary Psychology June, 1987;

Criticism Summer 1981, Spring 1984; French Review April 1978; Journal of Aesthetics and Art Criticism Fall 1981; Journal of Modern History December 1982; Modern Fiction Studies December 1982; Modern Language Review October 1973; New Statesman October 1986; Spectator March 12, 1977; Times Education Supplement October 10, 1986; Times Literary Supplement September 18, 1970; September 3, 1971; August 30, 1974; April 22, 1977; October 24, 1980; September 4, 1987; April 15–21, 1988; June 3–9, 1988; September 28, 1990; Western Humanities Review 1986.

*KUNZE, REINER (August 16, 1933–), German poet, novelist and translator, writes: "I was born in Oelsnitz (Erzgebirge). My father was a miner; my mother was a homeworker for the hosiery industry. From 1951 to 1955 I studied journalism and philosophy (history of literature, art and music) at the University of Leipzig. From 1955 to 1959 I held a teaching position there. Following political altercations that forced me to leave the university, I worked as an assistant mechanic in heavy machinery production. After my son Ludwig was born, I went through a divorce. In 1961 I married Elisabeth Mifka, a Czech medical doctor and dentist, and adopted her daughter Marcela. From 1962 to 1977 we lived in the German Democratic Republic (in Greiz, Thuringia). My wife worked as a jaw surgeon, and I was a freelance writer. However, most of my books could only be published in the Federal Republic, and in 1976, upon the publication of my prose work, *Die wunderbaren Jahre* (*The Wonderful Years*) by S. Fischer in Frankfurt am Main, I was excluded from the Writers Union. Political circumstances forced me to seek expatriation from the GDR. On April 13, 1977, we moved to the Federal Republic of Germany and settled near Passau (Bavaria).

"As a young person indoctrinated by state ideology from childhood on, I wrote verse that essentially illustrated this ideology and led me away from poetry; and yet, also dating from this period, there exist a few poems that are free of ideological delusions and coined, instead, by poetic images. Following a period of existential crises, during which I had become conscious of the inhumanity of the political regime I was committed to, I slowly discovered myself and began to trust my own eyes. Through my wife I got to know Czech poetry which had a lasting influence upon my use of imagery. I have been translating Czech poetry ever since."

—trans. T. Evans

Although Kunze's early poetry collec-

REINER KUNZE

tions—*die zukunft sitzt am tische* (the future sits at the table, 1955), *vügel über dem tau* (birds above the dew, 1959), *aber die nachtigall jubelt* (but the nightingale rejoices, 1962)—had received high praise in officially sanctioned reference works of the German Democratic Republic, he was, by the mid-1970s, reprimanded for the subjectively narrowed perspective and the distorted image of socialist society in his subsequent work (e.g., his satires of the bureaucracy). Influenced by Johannes R. Becher's poetic confessions, especially his books *Verteidigung der Poesie* (The defense of poetry) and *Macht der Poesie* (The power of poetry) which Kunze had read in the late 1950s, he came to the conclusion that poetry must be protected for its own sake and thus began to emancipate himself from the doctrine that poetry is ancillary to political ideology. His rejection of capital letters can be interpreted as a formal declaration that poetry is subject to different rules. To comply with ideology and to compromise would signal the end of art, a point made in a fable which Kunze wrote in 1960:

"The end of art"

You must not, the owl said to the heath cock,
you must not sing of the sun
the sun is not significant

The heath cock took
the sun out of his poem

You are an artist,
said the owl to the heath cock
And it was nice and dark.

—trans. T. Evans

°kūn´ se, rī´ nor

In his Afterword to *zimmerlautstärke* (1972; translated as *With the Volume Turned Down*) Kunze called the poem "a stabilizer," "a reference point of the self," "an act of gaining degrees of freedom inside and outside." However, the definitive breakthrough which also helped to establish Kunze before a wider audience, had occurred earlier, in his 1969 volume *sensible wege* (sensitive paths), dedicated to the people of Czechoslovakia and a protest against the invasion by Warsaw Pact troops the previous year. In his collection consisting of forty-eight poems and the cycle, "21 variations on the topic 'the mail'," Reiner Kunze openly sided with fellow authors who were persecuted by the authorities—Peter Huchel, Milan Kundera, Alexander Solzhenitsyn, and Jan Skácel to whom he is greatly indebted and whose works he had translated. Kunze avoids excessive emotion, relying instead on pithy observations or simple metaphors. In later poems reduction is carried even further, notably in the nocturnes from his 1973 volume *brief mit blauem siegel* (letter with a blue seal) published in Leipzig and almost completely ignored by the media in the German Democratic Republic but going through two editions of 15,000, each of which sold out within days:

"Nocturne II"

Sleep you don't come

You also
are afraid

In my thoughts you catch sight of
the dream your
murderer.

—trans. M. Hamburger

Kunze's images, according to P. J. Graves, "telescope into a single vivid picture a complete thought-sequence or a whole cluster of emotions. They are left without elaboration." The ambiguous title of Kunze's 1972 collection *With the Volume Turned Down* suggests, among other things, that poetry need not be loud and shrill in order to be heard. At the same time the title is a grim reminder that those who wish to listen to foreign broadcasts must be careful once again, lest they be denounced by neighbors as they had been during the Nazi period. Kunze's epigrammatic points, his subtle understatements, ironic hints and calm observations are reminiscent of the late Bertolt Brecht; but for his graphic use of metaphor Kunze, according to Peter Graves, claims a debt above all to modern Czech poetry. The opening cycle, "monologues with my monologue," finds its thematic sequel in a volume of short prose sketches, *Die wunderbaren Jahre*

(1976; translated as *The Wonderful Years*). The title of the collection is a quote from Truman Capote's *The Grass Harp*: "I was eleven, and then I was sixteen. Though no honors came my way, those were the lovely years" (the German translation reads *die wunderbaren Jahre*). The intention behind Kunze's title is highly ironic for, in part at least, his Wonderful Years unveil the aggressiveness of children growing up in a militaristic society, as for instance in the opening of a section entitled "Peace Children":

"Six-Year-Old"

He bores pins through toy soldiers. He shoves a pin into each belly until the point comes out of the back. He shoves it into the back until the point comes out of the chest.
They fall.
"And why *these* soldiers?"
"They are the others."

—trans. J. Neugroschel

In other sections of *The Wonderful Years*, Kunze chronicles the disheartening experiences of adolescents living in a world in which teachers, educators, policemen, and prosecuters are bent on intimidating or punishing nonconformist young people. Kunze does not preach, and he does not accuse; he merely registers. Comparable to his terse poems, the highly condensed documentary style and laconic tenor of his prose prove to be far more effective than passionate outcries or satirical renderings could ever be. Not all the texts in this collection focus on an oppressive educational system; some of Kunze's best prose pieces transcend the specifics of life in the German Democratic Republic and treat, with gentle humor and genuine insight, the pains of adolescence, its awkwardness and contradictoriness, or his teen-age daughter's infuriating and occasionally absurd logic as in "Fifteen"; following a description of his daughter's clothes ("She wears a skirt, it beggars description, for even one word would be too long") and her incredibly untidy room, Kunze continues as follows:

She's horrified of spiders. So I said: "There were two nests of spiders under your bed."
Her lilac-shadowed eyelids vanished behind popping eyeballs, and she started shrieking: "Eeeh! Yechh! Ugh! . . . And why do they have to build their nests under *my* bed?"
"No one ever bothers them there." I didn't want to hint any harder, and she *is* intelligent.
By evening, she had regained her inner equilibrium. Lying in bed, she had an almost supercilious air. Her slippers were on the piano. "I'm keeping them up there from now on," she said. "So the spiders can't crawl in."

—trans. J. Neugroschel

An actor, writer, and director a film version of *Die wunderboren Jahre* that attracted wide attention in West Germany for its political views. While many of Kunze's prose sketches and poems reflect his disapproval of German Democratic Republic–style socialism, his prime concern in writing is not to side with or against a particular political system. P. J. Graves emphasizes Kunze's commitment "to the defense of individual integrity in a hostile world, be it in the face of an overweening state . . . or of a wider feeling of vulnerability and powerlessness." It is the poet's task "to make the earth more inhabitable" (*With the Volume Turned Down*).

Prior to the publication of Kunze's poetry collection *auf eigene hoffnung* (at your own hope, 1981) critics wondered to what extent his writing might be affected by his move to the West in 1977. For the most part, *auf eigene hoffnung* as well as *eines jeden einziges leben* (everyone's one and only life, 1986) display stylistic as well as thematic continuity rather than innovation. As before, Kunze's single, pregnant metaphors are based on elemental words (*bells, bridges, apples, fish, birds, cocks, rain*), his poetic inspirations resulting from brief and precise observations made while travelling in Scandinavia, London, the Alps, France, Jerusalem, etc. A handful of texts that reflect the freedom of travel—, "leere schneestangen, norwegen, mitte september" (empty snow poles, norway, mid september), "Hallstatt mit schwarzem stift" (Hallstatt sketched in black) and "mit den eltern in den alpen" (with my parents in the alps) are among Kunze's most beautiful occasional poems whereas his 1980 cycle on the United States hardly transcends the tourist's narrow perspective. In a number of polemical poems in *auf eigene hoffnung*, the defense of poetry turns into the poet's self-defense against the culture industry of the West: Kunze refuses to deliver poetry at intervals that are dictated by marketing strategies. Attacking critics, politicians, ideologues, and church dignitaries, he claims in a poem consisting of just two lines: "They do not want your flight, they want / the feathers." Several new themes entered *eines jeden einziges leben* : life in a new house, concerns about the environment, the process of aging, and death.

P. J. Graves points out that Kunze remains independent of particular parties or groups. "If there is to be hope—and Kunze's work is infused with the defiant rejection of despair—it can only, in his view, be personal and individual." In a review of Kunze's *eines jeden einziges leben* in the *Times Literary Supplement* in 1988, Graves called him "one of Germany's most humane and sensitive poets." A volume of Kunze's essays on poetry, *Das weisse Gedicht* (The White Poems), was published in 1989.

Reiner Kunze is the recipient of numerous prizes and awards: Czech Writers Union Prize for Translators 1968; German Prize for Adolescent Literature (Federal Republic of Germany) 1971; Literature Prize of the Bavarian Academy of the Arts 1973; Mölle Prize for Literature (Sweden) 1973; Georg Trakl Prize in Poetry (Austria) 1977; Andreas Gryphius Prize 1977; Georg Büchner Prize 1977; Bavarian Film Prize 1979; Geschwister Scholl Prize 1981; Eichendorff Literature Prize 1984.

WORKS IN ENGLISH TRANSLATION: *With the Volume Turned Down, and Other Poems*, in Ewald Osers' translation, was published in 1973; another translation, by Lori Fischer, was published in 1981 with the title *With the Volume Down Low*. Joachim Neugroschel translated *The Wonderful Years* in 1977; it was also translated by Ewald Osers in 1978 as *The Lovely Years*. Selections from Kunze's poetry appear in Michael Hamburger's *German Poetry 1910–1975*, 1976, and in a special issue of Dimension in 1973. Several of his poems, translated by John Linthiceum, were published in The Literary Review, Fall 1989.

ABOUT: Contemporary Authors 93–96, 1980; Contemporary Literary Criticism 10, 1979; Dictionary of Literary Biography 75, 1988; Flores, J. Poetry in East Germany, 1971; Graves, P. J., (ed.) Three Contemporary German Poets: Wolf Biermann, Sarah Kirsch, Reiner Kunze, 1985. *Periodicals*—Encounter July 1978; New York Times Book Review April 24, 1977; New Yorker September 26, 1977; Publications of the Arkansas Philological Association (PAPA) 6, 1980; Selecta 3, 1982; Times Literary Supplement June 12, 1977; March 11, 1988.

LA GUMA, ALEX (February 20, 1925– October 11, 1985), South African novelist and short-story writer, was born in Cape Town, the son of mixed-race parents. His grandparents were all immigrants, of Indonesian, Malagasy, German, and Scottish extraction. The political activism of his father, a leading trade unionist and member of the South African Communist party, ensured that La Guma was intimate from an early age with left-wing anti-racist politics. He grew up in a working-class ghetto of Cape Town where the races mixed more freely than elsewhere in the country. At the age of thirteen, he volunteered unsuccessfully to join the International Brigade fighting fascism in Spain. He dropped out of high school and found employment as a warehouse hand, a factory worker, and a bookkeeper before becoming a journalist in 1957. After the Communist party was declared an illegal organization in 1950, La Guma was detained for months without trial on three separate occasions, charged with high treason along with

ALEX LA GUMA

155 other anti-racist leaders, and on acquittal was placed under a five-year house arrest. For that period he was barred from leaving his house, communicating with friends, writing journalism, and participating in politics. In 1966 he departed for England on an exit visa which forbade him to ever return. Abroad he worked in radio and insurance until serving, for eight years, as chairman of the London branch of the African National Congress. He moved to Cuba in 1982 where, until his death three years later, he served as chief representative of the African National Congress in the Caribbean.

Together with the poet Dennis Brutus, Alex La Guma is the best known of a generation of black South African writers who were driven into exile during the 1960s and early 1970s. He published fourteen short stories, five novels, and a travel book on the Soviet Union, along with an array of political essays on the liberation struggle. His first and most successful book, *A Walk in the Night and Other Stories* was, like all his subsequent writings, banned in South Africa. It is suffused with an empathy for outlaws and the socially disinherited—alcoholics, prisoners, prostitutes, the unemployed, and rebels against apartheid. In Nadine Gordimer's words, La Guma's protagonists "do not talk about inequality, they bear its weals." None more so than Michael Adonis, the leading character of the title story: thrown out of his job and hindered by the racial laws from getting another, he becomes a ghetto itinerant whose hopes disappear down a spiral of dissolution. The novella closes with his accidentally killing a white man and standing by as his friend, Willieboy, is blamed for the deed.

The short stories included in *A Walk in the Night* find La Guma at his most innovative. They are written largely in "Englikaans," the dialect blended of English and Afrikaans that is the staple of Cape Town's mixed-race ghettos. The stories bear out the observation of the American critic Bernth Lindfors that La Guma's characters exhibit "an unusual sensitivity or a sense of honor or morality which redeems them as human beings and raises them to heroic stature. These slum-dwelling heroes are victims of their environment and their passions. When they act, they do not exercise their own free will but rather they *react* to the pressures and forces working on them from within and without."

And a Threefold Cord, a less successful, somewhat episodic novel is again inhabited by slum-dwellers unable to escape the limits of their fundamentally reactive life. The setting is the ghetto of Windemere, a mound of human detritus and also a literal dump for garbage from the white suburbs, so that an entire section of the slum appears "like the back of a decaying monster, its scales of rotting paper, wood, offal, tin cans and indescribable filth, heaving and twitching in the stiff, damp breeze." Here, as in most of La Guma's fiction, the derelict landscape, depicted with minute naturalism, comes to dominate the novel. Indeed, the social protest in his writing tends to be achieved through accumulative depictions of the surface of the ghetto rather than through detailed inquiry into the psychology of its inhabitants:

> It could hardly be called a street, not even a lane; just a hollowed track that stumbled and sprawled between and around and through the patchwork of shacks, cabins, huts and wickiups· a maze of cracks between the jigsaw pieces of the settlement, a writhing battlefield of mud and straggling entanglements of wet and rusty barbed wire, sagging sheets of tin, toppling pickets, twigs and peeled branches and collapsing odds and ends with edges and points as dangerous as sharks' teeth, which made up the fencework around the quagmire of lots.

In his third book, *The Stone Country*, La Guma draws on his own experience of South African jail-life. Rigidly partitioned into black, "colored" and white cells, the prison stands as a microcosm for the rifts and graded privileges in the society at large. La Guma succeeds in creating one or two memorable inmates—notably the Casbah Kid, who awaits hanging on death row and of whom we are told that "vengeance slipped into his mind with the ease of the sprockets of an oiled wheel into the links of a greased chain." However, in the confines of this fictional prison La Guma has less scope to demonstrate his skill at evoking landscapes and the shallowness of his psychological interest is too much in evidence. As a consequence, the prisoners tend to come across as types rather than as fully individuated characters.

In the Fog of the Season's End marks a shift in La Guma's focus, as his depiction of the underground struggle against apartheid becomes inflected with tones of defiance absent from the earlier fiction. The novel conveys a full sense not only of the hazardous lives of guerrilla activists but also of how those guerrillas were created in the first place, through suffering ritual indignities under the migrant labor system and the pass laws, and being tortured in prison. The novel's primary character, Beukes, is the most autobiographical figure in La Guma's work. While commending the gentle prose and political commitments of *In the Fog of the Season's End*, Nadine Gordimer contends that La Guma "writes, like so many black exiles, as if life in South Africa froze with the trauma of Sharpeville . . . he cannot from abroad quite make the projection, at the deeper level, into a black political milieu that has changed so much since he left." His battle to stay in touch with the immediate, sensual realities of his remote homeland seems all the more urgent when one recalls that, despite nineteen years in exile, all his novels are set in South Africa.

La Guma's final novel, *Time of the Butcherbird*, is his most socially ambitious. It deals with the intersecting fates of South Africa's black, Afrikaans and English-speaking peoples, rather than restricting itself to the specific struggles of Cape Town's mixed-race community, as all his prior fiction had done. The novel is dedicated to "The Dispossessed" and charts both the forced removal of a black South African community from their ancestral lands and their defiance in the face of that decree:

> The dust settled slowly on the metal of the tank and on the surface of the brackish water it contained, laboriously pumped from below the sand; on the rough cubist mounds of folded and piled tents dumped there by officialdom; on the sullen faces of the people who had been unloaded like the odds and ends of furniture they had been allowed to bring with them, powdering them grey and settling in the perspiring lines around mouths and in the eye sockets, settling on the unkempt and travel-ceased clothes, so that they had the look of scarecrows left behind, abandoned in this place.

Threaded through this narrative of deracination is the story of the brooding personal revenge of Shilling Murile, a black laborer whose brother has been murdered by an Afrikaans farmer. Although Murile avenges his brother's death, it becomes clear by the end of the novel that isolated resistance to white tyranny is insufficient: the scale of the land's injustices requires, La Guma implies, a collective uprising.

La Guma stands as a primary influence on the naturalistic black South African novelists who burgeoned in the 1970s and 1980s. He has been particularly admired for the daring colloquialism of his dialogue, his robust evocations of the resilient human jetsam in Cape Town's ghettos, and for what his contemporary Lewis Nkosi describes as "the stunning precision of his observation and the bare-limbed economy of the prose." Moreover, as Nkosi observes, "the qualities which make La Guma's fiction so compellingly true and immediate are not simply its fidelity to its own source materials—which is a life of complete and naked brutality under a repressive regime—but the quiet exactness of its tone and the adequacy of its moral pressures."

PRINCIPAL WORKS: A Walk in the Night and Other Stories, 1962; And a Threefold Cord, 1964; The Stone Country, 1967; In the Fog of the Season's End, 1972; Time of the Butcherbird, 1979.

ABOUT: Abrahams, C. Alex La Guma, 1985; February, V. A. Mind Your Colour, 1981; Gordimer, N. The Black Interpreters, 1973; Nkosi, L. The Transplanted Heart, 1975; Parker, K. The South African Novel in English, 1978; Zell, H. M., C. Bundy, V. Coulon (eds.) A New Reader's Guide to African Literature, 2nd ed., 1983. *Periodicals*—New York Times Book Review January 12, 1986.

---

*LACOUTURE, JEAN (MARIE GÉRARD) (June 9, 1921–), French biographer, political scientist, sociologist, and journalist, was born in Bordeaux, the son of Antoine Lacouture, a surgeon, and the former Anne-Marie Servantie. He was educated by the Jesuits at the Collège de Tivoli in his native city, then in the law and arts faculties of the University of Bordeaux and in the law faculty of the University of Paris. He also holds a diploma from the École Libre des Sciences Politiques in Paris and a doctorate in sociology from the Sorbonne, the latter awarded in the late 1960s upon submission of the thesis that was to become the book *Quatre hommes et leurs peuples: Sur-pouvoir et sous-développement*, (Four Men and Their Nations: Excessive Power and Underdevelopment, 1969; translated as *The Demigods: Charismatic Leadership in the Third World*), one of the most remarkable and penetrating studies ever written of third-world political elites.

Although trained to be an attorney, Lacouture never practiced law. The first three decades of his career were spent as a working journalist. He was press attaché (1945–1947) on the general staff of General Philippe Leclerc, commander of French forces in Indochina, then held the same position (1947–1949) at the French high com-

JEAN LACOUTURE

mission in Morocco. He was diplomatic correspondent (1950–1951) for the left-wing journal *Combat* and for the daily newspaper *Le Monde* (1951–1953), then Egyptian correspondent for *France-Soir* (1954–1956). He returned to *Le Monde* for a long period of employment (1957–1975), first as chief foreign correspondent, then as general reporter. From 1961 to 1982 he was in charge of selecting the politics and sociology lists for the distinguished Parisian publishing house Editions du Seuil, where he founded and directed the collections "L'Histoire Immédiate" and "Traversée du Siècle." He taught political science in 1969–1972 at the Institute for Political Studies in Vincennes. Since his retirement from *Le Monde* he has been a full-time writer, and has become known as one of the most astute political biographers of his time.

Lacouture's first book (as well as several subsequent to it) was written with his wife, the former Simonne Grésillon, an expert on the Middle East, to whom he was married in 1951. *L'Egypte en mouvement* (Egypt on the Move, 1956; translated as *Egypt in Transition*) is an impressively thorough geopolitical study of modern Egypt, written the year of the epochal debacle over Suez and at the very apogee of President Gamal Abdel Nasser's political power and influence. It is basically a study of the Egyptian revolution of 1952 and its aftermath. The lengthy book's exhaustive detail, which makes it even today a valuable document for anyone interested in the inner workings of Nasserism and the origins of the contemporary Egyptian polity, is essentially the result of the Lacoutures' having lived and

worked in Cairo during the events described. Its English-language version was widely and very favorably reviewed. "A well-written, penetrating book," wrote Charles Issawi in *Saturday Review*, "the best by far yet written on postrevolutionary Egypt." James Morris in the *New York Times Book Review* called it "political reportage of brilliance: fair, scholarly, perceptive, often entertaining . . . fine journalism . . . a worthy example of the maturity and tolerance of the European tradition."

Other books written by Simonne and Jean Lacouture, most of them not available in English translation, include: *Le Maroc à l'épreuve* (Morocco's Ordeal, 1958); *Israel et les arabes: Le troisième combat,* (1967; translated as *Israel and the Arabs: The Third Combat*); *Les émirats mirages: Voyage chex les pétrocrates* (with Gabriel Dardaud; The Mirage Emirates: Journey among the Petrocrats, 1975); *Vietnam: Voyage à travers unre victoire* (Vietnam: Voyage in Time of Victory, 1976); and *En passant par la France* (By Way of France, 1982), the last a reflective tour of France in the aftermath of the Socialist election victory of 1981.

Since the 1950s Lacouture has been one of the major Western authorities on Indochina. His third book, written with the historian Philippe Devillers, was *La fin d'une guerre: Indochine 1954* (1960; revised by the authors and translated as *End of a War: Indochina, 1954*), a brilliant and, from the United States' point of view, entirely prescient study of the disastrous French experience in Vietnam. In an introduction written in early 1969, Lacouture describes the explicit parallelism between French and American aims in Vietnam: "with every passing day, the underlying continuity has become more evident. France fought to retain its influence in Vietnam through a ruling class tied to its interests; the United States launched its expeditionary force to secure victory for counterrevolution and to show the whole Third World that opting for the Marxist road to progress draws the vengeance of the Lord. A single thread of history links the two campaigns." The authors contend that the pervasive American passion for the anticommunist crusade has inured the American public to murderous military adventures among peoples they do not even begin to know or understand. They point to "this profound and disturbing ignorance among American politicians [which] led to an unconscious imitation of the French colonial way."

Le Vietnam entre deux paix (1965; translated as *Vietnam between Two Truces*) is a book that seemed more dated two decades later than its predecessor, but it had an essentially similar aim:

to show that the overwhelming presence of foreign forces in Vietnam obscured the true nature of the struggle being waged there, lessening the hope for the settlement of what was basically a local issue. Lacouture speaks frequently and uncompromisingly as a committed man of the left who has known Vietnam and its people for many years; for him, the long-term cost of the American intervention is clear: "the sight of Marines battling in Da Nang . . . drives to despair millions of people—in the West, in the uncommitted nations, and in the socialist world—who place their greatest hope in peaceful coexistence, which is the key to the liberalization of the totalitarian regimes."

Lacouture's experience in Indochina led him to write one of the most shocking, damning, and passionate books of the post–Vietnam War era. *Survive le peuple cambodgien!* (May the Cambodian People Survive!, 1978) was never translated into English. It had its origins in an article he published in 1976 in the *New York Review of Books* protesting the refusal of the new Cambodian government of Pol Pot and his Khmer Rouge to allow any foreign journalist into the country. The reason for this refusal, Lacouture gradually came to understand, was that nothing less than autogenocide was being practiced throughout the country. The book is "a cry of horror," in the words of the author, who expresses his "shame at having contributed, in however small a way, so feeble was the influence of the press, to the installation of one of the most oppressive powers that history has ever known." Lacouture also wrote the introduction to a grim, firsthand account of the Cambodian genocide, Y Phandara's *Retour à Phnom Penh* (Return to Phnom Penh, 1982), a native son's story of his voluntary return to revolutionary Cambodia and of his near extermination in Pol Pot's "reeducation camps."

Lacouture has also become known as an important authority on third-world political development. With the journalist Jean Baumier he wrote *Le poids du Tiers Monde: Un milliard d'hommes* (The Weight of the Third World: A Billion Men, 1962), an exploration of emergent political leadership in postcolonial societies. In *The Demigods*, he refined his position with a study of the careers—most of them at the time of publication no longer flourishing—of the Egyptian Nasser, Habib Bourguiba of Tunisia, King Norodom Sihanouk of Cambodia, and the Ghanaian Kwame Nkrumah. He poses at the outset the question: "We are told that the rise of a hero promotes the growth of national consciousness and gives a momentum to the struggles for economic development. But should this type of power, which is essential in the beginning, endure and become institutionalized? For what purpose, and in what ways?"

Lacouture's career as political biographer began with *De Gaulle* (1965) a short and extremely lively book written when the general was still in power as president of the French republic. It is not so much a complete biography as a speculation upon the forces and battles that made de Gaulle the most remarkable French politician of his generation. Lacouture had thus only a qualified conclusion to offer in summation of the man's career: "To some, he is only the flamboyant alibi for French political underdevelopment, and to others, the necessary agent of an abrupt transition into the industrial era: an operation they willingly qualify as Caesarean. So long as he lives, Frenchmen will feel they know the weight of this abusive man, this hypnotist who watches over their political sleep; but his greatness, true or false, will be measured more accurately when he is gone." Stanley Hoffmann wrote in the *New York Times Book Review*: "Rarely has a study succeeded in being so suggestive, perceptive and rich in so few pages. . . . Lacouture's range is unlimited, and his style a delight." De Gaulle himself was widely reported to have liked the book, which was anything but adulatory in its attitude to him, because it portrayed him primarily as a political man (*un homme politique*), not a military one.

Charles de Gaulle is also the title of Lacouture's most ambitious work to date, a monumental full-dress biography, nearly three thousand pages in all, which, complete with an extensive bibliography and a great many notes, was published in France in the nearly incredible space of only three years. Volume one, *Le Rebelle 1890–1944* (1984) appeared first, followed by volume two, *Le Politique 1945–1958* (1985), which won the prix des Ambassadeurs. Volume three is *Le Souverain 1959–1970* (1986).

The other biographies are no less magisterial, but treat men with whose accomplishments and political points of view the author might be thought to be more sympathetic. *Ho Chi Minh* (1967; translated as *Ho Chi Minh: A Political Biography*), was important in introducing the supreme leader of the Vietnamese revolution to his former French and then-current American enemies. "Of all men alive today," Lacouture wrote near the end of the book, "Ho is perhaps the one who has best shown the power of will, armed with an inexorable ability to wield power and rooted in national aspirations." This phrase was of course written before Ho's death in 1969. A revised French edition appeared in 1976, but was not translated into English. Here the author was able to offer a more balanced, posthumous assessment of Ho's career: "What is striking, finally, is the didactic will of the leader more than the concern of the man to leave of himself a flattering or even an exact picture."

Nasser (1971; translated as *Nasser: A Biography*) presents a complete account of the career of the great nationalist leader of Egypt from his boyhood through his military career and the revolutionary times he lived through and helped to make, to his death in 1970. It is not one of Lacouture's longer and more reflective biographies, but it succeeds in coupling an account of the man's life with the author's expert analysis of modern Egypt and the problems it faces. R. H. Nolte, writing in the *New York Times Book Review*, said that although the book was "impressionistic, sketchy, and with background and sidelights incomplete and much omitted, it is nevertheless deeply perceptive, lucid, and essentially fair to that prodigious man—triumph, failure, flaws and all."

André Malraux: Une vie dans le siècle (1973; translated in an abridged version as *André Malraux*) is Lacouture's largely successful attempt to take the measure of one of the great mythomaniacs of the century, the novelist, self-promoter, and minister of culture under President de Gaulle: "A writer with no followers, a 'loner' who has kept aloof from literary diplomacy and commerce since 1939, a writer of indefinable influence, . . . contemptuous of fashion and of stylistic or formal experiment, and quite happy to play the role of the man of action who has somehow wandered into literature, of the 'serious' man fallen prey to the futile malice of word-spinners, he is for many people, as for François Mauriac, 'the greatest living French writer and certainly the oddest.' But he himself has always questioned his greatness as a writer." Lacouture, wrote Mavis Gallant in the *New York Times Book Review*, "is not out to dynamite André Malraux but to circumscribe him. . . . If, at the end, the pieces seem more fragmented than ever the fault is not Lacouture's. He is dealing with a . . . character who may not want to be labeled." In the opinion of Roy McMullen in *Saturday Review*, Lacouture "was the right man for the job . . . of refocusing on this evasive personage. . . . The debunking, although courteously ironical, is ruthless." The biography won the Prix Aujourd'hui.

Léon Blum (1977) is a deeply admiring account of the charismatic intellectual who headed France's Popular Front government in the mid-1930s and who has always been regarded by people of the left—both inside France and abroad—as a wholly admirable and brilliant man of humane principle. The book is an official

biography, in that Lacouture had access to Blum's private papers and the cooperation of the family. It is especially evocative of the period of Blum's coming of age during the 1890s, when he was a budding *littérateur*, associating with André Gide, Marcel Proust, and Stéphane Mallarmé, and of the period just before World War I, when he was apprenticed politically to Jean Jaurès and emerged eventually in the very top echelons of the Socialist party.

A similarly adulatory account of another leftist French politician is Lacouture's *Pierre Mendès France* (1981) Mendès France held power only briefly (June 1954–February 1955) as prime minister during France's chaotic Fourth Republic, but his influence on France's political life and thought has been enormous. "He was a born Jacobin and secularist," writes the biographer; "he had been a model pupil of the public educational system and a brilliant student at the faculty of law and the School of Political Science. . . . He had been the youngest lawyer and the youngest deputy in France. He had been a secretary of state at thirty-one and a minister at thirty-seven. Everything in this background led toward his exercise of the highest and weightiest responsibilities." Lacouture is sympathetic and typically incisive about "PMF's" career as prime minister. The genre of political biography, wrote Robert O. Paxton in the *New York Review of Books*, is one in "which Lacouture has few peers. He is at his best here: warmly sympathetic toward an admirable person, and sensitive to the twists of system, personality, and chance that kept PMF from realizing his full possibilities."

Major works by Lacouture not translated into English include *François Mauriac* (1980), a lengthy politico-literary biography of a writer very little read in English-speaking countries but the most important figure in the French center-left Catholic tradition; and *Julie de Lespinasse: Mourir d'amour* (1980, with Marie-Christine d'Aragon), a biography of an extraordinary and nearly forgotten heroine of the Enlightenment, whose salon was frequented by d'Alembert, Condorcet, Marmontel, La Rochefoucauld, Turgot, and La Harpe. Her many amatory passions are recounted in great detail and her excellent letters are extensively quoted. Lacouture has published several collections of interviews—a kind of book more frequently encountered in continental Europe than in Britain or America. These include *Arabes & Israéliens: Un premier dialogue* (1974; translated as *Arabs & Israelis: A Dialogue*) in which he served as interlocutor for the Israeli historian Saul Friedländer and the Egyptian political scientist Mahmood Hussein, Norodom Sihanouk's *L'Indochine vue de Pékin*

(Indochina Seen from Peking, 1972); Georges Buis' *Les fanfares perdues* (Lost Fanfares, 1975); Alexandre Minkowski's *Le mandarin aux pieds nus* (The Barefoot Mandarin, 1975); and Lacouture's own engaging reflections on his life as a journalist, a series of interviews with Claude Glayman, *Un sang d'encre* (Ink for Blood, 1974).

Final signs, if any were needed, of Lacouture's exceptionally wide range of interests and great prolificity as a writer are his two volumes of sports commentary: *Signes du taureau: Chroniques 1965–1978* (1979), fifty-three wonderfully evocative articles on bullfighting, all save two previously published in *Le Monde*; and *Le rugby: C'est un monde* (1979), a similar collection on rugby football. "In sport, I am a marginal case," he told Claude Glayman in *Un sang d'encre*. "But I always write without ridicule. I publish technically elementary articles on rugby, as well as on the *corrida*. I aspire only to a simple evocation, which, without exasperating the specialists or causing them to make fun of me, may amuse interested readers. . . . I can bring to the description of a sport a certain concern for form and a certain disinterestedness which are not very widespread among those who have devoted themselves to it."

WORKS IN ENGLISH TRANSLATION: Francis Scarfe's translation of *Egypt in Transition* appeared in 1958. *End of a War: Indochina, 1954* was translated in 1969 by Alexander Lieven and Adam Roberts. In 1966 *Vietnam: Between Two Truces*, translated by Konrad Kellen and Joel Carmichael, and Francis K. Price's translation of *De Gaulle* were published. *Israel and the Arabs: The Third Combat* appeared in 1967, translator unidentified. Peter Wiles' translation *Ho Chi Minh: A Political Biography* was published in 1968. Patricia Wolf translated *The Demigods: Charismatic Leadership in The Third World* in 1970. *Nasser*, translated by Daniel Hofstadter, was published in 1973. In 1975 two translations—Alan Sheridan's *André Malraux* and Paul Auster and Lydia Davis' *Arabs and Israelis: A Dialogue*—were published. George Holoch translated *Léon Blum* in 1982 and *Pierre Mendès France* in 1985.

ABOUT: Contemporary Authors 101, 1981; Who's Who in France 1987–1988. *Periodicals*—America November 26, 1966; November 29, 1969; February 28, 1976; Annals of the American Academy May 1959; November 1969; Atlantic June 1966; Best Sellers October 15, 1966; July 1, 1973; April 1976; Book Week March 13, 1966; October 30, 1966; Book World July 7, 1968; Choice July 1966, December 1968, January 1969; March 1971, June 1976, March 1983, January 1985; Christian Century March 16, 1966; September 21, 1966; July 10, 1968; January 28, 1976; Christian Science Monitor December 2, 1958; May 19, 1966; July 27, 1968; Commonweal July 1, 1976; Current History March 1959; Economist October 1, 1966; July 19, 1969; Foreign Affairs July 1959; Library Journal March 1, 1966; May 15, 1966; September 15, 1966;

June 15, 1968; May 1, 1969; October 1, 1970; March 1, 1976; November 1, 1982; May 1, 1985; Manchester Guardian November 14, 1958; Nation May 2, 1966; February 14, 1976; New Republic April 16, 1966; February 21, 1976; April 8, 1985; New Statesman November 8, 1958; May 3, 1968; October 24, 1975; New York Review of Books November 17, 1966; September 11, 1969; March 4, 1976; January 20, 1983; June 13, 1985; New York Times Book Review December 14, 1958; May 13, 1966; December 18, 1966; August 4, 1968; August 24, 1969; August 19, 1973; January 11, 1976; December 26, 1982; April 21, 1985; New Yorker November 15, 1958; June 11, 1966; September 3, 1973; March 22, 1976; Newsweek March 14, 1966; July 15, 1968; November 23, 1970; December 29, 1975; Pacific Affairs Spring 1970; Political Science Quarterly March 1959, December 1966; Reporter June 2, 1966; Saturday Review December 27, 1958; April 9, 1966; November 12, 1966; January 30, 1971; January 24, 1976; Time July 19, 1968; Times Literary Supplement February 20, 1959; May 2, 1968; November 13, 1969; July 7, 1971; Virginia Quarterly Review Spring 1976.

L'AMOUR, LOUIS (DEARBORN) (March 22, 1908–June 10, 1988) American writer of Western fiction, was born in Jamestown, North Dakota, the youngest of seven children of Louis Charles and Emily (Dearborn) LaMoore. The spelling of his surname was his own choice, hardly calculated to attract readers of mass-market Western thrillers. The family name was originally L'Moore or Larmour, reflecting the French-Canadian background of one branch. He traced his ancestry back to the days of the earliest settlers of America and drew on his family's history for material in his Sackett novels of later years. L'Amour's father was a salesman of farm machinery, a veterinarian, also chief of police in Jamestown and a teacher in the local Methodist Sunday school; and his mother, who had trained to be a teacher before her marriage, was an amateur poet and expert storyteller. L'Amour liked to describe himself as "self-educated," although he had attended school regularly until he was fifteen. Mainly he educated himself with omnivorous reading and from listening to and absorbing all that went on around him. In his introduction to *The Sackett Companion*, L'Amour wrote of his boyhood in the West: "As a child I learned to listen and remember, and later, sitting around cow camps and in mining towns, I listened more than I talked. The men and women I met were survivors. Some survived by skill, some by chance, I learned, as my questions or comments helped revive memories. I had already acquired an interest in everything western."

From the ages of fifteen to nineteen, L'Amour drifted around the West in odd jobs: he did some amateur boxing, worked as a circus hand and a

LOUIS L'AMOUR

lumberjack, and finally shipped out to sea. In China he jumped ship and began wandering about the Far East on his own. According to his account he lived with bandits in Tibet and western China and had many colorful adventures. He also traveled in Africa. On his return to the United States he took some creative writing courses at the University of Oklahoma in Norman but never matriculated for a degree. He began his writing career as a book reviewer, and in 1939 published his first book—and his only collection of poems—*Smoke from This Altar*.

During World War II L'Amour served in a tank destroyer unit in France and Germany. He was honorably discharged from the army with the rank of first lieutenant in 1946. He settled in Los Angeles where he began writing Western stories for pulp magazines like *Texas Rangers* and *Thrilling Ranch Stories*, and he soon branched out to magazines with more general circulation like *Argosy*, *Collier's*, and the *Saturday Evening Post*. Like many other writers in the popular fiction market, he published under several names, among them "Jim Mayo" and "Tex Burns." (Under this name in 1950–1952 he published four post–Clarence Mulford *Hopalong Cassidy* novels.)

At the time of his death it was estimated that Louis L'Amour had published 101 books (novels, short-story collections, poetry, and works of nonfiction). Since then several additional works have appeared posthumously; and all his major titles are still in print. Statistics are plentiful: almost 200 million copies of his books are in circulation; as of 1981 he was one of the five best-

selling authors alive (in company with Harold Robbins, Barbara Cartland, Irving Wallace, and Janet Dailey); thanks to films and television dramatizations of his works, he probably reached a wider audience than any of these or of fellow Western writers like Zane Grey, Max Brand, and Ernest Haycox; his works have been translated into at least twenty foreign languages; he was the first author to receive both the National Gold Medal of the U.S. Congress (1983) and the Presidential Medal of Freedom (1984); at least two American Presidents—Jimmy Carter and Ronald Reagan—have been among his readers; he had a personal library of more than 8,000 books, diaries, maps, and explorers' notebooks, and biographical material on 2,000 gunfighters of the Old West—all of which he drew upon for his own work.

Critical commentary on Louis L'Amour tends to be patronizing. His huge sales, his prolificness, his formulaic plots, undistinguished prose style and undisguised didacticism make him suspect. Grudgingly or otherwise, however, reviewers recognize his work as a phenomenon of popular culture—American in origin but international in appeal. Michael T. Marsden, in a lecture to the American Historical Association in 1978 (published in *Arizona and the West*), found him an example of "how a writer can function as a cultural filter, creating what become artifacts of immense significance for understanding the complex nature of American culture." For Robert L. Gale he was "an anachronism [who] succeeds just the way Mother's Day, apple pie, baseball, Chevys, and Ronald Reagan do in these otherwise dyspeptic times: he extols the old-fashioned American virtues of patriotism, loyalty, unflinching courage, love of family, and a vision of the Old West both as the arena of the famous American second chance and also as mankind's last, best hope. All these elements may be corny, but they still ring true to the consuming public and thus sell well." His stories are packed with action, but, as Gale notes, there is "relatively little violence." While they have their share of love interest there is no explicit sex; indeed women are idealized. "In L'Amour's fiction," Marsden writes, "there is no greater Western sin than molesting a woman." He never hesitated to introduce passages of moralizing reflections, like this from *The Haunted Mesa* :

Each year our knowledge progresses, each year we push back the curtain of our ignorance, but there remains so much to learn. Our theories are only dancing shadows against a hard wall of reality. How few answers do we possess! How many phenomena are ignored because they do not fall into accepted categories! Ours is a world that has developed along materialistic, mechanistic lines, but might there not be others not just might there not be dozens of other ways, unknown and unguessed because of the one we found that worked?

The first of L'Amour's novels to appear under his own name was *Westward the Tide* in 1950. (Oddly enough, this novel was published in England and did not have an American edition until 1977.) Thereafter he published at least two and usually three novels every year. At the time of his death he left completed a collection of short stories, *Lonigan,* and two works of non-fiction—his detailed account of his research for the novels in his Sackett family saga and an autobiography, *Education of a Wandering Man.* Probably the best known of L'Amour's Westerns is *Hondo.* The novel is set in Arizona in the 1870s. Its hero, a dispatch rider and Indian scout, befriends a woman who has been deserted by her husband, and serves as a surrogate father to her young son. First published in 1953, *Hondo* was a stunning best-seller and swept L'Amour from the ranks of pulp writers into fame and prosperity. Over the years it has sold literally millions of copies. It was made into a very popular film in 1954 with John Wayne, Geraldine Page, Ward Bond, and James Arness. On the basis of its success L'Amour was signed by the paperback publisher Bantam, guaranteeing the widest possible distribution of his books (he was always cooperative with his publishers, making personal appearances all over the country to meet his readers and autograph his books). There have been many other motion picture adaptations of his novels; the most famous of them, however, was not adapted from one of his novels but was his adaptation of a film script by James R. Webb, *How the West Was Won* (1962), which starred James Stewart. L'Amour's novel of a shabby theatrical touring company venturing into the West, *Heller with a Gun,* was filmed as *Heller in Pink Tights* (1960), with Sophia Loren and Anthony Quinn. The film version of *Shalako* (1963) gave Sean Connery a chance to play a cavalry scout protecting some European tourists from the Apaches, and in *Catlow* (also 1963) Yul Brynner played a likable frontier outlaw. There have been television mini-series based on *Hondo* (1967–1968) and the Sackett novels—the latter, produced in 1979, was titled *Fair Blows the Wind.*

Although he was best known as a writer of American Westerns, L'Amour set his novels in many locales and in many periods of history. *Sitka* has the purchase of Alaska for its background. The Sackett family chronicle begins in Elizabethan England and moves across the Atlantic to New England, then gradually follows the American course of westward migration. The intrepid young hero of *The Walking Drum*

is a twelfth-century French adventurer who travels from his birthplace in Brittany to Spain and then to all manner of exotic scenes in the East—Kiev, Constantinople, Trebizond, and Baghdad. L'Amour did conscientious research for this book, supplying maps that trace his hero's travels, introducing historical figures like Averroës, and along the way citing an impressive list of references from Aristophanes, Virgil, Homer, and Arabian classics. At the other extreme are the hardboiled detective stories L'Amour wrote earlier in his career (some of these collected in 1983 in *The Hills of Homicide*) and his stories of adventure on the high seas and in wartime combat (some of these collected in 1980 in *Yondering*).

Wherever or whenever L'Amour's novels take place, they follow a basic pattern: a hero of great physical endurance, even greater moral probity, and some degree of romantic sensibility, confronts a challenge—outlaws, marauding Indians, the forces of nature—and survives, triumphant but humble. He is tough in action but tenderhearted and often surprisingly well read. He reveres nature, women and children, and although usually a "loner," he has a deep sense of commitment to the needs of others. An Indian-fighter when necessary, he nevertheless respects Indians when they are not warring enemies. At the beginning of the novel he is usually a drifter, a wanderer representative of the restless frontier spirit, but at the end, again representative of the ultimate destiny of the frontier, he becomes a settler, marrying and establishing a home and family. The movement is from epic to domestic—for L'Amour not a disillusioning experience but life-affirming. As a "self-appointed chronicler of the Western movement," John D. Nesbitt writes, " . . . Louis L'Amour is a self-styled historian and apologist for Western settlement."

Perceiving himself as a historian, L'Amour spared no pains to authenticate his stories with meticulously detailed accounts of plant and animal life, Indian lore and customs, genealogies, maps, scraps of miscellaneous information often introduced gratuitously. "Entertaining narrative effect is lost in favor of flat introduction of historical details and moral speeches," Nesbitt writes. But other readers enjoy L'Amour's "enthusiasm for detail and description." One such is the novelist Louise Erdrich, reviewing *Jubal Sackett* in the *New York Times Book Review* in 1985: "His stories are salted with authentic gleanings from old maps and geologic surveys, newspapers, pioneer diaries, anthropological works and courthouse records. From Jubal Sackett we learn the history of wild horses and of blue chicory, and what nourishing plants will save a reader from starvation. We also find

it how to tame a buffalo and make gunpowder
om scratch."

Nowhere is L'Amour's sense of history more
parent than in the novels that comprise the
ckett family saga. There are in fact three fam-
ies here—the Sacketts, who trace their ancestry
back to sixteenth-century Wales and in the
course of some eighteen novels span the American continent from the Jamestown colony to the
Far West of the 1870s; the Chantrys, who are descended from a sixteenth-century Irishman and
who move west after the Louisiana Purchase;
and the Talons, French-Canadians descended
from "a one-handed pirate." The families meet
occasionally as their paths cross in the novels. In
one instance at least they are united by a marriage. In their stories, L'Amour wrote, "which
will eventually become one story, there are casual meetings between the families. Occasionally
they will be associated in business, feud, or war,
and sometimes a character friendly with one
family will appear in the history of another. Or
perhaps they will have dealings with the same
enemies." Mainly what they have in common is
their continuity as registers of the opening of the
American continent.

L'Amour cited Balzac's *Comédie Humaine* as
a precedent for his work and planned to write
at least fifty novels in this project. He also provided "A Personal Guide to the Sackett Novels"
in *The Sackett Companion*—sorely needed if
one were to read through these novels in the order of their publication, which was not chronological. Replete with glossaries of characters
(both fictional and historical), places, ranches,
brands, rifles and pistols, saloons, restaurants, hotels, and books (references from the Bible and
the *Arabian Nights* to *The Pilgrim's Progress*,
The Deerslayer, and *Ivanhoe*), generously illustrated with maps of all the areas covered in the
narrative, and a double-page genealogical chart,
the book is an exhaustive record of as ambitious
a literary project as any in modern times.
Michael Marsden suggests that in conception
(though certainly not in execution) L'Amour's
triad of families "may well constitute a
Faulknerian series of interrelated characters and
events in the popular Western tradition.
L'Amour seems to be able to create in his readers
a feeling of belonging to a tradition; this in turn
provides L'Amour with a basis for a popular, organic fiction that creates a familiar yet ever unfolding world within the formulaic Western
world."

L'Amour made his home in Los Angeles—"a
rambling Spanish-style hacienda located on a
quarter-block off Sunset Boulevard," as Robert
Gale described it. He maintained a rigorous

work schedule, writing seven days a week for at
least six hours a day. He also traveled widely to
collect material for his books, and for several
years before his death he was involved in the development of Shalako, a reconstruction of an old
frontier town near Durango, Colorado. The
town is named for the hero of L'Amour's novel
Shalako who was so called after the Zuni rain
god. L'Amour was survived by his wife, the former Katherine Adams, whom he had married in
1956, and a son and daughter. Perhaps the best
and most succinct summary of his career was his
note on why he wrote the novel *Jubal Sackett* :
"I have always wished I could have been the first
man west, or one of the first to ride or walk in
that country when only the Indians were there,
to see it unblemished, unchanged, in all its original beauty. I came too late for that, so I wrote
a story about a man who did."

PRINCIPAL WORKS: For a full list of L'Amour's titles see
The Sackett Chronicle, 1988. Below is a selection of his
best-known works: Novels—Hondo, 1953; Heller with
a Gun; Kilkenny, 1954; The Burning Hills, 1956; Sitka,
1957; Shalako, 1962; High Lonesome, 1962; How the
West Was Won (adapted from screenplay by J. R.
Webb), 1963; Catlow, 1963; Kilrone, 1966; Down the
Long Hills, 1968; Fair Blows the Wind, 1978; Bendigo
Shafter, 1978; The Lonesome Gods, 1983; The Walk-
ing Drum, 1984; The Haunted Mesa, 1987. *Sackett
novels*—The Daybreakers, 1960; Sackett, 1961; Lando,
1962; Mojave, 1964; The Sackett Brand, 1965; Mustang
Man, 1966; The Sky-Liners, 1967; The Lonely Men,
1969; Galloway, 1970; Ride the Dark Trail, 1972;
Treasure Mountain, 1972; Sackett's Land, 1974; The
Man from the Broken Hills, 1975; To the Far Blue
Mountains, 1976; The Warrior's Path, 1980; Lonely on
the Mountain, 1980; Ride the River, 1983; Jubal
Sackett, 1985. *Collected short stories*—Yondering,
1980; Lonigan, 1988. *Poetry*—Smoke from This Altar,
1939. *Non-fiction prose*—Frontier, 1984; The Sackett
Companion: A Personal Guide to the Sackett Novels,
1988; Education of a Wandering Man, 1989.

ABOUT: Contemporary Authors New Revision Series 25,
1989; Contemporary Literary Criticism 25, 1983; Current Biography 1980; Dictionary of Literary Biography 25, 1981; Encyclopedia of Frontier and Western
Fiction, 1983; Gale, R. L. Louis L'Amour, 1985; Eris-
man, F. and R. W. Etulain (eds.) Fifty Western Writ-
ers: A Bio-Bibliographical Sourcebook, 1982;
L'Amour, L. The Sackett Companion, 1988; Educa-
tion of a Wandering Man, 1989; Nesbitt, J. D. *In*
W. T. Pilkington (ed.) Critical Essays on the Western
American Novel, 1980; Twentieth Century Western
Writers, 1982. *Periodicals*—Arizona and the West Au-
tumn 1978; Journal of American Culture Winter 1980;
New York Times June 13, 1988; New York Times Book
Review March 22, 1981; June 2, 1985; North Dakota
Quarterly Summer 1978; Roundup December 1970,
January 1976, February 1976; Smithsonian Magazine
May 1987.

LE GOFF, JACQUES (January 1, 1926–   ),
French medievalist, is the leading practitioner of
the "new history" or "new social history" inaugurated by the *Annales* school of Marc Bloch and
Lucien Febvre between the two World Wars.
Internationally recognized for his pioneering
scholarship in historical anthropology and the
history of mentalities (i.e. reconstructing the
thinking of people living in a given historical period, their assumptions, their reactions, their
own perceptions of the world around them), Le
Goff has been no less committed to encouraging
the appreciation of history outside of academia.
In addition to publishing several widely read
surveys, he has become a familiar figure in the
French press and on radio and television.

Born in the southern French town of Toulon,
not far from Marseille, Le Goff was the only
child of Jean and Germaine Ansaldi Le Goff. In
an autobiographical sketch written for his colleague Pierre Nora's *Essais d'égo-histoire* (Essays
in Self-History, 1987), Le Goff sketches the contrasting portraits of his taciturn father, a high-
school English teacher with strong anticlerical
feelings, and his outgoing mother, a piano teacher who remained devoutly committed to the
Catholic church; by mutual agreement, he notes,
they sent him to public school, but he received
a religious education until his first communion.
His adolescence coincided with the momentous
period between the Popular Front and the end
of World War II, and following the example of
his mother, who was involved with the Catholic
left, he joined the League Against Racism and
Anti-Semitism. When he was called up for the
Vichy government's compulsory work service,
he ran off to the Alps and joined a group receiving arms and medication parachuted by the
English, although he insists that the effort
was "a pseudo-Resistance rather than a real
Resistance."

Le Goff's fascination with medieval history
went back to his first year of high school and the
classes of Henri Michel (who later became one
of the leading historians of the French Resistance). While his interest in history remained
strong, he completed his high school studies in
French, Greek, and Latin literature, and following the Liberation, set out for Paris to study for
a degree in letters at the Sorbonne. In fact, this
plan lasted for two weeks: both the school and
the subject, he writes, "seemed so repulsive to
me that there was no possibility of continuing.
I may have almost missed out on becoming a historian, but the disappointment of the post-war
Sorbonne managed to bring me back to my true
calling." At this point he enrolled in the École
Normale Supérieure, where he was hardly more
satisfied with the instruction but profited from

JACQUES LE GOFF

the free time that cutting classes gave him to
plunge into Parisian cultural life. It was during
these university years, he recalls, that he established the work rhythm he has maintained ever
since: using his afternoons for museums and
movies, his nights for theater, concerts, and
bridge, and the solitary hours after midnight for
his own research and writing.

Following a chance encounter with an official
at the Ministry of Foreign Affairs in 1946, Le
Goff decided to participate in a Franco-
Czechoslovakian cultural exchange and spent a
year studying at the Charles University in
Prague. On his return, he completed his studies
at the École Normale Supérieure and embarked
on a "run-of-the-mill academic career" as a
high-school teacher in Amiens. A year later he
went off to Oxford with the dual aim of doing
research on medieval intellectuals and improving his English, but the atmosphere at the English university was no more appealing to him
than the Sorbonne had been, and the result was
"a blank year of my life." The next year, spent
at the École Française in Rome, was a welcome
contrast, but afterwards, when he found himself
back in Paris as a research assistant at the Centre
National de la Recherche Scientifique (CNRS),
the specter of Oxford came back to haunt him:
"If teaching without research is frustrating," he
realized, "research without teaching is dismal."

At this point he accepted a post as assistant to
Michel Mollat at the Faculty of Letters in Lille
and happily immersed himself in teaching, reading, and, for the first time, writing. His earliest
publication was *Marchands et banquiers du*

Moyen-Age (Merchants and Bankers of the Middle Ages, 1956), written for the popular reference series Que sais-je?. Following the format of the series, the text was necessarily more broad than deep, but nonetheless it was decidedly a work of social history, addressing the professional activities of medieval merchants and bankers, their political and social roles, moral and religious attitudes, and their impact upon the cultural of their times.

This first book was followed by another "brief and concise popularization" (in the words of Robert Lopez), *Les Intellectuels au Moyen-Age* (Intellectuals in the Middle Ages, 1957), which, according to Le Goff, was a "more personal effort" and thus "my first [real] work." Indeed, in a foreword to the 1985 edition, he informs readers that the text has not been revised because "the notion of the university milieu remains current, and in fact the basic viewpoint of this essay has been continuously confirmed and developed since 1957."

In 1958 Michel Mollat was appointed to the Sorbonne, but Le Goff was ineligible to succeed him at Lille because he had not completed his doctoral thesis. Reluctant to return to the CNRS, much less to high-school teaching, he took a teaching post at the Center for Historical Research—commonly known as the Sixth Section—of the École Pratique des Hautes Études, which was presided over by the doyen of French social history Fernand Braudel. As Le Goff comments in his autobiographical sketch, the Sixth Section was a possibility he had never explored before because he considered it "the promised land reserved for those who were endowed with an array of qualities I simply didn't have," and as a result, he adds, "I had the pleasure of entering the promised land and the additional pleasure of discovering that people were even happier there than I'd imagined."

This happiness, he explains, "came down to two things: freedom of research and intellectual exchanges." In addition to participating in the life of the École Pratique, he became part of an international community; particularly important were his contacts with Poland, where he not only established lasting ties with historians Witold Kula and Bronislaw Geremek but also met his future wife, Anna Dunin-Wasowicz, whom he married in 1962. Once these professional and personal elements of his life were in place, he recalls, he definitively abandoned the idea of doing a thesis in order to write—"a better use of the resources I'd accumulated"—and undertook his first major work, *La Civilisation de l'Occident Medieval* (1301, translated in 1988 as *Medieval Civilization*).

Commissioned for the *Great Civilizations* series, this 500-page, richly illustrated survey of the Western Middle Ages was again intended for an educated but nonspecialist audience. Characterized by Le Goff as "an attempt at synthesis," it combines a chronological survey with thematic essays ranging from "The Framework of Time and Space" and "Material Culture" to "Mentalities, Sensibilities, and Attitudes." As M. T. Clanchy pointed out in a *Times Literary Supplement* review of the belated English translation, the work "shows signs of age" in its focus on Western Europe to the exclusion of the Byzantine Empire, but the essays of the second part clearly anticipate Le Goff's preoccupations for the next twenty-five years, notably his desire "to describe medieval society in its own terms, to accept its imagination as a fact which must be integrated into the history of the period, just like political, social or economic facts."

Throughout the 1960s, Le Goff punctuated his teaching and research with a stream of contributions to colloquia and scholarly journals. In 1968, he began coproducing a weekly program, "History Mondays," for one of the major radio networks, and the following year, with Fernand Braudel's retirement from *Les Annales,* joined Emmanuel Le Roy Ladurie and Marc Ferro as a codirector of the venerable social-history journal. In 1972, when Braudel stepped down from the École Pratique as well, Le Goff was named president of the Sixth Section, and three years later, when this division was upgraded to the autonomous École des Hautes Études en Sciences Sociales, he became its first president.

One outcome of this professional engagement was *Faire l'histoire* (1974; partly translated as *Constructing the Past*), a three-volume anthology which he coedited with Pierre Nora. Bringing together some thirty essays by leading practitioners of the "new history," the work offered an extensive survey of the scope and possibilities of the discipline from the triple vantage of methodologies (quantitative history, history of preliterate and traditional societies, Marxist history, etc.), disciplines (art, archaeology, literature, demography, economics, religion, sciences, etc.), and themes (climate, the unconscious, myth, youth, the body, film, celebrations, etc.).

In this collective work, Le Goff's participation as "new historian" was limited to a single essay in the thematic volume, dealing with the history of mentalities. But three years later, his particular contribution to French social history was to become much clearer with the publication of eighteen of his essays written over the previous two decades in *Pour un autre moyen-âge: Temps, travail et culture en Occident* (For Another Middle Ages: Time, Work, and Culture in the West, 1976; translated as *Time, Work, and Culture in the Middle Ages*).

In a long and eloquent first-person introduction, Le Goff invokes the hindsight of a quarter-century to explain how he came to choose the Middle Ages as his field of study: first by default, in order to avoid the pitfalls he perceived in ancient and modern history, and then by design, with the conviction that the origins of modern social institutions could be traced back to the "long Middle Ages" that went from late Roman times to the Industrial Revolution. Describing the development of his intellectual concerns, he recalls how his initial passion for the Middle Ages was inspired by the writings of the nineteenth-century historian Jules Michelet, and how he then moved into the traditional history of ideas under the tutelage of Sorbonne professor Charles-Edmond Perrin before finally settling into cultural history under the triple influence (common to his entire generation) of the *Annales* school, Marxism, and ethnology. But here he acknowledges his particular debt of gratitude to economic historian Maurice Lombard at the École Pratique des Hautes Études "to whom I owe the main scientific, intellectual shock of my professional life"—the "revelation" of non-Western civilizations and the necessity of "a total history where material civilization and culture are integrated within the socioeconomic analysis of societies."

The essays that follow, grouped under the headings "Time and Work," "Work and Value-Systems," "Learned and Popular Culture," and "Toward a Historical Anthropology," demonstrate both the range and the evolution of Le Goff's interests, from the earliest study in the collection, dealing with "University Expenditures in Medieval Padua" (1956), to the latest, on "Symbolic Vassalage Rites" (1976). Although some reviewers noted obvious shortcomings in Le Goff's attempt at "total history"—notably the limited use of archaeology, legal codes, and philology, as well as the neglect of women's history ("conspicuous by its absence," according to Marcia Colish in the *Journal of Interdisciplinary History*), they were ultimately convinced by his evocation of "another" Middle Ages. As Robert Lopez wrote in the *Journal of Economic History*, coming after Le Goff's various works of synthesis and/or popularization, this collection of scholarly essays offered the "full measure of his talent" as "one of the most sensitive, imaginative, and erudite medievalists in France today."

With *La Nouvelle Histoire* (The New History, 1978), another collective work, which he coedited with Roger Chartier and Jacques Revel, Le Goff returned to the methodological underpinnings of the "new history," but now in a popular form (ten essays and a dictionary of common terms) intended for nonspecialist readers. In an interview with the Paris newspaper *La Croix* at the time, he insisted that the "new historians" did not see themselves in an adversarial position: "It's obvious that history didn't start with us, and that we come more to improve on the history that precedes us than to reduce it to nothing." But as his next monograph, *La Naissance de Purgatoire* (1981; translated as *The Birth of Purgatory*), demonstrated, the "new history" could be provocative nonetheless. In this full-scale inquiry into the history of mentalities, Le Goff takes on the notion of Purgatory—the "third place" between Heaven and Hell—as a "secular construction" that "presupposes and entails a substantial modification of the spatio-temporal frameworks of the Christian imagination." Central to his analysis is the tripartite vision ("thinking in threes") which he associates with the acceptance of the "third place," notably the division of society into three social orders, the appearance of an intermediary group of city-dwellers between lords and peasants, the interpolation of confession as a sacrament, placing the priest-confessor between believer and God.

The Birth of Purgatory provoked a wealth of critical responses, ranging from the modest suggestion that the subject at hand was not so much a "birth" as a "formation" or "crystallization" (Nathalie Zemon Davis in the *New York Review of Books*) to cries of "pure balderdash" in response to the idea that "thinking in threes" was related to the rise of the urban bourgeoisie (C. H. Lawrence in the *Times Higher Education Supplement*). For R. W. Southern, the attempt to equate the evolution of a word with that of a society was problematic. "At least in this case, I am not convinced that anything new came into existence with the new word . . . ," he wrote in the *Times Literary Supplement*. For Aaron Gurevitch, in the *Journal of Medieval History*, the role of the scholastics—Le Goff's medieval intellectuals, once again—had been overemphasized simply because more popular visions of Purgatory had been ignored; for Natalie Zemon Davis, the mentalities which Le Goff so vividly fleshed out still remained to be connected to more concrete structures, and "ironically, the very multiplicity of the connections he makes threatens to obscure the long-term historical forces that this book would lead us to believe were at work." But whatever the individual reservations and challenges expressed, the same reviewers were virtually unanimous in acknowledging the value of Le Goff's adventuresome work: "No serious reader of this wide-ranging account," wrote Robert E. Lerner in the *American Historical Review*, "will fail to be thoroughly engaged by it, seeing things that he or she has never seen before and disputing mentally with an author who prefers to be categorical and provocative."

Following *The Birth of Purgatory*, Le Goff published another work of synthesis, *L'Apogée de la Chrétienté* (The Apogee of Christendom, 1982), surveying Europe's long thirteenth century from 1180 to 1330 in a popular but incisive style that prompted Gérard Bessière to write in *La Vie*, "It's a delight to discover this great century . . . through the erudite, lucid, and thoroughly personal writing of Jacques Le Goff." The same year, he wrapped up five years' collaboration on the Italian Enciclopedia Einaudi, to which he contributed ten articles on history and history-writing, subsequently published in Italian as *Storia e memoria* (History and Memory, 1986) and in the original French as *Histoire et mémoire* (1988). Under France's new Socialist government, meanwhile, he was appointed to the Ministry of Education's project to "revive memory and give meaning to the history of France" and then served as head of the Commission for the Revival of History and Geography Teaching.

In 1985, Le Goff offered his more specialized readers a chance to catch up on his academic pursuits with *L'Imaginaire mediévale* (*The Medieval Imagination*), a collection of twenty articles, which, he wrote in the preface, was a kind of "sequel" to *Time, Work, and Culture in the Middle Ages*, intended to "clarify, extend, [and] deepen this pursuit of a renewed vision of medieval history." The themes of this second collection remain much the same—time ("the historian's privileged subject"), relations between popular and learned culture, an anthropological reading of history—but as the title makes clear, the reconstitution of material culture is hardly an end in itself, but a means of approaching the immaterial culture of the imagination. "To study the imagination of a society," Le Goff insists, "is to go to the heart of its consciousness and historical evolution." Thus he probes medieval attitudes toward "the marvelous," and toward aspects of time and space such as the Hereafter and the desert; he looks at medieval literature through the prism of historical anthropology, and perhaps most ambitiously, he takes on the subject of dreams and dreaming in the Middle Ages.

As with *The Birth of Purgatory*, the suggestiveness of Le Goff's arguments was seen as both the strength and weakness of his work. Commenting on the lengthy article on dreaming in early Christian society (which, Le Goff concludes, was a society of "blocked dreams"), Alexander Murray wrote in the *Times Literary Supplement* in 1986 that "this last suggestion is typical of many in [the] book: attractive, original, plausible, hypothetical, faintly anticlerical, and, equally faintly, tending to esotericism in the manner of its expression." At worst, Murray wrote, "Le Goff's 'other Middle Ages' can read like a house agent's description of one's own house: the approach is new, the language is new, but it is the same old house." But, he acknowledged, that "a fresh pair of eyes, after all, searching according to a new formula, can—and in this book often does—reveal a hidden cupboard here, an unused staircase there, and even, at times, a window no one has looked through before."

While most of the esays in *The Medieval Imagination* date from the period following *Time, Work, and Culture in the Middle Ages*, Le Goff chose to end the collection with a 1971 article entitled "Is Politics Still the Backbone of History?". This text, he indicates in the preface, was originally written for the American journal *Daedalus* and had drawn more interest abroad than in French circles, where, as he wrote at the time, politics, far from being the "backbone" of history, appeared to have become "an atrophied appendix, the rump of history." But now, nearly fifteen years later, he returned to the theme to argue for a "new" political history, or, as he has called it, a "political historical anthropology": a multi-dimensional reading of the political past that would treat its symbolic and imaginative aspects in combination with the great men and major events of traditional historiography.

This attempt at methodological synthesis is apparent in his next monograph, *La Bourse et la vic* (1986; translated as *Your Money or Your Life: Economy and Religion in the Middle Ages*), which reconsiders the subject of his first book, *Merchants and Bankers in the Middle Ages* in the light of *The Birth of Purgatory*. The focus of Le Goff's attention is now the usurer, whose improved prospects for the afterlife—i.e., Purgatory rather than Hell—are taken as an indication of changing relations of church and state in a society evolving from feudalism to capitalism. "The hope of escaping from Hell via Purgatory," he writes in the concluding lines, "permits the usurer to move thirteenth-century economy and society toward capitalism."

As various reviewers noted, Le Goff's use of sources (notably *exempla*, or moral tales) was once again quite imaginative, yielding what his colleague Jean-Claude Schmitt described in

Libération as "a lively, jam-packed book overflowing with ideas like a usurer's purse with coins." Somewhat more ambiguous, in the view of certain critics at least, was Le Goff's larger vision of the period, insofar as his emphasis on the mental and religious spheres ignored traditional economic interpretations, Marxist and otherwise. "There was a time," wrote Guy Bois in *La Quinzaine littéraire*, "when Le Goff, who, it should be noted in passing, owes a great deal to Marxism, posed the very real and difficult problem of relations between material and mental structures with more prudence and without throwing historical materialism overboard so casually." But, Bois concludes, "that time, obviously, is over."

Two years later, Le Goff himself seemingly put social history in the past tense in a *Times Literary Supplement* essay (April 14, 1989) entitled "After *Annales*: The Life as History." Indicating that his current project was a biography of King Louis IX, he acknowledged that historical biography was a far cry from the dominant trends of the past fifty years: "The thrust of the *Annales* school," he wrote, "was to study the development of economies, societies and civilizations in their underlying movements, to concentrate on analysis of structures and trends rather than on the narrative of events, and on the study of social groups rather than of individuals—still less great men." But picking up the threads of his 1971 *Daedalus* article ("Is Politics Still the Backbone of History?"), he made it clear that his notion of biography was not a reversion to traditional history but rather represented yet another form of synthesis, where political history is "inspired" by historical anthropology, and the life of the individual is cast within the collective history of the society.

Writing in *La Stampa* in 1987, Alberto Papuzzi describes Jacques Le Goff as "a kind of walking archive of the Middle Ages, an extraordinary machine which makes documents, ideas, and research into lucid scenarios." Le Goff himself suggests that "the chance of my career, basically, was to have been able to match up the concrete experiences of my life with the scientific and intellectual aspects of history proper." Two particular experiences that have affected his ideas as a historian, he indicates, were his administrative responsibilities with the Sixth Section and EHESS, which gave him first-hand knowledge of institutions, and the contact with his children (Barbara, born in 1967, and Thomas, born in 1970), which exposed him to youth.

His one professional disappointment, he says, is not having been invited to teach at the Collège de France, but he now considers his career to be

"complete." Alongside his scholarly work, he continues to promote a popular form of medieval history through public lecturing, participation in colloquia, newspaper and magazine articles, and making radio and television appearances; on the recommendation of his friend Umberto Eco, he served as historical advisor for the film version of *The Name of the Rose*—in his words, "a real lesson in humility." Politically, he remains active in human rights causes and has particularly close ties to Solidarity in Poland. In 1987 he was awarded the French National Prize for History.

WORKS IN ENGLISH TRANSLATION: Arthur Goldhammer has translated three major works by Le Goff: *Time, Work, and Culture in the Middle Ages*, 1980; *The Birth of Purgatory*, 1984; and *The Medieval Imagination*, 1988. Also published in 1988 were Julia Barrow's translation of *Medieval Civilization* and Patricia Ranum's translation of *Your Money or Your Life: Economy and Religion in the Middle Ages*. Le Goff's essay "Mentalities; A History of Ambiguities," translated by David Denby, is in *Constructing the Past: Essays in Historical Methodology*, edited by Le Goff and Pierre Nora, 1985.

ABOUT: Who's Who in France 1988–1989; Pierre Nora (ed.) Essais d'égo-histoire, 1987. *Periodicals*—American Historical Review December 1982; Journal of Interdisciplinary History Autumn 1981; Journal of Medieval History June 1983; Journal of Social History Fall 1982; La Quinzaine littéraire January 16, 1987; La Vie May 26, 1982; Libération November 4, 1986; New York Review of Books July 18, 1985; May 18, 1989; Télérama March 1, 1989; Times Higher Education Supplement March 8, 1985; Times Literary Supplement October 13, 1978, June 18, 1982, June 20, 1986, January 27, 1989, April 14, 1989.

*LE SUEUR, MERIDEL (February 22, 1900–), American writer of fiction, poetry, essays, biography, and autobiography, was born in Murray, Iowa, to William Wharton, a preacher, and Marion Lucy Wharton. She carries the name of her stepfather, Arthur Le Sueur, a prominent Socialist lawyer, whom her mother met in Fort Scott, Kansas, where both were teachers in a correspondence school for workers. Meridel Le Sueur also carries from her mother's family a long heritage of social commitment and political activism. Her maternal grandmother, who had settled as a homesteader in the Oklahoma Territory, worked vigorously for the Women's Christian Temperance Union. Her mother battled with equal energy for women's suffrage and the rights of labor to organize. She also, daringly for that era, left her husband and supported herself and her three children by running

°le sü´er

MERIDEL LE SUEUR

several small independent businesses, including a physical culture studio. With her second husband, Arthur Le Sueur, she moved to St. Paul, Minnesota where both continued their political activities; and young Meridel, who had grown up on the prairie and knew at first hand the joys and the hardships of rural life, was also early introduced to the struggles of the working class—farmer and factory worker alike. Her parents' home was a center for visiting social reformers, political radicals, labor organizers, progressives and social activists of all kinds, from Helen Keller, Clarence Darrow, and Eugene Debs to Lincoln Steffans and Ella ("Mother") Bloor. Another vital and enduring influence from her childhood onward was her friendship with and sympathy for the Native Americans who lived in the Midwest, the "Ancient People," as she called them in an autobiographical essay. She readily indentified with them rather than with the "Newly Come" and was especially sensitive to the plight of Native American women whose strength and endurance symbolized for her the struggles of her grandmother and her mother against repressive social and economic forces. "It was strange and wonderful," she wrote, "what these women had in common. They knew the swift linear movement of a changing society that was hard on women. They had suffered from men, from an abrasive society, from the wandering and disappearance of the family. They lived a subjective and parallel life, in long loneliness of the children, in a manless night among enemies."

Le Sueur had no formal academic education

beyond high school in Fort Scott. Her training as a writer began early, however, with the young country folk on the prairie: "I became a kind of village scribe, writing letters for those who could not write," she told an interviewer for *Ms.* magazine in 1975. A beautiful young woman, to judge from her photographs, she aspired to an acting career, but she never abandoned her social activism. In 1920 she went to New York to study at the American Academy of Dramatic Art and lived in an anarchist commune where she met Emma Goldman and other prominent radicals of the period. She joined the Communist party in 1924. Le Sueur's acting career was largely confined to the screen. In Hollywood she had small roles in silent films; her most glamorous but certainly hazardous job was as stunt woman for the heroine Pearl White in the long-running thriller-serial *The Perils of Pauline.*

Le Sueur's writing career began in the late 1920s when she returned to Minnesota, settling in St. Paul, which has been her home ever since. She traveled extensively over America as a journalist, reporting on strikes, migrant workers, the unemployed and impoverished, the struggles of Native Americans to preserve their land rights and ethnic identity. Le Sueur's journalism has much in common with her fiction. Both are deeply rooted in her own observations and experience and infused with outrage at the exploitation of the underclasses and compassion for their suffering. Both as a journalist and as a poet and novelist, Le Sueur writes with a passion and sensitivity that have little in common with conventional journalism. Blanche H. Gelfant, who wrote a Foreword to a new edition of Le Sueur's *North Star Country* in 1984, notes recurring images of seed, wheat and grain in all her work. Themes of nurturing, growth, survival, death, and rebirth dominate, whether it be in regional histories like *North Star Country* ("Many of the passages of history and oral telling were like grains of corn that are now sprouting in global heat and light," Le Sueur wrote in 1984 of this book that she had first published in 1945) or in her poetry and fiction. Here, as Elaine Hedges points out in *Ripening,* a recurring theme is the Greek myth of Demeter and Persephone—the loving earth mother's search for the daughter stolen from her by Pluto, the god of darkness and the underworld: "A celebration of that mother-daughter love," Hedges writes, "which patriarchy suppresses and an expression of women's traditional nurturing role."

In Le Sueur's earliest published short stories, some of them reprinted in the O. Henry and O'Brien annual collections of best short stories, young women come of age by first achieving independence from their bonds with their mothers only to develop new bonding relationships with their daughters and other women who share their problems. "Persephone," first published in *Dial* in 1927, retells the Demeter-Persephone myth in a midwest farm setting as a kind of prose poem. Describing the mother figure, here named Freda, Le Sueur writes: "In the spring we met her in the fields or in the thickets, where the first flowers were springing alone. In the full, golden light she comes towards us, full-bosomed, with baskets of wild berries hanging on her bright arms. When we run to her, she gives us gifts, berries, nuts, and wild fruits unknown to us."

Perhaps the most effective of these early stories is "Annunciation," which Le Sueur dedicated to her daughter, Rachel. It is a moving account of a desperately poor pregnant woman whose husband is unable to find work. Coarse and insensitive to her needs, he urges her to have an abortion, but she is determined to bear the child she is carrying. "Annunciation" is addressed to that unborn child: "Tonight, the world into which you are coming . . . is very strange and beautiful. That is, the natural world is beautiful. I don't know what you will think of man, but the dark glisten of vegetation and the blowing of the fertile land wind and the delicate strong step of the sea wind, these things are familiar to me and will be familiar to you. I hope you will be like these things."

In the 1930s, now married to Yasha Rabonoff and the mother of two daughters, Rachel and Deborah, Le Sueur became increasingly involved in political causes. She reported on the misery of life during the Depression for the *New Masses* and the *American Mercury*. The special interest of her journalism for today's readers is its focus on women in this period, many of them struggling to feed their families while their husbands were unemployed. Her best known work of journalism was an eye-witness report on the Minneapolis truckers' strike of 1934, "I Was Marching." Published in *New Masses* in September 1934, it is a highly personal account of her own reactions, her identification with the laboring masses, her resolution to work for radical change in American society, and a call to her fellow artists and writers to join her: "In these terrible happenings, you cannot be neutral now. No one can be neutral in the face of violence." She also wrote on-the-spot reports of the dust storms and droughts that impoverished farmers from Texas to North Dakota. In all these pieces, Le Sueur made no effort to disguise her rage at the economic system that she felt victimized these people and to express her deep compassion for them. It is highly charged, emotional journalism, but it is also honest in its presentation of the peo-

ple and events she observed. In "Women on the Breadlines," published in *New Masses* in 1932, she draws a series of vignettes of women in a free employment bureau waiting hopelessly for jobs. The essay concludes with her characteristic fervor: "It's not the suffering of birth, death, love that the young reject, but the suffering of endless labor without dream, eating the spare bread in bitterness, being a slave without the security of a slave." Two years later she published "Women Are Hungry" in the *American Mercury*. Here again she presents capsule sketches of women victims of the Depression—factory hands, domestic workers, teachers—all unemployed and destitute: "When you look at the unemployed women and girls you think instantly that there must be some kind of war. The men are gone away from the family; the family is disintegrating; the women try to hold it together, because women have most to do with the vivid life of procreation, food, and shelter. Deprived of their participation in that, they are beggars."

Although she wrote and published prolifically throughout the Depression era, Le Sueur herself was rarely far from poverty. Like many other writers of the period, she survived thanks to the New Deal's Federal Writers' Project, for which she worked at $90 a month collecting material for regional histories of the Middle West. As she recalled the experience in 1984: "The Federal Writers' Project in Minnesota consisted of editors whose papers had folded, free-lance writers of science fiction, advertising copy-writers—a wonderful motley crew who worked together toward the final goal, the state guide. There were about eighty on the project and we went amongst the people to find the true history of every county in the state. There was a project just to record the 'folk-says,' the model for this being instigated by B. A. Botkin in Oklahoma. We interviewed people who had lived to tell it in their own words without fancy grammar."

Le Sueur later drew on her experiences with this project when she wrote her history of the people of the Midwest—a history she tried to tell as much as possible in their own voices. Published as part of the American Folkways Series before tape recorders and television had become the tools of oral history, *North Star Country* was so far ahead of its time that its reviewers in 1945 challenged the whole conception of the book. Howard Mumford Jones asked, in the *Saturday Review of Literature*: "When is a book on American 'folkways' something more than wildly eccentric history? Why is the 'folkways' writer exempt from the usual canons of historical scholarship? And, by the way, what is a 'folkway' anyhow?" Jones conceded, however, that *North Star Country* is "a readable volume in anybody's terms." Stewart Holbrook, in the *New York Herald Tribune Books*, praised Le Sueur's "fine feeling for the right word" and her sense of drama and character, but he found the book "highly misleading" in its political tendentiousness: "From it a total stranger would get the impression that pretty much all of North Star Country is under mortgage to fat and grinning bankers; and that most of the farms had blown away in dust storms anyway. Both of these impressions mar a spirited and poetic book, and they are erroneous to a degree bordering on fantasy." Seen from a more contemporary perspective, however, *North Star Country* is an important book not for its documentation of anthropology or history but for what it reveals, as Gelfant wrote, of Le Sueur's "special sensibility as a writer, social critic, and iconoclastic woman." Collected here are the myths of the American Midwest—the tall stories told first by Native Americans, then by the farming settlers, and still later by the railroad and factory workers, all united in a common struggle to survive on the land. Interspersed with the prose are poems and ballads. Altogether it is, in Gelfant's words, "a strange mosaic of bits and pieces— highly political and yet poetic."

The same combination of social protest and poetry characterizes *Salute to Spring*, a collection of Le Sueur's short stories and journalism published in 1940. Politics is the dominating theme, but some of the stories are of genuine literary interest, comparable not only to the work of other American realists like Sherwood Anderson and Zona Gale but, in one instance at least, to D. H. Lawrence. This is "The Girl" (not to be confused with her novel of the same title)—a gripping study of a woman's awakening sexuality. Le Sueur, of unorthodox but middle-class background herself, captures the repression of a "respectable" woman, a school teacher, driving West alone, who reluctantly agrees to give a ride to a young drifter. Stirred by his strongly sexual presence beside her in the car yet inhibited by her fear, she rejects him. The story ends with his walking away from the car: "She drove around the curve, stopped, turned down the mirror and looked at her face. She felt like a stick and looked like a witch. Now she was safe—safe. She would never change, pure and inviolate forever; and she began to cry." *Salute to Spring* was one of the few of Le Sueur's works of this period to be read and reviewed outside her own political circles, and it impressed at least one reviewer, Alfred Kazin, favorably. "Miss Le Sueur," he wrote in the *New York Herald Tribune Books*, "is in some respects the most intense and self-consciously workmanlike artist proletarian literature has produced, and if the limitations and

bigotry of that literature only serve often to throw her own work into relief, she has positive virtues enough to remind us that an artist's will and fiber can be more important than the sources from which they are drawn."

In the late 1940s and the 1950s Meridel Le Sueur was one of many writers who came under the scrutiny of the House Un-American Activities Committee and of Senator Joseph McCarthy. Her left-wing sympathies, never for a moment concealed, made her a ready target for the wave of anti-Communist hysteria that swept the country. She was under FBI surveillance for some time, and in 1954 the House committee issued a subpoena for her, but it was never served. Ironically, during this period publishers who shunned her adult writing accepted for publication several books she wrote for children. These were drawn from American history and folklore, and they reflected her enduring interests in the oppressed and exploited. *Nancy Hanks of Wilderness Road*, for example, retells for children the story of an indomitable frontier woman who struggles courageously to raise her son: "You're goin' to be my loneliness made tall, my hunger walking, a friend to all in the wilderness, Abraham."

In urgent need of regular income Le Sueur worked as a waitress, in a garment sweatshop, and as an attendant for women in the Minneapolis State Asylum. She spent some time in the late 1950s in New Mexico and in Mexico, and she continues to spend part of every year in the Southwest. During the 1960s she actively supported the civil rights movement, the student rallies and anti–Vietnam War protests, and especially the demands of Native Americans for land rights. She found a whole new audience in the women's movement that emerged in the 1960s. Never in need of consciousness-raising herself, she at last had a large public and a real demand for her work. As a result, earlier works that were out of print or had never been published had a market. Her novel *The Girl*, written in 1939, finally found a publisher in 1977. She revised the manuscript extensively but in no way reduced the stark realism of its first-person narrative of a country girl who comes to the big city in the depths of the Depression. Never named herself, she gives a straightforward account of her life and the lives of other women Le Sueur knew in the 1930s. The man the girl loves and by whom she has a child is killed in a bank robbery. She suffers poverty, humiliation, and despair, but— thanks to the support of other women whose lives are even more terrible than hers—she survives and takes part in the fight for the struggle. In 1978, in an afterword to the novel, Le Sueur wrote: "This memorial to the great and heroic women of the Depression was really written by them. As part of our desperate struggle to be alive and human we pooled our memories, experiences, and in the midst of disaster told each other our stories or wrote them down."

A volume of Le Sueur's poetry, *Rites of Ancient Ripening*, was published in 1975. Most of her poems center on Native American culture and myths, but she has also written a long poem in support of Vietnamese women which Elaine Hedges includes in *Ripening*. Though in her late eighties, Le Sueur continues to write and, Hedges comments, "continues to communicate her unquenchably optimistic faith. Her terms of reference have changed since the 1930s, but her belief in the 'communal sensibility' and solidarity of the people . . . remains undiminished."

PRINCIPAL WORKS: *Fiction*—Annunciation, 1935; Salute to Spring, and Other Stories, 1940; Harvest: Collected Stories, 1977; The Girl, 1978. *Non-fiction*—North Star Country, 1945; Crusaders: The Radical Legacy of Marion and Arthur Le Sueur, 1955; Corn Village, 1970; Conquistadores, 1973; The Mound Builders, 1974. *Poetry*—Rites of Ancient Ripening, 1975. *Children's books*—Little Brother of the Wilderness: the Story of Johnny Appleseed, 1947; Nancy Hanks of Wilderness Road, 1949; Sparrow Hawk, 1950; Chanticleer of Wilderness Road: A Story of Davy Crockett, 1951; The River Road: A Story of Abraham Lincoln, 1954. *Selections*—Hedges, E. (ed.) Ripening: Selected Work, 1927–1980, 1982.

ABOUT: American Women Writers 2, 1980; Contemporary Authors New Revision Series 2, 1981; Gelfant, B. H. *Foreward to* North Star Country, 1984; Hedges, E. (ed.) Ripening, 1982; Who's Who in America, 1988–1989. *Periodicals*—Ms. August 1975; New York Herald Tribune Books June 9, 1940; December 16, 1945; New York Times Book Review April 4, 1982; Saturday Review of Literature January 5, 1946.

LEITHAUSER, BRAD (February 27, 1953–), American poet and novelist, was born in Detroit, the third of four sons of Harold Edward Leithauser, a lawyer, and Gladys Garner Leithauser, a biology researcher. He attended the Cranbrook School for Boys, Harvard College (bachelor's degree, 1975), and Harvard Law School (law degree, 1980). He won two university poetry awards as an undergraduate. In 1980 he married the poet Mary Jo Salter; together they traveled to Japan, where Leithauser was a research fellow from 1980 to 1983 at the Comparative Law Center in Kyoto.

Leithauser's first collection of poetry was *Hundreds of Fireflies*, a young man's book, somewhat self-conscious yet with a definite charm, a will to be engaging. There are poems

BRAD LEITHAUSER

about schooldays and law-school days, and numerous clever couplets, quatrains, or epigrams about insectivorous plants or the solar system or young love. He seems best here, most pleasing, as an observer of nature, a close looker who is enthralled and who struggles to be precise and meaningful, as in "A Quilled Quilt, a Needle Bed":

> Under the longleaf pines
> The curved, foot-long needles have
> Woven a thatchwork quilt—threads,
> Not patches, windfall millions
> Looped and overlapped to make
> The softest of needle beds. . . .
>
> It's a kind of pelt:
> Thick as a bear's, tawny like
> A bobcat's, more wonderful
> Than both—a maize labyrinth
> Spiraling down through tiny
> Chinks to a caked, vegetal
>
> Ferment where the needles
> Crumble and blacken. And still
> The mazing continues . . . Whorls
> Within whorls, the downscaling
> Yet perfect intricacies
> Of lichens, seeds and crystals.

The collection was very well received. Helen Vendler, in the *New York Review of Books*, remarked on "a welcome lightness and sweetness in" the poet's work. "Each of his poems repays rereading: most have a shapeliness of evolution that pleases all by itself; and on many pages the reader is struck by the writer's interest in playing with scale, a resource frequently ignored by poets." Robert B. Shaw, in *Poetry*, saw

Leithauser as "the sort of poet who collects and assimilates, giving each inconspicuous detail its due without inflating it, piling up exact observations with a freshness and prodigality like nature's own. He is one who, in Yeats's phrase, has attained 'right mastery of natural things.' One is reminded of earlier inspired accumulators: of [Marianne] Moore, of [Elizabeth] Bishop, perhaps most of [Richard] Wilbur. In these poets description can become almost microscopic; Leithauser emulates and even may outdo them at this."

Leithauser's Japanese experience was the inspiration for a handsome chapbook, the Sarabande Press' *A Seaside Mountain: Eight Poems from Japan*, which demonstrates better than any of his earlier work his ability to empathize with animals of all sorts, even human ones, drawing from his observation of them a kind of wisdom, or even strength, and demonstrating his characteristic sheer delight in observation. Here is "Hesitancy," about a meaningful confrontation at the zoo:

> For a start here's hesitancy
> played on a breezy afternoon
>   at the Kyoto zoo by an
> ostrich met with the offer
>   of a pretzel: a pink two-toed
> stalking to the fence, there to pin
>   upon the quailing child
>
>   the enlarged, enraged glare
>   of the born disciplinarian,
> while all the while the neck's
> spiral tube's atremble,
>   for the bird, too, is fearful. . . .
>
>   Through hesitancy we are placed
> in kinship with the scarred rat
>   as it hungrily sniffs at
> the broken cellar window;
>   elsewhere with the chary
> candy-striped spider as
>   with an evenhanded
>
>   sinister dexterity
> it sidesteps fatefully
> toward that wobble in the web
> that may mean prey, or
>   may mean predator.

For all this exactness and attractiveness of observation, however, the poem really has, as it reveals at the end, a metaphysical subject: our wish to believe in free will. Leithauser often shows himself to be, in Helen Vendler's phrase, "a poet interested in matter and spirit [she calls this 'a topic worthy enough but often rehearsed'], determinism and free will, who uses fine-grained description to bring these matters to conscious apprehension."

These Japan poems were included in Leithauser's next major collection, *Cats of the Temple*. In an introductory note, he expresses the hope that the book can be regarded as "a sibling companion" to his first collection—an understandable hope, considering how extremely well *Fireflies* was received. He was not granted his wish; many reviewers seemed actually hostile to what they almost unanimously perceived as a failure in his poetry to evince any signs of further development over half a decade of work. Richard Tillinghast, writing in the *New York Times Book Review*, saw "no artistic growth, no broadening of poetic vision" and decried Leithauser's "stance [of] poet as tourist. . . . one admires the virtuosity but wonders who is speaking and what emotions lie behind the richly wrought surfaces. This poetry resembles highly decorative wallpaper." Calvin Bedient, in *Sewanee Review*, remarked that in this collection Leithauser "generates only a modest emotional hum. . . . he is still practicing his scales, or playing over old Marianne Moore tunes and arrangements. When he is on his own, minus Moore, his restraint and caution prove a little dull, like his language. . . . Leithauser's narrative poetic model seems to be one of tepidly even communication; he conceives of poetry as polite discourse. His milk teeth do not break skin."

As a poet, Leithauser has been praised and blamed with equal vehemence for being an avatar of what has been termed the "neoconservative trend in modern poetry," in which, in Fred Muratori's words (*Library Journal*), "a reverence for technique, elegant and subtle rhyme structures, and a clean, contemporary diction characterize highly pictorial lyrics." His poetry is as easy to read, accessible, and amusing as any published in our day, yet some readers have felt, with D. J. Enright (*New Republic*), that "nature in Leithauser's verse might be even more engaging than it is if men and women were a little more to the fore."

Leithauser's novels share with his poetry a modest desire to be engaging and eschew any strong sense of challenging his reader. *Equal Distance* takes as its hero a twenty-three-year-old man, naive, irresolute, and utterly self-involved, on leave from law school who finds himself in Japan. He plays the carefully observant tourist (obviously a Leithauser specialty) in and around Kyoto, spends time with other foreigners, does not spend time with Japanese although he had intended to learn their language, and finally has an affair with a similarly footloose American woman. Ruth D. MacDougall, in the *Christian Science Monitor*, described the book as "a very first-novel first novel, yet so finished, so done with great good humor." Robert Jones, writing in *Commonweal*, however, thought that the author "spends more time saying things beautifully than thinking about what he says. . . . *Equal Distance* lacks the overriding intelligence, which prevents its story from becoming anything more than its narrowest surface. One wants to like Leithauser and to admire his talent, but he risks nothing."

Hence, Leithauser's second novel, has as its focus of interest Timothy Briggs, as blushingly naive a hero as has ever been presented in modern fiction, a chess prodigy from Indiana who in 1993 comes to Boston to play a match against a wisecracking computer chess program called ANNDY. He stays at the Totaplex, a lavish and stridently vulgar hotel with its own "multireligious center" which is owned by Congam (Conglomerate America? Con Game?), the fatuous, sinister corporation which is running the chess match as a publicity stunt. Timothy's family are all featured in his story, as are several Congam employees and a reclusive Japanese musical prodigy, never directly introduced into the narrative but referred to, who is in some ways a paradigm of Timothy himself. Intermittently throughout the story we witness the antics of a lunatic television evangelist given to shedding real blood in his telecasts, who at the end of the novel cuts his own throat at the climax of a hysterical, disjointed homily on the lies infesting the air breathed in America.

Hence has a somewhat cold, postmodern tone; it is a text-within-a-text, a novel that purports to contain a published novel, all things ripe for deconstruction. It possesses numerous curious elements and odd corners, meant to intrigue the ambitious reader but often never explained in any satisfactory way. For example, the events of the novel-within-the-novel are set in 1993, but the text itself is copyrighted 1997 and it is even suggested in the fictitious preface that it is a reprint by an organization called the Rearguard Press in Boston ("In the End was the word . . .") done in 2025, when books are practically obsolete, and several years after an event called the Shift has altered life as everyone has known it on Earth. Yet the Shift remains completely unexplained, and the dates are played with to no real purpose. "What Mr. Leithauser gains," Laura Shapiro writes in the *New York Times Book Review*, "by all this devising is a remarkable degree of control over our reading, the sort of control any author would love to exert. . . . [He] gives us lots to think about but, like the computer that writes symphonies, he ultimately bypasses the heart." Robert M. Adams, in the *New York Review of Books*, wrote: "*Hence* is a funny book without many laughs in it, a comic action (sort of) set in a cold, callous community, enacted by thin, gray puppets, and leading, if at all, to the most dispiriting of conclusions."

Leithauser held a Fulbright Fellowship in 1989 at the University of Iceland, where he taught courses in poetry. In October 1989 he was elected to the editorial board of the Book of the Month Club.

PRINCIPAL WORKS: *Poetry*—Hundreds of Fireflies, 1982; A Seaside Mountain, 1985; Cats of the Temple, 1986; Between Leaps: Poems 1972–1985, 1987; The Mail from Anywhere, 1990. *Fiction*—Equal Distance, 1985; Hence, 1989.

ABOUT: Contemporary Authors 107, 1983; Contemporary Literary Criticism 27, 1984. *Periodicals*—Book World February 21, 1982; Christian Science Monitor January 21, 1985; Commonweal March 8, 1985; Crosscurrents Spring 1986; Hudson Review Autumn 1986; Library Journal January 1, 1982; December 1984; February 1, 1986; January 1989; Nation April 12, 1986; New Republic April 14, 1982; January 21, 1985; October 27, 1986; May 8, 1989; New York Review of Books September 23, 1982; May 29, 1986; October 23, 1986; March 30, 1989; New York Times March 21, 1986; January 17, 1989; New York Times Book Review March 14, 1982; December 30, 1984; July 13, 1986; June 7, 1987; January 22, 1989; New Yorker March 11, 1985; Newsweek March 25, 1985; Poetry December 1982; Sewanee Review Winter 1988; Time March 15, 1982; Times Literary Supplement January 9, 1987; July 28, 1989.

LEONARD, ELMORE (October 11, 1925–), American novelist (nicknamed "Dutch" after a famous baseball player), was born in New Orleans, son of Elmore John, a salesman, and Flora (Rivé) Leonard. Leonard grew up in Birmingham, Michigan, outside of Detroit. He served in the South Pacific with the Navy for two years in World War II, then returned to Michigan and attended the University of Detroit, from which he received a Ph.B. in 1950 with a major in English. After graduating, Leonard turned his interest in writing to a career as an advertising copywriter, starting at the Campbell-Ewald agency. Resolved to continue fiction writing in his spare time, Leonard often rose at five in the morning, wrote till seven and then left for work. Occasionally he wrote while at work, keeping his writing in a drawer and closing the drawer when anyone came into his office.

Leonard's first works of fiction—short stories—were Westerns, a genre he chose because he liked Western movies. He had some success with these, and two of them were made into motion pictures: *3:10 to Yuma* (1957) and *The Tall T* (1957). Leonard published *The Bounty Hunters*, his first book, in 1953. In 1961, after many other Western stories and four more nov-

ELMORE LEONARD

els, including the much admired *Hombre* of 1961, Leonard left advertising as he had been wanting to since the early 1950s. He earned extra money by writing educational films for Encyclopedia Britannica in order to support his wife and at that time four children. The film rights to *Hombre* were bought by 20th Century–Fox in 1965 and a successful movie was made starring Paul Newman in 1967.

By the late 1960s, with some publishing and movie achievements behind him, Leonard was ready to return to full-time fiction writing and to expand into a new genre. He wrote his first crime novel, *The Big Bounce*. The writing of this novel marked more than a change in subject matter for Leonard. He told Ben Yagoda in a *New York Times Magazine* interview: "My New York agent took sick and while she was in the hospital she sent the manuscript to H. N. Swanson, the agent who had always handled my books in Hollywood. [Swanson had also been agent to Hemingway, Faulkner, Fitzgerald, and John O'Hara.] Swanie called me up and asked if I was the one who had written the book. When I said yes, he said 'Kiddo, I'm going to make you rich.'"

Swanson's prediction was not quite accurate for another fifteen years. While Leonard's sales were steady enough to keep him under contract, they were not meteoric. One problem was that his books were hard to categorize; they were crime novels, but not of the usual ilk. And, he told Bill Dunn in an interview for *Publishers Weekly*, "I've always taken exception to being placed in the mystery genre . . . I'm certainly

not right in the middle of the genre. I'm more on the edge, where a lot of everyday things are happening." For example, he rarely uses one continuing character as did Dashiell Hammett, John D. MacDonald, or Raymond Chandler. Leonard told Diane K. Shah in a *Rolling Stone* interview of how Delacorte, one of his publishers, tried in vain in their publicity efforts to link his novel *Unknown Man No. 89* with that of these other masters of the crime novel. Delacorte proclaimed it another Jack Ryan book, a character, they said, who has appeared in two other Leonard novels. But, as Shah writes, "Jack Ryan had been in only one other novel, *The Big Bounce*, and that had been ten years ago. Also, the ad said, 'Imagine Philip Marlowe serving a summons in Motown.' Leonard says, 'They're promoting my book using Raymond Chandler's character. How do you like that?' He looks indignant. 'My character would never say Motown.'"

This particularity regarding what a Leonard character would or would not say has led to his subsequent acclaim, fame and fortune. In an interview with Alvin P. Sanoff for *U.S. News and World Report*, Leonard traced literary influences upon him: "I don't come out of a tradition of private eyes or superspies. I wasn't influenced by Raymond Chandler and Dashiell Hammett. . . . Hemingway is the writer who influenced me the most. I studied his style, the way he used dialogue." He explained to Diane K. Shah his application of what he took from Hemingway: "I don't want it to sound like writing. I want you to get right into it and not be aware of me telling the story. My attitude toward the characters gives them a sound. I like all the people, think of them as kids. Or I think of a bank robber who's dominated by his wife. Here's this rough guy who at home is totally a wimp." As Leonard explained to Ben Yagoda, typically his villain "doesn't think he's doing an evil thing. I try to see the antagonist at another time—when he sneezes, say. I see convicts sitting around talking about baseball games. I see them as kids. All villains have mothers."

The spareness of Leonard's style, the iconoclastic nature of his heroes, and his richly textured, off-center villains earned him positive reviews before commercial success. The two met in 1983 with the publication of *Stick*, the story of Ernest Stickley, Jr. who had appeared first in Leonard's 1976 novel, *Swag*. J. D. Reed in *Time* described Stickley as "a dour Oklahoma hick who in *Swag* . . . conducts a doomed 100-day armed-robbery spree. Resurfacing in *Stick*, seven years and a prison term later, he has scarcely improved: he worships actor Warren Oates and thinks disco is dynamite." Reed assesses

Leonard as a stylist: "Although [he] is a master of the unexpected, violence is not his specialty. Leonard's principal virtues are a Panasonic ear and an infallible sense of character. His narrative tone is that of a man across the airplane aisle who has a good story to tell, if only he could trust you."

Leonard's research techniques are varied and unorthodox. Though he sometimes uses a research assistant to scout out a locale, he often relies on his close relationships with police departments. Leonard told Alvin Sarnoff of *Time*: "When I need background color, I sometimes spend time with the police. I have had good access ever since I did a story about the homicide squad for the *Detroit News*. . . . During the first few days I went through their files. . . . They would call me when they had a homicide. I would appear at the scene and follow them right through. There was a rapport immediately; they trusted me. . . . I would just sit in their squad room. Somebody would come in and say, 'What's Dutch doing here?' And they'd say: 'Leave him alone. He's listening.' . . . I also turn to the police when I need help with research on guns. . . . I'm insecure if I don't have a gun I can use in a story. I don't have any desire to fire guns, but they come in handy in a book." Leonard takes notes for dialogue constantly, picking it up from overheard conversations, television documentaries, wherever a peculiar jargon or slang can be heard. This attention to precision in recreating his characters' speech has played a large part in Leonard's warm reception from reviewers. In his *New York Times* review of *LaBrava*, in 1983, Christopher Lehmann-Haupt said, "As usual [Leonard's] dialog is so authentic that it dances off the page."

Leonard's productivity has always been high, with or without big sales and profiles in all the popular media. But as his steady stream of novels coincided with his newfound popularity, he became a publishing and publicity phenomenon. Seemingly out of nowhere, long-standing Leonard fans were now explaining in article after article what it was that put Elmore Leonard a cut above most crime writers. Stephen King found this avalanche of praise off-putting, as he writes in his *New York Times Book Review* article about *Glitz* in 1985: "My favorite crime novelist . . . is Jim Thompson. Thompson was rarely reviewed, but when he was he was excoriated . . . how does this bear on my Elmore Leonard block? Simple. I figured if so many critics liked him, he was probably a bore." That was before King had read *Glitz*. Having read it, he went to his local bookstore "and bought everything by Elmore Leonard I could find." He concluded that "Mr. Leonard is far from boring,

critical kudos or no." Of *Glitz* he wrote: "This is the kind of book that if you get up to see if there are any chocolate chip cookies left, you take it with you so you won't miss anything."

Glitz was received with fanfare and acclaim. The novel featured a vintage example of another trademark of Leonard's fictional technique, his unique villains. As Ben Yagoda wrote, "[Leonard] has created a gallery of compelling, off-the-wall villains unequalled in crime fiction." *Glitz*'s bizarre villain, Teddy Magyk, is a twisted, mother-dominated killer with a vendetta against Vincent Mora, the Miami-based cop protagonist. In his review, Stephen King called Magyk "one of popular fiction's really great crazies." In the *Times Literary Supplement*, Michael Wood describes Teddy Magyk further and gives a clear example of Leonard's gift for characterization: "We see the psychopath from the inside, follow the horrors of his thought without comment, the sheer levity in them making the horror really quite extreme. [Magyk] tips a drugged girl from a high balcony to her death and assesses her fall as if it were a competition dive: 'Nice execution, but 'ey, she didn't keep her feet together.'"

With *Bandits*, which appeared in 1987, Leonard tackled new geographic territory by setting the action in the city of his birth, New Orleans. Again, his attention to authenticity gained him critical praise. Walker Percy, a writer closely identified with his native city, wrote in the *New York Times Book Review*: "[Leonard's] New Orleans is done up with meticulous accuracy. The restaurants, the streets, bars, hotels are just right. . . . " The infallibly realistic dialogue is equally strong in the regional specifics required of a novel taking place in New Orleans. After quoting a piece of dialogue from the novel, Percy confirms: "Mr. Leonard's ear is sharp and accurate . . . sure enough, folks in West Feliciana Parish, which is next door to where I'm writing, could say that."

Leonard expanded his territory in other ways in *Bandits*. He included contemporary social and political circumstances in the construction of his plot, in this case by using the Nicaraguan revolution as a keystone. He told Alvin Sarnoff: "I find that I'm using more of what's going on around me —the Contras, former radicals— in my novels. . . . I was told once that putting such elements in a novel dates it because it won't mean anything to readers in years to come. But I'm not writing for years to come; I'm writing for next year when another book will be out."

This departure from the Leonard norm made *Bandits*, with its anti-Contra former nun and Somoza-following general, troublesome for some reviewers. "Nicaraguan politics, it turns out, may be a bit too heavy to be carried by the graceful pas de deux of Mr. Leonard's good guys and bad guys . . ." wrote Walker Percy. Christopher Lehmann-Haupt commented that "Mr. Leonard seems to be taking himself more seriously with his growing success. His more idealistic aims may not be altogether deplorable. But his books may take a little time to adjust to them."

Continuing in this topical vein, Leonard brought out *Freaky Deaky* in 1988. It focuses on two former radicals who in the late 1960s were arrested for bombing a Federal building, jumped bail, and vanished underground. In *Freaky Deaky* an often-used Leonard character, Chris Mankowski, plays protagonist, a basically straight cop whose idea of right and wrong is much less rigid than it was back when he was a rookie. Despite the political overtones, the disillusionment of the former radical activists who are now beginning to ask themselves if their cause was worth the effort, the plot revolves around money and conspiracy, as is the usual case in Leonard's novels, and thrusts its "hero" into the usual morally gray area where he must make painful choices. As Ken Tucker had pointed out in the *Village Voice* some years earlier, there is "a kind of wicked amorality in his [Leonard's] work. . . . The violence in his books is quick, quiet, and brutal; it's the kind that can strike you as being true and realistic even though the actions are utterly beyond your experience. Can an artist receive a higher compliment than that?" Cyra McFadden, in the *New York Times Book Reveiw*, found "the stage" of *Freaky Deaky* "crowded with as many rogues as *The Beggar's Opera*" and the pace as swift as "a cunning fox in front of the hounds." There is no lessening of pace in *Killshot*, which several reviewers hailed as Leonard at his best. Here a middle-aged couple who have witnessed a murder are fugitives not only from the trigger-happy killers but also from the forces of the law. The dizzyingly swift narrative, full of twists and surprises, "is only expedient," Ann Rule wrote in the *New York Times Book Review*, "but his *people* are real, with nary a stereotype in the pack." Again it is the sureness of his characterization, the authenticity of his dialogue, and his inside knowledge of how his characters live that make *Killshot*, in Rule's judgment, "pure, distilled vintage Leonard."

A methodical and disciplined worker Elmore Leonard writes on a daily nine-to-six schedule. He still lives in the town of Birmingham, Michigan, where he grew up. His first marriage, to Beverly Claire Cline, lasted from 1949 to 1977, when they were divorced. There are five children from this marriage. In 1979 he married Joan Leanne Lancaster.

PRINCIPAL WORKS: *Novels*—The Bounty Hunters, 1953; The Law at Randado, 1955; Escape from 5 Shadows, 1956; Last Stand at Saber River, 1957; Hombre, 1961; The Big Bounce, 1969; The Moonshine War, 1969; Valdez Is Coming, 1970; Forty Lashes Less One, 1972; Mr. Majestyk, 1974; Fifty-Two Pickup, 1974; Swag, 1976; Unknown Man No. 89, 1977; The Hunted, 1977; The Switch, 1978; Ryan's Rule, 1978; Gunsight, 1979; City Primeval: High Noon in Detroit, 1980; Gold Coast, 1980; Split Images, 1981; Cat Chaser, 1982; Stick, 1983; LaBrava, 1983; Glitz, 1985; Bandits, 1987; Freaky Deaky, 1988; Killshot, 1989; Get Shorty, 1990.

ABOUT: Contemporary Authors New Revision Series 12, 1984; Contemporary Literary Criticism 28, 1984; 34, 1985; Current Biography 1985; Who's Who in America 1988–89. *Periodicals*—Esquire, April 1987; Newsweek, April 22, 1985; New York Review of Books August 13, 1987; New York Times January 8, 1987, April 13, 1989; New York Times Book Review May 8, 1988, January 4, 1987, February 10, 1985, April 23, 1989; July 29, 1990; New York Times Magazine December 30, 1984; Publishers Weekly February 25, 1983; Rolling Stone February 28, 1985; Time May 28, 1984; Times Literary Supplement December 5, 1986; U.S. News and World Report March 9, 1987; Village Voice February 23, 1982.

LERNER, LAURENCE (DAVID) (December 12, 1925–), British poet, critic, and novelist, writes: "In 1947, Cape Town ceased to exist for me. I'd lived there for twenty-one years, the only child of a Jewish-English marriage, been indifferently educated at an Anglican school and then at the University of Cape Town, then gone back to my old school to teach, and finally left for England to continue my studies, without the slightest intention of returning to what I thought of as a cultural outpost and a political mess (though I didn't tell my mother that). I've been back three times: on the last visit, in 1978, I walked the streets in the clear winter sunshine, looking up at the granite face of Table Mountain, and realised that Cape Town had become a mythical city. A ghost child walked beside me, and I managed to write him one or two poems.

"When I left Cambridge I became a university teacher, first in what was then the Gold Coast, then in Belfast, then in 1962 to the newly founded University of Sussex, where my education really began. Teaching, as we all know, is the way to learn, and I found myself teaching the Modern European Mind, the History of Childhood, the Industrial Revolution and English Literature, Poetry, Science and Theology and so I learned. One day I saw a book in the

LAURENCE LERNER

university bookshop called *The Meaning of the Twentieth Century*, and I thought, it's probably got blank pages, but where else but Sussex would one see it.

"I got into the habit of going away from Sussex to teach in foreign parts—America, France, India, two wonderful years in Munich, now my favourite town after Brighton, but I always came back, and thought I would go on teaching there till I dropped. Then my wife retired after many years of teaching biology, and I was offered a chair at Vanderbilt, and we thought, why not. So now we pendulate between Brighton and Nashville—at one end the children, my books, the Fonthill Poets' group, at the other my students, my fine new colleagues, people wishing me a nice day in a rich Southern drawl. This will continue now till the permanent sabbatical comes.

"And writing? I seem to have spent my life wondering what sort of thing to write. Am I condemned, I kept asking, to write the fiction of a critic, the criticism of a poet, the poems of a novelist, never getting any of them right? Every now and then I've given up fiction, at which I've never been very successful, but then suddenly there was a story or even a novel demanding to be written.

"In moments of vainglory I think: I was put on this earth to write poems. And when I think that, of course, the poems won't come, or turn to dust on the page. So why do I go on writing them? I've sometimes compared my career as a poet to the history of medicine. It was not until late in the nineteenth century that doctors began to cure more people than they killed. Think of

the stupidity of humanity, paying all that good money to these dangerous quacks—and then think of the *List der Vernunft*, the hidden wisdom that made them go on doing it so that we would end up with the marvels of modern medicine. With a similar obstinacy perhaps I went on writing poems in the fifties and sixties until finally (as I now think) the poems were good enough to justify the effort I put into them. I have come to see there are a number of things I try to do in poems. One is to write straight from my own feelings—these are the poems that embarrass me most in the early volumes, but when they come off they are the most admired ('Under the Waterfall', 'Raspberries', 'Flesh'). One is to try and become someone else—hence one of my books is called *Selves*, and it and all subsequent books contain dramatic monologues. I went so far as to try and become a computer for a while, and this produced the two A.R.T.H.U.R. volumes, which computer people often enjoy, and many of my friends dislike. Part of what these books do is play word-games, which for me is the other delight in writing poetry.

"*Rembrandt's Mirror* begins with a sequence about my family, more autobiographical than any of the others. Yet poems are not autobiographies, and so I have inserted, more or less on principle, touches of fiction, and would hope that a reader couldn't tell the difference. The title poem is perhaps my favourite—it says what I think about the use of the self in art, and marks the fact that I once wanted to (but now never shall) write a whole book of poems about Rembrandt.

"I'd like to talk about my critical books, which usually get written because there's a problem I'm trying to clear up. The best is *Love and Marriage*, which got a mixed press. It's about how the Western literary tradition has depicted marriage (the institution) and love (the sentiment), compared with what we can know of the social reality. It's a sober academic book but I poured my heart into it: it derives from arguments with my children and my students on marriage today, from my love of Shakespeare and Fontane and Tennyson, from my ambivalence about the woman's movement, from my dislike of idealising the past to berate the present. It's a poor half-informed thing but mine own.

"When the poems stick (as lately) there are plenty of ideas for critical books—or the reverse. I'll go on writing."

———

Laurence Lerner's modest account above gives only a scant impression of his achievements. If he had been "indifferently educated" at St. George's Grammar School, Cape Town, this did not prevent him from receiving his B.A. in English and Latin with distinction in both (1944) and his M.A. with first class honors in English (1945), both from the University of Cape Town. He earned another B.A. at Pembroke College, Cambridge University, again with first class honors, this time in history and early English (1949). Meanwhile he had met and, in 1948, married Natalie Winch. They have four children.

After four years as a lecturer in English at the University College of the Gold Coast (1949–1953), he went to Queens University, Belfast, as lecturer first in extra-mural studies (1953–1957), then in English (1957–1962). His wanderings as a visiting lecturer or professor began in 1956, when he taught for a summer at the University of Dijon. He taught for twenty-two years at the University of Sussex, as lecturer, senior lecturer, reader, and finally (1970–1984) as professor of English, before joining Vanderbilt University as William R. Kenan Professor of English.

Lerner's first pamphlet, *Poems* (1955), was followed in 1959 by his first substantial collection, *Domestic Interior*, a Poetry Book Society Recommendation. Martyn Ford found it "very much of its time, not in the sense of being dated but in the way it captures that post-war mood of disillusionment and slightly genteel cynicism that one finds in the early poems of 'Movement' writers like Larkin, Amis and Robert Conquest. There's the same cool irony, the same sense of encroaching squalor, the same precise language put into scrupulously crafted, mostly traditional poetic forms." Arthur Terry, discussing the same collection in *Contemporary Poets*, wrote that many of its poems "are reactions to different environments; their strength lies not so much in description as in the way they establish a mental *rapport* with the external world, in which closely observed incidentals find their place in a wider pattern of experience."

Terry also discusses Lerner's first novel, *The Englishmen*, this time in *Contemporary Novelists*. It is, he says, "a study of racial prejudice in a South African school and its effect on the life of Richard Baxter, a young teacher who is planning to marry and emigrate to England. The 'Englishmen' of the title are two new members of staff—Franklin, a bluff but essentially conservative clergyman, and Tracy, a sophisticated and rebellious Cambridge graduate—whose arrival precipitates a series of conflicts which challenge the immature liberalism of the central character." Ultimately Baxter resolves to remain in South Africa to fight for racial justice.

"At both the personal and the public levels, the novel is a perceptive account of self-discovery," Terry writes.

Lerner says above that his critical books "usually get written because there's a problem I'm trying to clear up." The first of them, *The Truest Poetry*, attempts to clear up an extremely large problem: it is subtitled "An Essay on the Question, What Is Literature?" Lerner suggests that there are three ways in which literature may be considered valuable: because it gives us access to some kind of truth; because it expresses human emotions; or simply because it stimulates some sort of emotional response in the reader. The author is most suspicious of this last kind of writing—that which "aspires towards the condition of music"—and prefers the first: cognitive or truth-telling literature. The book was discussed in a front-page article in the *Times Literary Supplement* (May 6, 1960) which concluded that Lerner had written, "on a most difficult theme, a book light and brisk and yet packed with argument." Having established in *The Truest Poetry* his preference for "truth-telling" literature, Lerner discussed three practitioners of this mode in *The Truthtellers* · Jane Austen, George Eliot, and D. H. Lawrence. A reviewer in the *Times Literary Supplement* called this "a sound but somewhat pedestrian discussion" of these authors, and says that Lerner's conclusion is that "Jane Austen is a pre-Romantic, believing in the restraint of impulse; George Eliot is a positive Romantic, in whose work are released impulses of love and secular moral aspirations; D. H. Lawrence is a Romantic subversive, in whose works are released all those forces of cruelty, horror and egoism which Nietzsche depicted so well."

Lerner published a second volume of poems in 1964, *The Directions of Memory*. This seemed to Arthur Terry more adventurous in technique than the first book, also showing "a willingness to handle more difficult kinds of experience. Though one still occasionally feels that a poem has not found its ideal form, there is a more subtle sense of construction and a growing skill in the use of imagery." Several of the most striking poems deal with sexual relationships, sometimes from the woman's point of view. The most moving poem in the collection for Terry was "Years Later," a monologue in which a Jewish child deliberately aborted by its mother's Nazi torturers speaks of a sister who survived. Unlike Terry, P. N. Furbank found little of technical interest in the volume, but agreed that "Years Later" comes to life. Elizabeth Jennings also singled out this harrowing poem as "a real and original achievement," but thought that the majority of the others shared "the major weakness of much English poetry that is being written today"—that they are "merely moments of recollection held down like delicate and dead butterflies."

Martyn Ford, interviewing Lerner in the *South-East Arts Review*, remarked that "a recurrent feature of your collections of poetry is the division between those poems where the lyric voice speaks to us directly, for itself, and those where you take on other selves." *Selves*, in fact, was the title of Lerner's next collection of poems, which includes a whole section of monologues spoken by various victims of human cruelty—a laboratory rat, a battery-reared cockerel, a monkey used in some kind of feeding experiment ("Poor Monkey") who complains: "They do what they like, these doctors. You can't refuse. / We're primates! / You'd think we were Jews." "The Merman," in the same collection, seemed to H. S. Bhabra "at once a sustained act of literary criticism and an interrogation of human modes of perception": "When humans talk they split their say in bits / And bit by bit they step on what they feel. / They talk in bits, they never talk in all." Simon Rae agreed that "What makes the poem distinctive is Lerner's pursuit of the story's linguistic possibilities. He invents for the Merman not a new vocabulary, but convincing structures for his thought processes."

Continuing to ring the changes on his various modes of expression, Lerner next published another work of criticism, *The Uses of Nostalgia: Studies in Pastoral Poetry*. This had a very mixed reception. Its reviewer in the *Times Literary Supplement* wrote that, for Lerner, "pastoral is not so much literature as sociology, and anxiously interpreting the works he deals with so as to disclose various kinds of wishful thinking and bad faith, he belittles them." It seemed to this reviewer that Lerner's "diagnosis follows on from William Empson's" in *English Pastoral Poetry*, but "contributes no such novel insights." Alison Heinemann agreed, saying that "Lerner's unoriginal thesis—'nostalgia is the basic emotion of pastoral'—would sooner be forgiven were it not presented as an important idea." The poet Roy Fuller, however, found "much to admire here," though "it is the small-scale *trouvée* rather than any grand design that makes the best effect."

Lerner was asked by Martyn Ford about his "long-standing interest in science, psychology in particular," shown in poems like "Poor Monkey." He replied: "For me it's an aspect of the whole problem of being an academic and being a poet. . . . I have a lot of time for people who actually find out things we didn't know before. And that involves admiring people who are responsible and show careful judgement, whereas the poetic imagination is more likely to re-

spond to the irresponsible and the person who's got rather bad judgement." This conflict is implicit in one of Lerner's best-known books, *A.R.T.H.U.R.: The Life and Opinions of a Digital Computer*. A.R.T.H.U.R. (the Automatic Record Tabulator but Heuristically Unreliable Reasoner) is described by Ford as a member of "a very respectable tradition of naive narrators who, by virtue of their simplicity and openness, throw into relief human egotism and hypocrisy." These poems are, as H. S. Bhabra pointed out, "another of Lerner's appropriations of identity, lapped in irony" and offering "a very funny, intelligent view of the world from an inhuman, entirely rational, viewpoint." Some critics, like Simon Rae, found these "reflections on the idiosyncrasies of 'movers' (as opposed to 'metal people') not only amusing but "at times poignant."

Some of the ideas in Lerner's critical study of the social contexts of literature in his *Love and Marriage*—specifically the thesis that in the European literary tradition love and marriage are usually seen as "in a state of contest"—are given, he has said, "a kind of mischievous reworking" in the poems *A.R.T.H.U.R. and M.A.R.T.H.A.: The Loves of the Computers*. Simon Rae wondered "whether the joke of two computers falling in love ('I will hold your terminals in my sockets. Fill your circuits with my current' etc.) is sufficient to sustain a whole sequence . . . , but the poems are never without a certain ingenious wit." However, for H. S. Bhabra, this collection, unlike *A.R.T.H.U.R.*, "humanized his machines, damaging their, and his, integrity. What was a way of seeing becomes a simple joke."

The Man I Killed is generally recognized as Lerner's strongest collection to date; it was a Poetry Book Society Recommendation. Arthur Terry wrote that "the tone varies between humour, irony, and the deliberately flat statement of the horrific." He commended Lerner's "skill in counterpointing conversational rhythms against carefully controlled patterns of repetition" and identified "a verse pattern created largely by natural phrasing and the skilfull use of eye-rhymes and line breaks." John Mole found some "over-clever, modish work," but wrote that the collection's best poems "are among the most moving new work I have come across for some time. Lerner's method is to mix conversation with a carefully modulated rhetoric of cadence and repetition. Detail and orchestration lure the imagination towards a poem's central statement, giving it a sudden resonance." Thus, in the much-praised "Raspberries," the poet, whose loved one is "far and ill," is returned by the taste of the fruit he is eating to the day when "Our love unfolded in the taste of raspberries." And now the raspberries are

Tasting not only of death (I could bear that)
But of death and of you together,
The folder layers of love and the sudden future,
Tasting of earth and the thought of you as earth

As I go on eating, waiting for the news.

Nine of Lerner's essays "on literature and society," six of them previously published, were collected in *The Literary Imagination*. David Williams in the *New Statesman* called these "excellent pieces" by "a sensible, middle-ground man" about "how good imaginative writing comes to be written." A later critical book, *The Frontiers of Literature*, resumes from a different direction the theme of Lerner's first critical book—"the question, What Is Literature?" It is "an attempt to explore how literature impinges on, and overlaps with, the contiguous territories" of "history, crying, persuading, and play." By "crying" Lerner means writing that is primarily a discharge of emotion, like "confessional" poetry; "persuading" includes such didactic writings as sermons and political pamphlets; "play" encompasses nursery rhymes and nonsense verse. *Reconstructing Literature*, one of the half-dozen books that Lerner has edited, is a collection of essays by various hands opposing the poststructuralist approach to criticism and asserting the critic's right to look for meaning in the texts he studies, and to apply value judgments.

Lerner told Martyn Ford in 1980 of his intention to "do a book of poems about the Bible." The collection duly appeared in 1984 as *Chapter and Verse*. As H. S. Bhabra wrote in *Poetry Review*, it is "a series of retellings of biblical stories, mainly from the earlier part of the Old Testament," employing "a range of forms and measures from free verse to iambic pentameters and ballads. . . . Like the authors and editors of the original texts, Lerner is fascinated by the details of power politics, and his declared attitude of 'reverence without respect' allows him to use such details to explore the multiple ironies of grace. . . . Lerner also maintains his talent for entering unlikely or alien consciousness," with spectacular effect in his account of Jonah and the whale.

Bhabra also discusses Lerner's *Selected Poems*, which came the same year. Like Martyn Ford, Bhabra finds similarities between Lerner's poems and the early work of such "Movement" poets as Larkin and Amis; he shares "many of their concerns and techniques, some of their tone of voice . . . and some of their movement, a steady progress to the moralising of a perception or tale. . . . From the beginning, however, he showed an interest in the physically or emotionally foreign" and "these concerns have allowed him to insinuate himself into other

minds . . . : the insane, the alien, animals and, most of all, women. . . . His myths live." John Mole praised in Lerner's work "a clever, decent levelness of heart and mind with a sardonic edge."

A subsequent collection of verse, *Rembrandt's Mirror*, seemed to Michael O'Neill weakened by a tendency in some of the poems to confront their themes "in a head-on way. Certainly there are times when Lerner's work rests too securely in the grip of an originating idea." O'Neill was most impressed by the poems in this volume about family relationships, like "The Proposal," which "has the fierce helplessness in the face of experience which is typical of the collection's most impressive pieces."

Lerner's most recent novel is *My Grandfather's Grandfather*. It is narrated by Jeremy, a clever but unsuccessful young man, good at such useless things as philosophy and chess. Jeremy lives in Clapham with his mother and her father and relays his grandfather's tales about his forty years in South Africa as an employee of the Cape Town zoo, as well as the old man's recollections of his own grandfather, born in 1800. Jeremy suspects that many of these stories are fabrications but is sufficiently enchanted to set off for South Africa, at the end of the novel, with his lover Michael. John Mellors called it "a beautifully written book, deceptively easy to read, a subtle portrait of three generations of one family, the continuity and the contrasts, and Lerner can make you nostalgic for places you have never even seen."

PRINCIPAL WORKS: *Poetry*—Poems, 1955; Domestic Interior and Other Poems, 1959; The Directions of Memory, 1964; Selves, 1969; A.R.T.H.U.R.: The Life and Opinions of a Digital Computer, 1974; A.R.T.H.U.R. and M.A.R.T.H.A.: The Loves of the Computers, 1980; The Man I Killed, 1980; Chapter and Verse: Bible Poems, 1984; Selected Poems, 1984; Rembrandt's Mirror, 1987. *Novels*—The Englishmen, 1959; A Free Man, 1968; My Grandfather's Grandfather, 1985. *Critical works*—The Truest Poetry: An Essay on the Question, What Is Literature, 1960; The Truthtellers: Jane Austen, George Eliot, D. H. Lawrence, 1967; The Uses of Nostalgia: Studies in Pastoral Poetry, 1972; An Introduction to English Poetry: Fifteen Poems Discussed, 1975; Love and Marriage: Literature and its Social Context, 1979; The Literary Imagination: Essays on Literature and Society, 1982; The Frontiers of Literature, 1988. *As editor*—Poems of Milton, 1953; Shakespeare's Tragedies: A Selection of Modern Criticism, 1963; (with John Holmstrom) George Eliot and Her Readers: A Selection of Contemporary Reviews, 1966; Shakespeare's Comedies: A Selection of Modern Criticism, 1967; (with John Holmstrom) Thomas Hardy and His Readers: A Selection of Contemporary Reviews, 1968; The William Minard of English Literature, 1978; Reconstructing Literature, 1980.

ABOUT: Contemporary Authors New Revision Series 20, 1987; Contemporary Novelists, 3d ed., 1976; Contemporary Poets, 4th ed., 1985. *Periodicals*—Choice March 1980; Encounter June 1984; Listener March 5, 1964; August 8, 1985; London Magazine April 1964; Modern Fiction Studies Winter 1983; New Statesman September 1, 1972; June 13, 1980; August 21, 1982; South-East Arts Review Winter 1980–1981; Spectator March 27, 1964; Times Literary Supplement May 1, 1959; May 6, 1960; May 11, 1967; October 6, 1972; January 11, 1980; September 7, 1984; July 24, 1987.

REINHARD LETTAU

*LETTAU, REINHARD (September 10 1929–), German essayist and novelist, now a United States citizen, was born in Erfurt (in what would become the German Democratic Republic after World War II). He studied German and comparative literature as well as philosophy in Heidelberg and at Harvard and received a doctorate from Harvard in 1960 with a dissertation entitled "Utopia and the Novel." From 1955 to 1957 Lettau was assistant professor at Harvard; between 1957 and 1965 he taught as assistant and as associate professor at Smith College and as visiting professor at several other institutions. Between 1965 and 1967 he worked as a freelance writer in Berlin. On April 19, 1967 Lettau delivered a speech at the Free University of Berlin about the "mendacity and servility" of the West German press. In May he was suddenly threatened with expulsion. Although the expulsion order was canceled later, Lettau, who is considered one of the intellectual leaders of the 1968 student movement, left the Federal Republic of Germany. Since 1967 he has been professor of literature at the University of California, San Diego, as well as "poet-in-residence" at the University of Essen, West Germany. He is a member of the German chapter of PEN, and of the German Academy of the Arts. He married Mary Gene Carter in 1954; they have three children.

Lettau's volume of fifteen short stories, *Schwierigkeiten beim Häuserbauen* (Difficulties While Building Houses, 1962; translated as *Obstacles*) displays the author's talents on two levels. He writes in a seemingly traditional style, carefully working himself into a position where he is able to "explode" the narrative mode through a satirical punchline. There are no characters in his stories, instead there are types (such as "the ruler," "the magician," etc.). Lettau's humorous prose is shaped by his deep concern with the "puppet-on-a-string" behavior of people in modern society. He shows strong imagination in inventing fantastic and absurd realities. The maze, the labyrinth, and incomprehensible schemes are elements of his mysterious fictional world. In the story "Die Ausfahrt" (The Trip),

for instance, we find three friends who together buy a stagecoach for a trip. When they are about to depart, they cannot decide who is to be the coachman and who the passengers. After weeks of deliberation they decide on a non-solution: one is the coachman; the other two stand on the carriage-steps as grooms. The coach itself remains empty. The title story is about the deconstruction of a house: "A house is completed in the same way as a statue is by the sculptor, by subtraction rather than addition." In the end the construction workers build walls around the architect and stop working since nobody is giving them any instructions anymore.

In the collection of twenty-four extremely short prose pieces called *Auftritt Manig* (Enter Manig, 1963), Lettau playfully displays the various possible dimensions of his protagonist's personality. In an almost pedantic manner (for once devoid of satire and therefore written in a rather dry and barren style) he explores the possibilities of his character. Manig is no figure but rather a phantom, "released into the world as test person and reagent." An example: "Manig finds the street; he arrives at the house. The windows are lit up; he sees the party. There are two gentlemen involved in a conversation. One talks. The other talks. Both talk. . . . One shows the other his hand, the other one shows both hands. Manig knows enough; he turns around; so much for the party."

In his volumes *Feinde* (Enemies, 1968) and *Immer kürzer werdende Geschichten* (Stories, Becoming Shorter and Shorter, 1973), Lettau finds his way back to his specialty, satirical and

°let´ ou, rin´ här

grotesque portraits of (mostly) anonymous contemporaries. Taken together, these form a mosaic of awareness that defies traditional compositional expectations. The purpose of Lettau's aggressive style is clearly political, using wit and simplification to illuminate complex situations. Especially brilliant is his portrait of the student leader Rudi Dütschke ("Bildnis Rudi D."): "He talks while he writes, and while he writes, he talks. At the same time he listens to what others say. . . . He has to be able to prolong each step or to interrupt it instantly, so that he lives as if he were working on an endless, non-ending, continuously changing speech, extending forcefully in many directions."

In contrast to most of his associates of the 1968 movement, however, Lettau draws a clear distinction between literature and politics. "If I want to go into politics I use a rostrum to proclaim my ideas from." Politics, in his opinion, has to be followed by actions; literature does not.

As an essayist Lettau criticizes the media in *Täglicher Faschismus* (Daily Fascism, 1971) and *Amerikanische Evidenz aus 6 Monaten* (American Evidence from Six Months, 1971). An introductory essay is followed by documentation regarding the mighty and their crimes, with the details appearing in the American press. Taken out of context, these documents demonstrate such things as daily racial discrimination, police brutality, suppression of students' protests, etc. Of course, Lettau was criticized for these books on the grounds that his material was distorted and taken out of context. In 1978 he published a radio play, *Frühstücksgespräche in Miami* (*Breakfast in Miami*), which consists of dialogues in which South American dictators in exile inadvertently reveal the monstrosity of their lives and their responsibility for the economic disasters of their native lands.

Lettau has edited selections from the works of James Thurber, *Lachen mit Thurber* (Laughs with Thurber, 1963) and Franz Kafka, *Die Aeroplane in Brescia und andere Texte* (The Airplane in Brescia and Other Texts, 1977)—both writers who have had a distinct influence on his work. He has also written light verse full of puns and wordplay, collected in *Gedichte* (Poems, 1968). Other publications by Lettau include: *Die Gruppe 47. Bericht, Kritik, Polemik* (Editor: Group 47. Report, Critique, Polemics, 1967); *Dr. phil. Lettaus Sitten-Journal* (Journal of Morals by Reinhard Lettau, Ph.D., 1977); *Zerstreutes Hinausschaun. Vom Schreiben über Vorgänge in direkter Nähe oder in der Entfernung von Selbstähnlichem* (Looking Out, Absent-Mindedly. On Writing about Events in Direct Proximity or at a Distance from Self-Similarity, 1980), and

Herr Strich schreitet zum ÄuBersten. Geschichten. (Mr. Strich Goes the Limit [E. Dinter, ed.], 1982).

WORKS IN ENGLISH TRANSLATION: Ursula Molinaro translated *Obstacles* in 1965; this volume includes translations of the short prose pieces of his *Auftritt Manig*. A translation of *Enemies* by Agnes Rook was published in 1973. In collaboration with Julie Pradi, Lettau translated *Breakfast in Miami* in 1982.

ABOUT: Contemporary Authors New Revision Series 9, 1983; Dictionary of Literary Biography 75, 1988; Harris, C. P. Reinhard Lettau and the Use of the Grotesque, 1972; San Diego Union April 28, 1979; Times Literary Supplement July 10, 1969; October 10, 1971.

---

*LEVI, PRIMO (July 31, 1919–April 11, 1987), Italian memoirist, novelist, and poet, sent the following (in Italian) to *World Authors* in October 1986: "I was born in Turin in 1919. After completing the *liceo classico*, I began studies in chemistry at Turin University [in 1937] a short time before the Fascist racial laws [of 1938] forbade Jews access to academic status; I was graduated with honors in 1941. Following the German occupation of northern Italy, I joined a partisan band in the Val d'Aosta, but because of a secret denunciation was captured by the Fascist militia in December 1943. Recognized as a Jew, I was interned in a transit camp in Fòssoli, then in February 1944 was deported to the camp of Monowitz–Auschwitz. From our transport of 650 people, only fifteen men and nine woman survived. I was able to save myself by an exceptional combination of circumstances, among them my profession of chemist, which permitted me to work for a brief period in a laboratory. Liberated from the camp by the Soviets in January 1945, I was interned in Belorussia together with about a thousand other Italian civilian and military personnel. Our repatriation came only the following October, after an intricate voyage by rail of thirty-five days through nearly all the countries of Eastern Europe.

"Returning to Turin, I again took up my work as a chemist, but, impelled after a time by the duty to bear witness and by the need to free myself from the weight of my experiences, I quickly wrote up my prison recollections in the form of a memoir, *Se questo è un uomo* [*If This Is a Man*, first edition 1947, reprinted in an enlarged edition 1957; first English-language edition 1959]. Continually reprinted in succeeding years, this book has sold over half a million copies in Italy, has been adopted in schools in an annotated edition, has been translated into eight languages and adapted for the theater and radio,

°lā´ vē , prē´ mō

PRIMO LEVI

"In 1963 this book had as a sequel *La tregua* [The Truce; translated as *The Reawakening*], an account of the long voyage of repatriation. [It won the] Campiello Prize, was translated into seven languages and adapted for the radio; the two books together were published [in English] in the Penguin Modern Classics series and reprinted in 1966 in the Summit Books edition in the United States. In 1966 I published a collection of technological-fantasy narratives, *Storie naturali* [Natural Histories], Bagutta Prize 1967; other narratives on similar topics, *Vizio di forma* [Technical Error], appeared in 1971.

"In 1975 I ended my technical career, and in the same year published *Il sistema periodico* [*The Periodic Table*], a cycle of autobiographical accounts concentrating on my life as a chemist (Prato Prize, translated into three languages—another four translations are planned). In 1979 appeared *La chiave a stella* [*The Monkey's Wrench*] (Strega Prize), a novel in which a machine-fitter, in his workshop idiom, describes the adventures, defeats, and victories of his work as it developed in Italy and in distant countries. In 1981 appeared *La ricerca delle radici* [The Search for Roots], an anthology of my formative and favorite readings, and *Lilit*, a collection of stories on various subjects. In 1982, after a year of research, I published *Se non ora, quando?* [*If Not Now, When?*], an historical novel based in World War II telling of the journey of a Jewish partisan group from Russia to Italy. It received two out of the three most important Italian literary prizes, the Viareggio and the Campiello, and has been translated five times.

"In 1984, under the title *Ad ora incerta* [At an Uncertain Hour], appeared a collection of poetry (Carducci Prize 1985), and in the same year a *Dialogo* with the psysicist Tullio Regge. In 1985 *L'altrui mestiere* [The Crafts of Others] appeared, essays on various topics; in 1986, a collection of essays, *I sommersi e i salvati* [*The Drowned and the Saved*], which, forty years after the drafting of my first book, re-examined some themes relative to a man's subordination to extreme experiences. . . .

"From 1948 to 1975 I ran a resin and varnish factory near Turin and made numerous trips abroad. I contribute newspaper pieces to *La Stampa* of Turin; my articles appear in various Italian and foreign periodicals. I live in Turin. I was married in 1947; I have two children."
—trans. A. C. Kimmens

Detached, dispassionate, restrained, marked by an absence of bitterness and anger—these were the qualities cited by most reviewers of Levi's Auschwitz memoir, *If This Is a Man*. The book seemed to the reviewer for the *Times Literary Supplement* "the undramatized and therefore all the more moving account of the reactions of a highly sensitive and intelligent man to life in hell. . . . [It] is far more than accurate reporting. He has produced a work which commands both belief and comprehension. . . . What gives it greatness is that reading it one feels that it could not have been written in any other way. It has the inevitability of the true work of art." David Caute called it "a stark prose poem on the deepest sufferings of man . . . told without melodrama, without self-pity, but with a muted passion and intensity, an occasional cry of anguish, which makes it one of the most remarkable documents I have read."

Levi's journey home to Turin from Auschwitz, by truck, train, and cattle car, which lasted from January 27 to October 19, 1945, is the subject of *The Reawakening*. Once again, the author's marked lack of rancor and hatred seemed astonishing to reviewers. He "seems far less concerned," wrote Charlotte Saikowski, "with his own plight than with the experiences of those around him. He himself never emerges clearly as a personality; but through his sensitive, deftly drawn portraits one is introduced to a wonderful array of characters." David Dowler thought the book "grim, but at the same time heartening, reading. With a faith in human nature that is never facile or sentimental, he succeeds perfectly in communicating the vitality and even humor which men and women can show in the most dreadful conditions. It is Levi's strength

that he places his experiences within a firmly moral framework, so that in one fine passage early in the book he is able to express with moving conviction his belief that even the victims of the concentration camps, and their liberators, felt shame at their implication in a crime they had not committed." The Italian critic Sergio Pacifici called Levi "an 'occasional writer' *par excellence*, a man who writes not under the pressure of need or of contractual commitments, but when the inspiration truly moves him."

The Periodic Table is a book that could only have been written by a chemist. "I wanted to describe," Levi said in 1984, "to the nonprofessional what it's like to be a chemist. Every element brings a kind of 'click' for me. It triggers a memory." The tabulated system of elements formulated in the 1860s by the Russian D. I. Mendeleyev becomes for Levi a bridge between the world of things and the world of words, and thereby a means by which we may understand the universe and ourselves. There are twenty-one pieces in the book, each named after an element, yet the relation of the element to the theme of the piece constantly varies—it is sometimes symbolic, sometimes only a "trigger" or "click" which summons a reminiscence. The book begins with "Argon," one of the six "inert gases" which "do not combine"; it is an account of Levi's Jewish Piedmontese ancestors, of their attitude of "dignified abstention," of their peculiar dialect of Hebrew with Italian and Piedmontese inflections. The times they lived in, very definitely not the author's times, allowed them their dignity, permitted them to remain "inert," did not force them to "combine." With "Zinc" the author moves on to recollections of a chemistry class in Turin, where, under the direction of a detached, ironic professor, they are studying zinc, "a boring metal," "not an element which says much to the imagination," and one which in order to react requires the presence of impurities. The deft analogy to the condition of the Jews in Fascist Italy becomes clear: "Praise of purity, which protects from evil like a coat of mail; the praise of impurity, which gives rise to changes, in other words, to life." Alvin H. Rosenfeld thought *The Periodic Table* "not an angry or a brooding book. On the contrary, it is a work of healing, of tranquil, even buoyant imagination. The meditative power of [Levi's two earlier memoirs] is fully evident but is joined by a newly acquired power of joyful invention."

The successful publication of his novel *If Not Now, When?* in 1985, so soon after the favorable reception of *The Periodic Table*, meant the broadening and deepening of Levi's literary reputation in the English-speaking world. He had been known to some as one of the best practitioners of what in Italy is called *la letteratura concentrazionaria* (much of which he himself considered "bad literature"); in the mid-1980s, finally, he became famous in London and New York literary circles. "An unassuming man," wrote H. Stuart Hughes, "Mr. Levi strikes no poses; his eminence has arrived as an ever wider public discovered his integrity, his dignity, his humanity, and his exacting literary standards." *If Not Now, When?* tells the story of a band of Eastern European Yiddish-speaking Jews who late in World War II, by twos and threes, come together "along roads covered with blood" and determine to fight their way to Palestine. To do so they must battle the disintegrating yet always savage German military machine: they are thus the first Jews to organize themselves for combat "since Titus destroyed the Temple . . . a wretched aristocracy, the strongest, the smartest, the luckiest." Always a careful and economical delineator of character, Levi forces the reader to care deeply about each member of the ragged group, yet at the same time makes little effort to fire our interest by means of battle set-pieces: "This story is not being told," he sternly informs us, "in order to describe massacres." Some reviewers objected to the tone of the novel, which, though based on real events, did not represent a reality Levi knew first hand. David Denby disliked the writing's "incantatory and orotund rhythm . . . that approaches the banality of propaganda. . . . Levi needs to be a character himself in order to anchor his profoundest impressions of other people." To Anna Laura Lepschy, however, who knew the Italian original well, the author's "language, which has always had simplicity and precision, consciously acquired a coloring which was both biblical and popular, to give the feeling in Italian of the Yiddish world of the protagonists."

In *The Monkey's Wrench* Levi introduces us to Tino Faussone, a Turinese workman, master rigger of giant derricks and cranes, who travels the world trouble-shooting for huge construction projects. Levi meets Faussone in the Soviet Union, where the author-chemist had gone to do some trouble-shooting of his own, though on a considerably smaller scale. Faussone, though anything but voluble, somehow finds Levi easy to talk to; "I swear, you really want to know everything. . . . But you know someting? You're quite a guy, making me tell these stories that, except for you, I've never told anybody." Oil rigs in Alaska and Russia, suspension bridges in Calabria and India, he recounts all his adventures in an engaging, expansive, swaggering style. Along the way we learn much as well about Levi the chemist, the workman, and of the value he places on *il rusco*, everyday work: "If we except

those miraculous and isolated moments fate can bestow on a man, loving your work . . . represents the best, most concrete approximation of happiness on earth." Faussone, to the reader's considerable surprise, turns out to be, with all his gritty reality, a purely imaginary figure. Yet he is at the same time "perfectly authentic"—"a compound, a mosaic of numerous men I have met, similar to [him] and similar among themselves, in personality, virtue, individuality, and in their view of work and the world." Alfred Kazin concurred: "Everything in Mr. Levi's excellent book represents an eminently healthy character expressing itself as curiosity, intelligence, a love of man at his positive best—man at work." "Taken together," wrote Ian Thomson, *The Periodic Table* and *The Monkey's Wrench* signal a hitherto unprecedented bridging in contemporary Italian literature of the divide between science and art. (Levi never forgave Benedetto Croce his dictum that 'scientific problems are not real ones.')"

Levi's poetry, though by no means as significant as his prose, is another bridge between the scientist and the artist. It is a small body of work; *Ad ora incerta* (At an Uncertain Hour), the collection published in Italy in 1984, spans a forty-year period but includes only about sixty poems (plus a few translations). He was rather diffident about his poetry, confessing that it was something he felt more or less spontaneously and irrationally that he had to write—impelled, like the Ancient Mariner he quotes in the title of the volume, to express himself in verse at certain moments in his life. Reviewers generally agreed that his poetry did not rise to the highest levels of his prose. Still, as Peter Hainsworth wrote in the *Times Literary Supplement*, "they do throw into relief the tensions of his work—the rational, sceptical attitude toward what cannot be rationally explained, the refusal to forget what it would be simpler not to remember, the preservation of a humane and decorous style in the face of matter which is inhuman and obscene."

Levi's deep ties to his family and his city have often been remarked on. He continued to live in the same apartment in a stately old building on Corso Umberto in Turin that his family had occupied for three generations. He was much preoccupied with the failing health of his nonagenarian mother, and had himself been under treatment for depression following two prostate operations. Yet his devotion to precisely mining the past and his curiosity about the present seemed as unyielding and serene as ever. Nevertheless, on April 11, 1987, Levi left his fourth-floor apartment and hurled himself down the building's central stairwell to his death.

Suicide emerges quite suddenly as a major theme in Levi's writing among the meditative essays in *I sommersi e i salvati* (*The Drowned and the Saved*), a collection he completed shortly before his own death. He devotes a chapter of the book to Jean Améry, the Belgian philosopher who had been in Auschwitz with Levi, and who killed himself in 1978. For Holocaust survivors, Levi wrote in that chapter, "the period of their imprisonment (however long ago) is the center of their life, the event that, for better or worse, has marked their entire existence." He then quotes Améry: "He who has been tortured remains tortured. . . . He who has suffered torment can no longer find his place in the world. Faith in humanity—cracked by the first slap across the face, then demolished by torture—can never be recovered." After his death, several of Levi's friends alluded to a dream he would often describe: "I would see myself at the dinner table with my family or at work or in a green countryside. A relaxed atmosphere. And yet I felt a subtle anxiety, the sense of an imminent threat. Then as the dream proceeded, the scene dissolved. The family disappeared. There was no more work. No more countryside. I was still in the camp. And there was nothing real outside of the camp."

WORKS IN ENGLISH TRANSLATION: Stuart Woolf translated *If This Is A Man*, 1959, and *The Reawakening: A Liberated Prisoner's Long March Home through East Europe*, 1965. *The Periodic Table* was translated by Raymond Rosenthal in 1984. *If Not Now, When?* and *The Monkey's Wrench* (U.K. title *The Wrench*) were translated by William Weaver in 1985 and 1986. *Moments of Reprieve* was translated by Ruth Feldman, 1986. Published since Levi's death are another collection of essays, *Other People's Trades*, translated by Raymond Rosenthal in 1989; another collection of stories and essays, *The Mirror Maker*, also translated by Rosenthal, 1989; a collection of fables, *The Sixth Day and Other Tales*, translated by Rosenthal, 1990; and Levi's *Collected Poems*, translated by Ruth Feldman and Brian Swann, 1989.

ABOUT: Contemporary Authors 13, 1972; Grassano, G. Primo Levi (in Italian), 1981; Hughes, H. Stuart. Prisoners of Hope: The Silver Age of Italian Jews, 1924–1974, 1983; Lunetta, M. L'aringa nel salotto 1983; Zuccotti, Susan. The Italians and the Holocaust: Persecution, Rescue and Survival, 1987. *Periodicals*—Christian Science Monitor May 27, 1965; January 28, 1985; New Statesman March 19, 1960; August 13, 1965; New York Review of Books January 17, 1985; March 28, 1985; November 7, 1985; January 30, 1986; January 15, 1987; December 17, 1987; March 17, 1988; New York Times May 27, 1985; October 6, 1986; April 12, 1987; New York Times Book Review December 23, 1984; April 21, 1985; February 09, 1000; October 12, 1986; July 5, 1987; January 10, 1988; Saturday Review May 15 1965; Times Literary Supplement

April 15, 1960; March 29, 1985; August 22, 1986; June 5, 1987; October 2, 1987; April 14, 1989.

*LIDDELL, (JOHN) ROBERT (October 13, 1908–), British novelist, critic, and travel writer, was born in Tunbridge Wells, Kent, the eldest son of Major John Stewart Liddell of the Royal Engineers and the former Anna Morgan. He was educated at a noted public (i.e., private) school, Haileybury College (1922–1927), and in 1927 went up to Corpus Christi College, Oxford University. Liddell received his B.A. with first class honors in 1931 and a B. Litt. in 1933, when he was a Passmore Edwards Scholar. His M.A. followed in 1935.

Liddell began his career at Oxford, working as a senior assistant in the Department of Western Manuscripts in the Bodleian Library (1933–1938). He published his first novel, *The Almond Tree*, in 1938. It deals with the aging headmaster of a public school, working against time to complete his edition of St. Augustine, and the wife he has made his collaborator and condemned to finish his great work if he should die too soon. When she can no longer tolerate her husband's obsession and escapes to the South of France, he hires a secretary who, though less competent than his wife, is younger, more attractive, and more enthusiastic. Each of these three characters tells his or her own story in turn. A reviewer in the *Times Literary Supplement* was reminded of the relationship between Dorothea and Casaubon in George Eliot's *Middlemarch* but found the characters insufficiently individualized. Forrest Reid agreed that "the style remains the same" for each of the three narrators but, in spite of this technical failure, found "considerable psychological subtlety" in this first novel.

In 1939, after nearly ten years in the same university, Liddell spent a year as a lecturer at the University of Helsinki, Finland, beginning a long exile from England. After a year as a British Council lecturer in Greece, he went to the University of Alexandria in Egypt, lecturing there from 1941 to 1946. His second novel, called *Kind Relations* in Britain, *Take This Child* in the United States, was published in 1939. Covering the four years of World War I, 1914–1918, it tells the story of two boys whose mother is dead and whose father is an army officer serving in Egypt. The brothers are sent to live with relatives, and the book describes their experiences and reflections, centering on the elder brother, Andrew. Liddell's own father was an army officer and he is himself the elder of two brothers. This gives some weight to Roger Galway's suggestion that the novel is "on one uncommonly convincing that

ROBERT LIDDELL

one suspects the book to be largely autobiographical." Similar suspicions have occurred to reviewers of a good many of Liddell's novels. Galway comments: "A child's feelings about sex, religion, other children and the tiresome behaviour of grown-ups could hardly be more accurately reconstructed." Most reviewers agreed, praising the book for its "gentle insights," its avoidance of sentimentality, and its "many subtle touches."

In 1946 Liddell moved from Alexandria to the University of Cairo, teaching there as a lecturer until 1951 and in 1951–1952 as assistant professor. After that he returned to Greece, lecturing for the British Council for a further eleven years, and then joining the University of Athens as head of the English department (1963–1968). In 1947 he published *A Treatise on the Novel*, discussing with many examples the criticism of fiction, the novelist's range and values, the making of plot and characterization, and the value of descriptive "background" writing. Liddell holds that the latter had been too highly esteemed: "fiction is the delineation of character in action, and the landscape in the background is merely incidental." He asserts that "the novelist should be a humanist," and advocates the "pure novel" which eschews didacticism and concentrates on "human beings and their mutual reactions." The book's appendices include a small anthology of statements by novelists on their art, and an essay on the novels of Ivy Compton-Burnett, whom Liddell takes to be "of all English novelists now writing . . . the greatest and most original artist." *Some Principles of Fiction* appearing a few years later in 1953, is a more practical handbook, with chapters on subject matter, style, plotting, dialogue and, again, a collection of brief notes on these and other topics, most of them quotations from major novelists.

These two small books were reprinted in the United States in 1969 as *Robert Liddell on the Novel*. In his introduction, Wayne Booth suggests that Liddell's criticism has been neglected because of his "aggressive lack of system, his casual way of ignoring problems of logic and method that many American critics would worry over for hundreds of pages. No coherent theory of the novel is stated openly in these books, and I doubt that one could be extracted." Nevertheless, Booth writes, "by a steady habit of looking at his own experience as novelist and reader rather than at abstract rules . . . , he produces an astonishingly concentrated list of provocations to thought about fiction . . . few pages ever written about fiction are as stimulating as these."

Walter Allen, in his *Tradition and Dream* (1964), writes that Liddell's "attitude to fiction almost out-Jameses James in its austerity and is altogether too limiting for my taste." However, Liddell's "finest novel, *The Last Enchantments*, which is "closely related to . . . *A Treatise on the Novel* . . . is another matter." Allen says that "on the surface, the novel is composed largely of gossip over the teacups of North Oxford. The characters are scholars, minor men of letters, landladies, servants, members of the lunatic fringe of the University. The novel could scarcely have been written, one feels, without Jane Austen and Miss Compton-Burnett. Liddell catches a considerable part of their uncompromising, astringent qualities of wit and verbal precision; and the gradual stripping away of the pretensions of the central character, Mrs. Foyle, is very funny indeed. But also, explicit in the novel, is the analogy between Mrs. Foyle and Balzac's Goriot. . . . It is the index of Liddell's power and skill that he so successfully and movingly creates a female Goriot in terms of North Oxford tea-parties." *The Last Enchantments*, which appeared in Britain in 1948, was published the following year in the United States, where many reviewers shared Allen's enthusiasm. A. S. Morris called it "a book full of nostalgia . . . , wit, and exciting perception," and Hayden Carruth thought it the work of "a master stylist"—"together with the novels of Charles Williams, *The Last Enchantments* is the most exciting literary importation from England since the war." Not everyone agreed, however, and for V. P. Hass "too much of the book is devoted to silly conversation at silly, dreary teas. . . . It bored me excessively."

Liddell's next novel, *Unreal City*, made less of a stir. It is set in Alexandria towards the end of World War II. Its narrator, Charles, is a young English academic teaching at a French-administered college, but the central character is his friend Mr. Eugenides, an elderly Greek archaeologist, sentimental and homosexual, who becomes infatuated with a young corporal in the Royal Air Force. Francis King thought this "a beautifully evocative novel," but its reviewer in the *Times Literary Supplement* was less enthusiastic: "There is perhaps just enough material here for a novel, but Mr. Liddell does not seem altogether happy with it. His background scenes are lively and his writing has the combination of polish and humour and pointed observation his readers expect of him, but as a character his Mr. Eugenides is a failure. Mr. Liddell has been too tender with him; in his determination to give the poor old creature credit for the sincerity of his infatuation he slips into mawkishness."

Having criticized "the pictorial element in literature" in *A Treatise on the Novel*, Liddell says in *Contemporary Novelists* that he has himself "avoided descriptive writing in my novels, preferring to reserve it for my travel books." The first of these was *Aegean Greece*. Ian Scott-Kilvert wrote of it that "Mr. Liddell is a good example of the philhellene whose feeling for the country is perfectly balanced between the Greece of imagination and the Greece of experience. The Aegean lands he describes—the Saronic gulf, Northern Sporades, Cyclades and Dodacanese islands—are a part of Greece which does not easily yield up its secrets. . . . The author is a highly efficient and discriminating guide. . . . This is a book of real authority, as expert in modern Greece as it is in classical lore." Later works by Liddell in this genre include *Byzantium and Istanbul*, which is both a history of and a guide to the city; *The Morea*, dealing with the Peloponnese islands; and *Mainland Greece*. All were praised for their scholarship and the excellence of their descriptive prose, but irritated some reviewers on account of what one called their "singular aversion to almost every form of human contact."

Liddell's essay on Ivy Compton-Burnett in *A Treatise on the Novel* was extended several years later as *The Novels of Ivy Compton-Burnett*. He believes that "tyranny in family life" provides the subject matter of all fifteen of her novels. Accordingly his book has chapters on her "tyrants," on the impact of such domestic dictators on their environments and on their victims, on the "Chorus" of servants and other subsidiary characters in each novel, and on the texture of the author's prose. The book was rather coolly received, one reviewer complaining that "it does little more than list the main characteristics" of the novels, which are described in "over-ecstatic" terms. Liddell never met Ivy Compton-Burnett but for years maintained a remote kind of contact with her through her letters and, more often, those of a mutual friend, the novelist Elizabeth Taylor. *Elizabeth and Ivy*, published many years later, is an account of this relationship. Neither literary history nor theory, it portrays "both writers . . . in the manner of characters in a family memoir." Some critics pointed out that the book inevitably suffers from being based on correspondence, since letters reveal only what their authors choose to reveal. Christopher Hawtree found the memoir's discretion and restraint "merely frustrating (especially Liddell's repeated admission that he had detroyed the two novelists' correspondence)."

In 1959 Liddell returned to the novel with *The Rivers of Babylon*. Having written about an English academic in Alexandria in *Unreal City*, he now focuses on another such in Cairo. Since Liddell had himself taught in both cities, and since both characters are named Charles, it seems possible that both novels have an autobiographical element—especially since the Charles of *The Rivers of Babylon* is, again like Liddell himself, a novelist and a Roman Catholic. The story is set in the early 1950s and reaches its climax with that "Black Saturday" in 1953 when the Egyptian population, outraged by an incident in the Suez Canal Zone, rampaged through the city killing and destroying. The British staff at the university are told to go home but, at the end of the novel, it seems that Charles will be allowed to stay, though with his understanding of Cairo much altered. Apart from this, as one reviewer wrote, nothing much happens except that Charles forms Platonic attachments to some of his male students: "the matter of the novel is the eccentricities . . . of his acquaintances, plus some more or less smart conversation and a good deal about the position of the English in Egypt."

There were no more books until 1963, when Liddell published *The Novels of Jane Austen*. Each of her books is given a chapter in which such topics as social background, characterization, and theme receive separate treatment. No overall critical theory is advanced regarding any one novel or the works as a whole, and the book seemed to one reviewer no more than "a series of extended notes or commentaries." Some of these were very perceptive, but depended heavily "on the theory of composition advanced by Mrs. Q. D. Leavis in *Scrutiny*." The result was not an acceptable account of our present state of knowledge and in real truth "a responsible critical method" and "accuracy in purely factual details." D. W. Harding in the *New Statesman*

likewise found it "too much like the comfortable old academic attitude to Jane Austen."

Liddell's next novel, *An Object for a Walk*, centers on a heartless manipulator named Geoffrey Thwaite and his effect upon the lives of three people: Flora and Charles, who lose their virginity to him, and Hesther, who has the misfortune of marrying him. Each story is told in turn, and then coincidence brings Geoffrey together with all three of his victims during World War II in a refugee camp near Jerusalem. Geoffrey Thwaite bears a strong resemblance to one of Compton-Burnett's "tyrants" and a reviewer in the *Times Literary Supplement*, complaining of wooden characters and dated dialogue, found "the general tone . . . a blend of Jane Austen and Ivy Compton-Burnett, about both of whom Mr. Liddell has written. He manages their distancing coolness but lacks their wit." There were more comparisons with Compton-Burnett in reviews of *The Deep End*, set in the 1920s in an English prep school and dealing with the takeover attempt of a hypocritical clergyman. Wallace Hildick called it "a pleasantly diluted exercise in the grand manner," but more tasteful than original.

Stepsons, which followed a year later, was much more warmly received. It features in Elsa Faringdon another Compton-Burnett tyrant. A woman of Scottish birth but German descent, she becomes the second wife of an ineffectual army officer when he returns from service in Egypt after World War I. As Mary Borg wrote in the *New Statesman*, Elsa is full of good intentions but "an ignorant woman, steeped in fixed ideas of how to behave; stupidity and circumstance transform her into the stereotype villainness stepmother. . . . The book is an account of her marriage and the effect she has on her stepsons, employees and relations . . . in a style so lissom and sparkling that each sentence is a delight." Liddell and his brother also had an army father who served in Egypt during the Great War and made a second marriage, and Christopher Hawtree, describing the book as "potentially libellous," points out in the *Times Literary Supplement* that it is "a sequel to *Kind Relations* of 1939," in which also the father is named Faringdon.

Mr. Eugenides of *Unreal City* was reportedly modeled on Constantin Cavafy, and Liddell next published a critical biography of the great Greek poet, who worked for most of his life as a minor civil servant in Alexandria—a clerk in the Dantean "Third Circle of Irrigation." Derek Mahon wrote that Liddell "is scrupulous, sympathetic, erudite, and sometimes luminous, if a little over inclined to quote Ivy Compton-

Burnett. . . . What's missing is the man within. To his readers Cavafy is a hedonistic figure, a clinical if wistful sodomite with a rather jaundiced approach to social and political matters. To his friends he was a wit, a miser, a dirty old man. . . . Only once or twice do we see the warp of personality. As for the poetry itself, Mr. Liddell is excellent on both the erotic and the political poetry," though his translations "barely rise above the serviceable." The book appeared in the United States in 1977 and had a similar reception, though several reviewers found the discussions of Cavafy's poetry "superficial and diffuse."

Nor was there much enthusiasm for Liddell's *The Novels of George Eliot*. In it, as in *The Novels of Jane Austen*, he devotes a chapter to each of the novels, giving lengthy plot summaries and arguing that Eliot's "greatest achievement lies in those characters whose dilemmas stem from their high ethical aspirations." Laurence Lerner said that Liddell "writes with clarity and vigour" and his book "is lively, old-fashioned and provocative to the point of cantankerousness," but "all the insights are familiar and the critical method often consists of little except assertion."

After this string of lukewarm notices, or worse, there was a better reception for Liddell's *A Mind at Ease*—his book on Barbara Pym, whose work he had appreciated as early as 1940, and for his novel *The Aunts*, published in 1987 when he was almost eighty. The easy-going Miss Eliza Elwell and the cantankerous Mrs. Jane Keyworth live with Jane's arthritic but amiable husband George in an English spa town, perhaps Tunbridge Wells. The year is 1938 (when Liddell published his first novel). The ladies' activities and George's attempted escape with a masseuse are observed and recorded by their nephew Philip, who lives nearby with his old Oxford friend and one-time lover the Reverend James Freeling. For Linda Taylor, the interest of the novel lies less in the rather typecast aunts than "in the dialogues between Philip and James," who "preach a system of cosy Christian neutrality: justice tempered with mercy, duty to one's family, charity begins at home." Robert Liddell's strength as a novelist lies in his ability to convey a sense of period and society in the amiable argumentative speech of his characters." In Christopher Hawtree's opinion, Liddell's novels have been unduly neglected (a view also expressed by Wayne Booth regarding *Robert Liddell on the Novel*). Hawtree writes that "in his fiction Liddell has created a world so fully realized that each novel, whether set in England or abroad, appears to be as much part of an unobtrusive pattern as do those of his

friends, Barbara Pym, Elizabeth Taylor and Ivy Compton-Burnett."

Liddell has also written a radio play, *A Lesson from the Master* (1966) and published a number of translations. He is a Fellow of the Royal Society of Literature and has an honorary doctorate from Athens University. The author says that he is fluent in French and modern Greek, and reads Italian. His interests include European history, art and architecture, and cookery. His name is pronounced to rhyme with "middle."

PUBLISHED WORKS: *Fiction*—The Almond Tree, 1938; Kind Relations, 1939 (USA, Take This Child); The Gantillons, 1940; Watering Place (short stories), 1945; The Last Enchantments, 1948; Unreal City, 1952; The Rivers of Babylon, 1959; An Object for a Walk, 1966; The Deep End, 1968; Stepsons, 1969; The Aunts, 1987. *Critical works*—A Treatise on the Novel, 1947; Some Principles of Fiction, 1953 (Published with A Treatise on the Novel as Robert Liddell on the Novel, 1969); The Novels of Ivy Compton-Burnett, 1955; The Novels of Jane Austen, 1963; Cavafy: A Critical Biography, 1974; The Novels of George Eliot, 1977; Elizabeth and Ivy, 1986; A Mind at Ease: Barbara Pym and her Novels, 1989. *Travel*—Aegean Greece, 1954; Byzantium and Istanbul, 1956; The Morea, 1958; Mainland Greece, 1965. *As translator*—Old and New Athens, by Demetrios Sicilianos, 1960; A History of Modern Greek Literature, by Linos Politis, 1973; The Abbé Tigrane, by Ferdinand Fabre, 1988.

ABOUT: Allen, W. Tradition and Dream, 1964; Booth, W. *introduction to* Robert Liddell on the Novel, 1969; Borklund, E. Contemporary Literary Critics, 1982; Contemporary Authors 13–14, 1965; Contemporary Novelists, 1976; Who's Who, 1989. *Periodicals*—Choice June–August 1977; Encounter December 1977; Guardian February 24, 1939; Listener May 30, 1968; January 16, 1975; January 16, 1986; February 12, 1987; London Magazine July 1954; New Republic October 22, 1977; New Yorker August 1, 1977; New Statesman February 25, 1939; April 5, 1963; January 7, 1966; June 19, 1969; February 14, 1975; Spectator June 8, 1939; November 2, 1974; Times Literary Supplement June 25, 1938; November 2, 1940; July 28, 1945; August 1, 1952; October 23, 1953; February 11, 1955; May 14, 1955; June 27, 1958; June 15, 1959; February 22, 1963; December 8, 1966; October 28, 1977; January 23, 1987; Virginia Quarterly Review Summer 1977.

LISPECTOR, CLARICE (December 10, 1925–December 9, 1977), Brazilian novelist, short-story writer, author of "chronicles" and fiction for children, was born in Tchechelnik, Ukraine (now U.S.S.R.) while her parents, Pedro and Marian Lispector, were in the process of emigrating from Russia to Brazil. Arriving in Northeast Brazil some two months after the birth of their daughter, the couple eventually settled

CLARICE LISPECTOR

in 1929 in the city of Recife where Clarice entered school and wrote her first stories. In 1937 the family moved to Rio de Janeiro. In the same year, she completed her secondary studies at the Colégio Silvio Leite and published her first short story. In her teens, she continued to develop an intense interest in literature and eagerly read such authors as Dostoevsky, Virginia Woolf, Katherine Mansfield, and Herman Hesse, as well as the works of noted Brazilian writers such as Machado de Assis, Mário de Andrade, and Graciliano Ramos. Lispector attended law school in Rio while working as an editor for both a local news agency and the newspaper *A noite*. During the same period, she came into contact with some of the most innovative and experimental Brazilian writers of the period—most notably Antônio Callado, Lúcio Cardoso, Adonias Filho, and Cornélio Pena—many of whom took an interest in her work and encouraged her to keep writing. In 1943, while still in her teens, she graduated from law school, married a fellow student, and completed her first novel.

Perto do coração selvagem (Close to the Savage Heart), whose title was taken from Joyce's *Portrait of the Artist as a Young Man* and suggested by Lúcio Cardoso, was first published in 1944. It immediately proved both a financial and critical success, winning the Graça Aranha Prize within months of its appearance. The noted Brazilian critic Alvaro Lins commented upon its publication that this initial work by Clarice Lispector represented the first serious attempt at an introspective novel yet made" in the country, and another writer, Sérgio Milliet, affirmed

it as "our first novel in the spirit and technique of Joyce and Virginia Woolf." As Earl E. Fitz notes, *Perto do coração selvagem* "put her largely at odds with what was then being done in the Brazilian novel and short story. . . . Within the confines of Brazilian literary history, Clarice Lispector will always be remembered for moving prose fiction away from the rote regionalism and doctrinaire social realism of the 1930s, for showing that there were new ways to do it. When considered in this reformist context, Lispector shows her vital connection with the first generation of Brazil's modernist movement, a generation dominated by iconoclastic and highly experimental poetry as well as by a desire to be both international and nationalistic in theme and form."

In the same year of 1944, her husband entered the diplomatic corps, and the couple was soon dispatched to a post in Naples. In Europe, Lispector discovered the existentialist fiction of Jean-Paul Sartre and Albert Camus and began a new novel, *O lustre* (The Chandelier), which was published during a brief return to Brazil by the author in 1946. A third novel, *A cidade sitiada* (The Besieged City), appeared in 1949. The couple lived abroad for many years, including a sojourn in Berne, Switzerland and a period of eight years spent in Washington, D.C. Lispector separated from her husband in 1959 and, with her two children, returned that same year to live in Rio de Janeiro, her permanent place of residence until her death. During the years she spent mainly outside Brazil, Clarice Lispector also wrote a number of short stories, many of which were published in the magazine *Senhor* and some of which came out in book form as *Alguns contos* (Some Stories) in 1952. As Earl E. Fitz further notes, with the publication of *Alguns contos*, "Lispector immediately established herself as a powerful new force in Brazilian short fiction. . . . Her reputation as a technically demanding author rests largely, and with considerable justification, on her skills as a story writer rather than on her prowess as a novelist." In contrast to her rather loosely structured novels, the short stories are models of economic structure. Fitz points out, however, that thematically, "the pieces included in *Alguns contos* are cut from the same cloth as the earlier novels. We see the same penchant for psychological portraiture rather than action, the same lyrical ambience, and the same phenomenological connections between a person's mercurial inner world and the mysterious outer world that surrounds him."

Clarice Lispector began to receive widespread acclaim outside Brazil with the appearance of a collection of introspective and enigmatic short stories, *Laços de família* (1960, translated as

Family Ties, 1972). In these richly symbolic stories, women, ranging in age from adolescence to their eighties, confront challenges to their selfhood and experience moments of epiphany. According to the British critic John Gledson in the Times Literary Supplement: "Several of [these] stories are unforgetable, perhaps most obviously 'A imitação da rosa' ('The Imitation of the Rose'), a picture of a woman desperately and unsuccessfully trying to hold on to the few features in a blank world which might protect her from a relapse into 'the nervous breakdown' from which she has just emerged; or again, 'Feliz aniversário' ('Happy Birthday'), a picture of a loveless family party presided over by a crippled, resentful grandmother. These stories, like 'Amor' ('Love'), 'Começos de uma fortuna' ('The Beginnings of a Fortune'), and ['Os laços de familia' ('Family Ties')], are set in the middle-class milieu of Rio, and to a degree are specific to that world—for instance, one of the problems faced by Laura in 'The Imitation of the Rose' is how to deal with a maid to whom she herself feels inferior: the necessary mixture of authority and respect is something she is incapable of. Her trouble, and the trouble with many Lispector characters, is an overwhelming sensitivity. . . . " Another of the pieces from this collection, "O crime do professor de matemática" ("The Crime of the Mathematics Professor"), became one of the author's best known works of short fiction. A story of "guilt, obsession, and expiation" in which a male protagonist attempts to atone for a crime he believes he has committed, it first appeared in English translation in the American journal Odyssey.

Another of Clarice Lispector's major breakthroughs as an author came with the appearance of her fourth novel, A maça no escuro (1961; translated as The Apple in the Dark, 1967). This lengthy and complex work, in the words of Earl E. Fitz, "is a painstaking study of the birth and abandonment of a human consciousness. Profoundly symbolic and mythic, and written in an intense, lyrical style that recalls that of Djuna Barnes, Virginia Woolf, and Katherine Mansfield, A maça no escuro is really an ironic quest novel, one in which the erratic antihero protagonist ends up by embracing what he initially abjured." Introducing one of Lispector's few male central characters, the novel traces his difficult and finally humbling struggle for self-liberation. Fitz writes that A maça no escuro "advances the idea that while self-awareness is theoretically a worthy goal, it is difficult to recognize, achieve, and maintain. Indeed, it may even prove to be useless or dangerous in a society that stresses conformity in word and deed, unthinking allegiance to orthodoxy, and programmed behavior." He further notes that "although A maça no escuro contains much that links it thematically to Lispector's first three novels, its closely woven structure, its systematically metaphorical rendering of a consciousness in flux, and, above all, its intense phenomenological preoccupation with language make it stand apart from the works that came before it. In signaling that a new plateau of artistic achievement had been reached by its author, A maça no escuro anticipates the even more philosophical and lyrical novels that would follow . . . , [and] would help place Brazilian fiction on a par with the revolution in narrative that was sweeping through Spanish America, a revolution that would become known as the 'Boom' in Spanish American literature."

A paixão segundo G. H. (The Passion According to G. H., 1964) is Clarice Lispector's most hermetic and most difficult work. This novel is an extended monologue in which, as Nancy T. Baden explains in A Dictionary of Contemporary Brazilian Authors, a woman protagonist "is mesmerized by her unexpected encounter with a cockroach, a dreaded creature. Unable to move physically, her active mind searches for the meaning of existence as she tries to shed the passions and conventions of life. In a primitive, fetishistic sense, she consumes the creature in a rite of purification." As the "Passion" of the title suggests, there is a religious-mystical symbolism here. The narrator, unidentified except by her initials, begins her quest for self-knowledge when she enters her maid's back room and sees the cockroach: "The room had only one way in, and it was a narrow one: through the cockroach." At that moment she has a vision: "I had come in an 'I,' but the room then gave me the dimensions of 'she.' As though I were on the other side of a cube, the side that you don't see because you are seeing the front side." It is a vast, empty space, a desert, and her confrontation with the cockroach is a leap into the existential void:

> And I went toward that enticing madness. But my fear was not the fear of someone who was going toward madness and thus toward a truth—my fear was the fear of having a truth that I would come to despise, a defamatory truth that would make me get down and exist at the level of the cockroach. My first contact with truths always defamed me.

Not surprisingly, reviewers of the novel were reminded of Kafka, Sartre, and Camus. Suzanne Ruta wrote in the New York Times Book Review: "Lispector makes language the medium of both imprisonment and liberation, and the text is shaped in the form of a manual for meditation, a set of spiritual exercises leading at last to a more authentic relation with the world, the self and others. And she does it with an amazingly light and playful touch. She roots her French imports deep in Brazilian soil. The result is a luxuriant and fascinating hybrid."

With her reputation as one of Brazil's most outstanding narrators firmly established both within the country and in international literary circles by the early 1960s, Clarice Lispector continued to write prolifically until the end of her life. In 1964, the same year that *A paixão segundo G. H.* appeared, she published *A legião estrangeira*, a volume of short stories and journalistic pieces known in Brazil as "chronicles." This collection added to her international fame when, more than twenty years later, it was translated into English as *The Foreign Legion*. The stories are set mostly in Rio and again concern females who must confront social and emotional problems. In 1967, the same year in which she was severely burned in an apartment fire and immobilized for a period of several months, Lispector published the story, *O mistério do coelho pensante* (The Mystery of the Thinking Rabbit), which marked her debut as an author of children's literature. She published three other works for children: *A mulher que matou os peixes* (The Woman Who Killed the Fish, 1969), *A vida íntima de Laura* (Laura's Secret Life, 1974), and *Quase de verdade* (Almost True, 1978). *Uma aprendizagem ou o livro dos prazeres* (translated as *An Apprenticeship or The Book of Delights*), which won the *Golfinho de Ouro* Prize, appeared in 1969. Considered perhaps the "strangest" of Lispector's novels, this work has been described as existential within a socially relevant context.

During the early 1970s Clarice Lispector expanded her literary activities. She wrote a weekly column for the prestigious *Journal do Brasil*, did translations, and conducted interviews for news magazines. Nevertheless, she increasingly isolated herself from public life in Rio de Janeiro and gained a reputation as something of a recluse and an eccentric. At the same time, she began work on a book that took nearly three years to complete. The final product, described by Fitz as "sparely written but intensely poetic 'fiction' in monologue," appeared as *Água viva* (translated as *The Stream of Life*) in 1973. The following year she published her translation of Oscar Wilde's *The Picture of Dorian Gray* and spoke on "The New Hispanoamerican Narrative" at a convention in Cali, Colombia. In 1976, the year after the appearance of two minor works, *Visão do esplendor* (A Vision of Splendor) and *De corpo inteiro* (Sound of Body), Clarice Lispector was awarded first prize in the Tenth National Literary Competition for her

contribution to Brazilian literature. In 1976 she also represented Brazil at the World Witchcraft Congress at Bogotá, where she gave a lecture on her story "O ovo e a galinha" (The Chicken and the Egg).

Clarice Lispector's last major novel, *A hora da estrela* (*The Hour of the Star*), was published in 1977, the same year in which she learned that she was terminally ill with cancer. Fitz comments that, with this work, she produced a "novel that, structurally, represented a significant change from what she had previously done. . . . Lispector undertook in this novel a discussion of one of Brazil's most chronic and pressing social problems: the forced migration of people from the poverty-ridden Northeast to the overcrowded and overburdened industrial centers of the South. Although not entirely successful in its very conscious effort to join together a lyrically (and ironically) presented realization of self with a strong, socially oriented statement about how life in the Northeast cripples the emotional and intellectual growth of its people, *A hora da estrela* is an important work because it proves, as if proof were needed, that Lispector was both aware of and concerned about modern Brazil's social ills." The novel was made into a film with the same title. The author died in Rio on December 9, 1977, one day before her fifty-second birthday. *Para não esquecer* (In Order Not to Forget); *Un sopro de vida*; *pulsações* (A Breath of Life; Pulsations); and *A bela e a fera* (Beauty and the Beast) were published posthumously in 1978.

WORKS IN ENGLISH TRANSLATION: *Family Ties*, in Giovanni Pontiero's translation, was published in 1972. Pontiero has also translated *The Foreign Legion*, 1985, and *The Hour of the Star*, 1986. Gregory Rabassa translated *The Apple in the Dark* in 1967. *An Apprenticeship or The Book of Delights*, translated by Richard A. Mazzara and Lorri A. Parris, was published in the Texas Pan American Series in 1986. Ronald W. Sousa's translation of *The Passion According to G. H.* was published in 1988. *The Stream of Life*, in a translation by Elizabeth Lowe and Earl Fitz, was published in 1983 with a foreword by Hélène Cixous.

ABOUT: Cixous, H. Reading with Clarice Lispector, 1990; Contemporary Authors 116, 1986; Dictionary of Contemporary Brazilian Authors, 1981; Encyclopedia of World Literature in the Twentieth Century, rev. ed., III, 1981; Fitz, E. E. Clarice Lispector, 1985; Solé, C. A. and I. Abreu (eds.) Latin American Writers, III, 1989. *Periodicals*—Christian Science Monitor August 23, 1967; London Review of Books February 21, 1985; New York Times Book Review September 3, 1967; May 18, 1986; January 8, 1989; Saturday Review August 19, 1967; Times Literary Supplement January 15, 1971; April 30, 1986.

LIU BINYAN (also rendered as LIU PIN-YEN) (February 7, 1925–), Chinese journalist and writer, was born into a poor worker's family in Changchun, Jilin province, in the northeast region known as Manchuria. Much of his childhood was spent in the city of Harbin, Heilongjiang province, where his father held a factory job. The combination of Japanese influences (Japan being overlord of the then puppet Manchukuo government) and Russian (Harbin being a refugee haven for White Russians fleeing the Soviet Union) has clearly shaped the Liu Binyan of today. His father had worked in the Soviet Union, and from his childhood Liu learned firsthand the oppression of Japanese domination and the meaning of the October Revolution. His interest in international politics began at the age of twelve. His family's poverty combined with his yearning for a strong China stimulated his desire for learning. Not being able to attend school regularly, he managed to teach himself three foreign languages: Japanese, Russian, and English. He started to read Russian literature in its original language when he was very young. From that he went on to study Marxism. From reading he developed a strong urge to write, and he first saw his words in print in a local Chinese newspaper when he was fourteen. He dreamed of going to Shanghai, then the mecca of young people yearning for a more tolerant and liberal atmosphere, to pursue a writing career. For lack of travel funds he stopped in Peiping (now Beijing) and in 1940 became a scholarship student at the Catholic Furen Middle School. In school he was active in study groups (considered political activities) and was soon expelled. In desperation he enrolled in the Japanese-run Xinmin (New People) School. There, as the prize for winning a Japanese essay contest, he was given the unique opportunity to travel to wartime Japan in 1941.

Such benevolence had not altered his sense of outrage at the Japanese aggression. In 1943, at the age of eighteen, he moved to Tianjin and participated in the anti-Japanese underground work led by Communists. He formally joined the Communist party the next year, and remained a member until January 1987 when he was expelled from the Party.

Despite his lack of a formal education, he was able to make a living by teaching in primary schools and engaging in youth work. He stayed in Tianjin until 1946; then he returned to Harbin as a school teacher. In 1949, the year of the Communist triumph over all China, he was chosen as a member of a delegation to the International Youth Festival held in Hungary. In 1951, when he was assigned to work at *Zhongguo Qingnian Bao* (China Youth), the official organ of the

LIU BINYAN

Communist Youth League in Beijing, he started his journalistic career, first as a reporter, then as an editor. In 1956 he became a member of All China Writers' Union and published "Zai Qiaoliang Gongdi Shang" ("At the Bridge Worksite") and "Benbao Neibu Xiaoxi" ("Restricted Information from this Newspaper") in the monthly *Renmin Wenxue* (People's Literature) the same year. These stories, scathing criticisms of the Party's conservatism and its bureaucratic incompetence disguised as fiction, elicited a letter from Qin Chao-yang, then editor of *Renmin Wenxue*, praising Liu for having "broken new ground in realistic creation." The boldness and freshness of Liu's writing electrified the readers but brought only woes to the author. In 1957, Liu became one of the first victims of Mao Zedong's Anti-Rightist Campaign. Branded as "poisonous weed," he was forbidden to write and sent to farms in various provinces to do manual labor. In 1961 he returned to *Zhongguo Qingnian Bao*, not as an editor or a reporter, but to take charge of foreign language material in its reference room. He used the opportunity to study the Soviet Union.

For twenty-two years his voice was stifled. It was not until 1979, after he had been cleared of the Rightist label, that he published the now classic "Ren Yao Zhi Jian" ("People or Monsters?") in the September issue of *Renmin Wenxue* and came upon the literary scene with the force of a hurricane. Written in the form of a short story, his exposé of the large-scale corruption of a women's cadre in Heilongjiang province created an indignant stir among the public and shocked those in power in the government. The report took him three months of on-the-spot investigating and evidence-gathering to complete. When it was finally published in the generally liberated air of the post–Cultural Revolution era, Liu became a celebrity. Discussions of his report were held among readers and party cadres alike all over the country. With the sanction of the Party organ *Renmin Ribao* (People's Daily), which had engaged him as the paper's premier correspondent, he became a formidable roving investigative reporter in a country that rarely allows anyone such a free rein.

Liu's style of writing had its origin in the early 1930s when left-wing writers experimented with a new mode of reporting called *baogao wenxue* ("literature of reporting"), using dialogues and dramatization in place of cool, objective observations; its aim was to evoke emotion. One early classic example was Xia Yan's "Bao Shen Gong," a vivid description of the life of indentured laborers in Shanghai, then under the economic control of foreign capitalists. The essence of *baogao wenxue* resembles America's "new journalism" or "non-fiction novel," terms Liu was not unaware of. Liu Binyan was riding high, feared by bureaucrats and hailed as "Liu Qingtian" (Liu the Justice) by the people, until January 1987 when, deprived of a protector in the person of Hu Yaobang, recently ousted as the Party's general secretary, he was expelled from the Communist party along with another outspoken intellectual, the physicist Fang Lizhi. Stripped of his official title "Correspondent of *Renmin Ribao*," he remained a vice chairman of Zhongguo Zuojia Xiehui (Chinese Writers' Association, also known as All China Writers' Union). Hard-liners in the government called special sessions of journalists' associations to formally condemn him, but his colleagues refused, and thousands of readers wrote him offering encouragement and support.

Liu's numerous journalistic sketches and stories have been collected in anthologies and "selected works." His books in general are assured of a large readership, but the conservative English language journal *Chinese Literature* has not translated any of his work to date. One of his more recent controversial pieces is "Dierzhong Zhong-cheng" (Loyalty of the Second Kind), detailing the deeds of two non-Party members who decide that loyalty to the people supersedes loyalty to the Party. It was published in 1985 simultaneously in five different magazines and is still being read and discussed today. Another piece, "Wei Wancheng Maizang (The Unfinished Burial), published in Kaipan Wenxue, October 1986, attacked certain Party cadres' abuse of

power. Two of his more recent books are *Gaosu Ni Yi Ge Mimi* (To Tell You a Secret) and *Wodi Riji* (My Diary), both published in the fall of 1986 and both difficult to locate on the shelves of bookstores in China.

Liu has traveled to many countries. The first time he came to the United States was in 1982. In 1988, accompanied by his wife Zhu Hong, an editor, he began an extended stay in the United States, giving lectures at the University of California at Los Angeles. In 1988–1989 he was a Neiman Fellow at Harvard University. Following the ruthless suppression of the student uprising in Beijing's Tiananmen Square in June 1989, Liu Binyan emerged as a rallying point for exiled Chinese students and visiting scholars. In July 1989 he went to Paris to organize a Democratic Chinese Front with student leaders who had fled Beijing; he then returned to the United States to lecture on American campuses against the harsh repressive measures of the Chinese government.

Early in 1990, in collaboration with two fellow exiles, Ruan Ming, a political theorist, and Xu Gang, a poet, Liu published an account of these recent events—*Tell the World : What Happened in China and Why*. Later that same year he published a memoir, *A Higher Kind of Loyalty*, a candid account of his years as a loyal Communist party member and of his personal and painful struggle, as he puts it, "to see the light." It was not until the late 1980s and particularly the events of Tiananmen Square that Liu could make a complete break with the Party ideology: "I gave up my youth for the Communist Party in its struggle to seize state power. And now a handful of tyrants have betrayed the Party, turning themselves into enemies of the people in the real sense of the word." The first five essays collected in Liu's most recent book, *China's Crisis, China's Hope*, were delivered as lectures at Harvard in 1988–1989, before the events of Tiananmen Square, and express much of the disillusionment and disgust that fueled the student uprising; in the last two essays, however, Liu, writing in the aftermath of the massacre, affirms his hope for the future of the Chinese reform movement.

WORKS IN ENGLISH TRANSLATION: A translation of *People or Monsters? and Other Stories and Reportage from China after Mao* was edited by Perry Link in 1983; other translations of Liu's work may be found in Kai-yu Hsu's *Literature of the People's Republic of China*, 1980, and Hua-ling Nieh's *Literature of the Hundred Flowers*, 1981. *Tell the World* was translated by Henry L. Epstein 1990, and Zhu Hong translated *A Higher Kind of Loyalty: A Memoir by China's Foremost Journalist* in 1990. *China's Crisis, China's Hope* was translated by Howard Goldblatt in 1990.

ABOUT: K. Hsu. Literature of the People's Republic of China, 1980; H. Nieh. Literature of the Hundred Flowers, 1981; Who's Who in People's Republic of China, 2nd ed., 1987. *Periodicals*—New York Review of Books March 3, 1987; April 26, 1990; New York Times January 14, 1987; January 25, 1987; May 30, 1988; February 19, 1989; March 7, 1990; New York Times Book Review February 22, 1987; December 27, 1987; May 27, 1990.

LONGLEY, MICHAEL (July 27, 1939 –   ), Northern Irish poet, was born in Belfast and educated in that city's Malone Primary School and the Royal Belfast Academical Institution (1951–1958). He read classics at Trinity College, Dublin, receiving his bachelor's degree in 1963, after which he worked for seven years as a teacher in Blackrock, Belfast, and Erith, Northern Ireland. Since 1970 he has been assistant director for literature of the Arts Council of Northern Ireland.

Longley is perhaps the least widely known of the group of Northern Irish poets—the others are Seamus Heaney, James Simmons, and Derek Mahon (Paul Muldoon is occasionally added to the list, though younger by a decade than any of them)—who began publishing their work in the 1960s and who have urged on and nurtured one another in various poems and reviews in the decades since then. They constitute, in the words of D.E.S. Maxwell, writing in Douglas Dunn's critical anthology *Two Decades of Irish Writing*, "the first group of Ulster poets to have won recognition both as an identifiably regional group and as individuals." Longley began his published career modestly, with two pamphlets, *Ten Poems* and *Secret Marriages: Nine Short Poems*, and two collaborations, *Three Regional Voices* (also including poetry by Iain Crichton Smith and Barry Tebb) and *Room to Rhyme* (also including poems by Seamus Heaney and vernacular ballads and songs collected by David Hammond).

Longley's first important collection was *No Continuing City: Poems 1963–1968*, in which he presented thirty-four poems and introduced most of the themes that have continued to occupy his poetic attention. These include: an interest in classical learning and a desire to apply classical motifs to situations encountered in modern life ("Narcissus," "Persephone," "Circe," "Nausicaa," and "The Centaurs"); more than a passing interest in jazz and the great musicians of that genre ("Words for Jazz Perhaps," which includes poetic riffs on Fats Waller, Bud Freeman, Bessie Smith, and Bix Beiderbecke); an allied curiosity about North American legends and poets ("Emily Dickinson," "A Questionnaire for Walter Mitty," "Rip Van Winkle,"

and "Klondike"); a strong commitment to explore the Irish nature of his heritage, though emphatically not in the familiar and outmoded terms of the Celtic revival, twilight, or fringe ("The Hebrides," dedicated to Eavan Boland, "Dr Johnson on the Hebrides," and "Leaving Inishmore"); an informed and subtle commitment to creatures of nature ("The Osprey," "The Freemartin," and "Gathering Mushrooms"); a desire to ascertain his place within his family, to whom he often refers—parents (especially father), children, wife ("Epithalamion," "In Memoriam," and "Christopher at Birth"), and, finally, an open, generous, and friendly impulse toward his fellow Northern Irish poets. The most recent "troubles" in that province (they have continued for a generation) had scarcely begun when *No Continuing City* was published, but there are frequent reminders of unrest and discontent—even the title, a lament from Paul's Epistle to the Hebrews, has a sad significance—and a strong sense of poetry's entire inability to encompass the grotesque disarray presented by the world. In "To Derek Mahon," the collection's penultimate poem, there can be little doubt that "the poems we cannot write" refer specifically to the miseries, the "birthmarks" of Ulster:

> You alone read every birthmark,
> Only for you the tale it tells—
> Idiot children in the dark
> Whom we shall never bring to light,
> Criminals in their prison cells—
> These are the poems we cannot write.
>
> Though we deny them name and birth,
> Locked out from rhyme and lexicon
> The ghosts still gather round our hearth
> Whose bed and board make up the whole—
> Thief, murderer and clown—icon
> And lares of the poet's soul.

The reviewer of the collection for the *Times Literary Supplement*, unidentified as was then that review's custom but highly enthusiastic and probably (an Irish) partisan, lauded Longley's "open-faced and very welcome sense of humour: he has a touch of the Audenesque gift for reminding you, by an audacious placing of stresses within a normally slurred polysyllable, that a single word is itself an assembly. [See, for examples, the strategic placement of the words "Idiot" and "Criminals" in the poem quoted above.] And then there is his imagery, which is often well observed and clearly evoked. You see it without special glasses and sometimes it is sprung on you with a suddenness that draws a gasp." D.E.S. Maxwell commented that "Longley's first volume insists, directly and convincingly, on the capacity of art to renew the life it draws on."

An Exploded View: Poems 1968–72, thirty-nine in number, constitute further and deeper explorations of Longley's thematic interests. One subject not before given extended treatment, the violence in Ulster, is here dwelt on darkly and almost obsessively. The volume is dedicated ("For Derek, Seamus, and Jimmy") to Northern Irish poets—"We are trying to make ourselves heard / . . . Like the child who cries out in the dark." And one tripartite poem, "Letters," comprises an introduction and three epistolary addresses or apostrophes, one to each of the volume's dedicatees. The poem's introduction, "To Three Irish Poets," evokes "Blood on the kerbstones, and my mind / Dividing like a pavement, / Cracked by the weeds, by the green grass / That covers our necropolis . . ." and concludes with the poet's determination to "Claim this my country, though today / *Timor mortis conturbat me.*" In his third and most moving letter, "To Derek Mahon," Longley recalls how the guilt of indifference was banished as the two bourgeois poets had their eyes forcibly opened to the reality of working-class Belfast:

> We traced in August sixty-nine
> Our imaginary Peace Line
> Around the burnt-out houses of
> The Catholics we'd scarcely loved,
> Two Sisyphuses come to budge
> The sticks and stones of an old grudge,
>
> Two poetic conservatives
> In the city of guns and long knives,
> Our ears receiving then and there
> The stereophonic nightmare
> Of the Shankill and the Falls,
> Our matches struck on crumbling walls
> To light us as we moved at last
> Through the back alleys of Belfast. . . .

Yet the poem is, after all, about Ireland the multifarious, and he is able to end it with a masterful, healing, and sweetly comic evocation of his and Mahon's visit "years back, one Easter" to the Aran Islands, the Catholic, Gaelic-speaking epicenter of Irishness, where the "British" Ulstermen were forced to recognize their apartness, while at the same time they came to affirm the undeniable fact that, religion notwithstanding, they belonged there too:

> We were tongue-tied
> Companions of the island's dead
> In the graveyard among the dunes,
> Eavesdroppers on conversations
> With a Jesus who spoke Irish—
> We were strangers in that parish,
> Black tea with bacon and cabbage
> For our sacraments and pottage,
>
> Dank blankets drying up our Lent
> Till, perhaps, ourselves, we bent
> Our knees and cut the watery sod

> From the lazy-bed where slept a God
> We couldn't count among our friends. . . .

"Letters," in the words of Terence Brown (*Northern Voices*, 1975), "is obviously an attempt to write poetry that will absorb the impurities of a gravely infected colonial situation, and its success, which is mainly a matter of tone and emotional honesty, gives reason to hope that the imagination [as Longley expressed it in a memorable letter to the *Irish Times* of June 18, 1974] 'as an ordering agent . . . should survive its engagement with the "impure" just as the body is strengthened by inoculation.'"

The Ulster troubles also find their way into Longley's memories of his father—appropriately so, given that the strife enveloping the province has a history three centuries old, and the sectarian hatred has had to be relearned each generation, handed on from father to son. "In Memoriam," one of the most accomplished and deeply felt poems in *No Continuing City*, was an acceptance and evocation of his dead father's powerful presence ("your voice now is locked inside my head") and the father's revelations to his son just before his death of the confusion and horror of his military service in World War I. More of the same memories inform "Wounds" in *An Exploded View*: among the "pictures from my father's head— / I have kept them like secrets until now" is the ferocious anti-Catholicism of the all-Protestant Ulster Division, which was nearly annihilated at the Battle of the Somme. In the latter poem, however, present violence intrudes on and illuminates that of the past: among the uniformed dead buried alongside the old man the poet sees

> Also a bus-conductor's uniform—
> He collapsed beside his carpet-slippers
> Without a murmur, shot through the head
> By a shivering boy who wandered in
> Before they could turn the television down
> Or tidy away the supper dishes.
> To the children, to a bewildered wife,
> I think "Sorry Missus" was what he said.

Elsewhere in this second collection, many of the poems are, as always with Longley, short and sharp, brief images of experience more intensely felt for being worked at, as in the Yeatsian idyll "Swans Mating," a brilliant, light-filled recollection of a moment of close observation:

> Even now I wish that you had been there
> Sitting beside me on the riverbank:
> The cob and his pen sailing in rhythm
> Until their small heads met and the final
> Heraldic moment dissolved in ripples.
>
> This was a marriage and a baptism,
> A holding of breath, nearly a drowning,

Wings spread wide for balance where he trod,
Her feathers full of water and her neck
Under the water like a bar of light.

The Echo Gate: Poems 1975–79 comprises thirty-six typically well-crafted poems. Longley's themes are the same as before: "Wreaths" is a tripartite poem, memorials for a civil servant, a greengrocer, ten linen workers—only a few of the many murdered of Ulster; "Second Sight" is about his English ancestors and "Self-portrait" continues his witty exploration of his family connections; and "Thaw" is a haiku-like nature exercise, only four lines in length. Yet music and America seem to have lost their hold on his thematic consciousness, and his classical training, though perhaps evident enough in his careful versification and close attention to metrical detail, has this time yielded only an echo of Tibullus in the longer poem "Peace." More than ever, *The Echo Gate* attests to the poet's sense of Irishness, and two poems in particular show an Ulster Protestant's having come to terms of amusement, awe, and even admiration with the majority Irish Catholic culture. "Oliver Plunkett" is a memorial to the canonized Roman Catholic archbishop of Armagh, the last of his religion to be executed at Tyburn, in 1681, on politico-religious grounds, whose mummified head is kept in a glass reliquary in Drogheda Cathedral. And then there is the collection's longest and best poem, the masterful "Mayo Monologues," perhaps the most intensely imagined verse Longley has written, in which clarity of narrative line is closely united with lively compassion. The four monologues seem to be the spoken memories of southern Irish country people, simple enough personalities on the surface yet filled with self-knowledge and the basic understanding of their own lives: "Brothers" is an old man's speaking of his blind brother, now dead, whom he looked after in his later years; "Housekeeper" is an old woman's account of looking after another, the widow of her former employer, who treats her badly; "Self-heal" is a girl's tale of her blighted friendship with a retarded but sweet-tempered man; and "Arrest" is the searing tale spoken by a poor and solitary farmer who is taken away by the police to be "locked up in the institute / Because I made love to the animals." The poems are spare and unrhetorical, their artfulness almost invisible and the more noble and moving for that.

As part of his duties for the Arts Council of Northern Ireland, Longley edited *Under the Moon Over the Stars: Young People's Writing from Ulster*, selecting seventy-one poems from among 3,029 entries submitted by children from ages five to eighteen in a province-wide competition sponsored in 1970–1971 by the Arts Council. In his witty and graceful introduction, Longley speaks as a poet, with admirable candor, of the process of selection, being particularly sharp about "the 2,958 entries that I was unable to include": he had to wade through "an abundance of simpering pieties divided more or less evenly between dolls, pets and the infant Jesus. Very few poems of quality were written on religious topics, on large tragic themes like Aberfan, Biafra, Vietnam, East Pakistan, or on social problems like drugs and violence. This may be because the small arc of nascent lyric utterance is unable to bear such a load, or because such matters are really beyond the scope of the young writer. Indeed, only when the subject was approached in an oblique or idiosyncratic way was any contributor able to comment effectively on the violence and bloodshed which benight this tortured Province or, indeed, as one might suspect in some poignant cases, the writer's own street. . . . With those who laboured for hours only to have their efforts rejected, I commiserate: I too have suffered the same ignominy. And I urge those who dashed off in twenty seconds a few lines which happen to be included in this book, to feel no remorse. The Muse of Poetry is a fickle and wayward lady."

PRINCIPAL WORKS: *Poetry*—Ten Poems, 1966; Three Regional Voices (with I. Crichton Smith and B. Tebb), 1967; Room to Rhyme (with S. Heaney and D. Hammond), 1968; Secret Marriages, 1968; No Continuing City, 1969; Lares, 1972; An Exploded View, 1973; (with D. Abse and D. J. Enright) Penguin Modern Poets 26, 1975; Fishing in the Sky, 1975; Man Lying on a Wall, 1976; The Echo Gate, 1979; Selected Poems, 1963–1980, 1980; Patchwork, 1981; Poems 1963–83, 1986. *As editor*—Causeway: The Arts in Ulster, 1971; Under the Moon Over the Stars, 1971.

ABOUT: Brown, T. Northern Voices: Poets from Ulster, 1975; Contemporary Authors 102, 1981; Contemporary Literary Criticism 29, 1984; Dictionary of Literary Biography 40, 1985; Dawe, G. and E. Longley (eds.) Across a Roaring Hill: The Protestant Imagination in Modern Ireland, 1985; Dunn, D. Two Decades of Irish Writing: A Critical Survey, 1975; Ormsby, F. Poets from the North of Ireland, 1979.
Periodicals—Choice January 1978, June 1981; Encounter December 1973, December 1976; New Statesman December 5, 1969; February 18, 1977; January 11, 1980; Observer (London) August 22, 1976; December 9, 1979; January 27, 1980; Parnassus Fall–Winter 1981; Poetry Book Society Bulletin no. 103, 1979; Saturday Review December 26, 1970; Times Literary Supplement February 12, 1970; August 3, 1973; March 19, 1976; December 17, 1976; February 8, 1980; July 31, 1981; July 26, 1985.

*LOPATE, PHILLIP (November 16, 1943–), American novelist, poet, and essayist, was born in Jamaica Heights, New York City, the son of Albert Donald (a reporter) and Frances (Berlow) Lopate. He attended Eastern District High School in Brooklyn, where he edited the school's literary magazine, and upon graduating in 1960 entered Columbia College. At Columbia he was at first a prelaw student but later majored in English and minored in art history; in his senior year he was editor of the college's literary magazine, the *Columbia Review*, and president of Filmmakers of Columbia. During this year, too, he married Carol Bergman, and after his graduation in 1964 the couple (who were divorced in 1969) spent a year in Morocco and Spain where Lopate worked on a novel that was never published. Beginning in 1968 Lopate supported himself by teaching creative writing in the New York public school system. In 1971 he created and supervised the Arts Team Project at P.S. 75 in Manhattan under the auspices of the Teachers and Writers Collaborative, a federally-funded program.

At this time Lopate published two apprenticeship works—a novella, *In Coyoacan*, an experimental work influenced by Gertrude Stein's *Three Lives*, about a German immigrant family in Mexico between the 1930s and 1968; and, a year later, *The Eyes Don't Always Stay Open*, a collection of poetry of a psychological and at times lyrical nature. These books appeared in small-press editions and attracted little attention, but several years later Lopate came into sudden national prominence with *Being With Children*, about his teaching experiences in the Teachers and Writers Collaborative. The book won a Christopher Medal (1975) and occasioned over a hundred reviews and more than four dozen interviews.

Critical reception of the book was overwhelmingly favorable. Myra Cohn Livingston, in *Psychology Today*, remarked that "although this book is an account of teaching creative writing in the public schools, it is not the discussion of children's writing that makes *Being With Children* important. It is the rare ability of the author to see himself, with his frailties and strengths, his retrospection and introspection at work. It is his fine sense of humor, his profound desire to share the joys of creativity with children." Vivian Gornick, in the *New York Times Book Review*, was especially struck by Lopate's openness of approach and concern with the emotional content of communicating with the young. "What sets Lopate apart from other poets who have gone into the schools," she wrote, "is neither his preoccupation with the liberation of that famous children's 'imagination' nor his

PHILLIP LOPATE

ability to turn the children into poem factories but, rather, the enormous love and pleasure with which he feels the force of life persisting in children." In 1979 Lopate edited *Journal of a Living Experiment*, a collection of writing from the first ten years of Teachers and Writers Collaborative, including essays and reminiscences of such member/teachers as Anne Sexton, Hannah Brown, Kenneth Koch, and Herbert Kohl.

In 1976 *The Daily Round*, Lopate's second collection of poetry, was published. These poems are the plangent but by no means despairing expression of what Aram Saroyan, in the *Village Voice*, described as "the malaise of the unattached urban American." The title poem (which is dedicated to Osip Mandelstam) sounds the theme:

> Last cup of coffee
> Go slowly through the day
> Pick up the laundry on the way home from work
> Walk slowly through the grimy streets
> This is your last chance to see this life . . .

But it is a survivor's voice:

> My God, how I love this world
> Remember that the sun is yellow
> No matter what they try to tell you. . . .

We meet the speaker again in "Indigestible," trying to cheer up a friend in "a pre-suicidal mood" by inviting him out to dinner in a neighborhood delicatessen and in the process discovering his own melancholy: "But what is it that stops us when we're so near near to joy?" There is no answer, no dramatic conclusion. The friends part: "The next day he was still alive. / Still alive." As Sanyan wrote of these poems: "The self is a unit upon which it all rests, an accepting, humane, realistic self; the life in it need not be extravagant in display. It is on-going, a fact, and this is Lopate's real celebration, the life that is simply given" Hayden Carruth, in the *New York Times Book Review*, similarly noted the collection's prevailing tone of melancholy . . . [the poems] are lucid, consistent in tone, well and simply written, and—the acid test—they work. They move us."

Lopate's first novel, *Confessions of a Summer*, examines a triangular relationship between two young men in Manhattan—close friends—and the young woman they both love. Joseph McLellan, in the *Washington Post Book World*, commented that Lopate "approaches his time-worn subject with acute perceptions and mastery of style. The result is a psychological novel of considerable distinction." Wendy Levins, in *Library Journal*, also praised the work as "a narrowly focused but promising first novel; Lopate's exploration of the classic triangle is unpretentious, intelligent, and occasionally lyrical." Other critics, however, found the work disappointing. The reviewer for *Publishers Weekly* commented that "no matter how frequently Lopate praises his characters, they seem a rather unexceptional lot who offer little more than adolescent perceptions and a good deal of [the] dropping of famous philosphers' and writers' names (possibly to assure us that they are indeed brilliant). Lopate also tries to make them likable, but instead they strike us as selfish and childish in their convoluted affair."

In 1979 Lopate completed a Ph.D. in English education at Union Graduate School and left New York City to join the writing program at the University of Houston. His muse, however, seems to have remained in New York. *Bachelorhood: Tales of the Metropolis*, is a collection of essays and poems on the theme of bachelorhood as a way of life and type of urban sensibility. It is the work of a man who makes an inventory of the top drawer of his bedroom dresser "in a last attempt to understand the symbolic underpinnings of my character"; a man who "after so many years of living alone," adopts a cat (though he doesn't want one) and promptly becomes her slave; a New Yorker who reflects on the changing times in "Quiche Blight on Columbus Ave"; a writer for whom the genre of the personal essay exactly equates the condition of bachelorhood:

A bachelor's clinging to the minutiae of daily life has something puzzling and poignant about it, especially in

view of his being locked out of what society regards as the heart of the quotidian: family life. It is almost as if we were saying, We who are excluded from what you consider the central axis of social existence, the nursery and the conjugal hearth, will make a life out of the ephemeral impressions and bric-a-brac that chance throws our way.

Richard P. Brickner, in the *New York Times Book Review*, observed: "Despite the title, not all the pieces are about bachelorhood (of which Lopate, though once married for five years, is evidently a born practitioner), nor are they all about Lopate's bacheloric and city-boy personality, one of complex charm and exceptional intelligence, wittiness and talent. Lopate's book is often about matters commonly felt to be painful, such as disappointment or, perhaps more painful, having disappointment as a goal. Yet his artistic eye and ear, as well as his attitude, transform pain into something desirable, absorbing."

Against Joie de Vivre, another collection of Lopate's essays, demonstrated his mastery of this often unappreciated genre, in the judgement of reviewers. Lopate writes engagingly, "drawing us," Eva Hoffman commented in the *New York Times*, "into an absorbing dialogue with his own experience—and our own." Ranging from short, slight pieces on subjects like shaving a beard to meditations on serious subjects like the "power relations" between men and women, loneliness, disappointment, and melancholy, *Against Joie de Vivre*, as its title suggests, takes a cool, critical look at the American (and French) pursuit of happiness: "Over the years I have developed a distaste for the spectacle of *joie de vivre*, the knack of knowing how to live. Not that I disapprove of all hearty enjoyment of life. A flushed sense of happiness can overtake a person anywhere, and one is no more to blame for it than the Asiatic flu or a sudden benevolent change in the weather (which is often joy's immediate cause). No, what rankles me is the stylization of this private condition into a bullying social ritual." An essay, Lopate writes in an essay on essay writing, is the tracing of a writer's thoughts, "struggling to achieve some understanding." This precisely describes his method. Because he is candid, observant, and a graceful prose writer, he is a successful essayist. "The characteristic throughout [these essays]," Herbert Gold writes in the *New York Times Books Review*, "is that of a mind taking fresh thought. Meditation here doesn't mean a Zen emptying but an American filling up to abundance."

Lopate's novel *The Rug Merchant* appears to have evolved from the spirit that informs both *Bachelorhood* and *Against Joie de Vivre*. Its protagonist, Cyrus Irani, an Iranian immigrant, is a forty-four-year-old bachelor living on New York's Upper West Side. With "bachelor" sensibility, he is melancholic and introspective—at odds with the aggressive, materialistic world around him: "It was almost a point of pride with him to accept the provisional as the inevitable, and to find half-hidden crumbs of aesthetic satisfaction in whatever he was given." A dropout from Columbia graduate school where he had studied art and philosophy, he runs a small carpet shop in the heart of this rapidly gentrifying neighborhood. A crisis develops suddenly in his quiet life when his landlord triples his rent and he must confront the loss of his business. Characteristically, he drifts along until he does indeed lose his business—and almost loses his life. As his widowed mother wisely tells him: "You are evading the responsibility of doing something constructive with your life with the excuse that you have not the capacity for happiness." Reviews of the novel were favorable. Merle Rubin, in the *Christian Science Monitor*, called the work a "touching elegy to the city . . . [and] the interiority of the individual." Jerome Charnyn, in the *New York Times Book Review*, characterized *The Rug Merchant* as "a sad, tight lyrical song among the glittering ruins of Manhattan. Mr. Lopate never sentimentalizes Irani: some of us will see our own faces reflected in his luminous black eyes." The work was also praised by Robert Towers in the *New York Review of Books*, who remarked that "the novel lacks much drama. . . . The pace is slow and meditative in a way that some readers will find tedious. Others may be exasperated by Cyrus's passivity and resignation. I finished *The Rug Merchant*, however, with the sense that something memorable had been accomplished in the characterization of Cyrus and his city."

Lopate has said that the writers influencing his most are Dostoevsky, Céline, Chekhov, Cesare Pavese, Lionel Trilling, Rilke, Flaubert, Charles Lamb, Randall Jarrell, and Charles Reznikoff. "What interests me," he said, "are the personality problems, largesses, layers of rationalization, class background, speech patterns, sexual tropisms that make up a single person. . . . I don't consider myself an experimentalist . . . but a very traditional writer with a psychological bent. . . . I hate this modern emphasis on bodiless, neutral narrators, Inferno surrealism, stripped-bare syntax masquerading as punctilious craftsmanship. . . . I have to go back to what I love, to what first drew me to novels and prose: 1) that it gave you a world; 2) that it did that in the voice of a lively, worldly person you wanted to know."

PRINCIPAL WORKS: *Fiction*—In Coyoacan, 1971; Confes-

sions of a Summer, 1979; The Rug Merchant, 1987. *Poetry*—The Eyes Don't Always Want to Stay Open: Poems and a Japanese Tale, 1972; The Daily Round: New Poems, 1976. *Non-fiction prose*—Being with Children, 1975; Bachelorhood: Tales of the Metropolis, 1981; Against Joie de Vivre: Personal Essays, 1989.

ABOUT: Contemporary Authors 97–100, 1981; Contemporary Literary Criticism 29, 1984; Dictionary of Literary Biography, 1981. *Periodicals*—Christian Science Monitor May 20, 1987; Library Journal May 15, 1979; New York Review of Books June 25, 1987; New York Times May 24, 1989; New York Times Book Review November 2, 1975; August 7, 1977; July 22, 1978; October 11, 1981; March 8, 1987; May 14, 1989; Psychology Today December 1975; Publishers Weekly April 30, 1979; Village Voice January 24, 1977; October 14, 1981; Washington Post Book World July 16, 1979.

LOPEZ, BARRY HOLSTUN (January 6, 1945–), American essayist, naturalist and short-story writer, writes: "I was born in Port Chester, New York, and spent the first three years of my life in nearby Mamaroneck, New York, a small town on Long Island Sound. When I was three my family moved to the San Fernando Valley in southern California. It was here that I was first exposed to images that would profoundly affect me—wild animals on their own terrain, the Mojave Desert, the San Bernardino Mountains. The community we lived in, Reseda, was at that time in a state of transition. In a very few years the alfalfa haying operations, the horse pastures, the droves of sheep on the roads, the vast groves and orchards, the fields full of squash and melons were all gone.

"I raised a kind of pigeon as a boy of eight called tumblers, birds that flew up to a great height and then tumbled down, pulling out of the free fall just above the ground at the last moment. I wandered in the Santa Monica Mountains with my pals, often with a dog as a companion, and spent my summer days on the beach at Malibu and Zuma.

"Soon after we arrived in California my parents divorced. In 1955 my mother married Adrian Lopez and in 1956 my brother and I and my mother moved to New York City, where he lived. The change in social and economic circumstances was sharp for me, and at first disorienting. My barefoot days, the immediacy of a wild countryside, were gone; but in their place was something as exciting to me—the vitality of a city.

"I went to prep school in New York and then, at the age of seventeen, left for South Bend, Indiana, where I entered the University of Notre Dame. I began my studies there as an aeronauti-

BARRY HOLSTUN LOPEZ

cal engineer but switched my major to English at the end of my freshman year. I played soccer for two years at Notre Dame, worked at the college radio station as a newscaster and announcer, and acted in several plays. Beginning in my sophomore year, however, a position on the dean's list gave me the freedom to miss an occasional class and I began to travel extensively with my roommate over long weekends. We went up into Ontario and as far south as Louisiana. In the summer of 1964 my brother Dennis and I made a journey of some 6,000 miles in a pickup truck, out to the western United States and up into British Columbia and Alberta. It was the first time I'd been back to California, and I was exhilarated, brought back to life, by the landscapes of the West.

"The last part of the summer of 1964 I spent working as a wrangler at Triangle X Ranch in Jackson Hole, Wyoming. In the summer of 1965 I returned to wrangle horses there again. Earlier that year I had stayed with friends in Santa Fe, and I had a girlfriend in Salt Lake City. I was vaguely aware by then that though I was emotionally and spiritually at home only in the West, I missed there the intense intellectual conversation and passion for ideas I had come to know in the East.

"When I graduated from Notre Dame in 1966 I went to work briefly as a sales representative for New American Library and then as an editor. In June, 1967, I married Sandra Landers, whom I'd met as a senior at Notre Dame. We moved back to South Bend where she finished her undergraduate degree at St. Mary's College

and I entered Notre Dame's graduate school. In August, 1968, I received a Master of Arts in Teaching degree and Sandy and I moved out to Eugene, Oregon, where I entered the Master of Fine Arts program in creative writing at the University of Oregon. I thought that since I could not, it seemed, make a living as a writer— by this time I had published four or five stories, several book reviews, a handful of essays and some magazine articles—I would teach, and write as well as I could on the side. I left the program in frustration, however, after the first semester, and entered Oregon's School of Journalism. In 1970 I left that program too, two courses short of a master's degree, to write full time.

"In June of that year Sandy and I moved to a rural area on the McKenzie River in the Cascade Mountains in Oregon, where we have lived ever since. I was by then writing regularly for several magazines and had drafted the manuscript about the trickster figure that was published in 1978 as *Giving Birth to Thunder*. I continued to write for magazines and to string feature material for the *New York Times* and the *Washington Post*, and worked as well on *Desert Notes*, which was published by Andrews & McMeel in 1976. During the early seventies, Lewis Lapham at *Harper's*, Robley Wilson at the *North American Review*, and Jim Andrews of Andrews & McMeel gave me crucial encouragement.

"I still live in the same house and my work goes on as it has for the past eighteen years. Glancing back in my journals, I see that I still have the same handful of questions about the relationship between people and the landscapes they inhabit, about the issues of tolerance and dignity, about the spiritual dimension of life. I continue to pursue these questions in books, in essays and short stories, and I continue to travel. In 1985 I began to travel outside the United States for the first time since 1966, when I went to Europe. I went to Japan, to northern Hokkaido, and then to the Galápagos Islands, and then to Africa, to Antarctica, and China. These extensive journeys are the context of my work now."

———

In his 1986 speech accepting the American Book Award for non-fiction for *Arctic Dreams*, Barry Lopez said: "Even though I appear to write largely about other landscapes and animals, what is in my gut as a writer is a concern with the fate of the country I live in and the dignity and morality of the people I live with." Regarded today as a peer of Edwin Way Teale, Hal Borland, Loren Eisley, and other major American naturalist writers, Lopez has become the

voice of the conscience of many Americans who have turned to the shrinking wilderness for their faith in the future of humanity. In the natural landscape and in the animal life that populates it, he has discovered what he calls "the culture that contains all human culture." The moral dimensions of his work are in part at least the product of his early years. Raised as a Roman Catholic, he was early attracted to the contemplative life. He told Nicholas O'Connell in an interview that at one time he had considered entering a monastery. In 1966 he spent a month at the Gethsemani Monastery in Kentucky, of which Thomas Merton wrote so movingly in *The Seven Storey Mountain*. But Lopez denies that his purpose in writing is spiritual: "I don't think in terms of dividing the material from the spiritual." Rather, he seeks to explore the integration of the real and the mystical in nature.

The first book that brought Lopez to the attention of a large and appreciative reading public was his *Of Wolves and Men*, nominated for the 1980 American Book Award and a best-seller, that considers "the separate realities enjoyed by other organisms" and shows their peculiar relationship to the well-being of humankind itself. Speaking of a hybrid red wolf that he and his wife raised from the age of three weeks, Lopez writes: "I learned from River that I was a human being and that he was a wolf and that we were different. I valued him as a creature, but he did not have to be what I imagined he was. It was with this freedom from dogma, I think, that the meaning of the words 'the celebration of life' becomes clear."

Lopez never sentimentalizes or romanticizes animal life. He knows that wolves are wild and that they can kill. He also knows that a vast body of legend, superstition and ignorance have cruelly victimized them since ancient times. His attitude is realistic: "We have begun to see again, as our primitive ancestors did, that animals are neither imperfect imitations of men nor machines that can be described entirely in terms of endocrine secretion and natural impulses. Like us, they are generically variable, and both the species and the individual are capable of unprecedented behavior. They are like us in the sense that we can figuratively talk of them as beings, some of whose forms, movements, activities, and social organizations are analogous, but they are not more literally like us than are trees."

Of Wolves and Men is a balanced study of the real wolf, its physiology and habits, and of the archetypal image of the wolf in human culture. Illustrated with photographs and diagrams and enriched with the author's and others' first-hand observations of wolves in their natural habitat,

the book offers a soundly researched scientific study of wolves. It also surveys the history of wolves as part of "man's never-ending struggle to come to grips with the nature of the universe"—the wolf in mythology, folklore, fable and fairy tale, and the mysterious linking of men and wolves in the legendary werewolves. "In coming to terms with what we know and what we imagine about the wolf," Whitley Strieber wrote in the *Washington Post*, "Lopez has shed light on some painful truths about the human experience . . . he has made what we have done to the wolf a source of new knowledge about man." In the *New York Times Book Review* Bayard Webster called *Of Wolves and Men* "fascinating and often metaphysical . . . his book has a wealth of observations, mythology and mysticism about wolves that add a colorful part to the still unfinished mosaic that defines the wolf, the ancestor of the animal known as 'man's best friend.'"

The same sensitivity to environment, natural and human, figures in Lopez's short stories and reflective essays. *Desert Notes: Reflections in the Eye of a Raven* is a small book, less than one hundred pages, recounting impressionistically the experience of the desert, the narrator responding to it physically and spiritually. He writes about desert birds, a bath in the desert's hot springs, the luminosity of the desert sky, plants, insects, and the ancient Mound People who lived in the desert. The stories in *Winter Count* are slight and unplotted. They center mainly on epiphanies, and sketch lonely but self-sufficient people who cherish books and seashells and live inwardly rewarding lives: "We carry such people with us in an imaginary way," Lopez writes, "proof against some undefined but irrefutable darkness in the world." Lopez has also compiled a series of stories from Indian lore about the archetypal trickster-rogue Coyote, a combination of good and evil, who speaks for primitive human consciousness—*Giving Birth to Thunder, Sleeping with His Daughter: Coyote Builds North America*. The tales are written in a straightforward narrative, neither condescending nor in any way mannered, and rendering—as Barre Toelken writes in the Foreword to the book—"a personality profile and not the scholar's fossil."

The inspiration for *Arctic Dreams: Imagination and Desire in a Northern Landscape*, Lopez writes, was a visit he made to Alaska to study wildlife. Two minor incidents fascinated him. one was the sight, in the midnight light of the northern summer, of a flight of birds and a small herd of caribou crossing a river. The other took place not in the Arctic but in rural Michigan, where he came across the grave of a sailor who had died in an Arctic expedition in 1884. "The one, timeless and full of light, reminded me of sublime innocence, of the innate beauty of undisturbed relationships. The other, a dream gone awry, reminded me of the long human struggle, mental and physical, to come to terms with the Far North. As I traveled, I came to believe that people's desires and aspirations were as much a part of the land as the wind, solitary animals, and the bright fields of stone and tundra. And, too, that the land itself existed quite apart from these."

Modern technology has radically altered the landscape and the life of the native peoples. Lopez covers the geography, the history, and the bird and animal life of the Arctic with careful scholarly documentation. But he also studies what he calls "The Country of the Mind"—the challenge to the human imagination of ice, light and darkness, the aesthetics of the Arctic world. At the end of his own journey, looking over the Bering Sea from the tip of Saint Lawrence Island, Lopez writes that he bowed to the North in a gesture of respect and thanks: "When I stood I thought I glimpsed my own desire. The landscape and the animals were like something found at the end of a dream. The edges of the real landscape became one with the edges of something I had dreamed. But what I had dreamed was only a pattern, some beautiful pattern of light. The continuous work of the imagination, I thought, to bring what is actual together with what is dreamed is an expression of human evolution. The conscious desire is to achieve a state, even momentarily, that like light is unbounded, nurturing, suffused with wisdom and creation, a state in which one has absorbed that very darkness which before was the perpetual sign of defeat."

Edward Hoagland, who has himself written extensively about the American wilderness, described *Arctic Dreams* as a celebration of life, "a passionate paean to the Arctic" and the author as a "rhapsodist." For Michiko Kakutani in the *New York Times* it was "a book about the Arctic North in the way that *Moby Dick* is a novel about whales . . . he communicates to us a visceral sense of his own understanding and wonder, as well as an appreciation for this distant country that flickers insistently like a flashbulb after-image in our minds long after we've finished reading."

Lopez has had visiting professorships at Columbia University, Eastern Washington University, the University of Iowa, and Carleton College. He has twice had citations from the Christopher Foundation—for *Of Wolves and Men* and for *Arctic Dreams*, which also won the American Book Award. In 1986 he received an award in literature from the American Academy and Institute of Arts and Letters, and in 1987 he was named a Guggenheim Fellow. He holds an honorary Doctorate of Human Letters from Whittier College, California. His writings have been translated into many European languages as well as into Chinese and Japanese.

PRINCIPAL WORKS: *Non-fiction*—Giving Birth to Thunder, Sleeping with His Daughter: Coyote Builds North America, 1977; Of Wolves and Men, 1978; Arctic Dreams, 1986. *Short fiction*—Desert Notes, 1976; River Notes, 1979; Winter Count, 1981. *Collected essays*—Crossing Open Ground, 1988.

ABOUT: Contemporary Authors New Revision Series 7, 1982; 23, 1988; O'Connell, Nicholas (ed.) At the Field's End, 1988; Trimble, Stephen (ed.) Words from the Land, 1988; Who's Who in America 1988–1989. *Periodicals*—Denver Post, March 23, 1986; New York Times November 19, 1978; March 29, 1986; New York Times Book Review February 16, 1986; San Francisco Chronicle February 21, 1988; San Jose Mercury News March 16, 1986; Seattle Review Fall 1985; Washington Post November 27, 1978; November 24, 1986; Western American Literature Spring 1986.

*LU WENFU (March 23, 1928–   ), Chinese short-story writer, was born into a farming family in a village named Taixing on the north bank of the Yangzi River near the city of Suzhou. When he was a small child he already had many aspirations, none of which was to become a writer. At seven, he began to study the works of Confucius, which led him to an interest in books. He remembers that his mind was filled with childish imaginings: monsters and fairies, love and friendship, happiness and sadness, dastardly deeds and noble acts. He wanted so much to experience life that at sixteen he left the village to go to Suzhou to stay with his aunt. In that beautiful city, he became aware of the inequality among different classes of people. By the end of the war, in 1945, he became so disenchanted with the corrupt Kuomintang rule that upon his graduation from middle school, instead of going on to college, he went to the countryside to join the Communist forces. In 1949, after the Communist triumph, he came back to Suzhou with the victorious People's Liberation Army and started to work as a journalist on *Xin Suzhou Bao* (New Suzhou Daily). He was there eight years, during which time he also served as a correspondent for *Xinhua* (New China News Agency). Not satisfied with factual reporting, he tried his hand at fiction writing. His first attempt at a short story took him over a month to finish. He sent it to *Wenxue Yuekan* (Literary Monthly). Although the manuscript was rejected, the editor wrote

°loo wen foo

him an encouraging three-page letter. Greatly spurred, Lu submitted a second story, "Rongyu" (Honor), which was readily accepted and published with a complimentary review in the same issue of *Wenxue Yuekan*. He was then twenty-five.

Before long, his stories began to appear frequently in such magazines as *Renmin Wenxue* (People's Literature), *Mengya* (Sprout), and *Wenyi Yuebao* (Arts and Literature Monthly). His first collection of short stories, *Rongyu* (Honor), was published in 1956, and he was invited to become a member of the Chinese Writers' Union, East China branch. For the first time he went to Beijing, to attend the Union's first national conference, and there he met many promising young writers who later were to become household names.

One of his early stories, "Xiaohang Shenchu" (Deep Within a Lane), caused quite a sensation because at a time (during the Korean War) when most stories concerned arms production, heroism, model workers, sacrifices, etc., this one dealt with the life and loves of a prostitute. It was condemned by some critics as sentimental and petty bourgeois. By the spring of 1957, Lu had helped organize a professional writers' group under the auspices of the Jiangsu province branch of the Federation of Literary Art Circles. He left the newspaper and became a full-fledged *zhuanyi zuojia* (professional writer) stationed in Nanjing. In passionate discussions about the mission of the artist, he and his young writer friends decided that literature ought not to be used merely to sing praises, but should touch on all aspects of life. They also believed that literature ought not to be limited to Socialist Realism and that emphasis should be placed on human frailties rather than on political movements. And they argued that excessive class struggle had already destroyed normal human relationships and shattered the fabric of China's social life.

Such views were considered outrageously daring, even in the relatively relaxed atmosphere of the brief "Hundred Flowers Bloom" period. The young enthusiasts had planned a magazine to be called *Tansuozhe* (The Explorers), and an editorial expounding their ideas had already been written, when at the end of the year 1957 Mao launched his Anti-Rightist Campaign. Lu and his friends were instantly branded as "anti-party elements" and sent to farms and factories to work as laborers. Lu Wenfu went back to Suzhou to serve as an apprentice in a machine plant. (The incident, known as the "The Explorers Affair," was notorious in China's cultural circles in the late fifties.) For two years Lu worked at a lathe. He won the respect of his co-workers but was miserable at not being able to write.

In the summer of 1960, when cultural life revived, a professional writers' group was again set up in Jiangsu province. Since his work in the factory had been outstanding, Lu was judged fully reformed. He was transferred back to Nanjing to resume his position as a *zhuanyi zuojia*, but class struggle was everything then, and he found it hard to think and write creatively. He avoided the popular heroic style, wherein all characters were exaggerations, preferring to write about actual laborers, using his experience of three years in the factory. His stories soon caught the attention of readers and critics alike. He enjoyed a good reputation until 1964, when class struggle again came in vogue and writers' lives again were made miserable. Even with the blessing of Mao Dun, who was then editor of *Wenyi Bao* (Literary Gazette), the Party's literary organ, Lu could not avoid being hounded for "revisionist tendencies" in his writing. When an investigation into his past discovered his involvement in the Explorers Affair in 1957, he was roundly denounced, this time very severely. The attacks lasted some six months, with the newspapers in Suzhou devoting huge spaces to diatribes against him, accusing him of creating "mediocre" characters and advocating humanism instead of class struggle. His despair was such that he was almost driven to suicide, according to his own account.

In the summer of 1965 he was sent back to Suzhou and assigned to a cotton mill as a mechanic. Despondent, he stopped reading and writing altogether, finding solace in heavy drinking. Then came the worst period, the Cultural Revolution, during which he was consistently harassed, forced to confess his "crimes," and paraded through the streets with a placard around his neck. His fate even affected his relatives, and by late 1966, his whole family was given five days notice to leave Suzhou and go to the countryside. He, his wife, and their two small daughters settled in the poorest part of Jiangsu province, where they built a hut with their own hands and farmed for nine years. But Lu considered himself lucky in that many of his writer friends were exiled to the same area, so that he did not lack company; on many occasions they drank wine together and held heated discussions.

When the news of Mao's death and of the fall of the Gang of Four finally came in 1976, Lu and friends celebrated with a three-day drinking spree. After some twelve years of abstinence from writing, he picked up a pen again. For a while, the going was slow. He first tried out short essays and pieces of dialogues. Then he finished his first story in thirteen years, "Xianshen" (Dedication), which was quickly snatched up by the editors of the revived *Renmin Wenxu* (People's

Literature) and published in its April 1978 issue. It won an award as one of the best short stories of that year.

In his own words, it had taken Lu "five years, three rises and two falls" to enter this "unenviable" profession as a writer. Since then he has published often and won no less than four literary awards. He was elected a vice-chairman of the fourth congress of the Writers' Union, a prestigious and much-coveted position. In January 1985 he came to the United States as a member of the Chinese delegation invited by the International PEN to attend its 48th congress in New York. At one of the panel discussions he was asked by the audience whether he enjoyed creative freedom in China. His answer was affirmative. When asked whether Lu Xun, the great satirist, if he were alive today, would be allowed to write freely, his answer was: "Only Lu Xun himself could answer this question." When asked whether he himself, his speech, his work were subjected to censorship, he replied that no one but he himself censored his own writing, his own words.

Perhaps his best known work is "Meishijia" ("The Gourmet"), which was voted the best novella in 1984. It is a subtle, humorous tale of a man whose life, no matter what he does, is plagued by gluttony—before liberation, after, during the Cultural Revolution, and evidently forever.

WORKS IN ENGLISH TRANSLATION: *The Gourmet and Other Stories of Modern China*, 1987; *A World of Dreams*, 1988. (Translations are credited to Gladys Yang, William Jenner, Judith Burrows, Beth McKillop, and others.)

ABOUT: Who's Who in the People's Republic of China, 2nd ed., 1987.

LUDLUM, ROBERT (May 25, 1927), American novelist, was born in New York City, son of George Hartford (a businessman) and Margaret (Wadsworth) Ludlum. He spent his early childhood in the suburban community of Short Hills, New Jersey, until his father's death in 1934. Ludlum's mother was left sufficiently well off to send her son to a series of private schools in Connecticut. He received his primary education at the Rectory School, a junior boarding school for boys in Pomfret, then attended the Kent School and the Cheshire Academy. After appearing in school theatricals, he became stagestruck and in 1943, at sixteen, auditioned for and won a role on Broadway in *Junior Miss*, the long-running comedy by Jerome Chodorov and Jo-

ROBERT LUDLUM

seph Fields. Later in the same year he was part of the play's national touring company. In 1945, after graduating from the Cheshire Academy, he enlisted in the United States Marine Corps for a two-year tour of duty as an infantryman. Following his discharge in 1947, he enrolled at Wesleyan University, receiving his B.A. with distinction in 1951. In the same year he married Mary Ryducha, by whom he has three children—Michael, Jonathan, and Glynis.

Beginning in 1951, Ludlum worked as a professional actor, both in summer stock and on Broadway. Most of his acting assignments, however, were in television, where he appeared in 200 television plays, particularly for "Studio One," "The Kraft Television Theatre," and "Robert Montgomery Presents." "Usually," he has remarked, "I was cast as a lawyer or a homicidal killer. . . . But I got bored with the total lack of control an actor has, which is when I decided to become a producer." In 1956 Ludlum brought *The Owl and the Pussycat* and a revival of *The Front Page* to Broadway; and in 1957 he was producer at the North Jersey Playhouse in Fort Lee, New Jersey. Three years later, with the help of foundation grants, he established the Playhouse-on-the-Mall in Paramus, the first year-round legitimate theater in a suburban shopping mall. Here Ludlum featured stars of Broadway, Hollywood, and television in productions ranging from *Hamlet* to *Who's Afraid of Virginia Woolf?* The Playhouse-on-the-Mall was an immediate success, with an attendance of more than 140,000 in its first eight months alone. The Playhouse continued to flourish throughout the 1960s, but, discouraged by the repeated failure of adventurous productions, Ludlum decided to try his hand as a writer.

He found a lucrative sideline as the voice in television commercials, but his energies went chiefly into the writing of his first novel, *The Scarlatti Inheritance*, published in 1971, which became an immediate best-seller and a Book-of-the-Month Club alternate selection. Perhaps owing something to Ludlum's work in the theater, *The Scarlatti Inheritance* is a melodrama-thriller about an American heir to an industrial fortune, Ulster Scarlatti, who later appears, surgically altered, as Heinrich Kroeger, intimate of the German high command, financial backer of Hitler, and one of a group of tycoons bent upon possession of international power. The reviewer for *Time* commented that the "plot is kitsch, but does occasionally clutch, and the reader rests assured that the damned indeed are doomed." Martin Levin in the *New York Times Book Review* described the novel as "lurid melodrama" with thinly drawn characters but a suspenseful plot.

The Scarlatti Inheritance was quickly followed by two espionage thrillers with suburban American settings, *The Osterman Weekend* and *The Matlock Paper*. In *The Osterman Weekend*, John Tanner, a television news executive, invites three couples for a weekend at his New Jersey home in honor of his longtime friends the Ostermans. Before long, however, a CIA agent appears and Tanner becomes involved in a tug of war between the CIA and the international spy ring Omega, whose leader is believed to be one of Tanner's guests. William B. Hill in *Best Sellers* remarked that "the tale is tautly told and the writing is vivid . . . [but] the excitement is allowed to dissipate instead of crashing to a finale." The reviewer for *Library Journal* also faulted the ending, commenting that "as the action becomes more dramatic a hectic hysteria sets in and the plot dissolves into a porridge of nonsense." A film version of the novel was directed by Sam Peckinpah in 1983. *The Matlock Paper* is set at a college in Connecticut similar to Wesleyan where an English professor, James Matlock, becomes aware of a meeting of Nimrod, an international crime organization, on the campus, and is enlisted by the federal government to help in its destruction. "If action is what you want," Newgate Callendar commented in the *New York Times Book Review*, "action is what you get. The basic situation is unreal—indeed it's unbelievable—but a good writer can make the reader suspend his disbelief, and Ludlum is a good writer. Once one gets involved in this silly tale, the reviewer for *Library Journal* noted, "it is quite impossible not to finish it."

In his next novel, *The Rhinemann Exchange*, Ludlum returned to the period of World War II, where an exchange is to be made by the different sides of German gyroscopes for Allied industrial diamonds, and where espionage and intrigue are rife. The reviewer for the *New Yorker* belittled Ludlum's prose style ("reads like a Hearst feature writer of the twenties—staccato sentences, one sentence paragraphs"), yet conceded that the result was "reasonably entertaining." In the *New York Times Book Review*, Newgate Callendar remarked that the novel "has everything—espionage, professional killing, the Gestapo, the German high command, Zionists, Big Business, supercapitalists, infiltration, double-dealing. . . . it is written in breathless, edge-of-Armageddon prose that pants relentlessly along. But . . . a real storyteller is at work. You'll go along." *The Rhinemann Exchange* was adapted as an NBC television miniseries in 1977. Although often treated slightingly or even deplored by reviewers, Ludlum's thrillers regularly found their place at the top of the best-seller charts, and his next novel, *The Gemini Contenders*, was no exception, pushing Ludlum's hardcover and paperback sales past the ten million mark. Its story deals with the disappearance of a document, allegedly written by St. Peter, denying that Christ had been crucified—a document with the potential for unsettling the affairs of half the civilized world. Summing up the attitude of many critics, the reviewer for the *Times Literary Supplement* observed that "the initial premise of *The Gemini Contenders* is implausible, the plot improbable, the style florid, the characters unbelievable and the period details inaccurate. Nevertheless, Robert Ludlum has the ability to tell a story in such a way as to keep even the fastidious reader unwillingly absorbed."

Conspiracy with a paranoic tinge informs *The Chancellor Manuscript*, the premise of which is that J. Edgar Hoover did not die a natural death but was done away with by a group of highly-placed intellectuals. Many of Hoover's scandal-ridden private files are missing, and before long the novelist Peter Chancellor becomes involved in the mystery and is the repeated target of assassins. Barbara Phillips in the *Christian Science Monitor* found the novel deficient in many respects, yet gripping in its suspense. "There is no doubt," she observed, "that the book is entertaining. The characters are stock, the style melodramatic, the hero's durability preposterous. But the plotting's skillful, and the narrative races along with the speed of the expensive cars that Ludlum incomparably so lovingly into the plot." *The Holcroft Covenant* deals with a conspiracy in which the children of Nazi officials are spirited out of Germany before the end of the war, so that they may re-establish the Third Reich at some future time. This novel was frequently compared to Ira Levin's *The Boys from Brazil* (1976), usually to its disadvantage; Ludlum's book seemed to a number of reviewers to be burdened by a vastly overelaborated plot. Nevertheless, it provided the basis for a 1983 movie starring Michael Caine.

In *The Matarese Circle*, a Book-of-the-Month Club main selection, Ludlum's antagonists are an American intelligence agent, Brandon Scofield, and Vasili Taleniekov, a Russian spy, who pursue clues across several continents in a hunt for a terrorist organization responsible for the deaths of both the Soviet and American heads of state. Richard Freedman in the *New York Times Book Review* remarked that "the fans of Robert Ludlum, as numerous as the leaves on the trees, will delight in *The Matarese Circle*, which adheres strictly to formula. Others may feel that the novel is longer than its premise warrants and that the symmetry of the plot is more dogged than shapely." *The Bourne Identity* deals with a certain Carlos, head of a terrorist network, and an American counter-assassin, Jason Bourne, who suffers from amnesia. A number of critics felt that this was the best of Ludlum's novels. "*The Bourne Identity*," Michael Demarest summed up in *Time*, "is the most absorbing of Ludlum's . . . novels to date. His characters are complex and credible, his sleight of plot as cunning as any terrorist conspiracy. And his minutiae, from the rituals of Swiss banking to the workings of a damaged brain, are always absorbing. It is a Bourne from which no traveler returns unsatisfied."

Ludlum's novels of the 1980s, in addition to *The Bourne Identity*, include *The Parsifal Mosaic, The Aquitaine Progression, The Bourne Supremacy* and *The Icarus Agenda*, most of which employ international settings and all of which climbed to the top of the best-seller lists soon after their appearance. During the 1970s Ludlum also published three thrillers under pseudonyms—*Trevayne* and *The Cry of the Halidon* as Jonathan Ryder, and *The Road to Gandolpho* as Michael Shepherd; and these books too, even without the benefit of Ludlum's name, sold in large volume. *Current Biography* in 1982 described Ludlum as a "short thickset man with a ruggedly handsome face and longish gray hair . . . with an easy-going manner and a self-deprecating sense of humor." The Ludlums have a renovated, 200-year-old clapboard house overlooking Long Island Sound, where Ludlum likes to swim and fish. He also enjoys tennis and skiing.

PRINCIPAL WORKS: The Scarlatti Inheritance, 1971; The Osterman Weekend, 1972; The Matlock Paper, 1973; (as Jonathan Ryder) Trevayne, 1973; (as Jonathan Ryder) The Cry of the Halidon, 1974; The Rhinemann Exchange, 1974; (as Michael Shepherd) The Road to Gandolpho, 1975; The Gemini Contenders, 1976; The Chancellor Manuscript, 1978; The Holcroft Covenant, 1978; The Matarese Circle, 1979; The Bourne Conspiracy, 1980; The Parsifal Mosaic, 1982; The Aquitaine Progression, 1983; The Bourne Supremacy, 1986; The Icarus Agenda, 1988; The Bourne Ultimatum, 1990.

ABOUT: Contemporary Authors 33–36, 1978; Contemporary Literary Criticism 42, 1982; 43, 1987; Current Biography 1982; Dictionary of Literary Biography, 1983; Who's Who in America 1988–89, 1989. *Periodicals*—Best Sellers April 1972; Christian Science Monitor March 31, 1977; Library Journal March 1, 1972; March 1, 1973; New York Times Book Review April 4, 1971; May 6, 1973; October 27, 1974; April 8, 1979; New Yorker October 14, 1974; Time April 14, 1980; Times Literary Supplement October 1, 1976; Washington Post Book World March 19, 1978.

LYALL, GAVIN (TUDOR) (May 9, 1932–), British novelist, writes: "I was born and went to school in a suburb of Birmingham, Britain's second biggest city. The Second World War started when I was seven and obviously it must have had a big influence on me; perhaps I still haven't shaken off the unquestioning patriotism of the schoolboy who watched a squadron of German bombers fly over in perfect formation, who collected bits of anti-aircraft shrapnel and bomb casing, who helped sweep the windows off the floor when one bomb came too close. Balancing or contradicting this was the fact that my family were pacifist Quakers. I wasn't—I am told—allowed a toy gun until my parents realised this was just making other boys' guns glamorous. If I went in for self-analysis I could probably make something out of that.

"I was a good all-rounder at the big day-school I attended, winning the poetry and art prizes as well as being vice-captain of football and the track champion in my last year. My 'rebellion' was helping found the school's first jazz group (on drums: I tried several other instruments before realizing sadly that I have a tin ear). It all seemed pretty daring and way-out in Britain of the late forties.

"I was drafted into the Royal Air Force in 1951 and, suddenly seeing that two years weren't going to pass like a wet weekend, applied for pilot training and was lucky enough to get it. I spent a lot of my time being scared—I was only an average pilot, better suited to large aircraft than the early jet fighters I flew—but it was a very important time in my life. More im-

GAVIN T. LYALL

portant than Cambridge University, where I took an average degree in English literature (a degree that I now think shouldn't exist. examinations force the invention of arbitrary values. Literature should be studied—as opposed to read—only as an aspect of language or history). Cambridge seemed childish to my ex-military generation, but military training means you don't rebel, you study the regulations and sneak through the loopholes.

"Most of my work at Cambridge was on the student newspaper, then the best in Britain, and this led to a job on a national magazine when I graduated. Journalism seemed *real*, as flying had been, and my ambitions to write a novel or a great verse play (Bellerophon and Pegasus in a Battle of Britain setting) had faded. The only fiction I could see myself writing was a thriller. The magazine collapsed after a year and I married a reporter I'd met there, Katharine Whitehorn, who has since become Britain's leading woman columnist. There followed a few years of resigning or being fired from various organisations including the BBC, proving to myself that I wasn't a very good employee. During this time I started my first book, *The Wrong Side of the Sky*, based on my knowledge of flying but obviously more influenced by Chandler and Hammett than by the classic British adventure-story writers. I think several British writers at this time were seeking a European equivalent of the corrupt big city in the American genre. Some found it in the spy world, I in the arena of third-rate airlines, smuggling and gun-running.

"I made my last resignation (as aviation editor at the *Sunday Times*) and wrote six more books, all using one-off first-person characters as narrators. But towards the end of the seventies I was feeling rather jaded, and once caught myself thinking 'I can't do *that* in a Gavin Lyall book.' I don't recall what *that* was; the shock was in realising that I was type-casting myself.

"So I was looking for something new when I was asked to draft a TV story set in government circles. Research into how government works intrigued me (journalists, looking for the story of the day, seldom learn the underlying patterns of government), and when the TV project collapsed I was left with a group of fictional characters far better worked out and tested—in a succession of scripts—than any I had had when starting a book. But to fit them into a new book meant switching to third-person narration, and it took me six months of torn-up pages to achieve a confident 'voice.' Looking back at *The Secret Servant* I can now see how I was, not quite consciously, exploring the bounds of this new territory with constant shifts of viewpoint.

"I am now drafting my fifth Major Maxim story and enjoying having a repertory company of characters whose problems and relationships I can tackle at leisure, perhaps putting off something until the next book or even the one after. I don't see these as 'spy' thrillers; I see, with some sadness, that espionage and counter-espionage are now threads woven inextricably into the fabric of government world-wide. Or maybe, to those who knew, it has always been like this."

———

As an author of quality thrillers, Gavin Lyall travels in the company of John Le Carré and Len Deighton. But from the outset of his writing career, when he was being compared to Dashiell Hammett and Raymond Chandler and even, at one point, to James Bond's creator Ian Fleming, Lyall has been his own man. His uniqueness is in his craft rather than in his subject matter—his sharp characterization, crisp dialogue, and wry humor. As the *New York Times Book Review*'s resident thriller critic Newgate Callendar wrote in 1983: "Mr. Lyall has respect for language and for dialogue, much of which is spiced with upper-class wit or languid irony. There are no clichés. Characters are carefully shaped; plotting is logically worked out; backgrounds are authentic."

Until the publication of *The Secret Servant* in 1980, which introduced the spy-tracking Major Harry Maxim, Lyall had had different heroes and settings in each of his novels. Many of them drew on his own experience in the Far East and all of them showed expert knowledge of the countries in which they were set. *The Most Dangerous Game* has for its hero a commercial pilot working for mining companies in Finland on the Russian border, who becomes involved in international intrigue and is falsely accused of murder. In *Midnight Plus One*, Cane, a former gunrunner for the French Resistance in World War II, now a private detective, is hired to protect a Swiss financier who is a fugitive from his personal enemies and from the French police. Tough, yet sensitive enough to question the morality of the violence his work demands, Cane is a colorful hero who, the *New Yorker* reported, "earns his money in a satisfactorily blood-stained way, but he is not content merely to hold us breathless. He also treats us to helpings of robust humor." *Shooting Script* takes another airline pilot to the Caribbean and into a nest of intrigue involving violence, film-making (the pun of its title), a revolution, and the F.B.I. Martin Levin, in the *New York Times Book Review*, admired its hero: "What holds the novel neatly together is its hard-boiled aviator, a bitter young man whose charisma is sufficient to subdue some of the wilder nonsense." Hester Makeig wrote in the *Spectator*: "Gavin Lyall is a master of his craft, which is the expert setting of an *adventure* rather than a crime story. He has the gift of creating reader-involvement in the vivid events he portrays." In *Venus with Pistol* the hero, an antique gun dealer, plunges into the mazes of art collecting on a quest for a long-lost painting by Giorgione ("pistol," which in Giorgione's time meant coins or money, is another double-edged reference to the deadly danger of the quest). *Judas Country* is set in the Middle East. Its hero is a pilot flying a cargo plane loaded with what he thinks is champagne to Cyprus. He becomes involved in espionage, terrorism, blackmail, and murder—all delivered with maximum speed, tension, and hardboiled humor.

The Secret Servant begins with a meticulously planned suicide: "The trouble with dying was that you had to leave so many things unfinished. It was untidy." Its hero is the recently widowed Major Harry Maxim, "a military gentleman" of the Special Air Service, who is brought to No. 10 Downing Street to track down some defectors, spies, and moles—which of course he does. Fast with a gun yet delicate in conscience, Maxim is a distinctive personality in the current fiction crop of secret agents. One reviewer pointed out that he is "better born" than Len Deighton's Bernard Samson and "far more aggressive" than Le Carré's aging Smiley. Reviewers welcomed him and the book ("neat, literate and deliciously cynical," Peter Andrews characterized it in the *New York Times Book Review*), and they looked forward to a series of his adventures.

Its successor, *The Conduct of Major Maxim*, proved to be no disappointment. Marghanita Laski, in the *Listener*, hailed it as "a real pro job with which the reader can relax in perfect confidence of satisfaction"; and *The Crocus List*, with Maxim on the trail of some would-be assassins who plan to dispose of the President of the United States while he is on a visit to London, sustained the pace.

PRINCIPAL WORKS: The Wrong Side of the Sky, 1961; The Most Dangerous Game, 1963; Midnight Plus One, 1965; Shooting Script, 1966; Venus With Pistol, 1969, Blame the Dead, 1973; Judas Country, 1975; The Secret Servant, 1980; The Conduct of Major Maxim, 1983; The Crocus List, 1985; Uncle Target, 1988.

ABOUT: Contemporary Authors New Revision Series 26, 1989. *Periodicals*—Listener August 14, 1980; January 30, 1983; July 18, 1985; New York Times Book Review January 17, 1965; April 24, 1966; October 26, 1969; June 24, 1973; November 16, 1980; March 13, 1983; February 9, 1986; New Yorker July 17, 1965; November 17, 1980; Spectator May 13, 1966; November 22, 1969; Times Literary Supplement December 1, 1972; July 11, 1975; June 20, 1980; December 31, 1982; June 21, 1985.

MacEWEN, GWENDOLYN (September 1, 1941–November 30, 1987), Canadian poet, fiction writer, and translator, was born in Toronto to Alick James and Elsie Doris (Mitchell) MacEwen. She left school at eighteen, having already published one poem in the *Canadian Forum*, to devote herself to writing. She supported herself by working part-time in a children's library. By the early 1970s MacEwen was publishing her poems in literary journals, writing plays and documentaries for the Canadian Broadcasting Company, and giving readings of her work in Toronto coffee houses. Her readings were more often recitations because, as she told an interviewer in 1986: "I think it's kind of boring to watch a poet hiding behind a book and mumbling something over his glasses." In 1972 she and her second husband the Greek singer Nikos Tsingos, to whom she was married for six years, had their own coffee house, the Trojan Horse, in Toronto. (She had earlier married and been divorced from the Canadian poet Milton Acorn.)

"As a child and as a teenager," MacEwen told another interviewer, "I was always a loner and a dreamer, and I found that in my early and middle teens writing poetry was a way of organizing reality, of making reality make sense to me. . . . Writing poetry was my way of *controlling* reality." In later years MacEwen re-

GWENDOLYN MacEWEN

affirmed that belief. Her poetic vision was based in a solid reality but dominated by a mysticism she had absorbed from her studies in the writings of the Christian Gnostics, the seventeenth-century German mystic and theosophist Jacob Boehme, and the twentieth-century Swiss psychologist Carl Jung. Occasionally in composing a poem, she remarked, "I had a glimpse of a miraculous oneness, a wholeness. . . . [My poetry] is an attempt to convey to the reader this overwhelming sense of the oneness, the rightness, the wholeness of all life and all experience." She wrote, she said, "to create a bridge between the inner world of the *psyche* and the 'outer' world of things."

Like the ancient bards whose chants or hymns were intended to invoke "the mysterious forces which move the world and shape our destinies," MacEwen was a myth-maker: "I want to construct a myth," she wrote. The Canadian poet and novelist Margaret Atwood affirms that she did precisely that: "MacEwen is not a poet interested in turning her life into myth; rather she is concerned with translating her myth into life, and into the poetry which is a part of it." The result, in her early poetry in particular, was often obscurity. "I was at times baffled by my own metaphors and images toppling one upon the other." But as she matured, George Woodcock notes in *The Oxford Companion to Canadian Literature*, her poems acquired "a greater solidity of texture and concreteness of imagery, a sharper visualness, they reveal a preoccupation with time and its multiple meanings, with the ambivalences of existence, with the archetypal

patterns that emerge and re-emerge from ancient times to now, but also with the actual human lives that carry on in their mundane way within such patterns."

In 1962 MacEwen traveled to Israel and the Middle East. She learned enough Arabic to translate *The Call of the Curlew*, a novel by Taha Husayn, the Egyptian writer, but her translation was not published. In the Middle East she found new inspiration, and her poems based on that experience are expressions of an expanding consciousness of the mystical as it shines through the commercialized and trivialized reality of the holy sites. In "One Arab Flute," published in *The Shadow-Maker*, considered one of her finest volumes, she explores her reactions to the Holy Land: " . . . innocent as a postcard / among the dark robes and bazaars," she comes as an outsider with a vision of Christian faith. What she finds as she rides into Jerusalem, however, are "dead jeeps" lining the road. Yet among these "rusted wreaths of war," she reviews her faith: "you realize the City / lives /because it was destroyed."

Some years later MacEwen recalled her visit to Tiberius where she met an Arab who had ridden with T. E. Lawrence. This became the inspiration for her *T. E. Lawrence Poems*. In this volume she wrote in the voice of the soldier-adventurer himself, tracing his life from his boyhood in England through his spectacular career in Arabia to his imminent death in a motorcycle accident. One of the poems begins: "I did not choose Arabia; it chose me." Another reflects on the unity that exists even among different and often conflicting cultures:

Only God lives there in the seductive Nothing
That implodes into pure light. English makes Him
    an ugly monosyllable, but Allah breathes
A fiery music from His tongue, ignites the sands,
    invents a terrible love that is
The very name of pain.
                —"The Desert"

Greece was another profound influence on MacEwen's work. With her husband Nikos Tsingos she went to Greece not as a tourist but with some knowledge of the language and much sensitivity to the culture. She reported on that trip in a prose work *Mermaids and Ikons: A Greek Summer*. "Greece," she wrote, "presents a very real challenge to whoever goes there—a challenge to do more, to be more, to better the present moment in whatever way is possible, to improvise, to expand. To get things *off the ground.*" Although visiting the conventional tourist attractions—Athens, Mycenae, Mystras, Olympia—she saw and reported through the special filter of her imagination: "Sometimes I see Greek history in terms of a huge frieze of centaurs and humans—like the one from the temple of Zeus with its writhing, tangled group of figures fighting their way out of the stone. Great lusty bearded faces, hooves and hair and fullblown female breasts are arranged in a kind of controlled chaos as man struggles with horseman, his powerful, inner self. In a way, Greek passion is an endless battle with the centaur—a convoluted, internal war, a war declared upon time and mortality." One chapter in her book describes the visit she and her husband made to the poet Yannis Ritsos, some of whose poems they had translated. These, and her own version of Euripides' The Trojan Women, were published in 1981.

George Woodcock has pointed out that MacEwen's fiction, like her poetry, blends fantasy with history, personifying "the poetic dimensions of history." Julian the Magician drew on her readings in mysticism to portray a latter-day Christ figure, a young magician whose tricks are analogous to Christ's miracles and who suffers a similar fate. Julian's magic, Margaret Atwood notes, is "human alchemy"—the power of opening people's minds: "And the people believe because Julian lets them believe . . . he draws margins over which he knows their minds can jump; he unscrews hinges on all doors." A more daunting challenge was King of Egypt, King of Dreams, a fictional treatment of the life of the pharaoh Akhenaton who was allegedly the founder of monotheism. To this novel MacEwen appended a group of notes on the historical background and family relationships of the pharaohs, as well as a glossary of ancient names and terms. Akhenaton's tragedy, as she conceived it, was the failure of his imagination to grasp the duality of existence, the breadth of the vision that can embrace both good and evil, darkness and light. Critics, however, found no similar failure of imagination in MacEwen. They had detected qualities of fairytale even in Julian the Magician although the combination of the poetic and the mundane in that novel struck some of them as "undigested." In King of Egypt, King of Dreams the elements were far more successfully assimilated. The fantasy-fairytale spirit predominated. "It is, in fact, precisely when [it] abandons itself to nonsense and non sequitur that the novel becomes highly witty and enjoyable," George Jonas wrote in Saturday Night. Comparing her to Lewis Carroll, Jonas continued: "She is an absolute master of the genre; she does it subtly, and in a voice entirely her own."

MacEwen's first use of a Canadian setting was in a collection of short stories, Noman, where, Jan Bartley writes, she "integrates the magical and esoteric landscapes of Egypt, the Middle East, and Greece, with that of Canada." Her purpose, as in her poems, was "to reveal the mythic in the mundane—in short, to demonstrate that the ordinary is extraordinary." Even Canada is rendered extraordinary because she spells it "Kanada." Noman, as his name suggests, is a wanderer on a quest of self-discovery. In this volume and in its sequel Noman's Land surrealism seems to be superimposed on realism. In "Fire" a couple strip themselves of their worldly possessions in order to keep a fire burning in the huge fireplace of a house they have rented. In "Snow" a young Greek from the warm Mediterranean becomes enchanted by his first sight of snow in Kanada and literally sacrifices himself to it. MacEwen saw Canada as a magic land but also, realistically, as a nation divided spiritually and culturally. In one story in Noman, "Kingsmere," she recalled Canadian Prime Minister Mackenzie King who had faith in the future of a united Canada and, she writes, "tried to transplant Europe, to bring it here among the stark trees and silent trails." But, as she saw it, beyond the uniting arch that he would build lies the forest. The arch is not real: "this reconstruction of a past that was never yours, this synthetic history. . . . Here there is a tension between past and future, a tension so real it's almost tangible; it lives in the stone, it crackles like electricity among leaves."

Although MacEwen has received many honors as a Canadian writer—among them the Governor General's Award in 1970 for The Shadow-Maker, the A.J.M. Smith Poetry Award for The Armies of the Moon in 1973, and several Canada Council grants for writing—some critics regard her as a writer outside the mainstream of Canadian literature. But others argue that her work has a breadth that embraces both Canada and the world at large. D. G. Jones writes in his preface to her Earthlight: "Vertical in vision, oracular and metaphorical in mode, she speaks of a body of identity that is not so much social—political and general—as individual—sexual and mystical. . . . Such a vision is not apolitical. Though it does not discriminate English and French, Canadian and American, it allows her to speak with a collective voice few English-Canadian writers have managed."

Gwendolyn MacEwen died in Toronto at the age of forty-six. In 1986, the year before her death, she had been writer-in-residence at the University of Toronto. In spite of the recognition she had received in Canada, "her writing afforded her only slender means," the London Times reported in her obituary notice, "and the day before her death, she had to borrow from a friend to pay an unexpected bill."

PRINCIPAL WORKS: *Poetry*—The Rising Fire, 1963; A Breakfast for Barbarians, 1966; The Shadow-Maker, 1969; The Armies of the Moon, 1972; Magic Animals: Selected Poems, 1975; The T. E. Lawrence Poems, 1982; Earthlight: Selected Poems, 1982; Afterworlds, 1987. *Novels*—Julian the Magician, 1963; King of Egypt, King of Dreams, 1971. *Collected short stories*—Noman, 1972; Noman's Land, 1985. *Travel*—Mermaids and Ikons: A Greek Summer, 1978. *Children's books*—The Chocolate Moose, 1979; The Honey Drum, 1983; Dragon Sandwiches, 1986.

ABOUT: Atwood, M. Second Words, 1982; Bartley, J. Invocations: The Poetry and Prose of Gwendolyn MacEwen, 1983; Canadian Writers and Their Work 9, 1985; Contemporary Authors New Revision Series 22, 1988; Contemporary Poets, 4th ed. 1985; Dictionary of Literary Biography 53, 1986; Jones, D. G. *Preface to* Earthlight, 1982; Klinck, C. F. (ed.) Literary History of Canada, 2nd ed., 1976; Oxford Companion to Canadian Literature, 1983; Pearce, J. Twelve Voices: Interviews with Canadian Poets, 1980; Who's Who of Canadian Literature, 1983. *Periodicals*—Books in Canada July 1976; Canadian Forum January 1983; Saturday Night January 1972.

MAYNARD MACK

MACK, MAYNARD (October 27, 1909–   ), American scholar, critic, and educator, writes: "I was born in a very small town in southern Michigan. Its population at the time was usually given as 'five thousand Ethan Reynolds.' This meant 'five thousand and one,' the one being Reynolds, a town character alleged to feed entirely on whiskey and bananas. When I ran away from home at age five pulling my little wagon behind me, I shivered at the thought of meeting up with Reynolds. I had never seen him, but he stood in my fancy for everything that children better than the rest of us know is 'out there'—as threatening as it is inviting. Before I found him, alas, my parents found me and prudently sent me early to bed. Can that be why I have never altogether outgrown a naive belief in presences, quests, trials, dark towers, white goddesses, and other impedimenta of the Romantic imagination? If only I had been allowed to find Reynolds, probably slumped in a doorway smelling of overripe bananas, would it have made me a born-again realist? I hope not.

"Anyway, that little episode lingers in my mind as a synopsis of my performances as a writer. Always I have heard the mermaids singing, but always I have managed to persuade myself in time that they did not sing to me. The anxiety of my parents, later internalized as common sense, has always found me (out) before it was too late. So I have worn the bottoms of my trousers rolled and written about Shakespeare when with a little more nerve I could have been trying

to be Taylor the Water Poet, and about Pope when I might have been—who knows?—a triumphant Lewis Theobald. In compensation, I have been allowed to teach at Yale alongside some of the outstanding minds of my generation and have had the privilege of knowing generation after generation of gifted students—no bad fate.

"Many years ago I was asked for a thumbnail sketch of my life up to that time. Now, approaching the close of my seventh decade, I think it may still stand, with one or two very slight corrections:

"Born: Hillsdale, Michigan, 27 October 1909. Education: Yale—B.A. 1932; Ph.D. 1936. Career: Teacher, gadfly, and palace dwarf since 1936. Guru and sage since 1938. Dispenser of good advice since 1939. Terrifying example of what can happen, 1939–1978. Free spirit, 1978–1988.

"Author of large and dull books. Maker and maintainer of beautiful gardens. Husband to a lady (species all but extinct). Father of three, all teachers. Grandfather of eight, all uptaught.

"'Death, be not proud . . . .'"

More than forty years ago in an essay "On Reading Pope," Maynard Mack observed that "[Alexander] Pope is a poet more often written about than read and less often read than misread." Thanks however to his own lifetime of work on Pope, it is possible today to challenge Mack's statement. Pope is certainly read more widely today, and with more appreciation and understanding, than he was before Mack began writing about him. As editor Mack has established and annotated definitive texts of many of Pope's works in the Twickenham Edition (published by Yale University Press); as biographer he has written what is universally recognized as the definitive biography of Pope; and as critic he has corrected earlier misconceptions and firmly established Pope as a major poet for all ages: "Pope is anything but the poet of superficialities; on the contrary, he spent his whole life combating them, and with an exquisite decorum." Finally, as a teacher of literature Mack has trained several generations of scholars and critics (a number of whom acknowledged their indebtedness to him in a festschrift, *The Author in His Work: Essays on a Problem in Criticism*, edited by Louis L. Martz and Aubrey Williams (1978).

Maynard Mack is the son of Jesse Floyd and Pearl (Vore) Mack. In 1933, a year after taking his B.A. at Yale, he married Florence Brocklebank to whom he has dedicated most of his major books. Mack's entire professional career has been at Yale University, where he began to teach in 1936 in the English department, rising through the ranks from instructor to Sterling Professor of English in 1965. He has also held administrative posts as director of the humanities division, 1962 to 1964, and chairman of the English department, 1965 to 1968. From 1974 to 1977 he was director of the National Humanities Institute. He has honorary degrees from Duke University, Oberlin College, the University of Northern Michigan, Kalamazoo College, and Towson State University; among many other academic honors he has had Fulbright and Guggenheim fellowships and guest lectureships at universities in Canada, England, and America.

While Pope and his times has been the subject of most of Mack's study, he has also written extensively on satire, Elizabethan and Jacobean drama, and on Shakespeare. His *King Lear in Our Time* is a brief but carefully considered treatment of the play in terms of its stage history, its sources, and its appeal to us today. He briefly reviews historical and modern-day productions of the play, traces its roots to medieval romance, morality plays and visionary epics ("rather than to psychological or realistic drama, with which it has very little in common"), and, finally, reads the play as "a tragedy for our time . . . about the human condition, the state of man, in which the last of many mysteries is the enigmatic system of relatedness in which he is enclosed." In *Killing the King* Mack studies three of Shakespeare's plays in which regicide becomes a symbolic act for "competing visions of the nature of all action and indeed of all life"—*Richard II*,

Hamlet, and *Macbeth*. Tracing the idea of kingship in these plays to the dual conception of the character of the king as a mortal "natural body" and as a "body politic" that prevailed up to the Renaissance, Mack shows that "killing the king gradually becomes, then, in Shakespeare, a kind of lens in which all manner of political, social, moral, psychological, metaphysical, and religious questions are focused."

When in 1982 a large volume of Mack's essays was published as *Collected in Himself: Essays Critical, Biographical, and Bibliographical on Pope and Some of his Contemporaries*, Pat Rogers wrote in *Modern Language Review*: "Only a very considerable scholar with a sustained dedication to his subject could have produced a volume of such range, and at the same time such intellectual focus." Within the specialized area of Pope studies, Mack has indeed demonstrated remarkable range. Thanks to his training in classical languages he was able to edit and annotate Pope's translations of the *Iliad* and the *Odyssey*—"a work," he writes, "that at various times has seemed likely to remain in progress and at press as long as the siege of Troy combined with the wanderings of Odysseus." Equally expert in the social and political history of Pope's times, Mack has placed Pope within his total cultural as well as literary context. In *The Garden and the City* he wrote what Bertrand R. Bronson described in the *Yale Review* as "a kind of psychobiography of Pope and his sympathizers; an attempt to realize and revivify the intellectual and emotional ambience of the world they occupied." The book, an expansion of the Alexander lectures that Mack delivered at the University of Toronto in 1963, not only records with extensive documentation and illustration the building of Pope's country retreat at Twickenham, but shows, Mack writes in his Preface, "how one eighteenth-century writer, at any rate, managed to fashion from his personal experience and the literary past an enabling myth for himself and his work." In the country house with its elegant gardens and fanciful grotto designed by Pope himself, the poet created a private domain, a retreat from the political and social tensions that existed in his public life, "a true country of the mind." Patricia Meyer Spacks noted, in the *Journal of English and Germanic Philology*, that *The Garden and the City* was an important work of literary criticism: " in its skillful union and skillful distinguishing of 'Realities and Imagery,' it testifies to the enduring validity of literary scholarship."

Mack's more than forty years of study of Pope reached their culmination in his massive and magisterial *Alexander Pope: A Life*, "the first completed attempt . . . since 1900 to give a comprehensive account of the man and his times" (Preface). With close to nine hundred pages of text, one hundred pages of notes, and numerous illustrations, it is likely to remain the definitive biography for generations to come. The book interweaves critical discussion of Pope's poems with the biographical narrative. Mack is admiring but even-handed in his treatment of Pope's character, showing him as "exquisitely sensitive to criticism," mischievous, with an iconoclastic streak that made him many enemies—altogether a mixture of human qualities which in a man as brilliantly articulate as Pope inevitably produced scathing satire. In balance Pope emerges as thoroughly human and vulnerable, and, as Peter Martin wrote in his review in *Eighteenth Century Studies*: "The clarity, intriguing detail, precision, humanity, critical insight and largeness of view with which the author tells his story not only obliterate those old gossipy stories about [Pope], but also show him to be one of England's greatest moral poets."

The only reservation that some reviewers expressed was at what Lawrence Lipking in the *American Scholar* called "an overabundance of wisdom . . . the sheer high-mindedness of Mack's majestic biography." Others complained of a surfeit of anecdotes and allusions. John Wain, in the *New York Times Book Review*, wrote: "The merit is the sheer amount he knows. The fault is his inability to leave anything out." Ian Donaldson, however, in the *Times Literary Supplement*, found the style of the biography "comfortably pitched for the general reader who is prepared for the long haul through a thousand-page life . . . leisurely, genial, digressive, richly circumstantial."

In 1988 Mack was the principal speaker at the Yale festivities honoring the tricentenary of Pope's birth, which was celebrated with exhibits and programs about the poet and his work.

PRINCIPAL WORKS: Essential Articles for the Study of Alexander Pope, 1964, 1968; King Lear in Our Time, 1966; The Garden and the City: Retirement and Politics in the Later Poetry of Pope, 1731–1743, 1969; Essays on Pope, 1971; Alexander Pope: A Life, 1985. *As editor*—Twickenham Edition of Pope's Poetical Works: III (Essays on Man), 1950; VII–VIII (Iliad), IX–X (Odyssey), 1967; XI (Index), 1969; Pope's Essay on Man: Manuscripts of the Morgan and Houghton Libraries, 1962; The Last and Greatest Art: Some Unpublished Poetical Manuscripts of Alexander Pope, 1984.

ABOUT: Contemporary Authors 9–10, 1964. *Periodicals*—American Scholar Summer 1987; Eighteenth Century Studies Spring 1987; Hudson Review Summer 1986; Journal of English and Germanic Philology July 1970; Modern Language Review April 1984; New Statesman August 23, 1985; New York Times Book Review March 2, 1986; Times Literary Supplement November 2, 1984; September 13, 1985; Yale Review Summer 1970, Summer 1973.

MACK SMITH, DENIS (March 3, 1920 –   ), British historian of Italy, was born in London, the son of Wilfrid Mack Smith and Altiora Gauntlett Mack Smith. He was educated at St. Paul's Cathedral Choir School, London, Haileybury College, and Peterhouse, Cambridge University, where he was organ scholar and held also a scholarship in history. After a year (1941–1942) as assistant master at Clifton College, Bristol, he went to work for the government in London and passed his war service in the employ of various cabinet departments. Peterhouse elected him to a fellowship in modern history in 1947, and he remained there until 1962, when he was elected senior research fellow of All Souls College, Oxford, a position he still holds. He married Catherine Stevenson in 1963; they have two children.

The history of the Italian Risorgimento, the movement throughout the peninsula during the nineteenth century to achieve national unification and to forge a national identity, has always been Denis Mack Smith's special interest. His earliest book treated the two most powerful political men of the period: *Cavour and Garibaldi, 1860: A Study in Political Conflict*. This study analyzes the course of revolutionary politics in the year of civil war, during which Italy was transformed from a congeries of independent and squabbling statelets into a nation just short of territorial completeness. It was the hard and patient work of the dashing and romantic Giuseppe Garibaldi and the intellectual and statesmanlike Camillo Benso, conte di Cavour, which during a few dramatic months of 1860 brought the whole of the Kingdom in the Two Sicilies and much of central Italy under the banner of the House of Savoy. "The intention," writes Mack Smith in the book's preface, "has been to analyze a striking conflict of personalities and principles. . . . At the root of conflict was the problem of what political system would best suit a liberated Italy, and how to set about achieving it. This problem, in all its various aspects, raised what now seem to have been perhaps the most interesting and important questions in the whole of nineteenth-century Italian history. It was during these decisive months of 1860 in Sicily that the conflict over ends and means entered its sharpest phase, and became most dramatic and most complete."

The book, which was originally the Thirlwall

DENIS MACK SMITH

Prize essay at Cambrige in 1948, was termed an "excellent study" by G. A. Carbone in *American Historical Review*. D. P. Waley in the *Spectator* called it "a fascinating and very important book." "Mr. Mack Smith," he wrote, "tells the complicated story with verve and keeps it moving at a lively pace."

With another Cambridge historian of Italy, Moses I. Finley, Denis Mack Smith undertook to write a history of Sicily in three volumes, all of which appeared in 1968. *Ancient Sicily: To the Arab Conquest*, Finley's contribution to the endeavor, establishes the background for the events detailed in Mack Smith's two volumes *Medieval Sicily: 800 –1713* and *Modern Sicily: After 1713*. "To the register of misfortunes examined by Mr. Finley," wrote Gabriel Gersh in the *Saturday Review*, "Mack Smith adds the follies and crimes of twelve centuries, beginning with the Saracen invasion and concluding with the present-day Mafia activities. . . . The portrait of Sicily that emerges . . . is of a society fossilized in a state of feudalism."

Also in 1968 Mack Smith published *The Making of Italy 1796–1870*, a volume in the extensive series Documentary History of Western Civilization. In this book he selected, translated, and arranged in chronological order with brief introductions several dozen of the most important documents concerning the origin of modern Italy—diplomatic dispatches, letters, speeches and writings of such major participants as Giuseppe Mazzini, King Victor Emanuel I, and Massimo d'Azeglio, as well as Garibaldi and Cavour. In his introduction to the collection of doc-uments—which he calls "an outline history of the making of Italy"—Mack Smith recalls that the idea of Italy "had been in some people's minds for a long time before the nineteenth century. No doubt it was only a vague idea, and one without practical significance except to a select few; but national consciousness was not created out of nothing after 1800. . . . [Yet] the main obstruction in the way of the patriotic movement was not foreign governments; an even greater obstacle was the slowness of the great bulk of Italians to accept or even to comprehend the idea of Italy. . . . Even among intellectuals, the very concept of 'Italy' often continued to be distant and indefinite." The reviewer for *Choice* thought *The Making of Italy* "an excellent collection, unique in its field. . . . Many of the works excerpted are no longer available, especially in English."

Mack Smith next completed another documentary collection treating the same period, *Garibaldi*, a somewhat more focused book than its predecessor, and more impassioned as well, in that it considers—in Garibaldi's own words—the career of a fascinating national romantic hero, the most exciting and one of the most inspiring revolutionaries of his century. Garibaldi recounts his guerrilla apprenticeship in South America and his military campaigns on the Italian peninsula; he reveals his goals for a united Italy and for inter-European cooperation. Along with the words of "the great condottiere" himself, the author presents a series of contemporary opinions of Garibaldi, including those of Mazzini, Alexandre Dumas père, W. E. Gladstone, Alfred Tennyson, and Henry Adams, as well as those of the common citizens and soldiers who knew or served with him. *Garibaldi* was considered by William Courtney in *Library Journal* to be "an impartial account of a controversial and very human hero in Italian annals."

In *Victor Emanuel, Cavour, and the Risorgimento*, Mack Smith selects a number of controversial episodes and historical problems involving the king and his most successful prime minister and considers them in light of the documentation now available. The author expresses surprise in his preface at the extent to which his two principal figures are even today figures of legend rather than of historically verifiable fact; this is true even in Italy: "no critical study has been written of the monarch under whose rule this new nation was born and took shape. Instead his character has been concealed behind a smoke-screen of boring and gossipy panegyric. . . . Despite universal acceptance as the *padre della patria* and the *re galantuomo*, Victor Emanuel is entirely unknown to most Italians today except as a subject of anecdote and legend.

989. *Periodicals*—America No-
ican Historical Review October
February 1986; Annals of the
ovember 1954, July 1972; Best
hoice November 1968, October
ember 1976, December 1985;
ember 29, 1976; Christian Sci-
976; June 21, 1985; Economist
mber 20, 1976; February 27,
ory June 1986; Library Journal
1972; May 15, 1976; May 15,
lanchester Guardian May 14,
er 11, 1982; National Review
mber 12, 1982; New Republic
e 23, 1982; July 29, 1985; New
4; September 24, 1976; March
iew of Books October 5, 1972;
r 7, 1982; June 13, 1985; New
v June 20, 1976; May 16, 1982;
Yorker July 12, 1976; August
85; Newsweek June 14, 1982;
4; Social Studies April 1969;
nes (London) April 11, 1985;
ient August 6, 1954; April 9,
e 16, 1972; April 9, 1982; May
1989; Washington Post Book

MAN (FITZROY) (De-
ust 2, 1990), American ed-
uthor, the son of John
velyn Davidson Maclean,
Iowa, but when he was six
ly to western Montana,
and around Missoula. His
-born Presbyterian minis-
me. Mornings the elder
ading aloud from the Bi-
sworth, coupling tutorial
signments. Afternoons his
to roam the unspoiled
amily had settled, study-
auna. When the boy was
t officer haled him off to

clean worked part-time
ce. By then a dual influ-
rooted in his character:
consequence, he said, he
or a long time, maybe
education in a more for-
t to Dartmouth College,
in 1924. After teaching
ears, he returned to his
f Montana and Idaho,
a ranger from 1926 to

de on an academic ca-
thirty. Up to that time,
into the Forest Service

e man, with only enough of the
nd general background to make
elligible. Mussolini was neither
greatness thrust upon him but had
y out of obscurity by his own am-
ents. So well did he succeed that
ted more popular admiration than
ad received in the whole course of
y. . . . Italian fascism was more
ssolini. But the quirks of character
an were a crucial factor in both its
l failures. . . ."

omist reviewer called *Mussolini* a
raphy, erudite, subtle and constant-
." David Gilmour in the *New*
greed: "an exemplary political biog-
hat seems to make it unnecessary for
ackle the subject again."

hor received equally high critical
his next political biography, *Cavour*,
consideration of the greatest states-
he Risorgimento. "In March 1861,"
th writes in the preface, "a few weeks
avour's] death [at the age of fifty], the
of a new united kindgom was officially
ed after many centuries in which the
ninsula had been divided into separate
rd Palmerston [then British prime min-
ke for many contemporaries when he
a miraculous ending to one of the most
inary and romantic stories in the whole
ry." Mack Smith shows how Cavour de-
Italy's parliamentary system, following
cult and sometimes labyrinthine path, en-
alternately the support of both extremes
each other, and finally carrying into ef-
at pre-eminently difficult and almost par-
al operation, a conservative revolution."

e biography," wrote Merle Rubin in the
ian Science Monitor, "is particularly
in its illumination of the various factions
egions, not merely in Italy as a whole, but
within the Kingdom of Piedmont-
nia. . . . [Mack] Smith's scholarship is im-
able, his methods judicious." Raleigh Tre-
an in the *New York Times Book Review*
d the biography "an extraordinary saga of
eption, ruthlessness, blunders and turns of
une in the life of [Cavour]. . . . Mr. Mack
th has developed a smooth and urbane style
ich is extremely readable and effective."

Writing in the *Times Literary Supplement* in
89, David Gilmour pointed out that Italian re-
onse to Denis Mack Smith's studies of their
untry's history is divided between admiration
r his "mastery of sources and his discovery of
ew material" and resentment of his essentially
egative assessment. From at least 1959, when

he published the first edition of his *Italy: A Modern History*, he has taken a revisionist view of the Risorgimento, presenting it, Gilmour writes, "not as a heroic national struggle but as 'a civil war between the old and the new ruling classes' and as 'a movement not of the populace but of an elite.'" Thirty years later, in *Italy and Its Monarchy*, Mack Smith presented a similarly realistic and iconoclastic assessment of Victor Emmanuel II and his successors. The book offered his readers in Italy and abroad an opportunity to assess Mack Smith's overall contribution to the study of Italian history. Gilmour writes: "Even Mack Smith's detractors would admit that he has had a greater impact on Italian historiography than any contemporary historian. By destroying the musty complacencies of Risorgimento mythology, he forced Italian students to re-examine their own history . . . Denis Mack Smith's principal achievement is thus innovatory. His readability, range and judgment would by themselves place him in the top league of modern historians."

In addition to his works in English on modern Italian history, Denis Mack Smith, whose command of the Italian language is that of a cultivated native speaker, has also written and edited books in Italian: *Da Cavour a Mussolini* (1969), *Vittorio Emanuele II* (1972), *Un monumento al Duce* (1976), *Cento Anni di Vita Italiana attraverso il "Corriere della Sera"* (1978), and *L'Italia del Ventesimo Secolo* (1978). As editor he has introduced and published E. Quinet's *Le Rivoluzioni d'Italia* (1970), G. La Farina's *Scritti Politici* (1972), G. Bandi's *I Mille: Da Genova a Capua* (1981), and Francesco De Sanctis' *Un Viaggio Elettorale* (1983). Since 1962 he has been joint editor of the Nelson History of England. His works have won several literary awards, including the Duff Gordon Memorial Medal and the Wolfson Literary Award, both in 1977. From Italy have come the Serena (1960), Elba (1972), Villa di Chiesa (1973), Mondello (1975), Nove Muse (1976), and Rhegium Julii (1983) awards. He is a commendatore of the Ordine al Merito della Repubblica Italiana; in 1982 he was oratore ufficiale (official orator) della Repubblica di San Marino.

PRINCIPAL WORKS: Cavour and Garibaldi 1860, 1954; Garibaldi, 1957; Italy: A Modern History, 1959, rev. and enl. ed., 1969; Medieval Sicily, 1968; Modern Sicily, 1968; Victor Emanuel, Cavour and the Risorgimento, 1971; Mussolini's Roman Empire, 1976; Mussolini, 1981; Cavour, 1985; Italy and Its Monarchy, 1989. *As editor*—The Making of Italy 1796–1870, 1968; Garibaldi, 1969.

ABOUT: Contemporary Authors New Revision Series 17,

1986; Who's Who, 1[
vember 4, 1976; Amer[
1954, December 1972[
American Academy N[
Sellers October 1976; [
1969, April 1972, No[
Christian Century Sep[
ence Monitor July 8, 1[
January 1, 1972; Nov[
1982; June 8, 1985; His[
June 1, 1969; May 1,[
1982; May 1, 1985; N[
1954; Nation Septemb[
October 29, 1976; Nov[
September 11, 1976; Ju[
Statesman April 24, 19[
5, 1982; New York Rev[
August 5, 1976; Octobe[
York Times Book Revie[
September 1, 1985; Ne[
30, 1982; August 19, 19[
Spectator June 11, 195[
Time June 7, 1982; Tir[
Times Literary Supple[
1982; May 10, 1985; Jun[
10, 1985; October 13,[
World July 4, 1982.

*MACLEAN, NOR[
cember 23, 1902–Aug[
ucator, critic, and a[
Norman and Clara E[
was born in Clarinda, [
moved with his fam[
where he grew up in [
father, a strict Scottish[
ter, taught him at h[
Maclean devoted to re[
ble, Milton, and Word[
sessions with writing as[
young pupil was free[
woods near where the f[
ing the local flora and f[
ten, however, the truan[
the local school.

In his early teens Ma[
for the U.S. Forest Serv[
ence had become deepl[
books and nature. As a [
"was a divided soul f[
always." Continuing his[
mal pattern, he went ea[
where he took his B.A. [
English there for two y[
first love, the woods o[
working as a logger and[
1928.

Maclean did not deci[
reer until he was almost[
he had thought of going[

° mac lān´

His political significance has therefore been easy to ignore. . . . Cavour, too, has been preserved in part as a figure of legend, as someone who has had to be protected from the untempered winds of posthumous criticism. . . . The underlying theme [of the book] is the personal contribution which two very different individuals . . . made to the way that Italy became a nation."

Luigi Barzini thought Mack Smith's book "so rich in the new material he has gathered (or the material many of his Italian predecessors did not dare use) that he can often afford to leave out anecdotes and lines too well known to be recounted one more time. His books can be read with as much pleasure as good novels, at least by Italians who know the background. . . . Nevertheless Mack Smith is not Italian and his view of Italy is inevitably that of a twentieth-century, middle-class, northern Protestant scholar. Many of his censures seem inspired by an unconfessed desire to see Italy transform herself by magic into a law-abiding, tidy, fair-playing, decorous country."

Mack Smith next turned his attention to Benito Mussolini, the dictator whose rule (1922–1945) over Italy marked the world's earliest conscious experience with state facism. "The theme of this book," the author writes in the introduction to Mussolini's Roman Empire, the first of his two studies of the Duce, "is how Mussolini deliberately and even carefully steered his fascist movement into imperialism and into a succession of wars which eventually left Italy prostrate. . . . [The book's] prior assumption is that the nature of Mussolini's political career is better revealed by what fascism became than by how it began: ex fructibus eorum cognoscetis eos [by their fruits you will know them]. It is a study of political and military defeat and the reasons for that defeat."

C. S. Maier, writing in the New Republic, thought that Mack Smith's "reading of this period is ruthless but accurate and valuable, for he places the blame for Italy's war squarely on the reckless braggadocio and ugly annexationism of a regime that vaunted its military prowess as its final justification." James Joll, in the New York Times Book Review, called Mussolini's Roman Empire "a reminder of the inheritance of corruption, hypocrisy and deception with which the Italian state is saddled, some of which survived Mussolini's fall."

Mack Smith's Mussolini is the full-length study he had been working on for years. In contrast to Mussolini's Roman Empire, which the author had described as telling "the story of fascism in Italy," the later book is more strictly "a political biography . . . . The focus is on the public life of one man, with only enough of the wider context and general background to make his career intelligible. Mussolini was neither great nor had greatness thrust upon him but had to fight his way out of obscurity by his own ambition and talents. So well did he succeed that he . . . attracted more popular admiration than anyone else had received in the whole course of Italian history. . . . Italian fascism was more than just Mussolini. But the quirks of character in this one man were a crucial factor in both its successes and failures. . . . "

The Economist reviewer called Mussolini a "superb biography, erudite, subtle and constantly exciting." David Gilmour in the New Statesman agreed: "an exemplary political biography, one that seems to make it unnecessary for anyone to tackle the subject again."

The author received equally high critical praise for his next political biography, Cavour, his mature consideration of the greatest statesman of the Risorgimento. "In March 1861," Mack Smith writes in the preface, "a few weeks before [Cavour's] death [at the age of fifty], the existence of a new united kindgom was officially proclaimed after many centuries in which the Italian peninsula had been divided into separate states. Lord Palmerston [then British prime minister] spoke for many contemporaries when he called it a miraculous ending to one of the most extraordinary and romantic stories in the whole of history." Mack Smith shows how Cavour developed Italy's parliamentary system, following "a difficult and sometimes labyrinthine path, enlisting alternately the support of both extremes against each other, and finally carrying into effect that pre-eminently difficult and almost paradoxical operation, a conservative revolution."

"The biography," wrote Merle Rubin in the Christian Science Monitor, "is particularly strong in its illumination of the various factions and regions, not merely in Italy as a whole, but also within the Kingdom of Piedmont-Sardinia. . . . [Mack] Smith's scholarship is impeccable, his methods judicious." Raleigh Trevelyan in the New York Times Book Review called the biography "an extraordinary saga of deception, ruthlessness, blunders and turns of fortune in the life of [Cavour]. . . . Mr. Mack Smith has developed a smooth and urbane style which is extremely readable and effective."

Writing in the Times Literary Supplement in 1989, David Gilmour pointed out that Italian response to Denis Mack Smith's studies of their country's history is divided between admiration for his "mastery of sources and his dimensivity of immaterial" and resentment of his essentially negative assessment. From at least 1959, when he published the first edition of his *Italy: A Modern History*, he has taken a revisionist view of the Risorgimento, presenting it, Gilmour writes, "not as a heroic national struggle but as 'a civil war between the old and the new ruling classes' and as 'a movement not of the populace but of an elite.'" Thirty years later, in *Italy and Its Monarchy*, Mack Smith presented a similarly realistic and iconoclastic assessment of Victor Emmanuel II and his successors. The book offered his readers in Italy and abroad an opportunity to assess Mack Smith's overall contribution to the study of Italian history. Gilmour writes: "Even Mack Smith's detractors would admit that he has had a greater impact on Italian historiography than any contemporary historian. By destroying the musty complacencies of Risorgimento mythology, he forced Italian students to re-examine their own history . . . Denis Mack Smith's principal achievement is thus innovatory. His readability, range and judgment would by themselves place him in the top league of modern historians."

In addition to his works in English on modern Italian history, Denis Mack Smith, whose command of the Italian language is that of a cultivated native speaker, has also written and edited books in Italian: *Da Cavour a Mussolini* (1969), *Vittorio Emanuele II* (1972), *Un monumento al Duce* (1976), *Cento Anni di Vita Italiana attraverso il "Corriere della Sera"* (1978), and *L'Italia del Ventesimo Secolo* (1978). As editor he has introduced and published E. Quinet's *Le Rivoluzioni d'Italia* (1970), G. La Farina's *Scritti Politici* (1972), G. Bandi's *I Mille: Da Genova a Capua* (1981), and Francesco De Sanctis' *Un Viaggio Elettorale* (1983). Since 1962 he has been joint editor of the Nelson History of England. His works have won several literary awards, including the Duff Gordon Memorial Medal and the Wolfson Literary Award, both in 1977. From Italy have come the Serena (1960), Elba (1972), Villa di Chiesa (1973), Mondello (1975), Nove Muse (1976), and Rhegium Julii (1983) awards. He is a commendatore of the Ordine al Merito della Repubblica Italiana; in 1982 he was oratore ufficiale (official orator) della Repubblica di San Marino.

PRINCIPAL WORKS: Cavour and Garibaldi 1860, 1954; Garibaldi, 1957; Italy: A Modern History, 1959, rev. and enl. ed., 1969; Medieval Sicily, 1968; Modern Sicily, 1968; Victor Emanuel, Cavour and the Risorgimento, 1971; Mussolini's Roman Empire, 1976; Mussolini, 1981; Cavour, 1985; Italy and Its Monarchy, 1989. *As editor*—The Making of Italy 1796–1870, 1968; Garibaldi, 1969.

ABOUT: Contemporary Authors New Revision Series 17, 1986; Who's Who, 1989. *Periodicals*—America November 4, 1976; American Historical Review October 1954, December 1972, February 1986; Annals of the American Academy November 1954, July 1972; Best Sellers October 1976; Choice November 1968, October 1969, April 1972, November 1976, December 1985; Christian Century September 29, 1976; Christian Science Monitor July 8, 1976; June 21, 1985; Economist January 1, 1972; November 20, 1976; February 27, 1982; June 8, 1985; History June 1986; Library Journal June 1, 1969; May 1, 1972; May 15, 1976; May 15, 1982; May 1, 1985; Manchester Guardian May 14, 1954; Nation September 11, 1982; National Review October 29, 1976; November 12, 1982; New Republic September 11, 1976; June 23, 1982; July 29, 1985; New Statesman April 24, 1954; September 24, 1976; March 5, 1982; New York Review of Books October 5, 1972; August 5, 1976; October 7, 1982; June 13, 1985; New York Times Book Review June 20, 1976; May 16, 1982; September 1, 1985; New Yorker July 12, 1976; August 30, 1982; August 19, 1985; Newsweek June 14, 1982; Spectator June 11, 1954; Social Studies April 1969; Time June 7, 1982; Times (London) April 11, 1985; Times Literary Supplement August 6, 1954; April 9, 1982; May 10, 1985; June 16, 1972; April 9, 1982; May 10, 1985; October 13, 1989; Washington Post Book World July 4, 1982.

*MACLEAN, NORMAN (FITZROY) (December 23, 1902–August 2, 1990), American educator, critic, and author, the son of John Norman and Clara Evelyn Davidson Maclean, was born in Clarinda, Iowa, but when he was six moved with his family to western Montana, where he grew up in and around Missoula. His father, a strict Scottish-born Presbyterian minister, taught him at home. Mornings the elder Maclean devoted to reading aloud from the Bible, Milton, and Wordsworth, coupling tutorial sessions with writing assignments. Afternoons his young pupil was free to roam the unspoiled woods near where the family had settled, studying the local flora and fauna. When the boy was ten, however, the truant officer haled him off to the local school.

In his early teens Maclean worked part-time for the U.S. Forest Service. By then a dual influence had become deeply rooted in his character: books and nature. As a consequence, he said, he "was a divided soul for a long time, maybe always." Continuing his education in a more formal pattern, he went east to Dartmouth College, where he took his B.A. in 1924. After teaching English there for two years, he returned to his first love, the woods of Montana and Idaho, working as a logger and a ranger from 1926 to 1928.

Maclean did not decide on an academic career until he was almost thirty. Up to that time, he had thought of going into the Forest Service

°mac lān´

NORMAN MACLEAN

as a profession. What he wanted, however, was to make "companion pieces" of his twin passions for the western wilderness and for literature and writing. He decided that university teaching would leave him free to spend his summers in Montana, where in 1922 he and his father had built a log cabin on a tree-canopied site on the west shore of Seeley Lake, near the Big Blackfoot River. For most of his life, therefore, he was on the faculty of the English Department at the University of Chicago, beginning as an instructor in 1930. He took a Ph.D. there in 1940, and advanced through the ranks until he was named William Rainey Harper Professor of English in 1963, a title he held until his retirement in 1973. But he returned to Montana every summer: "my homeland," he called it; "I love it, I've always loved it and I always will." His devotion was returned when he was given honorary doctorates in letters from both Montana State University (1980) and the University of Montana (1981). Maclean was a dedicated teacher who loved the great university to which he belonged. Tutored by his wife, Jessie Burns, whom he married in 1931, he also developed a deep affection for the architectural and industrial beauty of Chicago, a place where a huge crane, "a giant in the sky," picks up things "as gracefully as a woman picks up a child."

Maclean's oeuvre consists basically of six widely disparate works: a military manual, two essays in literary criticism, two autobiographical essays, and the book on which his fame rests: *A River Runs Through It and Other Stories*. These six pieces develop along a spectrum whose

ous colors finally merge. All of them are an attempt to bring together the love of literature instilled in him by his Presbyterian father and the majestic natural setting in which this occurred. They become increasingly subjective as they move back in time; the influence of his father and his early background in Montana become more and more apparent.

The initial very objective piece is built on his experiences in the western forests as a logger, a surveyor, and a ranger. During World War II, concomitantly with his other duties at the University of Chicago, he wrote, with Everett C. Olson, *Manual of Instruction in Military Maps and Aerial Photographs* and became acting director of the Institute for Military Studies from 1943 to 1945. His next two works, however, were more literary: long essays that appeared in 1952 in an important volume edited by his mentor, colleague, and friend, Ronald S. Crane: *Critics and Criticism, Ancient and Modern*. The first of these, "From Action to Image: Theories of the Lyric in the Eighteenth Century," is a Longinian account of sublime thought, lofty passion, and the language by which they are expressed; and of the belief beginning to appear at the close of the eighteenth century that the poetic imagination can be expressed metaphorically in one form of composition as well as in another. The work is historical scholarship, but it furnishes a theoretical substructure to the poetic and rhythmic qualities that mark Maclean's famous novella, "A River Runs Through It." The second essay, however, is much more subjective: "Episode, Scene, Speech, and Word: The Madness of Lear." It is literary theory almost completely free of footnotes; Maclean is presenting, not the conclusions of other writers, but his own, using one of the greatest tragedies in all literature, *King Lear*, to illustrate the actions and characters that make tragedy operative and the language by which they are represented. Although the author is implicit rather than explicit, he is omnipresent as he analyzes how tragic literature is exemplified in Shakespeare's play.

There was then a long hiatus in Maclean's writing during which he devoted himself to teaching, garnering three prestigious awards endowed by Ernest Quantrell for excellence in undergraduate teaching, in 1932, in 1941, and in 1973, Chicago being the first university to establish such prizes on an annual basis. Although his approach was rigorous, his courses were extremely popular, with students sitting on the floor in jammed classrooms. After a few days he managed to bully those who were unregistered into leaving, and the rest settled down to a normal routine. They found that Maclean devoted extraordinary time and effort in grading their papers, his lengthy marginal comments indicating their strengths as well as their weaknesses. He made no attempt to be impartial about the literary works he was discussing. A passage that he found particularly impressive would cause him to lift his eyes heavenward and declaim "Wonderful lines, my friends! Wonderful lines!" Conversely, one that he considered banal would elicit a scornful gestures, his head turned sideways, his eyes closed, and his fingers pinching his nostrils together in wordless distaste. Perhaps the most dramatic event that occurred in any of his classes happened the day his students gathered for their final examination in literary criticism. He came in, announced quietly: "I have been telling you people all quarter that you must look for the key terms these critics use and analyze their writing for their underlying assumptions." He then turned and wrote the examination questions on the blackboard. As the class sat in silence reading them, one student slipped to the floor in a perfectly timed swoon.

If the passion for literature that animated Maclean's teaching made him demanding, he was also witty. A former student, M. E. Grenander, in an article about his teaching style in the *AAUP Bulletin*, described one of his broadcast lectures in which he constructed an Aristophanic comedy about the private lives of Chicago Mayor Ed Kelly and publisher William Randolph Hearst. A "scandalized announcer," it was reported, "cut his biting remarks off the air with the apology that 'the professor must be drunk.'" Maclean later wrote the author of the article a letter from his retreat in Montana giving the epilogue to this incident, which he said he had never forgotten. "When I came home that night," he said, "there was a fifth of Jack Daniel's Tennessee Sour Mash Whiskey sent special delivery by the piano player who had been substituted to finish the program. There was an accompanying note with his 'compliments and apologies.' So there is some truth in the report that 'the professor was drunk,' but it was not until late that evening."

Another feature of Maclean's attitude toward teaching—currently out of fashion—was his preference for subsidizing bright students on the basis of merit, regardless of need. In a letter to a prospective donor to the Norman Maclean Scholarship Fund, he wrote in high dudgeon, after a talented young poet he had sponsored was refused a scholarship to the University of Chicago because of her family's lower-middle-class income: "About students who have been given gifts, I feel they should be given more. I feel about them the way Notre Dame feels about fullbacks. We have to have students with gifts to perform our mission, and I am delighted if they will come for money."

After he retired, in June of 1973, Maclean decided to embark on a career of writing that used those "spots of time" in his own long life that had seemed memorable. His masters were Wordsworth, Browning, Gerard Manley Hopkins, Mark Twain, Robert Frost, Hemingway, and a little-known writer of western tales named Charlie Russell. His wife had died, and his two children, Jean Burns and John Norman, were grown. It was a fateful decision to make at the age of seventy. Looking back on it, years later, he remarked that it had involved enormous costs, not only the seven-day-a-week discipline involved—his substitute for "youth and genius and pure gift"—but also the sacrifice of friends, conviviality, and leisure-time activities.

All Maclean's post-retirement writing consisted of more-or-less fictionalized memoirs. Two of these, both involving his academic years, appeared in the *University of Chicago Magazine*. The first, "'This Quarter I Am Taking McKeon': A Few Remarks on the Art of Teaching," is a retrospective glance at his award-winning commitment to teaching undergraduates. Here he writes that the distinguishing characteristic of all great teachers, no matter what their styles may be, is that they are tough, that they care deeply "about something that is hard to understand," and that they can convey their pleasure in it "far better than most." Yet even in this essay, anchored in Dartmouth and the University of Chicago, Maclean concluded by harking back to his Presbyterian father. He closes with words that he thinks his father might have used: teaching is "the art of conveying the delight that comes from an act of the spirit, without ever giving anyone the notion that the delight comes easy."

Maclean's next memoir went back to 1928, his first year at the University of Chicago, when he became acquainted with one of the great scientists of the late nineteenth and early twentieth centuries, Albert Michelson, a former Navy officer whose measurements of the speed of light yielded the experimental data that enabled Einstein to create his theory of relativity. The first American to be awarded the Nobel Prize (1907), Michelson made the front pages of the nation's newspapers again in 1920, for his calculations of the diameter of the enormous distant star Betelgeuse. In 1928 Maclean was briefly associated with this "outstanding, strange and gifted man." It was an unlikely pairing: one of the two most famous physicists in the world and the brash "kid from Montana, a half-assed graduate student and teacher in English," whose knowledge of science and mathematics was limited to his observations of insects in the Montana woods and the trigonometry he had picked up as a surveyor. Michelson was a Renaissance man: not only a scientific genius, but also a talented billiards player, artist, and violinist. It is noteworthy that all these skills involve extraordinary gifts in the use of one's hands—Michelson was an experimental physicist, not a theorist—and Maclean has always admired those who use their hands skillfully. The "wonder" of Michelson, he said, was "what his head did with his hands." Years later, he told an interviewer: "I like to tell you about things that men and women can do with their hands that are wonderful."

Maclean's "'Billiards Is a Good Game': Gamesmanship and America's First Nobel Prize Scientist," was published in 1975. He remarked recently, "I think my story about him is one of the best things I ever wrote." In this lovingly detailed memoir of Michelson, Maclean moves back in his own life for the materials with which to construct his story. At its conclusion, as at the conclusion of his first one, he adverts to his youth, noting that his knowledge about Michelson stemmed in part from the fact that he was "brought up in pool halls and logging camps." And Michelson's stylish gift for words haunted him for years. Finally, Maclean introduces what were to become hallmarks of his autobiographical fictions: striking introductions and endings. The conclusion explains why the raw young graduate student was drawn to the world-famous scientist: "He was an artist and played many games well, especially those involving something like a cue, a brush, a bow, or, best of all, a box with slits and silvered mirrors. In that game he was playing with light and a star."

A River Runs Through It and Other Stories was published in 1976; the title piece was to become a classic. The first to be written, however, is a short story which comes second in the book: "Logging and Pimping and 'Your Pal, Jim.'" The protagonist is a young graduate student working summers in a logging camp with a burly partner who spends his winters reading library books and pimping. Although the narrator's Presbyterian father is mentioned, the story is primarily an amusing character study of "pal Jim," awesome in his powers of working, drinking, wenching, and presumably fighting, although his fellow sawyers are too overawed by his presence ever to put him to the test. A critical friend of Maclean's told him that he was "concentrating so on telling a story" that he didn't express his poetic love of the earth. But a striking feature of the novella "USFS 1919: The Ranger, the Cook, and a Hole in the Sky," the last story in the volume, is its poetic quality. The protagonist, a seventeen-year-old boy working for the summer with a Forest Service crew, sees the mountains of Idaho as "poems of geology." He greatly admires the ranger in charge of the crew, although

he instinctively hates the cook, a cardsharp during the winters. He is aware of beauty all around him, for "to all those who work come moments of beauty unseen by the rest of the world." He has a series of adventures that are a part of the "story" that has lodged in the mind of the elderly narrator: a dangerous fire, a narrow escape from a rattlesnake's strike, and a barroom brawl in an Idaho gambling den in which the boy is badly beaten up. In this story, too, his Presbyterian father comes to his mind with advice and counsel at key junctures of the tale.

The title story is the first novella in the collection, a poignant evocation of families whose members love even when they cannot understand or help each other, with the narrator and his wife both bound to siblings whose scapegrace exploits lead to pain and, in the case of Maclean's own brother, to death. A hard-drinking, street-fighting reporter in Helena, Montana, he was in his early thirties when he was found beaten to death in an alley. The only explanation for his murder is the warning a friendly police sergeant had given the narrator: Paul was "behind in the big stud poker game at Hot Springs. It's not healthy to be behind in the big game at Hot Springs. . . . At Hot Springs they don't play any child games like fist fighting." The only consolation the murdered man's brother and their preacher father can find in his death is that he must have died fighting; every bone in his right hand is broken.

It is not Paul's fighting, his drinking, or his gambling, however, by which the narrator remembers him; it is his superlative skill as a fly fisherman in the rushing glacial rivers of western Montana. The boys were taught by their father, who was only a good fisherman; Paul becomes a great one. Fly casting is a passion he feels so strongly and practices so constantly that his right arm, wrist, and hand have all become outsized, and the destruction of his magnificent casting hand contributes to the wrenching effect his death has on the reader. An inextricable part of the story is the Big Blackfoot River itself, whose beauty and power become symbols for the human passions that are acted out in and around it. One hot afternoon the narrator sits on its bank waiting for his brother and contemplating the river: "Even the anatomy of a river was laid bare. Not far downstream was a dry channel where the river had run once, and part of the way to come to know a thing is through its death. But years ago I had known the river when it flowed through this now dry channel, so I could enliven its stony remains with the waters of memory." This leads him to a meditation on reading "the waters of tragedy."

In "A River Runs Through It" Maclean's art has been so exquisitely tuned that the beginning and ending are already among those memorable statements that linger in the reader's mind, from the first sentence: "In our family, there was no clear line between religion and fly fishing" to its conclusion: "I am haunted by waters."

After the manuscript of the book was completed, its publication became a story in its own right. Turned down repeatedly by commercial eastern publishers, the manuscript was finally taken over by the University of Chicago Press in a unique venture: the first work of fiction it had ever published (in 1976). The gamble paid off. The book narrowly missed being awarded the Pulitzer Prize; recommended by the judges, it was passed over by the awards committee. But it was soon to become a classic. The reviewers— over 600 of them—were as enthusiastic as the publishers had been lukewarm. And the public was as avid as the reviewers, with over 130,000 copies sold by 1986. Chicago Press, having once committed itself to the book, published edition after edition. The title story appeared as a separate book in 1983, with photographs of the river by the author's son-in-law, Joel Snyder, a member of the University's art faculty, and a new essay by Maclean, "On the Edge of Swirls," describing the river, as nearly as it is possible for a human to do, from the viewpoint of the trout who live in it. (His brother Paul had hoped all his short life to learn to think like a trout.) And still another edition, illustrated with wood engravings by Barry Moser, was published in 1989.

Maclean himself had a moment of rare triumph in the publishing history of his book. Knopf, one of the publishers who had initially turned it down, wrote asking him for a chance to publish any other work he might be planning. His response concluded with a pungent paragraph, often quoted: "If it should ever happen that the world comes to a place when Alfred A. Knopf is the only publishing company left and I am the only author, then that will be the end of the world of books."

John Cawelti, in the *New Republic*, cited the "magical balance" of Maclean's stories: "Underneath the richness of particular details, there runs a wise and compassionate understanding of life and art forged through a lifetime of experience and learning and embodied in a prose that is richly colloquial yet highly controlled and which sometimes rises to extraordinary eloquence." James N. Baker, in *Newsweek*, called the stories "paeans to the harmonious unity of man and nature," eloquent and stylish. Eliot Fremont-Smith, in the *Village Voice*, classified the book as a "Literary Collectible,"

referring to its "magical probings of natural and human mysteries." In *New York Review of Books* Robert Sale said that Maclean as a Calvinist is "dedicated, not to work, as those who don't understand these matters like to think, but to the achievement of grace," and he called "A River Runs Through It" "an enchanted tale." According to Christopher Lehmann-Haupt, in the *New York Times*, "you have to keep staring at [its] surface . . . before you can make out the deeper things that lie underneath—and see past them to the depths where doomed mankind is transcending itself through art." Alfred Kazin, in the *Chicago Tribune*, wrote that it "officially takes its stand as the American classic it was affectionately recognized as from the first," praising its passages of "physical rapture in the presence of unsullied primitive America."

As an octogenarian, Maclean spoke of three projects he hoped to complete. One was the cinematic version of his novella, which film-makers had been clamoring vainly to do ever since it first appeared. He had resisted all of these demands, fearing that the movies would compromise his love poem to his family, until Robert Redford's Sundance Institute in Utah, where Maclean had spent a week in the summer of 1985, gave him a grant to write his own screenplay (he insisted on controlling the final product). He also worked for several years on a story about thirteen young parachuting smoke jumpers who were killed fighting the 1949 Mann Gulch forest fire in Montana (an episode referred to in *A River Runs Through It*). He had thought the research would take only a few months, but discovered that, because the families of the victims had sued the Forest Service, its records of the event were classified. Nevertheless, at the time of his death Maclean had finished this book—"Men and Fire," his second work of fiction—although it had yet to be published. Finally, Maclean hoped to write a book about his beloved wife of thirty-seven years, who had died of emphysema in 1968. But as he himself recognized, he was racing against time. Whether he completed all or any of these projects, he said, he had written what he wanted. "I have lived a blessed life."

PRINCIPAL WORKS: (with E. C. Olson) Manual of Instruction in Military Maps and Aerial Photographs, 1943; *essays in* Critics and Criticism, Ancient and Modern (ed. Ronald S. Crane), 1952; A River Runs Through It and Other Stories, 1976.

ABOUT: Contemporary Authors 102, 1981; Who's Who in America, 1988–89; O'Connell, Nicholas. At the Field's End: Interviews with Twenty Pacific Northwest Writers, 1987. *Periodicals*—AAUP Bulletin Winter 1954–55; Los Angeles Times June 25, 1986; New Republic May 1, 1976; New York Review of Books May 27, 1976; New York Times September 23, 1983; August 3, 1990; New York Times Book Review May 8, 1977; Newsweek August 30, 1976; Village Voice March 29, 1976; Wall Street Journal August 25, 1986.

*MAHAPATRA, JAYANTA (October 22, 1928–), Indian poet, translator, and short-story writer, writes: "The formidable white Englishman who first teased his alien English words into my schoolboy mouth has been dead now for three decades. I was the youngest (and poorest) among the thirty children in his class in the missionary school where I studied; through him I learnt to love the language I later began to use. The meager poetry I read (the prescribed course of Wordsworth, Keats, and Shelley in the senior Cambridge class) did not appear to have any noticeable effect; I strayed, lost touch with myself, studied physics, and never thought of looking at poetry for years. It was only much later, when I married a girl who loved poetry beyond measure, that a line of Keats would float into my mind, through dead walls and mysterious scientific symbols and the cruel clannish behavior of my people, like a stretched-out hand perhaps, bringing a little relief in having achieved a sense of direction.

"I was raised among simple people who believed (and still do) that things happen as they do because they happen as the consequence of things that have happened before, and that nothing can change the sequence of things. A deeper inner world of ancient thought and ritual closes in, from everywhere. And the people settle back peacefully into the deep-rooted tradition of their ancestors, even against the new education and technological advancement. All my life I've seen groups of mutilated lepers shuffle from house to house on Mondays (considered sacred by Hindus), when palmfuls of rice and coins are doled out to them. Life does not flounder like a tired old boat, but renews itself in an endlessly recurring cycle, as it has been for ages. Almost every year cyclones and floods sweep across coastal Orissa; and deaths are many. It becomes hard to believe that all those who die have reaped the consequence for what each one had done in his or her previous incarnation. One feels suspended between *nirvana* and the laws of loosening life. And perhaps one can only sit down to write a poem at midnight, perhaps idle songs of futility.

"My memories converge on a lone, conventional house at the village's end surrounded by aging, ominous-looking deodars, and coconut palms that stood at varying angles, dark sentinels

JAYANTA MAHAPATRA

to a childhood pattern. A wall went around; a door painted with cheap pitch opened into a narrow lane. I remember that door from the time I was seven: dark and sightless, it seemed to stand beyond it into something stranger. There it is, even today, in my dead father's house, as it stood years ago—when that pretty young cousin of mine used to bang away at the wood in the misty evenings to spare herself a merciless beating from her drunken husband. We had no electricity in the house; I recollect the oil lamps with their sooty flames swaying to the wind, looking almost human, obsequious; and the dreary wall, setting up its boundaries. Slowly with the passing of years, I soon found out that I was no longer *the* center of my world, but just one of many similar centers, of similar worlds—of my friends and neighbors. But it took me many painful years to realize that, many relationships, both real and imagined. And I learnt that every one of us is different from the others, and that no two people ever see life in exactly the same way. And that no individual can remain in isolation, but must learn to relate to those around him, must learn to communicate. This is especially true for a writer or poet—because a poet has to transmit his experience to others if his poetry is to *be*. And this is what the writing of poetry does to the poet: it makes him reach into himself to find out what he is, through the process of re-experiencing his own felt experience.

"Once, long ago, the footprints of my grandfather would have left their agitated trail on the unmade paths of this land; or he was suffering uncontrollably from hunger, away from the frayed fabric that famine had made of his life, and ultimately entering a new time of uncertainty and unease. It was the year 1866, a terrible period of drought and famine—when corpses by the hundreds were abandoned on the dry riverbeds, to the equally starving vultures and jackals. The year when Grandfather staggered into a mercy camp run by white missionaries, in a state of collapse—to embrace a new religion.

"Grandfather staked his claim to a place in the new social order. And I grew up between two worlds, probably unable to distinguish one from another. More than a century has gone by; but the menace of hunger still eats into our lives. Perhaps something keeps missing all the time, burdened as we are with the bewildering nucleus of love and hunger, sexuality and death. Something I feel I cannot escape from, making me reach for it in the poetry I write. And if these poems are inventions, they resemble longings amid the flow of voices, of footsteps, banging doors and uncertain laughter—toward a knowledge that everything around us comes out of the nowhere of life and death."

A poet and a scientist, a native Indian who writes in English, a modern town dweller whose subjects are often ancient and rural, Jayanta Mahapatra indeed lives in two worlds. The divisions of his life, however, do not necessarily account for the melancholy, subjective, and reflective nature of his poetry, but they may account for the uniqueness of his voice as a poet. Mahusudan Prasad, who collected a series of essays on him in *The Poetry of Jayanta Mahapatra: A Critical Study*, finds him "authentically Indian . . . rooted deeply in Indian socio-cultural heritage." Though his images are distinctly Eastern, his poetry is the product of an inner private world of his own construction that exists simultaneously with the actual world around him. These two worlds inevitably clash from time to time in his poetry, resulting sometimes in obscurity. In his early work in particular, Bruce King noted in *Contemporary Poets*, that "multiplicity of significances, dislocated, often baffling syntax, and disruption of grammar are held together rather by rich patterns of imagery and sound than by any clarity of argument or narrative."

Jayanta Mahapatra was born in the city of Cuttack in Orissa, the Indian state that is still his home, to Lemuel and Sudhansu (Rout) Mahapatra, and educated at English-language schools (his Indian language is Oriya). In 1946 he received a Bachelor of Science degree (with honors) from Ravenshaw College in Cuttack. He took a master's degree in physics (also with hon-

ors) from Patna University in 1949. In 1951 he married Jyotsna Rani Das; they have one son. After a year as subeditor of a newspaper in his hometown, he began teaching physics at Ravenshaw College in 1950. He has since taught at various engineering and technical colleges in Orissa, but mainly at Ravenshaw, until 1981 when he became reader in physics at Shailabala Women's College. Mahapatra was forty when he published his first volume of poetry. Since then, however, he has written prolifically. In addition to poetry, he writes short stories for the *Illustrated Weekly of India*. (One of these, "Bells for a Bull," a highly symbolic story of the fantasizing of a sexually frustrated woman, was published in *Contemporary Indian Short Stories*, edited by Ka Naa Subramanyan, 1977.) He has also translated three volumes of Oriyan poetry into English and published two collections of stories for children. In 1986 he told an interviewer that he had become so absorbed in his literary career that "physics has become a secondary occupation." Poetry, he says, "gives a direction to my movement of life."

Although he was not educated for a literary career, Mahapatra's early introduction to English poetry gave him a feeling for the English language, a sensitivity to its nuances and complexities. He found inspiration, he says, in many poets—American (Robert Penn Warren especially), European and Latin American—George Seferis, Pablo Neruda, Vicente Aleixandre, Rafael Alberti, and Juan Ramón Jiménez. Although some critics have traced echoes of T. S. Eliot in his thoughtful, melancholy poems on the fragmentation of modern life, Mahapatra says that he has read Eliot only in recent years. As a latecomer to poetry he is still exploring and discovering his voice. "When I began," he recalls, "I was so much obsessed by the feel for words, their sound qualities . . . [that] my first poems were in a way attempts in which the language left the ideas of the poems [implicit] . . . , lost in the depths of words." As his art matured, his notions of poetry changed: "Today I see that the idea behind the poem (or in the poem) is slowly beginning to surface, and my poems are perhaps being more direct ones."

The poems in Mahapatra's first collection *Close the Sky, Ten by Ten*, dedicated to his father, have been described as "exercise-poems," experiments in sound and wordplay. As S. K. Desai points out in "The Poetic Craft," an essay on his work, they operate outside the field of "normal logic" in what T. S. Eliot called "the logic of imagination," juxtaposing "the concrete and the abstract, the vague and the clear, the idea and the emotion." The book takes its title from the poem "Sanctuary" which plays on the contrast between the finite and the infinite:

now i close the sky
with a square ten by ten

the roof essential
hides the apocalyptic ideal

Some of the poems are fragmentary, for example "Woman":

Even
when she is

Even
when she is not

Others labor a poetic conceit, as in "Snakes":

At a distance you notice they are
things like rivers, floating as
on a map, black in summertime.
We watch, not used to their ways,
provoked to provoke the sudden spring
of coiled force within, sluggishly forward.
Cool winds slide up our moss-grown legs,
to hide us at first, then to hide
themselves. And we understand desire.

By 1976, with the publication of *A Rain of Rites*, Bruce King observes in his essay "The Shapes of Solitude" that Mahapatra "pulled his fragmented themes together into a more unified vision." That vision embraces all India but most specifically the ancient and poverty-ridden provinces of his native Orissa. Charles R. Larson, in *World Literature Today*, was so impressed with the sharpness of Mahapatra's images that he suggested an alternate title—"a thunderstorm of poetic surprises." He writes so fluently and vividly, Larson continued, "that many of his poems give the impression of having been animated by some private muse which exists solely to inspire him." The poems most often singled out by the critics are "Hunger," with its graphic image of a desperately poor fisherman selling his fifteen-year-old daughter into prostitution ("The fisherman said: will you have her, carelessly / trailing his nets and his nerves, as though his words / sanctified the purpose with which he faced himself"), and "The Whorehouse in a Calcutta Street," where again the poet's private fantasies confront the shocking reality of poverty and exploitation:

Walk right in. It is yours.
Where the house smiles wryly into the lighted street.
Think of the women
You wished to know and haven't.
The faces in the posters, the public hoardings.
And who are all *there* together,
those who put the house there
for the startled eye to fall upon,
where pasts join, and where they part.

The publication of Mahapatra's poems in

western journals (including *Critical Quarterly*, the *Times Literary Supplement*, the *Hudson Review*, *Poetry*, and the *Kenyon Review*, among others) in the mid-1970s brought him to the attention of a much larger public. In 1975 he received the Jacob Glatstein Memorial Award of *Poetry* magazine, and in 1976 he spent a year in the United States as visiting writer at the University of Iowa's International writing program. He traveled to Australia (1978) and Japan (1980) as a visiting writer; in 1985 he went to the U.S.S.R, as part of a cultural exchange; and in 1986 he traveled in Italy on a Rockefeller Foundation award.

In each of Mahapatra's subsequent volumes, critics have noticed a growing maturity and mastery. He remains, however, a poet of solitude. "He uses images exploratorily, to give shape to solitude," Bruce King writes, "especially to the various shifting, unstable desires, alienations, conflicts, complexities, hopes, memories, and imaginations which stir and flow through the mind. . . ." Subjective as he is, Mahapatra is very much a part of his society—not a regional poet but one who is consciously and articulately aware of the importance of his roots and their shaping power over his imagination. Orissa, with its ruined temples and long history "of broken empires and vanquished dynasties," figures in many of his poems. In *Waiting* (dedicated to Paul Engle, founder of the University of Iowa's writing program) Mahapatra describes one of the holiest pilgrimage sites in India, the temple of Puri:

At Puri, the crows.

The one wide street
lolls out like a giant tongue.

Five faceless lepers move aside
as a priest passes by.

And at the street's end
the crowds thronging the temple door;
a huge holy flower
swaying in the wind of greater reasons.
                              —"Taste for Tomorrow"

Critics have found an ambivalence in Mahapatra toward his country's past—his fascination with its mythology and tradition yet his ironic detachment from it ("Your silence, my land / grows / with an old petrified loneliness"). Some have suggested that being a Christian himself, he is more objective than his fellow Hindus. As an "insider-outsider," however, Mahapatra has the advantage of understanding what he does not necessarily worship. He is no more at ease with the present than he is with the past. A long poem in *A Father's Hours*, "The Twenty-fifth Anniversary of a Republic: 1975," comments bitterly on the "wasteland" of modern industrial India:

> What is wrong with my country?
> The jungles have become gentle, the women restless.
> And history reposes between the college-girl's breasts:
>   the exploits of warrior-queens, the pride pieced
>   together
> from a god's tainted amours. Is this where the
>   advantage lay?
> Mina, my pretty neighbour, flashes round and round
>   the gilded stage,
> hiding jungles in her purse, holding on to her divorce,
> and a lonely Ph.D.

One of Mahapatra's most ambitious works to date is a twelve-part, twenty-two-page poem entitled *Relationship*, for which he won the Sahitya Akademi Award in 1981, the first English-language Indian poet to do so. In *Relationship* he ponders the meanings of a crumbling ancient temple in Orissa. Deeply personal, the poem explores the poet's past, letting loose a flood of memories, summoning up images of dream and darkness, and questioning the meaning of life itself:

> would meaning remain
> in merely that a thing exists, in a single plain,
> in the helpless sips of loneliness we have made
> marooned on the stone, on the dark chariot of sun
> whose fevered granite wheels claw desperately
> at the strangled earth in our lives?

PRINCIPAL WORKS: *Poetry*—Close the Sky, Ten by Ten, 1971; Svayamvara and Other Poems, 1971; A Father's Hours, 1976; A Rain of Rites, 1976; Waiting, 1979; The False Start, 1980; Relationship, 1980; Life Signs, 1983; Dispossessed Nests, 1986; Selected Poems, 1987; Burden of Waves and Fruit, 1988; Temple, 1980. *General*—Orissa, 1989.

ABOUT: Contemporary Authors New Revision Series 15, 1985; Contemporary Poets, 4th ed., 1985; Prasad, M. (ed.) The Poetry of Jayanta Mahapatra: A Critical Study, 1986. *Periodicals*—Critical Quarterly Spring 1982; Hudson Review Winter 1977, Summer 1982, Summer 1986; Journal of South Asian Literature Summer–Fall 1984, Summer–Fall 1986; Kenyon Review Fall 1986; Parnassus Spring–Summer 1981; Poetry September 1977, November 1988; World Literature Today Autumn 1977, Spring 1987.

MALCOLM, JANET (193?–   ), American critic and journalist, was born in Prague, Czechoslovakia, the daughter of a psychiatrist. She was educated at the High School of Music and Art in New York and at the University of Michigan. Malcolm has been on the staff of the *New Yorker* since 1965 and her three books originally appeared in slightly different form in that magazine. She began her career with occasional

JANET MALCOLM

book reviews and a sort of glossy consumer column ("On and Off the Avenue"), but had something of a breakthrough in 1975 with the first in a series of columns on photography. These were mostly critical responses to events in the then burgeoning photography world of New York and elsewhere: museum and gallery shows of the work of Richard Avedon and Irving Penn, recently published studies of Alfred Stieglitz and Edward Weston, to cite a few examples. In 1980 Malcolm collected eleven of these pieces in *Diana & Nikon: Essays on the Aesthetic of Photography*. The title refers to two camera models, the cheap Diana and the expensive Nikon, which Malcolm takes to be emblematic of the bifurcating traditions of art photography. The primary tradition, as Malcolm sees it, is the painterly one initiated by Stieglitz and carried on by such masters as Weston, Evans, and Cartier-Bresson, which values "composition, design, tonal balance, and print quality." The counter-tradition, what Malcolm calls "the snapshot school," was initiated by Robert Frank with his seminal publication *The Americans* (1959), which welcomes instead "accidents of light, the messy conjunctions of shape, the randomness of the framing, the disorderliness of the composition." That the two traditions are not mutually exclusive, that in fact they inform each other in subtle, ambiguous ways, is the theme of one of the later essays, "Two Roads, One Destination." In her Preface Malcolm makes the somewhat startling admission that it was not until midway through the book that she felt she began to "get hold of the subject" and not until the

"Two Roads" piece that she untangled "some of its knottier issues." Despite this disclaimer, the book received mostly favorable reviews. Hilton Kramer in the *New York Times Book Review* identified Malcolm's discussion of the snapshot esthetic as the "intellectual center" of the book. "No other writer," he said, "has outlined this fateful development with quite the clarity or concision or eloquence that Miss Malcolm brings to it." He concluded: "Janet Malcolm is a very fine critic—the finest, perhaps, that the current photography boom has yet produced—and with this first book she easily takes her place among the most accomplished art critics now writing."

A very different conclusion was reached by Jed Perl in his formidable critique in *Art in America*. Perl objected to what he considered Malcolm's insensitivity to the "mysterious *mechanicalness* of photography," to her disproportionate attention to merely "fashionable" photographers like Avedon and Penn, and, most strenuously, to her "insistence that photography be understood before all else in relation to painting and printmaking," an insistence that "constricts and ultimately poisons Malcolm's approach." Perl's harsh judgments were decidedly a minority view, and his review of *Diana & Nikon* remains the roughest treatment that Malcolm has received for the book.

Malcolm's next two books were both concerned with psychoanalysis, a subject on which she has continued to write in the *New Yorker* and elsewhere. The focus of *Psychoanalysis: The Impossible Profession* is the pseudonymous, forty-six-year-old "Aaron Green," an analyst "of the most unswervingly Freudian sort" at the New York Psychoanalytic Institute. The book is divided between Aaron Green's extraordinarily frank, endlessly self-analytical conversations with Malcolm and Malcolm's own summaries of central psychoanalytic tenets, particularly the phenomenon of transference—"how we all invent each other according to early blueprints," as she put it. Malcolm's scrupulous, learned expositions of some very complicated concepts earned her universal praise; her "longish 'study guide to Freud's writings,'" wrote Brigid Brophy in the *London Review of Books*, "is the definitive answer to the beginner's question about where to begin." On the matter of Aaron Green, critics were divided. No one questioned Malcolm's journalistic skills in eliciting such fascinating confessions as Green's desire to be a beautiful woman or in portraying a driven, complex man. Yet the responses of readers to Green's personality tended to coincide (one supposes) with their attitudes toward orthodox Freudian analysis. To some, like R. Z. Sheppard in *Time*, Green seemed "an intelligent, sympathetic man . . .

defending the faith in an age of pill popping and package deals." To others, like Harold Bloom in the *New York Times Book Review*, he seemed "a garage mechanic of the mind, absurdly certain he is somehow Freud's true heir." One critic in the *New Statesman* made the seemingly outlandish but almost inevitable suggestion that Malcolm herself might have undergone some sort of transference experience with Green. This would at least make sense, she said, of Malcolm's "own confession that she finds psychoanalysts 'near saints'—and that *after* all her hours with Aaron and the tape-recorder, not before." At any rate, one finds Malcolm's description of their last interview—held, significantly, in Green's consultation room—strangely moving: "Aaron stared with displeasure into the middle distance, and I said nothing. The sound of a door slamming—heralding the patient whose arrival always ended our talks—broke the silence, and ended the final hour of our strange and remarkable encounter."

Where *Psychoanalysis: The Impossible Profession* approaches psychoanalysis through the sober, considered reflections of Malcolm and Aaron Green, *In the Freud Archives* does so through a cast of characters that would be at home in a Thomas Pynchon novel or a Jack Nicholson movie, as some of the reviews suggested. Malcolm's protagonist is Jeffrey Moussaieff Masson, described on the dust jacket as "a flamboyant, restless forty-two-year-old Sanskrit scholar turned psychoanalyst turned virulent anti-Freudian." Masson, who had improbably scaled the heights to become projects director of the Sigmund Freud Archives in 1980, provoked a storm of controversy by delivering a paper in New Haven in 1981 in which he attributed "the present-day sterility of psychoanalysis throughout the world" to Freud's early abandonment of the seduction theory in favor of the Oedipus complex. To Masson, Freud "shift[ed] the emphasis from a real world of sadness, misery and cruelty to an internal stage on which actors performed invented dramas for an invisible audience of their own creation." Briefly, the board of the Freud Archives, led by Masson's former mentor, the venerable K. R. Eissler, would have none of it, and Masson was removed from his post in October of 1981. "Would you make director of the archives someone who writes plain nonsense?" Eissler was quoted as saying in the *New York Times*. Masson was out of a job, but apparently unrepentant. In the same *Times* article he speculated with "inspired impudence" (Malcolm's words) on the effects he expected his discoveries would have on psychoanalytic practice. "They would have to recall every patient since 1901," he said, "It would be like the Pinto.

This is only part of the story. Malcolm interweaves an account of Masson's career before and after his fall with accounts of his touching but in the end painful relationship with Eissler, his edgy one with Anna Freud (for a time she gave him the run of her father's house in London but likened him to one of her dogs racing around and tearing up the garden), and, not least, his mutually suspicious one with Peter Swales, a former assistant to the Rolling Stones and self-described "punk historian of psychoanalysis." Swales had a few theories of his own about Freud, and for a while the two iconoclasts worked together until Swales broke off the relationship with a forty-five page single-spaced typewritten letter which Malcolm calls "a kind of masterpiece of invective."

Despite the farcical elements in this unlikely tale, *In the Freud Archives* is a serious, even scholarly examination of psychoanalytic theory and practice. Malcolm's informed discussion of Freud's theory of the Oedipus complex and infantile sexuality is as central to this book as was her discussion of transference to *Psychoanalysis: The Impossible Profession*. And like the earlier book, *In the Freud Archives* is a study in personality which reveals an alarming siege mentality among members of the psychoanalytic establishment. "Janet Malcolm tells the story with immense skill, moving about in time, fitting in her own interviews with and impressions of the flamboyant cast of characters among tracts of narrative reaching back into Freud's own lifetime," Anthony Quinton wrote in the *Times Literary Supplement*. Harold Bloom praised her "superb reportage," and most other critics concurred.

One person not impressed was Jeffrey Masson, who, in 1984, filed a $10.2 million libel suit against her, the *New Yorker*, and her publisher, Alfred A. Knopf, alleging that misquotations in the book had irrevocably damaged his career. The quotations to which Masson objected were among the few that Malcolm could not substantiate with tape recordings; her lawyers argued that nevertheless no misrepresentation had occurred because Masson was on record as having expressed similar sentiments elsewhere. The case was dismissed in 1987 by a federal judge who found no evidence that Malcolm had acted with malice or "with reckless disregard for the truth." Masson's appeal of the dismissal to a higher federal court was rejected in 1989. The *New York Times* on August 5, 1989 reported that this court "did not resolve whether Ms. Malcolm had changed her subject's words. But the court upheld the right of authors to alter statements of public figures as long as the changes do not misrepresent the speaker's meaning or are reason-able interpretations of what was said." One of the three appellate judges, however, filed a strong dissenting opinion, and in the fall of 1990 the Supreme Court agreed to consider whether the libel suit should be reinstated.

According to Malcolm, it was not the Masson proceedings but a longstanding concern with the interviewer/subject relationship that drew her to her next project, an investigation into a far better-known lawsuit in which a convicted murderer accused a journalist of abusing his trust and won a substantial out-of-court settlement. "The Journalist and the Murderer" appeared in two parts in the *New Yorker*, March 13 and March 20, 1989 and was published as a book in 1990. The journalist of the title is Joe McGinniss, author of *Fatal Vision* (1983), an account of the trial and ultimate conviction of Dr. Jeffrey MacDonald, a Marine Corps physician, for the murder of his wife and children. MacDonald had already been charged with these crimes when the contract for *Fatal Vision* was signed. He was eager to publish his story, both to assert his innocence and to defray some of his legal costs. McGinniss, for his part, was fascinated by the case and thought MacDonald had been wrongly accused; he was eager to write the book, a potential best-seller. He interviewed MacDonald extensively and during the trial sat in on the strategy sessions of the defense team. Privately he became convinced of MacDonald's guilt. McGinniss spent the next three years delving into the background of the case, maintaining all the while an ostensibly friendly relationship with the imprisoned MacDonald. The book he finally published, however, left no doubt where his allegiance lay, and MacDonald sued. McGinniss settled the case out of court for a reported $325,000 (*New York Times*, August 5, 1989).

Malcolm added an Afterword to *The Journalist and the Murderer* which itself provoked controversy, not only among journalists and lawyers but among readers concerned about the truth and accuracy of what they read. Responding to critics of her earlier *In the Freud Archives*, she denied that her criticism of McGinniss was in any way the response of "a guilty conscience" for her portrait of Masson: "The notion that my account of this case is a thinly veiled account of my own experience of being sued by a subject not only is wrong but betrays a curious naiveté about the psychology of journalists." She argues that there is a "moral ambiguity" in any relationship the journalist develops with his or her subject, a "false friendship" that is unhealthy because the journalist invariably has the upper hand: "The moral ambiguity of journalism," she writes "lies not in its texts but in the relationships out of which they derive—relationships that are invariably and inescapably lopsided." To that extent Malcolm implicates herself along with the rest of her colleagues in the opening paragraphs of her book: "Every journalist who is not too stupid or too full of himself to notice what is going on knows that what he does is morally indefensible. He is a kind of confidence man, preying on people's vanity, ignorance, or loneliness, gaining their trust and betraying them without remorse."

In a long and judicious review of *The Journalist and the Murderer* in the *New York Times Book Review*, Fred W. Friendly observed that Malcolm's criticism of her profession "no matter if exaggerated, should force all of us in the news business to re-examine our methods and manners." He approved her questioning the control that journalists exercise over their subjects but objected to her sweeping indictment of *all* journalists. "The manipulative reporter ambushes and entraps naïve, lonely, vulnerable prey who confuse attention with alliance. But the kind of fraternal relationship that Mr. McGinniss nourished with Dr. MacDonald over so many years is very rare indeed."

In addition to her four books, Malcolm has written numerous essays and book reviews on literary, artistic, and psychoanalytic subjects for the *New Yorker*, the *New York Times Book Review*, and the *New York Review of Books*. She lives in Manhattan with her husband, the photographer and *New Yorker* editor Gardner Botsford, and her daughter Anne.

PRINCIPAL WORKS: Diana & Nikon: Essays on the Aesthetic of Photography, 1980; Psychoanalysis: The Impossible Profession, 1981; In the Freud Archives, 1984; The Journalist and The Murderer, 1990.

ABOUT: Contemporary Authors 123, 1988. *Periodicals*—Art in America May 1980; London Review of Books April 15–May 5, 1982; New Statesman February 26, 1982; New York March 27, 1989; New York Review of Books March 1, 1990; New York Times August 5, 1989; October 5, 1990; New York Times Book Review May 4, 1980; May 27, 1984; February 25, 1990; Publishers Weekly September 4, 1987; Time September 28, 1981; Times Literary Supplement March 22, 1985.

MANDEL, ELI(AS WOLF) (December 3, 1922–   ), Canadian poet, critic, and anthologist, was born in Estevan, Saskatchewan, of Russian-Jewish immigrant parents. After service as a medical corpsman in World War II, he received bachelor's (1949) and master's (1950) degrees from the University of Saskatchewan and a doctorate in English (1957) from the University of

Toronto. He taught literature at the Collége Militaire Royal de Saint-Jean in Saint-Jean, Québec (assistant professor, 1953–1955; associate professor, 1955–1957), the University of Alberta (assistant professor, 1957–1959; associate professor, 1959–1963; professor, 1964–1967), and at York University in Toronto (associate professor, 1963–1964; professor, 1967–1980; professor of English and humanities from 1980).

Mandel's poetry is demanding and dark, filled with forebodings and unseen terrors. It contains very little joy, although a strong and seemingly spontaneous lyric impulse is constantly at his disposal. His earliest volume was *Trio*, which his poems shared with works by the poets Gael Turnbull and Phyllis Webb, and in which most of his contributions are characterized by images of madness, death, and the sadness of irrevocable change. *Fuseli Poems*, his first solo volume, was widely praised by Canadian reviewers for its vital language, energetic imagery, and careful structure, but the images are frequently of blood, murder, and overwhelming, incapacitating terror. *Black and Secret Man* contained thirty-three poems concerning, in the poet's own words, "objects of terror, sinister events, ominous places and whatever speaks out of darkness. It was written so that I could confront and recognize whatever is dark in human nature, and to discover how much of it is a reflection of self." The title poem finds him reflecting on some snapshots he took of "the garden here outside my home"—he finds them deeply sinister, redolent of "mortal murders" and hanged bodies. He instructs the reader, who may be innocently disposed to see them only as photographs, to beware of their hidden, terrible implications, using imagery straight from *Macbeth* :

> Now face the faces in the tree,
> The snarling wood, the years of treedom.
> Why, once when brains were out a man would die
> But now like maggot-pies and choughs and rooks
> A black and secret man of blood walks
> In the garden.
>   I never go there now.

So real does Mandel's terror seem that, the poems usually have the ability to convey fright to the reader, rather than amazement that someone so constantly terrified could ever write anything at all.

An Idiot Joy considers, among other problems and amid still much random terror, various ways of regarding poetry. The book's epilogue declares, in lines from "Crusoe," one of the collection's central poems,

> This was written for a foundling,
> alien, Greek, Hebrew,

in order not to go mad,
and for my keepers' sake,
that I might learn
singular love
no other is to blame.

The book's theme is the chaos and irrationality of the act of poetry: it is "a bad habit"; despite the poet's best intentions, "one by one my poems fall apart." Madness and savagery closely inhabit these poems, as do all manner of antisocial beings. The frustration engendered by living in society and by the limits governing political alternatives are so strong as to make the poet hysterical, mentally unhinged: "What scream issuing from the page / darkens my difficult, philosophic mind?" Yet he can still manage his old fierce irony, as in "Pictures in an Institution," a half-comical meditation on the ludicrous constraints to anything approaching true learning which confront a modern university:

Notice: the library is closed to all who read
any student carrying a gun
registers first, exempt from fines,
is given thirteen books per month,
one course in science, one in math,
two options
                    campus police
will see to co-eds' underwear

An Idiot Joy was the cowinner, with Alden Nowlan's Bread, Wine and Salt, of the Governor General's award for poetry in 1968.

There seemed at once a greater immediacy and less palpable terror in the poems collected in Stony Plain. A substantial portion of these sixty-two poems are memorials to personal heroes ("Oscar Wilde," "Albert Camus," "The Death of Don Quixote," "On the Death of Ho Chi Minh"), lively reflections on (then-) current events ("On the 25th Anniversary of the Liberation of Auschwitz," "The President and the Chairman Meet," "On the Cultural Revolution," "From 'The Pentagon Papers,'" "On the Renewal of Bombing in Vietnam December, 1972") or contemporary Canadian locales ("Ottawa October 70," "Saskatchewan Surveyor," the Wabamun poems). Mandel's apparently new preoccupations were welcome to most critics; Barry Cameron, in particular, writing in Canadian Forum, cited his progress "towards the laconic and minimal in style and expression and the mimetic fragmentation of form."

Among the poet's other collections should be noted Crusoe: Poems Selected and New, which includes much of his earlier work; and Out of Place, an account of his return to Saskatchewan, to the Estevan of his birth. He must admit to himself that he is out of place, not fully at home, in the vast prairie: "Whatever has been hidden here / remains of speech / the town lives / in its syntax we are ghosts". Yet the poet acknowledges that it is only from realizing a deep sense of place that we can find out who we are and what we are becoming. The book contains Ann Mandel's (the author's wife's) black-and-white photos of the area, strongly evocative of the northern plains with their empty spaces and desolate, abandoned houses. Life Sentence presents Mandel's journals of travels to the Canadian Rockies, France and Spain, Incan Peru, and India. These jottings are accompanied by twenty-nine new poems, many of them reactions to places and people encountered on his travels. He had, he says in the preface, been "trying to put together a book—new poems that seemed to me drawn to, compelled from questions of the kind we call political, various ways in which forms of inhumanity manifest themselves and then seek justification in the language of patriotism, revolution, law, virtue. I wanted a clear way of showing the great disorder in which I live, words that would be hard and pure enough to hold together the impure structures of our lives, something, as one of the spirits says to Yeats in his A Vision, 'purified of complexity.' I longed for clarity—and order." A second collection of his poems appeared as Dreaming Backwards: The Selected Poetry of Eli Mandel, 1954–1981.

As an anthologist and critic, Mandel has expanded many readers' ideas of Canadian literature, which is almost his only subject. Poetry 62, published in 1961, anthologized the selected work of twenty-three Canadian poets, of whom nine are francophone. He speaks in the preface of how encouraged he is by the richness and range of his country's poetry: "A lively poetry shatters limitations. It refuses to be contained by officialdom . . . for the simple reason that its life is change. And the present character of Canadian poetry is, above all, liveliness. Probably the most striking feature of contemporary Canadian poetry is its range of activity. It is now sufficiently varied to be represented in any number of ways—from the point of view of its articulate myth-makers, its passionate metaphysicians or its eloquent anarchists—and yet it leaves no impression that its energy is being dissipated in diversity. If anything, the opposite: one senses in it a gathering of forces for the performance of some unprecedented and enormously significant drama of the mind."

WORKS: Poetry—(with G. Turnbull and P. Webb) Trio, 1954; Fuseli Poems, 1960; Black and Secret Man, 1964; An Idiot Joy, 1967; Mary Midnight, 1971; Crusoe, 1973; Stony Plain, 1973; Out of Place, 1977; Life Sentence, 1983; Dreaming Backwards, 1983. Essays—Irving Layton, 1969; Another Time, 1977;

(with D. Taras) A Passion for Identity, 1986; The Family Romance, 1986. *As editor*—(with Jean-Guy Pilon) Poetry 62, 1961; Criticism, 1966; Five Modern Canadian Poets, 1971; Contexts of Canadian Criticism, 1971; Poets of Contemporary Canada, 1972; (with A. Mandel) Eight More Canadian Poets, 1972; (with D. Maxwell) English Poets of the Twentieth Century, 1972.

ABOUT: Contemporary Authors New Revision Series 15, 1983; Canadian Who's Who, 1989; Dictionary of Literary Biography 53, 1986. *Periodicals*—Canadian Forum November–December 1973; March 1978; Canadian Literature Autumn 1969; Dalhousie Review Fall 1960; Dandelion Fall–Winter 1983; Essays on Canadian Writing Summer–Fall 1980; Fiddlehead Spring 1978; Journal of Canadian Fiction Winter 1973; Saturday Night July 1973.

IVÁN MÁNDY

*MÁNDY, IVÁN (December 23, 1918–   ), Hungarian short-story writer, novelist, and playwright, writes: "I was born in 1918 in Budapest. In fact, that in itself contains my biography. I got everything from this city. My own world as well as the way I perceive the world of others.

"My first discovery came at the age of five or six, when I got to know an open-air corridor in the 'City' and a stairway. Then came the street and the square with the Jókai statue on it. Mór Jókai, the nineteenth-century classical novelist, always looked at me with timeless wisdom. Already then its original color had decayed to a strange greenish black. In some way, he seemed to believe in me. My schoolmasters and later my teachers, on the other hand, never believed in me at all. It's true, I didn't believe in them either. I felt that they were more interested in chastisement than in education. In the long run, I think I disappointed neither Jókai nor my teachers.

"My father was a journalist. Always in the middle of some gigantic conversation. (However, he was a journalist without a journal.) His way of life was not in the least bit altered by his marriage, which in fact broke up after a few years. My mother, the daughter of a post-office manager, watched with petrified dismay the mad whirlpool that surrounded my father. It really isn't surprising that she couldn't take it for very long. The scene of the conversation was sometimes our apartment on the third floor, sometimes a café, or somewhere on the street.

"In actuality, my father was a poet and a dreamer. He wanted to establish a theater, a circus, but most of all a newspaper. One of those real European-styled and standard newspaper. In fact he wanted to take Budapest, this sleepy city, and connect it to the blood circulation of

Europe! In the meantime, he really had no space to worry about little things, like earning money, etc. . . . He didn't even pay his rent and was very much insulted when they put us out on the street. In this way, the only normal home of my childhood disappeared.

"Next came the hotel period. From relatively fancy hotels to suburban lodgings. Here I got to meet all the has-been actors and acrobats, and of course those nice little streetwalkers. For the time being, the latter connections were only through my father.

"When did I start writing? Maybe when I said my final good-byes to school. That was way before my graduation. I have to confess that I am still way before graduation. My first attempts [at writing] were contained in a wrinkled checkered notebook. And then a slip of paper here, a slip there. . . . For a long time the editors held out. But I was so determined in my struggle that finally they were forced to give in. I used to sing marches to myself every time I started off to see one of the editors.

"At first, my short stories began appearing in the dailies. Later I broke the resistance of the weeklies, then the periodicals. The greatest honor was that Aladár Schöpflin, a much-respected critic, accepted one of my short stories in the periodical of the Franklin Society, the *Tükör* (Mirror). My first novelette was published. Never a thinner novelette! Never a prouder author!

"It's just that in the meantime everything exploded. The war broke out. The houses crumbled to their knees. Then in a huge cloud of smoke flew up in the air. The streets became twisted. I wasn't taken away to be a soldier. I wasn't sent to the front. My father ingeniously took care of that. Very likely, he knew a non-commissioned officer, who buried my draft notice. . . . It is very likely, in fact, that my father knew everybody. I took shelter in the basement of a hospital. I was surrounded by darkness. Fear, suspicion, and darkness. I thought I would never get out of there.

"But one day, the whole thing ended. I stood on the street, my back against the wall, the sun shining a bit timidly, a bit clumsily, as if not yet sure that the war had really ended.

"But we truly believed that something new was beginning to emerge. A more humane era in which war will never again be seen. And it was really so. . . . The cafés began opening amongst the ruins. They opened up and welcomed us in as we crawled out from the split-up streets. Mounds of coats on the chairs. There was no way we could afford the cloakroom. There we sat, twenty or thirty of us, around a single cup of coffee. We decided to establish a periodical. A periodical was founded at every table in the house. Along with a few old friends, we too created our own. The *Újhold* (New Moon). Where we obtained the money? How we got hold of a printer? Eternal mysteries.

"But still, this wasn't the most important thing. Those slips of paper! And to once again sit amongst them and start a short story! Six lines . . . every morning. The method is probably a bit disillusioning. It's true that before writing, I would sit for hours staring into thin air. And then the minute I felt the first sign of fatigue, I would stop. Once again I found myself staring into space. This was almost as important as writing itself.

"And the dreams! A slice of what we call reality—and my dreams! This is what gives the atmosphere and the essence of my short stories. My dreams are rather depressing. However, a Wednesday afternoon can be more terrifying than any dream. More terrifying and more improbable.

"The method . . . How did this so-called writer's method come to be? In a relatively naïve, almost infantile way. I started out with fairy tales. Already, even at the beginning I faltered. I simply couldn't get the action started. My imagination too had given up. The important things are always revealed in the very beginning. What I had left was observation. I had heard something about Maupassant. Maybe it was Flaubert who was advising the young Maupassant when he said: You must watch a tree up until the moment when it becomes different from all of the world's other trees. So I anchored

myself down in front of a tree. It was a simple, stalwart little tree. No matter how hard I tried, it didn't want to look any different from all the other trees. I stared at it for a long time, finding that I was slowly beginning to detest the poor little tree.

"At home I took out my double-backed notebook. I tried to write down what the tree looked like. No success.

"Then once I saw something. One of those really wrung-out figures. And then the tree appeared in front of me. This was worth more than any observation. For the first time I caught a glimpse of what is called inner reality. Not action, not imagination, not observation. What remains is an inner world. And, of course, what runs into this from our experience. The magic of an old shop, or a bulkhead, or a human face.

"In the years following 1945 two novels and a collection of my short stories were published. And in 1948 I received the highest literary award, the Baumgarten Prize.

"And then nothing.

"All of a sudden, the cafés and the periodicals disappeared. These were the 1950s. The age of Mátyás Rákosi's personality cult. Hungarian literature's most miserable period. Writers were no longer needed. Only those composition writers who dealt with the daily politics. Those who saw everything so bright and cheery.

"Iván Mándy the writer disappeared. Instead, there was Iván Mándy the rewriter. I rewrote everything and everybody. I styled the novels and short stories of all the idiotic amateurs. I have to admit, they didn't at all become any more bearable. Garbage is always garbage. I redid all of the foolish children's radio plays. All this, because I didn't want to starve to death. Naturally, I wasn't the only one. I was joined by all of my compatriots and friends who still believed in something. In man's freedom, in man's thought. And, of course, in literature.

"We never thought all this would ever end. But even in this situation I continued writing short stories. Without any hope of being published. These works were only allowed to be published during the period of consolidation following 1956. Slowly, I was once again accepted.

"The more important happenings of the 1960s: I got married; my wife is a doctor. In 1968 I received the Attila József Prize. During these years, the reader, too, was liberated. It was only then that I got to know the books of Hemingway, Faulkner, and Fitzgerald. I also became aware of the one person who next to Chekhov and Dostoevsky means the most to me, Sylvia Plath. It was of her that I wrote my only short-story-like study.

"And finally, what do I want? All in all what
could any writer want? To quote Géza Ott'
the greatest living Hungarian writer. Wh·
a novelist want? Hopefully, to write r

"With a modest modification. What
writer want? As surprising as it seems, to ·
According to the rules of his talent."

In January 1979, a radio interviewer opened
a discussion of Mándy's writings with the author
by noting that every one of his books is successful: viewers throng to films made from them; his
juvenile novels are the favorites of children; his
works are among the most frequently translated
in Europe; and he was awarded the Attila József
Prize when he turned sixty. Asked whether, in
light of these successes, he was content, Mándy
replied, "Yes. This is a fortunate time of my
life."

The way to this wide acceptance was, as he
states in his personal account, long and difficult.
His career began auspiciously enough during the
chaos of war and the turmoil following Hungary's defeat. His three short novels, *A csöszház*
(The Park Keeper's House, 1943), *Francia kulcs*
(Monkey Wrench, 1948), and *A huszonegyedik
utca* (The Twenty-First Street, 1948) as well as
his short-story collection, *Vendégek a palackban*
(Visitors in the Bottle, 1949), were generally considered exceptionally promising. However, the
dogmatic policies of the Rákósi régime, which
came into power in 1949, radically altered Hungary's literary climate, stifling the lively literary
expression that had emerged after the close of
the war. The rigid enforcement of the most schematic tenets of Socialist Realism abruptly ended
Mándy's opportunity to publish. All publishing
houses were nationalized, and approval of
manuscripts was vigilantly monitored. Authors
were expected to adhere to the prevailing party
ideology and to help socialism achieve victory in
the class struggle. Moreover, to attain strictly didactic aims, the style of a work had to be simple
and clear, so that the uneducated masses could
better comprehend and accomplish the goals of
socialism. Failure to comply did not necessarily
close every door to publication, especially not in
periodicals, but the slightest departure from the
dicta produced public accusations that the author had abandoned the nation, betrayed the
proletariat, become apolitical, or turned to romantic self-indulgence. The stringent enforcement of this cultural policy by loyal Marxist
critics in an atmosphere charged with political
threat and economic insecurity left open only
two paths to writers who did not believe in the
values of Socialist Realism. They could write

MÁNDY

on to anything or to nu
ship with another hu
in "insignificant hu
charge him with b
with trivial subject
man beings, thoug
ed his deep com
The purely p
Mándy's work
In 1963 Marx
acknowledge
fusing to su
however, o
tila József
had clea
read: "
these b
or for
than
that
ma
di
c

(1
but
extrac
ary life
entertaini.
impoverished
about lecturing
knowledge of to ·
who do not have an
are being taught. Fr.
stark social and politic
early 1950s—not his
narration—Mándy offers
rare insight into a time whe.
and out, many authors neverth.
faithful to "the rules of their talent.
later become major figures).

After the Soviet army crushed the 1·
ing and restored the Communist state, the
government, sensing the need for a safety ·
in its relations with writers, did not apply its ·
erary policy as strictly as Rákósi's arbiters had,
choosing instead to censure chiefly by controlling the number of copies printed. Mándy was
finally able to publish again, though printings in
his case were kept well under two thousand copies. Besides two of the four young-adult novels
comprising his *Csutak* series (1957–1968),
which, intended for "anyone ten years or older,"
soon became classics, two books of fiction for
adults appeared: *Idegen szobák* (Strange Rooms,
1957), a collection of short stories written over
an eight-year period, and *Fabulya feleségei* (Fabulya's Wives, 1959), a novel. These works indicated that Mándy would continue to explore the
places and people he had known intimately as a
child and young adult: the suburbs, the hotels,
the tenement houses, the second-hand clothing
stalls and the fleamarket that once existed in
Teleki Square and its environs, the coffeehouses,
the football fields, and the world of radio and
journalism—places inhabited mainly by drifters,
derelicts and social castaways, by has-been actors and actresses, failed professionals and intellectuals, all victims of vicissitudes that foredoom
them to make their way as best they can, suspended between the real and the unreal, overwhelmed by circumstances, and unable to hold

ture a satisfying relation-
an being. His absorption
an beings" led critics to
eing exclusively concerned
, wastrels and worthless hu-
some, like István Gáll, laud-
assion for the unfortunate.
litical assault of party-liners on
was aggressive and threatening.
t critics faulted him for failing to
the successes of socialism and report the revolution. Five years later,
the occasion of his receiving the At-
Prize, an enormous change in attitude
ly taken place. The official citation
. . . we feel that the one who wrote
oks made a holy vow never in any shape
or for any price to write anything other
he truth. From his first book to his latest,
s what he has written. . . . To work, to re-
faithful, and to write the truth as he
. . . , this is the reason why his work be-
me one of those very rare moments in Hun-
arian prose."

The publicaton of *Egyérintő* (The One-touch
Game, 1969), a 750-page anthology of selections
from his five books of short stories published
from 1949 to 1967, contributed to a much wider
appreciation of Mándy's creative powers. Reading the output of nearly twenty years within its
covers helped both critics and readers to overcome their tendency to dismiss his writings as
stylistically monotonous, one-dimensional in
characters, and devoid of useful human statement. They saw the many hues, the homogene-
ity of restrained tone, the blend of drama and
lyricism, the concreteness and word economy,
the use of atmosphere to unify the stories, and
the scenes flashing by as if projected on the silver
screen. Some reviewers also noted that the volume revealed significant modifications of earlier
practices, citing particularly a sharpening in his
narrative technique and a heightened realism.
Despite these changes, Mándy retains his economic style, the short, sometimes fragmentary
sentences so characteristic of his writings that, as
one reviewer observed, if Hungary has a prose
writer today "who can be unmistakably indentified on the basis of just one or two sentences,
Iván Mándy is that writer."

His landmark anthology *Egyérintő* includes
stories from *Régi idők mozija* (Old-Time Movies,
1967), remarkable evocations of the dream
world of the silents through the eyes of a boy approaching adolescence. They paint the picture
of a poor youth feasting on the magical world
projected on the screens of the little movie houses dotting Budapest in the twenties and thirties,

in which Mándy and his father habitually sought
a refuge from their own unsettled existence. The
youthful narrator recreates that fantasy world
beyond all historical reality in stories about movie stars, including Rudolph Valentino and Vilma
Banky, Greta Garbo and John Gilbert, the Gish
sisters, Charlie Chaplin, Erich von Stroheim,
Rin-Tin-Tin, Clive Brook ("the Great Bitter
One"), among many others. Foreign luminaries
enliven these pages. These stories and those in
Zsámboky mozija (Zsámboky's Movies, 1975), in
which Mándy's ever-present alter ego lives intimately as a member of the stars' families instead
of his parents', help to explain how the art of the
film happened to influence Mándy more extensively than any other Hungarian author.

In the 1970s, Mándy showed an increased interest in short-story cycles and novel-length
works. His *Mi van Verával?* (What's Up with
Vera?, 1970) and *Mi az öreg?* (What's Up, Old
Man?, 1972) reflect this tendency. In the first,
the characters in the story cycle are so connected
that the portrayal of a young girl completely uninhibited in her behavior and not defined by the
milieu of the 1960s comes close to being a novel,
while in the second, the material for a novel is
developed in the form of linked short-story accounts of a family's history, that of Mándy and
his parents, his most extensive retelling of their
life together. He also completed two novels in
this decade, drawing upon the dream techniques
of surrealism. *Egy ember álma* (One Man's
Dream, 1971) follows a character who dreams he
is a doctor during the historical events occurring
between the fall of the Hungarian Soviet Republic in 1919 and World War II, freeing Mándy in
a unique way from narrative restrictions to validate the absurdities present in the dream. *Álom
a színházban* (A Dream about a Theater, 1977),
in which Mándy summons up the chief characters from his earlier writings, portrays a playwright preparing for an opening who is tortured
by strange and depressing dreams stemming
from his anxieties about the success of the production.

Since 1975 Mándy has been increasingly preoccupied by concrete objects as distinct entities,
a trait already strongly present in his novels and
stories of the 1940s. Objects now move to the
center of his works as anthropomorphic presences, sharing in situations resembling those in
his short stories to develop recurring motifs. In
Tájak, az én tájaim (Land, My Lands, 1981), a
laundry, an elevator, a tobacco shop, furniture,
trams, and wash basins and water closets become
the means by which Mándy approaches his past.
For instance, the tobacco shop resurrects his
times in the suburbs, trams the stifling atmosphere of his childhood, and the wash basins and

water closets the pain he and his parents help-lessly inflicted on each other. His dramatic and lyrical treatment of furniture in *A bútorok* (The Furniture, 1978) makes that book of stories par-ticularly effective. In connection with this "novelette," Mándy maintains that pieces of fur-niture know much about people, that they par-ticipate in their lives and take on their sorrows, and that at times they even resemble them. He gives various sorts of furniture human disposi-tions and moods. Their most troubling experi-ence is to be cast out, to feel superfluous, and to sense their dissolution. Each brief story contrib-utes to the development of painful, truly human scenes.

On the other hand, the selections in *Átkelés* (Crossing, 1983) are miscellaneous. Even so, the epigraph of the opening story suggests a unify-ing principle in a greeting to the young genera-tion of Hungarian prosewriters: "An old player, who, however, will not yet leave the field, greets affectionately the young—but hardly youth-ful—members of the selected team." The stories are haunted by ghosts from Mándy's past, espe-cially his father's, and filled with objects. In a ra-dio play, the by-now legendary János Zsámboky dies, but his voice remains in the telephone and keeps on talking. In this volume is found Mándy's semi-fictional study of Sylvia Plath, built on his responses to photographs included in the edition of her letters edited by her mother. Also new is the treatment of recent historical events.

In his later years Mándy gained the admira-tion of Heinrich Böll, and in 1988 won the presti-gious Kossuth Prize. Critics keep reaching for images to praise him: his characters are "candleflames passing easily between the fingers," his stories "pieces of crystal etched from within." One reviewer places him among those few modern writers who make "no conces-sions to formal or substantial truth . . . and yet remain comprehensible and entertaining, even amusing," and claims that, unlike most other practitioners of the grotesque, "his visions are neither caricature nor satire, they do not express anger, bitterness, or despair but serve rather as a means to sympathy and even identification" with his simple heroes. And indeed, his compas-sion for the troubled, the trapped, the aban-doned, the lonely—whether human beings or objects, however ignoble, often ironically, mock-ingly portrayed—is the element that binds his prolific lifework into a harmonious whole.

WORKS IN ENGLISH TRANSLATION: Selected stories by Mándy were translated into English by Albert Tezla, 1988, with the title *On the Balcony.*

ABOUT: Tezla, A. Hungarian Authors: A Bibliographical Handbook, 1970. *Periodicals*—New Hungarian Quar-terly Winter 1980; World Literature Today Autumn 1981, Autumn 1984.

*MANO, D. KEITH (February 12, 1942–   ), American novelist, journalist, and playwright, writes: "I was born in New York City. For the first ten years of my life, we resided at 45 Thayer Street in Manhattan's Inwood section. I attended Hunter College Elementary School, and went on to Trinity High. I received a B.A. summa cum laude from Columbia College in 1963, and was the Kellett Fellow to Clare College, Cambridge. It was there that I began my first novel, *Bishop's Progress*, which was published when I was twen-ty-six.

"For twenty years, I was vice president of X-Pando Corporation, a family cement factory in Long Island City. From 1968 through 1973 I published a novel every year. I then spent nine years writing *Take Five*, which was published in 1982.

"During this long period I also wrote more than 600 magazine articles and columns. I have been book columnist for *Esquire*, film critic for *OUI* magazine and regular reviewer for the *New York Times Book Review*. I'm the only writer ever to be listed as contributing editor on the mastheads of both *Playboy* and *National Review* (for *NR* I have done a regular column, 'The Gimlet Eye,' for more than fifteen years).

"Recently I have begun writing for perfor-mance. In 1984 I wrote my first play, *Resistance*, which was performed at Writers Theatre and at The Williamstown Theatre Festival. I have also written episodes for *St. Elsewhere*.

"I am married to Broadway actress Laurie Kennedy, and I have two children, Roderick and Christopher, by a previous marriage.

"As a novelist I am a conservative, committed to Western traditions. I consider myself a Chris-tian writer, though some reviewers have called me a Christian pornographer. In my novels I have tried to relate traditional Christianity to the concerns of the modern world.

"*Bishop's Progress* dealt with progress and the Christian. *Horn* with civil rights and the Chris-tian. *War Is Heaven!* with the Christian and war. *The Death and Life of Harry Goth* with the Christian and death. *The Proselytizer* with the Christian and sexuality. *The Bridge* with the Christian and environmentalism. And *Take Five* presents a man who loses his five senses one after another, until he is left a shimmering spot in ab-solute nothingness—at which point one either finds God or goes mad. Or both.

°ma´ nō

D. KEITH MANO

"My novels are realistic in one sense. They deal very explicitly with sex, drugs and bodily functions. But reality is a subterfuge for me—well, all reality is a subterfuge. For me, real things are one term of a metaphor. The minor term—and they imply something greater. I haven't given up the medieval world view and the three-tiered universe."

———

In May 1988 on the eve of the off-Broadway opening of his play *Resistance*, D. Keith Mano described himself to an interviewer for the *New York Times*: "I'm a writer who gets a crazy vision and who follows it through." Whether his visions are crazy or prophetic is for the reader to decide, but Mano's stubborn determination to follow them through has cost him popular success and the income that accompanies it. After a brilliant early start with *Bishop's Progress*, Mano published five novels in five years—all of them with respectful critical attention but dismal sales records. When nearly ten years later his next novel, *Take Five*, was published, it followed the same course, with the result that he was unable to secure a contract for another novel. The problem, he speculates, is that "I've come to be associated with serious novels."

Serious in theme but also wildly eccentric and often full of black humor, his novels disturb even his most admiring critics. They are moral in the most profound sense, tackling religious and ethical issues that rarely figure in contemporary American fiction. Mano writes with passionate conviction, raging against what he sees as the erosion of Christian values by the liberalizing of American political and religious beliefs and institutions. For many years a member of the Episcopalian church, he came into conflict with his bishop over questions of the new liturgy, the ordination of women, and the open acceptance of homosexuality. (That bishop may have been the unnamed but "well known" liberal clergyman whom Mano described in one of his columns in the *National Review* as a man whose "grey-white hair has been blow-dried by, I guess, the winds of change.") In 1979 Mano left his church and joined the American Orthodox church, an offshoot of the Russian Orthodox church.

Bishop's Progress, with its title's echo of Bunyan's *The Pilgrim's Progress*, is the story of a prominent liberal Episcopalian clergyman who enters a hospital for heart surgery. Exposed not only to his own physical vulnerability but to the sufferings of others, he is confronted by the forces of science in the person of his attractive but threateningly Mephistophelean surgeon. The doctor seems to represent the forces of worldly humanism that have undermined modern-day Christianity. In contrast to him are the bishop's fellow patients whose needs convince him of the falsity of his own religious views. Humbled and contrite, the bishop repudiates his easy-going liberal Christianity and for the first time realizes the true nature of his faith and his vocation. A morality play in essence, the novel treats its spiritual subject in earthy physical detail. The reader is spared none of the clinical details of hospital treatment, and several reviewers complained that the gruesome descriptions detracted from the highminded themes of the book. But R. V. Cassill, in the *New York Times Book Review*, reconciled these apparent incongruities: "The luminous talents of D. Keith Mano have produced a work which is, at the same time, witty, disturbing, entertaining, grave, full of suspense, and a prolonged meditation on the riddle of faith in our epoch."

A clergyman also figures as the protagonist of Mano's second novel, *Horn*. This time he faces the sordid and terrifying realities of a church in Harlem and a Black Power movement headed by a former boxer who has a hornlike growth on his forehead. The real menace, however, is the liberal white minister of a neighboring church, and the central character comes to respect the black leader even as he rejects the man's radical philosophy. *Horn* is far more violent and grotesque than its predecessor, but in spite of its excesses it leaves "a residue of warmth," Stephen F. Caldwell wrote in the *New York Times Book Review*, a sense of human decency that surmounts self-serving hypocrisy. A similar but less clearly resolved confrontation occurs in *War Is Heaven!*, described by Frank Day in the *Dictionary of Literary Biography* as "Mano's apology for America's military role in Vietnam." The scene is a fictitious Central American country, and the novel sets an upright American army sergeant leading a small troop in combat with Communist guerrillas against a young black soldier who is bitterly opposed to the war. The mission fails and the sergeant dies, but the causes he advocates—religion and personal freedom—are affirmed. The book's "grandness of conception," Stephen F. Caldwell wrote in the *New York Times Book Review*, "tires and rubs instead of edifying, enlightening, pleasing, saving."

Absent from *War Is Heaven!* is the bizarre Rabelaisian humor that lightens other novels by Mano. Probably the best of them is *The Death and Life of Harry Goth*—"a funeral ship, heavily laden with pathos and parable . . . buffeted by howling gales of laughter," as Tom McHale described it in the *New York Times Book Review*. This chronicle of the Goth family—which owns a business that manufactures toilet brushes—is a saga of madness told in a series of grisly but often hilarious episodes. Harry Goth, one of five brothers, is misdiagnosed for a minor illness and believes that he is dying. He had wild adventures in funeral parlors, peep shows, and a monastery, while the other members of his family undergo even more nightmarish experiences. Mano, Geoffrey Wolff wrote in the *New York Times Book Review*, "loves those mutilated and misbegotten grotesques on call at penny wages from The Black Comedians' Theatrical Agency. For the sake of bet-you-can't metaphors, zanies abound, and dance all the Gothic steps. . . . Just a little too much is just enough for Mr. Mano. Not for him peace and quiet, the ordinary. He cherishes crises, calamity and farce; he drives at full throttle, straight pipes howling." According to Wolff, Mano's paradoxical fictions are characterized "by an unfashionable partiality toward the grand moral conundrum (What does it *all* mean?) and prose that is sometimes mannered, sometimes strained beyond its inherent strength, always fully-written, bold, inventive."

The inventiveness and exuberance that balance the grimness of Mano's vision are less conspicuous in *The Proselytizer*, a scathing portrait of a popular evangelist. More imaginative is *The Bridge*, set in the distant future after most of mankind has committed mass suicide in an excess of ecological zeal, convinced, Mano writes, "that man in good conscience can no longer permit this wanton destruction of our fellow creatures, whose right to exist is fully as great as

ours." The few surviving human beings are reduced to cannibalism in a grotesque parody of the Christian Holy Communion. Although some reviewers found Mano's satire effective—especially his barbs directed at group "sensitivity sessions"—they objected to his heavy-handedness. "His overdrawn characters tend to be mere mouthpieces for ideas," Martha Duffy wrote in *Time*. *Take Five*, published almost ten years later, showed no diminishment in Mano's boisterous style nor in the nightmare situations he is capable of inventing. Told in flashback by a character who has literally disappeared, having lost his five senses, the novel reconstructs a process of transcendence. "No man has ever found a crazier way to write a book about the Christian faith," Hugh Kenner commented in the *National Review*,

Mano has a longstanding interest in theater (while a graduate student in England he acted with the Marlowe Society) and is married to the actress Laurie Kennedy. *Resistance*, his first play, was written on a dare by his wife. Like his novels it pits the forces of good and evil against each other. The hero, a writer who has just won the Nobel Prize for Literature, is a devout Christian and an anti-Communist. When the fictional island in the Caribbean where he lives is taken over by a group of Communist insurgents, he is captured and confronted by a K.G.B. agent who attempts to force him to endorse the rebels. The play centers on the clash of two strong wills and the terrible pressures put on the writer to abjure his beliefs. Mano told an interviewer for the *New York Times* that his two principal characters "are great opponents because they have so much in common. So much of the Communist technique is borrowed from Christian technique; self-criticism sessions, for instance, are very similar to confession. The placing of one's rewards in the future; they both share that. And they both require a great deal of self-sacrifice from their devotees." *New York Times* drama reviewer Walter Goodman found the play more a "domestic drama" than "the duel of mind and spirit" one would have expected from the subject. "The writing," Goodman commented, "is smart, but to little effect . . . [with] wild swings from earnest encounters to melodramatic excesses to flat-out farce."

In his magazine writing Mano makes no more effort than in his novels to conceal his contempt for much that modern society stands for, but as in the novels he writes with such zeal and zest that even readers who strongly disagree with him enjoy reading him. C. H. Simonds, who interviewed him for the *National Review* in 1983, described him as hearty, "madly merry, on high simmer." At various times Mano has lived on an island in the Caribbean and in rural Rockland County in upstate New York, but his main base has always been New York City.

PRINCIPAL WORKS: Bishop's Progress, 1968; Horn, 1969; War Is Heaven!, 1970; The Death and Life of Harry Goth, 1971; The Proselytizer, 1972; The Bridge, 1973; Take Five, 1982.

ABOUT: Contemporary Authors 25–28, 1977; Contemporary Authors Autobiography Series 6, 1988; Contemporary Literary Criticism 2, 1974; 10, 1979; Dictionary of Literary Biography 6, 1980. Periodicals—National Review September 18, 1981; June 11, 1982; May 27, 1983; New York Review of Books June 10, 1982; New York Times May 29, 1988; June 8, 1988; New York Times Book Review February 18, 1968; March 9, 1969; June 21, 1970; March 14, 1971; April 23, 1972; May 23, 1982; Time September 10, 1973.

*MARECHERA,   DAMBUDZO   (1952– August 18, 1987), Zimbabwean novelist, short-story writer, and poet, established himself on the London literary scene, through both his writings and his defiantly marginal lifestyle, as the angry young man of colonial exile. Following independence he returned to Zimbabwe, but neither his rage nor his defiance abated, and after one more published work and numerous brushes with the Establishment, he succumbed to pneumonia at the age of thirty-five. Many of the details of Marechera's life, and often the most sordid ones, emerge from his writings, notably the novella "The House of Hunger" in the collection of the same name and his last published work, Mindblast. Born in the rural Rhodesian town of Rusape, he grew up with his nine brothers and sisters in a run-down three-room house. His father was a trucker, his mother a domestic, and, as he writes in "House of Hunger," their relationship was always troubled:

> I knew my father only as the character who occasionally screwed mother and who paid the rent, beat me up, and was cuckolded on the sly by various persons. He drove huge cargo lorries, transporting groundnut oil to Zambia and Zaire and Malawi. I knew that he was despised because of mother, and because he always wore khaki overalls, even on Sundays, and because he was quite generous with money to friends and enemies alike. The only thing was that he was an alcoholic.

The father died in an accident when Marechera was eleven, and his mother turned to prostitution to support the family. His own escape from the poverty and violence around him came through literature; it was, he recalls, the gap between the world he lived in and the ones he read about that impelled him to start writing. "I was

mesmerized by books at an early age," he indicates in Mindblast, adding with the deadpan irony that laces his works, "I obtained my first one—Arthur Mee's Children's Encyclopedia— at the local rubbish dump where garbage from the white side of town was dumped every day except Sundays." But, as he came to recognize, the very fact of knowing English cut him off from his family, and also from himself. Again, in "The House of Hunger" he recounts an incident where his autobiographical hero comes home one day full of excitement:

> I burst into the room and all at once exploded into my story, telling it restlessly and with expansive gestures, telling it to mother who was staring. A stinging slap that made my ear sing stopped me. I stared up at mother in confusion. She hit me again. "How dare you speak in English to me," she said crossly. "You know I don't understand it, and you think because you're educated—" She hit me again. "I am not speaking in Eng—" I began, but stopped as I suddenly realised that I was talking to her in English. I rushed out of the room. . . .

After attending a mission boarding school on scholarship, Marechera enrolled in the University of Rhodesia, where he edited a student magazine and published two small volumes of poetry but wound up getting expelled for his involvement in a riot over the wages of black workers on campus. He then received a scholarship to Oxford's New College and in 1974 set out for England. His mission-school background had left him with a strong respect for education, but at Oxford, "I was suddenly among people who didn't give a damn about hard work," he told the Guardian in a 1979 interview, adding, "You came out with your whole mind concussed." In reaction to the indifference of his tutors (in his words, "effortless guardsman doing the minimum), he tried to burn down New College, refused the administration's ultimatum that he undergo psychiatric treatment, and was expelled in 1977.

A brief stay at the University of Sheffield as writer-in-residence permitted Marechera to complete the manuscript that was to become The House of Hunger. He then made his way to London, where he sometimes hung out with Rastafarians, sometimes squatted in a North London tenement, and sometimes lived in the street, but always dragged his typewriter with him from place to place and kept writing. Finally, after three months in a Welsh jail (without typewriter) for possession of marijuana, he learned that The House of Hunger had been accepted for publication in Heinemann's African Writers Series.

This collection of stories set in pre-independence Rhodesia was, he later explained, "about the brutalisation of the individual's feel-

°ma re chér a, dam bŏod´ zō

ings, instincts, mental processes—the brutalisation of all this in such a way that you come to the point where, among ourselves in the Black urban areas, that is ordinary reality." Unlike more militant African fiction, Marechera's stories deal with neither the ruling white minority nor the fighters engaged in the liberation struggle, but rather, probe the deep inner states of people who are clearly extensions of himself— the young boy of "House of Hunger," a poet, a journalist, an academic in exile. In his view, he explained in a BBC interview, the problem in Southern Africa was to write

> about racialism, fascism, Black township life without appearing to write documentary novels, rather than actual fiction. I tried to find a style whereby I could actually use the facts which everybody knows in such a way that the fiction emanated, as it were, from the basic facts. In *The House of Hunger* I do not preach about politics, I do not preach about anything at all. I merely state what the House of Hunger, Zimbabwe, is like.

The resulting texts, as polished in their form as they were brutal in their content, sent waves through London's literary circles. As Angela Carter wrote in the *Guardian*, the stories were uneven in quality, "but it is rare to find a writer for whom imaginative fiction is such a passionate and intimate process of engagement with the world. A terrible beauty is born out of the urgency of his vision." And no less a writer than Doris Lessing (herself born in Rhodesia) began a lengthy review in *Books and Bookmen* with the observation: "The book is an explosion. It fuses a number of themes, any one of which would have been enough to make an ordinary adequate kind of book, in rage and poetry, laughter and obscenity." Writer and book, she continued, "are both in the nature of miracles. Hard for anyone to become a writer, but to do it against such handicaps?"

In spite of his success, Marechera himself remained impoverished, anguished, and, as he was soon to demonstrate, utterly contemptuous of the literary establishment now courting him. Named joint winner of the 1979 Guardian Prize for Literature, he turned the award ceremony into a brawl by throwing a stack of plates across the room followed by a chair apparently aimed at the *Guardian*'s literary editor. "I hadn't eaten anything for three days, and there were people eating themselves sick in my honour," he later commented in a *Sunday Times* interview.

A year later, Marechera was back in the same literary circles with *Black Sunlight*, a work that, in the words of *New Statesman* critic James Lasdun, "falls between fiction and chaos." A stream of consciousness and verbiage penned as a novel, *Black Sunlight* follows a photojournalist (point

edly named Christian) as he descends into the hell of a revolutionary guerrilla organization (Black Sunlight) which seeks to "transform the nature of available reality" by planting a bomb in a cathedral. Once again, the very explosiveness of the text—it culminates in a hallucinatory evocation of debauchery and death, followed by a list of all the authors who influenced Marechera, from Homer to Marinetti—drew the attention of the critics. But this time, there was a general consensus that, notwithstanding what Lasdun called "the makings of an extraordinary piece of fiction," the work did not really hold together. Marechera, wrote Faith Pullin in *British Book News*, demonstrated a "Burgess-like intoxication with language but does not yet possess Burgess' control and technique." Nonetheless, she concluded that if *Black Sunlight* was "often irritating in its exhibitionism . . . there is no doubt that it is the work of a writer of great potential and future achievement."

Shortly after the publication of *Black Sunlight* and (more to the point) eighteen months after Zimbabwe became independent, Marechera returned home. The occasion, or at least the free plane ticket, came from a TV program that was supposed to combine dramatized excerpts from *The House of Hunger* with a reportage on the author's reunion with his family. In an interview with the *Sunday Times* just before his departure, he announced that he was going because he wanted to find his mother and tell her what he'd been doing for the past ten years. Asked if he thought he'd fit in in Zimbabwe, he replied, "I don't know. I doubt it." The interviewer, Stephen Pile, commented that the writer was "probably the unhappiest person I have ever met."

True to form, Marechera arrived in the Zimbabwean capital, Harare, to learn that *Black Sunlight* had been banned for obscenity; he promptly blew up, disrupting the filming with a barrage of insults directed at the filmmaker and a member of the crew who was a former liberation fighter. The ban was subsequently lifted, but Marechera's life remained much as it had been in London—according to friends, he slept days, worked nights, and was usually dead drunk by morning. Often jobless and homeless, he spent considerable periods of time camped out in Harare's Cecil Square. When he was invited to a 1982 writers' festival in Berlin, he arrived without a passport and was jailed for nine hours, but wound up being escorted to the festival in a chauffeur-driven car and welcomed by fellow writers with a standing ovation. A year later, at the first Zimbabwe International Book Fair, his disruptive behavior got him another free ride, but this time it was in the car of a government minister, whose bodyguards apparently beat him up en route.

Marechera's literary outpourings of the period appeared in 1984 under the title *Mindblast, or the Definitive Buddy*, a collection of four short plays, a prose narrative, poems, and an appendix of excerpts from the journal he kept while living in Cecil Square. Just as *The House of Hunger* took its dual point of departure from the general situation in pre-independence Rhodesia and the writer's own experiences, *Mindblast* was an explosive response to the conditions Marechera found on his return—the independent state, its new elite, the general situation of the writer, and also his own abysmally negative experience. As he writes in the poem called "Throne of Bayonets":

> From all around I hear dark:
> Dread:
> > You think you are a poet
> > You are black and buggered

Published by a local press (before his departure from London, Marechera had been banned from the premises of Heinemann's following a brawl over royalties), the book was released in time for the second Zimbabwe Book Fair in August 1984; after an interview with two Dutch journalists, Marechera was arrested on the orders of the Central Intelligence Organization and detained, without charges, until the fair was over. According to David Caute, who devoted a lengthy essay, "Marechera and the Colonel: A Zimbabwean Writer and the Claims of the State," to the affair, neither Marechera's publisher nor his fellow writers nor even his lawyer came to his defense. "Marechera is a law unto himself," Caute observes. "Only the devil would write [him] a reference. His life is a model of bad behaviour but his intelligence acute, and his fiction is among the most arresting (if the pun may be excused) in contemporary Africa."

After the arrest, Marechera's publisher turned down his next novel, "The Depths of Diamonds," citing (rather unconvincingly, according to Caute) a limited audience and possible obscenity problems. He was also fired from a teaching job at People's College—"The CIO [Central Intelligence Organization] kept coming and questioning the staff and students to find out what I was saying about Antony and Cleopatra," he told Caute—and in a more direct form of harassment, he was beaten up by an army colonel in a Holiday Inn bathroom (thus the title of Caute's essay).

Along with his already precarious mental state, Marechera's health declined, and on August 18, 1987, he died in a Harare hospital. According to literary critic M. Z. Malaba, writing in the *Journal of Commonwealth Literature* after Marechera's death, "although he lacked the artistic discipline of [Zimbabwean writers] Mungoshi and Nyamfukudza, his flamboyant style caught the imagination of Europe." But, he continues, "what many Zimbabweans lament is his failure to channel his considerable talents in a more constructive manner." Yet for other observers, this departure from the norms of African literature was also his strength. In a 1986 essay, for example, his friend and literary biographer Flora Wild acknowledged that "his writing is full of contradictions and paradoxes. It disturbs the mind, it disrupts realities and patterns of thought so far taken for granted." But at the same time, she pointed out, "it creates pictures of striking beauty and lucidity, opening new horizons and dimensions of feeling, of grasping, of sensing life." And in an obituary for the *Journal of Commonwealth Literature*, another friend and critic, Robert Fraser, concluded that "Marechera's existence was one restless odyssey of risk . . . Peacock brilliant, his words were as vibrant on paper as in the flesh. *The House of Hunger, Black Sunlight, Mindblast* poured from his typewriter like sorties in some guerrilla campaign against the literal-mindedness of the bureaucrats and the insipid dullness of everything."

PRINCIPAL WORKS: The House of Hunger, 1978; Black Sunlight, 1980; Mindblast, or the Definitive Buddy, 1984. *Essay*—"Black and White: Why There Will Be Race Riots," Sunday Times August 10, 1980.

ABOUT: Caute, D. The Espionage of the Saints, 1986; Contemporary Novelists, 4th ed., 1986; Zell, H. M., C. Bundy, and V. Coulon. A New Reader's Guide to African Literature, 1983. *Periodicals*—African Literature Today 13, 1983; Books and Bookmen June 1979; British Book News, April 1981; Journal of Commonwealth Literature nos. 1 and 2, 1988; London Times January 24, 1982; August 20, 1987; New African April 1986; Times Literary Supplement January 2, 1981; World Literature Today Winter 1982.

MASON, BOBBIE ANN (May 1, 1940–   ), American novelist and short-story writer, writes: "Early in my childhood I was passionate about jigsaw puzzles, I concentrated intensely on them, and my mother tells how angry I would get when I got frustrated that the pieces wouldn't fit. My impulse to write owes something to the pleasure I enjoyed as a child fitting those pieces together in a coherent design. I have learned that writing is a discovery of designs, a piecing together of disparate parts into something that

BOBBIE ANN MASON

has a shape, a continuity, if not meaning. I seem to start with surfaces—physical details, settings, the particularities of daily life. In fooling around with them, I start on a quest for my characters' lives. What are their favorite foods and how do they dress? Just who are they? What do they care about? Eventually, I get into their emotional lives and ultimately the emotional content of the story emerges from somewhere in my subconscious. I have always found it difficult to start with a definite idea about a character, or even a definite emotion. If I start out to write about a marriage, say, that is troubled by a rebellious child, I can never quite find the setting or the physical characteristics that define their world. In so doing, I start going down other roads. But if I start with a pond that is being drained because of a diesel fuel leak, and a cow named Hortense, and some blackbirds flying over, and a woman in the distance waving, then I might get somewhere. I might find out that her marriage is in trouble because their child has just been arrested, but then I might not. It might be that she is waving to her husband to come quickly because she has just learned that her mother is ill, and she will have to make an urgent trip, far away. For me, writing is a way of exploring what is hidden, discovering a design, rather than imposing one on the world. What is especially interesting in these explorations is how chaotic everything is, how meaningless coincidences and superficial designs are. I like to think of myself as an adventurer, willing to confront the possibility that the pieces aren't going to fit together."

Born in Mayfield, Kentucky to Christie and Wilburn Arnett Mason and raised on a dairy farm, Bobbie Ann Mason is a writer of the "new" South. Her characters are not haunted by memories of the romantic antebellum South nor are they obsessed with the brooding guilt of their complex psyches. Working-class people—carpenters, truck drivers, saleswomen in the local drugstores—they are struggling with the routines and pressures of ordinary contemporary life. Their lives are defined by small circumstances. They are trying to cope with the problems of loneliness, disintegrating marriages, rebellious children, aging parents. They watch television, listen to country music and Bruce Springsteen, eat pizza and Doritos, shop at Kroger's and K-Mart, and are in no way remarkable other than in the simple fact of their humanity. Reviewers of Mason's work have found it ironic that most of her short stories were first published in magazines like the *New Yorker*, *Atlantic*, *Virginia Quarterly Review*, and *Paris Review*, where they were read and admired by a predominantly sophisticated, upper-middle-class public seemingly alien to the people she writes about. But as Robert Towers pointed out in the *New York Review of Books*, "she is one of those rare writers who, by concentrating their attention on a few square miles of native turf, are able to open up new and surprisingly wide worlds. . . ." Her recurring themes of "loss and deprivation, the disappointment of modest hopes," in David Quammen's phrase in the *New York Times Book Review*, are universal. "She portrays the disquieted lives of men and women not blessed with much money or education or luck, but cursed with enough sensitivity and imagination to allow them to suffer regrets." Mason herself describes her characters as "kind of naive and optimistic for the most part; they think better times are coming, and most of them embrace progress. But I think they reflect the tension that's in the culture between hanging on to the past and racing toward the future."

The "new" South is probably summed up in the reflections of Mason's character Leroy, a truck driver temporarily disabled by an accident, who in her story "Shiloh" reflects on the bewildering changes in the region where he has lived all his life: "Now that Leroy has come home to stay, he notices how much the town has changed. Subdivisions are spreading across Kentucky like an oil slick. The sign at the edge of town says 'Pop. 11,500'—only seven hundred more than it said twenty years before. Leroy can't figure out who is living in all the new houses. The farmers who used to gather around the courthouse square on Saturday afternoons to play checkers and spit tobacco juice have gone.

It has been years since Leroy has thought about the farmers, and they have disappeared without his noticing." Disaffected, unable really to communicate with his restless wife Norma Jean, both of them still grieving over the death of their baby some years earlier, Leroy helplessly contemplates the breaking up of their marriage: "Now Leroy has the sudden impulse to tell Norma Jean about himself, as if he had just met her. They have known each other so long they have forgotten a lot about each other. They could become reacquainted. But when the oven timer goes off and she runs to the kitchen, he forgets why he wants to do this."

Having majored in English and journalism at the University of Kentucky (B.A. 1962), with an M.A. in English from the State University of New York in Buffalo (1966), Mason did not begin writing fiction until she had completed a Ph.D. in English at the University of Connecticut in 1972. Her doctoral dissertation, published four years later as *Nabokov's Garden: A Guide to ADA*, was an impressively learned study of the imagery of gardens and insect life in Vladimir Nabokov's allusive and symbolic novel *Ada* in which she covered a wide ranging body of writing and painting—books on botany and entomology, the writings of the eighteenth-century naturalist Erasmus Darwin, Arabic erotica, the flower paintings of Jan Breughel and Hieronymus Bosch's "Garden of Earthly Delights," the English metaphysical poets—on all of whom Nabokov had drawn in his novel. Nothing could be more remote from this than the simple realism of her own fiction. But, as Mason told an interviewer for *Publishers Weekly* : "I was so sick of reading about the alienated hero of superior sensibility that I thought I would write about just the opposite."

The "opposite" certainly characterizes the background that Mason brought to her fiction. She grew up in the 1950s infatuated with pop culture, movies, country music, and early rock and roll. Sounding not unlike one of her characters, she recalled in an essay published in *A World Unsuspected* her experiences as a fifteen-year-old "fifties groupie"—organizing a fan club for a Kentucky singing quartet called the Hilltoppers: "I was a shy, backward, anti-social country kid living on a farm near Mayfield, Kentucky, a hundred and fifty miles from the nearest city, Nashville, but I was ambitious and determined to hit the big time—or at least meet somebody famous." After college she moved to New York for a few years and wrote for magazines like *Movie Stars, Movie Life,* and *TV Star Parade.*

This double life divided between academia

(she taught journalism part time at Mansfield State College in Pennsylvania from 1972 to 1979) and pop culture offered unique preparation for the fiction she began publishing in 1980 when her first story, "Offerings," appeared in the *New Yorker.* Her stories, like those of other *New Yorker* writers of her generation—the so-called "minimalists" Ann Beattie, Jayne Anne Phillips, Raymond Carver—are marked by much surface detail, mannerisms of style like open endings and the use of present-tense narrative—qualities which some reviewers fault as thin and superficial. But Mason's distinction, Michiko Kakutani pointed out in the *New York Times,* is "her desire to locate some sort of pattern or meaning in her people's spiritual malaise." She is more poignant and poetic than most of her contemporaries, but she is never sentimental, and she is often genuinely funny in capturing the speech and habits of her characters.

The publication of *Shiloh and Other Stories* and the generally enthusiastic critical reception of the book established Mason as one of the most promising of younger American writers. The title story had already been selected for the *Best American Short Stories of 1981*; the book won the Ernest Hemingway Foundation Prize for the best first fiction in 1982. It was also nominated for the National Book Critics Circle Award, the American Book Award, and the PEN/Faulkner Award. By 1983 another of her short stories, "Graveyard Day," was included in *Best American Short Stories* as well as in the annual anthology of best small-press writing, *The Pushcart Prize.* In 1986 her "Big Bertha Stories" was selected for the O. Henry Award. She has received grants from the National Endowment for the Arts (1983), the Pennsylvania Council on the Arts (1983), and the Guggenheim Foundation (1984).

In Country, Mason's first novel, is narrated by a seventeen-year-old Kentucky girl, Sam (Samantha), who drives with her uncle, a Vietnam veteran, and her grandmother to Washington, D.C. to see the Vietnam Memorial. Her father, whom she never knew, had been killed in Vietnam; her mother has remarried and begun a new life. Sam lives with her uncle, a chain-smoking, hard-drinking man who may be the victim of Agent Orange. Cool and self-possessed on the surface, devoted to pop culture and television, Sam remains a little girl at heart, hungry for love, curious about sex, longing to establish some kind of communion with her long-dead father and to find some meaning in the war in which he died. "It is a measure of Miss Mason's skill," Joel Conarroe wrote of *In Country* in the *New York Times Book Review,* "that despite her protagonist's minimal exposure to anything that is not banal she succeeds in communicating, persuasively, a movement toward adulthood and intellectual arousal." The banal certainly dominates Sam's physical world of video games, Burger Kings, Springsteen records, and a host of details that Anne Boston in the *Times Literary Supplement* characterized as "hick chic." Alice Brown, in the *New England Review*, found Mason's vision of America "terrifying, stripping, disheartening" and her characters inarticulate, "anaesthetized, paralyzed." But Michiko Kakutani praised the authenticity of her teenager's voice and the soundness of Sam's characterization: "She [Mason] has also understood and captured the ambivalence of youth: a young woman's craving for both knowledge and pristine ignorance, her need to be both idealistic and cool." *In Country* was made into a film in 1988, directed by Norman Jewison.

It is not only the young, however, who capture Mason's attention. Her short novel *Spence + Lila* focusses on the lives of an older farm couple trying to resist the changes of modern life and now confronting the reality of the wife's cancer. Mason told interviewer Mervyn Rothstein in the *New York Times Magazine* that the story is a kind of homage to her parents: "It's my journey back home." It is also a good deal more—a summary of her vision of life. As the aging husband faces the possible death of his wife, he reflects on the simple reality of being: "Everyone always wants a way out of something like this, but what he has here is the main thing there is—just the way things grow and die, the way the sun comes up and goes down every day. These are the facts of life. They are so simple they are almost impossible to grasp."

It is possible—as some of its reviewers suggested—that the facts of life are over-simple in *Spence + Lila*. While praising Mason's "superb ear for dialogue" and the "smooth, artful writing" of the novel, Frank Conroy, in the *New York Times Book Review*, raised a tantalizing question: "Are simple people really as simple as Spence and Lila suggest?" (Conroy's answer: "I don't think there are any simple people. Not down on the farm, not in the city, not anywhere.") Conroy complains of a kind of shallowness in these characters that prevents the reader from fully grasping their reality: "What happens in the novel is that we wind up watching Bobbie Ann Mason being moved by a love story. She seems to know something about these people that isn't there in the text; she knows, in any event, more than us, and even though we trust her, we feel to some extent abandoned. We feel uneasy, forced to peer around the author to catch quick glimpses of her characters." Michiko

Kakutani, in the *New York Times*, shared some of Conroy's disappointment, finding in *Spence + Lila* "a melodramatic predictability absent from Ms. Mason's earlier works." She was moved, however, by the author's "sure-handed ability to evoke Spence and Lila's life together on the farm that lends their story such poignance and authenticity." And in assessing Mason's collection of short stories, *Love Life*, published a year after *Spence + Lila*, Kakutani suggested that "one of her strengths as a writer [is] that she's able to look beyond the bluff facades of her characters and reveal the geography of their inner lives." Mason's stories, Kakutani concludes, "are not simply minimalist 'slice-of-life' exercises, but finely crafted tales that manage to invest inarticulate, small-town lives with dignity and intimations of meaning."

Although she continues to write mainly about the rural South and has, an interviewer noted, "a brisk Kentucky accent," Mason has lived for a number of years in rural Pennsylvania with her husband Roger Rawlings, a writer, and several cats.

PRINCIPAL WORKS: *Fiction*—Shiloh and Other Stories, 1982; In Country, 1985; Spence + Lila, 1988; Love Life, 1989. *Non-fiction*—The Girl Sleuth: A Feminist Guide to the Bobbsey Twins, Nancy Drew and Their Sisters, 1975; Nabokov's Garden, 1976.

ABOUT: Contemporary Authors New Revision Series 11, 1984; Contemporary Literary Criticism 43, 1987; Current Biography 1989; Harris, A. (ed.) A World Unsuspected: Portraits of Southern Childhood, 1987; Ryan, M. Stopping Places, 1984. *Periodicals*—Nation March 19, 1983; New England Review Summer 1986; New York Review of Books December 16, 1982; November 7, 1985; New York Times September 4, 1985; June 11, 1988; March 3, 1989; New York Times Book Review September 15, 1985; June 26, 1988; March 12, 1989; New York Times Magazine May 15, 1988; Publishers Weekly August 30, 1985; Time January 10, 1983; Times Literary Supplement April 18, 1986.

MATHEWS, HARRY (February 14, 1930 –), American novelist and poet, was born in New York City. His father, Edward Mathews, was an architect, and both his parents, Mathews has written, "had been born into and had remained dues-paying members of the world of Upper East Side WASP respectability." Influenced by his mother, Mary, his maternal grandfather, Henry Burchell, and several outstanding teachers, Mathews early developed a passion for poetry, especially the romantics and Browning, and for classical mythology and verse. He read widely throughout his childhood and began writing his own poetry while attending private

HARRY MATHEWS

schools in New York. He later attended Groton School in Massachusetts and enrolled at Princeton in 1947. After three terms, he enlisted in the Navy for a year, and during this time he married the artist Niki de Saint Phalle, who had been born in France and raised in New York. He then studied music at Harvard (B.A., 1952), where his literary attitudes were shaped by Eugene O'Neill, Jr., with whom he studied Greek tragedy, and by his friendship with such poets as William Meredith and W. S. Merwin. In July 1952 Mathews, his wife, and their baby daughter Laura left for France. There, after a year of musical studies, Mathews, who had quit writing poetry while at Princeton, decided to begin writing again. From 1954 to 1956 he and his family lived in Mallorca, where Mathews got to know the poet Robert Graves and where a son, Philip, was born. They then moved back to Paris and finally settled in the mountain village of Lans-en-Vercours. In 1960 Mathews' marriage ended, but he remained with his children until they had grown up. From 1974 to 1976 he lived in Venice, and after meeting the French writer Marie Chaix he returned to France to live with her and her two daughters. Since 1986 they have lived in Paris, though Mathews, since 1978, has spent half of each year teaching in the United States, at Bennington and at Columbia.

Mathews first published one of his poems in the *Hudson Review* in 1956. In the same year he met the poet John Ashbery, who became a close friend and a decisive influence on his work. Besides imparting a sense of imaginative and linguistic freedom in poetry, Ashbery introduced Mathews to the enigmatic and playful novels of Raymond Roussel, which offered Mathews a way of writing his own fiction. "Reading Roussel brought me several revelations," Mathews has written. "He demonstrated to me that psychology was a dispensable fashion, that the moral responsibilities of writing did not lie in respect of subject matter, and that the writing of prose fiction could be as scrupulously organized as Sir Philip Sidney's double sestina."

After one unsuccessful attempt at a novel, Mathews wrote *The Conversions*, which he has said was influenced by the mythological conjectures of Robert Graves as well as by the word-play and narrative caprices of Roussel. In 1961, Mathews, Ashbery, and Kenneth Koch founded the review *Locus Solus* (named after one of Roussel's novels), in which they published their own work and similarly experimental work during its two years of existence. *Tlooth*, Mathew's impudently inventive second novel, appeared in 1966. Another friendship crucial to his work began in 1970, when he met Georges Perec, a brilliantly eccentric French novelist. Perec introduced him to the group OuLiPo (Ouvroir de littérature potentielle, or Workshop of Potential Literature), which had been founded in 1961 by Raymond Queneau and François LeLionnais; Italo Calvino was another famous member. The group aimed to take a gamelike approach to literature by using elaborate and demanding formal devices; Perec's astonishing novel *La Disparation*, which employs only words that do not contain the letter e, is a notable example.

Mathews, whose work already showed a marked affinity for riddles, paradoxes, mazes, and strange cryptic fragments of learning and legend, took immediately to the group and its experiments. His verse and his shorter fiction, such as *Selected Declarations of Independence* and *Country Cooking and Other Stories*, show the influence most clearly. His third novel, *The Sinking of the Odradek Stadium*, shares with his first two a quest theme and what Mathews has called an "indirect, elaborate, and apparently frustrating approach to experience." This approach, he added, came out of his preoccupation with "the problem of knowledge: what it is, how it can be communicated, and also what it is not and how it can be belied." Mathews believed he had taken this theme as far as it could go, and his novel *Cigarettes*, though still formally intricate, is his most straightforward and realistic work of fiction, reflecting a desire to find mystery and meaning in ordinary human relationships rather than in permutations of language.

The narrative elusiveness inherent in Mathews' approach to fiction has prevented him from becoming a popular novelist, but he has had something of a cult reputation, and critics have found his baroque ambiguities and convolutions challenging and absorbing. His first novel, *The Conversions*, presents his characteristic themes and difficulties and was well received by reviewers. The anonymous narrator of the novel is given a ritual golden adze by an eccentric millionaire named Grent Wayl. The adze has seven mysterious scenes engraved on it, which seem to have both Christian and pagan significance. When Wayl dies, the narrator learns that his will bequeaths his entire fortune to the possessor of the adze, provided he can answer three riddles: (1) When was a stone not a king? (2) What was *La Messe de Sire Fadevant* ? (3) Who shaved the Old Man's beard? The riddles turn out to be connected with the scenes on the adze through multilingual puns and the existence of a secret religious society that used the adze in a coronation ceremony, but the narrator never quite solves them or the connected riddle of his own identity. His quest for the answers, through an exotically imaginative landscape rife with subtle clues and false scents, forms the body of the novel. Terry Southern, writing in the *Nation*, called it a quintessential "poet's novel," "where image, sound and an abstract interplay of values take precedence" and an insistence on a precise meaning would be beside the point. Calling it "a startling piece of work, laced with blue-burning imagery and crystal strands of insinuation," he evoked the digressive, mysterious, but also exuberantly comic texture of the novel: "Ludicrous hoax and cabal abound: nonexistent footnotes, reproductions of forged mss., sections of scientific and musicologist's esoterica, passages in Greek, Latin, Hungarian, obscure Slavic tongues, gibberish, and an eight-page chapter from a German novel—the translation of which must be closely checked against the original for possible error, that no clue be overlooked. The book is, of course, extremely funny."

The reviewer for the *Times Literary Supplement* also emphasized the book's purely imaginative and poetic virtues as opposed to conventional novelistic ones, calling it "fertile in linguistic skylarkings and fantastic invention. It is as exhilarating to read as a fireworks set-piece is to watch. . . . The human creatures which people this acrostic world . . . suit it as the Knave of Clubs suits his twelve fellow-travellers: they are not in any ordinary sense human, but they fit the milieu and strike appropriate attitudes. . . . Mingling not inappropriately with all this wizardry . . . there is a genuine and delightful vein of poetry and small, ancient-marinerish spurts of entrancing ballad narrative. Mr. Mathews is a delightful original."

The *Time* reviewer found the digressive parts greater than the whole: "it all hangs together after a fashion, but some of the pieces might better have stood alone. . . . In a strangely gripping passage, Mathews describes a heaven from which God has been banished. Its inhabitants run things as they did on earth; the rich and the powerful are welcomed, the poor and weak are persecuted. Mathews deftly turns everyday life into a nightmare. His symbolism is brilliant in fragments, but it spreads through the novel like crab grass and tends to choke the narrative."

No critic picked up on what Mathews has spoken of as the "religious underpinning" of *The Conversions*, though it was evinced in the passage about the God-bereft heaven and in the ritual background of the golden adze; since Mathews has said that religious significance was "mostly shoved out of sight" in his second novel, *Tlooth*, it is not surprising that critics tended to see it too in terms of a purely literary puzzle. "The whole novel is an elaborate game, a compound of absurd adventures, faked documents, diagrams and word puzzles," Peter Buitenhuis wrote in the *New York Times Book Review*. "There is little pretense of realism. Mathews has abandoned himself to an imagination full of strange lore and miscellaneous literary allusions." Apart from literary influences such as Swift and Poe, Buitenhuis thought the main influence on the novel was the celebrated Italian film director Federico Fellini, especially his mixture of fantasy and reality in 8½. But Buitenhuis felt that this technique did not work so well on the printed page: "The logic of printed words demands a minimal corresponding logic, a base of credibility, that the movie camera, through its greater flexibility, can ignore. . . . *Tlooth*, in spite of its creative experimentalism and its radical assault on reality . . . often loses the sustained interest required to make sense of its elusive complexity."

Tlooth turns, like *The Conversions*, on a quest, but this time it is a quest for revenge. The narrator (sexually ambiguous until the end) has had her career as a violinist ended by the unnecessary amputation of two fingers of her left hand and seeks revenge against the surgeon (also sexually ambiguous) who did it. This involves, among much else, a failed attempt to substitute a bomb for a baseball in a game taking place in a strange Siberian concentration camp where both protagonists, along with religious heretics such as "Defective Baptists" and "Resurrectionists," are imprisoned; the narrator's escape through several bizarre Asian mountain kingdoms; her being commissioned by a Venetian count to write a perversely imaginative pornographic film script which becomes interwoven with the narration; and a final opportunity for revenge as a result of the narrator's new vocation as a dentist. A somewhat baffled Granville Hicks wrote of *Tlooth* in the *Saturday Review*: "I am sure Mathews had fun writing the book, and I have had some fun reading it. He can write uncommonly well when he wants to, and he keeps this charade going, whatever it means. He creates one outrageous situation after another, and most of them he carries off effectively. In his inventiveness and erudition he is like Pynchon, Barth, and William Gaddis, but he seems less concerned with coherence than any of them."

Writing in *Harper's*, Roderick Cook found that the novel succeeded as pure fantasy, coherent or not: "while the method of telling it is quite sober, and the language plain, what actually happens is totally bizarre and wonderful. The descriptions that are blandly handed to you show an imagination and an ingenuity that are often just astonishing. . . . It is, for all its incidental excesses, fantasy, pure and simple."

Mathew's third novel, *The Sinking of the Odradek Stadium*, again involves a quest, this time for sunken treasure, as carried on in a series of letters exchanged by an American in Florida and his Southeast Asian wife in Italy. But as several critics noted, it is also about love, and the emotional temperature of the novel is thus raised above the rather chilly intellectual perplexity of his first two novels. Brain Stonehill in the *Chicago Review* found it superior "because the letters that pass between Twang and Zachary McCaltex are motivated not only by their greed for the Medici gold but also by a burning urge to throw down their pens and reading glasses, cross the ocean that separates them, and leap into each other's arms. Part of every letter is given over to expressions of longing, loneliness, or lust, and these passages provide an emotional depth and resonance that the other two novels lack." Although "much of the action consists of the perusal, translation, interpretation, and verification of a host of documents, maps, clues, and false leads," Stonehill found he was touched by the novel because it "is as much about feelings of love as about ideas of language."

Thomas R. Edwards made the same point in the *New York Review of Books* to modify his assessment of Mathews as a "coterie novelist, . . . a master of private jokes that most readers will feel annoyingly in the dark about": "For all of Zachary's stuffiness and Twang's not so hilarious difficulties with written English . . . , their letters are often openly and affectingly tender, where the earlier books almost entirely avoid the expression of strong or direct feelings. Unless

I've been had again, this seems a hopeful sign of mellowness to go along with Harry Mathews' immense elegance and skill."

Nevertheless, "ideas of language" remain an important theme of the book, as Irving Malin, noting allusions to Wittgenstein, pointed out in the *Review of Contemporary Fiction* : "We discover that, no matter how we move, we cannot free ourselves from the perplexities of language." Words "cannot point the way; they cannot *map* sunken treasure. . . . Yet words are the only things we can accept (according to Mathews) for our momentary salvation." And the salvation is ultimately comic. "*The Sinking of the Odradek Stadium* seems to me a comic masterpiece," wrote Edmund White in the *New York Times Book Review*, "as funny as Evelyn Waugh's *Scoop*, as intricate as Vladimir Nabokov's *Pale Fire*." Stonehill also detected an affinity to *Pale Fire*.

Cigarettes, Mathews' fourth novel, was published twelve years after *The Sinking of the Odradek Stadium*, and it is something of a departure in his work, perhaps reflecting, as he himself has noted, a time when "the focus of my life shifted from what I could learn by experiment to what I could learn by commitment." The novel retains something of the formal intricacy of his earlier works, but unsettling fantasy is replaced by unsettling reality. Lisa Zeidner, in the *New York Times Book Review*, remarked: "*Cigarettes* traces the connections among thirteen characters, between 1936 and 1963, in Saratoga Springs and Greenwich Village: artists, critics, gallery owners, patrons and society hangers-on. . . . Everyone knows everyone. It's a rough bunch to trust with a secret, and this crew harbors many. . . . " Each chapter examines the relationship between two of the characters— between parent and child, or siblings, or lovers, or friends. Since the chapters are not in chronological order, the novel is pieced together from various clues and revelations rather than unfolded through a plot. But beneath its structural intricacy, Zeidner wrote, "lurks a complex vision of parents and children, of how disappointments and dependencies are bequeathed from generation to degeneration. Mr. Mathews has the good sense to choose enigma over dogma."

Robert Towers, in the *New York Review of Books*, also thought that the novel succeeded because the complexity of form and relationship is never reduced to a simple moral: "As in an elaborate dance, the characters of *Cigarettes* step forward, perform their figure, and then step back—and on it goes until the formal but enigmatic pattern is completed, and we are back with the original narrator who has choreographed the whole spectacle. The themes that emerge are at least as numerous as the dancers. I suppose most of them could be summed up under the heading of the Vanity of Human Wishes. But one should not strain too hard after meanings—the pattern is enough. Though sad and painful things occur, the prevailing tone is more wistful than tragic, and there are many wonderfully droll interludes. The narrative voice throughout gives an impression of tight control; much more is told than dramatized, and the reader, while constantly informed and entertained, is not invited to come too close."

Yet the reader is invited to come closer in this novel than in Mathews' previous work, and this is what several critics stressed. "The narrative has weight and honesty, an answerability to the world (as in the account of Phoebe's acute hyperthyroidism and accompanying mental illness) which runs strikingly against the characteristic tendency of formalist *tour d'esprit* to dutiful playfulness, detachment, facile lightness, narrative irresponsibility and general inhumanity," wrote Galen Strawson in the *Times Literary Supplement.* And Lewis Warsh, writing in the *American Book Review,* found that "instead of the manic wit and the feeling of timelessness of the earlier books we have the suffering and abuse of real people in real time, and this return to earth, as it were (implying that the world we live in is as scary and insane as anything he could invent), results in his most beautiful and most hair-raising work."

Apart from Roussel, the novelist Mathews has most often been compared to is Thomas Pynchon, "who shares," Thomas R. Edwards wrote, "Mathews's interest in the messages that may be concealed in history, the necessity and absurdity of trying to make sense of a senseless world. They share too an interest in arcane scholarship, the technology of complex machines, and the subtleties of science, particularly medicine." But the differences are revealing: " . . . the dark intensities of Pynchon's nihilistic wit have no real counterpart in Mathews's lighter, brighter sense of fun. . . . (If one of his masters is the Beckett of *Watt,* another is surely [S. J.] Perelman)," wrote Edwards (and Mathews has in fact paid tribute to Perelman's inspired wordplay). Edmund White pointed out that "paranoia for Pynchon is the highest form of wisdom, the ultimate realism. For Mathews, however, interpretation is invariably misleading and facts refuse to yield their significance."

In any case, the appearance of *Cigarettes* prompted much different comparisons from White, who reviewed it in the *Review of Contemporary Fiction.* This time he invoked masters of social comedy like Jane Austen, F. Scott Fitzgerald, and Henry Green, and found two things particularly remarkable about it: "First, it is as involving as a nineteenth-century saga and as original as any modernist invention—a rare combination of readability and ingenuity. Second, it shows compassion toward characters usually slighted or ridiculed in contemporary fiction—the middle-aged and old, the successful, mothers, homosexuals, even sadists. Nor does it treat these characters with a governessy solicitude; rather it judges them on the basis of the good that they do and the happiness they feel and give."

Thus Mathews' work shows a remarkable range. It combines European formal and philosophical concerns with a sense of humor thoroughly American; it has evolved from the cosmic comedy of a world which, without God as the ultimate source of meaning, consists of overlapping but indecipherable messages, to the human comedy of mixed motives and missed connections. While remaining faithful to his interest in the way language both conveys and betrays the human quest for ultimate knowledge, Mathews has gradually accommodated more and more human feeling in his work, finding meaning in love and suffering as well as in the baffled pursuit of meaning.

PRINCIPAL WORKS: *Novels*—The Conversions, 1962; Tlooth, 1966; The Sinking of the Odradek Stadium, 1975; Cigarettes, 1987. *Collected short stories*—Country Cooking and Other Stories, 1977; Plaisirs singuliers, 1983. *Poetry*—The Ring: Poems 1956–59, 1970; The Planisphere, 1974; Selected Declarations of Independence (poetry and prose), 1977; Trial Impressions, 1977; Le savoir des rois: poèmes à perverbes, 1976; Armenian Papers: Poems 1954–1984, 1987. *Non-fiction prose*—Le Verger (memoir of Georges Perec), 1984; The Way Home: Collected Longer Prose, 1989.

ABOUT: Contemporary Authors Autobiography Series 6, 1988; Contemporary Authors New Revision Series 18, 1986; Contemporary Literary Criticism 52, 1989. *Periodicals*—American Book Review May–June 1988; Chicago Review Autumn 1982; Harper's November 1966; Nation September 29, 1962; New York Review of Books August 7, 1975, January 21, 1988; New York Times Book Review October 30, 1966, November 29, 1987; Review of Contemporary Fiction Fall 1987; Saturday Review November 12, 1966; Time June 15, 1962; Times Literary Supplement September 14, 1962; May 20–26, 1988; (Village) Voice Literary Supplement November 1987; September 15, 1989.

MATTHEWS, WILLIAM (PROCTOR)

(November 11, 1942–   ), American poet and essayist, writes: "It's fashionable for writers to complain about the mobility and deracination of American life, and to talk in autobiographical sketches about place and home and roots. It's easy to hear the loading of the moral dice. In American Sincere, the dialect in which such sketches are conventionally written, Latinate words like 'mobility' and 'deracination' are fancy-pants, and Anglo-Saxon words like 'place' and 'home' and 'roots' are honorific.

"But I've lived in Iowa, Ohio, Massachusetts, Connecticut, North Carolina, Colorado, Washington, Texas, and now in New York City, and I've travelled avidly.

"My father worked as a young man for the Department of Agriculture as a county agent in the Soil Conservation Service, and later for Children's International Summer Villages, a youth exchange program. My mother has always been a reader and a ponderer.

"My poems from the beginning have been about landscape, cities and memory; about love, marriage, and family life; about the nearly equal abilities of language to reveal and deceive; and about jazz and language and their relationships to emotional life.

"With the indispensable help of the translator Mary Feeney, I once co-translated a selection of prose poems from the great French poet Jean Follain. I recently collected the essays I've written to date that I care to preserve and published a book of them. Just now I'm working on a prose book, with some features of the essay and some of fiction, that begins with Sigmund Freud giving his 'Introductory Lectures on Psychoanalysis' at the University of Vienna Medical School in 1915. Of course I'm working on poems now, too.

"I learned from Peter Gay's wonderful biography that Freud usually wrote out his lectures in advance, then deliberately left the text at home when he went to give the lectures. It seems to me that in my modest way I've always done something rather like that. I write and write, pursuing something I can't even identify until I've written it, and then, armed with nothing better and nothing less than the experience of having just written it, I leave it behind and go on into the next ignorance and next curiosity.

"Lorca once wrote that setting out to write a poem was like entering a dark forest to hunt an animal. Probably. I've never hunted. And the wonderful American poet Robert Morgan has a character in one of his poems 'excited, as before a holdup.' No doubt, though I've never held anything or anyone up.

WILLIAM MATTHEWS

For writers to talk about the agonies of writing has always seemed to me more than a little self-advertising. I'd rather not. The difficulties are palpable and I hope I've seldom underestimated them. But what a gloomy and paranoid charisma a writer's life would have if it were not for the deep lure, nearly erotic, of the activity itself. Why else come back and back to the desk, not always with a trudge but often with a spry, pleased step of a lover wending a familiar and endlessly interesting path?

"Writers are disposed, probably by temperament, to talk either of freedom or of the acceptance of limitations. I'm not sure the two are opposite or even different. Whatever such catch phrases point to, a little helplessly and inarticulately, it has been in my life a powerful value, both fiercely personal and fiercely political, and whatever I know of it I've learned at the desk.

"I'm quite happy, as these brief notes will suggest, to talk about writing, the way opera buffs love to talk about singers and libretti. I've said nothing, really, about my poems. They'll have to speak for themselves. I trust that they can, but then once I'm done writing them, one by one, they're beyond any hope . . . I can have for them, and anyhow my fickle attentions have been turned to a new poem."

As practicing poet, editor of poetry journals, and teacher of creative writing, William Matthews has followed the vocation of poetry throughout his life. Born in Cincinnati, Ohio, to

William Proctor and Mary E. (Sather) Matthews, he received a B.A. from Yale in 1965 and an M.A. from the University of North Carolina in 1966. That same year he became one of the founders of Lillabulero Press and coeditor, with Russell Banks, of its poetry journal, a position he held until 1974. Since 1968, with only a few interruptions, he has taught at Wells College (1968–1969), Cornell University (1969–1973), Emerson College (1973–1974), Sarah Lawrence (1974), the universities of Colorado (1974–1978), Iowa (1976–1977), Washington (1978–1983), Houston (1981, 1983), and Michigan (1987). Since 1983 he has been on the English faculty of the City University of New York—at Brooklyn College from 1983 to 1985 and since 1985 at City College. Matthews has continued his editorial activities, serving on the editorial board for poetry of Wesleyan University Press from 1969 to 1973 and again since 1988. He was poetry editor of the *Iowa Review* (1976–1977) and guest editor for one issue of the *Indiana Review* in 1987, as well as a member of the literature panel of the National Endowment for the Arts (1976–1980), which he chaired during his last year in office. For four years (1985–1989) he was president of the Poetry Society of America. In 1983 he received *Poetry* magazine's Oscar Blumenthal Award and the State of Washington's Governor's Award for Literature. He has had fellowships from the National Endowment for the Arts (1974, 1983), the Guggenheim Foundation (1980–1981), the Ingram Merrill Foundation (1984), and a residency at the Rockefeller Foundation Center in Bellagio, Italy (1988).

Like most young poets Matthews experimented in a variety of styles, seeking his own voice. Unlike many, he appears to have found his early. Drawn to experimental poetry and surrealism, he favored free-form, short, imagistic verse, occasionally writing prose poems. Over the years he has moved toward a more formal structure, but he retains his essentially romantic subjectivity, exploring the mystery of the human self largely in terms of his own experience: nature, the American countryside, sports, jazz, and in more recent years childhood—his own in recollection and his children's. Divorced in 1974 from Marie Harris, whom he had married in 1963, he has two sons, William and Sebastian, who figure prominently in his poetry. "If I lived with my sons / all the year I'd be less sentimental / about them," he writes in "Moving Again" (from *Rising and Falling*). In fact, however, he is not sentimental. He writes of his children with the same meditative logic that dominates all his work, what Hugh Seidman, reviewing *Rising and Falling* in the *New York Times Book Review*, described as "an 'associative strategy':

the poem begins anywhere and evolves to a conclusion via a progression whose logic is more or less consistent, much as human life ranges between the extremes of pure chance and iron-clad predictability." In *A Happy Childhood*, a volume dedicated to his sons, he confronts human mortality itself:

> There's so little of swift time, and what time
> we have is so much like held breath, how could
> I or anyone be late? Think how fast
> the second half of life pays itself out,
> faster the smaller it grows, like tape:
> how, near the end, the fattened take-up reel
> scarcely turns at all.
>
>   —from "Tardy"

From the beginning of his career when he edited the poetry journal *Lillabulero*, Matthews has been identified with a group of poets—notably Robert Kelly, Robert Bly, W. S. Merwin, and James Wright—of the "deep image" movement. The phrase refers to a single strong image that evokes, in the unconscious of the poet and in turn of the reader, a wealth of feelings and associations. Such poetry, Robert Kelly wrote some years ago, "is the juncture of the experienced with the never-experienced. Like waking reality, it is the fulfillment of the imagined and the unimagined." One image resonates with others, but, as Kelly explains, the first image "will normally dominate all subsequent images and the poem as a whole, even when the reader seems to have forgotten it." In Matthews' "My Friends' Marriages Fly Apart Like Badly Designed Planes," for example, the tenuousness of marriage is explored in a series of images that expand and extend the simile of the title:

> The hills gleam shards.
> A bee's eye broken by refraction.
> Maybe lies keep the marriage up
>
> until they grow a sheath
> of ice.
>
> There's no way we can crash
> except together.
>
> We push through the wet night
>
> air, through the space we take up
> flying, carrying like a sack of mail
> our undelivered futures.

Although such poetry draws its power from free form and simplicity of language, the poet risks lapsing into mannerisms, into an excess of metaphors and similes. This was the principal critical objection to Matthews' early work. He "cuts his images with a razor," F. D. Reeve wrote in *Poetry* in 1971. "Where the blade has slipped the figure is scarred; where the hand held steady and moved patiently, calculatingly, the figure is crisply complete." In spite of these apparent excesses, most reviewers of Matthews' early work recognized an emerging talent. Of *Ruining the New Road*, his first major collection, the *Virginia Quarterly Review* commented: "Matthews is ever conscious of the risks we run in life and his meter and his metaphors take the kinds of chances real poetry needs if it is to succeed . . . this collection establishes him as an important poet with his own voice."

With his second and third volumes, *Sleek for the Long Flight* and *Rising and Falling*, Matthews demonstrated his gift for a poetry that is simple in language, spontaneous in feeling and, although intimate and personal, rich in associations that draw the reader immediately into the poem. In "Living among the Dead," he recalls his childhood curiosity about death with special poignancy because he is now a father:

> My sons and I are like some wine
> the dead have already bottled.
> They wish us well, but there is nothing
> they can do for us.
>
> To love the dead is easy.
> They are final, perfect.
> But to love a child
> is sometimes to fail at love
> while the dead look on
> with their abstract sorrow.
>
> To love a child is to turn
> away from the patient dead.
> It is to sleep carefully
> in case he cries.

Matthews takes a dim view of theme-hunting in poetry. In an essay published in *Fifty Contemporary Poets: The Creative Process* he wrote: "To say to a student that some poem is 'about illusion and reality' is to give the student a first and very crude way to think about the poem. That's fine, if it leads into the poem: words, silences, rhythms. But if the idea 'theme' becomes a place to stop and look and go no further, like a 'scenic overlook' at a park, then it's a useless idea. You have to go in." Going in involves the silences as much as the words of a poem. In a statement in *Contemporary Poets* Matthews wrote: "My poems hope to speak for themselves. Much of their speech would be silence. Just as an architect uses walls to organize space, I use the words of a poem to organize silences." As a poem representative of his work Matthews chose "Nurse Sharks" (from *Rising and Falling*). It is longer than most of his earlier poems and more anecdotal, but it is characteristic of the quiet, reflective quality of all his poems. "Nurse Sharks" begins with a circumstantial explanation that because sharks lack flotation bladders, they sleep in shallow waters or wedged into reef ledges:

> Once I woke a nurse shark (so named because it was
> thought to protect its young by taking them
> into its mouth). It shied from the bubbles I gave up
> but sniffed the glint the murky light made on my
>   regulator.

Swimming dangerously close, he senses his peril when he startles a group of sleeping sharks:

> I swirled around a stand of coral and swam
> fast to shore, startling the sharks to a waking frenzy:
> moil, water opaque with churned-up sand,
> gray flames burning out to sea. Last time I go diving
> alone, I promised myself, though I lied.

In his later collections Matthews has demonstrated a mature mastery of the meditative lyric, writing longer poems with heightened control and objectivity. There is also greater metrical variety. In *Foreseeable Futures* he writes some fifteen-line poems made up of five three-line stanzas, moving easily from pentameter to tetrameter and hexameter. In *Flood* the images are from nature but always, in some manner of association, related to the creative process itself. For example, in one poem the poet contemplates the serenity and silence of the waters:

> And if you should carry them with you
> like the memory of impossible errands
> and not know what you carry, nor how,
> so that you feel inelevably mute,
> as if from birth, then you will be apt
> for speech, for books, and you'll be glib
>
> though it torment you, and you'll rise
> to the sacraments of memory and lie down
> unable to forget what you can't name,
> and the wine in your glass will be ink.
> —from "The Waters"

These new poems, Peter Stitt wrote of *Flood* in the *Georgia Review*, "show the operation not just of a free and surprising imagination, but of a powerful and controlling intellect as well. The resulting poems are full of 'wit' in the best sense of the word, the sense exemplified by John Donne, say, though of course Matthews' poems are freer and more relaxed, being modern." It was Matthews' wit that also impressed Dick Allen, reviewing *Foreseeable Futures* in the *Hudson Review*. Hailing him as "our wittiest, funniest serious poet since [John] Berryman," Allen found Matthews more reflective than Berryman: " . . . a deeply playful and serious intelligence that acknowledges the failings of the world and is still generous with it—and with us." Similarly, Bonnie Costello observed some years ago, in her review of *Flood* in *Poetry*, that he "moves from outward observation to inward questioning," as does indeed most romantic poetry. What she found remarkable was his use, for example, of the flood motif in these poems as an image of "the creative urge" which "interests by the freshness and ease of its metaphysical resemblance." Another example from *Flood* of his metaphysical wit—seeing likenesses where there is no apparent likeness—is "An Airline Breakfast," in which he can even find "OK" "this wretched / and exhausted breakfast":

> The older I grow, the better
> I love to see what I can't see:
> The stars in the daytime,
> the idea of an omelet,
> the reasons I love what I love.
> It's what I can see I have to nudge
> myself to love, so wonderful
> is the imagination.

At the end of the 1980s Matthews celebrated his love of jazz in *Blues If You Want*, playing variations on the theme of creativity and the blues. From his boyhood, when he was learning to play the clarinet, he recalls

> . . . . I could swelter through an August
> afternoon—torpor rising from the river—and listen
> to J. J. Johnson and Stan Getz braid variations
> on "My Funny Valentine," and feel there in the room
> with me the force and weight of what I couldn't
> say. What's an emotion anyhow?

The jazz musician and the poet become one—as in "Every Tub," in which a player riding in a bus across the American landscape to another gig recalls once seeing a glorious sunrise. He feels inarticulate, unable to express its beauty in words:

> . . . It's as hard
> to describe now as it was to look at then,
> you've got to pay such fierce attention. See,
> the reason I'm a musician is, Language and I,
> we love each other but we never got it on,
> as the saying goes, we're just good friends
> though I surely love to talk.

PRINCIPAL WORKS: *Poetry*—Ruining the New Road, 1970; Sleek for the Long Flight, 1972; Rising and Falling, 1979; Flood, 1982; A Happy Childhood, 1984; Foreseeable Futures, 1987; Blues If You Want, 1989. *Essays*—Curiosities, 1989. *Translation*—(with M. Feeney) A World Rich in Anniversaries: Prose Poems of Jean Follain, 1979.

ABOUT: Contemporary Authors New Revision Series 12, 1984; Contemporary Literary Criticism 40, 1986; Contemporary Poets, 4th ed., 1985; Dictionary of Literary Biography 5, 1980; Heyen, W. (ed.) American Poets in 1976, 1976; Turner, A. T. (ed.) Fifty Contemporary Poets: The Creative Process, 1977; Who's Who in America 1988–1989. *Periodicals*—American Book Review March 1988; Choice September 1982; Georgia Review Fall 1982, Winter 1984; Hudson Review Autumn 1987; Library Journal April 1, 1982; New York Times Book Review October 21, 1979; Poetry July 1971, May 1983; Virginia Quarterly Review Autumn 1970.

McGINLEY, PATRICK (February 8, 1937–), Irish novelist, writes: "What I see as distinctive in my books reflects the life I knew in the remote glen in Donegal where I grew up. There people lived simply and precariously by hill-farming and inshore fishing. My father was a farmer and so was everyone else—apart from the priest, the schoolmaster and one or two lighthouse keepers. It was a close-knit, inward-looking community where gossip and speculation, character analysis and character assassination were so rife that by the time I was thirteen I had concluded that I knew pretty well everything that could be known about life, and I felt confident that anything I might have overlooked I could find out from my uncle who was more easy-going and more forthcoming under cross-examination than my father. It was an illusion that gave me an unwavering sense of security throughout my formative years. Life seemed solid and knowable: a shrewd man, by taking thought, could almost predict what was going to happen next. What mattered, I had learnt from my father, was strength of limb and purpose, practical commonsense, and a determination to pay one's way. It was a philosophy for men who labored on land and sea and whose livelihood provided no more than a meager sufficiency. It was perhaps typical of a community where everyone who lacked the skills of farming and fishing was seen as an outsider or at the very least 'different'.

"In the glen we were surrounded by hills to the north, south and east. The sea, which reached westwards all the way to America, seemed the easiest means of escape. The land was rocky and austere even in summer, and in winter it looked almost grim. On a good day the glen could look beautiful and serene, but good days are fairly rare on the west coast of Ireland, and now what I remember best is Atlantic mists enveloping the hills and the sea rising over the rocks along the shore. It was a landscape that lived for me. Every height and hollow had a name in Irish which I could translate into English while recalling the local legend about how the place had first got its name. During my boyhood the art of the *shanachie* (the folk story-teller) was already dying but I was born in time to hear tales of men who had seen mermaids combing their long hair on a rock before a storm, or of a poor man who had found a shilling he could never spend. The local folklore was inseparable from the landscape, and both acted strongly on my imagination. Later, when I came to read *A Midsummer Night's Dream* and *The Tempest*, I didn't find the magical events in them all that farfetched.

"Nearly everyone in the glen was bilingual in

PATRICK McGINLEY

English and Irish, though English was the language in everyday use. Most of the time we spoke a mixture of English and Irish, and it was a common trick of conversation to use an Irish word in an English sentence for emphasis or embellishment, or even for comic effect. We were all keenly aware that words are chameleons, and that an Irish word in an English sentence took color from its new environment and also shed a light of its own. Words were living things that danced and sang and changed their sense and sound in the company of other words or on the lips of different speakers. The sense of play I came to associate with language from an early age is still strong in me. All this, I feel, should have turned me towards poetry. Instead it was the urge to narrate that had to be appeased.

"After boyhood came university and its scientific interest in the oral culture I grew up with. Folklore motifs had to make sense. Explication ousted imagination for a while. The nimbus of magic dissolved; the music fled. It took me years to recover something of my childhood wonderment. The memories of my early life are now my most precious possession as a writer. They represent a world and a mode of living that is beyond the limits of my adult experience and demand to be explored for the simple reason that they haunt and vex."

Patrick McGinley was born in Glencolumkille, County Donegal, the eldest of five children. He attended St. Enda's College in Galway, which he describes as "a boarding school for as-pirant teachers or a prison-house for growing boys," and Galway University (1954–1957), where he studied English literature "under a professor who taught me more Anglo-Saxon than English. One thing I owe him is a love of Middle English poetry, which I still read with interest." After four years (1958–1962) of teaching secondary school in Ireland, McGinley went to London to work in publishing and journalism. In 1965 he spent a year in Australia where he wrote a first novel that never found a publisher. He resumed fiction writing in 1974 and *Bogmail*, his first published novel, appeared four years later. McGinley lives in Kent with his wife and son.

The "landscape that lived" for Patrick McGinley also lives in what one reviewer described as his "darkly comic novels about the Irish." In a comparison that seems remote but to McGinley's readers is oddly appropriate, Mordecai Richler wrote: "He knows his Irish bog as well as Isaac Bashevis Singer does the *shtetl*, and he can sing about it with something like the same magic." Even more than the land itself, McGinley knows the people: their language, their ancient folklore, and their stubborn roots in a tradition that continues into the present day to enrich their lives with humor even as it darkens them with violence. When his characters leave their bogland farms to live, as a few of them do, in Dublin or in London, they carry their heritage with them.

McGinley's first two novels, *Bogmail* and *Goosefoot*, were enthusiastically received by reviewers as "thrillers," but with a difference. *Bogmail* is not simply the story of a murderer who is being blackmailed or bogmailed. Since the murderer runs a village pub frequented by a group of wildly eccentric locals, the novel becomes a picture of a whole community in remote northwest Ireland. These are not the genial, hard-drinking, church-going country Irish of stereotype. Their talk is ringingly lyrical and authentic. It is also, as Robin W. Winks pointed out in the *New Republic*, "explicit and crude"; but, Winks continues, "the writing is so skilled, the power to evoke a sense of lush, green landscape so great, that one is fascinated with the perversities of the human character, perversities that seem all the more morbidly fascinating for being expressed in a lilting Irish voice." The central character, who commits a coldblooded murder with no pangs of conscience, nevertheless has the sensibility to listen raptly to a Robert Schumann cello concerto on his gramaphone and to reflect on the landscape he has known all his life:

> The old bog where his ancestors had cut their turf was derelict, the sites of the old turf stacks like graves, mounds of peat mould overgrown with rushes and here

and there a whitened stick of bog fir strewn among the heather and mountain grass. The old face of the bog was broken down by sheep's feet, rough weather and running water. Tufts of heather grew in crevices and the marks of the slane denoting the different spits were all gone, vanished into eternity, blown to dust by Atlantic winds. In a moment of lucidity he had a sense of centuries passing quickly while the long pull of his desperate existence seemed never-ending.

Closer to the conventional murder mystery but far darker in its implications is *Goosefoot*. The central character here is an intelligent and independent-spirited young woman fresh out of university with an honors degree in agricultural science, who elects to leave her farm home and family for a year of teaching in Dublin. Her decision proves a fatal one, but before its chilling conclusion *Goosefoot* introduces a host of colorful characters, city and country people, whose brilliant talk and often erotic actions constitute what Patricia Craig, in the *Times Literary Supplement*, calls "a celebration of Irish verbosity and virtuosity." Craig notes the novel's mixture of genres and reads it as a kind of parody of "the self-discovery novel, the Dublin pub novel, the idiosyncratic-Irish novel, the realistic rural novel, the whimsical novel, the aphoristic novel, the detective novel, and the romantic thriller." Another mystery-thriller is *Foxprints*, which, like *Goosefoot*, takes its central character away from rural Ireland to the city, in this case suburban London, and thrusts him into intrigue and murder. This novel struck Clancy Sigal, in the *New York Times Book Review*, as full of clever talk, but "obsessed with words. . . . His observations on suburbia are correct, if over-intellectualized."

McGinley's real strength as a novelist appears to be drawn from the soil of Donegal. *Foggage* (the title refers to grass which remains on the ground during winter) is an earthy and realistic study of a Donegal farmer whose ties to his land and family, specifically an incestuous relationship with his sister, lead to tragedy. The novel's power lies in its picture of routine rural life and the passive, near-animal existence of the central character. When he meets a woman of more refinement whom he comes genuinely to love, his past destroys the relationship. *Foggage*, Tom Paulin wrote in *Book World*, "belongs to [the] richly pessimistic tradition of vehement anti-pastoral . . . [it] has something which is compelling and exact—a disgusted comic despair which, just at times, is given a precise and almost theological structure." The shifting moods of comedy and tragedy are difficult to balance. Mordecai Richler, in the *New York Times Book Review*, felt that they "fail to mesh" and that the ending, with its suggestion of redemption,

"smacks of manipulation." Nevertheless, Richler concluded that "everything is redeemed by the high quality of the prose. Patrick McGinley is a very gifted man."

A recurring figure in McGinley's novels is the character who seeks to insulate himself, to lose his identity—in work, drink, sex, or sheer apathy—as if to prove his or (as in *Goosefoot*) her invulnerability. Such characters are doomed to frustration or destruction. In *The Trick of the Ga Bolga* an Englishman seeks escape from the tensions and pressures of World War II by retreating to a remote farm in Donegal: "He bought it not for shelter but for peace. He was sick of being jostled in shops by housewives with ration books, and he was sick of men who looked at him as if they had said less than they could. He was making a fresh start with a clean slate, and if anyone was going to write on the slate it would be himself. . . . " Ironically he is soon deeply involved with the community of strongly individualistic men and women and quite accidentally becomes a local hero. As the village schoolmaster tells him: "We want to believe you're good, and, as I told you before, what everyone believes must be true." Though set in contemporary times, the novel resonates with the mystery and enchantment of Irish folklore. The "ga bolga" itself is a weapon that was used by the legendary Cuchulain; it turns up here in a deceptive disguise until the protagonist learns bitterly what it really is. While he expressed reservations about the central character, "whose neurosis never comes convincingly into focus," and whose behavior remains "unaccountable," David Profumo, in the *Times Literary Supplement*, praised the novel's "often beautiful evocation of this particular type of Irish community. . . . The book is everywhere free from clichés of plot and expression, and is full of haunting peculiarities which accumulate to leave the impression of something mysterious and durable." Sheila MacLeod, in the *New Statesman*, was similarly impressed: "This is a strange, elusive novel which sometimes verges on the blarney, but is never less than excellently written and, once read, remains a powerfully haunting presence."

The premise of McGinley's novel *The Red Men* is as intriguing and as arbitrary as a fairy tale. A domineering old man gives each of his four sons a sum of money to invest for a year. At the end of that time, he will decide which of them has used the money in a way that best honors the family's legendary ancestors, the Red Men, and make that son his sole heir. Like most fairy-tale compacts, this one has unforeseen results. "The novel is indeed partly about the poverty of the family mythology," Jasper Rees wrote in the *Times Literary Supplement*. "The brothers have been brought up on tales of the Red Men; these bogus household gods have usurped the *shanachie*, the local historian, leaving the brothers to find out for themselves about the hill on the promontory shaped like two breasts. Maternal nature is integral to the novel because it teaches native wisdom to the headland's motherless children, whereas paternal ancestry delivers only 'a litany of little untruths.'" The brothers' schemes and adventures are sometimes mordantly funny, but Rees thought "the characters have to fight hard to be human" within the daunting formal constraints and symbolic overtones of the story.

PRINCIPAL WORKS: Bogmail, 1978; Goosefoot, 1982; Foggage, 1983; Foxprints, 1983; The Trick of the Ga Bolga, 1985; The Red Men, 1987; The Devil's Diary, 1988.

ABOUT: Contemporary Authors 120, 1987; Contemporary Literary Criticism 41, 1987. *Periodicals*—New Republic May 2, 1981; New Statesman August 30, 1985; New York Times Book Review August 2, 1981; December 25, 1983; July 21, 1985; Newsweek July 27, 1981; Times Literary Supplement February 11, 1983; September 7, 1984; September 13, 1985; March 27, 1987; Washington Post Book World December 18, 1983.

MELLERS, WILFRED HOWARD (April 26, 1914–), British musicologist, composer, and educator, was born to Percival and Hilda Maria (nee Lawrence) Mellers in Leamington Spa, England. He was educated at Leamington College and at Cambridge University, where he earned a B.A. in English Literature in 1936 and a B.Mus. in 1939. As a Cambridge undergraduate, Mellers was influenced by literary critic F. R. Leavis, whose interest in "the social background of the arts" and the interrelation among music, drama, and poetry have deeply affected Mellers' musicological writing.

After teaching music at Darlington Hall from 1938 to 1940, Mellers served as college supervisor in English and lecturer in Music at Downing College, Cambridge, from 1945 to 1948. He then worked as staff tutor in music at the extramural department of the University of Birmingham until 1960, when he became an Andrew Mellon Distinguished Professor of Music at University of Pittsburgh. He held that position until 1963, the year he was awarded an honorary Doctor of Music degree by the University of Birmingham. Mellers returned to England and in 1964 became the chairman of the newly established music department at the University of York. There he earned a reputation as an innovative and encouraging teacher, approaching "music as a human experience" and allowing students to learn through self-discovery.

In addition to teaching, Mellers has composed more than fifty pieces, many of them commissioned by music festivals and the BBC. Despite his stature as a composer, however, he has generally enjoyed greater renown as a writer. Like his university courses and his compositions, Mellers' writing demonstrates the breadth and depth of his knowledge, as well as his overriding interest in the social dimension and nature of artistic creation. His first book, *Music and Society*, traces the evolution of English music in a social context. Mellers explores why music styles flourished at some times, such as the Elizabethan Renaissance, and stagnated at others, notably during the British civil war of the mid-seventeenth century. With *Music and Society*, Mellers achieved early critical success. In the *Saturday Review*, Nan Cooke Carpenter described the study as "illumined by remarkable erudition combined with deep musical sensitivity and literary artistry. . . ."

At the beginning of his writing career, Mellers contributed frequently to magazines such as *Musical Times, Music Review*, and F. R. Leavis' *Scrutiny*, for which Mellers served as music editor for a time. Fourteen of his early articles, dealing with twentieth-century English, Central European, and French composers, were published collectively as *Studies in Contemporary Music*. The essays are notable for their historical and sociological perspective but, as critics pointed out, are somewhat uneven in quality and tone. The *Times Literary Supplement* reviewer commended Mellers' "catholicity of taste and sympathy" while maintaining that "the language is sometimes involved and sentences tend to become overladen with qualifying adjectives and clauses. . . ."

Mellers' next publication *François Couperin and the French Classical Tradition* was the first comprehensive study of the composer in English or French. The book presents Couperin within the artistic, political, and social world of the last two decades of Louis XIV's reign. In particular, Mellers examines the problem that resulted from "the moral tension between [Couperin's] passionate feeling and personal self-control." This tension, he argues, gave Couperin's music, which seems somewhat trivial at first glance, its substance and vigor.

Initially, *François Couperin* was well received. The *New Statesman and Nation* reviewer praised it as "distinguished by extreme thoroughness, together with a passionate love and deep understanding of a previously underestimated composer." The *Times Literary Supplement*, however, inferred from the presentation of data that Mellers had not fully digested all of them before beginning to write. Considered by some to be his best scholarly work, *François Couperin* was reprinted, in a revised and enlarged edition, in 1987. Ironically, a reviewer in the *Times Literary Supplement* found the study inadequate: "The imprecision of detail here . . . spoil[s] Mellers's work, and the human touches, charming though they are, do not compensate."

As Mellers acknowledges in many of his books, his writing has always been informed by his teaching. *Harmonious Meeting: A Study of the Relationship between English Music, Poetry and Theatre, c. 1600–1900* grew out of his classes at the University of Birmingham. The work, as indicated by its subtitle, examines the interrelationship among music, poetry, and drama in terms of its effect on artistic creativity in England. Part I traces the process by which music became inherently dramatic; Part II then outlines the process whereby literature and theater media became increasingly musical. Reviewers found *Harmonious Meeting* an enlightening and engrossing book because of the penetration and acute sensibility with which Mellers discusses particular works. *Spectator* reviewer Charles Reid, nonetheless, faulted Mellers for giving too little attention to the post-Handel period and for underrating Sir Arthur Sullivan in a sketchy argument.

In keeping with his broad tastes and knowledge, Mellers became one of the first European critics to take American music seriously. In *Music in a New Found Land*, he contends that American "art" music, jazz, and pop overlap and are equally important. He aims to reveal America and American life as they may be understood through American music. Discussing the compositions of Charles Ives, for example, Mellers writes that we

> have come to see that his integrity is synonymous with his experimental audacity—which springs from two related characteristics that are at the core of his Americanism. One is the pioneer's courage: his desire to hack a way through the forest since he has, indeed, no alternative. The other is that radical innocence of spirit without which—as we have seen in the literary figures—the pioneer could hardly embark on so perilous an adventure.

Music in a New Found Land won Mellers praise for his strong musicological grasp. In the *New York Times Book Review* Richard Franko Goldman extolled Mellers' "impressively wide knowledge of American music." The *Listener* critic proclaimed the 1987 reprint of the study "perceptive eloquent and judicious but criti-

cized Mellers for overlooking some major composers. An equally ambitious study, *Caliban Reborn: Renewal in Twentieth-Century Music*, derived from Mellers' visit to the United States. Based on a series of lectures Mellers gave at the University of Pittsburg, *Caliban Reborn* explores the "crisis" in twentieth-century music. Mellers attributes this crisis to humankind's inability to deal with the rapid changes it faces. He considers "in what, if any, ways these changes represent a radical departure from Western, European tradition, and if such a departure has occurred, to ask how much or how little it means." Reviewers acclaimed Mellers' erudition and insight in treating such a complex subject. Tim Souster of the *New Statesman*, however, found his "go-getting comparative style" disturbing because "its far-flung analogies tend not only to distort one's perspective of the value of the things which are compared, but to mask the high degree of selectivity which is fundamental to its approach."

Mellers narrowed his focus in his next study, *Bach and the Dance of God*. His thesis, however, is typically far-reaching: "no one with ears to hear can doubt that Bach was a religious composer, and that his religion springs from the depths of the human psyche, rather than from a topical and local creed." Mellers expounds this theme through his analysis of the key-signatures, tempi, rhythms, and the overall structure of specific movements of Bach's St. John Passion, B Minor Mass, unaccompanied cello suites, and Goldberg Variations, among other pieces. He also decodes Bach's music in terms of the visual, doctrinal, and numerical symbolism commonly used in the eighteenth century. In the *New York Times Book Review* Harold Schonberg called *Bach and the Dance of God* the "most unusual musical study of the year." "There are some fascinating speculations in this book," he continued, "but one has to enter the Mellers mind to respond, and many will dismiss the conclusions as the work of a learned crank." Another reviewer criticized Mellers for overemphasizing numerological symbolism but praised him for illuminating Bach's compositions with "his purely musical commentary and wealth of simple technical analysis and interpretation."

In 1983, Mellers produced a companion book, *Beethoven and the Voice of God*, with a similarly religious theme. He argues that all of Beethoven's music was a single evolving composition, an ongoing search for "a hidden song" that would conciliate the warring sides of the composer's tempestuous persona. Mellers supports his argument largely with evidence from Beethoven's later works such as his last six piano sonatas and *Missa Solomnis*. Like the Bach study,

Beethoven and the Voice of God impressed many critics as overly eclectic and not entirely convincing. *Listener* reviewer Hugo Cole questioned the connection between some of Mellers' ideas and his subject but nevertheless admired "the richness and variety of his own responses that give his books their special character. Mellers offers us a hundred keys to understanding—or at least, jingles the bunch before us as he is swept along on the tide of his own ideas."

Mellers took a more panoramic view of musical history in *The Masks of Orpheus: Seven Stages in the Story of European Music.* Through a detailed discussion of the myth of Orpheus as a musical subject, he again delves into the nature of artistic creation. While medieval people perceived Orpheus as attempting oneness with God, Mellers contends, "for high Renaissance man he was a humanist Hero asserting man's potential rivalry with the divine." The *Times Educational Supplement* reviewer called it "both fascinating and thought provoking."

Mellers' intellectual curiosity encompasses popular and rock music as well as classical forms. In *The Twilight of the Gods: The Beatles in Retrospect*, he argues that the Beatles were responsible for a radical shift away from chromatic, harmonically derived melodies to modal and pentatonic ones, reminiscent of medieval music and folksong. Originally delivered as a series of open lectures at the University of York, Mellers' argument depends largely on the systematic examination of the Beatles' albums. The book generated a wide range of critical responses. The *New York Times* reviewer concluded that "Mr. Mellers has raised some questions well worth considering, and on its own very idiosyncratic terms he has written a book well worth reading." In the *New York Times Book Review*, it was declared "a musical appreciation, too limited in scope to serve other functions." Another reviewer commended the ability to "set aside professional dignity and relax into enjoyment that marks Professor Mellers out as a man of unusually balanced and 'sociable' musical views."

Mellers' next study of popular music, *Darker Shade of Pale: A Backdrop of Bob Dylan*, investigates the black and Native American music that Dylan wove into his songs. Mellers first discusses white American folk, country, and pop music from the late nineteenth to the mid-twentieth century before analyzing Dylan's professional albums in depth. In general, reviewers agreed that *Darker Shade of Pale* made a valuable contribution to Dylan scholarship. The *Times Education Supplement* praised Mellers' "close and sober musical analysis." In the *Times Literary Supplement* Tony Russell hailed Mel-

lers' discussion of blues influence on Dylan's music but disparaged his discussion of Native American influence: "the reds stay resolutely under the bed."

Mellers again crosses the divide between "serious" and popular music in *Angels of the Night: Women Jazz and Pop Singers of the Twentieth Century.* Ranging in subject from Alabama gospel singer Vera Hall to performance artist Laurie Anderson, Mellers evaluates the role of personal experience in gospel, blues, jazz, country, soul, folk, rock, and pop music. *Angels of the Night* did not meet with unanimous praise. According to several critics, the book is unfocused and often marred by Mellers' erratic prose and questionable interpretations. "That a pupil of F. R. Leavis (as Mellers was)," declared Rupert Christiansen in the *Listener*, "could write that Kate Bush is 'a real mini-poet'—whatever that means—is, one can't help but feel, sign of a profound change in the climate of criticism." Brian Case's *Times Literary Supplement* review, however, applauded Mellers for his enormous range of tastes and knowledge and his sheer love of music.

Mellers has contributed articles to several musical encyclopedias and dictionaries, most notably *The Grove Dictionary of Music and Musicians.* In addition, he has written two volumes, *The Sonata Principle* and *Romanticism and the Twentieth Century*, of *Man and His Music*, a four-volume work that presents Western music within the context of Western culture.

Mellers remained the head of the University of York's music department until his retirement in 1981; the University subsequently made him professor emeritus. Since his retirement, he has worked part-time as visiting professor of music at the University of Keele (Staffordshire), City University (London), and Guildhall School of Music and Drama (London). He also guest lectures, performs concerts, and writes regularly for the *Times Literary Supplement* and *Early Music News.* In 1982, Mellers was awarded an honorary Doctor of Philosophy by the City University and named to the Order of the British Empire. A year later he was inducted as a Fellow of the Guildhall Society of Music and Drama. He has been married three times, to Vera Hobbes, Peggy Pauline Lewis, and Robin Hildyard, and has three daughters, Judith, Caroline, and Sarah.

PRINCIPAL WORKS: Music and Society, 1946; Studies in Contemporary Music, 1948; François Couperin and the French Classical Tradition, 1950; Music in the Making, 1951; Man and His Music (vol. 3, The Sonata Principle, and vol. 4, Romanticism and the Twentieth Century, 1957); Harmonious Meetings: A Study of the Relationship between English Music, Poetry, and Theatre, c. 1600–1900, 1965; Music in a New Found Land: Themes and Developments in American Music, 1964; Caliban Reborn: Renewal in Twentieth Century Music, 1967; Twilight of the Gods: The Beatles in Retrospect, 1973; Bach and the Dance of God, 1980; Beethoven and the Voice of God, 1983; A Darker Shade of Pale: A Backdrop of Bob Dylan, 1984; Angels of the Night: Women Jazz and Pop Singers of the Twentieth Century, 1986; The Masks of Orpheus: Seven Stages in the Story of European Music, 1987; Vaughan Williams and the Vision of Albion, 1989.

ABOUT: Contemporary Authors New Revision Series 4, 1981; Current Biography 1962; New Grove Dictionary of Music and Musicians 12, 1980; Who's Who, 1989. Periodicals—Listener June 23, 1983; October 30, 1986; March 3, 1988; Musical Times July 1984; New Statesman and Nation February 10, 1951; New Statesman March 22, 1968; New York Times July 4, 1974; New York Times Book Review May 16, 1965; September 22, 1974; December 6, 1981; Spectator May 28, 1965; Times Educational Supplement November 13, 1984; January 22, 1988; Times Literary Supplement December 15, 1950; April 12, 1974; December 7, 1984; November 7, 1986; November 20, 1987.

MICHAEL MEWSHAW

MEWSHAW, MICHAEL (February 19, 1943–), American novelist and non-fiction writer, was born in Washington, D. C., son of John Francis and Mary Helen (Dunn) Mewshaw, and grew up in East Riverdale, Maryland. He received his B.A., magna cum laude, from the University of Maryland in 1965, after having been editor of the campus literary magazine and a member of several honor societies, including Phi Beta Kappa. He received his M.A. from the University of Virginia in 1966, and in 1967 married Linda Kirby, by whom he has two sons, Sean and Marc. Mewshaw continued working on his Ph.D. until 1968, at which time he interrupted his doctoral studies to spend eighteen months in France on a Fulbright fellowship in creative writing. During this time he completed his first novel, Man in Motion, which tells the story of a young man named Matthew Hawley, who leaves his hometown in Maryland to acquire experience and become a writer. His travels, however, and the young woman he takes up with, lead to shattering disillusionment, and by the end he returns home to find his elusive identity through the girlfriend he left behind and his familial obligations. Like certain other reviewers, M. Cronan Minton in the Saturday Review found Man in Motion an "unpretentious first novel" with some brilliant scenes, and perhaps best in its evocation of the "funny-horrible" nature of Hawley's odyssey. The reviewer for the Virginia Quarterly Review found the novel inconclusive, but remarked that Mewshaw "writes well and easily, if not profoundly, on a familiar theme."

At the end of his Fulbright year, Mewshaw returned to the United States, completing his Ph.D. in 1970 and becoming assistant professor at the University of Massachusetts, where he taught creative writing and modern fiction from 1970 to 1971. In 1972 he published his second novel, Walking Slow, dealing with a young man recently returned to Washington, D.C. after a brief, abortive career in Vietnam; his life with a young woman, first in Washington and then in Los Angeles; and their eventual breakup. The reviewer for the Virginia Quarterly Review remarked that Mewshaw "has some claim to attention, even though his story offers no solutions to problems presented, resolves nothing, and essentially ends where it began. What commends the book is an enviable fluency in narration and a naturalism in handling dialogue." Although some reviewers commented slightingly on the novel, it was highly praised by Graham Greene, an influence on Mewshaw's fiction, who called it "one of the best black comedies I have read in years."

Declining an offer to join Stanford University's fiction workshop on a Wallace Stegner Fellowship, Mewshaw left America again for two years of travel in Europe, the Middle East, and North Africa. During this period he worked on a third novel, The Toll, published in 1974. This novel concerns a group of American hippie types in Morocco who, with the grandiose thinking of "revolutionary" youths of the 1960s, conspire to free a comrade from a local jail, where he is being held for possession of hash and an unregistered pistol. Ted Kuyler, an older man and veteran of the Korean War, also becomes involved in this doomed enterprise, which ends in betrayal and murder. The novel had a mixed reception. The reviewer for the *Times Literary Supplement* complained that with the exception of Kuyler, Mewshaw's characters were "virtually one-dimensional and our understanding of them—indeed, our desire to understand them—is correspondingly limited." Yet the *New Yorker*'s reviewer considered Mewshaw's success in the work "very considerable," and James R. Frakes in the *New York Times Review* called *The Toll* "one of the most thoroughing strippings-away of man's pretensions to humanity since *Last Exit to Brooklyn*." Many critics were impressed by Mewshaw's remarkable sense of place, as in his description of Moroccan market stalls displaying the slaughtered carcases of animals:

> At a couple of stalls camel heads hung from rusty hooks. Skinned down to the purpling meat and muscle, they still had their eyes and appeared perfectly serene, as though they weren't aware that their bodies had been severed. Below them, like dusty, rundown shoes outside a mosque, their feet stood in neat lines—calloused pads, bracelets of hair, and, extending to the shattered knees, slick pink joints of bone.

In 1973 Mewshaw became associate professor of English at the University of Texas at Austin, and in the following year, with a grant from the National Endowment for the Arts, completed a new novel, *Earthly Bread*. Set in Austin, it concerns a spiritually troubled priest, Father Amico, who is called in by a family that has arranged the kidnapping of their son, a Jesus freak, from a commune, and engaged the services of a noted deprogrammer, Noland Meadlow, to straighten the boy out. Father Amico, it is thought, may serve as a useful mediator between Meadlow and their son. The Austin motel where many of the events occur is rendered in terms of black comedy, its occupants including the former fat lady of a circus, her eccentric husband Zack, and a group of motel whores. But *Earthly Bread* remains, all the while, a novel of ideas. Does anyone, it asks, have the right to interfere with another's religious choices? Mewshaw thought not. Are the deterministic values of Meadlow to be preferred over the striving for a spiritual sense of life? The novel received mixed reviews. James G. Murray in the *Critic* thought that none of the "theological problems raised" were ever resolved, and that in the meantime the narrative lost momentum. But Eugene Chesnick in the *Nation* was impressed by Mewshaw's light-and-dark tale, placing him in "the tradition of Catholic comic novelists—O'Connor, J. F. Powers, Walker Percy."

Mewshaw spent 1975–1976 in Italy and ~ ca writing his novel *Land Without Shadow*, selected in 1979 by the *New York Times Book Review* as one of the year's best works of fiction. *Land Without Shadow* deals with an American film company on location in an African desert nation called Maliteta. The protagonist, a member of the company, discovers that disease and famine are decimating the members of a nearby refugee camp; but the existence of the camp has been kept secret by the government, and the question of whether or not to expose its shameful conditions becomes one of the moral problems faced by the protagonist. The reviewer for the *New Yorker* called *Land Without Shadow* "a strongly sardonic, sometimes affecting novel," and Dennis Pendleton in *Library Journal* found it "vivid and thought-provoking." Alan Cheuse in the *Nation* pointedly compared Mewshaw to Graham Greene in his attention to "problems of conscience." Mewshaw, he remarked, "attempts to work in the spirit rather than the letter of Greene's successes, creating first-rate adventure narration about believable characters set in an atmosphere of moral rigor."

Mewshaw was visiting artist and then writer-in-residence at the American Academy in Rome, 1975–1978, and in 1981 received a Guggenheim Foundation grant for fiction. His novel *The Year of the Gun* came out of that experience. Set in 1977, it concerns an American journalist on the staff of an English-language newspaper in Rome who fabricates a book about penetrating a cell of the Red Brigades, whose members are planning to kidnap Aldo Moro. When the Red Brigades learn of the book, the adventure plot begins to thicken. The reviewer for the *New Yorker* wondered if the situation was believable, but conceded that its "characters are fully constructed, its drive is irresistible, it has intelligent things to say about our age of violence and suspicion, and its depiction of the look and feel and fascination of Rome is almost beyond praise."

Mewshaw has also written books of nonfiction, including *Life for Death* about the imprisonment for life of a fifteen-year-old boy in Maryland for the shooting of his parents. Mewshaw's revelation of the shocking treatment of the youth by his parents and the dubious nature of his trial created a narrative, as Tom Buckley remarked in the *New York Times Book Review*, "that is almost Dickensian in intensity." *Short Circuit* is an exposé of the shady practices of the professional tennis circuit; and *Playing Away* is a journalistic account of the lure of Rome and the Mediterranean. In addition to these books, Mewshaw has published hundreds of articles and reviews in journals and newspapers. In an article in the *Nation* he commented on his preoccupation with traveling. "Personally," he remarked, "I would prefer to go places where at first I don't speak the language or know anybody, where I easily lose my direction and have no delusions that I'm in control. Feeling disoriented, even frightened, I find myself awake, alive, in ways I never would be at home. All my senses are suddenly alert, I can hear again, smell, see—and afterwards, if I'm lucky, I can write."

PRINCIPAL WORKS: Man in Motion, 1970; Walking Slow, 1972; The Toll, 1974; Earthly Bread, 1976; Land Without Shadow, 1979; Life for Death, 1980; Short Circuit, 1983; Year of the Gun, 1984; Blackballed, 1986; Money to Burn: the Story of the Benson Family Murders, 1987; Playing Away, 1988.

ABOUT: Contemporary Authors New Revision Series 7, 1982; Dictionary of Literary Biography, . . . winter 1976; Nation November . . . . Book Review

J. HILLIS MILLER

MILLER, J(OSEPH) HILLIS (March 5, 1928–   ), American scholar, critic, and educator, was born in Newport News, Virginia, to Joseph Hillis Miller, an educator and Baptist minister, and Nell (Critzer) Miller. He spent his early years in Lewisburg, Pennsylvania, where his father was Dean of Men at Bucknell University. The family later moved to upstate New York when the senior Miller became president of Keuka College, a Baptist institution; he later became New York State Associate Commissioner for Higher and Professional Education. With a staunchly Protestant family heritage, Miller attended Sunday school until he was a high school senior, but in later years, he told an interviewer in 1987, he felt that he had learned little about religion: "There was very little real teaching about what's going on in the Bible. . . . So, in one sense I had a religious upbringing, and in another sense I didn't. But what I *was* taught was a rigorous respect for truth, and some kind of vague assumption that the truth might be dark, ominous, not at all reassuring."

At Oberlin College, where Miller received a B.A. summa cum laude and was elected to Phi Beta Kappa in 1948, he had planned to major in physics, but courses in Renaissance literature under Andrew Bongiorno changed his academic direction. At Bongiorno's suggestion he studied Aristotle's *Rhetoric* for a whole semester, training himself in close reading and the analysis of

language. When Miller went to Harvard to begin graduate work, Bongiorno advised him to work with the literary scholar and critic Douglas Bush. Bush was the director of Miller's doctoral dissertation on Dickens, a work which later became his first book, *Charles Dickens: The World of His Novels*. After completing his M.A. (1949) and his Ph.D. (1952), Miller taught for a year at Williams College. In 1953 he accepted an appointment at Johns Hopkins University as an assistant professor of English. In the next twenty years he moved up in academic rank to professor of English and humanities. In 1972 he became professor of English at Yale University where, in 1979, he was named Frederick W. Hilles Professor of English and comparative literature. In 1986 he accepted a professorship in English and comparative literature at the University of California in Irvine, where he now lives. Miller married Dorothy Marian James in 1949. They have three children.

Although Miller has an international reputation as perhaps the most active and prolific of the American critics identified with the movement known as deconstructionism, he is also a prominent and influential figure in higher education. Both at Johns Hopkins and at Yale (where he was chairman of the English department from 1976 to 1979 and directed a number of summer seminars sponsored by the National Endowment for the Humanities), he has trained many graduate students who are now themselves teaching and engaged in criticism and scholarship. Long active in the Modern Language Association, he became its president in 1986,

Recondite as his own writing is, Miller has been much engaged with the practical realities of undergraduate teaching since the crisis years of the 1970s. His presidential address to the MLA, "The Triumph of Theory, the Resistance to Reading, and the Question of the Material Base," is both an impassioned defense of deconstructionism and a plea for strengthening education in the humanities. Speaking as a mediator between a "right-wing" attack on deconstructionism as destructive of traditional literary humanism and a "left-wing" condemnation of the movement as ahistorical and indifferent to the urgent needs of contemporary society, Miller replied "to those of the right . . . that deconstruction by no means destroys literary studies, nor has it caused or exacerbated some crisis in English studies or in humanistic studies generally. On the contrary deconstruction and literary theory generally are the only way to respond to the actual conditions—cultural, economic, institutional, and technological—within which literary study is carried on today." The teaching of expository writing to undergraduates remains a primary goal, but, as Miller sees it, "writing and reading are intimately related and deconstruction, as he writes in *The Ethics of Reading*, "is nothing more or less than good reading as such."

Miller's intellectual development can be traced in the stages of his academic career. At Harvard his dissertation reflected the influence of the New Criticism, the emphasis, that is, on close reading of literary texts as integral, self-contained works of art. During his long tenure at Johns Hopkins he discovered the Geneva school of phenomenological criticism—the writings of Georges Poulet in particular. This approach to literature focuses on the subjective nature of authorship. Rejecting questions of external form, the Geneva critics affirm (as Miller writes of Poulet in an essay on the Geneva school) that literature "is the embodiment of a state of mind . . . a certain mode of consciousness [that] has been brought into the open in a union of mind and words." In their emphasis on the author's consciousness and the critic's concern "for the subjective structure of the mind revealed by the whole body of an author's writing," the Geneva critics reverse the methodology of the New Criticism. At Yale, where Miller was a colleague of Harold Bloom, Geoffrey Hartman, and the late Paul de Man (all of them much influenced by the French deconstructionist critic Jacques Derrida), Miller moved from the so-called "criticism of consciousness" to deconstructionism. As Imre Salusinszky, interviewing Miller in *Criticism in Society*, put it: "Over the period you move from being a Poulet-influenced critic of consciousness, and of the

presence of reality in consciousness, to being a Derrida-influenced critic of language and of the absence of reality in language." To Donald Pease, surveying Miller's writings in *The Yale Critic*: "Several abrupt turns mark the critical career of J. Hillis Miller and withhold from his works that sense of stability and continuity that a lifelong pursuit of a single critical project might otherwise provide." He finds in Miller's career "a curious asymmetry, discernible most clearly in the disjunction between the critical position he claims to represent and the language he uses to describe that project. Throughout Miller's 'later' criticism we find traces and remnants of his earlier positions." Over all, however, Pease is impressed with the "coherence and integrity" of Miller's work in the sense that "if . . . he has failed to identify completely with any . . . critical position, this very fail... adequate repre... tions he is pursuing... Quarterly in the summer of 1980, its value "is not its coherence as theory but the fact that it has made possible new insights into what is going on in particular works even where that has been insight into the necessary blindness of the work to its own incoherence . . . ."

It is his persistent tendency to challenge, to deny, even to undermine received notions of literary study that makes Miller on the one hand so stimulating and on the other so exasperating to read. Reactions to his work, and that of the whole deconstructionist school, are rarely neutral. In the 1980s, a decade marked by a general indifference if not hostility to academic and intellectual theorizing, deconstruction has had a remarkable amount of coverage in the popular press, ranging from articles on the "Yale Mafia" (or the "boa-deconstructors") to outright political attacks on it as elitist, sterile, and even nihilistic. To all this Miller responded mildly in his MLA address that the "minimal obligations" of the academic profession are "to read carefully, patiently, and scrupulously, under the elementary assumption that the text being read may say something different from what one wants or expects it to say or from what received opinion says it says."

At the center of deconstruction is language itself. The primary motivation of his own critical studies, Miller writes in *Fiction and Repetition*, is "to devise a way to remain aware of the strangeness of language and to account for it." Language, the deconstructionists argue, is self-referential. That is, there are no fixed meanings with direct reference to "things as they are."

pers. In an article in the *Nation* he commented on his preoccupation with traveling. "Personally," he remarked, "I would prefer to go places where at first I don't speak the language or know anybody, where I easily lose my direction and have no delusions that I'm in control. Feeling disoriented, even frightened, I find myself awake, alive, in ways I never would be at home. All my senses are suddenly alert, I can hear again, smell, see—and afterwards, if I'm lucky, I can write."

PRINCIPAL WORKS: Man in Motion, 1970; Walking Slow, 1972; The Toll, 1974; Earthly Bread, 1976; Land Without Shadow, 1979; Life for Death, 1980; Short Circuit, 1983; Year of the Gun, 1984; Blackballed, 1986; Money to Burn: the Story of the Benson Family Murders, 1987; Playing Away, 1988.

ABOUT: Contemporary Authors New Revision Series 7, 1982; Dictionary of Literary Biography, 1981. *Periodicals*—Critic Winter 1976; Nation November 13, 1976; July 7, 1979; New York Times Book Review March 24, 1974; New Yorker July 30, 1984; Times Literary Supplement September 6, 1974; Virginia Quarterly Review Winter 1971, Summer 1972.

MILLER, J(OSEPH) HILLIS (March 5, 1928–), American scholar, critic, and educator, was born in Newport News, Virginia, to Joseph Hillis Miller, an educator and Baptist minister, and Nell (Critzer) Miller. He spent his early years in Lewisburg, Pennsylvania, where his father was Dean of Men at Bucknell University. The family later moved to upstate New York when the senior Miller became president of Keuka College, a Baptist institution; he later became New York State Associate Commissioner for Higher and Professional Education. With a staunchly Protestant family heritage, Miller attended Sunday school until he was a high school senior, but in later years, he told an interviewer in 1987, he felt that he had learned little about religion: "There was very little real teaching about what's going on in the Bible. . . . So, in one sense I had a religious upbringing, and in another sense I didn't. But what I *was* taught was a rigorous respect for truth, and some kind of vague assumption that the truth might be dark, ominous, not at all reassuring."

At Oberlin College, where Miller received a B.A. summa cum laude and was elected to Phi Beta Kappa in 1948, he had planned to major in physics, but courses in Renaissance literature under Andrew Bongiorno changed his academic direction. At Bongiorno's suggestion he studied Aristotle's *Rhetoric* for a whole semester, training himself in close reading and the analysis of

J. HILLIS MILLER

language. When Miller went to Harvard to begin graduate work, Bongiorno advised him to work with the literary scholar and critic Douglas Bush. Bush was the director of Miller's doctoral dissertation on Dickens, a work which later became his first book, *Charles Dickens: The World of His Novels*. After completing his M.A. (1949) and his Ph.D. (1952), Miller taught for a year at Williams College. In 1953 he accepted an appointment at Johns Hopkins University as an assistant professor of English. In the next twenty years he moved up in academic rank to professor of English and humanities. In 1972 he became professor of English at Yale University where, in 1979, he was named Frederick W. Hilles Professor of English and comparative literature. In 1986 he accepted a professorship in English and comparative literature at the University of California in Irvine, where he now lives. Miller married Dorothy Marian James in 1949. They have three children.

Although Miller has an international reputation as perhaps the most active and prolific of the American critics identified with the movement known as deconstructionism, he is also a prominent and influential figure in higher education. Both at Johns Hopkins and at Yale (where he was chairman of the English department from 1976 to 1979 and directed a number of summer seminars sponsored by the National Endowment for the Humanities), he has trained many graduate students who are now themselves teaching and engaged in criticism and scholarship. Long active in the Modern Language Association, he became its president in 1986.

Recondite as his own writing is, Miller has been much engaged with the practical realities of undergraduate teaching since the crisis years of the 1970s. His presidential address to the MLA, "The Triumph of Theory, the Resistance to Reading, and the Question of the Material Base," is both an impassioned defense of deconstructionism and a plea for strengthening education in the humanities. Speaking as a mediator between a "right-wing" attack on deconstructionism as destructive of traditional literary humanism and a "left-wing" condemnation of the movement as ahistorical and indifferent to the urgent needs of contemporary society, Miller replied "to those of the right . . . that deconstruction by no means destroys literary studies, nor has it caused or exacerbated some crisis in English studies or in humanistic studies generally. On the contrary, deconstruction and literary theory generally are the only way to respond to the actual conditions—cultural, economic, institutional, and technological—within which literary study is carried on today." The teaching of expository writing to undergraduates remains a primary goal, but, as Miller sees it, "writing and reading are intimately related" and deconstruction, as he writes in *The Ethics of Reading*, "is nothing more or less than good reading as such."

Miller's intellectual development can be traced in the stages of his academic career. At Harvard his dissertation reflected the influence of the New Criticism, the emphasis, that is, on close reading of literary texts as integral, self-contained works of art. During his long tenure at Johns Hopkins he discovered the Geneva school of phenomenological criticism—the writings of Georges Poulet in particular. This approach to literature focuses on the subjective nature of authorship. Rejecting questions of external form, the Geneva critics affirm (as Miller writes of Poulet in an essay on the Geneva school) that literature "is the embodiment of a state of mind . . . a certain mode of consciousness [that] has been brought into the open in a union of mind and words." In their emphasis on the author's consciousness and the critic's concern "for the subjective structure of the mind revealed by the whole body of an author's writing," the Geneva critics reverse the methodology of the New Criticism. At Yale, where Miller was a colleague of Harold Bloom, Geoffrey Hartman, and the late Paul de Man (all of them much influenced by the French deconstructionist critic Jacques Derrida), Miller moved from the so-called "criticism of consciousness" to deconstructionism. As Imre Salusinszky, interviewing Miller in *Criticism in Society*, put it: "Over the period you move from being a Poulet-influenced critic of consciousness, and of the presence of reality in consciousness, to being a Derrida-influenced critic of language and of the absence of reality in language." To Donald Pease, surveying Miller's writings in *The Yale Critic*: "Several abrupt turns mark the critical career of J. Hillis Miller and withhold from his works that sense of stability and continuity that a lifelong pursuit of a single critical project might otherwise provide." He finds in Miller's career "a curious asymmetry, discernible most clearly in the disjunction between the critical position he claims to represent and the language he uses to describe that project. Throughout Miller's 'later' criticism we find traces and remnants of his earlier positions." Over all, however, Pease is impressed with the "coherence and integrity" of Miller's work in the sense that "if . . . he has failed to identify completely with any single critical position, this very failure turns him into an adequate representative of a profession of critics trying to make sense of its loss of conviction." In deconstruction Miller has not found conclusive answers to the critical questions he is pursuing but, as he wrote in *Critical Quarterly* in the summer of 1980, its value "is not its coherence as theory but the fact that it has made possible new insights into what is going on in particular works even where that has been insight into the necessary blindness of the work to its own incoherence . . . ."

It is his persistent tendency to challenge, to deny, even to undermine received notions of literary study that makes Miller on the one hand so stimulating and on the other so exasperating to read. Reactions to his work, and that of the whole deconstructionist school, are rarely neutral. In the 1980s, a decade marked by a general indifference if not hostility to academic and intellectual theorizing, deconstruction has had a remarkable amount of coverage in the popular press, ranging from articles on the "Yale Mafia" (or the "boa-deconstructors") to outright political attacks on it as elitist, sterile, and even nihilistic. To all this Miller responded mildly in his MLA address that the "minimal obligations" of the academic profession are "to read carefully, patiently, and scrupulously, under the elementary assumption that the text being read may say something different from what one wants or expects it to say or from what received opinion says it says."

At the center of deconstruction is language itself. The primary motivation of his own critical studies, Miller writes in *Fiction and Repetition*, is "to devise a way to remain aware of the strangeness of language and to account for it." Language, the deconstructionists argue, is self-referential. That is, there are no fixed meanings with direct reference to "things as they are."

atre, c. 1600–1900, 1965; Music in a New Found Land: Themes and Developments in American Music, 1964; Caliban Reborn: Renewal in Twentieth Century Music, 1967; Twilight of the Gods: The Beatles in Retrospect, 1973; Bach and the Dance of God, 1980; Beethoven and the Voice of God, 1983; A Darker Shade of Pale: A Backdrop of Bob Dylan, 1984; Angels of the Night: Women Jazz and Pop Singers of the Twentieth Century, 1986; The Masks of Orpheus: Seven Stages in the Story of European Music, 1987; Vaughan Williams and the Vision of Albion, 1989.

ABOUT: Contemporary Authors New Revision Series 4, 1981; Current Biography 1962; New Grove Dictionary of Music and Musicians 12, 1980; Who's Who, 1989. *Periodicals*—Listener June 23, 1983; October 30, 1986; March 3, 1988; Musical Times July 1984; New Statesman and Nation February 10, 1951; New Statesman March 22, 1968; New York Times July 4, 1974; New York Times Book Review May 16, 1965; September 22, 1974; December 6, 1981; Spectator May 28, 1965; Times Educational Supplement November 13, 1984; January 22, 1988; Times Literary Supplement December 15, 1950; April 12, 1974; December 7, 1984; November 7, 1986; November 20, 1987.

MEWSHAW, MICHAEL (February 19, 1943–), American novelist and non-fiction writer, was born in Washington, D. C., son of John Francis and Mary Helen (Dunn) Mewshaw, and grew up in East Riverdale, Maryland. He received his B.A., magna cum laude, from the University of Maryland in 1965, after having been editor of the campus literary magazine and a member of several honor societies, including Phi Beta Kappa. He received his M.A. from the University of Virginia in 1966, and in 1967 married Linda Kirby, by whom he has two sons, Sean and Marc. Mewshaw continued working on his Ph.D. until 1968, at which time he interrupted his doctoral studies to spend eighteen months in France on a Fulbright fellowship in creative writing. During this time he completed his first novel, *Man in Motion*, which tells the story of a young man named Matthew Hawley, who leaves his hometown in Maryland to acquire experience and become a writer. His travels, however, and the young woman he takes up with, lead to shattering disillusionment, and by the end he returns home to find his elusive identity through the girlfriend he left behind and his familial obligations. Like certain other reviewers, M. Cronan Minton in the *Saturday Review* found *Man in Motion* an "unpretentious first novel" with some brilliant scenes, and perhaps best in its evocation of the "funny-horrible" nature of Hawley's odyssey. The reviewer for the *Virginia Quarterly Review* found the novel inconclusive, but remarked that Mewshaw "writes well and easily, if not profoundly, on a familiar theme."

MICHAEL MEWSHAW

At the end of his Fulbright year, Mewshaw returned to the United States, completing his Ph.D. in 1970 and becoming assistant professor at the University of Massachusetts, where he taught creative writing and modern fiction from 1970 to 1971. In 1972 he published his second novel, *Walking Slow*, dealing with a young man recently returned to Washington, D.C. after a brief, abortive career in Vietnam; his life with a young woman, first in Washington and then in Los Angeles; and their eventual breakup. The reviewer for the *Virginia Quarterly Review* remarked that Mewshaw "has some claim to attention, even though his story offers no solutions to problems presented, resolves nothing, and essentially ends where it began. What commends the book is an enviable fluency in narration and a naturalism in handling dialogue." Although some reviewers commented slightingly on the novel, it was highly praised by Graham Greene, an influence on Mewshaw's fiction, who called it "one of the best black comedies I have read in years."

Declining an offer to join Stanford University's fiction workshop on a Wallace Stegner Fellowship, Mewshaw left America again for two years of travel in Europe, the Middle East, and North Africa. During this period he worked on a third novel, *The Toll*, published in 1974. This novel concerns a group of American hippie types in Morocco who, with the grandiose thinking of "revolutionary" youths of the 1960s, conspire to free a comrade from a local jail, where he is being held for possession of hash and an unregistered pistol. Ted Kuyler, an older man and veteran of the Korean War, also becomes involved in this doomed enterprise, which ends in betrayal and murder. The novel had a mixed reception. The reviewer for the *Times Literary Supplement* complained that with the exception of Kuyler, Mewshaw's characters were "virtually one-dimensional and our understanding of them—indeed, our desire to understand them— is correspondingly limited." Yet the *New Yorker*'s reviewer considered Mewshaw's success in the work "very considerable," and James R. Frakes in the *New York Times Review* called *The Toll* "one of the most thoroughing strippings-away of man's pretensions to humanity since *Last Exit to Brooklyn*." Many critics were impressed by Mewshaw's remarkable sense of place, as in his description of Moroccan market stalls displaying the slaughtered carcases of animals:

> At a couple of stalls camel heads hung from rusty hooks. Skinned down to the purpling meat and muscle, they still had their eyes and appeared perfectly serene, as though they weren't aware that their bodies had been severed. Below them, like dusty, rundown shoes outside a mosque, their feet stood in neat lines—calloused pads, bracelets of hair, and, extending to the shattered knees, slick pink joints of bone.

In 1973 Mewshaw became associate professor of English at the University of Texas at Austin, and in the following year, with a grant from the National Endowment for the Arts, completed a new novel, *Earthly Bread*. Set in Austin, it concerns a spiritually troubled priest, Father Amico, who is called in by a family that has arranged the kidnapping of their son, a Jesus freak, from a commune, and engaged the services of a noted deprogrammer, Noland Meadlow, to straighten the boy out. Father Amico, it is thought, may serve as a useful mediator between Meadlow and their son. The Austin motel where many of the events occur is rendered in terms of black comedy, its occupants including the former fat lady of a circus, her eccentric husband Zack, and a group of motel whores. But *Earthly Bread* remains, all the while, a novel of ideas. Does anyone, it asks, have the right to interfere with another's religious choices? Mewshaw thought not. Are the deterministic values of Meadlow to be preferred over the striving for a spiritual sense of life? The novel received mixed reviews. James G. Murray in the *Critic* thought that none of the "theological problems raised" were ever resolved, and that in the meantime the narrative lost momentum. But Eugene Chesnick in the *Nation* was impressed by Mewshaw's light-and-dark tale, placing him in "the tradition of Catholic comic novelists—O'Connor, J. F. Powers, Walker Percy."

Mewshaw spent 1975–1976 in Italy and Africa writing his novel *Land Without Shadow*, selected in 1979 by the *New York Times Book Review* as one of the year's best works of fiction. *Land Without Shadow* deals with an American film company on location in an African desert nation called Maliteta. The protagonist, a member of the company, discovers that disease and famine are decimating the members of a nearby refugee camp; but the existence of the camp has been kept secret by the government, and the question of whether or not to expose its shameful conditions becomes one of the moral problems faced by the protagonist. The reviewer for the *New Yorker* called *Land Without Shadow* "a strongly sardonic, sometimes affecting novel," and Dennis Pendleton in *Library Journal* found it "vivid and thought-provoking." Alan Cheuse in the *Nation* pointedly compared Mewshaw to Graham Greene in his attention to "problems of conscience." Mewshaw, he remarked, "attempts to work in the spirit rather than the letter of Greene's successes, creating first-rate adventure narration about believable characters set in an atmosphere of moral rigor."

Mewshaw was visiting artist and then writer-in-residence at the American Academy in Rome, 1975–1978, and in 1981 received a Guggenheim Foundation grant for fiction. His novel *The Year of the Gun* came out of that experience. Set in 1977, it concerns an American journalist on the staff of an English-language newspaper in Rome who fabricates a book about penetrating a cell of the Red Brigades, whose members are planning to kidnap Aldo Moro. When the Red Brigades learn of the book, the adventure plot begins to thicken. The reviewer for the *New Yorker* wondered if the situation was believable, but conceded that its "characters are fully constructed, its drive is irresistible, it has intelligent things to say about our age of violence and suspicion, and its depiction of the look and feel and fascination of Rome is almost beyond praise."

Mewshaw has also written books of nonfiction, including *Life for Death* about the imprisonment for life of a fifteen-year-old boy in Maryland for the shooting of his parents. Mewshaw's revelation of the shocking treatment of the youth by his parents and the dubious nature of his trial created a narrative, as Tom Buckley remarked in the *New York Times Book Review*, "that is almost Dickensian in intensity." *Short Circuit* is an exposé of the shady practices of the professional tennis circuit; and *Playing Away* is a journalistic account of the lure of Rome and the Mediterranean. In addition to these books, Mewshaw has published hundreds of articles and reviews in journals and newspa-

Perhaps the clearest exposition of the deconstructionist position is in Miller's review (in *Diacritics*, Winter 1972) of M. H. Abrams' *Natural Supernaturalism*, a highly respected study of romantic literature which described the transformation or reformulation of Christian theology by the romantic poets into a natural and humanistic frame of reference. While praising the book for its scholarship, Miller argued that Abrams had "oversimplified the problem" with a narrow view of language as mimetic and of literary texts as having single, unequivocal meanings. Language, Miller writes, "is from the start fictive, illusory, displaced from any direct reference to things as they are. The human condition is to be caught in a web of words . . . ." The meaning of a passage of poetry is "multiple, vibrating, ambiguous. It cannot be reduced to a single, unequivocal statement." Elsewhere Miller refers to literary texts as "labyrinths" with the critic seeking the "Ariadne thread" in order to move through the twisting corridors of language. "Deconstruction as a mode of interpretation works by a careful and circumspect entering of each textual labyrinth. . . . [It employs] a subversive power," seeking that which is "alogical, the thread in the text in question which will unravel it all, or the loose stone which will pull down the whole building. . . . Deconstruction is not a dismantling of the structure of the text but a demonstration that it has already dismantled itself."

To this line of reasoning Abrams replied in an essay, "The Deconstructive Angel" (*Critical Inquiry*, Spring 1977), that if deconstructionist principles operate, "any history which relies on written texts becomes an impossibility." Language, Abrams wrote, "is a cultural institution that developed expressly in order to mean something," and a criticism that would deconstruct language "has nothing to do with our common experience of the uniqueness, the rich variety, and the passionate human concerns in works of literature, philosophy, or criticism." Other critics of deconstruction have similarly noted the paradox of a critical system that insists on the unintelligibility or "unreality" of language. Gerald Graff, for example, writes in *Literature Against Itself* (1979): "In a world in which nobody can look outside the walls of the prison house of language, literature, with its built-in confession of its self-imprisonment, becomes once again the great oracle of truth, but now the truth is that there is no truth."

Miller's criticism ranges widely over nineteenth- and twentieth-century literature, prose, poetry, and the novel. The most widely read and influential of his books remains *The Disappearance of God*, written while he was still working with the consciousness theories of the Geneva school. In this book Miller writes that there had been a time of harmony in Western civilization when "God, man, nature, and language participated in each other," and "the words of the poem incarnated the things they named." But after the Middle Ages fragmentation set in, a sharp division between the world and the thing, the word (signifier) and what it represented (the signified), subject and object: "The lines of connection between us and God have broken down, or God himself has slipped away from the places where he used to be. . . . As a result the nineteenth and twentieth centuries seem to many writers a time when God is no more present, and can only be experienced negatively, as a terrifying absence. . . . This splitting apart has been matched by a similar dispersal of the cultural unity of man, God, nature and language." Miller argues that the writers he is treating in *The Disappearance of God*—De Quincey, Browning, Emily Brontë, Matthew Arnold, and Gerard Manley Hopkins—all belonged to the tradition of romanticism, with a strong faith in God and an urgent need to "re-establish communication." As a result, they sought symbols that would establish "a new relation" between man and God, a new consciousness: "The artist is the man who goes out into the empty space between man and God and takes the enormous risk of attempting to create in that vacancy a new fabric of connections between man and the divine power. The romantic artist is a maker or discoverer of the radically new, rather than the imitator of what is already known."

The Disappearance of God hardly revolutionized the teaching of nineteenth-century literature, proposing essentially a displacement or shifting of consciousness that had been recognized by readers for many years. Reviewers also questioned Miller's selective approach, studying passages out of their context and often narrowly focusing on them rather than considering works as a whole. But, David DeLaura wrote in *Victorian Prose: A Guide to Research* (1973): "Miller's exceptional literary perceptiveness generally surmounts any incoherence in his controversial methodology, a difficult combination of formalist attention to style and existential or structuralist concern for the 'organizing form' in the consciousness of the author." There was a similar reaction to his *The Form of Victorian Fiction*, a study of literary form in the major Victorian novelists, in which Miller argues that "the novel is a structure of interpenetrating minds, the mind of the narrator as he beholds or enters into the characters, the minds of the characters as they behold or know one another. Not isolated consciousness, not consciousness at grips with natural objects, not consciousness face to face with God in meditation, but consciousness of the consciousness of others—this is the primary focus of fiction." Reviewers complained of Miller's "densely metaphysical" writing and his "difficult brilliance." Nevertheless there was consensus that it was a stimulating and provocative book that demanded much of the reader but was rewarding for its insights into the subjectivity of Victorian fiction.

In twentieth-century poetry as in nineteenth-century literature Miller discerned the same alienation from God, only now intensified to the Nietzschean "death of God." *Poets of Reality* discusses poets who began "with an experience of nihilism or its concomitants" and individually shaped their own new realities—Yeats, Eliot, Dylan Thomas, Wallace Stevens, and William Carlos Williams. It is the reshaping of their consciousness that Miller studies—a re-affirmation of the unity of a writer's work even in what appears to be the fragmented universe from which God has withdrawn. Even as late as 1982, in *Fiction and Repetition*, Miller continued to seek a sense of unity, if not univocal meaning, in literature. By this time a deconstructionist, he nevertheless sought—through a study of recurrences of rhetorical figures and images in a variety of novels ranging from Conrad's to Virginia Woolf's—"to account for the totality of a given work . . . the best critical essays are those which more or less overtly confront the question of what a total reading of the work at hand would be . . . a total accounting." Deconstruction has convinced him "that the specific heterogeneity of a given text can be exactly defined, even though a univocal meaning cannot be justified by the text."

Though some might call him a polemicist for deconstruction, since the mid-1980s Miller has moved increasingly into the position of a mediator, attempting, in response to its critics, to show its ethical as well as its intellectual bases. *The Linguistic Moment*, dedicated to the memory of Paul de Man, studies images of time in poetry from Wordsworth to Wallace Stevens, "moments of suspension within the texts of poems . . . when they reflect or comment on their own medium" and ultimately "dominate the functioning of the whole poem." Viewing these images as fundamental in literature, as they are in human life, he concludes that "literature is therefore inalienably ethical, philosophical, metaphysical, even religious." *The Ethics of Reading* expands upon this thesis with chapters on Kant, de Man, George Eliot, Trollope, Henry James, and Walter Benjamin. Miller begins by questioning the extent to which the act of reading itself is ethical, and proposes that "there is a necessary ethical moment in that act of reading as such, a moment neither cognitive, nor political, nor social, nor interpersonal, but properly and independently ethical." In passages from the authors under study he finds a relationship between storytelling and "universal moral law . . . even if that storytelling in one way or another puts in question or subverts the moral law." In the rhetorical study of literature as practiced by the deconstructionists, he discovers "the strange and difficult notion that reading is subject not to the text as its law but to the law to which the text is subject. The law forces the reader to betray the text or deviate from it in the act of reading it, in the name of a higher demand that can be reached only by way of the text."

In the summer of 1988 Miller engaged in a debate with the critic Tzvetan Todorov in the pages of the *Times Literary Supplement* (June 17–23) over the alleged Nazi sympathies expressed by Paul de Man during 1941–1942 when he was writing for a French student journal and two Belgian newspapers. De Man had been a disciple of the German philosopher Martin Heidegger who had openly professed his support for National Socialism. Claiming that the charges against de Man in the press were "extraordinary falsifications, misreadings, distortions and selective slanting of quotations," Miller wrote that in his early journalism de Man had been "by no means totally fascist, antisemitic, and collaborationist," and that he had not been named as a collaborator by French authorities after the war. Miller suggested that "the real target" was not de Man but deconstruction: "The real aim is to discredit that form of interpretation called 'deconstruction,' to obliterate it, as far as possible, from the curriculum, to dissuade students of literature, philosophy and culture from reading de Man's work or that of his associates, to put a stop to the 'influence' of 'deconstruction.'"

PRINCIPAL WORKS: Charles Dickens: The World of His Novels, 1958; The Disappearance of God: Five Nineteenth-Century Writers, 1963; Poets of Reality: Six Twentieth-Century Writers, 1965; The Form of Victorian Fiction, 1968; Thomas Hardy: Distance and Desire, 1970; Fiction and Repetition: Seven English Novels, 1982; The Linguistic Moment, 1985; The Ethics of Reading, 1986.

ABOUT: Arac, J., W. Godzich, W. Martin (eds.) The Yale Critics: Deconstruction in America, 1983; Borklund, E. Contemporary Literary Critics, 1982; Contemporary Authors 85–88, 1980; Dictionary of Literary Biography 67, 1988; Hartman, G. (ed.) Deconstruction and Criticism, 1979; Moynihan, R. A Recent Imagining, 1986; Salusinszky, I. Criticism in Society, 1987; Who's Who in America, 1988–1989. Periodicals—Critical Inquiry 3, 1977, 6, 1980; Criticism 24, 1982.

MORGAN, (GEORGE) FREDERICK

(April 25, 1922–), American poet, prose writer, translator, and editor, was born in New York City to John W. and Marion (Burt) Morgan. His father was a well-to-do manufacturer, and young Morgan, an only child, was educated in private schools—St. Bernard's in New York City and St. Paul's in Concord, New Hampshire He entered Princeton University in 1939 interested in studying music (piano and composition), but an interview in his freshman year with the poet and critic Allen Tate, then on the faculty, convinced him that literature and creative writing were his future. "He and I got along right from the start," Morgan told Peter Brazeau in an interview in 1979, "so I got into his course. That was a great breakthrough for me. I credit Allen with having probably done more for me than anyone else in terms of literary influence, not so much a poetic influence as an influence in getting me started on that road in my early reading and the development of my interest." After graduation in 1943, Morgan served in World War II from 1943 to 1945 in the Tank Destroyer Corps. On returning to civilian life, he made a definitive choice between literature and a career in business or law. With two fellow Princetonians, Joseph Bennett and William Arrowsmith, he founded a literary quarterly, the *Hudson Review*. First published in 1948, this journal has fulfilled the original aims of its founders: "Make the best new creative and critical works available, and give the reader an overall focus on literary developments, and on other arts in so far as possible, abroad as well as at home."

In its first year *Hudson Review* published the work of such distinguished writers as R. P. Blackmur, Wallace Stevens, Mark Schorer, Herbert Read, and Thomas Mann. Bennett and Arrowsmith eventually left the journal for other literary projects, but Morgan has remained its editor for over forty years. Since 1975 he has had a co-editor, the art critic Paula Deitz, his third wife, whom he married in 1969. During these years, Morgan wrote, as he says, "spasmodically." He found himself blocked as a poet: "It wasn't that I would try to write and couldn't; I kept putting off the writing. I had many poems begun but wasn't able to finish them, didn't spend the time. Most of my energy was diverted to *The Hudson Review*; I also had a lot of family responsibilities." Two earlier marriages, to Constance Canfield in 1942, and to Rose Fillmore in 1957, had ended in divorce. From his first marriage he had six children, one of whom, a son, committed suicide in 1968.

Within a few months of his son's death, Morgan began to write poetry. What was at least in part a therapeutic act proved to be in fact a turn-

FREDERICK MORGAN

ing point in Morgan's life. "The death of anyone who's very close shocks and hurts one," he told Brazeau, "but it makes one realize that whatever is important in one's life, one should start right now and do it. My son's death was a shattering blow that led to a whole series of changes in my life, of which my third marriage was the most rewarding. The resumption of my writing went along with these other changes; I see everything as having come together. They were all creative responses to that tragic event."

In 1972, at the age of fifty, Morgan published his first collection of poetry, *A Book of Change*. The volume received excellent reviews and a National Book Award nomination. Since then he has published a number of volumes of poetry and prose, as well as translations from French, Spanish, Italian, and ancient Greek and Latin poetry. This remarkable record of creativity is not as sudden as it appears. Morgan had devoted his career up to 1972 to reading, publishing, and encouraging the work of other poets. He had also for more than a decade been reading systematically in oriental religions, particularly the Hindu scriptures and the Chinese philosophers. *A Book of Change* echoed in its title the *I Ching*, and Morgan's poems share with these writings a strongly mystical and meditative quality. Another shaping influence on him was Ezra Pound whom he visited at St. Elizabeth's Hospital in Washington, D C, and whose work (the translation of the *Analects* of Confucius, *The Women of Trachis*, some of the *Cantos*) he published in the *Hudson Review*. Although he felt that Pound "was unquestionably somewhat deranged," he also found him "the most forceful and impressive person I have ever met." What he learned from Pound, he says, "broadened my sense of the tradition and the importance of translation."

The poems in *A Book of Change* reflect the many literary influences that Morgan had absorbed over the years, but these are thoroughly assimilated in a distinctly individual poetic voice. He works in a variety of forms—lyric quatrains, sonnets, triolets, long Whitmanesque lines, even prose poems. The most striking quality of these poems, according to several reviewers, is their openness and lucidity—the honesty and candor with which Morgan traces what Laurence Lieberman calls "the slow, irreversible growth of a second mental life—the fruition of a totally new sensibility." The book opens with a cool and serene lyric:

Two birds are perched in the midnight tree.
One whistles, hops and preens
his golden plumage ceaselessly;
he can't think what he means.

The other—motionless, discreet—
watches with golden eyes
till their twin radiances meet
in the profound sunrise.

But this is immediately followed by a poem dated July 30, 1968, in which his late son appears to him:

This was the first time I could dream of you,
or perhaps, the first time I had the strength to
    remember,
and I thank God for it and for the pain and the tears—
May they open my heart to the depths of life and death.

There are love poems, many of them directly addressed to Paula Deitz, and religious poems affirming his faith that "To live in the moment, each day as it comes, / requires a discipline and cleanliness." The God he confronts is a spirit of acceptance: "Count on nothing at all / except that I will love and try you hard." But this is a life-affirming resolution: "It's death to cling to me, but life to find me."

Deeply personal as *A Book of Change* is, it nevertheless addresses enduring and universal themes. "These are the age-old offices of poetry," Guy Davenport wrote in the *New York Times Book Review*, "and Mr. Morgan always writes with the age-old belief that poetry is a social bond, like language itself, and that poetry is the more meaningful for being public, transparent and eloquent."

Implicit in *A Book of Change* is the duality of the external natural world and the inner world of dream and spirit. Morgan's second collection, *Poems of the Two Worlds*, explores this duality

with what critics noted as even greater amplitude and an even surer grasp of poetic technique, meter, and sound. Hayden Carruth, in the *New Republic*, considers him a "religious" poet but not in any sectarian sense: "a man settled in his faith and happy in it." He draws deeply on memories of his past—sensitive evocations of his childhood ("A small boy is moving along a country road at night. He walks / alongside stone walls feeling their roughness intimately"), love affairs described in often erotic detail (Carruth calls him "very much a man-of-the-world . . . in either world"), but also celebrates the joys of his present life:

Joy to the fellows of my heart,
persons of woodland, of shore and sea—
joy to the brethren of my heart
dwelling in magnanimity.

—"The Word"

Stanley Kunitz compares him to the Chinese philosopher Lao-tse in his grasp of the fullness of all life, material and spiritual: "Eros is the proprietary spirit of Frederick Morgan's dominion. But he is also attended by his household gods, defenders of the daily life, who instruct him in the art of transforming ordinary experiences into sacred events, meditations, and celebrations."

Evident in Morgan's work since *Poems of the Two Worlds* is a movement toward poetic narrative in the form of parables and legends. Increasingly, in prose and poetry alike, he has focused on mystical experience, framed sometimes in Hindu, Chinese, Norse, or ancient Greek mythology, sometimes in simpler fairytale imagery. The title poem of *Death Mother and Other Poems* is addressed to a personal and personified Death seen as the mother image of primitive myth. She is the archetypal *femme fatale* in the literal rather than seductive sense:

You came as sleep, warily:
when I woke
things had a deep-blue look.

You disguised yourself as night, but
behind the stars
I saw dark flashes of your body.

And as for dreams—
how many you tried me with!
It seems you never weary of your
hopeful grim deceptions

as though I stood in need of such
visions of filth and blood
to move me to acknowledge your
dominion, mother.

At moments she is loving, "playful and sportive"; at other times she is terrifying. Like the Hindu Kali, she is goddess of both creation and destruc-

tion. Why do we mythologize death, the poet asks: "Why / get into talk of legends and deities / with all their paraphernalia?" The poet answers his question:

        All notions
    of continuance build up in us expectancy—
    and *that* is perhaps the answer: life
    as lived, responsive to its fiercest surge
    assumes its own indefinite extension . . .
    He has not fully lived, Lorenzo de' Medici said,
    who has not felt that other life to come—
    and yet one must not dwell on it too much
    or put on airs. The light goes out for sure

    and all the rest is images—in whose mind?

Poems of the Two Worlds contains a selection of short prose-poems, "Five Ballets," which are imaginative dream pieces—"Elves," "Demons," "Angels," "Pterodactyls," and "Nightwatchers." These anticipate the enigmatic prose parables of *The Tarot of Cornelius Agrippa*. In contrast to the clarity and firm resolution of his meditative, consolatory poems which struck some of his critics as didactic, the prose pieces are, in Morgan's words, "more tentative and exploratory. Poets have to be that, because they're really discovering themselves in the process of writing. Even the didacticism is for me, in a sense, a self-discovery. Often it's ironic." Each prose parable is printed opposite an illustration from a seventeenth-century tarot deck, and there is an oblique relationship between image and text. The prose itself is simple and unadorned. The time is the timeless world of the spirit—an innocent, natural world before mankind befouled it or perhaps after mankind destroys itself and the world is restored to its pristine condition. Sorcerers, angels, devils, talking animals, and mortal humans are the characters. In one parable an aging street magician confronts a younger image of himself in a mirror: "The two stood silent for many minutes—then as by a mutual consent, positions were instantaneously reversed. The one entered a realm of austere silence; the other resumed the journey, a journey that was no longer the same." In another a mortal tries to explain the meaning of love to a group of animals: "When you love," he tells them, "you know that existence has meaning and that you yourself are a part of that meaning." To this an elephant replies: "This feeling you have expressed is something we animals are continuously aware of from the very fact of being alive. It would appear that you men begin at somewhat of a disadvantage, and can only under special circumstances come to know life in its fullness."

Precisely what these parables mean Morgan himself is uncertain. Reading *The Tarot* for a radio taping, he recalls: "it struck me how really strange some of them are. I don't understand them, absolutely not. I could give a few clues as to what I was thinking of when I started, what imagery was in my mind, but then in expressing themselves they bring in materials I find unexpected and exciting. I have the feeling, 'My, could I really have written that?'" Readers of *The Tarot* have had similar reactions but recognized the haunting dream quality that the parables evoke. Dana Gioia wrote, in the *Southern Review*, "Somehow the demands of the parable form, the set interplay between his words and the illustrations of the cards. . . . all focused Morgan's imagination into creating an original and nearly perfect book." In *The Fountain and Other Fables*, another collection of his prose pieces, Morgan was less obscure, adopting the simple, forthright language of children's stories. They are not, however, simple fables in the manner of Aesop and La Fontaine. They are instead, as Monroe K. Spears observed in the *Sewanee Review*, more like "the modern open-ended fables of Borges, Kafka, Calvino . . . spare, concise, lucid, but with haunting and disturbing overtones." The fables, like his poetry, offer subtle variations on the theme of change and growth, dealing with the two worlds of reality and the imagination and the magician's (or poet's) power to fuse them. Spears writes: "These are fables whose meanings expand in the mind and are not exhausted by a single reading."

The publication of Morgan's *Poems: New and Selected* in 1987 gave his readers an opportunity to review his entire oeuvre up to that time. The volume contains twelve new poems, including one that is a collection of eight triolets, and selections from his earlier works. It is thus possible to see Morgan's development as a poet and a thinker over a span of fifteen years, to appreciate the variety but also the consistency of his work. The variety is apparent in the range of his subjects— from Greek and Norse myth to daily experiences of joy and pain to explorations of the mysteries of life and death—and in the equally broad scope of his translations. Robert Schultz observed, in the *Virginia Quarterly Review*, that in this collection Morgan "writes with equal gusto about theosophy and sex, about the fabulous and the quotidian, in verse free or formal, lyric or narrative." Read straight through, *Poems: New and Collected* reveals a poet who is essentially empirical, though fascinated by mysticism and mythology. Jerome Mazzaro, in the *Sewanee Review*, compares him to the philosopher F. H. Bradley in that "he senses a spiritual reality united in diversity and a harmonious system of experience that challenges imagination." Learned and abstruse as many of his points of reference are, Morgan writes a poetry of statement rather

than of image, achieving his effects, Schultz observes, "by accumulation of detail rather than crystallization, building by theme and illustration." In the first of the new poems in this volume, "Meditations for Autumn," Morgan writes: "Old names are out of fashion / and the new ones unconvincing; / one suffers nonetheless." His aim, according to Schultz, "has been to articulate his desire and to find a style by which a contemporary speaker can credibly explore the transcendent." In Daniel Hoffman's judgment of *Poems: New and Selected*, in the *Southern Review*, Morgan has succeeded in doing this: "Frederick Morgan's poems are unmistakable. He writes with a clarity, a seeming simplicity, in a style that enables him to dramatize the importunate themes of life, death and transcendence. He is a visionary poet, at once metaphysical and autobiographical, his grasp of mysteries as sure as his perception of the visible. The range and scope of the lyrics, fables, and dramatic monologues in this collection should make plain Morgan's stature as one of our most original and accomplished poets."

In 1982 Morgan lost his oldest daughter to cancer, and in 1990 his son Seth, who had survived drugs, alcohol, and prison to write a highly acclaimed novel, *Homeboy*, was killed in a motorcycle accident.

PRINCIPAL WORKS: *Poetry*—A Book of Change, 1972; Poems of the Two Worlds, 1977; Death Mother and Other Poems, 1979; Refractions, 1981; Northbook, 1982; Eleven Poems, 1983; Poems: New and Selected, 1987. *Prose*—The Tarot of Cornelius Agrippa, 1978; The Fountain and Other Fables, 1985.

ABOUT: Contemporary Authors 21, 1987; Contemporary Literary Criticism 23, 1983; Contemporary Poets, 4th ed., 1985; Hoffman, D. (ed.) Harvard Guide to Contemporary American Writing, 1979; Lieberman, L. Unassigned Frequencies: American Poetry in Review 1964–1977, 1977. *Periodicals*—New Republic May 15, 1976; New England Review Spring 1979; New York Times Book Review April 1, 1973; Sewanee Review Winter 1984, Spring 1986, Winter 1988; Southern Review Autumn 1979, Winter 1989; Times Literary Supplement July 2, 1982; Virginia Quarterly Review Winter 1988.

MORRIS, RICHARD B(RANDON) (July 24, 1904–March 3, 1989), American historian, was born in New York City, the son of Jacob Morris and the former Tillie Rosenberg. He attended public schools and was graduated cum laude from City College in 1924. After graduate work in history at Columbia University, he received his master's degree in 1925 and his doctorate in 1930. He began his teaching career in

RICHARD B. MORRIS

1927 at City College as instructor; he was assistant professor from 1932, associate professor from 1937, and full professor from 1947. In 1949 he became professor of history at Columbia, and from 1959 until his retirement in 1973 held Columbia's Gouverneur Morris chair in American history. He was departmental chairman from 1958 to 1961.

Morris has been a very widely published historian indeed; he was responsible, from the late 1920s onward, for several dozen books on various aspects of American history. Grouping these here according to subject gives some idea of the range of his interests and accomplishments as a historian.

Early in his career, Morris became interested in pre-Revolutionary legal history, at the time a virtually untouched area. *Studies in the History of American Law: With Special Reference to the Seventeenth and Eighteenth Centuries* is a pioneer book in its field, invaluable in suggesting to scholars beginning their inquiries the best ways to proceed. Most of the case records remained unpublished, a disability Morris addressed by his *Early American Court Records: A Publication Program*. A later, popular work which drew on his knowledge of American legal history was *Fair Trial: Fourteen Who Stood Accused, from Anne Hutchinson to Alger Hiss*. "Glaring deficiencies," he wrote in the preface to this book, "in the conduct and procedure of American criminal trials [have not yet] been eradicated." He held further that English trial practice has much to teach us.

The history of New York City was an interest

Morris shared with his mentor at Columbia, Evarts Boutell Greene. Together they published the seminal work *A Guide to the Principal Sources for Early American History (1600–1800) in the City of New York*. He then combined his pioneering interest in local and legal history in another book, *Select Cases of the Mayor's Court of New York City, 1674–1784*. During the 1930s Morris served as secretary of the committee on legal history of the American Historical Association, and in 1966–1973 was chairman of the New York Mayor's Task Force on Municipal Archives.

Morris was among the first American historians to pay serious attention to the history of labor—specifically, to the almost forgotten history of working men and women and their gradual attainment of dignity and justice in wage recompense and working conditions. His researches in the law and pre-Revolutionary history laid the foundation for *Government and Labor in Early America*, a book whose findings were supported by an examination of some twenty thousand cases, most of them unpublished. Other scholars had examined slavery and aspects of the free-labor and indentured-servant systems, but none before Morris had looked so closely at the sociolegal position of free and bound labor. "The experience of government with labor," he writes early in the book, "in the first two centuries of American history holds numerous clues to later developments and provides significant parallels to current patterns. Wage- and price-fixing and economic stabilization, the right of workers to take concerted action for their own advancement, child labor, absenteeism in industry, pirating of workers, restrictions on admission to a trade, restraints upon dismissals . . . constitute the core of the master-servant relations that were supervised by colonial and Revolutionary governments." Morris also edited *The U.S. Department of Labor Bicentennial History of the American Worker*, in which, along with five other authors, he examines the epochal struggle of working people in a new land; Morris' contribution to the volume is the first essay, "The Emergence of American Labor." The original Labor Department edition contains many evocative illustrations.

Morris was a tireless compiler and annotator of collections of documents—state papers, speeches, and other writings—especially destined for university students in American history. Among his books of this type were *Great Presidential Decisions: State Papers that Changed the Course of History*; *Basic Documents in American History*; *Significant Documents in United States History*; and *Basic Documents on the Confederation and the Constitution*. Other works that consist mainly of annotated readings are his two-volume, 1,350-page edition, with Henry Steele Commager, of *The Spirit of 'Seventy-Six: The Story of the American Revolution as Told by Participants* and *The American Revolution: A Short History*, two-thirds of which consists of "reading documents."

By the 1950s, Morris had become primarily interested in the political and diplomatic history of the American Revolution, and in particular the biographical study of several of the Founding Fathers. His short history of the Revolution, referred to above, was followed by an informative postscript to an edition of *The Autobiography of Benjamin Franklin*; a popular work, *The Making of a Nation: 1775–1789*; a short monograph, *A Letter from Henry Laurens to His Son, John Laurens, August 14, 1776*; a new introduction and notes to Sir George Otto Trevelyan's classic work, *The American Revolution* (1964 ed.); *The American Revolution, 1763–1783: A Bicentennial Collection* (1970); short political biographies of Franklin, Washington, Adams, Jefferson, Jay, Madison, and Hamilton in *Seven Who Shaped Our Destiny: The Founding Fathers as Revolutionaries*; *Witnesses at the Creation: Hamilton, Madison, Jay, and the Constitution*; and *The Forging of the Union 1781–1789*. Two books on the general topic of Revolutionary history remain among Morris' best-known works. *The Peacemakers: The Great Powers and American Independence* won Columbia University's Bancroft prize. The book goes beyond previous studies in its wide coverage of the peacemaking process and in its complete reassessment of the roles of the major participants. Morris explodes the myth of official French support for the Revolution and the Comte de Vergennes' often-alleged friendliness to the idea of American independence. He downgrades Franklin's importance in the treaty making, enhancing Jay's in the process: he shows that Jay, more than any of the other American negotiators, was responsible for securing the major concessions that won the peace. The negotiations, he notes, "began as an encounter between innocence and guile, but the Americans rapidly acquired a measure of sophistication sufficient for the task at hand." Not primarily a formal history of the American Revolution, *The Peacemakers* focuses on "the rival stakes of empire of the various belligerents caught up in a world war, of war aims that jeopardized the attainment of a durable peace and kept the issue of American independence in suspense until almost the very end." Morris studies the peacemakers themselves, "an extraordinary band of vibrant, subtle, prideful, and complex human beings, who tried to bend, or shape, or stretch, but, most of all, to dominate their world according to the set of national interests to which they were devoted." Samuel Flagg Bemis wrote in the *Saturday Review* that Morris "provides matchless descriptions of the purposes of intrigues of the various European chancelleries, superbly portraying the diplomatic personalities involved." In F. C. Brown's opinion in *Best Sellers*, "*The Peacemakers* represents one of the most monumental jobs of scholarly research imaginable. . . . [It] will be welcomed by scholars, students of diplomatic history and readers who enjoy minute historical detail."

Morris' second major work on Revolutionary history, *The Emerging Nations and the American Revolution*, studies a hitherto neglected aspect of the subject: the influences of the American political and social experience on European, South American, African, and Asian countries, noting especially the similarities in domestic and foreign policies of today's new nations to those of the early American republic. "For too long," Morris notes in the preface, "have Americans been content to view their revolution as a central experience in *their* national life and to ignore the liberation currents that the event set off throughout the world. If Americans themselves have held so parochial a view of the primary event in their history as a nation, they have been encouraged in their misconceptions by historians of revolutions who have rather consistently downgraded the American and hailed the French or the Russian or the Chinese as the transforming event of the modern world. The facts, as they are adduced in this book, do not support this assessment. . . . it was the American War for Independence that inaugurated the Age of Revolutions which has still not come to an end." The end of the book consists of the author's stirring plea to Americans to rediscover and employ their revolutionary tradition and its egalitarian ideals in solving problems at home and abroad.

Perhaps the greatest scholarly accomplishment of Morris' mature years consists of his work as editor of the papers of John Jay, the chief peace negotiator and first chief justice of the Supreme Court. Morris began his labors on the vast hoard of Jay papers, many of which were privately held and deposited specially at Columbia University in the late 1950s. A preliminary study, *John Jay, the Nation, and the Court*, was succeeded by the paper's first volume, *John Jay: The Making of a Revolutionary; Unpublished Papers 1745–1780*, covering Jay's early life, his years as a student and lawyer, his becoming a patriot, his nine-month presidency of Congress in the late 1770s, and his peace mission to Spain.

This was followed several years later by *John Jay: The Winning of the Peace; Unpublished Papers 1780–1784*, which considers the impasse created in the negotiations during Jay's long sojourn in Spain, the challenges to peacemaking in Paris in 1782, and the concluding of the peace and Jay's departure for home in May 1784. The historian Michael Kammen, writing in *Library Journal*, called Morris' work on the Jay papers "compelling, indeed lapidary. . . . [It] adds significantly to our understanding of American legal and constitutional development, as well as to our knowledge of politics and diplomacy in the Revolutionary era. . . . [It] also enhances our appreciation of Jay's complex personality; revealing the public figure as well as the refreshingly authentic family man." The papers, when fully published, will be four volumes in length.

Among Morris' other publications should be noted his editorship of the *Encyclopedia of American History*, first published in 1953, which was released in revised editions in 1961, 1965, 1970, 1976, and 1982. (The associate editor of the last two editions was his son, the City College historian Jeffrey B. Morris.) Also notable are his editorship, with Graham W. Irwin, of the *Harper Encyclopedia of the Modern World: A Concise Reference History from 1760 to the Present* and his authorship of two university textbooks, *USA: The History of a Nation* (written with William Greenleaf) and *America: A History of the People* (with Greenleaf and Robert Ferrell). He also edited, with Commager, the New American Nation series, a multivolume history of the United States, of which by mid-1988 some 40 volumes had been published. Morris edited the festchrift for Greene, *The Era of the American Revolution: Studies Inscribed to Evarts Boutell Greene* ; his own festchrift, *Perspectives on Early American History* (1973), was edited by Alden T. Vaughan and George Athan Billias.

Morris was visiting professor at Princeton (1948–1949), Hawaii (1957, 1976), New York University (1965–1966), the Free University of Berlin (1969), and the Hebrew University of Jerusalem (1969). In 1988 the Society of American Historians presented him with its Bruce Catton prize for lifetime achievement in the writing of history. Morris died in New York City at the age of eighty-four. He was survived by his wife, the former Berenice Robinson, and two sons.

WORKS: *Monographic works and collected essays*—Studies in the History of American Law, 1930, 1959; Historiography of America, 1600–1800, as Represented in the Publications of Columbia University Press, 1933; James DeLancey of New York: A Monograph, 1939; (with L. L. Snyder and J. E. Wisan), Early

American Court Records, 1940; Handbook of Civilian Protection, 1942; Government and Labor in Early America, 1946, 1965, 1975; Fair Trial, 1952, 1967; The American Revolution: A Short History, 1955; The Making of a Nation: 1775–1789, 1963; The New World: Prehistory to 1774, 1963; A Letter from Henry Laurens to his Son, John Laurens, August 14, 1776, 1964; The Peacemakers, 1965, 1970; The American Revolution Reconsidered, 1967; John Jay, the Nation, and the Court, 1967; The Emerging Nations and the American Revolution, 1970; Seven Who Shaped Our Destiny, 1973; Witnesses at the Creation, 1985; The Forging of the Union 1781–1789, 1987. *Textbooks and reference works*—(with E. B. Greene) A Guide to the Principal Sources for Early American History in the City of New York, 1929, 1953; (with J. S. Schapiro) Ancient and Medieval Times: From the Earliest Records to the Opening of the French Revolution, 1928, 1930, 1937; Encyclopedia of American History, 1953, 1961, 1965, 1970, 1976, 1982; Four Hundred Notable Americans, 1965; (with W. Greenleaf) USA: The History of a Nation, 1969; (with G. W. Irwin) Harper Encyclopedia of the Modern World, 1970; (with W. Greenleaf and R. Ferrell) America: A History of the People, 1971. *Compendia and edited books*—(with C. T. Bond) Proceedings of the Martland Court of Appeals, 1695–1729, 1933; Select Cases of the Mayor's Court of New York City, 1935; The Era of the American Revolution, 1939, 1965, 1971; (with L. L. Snyder) A Treasury of Great Reporting: "Literature under Pressure" from the Sixteenth Century to Our Own Time, 1949, 1962, (with L. L. Snyder) History in the First Person, 1951; (with L. L. Snyder) They Saw It Happen: Eyewitness Reports of Great Events, 1951; Basic Documents in American History, 1956, 1965; Alexander Hamilton and the Founding of the Nation, 1957, 1969; Basic Ideas of Alexander Hamilton, 1957, 1965; Great Presidential Decisions, 1960, 1965, 1966, 1973; (with J. L. Woodress) Voices from America's past, 1963; Trevelyan's The American Revolution, 1964; (with H. S. Commager) The Spirit of 'Seventy-Six, 1958, 1967; Significant Documents in United States History, 1969; The American Revolution: A Bicentennial Collection, 1970; Basic Documents on the Confederation and the Constitution, 1970; (with H. F. Graff) America at 200: Essays, 1975; John Jay: The Making of a Revolutionary, 1975; The U.S. Department of Labor Bicentennial History of the American Worker, 1976, 1983; John Jay: The Winning of the Peace, 1980.

ABOUT: Contemporary Authors New Revision Series 2, 1982; Who's Who in America, 1982–1983; Vaughan, A. T. and Billias, G. A. Perspectives on Early American History, 1973. *Periodicals*—America October 27, 1973; American Historical Review July 1930, July 1940, October 1946, April 1953, April 1975; Best Sellers October 15, 1965; Book Week October 10, 1965; Choice July/August 1976, February 1986; Harper's March 1970; Journal of American History December 1967, June 1975; Library Journal October 1, 1965; December 15, 1965; March 1, 1970; August 1973; April 15, 1976; September 1, 1985; New York Times May 8, 1988; March 6, 1989; New York Times Book Review November 14, 1965; November 25, 1973; February 22,

1976; November 17, 1985; June 14, 1987; Saturday Review November 1, 1952; October 2, 1965; August 19, 1967; August 15, 1970; Virginia Quarterly Review Autumn 1970, Summer 1976; Voice Youth Advocates April 1986.

MOTION, ANDREW (October 26, 1952–   ), English poet, critic, novelist, and biographer, was born in London, the older of the two sons of a prosperous brewer, also Andrew Motion, and Catherine Gillian Motion. As was and is the custom among the British landed gentry, he was sent away at the age of seven to a prep school that is recalled in "Skating," a memoir originally published in *Poetry Review* (September 1983). There he lived in fear "of doing badly at work, of being bullied," and his "school-days passed in a cringing inattentiveness. . . . Holidays, by contrast, were blissfully contented."

For Motion, "the only abiding thing, linking these isolated moments [of happiness] and suffusing the nothings between them, was the sense of my mother." She was a tall woman and "very beautiful." Motion and his younger brother Kit "were always proud of the way she looked, and enjoyed it. We used to creep into her bed in the morning as soon as my father had gone off to work. 'You're no good,' she'd tell me. 'You're a lamp-post.' (I was hopeless at cuddling.)" Their father, busy all week, spent most weekends as an officer with the Territorial Army, a voluntary militia somewhat resembling the National Guard: "Kit and I were very proud of him, but we didn't see a great deal of him."

Motion was a target for school bullies because he "looked like a sissy . . . with my fair hair, and I was clearly spoilt by my mother. . . . One Sunday afternoon a group of boys . . . tied me to a cedar tree, and beat me with bamboo canes. I still have the scars on my back—but I don't remember ever telling my mother. I wanted to be a success for her." Success eluded Motion in every area of prep-school life except sports, especially running, at which he excelled.

Motion's home life during vacations was equally unpropitious for a future writer. His parents owned very few books and his father claimed, "almost seriously," to have read nothing but half of Hammond Innes' *The Lonely Skier*. Motion himself "had a craze for Dennis Wheatley, then Hammond Innes, then Alistair MacLean, and eventually Ian Fleming—who was considered rather risqué." There was "no theatre, no art galleries, no concerts. . . . we led a typical landed life. It was extremely horsey." Nevertheless, during his last few vacations from prep school, Motion found himself writing sto-

ANDREW MOTION

ries: "They were giftless—melodramatic accounts of car accidents and Indian massacres—but I'd be pleased and surprised by them, and take them into my mother's bed in the morning to read them to her. 'Why are you so bloodthirsty?' she'd ask—and I'd never be sure whether this implied praise or blame. I can see now that my stories were ways of imagining the worst: ways of trying to prolong the idyll of her company by dreaming up some radically appalling alternative."

In 1965, when he was thirteen, Motion left his prep school and moved on to Radley College, a "public" school at Abingdon, in Berkshire. There he discovered that "learning wasn't as intimidating as I'd always imagined, and I relaxed. In fact I even started to be quite good at some things—especially English, which consisted largely of writing essays . . . and reading the First World War poets." Motion also made his first close friend and, staying with him during vacations, encountered "a society where it was perfectly normal—indeed, it was the done thing—to talk about books and paintings and so on."

In December 1968, while he was staying with a girl he hoped to seduce, the news came that his mother had been badly injured falling from her horse. Surgery to remove a bloodclot on her brain saved her life but left her with serious brain damage. She remained more or less comatose for three years, then gradually recovered her speech before dying, without having left the hospital, almost ten years after the accident. Blake Morrison has referred to "the haunting, guilt-ridden 'Freudian' coincidence that took

Motion away from home to the brink of his first sexual experience on the very day his mother had her accident," and Michael Hulse writes that "the tragedy that stopped his mother's life is in every way at the core of Andrew Motion's work."

After Radley College (1965–1970) and a summer of travel in France, Turkey, and Rhodes, Motion went up to University College, Oxford University, to read English. He graduated with first class honors, and stayed on to earn his M.Litt. In 1972, meanwhile, when he was only twenty, he had published his first pamphlet of poems, *Goodnestone: A Sequence*. In 1973 he was married to Joanna Jane Powell, who as Joanna Motion is a writer and reviewer. Two years later he received Oxford's Newdigate Poetry Prize for *Inland*. It is a long sequence of poems set in the early seventeenth century in the fens of East Anglia. Spoken by an unnamed villager, by the preacher Jesse Sease, and by others, it evokes the disruption of village life caused by the forced enclosure of common land. In the end the nameless speaker, displaced to a new village, is left "without past now, waiting for lights / to come on in foreign towns."

Motion began his career in 1977 as a lecturer in English at the University of Hull, teaching there until 1981, the year he won the Arvon-*Observer* prize for poetry. During his years at Hull, Motion began his friendship with the poet Philip Larkin, who was the university's librarian, and published three books, beginning in 1978 with his first important collection of verse, *The Pleasure Steamers*. It brought him both the Eric Gregory Award (1978) and the Cholmondeley Award (1979), and by 1983 had gone through three editions. Discussing this collection in *Southern Review*, David Middleton wrote that Andrew Motion "addresses the problem of how the mature mind can find and foster a civilized sensibility in a world in which Eliot's 'historical sense' is becoming a thing of the past. *The Pleasure Steamers* is divided into three sections. Part One [is] a miscellany of poems that examine the difficult English experience of the postwar welfare state against a (possibly) more glorious past, the relation of man to nature in the post-romantic era, and the idea of 'home' as the personal equivalent to cultural history."

The title poem may be taken as representative of this section. The pleasure steamers, as Middleton writes, are "tourist vessels taking their customers through an idealized but not wholly untrue English past"—one of the boats is said to have participated in the rescue of British troops (including the speaker's father) from Dunkirk in 1940. The poet himself shares neither his father's wartime danger nor "his cause," and nowadays the steamers are like "gaudy ghosts / with nowhere to haunt / but their past." They sail

for ever from here to the end
of a lost, inexhaustible century

where I may sometimes visit
but never stay, although
I discover at every return
I could have outlived myself there.

Part Two of *The Pleasure Steamers* reprints the sequence already published as "Inland," and Part Three consists of poems dealing directly with the accident and death of Motion's mother—his father driving every night, year after year, to visit her in the hospital ("A Dying Race"), her stored-away clothes ("In the Attic"), and, in five poems called "Anniversaries," the poet's own wintry journeys to the hospital on the anniversary of the accident, and the memories these evoke:

And I am still there,
seeing your horse return
alone to the open stable,
its rein dragging behind

a trail across the plough,
a blurred riddle of scars
we could not decipher then,
and cannot heal now.
                              —"Anniversaries: The First"

In an essay in Peter Jones and Michael Schmidt's *British Poetry Since 1970*, Blake Morrison described *The Pleasure Steamers* as combining "the best qualities of the departing '60s generation and the arriving '70s one." From the "minimalist" poetry associated with Ian Hamilton's *The Review* "he has learnt the value of 'withholding'. . . . *The Pleasure Steamers* is insubstantiality raised to a fine art. . . . But Motion also has a typically 1970s interest in the possibilities of a closely controlled syntax. In his case it has come through study of the work of Edward Thomas and through an affinity with Larkin—nostalgia, sadness and loss."

Andrew Motion's "study of the work of Edward Thomas" began at Oxford, where Thomas was the subject of his master's thesis. This developed into *The Poetry of Edward Thomas*, published in 1980. Andrew Nicholson in the *Yearbook of English Studies* (1983) called this "a major contribution" to Thomas studies, written with "great modesty and sensitivity." It represents the poet as "drawing much from the Georgians but also anticipating the Modernists in several important respects," although his aims are said to have been "evolutionary rather than revolutionary." Several of the features described

as characteristic of Thomas' poetry have also been found in Motion's: "the delicately unwound sentence, the tacit confession of alienation from stable harmony, and the tone of suggestive bafflement," as well as the "implied presence of a speaker" and a "passionate, but refined" patriotism.

Independence is a long poem spoken by a former engineer now retired to England after a career in India and the death in childbirth of his wife, whom he had married on India's Independence Day. Neil Corcoran noted in *Contemporary Poets* how the poem "returns again and again to images of loss, abandonment and estrangement and to a fundamental preoccupation with the final human loss, death, and its human response, grief." Corcoran called this poem "superbly complicated and inclusive," and many agree. Michael Hulse wrote that it "treats the concept of *home* without the self-indulgent emphasis . . . which is present at times in the poems in *The Pleasure Steamers*, and thus marks a move toward greater maturity and control." On the other hand Hulse found the poem "insensitive in its use of Indian history as local colour and stage props . . . and indeed the very conception of the piece seems in its condescending way to perpetuate colonial attitudes towards India."

In 1981 Motion succeeded Roger Garfitt as editor of *Poetry Review*, the quarterly journal of the Poetry Society. The following year he published his monograph on Philip Larkin. This brief study in Methuen's "Contemporary Writers" series attracted attention out of proportion to its length. Out of a close reading of Larkin's poems and novels, Motion argues that this outspoken opponent of literary modernism had failed to purge symbolist and modernist elements from his own work. Almost against his will, Larkin had achieved a synthesis between modernism and what Motion calls the "English line"—an achievement that could almost be seen as a continuation of the "evolutionary" process attributed by Motion to Edward Thomas. Most reviewers found the book both useful and persuasive.

There was a rather different response to Motion's other publication of 1982, *The Penguin Book of Contemporary British Poetry*, which he co-edited with Blake Morrison. Their introduction announced that a decisive "shift of sensibility" had "taken place very recently in British poetry"; that "after a spell of lethargy" in the 1960s and 1970s, "when very little—in England at any rate—seemed to be happening . . . a body of work has been created which demands, for its appreciation, a reformation of public taste." This reformation the editors sought to inaugurate with their "representative" and "didactic" anthology. The new poets, they claimed, had "exchanged the received idea of the poet as the . . . knowing insider for the attitude of the anthropologist or alien invader or remembering exile. . . . It is a change of outlook which expresses itself, in some poets, in a preference for metaphor and poetic bizarrerie to metonymy and plain speech; in others it is evident in a renewed interest in narrative."

The twenty poets in the anthology included six from Northern Ireland, where "the new spirit" had first made itself felt: Seamus Heaney, Derek Mahon, Michael Longley, Paul Muldoon, Tom Paulin, and Medbh McGuckian. Douglas Dunn and Tony Harrison represent "provincial and working-class" traditions. The so-called "Martian" poets—Craig Raine, Christopher Reid, and others—"share a delight in outrageous simile and like to twist and mix language in order to revive the ordinary." The "renewed interest in narrative" is exemplified in the work of James Fenton, Jeffrey Wainwright, and Motion himself.

The anthology was received with a good deal of dissatisfaction. Michael Schmidt, discussing the book in *PN Review*, was more moderate than many. He thought that the best poets in the anthology "fail to conform to the 'decisive shift of sensibility' that the editors are peddling," but that "what *is* profoundly contemporary about the anthology is the style of the introduction, the marriage of journalism and academic criticism, without the vigour of the one or the rigour of the other." And yet "the book, widely disseminated, reasonably priced, becomes canonical in the market-place. Excellence is, as so often, marginalised." Other critics found it reprehensible that an anthology of "contemporary British poetry" should find no place for the work of Philip Larkin, Ted Hughes, or Geoffrey Hill, and descried the black hand of a new "literary mafia."

In spite of such criticisms, the Penguin anthology has indeed become to some extent canonical—much used in schools and universities. Motion's appointment in 1983 as poetry editor of the publishing house of Chatto & Windus confirmed his status as a member of a new British poetic "establishment," along with Blake Morrison and Craig Raine, poetry editor at Faber & Faber.

In their introduction to the Penguin anthology, discussing the "renewed interest in narrative," Motion and Morrison defined this more closely as an interest in "describing the details and complexities of (often dramatic) inci-

dents, as well as in registering the difficulties and strategies involved in retailing them. . . . Contemporary poets write their stories with more reference to what the process involves. The fact of fictionalizing is relished as it is performed. . . . we are often presented with stories that are incomplete, or are denied what might normally be considered essential information. The reader is constantly being made to ask, 'Who is speaking?,' 'What are their circumstances and motives?,' and 'Can they be believed?'"

These considerations obviously apply to the narrative poems of Motion himself. He had shown an interest in the mode from the beginning—in "Inland" and in other poems in *The Pleasure Steamers*. The tendency was confirmed by *Secret Narratives* of 1983. Blake Morrison, writing in the *Yearbook of English Studies* (1987), suggested that "Motion's poetic development can best be understood as an attempt to escape his 'given' subject matter [his mother's accident and death] and its given mode, elegy, and to embrace the free inventions of narrative. . . . His narrative poems seethe with the power to invent, relish the act of fiction as it is being performed."

Thus, in a poem called "Open Secrets," a detailed anecdote that disturbingly associates adolescent sexuality and violent death (of a stag) is casually revealed to be an invention, made up to "kill" an hour: " . . . He was never / myself, this boy, but I know if I tell you his story / you'll think we are one and the same: both of us hiding / in fictions which say what we cannot admit to ourselves." Blake Morrison comments that "'hiding' for Motion takes the form of inhabiting lives which in their confidence, adventurousness, unscrupulousness, and even dishonesty are the opposite of the shy, vulnerable, integral, painfully honest 'I' of the early lyrics. Hence the rather desperately alien settings of the later work . . . and a set of characters in flight from themselves. But we come back to the same few inescapable emotions and the same searing self-knowledge. . . . Motion is attracted to characters and personae who know the ache and void of unrequited love . . . [the same emotions that underlie] his elegies for and memoir of his mother."

Motion's selected poems appeared the following year under the title *Dangerous Play*. These twenty-nine poems included no fewer than sixteen of the seventeen that had appeared in *Secret Narratives*, together with the prose memoir "Skating," seven new poems, and only six reprinted from *The Pleasure Steamers*. The collection, which received the John Llewellyn Rhys Memorial Prize, thus had the effect of underlining what Michael Hofmann called "Motion's ongoing poetic conversion, his move from lyric to narrative."

Writing in the *Times Literary Supplement* (January 11, 1985), Hofmann reported that "the new emphasis is on brushes with death, direct or indirect, real or imagined: with illness, murder, bereavement, war and revolution. . . . There is an almost total absence of poetic devices and effects. The vocabulary of poem after poem is simple and small. . . . It is a self-effacing, almost featureless style, entirely in the service of whatever scene or feeling is to be put over." For Hofmann, Motion is "not a descriptive writer" but "a *metteur-en-scène*, a designer. . . . What his poetry offers is the tension between the easy pleasure of reading him, and the weight and drama associated with his subjects."

For his next book, after so many imaginary biographies, Motion turned to a real one—or rather to three real ones. *The Lamberts* deals with three generations of an "inventive and exciting" family. George Lambert (1873–1930), settling in Edwardian London, became "the most famous Australian painter of his day." His son Constant (1905–1951), precociously brilliant as a composer, became musical director of the Sadler's Wells Ballet but drank himself out of his job and into an early grave. Constant's son Kit (1935–1981), inspired manager of The Who in the 1960s, died at the same age as his father of drink, heroin, and anything else he could get hold of. Motion argues that the Lamberts' creativity depended on "the very impulses which threatened to destroy it," and that "each child inherited—and exacerbated—the conditions and characteristics which had blighted his parents." Michiko Kakutani (*New York Times* April 29, 1987) found the book "both an exemplary family biography and an absorbing social history"; most reviewers agreed.

Another volume of poems followed in 1987, *Natural Causes*. As Ian Hamilton wrote in the *Times Literary Supplement* (October 9–15, 1987), "the verse-story genre is still prominent," but "the real strength of *Natural Causes* . . . is in its most directly personal poems. Motion has learned from his narrative excursions how to enrich the short lyric with some inexplicit jolts of drama—as in 'Hare Lip,' a strange, rather fearsome poem about fear. And throughout the book the sense of anticipated loss is even sharper than before. Motion the bereaved son is now a husband and a father. Having once lost everything, or so it must have seemed, he now—for a second time—has everything to lose. In the title poem 'Natural Causes' and in 'Hare Lip' and 'Firing Practice,' there is a resignation tinged with panic that reminds us of Philip Larkin, but with no attempt at any Larkin-like self-mockery":

> soon you will die,
> and not only you but this person
> you love, her children, everyone else;
> . . . no one prepared you for this—
> —"Firing Practice"

In a lighter vein, Motion's novel *The Pale Companion* (1989) concerned "adolescence, the shame of its incompleteness, and (less grandly) its embarrassments," according to Lorna Sage, who reviewed the book in the *Times Literary Supplement*.

Motion's first marriage was dissolved in 1983. In 1985 he married Janet Elisabeth Dalley. They have one son and live in London. Motion has remained at Chatto & Windus, becoming editorial director in 1985. His principal recreation is the cinema.

PRINCIPAL WORKS: *Poetry*—Goodnestone: A Sequence, 1972; Inland, 1976; The Pleasure Steamers, 1978; Independence, 1981; Secret Narratives, 1983; Dangerous Play: Poems 1974–1984, 1984; Natural Causes, 1987. *Criticism*—The Poetry of Edward Thomas, 1981; Philip Larkin, 1982. *Biography*—The Lamberts: George, Constant and Kit, 1986. *As editor*—(with Blake Morrison) The Penguin Book of Contemporary British Poetry, 1982.

ABOUT: Booth, M. British Poetry 1964 to 1984, 1985; Jones, P. and Schmidt, M. British Poetry Since 1970, 1980; Contemporary Poets, 4th ed., 1985; Who's Who, 1987. *Periodicals*—Critical Quarterly Autumn 1986; Encounter December 1983; Literary Review May 1986; New York Times April 29, 1987; PN Review 30, 1982, 32 1983; Poetry Review September 1983; Quarto March 1981; Southern Review 71 1 1981; Times Literary Supplement April 1, 1983; January 11, 1985; May 2, 1986; October 9–15, 1987; Yearbook of English Studies 1983, 1987.

MUNRO, ALICE (ANNE LAIDLAW) (July 10, 1931–   ), Canadian short-story writer and novelist, was born in Wingham, a small country town in Southwest Ontario, to Robert Eric and Anne Clarke (Chamney) Laidlaw. Her father, who had been a trapper in his youth, raised silver foxes for their pelts and when that failed, in 1948, worked as a foundry night watchman until he could return to farming, switching to turkeys. In his old age he wrote a novel about pioneer life in Canada. Her mother had been an elementary school teacher before marriage. The family, which eventually included another girl and a boy, lived on their farm on the outskirts of town; they were poor even by Depression standards, as were many of their rural neighbors.

Small towns like Wingham have been the setting for many of Alice Munro's stories, which vividly evoke both their buzzing collective life

ALICE MUNRO

and their hard-bitten parochialism. The isolation and narrow decency of country life were alleviated by what Munro has described as "a kind of ritualized wildness"—hockey, hunting, and reckless driving—but above all by gossip, scandal, and storytelling, amusements the more important in the absence of television. "Everybody in the community is on stage for all the other people," Munro explained to Mervyn Rothstein of the *New York Times*. "There's a constant awareness of people watching and listening. And—and this may be particularly Canadian— the less you reveal, the more highly thought of you are."

Alice Laidlaw attended the two-room Lowerton School from 1937 to 1939, then the Wingham Public School (1939–1944) and the Wingham and District High School (1944–1948). She was an able student and skipped a grade. When she was about twelve years old she decided to become a writer, a decision spurred, perhaps, by a family tragedy, for at about the same time her mother developed the first symptoms of the disease (Parkinson's) that would slowly destroy her (she died in 1959). In high school Alice Laidlaw began to stay in the classroom instead of going home for lunch and work on a novel, a tumultuous love-that-defies-the-grave romance owing a good deal to *Wuthering Heights*. This was a secret project; afraid of ridicule, she told no one of her ambitions and did her best to be popular with boys, neglecting, it seemed to her parents, the household arts she would need to be a good farm wife.

A farm wife, however, was not what she hoped to be, and after completing the basic high school course she went on to Grade 13, an additional year of education customary in her province for university-bound students. She won a scholarship and in 1949 entered the University of Western Ontario, in nearby London, where she majored in English with the announced intention of becoming a journalist—"a coverup. If I had said I wanted to be a writer, there would have been a difficult pause in the conversation." Scholarship students were then an anomaly at the university, which was referred to locally as "the country club," and Alice Laidlaw occasionally sold her blood to afford the necessary luxuries. She also published several stories in the campus literary magazine *Folio*, the first being "The Dimensions of a Shadow," a study of a spinster schoolteacher on the verge of madness.

She did not graduate from Western Ontario; instead, on December 29, 1951, she married a fellow student, James Munro, the scion of a well-to-do mercantile family (it was, according to one of their friends, a union of opposites). The couple moved to Vancouver, B.C., where he took a position with Eaton's department store and she worked in the public library until 1953, when their first child, Sheila, was born. A second daughter, Jenny, was born three and a half years later.

Munro has described her years as a suburban housewife and mother as a time of immense artistic frustration and gnawing self-doubt. Her husband was not averse to her writing—indeed, he was supportive—but she felt as though she were swimming against the tide. "In the 1950s, women's lives were both very enclosed and entirely open . . . ," she told Janet Watts of the *London Observer*. "You didn't have any privacy unless you were prepared to be very eccentric. And I was not. . . . I had a long training in duplicity and confidence, and I led a double life." Her models at this point included Eudora Welty and James Agee, and probably also Chekhov and the James Joyce of *Dubliners*; she threw out most of what she wrote but was satisfied with some of it and occasionally had stories accepted for publication in literary journals—*Queen's Quarterly*, *Canadian Forum*, and *The Tamarack Review*, whose editor, Robert Weaver, was especially encouraging; she also sold two stories to *Chatelaine*, a mass-market women's magazine. Munro's earliest stories were serious and competent but somewhat formulaic; they often relied upon the inherent drama of situation for their effects. By the end of the 1950s, however, she found herself able to go further—she had developed the distinctive voice of her mature style and discovered her subject matter close to home. "Before that it was probably 'I will be a writer';

and after that 'there are some things that have to be written by me,'" she told John Metcalf in an interview in the *Journal of Canadian Fiction*. In 1961 she took the drastic step of renting a room to use as an office, but this seemed to bring on a complete writer's block, and when James Munro decided to leave Eaton's, she suggested that they start a bookstore together. Munro's Books opened in Victoria in 1963. "When we moved to Victoria, the pressure was off. I was no longer working all day trying to write a novel. I was working in the bookstore, and it was a wonderful relief. Also, I talked to people all day. God, the isolation of housewives in those days! I love mindless chatter." With the birth of her third daughter, Andrea, in 1966, she stopped working in the store and began to assemble and revise the stories that would appear in her first collection.

The Dance of the Happy Shades was published by Ryerson, a Toronto firm, in 1968 with a foreword by Hugh Garner, an established Canadian writer. Only one of these fifteen stories is set in British Columbia (in a prototypical suburban development); the others are all set in the Southwest Ontario of Munro's childhood. They range in tone from the farcical "An Ounce of Cure," about a lovelorn babysitter's drunken spree, to the muted tragedy of "The Peace of Utrecht," about the guilty estrangement of two sisters who meet again after their mother's death. This story, first published in 1959 in *The Tamarack Review*, represented a breakthrough for Munro. It was her "first really painful autobiographical story" (autobiographical in emotion, though not in incident); it was "the first time I wrote a story that tore me up." "The Peace of Utrecht" is indeed a remarkable advance both for its depth of feeling and for its narrative technique. The narration does not follow the chronology of events but the movements of the younger sister's mind as she revisits her old home and recalls another time; it is a technique that allows the past to come forward with the power to surprise. In some of her early stories, Munro had shown an interest in the effects that could be achieved by a complex narrative voice, by having, for example, an older woman tell a story about herself as a young girl, so that two versions of the same person seem to be present at once. Freeing the narrative from the demands of strict chronology allowed for a more subtle interplay between voice and incident; it also focused attention firmly upon the characters' inner lives (and by extension upon the subjective nature of all narration). This was a technique Munro would return to, refine, and eventually adapt to third-person storytelling. But for the time being she was content to mine the autobiographical

material to which she had gained access in linear, first-person narratives. The stories in *Dance of the Happy Shades*—accessible, realistic, and blessed with a distinctive national flavor—were very much appreciated in Canada, where Munro's book won the Governor General's award for fiction. *Dance* was not so well liked in the United States, where it was released on the heels of her second book and suffered by comparison.

Lives of Girls and Women, like the later *Who Do You Think You Are?*, may be read as a novel, although some critics have argued that in both books the chapters are really more like linked short stories. *Lives* is a candid and high-spirited account of growing up in rural Canada, told in the retrospective first person by Del Jordan, now a grown woman and a writer, then a lively, questioning girl—"the bright one in her family, the one destined to break out of Jubilee and leave her friends—victims of ebbing curiosity and reduced expectations—for good and all," as Geoffrey Wolfe wrote in *Time*. Many details in this book are carried over from the later stories in *Dance*: the dog Major, the town Jubilee, the fraught relationship between mother and daughter, the fox farm. Carried over also are an easy, sustained command of the material, thick sensory detail, and convincing local color. Del's childhood and adolescence are crowded with incident and sharply observed characters, but the thread of the narrative is her gradual discovery of her own individuality as she experiments with religion and sex and measures herself against her classmates. In defining herself she is also separating from her roots, and by the time she is ready for university she has outgrown Jubilee, or so she thinks. The final chapter restores the town (and the past) to the condition of primal mystery, and permits the writing of a book that is not at all the exposé she had once imagined. "Del, looking back, tries to get it all just right," said Wolfe. "Nostalgia does not dampen her account, nor contempt deface it."

"*Lives* is one of those books I should really have written when I was younger," Munro told Beverley Slopen of *Publishers Weekly*. "It is the classic childhood, adolescence, breakthrough-into-maturity book. Every beginning writer has that material—and after that you're not sure what you can do. I went through a bleak period. And then I wrote the stories in the third book, *Something I've Been Meaning to Tell You*, almost desperately. I wasn't at all sure they worked." *Lives of Girls and Women* did work: it won the Canadian Booksellers International Book Year Award and was made into a television film in 1973 (Munro's daughter Jenny played the lead). It was not, however, much appreciated in Wingham, where Munro has been the subject

of aggrieved editorial comment in the local
paper.

By that time Munro, concerned about her father and stepmother's failing health, had returned to Ontario alone, taking up a temporary
position as writer-in-residence at her old university. Shortly thereafter she and James Munro
were legally separated. At the university, she re-
encountered the geographer Gerald Fremlin, an
older man whom she had known slightly in her
college days, and in 1976 they were married.
They moved into a farmhouse in Clinton, Ontario, about twenty miles north of Wingham, and
have lived there ever since, in great privacy.

Munro's third book, *Something I've Been
Meaning to Tell You*, contains six stories set in
the rural Ontario of her childhood (including two strong, semi-autobiographical pieces,
"Winter Wind" and "The Ottawa Valley"), and
seven set in aggressively up-to-date cities. In the
Toronto *Globe and Mail*, William French con-
gratulated the author on widening her range,
making the transition to "a new toughness, a
sense of the confusion and chaos of urban life,
the impermanence of man-woman relationships, especially in marriage, the conflict of
generations." Several of the stories are experiments in narrative, making use of fantasies and
unsent letters, or taking the point of view of a
puzzled or unreliable witness, inadvertently
blundering upon an unfathomable or unacceptable truth. These works are "persistently testing
what we know and how we know it," E. D. Blodgett wrote, adding that here "no position is
privileged." The title story, a rather unpleasant
tour de force, is told from the viewpoint of Et,
a spinster dressmaker, and concerns a romantic
triangle composed of her beautiful sister Char,
Char's gentle, foolish husband Arthur, and a
small-town Lothario named Blaikie Noble. But
behind this sensational tale, with its dark hints
of criminal passion, the reader can discern the
outline of another, subliminal triangle—
composed of Char, Arthur, and Et herself—and
perhaps a different crime. It is never clear what
actually occurred; Et can be (and has been) seen
as a deserving ugly duckling, a deceitful manipulator, or a defensive fabricator, one who will always reduce life's alarming possibilities to
skeletons in the closet (the skeletons may be
imaginary, but the closet is depressingly real).
The fabricator in "Material" is even more successful: a professional writer, he callously mis-
treats a neighbor woman, then immortalizes her
in fiction, much to the disgust of his ex-wife,
who cannot forget that she was his accomplice
in this project.

By contrast, *Something I've Been Meaning to
Tell You* also contains one of Munro's most popular old-fashioned stories, "How I Met My
Husband," about a fifteen-year-old domestic
slavey's crush on the barnstorming pilot who
flies into town one summer, fluttering the hearts
of the local ladies. A tribute to the resilience of
the young, it is told in a fresh, seemingly artless
manner that nevertheless draws neat distinctions
between townspeople and country folk, and between women who wait for romantic rescue and
women who get on with the business of living;
it has a surprise ending O. Henry might have envied. This story was also adapted for television.

Something I've Been Meaning to Tell You was
generally well received, although to Frederick
Busch, writing in the *New York Times Book
Review*, some of the stories seemed too thought-
out, or too ingratiating: "designed to win our
love rather than stun us with character or prose."
In *Canadian Forum*, Hilda Kirkwood compared
Munro to V. S. Pritchett in her ability to evoke
the first apprehensions of adult sexuality ("The
Found Boat," "Executioners") and added, "what
grips Alice Munro is the impossible emotional
dependence of women as she has known them,"
women who seem to be, as "Material" suggests,
"at the mercy" of life in a way that perhaps men
are not. *Something* assured Munro of a wider audience, for it attracted the attention of an American literary agent, Virginia Barber, who was
able to place most of her subsequent stories in
the *New Yorker* and the *Atlantic*, and to arrange
for her collections to be issued in the United
States by Knopf.

Munro's next book, *Who Do You Think You
Are?* (published in the United States as *The Beggar Maid: Stories of Flo and Rose*), returned to
the territory of *Lives of Girls and Women*. It is
a collection of linked short stories following the
life of Rose, who grows up in the poverty of rural
Hanratty, escapes to the wider world through
education, and promptly falls into an almost fatally proper marriage, succeeded by an almost
comically desperate struggle to establish herself
as a single mother, actress, and lover of various
unsatisfactory men. At last, however, Rose returns to Hanratty her own woman, to deal with
her now-senile stepmother Flo. If Rose is the
quintessential Munrovian heroine—engaging,
alert, and adventurous—Flo virtually embodies
the spirit of Hanratty: she is ignorant, watchful,
and derisive, a graduate and a professor of the
School of Hard Knocks. She is also, however,
fiercely independent, a whirlwind of energy and
a fountain of scandalous local history, scathing
commentary, and dubious folklore—she nour-
ishes her stepdaughter's imagination. When
Rose plunges into a more sophisticated world, a
world so distant from Hanratty that she must

"present" her own childhood to make it comprehensible to her smart new friends, it is precisely her provincial sturdiness, her long schooling as an outsider and secret dreamer, that enable her to negotiate the confusing and sometimes treacherous passage.

Munro received a second Governor General's award for *Who Do You Think You Are?*, which was also runner-up for the Booker Prize. On the jacket of the American edition, Margaret Laurence called the book "marvelously wise, funny and moving," and John Gardner wrote, "The psychological precision, even when Munro is dealing with the most minor characters, is a delight and the startling twists—for instance the unexpected leaps in time, the transformations of familiar characters . . . make the book what books ought to be, a little wild, a little mysterious."

In the opinion of some critics, *Who Do You Think You Are?* initiates a shift of emphasis in Munro's work. It recasts an autobiographical novel into third-person short stories, in which the themes of maturation and coming to terms with the past give way somewhat, in the latter half of the book, to questions of love and marriage, isolation and old age. It retains some of the sharp, almost impudent high spirits of *Lives of Girls and Women*, but the material is handled more selectively, more artfully. "Everybody's doing their own novel of their own lives," Munro told Rothstein. "The novel changes—at first we have a romance, a very satisfying novel that has a rather simple technique and then we grow out of that and we end up with a very discontinuous, discordant, very contemporary kind of novel. I think that what happens to a lot of us in middle age is that we can't really hang on to our fictions any more."

In *The Moons of Jupiter*, W. R. Martin wrote, "instead of being conspicuously vivacious, paradoxical, droll and divertive, Alice Munro's style has become sparer, more exact and incisive . . . less fizz, but more salt, in the narration." An unobtrusive symbolism governs several of the stories—to horrific effect in "The Turkey Season," in which a crew of men and women gut the birds that have been slaughtered for the holidays and attempt to draw out one another's sexual secrets; to steadying effect in the title story, in which the vast distances and natural order of the heavens seem to preside over the inter-generational conflicts and mortal risks of the foreground.

The stories in *The Moons of Jupiter* deal for the most part with older characters—some very old indeed, like Mrs. Cross and Mrs. Kidd, who inhabit a nursing home. But in general the characters are middle-aged. To William French,

"the dominant tone is a kind of poignant melancholy. . . . The women who tell the stories are usually in their 40s, fearful of losing their allure, caught between generations, worrying about their aging parents and maturing children" (occasionally, he thought, to claustrophobic effect). In the *New York Times Book Review*, however, Benjamin De Mott wrote that although the women's situations were familiar in fiction, "the freshness of Mrs. Munro's literary performance has little to do with situation, everything to do with character. . . . Occasionally the author fails to curb the garrulousness of one of her first-person narrators; occasionally . . . her comic bits seem predictable. But in the main her sense of style and craft is impeccable."

The pace of change accelerates in *The Progress of Love*, which also won a Governor General's award, as well as the Marian Engel Prize. Euphemia, the central character of the title piece, changes her name to Fame and makes her living as a real-estate agent, selling off old farmhouses like the one she grew up in; in "Circle of Prayer," a family heirloom is dropped into a dead classmate's coffin by an overwrought teenage girl (the family itself broke up several years earlier). "Unpolluted human love does not figure strongly in Alice Munro's stories," Janet Watts observed; " . . . She cannot help but see every scrap of her material—a face, a room, a marriage, a life—all the way round; and the most artfully draped illusion simply dissolves in the acid of her gaze. Her pages are lively with the noise and jostle of family life: yet her characters live, think and act in the silence of their solitude, the separateness of their warring perceptions." And Munro concurred: "What I want now in a story is an admission of chaos."

In a long article in the *New York Times Book Review*, Joyce Carol Oates placed Munro among such contemporaries as Peter Taylor, William Trevor, and Edna O'Brien—twentieth-century realists whose stories display some of the qualities of the nineteenth-century novel: three-dimensional characters who "behave, generally, like real people. That is, they surprise us at every turn, without violating probability"; pungent regional particulars; and an underlying moral seriousness—"[Munro's heroines have] the capacity to extract from frequently sordid experiences moral insights of a very nearly Jamesian subtlety and precision." Nevertheless, Oates thought that a few of the stories were not fully realized—" 'Eskimo' reads like an early draft"—and that several others were marred by self-conscious experimentation (the multiple viewpoints and time shifts in "White Dump," virtually an imploded novel; the broken-backed structure of "A Queer Streak"). In the London

Times Literary Supplement, Anne Duchêne also called the collection uneven, preferring however "the pared-down, more allusive contemporary stories to those with heavier traditional upholstery."

Reviews of Munro's 1990 collection, *Friend of My Youth*, were unequivocably favorable. "These stories are never too full—they give just enough," Robert Tower wrote in the *New York Review of Books*, while the reviewer for *Publishers Weekly* found it "difficult to do justice to Munro's magical way with characterization, or to her unerring control of her own resources: she writes about the forging and dismantling of friendships, marriages, families and solitudes with a trenchant knowledge of life and fiction as conspiring forces of creation." Several of these stories make brilliant use of the tale-within-a-tale. In "Five Corners," a nasty account of sexual blackmail flares up like a warning signal in the midst of what had been, up till then, a comfortable adulterous affair. Conversely, in "Pictures of the Ice," a carefully thought-out lie bestows upon the one person who recognizes it a badly needed sense of intimacy. "The haunting title story . . . ," Tower wrote, "begins with the narrator's recurring dream about her dead mother, and the reader anticipates a story about the relations between a mother and her daughter. But the narrative shifts into an account of two farm women, sisters, who belong to a sternly puritanical sect called the Cameronians, and their relation to the dour man—engaged to one sister, seduced by the other—who helps run the farm; in subject and atmosphere this material could almost have come out of a novel by Hardy." Told in a rapid, conversational manner, this tale-within-a-tale has an emblematic function: it serves as an object of contemplation for the narrator. She remembers how her mother would tell this story with the deepest respect, even reverence, for Flora, the jilted sister, who rose serenely above her humiliations, and how she herself as a teenager hated it, despising Flora as a monster of spiritual pride and sexual repression. "The odd thing," she realizes, "is that my mother's ideas were in line with some progressive notions of her times, and mine echoed the notions that were favored in my time. This in spite of the fact that we both believed ourselves independent, and lived in backwaters that did not register such changes. It's as if tendencies that seem most deeply rooted in our minds, most private and singular, have come in as spores on the prevailing wind, looking for any likely place to land, any welcome." And this humbling realization restores her mother to her as a whole person, free of the disfiguration of memory. A similar but more elusive moment of peace occurs

at the end of "Differently," after a headlong tale of friendship, passion, and betrayal that breaks every rule the heroine's writing instructor laid down in the opening paragraph.

"The wellspring of Munro's writing is the rhythms of spoken language," Heather Henderson wrote in *Maclean's*. "And when she deliberately fractures the classic structure of the short story, beginning at the end and drawing her characters back from experience to innocence, Munro's stories seem as natural as drawing a breath." The "spiraling" or "spatial" patterns of narrative that she favors—going back and forth in time, changing perspective, exploring memory, fantasy, and family history in a search for emotional truth—are in part a natural outgrowth of the way she works. She has said that she must have "starter dough from the real world" to invent a fictional world, and this may be something as simple as an overheard conversation. Once she has a "feeling" or "moment" in mind, "I go into it, and move back and forth and settle here and there and stay in it for a while. It's more like a house. . . . once I'm into it, I'll find out what happens. . . . A story is a spell, rather than a narrative."

Munro's stories concern what she knows or might know first hand—they are not set in future worlds or in extreme situations or among people wildly different from herself. Even the few set abroad (in countries that she has visited) center upon the Canadian visitor. She has often returned to material she has used in the past, to reshape and deepen it. "The Ottawa Valley," with its bleak confession of failure, is redeemed in "Friend of My Youth"; "Differently" has affinities with "Mischief" in *Who Do You Think You Are?*. Situations and character types recur in her fiction in new guises; indeed, if Munro's characters were actors, they would constitute a repertory company. Although she is not what is commonly called an adventurous writer, she has been bold and original in exploring the depths that lie beneath the surface of ordinary life, and in adapting her style to the demands of twentieth-century subject matter. She has no plans to write a novel, a form she says she does not understand, but several critics have remarked that her short stories have the power and variety of other writers' long books. Besides the awards mentioned above, Alice Munro received the Canada-Australia Literary Prize in 1977 and shared with Hugh Hood the 1974 award of the Ontario Council for the Arts; her story "Accident" won a gold medal from the National Magazine Awards Foundation, and a short film version of the early "Boys and Girls" won an Oscar in 1984.

PRINCIPAL WORKS: Dance of the Happy Shades, 1968;

Lives of Girls and Women, 1971; Something I've Been Meaning to Tell You, 1974; Who Do You Think You Are?, 1978 (U.S., The Beggar Maid: Stories of Flo and Rose, 1979); The Moons of Jupiter, 1982; The Progress of Love, 1986; Friend of My Youth, 1990.

ABOUT: Blodgett, E. D. Alice Munro, 1988; Carrington, I. de P. Controlling the Uncontrollable: The Fiction of Alice Munro, 1989; Contemporary Authors 33–36, 1978; Current Biography 1990; Frye, J. Living Stories, Telling Lives, 1986; Gadpaille, M. The Canadian Short Story, 1988; Gibson, G. Eleven Canadian Novelists, 1973; Lecker, R. et al. (eds.) Canadian Writers and Their Works, 1985; MacKendrick, L. K. (ed.) Probable Fictions: Alice Munro's Narrative Acts, 1983; Martin, W. R. Alice Munro: Paradox and Parallel, 1987; Metcalf, J. (ed.) Sixteen by Twelve, 1970; The Narrative Voice, 1972; Making It New, 1982; Miller, J. (ed.) The Art of Alice Munro: Saying the Unsayable, 1984; Twigg, A. For Openers: Conversations with 24 Canadian Writers, 1981; Who's Who 1988–1989. *Periodicals*—British Columbia Library Quarterly July 1971; Canadian Fiction Magazine September 1982; Globe and Mail (Toronto) May 25, 1974; November 11, 1978; October 16, 1982; Grand Street Autumn 1981; Journal of Canadian Fiction Fall 1972; Kitchener-Waterloo Record February 17, 1979; London Observer February 1, 1987; London Review of Books February 5, 1987; Maclean's September 22, 1986; Montrealer February 1962; Nation May 14, 1990; New York Review of Books May 17, 1990; New York Times February 16, 1983; September 3, 1986; November 10, 1986; March 9, 1990; April 17, 1990; New York Times Book Review October 27, 1974; March 20, 1983; September 14, 1986; March 18, 1990; Publishers Weekly August 22, 1986; January 19, 1990; Room of One's Own #4 1979; Time January 15, 1973; Times Literary Supplement (London) January 30, 1987; Wall Street Journal November 7, 1979.

MURRAY, LES(LIE) A(LLAN) (October 17, 1938–), Australian poet and essayist, writes: "Born at Nabiac, New South Wales, raised on parents' dairy farm at nearby Bunyah, in the farming and timbergetting country of the New South Wales north coast. Attended local schools, entered Sydney University in 1957. Majored in English and German; discontinued studies in 1960, returned to university in 1969 and gained B.A. degree that year. Began writing at university, worked on newspaper *Honi Soit*, co-edited university journals *Hermes* and *Arna* with Geoffrey Lehmann. Hitchhiked around Australia 1961–1962, worked in many jobs for brief periods. Married Valerie Morelli in 1962, moved to Canberra in 1963 to work for four years as science and technical translator at Australian National University. Went to Wales briefly in 1965 as Australian delegate to the British Commonwealth Arts Festival Poetry Conference, went to Europe again in 1967 and stayed until late 1968;

LES A. MURRAY

again worked in various survival jobs to support family and writing habit. On return, worked for prime minister's department, Canberra, till early 1971, left public service later that year to become full time free-lance author, has survived since then thanks to literary earnings, Literature Board fellowships, and wife's income as teacher. Couple has five children and lived quietly in Chatswood, Sydney, with frequent trips north to Bunyah and district, until 1986 when they moved back to his native region.

"From 1973 to 1979 Murray was acting editor of *Poetry Australia* magazine, and since 1978 he has been poetry reader and consultant to Angus and Robertson Ltd. He has also compiled and edited the *New Oxford Book of Australian Verse* (1986) and an anthology of Australian religious verse for Dove Communications of Melbourne. He contributed in large measure to the *Oxford Literary Guide to Australia* (1986). He has been writer-in-residence at the universities of New England, Stirling, Copenhagen, Newcastle, New South Wales, and La Trobe and at Sydney University. He has conducted reading tours in Australia, Europe, and the United States, sponsored in part by the Library of Congress. He has won a number of prizes, including the Grace Leven Prize for Best Book of Verse (1965 and 1980), the Captain Cook Bi-Centenary Prize for Poetry 1970, C. J. Dennis Memorial Prize for Poetry 1976, National Book Awards 1974 and 1984–1985, Australian Literature Society Gold Medal 1984, Mattara Prize (shared with Kevin Hart) 1980, the New South Wales Premier's Prize for Poetry 1984, and the Christopher Brennan Med-

al of the Fellowship of Australian Writers 1985.
Also in 1985 he was named winner of the Canada-Australia Prize and toured Canada reading
his poems. His volume *The Daylight Moon* won
the Australia National Poetry Award for 1988."

In a statement prepared for the *Bulletin* of the
Poetry Book Society of the United Kindgon, Les
A. Murray wrote: "In a way, the central theme
of my work is concern for the relegated and opposition to the relegators—which include words
such as *periphery*, *province*, *backward*,
primitive, *metropolitan*, *centre* and many more.
In a way, I'm grateful to have run into that ancient prejudice; it taught me to be wary of received attitudes. From there, it was only a short
step to opposing any and every Received Literary Sensibility. No one of those is ever commensurate with the whole truth. By no means all of
my poems are located in Bunyah, of course, but
to the extent that place is important among its
concerns, my home district is its centering
focus."

The Peasant Mandarin, the title of a collection
of Les A. Murray's prose essays, aptly describes
the character of this poet who is today recognized as (in the words of a fellow Australian
poet, David Malouf) "perhaps the most naturally
gifted poet of his generation in Australia."
"Mandarin" in the sense that he reflects the cultivated standards of a classical education and a
profound respect for tradition, Murray is also
the spokesman for a rugged anti-elite
"Australocentric" spirit that he proudly calls
"peasant." Unlike many of his contemporaries
who have found inspiration in the European and
American avant-garde, Murray has his own stern
and strict standards of "Australianness." As another distinguished Australian-born poet, Peter
Porter (who emigrated to England some years
ago), has written of him: "If the boring phrase
heard so often in Australia—'the cultural
cringe'—disappears, as I hope it will, then Murray will have been one of those who set it
packing."

In another of his essays, "The Human-Hair
Thread" (collected in his *Persistence in Folly*),
Murray traces "an Aboriginal presence in my
work almost from the start" back to his country
boyhood in Bunyah. There his father worked a
dairy farm which he was never able to buy. Deprived therefore of any heritage of land, Les
Murray grew up identifying with the Aborigines
who had lost their land to outsiders. In many of
his poems, most especially in a sequence of sixteen meditative poems "Walking to the
Cattle-Place" (published in *Poems against*

Economics), Murray reflects on the metaphysical nature of the land. "I set out to follow a cow,"
he writes in a commentary on what he calls his
"cow poems," "and I found a whole world, a spacious, town-despising grassland where Celt and
Zulu and Vedic Aryan were one in their
concerns." The poems are obscure in many of
their allusions, but the overall effect is strikingly
original and powerful. Written in the ambulatory rhythm of a country walk, the poems pose the
land as a "Middle Earth"—"the width of a
cow"—and the cow itself as sacred, as in the Sanskrit legends of the sacred cow:

> Around the sleeping house, dark cattle rubbing
> off on stiff corner joists their innocent felt
> And the house is nudged by a most ancient flow.
> I will wake up in a world that hooves have led to.

It is his dream to reclaim this land for his children:

> It will make them sad bankers.
> It may subtly ruin them for clerks
> This deeply involved unpickable knot of feeling
> For the furred, smeared flesh of creation, the hate, the
>   concern.

"A nation, a people, is always of more value
to the rest of mankind if it remains itself," Murray writes in *The Peasant Mandarin*. "Itself," in
his lexicon, is an Australia stripped of its acquired Western high technology and restored to
its natural landscape. In "Sydney and the Bush"
(in *Ethnic Radio*) he traces in simple quatrains
the history of Australia from its first colonial set-
tlements which from the outset separated and
alienated the white settlers from what should
have been their roots:

> When Sydney and the Bush first met
> there was no open ground
> and men and girls, in chains and not,
> all made an urgent sound.
>
> Then convicts bled and warders bred,
> the bush went back and back,
> the men of Fire and of Earth
> became White men and Black.

The poem ends grimly: "When Sydney and the
Bush meet now / there is no common ground."

Murray sounds a more hopeful note—the possibility of renewal and integration of spirit—in
"The Buladelah-Taree Holiday Song Cycle" (in
Ethnic Radio). This poem was inspired by a
translation of the Aboriginal "Moon-Bone
Cycle," and describes the return to the country
of townspeople on their holidays:

> for this is the season when children return with their
>   children
> to the place of Bingham's Ghost, of the Old Timber

Wharf, of
          the Big Flood That Time,
the country of the rationalized farms, of the day-and-
night
          farms, and the Pitt Street farms,
of the Shire Engineer and many other rumours, of the
tractor
          crankcase furred with chaff,
the places of sitting down near ferns, the snake-fear
places,
          the cattle-crossing-long-ago places.

The poem celebrates the experience of renewal and relearning that comes with the rediscovery of the land:

Now the sun is an applegreen blindness through the
swells,
          a white blast on the sea-face, flaking and
shoaling;
now it is burning off the mist; it is emptying the
density
          of trees, it is spreading upriver. . . .

Murray's poetic style defies easy description. He has been variously compared to Robert Frost for his measured restraint, to Ted Hughes and Seamus Heaney for his close, sympathetic but not sentimental observations of farm animals and of men at work on farms or in mills. "Murray's is a parochial poetry, much of it arising from a rural childhood in New South Wales," Blake Morrison wrote in the *Times Literary Supplement* in 1985, "but this parochialism gives it its strength and universality"; he sees Murray as "a poet of international stature." In Joseph Brodsky's judgment, "It would be as myopic to regard Mr. Murray as an Australian poet as to call Yeats an Irishman." Murray's language, often witty and inventive, ranges from the colloquial—capturing the idiom and rhythm of everyday Australian speech (sometimes to the bewilderment of European and American readers)—to a polish and elegance that have reminded some of his readers of classical poets like Virgil and Horace in their pastoral modes. The title of his first volume, *The Ilex Tree* (a collaboration with Geoffrey Lehmann), alludes to Virgil's *Eclogues*, and some of the poems published there reflect a similar timeless spirit:

Autumn is the winter's death,
He dries the rotted June rain in the earth,
Stiffens fat roots, ignites within the peach tree
Flower and seed. August is time to think
Of facing ploughshares, getting our new boots,
And of the first calves shivering in the grass
Still wet with birth-slime.
          —"A New England Farm, August 1914"

Murray is not, however, exclusively a regional and rural poet. He has lived in cities long enough to have mastered the language and imagery of urban life. In "The Police: Seven Voices" (in

Lunch & Counter Lunch), a sequence of poems characterizing the tough, rough-and-ready working city policeman, he catches the voice and authoritarian tone of his speakers: "I am a policeman / it is easier to make me seem an oaf / than to handle the truth." Handling his dangerous and often sordid duties he is brusque and businesslike: "if later goes all right / I am going to paint the roof of our house / on my day off." Significantly, one of his volumes is titled *The Vernacular Republic* and another *The People's Otherworld*, in which he describes bulldozers, drive-belts, film projectors "with a metaphoric zeal formerly reserved for cows and broad beans," Blake Morrison writes. His sophisticated rhymes and playful language are illustrated in poems like "Rhymes for a Small Capital" (in *Lunch & Counter Lunch*):

Citizens live in peace and honour
in Pearce and Higgins and O'Connor,
Campbellites drive Mercedes Benzes,
lobbyists multiply in Menzies . . .

Mow the parklands
gild the Mace
keep our Capital
upper case.

But Canberra's neither cold nor soulless
(except to those unsold, or coalless)
she has her delights—I won't distort 'em—
wide embassies of Spring and Autumn.

The recurring theme of urban versus country values is the subject of Murray's verse narrative *The Boys Who Stole the Funeral*, a sequence of 140 sonnets in which two boys steal the body of an old man from a funeral parlor in Sydney and transport it to the outback for burial in the man's native soil. Written out of Murray's passionate conviction that the spirit is, and must be, rooted in the land, the poem frames its message sharply. Thomas Shapcott, in *Australian Literary Studies*, had reservations about its "evangelical" fervor: "Les Murray presents his world as being clearly defined by necessary Rites of Passage. There are the Elect, and there are the Others. . . . But his country Eden is as uncomfortably stratified and suspicious as any claustrophobic centre of hypocrisy and bigotry." Nevertheless, Shapcott admired the energy and narrative skill of the poem, its depiction of the maturation through struggle and sacrifice of two young drifters. One boy is killed in what becomes an increasingly hazardous quest, but the other survives to undergo a ritual ceremony of manhood:

I ate a snake. I know that. A lot more happened
that I
          haven't
got to remember. But good. The bush is
tonight.

it'll kill you, but it's—decent. I think I learned that much.

Variations on by now familiar themes in Murray's work—the land, home, family, Australian history—appear in a collection of his poems, *The Daylight Moon*, published after he returned to live on his home farm in Bunyah. In contrast to the stark and bitter tone of *The Boys Who Stole the Funeral*, these later poems, Mick Imlah wrote in the *Times Literary Supplement*, are "good-humored and tolerant, the address muted, the technique undemonstrative, and the concerns are as large and impersonal as the continent that opens up in it." For Imlah, "Murray is revealed not only as the best but as the *most* Australian poet of the day . . . a poet resolutely at odds with much of the modern world, but increasingly at home with himself."

PRINCIPAL WORKS: *Poetry*—(with G. Lehmann) The Ilex Tree, 1965; The Weatherboard Cathedral, 1969; Poems against Economics, 1972; Lunch & Counter Lunch, 1974; Ethnic Radio, 1977; The Vernacular Republic, 1976, 1982; The Boys Who Stole the Funeral, 1980; The People's Otherworld, 1983; The Daylight Moon and Other Poems, 1987. *Prose*—The Peasant Mandarin, 1978; Persistence in Folly, 1984.

ABOUT: Contemporary Authors New Revision Series 11, 1984; Contemporary Literary Criticism 40, 1986; Contemporary Poets, 4th ed., 1985; Goodwin, K. Australian Poems in Perspective, 1979; Oxford Companion to Australian Literature, 1985. *Periodicals*—Australian Literary Studies May 1982; Journal of Commonwealth Literature, No. 1, 1982; London Magazine January 1967; New York Review of Books April 14, 1983; August 17, 1989; Poetry Australia December 1975, April 1979; Times Literary Supplement August 9, 1985; August 22, 1986; May 18, 1990.

*MUSCHG, ADOLF (May 13, 1934–), Swiss novelist, short-story writer, playwright, and essayist who writes in German, was born the son of a schoolteacher in Zollikon near Zürich. His half-brother was the late Walter Muschg, an internationally renowned professor of German literature at the University of Basel; his sister, Elsa Muschg, was a well-known author of children's books. He is married to the writer Hanna Johansen and has three sons, one from a previous marriage. He lives in Männedorf near Zürich.

In Zürich Muschg studied English and German literature with Emil Staiger and received a Ph.D. at the University of Zürich with a dissertation on the expressionist writer and artist Ernst Barlach. He taught briefly at a technical Gymnasium in Zürich. Between 1962 and 1964 he was a lecturer at the International Christian Uni-

ADOLF MUSCHG

versity in Tokyo. From 1964 to 1967 he was assistant to the program in German at the University of Göttingen, FRG. From 1967 to 1969 he taught at Cornell University and returned to Europe to take a teaching position at the University of Geneva. Since 1970 Muschg has been teaching as a professor of German at the Federal Institute of Technology (ETH) in Zürich. He wrote in a personal account in the *New York Times Book Review* in 1987:

I happen to write and teach German literature at the Swiss Federal Institute of Technology—a place with a few Nobels to its credit and the founding ambition, back in the mid-19th century, to become the preeminent Swiss university. But deep-rooted distrust of centralized education prevailed at the time, and so cotton barons and bankers of Zurich wound up with an engineering school presumed to pose less of a threat to the Swiss system of cultural checks and balances. The General Education program they initiated with an all-star cast of 1848 emigrés—some of them noted *hommes de lettres*, like the Italian literary critic Francesco de Sanctis—survives to this day, but so does the debate whether its quaint lack of "function" is an asset or a liability to a school working hard to stay abreast of the electronic revolution.

In a school catering to the general needs of future engineers, scientists and architects, there ought to be some leeway for irresponsible things—like creative writing. And there it is, as long as you take care to avoid a label that might compromise the academic solidity of the school. You have to show more, not less, respect for the still prevalent assumption that the writer has no place in a serious university community.

Muschg is a member of the Swiss Social Democratic Party. In 1975 he ran unsuccessfully as candidate for the Swiss Senate (Ständerat). From 1974 to 1977 he was a member of a Swiss government commission to prepare a total revision of

°moozhg

the Swiss constitution. In 1987–1988 he was called to Berlin to become research fellow at the prestigeous Wissenschaftsinstitut (Institute of Advanced Studies). He is a member of the German Academy of Arts (Akademie der Künste) in Berlin and the recipient of many literary prizes, including the Swiss Schillerpreis (1965), the Hamburger Lesepreis (1967), the Georg-Mackensen-Preis (1968), the C.-F.-Meyer-Preis (1968), and the Hermann-Hesse-Preis (1969).

Muschg became famous almost overnight with his first literary publication, the novel *Im Sommer des Hasen* (The Summer of the Hare, 1965). This novel is a sophisticated account of the adventures and personal self-discoveries of a group of Swiss travelers in Japan. It burst on the Swiss literary scene which at that time was almost totally overshadowed by the masterworks of the novelist Max Frisch and the playwright Friedrich Dürrenmatt. Muschg managed to establish himself with a style of his own, an ironically reflected search for identity, highlighted by brilliant and highly sophisticated insights from the author's awesome knowledge of world literature and of political and psychological theories. Although the plot is set entirely in Japan, *Im Sommer des Hasen* is scarce on exotic accounts of Japanese traditions and culture. Instead the novel reflects the transformation of bodies, minds, and characters taking place among the members of the Swiss tourist group under Japanese influence. Hired by a large Swiss firm, each of the participants is expected to write his individual account about "Japan in the widest sense" to be incorporated in a festschrift celebrating an important anniversary of the company. Muschg's novel consists of a long letter by the public relations manager of the company to its president in which he reports on the progress of the reports of the individual members of the delegation and the conversations he had with them while they explored Japan, and it ends with the manager's resignation. As his successor he nominates the only member of the delegation who did not write a report and who insisted that he fails "whenever I try to put my thoughts on paper. . . . I begin to formulate at a point when I have not understood at all; I accept a loss of consequences, and finally there it is in writing: never what I had in mind but something else which also reads quite nicely and is therefore useless."

Muschg's next novel *Gegenzauber* (Counter-magic, 1967) anticipates the political and cultural isolation of the New Left intellectuals during the 1968 student uprising. Again, as in *Im Sommer des Hasen*, a group of individuals experiences individual and collective isolation from the core of society. Their political engagement

turns out to be a narcissist disengagement in disguise. "We are different. We do not intend to change the world. . . . All we want is peace. Ours."

The author himself considers his third novel *Mitgespielt* (Played Along, 1969) a failure. Although he worked on it for almost ten years, this mystery story about a homosexual aesthete, Professor Hämmerli, who plays a role in the disappearance and reappearance of his favorite pupil Andrea, is too sleek and "designer-made" and offers too little resistance to an analytical approach. "Muschg furnishes his spaces instead of staking them out," wrote one of his critics.

Muschg's first play, the highly successful *Rumpelstilz* (Rumpelstiltskin, 1968), with the subtitle "A Middle-Class Tragedy," also deals with the strange bearings of a teacher's mind and introduces one of Muschg's favorite characters: the hypochondriac. In the play he is Professor Leu (Swiss-German for "lion"), who tyrannizes his entire family because he is under the impression that a little pain in his throat is the first symptom of a grave illness. In the end it is his quiet, long-suffering wife who dies of cancer while Mr. Leu goes on living healthily ever after. Muschg's obsession with health and illness and his preoccupation with teacher personalities surface again in his novel *Albissers Grund* (Albisser's Motive, 1974). Professor Albisser takes a shot at Mr. Zerutt, his psychiatrist, a gentleman with a dark past with whom he was in therapy for four years. The novel tells of the attempt of a court-appointed psychiatrist to unravel the biographies of Albisser and Zerutt and link them together. It turns out that under Zerutt's influence Albisser had joined a leftist apprentices' league and had become its "kitchen boy" and "driver of the revolution." He lost his middle-class standing by becoming a conscientious objector, forfeiting his job and going to jail for his convictions. He shoots at Zerutt because the psychiatrist has put too many obstacles in his path of self-discovery. When Zerutt asks him to "finally get serious with his biography" by dropping out of society and starting a commune in the south of France, Albisser refuses ("You taught me to live with my weakness. Here you got it!") and leaves Zerutt's hospital room.

In his play *Die Aufgeregten von Goethe* (The Excited Ones by Goethe, 1969) Muschg reinterprets and adapts a rather obscure early play by Goethe to reflect the contemporary political mood. Goethe's drama of a failed revolution resembles the 1968 uprising on the wane. "He is a theologian and a writer," says one of the characters. "They love to fight as long as they don't have to pay for it." The intellectual and the

revolution—very much the central political topic of the epoch, discussed by Sartre and others—
became one of Muschg's favorite subjects. It is
also the theme of his play *Kellers Abend. Ein
Stück aus dem 19. Jahrhundert* (Keller's Evening. A Nineteenth-Century Drama, 1975). The
title refers to a historic event, the inauguration
of Zurich's great nineteenth-century novelist
Gottfried Keller as Secretary of the canton of
Zürich in 1861. The event is authentic and so are
the figures on stage who assemble to celebrate
Keller's inauguration. They consist of a colorful
mixture of members of the Zurich government
and political immigrants, mostly former supporters of the 1848 revolution, among them Ferdinand Lasalle and Georg Herwegh, who play
silly games while the guest of honor, his back
turned to the audience, sits silently through the
whole evening. Only when Lasalle tries hypnosis
on Herwegh does Keller lose his composure; he
grips his chair and drives the frivolous guests out
of his house.

Muschg's attempt to grasp a historical event
and to pull it into a contemporary frame of reference and meaning is continued in another
book about Keller. The biography *Gottfried
Keller* (1977) is probably the finest book written
so far on the famous novelist. Muschg, who
seems to have learned a lot from Sartre's method
of telling the life story of the novelist Flaubert
(*L'Idiot de la famille*) by working his own biography into the account of the latter's life, analyzes the incredible odds in the life of Keller,
who grew up fatherless, was very tiny, and probably never made love to a woman. Nonetheless
he was the author of some of the most magnificent love stories in European literature.
Muschg's book on Keller is centered on the double meaning of *Schuld*, which in German implies "guilt" as well as "debt." Consequently,
Muschg uses psychoanalysis and economic theory ("early Marx and late Freud," as one of his
critics put it) as methods of interpretation. Keller
becomes a literary figure of Muschg's own making, a fact that was soon discovered and attacked
by professorial critics.

Muschg says he is "a leftist out of bad conscience, a conservative as far as tastes go,
brought up in the milieu of the establishment,
whom the rebels want to get rid of. If they do
succeed with my blessings, my blessings will not
mean anything anymore." His position between
establishment and revolution is displayed in radio plays such as *Das Kerbelgericht* (The Chervil
Trial, 1969; again a double meaning since it may
also imply "The Dish of Chervil"), which deals
with the street clashes in the 1960s between
young people and the Zurich police; the dreamlike love story without consequences *Why,*

Arizona (1977); and the political farce *Watussi.
Ein Stück für Zwei Botschafter* (Watusi. A Play
For Two Ambassadors, 1977, published together
with *Why, Arizona* and *Goddy Haemels
Abenteuerreise* in the 1982 volume *Übersee,*
Overseas), dealing with the consequences of a
real-life kidnapping of a Swiss ambassador. In
his TV play *High Fidelity oder Ein Silberblick*
(High Fidelity or Starry-Eyed, 1973) Muschg
discusses adultery and faithfulness in a typical
middle-class marriage.

In 1980 Muschg published his novel *Baiyun
oder die Freundschaftsgesellschaft* (Baiun, or
The Friendship Society). Like his first book it
deals with the reflections of a European tourist
group traveling in an exotic country, this time
China. The literary critics were not very kind to
this new attempt to use the old formula of seeing
an incomprehensible environment through the
eyes and minds of fictional figures (one of them
unmistakably resembling Max Frisch). To some,
Muschg's attempt to follow in the footsteps of
Georges Simenon in combining an exotic crime
story with cultural analysis and psychological insights ("Murder is a chance to surprise the survivors surviving. All of them") suffers from two
major flaws: the plot is overly ambitious and
eventually nebulous, and the author never quite
comes to grips (as he had in his earlier book) with
the culture of the host country (Muschg had
spent only two weeks in China, on a tourist visa).
However, other critics, such as Peter Demetz,
who calls *Baiyun* Muschg's "first true masterpiece of undisputed rank," have found Muschg's
"fatal gift of always saying too much" in this case
"controlled . . . with resolute energy."

In *Das Licht und der Schlüssel* (The Light and
the Key, 1984) we encounter, once more, the
psychiatrist Zerutt from *Albissers Grund*, only
this time he is called Constantin Samstag and has
turned into a therapist from Transylvania, a
Dracula figure, an "undead" who spends his
time bleeding the wives of cardiologists whom
he consults because of his own health problems
(imagined, of course). The rather dissolute
Dracula story is followed by thirteen essays in
letter form to Dracula's employer, a blind art
collector who has commissioned Samstag to
search for a lost still-life from the golden age of
Dutch painting. This pretext is used by the author to reflect on the appreciation of old masters
(the plot takes place in a rather stereotypical
Amsterdam) and the art of forgery. Michael Butler wrote in the *Times Literary Supplement*:
"These two narrative levels, however, are rapidly undermined by the proliferation of character
and incident, bitter ironies and complex jokes,
contemporary and historical controversies, and
above all by an extended disquisition on the na-

ture and fabrication of art itself. The incomparable Vermeer is set against the brilliant forger
Van Meegeren, the melancholy fate of Anne
Frank against the survival of the Nazi collaborator Pieter Menten. The result is a subtle and frequently confusing parody of the classical
German novel. What appears to be a welcome
unravelling of mysteries in the book's third section (simply entitled 'Novel') merely intensifies
the reader's puzzlement. Samstag and his employer turn out to be two halves of the same consciousness (character is too strong a word), and
the multiple stories spun from it to have no firm
root in any fictive reality. The novel turns re-
morselessly into a baleful commentary on its
own shaky aesthetic presuppositions."

In Switzerland Muschg appears as the quintessential intellectual of the generation immediately following Frisch and Dürrenmatt. As Demetz
puts it: "Whenever West German broadcasting
stations or Modern Language Association sections in America need a sober and enlightened
view of Swiss or central European intellectual
affairs, Muschg is inevitably invited." As a guest
lecturer in creative writing Muschg has toured
the United States and written the following
about his experiences:

> In painting or music there may still be a tradition from
> which the real master can abstract something new in the
> end. But in writing, the basic material words being
> signs—is already burdened with the conventions of expe-
> rience. These cannot go untested—and uncontested—if
> they are to render the author's own experience. There is
> no way *Ulysses* could have been written in the manner
> of Henry James, or Kafka's *Castle* as an exercise in good
> German. There can be no realism in contemporary liter-
> ature without the author being aware of the preestabli-
> shed—and prejudicial—"reality" of the signs he is using.
> It is by drawing consequences from this realization, cre-
> atively responding to it, that a writer becomes deserving
> of the title and of our attention.
>
> So the modern writer need not consciously reflect, or
> even understand, the development of modern physics,
> microbiology or social behavior—his style will show the
> change by creating symbolic equivalents. There is no re-
> turn to the fairy-tale realism of the latter-day Aristote-
> lians: they are innocents to the degree that they cannot
> even see what they are guilty of—the omission of the
> truth, or what truth can be captured in words. Setups like
> the Famous Writers' School are frowned upon by the av-
> erage European intellectual—and the reason for this
> contempt may be very silly. But you do not have to be
> a snob to accept that literature worth reading is too pre-
> cious—and too hazardous—to be left to professional
> writers.

When *The Blue Man*, the first book-length
sample of Muschg's work in English translation
(the title story obviously influenced by Ernst
Barlach's *Der blaue Boll*), appeared in 1985,
readers in the United States were confronted
with a collection of masterful short stories, all
dealing in one way or the other with Muschg's

central theme, "loneliness in the ice age of the
spirit." Muschg is contemporary Switzerland's
most prolific writer. Although his novels are long
and often meandering, some of his short stories
from collections such as *Fremdkörper* (Foreign
Bodies, 1968), *Liebesgeschichten* (Love Stories,
1972), *Entfernte Bekannte* (Distant Acquaintances, 1976), *Besuch in der Schweiz* (Visit to
Switzerland, 1978), *Noch ein Wunsch* (Another
Request, 1979), *Leib und Leben* (Body and Soul,
1981), and *Der Turmhahn* (The Steeple Cock,
1987) are small masterpieces of composition and
psychological insight.

It comes as no surprise that Muschg has also
excelled as an essayist, dealing from a theoretical
point of view with the major political, therapeutic, and literary problems of his times. The list
of his essay volumes is long: *Papierwände* (Paper
Walls, 1970; essay on Muschg's Japanese experiences, written between 1963 and 1970), *Fiktion
und Engagement, oder: kein letztes Wort auf
einem sehr weiten Feld* (Fiction and Engagement, or: No Last Word on a Very Large Field,
1972), *Von Herwegh bis Kaiseraugst—wie hal-
ten wir es als Demokraten mit der Freiheit*?
(From Herwegh to Kaiseraugst—do we, as democrats, side with freedom?, 1975; a lecture to
commemorate the 100th birthday of Georg Herwegh), *Geschichte eines Manuskripts* (History of
a Manuscript, 1977; a foreword to the novel
Mars by Fritz Zorn), *Besprechungen 1961–1979*
(Reviews 1961–1979, 1980), *Literatur als Thera-
pie? Ein Exkurs über das Heilsame und das
Unheilbare* (Literature as Therapy? A Digression about the Wholesome and the Incurable,
1981), *Die Tücke des verbesserten Objekts* (The
Perfidy of the Improved Object, 1981), *Goethe
der Einzige, Goethe als Beispiel* (Goethe the
Peerless, Goethe for Example, 1982), *Im Wasser
Flamme. Goethes Grüne Wissenschaft* (In the
Water Flame, Goethe's Green Science, 1985),
and *Goethe als Emigrant. Auf der Suche nach
dem Grünen bei einem alten Dichter* (Goethe as
Emigrant. In Search of the Green in the Work
of an Old Writer, 1986).

Muschg has also written a film script,
Deshima, 1987. In 1989 he was at work on a
modern version of *Parzival*.

WORKS IN ENGLISH TRANSLATION: Translation of shorter
works by Adolf Muschg have appeared in periodicals.
These include Michael Hamburger's "The Scythe
Hand or The Homestead" in Encounter in 1975; "Blue
Man" in Canto I, 1977, and "Reparations of Making
Good" in Canto II, 1978; "Brami's View" in Fiction VI,
1978. Marlis Zeller Cambon and Michael Hamburger's
translation of *The Blue Man* was published in 1985.

ABOUT: Cassell's Encyclopedia of World Literature,

1973; Columbia Dictionary of Modern European Literature, 1980; Contemporary Authors 85–88, 1980; Demetz, A. After the Fires, 1986; Dictionary of Literary Biography 75, 1988; Encyclopedia of World Literature in the 20th Century (rev. ed.) I, 1981. *Periodicals*—New York Times Book Review, May 19, 1985; Times Literary Supplement January 4, 1985.

SHIVA NAIPAUL

*NAIPAUL, SHIVA (February 25, 1945–August 13, 1985), Trinidadian novelist, short-story writer, and journalist, was born in Port of Spain, Trinidad (now Republic of Trinidad and Tobago), West Indies. He was the sixth of seven children of Seepersad and Droapate Naipaul, of Indian extraction and Hindu affiliation, and the couple's second son, the elder (by twelve years) being the distinguished author V. S. Naipaul. After schooling at St. Mary's College in Trinidad, Shiva Naipaul won an Island Scholarship to Oxford, where he attended University College (1964–1968) and studied Chinese. In 1967 he married a young Englishwoman, Jenny Stuart, and soon began a career as a writer. His first novel, *Fireflies*, published when he was twenty-five, received a number of awards—the Jock Campbell Award (the *New Statesman*), the Winifred Holtby Memorial Prize (from Britain's Royal Society of Literature), and the John Llewellyn Rhys Memorial Prize.

Fireflies chronicles the lives of three generations of a Hindu family in Trinidad, the well-to-do Khojas. The family's gradual decline is depicted in the marriage of one of its female members. She weds a bus driver, Ram Lutchman, and becomes disillusioned first with him and then with their sons, who cannot make anything of themselves. William Pritchard, in the *Hudson Review*, called the novel "impressively painstaking in its leisurely portrait of manners in Trinidad's Hindu community." The reviewer for the *Antioch Review* was impressed, too, by the novel's "fascinating accumulation of detail" which, although "quiet" and "restrained," creates a compelling interest in Naipaul's "remote and rarified world." Auberon Waugh hailed *Fireflies* as "a masterpiece . . . a delight and a miracle of enjoyment," and noted particularly its ambivalence of attitude. Naipaul, he wrote, satirizes the absurdities of his group "with conventional rigour but he is also keenly alive to the tragedy of its destruction, and it is this quality which makes his book so exceptional."

Fireflies was followed by *The Chip-Chip Gatherers*, which records the lives of two families, the Ramsarans and the Bholais, in a poor village in Trinidad. Egbert Ramsaran has risen from poverty through the success of his transport company, but cannot shake off the narrowness of his peasant attitudes, and his relations with the Bholais never achieve any common sense of purpose and understanding. The Bholais' son Julian flees this futile environment with a scholarship to England, but the Ramsaran's son Wilbert remains marooned in a "cannibal world of kinship." "If the book isn't quite as successful as the startlingly mature *Fireflies*," Martin Amis remarked, "it is because Mr. Naipaul has started to deal with the problem of focus. He is concentrating on nuance rather than ambiance, shaving down his sentences, holding his vast . . . comic talents carefully in check." The reviewer for the *Times Literary Supplement* found the novel excessively melancholy but skillful in its delineation of disorder and dislocation.

Rather than continuing with his novels of Trinidadian life, Naipaul devoted his energies in the 1970s to writing about conditions in various parts of the world, particularly in the Third World countries. His *North of South: An African Journey* gives his first-hand impressions of Kenya, Tanzania, and Zambia, located north of South Africa. John Darnton called *North of South* a "superbly written collection of hapless encounters—with rapacious officials, reckless taxi drivers, street hustlers, ideological robots and racist expatriates—strung together by the author's sardonic, often bilious observations. It is built on vignettes and cameo portraits." Roland Oliver also noted Naipaul's mordant wit, his novelist's power of vivid description and of characterization through reported dialogue." But a number of critics, and particularly Africanists, felt that Naipaul's portrait was one-sided and prejudicial. "The vignettes of the pathetically doomed Asians, of savagely cynical whites, of one long, hapless black-African comedy of errors," Eric Goldman observed, "too often have the quality of gallows humor. Eventually, we begin to weary of Naipaul's implacable pessimism."

Journey to Nowhere: A New World Tragedy, published in England as *Black and White,* deals with the mass suicide of Jim Jones and the members of his People's Temple in Guyana in 1978. Shortly after the event, Naipaul took part in a U.S. government–sponsored flight to Jonestown, and from his on-site observations and interviews with those associated with the massacre, prepared his narrative of tragic delusions. Especially emphasized are the culture of California and the cultist manias of the late 1960s and 1970s, which Naipaul believed had produced pastor Jones. Peter Schrag described the book as "a tough, intelligent, beautifully written account. . . . Naipaul has a flawless ear for the gobbledygook of Third World pretenders, encounter-group gurus, esties, obfuscating politicians and various other manipulators of rhetoric." Robert Coles, however, found Naipaul's conclusions too sweeping and biased," a leap "from one tragedy to another tragedy to the broadest possible social judgments."

Naipaul's third novel, *Love and Death in a Hot Country,* published in England as *A Hot Country,* draws from his observations of Guyana, which appears thinly disguised as Cuyama, a land so steeped in poverty and corruption as to leave his cast of characters virtually without hope. Nicholas Rankin remarked that "there is much voluptuous self-surrender to pessimism by the author . . . yet it does not mask Shiva Naipaul's other considerable talents as a novelist. He deftly captures place, mood and characters, and has not lost his eye for embarrassment and discomfiture." Charles Champlin admired the novel's "convincing atmosphere" but complained that the work contained too little story. There "is much talk but relatively little action. . . . Naipaul's book is a kind of sermon on political impotence, a despairing tract, bleak, fully captured and persuasive, on the high cost of history."

Naipaul's next book, *Beyond the Dragon's Mouth,* collected his short stories and a large number of his pieces of travel-social-political commentary written during the last decade and ranging over various parts of the world, including England, India, Iran, and Africa. John Krich found the stories, set largely in Trinidad, "accurate and convincing," and noted that they display superbly his "observational skills, his fine

ear for the rhythms of Caribbean street speech, his feel for the subtle traps and the cyclical logic of poverty. They are even touched here and there with genuine pity." But the Third World reportage was also highly praised, one reviewer calling it "literary journalism at its best." Ryszard Kapuscinski called attention to Naipaul's "obsession for discovering and unmasking false myths, hollow deities raised high on altars for no good reasons," and concluded "This book is splendid."

On August 13, 1985, in Sri Lanka, on the first leg of a trip to Australia, the subject of his next book, Shiva Naipaul died of a heart attack at the age of forty. *An Unfinished Journey,* published posthumously, contains six of his articles on subjects ranging from his relationship with his famous brother to the India of the Nehrus to the Australian aborigines. Of these articles the longest is his seventy-page account of Sri Lanka. John Gross remarked that this piece "shows him in top form. . . . The portrait of Tissa [a failed writer in Sri Lanka who is no longer convinced of the reality of his own existence] is comic and sad and rather frightening, and more than anything else in the book brings home what a subtle writer Mr. Naipaul could be at his best." John Avedon characterized these final, pessimistic pieces as "passionate works, bitterly funny, often brilliant, but essentially laments."

At his early death Naipaul was considered by many in Britain to be one of the most talented and wide-ranging authors of his generation. In a reminiscent article about him in the *New Republic,* Geoffrey Wheatcroft described him as "shaggy and bearlike in appearance—stocky and tending to be plump . . . intensely sensitive and sometimes prickly. [But] for those who knew him, Shiva could be the most warm and engaging of friends." In a similar vein, Alexander Chancellor, in the *Spectator,* pointed out that the portrait of Naipaul that may emerge from his writing, of a "solitary, gloomy, and self-obsessed person," was entirely misleading, for "he was one of the most companionable people I have ever met."

PRINCIPAL WORKS: *Novels*—Fireflies, 1971; The Chip-Chip Gatherers, 1973; Love and Death in a Hot Country (in U.K. A Hot Country), 1984. *Collected short stories*—Beyond the Dragon's Mouth; Stories and Pieces, 1985. *Non-fiction*—North of South: An African Journey, 1979; Journey to Nowhere: A New World Tragedy (in U.K. Black and White), 1981; An Unfinished Journey, 1987.

ABOUT: Contemporary Authors 110, 1984; 112, 1985; (obituary) 116, 1986; Contemporary Literary Criticism 32, 1985; 39, 1986; Contemporary Novelists, 1976; Dictionary of Literary Biography, 1985.

Periodicals—New Republic May 11, 1987; New Statesman April 20, 1973; New York Times Book Review
May 6, 1979; August 12, 1984; March 24, 1985; New
Yorker July 2, 1979; Spectator February 26, 1983; August 24, 1985.

NAYLOR, GLORIA (January 25, 1950–   ),
American novelist, writes: "I and my two sisters
were born in New York City, but my parents migrated from Robinsonville, Mississippi in 1949
where I, their oldest child, was actually conceived. So while my physical birth makes me a
native New Yorker, it was my conception in the
South that has played the more important role
in shaping my life as a writer. I inherited my
mother's consummate love of books, a love she
was not able to fully exercise in her youth because as a black the public libraries were barred
to her, and being from a family of sharecroppers
with eight children, books were a luxury that
they could not afford. So after working with her
family during the week, my mother would hire
herself out to do extra field work on her spare
Saturdays in order to obtain the pocket money
to send away to book clubs. This and other experiences promoted her desire to have all of her
children born in the North and to nurture their
interest, if any existed, to read and read and
read. I was the child to whom it was more than
an interest; exploring new worlds and new ideas
became bound up in the fiber of my being. I
used to be thrilled by just the smell and touch of
books, the sight of them lined up in rows and
rows on the library shelves. I can only imagine
what it must have been for my mother to have
those same feelings while living the life she did;
and when I did *imagine* it in my first novel, *The
Women of Brewster Place*, I like to think that it
was a tribute to her and other black women who
in spite of very limited personal circumstances
somehow managed to hold a fierce belief in the
limitless possibilities of the human spirit.

"And as a shy and introverted child, writing
became a way to allow myself, my spirit, to enter
into my own private feelings and those of others
to attempt to answer questions that I was too
timid to voice. My written words are my voice
in a sense, asking how is it that . . . ? We survive. We love. We hate. We hope. And ironically
I found that these far reaching questions are best
answered through the stories I grew up hearing
about life in Robinsonville, Mississippi, and
through the life that I experienced in New York.
It's an old formula: you reach the universal
through the particular. I believe it was Anthony
Burgess who said that a writer never mines from
any experiences after the age of ten. For myself

GLORIA NAYLOR

I can definitely concur up until the age of fourteen. Because it was at that time that my indiscriminate reading habits began to be honed and
I was introduced to the English classics and I
learned the difference between a simple voicing
of feelings and language. Language can be a
powerful tool, beautiful in and of itself, beyond
the telling of a story. There were the Brontës and
their unbridled passion, Austen and her satirical
restraint, Dickens and his social indignation,
while Thackeray stood aloof and made fun of
the genre by combining all of those elements. To
this day I believe that I'm still influenced by my
first introduction to the Victorian novel. I love
drama in a novel (perhaps even a bit of melodrama), evoking the physical environments, having
characters *feel* and calling shamelessly upon the
reader to feel with them. And then having
reached college and finally discovering that, in
spite of their absence in my formal educational
curriculum, there was a wealth of literature that
black American writers had been creating for
over a century—the two halves made the whole
that are now me. Learning about my literary
foremothers and forefathers and the validity of
the English language to my experiences (personal and historical) have provided me with more
material to mine than I will be able to use in a
lifetime. Yes, infinite possibilities lie between
the matrix of Afro-American-Woman."

———

Gloria Naylor has expressed some irritation
with critics, black and white alike, who insist
that the work of black writers should be

"definitive" of black experience. Being black is far more complex than any single writer or work can define. As black writers emerge into the American literary mainstream, she maintains, they confront a new challenge: "How do you keep your soul and still succeed in America? For the Afro-American," she told an interviewer for the *New York Times Book Review*, "regardless of where you climb on the ladder of success, there will be racism. Under these conditions, if you give up what centers you, what is unique in you—then you are lost. The greatness of this country is the uniqueness of its people. But there is pressure to amalgamate. And that is suicidal when it happens to the Afro-American."

Behind Naylor's work is a fierce moral urgency. Keenly sensitive to her identity as a black woman, she did not find her direction as a writer until, a student in a creative writing class at Brooklyn College, she read Toni Morrison's novel *The Bluest Eye*. Although she had been writing poetry and reading widely in English and American literature all her life, this book, "changed my life. I had been struggling along as a poet, afraid to make the transition from poetry to fiction, and struggling with a formal education that was deficient in any body of literature reflecting my black female existence as either subject or creator. And that one book fed both those needs."

After high school Gloria Naylor worked for seven years (1968–1975) as a missionary for the Jehovah's Witnesses in New York, North Carolina, and Florida. She entered college intending to prepare for a nursing career but soon switched to literature, supporting herself through her college years by working as a telephone operator in New York City hotels. In 1981 she received her Bachelor's degree in English from Brooklyn College; she went to Yale University to take an M.A. in Afro-American studies in 1983. At Yale she also took courses in the Women's Studies program: "I hoped that by combining the two I could find out what black women had been doing." By this time Naylor had discovered the richness of black women's writing—from the slave narratives of the past to the work of Zora Neale Hurston, Alice Walker, and Toni Morrison.

Although Naylor's novels have been compared to those of Walker and Morrison, reviewers have never failed to note their freshness and originality. *The Women of Brewster Place*, which won the American Book Award for the best first novel of 1982, is a book about female bonding in the context of racism and poverty. It is a community novel—in the literal sense that Brewster Place is a shabby, run-down, dead-end

street where poor black people live—and in the figurative sense that its women, as Naylor writes, "share a common oppression and, more importantly, a spiritual strength and sense of female communion that I believe all women have employed historically for their psychic health and survival."

There are seven separate but related stories in *The Women of Brewster Place*, each centering on a different representative character, making the fictional Brewster Place a kind of microcosm comprising all the varied experiences of black women in America. Naylor writes in an introductory chapter: "They were hard-edged, soft-centered, brutally demanding, and easily pleased, these women of Brewster Place. They came, they went, grew up, and grew old beyond their years. Like an ebony phoenix, each in her own time and with her own season had a story." The stories are linked by the street itself and also by the hard-won strength these women share, despite the diversity of their situations. In the dramatic climax of the novel, as the women gather to celebrate a block party, they unite in an act of liberation, tearing down the brick wall that has sealed off their street—a wall that Naylor has said symbolizes "simply the racism in this country." As a sudden rainstorm rages around them, they vent their feelings by chipping away at the wall—"with knives, plastic forks, spiked shoe heels, and even bare hands. . . . The bricks piled up behind them. . . . Suddenly, the rain exploded around their feet in a fresh downpour, and the cold waters beat on the top of their heads—almost in perfect unison with the beating of their hearts."

Close to life though Naylor's subject and characters are, *The Women of Brewster Place*, Annie Gottlieb wrote in the *New York Times Book Review*, "isn't realistic fiction—it is mythic. Nothing supernatural happens in it, yet its vivid, earthy characters . . . seem constantly on the verge of breaking out into magical powers. . . . Miss Naylor bravely risks sentimentality and melodrama to write her compassion and outrage large, and she pulls it off triumphantly." Other reviewers noted her ability to avoid the stereotypes of urban-ghetto fiction and her technical skill in using the street itself as her protagonist. They were also impressed with the tone of the book: "Naylor is not angry," William Bradley Hooper wrote in *Booklist*; "she writes with conviction and beautiful language, but spares the reader any bitterness. Characters are not puppets but exist and function as well-rounded personalities." There was a highly acclaimed four-hour television production of *The Women of Brewster Place* in March 1989, with Oprah Winfrey in a leading role.

Linden Hills, Naylor's second novel, dedicated to her parents Roosevelt and Alberta Naylor, again finds its center in a black community but is far more ambitiously conceived. Its structure, she acknowledges, was inspired by Dante's *Inferno*; it has many more characters than her first novel, and its theme is more daring and complex. Linden Hills is a "restricted" suburb, built and developed by a black family dynasty and now home to scores of upwardly mobile blacks. Racism and poverty hardly impinge on this enclave, where ambitious and successful blacks enjoy material comfort, even luxury. The price they are paying, however, is their souls. Having betrayed or sold out their natural heritage and culture, they suffer in "perverted Eden," a hell of their own creation. Naylor sustains her Dantean parallels throughout the book. The community itself is built along crescents or circles, that center on the home of the land's developer, one Luther (Lucifer?) Nedeed, whose family bought the land generations earlier. Satanic and destructive, Luther sets the tone for the violence and despair that dog the lives of the other residents. Yet grim as most of the action is in this novel, there is also humor and good will, especially in the two young black poets who do odd jobs in the community and act as observers and guides, somewhat in the manner of Dante and Virgil in their progress down to the depths of hell. They preserve a sense of balance, and retain their compassion and love of life, even as they witness horrors in the lives of the wealthy people who hire them: "Bloody noses had made them friends, but giving sound to the bruised places in their hearts made them brothers."

Linden Hills won praise from most reviewers, although some had reservations about its didacticism. Mel Watkins, in the *New York Times Book Review*, found it "an intriguing allegory, and for the most part Miss Naylor presents it with wit and insight into the [problems and] anxieties that plague assimilated blacks." Michiko Kakutani, in the *New York Times*, conceded that the narrative may lean too heavily "on baroque symbols and withheld secrets," but she felt that this weakness was redeemed "by the author's confident way with a story; her sassy, streetwise humor, her ability to empathize with her characters' dilemmas." In a long analytical article on the novel in *Contemporary Literature*, Catherine C. Ward pointed out the risks Naylor was taking: "*Linden Hills* is an uncomfortable and dangerous book which pricks the conscience. . . . Naylor has risked much by writing such a disturbing tale . . . she could lose a black audience that feels unjustly challenged and a white audience that thinks the novel's hard questions are not meant for them. Naylor also risks

offending modern sensibilities that regard an allegory about moral accountability [as] too medieval for their tastes. But because Naylor knows who she is, where she has been, and where she wants to go, she dares to tell her tale and dares the reader to reckon with it."

Naylor's fascination with the folklore that enriches black culture was the source of her third novel, *Mama Day*. In *Linden Hills* one of the characters recalls the visit to her home many years earlier of her great-aunt Miranda Day, known to the family as "Mama Day": "Coming with her cardboard suitcases, loose-fitting shoes, and sticky jars of canned whatever. Toothless but ready with a broad grin; almost illiterate but determined to give her very loud opinion regardless of the subject or the company." She is an embarrassment to her social-climbing Linden Hills relatives, but Naylor makes her the center of her new novel. As in *Linden Hills* there is a literary frame for the book. Here it is Shakespeare's *The Tempest*, as Miranda's name suggests, as does the setting of the first half of the novel—an island off the Georgia-Carolina coast, where Mama works her own brand of magic with love potions and spells. Settled originally by an African-born slave, the island is haunted by memories of the dark, ancient past. The center of the novel, however, is Mama Day's young grandniece and her ill-fated suitor, an ambitious Northern black. When its action moves to New York and concentrates on the young lovers, Bharati Mukerjee writes in the *New York Times Book Review*, the novel is weakened. "As long as the narrative confines itself to Mama Day and daily life on the bizarre island full of rogues, frauds, crazies, martyrs and clairvoyants, the novel moves quickly." But the New York sections become "set pieces . . . she is less proficient in making the familiar wondrous than she is in making the wondrous familiar." Nevertheless, Mukerjee concludes: "Gloria Naylor has written a big, strong, dense, admirable novel."

Gloria Naylor has taught writing courses at George Washington Univerity (1983–1984) and New York University (1986). In the fall of 1985 she was a cultural exchange lecturer in India for the United States Office of Information. That same year she received a fellowship from the National Endowment for the Arts. She lives in New York City.

PRINCIPAL WORKS: The Women of Brewster Place, 1982; Linden Hills, 1985; Mama Day, 1988.

ABOUT: Contemporary Authors 107, 1983; Contemporary Literary Criticism 28, 1984; Contemporary Novelists, 4th ed., 1986. *Periodicals*—Contemporary Literature Spring 1987; New York Times February 9,

1985; March 19, 1989; New York Times Book Review August 22, 1982; March 13, 1984; March 3, 1985; February 21, 1988; Publishers Weekly September 9, 1983.

NEWBY, (GEORGE) ERIC (December 6, 1919–), British travel writer and memoirist, was born in Barnes, west London, the only child of George Arthur Newby and Hilda Pomeroy Newby. He was educated at Colet Court, a London preparatory school, and at St. Paul's, one of the major British public schools.

Newby has always had the good fortune, not to mention the verbal wit and dexterity, to be able to turn most aspects of his varied career into books. He writes of his own life with apparent ease and good humor, rarely failing to find a retrospective laugh in past situations, not all of which can have seemed amusing at the time. He has not written much about his two years (1936–1938) with Dorland Advertising in London, but evidently was dissatisfied enough with his job there to resign in 1938 in order to begin what was to become a lifetime of extensive traveling. In 1938–1939 he served as apprentice and ordinary seaman aboard the *Moshulu*, a four-masted Finnish barque and one of the last sailing ships to be engaged commercially in the grain trade. This experience he recalled years later in two books: his first published work, *The Last Grain Race*, and, some years later, *Grain Race: Pictures of a Life Before the Mast in a Windjammer*. The latter book consists of hundreds of black-and-white photographs, copiously annotated by the author, taken during the ship's long last voyage. He lived, he explains in *Grain Race*, in extremely close quarters in the fo'c'sle with the other boys and the ordinary and able seamen. "The really big ships, of which *Moshulu* was one, had mostly been built in the nineties or early 1900s for the nitrate trade, at a time when steam was already a serious competitor. Although these ships were of immense size [the *Moshulu* was 5,300 tons dead weight], they were built so that they could be handled with the minimum number of men, and the accommodation was proportionate." He took "nearly all the photographs during my free watch below; many of them when I was done-in after long hours on deck, at the wheel or up in the rigging."

Newby's war service was a long one, beginning on his return from the sea with a stint in the Officer Cadet Training Unit at Camberley, Surrey. As a newly commissioned officer in the Black Watch Regiment, he was posted to India very early in the war, then back to the Mediterranean theater as a member of the Special Boat Section. He was captured off the coast of Sicily

ERIC NEWBY

in 1942 and spent the next three years in prisoner-of-war camps in Italy, Bohemia, and Bavaria. His time in Italy—during which he met his wife, Wanda, who was to accompany him on many of his subsequent travels—he describes in *Love and War in the Apennines*, a book whose events he divides into three distinct periods: "the one in which I was captured; the time I spent as a prisoner of war; and the third period when I was free after the Italian Armistice." He also describes the many ways he was helped by Wanda when he was in danger of being discovered by the Fascists or captured by the retreating Nazis. *Love and War* is certainly not a memoir full of heroic exploits and derring-do among brave Resistance fighters. "I finally decided to write the book," he explains, "because I felt that comparatively little had been written about the ordinary Italian people who helped prisoners of war at great personal risk and without thought of personal gain, purely out of kindness of heart. The sort of people one can still see today working in the fields as one whizzes down the Autostrada del Sole and on any mountain road in the Apennines."

Returning to the parental home after his war service (he was awarded the Military Cross in 1945), Newby suffered through two months of idleness following upon demobilization. His parents decided he must "do *something*," and so determined to make him a traveling salesman for their wholesale collection of readymade women's clothes, "a commercial venture of a sort that is now extinct." These adventures he describes in his very funny memoir of life in the British garment trade, *Something Wholesale*, which is both a kind of commercial and sporting biography of his father (1874–1956), a gruff, somewhat brutal sportsman—a rowing man—and an imperialist who insisted his only child be an "all-rounder," taking both a cold bath and "a thick ear" with equanimity, as well as an account of Newby's own unwilling immersion in the family business. "The hero of this book," he writes in the preface, "if it has one, is the man who, during the years it describes, was head of the dressmaking firm of Lane and Newby [founded in the 1890s]. . . . But this was my father in old age. We were separated by a great gulf of years, and when I was old enough to appreciate him the world which he knew and of which he was a part had passed away."

After ten years (1946–1956) in the business of selling women's dresses, the last year (after Lane and Newby had been forced to close) with the rather better known firm of Worth Paquin, Newby resigned once again to go traveling. This time, as he describes in *A Short Walk in the Hindu Kush*, he left with a friend from the British Foreign Service for Nuristan, in the extreme northeast of Afghanistan, bordering on Chitral and enclosed by the main range of the Hindu Kush mountains. (Even the passes there were all over 15,000 feet.) Neither of the friends, incredibly, had ever gone mountain climbing before. The book's climax is the intrepid pair's failure to climb Mir Samir, a most forbidding Afghan peak, and their subsequent meeting with the famous British explorer Wilfred Thesiger, who treated them with a mixture of kindness and contempt. The entire journey, literally from start to finish, reads like an endless nightmare, with every sort of problem travelers can encounter, some surmounted, some avoided, most endured. There is a great deal of "disaster and tragedy," all minutely described, not to mention the many "gastric disorders that were to hang like a cloud over our venture." Yet all is detailed, in typical Newby style, with unfailing wit and retrospective good humor. Gavin Maxwell, writing in the *New Statesman*, found *A Short Walk* "hilariously funny . . . highly readable and full of incident." "Immensely literate," agreed Jeanette Wakin in *Saturday Review*. "One of the most unusual exploration books of recent years. What's more, it's an extremely witty and funny book."

Newby worked in 1956–1959 for the London publishing firm of Secker & Warburg, who published his first two books. He then—unaccountably, given his earlier experiences, but most probably merely in order to earn money at a trade he knew well—returned to the garment business, serving in 1959–1963 as the central buyer for model dresses with the John Lewis Partnership, a principal British retailer. He quit this position to travel in India with his wife. *Slowly down the Ganges* is the amusing record of a 1,200-mile journey through northern India during the winter of 1963–1964. The book describes the great holy river "from the place where it enters the Plains of India to the Sandheads, forty miles offshore in the Bay of Bengal. . . . It is not an heroic story . . . we were too late for such feats, even if we had had the courage and determination to perform them. . . . It is not a book about India today; neither is it concerned with politics or economics. It is certainly not erudite. . . . It is about the river as we found it." The travelers were determined to make their journey by boat, and the first part of the book tells of this plainly doomed attempt to take a heavily laden boat that drew eighteen inches when empty down a river that in many places was only sixteen inches deep. Many painful days later and only a few miles down the river, the Newbys were obliged to abandon their dream and to proceed by other means of transportation, which eventually comprised such conveyances as train, bus, and bullock cart. Robin White, writing in the *New York Times Book Review*, appreciated the book's early part most of all: "the problems and delays combine to create a sort of 'African Queen' adventure on the Ganges, and it is in this section that Newby succeeds in drawing an intimate and fascinating portrait of place and people, capturing fully the feel of life along the river. . . . But as the crowded civilization from Banaras to Calcutta is approached, the lapses into historical summaries and tourist observations become more frequent. And ultimately one wishes that Newby had had to struggle with an impossible boat all the way."

Another long journey taken by the Newbys together is recounted in *The Big Red Train Ride*, a marathon of a trip on the Soviet rail system from Moscow to Nakhodka on the Sea of Japan in the spring of 1977. He dedicates the book "To the Peoples of Siberia, who have to live there," then warns in the acknowledgments that "Lynx-eyed rail enthusiasts may detect discrepancies in the distances given between some stations. Such discrepancies exist between official Russian and other timetables. They should address themselves to these authorities rather than to me." The book contains a convenient and well-drawn two-page map of the entire Soviet Union, showing the BAM Railway, then still under construction, the original and present routes of the Trans-Siberian Railway, and the route of what was formerly the Chinese Eastern Railway—all much discussed in the text. Despite this assistance provided to his readers, Newby later reported receiving "an immensely long and abusive letter from a reader who complained that the map . . . did not mark every station and halt on a line that is 5900 miles long and stretches over seven time zones."

In 1964–1973 Newby worked as travel editor for the London Sunday newspaper the *Observer* and as general editor of Time Off Books, a travel-guide list. He wrote *Time Off in Southern Italy.* With Diana Petry, he compiled two similar guidebooks, *Wonder of Britain: A Personal Choice of 480* and *Wonders of Ireland: A Personal Choice of 484.* Both books employ what the authors describe as "a frankly romantic approach to selection"; the wonders are both natural and man-made, and many are difficult to get to. They list the British wonders, generically, as "caves, churches, grottoes, castles, bridges, tombs, monuments, palaces, gardens, mazes, cliffs, whirlpools, woods, gorges, industrial remains, and eccentric constructions which the builders themselves would have been at a loss to explain the purpose of, if anyone had had the courage to ask them." The Irish wonders comprise "lonely islands, hidden loughs, huge precipitous cliffs, caverns, towers, abbeys, castles, churches, follies, industrial remains, tombs and memorials, great houses and demesnes, waterfalls, subterranean rivers, canals, cloud-capped mountains, passes, ancient woods, dolmens, crannogs, stone circles, cairns, earthworks, bridges, holy wells, crosses, Ogham stones, prehistoric cemeteries, and places of pilgrimage."

A Traveller's Life, despite its title, is declared by the author at the outset to be "not an autobiography. It concerns itself for the most part . . . with my life as a traveller in however modest a fashion from the time I was born more than sixty years ago." "Why do people travel?" he continues in his own light-hearted style. "To escape their creditors. To find a warmer or cooler clime. To sell Coca-Cola to the Chinese. To find out what is over the seas, over the hills and far away, round the corner, over the garden wall—with a ladder and some glasses you could see the Hackney Marshes if it wasn't for the houses in between, in the words of the old music hall song, the writer of which one feels was about to take off." As to his own reason for traveling, he quotes Evelyn Waugh's preface to *A Short Walk in the Hindu Kush*: to satisfy "the longing, romantic, reasonless, which lies deep in the hearts of most Englishmen, to shun the celebrated spectacles of the tourist and, without any concern with science or politics or commerce, simply to set their feet where few civilized feet have trod." "Though he denies the intention," writes Joseph Hone in the *Times Literary Supplement,* "Eric

Newby has written an autobiography purely in terms of his travels. . . . The result is an unusual but not entirely satisfying compromise—like a cake with two flavours. . . . That said, *A Traveller's Life* is none the less a feast. Newby has several crucial virtues lacking in more recently acclaimed travel writers. He is brief. . . . A lot of his effects lie between the lines. He . . . is one of the few travel writers who make you want to follow in his bootsteps."

Newby's recent books are *A Book of Travellers' Tales,* which he edited, excerpted, and annotated, and which forms a kind of sequel to *My Favorite Stories of Travel; Round Ireland in Low Gear,* an account of a sodden cycling holiday in midwinter; and *What the Traveller Saw,* a collection of essays illustrated by the author's photographs.

Newby was elected a fellow of the Royal Society of Literature in 1972 and of the Royal Geographical Society in 1975. He and his wife live near Wareham, in Dorset, on England's south-central coast.

PRINCIPAL WORKS: The Last Grain Race, 1956; A Short Walk in the Hindu Kush, 1958; Something Wholesale, 1962; Slowly Down the Ganges, 1966; Time Off in Southern Italy, 1966; Grain Race: Pictures of Life Before the Mast in a Windjammer, 1968; (with Diana Petry) The Wonders of Britain, 1968; (with Diana Petry) The Wonders of Ireland, 1969; Love and War in the Apennines, 1971; (with photographs by Raghubir Singh) Ganga, 1973; World Atlas of Exploration, 1975; Great Ascents, 1977; The Big Red Train Ride, 1978; A Traveller's Life, 1982; On the Shores of the Mediterranean, 1984; A Book of Travellers' Tales, 1985; Round Ireland in Low Gear, 1987; What the Traveller Saw, 1990.

ABOUT: Contemporary Authors 7–8, 1969; Who's Who, 1988–1989. *Periodicals*—Christian Science Monitor April 9, 1959; Library Journal April 15, 1959; September 1, 1967; December 1, 1977; September 1, 1982; Manchester Guardian November 14, 1958; New Statesman November 22, 1958; December 30, 1966; New York Times Book Review April 19, 1959; September 10, 1967; January 22, 1978; August 21, 1988; April 15, 1990; Newsweek August 14, 1967; August 23, 1982; Saturday Review June 13, 1959; Spectator January 23, 1959; Times Literary Supplement November 11, 1958; November 24, 1966; August 20, 1982; December 27, 1985; October 9, 1987.

NICHOLS, JOHN (TREADWELL) (July 23, 1940–   ), American novelist and essayist, writes: "I am half French, and I come from a fairly extensive family invested with all kinds of writers. My great-grandfather, Anatole Le Braz, was a noted poet and folklorist known as 'The Bard of Brittany.' A grandfather on the American side of the Atlantic, John T. Nichols (for whom I am named), was a famous naturalist who for many years was curator of fishes at the Museum of Natural History in New York, and many encyclopedic and scientific publications are full of his articles and reflections on the natural world. Myself, I began writing seriously when I was fourteen years old. My stories were all present-tense gangster epics full of raunchy slang, à la Damon Runyon. Later, after a trip to the Southwestern United States in 1957, I wrote my first novella-length work, about a young Chicano kid who leads his blind Indian grandfather up into the mountains to die.

"I attended Hamilton College in upstate New York between 1958 and 1962. While there I was no great shakes as a student, but I played football and hockey, ran track and cross-country, played my guitar with the folkies, acted in theatrical productions, wrote a humor column for the newspaper, and produced at least one novel a year on such topics as southern racism, blind blues singers in the New Orleans Storyville era, and innocent children descending into barbarism much like the youngsters of William Golding's *Lord of the Flies*.

"After college, I spent a year in Barcelona, Spain, living with my mother's mom, teaching English to Spaniards at the Instituto Americano, and working on a novel which came to be called *The Sterile Cuckoo*. I returned to New York in the spring of 1963, sold *The Sterile Cuckoo* in March of '64, and immediately took a bus to Guatemala to visit a friend. Though I spent but a short time in Guatemala, it was a turning point in my awareness of the world. And after I returned to New York and sold a second book, *The Wizard of Loneliness*, I became increasingly involved in the anti–Vietnam war movement. I went through a period of culture shock, overturned entirely many of my capitalist values, and begain trying to write a political fiction which had as its foundation an increasingly Marxist understanding of the world. But from 1965 to 1972 I had little success in merging this new politics with my art: I worked on six or seven novels that never saw the light of day.

"In 1969 I moved to Taos, New Mexico and for several years, on a purely volunteer basis, I wrote long muckraking articles about land and water struggles in Northern New Mexico for a journal called *The New Mexico Review*. I earned no money, but gained invaluable experience with the land, people, culture, and political shenanigans of the North. This eventually stood me in good stead, when, at the end of 1972, I blammed out *The Milagro Beanfield War* in a last-ditch effort to save what was by then an almost non-existent literary career. *Milagro* was published, it saved my 'career,' and although its messages are basically couched in humor, it represents an at least partially successful attempt to discuss such things as class struggle and cultural genocide in a way that is palatable to the North American reader.

"I believe strongly in a 'political' art. Remembering that Bertolt Brecht once said: 'Young man, reach for a book—it is a weapon.' For the past twenty years, in my work, in the organizing activities of my life, I have strongly advocated the necessity for a social conscience in the arts and humanities. I have little sympathy for an economic system based on planned obsolescence and conspicuous consumption, and find myself appalled at the values and policies of my nation in such negative adventures as its criminal attempts to overthrow the Sandinista revolution in Nicaragua.

"In 1980, purely by accident, I began to work on some film projects. I rewrote a Costa-Gavras film called *Missing*, and did two other pictures with him, concerning science and human values in the twentieth century, and a futuristic look at the outcome of nuclear war. I did a film with Karel Reisz that involved Haitian refugees and U.S. immigration policies, and did scripts of

Milagro for Robert Redford, and of my novel *The Magic Journey* for Louis Malle. At this writing [1986] I am working on a six-hour TV mini-series based on the life of Pancho Villa and the Mexican Revolution. I was married in 1985 to Juanita Wolf, and between us we have six assorted blood- and step-children, along with eight cats, and one very large chow named Mangus.

"Nelson Algren once wrote: 'I submit that literature is made upon any occasion that a challenge is put to the legal apparatus by a conscience in touch with humanity.' I buy that, and trust I always will."

When John Nichols bought an adobe house and settled near Taos, New Mexico in 1969 he was already an established writer with two novels published, one of them the very popular *The Sterile Cuckoo*. This book, with its portrait of a young college couple drifting into a turbulent love affair, caught the imagination of many young readers of the 1960s and the admiring attention of many book reviewers for the character of Pookie Adams, the fascinating oddball heroine. In Pookie readers found the lost generation of the 1960s: "Spunky as her efforts are to exorcise fear with force," Albert Goldman wrote in the *Nation*, "their ultimate effect is to make her 'a sterile cuckoo,' cut off from life by the comic persona she originally adopted to protect her deeply damaged personality." *The Sterile Cuckoo* was made into a motion picture with Liza Minelli as Pookie—a role for which she won an Oscar nomination.

The move to New Mexico changed the course of Nichols' life and career. His next book, after almost eight years of silence, was *The Milagro Beanfield War*, a story of the struggles of poor Chicanos to preserve their land and their rights against powerful Anglo business interests. The book and the novels which followed—*The Magic Journey* and *The Nirvana Blues*—comprise a New Mexico trilogy. Complementing them are several non-fiction books—*If Mountains Die, The Last Beautiful Days of Autumn, On the Mesa,* and *A Fragile Beauty.* "Different as the emphasis of each of these books may be," Nichols writes in his autobiographical introduction to *A Fragile Beauty,* "they all deal with questions of land, cultural ethics, problems of ecology, economics, history, and human survival."

Nichols writes that his love for the Southwest began in 1957 when he made a summer visit to Arizona and New Mexico. Though he spent the next years at schools in the East and then in Europe and New York City, he was never far from Spanish and Latin-American culture. He returned to New Mexico in 1969 not for its beauty or climate, but because of his political ideology: "New Mexico seemed to resemble a colonial country where political struggle could be as clearly focussed as it was in four-fifths of the rest of the world." Soon, however, he was as much caught up with the beauty of the land as with its social and economic problems: "The land was essential to the rhythm of life in Taos, and all of it was threatened by one form of development or another. Sadly, I quickly came to realize, the caretakers of the valley were being driven out."

The Milagro Beanfield War dramatizes the stuggle of a Chicano handyman to irrigate his half-acre beanfield. He does this by illegally diverting water from a creek. His example ultimately stirs up the whole community to organize against a giant development corporation that is driving them off the land and destroying their ancestral way of life. The story is as much fable and political allegory as it is realistic fiction, evoking from some of its critics comparisons not only to John Steinbeck for its sympathetic portrayal of impoverished farm workers but also to Gabriel García Márquez's *One Hundred Years of Solitude* for its use of the supernatural. (In fact Nichols did not read García Márquez until after he had written his book.) Milagro, Nichols writes at the beginning of the novel, "was a town whose citizens had a penchant not only for going crazy, but also for precipitating miracles." The citizens are driven into a stuggle which, considering the power of their opposition, is indeed "crazy." As their rebellion escalates, journalists and politicians become involved. But more interesting are the colorful Chicanos, with their legends and earthy humor, and the activist lawyer and VISTA worker from the East who enlist to support their efforts. Nichols wrote his first draft of this long novel in just five weeks, and even in its final version it retains a loose episodic structure. The unifying factor is the land itself, the consistent motif in this panorama of characters and incidents. Motley Deakin, in *Western American Literature*, finds the presentation "constantly shifting and, like the American humor of the frontier west, [it] may begin with a common reality, but gradually distorts that reality until the reader is left contemplating an absurdity that is both outrageous and amusing." Recognizing cinematic possibilities, several film companies took options on *The Milagro Beanfield War*, but it was not until 1986 that Robert Redford began shooting the movie. Nichols collaborated on the script with David Ward and wrote an account of its stormy filming in *A Fragile Beauty*. Released in early 1988, the film version was moderately successful, praised for its populist charm but faulted for its lack of dramatic tension. In the *Village Voice*, David Edelstein argued that the filmmakers had lightened the author's underlying pessimism and softened the "blood-crazy" texture of poor Chicano lives: the movie, he wrote, "cleaves to the supernatural/populist side of the book, dispensing with the flesh-and-blood cruelties that give Nichol's whimsy its mulelike kicks." (A film version of Nichols' second novel, *The Wizard of Loneliness*, about a young boy's coming of age in Vermont during World War II, was released in 1988.)

Nichols returned to the scene of Milagro in *The Magic Journey*, set in Chamisaville, "a soporific little town of relatively forgotten people." The theme again is the exploitation of the land and of the Chicanos who live on it—this time by a gaudy shrine dedicated to the "Dynamite Virgin." The novel is more serious and ambitious in scope than its predecessor, covering the years from the Depression of the 1930s through the rebellious years of the 1960s. Peopled with a large cast of colorful characters and narrated with exuberant energy, *The Magic Journey* nevertheless struck some of its reviewers as too obviously a "proletarian novel." Jeffrey Burke, in *Harper's*, found it weighed down by its "sober message." In contrast to *The Milagro Beanfield War*, "this work asks to be taken seriously . . . yet Nichols's creative energy runs so often to comic invention, to caricature instead of character, to spates of bathos and discursive high jinks, that he entertains far more than he instructs . . . the imbalance makes for ambivalence."

The Nirvana Blues, the final volume of the trilogy, continues the story of the selling-out of Chamisaville in the post-Watergate, post-Vietnam era, a period of cynicism and disillusionment. "America's answer to all of this," Nichols writes in the opening pages of the novel, "was more cars, more defense spending, more leach field, open-pit, and strip mining, more highways, more pork-barrel irrigation projects, less welfare, less ERA, more rape, more crime, more violence, more cops, more smog, more nuclear growth, more GNP, more GSA, more GOP." The tourists ("incoherent pilgrims") who flock now to Chamisaville are lost souls. "Somehow, word has gotten out that Chamisaville was the in place to go for religious, spiritual, sexual and organic-gardening kicks." As Lynn Z. Bloom pointed out in *Western American Literature*, *Nirvana Blues* depicts the final sell-out of the Chicanos and their culture to Anglo business. The hero (more accurately an antihero) dreams of saving the land but becomes hopelessly involved in the drug trade, and an old Chicano who clings stubbornly to his land is killed, a martyr to the cause. Bleak as the future

seems to be, Nichols does offer a note of hope in a whimsical epilogue. The central character, who has been gunned down after an attempted bank robbery, is offered a new soul and a new life. Yearning for "the Garden of Eden, Socialist style," his spirit is reborn among "the green hills and succulent valleys of a Communist country."

Nichols has written one other novel with a Chamisaville setting, but its subject is not the Chicano farmers. *A Ghost in the Music* is narrated by a young graduate student, the illegitimate son of a failed movie producer and former stuntman. The son flies from New York to New Mexico to help his father through a personal and professional crisis: "A high-risk player, he had spent his life teetering on the edge—of madness, bankruptcy, immense wealth, stardom." At first more exasperated than sympathetic, the graduate student comes gradually to understand and to love his father and to learn from him how to cherish life.

New Mexico also figures as the subject of several of Nichols' works of non-fiction. *If Mountains Die: A New Mexico Memoir* is a long reflective essay on his life in the Southwest, richly illustrated with photographs by William Davis. *On the Mesa* and *The Last Beautiful Days of Autumn,* both illustrated with Nichols' own photographs, are also personal records of the landscape, his friends, the books he loves, fishing, country walks. Mainly it is the land that Nichols celebrates because, as he writes near the end of *The Last Beautiful Days of Autumn*: "What I have to say about Taos pertains to everywhere. Taos is only a metaphor for that entire continent F. Scott Fitzgerald once imagined as the last piece of terrain wild and beautiful enough to be commensurate with our capacity for wonder."

PRINCIPAL WORKS: *Novels*—The Sterile Cuckoo, 1965; The Wizard of Loneliness, 1966; The Milagro Beanfield War, 1974; The Magic Journey, 1978; A Ghost in the Music, 1979; The Nirvana Blues, 1981; American Blood, 1987. *Non-fiction*—(with W. Davis) If Mountains Die, 1979; The Last Beautiful Days of Autumn, 1982; On the Mesa, 1986; A Fragile Beauty, 1987.

ABOUT: Contemporary Authors Autobiography Series 2, 1985; Contemporary Authors New Revision Series 6, 1982; Contemporary Literary Criticism 38, 1986; Dictionary of Literary Biography, 1982; Nichols, J. If Mountains Die, 1979; The Last Beautiful Days of Autumn, 1982; On the Mesa, 1986; A Fragile Beauty, 1987; Wild, P. John Nichols (Boise Western Writers Series), 1986. *Periodicals*—Harper's August 1978; Horizon April 1982; Journal of Popular Culture Summer 1973; Journal of the West April 1985; Nation February

8, 1985; New York Times March 18, 1988; New York Times Magazine December 27, 1981; Village Voice March 29, 1988; Western American Literature Fall 1985, Winter 1983.

give me this
our relatives the air
      floods
our rich friend
      silt

—from *Condensery*

*NIEDECKER, LORINE (FAITH) (May 12, 1903–December 31, 1970), American poet, was born in Fort Atkinson, Wisconsin, the daughter of Henry E. and Theresa (Kunz) Niedecker. She attended primary and secondary schools in Fort Atkinson, and from 1922 to 1924 was enrolled at nearby Beloit College. Her mother's deteriorating hearing caused Niedecker to return home. She married Frank Hartwig in 1928, but they separated two years later and were divorced in 1942. In Fort Atkinson Niedecker worked as a librarian from 1928 to 1930. During the Depression years she worked in Madison on the Federal Writers' Project which produced the *Wisconsin Guide*. From 1942 to 1944 she was a script writer for the local radio station, WHA. She then returned to Fort Atkinson, where from 1944 to 1950 she was a stenographer and proofreader on the staff of a regional journal, *Hoard's Dairyman*. Between 1957 and 1962 she had a job as a cleaning woman at the Fort Atkinson Memorial Hospital.

Niedecker's life and work are thus closely associated with southern Wisconsin. It was on Blackhawk Island, a sparsely populated island lying along the Rock River, between Fort Atkinson and Lake Koshkonong, that she spent most of her life. Her mother died in 1951, her father in 1954, and she inherited two houses on Blackhawk Island. The tribulations of renting, plumbing, foreclosure enter her poems, often with humor. In 1963 she was married a second time, to Albert Millen, a housepainter. They lived for a while in Milwaukee, but upon his retirement in 1969 they built their own house on Blackhawk Island. Except for trips to South Dakota and around Lake Superior, reflected in her poems, they remained on the island.

Marshland lies north of Blackhawk Island, and the Rock River rises in the spring: it is wild terrain. Niedecker has spoken of "red-winged blackbirds, willows, maples, boats, fishing (the smell of tarred nets), twittering and squawking noises from the marsh." Her closeness to her environment, her kinship with nature, is exemplified in her poetry:

Along the river
      wild sunflowers
over my head
      the dead
who gave me life

°nē´ dek ûr

At the beginning of her career, in the 1930s, she initiated a correspondence with the poet Louis Zukofsky, who became her lifelong friend and mentor. Niedecker once said that she would not have become a writer without the objectivist issue of *Poetry* magazine in February 1931, which Zukofsky edited. William Carlos Williams was her second major literary influence. Her poems were published during the 1930s in literary magazines and in *New Directions in Prose and Poetry*. In 1946 her first book, *New Goose*, was published by James A. Decker. In the 1950s she began a correspondence with Cid Corman, poet and editor of *Origin* and later her literary executor. Many of her poems were published in *Origin*; one issue featured her work.

Niedecker's second book did not appear until 1961 when *My Friend Tree* was published by a small press in Edinburgh. To Charles Tomlinson she wrote in 1966: "England is dear to my heart—notice of LN so much stronger than in this country." Basil Bunting called her "easily the finest female American poet." Zukofsky said, "I read only two modern women poets, [Marianne] Moore and Niedecker. One feels closer to Niedecker." Others have compared her to Emily Dickinson, noting her reticence, her self-imposed isolation from the outside world, the precision and concision of her verse. While her following among distinguished poets was strong, wide acknowledgment of her abilities came only after her death.

My Life By Water: Collected Poems 1936–1968 was published in London in 1970 and was the last book Niedecker proofread. Before it had come *North Central* in 1968 and *T&G* (the title from Lawrence Durrell's "Tenderness and Gristle") in 1969. Six years after her death Corman edited a selection of her poems, including some, he wrote, "that seem largely to have been 'abandoned' by the poet as perhaps not up to her best work." This was *Blue Chicory*, which appeared in 1976. In 1985 two influential posthumous volumes were published. These were *From This Condensery: The Complete Writings of Lorine Niedecker*, which included variants on poems as well as some of her radio plays and prose, edited by Robert J. Bertholf, curator of the Poetry Collection at the University of Buffalo, and *The Granite Pail: Selected Poems of Lorine Niedecker*, edited by Corman. Her letters to Corman from 1960 to

1970 were edited by Lisa Pater Faranda and published as *Between Your House and Mine* in 1987.

The uniqueness of Lorine Niedecker's verse is its tightness and precision, its musical structure (her poems, Michael Heller wrote in the *New York Times Book Review*, "seem to demand of the reader a concertgoer's attention as their often monosyllabic words play off assonance and dissonance, fuguelike rather than orchestral"), and a quality she called "condensery." In 1965 she wrote Cid Corman that "meaning has something to do with song—one hesitates a bit longer with some words in some lines for the thought or the vision—but I'd say mostly, of course, cadence, measure make song. And a kind of shine (or sombre tone) . . . that is of the same intensity throughout the poem. And the thing moves. But as in all poems, everywhere, depth of emotion condensed . . . ." As an objectivist poet, Niedecker moved beyond the imagism of Ezra Pound to emphasize the integrity of the poem as object. Objectivism, William Carlos Williams wrote, "concerned itself with an image more particularized yet broadened in its significance. The mind rather than the unsupported eye entered the picture." Characteristic of the poetry of this movement is her "Easter Greeting":

I suppose there is nothing
so good as human
immediacy

I do not speak loosely
of handshake
    which is

    ! of the mind
or lilies—stand closer—
smell

In his preface to *The Granite Pail* Corman described Niedecker as "a gracious, self-effacing woman, small and seemingly self-contained, with thick glasses she had worn since childhood. She was candid both with others and with herself, although never tactless, for she was always aware of others and she felt an almost palpable happiness in the privilege of their presences." Far from a somber personality, Niedecker was dubbed by Jenny Penberthy in the *Times Literary Supplement* "a poet whose humour (in both senses) is among the strongest reasons to read her." It was a quiet and subtle wit—homely yet allusive, as witness "Niedecker Weather":

Well—Milwaukee had
eleven and one
half inches of snow

but no rain. The niles

at street corners are
turning black. Ruskin

would have perished here,
but then, poor man, he
perished anyhow.

In the same article Penberthy noted Niedecker's "bookishness," which is "concealed behind the clear plain speech of her lines." Widely read, she especially enjoyed the letters of literary and historical figures—Jefferson and Adams (there is a long poem on Jefferson in *Blue Chicory*), Audubon, and among the Victorians Hopkins, Ruskin, William Morris, and Darwin. Her long poem on Darwin traces his voyage on the Beagle with passages from his letters—his ill health, his homesickness, the excitement of his discoveries, his conflicts with the *Beagle's* deeply religious Captain Fitzroy:

A thousand turtle monsters
drive together to the water
Blood-bright crabs

hunt ticks on lizards' backs
Flightless cormorants—
cold sea creatures—penguins

Seals here in tropical waters
Hell for Fitzroy
but for Darwin

paradise puzzle
with the jigsaw gists
beginning to fit.

Lorine Niedecker was the subject of a play by Kristin Thatcher, *Niedecker*, produced Off-Broadway in March 1989. Described by Stephen Holden in the *New York Times* as an "earnest low-key drama," its subject was the poet's second marriage, a happy one though it was shadowed by her working-class husband's lack of interest in her writing, which he called her "scribbling." Holden found the play "overly tidy domestic drama," but admired it as "a fully realized portrait of a marriage that flourishes because certain uncrossable boundaries on each side are tacitly respected."

PRINCIPAL WORKS: New Goose, 1946; My Friend Tree, 1961; North Central, 1968; T&G: Collected Poems 1936–1966, 1969; My Life By Water: Collected Poems 1936–1968, 1970; Blue Chicory, 1976; From This Condensery: The Complete Writing of Lorine Niedecker, 1985; The Granite Pail: Selected Poems of Loriner Niedecker, 1985; Between Your House and Mine: Letters of Lorine Niedecker to Cid Corman, 1960 to 1970, 1987.

ABOUT: Bertholf, R. J. *Introduction to* From This Condensery, 1985; Contemporary Authors New Revision Series 2, 1978; Contemporary Literary Criticism 10, 1979; Corman, C. *Editorial Note to* Blue Chicory, 1976, *Preface to* The Granite Pail, 1985; Dent, P. (ed.) The Full Note: Lorine Niedecker, 1983; Dictionary of Literary Biography 48, 1986; Dorn, E. *Introduction to* My Friend Tree, 1961; Heller, M. Conviction's Net of Branches, 1985; Williams, J. (ed.) Epitaph for Lorine, 1973. *Periodicals*—Choice May 1986, June 1986; Library Journal November 1, 1985; London Magazine April–May 1971; Nation April 13, 1970; March 15, 1986; New York Times March 19, 1989; New York Times Book Review February 13, 1977; January 29, 1986; Parnassus: Poetry in Review Spring–Summer 1977; Poetry May 1972; Times Literary Supplement February 27, 1968; September 6, 1985; September 25, 1987.

LEWIS NKOSI

*NKOSI, LEWIS (1936–   ), African novelist, journalist, essayist, and critic of African literature, was born in the Province of Natal, South Africa, and began his career as a journalist there when he started reporting for the *Ilanga lase Natal* (Natal Sun) in 1955. In 1956 he moved to Johannesburg to take up a position as a writer for *Drum* magazine. *Drum* had begun publication in 1951; by the end of the 1950s it had succeeded not only in changing the shape and tone of journalism in South Africa, but also in establishing itself as the voice of an entire generation of black urban dwellers in the nation. Besides Nkosi, regular contributors to *Drum* included such celebrated figures as Arthur Maimane, Todd Matshikiza, Bloke Modisane, Casey Motsisi, Ezekiel Mphahlele, Nat Nakasa, and Can Themba. In their work, as Nkosi subsequently observed, these writers "were alive, go-getting, full of nervous energy, very wry, ironic, and they brought to South African journalism a new vitality which none of the white writers had seemed capable of achieving."

The twelve years between 1948, when the Afrikaner National Party first came to power, and 1960, the date of the Sharpeville massacre— years which coincided with *Drum*'s rise—were epoch-making ones in South Africa. They were years of violence, retrenchment, and political defeat. The repression of Sharpeville brought the decade of the 1950s to an appropriate, if shocking, climax, inasmuch as it signaled the consolidation of apartheid and served as the pretext for the outlawing of all effective opposition to the state. *Drum* was one of the very few publications of the 1950s to report the events of the decade without flinching. Its coverage extended from strikes and riots and protest marches, through torture, urban squalor, and rural misery, to the treatment of farm and convict laborers, "forced removals," the enforcement of "pass laws," even the savage bulldozing of the black residential district of Sophiatown—where Nkosi lived—and its reconstruction as a whites-only zone under the cynical name of Triomf (Triumph).

Throughout the 1950s, *Drum* bore witness to the South African state's ferocious efforts to crush active resistance to apartheid. Yet the magazine's tone was by no means imbued with defeatism. On the contrary, the *Drum* style was upbeat, slick, unsentimental, jaunty, and streetwise. For the journalists of *Drum*, as for the leaders of the African National Congress and for black activists and intellectuals in general, the 1950s were not experienced as a time of defeat but as a time of opening and radical possibility. Writing subsequently about these years in *Home and Exile*, his first collection of essays on literature and social issues, Nkosi dubbed them "The Fabulous Decade": "It was a time of infinite hope and possibility. . . . It was a time when people of all races . . . joined together in a massive Defiance Campaign conducted along Gandhian lines, which resulted in hundreds of unresisted arrests but managed, in its own way, to frighten the Government out of its wits. . . . It was a time of thrust, never of withdrawal."

In 1960, Nkosi was awarded a Nieman Fellowship to study journalism at Harvard University. However, the South African authorities were prepared to issue him only a one-way exit permit. Nkosi has been barred from reentering South Africa ever since. Over the past thirty years, he has lived briefly in the United States, for an extended period in London, and is currently professor of literature at the University of Zambia. He served as literary editor for the London-based magazine *The New African* in the 1960s and has published journalistic articles in such newspapers and magazines as the *New Yorker*, the *New Statesman*, the *Guardian*, and *Black Orpheus*.

The bulk of Nkosi's non-fiction writing since 1970 has been critical and academic rather than journalistic and strictly topical. Yet his intellectual style, and his concerns and strategies as a writer, continue to reflect the protocols of his apprenticeship. The principles that were instilled in the young writer in the mid-1950s at *Drum* still inform Nkosi's critical practice today: courage and honesty, integrity and directness, cosmopolitanism and wit. Nkosi's critical writing is sharp-eyed and sinewy, scaled down, understated, and ironic. His delivery is measured and effective: muscular, uncluttered without ever becoming simplistic, and straightforward, with a tendency to harden on occasion into defiance. It is a delivery that eschews lavish gesture or the rhetoric of emotion without thereby eschewing passion and commitment.

Nkosi's cultural criticism has frequently provoked fierce argument. No position he has taken has proved to be as controversial as his stand on the matter of the social responsibility of the writer. At an African writers' conference in Sweden in 1967, the Nigerian writer Wole Soyinka spoke of the writer's vocation "[as] the record of the mores and experience of his society *and* as the voice of vision in his own time." Responding to this address, Nkosi rebuked Soyinka for his overestimation of the significance of writers in society. He argued that it was quixotic to attempt to retrieve the Romantic conception of poets as "unacknowledged legislators of the world." To Nkosi, it seemed merely tautological to encourage writers to be the bearers of a vision: "Every writer has a vision. Otherwise I do not see what he is doing writing." Against Soyinka, Nkosi urged writers to remain scrupulously conscious of their own limitations as social activists.

The thrust of Nkosi's critique of the rhetoric of commitment consisted in a defense of writing as a form of productive activity with its own relatively autonomous criteria of value and legitimacy. It was not that writers should not take up public positions or be concerned to represent history or the social world in their work. Rather, it was Nkosi's contention that the significance of a work could not be measured by either its political intentions or its author's status as a social activist. "There is a lot of committed literature, which is simply bad literature" he observed in his response to Soyinka—the problem here being that since it would be unacceptable to assess a writer's worth "by simply counting the number of guns he has carried to the revolutionary front," there is an urgent critical need at least "to separate the problem of gun running from the problem of wielding a pen."

Nkosi had earlier made much the same point in *Home and Exile*, in which he had taken issue with Jean-Paul Sartre's suggestion that, in certain specific socio-historical circumstances, the writer who is "on the side of the majority, of the two billion starving" might have to renounce literature for the time being "in order to educate the people." Nkosi's rebuttal of Sartre's position was economical and telling: "Unless he is variously talented the best way a writer can contribute anything of worth toward the development of his society is simply by writing—and writing as well as he knows how." The general point here was that it was necessary to distinguish the writer as a literary craftsman from the writer as a public citizen. The writer's effect on society would always be "accumulative rather than immediate."

Nkosi's critical practice fairly bristles with evaluations and assessments, advanced in a characteristically out-spoken vein. James Booth has noted that Nkosi's "lack of evasion is sometimes quite shocking"; and certainly he holds little back in his commentaries. He ringingly consigns the whole corpus of post-1945 British and American drama to the trash can of history, charging it with "having descended latterly into the appallingly low marshes of vigourless ineptitude and hysterically boring clichés." Nor is he averse to naming names, when the need seems to arise: he dismisses the short stories of the respected Ghanaian author, Ama Ata Aidoo, as "inadequate trivialities." He describes Modikwe Dikobe's historically important South African novel, *The Marabi Dance*, as a work "whose combination of bad taste, clumsy construction and wooden characterisation must seem, at least, to exceed anything we have yet encountered in African writing." And he speaks of Ezekiel Mphahlele, an erstwhile colleague of his on *Drum* and, like Nkosi himself, long a distinguished exile from South Africa,. as "a sometimes exasperatingly superficial thinker."

Nkosi has written extensively about African literature at the continental level. Yet he has remained especially interested in the field of black South African fiction, which he has tended to criticize for its failure to represent the actuality of life as it is lived by blacks in the society. In *Home and Exile* he argued: "With the best will in the world it is impossible to detect in the fiction of black South Africans any significant and complex talent which responds, with both the vigour of the imagination and sufficient technical resources, to the problems posed by conditions in South Africa." This "failure" on the part of black writers, he explained in *Tasks and Masks: Themes and Styles of African Literature*, was not the consequence of any political immaturity, but of a formal inability to phrase political vision imaginatively, to render it compelling not simply through its topicality, but in its own terms, as literature. In *Tasks and Masks*, Nkosi singled out three novelists who he felt had enjoyed limited success in this respect: Alex La Guma, Enver Carim, and Bessie Head. The achievement of these writers, he argued, lay in their plausible depiction of the "materiality of everyday existence."

It was precisely this depiction of the experience of life under apartheid that Nkosi himself set out to render in his own novel *Mating Birds*. In *The Rhythm of Violence*, a play written twenty years earlier, Nkosi had offered a portrait of Johannesburg familiar to any reader of *Drum* magazine. *Mating Birds* is not, however, a realist novel: it is concerned less with the material conditions of existence of its central protagonist, Sibiya—who is on death row, awaiting execution for the crime of having raped a white woman—than with his consciousness. This is the sort of subject that has always interested Nkosi. In *Home and Exile*, he spoke of the "spiritual chaos and confusion" to which apartheid necessarily condemned many black South Africans. In *Tasks and Masks*, he explored racial and sexual relations of power, above all when these involved a black man and a white woman in the context of a racist society like South Africa. Taking Carim's *A Dream Deferred* as his object, Nkosi drew attention in *Tasks and Masks* to the complexities of one particular exchange between a white woman, Marie de Villiers, and a black man, Letaka, the two central characters of Carim's novel. Carim had written: "She looked at him as white women of her country never do. She saw him." Nkosi glossed these lines as follows: "This act of 'seeing' is for the white woman in that situation the most revolutionary act; it is what the society, under normal circumstances, will not permit her; and this act of 'seeing' is, of course, an act of rebellion that is capable of freeing her if she will but permit herself to be freed from the shackles which society has so carefully woven around her. . . . [Society requires her] to 'forget the knowledge . . . of what she has seen,' which curtails any possibility for her own

personal liberation. She must deny the flash of recognition of Letaka as a human being capable of arousing a human response from her." The narrative outlined here, which unfolds from humanizing gaze and sexual attraction to revulsion and colonial or racist denial, becomes the narrative of Veronica, Sibiya's white victim in *Mating Birds*.

Despite its theoretical interest, Nkosi's novel is deeply flawed by an insistent inner failure of vision, in the form of a virulent and structuring sexism. *Mating Birds* fails as a novel because the central conceit upon which it is predicated cannot sustain the burden that Nkosi places upon it. In writing about *A Dream Deferred*, Nkosi had praised Carim for "perceiv[ing] the ambiguous position of white women as lying between oppressor and oppressed." In *Mating Birds* Nkosi tries to emulate Carim in this perception. He wants Veronica to emerge simultaneously as a conscious agent of Sibiya's destruction and a pawn in the service of the overarching racist order. She is to be puppeteer and puppet at the same time: on the one hand, orchestrating Sibiya's downfall; on the other, dancing to the tune of the dominant society's imperatives. Yet it is at this level of primary symbol that incoherence manifests itself. For Veronica is not credible as the active bearer of domination: Nkosi so naturalizes culturally constructed gender relations, he so relentlessly sexualizes Veronica, that the reader is invited only to see her archetypally as Woman, the natural and fitting object of Man's lust. And such a perception obliterates even the possibility of grasping Veronica's situation, simultaneously as oppressor and oppressed. The result is a novel that collapses in on itself. Henry Louis Gates, Jr., who reviewed the book for the *New York Times Book Review*, praised its "lyrical intensity" and "compelling narrative power," but objected: "At the novel's end, the master remains the master, and the slave remains a slave and is doomed to die; never does Sibiya, the slave to his obsession, become the master even of his own will. The ambiguities created by his own troubled story prevent the liberation that he and the reader eagerly seek from the novel's beginning." And Rob Nixon, in the *Village Voice*, judged *Mating Birds* "a book of bold psychological insight, but one marred by vexing sexual politics."

The masculinism that undermines *Mating Birds* as a novel is not absent from Nkosi's critical writing. But in his criticism, his qualities of conciseness, intellectual independence, and clearsightedness are never compromised. Nkosi's published output is already sufficient to insure his reputation as one of the most distinguished critics of African literature.

PRINCIPAL WORKS: Home and Exile, 1965; The Rhythm of Violence, 1965; The Transplanted Heart, 1975; Tasks and Masks: Themes and Styles of African Literature, 1981. *Novel*—Mating Birds, 1986.

ABOUT: African Book Publishing Record, 1977; Contemporary Authors 65–68, 1977; Contemporary Literary Criticism 45, 1987; A New Reader's Guide to African Literature, 1983. *Periodicals*—New Statesman August 29, 1986; New York Times Book Review May 18, 1986; Research in African Literatures 17, 1986; Southern Review January 1987; Times Literary Supplement August 8, 1986; Village Voice July 29, 1986; Washington Post Book World June 8, 1986; World Literature Today Spring 1983.

MARSHA NORMAN

NORMAN, MARSHA (WILLIAMS) (September 21, 1947–   ), American dramatist and novelist, was born in Louisville, Kentucky, the eldest of the four children of Bertha and Billie Williams, an insurance salesman. Both parents were Methodist fundamentalists, and her childhood was lonely, spent mainly in reading, writing stories, and playing with an imaginary companion. In high school she worked on the school newspaper and yearbook, and in her junior year she wrote a prize-winning essay on the biblical Job, "Why Do Good Men Suffer?", a title that curiously foreshadows the themes of her later work. On a scholarship Marsha Norman attended Agnes Scott College, a liberal arts school for women, in Decatur, Georgia. Because there was no creative writing program, she majored in philosophy, receiving her B.A. in 1969. She returned to Louisville and married Michael Norman, her former English teacher. They were divorced in 1974. In 1971 she took a master's degree in teaching at the University of Louisville.

During the Louisville years Norman taught disturbed adolescents at Kentucky Central State Hospital, an experience that she drew on for her first play, *Getting Out*. At the time, however, she did not contemplate writing as a career. She began teaching filmmaking in 1973 at the Brown School for gifted children and published occasional pieces, mostly written for children, in local newspapers. One of these pieces was the libretto for a musical about Thomas A. Edison and other American inventors.

By 1976 Norman was writing full time, contributing articles and book reviews to the *Louisville Times*, and she had met Jon Jory, the director of an outstanding regional theater group, the Actors Theatre of Louisville, who suggested that she write a play about "a painful subject," a striking departure from the upbeat, whimsical material she had been writing for children. Looking back at her experiences with disturbed teenagers at the Kentucky Central State Hospital, she conceived a character, a young woman who is released on parole from prison and must adjust to a new life. This was *Getting Out*, which Jory staged in the 1977 Louisville Festival of New Plays. Voted the best new play in a regional theater by the American Theatre Critics Association, it was included in *The Best Plays of 1977–1978*, the first non–New York production to be recognized in this annual volume.

Getting Out revolves around Arlene and Arlie, onstage at the same time, who represent the same person before, during, and after serving a prison sentence. Two actresses portray the conflicted heroine—Arlene in the present, free now but painfully bewildered and insecure as she struggles to make a life for herself, and Arlie, her rebellious younger self of the past. The theme of *Getting Out* is highly imaginative, but the dialogue, with its natural Kentucky flavor and its candor, give the play a quality of almost painful realism. "These disturbed or at least disheveled people," John Simon wrote of the characters in *New York Magazine*, " . . . have intelligence, wit, and pride. They are not sentimentalized, however; not easily reformed, and perhaps never redeemed. But they are brutally, sadly, and sometimes thrillingly real." Norman cast light on the genesis of the play, as well as on her own philosophy, in comments appearing in *Interviews with Contemporary Women Playwrights*. "My work with disturbed kids was perhaps the most valuable work I ever did," she said. "What you cannot escape seeing is that we are all disturbed kids. Emotionally disturbed children make extraordinary efforts to survive and be sane. . . . Watching those children cope with their terrors taught me to recognize it in myself and everybody else." The play ran at the Mark Taper Forum in Los Angeles (1978), at the Phoenix Theatre and the Theatre De Lys in New York (1978 and 1979, respectively), and garnered the John Gassner New Playwrights Medallion from the Outer Critics Circle, as well as the George Oppenheimer *Newsday* Playwriting Award.

There followed two years as playwright-in-residence, first at the Actors Theatre of Louisville (1978–1979) under a National Endowment for the Arts grant, and secondly at the Mark Taper Forum in Los Angeles (1979–1980) under a Rockefeller Foundation grant. During this time several of her plays were produced by these regional groups: *Third and Oak*, comprising two one-act plays, "The Laundromat," which later appeared on television, and "The Pool Hall"; *Circus Valentine* ; and *The Holdup*, which received a workshop production. In 1983 *The Holdup* went on to a staging by the American Conservatory Theatre in San Francisco.

In 1978 Marsha Norman married Dann C. Byck, Jr., a Louisville businessman who had been a founder and the first president of the Actors Theatre. In 1981 they moved to New York where Byck became a theatrical producer. He was one of the several producers who brought her next play, *'Night, Mother*, to the Broadway stage.

'Night, Mother, written in the summer of 1981, is a two-character play, and Norman wrote it with two actresses from Louisville in mind— Kathie Bates as the plain-looking and plain-speaking daughter Jessie and Anne Pitoniak as her mother. They created the roles on stage and played them during the play's long Broadway run. However, like all of Norman's plays, *'Night, Mother* originated in regional theater—first staged by the American Repertory Company in Cambridge, Massachusetts late in 1982, then moving to Broadway in the spring of 1983. Running only ninety minutes (with no intermission), it is a taut and gripping study of a suicide. Jessie, confronting what she regards as a failed and empty life, quietly tells her mother that she is going to kill herself, and while her mother sits by first disbelieving then desperately but ineffectually trying to stop her, she goes about her prepa-

rations for her death. The play received general acclaim, though there were a few fierce dissenters, and it won the Pulitzer Prize for drama in 1983. "A bitter but loving agon between mother and daughter . . . " wrote Thomas E. Luddy, "the play cuts directly to the heart and moves swiftly through shifting emotional and argumentative strategies to its preordained end: an offstage gunshot."

Critical opinion on *'Night, Mother* ranged from those who found it powerful and profound to those who, like Stanley Kauffmann in the *Saturday Review*, thought it "fundamentally a stunt." Richard Gilman, writing in the *Nation*, had reservations about its overall effect but praised the writing: "Norman writes cleanly, with wry humor and no bathos." Frank Rich, in the *New York Times*, found it "a shattering evening, but it looks like simplicity itself. . . . Miss Norman's play is simple only in the way that an Edward Hopper painting is simple." Jenny S. Spencer, in an article in *Modern Drama*, offered an extensive analysis of the play's appeal to women rather than to men. She suggested that women found the play intensely disturbing, realistic, and utterly riveting for the most part; but many men, unable to identify with the two characters, found it limited in focus. *'Night, Mother* was adapted for the screen by Marsha Norman and filmed in 1986, starring Sissy Spacek and Anne Bancroft, but much of its impact was lost in the screen version.

Since the highly successful stage production of *'Night, Mother*, Norman has written *Traveler in the Dark*, produced by the American Theatre Repertory Theatre in Cambridge in 1984 and at the Mark Taper Forum. It had a brief off-Broadway run in January 1990. The play is a study of a surgeon who, unable to save the life of a friend, suffers a crisis of faith. Norman has also written several screenplays and scripts for television.

Like *'Night, Mother*, Norman's first novel, *The Fortune Teller*, centers on a mother-daughter relationship, but the comparison ends there. She has a wider canvas in her novel— more characters, a complex plot involving the activities of the mother (a professional clairvoyant who encounters violence from an anti-abortion group) and the daughter's love affair with a man of whom the mother disapproves. Norman had originally planned *The Fortune Teller* as a play but turned to the form of the novel when she discovered that it gave her greater freedom "to include things like fire engines and sex, things you can't do onstage." Furthermore, as she told an interviewer in the *New York Times Book Review* : "The novel, for its old-time sense of storytelling, can sweep you up in the privacy of it. The theater is a communal event, like church. The difference is in constructing a mass to be performed for a lot of people and writing a prayer, which is just the longings of one heart." She sees an analogy between writing and fortunetelling: "You look into someone's life, read where they have been and predict what will happen to them. What Fay [the mother] does for her clients in *The Fortune Teller*, I've done for characters my whole writing life." Admirers of Norman's plays, however, were generally disappointed by the novel. Michiko Kakutani, in the *New York Times*, called it "contrived and heavy-handed," lacking the poignancy and emotional impact of her plays. "*The Fortune Teller* gives us only the sketchiest sense of its people's inner lives. They remain caricatures whose sole function, it seems, is to move the story line along dutifully and predictably." Amy Hempel, in the *New York Times Book Review*, enjoyed the book as "an entertainment, if not exactly literature." She noted the seriousness of Norman's feminism and its effective "mystic overlay," but, like Kakutani, she found the characters superficially rendered: "Their ways and exchanges are so familiar that *The Fortune Teller* ends up being a quick read that does not linger or make us think."

PRINCIPAL WORKS: *Plays*—Getting Out, 1979; 'Night, Mother, 1983. *Novel*—The Fortune Teller, 1987.

ABOUT: Betsko, K. and R. Koenig, Interviews with Contemporary Women Playwrights, 1987; Contemporary Authors 105, 1982; Contemporary Literary Criticism 28, 1984; Current Biography 1984; Dictionary of Literary Biography, 1984; Guernsey, Otis L. (ed.) Broadway Song and Story, 1986. *Periodicals*—American Theatre May 1984; Commonweal October 12, 1979; Daily News (New York) March 27, 1983; Library Journal September 1, 1983; Modern Drama September 1987; Ms. July 1983; Nation May 7, 1983; New Republic July 7, 1979; New York November 13, 1978; May 28, 1979; April 11, 1983; New York Times March 27, 1979; May 17, 1979; May 27, 1979; June 3, 1979; June 8, 1979; September 15, 1979; April 1, 1983; April 19, 1983; April 4, 1985; June 23, 1985; April 10, 1986; May 13, 1987; New York Times Book Review May 24, 1987; New York Times Magazine May 1, 1983; Newsday September 16, 1979; May 8, 1983; Newsweek May 28, 1979; Saturday Review September–October 1983; Time May 28, 1979; U.S. News & World Report June 8, 1987; Village Voice November 6, 1978; Washington Post April 30, 1983; Women's Wear Daily March 29, 1983; June 29, 1987; World Literature Today Spring 1984.

O'BRIEN, TIM (October 1, 1946–   ), American novelist and non-fiction writer, was born William Timothy O'Brien in Austin, Minnesota, the son of William T. (an insurance salesman) and Ava E. Schultz O'Brien. O'Brien grew up in Minnesota, first in Austin, and then, from the age of ten, in Worthington, three hundred miles distant. He matriculated at Macalester College in St. Paul, Minnesota, as a political science major, and during a summer program in Czechoslovakia wrote an unpublished novel. He received his B.A. degree, summa cum laude, from Macalester in 1968. Immediately after graduation, he was drafted into the U.S. Army and saw combat in Vietnam, receiving a Purple Heart for a shrapnel wound. In the course of his service with the 198th Infantry Brigade he was promoted to the rank of sergeant. After being discharged from the army in March 1970, O'Brien enrolled at Harvard University as a graduate student in government. During the summers of 1971 and 1972 he was an intern at the *Washington Post*, and he took a leave of absence from Harvard to serve as a national affairs reporter for the *Post* during the 1973–1974 academic year. He returned to Harvard from 1974 to 1976, but left to pursue a career as a novelist.

O'Brien's first book, *If I Die in a Combat Zone, Box Me Up and Ship Me Home*, portions of which first appeared in *Playboy*, the *Washington Post*, and Minnesota papers, is a memoir of his Vietnam experience. Central to the account is the intense conflict he suffered over whether to go or to escape to Sweden when he was called up in the draft and assigned to Vietnam. In the end, he went, but what he considered a failure of a certain kind of courage continued to trouble him. Critical reception of the book was favorable. The reviewer for the *New Yorker* called it a "controlled, honest, well-written account," and the reviewer for the *New Republic* found it "interesting and highly readable." Michael Casey, in *America*, remarked that what "especially distinguishes [the book] is the intensity of its sketches . . . , an intensity seldom seen in journalistic accounts of the war. . . . [Passages] cover the basic and advanced infantry training of the author, but the chapters on the infantry experience in Vietnam are the best in the book. Each is tightly written and holds its own independently." Annie Gottlieb, in the *New York Times Book Review*, commented that O'Brien "brilliantly and quietly evokes the footsoldier's daily life in the paddies and foxholes, evokes a blind, blundering war. . . . [He] writes—without either pomposity or embarrassment—with the care and eloquence of someone for whom communication is still a vital and serious possibility. . . . It is a

TIM O'BRIEN

beautiful, painful book arousing pity and fear for the daily realities of a modern disaster." Elaine Glover, in *Stand*, found O'Brien's narrative strategy particularly effective, observing that "the actual structure of the book (O'Brien moves easily backwards and forwards in time over the three years with which he is concerned) is most impressive. . . . But most of all, O'Brien conveys the sense of being trapped, of enforced participation."

Northern Lights, O'Brien's first novel, set in northern Minnesota, focuses upon two brothers, Harvey and Paul Perry, who become lost in a blizzard in the course of a long-distance skiing expedition. The struggle for survival of the pair, one of whom has served in Vietnam, once again raises issues of testing and courage. John Deck, in the *New York Times Book Review*, noted that O'Brien "tells the story modestly and neatly. For readers who abhor the media-inspired cadence and tone of many new novels, here is a crafted work of serious intent with themes at least as old as the Old Testament." Neil Hepburn, in the *Listener*, was especially struck by the long action sequence of the work. "The description of the epic ski-trek," he observed, "which makes up the central third of the book, is excellently done, slipping in and out between impressionism and straight narrative and very excitingly conveying the reality—almost the reality—of men past the end of their endurance." The reviewer for *Booklist* was also impressed by this section, but had reservations about other aspects of the book. "As is often the case in first novels," he commented, "there is a submerged issue—here the

conflict of the brothers' love around the memory of their dead father. That part of the novel does not come across very well, and the two wives are stick figures." Roger Sale, in the *New York Review of Books*, felt that in much of the novel O'Brien was writing too discernibly under the influence of Hemingway—"which is a shame, because O'Brien seems to have firsthand interests and sense of place, and, in one long stretch, shows himself to be a real writer, not a ventriloquist. . . . Freed from having to write much dialogue, O'Brien is free of Hemingway for more than a hundred pages, and the result is splendid clarity that is never nature writing, never heroics, never conscious understatement."

O'Brien's second novel, *Going After Cacciato*, portions of which first appeared in literary magazines and took the O. Henry Memorial Awards for 1976 and 1978, attracted widespread attention and won the 1978 National Book Award. This Vietnam war novel is told from the point of view of Paul Berlin, a soldier on guard duty who has reveries of going after Cacciato, a deserter, with other members of his unit—an imaginary trek that leads through Laos, India, Turkey, and Athens to Paris, where peace negotiations are being held. Doris Grumbach, in the *Chronicle of Higher Education*, remarked that in *Going After Cacciato*, O'Brien "has accomplished something of a miracle. By using the authentic and bloody details that he knows so well from the war he survived, he has created a narrative that borders on myth and theology, psychology and epic, a picaresque parable of the imagination. . . . Written with rare skill, in a style that alternates between earthy soldier-talk and elegant descriptive passages, full of scenes of horror and succeeded by humorous scenes, studded with believable and moving scenes and decency and courage . . . *Cacciato* contains the kind of truth that separates the shallow from fully realized and original fiction."

O'Brien's striking conception of the journey from Vietnam in imagination was faulted by some reviewers. Walter Clemons, in *Newsweek*, for example, declared it "an unworkable idea that nearly sinks the book." Michael Malone, in *Harper's*, thought that the "realistic" chapters were the strongest in the book. "They are so remarkably good," he wrote, "and so self-contained that the elaborate visionary plot in which they are placed strikes the reader as an afterthought, evocative, intelligent, and well-written, but a novelistic bridge with too many of its symbolic braces showing." John Updike, in the *New Yorker*, felt that the visionary journey as well as other aspects of the work had a studied effect. "For all is horrors," he observed, "Mr. O'Brien's Vietnam has a precious, bejewelled aspect; as the novel shuttles among its three loci—the actual war, the imagined flight, the long night of Paul Berlin at the observation post—there builds up a slightly insulating laquer of self-conscious art." And like certain other critics, Updike pointed out the influence of Hemingway on the novel, particularly of *A Farewell to Arms*, with its "separate peace" idyll of love and escape. Yet most of the reviewers found the fantasy journey the great success of the novel, which was variously called "one of the most original novels of the year" and "one of the finest books about the Vietnam war." John Gardner, in the *New Republic*, observed that in *Cacciato* the characters are "all larger than life, as well as vivid and simple as mythic figures or huge animated cartoon people and the idea of the novel is directly or seriously philosophical, not offhand: a systematic and exciting interpenetration of fact and imagination. It's a splendid book."

O'Brien's next novel, *The Nuclear Age*, moves back and forth in time from childhood in the 1950s to a world of the future set in 1995 to evoke the central character's growing obsession with nuclear annihilation. It had mixed reviews. "The problem for the readers," Gloria Norris remarked in *America*, "is that *The Nuclear Age* is uneven. The story of young William is absorbing. . . . But in adulthood, William grows fuzzier. Is he 'nutto' because that is the proper response of any decent man to escalating forces of death? Or is he merely, as he increasingly seems to the readers, a person who cannot get his feelings and ideas straight? *The Nuclear Age* is strongest when O'Brien is dealing with the world of the 1960s and the moral dilemmas and confusion of a young man in search of self-definition, and there it is often powerful." Like several other reviewers, Michiko Kakutani, in the *New York Times*, was impressed by the early scenes in the 1950s, but she too found the protagonist out of focus. The theme of the work, she remarked, is "presented as a didactic pastiche of R. D. Laing and Jonathan Schell, bereft of originality or persuasive passion. People do not normally spend every waking hour obsessing about abstractions like nuclear war or world-wide devastation, and Mr. O'Brien never makes William's hysteria real or convincing. He never captures his fear, his craziness or even his point of view; and since one cannot sympathize with William the way we did with the hero of *Cacciato*, he strikes us as little more than an aberration."

"Vietnam has never left Mr. O'Brien D.J.R. Bruckner wrote in the *New York Times* of April 3, 1990. The occasion for the article was the news that O'Brien was going back to Vietnam in June, officially for a conference of American and Vietnamese writers in Hanoi and personally so that he might see a monument commemorating the My Lai massacre. O'Brien had been in My Lai in 1969 when, a year after that tragedy, the news of it was finally released. In *The Things They Carried*, a collection of stories about the war and its victims, he again re-lives his wartime experience, in no way, however, finally exorcizing those terrible memories. "As you play with stories you find that whatever is said is not sufficient to the task," he told Bruckner. *The Things They Carried* records many voices that seem to be pouring out of the author's memory and creative imagination. "In Vietnam," he said, "men were constantly telling one another stories about the war. Our unit lost a lot of guys around My Lai, but the stories they told stay around after them. I would be mad not to tell the stories I know." There is a narrator in the book who is from time to time addressed as Tim or O'Brien, but he is a persona; while some details in his life correspond with the author's, others do not. As he writes: "I want you to feel what I felt. I want you to know why story truth is truer sometimes than happening truth." O'Brien describes his work as "a writer's book on the effects of time on the imagination . . . meant to be about man's yearning for peace."

Most of the reviewers of *The Things They Carried* found it indeed that—and more. They praised not only the painstaking graphic detail with which O'Brien brings the hideous past to life but also his stunning craft as a prose writer. For Michiko Kakutani in the *New York Times* the book "is an elegiac tribute to the powers of storytelling itself—a tribute that celebrates the transforming powers of the imagination, even as it acknowledges its limits." For Bruckner it has a Homeric quality "in the underlying assumptions about fate, in the enmity of the earth itself toward men in battle, in the sheer glory of fighting, in the boasting of young men." Robert R. Harris observed in the *New York Times Book Review* that *The Things They Carried* is not simply a powerful book about the Vietnam War but belongs "high up on the list of best fiction about *any* war."

In addition to the National Book Award for *Going After Cacciato*, O'Brien has received awards from the National Endowment for the Arts, the Massachusetts Arts and Humanities Foundation, and the Bread Loaf Writer's Conference. O'Brien, who is unmarried, lives in Boxford, Massachusetts.

PRINCIPAL WORKS: If I Die in a Combat Zone, Box Me Up and Ship Me Home, 1973; Northern Lights, 1974; Going After Cacciato, 1978; The Nuclear Age, 1985; The Things They Carried, 1990.

ABOUT: Contemporary Authors 85–88, 1980; Contemporary Literary Criticism 7, 1977; 19, 1981; 40, 1986; Dictionary of Literary Biography, 1981; *Periodicals*—America September 1, 1973; May 17, 1986; Book List September 15, 1975; Chronicle of Higher Education February 13, 1978; Listener April 1, 1976; New Republic May 12, 1973; December 3, 1977; New York Review of Books November 13, 1975; New York Times September 28, 1985; March 6, 1990; April 3, 1990; New York Times Book Review July 1, 1973; October 12, 1975; March 11, 1990; New Yorker July 16, 1973; March 27, 1978; Stand #3, 1974.

O'CASEY, BRENDA. See **ELLIS, ALICE THOMAS**

*ŌE KENZABURO (January 31, 1935–), Japanese novelist, short-story writer, and essayist, was born in a small village community in Shikoku, where his family had lived for generations. He was the third of seven children born to Oe Kōtaro and his wife Koseki. In 1944 Oe's father died in the Pacific War, and in the same year he also lost his grandmother who had taught him the art of oral performance. He attended local public schools for the first ten years of his education, but in 1951 transferred to a high school in Matsuyama City to get the advantages of a better education. After one year of intensive study at a preparatory school (*yobiko*) in Tokyo, he won admission to the University of Tokyo, where he received his B.A. in French literature in 1959.

Growing up in the turbulent years of the Pacific War, the young and sensitive Oe underwent a tremendous rite of passage. After the dropping of two atomic bombs in August 1945, Japan experienced a complete reversal. Literally overnight, the country was transformed from a totalitarian, militaristic state to a fledgling democratic nation, just as the Emperor switched his divine identity to that of a human being, becoming simply a cultural symbol of Japan. The majority of Japanese believed that, with General MacArthur as their conqueror, there were no questions to be asked about Japan's course of action. They had not questioned the Imperial power before, and it was now their lot to obey the new leader. Those who questioned the validity of the Emperor system at all were in the minority. This meant that at the age of ten Oe had to make an overwhelming adjustment of his own: from an overzealous patriotic boy ready to die as his father had for the Emperor to an angry, confused, humiliated, yet liberated boy of the new Japan. Even the elementary school he was attending changed its name and drastically re-

ŌE KENZABURO

vised its curriculum in 1947, in accordance with the reforms imposed by the occupation authorities. But within five years of the surrender, the democratization of Japan itself, underwent a swift change. Experimentation with diversity and free inquiry was cut short. The occupation forces began to crack down on the newly legalized Communist party, a turn of events which dumbfounded and disillusioned the idealistic Oe. These political changes had a lasting impact on his intellectual development.

A representative of the new postwar generation, Oe has been consistent in his passionate espousal of progressive causes ranging from nuclear disarmament to protection for whales. He has also spoken out on behalf of A-bomb victims, dissident writers, minorities, and the handicapped. He still carries with him the burden of the postwar disequilibrium and contradiction. Readers detect in his works an instinctive defense of the underdog side by side with a sense of discomfort at his own fragmented self afloat in an inconstant world. In addition to the changeable politics and social dislocations of postwar Japan, Oe had to cope with a personal handicap, the inferiority complex that continued to plague him. He was a shy country bumpkin plunged into the center of culture, Tokyo, and to compound his ordeal, he stuttered and spoke with a heavy Shikoku accent. He early on learned to express his sense of discomfort, insecurity, and vulnerability by writing, first during his high school days and more seriously in college. Writing for Oe was an enormously therapeutic vehicle for affirming his own identity and

°o′ wā

maintaining a semblance of order in his psyche. By challenging the Emperor-centered view of history, Oe also began to speak as the voice of the marginal on the peripheries of society.

One of his apprenticeship stories, "Kimyō na shigoto" (A Strange Job, 1957), won a Tokyo University May Festival prize and was later nominated for the Akutagawa Prize, the most important literary award given in Japan to relatively unknown writers. In the following year, another of his stories, "Shiiku" (Prize Stock, 1958), received that coveted prize. In the first-person narrative, a young boy tells a story of a black American pilot from a downed plane who is captured by villagers, and of how the boy and his younger brother try to communicate with the "prize stock." This story introduces for the first time Oe's "Macondo," an imaginary village "in the valley in the forest" modeled on his birthplace in Shikoku. Japanese critics praised the work for its powerful primordial imagery, raw energy, lyricism and the sharply-focused narrative style.

However, after this brilliant debut, Oe was a total disappointment to the same critics. He temporarily left the Edenic village community behind and moved on to the cutthroat world of the big city. His stories between 1958 and 1964 reflect the life of a college student in Tokyo, unable to fit in, aimless, politically ambiguous, sexually uninhibited, and with very little hope. Under the influence of Sartre whose work was Oe's B.A. thesis topic, and Professor Watanabe Kazuo who introduced Oe to French humanism, Oe found himself caught somewhere between existential despair and the Rabelaisian affirmation of life. *Warera no jidai* (Our Times, 1959), Oe's first book-length narrative, was an attempt to violate a literary taboo by using explicit sexual language. It was clear that he was far ahead of his times. The book offended the puritanical sensibilities of Japanese readers and critics, who condemned it as a "repulsive work."

Depressed but unrepentant, Oe chose not to tone down the use of sexually explicit language and created in succession three more "embattled cultural heroes": an ingratiating upstart who gives in to the establishment, in *Okurete kita seinen* (A Youth Who Came in Late, 1962); a Korean boy who commits a murder, in *Sakebigoe* (Outcries, 1962); and a charming picaro who lives by his wits, in *Nichijoseikatsu no bōken* (Adventures of Everyday Life, 1964). All these antiheroes wander in a potentially dangerous liminality, betwixt and between, no longer innocent boys but not quite grown-up. The student unrest of the 1960s was already evident in Oe's narratives. We also see a Japanese Huck Finn

trying to articulate his reluctance to grow up or accept the status quo. This suspicion of the adult world was already a motif in "Prize Stock" and became a major theme in *Memushiri kouchi* (Nip the Buds, Gun the Kids, 1957), a powerful story of evacuated reform schools boys who are manipulated and abandoned by villagers. Variations on this theme appear in later works such as *"Memushiri kouchi" saiban* (The Trial of "Nip the Buds, Gun the Kids," 1980) and *Natsukashii toshi e no tegami* (A Letter Written for the Nostalgic Year, 1987).

In February 1960 Oe married Yukari Itami, a younger sister of Jūzō Itami, the famous film director of *Tampopo, The Funeral*, and *A Taxing Woman*. In June 1963 Oe became the father of a baby boy, Hikari (which means "light"), who was born with a congenital abnormality of the skull. After undergoing several operations that spared him the fate of "leading the life of a vegetable," Hikari became a symbol of hope for Oe. He uses this autobiographical material as if he were a film director, shooting "retakes" in *Sora no kaibutsu aquwee* (Agwhee the Sky Monster, 1964); *Kojinteki na taiken* (1964; translated as *A Personal Matter*), a winner of the Shinchō Literary Prize; *Warera no kyōki o ikiru michi o oshieyo* (1969, translated as *Teach Us to Outgrow Our Madness*), a winner of the Noma Literary Prize. The birth of Hikari was the turning point in Oe's life and in his literary career. In the past his protagonists had tended to respond to the human tragedy with ennui, depression, alcoholism, or paranoia (all of which were reflected in the author's style); but the day-to-day problems of raising a handicapped child demanded self-discipline, courage, and a sharply focused sensitivity. Oe saw in the abnormality of Hikari contemporary man's fate in the mad world of the nuclear age. He began to identify with Hikari as someone on the periphery, at the same time as the important Other who would fill in the void and "activate his imagination." Bird, the protagonist in *A Personal Matter*, confronted with the inevitable choice of either eliminating his abnormal baby or living with it, finally says to himself: "It's for my own good. It's so I can stop being a man who's always running away. . . . All I want is to stop being a man who continually runs away from responsibility."

When the English translation of *A Personal Matter* appeared in 1968, American reviewers responded enthusiastically. The publication "marks the debut in English of an astonishing Japanese writer whose books deal with postwar youth with such uncompromising realism that he seems to have wrenched Japanese literature free of its deeply rooted, inbred tradition and moved it into the mainstream of world literature," wrote Robert and Tomi Hass in *Saturday Review*. In 1977, when *Teach Us to Outgrow Our Madness* was published in the United States, a reviewer for *Choice* called Oe "a brilliantly obsessive writer." Cornelia Holbert of *Best Sellers* hailed him as "a sophisticated and unerring writer, a great thinker and lover, not to be missed." Another reviewer recognized the significance of Oe's obsession: "Obsession in and of itself is hardly a guarantee of literary quality, but Oe is a supremely gifted writer," who is "able to 'fictionalize' the most significant elements of his life as few others, and his work has an enormous impact," wrote Ivan Gold in the *Washington Post*. Ann Redmon, in the *London Times*, marveled at Oe's creativity: "his personal fixation never contaminates his art. In the vaunted creative process, he has transcended himself and given us an access to liberty."

In two other major novels, *Kōzui wa waga tamashii ni oyobi* (The Waters Have Come in unto My Soul, 1973), a winner of the Noma Literary Prize, and *Pinchirannā chōsho* (The Pinchrunner Memorandum, 1976), Oe doggedly pursues his obsession: the growing-up of this insecure father, paired with his double, "the idiot son." This fantastical tale of a "switchover" demonstrates Oe's emotional development as he learned to cope with his personal tragedy. Also in this period, his literary imagination and technique matured greatly. He had already experimented with polyphony and multi-layered texts in *Chichi yo anata wa doko e ikuno ka?* (Father, Where Are You Going?, 1968) and *Manen gannen no huttobōru* (The Football Game of the First Year of Manen, 1967), a winner of the Tanizaki Junichiro Prize. (The title of the English translation is *The Silent Cry*.) As is typical with Oe, he made several significant intellectual rediscoveries in the course of his habitual voracious reading: Mikhail Bakhtin's "grotesque realism" and "carnivalization," Victor Turner's "communitas" and "marginality," Mircea Eliade's concept of the dyad of death and rebirth, trickster tales, and semiotics. Oe synthesized all of these ideas in one of the most ambitious and politically explicit of his novels, *Dōjidai geemu* (The Game of Contemporaneity, 1979). This long narrative takes the reader back to Oe's "Macondo," the village in the valley in the forest. Oe had first explored this journeying back to one's roots in *The Silent Cry* and again in *Ikani ki o korosu ka* (How to Kill a Tree, 1984) and *Natsukashii toshi e no tegami* (A Letter Written for the Nostalgic Year). He had also, in *Mizu kara waga namida o nuquitamoo hi* (The Day He Himself Shall Wipe My Tears Away, 1971), reacted against Yukio Mishima's ultraconservative vision of Imperial Japan (a vision

that had propelled Mishima to suicide in 1970). Both these themes—the primal village and the imperial past—were developed in *Dō jidai geemu* (The Game of Contemporaneity). Oe believed that a re-creation of Japan's mythical past—"when grass, trees, rocks and fierce *kami* [deities] uttered words," when a primeval chaos ruled the world—would generate "a culturally creative force." This was his attempt to "rearrange the Japanese cultural paradigm" centered on the emperor system. In an extremely daring feat, Oe pits a tiny Shikoku village against the mighty Empire of Japan, the former demanding complete independence, the latter expunging the village's past from official history. At the center of Oe's Macondo, "the village/nation/mini-cosmos," is a mythical creature, *kowasu hito* ("one who destroys"), who plays the role of a trickster, the source of regeneration and creative power. In her book, *The Marginal World of Oe Kenzaburo*, Michiko Wilson calls the novel "a gift to contemporary man who needs to recite a 'sacred' narrative at the end of the 'ritual process' that brings him into close rapport with the cosmic vision."

Oe carries his obsession even further in *M/T to mori no hushigi no monogatari* (The Tale of Marvel, M/T and the Forest, 1986) and "recycles" the entire text of *Dōjidai geemu*, this time in an oral tradition format. M stands for "matriarchy," T for "trickster." The Oe-like narrator relates a long story (404 pages) about the village in the valley, in an unusually colloquial style. The unhurried tone and much less complex raconteur manner indicate that the possible listener is a young boy or girl. Oe ends the novel by describing a musical composition entitled "The Forest of Marvel" by a retarded boy named Hikari. What Oe has in mind is a fantasy version of himself as an adult, making a gift to his younger readers, that of the myth and history of the village/nation/mini-cosmos, through his trickster intermediary Hikari.

Oe returns to this most precious of personal subjects, life with Hikari, in *Atarashii hito yo mezame yo* (Rouse up, O Young Men of the New Age!, 1983). Inspired by William Blake's *Prophecies*, Oe writes in a linked-short-story format of his delicate relationship with Hikari, now turning twenty, and also describes how a family copes with a handicapped child. Oe for the first time opted to tell his intimate story as an autobiographical fiction, a genre called the "I"-novel, enormously popular in Japan yet carefully avoided by Oe until now. It was as though he had snapped out of his paranoia and felt secure enough to share his inner thoughts with the reader. Japanese critics greeted the novel with enthusiasm. They named it the literary work of the year and awarded Oe the Osaragi Jirō Prize for non-fiction. One of the judges, the writer Inoue Yasushi, said in his comments: "For a number of years I have not been moved by a novel as much I have by this novel, or I have not come across a novel which sobered me up as much as it did while reading it. Nor have I read a novel whose author held me spellbound so long as he did after I finished reading it."

Although clearly one of the most articulate and political writers of contemporary Japan, Oe has never joined any political group or party. He is political in the sense that he feels strongly about his role as a writer in society, that both in his essays and speeches he discusses many of the socio-political issues people would rather avoid. He shares the same vision and political beliefs held by many authors of our times: Kurt Vonnegut, Jr., Günter Grass, Gabriel García Márquez, Ariel Dorfman, to name a few. Oe regards literature as transcultural and makes his position clearly known. Many of his later works draw their motifs from the classics of world literature: Dante, Blake, Dickens.

Romantic love is not represented in Oe's fiction, and female characters are usually relegated to secondary roles. Although Oe's women include a fertility goddess (Dōjidai geemu/The Game of Contemporaneity), a sex counsellor (A Personal Matter), a big sister/political sympathizer (The Pinchrunner Memorandum), and a mother who loses her child to her husband (The Pinchrunner Memorandum and The Waters Have Come in unto My Soul), these are not central figures in his stories. His first, and so far only, novel with a female protagonist is Jinsei no shinseki (Relatives of One's Life, 1989), which focuses on the mother of a retarded boy.

Oe is also the author of numerous essays on a wide range of topics, including literary criticism. Some representative essay collections are: Hiroshima nōto (Hiroshima Notes, 1965), Genshuku na tsunawatari (The Solemn Tightrope Walking, 1965), Kujira no shimetsu suru hi (The Day the Whales Shall Be Annihilated, 1972), Dōjidai to shite no sengo (Postwar as the Contemporaneity, 1973), Shōsetsu no hōhō (The Method of a Novel, 1978), Oe Kenzaburo dōjidai ronshū (An Essay on the Contemporary Age by Oe Kenzaburo, vols, 1981), Kaku no taika to "ningen" no koe (The Nuclear Conflagration and the Voice of "Man," 1982), Nihon gendai no yumanisto Watanabe Kazuo o yomu (Reading a Contemporary Japanese Humanist, Kazuo Watanabe, 1984), Saigo no shōsetsu (The Last Novel, 1988).

Oe has traveled abroad widely, was a visiting scholar at the Collegio de Mexico and the University of California at Berkeley. In 1989 the Belgium-based Europelia Arts Festival, which sponsors one of the major European cultural festivals, hosted Japan and named Oe the recipient of the Europelia Award. Besides Hikari, he has two other children, a son and a daughter.

WORKS IN ENGLISH TRANSLATION: Oe's novella "Prize Stock" was translated with the title "The Catch" by John Bester in Saeki Shoichi's anthology The Shadow of Sunrise in 1966 and reprinted in Shoichi's collection The Catch and Other War Stories, 1981. It appears as "Prize Stock" in John Nathan's translation and collection of Oe's stories titled Teach Us to Outgrow Our Madness, 1977, which also includes, in addition to the title story, "Agwhee the Sky Monster" and "The Day He Himself Shall Wipe My Tears Away." Nathan's translation of A Personal Matter was first published in 1968 and several times reprinted; John Bester's translation of The Silent Cry in 1974, also reprinted. A collection of Oe's essays on the aftermath of the bombing of Hiroshima (based on his visit to the city in 1963), translated by Toshi Yonezawa and edited by Donald L. Swain, appeared in 1981.

ABOUT: Contemporary Authors 97–100, 1981; Contemporary Literary Criticism 10, 1979; 36, 1986; Encyclopedia of World Literature in the 20th Century, rev. ed., III, 1986; Wilson, M. N. The Marginal World of Oe Kenzaburo, 1986. Periodicals—Choice December 1977; New York Times June 14, 1990; New York Times Book Review July 7, 1968; Saturday Review of Literature June 15, 1968; Studies in Short Fiction Fall 1974; Times (London) October 15, 1978; Washington Post Book World September 11, 1977.

*O'FAOLAIN, JULIA (June 6, 1932–   ), Irish novelist, short-story writer, and translator, writes: "I was born in London and brought home a year later to Ireland where, when I first began to talk, I astounded everyone by my English accent. I lost then later recovered it in a school elocution class and now think of this shifty voice as emblematic of a hybrid heritage. Our family name is a manifesto. My father was John Whelan until his teens when, Gaelicized as Sean O'Faolain, he joined the Republicans and eventually became their director of publicity in the civil war of 1922. O'Faolain was a nationalist, Whelan a scion of the British Empire and the cast-off identity reaches me through my birth certificate. O'Faolain is our everyday name; Whelan, an alias from a hectoring past, defines us on official registers. Englishness, though, haunts us too in more seductive ways—mostly through literature.

"My parents are writers and, when I was growing up, were at odds with the new Ireland, which had disappointed them by setting up a bigoted, fundamentalist Catholic regime. When

°ō f(w)ā´ lôn

JULIA O'FAOLAIN

I was nine, Sean founded a magazine in which, working from a hut in our garden, he assailed pillars of its priggish Establishment with the zest of a man playing skittles. Echoes of his polemics thundering around our house were my first formative influences. Simultaneously, however, I was subject to the principles of my school nuns whose Order, the Sacred Heart, harked back to the French Restoration and the 'union of altar and throne.' We had no throne in Ireland, so they made do by getting us to curtsy to the highest ranked among themselves so as to imbue us with a sense of hierarchy. Elitist and subtly worldly, they introduced me to French literature and I spent summers with a family picked by one of their sister houses in France.

"Here then were two incompatible ideals: order and ceremony or the ballady lure of revolution. Citizens of an ex-colony and bit-of-Third-World-in-the-First can find it hard to identify completely with the Western middle class. Many of us are disloyal members: detached, uneasy and ironic, and if we write this shows up in our writing, which is often an attempt to reconcile other forked messages bequeathed by our puritanical, playful, bruised and bemused, misogynist and spuriously cheerful tradition.

"I left when I was twenty. After spending six years at the universities of Dublin, Rome and Paris, I worked as a translator, teacher, short-order cook, etc., in London and Strasbourg, then met and married the historian Lauro Martines in Florence, where he was working on a Ph.D. for Harvard. Later we went to Reed College in Oregon, where he taught history and I taught

French, then back for four years to Florence, where he was a Fellow at the Villa I Tatti and I taught at the Scuola Interpreti, and after that we went to Los Angeles and London. Lauro has a chair at UCLA but our house is in London and we divide our time fairly equally between the two. We have one son.

"I visit Dublin regularly. Balky relations with reality continue to prevail there and gossip is so artful that fiction writers can find that their raw material is not raw at all but pre-prepared. People perform for each other and see each other as cards or characters. Blarney and mockery are the positive and negative charges of the electricity which turns them on and keeps them going, and the question cannot but arise: are all Irish fictions metafictions? 'We have a story for you,' Dublin friends will tell a writer. Or: 'There's a grand story about something that happened recently but you can't have it. So-and-so (another writer) is writing it up.'

"People as interested in narrative as this are not only participatory but also conniving readers whose sheer existence is a stimulus. Yet ours is finally an adversary relationship, since writers want to penetrate behind surfaces, and people who offer themselves as characters expect to be allowed to keep on their masks. In a nation of myth-makers, the demystifier's role is thrust on writers. There are many ways to assume it and mine tends to be a speeded-up, ironic realism. I need the quick pen-strokes of the caricaturist if I am to catch the shifts of my protean and manipulative 'characters.'

"Need I add that when I write about non-Irish people (Italians, French, Americans, or Ancient Gauls), I am apt to focus on the same sort of deceivers and self-deceivers as I knew back home? One becomes addicted to the stress which shaped one."

From her earliest published writings reviewers have noted Julia O'Faolain's skill in portraying and contrasting Anglo-Saxon, French, and Italian attitudes, in pinpointing with clear-eyed and deadly accuracy the subtle but profound differences in her characters' cultural backgrounds. O'Faolain is international and cosmopolitan in her own background. She grew up in the Irish home of her parents, the distinguished novelist, short story writer, and biographer Sean O'Faolain and Eileen O'Faolain, a writer of children's stories based on Irish folklore—where frequent visitors were Irish actors, artists, and writers like Frank O'Connor, Patrick Kavanagh, and Brendan Behan. Her education brought her into contact with, to use her own phrase, "two incompatible ideas"—first the strict and insular environment of a convent school in Dublin, then the freedom of university study (B.A. and M.A. from University College, Dublin, followed by study at the Sorbonne and the University of Rome). Married in Italy to an American scholar, she has in recent years lived a trans-Atlantic life. Although her novels and short stories have their settings in many cities—Dublin, Paris, Florence, Los Angeles—her roots as a writer remain firmly planted in Ireland. She is not a polemical writer, but if she has any "cause," it is the expression of a woman's right to make her own choices about her life. In one of her short stories, "Man in the Cellar," an English woman who has suffered physical and mental abuse from her Italian husband gets her revenge by imprisoning him in the cellar of their house. He is ultimately released unharmed, but the wife meanwhile has returned to England, a divorce, and a new life. She writes him a letter explaining her extraordinary behavior: "I had to fight back, even if I knew I would fail. . . . But, Carlo, I am not different from you. Being a female doesn't make me different. 'Feminine' strategies are responses to an objective situation: lack of power. There is no 'natural' love of subservience in women."

O'Faolain began her writing career with short stories, some of them published in the New Yorker. These are lean and compact, told in the cool detached manner of the satirist-observer with no emotional commitment. Her characters are mainly women discovering their potentialities—for good and also for evil, for intelligent choice and also for serious blunders. Transplanted usually from their homes to a foreign society, they enjoy their freedom but are sometimes betrayed by it. The results are often more wryly or balefully comic than tragic. In O'Faolain's first novel *Godded and Codded* (published in the U.S. as *Three Lovers*) a young Irish woman goes off to study at the Sorbonne and to have three love affairs and an abortion. Told with near clinical detail, the story is, however, not a sordid chronicle of wasted youth but a satirical portrait of the free swinging lifestyles of the 1960s in Europe. "[She] writes firmly," Sally Beauman observed in the *New York Times Book Review*, "with a voice all her own, the voice of her *New Yorker* stories expanded into a novel: well planned, intelligent, concise, more pointed than her father, with a cold female eye for the egocentricities of masculine behavior."

By the mid-1970s O'Faolain was recognized, Roger Garfitt wrote (in *Two Decades of Irish Writing*), as "an outstanding satirist of the affluent society . . . truly international in range." But Garfitt was not satisfied with categorizing her as a satirist. "To call Julia O'Faolain a sati-

rist . . . is to do her work only partial justice: it suggests the incisiveness of her talent—for wit and verbal devastation she has few equals among her contemporaries—but not the strength nor the subtlety of her concern. There is a power of mind behind her work, as well as an irreverently perceptive eye, that catches the intensity of human drives, the essential seriousness of the effort to live; without swallowing any of the trends in self-deception. She is an acute observer, who is involved at a level of concern deeper than the substance or sum of her observations."

The depth of Julia O'Faolain's concern is suggested by what are today regarded as her two most ambitious novels, *Women in the Wall* and *No Country for Young Men*. *Women in the Wall* marks a distinct departure from her contemporary subjects and satirical voice. It is an historical novel set in sixth-century Gaul. O'Faolain discovered her subject when she was doing research for a book she co-edited with her husband, the art historian Lauro Martines. *Not in God's Image* is a collection of excerpts from documents, laws, letters, and other writings from ancient Greece to the mid-nineteenth century on the role of women in European society. As the editors write in their Foreword: "By collecting testimonies left by men and—when possible—women who lived in those societies, [the book] aims at presenting a close-up picture of the lives of ordinary women from different social classes: of their status, social roles, degrees of freedom or tutelage, and of the mental conditioning which has survived to leave its residue in the attitude of our own times." In her readings in history, O'Faolain learned of Queen Radegunda, wife of a brutal Frankish warrior chieftain, who left him to found a religious order. From such fragmentary records as survive of this period she conceived a novel of stunning power. Radegunda herself succeeds in creating a haven of peace and order in a violent world, and she even achieves transcendence through a mystical union with Christ. But around her forces of human greed and factionalism work to destroy her achievement. Her protegée and designated successor Agnes has an illegitimate daughter who immures herself to expiate her mother's sin, and everywhere chaos and disorder set in. A young poet-priest, the seducer of Agnes, observes cynically the passing of the old order: "I was learning how Gaul was governed. Even disorder has its order—the only one future generations may know. Mine is perhaps uniquely cursed in that it retains a memory of true, institutional order, without any hope of its revival. Like the Garden of Eden, order was and was taken away: a sour and godly trick. All gone now. Illiteracy obliterates memory. The last image of the Roman experience survives in the language—Latin—and even that is crumbling like a weedy aqueduct, gnawed at by epidemics of prepositions which subvert its syntax as termites do timber."

Women in the Wall is by no means a conventional historical novel. There are few details of life in sixth-century Gaul. "Her concern," Maurice Harmon writes of O'Faolain (in *The Irish Novel in Our Time*), "is with the age-old paradoxes of human nature and her care is to allow character to reveal itself. . . . The nunnery is a microcosm for the tempests of the outside world." The wall is indeed symbolic. Laloge Pulvertaft, in the *Times Literary Supplement*, read it as "a symbol of the buried individuality of womankind." For Maurice Harmon, "All men and immured between the demands of the physical and the spiritual." Doris Grumbach, in the *New Republic*, found the book "wild, gaunt, bloody, tragic and wholly impressive." She wrote: "The force of language, the subtle and entirely successful recreation by means of it of the spirit as well as the events of Gallic life thirteen centuries ago . . . make *Women in the Wall* a remarkably modern historical novel, poignant and powerful."

In *No Country for Young Men* O'Faolain writes of the recent history of Ireland. It is a big, carefully structured novel centered on one Irish family from the 1920s to the present. Crowded into it are politics, violence, Irish-American relations, a murder mystery, romance, and madness. As in all her novels O'Faolain writes here with special insight into the lives of her women characters, Irish women married and unmarried, torn between old traditions and loyalties and their rights and needs in modern society. Several reviewers felt that O'Faolain had attempted to cover too much ground. "Such abundance of material is bound to get out of hand," Patricia Craig wrote in the *Times Literary Supplement*. Hermione Lee, in the *Observer*, detected a "schoolroom tone" in O'Faolain's treatment of Irish history: "At times the novel edges toward lecture topics." But she concluded that the book was redeemed by its lively plot: "And the novel's strong grasp of the relation between a family and a national history transcends its occasional imaginative sagginess." Julian Moynahan, in the *New York Times Book Review*, had no reservations about *No Country for Young Men*. He pronounced it a "stunning performance." In this novel, he wrote, O'Faolain "has hit her stride, using everything she knows." She certainly knows the complexities of current Irish politics and confronts these issues boldly. Comparing her to other contemporary Irish novelists who often stress only the comic and eccentric aspects of Irish life, Moynahan observed: "Julia O'Faolain

in her bitter, comprehensive realism has produced a book that has few if any parallels in contemporary Irish fiction and that must be read by all who care about 'that country' as it really is."

A realistically portrayed Los Angeles—freeways, mud slides, cultists, trendy lifestyles—is the scene of *The Obedient Wife*. Here an Italian wife, temporarily deserted by her businessman husband, struggles to raise a teen-age son and finally must decide between returning to a conventional bourgeois life in Italy with her husband or remaining in Los Angeles as the wife of a former priest. In her decision she discovers at last her own capacity for free choice. In *The Irish Signorina* another transplanted heroine, a young Irish girl, finds herself deeply involved in the lives of an old aristocratic Florentine family. These later novels, less ambitious in theme than *Women in the Wall* and *No Country for Young Men*, have been generally well received for their wit and shrewd observation of character. O'Faolain has not, however, abandoned historical research and more serious subjects. Her work in progress in the late 1980s was a novel about Pope Pius IX, the famous Pio Nono of the nineteenth century, who proclaimed the doctrine of papal infallibility.

PRINCIPAL WORKS: *Novels*—Godded and Codded (in U.S. Three Lovers), 1970; Women in the Wall, 1975; No Country for Young Men, 1980; The Obedient Wife, 1982; The Irish Signorina, 1984. *Collected short stories*—We Might See Sights! and Other Stories, 1968; Man in the Cellar, 1974; Daughters of Passion, 1982. *Translations*—(as Julia Martines) Two Memoirs of Renaissance Florence: The Diaries of Buonaccorso Pitti and Gregorio Dati, 1967; Chiaro, P. A Man of Parts, 1968. *As editor*—(with L. Martines) Not in God's Image: Women in History from the Greeks to the Victorians, 1973.

ABOUT: Contemporary Authors Autobiography Series 2, 1985; Contemporary Authors New Revision Series 12, 1984; Contemporary Literary Criticism, 1976; Dictionary of Literary Biography 14, 1983; Dunn, D. (ed.) Two Decades of Irish Writing, 1975; Rafroidi, P. and M. Harmon (eds.) The Irish Novel in Our Time, 1975. *Periodicals*—New Republic May 10, 1975; New York Times Book Review May 9, 1971; January 1, 1987; Observer June 1, 1980; Times Literary Supplement April 4, 1975; June 13, 1980.

OLDS, SHARON (November 19, 1942–), American poet, writes: "When I went back to the Sierra Nevadas for a week in the summer of 1986, I realized how important Northern California has been for me, what a strong sense of homeland I had—the ocean, the coastal range, the valley, the foothills, the mountains, the glacier lakes.

SHARON OLDS

"I was born in San Francisco in 1942. At age two, I was shown a book of ration stamps, and told this was to be our source of food now; I took the stamps away into a corner and ate them. I was always literal-minded and visually oriented. I lived near a school for the blind and sang in an Episcopal church choir with girls from that school. In the summer I went to Girl Scout camp. On special campfire nights, I would stand behind a Ponderosa pine and recite, in a loud quavery voice, homemade verses that began, 'I am the spirit of the tree.' I swam underwater as much as possible, and when no one was around I sometimes felt like a natural part of the earth. At fifteen, I went to boarding school near Boston and fell in love with the New England seasons and with New York City—like a mountain range made by people. After four years of college in the West, I came back to New York where I've lived ever since, on the Upper West Side of Manhattan, over the Hudson River.

"When I was a teenager I began to read a lot of poetry. I wrote in what Denise Levertov has recently named 'reusable forms' (Poetry East, Poetics issue, No. 20/21, Fall 1986). In college I studied languages—not linguistics but beginning grammar and vocabulary (French, Italian, German, Greek, Middle English). In graduate school I studied American literature. And in the home I studied love, nourishment, healing and pleasure. For many years now I've been a full-time mother and a full-time poet.

"For a long time I could not balance the elements of poetry: the beauty of language on the one hand, and on the other the believability of the voice (a regular person speaking). It took me even longer to feel my way toward speaking not just for myself. All along, the study of dance and the joy of dancing have helped me find my poems.

"Currently, I'm teaching at Brandeis in the fall, and Columbia or N.Y.U. in the spring, as well as a poetry workshop at Goldwater Hospital (a public N.Y.C. hospital for the severely physically handicapped), on Roosevelt Island. I've done some work on the PEN Freedom-to-Write committee and its Silenced Voices subcommittee, and follow the cases documented by Amnesty International and Helsinki Watch.

"The sources of poetry I think about these days are the need to release what's in us; the desire to make a new object (a new being, really) with its own particular beauty and power; the longing to know each other and be known by each other (the lessening of isolation); and the necessity of bearing witness for life, for the earth—to speak for oneself and for those who do not speak."

———

In 1986, in an article in the New York Times Book Review titled "American Poetry, Now Shaped by Women," Alicia Ostriker wrote: "The belief that true poetry is genderless—which is a disguised form of believing that true poetry is masculine—fails to recognize that writers necessarily articulate gendered experience just as they necessarily articulate the spirit of a nationality, an age, a language." Among the many American women poets who have emerged in the 1980s few articulate their gender more powerfully than Sharon Olds. Still, it would be misleading to label Olds a "feminist poet." She writes as a daughter, a woman, and a mother; but as the 1985 citation that accompanied the National Book Critics Circle Award for her second volume of poems, The Dead and the Living, read in part: "Olds writes of private and public traumas with a fierce commitment to the vulnerable—and with a saving wit. Hers is a voice like no one else's."

It is often an angry voice, tough and strident, but it can also be tender and loving. Satan Says, Olds' first collection, shocked several of its reviewers with the frankness of its language and the candor of its self-revelations. Lisel Mueller, in Poetry, expressed the reaction of many readers when she wrote: "She moves (and usually persuades) us by the very passion, even need, of her utterance. By the same token, she sometimes allows her rage to go out of control, using a voice so vehement, a language so hyperbolic, as to incur disbelief. . . . " But Mueller finds this problem only intermittent. "By far the greater number of her poems are believable and touching, and their intensity does not interfere with craftsmanship."

Satan Says, dedicated to the poet Muriel Rukeyser, is divided into four sections: Daughter, Woman, Mother, and Journey. The opening poem, "Satan Says," makes clear that the poems that follow are an act of exorcism: "I am trying to write my / way out of the closed box

> The pain of the locked past buzzes
> in the child's box on her bureau, under
> the terrible round pond eye
> etched around with roses, where
> self-loathing gazed at sorrow.

She is ambivalent about her parents: "I love them but / I'm trying to say what happened to us / in the lost past." Only through the open expression, in cruel obscene taunts that come through Satan's mouth, does she achieve, in the last line of the poem, "the suddenly discovered knowledge of love."

Bitterness is mingled with tenderness in the Woman section of *Satan Says* as the poet awakens to sexuality, love, and marriage. Love, she discovers, in "The Love Object," "can follow a woman / all the way into death and declare her / still herself." She can love fiercely but still retain her selfhood. After passionate lovemaking she sits beside her husband eating a meal—"a friend sits with a friend here" ("Primitive"). But it is motherhood that evokes Olds' deepest emotions. Linda Gregerson writes in *Poetry*: "Olds is an eloquent celebrant—I know no contemporary her equal here—of sexual love and its extrapolation in a mother's erotic ties to her children." In "Fish Story" she writes of bathing her daughter:

> those thighs like two fish, that whole
> glazed torso like a fish. . . .
>
> She could almost
> see the scales on this mermaid, this sleek
> stretching child, this glittering eel
> who used to be a shrimp in her sea—
> this woman she once had firmly in her body. . . .

In "The Mother" it is her little boy she is bathing:

> In the dreamy silence after bath,
> hot in the milk-white towel, my son
> announces that I will not love him when I'm dead
> because people can't think when they're dead. I can't
> think at first—not love him? The air outside the
> window is very black, the old locust
> beginning to lose its leaves already . . .
> I hold him tight, he is white as a buoy
> and my death like dark water is rising
> swiftly in the room. I tell him I loved him
> before he was born. I do not tell him
> I'm damned if I won't love him after I'm

dead, necessity after all being
the mother of invention.

Satan Says closes with Journey—a group of poems, most of which were inspired by a summer trip the poet made with her husband and her children to his former home in Nova Scotia. She summons up the ghost of her mother-in-law whom she never knew:

> You are not angry I am sleeping with your son,
> you are not angry we have given our daughter your name,
> you are not angry we are visiting here
> on the stone island where you died. You sit
> still and deep. The waves lift and
> cover the rocks.
>
> —from "Encounter"

In Olds' second volume, *The Dead and the Living*, winner of both the Lamont Poetry Prize and the National Book Critics Circle Award, public life claims her attention as strongly as private life. She still writes with bitterness and sometimes acerbic humor about her parents. One poem, dedicated to them, is "Possessed" and testifies to how much their memory haunts her. "I have never left," it begins:

> You think I left—I was the child
> who got away, thousands of miles,
> but not a day goes past that I am not
> turning someone into you.

She recalls "my bad grandfather" who "turned the lights out when we wanted to read" and her grandmother in a nursing home: "She'd crack / a joke sharp as a tin lid / hot from the teeth of the can-opener. . . ." But Olds' focus widens here to include the public outrages that every day confront us in photographs, newspapers, images on the television screen—grim, terrifying pictures from all over the world of atrocities, violence, starvation, race riots. These are counterpointed with a gallery of private images—her parents' divorce, a miscarriage she suffered, her little boy's awakening manhood at a children's party which she sees in metaphors of big business and war games. "The confidence of the best of these family portraits is astonishing," Harold Beaver wrote in the *New York Times Book Review*. "Only rarely does Miss Olds fall into cliché or sentimentality. . . . when the confessional drive is tamed to such life studies, it is not the agony we are likely to remember but the persistent comedy of human love."

Still haunted by her hostility toward her parents, Olds can now, however, move beyond herself. As Linda McCarriston wrote in the *Georgia Review*: "Olds presses outward to an inclusive understanding of suffering in the nuclear family. We endure reading the most painful of these poems because we hear in them not the voice of the victim—the child—but that of the adult daughter with children of her own, looking both forward and back, demanding justice." It is precisely Olds' self-awareness that gives her work its strength. David Leavitt wrote in the *Voice Literary Supplement* that "her poetry is remarkable for its candor, its eroticism, and its power to move." If her poetry has a weakness, Leavitt speculates, it is the absence in it of "the inchoate and the ineffable. . . . Olds' poems tend to be so complete that they leave the reader little to question or ponder."

The title of Olds' third volume, *The Gold Cell*, suggests the image of the primary unit of life, but as Alicia Ostriker points out in *Poetry*, it also implies "both entrapment . . . and pure treasure." Even more intense in its exploration of human sexuality than her earlier volumes, *The Gold Cell* expresses her revulsion at the brutality of family relations and her anxieties about safeguarding her children in a world of violence:

> The day my girl is lost for an hour,
> the day I think she is gone forever and then I find her,
> I sit with her awhile and then I
> go to the corner store for orange juice for her
> lips, tongue, palate, throat,
> stomach, blood, every gold cell of her body.
> —from "The Quest"

Only in her poems on mothering is the relentless savagery of her language abated, but even there, Anthony Libby noted in the *New York Times Book Review*, mothering is "a confrontation . . . with sickness, grotesque injury and the constant presence of death." Yet she leaves her readers, Alicia Ostriker wrote, with "a tacit moral imperative that we affirm as intensely as possible our biological existence and the attachment to others it implies, and that we hold life as absolutely precious." In *The Gold Cell*, more firmly than in her earlier collections, Olds celebrates the smallest, simplest things—something, she says:

> . . . I learned early to do, I am
> paying attention to small beauties,
> whatever I have—as if it were our duty to
> find things to love, to bind ourselves to this world.
> —from "Little Things"

Sharon Olds received a B.A. with distinction from Stanford University in 1964. In 1972 she took a Ph.D. in English from Columbia University with a dissertation on the prosody of the poems of Ralph Waldo Emerson. A Guggenheim Fellow in 1981–1982, she has taught writing at Sarah Lawrence, Columbia, New York University, Brandeis, and at the Poetry Society of Ameri-

ca and the Poetry Center of the New York YMHA. In 1989 she became director of New York University's Graduate School of Arts and Science Creative Writing Program. She has also given many poetry readings on college and university campuses.

PRINCIPAL WORKS: Satan Says, 1980; The Dead and the Living, 1984; The Gold Cell, 1987.

ABOUT: Contemporary Authors New Revision Series 18, 1986; Contemporary Literary Criticism 32, 1985; 39, 1986. *Periodicals*—Georgia Review Winter 1984; Ms. July 1984; New York Times Book Review March 18, 1984; March 9, 1986; March 22, 1987; Poetry June 1981, January 1987; (Village) Voice Literary Supplement March 1984.

OLIVER, MARY (September 10, 1935–), American poet, was born in Maple Heights, a suburb of Cleveland, Ohio, to Edward William Oliver, a teacher, and Helen (Vlasak) Oliver. She attended Ohio State University from 1955 to 1956 and spent another year, 1956–1957, at Vassar, but never completed a college degree. Except for a period when she lived at Steepletop, home of Edna St. Vincent Millay, working as secretary for Norma Millay, the poet's sister, and periods of teaching and travel abroad, she has lived in Provincetown, Massachusetts. From 1972 to 1973 she chaired the writing division of the Fine Arts Center in Provincetown; in 1980 and again in 1982 she was Mather Visiting Professor at Case Western Reserve University. She was poet-in-residence at Bucknell University and the University of Cincinnati in 1986. Until she received the Pulitzer Prize for poetry for *American Primitive* in 1984, Mary Oliver was little known outside a small circle of poets and poetry readers. Within that circle, however, she was much admired. The Poetry Society of America had awarded her its first prize in 1962 for one of her earliest published poems, "No Voyage." She also won the Shelley Memorial Award (1970), the Alice Fay de Castagnola Award (1973), and the Cleveland Arts Prize for Literature (1979). In 1972–1973 she held a fellowship from the National Endowment for the Arts, and in 1983–1984 she was a Guggenheim Fellow.

Mary Oliver's poems, published now over a period of some twenty-five years, read like a continuous and unswerving journey into the very heart of the natural universe. To categorize her, however, as a "nature poet" is as inadequate as it would be to describe Robert Frost (or William Wordsworth, for that matter) so simplistically. Like Frost, to whom she is often

MARY OLIVER

compared, Oliver uses simple language to explore sophisticated and complex states of mind and familiar, even homely, imagery to evoke sometimes dark, sometimes transcendentally joyous emotion. Her dedication to poetry seems to be epitomized in these lines from her "Entering the Kingdom" (in the collection *Twelve Moons*):

> The dream of my life
> Is to lie down by a slow river
> And stare at the light in the trees—
> To learn something by being nothing
> a little while but the rich
> Lens of attention.

From the outset of her career critics have regarded Oliver as much more than merely a lens or register of the nature she observes. Commenting on *The Night Traveler* in *Western Humanities Review* in 1979, Robert De Mott noted "an impressive declarative intelligence" in her work. The title of her Pulitzer Prize–winning *American Primitive* should not suggest, Linda Gregerson wrote in *Poetry*, "the helpless byproduct of rustic ingenuousness"; Oliver's poetry is primitive "only in the sense that it is originary, concerned and able to derive first principles before our eyes." Though she seeks to surrender herself to nature, it is with the sensitive responsiveness that Wordsworth called "a wise passiveness," alert to the significance of what she is experiencing. The title poem of her first collection, *No Voyage*, reveals a speaker who has in some way been wounded. She finds her life "wanting"—"On a cot by an open window / I lie like land used up, while spring unfolds." But there is a firm resolution to survive: "Let the dying go on, and let me, if I can, / Inherit from disaster before I move." She rejects a voyage of pure escape: "Here or nowhere I will make peace with the fact."

The rigorous emotional control that Oliver tried to exercise in some of these early poems struck some readers as excessive. Robert H. Glauber, in the *Prairie Schooner*, speculated: "Is there really blood and bone beneath this pale skin of verse? Control in a writer is admirable—especially in a young writer. But so is directness, passion, the determined pulse of young life." James Dickey, in the *New York Times Book Review*, wrote: "She never seems to be quite in her poems, as adroit as some of them are, but is always outside them, putting them together from the available literary elements."

The poems in Oliver's second collection, *The River Styx, Ohio*, have greater immediacy. They center on Middle America, the Ohio of her girlhood: landscape, Indian lore, family relationships. There is more sense of form in these lyrics and even occasional rhyme. Here her self-restraint is less inhibiting. Stanley Kunitz observed that her "tender evocations of an Ohio childhood read like an elegy for a lost heritage." In "Stark Boughs on the Family Tree," for example, she writes of her "thin ancestors [who] slowly fade / Under the flat Ohio skies." They were people, she finds, of no remarkable distinction or accomplishment, and she asks: "Why do I love them as I do?" Her answer is simple: " . . . they left the small / Accomplished, till the great was done"; and she recognizes that "They are the good boughs of my name."

With *The Night Traveler* Mary Oliver appears to have found her mature voice as a poet and a depth up to that time absent from her work. Her responses to nature now are richer and darker, more elemental but also more profound. These poems, Robert De Mott wrote, "will be familiar to anyone with an abiding interest in the nether world of dreams and the shadowy regions of the unconscious . . . [they] confront and often release the generative power of first forms residing in the human psyche." Animals, in particular, assume near-mythic dimensions. The bear prowling the dark forests is "The Night Traveler":

> But when he stops at your gate,
> Under the room where you lie half- asleep,
> You know it is not just anyone—
> It is the Night Traveler.

The bear image recurs in Oliver's later poems and becomes increasingly identified with the

poet herself. In *American Primitive* she becomes
one with the she-bear, following her into the forest on her quest for "the secret bin of sweetness
/ honey" . . . "a taste composed of everything
lost, in which everything / lost is found"
("Honey at the Table"). As she gorges herself on
honey she imagines the bear metamorphizing
into a bee—"an enormous bee / all sweetness
and wings" ("Happiness"). And finally, in "The
Honey Tree," the poet herself climbs the tree to
eat "chunks of pure light": "Oh, anyone can see
/ how I love myself at last! / how I love the
world!" Patricia Yaeger has analyzed these poems and others by Oliver in support of her thesis
that women writers devise strategies of language
in order to circumvent the restrictions imposed
on them by a male-dominated society and language. "In Oliver's poetry," Yaeger argues,
"women become appetitive, sexual, aggressive,
joyous, exotic beings who steal language happily,
who . . . unleash the language by placing
themselves at the point of commerce where old
social practices change." Feminist polemics,
however, have no role in Oliver's poetry. Her
"intoxication," her "honey-madness," is the joy
in nature that the release of language in poetry
allows her to express.

Dedicated to the memory of the Ohio-born
poet James Wright, who died in 1980, *American
Primitive* was acclaimed by Stanley Kunitz for
"the purity of its lyric voice, the loving freshness
of its perceptions, and the singular glow of a spiritual life brightening the pages." James Dickey,
who had expressed reservations about her earlier
work as self-consciously literary, found in
American Primitive "the enchantment of the
true maker." All traces of artifice seem to have
disappeared. As Linda Gregerson wrote, in
Poetry: "Hers are spare, lean poems of celebration, Sapphic in their lineaments and in their distillation of appetite, keenly disciplined to
luminous transcription of the visible, touchable,
edible world. Mary Oliver almost seems to have
taken pastoral, that most artificial of all literary
conventions, at its word, to have hied herself off
to the springs and the hills and found there the
sources of poetry."

Noting that it is always difficult to follow a
Pulitzer Prize volume, R. S. Bravard, in *Choice*,
judged that *Dream Work*, published three years
after *American Primitive*, met the challenge
successfully: "The work is sustained, varied, and
reflective of well-honed technique. . . . Oliver
is well on the way to becoming a major poet."
Part of her growth is her widening vision:

> You don't want to hear the story
> of my life, and anyway
> I don't want to tell it, I want to listen

> to the enormous waterfalls of the sun.
> And anyway it's the same old story—
> a few people just trying,
> one way or another,
> to survive.

> Mostly, I want to be kind.
> And nobody, of course, is kind,
> or mean,
> for a simple reason.
> !BAnd nobody gets out of it, having to
> swim through the fires to stay in
> this world.
>   —from "Dogfish"

The familiar natural world remains the principal subject of these poems, but in some she
ventures out into other areas—into music, for instance, in "Consequences," speculating on Beethoven's deafness, or, in "Robert Schumann,"
imagining the composer as a young man who has
just fallen in love, unaware of the madness that
awaits him. Contemporary history appears in
"1945–1985: Poem for the Anniversary," where
"In the films of Dachau and Auschwitz and Ber-
gen-Belsen / the dead rise from the earth / and
are piled in front of us . . . ."

"One of Ms. Oliver's hallmarks is plain
speech," David Kirby wrote of *Dream Work* in
the *New York Times Book Review*. "Ms. Oliver
points out that nothing is ever as simple as it
should be and therefore we should not talk it to
death." Kirby cites her poem "Stanley Kunitz,"
her tribute to a poet who also lives in Provincetown and who is a dedicated gardener. When
younger, Oliver had regarded him as a
Merlin—"strolling with important gestures /
through the garden / where everything grows so
thickly." Now, because she is mature, she knows
that a garden, like a poem, is not created effortlessly but demands patient, hard work: "raking
and trimming, stirring up . . . the wild and
shapeless air."

PRINCIPAL WORKS: No Voyage, and Other Poems, 1963;
The River Styx, Ohio and Other Poems, 1972; The
Night Traveler, 1978; Twelve Moons, 1978; American
Primitive, 1983; Dream Work, 1986; House of Light,
1990.

ABOUT: Contemporary Authors New Revision Series 9,
1983; Contemporary Literary Criticism 19, 1981; 34,
1985; Contemporary Poets, 4th ed., 1985; Dictionary
of Literary Biography 5, 1980; Who's Who in America
1988–1989; Yaeger, P. Honey-Mad Women: Emanci-
patory Strategies in Women's Writing, 1988.
Periodicals—Choice November 1986; Contemporary
Literature Spring 1989; Hudson Review Summer
1980; Library Journal January 15, 1965; June 1, 1986;
New York Times Book Review November 21, 1965;
October 21, 1979; October 12, 1986; Poetry October
1984, May 1987; Prairie Schooner Fall 1965; Virginian

Quarterly Review Winter 1987; Western Humanities
Review Spring 1979.

OSBORN, PAUL (September 4, 1901–May
12, 1988), American playwright and screenwriter, was born in Evansville, Indiana, the son of
Edwin Faxon Osborn, a Baptist minister, and
Bertha Judson Osborn. He grew up in Kalamazoo, Michigan, where his father had a church
post, and attended the University of Michigan,
earning a bachelor's degree in English (1923)
and a master's in psychology (1924). At Ann Arbor he formed a lasting friendship with Robert
Frost, who was then poet-in-residence. "The influence [of Frost] was subtle but strong," Osborn
said in 1962, "and perhaps can be summed up
by saying that he gave me the greatest respect
for the written word."

Following a stint as teaching assistant at Michigan, and still considering that he ought to pursue a career in electrical engineering, Osborn
suddenly discovered in himself the ability to
write for the theater. "I suppose," he told
Michiko Kakutani in a 1980 *New York Times* interview, "I was a rebel in the sense that I wanted
out of the environment. A lot of my old friends
back there were working in hardware stores or
banks, and that just wasn't for me. It wasn't theater itself that gripped me at first, it was the
need to get away from a life which sort of bored
me."

Osborn attended during 1927, on scholarship,
the well-known playwriting course given at Yale
University by George Pierce Baker and began
seriously to pursue his goal. His efforts were met
with conspicuous and rapid, though not at first
lasting, success: in November 1928, his first
three-act play, *Hotbed*, was given a full-scale
production on Broadway and was followed by
another New York production of his next play,
A Ledge, in November 1929. Neither play was
a critical or commercial success, but together
they formed the best possible on-the-job training
for an aspiring playwright, and they laid the
groundwork for his first Broadway success, the
smash-hit society comedy *The Vinegar Tree*, in
November 1930. He reminisced in a 1985 *New
York Times* interview with Stephen Harvey
about the failure of *Hotbed*, a tame play about
a young college teacher, the title of which seems
quite misleading today: "I'd written about people I knew, but I had to admit it was pretty dull.
So I supposed that the next time, I'd be better off
just making something up." He was working,
once having left New Haven for New York, at
"one job after another," Osborn told Margaret
Van Sant in 1984. "I think I was letting up the

PAUL OSBORN

gates of the railroad on Long Island, and the
woman who was going to do my first play, An-
toinette Perry [a legendary Broadway theatrical
director, for whom the Tony awards are named],
said what are you doing? And I said I had a job
and was working. She said, well, you've got a job
writing. And I said, yes, but I've got to eat. She
said, well, I wish you'd do something for me. I'll
give you a small allowance so you can quit your
job on the railroad and you just write. I said,
Okay, I'll take it! She was just delighted. I wrote
The Vinegar Tree then, and when I'd made
some money, I paid her all back."

"Making something up," in Osborn's phrase,
was perhaps the key to *The Vinegar Tree*'s success. It is a witty country-house comedy, very
much in the urbane, high-comic style of Philip
Barry, which concerns a scatterbrained woman,
played on Broadway by the accomplished far-
ceuse Mary Boland, who mistakes her younger
sister's lover for her own first love of decades
earlier. It enjoyed a long run on Broadway, directed by Winchell Smith and produced by
Dwight Deere Wiman, who was to produce
many of Osborn's theatrical successes of the
1930s (and who later produced the musicals of
Rodgers and Hart and the early ones of Rodgers
and Hammerstein). The play was well received
in London, and in 1933 was turned into a film,
Should Ladies Behave?, starring Alice Brady
and Lionel Barrymore. It was selected as one of
the ten best plays of the 1930–1931 New York
theatrical season.

Strangely, *The Vinegar Tree* marked the last
time (as well as the first) that an original play by

Osborn enjoyed a Broadway success its first time out. Of his subsequent original works, *Oliver, Oliver* had a short run on Broadway in 1934; *Tomorrow's Monday* was produced only in summer stock in 1936; *Morning's at Seven* played for just forty-four performances on Broadway beginning in November 1939; *Maiden Voyage* closed out of town in 1957; and *Film of Memory* received a modest, short-lived production in London in 1965.

During the 1930s, Osborn discovered a secure and profitable niche in the New York theatrical world as an adapter for the stage of the work of others, principally best-selling novelists. His first success in this genre was *On Borrowed Time* (1938), a long-running two-act adaptation of the novel of the same name by Lawrence Edward Watkin, a wistful comedy about a little boy who traps Death up a tree, a temporary occurrence during which nobody dies. This play marked Osborn's first of many collaborations with the director Joshua Logan and the set designer Jo Mielziner. His other major adaptative theatrical successes occurred during the 1940s and 1950s: *The Innocent Voyage* (1943), adapted from Richard Hughes' *A High Wind in Jamaica*); *A Bell for Adano* (1944, starring Fredric March, adapted from John Hersey's novel; *Point of No Return* (1951, starring Henry Fonda, adapted from John P. Marquand's novel); *The World of Suzie Wong* (1958, adapted from Richard Mason's novel). His last such work was the book for *Hot September*, a three-act musical adaptation of William Inge's play *Picnic*; it closed out of town in 1965.

Osborn's adaptations were deft and demanding theatrical work. The often unwieldy narrative of a novel, frequently encompassing dozens of major characters, had to be whittled and narrowed to yield tight dramatic action and streamlined, usually three-act, dramatic form. He learned, better than almost any such craftsman of his generation, how to keep and even refine a book's essential mood while at the same time tailoring the major characters who remained to the abilities of individual actors. A complete mastery of the literary original was obviously necessary, as was the confidence of the original novelist, along with a tireless willingness to rewrite again and again and to be a permanent fixture at every rehearsal. "In a way," he told Stephen Harvey in 1985 with characteristic self-effacement, "doing all these adaptations was much easier work. The characters always came first in my own plays, but with these novels, the structure and plot were already there to be rethought. It was a new kind of challenge. Still, I wish I hadn't agreed to do so many of them. I did them when I didn't have anything else to do." He remarked in a similar vein to Michiko Kakutani in 1980, "Sometimes, I wish I'd never done an adaptation. I liked to write original plays so much more, but the adaptations were so easy. Some one would come up and ask me to do one, and since I wasn't doing anything else, I'd end up doing it."

Osborn's adaptative skill also extended to films. He wrote, mainly from novelistic originals, more than a dozen well-received screenplays, of which the best known were *The Young in Heart* (1938, adapted from I.A.R. Wylie's *The Gay Banditti*); *Madame Curie* (1943, adapted from the biography of her mother by Eve Curie); *The Yearling* (1946, adapted from Marjorie Kinnan Rawlings's novel); *East of Eden* (1955, adapted from John Steinbeck's novel); *Sayonara* (1957, adapted from James A. Michener's novel); *South Pacific* (based on the musical by Richard Rodgers, Oscar Hammerstein, and Joshua Logan and on *Tales of the South Pacific* by James A. Michener); and *Wild River* (1960, adapted from William Bradford Hale's *Mud on the Stars* and Borden Deal's *Dunbar's Cove*). His screenplays for *East of Eden* and *Sayonara* were nominated for Academy Awards. Osborn spent several months of each year in Hollywood but always remained a permanent resident of the East Coast. "I never really held that snooty attitude so many playwrights had about Hollywood," he told Harvey. "I enjoyed working out there. It certainly wasn't the giddy life you were promised in those days. I'd go there for a few months a year, hole up in my office in the Selznick studios of MGM, and work very hard and fast. Sidney Franklin, the top producer at MGM in the '40s, was an awfully bright, literate man, and later on I loved working with Elia Kazan on *East of Eden* and *Wild River*. But California never really appealed to me, and I always felt my real work was in the theater."

No American playwright has had a more surprising and gratifying later career than Osborn. In April 1980 his 1939 original play *Morning's at Seven* was revived to enormous critical and popular success: its Broadway run the second time around lasted sixteen months and won him his first Tony award for best Broadway revival of 1980. "It was nice to get the Tony," he said after the 1981 awards presentation, "because I had really never even seen one." The play is a fond and somewhat slow-paced consideration of the lives of four late-middle-aged sisters. They have among them been the cause of much familial discord, and throughout the play this is hidden under apparent politeness based upon a thorough unwillingness to offend one another or to tell the truth about feelings, sexuality, or even family madness. Recalling the play's origins, in a 1980 interview with Christopher Sharp in *Women's Wear Daily*, Osborn said, "One day, in Kalamazoo, I was sitting in the house where I grew up and happened to look at all the members of the family sitting in backyards that adjoined our own backyard. I kept asking myself what kind of play could be created from the lives of all my aunts, uncles, and grandparents." The play was originally set in 1939, but Vivian Matalon, the director of its revival, moved it back to the year 1922, a simpler time, it seemed, in Midwestern America. Families, Osborn went on, "still talked to each other. There was a feeling too that writers could find extraordinary qualities in ordinary events. Sometimes, a simple question asked at a family dinner could turn into something extraordinary."

The play's renewed success pleased Osborn greatly, but he seemed to have been thoroughly unprepared for it. "I was never," he told Harvey, "a hell of a good salesman for my own work, and when they first talked about bringing *Morning's at Seven* back, I said, 'Oh God, they'll think it's so dated.' So it's all been something of a surprise." As to the reason why audiences of 1980 seemed thoroughly satisfied with the play and its message, whereas those of forty years earlier had not, he remarked in 1981, "Times, of course, have changed, and as I watched audience who attended [the revival], I noticed that young people seemed to enjoy it the most. It's a family play, . . . and on several occasions young people would come up to me and say, 'Geez, I wish it was that way now.' It's not merely nostalgia, it's the wish that things were a little more settled, more stable. There's not the unity today that once existed in family life." Walter Kerr, reacting to the revival, called it "a perfect production of a uniquely shaped play, merry and mellow and just possibly a bit mad. It's enchanting."

Tomorrow's Monday was given its New York premiere in October 1985 at the Circle Repertory Company. The following month *Oliver, Oliver* was produced by the Manhattan Theatre Club, directed by Vivian Matalon. Kent Paul, who directed *Tomorrow's Monday*, remarked that Osborn's "insight into American life goes beyond simple naturalism. I think it's astonishing the way *Tomorrow's Monday* prefigures so many important plays in its vision of the American family—from *The Glass Menagerie* to *'Night, Mother* and Lanford Wilson's Talley plays. And the characters are all written with a kind of gusto which is both theatrical and truthful at the same time." A revival of *The Vinegar Tree* by the York Theatre Company had a brief off-Broadway run in early 1988.

Osborn married Millicent Green, an actress, in 1939. They had one daughter. He died at his home in New York City at the age of eighty-seven.

WORKS PUBLISHED IN BOOK FORM: The Vinegar Tree, 1931; Oliver, Oliver, 1934; On Borrowed Time, 1938; Morning's at Seven, 1940; A Bell for Adano, 1945; The Innocent Voyage, 1946; Point of No Return, 1952.

ABOUT: Contemporary Authors 112, 1985; Who's Who in America, 1987–1988. *Periodicals*—Drama-Logue December 17, 1981; Los Angeles Herald Examiner December 5, 1981; Nation December 10, 1930; December 16, 1939; November 27, 1943; December 23, 1944; December 29, 1951; January 24, 1959; May 3, 1980; New Republic February 23, 1938; November 29, 1943; December 25, 1944; January 7, 1952; October 27, 1958; New York Times November 4, 1938; November 24, 1943; December 17, 1943; January 24, 1947; April 30, 1948; March 30, 1949; January 30, 1952; March 10, 1955; December 6, 1957; March 20, 1958; October 12, 1958; May 27, 1960; April 11, 1980; April 14, 1980; October 9, 1982; November 3, 1985; May 13, 1988; New Yorker December 16, 1944; December 22, 1951; October 25, 1958; April 21, 1980; Women's Wear Daily April 3, 1980.

*PADILLA, HEBERTO (January 20, 1932–   ), Cuban-born poet, novelist, translator, and journalist, now living in the United States, was born in Pinar del Río in western Cuba. He published his first book of poems at the age of sixteen, and the following year traveled to the United States, where he resided for lengthy periods until the overthrow of the Batista dictatorship in 1959. With the triumph of the revolution, Padilla left his Manhattan job as translator and teacher with Berlitz to become New York correspondent for Prensa Latina, the Cuban press agency. Within a few months, the revolutionary government called him back to Cuba, where he began work as cultural-affairs editor for the newly-created daily *Revolución*. During those first years, he also contributed to *Lunes de revolución*. Padilla helped found the Cuban Writers and Artists Union and served as director of its literature section and as a member of its editorial board. He was eventually made director of Cubartimpex, the state enterprise devoted to importing and exporting cultural properties, and was thus responsible for bringing many foreign books to Cuban readers. He also functioned as a representative of the Ministry of Foreign Trade (and as a foreign correspondent for Prensa Latina) in the Scandanavian countries, Great Britain, and the Soviet Union. At home or abroad, Padilla continued to write poetry throughout the early years of the Cuban Revolution. During this

ⁿpä de' ya, e ber' to

HEBERTO PADILLA

period, Casa de las Américas awarded an honorable mention to his collection *El justo tiempo humano* (The Right Moment for Humanity, 1962), and several of his other poems appeared in various anthologies.

J. M. Cohen, in *New York Review of Books*, describes Padilla's poetry during this period as "spare but romantic. . . . Padilla's predominant influences," he writes, "have been Blake, Wordsworth, and Byron, and those Russian poets who were strongly influenced by English romanticism. The outstanding sequence [of] The Right Moment for Humanity is 'The Childhood of William Blake,' a series of ten reflections on incidents in Blake's life and on his art." In this sequence, Cohen writes, "Padilla voices his fear that terror will eventually overcome the new Jerusalem that seemed to be coming forth in Cuba. This sequence is a social poem, but one of great depth and perspicacity." In a survey of Padilla's early work published in *Parnassus*, Elizabeth Macklin writes: "There is a sense of surprise in [these early] poems, of something unforeseen coming into view—approximating—and then sinking in. . . . Something closing in, taking you over, sweeping you maybe off your feet, maybe away completely. . . . Padilla regards the post-Batista changes: the wind tugging at the Coca-Cola signs; the Canada Dry courtesy clocks, 'stopped / at the old time.'"

By the late 1960s, however, Padilla had become something of a gadfly of the Cuban Revolution, increasingly skeptical of socialism and critical of Fidel Castro. In 1967 the poet put himself directly at odds with revolutionary au-

thorities by challenging the government's endorsement of a novel by the Cuban writer Lisandro Otero and by defending the work of the self-exiled novelist Guillermo Cabrera Infante. When Padilla's next book of poetry *Fuera del juego* (Outside the Game, 1968)—an angry attack on what he perceived as a repressed and regimented society—was awarded the Julian Casal Prize of the Writers and Artists Union, it was immediately condemned by *Verde olivo*, the official magazine of the Cuban army. Further efforts by the government to block the award produced a heated public controversy with the union, which eventually resulted in a severe tightening of the revolutionary regime's cultural policies. Following the subsequent loss of his standing with the Cuban government, Padilla took a job at the University of Havana.

Cohen identifies the poem *"En tiempos difíciles"* ("In Trying Times") as "perhaps the key to Padilla's growing resentment against thought suppression, and compulsory conformism of all kinds":

> . . . a dream
> (the great dream);
> they asked him for his legs
> hard and knotted
> (his wandering legs),
> because in trying times
> is there anything better than a pair
>   of legs
> for building or digging ditches?
> They asked him for the grove that
>   fed him as a child,
> with its obedient tree.
> They asked him for his breast,
>   heart, his shoulders.
> They told him
> that that was absolutely necessary.
> They explained to him later
> that all this gift would be useless
> unless he turned his tongue over to
>   them,
> because in trying times
> nothing is so useful in checking
>   hatred or lies.
> And finally they begged him
> please, to go take a walk.
> Because in trying times
> that is, without a doubt, the deci-
>   sive test.
>
> —trans. J. M. Cohen

In 1971, the "Padilla Case" was dramatically rekindled when the poet was briefly imprisoned and humiliated into making a public confession denouncing his own work and accusing several other writers, including his wife Belkis, also a poet, of antigovernment sentiment. The episode quickly produced a sharp reaction against the Cuban government by many noted figures of the international Left. Jean-Paul Sartre, Alberto Moravia, Susan Sontag, Carlos Fuentes, and fifty-six other European and American intellectuals signed a letter to Castro expressing their outrage. Padilla spent the rest of the 1970s translating the works of English romantic poets, unable to publish any of his own poetry or the novel on which he had been working. In 1980 he was allowed to leave Cuba and come to the United States, after Bernard Malamud, then president of the PEN American Center, and Senator Edward Kennedy's office interceded in his behalf.

Since moving to the United States, Padilla has published two major works in English translation. The first, *Legacies: Selected Poems*, collects poems he wrote in Cuba during his period of silence dating from 1971 and also includes several verses from the 1960s and early 1980s. As Gerry Clark notes in *Best Sellers* : "His early themes are personal and simple, dealing with love, dreams, and relationships (like the lovely, but unusual 'To Belkis, When She Paints'). Gradually, Padilla becomes more strident in his political opinion, writing poems of frank protest ('Don Gustano'). Some of his best work, however, deals with poetry and poets. . . . Whatever the theme, Padilla's writing is always rhythmic and forceful, and the images are crystal-clear. It is the sheer melodiousness of the poems, however, that is their strongest asset; the flow and ebb of the lines is unforced and perfectly metered, bringing each poem to a natural and satisfying conclusion. Poems this splendid, even after translation, are certainly of the highest order." Other critics, however, have found that politics placed too heavy a stamp upon Padilla's poetry. Lewis Hyde, for example, wrote (in the *Nation*) that *Legacies* reveals "a poet who has not been able to mine the richest veins of his sensibility because of the situation of his birth. [Padilla] is closer to W. H. Auden or Antonio Machado than, say, to Nicolás Guillén or Ernesto Cardenal. Left alone in London or Mexico City for the last twenty years, he might have given us a different group of poems—more poems on childhood, on sexual love, on the voices of the past, on landscape and spirit, and, yes, on politics, but political poems less busy adjusting their voices so as to slip between the slogans. . . . "

Padilla's novel *En mi jardín pastan los héroes* was smuggled out of Cuba by the author and was first published in Spain. It was translated into English as *Heroes Are Grazing in My Garden* in 1982. Michael Wood, in *New York Review of Books*, characterizes the book as "a novel of disappointment and creeping fear, of the hardening of revolutionary fervor into dogma, and of the pollution of private lives by politics." The novel introduces two men, brothers-in-law, living in Havana—an alcoholic novelist who is politically apathetic, and a translator, who is hopelessly ineffectual in his opposition to the Castro government. It is his delirious dream of "heroes of all sizes and ages—heroes suddenly as puzzled as clumsy, frightened children, heroes who moved like lancers to the sound of fife and flute," that gives the book its title. In the dream the heroes are chewing the grass he has been meaning to cut for days:

> They grazed—on all fours they cut the greenery with their teeth . . . they brandished their useless weapons, which would never again destroy. Children would come later, or a council of old men, under the clean vines returned to their original innocence, purged of history. He wanted this deluge to swallow everything—acts, speeches and apothegms, philosophers and enchanters, prophets and kings and secretaries—generals and bishops of all churches.

"It is a telling vision, an impossible peace," Wood writes, voicing a futility that anticipates the closing of the novel, with the two men "who at times seem like figments of each other's imagination, getting drunk and going swimming, incoherently sharing their helplessness."

Since emigrating to the United States in 1980, Heberto Padilla has as well become a fellow of the New York Institute for the Humanities at New York University and has been working on a translation of Maiakowsky's complete poetry. In 1990 he published a memoir, *Self-Portrait of the Other*. "My own life is not so very important," he said, "but I have been witness to many important events and many important people, and that's what the book [is] about."

WORKS IN ENGLISH TRANSLATION: A selection of Padilla's early poetry was translated by J. M. Cohen as *Sent Off the Field* in 1972. In 1982 Alastair Reid and Andrew Hurley translated *Legacies: Selected Poems*. The novel *Heroes Are Grazing in My Garden* was translated by Andrew Hurley in 1984. *Self-Portrait of the Other* was translated by Alexander Coleman, 1990.

ABOUT: Contemporary Authors 123, 1988; Contemporary Literary Criticism 38, 1986; Foster, D. W. (ed.) Dictionary of Contemporary Latin American Authors, 1975; Johnson, S. (ed.) Case of the Cuban Poet Heberto Padilla (Studies in Cuban Literature), 1978. *Periodicals*—Best Sellers May 1982; Nation January 23, 1982; New York Review of Books June 30, 1983; July 18, 1985; New York Times March 3, 1990; New York Times Book Review April 11, 1982; February 18, 1990; Parnassus Spring–Summer 1982; Time July 8, 1985.

PALMER, MICHAEL S(TEPHEN) (October 9, 1942–   ), American physician and writer of suspense fiction, writes "I am, I believe, a cogent argument for a liberal education. I entered

Wesleyan University in Connecticut as a potential history major, switched to Russian literature, and finally settled upon biology and pre-med. Along the way, I took seminars on Poe with Richard Wilbur and on war with Willard Wallace; I discovered that I could write reasonably well and that I could not draw or paint at all; I balanced classes in experimental cellular physiology with those in Near Eastern poetry and philosophy, and spent my evenings studying *mridanga*, a South Indian classical drum.

"My medical school, Case Western Reserve in Cleveland, stressed the humanistic aspects of medicine and encouraged us not to lose sight of the importance of balance in any physician's life. To that end, the school replaced grades and class rank with more subjective, but more accurate and less stress-inducing, personal faculty evaluations. Medicine as an art was emphasized at least as much as medicine as a science.

"The elements of a successful fiction writer: sensitivity, imagination, an open mind, a way with words, and uncompromising discipline, were present in me long before I thought about trying to write a book. When I finally did try, in late 1977, it was more out of curiosity than any burning desire to be published. Robin Cook, a classmate at Wesleyan, had recently published *Coma*, and after reading it, I set about writing a medical suspense novel of my own. One page a night (I was working 80 to 100 hours a week in private internal medicine practice on Cape Cod), my hobby became a book. And although the construction of that book was too faulty for publication, my writing—'an unusual sense of the dramatic,' one publisher called it—interested agent Jane Rotrosen enough to begin working with me.

"I continue to write because it is painful and exhilarating; difficult and challenging; and mostly, because it is a craft of progress, never perfection. The flashes of self-discovery—invariably surprises—are the purple hearts with which I am periodically rewarded for my efforts.

"I continue to practice medicine (now in an emergency-room setting) because I love the contact with people, the action, and the balance it brings to my life. The microcosm of the hospital provides a continuous flow of emotion—of triumph and tragedy, of pain and relief from pain—that exists nowhere else. It is my privilege to that energy, more than any other single element, that colors my writing, and makes it mine.

"'What is this person feeling at this moment?' is a question I ask with every page. Unless the answer to that question is crystal clear for each character, the novel will not work. Tacked on the wall around my desk are reminders to help keep me centered: Say What Thou Meanst; Always Tell a Story; Take Chances; A Character Must Never Fight, Never Choose, Until He is Good and Ready; and finally and most importantly, Relax."

————

The son of Milton (an optometrist) and May (Schoolnick) Palmer, Michael S. Palmer was born in Springfield, Massachusetts, and attended school in Springfield and Longmeadow, Massachusetts. After receiving his B.A. from Wesleyan University and his M.D., with honors, from Case Western Reserve in 1968, he was medical director, from 1969 to 1971, of the Cincinnati Free Clinic, of which he had been a cofounder. He returned to Massachusetts for a residency in internal medicine at Boston City Hospital and Massachusetts General Hospital. During this period, from 1971 to 1973, he was also a clinical instructor in medicine at Harvard and Tufts universities. He was in private practice in Falmouth, Massachusetts, from 1973 to 1979, when he assumed the practice of emergency medicine which he continues, dividing his time between the Boston area (Winchester Hospital) and Cape God (Falmouth Hospital).

Michael Palmer's writing career began as a hobby. Medicine was and remains a vital part of his life, and it is also the source of the best-selling thrillers he has written. "The hospital is like an oasis," he told a newspaper interviewer. "I work in the emergency room, where you can usually make a difference, where you usually know what is going on. I leave work after my long shift tired and exhausted, but I love it. I am revitalized by my work in the hospital." He has poured some of that restored energy into his books—with enough left over for a program of non-literary activities, including acting in summer stock, running, scuba diving, and playing the blues harmonica.

"I'm just writing a good read," Palmer told his interviewer. He had long been acquainted with other "good reads," having found relaxation from his medical duties in the fiction of John D. MacDonald, Robert Ludlum, and other writers of mystery and suspense fiction. The success of fellow physician and one-time fellow student Robin Cook's *Coma* and of the medical thrillers of Michael Crichton was a challenge for Palmer. "If Robin can do it, why can't I?" His breakthrough to best-sellerdom was not without effort, however. While his earliest efforts remained unpublished, they were promising enough to interest a literary agent who encouraged him to prepare an outline for a new novel.

The outline won him a contract and a substantial advance from Bantam Books, and he proceeded—after several persistent rewritings—to produce a best-seller, *The Sisterhood*. The marketing of this kind of book by a then unknown author was itself a story remarkable enough to be reported in the *New York Times Book Review* : "Since the author had no track record and was not known to the reading public, Bantam's marketing staff not only gathered prepublication blurbs from authors of block-buster books, but also printed up 11,000 'reading copies' of *The Sisterhood* and distributed them before publication to booksellers and others in a position to help the novel succeed." The result was, almost literally, an overnight success: five weeks on the *New York Times* mass-market best-seller list, eight weeks on *Publishers Weekly*'s list, over one million copies sold, and translations into eleven foreign languages.

The Sisterhood is the story of a young doctor who is wrongfully accused of murder when one of his patients dies of an overdose of morphine. To clear his name he tracks down a nationwide conspiracy—a group of nurses who have united in a plan to terminate the lives of hopelessly ill and suffering patients. Organized decades earlier for the idealistic aims of euthanasia, the "Sisterhood of Life" has become a sinister organization that murders for hire at the service of greedy or vengeful heirs of the victims. The action develops rapidly with all the "page turner" elements as the doctor and a sympathetic nurse close in on a psychopathic killer. "Palmer's novel will do nothing to enhance the reputation of the nursing profession," *Publishers Weekly* observed, but the reviewer concluded with praise of Palmer's inside medical knowledge and skill at constructing an absorbing plot: "Euthanasia will never again be an abstract subject to anyone who reads this grim, compelling tale."

Although not written in response to feminist protests over the portrait of women nurses in *The Sisterhood*, Palmer's next novel, *Side Effects*, restores a gender balance, having for its central character a brilliant and courageous young woman pathologist. She is trying to juggle the conflicting demands of her marriage and her career as well as to track down another conspiracy, this one even more powerful and sinister since it involves the entire pharmaceutical industry. The thriller ingredients are again all here—including mysterious computer technology, an international drug ring, and a former Nazi doctor who had once experimented on female victims in a death camp. *Side Effects* has the added interest of a timely domestic story of an endangered marriage. *Publishers Weekly* found the book "topical, fast-paced, and scary."

Michelle R. Koetke, in the *Sunday Independent North*, wrote: "Michael Palmer's tense, medically accurate, vivid suspense novel makes us care about the tattered relationships as much as the death threats in the offing. That *Side Effects* succeeds on both levels, makes it a richer, more satisfying novel and real advance in the genre."

Michael Palmer has homes in the Back Bay section of Boston and in Falmouth, on Cape Cod. He has two sons from his marriage to Judith S. Grass in 1964; they were divorced in 1972.

PRINCIPAL WORKS: The Sisterhood, 1982; Side Effects, 1985.

ABOUT: Contemporary Authors 114, 1985. *Periodicals*—New York Times Book Review October 3, 1982; Publishers Weekly July 9, 1982; March 1, 1985; Sunday Independent North March 24, 1985.

PASTAN, LINDA (OLENIK) (May 27, 1932–   ), American poet, was born in New York City to Jacob L. Olenik, a medical doctor, and Bess (Schwartz) Olenik. Her roots, she recalled in an autobiographical note for *American Poets in 1976*, were in the Bronx, though, she admits, "I used to ride on the Concourse Bus dreaming of complete escape—practicing my vowels and closing my ears to the Bronx speech surrounding me." She found some escape in obsessive childhood reading: "I dipped chilly toes into Emerson, swam with abandon in the buoyant waters of the nineteenth-century novel, almost drowned when I dove too early into Gide and Camus." She discovered poetry early and began writing her own poems: "It was as natural a process for me as growing breasts, it was part of my earliest womanhood." In her senior year at Radcliffe College (B.A. 1954) she won the Dylan Thomas Poetry Award given by *Mademoiselle* magazine, a contest in which Sylvia Plath was also a competitor.

In 1953, only just twenty, she married Ira Pastan, now a molecular biologist, and "turned my back on poetry and wrote little or nothing at all." She did manage, however, to take an M.L.S. at Simmons College in 1955 and an M.A. at Brandeis University in 1957. After the birth of her third child and first daughter she resumed writing poetry and has since won several awards for her work, including the Swallow Press New Poetry Series Award (1972), a grant from the National Endowment for the Arts (1972), the John Atherton Fellowship given by the Bread Loaf Writers' Conference (1974), the Poetry Society of America's Alice Fay di Castagnola Award (1977), and the American Book Award

LINDA PASTAN

poetry nomination for her *PM/AM* (1983). Currently on the staff of the Bread Loaf Writers' Conference, she has also taught in the M.F.A. program at American University. Though professionally an established poet, Pastan says that writing still involves an inner struggle: "The walk between the study and the kitchen is, in a sense, the longest walk I take. Guilt still lurks in one room, anger in the other—both are ghosts that I am determined to exorcise." Like so many other poets, Pastan has discovered that "poetry itself provides some of the solutions to the very problems it raises. By allowing myself to follow a poem wherever it wants to take me, I find that I often stumble upon truths about myself, my world, that I scarcely suspected I knew."

The title *The Imperfect Paradise*, Pastan's seventh collection of poems, might serve as an epitome of her whole poetic vision. Shadowing all human experience—in her case specifically the joys of love, motherhood, nature, intellectual discovery—is the ever-present threat of mutability, of change and loss. As she wrote in a characteristically spare lyric "Short Story":

In the short story
that is my life
the mother and the father
who were there from the beginning
have started to disappear.
Now the lover repeats
his one line, and the plot
instead of thickening
as it might, thins
almost to blank paper.
There is no epiphany.
Even an animal whose cry
seemed symbolic

has lapped its milk
and gone quietly
to sleep. And though
there is room for a brief
descriptive passage (perhaps
a snowfall, some
stiffening of the weather)
already
it is dark
on the other side
of the page.

A superficial reading of Linda Pastan's poetry might confirm the impression of bleak, unremitting despair that "Short Story" gives. But in fact she writes a poetry so lucid and balanced in its confrontation with human suffering and so full of emotional resilience and control that it is the sense of a paradise—however prone we are to lose it—rather than life's imperfections that emerges from her work. Sharing as her readers do both the pain and the pleasures of her daily existence, the response is one of recognition and acceptance of life's mystery and wonder. In 1978, in *Hudson Review*, Samuel Hazo described Pastan's poetry as "luminous." Apart from the competence of her technique, Hazo praised "the succinctness of final precision. . . . But succinctness is only half the story. The other and deeper half is vision. This is a woman with convictions; she is not satisfied to be mere litmus paper to the world."

Within the large framework of mutability, the major themes of Pastan's poetry are drawn from the immediacy of her life—nature, marriage, motherhood, her Jewish faith. The natural world with its cycles of change is an especially rich source of inspiration for her. She finds that nature "also helps to put things in a perspective that makes life more manageable. I live in an oak forest in Maryland and spend a lot of my time alone there, and I spend the summers on Nantucket, so my life is naturally focussed on the out-of-doors. . . . It will always surprise me how one thing, like a changing leaf, can feel at times comforting and at times threatening, depending on how you are looking at it."

Pastan's Jewish heritage reinforces her sense of continuity even in the flux of time. In "At the Jewish Museum" she responds to an exhibition of Lower East Side Jewish immigrant life at the turn of the century:

We can endure the eyes
of these children lightly,
because they stare
from the faces of our fathers
who have grown old before us.
Their hungers have always been
our surfeit. We turn again
from the rank streets, from
marred expectancies and laundry
that hangs like a portent

over everything.
Here in a new museum
we walk past all the faces
the cameras have stolen from time.
We carry them like piecework
to finish at home,
knowing how our childrens' sins
still fall upon the old Jew
in a coal cellar, on Ludlow street,
in nineteen hundred.

Marriage poses more subtle and challenging questions. Even in her first collection, *A Perfect Circle of Sun*, the spontaneous love between husband and wife ("We take an early walk and stop to kiss") is threatened by the poet's vision of the future:

I see beyond your head
two roses clenched like fists
against the kitchen wall
and think of tea brewing to bitterness
in its forgotten pot . . . .

— "Early Walk"

Love seems doomed in the very course of nature. In "Morning" the soon to be abandoned Queen Dido reflects:

Gravity is against us, pulling
our bodies apart;
September is against us,
pulling down summer leaf by leaf.

In *Aspects of Eve* Pastan probes the roots of male-female relationships. This is the Eve who must spin while Adam delves, assigned to a submissive role which she accepts with bitter resignation:

You are Odysseus
returning home each evening
tentative, a little angry.
And I who thought to be
one of the Sirens (cast up
on strewn sheets
at dawn)
hide my song
under my tongue—
merely Penelope after all.
Meanwhile the old wars
go on, their dim music
can be heard even at night.
You leave each morning,
soon our son will follow,
Only my weaving is real.

— "You Are Odysseus"

There are outbursts of frustration and rage. In "The Ides of March" she dreams of a liberating spring that "holds off":

Birds have eaten my path
of crumbs.
Who can promise that even spring
will blunder through the woods
home?

But essentially she acquiesces. In *Waiting for My Life*, another title that in one phrase captures the essence of her condition as a woman, a mother, and a poet, Pastan sees her existence as "The War between Desire and Dailiness," with the demands of her children ("spoons in the fists / of children, each beating / its own martial measure") in conflict with her desire to write. But the resolution is firm: "Let dailiness win."

To the extent that Pastan acquiesces in the demands of domesticity she has puzzled feminists, but she resists the easy temptation to assign blame to society's prescribed roles. She fiercely defends her integrity as the guardian of the home and family:

Who is it accuses us of safety,
as if the family were soldiers
instead of hostages,
as if the gardens were not mined
with explosive peonies,
as if the most common death
were not by household accident?

— "Who Is It Accuses Us?"

In a 1979 interview with *Poetic Miscellany* (published in *Acts of Mind*) Pastan put feminism in the perspective of the larger issues in poetry: "There are only really a few subjects in poetry: growing old, dying, intellectual or physical passion, the search for self or identity. The smaller subjects we might write about are just ways to get into those basic things. A good poet writes out of everyday life, and, right now, a good part of what a woman might write may be domestic in nature simply because women have been more involved in the domestic. As a woman changes, her poetry will change. The same will be true of men who do already occasionally write so-called 'men's poems' on domestic subjects."

Something of the same candor informs Pastan's use of metaphor. Here too her approach is spare and spontaneous. "I will usually begin a poem with a visual image (my imagination being very vivid)," she told *Poetic Miscellany*, "or sometimes with a line that has just come into my head. . . . the poem will suggest its own form to me, and if I keep myself receptive to it, I will eventually get it into the proper shape." Metaphor is simply her means of showing her reader familiar things in terms of something else, "in a way that you would not ordinarily have thought of putting two things together—then you have learned to see something as if for the first time, and you will see it in a fuller way. After all, what the poet tries to make you do is look freshly at the world."

Typical of Pastan's use of metaphor is "The Five Stages of Grief," in which death is a metaphor for loss—the loss of love, of faith, of youth, of one's children as they grow up. Her five stages are analogous to the stages that Dr. Elizabeth Kübler-Ross described in *On Death and Dying* as experienced by the terminally ill, only in Pastan's poem they are experienced by a woman confronting a crisis in her marriage:

> *Denial* was first.
> I sat down at breakfast
> carefully setting the table
> for two. I passed you the toast—
> you sat there. I passed
> you the paper—you hid
> behind it.

Following denial is anger, then depression ("a poor relation / its suitcase tied together / with string"), then hope in the form of compromise ("And all the time Hope / flashed on and off / in defective neon"), and at last acceptance:

> *Acceptance.* I finally
> reach it.
> But something is wrong.
> Grief is a circular staircase.
> I have lost you.

Still, the marriage endures. In *A Fraction of Darkness* the couple have reached a plateau of mature understanding: "So we try to give / our own lives to each other, to change / places a moment in the slow dance through time." The poet now looks at love wryly, with more than a trace of humor. In "Family Scene: Mid-Twentieth Century" she finds an old photograph of herself and her husband holding their pet dogs by their collars: "Marriage could be the caption, / which frees and confines at the same time." Looking back over their years of marriage, she speculates:

> And didn't it all work out? you ask,
> for there we are, twenty years into our marathon
> caught in black and white and smiling,
> and here we are now.
> Dumb luck, my father would have said,
>   who never quite approved of you.
> But who can ask for anything more of life
> than those strategies of the genes
> or the weather that we call luck?

Bruce Bennett, discussing *The Imperfect Paradise* in the *New York Times Book Review*, observed that overall Linda Pastan's poetry is neither depressing nor despairing. "What is more important, Ms. Pastan's unfailing mastery of her medium holds the darkness firmly in check." It is that control, plus "her own undiminished wonder and puzzlement at the exigencies of life," that led some of her readers to recall Emily Dickinson, a poet whom she greatly admires and to whom she paid tribute in a poem which, in its last lines, says as much about herself as it does Dickinson:

> We think of her hidden in a white dress
> among the folded linens and sachets
> of well-kept cupboards, or just out of sight
> sending jellies and notes with no address
> to all the wondering Amherst neighbors.
> Eccentric as New England weather
> the stiff wind of her mind, stinging or gentle,
> blew two half-imagined lovers off.
> Yet legend won't explain the sheer sanity
> of vision, the serious mischief
> of language, the economy of pain.
>
> —"Emily Dickinson"

PRINCIPAL WORKS: A Perfect Circle of Sun, 1971; Aspects of Eve, 1975; The Five Stages of Grief, 1978; Setting the Table, 1980; Waiting for My Life, 1981; PM/AM: New and Selected Poems, 1982; A Fraction of Darkness, 1985; The Imperfect Paradise, 1988.

ABOUT: Contemporary Authors New Revision Series 18, 1986; Contemporary Literary Criticism 27, 1984; Contemporary Poets, 4th ed., 1985; Dictionary of Literary Biography 5, 1980; Heyen, W. (ed.) American Poets in 1976, 1976; Jackson, R. (ed.) Acts of Mind: Conversations with Contemporary Poets, 1983; Lifshin, L. (ed.) Ariadne's Thread: A Collection of Contemporary Women's Journals, 1982. *Periodicals*—American Poetry Review January–February 1982; Hudson Review Autumn 1978; New York Times Book Review February 20, 1983; September 18, 1988; Parnassus Fall–Winter 1972; Poetry April 1986.

PATTERSON, (HORACE) ORLANDO

(June 5, 1940–   ), American sociologist and novelist, writes: "I was born in Savlamar, Jamaica, the remotest part of a small, discarded colony in an empire on the verge of collapse. As if that was not bad enough, my mother, a comely, strong-willed seamstress, decided two years after my birth that she had had enough of my father and his authoritarian ways and roving eyes. She moved with me to Kingston where she shared a matriarchal household with her two sisters and their mother. My earliest vague memories were of these women struggling with war-time scarcity. My first vivid memory was of a natural disaster indirectly caused by these scarcities. The dread typhoid struck my household as it had a great many other people in the weakened population. My grandmother and my youngest cousin died; another cousin was struck dumb. I was terrified. My mother said, 'Don't worry; we'll survive.' I stopped worrying and we survived. In essence, this pristine experience set the tone and pattern of my childhood.

"My mother moved back to the country when I was about five and I grew up in a dreary country town called May Pen, an ugly dust-bowl in an otherwise beautiful island. I was very lucky in my relationship with my mother. She often did the right things for the right reasons: empha-

ORLANDO PATTERSON

sizing the importance of schoolwork and making unusual effort to ensure that I received the right training and all the books I needed; genuinely interested in, and encouraging of, any and every sign of intellectual precocity on my part; fiercely ambitious for me, to the point where I simply came to assume that only the very best high school and colleges would be good enough for me even though we had no material basis for such expectations.

"She often also did the right things for the wrong reasons; for example, I was forced to eat countless fish-heads and swallow gallons of cod-liver oil because, by some kind of sympathetic magic, they were supposed to be good for my brain. She frequently did the wrong things for the right reasons; I was punished too frequently, and sometimes much too severely. Only in making one important and lasting decision did she do the wrong thing for all the wrong reasons. When I was twelve she reunited with my father thinking that a boy of my age needed the support and steady hand of a father. It was a disaster for her, although she stuck it out with him until his death. My years with my father were extremely unhappy and they came at a very vulnerable time in my education and intellectual development. But I survived that. My technique, perfected by the middle years of my childhood as a way of defending my own autonomy against my mother's powerful personality, was through escape in voluminous reading and excessive fantasy-play, both of which led naturally to writing and a passion for intellectual mind-play.

"My years at Kingston College, the Anglican high school, were critical. I was taught English culture and history, sang Anglican hymns in the Kingston College Boy's Choir and was both frightened and awed by the headmaster, who was also the Suffragan Bishop of Kingston, a small, proud man who wore a purple robe. I dealt with this heavy indoctrination into English civilization by the same means I had survived my mother and father—through withdrawal, fantasy, and intellectual reconstruction. Nothing I was learning had any direct relationship to my surroundings, and much of it was sheer imperialistic propaganda, for example the way in which the period of slavery in Jamaica was treated. This, however, was not a turn-off for me, as it was for so many of my schoolmates. Rather, I saw the content of my education as a fantastic edifice which I could skillfully absorb and interpret as a self-contained thing-in-itself, as I had done with myths and gods and novels from my earliest childhood. Studying English romantic poetry without having a clue what the English countryside looks like is a surprisingly effective way of coming to an appreciation of the autonomy of the literary text. History too was autonomous, as was geography. The unwitting philosophical effect of this bizarre education was a profound commitment to nominalism although I did not know then that that was the name of my prose.

"At the University of the West Indies I swung to the opposite extreme. I threw myself into nationalism and the politics of decolonization. I resented the irrelevance of my previous education and celebrated the realism of the folk. I became fascinated with the Rastafarian cult and their millenarian hope of return to the African motherland and wrote my first novel, *The Children of Sisyphus*, on them and their exilic vision. In consciously rejecting English culture, of course, I was merely welding myself more closely to it. I realized what was happening and developed an acute sense of the absurd. Inevitably I was ensnared by Camus, especially his book *The Myth of Sisyphus*.

"Inevitably, too, I had to go to England. I had a wonderful time at the London School of Economics where I became a member of the *New Left Review* board, reviewed for the *Times Literary Supplement*, published my first two novels and, after being appointed an assistant lecturer upon the completion of my dissertation, published my first academic work based on it: *The Sociology of Slavery: Jamaica 1655–1838*. At twenty-five I found myself on the faculty of one of England's greatest seats of learning, but I was yet to understand, much less come to terms with, the English. One day I met a beautiful, green-eyed Welsh woman who quickly disabused me of the idea that my dilemma was peculiarly West Indian. My English exile, my ambivalence toward the politely disruptive and acquisitive race that had made the very notion of home problematic, had been the fate of others, just across the western hills, for at least a thousand years. Realizing that there would be no quick solution to our problem, we turned to things romantic, got married, quit the L.S.E. and went back to Jamaica.

"That was a wonderful solution to my wife's cultural problems, but only the beginning of mine. Jamaica in 1967 was a materialist nightmare in which a conservative, modernizing government promoted policies which benefited a small, rapacious nouveau-riche elite, at the expense of a vast and burgeoning lumpen proletariat festering in stinking slums. When a radical colleague on the faculty of the University of the West Indies tried to lead discussions among the unemployed he was barred from the country. Upon our protests the troops were called to the campus. With my wife and infant daughter, Rhiannon, I left on a visiting associate professorship to Harvard. A year later, at thirty-one, I accepted a lifetime professorship in Harvard's department of sociology. My third novel, *Die the Long Day*, written on my return to Jamaica, was published the following year, a few months after the birth of my second daughter, Barbara. America was then in the throes of the ethnic revival movement, partly stimulated by the last, atavistic phase of the black civil rights movement. I saw hidden dangers in this development and came to terms intellectually with America by writing a critical treatise on the subject, *Ethnic Chauvinism: The Reactionary Impulse.* The work made me very unpopular with black and Jewish chauvinists. I dropped the subject. There were better reasons to be condemned and I was already involved with more important matters.

"In 1972 Michael Manley and his democratic socialist party had come to power. Manley had invited me to become his special advisor for social policy and development. For most of the seventies I divided my time between research on comparative slavery and teaching at Harvard and research and policy implementation aimed at alleviating urban poverty in Kingston. The Manley reforms failed dismally, including my own efforts in the crime-ridden slums of central Kingston. When he lost office in 1980 I went back to full-time research and in 1982 published a major work, *Slavery and Social Death.* Since then I have been working on a historical sociology of freedom in which I attempt to explain the origins and preeminence of freedom in the western world, my argument being that slavery ex-

plains both. When that work is completed I will return to the study of underdevelopment and urban poverty in the Caribbean. I will also return more seriously to the writing of fiction in the months ahead."

"It is scarcely an exaggeration to say that all of Orlando Patterson's published writings explore the theme of slavery." This apparently sweeping and therefore questionable generalization (by Bridget Jones in *Fifty Caribbean Writers*) proves on examination to be correct. Slavery is not the immediate subject of all of Patterson's work, but the ramifications of slavery— the complex and overlapping philosophical, moral and political questions of freedom of the will, human rights, ethnic identity, moral responsibility—are the central issues of both his fiction and his non-fiction. When he writes, in *Slavery and Social Death*, that "slavery and freedom are intimately connected, that contrary to our atomistic prejudices it is indeed reasonable that those who most denied freedom, as well as those to whom it was most denied, were the very persons most alive to it," he is commenting not only on the social institution of slavery, which most of us believe ceased to exist in the nineteenth century, but upon a condition of life which persists, though altered in form, to the present moment.

Patterson was only twenty-three when his first novel, *The Children of Sisyphus*, was published. Set in the slums of East Kingston, Jamaica, in 1959, it portrays in graphic detail the sordid, wretched lives of people who survive only because they are sustained by hope of some vague future paradise. In this novel the agency of their hope, which proves of course to be delusion, is the Rastafarian cult whose members preach a return to a homeland in Ethiopia. The people are deceived and betrayed by their leaders, but it is their power to endure stoically, to accept finally their existence in a world of absurdity and hopelessness, that gives them their dignity as human beings. Like the existentialist Albert Camus, whose *Myth of Sisyphus* inspired the title as well as the theme of his novel, Patterson here confronts the irrationality of the world with the simple fact of human endurance. Literally and metaphorically the Dungle, a garbage dump, is the center of his characters' lives. The novel begins with three garbage-men on their rounds in a donkey cart:

> They were like men possessed, up there above the city, wretched and lost. Abandoned to a fate which seemed to terrify them, partly because they were perpetually plagued with doubts of its existence, partly because they felt that if indeed it did exist, then in some bizarre way

they already knew what it was. Perhaps, the dismal blankness of their faces seemed to say, perhaps it was nothing more than the workings of the moment. Just them, the garbage-men, them and the empty terror of the uneventful, everlasting now.

Reviewers recognized the broad philosophical implications as well as the stark realism of *The Children of Sisyphus*. The first novel of a very young writer, it carried a burden of self-consciousness—too obvious an "authorial message," according to Kenneth Ramchand in *The West Indian Novel and Its Background*, and "luscious writing," according to C.L.R. James in the *New Left Review*. But Ramchand praised Patterson's picture of the Rastafarian cult as "an ambitious and enterprising attempt to translate social reality into some of its possibilities by fictional means"; and James, who found the novel "both good and serious," was similarly impressed that "Mr. Patterson's prose can tremble on the verge of going over the line but can never shake free from the discipline of the social structure and the sharp concrete realities in which it expresses itself." The struggles of the impoverished characters of *The Children of Sisyphus* are different from but no less intense than the struggle of the well educated young Jamaican of Patterson's second novel, *An Absence of Ruins*, who returns to his home from some years in London with a degree in sociology only to find himself alienated and unable to live in his native culture. The psychological slavery of this protagonist—his desire to escape from his mother, his wife, his homeland, and his self-loathing ("It is no longer, then, that I find life worthless, but that life has found me worthless")—have their parallel in the literal slavery that is the subject of Patterson's third novel, *Die the Long Day*, which is set in eighteenth-century Jamaica on a sugar plantation where a slave, Quasheba, fights heroically but tragically to save her daughter from a ruthless master.

The richly detailed historical background for *Die the Long Day* was familiar to Patterson from the extensive research he had done some years earlier for his doctoral dissertation. Published as *The Sociology of Slavery*, this is a comprehensive survey and analysis of slave society in Jamaica: "the first attempt," Patterson writes, "to analyze, in all its aspects, the nature of the society which existed during slavery in Jamaica, and in particular, to concentrate on the mass of the Negro people whose labor, whose skills, managed to maintain this system without breaking . . . under its yoke." Although the study is confined to Jamaica, it has much wider implications for colonial and social history. The islands of the West Indies, Patterson points out,

"are unique in world history in that they present one of the rare cases of a human society being artificially created for the satisfaction of one clearly defined goal: that of making money through the production of sugar." Hailed as "a major study of Jamaican slavery," *The Sociology of Slavery* cast new light on the whole structure of West Indian society. E. J. Hobsbaum, in the *Guardian*, found it "a lucid, densely packed and extremely intelligent analysis of slavery as a social institution . . . indispensable to all students of the West Indies before emancipation."

Several reviewers of *The Sociology of Slavery* expressed the hope that Patterson would extend his studies beyond the limits of Jamaica and the West Indies. This Patterson did, after many years of research, in *Slavery and Social Death: A Comparative Study*, covering not only African slavery but the entire concept and institution of slavery. As he points out in his Preface: "There is nothing peculiar about the institution of slavery. It has existed from before the dawn of human history right down to the twentieth century, in the most primitive of human societies and in the most civilized. There is no region on earth that has not at some time harbored the institution. Probably there is no group of people whose ancestors were not at one time slaves or slaveholders." Patterson documents this remarkable statement with studies of nearly 200 world cultures, from Africa, Asia, the Middle East, the Pacific, Northern Europe and the Western Hemisphere. What makes the book engrossing as well as informative reading is the fluency of Patterson's writing and his concern with "the symbolic aspects of slavery," seeing slavery "as a relation of domination rather than as a category of legal thought." Ultimately his book moves toward fundamental questions about the nature of freedom itself. He writes in the closing chapter: "Beyond the socio-historical findings is the unsettling discovery that an ideal cherished in the West beyond all others emerged as a necessary consequence of the degradation of slavery and the effort to negate it. The first men and women to struggle for freedom, the first to think of themselves as free in the only meaningful sense of the term, were freedmen. And without slavery there would have been no freedmen."

Of the many scholarly works on slavery that have been published in the last quarter century, David Brion Davis wrote in *New York Review of Books*, Patterson's *Slavery and Social Death* "is in many ways the crowning achievement" and will help "to set out the direction for the next decades of interdisciplinary scholarship." Michael Banton, in the *Times Literary Supplement*, commended the book not only for the range and depth of its historical research but also "for its suggestiveness of new problems." Because *Slavery and Social Death* raises questions about social inequality, Banton writes, "[it] throws a questioning ray upon the present as well." Stanley Aronowitz, in the *Voice Literary Supplement*, agreed that by studying slavery in the large context of world history from earliest times, Patterson sees slavery in a new light—"as a pre-figurative power over contemporary politics and social life." Although Robert Nisbet, in *Commentary*, questioned some of Patterson's concepts and generalizations (as well as his omission of such twentieth-century forms of slavery as the penal camps of the U.S.S.R.), he concluded: "This is a work of solid scholarship that will undoubtedly stand a long time before any effort is made to supersede it."

Deracination, the stripping away of the slave's status as an independent human being as well as of his ancestry and native culture, is the "social death" to which Patterson's title refers. It is also a pivotal issue in Patterson's most controversial book, *Ethnic Chauvinism: The Reactionary Impulse*. This book is addressed to a more immediate and topical question: the ethnic revival of the 1960s and 1970s. Patterson's survey of this phenomenon ranges widely over history and cultures, but it focuses most directly on ethnic movements in the United States, particularly among blacks and Jews. Confronting such sensitive areas as Afro-American studies in universities and Jewish identification with the state of Israel, *Ethnic Chauvinism* inevitably evoked lively response from readers and reviewers. Equally provocative is Patterson's thesis that "ethnicity . . . is an empty faith; it is a commitment to nothing more than the idea of itself." Irrational and divisive, it runs counter to what he considers the "one great idea which, however frequently suppressed, distorted, or violated, remains the supreme intellectual achievement of the [Western] civilization . . . the tradition of universalism, the idea of the brotherhood of mankind, the psychic unity of the human race, and the equality of man's or woman's worth."

Response to Patterson's book ranged from cautious approval to outright disapproval. Morris U. Schappes, in *Jewish Currents*, wrote: "Patterson wants to dissipate and disorient the entire ethnic upsurge and revival of the past 25 years and suck us all back into the cosmopolitan swamp in which he is floundering." But others, like Martin Glazer of Harvard University, compared the book to David Riesman's monumental studies of ethnicity of some thirty years earlier. (A former student and later a colleague of Riesman's, Patterson acknowledges his indebtedness to Riesman in the Preface to *Ethnic Chauvinism*.) Kenneth Clark, the eminent black sociologist, found the book "impeccable in its scholarship, thoughtful, tightly reasoned. But its outstanding quality is its courage in daring to confront fashionable neo-conservatism, to meet head on the insidiously anti-black position that seems to me inherent in the pro-ethnic posture."

Patterson is the son of Charles A. Patterson, a police detective, and Almina (Morris) Patterson. He received his B.Sc. degree in economics from the University of the West Indies on a Jamaican government scholarship and after some brief experience in social work for the Institute of Social and Economic Research in Jamaica, he went to England on a Commonwealth scholarship. He was awarded his doctorate in 1965. Patterson came to the United States as professor of sociology at Harvard in 1971, but he remains active in his research on social problems in the Caribbean. He has been a visiting scholar and professor at many institutions in the United States and abroad—among them the universities of Mainz and Trier, Cambridge, the West Indies, and Princeton. He has received several grants from the National Endowment for the Humanities, and in 1978–1979 he was a Guggenheim Fellow. He has been married since 1965 to Nerys Wyn Thomas whose assistance in translating Welsh and Irish documents and whose expertise on Celtic culture he acknowledges in his Preface to *Slavery and Social Death*.

PRINCIPAL WORKS: The Sociology of Slavery, 1969; Ethnic Chauvinism: The Reactionary Impulse, 1977; Slavery and Social Death: A Comparative Study, 1982. *Novels*—The Children of Sisyphus, 1964; An Absence of Ruins, 1967; Die the Long Day, 1972.

ABOUT: Contemporary Authors 65–68, 1977; Dance, D. C. (ed.) Fifty Caribbean Writers, 1986; Ramchand, K. The West Indian Novel and Its Background, 1970. *Periodicals*—Commentary April 1983; Guardian December 1, 1967; Jewish Currents October 1981; Nation December 31, 1977; New Left Review May–June 1964; New Republic February 11, 1978; New Statesman November 10, 1967; New York Review of Books February 17, 1983; New York Times Book Review September 10, 1972; Times Literary Supplement September 9, 1983; (Village) Voice Literary Supplement December 1982; Worldview April 1983.

*PAVLOVIĆ, MIODRAG (November 28, 1928–   ), Yugoslav poet, essayist, short-story writer, and playwright, was born in Novi Sad, the capital of the Yugoslav autonomous province of Vojvodina, to Branko and Kosara (Ilić) Pavlović. He studied medicine at the University of Belgrade, completing his studies in 1954, two years after the publication of his first book of poems, *87 Pesama* (87 Poems). He worked as a

päv´ lō vic´, mi´ ō dräg

MIODRAG PAVLOVIĆ

physician until 1956, when he decided to devote himself to literature. In 1959 he took a position as editor with the publishing house Prosveta in Belgrade and worked there until 1983. He is now retired, but takes part in the activities of the Serbian Academy of Sciences and Arts, of which he is a member. He is also a member of the Serbian Writers' Union and the Serbian PEN Club. Pavlović's poems have been translated into many languages, including French, English, German, Russian, Polish, Czech, Slovak, Slovene, Greek, Italian, Spanish, Romanian, Hungarian, Swedish, Hindi, Turkish, and Belorussian. His work has appeared in anthologies, literary magazines, and individual volumes.

Pavlović's eminence in Yugoslav letters is due, in part, to the impact that his first book, *87 Pesama*, made in 1952. It is a free-verse, "modernist" work that is "cool" rather than personal or romantic, that puts considerable distance between the regarding eye of the poet and the subject of his contemplation, which is conveyed by the "objective correlative." It is not by any means "confessional"—quite unlike the work of, say, Desanka Maksimović, who was writing, in traditional measures, highly personal poems of "witness" about the horrors of World War II at about the same time. Pavlović was not without emotion; and he, too, responded to the horrors of his time and place, but he did so by means of charged, economical, universalizing imagery. His technique was inspired by trends in the English-speaking world, particularly the work (which he knew well) of T. S. Eliot, W. B. Yeats, and W. H. Auden. In fact, he co-edited

and translated into Serbo-Croatian an anthology of contemporary English poetry in 1957 (with Svetozar Brkić).

It is a mistake to assume that Pavlović was attacked or harassed in the 1950s because his modernist technique did not conform to the officially approved realistic modes. Tito had broken with the Cominform in 1948, and "socialist realism," as opposed to ordinary realism, had made few converts among the writers and critics of the time. "Optimistic determinism" was not championed by any but a few doctrinaire Marxists. Moreover, most of the left-wing poets of the prewar era and the war years were, like Oskar Davičo, surrealists and did not endorse writing that was bent or distorted by didactic intent. Ivo Vidan of the University of Zagreb puts it in this way: "To be such an intransigent modernist as he [Pavlović] was in the early postwar years was certainly a position of independence and even perhaps courage. Yet for many decades now this kind of modernism has been totally uncontroversial politically. . . . Style and poetics have stopped being an ideological issue."

Representative of the poems in Pavlović's first book is one called "Underground":

On the wooden wall
a longlegged spider
hunts its own shadow
in the web

Down the rotten stairs
a yellow light
spits in the cellar

The cellar is deep
and sinks deeper
under the damp walls

A door
has shut someone
inside midnight

And an ant
looking like a man
raises his hand
at the bottom of the stairs

His cry
does not reach me

—trans. Stephen Stepanchev

The poem comes out of the pitiless, debasing experiences of World War II in Europe, when war and revolution destroyed the social fabric and made withdrawal from compassion a matter of survival, when alienation was commonplace. The cry of the "ant-man" does not reach the speaker. The cellar imagery, the environment of spider and ant, the yellow light spitting in the cellar, the door shutting someone inside midnight—all of this is shocking, depressing, and memorable. But the poem is not about a specific experience of the underground man; it is not a realistic account of a "true" incident. It is stripped, concise, objective. It represents symbolic action.

His technique now perfected, Pavlović moved on to subject matter unconnected with the immediate past. Like Robert Lowell, Randall Jarrell, and W. S. Merwin in the 1950s, he turned to myth and folktale archetypes for themes, choosing to begin with classical Greek mythology, the Slavs and Greeks having had close association in the Balkans since ancient times. In his *Mleko Iskoni* (Milk of Origin, 1962) Pavlović deals with familiar Greek myths, as the titles of some of the poems indicate: "The Birth of Aphrodite," "Agamemnon Appears," "Orestes at the Acropolis," "Persephone," and "The Son of Deucalion and Pyrrha Speaks." The most striking of these poems is the one entitled "Odysseus Speaks," in which the great warrior and sailor is represented as rejecting the harbors and temptations of the land in order to stay free. He wants to sail on forever: "They say I'm a seaman who has gone off course / but my secret is quite different: / in this way I'm saving myself from the land." This resolute refusal to dock in the harbor and yield to the responsibilities (and joys) of Ithaca calls up an image of Tennyson's "Ulysses," who also saw eternal seafaring as his destiny.

Having made his bow to Greece, Pavlović next turned to the history and mythology of his own people. The shift is evident in the collection *Velika Skitija* (Great Scythia, 1969), "Scythia" being the name sometimes given to the lands of the southern Slavs. (In fact, the Scythians were a non-Slavic people who roamed the steppes of southern Russia in ancient times.) The first poem in the collection, "The Slavs Beneath Parnassus," is transitional; it suggests that the Greek bards will accept the Slavs as "new sons" and teach them to sing: "our nakedness will be clothed in words like the birchtree with leaves in spring." What follows is a sequence of poems that focuses on events in the history of Serbia during the thirteenth and fourteenth centuries, when it was a powerful state rivaling Byzantium and aspiring to succeed it. For example, "The Conqueror of the Capital" is a dramatic monologue in which the ghost of Tsar Dushan speaks of entering Constantinople, his ultimate goal, only after his death "two hours' ride from the city." Actually, it was left to the Turks to conquer Constantinople. The manifest irony of the poem reminds one of the tone of C. P. Cavafy's poems on historical themes.

The crucial event of Serbia's medieval history was the battle of Kosovo Polje (Field of Black Birds) in 1389, when the armies of Prince Lazar engaged those of the Turkish Sultan Murat and lost. The result was five hundred years of occupation by the Turkish Empire and cultural oblivion, a time when the spirit of national resistance was fostered only by the heroic ballads of folk poets singing to the accompaniment of a single-stringed instrument called the *gusla*. The decisive defeat of 1389 underlies the psyche of Yugoslavs even today and seems to motivate them. Miroslav Krleža, a Croatian author, once said: "We are boring a tunnel through from the fourteenth century to the present." In *Velika Skitija* Pavlović deals with the national theme in such poems as "Speech on the Eve of Battle," "Conversation on the Battlefield," and "The Prince's Supper."

The poet's explorations of the Greek and Serbian past inevitably led him to a study of Christianity. In *Svetli i Tamni Praznici* (Light and Dark Holidays, 1971) he takes up such stories as that of the prodigal son and describes the exemplary lives of monks, martyrs, and Jesus. In *Hododarje* (Pilgrimage, 1971) he visits the holy places of history, East and West, and considers the ideas that animate them.

Pavlović's range kept widening. Archaeological discoveries in Vojvodina dating back to the Stone Age and the Early Bronze Age led him to a study of anthropological works on the prehistory of mankind all over the world. He became interested in archetypes, in links between cultures and between the historical record and the present. In his book *Karike* (Links, 1977), which consists of three cycles of poems, he explores links between myth and contemporary life, the past and the present, and the world of the living and the dead. This kind of linkage appears also in *Pevanja na Viru* (1977; translated as *Singing at the Whirlpool*) and *Divno Cudo* (A Divine Miracle, 1982). In *Bekstva po Srbiji* (Flights Through Serbia, 1979) he looks into Serbian history for standards by which to judge the present.

Pavlović justifies his preoccupation with myth and archetype in these terms: "Myths are the grammar of poetic thought, the grammar of imagination. . . . It cannot be otherwise: archetypes define man's basic relationships and these basic relationships come about in life and history." This emphasis on myth has led to a wave of interest in national history and cultural tradition in Yugoslavia, according to Aleksandar Petrov, who notes that, after all, the human psyche keeps creating new Hectors and new Agamemnons.

WORKS IN ENGLISH TRANSLATION: Collections of Pavlović's verse include Joachim Neugroschel's *The Conqueror in Constantinople*, 1976, Bernard Johnson's *The Slavs*

Beneath Parnassus, 1985, and Barry Callaghan's *A Voice Locked in Stone*, 1985. Barry Callaghan also translated *Singing at the Whirlpool*, 1983. English translations of his poems also appear in *Contemporary Yugoslav Poetry*, edited by Vasa D. Mihailovich, 1977. Stephen Stepanchev's translations of some of his poems are in *Sumac* 2, Winter–Spring 1970, and *Seneca Review* 4, December 1973.

ABOUT: Columbia Dictionary of Modern European Literature, 1980; Eekman, T. Thirty Years of Yugoslav Literature (1945–1975), 1978; Encyclopedia of World Literature in the 20th Century, rev. ed., 1983; Johnson, B. *Introduction to* The Slavs Beneath Parnassus, 1985; Marteau, R. *Afterword to* A Voice Locked in Stone, 1985; World Literature Since 1945, 1973. *Periodicals*—American Poetry Review January–February 1984; Books Abroad Autumn 1970, Spring 1972, Summer 1975; Canadian Slavonic Papers September 1978; Guardian December 19, 1985; Scottish Slavonic Review Spring 1986; Times Literary Supplement October 11, 1985; World Literature Today Spring 1977, Spring 1978, Winter 1981, Autumn 1986.

GEORGES PEREC

PEREC, GEORGES (March 7, 1936–March 3, 1982), French novelist, was born of Polish-Jewish parents in Paris. He lost his father on June 16, 1940, from untended war wounds, and was evacuated to Villard-de-Lans in the Vichy zone in 1942. His mother was deported by the German occupation authorities and died almost certainly at Auschwitz. Perec was brought up by his paternal aunt Esther and her husband David Bienenfeld, a well-to-do pearl trader. They returned to Paris in 1945 and formally adopted the nine-year-old Perec. His fragmentary memories of life before 1945 are recorded in his autobiographical work, *W ou le souvenir d'enfance* (1975; translated as *W or The Memory of Childhood*). Perec does not appear to have been entirely happy in his adoptive home and, after trying to run away (the escapade was narrated in a television film, *Les Lieux d'une fugue* [Runaway Places, 1975]), he was sent to board at the Collège Geoffroy Saint-Hilaire at Etampes, some forty miles south of Paris.

Georges Perec obtained his *baccalauréat* in 1954, after a final year under the philosophy teacher Jean Duvignaud, who introduced him to the literary circles of the Royaumont Centre, the periodical *Arguments*, and the *Nouvelle Nouvelle Revue française*. He pursued his studies first at the Lycée Henri IV (1954–1955) and then at the Sorbonne (1955–1956, history; 1956–1957, sociology) in increasingly desultory fashion. The serious depression he suffered in this period is the subject of the second-person narrative *Un Homme qui dort* (1967; translated as *A Man Asleep*). However, his decision to be a writer, which he had made at around the age of eighteen, never wavered.

Perec was drafted for the regular twenty-eight months' military service in January, 1958, and was trained as a paratrooper at airbases near Pau. His status as a war orphan exempted him from active service in Algeria and he was eventually transferred to headquarters staff in Paris, obtaining early release in December 1959. During this period he became a member of a left-wing group which took the name "La Ligne générale" in homage to the Soviet filmmaker Sergei Eisenstein. The group's aim was to develop a radical, Marxist aesthetic and to launch its own journal. Though the journal never appeared, many of the group's ideas found expression in articles (by Perec and others) on Alain Resnais' film *Hiroshima mon amour* and on realism in literature—articles which were published in various periodicals, including *Partisans*, in the early 1960s. Perec was not a supporter of the "new novel" of Alain Robbe-Grillet, and later comparisons between the two writers are usually based on misapprehensions about their respective aims.

In 1960, Perec and Paulette Petras moved into a flat on Rue de Quatrefages, in the Latin Quarter. They married shortly before leaving in October 1960 for a year in Sfax (Tunisia), where Paulette was employed as a teacher. Perec's first published novel, *Les Choses. Une Histoire des années soixante* (1965; translated as *Things. A Story of the Sixties*) bears obvious traces of this experience as well as of the lives of many of the Perecs' friends in Paris in the early 1960s. In

1962 Perec was appointed archivist at the Neurophysiological Research Laboratory attached to the Hôpital Saint-Antoine in Paris. He remained a professional archivist and information retrieval officer until 1979. It is probable that there are significant connections to be made between Perec's scientific and literary activities.

Most of Perec's writing prior to *Les Choses* has been lost. This short novel, as deeply molded by Flaubert's *Sentimental Education* as by Barthes' *Mythologies*, won the Prix Renaudot shortly after its publication in 1965 for its accurate observation of the social dilemma of a whole generation, the first in France to be confronted by massive consumerism. The novel's intentional ambiguity and controlled irony make it a literary achievement of a high order, irrespective of its value as a sociological document.

Perec abhorred the idea of "inspiration" and sought stimulus and support for his writing in formal constraints. In 1967 he became a member of the Oulipo (Ouvroir de Littérature Potentielle, "Workshop for Potential Literature"), founded in 1960 by Raymond Queneau and the mathematician François Le Lionnais. The Oulipo was devoted to exploring the creative potential of formal rules, both those attested to by past literature and those invented by the Oulipoists themselves and usually based on mathematics. Perec quickly proved himself the most brilliant verbal craftsman of the group, and perhaps of all time, in works such as *La Disparition* (Disappearance, 1969), written without the letter E; in *Les Revenentes* (Ghosts, 1972), written without the vowels a, i, o, u; and in the isogrammatic poetry of *Ulcérations* (1974) and *Alphabets* (1976). Perec was also associated from 1965 to 1970 with the artistic community of Le Moulin d'Andé in Normandy, but broke with it definitively in 1970.

Between 1968 and 1973 Perec brought his acute command of verbal form to the renewal of the German *Hörspiel*, or radio play. He wrote, in collaboration with his translator Eugen Helmle and the musician Philippe Drogoz, a series of experimental pieces of which the first, *Die Maschine* (1968), is now seen as the foundation stone of "das neue Hörspiel." Perec's involvement in the cinema dates from the early 1970s. Not all of his film scripts have been made into films, and many remain unpublished. His first film, codirected by Bernard Queysanne, is a remarkable recreation of his novel *Un Homme qui dort*, and won the Prix Jean Vigo in 1974. He went on to make *Les Lieux d'une fugue* (Runaway Places, 1975) unaided and, in 1979, with Robert Bober, a poignant two-hour television film on Ellis Island, also published as a book

(*Récits d'Ellis Island. Histoires d'errance et d'espoir*), in which he explores the meaning of his Jewish identity more fully than in *W ou le souvenir d'enfance*.

Between 1971 and 1975 Perec undertook his second analysis with J.-B. Pontalis, which ended by mutual agreement shortly after the publication of Perec's autobiographical novel *W ou le souvenir d'enfance*. This disturbing book recounts in alternating chapters two stories which at first seem to have nothing to do with each other, but which converge at the end on the horrifying vision of Nazi concentration camps. It is a powerful and moving memorial of the unspeakable loss which lies behind Perec's life and career as a writer. Its bizarre but convincing form represents an innovation in the art of autobiography as significant as Stendhal's *Life of Henry Brulard*.

Perec's concern to record his past and present experience of living gave rise also to *La Boutique obscure* (The Gloomy Shop, 1973), the transcription of 124 dreams of the period 1968–1973; to a major, as yet mostly unpublished project entitled *Lieux*; and to numerous shorter texts such as "Inventaire des aliments liquides et solides que j'ai ingurgités au cours de l'année 1974" (Inventory of the Liquid and Solid Foods I Consumed in the Course of the Year 1974) (in *Action poétique*, 1976). The most popular and haunting of Perec's writing about memory is *Je me souviens* (I Remember, 1978), a sequence of 479 numbered sentences all beginning "Je me souviens . . . ," recording micro-events of everyday life in the 1950s, none of them purely personal, none of them belonging to the domain of official history: pop songs, sporting heroes, advertising jingles, half-forgotten film stars, memories of the very web of social life presented without interpretation. *Je me souviens* has been adapted for the stage with great success by Sami Frey, and imitated in English by Gilbert Adair.

The main project occupying Perec after 1969, and occupying him intensely after Raymond Queneau's death in 1976, was the design and composition of *La Vie mode d'emploi* (1978; translated as *Life A User's Manual*). This huge novel, complete with index, chronology, and an alphabetical checklist of stories, describes the contents of the rooms in a Parisian apartment house as if the façade had been removed (one of its sources is Saul Steinberg's famous drawing of a New York apartment house with its façade removed, meticulously described by Perec in a long essay on space, *Espèces d'espaces*, in 1974). As it describes each room, chapter by chapter, it tells the stories of some of the people who live or lived there, or who had owned or made some of the objects contained within the description. One central story emerges, that of Percival Bartlebooth, an English millionaire, who had set out at the age of twenty-five to conduct his life according to a plan which would leave no trace. For ten years, he learns to paint watercolors from the painter Serge Valène, who is to some extent the narrator of the chapters set on the staircase. For twenty years he tours the world, painting one seascape a fortnight, each of which is mailed back to the craftsman Gaspard Winckler, who mounts the paintings and then cuts them into unique, 750-piece jigsaw puzzles. For the final twenty years of his life-plan, Bartlebooth reassembles the jigsaws, at the rate of one per fortnight, has the original watercolors reglued and separated from their backings by a special process, and returns the paintings to their places of origin, where they are dipped in a detergent solution and restored to their original state of blank paper.

Bartlebooth's self-effacing plan, like those of most of the hundreds of collectors, businessmen, racing cyclists, crooks, croupiers, diplomats, artists and craftsmen of every variety who people these pages, is thwarted. It is thwarted by blindness, in the first place; and it is thwarted with supreme cunning by the puzzle-maker Winckler, whose revenge on his paymaster is plotted— though it is only on a second reading that this can be noticed easily—from the very first chapter.

La Vie mode d'emploi is constructed from an interlocking set of formal constraints and can be seen as a vindication of the work of the Oulipo, as a fulfillment of the potential of potential literature. But it is not necessary to know its secret rules to read this masterpiece as a work of literature. It offers us no explicit instructions on how life should be used; but by showing such a teeming diversity of things and lives, and by showing both the necessity and the impossibility of conducting a plan or project to its conclusion, it says, obliquely, what it means to have "that ephemeral thing" called life.

Characteristic of all Perec's writing are the reuse of the actual words of other writers in new contexts and the inscription of details drawn from his own life and those of his friends in discreet, often secret ways. In La Vie mode d'emploi these techniques are used on a massive scale, and there is hardly a sentence in the work which is not predetermined by a constraint, a quotation, or a personal "intextus."

La Vie mode d'emploi won the Prix Médicis in 1978, and from 1979 Perec was able to live by his pen alone. He wrote a short novel about a forged painting in which other forged paintings are represented, Un Cabinet d'amateur (A Private Gallery, 1979), and (in collaboration) a film-script, Alfred et Marie, ou dites-le avec des fleurs (Alfred and Marie, or Say It with Flowers), in both of which names and stories from La Vie mode d'emploi are reused.

Apart from his work in films, on Récits d'Ellis Island and on Catherine Binet's Les Jeux de la Comtesse Dolingen de Gratz (The Games of Countess Dolingen de Gratz, 1980–1982) which he produced, Perec's main project in the last year of his life was a detective novel, entitled Cinquante-Trois Jours (Fifty-three Days) in homage to Stendhal, whose La Chartreuse de Parme was dictated in fifty-three days. He worked intensively on this novel during a period as writer-in-residence at the University of Brisbane in 1981, but was unable to complete it on his return to Paris because of ill health. He died of lung cancer in 1982.

Perec's achievements are so diverse and so spectacular as to defy any easy categorization. He was without doubt the greatest innovator of literary form of his generation. In life as in his work, he was a model of discretion and respect, all the while maintaining an irrepressible sense of humor. For all their formal complexity, many of his major works are joyous celebrations of life, and of the life of words. La Vie mode d'emploi was rightly hailed as a comic masterpiece when it appeared in English translation, and slighter pieces such as the stage play L'Augmentation and the spoof scientific article "Experimental Demonstration of the Tomatotopic Organization in the Soprano (cantatrix sopranica L.)" (written in quasi-English) must rank among the funniest pieces of wordplay ever invented.

Perec's culture, based on a traditional French education, was surprisingly international in its breadth; and his subtle engagement with the major intellectual issues of his time did not bind him narrowly to its passing fashions. He followed a unique and individual path, taking much from contemporary mentors such as Roland Barthes and Raymond Queneau, but much also from older and foreign writers in whom he found "a kind of kinship": Laurence Sterne, Thomas Mann, Malcolm Lowry, James Joyce, and Jules Verne are as important, in Perec's literary universe, as the standard French classics; Flaubert along with Herman Melville and Franz Kafka are sources less of inspiration than of examples and of textual practice. Among contemporary writers, he was closest to the American novelist Harry Mathews and to Italo Calvino, both also members of the Oulipo. As a result, and despite the special difficulties of translation, Perec's major works belong essentially to world literature rather than just to French.

It is too early to make an estimate of Perec's influence on other writers. What he offers is a new (though in fact very ancient) image of the writer's task as the modest exercise of a skill or craft. Like a carpenter or smith, Perec makes few theoretical statements about his difficult profession of working words into new shapes. His unpretentious but nonetheless formidable ability to handle words as things lies near the source of his creation of literary works of unparalleled power and originality, which succeed, by these unexpected means, in communicating a comprehensive vision of the world—a vision from which the artist himself is by no means absent.

WORKS IN ENGLISH TRANSLATION: *Les Choses. A Story of the Sixties* was translated by Helen R. Lane in 1967. A new translation by D. M. Bellos was published as *Things. A Story of the Sixties* in 1990. Bellos also translated *Life A User's Manual* in 1987 (with two chapters translated by Harry Mathews) and *W or The Memory of Childhood* in 1988. *A Man Asleep*, translated by A. N. Leak, was published in 1990. Translations of *La Disparition* (by G. Adair) and of Perec's plays and essays (by Bellos) are in progress.

In the summer of 1988 the Avignon Festival paid homage to Perec with "Galaxie Georges Perec," a program of films, exhibitions, radio broadcasts, workshops, and readings from Oulipo writings. Also presented were dramatizations of his *L'Augmentation, Je me souviens, W ou le souvenir d'enfance*, and *La Vie mode d'emploi*.

ABOUT: *Periodicals*—New York Review of Books June 16, 1988; New York Times November 26, 1988; New York Times Book Review November 15, 1987; January 8, 1989; Times Literary Supplement October 30, 1987; August 5, 1988; September 2, 1988; February 10, 1989. The Review of Contemporary Fiction is due to publish an issue devoted to Perec in Fall 1991.

PETRAKIS, HARRY MARK (June 5, 1923–), American novelist, short-story writer, and memoirist, was born in St. Louis, the son of the Rev. Mark Emmanuel Petrakis, a priest of the Eastern Orthodox Church, and Stella Christoulakis Petrakis. In *Stelmark: A Family Recollection* (1970), the son recounts how his father and mother emigrated from the island of Crete to America in 1916 to minister to a Greek immigrant coal-mining community in Price, Utah. After serving in parishes in Savannah, Georgia, and St. Louis, Father Petrakis was called to be pastor of a Greek Orthodox church in Chicago, where he remained until his death twenty-eight years later and where Harry and his several brothers and sisters grew up. His childhood memories, as he describes them,

HARRY MARK PETRAKIS

"tangled and ambulatory, had to do with what was almost totally Greek. Greek parents, Greek language, Greek food, Greek school, and Greek church. There were artifacts that belonged to the new land—candy and baseball, ice cream and movies. For the most part these existed as a kind of exotic bazaar outside the gates of the real city in which I lived."

Stelmark (the title is a conflation of his parents' Christian names) begins with Petrakis' childhood and ends with the acceptance in 1965, by Edward Weeks, editor of the *Atlantic Monthly*, of his story "Pericles of 31st Street," which "told of an old Greek vendor with a pushcart of hot dogs and peanuts, a defiant old man burning with pride in his heritage who teaches that pride to a group of storekeepers exploited by a landlord they were fearful of challenging." Petrakis had been writing and submitting stories unsuccessfully for ten years, and the *Atlantic* acceptance was a momentous turning-point for him, "the redeeming of my life, . . . the miracle of being born once again. . . . I felt like Lazarus," he said. Reprinted along with fifteen other stories, "Pericles" lent its title to Petrakis' first collection, published in 1965; the volume was nominated for a National Book Award. *Stelmark* also received very enthusiastic reviews. J. W. Hattman, writing in *Best Sellers*, called it "a work filled with humor, warmth, love, and wonderful people. It describes a kind of growing up that will never again be able to occur in this country, and it describes it in such a way that . . . [it seems] very unfortunate that it cannot still happen." To R. H. Donahugh, writing in *Library Journal*, "this short, really quite wonderful book" was "a celebration of life."

Nearly all of Petrakis' novels, as well as many of his short stories, treat the problems and joys attendant upon being an immigrant in America. It is, of course, a subject covered by several other writers, but none—not even William Saroyan, with whom he is often compared—have mined it so deeply as Petrakis, or for so long a period. His first novel, *Lion at My Heart*, describes the conflict between a staunchly Greek father and the elder of his two very American sons. *The Odyssey of Kostas Volakis* is the moving account of the coming to America of the title character and his wife Katerina. Their story extends from 1919 to 1954 and traces the progress of three generations through humble achievement and bitter family tragedy. The first chapter contains a wonderfully evocative contrast between Kostas and Katerina's wedding in Crete, just before their embarkation, and their disillusioning arrival in a dingy, miserable Chicago, "a region of grayness and gloom. Beyond a maze of tracks and shacks loomed the great gable-roofed mills. In the center of a group of stacks, a massive blast furnace lit the underbelly of the sky with flashes of flame. 'Here the black snow falls,'" said their cousin, who had come to meet them, "'Here there is never any daylight, and men work like tiny bugs beside the giant furnaces.'" The novel was well reviewed and won three prizes—the Friends of American Writers award, the Society of Midland Authors award, and the Friends of Literature award.

Among Petrakis' other novels are *A Dream of Kings* , about the life, loves, and sorrows of Leonidas Matsoukas, who appears to be, in his courageous attitude toward everything he faces, a grand, epic hero in the greatest Greek tradition. (This novel was also nominated for a National Book Award.) *In the Land of Morning* is a retelling, set in present-day Chicago, of the myth surrounding Electra and Aegisthus, Clytemnestra and Orestes. *The Hour of the Bell* is a historical novel set in 1820–1821, during the initial phase of the Greeks' ten-year struggle to free their country from Ottoman Turkish domination. Filled with blood, butchery, and betrayal, it examines the atrocities committed on both sides and goes far to explain the continuing animosity between Greeks and Turks. *Nick the Greek* tells the story of the legendary gambler Nicholas Andreas Dandolos, from his arrival in America in 1919 to his death in Los Angeles in 1966 and his epic funeral in Las Vegas. *Days of Vengeance* returns to Petrakis' favorite theme, emigration from Greece to America in the first decades of the twentieth century. *Ghost of the Sun* recounts the later life of Leonidas Matsoukas, the hero of

A Dream of Kings; to Robert H. Donahugh it seemed a gratifying sequel and "a most satisfying novel" in its own right.

Petrakis is a prolific writer of short stories, most of which have been collected into book form. They are frequently concerned with the Greek-American experience, with the tragedies and victories of an immigrant's daily life, and more often than not they are set in Chicago. The sixteen stories in *Pericles on 31st Street* were followed by eleven in *The Waves of Night and Other Stories*; twenty-eight appear in *A Petrakis Reader*, and thirty-four in *Collected Stories*. In a foreword to the last-named collection, the author writes of the "unusual appeal and joy" of short stories: "In the last couple of decades, the novels I've written have been gratifying and the main source of our support. But my attachment to the short story remains. From time to time the longing to write one is reawakened and I grope for a few opening lines. It's like pushing a small frail vessel out to sea. Will it stay afloat? Will the journey itself produce some magic of discovery? Nothing should be totally clear because the earth is a realm of infinite complexity, and unrequited love as well as unjustified suffering must be accepted as part of the mystery."

Petrakis has also written the screenplays for *A Dream of Kings* (with Ian Hunter, 1969) and *In the Land of Morning* (1974). In the early 1960s, for the television series *The Dick Powell Show*, he wrote the teleplays for "Pericles on 31st Street" (with Sam Peckinpah, 1961) and "The Judge" (with Bruce Geller, 1962). In 1978 he wrote the teleplay for Stephen Crane's "The Blue Hotel." He is also the author of *The Founder's Touch: The Life of Paul Galvin of Motorola* (1965), a flat, curiously eulogistic "official" biography of Galvin (1895–1959), a self-made man and the founder of a large U.S. electronics company, now defunct. *Reflections: A Writer's Life, A Writer's Work* (1983) is a continuation of the personal memoirs begun with *Stelmark*.

PUBLISHED WORKS: *Novels*—Lion at My Heart, 1959; The Odyssey of Kostas Volakis, 1963; A Dream of Kings, 1966; In the Land of Morning, 1973; The Hour of the Bell, 1976; Nick the Greek, 1979; Days of Vengeance, 1983; Ghost of the Sun, 1990. *Collected short stories*—Pericles on 31st Street, 1965; The Waves of Night and Other Stories, 1969; A Petrakis Reader, 1978; Collected Stories, 1987. *Non-fiction*—The Founder's Touch: The Life of Paul Galvin of Motorola, 1965; Stelmark, 1970; Reflections, 1983.

ABOUT: Contemporary Authors New Revision Series 4, 1981; Contemporary Novelists, 4th ed., 1986; Who's Who in America, 1988–1989. *Periodicals*—America June 8, 1963; October 8, 1966; Atlantic August 1959, December 1966, October 1976, September 1983; Best

Sellers June 1, 1963; October 1, 1966; June 15, 1969; September 1, 1970; March 15, 1973; January 1977; November 1983; Booklist January 15, 1987; Chicago Review Winter 1977; Chicago Sunday Tribune June 21, 1959; November 4, 1979; Choice July–August 1973, May 1987; Christian Science Monitor June 21, 1969; April 11, 1973; December 29, 1976; Kirkus Service April 1, 1959; March 15, 1978; September 1, 1979; June 1, 1983; Library Journal June 1, 1959; May 15, 1963; July 1966; June 15, 1969; October 15, 1970; March 15, 1973; December 1, 1976; June 1, 1978; December 15, 1979; August 1983; May 15, 1990; New York Herald Tribune Book Review August 16, 1959; June 23, 1963; New York Times Book Review June 28, 1959; August 11, 1963; October 2, 1966; June 29, 1969; September 13, 1970; March 11, 1973; October 3, 1976; August 28, 1983; Old Northwest December 1976; Saturday Review August 8, 1959; October 1, 1966; June 28, 1969; October 3, 1970; Sewanee Review July 1978; Times Literary Supplement March 11, 1960; Washington Post Book Week September 25, 1966; January 6, 1980.

JAYNE ANNE PHILLIPS

PHILLIPS, JAYNE ANNE (July 19, 1952–   ), American novelist, short-story writer, and poet, was born in Buckhannon, West Virginia, the middle child and only daughter of Russell Phillips, a contractor, and Martha Jane (Thornhill) Phillips, a schoolteacher. Growing up in a small and very provincial town, she learned early on the importance of defining oneself and one's private space by escaping into the world of reading and storytelling. She told an interviewer for *Publishers Weekly* in 1984 that "somehow very early I got the idea that language was some kind of private, secretive means of travel, a way of living your own life." Although she left Buckhannon and West Virginia when she finished college, she also acknowledges that a large part of herself is still rooted in her native state: "Family and tradition are what's important there. It's hemmed in by hills and valleys. People don't *leave* West Virginia." These two quite separate pressures—the urge to break away from one's roots and live a free and private life, and the need to return to one's roots in family and social structure—are reflected almost in counterpoint in Phillips' work.

By the time Jayne Anne Phillips entered West Virginia University in 1970 she was writing poetry, some of which she published in on- and off-campus literary magazines. She received her B.A. magna cum laude in 1974 and set out on a journey of self-discovery that took her eventually to the West Coast. Supporting herself with a variety of jobs but mainly working as a waitress, she drifted from California to Colorado, experiencing at first hand the rootless, affectless life of America "on the road"—street people, drug addicts, prostitutes, the cast-offs, rejects, and misfits of the 1970s. This—her own—generation, Phillips has observed, was different from the rebellious but goal-directed and idealistic generation of the 1960s: "unlike the people of the '60s, we didn't have a strong sense of goals, nor the illusion that we could make a difference." Crushed and demoralized by the accelerating war in Vietnam and the political scandals in Washington, she felt that "people began to experience a kind of massive ennui. People felt on their own. Kids dropping acid did it to obliterate themselves, not to have a religious experience. Only people with a strong sense of self came through."

Phillips' earliest stories—most of them short, impressionistic pieces that could be described as prose poems—are a sensitive register of this generation. She had learned from writing poetry the valuable lessons of precision and the compression of ideas in powerful images rather than extended narrative. The results are often no more than a single long paragraph, a fragment of story that nevertheless explodes with emotion. "The Powder of Angels, and I'm Yours," a mere two pages in *Black Tickets,* enters the ravaged mind of a young American girl who has been involved in drug-running in Colombia and ends up in a mental hospital in Washington:

> She could see Arlington Cemetery under gray pellets, rows of dumb stones. Embroidery. She pulled the thread in and out, working the plumed tail feathers. They asked her why she damned herself, they asked her why she didn't. All day Sunday the ministers came with their pamphlets. She liked to watch the priests in their feather-

stitched robes. Blessing their vials of water, they touched fingers to the foreheads of the monstrous. *Domine domine* they crooned, as each angel closed her eyes. . . .

Phillips launched her professional writing career modestly with the publication in 1976 of *Sweethearts*, a collection of one-page prose pieces, by a small press, Truck Press. Another small press, Vehicle Editions, published *Counting*, a second collection of short pieces, in 1978. Such ventures rarely approach commercial success, but *Sweethearts* won the Pushcart Prize, an award for small-press publications, in 1977 and led to her admission to the writing program at the University of Iowa, where she completed an M.F.A. in 1978. That same year she met Seymour Lawrence, an editor for Delacorte Press, at a writers' conference and submitted several of her stories for his consideration. These were accepted and published under the title *Black Tickets* in 1979 in both a hardcover trade edition and a quality paperback. The critical response to the book was enthusiastic, and the sales, for a first book by an unknown young author, were remarkable. *Black Tickets* won the endorsements of a number of distinguished writers, including Frank Conroy (who had been one of Phillips' teachers at Iowa), Annie Dillard, and Tillie Olsen, and was widely reviewed. In 1980 she received a signal honor from the American Academy and Institute of Arts and Letters which named her the first winner of the Sue Kaufman Prize for First Fiction.

Black Tickets contains twenty-seven stories that range in length from one and two paragraphs to substantial stories of close to twenty pages. They range just as widely in subject matter. About half of them explore the nightmares of drug abuse, disease, violence, and sexual abuse. The other stories focus on the more ordinary experiences of family life, but even here the atmosphere is heavily charged with tension as parents and children, husbands and wives, and lovers struggle to communicate with each other and achieve some sense of mutual understanding. "Characters and voices in these stories," Phillips writes in an opening note, "began in what is real, but became, in fact, dreams. They bear no relation to living persons, except that love and loss lends a reality to what is imagined." Phillips' imagined reality impressed reviewers with its vivid sensuous detail, its mastery—for so young a writer—of language, and its insights into human character. In this book, Michiko Kakutani wrote in the *New York Times*, "Jayne Anne Phillips stepped out of the ranks of her generation as one of its most gifted writers. Her quick, piercing tales of love and loss demonstrated a keen love of language and a rare talent for illuminating the secret core of ordinary lives with clearsighted unsentimentality."

One of the most enthusiastic admirers of *Black Tickets* was the novelist John Irving, who hailed Phillips, in the *New York Times Book Review*, as "a wonderful young writer, concerned with every sentence and seemingly always operating out of instincts that are visceral and true. . . ." Irving qualified his praise, however, with the observation that some of the stories in the collection—especially the short impressionistic pieces, "detract from the way the best of this book glows." He detected in them the self-consciousness of the student in a creative-writing class, "mere exercises in 'good writing.'" Irving was not the only reviewer of *Black Tickets* to note what Jeffrey Burke, in *Harper's*, called "an intentional display of range and virtuosity," and what Doris Grumbach, reviewing the book in *Books & Arts*, described as indulgence in "a certain fondness for ornate writing, which works less well than her stronger, more precise and simple rhetoric." The strongest stories in this collection, these reviewers agreed, were the longer and more developed narratives of family life. "I hope Miss Phillips is writing a novel," Irving commented, "because she seems at her deepest and broadest when she sustains a narrative, manipulates a plot, develops characters through more than one phase in their life. I believe she would shine in a novel."

Phillips appears to have responded to Irving's challenge in *Machine Dreams*, her first novel. Working slowly and painstakingly ("I work like a poet, really, one line at time," she told *Publishers Weekly*), she developed a group of characters, who also appear in the short story "Blue Moon," into a study of an American family living in a small town in West Virginia from the beginning of this century through the war in Vietnam. Although in no way autobiographical, *Machine Dreams* draws heavily upon its author's experience—the story includes a businessman father and career-minded mother who are incompatible and finally divorce (as Phillips' parents did); a bright and sensitive young daughter, Danner; a close and loving relationship with a younger brother; a childhood in rural West Virginia; the tragedy of the war in Vietnam, where her brother is shot down and reported missing in action (neither of Phillips' brothers, however, fought in Vietnam). The story shifts among several narrators—the parents recalling their parents and their earlier years, soldiers writing home from the fronts in World War II and later Vietnam, the brother Billy, and—the most articulate register—young Danner. Hers is the last narrative, and it emphasizes the grief and disillusionment that follow her experiences in the late 1960s, especially in reaction to her brother's death. She drifts around the country and experiments with drugs like so many of her generation; she is bitter about what she perceives as her country's betrayal of its own ideals. Nevertheless, her faith in family and her native roots sustain her: "But my parents are my country, my divided country. By going to California, I'd made it to the far frontiers, but I'd never leave my country. I never will."

Jonathan Yardley, in *Book World*, described *Machine Dreams* as "a heavily programmatic novel in which the various characters and their histories are meant to personify distinct aspects of twentieth-century American experience." Similarly, Phillips' panoramic survey of history condensed into a single family's history struck Michael Gorra, in the *Boston Review*, as harmful to the artistic integrity of the book: "I suspect that Phillips's interest in ventriloquism got the better of her: that in the attempt to create typical figures she tried to give each character's voice the autonomy it would have had as a short story in its own right, and so denied herself the omniscience and the irony that her form requires. The consequence of that autonomy is, paradoxically, to rob her characters of the individuality that could make one care about them. . . . Her characters are emblematic of their period, but only emblematic, symbols without substance. . . ." For Anne Tyler, in the *New York Times Book Review*, however, *Machine Dreams* had quite the opposite effect. She described it as "a patchwork quilt of American voices. Its shocks arise from small, ordinary moments, patiently developed, that suddenly burst out with far more meaning than we had expected. And each of these moments owes its impact to an assured and gifted author." And Michiko Kakutani, in the *New York Times*, expressed even more enthusiasm for the book, writing that *Machine Dreams* "not only ratifies [the] earlier accomplishment [of *Black Tickets*] but also establishes Miss Phillips as a novelist of the first order . . . a novel that succeeds in examining the intersection of public and private experience in America during the last four decades, without ever becoming didactic."

The "machine dreams" of the title refers to the dreams that haunt the father in the novel about his experiences in World War II when he drove a bulldozer over the corpses of Japanese soldiers. Machines become a metaphor for the American dream of power and progress that was so rudely shattered in the years following World War II. Metaphor figures again in the title story of her collection *Fast Lanes*. "Don't drive in the fast lanes unless you're passing," an experienced driver advises the narrator, a young woman returning home to West Virginia to see her dying father. She has been a waitress drifting around the country in the lost and alienated spirit of the times, one who has chosen to live her own life in the "fast lanes." But her three weeks' ride cross-country with a tough but kindly fellow drifter, an aging hippie himself, becomes a kind of journey into herself, and Phillips writes lyrically of her experiences on the road:

> But there was the windshield and the continual movie past the glass. It was good driving into the movie, good the way the weather changed, the way night and day traded off. It was good stopping at the diners and luncheonettes and the daytime bars, or even HoJo's along the interstates: an hour, a few hours, taking off as we'd walked in, as if we had helium in our shoes.

"Fast Lanes" had originally been published as a single story in an illustrated edition in 1984 by Vehicle Editions. It lent its title to a collection of seven Phillips stories published in 1987. These range from a rock star's monologue on his sad and frenzied life ("How Mickey Made It") to the reminiscences of a West Virginia country woman about her childhood devotion to her brother ("Bess"). Jay McInerney, writing in the *New York Times Book Review*, called *Fast Lanes* "a heterogeneous collection, stronger in parts than as a whole. . . . The reader seems to be watching a gifted writer develop a sense of voice and subject over the course of these stories." In the *New York Times*, Michiko Kakutani, who found the new book disappointing after the major achievement of *Machine Dreams*, described it as "a sort of space-filler between projects, intended to remind us of her presence." But for Paul E. Hutchinson, in *Library Journal*, the stories were up to the standards of her earlier books: "Phillips's perspective on contemporary life is refreshingly honest, her style engaging."

Her early critical and popular success has not changed Phillips' cautious and careful attitude toward her work. She told *Publishers Weekly*: "I'm the type of writer for whom writing is more painful than anything else, the kind of writer without the personal exuberance or ego orientation of those who are more like public performers. We are like acolytes, or novices, people who have put themselves at the mercy of something they surrender to completely." She cites as writers who have influenced her, "not for their style but their subject matters," Eudora Welty, Katherine Anne Porter, William Faulkner, and Edgar Lee Masters—"writers who wrote about materially disenfranchised people who had rich histories and myths, stories that are almost destinies in themselves."

Phillips has taught creative writing at a number of American colleges and universities, among these the University of Iowa, Humboldt State University in California, Boston and Brandeis universities, and Williams College. She married Mark Brian Stockman, a physician, in 1985. She has one son and two stepsons and lives in Brookline, Massachusetts. In addition to the Sue Kaufman award Phillips has received two fellowships from the National Endowment for the Arts (1978, 1985) and many awards for individual short stories. Her work appears in a number of short-story anthologies, including *The O. Henry Awards: Prize Stories 1980* and three collections of *The Pushcart Prize* —1978, 1980, and 1983. In 1981 she had a Bunting Institute Fellowship at Radcliffe College. In 1984 *Machine Dreams* received a National Book Critics Circle Award nomination, a Notable Book Citation from the American Library Association, and the *New York Times* Best Books of 1984 citation.

PRINCIPAL WORKS: *Novel*—Machine Dreams, 1984. *Collected short stories*—Sweethearts, 1976; Counting, 1978; Black Tickets, 1979; Fast Lanes, 1987.

ABOUT: Contemporary Authors 10, 1981; Contemporary Literary Criticism 15, 1980; 33, 1985; Contemporary Novelists, 4th ed., 1986; Dictionary of Literary Biography, 1980; Pearlman, Mickey (ed.) American Women Writing Fiction, 1989. *Periodicals*—Books & Arts November 23, 1979; Boston Review August 1984; Harper's September 1979; Library Journal March 15, 1987; New York Times June 12, 1984; April 11, 1987; New York Times Book Review September 30, 1979; July 1, 1984; May 3, 1987; Publishers Weekly June 8, 1984; Washington Post Book World June 24, 1984.

PLIMPTON, GEORGE (AMES) (March 18, 1927–), American writer and literary editor, was born in New York City, the oldest of four children of Francis T. P. Plimpton, a wealthy corporation lawyer and, in 1961–1965, deputy U.S. representative to the United Nations, and the former Pauline Ames. He was educated in private schools: St. Bernard's in New York and Phillips Academy in Exeter, New Hampshire, and at Harvard College, where he was editor of the humor magazine, the *Lampoon*. Plimpton interrupted his university career to serve in the U.S. Army in Europe from 1945 to 1948, then returned to Harvard, taking his bachelor's degree in English in 1950. After graduation he studied at King's College, Cambridge University, from which he earned a second bachelor's degree in 1952.

Plimpton went to Paris in the spring of 1952 to join in discussions with several friends— Harold Humes, Peter Matthiessen, Thomas Guinzburg, and Donald Hall—about launching

GEORGE PLIMPTON

a literary magazine. The result was the *Paris Review*, of which Plimpton became, and remains, editor-in-chief. "Soon," according to Gay Talese in *The Overreachers* (1965), "he could be seen strolling through the streets of Paris with a long woolen scarf flung about his neck, cutting a figure reminiscent of Toulouse-Lautrec's famous lithograph of Aristide Bruant. . . . Much of the editing of *The Paris Review* was done at sidewalk cafés by editors awaiting their turns on the pinball machine, [but] the magazine nonetheless became very successful because the editors had talent, money, and taste, and they avoided using such typical little-magazine words as 'Zeitgeist' and 'dichotomous,' and published no crusty critiques about Melville or Kafka, but instead printed the poetry and fiction of gifted young writers not yet popular." Among the writers whose first short stories were published in the magazine were Terry Southern, Philip Roth, Evan Connell, and even Samuel Beckett.

The very first issue of the *Paris Review*, in 1953, contained a long interview with E. M. Forster, even then the grand old man of English fiction, who was encouraged to reveal therein why he had not completed a novel since 1926. That interview was the first of many that the magazine would commission, publish, then collect into a distinguished series of books, *Writers at Work*, which by the mid-1980s had attained seven fat volumes, all save the first edited for publication in book form by Plimpton, who occasionally conducts an interview as well. His most famous contribution to the series was his interview with Ernest Hemingway, which appeared in the spring–summer issue of 1959. The formula for *Writers at Work* is unvarying: some middlingly well-known writer usually supplies the introduction; yet the interviews themselves are conducted by all and sundry—often by assistant professors of literature or magazine staffers. Sharply reviewing the second volume (1963), Wilfred Sheed wrote that the informattion contained in most of the interviews was neither better nor worse than Hollywood gossip: "I was mortally sick . . . of hearing about Hemingway's number-two pencils, and I felt they had about as much to do with literature as, say, whether Aldous Huxley slept in pajama tops or bottoms." He expressed regret for these remarks later, upon being asked to introduce the fourth volume (1976), by saying, "I did not yet realize that gossip is the very stuff of literature, the *materia prima* of which both books and their authors are made. From Homer to Bellow, gossip is simply what authors *do*, in books and out; and no fine distinctions are made between craft gossip and the wisdom of the keyhole." Francine du Plessix Gray, introducing the fifth installment (1981), characterized the contents of *Writers at Work* as "an ingenious literary genre . . . informally called the rewritten interview. . . . Is there anything more appealing than the offer of staging one's own portrait, choosing one's most advantageous expression and angle of profile? The success of [the series] is in part due to the great elasticity of its form, its remarkable hybrid of portrait and self-portrait. . . . *The Paris Review* may leave to posterity the richest document available on the craft of fiction in our time."

Plimpton returned to live in New York in the mid-1950s and began publishing the articles and books for which he is best known. He had always keenly followed American professional sports, and it occurred to him that he might use his influence to become not only an inside participant in that apparently closed world but also pals with some real American heroes; he then could write about the heady experience for the edification of the uncounted millions of his (male) fellow citizens who all their lives had yearned to be professional athletes for a day. He quickly secured the backing of Sid James, editor of *Sports Illustrated* magazine, for his first project, pitching to the eight best hitters from each baseball league in a postseason exhibition game at Yankee Stadium. "The point is," he told James, "that I would pitch not as a hotshot—that'd be a different story—but as a guy who's average, really, a sort of Mr. Everybody, the sort who thinks he's a fair athlete. . . . " His ruefully witty report of his adventure, which like all his other vicarious sporting attempts was in no sense an athletic suc-

cess, appeared in the April 1961 issue of *Sports Illustrated* and later, in an expanded form, as the book *Out of My League*. As did all of Plimpton's subsequent sports books, it enthralled and delighted the avid fans assigned to review it. Hemingway himself, sportsman nonpareil, in a blurb for the book, commented, "Beautifully observed and incredibly conceived, this account of a self-imposed ordeal has the chilling quality of a true nightmare. It is the dark side of the moon of Walter Mitty."

Plimpton's later first-hand professional sports experiences, all originally undertaken for *Sports Illustrated*, were recounted in several books. *Paper Lion* is about his on-field humiliations and the locker-room camaraderie he found as a temporary member of the Detroit Lions professional football team. *Bogey Man* is his account of a month spent on the professional golf tour, during which he passed most of his time worrying about his own game, his hopeless quest to lower his 18 handicap, and at odd moments, conducted what he freely conceded were fruitless, boring, and perfunctory interviews with the greatest names in golf, circa 1968. The experience was not at all like hanging around a football team, he decided. "There's not the same sense of camaraderie . . . and danger . . . and the drama, well, it's all *private* in golf, which is its strength." *Shadow Box* begins by recalling one of the author's first excursions into "participatory journalism," his lasting three rounds in the ring in 1959 against the then light-heavyweight champion, Archie Moore. The book gives an account of Plimpton's conversations about boxing with Hemingway, Norman Mailer, and Hunter Thompson. One critic, the nonsportsman Eileen Kennedy in *Best Sellers*, called it "self-indulgent . . . and rather sad." *Open Net* describes how the sportsman-author, by that time nearly sixty, sojourned with the Boston Bruins hockey team in their training camp, then played for five atypically nonviolent minutes as their goalie against the Philadelphia Flyers.

The descriptions in these books of being a temporary professional athlete have appeared to amuse a lot of Americans; the brief metamorphoses obviously hold endless fascination for Plimpton himself, who has made, as Leonard Bernstein once put it on the occasion in 1967 of the author's playing percussion for the New York Philharmonic, a lifelong profession out of being a permanent amateur. He has also written about (though not always in book form) taking part in a bullfight staged by Hemingway in 1954; losing a tennis match, 6-0, to Pancho Gonzales; losing a swimming meet to Don Schollander; and playing a rubber of bridge with Oswald Jacoby as his partner (they lost badly).

He made his film-acting debut as a Bedouin extra in *Lawrence of Arabia* in 1962, had a small speaking part in *The Detective* in 1968, played the mayor in Norman Mailer's film *Beyond the Law* in 1968, and played Bill Ford, owner of the Lions, in United Artists' release of *Paper Lion* in 1968, in which Alan Alda played the author.

Plimpton's other books—nonparticipatory—on professional football include *Mad Ducks and Bears*, which was originally intended as a manual on how to be an effective linebacker, by two exceptionally articulate Lion players: the offensive lineman John Gordy and the defensive lineman Alex Karras. Gordy was sure, he explained to Plimpton, that the book would be eagerly bought by the fifty million Americans (by his count) who had at one time or another played on the line of scrimmage. Yet it soon transpired that Plimpton's collaborators were not going to do their parts, so the book became, in his words, "an irreverent, roguish account of their lives as football players, full of anecdote, reminiscence and story, often tempered by grievance, but always with an underlying attitude of humor—as if their occupations were only acceptable in that light." *One More July: A Football Dialogue with Bill Curry* consists of tape-recorded reminiscences of the professional career of Curry, who played center first for the Green Bay Packers and then during his best seasons for the Baltimore Colts.

Other books on sports by Plimpton are *One for the Record: The Inside Story of Hank Aaron's Chase for the Home-Run Record*, a work overflowing with sportswriting hyperbole, in which the author calls the media event described in the title "a simple act of an unassuming man which touched an enormous circle of people, indeed an entire country. It provided an instant which people would remember for decades." The book consists of more than a hundred pages of similar memorials, followed by no fewer than forty pages of home-run-hitting statistics for Aaron and his chief historical rival, Babe Ruth. In *A Sports Bestiary*, Plimpton provides the consistently coy captions to the grotesque, witty drawings by Arnold Roth which illustrate in animal form various familiar terms used in connection with sporting events—the Sacrifice Fly, the Foul Tip, the Solid Left Hook, and others, including a particularly wicked one for the Gipper. *Sports!* is a coffee-table book of sports photographs by Neil Leifer, with captions by Plimpton.

Plimpton has collaborated, as editor, with Jean Stein on two books of tape-recorded oral history-as-biography. *American Journey: The Times of Robert Kennedy* comprises the thoughts and reminiscences of some two hundred individuals—chiefly those friends and supporters riding Robert Kennedy's funeral train from New York to Washington, but also the opinions of a few spectators who never knew the assassinated presidential candidate. "The concept of *American Journey*," writes Plimpton in the foreword, "was not to give a solid historical representation of an era. The technique used is occasionally almost the kaleidoscopic 'flicker' technique of films, in which a series of quick images of considerable variety provides an effect of wholeness. . . . The purpose . . . was . . . to record the impact of Robert Kennedy on the turbulent decade of the sixties." The editors also collaborated on *Edie: An American Biography*, which recounts by putting together snippets of recorded interviews with such people as Truman Capote, Andy Warhol, Gore Vidal, Patti Smith, Ivan Karp, John P. Marquand, Jr., and scores of others, the grim, even sordid life of Edie Sedgwick, a poor little rich girl who became a Warhol superstar, a drug addict, and a mental patient, and who died at the age of twenty-eight in 1971. "A readable and novelistic package," one critic called the book, and James Atlas in the *Atlantic* likened it to "listening to an all-night talk show; it has its longueurs, but enough memorable characters to keep us tuned in. . . . The snobbery of the rich and famous is nothing new; but it seems craven and pathetic in this chronicle."

For a time in the 1970s Plimpton held the appointive office of fireworks commissioner of New York City. *Fireworks* treats the history of the subject and its chief contemporary practitioners, mainly the Grucci family of Long Island, who manufactured and set off the official displays for New York's celebrations of the U.S. Bicentennial and the centenary of the Brooklyn Bridge. The text of the lavishly illustrated book was called "disjointed—jottings, really" by Fred Ferretti in the *New York Times Book Review*, while James Kaufmann termed its style "genial and chatty, . . . endearing and interesting."

The Curious Case of Sidd Finch is Plimpton's only novel, an expansion of a short story that originally appeared in *Sports Illustrated*. It recounts the stupendous and brief baseball career of the title character, an English orphan who, in the course of an unsuccessful search for his father's remains in the Himalayas, becomes an aspirant Buddhist monk and then, as a result of various Zen practices and meditations, is rendered capable of throwing a baseball 168 miles per hour. "Splendidly rendered," wrote A. Bartlett Giamatti in the *New York Times Book Review*, "with an experienced insider's knowledge, and the whole saga . . . is at once a parody of every player's as-told-to biography, a satire on professional sports, an extended (and intriguing) meditation on our national pastime, and a touching variant on the novel of education as Sidd learns of the world. . . . Mr. Plimpton's control is masterly."

Plimpton has published a juvenile book, *The Rabbit's Umbrella*, and with Christopher Hemphill edited *DV*, the fashion arbiter Diana Vreeland's obviously prerecorded collection of eccentric and insistent opinions. He has also been involved in various television specials, usually about sports and sports figures. He is active in many philanthropic causes, as a trustee for the public television station WNET (1973–1981), the National Art Museum of Sport (from 1967), the Police Athletic League (from 1976), the African Wildlife Leadership Foundation (from 1980), and the New York Zoological Society (from 1985); he serves on the board of directors of the National Tennis Foundation (from 1979), and the Squaw Valley Center for the Written and Dramatic Arts (from 1979). In 1988 he was chairman of the English Speaking Union's Books Across the Sea program. He was an associate fellow of Yale University's Trumbull College in 1967 and in the same year received the Distinguished Achievement Award of the University of Southern California. He has also won the Columbia University *Spectator*'s Blue Pencil Award (1981), the International Platform Association's Mark Twain Award (1982), and Long Island University's Chancellor's Award (1986). His honorary degrees are from Franklin Pierce (1968), Hobart Smith (1978), Stonehill (1982), and Pine Manor (1988) colleges and from Long Island (1984) and Southern California (1986) universities.

PRINCIPAL WORKS: *Non-fiction*—Out of My League, 1961; Paper Lion, 1966; The Bogey Man, 1968, repr., 1983; Mad Ducks and Bears, 1973; One for the Record, 1974; Shadow Box, 1976; One More July, 1976; (with N. Leifer) Sports!, 1978; (with A. Roth) A Sports Bestiary, 1982; Fireworks, 1984; Open Net, 1985; The Best of Plimpton, 1990. *Fiction*—The Rabbit's Umbrella (juv.), 1955; The Curious Case of Sidd Finch, 1987. *As editor*—Writers at Work, vol. 2, 1963; vol. 3, 1967; vol. 4, 1976; vol. 5, 1981; vol. 6, 1984; vol. 7, 1986; (with J. Stein) American Journey, 1970; Pierre's Book, 1971; The Fancy, 1973; (with J. Stein) Edie, 1982; (with C. Hemphill) DV, 1984.

ABOUT: Contemporary Authors 21–22, 1977; Current Biography 1969; Talese, G. The Overreachers, 1964. *Periodicals*—Atlantic December 1968, July 1982; Best Sellers December 1, 1968; December 15, 1970; January 1978; Booklist June 1, 1961; Book Week October 23, 1966; Book World November 3, 1968; Christian Science Monitor December 14, 1966; March 4, 1981; September 14, 1984; Commentary October 1967; Commonweal December 2, 1966; Economist June 12, 1971; Harper's July 1982; Library Journal April 1, 1961; November 1, 1966; December 15, 1966; December 1, 1968; November 1, 1970; November 1, 1973; November 15, 1973; August 1977; September 15, 1977; October 15, 1978; April 15, 1981; July 1982; October 15, 1982; September 1, 1984; December 1985; September 1, 1986; Life June 30, 1967; November 15, 1968; November 29, 1968; Ms. September 1982; Nation January 30, 1967; July 10–17, 1982; National Observer December 2, 1968; New Statesman June 18, 1971; October 13, 1978; July 31, 1981; New York Review of Books February 23, 1967; November 19, 1970; February 7, 1974; July 15, 1982; New York Times November 4, 1968; July 26, 1970; New York Times Book Review April 23, 1961; October 30, 1966; November 10, 1968; January 6, 1974; July 31, 1977; November 6, 1977; July 4, 1982; September 23, 1984; July 5, 1987; New York Times Magazine January 8, 1967; New Yorker May 20, 1961; November 12, 1966; February 13, 1971; December 6, 1971; December 17, 1973; August 22, 1977; December 12, 1977; November 24, 1985; Newsweek September 9, 1963; November 7, 1966; November 11, 1968; December 11, 1978; June 28, 1982; Saturday Review December 10, 1966; Time January 6, 1967; April 4, 1967; November 8, 1968; September 21, 1970; January 4, 1971; December 19, 1977; December 11, 1978; Times Literary Supplement October 1, 1971; September 5, 1986; March 20, 1987; Virginia Quarterly Review Spring 1967.

*POPESCU, DUMITRU RADU (August 19, 1935–), Romanian novelist and playwright, was born in Păușa, a village in Bihor county in the heart of the historical province of Transylvania. Both his mother, Maria Bentea (a native of Păușa), and his father, Traian Popescu, were local schoolteachers. He passed his childhood close to the Danube River in Danceu, his father's native village, where he attended elementary school, and went on to high school (1946–1952) in Oradea, a provincial center of industry and commerce near the Hungarian border. Then he went up to Cluj to study medicine. After three years in medical school, however, Popescu switched to Romanian studies, receiving his M.A. from the University of Cluj in 1961. By that time he had already published a number of short stories and two plays in literary periodicals, principally in the weekly *Steaua* (The Star) of Cluj. He began his professional writing career, after graduation, on the staff of *Steaua*, then under the editorship of A. E. Baconsky, a maverick and thorn-in-the-side of Communist officialdom. From 1970 to 1982 D. R. Popescu was editor of the Cluj *Tribune*; he then moved to Bucharest as editor of *Contemporanul*, a post he held until 1988, when he assumed the editorship of *România Literară*.

D. R. Popescu belongs to a generation who grew up under the Communist domination of

DUMITRU RADU POPESCU

Romania following World War II. He served his literary apprenticeship in the 1950s, a period of rigid Stalinist control that Romanians refer to as "the haunting decade" but emerged as a writer in the more relaxed and stimulating cultural atmosphere of the early 1960s. With the encouragement of *Steaua*'s editor Baconsky, he managed to keep his own work free of the formulas and clichés of Socialist Realism and established himself as a writer of remarkable industry and versatility, turning his hand not only to fiction but also to poetry, journalism, and critical essays; radio, stage, and television plays; and film scripts (these last mostly adaptations of his own short stories). A leading figure in Romanian cultural life, D. R. Popescu was a member of the central committee of the Romanian Communist party during the 1970s and 1980s and held an influential position in the Romanian Writers' Union, of which he became president in 1981.

Ironically, D. R. Popescu's recognition as a major writer was coextensive with the repressive Ceauşescu era (1965–1989). He published six volumes of his masterpiece, the "F cycle" of interrelated novels, in quick succession between 1969 and 1976, during a somewhat milder earlier stage of that dictatorship. The most powerful of these, *F* (1969) and *Vînătoarea regală* (1973; translated as *The Royal Hunt*), won the Writers' Union Prize. In the same period he scored a resounding success with his plays, one of which, *Aceşti îngeri trişti* (These Melancholy Angels, 1969) received the I. L. Caragiale Prize awarded by the Romanian Academy and three lesser awards.

The year 1977 marked a turning point for the worse in what was to be the most repressive regime in Romanian history. Popescu found himself in a equivocal position. As a writer-artist he was presumably dedicated to the free expression of the creative imagination. But as an establishment figure, president of the Writers' Union and an official of the Communist party, he could ill afford to take a public stand against censorship, suppression of civil liberties, and the persecution of some of his colleagues who had protested the tightening of totalitarian control. In his writings, however, he was able to explore the realities of his world under the cloak of myth and allegory. Nevertheless, when the Ceauşescu dictatorship was overthrown in December 1989, D. R. Popescu resigned from his office with the Writers' Union and as of early 1990 his fate was uncertain.

Probably the best known of contemporary Romanian writers and one of a dozen first-rate talents who succeeded in re-establishing ties with the great tradition of Romanian literature, Popescu has created his own fictional universe—a rural area, part real, part fantasy, where in close to mythic terms he explores the turbulent history of his own times. The novels of the "F cycle" —*F* (1969), *Cei doi kin dreptul Ţebei sau Cu faţa la pădure* (The Two by the Tzebea or Facing the Forest, 1973), *Vînătoarea regală* (The Royal Hunt, 1973), *O bere pentru calul meu* (A Beer for My Horse, 1974), *Împăratul norilor* (The Emperor of the Clouds, 1976), *Ploile de dincolo de vreme* (The Rains Beyond Time, 1976)—deal with the forced dissolution of privately-owned landholdings during the last years of Stalin's era and throughout Khrushchev's. Most of these lands were small farms, owned and worked by the peasants who had acquired them at the end of World War II, when the great landowners' estates were broken up and distributed among the peasantry by the victorious Red Army. As Popescu has noted in an essay, the peasantry—always the backbone of Romanian history—had borne the burden of World War II in both the Russian campaign and the battles for northern Transylvania. Their rewards were short-lived: drought, famine, and then the sweeping changes effected by the Communist party left them worse off than ever before. This is the real background of the chaos and violence that are depicted in near-fantastic terms in the "F cycle." Popescu creates a veritable inferno, a nightmare mixture of savagery and depravity comparable perhaps to the paintings of Hieronymus Bosch or, in the latest of his novels, *Oraşul îngerilor* (Angels' Town, 1985), to the work of Max Beckmann. Myth, magic, and superstition have replaced traditional moral and religious values. Anarchy prevails. Violent and sensational happenings—mysterious disappearances, grotesque metamorphoses, sudden deaths, epidemic disease—are rendered even more fantastic by Popescu's technique, which makes use of multiple points of view and unreliable narrators. The novels turn incessantly around the same characters and events, against much the same physical background, subverting the very reality they seem to be portraying.

Critics have been bemused by the "F cycle," caught off guard by the ambiguity and complexity of the novels. They cushioned their reactions by emphasizing the author's artistic technique, the grotesque absurdist fantasy, the baroque mannerisms. They debated the literary influences on Popescu, finding parallels to William Faulkner's darkly imagined yet realistically grounded Yoknapatawpha County and to the "magic realism" of Gabriel García Márquez's *One Hundred Years of Solitude*, among others. Popescu himself acknowledged a variety of influences, including Shakespeare, Montaigne, and Bakhtin. Author and critics alike seemed to be playing a game that distracted the official censors and permitted the individual reader to discover privately the stark truths in Popescu's vision of his native land.

Even in his writings for the theater—a much more public and exposed art—D. R. Popescu has been singularly successful in devising strategies of evasion and indirection. In staging his plays he invites both directors and audiences to take liberties with his text (by, for example, providing a play with as many as four different titles, each suggesting a different symbolic interpretation). He has published five volumes of plays, most of them in the absurdist mode, like the plays of his fellow Romanian Eugène Ionescu (who, however, has lived in Paris all his life), employing fantasy, indirection, and wit to cover incisive attacks on received ideas and the conditions of life in totalitarian societies.

In a later cycle of novels entitled *Viaţa şi opera lui Tiron B* (The Life and Works of Tiron B), Popescu adopts a different convention. *Iepurele şchiop* (The Limping Hare, 1980) purports to be a historical novel in the classic sense and introduces figures from real life. The author distances himself from the account by resorting to an intermediary—a journalist, Tiron B, who has ostensibly witnessed a trial that he describes in his diary. The novel had a cool critical reception, probably because, with the comedy and fantasy eliminated and the presence of Nicolae Ceauşescu as a character in the novel, critics felt themselves in an awkward position. In fact, Popescu's treatment of the dictator strikes a balance between fact and fiction, tantalizing and teasing the reader to judge independently and privately. The second volume in this cycle, *Podul de gheaţă* (The Ice Bridge, 1983), returns to the more imaginative and sensational spirit of his earlier novels and was well received. His novel of 1985, *Oraşul îngenrilor* (Angels' Town) is a complex work that successfully synthesizes realism and fantasy. The central characters are adolescents, too young to be actively involved in World War II but not too young to escape the horror around them. The book brings together Romanians, Hungarians, Jews, gypsies, Germans, and Serbs, and shows human values being forged amid ethnic tensions.

D. R. Popescu's works have been widely translated—in France, Germany, Italy, Sweden, India, and Japan, as well as in most of the countries of Eastern Europe—but only one novel from the "F cycle" is available in English. This is *The Royal Hunt*, described by its English translators as "one of the most successful artistic portrayals of mass terror in contemporary literature." The translation covers only one third of the original text, the episode that gives the title to the whole novel. Its subject is the devastation wrought on a peasant village by an epidemic of rabies. An allegory, it may be read on several levels of meaning. Literally it is an account of the plague by a young boy just coming to maturity and at the time only dimly aware of the profound meaning of the events he has witnessed. Now an adult, he is reporting his fragmentary memories of this terrifying episode to the son of one of its victims. What he records is the overthrow and destruction of a local Communist leader in an atmosphere of growing panic and anarchy. But the ritual hunt, the scapegoating, and the disease that transforms men into beasts can be read as metaphors for cruel and repressive social and political forces, and the allusions to actual events in recent Romanian history suggest that only the most obtuse readers could miss the powerful message of the book. As one of the characters in *The Royal Hunt* prophetically observes: "We need an epidemic so that people can forget about the disaster of the war and the misery that followed, and can forget that even now they don't have what they need in order to live, and can't have [it] as long as the old wounds aren't healed."

WORK IN ENGLISH TRANSLATION: J. E. Cottrell and M. Bogdan translated *The Royal Hunt* in 1985.

ABOUT: Cottrell, J. E. and M. Bogdan. *Introduction to The Royal Hunt*, 1985; Encyclopedia of World Literature in the Twentieth Century, rev. ed., III, 1983. *Periodicals*—Books Abroad Autumn 1974; New York

Times Book Review November 3, 1985; World Literature Today Spring 1977, Spring 1986.

PORTIS, CHARLES (December 28, 1933–   ), American novelist, was born in El Dorado, Arkansas, son of Samuel Palmer (a school superintendent) and Alice (Waddell) Portis. He graduated from high school in Arkansas in 1951 and in 1952 entered the U.S. Marine Corps; after serving in the Korean War he was discharged in 1955 with the rank of sergeant. He enrolled at the University of Arkansas in 1955, where he received his B.A. in 1958. Portis worked as a reporter in Memphis, Tennessee, in 1958, and in 1959–1960 for the *Arkansas Gazette* in Little Rock. He was then reporter and London correspondent for the *New York Herald Tribune* from 1960 until 1964, when he left to pursue creative writing. The writer Tom Wolfe, who knew him at that time, relates that "Portis quit cold one day; just like that, without a warning. He returned to the United States and moved into a fishing shack in Arkansas. In six months he wrote a beautiful little novel called *Norwood*."

Norwood tells the story of a marine, Norwood Pratt, who returns home to Ralph, Texas, to work as a filling station attendant and live with his sister Vernell. Vernell, however, marries an opinionated veteran named Bill Bird, who soon takes over the dwelling, and Norwood is only too happy to leave when Grady Fring the Kredit King asks him to drive a car to New York. Norwood obliges him, without knowing that the car is stolen. His adventures en route to New York and back involve him in much oddity, including a midget acquaintance and a talking chicken. A folk singer and good-hearted patsy, Norwood eventually finds a fiancée and a new life. Reviewers found the novel original and quite comical. Christopher Lehmann-Haupt commented that Portis "has written one of those books that make you laugh aloud. . . . What makes this tale very funny is the author's perfect ear for dialogue and Norwood's unstinting goodwill in a world of junk." Martin Levin in the *New York Times Book Review* remarked that Norwood "travels the same territory as Humbert Humbert: the neon desert invested with the tokens of midcentury America. But Mr. Portis's simple hero, unlike Mr. Nabokov's, is *with it*. Roller domes, bus stations, bowling alleys, chili parlors—these are his habitat and he thrives among them. . . . Mr. Portis does not patronize his comic book reading troubador; he marvels at him and touches his adventures along Route 67 with the magic of a fable."

Norwood was followed two years later by

CHARLES PORTIS

Portis' best-known novel, *True Grit*, related by Mattie Ross of Yell County, Arkansas. An unmarried, opinionated lady in 1928, Mattie recalls her experiences when she was fourteen and avenged the murder of her father in the Southwestern badlands by a Tom Chaney. Young Mattie enlists the aid of Rooster Cogburn, a U.S. marshal who once rode with Quantrill's border gang during the Civil War but has since become fat and forty, one-eyed and sloppy, and the two ride into the Indian territory where Chaney has taken refuge. After much bloodshed and many rollicking adventures, she confronts her enemy and with her old dragoon revolver sends "a lead ball of justice, too long delayed, into the criminal head of Tom Chaney."

Reviews of *True Grit* were overwhelmingly favorable. Charles Elliott, in *Life*, remarked that Mattie "is such a monumentally tough-minded believer in law and order and other bourgeois virtues that numerous Oklahoma malefactors (and I) will have a hard time forgetting her. Portis has the unusual ability to slide into a character so neatly you hardly know he's there. Portis may have his name on the title page of *True Grit*, but he doesn't come into it. Only Mattie does." Brian Garfield, in the *Saturday Review* observed that "*True Grit* is lively, uproarious high adventure. . . . Bred on McGuffey, the New Testament, and Horatio Alger, homely young Mattie is a hardy pioneer girl—tough, sassy, and free of self-doubt." The reviewer for *Time* agreed, remarking that "Portis has succeeded in creating in Mattie Ross a triumphant character, with true grit and sand, an original piece of Americana . . . and he has most vividly produced a true mock western."

True Grit, which was serialized in the *Saturday Evening Post*, became a best-seller, and was chosen as a Literary Guild bookclub selection. It was sold to Hollywood for $300,000, and adapted as a Paramount film in 1969, with John Wayne as the unkempt but doughty marshal Rooster Cogburn—a role that earned him an Oscar from the American Academy of Motion Pictures. With the commercial success of *True Grit*, Portis was relieved of the pressure of earning a living; since then he has published only two other novels. *The Dog of the South*, which followed, has as its hero Ray Midge, twenty-six, of Little Rock, Arkansas, whose restless wife Norma leaves home one day with Ray's Ford Torino and credit cards and joins her ex-husband, Guy Dupree, as he jumps bail on charges of writing threatening letters to the President. Ray sets out after them to get back his car and, incidentally, his wife. He tracks them across Mexico to Honduras, meeting a series of wacky characters along the way.

Larry L. King, in the *New York Times Book Review*, found the novel disappointing. "The yarn," he remarked, "works well enough in an amiable, low-key way as long as Ray Midge ambles through the Southwest and Mexico. But once he arrives in British Honduras, much of what follows appears to be little more than padding. Mr. Portis leads us to anticipate the moment when Midge catches up with his erring wife and her lover . . . but when he does find them we learn little more than a dime's worth of what they are about or what makes them tick." Yet many reviewers were enthusiastic about the novel. The reviewer for the *New Yorker* observed that Midge "is a cross between Buster Keaton and Don Quixote—innocent, generous to a fault, indefatigable, and perfectly deadpan—and . . . Charles Portis has blessed him with a supremely funny adventure." Walter Clemons, in *Newsweek*, found the narrative "a classic piece of American gab, in the line of Ring Lardner's 'The Golden Honeymoon' and Eudora Welty's 'Why I Live at the P. O.' Midge is gravely certain we will find every detail of his absurd junket interesting and each of his decisions logical. And so we do. He is a perfectly wonderful creation, and reading *The Dog of the South* is like being held down and tickled."

Portis' fourth novel, *Masters of Atlantis*, concerns a Lammar Jimmerson who, as a soldier in France during World War I, is inducted into the idiosyncratic Gnomon Society cult. The lore of this cult, supposedly handed down from the lost continent of Atlantis, becomes the source of the proselytizing mission of Jimmerson and his associates. They attempt to spread Gnomonism to all peoples, but as cult in-fighting ensues, a world of confidence men is comically exposed. Reviews of the novel were mixed. The reviewer for *Publishers Weekly* felt that the story was "slight," and "further undermined by the tone of self-affection and delight which runs gratingly unrestrained throughout." Beth Ann Mills in *Library Journal* noted that "con-men, crazies, and the super-credulous rush madly about in Portis' newest novel. . . . Those who enjoy deadpan comedy should get a good laugh here, but others may find it hard to care about what happens to Portis' madcap misfits." Yet Rudy Rucker in the *Washington Post Book World* found *Masters of Atlantis* "a funny and touching novel." Christopher Lehmann-Haupt in the *New York Times* stressed the beguiling quality of the hero's naïveté. "He is giving us," Lehmann-Haupt observed, "a picture of Main Street made silly, of Babbitry gone goofy. Yet for all its ridiculousness, there is a sweet dopey integrity to Lamar Jimmerson's innocence." Writing in the *Nation*, Thomas M. Disch also emphasized the naive appeal of the work. "Portis, like Dickens," he wrote, "takes an unashamed delight in grotesquery and freakishness and in the intractableness of stupidity, as though it were a poisonous weed to be marveled at."

Portis, a bachelor, lives in Little Rock, Arkansas. According to Gene Lyons in *Newsweek*, he is "a famous raconteur among his circle of old friends but shuns publicity and refuses to be cast in the role of the artist as seer."

PRINCIPAL WORKS: Norwood, 1966; True Grit, 1968; The Dog of the South, 1979; Masters of Atlantis, 1985.

ABOUT: Contemporary Authors New Revision Series 1, 1981; Dictionary of Literary Biography 6, 1980. *Periodicals*—Library Journal August 15, 1979; October 15, 1985; Life June 4, 1968; Nation November 30, 1985; New York Times October 7, 1985; New York Times Book Review July 24, 1966; July 29, 1979; New Yorker July 2, 1979; Publishers Weekly May 2, 1966; August 23, 1985; Saturday Review June 29, 1968; Time August 12, 1966; June 14, 1968; Washington Post Book World October 27, 1985.

PROSE, FRANCINE (April 1, 1947–), American novelist and short-story writer, was born in Brooklyn, New York, the daughter of Philip and Jessie Rubin Prose, both physicians. After earning a B.A. from Radcliffe in 1968 and an M.A. from Harvard in 1969, she traveled in India for a year and then returned to Harvard to teach creative writing. In 1973 her first novel was published.

FRANCINE PROSE

Judah the Pious was not the first novel that
one might have expected from a woman in her
mid-twenties who had spent much of her early
adulthood taking methedrine, sitting in at army
induction centers, and seeking enlightenment in
India. In place of autobiographical excursus or
social protest, *Judah the Pious* offered the reader
folklore, parable, and undisguised artifice. Its literary antecedents were to be found in Chaucer
and Isak Dinesen rather than in Jack Kerouac or
Thomas Pynchon. As in *The Canterbury Tales*
or *Seven Gothic Tales*, there is an outer and an
inner tale. The outer tale concerns Rabbi
Eliezer, an old, eccentric, faintly disreputable
scholar from the village of Rimanov (the time is
unclear), who is elected to go before the King of
Poland and argue for the restoration of Jewish
burial rights in an atmosphere of growing anti-
Semitism. Casimir, the lonely and inexperienced
sixteen-year-old king, is soon bewitched by the
rabbi's brusque but affectionate manner, especially when Eliezer abandons argument and
launches into an elaborate story about Judah Ben
Simon, a brilliant and handsome young naturalist whose scientific and spiritual investigations
take him deeper and deeper into a world where
reason and logic begin to lose their hold. This inner tale, which comprises the bulk of the novel,
is shot through with digression and all manner
of unlikely events until it dovetails neatly with
the outer tale which contains it. The burial
rights, needless to say, are restored, and the rabbi
at last disappears into the story that will contain
him.

Judah the Pious won the Jewish Book Council

Award in 1973 and is still one of Prose's most
highly regarded novels. D. Keith Mano found it
an "astounding" work, not for its prose, which
reads, he said, "like some bad translation of
itself," but for "the inherent, elemental force of
[the] narrative." It is, wrote Thomas Lask, "an
unusual and impressive effort, especially for a
first novel, notably successful in tone and overall finish, full of sudden delights and mocking
humor."

In the several novels that succeeded *Judah the
Pious* Prose continued to shun the autobiographical mode but perhaps, as Pearl K. Bell suggested, went "too far in the other direction."
Reviewing *The Glorious Ones*, about a commedia del l'arte troupe in seventeenth-century
Italy, Bell maintained that despite Prose's
"cleverly executed somersaults and cartwheels
through an obscure theatrical pocket of the past,
she fails to convince us that a razzle-dazzle stunt
is a solution to a young writer's pursuit of
originality." With *Household Saints*, Prose
seemed to find a subject and a milieu more ame-
nable to her imagination.

Household Saints is a family chronicle set in
Manhattan's Little Italy from the late forties to
the late sixties. The family in question is the San-
tangelos: Joseph, the patriarch, a local butcher
famous for his crafty business practices and for
having won his wife from his future father-in-
law in a pinochle game; Catherine, his prize
from the pinochle game, who becomes a loving
and devoted wife and tries, unsuccessfully, to
raise their daughter in the modern way, without
the religious obscurantism that has run on both
sides of the family; and Theresa, the stubbornly
unavailing object of her mother's efforts, more
interested in saints than in boys and inclined
more to sanctity than to sanity. The novel's
themes—the imperatives of family ties, the fine
line between fate and chance, between mysticism and madness—come together in a passage
late in the novel in which Joseph, coming to rescue Theresa from her boyfriend's apartment,
where she has lately been having conversations
with Jesus and Saint Theresa of Lisieux, reflects
on his troubles:

> Just one car, he caught himself thinking, just one car
> jumping over the center divider could settle their prob-
> lems for good. He crossed himself, looked around for
> some wood to knock on, and thought how little it takes
> to turn your life around. One minute, you're sitting on
> four aces. Your wife's upstairs cooking, your daughter's
> off at college, you're making good money in the shop.
> The next minute, you've got a handful of deuces and
> threes, and you're stuck in a cab coming back from a
> Brooklyn apartment where your daughter's been shack-
> ing up with her pimply boyfriend and losing her mind.
>   "Jesus Christ," he muttered.

"Like all fine novels," wrote Randolph Hogan in *The New York Times Book Review,* "*Household Saints* is an equation, everything held in delicate balance until the pieces fall into place with the certainty of algebra." Also impressed was Jean Strousse of *Newsweek,* who said, "Prose brings off a minor miracle of her own in the rare sympathy and detachment with which she gives life to this poignant story. She writes equally well about sausages and saints, documenting the madness and the grace of God in everyday life."

Prose followed *Household Saints* with *Hungry Hearts,* a parable about the relationship between life and art, reality and illusion. Its deliberately improbable plot concerns the travails of the Yiddish Art Theater as it travels through South America in the 1920s giving performances of Shloime Anski's classic play *The Dybbuk* to audiences very different from its appreciative hometown one on Manhattan's Second Avenue. More particularly, the story focuses on Dinah Rappoport, the young actress who plays the lead role of the passionate Leah and who finds herself possessed by her own dybbuk whenever she enacts her climactic scene of possession on stage.

Jerome Charyn, like other reviewers, was impressed but had reservations. "*Hungry Hearts,*" he wrote in *The New York Times Book Review,* "has the force of parable, the clear, clean line of prose without adornment. The book has a fine skeleton, but a skeleton isn't enough. All this business of life and art seems a little rehearsed. . . . For a novel about possession, *Hungry Hearts* is strangely unpossessed."

Some critics thought that Prose's wit bordered on if not actually degenerated into mere cutesiness and wisecracking in her next novel, *Bigfoot Dreams,* about the hard times of Vera Perl, a thirty-seven-year-old mother, estranged wife, and writer for a *National Enquirer*-like tabloid in New York called *This Week.* But Laura Shapiro of *Newsweek* was amused; she thought that "*Bigfoot Dreams* would make a perfect Woody Allen movie—with a woman, at long last, in the Woody Allen part." Whether this is a goal that a novelist ought to aspire to is a question that other critics might have debated; at any rate, *Bigfoot Dreams* was very much a matter of taste.

Prose's collection of short stories *Women and Children First* is comparatively circumscribed in tone and setting. In some ways resembling the more seriously alienated characters of Ann Beattie's fiction, the housewives, lawyers, photographers, and teachers of this book are mostly survivors from Prose's own generation, now on the brink of middle age, and thinking, as one of them does, "how the very worst moments of waiting for life to begin are better—much better—than knowing it already has." Not much in the way of outwardly dramatic circumstance happens in these stories: a man breaks up with his wife at a sushi bar; the father of a nonobservant Jewish family decides to become a Hasid; a married woman, talking to an old flame, suddenly feels "she's led her whole life wrong." Yet the pared-down realism of this book was, in the eyes of most critics, a gain in Prose's art, not a loss. "In the stronger tales," Michiko Kakutani wrote in the *New York Times,* "Ms. Prose seems to have sublimated her taste for the surreal and focused, instead, on what she once called 'the profound and fantastic heart of daily life.' The happy result is stories that glow with a burnished wisdom about the sorrows and satisfactions of domesticity, stories that use hardheaded journalistic observation and a mass of expertly orchestrated details to convey the texture of the everyday."

Francine Prose lives in upstate New York with her husband, Howard Michels, a sculptor whom she married in 1976, and their two sons. She has taught creative writing at Harvard, Sarah Lawrence, the University of Arizona, and the Iowa Writers' Workshop. In a piece called "Learning from Chekhov" that appeared in the 1988 *Fiction Writer's Market,* she gave the following advice to aspiring writers: "Forget about observation, consciousness, clearsightedness. Forget about life. Read Chekhov, read the stories straight through. Admit that you understand nothing of life, nothing of what you see. Then go out and look at the world."

PRINCIPAL WORKS: *Novels*—Judah the Pious, 1973; The Glorious Ones, 1974; Marie Laveau, 1977; Animal Magnetism, 1978; Household Saints, 1981; Hungry Hearts, 1983; Bigfoot Dreams, 1986. *Collected short stories*—Women and Children First, 1988.

ABOUT: Contemporary Authors 112, 1985; Contemporary Literary Criticism 45, 1987; Fiction Writer's Market, 1988. *Periodicals*—New Leader March 4, 1974; New York Times February 17, 1973; March 5, 1988; New York Times Book Review February 25, 1973; July 12, 1981; March 6, 1983; February 14, 1988; Newsweek August 3, 1981; July 21, 1986.

*RAKOSI, CARL (CALLMAN RAWLEY)

(November 6, 1903–), American poet and prose writer, writes: "I was born overseas. As a result, the first two languages I heard in my family were Hungarian and German. What special spin or tone that has given to my English I don't know. Nothing that I am aware of, but I

°ra kō´ sē

CARL RAKOSI

wouldn't bet on it. Next, I don't remember ever seeing my mother, don't remember her ever touching me or holding me when I was little. My father left her when I was only one year old and my brother Lester and I were brought up for the first six years of my life by her mother in a small town in southern Hungary. My mother lived somewhere in our house but always out of sight and hearing. Not that I felt anything was missing . . . no mother could have been more motherly than my grandmother . . . but it has left a great mystery in my biological past. A big chunk is missing, the part that would have told me who I am biologically. As a consequence, there has been a slight psychic discontinuity, both things which look as if they belong in the making of a poet-self.

"I have no memory of how I learned English. I was only six then and had joined my father and step-mother in Chicago. I must have picked it up on the playground from the other boys. All I remember is that one day I didn't know a word and the next thing I knew I was speaking it. In Gary, Indiana, where we moved next, the principal's office, after giving me a battery of tests, suddenly moved me two grades ahead of my age-group. This meant that all through grammar school I was the smallest kid in class and that in high school and university I was always two years younger than the others. I had no trouble keeping up with my school work but had to plug hard to keep in sports.

"We settled finally in Kenosha, Wisconsin. Like the other boys, I was out all day, playing baseball and soccer and basketball and ice hock-ey and running and swimming . . . not football, I was too light for that . . . fiercely engrossed, hating every minute I had to spend away from them to do house chores. In fact, I don't remember having any inner life until my junior year in high school when, after years of passing the public library on my way elsewhere, I decided to investigate that extraordinarily quiet building, looking like a graceful Grecian temple set in a small park, to find out what was inside. That is when Nietzsche and Huneker and Dickens and Tolstoy and Chekhov and Gorky . . . too many to mention them all . . . entered my life and I became spellbound, their junkie (we had no books at home), a kid with a secret life. A year later I wrote a paper on George Meredith for my English class. The teacher's notes in the margin showed extraordinary respect for my insight and rapport, and the dizzy thought raced through my mind that I might have been born to be one of that great company, that, in any case, my road lay in that direction. Then at the University of Chicago I wrote my first poems, and after that I knew that poetry was my calling. For the next three years at the University of Wisconsin I did nothing else and thought of nothing else. It became my identity, my very character, but just how this came about is beyond me.

"Coming after Pound and Eliot and Williams and Stevens, all of whom influenced me at first in different ways, the course I eventually took, after the usual years of groping and imitative work, led me to a kind of poetry that was called Objectivist. Associated with me in that name were Louis Zukofsky, George Oppen and Charles Reznikoff. You might say Pound's axioms on writing re-educated me, and whatever I wrote after that followed those axioms. They made such basic sense that they became my second nature. To all intents and purposes they were *my* principles and it became unthinkable for me to treat subject matter evasively or to use any word that did not (to use Pound's expression) 'contribute to its presentation.' Never, in other words, to be prolix or flaccid or unnecessarily abstract. Doing this, I found, made it safe to pour one's heart and mind into the writing.

"My poetry is, on the whole, lyrical and contemplative, grounded always in reality and character. When not lyrical, as in my *Americana* and *Droles de Journal*, it is satirical or humorous or ironic, little gremlins that can't make up their minds whether to laugh or curse. My prose is epigrammatic, towards which I seem always to be drawn."

———

Carl Rakosi was born in Berlin to Leopold Rakosi, a Hungarian watchmaker at that time in business in Germany, and Flora (Steiner) Rakosi. He spent his early years in Baja, a small town in Hungary. His mother suffered from mental depression, and he was raised by his maternal grandmother until the age of six when his father, who was by this time divorced, resettled in Chicago, remarried, and sent for him and his brother. He grew up in the midwest—Chicago; Gary, Indiana; and Kenosha, Wisconsin. Although his parents had little money, Rakosi managed with summer and part-time work to get a college education, taking a B.A. at the University of Wisconsin in 1924. He was by this time writing poetry and had published a few poems in the *Nation*, the *Little Review*, and Ezra Pound's *The Exile*. But having discovered that poetry and a degree in English were of little help in finding a job in the mid-1920s, Rakosi applied for a position as a social worker. In the years that followed, he drifted between social work and teaching, his heart set on a writing career that he could not afford to pursue.

Rakosi did social work in Cleveland and New York City, then returned to the University of Wisconsin for an M.A. in educational psychology in 1926. He spent a year teaching English composition at the University of Texas in Austin, two years teaching in a high school in Houston, a brief period in law school, and another training to be a psychiatrist. During this period he changed his name legally to Callman Rawley: "Rakosi was forever being mispronounced and misspelled, but the main reason was that I didn't think anyone with a foreign name would be hired, the atmosphere was such in English departments in those days." He retained Rakosi as his pen name under which all his writings have been published.

In 1932 Rakosi was invited by the poet Louis Zukofsky to contribute to an issue of *Poetry* that he was editing under Ezra Pound's sponsorship. Along with Zukofsky, George Oppen, and Charles Reznikoff, he became identified with the objectivist movement, writing a lean, unadorned, directly stated poetry. Rakosi was by now employed full time in social work. In 1940 he took a Master of Social Work degree at the University of Pennsylvania. From 1945 to 1968 he was executive director of Jewish Family and Children's Services in Minneapolis. Since retiring from social work, Rakosi has been a writer-in-residence at the University of Wisconsin (1969–1970) and Michigan State University in East Lansing. He received awards from the National Endowment for the Arts in 1969 and in 1972. Rakosi has also practiced privately as a psychotherapist. In recent years he has lived in San Francisco. He has been married since 1938 to Leah Jaffe, and they have two children.

During the years between 1933, when his first volume of poems was published, and 1941, when his *Selected Poems* appeared, Rakosi found it increasingly difficult to write poetry. He finally stopped writing poetry altogether: "I also stopped reading poetry," he said "I couldn't run the risk of being tempted." The demands of his job, especially in the critical years of the Depression, and the pressures of politics (for a brief period in the 1930s he was a Marxist) made it impossible for him to write anything except professional articles based on his social work. There was another gap in his creative output between 1941 and 1965, but since that time Rakosi has been remarkably productive, certainly putting the lie to the theory that poetry is an art of the young exclusively. Drawing upon experience enriched by his exposure as a professional social worker to the harshest realities of life, Rakosi writes with a mellowness that is realistic, not sentimental, forthright, outer-directed, and often richly humorous. An example is perhaps his best known poem, "Experiment with a Rat":

Every time I nudge that spring
                 a bell rings
and a man walks out of a cage
assiduous and sharp
                     like one of us
and brings me cheese.

How does he fall
               into my power?

As Diane Wakoski observed in *Contemporary Poets*, his poetry "feels like the language of a man who has been active all his life and now has comments about everything he has experienced, slightly wry and not at all uncritical, though delivered with friendliness."

Objectivist poets put their faith in the reality—the concreteness—of language, in the conviction that, as Michael Heller writes, words are "absolute symbols for objects, states, acts, interrelations, thought about them." They work against the romantic notion of the self or the ego as the center of the poet's consciousness. "The poet," Rakosi writes in one of the epigrammatic prose passages of *Ex Cranium, Night*, "is more modest than the ancient philosopher: he doesn't claim that what he has thought out is the ultimate reality." He achieves "objectification" in his poetry, Heller suggests, by the use of irony and distance. It is not that he is any less emotionally engaged, but that he is less self-involved (even when writing about his own observations and convictions), more engaged with the immediacy of his observation. In "The Lobster," for example, Rakosi observes with absolute objectivity:

> Eastern Sea, 100 fathoms,
> green sand, pebbles,
> broken shells.
>
> Off Suno Saki, 60 fathoms,
> gray sand, pebbles,
> bubbles rising.
>
> Plasma-bearer
> and slow-
> motion benthos!
>
> It radiates on
> terminal vertebra
> a comb of twenty
> upright spines
> and curls
> its rocky tail.
>
> Saltflush lobster
> bull encrusted swims
>
> backwards from the rock.

Perhaps the most striking characteristic of Rakosi's poetry is its compactness. Most of his poems are extremely short, and even when they run to two or more printed pages, their effect is of the tightest compression, of quintessences. "Man Contemplating a Rock" reads in its entirety:

> Incipit
>   the first
> philosopher
>   & ad
> infinitum

The beginning of a poem is the immediate perception of objects in reality. "Time to Kill" is simply a series of images perceived, as it were, at random:

> a man and his dog
>
> what fun
> chasing twigs
> into the water!

The poem continues with other images—"young girls bicycle by / in pairs and plaid shorts," "a gentle lake," an old man fishing, a plane flying overhead, and concludes:

> the poor small
> woodlouse
> crawls along
> the bark ridge
> for his life.

A poem that attempts to describe Rakosi's method of composition is "Shore Line," which opens meditatively: "We speak of *mankind.* /

Why not *wavekind* ?" and proceeds to a series of images perceived at the seashore—a small boy in a lifebelt sitting in a boat with a white and orange sail that is being sailed by his father; a fisherman throwing a fish back into the sea—

> This is the raw data.
> A mystery translates it
> into feeling and perception;
> then imagination;
> finally the hard
> inevitable quartz
> figure of will
>   and language.

Objectivist poetry does not exclude the poet's human presence. As L. S. Dembo observed in *Contemporary Literature* : "for Rakosi the true objectivist approach avoids the extremes of imagism, which he takes to be mere observation, and symbolism, which he believes seizes upon objects only as an excuse to express generalized moods." In "Services" Rakosi writes as a Jew at prayer:

> I, son of Leopold and Flora,
> also pray:
> I pray for meaning.
> I pray for the physical,
> for my soul needs no suppliant,
> I pray for man.
>
> And may a special providence look out
> for those who feel deeply.

Since resuming the writing of poetry in 1965, Rakosi told Dembo in an interview in 1968, he has been more committed to the "subject matter" and the "person" of the poet than he had been in his early work. He attributes this development to his "lifetime involvement with people in social work [which] might make me a poorer poet in some ways because I'm not so completely subsumed by language as I was then." He recognizes a joy in life which quite transcends poetry. In a poem of tribute to his wife, "Leah," for example, he begins by admitting that she does not belong in a poem:

> She is natural.
> She runs off
>   like rain water.
> I could not put her
>   under the hard master
> of an image
>   for my own need.
>
> So since poetry
>   is more abstract,
> more for its registrar,
>   give me her smile
> and let us hug
>   and romp
> in the plain life
>
> or I am lost!

PRINCIPAL WORKS: Two Poems, 1933; Selected Poems, 1941; Amulet, 1967; Ere-Voice, 1971; Ex Cranium, Night, 1975; My Experiences in Parnassus, 1977; Droles de Journal, 1981; History, 1981; Spiritus, I, 1983; Collected Prose, 1983; Collected Poems, 1986.

ABOUT: Contemporary Authors Autobiography Series 5, 1987; Contemporary Authors New Revision Series 12, 1984; Contemporary Poets, 4th ed., 1985; Hatlen, B. "Carl Rakosi and the Re-invention of the Epigram," in Rakosi, C. Collected Prose, 1983; Heller, M. Conviction's Net of Branches, 1985. Periodicals— Contemporary Literature Spring 1969; Iowa Review Winter 1971; New York Times Book Review January 28, 1968; November 16, 1975; March 8, 1987; (Village) Voice Literary Supplement January 13, 1987.

*RATUSHINSKAYA, IRINA (BORIS-OVNA) (March 4, 1954–), Soviet poet, short-story writer, memorist, and human rights activist, was born in Odessa. Her father was an engineer, and her mother taught Russian literature. She has one younger sister. Despite the fact that her mother was descended from the Polish gentry and the family lived in the Ukraine, Ratushinskaya's parents were officially registered as Russian nationals. When she was a child, her interest in her Polish roots, to which she was drawn by her grandparents, apparently caused friction between her and her conformist parents.

In 1971, Ratushinskaya began to study physics at the University of Odessa. She chose physics because it had remained relatively untainted by politics. As she told Ewa Kuryluk in an interview in the New York Review of Books: "At school I had been equally good in mathematics, physics, and literature. But I realized it was stupid to study the humanities in the Soviet Union. So I decided to change my female logic to a mathematical one. I understood that if I obtained a technical education, then this would open literature to me as well. In the Soviet Union people with technical professions are very much interested in literature and art. While people involved in the humanities are closed within their own fields." During her university years she had her first brush with the KGB. When she was nineteen, a KGB official tried to recruit her to fraternize with foreigners and report on their activities. She refused. In 1976, after graduation from the university, Ratushinskaya began to teach math and physics in secondary school and then became an assistant lecturer at Odessa Pedagogical Institute. She was interrogated by the KGB about an acquaintance who had applied to emigrate to Israel, and again she refused to cooperate. In 1977 she was asked to serve on the examination committee of the Pedagogical Insti-

IRINA RATUSHINSKAYA

tute and to discriminate against Jewish applicants. She turned down the post. As a consequence, she was reassigned to the laboratory staff and finally forced to leave her job.

Although Ratushinskaya began writing poetry when she was a child and had already gained some reputation for herself as a poet during her university years, she traces her serious commitment to poetry as a vocation to her discovery of the modernist tradition in Russian poetry at the age of twenty-four. In the essay "My Homeland" she describes this life-changing experience:

In a family of people basking in higher Soviet education, in schools girded in systematic controls, and in a literary world of deliberately half-baked books and journals, how could we have received any sense of other available culture? We never even knew of any "other" existing! So what a shock it was in my 24th year when I somehow happened to come across works of Mandelstam, Tsvetayeva, and Pasternak. I could have them but briefly, but I devoured them—and they literally threw me to my knees, physically shaking with delirium and fever. An abyss opened up before me and, unlike your normal nightmare where you can see yourself as an observer on the edge, I was thrown deep within, completely severed from whatever safe opening I'd come from. All my senses of history and literature were cracked and staggered. All the pent-up notions of who I might have been were stirred into motion. Was this the Polish spirit frolicking of its own accord now? I couldn't say. All I knew was that as long as I had been unable to take the Soviet religion seriously, there had never been any sense of anything to take its place. How could I go religion-seeking up there when I never even had my feet on the ground—in any homeland—down here? Clearly, I had not been looking for what now seemed to have found me. "It" had found me, as if a long-forgotten God had all along been buoying me up and guarding my soul when no one had been allowed to do this in all my years of childhood and youth.

> I covet that ten years I lost to my Soviet pseudo-education. . . . it was at 24, not 14, that I got a glimpse of our genuine culture and actual history. It was at 25, not 15, that I began to write. Yes, there were attempts before, writing attempts, but they were the mere scribblings of a child who through no fault of her own knew only half an alphabet.

In 1979, Ratushinskaya married Igor Gerashchenko, an engineer, and moved to Kiev to live with her husband. Since she could not obtain a residence permit, she could not find a job and so took up private tutoring in physics and math. In 1980, Ratushinskaya and her husband applied for permission to emigrate and were denied. The exile of Andrei Sakharov to Gorky convinced the couple to become involved in the struggle for human rights, and their first act was to write a letter protesting Sakharov's banishment. Their further activities included painstakingly photocopying banned books for dissemination as *samizdat*.

On December 5, 1981, Gerashchenko was fired from his engineering position, forcing him to take odd jobs repairing apartments and doing carpentry work to support the family. On December 10, the couple was arrested for the first time when they participated in the annual human rights demonstration in Pushkin Square in Moscow. They were given ten days each for "hooliganism," and Ratushinskaya served out her sentence in Butyrka Prison. On April 19, 1982, the door of their apartment was sprayed with a toxic substance, from which Ratushinskaya and her husband and three other people suffered mild poisoning. In the course of the following summer the apartment was ransacked four times. During the apple harvest, Ratushinskaya and Gerashchenko were offered jobs as farm laborers, giving the unemployed couple the opportunity to earn enough money in two months to keep them for an entire year. As they learned only later, however, the offer was a KGB provocation. Ratushinskaya was arrested on September 17, 1982 in the village of Lyshna, the other laborers having been specially selected as witnesses to testify against her. She was sent to a KGB prison and brought to trial after almost six months of imprisonment. The trial lasted only three days and, even by Soviet standards, represented a blatant violation of Ratushinskaya's rights. Her relatives were not allowed into the courtroom, and she was denied the right to choose her own counsel or to defend herself. On the day after her twenty-ninth birthday, she was sentenced under article 62 of the penal code of the Ukrainian SSR "for preparing and distributing anti-Soviet materials" to the maximum sentence of seven years of hard labor to be followed by five years of internal exile.

On April 12, 1983, Ratushinskaya was transported to Corrective Labor Colony ZhKh-385/3 at Barashevo in the Mordovian Autonomous Republic 330 miles southeast of Moscow. She was incarcerated in the "Small Zone," a separate compound for political prisoners and the only known settlement in the Soviet Union for female political prisoners.

Ratushinskaya spent the next three years in the "Small Zone" in inhuman conditions designed to break the spirit of resistance. She and her fellow prisoners were denied visits with their relatives; their correspondence was restricted; they were denied necessary medical care, and were confined for long periods of time in SHIZO, the acronym for the punishment isolation cell in which the women were kept on starvation rations, often in bitter cold. Even under these conditions, Ratushinskaya and her fellow prisoners struggled to maintain the vestiges of their human dignity, refusing to wear dehumanizing identification badges and going on hunger strikes in defense of their rights. Ratushinskaya continued to write poetry, and many of the over three hundred poems she wrote during her captivity were composed in SHIZO, scratched on a bar of soap and committed to memory before being erased to escape detection. In August 1984, she completed the poems in the collection *Vne limita* (translated as *Beyond the Limit*). The limit in the title refers to the limit of one letter every two months prisoners were allowed to write when confined in PKT, the prison within the camp.

Despite constant surveillance by guards and prison officials, Ratushinskaya was able to smuggle both her poems and camp news out to her husband. She became a *cause célèbre* in the West, with organizations such as PEN and Amnesty International campaigning for her release. In July 1986, she was transported to a KGB prison in Kiev, from which she was released on October 9, 1986, one day before the Soviet and American leaders met at the Reykjavik Summit. In November, Ratushinskaya and Gerashchenko applied for visas to travel abroad seeking medical care for Ratushinskaya, whose health had been seriously damaged by the rigorous conditions of her imprisonment. Their request was denied, but in December the decision was reversed, and on December 17, 1986, they left for London. Once there, their Soviet citizenship was revoked, forcing them to remain in the West. In recent years the couple have lived in London and in Chicago, where in 1988 she was poet-in-residence at Northwestern University.

Ratushinskaya's poetry straddles the seemingly antithetical poles of the individual's intensely private being, on the one hand, and her inevitable public or historical being on the other. In a poem which begins "And I don't know how they'll kill me," written in 1983 while she was in prison, the poet speculates on her own death, visualizing herself shot or tormented to death by the regime which has imprisoned her or, worse, imagining her heart wrenched out by the betrayal of those she loves:

And maybe, simply [they'll kill me]—in the form of a
     letter's news:
—You see . . . It turns out . . . Well, take cour-
     age . . .
We know you're strong . . . And how can I hold
     back my
     laughter
at those crumpled pages? How can one press
a hole, where just now there was a heart—
one's hands—already unneeded, unimportant?

But after this moment of doubt, she goes on to reaffirm her trust in her husband and friends:

Anyway, why am I chattering? That's not for me—
to assume doubt in my friends, my beloved—
to admit uncertainty! No is my only answer—
I refuse the assumption of greasepaint
on the most loyal in all the land,
most fierce, proud!
Well, what is it, wolf-like century? Curling
your snout like a beast?
Who's to be afraid of whom—do you know?
     Fire!

Recognizing the power of history to deform human relationships, the poet clings to ties, rendered fragile by distance and tyranny, for the strength to offer up her life in defiance of her enemies.

Just as history invades the sphere of the private in Ratushinskaya's poetry, so also, conversely, moments of intense beauty and domestic intimacy encroach on the harsh world of prison. Thus in another poem from 1983, beginning "I'll live through this, survive . . . ," the poet imagines how, once she's released, she'll answer those who ask her how she survived in prison:

And they'll ask: what helped us live,
without letters or news—just walls
and coldness in the cell, stupidity of official lies,
nauseating promises for betrayal.
And I'll tell about the first beauty which I saw in this
     captivity:
window in the frost! No spy holes, nor walls,
nor grating—no long suffering—
only bluish light in the smallest glass.
Whirling pattern—you can't dream of anything more
     enchanted!

By the same token, in a poem beginning "I'm sitting on the floor, leaning against the radiator," written toward the end of her first year in prison, the poet writes of "the sad story of Russia (or maybe we're just dreaming it?)," which includes

herself and another prisoner in SHIZO, her husband tuning a radio (presumably to an illicit station) in Kiev, and Mouse Mashka, a mouse tamed on breadcrumbs who shares her cell. Details like the pet mouse and the "prism-ice" of the window pane, evidence of Ratushinskaya's ability to preserve even in an isolation cell a vision imbued with childlike wonder, paradoxically render her prison world cosier and more intimate, while at the same time, by the force of contrast, throwing into relief the horror of her physical suffering.

While best known as a poet, Ratushinskaya works in prose as well. Her collection of short stories entitled *Skazka o trëkh golovakh* (translated as *A Tale of Three Heads*, 1986) comprises a series of fantastic tales which allegorically comment on the ills of Soviet life and history. Again here Ratushinskaya adopts a deliberately childlike angle of vision to make her point. For example, the title story, "A Tale of Three Heads," is cast as a fairy tale about a dragon with three heads. In the course of the brief tale (which is barely over two pages long), one of the dragon's heads consumes the other two in a transparent allegory of the history of Communist dictatorship in the Soviet Union. However, in an optimistic twist the story ends:

Until one day our dragon got lazy and caught its re-
     maining head in the train door at the last metro stop and
     was carted off to parts unknown.
     And so it should be, for what sort of fairy tale would
     this be without a happy ending?

However, Ratushinskaya's prison memoir, *Grey Is the Color of Hope*, is by far the most important of the poet's prose works. The memoir presents a compelling account of the poet's three years in a labor camp, focusing on the ongoing battle waged by the small but determined group of women political prisoners who inhabited the "Small Zone" to adhere to a strict moral code against the often sadistic attempts of camp officials to destroy their camaraderie. Inspired at least in part by Solzhenitsyn's *The Gulag Archipelago* (which Ratushinskaya cites gratefully as a textbook of sorts which prepared her for survival in the camps), *Grey Is the Color of Hope*, like its predecessor, is an act of memory and witness, preserving for posterity and announcing to a larger audience the atrocities committed by the Soviet government against its own people. Thus Ratushinskaya writes at the end of her introduction: "Even now, as I sit down to write this book, a small voice whispers at the back of my mind: leave it, forget about it, enough is enough! But I will remember. I know what must be done." Yet unlike the scope of Solzhenitsyn's massive historical opus, Ratushinskaya's canvas is more concentrated in time and space and belongs to a different and ostensibly "kinder" era. The very isolation of this small band of women—among the last political prisoners in the Soviet Union—renders their plight all the more poignant, and in her relation of their "small tragedies"—the pointless destruction of their beloved garden, the confiscation of letters from loved ones, the arbitrary cancellation of visits—Ratushinskaya achieves a powerful pitch of emotional intensity. Moreover, like Ratushinskaya's poetry, *Grey Is the Color of Hope* commemorates brighter moments as well, moments of communion and selflessness shared by fellow prisoners and moments of exhilaration when youth and the beauty of nature briefly overwhelm the harshness of prison existence. Thus Ratushinskaya relates how despite their weakened physical condition, the women decide to observe an ancient folk custom, dousing themselves with cold water and running naked and wet through the snow at Epiphany: "The snow burns my bare feet, the stars laugh at my protruding ribs, and joy bursts inside me like a small firecracker. Here are the buckets. The water feels quite warm. To avoid spilling water on the path (it's my turn to clear it tomorrow), I jump into a snowdrift and empty the bucket over myself there. After a searing moment, I no longer feel cold. Turning, I run back to the house. Halfway there I am unable to stop myself from waltzing instead of running. Tanya throws a towel over my shoulders. We do not need to look for reasons to laugh this night."

Ratushinskaya's poetry does not bear comparison with the most powerful voices in Russian poetry of the twentieth century, and her memoir must yield pride of place to Eugenia Ginzburg's haunting account of her incarceration and exile under Stalin, *Journey into the Whirlwind*, as well as to Solzhenitsyn. Nonetheless, her works represent a moving testimony to the indomitability of the human spirit and, as documents of recent times, serve as a reminder of those ills of the totalitarian system that survived into the Gorbachev era.

WORKS IN ENGLISH TRANSLATION: Two collections of Ratushinskaya's poems have appeared in English translation. The first, *Stikhi/Poems/Poemes*, translated by Meery Devergnas et al. and published in 1984, is a trilingual edition (Russian, English, French) which includes the essay "My Homeland" as well as selections of her poetry. The second, *Beyond the Limit/Vne limita*, published in 1987, is a dual-language edition (Russian and English) with translations by Frances Padorr Brent and Carol J. Avins. A dual-language edition of Ratushinskaya's short stories, *Skazka o trëkh golovakh/A Tale of Three Heads*, with translations by Diane Nemec Ignashev, was published in 1986, and

Grey Is the Color of Hope, translated by Alyona Kojevnikov, was published in 1988. *In the Beginning*, translated by Alyona Kojevnikov and published in 1990, is Ratushinskaya's memoir of her childhood and early years up to the time of her arrest in 1982.

ABOUT: Biographical Dictionary of the Soviet Union 1917–1988, 1989; Brent, F. Beyond the Limit, 1987; Current Biography 1988; Ignashev, D. *Foreword to* A Tale of Three Heads, 1986. *Periodicals*—Christian Science Monitor March 27, 1987; October 7, 1988; New York Newsday March 24, 1988; New York Review of Books May 7, 1987; June 1, 1989; New York Times June 28, 1987; New York Times Biographical Service March 24, 1987; New York Times Book Review October 30, 1988; Times Literary Supplement March 30, 1990; Washington Post May 14, 1987.

RENDELL, RUTH (BARBARA) (pseudonym BARBARA VINE) (February 17, 1930–   ), British writer of detective novels, psychological thrillers, and short stories, was born in London, the daughter of Arthur and Ebba (Kruse) Grasemann. She attended the Loughton County High School and worked as a reporter and sub-editor for independent West Essex newspapers before publishing her first crime novel in 1964. In 1950 she married Donald Rendell; they were divorced in 1975 but remarried two years later. They have one son. Rendell lives in Suffolk. Her most popular detective series—novels that have been hailed as solidly in the company of Dorothy Sayers, Agatha Christie, Ngaio Marsh, and Margery Allingham—center on the richly characterized Chief Inspector Reginald Wexford and his younger aide, Detective Inspector Mike Burden, and are set in the imaginary but very typical Sussex market town of Kings Markham. Kings Markham is not a tourist-brochure English village. Rendell insists: "The town is not at all like—I hate Agatha Christie so much, I can hardly bear to say the name of that village of hers—St. Mary Mead, where that awful Marple woman lives."

With more than thirty books now published, including three under the pseudonym "Barbara Vine," Ruth Rendell is regarded as not only one of the most prolific but also one of the most accomplished crime novelists writing in English, a peer of writers like Patricia Highsmith and P. D. James. In the course of her career, she has received one Silver and two Gold Dagger awards from the British Crime Writers Association, a special National Book Award from the Arts Council of Great Britain, and three Edgar Allan Poe awards from the Mystery Writers of America. She has been praised for her ingenious plotting—the hallmark of classic detective fiction—

RUTH RENDELL

and her penetrating insights into the darker side of human nature, more characteristic of the psychological crime novel. As early as 1981, writing in the *Times Literary Supplement,* Francis Wyndham observed that Rendell worked in two areas of crime fiction—"the classic puzzle, with a stable background and a recurring cast headed by a mildly eccentric detective and his more conventional subordinate; and the novel of pure suspense, in which a blundering innocent and a haunted psychopath become fatally entangled in a paranoid atmosphere of cross purposes and sinister coincidence."

Wyndham was not suggesting, however, that there was anything mechanical or formulaic in Rendell's large body of work. Rather, her novels have a basic structure, developed with many variations, in which a series of plausible and seemingly unrelated events and a group of seemingly average characters come together in a sudden and violent climax. Even in her earlier and more traditional detective novels her characterization is subtle and original. Rendell has said that she finds writing her Inspector Wexford books easier than the psychological suspense thrillers. Acknowledging Wexford's popularity she has said: "I get letters from women who would like to marry him if his wife ever dies!" But Wexford is no conventional leading-man hero. Douglas Johnson, in *London Review of Books,* describes him as "a character whose successes are due to the patient intelligence that compensates for growing old." He is sloppy, overweight, slow-moving, and, though at least on one occasion tempted to stray, he is a faithful

husband, a thoughtful, sensitive, and articulate man, having more in common with Georges Simenon's introspective Inspector Maigret than with the dazzling Lord Peter Wimsey of Dorothy Sayers' works. His assistant Mike Burden is also a fairly complex character. A widower with two young children to raise, he matures over the course of the novels, has love affairs, and finally remarries. The working relationship of the two detectives gives the novels considerable depth. As Jane S. Bakerman observed in the *Armchair Detective*: "The steady normality between the two men, their ability to balance affection and tension in a realistic fashion, greatly help to offset the horror of the ultimate rejection, the final non-affection, murder, around which each book is organized."

Both Wexford and Ruth Rendell came to fame in the early 1950s with her first book, *From Doon with Death.* The story begins with the murder of "an unprepossessing housewife" and involves the search for Doon, mysterious sender of letters and books. In his review in the *New York Times Book Review,* "Sergeant Cuff" lauded Wexford's competence and Rendell's "nice way of sketching various levels of life in Sussex." *Book Week*'s reviewer praised the "special quality" of Rendell's writing and called for more mysteries "of this high order." Wexford's challenging job demands all his resources—physical, emotional, and intellectual. In *A Guilty Thing Surprised* he stumbles upon a corpse in the woods, and, as the *Library Journal* sums it up, he must "search through many lives before he finds any pieces that stick together." Rendell here displays her firsthand knowledge of the English countryside and village life. The *Times Literary Supplement* praised the book as "a good murder story" which shows "care in creating people and place." Other Wexford novels have taken her detective as far afield as China, in *Speaker of Mandarin,* to solve a mystery back home in England. Here Rendell's allusions to classic Chinese poetry provide deftly interspersed clues, and in other Wexford novels there are allusions that reflect Rendell's extensive reading in all manner of subjects. In *An Unkindness of Ravens* Wexford must brush up on feminist terminology and Freudian psychology to tackle a murder that involves militant teenage feminists and the disappearance of a bigamist. The *Library Journal* stated that here Rendell has "a keen eye towards social observation . . . [and] offers sharp insights into feminism, pregnancy and the mother-child relationship." In *The Veiled One,* Rendell's fourteenth Wexford novel, she explores what the *New Statesman*'s reviewer calls "the dangerous life which goes on behind the veil of the everyday." Because the chief inspector is incapacitated, Detective Inspector Mike Burden is at the center much of the time. He struggles with Jungian jargon, pursues a paranoid young man, and finally acknowledges Wexford's superior wisdom. As in other of her novels, what might seem superfluous elements are so well assimilated that they prove to be essential to the unravelling of the puzzle.

Wexford and Burdon also figure in a number of Rendell's short stories. One of these, "The New Girl Friend," a grim and candidly told tale of sexual role-playing, received an "Edgar" in 1975. Like her full-length books, her stories are terse, tightly structured, and full of twists and surprises. Indeed, a common element linking her detective fiction with her psychological crime novels is her ability to startle and unsettle the reader who awaits an inevitable explosion of violence but can rarely anticipate the form it will take. As David Lehman wrote in *Newsweek*, Rendell "communicates an almost palpable sense of impending disaster."

Lehman, like a number of other reviewers of Rendell's work, prefers her psychological thrillers to the Wexford series, and in the 1980s she has seemed to move away from the pure detective genre, although she continues to publish in that area. Speculating in 1985 on her reasons for this change of direction, Douglas Johnson suggests that in fact it is more a natural development than a deliberate shift. Even in her detective novels she has raised questions of a profound nature on human identity, aberrant behavior, alienation: "The Wexford stories, like the thrillers, placed unthinkable events within an everyday context, explored confusions that revealed an apparently normal person to be abnormal." Johnson notes that many readers today reject the neat patterns of conventional detective fiction: "We want to be presented with the violence that lurks within the mundane, we want paranoia to be made plausible, we want to see those who are nourished on hatred, lives that are so suffused with boredom, pain and futility that they become unbearable. This is what Ruth Rendell has written about in her last two novels."

The novels to which Johnson refers are *The Killing Doll* and *The Tree of Hands*. In these, he points out, "there is violence but no mystery, no detection, no discovery, no revelation and no explanation of behaviour." Rendell holds her reader not with the contrivances of plot but with the complexities of her characters' inner lives. In *The Killing Doll* two unhappy children in a shabby house in a rundown neighborhood of North London live with adults with whom they simply can no longer communicate, and they are

drawn helplessly into a network of evil, imaginary and real. Even earlier, Rendell had explored the troubled emotional lives of alienated young people. In *A Judgement in Stone*, a book that "Newgate Callendar," in the *New York Times Book Review*, thought one of her best, she conjures up an alienated middle-class teenage intellectual: "Very slowly Giles closed his copy of the *Bhagavad Gita* which had been propped against the marmalade pot, and with a kind of concentrated lethargy extended himself to his full, emaciated, bony height. Muttering under his breath something that might have been Greek or, for all she knew Sanscrit, he let his mother kiss his spotty cheek." Giles and his stepsister Melinda are among the victims of an unfeeling, compulsive, illiterate housekeeper. The events leading up to mass murder here are gruesome but credible. As "Newgate Callendar" describes it: "Little by little a chip is added, with well-meaning people contributing to their own doom."

In *The Lake of Darkness* Rendell sketches her characters with details of the furnishings of a house that reveal the unsavory inhabitants. Although the rooms are "impeccably neat," the pervasive occult and eccentric vibrations suggest impending evil. Here, as in several other of her novels, there are hints of latent homosexuality and memories of disappointing sexual experience. Harriet Waugh wrote in the *Spectator* that *The Lake of Darkness* is above all "a well-constructed and deftly executed story." In *Make Death Love Me*, the central character, a mousey banker, is "poisoned . . . by the heady intoxication of literature." He flees a dismal suburban home and a vacuous existence for the excitement and distraction that London offers, but his romantic illusions render him ripe for theft, adultery, and death. In commenting on these psychological thrillers "Newgate Callendar" has noted Rendell's uncanny facility for getting inside her troubled characters' minds. The reader shares the sick vision of a demented killer as well as the flawed sight of so-called "normal" people. She creates a victim doomed by his own disturbed psyche but capable of inflicting disaster upon everyone around him. Still, our attention is focused on the victim, and Rendell withholds just enough from the reader to allow tension to mount steadily, even though we recognize the inevitability of the victim's fate.

As the decade of the 1980s closed, Rendell was continuing to publish Wexford novels, but critics (and apparently many of her readers) were giving more attention to her psychological crime novels. Partly, as Douglas Johnson had suggested, this may be because of a shift in public sensibilities; but it may also be because in this genre

Rendell has been able to employ her mastery of narrative technique in the service of a more subtle, profound, and terrifying mystery than any involved in the conventional detective story—the mystery of the human character.

In early 1990 American television audiences began watching dramatizations of Rendell's Wexford series with *Shake Hands Forever*. The author takes an active interest in the televising of her works, counsulting with writers and producers on scripts, costumes, and locations.

PRINCIPAL WORKS: *Novels*—From Doon with Death, 1964; To Fear a Painted Devil, 1965; In Sickness and Health, 1966; A New Lease of Death, 1967; Wolf to the Slaughter, 1967; The Secret House of Death, 1969; The Best Man to Die, 1969; A Guilty Thing Surprised, 1970; No More Dying Then, 1971; One Across, Two Down, 1971; Murder Being Once Done, 1972; Some Lie and Some Die, 1973; The Fear of Trespass, 1974; Shake Hands Forever, 1975; A Demon in My View, 1976; A Judgment in Stone, 1977; A Sleeping Life, 1978; Make Death Love Me, 1979; The Lake of Darkness, 1980; Death Notes, 1981; Put On by Cunning, 1981; Master of the Moor, 1982; Speaker of Mandarin, 1983; The Killing Doll, 1984; The Tree of Hands, 1984; An Unkindness of Ravens, 1985; Live Flesh, 1986; Heartstones, 1987; Talking to Strange Men, 1987; The Veiled One, 1988; The Bridesmaid, 1989; Going Wrong, 1990. *As Barbara Vine*—A Dark-Adapted Eye, 1986; A Fatal Inversion, 1987; The House of Stairs, 1989; Gallowglass, 1990. *Collected short stories*—The Fallen Curtain and Other Stories, 1976; Means of Evil, 1979; The Fever Tree and Other Stories, 1982; The New Girl Friend, 1986; Collected Short Stories, 1987.

ABOUT: Contemporary Authors 109, 1983; Contemporary Literary Criticism 28, 1984; Who's Who 1989. *Periodicals*—Armchair Detective April 1978; Library Journal March 1, 1985; September 1, 1986; June 15, 1987; London Review of Books March 7, 1985; New Statesman May 6, 1988; New York Times February 4, 1990; New York Times Book Review June 25, 1967; August 24, 1969; February 26, 1974; November 23, 1975; February 26, 1978; October 14, 1979; November 9, 1980; August 30, 1987; October 9, 1988; June 11, 1989; June 10, 1990; October 14, 1990; New Yorker July 6, 1987; Newsweek October 21, 1985; September 21, 1987; Saturday Review January 30, 1971; Time May 5, 1986; Times Literary Supplement February 23, 1967; April 23, 1970; July 23, 1982.

*REZZORI (D'AREZZO), GREGOR VON
(May 13, 1914–   ), a novelist and short-story writer in the German language, was born in Czernowitz (now the Ukrainian city of Chernovtsy), in the Austro-Hungarian province of Bukovina, which after World War I was merged into the kingdom of Romania. His Italian family name, Rezzori writes in his memoir *The Snows*

°retz´ ôr ē

GREGOR VON REZZORI

of Yesteryear, "derives from a fief in Sicily which, until the Bourbons, had belonged to the Holy Roman Empire of German Nations." The family belonged to a class of Germanicized minor nobility who always considered themselves at the apex of the myriad groups living along the frontiers of the decaying Austro-Hungarian Empire. Rezzori's parents were ill matched and separated while he was still a child. His father, Hugo, a civil servant, "a representative of the world of the Baroque who had landed in the wrong century," worked out his frustrations in hunting and the pursuit of women. In 1940, when the Russians took over Bukovina, he committed suicide. His mother—a woman of "wind-blown irrationality" and "delicate nervosity"—suffered a variety of probably imaginary illnesses and was neurotically overprotective of her children. Young Gregor was cared for mainly by a nurse whom he calls his "second mother." He was sent to a boarding school in Graz, in the Austrian province of Styria, then studied painting at the Kunstakademie in Vienna. He spent much of World War II in Vienna and Berlin, was not a soldier, and ended the war a penniless drifter.

Four of Rezzori's books have appeared in English. The first, *Ein Hermelin in Tschernopol* (An Ermine in Tchernopol, 1958; translated as *The Hussar*), is a vibrant, kaleidoscopic evocation of the imaginary city of Tchernopol, capital of the imaginary province of Teskovina. It is a city which "lies somewhere in the southeast of Europe . . . not a good, and certainly not a beautiful, city, but it was an extraordinarily intelligent one." The narrative is set at some time soon after the end of World War I; it is told, seemingly haphazardly and unconnectedly, in the first person, in an amused, indulgent, and ironic voice, by an adult recalling his childhood in Tchernopol and, even more memorable for him, the greater part of each year he spent idly with relatives in the foothills of the Carpathian Mountains.

Rezzori became intimately acquainted with the many peoples inhabiting this vast area, very little known in the West: "The blood of Dacians, Romans, Avars, Pechenegs, Kumans, Slavs, Hungarians, Turks, Greeks, Poles, Russians, and the Gepidae flowed in our veins. One could say, therefore, that Teskovina was 'ethnically very mixed' territory." Best of all, he loved the soft, undulating countryside, and the abrupt weather that was so much a part of it: "The first snow flurries, which came suddenly out of the east, drifted down on the magnificent blue-gold of autumn as, in their day, perhaps, the Pechenegs had descended on the cloisonné-columned halls of a Byzantine palace. To us, the snow seemed to taste of Asia." Various exotic characters are all passionately described: Miss Rappaport, the English governess; Mr. Alexianu, the Romanian tutor; Mr. Tarangolian, the country prefect and friend of the family; and the hussar of the English-language title, Major Nicholas Tildy de Szolonta et Voroshaza, whose story is "worth telling because he belonged to a species of human beings who are fast dying out—those who are masters of their own fate."

Most reviewers complained about the unconnected nature of the narrator's reminiscences; the word "exasperating" occurred more than once in their notices. Each of the many personages merits in the eyes of the narrator at least one lengthy, discursive story. Usually these allow the reader to form a comprehensive idea of the nature of a character, but this seems to occur at the expense of anything that could be termed, conventionally, a plot. The overall theme of the novel, however, is ever present and hard to miss: it is the inexorable decline and fall of the old Middle European order and the ways in which this momentous, thoroughgoing change unsettles even the lively, adaptable civilization of Tchernopol. "At its best," in the opinion of the reviewer for the *Kirkus Bulletin*, "this is writing as compact and many levelled as the most exciting poetry. . . . In stretches it is a great book; certainly a book for an intellectual audience, and one not to be read at a sitting."

Memoiren eines Antisemiten (1979; translated as *Memoirs of an Anti-Semite*) is undoubtedly Rezzori's best-known and most controversial work—its tendentious title alone guaranteed wide attention wherever the book appeared. The novel consists of five interconnected stories, all but one told in the first person in much the same disconnected tone as *The Hussar*, tracing the career from ardent, bedazzled youth to dyspeptic, disillusioned late middle age of a Central European fop, a man of elevated family, increasingly little money, and no political convictions. Gregor is the son of an intensely class-conscious minor aristocrat who is a monomaniacal hunter and a ferocious anti-Semite, a man who rarely lets an occasion pass without demonstrating his contempt for Jews in the rudest and most blatant ways conceivable. Each of Gregor's stories shows how he himself, in his dealings with Jews, has always, at all stages of his life, half-consciously internalized his father's prejudices. The book is thus a kind of chronicle of prejudice and its consequences; yet only in the last story, "Pravda," told in the third person, is the meaning of a life of prejudice made clear. Gregor is almost an old man, living in Rome with his third wife. His life has gone awry; nothing in his surroundings is comprehensible or fails to disgust him. He has lost a son, and even the cherished memory of the culture of *Mitteleuropa* is fading, incomplete, irrecoverable in anything like its totality. He is, he realizes at last, an alienated man who failed at crucial times in his life to make connections between emotional and sociopolitical realities. For all the Jews he befriended, for all the amusing, *gemütlich* fellow-feeling they shared with him, he was able to stand aside—an apparently acute observer, an aloof dandy—as his civilization crashed around him and the Jews, so integral a part of that civilization despite his father's claims, were taken away for extermination. His constant sang-froid is more chilling and sickening than any hysteria. There is always the underlying sense, in Gregor's accounts of the chaos swirling around him, that he himself after all had little to worry about. "During that summer and autumn of 1938, most of the Jews I knew went away. Some of them were arrested and locked up for a while, and came home with some rather gruesome stories about what was going on in the prisons of the Rossauerlände. Some disappeared, and we did not know whether they had been put in jail or had just fled at the last moment. All this was pretty awful, I had to admit. But one knew, after all, how people were—some being horrid, others really very nice—and those who got arrested were not always entirely innocent. A Jewish lawyer, telling about his cruel treatment at the hands of the SS, said proudly, 'But I was not arrested for just being a Jew. I am a criminal.'"

Rezzori's power of evocation in the stories is

often stupendous. In general feeling and in detail he captures the loveliness of the countryside in Bukovina in the 1920s; the half-Oriental, half-Slavic teeming squalor of Bucharest in the 1930s; the lively, polyglot café society of Vienna between the wars; and most fascinating of all, the banal, careless, quotidian quality of Central European anti-Semitism. In Vivian Gornick's view: "The man at the center of these stories is always on the verge of breaking through to some open understanding of his feelings about Jews; he keeps coming close, but never arrives. . . . He openly longs for prewar Europe, the only world he can ever understand or value, and retreats before our eyes into the cocoon-like dislocation he has always wanted to occupy."

An earlier novel of Rezzori's, much longer and more complex but not so finely formed as *Memoirs of an Anti-Semite*, is *Der Tod meines Bruders Abel* (1976; translated as *The Death of My Brother Abel*). This is an intricate and ambitious attempt, in over 600 pages, to portray the condition of Europe and European society from the end of World War I to the late 1960s. The narrator, who has much in common with those of the two books discussed above, is at the beginning of the novel in 1968 living in a seedy Parisian hotel composing scripts for "piglets" and "film weasels" while laboring intermittently and in increasing despair on fragments of a novel he has been unable to finish for nineteen years. We read these fragments, the "pieces, patches, sketches, notes" of his almost unbelievably eventful life. They take us, in no particular or chronological order, from his birth in the last year of World War I and his childhood in southeastern Europe through his youth in Vienna and his war service in the Romanian army; along the way, we glimpse all the hardships and deprivations attendant upon wartime and postwar devastation. "Rezzori's alter ego buttonholes you," according to Gabrielle Annan, in the *New York Review of Books*, "convinces you that what he has to say is not just important but vital, your great, your last, your only chance to understand what happened in and to Europe between 1918 and 1968."

This is a genuinely postmodern work of literature, in which plot and character and the reader's expectations regarding them are rigorously and constantly subordinated to theme and structure. The narrator, the author, identifies himself entirely with his book, sees himself, in fact, as the helpless creature of the *Zeitgeist*, the all-knowing, malignant spirit of the twentieth century: "As redeemers or wanton strivers, as geniuses or run-of-the-mill morons, we are tiny particles of some collective whole whose will we carry out—thereby fulfilling its destiny. None of our gestures can be dissociated from these states and currents, which furrow us like a wheat field in the wind—the wind of the *Zeitgeist*." It is all done with great brio, inventiveness, and a passion for language that attracts and persuades. Most reviewers were fairly convinced of the book's greatness, although, in a strikingly discordant note, S. S. Prawer, writing in the *Times Literary Supplement*, severely criticized the novel's "logorrhoea . . . too hyped-up, . . . too long . . . a work whose titillating and bitchy passages may beguile a railway journey, but which has neither the form nor the intellectual and moral substance to engage a more permanent interest."

Rezzori has written scripts for Volker Schlöndorf, among others, and has acted for Louis Malle. His works untranslated into English include stories about the imaginary country of Maghrebinien: *Maghrebinische Geschichten* (Maghrebinian Stories, 1953), *1001 Jahr Maghrebinien* (1001 Years of Maghrebinien, 1967), and *Der arbeitslose König* (The Unemployed King, 1981), the first two illustrated with dozens of his lively, spidery line drawings; four volumes of mordant sketches, *Idiotenführer durch die deutsche Gesellschaft* (Idiot Leaders in German Society, 1962–1965), also illustrated by the author; and several novels, from *Oedipus siegt bei Stalingrad* (Oedipus Conquers Stalingrad, 1954), subtitled *Ein Kolportageroman*, a dime-novel or penny-dreadful, to *Kurze Reise übern langen Weg* (A Short Trip on a Long Road, 1986).

PRINCIPAL WORKS IN ENGLISH TRANSLATION: *The Hussar* was translated by Catherine Hutter in 1960. Joachim Neugroschel translated *Memoirs of an Anti-Semite* in 1981, and *The Death of My Brother Abel* in 1985. Rezzori's memoir *The Snows of Yesteryear* was published in 1989 in a translation by H. F. Broch de Rotherman.

ABOUT: Contemporary Author 122, 1988; Contemporary Literary Criticism 25, 1983; Oxford Companion to German Literature, 2nd ed., 1986; Wer Ist Wer, 1988. *Periodicals*—Book World August 30, 1981; Choice February 1986; Christian Century August 31, 1960; Christian Science Monitor October 4, 1985; Kirkus Bulletin February 1960; Library Journal March 15, 1960; June 15, 1981; August 1985; Nation August 22–29, 1981; New Republic July 18, 1981; New York Herald Tribune Book Review March 29, 1960; New York Review of Books July 16, 1981; September 26, 1985; New York Times November 24, 1989; New York Times Book Review April 10, 1960; July 19, 1981; September 29, 1985; November 26, 1989; Newsweek July 13, 1981; Time April 11, 1960; September 14, 1981; Times Literary Supplement November 18, 1960; April 4, 1986.

RHODES, RICHARD (July 4, 1937–),
American novelist and non-fiction writer, was
born in Kansas City, Kansas, the younger son of
Arthur (a laborer) and Georgia (Collier) Rhodes.
A Hole in the World describes his early life.
When he was still a baby, his mother killed herself, and after a period of drifting, his father settled down with a second wife, an insanely
sadistic woman who beat, starved, and tormented her stepchildren until the authorities were
brought to intervene. Richard, by then aged
twelve, and his brother were sent to the Andrew
Drumm Institute in Independence, Missouri—a
farm run by the boys who lived there. After six
years at the Institute, during which he developed a genuine appreciation of farm life, he was
accepted at Yale University, from which he received his B.A. (cum laude) In 1959. In 1960
Rhodes married Linda Iredell Hampton, by
whom he has two children, Timothy James and
Katherine Hampton. They were divorced in
1974, and in 1976 Rhodes married Mary Magda-
lene Evans. Rhodes began his career as a writer
trainee for *Newsweek* in 1959. In 1960 he became a staff assistant for Radio Free Europe, in
New York City; and from 1960 to 1961 he was
an instructor in English at Westminster College,
Fulton, Missouri. For the next eight years—from
1962 to 1970—he worked as a publicity writer
and editor of in-house publications for Hallmark
Cards in Kansas City, Missouri. By 1970 he felt
confident enough to turn to writing full-time,
publishing articles for a variety of national magazines as well as fiction. From 1970 to 1974 he
was contributing editor for *Harper's* magazine,
and since 1974 for *Playboy*.

Rhodes' first book, *The Inland Ground: An
Evocation of the American Middle West*, was
published in 1970 to generally favorable reviews. Consisting of fifteen pieces of reportage
concerned with Kansas, Missouri, Nebraska, and
Iowa, it celebrates the independent spirit of the
prairie region. The essays are diverse, ranging
from a piece on hog-butchering and a coyote
hunt to biographical sketches of such notable native sons as Harry Truman and Dwight D.
Eisenhower. The reviewer for *Publishers
Weekly* considered it "an exceptional book," and
Thomas Goldwasser in the *Saturday Review* was
impressed particularly by the biographical
pieces, finding the sketch of Truman's return to
Missouri at the end of his presidency
"beautifully done."

Rhodes' second book, *The Ungodly: A Novel
of the Donner Pass*, is a fictionalization of actual
historical events. It is based on the wagon-train
expedition led by George Donner that left
Springfield, Illinois in April 1846 for California.
Through a series of mishaps and mistakes, the

RICHARD RHODES

party was forced to spend the winter in the Sierra Nevadas without sufficient provisions. Many
died of cold and hunger; others kept from starving by eating their dead. Reviews tended to fault
the novel in one respect or another. Phoebe Adams in the *Atlantic* commented that the book "is
stronger on maneuver than on characterization.
It is also aggravatingly languid until the final catastrophe, when the inchworm progress pays off
in detailed, slow-motion horror." Michael
Mewshaw in the *New York Times Book Review*
remarked that the novel "begins on a superficial
level, and stays there too long. There are monotonous weather reports, a proliferation of pointless anecdotes, and maddening shifts in point of
view. With dozens of people to deal with, Mr.
Rhodes might have been wiser to develop a few
of them in depth rather than skim through so
many interchangeable minds and emotions."

Holy Secrets, Rhodes' second novel, centers
upon Tom Haldane, a Kansas City gynecologist
whose thirteen-year marriage falls apart before
he eventually reestablishes his life. The work was
received rather coldly by reviewers, who complained that the narrative was frequently convoluted and pretentious. "Certain elements of
Tom's coming to terms with himself," Christopher Lehmann-Haupt commented in the *New
York Times*, "seem like clichés . . . [the actions
of certain characters] have quotation marks
around them, and one suspects they have been
forced to become clichés by the author's refusal
to let them be themselves." Much more favorably received was Rhodes' non-fictional *Looking
for America: A Writer's Odyssey*, which assem-

bles twenty of his magazine articles of the 1970s. Topics include skywriting, a New Mexico horse race, a trip West, a visit to the annual dances of the Osage Indians, and profiles of men in public life. Jack Forman in *Library Journal* found Rhodes at his best when writing about people. His finest pieces, he remarked, "deal with three men: J. Robert Oppenheimer, Edward Kennedy, and Gerald Ford—whose lives he dissects with preciseness and sometimes cruelty." The reviewer for the *Atlantic* commented that the collection "demonstrates that [Rhodes] is one of the best literary journalists now writing."

Rhodes returned to fiction with his third novel, *The Last Safari*, set in Africa. Its protagonist is Seth Crown, a white man raised by the Masai, a former hunter and guide who now owns a tourist camp in Tanzania. Twenty years earlier Crown's Masai wife had been raped and murdered by Boers on a rampage of racial hatred; but turmoil erupts again in more modern times when black terrorists led by a young man named Rukuma (who turns out to be Crown's own son) pillage the camp and kill the tourists. Reviews of the novel were decidedly favorable. Michael Malone, in the *New York Times Book Review*, remarked that "Mr. Rhodes evokes the 'brutal simplicity' of African land and life appreciatively, but without distortion and without the sensationalism that heated Robert Ruark's fiction about the same region." The reviewer for the *Atlantic* observed that Rhodes "lays out the bones of his tale in a spare prose that is deliberately (and sometimes ponderously) reminiscent of Hemingway . . . but the flesh of the book is fed by those qualities that have made Rhodes a first-rate essayist: a huge appetite for information, acute powers of observation, and the ability to find connections where none are obvious. . . . [This] is a serious novel that reads like a good mystery."

The Last Safari was quickly followed by *Sons of Earth*, a novel about astronaut Reeve Wainwright who walked on the moon but whose subsequent life has been harried by troubles. After he takes up a farming life near Kansas City, his adolescent son is kidnapped and held for ransom in an oversized coffin that is buried underground and has a life support system that will provide air and water for only a week. As Wainwright races to raise the ransom demand for $500,000 in gold, the deadline for saving his son rapidly approaches. Critics agreed that Rhodes had written a "high-voltage thriller" that, as the reviewer for *Publishers Weekly* remarked, "keeps the reading writhing in suspense right to the end." David Quammen, in the *New York Times Book Review*, found the psychotic kidnapper, Karl Grabka, who lusts after fame, however momentary or perverted, one of the striking successes of the work. "The actions and motivations of Karl Grabka throughout the tale," Quammen noted, "his febrile fantasies, the texture of his tawdry and disconnected life, are portrayed in a chillingly convincing and concrete way."

Rhodes' most notable book to date is the nonfictional *The Making of the Atomic Bomb*, which gained him widespread attention. A Book-of-the-Month Club selection, it won the 1987 National Book Award and the 1988 Pulitzer Prize. A work of 886 pages (including seventy pages of notes and bibliographic references), it traces the development of nuclear physics from the dawn of the twentieth century to the explosion of the first atom bombs at the end of World War II. Reviewers were frequently struck by Rhodes' grasp of the technical aspects of nuclear science, and his ability to convey them to the reader with a sense of drama—exemplified by his description of the first millisecond of the atomic age in New Mexico:

> The firing circuit closed; the X-unit discharged, the detonators at 32 detonation points simultaneously fired; they ignited the outer lens shell of Composition B; the detonation waves separately bulged, encountered inclusions of Baratol, slowed, curved, turned inside out, merged to a common inward-driving sphere; the spherical detonation wave crossed into the second shell of solid fast Composition B and accelerated; hit the wall of dense uranium tamper and became a shock wave and squeezed, liquefying, moving through; hit the nickel plating of the plutonium core and squeezed the small sphere shrinking, collapsing into itself, becoming an eyeball . . . .

William J. Broad in the *New York Times Book Review* remarked that *The Making of the Atomic Bomb* "is a major work of historical synthesis that brings to life the men and machines that gave us the nuclear age. . . . [It] is the best overview of the century's pivotal event." Solly Zuckerman in the *New Republic* observed that Rhodes "has taken infinite trouble to understand and to outline in simple language the principles of nuclear physics that are the foundation on which the story of the book rests. The personalities who move through this book come to life in a way that they are unlikely to have done had they been depicted by a scientist's pen. . . . I have no doubt that his book will stand for years to come as an authoritative account of the way our nuclear age started. Above all, lengthy though it is, it will be enjoyed as a magnificent read."

As several reviewers of Rhodes' *Farm: A Year in the Life of an American Farm* observed, the author was returning to his boyhood roots when he undertook to chronicle one year, 1986, in the life of a Missouri farming family (he gives them a fictitious name in the book). "I lived with the family on a daily basis," he told the *New York Times Book Review* in 1989. "I took an apartment for $75 a month in a nearby town. I was an unpaid hired hand with a notebook in my pocket. They live a life they deeply enjoy. It's really priceless. This family weathered the worst agricultural crisis since the 1930s. . . . They will never have to do what to them would be a fate worse than death—which would be to move to the city." A sympathetic but always conscientious journalist, Rhodes records in detail the hard but spiritually (though not financially) rewarding life of the modern-day American farmer. "Mr. Rhodes is clearly present in these pages," Christopher Lehmann-Haupt wrote in the *New York Times*. But why, Lehmann-Haupt asks rhetorically, should readers care about the trials of a farmer in the '80s? "We care because the author makes us care," he answers. Rhodes reports on the mechanics of farming, the pressures imposed on farmers by the large grain companies and by complex government regulations, the cruel treatment of hogs in the interests of fattening them for the market. "Mr Rhodes's chronicle is unvarnished, his vision acute," Maxine Kumin wrote in the *New York Times Book Review*.

Rhodes has been the recipient of numerous awards, including a Guggenheim Fellowship (1974–1975), a National Endowment for the Arts grant (1978), a Ford Foundation Fellowship (1981–1983), and an Alfred P. Sloan Foundation grant (1984). He lives in Kansas City, Missouri.

PRINCIPAL WORKS: Novels—The Ungodly: A Novel of the Donner Party, 1973; Holy Secrets, 1978; The Last Safari, 1980; Sons of Earth, 1981. *Non-fiction*—The Inland Ground: An Evocation of the American Middle West, 1970; Looking for America: A Writer's Odyssey, 1979; The Making of the Atomic Bomb, 1987; Farm: A Year in the Life of an American Farmer, 1989; A Hole in the World: An American Boyhood, 1990.

ABOUT: Contemporary Authors New Revision Series 1, 1981; 20, 1987; Who's Who in America 1988–1989. *Periodicals*—Atlantic August 1973, March 1979, April 1980; Library Journal January 15, 1979; New Republic August 22, 1988; New York Times December 30, 1977; September 21, 1989; New York Times Book Review July 29, 1973; March 9, 1980; August 9, 1981; February 8, 1987; September 24, 1989; October 28, 1990; Publishers Weekly September 7, 1970; April 10, 1981; Saturday Review January 9, 1971.

*ROA BASTOS, AUGUSTO (June 13, 1917–), Paraguayan novelist, short story writer, poet, film scriptwriter, and journalist, was born in the small village of Iturbe in the Guairá region of his native country. He grew up among

AUGUSTO ROA BASTOS

the peasantry, speaking both Spanish and the indigenous language of the region, Guaraní. In 1925, at the age of eight, he was sent to Asunción, the national capital, to attend a military academy. In the city, the young Roa was given access to the library of his uncle, the bishop of Asunción, which resulted in his first exposure to literature—most notably that of the Spanish Golden Age. He did not follow a military career, but before he reached the age of twenty, he had fought as a volunteer with the Paraguayan army in the savage Chaco War against neighboring Bolivia. In 1937 Roa Bastos finished his first novel, "Fulgencio Miranda," which was never published. After the war he pursued a career as a journalist. During the early 1940s he traveled among the *yerba maté* tea plantations of northern Paraguay collecting material as editorial secretary for the Asunción newspaper *El País*. His efforts resulted in the extensive documentation of the exploitation of plantation workers and—along with his experience in the Chaco War—provided him with much of the raw material for his first major novel, *Hijo de hombre* (1960; translated as *Son of Man*). Roa Bastos maintained his association with *El País* until 1947. In 1942 he published his first book, a collection of poetry entitled *El ruiseñor de la aurora* (The Nightingale of Dawn). He continued to write poetry throughout the 1940s and was also the author of a number of dramatic works that were presented in the capital. In 1944, Roa Bastos was awarded a fellowship by the British council to study radio and newspaper journalism in England. There he witnessed the final months of World War II and presented a series of radio programs on Latin American culture for the BBC. He also traveled to Paris, where he interviewed Charles De Gaulle and continued his radio broadcasts. In 1945 he took advantage of an invitation from the French ministry of information to travel throughout France and Africa. Roa Bastos returned to Paraguay in 1946 only to see his country engulfed in a bloody civil war by the beginning of the following year. As a result, the author—like thousands of his countrymen—sought political asylum in Argentina. In 1947, Roa Bastos settled in Buenos Aires, where he continued to live and work for many years until eventually taking up residence in France. He lived in Toulouse, where he taught at the University of Toulouse until his retirement in 1985. In February 1989, after the fall of General Alfredo Stroessner's government, he was invited by the new Paraguayan government to return to his native country; and, according to the *New York Times*, he indicated that he would accept the invitation.

In the forty years of Roa Bastos' exile from Paraguay, he returned to his native country from time to time on what he called "unauthorized visits." On his visit in 1982 he was arrested; his passport was confiscated and he was offically expelled. In 1986 he told Larry Rohter, in an interview in the *New York Times Book Review* : "They said I was a dangerous Marxist agitator who preaches subversion, when all I want is the possibility of a pluralist democracy, as has happened in Argentina, Brazil and Uruguay. Now I am one of only three citizens who is expressly forbidden to return." Rohter writes: "The irony is that [Roa's most famous work] *I the Supreme*, which Paraguayans regard as their greatest novel and which continues to circulate there despite its implied censure of the dictatorship of Gen. Alfredo Stroessner, was itself written while Mr. Roa Bastos was living in exile in Argentina. 'Exile has been for me an enormously enriching experience, and I don't hold any rancor against those who have exiled me,' said Mr. Roa Bastos, who has spent his years away from home as a film scriptwriter, professor and teacher of Guaraní. . . . 'I try to see exile not as a political sanction, as a punishment or restriction, but as something that has forced me to open to the world, to look at it in all of its complexity and breadth. The exile exists in a state of limbo, but he is also a privileged observer.'"

During the first years of his exile in Buenos Aires, Roa Bastos turned to the short story as a medium for voicing his social concerns. In 1953 he published his first collection of stories, *El trueno entre las hojas* (Thunder Among the Leaves). As David William Foster observes, these stories "with their emphasis on violence, on social injustice, and on the particular circumstances of the Paraguayan experience, anticipate the themes, language, and techniques of Roa's first published novel, *Son of Man.* . . . " Foster points out, however, that Roa, along with other Latin American writers, began to doubt the effectiveness of regionalism and social realism as "simply not an eloquent enough vehicle to represent the complex issue of the Latin American experience. Hence the interest in myth, in magical realism, in variants of European expressionism. . . . There is little doubt that Roa avails himself of the general principles of nonregionalist fiction. We realize this in his choice of a highly poetic language, the mixing of Spanish and Guaraní . . . , the use of exceptional circumstances that imply a meaning far beyond the surface texture of sequential events, and the creation of individuals that are less typical in a folkloristic sense and more figurative in a mythic one."

Hijo de hombre (Son of Man) won first prize in 1959 in an international competition sponsored by Editorial Losada, which published it the following year. As Robert H. Scott notes in the *Encyclopedia of World Literature in the Twentieth Century* : "Since its publication it has received universal acclaim as one of the best novels of the Latin American 'boom' era. Thematically and structurally it is an extension of the short stories, but its profoundly sensitive portrayal of human struggle, its symbolic and mythical qualities, and its understated style raise it to a higher artistic level." Considered to be "the national novel of Paraguay," *Son of Man* consists of seven distinct but subtly related narratives. It covers Paraguay's history from the nineteenth century to the present and is unified, Scott writes, by "the centrality of the Christ myth and the accompanying motifs of crucifixion-resurrection, heroism-betrayal, and the redeemed prostitute by which Roa Bastos is able to transmute Paraguayan reality into universal myth."

In 1960 Roa Bastos published another collection of poetry, *El naranjal ardiente* (The Burning Orange Grove). In 1960 he also wrote the screenplay for *Hijo de hombre*, which was recognized as film of the year in the Spanish language, and in succeeding years wrote movie scripts for a number of other major Latin American novels, including Miguel Angel Asturias' *El señor presidente.* In 1961 he directed the Writers Workshop sponsored by the Argentine Society of Writers and traveled to Germany to participate in another workshop with such other noted Latin American writers as Asturias and Jorge Luis Borges. Roa Bastos also returned to the short story in the 1960s and early 1970s. His best known collections of short fiction to appear after *El trueno entre las hojas* are *El baldio* (The Empty Field, 1966) and *Morencia* (Slaughter, 1969). In the words of Scott: "Most of Roa Bastos' [later] stories are set in rural or small-town Paraguay and deal with the oppressed poor; others have as their protagonists members of the middle class and take place in Asunción or Buenos Aires. . . . What stands out in these stories is man's heroic struggle for freedom, authenticity, and spiritual redemption in the face of what are seemingly hopeless circumstances. Tragically trapped by nature, society, and self, Roa Bastos' men and women are capable of self-redemption through solidarity and sacrificial death."

The work for which Roa Bastos is best known, however, is the lengthy and complex *Yo el Supremo* (1974; translated as *I the Supreme*). Praised by, among others, the renowned Mexican novelist Carlos Fuentes as "one of the milestones of the Latin American novel," *Yo el Supremo* is one of several works produced during the mid 1970s in the region which deal with the Latin American dictator. For this reason it is commonly compared with such masterpieces as Gabriel García Márquez' *El otoño del patriarca* (1975; translated as *The Autumn of the Patriarch*) and Alejo Carpentier's *el recurso del método* (1974; translated as *Reasons of State*). Unlike these novels, however, *Yo el Supremo* is based on a single identifiable historical figure, namely the Paraguayan despot Dr. José Gaspar Rodríguez Francia, who ruled his country as "Perpetual Dictator" from 1816 until his death at the age of seventy-four in 1840. The result, according to Fuentes in the *New York Times Book Review*, is "a richly textured, brilliant book—an impressive portrait, not only of El Supremo, but of a whole colonial society in the throes of learning how to swim, or how best not to drown. . . . This is Mr. Roa Bastos' dialogue with himself through history and through a monstrous historical figure whom he has to imagine and understand if he is ever to imagine and understand himself and his people."

As *New York Times* reviewer Michiko Kakutani explains: "In the case of *I the Supreme*, Mr. Roa Bastos has cleverly adopted the pose of 'compiler.' The novel, [the 'compiler'] writes, 'has been culled—it would be more honest to say coaxed—from some twenty thousand dossiers, published and unpublished, from an equal number of other volumes, pamphlets, periodicals, correspondences and all manner of testimony— gleaned, garnered, resurrected, inspected—in public and private libraries and archives.' The bulk of the book, however, takes the form of

Francia's own reminiscences . . . and for the most part, those reminiscences concern the dictator's attempts to answer the critics who accuse him of turning 'the nation into a doghouse stricken with hydrophobia'; to rationalize his actions, in short, to explain his life."

The novel, however, as Foster points out, is "neither documentary nor historical, although it does attempt to provide some illusion of the former. But unlike antiquarian historical novels, which are customarily characterized by the 'thesis' concerning the men and events they recreate, *I the Supreme* is neither a condemnation nor a revindication of Francia. Nor is it an objective novel, at least not in the sense of scholarly neutrality." Francia, speaking from his deathbed, reviews his life—often in a delirium that moves wildly from past to future, from reality to nightmare. Kakutani writes: "Though they lack the intense lyricism and strange magic found in García Márquez' work, these passages reverberate with a fierce surrealism—peopled with dwarfs, women warriors and clairvoyant animals; studded with Borgesian images of mirrors and labyrinths, mystical eggs and blankets made of batskin, and embroidered with subsidiary tales about madness, death and humiliation. . . . "

Yo el Supremo, in a manner characteristic of other contemporary Latin American works, is also a novel that enters into "structural" and semiological experimentation. Francia has no faith in language. "Forms disappear, words remain, to signify the impossible," he declares at one point. "No story can be told. No story worth the telling. But true language hasn't yet been born. Animals communicate with each other, without words. Better than we, who are so proud of having invented words out of the raw material of the chimerical. Without foundation. No relation to life." Kakutani points out that "Francia's words often seem to take on a life of their own that survives his own existence. . . . Just as his own public statements serve, at best, as a response to the 'outrageous falsehoods, wicked tricks and diabolical machinations' of his enemies, so his memoirs become fodder for the manipulations of successive generations. In fact, however cumbersome and rhetorical *I the Supreme* may often feel, the novel remains a prodigious meditation not only on history and power, but also on the nature of language itself."

Roa Bastos identifies *Yo el Supremo* as the second part of his "Paraguayan trilogy." He is currently at work on the final volume, which "covers a full century of Paraguay's tumultuous history, culminating in the opening in 1984 of the $16 billion Itaipú power plant, the world's largest, near Iguaçú Falls."

WORKS IN ENGLISH TRANSLATION: *I the Supreme*, in Helen Lane's translation of 1986, was the first of Roa Bastos' works to be published in the United States. It had earlier been translated into almost all the principal languages of the world, including Japanese and Chinese. The first English-language translation of his work was *Son of Man* by Rachel Caffyn, published in London in 1965.

ABOUT: Contemporary Literary Criticism 45, 1987; Encyclopedia of World Literature in the 20th Century 4, rev. ed., 1984; Foster, D. W. The Myth of Paraguay in the Fiction of Augusto Roa Bastos, 1969, *also* Augusto Roa Bastos, 1978; Foster, D. W. and V. R. Foster (eds.) Modern Latin American Literature 2, 1975. *Periodicals*—Book World (Washington Post) May 11, 1986; Commonweal May 23, 1986; New York Times April 2, 1986; New York Times Book Review April 6, 1986; New Yorker September 22, 1986; Times Literary Supplement August 15, 1975.

RODGERS, CAROLYN M(ARIE) (December 14, 1945–   ), American poet and fiction writer, writes: "I was born the last child of Clarence and Bazella. They hailed from Little Rock, Arkansas during the great migration with me in the womb. My older sisters and brother had all been born in the South. I was called the 'city slicker.'

"I grew up in Chicago right near 47th Street, home of the famous blues singers like Muddy Waters, Guitar Slim, and Howlin Wolf and the famed 708 Club. We lived in a small house, two doors down from an A.M.E. church (African Methodist Episcopal), where, after baptism, I spent much of my cognitive years. At the age of ten or eleven, the church bought a temple, and we marched, parade style, about twelve city blocks to it. The church was huge, and absolutely magnificent. It comfortably seated at least 1,000 people, with stained glass murals, a white altar with red velvet trimmings and natural wood chairs. The church was a former synagogue and it was so beautiful, we Negroes literally died and went to heaven there, singing the Hallelujah Chorus.

"In our first house on 47th Street, we had a yard all our own, unusual in Chicago with its huge building complexes and housing projects. In the summers, we tried to dig holes to Mexico, a feat I firmly believed possible. I read all the books in the nearby library by the time I was twelve years old. I especially liked biographies and fairy tales and pioneer stories. I sang in the young people's choir and, most important, I was enrolled by my mother in the Ethel Mimms Lucas School of Dramatic Arts, a school of 'elocutions.' There, I learned to memorize and dramatize the poetry of Negro authors like Paul Laurence Dunbar and Langston Hughes. Up until I was almost fifteen years old, I performed with great gusto and encouragement (monetary and verbal) at church affairs, teas, musicals and the like. I joined the drama club and the choir in high school, and I secretly began to write poems. After high school, I started playing the guitar and singing folk songs in coffee houses and for awhile, everyone, (including me) thought that I was going to be another Odetta rather than a Gwendolyn Brooks type. But the night life scared me away from singing professionally.

"After attending Hyde Park High School, I went to the University of Illinois, a Chicago junior college, and then on to Roosevelt University where I majored in English and minored in psychology. English never disappointed me. College was Shakespeare, Millay, Burns, Donne, Shelley, Keats, Eliot, and on and on. No Black authors, called Negro then. I read Baldwin on the side, fell in love with Martin Luther King, Malcolm X, and carried picket signs for our first Catholic president. While I was a student at Roosevelt, the English department had a reception for Gwendolyn Brooks, the first Negro author to ever win a Pulitzer. At that gathering, I approached her shyly and asked if she would look at some of my poems. She said, 'Yes.' It took me two years to get up enough courage to send her anything, but when I finally did, what she said about my work thrilled my heart. After that I began to send work out. Less than a year later, I was at a cocktail party for artists, and I met the editor of Johnson Publications Negro Digest. I asked him the same question I had asked Ms. Brooks. To make a long story short, he published me.

"I left college, one credit away from graduation. I began to work for the YMCA with high school dropouts. They provided a wealth of material, and I began to write more poems, short stories, and plays. Eventually, I decided to devote all my time and energies to writing, and I left the YMCA for the frightening world of the 'freelance writer.' People who had traveled that road ahead of me were there to catch me as I fell from sure paycheck grace. I began to travel around the country reading my poems at conferences, colleges, and bookstores, while submitting works to various magazines. It was wonderful, and very, very hard to do. In 1969, I began my teaching career. I had studied Afro-American literature on my own, and under the direction of two writing workshop leaders. I had met people like James Baldwin, LeRoi Jones, John O. Killens, and Margaret Walker at the home of Gwendolyn Brooks. They had shared their wealth of experiences in the small intimate groups we had congregated in.

"I began teaching first at Columbia College, went on to be an artist-in-residence at Albany State College, Malcolm X College and Indiana University. I continued writing and publishing and practically starving to death. In the year 1984, a most appropriate year, I decided to get a master's degree in English. Two and a half years prior to that, I had taken the one course I had needed for some twenty-odd years to get my B.A. I matriculated at the University of Chicago, and the degree was conferred. Oh happy day.

"I am still writing. I hope to always write. As early as nine years of age, I kept a diary, and I forgot to mention that even in junior college, I was published in the student literary magazine. The stuff I wrote almost makes me nauseous today, but I stand by it, stomach in check, and I can laugh about my ardor."

In 1968 Hoyt W. Fuller, Jr., the director of the Chicago Organization of Black American Culture, wrote in his introduction to her first book of poems, *Paper Soul* : "Carolyn Rodgers is a child of double words. She is an inhabitant of that construct most of us still recognize as middle-class America, an entity of special certainties and institutions; and at the same time she dwells among the spiritual and cultural revolutionaries who would shatter the weighty irrelevancies of that world, leaving stand only the solider outposts and bastions onto which a more humane edifice might be joined."

Over the next two decades Rodgers' work has matured and developed in new directions, but she remains essentially a poet "of double words" in the sense that she writes as a black poet expressing the pride of her identification with her race, and she also writes as a woman discovering her strength in sisterhood and female bonding. As a black activist she has learned to temper her rage without compromising her principles: "we are still hurting. / we are not free," she writes in "The Quality of Change" (in *The Heart as Ever Green*):

we have spent the years
talking in profuse & varied
silences to people
who have erected walls for themselves
to hear through.

The promises of recent history remain "words / synonyms?":

no change, status quo the same?
oh say, would you believe,
we are hoping again
for the change of ....
hi

the quality of
change.

As a woman she observes her sisters "clutch their men" tightly to "close peace in / close and sure, clutch":

the bias of their days dipped
in search & keep and life itself
clutching and caressing
reason and order
sanctity and peace.

—from "Untitled No. 1"

Rodgers' early poems, written in the fervor of the civil rights movement of the 1960s, reflect the excitement and defiance of young black people discovering their voices and finding an outlet in literature for their rage and frustration. A founding member of the Chicago Organization of Black American Culture, she met other young black writers and received encouragement from them as well as from established writers like Gwendolyn Brooks. *Paper Soul* contains a mixture of poems in what one critic described as "hip style– some in black English, others in formal English, all expressing youthful rebellion. She rejects the fundamentalist gospel religion of her family while affirming, however, a deep personal faith:

God—
they fear you, they hold you so
tight they squeeze the truth in you
out (you run wild in my soul).

—from "Testimony"

She is angry, keenly sensitive to the barriers that separate black from white society, writing bitterly for example of the campus of the University of Chicago where the Midway divides the affluent educated white society from the black ghetto of the South Side:

They say the slum is almost
cleaned and if you walk north
you won't have to look,
Think or even know that
It's there.

—from "Song to U. of C.—Midway Blues"

Rodgers' second collection, *Songs of a Blackbird*, elicited a less enthusiastic reception than had greeted *Paper Soul* in which the poet Don L. Lee (H. R. Madhubuti) found "glimpses of greatness." Both Lee and Dudley Randall acknowledge the continuing vitality of her work and its satirical wit: "i is uh revolutionist / i has uh blue newport dashiki . . . and we is saving to buy as many / Black businesses as we can." But they objected to certain mannerisms, especially the dialectal spelling which they found in compatible with the sophistication of the poems. Randall wrote: "The reader has only so much attention to give to a poem, and if he's distracted or puzzled by unfamiliar spellings, he has that much less attention for the poem." Lee concluded, however, that Rodgers' weaknesses in a few poems "only makes us more aware of her strength in others." Some of her most striking poems here are those in which she confronts her female identity:

> how do I put my self on paper
> the way I want to be or am and be
> not like any one else in this
> Black world but me?
>
> —from "Breakthrough"

Exploring and discovering herself in even greater depth characterizes the poems in *how i got ovah*, a volume which the *Library Journal* described as a transformation from "militant Black woman to a woman intensely concerned with God, traditional values, and her private self." When "little Willie" announces to Joe that "the revolution is dead. . . . Black is as tired as it is beautiful," Joe replies with analogies to flying in a plane—"you move so fast don't seem like you be moving at all"—and rest periods between rounds of boxing:

> now, Little Willie, Joe said
> I looks at it this way my man . . .
> the Revolution aint dead
> its tired,
> and jest resting.

She is also at peace with herself as a woman, more understanding of the old fashioned fundamentalist religion of her mother who "saved pennies / fuh four babies /college educashuns":

> My mother, religious-Negro, proud of
> having waded through a storm, is very obviously
> a sturdy Black bridge that I
> crossed over, on.
>
> —from "It Is Deep"

And she sees herself now as "more than a 'sister'":

> i saw a Woman. human.
> and black.
>
> i felt a spiritual transformation
> a root revival of love
> and i knew that many things
> were over
> and some me of—beauty—
> was about to begin.
>
> —from "Some Me of Beauty"

Here the poems reflect a self-assurance that comes with maturity. The voice is easier, more relaxed, even humorous (Angela Jackson, in her poem "Foreword" to the book, called Rodgers a "singer of sass and blues"), but still alert to the realities of American society.

These changes in outlook require no apology: Rodgers writes in an "Author's Note" in the volume that "where one has been makes where one is more meaningful." An even greater degree of assurance was apparent in *The Heart as Ever Green*. Once again she writes of feminism, love, religion, and black identity, but she seems more resolved to move forward not in strife but with calm determination. Reviewers noted the compassion, simplicity, and growing consciousness of nature as a source of faith and renewal:

> We now know why
> the fish swims away
> from his place of birth.
> we know now why
> it fights the rush
> of waters as it pressure points
> toward some unknown redestined place.
> if need be,
> we know now
> how.
>
> —"Spawning-to-Bring-Forth"

Rodgers' short fiction and essays have been published mainly in journals directed to a black audience—*Essence, Ebony, Black World, Negro Digest*. Her stories realistically portray life in black ghettos—the problems of school dropouts, teenage pregnancies, drug addiction. "In her stories as in her poetry," Jean Davis writes in the *Dictionary of Literary Biography*, "the dominating theme is survival, though she interweaves the idea of adaptability and conveys the concomitant message of life's ever-changing avenues for black people whom she sees as her special audience." Her work, both poetry and prose, appears in many anthologies of contemporary black literature, and she has given poetry readings at colleges and universities all over the United States. *how i got ovah* was a National Book Award nominee in 1976. She has also received the first Conrad Kent Rivers Writing Award (1969), an award from the Society of Midland Authors (1970), a grant from the National Endowment for the Arts (1970), and a Carnegie Award (1979).

PRINCIPAL WORKS: Paper Soul, 1968; Love Raps, 1969; Songs of a Blackbird, 1969; how i got ovah, 1975; The Heart as Ever Green, 1978; Translation, 1980; Eden and Other Poems, 1983.

ABOUT: Contemporary Authors New Revision Series 2, 1981; Contemporary Poets, 4th ed., 1985; Dictionary of Literary Biography 41, 1985; Lee, D. L. Dynamite Voices, 1971; Evans, M. (ed.) Black Women Writers, 1983. *Periodicals*—Library Journal July 1975; Publishers Weekly April 7, 1975; April 24, 1978.

RUBENS, BERNICE (July 26, 1928–),
Welsh novelist and filmmaker, grew up in Cardiff, Wales, the daughter of Eli and Dorothy
(Cohen) Rubens. She attended Cardiff High
School for Girls and University College, University of Wales, earning a B.A. (honors) in English
in 1947. After graduating, she taught at the
Handsworth School for Boys in Birmingham,
England, from 1948 to 1949, before becoming a
freelance screenwriter and documentary filmmaker.

A prolific novelist, seriously concerned with
problems of faith and self-definition in the modern world, Rubens regards herself as essentially
a spontaneous writer. In an interview with BBC
correspondent Rosemary Hartill in the late
1980s, she said: "I never consciously write anything. I am not conscious of what I intend to say,
what message, as it were, I intend to put over.
I don't have that kind of consciousness, and I'm
glad I don't. I think that if I did, the book
wouldn't work." As a fledgling novelist, Rubens
wrote from her own experience of growing up
in a Jewish family. Her first novel, *Set on Edge*,
concerns the Sperber family and its attempts to
marry off the spinster daughter Gladys. Rubens
focuses on the love-hate relationship between
Mrs. Sperber and Gladys, who is unable to leave
home even after her mother's death. John Coleman, in the *Spectator*, found this a "packed,
sharply written novel" though full of unlikable
characters; Rubens' intermittently "cruel, precise observation," he continued, attested to her
promise as a novelist. *Mate in Three*, Rubens'
second work, describes a simultaneously destructive and supportive relationship among a wife,
her husband, and his mistress. Critics again admired Rubens' style but thought that the book
was too schematic.

In *Madame Sousatzka*, Rubens tells the story
of Marcus Crominski, an accomplished child pianist, and the adults who figure prominently in
his life. Marcus' teacher, Madame Sousatzka, enhances his style with her Method, then becomes
reluctant to give him over to either his mother
or the crass impresario who wants to engineer
Marcus' success. The book received generally
good reviews. The *New Yorker* labeled it a
"strange little story" but admired Rubens' idiosyncratic supporting characters and complicated
and surprising plot. *Punch* reviewer R.G.G.
Price, however, called the book "too sugary," the
supporting characters unconvincing, and the story overly winsome "in its Jewish warmth and humour and colour and passion for the arts." The
novel was made into a film starring Shirley MacLaine in 1989, in an adaptation by the novelist
Ruth Prawer Jhabvala that changed the central
character into a young East Indian boy and set

BERNICE RUBENS

the scene in a very contemporary, rapidly deteriorating London neighborhood.

The Elected Member centers on the Zwecks,
a Jewish family whose destructive need for a
scapegoat is fulfilled by son Norman. A successful lawyer, Norman bends, then breaks under
their demands. He resorts to drug use, which
brings even greater censure from his father, a
rabbi, and his sister. As Rubens charts the
Zwecks' disintegration as a family, she fills in
past events, such as the late Mrs. Zweck's insistent lie that the family was happy and whole,
and another sister's elopement with a gentile. Finally, Norman collapses under his family's burden; the novel ends with his desperate prayer,
"Dear God, Look after us cold and chosen ones."
The novel won the 1970 Booker Prize, Britain's
highest literary award. It also earned acclaim
from most reviewers for its sensitivity, universality, and wit. Julian Mitchell called it "a remarkable achievement, easily the best of Miss Rubens'
four novels so far. . . . Above all, it is Miss Rubens' tenderness for the mad and broken which
makes her book a grave pleasure to read." The
New Statesman's David Haworth praised her
compassion and intelligence, singling her out as
"one of our finest Jewish writers." Despite their
overall endorsement of the book, however, reviewers found it flawed by clumsy flashbacks
and a lack of convincing writing in some scenes.

With her next novel, Rubens attempted to
"challenge myself to step outside that familiarity
of 'Jewish themes in a Jewish environment.'"
Sunday Best presents the witty, tongue-in-cheek
story of one day a meek transvestite George

Verrey Smith (he soberly teaches school the other six days). George buckles under the pressure of a spate of scandals and becomes Georgiana on a more regular basis. As he is forced to come to terms with his difficult childhood and cope with his frowzy wife and crazy mother, his female persona takes over completely. George narrates his own story until the takeover, after which Rubens employs a third-person narrator. Critics agreed that *Sunday Best* was not Rubens' best. Some missed the humor in earlier novels while others found the shifting narrative disruptive and uneven. Gerry Clark offered a more positive view in *Best Sellers*, calling the book "as entertaining an afternoon's divertissement as has been published in many a day." "The writing," he continued, "part straight-ahead narration and part first-person memoirs, is deceptively simple, and exceptionally clear."

Rubens again created a split-personality character in *Go Tell the Lemming*. Angela and her estranged husband David are reunited in Italy, where they have gone to work together on a film. The film's star, Daphne, is joined by her husband, and the two couples become involved in a series of infidelities and recriminations not unlike those in the script they are shooting. The hostility between the characters is heightened by Angela's dual personality, one side of which nurses rancor for David. Reviewers generally agreed that *Go Tell the Lemming* failed to achieve its potential. The *Listener*'s Roger Garfitt appreciated Rubens' "insight of feeling" and "several intelligent attempts to offset Angela's suffering, and create some perspective in the novel." However, he found the other characters stunted in development. The *Times Literary Supplement* similarly acknowledged the urgent emotions of Rubens' characters but felt that she had failed to create dramatic tension between them.

Loneliness and deprivation are frequent themes in Rubens' novels. In *I Sent a Letter to My Love* the main character, Amy Evans, a lifelong resident of a Welsh seaside town, seeks escape from her unloving mother and bachelor brother by advertising in a local paper for a "gentleman with similar needs"; only her brother responds. In *A Five-Year Sentence*, which was short-listed for the Booker Prize in 1978, another lonely, unmarried woman uses a diary, given her as a retirement present, as an outlet for her long-repressed sexuality. In both novels the central characters seem doomed to frustration and despair. Similarly, in *Birds of Passage* two elderly widows decide to seek the "something" that has eluded them in life by taking a luxury cruise, only to be victimized by a waiter who is a rapist. These novels won critical approval for their keen psychological insight and bitterly ironic humor, but they struck some reviewers as at times contrived. Edith Milton, for example, in the *New York Times Book Review*, wrote that the unhappy characters in *Birds of Passage* ultimately "look not only silly and small but also as though they had been manipulated by the author to serve her own frame of mind rather than their fictional necessities."

In other novels Rubens has moved far away from contemporary English setting. Java, where she traveled in 1969 while working on her documentary film *Stress*, is the scene of *The Ponsonby Post*, a black farce that examines critically the post-colonial collision of West and East. *Spring Sonata* is an even more ambitious and daring departure from conventional realism, having for its "hero" an infant genius, Buster Rosen; still *in utero*, Buster refuses to be born into the pain-inflicting world. Rubens presents Buster's story in excerpts from his journal, kept on a prescription pad snatched, along with a violin, during a fruitless cesarean. When Buster's relatives finally become convinced of his existence and musical talent, they scheme to take him and his mother on a concert tour. Buster's only escape is suicide, which he commits by severing his umbilical cord with his violin bow. Equally ambitious, though more realistic in subject matter, is Rubens' twelfth novel, *Brothers*. The book covers 150 years of history, focusing on the Bindels, a Jewish family. Rubens establishes her theme early in the book when Jakob Bindel tells his son and grandson that "only in the name of love is Death worthy, and friendship." Successive sets of brothers struggle to honor this directive in the face of disasters like pogroms and the Holocaust.

In her fiction of the mid-1980s Rubens has moved toward the mystery genre, but again she resists the traditional and conventional. *Mr. Wakefield's Crusade* tells the story of Luke Wakefield and his quest to solve the mystery of a letter that begins: "Dearest Marion, I have just returned from your funeral. I killed you, my dearest, as gently as I was able, and I buried you where no one will ever find you." *Our Father* introduces an adventuress/writer, Veronica Smiles, who falls in lust with God while trekking across the Sahara. She nonetheless marries Edward, a good if boring man. The plot becomes complicated when Veronica discovers that she is pregnant. Given her husband's sterility and her brief sexual encounter with a plumber who may have been God, she can only guess the baby's paternity. Meanwhile, she tries to come to terms with her own childhood in which she was caught between antagonistic parents, both now dead. These later novels have had mixed receptions, but reviewers agree that Rubens is always entertaining and challenging. Having once described herself as "open to the most radical changes in my thinking and outlook," she never fails to surprise and divert her readers.

Throughout her writing career, Rubens has continued to write and direct documentary films, which are often about the handicapped. Her honors include the 1969 Blue Ribbon Award of American Documentary Film Festival for her film *Stress* and a fellowship at the University of Wales. Rubens, who enjoys playing the piano and cello, lives in London with her husband Rudi Nassauer, also a writer, and their two daughters.

PRINCIPAL WORKS: Set on Edge, 1960; Mate in Three, 1966; Madame Sousatzka, 1962; The Elected Member, 1969; Sunday Best, 1971; Go Tell the Lemming, 1973; I Sent a Letter to My Love, 1975; The Ponsonby Post, 1977; A Five-Year Sentence, 1978; Spring Sonata, 1979; Birds of Passage, 1981; Brothers, 1983; Mr. Wakefield's Crusade, 1985; Our Father, 1987; Kingdom Come, 1990.

ABOUT: Contemporary Authors 25–28, 1977; Contemporary Literary Criticism 19, 1981; 31, 1985; Contemporary Novelists, 4th ed, 1986; Dictionary of Literary Biography 14, 1983; Hartill, R. (ed.) Writers Revealed, 1989; Who's Who, 1989. *Periodicals*—Best Sellers September 1980; Jewish Quarterly Autumn 1977; Listener November 15, 1973; November 8, 1979; December 17, 1981; New Leader July 30, 1979; New Statesman February 14, 1969; September 29, 1978; October 26, 1979; September 2, 1983; New York Review of Books July 20, 1975; New York Times November 29, 1987; New York Times Book Review May 6, 1979; June 20, 1982; November 17, 1985; December 27, 1987; New Yorker August 30, 1962; Punch December 5, 1962; Spectator December 23, 1960; Times Literary Supplement November 9, 1973; July 25, 1975; June 10, 1977; March 27, 1987; March 2, 1990.

RUMENS, CAROL (December 10, 1944–), English poet, novelist, playwright, editor, and critic, is the daughter of Wilfred Lumley and the former Marjorie Mills. She was born in Lewisham, in south London, and spent her childhood in the adjoining suburb of Forest Hill, where she had her primary education at St. Winifrede's Convent School. When she was about eleven the family moved further south to Croydon, on the outskirts of London. From 1955 to 1963 she attended Coloma Convent Grammar School there. She wrote verse from an early age and at sixteen became a reviewer for the *Croydon Advertiser* of local concerts.

In 1966 Carol Lumley entered Bedford College, University of London, as a student of philosophy. She was married a year later to David Rumens and, with the birth of their daughter Kelsey, left the university without a degree. Their second daughter, Rebecca, was born in 1968. She was thirty before she was able to go out to work, first in publishing as a publicity assistant (1974–1977), then as an advertising copywriter (1977–1981).

She had continued to write poetry during the years when her young children kept her at home and her first pamphlet of verse, *A Strange Girl in Bright Colours*, was published in 1973. These poems deal, not surprisingly and sometimes bitterly, with love and marriage, children and parenthood—with how "the trauma of marriage swallowed me," so that "my role is to wait / for the key in the lock, to serve the first clean kiss / and light up at a flick of my clitoris." ("Houses by Day")

John Press, in his article about Carol Rumens in the *Dictionary of Literary Biography*, places her "among the most talented" of "the generation who attained poetic maturity in the 1970s without the consciousness of belonging to a group." However, if she had allegiances to no specific literary movement, she could not entirely avoid the potent influence at that time of Sylvia Plath. In "An Essay on the Poetry of Carol Rumens" in *PN Review* in 1985, Anne Stevenson wrote that "no English-speaking woman beginning to write poetry in the 1960s, impressed by the work of Plath and Sexton, could altogether escape that diction of swaggering anguish, mixing college-girl paradox . . . with punchy colloquialisms . . . until the manner becomes almost a formula. But already by 1973 Carol Rumens . . . was moving beyond the poses of exercise poetry into . . . her [distinctive language] of trembling sensitivity."

The poet had remarked in her first collection that she was "interested in most forms of liberation, particularly women's and children's." The various imprisonments and circumscriptions of women, from Sappho and the Cumaean Sibyl to Charlotte Brontë and Anna Akhmatova, is the theme of the dozen poems in her second small book, *A Necklace of Mirrors*. Several of these poems were collected along with new work in Rumens' first major volume, *Unplayed Music*, in 1981. For the most part these poems deal with the ordinary concerns of family life and work in a London where "The pollen count rises in the afternoon. / An Arab child steals a lemon in Selfridges. / The discontent of the unions rumbles softly / like a pit disaster many miles away." ("Days and Nights")

By now, wrote Anne Stevenson, Rumens had "purged her poems . . . of hysteria and overwriting. A number of poems in *Unplayed Music* are as fine, technically and in terms of their human insight, as any minor verse written in this half-century. I would cite 'Coming Home,' 'Suburban,' 'Before These Wars,' 'Double Bed,' and 'A Marriage' as brilliant successes in what seems to be, beneath a veneer of contemporary women's attitudes, a deeply English tradition of observation and meditation. The wistfulness inherent in this tradition (Edward Thomas and Louis MacNeice belong to it) is enhanced, in Rumens' case, by the obvious delight she takes in making her poems into works of art."

Peter Bland, reviewing the collection in the *London Magazine*, also made the connection with Edward Thomas and found "a barely perceptible melancholy that threatens but never quite topples over into the sentimental. She is good at lifting the *music* of her work for a final stanza, while at the same time leaving the poem's moral considerations open-ended." In "Unplayed Music," the thrill of a possibly impending affair is concluded with:

All night in the small grey room
I'm listening for you, for the new music
waiting only to be played; all night I hear nothing
but wind over the snow, my own heart beating.

The red brick house in Forest Hill where Carol Rumens spent her first eleven years belonged to her grandparents and was shared with them, with their mentally damaged daughter, and with memories of another child the grandparents had lost in its infancy, as well as with Rumens' own parents. This haunted place became for Carol Rumens a "gingerbread house" in which her parents were imprisoned like Hansel and Gretel. It is evoked in the nine short poems collected in *Scenes From the Gingerbread House*. Dick Davis wrote of this sequence that the "poems are firmly and memorably put together, they make the claustrophobia of domestic emotion believably present and the language is never allowed to become limp or lachrymose. She is particularly good at using naturalistic detail so that it gently reverberates with symbolic connotative meaning." Davis quotes from the last poem in the set, "The Second Vision," in which her father's misty betrayed idealism, and his wish for his daughter to share it, are beautifully summed up by the way he points out to her distant objects she cannot make out:

—but I did see France
as we stood on the pier at Folkestone.
A smear of cloud where water
fainted into blue air,
it united us at last
in the one keen focus, stirred
a seeing at the back of my eyes.

In 1981 Rumens left advertising and became poetry editor of the literary magazine *Quarto*. She continued in that capacity with the *Literary Review* when, in 1982, it absorbed and replaced *Quarto*. In 1983–1985 she was also Creative Writing Fellow at the University of Kent. In 1983 her second major collection, *Star Whisper*, was a Poetry Book Society Choice.

Star Whisper is in three sections, the first dominated by a sense of exile and loss—domestic sometimes, as in "An Easter Garland," her elegy for her father—but most often in the context of Eastern Europe, for which Rumens feels a deep imaginative sympathy. The title poem reflects upon a passage in General Gourko's book *Wyna*, about his adventures during the 1930s in Siberia: "In my ears I heard all the time a sound as a trickle of corn, produced by the freezing of one's breath into hoar-frost; this music was locally called 'star whisper.'" The poem suggests that in the West, where we breathe more easily, our lives nevertheless lack the resonance of that cold music.

It seemed to Anne Stevenson that "here much of the English wistfulness disappears and is replaced by a laconic but highly disciplined pity. Influenced by the works of Middle European poets such as Miroslav Holub in Czechoslovakia and the Hungarian János Pilinszky, Carol Rumens retains her feminine voice, but extends her sympathies beyond Feminism in sinewy but heart-piercing poems. . . . Look, for instance, at the marvelous poem called 'The Hebrew Class,' in which she imagines a classroom . . . of Jewish children isolated in the innocence of 'grammatical laws' while a 'savage thaw of tanks' closes around them." The children's classroom

. . . is also history.
Consider your sweet compliance

In the light of that day when the book
Is torn from your hand,
And, to answer correctly the teacher's command,
You must speak for this ice, this dark.

In Stevenson's opinion, such poems avoid both what she calls "vicarious narrative" on the one hand and personal "confession" on the other, not serving "as a purge for vague guilts" but helping us "to understand ourselves and the world we have made" and taking "responsibility for individuality within the general horror."

The second section of *Star Whisper* comes home from Siberia to Regent's Park in London, where the pleasures and losses of love work themselves out against the background of John Nash's urban Arcadia. A number of poems in the third section also deal with love and marriage, and with the failure of both. John Press preferred these poems to those in the "Regent's Park Crossings" sequence, finding them "weightier and more emotionally satisfying. . . . 'Double Exposure,' a poem about a failed marriage, is a long, muted cry of pain. It is, however, not a moan of self-pity: the poet loses neither intellectual nor emotional control, observing with fine exactness the domestic interiors of a London suburb and the sleazy cosmopolitanism of the metropolitan streets. . . . There are other poems that show the poet's ability to assimilate into her art the hardness of the neon-lit city, as well as more tender poems about children and herself as a child."

There is a continuing preoccupation with Eastern Europe and Russia in the nineteen poems collected in *Direct Dialling*. Here the grief at the acuteness and universality of human suffering is so deep that most of these poems eschew the artifice of rhyme and, as Anne Stevenson wrote, press "beyond incident into an almost inarticulate region of moral shock." John Press regretted this departure but Stevenson found, in poems like "Outside Oswiecim" and "A Jewish Cemetery," "examples of how a poetic mode or style can be used with extraordinary power to transcend itself."

"Outside Oswiecim" has been much discussed. Oswiecim is the Polish name for Auschwitz and the poem, confronting the Holocaust, chooses to do so not in terms of the millions who died but of individuals, details:

Not 'the six million,' not 'the holocaust,'
not words that mass-produce, but names. One name;
Husserl's, perhaps. His favourite food, his new watch.

Jan Montefiore, in her *Feminism and Poetry* identifies the poem (by comparison with others on the same theme) as one that was, "as its title implies, written 'outside' the experience it commemorates: 'spoken' by a series of voices (the poet, the victims, even the fascists), it dramatizes its distance from its own material." John Cotton suggests in *Contemporary Poets* that it is precisely this distance from the events Rumens describes that "allows her to experience them imaginatively."

A *Selected Poems*, containing much new material as well as poems from earlier collections, was published in 1987. Elaine Feinstein, reviewing the book in the *Times Literary Supplement*, refers to Rumens' "allegiance to an Eastern European identity which, in her own life, can only be at one remove. And yet, reading her poems, it is impossible not to feel that she is in addition looking for a shape in the outside world that accounts for her own sense of displacement. It may

be that her very finest poems ("Letter from South London," for example) embody something else, a narrative exploration of the local commonplaces of her experience, and that it is in these, rather than in the poems with grander themes, that we find her own wry talent at its sharpest."

In fact Carol Rumens' interest in Eastern Europe may be traced back to a school friend who was Czech, about whom she wrote years later in her poem "Geography Lesson." In a letter to *World Authors* in 1989, Rumens wrote: "I became keen on Russian literature—I read *Dr. Zhivago* in my teens and was dazzled!" In the early 1980s her job for a London publisher took her to Prague, and she has since returned there and also visited Brno to give poetry readings. "I began learning Russian a few years ago and my interest is on practically every level—linguistic, literary, historical political." "Homesick" for a country she had never seen, Carol Rumens actually went to Russia for the first time in the spring of 1987. One result was *The Greening of the Snow Meadow*. The centerpiece of the book is her "scrapbook" of the visit, comprising her diary (in prose and verse), some of her own photographs, and sketches of Moscow and Leningrad by Jamie Jamieson-Black. There are three sequences of poems, all relating in some way to the Soviet Union and, finally, some translations of Mandelstam and Blok.

One source of the poet's attachment to Russia, wrote Sally Laird in the *Times Literary Supplement*, is the fact that "the 'you' of the opening poems is a Russian you, the Russia Rumens visits is a lover's birthplace." Laird found the diary "over-hasty" and "unexpectedly banal," revealing "Rumens' Russia—its light, its sadness, its obscure heroes—as the gift not of experience but of literature, imagination, love. It's a gift displayed in the poems' marvellous sense of winter, of the crunchy and sibilant sounds of Russian that are somehow the oral equivalent of winter's 'half-whisked whites' and hardnesses—and of softer consonants that mimic its slushy ending. . . . It's a tender ear that recreates these sounds. . . . Rumens' subtle exploration in these poems of her own attachment to Russia—both the thrill at its difference and the nostalgic wish to discover its human sameness—tells us something about the 'real' Russia as well as about Rumens' quest for 'home.'"

Russia is also the setting for Carol Rumens' first novel, *Plato Park* —in particular the Moscow world of cultural wheeling and dealing. The three central characters, like their author, are all "homesick" for worlds not their own. Arkady, a hack poet drudging on a Moscow literary mugazine, excessively admires everything British. The visiting English student Elizabeth represents for him all that Russia cannot give him. Elizabeth is herself infatuated with the "ice-and-fire barbarousness" of Russia, and with Ilya, a gifted musician robbed of his place at the Conservatory mostly through anti-Semitism.

The effects of these myopic encounters are traced through the characters' letters and journals over a number of years. A subplot concerns Boba, a feminist tortured by the KGB and then slowly murdered in a psychiatric "hospital," her diary dissolving into incoherence as the drugs destroy her mind. Arkady, defecting to England in pursuit of Elizabeth, is asked to smuggle out Boba's diary. Boyd Tonkin, in a *New Statesman* review, called the novel "a shade predictable," but concluded that "Rumens delivers her cargo of cross-cultural jokes with great aplomb and faultless timing."

Russia is also the background—figuratively, not literally—of Rumens' first play, *Nearly Siberia*, which was produced in Newcastle and in London (at the Soho Poly Theatre) in the fall of 1989. The scene is contemporary London, to which the heroine, a successful British journalist, brings her Russian lover. He, however, has emotional ties to his native land and to a Russian woman who is still there. With the coming of *glasnost* he has hopes of bringing his Russian lover to England and betraying the English woman, who is not pregnant with his child. Reviewing the play in the *Times Literary Supplement*, Lesley Chamberlain found it "a subtle analysis of the impact the Gorbachev era has had on the Russia-loving West," but lacking in dramatic power and convincing characterization. The heroine, Chamberlain writes, "is a cardboard person." Caught in a moral dilemma, haunted by her sentimental, romantic love for Russia, and tormented by the realization that her Russian lover is unfaithful, she becomes a symbol of crushed idealism. "If she were more real, the audience might well feel sorry for her in bed, and in love, and in love with Russia. . . . What *Nearly Siberia* gives us instead of character is sex and female anxiety."

Carol Rumens is also the author of a critical study of the novelist and short story writer Jean Rhys, and the editor of two verse anthologies: the Poetry Book Society's annual anthology for 1985, called *Slipping Glimpses*, and *Making for the Open: The Chatto Book of Post-Feminist Poetry: 1964–1984*.

In her introduction to *Making for the Open*, Rumens maintains that few anthologies of women's poetry published over the previous twenty years had been "solely, or even primarily concerned with excellence." Since it went "without saying" that "women have a voice, and the right to be heard," it was time to adopt a stricter criterion—"the stern art of poetry" itself. The anthology, containing "post-feminist" poems from twenty countries, was naturally not welcomed by some feminists, but impressed Michael Hofmann as "a conciliatory and hopeful book." He found it "full of discrimination, goodwill and adventure: an anthology to live with."

Carol Rumens has continued her work as poetry editor of the *Literary Review*. She is on the board of the Poetry Book Society and in 1984 won the Cholmondeley Award for poetry, given by the Society of Authors. The same year she was elected a Fellow of the Royal Society of Literature. The poet has said: "I do not belong to that school of thought which says in the face of extreme horror, suffered by others, one should be silent. On the contrary I believe that all the forces of imagination should be employed to speak of their suffering." In the opinion of Elaine Feinstein, "much of the pathos and courage of her poetry comes from the way she confronts experience with balance and control," in this way "finding an utterance which makes her one of the finest younger poets writing in England today."

Anne Stevenson agrees. She believes that Rumens' "gifts sometimes betray her into preciosity" and that "sometimes she too readily identifies with Middle-European *personae*." These "quibbles" apart, "Carol Rumens is one of a few women poets writing today whose seriousness is absolute but not closed; whose political beliefs are so enmeshed with her intelligence and sympathetic passions that it is impossible to consider the state of contemporary poetry in Britain without taking her work into account."

PRINCIPAL WORKS: *Poetry*—A Strange Girl in Bright Colours, 1973; A Necklace of Mirrors, 1979; Unplayed Music, 1981; Scenes from the Gingerbread House, 1982; Star Whisper, 1983; Direct Dialling, 1985; Selected Poems, 1987; The Greening of the Snow Beach, 1988; From Berlin to Heaven, 1989. *Fiction*—Plato Park, 1987. *Non-fiction*—Jean Rhys: A Critical Study, 1985. *As editor*—Slipping Glimpses: Poetry Book Society Anthology, 1985; Making for the Open: The Chatto Book of Post-Feminist Poetry, 1964–1984, 1985.

ABOUT: Contemporary Poets, 4th ed, 1985; Dictionary of Literary Biography 40, 1985; Montefiore, J. Feminism in Poetry, 1987. *Periodicals*—Guardian June 17, 1983; London Magazine July 1981, June 1985; New Statesman April 24, 1987; PN Review 37 1984, 46 1985; Times Literary Supplement April 3, 1981; November 29, 1985; November 20, 1987; March 31, 1989; October 13, 1989.

RUSSELL, (IRWIN) PETER (September 16, 1921–), British poet, translator, and editor, writes in 1990 from his home in Arezzo, Italy: "In 1925, then aged four, I decided that I would be, first and foremost, a poet. Later I learnt how the Muslim mystics call poetry the 'fruit of the Intellect' (*'aql*), and I noted that the Gospel of St John has Jesus say: 'The bread of God is that which cometh down from above and revivifies the world.' Jesus was the Logos. It has always seemed better to me to attempt an Imitation of Christ the Word, however ineptly and remotely, than to mimic the chatter around the kitchen sink.

"In 1968, at a loss for a final closure for a long poem I had written, I eventually found the words: 'Good writing is not enough'—a thought perhaps that Schools of Creative Writing might ponder. More recently I wrote that what we need is '*ideas*, not ideologies,' but since then, in addressing TV audiences I have come to realise that the 'revivification' comes from the Spirit, the Presence, the essential 'sense' rather than from the idea. The ideas can be left *implicit*. The emotion that the Spirit provokes is more meaningful than the verbal idea. Audiences are not dumb. 'Meaning' and the whole semantic syndrome are infinitely misleading. The post-Cartesian tradition has caused 'meaning' to be thought of as no more than the most economic and coherent restatement of what has already been said,—ideally a mathematical formula. Wittgenstein held that the meaning of words 'is the use that people make of them in a language.' Modern sociology, having progressively eliminated spirit, soul, mind and even consciousness, leaves us with nothing but an empty field of collective behaviour,—a pseudo-scientific view which simply does not correspond to the facts but which appeals to the rulers of States and of large corporations which want to control personalities as rigidly as they want to control molecules of washing-powder or plutonium.

"Because I have never kow-towed to the Left and its ideologies or to the pseudo-scientific sociological and linguistic theories of literature, I have been labelled by the incompetent 'of the extreme right.' There is no essential difference between the Right and the Left, any more than there is between Democrats and Republicans. The difference inheres only in which gang is momentarily in power—who will cut the cake. After a brief flirtation with the extreme left at the age of twenty-three, I had no further dealings with any political organisation whatever.

"For me, poetry revivifies, as no ideologies, slogans, propaganda, publicity or manifestoes or pills can ever revivify."

PETER RUSSELL

Peter Russell was born in Bristol, raised in Gloucestershire, and educated at private schools. "My first efforts in the poetic arts," he writes in a characteristic passage in the introduction to his collection *Elemental Discourses*, "were verse compositions in Latin and Greek at my preparatory school under a certain Mr. Sheffield and Mr. Richard Gordon, later of the Board of Education, both Oxford classicists. This was before Gilbert Norwood the treasonous clerk started to dismantle the old classical framework of English higher education in the 'thirties. Concurrently I wrote fiercely romantic Chattertonian imitations of Homer and Virgil and a series of sonnets, one for each bird on the British Bird List. There were four hundred of them, and I had actually seen and identified a large proportion of these species on my two-wheeled peregrinations all over Britain, but especially on my many long stays in the footsteps of Gilbert White, in and around Selborne."

At the age of eighteen, immediately upon his return from a summer holiday in Nazi Germany, he enlisted in the British Army and served throughout World War II in the European theater and later in the Far Eastern theater in the Indian Army, especially in Burma. After his demobilization in 1946 he read English at London University's Queen Mary College, where he was taught by James Sutherland and Norman Callan (he took no degree), then continued his career as a poet, which had begun in 1944 with the appearance of a 120pp. verse collection, *Picnic to the Moon*, a book later called by him a "mass of prosy scribble."

Despite having published well over thirty volumes of poetry, Russell is little known in his native Britain and almost completely unknown elsewhere. In part this neglect must be attributed to the ease with which he has made enemies in the world of modern poetry and to the fact that he has pursued his bêtes noires—academic poets, movement poets, poetasters, petty versifiers of all stripes, as well as communications experts and trend-followers—relentlessly over many years. Russell's friends and mentors in the late 1940s were well-established literary figures—they included Hugh MacDiarmid, Kathleen Raine, and Roy Campbell; during this period he lived in Italy and southern France and came to know Benedetto Croce, George Santayana, Max Beerbohm, and Richard Aldington, in addition to strengthening his longtime discipleship to Ezra Pound.

Russell's poetry varies widely in style and content. One of his compositions, a portmanteau "epic" called *Ephemeron* that he composed between August 1963 and February 1964, has never been published in full. Two-thousand-odd pages in length, it purports to be the account of everything that occurs in the poet's mind over a period of some thirty hours. Another poem, comparatively short at forty-two pages and highly regarded by Russell partisans, is *Paysages Légendaires*. The poem begins with an image of illumination:

Palladian villas and the changing seasons

An old man digging in the shade

The gold sun varnishes
The small viridian of the elms
And gilds the hidden cadmium of the glades. . . .

Written in the Italian Veneto in 1967–1968, the title refers, according to Richard Burns' introduction to the published version, to "those fleetingly glimpsed inner landscapes we all frequently pass through in fantasies, reflections, reveries and dreams, and some experience more vividly and precisely in moments of deep thought, love or contemplation. Inevitably, these landscapes are intimate and personal, rooted in autobiographical experience: this gives them their strength and authenticity. . . . [The poem] offers us a rich, complete network of themes that are both modern and rooted in the best of European (not *just* English) tradition. Russell's poetry has been enriched by an extremely wide reading in the literature, mysticism, philosophy and sciences of many languages."

In his many short poems, Russell has frequently evoked a Poundian feeling of classical severity, of restraint and stately regret, as in "The Fear of War," from *Omens and Elegies*, a lament over the ruin wrought by the war lately ended, and dread of war to come. He was among the earliest poets to envision the complete destruction that would result from nuclear war:

One more tomorrow all our deaths will be
Annihilated where that fatal tree
Spreads in the sun. Blossoms will fall
For the last time on the desolate city,

Where the Spring rejoicings are left by all
As superfluous where the mushroom ball
Breaks in the air—uncanny silence be
Where once blackbird and songthrush were.

Elsewhere his classicism is more playful, sometimes taking the form of a Catullan catch, or punchline, as in this untitled love poem written in 1959, from *Complaints to Circe*:

My sleepy dormouse lays her head
On my shoulder like a child:
The irksome day has long since fled—
The night was wild.

Her eyelids on her burning eyes,
Her head upon my breast has sunk:
I am enchanted by her sighs,—
Her haunting gentle snores,—she's drunk!

Russell has composed hundreds of epigrams over the years, collecting the best of them in *Epigrammata, Malice Aforethought or The Tumour in the Brain*. In his introduction to the book, entitled "Epigrammatics, or The Science of Speaking One's Mind," Russell writes, "As far as I can recall I have never sat down with the deliberate intention of writing an epigram. All of these pieces represent a sort of 'spot-reaction' to a limited but typical situation, generally negative. They are the reactions of the whole organism to a minute and perhaps trivial fragment of experience. . . . But really, as for *justifying* my low merriment I say with Iago 'puddings' to justification. Take them as fun or leave them. If you are not English you may find some of the humour painfully 'English' (especially if you read the *New Yorker* for your humour), but then I've always been English (though racially I am 99% Irish) and generally found it rather painful to be so." Epigrams allow Russell to indulge his passion for invective against the many enemies he has made. He is usually able to hit the mark in the neatest, most deadly way, as in this, written in Venice in December 1971:

To Certain (English) Neighbours

You kindly ask me in to tea and crumpets—
To watch your Telly, smell your filthy dog?
I'd rather pay my fond respects to strumpets,
Or pay a little visit to the bog . . .

Or, on a more famously inimical note, he writes:

On Being Called 'Infinitely Opaque' by H. M. McLuhan

Marshall McLuhan makes a *transparent* mistake
In calling all those who *see through* him—
OPAQUE. . . .

There is, finally, perhaps his most accomplished
epigrammatic parody, a "blare" against his dearest and most constant enemies, the bards of Academe:

  The Board's Blare

  Our Starver, Art without leaven,
  Bellowéd be thy Fame;
  Thy lingam come; thy will be gun,
  On Campus as it is in Tavern.
  Give us this day our Big Success.
  Review at length our vacuousness
  As we review those who evacuate with us.
  And read us not in Profundity;
  But circulate widely our Drivel:
  For Thine is the Foundation,
  The Grants and the Glory,
  For Sabbatical after Sabbatical.
                                    Eh, men?

As a translator, Russell has gone to school to
an expert of the genre in English, "the Old Master of the Blue Pencil," Ezra Pound. Pound had
dozens of comments to make about Russell's
most extended translating effort, the elegies of
Quintilius, an engaging poet of late classical antiquity whose urbane, conversational verse
strikes a note of deeply troubled, civilized ennui,
not to mention querulousness, all qualities which
found a ready echo in Russell's own poetic persona. Here is the opening of the second elegy, "The
Dispossessed," from the earliest (pre-Poundian)
published version, *Three Elegies of Quintilius*:

  Quintilius has moved: he found the heat
  Of Africa too much for an indolent smallholder.
  Recent proscriptions also threatened him
  (He said) with confiscation of his farm.
  So, taking the better of two evil courses
  (Poor Lycoris distraught at leaving so much behind)
  He has sold the little property at Sfax
  For a small price, and is come to Cagnes.

The six known elegies of the poet (not counting
the forty-eight on the papyrus discovered in
1968 at Aphrodisiapolis, still unedited), after
considerable reworking "*secondo* Pound," as
Russell put it, were published as *The Elegies of
Quintilius* in 1975. In addition to this Latinate
labor, Russell has also translated from Persian
several versions of the *qasida* of Khâqânî, entitled *The Ruins of Madâ'in*; from Italian, lyrics
of Camillo Pennati, *Landscapes*; and from Russian, *Poems of Osip Mandelshtam*, which includes one of the great Russian lyricist's most
moving poems, the infinitely sad Ovidian lament "Tristia":

  I love the way the thread is spun—
  The shuttle runs to and fro, the spindle hums—
  Look now—already like swansdown
  Barefooted Delia flies to meet you!
  O the meagre pattern of our life—
  Even our happiest words are threadbare!
  Everything has been of old and will be again:
  For us, only the moment of recognition is sweet.
                                    — (11. 17–24)

"For me," wrote Russell in his note on the poem
in *All for the Wolves: Selected Poems
1947–1975*, edited by Peter Jay, "these [last] two
lines . . . are among the most noble and solemn
and suggestive lines ever written in poetry, ancient, medieval or modern."

Of further note in Russell's long career is his
editorship from 1949 to 1956 of the quarterly
journal *Nine: A Magazine of Literature and the
Arts*, and his editorship of the festschrift *Ezra
Pound: A Collection of Essays . . . to Be Presented to Ezra Pound on his Sixty-fifth Birthday*,
a volume which included twenty pieces on the
works of Pound, at a time when the poet, still a
notorious figure in the postwar world, was approaching the midpoint of his incarceration in
St. Elizabeth's Hospital, Washington, D.C. The
roster of contributors includes T. S. Eliot, Edith
Sitwell, Allen Tate, George Seferis, Hugh Kenner, Marshall McLuhan, and Wyndham Lewis.
"Both the scholar's and the critic's approach to
a work of art are necessary ones," Russell wrote
in the introduction, "but it is well to remember—to quote an early letter of Mr. Pound's—
that scholarship and criticism are only 'hand-
maidens to the arts.' One of the best tributes to
a great poet is good criticism of his work, and if
these essays bring to a wider audience the actual
poetry of Ezra Pound, the true intention of both
scholarship and criticism will have been served."

In various prose works which have treated the
life and poetry of Peter Russell—in particular a
group of volumes edited by James Hogg and
published in 1981–1982 under the auspices of
the University of Salzburg—the poet frequently
discourses on the idea of "vitalism" in poetry,
"the philosophy of the new release, a poetry of
ideas, of feeling." As he wrote in the central lines
of *Paysages Légendaires*, "All that matters now
is poetry / In which the feeling is the thought."
He rails against the "mental *boutiques* and minimal art bazaars of the metropolis": "One of the
chief reasons for the pallidness of recent English
poetry is its failure to face up to 'feeling'";
"What we need is *ideas* not ideologies; original
thought not conformity . . . in short, the poetry
of the Creative Imagination." Yet for all this
doctrinaire certitude, and in many ways because
of it, he remains, near his seventieth year a figure the value of whose contribution to English

poetry "may be known," in Peter Jay's words, "to fewer people today than when he was active as an editor and publisher during the fifties and early sixties." According to his old friend and defender Kathleen Raine, "Peter Russell has, all these years, kept faith (as did his master Ezra Pound) with what is perhaps the greatest imaginative and philosophical conception of the European tradition, 'the Beautiful.' He is, like the Sufis, a poet of the drunkenness of the spirit."

Since 1989 Russell has concentrated on writing poetry and prose in the Italian language. He lives in what he describes as "an ancient Tuscan farmhouse," in Arezzo. In March 1990, only a short time after he was awarded the International Prize for Lyric Poetry, "Le Muse," of the city of Florence and was busy preparing copy for a new literary review in English and Italian, *Marginalia*, a fire in his home destroyed his library, manuscripts, notes, an archive of nearly fifty years. Undaunted by this disaster, Russell managed to produce three issues of *Marginalia* by August 1990.

PRINCIPAL WORKS: *Poetry*—Picnic to the Moon, 1944; Omens and Elegies, 1951; Descent, 1952; Three Elegies of Quintilius, 1954; Images of Desire, 1962; Elegy: Orpheus and Eurydice, 1962; Dreamland and Drunkenness, 1963; Complaints to Circe, 1963; The Spirit and the Body, 1963; Visions and Ruins, 1964; Agamemnon in Hades, 1965; The Golden Chain, 1970; Paysages Légendaires, 1971; The Elegies of Quintilius, 1975; Ephemeron, 1977; Theories, 1978; Acts of Recognition, 1979; Epigrammata, 1981; Elemental Discourses, 1981; Africa: A Dream, 1981; Selected Shorter Poems, 1982; All for the Wolves, 1984. *Translations*—Mandelshtam, O. Poems of Osip Mandelshtam, 1958; Pennati, C. Landscapes, 1964; Khâqânî, The Ruins of Madâ'in, 1973; Corbin, H. The Concept of Comparative Philosophy, 1981. *Prose*—Ezra Pound, 1950; (with K. Singh) G. V. Desani, 1952; Roy Campbell and Nine, 1981; Kathleen Raine: A Study, 1981; Edwin Muir's Poetry, 1981.

ABOUT: Contemporary Authors 97–100, 1981; Contemporary Poets, 4th ed., 1985; Hogg, J. (ed.) The Servant of the Muse: A Garland for Peter Russell on His Sixtieth Birthday, 1981; Hogg, J. (ed.) The Salzburg Peter Russell Seminar 1981/82, 1982; Hogg, J. (ed.) The Vitalist Reader, 1982.

*RYBAKOV, ANATOLY NAUMOVICH (January 1, 1911 [January 14, old style]–   ), Soviet novelist and children's writer, was born in Chernigov to an assimilated Jewish family named Aronson. His father was an engineer. In 1918 the family moved to Moscow and took up residence in the Arbat section of the city, where Rybakov spent the remained of his childhood.

ANATOLY NAUMOVICH RYBAKOV

He graduated from high school in 1928, worked for a time as a truck driver and chauffeur, and went on to study at the Moscow Institute of Transport Engineering. Rybakov was arrested in November 1933 during the uneasy period which preceded the full-scale terror inaugurated by Stalin in the wake of the assassination of the Leningrad Party boss Sergey Kirov in December 1934. After incarceration in the notorious Lubyanka and Butyrka prisons in Moscow, Rybakov was sentenced to three years in Siberian exile under the notorious article 58(10) of the Soviet Penal Code for "anti-Soviet agitation." "I was very depressed after the arrest," Rybakov has said, "for I had done nothing. But I soon found out from others that if you did nothing you only got three years. If I had done something, they would have given me ten years."

After serving out his sentence, Rybakov was allowed to return from Siberia but was barred from residence in large cities. He moved from place to place, taking such menial jobs as truckdriver and dance instructor until he was drafted into the Red Army in 1941, after Hitler's invasion of the Soviet Union. He served on various fronts as a transport officer in the Eighth Guards Army, fighting all the way to Berlin. His military service earned him medals and orders of the Fatherland War in the first and second degrees and the right to return home to Moscow after he was discharged from the army in 1946.

Rybakov in fact turned to writing while he was still in the army, shortly after the end of the war. While on leave, he visited the home in Moscow he had not seen in thirteen years of exile, wandering, and war. "Most of my friends had died, some in the war, some during the purges. I was seized by recollections about my youth. I had always wanted to write. I was 35 years old, and I understood that if I didn't start now I never would." Drawing on his childhood memories, Rybakov began his first novel, a children's adventure story, when he went back to Germany to serve out his term with the occupying forces and completed it after his return to the Soviet Union. *Kortik* (The Dagger, translated as *The Dirk*) was published in 1948. The novel, which is set in Moscow in the 1920s, traces two interwoven plot lines, both centering on a group of children who, like Rybakov himself during his childhood, live on the Arbat. The adolescent hero of the tale, Misha Polyakov, becomes embroiled in intrigue while visiting his grandparents in the village of Revsk during the civil war. He discovers a dagger which has been secreted by the good Bolshevik sailor Polevoy from the evil White officer Nikitsky. After Misha saves Polevoy from capture by Nikitsky's men, the sailor entrusts the dagger to him, and Misha takes it with him when he returns to Moscow with his mother. Back home, Misha and his friends—who coincidentally find themselves mixed up in a counterrevolutionary plot engineered by the villainous Nikitsky—doggedly pursue the mystery of the dagger and, in the end, solve it. The dagger, reunited with its sheath, contains an encoded message which proves to be the key to the cause of a mysterious explosion which destroyed a czarist battleship before the revolution. The nefarious Nikitsky is apprehended by the authorities, putting a stop to his anti-Soviet activities. In the parallel plot, Misha and his friends organize themselves into a unit of the then newly founded Communist youth group, the Pioneers.

The Dirk contains all of the obligatory elements of late Stalinist Socialist Realism. The characters are sharply distinguished along political lines as "good guys"—those who support the Soviet cause—and "bad guys"—those who oppose it. Misha himself functions as a conventional "Positive Hero," and we watch him grow from an unruly, if well-intentioned, boy into a loyal and politically conscious youth. However, despite the occasionally heavy-handed didacticism of the story—which at times reads like a textbook on how to become a good Pioneer—the portrayals of the children and their adventures have a charm which has endeared the book to successive generations of Soviet children. In the U.S.S.R. it was made into a movie, a feature-length cartoon, a TV special, and a play, the scenarios all written by Rybakov himself.

Following up on his early success, Rybakov continued to write works for children. In 1956, he wrote a sequel to *The Dirk* entitled *Bronzovaya ptitsa* (translated as *The Bronze Bird*), and the 1975 *Vystrel* (The Shot) completed the trilogy relating the adventures of Misha Polyakov and his friends in the 1920s. In a second trilogy for children—*Priklyucheniya Krosha* (Krosh's Adventures, 1960), *Kanikuly Krosha* (Krosh's Vacation, 1966), and *Neizvestnyi soldat* (Unknown Soldier, 1970)— Rybakov traces the adventures of his central character and first-person narrator, Serezha Krasheninnikov, nicknamed Krosh by his schoolmates. The three novels portray Krosh—at the ages of fifteen, sixteen, and eighteen respectively—as he grapples with the problems of coming of age in the Soviet Union in the late 1950s and early 1960s.

Rybakov's first novel for adults, *Voditeli* (Drivers), appeared in the journal *Okryabr'* in 1950 and received the Stalin Prize for literature in 1951. Drawing on his own earlier experiences as a driver, the author set the novel in a motor depot. While perhaps somewhat better than representative "production novels" of the late Stalin period in its fidelity to psychological detail and in its general readability, *Voditeli* nonetheless belongs to the genre of Stalinist ideological fiction in its subordination of personal relationships to problems of the workplace. The central character of the novel, the director of the motor depot, bears the same name, Mikhail Polyakov, as the hero of *The Dirk*. However, the older Polyakov, a full-fledged paragon of Communist virtue, appears wooden and uninteresting next to his youthful counterpart.

Rybakov published his second novel for adults, *Ekaterina Voronina* in *Novy mir* in 1955. The novel explores the life of river transport workers on the Volga, focusing on the title character's attempts to build a life for herself in the difficult postwar period. Clearly a product of the early "thaw" following Stalin's death, *Ekaterina Voronina* portrays characters who are morally and psychologically more complex than the characters in *Voditeli*, and the novel criticizes the type of Soviet bureaucrat who is insensitive to the individual emotional needs of his underlings. In a particularly daring scene which looks ahead to Rybakov's future works, Ekaterina finally decides to break with her boss, with whom she has become emotionally involved, because he refuses to acknowledge publicly his past acquaintance with a victim of the Stalin terror who has just returned from the camps.

Rybakov directly confronts the tragic legacy of Stalinism in his short novel *Leto v Sosnyakakh* (Summer In Sosnyaki, 1964). The author casts the work in something of the mold of a mystery story, centering around the sudden suicide of an older engineer who worked in the local factory and its connection with a young woman, Lilya Kuznetsova, whom, for unknown reasons, he summons to his deathbed. In the course of the plot we learn that Lilya's father was shot in the 1937 purges and that her mother's life was broken in the camps and exile. In the end it becomes clear that the engineer committed suicide out of guilt for having betrayed Lilya's father, destroying the family, almost two decades earlier. While certainly not of the literary quality of Solzhenitsyn's *One Day in the Life of Ivan Denisovich, Leto v Sosnyakakh* stands with that work as a testament to the greater openness which briefly reigned in Soviet publishing and intellectual life under Khrushchev.

Perhaps because of tighter controls over literature during the Brezhnev years, Rybakov returned to adult fiction only in 1978 with the publication of his novel *Tyazhelyi pesok* (translated as *Heavy Sand*). The novel is one of the few Soviet literary works to chronicle the atrocities committed against the Jewish population of the Ukraine by the German forces which occupied the area during World War II. Since official Soviet propaganda maintains that Jews suffered no more than other segments of the Soviet population at the hands of the Germans, the publication of *Heavy Sand* was something of a surprise, especially in the climate of growing anti-Semitism in the Soviet Union in the late 1970s. The novel did not, however, find its way into print without some difficulty. When the manuscript of *Heavy Sand* was rejected by the Soviet Union's premier literary journal, *Novy mir*, as too risky a project, Rybakov wisely offered it to the less prestigious journal *Oktyabr'*. The newly appointed editor of the journal, anxious to change the reactionary image *Oktyabr'* had acquired under its previous editor, agreed to publish *Heavy Sand*, although Rybakov had to make changes in the text to get it into print. Both the journal edition and the subsequent book edition of the novel sold out immediately, and copies of the book fetched high prices on the black market.

Although now largely overshadowed by the timely publication of Rybakov's recent *Deti Arbata* (translated as *Children of the Arbat*), *Heavy Sand* may justly be termed Rybakov's masterpiece. The novel marks a departure for Rybakov in at least two senses. First, *Heavy Sand* is the only one of Rybakov's works in which the major characters are Jewish. The author—who writes in Russian and knows no Yiddish or Hebrew—was prompted to explore his Jewish heritage by his own experiences during

the war. The plot was suggested to Rybakov by an acquaintance who related the story of his family to the author before the war. When Rybakov ran into his friend again after the war and asked about his family, he learned that they had perished. Only many years later did the writer sit down to write a novel based on their experiences, moving the action from Simferopol to his own native village of Chernigov and modeling the central figure of Jacob on his grandfather. "I invented nothing," he has claimed.

In *Heavy Sand* Rybakov also departs from his characteristic Realist or Socialist Realist aesthetic, adopting a manner reminiscent of the "magic realism" of Gabriel García Márquez's *One Hundred Years of Solitude* and coincidentally also centering his work on a matriarch who holds her family together over some four decades of war and revolution. *Heavy Sand* is built on Biblical allusion, its title drawn from Job 6:2–3: "Oh that my grief were thoroughly weighed, and my calamity laid in the balances together! For now it would be heavier than the sand of the sea: therefore my words are swallowed up." By the same token, the names of the major characters, Jacob and Rachel Rakhlenko, were inspired by the Old Testament patriarch Jacob and his beloved wife Rachel. Although occasionally marred, especially toward the end, by the intrusively didactic voice of the first-person narrator, the novel generally maintains a delicate balance between the haunting story of enduring love and the horrors of Nazi genocide which destroy the family but do not defeat its spirit.

Rybakov attracted international attention as a member of the "loyal opposition" who was willing to test the limits of official Soviet tolerance by speaking at the funeral of the renowned Soviet writer Yury Trifonov in 1981. In his eulogy he refused to pass over in silence, as had other speakers, the fact that Trifonov's father had been shot during the 1937 purge and his mother imprisoned in a labor camp. "A writer's real material comes from his sufferings," said Rybakov. "The truest memory is the kind that leaves scars on the heart."

Rybakov was finally catapulted to celebrity status with the publication of *Children of the Arbat* in 1987, a chronicle of the "scars" left on his own heart by the Stalin years. The novel, in which Stalin himself figures as a major character, has become symbolic of the cultural relaxation fostered by Gorbachev's policy of "glasnost" or openness and has arguably made Rybakov the most widely read and talked-about writer living in the Soviet Union today. Rybakov waited some twenty years to see his novel into print, resisting offers to publish it abroad because, as the author has said, "I wanted it to come out in Russia. I wanted my people to have it." The November 1966 issue of *Novy mir*, then under the liberal editorship of Aleksandr Tvardovsky, carried an announcement that the first part of *Children of the Arbat* would appear in the journal the following year. When the announced publication did not materialize, Rybakov went on to write the second part of the novel. Again in 1978 the journal *Oktyabr'* announced publication of the novel for 1979, and again the novel was not published, so Rybakov went on to write the third section of the novel. With each revision the role of Stalin grew. The whole novel finally appeared in the April, May, and June issues of the journal *Druzhba narodov* in 1987. *Children of the Arbat* rapidly became one of the most sought-after books in the Soviet Union, with people paying exorbitant black-market prices for the relevant issues of the journal or the book itself, or signing up for what might be years of waiting for library copies.

Like *The Dirk*, *Children of the Arbat* traces a double trajectory, but unlike the early novel it follows two separate casts of characters, whose fates only tangentially intersect. One plot line centers around Sasha Pankratov (who shares his name with a minor character in *The Dirk* trilogy), his family, and his circle of friends, all of whom grew up on the Arbat. By Rybakov's own admission, the key events of Sasha's life are drawn from the author's own biography. Thus, late in 1933, Sasha is arrested, like Rybakov himself, for a schoolboy prank, publishing satirical verses in the school newspaper, and is sentenced to exile in Siberia. Chapters focusing on Sasha's relationships with his friends, which grow more complex as his position worsens and the political atmosphere becomes more tense, alternate with chapters chronicling the intrigues of Stalin and his inner circle. The Stalin plot line culminates in the assassination of Kirov, which, Rybakov suggests, was engineered by Stalin himself to get rid of his popular rival. Sasha Pankratov's uncle Mark, a high-ranking Communist official, serves as the only direct plot link connecting the two spheres of characters and action. However, the true link between Stalin and the "children of the Arbat" lies in the very nature of the historical period as portrayed by Rybakov. Thus, as the juxtaposition of the two worlds in the novel shows, the psychology of terror initiated by Stalin filtered down to all levels of society, deforming the lives of an entire generation. A sequel to this novel, *Tridtsat' pyat' i drugie gody* (1935 and Other Years), published in *Druzhba narodov* in 1988, continues the chronicle of Sasha Pankratov and his era, and another novel (1944) is projected to complete the trilogy.

In understanding Rybakov's literary significance, the American reader might be well served by comparisons with such popular historical novelists as Herman Wouk and James Michener. However, such comparisons are limited in their value by the very different roles played by writers in Soviet and American society. Following the tradition of Russian writers as powerful moral spokesmen for their society, Soviet writers (with Rybakov among the most politically outspoken) have stood at the forefront of the changes rocking Soviet society under Gorbachev. By the same token, Soviet readers, starved for decades of accurate information about their country's history, have turned avidly to *Children of the Arbat* and other popular historical novels to fill in the gaps in their knowledge. By his own admission a writer not for the "elite," but for the "masses," Rybakov's importance lies in his ability to speak to and for his people at this crucial moment in history.

WORKS IN ENGLISH TRANSLATION: *The Dirk*, translated by David Skvirsky, was published by Foreign Languages Publishing House in Moscow in 1954, and the same publishing house issued *The Bronze Bird*, also rendered into English by David Skvirsky, in 1958. *The Dirk* is scheduled to be republished in the United States in 1990 or 1991. *Heavy Sand*, translated by Harold Shukman, was published in 1981, and *Children of the Arbat*, also translated by Harold Shukman, appeared in 1988.

ABOUT: Biographical Dictionary of the Soviet Union 1917–1988, 1989; Contemporary Authors 126, 1989; Contemporary Literary Criticism 23, 1983; Kasack, W. Dictionary of Russian Literature since 1917, 1988. *Periodicals*—Christian Science Monitor May 11, 1981; Life June 1988; London Times August 26, 1988; New York Times December 26, 1978; March 14, 1981; April 2, 1981; October 31, 1986; May 25, 1988; May 26, 1988; People June 27, 1988; Telegraph Sunday Magazine August 7, 1988; Time April 27, 1987; June 6, 1988; June 20, 1988; Wall Street Journal May 12, 1988; Washington Post June 3, 1988.

RYDER, JONATHAN. See **LUDLUM, ROBERT**

*EL-SAADAWI, NAWAL (October 27, 1932–), Egyptian fiction writer, essayist, playwright, psychiatrist, leading feminist in the Arab world, and president of the Arab Women's Solidarity Association, writes: "I was born in the village of Kafr Tahla by the river Nile in Egypt. My paternal grandmother was a poor peasant with nine daughters and one son (who became my father). She lost her husband [...] early in

al sa da wi, na wal

NAWAL EL-SAADAWI

life. He died of bilharziasis, which is a tropical parasitical disease that affects most peasants in Egypt. She worked hard in the field to enable her son to go to school and then to the university. When I was a child she told me that she starved herself to save money to pay the school fees for my father. She did not send any of her daughters to school. They are illiterate poor peasants in the village. Some of them educated their sons and daughters, but most of my cousins are peasants working in the field.

"My father was a very good student. He wanted to overcome poverty by education. He did. He graduated and got a good job in the Ministry of Education in Cairo and married my mother, the daughter of an upper-class military patriarch.

"My mother married my father without having seen him (except from behind the shutter). She wanted to marry anyone just to leave her father's house.

"I was brought up in this family. I was lucky to have such parents. They were much more progressive than other parents. They both believed in education and all of us (nine children), girls and boys, were sent to schools and then universities.

"I was very good in school. My father used to threaten us girls (we were six) that if any one of us failed in school she would be kept at home to wash the floor and marry.

"I became a medical doctor and worked in rural areas and in Cairo. I was not satisfied with my medical profession. I wanted to write and in fact I had been writing all the time since I was

a child. I published short stories and novels. I write in Arabic of course and I published my stories in newspapers and magazines and then in books.

"In 1970 I started writing on women's problems. My first non-fiction book *Al-Mar'a wa'l-jins* (Woman and Sex) created a lot of problems for me. In this book I touched on the untouchable, or the three taboos: 'Sex, religion, and class.'

"I lost my job in 1972 as Director General in the Ministry of Health. The health magazine which I edited was closed down. Under the rule of Sadat my books were censored and I was obliged to publish in Lebanon (Beirut). In 1981 I was put in prison by Sadat because of writings criticizing his politics. In my writings I was making links between the separated domains in life: political, economic, social, sexual, psychological, historical, etc. . . . I made the link between slavery, class and the patriarchal system. I was put on the blacklist and could not publish in Egypt or appear on T.V. or in the media.

"After Sadat's death I was released from prison by the new president (Mubarak). I published my recent books in Egypt. There is no censorship on books anymore but I am still on the blacklist, or the grey list as they call it now. As a writer and free thinker and feminist I am always in the opposition and never with the government or the establishment. I write for freedom, justice, and equality between people and between the sexes.

"My first husband was a medical doctor and I left him because he wanted me to serve him as a wife. My second husband was a man of law (a judge) and he came one day and said to me: 'You have to choose between me and your writing.' I chose my writing and left him. My third husband is a novelist and medical doctor. He is very progressive and a feminist. He translated some of my books into English. He plays, along with other progressive men, an important role in our Arab Women's Solidarity Association, which we founded in 1982.

"My last novel, *The Fall of the Imam*, was published in Cairo in 1987. Since then I have been receiving threats from unknown fundamentalist religious political groups. They say they will kill me because of my writings against a political religious leader (Imam). Then I received a telephone call from an official in the Ministry of Internal Affairs and he told me that security guards are appointed twenty-four hours a day in front of my house. Every day when I go out or into my home I see the security guard standing with his gun. Sometimes I have a vague feeling that he will shoot me from behind.

"I know now that to be a free and independent

writer you have to pay a very high price. But I prefer to pay the price and continue my creative writings.

"I have a lot of hopes for the future. Egypt will progress and be a leader in modern history as in ancient history. The Arab world will unite and lead in world progress.

"I have a daughter and a son. Both are creative writers. So we are a family of four creative people who have relationships based on equality and freedom."

It was only in the 1980s that Dr. Nawal el-Saadawi began to attract attention in the West, when the first translations of her essays and novels appeared in English and other European languages (including French, Italian, Portuguese, German, Dutch, Danish, Swedish, and Norwegian). But in the Arab Middle East, she has been known since the late 1950s as a writer whose short stories and novels gave a then rare fictional voice to the women of her culture. After the *succès de scandale* of *Al-Mar'a wa'l-jins* (Woman and Sex) in 1972, and the studies that were subsequently published in Beirut—*Al-Untha hiya al-asl* (Female Is the Origin, 1974), *Al-Rajul wa'l-jins* (Man and Sex, 1975), *Al-Mar'a wa'l-sira' al-nafsi* (Woman and Psychological Conflict, 1976)—a new generation of Arab intellectuals experienced what one Lebanese woman observer called the "revelation" of post-1968 feminism in their midst. Speaking to French journalists in 1982, she insisted that el-Saadawi "plays a very important role for Egyptian and Arab women, even those who aren't politically involved. Her writings influence the majority of Arab women," although, she added, "most Arab men criticize her, arguing that it's not time for the battle of the sexes and that women's issues shouldn't take priority over the national struggle."

Indeed, as el-Saadawi herself proudly acknowledges, her views have always been controversial and her stance oppositional. Following her studies at the Faculty of Medicine in Cairo in the early 1950s, she spent a decade practicing medicine in both the urban and rural areas of Egypt. In 1956, after completing a Master of Public Health degree at Columbia University in New York, she returned to Egypt to serve as director general of the Health Education department in the Ministry of Health, the appointment that, as she writes above, was terminated after the publication of *Al-Mar'a wa'l-jins* (Woman and Sex). At the end of the 1970s she began working for the United Nations as a coordinator of women's field programs, first in Ethiopia and

then in Lebanon, but she soon left the UN system because, she explained to British journalist Sarah Graham-Brown, there was "too much bureaucracy and discrimination against women . . . they do not believe very much in creativity. They want people who just obey."

Prior to *Al-Mar'a wa'l-jins* (which has undergone many reprints in Arabic but remains untranslated), el-Saadawi had published four collections of short stories and two novels, including the 1960 *Mudhakkirat tabbiba* (*Memoirs of a Woman Doctor*), which is considered to be the first modern feminist fiction in Arabic. (Published in Dutch in 1980, it has now been translated into English.) Part of a 1972 collection of short stories, *Al-Khayt wa'l-jidar* has been translated as *The Death of an Ex-Minister*. But in the course of the 1970s, el-Saadawi's writings took a more theoretical and polemical turn, as can be seen from her 1977 essay *The Hidden Face of Eve* (translated and edited by her husband, Sherif Hetata, in 1980), which not only takes on the "taboo" problems of Egyptian society—virginity and honor, female excision, prostitution, abortion, incest, child abuse—but attempts to situate this grim panorama of everyday experience in the larger economic and social context. While attacking female circumcision and other abuses practiced on the Arab woman, el-Saadawi takes pains to counter any facile equation of women's oppression with Eastern or more particularly Muslim society. Rather, in the various historical and sociological surveys that fill out the book, she argues for a root cause in "the class and patriarchal system that has ruled over human beings ever since slavery started to hold sway."

As Magali Morsi noted in a review of the French edition, *The Hidden Face of Eve* is written in a voice that is "vehement and sometimes, to be sure, disorganized, brandishing the argument like a cudgel rather than a foil," and even in the West, the book did not fail to provoke controversy. If American feminists like Robin Morgan welcomed it as "a cry of pain and rage, backed up by Saadawi's own solid scholarship, her sharp intellect, her wide cross-cultural reading and world travel, and her decades of personal experience," other readers more immersed in the Middle Eastern context took issue with the book's globalizing arguments. Magida Salman, for example, writing in the British political journal *Khamsin,* concluded that el-Saadawi's defense of Islam, accentuated in a special preface to the English edition, betrayed the mentality of "an Arab feminist who has fallen into the deep trap of nationalist justification and defensive reactions designed to prettify reality for the benefit of critical 'foreigners.'"

Such criticisms were fueled in the early 1980s by el-Saadawi's "cautiously optimistic" support for the Islamic Revolution in Iran, but ultimately she too was forced to concede the dashed hopes for a progressive Islam, especially with regard to women's rights; and in contrast with other Egyptian feminist organizations, her Arab Women's Solidarity Association, founded in 1982, has steered clear of alliances with Muslim women's groups.

In the course of the 1980s, the Western image of el-Saadawi the activist, based on *The Hidden Face of Eve* and obviously reinforced by her arrest in President Sadat's 1981 crackdown, was rounded out by the translation of three novels from the previous decade. *Al-Bahitha 'an al-hubb* (1974; translated as *Two Women in One*), looks at the dual patriarchy of family and state through the portrait of an eighteen-year-old medical student, Bahiah Shaheen, who escapes her father's domination through a romance that soon comes under the domination of the government when her boyfriend is arrested for political activities. She is married off to a man she does not love, runs away, plunges into political activity herself, and winds up in prison with her lover. A far more extreme rendering of the same themes is the haunting *Imra'a 'inda nuqta'l-sifr* (1976; translated as *Woman at Point Zero*). (It has also been published in a 1981 French translation, *Ferdaous, une voix d'enfer*, by Assia Djebbar and Assia Trabelsi.) Inspired by el-Saadawi's real-life encounter with an inmate in Qanatir Women's Prison while she was researching *Women and Psychological Conflict*, the novel recasts the conversations they had just before the woman was executed for the murder of her pimp and traces a lifelong chain of abuse at the hands of father, uncle, husband, employer, and a variety of male and female pimps. Yet another story of abuse and revenge, this time set in the Egyptian countryside, was *Mawt al-rajul al-wahid 'ala al-ard* (translated as *God Dies by the Nile*). In this allegorical indictment of the Sadat regime, political and patriarchal power coincide in the figure of a corrupt village mayor who finally receives his due from a simple peasant woman whose nieces he has seduced.

In her introduction to the French version of *Woman at Point Zero*, Assia Djebbar, herself a renowned Algerian novelist, stresses the literary qualities of el-Saadawi's text in order to signal what she sees as the emergence of women's expression in Arabic; in her view, "This is really a book about birth, the birth of speech." Indeed, in the case of all three translated novels, reviewers were struck by what Sue Dearden described as a "remarkable poetical-clinical style of language," which communicates far-reaching social commentary through concrete detail. *Two Women in One*, for example, opens with the telling observation that Bahiah Shaheen "stood with her right foot on the edge of the marble table and her left foot on the floor, a posture unbecoming for a woman." In *Woman at Point Zero*—as in the autobiographical passages of *The Hidden Face of Eve*—first-person descriptions offer irrefutable evidence for situations often experienced but rarely depicted.

The other aspect of these novels greatly appreciated by the critics was their universality, the way in which particular situations were used to convey more general truths. *Two Women in One*, wrote Barbara Harlow in *Choice*, is "embedded in the contemporary Egyptian context," but "nonetheless resonates with the larger issues which confront women throughout the Third World as well as in the West." Similarly, in his review of the French version of *Woman at Point Zero*, Mouloud Achour noted that the title character, Ferdaws, "could have remained without a nationality because, apart from the few details of the socio-cultural context, her story might have had the same outcome whether in the dismal cell of a Cairo prison or that of any other capital in the world."

Since she left the United Nations system in 1980, el-Saadawi has pursued her writing and related feminist activities full-time. In September 1981 she was among some fifteen hundred Egyptian men and women rounded up in President Anwar al-Sadat's crackdown on "instigators of sectarian rift"—mainly Muslim fundamentalists, but also a scattering of Christians and some members of the secular opposition like el-Saadawi. Following three months' detention in the same Qanatir Women's Prison where she had met Ferdaws nearly a decade earlier, she reworked her own prison experience into a play called *Al-Insan* (The People, 1983), translated into French by Magda Wassef as *Douze femmes dans Kanater* (Twelve Women in Qanatir, 1984). The title refers to el-Saadawi and her eleven cellmates, an unlikely assortment of women, ranging from "militant communists" to "the most fanatical Muslim fundamentalists," which, she writes in the preface, was "in some way, a microcosm of Egyptian society in the 1970s," reflecting "all the contradictions of that society but equally, its capacity to transform its defeats into victories."

This lengthy (nearly 250 pages) fictional account was followed by a volume of prison memoirs, *Mudhakkirat fi sijn al-nisa'* (1984; translated as *Letters from a Women's Prison*), where, in the chatty, often ironic tone of the diarist, she recounts the same sequence of events in the first person, interspersed with memories from her childhood. In an enthusiastic review for *Middle East* magazine, Nikki R. Keddie commented that "the book reads like a good novel," citing in particular the stranger-than-fiction ending where el-Saadawi was released from prison and immediately taken to meet the new Egyptian president, Hosni al-Mubarak, before being delivered to her home.

Continuing in this autobiographical vein, el-Saadawi has published two volumes of travel memoirs (*Rihlat awl al-'alam*, 1986). She has also written a second play, *Isis* (1986), which offers a feminist reading of the ancient Egyptian myth, and a satirical novel translated as *The Fall of the Imam*, which, in her words, is "about the fall of God, which certain political and social systems create. The fall of the caliph, whose role is both temporal and theological. It is the noisy fall of the Shah of Iran, Numeiry of Sudan, and Sadat of Egypt." *The Circling Song*, translated in 1989, was described by Sue Roe in the *Times Literary Supplement* as "a testament to artistic stamina and political courage . . . the oppressiveness of its atmosphere is a salient reminder that Western feminism is a relatively spacious and relaxed affair."

Nawal el-Saadawi lives in Cairo with her husband, but she maintains close ties with her village, where she heads a women's development project. Her dual careers, she insists, have "nourished" one another: "My knowledge of the medical sciences, my work in rural areas, my relations with male and female patients fed my writings with a deep and rich experience. . . . In the same way, my passion for writing, my love of art and my contemplation of life as it flowed past permitted me to see human beings in depth, helped me in my work as a medical doctor and made me realize the imperfections of my profession and its inability to cope with the fundamental problems of society and people."

WORKS IN ENGLISH TRANSLATION: Sherif Hetata translated *The Hidden Face of Eve* in 1980, *Two Women in One* and *God Dies by the Nile* in 1985, and *The Fall of the Imam* in 1987. *Woman at Point Zero* was translated by Osman Nusairi and Jana Gough in 1983; Nusairi and Gough also translated *Two Women in One* in 1985. Other translations are Marilyn Booth's *Memoirs from a Women's Prison*, Shirley Eber's *Death of an Ex-Minister* (short stories, 1987), and (translator not identified) *Memoirs of a Woman Doctor*, 1988, and *The Circling Song*, 1989. An excerpt from *Memoirs of a Woman Doctor*, "Growing Up Female in Egypt," translated by Fedwas Malti-Douglas, is in E. W. Fernea's anthology *Women and the Family in the Middle East*, 1985. Miriam Lowi's translation of a short story, *She Used to Be the Weaker*, is in *Index on Censorship*, March 1982.

ABOUT: *Periodicals*—Choice March 1987; Freedomways March 23, 1983; Index on Censorship March 1982; Khamsin 8, 1981; MERIP Reports March–April 1981; Middle East February 1987, August 1987; New York Times Book Review March 14, 1982; July 27, 1986; September 7, 1986; Race and Class Summer 1980; Times Literary Supplement, December 22, 1989; West Africa August 18, 1986.

SACKS, OLIVER (WOLF) (July 9, 1933–), British-born medical writer, was born in London, the son of Samuel Sacks and the former Elsie Landau, both physicians. He determined on medicine as a career from an early age, and in 1955, following national service, went up to Queen's College, Oxford, to read medicine. He took bachelor's degrees in medicine and chemistry in 1958. After residency at London's Middlesex Hospital, he continued his studies, with a specialty in neurology, at the University of California at Los Angeles. He became an instructor in neurology in 1965 at the Albert Einstein College of Medicine in New York City, where he is now professor of clinical neurology.

No other profession than the neurologist's, wrote Jerome Bruner, "is so implacably condemned to dwell in that restless and prismatic space that lies between mind and body. If to the philosopher the mind-body problem is a playground for fancy analytic footwork, for the neurologist it is a dilemma that compels the same kind of awesome respect that the mariner feels for the sea." Such a deep respect for the mysteries constantly offered up by his work has informed all of Sacks' writing; in confronting these mysteries, in delicately attempting to solve them, he has put to use, and steadily refined, an elegant, even poetic, discursive prose style. He has become, in Israel Rosenfield's words, "one of the great clinical writers of the 20th century."

Sacks' first book, *Migraine: The Evolution of a Common Disorder*, was extensively revised and republished fifteen years after its first publication as *Migraine: Understanding a Common Disorder*. It is an attempt to bring together, primarily for the lay reader, all the features of modern knowledge on a subject a general view of which has long been lacking. He understood the subject from the beginning as one of considerable complexity. "When I saw my first migraine patient," he writes in the preface, "I thought of migraine as a peculiar type of headache, no more and no less. As I saw more patients, it became apparent to me that headache was never the sole feature of a migraine, and later still, that it was not even a necessary feature of all migraines. I was moved, therefore, to inquire further into a subject which appeared to retical

OLIVER SACKS

before me, growing more complex, less capable of circumspection, and less intelligible, the more I learned of it. . . . After I had seen a thousand migraine patients, I saw that the subject made *sense.*" Sacks found it necessary "to employ a sort of continuous double vision, simultaneously envisaging migraine as a *structure* whose forms were implicit in the repertoire of the nervous system, and as a *strategy* which might be employed to any emotional, or indeed biological, end."

Migraine is a virtual miracle of concision: it contains exhaustive sections on the experience, occurrence, and basis of the disorder, and on therapeutic approaches to relief. There are glossaries of case histories and of terms, and a very complete bibliography and index, all in 270 pages. "Any layman," wrote W. H. Auden in a review of the first edition, "who is at all interested in the relation between body and mind, even if he does not understand all of it, will find the book as fascinating as I have. . . . Dr. Sacks discusses the physiological, biological, and psychological factors in migraine. His theories about its biological basis I found particularly interesting and suggestive." Rosenfield noted in reviewing the second edition that when the first appeared in 1970 "it was the first major study of the disorder" in almost a century. The book, he wrote, "should be read as much for its brilliant insights into the nature of our mental functioning as for its discussion of migraine."

After the excellent reception accorded *Awakenings*, a clinical study of the remarkable effects of a new drug, L-Dopa, on cases of postencephalitic Parkinsonism, Sacks turned for more than a decade to contributing to professional journals and, occasionally, to the British weekly *The Listener*. His next book, *A Leg to Stand On*, recounts his own slow recovery from the physical and mental effects of a broken leg he incurred in 1976 while mountain climbing in Norway. His description of the accident opens the book and is wonderfully well observed, both in his account of the outward, physical surroundings and his insight into the self-confident mindset of a robust young Englishman on holiday. Determined to climb the 6,000-foot mountain above Hardanger Fjord near Bergen in the space of one day, he sets out well before dawn. About halfway up, as he is rejoicing in the strength of his legs trained by years of exertion at sports, he passes a gate on which is nailed a sign in Norwegian, "Beware the bull!" Incredulous, he passes on, ever upward, making his way among great boulders, and on rounding one comes upon the seated bull: "It had a huge horned head, a stupendous white body and an enormous mild milk-white face. It sat unmoved by my appearance, exceedingly calm, except that it turned its vast white face up towards me. And in that moment it *changed*, before my eyes, becoming transformed from magnificent to utterly monstrous. The huge white face seemed to swell and swell, and the great bulbous eyes became radiant with malignance. The face grew huger and huger all the time, until I thought it would blot out the Universe. . . . It seemed now to be stamped with the infernal in every feature. It became, first a monster, and now the Devil."

At this sight the self-satisfied Englishman panics, turns, and bolts headlong back down the rocky path, then slips, falls, and suddenly experiences unbelievable pain. It occurs to him, the doctor, that someone has been seriously injured, then a second later he realizes that it is himself. Pulling himself together, he makes a diagnosis: "Muscle paralyzed and atonic—probably nerve injury. Unstable knee-joint—seems to dislocate backwards. Probably ripped out the cruciate ligaments." He also diagnoses his situation: he is alone, miles from human habitation, at an altitude where the nighttime temperature will drop well below freezing, even in that month of August. He then begins to fight for his life. Splinting his leg, he descends the mountain backwards, on all threes, witnessing with alarm as evening comes on the ebbing of his strength and consciousness due to cold and shock. Finally he is rescued, carried down the mountain, put into a local hospital, then flown back to London and placed in the care of a famous orthopedic surgeon. Then his ordeal begins in earnest. "A physician by profession, I had never found myself a patient before, and now I was at once physician and patient. I had imagined my injury . . . to be straightforward and routine, and I was astonished at the profundity of the effects it had: a sort of paralysis and alienation of the leg, reducing it to an 'object' which seemed unrelated to me; an abyss of bizarre, and even terrifying, effects. I had no idea what to make of these effects and entertained fears that I might never recover. I found the abyss a horror, and recovery a wonder; and I have since had a deeper sense of the horror and wonder which lurk behind life and which are concealed, as it were, behind the usual surface of health."

At the suggestion and with the encouragement of the eminent Soviet neuropsychologist Aleksandr R. Luria, to whom Sacks wrote in puzzlement "at these singular effects," he investigated over the years "some hundreds of patients, all with singular disorders of body-image and body-ego which were neurologically determined and essentially similar to my own." *A Leg to Stand On*, years in preparation, thus interweaves many themes: "the specific neuropsychological and existential phenomena associated with my injury and recovery; the business of being a patient and of returning later to the outside world; the complexities of the doctor-patient relationship and the difficulties of dialogue between them, especially in a matter which is puzzling to both; the application of my findings to a large group of patients; and the pondering of their implication and meaning—all this leading, finally, to a critique of current neurological medicine, and to a vision of what may be the neurological medicine of the future." Sacks concludes his preface by noting that the book "may be regarded as a sort of neurological novel or short story, but one which is rooted in personal experience and neurological fact." "The metaphor," wrote Jerome Bruner in his review of the book, "around which both Sacks' drama and his reflections revolve is the scotoma . . . [a] hole in experience, those pieces of self that evaporate, that escape the control of intention. . . ."

The Man Who Mistook His Wife for a Hat, and Other Clinical Tales is a collection of a couple of dozen case histories, most relatively short ones, concerning patients struggling with a variety of disabilities. These vignettes—many of which had been published from the early 1980s in the *New York Review of Books*—are grouped into four sections, entitled "Losses," "Excesses," "Transports," and "The World of the Simple." In his preface, Sacks confesses to feeling "a certain doubleness in me: that I feel myself a naturalist and a physician both; and that I am equally interested in diseases and people, perhaps, too, that I am equally, if inadequately, a theorist and

dramatist, am equally drawn to the scientific and the romantic, and continually see both in the human condition, not least in that quintessentially human condition of sickness—animals get diseases, but only man falls radically into sickness." He proceeds to deride modern case histories, which in his opinion "allude to the subject in a cursory phrase, . . . which could as well apply to a rat as a human being. To restore the human subject at the centre—the suffering, afflicted, fighting, human subject—we must deepen a case history to a narrative or tale: only then do we have a 'who' as well as a 'what,' a real person, a patient, in relation to disease—in relation to the physical." The study of such diseases requires "a new discipline," what Sacks calls "the neurology of identity [that] deals with the neural foundations of the self, the age-old problem of mind and brain."

In Sacks' view, the nineteenth century witnessed the high point of "the tradition of richly human clinical tales." The decline of the clinical narrative art accompanied "the advent of an impersonal neurological science." He considers the late works of his mentor Aleksandr Luria, in particular *The Mind of a Mnemonist* and *The Man with a Shattered World*, "attempts to revive this lost tradition." Sacks' own case histories are related to three venerable traditions: to the nineteenth-century one emulated by Luria; "to the tradition of the first medical historian, Hippocrates; and to that universal and prehistorical tradition by which patients have always told their stories to doctors." He goes on to write of "tales and fables" as well as case histories: "The scientific and romantic in such realms cry out to come together—Luria liked to speak here of 'romantic science.' They come together at the intersection of fact and fable, the intersection which characterizes . . . the lives of the patients here narrated."

J. K. Wing praised Sacks for having managed to convey "as few authors do nowadays a sense of continuity between the neurological and the psychiatric that has tended to be lost since the development of two separate professions. While the author is involved in his stories his virtues are paramount: excellent prose, a literary imagination, a talent for clinical (though not technical) exposition that is out of the ordinary; above all, a capacity to see through the eyes of people who have entered new worlds and must achieve new identities if they are to survive as truly human beings. His attempt to provide an overall philosophical framework is less satisfactory, because too far removed from the practicalities and limitations of medicine."

Michiko Kakutani, in the *New York Times*,

wrote, "Blessed with deep reserves of compassion and a metaphysical turn of mind, Dr. Sacks writes of these patients not as scientific curiosities but as individuals, whose dilemmas—moral and spiritual, as well as psychological—are made as complexly real to us as those of characters in a novel. It's not just that the strangeness of the stories in this volume often recalls works by writers as disparate as Jorge Luis Borges, Thomas Mann and Sherwood Anderson, but also that Dr. Sacks, like a novelist, is interested less in the manifestations of his people's conditions than in the consequences those conditions have on their inner lives."

Sacks draws on the same reserves of compassion and metaphysics to which Kakutani refers in his *Seeing Voices: A Journey into the World of the Deaf.* The sign language, literally the seeing voice, used by the prelingually deaf, Sacks argues in this book, has never been sufficiently recognized as the natural and unique language of the deaf. Educating deaf children in lip reading or the traditional signed English (corresponding to a literal translation of English words into hand symbols) deprives them of their natural freedom of expression, of their own culture as it were. *Seeing Voices* was in part inspired by the rebellion of students in 1988 at the only liberal arts college in the world for deaf students, Gallaudet College, in Washington, D. C. The students demanded that a deaf president be appointed. Their demonstrations won national and worldwide attention and were finally successful, bringing to the attention of what had been a largely indifferent public their right to be recognized not as handicapped or impaired but as citizens entitled to full civil rights. Sacks' enthusiasm for the students' cause and his defense of Sign as a language of the brain "fully comparable to speech . . . at once a most complex and yet transparent expression and transformation of speech" was praised by reviewers of the book. Reservations were expressed, however, because within its brief span (just under 200 pages) *Seeing Voices* did not fully and clearly develop his thesis or confront its practical difficulties. Anthony Burgess objected, in the *Times Literary Supplement*, that "those of us whose knowledge of sign language is limited to what we see as a kind of sideshow of the television news need something a little more pragmatic than deaf politics and neuropsychology." Paul West, taking a similar line in the *New York Times Book Review*, pointed out the difficulties for a Sign user in a society which does not understand the language. "Dr. Sacks, whose heart is in the right place, wants the deaf to have all they need, but most of all, their own natural and private language. He brings afresh to our attention

a problem that is never easily going to be solved."

PRINCIPAL WORKS: Migraine: The Evolution of a Common Disorder, 1970, rev. ed. published as Migraine: Understanding a Common Disorder, 1985; Awakenings, 1973; A Leg to Stand On, 1984; The Man Who Mistook His Wife for a Hat, 1985; Seeing Voices: A Journey into the World of the Deaf, 1989.

ABOUT: Contemporary Authors 53–56, 1975. *Periodicals*—American Scholar Summer 1985; Atlantic March 1986; Commonweal March 28, 1986; Library Journal June 15, 1971; February 15, 1986; Nation February 22, 1986; New Statesman June 29, 1984; December 13, 1985; New York Review of Books June 3, 1971; September 27, 1984; November 8, 1984; August 15, 1985; March 13, 1986; January 29, 1987; November 22, 1990; New York Times May 9, 1971; January 25, 1986; New York Times Book Review November 11, 1984; July 7, 1985; March 2, 1986; October 8, 1989; Times Literary Supplement February 7, 1986; January 19, 1990.

SANFORD, JOHN (B.) (May 31, 1904–), American novelist, memoirist, and writer on American history, was born Julian (originally Jacob) Lawrence Shapiro in New York City to parents of Russian-Jewish origin. He changed his name to John Sanford legally in 1940. His father, Philip D. Shapiro, was a lawyer; his mother, Harriet (Nevins) Shapiro, died when the boy was only ten, and he and a younger sister were raised by their maternal grandparents. Julian, however, always had a deep affection for his father and in later years a warm relationship developed between them.

Growing up in a relatively comfortable middle-class home in Harlem, he attended New York public schools and absorbed the street-life of New York in the pre–World War I era with its mixture of races, cultures, and social classes. A childhood friend was Nathan Weinstein, who was to become the novelist Nathanael West, author of *Miss Lonelyhearts* and *The Day of the Locust.* Young Shapiro entered Lafayette College in 1922 in spite of the fact that, having failed senior English, he lacked a high school diploma. He left after one year to drift around the United States, hitchhiking his way south and west, working in a variety of odd jobs, and even spending a short time in jail in the South for vagrancy. On his return to New York he managed to qualify for Fordham University Law School from which he received an LL. B. in 1927. He practiced law occasionally from 1928 to 1936 but was never much engaged in his profession. A chance meeting with his boyhood friend Nathanael West, now already a writer, and a small

JOHN SANFORD

family inheritance that made it possible for him to travel to Europe in 1930, convinced Shapiro that he too could be a writer. In London he boldly submitted a story to the *Criterion* which was edited by T. S. Eliot. Eliot rejected the story but encouraged him to continue writing. His first published stories were in little avant-garde magazines—*Tambour* in Paris, *Pagany* and the *New Review* in the United States.

In the summer of 1931 Shapiro and West rented a cabin in the Adirondack mountains where West completed *Miss Lonelyhearts* while Shapiro worked on his own first novel. On their return to New York City, West introduced Shapiro to the poet William Carlos Williams, who took a friendly interest in his work and published two of his stories in a magazine he edited, *Contact*. Williams' major influence on him, however, was to be felt some years later in the development of his style which he came increasingly to model on the vignette-type prose essays of Williams' now classic *In the American Grain* (1925). But in the 1930s and 1940s Shapiro wrote a terse, starkly realistic fiction in the naturalistic manner of Erskine Caldwell and James T. Farrell. His first novel, *The Water Wheel*, after many rejections from the larger trade publishers, was published by Dragon, a small press headed by the scholar-translator Angel Flores. Like so many first novels, it was a self-conscious and self-centered book, chronicling the experiences of a young man named John Sanford, a transparent disguise, whom, many years later in his memoirs *Scenes from the Life of an American Jew*, the author described as "law-clerk, sinner, ex-

convict, adolescent, grandson and legatee of a Litvak matchvendor." The *New York Times* dismissed *The Water Wheel* as the story of "an unpleasant weakling with a narcissus complex" but the reviewer also noted some "brilliant scenes" and "originality of style" in it. Shapiro had more encouragement from Williams' judgment that the book "is really written, it moves, it has the quality of a novel," and in the praise it received from James T. Farrell in *Esquire* and Alvah Bessie in *Scribner's*.

Although sales of *The Water Wheel* were practically nil, Shapiro was determined to pursue his career as a novelist. Two years later he published *The Old Man's Place*, set in the rugged Adirondack country where he had spent his summer with West. Here, and in some half dozen novels he published subsequently, some under the name John B. Sanford, some as John Sanford, he began to receive more critical attention. The reviews—many of which he reprints in his autobiographical memoir—were always mixed. There was praise for the realism of his portraits of hard-bitten country and working-class characters, his colorful and extravagant language, his compassion for the poor and oppressed, and his occasional flights of poetic prose. There was also censure, and often outrage, for his "shocking" frankness, his "cartoon characters" (Mark Schorer reviewing *The People from Heaven* in the *New York Times Book Review*), and "pseudo-tough, pseudo-poetic manner reminiscent of Steinbeck at his worst" (Richard Freedman on *The $300 Man*, in *Saturday Review*). Perhaps the fairest early assessment was John Chamberlain's, reviewing *The Old Man's Place* in the *New York Times*: "John B. Sanford gets excited about America, not for any ascertainable philosophical reasons, but simply because he loves its patterns and emotions. He is to the novel what the school of Thomas Benton or Grant Wood is to painting—a 'nativist' who takes a purely esthetic delight in the salt and savor, even in the occasional flaring brutality of the American character."

In 1936 Sanford received an offer from Paramount Pictures for an option on one of his short stories. He went to Hollywood at what then seemed a magnificent salary as a screenwriter and has lived in California ever since. Although his career brought him into contact with the rich and famous—glamorous screen stars, and writers like F. Scott Fitzgerald, William Saroyan, and his old friend Nathanael West (whose promising career ended abruptly with his death in an auto crash in 1940)—Sanford never saw any of his work materialize into a film. The richest reward for those years, he reports in his memoir, was his meeting with another screenwriter, Marguerite Roberts, to whom he has been married since 1938.

Long openly committed to the politics of the Left, Sanford paid a heavy price in the 1940s and 1950s when the Communist-hunting congressional committees of Representative Martin Dies and later of Senator Joseph McCarthy brought him and his wife under investigation for alleged subversive activities. As Sanford wrote in a note in the *New York Times Book Review* in 1982: "Called on to testify, we refused and were branded 'unfriendly witnesses.'" In 1951 they were both blacklisted, and although Marguerite Roberts returned to screenwriting some ten years later with, among other major films, her scenario for *True Grit*, starring John Wayne, Sanford was never able to regain a place as a writer for the screen or the popular trade publishers.

The bitter consequences of his blacklisting are recorded in the Introduction that Sanford wrote to a new edition of his most ambitious novel, *A Man Without Shoes*. He had completed this long book in 1947 and, he writes, "the sixteen seasons of the next four years were all of them winter. During that period, the book was submitted to some thirty publishers, and thirty-some times it was declined." Realizing at last that "I'd have to lay the book to rest or publish it myself," Sanford found a private printer, Saul Marks, who issued the novel in a beautifully designed format in 1951. Sanford continues the account: "When the work was completed, early in 1951, I thoughtlessly directed that the entire edition be delivered to my home. It was as if a cord of wood had been stacked in the hallway, and after a while, sales having hardly diminished it, it began to overwhelm me, and I had it moved into storage. There it has remained since the time of publication, so in a sense the book *was* buried after all."

A Man Without Shoes languished forgotten until 1982, when Black Sparrow Press issued 2,000 copies, with a new title page and Sanford's Introduction, and it was the subject of a long review-essay by Morris Dickstein in the *New York Times Book Review*. Although it cannot be said to have established or restored Sanford's reputation as a novelist, it awakened interest in his work and opened the way for the publication and wider recognition of his memoirs and his series of volumes on the American past. In the late 1980s, after years of obscurity, John Sanford was writing more prolifically and receiving more critical attention than at any other time in his life. The novel itself, in Dickstein's judgment, is flawed—tendentious, overwritten, and, from the standpoint of the 1980s, dated and naive in its populism and simplistic social views. But San-

ford's long record of political and social commitment, "the lived interaction between history and personal experience," as Dickstein describes it, "makes *A Man Without Shoes*, at its best, a memorable book to read and rediscover."

The central character of *A Man Without Shoes* (the title from the familiar saying: "I had no shoes and complained, but then I met a man without feet") is Daniel Johnson, and the novel is a minutely detailed record of his life from his conception to his early thirties. In some respects he is another projection of Sanford himself— growing up in Harlem, mingling with people of diverse races and backgrounds, drifting about the country, maturing into social awareness and political radicalism. But Johnson comes from a poor Irish family, his father a cab driver; he never attends college; he becomes actively involved in the protests against the executions of Sacco and Vanzetti (a cause of which Sanford himself was almost unaware at the time); and at the end he is planning to go to Spain to fight for the Loyalists in the Spanish civil war. For Dickstein it is "a fascinating document of its time," missing no detail of the turbulent American experience from World War I through the depression of the 1930s. Daniel Johnson is drawn as a representative figure. As he travels across the United States, Sanford inserts long passages reflecting on American history and biographies of Americans real and imaginary. There are soliloquies and flashbacks. "The whole book proceeds by montage or collage," Dickstein writes, "obviously indebted to the discontinuous techniques of John Dos Passos' multilayered novel *USA* but is told in a voice uniquely and distinctly Sanford's own."

In fact this technique had developed early in Sanford's writing. In his *Seventy Times Seven* of 1939, the story of a brutal Adirondacks farmer's vengeance on a rival, he had inserted passages of verse commenting on America's past— Custer's expedition into Montana, De Soto's quest for gold. In *Scenes from the Life of an American Jew*, addressing himself in the second person as he does throughout this memoir, he writes of that novel: "Thereafter you would speak directly, laminating your narratives with commentary on the unchristian episodes running through the course of the nation's expansion—a nation conceived in Christ that did not practice His preaching."

Sanford employs a similar manner, and a similar note of social protest, in the several volumes he has written on American history, using vignettes, little poetic-prose essays, and some free verse to sketch people and events in the American past from its earliest history—Eric the Red,

Columbus, the Pilgrims, the fathers of the American Revolution, the Civil War, all the way up to the atomic bombings of Hiroshima and Nagasaki. Originally conceived as a trilogy, then expanded to a fourth volume, the series comprises *A More Goodly Country*, a sweeping panorama of American history in portraits of Americans famous, infamous, obscure, often not identified by name, drawn from historical records, diaries, letters, newspapers; *A View from This Wilderness*, a similar survey, this time in terms of literary figures; *To Feed Their Hopes*, a gallery of American women; and *The Winters of That Country*, another collection of sketches of people and events from the Norse explorations to the Vietnam War. All the titles are taken from a single passage in William Bradford's *History of the Plymouth Plantation*: "The season it was winter, and they that know the winters of that country know them to be sharp and violent, and subject to cruell and fierce stormes. Neither could they go up to the top of Pisgah, as it were, to view from this willdernes a more goodly country to feed their hopes."

Sanford's imaginative re-creation of America in these volumes owes a debt to William Carlos Williams' *In the American Grain*, but, as Paul Mariani points out in his Foreword to *A View from This Wilderness*, he has written "a distinctive, idiosyncratic, iconoclastic masterpiece of American literature." Sanford writes a lusty, impressionistic prose that gives color if not historical authenticity to his work. For example, in *The Winters of That Country* he describes stockbrokers reacting to the Wall Street crash of 1929:

> How they leap and lunge, how they flay the air as though to throw their hands away! How they prance, how they mill in the moil, how they shrill and dance! And then a bell rings, and they curse and joke, they launch paper planes on the smoke and shivaree. A few launch themselves from a thirty-ninth floor, and they do not float. Halfway through a taxi-roof, they are members no more, and they may not trade in doves.

Reviewing *A More Goodly Country* in the *Christian Science Monitor*, Victor Howes observed: "In a prose that matches the time or the personality it depicts, Mr. Sanford . . . magnificently captures United States history in a series of vignettes featuring villains and heroes, enslavers and liberators. . . . He has brought to life a gallery of American figures persuasively, vividly, with a personal view that is by turns comic, tragic and ironic."

As history, Sanford's quartet makes no attempt to disguise its critical and ideological bias; as an expression of one man's passionate, if ambivalent, love for America, the volumes are stimulating and illuminating. Because he offers an

unabashedly personal view of history, he writes in terms of people and of the impact of events (wars, strikes, lynchings, protest movements) on people's lives. Probably the most interesting of this series are *A View from This Wilderness: American Literature as History* and *To Feed Their Hopes: A Book of American Women*. Sanford culls American literature from Columbus' log of his first sight of the New World to the suicide of the poet John Berryman in 1972. Almost no figure in the American literary canon, major or minor, is omitted, from Puritans like John Winthrop and John Eliot, through the Revolution with Madison, Jefferson, and Paine, to John Reed and Sacco and Vanzetti. Sometimes the subject himself speaks (Edgar Allan Poe: "Why did I marry my twelve-year-old cousin Virginia, whose mother was nearer my age, and in the hovels we shared with a cat, a bobolink, and a pair of canaries, did I ever see her naked . . . did I sink the sight in opium when drink was slow to drug me?"). Sometimes Sanford speaks as literary critic (on John O'Hara: "Words flooded from his arm. He had merely to point at paper, it seemed, and the spate would start, the freshet blow. Scenes would spread and stories run—a marvel, that fictive font of his").

Annette K. Baxter, in her Foreword, describes the purpose of *To Feed Their Hopes* as "nothing less than a panoramic raising of the national consciousness with respect to women in American life." Here again Sanford mixes real people and fictional characters, from Virginia Dare, Pocohontas, and Anne Hutchinson to Ethel Rosenberg and Eleanor Roosevelt, from Little Eva in *Uncle Tom's Cabin* to Ayn Rand's John Galt. Baxter is impressed with Sanford's understanding of feminism: "Sanford's view of women is of course a man's view, and it is valuable to us for being that. He demonstrates that it is possible for men, willing to equip themselves with knowledge, to scale the tangled emotional barbed wire between the sexes and cross over into understanding." An example is his vignette "Ad Libs by a Fictitious Character," in which Pearl, daughter of Hester Prynne, reflects bitterly on her father: "But Mr. Hawthorne seems to have been unaware of the second thing I saw . . . a second *A*, this one black . . . my begetter, the black letter A. Dimmesdale! . . . he let my mother alone to be stoned by eyes."

Sanford's autobiographical memoir *Scenes from the Life of an American Jew* runs to three volumes so far and chronicles his life in exhaustive detail. The title of its first volume, *The Color of the Air*, reflects his lifelong fascination with history: "The color of the air," he writes, "is a fast color, for history does not fade." Like most of his works it is written in scenes, almost cinematic in form, with short "takes" and flashbacks and interspersed with historical vignettes. The third volume, *A Very Good Land to Fall With*, concludes with the dropping of the A-bomb in 1945, but Sanford expects to continue the account in future books. He covers much ground here that he had covered in his earlier works, and the piling up of detail tends to weaken the dramatic effectiveness of the work. But he offers a lively and revealing, if somewhat narrowly slanted, record of his times. Volume I impressed Robert Gorham Davis, in the *New York Times Book Review* in 1985, with its "masterly powers of evocation . . . [that] give this neglected author a distinctive enough identity to stimulate a reexamination, both political and literary, of all his writings."

PRINCIPAL WORKS: *Novels*—The Old Man's Place, 1935; Seventy Times Seven, 1939; The People from Heaven, 1943; A Man Without Shoes, 1951, 1982; The Land that Touches Mine, 1953. *As Julian L. Shapiro*—The Water Wheel, 1933. *Collected short stories*—Adirondack Stories, 1976. *Historical vignettes*—A More Goodly Country, 1975; A View from This Wilderness, 1977; To Feed Their Hopes, 1980; The Winters of That Country, 1984. *Memoirs*—Scenes from the Life of an American Jew: I, The Color of the Air, 1985; II, The Waters of Darkness, 1986; III, A Very Good Land to Fall With, 1987.

ABOUT: Baxter, A. K. *Foreword to* To Feed Their Hopes, 1980; Contemporary Authors 123, 1988; Mariani, P. *Foreword to* A View from This Wilderness, 1977; Sanford, J. Scenes from the Life of an American Jew, 3 vols., 1985–1987. *Periodicals*—Christian Science Monitor April 30, 1975; Library Journal June 15, 1975; Literary Review Summer 1985; New York Times Book Review July 11, 1982; November 10, 1985.

*SÁNTA, FERENC (September 4, 1927–   ), Hungarian novelist and short-story writer, writes: "I was born in the Transylvanian city of Brassó (since 1921 a part of Romania). My childhood was spent in great poverty, but frankly I can, in retrospect, only be thankful for this fate: humanistic compassion and responsibility to one's fellows is stronger among the poor than among anyone else. I was taught that it is my duty to help others and it seems only natural to me that others should help me too. As for my education, I attended Unitarian and Reformed colleges, but I never finished these studies. At that time I reasoned that school took too much time away from learning and there was more than a little truth to this. From the age of fourteen on I was a constant visitor to the library. I read my first book at six and since then never a day passed that did not include some reading. I

FERENC SÁNTA

would skip school to go and sit in some university reading room where I could stay until late afternoon. I might try to somehow explain this disgust of mine with school: they tried to teach me Latin grammar when I had already long before read Plutarch, Lucan, Tacitus in the mother tongue. The same was the case with the Greeks—long since had I read in entirety Homer and Aristophanes when they tried to beat the Greek alphabet into my head. Today, of course, I would gladly sit again on those benches and honestly, I would excel even at mathematics!

"I married early and well, and this has proven one of the most important elements of my life. I have four sons and already fourteen grandchildren, which is all as it should be! Upon getting married, as I knew nothing but literature, philosophy, and history but had nothing in the way of qualifications, I went to work in a mine in the vicinity of Budapest. I could have obtained some little desk job, but I really did not like the idea. It seems to me that I was a free-minded and independent person even at that young age, as I certainly am now. Helping to maintain that state of mind has been my unfailing disbelief that any one political, philosophical, or religious institution, organization, or the like can provide the answer to all the world's problems. These things do nothing for the human condition. Rather I believe that there are certain absolute moral truths and 'eternal ethical norms' according to which we must live. These ethical norms are not relative, but rather have constant voices, universal and innate. Only under extraordinarily inhuman conditions can their development in the young

°shän´ ta, fe´ rents

be crippled, unless one consciously 'decides to become a villain.' I speak now about conscience. Frederick the Great once wrote to Voltaire that he could not observe the attribute of goodness in a baby, whereupon Voltaire responded that 'neither can one see the moustache on a baby boy, yet when the time will come that will make known its presence.' Similarly I believe that the conscience is always capable of directing us in the matters of life and we always know whether our actions are right or wrong. Call it a daemon, a categorical imperative, or what you will but there it is inside us. For this reason I maintain that one can only remain deprived of human dignity and free will for a short time—sooner or later his conscience will protest.

"I worked in a number of factories and was a soldier as well (fortunately only in peacetime); then in 1954 after the death of Stalin there emerged in Hungary a generation of young writers, myself among them. In 1956 I published my first collection of short stories, in the same year as the terrible and cruel struggle within Hungary. I myself was a member of the directorship of the Petőfi Circle, a forum of young Hungarian intellectuals seeking political reform, from 1955 on. After the 1956 tragedy I went to work in yet another factory and only in 1961 was my next book published. I have never regretted my long silence. Then I had already worked in the library of the Institute of Literary Studies (an institute of the Hungarian Academy of Sciences).

"My literary career was begun with the publication of 'Sokan voltunk' ['Too Many of Us,' a short story] in 1954. It was followed by seven books, the first in 1956 and the last in 1970. My books have been published in several languages, including all socialist countries.

"Two films based on my novels (Az ötödik pecsét [translated as The Fifth Seal] and Húsz óra [Twenty Hours]) were awarded the first prize at the Moscow Film Festival, whereas a TV-film based on 'Halálnak halála' ['No More Dying Then,' a short story] at the Monte Carlo Festival won the Golden Nymph and the prize of the Roman Catholic Church."

Readers enthusiastically received Sánta's short story "Sokan voltunk" in which the narrator recollects from his childhood the events surrounding the death of his grandfather who chose to die to ease the poverty of the family. Critics, looking back on the story years later, concluded that its symbolic representation of reality marked a significant development in postwar Hungarian fiction. Not only did it differ from the critical realism of such influential predecessors as Kálmán Mikszáth (1847–1910) and Zsigmond Móricz (1879–1942) and even from the fiction of József Nyírö (1889–1953) and Áron Tamási (1897–1966) to whom Sánta has acknowledged his debt; perhaps more importantly, it did not obey the dicta of schematism, which was being imposed on writers during the first half of the 1950s in the name of Socialist Realism. Later, in answer to criticism of his use of symbols in his first novel, Az ötödik pecsét (The Fifth Seal, 1963), Sánta contended that "Literature must not copy life. Instead, it must compress the most important matters into their purest and sharpest form, when symbols are required for their expression, so that the work will shock and lead the reader through a catharsis and thus mold him."

The short stories in Sánta's first collection, Téli virágzáz (Winter Blossoming, 1956), most of them written in a two-year period, already show three permanent traits. Besides the symbolic mode, these stories of poverty, based on his personal experiences, show the influence of the folk literature of the ancient Seklers of Transylvania, where Sánta lived until his parents moved to Hungary in 1945. They use the cadences and lyrical concreteness, the abrupt transitions, the taut sentences, the dramatic dialogue, and the sparseness of narrative detail typical of folk tale and ballad, elements that would remain, though subdued, a feature of Sánta's style when he turned from peasants to other characters struggling with ethical decisions in his later, no longer autobiographical, fiction. The third trait of the early stories is their dramatic form. Aiming at uncovering the essentials of human integrity in these stories, Sánta forces his characters to make painful choices, as, for example, in "Kicsi madár" (Little Bird), whose boy protagonist chooses to sing to a hated kulak in order to make money to buy medicine for his sick sister. Reviewers gave the collection a mixed reception. Some wondered whether Sánta's vision would be limited to a rather intuitive and emotional treatment of childhood, while others, finding the first stories the best, feared that a decline in his creativity was already evident.

Sánta, however, was deciding upon his future path as a writer. The 1956 uprising and its violent suppression by the Soviet Army deeply depressed him, and the next two or three years were most critical to his growth. Rethinking his themes and techniques, Sánta decided to make direct, critical statements about the 1950s and the events of October and November 1956 in a disciplined and intellectual prose, a change in substance and style that took some time for him to accomplish. Adapting the principle of creative ity he found in Paul Valéry's *Introduction à la méthode de Léonard da Vinci* (1895), Sánta undertook writing tasks he found distasteful, even some unsuited to his talents, to spur himself on to new achievements. He resisted, he tells us, emotions flowing from his own experiences onto the page almost without any intervention of thought; instead, he sought out themes that emerged from his personal convictions but possessed enough emotional potential to nourish his creative powers, the major one being his antifascism. He also presented issues more objectively; he now learned, he says, to "invent with a consciously operative and functioning imagination those incidents and characters most suited to the projection of thought." The shift in point of view and the deliberate composition diminished the lyrical, ballad-like flow; now the language projected the intellect and not solely the main emotion based on personal experience.

His second short-story collection, *Farkasok a küszöbön* (Wolves at the Threshold), published five years after the first, exhibits clear signs of these changes. The somewhat static and familiar world of the first collection is mostly absent. He now observes a wider array of characters objectively in complex decision-making situations of a completely fictional nature. Previously, ordinary men and women making their way through material and moral crises of daily life underwent tests of their capacity for ethical growth; now, in addition, in the cycle of five stories called "Olasz történet" (An Incident in Italy) and opening the collection, ordinary human beings are plunged into self-appraisal by the relentless cruelty of life and by the physical and psychological threats of fascism, especially its appalling deadening of the human conscience and perversion of human judgment. The world Sánta portrays is bleak; it is without a community supporting acts of integrity, and even the protagonists, repelled by the inhumanity surrounding them, pursue ethically laudable ends in isolation and rather pointlessly. In "An Incident in Italy," the nameless young protagonist chooses certain starvation instead of a job as a lion-tamer because he cannot tolerate a position of authority based upon force and conditioning, and in "Kicsik and nagyok" (Little Ones and Grownups), two children trying to imitate their parents are unable to reenact the cruelties they have observed their parents inflicting on each other. Though all the stories in the cycle expose in some way the terrors of fascism, two engage the theme exclusively, "Nácik" (Nazis) and "Müller család halála" (The Müller Family's Death). The first portrays a little boy's chilling confrontation with German soldiers who force him to call a dog a goat; the second tells of a German who, accepting fascism because it enables

him to support his family, ultimately becomes himself a victim of its bestiality.

Hereafter, Sánta wrote only four short stories, the last in 1963, which are included in his final collection, *Isten a szekéren* (God in the Wagon, 1970). They follow familiar thematic and stylistic lines but delve more deeply into issues of the times. "Az öreg és a fiatal" (The Young and the Old) concerns the transmission of values in its portrayal of an impatient hangman giving on-the-job training in the technique of his craft to an apprentice, and the title story recounts an initially skeptical peasant's tender response to the "Lord God," who has been wearied and depressed by His sojourn on earth. The remaining two stories further explore the evils of fascism. "A veder" (The Pail), its profusion of details aiming for the special effects of a slow-motion camera, depicts the paralyzing rigidity of the fascist temperament through a German sentry's paranoid behavior. "Halálnak halála" (translated as "No More Dying Then") celebrates the triumph of humanistic values over death (the ultimate weapon of fascism) when two prisoners from the Hungarian underground, being led to certain execution by a single armed soldier, choose instinctively to save the guard's life rather than their own, to his consternation. A reviewer ranked this volume, which contains all but one of the stories Sánta has published, among the foremost accomplishments in the history of the Hungarian short story and regretted it did not include anything not published previously.

Sánta's three novels mark the latest phase of his development. These parabolic short novels apply a sharp scalpel to the Hungarians' experiences with domestic fascism and Stalinism. *The Fifth Seal* takes up the necessity of acting against the abuse of power regardless of the risk it entails; *Húsz óra* (Twenty Hours, 1964) explores the political causes leading Hungarians in a village to turn against each other violently during the 1956 uprising; and *Az áruló* (The Traitor, 1966) tests the value of revolution as an authentic instrument of social reform. Sánta's extensive use of dialogue in these novels pushes action and description into the background, in order to lay out ethical alternatives for the characters. Each work is, however, technically different: *The Fifth Seal*, set in Budapest at the close of the Second World War, is devoted mostly to a Socratic dialogue between four ordinary men in a tavern struggling with the moral dilemma offered by the hypothetical choice of being an abject slave or an all-powerful pharaoh, thus giving through contrast a dramatic impact to the brutality the participants suffer at the hands of Hungarian fascists at the end of the novel; *Húsz óra* uses reportorial investigation to interlace events that occurred over two decades in the village where the violence happened; and *Az áruló* resurrects from their graves four participants in the Hussite Wars, summoned by an author living in the atomic age to debate their past actions on the basis of their differing attitudes toward life, namely: a Hussite soldier who is a zealous advocate of revolutionary violence, a monk who believes in a hedonism verging on cynicism, a student soldier who thinks reform is the antidote to every uprising, and an old peasant who, accepting his fate and believing nothing will ever change, wants only to save for himself whatever he can under prevailing circumstances.

In a 1979 interview occasioned by the republication of the three novels, Sánta states that each novel examines the connection between power and mankind, or, basically, the ways in which corrupt power leads human beings into evil. According to him, all three novels verify the fact that fanaticism is the root of all evil. To him, it is incontrovertible that individuals who hold their personal convictions to be the truth will never subject themselves to the control of the people. This unhappy fact, he is convinced, is the greatest cause of human suffering because it fosters apathy and thus gives fanaticism the power to rule. In the novels, he was ultimately searching, Sánta asserts, for the way human honor can survive in its historical conflict with fanaticism.

In all his works, Sánta searches for the ethical norms of humanistic thought because, in his view, new ethical standards have not yet sufficiently emerged to replace the religious values that were swept away by the tragic historical events of the present century. In the past, persons knew exactly what moral principles they were violating; today, they no longer do. Sánta tries to fill this void with the following standard of humanity: "anything that abases, injures, or destroys man is sinful." His protagonists come face to face with this standard, to be judged by the rigor with which they measure up to it. However, Sánta tests them with an optimism founded in his confidence about man's native capacity to measure up to the edicts of "eternal ethical norms." In the long run, the forces of evil lack the power to cripple mankind permanently, for goodness is, he insists, so deeply imbedded in human nature that the conscience unfailingly points to the solution of every ethical dilemma perplexing mankind. The voice of conscience, silent when humans are performing acts of goodness, instantly protests when they are about to commit an evil act. Moreover, the conscience intervenes freely and independently, not instructed by a particular philosophical or ethical system, for it can . . . instantly distinguish and

measure everything and unerringly determine our proper behavior on its own." This is not to say that Sánta underestimates the role of judgment in the creation of moral behavior. On the contrary, judgment is, like the conscience, natural to man; indeed, to judge is "the most natural of /man's/ rights," whose free exercise is essential to "his good health." He proclaims the sanctity of every man's right to exercise his personal judgment in heeding his conscience.

In a 1967 interview, Ferenc Sánta had already claimed supremacy for writers in exercising this right of judgment. In his view, it is even more important for artists and writers to preserve "their independence of thought against the extremes of alluring and revolting passions" and to guard constantly "their freedom to strive for the act of rational and correct judgment." Because the writers' quest for truth protects man from the fanatical extremes contending for control over his judgment, they must pursue their literary mission vigilantly. The writer's most pressing function is "to curb—while we still can—the opposing animosities" of contending ideologies. Calling this role "the greatest imperative of our age" and "anyone who shirks it guilty," he implores writers to "stand in the way of the obsessed . . . /to/ discredit the hideous, degenerate, and sick logic of the accursed. The light of reason must be shone upon them, for they shall be destroyed by it, even as poisonous vegetation is destroyed by the sun."

The passion with which Sánta declares his views of the writer's authority and the function of literature contributes to the perplexity about his self-imposed silence since the publication of *Az áruló* in 1966. Sánta finally addressed the question in a 1986 interview. His first silence, from 1956 to 1961, had been a time for him to search for valid statements to make about the disastrous events of the fifties. The second silence, he reveals, was made more difficult by his bitterness at the state of his country. He was distressed not only by the moral decline produced by improvements in the economy in the 1960s but also (and especially) by the high suicide and death rates and alcoholism of his people and by his grave doubts about the political system that created the "unspeakably bad" situation in the name of socialism.

His deep bitterness gravely hampered his efforts to assess the moral condition of the people as a member of the national community. He wrote many bitter pieces but threw them away; in addition, he lacked the strength to find the word with which to close a piece and lost the hope of beginning one armed with the power of truth. Incapable of exercising a balanced, objective judgment, he could not write himself out of his bitterness and feeling of hopelessness. "What possibilities lay open to me? Either to write, as so many did, about sparrows and springtime or when I am in a bad mood about autumn and winter, in order to make money? Or simply . . . to write myself out of my bitterness but without attaching hope to it?" Then his rereading the history of Hungary taught him again that despite numerous struggles and destructive goals, Hungarians still survive. "We proved that somehow the value of a person, of a nation is characterized not only by what they give to the world but also by what they are capable of receiving. And that this people's intelligence and talent were capable of enormous trials and able to survive numerous tragedies." At this, his juices began to stir again, and he was filled with the pride of a person or nation that has accomplished great works. And so "my first novel in many years will appear next year, and it will be followed by one or two more."

As of October 1989, the novel remains a promise, but when it is published, the public will read it eagerly to learn what this troubled, complex, and sometimes volatile man, never in harmony with his times, will say about dramatic changes his country has undergone in the more than twenty years since he last spoke up—an author who with other members of his generation faced, in his own words, "the throes of socialism, . . . put an end to taboo-themes, to schematism, . . . and flung open and spread the door wide for literature" in postwar Hungary.

WORKS IN ENGLISH TRANSLATION: Selected stories by Sánta were translated into English by Albert Tezla, 1985, with the title *God in the Wagon*; *Az ötödik pecsét* (1963), a novel, was translated into English by A. Tezla in 1986 with the title *The Fifth Seal*. Translations of some stories and an interview done in 1967 are published in Albert Tezla's *Ocean at the Window: Hungarian Prose and Poetry since 1945*, 1980.

ABOUT: Tezla, A. Hungarian Authors: A Bibliographical Handbook, 1970; Tezla, A. Ocean at the Window, 1980. *Periodicals*—Hungarian PEN 1984.

SCHAEFFER, SUSAN FROMBERG (March 25, 1941–), American novelist and poet, was born in Brooklyn, New York, daughter of Irving and Edith (Levine) Fromberg. She grew up in Brooklyn and on Long Island, and received all three of her degrees from the University of Chicago—B.A. 1961; M.A., with honors, 1963; and Ph.D. in English literature, with honors, 1966. She wrote her doctoral dissertation on the novels of Vladimir Nabokov. After receiving

SUSAN FROMBERG SCHAEFFER

her Ph.D., Susan Fromberg remained in Chicago for several years, as instructor in English at Wright Teachers College, 1964–1965, and as assistant professor at the Illinois Institute of Technology, 1965–1967. Since then she has taught in the English department at Brooklyn College, City University of New York. In 1970 she married Neil J. Schaeffer, who was also teaching in the English department at Brooklyn College (and was its chairman in the 1980s), and by whom she has two children. In the course of her career she has also been guest lecturer at the University of Chicago, Cornell University, the University of Arizona, the University of Maine, Yale University, the University of Texas, and the University of Massachusetts. At the same time Schaeffer has had a remarkably prolific career as a writer. She has published five volumes of poetry (one of which was nominated for a National Book Award), a collection of short stories, and two children's novels, but she is best known and has attracted most attention as a novelist.

Schaeffer's first novel, *Falling*, which deals with a young woman who grows up in Brooklyn and attends graduate school at the University of Chicago, presumably draws from her personal experience but was regarded by reviewers as a work transcending the merely personal. Writing in *Time*, which selected *Falling* as one of the ten best novels of 1973, R. Z. Sheppard remarked that the success of *Falling* was "no mean achievement, because [Schaeffer] has chosen . . . material long since worn to clichés—Elizabeth's immigrant Jewish grandparents, the New York middle-class scene, an unsuccessful engagement, a suicide attempt, and a prolonged psychoanalysis. . . . The author handles this with great credibility, tact and humor. But Elizabeth is more than a fleshed out case history because she has a strong character." Pearl K. Bell in the New Leader agreed with Sheppard's appraisal, and elaborated upon it. "The astonishing thing about Susan Fromberg Schaeffer's superb first novel," she observed, " . . . is that she emerges in triumph from a risk that most young authors would not even consider worth taking. Stubbornly fixing her penetrating sights on material that anyone knows has been done to death—Jewish life in Brooklyn, graduate school, . . . and scrabbling in the family dirt for the Holy Grail of the self, Mrs. Schaeffer has managed to establish a marvelously original claim to these tattered topics. She is a writer of uncommon talent and honesty, blessed with a natural command of humor and perception, and she has crafted one of the most engaging and genuinely funny books I've read in years."

Schaeffer's second novel, Anya, a Book-of-the-Month Club selection, attracted even greater attention. In this work, Schaeffer selected material of which she could have had no first-hand acquaintance whatever—the destruction of the Jews in Vilna, Poland in the late 1930s. In the novel, Schaeffer employs two different time frames, Vilna in the thirties when Anya Savikin is a medical student, and New York in 1973 where Anya, trapped in a depressing marriage, looks back upon the past. John Skow in Time commented that the "overwhelming impression left by this rich and brooding novel of wartime Poland is of an actual life agonizingly remembered, not of events and characters cut and fitted to the pattern of a story. . . . The author's account of Anya's war years is detailed and obsessive, a daily rediscovery of the same obsessive pain." Elaine Reuben in the New Republic remarked that "Schaeffer's voice has the elegiac quality of a medium as she re-creates the world of Vilna's Jewish bourgeoisie . . . an achievement of power and importance." Alan Mintz in Commentary was also impressed by the evocative power of the work, but he felt that "the spaces which come to life in this novel are essentially domestic. The Savikins' apartment in Vilna is so intensely imagined that each piece of furniture gives off endless recollections of family life." He faulted the novel, however, for repetition and formlessness. "Every stage in Anya's trek through Eastern Europe," he commented, "is lavished with the same attention. . . . There is, moreover, something suffocating and constricted in the relentless focus on the family, made even more so by the way in which male characters are overshadowed and effaced by the women, and relations between men and women go virtually unrepresented."

Time in Its Flight, another Book-of-the-Month Club selection, is a huge work, nearly 800 pages long, recounting the life of the Steeles in Vermont from pre–Civil War times to the 1960s, but set largely in the nineteenth century. Reviews of the novel were mixed. Patricia Meyer Spacks in the Hudson Review found that it possessed "undeniable power derived partly from its relentless accumulation [of authentic detail]." Spacks went on to comment, however, that despite "all her exactness, her rural Vermont does not live like Singer's Warsaw; it informs the intellect more fully than the imagination. And the meticulous account of a family's individual and collective experience almost inevitably creates a certain tedium. So many births, deaths, illnesses, love affairs: the reader begins to feel the limitations rather than the variety of human possibilities." Lynne Sharon Schwartz in the Saturday Review remarked, similarly, that Schaeffer's "attempt to render a photographic reality of affectionate family size . . . yields tedium. When Schaeffer is not patronizing her characters or reminding the reader how lovable they are in their quirkiness, her writing can be taut and vigorous. . . . These are small gems in a framework too lax and comprehensive to sustain excitement."

Schaeffer's next novel, Love, is also a family saga, this time dealing with two Jewish immigrant families, the Lurias and the Romanoffs, from the turn of the century through 1978. Many reviewers felt that it carried authority but tended to be diffuse and, at times, sentimental. Attracting more attention was Schaeffer's The Madness of a Seduced Woman, a 600-page novel set in Vermont at the turn of the century. In this work, Schaeffer traces the experience of Agnes Dempster, who at sixteen leaves her family of eccentric farmers in North Chittenden to become a seamstress in Montpelier; there she falls in love with Frank Holt, a sculptor, and when he does not reciprocate her passion shoots not him but the woman he is seeing and then herself. Agnes, who survives her wound to stand trial for murder, becomes a study by Schaeffer into questions of passion and deception, fate and free will, biology and cognition. Elizabeth Ward in the Washington Post Book World considered the novel "an uncannily gripping story" that asked the reader to "define the wavering line between love and obsession, fruitful commitment and destructive dependence." Rosellen Brown in the New York Times Book Review, however, felt that Schaeffer's ideas were not clearly thought out. Agnes' recognition that her error had been her dependency on Frank, she wrote, "is a description of a symptom, not a cause. Surely Mrs. Schaeffer has not spent hundreds of pages documenting Agnes' hereditary willfulness only to end with such a tepid and conventional rebuke."

Among Schaeffer's more recent novels, *Mainland* and *The Injured Party* both deal with the nervous breakdown of a novelist-heroine in mid-life, and her withdrawal from the outer world to find a reintegration of personality. A number of reviewers found *The Injured Party* disappointing. Wendy Brandmark in the *New Statesman* remarked that "Schaeffer's ability to pull us into the complex emotional lives of her characters is not apparent in *The Injured Party*. We are too conscious of the writer watching the characters watch themselves to get involved. *The Injured Party* is not so much a novel as an exquisitely written testimony, a critical analysis of a breakdown." Moving radically away from the subjectivity of these novels, Schaeffer turned next to the Vietnam War, writing in *Buffalo Afternoon* a remarkably imaginative re-creation of the combat and post-combat experiences of Pete Bravado, an Italian boy from Brooklyn, who is drafted and sent to Vietnam. There he confronts—and she reconstructs with remarkable and harrowing detail—the unremitting horror of combat. All this is background to the postwar trauma he suffers when he returns home. Describing the book as no less than a "coup," Nicholas Proffitt in the *New York Times Book Review* marvelled at its authenticity. In fact Schaeffer had over a two-year period interviewed fifteen Vietnam combat veterans, but hers is more than a faithful journalistic report. Proffitt wrote that *Buffalo Afternoon* "goes right at the war, like Pete Bravado, the young soldier whose story it tells, trying to take its objectives with a frontal assault. And take them it does. *Buffalo Afternoon* is one of the best treatments of the Vietnam War to date, and all the more impressive for the fact that its author never heard a shot fired in anger or set foot in that country."

Schaeffer is Briecklundian professor of English at Brooklyn College, and director of its Creative Writing Program. Interviewed in *Publisher's Weekly* in 1983, she spoke of the unusual way in which she writes her novels. "I don't start to write," she commented, "until I know what the book is about from beginning to end, scene by scene. When I actually begin writing, something strange happens. I become enveloped in a kind of conflagration, a burning to get the book out of my system. I write the book all the way through, stopping as little as possible. I sleep only two or three hours a night. All the energy I might release if I wrote a little at a time builds up and spills out almost beyond my

control." Once the draft is completed, she makes a revision, but never using pen or pencil. "Only actually retyping the book," she notes, "allows the creative process to begin again."

PRINCIPAL WORKS: *Novels*—Falling, 1973; Anya, 1974; Time in Its Flight, 1978; Love, 1981; The Madness of a Seduced Woman, 1983; Mainland, 1984; The Injured Party, 1986; Buffalo Afternoon, 1988. *Poetry*—The Witch and the Weather Report, 1972; Alphabet for the Lost Years, 1976; Granite Lady, 1974; Rhymes and Runes of the Toad, 1975; The Bible of the Beasts of the Little Field, 1980. *Collected short stories*—The Queen of Egypt and Other Stories, 1980. *Children's novels*—The Dragons of North Chittendon, 1986; The Four Hoods and Great Dog, 1988.

ABOUT: Contemporary Authors 49–52, 1975; Contemporary Novelists, 4th ed., 1986; Pearlman, M. (ed.) American Women Writing Fiction, 1989; Who's Who of American Women: 1989–1990, 1988. *Periodicals*—Commentary March 1975; Hudson Review Winter 1978–1979; New Leader August 6, 1973; New Republic June 18, 1975; New Statesman December 5, 1986; New York Times Book Review May 22, 1983; May 21, 1989; Publishers Weekly April 8, 1983; Saturday Review June 24, 1978; January 1981; Time June 18, 1973; October 14, 1974; Washington Post Book World June 12, 1983.

SCHICKEL, RICHARD (WARREN) (February 10, 1933–   ), American film critic, was born in Milwaukee and raised in Wauwatosa, Wisconsin, the son of Edward John Schickel and the former Helen Hendricks. After attending local public schools, he received his bachelor's degree, with a major in political science and history, from the University of Wisconsin in 1956. He almost immediately left for New York City, where he landed a junior reporter's job on the magazine *Sports Illustrated*. He worked there for a year before continuing his progression through a series of jobs in the New York–based media. He worked for the now-defunct magazines *Look* (1957–1960) and *Show* (1960–1964); for the NBC-TV weekly series "Sunday" (1963–1964); and as a consultant for the Rockefeller Brothers Fund (1963–1965) and the Rockefeller Foundation (1965). For the last organization, he produced one of the first of his many books, *The Long Road to College: A Summer of Opportunity*, a report on a summer of college-preparedness training for black students conducted in 1964 at Oberlin and Dartmouth colleges and Princeton University.

Schickel had always, even as a child, been fascinated with films and film stars. He saw Walt Disney's *Snow White* at the age of five and loved it intensely. "You can date me easily," he told a

RICHARD SCHICKEL

colleague in 1967. "I can remember the exact year—1943—that the Friday night kids' movie went from 8 to 10. My first critical act, at age 11, was getting booted out of the theater for criticizing a Dennis Morgan western. Foot-stomping and yelling were, I recall, the current critical device." He began film reviewing in 1965, after he had been a professional writer for ten years. *Life* magazine hired him as its film critic; before that periodical stopped publication in 1972, he saw thousands of movies and wrote hundreds of film reviews, virtually none more than five hundred words in length, many considerably shorter. He then moved to *Time*, where he has continued to review films. Time-Life house style has strongly influenced the kind and form of reviews Schickel writes: his critical pieces are always decisively pro or con and are expressed in a highly colored prose sometimes at variance with the tone of the film in question. He described his approach to his job in a sidebar profile that appeared in *Life* in 1967, written by the magazine's managing editor, George P. Hunt: "He never takes notes or sees a film twice. 'The audience can't,' he says. 'Why should I?' He can instantly tell you who played what part and when and, when pressed, will quote endless dialogue from film he has seen years ago. . . . He carries around four or five unreviewed movies in his head at all times and prefers to wait a week or more before writing about any of them. 'What sticks in your head is what's worth mentioning,' he says. 'Besides, it gives you a chance to change your mind, which I do constantly.'"

He republished eighty-six of his late reviews in

Second Sight: Notes on Some Movies 1965–1970. A more expansive and perhaps congenial format for Schickel's evident passion for American films has been the filmographies and biographies he has written on some of the great movie figures. He first turned his attention to a man who became quite literally a legend in his own time, the elder Douglas Fairbanks. *His Picture in the Papers: A Speculation on Celebrity in America Based on the Life of Douglas Fairbanks, Sr.* is a short account of the star-celebrity system as it developed in Hollywood during the silent-film era. He was clearly much taken with the glamour of his subject. "Watching him," he writes in Chapter 1, " . . . one feels as one does watching an old comedy by Keaton or Chaplin: that somehow we have lost the knack, not to mention the spirit, for what they did, and that the loss is permanent. . . . Fairbanks was . . . always—triumphantly, irritatingly, ingratiatingly—Fairbanks, both on the screen and away from it. Indeed, there is about his career a certain inevitability; one can't quite imagine what he would have done with himself if the movies had not come into existence and provided him with precisely the kind of showcase his spirit and talents required." Schickel also supplied the introduction and captions for *The Fairbanks Album: Drawn from the Family Archives by Douglas Fairbanks, Jr..*

Schickel's next book-length treatment of a silent-film star was *Harold Lloyd: The Shape of Laughter*, an attempt to rehabilitate the reputation of a man he considers to be unjustly forgotten. He analyzes the factors that have condemned Lloyd to the "fringe of cinematic consciousness": "It seems to me self-evident," he writes in Chapter 1, "that any performer who achieved and sustained over a period of years the enormous popularity that Lloyd enjoyed must have had virtues that his more recent critics have ignored." The overriding virtue of his work is "that it is simply and consistently more hilarious than the work of any contemporary other than Keaton."

The author's other major filmography is *Cary Grant: A Celebration*, which appeared on the eightieth birthday of the great romantic and comedic leading actor. In addition to numerous captioned still shots from films and studio publicity photos, the book contains brief analyses of each of Grant's seventy-two films. Schickel also produced a volume, *Gary Cooper*, consisting not of stills but of dozens of carefully and languidly posed portrait photographs showing the "perfect masculine grace" of Cooper, "the only truly beautiful actor who did not spoil the effect of his handsomeness by seeming vain or self absorbed." He was "demonstrably . . . the

greatest star of his era and one of the two or
three greatest stars in the history of the sound
film." Cooper "had his minimalist mannerisms, . . . mostly his art consisted of a show of
artlessness. . . . He made as little fuss as possible over his craft, and appears to have been the
least egocentric of actors. . . . With each passing year the time and place that formed Gary
Cooper recede more deeply into the past, assur-
ing us that we will not see his like again, doom-
ing us to be forever bereft of that profound
reassurance we found in his heart-breaking reserve. . . . Our oldest, fondest dreams have, for
some of us, a resonance that no reality, however
vividly it stirs the memory, can ever truly
match." Such eulogistic, uncritical writing about
film stars has become something of a Schickel
trademark.

Another publication, *Striking Poses: Photographs from the Kobal Collection*, consists of
dozens of briefly captioned color photos of most
of the screen stars of the 1940s, many in false and
utterly ridiculous poses, degrading both to them
and their industry. It was in the stills studio,
Schickel writes in an introduction to this collection, "more than anywhere else on the lot, that
image subsumed individuality and a person was
made to feel that he or she was only a paper-doll
persona up in a cardboard sky, representing not
his or her own uniqueness, but a corporate version of it, something being cut and shaped to fit
a predetermined mold, a salable type."

Schickel's major film biography, the product
of more than a decade of research, is *D. W. Griffith: An American Life*, which, in almost 700
pages, follows the great silent-film director's career from his reluctant entry into films in 1908
to his involuntary retirement in 1931. In his introduction, the author describes in great detail
the many difficulties his subject presented him
with: "Griffith, though he gave many interviews
and caused much publicity about himself to be
generated, had two personal characteristics that
are a biographer's despair; he was both secretive
and a mythomaniac. . . . About almost every
significant aspect of his activities he maintained
a profound silence, which he later covered with
an excess of explanations that nearly always
tended toward the grandiose and the improbably noble. . . . The Griffith biographer is
forced to sift through mounds of misinforma-
tion, trusting his own common sense, critical intelligence and speculative abilities in order to
arrive at a plausible and coherent historical
narrative." The biography received mainly favorable reviews. Sam Kaplan in the *Nation*
called it "thorough and intelligent," and the director Peter Bogdanovich, writing in the *New
York Times Book Review*, praised Schickel for

keeping "a firm hand on the story of Griffith's
personal life without ever losing historical perspective—no mean feat, since the birth and
growth of the movies in America is the crucial
background of the sprawling tale."

*The Men Who Made the Movies: Interviews
with Frank Capra, George Cukor, Howard
Hawks, Alfred Hitchcock, Vincente Minnelli,
King Vidor, Raoul Walsh, and William A
Wellman* grew out of Schickel's participation for
public television as writer, director, and producer of a special of the same name, aired in 1973.
He greatly respects the directors whose interviews make up the book and the series. Most of
all, he admires their "attitude [which] was composed of a toughness that was never harsh, a
pride in achievement that was never boastful, a
self-reliance and an acceptance of the difficulties under which they had labored—and of the
flops they cheerfully admitted they had made—
which contained neither self-pity nor a desire to
blame others—producers, the studio system,
their actors or writers—for the things that had
gone wrong." Other television specials, in the
production and writing of which Schickel has
participated, are "Life Goes to the Movies"
(1976), "Funny Business" (1978), "Into the
Morning: Willa Cather's America" (1978), "The
Horror Show" (1979), "SPFX" (1980), and
"James Cagney: That Yankee Doodle Dandy"
(1981).

Among Schickel's other books are a novel,
Another I, Another You, on the subject of adultery and divorce; *Singled Out*, a sort of survival
guide for perplexed American divorced people;
and an attack on the worship of famous people
in America, *Intimate Strangers: The Culture of
Celebrity*. He has also written and revised a
well-known debunking study of Walt Disney
Enterprises, *The Disney Version: The Life,
Times, Art and Commerce of Walt Disney*, a
book which the moguls at the Disney company
were particularly eager not to see published, and
which, in the end, had to come out without a single accompanying (copyrighted) photograph.

WORKS: *Non-fiction*—The World of Carnegie Hall,
1960; The Stars, 1962; Movies: The History of an Art
and an Institution, 1964; The Long Road to College,
1965; The World of Goya 1746–1828, 1968; The Disney Version, 1968, rev. ed., 1985; Second Sight, 1972;
His Picture in the Papers, 1973; Harold Lloyd, 1974;
The Men Who Made the Movies, 1975; The World of
Tennis, 1975; Singled Out, 1981; Cary Grant, 1984; D.
W. Griffith, 1984; Intimate Strangers, 1985; Gary Cooper, 1985; Striking Poses, 1987. *Juvenile*—The Gentle
Knight, 1964. *As coauthor*—(with Lena Horne) Lena,
1965; (with Bob Willoughby) The Platinum Years,
1974; (with Douglas Fairbanks, Jr.) The Fairbanks Album, 1976; (with Michael Walsh) Carnegie Hall, 1987.

As coeditor—(with John Simon) Film 67/68, 1968. *Fiction*—Another I, Another You: A Love Story for the Once-Married, 1978.

ABOUT: Contemporary Authors New Revision Series 1, 1981; Who's Who in America, 1989–1990. *Periodicals*—America June 22, 1968; November 11, 1978; Best Sellers May 15, 1968; August 1, 1968; February 15, 1974; May 1976; Choice December 1968, May 1974, June 1975, July–August 1976, October 1976, September 1984; Christian Science Monitor May 23, 1968; May 22, 1984; August 5, 1985; Commentary September 1968; Commonweal June 12, 1968; October 18, 1968; May 22, 1974; Economist May 5, 1984; June 21, 1986; Harper June 1968; Library Journal April 15, 1968; August 1975; January 15, 1976; April 15, 1978; April 1, 1981; November 1, 1983; April 1, 1984; May 1, 1985; Milwaukee Journal March 3, 1974; Nation April 7, 1984; National Review March 15, 1974; November 1, 1985; New Republic July 6, 1968; May 30, 1981; April 23, 1984; May 27, 1985; New Statesman February 25, 1977; New York Times Book Review May 5, 1968; April 9, 1978; July 19, 1981; December 4, 1983; April 8, 1984; March 17, 1985; New Yorker May 25, 1968; Playboy January 1965; Saturday Review May 9, 1974; Time May 31, 1968; May 1, 1978; May 25, 1981; April 9, 1984; April 8, 1985; Times Literary Supplement December 16, 1965; July 2, 1976; June 15, 1984; July 11, 1986; Virginia Quarterly Review Winter 1977.

LYNNE SHARON SCHWARTZ

SCHWARTZ, LYNNE SHARON (March 19, 1939–), American novelist and short-story writer, writes: "I wrote my first stories at the age of seven and I sometimes think they were my best work, that is, the most unfettered, clear, and free in their peregrinations through reality and fantasy. Unfortunately they are lost—perhaps I didn't value them sufficiently to save them. Those stories unabashedly took on themes such as the creation of the earth and human beings, the nature of God (a 'kind scientist,' I remember, was my designation), the transformation of evil into good—all of them matters that might give pause to a more sophisticated writer.

"After that time, for twenty-five years or so, life seemed to close in. Outwardly the boundaries were stretching—I went to school, made friends, read, married, traveled. But the inner landscape, the landscape of possibility and initiative, narrowed. The pressures of convention and conformity had immense force during the time I grew up, the nineteen-fifties, and in the place, Brooklyn, New York, where urbanity and provinciality, incarnate in the decent, poignant ambitions and values of second-generation Eastern European Jews, made a troubling mix. As a result, all the tasks of my life since seem to merge in the one task of making myself a writer, which meant breaking free of what was expect-

ed of me and creating a new self, a new life, or rather, allowing the seven-year-old with the intrepid imagination to take power again.

"Despite the breaking away, the sources of writing, for me, anyway, remain in childhood. In family and its largest meanings, literal and metaphorical. My father was an intensely verbal, passionate, generous-hearted and short-tempered man. In his rages, whose deepest source remains a mystery, words erupted from him with fervor and truth and frightening eloquence; I think it was while listening to him, feeling half-scared and half-fascinated, that I absorbed the potent and complex connection between passion and language, the impulses that inform my work. My mother was quite different—tolerant, instinctive in her responses, less exacting, compassionate, and above all, theatrical—a woman whose presentation of self was magnetic and colorful. From her I absorbed spiritual and emotional latitude, and the notion of the artist as performer, one who projects an image of self-in-the-world: how it is to be here, breathing and feeling and mortal. Of course becoming a writer entails going beyond the experience of one self to embrace all others, but the self is the start.

"Because I was articulate and did well in school and read a great deal, my parents encouraged me to become a teacher. 'Teacher' was what clever girls became. But I knew early on that that was not my vocation. There was something else, though I didn't know its name. 'Writer,' in our world, was not something anyone did with her life. It took me twenty-five years to find that it could be done, and to learn how. I was bred to passivity. It was no one's malevolence or deliberate repression, but the time and the place and the social circumstances. A writer, I had to discover, is an activist: actively seeing, feeling, touching, connecting, and changing. Above all, actively taking possession of language like an ardent lover. In my early thirties, I wrenched myself out of passivity and became an activist. I wrote once again. Other writers may be impelled or inspired by topics or issues; I was impelled by a general defiance, and by words. No matter what I have written about—and I have tried, as my writing has developed, to write about larger and larger things—I have always written primarily out of love and reverence for words and what they can do. They are not simply a means of expression, a translation of emotion or thought; in the writing they *become* the reality, and more fertile than most others.

"My early works are very private—the intricacies of the inner lives of a few characters. Not only is this purview natural for a beginning writer; it is also easier to control technically. With time and experience and courage I have enlarged what I write about, and focused more on the social context, the outer meshing with the inner, as it were, for a more accurate and thorough rendering of the texture of experience. All of my work has been critical of social pressures that smother the human spirit, and has scrutinized the results of such repression. Indeed it has been anarchic in spirit, although in my early books, for whatever reason, the anarchism was tame and scarcely recognizable. Only lately has it shown itself clearly. In *The Melting Pot and Other Subversive Stories*, each story questions and undermines its characters' moral and ideological premises, and probably unsettles the reader. So much the better. Good writing does not lull the spirit but quickens it, does not tether the imagination to what is already known, but frees it for quest."

The daughter of Jack M. Sharon, a lawyer and accountant, and Sarah (Slatus) Sharon, Lynne Sharon was educated at Barnard College (B.A. 1959) and Bryn Mawr (M.A. 1961). She married Harry Schwartz, a city planner, in 1957; they have two daughters. She seems almost to have drifted into a writing career—from editorial work, writing publicity for a public housing program, teaching English at Hunter College in New York City and at New York University, doing graduate work at New York University in comparative literature. Just at the point of selecting a subject for her doctoral dissertation,

Schwartz resolved to pursue her long-dreamed-of goal of creative writing. It was not an easy decision for a young, middle-class American woman who had been raised in the standards and values of the 1950s. As she recalled in an article in *Barnard Alumnae*: "Back then the notion of inventing a life and a life's work, rather than accepting those given us, required first a certain vision of possibilities, which we lacked, and second, taking ourselves very seriously indeed. . . . Unprepared as I thus was, when I grasped what I needed to do in order to be a writer, I tried to yank my life out of its accustomed path. With a sense of recklessness I became an activist: I wrote."

What Schwartz wrote were short stories, published in the *Ontario Review, Transatlantic Review, Redbook,* and other magazines. These received considerable recognition, several selected for anthologies like *Best American Short Stories* (1978, 1979) and *O. Henry Prize Stories* (1979). One of her stories, "Lucca," won an award from Vanguard Press in 1974 and another, a story of two young lovers, Caroline and Ivan, "Rough Strife," won an award from the Lamport Foundation in 1977. This story came to the attention of Ted Solotaroff of Harper & Row, who encouraged her to weave her by now several stories about Caroline and Ivan into a novel which became *Rough Strife*, winner of American Book Award and PEN/Hemingway nominations for best first novel of 1981.

Rough Strife is the story of the turbulent yet basically solid relationship between two highly intelligent and sensitive people. Their twenty years of marriage are a series of emotional highs and lows—periods of lyrical romantic interludes, periods of chilly alienation. Caroline is a brilliant mathematician, Ivan a gifted and successful art historian. They live a comfortable upper-middle class life on New York's gentrified Upper West Side, and they have two daughters. But although they have active lives and a circle of equally talented and successful friends, the marriage is curiously isolated, set off like some specimen under a microscope. "Lynne Sharon Schwartz registers the fluctuations of marital feeling with the fidelity of a Geiger counter," Katha Pollitt wrote in the *New York Times Book Review*. "The problem is, the emotional dynamics of Caroline's marriage are not interesting enough to bear the close inspection Miss Schwartz bestows." The result, Pollitt continues, is that in order to sustain interest she magnifies small incidents into melodrama and "inflates her language beyond proportion." Narrow as the focus of the book is, its examination of modern marriage, largely from the woman's point of view, was judged by most critics to be sensitive and perceptive. "Without sentimentality or bitterness," Lore Dickstein wrote in *Ms.*, ". . . it all rings true: the crises and the dull spells, the falling in and out of love with the same person, the struggle of creating an enduring partnership." The reviewer for the *Library Journal* found the book "a portrait of life during the past two decades that rings true"; and Dorothy Wickenden, in the *New Republic*, judged the characters believable though "precious." *Rough Strife*, she summed up, "is a wise novel, rewarding in its honesty and clarity of vision."

Balancing Acts represents another facet of Schwartz's realism. Here her principal characters are far removed from the "precious" world of intellectual Manhattan. They are a seventy-four-year-old widower who is a retired circus acrobat-juggler and a restless, disaffected adolescent girl whom he meets when he volunteers to coach a high school gymnastic team. The environment of these characters is narrow but less enclosed than the rarefied background of *Rough Strife*, and in her picture of both the senior citizens' home where the old man lives and the cluttered average life of the teenager's family Schwartz displays her gift for simple unadorned realism. Critical response to the novel varied from reviews that found the book charming and moving to others that rejected it as sentimental and contrived. Judith Gies struck a balance herself in *Saturday Review* by noting the appropriateness of the title which suggests the parallel betweeen the old man's learning to relinquish life and the young girl's learning to accept it. "Each is looking for transcendence, a way to escape the law of gravity. What they find, as they jostle each other's lives, is a precarious sense of balance." She complained, however, that the symmetry is excessive and that "the novel seldom soars . . . the central metaphor is polished to an insistent shine."

Schwartz's most ambitious novel to date is *Disturbances in the Field* in which she returns to the Manhattan scene and a marriage like that of the couple in *Rough Strife*. In *Disturbances in the Field*, however, her principal characters have a far broader emotional range and considerably more psychological depth. For Carole Cook, in *Commonweal*, it is "just such a novel as Henry James would have approved, being not so much a story, moral or otherwise, as the execution of an entire unique world out of a generous accumulation of detail, character, and incident. . . . It has the total quality of reality, in all its untidiness and muddlement and mulish resistance to logical formula. It is a novel in which an intensely rich and complex mind radiates out from the hub of its subjective center.

That "subjective center" is Lydia Rowe, a highly intelligent and well educated woman gifted not only with a talent for music (she is a pianist in chamber music groups) but also with what appears to be an almost blessed life—a loving husband who is himself a gifted painter, four charming children, and a group of loyal college friends. Well schooled in philosophy, Lydia believes in living the examined life, in achieving a kind of perfection of form in an emotionally balanced life of reason. The tranquility of her life is shattered when her two younger children are killed in a bus accident, and she and her surviving family must confront their loss. In a sense, as Anatole Broyard observed in the *New York Times Book Review*, Schwartz wrote two books here. He finds the first half labored and self-consciously intellectual with the characters discussing philosophy and music "like the undigested lessons of an intellectual *nouveau riche*." But after the deaths of the children, Broyard writes, the book moves "beyond literature and philosophy to a tough, battered truth." For Carole Sternhell in the *Voice Literary Supplement*, the book was "luminous," with the quality of the chamber music Lydia plays, creating "a balance, a harmony of ideas, despairing in order to affirm." In their loss Lydia and her family are at first bitterly divided, but ultimately she at least is strengthened. "It is a tribute to Schwartz's skill," Sternhell writes, "that she tells this story without melodrama or excess, that she never forgets the exuberance at the heart of poignancy."

Although she began her career as a short story writer, it was not until after she had published three novels that Schwartz published her first collection of short stories, *Acquainted with the Night*. The stories here range in genre from simple domestic realism to fantasy, but in all of them fundamentally decent people try to cope with the uncertainties of life—from a middle-aged man's anxieties during a single night of insomnia ("Acquainted with the Night") to the problems of the woefully confused and self-absorbed parents of a troubled young son ("The Age of Analysis"), and the well meaning efforts of a suburban New York family to establish a friendly relationship with their daughter's black music teacher ("The Middle Classes"). All of the stories are characterized by objectivity and restraint. "The Middle Classes," for example, Schwartz told an interviewer for *Publishers Weekly*, was not written as a story about race relations: "I wanted to write about my piano teacher and my old block. I really mean to bring in the whole world, but it doesn't come in the form of political statements." Similarly, what struck several reviewers as a distinct bias against psychoanalysis in "The Age of Analysis" was, she says, not an intentional attack but a reflection on "the way the values and methods and jargon have penetrated people's lives so that they live according to this." Schwartz's short stories, both in *Acquainted with the Night* and in her second collection *The Melting Pot and Other Subversive Stories*, have had mixed receptions, some reviewers missing the irony and poignancy they found in her novels, but most of the stories exemplify what Perri Klass in the *New York Times Book Review* describes as her special "skill at using the small intricacies of daily life to tell stories about big subjects." In her second volume, Klass writes, "Lynne Sharon Schwartz writes cleanly and with compassion. Her voice is strong, even as her stories are varied and her images are compelling."

In 1989 Lynne Sharon Schwartz published a novella (146 pages), *Leaving Brooklyn*, that, while not in any plot detail autobiographical, draws heavily on her childhood in post World War II Brooklyn. Sven Birkerts, in the *New York Times Book Review*, described it as "an invention masked as a memory." The central character is a sheltered middle-class fifteen-year-old Jewish girl who has a vision problem of real but also metaphoric significance: one eye functions normally, the other gives her an unsteady vision "where the common, reasonable laws of physics did not apply, where a piece of face or the leg of a table or frame of a window might at any moment break off and drift away." Her parents take her to an ophthalmologist for treatment, and a close relationship develops between them. This is more than the young girl's sexual initiation. It marks her coming of age emotionally as well, a subject Schwartz treats with insight and delicacy. Birkerts observes: "Ms. Schwartz . . . writes with confidence and stylistic dash. Whether she is describing the hermetic milieu of her Brooklyn—its shops and living rooms and street-corner exchanges—or the edgy dreaminess of the adolescent psyche, she catches both the outer contours and the inner propulsions of her subject."

Schwartz has written one non-fiction book, *We Are Talking about Homes*, a detailed account of the struggles of the tenants (including herself and her family) of an apartment building owned by Columbia University to force their landlord to restore their homes after a damaging fire.

PRINCIPAL WORKS: *Novels*—Rough Strife, 1980; Balancing Acts, 1981; Disturbances in the Field, 1983; Leaving Brooklyn, 1989. *Collected short stories*—Acquainted with the Night, 1984; The Melting Pot and Other Subversive Stories, 1987. *Non-fiction*—We are Talking about Homes: A Great University against its Neighbors, 1985.

ABOUT: Contemporary Authors New Revision Series 103, 1982; Contemporary Literary Criticism 31, 1985; Schwartz, L. S. We Are Talking about Homes, 1985. *Periodicals*—Barnard Alumnae Spring 1981; Commonweal November 4, 1983; Library Journal June 15, 1980; Ms. June 1980; New Republic June 14, 1980; New York Times October 28, 1983; New York Times Book Review June 15, 1980; April 30, 1989; Publishers Weekly August 3, 1984; Saturday Review June 1981; (Village) Voice Literary Supplement October 1983.

*SCLIAR, MOACYR (March 23, 1937–), Brazilian novelist, short-story writer, and journalist, was born in Porto Alegre, capital of the country's southernmost state, Rio Grande do Sul. The son of Jewish immigrants, he spent much of his early life in the predominantly Jewish neighborhood of Bom Fim in Porto Alegre. He began his formal education at the School of Education and Culture, and later graduated from a local Catholic high school. He completed his studies at the School of Medicine of the Federal University of Rio Grande do Sul in 1962 and has been a practicing physician in public health in his native city since 1969.

Moacyr Scliar began his literary career in the early 1960s. His short fiction first appeared in anthologies and journals, and by 1963 he had published an entire collection of stories entitled *Tempo de Espera* (Time of Expectation) in conjunction with another young southern Brazilian writer, Carlos Stein. He first achieved national recognition in 1968 with the appearance of his second volume of short stories, *O Carnaval dos Animais*. As one critic later noted: "Initially, much was made of this book as a sort of bestiary in the manner of [Jorge Luis] Borges, to whom Scliar, moreover, compared himself on several occasions, particularly because of his stories marked by footnotes and asides in which the character or the narrator-character humorously comments on the narrative itself." Translated as *The Carnival of the Animals* in 1985, this collection has been well received by critics in the United States. As Douglas Day notes in the *New York Times Book Review*: "In the lead story, 'The Lions,' millions of lions roam Africa, threatening by their numbers all of Europe and America. They must be destroyed. A nuclear explosion kills most; a herd of poisoned and programmed gazelles (gazelles! the gentlest of creatures!) disposes of most of the rest of the lions; and hunters 'equipped with sophisticated and ultra-secret weapons' do the rest—except for one last lion cub, shot in a zoo by a madman." It is clear that in these fantastic stories the terrible suffering of the animals at the hands of cruel human beings reflects the Holocaust. Douglas Day compares

°sklēr, mwä sēr´

MOACYR SCLIAR

Scliar's vision to Jonathan Swift's: "He does terrible things to his humans, and worse to his animals, those passive victims of the victimized humans. One laughs with him, but make no mistake about it: Mr. Scliar is a tough writer, one of the bitterest to come out of Latin America in a long time."

Scliar's second book, the short novel *A Guerra do Bom Fim* (The War of Bom Fim, 1972), prefigures much of his later fiction with the presence of a Brazilian Jewish protagonist and its use of what has been described by various commentators as "typical Jewish humor." The setting of this novel is likewise characteristic of much of Scliar's subsequent work in that it takes place in the author's home city of Porto Alegre. It relates the story of a youth growing up in Bom Fim during the Second World War and depicts the rise of a Jewish middle class which eventually enlists itself in the cause of Israeli Zionism. His *O Exército de um Homem Só* (1973; translated as (*The One-Man Army*) is, in the words of Antonio Hohlfeldt in *A Dictionary of Contemporary Brazilian Authors*, "the story of Captain Birobidjan, a Jew in Porto Alegre who, attacked by madness, goes from being a major real estate agent to retirement in a remote district where he wants to start a utopic city in which the inhabitants, men and animals, will have absolute social equality." *Os Deuses de Raquel* (The Gods of Raquel, 1975) introduces the female protagonist—in this instance, the daughter of Israeli immigrants to Porto Alegre—to the fiction of Scliar, and, along with his later *O Ciclo das Águas* (The Cycle of Waters, 1977), which deals

with a Jewish street prostitute in the same city, is considered among his most serious works.

By the mid-1970s Moacyr Scliar had clearly shown himself to be a writer concerned with ethnic issues, but, as Hohlfeldt notes in reviewing the author's earliest literary production, "the selection of a Jewish character reveals much more a specific critical choice—the marginal individual of the lower middle class—than a selection based simply on race." He goes on to state regarding these initial works that "Scliar's style, which is related to the fantastic realism that characterizes the contemporary Latin American novel, may be considered his second major contribution to Brazilian literature. However, far from being simply a stylistic choice, it is the proper form of expression for a vision of a chaotic world, a vision whose critical perspective includes a moral position such as we find with all humorists in the history of art. Social climbing, the Darwinian theory of the survival of the fittest, free competition, told with a humor and irony that spares nothing, are the concerns of this writer, whose narratives (which are never extensive) are built on an objective and direct style that the author admits to being his chief goal."

Scliar's popularity in his native country increased during the latter half of the 1970s as he returned to the short story as an effective means of combining the same type of ironic humor and what is often described as "Kafkaesque" fantasy with an acute but subtle social and political awareness. He published two more volumes of stories in 1976: *A Balada do Falso Messias* (The Ballad of the False Messiah), whose lead story, as the collection's title suggests, deals with a self-proclaimed Jewish Messiah named Shabtai Zvi, and *Histórias da Terra Trêmula* (Stories of the Trembling Earth). During the same period, Scliar also continued to write a weekly column for the Porto Alegre daily *Zero Hora*, as well as contributing to various other Brazilian and foreign newspapers and literary periodicals. He published two minor short novels in 1977 and 1978, and the following year produced his fourth collection of short stories, *O Anão no Televisor* (The Dwarf in the Television Set). He likewise maintained his full-time medical practice "with great difficulty," as he describes it, "but also with great satisfaction."

It has been mainly during the 1980s, however, that Scliar has produced his most highly acclaimed work and has achieved an international reputation as one of Latin America's most brilliant writers. As his fiction has become known to readers in the United States, he has been increasingly compared to such American authors as Malamud, Roth and Bellow. As Voluminous

(1979; translated as *The Volunteers*) is Scliar's third novel to be translated into English. It is described by one reviewer as "a spare, elegiac tale," in which the author "continues to probe the ethnic diversity of Brazil with a singular cast of nimbly and graphically limned characters. On a December night in 1970, the tugboat *Voluntários* sets sail from Porto Alegre; its mission is to bring the dying Benjamin, who is nostalgic for a Wailing Wall that he has never seen, to the legendary city of Jerusalem. The motley crew includes a prostitute; a Palestinian Maronite Christian who left Jerusalem after the Six-Day War; a preacher of a new religious sect, the followers of which are to build a Christian kingdom in Jerusalem; a captain who hasn't navigated a boat in years; and Paulo, the narrator, a self-described 'son of the Portuguese bar owner, this goy.'" Another of Scliar's better known novels is his *O Centauro no Jardim* (1980; translated as *The Centaur in the Garden*). Generally considered one of his best efforts in "fantastic realism," it is the first-person narrative of a Brazilian Jew born with the body of the mythical creature named in the title and relates his tragicomic adventures in northern Africa and Europe, as well as in modern day Rio Grande do Sul and São Paulo. This work is perhaps best described as a type of existential allegory with many of the political and social overtones which mark much of the author's earlier work. The short novel, *A Festa no Castelo* (The Celebration in the Castle) is a more overtly political allegory published in 1982, following the appearance of the novellas *Max e os Felinos* (translated as *Max and the Cats*) and *Cavalos e Obeliscos* (Horses and Obelisks) in 1981.

Scliar's novel of 1983, *A Estranha Nacão de Rafael Mendes* (translated as *The Strange Nation of Rafael Mendes*), has been translated into English and has been praised by a number of critics in the United States. Herbert Gold describes it as a "bemusing" novel in which: "Rafael Mendes, a harassed financier, husband, father—his company is going under, his wife is out of her mind, his daughter is deep into the usual adolescent sexual and religious outrageousness—discovers peculiar news about his ancestors. The story within the story is contained in the notebooks of his father, also named Rafael Mendes, which tell of the many Rafael Mendeses from whom they descend, all the way back to the prophet Jonah throwing claustrophobic tantrums in the belly of a commodious but odoriferous whale. The strange nation of the title is, of course, the nation of Israel. . . . We're in a world of Brazilian yuppies, although the book takes place at a time when Generalissimo Franco lies dying in a coma and the word yuppie has yet to be born. We're also in a world of prophets, although 'they are only interested in foretelling the future, and what do we care about the future? In the future we'll all be dead.'"

Scliar is also the author of two volumes of "crônicas"—the name given to a genre of short journalistic pieces practiced by many contemporary Brazilian writers. His collection of stories *O Olho Enigmático* (*The Enigmatic Eye*) was published in 1986. Moacyr Scliar has received numerous prizes for his fiction in his native Brazil and has been published in France, Germany, and Spain, as well as in the United States. *The Centaur in the Garden* is scheduled to be translated and published in Finland, Sweden, and Israel. The author sums up his goals as a writer in the following statement: "I have at least two tangible reasons (beyond the intangible ones) for dedicating myself to this strange habit of writing. For one thing, I make up part of the unstable and uneasy Brazilian middle class; for another, I owe to my Jewish origins the permanent feeling of wonderment that is inherent to the immigrant and the cruel, bitter, and sad humor that through the centuries has served to protect Jews against despair. It is at the level of language, however, that these impulses are able to produce their effects. It is in language that I have faith, as a vehicle for esthetic expression and also—and above all else—as an instrument for changing the world in which we live."

WORKS IN ENGLISH TRANSLATION: Eloah F. Giacomelli has been Scliar's principal English translator with *The Carnival of the Animals* and *The One-Man Army* in 1985, *The Strange Nation of Rafael Mendes* in 1987, and *The Volunteers* in 1988; *The Enigmatic Eye*, Giacomelli's translation of a collection of Scliar's short stories, was published in 1989. Margaret Neves translated *The Centaur in the Garden* in 1985. The novella *Max and the Cats* was translated by Eloah F. Giacomelli in 1990.

ABOUT: Foster, D. W. and R. Reis (eds.) A Dictionary of Contemporary Brazilian Authors, 1981. *Periodicals*—Modern Language Journal 64, 1980; New York Times July 11, 1990; New York Times Book Review April 4, 1986; January 31, 1988.

SEGAL, LORE (GROSZMANN) (March 8, 1928–), American (Austrian born) novelist, children's writer, and translator, writes: "I was ten years old when I came to England with a children's transport and executed my first intentional piece of 'writing.' It was a letter that moved a refugee committee to get my parents out of Hitler's Vienna—a proof that bad art makes things happen. It was a tear jerker full of

LORE SEGAL

very symbolic winter roses that kept blooming through the snow, and a lot of sunsets.

"Some years ago I happened upon one of those old school books with purple covers and a white label with a red border in which English school children did their home work. I had filled its thirty-six lined pages with my Hitler story. I recall the impetus very clearly: we call it bearing witness. I remember my irritation—a sort of horror—that my good new foster parents had so little sense of what was, at that very instance, happening in that other world. The clever youngest of the six grown-up daughters became my friend and got what I had written translated into English: another lot of sunsets. I remember, acutely, the urge to inject what I felt to be missing in what I had put down. I remember the feel of not having got it all said at all.

"My parents arrived and my father was interned as an enemy alien. I was twelve; we were once more on the move, and I was throwing up. I remember, between bouts, lying on a bed in a narrow room at the head of a steep stair. My mother was reading me *David Copperfield*, and I knew that that's what I was going to do. I was going to be a writer. The word 'writer' came to me with the shock of revelation. I did not, at that time, connect with it what I had doing since I was ten.

"I'm not sure that my subject has changed, though it has taken several forms. The impetus is the same—the passion, truly, to get whatever it is, said, to get all of it said, and to get it as formally and feelingly right as a Bach fugue. Sunsets not permitted."

———

Lore Segal was born in Vienna and spent the first ten years of her life in the comfortable middle-class household of her father, Ignatz Groszmann, an accountant, her mother Franzi (Stern) Groszmann, and a loving family of uncle, aunts, and grandparents. Calamity fell swiftly with the Nazi occupation of Austria in 1938. Her parents managed to send her to England along with hundreds of other refugee children. There she lived in a succession of foster homes, cared for by kindly but to her essentially alien English hosts. Although her parents also later found refuge in England, she had no real home. Her father, released from an enemy alien camp, was in ill health. While he struggled in menial jobs, it was her mother who held the family together by working as a cook and housekeeper and occasionally giving piano lessons. Young Lore grew up living in "other people's houses," but she got a good education and won a scholarship to Bedford College, University of London, from which she received her B.A. in 1948. By this time her father was dead and her mother had emigrated to the Dominican Republic, where Lore joined her to await the visas that would admit them to the United States. In 1951, with her mother, she joined her uncle and grandmother in New York City.

Other People's Houses, Segal's first book, is her memoir of these experiences. It is classified as a novel but told with the candor of straight autobiography. It is also told with the unadorned simplicity and honesty of the child Lore Segal was—self-centered and coolly observant, disarmingly frank, unsentimental but keenly sensitive to both the strengths and the weaknesses of the adults around her. "On the surface," Richard Gilman wrote of the book in the *New Republic*, "it is an account of flight from the Nazis, of displacement and transplantation; but beneath that it contains an extraordinarily subtle rendering of the self, a tracing of its parabola through growth, time, and the succession of places, a tracking down of the ways in which personal history managed to survive the mortal shame and sorrow of the era that enclosed it."

Segal had taught English in the Dominican Republic; in New York she worked in a variety of jobs from file clerk in a shoe factory to public relations and commercial art, to free-lance writing. In 1961 she married David I. Segal, an editor, by whom she had two children. It was for them that she made up and later wrote the stories that established her as a children's writer. With a blend of earthy humor and fantasy, her stories, as G. A. Woods wrote in the *New York Times Book Review*, "reflect the warmth and naturalness of family life with gentle mirth." In 1970 *Tell Me a Mitzi*, with Harriet Pincus' ap propriately wise and funny illustrations, won both the American Library Association's Notable Book Award and *Book World*'s Children's Book Festival Prize. Composed of three short and simple tales about little Mitzi, her parents and her baby brother, it delighted adults almost as much as it did children. Selma G. Lanes noted that *Tell Me a Mitzi* is a "poetic, bittersweet grasp, both in text and pictures, of the fragile will-o'-the-wisps of adventure and misadventures that comprise the flavor of childhood." But Zena Sutherland, in the *Saturday Review*, cautioned that parents should read the book to themselves first, "so they won't break up while reading it to the children." The same blend of humor and honest realism has given her subsequent books for children an almost equal appeal for adults. *The Story of Mrs. Lovewright and Purrless Her Cat* charmed as sophisticated a reviewer as the English novelist Fay Weldon who wrote in the *New York Times Book Review* that it "chooses to present us not with a cute and lovable pet but a wild and untractable cat, in which response and love is gained with difficulty. . . . It is a view of things closer to the child's own experience of life than that usually offered in the cozy world of juvenile fiction."

The whimsy but also the palpable core of reality in Segal's work made her an ideal collaborator for the artist Maurice Sendak, who had long wanted to illustrate some of the *Household Tales* of the brothers Grimm. Her translation from the German of twenty-three of those tales, along with four translated by Randall Jarrell, provided the text for Sendak's illustrations in *The Juniper Tree, and Other Tales from Grimm*. "There was no translation I could work with," Sendak said, until he came upon Segal's, and according to Walter Clemons in *Newsweek* the result was Sendak's best work up to that time. Long softened and sentimentalized, in Segal's translation the Grimm stories, with Sendak's complementary illustrations, are unrelentingly frightening, grotesque and enchanting, with what Gabrielle Annan described in the *Times Literary Supplement* as "a gnarled effect which is not unpleasant or unsuitable." Alison Lurie, in the *New York Times Book Review*, recognized this as "the edition of Grimms's tales we need and deserve at this place in time and history. Stylistically it is a pleasure to read." When Lore Segal undertook, perhaps even more boldly, to write a children's version of the Old Testament using English and German translations in *The Book of Adam to Moses* (with Leonard Baskin's illustrations), she wrote in her introduction that she wanted her young readers to meet characters who "are sometimes faithful and sometimes disobedient; they get hungry, they want children;

have friendships; grieve when they are unloved; they work, despair, murder, go mad." For Mary Gordon, reviewing this book in the *New York Times Book Review*, Segal achieves this goal "in language that is rhythmic, appropriate to its shifting levels of diction, and yet not inaccessible to the children who should have this treasure for their own."

The characters in Segal's adult fiction are only one remove from her children's world. To be sure, they encounter many of the realities of contemporary adult life—sex, alcohol, drugs, racism. But they are seen always in an aura of enchantment that is both funny and, because their world is after all real, sad. *Lucinella* is a kind of fairy tale set, however, in the real or at least recognizable world of New York literary society. Lucinella is a young poet, "twenty going on forty," who is rapidly "turning into a Russian novel." She goes to Yaddo, the colony for artists, musicians, and writers in upstate New York, where the novel begins: "Lucinella is my name. I wear glasses. It's my first visit here and I'm in love with five poets, four men, one woman, and an obese dog called Winifred." With fairy-tale logic Lucinella's life and career spin through the New York literary scene, capturing with sharp but not caustic satire the foibles of the avant-garde of the 1950s and 1960s. Reviewers found the novel entertaining but limited in its audience appeal. Suzanne Juhasz, in the *Library Journal*, wrote: "The wit is deft and accurate; the style mingles comic fantasy with social commentary, as not only literary people but literary attitudes about art and reality are mocked." But Phyllis Birnbaum commented in *Saturday Review*: "One suspects that only those who commute exclusively within these intense literary circles will be able to sustain an interest in Lucinella and her friends."

Near the end of *Other People's Houses* Lore Groszmann, as she then was, takes a creative writing course at the New School for Social Research and meets her first Americans. Among them is "a middle-aged Negro called Carter Bayoux, who dominated the class with his powerful presence and silence." They become good friends, but we hear no more about him. Carter Bayoux disappeared from her life, but not from her imagination. He turns up again, this time in a wholly fictitious work, *Her First American*, as the hero/anti-hero who introduces Ilka Weissnix, a young immigrant from Austria, to an improbable yet oddly real America. Through Carter, once a distinguished writer, United Nations correspondent, and lecturer, now rapidly drinking himself to death, Ilka encounters a colorful assortment of Americans from black Gospel singers to white liberals of the 1950s. Thanks to what Carolyn Kizer, in the *New York Times Book Review*, calls "Mrs. Segal's faultless ear for dialogue," her readers participate in a kaleidoscope of experiences all of which thrust Ilka into a dizzying American culture. *Her First American* is at once funny, as Ilka struggles with the English language and stolidly accepts the madness she sees around her, and sad, as she watches Carter's rapid self-destruction. It is also "delicately observant," in one reviewer's phrase, in its treatment of Jewish-black relations. Carolyn Kizer summed it up: "Essentially this novel is about how we behave to one another and the consequences of that behavior. It's about how we lose by winning, how we are educated by loving, how we change and are changed by everyone we know. Mrs. Segal, in her mix of history, memory and invention, and the ruthless honesty which had always characterized her work, shows us ourselves, and reveals herself."

Lore Segal, now widowed, lives in New York but commutes weekly to teach writing at the University of Illinois at Chicago Circle. She has also taught at Columbia University, Bennington College, and Princeton. In 1965–1966 she was a Guggenheim Fellow, and she has had grants from the National Council of the Arts and Humanities and other foundations.

PRINCIPAL WORKS: *Novels*—Other People's Houses, 1964; Lucinella, 1978; Her First American, 1985. *Children's books*—Tell Me a Mitzi, 1970; All the Way Home, 1973; Tell Me a Trudy, 1978; The Story of Old Mrs. Brubeck and How She Looked for Trouble and Where She Found Him, 1981; The Story of Mrs. Lovewright and Purrless Her Cat, 1985; The Book of Adam to Moses, 1987. *Translations*—(with R. Jarrell) Morgenstern, C. Gallows Songs; Grimm, W. and J. The Juniper Tree and Other Stories, 1973.

ABOUT: Contemporary Authors New Revision Series 5, 1982; Lanes, S. G. Down the Rabbit Hole, 1976; Something About the Author 4, 1973; Segal, L. Other People's Houses, 1964. *Periodicals*—Library Journal November 1, 1976; New Republic December 12, 1964; August 5, 1985; New York Times Book Review May 17, 1970; November 4, 1973; May 19, 1985; November 10, 1985; November 8, 1987; Saturday Review July 25, 1970; Times Literary Supplement September 20, 1974.

*****SEMPRUN (Y MAURA), JORGE** (December 10, 1923–   ), Spanish novelist, screen writer, memoirist, and government official, appointed Minister of Culture in 1988, was born in Madrid into a family with a distinguished history of government service. His father, José María Semprun y Gurrea, held prominent civil office in the Spanish Republican government and represented his country in diplomatic posts in Rome and

JORGE SEMPRUN

The Hague. His mother, Susanna, was the daughter of Antonio Maura (d. 1925), who had served as a member of the Spanish legislature and for several terms as prime minister of Spain during the first quarter of the twentieth century. The family heritage of liberal Catholicism and liberal politics drove them into exile in France in 1936 when the Spanish civil war broke out. Jorge Semprun received most of his education in Paris at the Lycée Henri IV and at the Sorbonne, where he later took a master's degree in Latin.

With the outbreak of World War II and the German occupation of his adopted country, young Semprun joined the *maquis*, the underground French Resistance. He was captured by the Nazis and imprisoned in the notorious Buchenwald camp from 1943 until the Allied victory in 1945. Semprun describes these years and the turbulent ones that followed in his *Autobiography of Federico Sanchez and the Communist Underground in Spain* : "At the age of eighteen you immersed yourself, gladly and gaily, in the clandestine activity of the anti-Nazi Resistance. You endure, without major problems, with inexhaustible intellectual curiosity, the concentration-camp experience at Buchenwald. You plunged once again, with a sort of wild *joie de vivre*, into the Spanish underground after 1953."

Federico Sanchez is one of several names that Semprun assumed during the years when he worked as an underground agent first for the French Resistance, later for the Spanish Communist party. Disguise, displacement and the constant threat of arrest and/or violent death are the motifs of his autobiography, his novels, and the several internationally known film scenarios he has written. In these Semprun, or a fictional persona, is a hunted and a haunted man— hunted by agents of the Nazis and subsequently by agents of Generalissimo Franco's dictatorship in Spain; haunted by the memories of his disillusionment and break with the Communist party. He had joined the Party in 1947 when he was living in Paris, still an exile from his native land. He did not in fact legally visit Spain until 1967, but from 1953 to 1964 he made many trips across the border under assumed names as a Communist agent. Over the years he became increasingly disenchanted with what he called "the rigidity of Stalinism" that persisted long after Stalin's death. He began to feel that the Spanish Communist party failed to understand and promote the real needs of the Spanish people, and he was bitterly disillusioned by the fates of fellow Party members in the Iron Curtain countries of Eastern Europe. His final break with Communism came in 1964 when he was expelled from the Party. He continued, however, in his writing to explore his mind and conscience during the years that he had been a loyal Communist. Addressing himself as Federico Sanchez in the *Autobiography*, he writes:

> . . . between 1945, when you came back from Buchenwald, and June 1953, the date of your first clandestine trip to Spain, it cannot be said, in all truth, that you were an exemplary militant. You have always been bored by the nostalgic, victory-shall-be-ours platitudes of exile; the beatific murmurs of meetings completely out of touch with any sort of social reality; the manipulation of a ritualistic Marxist language, as though the essential task were to keep a prayer wheel turning. When all is said and done, the day-to-day aspect of politics has always bored you; politics has interested you only as risk and as total commitment. In other words, admit it once and for all and be damned: you have never been a proper militant.

In 1947 Semprun worked in Paris for UNESCO as a translator (he is fluent in French, Spanish, and German) and eked out a living with free-lance writing. He also wrote poetry during this period which he describes in the *Autobiography* as "dripping with Stalinist-lyrical sincerity and alienated religiosity." Some of these poems—notably one celebrating the heroine of the Spanish civil war La Pasionaria (Delores Ibárurri)—are included in the book. Semprun did not become fully engaged in writing, however, until after his break with the Communist party. La Pasionaria, who had hailed him as a hero in 1947, now denounced him as a "hare-brained intellectual." An intellectual indeed Semprun has been from his youth, when he read Hegel, Marx, and George Lukács. He writes of himself: "In those days you were not

yet a Stalinized intellectual; that is to say, you had kept your critical spirit, your capacity for negation, that creator of conflicting affirmations. You did not have a sacralized vision of the party you had just joined. You thought of it as an instrument of revolutionary struggle, one among others, certain aspects of which could be questioned and were always modifiable. Your Stalinization came later." It was as an intellectual, thinking independently and critically, that he finally came to the conclusion that "the Party had been turned into an end in itself, into a devouring metaphysical entity, whose principal vocation is its own preservation. And this implies that elements of a critical loyalty—religious bonds—predominate over rational elements."

Once freed from his political commitments, Semprun began to review his experiences as a Communist activist and prisoner in a series of novels, all written in French. The first of these was *Le grand voyage* (1963; translated as *The Long Voyage*), a harrowing account of a five-day train journey, packed into a padlocked boxcar with 120 other political prisoners from France to a Nazi concentration camp: "The train whistles in the Moselle Valley, and I let my light memories take wing. I'm twenty, I can erase all kinds of things from my life. Fifteen years from now, when I write about the voyage, it will be impossible. Or at least I suspect it will. Not only will things weigh something in your life, they'll have a weight of their own. Fifteen years from now memories won't be so light." The narrator will survive two years in the camp because he is young and strong and because he is a political prisoner, not a Jew destined for extermination. *The Long Journey* won the Prix Formentor in 1963. Reviewers of the English translation were mixed in their reception. Stanley Kauffmann, in *New York Review of Books*, judged it "an honorable and humane work," but he found it less emotionally engaging than its subject warranted—the result, he felt, of "insufficient artistic ability." But R. D. Spector, in *Book Week*, wrote: "Whether as art or instruction, his novel is a triumph of honesty and technique."

Almost twenty years later Semprun returned to his Buchenwald memories for another novel, *Quel beau dimanche!* (1980; translated as *What a Beautiful Sunday!*). In this far more subtly and intricately developed book, Semprun moved freely back and forth in time to describe not only his own experiences as a prisoner but also to explore existential questions of freedom and responsibility. Buchenwald is near Weimar, once the center of German culture, where Goethe had lived. The novel begins with the narrator— clearly a projection of Semprun's self— contemplating a tree near the camp, a spot where Goethe might have held his famous conversations with Eckermann. It is Sunday and he is returning to the camp from a labor assignment, but for a moment—which expands into the whole book—he experiences a liberation of spirit that will ultimately insure his survival. In a pattern of free association that a Hungarian scholar, Peter Egri, traces back to Semprun's reading of Proust, Sartre, and William Faulkner, he relives his early life, his deportation to the camp, the activities of his fellow political prisoners, most of them Communists. Years later, as he writes this book, Semprun can identify with all victims of repression. The glimpse of the winter sky over the Gare de Lyon in Paris sends his sympathetic imagination into the *gulags*, and he now understands Solzhenitsyn's *A Day in the Life of Ivan Denisovitch* and Varlam Shalamov's *Kolyma Tales* as he never had before. His renunciation of Communism becomes all the more significant as he realizes his own complicity in those early years when he had believed that as a Communist he was "in the camp of the just"—"whereas the ideas for which I thought I was fighting, the justice for which I thought I was fighting, was serving at the same time to justify the most radical injustice, the most absolute evil: the camp of the just had created and was running the Kolyma camp."

What a Beautiful Sunday!, Robert Boyers wrote in a long review in the *Times Literary Supplement*, is "a more compelling and original book" than *The Long Voyage*, " . . . more artful and more discursive and ultimately more serious." Semprun's many years of political engagement and many subsequent years of reflection on that activity have enriched his understanding—to the extent that it can ever be understood—of the Holocaust. As Boyers writes:

> Semprun's aim, in *What A Beautiful Sunday!*, is not to account for the Holocaust or for the willing complicity of persons like himself in the crimes of Stalin and his successors. Neither is it to evoke suffering or to apologize or get even. His aim is to show how a man endowed with great intelligence and passion can think about something for many years without feeling that he has accounted for it and without abandoning the belief that politics is an indispensable aspect of our capacity to deal with our condition.

Men whose destinies are indelibly stamped with their political histories are the subjects of most of Semprun's novels. In *La deuxième mort de Ramón Mercader* (1969; translated as *The Second Death of Ramón Mercader*), winner of the Prix Femina, Semprun again uses free association and intricate narrative structure, here showing the influence of Alain Robbe-Grillet and the *nouveau roman*. Opening with a single sentence that runs eleven lines, he places his central character simultaneously in the shadowy world of a painting he is looking at in a museum—Vermeer's "View of Delft" (a painting much admired by Proust's Swann)—and in the sordid intrigue of twentieth-century international espionage. Ramón Mercader also happens to be the name of the assassin of Leon Trotsky. Semprun's character is apparently an agent of the Soviet government now working in Amsterdam; he becomes the center of sinister and complex intrigue involving Soviet agents, the Dutch secret police, and the CIA. With a framework, in the judgment of S. J. Laut in *Book Week*, "in the best tradition of Maugham, Greene, and Simenon," the book is "a metaphor for the corruption, the fear, the uncertainty, the meaninglessness and the violence of today . . . a splendid tour de force." J. Y. Kelly wrote in *Library Journal* that "the real suspense lies in the stylistic surprises of this experimental work." Semprun has published two other novels in French. *L'Algarabie* (1981) is the story of the last day in the life of a Spanish emigré in Paris, leading a clandestine life without identity papers or hope for the future. Its title—French-Arabic for "gibberish"—reflects the sense of confusion of identity that emigrés feel. Semprun says that the book, over ten years in the writing, reflects his own confusion of nationality; it was written alternately in Spanish and in French. *La montagne blanche* (The White Mountain, 1986) introduces three middle-aged men, reunited for a short holiday in 1982, reviewing their lost dreams of a utopian future for Europe as well as their interwoven lives and loves.

Semprun wrote his first screenplay at the invitation of the French film director Alain Resnais who had read *The Long Voyage* and been struck by what he considered its remarkably cinematic techniques—the striking visual images and the use of flashbacks and flashforwards. Resnais' film *La guerre est finie* (*The War Is Over*), which starred Yves Montand, is the story of a veteran of the Spanish civil war and the French Resistance for whom war never seems to end. Released in 1966, it won international acclaim. In 1974 Semprun again collaborated with Resnais on a film based on the life of Alexander Stavisky, who had emigrated to France penniless after the Russian Revolution. Stavisky became a notorious figure in international society, a swindler and con-man who made and lost fortunes and lived a lavish and colorful life until his past caught up with him. Faced with ruin, he committed suicide (or possibly was murdered) in 1934. *Stavisky*, with Jean-Paul Belmondo in the title role, was widely admired in the United States and abroad for its elegant style and its striking evocation of the decadence of European society on the eve of World War II, but it did not have the popular success of the earlier film. In 1968 Semprun wrote the screenplay for director Constantin Costa-Gavras' *Z*, co-starring Montand and Jean Trintignant—a film which traces in flashbacks the assassination of a Greek political activist. It was an international success and won Hollywood's Academy Award for the best foreign film of 1969. He has also written the screenplays for Costa-Gavras' *L'aveu* (*The Confession*) in 1972, the story of a Communist bureaucrat forced to testify against his associates, and in 1975 *État de siège* (*State of Siege*), about the political kidnapping of a United States official in Latin America. Working with the expatriate American director Joseph Losey, he wrote *Les routes du sud* (*The Roads to the South*), released in 1978 and starring Yves Montand; it was generally considered an inferior sequel to *La guerre est finie*. In 1972 Semprun himself wrote and produced a documentary film on the memories of people who had lived through the Spanish civil war, *Les deux* (The Two). He regards all his film work as literature, with the same function as his novels—namely, as he told an interviewer for the film magazine *Cinéaste* in 1979—as "that which transforms culture and, through the process, society . . . [it] must above all set itself up as an end and not as a means." The goal, he insists, is realistic, not idealistic. "Literature is not a privileged activity separated and alienated from the real world. Even the most abstract writers still bear witness to reality."

Married to Colette Leloup and the father of two children (one son from an earlier marriage), Semprun made his home in Paris until the late 1980s when he was invited to return to Spain and accept public office. In July 1988 he was appointed Minister of Culture in the government of Prime Minister Felipe Gonzalez Márques, a post he accepted with some hesitation. When the possibility of such an appointment was first raised he told an interviewer, "It is unthinkable." Yet he also reflected: "At times I think that few years remain and I ought to return to Spain to do something." Once committed to his responsibilties, he plunged into his work with his characteristic energy. He immediately began work on plans for the great international celebrations of 1992 when Barcelona will host the Summer Olympics, Seville will have an exposition celebrating the 500th anniversary of Columbus' discovery of the New World; and Spain will fully enter the European Economic Community. He was also engaged in supervising the installation in Madrid of the art treasures of the Thyssen-Bornemisza collection and the renovation of the Prado.

WORKS IN ENGLISH TRANSLATION: *The Long Voyage*, in Richard Seaver's translation, was published in 1964. Seaver also translated Semprun's screenplay *Stavisky* in 1975. Len Ortzen translated *The Second Death of Ramón Mercader* in 1973. *What a Beautiful Sunday!* was translated by Alan Sheridan in 1980. *The Autobiography of Federico Sanchez and the Spanish Underground in Europe*, the only one of Semprun's major works first published in Spanish rather than French, was translated by Helen R. Lane in 1979.

ABOUT: Contemporary Authors 111, 1984; Egri, P. Studia Romanica 4, 1969; Georgakas, D. (ed.) Cinéaste Interviews, 1983; Semprun, J. The Autobiography of Federico Sanchez, 1979. *Periodicals*—Best Sellers October 1, 1973; History Today October 1980; Library Journal December 15, 1973; September 15, 1982; New Statesman March 2, 1973; New York Herald Tribune Book Week May 10, 1964; New York Review of Books May 8, 1964; New York Times August 9, 1988; October 23, 1990; New York Times Book Review May 3, 1964; New Yorker August 8, 1964; Salmagundi Fall 1983; Times Literary Supplement November 11, 1983; World Literature Today Winter 1979.

SETON, CYNTHIA PROPPER (October 11, 1926–October 23, 1982), American novelist and essayist, was born in New York City, the daughter of Karl and Charlotte (Janssen) Propper. After graduating from the Fieldston School, she matriculated at Smith College, where she received her B.A. degree in 1948. In 1949 she married Paul H. Seton, a psychoanalyst, by whom she had five children—Anthony, Julia, Margaret, Jennifer, and Nora. She was a columnist for the *Washington Post* in 1959–1960, and thereafter, for twelve years, for the *Berkshire Eagle* in Pittsfield, Massachusetts. Her first book, *I Think Rome Is Burning*, a collection of her columns, was followed by two collections of essays, *A Special and Curious Blessing* and *The Mother of the Graduate*, which discuss the problems of family life and marriage against the background of the Vietnam War.

In 1971, Seton published her first novel, *The Sea Change of Angela Lewes*, the protagonist of which is the wife of a professor at Smith, a mother, and a secret writer. In a middle-aged "sea change," she achieves new independence, new confidence, begins to feel her uniqueness. Although reviews were generally favorable, often describing the novel as "intelligent" and "engaging," the reviewer for *Publishers Weekly* felt that Seton "raises but doesn't answer some nagging questions." Susan Burke, in *Best Sellers*, remarked that "Mrs. Seton seems to have carried her characters with her for years, [setting them down here] in outline form, as if they were solutions to geometry problems. . . . Perhaps she is too possessive of her people, and doesn't want to tempt our misinterpretation." She was also puzzled by many discernible likenesses between the protagonist's life and Seton's own. "You wonder, and you mind," she commented, "because it's hard to know what she means by doing that. . . . But this is Mrs. Seton's first novel. Maybe the next one (and hopefully there will be a second) will give us an answer."

The Half-Sisters, a Book-of-the-Month Club selection, focuses upon two girls, Erica and Billie, who have the same father but different mothers, and their contrasted experiences through life. In their childhood in the 1930s, they spend idyllic summers together at a Long Island beach, then are separated for years. They meet there again as young women about to have their first sexual experiences, and are both attracted to the same man. The last section, in 1970, brings them back to the same beach, as women in their forties whose lives have turned out differently than they had hoped. Margaret Atwood, in the *New York Times Book Review*, characterized the work as a "delightful novel, jaunty as a roadster and with something of a period flavor. . . . Listening to Cynthia Propper Seton recount [the two women's] ups and downs, their betrayals, dishonesties, loyalties and illuminations, is like listening to a witty, well-traveled, sophisticated and slightly eccentric rich aunt gossiping and passing judgments upon her acquaintances, a fascinating pastime when the aunt has the flair, style, and pithiness of the author. . . . The overview that emerges is a comic one, although muted by a sense of great futilities lying beyond its perimeters."

Seton's next novel, *A Fine Romance*, which was nominated for a National Book Award, made an even stronger impression. In this work, two American families converge in an eight-day package tour of Sicily, in the course of which the reader sees the nature and the limitations of Kitty Winters' marriage to her husband Gerard. Peter Prescott, in *Newsweek*, commented that Seton "writes about intelligent people who have read good books, are capable of good argument and aware that they do not always say quite what they mean. . . . Good novels about workable marriages are almost extinct today, but Seton's is one: it is witty, observant and precise— and, oddly, for a story by a feminist, it offers more sympathy to the good, dull husband than to the resigned, uncomfortable wife." Peter La Salle, in *America*, also praised *A Fine Romance* as a "novel of manners in which much of the insight sparkles in delightfully intelligent conversation. All the characters discover a little more about themselves by the story's end, especially Dr. Winters and his wife. She also provides

superb portraits of the Winters children, wide-eyed and lovably goofy, and, in the novelist aunt, offers intriguing thoughts on fiction writing in general. On the whole, a deft, handsome piece of work."

A Fine Romance was followed by *A Glorious Third*, which resembles it in some respects, particularly in its dealing with a modern marriage in mid passage and a trip abroad. Its central figure, Celia Webb Dupont, a 45-year-old mother of five and wife of an executive, decides in 1968, a period of change and global unrest, to make her remaining years the "glorious third" portion of her life. She goes with her husband to France to immerse herself in culture. While there both Celia and her husband engage in flirtations, he with a young feminist who is treated satirically, but in the end their marriage not only survives but is stronger for the experience. Lynne Sharon Schwartz, in the *Saturday Review*, described the novel as "a gem of a comedy. With delectable wit and a glittering style, Seton examines the leisured urban upper-middle class, its guilts and self-deceptions, its integrity, poignant strivings, and resignation. [But] *A Glorious Third* is more surface than depth, more Oscar Wilde than Jane Austen. . . . It suffers from an overlong beginning, sketchy middle, and sudden, far-too-cozy ending." Helen Yglesias, in the *New York Times Book Review*, admired Seton's gifts as a needle-sharp satirist, but believed that the novel's "cool, ironic atmosphere" prohibited any "blood passions." "Despite all the author's skill," she observed, "some readers will finish the book intensely irritated by the world of its essentially light-hearted, self-satisfied, comfortable creatures."

A Private Life involves another jaunt to France when Fanny Foote, who works for a feminist magazine, is assigned by her editor to uncover the story behind her aunt Fanny's sudden departure from America and subsequent life abroad with a companion named Lútecie—an apparent (though, as it turns out, not actual) latter-day version of Gertrude Stein and Alice B. Toklas. Writing in the *Washington Post Book World*, Alice Adams commented that "there is a certain sort of novel for which a certain sort of dedicated novel reader will yearn. We want, then, a fairly light but highly intelligent amusement: an early Mary McCarthy novel, say; a Muriel Spark; anything by Barbara Pym. . . . And this novel, along with Seton's other books, certainly approaches the excellence of those books mentioned . . . by McCarthy, Spark, or Pym." William Pritchard, in the *Hudson Review*, remarked that "Over the past six years, Cynthia Seton has produced three deftly written novels about men and women—and children—in very much the contemporary world of ideas and assumptions about marital fidelity, feminism, 'finding' oneself, and all those other important and sometimes boring issues. But in *A Fine Romance . . .* , in *A Glorious Third . . .* , and now in *A Private Life*, she refuses ever to become boring about them, since everything is invariably touched by her wit and made thereby lively, alive. This may have to do with the fact that . . . Mrs. Seton looks on her own stories without solemnity, and is therefore wary of bringing things together in rousing good ways. Subtlety is the mode, and surprise is usually the result. She should be read."

A Private Life was the last of Seton's distinctive novels. After having battled Hodgkin's disease for eleven years, she died in Northampton, Massachusetts in October 1982, at the age of fifty-six, of acute leukemia.

PRINCIPAL WORKS: I Think Rome Is Burning, 1962; A Special and Curious Blessing, 1968; The Mother of the Graduate, 1970; The Sea Change of Angela Lewes, 1971; The Half-Sisters, 1974; A Fine Romance, 1976; A Glorious Third, 1979; A Private Life, 1982.

ABOUT: Contemporary Authors New Revision Series 7, 1982; 108 (obituary), 1983; Contemporary Literary Criticism 27, 1984. *Periodicals*—America June 25, 1976; Best Sellers September 1, 1971; Christian Science Monitor April 18, 1979; Hudson Review Spring 1982; Library Journal July 1971; June 15, 1974; Newsweek May 17, 1976; New Yorker June 28, 1976; New York Times (obituary) October 24, 1983; New York Times Book Review May 25, 1974; February 18, 1979; Publishers Weekly June 21, 1971; February 25, 1974; Saturday Review March 17, 1979; Washington Post Book World February 25, 1979; May 16, 1982.

*SHABTAI, YAAKOV (1934–August 4, 1981), Israeli dramatist and fiction writer, is best known for the two novels he produced just before his premature death at The age of forty-seven. With these long, emotionally charged meditations on life, death, and life after death, Shabtai arrived at a distinctive form of literary expression that Robert Alter, in the *New York Times Book Review*, hailed as "a revolution in Hebrew prose."

The son of a construction worker, Shabtai was born and raised in the Jewish city of Tel Aviv, Palestine during the British Mandate. When he was sixteen—two years after the creation of the state of Israel—he went to work on a kibbutz for the summer and met his future wife, Edith, who was then fifteen. After he finished high school in Tel Aviv, the two of them went to another kibbutz, where he completed his military obliga-

tion. They were married in 1954 and for the next ten years lived on the kibbutz where they had met.

During this time Shabtai was mainly involved in farming, but he began to write on the side and published his early short stories in the Israeli daily *Ha'aretz*. At his wife's urging, they left the kibbutz in 1964 and moved to Tel Aviv so that he could pursue his writing career. Four years later he submitted his first play, *Crown Crazy*, to the state theater, Ha-cameri, where it was staged by Samuel Bunimi in 1969. As the title suggests, albeit obliquely, *Crown Crazy* was a portrait of the biblical king David, who, according to Shabtai, was "not someone whose desires can be stuffed into a dwarf. He is alive, human, complex, and full of appetites. Everything about him is extra large, as with a real king. A lot of love and hate, a lot of ambition, of regrets, a lot of man."

Two years later, at the age of thirty-seven, Shabtai suffered his first heart attack. The following year he published a collection of short stories, *Uncle Peretz Takes Off*, that Robert Alter described as a "stylistic trailblazer" for their deft synthesis of spoken and literary Hebrew. Nonetheless, Shabtai himself was at that time committed primarily to the theater: "He saw himself first and foremost as a playwright," his wife recalled in an interview with Israeli critic Gideon Ofrat. "His writing of stories accompanied his writing of plays." In the early 1970s he became resident dramaturge at the Haifa Theater, where he collaborated with director Michael Alfredo on a number of adaptations and original plays. Like *Crown Crazy*, these works were mostly set in the past—adaptations of Machiavelli's *Mandragola* and *The Asses* of Plautus staged as commedia del l'arte improvisations, a *Life of Caligula* written for one actor and chorus, *Don Juan and His Friend Shippel* (1976) set in contemporary Haifa but evoking the seventeenth-century Don Juan. "I would like to write about the here and now, but somehow it doesn't work out," Gideon Ofrat quotes Shabtai as saying in *Modern Hebrew Literature*. "The distance enables me to get deeper into the characters." But according to Ofrat, Shabtai's most successful venture in the domain of theater, and "one of the finest plays ever to have been written in Israel," was *The Spotted Tiger* (1974), set in the writer's native Tel Aviv in the 1920s. Based on his own short story "A Private and Scary Spotted Tiger," the play was a realistic drama with autobiographical overtones and, in Ofrat's view, benefited considerably from the direct connections to his life and his prose writing.

°shâb tī´, yâ´ kov

In any event, with the publication of his first novel in 1977, the "moderately successful playwright," as Alan Lelchuk characterizes him in the *New York Times Book Review*, became a leading figure on the Israeli literary scene. *Zikhron devarim* (translated as *Past Continuous*) literally means "remembrance of things," and like Proust's *Remembrance of Things Past* which it obviously evokes, Shabtai's stream-of-consciousness narrative (completely unparagraphed in the nearly three-hundred-page Hebrew original) moves in and out of time on the momentum of memory. The scope and tenor of the "action" are tersely defined in the first sentence: "Goldman's father died on the first of April, whereas Goldman himself committed suicide on the first of January." But within this limited span of time and death, Shabtai effectively recreates an era. Moving back and forth between the passing of Israel's older generation of East European idealists (Goldman the father) to the impasse of their sons (Goldman and his decadently depressive sidekicks Cesar and Yisrael), he establishes a dismal chronicle of decline. "No kibbutz utopias here, no Jerusalem mystique, no Zionist uplift, no sabra heroics, in other words, no magical society," wrote Lelchuk. "Instead, it is a portrait with Balzacian breadth—of a family and a people in trouble, lives lived at the end of a lofty dream gone haywire, paradise exploding." As he wryly noted, it was "not an easy read, nor what one would call entertaining," and in his view, there were times when Shabtai was "the servant of his material and not its master." But nonetheless, he, like others, hailed *Past Continuous* as the best literary portrait of Israeli society to date.

Shabtai was still basking in this aura of praise—and prizes—when he undertook his second novel, *Sof davar* (translated as *Past Perfect*). Seemingly engaged in a race against death—he had suffered another serious heart attack—he spent a full eight hours a day writing and rewriting the text, with the result, as Rochelle Furstenberg comments in her review of the English version, that the novel "merges the life of the writer with his work as few books do." Although it begins in the panoramic mode of *Past Continuous*, it quickly comes to focus on a single character, the autobiographical Meir, a forty-two-year-old engineer who is dying. Just as Goldman's death was preceded by that of his father, Meir senses the imminence of his own demise following the death of his mother, which, Shabtai writes in his typically meandering prose, "had exposed him to the terrible dangers of existence, and mainly to death, from which, simply by her presence, she had protected him, and he said to himself that now that she was dead, it was his turn to die." With this recognition, Meir

abandons himself to sexual fantasy (sadly unfulfilled) and, in the breach, a spree of oral gratification worthy of King David with his "appetites." In the end, which follows a stroke in a London bookstore, Meir comes to terms with his mortality and, in a final, visionary coda, passes through death to a new life.

According to his wife, Shabtai originally intended to call the novel "The Departure"; in March 1981, while he was editing the various drafts of his twelve-hundred-page manuscript, he decided instead on *Sof davar* (literally "the end of the matter"), which comes from the end of the biblical book of Ecclesiastes, the so-called Wisdom of Solomon. Two weeks later he suffered a final heart attack and died. By that time, he had completed the revision of two of the book's four chapters; with the help of critic Dan Meron, his wife went through the multiple versions of the other two chapters and, after two years' work, arrived at the 235-page novel that was published in 1984 with her own Afterword. In his review of the English translation, Robert Alter notes that the resulting text bears no traces of this posthumous effort, although, in his view, it is not a "masterpiece" like *Past Continuous*. For Alter, the work does not always transcend Shabtai's "private obsession" with illness and death to arrive at "a larger vision of human life." Nonetheless, he, like other reviewers, was ultimately drawn into Shabtai's world with the last twenty-five pages, "a prose-poem imagination of the world beyond the dread of death, dislocation, and despair," which he found "almost worthy of comparison with Molly's soliloquy at the end of *Ulysses*."

Alan Lelchuk, who visited Shabtai in his modest Tel Aviv apartment, recalls him as someone with "a youthful spirit, an eye for mirth, and a taste for literature." But where his writing was concerned, he was serious to the point of obsession: according to his wife, Edith, he read and studied every sentence of his manuscripts—*Past Perfect* was rewritten four times—"with a compulsive tendency to examine them anew, again and again, changing the order of the words, their rhythm, with . . . a terrifying sense of artistic responsibility."

WORKS IN ENGLISH TRANSLATION: *Past Continuous* (1985) and *Past Perfect* (1987) were both translated by Dalya Bilu. An excerpt from *Past Perfect* appears in *Modern Hebrew Literature*, Spring–Summer 1985.

ABOUT: Modern Hebrew Literature Spring–Summer 1985, Spring–Summer 1986; New York Review of Books October 10, 1985; New York Times Book Review April 21, 1985, August 9, 1987; Times Literary Supplement April 20, 1990; World Literature Today Spring 1986.

SHAPIRO, HARVEY (January 27, 1924–),
American poet and editor, writes: "It is difficult
for me to explain myself. If my poems cannot do
it for me—why else did I send them out into the
world?—how can I, limited as I am by this humdrum mind that can barely make its way
through the day, except when liberated (or energized or lifted up) by the process of writing poems.

"Writing. To clarify a confusion. I think the
confusion begins with my parents who arrived
in America (my mother as a young girl, my father as an adolescent) from some mud village
outside of Kiev, and never could figure out what
they were to do in this New World. My mother
finally settled for the iron codes of the bourgeois
suburbs, and never questioned those values; they
were handed down to her on Sinai. My father
thought America meant the romance of business, and prospered in that belief, until he went
bankrupt.

"I see myself following my father's ghost
through the same streets of New York City, beset
like him by the same dislocation, the same cultural shock. But I react differently. My life has
given me a completely different set of instruments to help me find my way.

"I was the first member of my family to go to
college. Indeed, thinking back on my childhood
I can't recall any adult of my knowing who had
gone to college. I went to Yale, and then after little more than a year there went into World War
II. So my points of reference from then on were
completely different from those of my parents.
I had written poems and stories in childhood but
had never thought of myself as a writer. At Yale,
before the war, I was an International Relations
major. Now I don't even know what that means
or where I thought it would lead me. Maybe into
a foreign post for the State Department, a most
unrealistic notion, given what I know now about
my lack of diplomacy. After the war, I knew I
wanted to write poetry.

"What had happened? Maybe the passage of
time—three years. Maybe the experience of
combat. I flew thirty-five missions over Germany and Austria as a gunner in a B-17. Some clari-
fying chill (high altitude, the possibility of
dying) must have reached me on those flights.
Anyway, I never wavered after that, and poetry
has been the one consistent thread in my adult
life.

"Working to support my poetry, mainly as a
journalist, sometimes as a teacher, I have always
led a bourgeois life. By choice not by chance. My
earliest coherent image of the artist, I think,
came out of Thomas Mann's short story 'Tonio
Kroger,' and it was that of the dissident, un-at-

HARVEY SHAPIRO

home spirit who blended into the middle class
for protection while he did his real work in secret and out of another life completely. Something like that. It was not an unusual image for
someone of my generation. William Carlos Williams, poet and pediatrician, and Wallace Stevens, poet and insurance executive, were my
models. And indeed it seemed to me, even later,
that the younger poets who interested me—
Robert Lowell, Randall Jarrell, Delmore
Schwartz, John Berryman—were all leading that
sort of life. I did not suspect the breakdowns and
suicides that were to follow.

"In any case, much of my poetry has a middle
class frame; that's the plot. A man walks through
the streets of his life, observing, trying to figure
it all out. In some of the poems the man is Jewish;
that's my tribal identity. I don't mean to say that
my work has had a program, except for one brief
period when I think I was consciously trying to
mine my tribal inheritance (the period of my
book *Mountain, Fire, Thornbush*). It is simply
the picture I get of it, looking back on it. This
battle report of a struggle so many face in so
many American cities.

"Recently I came across something Emily
Dickinson wrote in a letter justifying her work:
'The Sailor cannot see the North, but knows the
Needle can.' Just so, I have always trusted the
poems to find their direction."

———

Harvey Shapiro was born in Chicago to Jacob
Shapiro, a businessman, and Dorothy (Cohen)

Shapiro. He completed his B.A. at Yale in 1947 with time out for service in the U.S. Army Air Force, for which he won a Distinguished Flying Cross. After taking an M.A. from Columbia in 1948 he taught English at Cornell University for two years and spent a year as creative writing fellow at Bard College in Annandale-on-Hudson, New York. In 1955 Shapiro joined the editorial staff of *Commentary*. From 1956 to 1975 he was an editor for the *New Yorker*, with one year off (1968) on a Rockefeller Foundation fellowship in poetry. In 1975 he became editor of the *New York Times Book Review*, a post he held until 1983 when he was appointed deputy editor of the *New York Times Magazine*. He married Edna Lewis Kaufman, a psychologist, in 1953; they have two sons and live in Brooklyn, New York.

Shapiro has not enjoyed the luxury of a full-time career as a poet. As a result he has produced a relatively small amount of poetry, much of that not widely reviewed. Nevertheless Shapiro is recognized as a significant voice in contemporary American poetry, one who expresses the sensibilities of the urban middle-class American intellectual and, more particularly, of the contemporary American Jew. Tracing his development over the more than three decades that he has been publishing, critics have observed changes in Shapiro's style and tone, but they have also found a distinct continuity. His early verse was more formal and imagistic than his later work, but from the beginning Shapiro wrote with simplicity and candor. David Ray, reviewing *The Light Holds* in 1984 for the *New York Times Book Review*, summed up his achievement: "His poems withhold little, they share with the reader an unmistakable loneliness, a search for love, a fight against depression and despair and a response to the bewildering assaults of pop culture." Poetry serves him as what Ray calls "a vehicle for redemption and understanding." As early as 1953, in his first collection *The Eye*, Shapiro was seeking to draw meaning and shape from his experience. Writing of the death of his grandmother, he recalls her from his childhood memories:

> My grandmother drank tea, and wailed
> As if the Wailing Wall kissed her head
> Beside the kitchen window:
> While the flaking, green-boxed radio
> Retailed in Yiddish song
> And heartache all day long.
> Or laughter found her,
> The sly, sexual humor of the grave.

A seemingly banal, empty life, he grasps now that it was nevertheless worthy of celebration.

> I sing her a song of praise.
> She meddled with my childhood
> Like a witch, and I can meet her
> Curse for curse in that slum heaven where we go
> When this American dream is spent—
> To give her a crust of bread, a little love.

With the publication of *Mountain, Fire, Thornbush*, which, Hayden Carruth wrote, "contains poems of Jewish life so cogent and expressive that they must be irresistible to anyone," and *Battle Report* in the 1960s, Shapiro came to the attention of a small but appreciative readership. *Battle Report* included poems that define his own poignant vision of poetry—"News of the World," for example, that begins: "The past, like so many bad poems, / Waits to be reordered, / And the future needs reordering too." In his despair at his inability to fill such needs ("angling for direction"), he recalls how the Homeric favored found hope in hearing the voice of a god or goddess. The poem ends: "Turning to a friend, / I ask again / For news of the world." Thus resolved in his vocation as a poet, he discovers the significance of words and he quotes from a Hebrew scholar:

> "The word moves a bit of air,
> And this the next, until it reaches
> The man who receives the word of his friend
> And receives his soul therein
> And is therein awakened"—

As a poet Shapiro reflects that he is "not yet on the first / Rung . . . to move a bit of air," but he does not lose hope:

> If a man ask, can he have
> This thing, whether it be
> An infusion of souls, or souls,
> Steadfast to complete the journeying?
> Words moving a bit of air
> So that the whole morning moves.
>   —from "Spirit of Rabbi Nachman"

In his review of *Battle Report* in the *Nation*, David Ignatow found these mature poems of Shapiro far more uncompromising and firm in resolution than this earlier work. "They spring from a dual vision in the poet of disillusionment, and regeneration born from disillusionment." Reliving his combat experiences in *Battle Report* or confronting his own mortality as he approaches middle age, Shapiro is now in control. As Ignatow reads him: "To live is to endure and it is through endurance that we manifest the energy of life." Nowhere is this faith more apparent than in Shapiro's poems on Judaism. Hayden Carruth conjectures that Shapiro is not religious "in the ordinary sense," at least in terms of strict orthodoxy. Rather, he treats religious themes "with a familiar if edgy worldliness that often amounts to skepticism or even cynicism, but that never quite lets go of the religious handle." An example is "Ditty" (from *This World*):

Where did the Jewish god go?
Up the chimney flues.
Who saw him go?
Six million souls.
How did he go?
All so still
As dew from the grass.

Harold Bloom, on the other hand, attributes this apparent worldliness to the restraint and spareness of Shapiro's languages, much of which Bloom traces to the influence of one of the poets Shapiro most admires—William Carlos Williams—as well as to others like Charles Reznikoff, Louis Zukofsky, and George Oppen. Bloom writes that "the deep reader in me wants more, and laments the attachment of Shapiro to so minimal a modernist tradition, so sadly lacking in the rhetorical resources that his insights desperately require." Others, however, accept Shapiro's tendency to internalize his faith as simply characteristic of the modern psyche. Jascha Kessler, for example, writes in a review of Shapiro's *This World* in the journal *Midstream* : "I take his minimal succinctness as the sign of his strength and health, even when he seems most helpless; it is one measure of his truth as a poet. Were he more rhetorical, his makings might seem suspect, at least to me."

Shapiro writes in another poem ("A Short History") "Urbanity obscures the mystery." Here, R. Barbara Gitenstein suggests, "Harvey Shapiro argues that in the modern world urbanity destroys the meaning of creation by destroying the mystery . . . man forgets that the creation began in destruction and through the auspices of language, the Hebrew alphabet particularly." The first letter of the Hebrew alphabet is *aleph*, which is related to the Hebrew word for "ox." In a poem titled "Aleph" (in *Battle Report*) Shapiro traces the creation of language. "Oxhead," it begins, "working in / The intelligence. First sign, / Alphabet's wedge." Followed by the other characters of the alphabet, all of them images ("house, fish, / Man praying, palm of hand"), the poem moves on to the Greek alphabet:

But to return to first
Signs when the world's
Complex—
The head of an ox
Blunt, blundering,
Withal intelligencer
Pushing forward, horns raised
Stirring the matter
To make a beginning
For Amos, Homer,

And all who came first
In that sign.

Modern life and our language, Shapiro suggests in another religious poem, "Mountain, Fire, Thornbush," have tamed the religious ecstasy of Moses:

. . . We are
Only a step from discursive prose
When the voice speaks from the thornbush
Mountain, fire, and thornbush
Supplied only with these, even that aniconic Jew
Could spell mystery.

As Grace Schulman, reviewing his *Lauds* in the *Nation*, sees it, Shapiro's vision is one of a drifting chaotic world, but a world "that can be redeemed by art, sanctified by illumination." Transfiguration and transcendence are still possible in the very actuality of everyday commonplace life: "Shapiro praises things of the world with faith that song is a way of apprehending ideal beauty." Whether celebrating life with ironic humor, as in the poem "Considering" (in *The Light Holds*):

Like the man who walked
his three-legged dog
in Central Park—
pride and pathos
struggling in his face—
I consider my life
and my art.

or with genuine religious awe, as in the closing lines of "A Jerusalem Notebook" (also in *The Light Holds*):

I cannot dissever my happiness from language
or from your body. Light a candle for me
at the false tomb of David. I am of that line.

If I forget my happiness, let me be dust.
Jerusalem, here I am going up again.
It is your moon, your labyrinths, your desert
Crowding east where the sun waits.

Shapiro reveals himself as, in Jascha Kessler's words, "a man who realizes that he has been struck a mortal blow, who seems stunned though conscious, yet manages to pursue his life efficiently enough to convince us he remains sound and whole."

PRINCIPAL WORKS: The Eye, 1953; The Book and Other Poems, 1955; Mountain, Fire, Thornbush, 1961; Battle Report, 1966; This World, 1971; Lauds, 1975; Lauds & Nightsounds, 1978; The Light Holds, 1984; National Cold Storage Company: New and Selected Poems, 1988. *Novel*—(with Paulett Tumay) Murder in SoHo, 1987.

ABOUT: Bloom, H. Figures of Capable Imagination,

1976; Carruth, H. Working Papers: Selected Essays and Reviews, 1982; Contemporary Authors New Revision Series 15, 1985; Contemporary Poets, 4th ed., 1985; Gitenstein, R. B. Apocalyptic Messianism and Contemporary Jewish-American Poetry, 1986; Who's Who in America 1989–1990. *Periodicals*—Midstream April 1972; Nation April 24, 1967; September 13, 1971; May 22, 1976; New Leader July 9–23, 1984; New York Times Book Review April 1, 1984; December 11, 1988; Poetry January 1972.

SHAPIRO, JULIAN LAWRENCE. See SANFORD, JOHN B.

SHARPE, TOM (THOMAS RIDLEY) (March 30, 1928–), British novelist and playwright, was born in Holloway, London, the son of a Unitarian minister, the Reverend George Coverdale Sharpe, and the former Grace Egerton Browne. He attended Lancing College, served in the Royal Marines (1946–1948), and read history and social anthropology at Pembroke College, Cambridge, taking his degree in 1951. He emigrated to South Africa the year of his graduation and was successively a social worker in Soweto, near Johannesburg (1951–1952), a teacher in Pietermaritzburg (1952–1956), and a photographer (1956–1961). He wrote nine plays while living in South Africa; only the last of them, "The South African," was produced (in London), provoking official outrage in South Africa and leading to his imprisonment and deportation. Back in Britain again, he worked as history lecturer at the Cambridgeshire College of Arts and Technology in 1963–1971. Since 1971 he has been a full-time writer.

Sharpe's novels are bitingly, satirically comic, with a sense of general misanthropy that may leave the reader quite unsettled. He has hardly ever created a noble or forthright character: his books are thickly populated with characters who are either downright wicked or whose attempts to prevail over the muddle of their lives are clouded with impure motives of narrow self-interest. The guiding technique throughout his work is slapstick farce, backed up by a fair amount of obsessive sexuality and cloacal detail. Such motifs have ensured for his books extreme popularity in Britain (his U.S. audience is a small one); critics have been fond of comparing him to Evelyn Waugh and P. G. Wodehouse, although his popularity after two decades of writing and a dozen published novels is rather narrower than that of either of those authors.

Sharpe's first two books, the only ones set in South Africa, are his nearest approaches to seri-

TOM SHARPE

ous political satire. *Riotous Assembly* and *Indecent Exposure* both take place in Piemburg, like Pietermaritzburg an English enclave in the middle of a solidly Afrikaner province. Both feature the bumbling exploits of Kommandant van Heerden of the South African Police Force, the police chief of Piemburg, a brutal hater of blacks but an indiscriminate lover of all things English. In the first book he attempts to solve the murder of the Zulu cook to a much-admired (by him) English family, the Hazelstones. In the second, his rival assistant, the grim Lieutenant Verkramp, a Boer ideologue and an inveterate anglophobe, employs aversion therapy in a fanatical attempt to cure the Piemburg police of compulsive sexual relations with blacks. Identities and sexual roles are constantly reversed in both books, which are less attacks on apartheid than sendups of the Afrikaner-English rivalry and the contemporary abuse of psychiatry: "There didn't seem," in the words of *Riotous Assembly*'s omniscient, amused narrator (another constant in Sharpe's books), "to be any significant difference between life in the mental hospital and life in South Africa as a whole. Black madmen did all the work, while white lunatics lounged about imagining they were God." All British reviewers were full of praise for both books and for their author's "exuberant yet beautifully controlled sense of devastating farce," in the words of Anthony Thwaite in the *Observer*. American reviewers were less uniformly charmed. "The pranks quickly get tiresome, wrote Stephen Hathaway in the *New York Times Book Review*. "Face it South African police are not Keystone Kops and the brutal metaphysicians of apartheid are certain to remain indifferent to this aggregation of puerile sight gags."

No fewer than seven of Sharpe's "British" novels have as their primary target the foibles of academic life. The phrases "campus novel" and "campus satire" have been used to refer to this peculiarly British subgenre; but Sharpe's contributions to it are quite unlike the cozy British academic comedies of David Lodge and Malcolm Bradbury, whose points of view and characters are those of insiders. Sharpe considers academics a very low form of humanity indeed, and he writes about them not as one of them, but acidly and from an angry distance. *Porterhouse Blue* concerns an intrigue-ridden Cambridge college, bloated with privilege and staffed by fools, whose new master, a failed Labour politician, is utterly undone in his schemes to force the hidebound institution into accepting late twentieth-century academic progress, or what passes for it. *Wilt, The Wilt Alternative,* and *Wilt on High* feature the misadventures of Henry Wilt, a Walter Mitty–like fantasist, a low-grade lecturer in "liberal studies" at a low-grade technical college. His colleagues and students alike are appallingly stupid and vulgar; his wife, sexually insatiable and a devotee of all things "organic," laces his beer with home-made aphrodisiacs; his quadruplet daughters are monstrous parodies of the worst that children can become. Wilt develops a violent mistrust of all authority, organized or (more usually) disorganized, and a deep hostility to any form of theoretical knowledge. Once in power at Fenland Tech, he eliminates novels from the college's syllabus in favor of courses on beer making, preparing fraudulent tax returns, and coping with the ignorant malice of the police. *The Great Pursuit* takes as its targets the perpetrators of pretentious academic literary criticism and greedy, soulless publishers. *Vintage Stuff* pokes fun at mediocre British preparatory schools, where the masters, too ignorant to have serious thoughts about academic matters, spend all their time either plotting against one another or tilting at windmills. *Ancestral Vices* strikes blows against both left-wing academics and right-wing capitalists, with the cruel and loutish English upper class thrown in for good measure.

One of Sharpe's cleverest satires is *Blott on the Landscape,* in which Sir Giles Lynchwood, member of Parliament and an impotent misogynist, concocts a scheme to run a motorway through his rural constituency and the ancestral estate of his hated wife, Lady Maud. She takes on her gardener, the eponymous Blott, as chief ally against her husband and the property developers. After Sir Giles is eaten by the lions in the safari park set up by his wife, Blott succeeds to the property, winning the title, Lady Maud, and his late master's parliamentary seat in the kind of tables-turned ending characteristic of many of Sharpe's novels. To Peter Ackroyd, writing in the *Spectator, Blott* "is better than it really ought to be. . . . There are some extremely funny scenes, which actually seem funnier in retrospect than they did at the time, and over it all hangs the air of mild prurience which is so necessary in matters of humor."

The Throwback is a novel into which Sharpe has thrown most of his peculiar comic arsenal. The characters are uniformly repulsive, their sexual oddities fit them neatly. The hero, Lockhart Flawes, is a naive country gentleman who seems to come straight out of the eighteenth century; his being forced to come to terms with modern life provides the momentum for the endless series of disasters that occur throughout the novel. The Sharpeian puns are likewise nonstop, as are the characteristically tasteless practical jokes: dogs are variously dismembered and left to rot or made to run amok on LSD, and sexual outrages are visited on spinsters and a vicar's wife. Death, too, as in the other novels, is merely another comic device.

With the aid of scripts by the novelist Malcolm Bradbury, both *Blott on the Landscape* and *Porterhouse Blue* have been made into television mini-series by the BBC (the former in 1985, the latter in 1987) and achieved great success with the British viewing public. The Wilt books inspired *The Misadventures of Mr. Wilt,* a 1990 film directed by Michael Tuchner.

PRINCIPAL WORKS: Riotous Assembly, 1971; Indecent Exposure, 1973; Porterhouse Blue, 1974; Blott on the Landscape, 1975; Wilt, 1976; The Great Pursuit, 1977; The Throwback, 1978; The Wilt Alternative, 1979; Ancestral Vices, 1980; Vintage Stuff, 1982; Wilt on High, 1984. *Plays*—Pitch Pine and Brass Handle, 1982; Too Many Pebbles, 1982; When We Practice to Deceive, 1982.

ABOUT: Contemporary Authors 122, 1988; Contemporary Literary Criticism 36, 1986; Dictionary of Literary Biography 14, 1983; Who's Who, 1989. *Periodicals*—Book World March 5, 1976; June 10, 1984; March 3, 1985; Books and Bookmen June 1971, June 1973, April 1976, August 1979, November 1982, July 1983, December 1984; Critique Winter 1984; Encounter July 1974; Guardian Weekly August 5, 1979; Listener May 13, 1971; March 4, 1976; April 14, 1977; March 30, 1978; August 2, 1979; November 6, 1980; November 18, 1982; October 11, 1984; London Review of Books December 20, 1984; New Statesman May 24, 1974; May 23, 1975; March 4, 1976; March 24, 1978; August 3, 1979; October 10, 1980; November 7, 1980; November 12, 1982; New York Times February

6, 1985; New York Times Book Review May 12, 1985;
May 17, 1987; Observer March 25, 1973; April 14,
1974; February 29, 1976; November 14, 1982; May 15,
1983; September 30, 1984; Punch March 21, 1973;
June 4, 1975; March 22, 1978; September 8, 1982; November 3, 1982; October 24, 1984; Spectator May 15,
1971; May 24, 1975; March 6, 1976; March 25, 1978;
December 20, 1980; November 10, 1984; Time November 11, 1974; Times Literary Supplement July 2,
1971; April 19, 1974; May 23, 1975; March 25, 1978;
December 7, 1979; November 14, 1980; November 12,
1982; October 12, 1984; June 26, 1987.

SUSAN SHEEHAN

SHEEHAN, SUSAN (August 24, 1937–),
American journalist, is the daughter of Charles
and Kitty C. (Herrman) Sachsel. Born in Vienna,
Austria, she came to the United States in 1941
and became a naturalized citizen in 1946. After
completing a B.A. at Wellesley College in 1958,
Sheehan spent two years as an editorial researcher for Esquire-Coronet, a magazine publisher in
New York City. She then worked as a freelance
writer from 1960 to 1962, when she became a
staff writer at the New Yorker, a position she
continues to hold.

Sheehan has won her reputation as a writer of
nonfiction, works which have been characterized as "advocacy journalism." She wrote her
first book, Ten Vietnamese, while in Vietnam
with her husband, Neil Sheehan, then a New
York Times foreign correspondent. Surrounded
by journalists who covered the official side of the
war, Sheehan decided to report on its everyday,
human aspect:

> . . . few of the ordinary people of Viet Nam are written
> about: they don't hold press conferences, they don't com-
> mand troops, and they don't plot coups d'état. They are
> unable to speak English or French, and they lack the ser-
> vices of interpreters. To me their absence from most ac-
> counts of the war seemed regrettable. It was these
> Vietnamese—the people I've heard called "the ninety-
> five per cent that don't count"—who interested me, for
> the war is being fought over them and they are its chief
> participants and chief victims.

Overcoming problems such as language barriers, inadequate transportation, limited accom-
modations, and the danger of delving into the
Viet Cong side of the story, Sheehan sought out
her subjects by "roaming the countryside." During a nine-month period she conducted and
wrote up interviews with a variety of people,
including a peasant, a landlord, a refugee, a politician, a Buddhist monk, a South Vietnamese soldier, a Viet Cong, and a North Vietnamese
prisoner. Except for providing simplified background information, Sheehan allowed her ten
Vietnamese to relate their own stories.

Reviewers commended Sheehan for present-

ing an alternative view of Vietnam but questioned her matter-of-fact approach and her
knowledge of the country and its complex politics. The Times Literary Supplement reviewer
noted that the book is "readable in spite of
a curiously false-naive style," adding that
"Sheehan's own contributions must be treated
with caution." Gavin Young, writing in the New
York Times Book Review, called Ten
Vietnamese "one of the most revealing books yet
written about Vietnam." Nevertheless, Young
criticized Sheehan's selectivity, particularly her
neglect of Vietnamese who resented American
interference, and contended that Sheehan's "flat
'let-them-speak-for-themselves' New Yorker
technique" did not do justice to her subject.

Like most of Sheehan's books, her second, A
Welfare Mother, began as a New Yorker
"profile." After convincing the magazine to publish an article about Hispanic welfare recipients,
Sheehan decided that focusing on one individual
would provide her story with more vividness and
"felt truth," if fewer "facts." Through the Department of Social Services, she found a willing
subject, Carmen Santana, a Puerto Rican woman
who lived in Brooklyn with her lover and four
of her nine children. Sheehan researched her
topic for two and a half years, gathering first-
hand information about Mrs. Santana's childhood, family, environment, and employment
history. In the end, Sheehan depicted a woman
forced by circumstances to go on "the welfare,"
who adroitly cheated the system on which she
now relied. A Welfare Mother was praised for
its clear and detailed presentation of a largely ig-

nored subject. Susan Jacoby, however, in the *New York Times Book Review* raised several doubts about the study, describing it as "a profoundly disturbing example of the way in which the best journalistic intentions can be thwarted by the barrier between reporters and people who do not hold the same values or enjoy a similar standard of living."

In *A Prison and a Prisoner*, Sheehan again reported on a system by focusing on an individual who lives within it. The book revolves around George Malinow, a repeat offender and long-term prisoner, and includes accounts of his prison life, his previous crimes, and his childhood. As with her earlier works, Sheehan immersed herself in her topic, spending long days and even nights at the Green Haven Correctional Facility in Beckman, New York, observing and interviewing inmates, guards, and administrators. Her descriptions of Green Haven range from its menus, remedial classes, and visiting rights to its thriving black market in contraband goods, prisoner violence, and prisoner abuse. She also provides background material on the New York prison system and the "liberalizing" changes made after the Attica riots. Sheehan refrains from passing judgment on either Malinow or the prison system. In conclusion, however, she writes that Malinow, awaiting parole once again, "doesn't believe in rehabilitation, but he knows that since he was last sent to prison people have responded to him with kindness and love, and that he has a different outlook, and that is what counts." *A Prison and a Prisoner* won a Gavel Award from the American Bar Association and accolades from critics, who called it a "marvelous work of detailed reporting" and "perhaps the best survey of life behind bars." *New York Times* reviewer Anatole Broyard had some reservations about the book, however, characterizing it as an "accurate but curiously passive picture of the current issues in prison management."

Is There No Place on Earth for Me? has proven to be Sheehan's most successful and affecting book to date. It chronicles the life of "Sylvia Frumkin," an intelligent, strong-willed, schizophrenic young woman. Sheehan conducted research by accompanying Sylvia everywhere, including the psychiatric ward of a state mental hospital, a transitional residence, and the home of Sylvia's parents. In addition, she studied Sylvia's files and interviewed those involved in her case in order to reconstruct the history of Sylvia's mental illness. Her account raises questions about the success of deinstitutionalization, the competence of many psychiatrists, the burdens placed on hospital and social service staff, and the efficacy of psychopharmacology. Sheehan depicts graphically the impact of Sylvia's disease on her parents and sister and, moreover, on Sylvia herself:

> She became upset again on Saturday evening. She took her clothes off, refused to go to bed, banged on many of the doors in the ward, kept the other patients awake, and insisted that she needed a blood test, because she might be pregnant. At eleven o'clock, she was given an injection of Thorazine and was put into seclusion. The nurse management team was called over twice to help with her; the doctor on night duty renewed the seclusion order twice. Miss Frumkin spent the night singing, laughing, and talking to herself.

The study earned Sheehan wide acclaim. She won a Mental Health Media Award in 1981, the Pulitzer Prize for best nonfiction work in 1982, and a nomination for the American Book Award for general nonfiction in 1983. *New York Times Book Review* critic Maggie Scarf lauded Sheehan's "beautifully written chronicle." Ellen Sweet, writing in *Ms.*, approved of Sheehan's focus on the bright, articulate, and pathetic Sylvia Frumkin. In the *New Republic* Dr. Willard Gaylin, a practicing psychoanalyst and professor of psychiatry, praised the book as "brilliantly documented, if overly detailed." Gaylin criticized Sheehan's disparagement of the drug therapy given to Frumkin, however, noting that no consensus had been reached concerning the proper use of antipsychotic drugs. He concluded his review with the hope that Sheehan would "one day free herself from her identity as a *New Yorker* reporter" and tap her inner resources more fully.

In keeping with her reputation for reporting on systems, Sheehan next explored state care for the elderly. *Kate Quinton's Days* describes the travails of an eighty-year-old widow suffering from osteoarthritis and unable to care for herself. Sheehan followed the case from January 1982 to February 1983, during which time Quinton almost went into a nursing home but instead was chosen to participate in an experimental program designed to provide the elderly with home nursing care. Sheehan narrates Quinton's struggle to remain with her daughter Claire, herself disabled by a spinal injury. While the narrative highlights both women's fight to maintain their independence, Sheehan also describes many of the people who enter their lives, from bureaucrats to home attendants. In addition, she includes a summary on the debate between nursing home and home care advocates, complete with statistics on costs.

Sheehan's account of Kate Quinton's situation and of the services available to New York City's elderly impressed reviewers with its lucidity and timeliness. *Psychology Today* reviewer Wray Herbert found it "an affirmative, at times even upbeat, story." Sheehan, he asserts, "has constructed a far more powerful argument for home care than any statistics could provide." "In the journalistic tradition of Orwell," Merle Rubin wrote in *The Christian Science Monitor*, "Sheehan has achieved power through directness and clarity."

Kate Quinton's Days prompted Michele Souda, in the *Nation*, to analyze Sheehan's work more closely and critically:

> Sheehan operates as something of a *cinema verité* director: she lets the camera (in this case the pen) roll and edits later, pruning and rearranging her material. She will, in the process, convert many of her interviewees' words into indirect discourse, a technique that lends itself to summary and economy but also allows for the careful, sometimes inappropriate superimposition of the writer's attitudes and conclusions on the less self-conscious words of the speaker.

Because Sheehan has "the novelist's eye and ear," Souda continued, she has increasingly allowed narrative to overcome documentary, characters to overcome facts and figures. While this fictional quality tends to raise questions about the "truth" in her work, it endows her writing with "the symmetry and poetry of narrative, and from such symmetry comes the impact of Sheehan's journalistic statement."

Sheehan brought this same journalistic technique to a vastly different subject in *A Missing Plane*. In reconstructing the events that surrounded the fatal crash of a U.S. Army Air Force bomber during World War II, she also revivifies the plane's pilot, Second Lieutenant Robert Allred, and the twenty-one male passengers who died with him. Sheehan devotes one section of the book to the discovery of the plane and the recovery of the victims' remains in the early 1980s, another to the painstaking identification of the human remains by a physical anthropologist, and the last to a biography of Allred. In the final section, she presents her recreation of Allred's last flight, intended to take him and his men from Port Moresby, New Guinea, to their base at Nadzab, located on the other side of the Owen Stanley Range. Allred took a short cut over the mountain range, flew into a cloud, and crashed into a mountainside. Reviewers applauded Sheehan's meticulous, insightful, and intriguing reconstruction. In the *New York Times Book Review*, Eric Lax praised her for serving "the higher purpose of accounting for any man killed in war, no matter how long it takes." *Publishers Weekly* found it "hard to say which phase of Sheehan's re-creations is more remarkable."

In addition to her work for the *New Yorker*, Sheehan has written for the *New York Times*,

Atlantic Monthly, New Republic, Harper's and *McCalls*. She has participated on a number of committees and panels, including the literature panel of the District of Columbia Commission on Arts and Humanities (1979–   ) and the advisory committee on employment and crime of the Vera Institute of Justice (1978–   ). She has also served as a consultant for the 42nd Street redevelopment project for the New York City Department of City Planning and as a judge for the Robert F. Kennedy Journalism Awards (1980, 1984). In 1984, she received a Distinguished Alumni Award from Wellesley College.

Susan and Neil Sheehan were married in 1965 and spent their honeymoon in Saigon where she wrote *Ten Vietnamese*. Both their careers advanced rapidly in the following years, with Neil Sheehan making his name as the *New York Times* reporter to whom Daniel Ellsberg gave the Pentagon Papers in 1971. It was Susan Sheehan who suggested to her husband that he write a book about the colorful and controversial Lieutenant Colonel John Paul Vann, an American military adviser in Vietnam, who was killed in a helicopter crash in 1972. "I'm always making suggestions to my husband that I later regret," she wrote in an article, "When Will the Book Be Done?", in the *New York Times Magazine*. In the end she had no reason to regret her suggestion. Neil Sheehan's biography of Vann, *A Bright Shining Lie: John Paul Vann and America in Vietnam* was published in 1988 to critical acclaim, and it won both the Pulitzer Prize and the National Book Award. But the sixteen-year interval between her suggestion and the publication of *A Bright Shining Lie* was a period of painful trial for both Sheehans. Neil Sheehan was struggling to write the book against formidable odds—a libel suit, ultimately dismissed, for his first book, *The Arnheiter Affair* (1972), and an automobile accident that left him severely injured. Susan Sheehan, as she writes in her *Times Magazine* article, was herself "close to the edge" from overwork, bouts of ill health, and worry about finances. She was, moreover, going through a crisis in her own career. Having committed herself to writing a biography of Alfred A. Knopf, the publisher, and having done considerable research on her subject, she discovered that "my heart was no longer in the Knopf biography" and that she was happier writing her *New Yorker* pieces. Her account of these lean and painful years has a happy ending with the triumphant success of *A Bright Shining Lie*. "If at times the price seemed high," she writes, "well, few people ever have the chance to spend sixteen years doing what they want to do."

The Sheehans live in Washington, D.C. They have two grown daughters.

PRINCIPAL WORKS: Ten Vietnamese, 1967; A Welfare Mother, 1976; A Prison and a Prisoner, 1978; Is There No Place on Earth for Me?, 1982; Kate Quinton's Days, 1984; A Missing Plane, 1986.

ABOUT: Contemporary Authors New Revision Series 12, 1984; Who's Who on the East Coast 1986; Writers Directory 1988–1990. *Periodicals*—Christian Science Monitor September 11, 1984; McLeans September 20, 1982; Ms June 1982; Nation November 24, 1984; New Republic May 12, 1982; New York Times May 13, 1978; New York Times Book Review April 16, 1967; August 8, 1976; May 2, 1982; October 19, 1986; New York Times Magazine April 15, 1990; Psychology Today November 1984; Publishers Weekly August 22, 1986; September 2, 1988; Times Literary Supplement October 5, 1967.

SHEN JUNG or **SHEN RONG**. See **CHEN RONG**

SHEPHERD, MICHAEL. See **LUDLUM, ROBERT**

SIMMONS, JAMES (STEWART ALEXANDER) (February 14, 1933–), Northern Irish poet, writes from his home near Belfast: "James Simmons was born in Londonderry, Northern Ireland, son of a cultivated liberal stockbroker. He grew up in comfortable circumstances in a musical household during the Second World War. At the age of eleven he was sent to Campbell College as a boarder, where he enjoyed sport, but became modestly rebellious in his later teens, pacifist, agnostic, and sexually liberated so that he was not welcomed back to the school for a final year in which he might have tried for university scholarships. His passion was singing popular songs, but he was also dabbling in verse, and after he left school determined to be a writer and/or singer. In pursuit of these aims he spent several years in London until he married [Laura Stinson] in 1955. During his wanderings he had met Prof. Bonamy Dobrée, who offered him entry to Leeds University if he could find the money. His wife worked for a year and thereafter they existed on educational grants. Leeds [from which Simmons received a bachelor's degree in English in 1958] was the most brilliant of the English universities at that time, with Geoffrey Hill, Thomas Blackburn, and Arnold Kettle on the staff and Wole Soyinka and Tony Harrison among the students.

"Although Simmons had already published poems this was his first experience of a genuine-

JAMES SIMMONS

ly cultivated society. The plain living and exalted ambitions of his colleagues impressed him deeply. He edited a weekly poetry magazine *Poetry and Audience* and an anthology *Out on the Edge*. His first child, Rachael, was born in Leeds.

"When he graduated, to avoid army service, he found employment in a Quaker school in Lisburn, Northern Ireland, where the rest of five children by his first wife were born. In the school he initiated a tradition of producing plays from which came some professional actors (including Ian McIlhenny). Two of his pupils have become writers, Sam McBratney and Michael Dibdin, who recently won the Silver Dagger Award for crime writing. He also helped to found a Society for Teachers of English, began to broadcast songs and poems, and met the slightly younger writers who helped to form the 'Ulster Renaissance': Seamus Heaney, Derek Mahon, and Michael Longley.

"In 1963 he joined Tony Harrison at Ahmadu Bello University in Nigeria, where good work was done in encouraging drama. They wrote together *Aikin Mata* for the students (1966). Simmons and his family left Zaria in 1967 because of deteriorated conditions due to the civil war. The pamphlet *No Ties* is based on an affair he enjoyed when his family had gone home ahead of him. The marriage had begun to deteriorate in Africa, although it did not finally break down until the 1970s.

"The pamphlet *Ballad of a Marriage* was published by Festival Publications in 1966. The start of the Belfast Festival was another symptom of the amazing blossoming of cultural life in Northern Ireland. It suddenly became apparent that there were poets, painters, and musicians of distinction in a province often described as a cultural wilderness. The brilliant painter Colin Middleton had been art teacher at Friends' School when Simmons was there. Poets and painters showed considerable interest in each other's work. Sean O'Riada brought the Chieftains to play in Belfast; the Northern poet, John Montague, gave them their title. Van Morrison was singing in local bars, the flautist James Galway was learning his skills in Orange bands.

"In May 1968 Simmons founded *The Honest Ulsterman*, perhaps the most vital of Irish literary magazines, which is still appearing under later editors. In it the early poems of Derek Mahon, Paul Muldoon, Seamus Heaney, et al. appeared, and a host of lesser talents. It also included prints by contemporary artists.

"Simmons' poetic career became more public in 1967 when the Bodley Head published *Late But in Earnest*, which was praised by Graham Greene. That august house also published *In the Wilderness* (1969) and *Energy to Burn* (1971). In 1968 Simmons was appointed lecturer at the New University of Ulster (now the University of Ulster) in Coleraine. Here he did more distinguished work in drama, climaxing in a performance of King Lear which for some discriminating judges is the finest interpretation of that great role. An excess of interests is sometimes thought to have been a fault in Simmons' career: actor, director, poet, songwriter, singer, painter, editor, critic, teacher, sexual therapist, 'a legend in his own time.'

"His next five volumes of poetry were published by the Blackstaff Press in Belfast, a further example of cultural revival in the province: *The Long Summer Still to Come* (1973), *West Strand Visions* (1974), *Judy Garland and the Cold War* (1976), *Constantly Singing* (1981), and *From the Irish* (1984). These have had mixed reactions, dismissive and adulatory. He might be the best of the Irish poets or not worth reading. In his critical work he has had limited praise for famous contemporaries like John Montague and Seamus Heaney, which produces a hostile reaction. Heaney, who is a friendly acquaintance, has never mentioned Simmons' name in print, though he is usually generous with puffs for poets, musicians, painters, etc.

"There are three L.P.s of Simmons singing his songs, *City and Eastern*, *Love in the Post*, and *The Rostrevor Sessions*. His amazing settings of Yeats' poems are known only to the lucky few. Only *The Rostrevor Sessions* is easy to get hold of, from Spring Records, Rostrevor, Northern Ireland.

"Of his plays, only the collaboration with Harrison has been printed. His work appears in most of the anthologies of Irish poetry except the disgraceful Muldoon selection for Oxford. In 1976 B.C.C.-TV 'Omnibus' made a twenty-minute programme of his life and work which is worth looking at. There is a magnificent interview on Irish T.V. in the series 'Hanly's People,' but it may not have been recorded.

"His great critical book on Sean O'Casey was published by Macmillan (London) in 1983 and is his only book available in America. [Also in 1983 Simmons retired from the New University of Ulster Coleraine, where he had been for several years lecturer in Anglo-Irish literature.] In the early 1980s he married his longtime mistress Imelda Foley, sister of the poet. They had one marvellous child, Anna. Imelda left him after five years, 'overpowered by rectitude and genius,' and he is at present deeply satisfied with the brilliant young American poet, Janice Fitzpatrick, since 1987. She is of true New England stock and likely to stick with him till death. They have one fine boy, Ben Simmons (b. 26/7/88), who had great difficulties at birth (esophageal atresia) but is now thriving. On going to press Simmons' new collection *War on Want* has been turned down by the publisher who brought out *Poems, 1956–1986*, Gallery Books, Dublin, and Bloodaxe Books, Newcastle upon Tyne, England. This selection from all his previous work won many awards and is his only available book. The two poets live together in a coastguard's cottage in Island Magee, not far from Belfast, where they are starting an arts centre, the Poets House. It is an extraordinarily beautiful spot with panoramic views of the Irish Sea across to Ailsa Craig and the Mull of Kintyre. You should visit them."

Among the several frequently recurring themes in the poetry of James Simmons, none is more painfully explored than married life, its betrayals and disappointments. The sad bitterness of love as it is traduced and turns to hate is one of the emotions he apparently finds it easiest to contemplate and to communicate. The poet confesses to recurrent, angry fantasies of strange men making love to the woman who will be his wife, acts which, imagined later and often, thereby ruin his marriage for him. For example, he writes in "Husband to Wife":

When I consider how your life was spent
before we met, I see a parked car
where some man took you down, with your consent,
and helped to make you what you are

The first stanza of "Memorials of a Tour of Yorkshire" shows the other side of the coin of the poet's marital relationship:

I think this student is called Jane
who leans against me in the booth,
her lips wet with the dirty rain
of Leeds. The flattery of youth
is pleasing to an aging poet who
is waiting for his trunk call to go through.

The poet has written on occasion of the incessant violence in his Ulster homeland. "The Ballad of Gerry Kelly: Newsagent" and "Claudy," both traditional Irish ballads about routine outrages committed by the Men of Violence, are effective and affecting. Yet Simmons is very conscious of being an "Ulster Protestant," and thus refers to himself often; he appears to have little sympathy for the Catholics of the beleaguered province.

The man next door, a Catholic,
His small wage acquires
From children's encyclopedias
Sold to reluctant buyers.

His wife, next door, is also
A Catholic, she bears
A child almost every year;
They sometimes come in pairs. . . .

The priest is full of sympathy
When, having drunk more
Than usual, the husband throws
His family through the door. . . .
                              "If the Cap Fits"

In the short collection *No Land Is Waste, Dr Eliot*, Simmons contrasts his own gargantuan appetite for life and love with the strangled, dessicated ways he imputes to T. S. Eliot. He writes in a note that "what unifies these poems is their reaction against the refined anti-life feeling most famously exemplified by Eliot's *The Waste Land*. However, I am not attacking the man, he had the measure of his own poem."

Simmons' only published prose work of criticism, *Sean O'Casey*, was part of the Macmillan Modern Dramatists series. He treats the entire career of O'Casey (1880–1964), whom he describes in his first chapter as "emphatically a working-class writer. It is part of his originality that we feel, in his best plays, that the insulted and injured are allowed to speak in their own voice, perhaps for the first time in our literature." Simmons' own drama, *Aikin Mata*, written with Tony Harrison, is a translation and adaptation of Aristophanes' *Lysistrata*, with Nigerian names and characters, but retaining much of the ancient Greek dramatic situation.

Direct to the point of bluntness, candid often to the point of aggressive insult, James Simmons

has evoked angry reactions from some of his reviewers. Like other, notably Irish, ironists, he delights in paradox, specifically (as Terry Eagleton wrote of him in the *Times Literary Supplement* in 1975) "the paradox of an essentially subversive wit." He is, nevertheless, highly regarded by many readers for what John Cotton, in *Contemporary Poets*, calls "his basic humanity, and his sympathy and preference for the human condition however fallible and whatever its faults." Edna Langley, in an introduction to a collection of his poems, wrote: "In the poetry of James Simmons art and life never look like becoming polite strangers. Their intimacy declares itself through the effortlessly natural tones of the poet's voice . . . the poems have an air of very immediately addressing the reader out of the immediacy of experience." Beneath the flippancy is a strong moral-didactic impulse. Gavin Ewart, in the *Times Literary Supplement* in 1978, observed: "One part of his imagination desires to change the world, not simply to stage it as it is." Peter Porter, in the *Observer* in 1985, offered as balanced a judgment as is likely to be rendered on Simmons' work to date: "To be pro–booze-and-sex, 'on the side of life' and the rest of it, and not seem strained, is Simmons's achievement. I suspect that many years from now his handling of the vernacular will seem one of the lasting styles of a very confused literary period."

PRINCIPAL WORKS: *Poetry*—Ballad of a Marriage, 1966; Late but in Earnest, 1967; In the Wilderness, 1969; Ten Poems, 1969; No Ties, 1970; Energy to Burn, 1971; No Land Is Waste, Dr Eliot, 1972; The Long Summer Still to Come, 1973; West Strand Visions, 1974; Judy Garland and the Cold War, 1976; The Selected James Simmons, 1978; Constantly Singing, 1980; From the Irish, 1985; Poems, 1956–1986, 1986. *Drama*—(with T. Harrison) Aikin Mata, 1966. *Non-fiction*—Sean O'Casey, 1983.

ABOUT: Contemporary Authors 105, 1982; Contemporary Poets, 4th ed., 1985; Contemporary Literary Criticism 43, 1987; Dawe, G. and E. Longley (eds.) Across a Roaring Hill: The Protestant Imagination in Modern Ireland, 1985; Dictionary of Literary Biography 40, 1985; Longley, E. *Introduction to* The Selected James Simmons, 1978. *Periodicals*—Encounter February 1981; Observer October 19, 1980; September 1, 1985; Times Literary Supplement February 28, 1975; July 28, 1978; January 23, 1981; April 27, 1984.

SIMON, KATE (GROBSMITH), (December 5, 1912–February 4, 1990), American travel writer and memoirist, wrote: "I was born at the opening of World War I in a poor Jewish family of Warsaw. My grandfather, a tinsmith, died

KATE SIMON

young but the family of several children were, though undereducated, quick to learn skills and contribute to the household. My mother, with one year of education, became an apprentice, at the age of eight, in a corset factory. In time she learned all the skills involved and opened her own very successful shop. She continued to help support her mother and younger siblings with whom we lived after I and my brother were born and my father gone off to America, with the promise of sending for us almost immediately.

"Whether it was a question of money or the fact that my father enjoyed his temporary bachelorhood, my brother was born in his absence and I already four when we met at Ellis Island. (I was one year old when he left.) Like many war-time children my brother was malnourished and rachitic and I had the sole care of him on the journey from Warsaw to Rotterdam—to board the steamer *Susquehanna*—while my mother arranged the many stages of our trip, fed us and found us temporary shelters. It was an enormous responsibility for a four-year-old, and the intense, wary attention to all details, to places, to faces, to voices, to new words, may have been the very first habits that became characteristics of the travel writer I later became. My first steady habitat was a mixed community of immigrants in the Bronx, the matter of my first autobiographical book, *Bronx Primitive*. The difference of habits, language, religion, female information exchanged on the streets, became matters that further fed my curiosity and sharpened the travel writer's need to record and comment on, though silently at the time.

"In early adolescence I left home and the Bronx sustaining myself on a variety of jobs—teaching, modeling, baby-sitting, working as a library assistant and a number of miscellaneous etceteras. Out of trying on various personae, of avidly picking up information—mainly from helpful teachers—when and where I could, I began to develop a courageous (though actually often filled with fear) role of explorer of the city and all it had to offer in the Depression years, from fathers selling apples, to the WPA theater, to general radicalism, to long, inexpensive talking sessions at Village cafeterias.

"All this and much more, including the character and quality of Hunter College as I then knew it, became the material for the second volume of autobiography, *A Wider World*. Before the autobiographies there were many other books, mainly of travels—New York, Mexico, Italy, England, Rome, Paris, London and a history of Fifth Avenue. This stream began with a trickle which was a challenge to write an unusual guide book of New York. It was successful, became a sort of classic of its type, and its fame led to offers to write the other travel books.

"In the course of my travels in Italy, I became fascinated by the court of the Gonzaga of Mantua whose story should soon be ready for editorial review and ultimate publication [published in 1988 as *A Renaissance Tapestry*].

"I am frequently asked why a travel writer should turn to autobiography. My immediate answer is that artists use varieties of media, composers work in several disparate forms—why not writers? However, I see the autobiographies as a certain kind of travel book too, recording times and places, with myself as prime observer, as I might observe and record Siena or Rome or Paris."

———

"I must have started being a travel writer when we first came to America," Kate Simon told an interviewer for the *New York Times Book Review* in 1986. Arriving as a four-year-old with her mother and younger brother, she early learned the necessity for observing, noting, and recording everything that was happening around her. For that reason her travel writings and her memoirs have a special pungency. "Simon is gifted with almost cinematic visual recall," Sybil S. Steinberg wrote in *Publishers Weekly*. "Details of place and atmosphere, of appearance and character are augmented by an ability to recall smells, tactile sensations, and weather." In her two volumes of memoirs, *Bronx Primitive : Portraits in a Childhood* and *A Wider World : Portraits in an Adolescence*, both highly praised by reviewers, she evokes a whole lost world of Jewish life in New York in the 1920s and 1930s—the economic struggles of working-class families, their efforts and those of their children to adapt to a new and foreign culture. Kaila, as she was then known, grew up in a mixed ethnic neighborhood in the southeast Bronx, went to public schools that imposed strict standards of study and behavior, loved her warm-hearted mother and younger brother and sister, battled with her demanding father, and developed into a sensitive writer who communicated her sense of the past in vivid prose:

> The shapes of things changed in the summertime. The smoke from the hat factory next door became fat and slow, oozing like a chorus of fat ladies in pink, blue, yellow, purple dresses. The edges of buildings shook and melted. Cold, dry faces opened and glistened with sweat. The spikey park flowers bent and hung. The sidewalks sweated, the walls sweated, and out of the heat and wetness came heavily ornate, lazy bunches of grapes, the opulent shine and smell of plums, the rubies of pomegranite seeds set in their yellow embroidery. (When I came to know Keats' 'Ode to Autumn' and the Ingres women in his 'Turkish Bath,' they became again the languid airs and shapes of my childhood summers.)

Kate Simon's independence of spirit asserted itself early. At thirteen, after a spectacular quarrel with her father over her refusal to spend four hours a day practicing piano, she became virtually self-supporting: "My boundaries of school, library, movies, and home had become too tight, like outgrown shoes," she writes in *A Wider World*. "Packing a bundle of fear, courage, and practiced stubbornness, I was readying for exploration." Meanwhile, however, there was high school and college, through which she supported herself with a variety of jobs. Graduating from New York City's then tuition-free Hunter College in the depths of the Great Depression when the lists for English teaching appointments were closed, Simon worked as a secretary for the Book of the Month Club, on a house organ for a printing company, and as a general assistant at *Publishers Weekly*. She began her writing career with book reviews for the *New Republic* and the *Nation* and more or less stumbled into travel writing when a friend showed her a guidebook to expensive London restaurants. The idea occurred to her to write a guide to inexpensive New York eating places and grew at last into her first book, *New York Places and Pleasures*.

The volume was an immediate success and has since gone through several editions. Gerald Gottlieb hailed it in the *New York Herald Tribune Book Review* as "cheerful, democratic, enterprising, engaging, ingenious, romantic and altogether unhackneyed." Competing with many other guides to New York, Simon's book stood out for both its readability and its commonsense recommendations—qualities that have made her subsequent travel guides equally successful. Writing on New York she emphasized the dizzying pace of life—"The writer on New York City writes on swiftly rushing waters"—but this is not an impressionistic essay. The book begins with a history of the city, proceeds to practical advice on transportation, places to visit, shopping, dining, entertainment, and ends with an appendix—an alphabetical list of addresses for everything from organically grown Adzuki beans to Zithers. Simon delighted in exploring ethnic neighborhoods and seeking out obscure but colorful spots that tourists usually miss. In the United States or abroad, she made a point of talking to people and communicating to her readers the human character of a neighborhood or a city. In her third book, *New York*, a collection of Andreas Feininger's photographs interspersed with her own short pieces, she wrote: "As the city spurs its citizen to quickness, it tempts him to an uneasy tolerance and teaches him, no matter what innate pugnacity, to try to be a peaceable man. For practice it offers him a gratifying set of arenas, a heady alternation of small defeats and the triumph of survival."

With the publication of her second travel book, *Mexico Places and Pleasures*, Simon won J. C. Furnas' personal travel book award— "popularly known as Ulysses," he wrote in the *New York Times Book Review*, "for charm and virtuousity . . . [she is] clearly a lady of common sense and reliable counsels." London, Paris, Rome followed—all well received. The English historian J. H. Plumb hailed her for having made "one of the dullest forms of literature a brilliant work of art." It was not only the cosmopolitan centers, however, that fascinated Simon. She also sought out "the places in between." *England's Green and Pleasant Land* deliberately excludes London and the large industrial cities to concentrate on leisurely exploration of the English countryside, sleepy villages and market towns that tourists rarely visit. Similarly, in *Italy : The Places in Between* she recommended side trips from each of the major tourist centers that bring the traveller to the real heart of Italy—Siena and its environs, Lucca, Viterbo, Gubbio, Mantua. "Whether she is describing Etruscan tombs or an aproned guide flicking dust from a balustrade, she bombards us with details as voluminous as pasta," C. W. Casewit writes in *Book World*, "history, ancient and modern, travel information and, thankfully, personal observation."

Mantua is the scene of Kate Simon's *Renaissance Tapestry*, a departure from her travel writings into pure history. Her subject is the powerful Gonzaga family who ruled the city-state from the mid-fourteenth to the early seventeenth century. Princes, statesmen, and warriors, the family is probably most alive for us in their function as art patrons. Simon used the image of tapestry to show the interweaving of politics, art, and personal history. Castiglione and Machiavelli figure here not as members of the Gonzaga households but as recorders of the spirit of the Italian Renaissance. An amateur painter herself, Simon wrote appreciatively and knowledgeably of Italian art. Regretting only that the book was inadequately illustrated, Herbert Mitgang, in the *New York Times*, praised *A Renaissance Tapestry* : "Delving into the past through paintings, sculpture and tapestries as well as manuscript records, Miss Simon has put her reporting abilities to work, filling in the historical blanks. With great imagination, she dares to interpret characters and events by studying the figures, their weapons, their cruel or handsome faces, their posturings."

The third and final volume of Kate Simon's memoir, *Etchings in an Hourglass*, was published posthumously in the summer of 1990. The book was written after she had learned that she was terminally ill and is a free-ranging narrative, a series of recollections ("the organization is as chaotic as memory usually is," Doris Grumbach wrote in the *New York Times Book Review*) of travel, of friends and love affairs covering the span of her life. It completes the self-portrait of a woman who described herself as "so enamored of life, of its vagaries, its soaring flights and precipitous depths, that I promised myself I would experience everything, stipulating no qualities good or bad, and it has pretty much all happened."

Kate Simon was married twice—to Dr. Stanley Goldman, who died in 1942 and from whom she had a daughter who died in 1954, and to the publisher Robert Simon, from whom she was divorced in 1960. She died at her home in New York City at the age of seventy-seven.

PRINCIPAL WORKS: New York Places and Pleasures, 1959; Mexico Places and Pleasures, 1962; New York (photos by A. Feininger), 1964; Kate Simon's Paris, 1967; Kate Simon's London, 1968; Italy: The Places in Between, 1970; Rome Places and Pleasures, 1972; England's Green and Pleasant Land, 1974; Fifth Avenue: A Very Social History, 1978; Bronx Primitive, 1982; A Wider World, 1986; A Renaissance Tapestry: The Gonzagas of Italy, 1988; Etchings in an Hourglass, 1990.

ABOUT: Contemporary Authors 115, 1985; Simon, K. Bronx Primitive, 1982; Simon, K. A Wider World, 1986. *Periodicals*—Book World April 12, 1970; New York Herald Tribune June 14, 1959; New York Times February 15, 1986; April 5, 1988; February 5, 1990; New York Times Book Review June 2, 1963; May 22,

1982; 02080001 February 23, 1986; April 10, 1988; August 19, 1990. Publishers Weekly May 24, 1982.

SMITH, DAVE (DAVID JEDDIE) (pseudonym SMITH CORNWELL) (December 19, 1942–   ), American poet, short-story writer, novelist, and critic, writes: "My ancestors were Virginians from the area of Lynchburg, but were people who found a need to move their generations into the mountains of West Virginia and Maryland. None seem to have thrived particularly. My grandparents were B&O railroad people in Cumberland, Maryland. The Great Depression drove my mother's parents south to Baltimore where, toward the end of those hard times, my grandfather Cornwell got work, went to night school, and made himself a mustang engineer. In time he took the family to Portsmouth, Virginia. I grew up in the truck farming community of Churchland and around the waterfronts of what is commonly called Tidewater.

"My father was killed in an automobile accident when I was seventeen and my grandmother, the linchpin of the family, died of a heart attack when I was twenty-two. The remaining history of my family is like the exploding down of a milkweed pod. We are a record of self-contained but scarcely managed troubles, an unraveling whose parts occasionally collide as gently as possible. In my own life I have married, engendered three children, lived in six states in twenty years, taught college literature and writing, and eventually found my way back to my home ground. Yet whatever evidence of continuity I sought is in the mind seeking connections, patterns.

"What I have learned is that the patterns in my life are those of my ancestors and seem both deeply sad and inescapable. To be aware of them is to be drawn to what would be glibly called a tradition, yet one wants it to be that, to be a history with significance and lessons and effect. One wants a language to make that awareness live. This is an obligation, a responsibility. All I have written or am likely to write consists of the tale of human obligations—those honored and those not—and their costs. The sweet beauty of life and the wretched recognition of its brevity account for whatever may be said of my subjects, and I need make no further attempt to summarize.

"Of style in my writing, it might be said to be based on the assumption that anyone's life is a series of haphazard events each one of which potentially reveals a common and ultimate reality. This reality is all we want but it seldom grants itself in a single phrase, however memorable.

DAVE SMITH

Rather, it appears to emerge from the trance of cadences that only poetry, and the chanciest, can put in our mouths. This poetry, dramatically constructed, wants to speak the actual-seeming, but always uncommon, dialect of a man urgent with passion impelled by the explicit themes of his time. These would include everything we can call lovelessness—that which is deadly to the human spirit, as is loneliness, ignorance, prejudice, simple malice, and more.

"In short, I have tried to write as one who looked hard and steadily and said a little of the truth in speech directly understandable without exegesis or possession of degrees. But a speech that dignified the art of poetry as much as the lives of its attendants. That I imagine to be the writer's obligation beyond all else. His delight consists of honestly satisfying himself that his effort has been unstinting—for he knows from the start that his only result will be failure. In this, too, he will repeat the shapes of the ancestors and the unborn, trying simply to know what life means that means so utterly much. I have tried to write well enough to earn the trust of each man and woman who knows, but can bear reminding, that our struggle is always and ever for freedom, a thing that may be sung when it cannot be said."

In an interview with Peter Balakian collected in *Local Assays*, Dave Smith speaks candidly and thoughtfully of what region, specifically the South, means to him. Cautious of labels and easy generalizations, he acknowledges only that "to be a Southern writer is merely an accident of birth, though it does reflect certain cultural and aesthetic traditions—either in practice or rejection." But beyond accident is the choice that Smith has made to return to his home ground, Tidewater Virginia. Before making that choice he tested "the limits of what I could do" by living in and writing about other parts of the country, notably the West, in *Goshawk, Antelope*.

Smith grew up in what he calls "a prototypical American family . . . always on the move." The son of Ralph Gerald Smith, a naval engineer, and Catherine (Cornwell) Smith, he was even as a child on intimate terms with men who hunted and loved sports, and he early developed his sense of what in another essay he calls "the community of character, that man or woman in action and in spirit attaining as near as possible to nobility before being ignobly crunched by the adversity that is inescapable." For that reason, perhaps, his mature poetry, as Helen Vendler writes, "dwells on strenuousness and on obliteration—the strenuousness of building, fishing, giving birth; the obliteration of shipwreck, disease, drunkenness, unemployment, death . . . [he is] a heavy poet, serious, burdened, sometimes angry, full of life's effort." In a memory poem, "The Tire Hangs in the Yard," he comes upon a tire which he used as a swing when he was a child, and he sees his whole life as one of "hanging in darkness": "We pass also, and are blind, into the years like trees / holding their scars, half-healed. . . . ":

> Where do they go who once were with us on this
>   dream road,
> who flung themselves like seed under berry-
> black nights, the faces black-clustered,
> who could lean down and tell us
> what love is and mercy . . . .

Memory for Smith evokes profound but not always solemn reflection. The past was a proving ground for the man and for the poet-to-be. In purely personal terms, as expressed in his poem "Roundhouse Voices," it frames itself in a recollection of an uncle, who now lies dead, and who years before had coached him in baseball on the forbidden grounds of a railroad roundhouse:

> In the full glare of sunlight I came here, man-tall but
>   thin
> as a pinstripe, and stood outside the rusted fence
> with its crown of iron thorns while
> the soot cut into our lungs with tiny diamonds.
> I walked through houses with my grain-lovely slugger
> from Louisville that my uncle bought and stood
> in the sun that made its glove soft on my hand
> until I saw my chance to crawl under and get past
> anyone who would demand a badge and a name.

He sneaks into the roundhouse:

The guard hollered that I could get the hell from
　　there quick
when I popped in his face like a thief. All I ever wanted
　　to steal was life and you can't get that easy
in the grind of a railyard.

Now looking at his uncle in his coffin, he wonders "what good did all those hours of coaching
do?" What came of it is that he is a poet and
must look to language to express his grief,
"trying to say back that life . . . words/ that
won't let us be what we wanted, each one / chas-
ing and being chased by dreams in the dark."

The past is also rich with history for Smith,
who is sensitive to his Southern heritage. "I think
what it really means to be a Southern writer," he
told Balakian, "is not so much a matter of geographical orientation but of the immediate and
felt reality of history in a place." Identifying
Walt Whitman as "the greatest American poet
yet," he has written several poems on Civil War
sites and their enduring significance. On the battlefield of Fredericksburg where "The big steel
tourist shield says maybe / fifteen thousand got
it here," he reflects bitterly:

If each finger were a thousand of them
I could clap my hands and be dead
up to my wrists. It was quick
though not so fast as we can do it
now, one bomb, atomic or worse,
the tiny pod slung on wingtip,
high up, an egg cradled
by some rapacious mocking bird.

From his earliest publications Smith has impressed his readers with the distinctiveness of his
poetry, its density and lyrical richness—work,
Vendler writes, "of a man writing dense verse
out of hard moments." Because he packs so
much into the verse, the effect is one of
"wonderfully constructed momentum." More
than one critic has compared his poetry to the
prose of William Faulkner. Among poets he
most admires—besides Whitman—are Gerard
Manley Hopkins (Smith is fond of combining
words and inverting syntax), Robert Penn Warren, Robert Lowell, James Dickey, James
Wright. While it would not be accurate to characterize him as a narrative poet, individual people and their fates figure prominently in his
work, especially the strong, hard-working fishermen of the mid-Atlantic coast. Michael Heffer-
nan, writing in *Commonweal* of his early
volume *The Fisherman's Whore* with its stark
picture of shipwreck and human cannibalism,
noted his "eye for detail and human nuance not
unlike Faulkner's or Robinson Jeffers'."
Cumberland Station impressed Dana Wier, in
the *Hollins Critic*, as "a densely populated book,
a rich presentation of America's people, culture,

and landscape." For Calvin Bedient, however, in
the *Chicago Review*, the poems, though they
showed "a potentiality for greatness," were imprecise and "churn on almost like prose, without
lingering delicacies of ear."

Other critics have faulted some of Smith's
work for haste and "unnecessary ornamentation." Fred Chappell, writing on *In the House
of the Judge* for *Western Humanities Review*,
found the poems "overlaid with a heavy veneer
of false elegance." And Charles Molesworth, reviewing *The Roundhouse Voices* for the *Nation*,
cautioned that although Smith "has a distinctive
style, a subject matter and a gravity of language
and sensibility that is worth our attention," there
is a certain "emotional aphasia" in this volume
"that keeps the poems from enacting any transformation or transcendence." But Bruce Weigl,
in *TriQuarterly*, finds a growing mastery in each
succeeding volume. Of *Goshawk, Antelope*, poems mainly inspired by Smith's residence in the
West, Weigl writes: "What Smith most dramatically demonstrates in this book and what sets
him apart from most of his contemporaries and
elevates his work to the level of national importance is simply his ability to get better and
better."

Smith's novel *Onliness* (its title from a popular
song: "Save my love for sorrow, / I gave you my
onliness, / Come and give me your tomorrow")
has for its central character a none-too-bright giant of a man. He finds work in a garage in a little
backwoods Virginia town where his boss, who
becomes a kind of surrogate father to him, is
fighting to save his rundown shop from local real
estate developers. On the surface *Onliness*, Alan
Bold writes in the *Times Literary Supplement*,
"has all the ingredients of all-American fiction:
the dumb ox, the whore with a heart of gold, the
seductive Southern belle, the isolated garage, the
doomed dream, the token black, the consumer-
oriented fetishism, the obligatory violence." But
underneath, Bold observes, the story is an allegory of innocence and idealism pitted against society's sordid materialism. Tom O'Brien, in the
New York Times Book Review, calls it "a provocative, exuberant, at times hilarious, at times
touching but uneven first novel." Its strengths
are the "extraordinary human riches in this
wrench-and-fender setting of a father-son tale,"
and the way Smith transforms his material "into
the stuff of myth and symbol." Its weaknesses,
according to O'Brien, are its slow pace, strained
narrative voice, and an excess of eccentric characters.

Smith has also published a collection of essays
and reviews, *Local Assays: On Contemporary
American Poetry*. Among the most interesting

pieces here are his comments on the teaching of creative writing, among them: "I try to give my students patience, attention, intensity, honesty, and the lessons of my own experience. . . . Teaching for me is largely a matter of developing an attitude toward experience." Smith began his career as a high school teacher of English and French and football coach in Poquoson, Virginia, just after receiving his B.A. from the University of Virginia in 1965. He taught English as a teaching assistant while working for his M.A. at Southern Illinois University (1969) and at Ohio University from which he received his Ph.D. in 1976. At that time, having already published several volumes of poetry, he began teaching creative writing and directing creative writing programs at the University of Utah (1976–1980), the State University of New York at Binghamton (1980–1981), and the University of Florida (1981–1982). He returned to his native state where since 1982 he has been professor of English at Virginia Commonwealth University. He lives in Richmond. In 1966 he married Deloras Mae Weaver. They have three children. Smith has given lectures and readings at many colleges and universities and received, among other honors, an award from the American Academy and Institute of Arts and Letters (1979), a Guggenheim fellowship (1981), and fellowships in poetry from the National Endowment for the Arts (1976, 1981). He was a finalist for the Pulitzer Prize for two of his volumes—*Goshawk, Antelope*, and *Dream Flights*. Under the pseudonym Smith Cornwell, Smith has published stories, poems, and articles in periodicals including *The Nation, Shenandoah, Southern Review*, and *Prairie Schooner*.

PRINCIPAL WORKS: *Poetry*—Bull Island, 1970; Mean Rufus Throw Down, 1973; The Fisherman's Whore, 1974; Cumberland Station, 1977; Goshawk, Antelope, 1979; Dream Flights, 1981; Homage to Edgar Allan Poe, 1981; In the House of the Judge, 1983; The Roundhouse Voices: Selected and New Poems, 1985. *Fiction*—Onliness, 1981; Southern Delights (short stories), 1984. *Non-fiction prose*—Local Assays, 1985. *As editor*—The Pure Clear Word: Essays on the Poetry of James Wright, 1982.

ABOUT: Contemporary Authors New Revision Series 1, 1981; Contemporary Literary Criticism 22, 1982; 42, 1987; Contemporary Poets, 4th ed., 1985; Dictionary of Literary Biography 5, 1982; Smith, D. Local Assays, 1985; Vendler, H. Part of Nature, Part of Us: Modern American Poets, 1980. *Periodicals*—Chicago Review Autumn 1977; Commonweal August 15, 1975; Georgia Review Spring 1980; Hollins Critic October 1977; Hudson Review Autumn 1981; Nation October 5, 1985; New York Times Book Review November 15, 1981; Poetry August 1982; Sewanee Review Summer 1983; Times Literary Supplement November 27, 1981;

May 22, 1987; TriQuarterly Fall 1985; Western Humanities Review Autumn 1983.

SMITH, DENIS MACK. See **MACK SMITH, DENIS**

*SOUSTER, RAYMOND (pseudonyms JOHN HOLMES and RAYMOND HOLMES) (January 15, 1921–), Canadian poet and novelist, writes: "I was born, the first of two children, to Austin Holmes Souster and Norma Rhodesia Baker Souster, in Toronto, Canada. As all Canadians are immigrants of one generation or another, my grandparents were no exception; my maternal grandmother being born in County Antrim, Ulster, and my paternal great-grandfather in Fenny Stratford, near Stratford-on-Avon, England. My mother and father were both born and raised in Toronto, and met shortly before he went overseas with the Canadian Army in 1916 in World War One. When he returned to Canada in 1920 they were married, and I was the first child to arrive, my brother Kenneth following two years later.

"I attended local public schools in Toronto's Runnymede district, then went on to University of Toronto Schools and Humberside Collegiate Institute, graduating from the latter in 1939. It was at U.T.S. that I first became exposed to poetry in a meaningful way, reading every book of verse in its well-stocked library. That and my already acquired addiction to sandlot baseball were to become two large obsessions in my life, and are still very much a part of me.

"My father had earned a steady but very modest salary as a bank clerk since the age of fifteen. When I graduated from high school it was decided that it was time I began earning my own living. As Canada along with the rest of the world was still deep in the grip of a merciless depression, jobs were scarce, and I considered myself lucky to be accepted as a junior clerk by one of Canada's five Chartered banks. On September 1, 1939, I began work at the bank as news swept through the city that Hitler and his hordes had invaded Poland.

"On September 9 Canada declared war on Germany and recruiting began immediately for the armed forces. The conflict seemed very remote to me, though I hated everything that Hitler and Nazism stood for. However, with my poor eyesight and flat feet I had no illusions about being accepted in any combatant role. Mastering a new job, writing more and more verses, pitching junior sandlot baseball kept me

RAYMOND SOUSTER

from thinking too much about the conflict then raging. So that it wasn't until 1941 that I enlisted as an airman second class in the Royal Canadian Air Force. Being classed as unfit aircrew I was given the choice of three ground trades open at the time, and was sent out of town to train as an equipment assistant, or storekeeper. This in itself was a major event in my life, as I had never been previously away from Toronto for more than a day or two at a time. Upon graduation from Technical Trade School I was posted to an air base at Sydney, Nova Scotia, on Canada's East Coast, where I remained for the next two years. Here I sharpened my skills at poetry in my spare time, writing much and reading even more. A year spent at another air base in neighboring New Brunswick, then a short posting to England and a Yorkshire airdrome, completed my war service. The day the bomb was dropped at Hiroshima I was at Dartmouth, Nova Scotia, as a member of the R.C.A.F.'s Eagle Force of volunteers poised to go to the Far East for the war with Japan. Three short days later I became a civilian again.

"Re-entering the service of the bank that November, I remained working with that institution until my retirement forty-five years later in 1984, spending all that time in the same downtown Toronto location! In 1947 I married Rosalia Lina Geralde, a fellow clerk in my office, and next year we will celebrate our fortieth wedding anniversary.

"Looking back now over the years I have labored at my craft, certain dates, places, publications, activities but above all, people, come to mind and stand out strongly, beginning with my first published poem in the *Toronto Star* of 1935 at the age of fourteen. Five years later came the publication of my first poem in a national magazine, *The Canadian Forum*, and the important encouragement of Earle Birney, still one of my staunch supporters. While stationed in the air force at Sydney in 1942 I became contributing editor of an informal mimeographed semi-monthly called *Direction* which was published without official approval or knowledge, and whose last issue appeared after the war. In the following year I met John Sutherland, Louis Dudek and Irving Layton while on leave in Montreal, a major event in my development as a poet. It was in John Sutherland's *First Statement* magazine that my poem "The Hunter" appeared, marking the beginning of an association which lasted until his untimely death. Nineteen forty-four saw my first appearance in book form in Ryerson Press' anthology of verse, *Unit of Five*. In 1946 John Sutherland's First Statement Press issued my first book, *When We Are Young*, while in 1947 my first commercially published book titled *Go To Sleep, World* appeared through Ryerson Press.

"An important early association beginning in the early fifties was a correspondence with the American poet and editor Cid Corman, of Boston, publisher of *Origin* magazine. Through him I first became aware of a whole new generation of American poets then making their first beginnings. Robert Creeley, Charles Olson and Denise Levertov were the most important influences for me, and when I initiated poetry readings in Toronto not too long afterwards at the Greenwich Gallery (1957), these poets were among those who made the pioneer trip up to Canada. Then in 1964 my most widely circulated book, *The Colour of the Times*, a collected poems up to that time, appeared, for which I received the Governor General's Award for Poetry in English, the Canadian equivalent of the American Pulitzer Prize or National Book Award. Finally, in 1969, after several more books published by Toronto houses, my first book issued by Oberon Press of Ottawa, *So Far So Good*, appeared. Since then they have published fourteen more books of mine in what has become a very rewarding partnership.

"I have earlier mentioned my involvement with the little magazine *Direction* while still in air force blue. In 1952, because I felt very isolated in the literary community of the period, I began editing *Contact*, a mimeographed poetry magazine. That was also the year that the first poetry publication of Contact Press appeared, and I continued to be associated with it over the next decade and a half. In 1957, with the help of Cid Corman, I began a second little magazine of poetry, *Combustion*, to which many American poets contributed poems.

"In 1969 I took part in the formation of the League of Canadian Poets, and was its first elected chairman, serving for four years in this capacity. I am now a Life Member of this vital organization.

"Besides the already-mentioned Governor General's Award for Poetry in English, I have been pleased to receive the President's Award of the University of Western Ontario, the Centennial Medal of Canada, the Canadian Silver Jubilee Medal honoring Queen Elizabeth II, and the City of Toronto Books Award."

A distinguishing feature of the work of the young Canadian poets who emerged just after World War II, according to David Stouck, is that "they were urban-centered, concerned with Canada as a society rather than a landscape." Certainly this is true of the poetry of Raymond Souster, who for more than forty years has lived and worked in Toronto and found his sources of inspiration there. It is a disarmingly simple, "low-key poetry," as he describes it himself, a poetry others have described as one of "understatement and economy." Rejecting so-called "academic" poetry, Souster has opted for a populist voice—the spokesman for plain-talking working people who enjoy jazz, baseball, and sex—"whole-hearted and harmonious sex, the best in Canadian literature," Munro Beattie writes in the *Literary History of Canada*. "I don't want to be known to my fellow workers as a poet," Souster told an interviewer. "I'm more interested in those little moments of truth that occur in the unlikely places, the private places."

In his early work Souster reflected the influences of the poets he most admired—Philip Larkin (who, like him, was urban and a jazz enthusiast), Charles Olson, and William Carlos Williams (who also drew on the towns they lived in—Gloucester, Massachusetts, and Paterson, New Jersey—for their material). Like them he affirms the values of the ordinary and the commonplace in simple lyrics and sharply observed images. In the early 1950s, for example, he wrote "Old Woman in Hospital Eating Breakfast":

> Slowly
> carefully
> painstakingly
> she turns the spoon
> within the open
> end of the egg
>
> And slowly
> carefully

> painstakingly
> lifts the spoon
> to her eagerly-waiting
> mouth.

"Singing small," in critic Mike Doyle's phrase, Souster writes a poetry that one critic has called "Wordsworthian." To the extent that it appears spontaneous, draws on "incidents and situations from common life," and is written in the language of "a man speaking to men," the comparison is appropriate. A representative poem from the mid-1970s is "Queen Anne's Lace":

> It's a kind of flower
> that if you didn't know it
> you'd pass by the rest of your life.
>
> But since it's pointed out
> you'll look for it always,
> even in places
> where you know it can't possibly be.
>
> You will never tire
> of bending over to examine,
> to marvel at this,
> the shyest filigree of wonder
> born among grasses.
>
> You will imagine poems
> as brief, as spare,
> so natural with themselves
> as to take breath away.

The nature that Souster celebrates is refracted through urban eyes and with humor, as in "For the Birds":

> These mornings
> (damn 'em)
> they start coaxing up the dawn
> at 5 AM,
>
> and after all
> that extravagant fanfare
> it either rains
> or is eighty-five in the shade.

Souster has had a lifelong love-hate relationship with his native city, Toronto. Appalled by its urban blight, the omnipresence of drifters, the homeless, drunks, drug addicts, and prostitutes, he is nevertheless fascinated by the spectacle of humanity that the city offers. In "Yonge Street Saturday Night," he writes:

> Except when the theatre crowds engulf the sidewalk
> at nine, at eleven-thirty
> this street is lonely, and a thousand lights
> in a thousand store windows
> wouldn't break her lips into a smile.

He notes the bums, the lovers, and the idle walkers like himself—"walking as though we were honestly going somewhere." They are all seeking

something perhaps that will make us smile
with a strange new happiness,
a lost but recovered joy.

Souster's critics have sometimes detected and objected to a note of didacticism in his work. They find this disturbing, however, only when, as it does at times, his moral earnestness leads to diffuse and careless expression. Hayden Carruth, writing in the *Tamarack Review* in 1965, accused him of sentimentality, haste, and carelessness: "[We] know from his best work that he can manage the poetic line with delicacy and intelligence. But many too many poems move in thumping gait, resulting in a complete loss of tension and of the line-value as the fundamental unit of the poem." But at his best, Carruth continued, Souster writes in "true, simple terms . . . without . . . the least artifice or condescension." George Jonas, in *Saturday Night*, had similar complaints against his didacticism in his political poetry of the late 1960s. Outraged at the American role in Vietnam, for example, Souster sounded an uncharacteristic note of shrillness—"America / your time is running out fast . . . ," he wrote in "Death Chant for Mr. Johnson's America" in 1968. According to Jonas: "This is bad, because Souster's main asset as a poet is not inventiveness of form or profundity of thought, but emotional honesty and integrity. Normally he is not trying to be clever, current or fashionable; he means what he says and makes the reader believe him."

In his strongest poems of political protest Souster writes with sharply focused irony, as in "The Bourgeois Child," of the 1950s:

I might have been a slum child,
I might have learned to swear and steal,
I might have learned to drink and whore.

But I was raised a good bourgeois child
and so it has taken me a little longer.

or in "Money Talks," published in 1962:

Money talks
so they say;

sometimes with the soft
persuasiveness of the pimp,
sometimes with the quick
deep cut of the lash,

but more often than not
when it's finally finished,
it really hasn't said
anything at all.

Souster has published two novels under pseudonyms—as "Raymond Holmes," *The Winter of Time*, and as "John Holmes," *On Target*. Both draw on his wartime experiences.

PRINCIPAL WORKS: The Collected Poems of Raymond Souster, 1940–1986 (5 volumes), 1980–1984; Going the Distance, 1983; Jubilee of Death, 1984; Queen City, 1984; It Takes All Kinds, 1986. *Novels*—(as "Raymond Holmes") The Winter of Time, 1949; (as "John Holmes") On Target, 1972.

ABOUT: Contemporary Authors New Revision Series 13, 1984; Contemporary Literary Criticism 5, 1976; 14, 1980; Contemporary Poets, 4th ed., 1985; Davey, F. Louis Dudek & Raymond Souster, 1980; Geddes, G. and P. Bruce. 15 Canadian Poets plus 5, 1978; Klinck, C. F. (ed.) Literary History of Canada, 1965; Meyer, B. and B. O'Riordan (eds.) In Other Words: Interviews with Fourteen Canadian Writers, 1984; Stouck, D. Major Canadian Writers: A Critical Introduction, 1984; Toye, W. (ed.) Oxford Companion to Canadian Literature, 1983; Whiteman, B. Raymond Souster: A Descriptive Bibliography, 1984. *Periodicals*—Canadian Banker August 1984; Canadian Literature Autumn 1972, Winter 1974; Saturday Night December 1971; Tamarack Review Winter 1965.

SPENCE, JONATHAN D(ERMOT) (August 11, 1936–   ), American sinologist, was born in Surrey, England, the son of Dermot Gordon Chesson Spence and the former Muriel Crailsham. After service in the British army in 1954–1956, he received a bachelor's degree from Cambridge University in 1959—he was a member of Clare College—and a doctorate in history from Yale University in 1965; since then he has taught Chinese history in Yale's history department. He has been full professor since 1971 and is currently the holder of the George Burton Adams chair in history. He has also been chairman of his department as well as of the humanities division at Yale.

Spence's doctoral dissertation, written under the direction of Professors Arthur and Mary Wright, became his first published book, *Ts'ao Yin and the K'ang-hsi Emperor, Bondservant and Master*. This was one of the first Western studies on any aspect of the Ch'ing (Manchu) dynasty's first century. The book deals with the life of the Ch'ing official Ts'ao Yin (1658–1712); as the author writes in his introduction, it "attempts to relate his life to the institutions of his time, and to give equal recognition to those institutions. . . . What is of importance to me is not so much where Ts'ao Yin was on a certain day, or what he felt at a certain time, but what it means when we read in the official Chinese histories that he was a bondservant, a textile commissioner, a salt censor." Beginning with Ts'ao Yin's great-grandfather in the Manchu era of the early seventeenth century, it studies the whole turbulent Ch'ing dynasty; "This was not simply a time for new men, but rather a time for

JONATHAN D. SPENCE

the old men tied to the new; what more admirable in 1675 than to be a Manchu bondservant with a classical Chinese education? This Ts'ao Yin was. . . . He was not one of the great officials of the Ch'ing dynasty, nor even a major figure in the K'ang-hsi reign. His importance lies rather in what the course of his life can tell us about the society in which he lived and the institutional framework within which he operated."

The work received Yale's John Addison Porter Prize in 1965, and as a book was generally favorably reviewed. Yushu Pu, writing in *Library Journal*, called it "a notable work of critical scholarship based on original sources." The reviewer for the *Yale Review* thought that Spence had found "a whole new kind of social mobility in the early Ch'ing dynasty. . . . [His] initial contribution to the field of Chinese history and the study of living institutions will likely be a lasting one."

To Change China: Western Advisers in China 1620-1960 comprises a series of biographical-critical studies of very different men, who are united by the fact that they placed their technical skills at the disposal of the Chinese. "At the beginning of the period" covered, Spence writes in his introduction, "they brought knowledge of the stars and of planetary motion; at the end, they introduced the Chinese to aerial warfare and the mysteries of the atom." He chooses sixteen out of the hundreds of men whose careers are still remembered—astronomers, soldiers and doctors, administrators, translators, engineers, one professional revolutionary organizer— " . . . their cumulative lives have a curious con-

tinuity. They experienced similar excitement and danger, entertained similar hopes, learnt to bear with similar frustrations, and operated with a combination of integrity and deviousness. They bared their own souls and mirrored their own societies in their actions, yet in doing so they highlighted fundamental Chinese values. And they speak to us still, with a shared intensity, about the ambiguities of superiority, and about that indefinable realm where altruism and exploitation meet." Among those whose stories are considered are the seventeenth-century Jesuit missionary-astronomers Adam Schall and Ferdinand Verbiest; the mid-nineteenth-century Protestant missionary-physician Peter Parker; the American military adventurer Frederick Townsend Ward and his British counterpart Charles George "Chinese" Gordon, the latter of whom helped direct the wholesale and appalling destruction of the imperial summer palace in 1860 and helped put down the Christian-inspired Taiping Rebellion in 1863; Mikhail Borodin, the Russian revolutionary who tried vainly to export the principles of the Comintern into China in the 1920s; and Generals Claire Chennault, Joseph Stilwell and Albert Wedemeyer, American commanders in the Sino-Burmese theater during World War II.

John King Fairbank, the dean of American Sinologists, called *To Change China* "a fascinating popular book." Writing in the *New York Review of Books*, he went on to describe the work's theme as "the conflict between Western and Chinese values, specifically between the aims of the foreigners and those of their Chinese employer-advisees, at the same time as they find a common if temporary bond in technology." H. L. Kahn, in the *New York Times Book Review*, called Spence's book "a series of finely wrought mini-memoirs, . . . absorbing, . . . serious historical entertainment at its best."

One of Spence's best-known books is a fascinating literary exercise, *Emperor of China: Self-Portrait of K'ang-hsi*, a successful attempt to fuse the fragmentary writings of the greatest of the Manchu emperors (r. 1661-1722) into an autobiography. The author's purpose in this endeavor, he writes in the introduction, "is to gauge the dimensions of [K'ang-hsi's] mind: what inner resources did he bring to the task of governing China? What did he learn from the world around him, and how did he view his subjects?" Spence divides the book into the five chapters or categories into which K'ang-hsi's thoughts seemed naturally to fall. These are "In Motion," constructed of the emperor's ideas as he moved across his dominions, "and of his awareness of the richness and variety of the country he ruled"; "Ruling," K'ang-hsi's reflections on the im-

mensely complicated task of governing seven-teenth-century China; "Thinking," which "required openness and flexibility," recounts his exuberant curiosity about all forms of learning, his "endless delight in finding out what things were made of and how they worked"; "Growing Old," showing "how closely K'ang-hsi was aware of the body as fallible and how he carried this awareness into an interest in diet, illness, medicine and memory"; and "Sons," with its tone of intrigue and suspicion regarding the heir-apparent and other members of the large imperial family. The last chapter is "Valedictory," being a translation of K'ang-hsi's farewell address to his court in 1717. The main appendix consists of seventeen letters written by the emperor to Ku Wen-hsing, the chief eunuch, in the spring of 1697, a unique sequence of imperial letters written in informal style to a trusted courtier relating traveling details and other experiences.

Emperor of China was widely and favorably reviewed. A. J. Nathan, writing in *Library Journal*, called the translation "masterfully restrained, reflecting as nearly as English can the balance and informal dignity of the Chinese." V. S. Pritchett, in the *New Yorker*, remarked that Spence's "graceful arrangement of the material does not lose the accidental quality of nature. . . . One is left astonished by the sight of a Son of Heaven who for the first time—as far as we know—is fascinated by himself as a man."

"As I was writing about the emperor," Spence revealed in an interview in 1984, "I began to wonder who would be the exact opposite: a poor man—no, a poor woman." His next book, *The Death of Woman Wang*, is an attempt to write Chinese local history, based on his study of documents concerning the county of T'an-ch'eng in the northeastern Chinese province of Shantung during the years 1668 to 1672. "The focus," he explains in his introduction, "is on those who lived below the level of the educated elite: farmers, farm workers, and their wives, who had no bureaucratic connections to help them in times of trouble and no strong lineage organizations to fall back on." Spence studies the "small crises" in the lives of these people—their work on the land, local violence, the struggles of individual women. "I say these crises were 'small,' but that is only true in the context of the overall historical record. To the people actually involved they were of absolute, fatal importance." Spence was obliged to rely upon the sketchy memoirs of a local magistrate and partial accounts of local history. "It is always hard to conjure up from the past the lives of the poor and the forgotten; and the Chinese thoroughness in the spheres of state and county historiography has ironically been accompanied by the nonpreservation of most local

records." He adds a moving coda—very much in the Chinese style—of the meaning for him of the life of this long-forgotten woman: "My reactions to woman Wang have been ambiguous and profound. She has been to me like one of those stones that one sees shimmering through the water at low tide and picks up from the waves almost with regret, knowing that in a few moments the colors suffusing the stone will fade and disappear as the stone dries in the sun. But in this case the colors and veins did not fade; rather they grew sharper as they lay in my hand, and now and again I knew it was the stone itself that was passing on warmth to the living flesh that held it."

Spence's "great achievement," according to Paul Berman in *Harper's*, "is to have revealed something about the literary possibilities of historical scholarship. . . . [His] literary experimentalism could reasonably be said to constitute an avant-garde in the stodgy field of history." T. H. White, writing in the *New Republic*, declared that Spence "shows himself at once historian, detective, and artist. . . . [He] makes history howl. Cutting swatches of trials, episodes, case histories from his materials. Spence bodies forth better than anybody else I have ever read the brutality, cruelty, and horror that underlie modern Chinese history."

Spence's foray into modern Chinese history, *The Gate of Heavenly Peace: The Chinese and Their Revolution, 1895–1980*, is a biographical-critical study of a small number of the thousands of men and women who were caught up in the seemingly endless process of violence and renewal that characterized the Chinese revolution. With his next book he returned to the earlier period of Chinese history he has made his own, *The Memory Palace of Matteo Ricci*, a stirring chronicle of the experiences of Matteo Ricci, S.J., the Italian-born, Portuguese-speaking Jesuit resident/missionary in late Ming-dynasty China, who lived in many parts of the country from 1583 until his death in 1610. He was acquainted with men of great power and learning, was an artist, but is best known for five compositions in Chinese, a language he learned to perfection. These were: a map of the world (1584, 1602); *Treatise on Friendship* (1595); the catechism *True Meaning of the Lord of Heaven* (1603); books 1-6 of Euclid's *Elements of Geometry* (1607); and *Treatise on the Mnemonic Arts* (1596). The last work forms the cornerstone of Spence's book, for Ricci had a phenomenally well-trained memory. "In 1596," the author begins, "Matteo Ricci taught the Chinese how to build a memory palace. He told them that the size of the palace would depend on how much they wanted to remember: the most ambitious

construction would consist of several hundred buildings of all shapes and sizes; 'the more there are the better it will be,' said Ricci, though he added that one did not have to build on a grandiose scale right away. . . . In summarizing his memory system, he explained that these palaces, pavilions, divans, were mental structures to be kept in one's head, not solid objects to be literally constructed out of 'real' materials. . . . The real purpose of all these mental constructs was to provide storage spaces for the myriad concepts that make up the sum of our human knowledge." Spence goes on to describe Ricci's career in China, developing an overall picture of Jesuit and Christian influence in sixteenth- and early seventeenth-century China.

"What [Spence] has actually written," wrote Paul Robinson in the *New York Times Book Review*, "while still centered on Ricci, more nearly resembles the portrait of an age, and it is perhaps as remarkable for its form as its content. It is organized about a series of visual representations—four of them imaginary, four actual pictures—that creates a richly layered and complex impression of Ricci's world, while also introducing us to a conception of memory that categorically sets that world apart from our own."

Something like the reverse of Matteo Ricci's eminently successful travels in China was the fate of John Hu, the subject of Spence's *The Question of Hu*. This is a short and very readable account of a Chinese convert to Christianity, who traveled to Europe in 1722 as a copyist-assistant to Father Foucquet, a Jesuit missionary returning to his homeland after many years in China. Hu's inability to speak any European language and to adjust to European customs led him into many painful, and sometimes ludicrous, situations. His behavior seemed so eccentric to the Parisians that he was committed to Charenton, the notorious hospital for the insane. Hu's "question," when finally addressed in Chinese, was simply, "Why have I been locked up?" But as Angeline Goreau wrote in a very favorable notice in the *New York Times Book Review* : "*The Question of Hu* also addresses the larger question of how we define madness and to what degree the madhouse was the instrument of social control. *The Question of Hu* must also be read as the question of 'who?'—a subtle and complex evocation of the way in which identity is bound up in culture . . . what does it mean to interpret another culture? In the same way that he used Ricci's memory palace as a metaphor for the writing of history, Mr. Spence uses Hu's story to examine the act of 'translation.'"

In 1990 Spence published what has been described as a "monumental new history." This was *The Search for Modern China*, a sweeping but also richly detailed survey of Chinese history from the passing of the Ming dynasty in the early 1600s to the crushing of the democracy movement of June 1989. A recurring theme that Spence traces through those four centuries is the Chinese struggle for a civil society governed by a body of law and separate from autocratic state control. "We can see how often the Chinese people, operating in difficult or even desperate circumstances, seized their own fate and threw themselves against the power of the state," Spence writes in the preface. His book shows how deeply rooted Chinese cultural traditions as well as actions of the ruling classes themselves have frustrated these attempts. His broad perspective, fortified with extensive scholarship and enlivened with profiles of major figures of Chinese history and liberal quotation from popular and classic Chinese literature, won high praise from both Sinologists and general readers. Christopher Lehmann-Haupt in the *New York Times* suggested that *The Search for Modern China* "will undoubtedly become a standard text on the subject." He also emphasized its readability as historical narrative, "always lively, always concrete, always comprehensible, no matter how complex the issue." In the *New York Review of Books* John K. Fairbank wrote that this huge book (close to 900 pages) "is given coherence by the fact that Professor Spence himself, as a humanist concerned with the particular impressions and motives of different people, has time after time worked his way down to the documentary ground floor of history. As a writer of great literary skill, he constructs a narrative that leaves out inconsequential names and details while conveying the mood of the times and the concerns of both the Chinese elite and the public."

Spence has received several awards and prizes, including the Christopher Award (1975), Yale University's DeVane Teaching Medal (1978), the *Los Angeles Times* Book Award (1982), and the Vursell Prize of the American Academy and Institute of Arts and Letters (1983). He was a Guggenheim fellow in 1979–1980 and is a member of the American Academy of Arts and Sciences, the Association of Asian Studies, and the American Historical Association.

PRINCIPAL WORKS: Ts'ao Yin and the K'ang-hsi Emperor, 1966; To Change China, 1969; Emperor of China, 1974; The Death of Woman Wang, 1978; The Gate of Heavenly Peace, 1981; The Memory Palace of Matteo Ricci, 1984; The Question of Hu 1989; The Search for Modern China, 1990. *As editor*—Ch'ing shih Wen t,

1965–1973; (with John E. Wills, Jr.) From Ming to Ch'ing: Conquest, Region, and Continuity in Seventeenth-Century China, 1979.

ABOUT: Contemporary Authors 21–24, 1977; Who's Who in America 1989–1990. *Periodicals*—America November 16, 1974; February 9, 1985; American Historical Review July 1967, June 1979, June 1980; Atlantic June 1974; Book World August 17, 1969; Choice July 1967, September 1969, October 1974, December 1978, December 1979, February 1982, June 1985; Christian Science Monitor September 14, 1978; March 12, 1979; November 9, 1981; Commonweal October 19, 1984; Harper's August 1978; Library Journal November 15, 1966; May 15, 1969; November 1, 1974; June 1, 1979; September 15, 1981; December 1984; Nation September 2, 1978; December 19, 1981; December 29, 1984; New Republic June 3, 1978; October 14, 1981; June 10, 1985; New Statesman October 24, 1969; August 4, 1978; New York Review of Books June 5, 1969; November 28, 1974; May 18, 1978; February 18, 1982; June 13, 1985; New York Times May 10, 1990; May 31, 1990; New York Times Book Review July 13, 1969; May 26, 1974; June 11, 1978; October 18, 1981; November 25, 1984; December 18, 1988; May 13, 1990; New Yorker November 4, 1974; June 5, 1978; June 17, 1985; Newsweek June 24, 1974; May 22, 1978; November 9, 1981; Quill & Quire February 1985; Saturday Review October 1981; Times Literary Supplement March 16, 1967; October 20, 1978; December 7, 1979; September 27, 1985; November 24, 1989; Virginia Quarterly Review Spring 1979; Yale Alumni Magazine October 1984; Yale Review March 1967, October 1969, Spring 1979, Summer 1982.

SPINRAD, NORMAN (RICHARD) (September 15, 1940–), American author of science-fiction novels and short stories, writes: "I was born in New York City in 1940, grew up in the Bronx, attended the Bronx High School of Science, graduated CCNY in 1961, saw my first publication in 1963, had my last wage-slave job in 1965, and have been a full-time writer ever since.

"Upon graduation from college and acceptance at Fordham Law School, I tripped around Mexico for a couple of months and returned with the vision and resolution that I would be a writer, period. Instead of going to law school, I rented a cheap roach-infested beatnik pad in the East Village, and wrote, paying the rent by working part-time in a custom leather shop and a custom carpentry shop owned by supportive friends. I survived a whole month as a Welfare Investigator in Bedford-Stuyvesant and half a year as a literary agent.

"I split to California in 1966, moved to London in 1969, where my novel *Bug Jack Barron* and my own person were denounced in Parliament as 'degenerate,' returned to Los Angeles in

NORMAN SPINRAD

1969. In the period 1969–1972, in addition to writing fiction, I was a mainstay of the underground press as a political writer and film-reviewer in the *Los Angeles Free Press* and the *Los Angeles Staff*, where I got to meet all too many members of the Manson Family, became embroiled in the Eldridge Cleaver–Timothy Leary affair, and participated in a publishing coup against the porn mafia. During this period, I also briefly had a radio phone show on KPFK. I moved back to New York in 1975, returned to Los Angeles in 1983, sang on a single recorded in Paris in between, and now here I am.

"What does all this have to do with the fact that the core of my work is science fiction? What indeed? Most 'science-fiction writers' segue into writing science fiction out of their adolescent involvement in the science-fiction subculture, but I arrived at wherever I am along an entirely different vector. Early on, I was as deeply influenced by Norman Mailer, William Burroughs, Thomas Pynchon, and Henry Miller as by Theodore Sturgeon, Alfred Bester, and Philip K. Dick. If I was part of any subculture it was the bohemian Greenwich Village subculture, and later on its mass market transmogrification in the Counterculture.

"It was my vision from the very outset that science fiction, being at least theoretically the fiction of the infinite possible by definition, had within it the possibilities for literature on the highest possible level, and this is the goal I have pursued within the form ever since.

"It is the synergetic convergence between these two strains of influence, between the visionary impulse of science fiction and the hipster angle of vision, between the analytical extrapolation of science fiction and the Dionysian stream of American letters, between the Bronx High School of Science and the East Village and the Haight, between the things of the intellect and the things of the spirit, which, I suppose, has given my fiction what uniqueness it has. As science fiction, it is uncharacteristically experimental in form and style, uncharacteristically political, uncharacteristically sexual, uncharacteristically somewhat mystical in places. As so-called 'mainstream fiction,' it is peculiarly future-oriented, scientifically and technologically literate, and concerned thematically with macro-politics.

"Yes, I do write science fiction, am quite conversant with the literary history of the genre, teach science-fiction writing, and have written hundreds of thousands of words of criticism on the subject. But I also feel that I am writing in another American tradition as well, one that runs from William James, through Walt Whitman, Henry Miller, early Pynchon and some Mailer, on into its golden age in the late 1950s and early 1960s with the Beats like William Burroughs and Jack Kerouac, seeming to peter out in Ken Kesey, Richard Farina, and *Easy Rider*.

"What this tradition really represents and why it is in its current critical and popular eclipse would take far more space than is alotted for this essay to explicate. But I do feel that to the limits of my ability I am carrying it forth too. And that its next evolutionary step must come through science fiction. (See *Child of Fortune*.)

"We have multiplied our senses, gotten our hands on the fire of the gods, seen deeply into our own psyches, taken our first step out into the universe, fractured all previous cultural patterns, polluted the biosphere, and unleashed the chaos of our own sexuality. Soon we will be the masters of our own DNA, venture out into space, learn whether or not we are alone in the galaxy, and/or exterminate life on this planet. We are passing through what is not merely the greatest transformation crisis in the history of our species but what must be the most crucial confrontation between spirit and science, universe and sentience, that sapient species anywhere must negotiate on their way to long-term stability.

"That's why I write science fiction.

"These days, what else is there?"

For some years now Norman Spinrad has been engaged in a campaign to correct and clarify the definition of what is commonly called "science fiction." One of its foremost contemporary practitioners, he is also one of its most thoughtful and articulate critics. In popular usage "science fiction" is simply a publisher's trade designation, a loose term for a literature of fantasy that draws upon the technology of modern science for some of its frame of reference. In fact, science fiction—or at least the science fiction of the so-called "New Wave," launched in England by Michael Moorcock, J. G. Ballard, and others—aims to be a new form of the experimental modern novel, free of the conventions that have rendered so much science fiction mere hack or pulp writing. Not only does the New Wave seek to subvert a traditional literary genre by shunning conventional narrative, plot, dialogue, and introducing hitherto taboo subjects like explicit sex and violence, but it also attempts to confront the most serious and disturbing political and social issues of the times with techniques of satire and black humor. Because science fiction gives us, in Spinrad's words, "an illusion of verisimilitude around imaginary content," it is in no substantial way different from other good fiction. Indeed, in its best examples, science fiction—or "speculative fiction" as Spinrad prefers to call it—"transcends other great literature. Science fiction has the potential not merely to describe existing realities, but actually to *create* realities . . . as a style of consciousness, a philosophy of the nature of reality, a series of camera-angles on the universe" ("Rubber Sciences").

Whether Spinrad has achieved in his own writings the lofty goals he assigns to science fiction remains a matter for critical debate. His earliest works were admired for their inventiveness but remained within the tradition. *The Solarians*, for example, was a "space opera" about a galactic war between humanity and a ruthless enemy from another planet. *Agent of Chaos* is another treatment of the threatened destruction of planet earth by enemies in outer space. Both novels attracted attention, however, for their implicit political commentary, much of it reflecting the unrest of the 1960s. It was a more lurid and controversial book, however, that brought Spinrad wider recognition, not all of it favorable—*The Men in the Jungle*. The central character of this novel is a revolutionary who finds a new planet to rule—Sangre—which, as its name suggests, is a nightmare society where cannibalism, torture, and every other form of savagery are practiced (and described in explicit detail). Reviewers for the most part agreed that Spinrad was not exploiting violence for its own sake but none too thinly alluding to the atrocities of the Vietnam War. "The action is fast, bloody, sexy, and compelling," Robert W. Haseltine wrote in *Library Journal*. "The theme seems to be that, given an environmental setting where the finer parts of man's character cannot develop, the sado-masochist will be in the fore." Haseltine found the novel "very well done" of its kind. But Jan Slavin, in *Luna Monthly*, was uncertain as to whether Spinrad was satirizing sexsadism books or seriously condemning contemporary violence: "Perhaps he is trying to hold up a mirror to the great amount of violence, perversion and even blood-lust that is present in the world today. But that mirror seems warped, and rather than reflecting or shocking into action . . . it only disgusts, or titillates, depending on your sensibilities."

Spinrad's first widely noticed novel was *Bug Jack Barron*, which outraged some Establishment figures in both Britain and the United States for its bold attack on media domination, but impressed other readers with its wit and chilling picture of the imminent dangers of television. Jack Barron is a TV talk show host on a call-in show (Spinrad's imaginary "videophones" of 1969 foreshadowed some uncomfortable realities of the 1980s). He becomes involved with a multibillionaire who is determined to assure his immortality with what appears to be cryogenics but actually involves organ transplants from children. The American scene of the very near future that is depicted here is wildly absurd but also chillingly close to reality in its implications. For the *Times Literary Supplement*'s reviewer, "Mr. Spinrad writes with verve and has a lively ear for current idiom. His 'political science fiction' has a deadly plausibility." *Bug Jack Barron* won Spinrad a Hugo nomination in 1970. The same year he received another Hugo nomination for a teleplay, "The Doomsday Machine" that he wrote for "Star Trek."

Probably the best known of Spinrad's novels to this day is *The Iron Dream*, which received a National Book Award nomination in 1973. It is daring in its imaginative conception and, in the judgment of many reviewers, brilliantly brought off. H. Bruce Franklin, writing in *Book World*, called it "a highwater mark of New Wave science fiction." *The Iron Dream* is an absolutely straight-faced send-up of a sciencefiction novel written by one Adolf Hitler, "Lord of the Swastika." It begins with a list of other science-fiction titles by Hitler, including "The Master Race" and "Tomorrow the World", and a biographical introduction which up to a point is factually correct. But this Adolf Hitler, we learn, emigrated to New York in 1919, learned English, supported himself as a sidewalk artist until he became a successful illustrator for sciencefiction magazines. From 1935 to his death in 1953 he wrote novels, the most successful of which was "Lord of the Swastika". The novel begins by introducing its superman hero, Feric

Jaggar, a blue-eyed blond Aryan: "Feric Jaggar looked every inch the genotypically pure human that he in fact was. . . . The sight of Feric put mutants and mongrels in their place, and for the most part they kept to it." Later, when he achieves power, he is greeted with salutes and calls of "Hail Jaggar!" The story is full of brutal detail, violence, skull and bone smashing, as he conquers the world, scours his enemies (the Zinds) from the face of the earth, and prepares to conquer outer space. At the end of the novel there is an Afterword by a Professor Homer Whipple, a mock scholarly-critical discussion of the book which, we are told, won the Hugo award as the best science-fiction novel of 1954. The book has had a great impact on American society, Whipple notes—the swastika motif has been widely adopted and groups like the Christian Anti-Communist Legion, motorcycle gangs, and the American Knights of Bushido are being organized to imitate Jaggar's forces. Whipple is uneasy about this tremendous success: "There is admittedly a certain raw power in many passages of the novel, but this seems more the result of psychopathology than of conscious, controlled literary craftsmanship." Nevertheless even he is impressed with its "grand guignol pageantry." Although he finally dismisses the whole thing as irrational ("Obviously, such a mass national psychosis could never occur in the real world"), the reader is left with the chilling realization that such horrors can happen in the real world. As Franklin writes: "At the very least, *The Iron Dream* must be admired as a remarkable tour de force, a dazzling display of ingenuity and originality. But it is much more than that, for it forces us to confront elements of fascism within our own culture low and high."

Franklin concludes his review of *The Iron Dream*, written in 1982 when the novel was reissued, with the observation: "Unhappily, *The Iron Dream* seems at least as timely today as it did a decade ago." The question of Spinrad's timeliness has always loomed large. Much of his work, including a number of highly praised short stories, was a product of the 1960s and 1970s, and the blander climate of the 1980s has not proved as stimulating to Spinrad. *The Void Captain's Tale*, involving an interstellar flight piloted by a woman who is seeking "the ultimate experience"—union with the universe—is constructed on several levels of meaning and introduces a new synthetic language not unlike Anthony Burgess' invented *patois* in *A Clockwork Orange*. For Howard Waldrop in *Book World*, this is Spinrad's "best book" and a sign of his growing maturity as a novelist. Other readers, however, found it obscure. Gerald Jonas, in the *New York Times Book Review*, wrote that "this is science fiction as self-conscious art—perhaps 'artifice' would be a better word. . . . As with all artifice, *The Void Captain's Tale* depends on the cooperation of the audience for its effects." *Child of Fortune* returns to the interstellar scene of *The Void Captain's Tale* and again uses the polyglot language he had introduced in the earlier novel. His central character is again a young woman whose nervous sensibilities are connected with her sexual experiences in very bizarre ways. Gerald Jonas was unreservedly enthusiastic in his review. Though he judged the opening chapters—in which the heroine explores the wonders of several planets—rather hard going, once into the story he found it "marvelous," especially in its evocation of a gigantic blooming forest. Tom Easton, in *Analog Science Fiction/Science Fact*, described *Child of Fortune* as a picaresque novel "that may well be science fiction's equivalent of Fielding's *Tom Jones*, a long, witty, wonderful tale of maturation." In this novel, he feels, Spinrad has truly come into his own as an "honored elder" of the storyteller's tribe.

Spinrad's non-fiction includes a collection of short pieces he wrote for magazines in the 1960s, *Fragments of America*—"different-but-somehow-connected fragments of that confused and kaleidoscopic mosaic that is modern American civilization," as he described them in his introduction. His writings on science fiction include the essay "Robber Sciences," which is included in *The Craft of Science Fiction*, edited by Reginald Bretnor (1976), another essay on the filming of John Brunner's *Stand on Zanzibar* in *SF: The Other Side of Realism*, edited by T. D. Clareson (1971), and his introductions to two science-fiction anthologies which he edited—*The New Tomorrows* (1971) and *Modern Science Fiction* (1974).

PRINCIPAL WORKS: *Novels*—The Solarians, 1966; The Men in the Jungle, 1967; Agent of Chaos, 1967; Bug Jack Barron, 1969; The Iron Dream, 1972; Passing through the Flame, 1975; Riding the Torch, 1978; A World Between, 1979; The Void Captain's Tale, 1983; Child of Fortune, 1986; Little Heroes, 1987. *Collected short stories*—The Last Hurrah of the Golden Horde, 1970; No Direction Home, 1976; The Star Spangled Future, 1979. *Non-fiction*—Fragments of America, 1970; Staying Alive: A Writers' Guide, 1983; Other Americans, 1988.

ABOUT: Contemporary Authors New Revision Series 20, 1987; Contemporary Literary Criticism 46, 1988; Dictionary of Literary Biography 8, 1981; Magill, F. N. (ed.) Survey of Science Fiction Literature 1, 3, 1979; Smith, C. C. (ed.) Twentieth-Century Science Fiction Writers, 2d ed., 1986. *Periodicals*—Analog Science Fiction/Science Fact December 1985; Book World July 25, 1982; February 27, 1983; Library Journal March 1, 1967; Luna Monthly July 1970; New York Times Book Review May 22, 1983; September 8, 1985; Publishers Weekly January 2, 1981; Times Literary Supplement March 26, 1970.

STANDER, SIEGFRIED (August 26, 1935–), South African novelist and journalist, writes: "Are there, after all, dark waves that influence the lives of the unborn? I was born in the Karoo (a Khoi-Khoin word meaning, roughly, 'The Dry Place'), the arid plateau that guards the southern entry to Africa. But at the age of two months, so I am told, I was taken over the mountains to the sea. By choice I have spent most of my life living close to the ocean, yet the greater part of my work has been set in desert landscapes.

"That ambivalence is possibly reflected in my work. I am of part Afrikaner descent—a mixture of German and Dutch and Huguenot and God knows what else—and part English and Scottish. But Africa is all I know. I write in English, yet my subject matter more often than not is the pride and prejudice of the Afrikaner, an attitude of mind for which I have understanding and even sympathy, but very little patience. Perhaps what I'm after is to try to explain the contradictions of being what I am, where I am. It is not easy to judge.

"However, all this seems a somewhat portentous analysis of a writing career that has been devoted essentially to the telling of stories. There are a lot of stories to be told about this part of Africa. I hope to live to tell a few more.

"My parents, both teachers, chose, for reasons still obscure to me, to leave their home in the hills and forests of the Outeniqualand to make their lives for almost a quarter of a century in a small Karoo hamlet. The region was primitive and poor then, but my sisters and I were privileged children, relatively sheltered from the hardships our neighbours endured. My father died when I was seven and we left the Karoo: for ever, as it turned out. Some impressions must have stuck, however, for I have used a background of deprival in novels as stories with other settings. Oddly, I have never written about the Karoo; the desert I 'adopted' is the Kalahari, and I only came to know it after I met my wife, Jo, who comes from those parts.

"I can fairly claim that writing was my earliest ambition. I started my first novel while still at school (it was hopelessly immature, needless to say) and although I studied law for a time my persistent dream was to become a writer. I achieved it by way of journalism and in spite of

SIEGFRIED STANDER

contrary evidence still believe this to be the finest school for teaching precision of language, brevity of style and accuracy of observation. I was fortunate enough to win the C.N.A. [Central News Agency] Literary Award with my first (adult) novel and achieved modest critical success with this and subsequent books. I left journalism in 1969 to give my time to full-time writing. Although fiction is my first preference I have had to turn to producing works of nonfiction from time to time in order to make a living.

"I have travelled extensively in Southern Africa, but not, to my regret, very widely elsewhere. My country is a land in conflict and it is an unhappy fact that conflict and confrontation are the raw materials of a writer's craft. However, I have tried, within my limits, to remain objective about South Africa's problems and have always shied away from propaganda and 'statements.' Proselytism bores me; I see no reason to inflict boredom on others."

———

Siegfried Stander characterizes his work as essentially "the telling of stories," and William Plomer, the South African–born English novelist, called him "a compulsive story teller." The stories he tells in a lean and unadorned prose resonate with the land itself—especially the rugged, dangerous, and still wild bush and desert of the Kalahari where men and animals alike struggle for survival. Born in Rietbron, Cape Province, to Adam Johannes and Janet Selina (Derbyshire) Stander, Siegfried Stander went to

high school in Port Elizabeth and attended the University of South Africa as an extramural student from 1952 to 1954. From 1955 until 1969 he worked as a journalist in Port Elizabeth and in Cape Town, except for one year, 1959, when he farmed in Bechuanaland. He married Jo Heydenreich, a medical practitioner, in 1957. They have two children and make their home in Port Elizabeth.

In 1973 a reviewer of Stander's *Leopard in the Sun* in the *Times Literary Supplement* complained of "his tame response to the human situation in his country" and faulted him for writing "escapist" fiction, adventure stories which do not confront South Africa's single most critical problem, apartheid. In fact, Stander's novels, especially his recent work, reflect deep sensitivity to this issue, but they do so in an oblique way. Nature conditions the lives and actions of his characters. In nature both humans and animals are tested in ways that reflect the tragic dilemmas of his country.

The first novel by which Stander became known to an international readership was *The Horse*, the story of a magnificent white stallion orphaned as a colt and adopted and nurtured by a zebra mare who had lost her own foal. The horse becomes the leader of the zebra herd but is pursued to his death by a white ivory hunter. The book was marketed to a juvenile as well as an adult public and indeed in its simple, forthright narrative it appeals to young readers. But as Alice McCahill recognized in her review in *Best Sellers, The Horse* is more than a simple animal tale: "It is about courage and nobility and the indefinable quality that makes for trust and leadership. It is about the wild creatures of the world, about their relationship to man, and their wonderful, mysterious place in God's universe." Reviewers of *The Horse* were impressed with Stander's acute understanding of animal behavior. There is no sentimentalizing or anthropomorphizing in the novel. "There is hardly a false or strained detail," a *Times Literary Supplement* reviewer wrote. "Most appealing is his determination *not* to make animal life carry a heavy or obvious weight of human meaningfulness."

Although wild animals figure importantly in a number of his other novels, Stander has focused more intensely on human characters in subsequent novels. *The Fortress* is the first of a projected trilogy about colonial South Africa. It is set in German West Africa in 1914 where two men come into conflict. One is a middle-aged, peace-loving engineer, the district manager, married to a younger wife who is bored and unhappy in her bleak surroundings. The other is a younger Prussian officer, arrogant and hot-tempered, also unhappily married, who comes to the fortress in charge of frontier defense. Conflict between them is inevitable, a clash that reflects not only their personal differences but the ideological divisions of colonialism. Forced to become allies to defend the region against the British, the men lead a camel patrol through the Kalahari. They encounter Boer parties under Jan Niemand's leadership, Bushmen and Hottentot warriors, and finally the British in an action-packed adventure story. Published five years later, *Flight from the Hunter* is set in contemporary times and though also full of action and violence, it concentrates more narrowly on the psychology of its central character, Leroux, a successful Canadian animal photographer who has come to South Africa to photograph wild animals. While flying over the bush with his young pilot and a girl he has picked up in a bar the night before, they are shot down by poachers. The pilot is killed and Leroux and the girl are taken hostage. Self-confident of his macho image, Leroux soon discovers his helplessness, even while his captors, in their desperate attempt to escape, are simultaneously discovering their own weaknesses. At the violent climax Leroux finds himself a coward, having failed to save the life of a black native who has helped him. He has also, in some way he dimly begins to perceive, failed the girl, and he leaves Africa realizing "that there are more ways of betrayal than the Judas act of leaving a man to his death." "It is one of those fate-has-linked-us-together books," the *New York Times Book Review*'s "Newgate Calendar" wrote: "Stander does not work in black-and-white patterns; his photographer is like most of us—part coward, part hero. Very well done."

The most ambitious of Stander's novels to date is *Into the Winter*. Here he confronts the issue of apartheid in unmistakable terms. "On its simplest level," Alan Cowell wrote in the *New York Times Book Review*, "*Into the Winter* is about race, specifically the troubled relationship between emergent black Africa and white resistance, or indifference, to the new order." Pitted against each other at the outset are a young black game warden, educated at the London School of Economics and uneasily adjusting himself to the power of a newly established black-ruled country bordering on still-white South Africa, and an old white Afrikaner cattle drover whom he arrests for an accidental killing. In the course of their arduous journey out of the bush the two men develop a curious bond that transcends their racial and cultural differences. The black man protects his prisoner from a black "special police" force, and the white man protects him from a group of belligerent whites at a bar. The

story, however, finds deeper significance in a parallel journey of an aged bull elephant toward his death place and a buffalo who follows him out of some mysterious instinct of fellowship. Animals and men are creatures of the same nature. Stander writes:

> Although the two old animals, the elephant and the buffalo, had already travelled many miles together, there was nothing in their mutual bearing to indicate companionship. They grazed separately, often drank separately and even on the march were seldom close together. The buffalo would trudge along, head swinging, eyes fixed short-sightedly on the ground in front of him, far over on the flank. The elephant, for his part, seemed unaware of the existence of the other. They were comrades only in the sense that they had chosen not, for the present, to be adversaries.

There is no sentimentally happy conclusion to this journey for either man or beast, and the novel offers no easy answers to the tragic problems it explores; but as Cowell points out, it provokes "disturbing questions" and examines them with candor and sympathy.

Stander collaborated on three novels with the late Dr. Christiaan Barnard, the internationally famous surgeon who performed the first heart transplant in 1967. Reviewers found these typically "doctor books" with much clinical detail and conventional plotting. One of them, *The Unwanted,* however, again pairs two men, both brilliant doctors and researchers, friends from childhood. One is a white South African heart surgeon, the other a "colored" geneticist whose family had been in service to the white man's family. They establish a bond of friendship and professional collaboration, but must work against a multitude of subtle and overt pressures, including apartheid.

PRINCIPAL WORKS: *Novels*—This Desert Place, 1961; The Emptiness of the Plains, 1963; Strangers, 1965; The Journeys of Josephine, 1968; The Horse, 1968; The Fortress, 1972; Leopard in the Sun, 1973; Flight from the Hunter, 1977; Into the Winter, 1983; (with C. Barnard) The Unwanted, 1974; In the Night Season, 1978; The Faith, 1984. *Non-fiction*—Tree of Life, 1983; Like the Wind, 1985; The Watering-place, 1987.

ABOUT: Contemporary Authors New Revision Series 19, 1987. *Periodicals*—Best Sellers March 1, 1969. New York Times Book Review March 11, 1973; November 16, 1975; November 27, 1977; June 25, 1978; February 3, 1985; Times Literary Supplement May 18, 1973; March 19, 1976; April 29, 1977.

STEEL, RONALD (LEWIS) (March 25, 1931–), American political scientist and biographer, writes: "Why people become writers is

RONALD STEEL

probably as much of a mystery as why they do anything else. One reason might be to try to make sense of the world—at least for oneself. And also to try to make sense of oneself. I think that applies to me.

"I grew up amidst cornfields in northern Illinois feeling, like many children, that I didn't quite belong where I was, but without any sense of where I might properly fit. I did the usual things boys do in small towns: rode my bicycle, trapped small animals, went to basketball games. I did a lot of reading, but mostly in secret so that I wouldn't be considered 'bookish' by regular guys. I was also aware, as one of the few Jews in a very small farm town, that this was considered an extremely odd and exotic thing to be—though beyond that I didn't know what to make of it.

"Like a lot of people who grow up in small towns, I thought it was a place to escape from when one grew up. And I did. I lived in New York and Paris and London, and in a dozen other places across the globe that for a time I called home. All those places shaped me in one way or another. But somewhere along the way I also stopped trying to escape from the small town. Confinement, I've come to think, lies more in the head than in the place, and I no longer think it a sign of moral (or any other kind of) superiority to live in a city rather than a village.

"I've learned that there are many different ways to live, and I've lived some of them. I've been a student, a soldier, a wanderer, a house-sitter, a translator, a diplomat, an editor, a journalist, and most recently, a college professor. Al-

though the combination looks a bit odd on paper, somehow for me they all seem to fit together neatly, though assuredly not inevitably. A different decision here or there could, I realize, have taken me down quite different paths. Although maybe the choice is not so free as I imagine, and we make the decisions we do because of some untinkerable inner mechanism.

"For example, early in the 1970s I rather casually agreed, at a publisher's urging, to write a book about Walter Lippmann, the nation's leading political columnist and public philosopher. I thought this would give me a chance to comment on foreign policy, as I had in two earlier books written mostly in Europe, from a somewhat different and more American angle.

"What I hadn't counted on was that I would be drawn deeply into the mystery of my subject's personality, that I would become absorbed by American history (about which I was abysmally ignorant), and that I would spend nearly a decade trying to unravel the links between personality and politics. I became a biographer, which I had never quite intended, a scholar who burrowed for years in the archives of a great library, and most surprising of all, a professor—a career I had never seriously considered since leaving graduate school in a huff.

"Was all this accidental? Had I not chosen to writen about Lippmann, or someone like him, would I have gone off to Hollywood to write screenplays, or to Washington to read urgent cables and write secret memos? Perhaps for a time. There are so many different ways to live, for a time. But I think I wrote the kind of book I did— which was not at all the one I intended—because of some need or compulsion I was hardly aware of myself. A writer's life may determine his choice of material, but sometimes it is the other way around as well.

"Now I no longer think of myself as a journalist, as I once did, but as a college professor and a writer who has the rare luxury to pursue his interests. Being a writer is such a curious and privileged, demanding and also rewarding, career that one does it and is glad for the opportunity to do so. This is especially true if one is so fortunate as to be able to do his work, as writers in so many countries are not, without fear of censor, reprimand or punishment—except, of course, from one's readers."

———

Ronald Steel was born in Morris, Illinois. He graduated from Northwestern University in 1953, did graduate study for a short time at the Sorbonne, and earned a master's degree in political science from Harvard University in 1955. After a year as vice-consul in the U.S. Foreign Service (1957–1958) and a stint as editor for Scholastic Magazines in New York City (1959–1962), Steel became a full-time writer.

His first book, *The End of Alliance: America and the Future of Europe* explored the inconsistency and obsolescence of U.S. foreign policy, in particular its rigid anti-Sovietism, and stated the case for its drastic revision. In his introduction, Steel writes: "In . . . this book I have tried to assess Europe's new resistance to America, not to praise it; to discuss the collapse of the old alliances, not to bemoan it. In questioning entrenched assumptions, one is often forced to play the devil's advocate, a role which, I trust, is not quite the same as being that advocate." In six chapters, *The End of Alliance* treats the erosion of the postwar consensus, the functional limits of the Atlantic alliance, the problem of a divided Germany, and the changing nature of the U.S.-U.S.S.R. superpower rivalry. The book was called "absolutely first-rate" by T. H. White. "A major work of analysis and study—fresh, hard, and immensely valuable as a contribution to the re-examination of American diplomatic purpose." John Freeman concurred: "It is not necessary to agree with all the conclusions of this brilliant little essay to appreciate Mr. Steel's quality. At times he pushes his arguments, as it seems to me, too far—ingeniously revealing trends or hazards and then constructing a further argument upon them as if they were present facts. But that is the occupational fallibility of the committed advocate. *End of Alliance* establishes Mr. Steel as a most quick-witted and pungent pamphleteer. A lot of what he writes is sensible, and surprisingly little of it is yet spoken about in polite company."

Pax Americana continued Steel's mordant analysis of U.S. foreign policy; in general it examines how the American empire came about, how it is maintained, why it appears justified to many Americans, and what the price of its pursuit might be. The book's title in particular, the author recalls, comes from an address by President John F. Kennedy in June 1963 "when he urged his countrymen to re-examine the inherited attitudes of the cold war: 'What kind of peace do we seek? Not a Pax Americana enforced on the world by American weapons of war . . . not merely peace for Americans but peace for all men and women—not merely peace in our time but peace in all time.'" The book won high praise: Henry Steele Commager thought it "all in all the most thorough, the most ardent and, to my mind, the most persuasive critique of American foreign policy over the last twenty years that has yet appeared. . . . One theme runs through almost all the chapters of this book: the theme

of American obsession with the Communist menace." William Pfaff strongly agreed: "*Pax Americana* will not be a popular book in Administration circles, which is a pity. Ronald Steel's journalism—edged, witty, and polemical—has drawn too much blood, his influence on the Senate foreign policy rebels has been too pronounced. . . . [He] makes a general argument on policy that avoids bitterness, is alive to the predicaments and dilemmas of government and deserves the attention of men in power."

By the time of the publication in 1971 of *Imperialists and Other Heroes: A Chronicle of the American Empire*, a collection of separate articles on foreign policy all first published in the *New York Review of Books*, Steel had begun the ten years of research that culminated in one of the most discussed political biographies of the early 1980s. *Walter Lippmann and the American Century*, generally considered exhaustive and authoritative, is the passionately engaged study of the life (1889–1974) and career of the eminent American political commentator and columnist, confidant of every president from Woodrow Wilson to Lyndon Johnson, and probably the twentieth century's most influential journalist. Lippmann's was, in the words of Van Wyck Brooks, "the most brilliant career ever devoted in America to political writing." Steel saw him also as "a moralist and public philosopher." Lippmann, Steel wrote in his Introduction, "began his career in the halcyon days before the First World War, when human progress seemed unlimited and inevitable, when poets danced in the squares and science promised a life of leisure and abundance for all. He ended it with the trauma of Vietnam, the shame of Watergate, and rioters running through the streets. . . . Influence was Lippmann's stock in trade, was what made him a powerful public figure. . . . He commanded no divisions, but he did have an enormous power over public opinion." In the columnist's last years, Steel writes, "instead of bowing out gracefully as the elder statesman of American journalism, he became involved in the most vituperative fight of his career. Outraged by the destructiveness and the obsessions of the Vietnam War, he turned bitterly against the administration—one whose highest echelons were staffed by those who admired and flattered him. He became emotionally involved in the war, . . . [it] rekindled his sense of outrage. It was perhaps his finest hour."

Steel came to know Lippmann well during the early years of research and was given unrestricted access to his papers, housed at Yale University. "It might seem," he wrote in a reminiscence in 1985, "that it is a wonderful break for a biographer to know the subject of his work. In a way it is. But in another way it complicates things. An intruder steps between the writer and his work, an intruder who can't easily be chased away because he, as subject, has every right to be there. There were times when I actually tried to avoid Lippmann so that I could see him as someone other than the person across the table." The more Lippmann demurred at revealing things about his life that he considered "personal," the more obsessed Steel became about getting at all the truth. "Increasingly," he continued, "I realized that I could not merely tell *his* story. Rather, I would have to tell my story about him. Inevitably that would put us into competition and even into conflict. He would want his story told in a certain way, although he would never have said so directly. That is what he had meant by his admonition that I not get too personal." The death of his subject in 1974 finally allowed Steel the distance to complete his book; Lippmann, his biographer believed, had "long since made his peace with himself and was willing to let others make their judgments as they would. He did not seem particularly concerned with posterity. He had done the best he could, and beyond that no one could ask more." What Steel learned from his subject is "that one can be a part of one's time without surrendering to it, that even accomplishments such as his are three parts hard work to one part genius, and that the greatest pitfall is not worldly fame but ceasing to care about making a difference."

Walter Lippmann and the American Century won, among other prizes, the Bancroft Prize of Columbia University, the National Book Critics Circle Award for non-fiction, and the American Book Award for biography. Its critical reception was divided, generally along political lines, with the left accepting it as a true picture of an American original, and the right accusing Steel of imposing his own views on the more moderate ones of his subject. Joseph Epstein's views are characteristic of the latter opinion: he found the book full of "revisionist presuppositions, assumptions and notions . . . a political biography in the full sense of the term . . . written out of a quite specific political point of view." Kenneth Lynn was in strong agreement with this essentially political judgment: "One would expect that [Steel] would be at his best in demonstrating how remarkably well Lippmann's political commentaries have stood the test of time. Steel, however, is an ideologue whose approach to the issues of twentieth-century American politics is as predetermined as Lippmann's was exploratory." A friendlier, less ideological assessment of the biography was offered by J. C. Harsch: "I lived through the Lippmann period. I thought I understood most of the events. I understand them

better for having relived them through the Lippmann story. . . . This is a book of first importance and should be read by anyone wanting a clearer sense of how America got to where it finds itself today." Anthony Lewis thought the book candid and balanced: "Steel does not flinch from unpleasant facts or critical judgments. He has mastered an enormous amount of material and presents it with clarity and pace. "

Steel was the editor of several volumes in the Wilson Reference Shelf series, including *Federal Aid to Education, Italy, North Africa,* and *New Light on Juvenile Delinquency.* He has been visiting fellow at Yale University (1971–1973) and the Woodrow Wilson International Center for Scholars (1984–1985) and visiting professor at Wellesley (1978), Texas (1977, 1979, 1980, 1985), Rutgers (1980), UCLA (1981, 1986), Dartmouth (1983), and Princeton (1984).

PRINCIPAL WORKS: The End of Alliance, 1964; (with George H. T. Kimble) Tropical Africa Today, 1966; Pax Americana, 1967, rev. ed., 1970; Imperialists and Other Heroes, 1971; Walter Lippmann and the American Century, 1980. *As editor*—Federal Aid to Education, 1961; Italy, 1963; North Africa, 1967; New Light on Juvenile Delinquency, 1967.

ABOUT: Contemporary Authors New Revision Series 7, 1982; Who's Who in America 1989–1990. *Periodicals*—America May 23, 1964; American Political Science Review September 1964; Best Sellers August 15, 1967; Book Week April 26, 1964; July 16, 1967; Choice January 1968; Christian Century July 26, 1967; Christian Science Monitor August 3, 1967; September 8, 1980; Columbia Journalism Review September–October 1980; Commentary October 1980; Commonweal June 26, 1964; October 27, 1967; November 7, 1980; Economist September 20, 1980; Foreign Affairs Fall 1980; Journal of American History September 1964; Journal of American Studies December 1981; Library Journal April 15, 1964; September 15, 1964; May 15, 1967; April 15, 1971; September 1, 1980; Nation September 11, 1967; November 8, 1980; New Republic July 22, 1967; August 16, 1980; New Statesman July 3, 1964; New York September 15, 1980; New York Review of Books September 10, 1964; October 9, 1980; New York Times August 22, 1980; New York Times Book Review March 29, 1964; July 16, 1967; September 12, 1971; August 24, 1980; Newsweek July 24, 1967; September 8, 1980; Pacific Affairs Fall–Winter 1967–1968; Saturday Review July 3, 1971; September 1980; Time September 8, 1980; Times Literary Supplement July 2, 1964; August 3 1967; February 20, 1981; Virginia Quarterly Review Winter 1968; World Politics October 1964, October 1968.

STONE, LAWRENCE (December 4, 1919–), British-born American historian, was born in Epsom, Surrey, the son of Lawrence Frederick Stone, an artist, and Mabel Julia Annie Reid Stone. He attended Charterhouse, a major public school, spent part of 1938 at the Sorbonne, then went up to Christ Church, Oxford University, where he read history for two years. In 1940, upon the outbreak of World War II, he left Oxford and received a commission in the Royal Naval Volunteer Reserve, serving until demobilization in 1945. He took a first in history on an accelerated course in 1946 and was awarded the Bryce research studentship at his college, after which he was elected lecturer in history at University College (1947–1950) and fellow in modern history at Wadham (1950–1963). In 1960–1961 Stone was a visiting member of the institute for Advanced Study at Princeton, and two years later left Oxford to take up a professorship in the history department at Princeton, where he has remained ever since; he was chairman in 1967–1970 and founding director in 1968 of the influential Shelby Cullom Davis Center for Historical Studies.

Under Stone's guidance, the Princeton history department has in recent years achieved international renown. The shared historical concerns and similar historiographic methods of the department's leading members—Peter R. L. Brown, Natalie Zemon Davis, Robert C. Darnton, and Carl E. Schorske, among others—can be traced to their general appreciation of what has been called "the new history." At Princeton occurred the first successful transplantation into the English-speaking world of the preferences of the French Annalistes for social and economic as opposed to traditional political history. The pioneering work of these French historians—among them are Marc Bloch, Lucien Febvre, Fernand Braudel, Michel Foucault, Philippe Ariès, Emmanuel Le Roy Ladurie, and Georges Duby—had been greatly admired by Stone since his undergraduate days, and Princeton has come to be considered the primary American outpost of the French school and its central insistence that history and its practitioners must look beyond "mere events" to consider the effects of deeper climatic, ecological, economic, and mental conditions. In his own work, Stone has taken these new concerns to heart, and by so doing has revolutionized his generation's understanding of early modern England.

Stone's first book seems anomalous in his career, but is still no less influential for that. *Sculpture in Britain: The Middle Ages* was one of the earliest volumes to appear in the Pelican History of Art series. The author demonstrates a remarkable grasp of art-historical terminology

LAWRENCE STONE

and is able again and again to bring into play his understanding of how wider historical forces shaped our present understanding of English medieval sculpture. Early in the book the author imagines the wealth of art that has disappeared: "sculptural losses far exceed those of architecture and are equalled only by those of mural paintings and glass. . . . The result of the destruction of well over ninety percent of English medieval religious imagery is to make it all but impossible to reconstruct the work of individual artists and gravely to distort our vision of the past."

With his next book, Stone began the close scrutiny of the early modern English political, economic, and social ascendancy which was to become his life's work. *An Elizabethan: Sir Horatio Palavicino* is a full-length biographical study of "a man who was primarily a business magnate . . . the last but one of a long line of Italian financiers who for 400 years had served the English crown." Stone's examination of his career, he writes in his Introduction, "leads into strange and sometimes untrodden paths of high finance and government borrowing, big business and world monopoly, diplomacy and espionage, land management and social transformations, policy-making and party politics at home and abroad." The evident note of eagerness here to explore new historical ground recurs throughout Stone's career.

The Crisis of the Aristocracy 1558–1641 is considered by many admirers of Stone's work to be his greatest book. It is a massive, magisterial study offering "a new explanation of the central event of modern English history—the breakdown of monarchical and aristocratic government in 1640–1641 and its re-establishment on terms in 1660 and 1688." Stone's description of the goals of the book in the Introduction is revealing of his historical priorities, which were fairly fixed even in the mid-1960s: "This book sets out to do two things: firstly to describe the total environment of an elite, material and economic, ideological and cultural, educational and moral; and secondly to demonstrate, to explain, and to chart the course of a crisis in the affairs of this elite that was to have a profound effect upon the evolution of English political institutions. It is therefore at once a static description and a dynamic analysis; it is a study in social, economic, and intellectual history, which is consciously designed to serve as the prolegomenon to, and an explanation of, political history." The reviewer for the *Economist* wrote that Stone's treatment of personalities "is robust and vivid. . . . [He] writes with unflagging verve and his vigorous style is enlivened by telling modern analogies, so that the reader is never wearied by the details so extensively marshalled."

After republishing three articles concerning the historiography and interpretation of *The Causes of the English Revolution 1529–1642,* Stone turned his attention to a study of aristocratic family life in early modern England which expands upon the concerns expressed in *The Crisis of the Aristocracy. Family and Fortune: Studies in Aristocratic Finance in the Sixteenth and Seventeenth Centuries* consists of two parts, the first being an exhaustive study of the finances of the Cecils, earls of Salisbury from 1590 until 1733, including their acquisition of extensive land, their building of Hatfield House in 1607–1612, their development of some of their London lands, their consolidation of their estates, and their decay due to civil war and internal family crises. Part Two, "Other Families," comprises shorter accounts of the Manners, earls of Rutland, 1460–1660; the Wriothesleys, earls of Southampton, 1530–1667; the Berkeleys, lords Berkeley, 1500–1680; and the Howards, earls of Suffolk, 1574–1745. When *The Crisis of the Aristocracy* was published, the author explains in the Introduction, "several critics complained of the absence of any detailed chronological studies of specific families by which it would be possible to trace the varying effects on these families of fertility, marriage, court service, conspicuous consumption, estate administration, debt, legal provision, and industrial and commercial entrepreneurship. . . . These particular families have been selected, not necessarily because of their typicality, but rather because of the wealth of surviving but unpublished documentation about them. . . . These are families living on a heroic scale, streaking up to the heights, and sometimes plunging down again with the spin of Fortune's wheel." The reviewer for the *Times Literary Supplement,* noting that Stone dedicates the book to "the owners of private family archives who have so generously made them available to serious scholars," concludes, "They deserve his gratitude, since he does nothing to conceal the slime from which these ancient families originated. Themes linking the essays are the role of court office in founding—or retrieving—the fortunes of a family, how far this amounted to 'corruption,' and what it contributed to the origins of the English civil war. . . . [The book] contains a great deal for historians to ransack and brood over."

Another family study, somewhat more widely based, is *The Family, Sex and Marriage in England 1500–1800.* The 800-page book, Stone writes in his Introduction, records "vast and elusive cultural changes [that] expressed themselves in changes in the way members of the family related to each other, in terms of legal arrangements, structure, custom, power, affect and sex. The main stress is on how individuals thought about, treated and used each other, and how they regarded themselves in relation to God and to various levels of social organization, from the nuclear family to the state. The microcosm of the family is used to open a window on to this wider landscape of cultural change." The book attempts to describe what is in the author's view a quite recent fundamental shift in basic human feelings. In the opinion of the reviewer for the *Economist,* the book would interest a far wider audience, because of its more popular subject matter, than any of Stone's previous books. "It provides an excellent review of child-rearing practices over three centuries. . . . [It] is full of fascinating information—on contraception, abortion, veneral disease cures of the past and breast-feeding taboos."

With his wife, Jeanne Caecilia Fawtrier Stone, the author next published as challenging and revisionist a book as any he has written. *An Open Elite?: England 1540–1880* examines patterns of conservation and acquisition of property, and consequently of political influence, within the elite. Studying the emergence of the middle-class entrepreneur and his assimilation into English landed society, the Stones write that England has long been perceived as "'an open elite.' . . . This is a paradigm readily accepted both by liberal and by Marxist social historians, even if they have drawn different moral conclusions from it. . . . The self-made man was made dizzy by the lure of charm, grace, favour, and an entree into the company of the elite. . . . According to accepted wisdom, this was how the landed elite of England perpetuated their political and social hegemony and their economic property rights through and beyond the great transformations of the industrial revolution and the advent of participatory democracy. Such were the perceptions of contemporaries, and such are the opinions of most modern historians. But what were the facts?" The facts—as adduced by the Stones with the aid of a computer, and presented partly by means of sixty-four tables, a wealth of appendixes, and much other apparatus—boldly challenge the great untested myth of the open elite. The important thing about the book, in the opinion of David Cannadine, writing in the *New York Review of Books*, "is the authors' breadth and bravery in taking on all of postmedieval English history. . . . At the very least, it provides the first quantitative basis for analyzing the landed classes of England in their years of wealth, power, and glory. More broadly, it is offered as a major reassessment of the social, political, and economic history of England since the Reformation. Either way, it is the most important, exciting, and original book on the English landed elite to have appeared since *The Crisis of the Aristocracy*. There can be no higher praise than that."

WORKS: Sculpture in Britain: The Middle Ages, 1955, rev. ed., 1972; An Elizabethan: Sir Horatio Palavicino, 1956; The Crisis of the Aristocracy 1558–1641, 1965; The Causes of the English Revolution 1529–1642, 1972; Family and Fortune: Studies in Aristocratic Finance in the Sixteenth and Seventeenth Centuries, 1973; The Family, Sex and Marriage in England 1500–1800, 1977; The Past and the Present, 1981; (with J.C.F. Stone) An Open Elite?: England 1540–1880, 1984; The Road to Divorce: England 1530–1987, 1990. *As editor*—The University in Society (vol. 1, Oxford and Cambridge from the 14th to the Early 19th Century; vol. 2, Europe, Scotland, and the United States from the 16th to the 20th Century), 1975; Schooling and Society: Studies in the History of Education, 1976.

ABOUT: Contemporary Authors 13–16, 1975; Who's Who, 1989–1990. *Periodicals*—American Historical Review October 1965, October 1973, December 1974; American Sociological Review June 1966; Choice October 1973, February 1974, May 1978, November 1981, November 1984; Economist May 1, 1965; July 21, 1973; October 8, 1977; Encounter April 1973, December 1981, January 1985; English Historical Review July 1966, October 1973; History February 1982; Library Journal February 1, 1973; Manchester Guardian July 8, 1955; Nation August 13, 1955; New Republic July 8–15, 1978; September 30, 1981; New Statesman July 30, 1955; May 21, 1965; August 4, 1972; September 7, 1984; New York Review of Books July 7, 1966; November 24, 1977; December 20, 1984; New York Times Book Review December 25, 1977; January 10, 1982; New York Times Magazine April 19, 1987; Polit-

ical Science Quarterly June 1966; Spectator July 29, 1955; Times Literary Supplement August 19, 1955; April 7, 1966; September 29, 1972; July 13, 1973; October 21, 1977; April 30, 1982; September 7, 1984.

STRAUSS, BOTHO (December 2, 1944–   ), German playwright and novelist, was born in Naumburg/Saale (in what was later in the German Democratic Republic), the son of a nutritional consultant. Strauss attended public schools (*Gymnasium*) in West Germany and spent five semesters studying sociology, theater, and German literature in Cologne and Munich. He began but never completed a dissertation on Thomas Mann and theater. From 1967 to 1970 he made his mark as a contributing editor and critic for the journal *Theater heute*. The numerous essays he wrote in this capacity reflect his early interest in the complex relationship between aesthetics and politics. From 1970 to 1975 this interest was pursued further in his dramaturgical contributions to various plays performed by the Schaubühne in Berlin (formerly Am Halleschen Ufer), where Strauss often collaborated with the influential director Peter Stein.

Although two of Strauss' plays, *Die Hypochonder* (The Hypochondriacs, 1972), and *Bekannte Gesichter, gemischte Gefühle* (Familiar Faces, Mixed Feelings, 1974), were performed on West German stages in the early 1970s, it was not until the middle of the decade that this versatile author was recognized as a significant literary force. Upon publication of *Die Widmung : Eine Erzählung* (1977; translated as *Devotion*), Marcel Reich-Ranicki, feuilleton editor for the widely read *Frankfurter Allgemeine Zeitung*, proclaimed that Strauss might well be the author to write the representative novel of his generation. For both his plays and his prose Strauss has won numerous awards, including a Villa Massimo Fellowship to Rome (1976) as well as two prizes from the prestigious Bavarian Academy of Arts (1981 and 1987).

The ambivalences and paradoxes that figure throughout Strauss' oeuvre have rendered him extremely controversial. There are those who decry his alleged fascination with cultural pessimism and melancholy nihilism as old-fashioned, while others worship him as the aesthetic elite's brilliantly morose prophet of doom and despair. Most of his characters teeter on the brink of disaster or absurdity, trapped in a no-man's-land between the sublime and the profane. When the protagonist of *Die Widmung* quits his job and locks himself in his apartment to await the unlikely return of the girlfriend who has aban-

BOTHO STRAUSS

doned him, critics were quick to label Strauss a representative of the "new subjectivity" trend in literature, one that supposedly ranked private concerns over political issues, the so-called "retreat into the private sphere." While much of West German culture in the 1970s did evince a reaction against the political abstractions and generalizations propagated by the student activists of the late 1960s and early 1970s, it is misleading to read any Strauss text at face value. *Die Widmung* in fact makes repeated use of the situational image riddle (rebus) to challenge the assumption of any purely private subjectivity. On several intricately interwoven levels the text explores the status of literary language in an industrialized age in which the media cultivate not an integrated subject but fragmentation and disintegration.

For Strauss this disintegration signifies both calamity and opportunity. The calamity has to do with what he regards as an insidious abrogation of historical consciousness, while the opportunity lies in blazing new epistemological trails. This explains Strauss' interest in French poststructuralist theory, especially in Michel Foucault's archaeological concept of knowledge. In this account, cognitive insights, which ensue from attention to the particular, are subject to illuminating multiplication, not stultifying homogenization. Strauss always catches his readers by surprise when he incorporates into his texts seemingly insignificant details of mundanity, as for example when the male protagonist in *Kalldewey, Farce* (1981) is dismembered by a washing machine, not the mythological maenads

one would expect. This uncomfortably simultaneous insistence on profundity and banality indicates, furthermore, an implicit rejection of Theodor W. Adorno's notion of aesthetic autonomy. For Adorno, a major proponent of the Frankfurt School of Critical Theory whose radical thought influenced Strauss greatly, art is always infused with sociality, but only good art manages to resist the status quo by virtue of a negative dialectic. Strauss no longer concedes that this type of aesthetic autonomy is possible. His texts articulate a response and a challenge to the postmodernist tendency to dissolve the distinctions between the literary and the real.

A recurring theme in Strauss' work, the dissolution of boundaries, figures already in *Marlenes Schwester* (Marlene's Sister, 1974), a short prose piece in which one also detects Romantic elements in Strauss' style and motifs. The fantastic tale of a vampire community punctuates the banal yet eerie account of two adult sisters who cannot live with or without each other. The disease from which Marlene's sister suffers but does not expire finds a later echo in the strange debilitating disease that afflicts the protagonist's daughter in *Rumor* (1980; translated as *Tumult*). Likewise, the playful, at times even comical rejection of linear temporality and narrative authority evidenced in *Marlenes Schwester* is developed further in virtually all of Strauss' subsequent writings.

Theorie der Drohung (Theory of Threat, 1975) and *Rumor* are oddly reminiscent of the works of Max Frisch, the Swiss novelist and dramatist. In the former a mental patient claims to know the identity of the narrator, an identity he initially rejects, much like Frisch's Stiller. In the latter, Strauss weaves another fantastic tale, this time replete with psychological motifs, to question the authenticity of language, authorship, and identity. Frisch's *Homo faber* would seem to be one of the predecessors of *Rumor*, in which Bekker returns to his former place of employment, the alienating Institute for News, as well as to an incestuous attraction to his adult daughter. Whereas Frisch explores narration as a means to making moral choices in history, Strauss' characters have no integrated center from which they could make such forays. In *Rumor* Strauss indicts the increasingly depersonalized social organization of knowledge in advanced capitalism. Bekker is the "thwarted warrior" who does not know quite how to do battle with the ubiquitous Institute, the "outhouse of the mind," that threatens the annihilation of historical consciousness by specializing in compartmentalized "know-how" and thoroughly degrading its employees. *Rumor* is the first of Strauss' texts in which the German legacy of the

Third Reich is accorded explicit significance. The stepson of the former Nazi officer is, however, at best an ineffective agent of socio-political resistance. Fool or visionary? The reader is never sure which. At the conclusion of the novel, in a transformation similar to Gregor Samsa's metamorphosis, Bekker is reduced to creature-like habits, incoherent babbling, and heavy breathing. At a crucial juncture the narrator abdicates his authority as well, so that *Rumor* effectively questions the viability of literature in contemporary industrialized society.

Not surprisingly, *Paare, Passanten* (Pairs, Passers-By, 1981) signifies a marked deviation from Strauss' earlier prose style. Here the storyteller yields to the cultural commentator, whose essays, aphorisms, and impressions of everyday life often contradict each other. The fact that Strauss' texts demand a critical reader is especially noteworthy given that, in *Paare, Paasanten* at least, primary themes are the loss of history in an age of widespread computerization, the impending threat of nuclear catastrophe, and the farewell to any illusions as to the ultimate significance of literature in a society in which the social function of literature has been seriously curtailed. *Niemand anderes* (No One Else, 1987) is comparable in style and motif, although here, as in all of Strauss' more recent works, one notes a growing insistence on the quest for something that might vaguely be termed spiritual or aesthetic transcendence. This has led some critics to denounce Strauss again for what they consider his reactionary tendencies. And yet, even in *Der junge Mann* (1984; translated as *The Young Man*), a lengthy "Romantic-Reflection-Novel," the protagonist's quest for visionary illumination is inextricably grounded in references to the mundane (Pacman games, for example). Leon Pracht is initiated into the world of theater, but unlike the Tower Society that Goethe's Wilhelm Meister encounters, the Tower here is a high-rise hotel housing the protagonist's idol, a has-been from whom Leon is finally glad to escape. This novel, characteristically self-reflective, is full of allegories, Romantic excursions, and erotic grotesques. Strauss indulges in the narrativity that his earlier works seemed to question. The many allusions to the German tradition of the *Bildungsroman* are marked both by a desire to recapture an aesthetic vision and by the knowledge that the need for such transcendence in today's world is always in danger of becoming ideology.

Strauss' dramatic oeuvre echoes many of the same themes found in his prose, albeit with a more pronounced emphasis on mythological and fantastic elements. The playwright first caught the critics' eye with *Trilogie des Wiedersehens*

(Reunion Trilogy, 1976), in which an exhibit of neo-realist paintings provides the foil for a sociopsychological study of the visitors to the exhibit. Critics have noted the influence of Maxim Gorky's *Summer Guests*, for a German stage production of which Strauss served as dramaturge. Strauss' subsequent plays move even further away from classical and mimetic traditions; allusions to absurdist theater are frequent, as in *Kalldewey, Farce*, which harks back to Samuel Beckett's *Waiting for Godot*. *Gross und klein: Szenen* (1978; translated as *Big and Little*) brought Strauss his first great success on stage with the endearing and repulsive character of Lotte, played by Edith Clever in Berlin and in the 1980 film production. This "disgusting angel" passes from one unlikely station to another in search of love and meaning, finding none. Her real discourse is with God, a silent partner whose agency she is supposed to enact. But Lotte also resists her entrapment in the symbolic order and hence is left searching for that which she, as a fallen angel, can no longer symbolize. Strauss pursues a "theater of consciousness" (the word stems from the German author Martin Walser) versus one of documentation, but he does not psychologize. Rather, he startles the spectators with "characters" such as a tent or a larger-than-life-sized book that bleeds. The quest of meaning proceeds only on the premise that all meaning and signs are suspect.

The East German playwright Heiner Müller once said of Strauss' plays that history appears in them only as a blank. Many read his preoccupation with mythological motifs and older works of art in this vein. In *Kalldewey, Farce* we see a modern-day Orpheus and Eurydice encounter a punk lesbian couple from Berlin with allusions to Mozart's *Magic Flute* in the background. *Der Park* (The Park, 1983) takes Shakespeare's *A Midsummer Night's Dream* as its reference point. Here mythological creatures descend to the human realm, only to be disappointed in the lethargy and apathy they find. The teacher in *Die Fremdenführerin* (The Tourist Guide, 1986) vacations in Greece in order "to reach a decision," but when he cannot keep the woman he thinks he has claimed, the text turns her into a mythological allusion. Although myth does not figure very strongly in Strauss' three more recent plays—*Besucher* (Visitors, 1988), *Die Zeit und das Zimmer* (Time and the Room, 1988), and *Sieben Türen: Bagatellen* (Seven Doors: Things of No Consequence, 1988)—they all address a troubled relationship between social time and historical consciousness. A play that reflects on its own possibilities (or lack thereof) for realist theater, *Besucher* obfuscates the distinction between theater and "reality." The play within the play never moves past a particular scene that the actors rehearse over and over again; the "real" play ends with its own beginning. Similarly, time is askew and reality suspended in *Die Zeit und das Zimmer*. The passer-by motif of *Paare, Passanten* and *Niemand anderes* finds an echo here when two men in an apartment conjure up the presence of strangers they see on the street as they speak about them. The initially barren apartment is soon filled with peculiar, intertwining stories, but it is a point of no-history, since no one knows any more how their stories (histories) fit together. Similarly, *Sieben Türen* ends with the proclamation of the "Zero Hour."

Yet even this last term is, self-consciously, a historical one (referring to the much disputed "new beginning" after the fall of the Third Reich). In a philosophical treatise that Strauss surely knows (*Dialectic of Enlightenment*, 1947), Max Horkheimer and Theodor W. Adorno argued during and after the war that the historical tendency of the Enlightenment has been to eradicate difference, that Enlightenment itself had turned into its opposite: myth. While Strauss is often accused of cultivating new and old myths instead of historical awareness, he knows too well that contemporary West German society cannot sustain either myth *or* Enlightenment. He looks for history in the cracks between the two. If the German critical theorists have argued that the Enlightenment annihilates all difference, the poststructuralists contend that difference is the structural foundation for all social phenomena. Strauss' prose as well as his plays can be read as an attempt to explore the extent to which a society of mass consumerism can allow for genuine difference, for a critical historical consciousness in spite of all social developments to the contrary. His works will undoubtedly be subject to varied and controversial readings for a long time to come, but even now his international reputation rivals those of Peter Handke and Thomas Bernhard, with whose works his writing is often compared.

WORKS IN ENGLISH TRANSLATION: English translations of Botho Strauss' writings include Anne Cattaneo's *Big and Little* in 1979; Sophie Wilkins's *Devotion*, 1979; Michael Hulse's *Tumult*, 1984; and Edna McCown's *The Young Man: A Novel*, 1989.

ABOUT: Adelson, L. Crisis of Subjectivity, 1984; Bullivant, K. (ed.) The Modern German Novel, 1987; Columbia Dictionary of Modern European Literature, 1980; Contemporary Literary Criticism 22, 1982; DeMeritt, L. New Subjectivity and Prose Forms of Alienation, 1987; Demetz, P. After the Fires, 1986. *Periodicals*—Antigonish Review 66–67, 1986; German Quarterly 57, 1984; Germanic Review 61, 1986; Monatshefte 78, 1986; 79, 1987; New German Critique 30, 1983; New York Times March 19, 1989; Times Literary Supplement May 2, 1980; February 22, 1985; October 9, 1985; April 24, 1987; World Literature Today Summer 1977; Winter 1979; Summer 1979.

*SUKENICK, RONALD (July 14, 1932–), American novelist, short-story writer, and critic, was born in Brooklyn, New York, the son of Louis and Ceceile Frey Sukenick. He graduated from Cornell University in 1955 and received his M.A. (1957) and Ph.D. (1962) from Brandeis University. In 1961 he married Lynn Luria, a poet. He has been director of the creative writing program at the University of Colorado in Boulder since 1972. He has also taught at Sarah Lawrence College and been writer-in-residence at the University of California, Irvine, and at Cornell. He lives in Boulder and Ben Lomond, California. In 1974 Sukenick joined with Jonathan Baumbach and a group of other novelists to found the Fiction Collective, a cooperative project that publishes non-traditional fiction ordinarily not handled by commercial trade publishers. In 1977 he became the publisher of *American Book Review*, which, like Fiction Collective, serves the interests of experimental and countercultural writers by offering an "alternative" to such established reviewing journals as the *New York Times Book Review* and the *New York Review of Books*.

Since the late 1960s Ronald Sukenick has been among the most prominent American writers of avant-garde or experimental fiction. Although he has pursued a successful academic career, he spent a number of years living a bohemian life in Greenwich Village and the Lower East Side of Manhattan during the 1950s and '60s, and he has tried to retain the countercultural inspiration of his work. Specifically, while work such as his renounces the conventional portrayal of social reality and social problems, it has in his view the social function of undermining the "consensual reality" established by mass-market fiction and other media. It thus maintains an adversarial, radical role, even while the bohemian adversarial culture has disappeared or has been assimilated by the consumer culture, rendering such literary labels as "underground" or "experimental" obsolete.

The radical character of Sukenick's work consists chiefly in its attempt to convey and adhere to the flow of immediate experience, to be spontaneous and unpremeditated. It is thus at the opposite end of the scale from more formalistic experimental fiction, such as the work of Georges Perec and the Oulipo group in Paris during the 1960s and 1970s, which relied on the

°sook´ e nik

RONALD SUKENICK

application of rigorous arbitrary rules and re-nunciations, as in a challenging, esoteric game. While Sukenick's work often has a playful, gamelike quality, as in the descending order of chapters and correspondingly diminishing prose in *Out*, the game seems improvised, the rules made up as he goes along, and liable to change at any moment. The stress on improvisation, spontaneity, and casual, free-flowing experience reveals Sukenick's roots in the Beat movement and the Greenwich Village bohemia of the 1950s, with their devotion to progressive jazz, free-form poetry, sexual and hallucinatory ex-periments, and spur-of-the-moment artistic in-spiration. If more or less conventional narrative devices or expectations emerge in Sukenick's work, they are there only to be quickly sabo-taged in order to shock the reader into a renewed awareness of immediate experience, including the experience of writing and reading. What this means in practice is that Sukenick's own favorite character is himself, often surprised in the act of writing, and the material improvised upon is fre-quently autobiographical. But the tone is usually less introspective than ironic and picaresque. With Sukenick in his various guises and disguises comes a milieu which is often bohemian and countercultural in its atmosphere and preoccu-pations. Thus the author, amid parodies, impro-visations, typographical whimsies, and general rejection of realism, still manages to offer the reader a slice of life, a sense of a certain Ameri-can time and place.

Sukenick's first novel, *Up*, is an exuberant mélange of wordplay, parody, and narrative tangents and fragments with a rather conven-tional core: the story of a Jewish boy from Brook-lyn who after numerous adolescent trials becomes a teacher and writer—that is, a teacher and writer named Ronald Sukenick who is writ-ing a novel called *Up*. The novel is self-reflective to the point of containing its own review—a neg-ative one, which condemns it because its main character is too closely identified with its author. The book ends with a description of the party celebrating its own publication, with Sukenick and his wife in attendance. In the *Saturday Review* Edward M. Potoker praised both its comic inventiveness and its serious concerns, calling it "one of the funniest books of the season, a hilarious outburst of wild comedy that mocks the pretensions of the young" but that also has "a solid intellectual substratum . . . in which se-rious points are made coolly and without the pontifical solemnity some cultural historians require." Potoker was reminded of two earlier literary misfits: "Unconventional in the tradition of Sterne's *Tristram Shandy*, *Up* also recalls the eccentric books of Ronald Firbank." His only ob-jection was to the treatment of the familiar up-from-Brooklyn material: "On one level *Up* is a Jewish novel and a rather dreary one, for Suken-ick doesn't want to write a Jewish novel repeat-ing what Bellow, Malamud, and Roth have done and overdone. . . . When Sukenick deals with his Jewishness directly he is usually sentimental or pathetic, sometimes even bitter. When he deals with it indirectly he tends to create weak parody and burlesque." But Potoker thought the novel more than made up for these defects with its assemblage of "whacky characters" and the controlling comic sensibility that unites its in-congruous fragments: "Out of broad humor and a sense of structural irony, Sukenick balances the sentimental, the emotional, and the pathetic with the obscene, the trivial, and the absurd."

In *Harper's* Irving Howe conceded Sukenick's virtuosity but found it insufficient to lift the nov-el above its trivial subject matter. Sukenick, he said, "can do just about anything with words. He can turn out a parody, a burlesque, a pastiche, a bit of genre realism, a modernist set piece; he has a fine gift for mimicry . . . he has absorbed the lessons of Joyce and the influence of Bellow; he has done just about everything except write a good novel. . . . It really ought to be great fun, an exuberant outpouring of comic genius, mocking the banalities of the age and the preten-sions of the young. But alas, no. . . . effective satire cannot be written about a world that is sil-ly rather than evil, characters who are pip-squeaks rather than ominous." In direct reply in the *New York Times Book Review*, Raymond A. Sokolov accused Howe of an outdated hankering after "classics, shapely masterpieces." He went on to defend the novel as something *sui generis*: "Though it pretends to be autobiographical (and is to a certain extent), *Up* is really a work of literary criticism in, very loosely speaking, novel form. For those in the know, it will be a picnic of assorted delicacies, nearly all of them to be eaten with tongue in cheek." And in his *New York Times* review, Thomas Lask concluded that *Up* did rise above its conventional material: "Perhaps the substance of the book is not new and Mr. Sukenick reminds us that he hasn't forgotten any of the authors from Homer to Joyce he has read. But he has at least refused to play it safe and made something fresh and crisply readable from matter that could have been jaded and tired."

Sukenick's second novel, *Out*, lacks even the minimal narrative coherence and the identifiable central figure of *Up*. "It is really the imagery which holds the book together," wrote Tom Johnson in the *Village Voice*, "and it holds together very well, despite the absence of logical threads, social messages, character development, and other conventions. Stick-ups and seductions occur with fair regularity. Fuses and sticks of dynamite occur throughout the book, usually as phallic symbols. Countdowns, numerological symbols, cryptic messages, pig Latin, tongues, and spy-story references are scattered throughout the book. The many characters frequently change their names and seldom stay around for more than a chapter." The only real development in the novel is the gradual disappearance of prose on the page, as the chapters, numbered ten to one in descending order, each contain a corresponding number of lines per page, so that chapter five has five lines per page, chapter four four lines, until the book, echoing the title, peters "out" at the end, the last page containing only the letter *o*.

The formal shape of Sukenick's third novel, *98.6*, is a triptych. The first section, titled "Frankenstein," is a collage of atrocities, made up of juxtaposed newspaper accounts and historical fragments of crimes and war; the second section, called "The Children of Frankenstein," is about a utopian commune of escapees from the monstrous world of the first, including a character named Ron Sukenick who is writing a novel about the commune as the commune itself disintegrates; the third section, "Palestine," offers a prophetic Israel as an alternative, perhaps purely imaginary, to the failed realities of the first two sections. Paul D. McGlynn, in the *Southern Humanities Review*, found the book flawed by its tendency "to thump the reader over the head with a Myth," but also found much to praise. Sukenick's prose style is fast, nervy, exciting,

like Mailer and even Kerouac at their best; the comedy nearly always works. . . . Sex and violence, instead of being mere juvenile exhibitionism, create the narrative rhythms, and character, in turn, creates the sex and violence. . . . Sukenick's recurrent images are the sea, spouting whales, motion and stasis, very appropriate to the creation-redemption-apocalypse structure. . . . The vision is genuinely universal."

Long Talking Bad Condition Blues consists of a completely unpunctuated text whose speech rhythms are established by pure sound and by spacing on the page. Peter Quartermain in the *Chicago Review* called it a tour de force and a "brilliant book"—"racy, colloquial, comic, readable; it is a prose in which the reader feels instantly at home . . . and in which on reflection he finds himself homeless" like the outcasts on an island who are the book's ostensible subject. The novel is, he concluded, "a vision of hell, very funny, highly readable, and at the same time deeply moving: people caught in inertia, hanging around waiting for something to happen like teenagers in a suburban shopping mall."

Sukenick reappears as his own protagonist in *The Endless Short Story*, which Lois Gordon called his "most lyrical fiction" in her *New York Times Book Review* article. "It lacks the violence and defiance of, say, '*Up*,' '*Out*' or '*98.6*,' although it retains the author's favorite visual effects and disjunctures of language and punctuation." Following Sukenick as he returns to Brooklyn and visits California and Paris, the book is really, according to Gordon, an "interiorized journey": "Early on, Mr. Sukenick stands at the peak of the Colorado Rockies, reflecting with a certain equanimity on the 'endless short story' of his life. Disparate sequences, in diverse styles, convey his preoccupations with birth, death and the deterioration of love; he is, above all, committed to his art." And the art in this case is successful, she thought; the novel is "a beautiful and poetic work, funny, intellectually challenging and unexpectedly moving."

Sukenick has published one other novel, *Blown Away*, a disjointed tale of Hollywood intrigue in which Gerald Jay Goldberg, writing in the *New York Times Book Review*, detected a "lethal loss of fictional energy," and a collection of stories, *The Death of the Novel and Other Stories*, in which Sukenick's characteristic verbal and formal play and characteristic character—Sukenick himself—are used to brilliantly varied effect; one critic, Timothy Dow Adams, thought that the stories sustained Sukenick's improvisational method better than any of the novels. A memoir of Greenwich Village in the 1950s and

1960s titled *Down and In: Life in the Underground* was published in 1987; it was intended, Sukenick explained, to "revalidate" the countercultural ethos that by the 1980s was being denigrated or misunderstood.

Sukenick's critical writing can also be seen as an attempt to defend and revalidate the countercultural commitment to spontaneity and improvisation that has provided inspiration for his own fiction—notably his *In Form: Digressions on the Art of Fiction.* But here Tony Tanner, in the *New York Times Book Review,* found him repeating himself: "for a writer who attaches so much importance to flow, motion, generation, improvisation and so on, the attitudes and prescriptions . . . are disappointingly static, reiterative." He quotes Sukenick as saying in an interview, "I'm like a fisherman with a fast boat that keeps pulling in fish and throwing them overboard. I like to travel light." Tanner comments, "The trouble is, it is invariably the same fish he pulls in. Arguably Mr. Sukenick travels rather *too* light." Sukenick also published a revision of his Ph.D. dissertation on Wallace Stevens as *Wallace Stevens: Musing the Obscure,* a book praised by Denis Donoghue in the *New York Review of Books* for its refusal to seek a theoretical or philosophical unity in Stevens' poems. It is probable that no such unity can be found in Sukenick's own art; it is as incongruously diverse as the contemporary experience it aims to be faithful to.

PRINCIPAL WORKS: *Novels*—Up, 1968; Out, 1973; 98.6, 1975; Long Talking Bad Condition Blues, 1979; The Endless Short Story, 1986; Blown Away, 1987. *Collected short stories*—The Death of the Novel and Other Stories, 1969. *Memoir*—Down and In: Life in the Underground, 1987. *Criticism*—Wallace Stevens: Musing the Obscure, 1968; In Form: Digressions on the Art of Fiction, 1985.

ABOUT: Bellamy, J. D. (ed.) The New Fiction: Interviews with Innovative American Writers, 1974; Contemporary Literary Criticism 3, 1973; 4, 1975; 6, 1976; 48, 1988; Contemporary Authors 25–28, 1977; Dictionary of Literary Biography Yearbook 1981; Klinkowitz, J. The Self-Apparent Word, 1985; Kutnik, J. The Novel as Performance, 1977; Nagel, J. American Fiction, 1977; Pearce, R. The Novel in Motion, 1983; Waugh, P. Metafiction, 1984. *Periodicals*—Chicago Review Autumn 1980; Harper's May 1968; New York Review February 1, 1968; New York Times June 22, 1968; September 25, 1969; New York Times Book Review July 14, 1968; January 27, 1985; November 16, 1986; March 15, 1987; November 1, 1987; Saturday Review, July 6, 1968; Sewanee Review Winter 1984, Spring 1986; Southern Humanities Review Winter 1977; Village Voice November 29, 1973.

SWIFT, GRAHAM (May 4, 1949–   ), British novelist and short-story writer, was born in London, son of a civil servant. He attended Dulwich College, 1960–1967, and Queen's College, Cambridge University, 1967–1970, from which he received his B.A. and M.A. degrees. Swift taught English in London schools of education for nine years, becoming a full-time writer in 1983. His first novel, *The Sweet Shop Owner,* was considered an impressive debut and was widely praised. The novel depicts the life of Willy Chapman, set up in a small business by his late wife, from whom he was alienated, and his narrow, circumscribed life involving an estrangement from his daughter as well. The work takes place within a single day, but through shifts in time reveals the whole pattern of his life.

Frank Rudman in the *Spectator* was impressed by the novel, remarking that "the Chapman family's bitter history is brilliantly chronicled by Graham Swift who captures the essence of the small, modest but obliging variety of family establishments that made up High Street business before the remorseless blight of supermarkets and building society boxes squashed them out of existence." Michael Gorra, in the *New York Times Book Review,* praised especially the method by which "in moving through Willy's memory with all the skill of an impressionist master like Ford Madox Ford, Mr. Swift makes that day contain all the others." Gorra went on to say that Swift's narrative "produces a terrifying and painfully sad sense of the way time's passage makes the walls of life close in. To me that sense far outweighs the novel's main weakness—its defective analysis of the emotional web within Willy's family. . . . *The Sweet Shop Owner* is on the whole a remarkable novel. . . . There is a touch of Joyce in Graham Swift's revelation of the hidden poetry of small men's lives." A dramatized version of the novel was performed at the Brighton Festival in 1989.

Shuttlecock also deals with alienation and the impingement of the past upon the present, but its form is different from that of *The Sweet Shop Owner.* In *Shuttlecock,* a man named Prentis works in police archives filing "useless" data from closed investigations. One of the files relates to the war record of his father, who lies in a London hospital unable to speak. During World War II, while in the French Resistance, he had been captured and interrogated by the S.S., an experience recorded by him in his espionage memoir "Shuttlecock." But the question is now raised as to whether his father had not, in fact, broken down and collaborated with the Gestapo for his "escape." Larger issues of the reliability of history, of the transmission of meaning and order, are eventually raised as part of a

GRAHAM SWIFT

philosophical questioning framed by Prentis' experience.

Reviewers were again impressed by Swift's narrative gifts. Richard Boston in *Punch* commented that "the connections between Prentis' professional and personal lives are delineated with great skill, and the quality of the writing is consistently high." John Mellor in the *London Magazine* described Prentis' work at the office as "Kafkaesque," and proposed that the novel's theme was that "knowledge is dangerous and breeds unhappiness and that only ignorance enables us to enjoy life." He noted, too, how *Shuttlecock* works effectively on different levels. "It is a novel about ideas," he remarked, " . . . [and] it is an entertaining psychological mystery-thriller."

Learning to Swim is a collection of eleven of Swift's short stories, published previously in a number of British magazines; and all but one of them are narrated in the first person. The collection drew mixed reviews. "These stories," Jonathan Penner wrote in the *Washington Post Book World*, "are of thoroughly mixed merit. Swift writes grand scenes, magical paragraphs—and finds as many ways to fail as succeed. His story collection looks like the laboratory of a novelist." Byrn Caless, in *British Book News*, was struck by the bleakness of the tales. "What I find difficult to accept," Caless commented, "is that such blighting is so universal and so unremitting. . . . [Most] of the stories are stark statements against which *The Waste Land* seems positively frivolous." Alan Hollinghurst, in the *Times Literary Supplement*, however, found the

stories enigmatic in the way that challenged the reader. "Swift's precision," he observed, "is a vindication of artistic pleasure in the description of a world in which opportunities for pleasure have dwindled away."

Swift's third novel, *Waterland*, brought him into prominence. A finalist for England's prestigious Booker Prize, it won the *Guardian* Fiction Prize and the Geoffrey Faber Memorial Prize in 1983. Its narrator, Tom Crick, is about to be phased out as a history teacher (history itself is to be assimilated into a vaguely defined "general studies" program) at an English school. On his final day, instead of lecturing to his students on the French Revolution, he lectures on the fens, a kind of watery wasteland, and on the two families from which he is descended. The narrative is complex in structure, and includes digressions on the natural history of eels and on Crick's discovery at sixteen of a boy's body floating in the lock tended by his father. Yet Swift's diverse material is absorbing and never loses its clarity.

The meaning of *Waterland*, M. J. Fitzgerald maintains in his sketch of Swift in *Contemporary Novelists*, is that man is "not part of a progressive History nurtured by reason, but of a natural history which 'doesn't go anywhere,' that all the particular complexities of human endeavour and curiosity are nothing more than dredging machines, and the only important thing is to have 'tried and so prevented things slipping,' not to have 'let the world get any worse.'" Michael Wood, in *New York Review of Books*, remarked that *Waterland* "is a formidably intelligent book, rather cumbersome at times, quite often a little too solemn for its own good. The ghosts of Faulkner, Günter Grass, and García Márquez stamp about in it rather heavily. Nonetheless, it is the most powerful book I have read for some time." Also impressed by the book, Michael Gorra, in the *New York Times Book Review*, declared that *Waterland* established Swift "as one of the brightest promises the English novel now has to offer."

Out of This World is about the alienation of children from their parents in two successive generations. Linda Gray Sexton in the *New York Times Book Review* felt that the book "deserves to be ranked at the forefront of contemporary literature"; but other reviewers considered the novel overly schematic and lacking in humor. John Bemrose in *Maclean's* commented: "As in his fine earlier novel *Waterland*, Swift tries to show how private lives are bound up with the events of history. But while his competence at interweaving the themes is impressive, his novel lacks impact. The first person reminiscences of both Harry and Sophie are too sketchy to give the real past substance. As a result, *Out of This World* remains a very cerebral book that describes strong emotion while failing to communicate it."

In addition to his other prizes, Swift was given the Royal Society of Literature Winifred Holtby Award in 1984. A profile article in *Newsweek* describes Swift as "skinny, soft-spoken, funny and highly intelligent" and notes that "he lives in London south of the Thames, a region that his companion, a witty young woman named Candice Rodd (to whom *Waterland* is dedicated), explains is 'not quite chic, just yet. We have a local paper that constantly features the celebrities who've moved in. But the tone is rather defensive.'"

PRINCIPAL WORKS: The Sweet Shop Owner, 1980 (U.S., 1985); Shuttlecock, 1981 (U.S., 1984); Learning to Swim, 1982 (U.S., 1985); Waterland, 1983 (U.S., 1985); Out of This World, 1988.

ABOUT: Contemporary Authors 117, 1986; Contemporary Literary Criticism 41, 1987; Contemporary Novelists, 1986. *Periodicals*—British Book News December 1982; London Magazine November 1981; Maclean's April 25, 1988; Newsweek April 30, 1984; New York Review of Books August 16, 1984; New York Times Book Review June 23, 1985; September 11, 1988; Times Literary Supplement August 27, 1982; Washington Post Book World April 14, 1985.

---

*SZABÓ, MAGDA (October 5, 1917–), Hungarian novelist and playwright, was born in Debrecen, an agricultural and trade center located on the edge of the Great Plain in Southeastern Hungary. Her father, nearly forty when she was born, was secretary to the mayor, then deputy city clerk, later deputy to the alderman for culture, and city alderman; when he retired he was associate judge of the Orphan's Court. Her mother, who first aspired to be a dancer and then a concert pianist and who was thirty-three when she gave birth to Magda, had been a teacher but settled into being a wife and mother, though she, like her husband, wrote poems and short stories. Magda Szabó's parents exploited every opportunity to give her a sense of the history and culture of Debrecen, long associated with the country's literary traditions, famous as a citadel of Protestantism in a nation of Catholics, and revered as the center of Hungary's rebellion against the Habsburgs in 1848–1849. During regular walking tours of the city, they stopped at houses to tell her of the poets, writers, and patriots who had lived in them, and paused on streets to recount the dramatic historical events that had taken place on them. Through

MAGDA SZABÓ

accounts of her family's history they also taught her to revere her forebears, "to feel them in my genes." Szabó detested her mother's family for the cruel way they had treated her mother but enjoyed visiting with her father's family.

Among several uncles on her father's side, she found Emil particularly delightful, a musician who was Bartók's and Kodály's student and from whom she first heard of authentic Hungarian folk music. He knew several ancient languages and, as an amateur Egyptologist, helped her to draw hieroglyphics; he also explained how music originated and why composers do not need an instrument to compose music, all exotic bits of knowledge that nurtured her active imagination. She was taken to the movies—she wrote an imaginary version of Al Jolson's *The Singing Fool* when her parents did not let her see it—and to plays regularly, sometimes one play in the afternoon and another in the evening. Original stories were told daily, with her parents alternating in inventing twists and turns in character and plot. Her parents did everything to encourage her development into an exceptional child without warping her personality. She recited poems, wrote verses when she barely knew the letters of the alphabet, and carved her rhymes on a door before she had really learned to write. A scrawny, sickly child, she was not admitted to the first grade of elementary school. Her mother taught her everything the year's study plan required in such a playful, entertaining way that all the teaching she encountered thereafter seemed pale and boring to her.

Because her autobiography ends with her

tenth year, much less information is available about her twelve years in the Dóczi Institute for Young Ladies. However, she does report on her experiences in the Girl Scouts, which she despised fiercely, and on learning to speak Latin with the help of her father after she had mastered its basic grammar in school. She has warmly acknowledged her lasting debt to a teacher, György Szondy, also a journalist, for organizing her reading of world literature and also for treating her, fourteen at the time, as an equal. It was for her, she says, a time of serious learning and of forming many friendships.

After graduating with distinction in 1935, she entered the university in Debrecen to become a teacher of Latin and Hungarian. But before beginning her studies, she spent the first of several summers in Vienna in a boarding school, mastering the German language and coincidentally acquiring an early understanding of the Nazi threat. Her five years at the university were "the most harmonious and the happiest of my life." Upon completing a thesis on cosmetics during the Roman Period, she obtained her doctorate with distinction in 1940. She immediately accepted a position as an hourly lecturer and then as an assistant teacher at the Dóczi Institute; but fearing she could not obtain a permanent position, she became in 1942 a Latin and history teacher at the Reformed Church's Secondary School for Girls in Hódmezővásárhely, near Szeged in Southwestern Hungary, with the stipulation that she complete work in history, a requirement she met in medieval history in two years. She considers her two years at this school among the most enriching she has ever known in her profession.

After the war, on March 1, 1945, she accepted a teaching position at the Mihály Fazekas Public Secondary School, but she moved, instead, to Budapest at the urging of an influential friend who promised her a post as head of the film or literature section in the government being formed at the time to begin Hungary's rehabilitation. On April 4 she was named head of the film section; she next served in the literary department and then later as secretary in the office of the deputy secretary of the Ministry of Religion and Education, which afforded her the opportunity to know everyone engaged in cultural matters. For writers the period from 1945 to 1948 was euphoric: "Until 1948," she writes, "it was a time with cherished memories of the giggling of young joy, passion for life, exuberant gaiety, never flagging hope, ecstasy." In the atmosphere of complete freedom, she helped to build an education program along new intellectual lines and to establish support for the arts. She joined the circle of writers affiliated with the progressive

periodical *Új Hold* (New Moon) that sought to introduce recent western literary trends into Hungary's literature, and she came to know writers who, like herself, would become major figures in the post-1956 literary scene: poets Ágnes Nemes Nagy, János Pilinszky, and György Rába, and prosewriter Iván Mándy. In 1947 she met her husband, Tibor Szobotka, a writer, literary historian, and translator, at a reception for Stephen Spender hosted by the Writers' Union. She made her debut as a writer not only with poems in literary journals but with two books of verse: *Bárány* (Lamb, 1947) and *Vissza az emberig* (Back to Mankind, 1949). These poems, which she had carried to Budapest in her luggage, reflected the terrors of the war and a reckoning with the catastrophe. In the image of the lamb she mourned the sacrificial victims of human bestiality; in the second volume she pleaded for a return to the humanistic heritage of western civilization, to the moral imperatives of the Roman world she knew so well.

However, the darkness descending upon Hungary's literary life with the advent of Mátyás Rákosi's Communist government and personality cult soon enveloped her as it did so many progressive writers, beginning a period one literary historian called the "lean years of Hungarian literature." The prize the trustees of the Baumgarten Foundation awarded her for *Bárány*, whose publication the foundation had subsidized, was revoked and given to another author on the orders of József Révai, the régime's arbiter of Marxist literary policy, which variously penalized all writers who showed signs of not following the tenets of schematism. Also, she was summarily dismissed from the ministry and declared unqualified to teach at the secondary school level. Fortunately, she became a teacher at a general school for boys and then a supervisor of practice teaching at a general training school for teachers until 1959, when she began to make a living entirely with her writings.

Szabó's name was not to appear in print for ten years, except as a translator, and many thought she had permanently vanished from the literary scene. In reality, like others excluded from the nation's creative life, she wrote for her "desk drawer" as well as for her students for the next nine years, until 1958, when, given the less rigid control of the national publishing houses after the 1956 uprising, what she had written during the long period of public silence poured into print. Two books of her poems appeared in 1958: *Neszek* (Noises), a collection, and *Bárány Boldizsár* (Boldizsár the Lamb), a poetic tale for children. But her predilection for prose fiction manifested itself at this time. Between 1958 and 1960 three of her novels for adults were published, as well as two novels for adolescents. During this period she continued to write poetry, but in a commentary on the collection of her poems issued in 1975, Szabó says she would not have published the verses even if the opportunity to do so had been present when she wrote them. She kept sending her poems to her mother, asking her to read them and then to burn them, but on her mother's death in 1967, she found them all in a drawer and included a selection in the 1975 edition. Szabó had already begun, she reports, to turn her attention increasingly from the subjective, highly personal sphere of the lyric to the life and thoughts of others. Recognizing that the analysis and understanding of the world existing outside herself was, as she puts it, at least as interesting as the thoughts and feelings she projected from within herself, she chose fiction as her preferred genre.

Freskó (Fresco, 1958) and *Az őz* (1959; translated as *The Fawn*) contained the basic strands of her novels: psychological conflicts arising from social causes, strong and weak women from the provincial or bourgeois classes caught up in the times, the probing of characters through the interior monologue, plots crafted to build tension, and a supple style. In *Freskó*, a funeral forces the alienated members of a Calvinistic intellectual family in the provinces, hardly touched by any sense of their own evanescence, to take stock of themselves as they await the arrival of a young woman, who, unlike them, had escaped to Budapest from the oppressive family atmosphere that has permanently deformed their spirits. Szabó traces their relationships in the thirteen hours taken up by the novel through interior monologues that blend the past and present, by means of flashbacks, a technique, critics were quick to observe, rare in the Hungarian novel at the time. *Az őz*, set in Hungary after 1945, opens with Eszter, an actress, telling her life-story to her dead lover while sitting on his grave, framing her grief within juxtapositions of the past and the present in a solitary monologue. Eszter is a strong woman isolated from her social class. With her atypical life closing all doors to intimacy, she relies solely on herself, and obeying her own laws, turns ever inward, only to increase her painful isolation. Both novels were generally well received abroad. In Hungary, reviewers praised the care with which Szabó had developed the characters, but some hoped that, in keeping with Socialist Realism, she would turn to more recent and clearer conflicts and create more positive heroes as models for her readers.

Three works completed the first phase of Szabó's development as a novelist: *Disznótor* (1960; translated as *Night of the Pig-Killing*),

Pilátus (Pilate, 1963), and *Danaida* (Danaid, 1964). In *Disznótor*, set in a Transdanubian town in 1955, the cultures of once-rich landowners and artisans clash in the marriage of a former soapmaker, János Tóth, to a former aristocrat, Paula Kemery. The novel is concerned with the changes events have wrought in the economic status, personal values, and attitudes of its characters, whose bitterness at being victimized by history has not diminished with the passage of time. Events, dramatically compressed into a single day, compel Tóth to perceive the sham of his marriage and, overwhelmed by the insight, to kill his wife on the eve of the traditional feast. Szabó again resorts to the interior monologue, but this time she uses objective narration more extensively than in *Freskó* and *Az őz*. In *Pilátus* (Pilate, 1963), Szabó explores one of her major themes: the relationship between generations. In this novel, Iza, a woman physician, assumes complete custody of her recently widowed mother. Unable to communicate, to find words to express their responses to their new relationship, neither can convey to the other her true feelings about the difficulties she is experiencing. Iza responds generously to her mother's needs, but from a sense of duty, not love. Sensing the lack of love, her mother decides her life is superfluous and commits suicide. The tragic collision between two very different ethical worlds prevents the mother and daughter from building a genuine relationship. In *Danaid*, which takes place in the 1930s, Szabó deals with the predicament of persons who, constantly sacrificing themselves, are absorbed into the lives of others without imprinting any trace of their individuality on the world. Departing from her previous passionate women characters, she develops the motif through Katalin, a provincial archivist. Lacking self-confidence and believing she can make others forget her insignificance by constantly serving their needs, she fails to understand that this very suppression of the self is the flaw that keeps her from knowing true companionship. *Danaid* is the first of Szabó's novels in which the characters are not presented through extensive interior monologue. As a critic notes, Szabó now "observes, views, describes, and displays the protagonists but retains the right to be a spectator; in other words, she changes her objectives and conveys her displeasure and judgment through stresses and emphases; indeed, she unveils her characters' flaws and improper and foolish behavior, thus naturally enlarging the novel's dimension."

In the second half of the 1960s, Szabó concluded that she no longer had anything of value to say about the struggles of lonely, troubled women seeking a place in Hungary's socialist society and solutions to the moral issues they were facing. Accordingly, her next novel, *Mózes egy, huszonkettő* (Moses 1:22, 1967) delineates the polar conflict between generations. With the Abraham and Isaac story as referent, Szabó portrays the young as yearning for a world different from the one they inherited and demanding the right to form beliefs untainted by their parents' fears and compromises. *Katalin utca* (Katalin Street, 1969) is a synthesis of everything she had tried to develop in all her previous novels. Its theme—the impact of historical change on individuals even when they do not take note of the events around them—is found in her other works, but this time the connections developed between philosophical outlook and historical occurrence enlarge its dimension. The members of the family, barely able to breathe in the bleak atmosphere, have closed the doors to each other's personalities. Irén Elekes, the chief character, has been crushed by history but fails to see the cause of her misfortune. Immersed in herself, she does not realize that she must change in order to give her life a fresh direction.

To date, two very different novels round out Szabó's work in the genre: *Szemlélők* (Spectators, 1973) and *Régimódi történet* (An Old-Fashioned Story, 1977). The first, which, according to a critic, continues the narrative technique of *Katalin Utca* in the manner of a "rhythmic canon," examines the large question of the true identity of Hungary, as well as other East European nations. Through conflicts in a love affair between a West European man and an East European woman—her first truly intellectual woman protagonist—Szabó tries to discover what the real nature of the peoples living in the region is and how they will eventually view their tumultuous history and heal the psychological and ethical dilemmas that plague them. *Régumódi történet*, on the other hand, is a fictionalized account of her mother's stifled life in her family, the Jablonczays. A reviewer in *World Literature Today* called it a sensitive portrait of her mother and "the masterful reconstruction of the drama tearing apart the Jablonczay family through repeated battles between the forces of pragmatism and imagination, puritanism and profligacy, dour discipline and litertarian escapades." And it is a compassionate tribute to the parents Szabó loved so dearly.

Between 1958 and 1970 Szabó also published several novels for adolescents, all very popular. *Mondják meg Zsófikának* (translated as *Tell Sally*), which appeared in 1958, the same year as *Freskó*, and which Szabó adapted for the stage in 1971 seeks to inculcate in teenagers a sense of responsibility, feelings of compassion, and a

readiness to help others. *Szigetkék* (Island-Blue, 1959) envisions an island utopia so civilized that "technological progress" cannot destroy human relationships. *Álarcosbál* (The Masked Ball, 1961) warns teenagers of the great danger they face if they withdraw into a private world, while *Születésnap* (The Birthday, 1962) informs them about the first disappointments they are likely to encounter on reaching long-yearned-for adulthood. *Tündér Lala* (Lala the Fairy, 1968) relates the story of the son of a fairy queen who, unlike the little boy in *Szigetkék* who longs for a perfect society, wants to leave the fairy kingdom for the company of ordinary beings because he realizes that fulfilling a desire produces joy only if one has to struggle to achieve it; and *Abigél* (Abigail, 1970) aims at helping teenagers to understand the past through the story of a fifteen-year-old girl attending a boarding school in a small Hungarian town in the early 1900s.

It was the drama, however, that became her second genre. A love for the theater emerged early in her life. In Debrecen she had organized a little theater company among her schoolmates and written pieces for them to perform on school holidays, a practice she followed while she was a schoolteacher; in a short essay published in a cultural periodical in 1983, she traces the roots of her deep attachment to the drama to her family. Her first play, *Kigyómaras* (The Snake Bite, 1960), generally acknowledged as demonstrating her understanding of the living stage, takes its theme and characters from *Disznótor*, while her second play, *Leleplezés* (The Unveiling, 1962), uses the basic theme of *Az öz*. Reflecting the need for fresh themes she sensed in the mid-1960s, she has turned to persons and events from Hungary's troubled history, a tendency that continues in her plays. *Fanni hagyományai* (Fanny's Posthumous Papers, 1964) is based on a novel of sentiment by József Kármán, first published in 1794. Szabó's treatment of the heroine's unhappy love and death is more than an adaptation, however; writing the play for the 170th anniversary of the ill-fated Jacobin conspiracy led by Ignác Martinovics, a philosopher and Franciscan monk, she presents the unfortunate Fanny amid the setting and problems of provincial Hungary near the end of the eighteenth century and in the process removes much of the sentimentalism with which its original is awash. *Kiálts, város!* (Cry Out, City!, 1973), set in the opening years of the seventeenth century in Szabó's birthplace, probes the conflict between the two sides of Calvinism: its early progressive intellectualism and its eventual dogmatic rigidity and sternness. *Az a szép, fényes nap* (That Lovely, Sunny Day, written in 1974 and first staged in 1976) is the first of four successive plays that revive critical times from an even more distant past, in this case the linking of pagan Hungary to Christian Europe by Prince Géza and Vajk, the later King Stephen, to produce the painful but beautiful birth of a new world for their country. Next, a trilogy confronts the question of Hungary's place in the flow of history: *A meráni fiú* (The Boy of Meran, 1981), *A csata* (The Battle, 1981), and *Béla király* (King Béla, 1983). The first play embraces the events that preceded the thirteenth-century Mongol invasion and its consequences for Hungary; the second portrays the tragic change of a cultured Hungary into a land of savagery by that invasion; and the third depicts the reconstruction of the nation through the skills of an ironhanded and politically astute king. In the trilogy Szabó points to several national weaknesses which, she holds, Hungary's history reveals, including tendencies toward prejudice, lack of political resilience, and difficulty in perceiving the realities of historical situations. Her technique shows hardly any trace of tendencies present in contemporary drama, but the success of her plays at the box office proves their appeal to a large audience. They were published in collected editions in 1966 and 1975.

Szabó's oeuvre includes other genres as well. To her stage plays must be added the dramas she wrote for radio in the 1960s: *Hallei kirurgus* (The Chirurgeon of Halle, 1963), in which Handel's aging father finally realizes he must accept the prodigal's desire for a musical career and not impose that of a lawyer or judge on him, a situation reflecting one of Szabó's generational themes at that time; *A rab* (The Prisoner, 1965), which draws on the writings of Ferenc Kazinczy, a leading figure of the Hungarian Enlightenment, to find in his last days as a political prisoner an example of faith overcoming hardships and barriers to human liberty; and *Békekötés* (Peace Pact, 1965), which, using the theme of *Pilate*, presents the problems of a widow made dependent by her son's death in battle on two daughters who are unable to get along with each other.

She also wrote short stories early in her career. The eighteen stories collected in *Alvók futása* (Sleepers' Escape, 1967) are variations on the theme of generations in conflict because they fail to understand each other. To a reviewer who found the stories morbid, she was delighted to proclaim she is a necrophobe, not a necrophile. "Why should [they] have been cheerful, tell me why? What were my experiences like? Death constantly accompanied us and took, one after the other, those most precious to me. I was helpless and so was my love." She has published two accounts of her travels in Europe: *Hullámok kergetése* (The Pursuit of the Waves, 1965), re-

cording her observations of several European countries, and *Zeusz küszöbén* (On Zeus's Threshold, 1968), bringing into play her longstanding affection for classical civilization through her account of a trip to Greece in the summer of 1966. *Ókút* (Fountainhead), a candid account of the first ten years of her life, appeared in 1970. *Kívül a körön* (Outside the Circle, 1980), a 600-page collection of previously published essays and studies which sold out in days, consists of her writings on Hungarian literary history and aesthetics and on Hungarian authors no longer familiar to most of her fellow countrymen. The publication brought praise for her basic knowledge about the "sovereign" use of material and method and for her outlook as a woman on the literature of her nation. In 1983 she eulogized her late husband by publishing the writings he had left behind under the title *Megmaradt Szobotkának* (This Remained for Szobotka). His writings comprise about one fourth of its content; Szabó adds the remainder to complete his "memoir." Basing her narration on extant materials and her own life with the author, she paints a portrait of her husband's struggle to achieve deserved recognition as a novelist with an awareness that he "left every secret of his life here and turned himself over to me completely." In a 1983 interview concerned with turning points in her life and career, she called her husband's death the most fateful: "I had to learn to become the wife of a deceased husband."

Szabó's has been a long and prolific career. She is immensely popular in Hungary, and her works have been translated into twenty-six foreign languages. The list of the Baumgarten Prizes now includes her name for 1949, and two prestigious awards have followed: the Attila József Prize in 1959 and the Kossuth Prize in 1978.

WORKS IN ENGLISH TRANSLATION: *Mondják meg Zsófikának* was translated into English by Ursula McLean in 1963 with the title *Tell Sally*; *Az öz* by Kathleen Szasz in 1963 with the title *The Fawn*; Szasz also translated *Disznótor* in 1966 as *Night of the Pig-Killing*.

ABOUT: Tezla, A. Hungarian Authors: A Bibliographical Handbook, 1980. *Periodicals*—America September 21, 1963; Herald Tribune Book Review August 25, 1963; Kirkus Review November 1, 1965; Library Journal November 15, 1963; January 15, 1966; Nation November 9, 1963; New Statesman August 20, 1965; Saturday Review September 21, 1963; Times Literary Supplement May 24, 1963; World Literature Today Summer 1978.

*SZYMBORSKA, WISŁAWA (July 2, 1923–   ), Polish poet, was born in Bnin in Western Poland. In 1931 she moved to Krakow. She studied Polish literature and sociology at the Jagiellonian University in Krakow from 1945 to 1948. In 1953 she joined the Krakow literary weekly *Zycie literackie* as poetry editor and columnist.

Szymborska has published eight volumes of poetry: *Dlatego Zyjemy* (That's Why We Are Alive, 1952), *Pytania zadawane sobie* (Questioning Oneself, 1954), *Wołanie do Yeti* (Calling the Yeti, 1957), *Sól* (Salt, 1962), *Sto pociech* (A Hundred Joys, 1967), *Wszelki wypadek* (Chance, 1972), *Wielka liczba* (A Great Number, 1976), *Poezje* (Poems, 1977), and *Ludzie na moście* (People on a Bridge, 1986). Some of these titles rely on word-play which it is impossible to render elegantly into English. Two collections of her book reviews entitled *Lektury nadobowiazkowe* (Extra-curricular Readings) appeared in 1973 and 1981. Szymborska's poetry has been translated into French, German, Russian, Czech, Hungarian, and Dutch, as well as English.

Introducing Szymborska's selection *Poezje* in 1977, the critic Jerzy Kwiatkowski described her book as "one of the most important in contemporary Polish poetry. An amazing simplicity and communicatibility. The use of narrative and anecdote. A complete unpretentiousness. Yet at the same time—intellectually the most ambitious work, a poetic world with the most interesting mode of existence." This judgment has since been generously endorsed and confirmed by other critics, as well as by the general public.

In spite of the warm critical reception of her work, Szymborska's road to pre-eminence and acclaim was slow. Her first two volumes reflect the political simplicities and evasions of the Stalinist era and are hard to distinguish formally, stylistically, or linguistically from the general mass of mediocre verse produced at the time. The 1957 volume signals her break with the naiveties of her youth which are examined in her poem "Rehabilitation," in which she observes that Poles are engaged in an on-going debate trying to understand why so many able writers succumbed to the communist government's call to participate in the creation of a dreary and often dishonest social-realist literature during 1947–1957. Was it fear? Was it a desire to ingratiate oneself with those in power in exchange for certain privileges? Was it a contagious disease? Or was there—as the influential critic Artur Sandauer wrote in an essay on Szymborska—a deep desire to help entrench the new dispensation which, by its very promise to re-establish order and stability, easily appealed to a population which had just emerged from violence of World War II?

Because of the strength of nineteenth-century Polish romantic poetry and the fact that recent Polish history has favored confessional verse—emotionally, religiously, and patriotically committed—of a kind perfected by the romantics, the classical tradition has at best played a supporting role in contemporary Polish poetry, as in the work of Zbigniew Herbert and Czesław Miłosz. But the distinguishing features of Szymborska's mature work are those of the eighteenth-century Enlightenment: detachment, wit, erudition lightly employed, verbal brilliance centered not on elaborate metaphorical structures but on an exploitation of the punning possibilities of ordinary speech, an ability to handle narrative and ideas in a fresh and arresting manner. At the same time, her poetry is permeated with a Nietzschean exuberance, a joyful drive and energy which banish any suspicions that she is shackled by conventions of classical decorum. The poet and critic Krzysztof Karasek has aptly described as Mozartian her "joy arising from the play of intellect and imagination."

Like the detached, impersonal god of eighteenth-century Deism who was perceived as retreating into outer space, a watchmaker who had constructed a wondrously intricate clock which he left to its own devices after winding it up for eternity, Szymborska observes the earth, the creatures and objects found on it, as it were from outer space. Her training in scientific method doubtless accounts for Szymborska's clinical objectivity and voracious curiosity: "I read books on science, history and anthropology. I read lexicons and guide-books," she said in an interview, and the range of her book reviews—from cookery, tourism, gardening, and witchcraft to art history, T. S. Eliot's cat poems, and Edward Lear's nonsense poems bears this out. Szymborska imports all this bric-à-brac into her poetry. "There is no lack of subjects," she says, adding, "I would like each of my poems to be different," in contrast to those poets who "spend their lives effectively writing one long poem split into little bits." In this she most radically departs from her Enlightenment aesthetic, which claimed that it was proper for God to create everything but that the human artist had to confine himself to certain carefully defined topics. But Szymborska writes as a divine creator of the joys of creation ("The joys of writing / The ability to make things last" and "I've thought out the world, second edition / Second corrected edition"), of how her imagination, employing words rather than clay, can conjure objects and situations out of the air:

Where is this written doe running through the written
    forest?
Does she want to drink from the written water
reflecting her mouth like carbon paper?
    . . . In a drop of ink, quite a few hunters
wait, squinting,
to surround the doe, to shoot.

—trans. Sharon Olds

She can recreate the sordid and wretched
phenomenon of modern terrorism:

The bomb will explode in the bar at twenty past one.
Now it's only sixteen minutes past.
Some will still have time to enter,
some to leave.

The terrorist's already on the other side.
That distance protects him from all harm
and well it's like the pictures:

A woman in a yellow jacket, she enters.
A man in dark glasses, he leaves.
Boys in jeans, they're talking.
Sixteen minutes past and four seconds.
The smaller one he's lucky, mounts his scooter,
but that taller chap he walks in . . .

—trans. Adam Czerniawski

She can generate numberless reasons why
Lot's wife looked back:

I looked back supposedly curious . . .
I looked back regretting the silver dish.
Through carelessness—tying a sandal strap
In order not to keep staring at the righteous nape
of my husband, Lot. . . .
I looked back when setting down the bundle.
I looked back in terror where to step next . . .

—trans. Adam Czerniawski

She can understand the inability of modern
German youth to confront their country's recent
brutal past:

Conceived on a mattress of human hair,
Gerda, Erica, perhaps Margarette.
She doesn't, really doesn't know anything about it.
That kind of knowledge is impossible
to accept or transmit.
The Greek Furies were simply too just.
We'd be put off today by their winged savagery.

—trans. Jan Darowski

She can weave a dazzling aerobatic display
round the figure π:

The longest snake on earth breaks off after several metres.
Likewise, though at greater length, do fabled snakes.
The series comprising π
doesn't stop at the edge of the sheet,
it can stretch across the table, through the air,
through the wall, leaf, bird's nest, clouds, straight to
    heaven . . .

—trans. Adam Czerniawski

The poet-watchmaker can put on her sardonic intergalactic voice to mock humanity's hopelessly desperate attempts to arrest the flow of
time:

A strange planet with its strange people
They yield to time but don't recognise it.
They have ways of expressing their protest,
they make pictures, like this one for instance . . .
You see a boat sailing laboriously upstream.
You see a bridge over the water and people on the
bridge.
The people are visibly quickening their step,
because a downpour has just started . . .
The point is that nothing happens next . . .
The boat sails on motionless.
The people on the bridge
Run just where they were a moment past. . . .

—trans. Adam Czerniawski

Here, in "People on a Bridge" (the title of a
print by the Japanese artist Hiroshige Utagawa),
the poet has a picture as a springboard for her
metaphysical speculation, exploiting our amazement at the stillness an artist can achieve in the
midst of an inexorable flow of time. Pictures, by
their power to compel our attention, their immediacy, their ability to subvert our beliefs regarding what is seen and what exists, inevitably
appeal to Szymborska's puzzled curiosity about
the world and enable her to throw our daily reality into relief. Her "Breughel's Two Monkeys"
serves to confront humans with the animal kingdom; "Pietà" employs the reference in the title
to traditional representations of Christ's passion
to highlight a modern maternal tragedy; a description of a joyous medieval chivalric miniature leads to a reminder of the equally
obsessively depicted—but here disguised—
horror of hell; in "Byzantine Mosaic" the asceti-
cally portrayed characters are made to express
their suitably ascetic thoughts; in "Landscape"
the viewer literally steps into a hallucinatorily
depicted scene, of a kind perfected by the Dutch
masters. The photographic album, a museum of
artifacts, and the cinema are also exploited by
the poet to explore time, memory, and existence.

"Should someone classify my work as 'wom-
en's poetry' I would not be too upset, but I am
not concerned to make an issue of this fact,"
Szymborska declared. But because in so many of
her poems she invents a persona or enters the
mind of a historical, legendary, or imagined
character, it is not surprising that portrayals of
women are often found in her work: not only
Lot's wife, but Cassandra, Mary Stuart, and
Queen Elizabeth, the women painted by Rubens; there is a "Portrait of a Woman" and "In
Praise of My Sister"; there are poems about
childhood and motherhood. Polish grammar can
distinguish the speaker's gender (a nightmare
for a translator into English) and Szymborska's

unattributed monologues make it clear that a woman is speaking. In the following "Homecoming," the grammar itself indicates a female perspective on the male as eternal child:

> He was back. Said nothing.
> But it was clear something had upset him.
> He lay down in his suit.
> Hid his head under the blanket.
> Drew up his knees.
> He's about forty, but not at this moment.
> He exists—but only as much as in his mother's belly
> behind seven skins, in protective darkness.
> Tomorrow he is lecturing on homeostasis
> in metagalactic space travel.
> But now he's curled up and fallen asleep.
> —trans. Adam Czerniawski

Thus, however determinately Szymborska may wish to strive for an interstellar perspective, this last poem especially illustrates her involvement with humanity. She cannot in the end escape the somber truth that she is part of the variety of situations she so coolly chronicles. This ambiguity of her situation (part divine, part human) endows her work with tension and richness.

Echoing Rainer Maria Rilke's "Just once / everything, only for once. Once and no more. And we too / once. And never again," Szymborska asks "Why only once as myself?" in a poem suitably entitled "Wonderment," which in turn echoes Plato's observation that philosophy begins in wonder. As poets, Rilke and Szymborska pose the question personally, just as the philosopher Leibniz poses it in general terms ("Why is there something rather than nothing?"). Herein in brief lies the essential distinction between the two modes of discourse. The danger for Szymborska emerges in her occasional failure to find a suitably particularizing story for a concept— memory, the passing of time, the puzzles of perception—which she wants to use as a core for a poem. As she has said, for her the difficulty is not finding a subject for a poem—there are plenty about—but "presenting [the subject] as a problem." Here she admits to an intellectualist approach which has confined some of her poems to somewhat arid argument. The critic Piotr Kuncewicz asks, "Is a poet a magus or only an interpreter?" and replies, "Szymborska has failed to reach myth-creating forms. There are only traces and echoes of what might have been." Szymborska's aspirations are very high and where she succeeds the results are brilliant.

WORKS IN ENGLISH TRANSLATION: *Sounds, Feelings, Thoughts: Seventy Poems by Wisława Szymborska* was translated by Magnus J. Krynski and Robert A. Maguire in 1981. Selections from her poetry appear in the following collections: Celina Wieniewska (ed.) *Polish Writing Today*, 1967; Czesław Miłosz (trans.)

Postwar Polish Poetry, 3d. ed., 1983; Adam Czerniawski (trans.) *The Burning Forest: Modern Polish Poetry*, 1988; Susan Bassnett and Piotr Kuhiwczak (trans.) *Ariadne's Thread: Polish Women Poets*, 1988. There are also translations in periodicals—*Modern Poetry in Translation*: Poland, No. 23–24, Spring 1975, and translations by Grazyna Drabik, Austin Flint, and Sharon Olds in *Quarterly Review of Literature* 24: Poetry Series 4, 1982.

ABOUT: Columbia Dictionary of Modern European Literature, 1980; Encyclopedia of World Literature in the 20th Century, rev. ed., IV, 1984; Levine, M. G. Contemporary Polish Poetry 1925–1975, 1981; Stankiewicz, W. J. The Tradition of Polish Ideals, 1981. *Periodicals*—Cambridge Quarterly 16, 1987; Encounter May 1988; New York Review of Books October 21, 1982; Rialto Winter 1987/1988.

*TAKAMURA KŌTARŌ (March 13, 1883– April 1, 1956), Japanese sculptor, painter, writer, translator, and poet, was born in Tokyo, the first son of Takamura Kōun and his wife Waka. Takamura Kōun (1852–1934) was an accomplished craftsman specializing in Buddhist art. But at the time of Kōtarō's birth the family fortunes were at low ebb, in part because the Imperial Restoration of 1868 had brought with it a change in the state religion, from Buddhism to Shintoism, and the consequent denigration of all things related to Buddhism. In 1889, however, Okakura Tenshin (1862–1913), later to become the curator of Oriental arts at the Boston Museum of Art, persuaded Kōun to join the faculty of the Tokyo School of Fine Arts. Okakura and the American philosopher and art critic Ernst Fenollosa had just established the school in order to promote indigenous Japanese art and counter the Western influences that were flooding the country as it ended its 250 years of isolation. From then on Kōun's fame and prestige steadily increased. His wood carving "Old Monkey" attracted attention at the Chicago World Fair in 1893. Among his sculptures still on public display are the bronze equestrian statue of the prewar nationalist hero Kusunoki Masashige (1294– 1336), which is in front of the Imperial Palace, and the bronze statue of the statesman Saigō Takamori (1827–1877), which is in Ueno Park.

Takamura Kōtarō, following tradition, was expected to make sculpture his profession and as a young boy he seemed to take to it naturally. He went on to study it at the Tokyo School of Fine Arts where his father taught. While still a student there he was encouraged to study Western sculpture first-hand. In early 1906 he went to New York, attended the National Academy of Design, and worked briefly for Gutzon Borglum, the American sculptor of Mount Rushmore

°tā kä mu´ rä kō tä´ rō

TAKAMURA KŌTARŌ

fame. At the Art Students League of New York he won a scholarship, and in June 1907 moved to London; there he became friends with Bernard Leach, who later went to Japan and became a great potter. The following June Takamura moved to Paris where he lived for about a year. (Later he learned that above his basement apartment had lived the German poet Rainer Maria Rilke, then the secretary of Auguste Rodin, whom Takamura greatly admired and had vainly attempted to meet.) After traveling to Italy and briefly revisiting London, Takamura returned to Japan at the end of June 1909.

The sojourn abroad and direct experience of Western culture and art had complex effects on Takamura. His sentiments as he returned to his country are tersely expressed in a free-verse poem he published in early 1911, entitled "Netsuke no Kuni" ("The Country of Netsuke"), which characterizes the typical Japanese as a human specimen physically, mentally, and culturally inferior to the European:

Cheekbones protruding, lips thick, eyes triangular, with
a face like a netsuke carved by the master
    Sangorō
blank, as if stripped of his soul
not knowing himself, fidgety
life-cheap
vainglorious
small & frigid, incredibly smug
monkey-like, fox-like, flying-squirrel-like, mudskipper-
like, minnow-like, gargoyle-like, chip-from-a-cup-like
    Japanese

            —trans. Hiroaki Sato

The last line consists of traditional curse-words. Frustrated by the pervasive backwardness that he saw in his compatriots and their culture, Takamura threw himself into the deliberately indulgent activities of Pan's Club, a gathering set up by a group of self-styled "decadent" writers and artists. At the same time his indignation and sense of inferiority moved him to assume a missionary fervor in informing the Japanese public of the thoughts and behavior of Western artists and poets. Although he had dissociated himself from Pan's by early 1913, he continued through much of his life to translate and write about the many Europeans and Americans he admired. To name only those whose words, poems, and ideas he published in book form, they are Rodin ("Sayings," 1916; "More Sayings," 1920; a biography, 1927); Van Gogh (Elizabeth's "Memoirs," 1921); Whitman ("Diary Excerpts," 1921); Verhaeren (Les Heures Claires, 1921; Les Flammes Hautes, 1925; selected poems, 1953); and Romain Rolland (Liluli, 1924). In 1926 he and several writers formed the Association of Friends of Romain Rolland.

His Western experiences also made him resolve to pursue sculpture as "an artist," rather than as a craftsman like Kōun. That decision ironically forced him to rely on his father's largesse as long as the latter was alive. He earned money, for example, by making models for Kōun's sculptures. His own work reflected the dichotomy between his classical Japanese training and his desire to be "artistic" in the European sense. He produced two distinct types of work: skillfully executed wood-carvings of insects, animals, fruit, and fish, which are much in the traditional mode, and bronze sculptures of human hands and heads, which show the powerful influence of Rodin. Despite this ambivalence, Takamura Kōtarō played a pivotal role in molding modern sculpture in Japan. He was also an accomplished painter.

His foreign experiences affected Takamura in poetry as well. He had begun writing and publishing verses in the traditional forms of 5-7-5-syllable haiku and 5-7-5-7-7-syllable tanka as early as age 17, when his haiku won first prize in a contest sponsored by a national daily. In New York, however, he started writing longer poems in "new style." At that time "new-style" poems, which had come into being in the late nineteenth century under the influence of Western poetry, were still being composed in classical Japanese and mainly in various combinations of 5 and 7 syllables. Takamura's early pieces were no different, but it did not take him long to begin experimenting. In late 1909 he published a Whitmanesque free verse using the vernacular, called Nioi (Smell). Netsuke no Kuni, cited above, followed.

Among his early attempts to write poems free from syllabic constraints and in colloquial Japanese, —N Joshi ni (—To Lady N), published in July 1912, stands out as particularly successful. Takamura changed the title to Hito ni (To Someone) and revised the content extensively when he included it in his first collection of poems, Dōtei (Journey), in 1914. That book, published with the money his father had given him, was to become one of the two landmarks in modern Japanese poetry showing the mastery of colloquial language. (The other is Tsuki ni Hoeru [Howling at the Moon] by Hagiwara Sakutarō [1886–1942], published in 1917.)

—N Joshi ni also proved prophetic. Opening with the remonstration, "No, no, I don't like it / your going away—," it was addressed to Naganuma Chieko (1886–1938), a painter and a member of the feminist Blue Stocking Society, whom Takamura had met in late 1911. Married two years later, they set out living as artists on an equal footing, an unusual arrangement in Japan then or now. For many years their life together was outwardly uneventful, although, as the pressures of his art work increased, Takamura left more household chores to Chieko and that meant, he acknowledged, a greater artistic sacrifice on her part. In August 1931 she showed symptoms of schizophrenia for the first time. In July 1932 she attempted suicide and was hospitalized for three weeks. Thereafter her schizophrenia worsened steadily. Normally a quiet woman who tended to withdraw into herself (though physically active in tennis, bicycling, and riding), she now ranted, threw things at people, and harangued in the streets. Takamura valiantly tried to care for her in their home but in February 1935, exhausted, he put her in a hospital. There Chieko began making paper cutouts and collages, an activity she continued until her death in October 1938, even though her condition did not improve enough to warrant release. Takamura's poem about his last meeting with her is entitled "Remon Aika" ("Lemon Elegy"):

So intensely you had been waiting for lemon.
In the sad, white, light deathbed
you took that one lemon from my hand
and bit it sharply with your bright teeth.
A fragrance rose the color of topaz.
Those heavenly drops of juice
flashed you back to sanity.
Your eyes, blue and transparent, slightly smiled.
You grasped my hand, how vigorous you were.
There was a storm in your throat
but just at the end
Chieko found Chieko again,
all life's love into one moment fallen.
And then once
as once you did on a mountain top you let out a great
   sigh
and with it your engine stopped.

By the cherry blossoms in front of your photograph
today, too, I will put a cool fresh lemon.
                                        —trans. Hiroaki Sato

This poem and about thirty others, along with Takamura's essays on Chieko's life and her paper cutouts, were collected in his second book of poems, Chieko Shō (Selection of Writings about Chieko), published in 1941. The selection, later expanded, is probably the most widely read book of poems in Japan; its editions are often adorned with a sampling of Chieko's paper cutouts.

If Takamura's poetry cannot be thought of without Chieko, it is also inexorably linked to sculpture. A man who considered himself to be more a sculptor than a poet throughout his life, he often described the act of carving and sculpting in his poems. One such poem, written in 1911, is called "Chichi no Kao" ("My Father's Face")

When I make my father's face with clay,
below the window in twilight
my father's face is sad and lonely.

Its shadings, having some resemblance to my face,
are eerie, the law terrifying,
and the old age of my soul, nakedly
manifest, unexpectedly startles me.
My heart, eager to see what it fears,
looks at the eyes, the wrinkles on the forehead.
My father's face that I made
remains deeply silent like fish
yet tells, alas, of its painful days of the past.

Is it the dark cry of steel
or the ghost's voice of Hamlet I saw in the West?
Its piercing echo, though without rancor,
seeps into my nails and throbs like whitlow.

When I make my father's face with clay,
below the window in twilight
the mysterious lineage of the blood whispers . . .
                                        —trans. Hiroaki Sato

Takamura wrote few poems while Chieko was gravely ill. But his output began to increase from about the year she died, and with the onset of World War II in 1939, acquired an overtly militaristic tone. By the end of the war he had written a large body of poems upholding Japan's nationalistic causes. The majority of them were published in Oinaru Hi ni (The Great Day), in 1942; Ojisan no Shi (Uncle's Poems), in 1943; and Kiroku (Record), in 1944. When the Patriotic Association for Literature was set up in 1942, he became its director of poetry, thereby making himself a conspicuous "collaborator" among men of letters. As a result, following Japan's defeat he was accused, not under the law but by fellow writers, of "war responsibilities." In reaction he wrote a series of twenty poems under the title of Angu Shōden (A Brief History of Imbecility), which he published in 1947. Though obviously an apologia, the sequence is also a moving summation of an artist's experiences during the most turbulent period of modern Japanese history. To make up for his contribution to the war, he also remained, as a form of self-exile, in the remote part of northern Japan where he had moved after his house in Tokyo was bombed. He did not return to Tokyo until 1952, when he accepted a commission to build a statue to commemorate the people who helped establish Towada National Park. The bronze statue, of twin nudes, was completed and erected in October 1953. Not long afterward his chronic tuberculosis worsened and he did not recover, though he remained active to the end. During the postwar period, he published *Tenkei* (A Type), in 1950; *Chieko Shō: Sono Go* (*Chieko Shō:* Afterward), in 1950; and selected poems in 1955. A year after his death, his "complete writings" began to be published in an edition of eighteen volumes, concluded the following year.

WORKS IN ENGLISH TRANSLATION: Soichi Furuta's translation of *Chieko's Sky* was published in 1978, and Hiroaki Sato's *Chieko and Other Poems of Takamura Kōtarō* appeared in 1980. Sizable selections are in Sato's *Ten Japanese Poets*, 1973, and Sato and Burton Watson's *From the Country of Eight Islands*, 1981. A nearly full listing of translated poems may be found in Makoto Ueda's *Modern Japanese Poets* published in 1983.

ABOUT: Encyclopedia of Japan, 1984; Keene, D. Dawn to the West: Japanese Literature in the Modern Era, II, 1984; Ueda, M. Modern Japanese Poets and the Nature of Literature, 1983. *Periodicals*—Parnassus Spring/Summer 1981.

*TANIKAWA SHUNTARŌ (December 15, 1931–), Japanese poet, essayist, script-writer, and translator of nursery rhymes, writes: "I was born in Tokyo by cesarean section. Many people claim that children born thus will be unusually bright but lacking in stamina. I've no reason to think otherwise. As a child, I suffered from a coronary valvular problem and so things like marathon races were out of the question. Even today I have no interest in long, drawn-out matters, like epic poems. The valvular problem, however, seems to have healed of its own accord.

"I was born the only child of Tetsuzō Tanikawa who went on to become, in people's judgment, one of modern Japan's most distinguished philosophers. My father was important to me, for when I browsed in his study I found an encyclopedia from which I learned all I then knew about sex.

"Among childhood experiences, one was especially significant. Early one morning I was

TANIKAWA SHUNTARŌ

standing in our garden on a lawn drenched with dew. The sun was ascending behind a tree in the neighbor's garden (we call it the 'false acacia tree'). In those moments something came to life inside of me that I'd never felt before. I now think that 'something' was poetry. That night I wrote in my diary, 'Today for the first time in my life I felt that the morning was beautiful.'

"Looking at the past, I'd say there's really nothing I want to forget. I've no sense of 'if only this or that.' Not that I deliberately set out to plan my life in that way; and not that I had a terrifically iron will either. It's just that I'm unable to feel regret about anything in my past. And maybe that's why I'm no good with dates or of conceiving of my past in terms of dates. I don't feel that anything in my life has been concluded; sometimes I feel that I'm still in my childhood. You might think of it this way, that maybe I have nothing pleasant enough to remember. Past? Future? I live entirely in the present.

"What was always remarkably strong for me was the bonding between my mother and me. When I became a young man and decided that I could and would launch out on my own I did so in reaction against that maternal bonding. I recall the passion with which I determined to be independent and I am still filled with that determination.

"When a junior high-school classmate introduced me to poetry I of course had no idea that I wanted to be a poet. Literature wasn't much on my mind at that time. As a matter of fact, it isn't very important to me now either. It's the human experience that lies behind literature

that interests me. Literature is a mere reflection. Isn't it the same with a lot of academic subjects? I didn't like school at all in those days and the social changes that took place after the war really pleased me.

"I don't remember exactly how I felt when I first started writing poetry but I know that little by little I did almost nothing else. I'm sorry to say in fact it became my sole pursuit. Why? Well, I don't actually like poetry very much but I felt that writing poems was the only thing I *could* do. The idea of going to college repulsed me. I refused to enroll. Two notebooks filled with my poems, however, convinced my parents that I was serious about being a poet and so they accepted my decision.

"I had begun writing quite a lot in my late teens. Maybe the way I got into poetry wasn't so bad after all, for I came to it directly, frankly, objectively—without academic biases. I wasn't starry-eyed or sentimental but just wrote poems the way other kids rode bikes or played Ping Pong. It was an easy game.

"For good or for ill, for forty years now publishers have kept soliciting my work and I've sold my poems like merchandise. Maybe that is why I've kept my writer's nose to the grindstone. Otherwise unemployed, I depend on writing for my wherewithal and although income is a first consideration there's more to it than money, I'm in some public demand.

"However few my readers, those I do have create a role in society for me which makes me at once economically and psychologically stable. As for readers, I want to entertain without flattering them. I don't want to instruct them—just communicate with them. Writing is my only true link to my contemporaries. And I will write nothing unless I am inwardly compelled. What I write for myself and what I write for the public are one and the same. That is the very function, the purpose, of words."

Shuntarō Tanikawa is a leading representative of and spokesman for a generation of Japanese poets who came to maturity after World War II, open and sensitive to what for so many generations had been foreign to Japan— Western popular culture and a recognition of the inter-relatedness of all cultures and human values. Barely into his teens, a schoolboy in Tokyo, he was witness to the devastation of the closing years of the war. Although his father and his mother, a gifted pianist, raised him in a rich cultural environment where he developed a passion for classical Western music, especially for Beethoven, he grew up with a sense of crumbling

traditions and values. "It was a period of a of vacuum for us," he has written of his ge tion, "and nobody knew what to believe. decision not to go to college, usually the ce of political activism in Japan, further isola him. He describes his state of mind at that ti in a poem called "Growth":

age three
there was no past for me

age five
my past went back to yesterday

age seven
my past went back to topknotted samurai

age eleven
my past went back to dinosaurs

age fourteen
my past agreed with the texts at school

age sixteen
I look at the infinity of my past with fear

age eighteen
I know not a thing about time

Tanikawa began writing poetry with no serious ambitions of becoming a writer, but by 1950 he was publishing poems in a prominent literary journal, *Bungakkai* (Literary World). Two years later he published his first volume, *Nijuoku konen no kodoku* (Twenty Billion Years of Loneliness). Meanwhile he had also begun a career, more lucrative than any young poet's, of writing lyrics for popular music, and this brought him into touch with a far larger audience than his poetry had ever done. Excited by the possibilities of the mass media, Tanikawa was soon writing for radio, film, stage, and television. His first marriage, in 1954, was to Kishida Eriko, herself a poet and the daughter of the playwright Kishida Kunio. The marriage ended in divorce in 1956. In the following year he married Ookubo Tomoko, an actress; they were separated in 1981. From this marriage Tanikawa has two children, a son and a daughter. It was for his own family that he wrote his first children's stories, poems, and plays. These have had enormous popularity in Japan. He has also translated children's classics from Mother Goose to the Peanuts comics into Japanese.

Tanikawa is today considered Japan's most popular poet. He enjoys a celebrity accorded in the Western world only to superstars. He has also won international recognition. He has traveled in Europe and in the United States on fellowships from the Japan Society, and he has represented his country at many international gatherings, among them the International Poetry Festival held at the Library of Congress in

Washington, D.C. in 1970, Poetry International 1977 in Rotterdam, and the Japanese Poetry Festival in New York City in 1985. At home he has received the Japan Disc Grand Prix, an award from the Japan Phonograph society for a song recording (1962), the Japan Translation Culture Prize for his translation *Maza Gusu uta* (Mother Goose rhymes), and several literary awards for his poetry.

Tanikawa writes on a businesslike schedule in his own studio-office, producing an astounding amount of work. His great popularity, as well as his productivity, have led some critics to question the artistic merit of his poetry. Geoffrey O'Brien, reviewing his *Selected Poems* in the *Village Voice*, finds that the collection "contains more than its share of banal, sentimental, or harried work . . . the more homiletic verses here verge on Rod McKuen." Nevertheless O'Brien is convinced that Tanikawa "is capable of much better," and in his best work "reaches a darker, more meditative vein, focussing with tactile immediacy on the futilities and momentary pleasures of existence." Harvey Shapiro, writing of the same volume in the *New York Times*, found Tanikawa's "the voice of a major poet." Shapiro was especially struck by Tanikawa's fascination with the American West, to which he was introduced by American films. He has written on folk heroes like Billy the Kid:

> In killing, I tried to make sure of men and myself
>   my
> youthful way of proving was studded in colors of blood
>   but with
> the blood of other men I couldn't paint away the blue
>   sky   I
> needed my own   I got it today . . . .

There is indeed no question that Tanikawa has made an important contribution to modern Japanese poetry. He has also enlightened the Western public to the changing character of Japanese poetry, a good deal of which has moved away from the traditional forms of the tanka and the haiku with their strict syllabic prosody. Since the beginning of the twentieth century, Japanese poets, many of them under European influence, have experimented in other forms. Tanikawa is well read in European literature (except, he admits, "I have never read Marx and Freud"). He cites among influences upon him a varied group ranging from Albert Camus, Eugène Ionesco, Luigi Pirandello, and Federico García Lorca to popular French lyricist poets like Robert Desnos and Jacques Prévert. Early in his career he studied Rainer Maria Rilke's poems in Japanese translations and attempted to write in sonnet form. An example, from his *Rokujū no sonetto* (Sixty Sonnets, 1953), is his Sonnet 58:

> Because of remoteness
> Mountains can become mountains,
> When stared at too closely
> A mountain comes to resemble myself
>
> Vast landscapes bring men to a halt,
> Then men become aware of being surrounded
>   by profuse remotenesses,
> They are always
> Remotenesses that make men men.
>
> Yet man inside himself
> Possesses a remoteness
> Therefore man continues on to yearn . . .
>
> Occasionally man cannot exceed the place
>   that transgresses every remoteness,
> Without being seen anymore
> Man at such times becomes the landscape.

At the heart of all Tanikawa's work, whether addressed to a large popular audience or to more sophisticated readers of poetry, is what Geoffrey O'Brien cites as "the directness of his tone, which can seem that of a relaxed and confiding friend. The popularity of such low-keyed intimacy reminds us that Japanese poetry still values the sincere and spontaneous more highly than the ironically deconstructed." As James R. Morita sums it up in *World Literature Today*: "Tanikawa consciously (and conscientiously) seeks an audience for his poetry in the masses. He writes song lyrics, satirical verses for newspapers and comedies for the theatre. His language, often tinged with humor and pathos, is eminently facile not only to the ears but also to the eyes and mind of the reader. Evidently, he has the rare ability to see simplicity in what is quite complex and hope in what is actually deplorable. His concern is, in broad terms, humanitarianism."

WORKS IN ENGLISH TRANSLATION: *The Selected Poems of Shuntarō Tanikawa* translated by Harold Wright was published in 1983. All translations quoted above are Wright's. Individual volumes in translations by William I. Elliott and Kawamura Kazuo include *With Silence My Companion* (1970, *Tabi*—poems inspired by his eight months of travel in the West in 1963), published in 1975; *At Midnight in the Kitchen I Just Wanted to Talk at You* (1975, *Yonaka ni daidokoro de boku wa kimi ni hanashi kaketakatta*), published in 1980, and *Coca-Cola Lesson* (1980, *Kokakōra ressun*), 1986.

ABOUT: Contemporary Authors 121, 1987; Encyclopedia of Japan, 1983; Wright, H. *Afterword to* Selected Poems of Shuntarō Tanikawa, 1983. *Periodicals*—New York Times November 12, 1983; Village Voice February 28, 1984; World Literature Today Summer 1984.

TAYLOR, CHARLES (November 5, 1931   ), Canadian philosopher, writes: "I was

born and brought up in Montréal, in a family part English- and part French-speaking, at a time when people in Canada still looked towards the European mother-countries which had founded ours. My father felt very keenly the attachment to Britain, my maternal grandfather (rather rare among French Canadians) had a strong affinity to France. It was almost foreordained that I would want to study in both metropolitan countries when I came of age. From all of this, background and study, Canada emerged for me not only as a nation, more or less like others, but also as a standpoint from which to view the world.

"One way that you see things through the prism of a Montréal childhood accentuates language. I would say: it gives language its full significance in human life, not just a medium of representation and communication, but what gives shape to human existence. It was just obvious that what you could say, think, feel, find funny, be dramatic about, was different in each language. The mode of expression helped constitute what was expressed. It doesn't take one long to generalize beyond the two cases, and to realize that each such medium, each culture, encapsulates and conserves its own way of experience, thought and sensibility; something analogous to another world, with its own unfamiliar coloration. To be able to explore these worlds is a delight and a fascination. If I could be guaranteed 250 years of life, I would spend a good century learning all the languages I could.

"Another crucial formative fact was the garden—really fairly spacious grounds—where I spent my childhood. I understand the image of paradise. It wasn't that I was terribly happy there: I don't remember my time as a child either as specially happy or the reverse. But I knew very early that the secret is somewhere there, and I came to see later how we are both linked with it and separated from it by time.

"The link we make in language. And so in another way, too, language as expression, language as world-making has become central to me. In which I find myself in the very mainstream of twentieth-century culture. Through my idiosyncratic route, I came to the common question. We are all obsessed with language. But we understand it in radically diverse terms.

"With the right gifts, these concerns could have made a poet, but as things were I was drawn into philosophy, from which I have yet to emerge. I have tried to make sense of all this in the clearest prose I can master. Humans as cultural animals endowed language are protean beings, and yet there is such a thing as human nature, a range of potentialities which are pecu-

liarly ours. We have been busy realizing a certain sub-set of these in the modern West, which we are tempted at times to take as the very epitome of human nature, at other times to see as a loss, a forgetting of what earlier cultures enjoyed. I don't think we have yet found the terms to come to grips with this: to express the inescapably particular in relation to the universal in human life; and above all to see our own Western culture in this relation, without chauvinism, but without recoil in self-depreciation either.

"I don't find myself at home in any of the popular views about modernity: either the upbeat endorsements of the Enlightenment project, or the gloomy inventories of irreparable loss. Or rather, I agree too much with both. Modernity has brought freedom, inwardness, a concern for rights, equality, universal welfare, the self-awareness of the creative imagination. And at the same time, these are linked to areas of darkness: among others, a reductive understanding of human life which flattens inwardness, trivializes freedom, and numbs the imagination. How are these connected? For the unqualified proponents of Enlightenment, there is no darkness to explain; for the straight-line counter-Enlightenment, the darkness is the nemesis following the hubris of freedom. But I can't agree with either, and am still looking for the answer.

"I have a hunch that I speak for more than myself. I think we are all more ambivalent about modernity than the partisan theories allow. We just need to be able to release the full range of our responses. In fact, one of the most striking things about modernity is its tendency to repress the spiritual. We are the first civilization where masses of people deny all religious sense, and this is considered normal. In my view, what we see here is a powerful repression, where spiritual life is being denied, paradoxically, for spiritual reasons. We need to release the spiritual, which I for my part see as a love of God which rises in every human being. And that means, to find new language for it.

"And so once again, I see language as expression, language which makes a human world, at the very heart of our predicament."

————————

Charles Taylor's uniqueness among contemporary philosophers, Richard Rorty suggested in a review of Taylor's *Philosophical Papers* in the *Times Literary Supplement*, is that "he is so well read, and so intellectually curious, that he is remarkably good at what [Hans Georg] Gadamer calls 'fusing horizons'—coalescing two perspectives into a single synoptic view, melding two vocabularies into a larger and richer language."

Those vocabularies are, on the one hand, the rigorous analytical discourse of mathematics and the natural sciences and, on the other, the intuitive or subjective discourse of interpretation or hermeneutics. Taylor's aim, as Rorty sees it, "is to show that human beings (or, more generally, agents) are metaphysically distinct from the rest of the universe, and therefore need to be understood hermeneutically rather than 'scientifically.'"

Essentially, as Michael Ignatieff wrote in the Canadian journal *Saturday Night*, Taylor's whole career has been a search for "the reconciliation of opposites—Marxism and Catholicism, liberalism and socialism, English analytical philosophy and French and German metaphysics." A humanist in the most traditional sense of one who is committed to the study of human welfare and values, he rejects notions of scientific analysis of humankind—behaviorism, for example, or artificial intelligence, which purport to explain and predict human activity. Yet he is also committed to a social philosophy which would strike many traditional thinkers as radical. Although he has spent his entire professional life in academia, he also served as vice president of the New Democratic Party of Canada from 1965 to 1973, during which he led an unsuccessful attempt to unite French- and English-speaking Canadians. He defined his political philosophy in *The Patterns of Politics* in 1970, challenging the liberal-consensus politics of then Prime Minister Pierre Trudeau and arguing for a socialist system under which "the autonomy and power of the corporate system [would] have to be brought more into line with social needs and goals."

Taylor's controversial but balanced social philosophy—with its advocacy of tolerance, free speech, and civil rights, and its criticism of the laissez-faire capitalism that, in his view, permits exploitation and inequality—developed early. The son of an industrialist, Walter Margrave Taylor, and Simone Beaubien Taylor, he attended McGill University (B.A. 1952), then went on to Oxford as a Fellow of All Souls College to study philosophy. In the formal and conservative setting of the Oxford of that time, Taylor was regarded as a radical and an anomaly—a Catholic who leaned toward Marxism. With a group of fellow students—including E. P. Thompson, who was to become a leading Marxist historian—he founded the *Universities and Left Review*, which later became the *New Left Review*. After receiving an M.A. (1960) and a D. Phil. (1961) from Oxford, Taylor returned to McGill, where he has taught philosophy and political science since 1961. He has also been Chichele Professor of Social and Political Theory at Oxford (1976–1981) and visiting professor at Princeton (1965) and at Berkeley (1974). In 1981–1982 he was a member of the Institute for Advanced Study at Princeton. Married since 1956 to Alba Romer, an artist, he has five children and lives in Montreal.

It is in moral and social philosophy rather than political theory that Taylor has won his major reputation. Mediating between what is now considered the philosophical "right"—i.e. the adaptation of the methods of the natural sciences to the social sciences—and the philosophical "left"—the rejection of humanism and idealism altogether, Taylor follows the example of the eighteenth-century German philosopher Hegel, "attempting nothing else," Rorty writes, "than a synthesis of moral reflection with intellectual history, one which will do for our time what Hegel did for his." Taylor's *Hegel* and his *Hegel and Modern Society* aim, he writes, "to produce not just an exposition of Hegel, but a view of the ways in which he is relevant and important to contemporary philosophers." Taylor finds Hegel's political philosophy especially timely on the troubling question of personal freedom and its limits in a complex modern industrial society. As he sees it, Hegel's work combines two ideals of romanticism: "The aspiration to radical autonomy on one hand, and to expressive unity with nature and within society on the other," aspirations shared by many modern thinkers but difficult to reconcile.

This problem was the basis for a series of lectures Taylor delivered at the University of Delhi in 1981 and published as *Social Theory and Practice*. Here he defined the issue as "a powerful tendency in modern technological civilizations to assimilate human to natural science, and thus in a way to assimilate man to things, sometimes even to understand ourselves on the model of machines. This tendency is dangerous and destructive because human beings live by their self-interpretations. It is a matter of vital necessity to get ourselves right—or at least not to entertain too distorted a picture of ourselves." Defining selfhood or personhood thus becomes Taylor's goal, although he is quick to acknowledge that "there can be no absolute understanding of what we are as persons." We define ourselves by interpreting ourselves. As he writes in the Introduction to *Philosophical Papers*, a collection of essays and lectures that covers some fifteen years of his career, "to be a full human agent, to be a person or a self in the ordinary meaning, is to exist in a space defined by distinctions of worth. A self is a being for whom certain questions of categoric value have arisen and received at least partial answers." Questions of worth or value cannot be treated scientifically:

"What it is to possess a liver or a heart is something I can define quite independently of the space of questions in which I exist for myself, but not what it is to have a self or be a person."

The strength of Taylor's *Philosophical Papers*, Michael J. Shapiro writes in the journal *Political Theory*, is their "doctrinal dimension": "Alongside Charles Taylor the critic of empiricism stands Charles Taylor the hermeneutically oriented political philosopher, and hovering in the background, directing these two, is Charles Taylor the moralist, advocating communitarianism over social atomism and the integrity of the human subject against what he sees as immoralist Nietzsche-inspired views of a fragmented subject." Shapiro, however, criticizes Taylor for allowing "his moral code [to] overmaster his analytical one," for clinging to eighteenth-century Enlightenment thinking and "a traditional Christian ethic leavened with some of the language of a German speculative philosophy." Others, among them the British philosopher Ernest Gellner, have questioned his communitarianism and distrust of individualism as "naive" and posing the risk of authoritarianism. Nevertheless, as Shapiro concludes: "In general, Taylor displays a philosophical sophistication, political sensitivity, and, not insignificantly, an admirable humanitarian concern with those whose relatively poorer shares of public goods are either ignored or justified within the unreflective doctrines of individualism."

In 1989 Taylor published a book on which he had worked for a number of years, a long and wide-ranging study of morality in the modern world, *Sources of the Self: The Making of the Modern Identity*. The book reaffirms his faith in the human capacity for reason and making moral judgments—what he calls "the affirmation of ordinary life." It is in the daily routines of work and personal domestic life, not necessarily in the rarefield atmosphere of philosophical thought, that human beings confront and make their choices between good and evil. Moving from Plato to Nietzsche to Foucault and Derrida and drawing as well upon poetry and art, Taylor traces the history of moral theory into the modern era in which the bases of all moral values appear to be disintegrating. His essentially sanguine view of the prospects of the modern self does not deny the evil and destruction of which humanity is capable. Rather, as he writes at the close of the book: "There is a large element of hope. It is a hope that I see implicit in Judaeo-Christian theism (however terrible the record of its adherents in history), and in its central promise of a divine affirmation of the human, more total than humans can ever attain unaided."

Sources of the Self was praised by its reviewers as an enlightening and stimulating book. For the psychologist Jerome Bruner it "is surely one of the most important philosophical works of the last quarter of a century . . . Charles Taylor emerges as one of the truly great practitioners of philosophy in our century." Jeremy Waldron, in the *Times Literary Supplement*, expressed some reservations over Taylor's "speculations at the end of the book on religious belief and the spiritual dimensions of human life," but he found it "an engaging book. Few have Taylor's talent for writing clearly, even colloquially, while preserving a sense of the difficulty and depth of the material."

PRINCIPAL WORKS: The Explanation of Behavior, 1964; Patterns of Politics, 1970; Hegel, 1975; Hegel and Modern Society, 1979; Social Theory as Practice, 1983; Philosophical Papers, 2 vols. (I. Human Agency and Language; II. Philosophy and the Human Sciences), 1985; Sources of the Self: The Making of the Modern Identity, 1989.

ABOUT: Contemporary Authors New Revision Series 11, 1984; Canadian Who's Who 1988; Nielsen, K. *in* Held, V., S. Morgenbessor, T. Nagel (eds.) Philosophy, Morality and International Affairs, 1974. *Periodicals*—Political Theory May 1986; Saturday Night December 1985; Times Literary Supplement December 6, 1985; March 23, 1990.

TAYLOR, HENRY (SPLAWN) (June 21, 1942–   ), American poet and critic, writes: "I was born in the farm country of Loudoun County, about fifty miles west of Washington, D.C., and I grew up there, attending local schools until I was fifteen. My father was a dairy farmer in those days; I think that, though he was good at it, my vicarious experience of his work turned me away from it; I learned at an early age that I would not follow my father into a way of life that he and generations of his forebears had been following on the same land since the 1790s. Whether he wanted to or not, he encouraged me in this decision; my parents are both well-educated people, and taught me early to read poems aloud as if they meant something. In my second book, there is a poem called 'To Hear My Head Roar' which recounts some of my early struggles with learning poems by heart and saying them before schoolmates; in it, I acknowledge that I was following my father's footsteps in that direction, instead of in another.

"But growing up in the country, with one set of grandparents nearby, and my maternal grandfather not far away, and being allowed to participate in adult conversations from an early

HENRY TAYLOR

age, gave me a background that I have drawn on ever since. Many of the stories my poems tell are versions of things I have been hearing about all my life; and many of the attitudes I take toward my work are attitudes I first learned while operating a piece of farm machinery, or working with horses.

"Horses, in fact, were central to my life until I was in my early twenties; my sisters and I had various ponies and horses around the place, and our parents (well, my mother, to be truthful, has always been a touch nervous about the horses; but she has put up with their presence with unique grace) started us foxhunting, showing in small local horse and pony shows, and generally being as horsy as we could be without spending enormous fortunes, which we did not have. Many of my poems draw heavily on that experience.

"When I was in the tenth grade, I went off to George School, a Quaker school in Bucks County, Pennsylvania. I had grown up in the Religious Society of Friends, and knew that my grandmother and my father, as well as numerous cousins, aunts, etc., had gone to George School. When I got there, I wasn't ready; I found myself among urban sophisticates, and was keenly aware of my comparatively provincial background. I wouldn't be fifteen again for anything. But George School was where I began to get a whiff of what literature was like; it was also where I encountered Eugénie Vickery and John Carson, two of the finest teachers who ever lived. Madame Vickery took us through Molière by the end of our third year of French, and Mr.

Carson inspired in me what I have to call a passion for the study of biology.

"I attended the University of Virginia; my grades at George School were low enough that I was admitted very tentatively and provisionally; but the scores I earned on biology and French achievement tests got me an invitation to join the first group of Echols Scholars at the University. I got these contradictory letters about three weeks apart, and still have them. At the University, I found the biology labs uninhabitable (they have since been handsomely replaced), so I backed into English as a major, though I took graduate French courses throughout my undergraduate years. There were two people at Virginia who helped me most to see how to go in the direction I was thinking I might take; one was Richard Dillard, then a graduate student in English, and the other was George Garrett, who came there my third year to teach creative writing. What my life would have been without their friendship I cannot imagine. Dillard encouraged me to take a Master's in Creative Writing at Hollins College, where he was by then teaching; there I had the close and invaluable guidance of Louis Rubin and William Jay Smith. There also I met my wife Frannie; we married in 1968, and she has become, among many treasured roles, my most reliable first reader.

"Since those student days, I have been a full-time professor, with occasional leaves of absence to write. I live now where I grew up, and continue to find that landscape the most evocative of any I have lived in."

———

In 1986 Henry Taylor's *The Flying Change* won the Pulitzer Prize for poetry and brought to national attention a poet who, for almost twenty years, had been publishing a poetry distinguished for its quiet and elegant expression of the mysterious but intimate bonds between man and nature. Taylor is no more a "nature poet" than was Robert Frost, to whom he has sometimes been compared. He sees nature with clear, unenchanted eyes and sees man's groping efforts to come to terms with it as an on-going struggle with profound moral implications. In "Riding a One-Eyed Horse" he instructs his reader in how to guide an animal for whom "One side of his world is always missing." The rider must be carefully controlled:

Your legs will tell him not to be afraid

if you learn never to lie. Do not forget
to turn his head and let what comes come seen:
he will jump the fences he has to if you swing
toward them from the side that he can see

and hold his good eye straight. The heavy dark
will stay beside you always; let him learn
to lean against it. It will steady him
and see you safely through diminished fields.

George Garrett, the poet and Taylor's former
teacher, notes in the *Dictionary of Literary
Biography* that place (for Taylor the rolling Virginia countryside), the tradition of solid family
continuity, and the Quaker religion are
"essentials" of his art. To this Garrett adds his experience with horses who have indeed become
a kind of surrogate for Taylor's emotions and
even for his poetic technique: "I think in terms
of analogies to equitation when I'm writing.
Nerve and touch, and timing."

Taylor's first collection, *The Horse Show at
Midnight*, was published when he was still in his
early twenties. It introduced a poet of distinct
promise and, in some of the poems, impressive
maturity and technical skill. The long title poem
is a remarkable imaginative exercise—a narrative in the form of two monologues recalling a
great horse show held earlier in the day. One is
told from the point of view of The Rider, the
other The Horse. For both the show is more than
a test of strength and courage. It is an affirmation of the spiritual bond that unites all creatures
in nature—human and animal. In riding they
have become one. The Rider dreams of that moment of unity but is unable to reconstruct it:

One horse only stays with me
Straining to hear a command
That I am unable to utter.

He is left finally alone with his human mortality:

The empty ring does not echo
And the horse has left no hoofprints.
In the moonlight, alone, I sink down
Kneeling in nothing but bones
And I call to my horse once again
But the ring and the grandstand are quiet.

But back in his stable The Horse accepts his mortality with quiet faith:

This man is only partly a rider
And the rider in him is within me.
Helpless, grief-stricken, and alone,
He kneels out there in the moonlight
With only his bones for a body,
His heart singing deeply within
A shape that moves with new life.
I believe in the singing, and sleep.

Another poem from *The Horse Show at
Midnight* that was singled out for praise in the
Times Literary Supplement's review of the
book is "A Blind Man Looking His House".

The tall clock in the hallway strikes
The half-hour chime:
Twelve-thirty. Now the hour has come
For footsteps in the dark, that like
To wander through this house from room to room.

My wife and I live here alone,
So my wife thinks;
But in the dark my dark eye blinks,
Down passageways of pure unknown
The hunter starts to stalk, and my heart sinks . . . .

Groping his way through his house he feels a
nameless terror: "There is no safe place for me
any more." The poem ends:

Time and again my wife has said
No one is there;
But in the weather of despair
As I climb up through dark to bed
I hear his step behind me on the stair.

Taylor's vision of the American countryside is
realistic, not bucolic. "It is the two sides, the
beastly and the beautiful that Taylor reveals in
these artfully crafted lyrics," Joseph Parisi wrote
in *Booklist* of the poems in *The Flying Change*.
Of his earlier collection, *An Afternoon of Pocket
Billiards*, Kelly Cherry observed in *Book
Forum*: "There is no sentimentality here, no
easy relaxation into extremes, but a careful balancing between points, like a mathematical
wave plotted between upper and lower quad-
rants around an invisible horizontal bisector, a
graceful dancing curve." In "Somewhere Along
the Way" (in *The Flying Change*) the speaker
stops on the road to ask directions of an old farmer: "Rust is lifting the red paint from his barn
roof, / and earth hardens over the sunken arc /
of his mower's iron wheel." Having gotten his directions, he lingers listening:

a little while longer to the soft click
of the swaying grain heads soon to be cut,
and the low voice, edged with dim prophecy,
that settles down around you like the dust.

Somber as much of Taylor's poetry is, there
is also a distinct element of humor in some of it.
This is reflected in his parodies—good-natured
but deadly accurate—of contemporary poets. In
The Horse Show at Midnight he has a number
of these—on James Dickey (a poet whose influence he acknowledges), J. V. Cunningham,
Howard Nemerov, Robert Creeley, Denise
Levertov, James Wright, Robert Bly, and
George Garrett. At the time Taylor was writing
these, he told John Graham in an interview in
The Writer's Voice, "I was trying to find my
own voice . . . unless you do imitations you
don't really find out what it is." But more fundamental is the controlled balance between sorrow
and humor that marks many of his poems. As he

explains in a prose note to his poem "The Flying Change," equestrians learning to canter discover that a horse can suddenly change leads: "The aim of teaching a horse to move beneath you is to remind him how he moved when he was free." From this Taylor has learned a lesson as a poet: "I hold myself immobile in bright air, / sustained in time against the flying change." The trick is equilibrium.

Taylor achieves this balance sometimes within a single long poem. "An Afternoon of Pocket Billiards," for example, is a meditation on the speaker's unhappy love affair or marriage. He is playing billiards in a noisy hall, aware of his false moves and bad luck:

> . . . I turn back, but am caught
> between my past and the shifting design
> on a green field of order where I wait
> for time and strength of will to dissipate
>   these shapes that coil and turn
> above the hush and click of herded spheres.

But balancing his despair is a kind of rueful humor. Like the play of chance that dictates his game, he waits:

> for the game's random shifts to bring you back,
> high and low, striped and solid balls rotate.
> I chalk my cue and call for one more rack,
> listening for the words to an old song
> I learned too long ago: "I may be wrong,
>   but I'll be right someday."

Henry Taylor is the son of Mary (Splawn) and Thomas Edward Taylor, a high school principal who also operated a large family farm. He received his B.A. in 1965 from the University of Virginia and an M.A. from Hollins College in 1966. After two years as an instructor at Roanoke College in Salem, Virginia, Taylor joined the English department at the University of Utah, where he taught from 1968 to 1971 and directed the university's annual writers' conferences from 1970 to 1972. In 1972 he became an associate professor of literature at American University in Washington, D.C. Since 1976 he has been professor of literature there, teaching and directing the M.F.A. program in creative writing and the American studies program. In addition to the Pulitzer Prize, Taylor has twice had fellowships from the National Endowment for the Arts (1978, 1986) and a grant from the National Endowment for the Humanities (1980–1981). In 1984 the American Academy and Institute of Arts and Letters awarded him its Witter Bynner Prize. His first marriage in 1965 ended in divorce in 1967. In 1968 he married Frances Ferguson Carney.

PRINCIPAL WORKS: *Poetry*—The Horse Show at Midnight, 1966; Breakage, 1971; An Afternoon of Pocket Billiards, 1975; Desperado, 1979; The Flying Change, 1985. *As editor*—Poetry: Points of Departure, 1974; The Water of Light: Miscellany in Honor of Brewster Ghiselin, 1976. *As translator*—(with R. A. Brooks) Euripides' Children of Herakles.

ABOUT: Contemporary Authors 33–36, 1978; Contemporary Authors Autobiography Series 7, 1988; Contemporary Literary Criticism 44, 1986; Dictionary of Literary Biography 5, 1980; Garrett, G. (ed.) The Writer's Voice, 1973; Who's Who in America Supplement 1987–1988. *Periodicals*—Book Forum 3, 1977; Booklist March 15, 1986; New York Times Book Review May 4, 1986; Poetry March 1987; Southern Review October 1986; Times Literary Supplement August 18, 1966; Western Humanities Review Spring 1971; Virginia Quarterly Review Summer 1976.

TENNANT, EMMA (CHRISTINA) (pseudonym CATHERINE AYDY) (October 20, 1937–   ), British novelist and journalist, writes: "I was born in London but taken straight up to Scotland, to a fake baronial castle built by my great-grandfather, where in a remote valley and left alone for long stretches of time I stayed until after the end of the war. I was alone a lot because my father was head of the SOE [Special Operations Executive, a branch of British intelligence] in Cairo and was busy trying to help the *andartes*, the Communist guerrillas of Northern Greece, from being betrayed by Winston Churchill in the drive to restore the monarchy there. I suppose some of all this must have filtered through: that someone who didn't necessarily hold strong political views (which my father didn't, having been brought up in the family tradition of Liberals) was still prepared to risk a good deal if promises were broken, as in the case of the Greek resistance and Churchill they were. In the event, he lost his job and came back permanently to Scotland, where he dedicated his energies to building me a Georgian doll's house, as different as could possibly be from the Gothic folly where we were immured and perhaps symbolic too, for all one knows, of the Ibsenite struggle that was to ensue in my case between the need to settle down and raise a family and a need equally strong to write.

"Scotland, then, was the lost Eden of my childhood. 'Caledonia stern and wild / Fit Nurse for a Poetic Child' could certainly be applied to me: growing up in a glen where the ancient birch trees facing my bedroom window were those of the Ettrick Forest, a place immortalized by James Hogg, the shepherd and self-taught genius. Here, people foolish enough to wander were transformed into three-legged stools or hopping birds; there was a fairy ring that had

EMMA TENNANT

that pale green translucent moss of enchanted circles; and then the forestry commission said my father had to cut it down! So my memories of childhood are also of a brisk transition from magic to reality, of alone-ness to security and protection. And perhaps, too, that sense of the 'other' peculiar to Scotland, it being argued by some Scots that to grow up in one culture and then to go south for employment—or abroad—is to be transformed, like one of Hogg's Ettrick strollers, into two people. Certainly the Double came to Scotland—via Hoffmann and the German metaphysical writers—rather than to England; and James Hogg's masterpiece *The Confessions of a Justified Sinner* was the first novel to reflect its entry—followed later, of course, by Stevenson's Jekyll and Hyde. My own attempt to come to terms with this doubleness was a novel, *The Bad Sister*, which shows a woman confronting her double and, instead of Hogg's exposition of the dangers of the repressions of Calvinism, gives the heroine the indoctrination (and thence the justification to murder her father) of extreme separatist feminism.

"All this, however, only came to me when I was in my mid-thirties. In the meantime I had gone south to London, school, marrying, children, work in journalism. I always wrote, but found efforts at realism were in no way repaid with success: I had grown up in too different a surroundings, for one thing, from the English middle-class—or Northern working-class for that matter—which were the subject of pretty well all contemporary novels in the fifties and sixties. Also I could find no way of expressing

my sense of otherness as a woman; and, while much appreciating Doris Lessing's *The Golden Notebook*, I had no ability—or desire—to describe life in that way. It became gradually clear to me, after meeting British science-fiction writers—J. G. Ballard amongst them—that a way to the centre for me lay in the fantastic; and despite the very deep loathing of the British literary establishment for any writing that could be so described, I set out to read as many Latin American and Central European writers as possible, finding confirmation in such works as Bulgakov's *The Master and Margarita* and the writing of Bruno Schulz, that there was nothing inherently 'silly,' as the English would have it, in showing the world through lenses both fantastic and real: that the English were indeed limited by a creative feebleness and love of irony which left them out of the most interesting writing, all going on in other parts of the world. Since then, of course, 'magic realism' has taken root in Britain and the scene has much changed: some of this change, I hope, being due to the literary newspaper *Bananas* which I edited from 1975–1978 and which was strongly in favour of this kind of writing.

"Having written several novels of this kind, I am now embarking on a sequence of novels, set in England from the mid-fifties to the mid-eighties and showing the extraordinary political and social changes, not least the changes in the lives of girls and women. It is very challenging, and I hope it will be humorous in style."

———

Although she has lived almost her entire adult life in London, the ruling spirit of Emma Tennant's eccentric but eminently lively and imaginative fiction is the wild and remote Scotland of her childhood. Whether set in realistically recognizable contemporary London or in country houses in England or Ireland or on a tropical island in the West Indies, her novels carry a freight of both innocent whimsy and ominous witchcraft; they blend the supernatural and the real in a mixture comparable in contemporary English writing only to the work of Angela Carter and in world literature to such writers as Bruno Schulz, Gabriel García Márquez, and Cynthia Ozick. Tennant chose the novel rather than poetry as her medium because, she told John Haffenden, that form gives her "elbow room" for her wide ranging imagination and "the feeling that anything might happen next, as long as you can also keep control of what is going to happen next." Reviewers of her books are divided on whether she is essentially a traditional story teller, a spinner of fantasy tales that hold the reader fascinated even while they defy logic and common sense, or a pioneer in the newer mode of the anti-novel, parodying or subverting conventional genres of fiction. Her readers would likely agree, however, with Peter Lewis, in *Contemporary Novelists*, that "her work is strongly individual, the product of an intensely personal, even idiosyncratic, attempt to create an original type of highly imaginative fiction."

It is that powerful strain of individualism that caused Tennant to rebel, even in her girlhood, against the conventions of her upper-class society. Born in London to Christopher Grey, 2nd Baron Glencommer, and Elizabeth (Powell) Tennant, Lady Glencommer, she spent her early childhood in the family's imposing baronial home to Scotland, about thirty miles south of Edinburgh. Her first education was at a village school—"a Scottish education—meaning that you are taught to read in three weeks, and no nonsense about it." Her rebellion began when her family moved to London and sent her to the fashionable St. Paul's Girls' school, which she insisted on leaving at fifteen. Transferred to a small finishing school in Oxford, she received an excellent education in languages and art history and continued her studies in art history for a year in Paris at the Louvre. Typical of young women of her class in the 1950s, she did not go to university but instead made her debut. She was duly presented at court in 1956 (an occasion on which debutantes were so nervous, she recalls, "anyone would think we were due to audition for Lady Macbeth"). In 1957 she married Sebastian Yorke, son of the novelist Henry Green.

Emma Tennant's first novel, *The Colour of Rain*, was published when she was only twenty-four. She used a pseudonym, Catherine Aydy, partly, she said, because there were identifiable characters in the book and partly out of sheer whimsy. Written largely in dialogue, in a style much influenced by the novels of her father-in-law, the book was drawn from her own disenchantment with shallow upper-class London society. She had already published some short stories in the *Listener* and the *New Statesman* and done some travel writing for *Queen* magazine. By 1966, now divorced, she was feature editor of the London *Vogue*. She continued to be active in journalism during the next decade and founded and edited her own literary quarterly, *Bananas*, which published both established writers and relative unknowns like Angela Carter, J. G. Ballard, Beryl Bainbridge, and Thomas Disch. Tennant herself did not return to novel-writing, however, until she discovered science fiction in the early 1970s and met two of its most successful practitioners, Michael Moorcock and

J. G. Ballard: "they told me that I must be professional, structure a book in four parts of 40 pages each, introduce and develop characters in situation, and then lead up to climax or catastrophe."

Her first venture in this imaginative genre, *The Time of the Crack*, provides the catastrophe but is nowhere so rigidly schematized as her formula suggests. Set in a London of the future and written in a simple, almost childlike prose, it poses an apocalyptic disaster—a crack in the Thames riverbed causes the destruction of half of London and threatens eventually to swallow the entire southern part in England. Horrifying as the situation appears to be, Tennant presents it with such whimsical humor that one reviewer compared the book to Lewis Carroll working with H. G. Wells' material. Her central character is a bunny from the Playboy club who manages to survive. She encounters a band of women led by the militant feminist Medea Smith who have discovered a new freedom in this disaster: "Sisters," Media preaches, "we are preparing ourselves to reach the Other Side. There will be tribulations, as our oppressors will try to stop us. But let me tell you what awaits us there. A matriarchal society. More than equal pay and educational opportunities. Liberation from childbirth and child care." While the former bunny ponders: "How can you have a matriarchal society, if that means the mothers running things, and not have children?," other survivors try to make their way through the nightmarish ruins of London with the insouciance of characters in *Alice in Wonderland*.

Whether *The Time of the Crack* was science-fiction fantasy or a serious political allegory was debated by its reviewers. Peter Lewis compared it to *Nineteen Eighty-Four* as "in its bizarre way a 'condition of England' novel projecting onto the immediate future current obsessions with decline and fall, and literalizing the metaphor of national disintegration." The reviewer for the *Times Literary Supplement*, on the other hand, preferred to read it as "a comic apocalypse . . . [that] does manage to say a few pertinent things about the society in which we live." Tennant's next novel, *The Last of the Country House Murders*, is also set in a future in which the prospects of English society are very grim. A parody, as the title suggests, of country-house detective novels, this one poses the dilemma of an aristocratic estate owner who contrives his own murder in order to turn his house into a lucrative tourist attraction. Swinging wildly between fantasy and realism, the book was well received as a minor but entertaining satire. *Hotel de Dream* even more directly enters the dream life of a group of shabby, frustrated people who live in a cheap Kensington rooming house. Their escapes into dream fantasy collide with the equally bizarre reality of London life in "a trip to chaos and absurdity," as the *Times Literary Supplement* reviewer noted. Other reviewers were impressed with the ingenuity of a plot that introduces a woman novelist whose characters also have dream lives, and with Tennant's skill, as Harriet Waugh wrote in the *Spectator*, "both in weaving . . . complex and different dimensional threads into one cohesive whole and in successfully making the reader part of this strange comic world."

Up to this point in her career Emma Tennant had made her reputation for what James Brockway, in *Books and Bookmen*, called "contemporary cleverness." The question of whether she could write works of greater substance was resolved to the satisfaction of most of her reviewers with *The Bad Sister* in 1978. In this ambitiously conceived novel, Tennant set out to write her own twentieth-century feminist version of the nineteenth-century Scot James Hogg's *Private Memoirs and Confessions of a Justified Sinner* (1824), as she was later (in 1989) to do with Robert Louis Stevenson's even better known novel of the double in her *Two Women of London: The Strange Case of Ms. Jekyll and Mrs. Hyde.* Hogg's haunting story of a fanatical Scotsman so imbued with Calvinism that he deludes himself into believing he has a double and ends up murdering his mother and brother is mirror-reversed by Tennant into a chilling portrait of a woman's madness and of the excesses to which militant feminism may go. As she told Haffenden: "I think the lack my book deals with is that to pursue the feminist position, to become aware of the loss of the masculine principle in you, and then to murder it—by murdering paternalist society—is no answer. It's self-defeating." The feminist leader in *The Bad Sister* is a diabolical creature, part woman, part witch, who possesses and consumes the soul of the novel's central character, Jane Wild. According to a psychiatrist's report, amply supported by her own journal which forms the center of the book, Jane is "a schizophrenic with paranoid delusions . . . an example of the narrow borderline between depth psychology and occultism; in her case the alternation of the rational and the irrational is particularly stressed by the introduction of the supernatural." Jane's journal is a record of the delusions of doubleness—her tormenting sense of her "otherness"—so graphic and compelling that the reader rejects any scientific diagnosis. A successful film critic living with her lover Tony, who is attentive though apparently attracted to other women, Jane is not herself a particularly victimized woman, although she lives next door to a home for abused

women and a lesbian bar, and her mother had been seduced and abandoned by her upper-class father. Jane's cause is exploited by the militantly feminist Satan-witch Meg, and she sees her legitimate half-sister as not only her other self but also as a rival for her lover's affections: "If she was half of me then she was incomplete, the half that was me she yearned for, her dreams of me were as much an invention as mine were of her. We envied and pitied each other, we begged for our fullness. Yet the joke in the whole matter was that these two halves were quite arbitrary— Tony, by needing us both, had split us in this way. It wasn't a difficult thing to do. The Muse is female, and a woman who thinks must live with a demented sister. Often the two women war, and kill each other."

A less malevolent, indeed almost a benign supernaturalism pervades two other novels by Tennant. *Wild Nights*, dedicated to her younger brother Colin with whom she shared her childhood in Scotland, is told from the point of view of an imaginative child who sees her odd but unremarkable relatives in a haze of fantasy. There are her aunts who bring with them when they visit an aura of enchantment that transforms nature: "When my aunt Zita came, there were changes everywhere. The days outside, which were long and white at that time of the year, closed and turned like a shutter, a sharp blue night coming on sudden and unexpected as a finger caught in a hinge." And there is Uncle Wilhelmina, who "seemed to lean against the wind as if it were a stuffed bolster and could be depended on to support him." *Wild Nights* has no plot. In the shorter second part of the novel the family goes to the south of England on a visit but returns to the darkness of the north because "my father wanted the intransigence of the north, the one, stubborn view." *Wild Nights* is Tennant's personal myth. In *Alice Fell* she turns to Greek myth, recasting the story of Persephone, who disappears into the underworld, and her mother Demeter, who searches for her. In Tennant's version, Alice (who combines elements of Persephone with Lewis Carroll's Alice) is born in the late 1950s, just at the time of the crisis in Suez, "when England was trying to hold on, to keep what remained to it of the imperial dignity of the past." She comes of age with "a new race of young men, in black leather jackets and badgers' faces," and her underworld is London's Soho, where she becomes a prostitute. But like Persephone she is found by her mother and returned to her home. Reviewers noted a new poignant, poetic quality in the writing of *Alice Fell*. For Carol Rumens in the *Times Literary Supplement* it had a "painterly" effect, the characters like figures in a medieval tapestry.

For Bernard Levin in the (London) Sunday *Times*, it was "a strange and very beautiful book, a sort of elegy for England in the 1950s and 60s."

Tennant's later novels, as she writes above, deal more directly with contemporary English society and women's role in it. One, however, *Black Marina*, is a political novel set in the West Indies, on an island that appears to be modeled on Grenada. There the narrator, a stranded hold-over from the swinging sixties, tends bar and gets involved in intrigue and violence fomented by Marxist revolutionaries and C.I.A. agents.

For the most part Tennant's work continues to draw imaginatively on literary sources as well as contemporary events. The title of her psychological thriller *Woman Beware Woman* (published in the United States as *The Half-Mother*) evokes the festering darkness of Jacobean tragedy, in particular Thomas Middleton's *Women Beware Women*, with its gallery of corrupt and manipulative female characters; Tennant's story, however, is set in twentieth-century Ireland and owes its direct inspiration to a nineteenth-century novel, Prosper Merimée's *Colomba*: "I see the book as an interplay between three very different women, as concerning treachery on public and private levels," Tennant told John Haffenden. For her it is neither feminist nor anti-feminist but a story "about the horrors of the 'perfect' family, and what in fact goes on underneath, the entrapments and the tensions." *Queen of the Stones*, about a group of schoolgirls lost in a fog and reverting to their own form of savagery, is another mirror-reversal, this time on William Golding's *Lord of the Flies*; and *The Adventures of Robina: By Herself*, with its teasing title page "edited by Emma Tennant," while set in the 1950s, was inspired, she writes, by "reading such masterpieces as Defoe's *Roxana*, Smollett's *Peregrine Pickle*, and the Journals of James Boswell."

Emma Tennant lives in London and summers in a cottage in Thomas Hardy country in Dorset. She has a son from her first marriage and two daughters from subsequent marriages. She was elected Fellow of the Royal Society of Literature in 1982.

PRINCIPAL WORKS: The Time of the Crack, 1973 (re-issued as The Crack, 1978); The Last of the Country House Murders, 1974; Hotel de Dream, 1976; The Bad Sister, 1978; Wild Nights, 1979; Alice Fell, 1980; Queen of Stones, 1982; Woman Beware Woman (in U.S. The Half-Mother), 1983; Black Marina, 1985; The Adventures of Robina: By Herself, 1986; The House of Hospitalities, 1987; A Wedding of Cousins, 1988; The Magic Drum, 1989; Two Women of London: The Strange Case of Ms. Jekyll and Mrs. Hyde, 1989; Sisters and Strangers: A Moral Tale, 1990. As Catherine Aydy—The Colour of Rain, 1964. *Children's*

books—The Search for Treasure Island, 1981; The Ghost Child, 1984.

ABOUT: Contemporary Authors New Revision Series 10, 1983; Contemporary Literary Criticism 13, 1980; Contemporary Novelists, 4th ed., 1986; Dictionary of Literary Biography 14, 1983; Haffenden, J. Novelists in Interview, 1985; Malzahn, M. Aspects of Identity: The Contemporary Scottish Novel (1978–1981), 1984; Smith, C. D. (ed.) Twentieth Century Science Fiction Writers, 2nd ed., 1986; Who's Who, 1990. *Periodicals*—Books and Bookmen January 1977; New York Times Book Review May 5, 1985; Spectator July 24, 1976; (London) Sunday Times November 16, 1980; Times Literary Supplement June 15, 1973; July 11, 1980; June 21, 1985; January 24, 1986; September 18, 1987; September 30, 1988; June 16, 1989; July 13, 1990; September 21, 1990.

THOMPSON, E(DWARD) P(ALMER) (February 3, 1924–), British historian and antinuclear activist, was born in Oxford, the second son of Edward John Thompson, poet, novelist, and historian, who had served for several years as an educational missionary in India, where he had become personally acquainted with many of the fathers of Indian nationalism. Young Edward's mother, T. Jessup Thompson, was an American, descended from a long line of missionaries who were famous throughout the Middle East: her grandfather, Henry Jessup, described his adventures there in a well-known nineteenth-century memoir, *Fifty-three Years in Syria*.

Edward and his brother Frank spent their childhood in a house on Boars Hill, near Oxford, where frequent visitors were Robert Bridges, John Masefield, Gilbert Murray, and Sir Arthur Evans, and where Rabindranath Tagore, Mahatma Gandhi, and Jawaharlal Nehru all stayed when in Engalnd. "E. P.," as he came to be called to distinguish him from his father, was educated at Kingswood, a Methodist public school in Bath, then won a scholarship in 1941 to Corpus Christi College, Cambridge, where he started in literature but switched to read history. Like those of most of his contemporaries, his university career was cut short by World War II; he was commissioned an officer in the army and fought in Italy and France. He returned to Cambridge in the immediate postwar years to finish his degree, taking a first in history in 1946, but also spent some time in Yugoslavia and Bulgaria as a volunteer, rebuilding railroads and doing basic reconstruction work. He has always acknowledged this experience as vital in shaping his understanding of the nature of popular collective struggle. His first book, written with his mother, was *There Is a Spirit in Europe . . . :*

E. P. THOMPSON

A Memoir of Frank Thompson, a moving account of the life and early death of his brilliant and gifted brother, who, with a group of Bulgarian partisans, was killed by the Nazis in 1944 and is officially a National Hero of Bulgaria.

At Cambridge, following the war, Thompson met his wife, Dorothy, who is also a historian and who has been for many years a lecturer in modern history at Birmingham University. She is the leading British historian of the Chartist movement. During the late 1940s and early 1950s, both Thompsons were active members of the British Communist party and its Historians' Group. In 1948 they left Cambridge and moved to Halifax, Yorkshire, where E. P. took up a lectureship in the extramural studies department at Leeds University and also taught with the Workers' Educational Association. He remained at Leeds until 1965, latterly as senior lecturer and reader, then for six years was reader in social history and director of the Centre for the Study of Social History at the new University of Warwick. Since 1972 he has been self-employed as a writer, historian, and social activist.

William Morris: Romantic to Revolutionary, published in 1955, was Thompson's first major work of history. It remains even today the most comprehensive and balanced biography of the protean poet, designer, and social theorist, and illuminates the broad sweep of late-nineteenth-century British cultural history, including the Gothic Revival, the Arts and Crafts movement, industrial capitalism, and Victorian tastes and manners. In an interview with Mike Merrill in 1976, discussing the circumstances surrounding

his writing of the book, Thompson said, "I was preparing my first classes. I was teaching as much literature as history. I thought, how do I, first of all, raise with an adult class, many of them in the labor movement—discuss with them the significance of literature to their lives? And I started reading Morris. I was seized by Morris. I thought, why is this man thought to be an old fuddy-duddy? He is right in with us still. . . . it ended up being an 800-page book. Morris seized me. I took no decision. Morris took the decision that I would have to present him. In the course of doing this I became much more serious about being a historian." He went on in the interview to describe the book as being "in a central respect, an argument about the Romantic tradition and its transformation by Morris." Its point is "that Morris was an original socialist thinker whose work was complementary to Marxism." *Time* magazine called the book "not only the standard biography of Morris; it makes us realize . . . how completely admirable a man this Victorian was—how consistent, how honest to himself and others, how incapable of cruelty or jargon and, above all, how free." The author, according to the *New York Times Book Review*, "has the distinguishing characteristic of a great historian: he has transformed the nature of the past, and it will never look the same again; and whoever works in the area of his concerns in the future must come to terms with what Thompson has written. . . . His book is indispensable."

Thompson's next book, *The Making of the English Working Class*, is considered by many historians to be among the century's greatest works of social history. It tells the intricate and little-known story of the transformation, between 1790 and 1832, of the inchoate English laboring poor into the English working class. "In the 1790s," Thompson explains early in the 958-page book, "something like an 'English Revolution' took place, of profound importance in shaping the consciousness of the post-war [Napoleonic Wars] working class. It is true that the revolutionary impulse was strangled in its infancy; and the first consequence was that of bitterness and despair. The counter-revolutionary panic of the ruling classes expressed itself in every part of social life; in attitudes to trade unionism, to the education of the people, to their sports and manners, to their publications and societies, and their political rights. . . . England differed from other European nations in this, that the flood-tide of counter-revolutionary feeling and discipline coincided with the flood-tide of the Industrial Revolution. . . . The 'natural' alliance between an impatient radically minded industrial bourgeoisie and a formative proletariat was broken as soon as it was formed." The book is strongly concerned with the peculiarly English idea of class, an idea which, even today, permeates both consciously and unconsciously much of British social discourse. "I am convinced," the author continues, "that we cannot understand class unless we see it as a social and cultural formation, arising from processes which can only be studied as they work themselves out over a considerable historical period. In the years between 1780 and 1832 most English working people came to feel an identity of interests as between themselves, and as against their rulers and employers. . . . the working-class presence was, in 1832, the most significant factor in British political life." Thompson's passion for his subject and his intense sympathy for the poor so grievously wronged in the past is everywhere evident: "I am seeking to rescue the poor stockinger, the Luddite cropper, the 'obsolete' hand-loom weaver, the 'utopian' artisan, and even the deluded follower of Joanna Southcott, from the enormous condescension of posterity." The reviewer for the *Times Literary Supplement*, expressing an opinion shared by most historians, called *The Making of the English Working Class* "a portent. Just as new orthodoxies seemed to be settling down on the pre-Chartist period working-class history, a fresh, lively mind has ranged over the whole field and shown that new scholarship is not incompatible with old enthusiasm and commitment. . . . Mr. Thompson's deeply humane imagination and controlled passion help us to recapture the agonies, heroisms and illusions of the working class as it made itself: no one interested in the history of the English people should fail to read his book."

In 1971, along with Eileen Yeo, Thompson published *The Unknown Mayhew: Selections from the Morning Chronicle 1849–1850*. This book consists of newspaper reports written early in the career of Henry Mayhew, the much-celebrated yet strangely little-known author of the acclaimed *London Labour and the London Poor* (1861–1862), a landmark exposé of the miserable and appalling conditions endured by the Victorian urban poor. The reviewer for the *New Republic* called the reports by Mayhew reprinted in this book "milestones in the history of social reportage, . . . an extraordinary series of documents. . . . [Thompson and Yeo] have written substantial introductions so that we get a good idea what sort of life Mayhew lived, how and under what circumstances he went about doing the work, . . . and what he hoped to accomplish as a social investigator."

Thompson's other major work of historical scholarship is *Whigs and Hunters: The Origin of the Black Act*, which he calls "an experiment in historiography, although not of a kind which is likely to meet with approval." It is an account of the very bad relations between rulers and the ruled in the second quarter of the eighteenth century, and is suffused with the high indignation for which this historian has come to be admired. "The British state," he writes near the beginning of the book, "all eighteenth-century legislators agreed, existed to preserve the property and, incidentally, the lives and liberties, of the propertied." The so-called "Black Act," enacted by Parliament in 1723, created some fifty new capital offenses against property and, Thompson writes, "signalled the onset of the flood-tide of eighteenth-century retributive justice. Its passage suggests not only some shift in legislative attitudes, but also perhaps some complicity between the ascendancy of the Hanoverian Whigs and the ascendancy of the gallows." Lawrence Stone, writing in the *New York Review of Books*, praised Thompson for his "meticulous skill and painstaking attention to detail. . . . [He] has brilliantly elucidated the factual background to this Act. Where I disagree is over his claims about the especially malevolent, self-interested, and corrupt character of English government in the 1720s."

Thompson left the Communist party in 1956 along with 10,000 of his fellow members following the Soviet supression of the Hungarian revolution; he has since been a member of the British Labour party. He has had a long and distinguished career as a political commentator; his regular articles for such publications as the *Guardian* and *New Left Review*, and especially his books, have often pervasively influenced Labour's frequent debates on public issues. For about a decade from the late 1970s Thompson abandoned historical studies altogether in order to devote all his time to the Campaign for Nuclear Disarmament and its affiliated organization, European Nuclear Disarmament. He has for some time been among the leadership of both groups. He has brought the same passion and the same talent for principled, meticulous, and finely informed denunciation to his antiwar work that he has shown in the best of his historical writing. Collections of his essays include *The Poverty of Theory & Other Essays* and *Writing by Candlelight*; but as a political writer Thompson is perhaps best appreciated in his full-length treatments of what he considers the most important themes of our time: *Zero Option*, which advocates a nuclear-free Europe; *Double Exposure*, a narrative of the struggle of the world's nonaligned peace movement during the early 1980s; and *The Heavy Dancers*, a dark meditation on the world's apparent, quasi-conscious preparations for "the ultimate war."

He has also edited and contributed to several books on contemporary peace issues, including *Protest and Survive*, written in direct response to the British government's pamphlet *Protect and Survive*, which advocated civil-defense measures in the event of a nuclear war; *Exterminism and Cold War*; *Star Wars: Science-Fiction Fantasy or Serious Possibility?*; and *Prospectus for a Habitable Planet.*

In 1988 Thompson published his first novel, *The Sykaos Papers*, in which a poet-explorer from a distant planet comes to Earth; he observes the alien planet, and is in turn observed by its largely heedless inhabitants in discordant, intrusive ways that prove ultimately catastrophic. In an interview at the time of the novel's publication, the author remarked that he has begun again to work on his long-awaited study of William Blake, which will be among the first to place the great visionary poet, draftsman, and engraver firmly within the English political life of his time.

Thompson has been visiting professor at the State University of New York at Buffalo (1966), New York University (1968), the University of Pittsburgh (1975), Rutgers University (1976), and Brown University (1980–1981). He has been Alexander lecturer at the University of Toronto (1978), Camp lecturer at Stanford (1981), Bertrand Russell lecturer at McMaster University (1985), and Montgomery fellow at Dartmouth (1983). He holds honorary doctorates from Hull (1981) and the Open University (1982), and is a fellow of the Royal Historical Society and the Royal Society of Literature. He and his wife have lived for many years in the Worcestershire countryside.

PRINCIPAL WORKS: *History and non-fiction*—(with T. Jessup Thompson) There Is a Spirit in Europe . . . : A Memoir of Frank Thompson, 1947; The Struggle for a Free Press, 1952; William Morris: Romantic to Revolutionary, 1955, rev. ed., 1976; The Making of the English Working Class, 1963; Whigs and Hunters: The Origin of the Black Act, 1975; The Poverty of Theory & Other Essays, 1978; Writing by Candlelight, 1980; Zero Option, 1982; Beyond the Cold War, 1982; Double Exposure, 1985; The Heavy Dancers, 1985. *As editor*—The Railway: An Adventure in Construction, 1948; Out of Apathy, 1960; (with Stuart Hall and Raymond Williams) May Day Manifesto, 1967; Warwick University Ltd: Industry, Management and the Universities, 1970; (with Eileen Yeo) The Unknown Mayhew: Selections from the Morning Chronicle 1849–1850, 1971; (with Douglas Hay, Peter Linebaugh, John G. Rule, and Cal Winslow) Albion's Fatal Tree: Crime and Society in Eighteenth-Century England, 1975; (with Jack Goody and Joan Thirsk) Family and Inheritance: Rural Society in Western Europe, 1200–1800, 1976; (with Dan Smith) Protest and Survive, 1980; Exterminism and Cold War, 1982; Star Wars: Science-

Fiction Fantasy or Serious Possibility?, 1985; (with Dan Smith) Prospectus for a Habitable Planet, 1987. *Poetry*—Infant and Emperor, 1983. *Fiction*—The Sykaos Papers, 1988.

ABOUT: Anderson, Perry. Arguments within English Marxism, 1980; Inglis, Fred. Radical Earnestness: English Social Theory, 1880–1980, 1982; Kaye, Harvey J. The British Marxist Historians: An Introductory Analysis, 1986; MARHO, The Radical Historians Organization. Visions of History, 1983; Palmer, Bryan. The Making of E. P. Thompson, 1981. *Periodicals*—America January 15, 1983; American Historical Review October 1964; Book Week May 10, 1964; Book World June 13, 1971; Booklist; June 1, 1962; Bulletin of the Atomic Scientists October 1983; Canadian Forum February 1981; Choice October 1976, October 1977, January 1986; Christian Science Monitor May 2, 1986; Commentary July 1964, January 1983; Commonweal July 1964; Contemporary Sociology July 1980; Economist February 15, 1964; October 18, 1975; April 23, 1977; December 2, 1978; June 1, 1985; Encounter January 1981; Harper's February 1983; Library Journal April 15, 1962; March 15, 1964; August 1976, August 1977; November 15, 1981; November 15, 1982; November 1, 1985; Nation April 6, 1964; July 9, 1977; New Republic April 11, 1964; October 30, 1971; June 4, 1977; February 2, 1980; December 27, 1982; New Statesman November 29, 1963; October 10, 1975; May 30, 1980; July 11, 1980; April 5, 1985; New York Review of Books April 16, 1964; July 22, 1971; February 5, 1976; July 14, 1977; New York Times Book Review May 15, 1977; November 14, 1982; September 25, 1988; New Yorker June 6, 1964; June 27, 1977; Radical History Review Fall 1976; Saturday Review June 25, 1977; Scientific American January 1965; Studies in Political Economy Fall 1982; Time June 27, 1977; Times Literary Supplement December 12, 1963; January 30, 1976; March 29, 1985; Virginia Quarterly Review Summer 1964.

THOMPSON, FLORA (JANE TIMMS) (December 5, 1876–July 21?, 1947), British memoirist and novelist, was born in the Oxfordshire village of Juniper Hill, in the parish of Cottisford, the eldest of ten children of a stonemason, Albert Timms, and Emma (Lapper) Timms and spent most of her life in small provincial towns and villages. She published only three books, all late in her life, but at the time of her death, as Margaret Lane observes, "her fame [had] spread to an extent of which she herself, had she been foretold, would have been incredulous." To this day her faintly fictionalized records of her early years in the trilogy *Lark Rise* (1939), *Over to Candleford* (1941), and *Candleford Green* (1943) remain small classics of English rural life in the last three decades of the nineteenth century, read in British schools as documentary history and by an admiring public for their simple charm and nostalgia.

FLORA THOMPSON

Recent scholarship has challenged the accuracy of Thompson's local history and emphasized her "special pleading" for a long vanished past. Writing from memory so many years after the events she described and at a time of general world upheaval and despair in the late 1930s and early 1940s, she could scarcely resist painting the past in a modestly golden light: "people were poorer and had not the comforts, amusements, or knowledge we have today; but they were happier . . . they knew the now lost secret of being happy on little." But she never claimed absolute accuracy for her work; she changed names of people and places, compressed and combined family histories, passed lightly over sordid matters like crime, madness, and alcoholism. In the subtitle to *Over to Candleford* she wrote: "The following is intended less as autobiography than as a record of the impressions of a child brought up in a remote country hamlet in the eighteen-eighties. It is written in the third-person because the writer can best see objectively, across the gulf of time and war and change, the child who was herself moving in that now vanished world."

Laura, the persona of her books, is, however, the virtual double of Flora Thompson, and her remarkable memory, as well as her sensitivity to her natural surroundings, evokes that lost past so vividly that the essential truths of her books cannot be denied. Certainly the details of Laura's life are faithful to what is known of her creator's life. It was a happy childhood, with a stern but loving mother, a devoted younger brother-companion Edmund (Edwin in real life), a closely knit community, the security of ancient but still observed traditions and customs (games, May Day, harvest feasts), and the freedom of the beautiful Oxfordshire countryside. A quiet child, she looked and listened, absorbing both nature and human nature. Her memory, while selective, also embraced the poverty around her. Food was coarse, clothes shabby, sanitation primitive, child mortality dismaying (four of her brothers and sisters died in childhood), education minimal. To the child Laura "the hamlet once appeared as a fortress," but the adult Thompson adds that "the hamlet was indeed in a state of siege, and its chief assailant was Want."

Like all village children, Laura/Flora attended the small local school, three miles from her home, that taught only the three R's, some Bible stories, and sewing, until the age of twelve, when the boys left to learn a trade or to farm and the girls went off to do domestic work in neighboring communities. But an early passion for reading and writing set her apart from other children. Though her parents were uneducated and had few books in the home, she managed to find books and read everything at hand from local newspapers to popular romances that circulated among the neighbors. Later, visiting her somewhat more prosperous cousins in nearby Buckingham (Candleford), she was introduced to books in their home. Her uncle, a shoemaker, encouraged her to read aloud to him while he worked in his shop and thus she discovered *Pamela*, *Cranford*, *Villette*, and other classics. Her reading was supplemented with the age-old traditions of reciting and singing poems and songs that delighted her and that she recorded later in her books. "I cannot remember a time," she wrote in a posthumously published memoir "Heatherley," "when I did not wish and mean to write. My brother and I used to make up verses and write stories and diaries from our earliest years, and I had never left off writing essays for the pleasure of writing. No one saw them; there was no one likely to be interested."

At fourteen Laura/Flora went to work as assistant to the postmistress at nearby Fringford (Candleford Green). She not only sorted mail, sold stamps, and operated the then-new telegraph equipment, but also, for a time, delivered the mail to neighboring farms, enriching her imagination with insights into the lives of a variety of local people. Her trilogy ends with her departure at age twenty from Candleford Green: "driven on by well-meant advice both from without and from within by the restless longing to see and experience the whole of life . . . ." But in fact the post office remained her working place for many years to come. She moved on to a somewhat larger town, Grayshott, in Hampshire. Grayshott was something of a literary cen-

ter where writers spent their holidays. Among her clients at the post office were Arthur Conan Doyle, Richard Le Gallienne, and George Bernard Shaw. But Laura/Flora was merely a spectator on this literary scene.

At twenty-four Flora Timms married a postal clerk, John Thompson, and they settled in Bournemouth on a limited income which left her barely enough for the penny tram fare to the local public library. She was conspicuously silent in her memoirs about her marriage and family life, but Margaret Lane, who interviewed her daughter Winifred years later and had access to her unpublished papers at the University of Texas at Austin, reports that the marriage was not happy. Domestic responsibilities were heavy; there were three children, and she had to assist her husband in his post office duties. Moreover, he was not sympathetic to her literary interests, and she was obliged to write secretly in what little time she could find.

It was not until she won a prize contest with an essay on Jane Austen that Flora Thompson had the courage to send out her articles and short stories to local magazines. When these were accepted and she began to receive small payments for her writing, she at last felt that "I had earned the right to use my scanty leisure as I wished." Even then, however, financial need forced her to write mainly what she called "small, sugared love stories." Her ambition was to be a poet, but she wryly observed (still in Laura's voice), "the pen she had taken for a sword had turned in her hands into a darning needle." The evidence of her talent as a poet, collected in a small volume *Bog Peat and Myrtle* that she managed to publish in 1921 (some of these poems are reprinted in her posthumous *A Country Calendar*), suggests that her real poetry was in her simple, sensitive prose.

Thompson continued and extended her literary activities in the years between the two World Wars. She published a series of nature sketches (later collected in *A Country Calendar*) in a little magazine, *The Catholic Fireside*. She was a ghost writer for a big game hunter who was writing his memoirs of Africa, and she founded a literary society for postal workers, the Peverel Society, which circulated the writings of their members privately but did not publish them at the time. In 1928 John Thompson was transferred to Dartmouth where Flora began writing the sketches of her childhood which became *Lark Rise*. One of these, "Old Queenie," a portrait of an eccentric old lady in Juniper Hill who practiced the ancient craft of lace-making while she lovingly tended her swarming beehives, was published in *The Lady* in 1937. An-

other sketch, "May Day," appeared in the *Fortnightly Review*. Encouraged by this success, Thompson sent these to Sir Humphrey Milford of Oxford University Press who urged her to assemble a volume, and in 1939, on the eve of World War II, *Lark Rise* was published. It was followed swiftly by *Over to Candleford* and *Candleford Green*, written, she recalled, "under difficulties . . . several of the passages to the sound of bombs falling."

If these books were misread as social history, they were nevertheless, an achievement of evocation and resurrection—not of precise detail perhaps, but of the illusions which supported and sustained English society in some of the darkest days of its history. This achievement was conveyed, H. J. Massingham writes, "through so delicate a mastery, with so beguiling an air and by so tender an elegy, that what she has to tell is 'felt along the heart' rather than as a spectacular eclipse." Thompson's success came too late for her to enjoy it: "Twenty years ago I should have been beside myself with joy, but I am now too old to care much for the bubble reputation." The wars had brought personal tragedy—her brother Edwin killed in action in World War I, her younger son Peter in World War II. In spite of failing health, she continued to write, completing a novel, *Still Glides the Stream*, only shortly before her death. A characteristically quiet book, it recounts the visit of Charity Finch, a middle-aged school teacher, to the Oxfordshire village of her childhood which she has not seen in many years. She finds little changed. The story centers mainly on her uncle and distant cousins, village romances—nostalgic but not sentimental—and gossip. Reviews were appreciative, but the book was quickly forgotten.

Lark Rise to Candleford, however, retains its place in English rural literature—from nineteenth-century classics like Miss Mitford's *Our Village* and Mrs. Gaskell's *Cranford* through recent works like Ronald Blythe's *Akenside*. It has been reissued several times in illustrated editions, including an abridged *Illustrated Lark Rise to Candleford* (1983) with numerous flower prints, Bewick engravings, and reproductions of Victorian genre paintings, which was a bestseller. In 1973 it appeared as a Penguin paperback, reprinted in 1984. As recently as 1978 *Lark Rise* was dramatized by Keith Dewhurst and produced at the National Theatre in London. Centering on a single day when Laura is ten and her brother eight, the play incorporated a number of characters from the book along with their songs in a lively production that reviewers compared to Dylan Thomas' *Under Milk Wood*. But its survival as a book depends neither on its dramatic nor its sociological value but on a qual-

ity that Thompson herself described in a passage in *Still Glides the Stream* : "The world of her childhood had been a narrow world, inhabited by simple people whose lives had been restricted by poverty and other hardships and deprivations; yet it had held something of beauty, of unselfconscious simplicity and downright integrity, that seemed to her worthy of remembrance."

PRINCIPAL WORKS: Lark Rise, 1939; Over to Candleford, 1941; Candleford Green, 1943; Lark Rise to Candleford 1945; A Country Calendar and Other Writings, 1979; (with Julian Shuckburgh) The Peverel Papers, 1986. *Novel*—Still Glides the Stream, 1948. *Poetry*—Bog Peat and Myrtle, 1921.

ABOUT: Clive, J. Not by Fact Alone: Essays on the Writing and Reading of History, 1989; Lane, M. Purely for Pleasure, 1969; Flora Thompson, 1976; *Introduction to* A Country Calendar, 1979; Massingham, J. H. *Introduction to* Lark Rise to Candleford, 1973, 1984. *Periodicals*—New York Times Book Review July 21, 1974; (London) Times July 21, 1947; Victorian Studies 29, Autumn 1985.

HUNTER S. THOMPSON

THOMPSON, HUNTER S(TOCKTON)
(July 18, 1939–   ), American journalist, is one of the best known—some would say most notorious—of the practitioners of the New Journalism. This genre originated in the 1960s and purported to liberate the journalist from the demands of impersonality and objectivity of straight reporting. The New Journalist assumes the role not of witness-reporter but of actor-participant in the events being covered, and the result is a literary hybrid that combines the actuality and topicality of straight reporting with the excitement and emotional appeal of fiction. In 1973 Joseph Kanon wrote of Thompson in the *Saturday Review* : "We turn to his work not for 'objective' reporting . . . but to watch an interesting sensibility engaged in high drama."

Hunter S. Thompson was born in Louisville, Kentucky to Jack R. and Virginia (Ray) Thompson. His father was an insurance agent. Thompson had no formal education beyond the public schools of Louisville. He got his first taste of journalism during his two years in the United States Air Force covering sports for an Army newspaper at Fort Eglin, Florida. Describing himself (in *The Great Shark Hunt*) as "a morale problem," he was honorably discharged in 1958, "after one of the most hectic and unusual Air Force careers in history." "Hectic" and "unusual" remain the operative words for Thompson's professional life—at least as it has emerged in his semiautobiographical, semi-fictitious books.

Thompson held—usually only briefly—a number of jobs on small-town newspapers, *Time* magazine, and a bowling magazine in Puerto Rico. In 1960 he settled in the heart of the then flourishing Beat culture in San Francisco to write a novel, but he was soon on the road again, this time as Caribbean correspondent for the *New York Herald Tribune*. By 1961 he was reporting from South America on smuggling, banditry, and other colorful subjects for several North American news outlets. For two years he was South American correspondent for the *National Observer*. By 1963 Thompson was back in San Francisco freelancing and working on the unfinished novel. He supplemented his writing income by driving a cab. On the scene during the tumultuous days of the Free Speech movement at the University of California at Berkeley and right in the center of the hippie drug scene, Thompson found plenty of material to report on for the *Nation*, the *New York Times Magazine*, *Harper's*, *Scanlan's* and other journals. In his reports he caught the quintessential excitement of the period, the momentum of what he would later describe as "a high and beautiful wave." Looking back on the scene almost a decade later in *Fear and Loathing in Las Vegas*, he wrote:

San Francisco in the middle sixties was a very special time and place to be a part of. Maybe it *meant something*. Maybe not, in the long run . . . but no explanation, no mix of words or music or memories can touch that sense of knowing that you are there and alive in that corner of time and the world. Whatever it meant . . . it seems entirely reasonable to think that every now and then the energy of a whole generation comes to a head in a long fine flash, for reasons that nobody really understands at the time—and which never explain, in retrospect, what actually happened.

On the suggestion of Carey McWilliams, the editor of the *Nation*, in 1965 Thompson wrote an article on motorcycle gangs that changed the course of his career. A report on the Hell's Angels riders who had been the subject of a 1954 film *The Wild Ones*, starring Marlon Brando, Thompson's article caught the attention of several publishers, and Random House offered him a contract for a book on the subject. In a note to that book, *Hell's Angels: A Strange and Terrible Saga*, published in 1966, Thompson acknowledged McWilliams" "ideas and suggestions [that] gave the book a framework and perspective that it might not otherwise have had."

Thompson spent a year not merely observing but riding with the Hell's Angels, eating, drinking with them, taking the same risks, including several painful accidents and, on Labor Day, 1966, a beating and stomping "by four or five Angels who seemed to feel I was taking advantage of them. A disagreement suddenly became very serious." His life was saved only by the intervention of another member of the gang. Altogether it was a brutal experience which he described as "a bad trip . . . fast and wild in some moments, slow and dirty in others, but on balance it looked like a bummer. On my way back to San Francisco, I tried to compose a fitting epitaph. I wanted something original, but there was no escaping the echo of Mistah Kurtz' final words from the heart of darkness: 'The horror! The horror! . . . Exterminate all the brutes!'"

Such combinations of street argot and literary allusion are characteristic of Thompson's writing style. *Hell's Angels* begins as straight journalism with reports on the nature and number of motorcycle gangs nationally but soon moves to personality profiles of gang members, with vivid reconstruction of their lives, backgrounds, and activities. Thompson traces their history from their emergence in the 1950s to 1965 when, he writes, "they were firmly established as all-American bogeymen." Although he was himself actively involved with the Angels, he remained essentially an observer, shrewdly recognizing their vulnerability beneath their posturing macho image; for him they were in some measure a creation of the national press. While he neither sentimentalized nor romanticized them, Thompson saw the Angels as essentially drifters, uneducated, usually unemployed, leading empty, hopeless lives alienated from the mainstream of American society: "Their world is so rife with hostility that they don't even recognize it. They are deliberately hard on most strangers, but they get bad reactions even when they try to be friendly. I have seen them try to amuse an outsider by telling stories which they consider very

funny—but which generate fear and queasiness in a listener whose sense of humor has a different kind of filter." An Angel achieves selfhood only on his motorbike: "His motorcycle is the only thing in life he has absolutely mastered. It is his status symbol, his equalizer. . . . Without it, he is no better than a punk on a street corner. And he knows it."

Most reviewers of *Hell's Angels* recognized a fundamental thoughtfulness and seriousness in the book, although several expressed reservations about Thompson's lurid style and his tendency to shift responsibility for their outlaw behavior from them to society as a whole. For Richard M. Elman, in the *New Republic*, the book was "a tendentious but informative participant-observer study of those who are doomed to lose." As a projection of a violence-prone America, in Elman's view, *Hell's Angels* "is a hairily comic metaphor for a society getting just about what it deserves for napalming Vietnamese and instituting privileges for everybody except those who need it most; and it's a metaphor which, even in its grotesque nonsensicality, manages to scratch a bit of the truth off the American veneer. . . . "

What was "comic metaphor" in *Hell's Angels* became hallucinogenic nightmare in Thompson's *Fear and Loathing in Las Vegas*. His best known book, it lives up to its subtitle "A Savage Journey to the Heart of the American Dream." The journey began in two articles Thompson wrote for *Rolling Stone* magazine in the early 1970s. Assuming the persona of one Raoul Duke, a hard-drinking drug-using journalist assigned to cover an auto race and simultaneously a convention on drug law enforcement, Thompson had the advantage of playing two roles at once—the observing reporter writing the book and the leading actor in it. Duke, accompanied by a drunk and drug-crazed Samoan lawyer friend Dr. Gonzo (actually a Chicano lawyer, Oscar Acosta), is sent to Las Vegas to cover a story. "But what *was* the story?" he asks. "Nobody had bothered to say. So we would have to drum it up on our own. Free enterprise. The American Dream. Horatio Alger gone wild on drugs in Las Vegas. Do it *now*: pure Gonzo journalism."

Gonzo—a word of no particular meaning used by a fellow journalist to describe Thompson's style—caught on as a name for a new kind of journalism—one that Thompson defined in *The Great Shark Hunt* as "a style of 'reporting' based on William Faulkner's idea that the best fiction is far more *true* than any kind of journalism—and the best journalists have always known this." In an era which saw the birth of a so-called "New Journalism" associated with the highly charged anti-establishment fervor of Norman Mailer's *The Armies of the Night* (a report on the anti–Vietnam War movement), and the wildly unorthodox reporting on pop culture by Tom Wolfe in *The Electric Kool-Aid Acid Test*, Thompson's work stood out and apart as the ultimate extreme. John Hellmann described it aptly in *Fables of Fact* as "journalism which reads as savage cartoon." Thompson does not describe the drug culture so much as he gives the effect of the drug experience itself. "The book's highest art is to be the drug it is about," Crawford Woods wrote in the *New York Times Book Review*. "To read it is to swim through the highs and lows of the smokes and fluids that shatter the mind, to survive the terror of the politics of unreason."

In literary terms *Fear and Loathing in Las Vegas* is a road novel, its ancestry going back far beyond Jack Kerouac's *On the Road* of 1957 to *Don Quixote*, if not even earlier to the *Odyssey* (one reviewer compared Duke's lawyer-companion Dr. Gonzo to Sancho Panza). It has an outlaw or socially rejected hero on a quest for self-fulfillment in a narrative (the book cannot be said to have a plot) that takes him through a series of bizarre adventures. The difference is that while classic heroes from Don Quixote to Huckleberry Finn operate within some kind of personal value system, however unconventional, Duke operates in a meaningless, chaotic, near-psychedelic delirium which may or may not be America in mid-century. He writes:

> Every now and then when your life gets complicated and the weasels start closing in, the only real cure is to load up on heinous chemicals and then drive like a bastard from Hollywood to Las Vegas. To *relax*, as it were, in the womb of the desert sun. Just roll the roof back and screw it on, grease the face with white tanning butter and move out with the music at top volume, and at least a pint of ether.

At the outset of the journey, racing and rapidly burning out the engine of his rented car, "the drugs began to take hold. . . . And suddenly there was a terrible roar all around us and the sky was full of what looked like huge bats, all swooping and screeching and diving around the car, which was going about a hundred miles an hour with the top down to Las Vegas." Thompson's drug-induced hallucinations are brought to graphic life in the grotesque illustrations that a British artist, Ralph Steadman, provided for this and his later books—twentieth-century Hieronymus Bosch visions of human and inhuman depravity. Yet for all its nightmare quality, *Fear and Loathing in Las Vegas* never completely loses touch with what Thompson calls "the socio-psychic factor." As Hellmann observes: "These authorial inversions of the conventional reporter's approach to actuality and the traditional American hero's search for fulfillment result from a single response to the unreality of contemporary America. For Thompson, the landscape of America in the 1970's is itself hallucinatory, and Las Vegas, America's dream city, epitomizes it."

Assuming the persona now of Dr. Hunter S. Thompson he continued his pursuit of "the socio-psychic factor" in *Fear and Loathing on the Campaign Trail '72*, a collection of reports written for *Rolling Stone* during the 1972 presidential campaign. In typical gonzo fashion Dr. Thompson mixes fact and fantasy, from time to time inventing stories about the candidates and the journalists covering them but in some odd way vividly capturing the frantic machinations involved in the election of an American president. Thompson made no pretense of concealing his hatred for most establishment politicians—especially Richard Nixon—and his sympathies for the Democratic nominee George McGovern. In a long analytical piece in the *Columbia Journalism Review*, Wayne C. Booth compared the book with Theodore White's *The Making of the President 1972*, not always to Thompson's disadvantage. He finds that both "offer, finally, a journalism that aspires to the condition of history," and that neither succeeds. Thompson's style (in Booth's words "tough-guy gush"), he suggests, is his major weakness: "At his best, he can cover a lot of ground fast, and he can be both vivid and very funny. But spontaneity is perhaps the hardest of all stylistic effects to maintain. At his worst, Thompson reads like a bad parody of himself, the clichés worn out by the effort to look brand new."

By the mid-1970s there were signs that Thompson had indeed exhausted much of the spontaneity and shock-effect that had marked his early work. He continued to report on sporting events and politics for *Rolling Stone* until 1976, when a disagreement over presidential candidate Jimmy Carter, whom Thompson appeared to admire, led to his break with the magazine. The pieces he wrote for *Rolling Stone* and other journals during the 1970s are collected in *The Great Shark Hunt: Strange Tales from a Strange Time*. For many reviewers in 1979 the book was a striking example of obsolescence. "Apocalypse has come and gone and what will the psychedelic writers do now?" Garry Wills asked in the *Washington Post Book World*. "Did they flame out, like their decade?" Taking a particularly negative view was Joseph Nocera in the *Washington Monthly*. His title was his thesis—"How Hunter Thompson Killed New Journalism," and he accused Thompson and his peers of "cultural arrogance," exploiting the countercultural style. New Journalists, Nocera writes, promised a form "that would merge fact-writing and opinion-writing, a style you might idealistically call truth-writing. But more than anyone else, Hunter Thompson has damaged and discredited New Journalism's promise. Instead of being exhilarated by his freedom, he was corrupted by it. Instead of using it in the search for truth, he used it for trivial self-promotion."

In the 1980s Thompson himself became a cartoon figure as Raoul Duke in Gary Trudeau's comic strip *Doonesbury*. As Dr. Hunter S. Thompson he was also the subject of a film, *Where the Buffalo Roam*, in 1980 in which Bill Murray starred. Thompson's two books of the decade received far less attention than his earlier work. In *The Curse of Lono* he and Ralph Steadman, his illustrator, go to Hawaii to cover a running marathon and find themselves in a savage land straight out of the geography of their frenzied imaginations, in which at some point Thompson identifies himself with the ill-fated explorer Captain Cook. Though he found "some stylish and funny passages" in the book, Charles Haas, in the *New York Times Book Review*, judged that *Lono* is not nearly the sharp entertainment that *Fear and Loathing* is. . . . His Hawaii is a mix of cheap tourism, constant racial violence, boom and bust, and storms that turn the book into a sullen chronicle of a rained-out vacation." *Generation of Swine: Tales of Shame and Degradation in the '80s*, a collection of Thompson's columns originally published in the *San Francisco Examiner*, offers a more sober but still feisty Thompson who quotes W. H. Auden and the Book of Revelation: " . . . it is not because I am a biblical scholar, or because of any religious faith, but because I love the wild power of language and the purity of the madness that governs it and makes it music." After prophesying apocalypse, he proceeds to "Let the good times roll" with acidulous commentary on American life in the 1980s. Kenneth Kister, in *Library Journal*, wrote that the book "tries to recapture the old ebullience, but much of it falls flat. Still, Thompson's fans—there are many—will savor his wild words on Ted Kennedy, Gary Hart, Al Haig, Ollie North, George Bush, TV preachers, et al." A more enthusiastic reception came from Michael E. Ross, in the *New York Times Book Review*, who wrote that Thompson proves again "that he is one of our most incisive, insightful and hilarious social critics. . . . With *Generation of Swine* Mr. Thompson shows himself to be an outlandish, skeptical Jeremiah. But one harbors a suspicion that his is the kind of unvarnished, crazy wisdom that is valuable in these times. In moderation, of course."

In contrast to the frantic life-styles of his various personae, Thompson has lived for many years on a remote farm in Woody Creek, Colorado, not far from Aspen. He has been married since 1963 to Sandra Dawn, and they have one son, Juan. By his own account in a note appended to *Fear and Loathing in Las Vegas*, "his life style was severely altered" in 1968 when he became involved in "The Aspen Freak Power Uprising" and ran for county sheriff, losing in a very close election. "Meanwhile the author continues to work his own strange tangents, seemingly oblivious of public outrage, acclaim or criticism of any sort. He is known to a handful of friends as a compulsive hermit with an atavistic fondness for the .44 Magnum and extremely amplified music." Responding to an interviewer from *Rolling Stone* in late 1987 who asked, "Why are you a journalist?" Thompson said: "I would not be anything else, if for no other reason that I'd rather drink with journalists. Another reason I got into journalism, you don't have to get up in the morning."

In May 1990 Thompson was ordered to stand trial in Aspen on felony and misdemeanor charges following a search of his house during which some drugs and explosives were found. The charges were dropped, however, when prosecutors admitted that their case was not strong enough to pursue. Thompson reacted to these events with characteristic aplomb, announcing that he would cover his own trial for *Rolling Stone* ("I'm sure my lawyers will go nuts"). The *New York Times* of May 22, 1990 quoted his press agent to the effect that this latest notoriety would benefit Thompson's lecturing career. "It's really increased the interest in Hunter on college campuses. He's already booking into the fall."

PRINCIPAL WORKS: Hell's Angels: A Strange and Terrible Saga, 1966; Fear and Loathing in Las Vegas: A Savage Journey to the Heart of the American Dream, 1972; Fear and Loathing on the Campaign Trail '72, 1973; The Great Shark Hunt: Strange Tales from a Strange Time, 1979; The Curse of Lono, 1983; Generation of Swine: Tales of Shame and Degradation in the '80s, 1988.

ABOUT: Contemporary Authors 23, 1988; Contemporary Literary Criticism 9, 1978; 17, 1981; 40, 1986; Crouse, T. The Boys on the Bus, 1974; Current Biography 1981; Dickstein, M. The Gates of Eden: American Culture in the Sixties, 1977; Hellmann, J. Fables of Fact: The New Journalism as New Fiction, 1981; Klinkowitz, J. The Life of Fiction, 1977; Vonnegut, K. Wampeters Foma and Granfalloons, 1974; Who's Who in America 1988–89. *Periodicals*—Columbia Journalism Review November–December 1973; Library Journal August 1988; New Republic February 25, 1967; August 25, 1979; New York Times May 22, 1990; May 31, 1990; New York Times Book Review July 11, 1971

January 15, 1984; August 14, 1988; Rolling Stone November 5– December 10, 1987; Saturday Review April 21, 1973; Washington Monthly April 1981; Washington Post Book World August 19, 1979.

TINDALL, GILLIAN (ELIZABETH) (May 4, 1938–   ), British novelist, historian, and biographer, was born in London to D. H. Tindall and U.M.D. Orange. She read English at Lady Margaret Hall, Oxford University, earning a B.A. (with honors) and an M.A. Tindall also studied art at the Sorbonne, acquiring both fluency in French and a lasting affinity for France.

The author drew on her first-hand knowledge of Paris in her first two novels, *No Name in the Street* and *The Water and the Sound*. *No Name in the Street* charts the maturation of Jane, a nineteen-year-old half-French Briton. During an extended stay in the Left Bank of Paris, Jane's happiness begins to disintegrate when she learns that her French lover Vincent has an English male lover and that she is pregnant. Once her heroine has made these troubling discoveries, Tindall explores Jane's struggle to understand and accept them. *The Water and the Sound*, also set in Paris, centers on a young English novelist, Nadia, who seeks to elucidate her late parents' shadowy past. Through a wide range of secondary characters, Tindall slowly brings together the bohemia of the parents' pre–World War II generation and the daughter's of the 1960s. Reviewers praised Tindall's portrayal of people and places in both novels. The *Times Literary Supplement* reviewer of *No Name in the Street* thought Tindall had "a good ear for everyday speech and a gift for quick sketches of people and places" but found the novel ponderous in its opening section and over-informative throughout. *The Water and the Sound* was acclaimed for its strong prose and ingenious framework. The *New York Times Book Review*, however, observed that "what Miss Tindall builds on [the framework] is a rococo structure as ornate as an opera libretto." The *Times Literary Supplement* found the ultimate truth about Nadia's parents contrived, so that "this otherwise brilliant novel is forced."

Tindall's next novel, *The Youngest*, was described by one reviewer as "a kind of psychological detective story of the soul." The soul in question belongs to Elizabeth, an educated, sensitive woman who has carefully and selfishly controlled her life and family. When she gives birth to a severely deformed baby, she impulsively smothers it. As Elizabeth becomes increasingly disturbed by her act, she realizes that she has always smothered whatever she cannot cope

GILLIAN TINDALL

with because of her self-absorption and craving for independence. As the novel progresses, it becomes clear that the deformed baby symbolizes Elizabeth's disfigured character. The work received mixed reviews, some finding it marred because the social dilemma dominates the fiction. Others, however, praised its sensitive treatment of a difficult subject. "In its complexity and insight," the *Times Literary Supplement* observed, "this is Miss Tindall's best book so far."

Tindall again uses a death in the family as the beginning of a painful process of self-discovery in *Someone Else*. After seven years of marriage and one of motherhood, Joanna Roux is suddenly widowed. Prompted by the insights of supportive friends, she begins to reinterpret her marriage and finds herself facing an identity crisis. Several reviewers characterized the novel as a soap opera, but a "very creditable one that deserves a good audience," according to Sara Blackburn of *Book World*. Blackburn also praised Tindall for not trying to make the book loftier than its premise allowed. While Angela Ambrose, in *America* magazine, objected to Joanna's superficiality, in the *Library Journal* Grace Mainzinger noted that Tindall's "talents are seen at their best in the development of the character Joanna."

In *Fly Away Home*, Tindall chronicles her heroine's personal odyssey from self-doubt to acceptance through the medium of the woman's diary. Anatonia Boileau, an Englishwoman married to a French Jew, attributes her unhappiness to a prolonged lack of personal growth. She attempts to work through her troubling past in her journal. However, it takes a visit to an old lover in Israel and several personal tragedies before Anatonia realizes she cannot go back to the past and finally returns to her husband. Winner of the 1972 Somerset Maugham Award, *Fly Away Home* provoked mixed reactions among reviewers. Clive Jordan, in the *New Statesman*, summed it up as "a serious, valid and occasionally moving attempt to reproduce the texture of a life," an attempt foiled, however, by "measured, flat, undemonstrative, analytic" language. The *Times Literary Supplement* found Anatonia insufficiently spontaneous in her self-absorption, but her critical intelligence "provides some sparkling comment on the external events that colour her diary."

The author created her first male protagonist in *The Traveller and His Child*. The traveller, Robert, has recently been divorced by his American wife, who has taken their son Robbie to live in the States. Although Robert does not acknowledge his grief over losing Robbie, it prompts him to kidnap a seven-year-old boy. As the pair travel through France, however, Robert perceives the harmfulness of his behavior, relinquishes the child, and earns forgiveness. *The Traveller and His Child* fared well critically. Max Egremont, in *Books and Bookmen*, noted that although Tindall reveals Robert's discovery slowly, "we follow her attentively every inch of the way." In the *New Statesman* Valentine Cunningham remarked on the calculated quality of the novels; Tindall, however, "lays bare the pains and ambivalence of her domestic scenes with unflinching exactitude."

In 1973, Tindall's first collection of short stories, *Dances of Death*, was published. In the preface, Tindall describes the collection's theme as "the ordinariness of death, the awkward mystery, within the context of daily life," a subject she believes deserves more attention from novelists. She approaches her theme in a variety of ways; in "Heraclitus," for example, a man deifies an old war comrade who he thinks is dead. "The Secret of a Joyful Life" deals with life and death at a second-rate boarding school. While critics commented on Tindall's fine style and intelligence, many felt the common theme rendered the stories self-conscious and predictable, with death serving as a gimmick. According to the *Times Literary Supplement* reviewer, "One's subconscious concentration on the thematic treatment in [her] stories becomes something of a game in which dramatic rather than naturalistic irony predominates."

Having written six novels and many short stories, in 1974 Tindall assumed the role of literary biographer. *The Born Exile: George Gissing* ana-

lyzes the life and work of the Victorian novelist best known for *New Grub Street*, a study of nineteenth-century hack writers. Tindall proposes that Gissing's self-destructiveness and unhappiness were self-imposed to some extent, and that he sought disastrous relationships with women because they offered him "an escape downward" from his failed academic career. Without suggesting that Gissing's novels are autobiographical, she probes the connections between the novelist's personal life and his writings, which often describe the kind of squalor and misery he himself experienced. The biography impressed reviewers with its thorough and intelligent treatment of Gissing's works. In the *New York Times Book Review*, Peter Stansky praised Tindall's knowledge of Gissing's works and their reflection of his psychology, personal history, life, and environment. Her familiarity with current scholarship and previous work on Gissing also commanded Stansky's respect. The *Times Literary Supplement* reviewer contended that the idea of downward escape remains conjectural, but conceded that Tindall documents it with "convincing detail and with great sympathy."

A Handbook on Witches, Tindall's first historical work, surveys witchcraft in England from the Middle Ages to circa 1700. Drawing on scholarly studies, popular literature, and folklore, Tindall considers the black arts, familiars, orgies, charms, and witchcraft's origins in ancient religions. Furthermore, she offers a critical discussion of the role of the Christian churches in fanning the flames of the witch mania. Reviewers described the book as a good introduction to the subject. In the *New Statesman* Stevie Smith commended Tindall's "candid forthrightness and good sense," even though they were "often slangily expressed." The *Christian Century*'s critic acknowledged the book as a source for the uninitiated but questioned the need for yet another study of witchcraft.

Tindall wrote as an urban historian in *The Fields Beneath: The History of One London Village*, which chronicles the life of Kentish Town from an inner suburb of London during the times of William the Conqueror to little more than a thoroughfare after the advent of the railroad. Tindall, a long-time resident of the area, argues that places like Kentish Town, although historically prosaic, were still the loci of social upheaval and physical dislocation and may reveal more of the past than better-known sites. The study was lively and concerned local history, but some reviewers thought it inadequate as rigorous historical scholarship (one demoted it from "a new approach to urban history," as touted by the publisher, to urban an cial history). In the *New Statesman* V. S. Pritchett praised the effort of recovering the local history of London's less elegant areas and noted that Tindall "has a sharp mind and eye and is an excellent local historian of the new kind because she belongs." Valerie Pearl of the *Listener* described the book as splendidly fluent and readable, but impressionistic and often unsubstantiated.

Bombay, the setting of a short story in Tindall's collection *The China Egg*, was the subject of her full-scale history, *City of Gold: The Biography of Bombay*. Surveying the city's past from the seventeenth century to the present, she focuses on its architecture and British roots. She draws on old memoirs and diaries to portray those who shaped Bombay and takes her readers on a guided tour of the present-day city, including its slums. "There is wretched poverty in Bombay," she notes, "but it is not hopeless poverty." As with her history of Kentish Town, reviewers found *City of Gold* insightful, intelligent, and well-researched. A writer in the *New Statesman* described Tindall as an "insatiably curious novelist and historian, [who] does not rest until she gets to the origins of whatever interests her." Although he detected some inaccuracies in the architectural sections, the *Spectator*'s Gavin Stamp summarized the work as unpatronizingly wise and perceptive urban history. "The refreshingly provocative side of the book lies in Miss Tindall's attitude towards the urban sprawl. On the whole she is *for* it," John Grigg observed in the *Listener*.

In recent novels like *To the City* and *Give Them All My Love*, Tindall combines history and fiction by delving into the pasts of protagonists Joe Beech and Tom Ferrier, respectively. In *To the City*, Beech returns from England to Vienna, which he fled forty-five years ago during the Holocaust. The visit jolts Beech into recalling his past, and he becomes haunted by memories of his father, mother, and sisters, all killed by the Nazis. The hero of *Give Them All My Love*, Tom Ferrier, also attempts to confront the past. A self-aware and self-controlled narrator, he reveals how he became obsessed by the idea that his daughter's death, apparently a tragic accident, was in fact a premeditated murder, and how he was then drawn toward committing murder himself. Generally, reviewers found more to fault in *To the City* than in *Give Them All My Love*. In the *Times Literary Supplement*, Jo-Ann Goodwin lamented Tindall's concentration on Beech's pre-Vienna *angst* at the expense of the actual visit to Vienna. Furthermore, she found that "the writing is drab and suffers from a lack of proper pacing—this is unfortunate, as Gillian Tindall's initial ideas are promising." An-

other *Times Literary Supplement* reviewer, Alan Hollinghurst, gave high marks to *Give Them All My Love*, calling it "tightly controlled." The novel, he added, possesses "keen moral insight" and "a beautiful economy of means," so that "all the material will be exploited and recalled again" in the building of Ferrier's obsession.

In addition to writing fiction, history, and biography, Tindall contributes to the *London Times*, *New Society*, the *Observer*, the *Manchester Guardian*, the *New Statesman*, and the *London Evening Standard*. She has also translated Renée Masson's *Number One* (1964) and written a children's book, *The Israeli Twins* (1963), and a radio play. Tindall is married to Richard G. Lansdown, a psychologist, and has one son, Harry. Her avocations include keeping house and foreign travel.

PRINCIPAL WORKS: *Novels*—No Name in the Street, 1959; The Water and the Sound, 1961; The Youngest, 1967; Someone Else, 1969; Fly Away Home, 1971; The Traveller and His Child, 1975; The Intruder, 1979; Looking Forward, 1983; To the City, 1987; Give Them All My Love, 1989. *Collected short stories*—Dances of Death, 1973; The China Egg, 1981. *Non-fiction*—A Handbook on Witches, 1966; The Born Exile: George Gissing, 1974; The Fields Beneath: The History of One London Village, 1977; City of Gold: The Biography of Bombay, 1982; Rosamond Lehmann: An Appreciation, 1985.

ABOUT: Contemporary Authors New Revision Series 11, 1984; Contemporary Literary Criticism 7, 1977; Contemporary Novelists, 4th ed., 1986; Who's Who 1989. *Periodicals*—America February 21, 1970; Books and Bookmen October 1975; Christian Century February 23, 1966; Library Journal September 18, 1969; Listener September 16, 1977; October 27, 1977; March 11, 1982; New Statesman August 6, 1966; July 2, 1971; June 27, 1975; April 16, 1982; New York Times Book Review July 29, 1962; Spectator July 10, 1971; April 10, 1982; Times Literary Supplement October 2, 1959; July 7, 1961; July 16, 1971; July 20, 1973; February 22, 1974; May 8, 1987; May 5, 1989; Washington Post Book World January 4, 1970.

TODOROV, TZVETAN (March 1, 1939–   ), Bulgarian-born literary critic and theorist, now living in France, writes: "In 1987 my past life will consist of two halves of equal length: I was born in Bulgaria forty-eight years ago, and I left my country at the age of twenty-four. This is pure coincidence, of course, but I think it reflects something concerning my identity, which I can only describe as a series of divisions in 'halves' (actually more than two).

"The simplest, for that matter, is the division

TZVETAN TODOROV

Among contemporary literary theorists, Tzvetan Todorov has won distinction for his many significant contributions toward a "poetics" of literature based not upon interpretation but upon a study of the structure and conventions of literary discourse. "If there can be a science of literature," Robert Scholes wrote of Todorov's early work, "critics like Todorov . . . will bring it into being." Poetics, Todorov writes in his *Introduction to Poetics*, is not "the description of a particular work, the designation of its meaning, but the establishment of general laws of which the particular text is the product." His poetics is rooted in his study of the laws and principles, i.e. the structure, of language itself. He defines it as "a science of literature, in opposition both to interpretation of individual works (which deals with literature but does not constitute a science) and to the other sciences, such as psychology or sociology, in that it institutes literature itself as an object of knowledge, whereas previously literature was considered as one manifestation among others of the psyche or of society."

Bulgarian-born, the son of Todor Borov, a university professor, and Haritina (Peeve) Todorova, a librarian, Tzvetan Todorov studied Slavic philology at the University of Sofia (M.A. 1961) and acquired a solid background in the critical theory known as Russian formalism, which emphasized the study of form, as opposed to content, in literature. Since 1963 he has lived in Paris. He married Martine van Woerkins, a writer, in 1972. At the University of Paris (where he became *docteur de troisième cycle* in 1966 and *docteur d'état* in 1970) Todorov came under the influence of Roland Barthes and the school of structuralism then emerging into international prominence. As a student of Barthes, he began contributing articles to *Communications*, a journal published by the École Practique des Hautes Études, and he began to formulate his own critical position as a kind of bridge between Russian formalism, its modifications by the Prague school of criticism, and French structuralism. In 1970 Todorov became the founder and editor of the influential journal of literary theory *Poétique*. With Hélène Cixous and Gérard Genette, his colleagues on the journal, he called for an opening of the literary canon to embrace all forms of communication from folklore to the mass media and to break down the barriers between literature as belles lettres and popular culture. Also widely read in German and Anglo-American literature and literary theory, Todorov has a uniquely cosmopolitan background. Peter Brooks writes: "He stands as an important figure of transmission and integration, someone whose reach towards a poetics of

between the Bulgarian and the Frenchman. During the first twenty-four years, I lived with my parents, graduated first from high school, then from university, and worked for two years. During the next twenty-four years, I lived (only with a few interruptions) in Paris, married, had children, wrote books and sometimes taught. I am no longer a pure Bulgarian, and I will never be a pure Frenchman; I experience this impurity as a blessing rather than as a curse; I would feel impoverished if either of these two halves were missing.

"I feel equally divided between my activities as a writer and as a scholar. I spent most of my working time learning: always reading new books, improving my acquaintance with this or that part of history. However, my profession is to write books, not to collect information, and for me the difference is a vast one; and although I write essays rather than fiction or poetry, the enterprise is not less risky. The genre that I presently specialize in is also hybrid: reflections on history, exemplary narratives. I must add that I became aware of this at the age of forty only: in the humanities, I am afraid, the years of apprenticeship last a particularly long time—if, indeed, they ever end.

"And if I had to describe my life-philosophy, I would again need to refer to some admixture: something like a non-resigned pessimism. In a world that frequently seems to me to be moving from bad to worse, I continue to believe it is possible to strive for (some) good."

the greatest generality is informed by a grasp of the diverse traditions of literary theory since Aristotle."

Todorov's first published book, *Théorie de la littérature* (1965), was his French translation of a collection of writings by the Russian formalist critics that made their work accessible for the first time to many Western critics. Appointed to a research position at the Centre National de la Recherche Scientifique in Paris in 1968, Todorov collaborated with Oswald Ducrot on *Dictionnaire encyclopédique des sciences du langage* (1973; translated as *Encyclopedic Dictionary of the Sciences of Language*). A timely and useful contribution to the emerging interest in critical theory in the 1960s and 1970s, the book contains some fifty articles, arranged conceptually and beginning with a history of modern linguistics and an analysis of the branches of linguistic study, followed by entries on poetics, stylistics, and the philosophy of language. Todorov's specific contributions were articles on sociolinguistics, rhetoric, stylistics, poetics, semiotics, and literary genres.

Although his earliest writings had not been translated into English, Todorov's work came to the attention of many English and American critics who were especially impressed with his perceptive and wide-ranging studies of fiction. His *Littérature et signification* (1967) was a study of Choderlos de Laclos' intriguing novel of 1782, *Les Liaisons Dangereuses*. An epistolary novel, this book raises many questions about signification—what the letter writers say, what they mean, what they signify to their recipients inside the novel and to the reader outside the novel. "Every work, every novel, tells through its fabric of events the story of its own creation, its own history," Todorov wrote, and he showed how the devious schemes of seduction and betrayal in that novel create themselves as they develop in the letters. This was followed by the even more closely analytical *Grammaire du Decameron* (1969), which actually worked out a grammar of narrative form from a study of Boccaccio's famous tales. A "grammar of narrative," Todorov points out, leads to the understanding of a "universal grammar." He writes: "Not only all languages but all signifying systems conform to the same grammar. It is universal not only because it informs all the languages of the universe, but because it coincides with the structure of the universe itself." In Todorov's grammar of narrative there are three elements: the semantic (the content of the work), the syntactic (the combinations of various units of discourse within the work that move the narrative forward), and the verbal (the rhetoric by which the story is told—style, tone, diction, per-

spective, etc.). Todorov further divides the syntactic into propositions (the basic actions of the plot) and sequence (the combination of propositions). Out of this a working grammar emerges in which the characters in a story function as nouns, their attributes as adjectives, and their actions as verbs. Each of these terms is further broken down into its grammatical components and functions—the categories of propositions (actions which modify, transgress, punish, etc.) and of sequence (temporal, logical, spatial).

An approach to fiction as schematic as this may appear to ignore the aesthetic and emotional responses to literature. But Todorov's methodology has broad social, cultural, and historical contexts. He reads the *Decameron,* for example, as a bold break with medieval tradition, reflecting a liberalizing and individualist spirit that anticipated the Renaissance. John Bayley, who describes much of Russian formalism, structuralism, and deconstructionism as "a game with linguistic properties and characteristics which determine the game's output . . . [a] sterilizing of the critical field," nevertheless finds in Todorov's work "a new approach, a new technique of reading [that] is genuinely educational; it enlarges the possibilities of appreciation and understanding." He considers Todorov himself "the most humane . . . and accessible of the new-style critics."

Complex as Todorov's theorizing may be, his writing style is remarkable for its lucidity, and he is careful to offer his readers ample and specific illustrations of his points. An example is his genre study *The Fantastic*, first published in 1970 as *Introduction à la littérature fantastique*. Drawing upon an enormous range of reading from German, French, and English literature, cutting across the literary hierarchy from Henry James and Edgar Allan Poe to Agatha Christie, Todorov seeks not so much to define the fantastic as to account for its existence:

In a world which is indeed our world, the one we know, a world without devils, sylphides, or vampires, there occurs an event which cannot be explained by the laws of this same familiar world. The person who experiences the event must opt for one of two possible solutions: either he is the victim of the illusion of the senses, of a product of the imagination—and laws of the world then remain what they are; or else the event has indeed taken place; it is an integral part of reality—but then this reality is controlled by laws unknown to us. Either the devil is an illusion, an imaginary being; or else he really exists, precisely like other living beings—with this reservation, that we encounter him infrequently. The fantastic occupies the duration of this uncertainty. Once we choose one answer or the other, we leave the fantastic for a neighboring genre, the uncanny or the marvelous. The fantastic is that hesitation experienced by a person who knows only the laws of nature, confronting an apparently supernatural event.

As a genre the fantastic flourished from the late eighteenth through the nineteenth century when, according to Todorov, the supernatural was a medium for expressing subjects (such as social and sexual taboos) that could not be introduced in realistic terms. "Sexual excesses," he writes, "will be more readily accepted by any censor if they are attributed to the devil." Twentieth-century writers, however, have been liberated from such restraints: "Psychoanalysis has replaced (and thereby made useless) the literature of the fantastic. . . . The themes of fantastic literature have become literally the very themes of the psychological investigations of the last fifty years." To illustrate, among other examples, Todorov cites Franz Kafka's short story "The Metamorphosis." When Gregor Samsa awakens one morning as a gigantic insect, there is nothing of the marvelous or miraculous signified. His family, even Gregor himself, come to accept the condition because the world in which they live is as abnormal and bizarre as the event itself. Similarly, most contemporary science fiction is not fantastic or marvelous because "we can no longer believe in an immutable, external reality." In such a world "the fantastic becomes the rule, not the exception."

Poétique de la prose (1971; translated as *The Poetics of Prose*), a collection of sixteen of Todorov's essays written during the 1960s, applies the complex and to many readers obscure theories of structuralist criticism to specific works of literature—a number of popular detective stories, the *Odyssey*, the *Arabian Nights*, the *Quest of the Holy Grail*, and a group of stories by Henry James. The familiarity of these examples and the clarity of his writing, Jonathan Culler observes, make Todorov "of all those working in the French tradition, the most immediately accessible and attractive to the nonspecialist reader." Todorov argues in his chapter "How to Read" that there are three possible approaches to reading: projection (in which the reader imposes a theory upon the text—e.g. a Marxist or a Freudian reading), commentary (explication, close reading), and poetics (a search for the general principles that manifest themselves in the text). However, poetics does not impose laws or rigid criteria: "by locating the universal features of literature within an individual work, we merely illustrate, to infinity, premises we will have already posited. A study in poetics, on the contrary, must come to conclusions which complete or modify the initial premises." In Todorov's view, reading is an active process which "presupposes poetics; in poetics it finds its concepts, its instruments." There is no single prescribed way of reading no single "right" reading. As Culler writes: "Reading involves,

rather, the discovery of how a given work employs, modifies, parodies, and implicitly comments upon the signifying procedures defined by poetics. What Todorov calls reading is in fact a criticism guided and informed by poetics."

In his pursuit of the study of the universal structure of language, Todorov has given much attention to the study of signs and symbols. Two of his major works in this area are *Symbolisme et interpretation* (1978; translated as *Symbolism and Interpretation*) and *Théories du symbole* (1977; translated as *Theories of the Symbol*). The first of these is a historical survey of the writings on symbolism from the Church Fathers through the nineteenth century. Recognizing the multiplicity of theories of interpretation that have emerged over the centuries and continue to emerge in the present day, Todorov asks, "What position must one occupy in order to be capable of describing *all* interpretive strategies?" The answer, he believes, lies in mediating among them and acknowledging their coexistence. It is his hypothesis that each one contains "a measure of truth." *Theories of the Symbol* examines and analyzes writings on symbolism from Augustine through the German romantics into the twentieth century with Freud, Ferdinand Saussure, and Roman Jakobson. The special value of the book, several of its reviewers observed, is its consideration of symbolism as treated in such diverse disciplines as aesthetics, literary criticism, linguistics, anthropology, and psychoanalysis.

In recent years Todorov appears to be moving toward a larger, more historically and humanistically based theory than that held by other poststructuralist critics. Evidence of this includes his *Mikhail Bakhtine: le principe dialogic* (1981; translated as *Mikhail Bakhtin: The Dialogical Principle*), a close and sympathetic study of the Russian critic who rejected formalism and stressed the importance of the historical and ideological context of a work, and his philosophical-historical *La conquête de l'Amérique: la question de l'autre* (1982; translated as *The Conquest of America: The Question of the Other*). In preparation for this book, which Anthony Pagden in the *Times Literary Supplement* describes as "a study of the semiotics of the encounter between Europeans and Amerindians in sixteenth-century Mexico and the Caribbean," Todorov read many contemporary records of the exploration of the New World—the letters and journals of Christopher Columbus, Cortéz, Bartolomeo de Las Casas, Diego Durán, Bernardino de Sahagún. He discovered, as he writes in an account of his research (in his *Introduction to Poetics*), that "the sixteenth-century texts, already highly discrepant among themselves, reveal an image structured very differently from the way it will appear in the eighteenth century (or in the twentieth century)." If we are to understand the past of any culture, we must know how to read its signs—in written language, as is the case with Europeans, or in rituals, social customs, dress and gestures, as in the case of the Indians. By doing this, Todorov suggests, we extend our understanding of our own culture as well as the culture of others. "We can discover the other in ourselves, realize we are not a homogeneous substance radically alien to what is not us." His conclusion is far-reaching: "We are like the conquistadors and we differ from them; their example is instructive but we shall never be sure that by *not* behaving like them we are not in fact on the way to imitating them, as we adapt ourselves to new circumstances. But their history can be exemplary for us because it permits us to reflect upon ourselves, to discover resemblances as well as differences; once again self-knowledge develops through knowledge of the Other."

WORKS IN ENGLISH TRANSLATION: Most of the English translations of Todorov's works have been done by Richard Howard and Catherine Porter. Howard translated *The Fantastic: A Structural Approach to a Literary Genre* (1973), *The Poetics of Prose* (1977), *Introduction to Poetics* (1981), and *The Conquest of America* (1984). Catherine Porter has translated his collaboration with Oswald Ducrot, *Encyclopedic Dictionary of the Sciences of Language* (1979), as well as *Theories of the Symbol* (1982), *Symbolism and Interpretation* (1983), and *Literature and Its Theorists* (1987). *Mikhail Bakhtin*: The *Dialogical Principle* was translated by Wlad Godzich (1984).

ABOUT: Bayley, J. The Order of Battle at Trafalgar and Other Essays, 1987; Brooke-Rose, C. A Rhetoric of the Unreal: Studies in Narrative and Structure Especially the Fantastic, 1981; Brooks, P. *Introduction to Todorov's Introduction to Poetics*, 1981; Contemporary Authors 73–76, 1978; Culler, J. *Foreword* to Todorov's Poetics of Prose, 1977; Hawkes, T. Structuralism and Semiotics, 1977; Jefferson, A. and D. Robey. Modern Literary Theory, 2nd ed., 1986; Scholes, R. Structuralism in Literature: An Introduction, 1974; Spilka, M. (ed.) Towards a Poetics of Fiction, 1977; Valdes, M. J. and O. J. Miller (eds.) Interpretations of Narrative, 1978. *Periodicals*—Comparative Literature Summer 1983; London Review of Books October 7, 1982; New York Review of Books September 19, 1984; October 23, 1986; New York Times Book Review August 5, 1984; January 10, 1988; Times Literary Supplement October 1, 1982.

TOMKINS, CALVIN (December 17, 1925–), American art critic, was born in Orange, New Jersey, the son of Frederick Tomkins and the former Laura Graves. He received his bachelor's degree from Princeton University in

CALVIN TOMKINS

1948. He was employed as a New York–based news reporter for Radio Free Europe (1953–1957) and as reporter, then general editor for art, music, and religion on *Newsweek* magazine (1957–1961). Since 1961 he has been on the staff of the *New Yorker*; during much of that time he has been, as successor to Harold Rosenberg, the magazine's critic of modern art, and is generally considered one of the most careful and level-headed of the art world's many chroniclers of the avant-garde.

Tomkins' writing career got off to an uncertain start in 1951 with the publication of his only novel, *Intermission*. It is the story, told in what a *New Yorker* critic termed "flat, discouraged prose," of two wealthy New Jersey brothers who travel out to Santa Fe to visit a college friend. They find, to their bemusement, that he is living with an older, married woman, and the novel is an account of the unsettling effects of this discovery. Charles Lee, writing in the *Saturday Review of Literature*, called *Intermission* "fluently written," but went on to complain, "The trouble with . . . [the] novel is that it tries to make a lost generation out of a generation that found itself years ago. It tries to deal in Jamesian subtleties with characters who are hollow rather than deep. It is an intermission almost without a play."

During his stint at *Newsweek*, which then had no full-time art critic, Tomkins had written several articles on art and had developed a serious curiosity about the contemporary art world. Upon his move to the *New Yorker*, he began to publish profiles, a biographical critical form for which the magazine is famous, on some of the better-known modern artists. His profiles on the proto-cubist and sculptor Marcel Duchamp, the musician John Cage, the sculptor Jean Tinguely, and the pop artist Robert Rauschenberg were gathered together with a short introduction in *The Bride and the Bachelors: The Heretical Courtship in Modern Art*. The author, in presenting his subjects, attempts to abolish the Olympian stance which artists are popularly supposed to adopt vis-à-vis the public. The four men are to Tomkins as near as possible to being "just folks"; he writes about them calmly, with as much equanimity as he can muster. "In suggesting that there may be a common design underlying the work of the four artists discussed in this book, it should be understood that I do not wish to entangle anyone in my design, least of all the subjects themselves. . . . The most striking of [their] shared attitudes is a belief that art is not half so interesting or important a business as daily life. The religion of art, with its agonies and ecstasies so dear to popular fiction, strikes these men as an absurd pretense. Their attention is turned outward on the world around them, not inward upon their own reactions to it . . . ."

The even tone of Tomkins' book greatly annoyed two establishment art critics. Max Kozloff, writing in the *Nation*, attacked the *New Yorker*: "Being a champion of WASP taste, notorious for the tepidness with which it receives anything vital in the arts, the magazine here imposes a shockingly casual accent on the biographies of some rather subversive individuals. And yet, even if delivered in Tomkins's inimitable teatime tone, there is a mass of new material here that any scholar or critic would welcome. . . . As is proper, Duchamp dominates the proceedings. A cautionary note appears in the master's disdain for commercialism, and one of the major themes of this book is the conviction of its protagonists that life is more important than art, sensibility more important than sales." Hilton Kramer, in the *New York Review of Books*, directed his criticism at the author himself: the four profiles, in his opinion, "constitute . . . [a] straightforward exercise in legend-mongering. . . . [The book's] success is directly attributable to its author's total lack of intellectual involvement with either the art in question or, indeed, with aesthetics as such."

Undeterred by such an unfavorable reaction to his first book on art, Tomkins continued to write on the subject for the *New Yorker*. His next book, *The World of Marcel Duchamp*, was part of the Time-Life series on artists of world importance. Duchamp, in Tomkins' view, exerted "the most potent influence on the diverse, antitraditional arts of the mid 20th century. The book

is more than an account of Duchamp's career: it is actually a survey of the avant-garde art movements of the half-century preceding its publication, including cubism, dada, futurism, surrealism, pop, and op.

Tomkins contributed an influential and eerily prophetic essay, "Raggedy Andy," to John Coplans' short but seminal retrospective examination, *Andy Warhol* (1969), the first of many books on the subject. Concentrating on the limitations and personalization of Warhol's brand of art-making, Tomkins wrote, "A great deal of what took place in America during the last decade is missing, of course, from Warhol's house of mirrors. He has had nothing whatsoever to say to the young militants, the activists on either side of our contemporary conflicts. Participation, confrontation, martyrdom do not interest him: nobody at The Factory today would dream of going on a peace march, and if Andy contributes a painting to a liberal benefit it is only because a refusal would be awkward and un-cool. And no one in the history of cool has ever been cooler than Andy." Commenting on Warhol's pale, blond, and otherworldly appearance, Tomkins quotes one of the artist's friends: "'One of the things he would have liked most was to have been beautiful.' Perhaps he is. At the moment, though, what we seem to see reflected in that strange face is a sickness for which there may be no cure. This is the new shudder brought by Warhol's art. Andy, in what one fervently hopes is just another put-on, begins to look more and more like the angel of death."

Merchants and Masterpieces: The Story of the Metropolitan Museum of Art is the official centennial history of America's greatest art museum, written by Tomkins with the full support of the trustees, staff, and archival resources of the institution. He divides the book into four parts: "Men of Fortune and Estate," "A Climate for Acquisition," "Curators and Collectors," and "The Masses Arrive." The point of his book is the democratization of the museum and its goals: "Now that the mass public has been drawn into the temple, not even the elitist critics expect it to go away. Its presence, in fact, may be the clearest sign that the Metropolitan's real work has only just begun." The history was well received.

Tomkins' other writings on art include the principal article in David Bourdon's compendium *Christo: "Running Fence," Sonoma and Marin Counties, California 1972-76* (1978), an immense, 694-page book outlining in almost unbelievably minute detail each step in the construction of *Running Fence*, the Bulgarian artist Christo's nylon and aluminum construction that briefly traversed a portion of northern California in 1976. Included in the book, alongside such mementos as the facsimile reproduction of the hundreds of pages of Sonoma County's "Environmental Impact Report (Draft)," is Tomkins' highly laudatory article, "Christo's Public Art: How to Win Friends, Outlast Enemies, and Make the Social Structure Work for You in Northern California." "The entire process," the author concludes, "was the work of art, then—four years of planning and organizing, vast expenditures of imagination and money, an incredibly complex marshalling of forces and energies on many levels. And yet, beyond the process, there was that amazing visual image. The ephemeral end product, the great white fence, was far more beautiful than anyone, even Christo himself, had anticipated. . . . The landscape concentrated by *Running Fence* became more memorable than real."

Off the Wall: Robert Rauschenberg and the Art World of Our Time, a full-length critical biography of the artist, brought Tomkins back to the study of a figure he had written about extensively early in his career. The book is more than a return; it is a reworking and updating of material previously published as *New Yorker* profiles and already collected in *The Bride and the Bachelors*. It looks at the successes and failures, the friendships and enmities, and even the deaths in the world of Rauschenberg and others prominent in the New York art scene of the 1950s and 1960s. *The Scene: Reports on Post-Modern Art* attempts to categorize and explain the social and aesthetic involvements of modern artists. It is a complex subject, resistant to full explication, but Tomkins' restrained prose style and his inclination to report on rather than analyze the work of contemporary artists leaves him "free," in the words of Mary Ann Tighe in the *Washington Post Book World*, "to cover territory that is foreign to criticism. Unencumbered by aspirations to higher significance, he deals with the practical problems of making art today."

Tomkins has written two notable books that have nothing to do with the modern artistic avant-garde. *Eric Hoffer: An American Odyssey* is a full-scale encomium based on his three-part *New Yorker* profile of the American working-class social philosopher, the self-educated, aphoristic author of *The True Believer*. But Tomkins' best book in the opinion of many, and certainly his best-known, is *Living Well Is the Best Revenge*, a spare, slender, intensely admiring study of the flamboyant lives of Gerald and Sara Murphy, pioneer American expatriates in France during the 1920s. The book describes their life together as well as their friendships— with Scott and Zelda Fitzgerald (the Murphys were the models for Nicole and Dick Diver in *Tender Is the Night*), Ernest Hemingway, John Dos Passos, Archibald MacLeish, Cole Porter, Picasso, Léger, Diaghilev, Stravinsky, Braque, Derain, and Bakst. Tomkins is adroit at catching the precise nuances of his characters in their scene: "American expatriate life in Paris in the twenties was, in general, one of rather self-conscious intellectual ferment. For the Murphys, however, it was something different. Older by a decade than most of their fellow expatriates, and leading a relatively stable existence that centered largely on their children, they had little in common with the determined bohemianism of many of the Americans in Montparnasse. Most of their friends were married couples with children, who, like them, had come to live in Paris primarily because of a profound discontentment with American life." The final chapter, "Ten Paintings," is Tomkins' account of practically the entire artistic output of Gerald Murphy, which he considers "amazingly contemporary, . . . fresh, original, and full of authority."

The book occasioned generally favorable criticism: the novelist Louis Auchincloss, writing in the *New York Times Book Review*, called it "a beautiful and evocative memoir. . . . Short as this book is, . . . it is still just a few pages too long. Because, toward the close, the nagging idea begins to intrude: isn't the good life better to live than to read about? And so one is ready at last to turn to the greater reality of fiction, as opposed to past fact, and to reopen *Tender Is the Night*. It is absorbing reading on top of Tomkins's revelations."

Tomkins has been married three times. With his second wife, Judy Johnston, he wrote *The Other Hampton*. His third wife is the writer Susan Cheever, daughter of John Cheever, the short-story writer and longtime contributor to the *New Yorker*.

PRINCIPAL WORKS: The Bride and the Bachelors, 1965; The Lewis and Clark Trail, 1965; The World of Marcel Duchamp, 1966, rev. ed., 1968; Eric Hoffer, 1969; Merchants and Masterpieces, 1970, revised 1989; Living Well Is the Best Revenge, 1971; (with Judy Johnston) The Other Hampton, 1974; The Scene, 1976; (with David Bourdon) Christo: Running Fence, 1978; Off the Wall, 1980; Post- to Neo-: The Art World of the 1980s, 1988. *Fiction*—Intermission, 1951.

ABOUT: Contemporary Authors New Revision Series 8, 1983; Who's Who in America 1988–1989. *Periodicals*—Art in America September 1980; Best Sellers April 15, 1970; July 15, 1971; November 1976; Book Week May 9, 1965; Chicago Tribune August 12, 1951; Chicago Tribune Book World May 15, 1980; Choice September 1967; Christian Science Monitor August 14, 1965; July 15, 1971; September 8, 1976;

Commonweal September 7, 1951; October 8, 1965; Economist May 20, 1972; Harper's September 1971; Library Journal August 1951; November 15, 1965; April 15, 1967; July 1967; April 15, 1970; September 15, 1971; May 15, 1980; Nation December 20, 1965; Natural History November 1966; New Republic October 23, 1976; June 21, 1980; New Statesman October 22, 1965; New York Herald Tribune Book Review September 2, 1951; New York Review of Books June 17, 1965; May 8, 1969; January 27, 1972; New York Times August 12, 1951; June 25, 1971; May 31, 1980; New York Times Book Review August 26, 1951; April 12, 1970; July 18, 1971; July 25, 1976; May 25, 1980; June 28, 1981; New Yorker September 29, 1951; April 18, 1970; Newsweek June 22, 1970; July 19, 1971; December 10, 1979; Saturday Review of Literature August 25, 1951; July 24, 1971; Time July 19, 1971; Times Literary Supplement January 20, 1966; Virginia Quarterly Review Summer 1972, Autumn 1980; Washington Post Book World June 27, 1971; August 5, 1979; August 10, 1980.

STEPHEN TOULMIN

TOULMIN, STEPHEN (EDELSTON)

(March 25, 1922–), British philosopher, was born in London, the son of Geoffrey Edelston Toulmin, a company secretary, and the former Doris Holman. He was educated at the Oundle School and King's College, Cambridge University, from which he received a degree in physical sciences in 1943. From 1942 to 1945 he performed his war service as a junior scientific officer in a research establishment of the Ministry of Aircraft Production. Toulmin returned to Cambridge immediately after the war and began the study of philosophy, a subject for which he had had no undergraduate preparation. He studied under the eminent philosophers Ludwig Wittgenstein and John Wisdom, held a research studentship at King's from 1947 to 1951, and took his doctorate in 1948. He was then successively university lecturer in the philosophy of science at Oxford (1949–1955), professor of philosophy at Leeds (1955–1959), director of the Unit for the History of Ideas at the Nuffield Foundation, London (1960–1965); he came to the United States as professor of philosophy at Brandeis University (1965–1969), and subsequently was professor of philosophy at Michigan State (1969–1972), and senior lecturer in social thought and philosophy at the University of Chicago (1973–1986). Since 1986 he has been Avalon professor of the humanities at Northwestern University.

Toulmin's first book was *An Examination of the Place of Reason in Ethics*. He claims in the introduction to have "taken up the discussion" of his theme where Francis Bacon in *The Advancement of Learning* left off. "But I have also extended its range for, where he confined himself

to pointing out the limitations of some of the more common ethical arguments, I have tried to discover, more generally, what it is that gives these arguments such value and scope as they possess. This has meant going at considerable length into the nature of reasoning and the foundations of logic. . . . " In the structure of the book Toulmin considers the problem from the point of view of the traditional approaches (objective, subjective, and imperative); of logic and life (with its sections "Reasoning and its uses," "Experience and explanation," and "Reasoning and reality"); the nature of ethics ("Is ethics a science?", "The function and development of ethics," "The logic of moral reasoning," and "Ethics and society"); and the boundaries of reason ("Philosophical ethics" and "Reason and faith"). In a new introduction to a reprinting of the book in 1986, Toulmin recalls it as "the work of a philosophical tyro," but adds that "having been trained as a natural scientist, I had always hoped to relate philosophical issues to practical experience, and could never wholly side with Hume the philosopher against Hume the backgammon player. . . . After hearing Wittgenstein's skeptical arguments several hours a week for eighteen months, I could not just take the accepted program of 'metaethics' on trust. Instead, I looked for a way of moving beyond the problems to which that program gave rise . . . into the realm of practical moral reasoning."

In 1953 Toulmin published *The Philosophy of Science: An Introduction*, a short treatment of a subject which in those days had been very little explored in English. "The philosophy of science," he explains at the beginning of the book, "has . . . been taken to cover a wide variety of things, ranging from a branch of symbolic logic to the propagation of secularist gospels. . . . The knot of problems on which I have concentrated seems to me to underlie the whole range of topics constituting [the subject]: without some understanding of these issues one can, for instance, neither assess the relevance of mathematical logic to the sciences, nor appreciate the true status of those 'religions without revelation' sometimes built upon them. At any rate, I have tried whenever possible to deal with the problems the layman finds puzzling when he reads about the exact sciences." Richard Wollheim wrote in the *New Statesman* that Toulmin "has most decidely a case to argue, and he argues it clearly and eloquently. . . . [His] exposition is certainly clearer and more cogent than earlier versions of the same view."

The Uses of Argument is an elementary text in analytical philosophy which Toulmin wrote while professor at Leeds. In his introduction he pointed out that the book's intentions are radical, "but the arguments in it are largely unoriginal. . . . The purpose of these studies is to raise problems, not to solve them; to draw attention to a field of inquiry, rather than to survey it fully; and to provoke discussion rather than to serve as a systematic treatise." The problems he raises concerning argument are in a sense *logical* problems: "Perhaps they had better be described as problems *about* logic; they are problems which arise with special force not within the science of logic, but only when one withdraws oneself for a moment from the technical refinements of the subject, and inquires what bearing the science and its discoveries have on anything outside itself—how they apply in practice, and what connections they have with the canons and methods we use when, in everyday life, we actually assess the soundness, strength and conclusiveness of arguments."

During his time at the Nuffield Foundation, Toulmin published several books, the first of which was *Foresight and Understanding: An Enquiry into the Aims of Science*, a series of essays comprising a revision and expansion of his Mahlon Powell lectures delivered at Indiana University in the spring of 1960. Toulmin was then for the first time working in America; he was during 1959–1960 visiting John Dewey professor of philosophy at Columbia. "The present enquiry," the author writes in the first lecture, "attempts something very hard—to focus on science something of the insider's judgment and the outsider's breadth of vision alike. . . . Still, certain general questions about science remain which, though not immediately urgent for the working scientist, are none the less worth asking. . . . Our central concern here will be with questions of just this sort. We must try to categorize the *aims* of science: to give, that is, some account of the distinctive purposes and goals properly pursued in scientific enquiry."

"What is science for?" wrote Robin Clarke in the *Spectator*, "With great success Stephen Toulmin has failed to answer the intended question of his book. . . . His failure is brilliant and assures him his place as an historian of science. . . . This success of failure is throughout at pains to emphasize that the scientific image of other ages formed by the intellectual spectacles of our own age is not a clear one."

With the science historian June Goodfield, his wife, Toulmin began during the 1960s for the Nuffield Foundation a projected four-volume exposition called "The Ancestry of Science." Volume 1, *The Fabric of the Heavens: The Development of Astronomy and Dynamics*, emphasizes the contributions of astronomy and dynamics to early cosmological thinking. In their discussion of cosmology, the authors take the subject from its Babylonian origins through its Copernican and Newtonian refinements to the mid-twentieth-century exegeses of scientific theory. The reviewer for the *Times Literary Supplement* thought the book "full of intellectual excitement, and much of its most telling and vivid argument rests on quite recent archaeological and other research."

In Volume 2, *The Architecture of Matter*, the authors undertake a survey of the chemistry, physics and physiology of material things from the beginnings of science up to the present age. "This time our story," they write in the introduction, "is both vast and largely unfamiliar. To the best of our knowledge, in fact, this is the first recent attempt to give a coherent general account of the whole field we have called 'matter-theory' . . . as it has evolved since the very beginnings of science." C. C. Gillispie, in the *New York Times Book Review*, thought this volume "an even abler work [than its predecessor]—as useful, . . . but more original and absorbing. . . . The Toulmins achieve what has eluded most writers, a sane and plausible account of alchemy. . . . It is that rare achievement, a lively book which at the same time takes the fullest possible advantage of scholarly knowledge, both on the part of the authors and the many colleagues whom they generously cite."

At the start of Volume 3, *The Discovery of Time*, the authors write, "Having surveyed elsewhere man's changing ideas about the layout, workings and occupants of the natural world, we are here concerned with its 'life-story,' and have

attempted to depict the gradual emergence of a continuing sense of history out of earlier mythological and theological systems." In the course of the two earlier volumes, they continue, "we were mapping the development of ideas whose place was securely within the natural sciences, and which overlapped only marginally into other regions of intellectual enquiry. In the area of historical ideas, by contrast, we have found ourselves continually driven outwards from natural science proper into other disciplines." The book was reviewed rather severely in the *New Statesman* by Moses I. Finley, the noted Cambridge historian. In his opinion, it "surveys a single well-trodden field, how modern western man came to think in evolutionary terms about himself and the cosmos, how he 'discovered' history, human and 'natural.' . . . This [book] is not informed by any important fresh insights that I can see, nor is the use of language precise enough for the subject."

In Volume 4, which was to have been "Science and Its Environment," the authors intended "to set the intellectual genealogies examined in the earlier books into their own historical contexts, and consider what can be done to characterize in general terms the processes of 'give and take' by which scientific thought has continually interacted with the wider social and cultural environment." This volume of the series, however, has not been published.

Toulmin's most widely read book is probably *Wittgenstein's Vienna*, written with the historian Allan Janik at a time when popular interest in the Austro-British linguistic philosopher was at its peak. Yet the book, the authors write in the introduction, was not intended as a biography of Wittgenstein. "Instead, we are concerned with one specific problem [to what extent is the philosopher's originality a product of Viennese philosophical preoccupations?]. . . . A hypothetical solution to the problem . . . will serve to reestablish the significance of links between Wittgenstein and the Viennese, German-language thought and art of his time that have been obscured as a result of his later associations with the English-speaking philosophers of . . . Cambridge and Cornell." J. G. Garrison wrote in the *Christian Science Monitor* that the book "is primarily about Vienna from roughly 1875 to 1925, the Vienna into which Wittgenstein was born, where his particular outlook was formed, and whose peculiar intellectual atmosphere underlay the philosopher's deeply moralistic and distrusting nature." The reviewer for the *Economist*, however, thought that the analysis in chapters 6 and 7 of Wittgenstein's philosophical thought, "though it contains some welcome critical hints, is at once too murky and too superficial to be of much value."

Cosmopolis: The Hidden Agenda of Modernity is a far-ranging inquiry into the origins and development of the modern worldview. "With refreshing straightforwardness," T. K. Rabb wrote in the *Times Literary Supplement*, "[Toulmin] tells us that the modern world began in the first third of the seventeenth century, and that its problems were caused by the lust for certainty and stability that preoccupied those particular decades. In his view, the figures who created and consolidated the vision of man, society and nature that held sway in the West for the next 300 years—Descartes, Hobbes, Louis XIV and Newton—tied our instincts and inclinations with bonds that we are only now learning to break." Although Rabb thought that Toulmin sometimes oversimplified modern history in the service of his thesis, or in an attempt to cover the ground too rapidly, he found the range of reference "astonishing" and the book as a whole provocative and often eloquent.

PRINCIPAL WORKS: An Examination of the Place of Reason in Ethics, 1953; The Philosophy of Science, 1953; The Uses of Argument, 1958; Foresight and Understanding, 1961; The Riviera, 1961; (with J. Goodfield) The Fabric of the Heavens, 1961; (with J. Goodfield) The Architecture of Matter, 1962; Night Sky at Rhodes, 1963; (with J. Goodfield) The Discovery of Time, 1965; Wittgenstein's Vienna, 1973; Knowing and Acting, 1976; (with A. Janick and R. Rieke) An Introduction to Reasoning, 1979; The Return of Cosmology, 1982; (with A. R. Jonsen) The Abuse of Casuistry, 1987; Cosmopolis: The Hidden Agenda of Modernity, 1990. As editor—Seventeenth Century Science and the Arts, 1961; Norwood Russell Hanson, What I Do Not Believe, 1971.

ABOUT: Contemporary Authors New Revision Series 20, 1987; Who's Who 1988–1989. Periodicals—Book Week August 9, 1964; August 1, 1965; Christian Science Monitor April 7, 1964; May 9, 1973; Economist June 2, 1973; Encounter August 1973; Guardian December 29, 1961; Library Journal November 1, 1961; March 1, 1962; March 1, 1963; April 1, 1964; May 15, 1965; November 15, 1972; National Review October 26, 1973; New Statesman March 28, 1953; March 30, 1962; June 11, 1965; New York Times Book Review April 28, 1963; March 8, 1964; October 24, 1965; September 2, 1973; New Yorker November 6, 1965; July 23, 1973; Newsweek April 16, 1973; Saturday Review of Society May 1973; School & Society February 21, 1953; Scientific American July 1963; Spectator July 10, 1953; January 5, 1962; Time March 19, 1973; Times Literary Supplement March 13, 1953; February 17, 1961; January 12, 1962; April 26, 1963; November 28, 1963; August 17, 1973; June 29, 1990; Virginia Quarterly Review Autumn 1964; Wilson Library Bulletin May 1962.

*TSALOUMAS, DIMITRIS (October 13, 1921–), Greek poet and translator, now living in Australia, writes: "I was born on the Dodecanese island of Leros in the Aegean Sea. In 1922, almost on my first birthday, Mussolini marched on Rome and began to take steps towards realizing his mad dream of resurrecting the Roman Empire. The temporary occupation arrangements of the Dodecanese, seized by the Italians in 1912 during the Italo-Turkish war, were immediately denounced and the islands were formally annexed and later renamed the Italian Islands of the Aegean. Thus I grew up under the tender wing of the Fascist eagle in an almost continuous state of loathing and hatred for the blackshirts, shared by every other islander with the exception of a few collaborators and spies. Italy collapsed in 1943, and we spent the rest of the war in the benevolent custody of the Nazis.

"The authorities were never successful in winning the hearts of the Dodecanesians, but on the personal level relations between Greeks and Italians were reasonably friendly on the whole, even when De Vecchi, Mussolini's old mate, was appointed governor in the middle thirties and embarked on a program of suppression and de-hellenization of the islands. De Vecchi was an arrogant fool who only succeeded in intensifying the antagonism and hatred of the islanders and in getting us all involved in anti-Fascist activities that were to prove detrimental to their war effort in that sector of their operations.

"During De Vecchi's governorship travel between the islands and Greece became almost impossible; books were unavailable and Greek schools were closed. Thus, after my eighth year at the Greek school of Leros, I found myself on a permanent holiday without much to do. Sheer boredom and my passion for reading made me take up the study of the Italian language. The temptation of all those books in the excellent shops that catered for the needs of thousands of troops, technicians and administrative staff was too much to resist. I enrolled in the Italian high school and from there went to the capital island of Ródhos to complete my education at the Liceo Classico and at the School of Music, where I studied the violin. To my Italian teachers and friends I owe, among other things, the discovery of the world of music and poetry.

"In 1942 I returned to fortress Leros. That was the end of my formal education, but I was full of ambition and hope. Unfortunately, there is little one can do on a tiny island cut off from the rest of the world at war. It was as much as one could do to keep alive. But this struggle for survival did not end with the war. It continued throughout the forties, and it was indeed during those years that real hardship began for me and

DIMITRIS TSALOUMAS

many of my friends, especially with the handing over of the Dodecanese to Greece and the arrival of the Greek gendarmerie, who found us on the wrong side of their politics. It was a period of persecution and unremitting harrassment for anyone suspected of anti-royalism and even anti-Fascist activities, past or present. All this was bitterly disappointing but not entirely unexpected, considering the kind of government the allies prescribed, installed and supported, and the elements out of which its gendarmerie was constituted under the guidance of the various British missions that were implementing Churchill's cold war policies. I thought I could not survive in that climate and migrated to Australia in 1952. I resumed my formal studies in Melbourne, where I joined the Victorian Education Department and taught at various high schools from 1959 to 1982.

"I began to write poetry in the years of frustration after the war but stopped soon after the publication of two short collections before I left for Australia. It wasn't until the middle sixties that I resumed writing, partly because I felt a great urge to do so, and partly because I no longer found satisfaction in the internationally uniform poetic idiom of the times. My ambition was to restore, for myself, meaning and dignity to an art which, as it seemd to me then, was becoming effete and degenerate by the extreme romanticism of the vast majority of its practitioners. Whether I've been successful or not is beside the point. To me it was a matter of private, strictly personal urgency. I never tried to influence or even let others know what I was doing. I kept on

the path I had chosen, guided by an unshakeable faith in the power of *poetry*, the creative power of the imagination in general. I simply believed, as I still believe, that without it life would be poor and meaningless. It seems to me that even our experience of suffering is enhanced by it. This is how I put it in one of the two pieces I addressed to the reader in *The Book of Epigrams*:

TO THE READER—II

If when you walk through the mist you notice birds
   ablaze like pomegranates
in the window and on the bearded roof of winter,
   if sometimes the dark tunnels
let you out on to the balconies of the Amazon
   to see without fear flesh-eating leaves
swallowing alive the straying beams of the sun,
   and if your rights are trampled
or for your country's sake you're led away
   to gaol and see how blood sets fire
to the wilderness in the people's eyes,
   then know that you are indebted to me, that if you doff
the music I clothed you in, the shudder will crack you,
   the mists will flood you, and you'll perish.
                    —trans. Philip Grundy

"My first book since I arrived in Australia was published in 1974, and I worked in isolation and obscurity producing another six till 1983, when a book of English translations from my work appeared in Melbourne and my name was heard of beyond the narrow circle of my friends and a handful of readers in Greece."

———

In awarding him the First Prize for Australian Literature in 1983, the judges of the National Book Council welcomed Dimitris Tsaloumas to the company of Australian poets. "We did not know you in your poet's infancy, Dimitris," the judges wrote, but "we welcome you in your splendid maturity." The occasion for this award was the publication of a bilingual edition of Tsaloumas' poems, *The Observatory*. Tsaloumas is one of a number of Greek poets who have left their native land but continue to write in their native language (though fluent in the languages of their adopted countries). In his case, however, there was a long period of silence from 1952, when he emigrated to Australia, until the mid-1960s, when he resumed the writing of poetry. Since then, however, Tsaloumas has written a substantial amount of poetry in Greek (some of which he has himself translated into English) and he has also translated a considerable amount of contemporary Australian poetry into Greek.

Although Tsaloumas has made his career and his home in Australia for close to forty years, his poetry remains distinctly Greek and distinctly individual in its spirit. His readers agree that he

is not an "easy" poet. "His poems are characterised by multiple viewpoints and deliberate surprises. The shifts are not always clearly sign-posted," Geoffrey Lehmann wrote in the *Sydney Morning Herald* in 1983. More recently Peter Levi noted, in the *Times Literary Supplement*: "It is not really possible to place Tsaloumas accurately by reference to other writers. He is something that was missing, and happy the language that possesses such a poet. The poems are not always easy; they belong to the modern movement. But they are memorable."

They are memorable, among other reasons, for their bold, forthright expression of the grim truths of life as Tsaloumas perceives them. He speaks for the generation of Greeks who were bitterly disillusioned by the fate of their country in the aftermath of World War II—a generation, Levi writes, "with whom he shares a seriousness, a demotic vigour of phrase and a laconic lyricism." This spirit is illustrated in one of his longer poems, "The Sick Barber," which takes place on the island of Patmos during the war. The poet recalls the bleak, wintry atmosphere, bad news of the war, the misery of life: "On days like this / drunkards' noses turn blue, / doors slam and sounds are heard / in the empty houses of the rich." In spite of his failing health, however, the barber remains cheerful: "If I had some wine like yours / I'd fill my pitcher / and go outside to sit in the yard / and chat with the sparrow." The poem ends with his death from tuberculosis:

The barber won't get up again,
not now not in spring
however warm the days.
The pretty serenades and
the Waves of the Danube
hang now from the nail
along with the washed-out smells
above the basin-stand
with the barbers-shop debris,
dirty lather, stale bristles,
cigarette butts.
Further along, on another nail,
the striped cloth, greasy
where it fastens round the neck,
and a shudder runs down the spine of time.
                    —trans. Philip Grundy

Like many other contemporary poets, Tsaloumas sees in the disappearance of classical mythology a parallel to the alienation of the human spirit today. Reviewing his *Book of Epigrams* in *World Literature Today*, John E. Rexine comments on the deep passion yet the restraint with which Tsaloumas confronts his sense of loss. He writes, Rexine says, "from the vantage point of one who has himself lost his own world and is feverishly seeking to find another he can call his own . . . He can deftly interweave his an cient and Byzantine Greek past with the dilemma of living an agonizing modern life in a vast continent at the very end of the world of the diaspora." In "Observations of a Hypochondriac" he reflects:

> The poets who, singing in bygone ages,
> extolled immortal love, and the prophets
> who heard God's voice from the scaffoldings
> of the world, never knew the depression that is ours
> who, locked up the whole day,
> study the woodworm in the cavities of time.
>
> —trans. Philip Grundy

Tsaloumas writes as a man who has known political betrayal and responds now with an ironic, almost humorous, detachment, as in "The Holy Inquisition":

> Well, they took me and put me on this stool
> and looked at me sadly. They bring me tea
> and mournfully inquire, the President that is,
> what I've got up my sleeve. My arm, says I, and
> he thinks about that. Then asks me if I believe,
> and in what God, and I tell him none,
> naturally, and that upsets him no end. Then
> why do they come and tell us you blaspheme?
> God knows! One day I'll tear my clothes,
> I'll burn my cage. And they let me go.
> No torture, no nothing. Nothing, I tell you.
> Tomorrow I'll go there early
> and if they don't let me in I'll raise hell.
>
> —trans. Philip Grundy

But transcending his bitterness is an almost serene faith. He has found his place in Australian society, and he has not lost his memories of his Greek heritage. In "Consolation," a poem addressed to a friend who has suffered a loss, he advises resignation: "Yet to have held something in your hands / is worth the bitterness of losing it."

WORKS IN ENGLISH TRANSLATION: Two volumes of Tsaloumas' verse are available in English: a selection from seven volumes of his poems in Greek from 1974 to 1983, *The Observatory* (1983), edited by Philip Grundy with translations by Tsaloumas himself, Grundy, and Margaret Carroll, and *The Book of Epigrams* (1985), translated by Grundy. Tsaloumas published a collection of his translations into Greek of *Contemporary Australian Poetry* (1985).

ABOUT: Oxford Companion to Australian Literature, 1985. *Periodicals*—Sydney Morning Herald May 25, 1985; Times Literary Supplement October 4, 1985; World Literature Today Summer 1986.

TS'AO YÜ. See **CAO YU**

TURNER, FRED(ERICK) (November 19, 1943–), British-born poet, novelist, and essayist, now living in the United States, writes: "In 1977, in my thirty-fourth year, I received a gift which becomes more astonishing to me as I begin to understand its rarity, its undeservedness, and its effects. The gift was a whole year of almost perfect happiness; not merely a material contentment and a physical well being (though it was there as well), but an almost daily experience of spiritual rapture, personal intimacy with those whom I loved and who loved me, overwhelming intellectual enlightenment and imaginative and creative liberation. That year is celebrated in my book of poems and aphorisms *The Garden*, but it is in many ways also the source of my subsequent work: my two epic poems *The New World* and *Genesis*, my book of essays *Natural Classicism*, my lyric poetry, my scientific and philosophical studies, and my activities as an editor and teacher.

"One of the integral characteristics of that period of epiphany was the strong sense that *this* was paradise, and that I could ask for no more, having been given so much more than I could possibly deserve. Together with this feeling was a knowledge that I could prolong the experience if I wished, but that to do so would not be right. I must return to the world of uncertainty, contingency, struggle and dependence on social judgments, and embody the spirit of the experience in such forms as might trigger it in others.

"I myself had been brought to the brink of that experience by reading Pasternak's *Doctor Zhivago* and *My Sister, Life*, Tolstoy's *Anna Karenina*, the mystical poems of Yeats, Eliot, Dickinson, Blake, St. John of the Cross, and the works of Sappho, Murasaki, Homer, Rabelais, and Shakespeare; and by meditation on the music of Bach and Mozart, the philosophy of Plato, Wittgenstein, Nietzsche, and Whitehead, and the new scientific breakthroughs in physics, cosmology, evolution, psychophysics, and neurochemistry. It was my task to communicate that experience to others.

"So I plunged into a decade of intense labor. It included the articulation of a new philosophical paradigm of the physical/spiritual universe, the revival of the old *Kenyon Review* as a means to communicate with others who might have discovered or be ready to discover the new visions for themselves, a major attempt at Kenyon College and at the University of Texas at Dallas to reshape the academy in such a way as to remove the barriers to insight, and a series of long narrative poems. This work, and the commitments and attachments of bringing up a family, felt like a return to the struggle and anxiety of the world; but there was also a new delight in the

FRED TURNER

of absurd and delightful comedy which seems to dog my footsteps."

———

karmic embodiment of the vision I had been given. Moreover, my most personal relationships, especially my marriage, were and are saturated with the feeling of epiphany; and the many reverses and attacks that I endured in those years were sweetened by the sense of that garden that lay just around the corner of every moment.

"The mission which I seem to have been given was to restore to my culture that sense of spiritual joy and hope that it had lost. Four parallel paths to this goal offered themselves. The first was the celebration of the miraculous beauty and unity of the universe and the human being as revealed by science, especially in an expanded theory of evolution. The second was the expression of that vision in a literature which would be transformed and enriched by being reconnected to its ancient and panhuman genres and forms: epic, ritual, meter, narrative. The third was the reopening of the discipline of theology to include the most rigorous and imaginative science, the ancient worldviews of animism, totemism, and polytheism, and the insights of the mystics. And the fourth was a change in the fundamental socio-cultural paradigms, including the reorganization of the academy without academic departments, the perception of humankind as that part of nature designed to be its gardener, and a refounding of economics on a unified philosophy of value. Obviously this work required also a reinterpretation of human history.

"There is something in a synopsis that denatures and solemnifies. I am aware that this summary fails to capture much of the subjective flavor of my life, especially the persistent theme

Fred Turner was born in Northamptonshire, England to Edith and Victor Witter Turner, a distinguished anthropologist. He spent three years of his boyhood in Zambia while his father did fieldwork for a doctoral degree. Young as he was, the exposure to tribal cultures, myths, and rituals influenced him greatly. On his family's return to England, young Turner, then eleven, found it difficult to adjust to the bland social and cultural life of the 1950s. By early adolescence, he told Wade Newman in an interview in *Southwest Review*, he was a rebel against "the prevailing Dustbin School in England . . . which equated realism with that which was miserable and disgusting, and sort of depressing, dispiriting and discouraging." He found refuge in mysticism, in religion (his family had converted to Catholicism), and in reading, especially science fiction and the poetry of Gerard Manley Hopkins. Turner's earliest poems were often experiments in Hopkins' unique metrical system of sprung rhythm.

At Christ Church, Oxford, Turner specialized in Shakespeare and Elizabethan literature. A visit to the United States in 1961 impressed him with the vitality of the "new" world. He returned to Oxford to complete his education (B.A. 1965, B. Litt. 1967, M.A. 1967) but emigrated to America in 1966 with his wife Mei Lin Chang, whom he had met as a student of modern languages at Oxford. They settled in Santa Barbara where, at twenty-three, he became an assistant professor of English at the University of California and director of the Santa Barbara Poetry Festival. Two years later he published his first collection of poems, *Deep Sea Fish*. In 1971 Turner published the thesis he had written at Oxford under Dame Helen Gardner, *Shakespeare and the Nature of Time*, a study of "the central problems of man's temporal nature and his relationship with his environment of time" in Shakespeare's sonnets and eight of his plays.

In 1972 Turner became associate professor of English at Kenyon College where for many years the important critical journal *Kenyon Review* had been published. With colleagues at Kenyon Turner revived the journal and served as its editor from 1978 to 1983. In 1983 he spent a year in England as visiting professor of English at the University of Exeter, and in 1985 he joined the faculty of the University of Texas at Dallas as Founders Professor of Arts and Humanities. He lives in Dallas with his wife and two sons and has traveled widely in Europe and the United States giving poetry readings and lectures.

Though Turner has written in a variety of genres—lyrical and narrative poetry, literary criticism and scholarship, science fiction—he has had a consistent vision and goal in all his work. This has been to pursue what, in *Natural Classicism*, he calls "a science of beauty"—a conviction "that beauty can be a legitimate subject of scientific investigation, and that such a science will offer powerful solutions to problems in other disciplines, and a richer understanding of the world." To this end Turner has written a visionary poetry, moving from an early lyricism that echoed his "inherited culture" of classicism and romanticism to long narrative and epic poems that attempt to demonstrate (as he writes in his Introduction to his epic poem *The New World*) "that a viable human future, a possible history, however imperfect, does lie beyond our present horizon of apparent cultural exhaustion and nuclear holocaust. Art has the world-saving function of imaginatively constructing other futures that do not involve the Götterdämmerung of mass suicide; because if there is no imaginative future, we will surely indeed *choose* destruction, being as we are creatures of imagination."

Turner's early poems collected in the aptly titled *Between Two Lives* reflect his growing awareness of both his strangeness as a foreigner in an "exotic" new land, America (in "Santa Barbara, 1970" he sees himself as "an inhabitant, an / inexplicable local of this foreign land") and of his ability to merge into spiritual union with the universe:

as a boy, I
would feel sometimes the world as a totality, a single
note,
my awareness penetrating the walls of my room. . . .
—from "The Music"

The political unrest of the 1970s, particularly among American students, alienated him even further from his own generation which, he told Newman, "grew up on modernism . . . the drab, imitative modernism of the sixties and seventies." He addressed that generation in "The Riots, 1968–1969":

Your epiphanies, my God, are maybe sweet
to your converted, and your poison meat
to those who know their need. My hands
are not so strong, my eyes fail in your lands.
They whose fists now seem uplifted to my head
may be the Satans without whose blessing I am dead.

Turner is one of the founders of a new literary movement, Expansionism, that affirms its opposition to modernism and seeks to restore to the arts "the great classical forms . . . tonality, the figurative, the representational in the visual arts, and meter and the great poetic genres, and plot in the novel." He looks to Homer, Virgil, Dante, Shakespeare, and Milton rather than to twentieth-century poets and novelists as writers who "were able to do what people really need and want: that is, stories, myths, and situations in which they can learn what happens next, and characters with whom they can identify. If poetry can give people that, I think people will read poetry." Turner himself therefore began to compose narrative verse in long, carefully metered lines, usually pentameter, varying the five heavy stresses with ten lighter ones and varying the tone, as in the Homeric epic, with deliberate shifts from high to low style.

There are some narrative poems in *Between Two Lives*, but Turner's first really extensive use of the form was in *The Return*, a first-person narrative by an American reporter covering the Vietnam war:

By the banks of the Mekong River there still stands
a ragged geodesic dome built by the crack
shelter group of the Army Corps of Engineers.
Some of its panels are beaten out, some reflect
in jungle bluenesses, shards of bright moonlight.

He meets and falls in love with a young Chinese-American woman who works with him as a photographer. They become involved in a secret investigation of a drug operation, are captured by drug dealers and in desperate danger. They manage to escape through India and finally return to a materialistic American society that seeks to exploit their adventures in sensational books. The poem ends, however, in a spirit of peace and reconciliation. The couple marry and find their place in a small midwest American town:

Not that we live in great solemnity.
We're happy, are not much concerned for
permanence.
Those who, disposed to find us odd or dull, leave us
alone, find us well pleased to be ignored. Those who
are skeptics of our happiness—let them be
happier than we and then surely in their content
they could not grudge us our joining in their
happiness.

The Return was published with a Preface by the well-known critic George Steiner who noted the difficulty first of writing and then of finding an audience for the long poem today. "Fred Turner," he wrote, "reclaims for poetry its antique privilege of heroic action, its right and, perhaps, primal compulsion to tell a story more sharply, with more economy than can that later idiom which is prose." Turner reclaimed that privilege on a far larger and more ambitious scale in his *The New World: An Epic Poem* of nearly two hundred pages. Here, in a narrative set in an America of the distant future (it begins in 2376 A.D.), he frankly acknowledges as his models the epics of classical literature. He writes in his Introduction: "American culture is celebrated in *The New World* as *Beowulf* celebrates the Nordic, Virgil the Roman, and Homer the Greek. . . . *The New World* represents a swing of the epic poem away from the self-regard or self-concern of Wordsworth's *Prelude* and Eliot's shattered mini-epic *The Waste Land* toward a new kind of outward glance at the world." He is equally candid about the poem's anti-modernism. Its theme, he writes, "is the discovery of a third mode of knowledge, belief, and commitment that transcends the contemporary dilemma of fanatical blind faith and affectless hedonism." In *The New World* the human race survives in a world depleted of its natural resources. Many of its citizens have emigrated to other planets and the remaining ones live in a high-tech society ruled by violent matriarchies and fanatical theocracies, policed by mounted knights in armor who fight with state-of-the-art laser equipment. But the poem adheres strictly to the conventions of the classic epic. It begins "I sing of what it is to be a man and woman in our time" and proceeds to an invocation of the muse (here "wind of the spirit")—"lend me your lightning, apocalypse yourself, let me see / one pattern of the whole, and clothe my poem in words." It incorporates other epic conventions—a brave young hero on a quest, stories within stories, battle scenes:

> The order is given, the head of the enemy column
> has passed through a bend in the valley; the first wedge
> breaks into movement, crests the top of the rise,
> and canters on down.

The hero, living in the ruined city of Hattan Riot (Manhattan), sets off with his mother on a perilous journey through the "Mad county" of Vaniah (Pennsylvania) on a quest for freedom in Ahiah (Ohio). Like most epic heroes, he is killed at the end in an act of treachery, but he leaves behind a family and a son who will carry on his mission.

The New World received wide critical attention, partly because of its ambitious scheme but also because of its science fiction elements. "His poem," Paul O. Williams wrote in the *Christian Science Monitor*, "is an entertainment, a delight, a wry and penetrating comment on human behavior, and a sizable narrative experience." But Williams found its weakness in its size: "the story sometimes overwhelms the projected length of the poem, causing Turner to summarize large

and important sections of narrative, to allow vital scenes to happen offstage and merely be reported later." For Robert B. Shaw in *Poetry* the plot was "spasmodic," the characters unreal, and the verse "for long stretches barely distinguishable from prose." William Logan, in the *New York Times Book Review*, also found problems in the verse: "When the verse of *The New World* is confined to the luxuriance of nature or the special effects of battle, it has the texture and visual attention derived from its particular details. Given the poet's philosophical and literary ambition, the practice elsewhere produces a line indistinguishable from prose and therefore almost incapable of subtlety as a poetic medium."

Reviewers of Turner's science-fiction prose novel *A Double Shadow* had no such reservations, however, and were almost uniformly delighted with his imaginative ingenuity, fusing Greek and Japanese myths with a romantic love story, all set in a futuristic Martian society ruled by a "femarchy"—goddesses who, Turner writes, "act as umpires, constitute a final court of appeal in aesthetic disputes, and officiate at the various festivals that are held at leaf-fall and cherry blossom time in different parts of the planet." Frederick Patten, in *Library Journal*, found *A Double Shadow* "one of the best science fiction novels of the year, if not the decade." The reviewer for *Publishers Weekly* compared it to Vladimir Nabokov's *Pale Fire* in that the narrator is a fictional author who is writing a wildly imaginary history. An ineffectual man, aware of his wife's infidelity, he describes himself as "a cowardly intellectual." At the end of his vastly complicated story, he confesses that it has gotten away from him "into green and geometric jungles of myth, where everything is structure and all self and particularity is lost."

This closing of *A Double Shadow* describes and parodies the trends in modern literature that Turner has criticized severely in many of his critical essays. These are collected in *Natural Classicism: Essays on Literature and Science*, in which Turner rejects deconstructionism and all theories of literature that deny the authority of the text and argue that literature is open-ended, flexible, and subject to multiple interpretation. "Great literature," Turner writes, "is the achievement of unmistakable clarity and intelligibility in the teeth of the proclivity of every word, every sentence, to collapse entropically into divine indeterminacy." Another essay in this collection, "The Neural Lyric: Poetic Meter, the Brain and Time," originally published in *Poetry* (August 1983) where it won the Levinson Prize, argues that language in the form of metered verse is more accessible to the human brain than unmetered verse. Drawing upon the research of the German neurophysicist Ernst Pöppel, Turner analyzes the functions of the parts of the human brain as they control our powers of reasoning and comprehension: "By means of metrical variation the musical and pictorial powers of the right-brain are enlisted by meter to cooperate with the linguistic powers of the left, and by auditory driving effects the lower levels of the nervous system are stimulated in such a way as to reinforce the cognitive functions of the poem, to improve the memory, and to promote physiological and social harmony. Metered poetry . . . may thus act as a technique to concentrate and reinforce our uniquely human tendency to make sense of the world in terms of values like truth, beauty, and goodness."

PRINCIPAL WORKS: *Poetry*—Deep Sea Fish, 1968; Between Two Lives, 1972; Counter-Terra, 1978; The Return, 1981; The New World, 1985; The Garden, 1985; Genesis, 1988. *Prose*—Shakespeare and the Nature of Time, 1971; Natural Classicism, 1986. *Novel*—A Double Shadow, 1978.

ABOUT: Contemporary Authors New Revision Series 12, 1984; Dictionary of Literary Biography 40, 1985. *Periodicals*—Christian Science Monitor February 4, 1986; Library Journal June 15, 1978; Poetry April 1986; Publishers Weekly April 13, 1978; New York Times Book Review October 27, 1985; Southwest Review Summer 1986; Times Literary Supplement March 29, 1974.

LUISA VALENZUELA

*VALENZUELA, LUISA (January 23, 1944–), Argentinean novelist and short story writer, now living in New York City, writes: "My childhood was spent in the presence of the great Argentine writers of the time (Borges, Sabato, Nale Roxlo, Peyrou). That is why, obviously, if not my vocation, my ambition was to be a painter. Or a mathemetician. The sharpness of colors and numbers dazzled me. It is true that the writings of Luisa Mercedes Levinson, my mother, also dazzled me. But I wanted to follow another very distinct path. I was a voracious and eclectic reader from the time I was a small girl, and even though I pretended to read the great literature, Emilio Salgari was my favorite author. His adventure novels launched me into the streets and, on turning the corner, the vacant lot would turn into dense jungle where Sandokan, the Tiger of Malaysia, would appear. I used to concoct long and dangerous journeys while I was glancing at my mother in her bed, writing, surrounded by papers. It took me a long time to understand the implicit activity in this apparent passivity, and not because I lacked the necessary

imagination—on the contrary. My imagination was a motor that obliged me to act. So, from the age of five when I first ran away from home, so to speak, until age seventeen when finally I turned myself in, it seems I had been running away from words. Or rather, running away from the awareness of the dominion that words exercise over all of us. But no one can truly flee, and least of all the author of these lines, who made her first pun when she was barely two years old.

"Poking around in childhood, something I rarely do, for I am not in the least an autobiographical writer, I find two incidents which may have pushed me into literature head first:

"1) I had a sister ten years older than I, who in my tender youth read me horror stories in order to make me eat. I would open my mouth in fright and she would stuff it. I swallowed my fear and my fascination along with the food. During one memorable lunch my mother interrupted the reading, suggesting that perhaps the story was too scary for a child. That same night I hallucinated that the woman in the story, with her brains popping out of her head, was entering my room with an axe in her hand. I was never able to find out the ending of that story or the fate of the protagonists. Even until now, I search for the dénouement.

"2) When I was in the sixth grade, the teacher asked my mother to help me with my school compositions. 'Your daughter is so good in mathematics and science, it's a shame that she doesn't write easily,' she must have told her. My mother, the well known writer, tried to write the text in what she believed to be the style of an eleven-year-old. It struck me as so sickeningly sweet, so removed from my personality, that from that time on I decided to assume responsibility for my own writing.

"Mine seems to be a history of precociousness and why not. In this adventure of writing perhaps it is easier to plunge in when one is very young. At age seventeen I wrote my first real story, which the novelist Juan Goyanarte published in his (then) distinguished literary magazine *Ficcion*. Goyanarte said that I had the stuff of a novelist and insisted I should give it a try. I thought I would never have the patience for such an endeavor, until shortly thereafter, I got married and went to live in France, where my daughter was born. In Paris, between the 'trotteuses' who walked the streets in front of our apartment near the Bois de Boulogne, and my very painful nostalgia for Buenos Aires, *Hay que sonreir* (*Clara*, in the English version) came into being. In France I also wrote or conceived the first stories of *Los heréticos* (The Heretics). Sometimes I think that the strangeness of living abroad is the motor for my writing. Like a perpetual search that extends from the blank page to the map of the world. My first shock at confronting New York was what gave birth to *El gato eficaz* (Cat-o'-nine-deaths). My stay in Barcelona unleashed the novel *Como en la guerra* (He Who Searches), in which mythical Argentines move around an even more mythical Barrio Gotico. With this novel, I began to realize that literature could be dangerous, but it was still at the margin of real danger. The rest came immediately afterwards, upon my return to Buenos Aires in 1974, when the paramilitary violence was already being unleashed. I realized then that it was necessary for me to write in order to achieve an understanding of that reality which was so foreign to what I had left behind two years earlier. In one month, I produced the stories in *Aqui pasan cosas raras (Strange Things Happen Here)*. I wrote them in cafes, reacting to the generalized paranoia and fear, and thinking that I should write in illegible handwriting so that no one could read over my shoulder (the writer as witness? the writer as antenna?). Writing about it, unfortunately, does not stop the horror, and the spiral of violence and state terrorism reached a point in Argentina where one could continue writing but could not show the product even to one's most intimate friends, for fear of endangering them. That happened to me with the narrative *Cambio de armas (Other Weapons)* and so I decided to go away in order not to fall into self-censorship. An invitation to be a writer in residence for a semester at Columbia University at the beginning of 1979 gave me the pretext to leave. Later I would see where I

would head. But New York is a vice, and I was hooked. For the time being, I return to Argentina only intermittently. *Cola de lagartija* (*The Lizard's Tail*), that fable about power, repression and (confounded, confused) sex, could be written only many kilometers away from the scene of the crime. But now that I am writing a novel that takes place in New York, with Argentine protagonists, perhaps I need to distance myself once again. Exile can be devastating, but the perspective and separation refine the marksmanship."

———

Luisa Valenzuela was born in Buenos Aires, Argentina. She began her career as a writer and journalist at an early age. Her first stories were published in *Quince Abriles* and *Ficcion* and she worked as a journalist for publications such as *Esto Es, Atlantida,* and *El Hogar*. She later moved to Paris where she worked for Radio Television Française writing programs. In 1964, after returning to Argentina, she became the assistant editor of the *La Nacion* sunday supplement. She received the Kraft Award for journalism in 1965. Argentina's Instituto Nacional de Cinematografia presented her with an award for her script "Clara," based on her novel *Hay que Sonreir* (1966). In 1969–1970, she received a Fullbright Grant to participate in the International Writers Program in the University of Iowa. In 1979, she moved to New York City where she has been a writer-in-residence at Columbia University, Center for Inter-American Relations and at City University of New York–Racata Writers Workshop. She received a Guggenheim Fellowship in 1983, is a fellow of the New York Institute for Humanities and a member of the Freedom to Write Committee of PEN American Center. She is currently conducting a creative writing workshop at New York University, Writing Division.

Luisa Valenzuela is described as "one of the significant authors to have emerged in Argentina since the 'boom' in Latin American literature of the 1960's." Her fiction—written in a style "marked by the dazzling ellipses, bizarre fantasy and baroque textures we have come to associate with Latin American prose"—is also cited as belonging to "the remarkable constellation of fiction that emerged from the violent, irrational and tortuous reality of Argentina in the 1970s." Much of her best work shows the influence of expressionism and surrealism, which has led numerous critics to define it within the boundaries of so-called Latin American "magic realism." For at least one North American critic, "Valenzuela's use of magic realism emphasizes the surreal and bizarre more so than does the fiction of such pioneers of the technique as Gabriel García Márquez and Julio Cortázar." Other critics emphasize Valenzuela's focus on Latin American sociopolitical issues. Among the themes identified as most common in her work are those of "violence, political oppression, and cultural repression, especially as the latter relates to women." In terms of literary technique, Valenzuela is best known for her "experiments with narrative structure through a constantly shifting point of view and through self-conscious language that examines the creative process of art," and for her use of "humor, irony, neologisms, and Argentinean slang." Much of her fiction is defined as feminist, presenting "satirical views of the relations between the sexes."

Valenzuela's first novel, *Hay que sonreir* (Something to Smile About, 1966), is the story of a simple, childlike country girl who comes to Buenos Aires with a dream—to see the ocean and to achieve some sense of selfhood and spirituality. But in a society that demands woman's passive acceptance of male domination she can survive only by becoming a prostitute, using her body (the physical) rather than her head (the spiritual). Betrayed by the man she idealizes, she becomes the victim of an exploitive fortune-teller and suffers a final indignity when the fortune-teller decapitates her. Praised by many reviewers for its "infusion of magic realism into [a] conventional structure," the novel was translated into English and published with selections from Valenzuela's collection of stories from the same period, *Los heréticos* (The Heretics), as *Clara: Thirteen Short Stories and a Novel.*

Strange Things Happen Here: Twenty-Six Short Stories and a Novel brings together translations of two more of Valenzuela's early works: the novel *Como en la guerra* (As in the War, 1977; translated as *He Who Searches*) and the collection of short stories written in the period immediately following the author's return to Argentina in 1974. *He Who Searches* is narrated by an Argentinean psychiatrist who lives in Barcelona but returns to Buenos Aires in search of a prostitute he had known there fifteen years earlier. He finds his native land torn by revolution and poverty and—at last—the mysterious prostitute herself, now apotheosized as Eva Perón. In both the novel and short stories the horrors of a fascist dictatorship and the cruel repression of women are depicted in stark, nightmarish detail and blunt language In the words of Amanda Heller, in the *Atlantic Monthly*, the often very short pieces which make up *Strange Things Happen Here* "offer a surrealistic picture of life in a fascist state. Though the themes of the stories vary from sex to politics to philosophical quest, in each one the threat of violence lurks close to the surface. Valenzuela's Argentina is a place where any ordinary parcel may contain a bomb, where any car may belong to the secret police, where even the conversation of children turns to talk of guns. . . . On the whole, . . . the collection gives a vivid, eerie, and affecting sense of life in a society where a cruel tension is the governing condition."

Valenzuela's first important work to be published after her departure from Argentina in 1979 was *Cambio de armas* (Exchange of Arms, 1982; translated as *Other Weapons*). Political and sexual domination figures everywhere in these stories which, Margery Resnick writes in the *New York Times Book Review*, "chronicle female desire in tightly circumscribed worlds where women's lives are largely ruled by their exotic dreams." The title story is the narrative of a woman who is imprisoned and sexually humiliated by her jailer, called "the Colonel," toward whom she has ambivalent feelings. Resnick writes: "Miss Valenzuela never loses her grasp on the interplay of dependence and power that rules these men and women. . . . If this relationship, with its trappings of sadomasochism, expresses the universal state of men and women, then Miss Valenzuela's vision is a stark one indeed. Her images of cruelly manipulated women are not softened by the subsequent revelation that reverses male-female roles, and the larger political resonances that generally mark this writer's work can only be faintly heard."

Cola de lagartija (1984; translated as *The Lizard's Tail*) is considered by some critics to be Valenzuela's most important work. Also written since her arrival in New York City, this work is characterized as a novel in which "fantasy, myth, magical transformations, bizarre ritual [and] caustic satire prevail over any semblance of conventional narrative, much less plot." Considered a political roman à clef, the novel has for its central character someone apparently modeled on one of Isabel Perón's advisers; the book was not published in Argentina for obvious reasons. Designated "Minister of Social Well Being," he is a sorcerer, a kind of witch doctor with uncanny sexual powers. He tells his own story in a wildly surrealistic, stream-of-consciousness style that makes it difficult for the reader to distinguish between fantasy and reality. In Allen Josephs' opinion, in the *New York Times Book Review*, "[Valenzuela's] attempt at virtuosity tends to undermine the novel. In order to convince the reader of the Sorcerer's madness and narcissistic depravity, she resorts to surrealism, hyperbole, and self-indulgent prose." While conceding that the narrative technique is knotted and obscure, other reviewers, however, found *The Lizard's Tail* fascinating. Anne Marie Schultheis, in *Best Sellers*, wrote: "In spite of the density of the novel, Valenzuela does communicate well her ideas on power, politics, and magic through the form of magical realism. Her achievement lies in this blend of fact and fantasy."

Perhaps the best overall summary of Luisa Valenzuela's importance within contemporary Argentine fiction is one offered by the novelist Julio Cortázar in *Review:* "Courageous—with neither self-censorship or prejudice—careful of her language—which is excessive when necessary but magnificently refined and modest as well, whenever reality is—Luisa Valenzuela travels through her various books, lucidly charting the seldom-chosen course of a woman deeply anchored in her condition, conscious of discriminations that are still horrible all over our continent, but, at the same time, filled with a joy in life that permits her to surmount both the elementary stages of protest and an overestimation of women in order to put herself on a perfectly equal footing with any literature—masculine or not. To read her is to enter *our* reality fully, where plurality surpasses the limitations of the past; to read her is to participate in a search for Latin American identity, which offers its rewards beforehand. Luisa Valenzuela's books are our present but they also contain much of our future; there is true resplendence, true love, true freedom on each of her pages."

WORKS IN ENGLISH TRANSLATION: Luisa Valenzuela's novel *The Lizard's Tail* was translated by Gregory Rabassa in 1983. Collections of her shorter fiction include *Clara: Thirteen Short Stories and a Novel* by Hortense Carpentier and J. Jorge Castello, 1976; *Strange Things Happen Here: Twenty-Six Short Stories and a Novel* by Helen Lane, 1979; *Other Weapons: Novellas* by Deborah Bonner; and a selection of her stories from previous anthologies, as well as some new work, by six different translators (Hortense Carpentier, J. Jorge Castello, Helen Lane, Christopher Leland, Margaret Sayers Peden, and David Unger), *Open Door*, 1988.

ABOUT: Contemporary Authors 101, 1981; Contemporary Literary Criticism 31, 1985; Marting, D. E. (ed.) Women Writers of Spanish America, 1987; Solé, C. A. and M. I. Abreu (eds.) Latin American Writers II, 1989. *Periodicals*—Atlantic Monthly July 1979; Best Sellers November 1983; New York Times Book Review July 1, 1979; October 6, 1985; October 30, 1988; Review 24, 1979; Studies in Short Fiction Spring 1980; World Literature Today Summer 1983.

VINE, BARBARA. See **RENDELL, RUTH**

VLIET, R(USSELL) G. (1929–May 11, 1984), American novelist, poet, and playwright, was born in Chicago, the son of a naval medical officer. He lived as a child in American Samoa and as an adult in various parts of the American Southwest, in New England, and, during 1968–1970, in Yautepec, Mexico. He earned bachelor's (1951) and master's (1952) degrees from Southwest Texas State College in San Marcos, and attended Yale University School of Drama for graduate work in 1955–1956, studying under Robert Penn Warren and Lemist Esler.

Vliet began his writing career as a playwright, and although few of his plays were published in book form, some of them won awards, notably *The Regions of Noon*, which was named play of the year by the Southeastern Theatre Conference in 1961. As early as 1954, one of his teachers had told him he was more novelist than playwright, but he nevertheless spent the next ten years trying to write plays and succeeding more often than not, always insisting, with that stubbornness which everyone who knew him remarked as one of his outstanding traits, that *Rockspring*, a slender novel written in 1963–1964 but not published until 1974, was a kind of fluke in the progress of his dramatic-poetic career. He eventually accepted and worked with his novelistic gifts, and most critics now consider them to be the greatest ones he possessed.

Rockspring takes place in western Texas and northern Mexico in the 1880s; it is the story of the kidnapping of a fourteen-year-old blond girl, a farmer's illiterate daughter, by two Mexicans and an Indian and of her eventual deliverance by one of her Mexican abductors, with whom she has fallen in love. Lee Sullenger, writing in *Library Journal*, commented on the "well-developed . . . ironic theme of evil changing into good, then becoming evil again. [The novel is] a fast-paced story of cultural clash, with accurate use of detail, and with characterization that is stark, lean, and very convincing." Vliet's painstaking recreation of frontier life was particularly singled out for praise by other critics, and this characteristic of his writing was to serve him faithfully in his subsequent fictional work.

Vliet's second novel, *Solitudes*, is also set in the Texas of the 1880s. It is the story of Claiborne Sanderlin, a wild young man, a being of pure instinct, illiterate and coarse, living in a state of nature. In a moment of violence, he shoots and kills an old Mexican rancher who has seen and might tell about the cattle-rustling operation Clabe is

R. G. VLIET

participating in. From this point, quite early in the novel, Clabe has a vision to follow, for before being shot the Mexican had shown him a photograph of a woman in a white dress. The young man feels compelled to seek her out, to understand why he killed the man who had her photo, although he does not know why he is obeying this compulsion. His journey is an epic wandering, filled with stray thoughts, memories of his sad, abused childhood; there remains always in his mind the young woman in the white dress, and the mystery she represents. He suffers from epilepsy but understands that disease only as a dreaded blackness. Finally he discovers the woman, Soledad, and in his final confrontation with her he also confronts himself, his reason for killing the old man, and his very reason for being. "Clabe's point of view," wrote W. S. Di Piero in *Commonweal*, "which governs the book, is so seamless that we are finally one with him when he reaches the luminous conclusion about himself: that his violence against others is an act of self-hatred bred by unknowing. From dread and murder the novel moves convincingly toward compassion and mercy. It is a tale about grace hard won, and about how self-knowledge finally redeems a man from his own worst instincts." Peter Glassman wrote in the *Hudson Review*: "Particularly, I admire Vliet's prose. His language is provokingly inventive, remarkable in its images, lithe and intriguing in its patterns of sound. Few other of our writers enjoy so full and responsible a relation with nature, . . . have so quick an ear for idiom and argot, . . . possess so swift and fresh a feeling for human ec-

centricity, so active a love for the multiformity of our kind."

Solitudes experienced a difficult transit from manuscript to printed book, and Vliet was far from satisfied with the version published by Harcourt, Brace, Jovanovich in 1977. In 1986, two years after his death, Texas Christian University Press brought out a definitive edition, entitled *Soledad, or Solitudes*, comprising much new material omitted from the first edition. His wife, Ann Vliet, wrote in the introduction to the restored version: "I typed out the new manuscript from his revised text and was amazed at what a good book it now was: the narrative line was perfectly clear, the detail that was left seemed to fall into its natural place, the disparity between styles disappeared into a rich organic form. Left alone to percolate in the back of Russ's mind, it had finally become what it could be."

"To get a literature of the Southwest," Vliet once said, "to get an *image* of the Southwest, we are going to have to have poems and novels of such high linguistic and intuitive capabilities as to be able to probe and release, in their own idiom—reflecting the sky they are under and the land they are on, the past they come from and the present they are in—the individual communal psyches that, though they are at once all men, are also, and especially, of *this* time, *this* place." His third novel, *Scorpio Rising*, published posthumously, is set largely in the late nineteenth and early twentieth centuries on the Edwards Plateau, in and around the town of Alto Springs, the fictional counterpart of Rocksprings, which is the county seat of Edwards County, Texas. The story opens in the mid-1970s, with a portrait of Rudy Earl Castleberry, a young Texan who is living and working unhappily in Massachusetts. His journey back home to the Texas hill country is accompanied by an abrupt shift in the novel's focus back to the time of his grandmother, Victoria Ann, who in the early twentieth century, before dying young, became part of a plot involving blackmail, murder, and the birth of a deformed child. Rudy's connection, actual and spiritual, to the violence and passion of the past is the underlying theme of the novel, but as with Vliet's other fiction, its greatest strength consists of its careful, realistic description of life in rural Texas at the turn of the century. "The monologue tone of the first [part of the novel]," wrote Wendy Lesser in the *Hudson Review*, "is not merely an artistic tic, but a well-founded presentation of character, and it enables the people around Rudy as well as the narrator himself to come fully to life. The lush style of the second [part], with its heavy share of italicized material, might seem pretentious and overbearing in less skilled hands, but Vliet knows exactly how far he can go and he never lets the tone become melodramatic. The two styles are both authorial disguises, in the sense that they contain numerous idiomatic expressions representing the thought and language of their characters. But this technique never seems condescending; on the contrary, the language of the novel is especially rich *because* it stems from local idioms and individual viewpoints." Gary Davenport, writing in the *Sewanee Review*, called *Scorpio Rising* "the most powerful and successful recent exemplar" of a novelistic genre he calls "the heartlander in search of his roots," one which "deals with the initiation or emergence of a young person from the American West, . . . and specifically with his attempt to place himself in the traditions of his family and his fellow regionals. . . . Vliet's prose style is poetic, and often effectively so: large tracts of the second part typographically resemble modern verse, and they make use of its abrupt cuts and imagistic fragmentation as well."

Vliet's poetry pays the same close attention as does his fiction to sharp regional detail and to accuracy of idiom. *Events & Celebrations*, published in 1966, collects a great variety of verse-form and prose poems written over the decade previous to the book's publication. The most notable poem is the twenty-part "Clem Maverick," the story told by various of his friends of a country-and-western balladeer who died a legend at the age of twenty-nine after an intense, raucous life. The Maverick poems were slightly revised and expanded and issued in a woodcut-illustrated book of their own (*Clem Maverick: The Life and Death of a Country Music Singer*) in 1983. Dan Jaffe, reviewing *Events & Celebrations* in *Saturday Review*, wrote, "Satirical and sorrowful, [the Maverick] poems provide one with a sense of the way in which the public world infringes on the private life of an unsophisticated man, and how he in turn affects others. Our view is from the outside, but always there is a sense of inner tragedy."

Subsequent poetry collections were *The Man with the Black Mouth* and *Water and Stone*. The title poem of the latter collection is really a verse drama, in feeling a kind of Japanese No play, in which ghosts address one another about the drowning death of an eleven-year-old boy. The characters in the play were picnickers who failed to rescue him, and their lives were ruined by the failure, as each person, now a ghost, sees it. "The poem," wrote Joscha Kessler in the *Los Angeles Times*, "is beautifully done, spare and poignant, and would, I believe, act well, like Yeats' poetic plays. It hints at other tragic stories

immanent in most of the poems of this collection, a rich and fine achievement."

PRINCIPAL WORKS: *Fiction*—Rockspring, 1974; Solitudes, 1977, rev. ed. published as Soledad, or Solitudes, 1986; Scorpio Rising, 1985. *Poetry*—Sand Is the Tool, 1953; Events & Celebrations, 1966; The Man with the Black Mouth, 1970; Water and Stone, 1980; Clem Maverick, 1983.

ABOUT: Contemporary Authors 37–40, 1972; 112, 1985; Contemporary Literary Criticism 22, 1982; Contemporary Poets, 3d. ed., 1980. *Periodicals*—Atlantic June 1974; Best Sellers August 1, 1974; May 1985; Book Week July 10, 1966; March 2, 1986; Booklist March 15, 1985; Choice November 1966; Commonweal December 23, 1977; Harper's December 1980; Hudson Review Autumn 1977; Autumn 1980; Autumn 1985; Library Journal June 1, 1966; June 15, 1974; April 15, 1980; March 15, 1985; Los Angeles Times November 9, 1980; New York Times Book Review August 18, 1974; May 5, 1985; Newsweek April 1, 1985; Saturday Review October 15, 1966; Sewanee Review April 1986; Virginia Quarterly Review Autumn 1966; Western American Literature Spring 1986.

WALKER, MARGARET (ABIGAIL) (July 7, 1915–   ), American poet, novelist, and biographer, was born in Birmingham, Alabama, to a Jamaican-born Methodist minister, Sigismund Walker, and Marion (Dozier) Walker, a music teacher. She grew up in an economically poor but culturally rich family. From her father she early acquired a taste for classical literature, the Bible, and Shakespeare. From her mother she learned about her American black heritage in music; and from her maternal grandmother she heard black folktales and stories of her ancestors who had been slaves—material that years later was to inspire her novel *Jubilee*.

Growing up in the early days of the Roosevelt–New Deal era, Margaret Walker attended Northwestern University funded partly by assistance from the NYA (National Youth Administration). After receiving her B.A. in 1935 she worked for the WPA (Works Progress Administration) as a junior writer at $85 a month. Along with numbers of other young writers—Saul Bellow, Nelson Algren, Willard Motley, Richard Wright—she was assigned to the preparation of a State of Illinois Guidebook. Such projects not only helped artists and writers survive the rigors of the depression of the 1930s, but also brought together talented young people who encouraged and influenced each other. An example was Margaret Walker's friendship over some three and a half years with Richard Wright. "When I first met Wright," she told Nikki Giovanni in *A Poetic Equation*, "I was impressed

MARGARET WALKER

with his genius and his talent as a writer. But he was still in the crude stage in that he could not spell or punctuate and he gave his things to me to read, revise, and type." At that time Walker was working on a novel of her own, never published, about a young black woman driven into prostitution by the conditions of urban slum life. Walker sees a similarity between her story and the opening sections of Wright's *Native Son*, which also describe the squalor of such surroundings.

In 1939, having worked for the WPA the maximum time allowed under the law, Margaret Walker lost her job. By this time she had resolved upon a career in writing and teaching, in preparation for which she enrolled at the University of Iowa for a master's degree. Under the direction of Paul Engle, the Iowa Writers' Workshop gave her encouragement to explore the history and folklore of black people in America. Although she had already—from the age of nineteen in fact—conceived a novel about her slave ancestors, she worked on poetry for her thesis, receiving an M.A. in 1940 for a manuscript that was later to be published as *For My People*.

With the publication of *For My People* as winner of the Yale Younger Poets Series Award in 1942, Margaret Walker's career as a writer was dramatically launched. She was one of the youngest black poets ever to have been published and, more remarkable, she was the first black woman poet to have been nationally honored. (The first Pulitzer Prize for Poetry awarded to a black woman went to Gwendolyn Brooks

in 1950 for *Annie Allen*.) *For My People* was published with a Foreword by Stephen Vincent Benét, who hailed the honesty and versatility of her work: " . . . in whatever medium she is working, the note is true and unforced. There is a deep sincerity in these poems—a sincerity at times disquieting. For this is the song of her people, of her part of America." A small book containing only twenty-six poems, it was, nevertheless, as Eugene B. Redmond observed in *Drumvoices*, "one of the most influential by a black poet." Its bold affirmation of the rights and stature of her people, its humorous and earthy portraits of archetypal figures from black folklore, and its sensitive insights into Walker's own childhood found an audience that until then had had a very limited perception of black culture. Still in print years later in the early 1970s when the civil rights movement had effected profound changes in American society, *For My People* continued to move and inspire readers. In *Black World* in 1971 Paula Giddings noted Walker's ability to "touch and feel the life-force of her history. . . . Her protest against white actions or Black inaction and, even more importantly, the manifestation of her love for Black people . . . are important keys to our struggle." Some years later Eugenia Collier wrote of the book, in *Black Women Writers*: "It melts away time and place and it unifies Black listeners. Its power is as compelling now as it was forty-odd years ago when it was written, perhaps more so as we have experienced the flood tide and the ebb tide of hope. The source of its power is the reservoir of beliefs, values, and archetypal characters yielded by our collective historical experience. It is this area of our being which defines us, which makes us a people."

The title poem of the volume, "For My People," has become Margaret Walker's signature poem. Written in a kind of Whitmanesque free verse, it achieves its effects, Dudley Randall wrote in *The Black Aesthetic*, "by the sheer overpowering accumulation of a mass of details, delivered in rhythmical parallel phrases." An ode, as it were, to an oppressed people, it begins:

> For my people everywhere singing their slave songs
>   repeatedly: their dirges and their ditties and their
>   blues and jubilees, praying their prayers nightly
>   to an unknown god, bending their knees humbly
>   to an unseen power;
>
> For my people lending their strength to the years, to the
>   gone years and the now years and the maybe
>   years, washing ironing cooking scrubbing
>   sewing mending hoeing plowing digging planting
>   pruning patching dragging along never gaining
>   never repeating never knowing and never
>   understanding;

The poem voices anger but also faith and hope:

For the cramped bewildered years we went to school to
   learn to know the reasons why and the answers
   to and the people who and the places where and
   the days when, in memory of the bitter hours
   when we discovered we were black and poor and
   small and different and nobody cared and
   nobody wondered and nobody understood;

and moves to a prophetic conclusion:

Let a new earth rise. Let another world be born. Let a
   bloody peace be written in the sky. Let a second
   generation full of courage issue forth; let a
   people loving freedom come to growth. Let a
   beauty full of healing and a strength of final
   clenching be the pulsing in our spirits and our
   blood. Let the martial songs be written, let
   the dirges disappear. Let a race of men
   now rise and and take control.

Elsewhere in *For My People* Walker writes a
deeply personal poetry. Recalling her roots in
"Dark Blood" she reflects on her "bizarre beginnings in the old lands"—jungles, the sea, wan-
derlust and her desire to travel "to the tropical
lands of my birth." But she knows that she will
return "to the littered streets and the one-room
shacks of my old poverty, and blazing suns of
other lands may struggle then to reconcile the
pride and pain in me."

Margaret Walker did not publish another volume of poetry for more than twenty years. During that time she began what was to be a long
teaching career. Her first position was on the
English faculty of Livingstone College, in Salisbury, North Carolina in 1941–1942. She taught
at West Virginia State College from 1942 to
1943 and returned to Livingstone in 1945 as professor of English. In 1949 she became professor
of English at Jackson State College in Jackson,
Mississippi, where she remained until her retirement in 1979. In 1968 she was appointed director of Jackson's Institute for the Study of the
History, Life, and Culture of Black Peoples.
During this period she also traveled to many colleges lecturing, conducting writing workshops,
and reading her poetry. In 1969 she spent a semester at Northwestern University as visiting
professor of creative writing.

In 1943 Margaret Walker married Firnist
James Alexander, a disabled war veteran; he
died in 1980. They had two sons and two daughters. Throughout the 1940s and 1950s she pursued her research for what was to become her
most famous book, the novel *Jubilee*. "Long before my story had a name," she recalled in an essay "How I Wrote *Jubilee*," "I was living with it
and imagining its reality." A fragment begun in
1934 was put aside but not forgotten. In 1944 a
fellowship from the Rosenwald Foundation subsidized a year of research in archival records. In
1948 Walker prepared her first outline for the

book. The research was completed with a Ford
Fellowship in 1953 when she began her travels
to libraries and local records offices in North
Carolina and Georgia. The stories she had heard
in childhood from her grandmother began to
take shape as history—both of the South before,
during, and just after the Civil War and of her
own roots in that history. "I was simply determined to substantiate my material, to authenticate the story I had heard from my
grandmother's lips." She completed a draft of
the novel in 1953 at Yale University, working
under Norman Holmes Pearson, but in the next
several years family responsibilities, frequent
bouts of ill health, and heavy teaching duties
prevented her from revising the book. Not until
1961 was she able to resume work on it. In that
year she returned to the University of Iowa to
begin work on a Ph.D. Here she took courses in
history, read Tolstoy's *War and Peace* and Sir
Walter Scott's historical novels, and—under the
direction of novelists R. V. Cassill and Vance
Bourjaily—completed *Jubilee* as her doctoral
dissertation. The degree was awarded in 1965,
and the novel was published the following year.

Jubilee takes its title from a spiritual, "Do you
think I'll make a soldier?/In the year of
Jubilee?," and each of its fifty-eight chapters begins with an excerpt from a traditional black
song. It is a long and densely packed novel offering a panoramic view of the South from antebellum to Reconstruction times, told by an omni
scient narrator and centering on the life of a
black woman named Vyry who is closely modeled on Walker's great-grandmother, Margaret
Duggan Ware. Vyry is the child of a slave and
a white plantation owner in Georgia. She has
light skin, grey-blue eyes and sandy hair and
could pass as white, but she is raised as a slave
in the kitchen of her father's household and suffers the humiliations and physical abuse of slavery (including a brutal beating by an overseer).
She grows up uneducated but wise, a compassionate and indomitable woman, fighting for her
children and achieving dignity and self-respect.
She falls in love with a well educated, self-
supporting, free black man, Randall Ware (the
real name of Walker's grandfather), who is unable to buy her freedom. Nevertheless, they
marry and have two children before they are
separated by the chaotic events of the Civil War.
In the aftermath of the war—the plantation ravaged—Vyry accepts the protection and the love
of an illiterate, hardworking black ex-slave and
lives as his wife. They move to Alabama, where
in the Reconstruction era they try to establish a
farm and a home for themselves and their children, but they encounter floods, the exploitation
of sharecropper landlords, and the hostility of

the Ku Klux Klan. Finally, thanks to Vyry's skill as a "granny" (midwife), they are accepted as free people in an Alabama community. They settle on a small piece of land, build a house, and look forward to a future that promises hard work but also independence and a measure of dignity. At this point Ware, who had been searching for his wife for many years, turns up seeking to reclaim her. Vyry makes a difficult but apparently wise choice and the novel ends on a note of hope and reconciliation.

As a historical novel *Jubilee* offers a faithful and detailed picture of plantation life and the struggles of the agrarian black poor. Walker's point of view is always that of the black, but while many of the Southern white characters— from plantation owners to overseers to poor whites—are represented as hostile or, at best, indifferent to the plight of black people, she introduces some sympathetic white characters. The free man Randall Ware is implacable in his resentment and distrust of whites, but Vyry remains understanding and forgiving: "We both needs each other. White folks needs what black folks got just as much as black folks needs what white people is got, and we's all got to stay here mongst each other and get along, that's what." She is sustained by her simple but strong religious faith and her generous capacity for love. Walker writes: " . . . she was touched with a spiritual fire and permeated with a spiritual wholeness that had been forged in the crucible of suffering. . . . Peasant and slave, unlettered and untutored, she was nevertheless the best true example of the motherhood of her race, an ever present assurance that nothing could destroy a people whose sons had come from her loins."

From her earliest drafts of the novel Walker recognized the challenge of integrating the complex history of the period with a lively fictional narrative. Large chunks of history are introduced in the narrator's voice although she never loses the thread of the story. Many reviewers of *Jubilee* found her technique seriously flawed. Arthur P. Davis, in *From the Dark Tower*, complained that too much was crowded into the book: "She has made use of practically every stock myth, legend, and situation that we have ever met before. . . . Miss Walker has not fused the material sufficiently; she often *tells* when she should *render*, and she has not developed many of her characters fully enough. As a result of these shortcomings, one leaves the novel impressed by the tremendous possibilities the material offers, but is saddened by the novelist's failure to make it come fully alive." Wilma Dykeman, in the *New York Times Book Review*, had similar complaints about stereotypical characters and Walker's tendency to catalogue rather than dramatize the action. But Dykeman praised the book's "ring of artistic truth," and Abraham Chapman, in *Saturday Review*, had high praise for "the colorful and musical speech" of the black characters that "transcends the stilted prose of the narrator." Such critical reservations had little effect on the sales of *Jubilee*, which went into many editions and remains a popular favorite to this day.

In the changing political and social climate of mid-century American life, Margaret Walker has become identified with an older generation of black writers who were as deeply committed to the cause of racial justice as their younger peers but spoke in a gentler voice. The generational gap is graphically demonstrated in *A Poetic Equation: Conversations Between Nikki Giovanni and Margaret Walker*. Their candid conversations, taped in 1972 and 1973, ranged over the politics, literature, and personal experiences of the two women; the tone moves from sometimes angry debate to laughter and expressions of affectionate sisterhood. Giovanni is unrelenting in her distrust of white people. Walker, not nearly so sanguine in 1972 as her Vyry was in *Jubilee*, has nevertheless kept her essential faith. "Before I die," she told Giovanni:

> I want to make a certain statement about what our life is like here, but I want to add something that's not just about black people. I believe deeply in a common humanity. The black man belongs to the family of man. One part of that family is out of control—like a virus or cancer—and that is the white man. He and his technological society are bent on destroying the world. . . . But I *don't* believe that all the white people in the world are not good. There are some people of good will.

Walker's faith had been sorely tested in the violence of the preceding few years. In *Prophets for a New Day*, poems published in 1970, she spoke out forcefully. Most of the poems were inspired by specific events: the murders of Malcolm X and the three young civil rights workers Andrew Goodman, Michael Schwerner, and James Chaney; the bombings of churches; the demonstrations against public school integration. "Jackson, Mississippi" addresses her home town as "City of tense and stricken faces . . . / City of barbed wire stockades / and ranting voices of demagogues." In "Birmingham" she writes that "My life dies best on a southern cross / Carved out of rock, with shooting stars to fire / The forge of bitter hate." Her voice is passionate, even militant, but it remains staunchly Christian. Her imagery is heavily biblical. The Old Testament prophets Jeremiah, Isaiah, and Amos are identified with contemporary figures like Martin Luther King. A lighter note is struck in the volume, however, in a poem that also has

racial symbolism—"The Ballad of the Hoppy Toad." In dialect and rhythmic ballad meter she draws on black folklore and superstition in the story of "the goopher man," who has put a curse, a spirit taking the shape of a "hoppy toad," on the speaker. With the aid of wise old Sis Avery, she exorcises the spirit:

> Don't want to burn his picture
> Don't want to dig his grave
> Just want to have my peace of mind
> And make that dog behave.

In *October Journey* three years later she celebrated black poets and leaders like Harriet Tubman, Mary McLeod Bethune, Gwendolyn Brooks, and Paul Lawrence Dunbar. Here, overall, her tone is melancholy and despairing of the future. The title poem describes a train journey taken by the poet into her southern homeland. Cheered at first by the brilliant autumn foliage, she grows increasingly depressed as she travels south:

> The clock runs down
> timeless and still.
> The days and nights turn hours to years
> and water in a gutter marks the circle
>   of another world,
> hating, resentful, and afraid,
> stagnant, and green, and full of slimy things.

Walker's long awaited biography *Richard Wright: Daemonic Genius*, subtitled "A Portrait of the Man, a Critical Look at His Work," was published in 1988. "This book is both a memorial for the man and testimonial to the wonderful friendship we shared more than fifty years ago," she writes in her dedication. Drawing not simply on her memories of Wright but upon many years of research, she described her method here as "that of a research scholar. I am not a detective." Her preparation for the book began in 1971 when she participated in a seminar on Wright at the University of Iowa. With grants from the National Endowment for the Humanities (1972) and the Ford Foundation (1979–1980), she worked through the Wright archives at Yale University and read virtually everything he wrote and everything that has been written on him. The result is a thoroughly documented account with many pages of notes and a concluding "Bibliographical Essay and Guide to Wright Studies." Walker describes her approach as psychobiographical, "since psychology was his deepest interest as a key to the creative, the sexual, and the actual or psychological man." She sees Wright as a "daemonic" figure, "compulsive and driven by demons." Her own friendship with him had ended abruptly and painfully, the result, she feels, of misunderstanding and the

alienation and ambivalence that ruled his personal and creative life: "He was a writer of great power and great passion but, nevertheless, a human being with the same weaknesses and flaws of all human beings." She portrays him as vulnerable and insecure, carrying throughout his life the burden of his memories of a violent and desperately poor early life and an even greater burden of self-hatred, reflected—as Milton Meltzer points out in his review of the book in *Library Journal*—in the "negative treatment of women, especially black women, in his work . . . and . . . his misunderstanding of black Africa." Meltzer found the book "somewhat pedantic" in its heavy scholarship, but concluded that it "adds fresh information and helpful insights to current biographies of Wright." The reviewer for *Publishers Weekly* hailed it as "this excellent, flesh-and-blood portrait [that] gets closer to the inner man than any previous volume."

PRINCIPAL WORKS: *Poetry*—For My People, 1942; Prophets for a New Day, 1970; October Journey, 1973. *Fiction*—Jubilee, 1965. *Non-fiction*—How I Wrote "Jubilee," 1972; (with N. Giovanni) A Poetic Equation: Conversations between Nikki Giovanni and Margaret Walker, 1974; Richard Wright: Daemonic Genius, 1987; How I Wrote "Jubilee" and Other Essays on Life and Literature, 1989.

ABOUT: Contemporary Authors New Revision Series 26, 1989; Contemporary Literary Criticism 1, 1973; 6, 1976; Davis, A. P. From the Dark Tower: Afro-American Writers 1900–1960, 1974; Dictionary of Literary Biography 76, 1988; Evans, M. (ed.) Black Women Writers 1950–1980, 1983; Gayle, A. (ed.) The Black Aesthetic, 1971; Redmond, E. B. Drumvoices: The Mission of Afro-American Poetry, 1976; Tate, C. (ed.) Black Women Writers at Work, 1983; Walker, M. How I Wrote "Jubilee," 1972; A Poetic Equation, 1974. *Periodicals*—Black World December 1971; Choice July 1974; Christian Science Monitor September 29, 1966; Library Journal February 15, 1971; November 1, 1987; New York Times Book Review September 25, 1966; August 14, 1988; Publishers Weekly October 14, 1988; Saturday Review September 24, 1966.

*WALSER, ROBERT OTTO (April 15, 1878–December 25, 1956), Swiss poet, novelist, writer of short prose and short plays, was born in Biel, twenty miles northwest of Berne, the seventh of eight children. Because of the family's financial difficulties, he had to leave school at the age of fourteen and begin an apprenticeship with a local bank. His mother, who had been emotionally unstable for some time, died in 1894. Upon completion of his training in 1895

°väl´ zor

he first moved to Basel and then to Stuttgart where he joined his brother Karl, who was to become a well-known painter, book illustrator, and set designer for Max Reinhardt after the turn of the century. Walser had aspired to a stage career, but following a disastrous audition with the famous actor Josef Kainz he decided to bury this ambition. The next decade he spent mainly in Switzerland, holding dozens of jobs and changing his whereabouts countless times; he worked in banks, in an unemployment office, in a rubber factory, in a brewery, leading the life of the "little guys," the lowly employees and clerks—pushed around and alienated—who were to reappear in so many of his later works. He was also assistant to an engineer turned inventor on the brink of bankruptcy—an experience that Walser drew on in his second novel. In 1898 a selection of his poems was published in *Der Bund*, a Bernese daily. These poems attracted the attention of Franz Blei, a prominent man of letters who helped Walser establish professional contacts in Munich, above all with writers associated with the influential Jugendstil magazine *Die Insel*. Soon after the publication of his first book, *Fritz Kochers Aufsätze* (Fritz Kocher's Essays, 1904), Walser moved to Berlin. Through his brother Karl, who had settled there, he met among others Bruno and Paul Cassirer, Samuel Fischer, Maximilian Harden, Walther Rathenau, Frank Wedekind and Hugo von Hofmannsthal. In quick succession Walser wrote three novels, all of them published by Bruno Cassirer: *Geschwister Tanner* (The Tanner Siblings, 1907) which was enthusiastically received by Christian Morgenstern, then editor at Cassirer's; *Der Gehülfe* (The Assistant, 1908), and—based upon Walser's brief experience as a student in a school for butlers—*Jakob von Gunten* (1909), which was to become one of Franz Kafka's favorite books. Furthermore, a bibliophile edition of his poems appeared in 1909, and numerous short prose pieces were accepted by vanguard newspapers and periodicals and later collected in books: *Aufsätze* (Essays, 1913), *Geschichten* (Stories, 1914), *Kleine Dichtungen* (Small Compositions, 1914). In short, Walser's beginnings as a young writer seemed quite auspicious; however, following a profound crisis the exact nature of which remains conjectural—practically nothing is known of the circumstances surrounding his life from 1909 to 1912—Walser returned to Biel in 1913 where, for nearly eight years, he lived on a shoestring in a stark and chilly attic room in the Hotel Blaues Kreuz: a typically Walserian alternative to life in the Ivory Tower. For the most part he kept aloof from fellow writers in Switzerland, and World War I further isolated him from his readers in Germany. Through his

sister Lisa, a teacher in a school nearby, he met Frieda Mermet, whom he "courted" for a few years: they visited each other; they went on outings and corresponded. Seemingly content to be his surrogate mother and "mistress" at a distance no doubt established on his terms, she mended and laundered his clothes and, unfailingly and for decades, kept providing him with those care packages that have become legendary among Walser readers and scholars. From Biel Walser ventured forth on his famous *Spaziergänge*, i.e. his walks that led him to the surrounding countryside, to villages and small towns of Central Switzerland and that inspired the prose sketches he continued to write for newspapers and to publish in 1917 in book form: *Der Spaziergang* (The Walk), *Prosastücke* (Prose Pieces), *Kleine Prosa* (Small Prose). *Poetenleben* (A Poet's Life) followed in 1918 and *Seeland* in 1919. The idyllic tenor of the works written during the Biel period (which coincided with World War I and the October Revolution) gained him the mistaken reputation of a writer turned shepherd boy. Apolitical as his writings were—marked by chatty arabesques, irritating disgressions, and absurdly courteous flowery language, these texts provide a critical counterreality to a world at war. In 1921 Walser moved to Berne where he held a job as assistant librarian in the State Archives only to return to free-lance writing six months later and to resume the nomadic patterns of his youth, moving from one rented room to the next fifteen times within eight years. *Die Rose* (The Rose, 1925), a prose collection, was Walser's last book to be published during his lifetime. The fourth novel that has survived, "*Der Räuber*"-*Roman* (The Robber, 1925), did not appear until 1972. It was one of over 500 texts written in pencil in a minuscule script during the Berne years. Walser, once again suffering from a severe crisis of existential proportions, had devised this "pencil method," as he called it, in order to overcome his writer's block. After Walser's death most of the microscripts, initially thought to be in a secret code, were deciphered thanks to the painstaking labor of a few scholars. In the late twenties Walser began to have acute anxiety attacks and "to hear voices"; he eventually agreed to enter the Waldau, an asylum at the outskirts of Berne in 1929. Living within this "monastery of modernity," to quote Elias Canetti, his condition—initially diagnosed as schizophrenia—improved quickly; he was free to move about town, resumed his writing and published in newspapers. By 1933 Walser was no longer considered a clinical case. Yet at the request of his beloved sister Lisa, for reasons that remain dubious to this day and against his own vehement protests, Walser was transferred to an

institution in Herisau, a small town in remote eastern Switzerland. During the remaining twenty-three years of his life, Walser kept his vow never to write another line if he were brought to Herisau. "I am not here to write; I am here to be mad," he said to Carl Seelig, his legal guardian upon Lisa's death in 1944. Seelig was a journalist from Zurich who had taken an early interest in Walser and regularly visited him in Herisau. His account of their conversations provides plenty of reason to question the good judgment and the motives of those who continued to declare Walser "insane." By publishing several new collections of his works as well as reprints, Seelig saw to it that Walser had at least a slender income and would not be altogether forgotten during the long years of his silence. In 1956 Robert Walser died from a heart attack while out on a walk on Christmas Day. Farm children playing in the fields near their home found him stretched out in the snow.

Although never belonging to a school or movement and only rarely expounding on his aesthetics, Walser, like other early twentieth-century artists and writers, searched for new forms that would adequately express a radically altered perception of the world. His "naiveté," like the painter Henri Rousseau's, is based on conscious artistic volition and goes hand in hand with his rejection of conventionally perceived reality; with Rousseau he also shares the suspension of rational expectation, the blending of dream and reality, and the telescoping of different moments in time. Frequently, Walser created the impression of not knowing how to write, of starting from scratch: in *Fritz Kochers Aufsätze*, a collection of school compositions supposedly written by a youngster and ingénu, a favorite persona of Walser; or in some of his utterly simple, early poems that have freed themselves from *Jugendstil* ornamentation. Walser's perception of time is ahistorical; time is no longer an objective, causal progression from past to present to future. He shares with his contemporaries a revolt against nineteenth-century historicism and the repudiation of memory insofar as it entails organized logical conservation of past experiences. In *Geschwister Tanner*, Kaspar, the brother of the protagonist and a painter, wonders what the point would be of going to Italy to improve his painting by learning from the past. Simon tears up his childhood recollections because they are useless, and in his speech at the end of the novel he says he is stepping carelessly on his memories in order to run the more freely. Josef Marti in *Der Gehülfe* destroys the diary he has started to write, and Jakob von Gunton is virtually incapable of putting together his kind of novel. When after several failed attempts he finally

does manage to hand in the account of his life, it defies average expectations altogether. Although called "A Diary," *Jakob von Gunten* leaves the reader at a loss as to when the individual entries were made and as to how much time has elapsed from one entry to the next. With the demise of the time structure characteristic of diary-keeping, *Jakob von Gunten* becomes in a very real sense a *journal intime*, not registering the objective and measurable process of time but mapping the explorations by way of dreams and daydreams into the inner chambers of Jakob's own self and of the few he really cares about. Jakob von Gunten perceives time in spatial terms, as a mosaic design of sorts: "How peculiar that was. The particular weeks eyed one another like small glittering gems." Susan Sontag's observation that Walser "spent much of his life obsessively turning time into space" is apt. As Walser put it himself in "The Walk," he is not interested in journeys; what he is engaged in is a "fine circular stroll," a walk, in other words, that takes him back to where he started; thus time, too, is bent into a two-dimensional geometric shape.

Repeatedly, in Walser's works, objects begin to emancipate themselves from the subject who categorized them; things we normally perceive around us in stasis begin to act independently of our volition. In *Der Gehülfe*, Mr. Tobler's absurd and doomed inventions—an advertising clock and a vending machine selling ammunition—keep beckoning to Joseph Marti in an irritated yet pleading manner. Trees keep an eye on what Simon Tanner and his brother are up to. In "Welt," a prose piece written in 1902, mountains are heaving up and down, trees are flying through space like giant birds, buildings bump into each other like drunkards. Taking mercy on this helter-skelter world, God stuffs this chaos into a bag to let it disintegrate into nothingness. In "Die Stadt," written in 1914, pale houses stare at the visitor with displeasure, and windows keep grimacing. Not only has the town become a wasteland, a lugubrious replica of what it once was, but the universe, too, is out of joint. In a variation to the Grandmother's tale in Georg Büchner's *Woyzeck*, Walser pursues the thought of a cosmic fraud to its worst possible consequence: gone are the stars, gone is the moon, gone is the sun; all stellar and planetary points of orientation have vanished. Walser also describes states of mind taking on shape and becoming active agents. In *Der Gehülfe* the anxiety haunting various members of the Tobler household taps quietly at the window panes, lifts up curtains to peer into the living quarters, and keeps standing in doorways to remind everyone passing by of the feeling of precariousness. By literally turning a character inside out, Walser has moods and emotions act from the outside on the person who generated them in the first place. When Mr. Tobler hears from his attorney that his bankruptcy can no longer be averted, he is thrown on a chair, "as if tons had crashed down on him, as if fists were pressing upon him, as if weights were lying on his neck, live weights, swaying, ringing, and pushing in sudden violent anger." In passages like these, the visible manifestations of anxiety and terror are portrayed by Walser with the hyperagitated plasticity that a decade later would become the hallmark of expressionism.

Like Robert Musil in his *Man Without Qualities*, Walser accepts "the present as hypothesis." Consequently his artistic imagination can freely create visions of what might have taken place instead of what in fact did take place—or what there might be rather than of what there is. In his novels, passages in the subjunctive run on for pages. Somersaulting in and out of the hypothetical, Walser debunks some of the plots of classical literature: Schiller's *Kabale und Liebe* need not have been a tragedy; Ibsen's Nora need not necessarily have slammed the door behind her, walking out on her marriage the way she did—Helmer might just as well have called her back and suggested she fix him hashed potatoes instead. If Walser's Nora is content in the end, it is "because Helmer had said something unexpected" (*Die Rose*). Such whimsical play with the possible, these ventures into the realm of the hypothetical confront the reader with a counterreality that provides not only for a "change of air," but also, and more importantly, for a change of viewpoint.

Walser's work of the twenties and early thirties, all too frequently and conveniently labelled as psychopathological in the past, is highly experimental. Approximating the *écriture automatique* of the surrealists, many texts are structured by homophones and compulsive rhymes; what appears to be silly or downright nonsensical at first sight is in fact a subversive strategy that allows Walser to criticize not only conventional patterns of speech but also social behavior and politics under the tyranny of consent. Considering his art of montage, the acrobatics of his puns, the shock effect he creates by challenging "good taste" and taboo topics, and the frequent introduction of metaliterary discourse at the expense of plot, Walser is indeed—to quote Mark Harman—"a quirky one-man avant-garde." His sharp criticism of the culture industry, of mega-writers and bourgeois intellectual consumerism should not be dismissed as sour grapes stemming from an author whose readers had dwindled away; similar concerns were raised by André Breton and Walter Benjamin in

the 1920s. Walser had opted to steer away from "Zilch, the Cat": "Zilch is a kind of factory or industrial enterprise, for which writers produce and deliver daily, perhaps even hourly, with steadfast zeal. . . . All that is achieved goes to her first; she eats with relish, and only what lives on and works despite her is immortal."

Most critics agree that Walser frustrates and also tantalizes his readers by ultimately eluding them. While highly self-reflective, even confessional at times, Walser hides behind a myriad of first-person narrators: page boys and office clerks, children and women—single or married, young or old, proletarian or aristocratic; behind "real" people and characters lifted out of plays and novels; clowns and writers—Büchner, Kleist, Hölderlin, Lenau, Brentano, to name just a few. To be sure, Walser once remarked that his entire work is a kind of novel in progress, a "me-book, cut up into countless small segments." While this observation may aptly describe his method of writing, it says little about Walser himself, and we will never know for certain who this "me" was that spoke with so many voices and wore so many guises. Yet he had given his readers and critics fair warning: "Nobody has the right to treat me as if he knew me." *Why* did Walser write? Perhaps in order to constantly reassure himself that by writing he could provide structure to the chaos within himself. Walter Benjamin suggested that Walser's figures "have put madness behind them and can thus remain so laceratingly, inhumanly, and unfailingly superficial. If we wish to find one word to describe what is pleasing and uncanny about them, we might say: *they are all cured.*" Leading the life of a recluse, he may have won from writing, at least during the Berne years, his only proof that he lived at all: "One day some fragrance or other will issue from my being and my beginning. . . . " (*Jakob von Gunten*).

Robert Walser has ceased to be "a literary rumor" (as Martin Walser, his German namesake, put it in the 1960s) and is rapidly emerging as an important figure in twentieth-century literature. The 1978 paperback edition of his works in twelve volumes, complete with critical notes, as well as the elaborate celebrations on his centennial in Zurich, Berlin, and elsewhere, were indications of Walser's growing recognition by the reading public. Walser has attracted ever-growing interest in Italy, the Netherlands, Spain, Poland, and China, and as recently as 1982 a collection of his works in English translation, introduced by Susan Sontag, helped to bring him to the attention of American readers as well. In part the rediscovery of Walser has to do with his influence on Kafka, first noted by Robert Musil, and with the growing impact on contemporary theory of Walter Benjamin, who as early as 1929 had written a most elucidating and poignant essay on Walser. But the current Walser renaissance also endeavors to establish his relevance for today's reader. Thus Martin Walser has drawn attention to the essentially contemporary quality in the works of Robert Walser, to their relativism, their elusiveness, and their radical, all but innocuous stylistic reduction; Horst Denkler has commented upon certain affinities between the alienated German youth of the late 1970s and Robert Walser, who three quarters of a century earlier turned his back upon bourgeois society to opt instead for the life of a drop-out with all the consequences such a choice would and eventually did entail: poverty, isolation, and the lack of fame.

According to Christopher Middleton, his brilliant translator, Walser "risked all rather than compromise and was broken eventually." The life of this "great artist in language" has inspired many contemporary authors to "Walseresque" approximations, combining fiction and documentary, essay and hagiography; his fate has come to be seen, moreover, as paradigmatic of the condition of literature in our modern/postmodern society.

WORKS IN ENGLISH TRANSLATION: English translations of Robert Walser's writings include Christopher Middleton's *The Walk and Other Stories* (1957) and *Jakob von Gunten* (1969); Christopher Middleton's (et al.) *Selected Stories* (1982); Walter Arndt's, Mark Harman's (et al.) selected stories, poems, and fairy-tale plays in *Robert Walser Rediscovered* (1985). The collection *"Masquerade" and Other Stories* was translated by Susan Bernofsky (1990).

ABOUT: Avery, G. C. Inquiry and Testament: A Study of the Novels and Short Prose of Robert Walser, 1968; Cardinal, A. The Figure of Paradox in the Works of Robert Walser, 1982; Columbia Dictionary of Modern European Literature, 1980; Hamburger, M. From Prophecy to Exorcism. The Premises of Modern German Literature, 1965; Harman, M. (ed.) Robert Walser Rediscovered, 1985; Sontag, S. *Introduction to Walser's Selected Stories,* 1982. *Periodicals*—Comparative Criticism 6 (1984); The German Quarterly 57 (1984); Modern Language Quarterly 24 (1963); Modern Language Review 78 (1983); New Orleans Fall, 1989; Orbis Litterarum 37 (1982); Revue des Langues Vivantes 23 (1958).

*WANG MENG (October 15, 1934–   ), Chinese short-story writer, novelist, and political activist, was born in Beijing (then Peiping) to a family of intellectuals. His father was a university instructor and his mother a primary school teacher and librarian. From his childhood he

WANG MENG

was radicalized by the chaos and poverty brought on by the Japanese invasion of China. He participated in Communist-led underground activities while in middle school, and in 1948, when he was only fourteen, he joined the Young Pioneers of the Communist party. By 1949, the year of the Communist triumph over the China mainland, he had become a functionary at the headquarters of the Young Pioneers in Beijing and was sent to the Communist Youth League cadre school to study political theory. He advanced so fast in the Communist youth apparatus that by 1950 he was elected deputy secretary of one of the League's district committees. His interest in books prompted him to engage in creative writing. When his first novel *Qingchun Wansui* (Long Live Youth) was serialized simultaneously in Shanghai's *Wen Hui Bao* (Wen Hui Daily) and Beijing's *Beijing Ribao* (Beijing Daily) in 1954, he received much praise, especially from young people. Wang Meng was only nineteen then, and his novel reflects the life of middle-school students in the early days of the People's Republic, filled with youthful enthusiasm and revolutionary spirit. The Party's role in the building of a new nation is extolled in the story, which exudes such optimism that both the literary establishment and the Party hierarchy took note of the young writer. His first short story "Xiao Duoer" (Little Beanie), often erroneously reported as his very first published work, actually appeared in print a year later, in the November 1955 issue of *Renmin Wenxue* (People's Literature).

Wang Meng has said that his fame really began with a 27,000-word story "Zuzhibu Xinlai De Qingnianren" ("A Young Man Arrives at the Organization Department"), published in the September 1956 issue of *Renmin Wexue*. The story, a realistic portrayal of the clash between youthful, idealistic revolutionaries and older, entrenched Party bureaucrats, inevitably aroused the ire of many, leading to a series of debates. Despite the fact that the manuscript had been rewritten numerous times at the magazine editors' suggestion, attacks were virulent. *Wenyi Xuexi* (Literary Studies), the official organ of the Communist Youth League, for example, published some forty critiques of the story in a three-month period, claiming that a total of over a thousand critical pieces had been received, a majority of which accused the author of distorting the Party organization and the image of veteran Party cadres. Only a few authors, including Liu Binyan, dared to support Wang Meng as a creative artist. The controversy was such that Mao Zedong himself became involved by injecting in a speech given at the Supreme State Conference in February 1957 a call for a further relaxation of control over public expression. He referred to "A Young Man Arrives at the Organization Department" as an example to encourage the on-going Hundred Flowers movement. Mao's speech even caused Zhou Yang, the generally acknowledged "literary czar" of Communist China, to reverse his previous position. But Wang Meng's good fortune did not last long. By the end of 1957, at the height of the anti-rightist campaign, he was accused of being an anti-Party element and was sent to the countryside to undergo "reform through labor." He was there five years, leaving his newly-wed bride in Beijing. In 1962, he was transferred back to Beijing to teach Chinese literature at Beijing Teachers College. The next year he was again banished, to the Uighur Autonomous Region in Xinjiang Province in the northwest "to experience and to learn from life" in local agricultural communes. He did not waste the time. In the fifteen years he was in the region, he mastered the Uighur language and translated a number of Uighurian stories into Chinese. By 1976, he began to publish short stories again, many of which won prizes. Well-known works include: "Zui Baogui Di" (The Most Precious), which won the best short story prize in 1978; "Youyou Cuncaoxin" ("The Barber's Tale"), which won the same prize in 1979; "Hudie" ("The Butterfly"), judged by *Wenyi Bao* (Literary Gazette), the official Communist literary organ, as one of the best novelettes of the 1977–1980 period. Other stories that have been translated into English are "Shuoke Yingmen" ("A Spate of Visitors"), "Ye De Yan" ("A Night in the City"), "Chun Zhi Sheing"

("Voices of Spring"), "Ru Ge De Xingban" ("Andante Cantabile"), and "Lun Xia" ("Under the Wheel"). Of these, two were particularly singled out for criticism: "A Night in the City" and "Voices of Spring." Wang Meng was accused of experimenting with the "decadent stream of consciousness method" in his writing. The time was 1981, and "stream of consciousness" was indeed in vogue among a few daring writers, as foreign literature began to flood China after the normalization of Sino-American relationships in 1979. Wang Meng had begun to read American books. Later, in one of his numerous interviews with newspaper reporters, he mentioned that he was particularly impressed by the works of Hemingway, John Cheever, and Joyce Carol Oates.

Brought back to Beijing in 1979 after the triumph of Deng Xiaoping, Wang Meng was invited to become a member of the All China Writers' Union, assuming the status of *zhuanyi zuojia* (professional writer), and was soon elected to the Union's executive council, a prestigious position. His fame established, he began to receive invitations from abroad. His first visit to the United States was in the fall of 1980, as a participant of the International Writing Program at the University of Iowa. In the few weeks he spent on the university campus, he quickly picked up enough English to carry on daily conversations with his new friends, his linguistic talent having already been proven during his exile in the Uighur Region. Arriving in New York, he was asked by E. J. Kahn of the *New Yorker* at an interview at the Algonquin Hotel what he had been doing in America. Wang Meng replied: "Eating and meeting." His knack for rhyme in a newly-learned language greatly amused the veteran journalist. At a reception later, he was found conversing animatedly with Paule Marshall, perhaps the first black author with whom he had ever spoken directly. He was in New York again in January, 1986 as a guest of the 48th International PEN Congress. Its theme being "The Imagination of the State and of the Writer," Wang Meng was called upon to speak as a representative of a socialist country. He said he did not think that the state and the writer were necessarily adversaries and that a writer was much like a ship in the waters of the state. It is this kind of smooth diplomatic skill that prompted his rapid rise in the Communist hierarchy. In June 1986 he was appointed Minister of Culture.

Writer-colleagues were pleased that a creative writer had been appointed, firmly on the record as favoring creative freedom. But then, as a bureaucrat representing the government, Wang Meng was compelled to state that the Party must maintain the power to limit the dissemination of views considered inimical to its basic policies. He found no release from this dilemma. He took up the official title with great reluctance. As Timothy Tung reported in a letter to the *New York Times* (September 5, 1989): "In the three years that Wang Meng was Culture Minister, he was never comfortable in his exalted position. Not only did official duties pull him away from his beloved occupation of writing, but also bureaucratic routine bored him and kept him apart from his literary friends, who naturally regarded him with a suspicious eye." Following the massacre at Tiananmen Square in June 1989 and its repressive aftermath, Wang Meng quietly removed himself from the public scene by checking into a hospital, but he was dismissed from his government post in the late summer of 1989.

WORKS IN ENGLISH TRANSLATION: A collection of Wang Meng's short stories, *The Butterfly, and Other Stories*, was published in paperback by Panda Books in 1983. The English language periodical *Chinese Literature* has published some of his stories; one, "A Fervent Wish," appears in *Prize-Winning Stories from China, 1978–1979*, published by the Foreign Language Press in Beijing, 1981. Excerpts from "A Young Man Arrives at the Organization Department" are published in Kaiyu Hsu's *Literature of the People's Republic of China*, 1980, and in Hualing Nieh's *Literature of the Hundred Flowers*, II, 1981 (which also includes his essay on the reception of the story in China). In 1990 a novella that he had written in 1979 was published in Wendy Larson's translation as *A Bolshevik Salute: A Modernist Chinese Novel*.

ABOUT: Hualing Nieh (ed.) Literature of the Hundred Flowers, II, 1981; Rui An. *Preface to* The Butterfly, and Other Stories, 1983; Who's Who in the People's Republic of China, 2nd ed., 1987. *Periodicals*—Nation October 30, 1984; New York Times June 26, 1986; September 5, 1989; September 19, 1989; New York Times Book Review August 9, 1987; March 18, 1990.

WASSERSTEIN, WENDY (October 18, 1950–), American playwright, was born in Brooklyn, New York, the youngest of four children of Morris Wasserstein, a prosperous textile manufacturer, and the former Lola Schleifer, who had both arrived in the United States as children in the 1920s. She was raised on Manhattan's Upper East Side, attended the exclusive Calhoun School, took dancing lessons every Saturday morning at a class run by the famous choreographer June Taylor, and was afterwards permitted to attend a Broadway matinée performance every Saturday afternoon. She moved on to Mount Holyoke College in Massachusetts, ma-

WENDY WASSERSTEIN

joring in history; she took her bachelor's degree in 1971.

Wasserstein's connection to the theater began in earnest after her sophomore year in college, when she took a summer playwriting course at Smith College, an experience she has described as "confidence-building." After 1971, living in New York, she studied creative writing under Joseph Heller and Israel Horovitz at City College of the City University of New York. While following Horovitz's playwriting course, she had her first play, *Any Woman Can't*, produced Off Broadway in 1973 by Playwrights Horizons, a nonprofit theater group with an international reputation for nurturing playwriting talent, with which she has continued to be associated. "I am very lucky," she remarked in *Interviews with Contemporary Women Playwrights*, "because [Playwrights Horizons] is my home, and it has made a tremendous difference to me, having someplace that I know I can work out of. I've had a long association with the people there. Life is competitive, but Playwrights Horizons is not. It is a community, and that has always been very important to me." With great trepidation, she entered Yale University's School of Drama, where her work was mainly of the collegiate revue variety. With David Hollister she wrote a musical, *Montpelier Pa-zazz*, which Playwrights Horizons produced in 1975. With Christopher Durang, who has remained a close friend, she wrote for the Yale Cabaret group in the 1977–1978 season a musical revue, *When Dinah Shore Ruled the Earth*, which the collaborators later made into a film. She took her master's degree in fine arts from Yale in 1976.

Uncommon Women and Others was Wasserstein's first solo theatrical success. An exuberant, comic view of life in an elite women's college during the early 1970s, when feminism was causing many women to question most of the previously settled opinions about their lives, the two-act work progressed from a workshop production at the National Playwrights Conference to a full-scale off-Broadway production by the Phoenix Theater Company which opened in November 1977 at the Marymount Manhattan Theater. The play concentrates on the interreaction of six former classmates at a Mount Holyoke reunion six years after graduation—a cross-section of young women intellectuals of their time. "We see them," wrote Richard Eder in a review of the New York performance in the *New York Times*, "in flashbacks. . . . Only a small part of the focus is upon the changes that have taken place since [graduation]; the time has not been long enough for them to be very great. The main emphasis is upon the lacerations, hopes, despairs and confusions that the times inflict upon these students at a hatchery for 'uncommon women,' where walls have turned porous and all the winds blow through." Eder acknowledged the pervasive hilarity of the play, but singled out for special praise Wasserstein's sense of compassion for her women: "She lets her characters—some of them, anyway—get away from her and begin to live and feel for themselves."

The author herself has remarked on the play's autobiographical element: "I've always thought that *Uncommon Women* was me split into nine parts. . . . I find it difficult to write autobiographical characters. There aren't good guys and there aren't villains in my plays. If I were to say there's a problem with my writing, it's typified by the line in *Uncommon Women* when one character says, 'Sometimes it's difficult having sympathy with everyone's point of view.' I have been accused of being too generous to the other, less autobiographical characters in my plays, but in fact, it is hardest for me to be generous to the character that is closest to me." That character is Holly, one of the two most "creative" women in the group. Holly's honesty of portrayal is one reason the play never moved to Broadway, according to the playwright: "The producer told me that at the end of the play things should be different. He said the play was too wistful. He thought that at the end, when everyone asks Holly, 'What's new with you?' she should pull out a diamond ring and say, 'Guess what? I'm going to marry Dr. Mark Silverstein.' I thought, 'Well, she'd have to have a lobotomy, and I'd have to have a lobotomy too.' So the play never went to Broadway."

In another vignette revealing the loss of direc-

tion feminism has suffered among the goal-oriented college students since her own college days, Wasserstein talked about a production of *Uncommon Women* at Mount Holyoke: "I asked some of the students there what they thought about the play. One of them said, 'Well, we think it's a nice *period* piece.' I said, 'Who do you think I am, Sheridan?' I mean, I had been studying there only eight years before! Then the women told me that unlike my characters, they knew what they wanted: to go to business school, or earn Ph.D.s or get married. I did think to myself, 'This is becoming like Amherst College during the fifties. What's so great about that?'"

Wasserstein's next theatrical success was *Isn't It Romantic*, another two-act play about two long-term college friends and their ways of growing up, solving in their own fashions the problems posed by careers, personal and sexual relationships, and the demands of their families that they live their lives more or less according to convention. By the end of the play the supportive relationship between Janie Blumberg, a freelance writer, Jewish and chronically overweight, who has landed a job with "Sesame Street," and Harriet Cornwall, an account executive with Colgate Palmolive, WASP and svelte, has arrived at a breakup over Harriet's decision to marry a man she hardly knows and doesn't love. "What do you do?" Janie explodes at Harriet at the end of their ultimate confrontation. "Fall in with every current the tide pulls in? Women should live alone and find out what they can do, put off marriage, establish a vertical career track, so you do that for a while. Then you almost turn thirty and *Time Magazine* announces 'Guess what girls, it's time to have it all.' Jaclyn Smith is married and pregnant and playing Jacqueline Kennedy. Every other person who was analyzing stocks last year is analyzing layettes this year. So you do that. What are you doing, Harriet? Who the hell are you? Can't you conceive of some plan, some time management scheme that you made up for yourself? Can't you take a chance?"

By most accounts, *Isn't It Romantic*, which opened in May 1981 off-Broadway at the Phoenix Theater to very mixed reviews, was greatly improved during the year Wasserstein worked on it under the guidance of André Bishop, artistic director of Playwrights Horizons, and Gerald Gutierrez, the house's principal director. The revised version, which focuses more on Janie and on her discovery of her own need for emotional maturity, was a resounding success with the critics on its opening at Playwrights Horizons in December 1983. It moved to a large off-Broadway theater and ran for a total of 733 performances.

In the mid-1980s Wasserstein produced two memorable teleplays for the Public Broadcasting System. For the Great Performances series she adapted a dark short story by John Cheever, "The Sorrows of Gin." For the series Trying Times she wrote a short original play, "Drive She Said," in which a somewhat repressed art-history professor, a specialist on the Fabergé egg, loses her medievalist academic boyfriend to a sex-kitten TV star, then comes to the conclusion that learning to drive will solve all her problems. In a hilarious reversal of feminist expectation, it does: she not only becomes a famous beauty queen, she actually falls in love with her driving instructor and by a complete fluke passes her driving test.

In 1986 Wasserstein told an interviewer: "I hope to write a play that is going to be a history of the Women's Movement, which is a serious thing to take on. I want to write about someone who went through it and how it affected them personally—I want to explore the reverberations. Because I want to understand, and sometimes I understand better by writing." That play, at the time of the interview in an obviously early stage of gestation, was *The Heidi Chronicles*, by general agreement Wasserstein's most complex, accomplished, and successful dramatic work. In it another art historian, Dr. Heidi Holland, delivers a lecture in 1988 about neglected women artists. The play then goes back twenty-five years to follow Heidi and some of her friends—male as well as female—from a high school dance in 1964 back to the present. In its sweep and movement, the play recounts the struggles of the women's movement from the dark days of the unenlightened 1960s through the consciousness-raising groups and sense of solidarity of the 1970s to the 1980s, when the slogan was "have it all" and the price to be paid was alienation. This feeling of alienation—that the women's movement set up expectations it simply never began to fulfill—is closely analyzed in *Heidi*. Wasserstein explained it in a trenchant interview with Mervyn Rothstein in the *New York Times* just before her play opened: "If we were all in this together, why does it feel so separate now? What is that feeling of being stranded, of being alone? What happened to these movements? What happened to this feeling of a generation together? . . . Sometimes I see these *Good Housekeeping* ads for a return to traditional values, and I see these mothers in their pearls and little dresses, and I just think, 'What's happened? How has all this happened?' I read all the stuff about a kinder, gentler life, and all of that, and I find it very upsetting. Are they saying that the women who decided to fulfill their potential have made a mistake? That's completely unfair.

It makes you feel stranded. It makes you feel part of a tidal wave." She makes the point in the play, most memorably, near the end as Dr. Holland gives a speech, a tour de force of dramatic writing, to her high school alumnae association on the topic "Women, Where Are We Going?" She tells them of a locker-room encounter with her exercise-class teacher, in which she confesses to being very unhappy—"I'm afraid I haven't been happy for some time." Then she looks out at her audience: "I don't blame the ladies in the locker room for how I feel," she continues. "I don't blame any of us. We're all concerned, intelligent, good women. It's just that I feel stranded. And I thought the whole point was that we shouldn't feel stranded. I thought the point was we were all in this together." *Heidi* offers no pat answers or solace for this feeling of loss. "At the beginning of her journey," Mel Gussow wrote in a review of the play for the *New York Times*, "Heidi is adamant that she will never be submissive, especially to men. To our pleasure the endearing character finally finds selfless fulfillment. Following the chronicles of Heidi, theatergoers are left with tantalizing questions about women today and tomorrow."

Heidi received uniformly enthusiastic reviews on its opening at Playwrights Horizons. It won the Tony award, the Dramatists Guild award, and the Pulitzer prize for best play of the 1988–1989 season. Moving from off-Broadway to the Plymouth Theater, it settled in for a long and profitable Broadway run.

PRINCIPAL PUBLISHED WORKS: *Plays*—Uncommon Women and Others, 1978; Isn't It Romantic, 1984; The Heidi Chronicles and Other Plays, 1990. Essays—Bachelor Girls, 1990.

ABOUT: Betsko, K. and R. Koenig (eds.) Interviews with Contemporary Women Playwrights, 1988; Contemporary Authors 121, 1987; Contemporary Literary Criticism 32, 1985; Current Biography 1989; National Playwrights Directory, 2nd ed., 1981; Who's Who of American Women, 1984. *Periodicals*—Nation February 18, 1984; New York November 22, 1977; June 29, 1981; New York Times December 16, 1983; January 1, 1984; January 3, 1984; December 11, 1988; December 12, 1988; February 28, 1989; May 7, 1989; New Yorker June 22, 1981; June 13, 1983; December 26, 1983; Variety June 17, 1981.

WELCH, JAMES (November 18, 1940 –   ), American novelist and poet, was born in Browning, Montana and spent much of his childhood on the Blackfeet and Fort Belknap reservations in that state. Although he has almost as much Irish blood as Indian (Blackfoot on his father o side, Gros Ventre on his mother's), Welch's work is resolutely "Indian-oriented," and he has described himself as both an "Indian writer" and "an Indian who writes." Welch attended colleges in Montana and Minnesota, eventually receiving a B.A. from the University of Montana in 1965, but although he had written some prose pieces, it was not until he entered the M.F.A. program at Montana that he began to make himself a writer. One of his professors there was the poet Richard Hugo, who plunged him into a crash course in poetry and gave him the invaluable advice, "Write about what you know." (Years later Welch paid tribute to his mentor by coediting Hugo's posthumous autobiography, *The Real West Marginal Way*.) For seven or eight years thereafter Welch worked on his poetry, the result of which labor was his first book and only collection of poems.

Riding the Earthboy 40 (the title refers to forty acres of farm that Welch's father once leased from the Earthboy family), was widely considered an impressive debut, although it was not much noticed until its reissue by a major publisher (Harper & Row) in 1975, after the success of his first novel, *Winter in the Blood*, in 1974. These short, sometimes cryptic poems move from elegy to comedy, from rage to acceptance, scrupulously avoiding sentimentality or stereotype in their treatment of Native American themes. At least one critic, Robert Holland in *Poetry*, thought that the poems scrupulously avoided *feeling* as well and that the book did "little service either to poetry or to the American Indian," but Welch did not have many such reviews. The most widely anthologized poem in the collection is "The Man from Washington," about an official from the Bureau of Indian Affairs who promised:

> that life would go on as usual,
> that treaties would be signed, and everyone—
> man, woman and child—would be inoculated
> against a world in which we had no part,
> a world of money, promise and disease.

Of *Riding the Earthboy 40* Joseph Bruchac wrote, "With irony and honesty, James Welch has approached being an Indian and being a poet in contemporary America and come out of it with poems which are always memorable and in some cases close to great. It seems certain that he will continue to be a vital force in American writing, not just as an Indian or a poet, but as both." Welch has remained a force in American writing, but not as Bruchac predicted. Since *Riding the Earthboy 40* he has published no verse and has turned exclusively to prose fiction.

Welch began writing fiction because of his desire to describe the Highline country of Montana "in an extended way." His poems, he told Nicholas O'Connell in *At the Field's End*, "just weren't doing it. They were like snapshots. They would get pieces of it, but never the whole scope of the thing." So he began constructing a first-person narration around "a main character who is part of that country but is fairly sensitive, who has a good eye." Never much interested in plot, Welch left the situation quite simple, even after extensive revisions undertaken at the suggestion of William Kittredge, his former teacher at the University of Montana. *Winter in the Blood*, as the book came to be called, describes a week or so in the life of an unnamed Blackfoot man in his early thirties as he talks with his recently remarried mother about the past, works occasionally as a farmhand, drifts from bar to bar in the small cities and towns of northern Montana, and half-heartedly searches for a former girlfriend that he is not sure he wants to find. What gives this tale of anomie and rootlessness its special power, aside from Welch's spare, laconic prose, is its placement within the context of contemporary Native American life. "We are accustomed to speak of alienation as the pervasive theme of twentieth-century American fiction," wrote Blanche H. Gelfant in the *Hudson Review,* "but the alienation of the middle-class white man seems a whining, self-pitying pose beside the experience of the American Indian, separated as he is from his land, his traditions, his people, his customs, his past; separated as he is from himself." For Gelfant, *Winter in the Blood* was "a simple and striking story about death—the death of a people, a tradition, a land, a river, a promise. We must read it to our despair." Other readers, however, saw glimmers of hopefulness in the novel's grim comedy and even an "opening onto light" in its climactic scene of familial reconciliation. Here at last the narrator finds a connection to the past and his Indian heritage when he discovers than an ancient, blind Blackfoot man named Yellow Calf is actually his grandfather and the literal savior of his family line, a secret the old man reveals to him indirectly in a moment of shared communion. With this scene, wrote Reynolds Price, the narrator achieves "a recovery of the past; a venerable, maybe lovable, maybe usable past." The conclusion of *Winter in the Blood* is perhaps deliberately ambiguous and has been interpreted in quite different ways, yet Welch's first novel was acclaimed by critics of all persuasions. In his *New York Times Book Review* piece, Price concluded: "Few books in any year speak so unanswerably, make their own local terms so thoroughly ours. *Winter in the Blood*—in its young crusty dignity, its grand bare lines, its comedy and mystery, its clean pathfinding to the center of hearts—deserves more notice than good novels get."

Welch's second novel, *The Death of Jim Loney*, shares with its predecessor the vast, desolate setting of northern Montana, a tightly reined-in prose style, and a protagonist far gone into an alienation that he cannot comprehend. But if *Winter in the Blood* allows its protagonist the possibility of spiritual recovery, *The Death of Jim Loney* moves inexorably to the fulfillment of its title. Jim Loney is a thirty-five-year-old "half-breed" who feels estranged from both the white and Indian worlds, not to mention from himself. He works as a farmhand when he needs to, but as the novel opens is spending more and more time alone, drinking and brooding. Yet Loney is loved: by a young schoolteacher named Rhea from a wealthy Texas family, and by his older sister Kate, a successful professional living in Washington, D.C., who responds to her brother's "crisis of spirit" by offering to take him back with her. By the time the two women join forces, however, Loney is unreachable; and after he kills an old Indian friend in what is possibly *not* a hunting accident, he becomes a fugitive and can only wait for a ritualistic death at the hands of a sadistic reservation policeman.

For all the novel's despair, the possibility remains that Loney's acceptance and planning of his death may be an affirmation of the self, the only form of affirmation available to him. The language of the final paragraph, at least, has a delicately poised symbolism that could be read in more ways than one:

> This is what you wanted, he thought, and that was the last thought left to him. He stood and he felt a dimness in his head and he took two steps and he felt something sharp in his stomach as though someone had jabbed him with a stick. And he fell, and as he was falling he felt a harsh wind where there was none and the last thing he saw were the beating wings of a dark bird as it climbed to a distant place.

"The novel is not a very happy or a very hopeful one," wrote Paul N. Pavich, an understatement that no critic would have quarreled with. Despite mostly favorable reviews, some critics found it less compelling than *Winter in the Blood*. "Though persistently and powerfully James Welch," wrote Kenneth Lincoln, "*The Death of Jim Loney* seems more self-consciously interior, less gutsy in detail than *Winter in the Blood*. The second novel's focus is less sharp, with less sense of place, ear for dialogue, and particularizing narrative voice." And yet Lincoln remained impressed by the authenticity of Welch's portrayal of contemporary Indian life. "This novel," he said, "is almost too real."

Welch's third novel, *Fools Crow*, was a major departure for him. Starting with family stories about a great-grandmother who survived a massacre by the United States Army in the 1870s and immersing himself in research and interviews, Welch composed an ambitious historical novel about one branch of the Montana Blackfeet called the Pikuni in the years just after the Civil War. This was a tragic period for the Blackfeet; their tribal traditions and their very lives were lost to smallpox, hunger, internal dissension, and slaughter by white soldiers. These terrible events are seen through the eyes of White Man's Dog, a young warrior who in the course of the novel becomes the tribal leader Fools Crow. In the end Fools Crow realizes that he and his people are powerless against the Napikwans (whites), and yet he keeps the faith: "For even though he was, like Feather Woman, burdened with the knowledge of his people, their lives and the lives of their children, he knew they would survive, for they were the chosen ones."

What gives the novel its unusual texture is Welch's incorporation of Indian mythology into the daily lives of its characters. In one pivotal scene Fools Crow travels for three days to meet with Feather Woman, an all-knowing deity who reveals to him in a vision the fate of his people—a vision so horrible that Fools Crow can never fully reveal it himself. Peter Wild considered this interpenetration of different levels of reality "the book's major accomplishment." "To say that [Welch] keeps dreams and events working nicely in tandem," he wrote in *The New York Times Book Review*, "would be a misstatement of what finally is an unpredictable series of natural and supernatural interactions; yet the relationship always is there, the real world blending into the unreal until neither we nor the characters themselves can tell the difference." Writing so completely from within the Indian viewpoint, however, carried certain risks that Welch did not always overcome; as Louis D. Owens put it, "at times, the carefully articulated speech of the author's Blackfeet is inevitably reminiscent of the stilted Oxfordian verbiage found in romantic treatments of Indians from James Fenimore Cooper to the Hollywood Western." Yet Owen had no doubts about Welch's achievement. "Rescuing this novel from such guilt by association," he went on to say, "is a hardness and precision of language lacking in nearly every other fictional attempt to render Indian speech in English, an absolute certainty of voice."

James Welch lives in Missoula, Montana with his wife Lois, who was his coeditor on the Richard Hugo autobiography. He has worked variously as an Indian firefighter, counselor, and teacher, but for some years has written full time

PRINCIPAL WORKS: *Poetry*—Riding the Earthboy 40, 1971 (rev. ed., 1975). *Novels*—Winter in the Blood, 1974; The Death of Jim Loney, 1979; Fools Crow, 1986. *As editor*—(with Lois Welch and Ridley Hugo) The Real West Marginal Way: A Poet's Autobiography, 1986.

ABOUT: Bruchac, J. Survival This Way: Interviews with American Indian Poets, 1987; Contemporary Authors 85–88, 1980; Contemporary Literary Criticism 6, 1976; 14, 1980; 52, 1989; Contemporary Poets, 4th ed., 1985; O'Connell, N. At the Field's End: Interviews with Twenty Pacific Northwest Writers, 1987; Velie, A. R. Four American Literary Masters: N. Scott Momaday, James Welch, Leslie Marmon Silko, and Gerald Vizenor, 1982. *Periodicals*—American Indian Culture and Research Journal 1, nos. 1 & 2, 1980; Hudson Review Summer 1975; Los Angeles Times Book Review December 14, 1986; New York Times Book Review November 10, 1974; November 14, 1986; Poetry February 1977; Western American Literature November 1980.

EDMUND WHITE

WHITE, EDMUND (January 13, 1940–   ), American novelist and non-fiction writer, was born in Cincinnati, Ohio, son of Edmund Valentine and Delilah (Teddlie) White, who were, respectively, an engineer and a psychologist. After receiving his B.A. from the University of Michigan in 1962, he moved to New York City where he was a staff writer for Time-Life, Books Division, from 1962 to 1970. In 1963 he had a play, "The Blue Boy in Black," performed at the Masque Theater, and subsequently in the 1960s wrote novels in which he could interest no publisher. From 1972 to 1973, he was senior editor at the *Saturday Review*; and in 1973 received an Ingram Merrill grant for fiction and published his first novel, *Forgetting Elena*. The novel takes place on a mysterious resort island, never clearly specified but suggesting Fire Island, where the hero-narrator, who has lost his memory, attempts to understand the rules of etiquette that govern its manners. Self-discovery in this rarified world is regarded as bad form.

Forgetting Elena was praised by Arthur Cooper in *Newsweek* as "a novel with the intricate texture of a spider's web and the mood of Alain Resnais's enigmatic film *Last Year at Marienbad*. . . . As a writer, White possesses the rare combination of a poetic sense of language and an ironic sense of humor. His characters are carved wickedly from fashion magazines; he succeeds in making them look foolish, in satirizing them for believing that 'all these fads and styles are so desperately important.' *Forgetting Elena* is one of the most finely worked and satisfying novels to appear in some time." After *Elena*, White worked for five years on a novel rejected by twenty-two publishers.

"No one," he later told an interviewer, "was interested. It was turned down by everyone in New York. It was probably the most crushing blow of my life." He then wrote, with Charles Silverstein, *The Joy of Gay Sex*, a popular manual with a liberated attitude toward sexuality, and his first public acknowledgment of his homosexuality. In the following year, after being rejected by twelve publishers, his novel *Nocturnes for the King of Naples* was brought out with an endorsement on its jacket by Gore Vidal: "A baroque invention of quite startling brilliance."

Nocturnes consists of eight mood pieces, or monologues, addressed to a lost lover, evidently an older man now dead, who awakened the narrator to the possibilities of sexual friendship. Some reviewers were puzzled by the stylized nature of the book and tended either to like it extravagantly or not to care for it at all. One of those who liked it very much was J. D. McClatchy in *Shenandoah*. "The astonishing stylistic virtuosity of *Nocturnes*," he commented, "may distract an absorbed or careless reader from White's power that dominates his moving portrait of refracted feeling. . . . *Nocturnes* is a brilliant, provocative, and commanding achievement." John Yohalem in the *New York Times Book Review*, however, found White's prose "narcissistic," and its "erotic faun" narrator and other eccentric characters "unsympathetic."

From 1977 to 1979, White taught creative writing at Johns Hopkins University, and in 1980 published a non-fiction work, *States of Desire: Travels in Gay America*, an account of gay men and their lifestyles in many different parts of the country. Reviews were generally favorable. Although expressing some reservations, Walter Clemons in *Newsweek* acknowledged that White's book was "consistently entertaining and often funny. . . . He shrewdly notes regional variances in gay status, aspiration, fantasy and self-hatred in more than twenty cities. . . . his novelistic gifts—curiosity about character (his own as well as others'), an alert ear and eye for revelatory detail—make this book absorbing." Paul Cowan in the *New York Times Book Review*, however, complained that White never explores the feelings of those he interviews "to the point where his characters become real or his own half-hidden commitments and doubts begin to surface. That's probably one reason why his journey doesn't seem to furnish him with any lasting personal discoveries." The gay America described in White's book was soon to be irrevocably altered by the AIDS epidemic; the author was one of the founders, the following year, of Gay Men's Health Crisis, a volunteer organization formed to educate the public and care for victims of the disease.

In 1981–1982, White was executive director of the New York Institute for the Humanities, a scholarly group sponsoring seminars, lectures, and roundtable discussions, based at New York University and supported by the school and national grants; and in 1981–1983 was adjunct professor of creative writing at Columbia University School of the Arts. His third novel, *A Boy's Own Story*, appeared in 1982. Set in the 1950s, it deals in partly autobiographical form with a boy's prep school years and dawning recognition of his homosexuality. Reviews were generally quite favorable. Catherine R. Stimson, in the *New York Times Book Review*, wrote: "This book is as artful as his two earlier novels but more explicit and grounded in detail, far less fanciful and elusive. . . . Balancing the banal and the savage, the funny and the lovely, [White] achieves a wonderfully poised fiction." The reactions of Alan Hollinghurst, in the *Times Literary Supplement*, were more mixed. "Many of White's observations," he commented, "are piercingly acute, his ruminations subtle and irresistible. His settings—schools, summerhouses, medium-sized towns—are poignantly caught." But he was irritated by White's elaborate metaphors—"the night, intent seamstress, fed the fabric of water under the needle of our hull," "the terrible, decaying Camembert of my heart," "the torso flowering out of the humble calyx of his jeans." It seemed to him that White's prose was often marred by "preciosity and artiness."

White's next novel, *Caracole*, marked a return to the highly stylized manner of *Elena* and

Nocturnes. The novel is not set in any exact time or in any exact place, although Venice and Paris are the apparent models for the city, where the principal characters—Mateo, Angelica, Gabriel, Edwige, and Mathilda—come together and drift apart. To some reviewers, *Caracole* was a triumph of high style—witty, elegant, enigmatic, more European than American. Writing in the *Nation*, Phyllis Rose remarked: "If you want to know about the complexities of a small, closed social system and if Stendhal's Parma seems too remote, try White's portrait of an imaginary city. . . . More than most American writers, White is divided between . . . two impulses, old-fashioned realism and modernist artifice. . . . *Caracole* appeals to me precisely because of its unique mixture of artifice and realism." Other reviewers, like Stanley Reynolds in *Punch*, felt that White's work was comparable less to Proust (a White favorite) than to Ronald Firbank. "There is," Reynolds remarked, "a constant straining after effect which, in a novel of over 300 pages, is finally exhausting."

The Beautiful Room Is Empty, a sequel to *A Boy's Own Story*, deals with White's protagonist in his college years at the University of Michigan (where he compulsively cruises student union lavatories), his arrival in New York in the late 1950s, and his affair with a student named Sean. He appears at the end at the Stonewall disco in the Village on the eve of gay consciousness. Peter Prescott, in *Newsweek*, called *The Beautiful Room Is Empty* "a brilliant book, informed by White's adroit, astringent comic sense," and other critics also praised the novel generously. But many reviewers objected to the book's stereotyped characters and situations, and "inert" episodic structure. *The Darker Proof*, which appeared in the same year, is a collection of two stories by White and four by Adam Mars-Jones dealing with gay life in the age of AIDS. Alan Hollinghurst, in the *Times Literary Supplement*, was especially impressed by White's stories, which "resonate with dreamlike echoes. . . . 'An Oracle' is the finer achievement, but both stories have endings of faultless eloquence. They are fraught, romantic works, and they convince you that they need to be like that."

White plans two further novels as sequels to *A Boy's Own Story* and *The Beautiful Room Is Empty*, which will take his protagonist through the hedonist 1970s and the AIDS-menaced world of the 1980s. He has lived in Paris in recent years but is now a visiting professor at Brown University, where he teaches courses in creative writing and the works of Jean Genet.

PRINCIPAL WORKS: Fiction—Forgetting Elena, 1973; Nocturnes for the King of Naples, 1978; A Boy's Own Sto-

ry, 1982; Caracole, 1985; The Beautiful Room Is
Empty, 1988; The Darker Proof, 1988. *Non-fiction*—(with C. Silverstein) The Joy of Gay Sex,
1978; States of Desire: Travels in Gay America, 1980.

ABOUT: Contemporary Authors New Revision Series 3,
1981; Contemporary Literary Criticism 27, 1984.
Periodicals—Nation January 5, 1974; November 16,
1985; New York Times Book Review February 3,
1980; February 24, 1980; October 10, 1982; Newsweek
April 30, 1973; February 11, 1980; March 21, 1988;
Publishers Weekly September 24, 1982; Shenandoah
Fall 1978; Time July 30, 1990; Times Literary Supplement August 19, 1983; January 22, 1988.

WHITMAN, RUTH (BASHEIN) (May 28,
1922–), American poet and translator, writes:
"I sold my first poem at the age of eleven in
1933, in the midst of the Depression. With the
five dollars I was paid for that poem by *Young
America*, I bought a copy of Louis Untermeyer's
British and American Poets. Reading the anthology from cover to cover, I thought 'This is where
I want to belong.'

"Growing up in a first-generation Russian-Jewish household, I constantly heard a barrage
of languages—Yiddish, Russian, English—spoken by my parents and grandparents. Everyone talked loudly and passionately day and night
around the kitchen table. My grandfather sang
Russian lullabies to me, and I can still remember
some of the words and tunes. Those grandfatherly serenades surely had something to do with my
obsession with poetry.

"In the summer of 1941 my English professor
at New York University suggested I apply for a
scholarship to the Bread Loaf School of English
Summer School. In the seductive Green Mountains of Vermont I sat at the, knee of Robert
Frost, was introduced to the 'World's Body' by
John Crowe Ransom, and sat on the lap of young
Theodore Roethke whenever we drove down the
mountain to the Middlebury Tavern. I vowed
never to return home to New York. A young
Harvard poet invited me to elope with him to
prewar Cambridge.

"I had been writing and imitating since I was
sixteen—first because I fell in love with Walt
Whitman, then Emily Dickinson, then John
Donne, then W. B. Yeats—an eclectic kind of
self-education. I knew I was one of the last romantics, and must look for ways to modify that
disposition by reading Williams and Pound, Eliot and Auden, Levertov, Creeley, Rich, Kunitz,
and Ammons. Nothing in the world seems to me
more beautiful than the way that a concrete fact
or object suddenly leaps beyond itself into metaphor. I believe that music occupies the same

RUTH WHITMAN

world of metaphysical transcendence, and my
deepest (and probably impossible) desire is to
write poetry that parallels the metaphysical precincts of music.

"Married and living in Cambridge, Massachusetts, I was first a student, then a graduate student, and then a dropout. I had stopped writing,
for the first and only time in my life. Sitting on
the rocks in Pigeon Cove one March in 1947, in
sight of T. S. Eliot's 'Dry Salvages,' I made a major decision. Graduate school was death to poetry. I wanted books of poems and babies. The
babies—three of them—came before the books.
I found myself with a household to run, a husband in graduate school, money to earn, and,
like 'rowing against the tide,' the drive to write
poetry. I did most of my writing between 2 a.m.
and 6 a.m. When my youngest child was two, I
went to the MacDowell Colony for two weeks
and wrote my first book. Six years later a fellowship to the Bunting Institute at Radcliffe College
gave me a place to work and money to live on
for two years, in the company of high-powered
creative women. While I was there my second
collection, *The Marriage Wig*, was published
and received the Kovner Award and the Alice
Fay di Castagnola Award. I also finished a third
collection and a second book of translations of
Yiddish poetry.

"For the past twenty years I have been especially interested in exploring the lives of heroic
and remarkable women. These have included
Lizzie Borden (*The Passion of Lizzie Borden*),
the pioneer woman Tamsen Donner (*Tamsen
Donner: A Woman's Journey*), and most recent-

ly, the Israeli parachutist, Hanna Senesh, who was part of a rescue mission from Palestine to Hungary in 1944 (*The Testing of Hanna Senesh*). I have now begun to study the life of Queen Hatshepsut, the only woman pharaoh in Egyptian history. I have been fascinated by the enigma of Hatshepsut's personality since the 1940s. Between then and now I had already written several poems about her. In 1985 I was able to visit Egypt during a Fulbright Fellowship to Jerusalem, and to look at her sites in Thebes, Karnak, Luxor, and the Valley of the Kings. With each of my last three books, it has been very important to me to see the landscape I was writing about, in order to enter into the life of another time and place. I was fortunate, when I was writing in 1975 about the experience of Tamsen Donner in 1846, to receive a grant from the National Endowment for the Arts so that I could follow her trail across the American continent from Illinois to California.

"Many of my poems have been set to music. *Tamsen Donner* has been made into a dance/theater piece that was performed in Boston in 1982, 1984, and 1986. It has also been adapted for the stage and filmed for television. *Lizzie Borden* has been set as an opera and also performed several times in New York and San Diego. This is a source of satisfaction to me since I believe that my particular lyric voice is essentially musical, a belief that seems to be corroborated by several contemporary composers.

"I have always believed that the purpose of poetry is to celebrate human experience, and in my case, it is not only my own personal experience that I want to universalize, but more importantly, the experience of other human beings, not only in my era but in other eras as well. I see it as my special obligation to illuminate these lives in poetry."

———

In 1982 Ruth Whitman published a handbook for aspiring poets, *Becoming a Poet: Source, Process, and Practice*, full of sensible advice based on her own career. "Becoming a poet," she wrote, "is not a casual accident. Nor is it a sudden ascension into heaven on the wings of sheer aspiration." For Ruth Whitman it had its sources in her early love for language and reading, a solid academic education, and the heady atmosphere of Bread Loaf where in 1941 she met her first husband, Cedric Whitman, a classical scholar. They married that same year and she completed her undergraduate studies at Radcliffe, majoring in Greek and English, in 1944. In 1947 she received an M.A. from Harvard. During these years and through the 1950s she had two

daughters, worked as an editor for Houghton Mifflin and Harvard University Press and as a free-lance editor, and published poems in a number of journals.

In 1985 Whitman wrote: "In writing poetry my purpose has changed from celebrating my own cycle of experience to bearing witness to the experience of other men and women." Her early works, first collected in 1963 in *Blood and Milk Poems*, were, as Richard Damashek observed in *Contemporary Poets*, "personal, subjective, and strongly formal." Short lyrics mainly, they showed a mastery of striking images and musical sound:

> Strewn on the sand, a pride of nuns—
> Apart from the herd, adrift on the beach,
> Undone to their chins, with legs laid bare—
> Spread out their wintry souls to bleach,
> Smiled the sun their orisons,
> And hid their bandaged hair.
> —from "Nuns on the Beach"

With her second collection, *The Marriage Wig and Other Poems*, it was clear that Ruth Whitman's range of real and imagined experience had widened to include not only poems of personal experience—motherhood, her love of nature, her travels in Greece and Egypt—but poems inspired by her Jewish heritage. Both the title poem and other related ones ("Cutting Rapunzel's Hair," "The Nun Cuts Her Hair," "Cutting the Jewish Bride's Hair") explore the symbolism of woman's identity. "The Marriage Wig" refers to the custom of cutting the hair of Orthodox Jewish women when they marry so that their husbands will not be distracted by their physical beauty from the spiritual sanctity of marriage. "I blind you with my hair," the bride says, citing the Mishnah. But she ponders, "To any man not blind, a wig is false," and she raises the challenge:

> It's to possess more than the skin
> that these old world Jews
> exacted the hair of their brides.
>   Good husband, lover of the Torah,
>   does the calligraphy of your bride's hair
>   interrupt your page?
>
> Before the clownish friction of flesh
> creating out of nothing
> a mockup of its begetters,
> a miraculous puppet of God,
> you must first divorce her from her vanity.
>
> She will snip off her pride,
> cut back her appetite to be devoured,
> she will keep herself well braided,
> her love's furniture will not endanger you
>   but this little amputation
>   will shift the balance of the universe.
> —"Cutting the Jewish Bride's Hair"

Reviewers of Whitman's poems up to this point in her career admired her "delicacy of perception" and her sensitivity to nature. Robert D. Spector, in *Saturday Review*, praised "her feminine sensibility" and her technical mastery: "The verse itself has a deceptive simplicity, hiding allusiveness behind a straightforward style and unaffectedly uniting rhythm and subject matter." But Mona Van Duyn, also writing of *The Marriage Wig*, in *Poetry*, felt that she had not yet realized her potential: "The most consistent fault of Miss Whitman's poems, I think, is some sort of lack of effort, a misplaced confidence in the fact that simply by printing her feelings or thoughts on a page she will 'catch and hold' a reader's interest, empathy, admiration." Such criticism did not apply, however, to Whitman's collection published five years later, *The Passion of Lizzie Borden: New and Selected Poems*. The striking title poem reveals her powers of imaginative identification with other people, portraying the notorious accused ax-murderer of her father and stepmother not as an innocent, maligned victim, but as a deeply repressed woman who finds fulfillment in terrible violence:

In the August heat
she irons handkerchiefs for her stepmother,
heating the iron on the kitchen fire
in the black stove.

The center of the earth is always boiling,
and she must have the trick of eye to see
how she can liquefy
stones, trees,
slash air so she can breathe,
take life to make life, break
the blind wall open with her fist.

This volume also contains some of Whitman's best known and most frequently anthologized poems, including the memorable "Castoff Skin":

She lay in her girlish sleep at ninety-six,
small as a twig.
Pretty good figure,

for an old lady, she said to me once.
Then she crawled away, leaving
a tiny stretched transparence

behind her. When I kissed her paper cheek
I thought of the snake,
of his quick motion.

As Whitman has matured as a poet she has increasingly moved toward what she describes as "bearing witness" to others' lives. *Tamsen Donner: A Woman's Journey* was inspired by the tragic fate of a group of Americans traveling in a wagon train to California in 1846. Lost in a snowstorm in the Sierras and starving, some resorted to cannibalism. A few managed to find their way to safety, but Tamsen Donner chose to remain behind and perish with her husband who had been badly injured. Whitman received a grant from the National Endowment for the Humanities which enabled her to travel the route of the Donner party. "During the trip," she writes, "I kept a journal, as I knew she had done. I discovered—what I already knew—that in a poet's journal, prose passages become interlinked with lyrics, like recitative and aria, and these together help to weave back and forth, between immediate and symbolic levels of reality." Interspersing prose and poetry, Whitman recreates this grim episode with delicacy and portrays in Tamsen Donner a woman of extraordinary vision and courage:

If my boundary stops here
I have daughters to draw new maps on the world,
they will draw the lines of my face
they will draw with my gestures my voice
they will speak my words thinking they have invented
  them

they will invent them
    they will invent me
I will be planted again and again
I will wake in the eyes of their children's children
they will speak my words.

Another imaginative re-creation of an extraordinarily courageous woman is Whitman's *The Testing of Hanna Senesh*, the twenty-three-year-old Jewish girl who enlisted as a British Intelligence volunteer and was parachuted behind enemy lines in Yugoslavia, captured in Hungary, tortured and executed by the Nazis in 1944. Hungarian-born herself, Senesh had lived in a kibbutz in what was then still Palestine. In reconstructing the last months of her life, Whitman interviewed people who had known her, and she went to Jerusalem in 1977 and again in 1979 and 1981. She translated some of the young woman's own Hebrew poetry and her farewell letter to her mother. The rest, Whitman writes, is "my re-creation of what she might have written during the last nine months of her life." Powerful and moving as Senesh's story is, it is not altogether solemn. Whitman expresses the youthful zest and vigor of her heroine, her delight in nature and in the joyous celebrations she shared with others even in times of peril, her quiet courage and faith:

There's a fire in me
it must not go to waste.

Sitting in the snow,
I fan it with my breath.

I cup it in my hands:
it must not be lost.

g to end," as one re-
down Philadelphia's
e unstable activist and
on scheme, remarks,
killing us, whittling
woman, a baby at a
sitting on our asses
thers received most-
igh in retrospect it
work in Wideman's

sed before he pub-
nan learned or re-
ith which to talk
language was, es-
at Wideman had
ewood, and most
ith accomplished
ding Place, pub-
Damballah was a
ed short stories
acters, from the
n escaped slave
od in the 18ea
nater French,
of the jazz age.
, figures promi-
about the rela-
a young man o
) and the recli
ho takes him
, Bess. Per
Damballah br
ideman. Compa
Damballah to Je
kins wrote, "Lik
used a narrative
on and dream se-
te poetic portrait of
people. . . . The in-
as disparate as they
ogether as a remark
montage of black life
rations."
delved further into the
liscovered in his previ-
d by "Doot," a young
Wideman himself, it tells
es' fatal return to Home-
on the lam, his violent
the police, and the ways
truggle to keep his story
Wideman's fiction, how-
nt to texture, and the tex-
u Yesterday is dense with
of jazz and blues songs,
d the endless permutations
Still the most highly regard-

/
,
m
ly
ely
to
em
raft,
own.
etry is
er time be-
chusetts and
o daughters
ed in 1958.
Houghton
4, she mar-
6. Long ex-
e writing,
poet-in-
nd uni-
Rad-
y at
the
t.

WIDEMAN, JOHN EDGAR (June 14, 941–), American novelist and literary and social critic, was born in Washington, D.C., one of five children of Edgar and Betty (French) Wideman. Wideman spent the formative part of his childhood in Homewood, a black district in Pittsburgh, Pennsylvania, where both sides of his family had deep roots. With its complex mores and traditions and its gradual decline from a stable and supportive black community into an embattled ghetto, Homewood has provided Wideman with his richest source of material and is the setting of at least four of his books.

Wideman's father was a waiter, and his son has described his parents as "an ideal combination of laissez faire— 'Do what you want, but do it well,' they said. They never gave any indication that I should not attempt to do anything." When he was ten the family moved to the predominately white, upwardly mobile neighborhood of Shadyside, the first of many such disjunctions between the black and white worlds that Wideman was to experience in his youth. In high school he excelled as a student and as an athlete, and in 1959 he was admitted on scholarship to the University of Pennsylvania in Philadelphia. Despite a certain discomfort that he felt at being one of a handful of black students in an overwhelmingly white school (a feeling he tried to hide from himself as from well as others), Wideman achieved an exemplary record at college, becoming an all-star basketball player and graduating Phi Beta Kappa as an English major. In 1963 he became the second black American to win a Rhodes Scholarship; he spent the three years of his study at Oxford University, where he wrote a thesis on the eighteenth-century novel and was captain and coach of the basketball team. Returning from Oxford with a bachelor of philosophy degree, Wideman spent the 1966–1967 academic year as a fellow of the Creative Writing Workshop at the University of Iowa.

A Glance Away, Wideman's first novel, published in 1967, the year he joined the English culty at the University of Pennsylvania, was ry much a reflection of the advanced literary ning he had received. Neither it nor its suc-or, *Hurry Home*, was overtly concerned with of racial injustice, nor had Wideman yet ered the fictional possibilities of Home-both novels being set largely in unnamed n cities. Instead Wideman used a variety rnist techniques—interior monologue, g of chronology, incorporation of sec-texts"—to embody his characters' elf. In the first novel Eddie Lawson, rug addict whose decision to stay ed by a white, homosexual English nd Robert Thurley, provides the

JOHN EDGAR WIDEMAN

focus for a series of Camus-like questionings of purpose; in the second Cecil Braithwaite, a black law student who works as a janitor, accepts the invitation of a guilt-ridden white artist named Webb to accompany him on a tour of Spain and Italy, where Cecil's experience of the monuments of western (and later African) civilization precipitates a reevaluation of his individual and cultural identity. Both novels were notable for sympathetic and complex portrayals of white characters (Thurley and Webb); somewhat unusually for a young black writer in the late sixties, Wideman placed art firmly above ideology. The two books impressed critics as achieved works of fiction, all the more noteworthy for having been written by an author so comparatively young. Of *A Glance Away*, Iain Bamforth wrote in the *Times Literary Supplement*: "There is little in the novel which betrays it as the work of a young man—an occasionally ponderous symbolism, perhaps—and far more which impresses with its stylistic maturity."

More realistic in approach than *A Glance Away* and *Hurry Home*, *The Lynchers* revealed the influence of major black writers like Jean Toomer and Richard Wright, until then not much of a presence in Wideman's work. Moreover, the story itself—about a failed plot by four black men of different backgrounds to murder a racist white policeman for crimes against their people—focused on specific issues in black American culture rather than on the more general existential preoccupations of Wideman's first two novels. Though not polemical, *The Lynchers* was an angry book, "pulsat[ing] with

frustration from beginnir
viewer put it. Walking
South Street, Littleman, th
originator of the retaliati
"This street means they're
away day by day a man,
time. And most of us just
wasting our time." *The Lyn*
ly favorable reviews, altho
seems a clearly transitional
career.

In the eight years that pa
lished his next books, Wider
learned "a new language w
about [his] experience." This
sentially, the black English th
heard on the streets of Hom
critics agreed that he used it w
fluency in *Damballah* and *Hi*
lished simultaneously in 1981.
collection of twelve interrela
about various Homewood char
semi-legendary Sybele Owens,
who helped to found Homewo
(and was in fact Wideman's r
great-great-grandmother), to J
rowdy but benevolent patriarch
One of John's grandsons, Tommy
nently in *Hiding Place*, a novel
tionship that develops between
the run from the law (Tommy
sive, misunderstood woman w
his great-grandmother's siste
more so than *Hiding Place*,
new and fertile ground for W
ing Wideman's methods in
Toomer's in *Cane*, Mel Wa
Toomer, Mr. Wideman ha
laced with myth, superstit
quences to create an elabor
the lives of ordinary black
dividual 'parts' or stories,
may initially seem, work
ably vivid and coherent
over a period of five gen

Sent for You Yesterday
territory Wideman had
ous two books. Narrate
black writer not unlike
the story of Albert Wilk
wood after seven year
death at the hands of
those closest to him
alive. As with most o
ever, plot is subservi
ture of *Sent for Yo*
digression, snatches
dream sequences, a
of black street slang

ed of Wideman's novels, it won the 1984 PEN/ Faulkner Award. In his *Washington Post Book World* review, Garrett Epps wrote, "Wideman has a fluent command of the American language, written and spoken, and a fierce, loving vision of the people he writes about. Like Faulkner's, Wideman's prose fiction is vivid and demanding."

In the dedication of *Damballah*, Wideman wrote that he conceived of the stories as letters from home to his younger brother Robby, serving a life sentence without parole in a Pennsylvania prison for his role in a 1974 robbery in which a man was killed (though not by him). In *Brothers and Keepers* Wideman went back to his brother's story and to his own. This mix of memory, imagination, feeling and fact"—Wideman's only work of nonfiction— examines with painful honesty the divergent paths that the two brothers have taken from the same source. "Why Robby there behind bars— why me here?" Wideman asks, knowing that the question can never be fully answered. While he does not excuse the tragic waste of his brother's life, he is at least as hard on his own. Recalling Robby's furtive visit to him in Laramie, Wyoming (where Wideman was living and teaching) on the night before his capture, he writes, "I'd come west to escape the demons Robby personified. I didn't need outlaw brothers reminding me how much had been lost, how much compromised, how terribly the world still raged beyond the charmed circle of my life on the Laramie plains." The brothers *do* work towards an understanding of Robby's plight and their separate fates, and Robby's gradual acquisition of self-knowledge is paralleled by Wideman's own. Yet they are ultimately separated by iron bars and all the systematic humiliations of prison life. In a letter from Robby that concludes the book, he informs his older brother that his appeal for a retrial has been again denied.

Although Christopher Lehmann-Haupt was put off by what he considered "its many whining, posturing passages," Ishmael Reed thought *Brothers and Keepers* "a rare triumph in its use of diverse linguistic styles." Speaking of the juxtaposition of Robby's vivid, colloquial speech with Wideman's more formal, literary manner, Reed said, "the result is a book that has the impact of reading Claude Brown's powerful *Manchild in the Promised Land* and James Weldon Johnson's elegant *The Autobiography of an Ex-Colored Man* in alternating paragraphs."

After the powerful self-examination and social criticism of *Brothers and Keepers*, Wideman's return to fiction with *Reuben* struck some readers as disappointing. Once again set in

Homewood, the novel revolves around the figure of Reuben, an aging, hump-backed lawyer living in an abandoned trailer who does what little he can for other, virtually disenfranchised blacks caught in legal entanglements. Reviewers like Richard Gibson and Walter Kendrick considered *Reuben* Wideman's weakest work to date. "The plot is slender and social complexities are reduced to monochromatic monotony," wrote Gibson, and Kendrick suggested that Wideman might have mined the Homewood vein "to depletion."

A better reception was accorded Wideman's collection of twelve stories, *Fever*. Here, especially in the powerful title story, he explored a new vein—American history. "Fever" takes place in Philadelphia during the yellow fever epidemic of 1793–1794, during which blacks worked side by side with whites to fight the ravages of the disease. The literal plague symbolizes the fundamental sickness of racism, and Wideman's metaphoric fever ranges over American history from eighteenth-century Philadelphia to the 1985 police action in the same city against the black group MOVE, which led to a devastating fire. As a black doctor treating the yellow fever victims observes: "Fever grows in the secret places of our hearts, planted there when one of us decided to sell one of us to another." The other stories in *Fever* are set in the twentieth century, but, as Clarence Major wrote in the *Washington Post Book World*, "in one way or another they echo the sentiment of the fever metaphor." They share a common theme that Herbert Mitgang defined, in his *New York Times* review, as "the efforts of blacks and whites to develop friendships and the difficulties, even with good will, of penetrating each other's worlds." Mitgang felt that overall the stories "are fragmentary in their plots, strained in writing and not always able to persuade the reader to suspend disbelief." But for Susan Fromberg Schaeffer, in the *New York Times Book Review*, Wideman's achievement here was to take the idea of human equality and kinship "from the world of concepts and, through the alchemy of his prose, convert it to flesh-and-blood truth."

Wideman has said that he finds teaching "a nice counterbalance to the loneliness and isolation you're necessarily involved in when writing fiction," and his parallel career as an English professor has taken him from the University of Pennsylvania to the University of Wyoming and, most recently, to the University of Massachusetts in Amherst. He has written essays on various aspects of black literature for such publications as the *American Scholar* and *American Poetry Review*. Wideman married Judith Ann Goldman in 1965, he and his wife have three children: Daniel, Jacob, and Jamila. Tragic circumstances overtook the Wideman family in 1986 when Jacob Wideman, then sixteen, was arrested for the murder of a traveling companion after a camping trip in Maine. Two years later he pleaded guilty and was sentenced to life imprisonment. This personal loss forms a part of Wideman's most recent novel, *Philadelphia Fire*.

PRINCIPAL WORKS: *Fiction*—A Glance Away, 1967; Hurry Home, 1970; The Lynchers, 1973; Damballah, 1981; Hiding Place, 1981; Sent for You Yesterday, 1983; Reuben, 1987; Fever: Twelve Stories, 1989; Philadelphia Fire, 1990. *Non-fiction*—Brothers and Keepers, 1984.

ABOUT: Contemporary Authors New Revision Series 14, 1985; Contemporary Literary Criticism 5, 1976; 34, 1985; 36, 1986; Contemporary Novelists, 4th ed., 1986; Dictionary of Literary Biography 33, 1984; O'Brien, J. (ed.) Interviews with Black Writers, 1973. *Periodicals*—Black World June 1975; New York Times May 16, 1984; October 29, 1984; September 4, 1986; October 18, 1988; December 5, 1989; New York Times Book Review April 11, 1982; November 11, 1984; January 13, 1985; November 8, 1987; January 24, 1988; December 10, 1989; September 30, 1990; Publishers Weekly November 17, 1989; Time October 1, 1990; Times Literary Supplement January 16, 1987; August 5–11, 1988; Washington Post Book World July 3, 1983; November 5, 1989.

*WIENERS, JOHN (JOSEPH) (January 6, 1934–), American poet, was born in Boston, the son of Albert Eugene Wieners, a laborer, and the former Anna Elizabeth Laffan, a domestic worker. Raised in the Roman Catholic church, he attended the local public schools and Jesuit-run Boston College, where he majored in English and from which he took his bachelor's degree in 1954. He worked for a time in Harvard University's Lamont Library. One night in September 1954, he heard Charles Olson read his poetry at the Charles Street Meeting House. The following spring he enrolled as a student at Olson's Black Mountain College, an experimental institution in North Carolina, where the faculty included the poets Robert Duncan and Robert Creeley, the painters Robert Motherwell and Josef Albers, the choreographer Merce Cunningham, and the composer John Cage.

Wieners stayed in North Carolina until the summer of 1956, when he returned to Boston and his library job. He soon published the first issue of a little magazine, *Measure*, which was to appear in two further issues up to the summer of 1962, and which included the work of poets connected with the Black Mountain school as

JOHN WIENERS

well as those who were Wieners' friends from Boston and California.

Wieners' connection with the Beats, of which movement he is considered an important, though not a founding, member, began when he traveled to San Francisco in mid-1956. There, through Duncan, he met Allen Ginsberg, Jack Kerouac, Michael McClure, David Meltzer, Philip Lamantia, and others. His closest friends, however, were the painters Robert LaVigne and Wallace Berman. Wieners' first book of poetry, *The Hotel Wentley Poems*, consists of eight lyrics written from June 15 to June 23, 1958. They lay open youth's intensity of feeling, and manifest an accomplishment in the poet's craft that Duncan and Olson had already found remarkably precocious. They are all poems about love, even though their titles ("A Poem for Record Players," "A Poem for Vipers," "A Poem for Museum Goers," "A Poem for the Insane," and so forth) may suggest otherwise, and there is none of the happiness or joy of youth in them, but an intense meditation on bitter reality, a study of love gone bad, and desolation, and the pain of a young poet cursed by the strength of his vision and aware of what it is taking out of him. These feelings come together triumphantly in the longest of them, the seven-part "A Poem for Painters":

> Our age bereft of nobility
> How can our faces show it?
> I look for love.
>   My lips stand out
> dry and cracked with want
>   of it.

> Oh it is well. . . .
>
> I held love once in the palm of my hand.
>   See the lines there.
>   How we played
> its game, are playing now
> in the bounds of white and heartless fields.
>   Fall down on my head,
> love, drench my flesh in the streams
>   of fine sprays. Like
>   French perfume
>   so that I light up as
>   mountain glories and
> I am showered by the scent
>   of the finished line.

The poem's last stanza is considered by some critics and fellow poets to be as poignant and powerful as any verse of our times. Robert Creeley describes this passage as "words [that] became our own . . . There was nothing else to shelter or protect him."

There was, in Denise Levertov's and Allen Ginsberg's opinion, even better poetry to come from Wieners, although the cost to the poet was evidently high. Worn out and miserable, he left the West Coast to return to Boston in 1959, where he was hospitalized for the first of several occasions in a mental asylum. The fifty-two poems in *Ace of Pentacles* were written, for the most part, in Boston and also in New York, where he lived from 1961 to 1963, for much of the time sharing an apartment with the prose writer Herbert Huncke, like him addicted to hard drugs, a homosexual, and bitter and despairing about life. (He calls him in "For Huncke" from *Selected Poems* "The guide and wizard I would worship and obey, / my guardian teacher, who knows how to stay / alive on practically nothing in the city / until help comes, usually from a stranger or youth.") Everything seems cursed in this collection, and the degradation the poet experiences is not stinted in the description. Wieners' self-revealed life, to Levertov, writing in *Poetry*, is one "unusually defenseless against grief and disaster. . . . [Yet] there is never any sense that he capitalizes on dramatic events or is dependent on them for his poetry; he doesn't see them as dramatic. What moves us is not the darkness of the world in which the poems were written, but the pity and terror and joy that is beauty in the poems themselves. When there is no song, no honey on the lips, only the presentation of drama, it can happen that the subject matter itself is invested with a false glamor. In Wieners the glamor is the word-music itself. I am brought to remember Orpheus, who did not sing *about* hell: he was *in* hell, and sang there, leading the way out." The central sequence in *Ace of Pentacles* (named after the tarot card symbolizing triumph over suf-

fering) is undoubtedly "The Ages of Youth," the pivotal poem of which is "The Acts of Youth," in which the devastating sadness and waste of life become nearly too much to bear, but are finally, by a mighty act of poetic volition, made into art:

> And with great fear I inhabit the middle of the night
> What wrecks of the mind await me, what drugs
> to dull the senses, what little I have left,
> what more can be taken away? . . .
>
> So I turn on the light
> And smoke rings rise in the air.
> Do not think of the future, there is none.
> But the formula all great art is made of.
>
> Pain and suffering. Give me the strength
> to bear it, to enter those places where the
> great animals are caged. And we can live
> at peace by their side. A bride to the burden
>
> that no god imposes but knows we have the means
> to sustain its force unto the end of our days.
> For that is what we are made for; for that
> we are created. Until the dark hours are done.
>
> And we rise again in the dawn.
> Infinite particles of the divine sun, now
> worshipped in the pitches of the night.

The strong strain of traditional religious imagery here, juxtaposed with the impedimenta of drugged desolation, produce a powerful poetic charge, echoing Keats and Whitman at their clearest and most illuminating.

Wieners' despair, anguished terror, and brutal honesty are too strong for even the small coterie of readers who appreciate modern American poetry: he has never been a popular poet. But other poets have always considered him one of the very best and purest voices America has produced in the twentieth century. To Robert Creeley, Wieners' poetry "has an exceptional human beauty. . . . There is in it such a commonness of phrase and term, such a substantial fact of daily life transformed by the articulateness of his feelings and the intensity of the inexorable world that is forever out there waiting for any one of us. . . . Against the casual waste of our usual lives, his has proved a cost and commitment so remarkable. He has given everything to our common world."

The mid-1960s were a productive period for Wieners. In 1965–1967, at the suggestion of Charles Olson, he enrolled as a graduate student in the State University of New York at Buffalo. He worked there as teaching assistant to Olson, who held the chair of poetics in the university. Many of their fellow poets came to Buffalo as visiting professors, including Duncan, Ginsberg, Creeley, Gregory Corso, and Ed Sanders. Pressed *Wafer*, *Asylum Poems* and *Nerves* showed no slackening of force, rather a lengthening of the poetic line, and a more sustainedly lyrical strain. Olson invited Wieners to accompany him to the Spoleto Festival in June–July 1965, one of his rare trips outside the United States. He there met Ezra Pound. (A remarkable photograph exists of Wieners walking in the Piazza San Marco, Venice, between Olson and Pound.) He described his first sighting of Pound in a resonant passage of discursive prose: "His eyes were like stone. They pierced me from a distance. I felt I was in the presence of a god and afraid to look. . . . It seemed strange, that the world, which had flocked to him earlier, now left him alone, and looked idly on across the square. . . . I felt I was in the presence of a Chinese sage or mandarin. His hair was of the finest silk spun, a cocoon I thought, and when he rose to go, uttering no words one can hear, I thought, 'He goes into the door of life, not death.'"

The pain of living did not lessen for Wieners during the 1970s. He moved in 1971 to a rooming house on Joy Street on Beacon Hill, behind the Massachusetts state capitol. Between periods of institutionalization, he continued sporadically but prolifically to write verse, which became, for the most part, increasingly obscure. *Behind the State Capitol, or Cincinnati Pike*, at more than two hundred pages, is considered by Wieners to be a single, unitary poem. "Children of the Working Class" shows him at his most bitter and pestilence-obsessed. It was written "from incarceration, Taunton State Hospital, 1972":

There has never been a man yet, whom? no matter
  how wise
can explain how a god, so beautiful he can create
the graces of formal gardens, the exquisite twilight
  sunsets
in splendor of elegant toolsmiths, still can yield the horror of

dwarfs, who cannot stand up straight with
  crushed skulls,
diseases on their legs and feet unshaven faces and
  women,
worn humped backs, deformed necks, hare lips,
  obese arms
distended rumps, there is not a flame shoots out
  could ex-
tinguish the torch of any liberty's state infection.

1907. My Mother was born, I am witness t-
o the exasperation of gallant human beings at g-
od, priestly fathers and Her Highness, Holy Mother the
  Church
persons who felt they were never given a chance, had n-
o luck and were flayed at suffering.

   . . . I am witness
not to Whitman's vision, but instead the
poorhouses, the mad city asylums and relief worklines. Yes, I am witness not to
God's goodness, but his better or less scorn.

During the 1970s Wieners became politically engaged, joining the struggles against the Vietnam War and in favor of racial and sexual rights and equality. After 1975 he stopped writing for about eight years, telling those who asked that "poetry is not my calendar" and "I am living out the logical conclusion of my books." And these were out of print. He began writing again about 1983, bringing out the collection *She'd Turn on a Dime*. Working with the editor Raymond Foye, he published, at the urging of Ginsberg and under the auspices of California's Black Sparrow Press, two volumes, *Selected Poems 1958–1984*, which includes corrected and complete versions of all of his collections, and *Cultural Affairs in Boston: Poetry & Prose 1956–1985*, including much uncollected poetry and some exceptionally lucid descriptive prose. "John Wieners' glory," wrote Allen Ginsberg in a foreword to the former volume, "is solitary, as pure poet—a man reduced to loneness in poetry, without worldly distractions—and a man become one with his poetry. A life in contrast to the fluff and ambition of Pulitzer, National Book Awardees, Poetry Medalists from the American Arts & Letters & Poetry Academies—harmless bureaucratic functionaries among themselves, until the holders of these titles deny the pure genius of poets like John Wieners, . . . till such books as this emerge from obscurity of decades, to reveal the true light of genius in the poem."

PRINCIPAL WORKS: The Hotel Wentley Poems, 1958 (rev. ed. 1965); Of Asphodel, In Hell's Despite, 1963; Ace of Pentacles, 1964; Chinoiserie, 1965; Gardenias (For Billie Holiday), 1966; Pressed Wafer, 1967; A Letter to Charles Olson, 1968; Unhired, 1968; Asylum Poems (For my Father), 1969; Youth, 1970; Nerves, 1970; Woman, 1972; Selected Poems, 1972; Playboy, 1972; The Lanterns Along the Wall, 1972; Hotels, 1974; Behind the State Capitol, or Cincinnati Pike, 1975; She'd Turn on a Dime, 1984; Selected Poems 1958–1984, 1986; Cultural Affairs in Boston, 1988.

ABOUT: Contemporary Authors 15–16, 1975: Contemporary Literary Criticism 7, 1977; Contemporary Poets 4th ed., 1985; Dictionary of Literary Biography 16, part 2, 1983; Levertov, D. The Poet in the World, 1973. *Periodicals*—American Book Review March–April 1987; Big Table no. 4, 1960; Book Week January 3, 1965; Contemporary Literature vol. 16, no. 1, Winter 1975; Nation May 31, 1965; New York Times Book Review November 23, 1986; Parnassus Spring–Summer 1973; Times Literary Supplement May 21, 1971.

WILCOX, JAMES (April 4, 1949–), American novelist and short-story writer, writes: "Although I was born and raised in Hammond,

JAMES WILCOX

Louisiana, a small town about an hour's drive from New Orleans, my father was born in England and my mother in Milwaukee, Wisconsin. Since Southern society puts a premium on one's family background, I could not help feeling a little out of the mainstream, having no great-great-grandfathers to boast of who had served in the War Between the States. Indeed, I was looked upon with suspicion in grade school when I ventured to say that the Rebel cause had been tainted by slavery.

"In another area I also felt on the periphery, and this was religion. My father was a Methodist, my mother a Catholic, who had signed a paper promising to raise her children—there turned out to be five—as Catholics. Once I was given a holy card by a nun that caused my father some distress. It was a prayer for the conversion of a Protestant. In high school I became the church organist at the First Methodist Church, where my father was choir director. I couldn't help feeling, even at that late age, that there was something unsettling about helping out at a Protestant service.

"In the South at that time a boy found popularity through sports, mainly football, basketball, and baseball. My father had another agenda in mind for his children. As Head of the Music Department at Southeastern Louisiana College, he wanted each of his children to love music and master at least one instrument. I could not be more grateful to him today, since I now spend many hours at the piano playing Chopin, Ravel, Bach, Prokofiev, Scriabin. At the time, though, in high school, I couldn't help feeling self-

conscious about being the only cellist in the entire student body—indeed, the entire town. In 1964, as a freshman, I became a member of the Baton Rouge Symphony and would drive the forty-five miles up and back from Baton Rouge for evening rehearsals and concerts. The money I earned was saved for college. Strangely enough, though I was a musician who genuinely loved classical music (and secretly despised rock and roll), I did manage to get elected president of the student body and to have many friends.

"In 1967 I went to Yale, a member of the Class of '71. It took me a long while to adjust to school in the East. Not only was I physically cold much of the time, but also I felt a slight chill in the air as far as friendship went. I was miserable, homesick for my friends back home, the warmth of Southern hospitality. When I first arrived on the Old Campus, we were required to wear ties to the dining halls and rather strict parietal hours were enforced. This all changed quite rapidly. Soon the campus was a hotbed of protests and strikes. The Vietnam War, the Bobby Seale trial, the dining hall workers' wages, all of these were hotly debated by students and faculty while the more radical element dodged tear gas. During this time I never lost interest in my studies. My sophomore year I was in a creative writing seminar headed by the Dean of Silliman, John J. E. Palmer, who was also the editor of the *Yale Review*. The year after I was in another creative writing seminar, this time with Robert Penn Warren. Mr. Warren agreed to be my tutor for my senior year project, which was writing a novel. (Mercifully, the novel was never published. It is quite dreadful.) I also wrote lengthy essays on Whittier and Roethke (for Harold Bloom), on Racine's *Athalie* and Revelation, and on the development of language in children and also on the language of schizophrenia.

"In 1971, after being graduated from Yale and spending some time in Europe, I was hired as an editorial assistant at Random House. I was privileged to be working with Albert Erskine, who had been Faulkner's editor, as well as John O'Hara's, Malcolm Lowry's, Eudora Welty's, among others. I assisted Mr. Erskine in the preparation of *Flags in the Dust* from Faulkner's own manuscript and typescript. Later, as an assistant editor and then an associate editor, I worked in conjunction with more senior editors with authors as diverse as Dr. David Reuben, Hunter S. Thompson, James Michener, Hugo Black, Jr., Dr. William Nolen, and Timothy Crouse.

"After one year as an associate editor at Doubleday, I decided that I wanted to devote myself full-time to writing. Even though I had never published anything before, I resigned my post

tion and began supporting myself with part-time jobs while writing one short story after another. When two of these had been accepted by the *New Yorker*, I started my first novel. I have now completed four novels set in Louisiana and am working on my fifth. In 1986 I was a recipient of a Guggenheim Fellowship. "

James Wilcox's Tula Springs, Louisiana is a country of the imagination. Like other fictional communities ranging from Anthony Trollope's Barsetshire to William Faulkner's Yoknapatawpha County, it has a base in its creator's own life. Because Wilcox writes as an American Southerner—drawing his material from a region that has a more distinct definition in American literature than any other part of the United States—he invites comparison with a battalion of modern Southern writers—Faulkner, Eudora Welty, Flannery O'Connor, and, closer to home in Louisiana, Walker Percy and John Kennedy Toole. However, Wilcox's distinction as a writer is at best distantly related to the achievement of any other Southern writer. He is indeed Southern; his characters are shaped in their individuality by the region in which they have their roots. But they owe little to their literary antecedents. It is significant that most reviewers of his novels have singled out for praise characteristics that are universal rather than regional: his sense of comedy ("Mr. Wilcox has real comic genius," Anne Tyler wrote of his first book, *Modern Baptists* in the *New York Times Book Review*) and his compassion for the frailties of human nature ("Foibles, he suggests, aren't what make us weak"; Dan Cryer wrote of *Sort of Rich* in *New York Newsday*, "they make us deeply human").

Modern Baptists introduces Tula Springs and a large cast of characters, many of whom reappear in his later novels. Through this once-prosperous logging town, an abandoned railroad track runs parallel to the main street, now itself reduced to a tin-roofed laundromat, empty store fronts, auto repair shops, and "a shoe store that never has the size you wanted." The town is still nevertheless, a living American community with a nearby shopping mall, a Wal-Mart, a new BurgerMat, and all the other amenities of the 1980s. Its citizens have air-conditioning, television sets, and microwaves. As Michiko Kakutani described Tula Springs in the *New York Times* in 1989, it is "one of those peculiar outposts of the New South—half suburb, half small town, poised between a quickly receding pastoral past and a greedy consumerist future. "

"Bobby" Pickens, the hero—more accurately, the anti-hero—of *Modern Baptists*, is a represen-

tative, almost archetypal character in Wilcox's fictional community. A mild-mannered bachelor of forty-one, he loses his job as assistant manager of the Sonny Boy Bargain Store and briefly entertains the idea of becoming a preacher in a church of his own for modern Baptists: "Baptists who were sick to death of hell and sin being stuffed down their gullets every Sunday. There wasn't going to be any of that old-fashioned ranting and raving in Mr. Pickens's church. *His* Baptist church would be guided by reason and logic." In the course of the novel Bobby learns that human beings simply cannot live by reason and logic, especially if they live in Tula Springs.

Misunderstandings, mistaken identities, and misguided hopes and ambitions are the devices of farce; Wilcox uses these liberally in *Modern Baptists* and the novels that have followed it. Yet, as Anne Tyler observed in her review of this first book: "What makes them work here is that Mr. Wilcox knows exactly how far to take them. " His characters have a genius for little except bungling and muddling their lives. "They're people waiting dismally for something to fall on them, and just about everything does," Tyler writes. Yet they have a remarkable resiliency. Their random mishaps and misadventures prove to be not random but part of a careful design on the author's part. J. O. Tate, in the *National Review*, describes Wilcox's fictional technique as one of "surreal transcription"— giving the illusion of dream, even nightmare at times, but operating within the novelist's carefully controlled realism. Reviewers of his novels have almost unanimously noted and praised his ability to skirt the absurdist and to turn farce and satire into good-natured, even compassionate humor. British reviewers in particular have singled out this quality of good humor in Wilcox's work. Sheila MacLeod wrote, in the *New Statesman*, of *North Gladiola* : "Although all the characters are mocked, they condemn themselves with endearing guilelessness out of their own mouths. Precision without cruelty is rare in humour, but James Wilcox achieves it consistently and with seeming effortlessness. "

Lisa Zeidner observed in a review of Wilcox's second novel, *North Gladiola*, in the *New York Times Book Review*, that unlike writers who tend to portray the modern South in either the grim Gothic manner or with the broad strokes of farce and absurdist humor, Wilcox "has just the right combination of affection for and detachment from his characters for writing comedy." It is a combination that gives him the ability to root his characters so firmly in their social environment that he can bring them to credible life even while portraying them as, at times at least, clowns and buffoons. Essentially, as Francine

Prose pointed out in a review of *Sort of Rich* in the New York weekly *7 Days*, Wilcox is writing comedy of manners: "Reading Wilcox (like Austen or Pym), we are persuaded of how much meaning resides in the mundane, of how emblematic the small gesture may be. The domestic is, after all, the arena in which most of us operate, and the challenge for the novel of manners is to uncover its mysteries, its beauties, its follies, and (perhaps most important) its bravery; to be at once satiric and in awe of the dignity of the ordinary."

To read *North Gladiola* as a comedy of manners is to see how rich in social satire that genre can be. At fifty-seven Mrs. Ethyl Mae Coco—long married, the mother of six, a Catholic convert of ardent but sometimes fragile faith—is trying to bring culture to Tula Springs with a string quartet, the Pro Arts, which plays everything from Mozart and Haydn to the love song from *Dr. Zhivago* and a medley from *Cats*. A diligent cellist herself, she bravely marshals her fellow musicians—among them a forty-nine-year-old Korean graduate student writing a dissertation on the Marxist and Freudian implications of tourism—into engagements at the new local BurgerMat (where opening night is a black-tie affair), Dick's China Nights ("the most expensive restaurant in Tula Springs, offering a variety of Mandarin and Polynesian specialities, along with a full selection of French and traditional American dishes, including diet hot dogs"), the state mental hospital, rodeos, and beauty pageants. She worries about her nearly senile husband, the turbulent lives of her highly individualistic children, her neighbors, a mentally retarded boy, her wavering religious faith, and the collapsing state of the world in general. But, desperate as her situation appears to be, the reader can never abandon hope in her capacity to survive. Reflecting that she would like to receive letters from her children "telling her that everything was fine, everyone missed her and wished she was there," she formulates a theory about hypocrisy: "if you kept pretending long enough and hard enough, your good humor eventually took on a reality of its own and ceased being hypocritical. In a sense this was precisely what the saints did—*willed*, in the face of every sort of suffering and distraction, their good humor, thus making hypocrisy, in a way, the root of all good."

Tula Springs has remained the center of Wilcox's novels of the late 1980s, but the always large cast of characters in his books has been expanded to include a handsome young dental student from New Jersey (in *Miss Undine's Living Room*) and a Radcliffe-educated intellectual from New York (in *Sort of Rich*). As outsiders

they are exposed to culture shock. The heroine of *Sort of Rich*, newly married to the richest man in Tula Springs, has a particularly trying time adjusting herself to the strange and eccentric characters she meets. Both novels have intricate plots—mystery and intrigue based more on misunderstanding than genuine guile; but all the details fall in place at the end. In *Miss Undine's Living Room*, the living room itself, belonging to a retired schoolteacher (who is really *Mrs.* Undine) is the scene where, at the end, four woman vie for the attention of the handsome dentist. Both novels are quite distinctly modern comedies of manners, with hints of murder, suicide, adultery, psychopathology, and political corruption. But a certain elemental good will prevails.

Reviewers for the most part have received each succeeding novel by Wilcox as a stride forward in his work, citing his increasing mastery of plot and characterization. "Each time out," Walter Kendrick wrote of *Miss Undine's Living Room* in the *Village Voice*, "Wilcox gets better—subtler, more complex, closer to the fusion of poetics and joy that makes for the highest comedy." There were, however, some reservations in Rosemary Daniell's review of the same novel in the *New York Times Book Review*: "The story, told from several points of view, answers every question, is fulfilled in almost every detail. Still, some moments ring less true than others." Some of the scenes, she felt, move too swiftly—"as though some emotional steps are missing." Michiko Kakutani, reviewing *Sort of Rich* in the *New York Times*, found in both it and the earlier *Miss Undine's Living Room* "implausible narrative contrivances that turn characters into passive pawns in Mr. Wilcox's hands, and their motivations are clumsily explicated in asides delivered by psychiatrists and friends." She also detected, in the second half of the novel, an effort on the author's part "to explore some of the more somber aspects of life in Tula Springs."

PRINCIPAL WORKS: Modern Baptists, 1983; North Gladiola, 1985; Miss Undine's Living Room, 1987; Sort of Rich, 1989.

ABOUT: Contemporary Authors 125, 1989. *Periodicals*—London Review of Books March 1, 1984; National Review August 23, 1985; New Statesman August 30, 1985; New York Times June 13, 1989; New York Times Book Review July 31, 1983; June 30, 1985; October 8, 1987; May 28, 1989; 7 Days May 17, 1989; Newsweek June 10, 1985; Times Literary Supplement June 29, 1984; Village Voice August 25, 1987.

WILLIAMS, THOMAS (ALONZO) (November 15, 1926–October 23, 1990), American novelist and short-story writer, contributed the following autobiographical statement to *World Authors*: "I was born in Duluth, Minnesota. My mother was a Marvin—a family that more or less founded the town and constituted much of its churchly and commercial gravity. My father's family had originally come from Duluth, but he was born in Glendive, Montana, in 1896. When he was about six his father, who did something for the railroad, disappeared on business in San Francisco. His mother, Addie Wilkinson Williams, by all accounts a fine and heroic woman, sold the horses (she had lost the house and never got the insurance money), and took her five living children back to Duluth and raised them. My father, being the oldest boy, had to work and his schooling was spotty, though he later did many things in business, was a newspaper editor and owner, was head of swimming instruction for the state, was an accountant, a columnist ('Just a Thinkin',' by Tom A. Williams), a justice of the peace, and finally in middle-age went to theological school and became a Protestant minister in Pasadena, California, where he raised another family. My mother went to Macalester College. My parents were divorced when I was ten and my mother went to New York City where, after many adventures, she met and was later married to a failed professor (Ph.D. Heidelberg) and political candidate (City Fusion Party) who was a member of an ancient New Hampshire family named Clough. He was designated by his family to return to Lebanon, New Hampshire to save the family lumber business, which was on the verge of bankruptcy. He didn't want to do this, but he did, and in fact made quite a lot of money. He died at forty-three of cancer of the brain, leaving my mother enough money so that she could spend and travel and generously give until she died in 1983 in Arizona at the age of eighty-three, nearly broke.

"I mention these events because they seem to have enhanced and mystified my relationship to my country, my times, and to my own life. I must also mention an uncle and aunt who gave this wanderer love and a sense of the possible steadiness of love. There was also my time in the U.S. Army, 1944–1946, here and overseas, and later a marriage that has lasted thirty-five years, and two children now grown up and into their lives. I feel 'American,' though not exactly in the sense my D.A.R. aunt meant when she informed me that I was a 'Mayflower descendant.' It's more that no part or people of my country, no violence, selfishness or generosity, seems alien or far away. Certainly not in New England, where I was taken as a child against my will (as all chil-

THOMAS WILLIAMS

dren are taken against their unconsulted wills), and where I remain. I've never felt that I must document my times; it's more that without being able to help it I embody certain definitions, and if I write well enough everything will somehow be revealed. And so it all comes to language itself. Words, their juxtapositions and interstitial silences—these are the mysteries that make me curious enough to write.

"As for audience, there are those who admire my work, and there are those who rather vociferously don't. It is in this area, where sympathy, or its possibility, meets with theory and just plain dislike, where I am at a loss, and where I've probably spent too much time brooding, and making sterile aphorisms I'll never include in fiction, such as 'Experimentalism is the last refuge of the tin-eared.' This is a weakness and a waste.

"I teach writing and literature at the University of New Hampshire, and have for nearly thirty years. The University has been generous, yet demanding of time. As a person I want to be free to enjoy what is left of a beautiful world, and as a writer I want to be free to work, but from my students come the multitudinous pages I must take to heart or have no heart. So I take what time there is, as we all do."

In 1979 Donald Hall wrote, in the *National Review*: "If I call Thomas Williams the best unknown novelist in America, it is my disingenuous attempt to gain your attention. He is hardly unknown—with seven novels, a book of stories, and one fat prize." The "fat prize" was the 1975 National Book Award for *The Hair of Harold Roux*. Hall was correct in prodding the fiction-reading public, for Williams remained an admired but not widely known novelist. A fellow novelist, Stephen King, observed in *Book World* in 1986: "Thomas Williams is not a name, like that of Philip Roth or Saul Bellow or Joyce Carol Oates. . . . Yet he may be our best living novelist, because of some curious interior tension in the actual creation of his stories—the dirty hammer-and-anvil job of putting words down on pieces of paper."

The actual process of writing intrigued Williams. He was a teacher of writing as well as a practicing novelist, and several generations of students at the University of New Hampshire apparently benefitted from the experience of working with him. The tension to which King refers, the struggle of the novelist to bring order and coherence to experience—real or imagined—is articulated in the opening pages of *The Hair of Harold Roux* where a middle-aging professor-novelist sits in his study, sometime in the early 1970s, trying to write a novel about his past:

> Aaron Benham sits at his desk hearing the wrong voices. The human race he has been doomed to celebrate seems to be trying to prove to him that nothing is worthwhile, nothing at all. He sits in his small study surrounded by the interesting, haphazard fragments of the business of his life—books, stacks of old galley proofs, knives, pencils, pen, typewriter, dictionaries, shelves of old and new quarterly magazines, catalogs, incunabula.

At this moment he despairs for the world, and for the novelist. "But right now it seems to him that his world, with a temporary remission now and then, is departing on a long slide away from any sort of rational middle. . . . Nobody is listening to anybody else. He wonders if he stands between chaos and that other order, the order of death—wonders if there is still a place to stand."

Williams' fictional Aaron Benham never quite resolves the problem, though he writes a transparently autobiographical novel within the novel. (That novel, also titled "The Hair of Harold Roux," is the story of a college student who will someday become a novelist.) But woven into the fabric of *The Hair of Harold Roux* are a series of complex plots and characters, a haunting fairy tale that Benham spins for his young children, Aaron's own stable but troubled marriage, the problems of one of his students who is on drugs, and those of a colleague who will be denied ten ure because he cannot bring himself to write a doctoral dissertation. And the novel inside this novel introduces a large group of characters with

their own problems, not least of whom is the other would-be novelist, Harold Roux, prematurely bald and wearing the wig that gives both novels their title. Complicated and confusing as all this seems, Williams managed to write a lucid book—"an entertaining, skilfully organized novel," the reviewer for the *Times Literary Supplement* judged it. "None of the multitudinous characters is miniaturized," R. V. Cassill wrote in *Book World*. "All the scenes are fully wrought, not merely exploited for chance lines, contrasts, or quick effects. Everywhere the language flows from the purest vernacular to the elevation demanded by distilled perceptions. Our largest sympathies are roused, tormented and consoled."

Although this novel won high praise, Williams was correct in pointing out that there are those who "rather vociferously" dislike his work. The reception of most of his books has swung between enthusiastic admiration and cautious reserve with a few outright condemnations. One weakness cited is his tendency to assume moral stances that some reviewers regard as self-indulgent or sentimental. His love stories, though often narrated with explicit sexual detail, are romantic, almost idyllic. Even his first novel, *Ceremony of Love*, which drew heavily on his experiences in occupied Japan after World War II, appealed to Herbert Mitgang in the *New York Times* as a romance showing "possibilities [that] intrigue the imagination," though otherwise he found the novel awkward and melodramatic. Perhaps Williams' most severe critic was the late John Gardner who, in the *New York Times Book Review* in 1977, referred to him as "more a preacher and entertainer than a serious novelist." Gardner, however, was reviewing a novel unique among Williams' works, an allegorical fantasy, *Tsuga's Children*, which is an expansion of the bedtime tale Aaron Benham tells his children in *The Hair of Harold Roux*.

Except for his first novel and *Tsuga's Children*, almost all of Williams' fiction is set in Leah, New Hampshire, an imaginary New England town explored so thoroughly that some reviewers call it his Yoknapatawpha County. *Town Burning*, Williams' second novel, centers on the difficulties of adjustment of a World War II veteran who returns to a small New Hampshire town after living in Paris. Chad Walsh, in the *New York Herald Tribune Books*, called it "an authentic picture of northern New England." The same town, Leah, is the scene of *The Night of Trees*, in which a father and son, returning for a hunting trip, both of them at critical periods in their lives, find some self-definition and a kind of meaning

Williams' first real critical success was *Whipple's Castle*, a chronicle of a family whose lives in this town are traced from the depression through the years of World War II and the Korean War. Richard Rhodes, in *Book World*, hailed this novel as "a masterpiece . . . [that] speaks to the American experience of place and local tradition which our urban fiction has recently neglected. . . . Williams [writes] coolly, from the deepest resources of reason, from a kind of post-analytic health of the imagination." In *The Followed Man* he again brought his hero, a desperately unhappy man trying to recover from the deaths of his wife and children in an air crash, back to New Hampshire to confront his past. Donald Hall, in the *National Review*, pronounced this book "Williams' best novel, strong, beautiful, and harrowing."

There was a gap of eight years between *The Followed Man* and *The Moon Pinnace*. The time was obviously well spent in shaping and maturing his art because the novel was widely praised as his best work to date. Leah is again the scene, and the main narrative line is a romantic love story which begins in 1948 with the hero, returning from college and service in World War II, falling in love with a local girl who is bright and capable, but already trapped in her drab lower-middle-class milieu. A single summer changes the destinies of the lovers. The young man drives his motorcycle out west, where he discovers his father and a half-sister of whose existence he had been unaware. The young woman works as the manager of a lakeside resort where she encounters a group of bizarre European emigrés. At the end of the summer, the two young people are reunited, mature and convinced of their love. The novel ends with a brief scene some thirty-six years later. Long and still happily married, the couple go sailing on a lake, and the hero reflects on his life and on the life of his country: "He can't define his country because it is the air he breathes, the water (becoming acidic, oh, woe) he swims in. In a way, he and Dory are his country. He even has a battle star for having fought for it. . . . But his country, his life—how can he define it, them? A black man or woman can now take a leak in Utah; that's no small thing. Hold on to that."

"Mr. Williams's fictional strategy is not always successful," Christopher Lehmann-Haupt wrote in the *New York Times*. The "moral focus" of the novel is at times obscure and there is "near sentimentality" and excessive violence. Still, Lehmann-Haupt concludes, "his characters are wonderfully solid and individual on the page, especially his New Hampshirites. His prose aches with its tenderness for human vulnerability." For Stephen King *The Moon Pinnace* was re-markable for its transformation of a sentimental love story into real literature: "To make something real and rewarding from this bunch of hoary American clichés is the risk Williams takes; his success is breathtaking. He takes the stuff of all those hokey postwar B-movies and turns it into a love story that is both artistic and as sweetly artless as its main characters." The "moon pinnace" of the title refers to a small boat shaped like a crescent moon. It alludes also, through its Latin translation *phaseolus lunatus*, to the lima bean (*Phaseolus limensis*), a vegetable which has a curiously symbolic role in this novel.

Williams published a number of short stories in *Esquire*, the *New Yorker*, *Kenyon Review*, and other journals. Some of these were selected for the *O. Henry Prize Stories* and *Best American Short Stories*. He had a Guggenheim Fellowship and a Dial Fellowship for fiction in 1963 and a Rockefeller grant for creative writing in 1968. He was married in 1951 to Elizabeth May Blood; they had a daughter and a son.

PRINCIPAL WORKS: *Novels*—Ceremony of Love, 1955; Town Burning, 1959; The Night of Trees, 1961; Whipple's Castle, 1969; The Hair of Harold Roux, 1974; The Followed Man, 1978; The Moon Pinnace, 1986. *Short stories*—A High New House, 1963.

ABOUT: Contemporary Authors New Revision Series 2, 1981; Contemporary Literary Criticism 14, 1980; Who's Who in America 1987–1988. *Periodicals*—Book World (Washington Post) January 26, 1969; May 19, 1974; July 6, 1986; Esquire July 1974; National Review January 19, 1979; New York Herald Tribune Books October 25, 1959; November 26, 1961; New York Times June 5, 1955; July 1, 1986; New York Times Book Review May 15, 1977; Times Literary Supplement June 6, 1975.

WILSON, A(NDREW) N(ORMAN) (October 27, 1950–   ), British novelist, biographer, editor, and critic, was born in Stone, Staffordshire, the son of Norman Wilson, a director of the Wedgwood pottery firm, and the former Jean Dorothy Crowder. He was at first sent to school in Stone to Roman Catholic Dominican nuns, an experience he found painful, then to a preparatory school in Great Malvern, Worcestershire, that he found even more unpleasant, and finally to Rugby. He read English at New College, Oxford, taking his degree in 1972. The previous year, still an undergraduate, he married Katherine Duncan-Jones, a woman considerably his senior and one of the most brilliant dons in Oxford, a specialist in Renaissance English literature, fellow of Somerville College, and

A. N. WILSON

niece of the undisputed ruler of the English faculty, Professor Dame Helen Gardner.

Wilson won two university awards, the Chancellor's essay prize in 1971 and the Ellerton prize in theology in 1975. He had an extensive but somewhat unfocused teaching career throughout the 1970s, first for the Edward Greene tutorial agency, then as freelance tutor for St. Hugh's and New colleges, finally as junior English master at the Merchant Taylors' School. In 1973 he began studies for the Anglican priesthood at St. Stephen's House, but abandoned that intention after a year.

Wilson's extremely prolific published literary career began in the late 1970s and has continued unabated into the 1990s, often at the rate of more than a book a year. His authorial stance, always very salient in his works, combines a critical, satiric view of British society with a marked disinclination to sympathize with his characters, who often act foolishly, unreflectively, and against what one would consider their best interests. He does not scruple to conceal his politics, which could be described as old-style Tory and strongly anti-Socialist, or his religion, High Church Anglicanism.

The first of Wilson's many novels was *The Sweets of Pimlico*, which explores the strange, asexual attraction between a young Englishwoman and an elderly German aristocrat. It introduces many of the themes that have recurred in Wilson's fiction, including class obsession, homosexuality and its place in English society, and the varied nuances between types of Catholicism, Anglo- and Roman religious themes were

uppermost in Wilson's next two novels, *Unguarded Hours* and *Kindly Light*, both of which chronicle the career of the hapless Norman Shotover, who pursues a clerical life for lack of any more pressing vocation, after meandering equally aimlessly through a few years at university. The extremely eccentric minor characters in these novels demonstrate the author's great skill at such comic creations; these include a few severely alcoholic clergymen, harmlessly lunatic aristocrats, and extremist academics. Reviewing *Unguarded Hours* in the *Times Literary Supplement*, Michael Neve called the author "a gentle Anglican moralist."

The Healing Art was said to break new ground for Wilson in terms of his being able to demonstrate empathy for his principal characters, but their comic foolishness usually claims the upper hand. It is the story of Pamela Cowper, an Oxford don mistakenly told in a medical-bureaucratic muddle that she is dying of cancer—she is in fact in perfect health, while Dorothy, a working-class woman treated at the same time, wastes away amid smug medical reassurance. The novel concentrates on Pamela, her High Church connections, a lesbian affair, and her eventual marriage to a priest nicknamed Sourpuss, while Dorothy, greatly condescended to by her family, the medical profession, as well as the author, is allowed to expire in gruesome, unedifying misery.

In *Who Was Oswald Fish?*, the city council of Birmingham has decided to demolish a nineteenth-century church in the Gothic Revival style, the only surviving work of the obscure Oswald Fish. The architect's reputation thus enjoys a revival of interest, and through his rediscovered, scandalous diaries most of the novel's characters are shown to be part of his family tree. Douglas Dunn in *Encounter* called this novel "a study, both comic and pathetic, of families and interrelationships, of the bizarre weave of English life extending into Europe and the Empire, with its tragedies, ambitions, pettiness, contrasts and extremes, a family saga in shorthand." A. S. Byatt, however, writing in the *Times Literary Supplement*, referred to her distaste for the book and for Wilson's work in general: " it is not really a novel so much as a sort of candy-floss with a bitter after-taste. A. N. Wilson displays a gossipy, sneering contempt for his world, his characters and his readers. . . . he is somehow frivolously merciless. . . . He treats life and death with a flip sneer. His reputation is now considerable. I don't quite understand why."

Wise Virgin is the grim yet comic story of Giles Fox, a Miltonic figure, a British librarian and scholar who is blind, a widower, working

wives to death and his eyesight to disease. He is attracted to his new research assistant, and soon comes to love her. He places great trust in his work and in his virginal daughter, but his book, when it appears, is cruelly dismissed by academic reviewers and his daughter falls hopelessly in love with a scheming homosexual. Bruce Allen in the *Christian Science Monitor* called Wilson "a novelist who knows his business" and the novel "a formidably skillful book." Peter Prescott in *Newsweek* agreed: "In presenting his comedy, Wilson never stoops for a broad effect, never lays calamities upon his characters. Instead, while cutting down their fondest hopes, he takes pains to show how their discomforts arise from what these people are."

Scandal; or, Priscilla's Kindness concerns a plot to destroy the fast-rising political career of Derek Blore, government minister, involving a prostitute and incriminating photographs. The affair becomes a national scandal despite the efforts of Blore's beautiful and saintly wife, Priscilla. The characters' sexual peculiarities are typically made much of, yet the author's usual comic verve occasionally seems to falter in the face of such welters of sinfulness. Whitney Balliett in the *New Yorker* called *Scandal* "full of fine Dickensian figures modernized. . . . Wilson ticks off a lot of things—the English caste system, greed, stupidity, cruelty, and hypocrisy." Michael Wood in the *New York Times Book Review* thought this book "a little tired, slacker than Mr. Wilson's earlier novels. But at its best his writing combines, to adapt a phrase from the book, an arrogant beauty with a sense of its own comedy."

Wilson's next novel, *Gentlemen in England: A Vision*, broke new ground in his treatment of English society. Set in middle-class Victorian England, it revolves around the Nettleship family and the extreme emotional turmoil which besets them. The father, a geologist, has lost his faith in God, and his wife has not spoken to him for fifteen years. Their children, as unhappy as their parents, attempt unsuccessfully to understand their muddled world. The humor here is muted, the tone of Victorian pastiche at times clearly overpowering it. The book did not please all its reviewers. Laurie Spector Sullivan, writing in *Library Journal*, claimed to discern a "curiously leaden tone" pervading it: "it may be the attempt at arch humor, but it has a soporific effect." John Sutherland in the *Times Literary Supplement* complained about Wilson's fiction in general: reading his novels, he wrote, "is an unrelaxing experience. They do not seem to like us very much and one constantly strains to catch the tone." Yet he admired the book, calling it "an admirable historical fiction from a writer who

must by now be considered foremost in his generation."

Love Unknown, Wilson's ninth novel, is set in London and Paris as it follows the lives of three Englishwomen from young adulthood into middle age, dealing with the author's usual themes of friendship, love, and infidelity. Webster Schott in the *New York Times Book Review* called it "a traditional English comic novel that escapes its boundaries. It becomes an acidic commentary on sex, love, and religion." John Melmoth, however, in the *Times Literary Supplement*, criticized it for being "so self-conscious that it lacks any real sense of its own identity. . . . too esoteric in its concerns, too cool for comfort, it musters style in the place of substance, ambivalence in the place of complexity." *Incline Our Hearts* is narrated by a sour young man, a middle-class snob; the novel attains a certain Proustian tone, though not Proust's intensity, by the narrator's realization, in the words of David Nokes in the *Times Literary Supplement*, that "the *dramatis personae* of childhood are as much creations of the imagination as of the memory." A sequel, *A Bottle in the Smoke*, carries the narrator out into his first jobs and his first marriage, achieving a mixture of comedy and sadness, and a third volume is promised.

As a biographer, Wilson has shown himself almost as productive and indefatigable as in his fictional efforts. *The Laird of Abbotsford: A View of Sir Walter Scott* "is an attempt," the author declares in the preface, "to read Scott's life and work as complementary to one another. Between the work and the life, as between the works themselves—poems, historical novels and medieval romances—I find harmonies where other critics see only unevenness and discord. . . . No one can meditate on Scott for long without a sense that life is richer and fuller for his having lived; that his sheer goodness, as a man and as an artist, have permanently extended the limits which human genius and virtue may hope to touch." There are chapters on Scott's religion, his heroines, his medievalism, and his critics, on his belief in love and friendship and on his ideal of the man of action. Wilson is always fair to and admiring of his subject, but honest as well, as when he criticizes Scott's "obsession with the past, his desire to cocoon himself in an artificial world of gothick battlements, tartans and thumbscrews." Despite all Scott's foibles, however, Wilson believes him "the greatest single imaginative genius of the nineteenth century." According to the reviewer for the *Economist*, "After all the ingenious analysis of Scott's intellectual standing of the past 50 years, Mr. Wilson is content to enjoy him. Few books of literary criticism in this disillusioned age have been so full of infectious enthusiasm." Wilson edited Scott's *Ivanhoe* for the Penguin Classics series in 1982.

Wilson's *The Life of John Milton* is a short, pithy biography, surveying his subject from his London boyhood in Bread Street through the majestic compositions of his maturity to his old age, blindness, and death. Scholars of seventeenth-century literature, and especially Miltonists, judged the book harshly. For Christopher Hill, writing in the *New Statesman*, the book was "jauntily" written, but "begins to stumble" when dealing with Milton's political career: "Factual errors abound. . . . Mr. Wilson's own aesthetic contempt for political commitment makes him want to deny it to the poet. . . . For [Milton] the English Revolution was God's Cause. This conviction was central to his life, and therefore to his poetry."

Hilaire Belloc is a much longer and apparently more deeply researched biography. Belloc, a Roman Catholic man of letters and one of the most popular and controversial English writers of the early twentieth century, is hardly remembered today; even many English Roman Catholics are deeply embarrassed by the recollections of his discreditable views. Wilson admires him extravagantly: "His greatness really consisted not even so much in what he said as in what he was. There was no one else in the history of the world remotely like him. He was more strongly, more vigorously, more riotously, more intolerably *himself* than almost any other human being. . . . The experience may be crude, but it is unforgettable." This crudeness—Belloc's liking for blatant effrontery, his extreme political heterodoxy and intolerance, his violently expressed anti-Semitism—is given full expression, as are also the refined qualities of the man's writings, both prose and poetry, and the extent to which Belloc was apparently loved by his many friends. The biography was generally well received, although Wilfred Sheed in the *New York Times Book Review* criticized the author for "repeating his favorite quotes and anecdotes once too often, which suggests that he . . . may have gone light on his research; and he tends, in a style common to recent pop biographies, to summarize his subject's character traits again and again, long after we seem to have got a good grasp on them." Noel Annan, in the *Times Literary Supplement*, wrote that Wilson "confounds criticism of Belloc by the frankness with which he draws attention to Belloc's intolerable failings and the shrewdness by which he makes them intelligible." In 1984 Wilson edited Belloc's *The Four Men* (1912), which Bernard McCabe in the *New York Review of Books* called "an unaccurate

tively whimsical and loquacious celebration of Sussex" full of "a false Edwardian heartiness about the ways of country folk."

In preparation for his biography *Tolstoy* Wilson spent several years acquiring a reading knowledge of Russian. His interest in the great Russian began, he notes at the beginning of the lengthy book, in 1967 "when I heard R. V. Sampson [author of *Tolstoy : The Discovery of Peace*, 1973] talking about Tolstoy. . . . I was amazed that anyone could speak of a novelist as if he were divine, but pretty quickly became excited by the Tolstoyan ideas which Professor Sampson expounded. That excitement, and that amazement, continue to this hour. I have never got over Professor Sampson's lecture." He goes on to write in the foreword of Tolstoy's being born into "the very highest social rank," a fact which allowed him, all his life, the freedom to speak his mind to Russia's often tyrannical rulers without suffering the severe punishment accorded to other rebels. "At various points in the last two decades of his life it seriously began to look as though Tolstoy's was the only voice which the Russian Government did not dare to muzzle. So long as he was there, huge numbers of Russians felt that it was not quite impossible to believe in the prospect of individual liberty, the survival of individual dignity in the face of a cruel, faceless, bureaucratic tyranny. . . . In Tolstoy, successive Tsars and their advisers recognised that they had a literary monument too large to dislodge." The biography was received unfavorably by several critics. Sara Maitland, in the *New Statesman*, complained that "Wilson finds Tolstoy silly. . . . It is very odd to commit yourself to over 500 obviously conscientiously researched pages on someone whom you think is a misguided nit-wit. . . . The book is riddled with petty sneers, [and] in short, is not a lot of help for anyone who wishes to engage with the complex history of Russian 19th-century radicalism, or with the vast and complex personality of Tolstoy." Paul Stuewe, in *Quill & Quire*, thought that Wilson had "badly overreached himself. . . . His tone is often irritatingly flippant— all opportunities for punning and word-play are aggressively embraced. . . . Most damningly, no coherent portrait of the Russian writer emerges." On the other hand, the *Economist* reviewer had high praise for the book, calling it "among the most impressively intelligent biographies ever written."

Wilson's characteristic fascination with complex and ambivalent subjects drew him next to C. S. Lewis, whose distinguished scholarship in medieval and Renaissance literature is less widely appreciated today than his children's books (the Narnia chronicles) and his writings on reli-

ics, morality, and religion. It is the latter that have transformed the reticent Oxford don into a kind of cult figure, and, pursuing that paradox, Wilson travelled to Illinois (where there is a Lewis archive-museum at Wheaton College) and to Monrovia, California, where a local Episcopal church has a stained glass window in his memory. Although he had never met Lewis, Wilson had the Oxford background requisite to place him in his academic context. The result is a biography, *C. S. Lewis*, that emphasizes the paradox of Lewis' character and reputation. Wilson writes: "This phenomenon can only be explained by the fact that his writings, while being self-consciously and deliberately at variance with the twentieth century, are paradoxically in tune with the needs and concerns of our times." Wilson's treatment of his subject is at once iconoclastic—challenging "the image of an evangelical Lewis," ascetic and celibate—and sympathetic, with high praise for his literary histories and respect for his personal and spiritual struggles. "We do Lewis no honour to make him into a plaster saint," he writes, "and he deserves our honour." *C. S. Lewis* was well received. David Nokes, in the *Times Literary Supplement*, found it "lively, witty, and written with Wilson's customary flair." Comparing the book to many others that have been published on Lewis, Penelope Fitzgerald observed, in the *New York Times Book Review*, that none of these "have been as brilliant or as edgily sympathetic as this one." And Christopher Lehmann-Haupt concluded his review in the *New York Times* : "In allowing one to glimpse that myriad-eyed self, Mr. Wilson has written a biography that is literature."

In addition to his adult novels, Wilson has produced books for young readers. *Stray* is written from the point of view of Pufftail, a proud old alley cat who is telling the appalling yet intriguing story of his eventful life to his grandson. The author enters the minds and feelings of his feline characters with remarkable ease; he writes on the book's dust jacket, "I can think of many ways in which I would be a better person if I were more like my cats. But I cannot think of a single way in which my cats would be any better for being more like me. *Tabitha* is a collection of stories about Pufftail's daughter. David Profumo, in the *Times Literary Supplement*, wrote of *Stray*: "it is a measure of A. N. Wilson's psychological subtlety that after twenty chapters of his feline biography the present reviewer (if not an ailourophobe, then a confirmed cynic and dog-lover) found he had been converted."

Wilson has also written High Church apologetics: *How Can We Know: An Essay on the Christian Religion* and, a collaborative effort with Charles Moore, editor of the *Spectator*, and

Gavin Stamp, architecture critic: *The Church in Crisis*. Thirty-nine of Wilson's miscellaneous pieces, written over ten years and most originally published in the *Spectator* (of which weekly he was in 1981–1983 literary editor) appeared as *Penfriends from Porlock* in 1988. In 1989 he did a series of television documentary programs for the *BBC*, "Eminent Victorians," the title and theme borrowed from Lytton Strachey's iconoclastic work; these programs were the basis for Wilson's 1990 book.

The author won the John Llewelyn Rhys memorial prize twice, in 1978 for *The Sweets of Pimlico* and in 1981 for his Scott biography. *The Healing Art* is his most prize-winning work to date, taking in 1981 the Somerset Maugham award, the Southern Arts prize, and the Arts Council National Book award. *Wise Virgin* won the W. H. Smith literary award in 1983. Wilson was elected a fellow of the Royal Society of Literature in 1980.

PRINCIPAL WORKS: *Fiction*—The Sweets of Pimlico, 1977; Unguarded Hours, 1978; Kindly Light, 1979; The Healing Art, 1980; Who Was Oswald Fish?, 1981; Wise Virgin, 1982; Scandal, 1983; Gentlemen in England, 1985; Love Unknown, 1986; Incline Our Hearts, 1988; A Bottle in the Smoke, 1990. *Juvenile fiction*—Stray, 1987; Tabitha 1989. *Non-fiction*—The Laird of Abbotsford, 1980; The Life of John Milton, 1983; Hilaire Belloc, 1984; How Can We Know, 1985; (with C. Moore and G. Stamp) The Church in Crisis, 1986; The Lion and the Honeycomb, 1987; Tolstoy, 1988; Penfriends from Porlock, 1988; C. S. Lewis, 1990. Eminent Victorians, 1990. *As editor*—Scott, W. Ivanhoe, 1982; Stoker, B. Dracula, 1983; Belloc, H. The Four Men, 1984.

ABOUT: Contemporary Authors 122, 1988; Dictionary of Literary Biography 14, 1983; Who's Who 1989–1990. *Periodicals*—America September 17, 1983; American Scholar Autumn 1985; Atlantic September 1984; Book World July 1986; Choice November 1980, June 1983, January 1985; Christian Science Monitor November 29, 1983; January 11, 1985; March 19, 1986; August 5, 1987; Commentary November 1984; Commonweal October 5, 1984; Economist June 28, 1980; February 5, 1983; April 28, 1984; July 23, 1988; Encounter January 1982, July–August 1983; Library Journal May 15, 1983; July 1983; November 1, 1983; September 15, 1984; October 1, 1984; February 1, 1986; May 15, 1987; August 1988; Nation December 3, 1983; New Republic May 23, 1983; March 17, 1986; New Statesman August 22, 1980; October 23, 1981; October 29, 1982; January 21, 1983; September 16, 1983; May 4, 1984; September 6, 1985; June 3, 1988; New York Times March 12, 1986; May 16, 1987; August 10, 1988; January 10, 1989; February 19, 1990; July 6, 1990; New York Times Book Review November 27, 1983; September 2, 1984; February 17, 1985; March 9, 1986; June 14, 1987; August 28, 1988; February 26, 1989; February 18, 1990; New York Review of

Books November 7, 1985; November 24, 1988; February 19, 1990; New York Times Book Review February 18, 1990; Newsweek October 31, 1983; September 12, 1988; New Yorker January 14, 1985; Quill & Quire October 1988; Saturday Review November–December 1984; Times December 5, 1983; November 5, 1984; March 17, 1986; June 8, 1987; August 15, 1988; Times Literary Supplement October 3, 1980; October 23, 1981; November 5, 1982; February 4, 1983; September 9, 1983; April 27, 1984; November 5, 1984; September 6, 1985; August 29, 1986; April 3, 1987; January 15, 1988; September 2, 1988; February 16, 1990; August 31, 1990; World Literature Today Spring 1985.

WILSON, AUGUST (April 27, 1945–   ), American playwright, was born in Pittsburgh, Pennsylvania, the son of Daisy Wilson, a fiercely determined, hard-working black woman who had moved to Pittsburgh from North Carolina and who gave her six children a positive racial identity as well as keeping them healthy, fed, and educated, all from the confines of a cold-water, walk-up apartment in a poor section of the city. His father, for whom he was named, was white, of German extraction, a baker by trade, and an infrequent, sporadic presence in the household.

The youth's school days were not a successful experience. Raised a Catholic, he found his brief attendance at parochial high school especially brutal: "I started," he explained in 1984 to Michael Feingold in an interview in the *Village Voice*, "at Central Catholic High School. . . . I was the only black in the school, first of all. . . . [It] was really the first time I had confronted anything like racism, actually. I would come to school and there would be a note on my desk that said 'Go home, nigger.' And every morning, like clockwork, I would just pick it up and throw it away. . . . It wasn't a very good experience. I got into a lot of fights. One particular day there was, like, forty-some kids waiting outside after school for me, the principal had to send me home in a cab. And I just said, this is not what I want to do, I don't care to go to school here." Transferring to the local public high school, he soon had an equally alienating experience. His new history teacher, upon reading a paper on Napoleon which Wilson had written, gave him a grade of A+/F, telling him he did not believe the boy could have written it, and that the failing grade would stand unless he could prove he did. The young writer threw the paper into the wastebasket and simply stopped going to school in protest at this injustice.

A dropout at fifteen, Wilson began working at a succession of menial jobs, but he had already, at least three years earlier, discovered the liter-

AUGUST WILSON

ary riches of the public library. He read the works of Ralph Ellison, Langston Hughes, and Richard Wright; these and other American writers constituted his real education. In 1965 his sister Freda, then a student at Fordham University, sent him twenty dollars for having written for her a term paper, "Two Violent Poets: Carl Sandburg and Robert Frost." With the money he bought his first typewriter, turning another corner as a serious writer. The first thing he typed was his own name—"to see what it would look like in print," he remarked later. He was reading heavily in American poetry, and eventually succeeded in having some of his own work published in the little magazines *Black World* (Summer 1971) and *Black Lines* (September 1972).

Caught up in the explosion of black consciousness of the late 1960s, Wilson came to consider himself a black nationalist, and still does. In 1968, with the playwright Rob Penny, he founded a troupe in Pittsburgh called Black Horizons Theatre in order "to politicize the community," he said in 1987 in an interview with Samuel G. Freedman in the *New York Times Magazine*. "I wasn't writing any plays then. I was directing—I mean, I didn't know how to do that either. I'd never even seen a play. We did Baraka, we did Bullins, we did whoever was out there during that brilliant time. I didn't even think about writing one myself until much later." The angry, didactic works of the black theater of the 1960s and early 1070s contrast starkly with the theatrical voice that Wilson developed later in his deeply introspective examinations of the black experience in America.

After a visit to St. Paul, Minnesota, in 1978 to visit Claude Purdy, a friend who had worked in the theater in Pittsburgh before becoming director of Penumbra, a black theater group in St. Paul, Wilson himself moved to Minnesota, attracted by its friendly, relaxed atmosphere. He obtained a job almost immediately, of a sort any aspiring playwright would delight in: writing plays for a small theater troupe established in the anthropology wing of the Science Museum of Minnesota. He recalls having trouble in those days with dialogue: it was "too poetic," he remarked in an interview with ABC correspondent Bob Brown broadcast December 9, 1988, on the program *20/20.* "I was trying to force words into the mouths of characters. I thought you had to change the language in order to make the characters meaningful." "How do you make them talk?" he asked Purdy. "You don't," his friend replied. "You listen to them." Removed from the streets of his youth, he was finally able to hear, clearly and as if for the first time, the strong, cadenced talk of the black people he had grown up among. Michael Feingold remarked in 1984 on the striking disparity between Wilson's "refined, low-toned speech and the flamboyant vernacular of his characters. . . . It's high praise to a playwright's imagination . . . when his lines are memorable in inverse proportion to the likelihood of his saying them himself." His first play, written at Purdy's urging, was *Jitney,* a two-act drama set in a Pittsburgh gypsy-cab company. It received its first performance in his home town in 1982 by the Allegheny Repertory Theater. Another early dramatic work, *Fullerton Street,* also had a Pittsburgh setting. Wilson's first major play, *Ma Rainey's Black Bottom,* had its origin in a record he bought in 1965 of the great blues singer Bessie Smith. He learned that Smith had taken lessons from the blues pioneer Gertrude (Ma) Rainey, whose voice exists for us now on only a few early recordings. The playwright already knew about the importance of the blues in black life. Among his earliest influences, he told *New York Newsday* in 1987, "the blues would be the first. . . . I see the blues as a book of literature and it influences everything I do. . . . Blacks' cultural response to the world is contained in the blues." During the course of the play, Ma Rainey often reflects on the meaning of the blues: "White folks don't understand about the blues. They hear it come out, but they don't know how it got there. They don't understand that's life's way of talking. You don't sing to feel better. You sing 'cause that's a way of understanding life."

The play takes place in March 1927, in a cheap recording studio in Chicago where Ma Rainey has come with her band to record some of her best-known songs. A figure of enormous size and authority, she is temperamental and demanding, treating her white manager, the white record company owner, and the white sound engineer with withering contempt: she knows very well that it is her musical talent that puts money into their pockets. Speaking to Cutler, the elderly trombonist who leads her band, she says of the whites, "Wanna take my voice and trap it in them fancy boxes with all them buttons and dials . . . and then too cheap to buy me a Coca-Cola. And it don't cost but a nickel a bottle. . . . They don't care nothing about me. All they want is my voice. . . . As soon as they get my voice down on them recording machines, then it's just like if I'd be some whore and they roll over and put their pants on. Ain't got no use for me then. I know what I'm talking about." The play's overt theme, the white exploitation of black musical artists, mirrors a second, deeper one: the inability of blacks—and of artists—to make common cause in the face of their exploiters. Each of the band members reflects a different point of view of the way American racism has harmed black people, and the melodramatic violence of the ending affirms the simple fact that some people, like the young black trumpeter Levee, have endured more racism in their lives than is humanly bearable.

Wilson completed *Ma Rainey* in late 1981. It received a staged reading under the auspices of the National Playwrights Conference the following summer at the Eugene O'Neill Theater in Waterford, Connecticut. Wilson became friends with the conference's director, Lloyd Richards, who is also director of the Yale Repertory Theater in New Haven and dean of the Yale School of Drama, and a powerful figure in the American black theater. Richards recalls first thinking of the play's author as "a new voice. A very important one. It brought back my youth. My neighborhood. Experiences I had." Wilson was helped by Richards to polish the play, and it eventually had a successful run in New Haven in 1984. On October 11, 1984, it opened at the Court Theater on Broadway and ran for 275 performances before closing the following June, winning the New York Drama Critics Circle Award for best play of 1984–1985 as well as several Tony nominations. It was published in book form in 1985 by New American Library.

The playwright began writing his next play, *Fences,* before *Ma Rainey* had even been staged at the Yale Repertory. He wrote the first scene on a bus from the O'Neill Theater Center in Waterford to New York. "I remember thinking," he said in 1985, "'what do I do now?' So I immediately started *Fences.* I didn't want to allow that pressure to build." With his new project, Wilson revealed his overall aim as a playwright: to tell of the encounter, decade by decade, of the released black slaves and their descendants with a vigorous, ruthless, growing America. *Fences* "encompasses the 1950s," writes Richards in an introduction to the New American Library edition of the play (1986), "and a black family trying to put down roots in the slag-slippery hills of a middle American urban industrial city that one might correctly mistake for Pittsburgh, Pennsylvania." The author precedes the published version of his play with a note in which he compares the treatment accorded "the destitute of Europe" and "the descendants of African slaves" in the great cities of America at the turn of the century. For the Europeans, "the city grew. It nourished itself and offered every man a partnership limited only by his talent, his guile, and his willingness and capacity for hard work. [It was] a dream dared and won true." American blacks, however, "were offered no such welcome or participation. . . . The city rejected them and they fled and settled along the riverbanks and under bridges in shallow, ramshackle houses made of sticks and tar-paper. They collected rags and wood. They sold the use of their muscles and their bodies. They cleaned houses and washed clothes, they shined shoes, and in quiet desperation and vengeful pride, they stole, and lived in pursuit of their own dream. That they could breathe free, finally, and stand to meet life with the face of dignity and whatever eloquence the heart could call upon."

Fences, the final version of which is in two acts and nine scenes, takes place in 1957 (the final scene occurs eight years later). It is about Troy Maxson, son of an Alabama sharecropper, who knows he is a failure and takes his frustration out on everyone around him, including his wife and his young son, Troy, who leaves home at fourteen. Troy learns violence from his father, but also the value of work and the fact that a man must always, come what may, take responsibility for his family. The elder Troy, who works as a garbage collector, is a first-rate amateur baseball player, but he has learned the bitter lesson that even his superior skills in sports are of no value in segregated America. "He learns," writes Richards, "that he must fight and win the little victories that—given his life—must assume the proportion of major triumphs. He learns that day to day and moment to moment he lives close to death and must wrestle with death to survive. He learns that to take a chance and grab a moment of beauty can crumble the intricate fabric of an intricate value system and leave one desolate and alone." In the course of the play he alienates both his son, driving him away from the family house, and his patient wife of eigh-

teen years, by fathering a child by another woman. Yet they both consider Troy the greatest force in their lives, and, in truth, he dominates every facet of the play with a huge, elemental physical presence and strength of character. He sees his hard-working life as an epic battle against Death, with whom he has fought often, titanically, in the past. The play's principal metaphor is the fence which he is constantly preparing to build around his yard, and which he never actually completes. His apostrophe to Death in the middle of Act II is his final, enraged challenge to his lifelong adversary, who has just taken the life of Alberta, the woman who died giving birth to his child:

> Alright, Mr. Death. See now . . . I'm gonna tell you what I'm gonna do. I'm gonna take and build me a fence around this yard. See? I'm gonna build me a fence around what belongs to me. And I want you to stay on the other side. See? You stay over there until you're ready for me. Then you come on. Bring your army. Bring your sickle. Bring your wrestling clothes. I ain't gonna fall down on my vigilance this time. You ain't gonna sneak up on me no more. . . . This is between you and me. Man to man. You stay on the other side of that fence until you ready for me. Then you come up and knock on the front door. Anytime you want. I'll be ready for you.

Fences took a route to Broadway remarkably similar to that of its predecessor. It received a staged reading in the summer of 1983 in Waterford, its first full-scale performance at the Yale Repertory in 1985, and opened to rave reviews at the 46th Street Theater on March 26, 1987. Before its New York opening, it was produced at the Goodman Theater, Chicago, the Seattle Repertory Theater, and by Carole S. Hays in San Francisco. It took in $12 million in the first year of its New York run, winning the Tony Award, the New York Drama Critics Circle Award, and the American Theater Critics Award for best play of the 1986-1987 season, as well as three other Tony awards and, in April 1987, the 1987 Pulitzer Prize for drama.

As part of Wilson's ambitious plan to write a history in drama of the black experience in America, the play that followed *Fences*, *Joe Turner's Come and Gone*, moves back in time to 1911. Set in a Pittsburgh boarding house, it is the story of Herald Loomis, a large, brooding, mysterious man who has just been released from his bondage of seven years of indentured servitude to Joe Turner (who never appears in the play) for a gambling debt. Herald Loomis turns up at the boarding house with his little daughter. He is seeking his wife who disappeared some years before, and he is also seeking some inner peace that will soothe his rage and restore him to the faith he once had. The other boarders are a married ful-

What holds them together is the distant memory of Africa, slave ships, and the bondage of slavery. Some are holding their own in a working-class society, fighting in their modest way for economic status and dignity. Some are losers; some are simply cheerful survivors; and some have found escape in evangelical religion. All of them have a brief moment of revelation in a powerfully staged and joyous juba dance. Loomis finds his wife and there is some hope that he will someday find his soul, but the ending of the play is unresolved. Produced in New York in the spring of 1988, *Joe Turner's Come and Gone* was generally well received by the critics, but it was not a box office success.

Another of Wilson's plays opened on Broadway in 1990 after several performances at regional theaters. *The Piano Lesson* is set in the 1930s and dramatizes a family conflict over values—a dispute over an old and cherished piano that has symbolic importance to the family but could realize a large sum of money if sold. The play's theme, Wilson told a *Chicago Tribune* interviewer in 1987, is "What do you do with your legacy? There's 130 years of family history in the piano that you see on stage. What does the family do with it?" *The Piano Lesson*, however, is more than a simple domestic drama. As Frank Rich wrote in his review in the *New York Times*, the play "is joyously an African-American play: it has its own spacious poetry, its own sharp angle on a nation's history, its own metaphorical idea of drama and its own palpable ghosts that roar right through the upstairs window of the household where the action unfolds." A critical and popular success, *The Piano Lesson* won Wilson his second Pulitzer Prize and his fourth Drama Critics Circle Award.

Wilson, who has become a millionaire from his writing, can often still be seen, even after all his success, sitting at the end of the bar in Sweeney's Pub in St. Paul, writing on a yellow legal pad and smoking endless cigarettes. "Writing is a solitary occupation," he says "and I fight against being solitary." Among the most profound of the influences on his work are the paintings of the black artist Romare Bearden—both *Joe Turner* and *The Piano Lesson* took their titles from Bearden canvases. For Wilson, the artist represents "the first time I encountered anyone who dealt with black life in a large way. He shows through his work a black life that has its own sense of self, its own fullness, and he does this in terms of myth and ritual. . . . I try to define ritual that's attendant on everyday life, to uncover and expose it. It exists in ordinary life, anyway; you just don't always recognize it." Asked by Brown what he most wanted to be remembered for, Wilson replied, "Honesty. That is the most difficult thing. Being able to face yourself. You must be willing to confront whatever you find there. That's the great thing. You spend years of your life rassling with something you're afraid of and you find that your spirit has gotten larger."

PRINCIPAL WORKS: Ma Rainey's Black Bottom, 1985; Fences, 1986; Joe Turner's Come and Gone, 1988; The Piano Lesson, 1990.

ABOUT: Contemporary Authors New Revision Series 12, 1988; Contemporary Literary Criticism 39, 1986, 50, 1988; Current Biography 1987. *Periodicals*—Chicago Tribune September 16, 1984; October 15, 1984; February 9, 1986; April 10, 1987; June 8, 1987; Christian Science Monitor October 16, 1984; March 27, 1987; Commonweal May 22, 1987; Ebony November 1987; Essence August 1987; Nation December 8, 1984; New Leader April 6, 1987; New York April 6, 1987; New York Newsday October 7, 1984; March 27, 1987; April 20, 1987; New York Post October 12, 1984; March 27, 1987; New York Times April 11, 1984; April 13, 1984; October 12, 1984; October 22, 1984; May 6, 1986; May 14, 1986; June 20, 1986; March 27, 1987; April 5, 1987; April 9, 1987; April 17, 1987; May 7, 1987; April 15, 1990; April 17, 1990; New York Times Magazine March 15, 1987; New Yorker October 22, 1984; Newsweek October 22, 1984; Saturday Review January–February 1985; Time April 27, 1987; Village Voice November 27, 1984; April 7, 1987; Washington Post November 18, 1984; May 20, 1986; April 15, 1987; June 9, 1987; October 4, 1987.

WILSON, WILLIAM S(MITH) (April 7, 1932–   ), American short-story writer, novelist, and essayist, writes: "I was born in Baltimore, Maryland, to a mother, May Grubert, who had stopped school in the ninth grade to go to work, but who continued her self-education the rest of her life, reading the great Russian novels while pregnant with me. She was born into an Irish Catholic family, but left the religion early. When my sister and I were sufficiently grown, she studied art and became a successful artist under the name May Wilson. My father, William S. Wilson, Jr., was born on the then remote Eastern Shore of Maryland, to parents who had left their family religions, and later divorced. He was self-supporting from an early age. Marrying quite young, he went to law school at night in Baltimore, and practiced as a lawyer, active in legislative work for more than sixty years. I started elementary school in Baltimore in a working-class section, still unable to speak clearly because of an impediment; in first grade I received some help in school, and had a tutor at home on Saturday, so that by second grade I could speak intelligibly albeit mechanically. In 1941 we moved to

WILLIAM S. WILSON

a suburb, where I completed grade school and high school. By the end of high school, we lived in outright country, with sheep, chickens, and turkeys, and a large swimming pool which I think influenced my prose style. I started writing a dictionary of operational definitions, wrote the graduation-ceremony pageant, and was president of the senior class. I also acted in two plays in professional summer stock, sufficient experience to see that I had neither talent for nor interest in acting, and not much sympathy for theatricality in art.

"I started at the University of Virginia with thoughts of law school. I enrolled in the remarkable two-year Honors course in philosophy, with no classes, but a two-year history of philosophy. I wrote almost weekly papers, and then a thesis, for my patient tutors, which was useful practice in handling abstract terms. The philosophic training was strongest in critical thinking, with so much logical positivism and empiricism the first year that I brought the second year around to the philosophy of science. I still work out of problems I explored then, and probably read more philosophy than fiction. However, the graceful Nancy Hale was a presence on the Grounds, at every opportunity telling me to read Flaubert, and I did that, once browsing during a fraternity roughhouse and enjoying a moment of illumination that I still draw on.

"I continued on to Yale University for graduate work in English literature, fleeing after the first year. . . . Returning to Yale a year later, I hung on for two years of classes, making visits to friends in New York City, among them the artist Ray Johnson, whose New York Correspondence School of Art has influenced much of my life, and work. The Yale Art Gallery, with its frequent lectures, was a glorious refuge from my problems with the official program in literature. I taught at the University of Delaware for a year, then returned to Yale to write my dissertation on a long poem by Geoffrey Chaucer, reading it as an allegory of the intellectual methods of grammar, rhetoric, and logic.

"In September 1959 I married and started teaching at Bowdoin College, writing stories that were to be parts of a novel that would never be assembled together in one place at one time, and deservedly, they never were. My thinking about fiction was strongly influenced by a passionate attachment to contemporary painting, and was answerable to achievements in the philosophy of science. We moved to New York City where I began teaching at Queens College in 1961. Twin daughters were born and three years later a son. Within a year of his birth, I was a single parent, and quite busy, writing only a few essays on art.

"I had been writing stories and such from childhood, and had won a prize for fiction in college, but only with the encouragement of Joseph McElroy did my stories start to appear. Thirteen were collected in a book, and several have now been translated into French. The titles are usually one uncapitalized word, like a dictionary entry, since I think of each story as defining a word by using it to point with at a complex situation. These stories reflect my interests in scientific and intellectual methods, and the ways in which the methods of thinking produce and shape the object of thought. The stories are a form of science fiction, usually set in an indefinite future. In 1982 I published an epistolary future-fiction Utopian novel, *Birthplace: moving into nearness*, which was nominated for the PEN-Faulkner Award, and called a "philosophic poem" by the *New York Times*. Through these years I have published a group of essays on Chaucer; many essays on contemporary visual artists, and in press are essays on Robert Altman's film, *Nashville*; an essay on the logic of postmodernism, 'And/or: one or the other, or both,' and an essay on Harold Brodkey."

———

"If you are going to know my books," William S. Wilson writes in his short story "métier: why I don't write like Franz Kafka," "you need to know what I know." It is not easy to know Wilson's books, and to aspire to the breadth of his knowledge is a daunting prospect. But to the extent that Wilson's writings are the products of what he knows, the experience of knowing his books is as rewarding as it is demanding. Wilson calls his stories "science fiction," though they rarely adhere to the conventions of that genre. Rather, as the novelist Joseph McElroy has pointed out, they are science fiction in that "the root sense of *science* is *knowing*." In the eighteenth century such writing would have been described as philosophical fiction (*conte philosophique*), not because it upholds a particular philosophy but because it explores the nature of truth and reality, as opposed to stories that attempt to imitate reality. McElroy suggests that "one meaning of Wilson's stories is definition—the setting of . . . limits in the compilation of some dictionary of experience." Wilson suggests still another—that the meaning of his fiction "is in the experience of figuring out how to read it." He writes, in an essay "loving/reading" (*Antaeus*, Autumn 1987): "A writer of fiction, and of poems, renders a reading of existence, for the way that the author's 'reading' is to be read is a model or example or lesson in how existence is to be read. The meaning of writing is the style of reading that it teaches."

Wilson writes that his "passionate attachment" to contemporary art has indeed influenced his fiction. His mother, May Grubert Wilson, was a painter and sculptor, largely self-taught and known especially for her assemblages. Though she did not begin to exhibit professionally until late in her life, she early transmitted her sense of form and color to her son. In an article on Cézanne that Wilson published in *Antaeus* (Spring 1985) he writes of his early years that the great painter's "visual thinking . . . emerged to affect the texture of our daily lives." Cézanne's use of color planes to create effects of space produces a feeling of immediacy that is outside of time and reflects, Wilson writes, his rapport with his world. For Wilson, the writer, like the painter, works with planes: "I read a novel and see that the author has shifted or violated planes, that is, has changed the plane of focus; errors in point of view, in my vocabulary, are violations of the focal plane, as when a writer suddenly goes beyond a speech into the thoughts of a character, into a mental plane . . . The meaning of a work of art seems to me to emerge from the relations among planes—stable or unstable, open or closed, systematic or unsystematic."

The short stories collected in Wilson's first book, *Why I Don't Write like Franz Kakfa*, are definitions, as their one-word uncapitalized titles indicate: "love," "marriage," "men," "women," etc. They are hardly narrative, nor do they introduce recognizable characters; but they are carefully constructed and move forward with a sometimes deadly logical progression.

McElroy aptly describes them as "haunted essays which seem to say a story should be as well written as an essay, thought through as thoroughly as it is thought up." They focus on the limits of meaning, as definitions do, with the logic and precision of mathematical theorems. The story "love" is a dialogue in which the lovers explore the logical possibilities of their relationship. One argues that love is an illusion; therefore, it cannot exist. The other argues that because we feel it, love exists: "It feels objective to me. I am constrained to think of you in a certain way, and I have feelings for you, new feelings, which are like theorems that come into existence as they are proved. We don't have our feelings until we examine them and find out what they are." In "marriage" a man and a woman are joined by delicate surgery that literally makes—and therefore entraps—them as one; and in "men" a man is so driven by his passion for knowledge that he seeks "to know how it feels to witness my own death." He submits to the gradual amputation of his bodily parts as "an introduction into the discontinuations and discontinuities of death." The story "métier" takes the form of an interview in which the author answers the question "Why is my writing not like Franz Kafka's?" The author is precise, an edge pedantic and sarcastic, but he makes clear that he is his own man and writes like no one else because he writes "in order to find the boundaries of my beliefs—to learn to read how I read existence." His stories mirror nothing: "They are like shards of glass in a glazier's bin, the scraps that fall when a sheet of glass is cut to specifications." All writers, he insists, "will be the source of their own law."

Reviewers of *Why I Don't Write like Franz Kafka* were impressed with "the intellectual texture" (Kenneth Baker's phrase in the *New York Times Book Review*) of Wilson's work, but their judgments on the book ranged from exasperation to qualified approval. J. D. O'Hara, in *Library Journal*, objected that "manner smothers matter; the implications of such themes are left folded, lost in a welter of scientific blather about method," and the *New Yorker*'s reviewer confessed to bafflement: "Wilson has obviously read widely, and his stories often take us into disagreeable corners of knowledge without giving us anything in reward." As sympathetic a reader of Wilson as Joseph McElroy conceded that "there are moments in his stories which Wilson seems to me to have 'made' so much of his experience that we may be too much less aware of a weight of accrued, particular knowledge of the world than we are of the thinking subject's conscious operations. These operations, for all their generous refusal to be secret, tricky, or condescending to the reader, are sometimes so near to domineering that the reader may feel that some thinness or curtailment is being disguised." Nevertheless, McElroy concludes that Wilson's work may herald a new form of fiction which he calls "abstract naturalism": "But whatever we call them, his stories are so firm, so precise, so explicit, and so dialectically rich that they call into question the standards by which most fiction is written."

The publication of Wilson's novel *Birthplace: moving into nearness* and its nomination for a PEN-Faulkner Award confirmed the expectations of his readers that he would move on to fiction of larger dimensions. *Birthplace* is a family history told in the form of letters that are collected in one long letter, the length of the entire novel, written by Salathiel to his grandson Octavio. Himself grandson-son-father, Salathiel is "the librarian of time, able to see and to feel with my hands the shape of things to come ever being reshaped." The integrating theme of the novel, however, is not the family but time itself—not calendar time but the movement of human life toward renewal or rebirth. In an epigraph Wilson quotes Wallace Stevens:

> The accent of deviation in the living thing
> That is its life preserved, the effort to be born
> Surviving being born, the event of life.

Salathiel rejects sequential narrative: "This seems to be a story, Octavio, that had no particular place to start; a story that has changed in the telling, even as the telling has made changes; and a story with no particular place to end. I have tried to tell you of our rapports." Salathiel is an old man, although he has just become a father again, and he has discovered his place in the "historical process" of growth and renewal: "I found my definition of thinking long ago amidst the impurities of a tainted philosopher, Martin Heidegger: *moving into nearness.*" What brings him and his family into this condition is language, "our republic of letters"—the form of communication that unites his family—and, we must assume, humanity. (The novel is divided into two parts significantly titled "Correspondence" and "Coherence.")

Like many so-called "modernist" novels, *Birthplace* is about the act of artistic creation rather than about the acts of its characters. Its "true subject," Jonathan Baumbach wrote in the *New York Times Book Review*, "is the relationship of language to the workings of the imagination." The characters write letters to each other not for immediate communication but for delivery in the future; the letters help them to discover their pasts and to create their futures. They span time from mid-twentieth century to the near future on a calendar invented by Wilson and cover space from Baltimore to a Caribbean island called Primavera on a map invented by Wilson. The writers include, besides Salathiel, his children and grandchildren, all of them named echo-names from Shakespeare, perhaps Virginia Woolf, certainly Wilson's imagination. Orlando is a would-be novelist, Olivia a filmmaker, Aurelia a scientist, Oliver a poet of sorts. From these letters we gradually infer the family's and the island's history, its delivery from a tyrannical patriarch Kwant (who "disallowed plastic, chewing gum, bulkheads, newspapers, floral-print fabrics, and, as he announced one night dramatically, 'semioticians'") by a Mayan Indian Delenda Kinh who appears mysteriously from the sea. Liberated to pursue their interests, the letter writers grow and develop: "They found their lives most real when they discovered in them correspondences with each others' lives. . . . They built relations into rapport—each so different from the others—and they influenced each other so fluctuatingly that the differences among them were always the same differences. . . . "

For all its discontinuities, *Birthplace* is neither obscure nor excessively challenging to a thoughtful reader. It is not, however, emotionally engaging—at least for Caryn James, reviewing it in the *Village Voice*, who wrote: "Wilson tries hard to make us care about these people, but for all its ambitious linguistic devices, *Birthplace* is really someone else's family album, and a little of that goes a long way." Jonathan Baumbach, however, hailed it as "an eccentric, often brilliant first novel." Though he judged it uneven and "self-conscious," falling sometimes into "tedious repetition," Baumbach concluded: "Still, this odd species of experimental fiction sustains itself at an impressively high level much of the time. What moves us in this work are the esthetic qualities and not tragic events, not what happens to the characters but the language and form in which events are revealed. *Birthplace* is a long philosophical poem in the guise of utopian fiction."

Principal Works: *Collected short stories*—Why I Don't Write Like Franz Kafka, 1977. *Novel*—Birthplace: Moving into Nearness, 1982.

About: Contemporary Authors 81–84, 1979. *Periodicals*—Antaeus Autumn 1975; La Nouvelle de Langue anglaise: The Short Story, V: Rencontres internationales, 1988; Library Journal November 15, 1977; New York Times Book Review January 1, 1978; August 8, 1982; New Yorker February 13, 1978; (Village) Voice Literary Supplement December 1989.

WITTKOWER, RUDOLF (June 22, 1901–
October 11, 1971), German-American art historian, was born in Berlin, the son of Henry Wittkower and his wife. He studied at Munich and
Berlin universities, taking his doctorate from the
latter in 1923. After his marriage that same year
to Margot Holzmann, who was to serve as collaborator in many of his published works, the couple spent the next decade in Rome, where he was
assistant and research fellow at the Bibliotheca
Hertziana.

In the mid-1920s Wittkower was commissioned to revise the old Baedeker guide to Rome.
The new edition, published in 1927, required, in
Margot's words, "a re-appraisal not only of all
the Baroque art and architecture but also of delicious *trattorie* and *osterie* in and near Rome." In
addition to this first-hand course in the appreciation of Italian Baroque art and architecture,
Wittkower also found time for collaboration
with the senior scholar Ernst Steinmann on
the monumental *Michelangelo Bibliographie
1510–1926*, published in Leipzig in 1927, as well
as his first of several studies of Gian Lorenzo
Bernini, the Baroque artist the recovery of
whose reputation owes everything to Wittkower's lifelong labor; this preliminary work was
Die Zeichnungen [Drawings] *des G. L. Bernini*.
In the 1970 reprint by Collectors Editions of the
1931 Berlin first edition, Wittkower recalled
that the original enterprise, which he undertook
with the help of his fellow assistant at the Hertziana, Heinrich Brauer, "seemed foolhardy and
could only be explained by infatuation carrying
away two enthusiastic youths. It seemed a bad
augury that [Bernard] Berenson [the greatest art-
historical arbiter of his time but decidedly no
lover of the Baroque], to whom I had shown the
photographic material when the corpus was approaching completion, confessed to feeling
physically sick after having been submitted to
this trial."

Wittkower returned to Germany in 1933 and
served briefly as lecturer in art history at Cologne University, but was forced to relinquish
that post by the Nazi regime. He and his wife
emigrated to Britain, where he immediately
joined the staff of the Warburg Institute. While
in Italy he had met Aby Warburg and Erwin
Panofsky, and had first become aware through
them of the importance of the new ancillary discipline of iconographical studies. Wittkower
taught at the institute from 1934, holding the
Durning-Lawrence professorship in the history
of art at the University of London from 1949 until 1956, when he left to join the art and architecture department of Columbia University. In
New York he was chairman of the department
from his arrival until his retirement in 1969,

RUDOLF WITTKOWER

when he was awarded the emeritus Avalon
Foundation professorship in the humanities.

His publications were at first, as is common
with art historians, somewhat slow in appearing,
but they improved greatly in quantity and originality in the 1950s. He assisted his Warburg colleague Fritz Saxl with *British Art and the
Mediterranean*, a record of a popular photographic exhibition mounted by the institute in
1941, "At a period," according to the authors' introduction, "when inter-European relations
were disrupted by the war, it was stimulating to
observe in the arts of [Britain] the agelong impact of the Mediterranean tradition on the British mind. . . . Every section bears witness to the
extent to which English art is indebted to Greece
and Italy, and should show the fascinating transformation which the foreign elements have undergone as soon as they were introduced." The
small book *Architectural Principles in the Age of
Humanism* "was given," on its initial appearance
in 1949, Wittkower recalls in his preface to the
revised edition (1965), "a very friendly
reception." Kenneth Clark wrote in the
Architectural Review that the book's first result
was "to dispose, once and for all, of the hedonist,
or purely aesthetic, theory of Renaissance
architecture." The author goes on, "This defined
my intention in a nutshell. The book is concerned with purely historical studies of the period 1450 to 1580, but it was my most satisfying
experience to have seen its impact on a young
generation of architects. . . . The structure of
the book is simple. Two chapters on (what constitute in my view) the central problems of Re-

naissance architecture—the meaning of church architecture and the proportional organization of buildings—frame the two chapters on [Leon Battista] Alberti and Andrea Palladio, who were equally great as theorists and practitioners and mark the beginning and end of the period under review."

Wittkower's first important monograph, the relatively short but information-packed *The Drawings of the Carracci in the Collection of Her Majesty the Queen at Windsor Castle*, was begun during World War II at the suggestion of Anthony Blunt. The catalogue, in the author's words, "is concerned with the work of three clearly distinct personalities, whose temperaments, intellectual endowments and artistic aims were different enough. But few critics are, at present, able to discriminate between the three important members of the family," the brothers Agostino and Annibale and their cousin Lodovico, Bolognese artists who were active from the late sixteenth into the first decade of the seventeenth centuries (in the case of the brothers) and to 1619 (in the case of the cousin). The monograph was very well received. Lawrence Gowing, writing in the *New Statesman*, called it "the only discussion in English of the family, and the only study anywhere of Annibale's whole career, as well as an exemplary catalogue. . . . The dust is blown off with a vengeance, and in the drawings Annibale, at least, is seen vividly at very close quarters; so close is he, and so much more comprehensible to us in relation to his times than are the masters of the High Renaissance, that lessons may perhaps be learned here which are now beyond our reach elsewhere."

The author's groundbreaking work on the Carracci was followed only three years later by his most important monograph, *Gian Lorenzo Bernini*. The work's subtitle, *The Sculptor of the Roman Baroque*, indicated the limitation of its approach, but Bernini the sculptor had never before been given a comprehensive treatment in English, and the book's two subsequent revisions have served to confirm and maintain its preeminence. "I have made an attempt," wrote Wittkower, "at interpreting Bernini's sculptural work in the spirit in which, I believe, it was created. He was the most fertile and the most accomplished artistic exponent of seventeenth-century Catholicism, and the strength of his own religious conviction no less than the general fervour of post-Tridentine Catholicism form the background against which his art must be seen." The book is an entirely successful attempt to restore the gleam to the reputation of Bernini as *uomo universale*, an artist of all-around performance "in line of succession to the great Renaissance artists—and probably the last link in that chain."

His fame had sunk very low indeed, as he had predicted, in the two centuries after his death. Indeed, in a famous piece of invective, John Ruskin, contemplating the sculptor's work in the late nineteenth century, declared it "impossible for false taste and base feeling to sink lower." Wittkower comments, "As if this slaughter of a great master's fame upon the altar of dogmatic ideas was not enough, those who in more recent time fanatically advocated 'truth to material' and 'functional art' regarded Bernini and all he stood for as the Antichrist personified." Lawrence Gowing in the *New Statesman* praised the monograph highly. Wittkower, he wrote, "has studied the artist for a lifetime: he must have forgotten more about Bernini than most of us will ever know, and it is an achievement that the gulf should be so seldom evident. The positive temper of his writing, as much as the massive learning, is a continual pleasure."

Wittkower's most considerable work of art-historical synthesis first appeared in 1958. This was *Art and Architecture in Italy 1600 to 1750*, which, he remarks in the foreword, "is concerned with the Italian Baroque period in the widest sense, but not with the European phenomenon of Neoclassicism. . . . Instead of saying little about many things, I attempted to say something about a few things, and so concerned myself only with the history of painting, sculpture, and architecture." Although the volume is comprehensive and magisterial, it suffers by comparison with many in its distinguished series, the Pelican History of Art, to the extent that its subject covers a period and place the art and architecture of which, although of undoubted quality and interest, have never in the modern age experienced any sort of genuine popularity.

With his wife, Wittkower collaborated on two important books, one of which approached the condition of being a popular work for a mass audience. This was *Born under Saturn: The Character and Conduct of Artists—A Documented History from Antiquity to the French Revolution*. "In recent years," the authors write in the introduction, "more work has been devoted to the problems of the artist's personality and the mysterious springs of his creative power than ever before in history. . . . More often than not psychologists, sociologists, and, to a certain extent, art critics agree that certain marked characteristics distinguish the artist from 'normal' people. The 'otherness' of artists is also widely accepted by the general public. Though comparatively few laymen are really in a position to judge from historical knowledge or personal experience, there is an almost unanimous belief among them that artists are, and always have been, egocentric, temperamental, neurotic, rebellious, unreliable, licentious, extravagant, obsessed by their work, and altogether difficult to live with. . . . Our main concern was to investigate when, where, and why an image of the typical artist arose in people's minds, and what its distinguishing traits and varying fortunes have been." Stopping short of the relative artistic chaos of the French Revolution and the Romantic period, the book offers few solid conclusions. On the subject of the origins of the popular idea of the typical artist, the Wittkowers found so many contrasts of good and bad business sense, wastrels and misers, lovers of conviviality and solitude, great lovers and celibates, that there was no final answer to be had. John Canaday, writing in the *New York Times Book Review*, remarked that the Wittkowers' "feats of scholarship and compression are impressive enough . . . in this giant popcorn-ball of a book. . . . In looking over the records [they] have questioned such anecdotal historians as Vasari, who was better at telling a good story about an artist than at checking it for veracity. . . . There are good comments on the artist's position in society, his methods of work, and the artist-patron relationship. . . . [The authors] have a wonderful time and so should the reader."

The Wittkowers' other major collaboration was *The Divine Michelangelo: The Florentine Academy's Homage on His Death in 1564*, which is a facsimile edition, with introduction, translation, and annotation, of *Esequie del Divino Michelagnolo Buonarroti* (Florence, 1564). This is a fascinating monograph-cum-translation, detailing the arduous planning, chiefly by Giorgio Vasari, to memorialize Michelangelo among his fellow Florentines after his death in Rome in 1564 at an advanced age. The Wittkowers' introduction is chiefly remarkable for the account of the relative indifference of Duke Cosimo de' Medici and the jealous rivalry and even sabotage committed during the Academy's planning sessions by various eminent artists, including Benvenuto Cellini and Bartolommeo Ammannati.

Soon after his retirement, Wittkower took up the Kress professorship-in-residence at the NationalGallery of Art in Washington, D.C., where or a year he supervised the work of young scholars. His sudden death in the autumn of 1971 occurred at the beginning of a period he hoped would be fruitful for him: he had many projects in hand, completion of which had been forestalled by the intense pressure of administrative and supervisory work. In the event, it fell to his widow to organize all of his *disjecta membra* for publication, and this she proceeded to do, accomplishing much over the next decade. The books included four volumes of Wittkower's collected essays, most previously published but some existing only in notes. *Palladio and Palladianism* consists of thirteen essays, of which six are on Andrea Palladio, two on Inigo Jones, and three on Richard Boyle, third Earl of Burlington; there are also a valuable conspectus of the English literature on architecture and a seminal piece of the sort that Wittkower did best, "Classical Theory and Eighteenth-Century Sensibility." *Studies in the Italian Baroque* contains fifteen articles, of which four are on Bernini, three on Giovanni Battista Piranesi, two on Bernardo Vittone, and one each on Guarino Guarini, Francesco Borromini, Carlo Rainaldi, and Pietro da Cortona. The third volume is *Allegory and the Migration of Symbols*, fourteen essays on hieroglyphics, the arts of the East, and iconographical studies in general, which had remained an abiding interest of Wittkower's since the 1920s. The fourth and last in the series, *Idea and Image: Studies in the Italian Renaissance*, presents ten essays on Renaissance topics, including two on Michelangelo and one each on Filippo Brunelleschi, the young Raphael, and Giorgione, and a piece on "The Changing Concept of Proportion" among late medieval and Renaissance architects.

Other volumes appearing under Margot Wittkower's curatorship included *Gothic vs. Classic: Architectural Projects in Seventeenth-Century Italy*, comprising the Charles T. Mathews lectures for 1971–1972, which Wittkower had just begun to present, under the joint auspices of the School of Architecture at Columbia and the Metropolitan Museum of Art, at the time of his death. *Sculpture: Processes and Principles* is a recension of the twelve lectures given by Wittkower as Slade professor of fine arts at Cambridge University for the academic year 1970–1971.

The two-volume festschrift, edited by Douglas Fraser, Howard Hibbard, and Milton J. Lewine, *Essays Presented to Rudolf Wittkower on His Sixty-Fifth Birthday* (1967), has remained a highly important collection of documents in the two fields of Wittkower's specialization. There are twenty-six contributions to volume one, *Essays in the History of Architecture* and thirty-nine to volume two, *Essays in the History of Art*. The essays, write the editors in their preface, "are designed to deal with subjects in each of the overlapping categories into which most of his published work falls: the migration and interpretation of symbols, problems of proportion and perspective, the iconographic interpretation of art, Italian Renaissance sculpture and architecture, Baroque art in all its manifestations, Palladio and Palladianism, and English architecture. Many of these essays expand our knowledge in these various fields; others refine ideas or explore new aspects of material Wittkower has worked on. But it is safe to say that a majority of these essays could never have been written without his pioneering work in such fields as the Italian Baroque, which opened the way to modern interest and scholarship."

Having won its Serena medal in 1957, Wittkower was elected a fellow of the British Academy in 1958. He was also fellow or honorary fellow of the American Academy of Arts and Sciences (from 1959), the Accademia di Belle Arti, Venice (1959), the Accademia dei Lincei, Rome (1960), the Royal Institute of British Architects (1965), and the Royal Society of Architecture (1970). He was a corresponding member of the Max Planck Institute in Göttingen and retained his ties to the Bibliotheca Hertziana, Rome. He was awarded honorary degrees by Columbia, Duke, and Leeds universities.

PRINCIPAL WORKS: (with E. Steinmann) Michelangelo Bibliographie, 1927; (with H. Brauer) Die Zeichnungen des G. L. Bernini, 1931; (with T. Borenius) Sir Robert Mond's Collection of Drawings, 1935; (with F. Saxl) British Art and the Mediterranean, 1948; Architectural Principles in the Age of Humanism, 1949; The Artist and the Liberal Arts, 1952; The Drawings of the Carracci, 1952; Gian Lorenzo Bernini, 1955; Art and Architecture in Italy 1600–1750, 1958; (with M. Wittkower) Born under Saturn, 1962; Disegni de le Ruine di Roma, 1963; (with M. Wittkower) The Divine Michelangelo, 1964; La Cupola di San Pietro, 1964; Gothic vs. Classic, 1974; the collected essays, ed. by M. Wittkower, including Palladio and Palladianism, 1974, Studies in the Italian Baroque, 1975, Allegory and the Migration of Symbols, 1977, and Idea and Image, 1978; Sculpture, 1977.

ABOUT: Essays Presented to Rudolf Wittkower on His Sixty-Fifth Birthday, 1967; Who's Who 1971–1972. Periodicals—Art Bulletin June 1978; Best Sellers April 1979; Choice June 1967, July–August 1974, October 1974, April 1976, March 1978, September 1979; Library Journal January 1, 1954; March 1, 1956; February 15, 1967; June 1, 1974; October 1, 1977; January 1, 1979; Economist August 27, 1977; New Statesman March 28, 1953; December 17, 1955; New York Herald Tribune Book Review December 4, 1955; August 18, 1963; New York Times December 11, 1955; October 12, 1971; New York Times Book Review August 11, 1963; Saturday Review June 6, 1953; Times Literary Supplement December 23, 1955; May 24, 1974; October 11, 1974; November 7, 1975; March 18, 1977.

WOLFE, GENE (RODMAN) (May 7, 1931–), American science fiction writer, was born in Brooklyn, New York, the son of Roy Emerson Wolfe, a salesman, and the former Mary Olivia Ayres. He was educated in local schools

GENE WOLFE

and attended Texas A & M University in 1949 and 1952, eventually, in 1956, taking a bachelor of science degree in mechanical engineering from the University of Houston, which he attended under the G.I. bill. He has worked at two successive full-time jobs throughout his writing career, first as project engineer with Procter & Gamble (1956–1972), then (from 1972) as senior editor for Plant Engineering magazine, a trade journal. He served with the United States Army in Korea in 1952–1954, and was awarded the Combat Infantry badge.

Wolfe began writing science fiction only in the mid-1960s. His first story, "Mountains Like Mice," appeared in World of If in 1966. From that time on, he became an extremely prolific contributor to several science-fiction publications, including the Magazine of Fantasy and Science Fiction, Isaac Asimov's Science Fiction Magazine, Analog Science Fiction/Science Fact, Galaxy, and, especially, the Orbit series edited by Damon Knight. Knight befriended Wolfe and helped him edit and refine his early work; Wolfe thanked him for his faithfulness in his introduction to The Fifth Head of Cerberus, three interconnected stories all originally published in Orbit, jokingly recalling how Knight, "one well-remembered June evening in 1966, grew me from a bean."

Wolfe's early novels were recognized as competent neophyte work, but received little praise even in the critically lenient science-fiction press. Reviewing Operation Ares, a novel set in a grim, utilitarian future, Joanna Russ protested in the Magazine of Fantasy and Science Fiction that it "is going to do the author's reputation a disservice some day. . . . *Ares* is far below Wolfe's best. It is a convincing, quiet, low-keyed, intelligent book that somehow fades out into nothing." *Peace*, a more conventional novel about a sick, elderly man who, under the influence of psychological counseling, tells four interrelated stories of his childhood, relatives, and friends, was described as "work to read" and "esoteric" by the *Choice* reviewer. Jack Tootell in *Library Journal* called the novel "atmospheric in its evocations, sharp and clear in its characters, and in parts skillfully handled. But its episodic structure misses the tensions of a developing plot."

Wolfe's career as a science-fiction and fantasy writer of real renown in the field is generally considered to have begun with the publication of the first volume of his tetralogy, The Book of the New Sun. These are picaresque novels about the wanderings, battles, loves, failures, and triumphs of one Severian, who tells his saga in the first person in a fluid yet markedly stilted prose, quite characteristic of the swords-and-sorcery subgenre of fantasy fiction. The setting and characters seem vaguely medieval in tone, although the story is presumably meant to occur in the distant future, on an Earthlike planet revolving around a dying sun. At the beginning of the first novel, *The Shadow of the Torturer*, Severian is a young man apprenticed to the Guild of the Torturers, an organization (like much else in the series it has fallen far from a dimly grasped former greatness) which must punish and execute state prisoners. Much of the first book's narrative comprises an elaborate description of the City Imperishable and its grim Citadel: a good deal of the action takes place in deserted mausoleums and there is much byplay about the cruel treatment meted out to the impoverished, ignorant common people by those who consider themselves their betters—among them the hero and his companions. In punishment for falling in love with a prisoner (or "client," as such miserable people are called) and then killing her before she can be further tortured, Severian is sent away from the Citadel. At the conclusion of the first book he is about to begin this far-flung exile: "it was to lie outside the City Imperishable and among the forests and grasslands, mountains and jungles of the north."

Professional critics of science fantasy (most are themselves authors in the genre) were delighted with the tetralogy's first installment. Algis Budrys, writing in the *Magazine of Fantasy and Science Fiction*, thought that "Wolfe is clearly writing one book with four aspects. Thus, while the whole will very likely be far greater than the sum of its parts, no one part is whole.

It is also not dispensable." James Gunn, in the *Washington Post Book World*, wrote that Wolfe "has turned to the writing of long, well-textured, colorful science fantasy after an earlier career dedicated mostly to short fiction that was usually difficult, often ambiguous, sometimes obscure, and always skillfully written."

The tetralogy's other volumes followed in quick succession, all recounting the further adventures of Severian. In *The Claw of the Conciliator* he journeys toward his exile and his new role as public executioner in Thrax, the City of Windowless Rooms. *The Sword of the Lictor* sees him reunited with his lover Dorcas and freshly arrived at Thrax. By the end of *The Citadel of the Autarch*, Severian has returned to the City Imperishable and has himself become Autarch, supreme ruler of the southern Commonwealth. The structure of The Book of the New Sun becomes increasingly episodic as the series progresses. There is a great profusion of characters constantly being introduced; most have single, Latinate names and they are difficult for the reader to keep separate. After a few chapters consisting of their interposed stories and the events surrounding them, the new characters disappear, abandoned by the wandering Severian. Once again, those critics partial to this sort of writing were enthusiastic in their appreciation: "a major landmark of contemporary American literature, . . . a genuine marvel," wrote "R.G." in *Booklist*; John Clute, in *Book World*, held that Wolfe "must be taken as attempting something analogous to Dante's supreme effort, . . . a novel that makes sense in the end only if it is read as an attempt to represent the Word of God." Such hyperbole has become a commonplace in his peers' reaction to Wolfe's work.

Further adventures of Severian, all remarkably similar in tone, style, and format to those in the earlier four books, are recounted in *The Urth of the New Sun*. Wolfe changed his focus in *Soldier of the Mist*, a novel purporting to be the author's translation of a scroll recounting events in ancient Greece in 479 B.C., reporting "Greece as it was reported by the Greeks themselves," and telling the story of the culmination of the Persian Wars.

In 1973, Wolfe won the Nebula award, presented by the Science Fiction Writers of America, for the best science-fiction novella of the year, "The Death of Doctor Island." *Peace* won the Chicago Foundation for Literature award in 1977, and his "The Computer Iterates the Greater Trumps" was awarded the Rhysling award for science-fiction poetry in 1978. The Book of the New Sun tetralogy won the World Fantasy award. The author is a long-time member of the Science Fiction Writers of America, the Authors Guild, PEN, and World Science Fiction, and has served as president of the Science Fiction Poetry Association.

WORKS: *Novels*—Operation Ares, 1970; Peace, 1975; The Devil in a Forest, 1976; The Book of the New Sun tetralogy: The Shadow of the Torturer, 1980; The Claw of the Conciliator, 1981; The Sword of the Lictor, 1981; The Citadel of the Autarch, 1982; Free Live Free, 1985; Soldier of the Mist, 1986; The Urth of the New Sun, 1987. *Short fiction*—The Fifth Head of Cerberus, 1972; The Island of Doctor Death and Other Stories, 1980; Gene Wolfe's Book of Days, 1981; The Castle of the Otter, 1982; The Wolfe Archipelago, 1983; Endangered Species, 1989.

ABOUT: Contemporary Authors New Revision Series 6, 1981; Contemporary Literary Criticism 25, 1983; Dictionary of Literary Biography 8, 1981. *Periodicals*—Best Sellers April 1982; Book World May 25, 1980; March 22, 1981; January 24, 1982; January 30, 1983; November 27, 1983; October 26, 1986; August 28, 1988; October 25, 1988; Booklist November 1, 1982; June 15, 1986; September 1, 1987, September 15, 1988; Choice October 1975; Christian Science Monitor January 27, 1988; Fantasy Newsletter December 1981; December 1982; Library Journal June 15, 1975; December 15, 1982; November 15, 1986; October 15, 1987; Magazine of Fantasy and Science Fiction April 1971, May 1978, May 1980, June 1981, April 1983, January 1984, November 1985, February 1987, March 1988; New Statesman November 28, 1986; January 15, 1988; New York Times Book Review July 13, 1975; September 12, 1976; May 22, 1983; November 6, 1983; November 24, 1985; December 20, 1987; Observer (London) August 23, 1987; Riverside Quarterly August 1973; Times Literary Supplement January 15, 1988; Voice of Youth Advocates August 1983, February 1987, April 1988.

*YANG JIANG (pen name of Yang Jikang) (July 17, 1911–), Chinese playwright, essayist, and memoirist, writes (in 1986): "I was born into an old scholarly family. My father was an eminent jurist as well as a philologist. He was the first Chinese to obtain a degree in law at the University of Pennsylvania, U.S.A., and his thesis *The Commercial Code of Japan* (written in English) was published in 1911 in the University of Pennsylvania Law Series (No. 1). When I was twelve, he retired from public life and settled down in Soochow to practice law. I studied in Soochow and graduated with a B.A. degree majoring in political science from the American missionary Soochow University in 1932. During my last year there, the university closed down in consequence of student agitation, and I was permitted to finish my studies as a guest student at at

YANG JIANG

the National Tsinghua University in Peking (now Beijing). The following year, having passed a rather severe examination, I was admitted to Tsinghua as a postgraduate in the Department of Foreign Languages and Literature.

"It was in 1932 that I met at Tsinghua my future husband, Qian Zhongshu. We were married in 1935 and then went abroad for advanced studies in England and France. We returned to China in 1938 when the Sino-Japanese War was raging. Both our parental homes had been pillaged and our families were taking refuge in Shanghai. My husband went alone to the interior of China to teach in the universities. I was elected to be the principal of a girls' high school which was originally my alma mater in Soochow and at that time had its temporary quarters in the French Concession in Shanghai. The school was closed in 1941 after Pearl Harbor.

"In 1942 I started to write plays under the pen name 'Yang Jiang.' The plays were performed and had a very good press. When the World War II came to an end, I became a professor in the Department of Western Literature in the Roman Catholic Aurora College for Women in Shanghai. My essays and stories written at that time were published in well-known periodicals.

"After the liberation of Shanghai in 1949, my husband and I both were both were offered professorships in Tsinghua University. In 1952, upon the nation-wide reorganization and amalgamation of the institutions of higher education, I became a research fellow in the Foreign Literature Section of the newly-founded Institute of Literature. The Section expanded until it finally became the full-fledged Institute of Foreign Literature in the Chinese Academy of Social Sciences in 1964, and I have remained a member.

"A part of my work in the Institute consists in the translation of foreign literary classics into Chinese. For my versions of *Lazarillo de Tormes* and *Don Quixote*, I was awarded La Orden Civil de Alfonso X el Sabio by the King of Spain in 1986.

"After the fall of the Gang of Four, my essays in literary criticism, once considered 'poisonous weeds,' were collected and published. I wrote and published a collection of short stories, a sketchbook of my life in a cadre school, as well as some reminiscences and essays (see the list of my published works below). At the age of seventy-five, I am writing a novel, wondering all the while whether I will be able to finish it.

"I am happily married and have one daughter."

Yang Jiang is famous for her memoirs of the Cultural Revolution days, *Ganxiao Liuji* (1981). It has had three English translations, variously titled as *A Cadre School Life: Six Chapters* (1982), *Six Chapters from My Life "Downunder"* (1984), and *Six Chapters of Life in a Cadre School* (1986). The title in Chinese invokes the memory of another recording of a Chinese intellectual's life, *Fusheng Liuji* (Six Chapters from a Floating Life), written almost two centuries ago by Shen Fu, a disgruntled Confucian litterateur in the Qing Dynasty who was unhappy with his aimless life. There is no doubt that Yang Jiang had Shen Fu's book, a minor classic, in mind when she wrote and titled her own memoirs of the life in a Communist cadre school during the Cultural Revolution. The two lives were, of course, entirely dissimilar, but it is astonishing to discover that Yang Jiang has captured Shen Fu's melancholy mood, helpless resignation in the face of a gloomy reality. In depicting the inhuman sufferings of these sensitive and humbled intellectuals, *Ganxiao Liuji* does not scream in agony; it merely whispers the pain. Yang Jiang's style is simple and direct. She is sardonic, self-deprecating, sometimes even bitterly humorous. She never pointedly accuses the torturers to their faces, but the effect can be devastating. Her writing is so controlled that even a most touching scene of love expressed wordlessly between herself and her husband seems to be extraordinarily ordinary. Her dry understatement is exemplified by her observation that "the [human] waste produced in the cadre school was the best around," illustrating that these unfortunates, even at their lowest, could comfort themselves with the notion that they at least contributed something to the welfare of the nation—much in the spirit of Lu Xun's character Ah Q.

The West has long been awaiting a Chinese book of reminiscences of life under Mao's erratic rule on the scale of Alexander Solzhenitsyn's Nobel Prize–winning *Gulag Archipelago*. *Ganxiao Liuji*, a slim volume of some 60,000 words, is not that book. But Yang Jiang's subtlety and air of resignation seem to fit the present Chinese mood. So far, no published works depicting the horrors of the Cultural Revolution have proven better than *Ganxiao Liuji*. And in its English translations it will certainly become an important part of Western understanding of the Chinese puzzle called the Great Proletarian Cultural Revolution. Perhaps nothing says better what the Chinese reading public is thinking than the words of Qian Zhongshu, Yang Jiang's husband, the distinguished essayist and novelist (author of *Fortress Besieged*), who writes in the Foreword: " . . . Yang Jiang asked me to look over the manuscript. I felt that she should have written one more chapter, which we can . . . call 'A Sense of Shame: Participating in Political Campaign.'"

Yang Jiang started out as a playwright, producing her first play *Chenxin Ruyi* (As You Desire), a comedy, in 1944 when she lived in the French Concession of Shanghai under Japanese occupation. Its success was followed by another comedy the following year, *Nonzhen Chenjia* (The Cheat). Her third play, *Youxi Renjian* (The World at Play), failed. Yang Jiang also wrote critical essays on Chinese and Western literature, collected in a 1979 volume titled *Chunni Ji* (Spring Soil), and translated into Chinese the Spanish classics *Gil Blas* (1956), *Don Quixote* (1978), and *Lazarillo de Tormes* (1986).

WORKS IN ENGLISH TRANSLATION: *A Cadre School Life: Six Chapters* was translated by Geremie Barmé in 1982; *Six Chapters from My Life "Downunder"* by Howard Goldblatt in 1984; *Six Chapters of Life in a Cadre School* by Djang Chu in 1986. The last play Yang Jiang wrote, *Fengxu* (1947), was translated by Edward Gunn in his *Twentieth Century Chinese Drama: An Anthology*, 1983.

ABOUT: New Republic January 23, 1984; Times Literary Supplement June 24, 1983; World Literature Today Winter 1985.

*YASUOKA SHŌTARŌ (May 30, 1920–   ), Japanese short- story writer and novelist, was born in Kōchi City on the island of Shikoku. His father, Akira, studied to become a veterinarian for the Japanese army, a "horse doctor," as his

°yä sū ō´ kä shō tä´rō

YASUOKA SHŌTARŌ

unimpressed wife, Tsune, would later remark disparagingly. Although Kōchi remains imbedded in Yasuoka's mind and writing as his hometown, he never spent more than two consecutive months there throughout his life. When his father qualified to treat military animals, the family began moving around on assignments, and by the time Yasuoka reached his fifth birthday, his family had already moved five times. In 1925, they were dispatched to Seoul, where they remained for four years. Yasuoka was initially enrolled in elementary school in Korea, but more inevitable transfers came, and during the first four grades he attended six different primary schools in three different cities and two separate countries. By his own account, he had no friends, lost confidence in his ability to perform scholastically, and suffered repeated embarrassment, since he would have barely learned to comprehend and speak the local dialect when he would be carted off to another city.

Yasuoka's miserable performance in school—he consistently ranked among the worst students in his class—was a particular disappointment to his mother. She felt she had married beneath her status and cultural level, and the humiliation she experienced over Akira's lackluster profession she translated into exaggerated hopes for her only son. When he proved himself unable to fulfill her dreams, her disappointment filled him with guilt; at the same time it prompted him to surround himself with "bad company" (the title of one of his later short stories) and actively seek new lows of dissipation and failure. At the crux of his history work is the impulse to barter re-

peated personal failure into artistically restructured success.

In January of 1934, Yasuoka's parents decided that firm action was necessary to effect a change in the boy's school performance. He was sent to live with the chief priest of a Buddhist temple, a man who was also his instructor in the Chinese and Japanese classics. For two years he boarded at the religious sanctuary, where he was expected to work alongside monks and devote himself to his studies while the chanting of sutras echoed in his ears. The experience enabled Yasuoka to squeeze a diploma from his middle school, but he spent more time frequenting movie theaters and coffee shops than the classroom.

After graduation from middle school, Yasuoka failed his entrance exams to three different higher schools. Shortly after he failed his first examination, his father was transferred to central China, but because Japan was now engaged in full-scale battle on the continent, this time mother and son chose to remain alone together in Japan. Except for a few brief furloughs when his father returned home, Yasuoka saw nothing of the man until the defeat eight years later.

With his father out of the picture and the likelihood that his relationship with his mother would become increasingly stifling, Yasuoka and his friends formed a "Fūten Club" (which can be interpreted either as the "Insanity Club" or the "Juvenile Delinquents Club"). Their pranks, practical jokes and acts of decadence were modeled after the chief cultural bohemians of the day, Tanizaki Junichirō and Nagai Kafū; in a broader sense, however, they were a reaction not only against the oppressiveness of home, but also against the mounting influence of the Japanese military in domestic politics and the restrictions that were being placed upon intellectual dissent. Yasuoka's generation has been identified as something of a "lost" generation in Japan, since most of its members hovered near adulthood at the opening of the Pacific War, too young to have gained familiarity with Marxist doctrine but slightly too old to accept fully the militaristic propaganda of the thirties and forties.

Yasuoka spent the early war years formally enrolled in the Department of Literature at Keiō University, but instead of attending classes, he whiled away his time reading quasi-pornographic illustrated novels from the nineteenth century and learning to sing jōruri, the theatrical chanting style also linked to Japan's period of early-modern dandyism. The month that Pearl Harbor was attacked, Yasuoka published his first short story—appropriately enough, it was a sword-slashing adventure story set in the past, and has been lost—in a coterie journal he had started with a group of friends.

Yasuoka retained a student draft deferment until March of 1944, when, just before his twenty-fourth birthday, he was called into active service in the Japanese Army. He was sent to Manchuria for basic training, but he developed a ferocious case of diarrhea ("I grew ever more fondly attached to the latrine. It was the only place where I could relax; crouched there in the toilet I felt my only sense of fulfillment in life. I thought how nice it would be if I could have all three meals and then sleep there at night," he has written). In August of 1944, just six months after he was drafted, Yasuoka contracted a serious lung ailment and was placed in a military hospital. The following day his regiment was transferred to the Philippines, where every last man was annihilated in the fierce fighting at Leyte ·between October and December. Yasuoka, the sole survivor of that battalion, spent the final year of the war being transferred—as he had been in his school days—from one Manchurian military hospital to another. Finally he was sent back to Japan in March of 1945.

Yasuoka's father was not repatriated from the battlefield until nearly a year after the surrender, so Yasuoka and his mother moved into a rented house at Kugenuma, looking out over the Bay of Sagami. He tried working at several odd jobs, playing broker for a black market operation and sweeping floors in the building where General MacArthur's general headquarters was located. But severe recurrent back pains soon made it impossible for him to continue working. His condition was diagnosed as spinal caries (Pott's disease), a partial destruction of the vertebrae brought on by tubercular infection. Yasuoka went to bed, and he and his mother lived off the money sent to them from his father's government pension.

The return of a broken, humiliated patriarch to the home in May of 1946 triggered Yasuoka's first tangible recognition of Japan's defeat. His father puttered aimlessly around their borrowed garden even after his pension checks stopped coming. His wife's scorn for him intensified, and she longed for the days when she had been alone with her son. Yasuoka had to get out of his sickbed and try to find part-time work to hold the crumbling family unit together. He spent some time as a "house guard," hired by the Occupation to keep watch over houses that had been temporarily vacated by U.S. military personnel. "It was the only job where I could work half lying down," Yasuoka has noted. While he guarded the deserted homes, Yasuoka managed to regain admittance to Keiō University, more out of boredom than a thirst for knowledge. One of his classmates, Endō Shūsaku, recalls that "Yasuoka . . . appeared in the classroom dressed in a military uniform, but only on days when he was trying to sell more American tobacco or soap."

In February of 1949, just before his thirtieth birthday, Yasuoka's health took a sharp turn for the worse. He was no longer able to work and had to go straight to bed, wearing a painful and awkward corset that he would not be able to remove for six years. But total immobility meshed with his personality, and he insists he never once felt bored or restive throughout the many months he was forced to lie in bed. "Finding myself totally useless to society," he has written of those days, "I spent several years marinating something within myself, much the way pickled vegetables age in a fermenting tub in the bowels of a musty storage shed. . . . Between the ages of twenty-five and thirty I almost never took a bath; I lay motionless in my dust-covered bedding. . . . Although I considered myself an unreliable individual, I couldn't put my trust in anything outside myself either. I knew I had to cling to my own unreliability for as long as I lived. In an attempt to take hold of that unreliable something within me and set it before my eyes, I decided I must try to capture it in writing on the paper that lay beside my pillow."

Yasuoka commenced his writing career from his sickbed, and in 1951 one of his stories, "Garasu no Kutsu" (The Glass Slipper), received considerable attention, and along with two stories from the following year, "Shukudai" (Homework) and "Aigan" (Prized Possessions) was nominated for the important Akutagawa Prize. These stories, set in childhood and early adulthood and focusing upon the private humiliations and degradations, always tempered with a dose of masochistic humor that echoed Japan's national humiliation of defeat and occupation, are vivid depictions of the psychology of failure. The novelist Mishima Yukio suggested that the tone in Yasuoka's work derives from "a Chekhovian tenderness of mind and self-pity."

Yasuoka quickly became one of the central figures in a new literary gathering known as the "Daisan no Shinjin" (Third Generation of New Writers), but even as his career began to burgeon, his family was collapsing. His parents were forced to move out of their rented home in October of 1952. Rather than accompany them back to the family home in Kōchi and thereby interrupt his literary activities, he sent them back alone. Separation from her son snapped the final ties his mother had with sanity. She fell victim to paranoid delusions after her arrival in Kōchi and had to be placed in a mental institution looking out on the bay, where she spent the remainder of her life.

In 1953, Yasuoka received the Akutagawa Prize for two stories, "Inki Na Tanoshimi" (Gloomy Pleasures) and "Warui Nakama" (Bad Company). The following year, amid increasing success as a writer, he was finally able to put the bleakness of the early postwar years behind him. His spinal caries having healed, he removed his miserable metal corset, and he was married to Hiraoka Mitsuko. But success remained an uncomfortable burden to him. A certain stale familiarity began to steal across his stories, which were consistently drawn from personal experience, and a few attempts to produce surrealistic variations on his themes were diffuse and poorly received. Compounding his frustration was the need to make several trips to Kōchi to attend to his mother; in March of 1955 he helped make the arrangements to commit her to the asylum.

It was nearly a year before Yasuoka produced a major work of literature. *Tonsō* (Flight, 1956) was described as his first full-length novel, though in reality it was a patchwork, an account of his inept career as a soldier stitched together with an almost verbatim copy of an earlier short story describing the military hospitals in which he had waited out the end of the war. Despite its uneasy construction, *Tonsō* vividly depicts the emotional quandary of a young recruit who has no desire to serve his country and who seeks refuge from "daily life" in the barracks by retreating into the latrine where he can be in a "tiny world off in a corner that belonged to him alone."

The material for Yasuoka's most impressive literary work was derived once again from personal tragedy. In July of 1957, he and his father were present in the seaside asylum when his mother died. Two years later he parlayed the experience into one of the most moving short novels of the postwar period, *Kaihen no Kōkei* (also titled *Umibe no Kōkei*; translated as *A View by the Sea*). The humor of the early stories is drained from this work, which focuses on the self-interested son as he begrudgingly watches over his blind, dying mother for the last nine days of her life. The novel is a landmark in the development of personal fiction in Japan; it inherits the traditions of autobiographic detail from Yasuoka's predecessors, but the narrow, biased "view" which the reader sees through the son's eyes is tempered by a more detached narrative which exudes sympathy for the other characters. The failure of the son to comprehend his own complicity in the collapse of his family is painful, but the portraits which emerge of an inept but loving father and a victimized mother are warm and memorable. As Anthony H. Chambers noted in the *New York Times Book Review*, Mr. Yasuoka has transcended the limi-

tations of autobiographical fiction by maintaining just enough distance between himself and the young man to let us see what the young man cannot—his role in the collapse of his family and his mother's insanity."

At the invitation of the Rockefeller Foundation, Yasuoka and his wife spent six months in 1960 in the United States, primarily in Nashville. Yasuoka's memoir of the visit, *Amerika Kanjō Ryokō* (A Sentimental Journey to America, 1962), suggests that he was most sensitive to the racial discrimination he encountered, which he felt extended to himself, but the work is also a lively outsider's view of America in the 1960s.

Yasuoka labored for five years over his next novel, *Maku ga Orite Kara* (After the Curtain Falls, 1967), a work which pursues the motif of family collapse into the marriage of a son whose mother had died insane. In style and construction it rivals *A View by the Sea*, but in overall effect it does not surpass the earlier novel. An act of adultery committed abroad, and the protagonist's desire to halt the passage of time while an airplane is taking him back to confess to his wife, are the motifs at the center of Yasuoka's next novel, *Tsuki wa Higashi ni* (The Moon Is to the East, 1971). It could be described as Yasuoka's "last" novel; since its publication, he has devoted himself exclusively to short stories, essays on literature, film, and society, and a series of highly literary, meticulously researched re-creations of the past, especially the history of his ancestors in Kōchi during the turbulent years surrounding the Meiji Restoration of 1868. Yasuoka's interest in the past began to be evident in the short story collections *Hashire Tomahōku* (Run, Tomahawk!, 1973) and *Hōhishō* (Selections on Farting, 1979), became overt when he agreed to work as cotranslator on the Japanese version of Alex Haley's *Roots* in 1977, and culminated in a new pinnacle in Yasuoka's work with the 1981 publication of the lengthy investigation of his own Kōchi roots, titled *Ryūritan* (A Tale of Wanderers). This quasi-novel received the Grand Prize for Japanese Literature. Since then, Yasuoka has kept his eyes firmly fixed upon the past, publishing in 1984 another documentary work, *Daiseikimatsu Sākasu* (The Grand Fin-de-siècle Circus), following the steps of a Japanese circus troupe which traveled through Europe and the United States in the middle of the nineteenth century.

The ironic self-portrait which Yasuoka has created in his fiction, especially in his finely crafted short stories, provides a detailed look at the confusion and humiliation of a young Japanese man at a time when his country was involved in war and then subjected to total defeat and foreign occupation. His characters, and the situations in which they find themselves, are vivid re-creations of those traumatic times. At the same time, Yasuoka has successfully broken the mirror of self-reflection that limited the perspectives in earlier Japanese autobiographical fiction, and has provided in his stories "a second pair of eyes" to scrutinize all the follies and shortcomings of his characters. He has, in this manner, opened up the dimensions of the prose narrative and infused it with a healthy, if painful, dose of irony.

WORKS IN ENGLISH TRANSLATION: *A View by the Sea*, along with five early short stories, was translated by Kären Wigen Lewis in 1984; "The Glass Slipper" and "The Pawnbroker's Wife" were translated by Edward Seidensticker in 1961; "Prized Possessions" was translated by Edwin McClellan in 1977.

ABOUT: Encyclopedia of Japan, 1984; Gessel, V. C. The Sting of Life: Four Contemporary Japanese Novelists, 1989; Nihon Kindai Bungaku Daijiten, 1984. *Periodical*—New York Times Book Review October 7, 1984.

*YOSHIYUKI JUNNOSUKE (April 13, 1924–   ), Japanese novelist and short-story writer, was born in Okayama City as the eldest son of a family with rich aesthetic ties. His father, Yoshiyuki Eisuke (1906–1940), established himself in the 1920s as a leading avant-garde novelist, experimenting with a unique style combining elements of dadaism and modernism. But after a few years he abruptly abandoned his literary career, trashing every book in his library except three of his own composition, and took a job as a stockbroker. Two of Junnosuke's younger sisters also became involved in the arts: Kazuko became an actress, and Rie (b. 1939) started out as a poet and won the Akutagawa Prize for fiction with her 1981 story, "Chiisana Kifujin" (The Little Lady). Junnosuke's mother ran the first Western-style beauty salon in Japan.

In 1927 the family moved to Tokyo, where Yoshiyuki attended primary and middle schools. When he was sixteen, his father died of a sudden heart attack. In 1942 Yoshiyuki enrolled in the department of literature at Shizuoka Higher School in his native province, but he resented the mounting emphasis on military drills and supervision in Japanese schools. Later he would write, "The table tennis club I belonged to was shut down because it was an 'enemy sport,' and the ping-pong table was hauled into the cafeteria and used as a lunch table. I was furious, but there was nothing I could do about it." Unable to put up with such incursions on his freedom, Yoshi-

yuki decided to take a leave of absence from school and persuaded a doctor to give him a letter certifying a nonexistent heart condition. During this brief sabbatical he became absorbed in the reading of literature and wrote some poems and essays of his own.

In August of 1944, despite his medical excuse, Yoshiyuki was drafted into the Japanese infantry, but three days after his induction the army's medical examiner discovered that he was suffering from bronchial asthma, and Yoshiyuki was sent back home the following day. He has continued to suffer from severe asthmatic attacks throughout his life. The following April he enrolled in the English literature department of Tokyo University. In May, just three months before the war ended, the family residence in Tokyo was destroyed by the fires resulting from an Allied air raid; Yoshiyuki fled the burning house carrying only a notebook in which he had composed fifty verses.

He moved into an apartment and continued to enroll in classes, but his consuming interest after the war was to edit and publish a small coterie literary magazine. He was successful in bringing out three issues of a journal which he called *Ashi* (Reeds), where he first put a story, "Yuki" (Snow), into print. He joined the publication staffs of several other little magazines and continued to publish stories that he had written but had been unable to print during the war years, as well as new works. In the fall of 1947, unable to afford his studies any longer, he dropped out of school and took a job as a reporter for a cheap scandal magazine, *Modan Nihon* (Modern Japan). He worked with the magazine as a pulp journalist for six years but continued to write stories and submit them for publication. The air of decadence and damp sensuality that hovers over even the finest of Yoshiyuki's later writings can be partially attributed to his years with this journal.

After the war many young Japanese writers banded together under the auspices of Marxist thought, persuaded that the political and aesthetic guidance provided by leftist philosophy was the proper direction for their defeated nation. Yoshiyuki, however, remained detached, disengaged from all such movements. "The postwar clique of authors," he wrote, "spent their youth in league with communism, but mine was spent very differently. As a result, my concerns are unlike theirs. During the war, I couldn't bring myself to sacrifice my life for the sake of any single philosophy, even if its ideals might be realized at some point in the future. Many willingly made that sacrifice, but the very thought repelled me. The idea of becoming a sacrifice

°yō shē yû´ kē jû nō soo´ kē

gave me no pleasure. . . . Communism enjoyed a great wave of popularity shortly after the war. . . . But the innate resistance I felt toward it was the same resistance I had felt toward the militarism of the war years. I could not bear the thought of putting on another uniform when I had just taken off the previous one and thereby liberated my individuality. Neither did I care for the thought of martyring myself for the sake of some ideal that might possibly be realized in some distant future." The secularism and focus upon gratifications of the present moment in Yoshiyuki's literature, so reminiscent of the softly decadent erotic Japanese prose of the early nineteenth century, reflect his suspicion of ideology.

In 1950, at the age of twenty-six, Yoshiyuki published the story which he regards as his debut work, "Bara Hambainin"(Flower Seller); it is infused with the blend of poetic sensitivity and erotic desire that has remained Yoshiyuki's hallmark and special province throughout his career. Yoshiyuki's first published novel, *Genshoku no Machi* (Street of Primary Colors, 1951), was nominated for Japan's most important award for newcomers, the Akutagawa Prize. Two more of his stories from the following year were nominated for the same prize, but in late 1952 Yoshiyuki was diagnosed as suffering from tuberculosis, and in the spring of 1953 he resigned from the publishing house which sponsored *Modan Nihon* and went into a hospital for treatment. He was recovering from surgery which removed his left lung when he received word that his short story "Shūu" (1954; translated as "Sudden Shower" in 1972) had won the Akutagawa Prize. Both *Genshoku no Machi* and "Shūu" are set in the world of prostitutes, a frequent setting for Yoshiyuki's studies of human interrelations. Ever a shadowy opponent of the establishment, whether it be political or literary, he is most at home writing of the engagements between social mavericks beyond the fringes of acceptability. Having viewed the corruption of public institutions, Yoshiyuki's characters reject them as inherently hypocritical and seek for a paradoxical "purity" in the fleeting, uncomplicated sexual encounters between prostitutes and their clients. In works such as *"Shūu,"* however, the unsullied physicality of that relationship frequently teeters on the brink of collapse when either the man or the woman begins to develop an emotional attraction to, and hence entanglement with, a single partner. The celebrated novelist Mishima Yukio, an avid devotee of Yoshiyuki's style, wrote of this story: "The delicacy of Yoshiyuki's language and sensibility is probably more subtle and sophisticated than that of any Japanese writer since the war [This] is not just a love

story; Yoshiyuki gives us first-hand experience of the woman's sensuality and we are made to feel somehow like skin-divers on the sea-bed of man's passions and emotions. Yoshiyuki's attitude to the woman is elegant and relaxed, and yet has an element of sharpness that disturbs and unnerves. The lyricism of Yoshiyuki's writing is semi-neurotic and, by restricting his subject, he is able to convey a deeply sensual experience in a world as confined as a bath-tub. The *idée fixe* of Japanese youth today—that love is impossible and impracticable—lies deep at the root of Yoshiyuki's thinking." Another representative story in this mode is "Shōfu no Heya" (1958, A Prostitute's Room; translated as "In Akiko's Room"), of which Howard Hibbett has written, "Yoshiyuki writes of the world of outcast women both as a refuge from the hypocrisies of ordinary society and as an irresistibly alluring setting for romantic self-degradation. . . . Yoshiyuki prefers to keep a discreet distance from his characters. . . . The cool, polished surface of his fiction faithfully reflects a world of mingled frivolity and futility."

During his convalescence, Yoshiyuki in early 1953 had been instrumental in organizing a new, informal literary gathering of writers who had recently made their debuts. Originally sponsored by the journal *Bungakkai* (The Literary World), this meeting brought together writers who would later be labeled the "Daisan no Shinjin" (Third Generation of New Writers) and included such important figures as Yasuoka Shōtarō, Endō Shūsaku, Shimao Toshio, Kojima Nobuo, and Shōno Junzō. The writers and editors who organized the group looked upon Yoshiyuki as an able adviser, since he seemed to have the greatest familiarity with contemporary literature, but Yoshiyuki himself, referring to one afternoon when three other young writers gathered at his apartment, has described the haphazard manner in which the group was assembled: "The editors at *Bungakkai* . . . asked us to agree upon a list of ten writers and five critics. . . . So we wrote down the names of the ten people we thought should be invited on the left side of a sheet of paper; any other names that came up went into the right column. In our selection, we did our best to choose solely on the basis of the value of their writings."

After his release from the hospital in October of 1954, Yoshiyuki spent the next two years in bed recuperating, but his newfound popularity after receipt of the Akutagawa Prize kept requests from major journals flooding in. His most important work from this period was a series of interrelated short stories eventually collected under the title *Honoo no Naka* (Within the Flames, 1956). Like many of Yoshiyuki's works (and, it should be noted, like those of many of his contemporaries in the Third Generation), this book is structured like an autobiographical novel, and indeed many of the episodes in the work can be directly traced to Yoshiyuki's own experiences during the war years. But unlike prewar practitioners of the so-called "I-novel" genre, Yoshiyuki blends fact with fabrication, selecting and shaping his materials, and presenting his stories in a style which creates a vivid mood of intermingled corruption and sincerity unlike anything his predecessors in the form had created. According to Miura Shumon, one of Yoshiyuki's contemporaries in the Third Generation, "Yoshiyuki is known to postwar writers as an epicure. While his inward-looking works reveal an almost excessive aestheticism, they differ from prewar I-novels. The writers who constituted the mainstream of prewar pure literature were young, as were most of their readers. Consequently, their works tended toward exploration of the meaning of life. But Yoshiyuki sees the world in terms not of moral values but of aesthetic values. In his works he explores that vague border area where aesthetic distinctions are blurred."

"Kigi wa Midori ka" ("Are the Trees Green?") was published in 1958. It is the story of a nightschool teacher whose romantic feelings toward one of his students are intertwined with memories of his childhood with his late father. Near the beginning of the story is a typical Yoshiyuki passage:

> When he looked out on the shrouded town, he would experience two different emotions. One was a feeling of ennui at the thought of having to go down into the town. It was oppressive just to think of the monotonous work waiting for him there. How much better if he could retrace his steps from the bridge, return to his room, crawl under the bedding, and go back to sleep. The other was a stimulus at the thought of descending into the unfathomable, shadowy depths of the mist. He would have one or the other of these feelings, varying with the day. Whichever one he experienced would serve him as a barometer to measure his own mental state.

Another work, "Kinjū Chūgyo" ("Birds, Beasts, Insects and Fish," 1959), once again suggests, in the story of a pessimistic man who works for a collapsing publishing company and finds his only relief from the tedium of his life in the love and pain he shares with a young woman, that sensual pleasure is the only means to validate existence in the modern world. This theme is explored and expanded in such novels as *Yami no Naka no Shukusai* (Festival in the Dark, 1961), a semi-autobiographical work describing the collapse of a marriage after the husband falls in love with an actress, and *Kōru Gāru* (Call Girl, 1962).

In 1963 Yoshiyuki published one of his most widely discussed novels, *Suna no Ue no Shokubutsugun* (Vegetation on the Sand), an attempt to capture middle-aged human sexual behavior at the moment when it touches upon larger questions of the meaning of an individual life and the quest for self-fulfillment. Yoshiyuki lectured for one year, 1964–1965, in the art department at Nihon University, on the history of Dadaism. His 1965 short story collection, *Fui no Dekigoto* (An Unexpected Occurrence), received the Shinchōsha Literary Prize. In that same year, Yoshiyuki's collected short stories were published in five volumes.

Yoshiyuki's next major novel, *Hoshi to Tsuki wa Ten no Ana* (The Stars and Moon Are Holes in the Sky, 1966), which received a literary prize from the Ministry of Education, shares with his earlier works a focus on the various aspects of human psychology which find their expression in sexual activity—in this case, in the sadistically erotic relationship between a middle-aged writer and a schoolgirl—but it also expresses his feelings about the loss of his father to death and his emotional break with his mother.

Perhaps the best known of Yoshiyuki's novels both in Japan and abroad is *Anshitsu* (1969; translated as *The Dark Room*). Once again the protagonist is a middle-aged novelist weary of life, and even more wary of emotional contact since the death of his wife. He spends his days in idle dalliance with prostitutes, their physical couplings becoming more and more twisted and sadomasochistic, but all the more attractive to him, especially after he meets one who is sterile. The opportunity to push his sexual drives to the limit in verification of his existence without the potential for perpetuating the cycle by impregnating his partner comes to seem the ultimate in self-fulfillment. But though he eventually tires and comes to fear his association with the woman, he finds himself continually drawn to her "dark room." For all the starkness of erotic detail in the novel, Yoshiyuki elevates it above the level of prurience by providing a detached perspective, a suggestion that the existential fulfillment of the protagonist's carnal desires is the source of much of the stagnation and lethargy that he feels emotionally. The novel, which received the Tanizaki Prize for literature, has been described by Howard Hibbett as "a nihilistic account of a man's attempt to escape depression through sex. [It] has a fastidious delicacy recalling the elegant 'soft literature' of the later Edo period. The urbane refinement of [Yoshiyuki's] astringent prose style is much admired."

In 1971 Yoshiyuki's collected works were published in eight volumes. The following year he was plagued by a variety of physical ailments, and produced only a quasifictional account of his travels around the United States and Europe with his lover, *Shimetta Sora, Kawaita Sora* (Damp Skies, Dry Skies). His 1974 story collection, *Kaban no Nakami* (*Personal Baggage*), was widely hailed as a stylistic masterpiece and received the Yomiuri Literary Prize. The most important of his recent novels is *Yūgure Made* (Until Dusk, 1978), another inquiry into the interpersonal significance of sexual relationships, this time about an aging man's obsessive need to have guarantees of his young lover's emotional rather than physical virginity; it was awarded the Noma Prize.

Yoshiyuki has also been an active writer of entertainment novels: his writings for the popular audience were anthologized in eleven volumes in 1976; he is a renowned essayist, his *Watakushi no Bungaku Hōrō* (My Literary Wanderings, 1965) being a particularly illuminating reminiscence of the literary world of the 1950s and 1960s; and he has also devoted much of his energy to the work of translation. In addition to translating four stories from Henry Miller's *Nights of Love and Laughter*, he also published a complete Japanese rendition of Miller's *Insomnia or The Devil at Large* in 1975. Between 1981 and 1982, he did modern Japanese translations of two erotic masterpieces, *Kōshoku Ichidai Otoko* (The Life of an Amorous Man) and *Kōshoku Ichidai Onna* (The Life of an Amorous Woman), by the seventeenth-century author, Ihara Saikaku. Yoshiyuki's is one of the most distinctively flavored, independent voices in Japanese letters today.

WORKS IN ENGLISH TRANSLATION: "Sudden Shower" was translated by Geoffrey Bownas in 1972; *The Dark Room* and "Personal Baggage" were translated by John Bester in 1975 and 1976, respectively; "In Akiko's Room" was translated by Howard Hibbett in 1977; "Birds, Beasts, Insects and Fish" was translated by M. T. Mori in 1981; "Are the Trees Green?" was translated by Adam Kabat in 1985; "Scenes at Table" was translated by Geraldine Harcourt in 1985.

ABOUT: Encyclopedia of Japan, 1984.

*ZHANG JIE (also rendered as CHANG CHIEH), (April 27, 1937–   ), Chinese novelist, short-story writer, and essayist, writes: "I was born in Beijing. My childhood was grim with no toys or flowers, hardly any sweets or fruit or even enough to eat. The deepest impression of my childhood was hunger. A few months after my birth my father left my mother and me. Having a new wife he took no responsibility for

ZHANG JIE

us. In our feudal country there was no law against this.

"I was brought up in utter poverty. That made me prize the warmth of human companionship, made me often mistake a flicker of light or malicious deception for heartfelt warmth which I tried to repay a hundred-fold. Although this was one of the main reasons for my unhappiness I never regretted it or learned my lesson. Instead I sometimes considered that this suffering had enriched me. All human beings, especially writers, have to experience failure.

"These circumstances made me sensitive to all injustice and inequality between rich and poor, men and women, in terms of moral character and human dignity. I determined to fight injustice all my life, willing to sacrifice everything for this. I started writing late in life after fighting against poverty, humiliation, oppression and prejudice. Actually my experience was not unlike my mother's so many years before. But knowledge gave me strength. I finally broke my shackles. Although some people cursed me as if I were a witch, it pleased me to know that my pen had got under their skin. I continue to write for my ideal, to fight all injustice and inequality.

"Isn't this childish and ridiculous?

"What is the difference between a writer and a psychotic? Can I guarantee that I understand this world and everyone in it including myself? How well do I understand myself? How well understood am I?

"Now I have many readers. My works have been published in England, France, West Ger-

°tsäng chēe

many, East Germany, Holland, Norway, Denmark, Finland, Sweden, Brazil, and the Soviet Union. Yet walking alone sometimes on a cobbled street, my shoes beat out a rhythm on the cobbles, and echoing that rhythm I ask: Who knows you? Who knows you? Who knows you? . . .

"The answer comes back: No one, no one, no one . . . ."

When her novel *Chenzhong De Chibang* (translated as *Leaden Wings* and *Heavy Wings*) first appeared in 1981, Zhang Jie had difficulties in ordering reprints despite the large demand from readers. It was a lesson she would not soon forget. The novel deals with problems in China's new industrial policy. It depicts conflicts between the doers (reformers) and those resisting change, and some of the characters were too closely identified with certain cadres of a certain industry for comfort. Only a few years after the ending of the Cultural Revolution, in the year 1981, official indifference and inaction were still the norm. Zhang Jie was all too familiar with such hostility. Only two years before, her short story "Ai, Shi Bu-neng Wangji De" ("Love Must Not Be Forgotten") had caused great consternation among the bureaucrats, whose displeasure was triggered by ideological dogmatism as much as by male chauvinism. Zhang Jie was the first Chinese author (and a woman at that) who dared to touch upon the subject of love—in this case a woman's longing for a married man. Readers devoured the story after two decades of reading about love for the country, love for Chairman Mao, and love for machines, etc. The author became an instant celebrity. "Love Must Not Be Forgotten" was written in first person and, although the narrator's story is about her mother, readers in China conveniently assume the work is autobiographical. In the summer of 1982, an American visitor put up this question to her, to which she replied, not exactly in a direct fashion: "Writing must be a result of an accumulation of life experience. I've met people of all shades and forms. I don't use one particular person as the base for characterization, but a combined impression of many whom I've observed. I pick out touching traits of each person and put them together to create a character who in turn moves the reader. Using one single person as model is too thin, too simplistic. The art is to mix together characteristics of many and then to select and create."

Zhang Jie's father was a schoolteacher in Beijing (then Peiping) who abandoned her soon after she was born and left her mother for another woman. She was brought up in poverty by a mother who taught in primary school and was inspiring enough to plant in her an interest in books. By the year she was ready for college, China was already firmly under a new, revolutionary government. Her desire to go to Beida (Beijing University) to study literature was thwarted by the government policy of assigning students to learn subjects considered in great national need. She did not go to the legendary Beida, nor was she given a chance to study literature. Later she wrote that when the notice of enrollment came from the economics department of Renmin Daxue (People's University) she wept bitterly. After graduation, her first job, assigned by the government, was as a statistician at the First Technical Industrial Department in Beijing. When hard times came, like millions of other educated Chinese, she was *xiafang* (sent down to farms or factories) to spend years in Fujian Province in the south, working in an electrical components factory.

It was only after her return to Beijing that she began to write stories. For a time she also wrote film scripts for the Beijing Film Studio. As a celebrated author now she has attained the status of *zhuanyi zuojia* (professional writer), being a member of the All China Writers' Union. After a visit to the United States in 1982 she produced a collection of impressions, *Fang Mei Sanji* (Notes on a Journey to the U.S.), in which she makes sardonic comments on American mores. But it took an American writer, Annie Dillard, to capture Zhang Jie's passion. Dillard happened to catch an exchange between the demure Chinese writer and the American poet Allen Ginsberg: "I witness only the climax: 'Mr. Ginsberg!' Zhang Jie is leaning forward fiercely over the interpreter's knees. Her slender shoulders are squared. 'You should not think only of yourself! You must live and work so as to fulfill your obligations! Have your goals firmly in your mind. You should not take drugs! Think of your responsibility to society. As for myself, my goals are always clear. My mind is never confused!'"

Zhang Jie's impatience is evident in her outspoken *As Long as Nothing Happens, Nothing Will* where her targets are hypocrisy, political intrigue, nepotism, bureaucratic inefficiency, and sexual maneuvering. Though she is realistic enough to know that the world is not perfect, she defines her goal as a writer in idealistic terms—"to instill confidence and courage in the people." Obviously unable to reconcile such ideals with the repressive measures of the Chinese government in recent years, Zhang Jie has become a voluntary exile. In 1990 she was teaching at Wesleyan University in Connecticut.

WORKS IN ENGLISH TRANSLATION: A collection of Zhang Jie's stories, *Love Must Not Be Forgotten*, was translated with an introduction by Gladys Yang in 1986. An English translation of *Leaden Wings* was published in China in 1987; in 1990 a new translation by Howard Goldblatt was published under the title *Heavy Wings*. *As Long as Nothing Happens, Nothing Will* was translated in China in 1988. One of Zhang Jie's short stories, "Who Knows How to Live," is in *Prize-Winning Stories from China, 1978–1979*, published by the Foreign Language Press in Beijing, 1981.

ABOUT: Dillard, A. Encounters with Chinese Writers, 1984; Who's Who in People's Republic of China, 2nd ed., 1987. *Periodicals*—New York Times March 7, 1989; U.S.-China Review May–June 1984, January–February, 1985.

*ZHANG XIANLIANG (also rendered as CHANG HSIEN-LIANG) (1936–), Chinese short-story writer and novelist, was born into a middle-class family in Nanjing, the former Nationalist capital, where his father was a Kuomintang official and also managed a number of large enterprises including a shipping company. His class background was to be a handicap in his young life once the Communists took over. In 1952, his father was arrested and accused of spying. The father died while serving his sentence, and the son moved to Beijing and enrolled in a middle school. Independent in his thinking even then, he joined a juvenile group called "Qi Xiongdi" (Seven Brothers) and was expelled from the school in 1954 for "hoodlum activities." Not being able to continue his education, he volunteered to go to the remote northwestern region of Ningxia to work. In 1956, he became a teacher at the Cadres' Culture School under the auspices of the Gansu Provincial Party Committee. It is not clear whether that was the year he joined the Communist party.

Zhang became interested in literature at a very young age. At thirteen he began to write poems. He already had had three poems published and was hailed as one of the most promising young poets before the appearance of his long lyric "Da Feng Ge" (Song of the Great Wind) shocked the literary world in 1957. It was first published in the July issue of *Yan He* (Yan River) but was instantly picked up by *Renmin Ribao* (People's Daily), and thus assured a huge readership. Soon Mao Zedong started the anti-rightist campaign and the poem "Da Feng Ge" came under virulent attack by literary bureaucrats. Zhang later was to explain that during the "Hundred Flowers" period, like all other young Chinese, he was enthusiastic over China's future as a new nation, but his extolling of the coming

of the new era was interpreted by the bureaucrats as wishing for a return of the old times. He was accused of being a rightist and sent to a labor camp for reform. From then on he was in and out of the labor camp and jail numerous times. Released from the camp in 1961, by the next year, in the atmosphere of "continuous class struggle," he had been branded an "anti-revolution element" and sent to jail for three more years. In 1965, a new "Campaign for Socialist Education" started and he was *xiafang* (sent down) to a commune for three years. During the height of the Cultural Revolution in 1968, he was again locked up; this time the label was "antirevolutionary-revisionist." He was released and rearrested in 1970. In 1972 he was set free as an aftermath of the Lin Biao Affair (a plan to assassinate Mao), but not until 1979 was he formally rehabilitated.

In discussing with an interviewer those twenty-two years of horrible yet absurd experience, he did not seem resentful. His explanation may speak for most of those who had endured similar hardships: "In the beginning, I did not consider myself as anti-Party or anti-socialist, because I believed the Party could never be wrong. After much self-examination and self-criticism, I even began to believe I actually had sinful thoughts in my blood." He remembered that in 1960 the great famine brought on by Mao's Great Leap Forward campaign shocked him into a rude awakening that what China practiced then was "not true socialism." That was the moment he began to realize that he, "the rightist," might not be wrong and that it was possible that the Party had erred.

When he began to write again in 1979 he was already a middle-aged man full of stories to tell. He joined the editorial staff of a literary magazine called *Shuofang* (The North), which printed his first short story "Ling Yu Rou" (Soul and Body). Winning the award as one of the best short stories in 1980, "Ling Yu Rou" later became known as "Mu Ma Ren" (A Herdsman's Story) which was made into a popular movie and elevated Zhang to the rank of a national celebrity. His other works include "Xiao Er Bu La Ke" (Bitter Springs), depicting the life of a truck driver in the Ningxia Uighur region; "Lu Hua Shu" (Mimosa), telling the story of a young man just released from prison; "Long Zhong" (The Dragon Seed) and "He De Zisun" (Children of the River), both based on his life among the Uighurs in the northwest province of Gansu; and the novel *Nanren De Fengge* (The Way to Be a Man), said to be semi-autobiographical.

His best known work is the novella *Nanren De Yiban Shi Nüren* (Half of Man Is Woman), which, when first published in China in 1985, caused alarm and controversy for its audacity in depicting sexuality as man's basic instinct. This story of life in the Chinese gulag is undoubtedly autobiographical. Zhang Yonglin, the central character, bearing the same family name as the author's, also spends some twenty years in labor camps. While he is working in a rural commune, his chance encounter with a beautiful woman bathing nude in the river revives his yearning for a new life. Eight years later, when they meet again and marry, he realizes that the unintellectual, unromantic farm woman is not at all the woman he has idealized. Impotence ensues, symbolizing the powerlessness of people in other spheres, such as prison.

In an unusual, self-promoting article entitled "Please Buy *Selected Stories of Zhang Xianliang*" published in Shanghai's *Wen Hui Bao* (Wen Hui Daily), Zhang ridicules his critics for such cliché-ridden criticisms as "full of salacious thoughts," "unhealthy depiction of animal desire," "unfit for young readers," etc. Quoting Marx, Engels, and Lenin, he claims that "communism is not asceticism," that "the relationship between sexes is the highest form of life's force" and that he has intended to make use of honesty in his works "to challenge hypocrisy created by suppression."

Tall, agile, and completely uninhibited in words and in action, Zhang is the center of attention in any kind of social gathering. He speaks freely and unreservedly. At a dinner party given by the International Writing Project of the Uni-

versity of Iowa in 1987, he did a wild solo disco dance on the dance floor. He has visited the United States several times. In a speech entitled "The Artistic Quest of China's Authors Today," during one of the visits, he commented on what was wrong with China's creative writing: "The great majority of contemporary Chinese literary works neglect a most important law of the use of the language: economy. Our language is short on ambiguity, subtle hints and multiple meanings. It is short on understatement and humor. Writers tend to write down everything that is in their minds, leaving nothing to the reader's own imagination." He feels that China's creative writing has been dormant for at least twenty years and now, reawakening, must compete with literature of other countries. Chinese writers can achieve that goal only by "faithfully portraying the life and the value of the Chinese people and China's historical progress and evolution." He was opposed to the past literary policy of the Communist party: "Writings that deal only with positive, happy subjects can only produce conceptualized, formula writing."

WORKS IN ENGLISH TRANSLATION: *Mimosa and Other Stories*, 1985, was translated by Gladys Yang, W.J.F. Jenner, et. al. *Half of Man Is Woman*, 1988, was translated by Martha Avery.

ABOUT: Who's Who in the People's Republic of China, 2nd ed., 1987.

List of Authors by Nationality

ALGERIAN
Assia Djebar

AMERICAN
Edward Abbey
Alice Adams
Renata Adler
Robert Alter
Max Apple
Rudolf Arnheim (German-born)
Dore Ashton
Paul Auster
Russell Banks
Frederick Barthelme
Michael Benedikt
Jeremy Bernstein
Alfred Bester
Stephen Birmingham
Sissela Bok (Swedish-born)
T. Coraghessan Boyle
Harold Brodkey
Victor H. Brombert
William Bronk
Jerome S. Bruner
Philip Caputo
Fred Chappell
Amy Clampitt
I. Bernard Cohen
Frank Conroy
Robin Cook
Ann Cornelisen
Ronald S. Crane
Robert Darnton
Donald Davidson
Natalie Zemon Davis
Paul de Man (Belgian-born)
Edwin Denby
Philip K. Dick
Owen Dodson
Ellen Douglas
Rita Dove
Elizabeth Drew
Norman Dubie
Christopher Durang
John Ehle
Nora Ephron
Joseph Epstein
Louise Erdrich
Amitai Etzioni (German-born)

Raymond Federman (French-born)
Frances Fitzgerald
Thomas Flanagan
Carolyn Forché
Richard Ford
Paula Fox
Tess Gallagher
Howard Gardner
Martin Gardner
Clifford Geertz
Brester Ghiselin
Ellen Gilchrist
Mark Girouard
Albert Goldbarth
Ellen Goodman
Arthur Gregor (Austrian-born)
Doris Grumbach
A. R. Gurney, Jr.
Rosa Guy (Trinadadian-born)
Barry Hannah
Robert L. Heilbroner
Beth Henley
Jamake Highwater
Gertrude Himmelfarb
Alice Hoffman
Douglas R. Hofstadter
Rachel Ingalls
Albert Innaurato
Denis Johnson
Robert Kelly
Joseph Kerman (British-born)
Jamaica Kincaid (Antiguan-born)
Stephen King
Louis L'Amour
Meridel Le Sueur
Brad Leithauser
Elmore Leonard
Phillip Lopate
Barry Holstun Lopez
Robert Ludlam
Maynard Mack
Norman MacLean
Janet Malcolm
D. Keith Mano
Bobbie Ann Mason
Harry Mathews
William Matthews
Michael Mewshaw
J. Hillis Miller

Frederick Morgan
Richard B. Morris
Gloria Naylor
John Nichols
Lorine Niedecker
Marsha Norman
Tim O'Brien
Sharon Olds
Mary Oliver
Paul Osborn
Michael S. Palmer
Linda Pastan
Orlando Patterson (Jamaican-born)
Harry Mark Petrakis
Jayne Anne Phillips
George Plimpton
Charles Portis
Francine Prose
Carl Rakosi (Hungarian-born)
Richard Rhodes
Carolyn M. Rodgers
John Sanford
Susan Fromberg Schaeffer
Richard Schickel
Lynne Sharon Schwartz
Lore Segal (German-born)
Cynthia Propper Seton
Harvey Shapiro
Susan Sheehan
Kate Simon
Dave Smith
Jonathan D. Spence
Norman Spinrad
Ronald Steel
Lawrence Stone (British-born)
Ronald Sukenick
Henry Taylor
Hunter S. Thompson
Calvin Tomkins
Fred Turner (British-born)
R. G. Vliet
Margaret Walker
Wendy Wasserstein
James Welch
Edmund White
Ruth Whitman
John Edgar Wideman
John Wieners
James Wilcox
Thomas Williams
August Wilson
William S. Wilson
Rudolf Wittkower (German-born)
Gene Wolfe

ARGENTINEAN
Humberto Costantini
Luisa Valenzuela

ARMENIAN
Gevorg Emin

AUSTRALIAN
Jessica Anderson
Thea Astley
Peter Carey
Xavier Herbert
Robert Hughes
Elizabeth Jolley
Les A. Murray

AUSTRIAN
Ernst Jandl

AUSTRO-HUNGARIAN
Gregor von Rezzori

BRAZILIAN
Autran Dourado
Clarice Lispector
Moacyr Scliar

BRITISH
Peter Ackroyd
Robert Aickman
Martin Amis
Anthony Bailey
Julian Barnes
Rachel Billington
William Boyd (Ghana-born)
Asa Briggs
Humphrey Carpenter
Angela Carter
Caryl Churchill
Richard Cobb
Isabel Colegate
Barbara Comyns
Peter Conrad
Freeman J. Dyson
Terry Eagleton
Alice Thomas Ellis
Stuart Evans
James Fenton
Eva Figes (German-born)
Roy Fisher
Ken Follett (Welsh-born)
Margaret Forster
P. N. Furbank

Victoria Glendinning
Christopher Hampton
David Hare
Tony Harrison
David Hughes
Gabriel Josipovici
John Keegan
Laurence Lerner
Robert Liddell
Gavin Lyall
Denis Mack Smith
Wilfrid Howard Mellers
Andrew Motion
Eric Newby
Ruth Rendell
Bernice Rubens
Carol Rumens
Peter Russell
Oliver Sacks
Tom Sharpe
Graham Swift
Emma Tennant
E. P. Thompson
Flora Thompson
Gillian Tindall
Stephen Edelston Toulmin
A. N. Wilson

CANADIAN
Robert Bringhurst
Timothy Findley
Daryl Hine
Hugh Hood
Gwendolyn MacEwen
Eli Mandel
Alice Munro
Raymond Souster
Charles Taylor

CHILEAN
Isabel Allende
Maria Luisa Bombal

CHINESE
Ai Qing
Cao Yu
Chen Rong
Feng Jicai
Liu Binyan
Lu Wenfu
Wang Meng
Yang Jiang
Zhang Jie
Zhang Xianliang

CUBAN
Heberto Padilla

CZECHOSLOVAKIAN
Saul Friedlander (Czech-Israeli)
Ivan Klíma

EGYPTIAN
Andrée Chedid (writes in French)
Tawfiq al-Hakim
Nawal el-Saadawi

FINNISH
Paavo Haavikko

FRENCH
Philippe Ariès
René Crevel
Julia Kristeva
Jean Lacouture
Jacques Le Goff
Georges Perec
Tzvetan Todorov (Bulgarian-born)

GERMAN
Jurek Becker
Michael Ende
Hans-Georg Gadamer
Gert Hofmann
Walter Kempowski
Reiner Kunze
Reinhard Lettau
Botho Strauss

GREEK
Manolis Anagnostakis
Dimitris Tsaloumas

GUADELOUPAN
Jean-Louis Baghio'o
Maryse Condé

HUNGARIAN
Sándor Csoóri
Iván Mándy
Magda Szabó
Ferenc Sánta

INDIAN
Bhabani Bhattacharya
Jayanta Mahapatra

INDO-PAKISTANI
Zulfikar Ghose

IRISH
Molly Keane
Patrick McGinley
Julia O'Faolain

ISRAELI
Yaakov Shabtai

ITALIAN
Dario Fo
Carlo Ginzburg
Primo Levi

JAPANESE
Ariyoshi Sawako
Enchi Fumiko
Ibuse Masuji
Inoue Yasushi
Ōe Kenzaburo
Takamura Kōtarō
Tanikawa Shuntarō
Yasuoka Shōtarō
Yoshiyuki Junnosuke

NEW ZEALANDER
Lauris Edmond
Keri Hulme

NIGERIAN
Elechi Amadi

NORTH IRISH
John Hewitt
Michael Longley
James Simmons

PARAGUAYAN
Augusto Roa Bastos

POLISH
Janusz Głowacki
Tadeusz Konwicki
Wisława Szymborska

ROMANIAN
Ion Caraion
Dumitru Radu Popescu

RUSSIAN
Mikhail Mikhailovich Bakhtin
Sergey Dovlatov
Vasily Grossman
Irina Ratushinskaya
Anatoly Naumovich Rybakov

SCOTTISH
Robin Fulton
Alasdair Gray
Stuart Hood

SOUTH AFRICAN
Dennis Brutus
Christopher Hope
Alex La Guma
Lewis Nkosi
Siegfried Stander

SPANISH
Jorge Semprun

SWISS
Jürg Federspiel
Adolf Muschg
Robert Otto Walser

TRINIDADIAN
Michael Anthony
Shiva Naipaul

WELSH
Gillian Clarke

YUGOSLAVIAN
Miodrag Pavlović

ZIMBABWEAN
Dambudzo Marechera

Acknowledgments

The lines from the poem "Among School Children" on pages 5–6 are from *London Lickpenny* (London: Ferry Press, 1974) by Peter Ackroyd

The lines beginning "Still, it might be beautiful . . ."; the elegy "Harris 1944"; and the lines beginning "Upright and lonesome . . . ," "Intransigent, inaccessible, always ready. . . .," "Words must be hammered . . . ," and "So be it. . . ." on pages 32–33 are all from *The Target* (NY: Pella, 1980) by Manolis Anagnostakis, translated by Kimon Friar

The lines from "Scribe," "Wall Writing," and "Shadow to Shadow" on page 56 are from *Wall Writing* (Great Barrington, MA: The Figures, 1976) by Paul Auster

The lines from "Victoria Falls" on page 79 are from *Changes: A Chapbook* (Detroit: New Fresco, 1961) by Michael Benedikt

The lines from "Country Living" on page 80 are from *Sky* (Wesleyan University Press, 1970) by Michael Benedikt

The lines from "Taxidermy" on page 80 are from *Mole Notes* (Wesleyan University Press, 1971) by Michael Benedikt

The lines beginning "Am I doomed . . ." on pages 80–81 are from *The Badminton at Great Barrington; or Gustave Mahler and the Chattanooga Choo-Choo* (University of Pittsburgh Press, 1980) by Michael Benedikt

The lines from "Deuteronomy" and "Parmenides" on page 108 are from *The Beauty of the Weapons: Selected Poems 1972–1982* (Toronto: McClelland and Stewart Ltd., 1982) by Robert Bringhurst

The lines from "Saraha" on pages 108–109 are from *Pieces of Map, Pieces of Music* (Toronto: McClelland and Stewart Ltd., 1986) by Robert Bringhurst

The lines from "The Tree in the Middle of the Field," "How Indeterminacy Determines Us," "The World in Time and Space," and "Truth as a Far Country; as a Piteous Ogre" on page 115 are from *The World, the Worldless* (NY: New Directions, 1964) by William Bronk

The lines from "The Effect of Cause Dispaired" on page 116 are from *Silence and Metaphor* (NY: Elizabeth Press, 1975) by William Bronk

The lines from "Getting Older" on page 116 are from *Manifest; and Furthermore* (Berkeley: North Point Press, 1987) by William Bronk

The lines from "My House New-Painted" on page 117 are from *Life Supports* (Berkeley: North Point Press, 1981) by William Bronk

The lines from "Sirens, Knuckles, Boots" and "I Must Speak" on pages 123–124 are from *Sirens, Knuckles, Boots* (Ibadan, Nigeria: Mbari Publications, 1963) by Dennis Brutus

The lines beginning "vague heroism . . . " and "I cut away . . . " on page 124 are from *Letters to Martha, and Other Poems from a South African Prison* (London: Heinemann Educational, 1968) by Dennis Brutus. Reprinted by permission of Heinemann Educational Books Ltd. and from Hill and Wang, a division of Farrar, Straus and Giroux, Inc.

The lines from "Flying to Denmark" on page 125 are from *A Simple Lust* (London: Heinemann Educational Books Ltd. and NY: Hill and Wang, a division of Farrar, Straus & Giroux, Inc., 1973) by Dennis Brutus

The lines from "Song from the Occupation Time," "She Who Tarries in the Land of Winds," and "De-ornamentation" on pages 132–133 are from *Poems* (Athens: Ohio University Press, 1981) by Ion Caraion, translated by Marguerite Dorian and Elliott B. Urdang

The lines from "Rimbaud Fire Letters to Jim Applewhite" and from "My Grandmother Washes Her Feet" on page 146 are reprinted by permission of Louisiana State University Press from *Midquest* by Fred Chappell. Copyright © 1981 by Fred Chappell

The lines beginning "First, erase your name . . . " on page 150 are from *Women of the Fertile Crescent* (Washington, D.C.: Three Continents Press, 1978) by Andrée Chedid, translated by Samuel Hazo and Mirène Ghossein

The lines from "Fog," "Salvage," and "Beethoven, Opus III" on page 156 are from *Kingfisher* (NY: Alfred A. Knopf, Inc., 1983) by Amy Clampitt

The lines from "Urn-Burial and the Butterfly Migration" and "What the Light Was Like" on page 156 are from *What the Light Was Like* (NY: Alfred A. Knopf, Inc., 1985) by Amy Clampitt

The lines from "In Pisgah Graveyard" and "Lunchtime Lecture" on page 158 are from *The Sundial* (Dyfed, U.K.: Gomer Press, 1978) by Gillian Clarke

The lines from the title poem and "Sheila na Gig at Kilpeck" on page 159 are from *Letter From a Far Country* (Manchester: Carcanet Press, 1982) by Gillian Clarke

The lines from "City Without Smoke" on page 209 are from *Complete Poems* by Edwin Denby, copyright © 1986 by Full Court Press. Reprinted by permission of Random House, Inc. and the Robert Cornfield Literary Agency

The lines from "Black Mother Praying" on page 218 are from *Powerful Long Ladder* by Owen Dodson. Copyright © 1946 by Owen Dodson. Reprinted by permission of Farrar, Straus & Giroux, Inc.

The lines beginning "Don't pay attention . . . " on page 219 are from *The Confes-*

The lines from "Answering a Letter from a Younger Poet," "Sea," "The Catch," and "For the Eighth Decade" on pages 343–344 are from *Windrose: Poems, 1929–1979* (University of Utah Press, 1980) by Brewster Ghiselin

The lines from "Hospital" on page 361 are from *Coprolites* (NY: New Rivers Press, 1974) by Albert Goldbarth

The lines from "The Lost First Decade" on page 361 are from *Jan. 31* (NY: Doubleday, 1974) by Albert Goldbarth

The lines from "Blackout" on page 367 are from *Octavian Shooting Targets* (NY: Dodd Mead, 1954) by Arthur Gregor

The lines from "Words of the Pilgrim" on page 368 are from *Embodiment and Other Poems* (NY: Sheep Meadow Press, 1982) by Arthur Gregor

The lines from "The Birthplace" and "The Finnish Cycle" on pages 381–382 are from *Snow in May: An Anthology of Finnish Writing 1945–1972* (London: Associated University Presses, 1978) by Paavo Haavikko, translated by Anselm Hollo

The lines from "Winter Palace" on pages 382–383 are from *Paavo Haavikko and Tomas Tranströmen Selected Poems* (1968) by Paavo Haavikko, translated by Anselm Hollo

The lines from "Heredity," "Them & [uz]," "Litererchewer," and "Book Ends" on pages 399–400 are from *Continuous* (London: Rex Collings, Ltd., 1981) by Tony Harrison

The lines beginning "and being a man of doubt . . ." on page 400 are from *A Kumquat for John Keats* (Newcastle upon Tyne: Bloodaxe Books, 1981) by Tony Harrison

The lines from "I write for . . . ," "Neither an elegy nor a manifesto," "Conacre," "O country people," "Once Alien Here," and "The Colony" on pages 411–412, 413 are from *The Selected John Hewitt* (Belfast: Blackstaff Press, 1981) by John Hewitt

The lines from "The Response" on page 412 are from *Collected Poems 1932–1967* (McGibbon & Kee, 1968) by John Hewitt. Reprinted by permission of Blackstaff Press

The lines beginning "Grey sea, grey sky, . . ." on page 413 are from *Kites in Spring* (Belfast: Blackstaff Press, 1980) by John Hewitt

The lines beginning "For me, as for anyone . . ." on page 421 are from *Academic Festival Overtures* (NY: Atheneum, 1985) by Daryl Hine

The lines beginning "Morning like a dangling participle . . ." on page 422 are from *Daylight Saving* (NY: Atheneum, 1978) by Daryl Hine

The lines from "Bluebeard's Wife" on page 422 are from *The Wooden Horse* (NY: Atheneum, 1965) by Daryl Hine

The lines from "Epilogue: To Theocritus" on page 422 are from *Theocritus: Idylls and Epigrams* (NY: Atheneum, 1982) by Daryl Hine

The lines from "The Flight of the White South Africans" on page 439 are from *Cape Drives* (London: London Magazine Editions, 1974) by Christopher Hope

The lines from "ode auf n" on page 459 are from *Laut und Luise* by Ernst Jandl, Gesammelte Werke in drei Banden © 1966, 1985 by Luchterhand Literaturverlag, Frankfurt/Main

The lines from "No Music Please" on pages 459–460 are from *No Music Please* (London: Turret Books, 1967) by Ernst Jandl, translated by Georg Rapp

The lines from "Checking the Traps" on page 462 are from *The Man Among the Seals* (Iowa City: Stone Wall Press, 1969) by Denis Johnson. Reprinted by permission of the Robert Cornfield Literary Agency

The lines from "The Boarding" on page 463 are from *The Incognito Lounge and Other Poems* by Denis Johnson. Copyright © 1982 by Denis Johnson. Reprinted by permission of Random House, Inc.

The lines from "Style is Death" on page 477 are from *Finding the Measure* (Los Angeles, CA: Black Sparrow Press, 1968) by Robert Kelly

The lines from "Of Winter's Birds" on page 477 are from *Lunes/Sightings* (NY: Hawk's Well Press, 1964) by Robert Kelly and Jerome Rothenberg

The lines beginning "suburbs of the one great city . . ." on page 478 are from *The Common Shore* (Los Angeles, CA: Black Sparrow Press, 1969) by Robert Kelly

The lines from "Nocturne II" on page 501 are from *German Poetry 1910–1975* (Manchester: Carcanet New Press, 1976) by Reiner Kunze, translated by Michael Hamburger. Reprinted by permission M. Hamburger

The lines from "Peace Children" and "Fifteen" on page 501 are from *The Wonderful Years* (NY: George Braziller, Inc., 1977) by Reiner Kunze, translated by Joachim Neugroschel

The lines from "A Quilled Quilt, a Needle Bed" on page 520 are from *Hundreds of Fireflies* (NY: Alfred A. Knopf, Inc., 1982) by Brad Leithauser. Reprinted by permission of Alfred A. Knopf, Inc.

The lines from "Hesitancy" on page 521 are from *A Seaside Mountain: Eight Poems from Japan* (Charlotte, NC: Sarabande Press, 1985) by Brad Leithauser

The lines from "Poor Monkey" and "The Merman" on page 528 are from *Selves* (London: Routledge & Kegan Paul, 1969) by Laurence Lerner

The lines from "Raspberries" on pages 528–529 are from *The Man I Killed* (London: Secker & Warburg, 1980) by Laurence Lerner

The lines from "To Derek Mahon" on page 544 are from *No Continuing City: Poems 1963–1968* (London: Gill & Macmillan, 1969) by Michael Longley

The lines from "Letters," "Wounds," and "Swans Mating" on pages 545–546 are from *An Exploded View: Poems 1968–72* (London: Gollancz, 1973) by Michael Longley

The lines from "The Daily Round" and "Indigestible" on pages 547–548 are from *The Daily Round: New Poems* (NY: Sun, 1976) by Phillip Lopate

mouse . . ." on page 728 are from *Complaints to Circe* (London, 1963) by Peter Russell

The lines from "To Certain (English) Neighbours," "On Being Called 'Infinitely Opaque' by H. M. McLuhan," and "The Board's Blare" on pages 728–729 are from *Epigrammata, Malice Aforethought or The Tumour in the Brain* (Salzburg Studies, 1954) by Peter Russell

The lines from "The Dispossessed" on page 729 are from *Three Elegies of Quintilius* (Tunbridge Wells: Pound Press, 1954) by Peter Russell

The lines from "Tristis" on page 729 are by Osip Mandelshtam; the translation is by Peter Russell, taken from his book *All for the Wolves: Selected Poems 1947–1975* (Redding Ridge, CT: Black Swan Books, 1984)

The lines from "Death of a Grandmother" on page 769 are from *The Eye* (Swallow, 1953) and reprinted in *National Cold Storage Company: New and Selected Poems* (Wesleyan University Press, 1988) by Harvey Shapiro

The lines from "News of the World" on page 769 are from *Battle Report*, copyright © 1965 by Harvey Shapiro. Reprinted by permission of University Press of New England

The lines from "Spirit of Rabbi Nachman," "Aleph," and "Mountain, Fire, Thornbush" on pages 769–770 are from *Battle Report* (Wesleyan University Press, 1966) by Harvey Shapiro. Permission to reprint from Harvey Shapiro

The lines from "Ditty" on page 770 are from *This World*, copyright © 1965 by Harvey Shapiro. Reprinted by permission of University Press of New England

The lines from "Considering" and "A Jerusalem Notebook" on page 770 are from *The Light Holds*, copyright © 1984 by Harvey Shapiro. Reprinted by permission of University Press of New England

The lines from "Husband to Wife" and "If the Cap Fits" on pages 777, 778 are from *Late But in Earnest* (London: Bodley Head, 1967) by James Simmons

The lines from "Memorials of a Tour of Yorkshire" on page 778 are from *Energy to Burn* (London: Bodley Head, 1971) by James Simmons

The lines from "The Tire Hangs in the Yard," "Roundhouse Voices," and "On a Fieldtrip at Fredericksburg" on pages 782–783 are from *The Roundhouse Voices* (NY: Harper & Row, 1985) by Dave Smith. Reprinted by permission of University of Illinois Press

The lines from "Old Woman in Hospital Eating Breakfast," "Queen Anne's Lace," "For the Birds," "Yonge Street Saturday Night," "Bourgeois Child," and "Money Talks" on pages 786–787 are from *Collected Poems of Raymond Souster, 1940–1986* (Ottawa: Oberon Press, 1980–1986) by Raymond Souster

The lines beginning "The joys of writing . . ." on pages 815–816 are from *Quarterly Review of Literature* 23: Poetry Series 4 (1982)

by Wisława Szymborska, translated by Sharon Olds

The lines beginning "The bomb will explode . . . ," "I looked back . . . ," "The longest snake on earth . . . ," and the lines from "People on a Bridge" and "Homecoming" on pages 816, 817 are from *The Burning Forest: Modern Polish Poetry* (Newcastle upon Tyne: Bloodaxe Books, 1988) by Wisława Szymborska, translated by Adam Czerniawski

The lines beginning "Conceived on a mattress . . ." on page 816 are from *Modern Poetry in Translation* No. 23–24 (Spring 1975) by Wisława Szymborska, translated by Jan Darowski

The lines from "The Country of Netsuke," "Lemon Elegy," and "My Father's Face" on pages 818–819 are from *Chieko and Other Poems of Takamura Kōtarō* (Honolulu: University of Hawaii Press, 1980) by Takamura Kōtarō, translated by Hiroaki Sato

The lines from "Growth," the lines beginning "In killing, I tried to make sure . . . ," and the lines from "Sonnet 58" on pages 821, 822 are excerpted from *The Selected Poems of Shuntarō Tanikawa*, copyright © 1983 by Shuntarō Tanikawa, translated by Harold Wright. Reprinted by permission of North Point Press

The lines from "Riding a One-Eyed Horse" and "An Afternoon of Pocket Billiards" on pages 826–827, 828 are from *An Afternoon of Pocket Billiards* (University of Utah Press, 1975) by Henry Taylor

The lines from "The Horse Show at Midnight" and "A Blind Man Locking His House" on page 827 are from *The Horse Show at Midnight* (Louisiana State University Press, 1966) by Henry Taylor

The lines from "Somewhere Along the Way" and "The Flying Change" on pages 827, 828 are from *The Flying Change* (Louisiana State University Press, 1985) by Henry Taylor

The lines from "To the Reader II," "The Sick Barber," "Observations of a Hypochondriac," "The Holy Inquisition," and "Consolation" on pages 855–856 are from *The Observatory* (University of Queensland Press, 1983) by Dimitris Tsaloumas, translated by Philip Grundy

The lines from "The Music" and "The Riots 1968–1969" on page 858 are from *Between Two Lives*, copyright © 1972 by Fred Turner. Reprinted by permission of University Press of New England

The lines beginning "By the banks of the Mekong River . . ." on page 858 are from *The Return* (Woodstock, VT: Countryman Press, 1981) by Fred Turner

The lines beginning "I sing of what it is . . ." on page 859 are from *The New World* (Princeton University Press, 1985) by Fred Turner

The lines from "For My People" on pages 866–867 are from *For My People* (New Haven: Yale University Press, 1942) by Margaret Walker

The lines from "Jackson Mississippi," "Birmingham," and "The Ballad of the Hoppy Toad" on pages 868, 869 are from *Prophets for a New Day* (Detroit: Broadside Press, 1970) by Margaret Walker

The lines from "October Journey" on page 869 are from *October Journey* (Detroit: Broadside Press, 1973) by Margaret Walker

The lines from "The Man from Washington" on page 878 are from *Riding the Earthboy 40* (NY: World Publishing, 1971) by James Welch

The lines from "Nuns on the Beach" on page 883 are from *Blood and Milk Poems* (NY: October House, 1963) by Ruth Whitman

The lines from "Cutting the Jewish Bride's Hair" on page 883 are from *The Marriage Wig and Other Poems*, copyright © 1968 by Ruth Whitman, reprinted by permission of Harcourt Brace Jovanovich, Inc.

The lines from the title poem and "Castoff Skin" on page 884 are from *The Passion of Lizzie Borden* (NY: October House, 1973) by Ruth Whitman

The lines beginning "If my boundary stops here . . ." on page 884 are from *Tamsen Donner: A Woman's Journey* (Cambridge: Alicejamesbooks, 1977) by Ruth Whitman

The lines beginning "There's a fire in me . . ." on pages 884–885 are from *The Testing of Hannah Senesh* (Detroit: Wayne State University Press, 1986) by Ruth Whitman

The lines from "A Poem for Painters," "The Acts of Youth," and "Children of the Working Class" on pages 888–889, 890 are reprinted from *Selected Poems: 1958–1984* with the permission of Black Sparrow Press. Copyright © 1958, 1964, 1975 by John Wieners

The lines from "For Huncke" on page 889 are reprinted from *Cultural Affairs in Boston: Poetry & Prose 1956–1985* with the permission of Black Sparrow Press. Copyright © 1988 by John Wieners

Picture Credits

Edward Abbey: photo by Jay Dusard, courtesy Henry Holt and Company; *Peter Ackroyd*: courtesy Hamish Hamilton Ltd.; *Alice Adams*: photo © Thomas Victor; *Renata Adler*: photo by Richard Avedon, courtesy Alfred A. Knopf; *Ai Qing*: courtesy of the author; *Robert Aickman*: photo © London Times, courtesy Kirby McCauley Ltd.; *Isabel Allende*: Photo © Peter Peitsch, courtesy of the author; *Robert Alter*: photo by Ed Kirwan, courtesy Simon and Schuster; *Elechi Amadi*: courtesy Heinemann International; *Martin Amis*: photo by Miriam Berkley; *Manolis Anagostakis*: courtesy of the author; *Jessica Anderson*: photo by Reece Seannell, courtesy of the author; *Max Apple*: photo by Jerry Bauer; *Ariyoshi Sawako*: courtesy Japan Foreign-Rights Centre; *Rudolf Arnheim*: courtesy of the author; *Dore Ashton*: photo © Greg Schaler 1989, courtesy of the author; *Thea Astley*: courtesy G. P. Putnam's Sons; *Paul Auster*: photo © Françoise Schein.

Anthony Bailey: photo © Rollie McKenna; *Russell Banks*: photo by Thomas Victor; *Julian Barnes*: photo © Miriam Berkley; *Frederick Barthelme*: photo by Rie Fortenberry; *Jurek Becker*: photo by Ashkan Sahihi; *Michael Benedikt*: photo by Robert Turney, courtesy of the author; *Alfred Bester*: photo by Roger Field, courtesy of Kirby McCauley Ltd.; *Bhabani Bhattacharya*: AP/Wide World Photos; *Rachel Billington*: photo by Jerry Bauer; *Stephen Birmingham*: photo by Jeffrey Kauck; *Sissela Bok*: courtesy of the author; *Maria Luisa Bombal*: New York Times Pictures; *William Boyd*: photo by Jerry Bauer; *T. Coraghessan Boyle*: photo © Pablo Campos 1988; *Asa Briggs*: courtesy of the author; *Robert Bringhurst*: photo by Beatrice Dowd, courtesy of Copper Canyon Press; *Harold Brodkey*: photo © Jerry Bauer; *Victor H. Brombert*: photo by R. P. Matthews; *William Bronk*: photo © Saratoga Illustrated; *Jerome S. Bruner*: Stanley Seligson Photography; *Dennis Brutus*: Africa Network.

Cao Yu: photo by Shen Jun, courtesy of the author; *Philip Caputo*: photo © Lawson Little 1986; *Ion Caraion*: courtesy Mylabris Press; *Peter Carey*: photo by Thomas Victor; *Humphrey Carpenter*: photo by Billett Potter, courtesy of Houghton Mifflin Company; *Angela Carter*: photo © Tara Heinemann 1984; *Fred Chappell*: courtesy of the author; *Caryl Churchill*: photo by Paul Harter; *Amy Clampitt*: photo © Thomas Victor; *Richard Cobb*: photo by Jerry Bauer; *I. Bernard Cohen*: Robert Reinhold/New York Times Pictures; *Isabel Colegate*: photo by Jerry Bauer; *Barbara Comyns*: courtesy of the author; *Frank Conroy*: photo by Andrew Lautman; *Robin Cook*: photo by Barbara Ellen Cook; *Ann Cornelisen*:

courtesy of the author; *Humberto Costantini*: photo by Fiora Bemporad; *René Crevel*: photo © Bernice Abbott, courtesy Watkins/Loomis Agency, Inc.; *Sándor Csoóri*: courtesy Artisjus (Budapest).

Robert Darnton: courtesy Los Angeles Times; *Donald Davidson*: courtesy University of California, Dept. of Philosophy; *Natalie Zemon Davis*: Sauro/New York Times Pictures; *Paul de Man*: courtesy Yale University; *Owen Dodson*: courtesy of the author; *Ellen Douglas*: Ellen Douglas; *Autran Dourado*: courtesy of the author; *Rita Dove*: photo by Fred Viebahn, courtesy of the author; *Sergey Dovlatov*: Conrad/New York Times Pictures; *Elizabeth Drew*: photo by Stanley Tretick; *Norman Dubie*: photo by Chris Pichler; *Christopher Durang*: photo by Jerry Bauer; *Freeman J. Dyson*: courtesy of the author.

Terry Eagleton: courtesy of the author; *Lauris Edmond*: courtesy of the author; *John Ehle*: photo by Nicholas Dean; *Alice Thomas Ellis*: courtesy of Viking Press; *Gevorg Emin*: courtesy of the author; *Michael Ende*: photo by Jerry Bauer; *Nora Ephron*: photo © Thomas Victor; *Joseph Epstein*: courtesy W. W. Norton; *Louise Erdrich*: photo by Michael Dorris, courtesy Henry Holt and Co.; *Amitai Etzioni*: photo by Ankers Photographers, Inc.; *Stuart Evans*: courtesy of the author.

Raymond Federman: courtesy of the author; *Jürg Federspiel*: photo by Torricelli; *James Fenton*: photo by Joyce Ravid; *Eva Figes*: photo by Jerry Bauer; *Timothy Findley*: photo by Elisabeth Feryn; *Roy Fisher*: photo by Laurence Spartham; *Frances Fitzgerald*: photo by Stuart Bratesman; *Thomas Flanagan*: Shavel/New York Times Pictures; *Dario Fo*: photo by Corrado M. Falsini; *Ken Follett*: courtesy of the author; *Carolyn Forché*: photo by Jerry Bauer; *Richard Ford*: photo by Kristina Ford; *Margaret Forster*: photo by Frank Herrmann, courtesy of the author; *Paula Fox*: photo © Jerry Bauer; *Saul Friedlander*: photo by Jerry Bauer; *Robin Fulton*: courtesy of the author.

Hans-Georg Gadamer: German Information Center; *Tess Gallagher*: photo by Jim Heynen; *Howard Gardner*: courtesy of the author; *Martin Gardner*: photo © Jennifer Walsh; *Clifford Geertz*: photo by Herman Landshoff; *Brewster Ghiselin*: courtesy of the author; *Zulfikar Ghose*: photo by Helena de la Fontaine; *Ellen Gilchrist*: photo by Jerry Bauer; *Carlo Ginzburg*: photo by Jerry Bauer; *Victoria Glendinning*: photo by Caroline Forbes; *Janusz Głowacki*: photo by Jerry Szczesny; *Albert Goldbarth*: photo by Betty Gottlieb; *Ellen Goodman*: AP/Wide World; *Arthur Gregor*: courtesy of the author; *Vasily Grossman*:

courtesy of the author; *Doris Grumbach*: photo by Jerry Bauer; *A. R. Gurney, Jr.*: courtesy of the author; *Rosa Guy*: courtesy Gerard W. Purcell Associates, Ltd.

Paavo Haavikko: photo by Irmeli Jung; *Christopher Hampton*: photo by Jerry Bauer; *Barry Hannah*: photo by Robert Jordan; *David Hare*: compliments of Margaret Ramsay Ltd.; *Tony Harrison*: courtesy Peters, Fraser and Dunlop; *Robert L. Heilbroner*: courtesy of the author; *Beth Henley*: courtesy of the author; *Xavier Herbert*: courtesy of the Australian Information Service; *John Hewitt*: photo by Dermott Dunbar (Blackstaff Press); *Jamake Highwater*: William Coupon; *Gertrude Himmelfarb*: courtesy City University Graduate School; *Daryl Hine*: photo by Denise Saenni; *Alice Hoffman*: photo © Thomas Victor 1982; *Gert Hofman*: photo by Isolde Ohlbaum; *Douglas R. Hofstadter*: courtesy of the author; *Hugh Hood*: photo by Noreen Mallory; *Stuart Hood*: courtesy of the author; *Robert Hughes*: photo © Timothy Greenfield-Sanders; *Keri Hulme*: New York Times Pictures.

Rachel Ingalls: Cam Press/New York Times Photos; *Albert Innaurato*: courtesy Martha Swope Associates; *Inoue Yasushi*: The Image Bank.

Ernst Jandl: courtesy of the author; *Denis Johnson*: photo by Jerry Bauer; *Elizabeth Jolley*: photo by Tania Young; *Gabriel Josipovici*: courtesy of the author.

Molly Keane: photo by Liam White; *John Keegan*: photo by Mark Gerson, courtesy Viking; *Robert Kelly*: photo by Mary Moore Goodlett; *Joseph Kerman*: courtesy Harvard University Press; *Jamaica Kincaid*: photo © Mariana Cook 1988; *Stephen King*: photo by James Leonard; *Ivan Klíma*: courtesy Dilia Vysehradska; *Taduesz Konwicki*: photo by Thomas Victor; *Julia Kristeva*: photo by Jerry Bauer; *Reiner Kunze*: courtesy of the author.

Alex La Guma: photo by George Hallett; *Jean Lacouture*: Cam Press/New York Times Pictures; *Louis L'Amour*: AP/Wide World Photos; *Jacques Le Goff*: photo by Jacques Robert; *Meridel Le Sueur*: photo by Jerome Liebling, courtesy of the author; *Brad Leithauser*: photo by Jerry Bauer; *Elmore Leonard*: photo by Joan Leonard; *Laurence Lerner*: courtesy of the author; *Reinhard Lettau*: courtesy German Information Center; *Primo Levi*: photo by Marco Sorrentino; *Robert Liddell*: New York Times Pictures; *Clarice Lispector*: courtesy of New Directions Publishing; *Liu Binyan*: courtesy Timothy Tung; *Phillip Lopate*: Sally Gall/New York Times Pictures; *Barry Holstun Lopez*: photo by Jerry Bauer; *Robert Ludlam*: photo by Michelle Ryder; *Gavin Lyall*: photo by Jerry Bauer.

Gwendolyn MacEwen: photo by Dimitri Andri Koglov, courtesy of the author; *Maynard Mack*: courtesy Yale University; *Denis Mack Smith*: New York Times; *Norman Maclean*: photo by Joel Snyder; *Jayanta Mahapatra*:

courtesy of the author; *Janet Malcolm*: photo by Jerry Bauer; *Iván Mándy*: courtesy Artisjus (Budapest); *D. Keith Mano*: courtesy of the author; *Bobbie Ann Mason*: photo by Thomas Victor; *Harry Mathews*: photo by Miriam Berkley; *William Matthews*: photo by Star Black; *Patrick McGinley*: courtesy of the author; *Michael Mewshaw*: photo by Jerry Bauer; *J. Hillis Miller*: courtesy Queens College; *Frederick Morgan*: courtesy of the author; *Richard B. Morris*: AP/Wide World Photos; *Andrew Motion*: photo by Jerry Bauer; *Alice Munro*: courtesy Canadian Consulate General; *Les A. Murray*: courtesy of the author; *Adolf Muschg*: New York Times Pictures.

Shiva Naipaul: photo by Jerry Bauer; *Gloria Naylor*: photo © Donna DeCesare; *Eric Newby*: photo by Sonia Newby; *John Nichols*: photo by Juanita Wolf; *Lorine Niedecker*: photo © Jonathon Williams, reprinted by permission of North Point Press; *Lewis Nkosi*: courtesy Constable Publishers; *Marsha Norman*: courtesy William Morris Agency.

Tim O'Brien: AP/Wide World; *Ōe Kenzaburo*: courtesy Serpent's Tail Press; *Julia O'Faolain*: photo by Mark Gerson, FHP; *Sharon Olds*: photo by Thomas Victor; *Mary Oliver*: photo by Molly Malone Cook; *Paul Osborn*: M. A. Barcelona/New York Times Pictures.

Heberto Padilla: photo by Jerry Bauer; *Linda Pastan*: courtesy of the author; *Orlando Patterson*: photo by Anthony Bottone, M.D., courtesy Harvard University Press; *Miodrag Pavlović*: courtesy of the Language Studies Centre, London School of Economics & Political Science; *Georges Perec*: photo by Anne de Brunhoff; *Harry Mark Petrakis*: photo by George Nicholson, NYC; *Jayne Anne Phillips*: photo by Jerry Bauer; *George Plimpton*: photo by Anthony Edgeworth; *Dimitru Radu Popescu*: courtesy Stefan Stonenescu; *Charles Portis*: New York Times Pictures; *Francine Prose*: photo by Miriam Berkley.

Carl Rakosi: courtesy of the author; *Irina Ratushinskaya*: courtesy Northwestern University Press; *Ruth Rendell*: photo by Jerry Bauer; *Gregor von Rezzori*: Edoardo Fornacianra/New York Times Pictures; *Richard Rhodes*: courtesy of the author; *Augusto Roa Bastos*: AP/Wide World Photos; *Bernice Rubens*: photo by Jerry Bauer; *Peter Russell*: courtesy Harper & Row; *Anatoly Naumovich Rybakov*: AP/Wide World Photos.

Oliver Sacks: photo by Alex Gotfryd; *Nawal el-Saadawi*: courtesy of the author; *John Sanford*: courtesy Harper & Row; *Ferenc Sánta*: courtesy Artisjus (Budapest); *Susan Fromberg Schaeffer*: photo by Jerry Bauer; *Richard Schickel*: photo by N. Kaye, New York Times Pictures; *Lynne Sharon Schwartz*: photo by Thomas Victor; *Moacyr Scliar*: photo by Miriam Berkley; *Lore Segal*: photo by Marilyn McLaren; *Jorge Semprun*: AP/Wide World Photos; *Harvey Shapiro*: photo by Bill Aller; *Tom Sharpe*: photo by Jerry Bauer; *Susan*